MAP PAGES

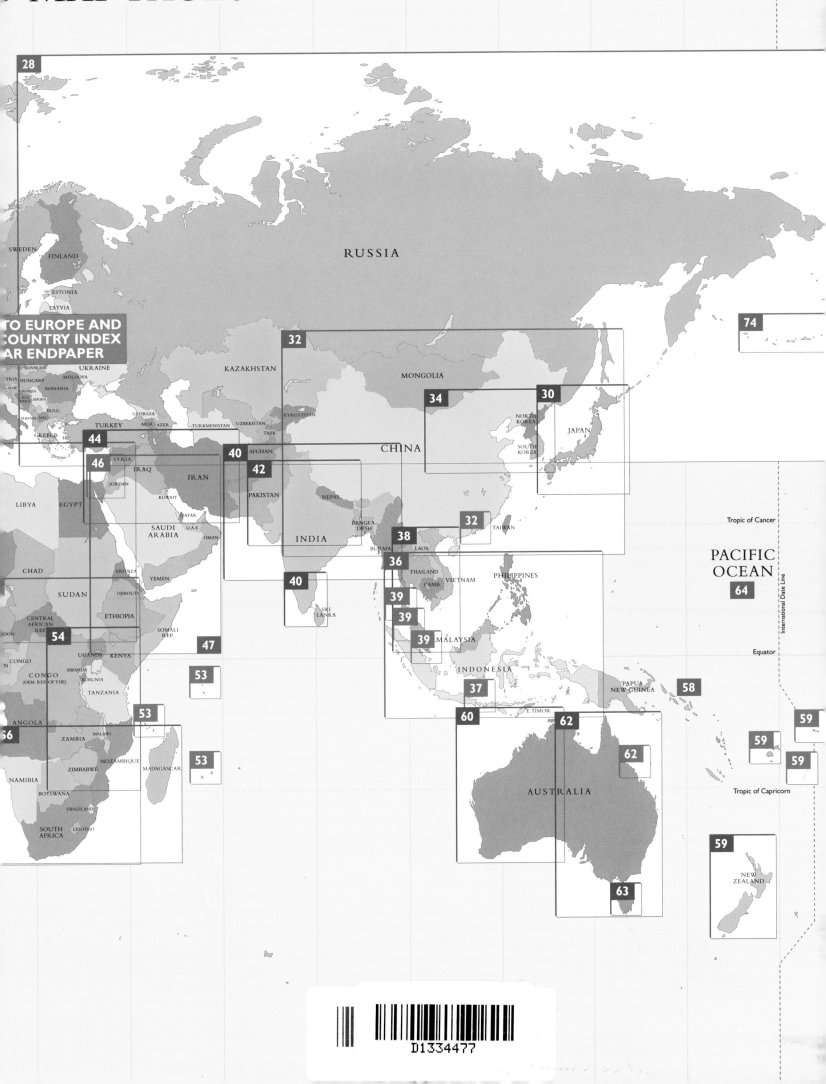

28

74

32

34

30

44

46

40

42

32

38

36

40

39

39

39

47

53

54

53

53

37

58

59

59

59

60

62

62

64

63

59

SWEDEN

FINLAND

ESTONIA

LATVIA

RUSSIA

UKRAINE

SLOVAK REP.

TRIA MOLDOVA

HUNGARY

SLOV. ROMANIA

CROATIA

BOS. SERBIA

HERZ.

ALBANIA MAC.

BULG.

GREECE

GEORGIA

TURKEY

ARM. AZER.

TURKMENISTAN

UZBEKISTAN

KAZAKHSTAN

KYRGYZSTAN

TAJIK.

MONGOLIA

NORTH
KOREA

JAPAN

SOUTH
KOREA

CHINA

SYRIA

IRAQ

IRAN

AFGHAN.

JORDAN

KUWAIT

PAKISTAN

NEPAL

BANGLA-
DESH

TAIWAN

LIBYA

EGYPT

SAUDI
ARABIA

U.A.E.

QATAR

OMAN

INDIA

BURMA

LAOS

THAILAND

VIETNAM

CAMB.

PHILIPPINES

Tropic of Cancer

PACIFIC
OCEAN

CHAD

ERITREA

YEMEN

SRI
LANKA

SUDAN

DJIBOUTI

CENTRAL
AFRICAN
REP.

ETHIOPIA

SOMALI
REP.

OON

UGANDA KENYA

CONGO

RWANDA

BURUNDI

TANZANIA

MALAYSIA

INDONESIA

PAPUA
NEW GUINEA

ANGOLA

ZAMBIA MALAWI

MADAGASCAR

E. TIMOR

MOZAMBIQUE

ZIMBABWE

NAMIBIA

BOTSWANA

SWAZILAND

SOUTH
AFRICA

LESOTHO

AUSTRALIA

NEW
ZEALAND

International Date Line

Equator

Tropic of Capricorn

D1334477

PHILIP'S

WORLD ATLAS

Philip's are grateful to the following for acting as specialist geography consultants on '*The World in Focus*' front section:

Professor D. Brunsden, Kings College, University of London, UK
Dr C. Clarke, Oxford University, UK
Dr I. S. Evans, Durham University, UK
Professor P. Haggett, University of Bristol, UK
Professor K. McLachlan, University of London, UK
Professor M. Monmonier, Syracuse University, New York, USA
Professor M-L. Hsu, University of Minnesota, Minnesota, USA
Professor M. J. Tooley, University of St Andrews, UK
Dr T. Unwin, Royal Holloway, University of London, UK

THE WORLD IN FOCUS
Cartography by Philip's

Picture Acknowledgements
Robin Scagell/Galaxy page 3

Illustrations: Stefan Chabluk

WORLD CITIES
Cartography by Philip's

**Page 10, Dublin: The town plan of Dublin is based on Ordnance Survey Ireland by permission of the Government Permit Number 8621.
© Ordnance Survey Ireland and Government of Ireland.**

Page 11, Edinburgh, and page 15, London: This product includes mapping data licensed from Ordnance Survey® with the permission of the Controller of Her Majesty's Stationery Office. © Crown copyright 2010. All rights reserved. Licence number 100011710.

All satellite images in this section courtesy of Fugro NPA Ltd, Edenbridge, Kent, UK (www.satmaps.com).

Published in Great Britain in 2010 by Philip's,
a division of Octopus Publishing Group Limited
(www.octopusbooks.co.uk)
Endeavour House, 189 Shaftesbury Avenue, London WC2H 8JY
An Hachette UK Company (www.hachette.co.uk)

Copyright © 2010 Philip's

Cartography by Philip's

ISBN 978-1-84907-103-1

A CIP catalogue record for this book is available from the British Library.

Printed in Hong Kong

Details of other Philip's titles and services can be found on our website at:
www.philips-maps.co.uk

PHILIP'S

WORLD ATLAS

IN ASSOCIATION WITH
THE ROYAL GEOGRAPHICAL SOCIETY
WITH THE INSTITUTE OF BRITISH GEOGRAPHERS

Contents

World Statistics

Countries   vi
Physical Dimensions   vii
User Guide   viii

The World in Focus

Planet Earth   2–3
Restless Earth   4–5
Landforms   6–7
Oceans   8–9
Climate   10–11
Water and Vegetation   12–13
Environment   14–15
Population   16–17
The Human Family   18–19
Wealth   20–21
Quality of Life   22–23
Energy   24–25
Production   26–27
Trade   28–29
Travel and Tourism   30–31

World Cities

Amsterdam   2
Athens   2
Atlanta   3
Baghdad   3
Bangkok   3
Barcelona   4
Beijing   4
Berlin   5
Boston   6
Brussels   6
Budapest   7
Buenos Aires   7
Cairo   7
Cape Town   8
Copenhagen   8
Chicago   9
Delhi   10
Dublin   10
Edinburgh   11
Guangzhou   11
Helsinki   11
Hong Kong   12
Istanbul   12
Jakarta   12
Jerusalem   13
Johannesburg   13
Karachi   13
Kolkata   14
Lagos   14
Las Vegas   14
Lima   14
London   15
Lisbon   16
Los Angeles   16
Madrid   17
Manila   17
Melbourne   18
Mexico City   18
Miami   18
Milan   19
Moscow   19
Montréal   20
Mumbai   20
Munich   21
New Orleans   21
New York   22
Orlando   23
Osaka   23
Oslo   23
Paris   24
Prague   25
Rio de Janeiro   25
Rome   26
San Francisco   26
St Petersburg   27
Santiago   27
São Paulo   27
Seoul   27
Shanghai   28
Singapore   28
Stockholm   29
Sydney   29
Tokyo   30
Tehran   31
Toronto   31
Vienna   32
Warsaw   32
Washington   33
Wellington   33
Index to City Maps   34–39
World Cities Satellite Images   40–48

World Maps

Map Symbols   1

The World: Political
1:95 000 000   2–3

Arctic Ocean
1:35 000 000   4

Antarctica
1:35 000 000   5

Europe

Europe: Physical
1:20 000 000   6

Europe: Political
1:20 000 000   7

Scandinavia 1:6 000 000
Iceland 1:6 000 000
Færoe Islands 1:6 000 000

                                             8–9

Ireland 1:2 000 000

                                             10

Scotland 1:2 000 000
                                             11

England and Wales
1:2 000 000
                                             12–13

British Isles 1:5 000 000
                                             14

Netherlands, Belgium and
Luxembourg 1:2 500 000
                                             15

Central Europe 1:5 000 000

                                             16–17

Eastern Europe and Turkey
1:10 000 000
                                             18–19

France 1:5 000 000
                                             20

Spain and Portugal
1:5 000 000

                                             21

Italy and the Balkan States
1:5 000 000
                                             22–23

The Balearics, the Canaries and
Madeira 1:1 000 000 / 1:2 000 000
                                             24

Malta, Crete, Corfu, Rhodes
and Cyprus
1:1 000 000 / 1:1 300 000
                                             25

Asia

Asia: Physical 1:47 000 000   26

Asia: Political 1:47 000 000   27

Russia and Central Asia
1:20 000 000
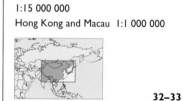
                                             28–29

Japan 1:5 000 000

                                             30–31

China and the Far East
1:15 000 000
Hong Kong and Macau 1:1 000 000

                                             32–33

Northern China and Korea
1:6 000 000
                                             34–35

Indonesia and the Philippines
1:12 500 000
Java and Madura 1:7 500 000
Bali 1:2 000 000
                                             36–37

Mainland South-east Asia
1:6 000 000
Ko Phuket 1:1 000 000
Ko Samui 1:1 000 000
Pinang 1:1 000 000
Singapore 1:1 000 000
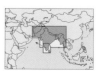
                                             38–39

South Asia 1:10 000 000
                                             40–41

Northern India, Pakistan and Nepal
1:6 000 000
Jammu and Kashmir 1:6 000 000

42–43

The Middle East
1:7 000 000

44–45

The Near East 1:2 500 000

46

Arabia and the Horn of Africa 1:15 000 000

47

Africa

Africa: Physical
1:42 000 000   48

Africa: Political
1:42 000 000   49

Northern Africa
1:15 000 000
Azores 1:15 000 000
Cape Verde Islands 1:10 000 000

50–51

Central and Southern Africa
1:15 000 000
Seychelles 1:2 500 000
Réunion 1:2 500 000
Mauritius 1:2 500 000
Comoros 1:8 000 000

52–53

East Africa 1:8 000 000

54–55

Southern Africa
1:8 000 000
Madagascar 1:8 000 000

56–57

Australia and Oceania

Australia and Oceania: Physical and Political
1:50 000 000   58

New Zealand 1:6 000 000
Samoan Islands 1:6 000 000
Fiji 1:6 000 000
Tonga 1:6 000 000
Tahiti and Moorea 1:1 000 000

59

Western Australia
1:8 000 000

60–61

Eastern Australia
1:8 000 000
Torres Strait 1:8 000 000
Whitsunday Islands 1:2 500 000
Tasmania 1:8 000 000

62–63

Pacific Ocean
1:54 000 000   64–65

North America

North America: Physical
1:35 000 000   66

North America: Political
1:35 000 000   67

Canada 1:15 000 000

68–69

Western Canada 1:7 000 000

70–71

Eastern Canada 1:7 000 000

72–73

United States 1:15 000 000
Hawai'i 1:15 000 000
Alaska 1:15 000 000

74–75

United States – West
1:6 700 000

76–77

Central and Southern California and Western Washington
1:2 500 000

78–79

United States – Midwest and North-east
1:6 700 000

80–81

North-eastern United States
1:2 500 000

82–83

United States – South
1:6 700 000

84–85

Mexico 1:8 000 000

86–87

Central America and the West Indies 1:8 000 000
Jamaica 1:3 000 000
Guadeloupe 1:2 000 000
Martinique 1:2 000 000
Puerto Rico 1:3 000 000
Virgin Islands 1:2 000 000
St Lucia 1:2 000 000
Barbados 1:2 000 000

88–89

South America

South America: Physical
1:35 000 000   90

South America: Political
1:35 000 000   91

South America – North
1:16 000 000
Trinidad and Tobago 1:2 500 000

92–93

Central South America
1:8 000 000

94–95

South America – South
1:16 000 000

96

Index to World Maps
97–176

World Statistics: Countries

This alphabetical list includes the principal countries and territories of the world. If a territory is not completely independent, the country it is associated with is named. The area figures give the total area of land, inland water and ice. The population figures are 2009 estimates where available. The annual income is the Gross Domestic Product per capita in US dollars. The figures are the latest available, usually 2009 estimates.

Country/Territory	Area km² Thousands	Area miles² Thousands	Population Thousands	Capital	Annual Income US $
Afghanistan	652	252	28,396	Kabul	800
Albania	28.7	11.1	3,639	Tirana	6,200
Algeria	2,382	920	34,178	Algiers	7,100
American Samoa (US)	0.20	0.08	66	Pago Pago	8,000
Andorra	0.47	0.18	84	Andorra La Vella	42,500
Angola	1,247	481	12,799	Luanda	8,800
Anguilla (UK)	0.10	0.04	14	The Valley	8,800
Antigua & Barbuda	0.44	0.17	86	St John's	18,100
Argentina	2,780	1,074	40,914	Buenos Aires	13,800
Armenia	29.8	11.5	2,967	Yerevan	5,900
Aruba (Netherlands)	0.19	0.07	103	Oranjestad	21,800
Australia	7,741	2,989	21,263	Canberra	38,500
Austria	83.9	32.4	8,210	Vienna	39,400
Azerbaijan	86.6	33.4	8,239	Baku	9,900
Azores (Portugal)	2.2	0.86	236	Ponta Delgada	15,000
Bahamas	13.9	5.4	308	Nassau	29,800
Bahrain	0.69	0.27	729	Manama	38,400
Bangladesh	144	55.6	156,051	Dhaka	1,600
Barbados	0.43	0.17	285	Bridgetown	18,500
Belarus	208	80.2	9,649	Minsk	11,600
Belgium	30.5	11.8	10,414	Brussels	36,600
Belize	23.0	8.9	308	Belmopan	8,200
Benin	113	43.5	8,792	Porto-Novo	1,500
Bermuda (UK)	0.05	0.02	68	Hamilton	69,900
Bhutan	47.0	18.1	691	Thimphu	6,200
Bolivia	1,099	424	9,775	La Paz/Sucre	4,600
Bosnia-Herzegovina	51.2	19.8	4,613	Sarajevo	6,300
Botswana	582	225	1,991	Gaborone	12,100
Brazil	8,514	3,287	198,739	Brasília	10,200
Brunei	5.8	2.2	388	Bandar Seri Begawan	50,100
Bulgaria	111	42.8	7,205	Sofia	12,600
Burkina Faso	274	106	15,746	Ouagadougou	1,200
Burma (Myanmar)	677	261	48,138	Rangoon/Naypyidaw	1,200
Burundi	27.8	10.7	9,511	Bujumbura	300
Cambodia	181	69.9	14,494	Phnom Penh	1,900
Cameroon	475	184	18,879	Yaoundé	2,300
Canada	9,971	3,850	33,487	Ottawa	38,400
Canary Is. (Spain)	7.2	2.8	1,682	Las Palmas/Santa Cruz	19,900
Cape Verde Is.	4.0	1.6	429	Praia	3,900
Cayman Is. (UK)	0.26	0.10	49	George Town	43,800
Central African Republic	623	241	4,511	Bangui	700
Chad	1,284	496	10,329	Ndjaména	1,500
Chile	757	292	16,602	Santiago	14,700
China	9,597	3,705	1,338,613	Beijing	6,500
Colombia	1,139	440	43,677	Bogotá	9,200
Comoros	2.2	0.86	752	Moroni	1,000
Congo	342	132	4,013	Brazzaville	4,200
Congo (Dem. Rep. of the)	2,345	905	68,693	Kinshasa	300
Cook Is. (NZ)	0.24	0.09	12	Avarua	9,100
Costa Rica	51.1	19.7	4,254	San José	11,300
Croatia	56.5	21.8	4,489	Zagreb	17,600
Cuba	111	42.8	11,452	Havana	9,700
Cyprus	9.3	3.6	1,085	Nicosia	21,200
Czech Republic	78.9	30.5	10,212	Prague	25,100
Denmark	43.1	16.6	5,501	Copenhagen	36,200
Djibouti	23.2	9.0	725	Djibouti	2,800
Dominica	0.75	0.29	73	Roseau	10,200
Dominican Republic	48.5	18.7	9,650	Santo Domingo	8,200
East Timor	14.9	5.7	1,132	Dili	2,400
Ecuador	284	109	14,573	Quito	7,300
Egypt	1,001	387	78,867	Cairo	6,000
El Salvador	21.0	8.1	7,185	San Salvador	6,000
Equatorial Guinea	28.1	10.8	633	Malabo	36,100
Eritrea	118	45.4	5,647	Asmara	700
Estonia	45.1	17.4	1,299	Tallinn	18,800
Ethiopia	1,104	426	85,237	Addis Ababa	900
Faroe Is. (Denmark)	1.4	0.54	49	Tórshavn	31,000
Fiji	18.3	7.1	945	Suva	3,800
Finland	338	131	5,250	Helsinki	34,900
France	552	213	64,058	Paris	32,800
French Guiana (France)	90.0	34.7	203	Cayenne	8,300
French Polynesia (France)	4.0	1.5	287	Papeete	18,000
Gabon	268	103	1,515	Libreville	13,700
Gambia, The	11.3	4.4	1,778	Banjul	1,300
Gaza Strip (OPT)*	0.36	0.14	1,552	–	3,100
Georgia	69.7	26.9	4,616	Tbilisi	4,500
Germany	357	138	82,330	Berlin	34,200
Ghana	239	92.1	23,888	Accra	1,500
Gibraltar (UK)	0.006	0.002	29	Gibraltar Town	38,200
Greece	132	50.9	10,737	Athens	32,100
Greenland (Denmark)	2,176	840	58	Nuuk	34,700
Grenada	0.34	0.13	91	St George's	12,700
Guadeloupe (France)	1.7	0.66	453	Basse-Terre	7,900
Guam (US)	0.55	0.21	178	Agana	15,000
Guatemala	109	42.0	13,277	Guatemala City	5,200
Guinea	246	94.9	10,058	Conakry	1,100
Guinea-Bissau	36.1	13.9	1,534	Bissau	600
Guyana	215	83.0	753	Georgetown	3,900
Haiti	27.8	10.7	9,036	Port-au-Prince	1,300
Honduras	112	43.3	7,834	Tegucigalpa	4,200
Hungary	93.0	35.9	9,906	Budapest	18,800
Iceland	103	39.8	307	Reykjavik	39,800
India	3,287	1,269	1,156,898	New Delhi	3,100
Indonesia	1,905	735	240,272	Jakarta	4,000
Iran	1,648	636	66,429	Tehran	12,900
Iraq	438	169	28,946	Baghdad	3,300
Ireland	70.3	27.1	4,203	Dublin	42,200
Israel	20.6	8.0	7,234	Jerusalem	28,400
Italy	301	116	58,126	Rome	30,200
Ivory Coast (Côte d'Ivoire)	322	125	20,617	Yamoussoukro	1,700
Jamaica	11.0	4.2	2,826	Kingston	8,300
Japan	378	146	127,079	Tokyo	32,600
Jordan	89.3	34.5	6,269	Amman	5,300
Kazakhstan	2,725	1,052	15,399	Astana	11,400
Kenya	580	224	39,003	Nairobi	1,600
Kiribati	0.73	0.28	113	Tarawa	5,300
Korea, North	121	46.5	22,665	Pyŏngyang	1,800
Korea, South	99.3	38.3	48,509	Seoul	27,700
Kosovo	10.9	4.2	1,805	Pristina	2,300
Kuwait	17.8	6.9	2,693	Kuwait City	55,800
Kyrgyzstan	200	77.2	5,432	Bishkek	2,100
Laos	237	91.4	6,834	Vientiane	2,100

*OPT = Occupied Palestinian Territory

Country/Territory	Area km² Thousands	Area miles² Thousands	Population Thousands	Capital	Annual Income US $
Latvia	64.6	24.9	2,232	Riga	14,500
Lebanon	10.4	4.0	4,017	Beirut	11,500
Lesotho	30.4	11.7	2,131	Maseru	1,500
Liberia	111	43.0	3,442	Monrovia	500
Libya	1,760	679	6,324	Tripoli	14,600
Liechtenstein	0.16	0.06	35	Vaduz	122,100
Lithuania	65.2	25.2	3,555	Vilnius	15,000
Luxembourg	2.6	1.0	492	Luxembourg	77,600
Macedonia (FYROM)	25.7	9.9	2,067	Skopje	9,000
Madagascar	587	227	20,654	Antananarivo	1,000
Madeira (Portugal)	0.78	0.30	241	Funchal	22,700
Malawi	118	45.7	15,029	Lilongwe	900
Malaysia	330	127	25,716	Kuala Lumpur/Putrajaya	14,700
Maldives	0.30	0.12	396	Malé	4,200
Mali	1,240	479	13,443	Bamako	1,100
Malta	0.32	0.12	405	Valletta	23,800
Marshall Is.	0.18	0.07	65	Majuro	2,500
Martinique (France)	1.1	0.43	436	Fort-de-France	14,400
Mauritania	1,026	396	3,129	Nouakchott	2,100
Mauritius	2.0	0.79	1,284	Port Louis	12,400
Mayotte (France)	0.37	0.14	224	Mamoudzou	4,900
Mexico	1,958	756	111,212	Mexico City	13,200
Micronesia, Fed. States of	0.70	0.27	107	Palikir	2,200
Moldova	33.9	13.1	4,321	Kishinev	2,400
Monaco	0.001	0.0004	33	Monaco	30,000
Mongolia	1,567	605	3,041	Ulan Bator	3,400
Montenegro	14.0	5.4	672	Podgorica	9,800
Morocco	447	172	31,285	Rabat	4,600
Mozambique	802	309	21,669	Maputo	900
Namibia	824	318	2,109	Windhoek	6,400
Nauru	0.02	0.008	14	Yaren	5,000
Nepal	147	56.8	28,563	Katmandu	1,200
Netherlands	41.5	16.0	16,716	Amsterdam/The Hague	39,000
Netherlands Antilles (Neths)†	0.80	0.31	227	Willemstad	16,000
New Caledonia (France)	18.6	7.2	228	Nouméa	15,000
New Zealand	271	104	4,213	Wellington	27,700
Nicaragua	130	50.2	5,891	Managua	2,800
Niger	1,267	489	15,306	Niamey	700
Nigeria	924	357	149,229	Abuja	2,400
Northern Mariana Is. (US)	0.46	0.18	51	Saipan	12,500
Norway	324	125	4,661	Oslo	59,300
Oman	310	119	3,418	Muscat	20,300
Pakistan	796	307	174,579	Islamabad	2,600
Palau	0.46	0.18	21	Melekeok	8,100
Panama	75.5	29.2	3,360	Panamá	11,900
Papua New Guinea	463	179	5,941	Port Moresby	2,300
Paraguay	407	157	6,996	Asunción	4,100
Peru	1,285	496	29,547	Lima	8,600
Philippines	300	116	97,977	Manila	3,300
Poland	323	125	38,483	Warsaw	17,800
Portugal	88.8	34.3	10,708	Lisbon	21,700
Puerto Rico (US)	8.9	3.4	3,966	San Juan	17,100
Qatar	11.0	4.2	833	Doha	121,400
Réunion (France)	2.5	0.97	788	St-Denis	6,200
Romania	238	92.0	22,215	Bucharest	11,500
Russia	17,075	6,593	140,041	Moscow	15,200
Rwanda	26.3	10.2	10,746	Kigali	1,000
St Kitts & Nevis	0.26	0.10	40	Basseterre	18,800
St Lucia	0.54	0.21	160	Castries	10,900
St Vincent & Grenadines	0.39	0.15	105	Kingstown	18,100
Samoa	2.8	1.1	220	Apia	4,700
San Marino	0.06	0.02	30	San Marino	41,900
São Tomé & Príncipe	0.96	0.37	213	São Tomé	1,400
Saudi Arabia	2,150	830	28,687	Riyadh	20,300
Senegal	197	76.0	13,712	Dakar	1,700
Serbia	77.5	29.9	7,379	Belgrade	10,400
Seychelles	0.46	0.18	87	Victoria	19,400
Sierra Leone	71.7	27.7	5,132	Freetown	900
Singapore	0.68	0.26	4,658	Singapore City	50,300
Slovak Republic	49.0	18.9	5,463	Bratislava	21,100
Slovenia	20.3	7.8	2,006	Ljubljana	28,200
Solomon Is.	28.9	11.2	596	Honiara	2,600
Somalia	638	246	9,832	Mogadishu	600
South Africa	1,221	471	49,052	Cape Town/Pretoria	10,000
Spain	498	192	40,525	Madrid	33,700
Sri Lanka	65.6	25.3	21,325	Colombo	4,500
Sudan	2,506	967	41,088	Khartoum	2,300
Suriname	163	63.0	481	Paramaribo	8,800
Swaziland	17.4	6.7	1,337	Mbabane	4,400
Sweden	450	174	9,060	Stockholm	36,800
Switzerland	41.3	15.9	7,604	Bern	41,600
Syria	185	71.5	21,763	Damascus	4,700
Taiwan	36.0	13.9	22,974	Taipei	30,200
Tajikistan	143	55.3	7,349	Dushanbe	1,800
Tanzania	945	365	41,049	Dodoma	1,400
Thailand	513	198	65,998	Bangkok	8,100
Togo	56.8	21.9	6,032	Lomé	900
Tonga	0.65	0.25	121	Nuku'alofa	4,600
Trinidad & Tobago	5.1	2.0	1,230	Port of Spain	23,300
Tunisia	164	63.2	10,486	Tunis	8,000
Turkey	775	299	76,806	Ankara	11,200
Turkmenistan	488	188	4,885	Ashkhabad	6,700
Turks & Caicos Is. (UK)	0.43	0.17	23	Cockburn Town	11,500
Tuvalu	0.03	0.01	12	Fongafale	1,600
Uganda	241	93.1	32,370	Kampala	1,300
Ukraine	604	233	45,700	Kiev	6,400
United Arab Emirates	83.6	32.3	4,798	Abu Dhabi	41,800
United Kingdom	242	93.4	61,113	London	35,400
United States of America	9,629	3,718	307,212	Washington, DC	46,400
Uruguay	175	67.6	3,494	Montevideo	12,600
Uzbekistan	447	173	27,606	Tashkent	2,800
Vanuatu	12.2	4.7	219	Port-Vila	4,800
Venezuela	912	352	26,815	Caracas	13,200
Vietnam	332	128	88,577	Hanoi	2,900
Virgin Is. (UK)	0.15	0.06	24	Road Town	38,500
Virgin Is. (US)	0.35	0.13	110	Charlotte Amalie	14,500
Wallis & Futuna Is. (France)	0.20	0.08	15	Mata-Utu	3,800
West Bank (OPT)*	5.9	2.3	2,416	–	2,900
Western Sahara	266	103	405	El Aaiún	2,500
Yemen	528	204	22,858	Sana'	2,500
Zambia	753	291	11,863	Lusaka	1,500
Zimbabwe	391	151	11,393	Harare	200

† Plans have been announced to dissolve the Netherlands Antilles as a political entity in October 2010. The five islands will then each have a new constitutional status within the Kingdom of the Netherlands.

World Statistics: Physical Dimensions

Each topic list is divided into continents and within a continent the items are listed in order of size. The bottom part of many of the lists is selective in order to give examples from as many different countries as possible. The order of the continents is the same as in the atlas, beginning with Europe and ending with South America. The figures are rounded as appropriate.

World, Continents, Oceans

	km²	miles²	%
The World	509,450,000	196,672,000	–
Land	149,450,000	57,688,000	29.3
Water	360,000,000	138,984,000	70.7
Asia	44,500,000	17,177,000	29.8
Africa	30,302,000	11,697,000	20.3
North America	24,241,000	9,357,000	16.2
South America	17,793,000	6,868,000	11.9
Antarctica	14,100,000	5,443,000	9.4
Europe	9,957,000	3,843,000	6.7
Australia & Oceania	8,557,000	3,303,000	5.7
Pacific Ocean	155,557,000	60,061,000	46.4
Atlantic Ocean	76,762,000	29,638,000	22.9
Indian Ocean	68,556,000	26,470,000	20.4
Southern Ocean	20,327,000	7,848,000	6.1
Arctic Ocean	14,056,000	5,427,000	4.2

Ocean Depths

Atlantic Ocean

	m	ft
Puerto Rico (Milwaukee) Deep	8,605	28,232
Cayman Trench	7,680	25,197
Gulf of Mexico	5,203	17,070
Mediterranean Sea	5,121	16,801
Black Sea	2,211	7,254
North Sea	660	2,165

Indian Ocean

	m	ft
Java Trench	7,450	24,442
Red Sea	2,635	8,454

Pacific Ocean

	m	ft
Mariana Trench	11,022	36,161
Tonga Trench	10,882	35,702
Japan Trench	10,554	34,626
Kuril Trench	10,542	34,587

Arctic Ocean

	m	ft
Molloy Deep	5,608	18,399

Southern Ocean

	m	ft
South Sandwich Trench	7,235	23,737

Mountains

Europe

		m	ft
Elbrus	Russia	5,642	18,510
Dykh-Tau	Russia	5,205	17,076
Shkhara	Russia/Georgia	5,201	17,064
Koshtan-Tau	Russia	5,152	16,903
Kazbek	Russia/Georgia	5,047	16,558
Pushkin	Russia/Georgia	5,033	16,512
Katyn-Tau	Russia/Georgia	4,979	16,335
Shota Rustaveli	Russia/Georgia	4,860	15,945
Mont Blanc	France/Italy	4,808	15,774
Monte Rosa	Italy/Switzerland	4,634	15,203
Dom	Switzerland	4,545	14,911
Liskamm	Switzerland	4,527	14,852
Weisshorn	Switzerland	4,505	14,780
Taschorn	Switzerland	4,490	14,730
Matterhorn/Cervino	Italy/Switzerland	4,478	14,691
Grossglockner	Austria	3,797	12,457
Mulhacén	Spain	3,478	11,411
Zugspitze	Germany	2,962	9,718
Olympus	Greece	2,917	9,570
Galdhøpiggen	Norway	2,469	8,100
Ben Nevis	UK	1,342	4,403

Asia

		m	ft
Everest	China/Nepal	8,850	29,035
K2 (Godwin Austen)	China/Kashmir	8,611	28,251
Kanchenjunga	India/Nepal	8,598	28,208
Lhotse	China/Nepal	8,516	27,939
Makalu	China/Nepal	8,481	27,824
Cho Oyu	China/Nepal	8,201	26,906
Dhaulagiri	Nepal	8,167	26,795
Manaslu	Nepal	8,156	26,758
Nanga Parbat	Kashmir	8,126	26,660
Annapurna	Nepal	8,078	26,502
Gasherbrum	China/Kashmir	8,068	26,469
Broad Peak	China/Kashmir	8,051	26,414
Xixabangma	China	8,012	26,286
Kangbachen	Nepal	7,858	25,781
Trivor	Pakistan	7,720	25,328
Pik Imeni Ismail Samani	Tajikistan	7,495	24,590
Demavend	Iran	5,604	18,386
Ararat	Turkey	5,165	16,945
Gunong Kinabalu	Malaysia (Borneo)	4,101	13,455
Fuji-San	Japan	3,776	12,388

Africa

		m	ft
Kilimanjaro	Tanzania	5,895	19,340
Mt Kenya	Kenya	5,199	17,057
Ruwenzori (Margherita)	Ug./Congo (D.R.)	5,109	16,762
Meru	Tanzania	4,565	14,977
Ras Dashen	Ethiopia	4,533	14,872
Karisimbi	Rwanda/Congo (D.R.)	4,507	14,787
Mt Elgon	Kenya/Uganda	4,321	14,176
Batu	Ethiopia	4,307	14,130
Toubkal	Morocco	4,165	13,665
Mt Cameroun	Cameroon	4,070	13,353

Oceania

		m	ft
Puncak Jaya	Indonesia	5,029	16,499
Puncak Trikora	Indonesia	4,730	15,518
Puncak Mandala	Indonesia	4,702	15,427
Mt Wilhelm	Papua New Guinea	4,508	14,790
Mauna Kea	USA (Hawai'i)	4,205	13,796
Mauna Loa	USA (Hawai'i)	4,169	13,681
Aoraki Mt Cook	New Zealand	3,753	12,313
Mt Kosciuszko	Australia	2,228	7,310

North America

		m	ft
Mt McKinley (Denali)	USA (Alaska)	6,194	20,321
Mt Logan	Canada	5,959	19,551
Pico de Orizaba	Mexico	5,610	18,405
Mt St Elias	USA/Canada	5,489	18,008
Popocatépetl	Mexico	5,452	17,887
Mt Foraker	USA (Alaska)	5,304	17,401
Iztaccihuatl	Mexico	5,286	17,343
Mt Lucania	Canada	5,226	17,146
Mt Steele	Canada	5,073	16,644
Mt Bona	USA (Alaska)	5,005	16,420
Mt Whitney	USA	4,418	14,495
Tajumulco	Guatemala	4,220	13,845
Chirripó Grande	Costa Rica	3,837	12,589
Pico Duarte	Dominican Rep.	3,175	10,417

South America

		m	ft
Aconcagua	Argentina	6,962	22,841
Bonete	Argentina	6,872	22,546
Ojos del Salado	Argentina/Chile	6,863	22,516
Pissis	Argentina	6,779	22,241
Mercedario	Argentina/Chile	6,770	22,211
Huascarán	Peru	6,768	22,204
Llullaillaco	Argentina/Chile	6,723	22,057
Nevado de Cachi	Argentina	6,720	22,047
Yerupaja	Peru	6,632	21,758
Sajama	Bolivia	6,520	21,391
Chimborazo	Ecuador	6,267	20,561
Pico Cristóbal Colón	Colombia	5,800	19,029
Pico Bolivar	Venezuela	5,007	16,427

Antarctica

		m	ft
Vinson Massif		4,897	16,066
Mt Kirkpatrick		4,528	14,855

Rivers

Europe

		km	miles
Volga	Caspian Sea	3,700	2,300
Danube	Black Sea	2,850	1,770
Ural	Caspian Sea	2,535	1,575
Dnepr (Dnipro)	Black Sea	2,285	1,420
Kama	Volga	2,030	1,260
Don	Black Sea	1,990	1,240
Petchora	Arctic Ocean	1,790	1,110
Oka	Volga	1,480	920
Dnister (Dniester)	Black Sea	1,400	870
Vyatka	Kama	1,370	850
Rhine	North Sea	1,320	820
N. Dvina	Arctic Ocean	1,290	800
Elbe	North Sea	1,145	710

Asia

		km	miles
Yangtze	Pacific Ocean	6,380	3,960
Yenisey–Angara	Arctic Ocean	5,550	3,445
Huang He	Pacific Ocean	5,464	3,395
Ob–Irtysh	Arctic Ocean	5,410	3,360
Mekong	Pacific Ocean	4,500	2,795
Amur	Pacific Ocean	4,442	2,760
Lena	Arctic Ocean	4,402	2,735
Irtysh	Ob	4,250	2,640
Yenisey	Arctic Ocean	4,090	2,540
Ob	Arctic Ocean	3,680	2,285
Indus	Indian Ocean	3,100	1,925
Brahmaputra	Indian Ocean	2,900	1,800
Syrdarya	Aral Sea	2,860	1,775
Salween	Indian Ocean	2,800	1,740
Euphrates	Indian Ocean	2,700	1,675
Amudarya	Aral Sea	2,540	1,575

Africa

		km	miles
Nile	Mediterranean	6,695	4,160
Congo	Atlantic Ocean	4,670	2,900
Niger	Atlantic Ocean	4,180	2,595
Zambezi	Indian Ocean	3,540	2,200
Oubangi/Uele	Congo (D.R.)	2,250	1,400
Kasai	Congo (D.R.)	1,950	1,210
Shaballe	Indian Ocean	1,930	1,200
Orange	Atlantic Ocean	1,860	1,155
Cubango	Okavango Delta	1,800	1,120
Limpopo	Indian Ocean	1,770	1,100
Senegal	Atlantic Ocean	1,640	1,020

Australia

		km	miles
Murray–Darling	Southern Ocean	3,750	2,330
Darling	Murray	3,070	1,905
Murray	Southern Ocean	2,575	1,600
Murrumbidgee	Murray	1,690	1,050

North America

		km	miles
Mississippi–Missouri	Gulf of Mexico	5,971	3,710
Mackenzie	Arctic Ocean	4,240	2,630
Missouri	Mississippi	4,088	2,540
Mississippi	Gulf of Mexico	3,782	2,350
Yukon	Pacific Ocean	3,185	1,980
Rio Grande	Gulf of Mexico	3,030	1,880
Arkansas	Mississippi	2,340	1,450
Colorado	Pacific Ocean	2,330	1,445
Red	Mississippi	2,040	1,270
Columbia	Pacific Ocean	1,950	1,210
Saskatchewan	Lake Winnipeg	1,940	1,205

South America

		km	miles
Amazon	Atlantic Ocean	6,450	4,010
Paraná–Plate	Atlantic Ocean	4,500	2,800
Purus	Amazon	3,350	2,080
Madeira	Amazon	3,200	1,990
São Francisco	Atlantic Ocean	2,900	1,800
Paraná	Plate	2,800	1,740
Tocantins	Atlantic Ocean	2,750	1,710
Orinoco	Atlantic Ocean	2,740	1,700
Paraguay	Paraná	2,550	1,580
Pilcomayo	Paraná	2,500	1,550
Araguaia	Tocantins	2,250	1,400

Lakes

Europe

		km²	miles²
Lake Ladoga	Russia	17,700	6,800
Lake Onega	Russia	9,700	3,700
Saimaa system	Finland	8,000	3,100
Vänern	Sweden	5,500	2,100

Asia

		km²	miles²
Caspian Sea	Asia	371,000	143,000
Lake Baikal	Russia	30,500	11,780
Tonlé Sap	Cambodia	20,000	7,700
Lake Balqash	Kazakhstan	18,500	7,100
Aral Sea	Kazakhstan/Uzbekistan	17,160	6,625

Africa

		km²	miles²
Lake Victoria	East Africa	68,000	26,300
Lake Tanganyika	Central Africa	33,000	13,000
Lake Malawi/Nyasa	East Africa	29,600	11,430
Lake Chad	Central Africa	25,000	9,700
Lake Bangweulu	Zambia	9,840	3,800
Lake Turkana	Ethiopia/Kenya	8,500	3,290

Australia

		km²	miles²
Lake Eyre	Australia	8,900	3,400
Lake Torrens	Australia	5,800	2,200
Lake Gairdner	Australia	4,800	1,900

North America

		km²	miles²
Lake Superior	Canada/USA	82,350	31,800
Lake Huron	Canada/USA	59,600	23,010
Lake Michigan	USA	58,000	22,400
Great Bear Lake	Canada	31,800	12,280
Great Slave Lake	Canada	28,500	11,000
Lake Erie	Canada/USA	25,700	9,900
Lake Winnipeg	Canada	24,400	9,400
Lake Ontario	Canada/USA	19,500	7,500
Lake Nicaragua	Nicaragua	8,200	3,200

South America

		km²	miles²
Lake Titicaca	Bolivia/Peru	8,300	3,200
Lake Poopo	Bolivia	2,800	1,100

Islands

Europe

		km²	miles²
Great Britain	UK	229,880	88,700
Iceland	Atlantic Ocean	103,000	39,800
Ireland	Ireland/UK	84,400	32,600
Novaya Zemlya (N.)	Russia	48,200	18,600
Sicily	Italy	25,500	9,800
Corsica	France	8,700	3,400

Asia

		km²	miles²
Borneo	South-east Asia	744,360	287,400
Sumatra	Indonesia	473,600	182,860
Honshu	Japan	230,500	88,980
Sulawesi (Celebes)	Indonesia	189,000	73,000
Java	Indonesia	126,700	48,900
Luzon	Philippines	104,700	40,400
Hokkaido	Japan	78,400	30,300

Africa

		km²	miles²
Madagascar	Indian Ocean	587,040	226,660
Socotra	Indian Ocean	3,600	1,400
Réunion	Indian Ocean	2,500	965

Oceania

		km²	miles²
New Guinea	Indonesia/Papua NG	821,030	317,000
New Zealand (S.)	Pacific Ocean	150,500	58,100
New Zealand (N.)	Pacific Ocean	114,700	44,300
Tasmania	Australia	67,800	26,200
Hawai'i	Pacific Ocean	10,450	4,000

North America

		km²	miles²
Greenland	Atlantic Ocean	2,175,600	839,800
Baffin Is.	Canada	508,000	196,100
Victoria Is.	Canada	212,200	81,900
Ellesmere Is.	Canada	212,000	81,800
Cuba	Caribbean Sea	110,860	42,800
Hispaniola	Dominican Rep./Haiti	76,200	29,400
Jamaica	Caribbean Sea	11,400	4,400
Puerto Rico	Atlantic Ocean	8,900	3,400

South America

		km²	miles²
Tierra del Fuego	Argentina/Chile	47,000	18,100
Falkland Is. (E.)	Atlantic Ocean	6,800	2,600

User Guide

The reference maps which form the main body of this atlas have been prepared in accordance with the highest standards of international cartography to provide an accurate and detailed representation of the Earth. The scales and projections used have been carefully chosen to give balanced coverage of the world, while emphasizing the most densely populated and economically significant regions. A hallmark of Philip's mapping is the use of hill shading and relief colouring to create a graphic impression of landforms: this makes the maps exceptionally easy to read. However, knowledge of the key features employed in the construction and presentation of the maps will enable the reader to derive the fullest benefit from the atlas.

Map sequence

The atlas covers the Earth continent by continent: first Europe; then its land neighbour Asia (mapped north before south, in a clockwise sequence), then Africa, Australia and Oceania, North America and South America. This is the classic arrangement adopted by most cartographers since the 16th century. For each continent, there are maps at a variety of scales. First, physical relief and political maps of the whole continent; then a series of larger-scale maps of the regions within the continent, each followed, where required, by still larger-scale maps of the most important or densely populated areas. The governing principle is that by turning the pages of the atlas, the reader moves steadily from north to south through each continent, with each map overlapping its neighbours.

Map presentation

With very few exceptions (for example, for the Arctic and Antarctica), the maps are drawn with north at the top, regardless of whether they are presented upright or sideways on the page. In the borders will be found the map title; a locator diagram showing the area covered; continuation arrows showing the page numbers for maps of adjacent areas; the scale; the projection used; the degrees of latitude and longitude; and the letters and figures used in the index for locating place names and geographical features. Physical relief maps also have a height reference panel identifying the colours used for each layer of contouring.

Map symbols

Each map contains a vast amount of detail which can only be conveyed clearly and accurately by the use of symbols. Points and circles of varying sizes locate and identify the relative importance of towns and cities; different styles of type are employed for administrative, geographical and regional place names. A variety of pictorial symbols denote features such as glaciers and marshes, as well as man-made structures including roads, railways, airports and canals.

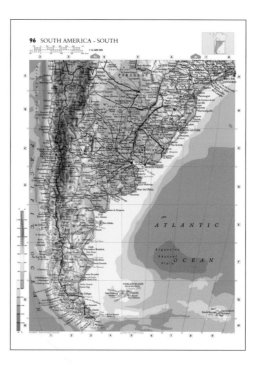

International borders are shown by red lines. Where neighbouring countries are in dispute, for example in the Middle East, the maps show the *de facto* boundary between nations, regardless of the legal or historical situation. The symbols are explained on the first page of the World Maps section of the atlas.

Map scales

The scale of each map is given in the numerical form known as the 'representative fraction'. The first figure is always one, signifying one unit of distance on the map; the second figure, usually in millions, is the number by which the map unit must be multiplied to give the equivalent distance on the Earth's surface. Calculations can easily be made in centimetres and kilometres, by dividing the Earth units figure by 100 000 (i.e. deleting the last five 0s). Thus 1:1 000 000 means 1 cm = 10 km. The calculation for inches and miles is more laborious, but 1 000 000 divided by 63 360 (the number of inches in a mile) shows that the ratio 1:1 000 000 means approximately 1 inch = 16 miles. The table below provides distance equivalents for scales down to 1:50 000 000.

LARGE SCALE		
1:1 000 000	1 cm = 10 km	1 inch = 16 miles
1:2 500 000	1 cm = 25 km	1 inch = 39.5 miles
1:5 000 000	1 cm = 50 km	1 inch = 79 miles
1:6 000 000	1 cm = 60 km	1 inch = 95 miles
1:8 000 000	1 cm = 80 km	1 inch = 126 miles
1:10 000 000	1 cm = 100 km	1 inch = 158 miles
1:15 000 000	1 cm = 150 km	1 inch = 237 miles
1:20 000 000	1 cm = 200 km	1 inch = 316 miles
1:50 000 000	1 cm = 500 km	1 inch = 790 miles
SMALL SCALE		

Measuring distances

Although each map is accompanied by a scale bar, distances cannot always be measured with confidence because of the distortions involved in portraying the curved surface of the Earth on a flat page. As a general rule, the larger the map scale (i.e. the lower the number of Earth units in the representative fraction), the more accurate and reliable will be the distance measured. On small-scale maps such as those of the world and of entire continents, measurement may only be accurate along the 'standard parallels', or central axes, and should not be attempted without considering the map projection.

Latitude and longitude

Accurate positioning of individual points on the Earth's surface is made possible by reference to the geometrical system of latitude and longitude. Latitude *parallels* are drawn west–east around the Earth and numbered by degrees north and south of the Equator, which is designated 0° of latitude. Longitude *meridians* are drawn north–south and numbered by degrees east and west of the *prime meridian*, 0° of longitude, which passes through Greenwich in England. By referring to these co-ordinates and their subdivisions of minutes ($\frac{1}{60}$th of a degree) and seconds ($\frac{1}{60}$th of a minute), any place on Earth can be located to within a few hundred metres. Latitude and longitude are indicated by blue lines on the maps; they are straight or curved according to the projection employed. Reference to these lines is the easiest way of determining the relative positions of places on different maps, and for plotting compass directions.

Name forms

For ease of reference, both English and local name forms appear in the atlas. Oceans, seas and countries are shown in English throughout the atlas; country names may be abbreviated to their commonly accepted form (for example, Germany, not The Federal Republic of Germany). Conventional English forms are also used for place names on the smaller-scale maps of the continents. However, local name forms are used on all large-scale and regional maps, with the English form given in brackets only for important cities – the large-scale map of Russia and Central Asia thus shows Moskva (Moscow). For countries which do not use a Roman script, place names have been transcribed according to the systems adopted by the British and US Geographic Names Authorities. For China, the Pin Yin system has been used, with some more widely known forms appearing in brackets, as with Beijing (Peking). Both English and local names appear in the index, the English form being cross-referenced to the local form.

THE
WORLD
IN FOCUS

Planet Earth	2	Water and Vegetation	12	Quality of Life	22
Restless Earth	4	Environment	14	Energy	24
Landforms	6	Population	16	Production	26
Oceans	8	The Human Family	18	Trade	28
Climate	10	Wealth	20	Travel and Tourism	30

Planet Earth

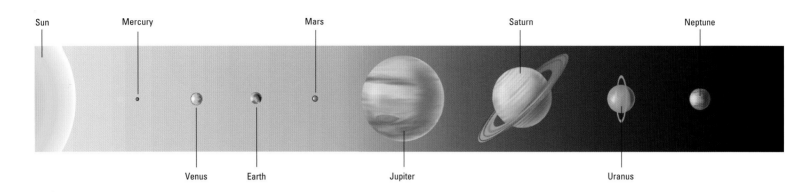

The Solar System

A minute part of one of the billions of galaxies (collections of stars) that populate the Universe, the Solar System lies about 26,000 light-years from the centre of our own Galaxy, the 'Milky Way'. Thought to be about 5 billion years old, it consists of a central Sun with eight planets and their moons revolving around it, attracted by its gravitational pull. The planets orbit the Sun in the same direction – anti-clockwise when viewed from above the Sun's north pole – and almost in the same plane. Their orbital distances, however, vary enormously.

The Sun's diameter is 109 times that of the Earth, and the temperature at its core – caused by continuous thermonuclear fusions of hydrogen into helium – is estimated to be 15 million degrees Celsius. It is the Solar System's only source of light and heat.

Profile of the Planets

	Mean distance from Sun (million km)	Mass (Earth = 1)	Period of orbit (Earth days/years)	Period of rotation (Earth days)	Equatorial diameter (km)	Number of known satellites*
Mercury	57.9	0.06	87.97 days	58.65	4,879	0
Venus	108.2	0.82	224.7 days	243.02	12,104	0
Earth	149.6	1.00	365.3 days	1.00	12,756	1
Mars	227.9	0.11	687.0 days	1.029	6,792	2
Jupiter	778	317.8	11.86 years	0.411	142,984	63
Saturn	1,427	95.2	29.45 years	0.428	120,536	62
Uranus	2,871	14.5	84.02 years	0.720	51,118	27
Neptune	4,498	17.2	164.8 years	0.673	49,528	13

* Number of known satellites at mid-2010

All planetary orbits are elliptical in form, but only Mercury follows a path that deviates noticeably from a circular one. In 2006, Pluto was demoted from its former status as a planet and is now regarded as a member of the Kuiper Belt of icy bodies at the fringes of the Solar System.

The Seasons

Seasons occur because the Earth's axis is tilted at an angle of approximately 23½°. When the northern hemisphere is tilted to a maximum extent towards the Sun, on 21 June, the Sun is overhead at the Tropic of Cancer (latitude 23½° North). This is midsummer, or the summer solstice, in the northern hemisphere.

On 22 or 23 September, the Sun is overhead at the Equator, and day and night are of equal length throughout the world. This is the autumnal equinox in the northern hemisphere. On 21 or 22 December, the Sun is overhead at the Tropic of Capricorn (23½° South), the winter solstice in the northern hemisphere. The overhead Sun then tracks north until, on 21 March, it is overhead at the Equator. This is the spring (vernal) equinox in the northern hemisphere.

In the southern hemisphere, the seasons are the reverse of those in the north.

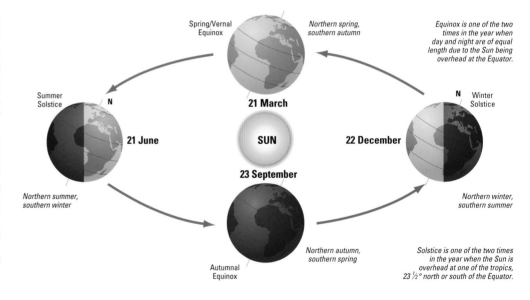

Day and Night

The Sun appears to rise in the east, reach its highest point at noon, and then set in the west, to be followed by night. In reality, it is not the Sun that is moving but the Earth rotating from west to east. The moment when the Sun's upper limb first appears above the horizon is termed sunrise; the moment when the Sun's upper limb disappears below the horizon is sunset.

At the summer solstice in the northern hemisphere (21 June), the Arctic has total daylight and the Antarctic total darkness. The opposite occurs at the winter solstice (21 or 22 December). At the Equator, the length of day and night are almost equal all year.

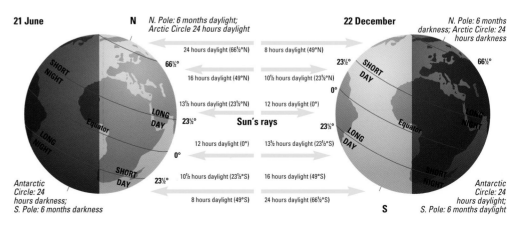

Time

Year: The time taken by the Earth to revolve around the Sun, or 365.24 days.

Leap Year: A calendar year of 366 days, 29 February being the additional day. It offsets the difference between the calendar and the solar year.

Month: The 12 calendar months of the year are approximately equal in length to a lunar month.

Week: An artificial period of 7 days, not based on astronomical time.

Day: The time taken by the Earth to complete one rotation on its axis.

Hour: 24 hours make one day. The day is divided into hours a.m. (ante meridiem or before noon) and p.m. (post meridiem or after noon), although most timetables now use the 24-hour system, from midnight to midnight.

Sunrise

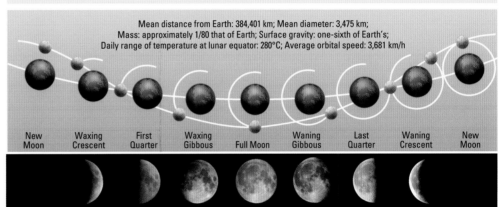

Sunset

The Moon

The Moon rotates more slowly than the Earth, taking just over 27 days to make one complete rotation on its axis. This corresponds to the Moon's orbital period around the Earth, and therefore the Moon always

Phases of the Moon

Mean distance from Earth: 384,401 km; Mean diameter: 3,475 km; Mass: approximately 1/80 that of Earth; Surface gravity: one-sixth of Earth's; Daily range of temperature at lunar equator: 280°C; Average orbital speed: 3,681 km/h

| New Moon | Waxing Crescent | First Quarter | Waxing Gibbous | Full Moon | Waning Gibbous | Last Quarter | Waning Crescent | New Moon |

presents the same hemisphere towards us; some 41% of the Moon's far side is never visible from the Earth. The interval between one New Moon and the next is 29½ days – this is called a lunation, or lunar month.

The Moon shines only by reflected sunlight, and emits no light of its own. During each lunation the Moon displays a complete cycle of phases, caused by the changing angle of illumination from the Sun.

Eclipses

When the Moon passes between the Sun and the Earth, the Sun becomes partially eclipsed (1). A partial eclipse becomes a total eclipse if the Moon proceeds to cover the Sun completely (2) and the dark central part of the lunar shadow touches the Earth. The broad geographical zone covered by the Moon's outer shadow (P), has only a very small central area (often less than 100 km wide) that experiences totality. Totality can never last for more than 7½ minutes at maximum, but is usually much briefer than this. Lunar eclipses take place when the Moon moves through the shadow of the Earth, and can be partial or total. Any single location on Earth can experience a maximum of four solar and three lunar eclipses in any single year, while a total solar eclipse occurs an average of once every 360 years for any given location.

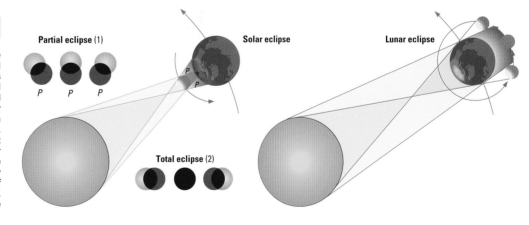

Tides

The daily rise and fall of the ocean's tides are the result of the gravitational pull of the Moon and that of the Sun, though the effect of the latter is not as strong as that of the Moon. This effect is greatest on the hemisphere facing the Moon and causes a tidal 'bulge'.

Spring tides occur when the Sun, Earth and Moon are aligned; high tides are at their highest, and low tides fall to their lowest. When the Moon and Sun are furthest out of line (near the Moon's First and Last Quarters), neap tides occur, producing the smallest range between high and low tides.

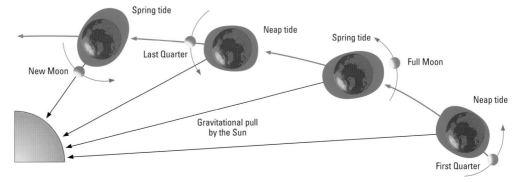

Restless Earth

The Earth's Structure

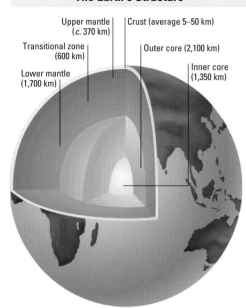

- Upper mantle (c. 370 km)
- Crust (average 5–50 km)
- Transitional zone (600 km)
- Outer core (2,100 km)
- Lower mantle (1,700 km)
- Inner core (1,350 km)

Continental Drift

About 200 million years ago the original Pangaea landmass began to split into two continental groups, which further separated over time to produce the present-day configuration.

180 million years ago

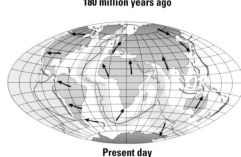

135 million years ago

- ▬ Trench
- ▬ Rift
- New ocean floor
- Zones of slippage

Present day

Notable Earthquakes Since 1900

Year	Location	Richter Scale	Deaths
1906	San Francisco, USA	8.3	3,000
1906	Valparaiso, Chile	8.6	22,000
1908	Messina, Italy	7.5	83,000
1915	Avezzano, Italy	7.5	30,000
1920	Gansu (Kansu), China	8.6	180,000
1923	Yokohama, Japan	8.3	143,000
1927	Nan Shan, China	8.3	200,000
1932	Gansu (Kansu), China	7.6	70,000
1933	Sanriku, Japan	8.9	2,990
1934	Bihar, India/Nepal	8.4	10,700
1935	Quetta, India (now Pakistan)	7.5	60,000
1939	Chillan, Chile	8.3	28,000
1939	Erzincan, Turkey	7.9	30,000
1960	S. W. Chile	9.5	2,200
1960	Agadir, Morocco	5.8	12,000
1962	Khorasan, Iran	7.1	12,230
1964	Anchorage, USA	9.2	125
1968	N. E. Iran	7.4	12,000
1970	N. Peru	7.8	70,000
1972	Managua, Nicaragua	6.2	5,000
1974	N. Pakistan	6.3	5,200
1976	Guatemala	7.5	22,500
1976	Tangshan, China	8.2	255,000
1978	Tabas, Iran	7.7	25,000
1980	El Asnam, Algeria	7.3	20,000
1980	S. Italy	7.2	4,800
1985	Mexico City, Mexico	8.1	4,200
1988	N.W. Armenia	6.8	55,000
1990	N. Iran	7.7	36,000
1993	Maharashtra, India	6.4	30,000
1994	Los Angeles, USA	6.6	51
1995	Kobe, Japan	7.2	5,000
1995	Sakhalin Is., Russia	7.5	2,000
1997	N. E. Iran	7.1	2,400
1998	Takhar, Afghanistan	6.1	4,200
1998	Rostaq, Afghanistan	7.0	5,000
1998	Izmit, Turkey	7.4	15,000
1999	Taipei, Taiwan	7.6	1,700
2001	Gujarat, India	7.7	14,000
2002	Baghlan, Afghanistan	6.1	1,000
2003	Boumerdes, Algeria	6.8	2,200
2003	Bam, Iran	6.6	30,000
2004	Sumatra, Indonesia	9.0	250,000
2005	N. Pakistan	7.6	74,000
2006	Java, Indonesia	6.4	6,200
2007	S. Peru	8.0	600
2008	Sichuan, China	7.9	70,000
2010	Haiti	7.0	230,000

Earthquakes

Earthquake magnitude is usually rated according to either the Richter or the Modified Mercalli scale, both devised by seismologists in the 1930s. The Richter scale measures absolute earthquake power with mathematical precision: each step upwards represents a tenfold increase in shockwave amplitude. Theoretically, there is no upper limit, but most of the largest earthquakes measured have been rated at between 8.8 and 8.9. The 12–point Mercalli scale, based on observed effects, is often more meaningful, ranging from I (earthquakes noticed only by seismographs) to XII (total destruction); intermediate points include V (people awakened at night; unstable objects overturned), VII (collapse of ordinary buildings; chimneys and monuments fall), and IX (conspicuous cracks in ground; serious damage to reservoirs).

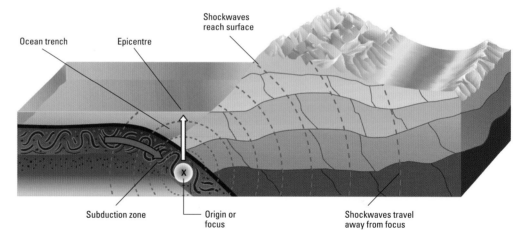

- Shockwaves reach surface
- Ocean trench
- Epicentre
- Subduction zone
- Origin or focus
- Shockwaves travel away from focus

Structure and Earthquakes

- Mobile land areas
- Submarine zones of mobile land areas
- Stable land platforms
- Submarine extensions of stable land platforms
- Mid-oceanic volcanic ridges
- Oceanic platforms

1976 ○   Principal earthquakes and dates (since 1900)

Earthquakes are a series of rapid vibrations originating from the slipping or faulting of parts of the Earth's crust when stresses within build up to breaking point. They usually happen at depths varying from 8 km to 30 km. Severe earthquakes cause extensive damage when they take place in populated areas, destroying structures and severing communications. Most initial loss of life occurs due to secondary causes such as falling masonry, fires and flooding.

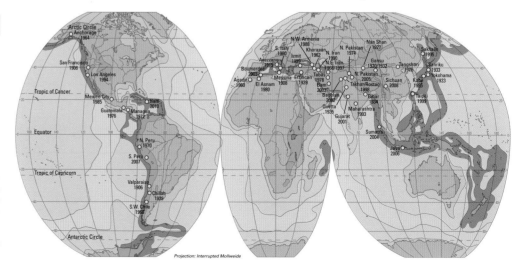

Projection: Interrupted Mollweide

Plate Tectonics

— Plate boundaries   PACIFIC Major plates

➤ Direction of plate movements and rate of movement (cm/year)

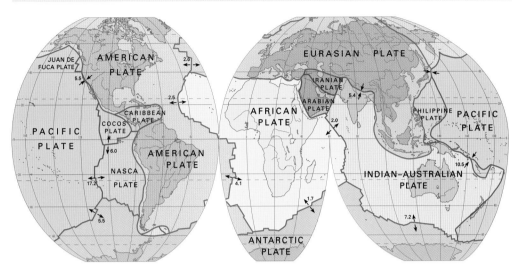

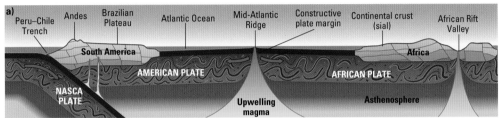

a)
Peru–Chile Trench | Andes | Brazilian Plateau | Atlantic Ocean | Mid-Atlantic Ridge | Constructive plate margin | Continental crust (sial) | African Rift Valley

South America

AMERICAN PLATE

NASCA PLATE

AFRICAN PLATE

Africa

Upwelling magma

Asthenosphere

The drifting of the continents is a feature that is unique to planet Earth. The complementary, almost jigsaw-puzzle fit of the coastlines on each side of the Atlantic Ocean inspired Alfred Wegener's theory of continental drift in 1915. The theory suggested that the ancient supercontinent, which Wegener named Pangaea, incorporated all of the Earth's landmasses and gradually split up to form today's continents.

The original debate about continental drift was a prelude to a more radical idea: plate tectonics. The basic theory is that the Earth's crust is made up of a series of rigid plates which float on a soft layer of the mantle and are moved about by continental convection currents within the Earth's interior. These plates diverge and converge along margins marked by seismic activity. Plates diverge from mid-ocean ridges where molten lava pushes upwards and forces the plates apart at rates of up to 40 mm [1.6 in] a year.

The three diagrams, left, give some examples of plate boundaries from around the world. Diagram (a) shows sea-floor spreading at the Mid-Atlantic Ridge as the American and African plates slowly diverge. The same thing is happening in (b) where sea-floor spreading at the Mid-Indian Ocean Ridge is forcing the Indian–Australian plate to collide into the Eurasian plate. In (c) oceanic crust (sima) is being subducted beneath lighter continental crust (sial).

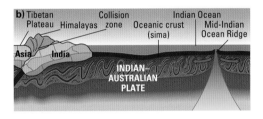

b) Tibetan Plateau | Himalayas | Collision zone | Oceanic crust (sima) | Indian Ocean | Mid-Indian Ocean Ridge

Asia   India

INDIAN–AUSTRALIAN PLATE

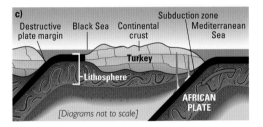

c)
Destructive plate margin | Black Sea | Continental crust | Subduction zone | Mediterranean Sea

Turkey

Lithosphere

AFRICAN PLATE

[Diagrams not to scale]

Volcanoes

Volcanoes occur when hot liquefied rock beneath the Earth's crust is pushed up by pressure to the surface as molten lava. Some volcanoes erupt in an explosive way, throwing out rocks and ash, whilst others are effusive and lava flows out of the vent. There are volcanoes which are both, such as Mount Fuji. An accumulation of lava and cinders creates cones of variable size and shape. As a result of many eruptions over centuries, Mount Etna in Sicily has a circumference of more than 120 km [75 miles].

Climatologists believe that volcanic ash, if ejected high into the atmosphere, can influence temperature and weather for several years afterwards. The 1991 eruption of Mount Pinatubo in the Philippines ejected more than 20 million tonnes of dust and ash 32 km [20 miles] into the atmosphere and is believed to have accelerated ozone depletion over a large part of the globe.

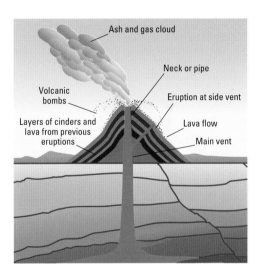

Ash and gas cloud

Neck or pipe

Volcanic bombs

Eruption at side vent

Layers of cinders and lava from previous eruptions

Lava flow

Main vent

Distribution of Volcanoes

Volcanoes today may be the subject of considerable scientific study but they remain both dramatic and unpredictable: in 1991 Mount Pinatubo, 100 km [62 miles] north of the Philippines capital Manila, suddenly burst into life after lying dormant for more than six centuries. Most of the world's active volcanoes occur in a belt around the Pacific Ocean, on the edge of the Pacific plate, called the 'ring of fire'. Indonesia has the greatest concentration with 90 volcanoes, 12 of which are active. The most famous, Krakatoa, erupted in 1883 with such force that the resulting tidal wave killed 36,000 people, and tremors were felt as far away as Australia.

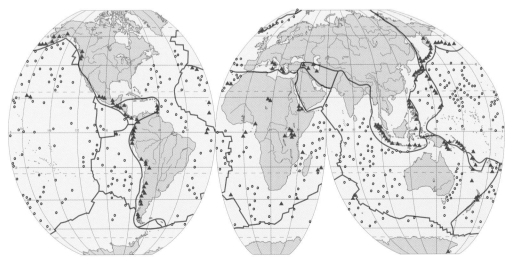

○ Submarine volcanoes

▲ Land volcanoes active since 1700

— Boundaries of tectonic plates

Landforms

The Rock Cycle

James Hutton first proposed the rock cycle in the late 1700s after he observed the slow but steady effects of erosion.

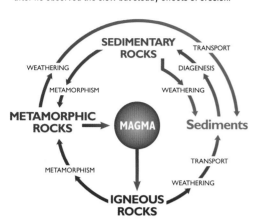

Above and below the surface of the oceans, the features of the Earth's crust are constantly changing. The phenomenal forces generated by convection currents in the molten core of our planet carry the vast segments or 'plates' of the crust across the globe in an endless cycle of creation and destruction. A continent may travel little more than 25 mm [1 in] per year, yet in the vast span of geological time this process throws up giant mountain ranges and creates new land.

Destruction of the landscape, however, begins as soon as it is formed. Wind, water, ice and sea, the main agents of erosion, mount a constant assault that even the most resistant rocks cannot withstand. Mountain peaks may dwindle by as little as a few millimetres each year, but if they are not uplifted by further movements of the crust they will eventually be reduced to rubble and transported away.

Water is the most powerful agent of erosion – it has been estimated that 100 billion tonnes of sediment are washed into the oceans every year.

Three Asian rivers account for 20% of this total: the Huang He, in China, and the Brahmaputra and the Ganges in Bangladesh.

Rivers and glaciers, like the sea itself, generate much of their effect through abrasion – pounding the land with the debris they carry with them. But as well as destroying they also create new landforms, many of them spectacular: vast deltas like those of the Mississippi and the Nile, or the deep fjords cut by glaciers in British Columbia, Norway and New Zealand.

Geologists once considered that landscapes evolved from 'young', newly uplifted mountainous areas, through a 'mature' hilly stage, to an 'old age' stage when the land was reduced to an almost flat plain, or peneplain. This theory, called the 'cycle of erosion', fell into disuse when it became evident that so many factors, including the effects of plate tectonics and climatic change, constantly interrupt the cycle, which takes no account of the highly complex interactions that shape the surface of our planet.

Mountain Building

Mountains are formed when pressures on the Earth's crust caused by continental drift become so intense that the surface buckles or cracks. This happens where oceanic crust is subducted by continental crust or, more dramatically, where two tectonic plates collide: the Rockies, Andes, Alps, Urals and Himalayas resulted from such impacts. These are all known as fold mountains because they were formed by the compression of the rocks, forcing the surface to bend and fold like a crumpled rug. The Himalayas were formed from the folded former sediments of the Tethys Sea, which was trapped in the collision zone between the Indian and Eurasian plates.

The other main mountain-building process occurs when the crust fractures to create faults, allowing rock to be forced upwards in large blocks; or when the pressure of magma within the crust forces the surface to bulge into a dome, or erupts to form a volcano. Large mountain ranges may reveal a combination of these features; the Alps, for example, have been compressed so violently that the folds are fragmented by numerous faults and intrusions of molten igneous rock.

Over millions of years, even the greatest mountain ranges can be reduced by the agents of erosion (most notably rivers) to a low rugged landscape known as a peneplain.

Types of faults: Faults occur where the crust is being stretched or compressed so violently that the rock strata break in a horizontal or vertical movement. They are classified by the direction in which the blocks of rock have moved. A normal fault results when a vertical movement causes the surface to break apart; compression causes a reverse fault. Horizontal movement causes shearing, known as a strike-slip fault. When the rock breaks in two places, the central block may be pushed up in a horst fault, or sink (creating a rift valley) in a graben fault.

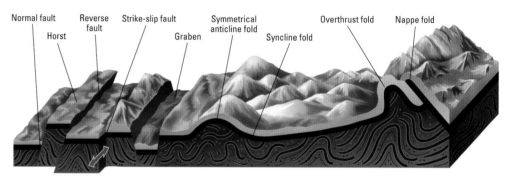

Types of fold: Folds occur when rock strata are squeezed and compressed. They are common, therefore, at destructive plate margins and where plates have collided, forcing the rocks to buckle into mountain ranges. Geographers give different names to the degrees of fold that result from continuing pressure on the rock. A simple fold may be symmetric, with even slopes on either side, but as the pressure builds up, one slope becomes steeper and the fold becomes asymmetric. Later, the ridge or 'anticline' at the top of the fold may slide over the lower ground or 'syncline' to form a recumbent fold. Eventually, the rock strata may break under the pressure to form an overthrust and finally a nappe fold.

Continental Glaciation

Ice sheets were at their greatest extent about 200,000 years ago. The maximum advance of the last Ice Age was about 18,000 years ago, when ice covered virtually all of Canada and reached as far south as the Bristol Channel in Britain.

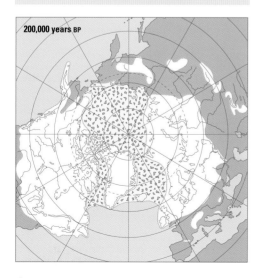

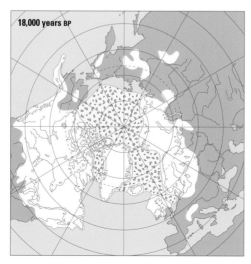

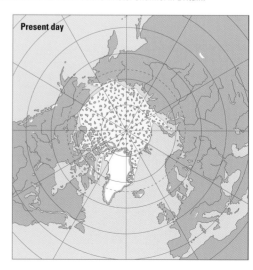

Natural Landforms

A stylized diagram to show some of the major natural landforms found in the mid-latitudes.

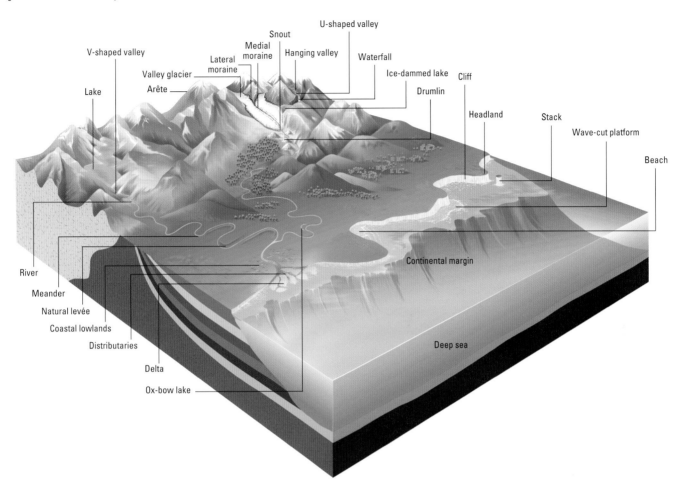

Desert Landscapes

The popular image that deserts are all huge expanses of sand is wrong. Despite harsh conditions, deserts contain some of the most varied and interesting landscapes in the world. They are also one of the most extensive environments – the hot and cold deserts together cover almost 40% of the Earth's surface.

The three types of hot desert are known by their Arabic names: sand desert, called *erg*, covers only about one-fifth of the world's desert; the rest is divided between *hammada* (areas of bare rock) and *reg* (broad plains covered by loose gravel or pebbles).

In areas of *erg*, such as the Namib Desert, the shape of the dunes reflects the character of local winds. Where winds are constant in direction, crescent-shaped *barchan* dunes form. In areas of bare rock, wind-blown sand is a major agent of erosion. The erosion is mainly confined to within 2 m [6.5 ft] of the surface, producing characteristic mushroom-shaped rocks.

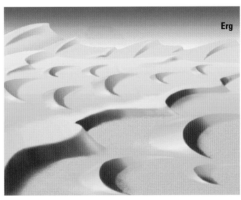

Surface Processes

Catastrophic changes to natural landforms are periodically caused by such phenomena as avalanches, landslides and volcanic eruptions, but most of the processes that shape the Earth's surface operate extremely slowly in human terms. One estimate, based on a study in the United States, suggested that 1 m [3 ft] of land was removed from the entire surface of the country, on average, every 29,500 years. However, the time-scale varies from 1,300 years to 154,200 years depending on the terrain and climate.

In hot, dry climates, mechanical weathering, a result of rapid temperature changes, causes the outer layers of rock to peel away, while in cold mountainous regions, boulders are prised apart when water freezes in cracks in rocks. Chemical weathering, at its greatest in warm, humid regions, is responsible for hollowing out limestone caves and decomposing granites.

The erosion of soil and rock is greatest on sloping land and the steeper the slope, the greater the tendency for mass wasting – the movement of soil and rock downhill under the influence of gravity. The mechanisms of mass wasting (ranging from very slow to very rapid) vary with the type of material, but the presence of water as a lubricant is usually an important factor.

Running water is the world's leading agent of erosion and transportation. The energy of a river depends on several factors, including its velocity and volume, and its erosive power is at its peak when it is in full flood. Sea waves also exert tremendous erosive power during storms when they hurl pebbles against the shore, undercutting cliffs and hollowing out caves.

Glacier ice forms in mountain hollows and spills out to form valley glaciers, which transport rocks shattered by frost action. As glaciers move, rocks embedded into the ice erode steep-sided, U-shaped valleys. Evidence of glaciation in mountain regions includes cirques, knife-edged ridges, or arêtes, and pyramidal peaks.

Oceans

The Great Oceans

Relative sizes of the world's oceans

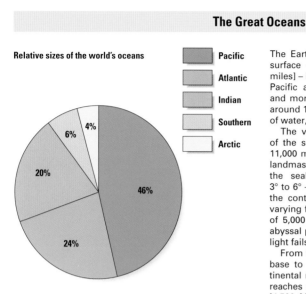

Legend:
- Pacific
- Atlantic
- Indian
- Southern
- Arctic

Pie chart values: 46%, 24%, 20%, 6%, 4%

From ancient times to about the 15th century, the legendary 'Seven Seas' comprised the Red Sea, Mediterranean Sea, Persian Gulf, Black Sea, Adriatic Sea, Caspian Sea and Indian Sea.

The Earth is a watery planet: more than 70% of its surface – over 360,000,000 sq km [140,000,000 sq miles] – is covered by the oceans and seas. The mighty Pacific alone accounts for nearly 36% of the total, and more than 46% of the sea area. Gravity holds in around 1,400 million cubic km [320 million cubic miles] of water, of which over 97% is saline.

The vast underwater world starts in the shallows of the seaside and plunges to depths of more than 11,000 m [36,000 ft]. The continental shelf, part of the landmass, drops gently to around 200 m [650 ft]; here the seabed falls away suddenly at an angle of 3° to 6° – the continental slope. The third stage, called the continental rise, is more gradual with gradients varying from 1 in 100 to 1 in 700. At an average depth of 5,000 m [16,500 ft] there begins the aptly-named abyssal plain – massive submarine depths where sunlight fails to penetrate and few creatures can survive.

From these plains rise volcanoes which, taken from base to top, rival and even surpass the tallest continental mountains in height. Mauna Kea, on Hawai'i, reaches a total of 10,203 m [33,400 ft], some 1,355 m [4,500 ft] higher than Mount Everest, though scarcely 40% is visible above sea level.

In addition, there are underwater mountain chains up to 1,000 km [600 miles] across, whose peaks sometimes appear above sea level as islands, such as Iceland and Tristan da Cunha.

The Ocean Depths

Average and maximum depths of the world's great oceans, in metres

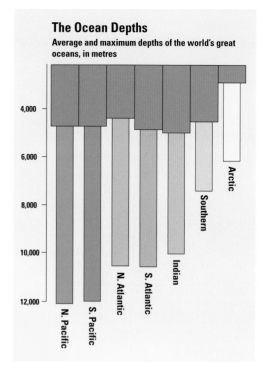

Bar chart labels (depth axis): 4,000 / 6,000 / 8,000 / 10,000 / 12,000

Ocean labels: N. Pacific, S. Pacific, N. Atlantic, S. Atlantic, Indian, Southern, Arctic

Ocean Currents

January ocean currents (Northern Hemisphere: winter; Southern Hemisphere: summer)

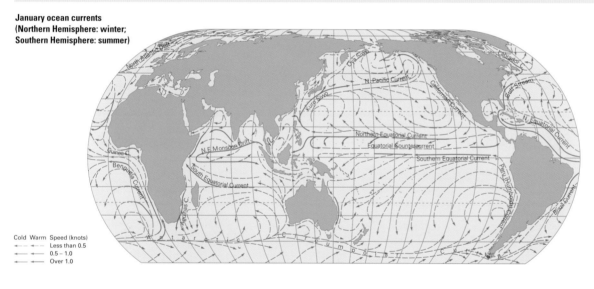

Cold Warm Speed (knots)
- Less than 0.5
- 0.5 – 1.0
- Over 1.0

July ocean currents (Northern Hemisphere: summer; Southern Hemisphere: winter)

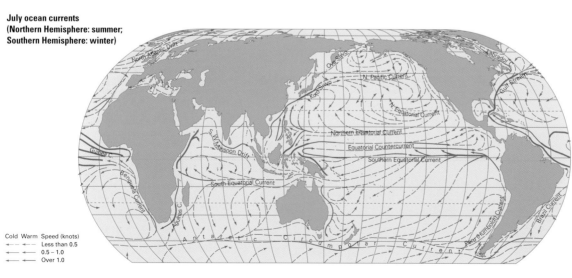

Cold Warm Speed (knots)
- Less than 0.5
- 0.5 – 1.0
- Over 1.0

Moving immense quantities of energy as well as billions of tonnes of water every hour, the ocean currents are a vital part of the great heat engine that drives the Earth's climate. They themselves are produced by a twofold mechanism. At the surface, winds push huge masses of water before them; in the deep ocean, below an abrupt temperature gradient that separates the churning surface waters from the still depths, density variations cause slow vertical movements.

The pattern of circulation of the great surface currents is determined by the displacement known as the Coriolis effect. As the Earth turns beneath a moving object – whether it is a tennis ball or a vast mass of water – it appears to be deflected to one side. The deflection is most obvious near the Equator, where the Earth's surface is spinning eastwards at 1,700 km/h [1,050 mph]; currents moving polewards are curved clockwise in the northern hemisphere and anti-clockwise in the southern.

The result is a system of spinning circles known as 'gyres'. The Coriolis effect piles up water on the left of each gyre, creating a narrow, fast-moving stream that is matched by a slower, broader returning current on the right. North and south of the Equator, the fastest currents are located in the west and in the east respectively. In each case, warm water moves from the Equator and cold water returns to it. Cold currents often bring an upwelling of nutrients with them, supporting the world's most economically important fisheries.

Depending on the prevailing winds, some currents on or near the Equator may reverse their direction in the course of the year – a seasonal variation on which Asian monsoon rains depend, and whose occasional failure can bring disaster to millions of people.

World Fishing Areas

Main commercial fishing areas (numbered FAO regions)

Catch by top marine fishing areas, million tonnes (2006)

1.	Pacific, NW	[61]	21.2	22.6%
2.	Pacific, SE	[87]	14.7	15.7%
3.	Pacific, WC	[71]	10.7	11.4%
4.	Atlantic, NE	[27]	9.7	10.3%
5.	Indian, E	[57]	5.6	6.0%
6.	Indian, W	[51]	4.4	4.7%
7.	Atlantic, EC	[34]	3.5	3.7%
8.	Pacific, NE	[67]	3.1	3.3%
9.	Atlantic, NW	[21]	2.2	2.3%
10.	Atlantic, SW	[41]	1.8	1.9%

 Principal fishing areas

Leading fishing nations

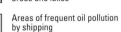

China 16.3% Peru 8% Indonesia 5.4% USA 5.3% Japan 4.7% India 4.4% Chile 4.2%

World total (2007): 90.1 million tonnes
(Marine catch 90.3% : Inland catch 9.7%)

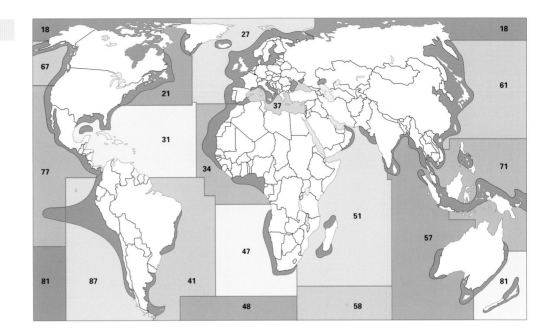

Marine Pollution

Sources of marine oil pollution

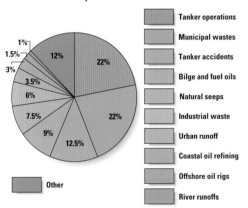

1% 1.5% 3% 3.5% 6% 7.5% 9% 12.5% 22% 22% 12%

- Tanker operations
- Municipal wastes
- Tanker accidents
- Bilge and fuel oils
- Natural seeps
- Industrial waste
- Urban runoff
- Coastal oil refining
- Offshore oil rigs
- Other
- River runoffs

Oil Spills

Major oil spills from tankers and combined carriers

Year	Vessel	Location	Spill (barrels)*	Cause
1979	Atlantic Empress	West Indies	1,890,000	collision
1983	Castillo De Bellver	South Africa	1,760,000	fire
1978	Amoco Cadiz	France	1,628,000	grounding
1991	Haven	Italy	1,029,000	explosion
1988	Odyssey	Canada	1,000,000	fire
1967	Torrey Canyon	UK	909,000	grounding
1972	Sea Star	Gulf of Oman	902,250	collision
1977	Hawaiian Patriot	Hawaiian Is.	742,500	fire
1979	Independenta	Turkey	696,350	collision
1993	Braer	UK	625,000	grounding
1996	Sea Empress	UK	515,000	grounding
2002	Prestige	Spain	463,250	storm

Other sources of major oil spills

Year	Vessel	Location	Spill (barrels)*	Cause
1983	Nowruz oilfield	Persian Gulf	4,250,000[†]	war
1979	Ixtoc 1 oilwell	Gulf of Mexico	4,200,000	blow-out
2010	Deepwater Horizon	Gulf of Mexico	3–8,700,000[†]	blow-out

* 1 barrel = 0.136 tonnes/159 lit./35 Imperial gal./42 US gal. [†] estimated

River Pollution

Sources of river pollution, USA

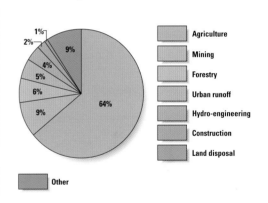

1% 2% 4% 5% 6% 9% 9% 64%

- Agriculture
- Mining
- Forestry
- Urban runoff
- Hydro-engineering
- Construction
- Land disposal
- Other

Water Pollution

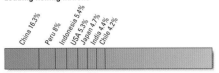

Severely polluted sea areas and lakes

Polluted sea areas and lakes

Areas of frequent oil pollution by shipping

▲ Major oil tanker spills

▲ Major oil rig blow-outs

▼ Offshore dumpsites for industrial and municipal waste

Severely polluted rivers and estuaries

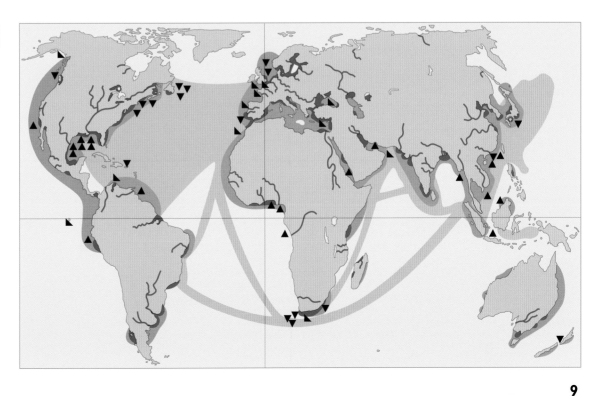

The most notorious oil rig blow-out of recent years occurred when the BP rig 'Deepwater Horizon' exploded on 20 April 2010. It is estimated that between 3,000,000 and 8,700,000 barrels of crude oil were spilled into the Gulf of Mexico, making it the world's second worst oil spill in history (after the Lakeview Gusher, California, of 1910).

Climate

Climate Regions

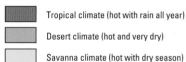

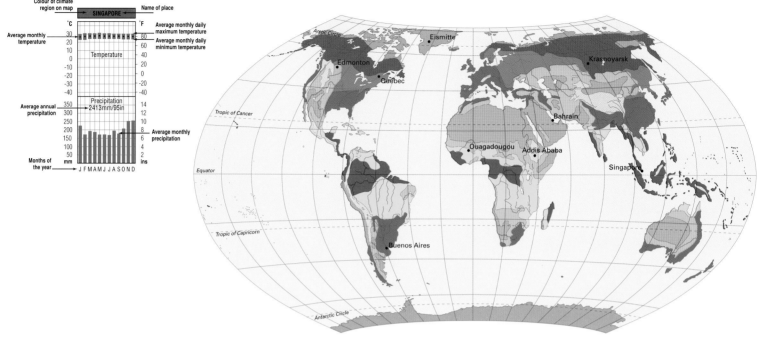

Tropical climate (hot with rain all year)	Steppe climate (warm and dry)	Subarctic climate (very cold winter)
Desert climate (hot and very dry)	Mild climate (warm and wet)	Polar climate (very cold and dry)
Savanna climate (hot with dry season)	Continental climate (wet with cold winter)	Mountainous climate (altitude affects climate)

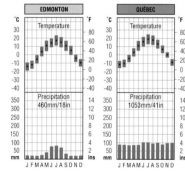
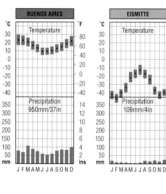
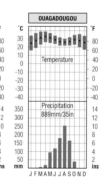
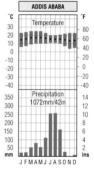
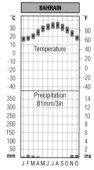
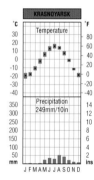
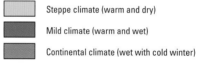
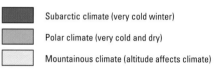

Climate Records

Temperature

Highest recorded shade temperature: Al Aziziyah, Libya, 57.7°C [135.9°F], 13 September 1922.

Highest mean annual temperature: Dallol, Ethiopia, 34.4°C [94°F], 1960–66.

Longest heatwave: Marble Bar, W. Australia, 162 days over 38°C [100°F], 23 October 1923 to 7 April 1924.

Lowest recorded temperature (outside poles): Verkhoyansk, Siberia, –68°C [–93.6°F], 7 February 1982.

Lowest mean annual temperature: Polus Nedostupnosti, Pole of Cold, Antarctica, –57.8°C [–72°F].

Precipitation

Driest place: Quillagua, Chile, mean annual rainfall 0.5 mm [0.02 in], 1964–2001.

Wettest place (average): Mt Wai-ale-ale, Hawai'i, USA, mean annual rainfall 11,680 mm [459.8 in].

Wettest place (12 months): Cherrapunji, Meghalaya, N. E. India, 26,461 mm [1,042 in], August 1860 to July 1861. Cherrapunji also holds the record for the most rainfall in one month: 2,930 mm [115 in], July 1861.

Wettest place (24 hours): Fac Fac, Réunion, Indian Ocean, 1,825 mm [71.9 in], 15–16 March 1952.

Heaviest hailstones: Gopalganj, Bangladesh, up to 1.02 kg [2.25 lb], 14 April 1986 (killed 92 people).

Heaviest snowfall (continuous): Bessans, Savoie, France, 1,730 mm [68 in] in 19 hours, 5–6 April 1969.

Heaviest snowfall (season/year): Mt Baker, Washington, USA, 28,956 mm [1,140 in], June 1998 to June 1999.

Pressure and winds

Highest barometric pressure: Agata, Siberia (at 262 m [862 ft] altitude), 1,083.8 mb, 31 December 1968.

Lowest barometric pressure: Typhoon Tip, Guam, Pacific Ocean, 870 mb, 12 October 1979.

Highest recorded wind speed: Bridge Creek, Oklahoma, USA, 512 km/h [318 mph], 3 May 1999. Measured by Doppler radar monitoring a tornado.

Windiest place: Port Martin, Antarctica, where winds of more than 64 km/h [40 mph] occur for not less than 100 days a year.

Climate

Climate is weather in the long term: the seasonal pattern of hot and cold, wet and dry, averaged over time (usually 30 years). At the simplest level, it is caused by the uneven heating of the Earth. Surplus heat at the Equator passes towards the poles, levelling out the energy differential. Its passage is marked by a ceaseless churning of the atmosphere and the oceans, further agitated by the Earth's diurnal spin and the motion it imparts to moving air and water. The heat's means of transport – by winds and ocean currents, by the continual evaporation and recondensation of water molecules – is the weather itself. There are four basic types of climate, each of which can be further subdivided: tropical, desert (dry), temperate and polar.

Composition of Dry Air

Nitrogen	78.09%	Sulphur dioxide	trace
Oxygen	20.95%	Nitrogen oxide	trace
Argon	0.93%	Methane	trace
Water vapour	0.2–4.0%	Dust	trace
Carbon dioxide	0.03%	Helium	trace
Ozone	0.00006%	Neon	trace

El Niño

In a normal year, south-easterly trade winds drive surface waters westwards off the coast of South America, drawing cold, nutrient-rich water up from below. In an El Niño year (which occurs every 2–7 years), warm water from the west Pacific suppresses up-welling in the east, depriving the region of nutrients. The water is warmed by as much as 7°C [12°F], disturbing the tropical atmos-pheric circulation. During an intense El Niño, the south-east trade winds change direction and become equatorial westerlies, res-ulting in climatic extremes in many regions of the world, such as drought in parts of Australia and India, and heavy rainfall in south-eastern USA. An intense El Niño occurred in 1997–8, with resultant freak weather conditions across the entire Pacific region.

Normal year

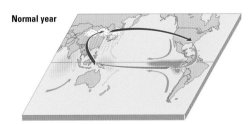

El Niño event

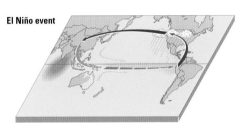

Beaufort Wind Scale

Named after the 19th-century British naval officer who devised it, the Beaufort Scale assesses wind speed according to its effects. It was originally designed as an aid for sailors, but has since been adapted for use on the land.

Scale	Wind speed		Effect
	km/h	mph	
0	0–1	0–1	**Calm**
			Smoke rises vertically
1	1–5	1–3	**Light air**
			Wind direction shown only by smoke drift
2	6–11	4–7	**Light breeze**
			Wind felt on face; leaves rustle; vanes moved by wind
3	12–19	8–12	**Gentle breeze**
			Leaves and small twigs in constant motion; wind extends small flag
4	20–28	13–18	**Moderate**
			Raises dust and loose paper; small branches move
5	29–38	19–24	**Fresh**
			Small trees in leaf sway; wavelets on inland waters
6	39–49	25–31	**Strong**
			Large branches move; difficult to use umbrellas
7	50–61	32–38	**Near gale**
			Whole trees in motion; difficult to walk against wind
8	62–74	39–46	**Gale**
			Twigs break from trees; walking very difficult
9	75–88	47–54	**Strong gale**
			Slight structural damage
10	89–102	55–63	**Storm**
			Trees uprooted; serious structural damage
11	103–117	64–72	**Violent storm**
			Widespread damage
12	118+	73+	**Hurricane**

Conversions

°C = (°F − 32) × 5/9; °F = (°C × 9/5) + 32; 0°C = 32°F

1 in = 25.4 mm; 1 mm = 0.0394 in; 100 mm = 3.94 in

Temperature

Average temperature in January

Temperature

- 30°C
- 20°C
- 10°C
- 0°C
- −10°C
- −20°C
- −30°C
- −40°C

Average temperature in July

Temperature

- 30°C
- 20°C
- 10°C
- 0°C
- −10°C

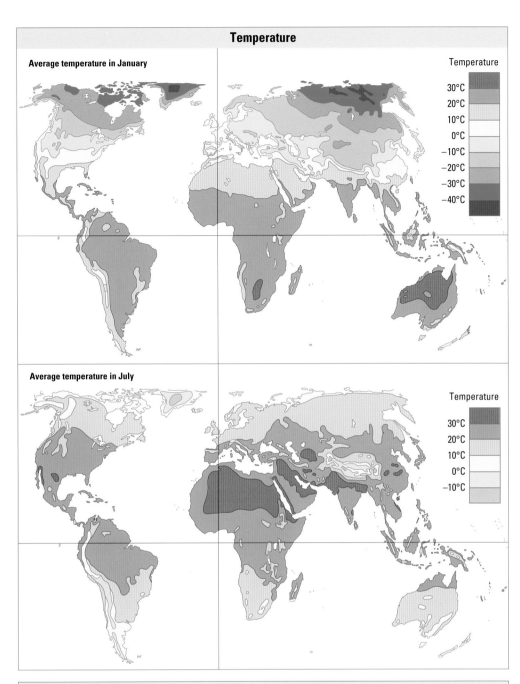

Precipitation (Rainfall and Snow)

Average annual precipitation

- 3,000 mm
- 2,000 mm
- 1,000 mm
- 500 mm
- 250 mm

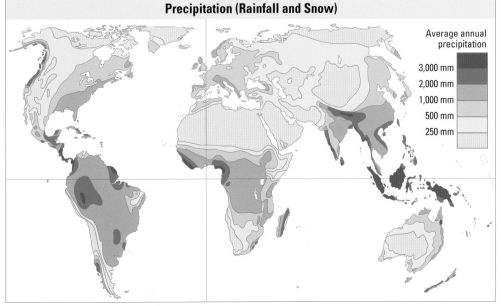

Water and Vegetation

The Hydrological Cycle

The world's water balance is regulated by the constant recycling of water between the oceans, atmosphere and land. The movement of water between these three reservoirs is known as the hydrological cycle. The oceans play a vital role in the hydrological cycle: 74% of the total precipitation falls over the oceans and 84% of the total evaporation comes from the oceans.

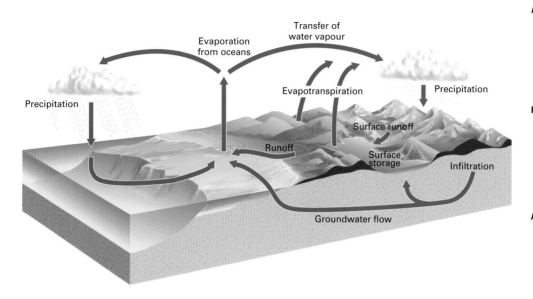

Water Distribution

The distribution of planetary water, by percentage. Oceans and ice caps together account for more than 99% of the total; the breakdown of the remainder is estimated.

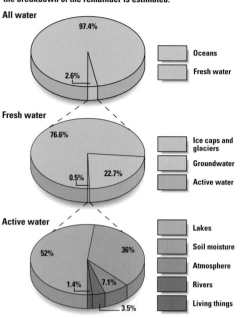

All water — 97.4% / 2.6% — Oceans / Fresh water

Fresh water — 76.6% / 0.5% / 22.7% — Ice caps and glaciers / Groundwater / Active water

Active water — 52% / 36% / 1.4% / 7.1% / 3.5% — Lakes / Soil moisture / Atmosphere / Rivers / Living things

Water Utilization

Domestic ■ Industrial ■ Agriculture □

The percentage breakdown of water usage by sector, selected countries (2007)

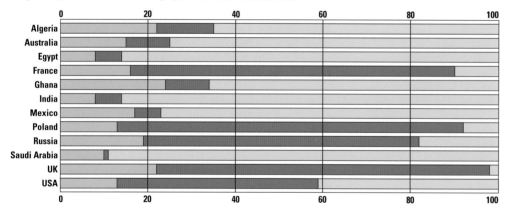

	0	20	40	60	80	100
Algeria						
Australia						
Egypt						
France						
Ghana						
India						
Mexico						
Poland						
Russia						
Saudi Arabia						
UK						
USA						

Water Usage

Almost all the world's water is 3,000 million years old, and all of it cycles endlessly through the hydrosphere, though at different rates. Water vapour circulates over days or even hours, deep ocean water circulates over millennia, and ice-cap water remains solid for millions of years.

Fresh water is essential to all terrestrial life. Humans cannot survive more than a few days without it, and even the hardiest desert plants and animals could not exist without some water. Agriculture requires huge quantities of fresh water: without large-scale irrigation most of the world's people would starve. In the USA, agriculture uses 41% and industry 46% of all water withdrawals.

According to the latest figures, the average North American uses 1.3 million litres of water per year. This is more than six times the average African, who uses just 186,000 litres of water each year. Europeans and Australians use 694,000 litres per year.

Water Supply

Percentage of total population with access to safe drinking water (2006)

- 100% with safe water
- 90 – 100% with safe water
- 80 – 90% with safe water
- 70 – 80% with safe water
- 60 – 70% with safe water
- Less than 60% with safe water
- No data available

Least well-provided countries

Madagascar	47%	Mozambique	42%
Nigeria	47%	Niger	42%
Congo (Dem. Rep.)	46%	Papua New Guinea	40%
Equatorial Guinea	43%	Somalia	29%
Ethiopia	42%	Western Sahara	26%

Natural Vegetation

Regional variation in vegetation

- Tundra and mountain vegetation
- Needleleaf evergreen forest
- Mixed needleleaf evergreen and broadleaf deciduous trees
- Broadleaf deciduous woodland
- Mid-latitude grassland
- Evergreen broadleaf and deciduous trees and shrubs
- Semi-desert scrub
- Desert
- Tropical grassland (savanna)
- Tropical broadleaf rainforest and monsoon forest
- Subtropical broadleaf and needleleaf forest

The map shows the natural 'climax vegetation' of regions, as dictated by climate and topography. In most cases, however, agricultural activity has drastically altered the vegetation pattern. Western Europe, for example, lost most of its broadleaf forest many centuries ago, while irrigation has turned some natural semi-desert into productive land.

Land Use by Continent (2007)

- Forest
- Permanent pasture
- Permanent crops
- Arable
- Other

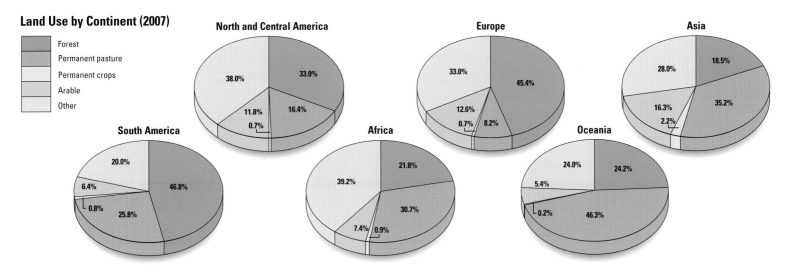

North and Central America: 38.0%, 33.0%, 16.4%, 11.8%, 0.7%

Europe: 33.0%, 45.4%, 12.6%, 8.2%, 0.7%

Asia: 28.0%, 18.5%, 35.2%, 16.3%, 2.2%

South America: 20.0%, 46.8%, 25.8%, 6.4%, 0.8%

Africa: 39.2%, 21.8%, 30.7%, 7.4%, 0.9%

Oceania: 24.0%, 24.2%, 46.3%, 5.4%, 0.2%

Forestry: Production

Forest and woodland (million hectares)		Annual production (2008, million cubic metres)	
		Fuelwood	Industrial roundwood*
World	**3,869.5**	**1,891.5**	**1,556.7**
Europe	1,039.3	152.5	504.6
S. America	885.6	200.9	185.7
Africa	649.9	637.6	70.3
N. & C. America	549.3	131.5	500.3
Asia	547.8	753.7	243.3
Oceania	197.6	15.9	52.4

Paper and Board

Top producers (2008)**		Top exporters (2008)**	
China	83,685	Germany	13,254
USA	80,178	Finland	11,851
Japan	28,360	USA	11,707
Germany	22,842	Canada	10,910
Canada	15,773	Sweden	10,579

* roundwood is timber as it is felled
** in thousand tonnes

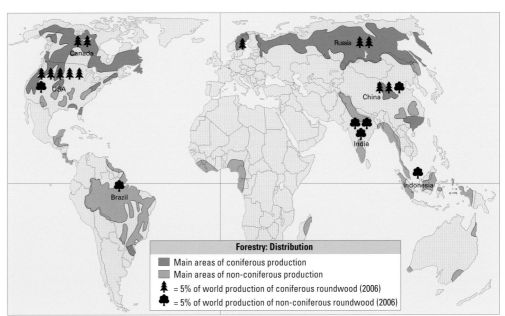

Forestry: Distribution

- Main areas of coniferous production
- Main areas of non-coniferous production
- 🌲 = 5% of world production of coniferous roundwood (2006)
- ♣ = 5% of world production of non-coniferous roundwood (2006)

Environment

Global Warming

Carbon dioxide emissions in tonnes per capita (2008)

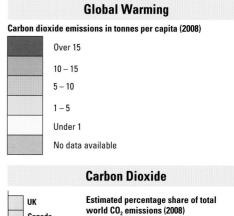

- Over 15
- 10 – 15
- 5 – 10
- 1 – 5
- Under 1
- No data available

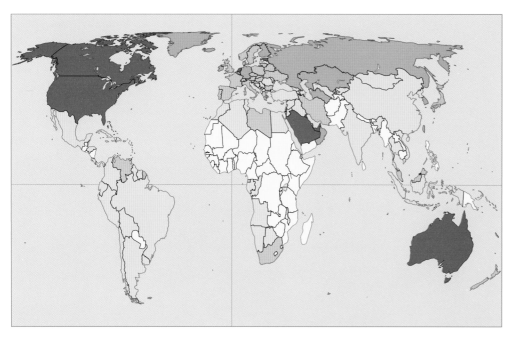

Carbon Dioxide

Estimated percentage share of total world CO_2 emissions (2008)

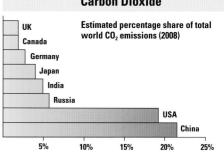

- UK
- Canada
- Germany
- Japan
- India
- Russia
- USA
- China

5%   10%   15%   20%   25%

Predicted Change in Precipitation

The difference between actual annual average precipitation, 1960–1990, and the predicted annual average precipitation, 2070–2100. It should be noted that these predicted annual mean changes mask quite significant seasonal detail.

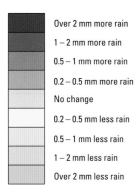

- Over 2 mm more rain
- 1 – 2 mm more rain
- 0.5 – 1 mm more rain
- 0.2 – 0.5 mm more rain
- No change
- 0.2 – 0.5 mm less rain
- 0.5 – 1 mm less rain
- 1 – 2 mm less rain
- Over 2 mm less rain

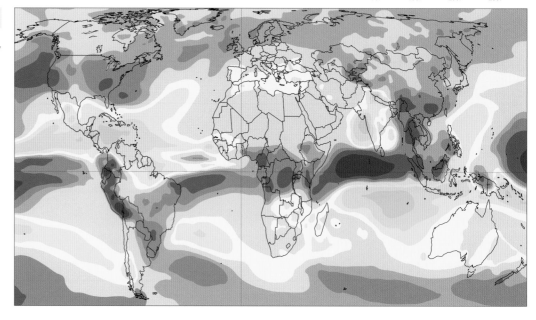

Predicted Change in Temperature

The difference between actual annual average surface air temperature, 1960–1990, and the predicted annual average surface air temperature, 2070–2100. This map shows the predicted increase, assuming a 'medium growth' of global economy and assuming that no measures are taken to combat the emission of greenhouse gases.

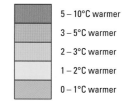

- 5 – 10°C warmer
- 3 – 5°C warmer
- 2 – 3°C warmer
- 1 – 2°C warmer
- 0 – 1°C warmer

Source: The Hadley Centre of Climate Prediction and Research, The Met. Office

14

Projected Change in Global Warming

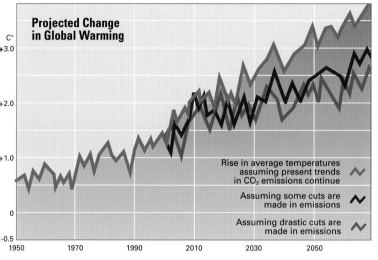

C°
+3.0
+2.0
+1.0
0
-0.5

1950   1970   1990   2010   2030   2050

Rise in average temperatures assuming present trends in CO₂ emissions continue

Assuming some cuts are made in emissions

Assuming drastic cuts are made in emissions

Possible Effect of Sea Level Rise in Florida

Sea levels have risen worldwide by about 2 cm since 1900. If CO₂ emissions continue at the same rate, the sea level is expected to rise by 7.4 m by 2200. The map shows the dramatic effects that such a rise could have on the southern part of Florida in the USA.

Submerged land area if sea level rises 4.5 m

Submerged land area if sea level rises 7.4 m

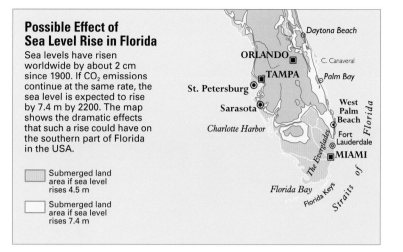

Daytona Beach
ORLANDO
C. Canaveral
TAMPA
Palm Bay
St. Petersburg
Sarasota
West Palm Beach
Charlotte Harbor
Fort Lauderdale
MIAMI
Florida Bay
Florida Keys
Straits of Florida
The Everglades

The Greenhouse Effect

Carbon dioxide is increased by burning fossil fuels and cutting forests

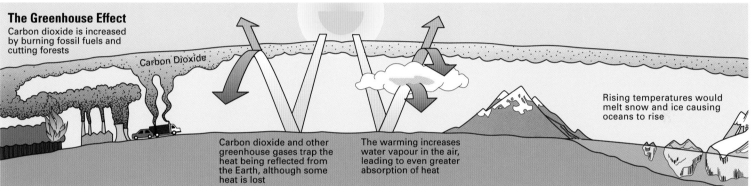

Carbon Dioxide

Carbon dioxide and other greenhouse gases trap the heat being reflected from the Earth, although some heat is lost

The warming increases water vapour in the air, leading to even greater absorption of heat

Rising temperatures would melt snow and ice causing oceans to rise

Desertification

Existing deserts

Areas with a high risk of desertification

Areas with a moderate risk of desertification

Former areas of rainforest

Existing rainforest

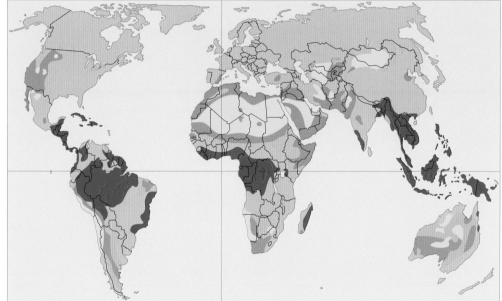

Forest Clearance

Thousands of hectares of forest cleared annually, tropical countries surveyed 1980–85, 1990–95 and 2000–05. Loss as a percentage of remaining stocks is shown in figures on each column. Gain is indicated as a minus figure.

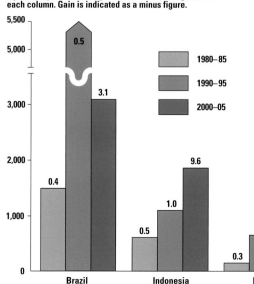

5,500
5,000
3,000
2,000
1,000
0

1980–85
1990–95
2000–05

Brazil: 0.4, 0.5, 3.1
Indonesia: 0.5, 1.0, 9.6
India: 0.3, 0.0, 0.7
Burma: 0.3, 1.4, 4.7
Thailand: 2.4, 2.6, 2.0
Vietnam: 0.7, 1.4, -12.2
Philippines: 1.0, 3.5, 4.2
Costa Rica: 4.0, 3.0, -0.6

Deforestation

The Earth's remaining forests are under attack from three directions: expanding agriculture, logging, and growing consumption of fuelwood, often in combination. Sometimes deforestation is the direct result of government policy, as in the efforts made to resettle the urban poor in some parts of Brazil; just as often, it comes about despite state attempts at conservation.

Loggers, licensed or unlicensed, blaze a trail into virgin forest, often destroying twice as many trees as they harvest. Landless farmers follow, burning away most of what remains to plant their crops, completing the destruction. However, some countries such as Vietnam and Costa Rica have successfully implemented reafforestation programmes.

15

Population

Demographic Profiles

Developed nations such as the UK have populations evenly spread across the age groups and, usually, a growing proportion of elderly people. The great majority of the people in developing nations, however, are in the younger age groups, about to enter their most fertile years. In time, these population profiles should resemble the world profile (even Nigeria has made recent progress by reducing its birth rate), but the transition will come about only after a few more generations of rapid population growth.

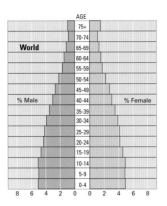

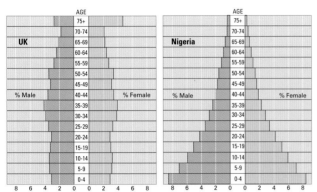

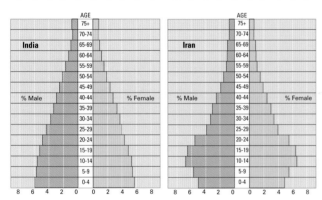

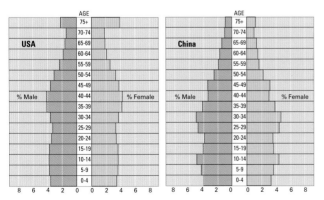

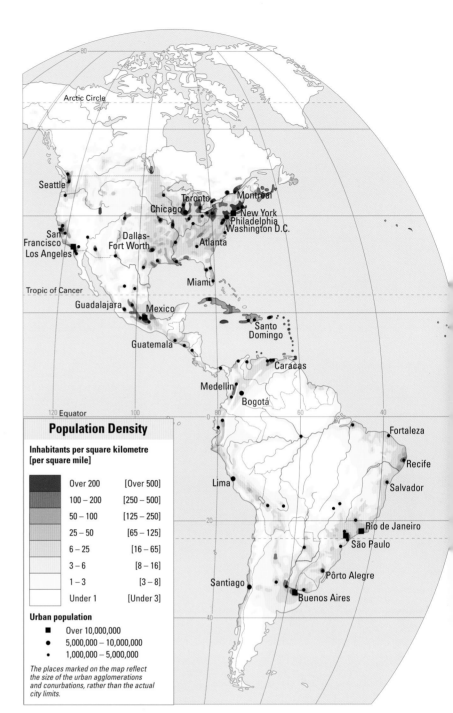

Population Density

Inhabitants per square kilometre [per square mile]

Over 200	[Over 500]
100 – 200	[250 – 500]
50 – 100	[125 – 250]
25 – 50	[65 – 125]
6 – 25	[16 – 65]
3 – 6	[8 – 16]
1 – 3	[3 – 8]
Under 1	[Under 3]

Urban population

- ■ Over 10,000,000
- ● 5,000,000 – 10,000,000
- • 1,000,000 – 5,000,000

The places marked on the map reflect the size of the urban agglomerations and conurbations, rather than the actual city limits.

Most Populous Nations, in millions (2009 estimates)

1.	China	1,339	9. Russia	140	17. Turkey	77
2.	India	1,157	10. Japan	127	18. Congo (Dem. Rep.)	69
3.	USA	307	11. Mexico	111	19. Iran	66
4.	Indonesia	240	12. Philippines	98	20. Thailand	66
5.	Brazil	199	13. Vietnam	89	21. France	64
6.	Pakistan	175	14. Ethiopia	85	22. UK	61
7.	Bangladesh	156	15. Germany	82	23. Italy	58
8.	Nigeria	149	16. Egypt	79	24. South Africa	49

Continental Comparisons

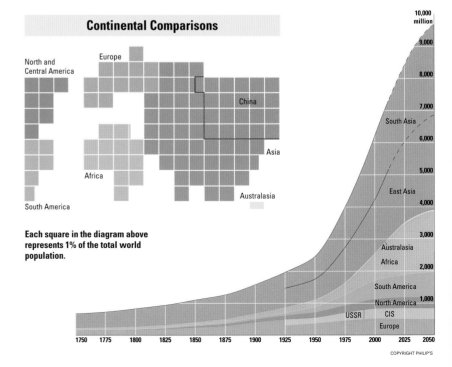

Each square in the diagram above represents 1% of the total world population.

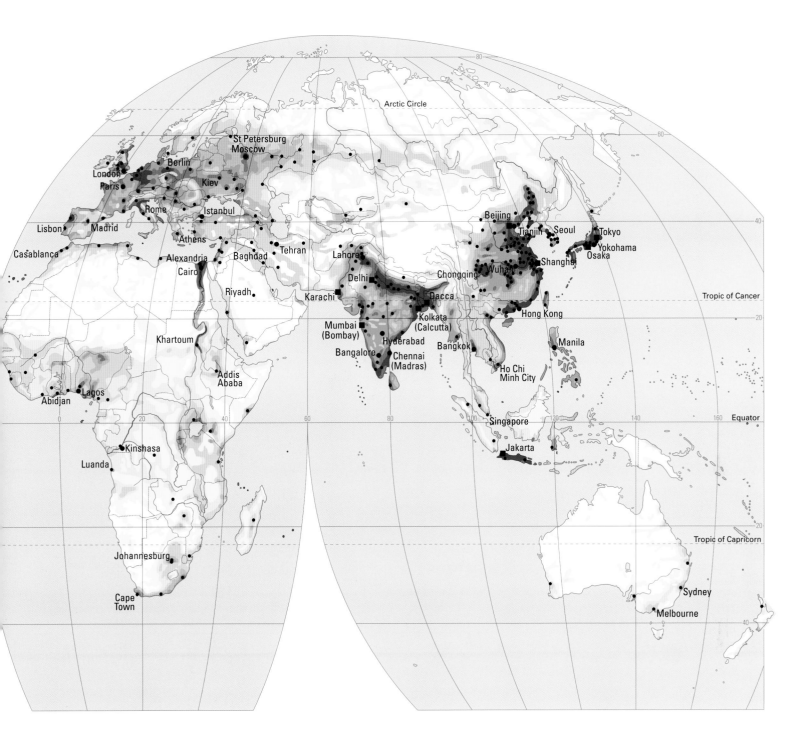

Arctic Circle

St Petersburg
Moscow
Berlin
London
Paris
Kiev
Rome
Istanbul
Lisbon
Madrid
Athens
Casablanca
Alexandria
Baghdad
Tehran
Lahore
Beijing
Cairo
Tianjin
Seoul
Tokyo
Yokohama
Osaka
Wuhan
Shanghai
Delhi
Chongqing
Riyadh
Karachi
Dacca
Tropic of Cancer
Khartoum
Kolkata
(Calcutta)
Hong Kong
Mumbai
(Bombay)
Hyderabad
Bangalore
Chennai
(Madras)
Bangkok
Manila
Addis
Ababa
Ho Chi
Minh City
Lagos
Abidjan
Singapore
Equator
Kinshasa
Jakarta
Luanda
Johannesburg
Tropic of Capricorn
Sydney
Cape
Town
Melbourne

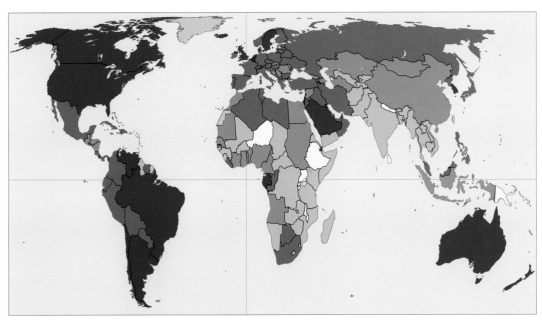

Urban Population

Percentage of total population living in towns and cities (2009)

	Over 80%
	60 – 80%
	40 – 60%
	20 – 40%
	Under 20%
	No data available

Most urbanized		Least urbanized	
Singapore	100%	Burundi	11%
Kuwait	98%	Papua New Guinea	13%
Belgium	97%	Uganda	13%
Qatar	96%	Trinidad & Tobago	14%
Malta	95%	Sri Lanka	15%

17

The Human Family

Predominant Languages

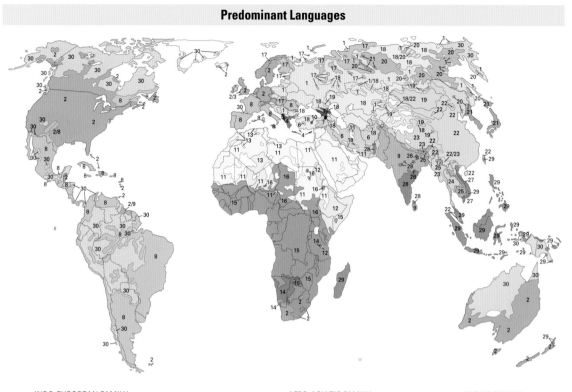

Languages of the World

Language can be classified by ancestry and structure. For example, the Romance and Germanic groups are both derived from an Indo-European language believed to have been spoken 5,000 years ago.

First-language speakers, in millions (2008)
Mandarin Chinese 845, Spanish 329, English 328, Arabic 221, Hindi 182, Bengali 181, Portuguese 178, Russian 144, Japanese 122, German 90, Javanese 85, Wu Chinese 77, Telugu 70, Vietnamese 69, Marathi 68, French 68, Korean 66, Tamil 66, Punjabi 63, Italian 62.

Distribution of Living Languages

The figures refer to the number of languages currently in use in the regions shown

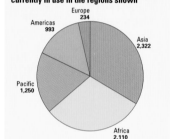

Europe 234
Americas 993
Asia 2,322
Pacific 1,250
Africa 2,110

INDO-EUROPEAN FAMILY

1 Balto-Slavic group (incl. Russian, Ukrainian)
2 Germanic group (incl. English, German)
3 Celtic group
4 Greek
5 Albanian
6 Iranian group
7 Armenian
8 Romance group (incl. Spanish, Portuguese, French, Italian)
9 Indo-Aryan group (incl. Hindi, Bengali, Urdu, Punjabi, Marathi)
10 CAUCASIAN FAMILY

AFRO-ASIATIC FAMILY

11 Semitic group (incl. Arabic)
12 Kushitic group
13 Berber group

14 KHOISAN FAMILY

15 NIGER-CONGO FAMILY

16 NILO-SAHARAN FAMILY

17 URALIC FAMILY

ALTAIC FAMILY

18 Turkic group (incl. Turkish)
19 Mongolian group
20 Tungus-Manchu group
21 Japanese and Korean

SINO-TIBETAN FAMILY

22 Sinitic (Chinese) languages (incl. Mandarin, Wu, Yue)
23 Tibetic-Burmic languages

24 TAI FAMILY

AUSTRO-ASIATIC FAMILY

25 Mon-Khmer group
26 Munda group
27 Vietnamese

28 DRAVIDIAN FAMILY (incl. Telugu, Tamil)

29 AUSTRONESIAN FAMILY (incl. Malay-Indonesian, Javanese)

30 OTHER LANGUAGES

Predominant Religions

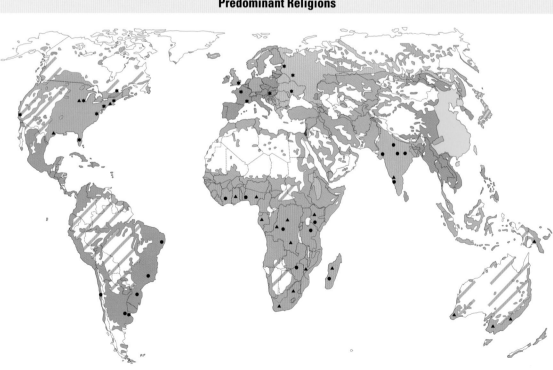

Religious Adherents

Religious adherents in millions (2006)

Christianity	2,100	Hindu	900
Roman Catholic	1,050	Chinese folk	394
Protestant	396	Buddhism	376
Orthodox	240	Ethnic religions	300
Anglican	73	New religions	103
Others	341	Sikhism	23
Islam	1,070	Spiritism	15
Sunni	940	Judaism	14
Shi'ite	120	Baha'i	7
Others	10	Confucianism	6
Non-religious/		Jainism	4
Agnostic/Atheist	1,100	Shintoism	4

▲ Roman Catholicism

Orthodox and other Eastern Churches

• Protestantism

Sunni Islam

Shi'ite Islam

Buddhism

Hinduism

Confucianism

★ Judaism

Shintoism

Tribal Religions

United Nations

Created in 1945 to promote peace and co-operation, and based in New York, the United Nations is the world's largest international organization, with 192 members and an annual budget of US $4.2 billion (2008–9). Each member of the General Assembly has one vote, while the five permanent members of the 15-nation Security Council – China, France, Russia, UK and USA – each hold a veto. The Secretariat is the UN's principal administrative arm. The 54 members of the Economic and Social Council are responsible for economic, social, cultural, educational, health and related matters. The UN has 16 specialized agencies – based in Canada, France, Switzerland and Italy, as well as the USA – which help members in fields such as education (UNESCO), agriculture (FAO), medicine (WHO) and finance (IFC). By the end of 1994, all the original 11 trust territories of the Trusteeship Council had become independent.

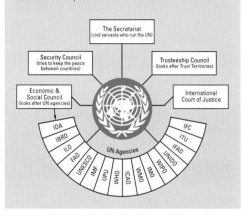

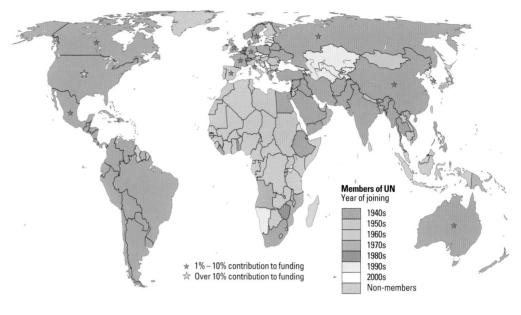

Members of UN
Year of joining

- 1940s
- 1950s
- 1960s
- 1970s
- 1980s
- 1990s
- 2000s
- Non-members

★ 1%–10% contribution to funding
☆ Over 10% contribution to funding

MEMBERSHIP OF THE UN From the original 51, membership of the UN has now grown to 192. Recent additions include East Timor, Switzerland and Montenegro. There are only two independent states which are not members of the UN – Taiwan and the Vatican City. All the successor states of the former USSR had joined by the end of 1992. The official languages of the UN are Chinese, English, French, Russian, Spanish and Arabic.

FUNDING The UN budget for 2008–9 was US $4.2 billion. Contributions are assessed by the members' ability to pay, with the maximum 22% of the total (USA's share), and the minimum 0.001%. The 27-member EU pays nearly 39% of the budget.

PEACEKEEPING The UN has been involved in 64 peacekeeping operations worldwide since 1948.

International Organizations

ACP African-Caribbean-Pacific (formed in 1963). Members have economic ties with the EU.

APEC Asia-Pacific Economic Co-operation (formed in 1989). It aims to enhance economic growth and prosperity for the region and to strengthen the Asia-Pacific community. APEC is the only intergovernmental grouping in the world operating on the basis of non-binding commitments, open dialogue, and equal respect for the views of all participants. There are 21 member economies.

ARAB LEAGUE (formed in 1945). The League's aim is to promote economic, social, political and military co-operation. There are 22 member nations.

ASEAN Association of South-east Asian Nations (formed in 1967). Cambodia joined in 1999.

AU The African Union replaced the Organization of African Unity (formed in 1963) in 2002. Its 53 members represent over 94% of Africa's population. Arabic, English, French and Portuguese are recognized as working languages.

COLOMBO PLAN (formed in 1951). Its 25 members aim to promote economic and social development in Asia and the Pacific.

COMMONWEALTH The Commonwealth of Nations evolved from the British Empire. Pakistan was suspended in 1999, but reinstated in 2004. Zimbabwe was suspended in 2002 and, in response to its continued suspension, Zimbabwe left the Commonwealth in 2003. Fiji Islands was suspended in 2006 following a military coup. Rwanda joined the Commonwealth in 2009, as the 54th member state, becoming only the second country which was not formerly a British colony to be admitted to the group.

EU European Union (evolved from the European Community in 1993). Cyprus, the Czech Republic, Estonia, Hungary, Latvia, Lithuania, Malta, Poland, the Slovak Republic and Slovenia joined the EU in May 2004; Bulgaria and Romania joined in 2007. The other 15 members of the EU are Austria, Belgium, Denmark, Finland, France, Germany, Greece, Ireland, Italy, Luxembourg, Netherlands, Portugal, Spain, Sweden and the UK. Together, the 27 members aim to integrate economies, co-ordinate social developments and bring about political union.

LAIA Latin American Integration Association (1980). Its aim is to promote freer regional trade.

NATO North Atlantic Treaty Organization (formed in 1949). It continues despite the winding-up of the Warsaw Pact in 1991. Bulgaria, Estonia, Latvia, Lithuania, Romania, the Slovak Republic and Slovenia became members in 2004.

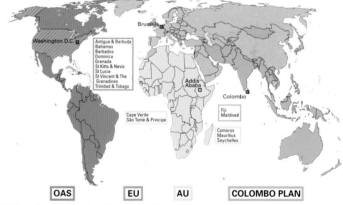

OAS | EU | AU | COLOMBO PLAN

OAS Organization of American States (formed in 1948). It aims to promote social and economic co-operation between countries in the developed North America and developing Latin America.

OECD Organization for Economic Co-operation and Development (formed in 1961). It comprises 30 major free-market economies. Poland, Hungary and South Korea joined in 1996, and the Slovak Republic in 2000. The 'G8' is its 'inner group' of leading industrial nations, comprising Canada, France, Germany, Italy, Japan, Russia, the UK and the USA.

OPEC Organization of Petroleum Exporting Countries (formed in 1960). It controls about three-quarters of the world's oil supply. Gabon formally withdrew from OPEC in August 1996.

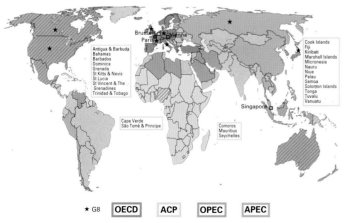

★ G8 | OECD | ACP | OPEC | APEC

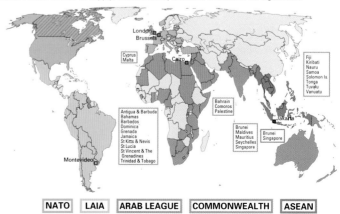

NATO | LAIA | ARAB LEAGUE | COMMONWEALTH | ASEAN

Wealth

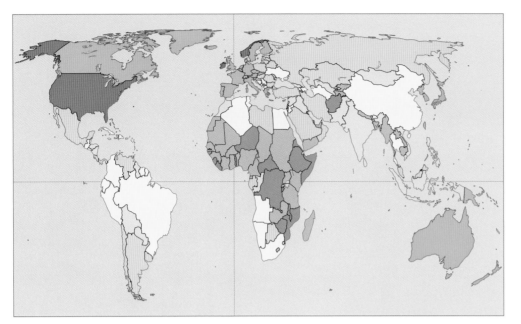

Levels of Income

Gross National Income per capita: the value of total production divided by the population (2009)

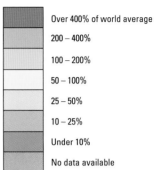

- Over 400% of world average
- 200 – 400%
- 100 – 200%
- 50 – 100%
- 25 – 50%
- 10 – 25%
- Under 10%
- No data available

Wealth Creation

The Gross National Income (GNI) of the world's largest economies, US $ million (2008)

1.	USA	14,466,100	21.	Indonesia	458,200
2.	Japan	4,879,200	22.	Poland	453,000
3.	China	3,899,300	23.	Norway	415,200
4.	Germany	3,485,700	24.	Austria	386,000
5.	UK	2,787,200	25.	Saudi Arabia	374,300
6.	France	2,702,200	26.	Denmark	325,100
7.	Italy	2,109,100	27.	Greece	322,000
8.	Spain	1,456,500	28.	Argentina	287,200
9.	Brazil	1,411,200	29.	South Africa	283,300
10.	Canada	1,390,000	30.	Venezuela	257,800
11.	Russia	1,364,500	31.	Finland	255,700
12.	India	1,215,500	32.	Iran	251,500
13.	Mexico	1,061,400	33.	Ireland	221,200
14.	South Korea	1,046,300	34.	Hong Kong	219,300
15.	Australia	862,500	35.	Portugal	218,400
16.	Netherlands	824,600	36.	Colombia	207,400
17.	Turkey	690,700	37.	Thailand	191,700
18.	Switzerland	498,500	38.	Malaysia	188,100
19.	Belgium	474,500	39.	Israel	180,500
20.	Sweden	469,700	40.	Nigeria	175,600

The Wealth Gap

The world's richest and poorest countries, by Gross National Income (GNI) per capita in US $ (2008)

Richest countries			Poorest countries		
1.	Luxembourg	64,320	1.	Congo (Dem. Rep.)	290
2.	Norway	58,500	2.	Liberia	300
3.	Kuwait	52,610	3.	Burundi	380
4.	Macau (China)	52,260	4.	Guinea-Bissau	530
5.	Brunei	50,200	5.	Eritrea	630
6.	Singapore	47,940	6.	Niger	680
7.	USA	46,970	7.	Central African Rep.	730
8.	Switzerland	46,460	8.	Sierra Leone	750
9.	Hong Kong (China)	43,960	9.	Mozambique	770
10.	Netherlands	41,670	10.	Togo	820
11.	Sweden	38,180	11.	Malawi	830
12.	Austria	37,680	12.	Ethiopia	870
13.	Ireland	37,350	13.	Rwanda	1,010
14.	Denmark	37,280	14.	Madagascar	1,040
15.	Canada	36,220	15.	Mali	1,090
16.	UK	36,130	16.	Nepal	1,120
17.	Germany	35,940	17.	Uganda	1,140
18.	Finland	35,660	18.	Burkina Faso	1,160
19.	Japan	35,220	=	Chad	1,160
20.	Belgium	34,760	20.	Comoros	1,170

Continental Shares

Shares of population and of wealth (GNI) by continent

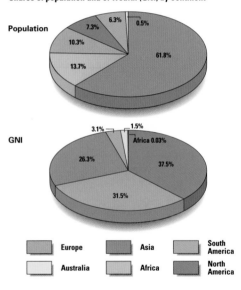

Population

6.3% | 0.5%
7.3%
10.3%
13.7%
61.8%

GNI

3.1% | 1.5%
Africa 0.03%
26.3%
37.5%
31.5%

- Europe
- Asia
- South America
- Australia
- Africa
- North America

Inflation

Average annual rate of inflation (2009)

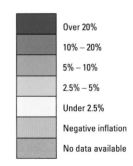

- Over 20%
- 10% – 20%
- 5% – 10%
- 2.5% – 5%
- Under 2.5%
- Negative inflation
- No data available

Highest average inflation		Lowest average inflation	
Seychelles	34%	Qatar	−3.9%
Mongolia	28%	Ireland	−3.9%
Venezuela	27%	San Marino	−3.5%

International Aid

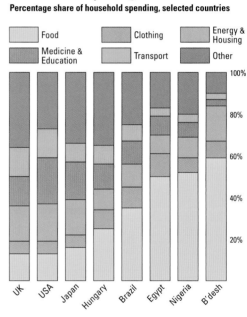

Official Development Assistance (ODA) provided and received, per capita (2007)

Over $100 per person
$50 – $100 per person
$20 – $50 per person
} Providers

Under $10 per person
$10 – $25 per person
$25 – $50 per person
Over $50 per person
} Receivers

No data available

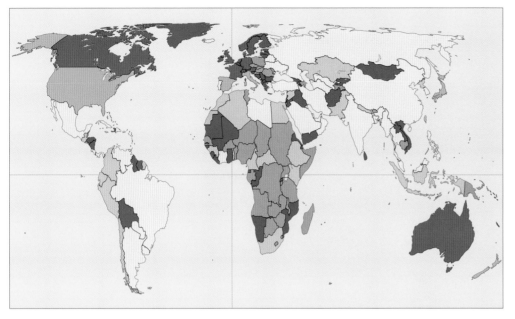

Debt and Aid

International debtors and the aid they receive

Although aid grants make a vital contribution to many of the world's poorer countries, they are usually dwarfed by the burden of debt that the developing economies are expected to repay. It is estimated that the total debt burden of developing countries is US$523 billion.

Debt, US $ per capita (2007)

Aid, US $ per capita (2007)

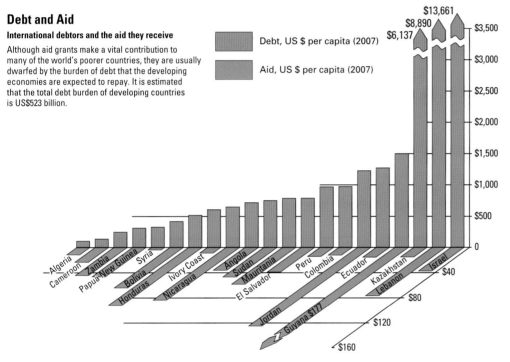

Distribution of Spending

Percentage share of household spending, selected countries

Food
Medicine & Education
Clothing
Transport
Energy & Housing
Other

UK   USA   Japan   Hungary   Brazil   Egypt   Nigeria   B'desh

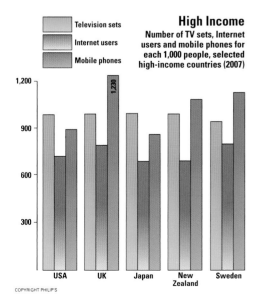

High Income

Television sets
Internet users
Mobile phones

Number of TV sets, Internet users and mobile phones for each 1,000 people, selected high-income countries (2007)

USA   UK   Japan   New Zealand   Sweden

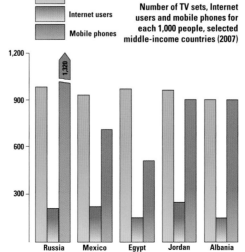

Middle Income

Television sets
Internet users
Mobile phones

Number of TV sets, Internet users and mobile phones for each 1,000 people, selected middle-income countries (2007)

Russia   Mexico   Egypt   Jordan   Albania

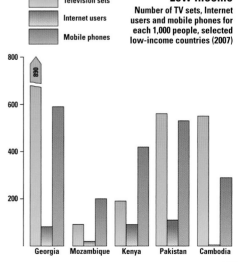

Low Income

Television sets
Internet users
Mobile phones

Number of TV sets, Internet users and mobile phones for each 1,000 people, selected low-income countries (2007)

Georgia   Mozambique   Kenya   Pakistan   Cambodia

21

Quality of Life

Daily Food Consumption

Daily Food Consumption

Average daily food intake in calories per person (2005)

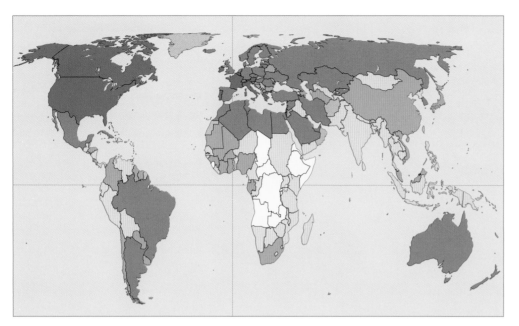

- Over 3,500 calories per person
- 3,000 – 3,500 calories per person
- 2,500 – 3,000 calories per person
- 2,000 – 2,500 calories per person
- Under 2,000 calories per person
- No data available

Hospital Capacity

Hospital beds available for each 1,000 people (2007)

Highest capacity		Lowest capacity	
Japan	14.1	Angola	0.1
Belarus	11.1	Cambodia	0.1
Russia	9.7	Malawi	0.1
Ukraine	8.7	Senegal	0.1
South Korea	8.6	Ethiopia	0.2
Czech Republic	8.4	Nepal	0.2
Germany	8.3	Bangladesh	0.3
Azerbaijan	8.1	Guinea	0.3
Lithuania	8.0	Madagascar	0.3
Hungary	7.9	Mali	0.3
Kazakhstan	7.8	Afghanistan	0.4
Austria	7.6	Chad	0.4
Latvia	7.6	Sierra Leone	0.4
Malta	7.6	Benin	0.5
Iceland	7.5	Nigeria	0.5

Although the ratio of people to hospital beds gives a good approximation of a country's health provision, it is not an absolute indicator. Raw numbers may mask inefficiency and other weaknesses: the high availability of beds in Belarus, for example, has not prevented infant mortality rates over three times as high as in the United Kingdom and the United States.

Life Expectancy

Years of life expectancy at birth, selected countries (2009)

The chart shows combined data for both sexes. On average, women live longer than men worldwide, even in developing countries with high maternal mortality rates. Overall, life expectancy is steadily rising, though the difference between rich and poor nations remains dramatic.

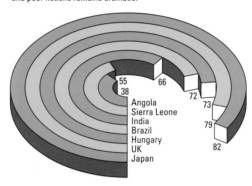

55
38
66
72
73
79
82

Angola
Sierra Leone
India
Brazil
Hungary
UK
Japan

Causes of Death

Causes of death for selected countries by percentage

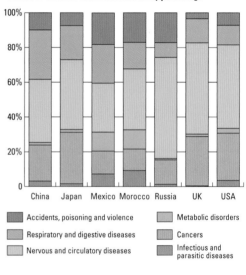

China, Japan, Mexico, Morocco, Russia, UK, USA

- Accidents, poisoning and violence
- Respiratory and digestive diseases
- Nervous and circulatory diseases
- Metabolic disorders
- Cancers
- Infectious and parasitic diseases

Infant Mortality

Number of babies who died under the age of one, per 1,000 live births (2009)

- Over 100 deaths per 1,000 births
- 50 – 100 deaths per 1,000 births
- 20 – 50 deaths per 1,000 births
- 10 – 20 deaths per 1,000 births
- Under 10 deaths per 1,000 births
- No data available

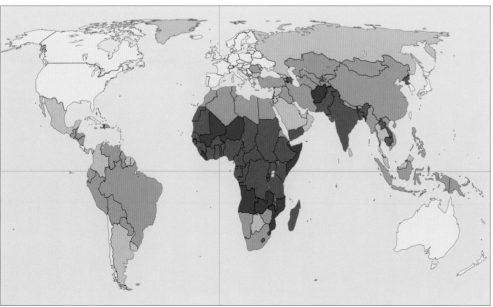

Highest infant mortality		Lowest infant mortality	
Angola	180 deaths	Japan	3 deaths
Afghanistan	153 deaths	Iceland	3 deaths
Liberia	138 deaths	France	3 deaths

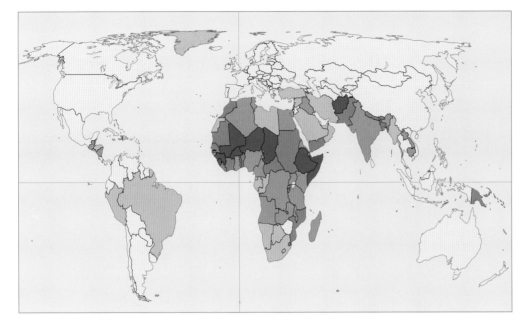

Illiteracy

Percentage of the total adult population unable to read or write (2007)

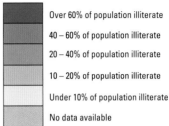

- Over 60% of population illiterate
- 40 – 60% of population illiterate
- 20 – 40% of population illiterate
- 10 – 20% of population illiterate
- Under 10% of population illiterate
- No data available

Countries with the highest and lowest illiteracy rates

Highest		Lowest	
Burkina Faso	87	Australia	0
Niger	83	Denmark	0
Mali	81	Finland	0
Sierra Leone	69	Liechtenstein	0
Guinea	64	Luxembourg	0

Fertility and Education

Fertility rates compared with female education, selected countries (2008)

- Percentage of females aged 12–17 in secondary education
- Fertility rate: average number of children borne per woman

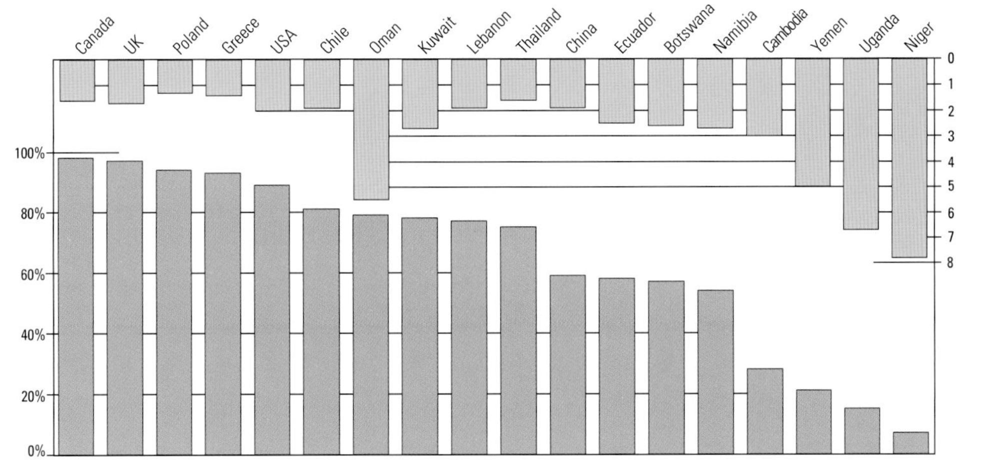

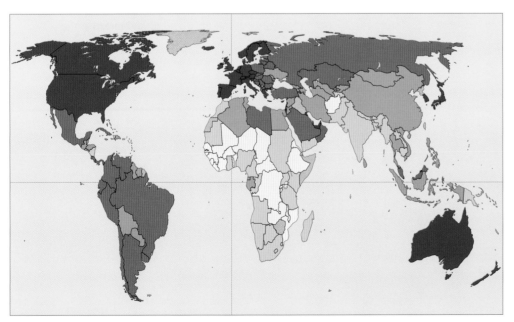

Living Standards

At first sight, most international contrasts in living standards are swamped by differences in wealth. The rich not only have more money, they have more of everything, including years of life. Those with only a little money are obliged to spend most of it on food and clothing, the basic maintenance costs of their existence; air travel and tourism are unlikely to feature on their expenditure lists. However, poverty and wealth are both relative: slum dwellers living on social security payments in an affluent industrial country have far more resources at their disposal than an average African peasant, but feel their own poverty nonetheless. A middle-class Indian lawyer cannot command a fraction of the earnings of a counterpart living in New York, London or Rome; nevertheless, he rightly sees himself as prosperous.

The rich not only live longer, on average, than the poor, they also die from different causes. Infectious and parasitic diseases, all but eliminated in the developed world, remain a scourge in the developing nations. On the other hand, more than two-thirds of the populations of OECD nations eventually succumb to cancer or circulatory disease.

Human Development Index

The Human Development Index (HDI), calculated by the UN Development Programme (UNDP), gives a value to countries using indicators of life expectancy, education and standards of living (2007). Higher values show more developed countries.

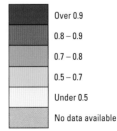

- Over 0.9
- 0.8 – 0.9
- 0.7 – 0.8
- 0.5 – 0.7
- Under 0.5
- No data available

Highest values		Lowest values	
Norway	0.971	Niger	0.340
Australia	0.970	Afghanistan	0.352
Iceland	0.969	Sierra Leone	0.365
Canada	0.966	Central African Rep.	0.369
Ireland	0.965	Mali	0.371

Energy

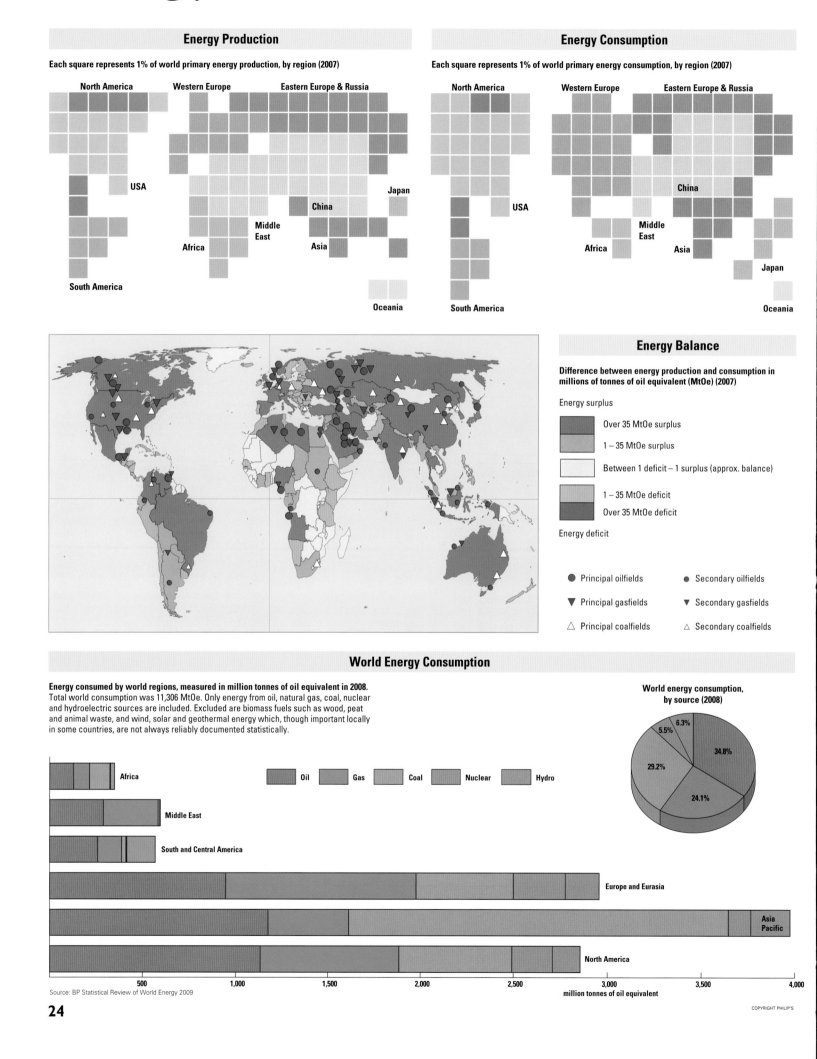

Energy Production

Each square represents 1% of world primary energy production, by region (2007)

North America
Western Europe
Eastern Europe & Russia
USA
Japan
China
Middle East
Africa
Asia
South America
Oceania

Energy Consumption

Each square represents 1% of world primary energy consumption, by region (2007)

North America
Western Europe
Eastern Europe & Russia
China
USA
Middle East
Africa
Asia
South America
Japan
Oceania

Energy Balance

Difference between energy production and consumption in millions of tonnes of oil equivalent (MtOe) (2007)

Energy surplus

Over 35 MtOe surplus

1 – 35 MtOe surplus

Between 1 deficit – 1 surplus (approx. balance)

1 – 35 MtOe deficit

Over 35 MtOe deficit

Energy deficit

● Principal oilfields   ● Secondary oilfields

▼ Principal gasfields   ▼ Secondary gasfields

△ Principal coalfields   △ Secondary coalfields

World Energy Consumption

Energy consumed by world regions, measured in million tonnes of oil equivalent in 2008.
Total world consumption was 11,306 MtOe. Only energy from oil, natural gas, coal, nuclear and hydroelectric sources are included. Excluded are biomass fuels such as wood, peat and animal waste, and wind, solar and geothermal energy which, though important locally in some countries, are not always reliably documented statistically.

World energy consumption, by source (2008)

6.3%
5.5%
34.8%
29.2%
24.1%

Oil   Gas   Coal   Nuclear   Hydro

Africa

Middle East

South and Central America

Europe and Eurasia

Asia Pacific

North America

500   1,000   1,500   2,000   2,500   3,000   3,500   4,000

million tonnes of oil equivalent

Source: BP Statistical Review of World Energy 2009

Energy

Energy is used to keep us warm or cool, fuel our industries and our transport systems, and even feed us; high-intensity agriculture, with its use of fertilizers, pesticides and machinery, is heavily energy-dependent. Although we live in a high-energy society, there are vast discrepancies between rich and poor; for example, a North American consumes six times as much energy as a Chinese person. But even developing nations have more power at their disposal than was imaginable a century ago.

The distribution of energy supplies, most importantly fossil fuels (coal, oil and natural gas), is very uneven. In addition, the diagrams and map opposite show that the largest producers of energy are not necessarily the largest consumers. The movement of energy supplies around the world is therefore an important component of international trade.

As the finite reserves of fossil fuels are depleted, renewable energy sources, such as solar, hydro-thermal, wind, tidal and biomass, will become increasingly important around the world.

Nuclear Power

Major producers by percentage of world total and by percentage of domestic electricity generation (2008)

Country	% of world total production	Country	% of nuclear as proportion of domestic electricity
1. USA	31.0%	1. France	77.5%
2. France	16.1%	2. Lithuania	75.6%
3. Japan	9.4%	3. Slovak Rep.	56.7%
4. Russia	5.9%	4. Belgium	55.4%
5. South Korea	5.5%	5. Ukraine	45.5%
6. Germany	5.4%	6. Slovenia	42.2%
7. Canada	3.4%	7. Sweden	41.9%
8. Ukraine	3.2%	8. Armenia	40.7%
9. China	2.5%	9. Switzerland	40.2%
10. Sweden	2.3%	10. Hungary	37.2%

Although the 1980s were a bad time for the nuclear power industry (fears of long-term environmental damage were heavily reinforced by the 1986 disaster at Chernobyl), the industry picked up in the early 1990s. Sixteen countries currently rely on nuclear power to supply over 25% of their electricity requirements. There are over 400 operating nuclear power stations worldwide, with over 100 more planned or under construction.

Hydroelectricity

Major producers by percentage of world total and by percentage of domestic electricity generation (2007)

Country	% of world total production	Country	% of hydroelectric as proportion of domestic electricity
1. China	14.3%	1. Lesotho	100%
2. Brazil	12.3%	= Bhutan	100%
3. Canada	12.2%	= Paraguay	100%
4. USA	8.3%	4. Mozambique	99.9%
5. Russia	5.8%	5. Congo (Rep. Dem.)	99.7%
6. Norway	4.4%	6. Nepal	99.5%
7. India	4.1%	7. Zambia	99.4%
8. Venezuela	2.8%	8. Norway	98.7%
9. Japan	2.4%	9. Tajikistan	97.9%
10. Sweden	2.2%	10. Burundi	97.8%

Countries heavily reliant on hydroelectricity are usually small and non-industrial: a high proportion of hydroelectric power more often reflects a modest energy budget than vast hydroelectric resources. The USA, for instance, produces only 6% of its power requirements from hydroelectricity; yet that 6% amounts to almost half the hydropower generated by most of Africa.

Fuel Exports

Fuels as a percentage of total value of exports (2007)

- Over 50%
- 10 – 50%
- 1 – 10%
- Under 1%
- No data available

In the 1970s, oil exports became a political issue when OPEC sought to increase the influence of developing countries in world affairs by raising oil prices and restricting production. But its power was short-lived, following a fall in demand for oil in the 1980s, due to an increase in energy efficiency and development of alternative resources. However, with the heavy energy demands of the Asian economies early in the 21st century, both oil and gas prices have risen sharply.

Conversion Rates

1 barrel = 0.136 tonnes or 159 litres or 35 Imperial gallons or 42 US gallons

1 tonne = 7.33 barrels or 1,185 litres or 256 Imperial gallons or 261 US gallons

1 tonne oil = 1.5 tonnes hard coal or 3.0 tonnes lignite or 12,000 kWh

1 Imperial gallon = 1.201 US gallons or 4.546 litres or 277.4 cubic inches

Measurements

For historical reasons, oil is traded in 'barrels'. The weight and volume equivalents (shown right) are all based on average-density 'Arabian light' crude oil.

The energy equivalents given for a tonne of oil are also somewhat imprecise: oil and coal of different qualities will have varying energy contents, a fact usually reflected in their price on world markets.

Energy Reserves

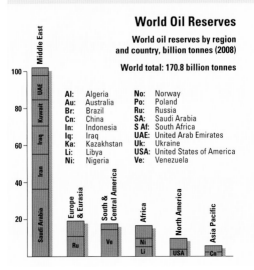

World Oil Reserves

World oil reserves by region and country, billion tonnes (2008)

World total: 170.8 billion tonnes

Al:	Algeria	**No:**	Norway
Au:	Australia	**Po:**	Poland
Br:	Brazil	**Ru:**	Russia
Cn:	China	**SA:**	Saudi Arabia
In:	Indonesia	**S Af:**	South Africa
Iq:	Iraq	**UAE:**	United Arab Emirates
Ka:	Kazakhstan	**Uk:**	Ukraine
Li:	Libya	**USA:**	United States of America
Ni:	Nigeria	**Ve:**	Venezuela

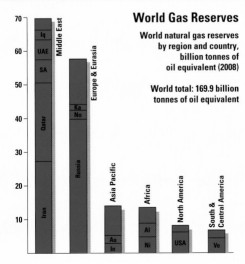

World Gas Reserves

World natural gas reserves by region and country, billion tonnes of oil equivalent (2008)

World total: 169.9 billion tonnes of oil equivalent

World Coal Reserves

World coal reserves (including lignite) by region and country, billion tonnes (2008)

World total: 826.0 billion tonnes

Production

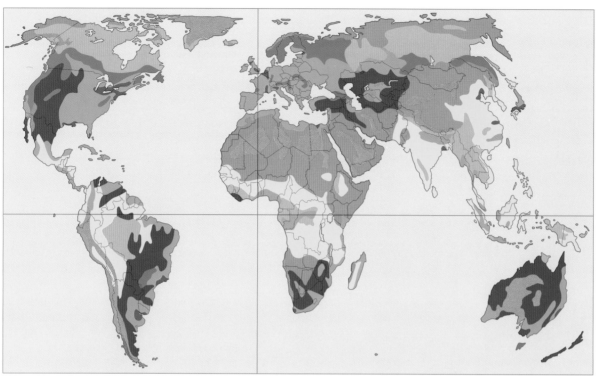

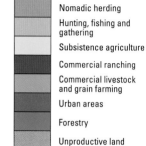
Staple Crops

Wheat

China 16.3% India 11.4% USA 9.9% Russia 9.2% France 5.1% Canada 4.1% Germany 3.6%

World total (2008): 689,946,000 tonnes

Maize

USA 37.4% China 20.2% Brazil 7.2%

World total (2006): 822,713,000 tonnes

Oats

Russia 22.6% Canada 16.6% USA 5.0% Poland 4.9% Australia 4.9% Finland 4.5% Spain 4.5%

World total (2008): 25,785,000 tonnes

Millet

India 31.8% Nigeria 25.4% Niger 10.9% China 5.1%

World total (2008): 35,651,000 tonnes

Rice/Paddy

China 28.2% India 21.6% Indonesia 8.8% Bangladesh 6.8% Vietnam 5.7% Burma 4.5% Thailand 4.4%

World total (2008): 685,013,000 tonnes

Potatoes

China 18.2% India 11.0% Russia 9.2% Ukraine 6.2% USA 6.0%

World total (2008): 314,140,000 tonnes

Soybeans

USA 34.9% Brazil 25.9% Argentina 20.0% China 6.7%

World total (2008): 230,953,000 tonnes

Cassava

Nigeria 19.1% Thailand 11.8% Brazil 11.1% Indonesia 9.3% Congo Dem Republic 6.4% Ghana 4.1%

World total (2008): 232,950,000 tonnes

Sugars

Sugar cane

Brazil 37.2% India 20.0% China 7.2% Thailand 4.2% Pakistan 3.7% Mexico 2.9%

World total (2008): 1,743,093,000 tonnes

Sugar beet

France 13.3% Russia 12.7% USA 11.8% Germany 10.1% Turkey 6.8% Ukraine 5.9% China 4.4% Poland 3.8%

World total (2008): 227,585,000 tonnes

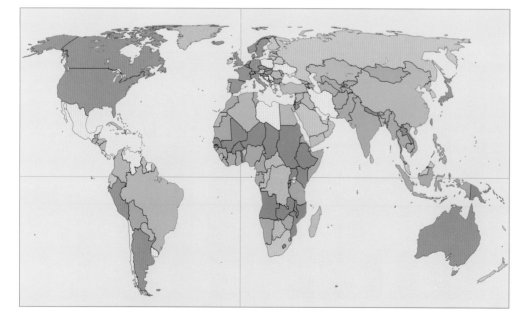

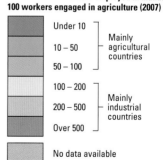
COPYRIGHT PHILIP'S

Mineral Production

Aluminium
China 33.8% | Russia 9.7% | Canada 8.0% | USA 6.8% | Australia 5.1% | Brazil 4.3% | Norway 3.5%

World total (2008): 39,000,000 tonnes (refined metal)

Bauxite
Australia 29.9% | China 17.1% | Brazil 10.7% | India 10.3% | Guinea 9.0% | Jamaica 6.8% | Russia 3.1% | Venezuela 2.7% | Surinam 2.6% | Kazakhstan 2.4%

World total (2008): 205,000,000 tonnes

Chromium
S. Africa 44.9% | Kazakhstan 17.1% | India 15.4%

World total (2008): 21,500,000 tonnes

Copper
Chile 36.1% | Peru 7.7% | USA 7.6% | China 6.1% | Indonesia 5.7% | Australia 5.0% | Russia 4.8%

World total (2008): 15,400,000 tonnes

Diamonds
Congo (Dem. Rep.) 29.9% | Australia 23.4% | Russia 19.5% | S. Africa 11.7% | Botswana 10.4%

World total (2008): 169,000,000 carats

Gold
China 11.8% | S. Africa 10.8% | Australia 10.5% | USA 10.2% | Peru 7.3% | Russia 6.7%

World total (2008): 2,340,000 kg (metal content)

Iron Ore
China 34.8% | Brazil 17.5% | Australia 14.7% | India 8.9% | Russia 5.2% | Ukraine 3.3% | USA 2.6%

World total (2008): 2,030,000,000 tonnes

Lead
China 39.1% | Australia 16.8% | USA 10.7% | Peru 9.0% | Mexico 2.6%

World total (2008): 3,840,000 tonnes

Manganese
S. Africa 20.6% | Australia 20.2% | China 15.9% | Gabon 11.8% | Brazil 7.4% | India 7.1%

World total (2008): 12,600,000 tonnes

Mercury
China 60.6% | Kyrgyzstan 18.9%

World total (2008): 1,320,000 tonnes (metal content)

Nickel
Russia 16.9% | Canada 15.3% | Indonesia 13.8% | Australia 9.7% | New Caledonia 7.5% | Colombia 6.1% | China 5.1%

World total (2008): 1,660,000 tonnes

Silver
Peru 16.6% | Mexico 14.2% | China 12.8% | Australia 8.9% | Chile 9.2% | Poland 6.2%

World total (2008): 20,400 kg (metal content)

Tin
China 41.4% | Indonesia 31.3% | Peru 12.0% | Bolivia 5.4% | Brazil 2.9%

World total (2008): 326,000 tonnes

Uranium
Canada 20.5% | Kazakhstan 19.4% | Australia 19.2% | Namibia 10.0% | Russia 8.0% | Niger 6.9%

World total (2008): 43,800 tonnes

Zinc
China 26.6% | Australia 13.9% | Peru 13.2% | Canada 5.7% | USA 7.4% | Mexico 3.9% | Kazakhstan 3.5%

World total (2008): 10,900,000 tonnes

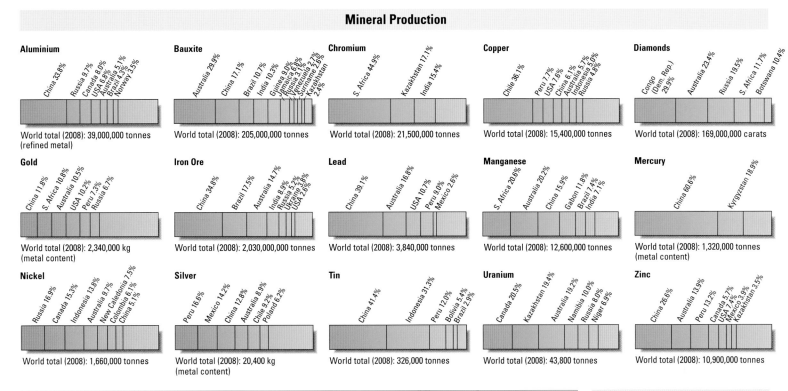

Mineral Distribution

The map shows the richest sources of the most important minerals (major mineral locations are named)

- ● Bauxite
- ◖ Chromium
- □ Cobalt
- ▢ Copper
- ◆ Diamonds
- ▽ Gold
- ● Iron ore
- ▲ Lead
- ▲ Manganese
- ▽ Mercury
- ▲ Molybdenum
- ▪ Nickel
- ▽ Potash
- ◠ Silver
- ▽ Tin
- ▽ Tungsten
- ◆ Zinc

The map does not show undersea deposits, most of which are considered inaccessible.

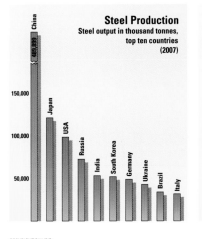

Steel Production
Steel output in thousand tonnes, top ten countries (2007)

China 489,899; Japan; USA; Russia; India; South Korea; Germany; Ukraine; Brazil; Italy

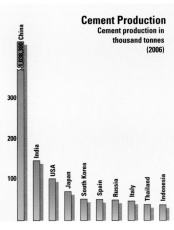

Cement Production
Cement production in thousand tonnes (2006)

China 1,038,300; India; USA; Japan; South Korea; Spain; Russia; Italy; Thailand; Indonesia

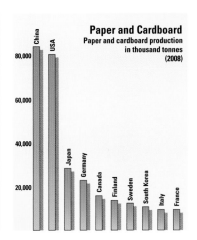

Paper and Cardboard
Paper and cardboard production in thousand tonnes (2008)

China; USA; Japan; Germany; Canada; Finland; Sweden; South Korea; Italy; France

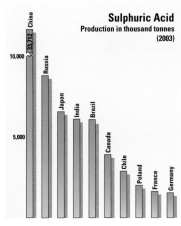

Sulphuric Acid
Production in thousand tonnes (2003)

China 33,712; Russia; Japan; India; Brazil; Canada; Chile; Poland; France; Germany

27

Trade

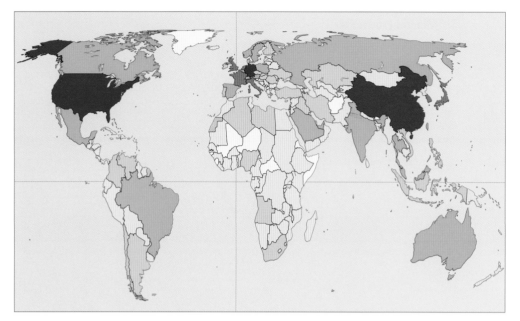

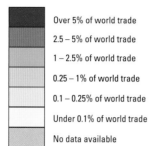
Countries with the largest share of world trade

1. China	9.86%	6. Netherlands	3.28%
2. Germany	9.80%	7. Italy	3.05%
3. USA	8.21%	8. South Korea	2.93%
4. Japan	4.26%	9. UK	2.90%
5. France	3.77%	10. Hong Kong (China)	2.70%

The Main Trading Nations

The imports and exports of the top ten trading nations as a percentage of world trade (2006). Each country's trade in manufactured goods is shown in dark blue

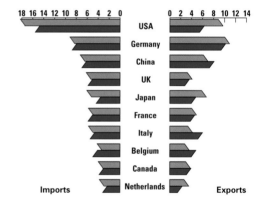

Imports   Exports

Major Exports

Leading manufactured items and their exporters

Motor Vehicles
World total (2008): US$ 3,355,798 million

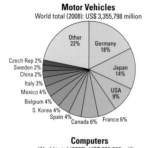

Telecommunications Gear
World total (2008): US$ 1,619,703 million

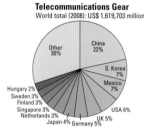

Petrol Products
World total (2008): US$ 1,819,371 million

Computers
World total (2007): US$ 236,396 million

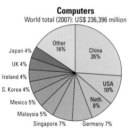

Electrical Components
World total (2008): US$ 5,333,323 million

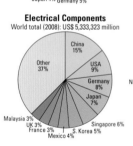

Pharmaceuticals
World total (2008): US$ 1,238,425 million

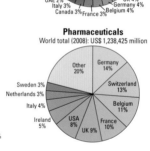

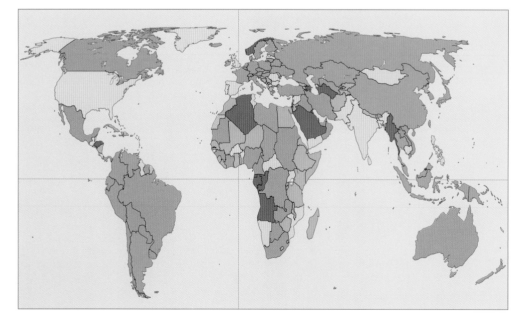

Balance of Trade

Value of exports in proportion to the value of imports (2009)

Imports exceed exports by:

- More than 40%
- 20 – 40%
- 20% either side
- 20 – 40%
- More than 40%
- No data available

Exports exceed imports by:

The total world trade balance should amount to zero, since exports must equal imports on a global scale. In practice, at least $100 billion in exports go unrecorded, leaving the world with an apparent deficit and many countries in a better position than public accounting reveals. However, a favourable trade balance is not necessarily a sign of prosperity: many poorer countries must maintain a high surplus in order to service debts, and do so by restricting imports below the levels needed to sustain successful economies.

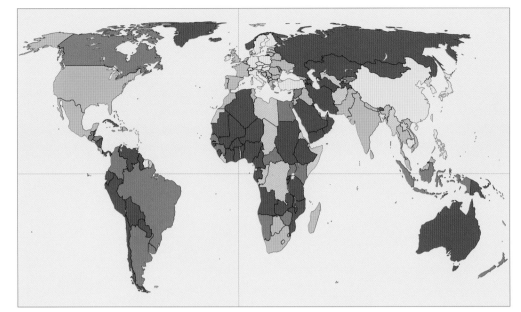

Trade in Primary Exports

Primary exports as a percentage of total export value (2008)

- Over 75%
- 50 – 75%
- 20 – 50%
- Under 20%
- No data available

Primary exports are raw materials or partly processed products that form the basis for manufacturing. They are the necessary requirements of industries and include agricultural products, minerals, fuels and timber, as well as many semi-manufactured goods such as cotton, which has been spun but not woven, wood pulp or flour. Many developed countries have few natural resources and rely on imports for the majority of their primary products. The countries of South-east Asia export hardwoods to the rest of the world, while many South American countries are heavily dependent on coffee exports.

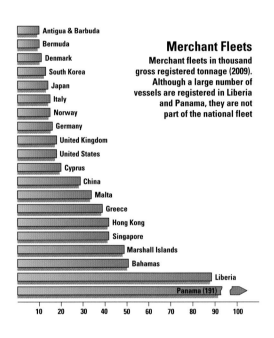

Merchant Fleets

Merchant fleets in thousand gross registered tonnage (2009). Although a large number of vessels are registered in Liberia and Panama, they are not part of the national fleet

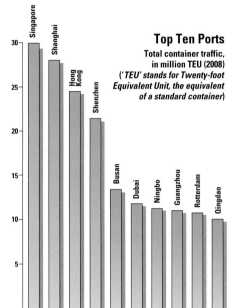

Top Ten Ports

Total container traffic, in million TEU (2008) ('TEU' stands for Twenty-foot Equivalent Unit, the equivalent of a standard container)

Types of Vessels

World fleet by type of vessel (2009)

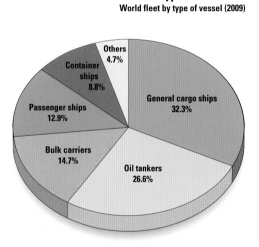

- Others 4.7%
- Container ships 8.8%
- Passenger ships 12.9%
- Bulk carriers 14.7%
- General cargo ships 32.3%
- Oil tankers 26.6%

Exports Per Capita

Value of exports in US $, divided by total population (2009)

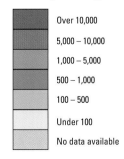

- Over 10,000
- 5,000 – 10,000
- 1,000 – 5,000
- 500 – 1,000
- 100 – 500
- Under 100
- No data available

Countries with highest exports per capita

San Marino	$153,413
Svalbard (Norway)	$93,573
Liechtenstein	$71,057
Singapore	$52,603
Hong Kong (China)	$46,335
Qatar	$44,919

Travel and Tourism

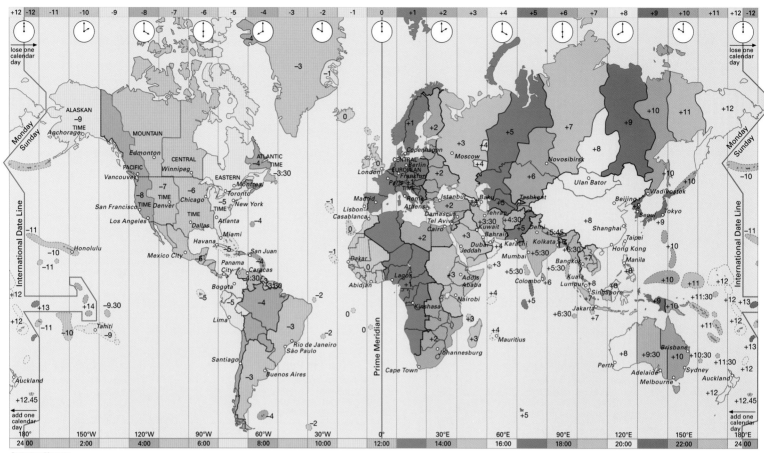

Projection: Mercator

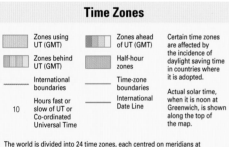

Time Zones

Zones using UT (GMT)	Zones ahead of UT (GMT)	Certain time zones are affected by the incidence of daylight saving time in countries where it is adopted.
Zones behind UT (GMT)	Half-hour zones	
International boundaries	Time-zone boundaries	Actual solar time, when it is noon at Greenwich, is shown along the top of the map.
10 Hours fast or slow of UT or Co-ordinated Universal Time	International Date Line	

The world is divided into 24 time zones, each centred on meridians at 15° intervals, which is the longitudinal distance the sun travels every hour. The meridian running through Greenwich, London, passes through the middle of the first zone.

Rail and Road: The Leading Nations

Total rail network ('000 km)	Passenger km per head per year	Total road network ('000 km)	Vehicle km per head per year	Number of vehicles per km of roads
1. USA 233.8	Japan 1,891	USA 6,378.3	USA....................12,505	Hong Kong 287
2. Russia 85.5	Switzerland 1,751	India 3,319.6	Luxembourg 7,989	Qatar....................284
3. Canada 73.2	Belarus 1,334	China 1,765.2	Kuwait.................7,251	UAE.......................232
4. India 63.1	France 1,203	Brazil 1,724.9	France 7,142	Germany 195
5. China..................60.5	Ukraine.................1,100	Canada.............1,408.8	Sweden..............6,991	Lebanon 191
6. Germany.............36.1	Russia.................1,080	Japan 1,171.4	Germany 6,806	Macau.................172
7. Argentina 34.2	Austria.................1,008	France 893.1	Denmark 6,764	Singapore 167
8. France.................29.3	Denmark 999	Australia 811.6	Austria................6,518	South Korea 160
9. Mexico.................26.5	Netherlands 855	Spain 664.9	Netherlands 5,984	Kuwait 156
10. South Africa.........22.7	Germany 842	Russia 537.3	UK 5,738	Taiwan 150
11. Brazil..................22.1	Italy 811	Italy 479.7	Canada 5,493	Israel 111
12. Ukraine 22.1	Belgium 795	UK 371.9	Italy......................4,852	Malta 110

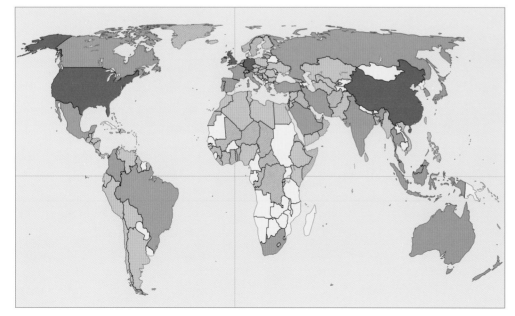

Air Travel

Number of air passengers carried (2008)

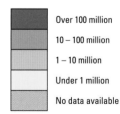

	Over 100 million
	10 – 100 million
	1 – 10 million
	Under 1 million
	No data available

World's busiest airports (2009) – total passengers
1. Atlanta (Hartsfield Internat'l)
2. London (Heathrow)
3. Beijing (Capital Internat'l)
4. Chicago (O'Hare Internat'l)
5. Tokyo (Haneda)

World's busiest airports (2009) – international passengers
1. London (Heathrow)
2. Paris (Charles de Gaulle)
3. Amsterdam (Schipol)
4. Hong Kong (International)
5. Frankfurt (International)

Destinations

- Cultural and historical centres
- Coastal resorts
- Ski resorts
- Centres of entertainment
- Places of pilgrimage
- Places of great natural beauty
- Popular holiday cruise routes

Visitors to the USA

Overseas arrivals to the USA, in thousands (2006)

1. Canada	15,995
2. Mexico	13,400
3. UK	4,176
4. Japan	3,673
5. Germany	1,386
6. France	790
7. South Korea	758
8. Australia	603
9. Italy	533
10. Brazil	525

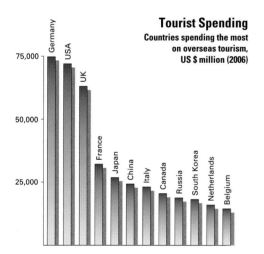

Tourist Spending

Countries spending the most on overseas tourism, US $ million (2006)

Importance of Tourism

	Arrivals from abroad (2006)	% of world total (2006)
1. France	76,001,000	9.0%
2. Spain	55,577,000	6.6%
3. USA	46,085,000	5.4%
4. China	41,761,000	4.9%
5. Italy	36,513,000	4.3%
6. UK	29,970,000	3.5%
7. Germany	21,500,000	2.5%
8. Mexico	20,617,000	2.4%
9. Turkey	20,273,000	2.4%
10. Austria	19,952,000	2.4%
11. Russia	19,940,000	2.4%
12. Canada	19,152,000	2.3%

The 846 million international arrivals in 2006 represented an additional 43 million over the 2005 level – making a new record year for the industry. Growth was common to all regions, but particularly strong in Asia and the Pacific, and in the Middle East.

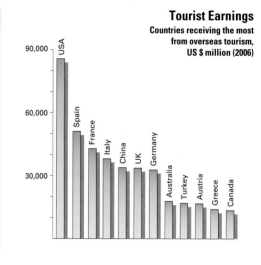

Tourist Earnings

Countries receiving the most from overseas tourism, US $ million (2006)

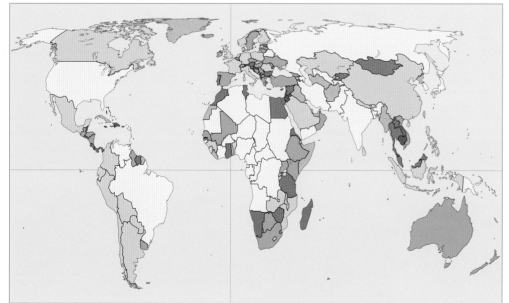

Tourism

Tourism receipts as a percentage of Gross National Income (2006)

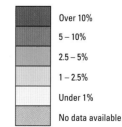

- Over 10%
- 5 – 10%
- 2.5 – 5%
- 1 – 2.5%
- Under 1%
- No data available

WORLD CITIES

AMSTERDAM	2	HONG KONG	12	MUMBAI	20	TEHRAN	31
ATHENS	2	ISTANBUL	12	MUNICH	21	TORONTO	31
ATLANTA	3	JAKARTA	12	NEW ORLEANS	21	VIENNA	32
BAGHDAD	3	JERUSALEM	13	NEW YORK	22	WARSAW	32
BANGKOK	3	JOHANNESBURG	13	ORLANDO	23	WASHINGTON	33
BARCELONA	4	KARACHI	13	OSAKA	23	WELLINGTON	33
BEIJING	4	KOLKATA	14	OSLO	23		
BERLIN	5	LAGOS	14	PARIS	24	INDEX	34–39
BOSTON	6	LAS VEGAS	14	PRAGUE	25		
BRUSSELS	6	LIMA	14	RIO DE JANEIRO	25		
BUDAPEST	7	LONDON	15	ROME	26	WORLD CITIES	
BUENOS AIRES	7	LOS ANGELES	16	SAN FRANCISCO	26	SATELLITE IMAGES	
CAIRO	7	LISBON	16	ST PETERSBURG	27	CAPE TOWN	40
CAPE TOWN	8	MADRID	17	SANTIAGO	27	KARACHI	41
COPENHAGEN	8	MANILA	17	SÃO PAULO	27	LONDON	42
CHICAGO	9	MELBOURNE	18	SEOUL	27	MELBOURNE	43
DELHI	10	MEXICO CITY	18	SHANGHAI	28	NEW ORLEANS	44
DUBLIN	10	MIAMI	18	SINGAPORE	28	NEW YORK	45
EDINBURGH	11	MILAN	19	STOCKHOLM	29	SAN FRANCISCO	46
GUANGZHOU	11	MOSCOW	19	SYDNEY	29	SANTIAGO	47
HELSINKI	11	MONTRÉAL	20	TOKYO	30	TOKYO	48

CITY MAPS

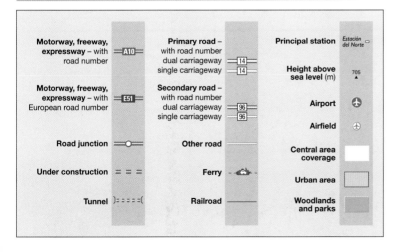

Motorway, freeway, expressway – with road number — A10

Motorway, freeway, expressway – with European road number — E51

Road junction

Under construction

Tunnel

Primary road – with road number
dual carriageway — 14
single carriageway — 14

Secondary road – with road number
dual carriageway — 96
single carriageway — 96

Other road

Ferry

Railroad

Principal station — Estación del Norte

Height above sea level (m) — 705

Airport

Airfield

Central area coverage

Urban area

Woodlands and parks

CENTRAL AREA MAPS

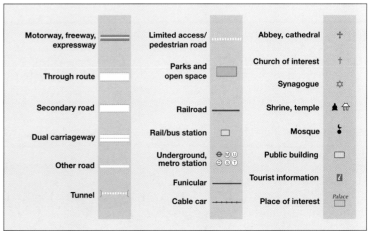

Motorway, freeway, expressway

Through route

Secondary road

Dual carriageway

Other road

Tunnel

Limited access/ pedestrian road

Parks and open space

Railroad

Rail/bus station

Underground, metro station

Funicular

Cable car

Abbey, cathedral — †

Church of interest — †

Synagogue — ✡

Shrine, temple — ⛩

Mosque

Public building

Tourist information — i

Place of interest — Palace

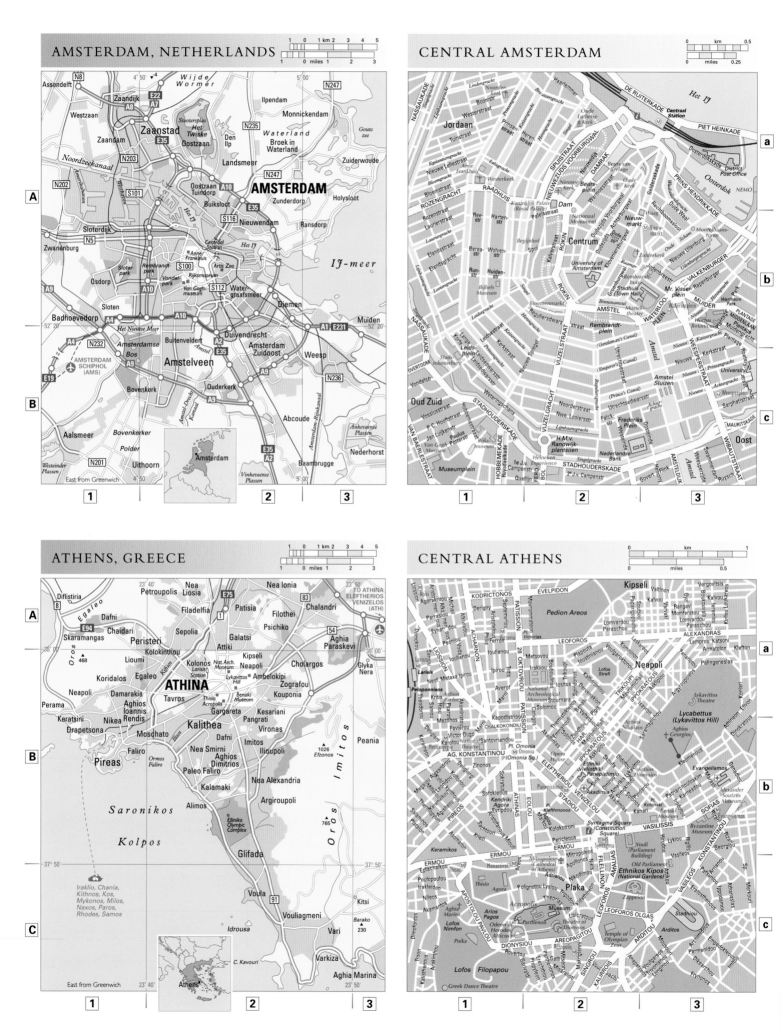

COPYRIGHT PHILIP'S

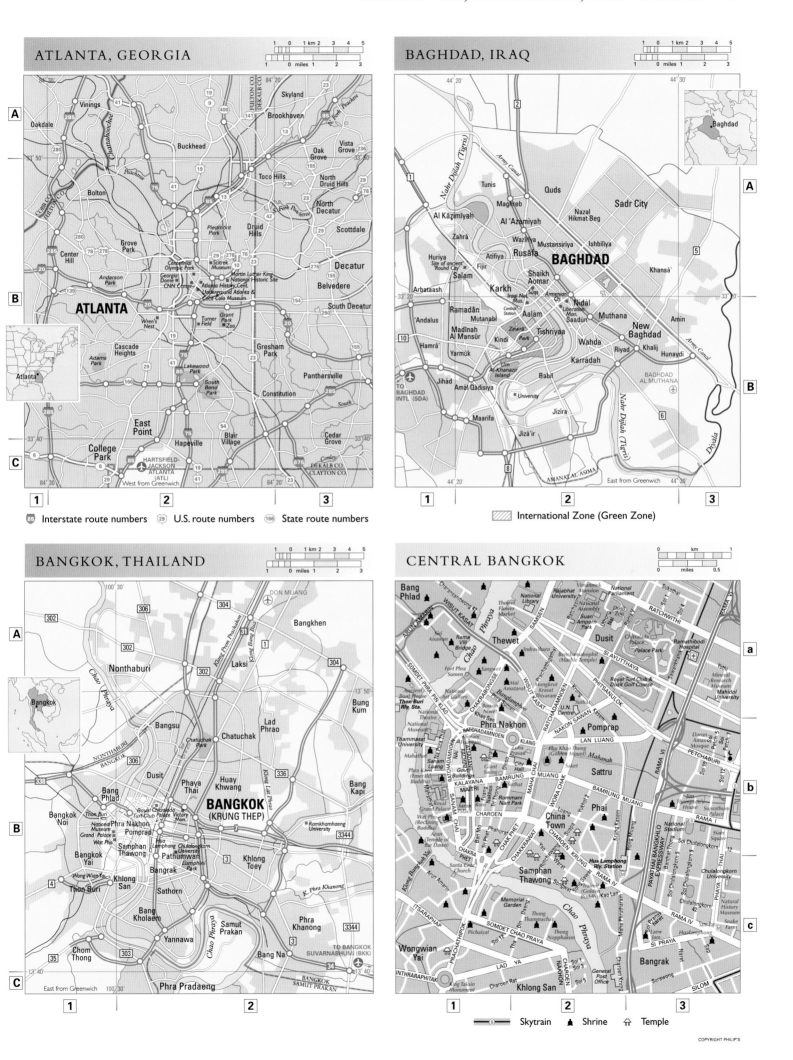

ATLANTA, GEORGIA

1 0 1 km 2 3 4 5
1 0 miles 1 2 3

A

Vinings
Oakdale
285
41
Skyland
Brookhaven
85
N. Fork Peachtree
400
141
9
19
23

Buckhead
13
Oak Grove
Vista Grove 236

280
33° 50'
Bolton
19
155
Toco Hills
North Druid Hills
236
78
209
75
41
13
North Decatur
S. Fork Peachtree
42
Scottdale
29

139
Grove Park
Piedmont Park
Druid Hills
29
278
278
155
Decatur

B
78 278
Center Hill
285
Centennial Olympic Park
10
Sciitrek Museum
Martin Luther King National Historic Site
Belvedere
154
33° 20'

20
Georgia Dome/CNN Center
Atlanta History Cent.
Underground Atlanta & Coca-Cola Museum
20
South Decatur
260

ATLANTA
Wren's Nest
Turner Field
Grant Park Zoo
19
154

Adams Park
Cascade Heights
41
75
Lakewood Park
23
Gresham Park
155
20

Atlanta
166
29
South Bend Park
Constitution
285

East Point
54
75
Blair Village
Pantherville

33° 40'
6
College Park
6
Hapeville
75
285
Cedar Grove
33° 40'

C
285
29
HARTSFIELD-JACKSON ATLANTA (ATL)
19
41
Conley
675
DEKALB CO. CLAYTON CO.

84° 30'
West from Greenwich
84° 20'
23

1   **2**   **3**

85 Interstate route numbers   29 U.S. route numbers   166 State route numbers

BAGHDAD, IRAQ

1 0 1 km 2 3 4 5
1 0 miles 1 2 3

Baghdad

44° 20'
2
44° 30'

Nahr Dijlah (Tigris)
Army Canal

A
1
Tunis
Quds
Sadr City
33° 20'

Maghteb
Nazal
Hikmat Beg

Al Kāzimīyah
Al 'Azamīyah
Khansā'
5

Zahrā
Wazīriya
Mustansiriya
Ishbiliya

Huriya
Site of ancient Round City
Atifiya
Rusāfa
BAGHDAD

Arbataash
Fijir
Salam
Shaikh Aomar
Suq
Armenian Ch.

Iraqi Nat. Mus.
Central Station
Zawrā' Park
Nidal
Liberation Mon. Saadūn
Amin

B
'Andalus
Ramadān
Karkh
Aalām
Tishriyaa
Muthana
New Baghdad
Army Canal
33° 20'

10
Hamrā
Mutanabi
Kindi
Wahda
Amin

Madīnah Al Mansūr
Yarmūk
Riyad
Khalij
Karrādah
Hunaydi

Jihād
Um Al-Khanazir Island
Babil
Nahr Dijlah (Tigris)
Diyala

TO BAGHDAD INTL (SDA)
Amāl Qādisiya
University
Jizira
6
B

8
Maarifa
Jizā'ir
BAGHDAD AL MUTHANA

44° 20'
AMANAT AL. ASIMA
East from Greenwich
44° 30'

1   **2**   **3**

International Zone (Green Zone)

BANGKOK, THAILAND

1 0 1 km 2 3 4 5
1 0 miles 1 2 3

Bangkok

100° 30'
302
306
304
DON MUANG

A
Chao Phraya
Khlong Prem Prachakon
31
Bangkhen

302
Nonthaburi
304
Laksi

13° 50'
302
Bangsu
336
Chatuchak Park
Chatuchak
Lad Phrao
Bung Kum

338
NONTHABURI
BANGKOK
306
Dusit
Phaya Thai
Huay Khwang
Klong Lat Phrao
Bang Kapi

B
Bang Phlad
Royal Chitralada Palace Turf Club & Palace
BANGKOK (KRUNG THEP)
Victory Mon.
Ramkhamhaeng University
3344

Bangkok Noi
National Museum
Phra Nakhon
Grand Palace
Pomprap
Hua Lamphong
Chulalongkorn University
3
Khlong Toey

Wat Pho
Samphan Thawong
Pathumwan
Lumphini Park

Bangkok Yai
Bangrak

4
Wong Wian Yai
Khlong San
Sathorn
K. Phra Khanong

Thon Buri
Bang Kholaem
Phra Khanong
3344

Yannawa
Chao Phraya
Samut Prakan
Bang Na
34
TO BANGKOK SUVARNABHUMI (BKK)

C
35
Chom Thong
303
Phra Pradaeng
BANGKOK SAMUT PRAKAN

13° 40'
East from Greenwich
100° 30'

1   **2**

CENTRAL BANGKOK

0 km 1
0 miles 0.5

Bang Phlad
Charansanitwong 43
Vimanmek Mansion
National Parliament
RAMA V

WISUT KASAT
Thewet Flower Market
National Library
Rajabhat University
National Assembly
Suan Amporn Park
Dusit Zoo
RATCHWITHI

a
ARUN AMARIN
Chao Phraya
Thewet
Rama VIII Bridge
Indravarharn
Dusit
Chitralada Palace
Chitralada Palace Park
Ramathibodi Hospital

Si Aisawan
SOMDET PHRA PIN KLAO
SAMSEN
Benchamabophit (Marble Temple)
SI AYUTTHAYA
Yothi
Mineral Research Museum
Mahidol University

Ancient Boat House
National Art Gallery
Thon Buri Rly. Sta.
Fort Phra Sumen
Mai Amatarot
Mongkrut Krasat
Royal Turf Club & Dusit Golf Course
PHITSANULOK

National Theatre
National Museum
Bowon Niwet
U.N. Centre

WISUT KASAT
Sangwet
Banglamphoo

b
Thammasat University
Phra Nakhon
RATCHADAMNOEN
NAKON SAWAN
Pomprap
RAMA VI

Mahathat
Sanam Luang
Loha Prasad
Wat Saket
Darun Aman Mosque
PETCHABURI

Phra Kaeo (Emerald Buddha)
Giant Swing
Phu Khao Thong (Golden Mount)
Mahanak
PETCHABURI

Royal Grand Palace
Govt Buildings
City Hall
LAN LUANG
Jim Thompson's House
Suprathara Mosque

KALAYANA
Sanam Chai
MAITRI
Rommani Nart Park
BAMRUNG
Sattru

CHAROEN
Wat Pho (Reclining Buddha)
Arun (Temple of the Dawn)
WORA CHAK
Phai
BAMRUNG MUANG
National Stadium
Siam Square
RAMA I

c
ITSARAPHAP
Santa Cruz Church
CHAKRAWAT
China Town
CHAROEN KRUNG
Chulalongkorn University
Natural History Museum

Klong Bang Luang
Arun Amarin
Yaowarat
RAMA IV
Snake Farm

Memorial Garden
Samphan Thawong
Hua Lamphong Rly. Station

Wongwian Yai
Pichaiyat
Thong Thammachat
Chao Phraya
General Post Office
Bangrak

King Taksin Monument
Charoen Rat
Khlong San
SI PRAYA
SILOM
Surawong

1   **2**   **3**

━S━ Skytrain   ▲ Shrine   ⚎ Temple

COPYRIGHT PHILIP'S

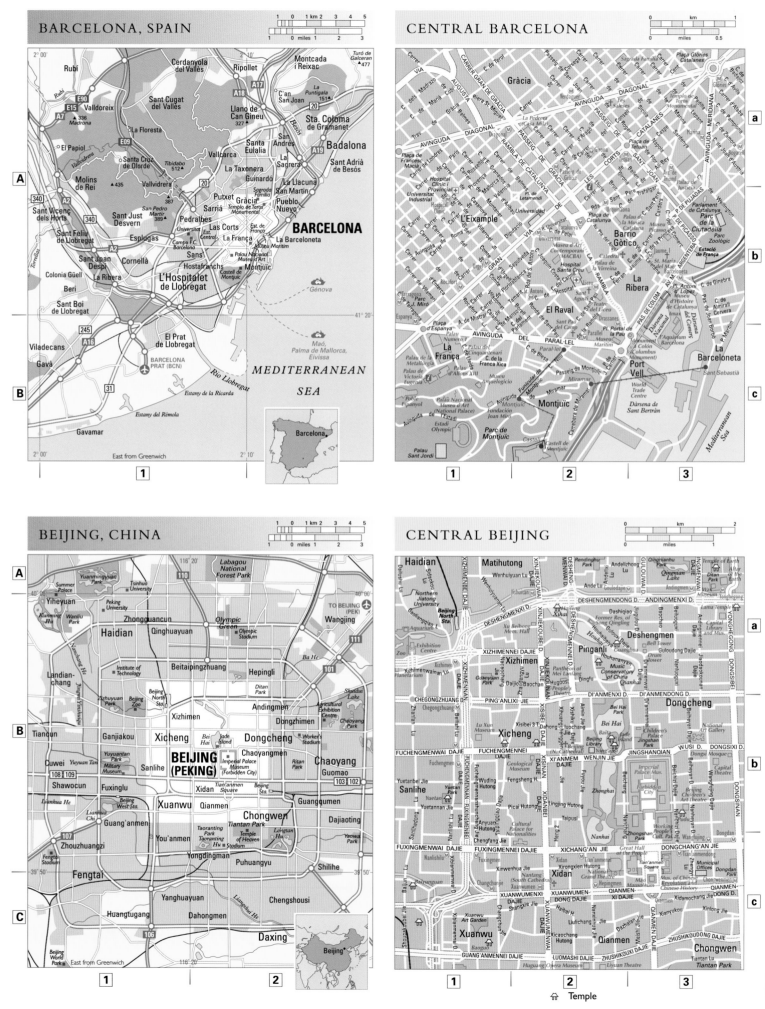

BARCELONA, SPAIN

CENTRAL BARCELONA

BEIJING, CHINA

CENTRAL BEIJING

Temple

BERLIN, GERMANY

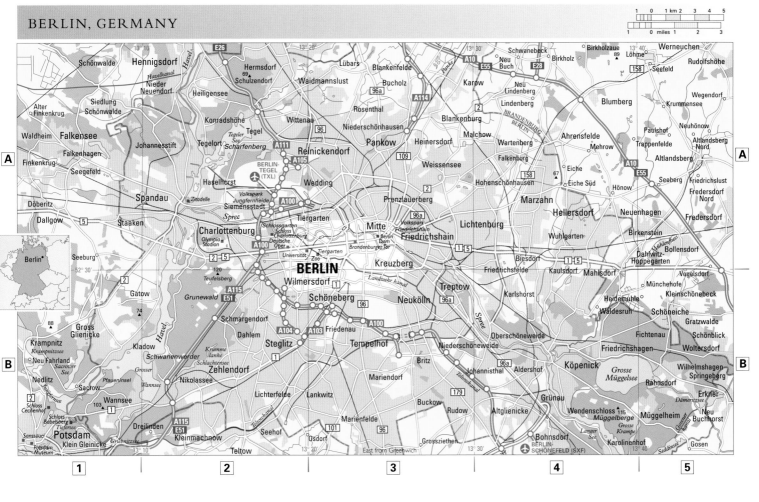

CENTRAL BERLIN

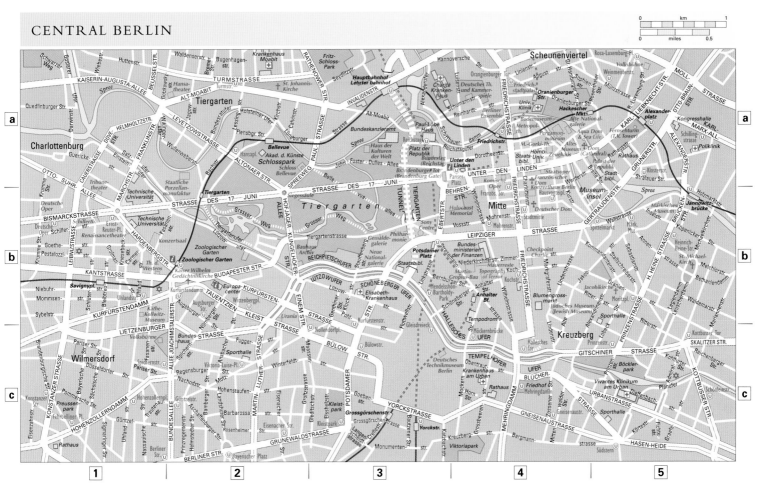

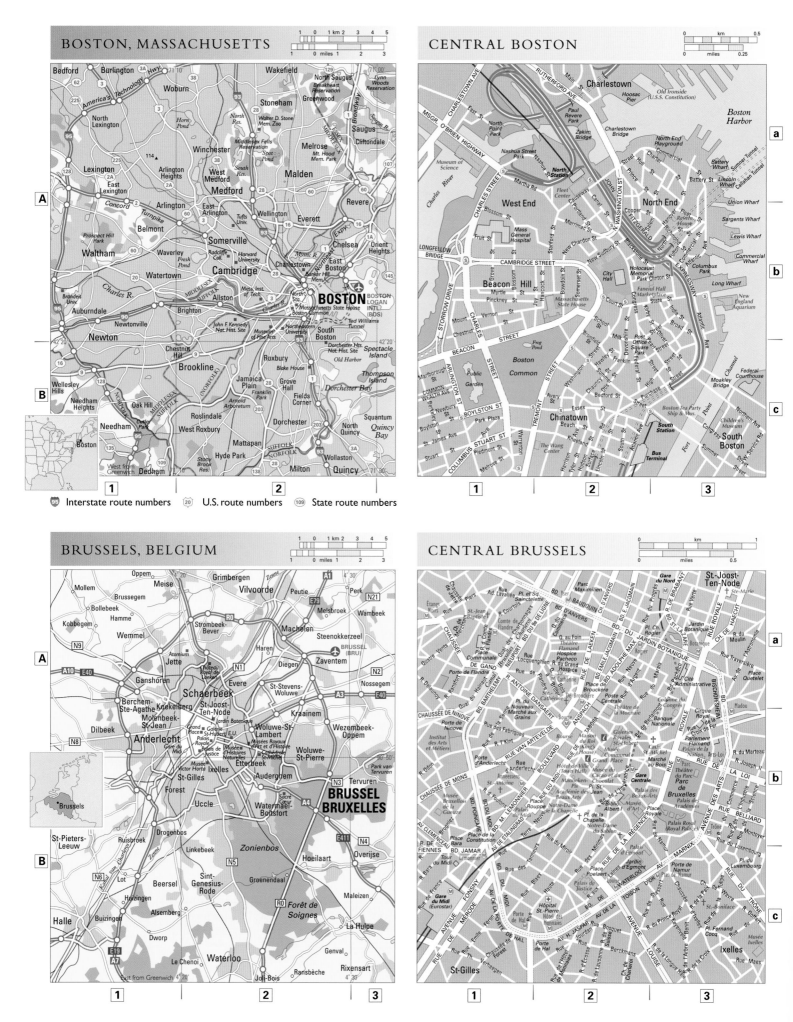

BOSTON, MASSACHUSETTS

CENTRAL BOSTON

95 Interstate route numbers   20 U.S. route numbers   109 State route numbers

BRUSSELS, BELGIUM

CENTRAL BRUSSELS

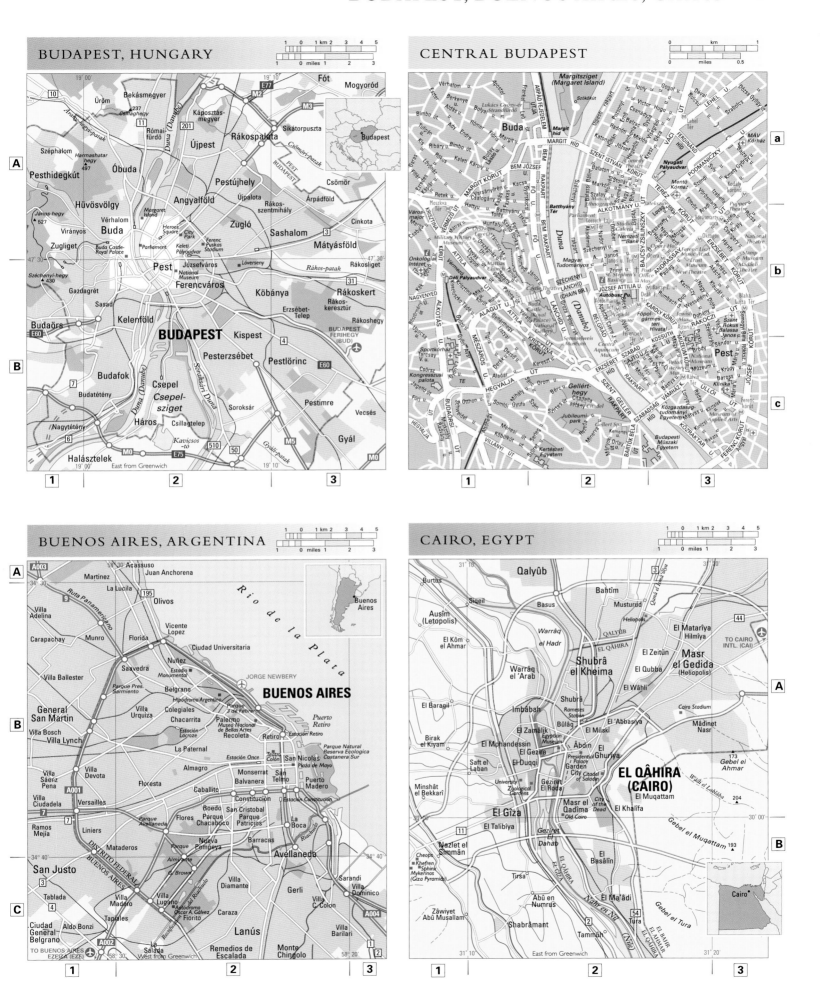

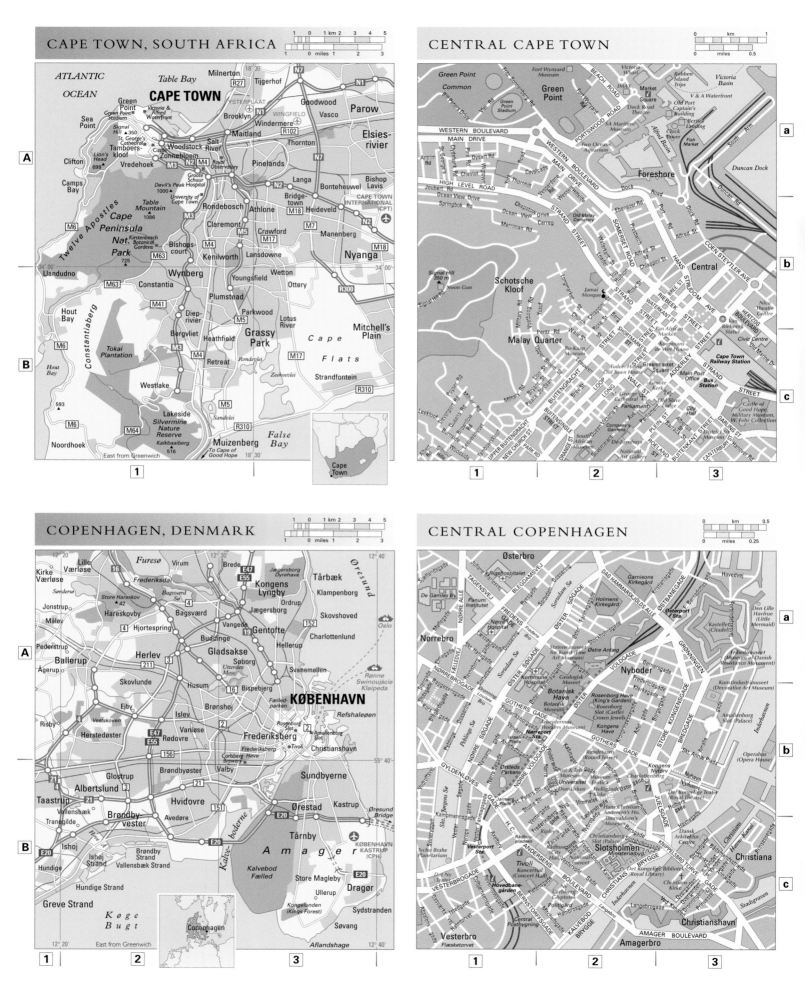

CHICAGO, ILLINOIS

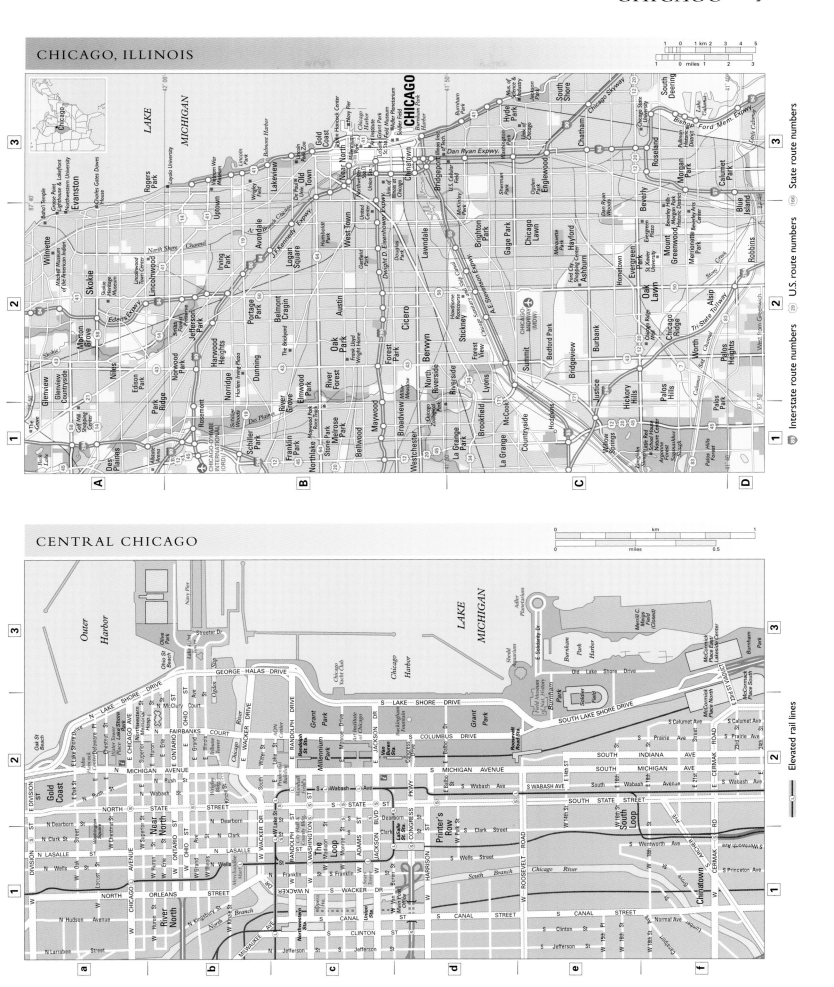

State route numbers (166)

U.S. route numbers (20)

Interstate route numbers (85)

CENTRAL CHICAGO

Elevated rail lines

COPYRIGHT PHILIP'S

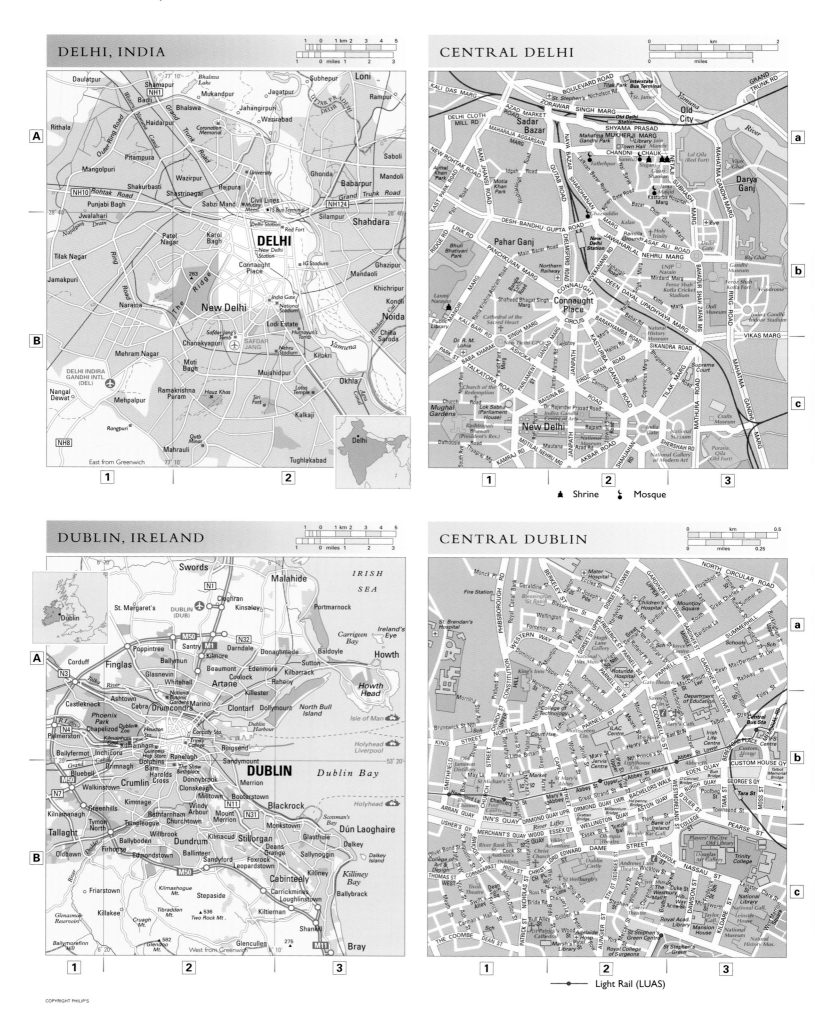

DELHI, INDIA

CENTRAL DELHI

▲ Shrine   ♪ Mosque

DUBLIN, IRELAND

CENTRAL DUBLIN

Light Rail (LUAS)

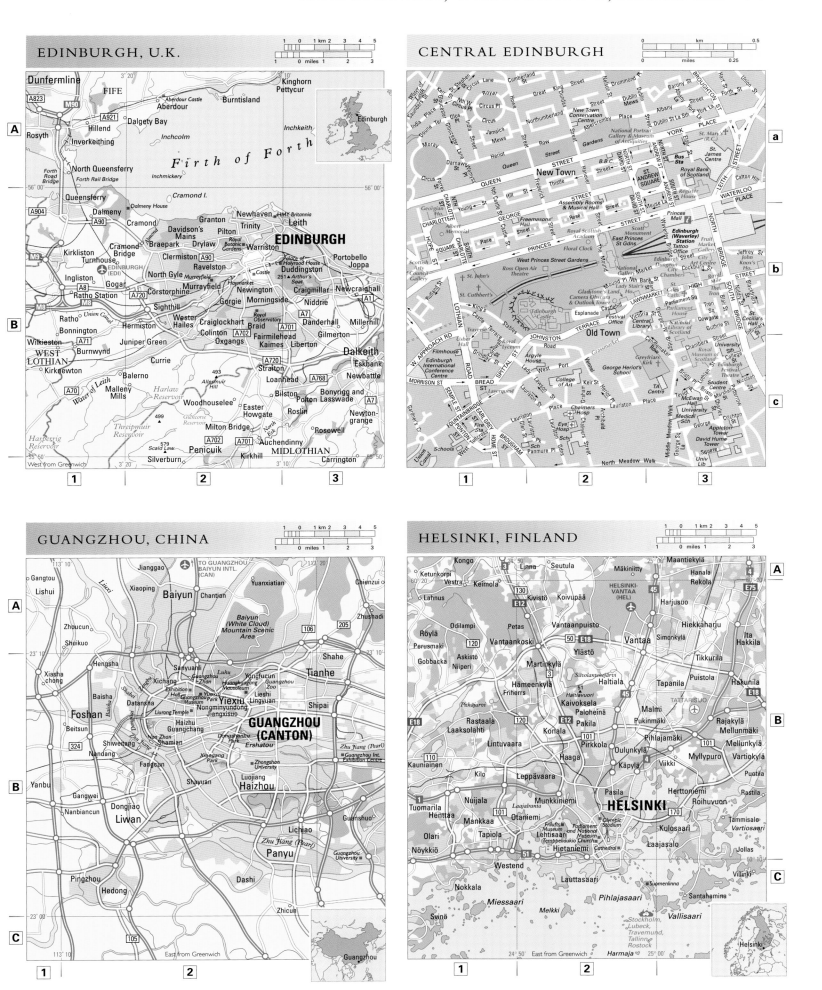

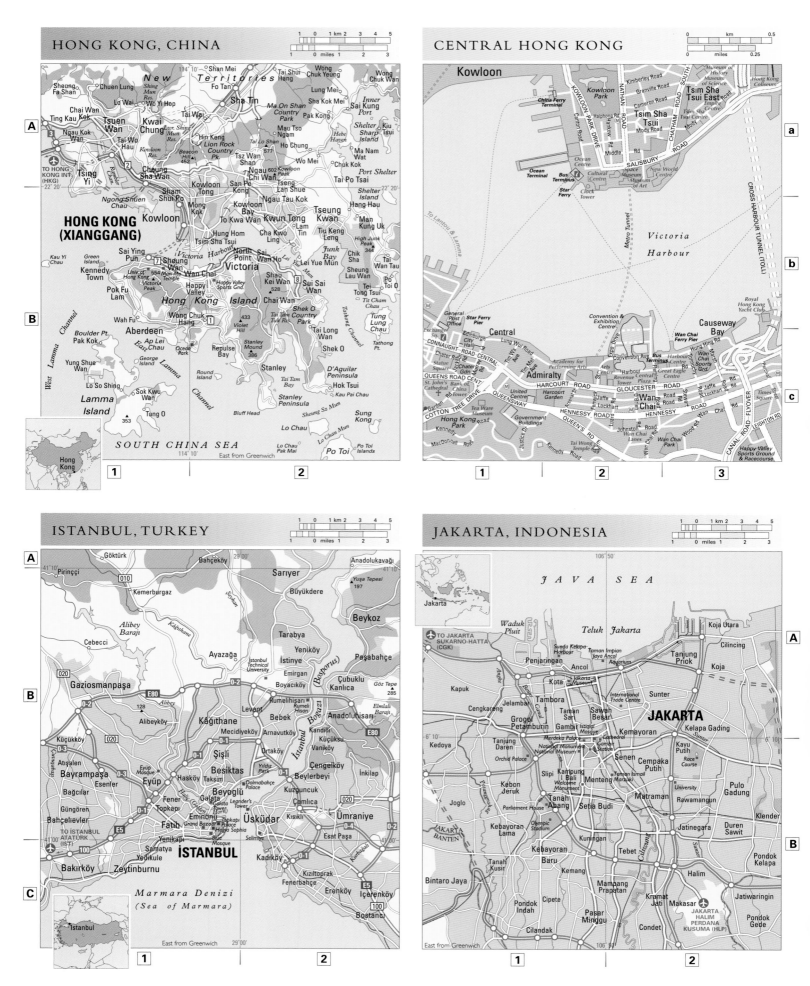

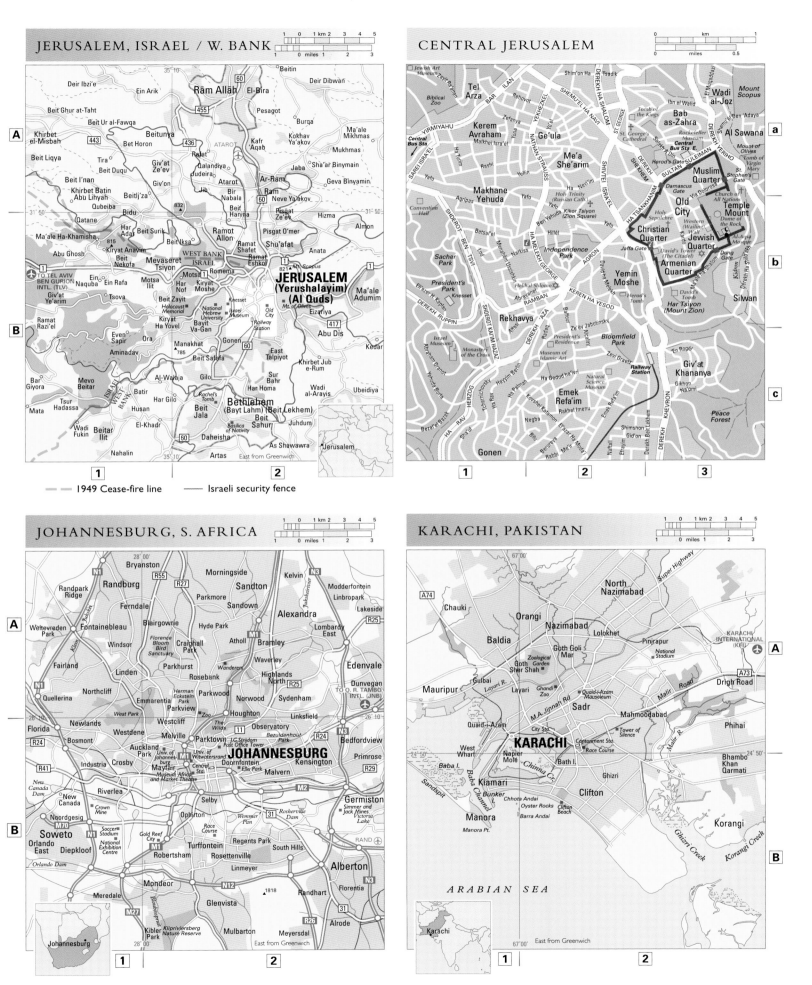

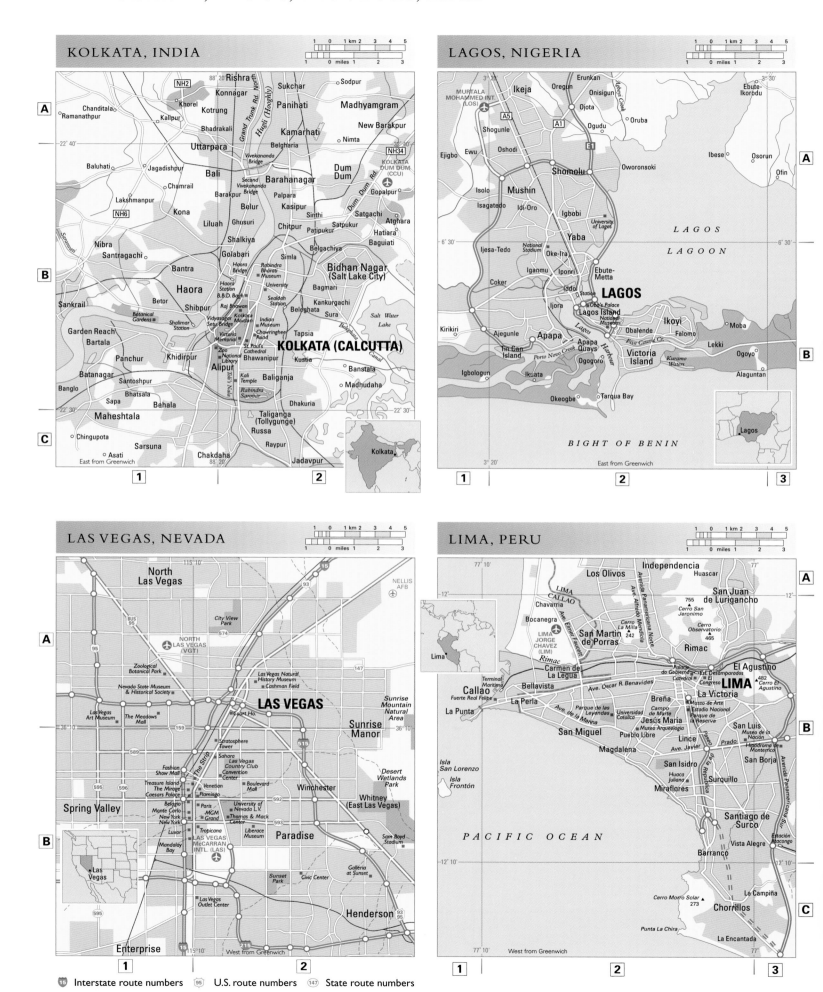

KOLKATA, INDIA

Rishra
Sopdur
Sukchar
Konnagar
Panihati
Madhyamgram
Khorel
Chanditala
Kotrung
Ramanathpur
Kalipur
Bhadrakali
Kamarhati
New Barakpur
Uttarpara
Vivekananda Bridge
Belgharia
Nimta
KOLKATA DUM DUM (CCU)
Baluhati
Jagadishpur
Bali
Barahanagar
Dum Dum
Lakshmanpur
Second Vivekananda Bridge
Palpara
Dum Dum Rd.
Chamrail
Barakpur
Kasipur
Gopalpur
NH6
Kona
Belur
Ghusuri
Sinthi
Satgachi
Atghara
Nibra
Shalkiya
Chitpur
Patipukur
Satpukur
Hatiaria
Santragachi
Golabari
Simla
Belgachiya
Baguiati
Haora Bridge
Rabindra Bharati Museum
University
Bantra
Haora Station
Bidhan Nagar (Salt Lake City)
Haora
B.B.D. Bagh
Sealdah Station
Bagmari
Betor
Raj Bhawan
Indian Museum
Kankurgachi
Shibpur
Beleghata
Sura
Sankrail
Botanical Gardens
Shalimar Station
Kolkata Maidan
Chowringhee Road
Tapsia
Salt Water Lake
Garden Reach
Vidyasagar Setu Bridge
St. Paul's Cathedral
KOLKATA (CALCUTTA)
Bartala
Victoria Memorial
Bhawanipur
Kustia
Zoo
National Library
Banstala
Panchur
Khidirpur
Alipur
Kali Temple
Baliganja
Batanagar
Santoshpur
Rabindra Sarovar
Madhudaha
Banglo
Bhatsala
Sapa
Behala
Dhakuria
Maheshtala
Taliganga (Tollygunge)
Chingupota
Russa
Sarsuna
Raypur
Asati
Chakdaha
Jadavpur
East from Greenwich

Kolkata

LAGOS, NIGERIA

Erunkan
Ikeja
Oregun
Onisigun
Ebute-Ikorodu
MURTALA MOHAMMED INT (LOS)
Ojota
Oruba
Shogunle
Ogudu
A5
A1
Ejigbo
Ewu
Oshodi
Oworonsoki
Ibese
Osorun
Isolo
Shomolu
Ofin
Mushin
Ofin
Isagatedo
Idi-Oro
Igbobi
University of Lagos
LAGOS LAGOON
Ijesa-Tedo
National Stadium
Yaba
Oke-Ira
Iganmu
Iponri
Coker
Ebute-Metta
Iddo
Oba's Palace
LAGOS
Kirikiri
Ijora
Lagos Island
National Museum
Ajegunle
Apapa
Obalende
Ikoyi
Tin Can Island
Apapa Quays
Falomo
Moba
Lagos Harbour
Lekki
Igbologun
Ogogoro
Victoria Island
Ogoyo
Ikuata
Porto Novo Creek
Kuramo Waters
Alaguntan
Okeogbe
Tarqua Bay

BIGHT OF BENIN
East from Greenwich

Lagos

LAS VEGAS, NEVADA

North Las Vegas
NELLIS AFB
BUS 95
City View Park
574
NORTH LAS VEGAS (VGT)
93
15
95
Zoological Botanical Park
147
Nevada State Museum & Historical Society
Las Vegas Natural History Museum
Cashman Field
LAS VEGAS
Las Vegas Art Museum
The Meadows Mall
159
Court Ho.
Sunrise Mountain Natural Area
Stratosphere Tower
515
Sunrise Manor
589
Fashion Show Mall
Sahara
Las Vegas Country Club Convention Center
Desert Wetlands Park
595
596
Treasure Island The Mirage Caesars Palace
Venetian
Boulevard Mall
592
Winchester
Spring Valley
Bellagio
Monte Carlo
New York New York
Paris
MGM Grand
University of Nevada L.V.
Whitney (East Las Vegas)
Luxor
Tropicana
Thomas & Mack Center
593
Liberace Museum
Mandalay Bay
LAS VEGAS McCARRAN INTL. (LAS)
Paradise
Sam Boyd Stadium
Las Vegas
Galleria at Sunset
Sunset Park
Civic Center
Las Vegas Outlet Center
Henderson
93 95
Enterprise
15
215
West from Greenwich

Las Vegas

LIMA, PERU

Independencia
Los Olivos
Huascar
LIMA CALLAO
Chavarria
San Juan de Lurigancho
Cerro San Jeronimo
Bocanegra
Avenida Panamericana Norte
San Martin de Porras
Cerro Observatorio
LIMA JORGE CHAVEZ (LIM)
Rimac
Rimac
El Agustino
Terminal Maritimo
Palacio do Gobierno
Est Desamparados
Congreso
LIMA
Callao
Carmen de La Legua
Cerro El Agustino
Fuerte Real Felipe
Bellavista
Catedral
La Victoria
La Punta
La Perla
Breña
San Luis
Ave. Oscar R. Benavides
Campo de Marte
Estadio Nacional
Parque de las Leyendas
Universidad Catolica
Jesús Maria
Parque de la Reserva
San Miguel
Museo Arqueológia
Lince
San Borja
Ave. de la Marina
Pueblo Libre
Magdalena
Ave. Javier
Hipodromo de Monterrico
Isla San Lorenzo
San Isidro
Huaca Juliana
Surquillo
Isla Frontón
Miraflores
PACIFIC OCEAN
Santiago de Surco
Vista Alegre
Estación Atocongo
Barranco
Cerro Morro Solar
La Campiña
Chorrillos
Punta La Chira
La Encantada
West from Greenwich

Lima

15 Interstate route numbers   95 U.S. route numbers   147 State route numbers

COPYRIGHT PHILIP'S

LONDON, U.K.

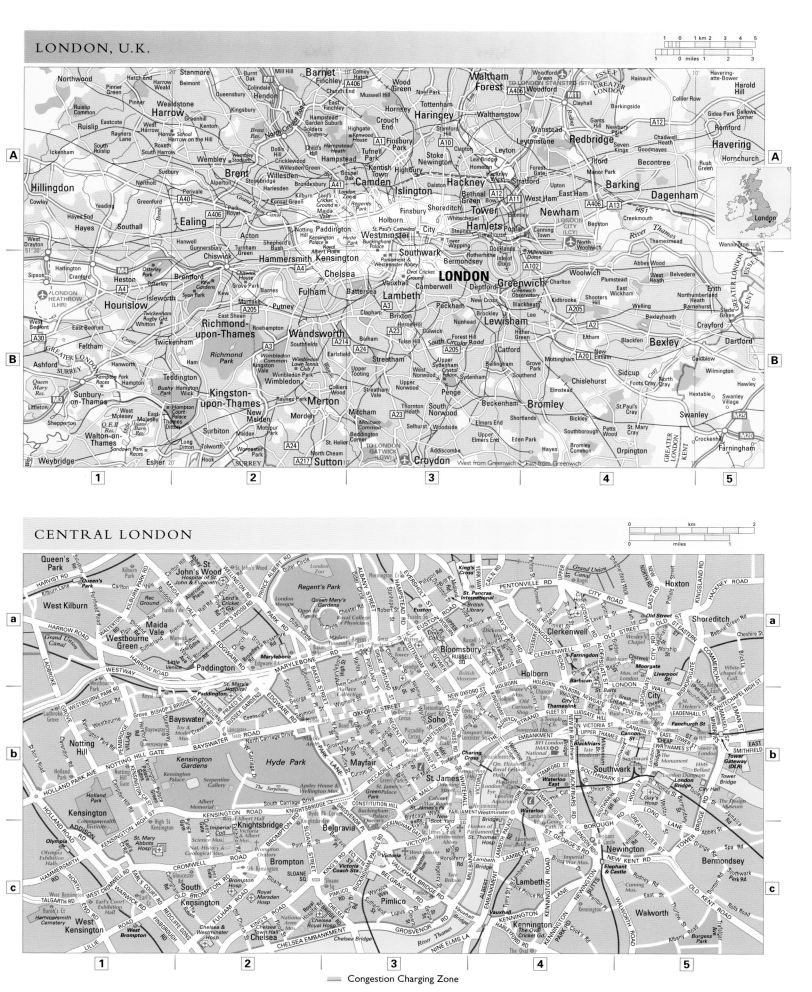

1   0   1 km 2   3   4   5
1   0 miles 1   2   3

A

B

1   2   3   4   5

CENTRAL LONDON

0   km   2
0   miles   1

a

b

c

1   2   3   4   5

▬ Congestion Charging Zone

COPYRIGHT PHILIP'S

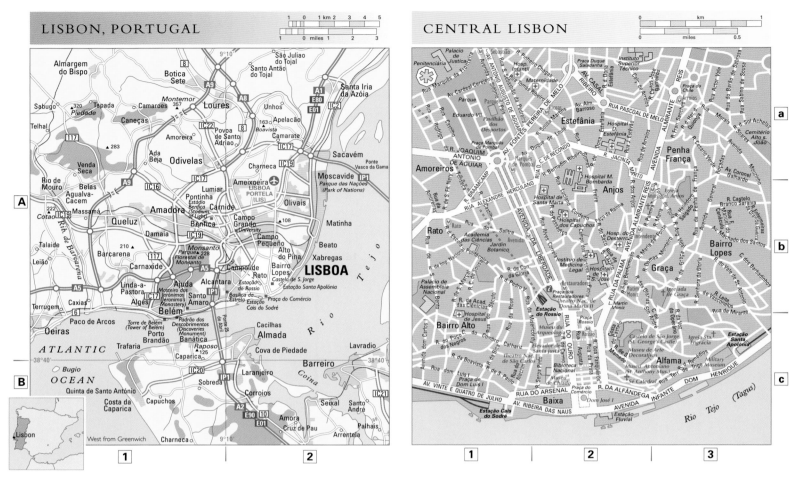

LISBON, PORTUGAL

CENTRAL LISBON

LOS ANGELES, CALIFORNIA

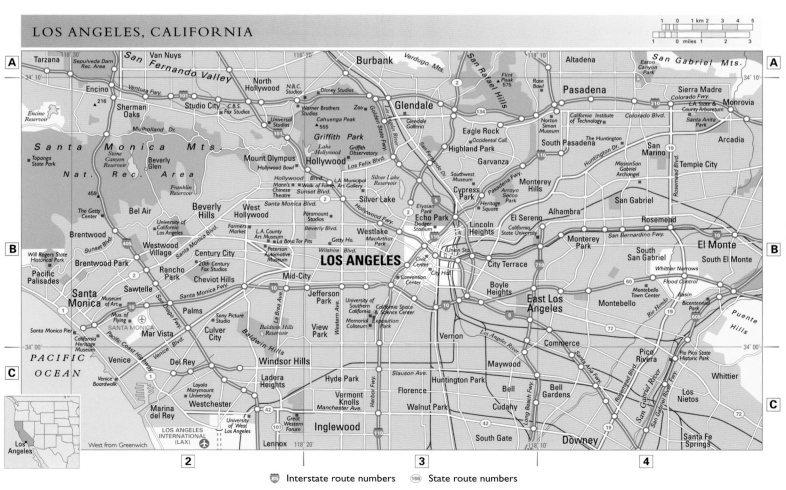

85 Interstate route numbers   166 State route numbers

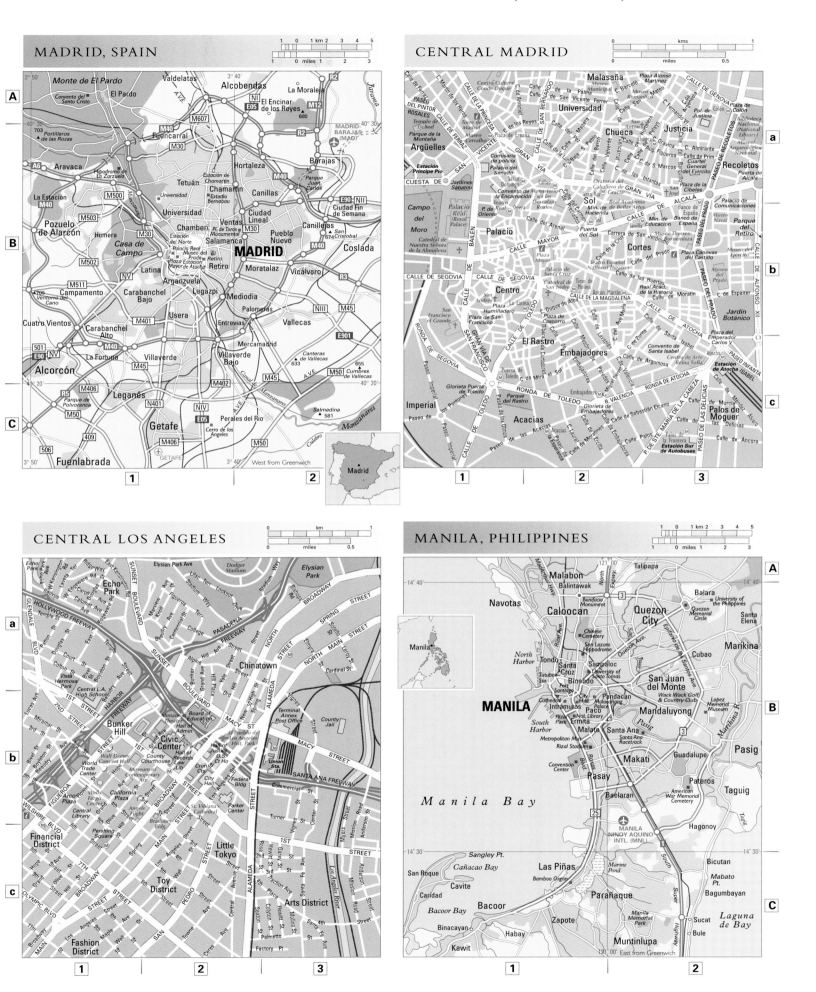

MADRID, SPAIN

1 0 1 km 2 3 4 5
1 0 miles 1 2 3

Monte de El Pardo
Valdelatas
Alcobendas
La Moraleja
R2
A 3° 50'
Convento del Santo Cristo
El Pardo
N1
El Encinar de los Reyes
M12
680
E05
AVE
40° 40'
703 Portilleros de las Rozas
M607
Fuencarral
M30
R2
MADRID BARAJAS (MAD)
40° 30'
A6 Aravaca
Hipódromo de La Zarzuela
Hortaleza
Barajas
Estación de Chamartín
M40
Tetuán
Estadio Bernabéu
Canillas
E90 N11
Universidad
Chamartín
Ciudad Lineal
Ciudad Fin de Semana
N11
La Estación
M40
Pozuelo de Alarcón
M503
Chamberí
Ventas
Pl. de Toros Monumental
Canillejas
674 San Cristóbal
M30
B
Humera
Salamanca
Pueblo Nuevo
Coslada
M502
Casa de Campo
Estación del Norte Palacio Real Museo del Prado Plaza Estación Mayor de Atocha
MADRID
M40
Latina
Retiro
Moratalaz
Vicálvaro
NV
Arganzuela
Legazpi
R3
Carabanchel Bajo
Mediodía
Campamento
M511
Usera
Palomeras
N111
M45
M401
Cuatro Vientos
Carabanchel Alto
Entrevías
Vallecas
E901
501
E90 NV
M40
La Fortuna
Villaverde
Mercamadrid
655
Alcorcón
M45
Villaverde Bajo
Canteras de Vallecas
633
Cumbres de Vallecas
Salmedina 581
40° 20'
C
M406
Leganés
M402
M45
M50
R5 Parque de Polvoranca
N401
Getafe
M50
409
M406
Perales del Río
Cerro de los Ángeles
M50
506
Fuenlabrada
GETAFE
3° 50'
3° 40'
West from Greenwich

Madrid

1 **2**

CENTRAL MADRID

0 kms 1
0 miles 0.5

CENTRAL LOS ANGELES

0 km 1
0 miles 0.5

MANILA, PHILIPPINES

1 0 1 km 2 3 4 5
1 0 miles 1 2 3

Manila

COPYRIGHT PHILIP'S

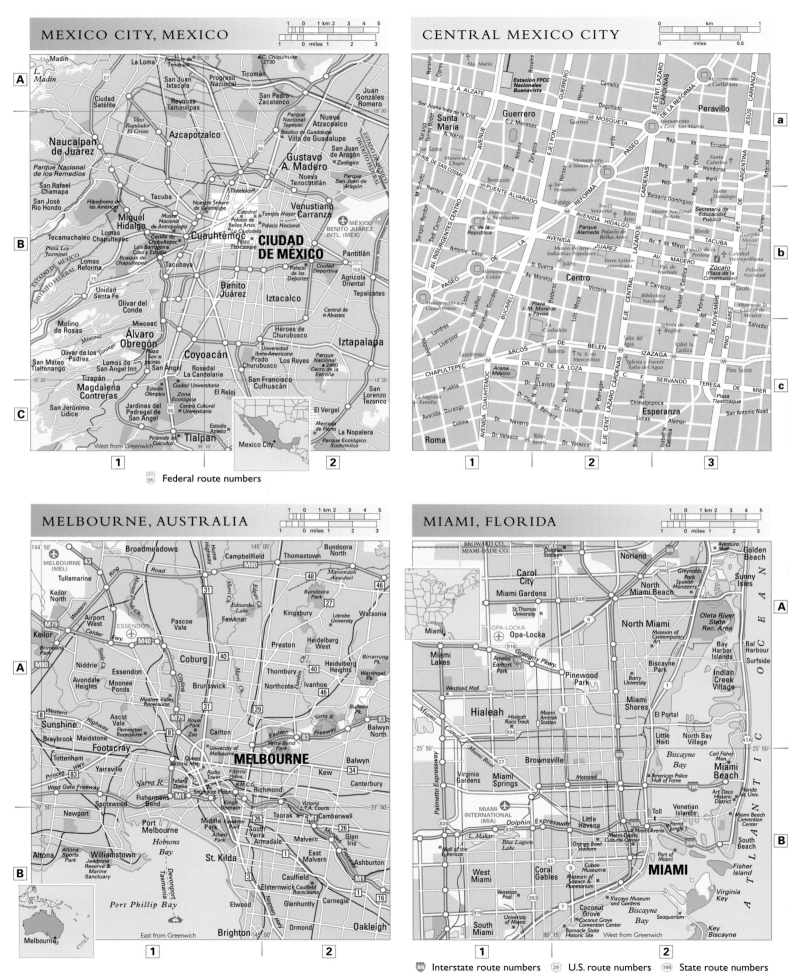

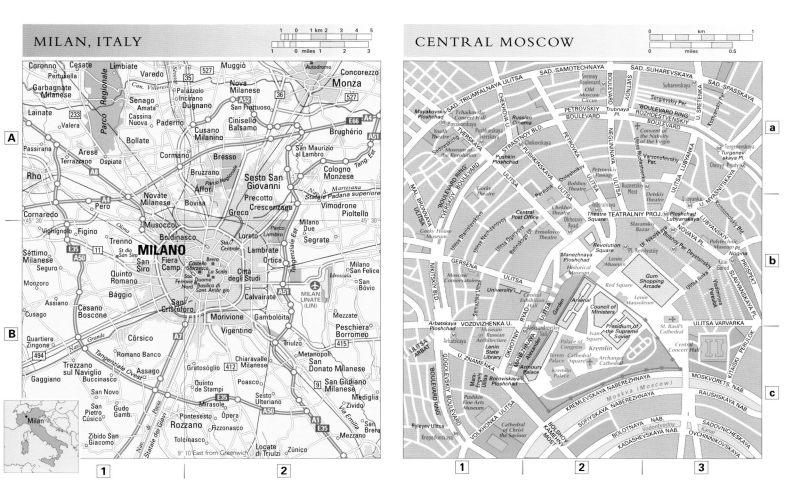

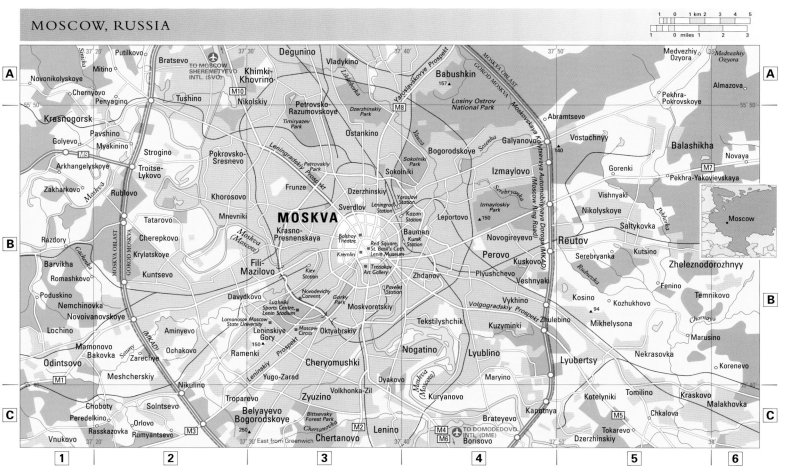

COPYRIGHT PHILIP'S

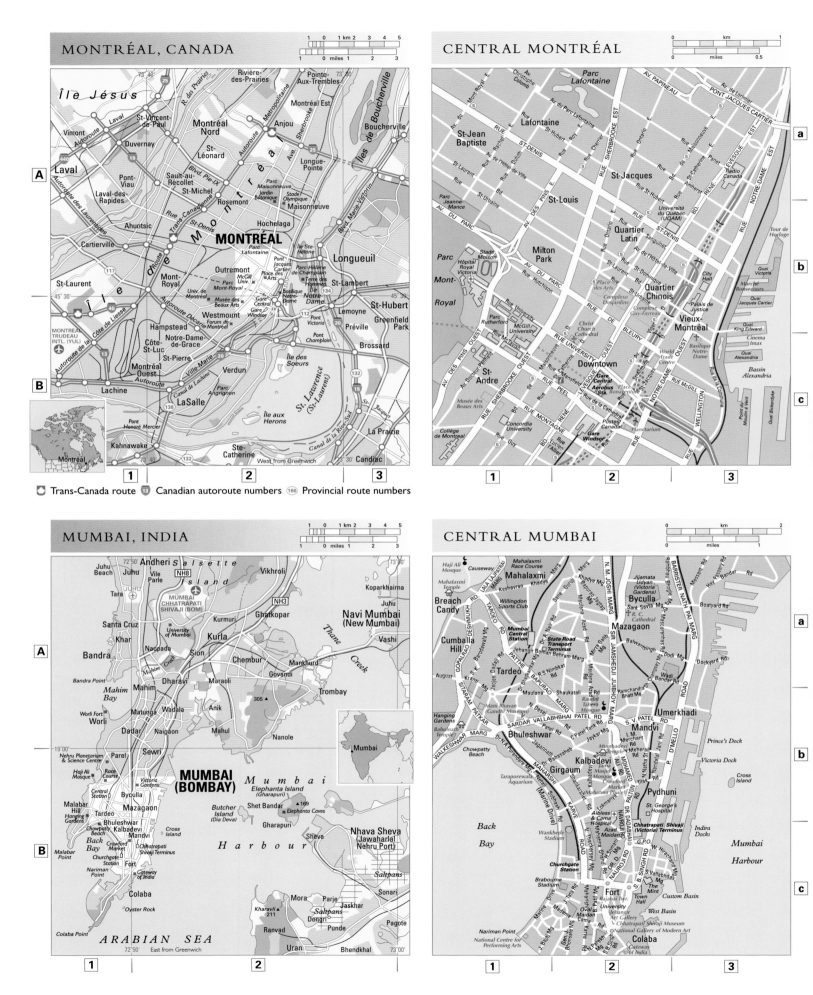

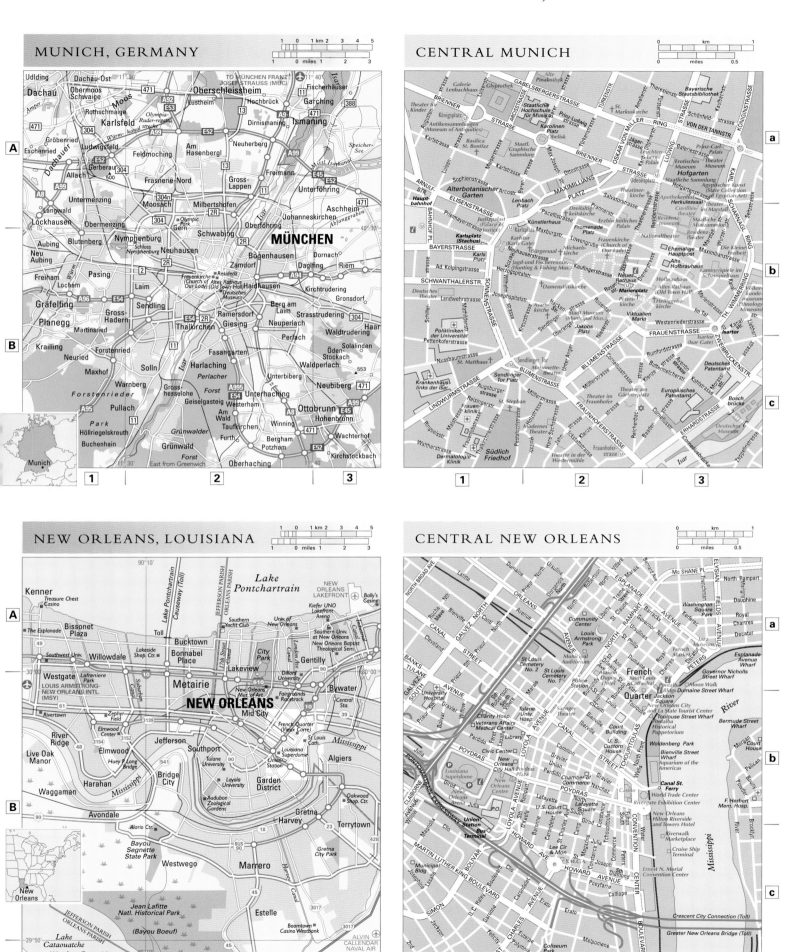

NEW YORK, NEW YORK

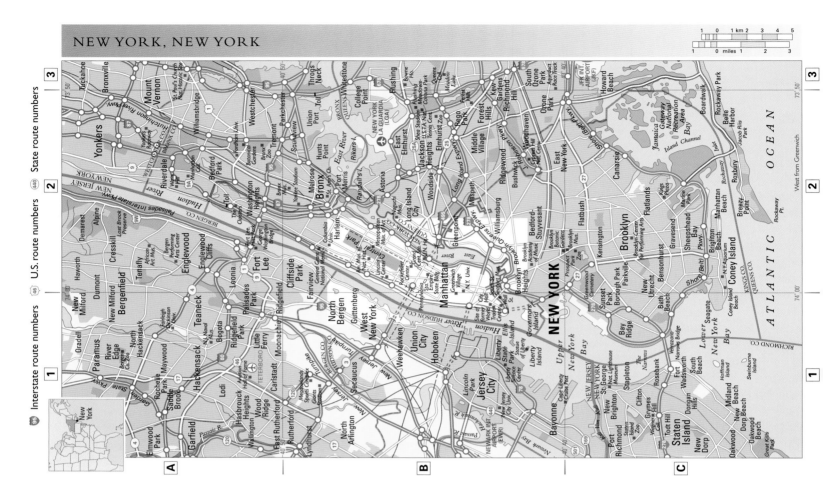

CENTRAL NEW YORK

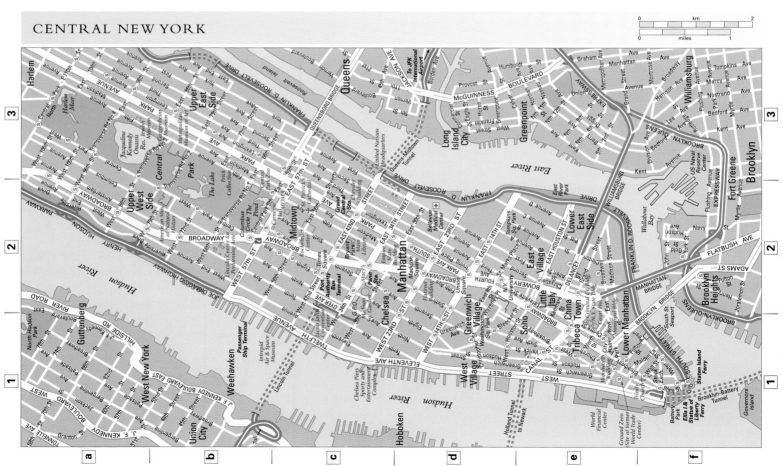

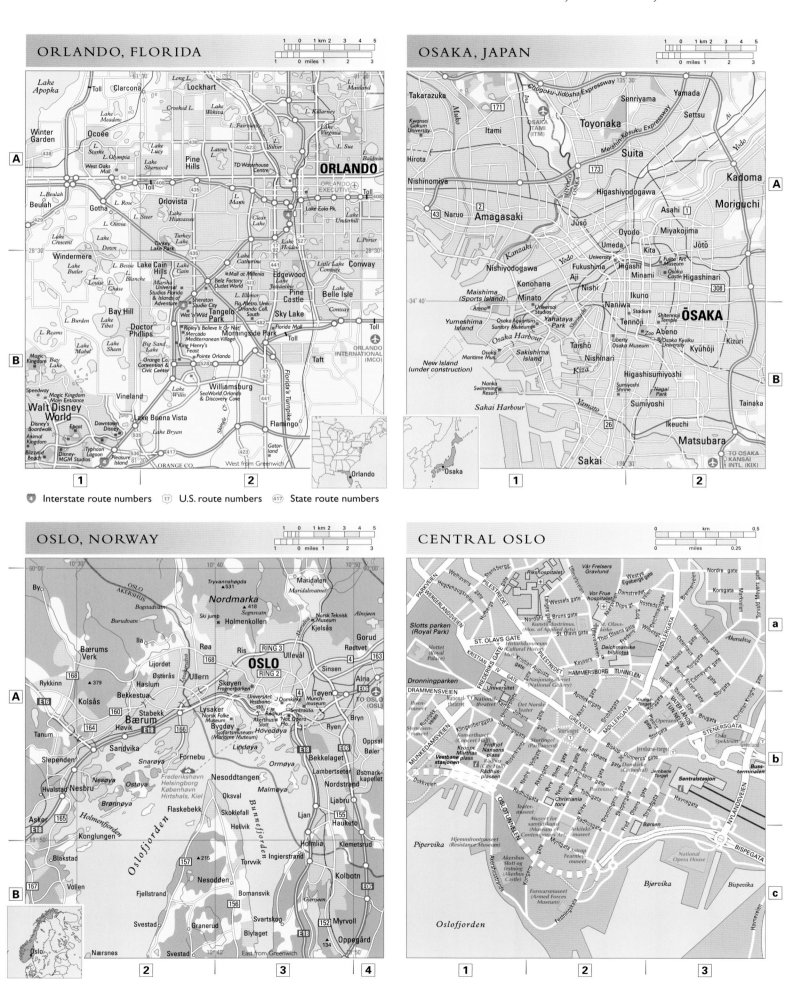

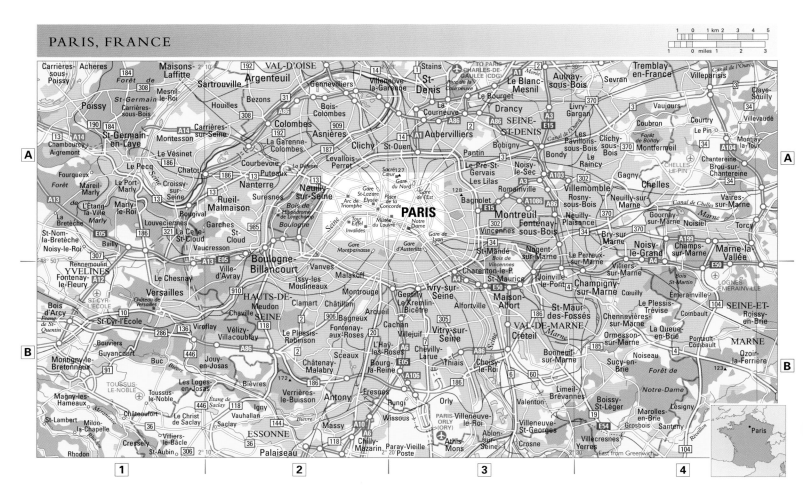

PARIS, FRANCE

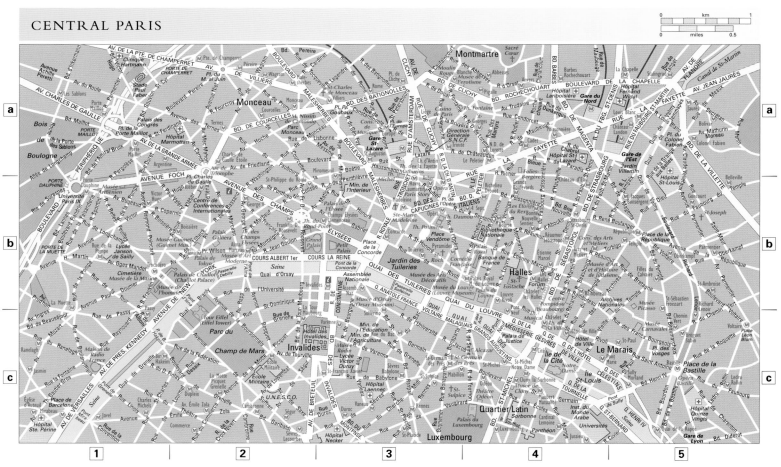

CENTRAL PARIS

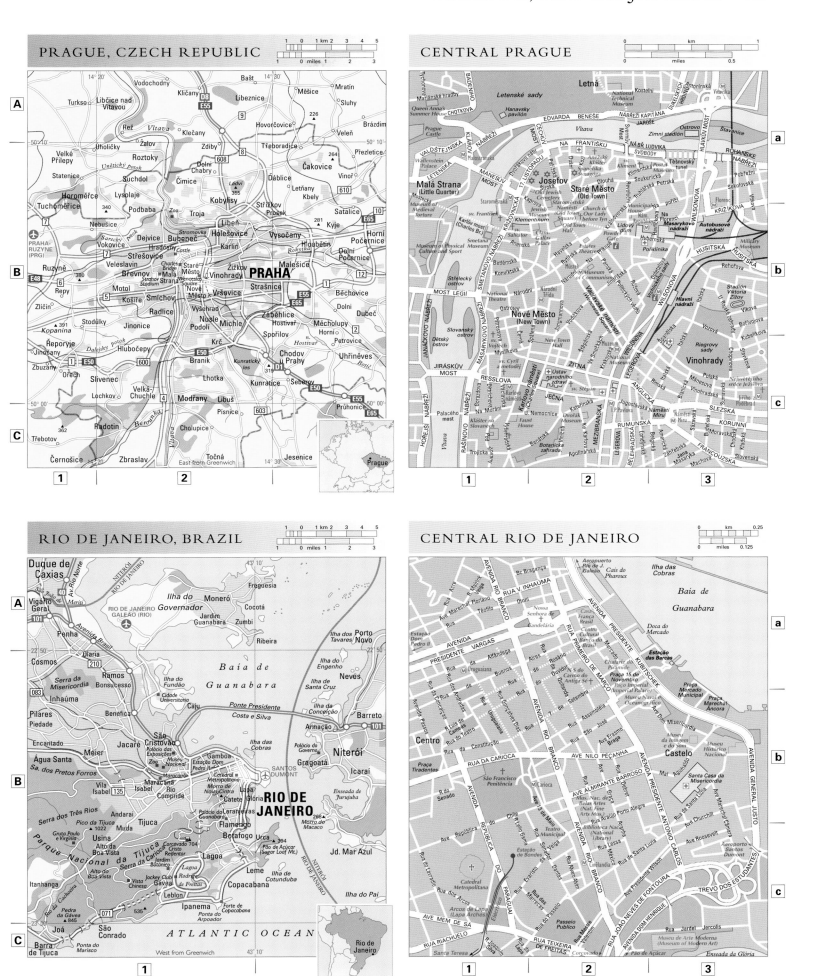

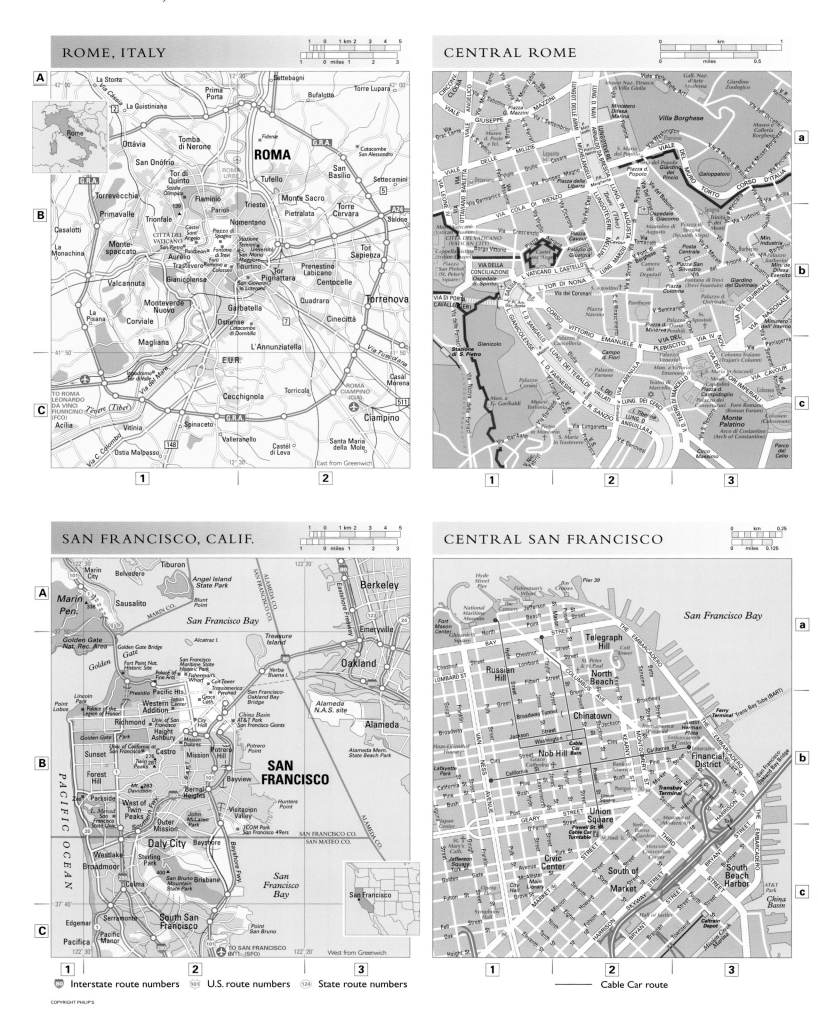

ROME, ITALY

CENTRAL ROME

SAN FRANCISCO, CALIF.

CENTRAL SAN FRANCISCO

🛣️ **80** Interstate route numbers   **101** U.S. route numbers   **124** State route numbers

—— Cable Car route

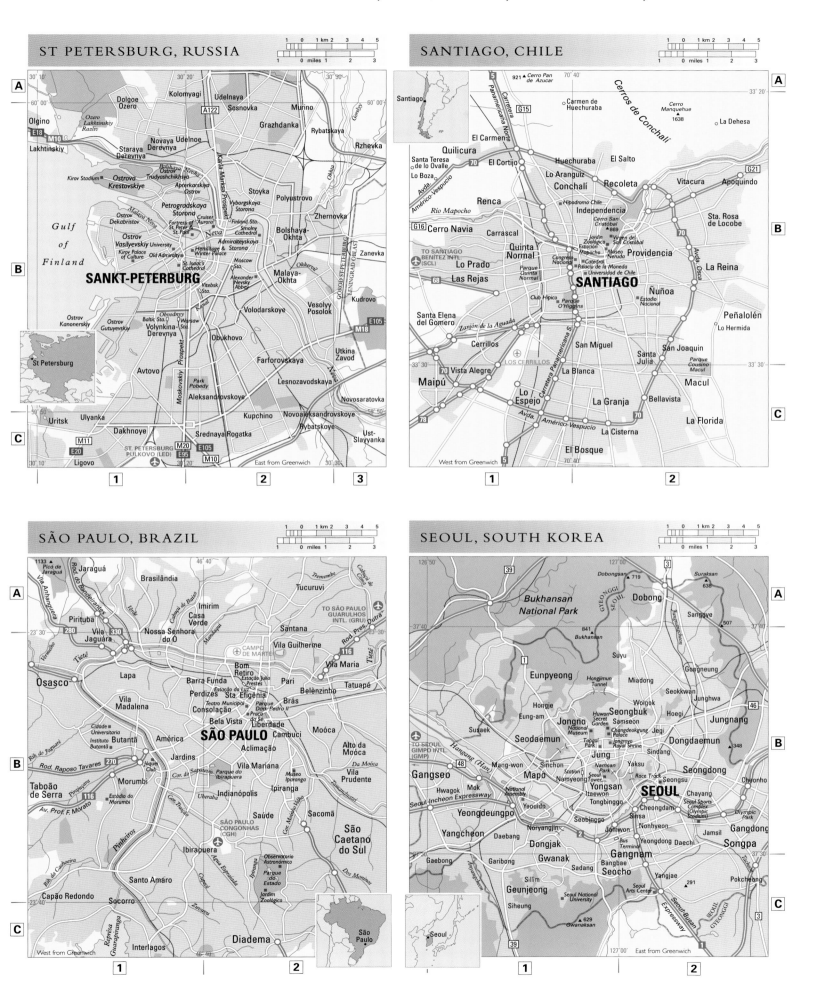

ST PETERSBURG, RUSSIA

1 0 1 km 2 3 4 5
1 0 miles 1 2 3

30° 10' 30° 20' 30° 30'

A

60° 00' 60° 00'

Olgino
Ozero Lakhtinskiy Razliv
E18 M10
Lakhtinskiy
Staraya Derevnya
Novaya Udelnoe Derevnya
Kolomyagi
Udelnaya
Sosnovka
Murino
A122
Grazhdanka
Rybatskaya
Rzhevka

Kirov Stadium
Ostrova Krestovskiye
Bolshaya Nevka
Ostrov Trudyaschikhsya
Apterkarskiya Ostrov
Petrogradskaya Storona
Vyborgskaya Storona
Stoyka
Polyustrovo
Fortress of St. Peter & St. Paul
Cruiser Aurora
Finland Sta.
Zhernovka

Ostrov Dekabristov
Ostrov Vasilyevskiy University
Kiров Palace of Culture
Malaya Neva
Hermitage & Winter Palace
Admiralteyskaya Storona
Smolny Cathedral
Bolshaya-Okhta
Zanevka

B
Gulf of Finland
Old Admiralty
St. Isaac's Cathedral
Moscow Sta.
Alexander Nevsky Abbey
Okkервel
Malaya-Okhta

SANKT-PETERBURG
Vitebsk Sta.
Neva
Volodarskoye
Vesolyy Posolok
Kudrovo

Ostrov Kanonerskiy
Ostrov Gutuyevskiy
Obvodnyy Kanal
Baltic Sta.
Warsaw Sta.
Volynkina-Derevnya
E105

Avtovo
Obukhovo
Farforovskaya
Utkina Zavod

Park Pobedy
Moskovskiy Prospekt
Aleksandrovskoye
Lesnozavodskaya
Novosaratovka

St Petersburg

59° 50' 59° 50'

Uritsk
Ulyanka
Dakhnoye
Kupchino
Novoaleksandrovskoye
Rybatskoye
Ust-Slavyanka

C
M11
Srednaya Rogatka
M20
ST. PETERSBURG PULKOVO (LED)
M18
Ligovo
E20
E95
E105
M10

30° 10' East from Greenwich 30° 30'

1 2 3

SANTIAGO, CHILE

1 0 1 km 2 3 4 5
1 0 miles 1 2 3

A
5
921 Cerro Pan de Azucar
70° 40'
Carmen de Huechuraba
Cerros de Conchalí
Cerro Manquehue 1638
La Dehesa
33° 20'

Santiago
Carretera Panamericana Norte
G15
El Carmen
Quilicura
Santa Teresa de lo Ovalle
G21
Lo Boza
El Cortijo
70
Huechuraba
El Salto
Lo Aranguiz
Conchalí
Recoleta
Vitacura
Apoquindo

Américo-Vespucio
Rio Mapocho
Renca
Hipódromo Chile
Independencia
Sta. Rosa de Locobe

B
G16
Cerro Navia
Carrascal
Jardín Zoológico
Cerro San Cristóbal 869
Virgen del San Cristóbal
70
La Reina

68
Lo Prado
Quinta Normal
Estación Mapocho
Congreso Nacional
Catedral
Museo Neruda
Providencia
Avda. Osa

Las Rejas
Parque Quinta Normal
Universidad de Chile
Palacio de la Moneda
SANTIAGO
Ñuñoa

Club Hipico
Parque O'Higgins
Estadio Nacional
Peñalolén

Santa Elena del Gomero
Zanjón de la Aguada
San Miguel
San Joaquin
Lo Hermida

Cerrillos
Santa Julia
Parque Cousiño Macul

33° 30'
70
Vista Alegre
LOS CERRILLOS
La Blanca
Santa Julia
Macul
33° 30'

Maipú
78
Lo Espejo
Carretera Panamericana S
La Granja
Bellavista
Avda. Américo-Vespucio
70
La Florida

C
La Cisterna
El Bosque
5
West from Greenwich
70° 40'

1 2

SÃO PAULO, BRAZIL

1 0 1 km 2 3 4 5
1 0 miles 1 2 3

46° 40'

A
1133 Pico de Jaraguá
Rod. do Bandeirantes
Jaraguá
Brasilândia
Tucuruvi
Tremembé
Cabeça de Cima
Vila Anhanguera

23° 30'
280
Pirituba
Casa Verde
Imirim
Santana
TO SÃO PAULO GUARULHOS INTL. (GRU)
Rod. Pres. Dutra

330
Vila Jaguára
Nossa Senhora do Ó
Tietê
Mombaça
Campo de Marte
Vila Guilherme
116
Tietê

Osasco
Lapa
Barra Funda
Bom Retiro
Estação Julia Prestes
Pari
Vila Maria
Tatuapé

Vila Madalena
Perdizes
Sta. Efigênia
Estação da Luz
Belénzinho
Brás

Cidade Universitária
Consolação
Teatro Municipal
Parque Dom Pedro II
Praça da Sé
Mooca

B
Instituto Butantã
Butantã
América
SÃO PAULO
Liberdade
Cambuci
Alto da Mooca

Rod. Raposo Tavares
270
Jardins
Aclimação
Da Mooca

Taboão de Serra
Jóquei Club
Vila Mariana
Museu Ipiranga
Vila Prudente

116
Morumbi
Parque do Ibirapuera
Indianópolis
Ipiranga

Estádio do Morumbi
Av. Prof. F. Morato
Saúde
Sacomã

Pinheiros
SÃO PAULO CONGONHAS (CGH)
Ibirapuera
Observatório Astronômico
São Caetano do Sul

23° 40'
Santo Amaro
Parque do Estado
Jardim Zoológico
Dos Meninos

C
Capão Redondo
Socorro
Represa Guarapiranga
Diadema
46° 40'
São Paulo

West from Greenwich
Interlagos

1 2

SEOUL, SOUTH KOREA

1 0 1 km 2 3 4 5
1 0 miles 1 2 3

126° 50' 127° 00'

A
39
3
Dobongsan 719
Suraksan 638
Bukhansan National Park
GYEONGGI SEOUL
Dobong
Sanggye
507
37° 40'
1
Bukhansan 841
Suyu
Gongneung

Eunpyeong
Hongjimun Tunnel
Miadong
Seokkwan
Junghwa

Hongje
Wolgok
Seongbuk
Hoegi
46

B
Eung-am
Huwon Secret Garden
Jongno
National Museum
Changdeokgung Palace
Jegi
Jungnang
348

TO SEOUL GIMPO INTL. (GMP)
Hangang (Han)
Susaek
Seodaemun
Top-gol Park
Jongmyo Royal Shrine
Dongdaemun

48
Jung
Sindang
Seongdong

Gangseo
Mang-won
Sinchon
Station
Namsan Park
Yaksu
Seongsu

Hwagok
Mok
Namdaemun
Seoul Tower
Itaewon
Race Track
Cheonho

SEOUL
National Assembly
Yongsan
Chayang
Seoul Sports Complex
Olympic Stadium

Yeongdeungpo
Seoul-Incheon Expressway
Yeouido
Tongbinggo
Cheongdam
Sinsa
Nonhyeon
Gangdong

37° 30'
Yangcheon
Noryangjin
Seobinggo
Bus Terminal
Yeongdong Daechi
Jamsil
Songpa

Daebang
Dongjak
Jamwon
Gangnam
Bangbae
Yangjae

Gaebong
Garibong
Gwanak
Sadang
Seocho
291
Pokcheong

Sillim
Geunjeong
Seoul National University
Seoul Arts Center
Seoul-Busan Expressway
GYEONGGI SEOUL

C
Siheung
629 Gwanaksan
127° 00' East from Greenwich

Seoul

1 2

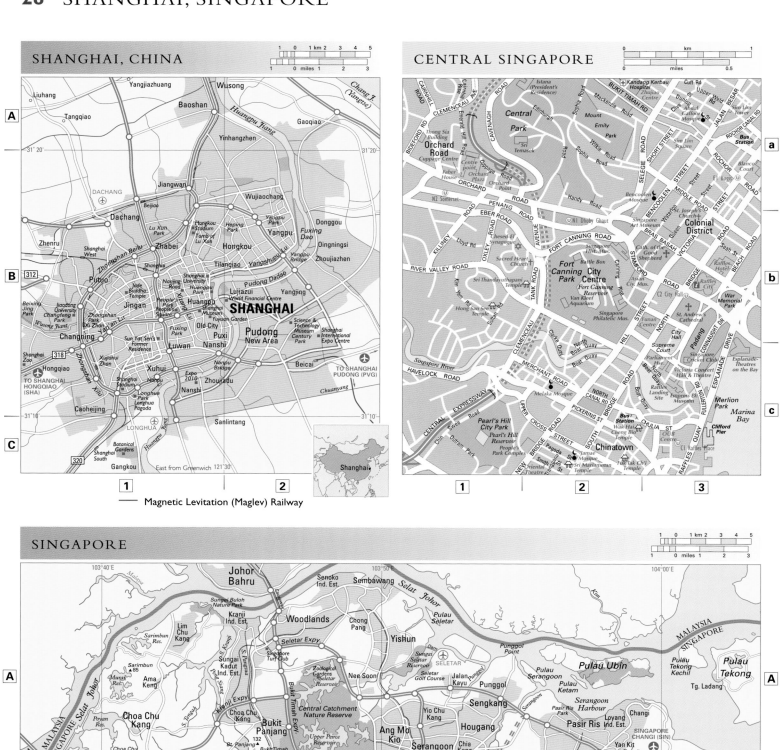

COPYRIGHT PHILIP'S

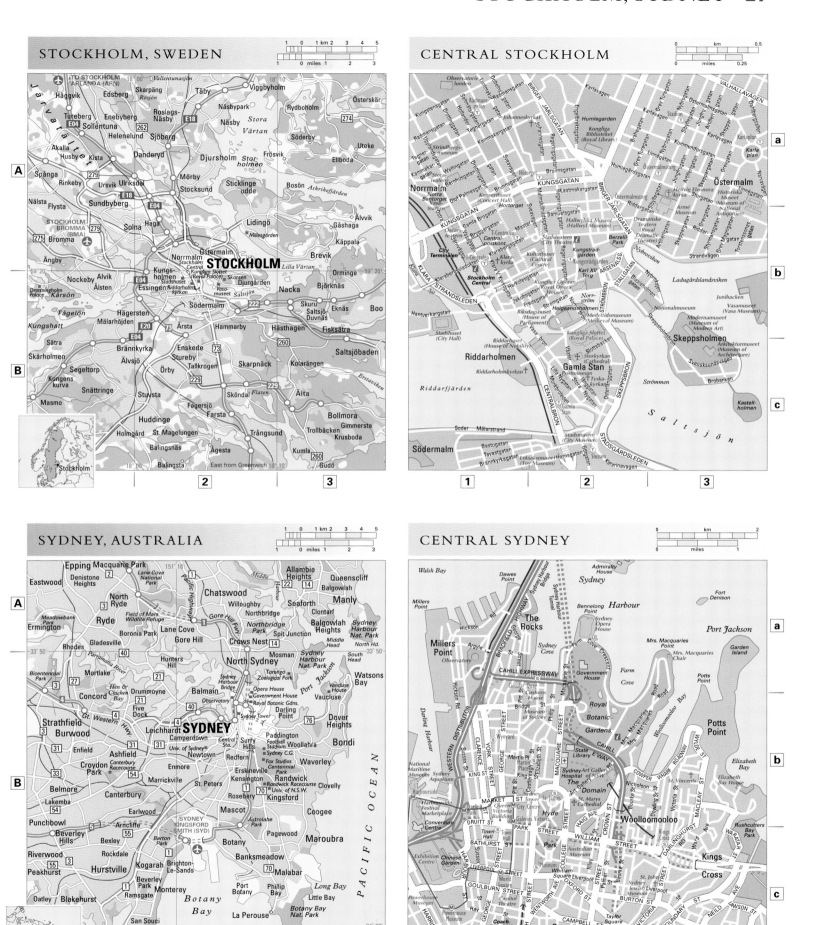

STOCKHOLM, SWEDEN

CENTRAL STOCKHOLM

SYDNEY, AUSTRALIA

CENTRAL SYDNEY

—Ⓜ— Monorail

TOKYO, JAPAN

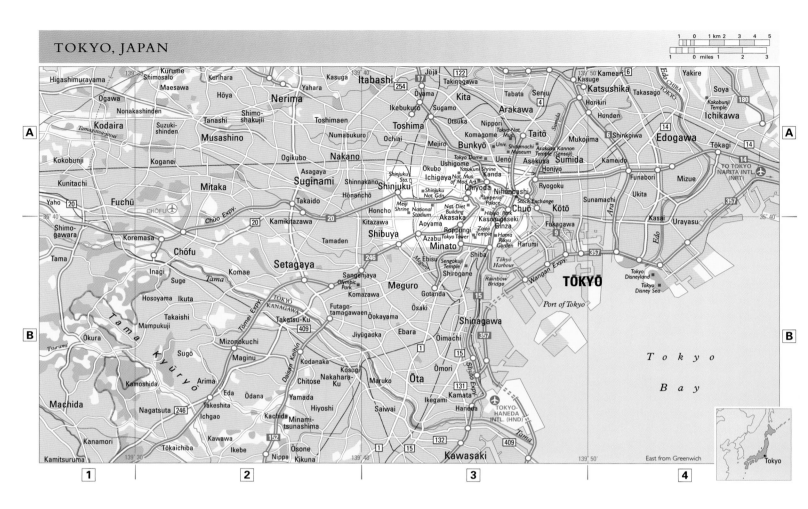

CENTRAL TOKYO

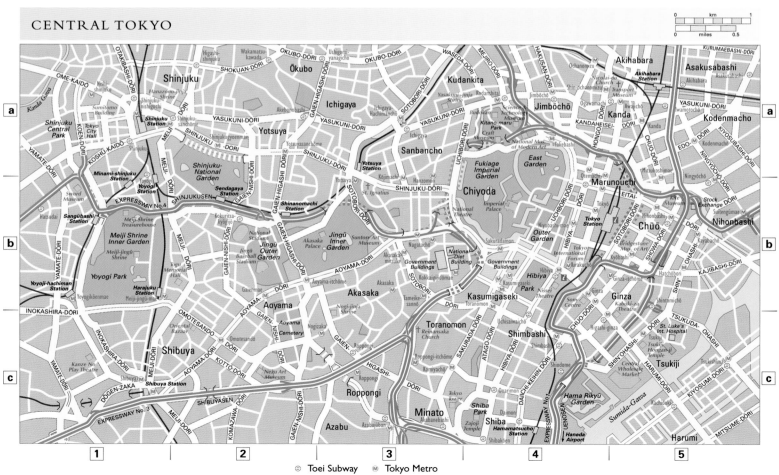

⊖ Toei Subway   Ⓜ Tokyo Metro

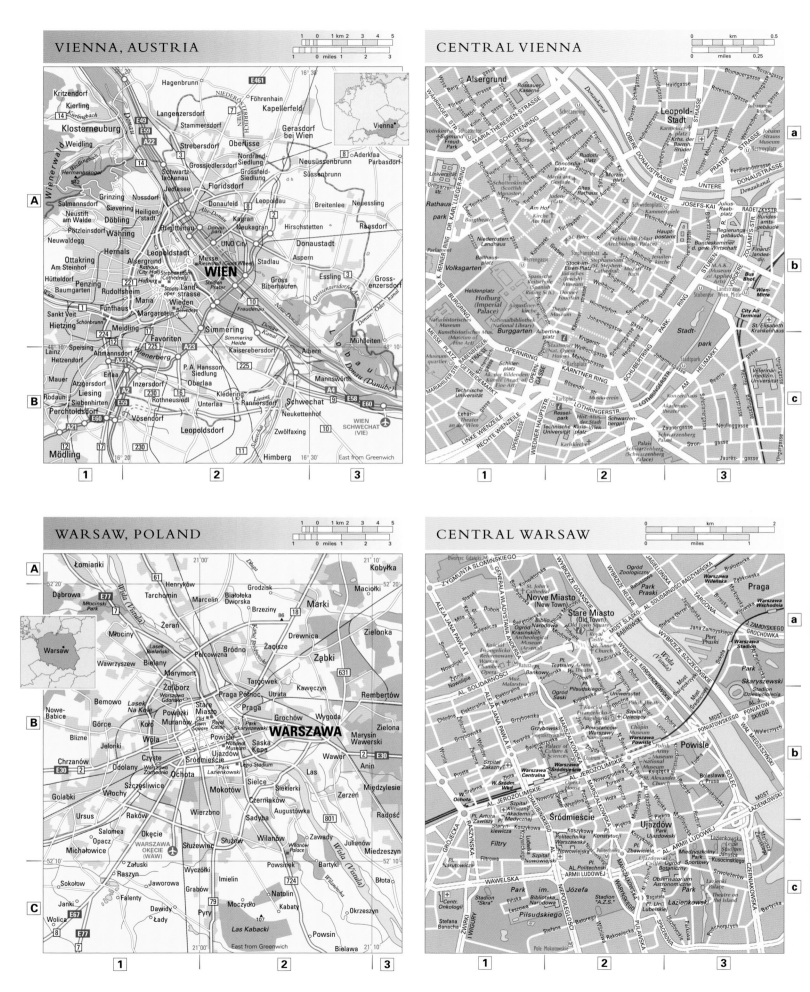

WASHINGTON D.C.

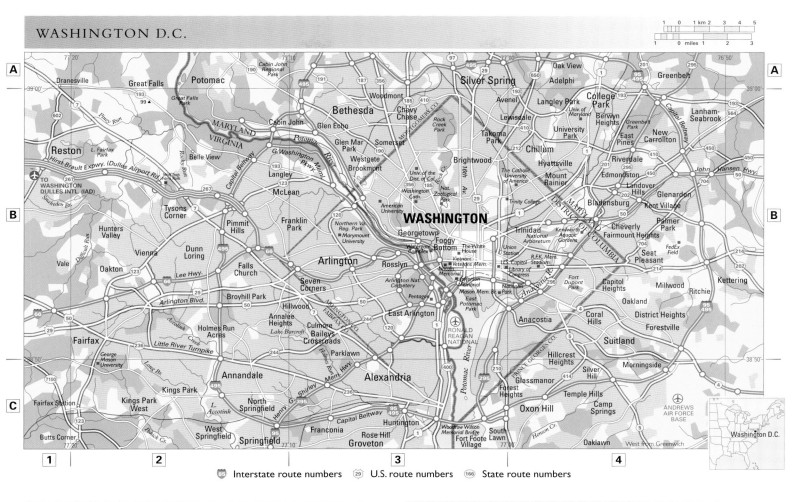

Interstate route numbers   U.S. route numbers   State route numbers

CENTRAL WASHINGTON

WELLINGTON, NEW ZEALAND

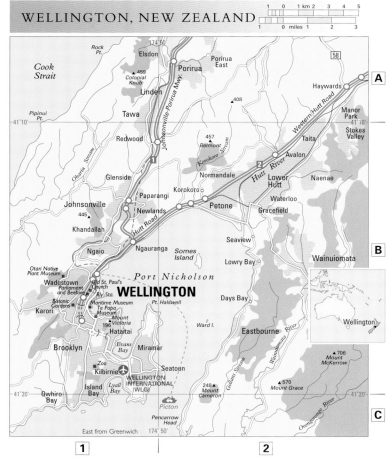

INDEX TO CITY MAPS

The index contains the names of all the principal places and features shown on the City Maps. Each name is followed by an additional entry in italics giving the name of the City Map within which it is located.

The number in bold type which follows each name refers to the number of the City Map page where that feature or place will be found.

The letter and figure which are immediately after the page number give the grid square on the map within which the feature or place is situated.

The letter represents the latitude and the figure the longitude. The full geographic reference is provided in the border of the City Maps.

The location given is the centre of the city, suburb or feature and is not necessarily the name. Rivers, canals and roads are indexed to their name. Rivers carry the symbol → after their name.

An explanation of the alphabetical order rules and a list of the abbreviations used are to be found at the beginning of the World Map Index.

A

Aalām *Baghdad* **3** B2
Aalsmeer *Amsterdam* **2** B1
Abbey Wood *London* **15** B4
Abcoude *Amsterdam* **2** B2
Åbdin *Cairo* **7** A2
Abeno *Osaka* **23** B2
Aberdeen *Hong Kong* **12** B1
Aberdour *Edinburgh* **11** A2
Aberdour Castle *Edinburgh* **11** A2
Abfanggraben → *Munich* **21** A3
Ablon-sur-Seine *Paris* **24** C3
Abramtsevo *Moscow* **19** B3
Abu Dis *Jerusalem* **13** B2
Abû en Numrus *Cairo* **7** B2
Abu Ghosh *Jerusalem* **13** B1
Acassuso *Buenos Aires* **7** A2
Accotink, L. *Washington* **33** C2
Accotink Cr. → *Washington* **33** B2
Achères *Paris* **24** A1
Acilia *Rome* **26** C1
Aclimação *São Paulo* **27** B2
Acropolis *Athens* **2** B2
Acton *London* **15** A2
Açúcar, Pão de *Rio de Janeiro* **25** B2
Ada Beja *Lisbon* **16** A1
Adams Park *Atlanta* **3** B2
Addiscombe *London* **15** B3
Adelphi *Washington* **33** A4
Adler Planetarium *Chicago* **9** B3
Admiralteyskaya Storona *St. Petersburg* **27** B2
Åffori *Milan* **19** A2
Aflandshage *Copenhagen* **8** B3
Afsarīyeh *Tehran* **31** B2
Agboyi Cr. → *Lagos* **14** A2
Ågerup *Copenhagen* **8** A1
Ågesta *Stockholm* **29** B2
Aghia Marina *Athens* **2** C3
Aghia Paraskevi *Athens* **2** B2
Aghios Dimitrios *Athens* **2** B2
Aghios Ioannis Rendis *Athens* **2** B1
Agincourt *Toronto* **31** A3
Agra Canal *Delhi* **10** B2
Agricola Oriental *Mexico City* **18** B2
Água Espraiada → *São Paulo* **27** B2
Agualva-Cacem *Lisbon* **16** A1
Ahrensfelde *Berlin* **5** A4
Ahuntsic *Montreal* **20** A1
Ai → *Osaka* **23** A2
Aigremont *Paris* **24** A1
Air View Park *Singapore* **28** A2
Airport West *Melbourne* **18** A1
Ajegunle *Lagos* **14** B2
Aji *Osaka* **23** A1
Ajuda *Lisbon* **16** A1
Akalla *Stockholm* **29** A1
Akasaka *Tokyo* **30** A3
Akbarābād *Tehran* **31** A2
Akershus Slott *Oslo* **23** A4
Al 'Azamīyah *Baghdad* **3** A2
Al Quds = Jerusalem *Jerusalem* **13** B2
Al-Walaja *Jerusalem* **13** B1
Alaguntan *Lagos* **14** B2
Alameda *San Francisco* **26** B3
Alameda Memorial State Beach Park *San Francisco* **26** B3
Albern *Vienna* **32** B2
Albert Park *Melbourne* **18** B1
Alberton *Johannesburg* **13** B2
Albertslund *Copenhagen* **8** B2
Alcántara *Lisbon* **16** A1
Alcatraz I. *San Francisco* **26** B2
Alcobendas *Madrid* **17** B2
Alcorcón *Madrid* **17** B1
Aldershot *Berlin* **5** B4
Aldo Bonzi *Buenos Aires* **7** C1
Aleksandrovskoye *St. Petersburg* **27** B2
Alexander Nevsky Abbey *St. Petersburg* **27** B2
Alexandra *Johannesburg* **13** A2
Alexandra *Singapore* **28** B2
Alexandria *Washington* **33** C3
Alfortville *Paris* **24** B3
Algés *Lisbon* **16** A1
Algiers *New Orleans* **21** B2
Alhambra *Los Angeles* **16** B4
Alibey → *Istanbul* **12** B1
Alibey Baraji *Istanbul* **12** B1
Alibeyköy *Istanbul* **12** B1
Alimos *Athens* **2** B2
Alipur *Kolkata* **14** B1
Allach *Munich* **21** A1
Allambie Heights *Sydney* **29** A2
Allermuir Hill *Edinburgh* **11** B2
Allstate Arena *Chicago* **9** A1
Allston *Boston* **6** A3
Almada *Lisbon* **16** A2
Almagro *Buenos Aires* **7** B2
Almargem do Bispo *Lisbon* **16** A1
Almirante G. Brown, Parque *Buenos Aires* **7** C2
Almon *Jerusalem* **13** B2
Almond → *Edinburgh* **11** B2
Alna *Oslo* **23** A4
Alnsjøen *Oslo* **23** A4
Alperton *London* **15** A2
Alpine *New York* **22** A2
Alrode *Johannesburg* **13** B2
Alsemberg *Brussels* **6** B1

Alsergrund *Vienna* **32** A2
Alsip *Chicago* **9** C2
Ålsten *Stockholm* **29** B1
Ålta *Stockholm* **29** B3
Altadena *Los Angeles* **16** A4
Alte-Donau → *Vienna* **32** A2
Alter Finkenkrug *Berlin* **5** A1
Altes Rathaus *Munich* **21** B2
Altglienicke *Berlin* **5** B4
Altlandsberg *Berlin* **5** A5
Altlandsberg Nord *Berlin* **5** A5
Altmannsdorf *Vienna* **32** B1
Alto da Boa Vista *Rio de Janeiro* **25** B1
Alto da Mooca *São Paulo* **27** B2
Alto do Pina *Lisbon* **16** A1
Altona *Melbourne* **18** B1
Alvik *Stockholm* **29** B1
Alvin Callendar Naval Air Station *New Orleans* **21** B2
Älvsjö *Stockholm* **29** B2
Am Hasenbergl *Munich* **21** A2
Am Steinhof *Vienna* **32** A1
Am Wald *Munich* **21** B2
Ama Keng *Singapore* **28** A2
Amadora *Lisbon* **16** A1
Amagasaki *Osaka* **23** A1
Amager *Copenhagen* **8** B3
Amål Qâdisiya *Baghdad* **3** B2
Amalienborg Slot *Copenhagen* **8** A3
Amata *Milan* **19** A1
Ambelokipi *Athens* **2** B2
Ameixoeira *Lisbon* **16** A1
América *São Paulo* **27** B1
American Police Hall of Fame *Miami* **18** B2
American Univ. *Washington* **33** B3
Amin *Baghdad* **3** B2
Aminadav *Jerusalem* **13** B1
Amirābād *Tehran* **31** A2
Amora *Lisbon* **16** B2
Amoreira *Lisbon* **16** A1
Amper → *Munich* **21** A1
Amstel-Drecht-Kanaal *Amsterdam* **2** B2
Amstelveen *Amsterdam* **2** B2
Amsterdam *Amsterdam* **2** A2
Amsterdam ✈ (AMS) *Amsterdam* **2** B1
Amsterdam-Rijnkanaal *Amsterdam* **2** A2
Amsterdam Zuidoost *Amsterdam* **2** B2
Amsterdamse Bos *Amsterdam* **2** B1
Anacosta *Washington* **33** B4
Anacostia *Washington* **33** B4
Anadoluhisarı *Istanbul* **12** B2
Anadolukavağı *Istanbul* **12** A2
Anata *Jerusalem* **13** B2
Ancol *Jakarta* **12** A1
'Andalus *Baghdad* **3** B1
Andarai *Rio de Janeiro* **25** B1
Anderlecht *Brussels* **6** A1
Anderson Park *Atlanta* **3** A2
Andingmen *Beijing* **4** B2
Ang Mo Kio *Singapore* **28** A3
Ångby *Stockholm* **29** A1
Angel I. *San Francisco* **26** A2
Angel Island State Park △ *San Francisco* **26** A2
Angke, Kali → *Jakarta* **12** A1
Angyalföld *Budapest* **7** A2
Anik *Mumbai* **20** A2
Anin *Warsaw* **32** B2
Anjou *Montreal* **20** A2
Annalee Heights *Washington* **33** B2
Annandale *Washington* **33** C2
Anne Frankhuis *Amsterdam* **2** A2
Antony *Paris* **24** B2
Aoyama *Tokyo* **30** B3
Ap Lei Chau *Hong Kong* **12** B1
Apapa *Lagos* **14** B2
Apapa Quays *Lagos* **14** B2
Apelação *Lisbon* **16** A2
Apopka, L. *Orlando* **23** A1
Apoquindo *Santiago* **27** B2
Apterkarskiy Ostrov *St. Petersburg* **27** B2
Ar Kazimiyah *Baghdad* **3** B1
Ar Ram *Jerusalem* **13** A2
Ara → *Tokyo* **30** A4
Arakawa *Tokyo* **30** A4
Arany-hegyi-patak → *Budapest* **7** A2
Aravaca *Madrid* **17** B1
Arbataash *Baghdad* **3** A1
Arc de Triomphe *Paris* **24** A2
Arcadia *Los Angeles* **16** B4
Arcueil *Paris* **24** B2
Arese *Milan* **19** A1
Arganzuela *Madrid* **17** B1
Argenteuil *Paris* **24** A2
Argiroupoli *Athens* **2** B2
Argonne Forest *Chicago* **9** C1
Arima *Tokyo* **30** B2
Arlanda, Stockholm ✈ (ARN) *Stockholm* **29** A1
Arlington *Boston* **6** A1
Arlington *Washington* **33** B3
Arlington Heights *Chicago* **9** A1
Arlington Nat. Cemetery *Washington* **33** B3
Armação *Rio de Janeiro* **25** B2
Armadale *Melbourne* **18** B2
Armour Heights *Toronto* **31** A2
Arncliffe *Sydney* **29** B1
Arnold Arboretum *Boston* **6** B2

Árpádföld *Budapest* **7** A3
Arrentela *Lisbon* **16** B2
Arroyo Seco Park *Los Angeles* **16** B3
Årsta *Stockholm* **29** B2
Artane *Dublin* **10** A2
Artas *Jerusalem* **13** B2
Arthur's Seat *Edinburgh* **11** B3
Arts, Place des *Montreal* **20** A2
As Shawawra *Jerusalem* **13** B2
Asagaya *Tokyo* **30** A2
Asahi *Osaka* **23** A2
Asakusa *Tokyo* **30** A3
Asati *Kolkata* **14** A2
Aschheim *Munich* **21** A3
Ascot Vale *Melbourne* **18** A1
Ashbridge's Bay Park *Toronto* **31** B3
Ashburn *Chicago* **9** C2
Ashburton *Melbourne* **18** B2
Ashfield *Sydney* **29** B1
Ashford *London* **15** B1
Ashtown *Dublin* **10** A2
Askisto *Helsinki* **11** B1
Askrikefjärden *Stockholm* **29** A3
Asnières *Paris* **24** A2
Aspern *Vienna* **32** A2
Assago *Milan* **19** B1
Assendelft *Amsterdam* **2** A1
Assiano *Milan* **19** B1
Astoria *New York* **22** B2
Astrolabe Park *Sydney* **29** B2
Atarot *Jerusalem* **13** A2
Atarot ✈ (JRS) *Jerusalem* **13** A2
Atghara *Kolkata* **14** B2
Athens *Athina* **2** B2
Athina *Athens* **2** B2
Athína ✈ (ATH) *Athens* **2** A3
Athínai = Athens *Athens* **2** B2
Athis-Mons *Paris* **24** B3
Athlone *Cape Town* **8** A2
Atholl *Johannesburg* **13** A2
Atifiya *Baghdad* **3** A2
Atişalen *Istanbul* **12** B1
Atlanta *Atlanta* **3** B2
Atlanta ✈ (ATL) *Atlanta* **3** C2
Atlanta Hartsfield Int. ✈ (ATL) *Atlanta* **3** C2
Atlanta History Center *Atlanta* **3** B2
Atlanta Zoo *Atlanta* **3** B2
Atomium *Brussels* **6** A2
Attiki *Athens* **2** A2
Atzgersdorf *Vienna* **32** B1
Aubervilliers *Paris* **24** A3
Aubing *Munich* **21** B1
Aubrak *Bangkok* **3** B2
Auburndale *Boston* **6** A1
Auchendinny *Edinburgh* **11** B2
Auckland Park *Johannesburg* **13** B1
Auderghem *Brussels* **6** B2
Augustówka *Warsaw* **32** B2
Aulnay-sous-Bois *Paris* **24** A3
Aurelio *Rome* **26** B1
Ausim *Cairo* **7** A1
Austerlitz, Gare d' *Paris* **24** A3
Austin *Chicago* **9** B2
Avalon *Wellington* **33** B2
Avedore *Copenhagen* **8** B2
Avellaneda *Buenos Aires* **7** C2
Avenel *Washington* **33** B4
Avondale *Chicago* **9** B2
Avondale *New Orleans* **21** B1
Avondale Heights *Melbourne* **18** A1
Avtovo *St. Petersburg* **27** B1
Ayazağa *Istanbul* **12** B1
Ayer Chawan, Pulau *Singapore* **28** B2
Ayer Merbau, Pulau *Singapore* **28** B2
Azabu *Tokyo* **30** B3
Azcapotzalco *Mexico City* **18** B1
Azteca, Estadia *Mexico City* **18** C2
Azúcar, Cerro Pan de *Santiago* **27** A1

B

Baambrugge *Amsterdam* **2** B2
Baba Channel *Karachi* **13** B1
Baba I. *Karachi* **13** B1
Babarpur *Delhi* **10** A2
Babushkin *Moscow* **19** A3
Back B. *Mumbai* **20** B1
Baclaran *Manila* **17** B1
Bacoor *Manila* **17** C1
Bacoor B. *Manila* **17** C1
Badalona *Barcelona* **4** A3
Badhoevedorp *Amsterdam* **2** A1
Badli *Delhi* **10** A1
Bærum *Oslo* **23** A2
Bağcılar *Istanbul* **12** B1
Bággio *Milan* **19** B1
Bâgh-e-Feyz *Tehran* **31** A1
Baghdad *Baghdad* **3** A2
Baghdad al Muthana ✈ (BGW) *Baghdad* **3** B2
Baghdad Int. ✈ (SDA) *Baghdad* **3** B1
Bagnolet *Paris* **24** A3
Bagneux *Paris* **24** B2
Bagsværd *Copenhagen* **8** A2
Bagsværd Sø *Copenhagen* **8** A2
Baguiati *Kolkata* **14** B2
Bagumbayan *Manila* **17** C2
Baha'i Temple *Chicago* **9** A2
Bahçeköy *Istanbul* **12** A1
Bahçelievler *Istanbul* **12** B1

Bahtīm *Cairo* **7** A2
Baile Átha Cliath = Dublin *Dublin* **10** A2
Baileys Crossroads *Washington* **33** B3
Bailly *Paris* **24** A1
Bairro Lopes *Lisbon* **16** A2
Baisha *Guangzhou* **11** B2
Baiyun *Guangzhou* **11** A2
Baiyun Hill *Guangzhou* **11** B2
Baiyun Mountain Scenic Area *Guangzhou* **11** A2
Bakırköy *Istanbul* **12** C1
Bal Harbor *Miami* **18** A2
Balara *Manila* **17** B2
Baldia *Karachi* **13** A1
Baldoyle *Dublin* **10** A3
Baldwin, L. *Orlando* **23** A2
Baldwin Hills *Los Angeles* **16** B2
Baldwin Hills Res. *Los Angeles* **16** B2
Balgowlah *Sydney* **29** A2
Balgowlah Heights *Sydney* **29** B2
Balham *London* **15** B3
Bali *Kolkata* **14** B1
Baliganja *Kolkata* **14** B2
Balingsnäs *Stockholm* **29** B2
Balingsta *Stockholm* **29** B2
Balintawak *Manila* **17** B1
Ballerup *Copenhagen* **8** A2
Ballinteer *Dublin* **10** B2
Ballyboden *Dublin* **10** B2
Ballybrack *Dublin* **10** B3
Ballyfermot *Dublin* **10** A1
Ballymorefinn Hill *Dublin* **10** B1
Ballymun *Dublin* **10** A2
Balmain *Sydney* **29** B2
Balnahati *Kolkata* **14** B1
Balvanera *Buenos Aires* **7** B2
Balwyn *Melbourne* **18** A2
Balwyn North *Melbourne* **18** A2
Banática *Lisbon* **16** A2
Bandra *Mumbai* **20** A1
Bandra Pt. *Mumbai* **20** A1
Bang Kapi *Bangkok* **3** B2
Bang Na *Bangkok* **3** B2
Bangbae *Seoul* **27** C1
Bangkhen *Bangkok* **3** A2
Bangkok *Bangkok* **3** B2
Bangkok Don Muang Int. ✈ (BKK) *Bangkok* **3** A2
Bangkok Noi *Bangkok* **3** B1
Bangkok Yai *Bangkok* **3** B1
Banglo *Kolkata* **14** B1
Bangrak *Bangkok* **3** B2
Bangsu *Bangkok* **3** A2
Banks, C. *Sydney* **29** C2
Banksmeadow *Sydney* **29** B2
Bantala *Kolkata* **14** B2
Bantra *Kolkata* **14** B1
Baoshan *Shanghai* **28** A1
Bar Giyora *Jerusalem* **13** B1
Barahanagar *Kolkata* **14** B2
Barajas *Madrid* **17** B2
Barajas, Madrid ✈ (MAD) *Madrid* **17** B2
Barakpur *Kolkata* **14** A2
Barcarena *Lisbon* **16** A1
Barcarena, Rib. de → *Lisbon* **16** A1
Barcelona *Barcelona* **4** A2
Barcelona-Prat ✈ (BCN) *Barcelona* **4** A1
Barcroft, L. *Washington* **33** B3
Barking *London* **15** A4
Barkingside *London* **15** A4
Barnes *London* **15** B2
Barnet *London* **15** A2
Barra Andaí *Karachi* **13** B2
Barra Funda *São Paulo* **27** B2
Barracas *Buenos Aires* **7** B2
Barrackpur = Barakpur *Kolkata* **14** A2
Barranco *Lima* **34** B2
Barreiro *Lisbon* **16** B2
Barreto *Rio de Janeiro* **25** B2
Bartala *Kolkata* **14** B1
Barton Park *Sydney* **29** B1
Bartyki *Warsaw* **32** C2
Basus *Cairo* **7** A2
Batanagar *Kolkata* **14** B1
Bath Beach *New York* **22** C1
Bath I. *Karachi* **13** B2
Batir *Jerusalem* **13** B1
Batok, Bukit *Singapore* **28** A2
Battersea *London* **15** B3
Bauman *Moscow* **19** B3
Baumgarten *Vienna* **32** A1
Bay, L. *Orlando* **23** B1
Bay Harbor Islands *Miami* **18** A2
Bay Hill *Orlando* **23** B1
Bay Ridge *New York* **22** C1
Bayit Va-Gan *Jerusalem* **13** B2
Bayonne *New York* **22** B1
Bayou Boeuf *New Orleans* **21** A1
Bayou Segnette State Park → *New Orleans* **21** B2
Bayrampaşa *Istanbul* **12** B1
Bayshore *San Francisco* **26** B2
Bayt Lahm *Jerusalem* **13** B2
Bayview *San Francisco* **26** B2
Bāzār *Tehran* **31** A2
Beach Channel *New York* **22** C3
Béchovice *Prague* **25** B3
Beck L. *Chicago* **9** A1
Beckenham *London* **15** B3

Beckton *London* **15** A4
Becontree *London* **15** A4
Beddington Corner *London* **15** B3
Bedford *Boston* **6** A1
Bedford Park *Chicago* **9** C2
Bedford Park *New York* **22** A2
Bedford Stuyvesant *New York* **22** B2
Bedford View *Johannesburg* **13** B2
Bedok *Singapore* **28** B3
Bedok Res. *Singapore* **28** A3
Behala *Kolkata* **14** B1
Bei Hai *Beijing* **4** B2
Beicai *Shanghai* **28** B2
Beijing *Beijing* **4** B1
Beit Duqu *Jerusalem* **13** A1
Beit Ghur at-Tahti *Jerusalem* **13** A1
Beit Ghur el-Fawqa *Jerusalem* **13** A1
Beit Hanina *Jerusalem* **13** B2
Beit Ij'za *Jerusalem* **13** A1
Beit Iksa *Jerusalem* **13** A1
Beit I'nan *Jerusalem* **13** A1
Beit Jala *Jerusalem* **13** B2
Beit Liqya *Jerusalem* **13** A1
Beit Nekofa *Jerusalem* **13** B1
Beit Sahur *Jerusalem* **13** B2
Beit Sofafa *Jerusalem* **13** B2
Beit Surik *Jerusalem* **13** B1
Beit Ur al-Fawqa *Jerusalem* **13** A1
Beit Zayit *Jerusalem* **13** B1
Beitaipingzhuan *Beijing* **4** B1
Beitar Ilit *Jerusalem* **13** B1
Beitin *Jerusalem* **13** A2
Beitsun *Guangzhou* **11** B2
Beitunya *Jerusalem* **13** A2
Bekasi *Jakarta* **12** B2
Bir Nabala *Jerusalem* **13** A2
Birak el Kiyam *Cairo* **7** A1
Békásmegyer *Budapest* **7** A2
Bekkelaget *Oslo* **23** A4
Bekkestua *Oslo* **23** A2
Bel Air *Los Angeles* **16** B2
Bela Vista *São Paulo* **27** B2
Bélanger *Montreal* **20** A2
Belas *Lisbon* **16** A1
Belém *Lisbon* **16** A1
Belém, Torre de *Lisbon* **16** A1
Belenzinho *São Paulo* **27** B2
Belgachiya *Kolkata* **14** B2
Belgharia *Kolkata* **14** A2
Belgrano *Buenos Aires* **7** B2
Bell *Los Angeles* **16** C3
Bell Gardens *Los Angeles* **16** C4
Belle Harbor *New York* **22** C2
Belle Isle *Orlando* **23** B2
Belle View *Washington* **33** C3
Bellingham *London* **15** B3
Bellwood *Chicago* **9** B1
Belmont *Boston* **6** A1
Belmont *London* **15** B2
Belmont, Mt. *Wellington* **33** A2
Belmont Cragin *Chicago* **9** B2
Belmont Harbor *Chicago* **9** B3
Belmore *Sydney* **29** B1
Belur *Kolkata* **14** B2
Belvedere *Atlanta* **3** B3
Belvedere *London* **15** B4
Belvedere *San Francisco* **26** A2
Belyayevo Bogorodskoye *Moscow* **19** C2
Bemowo *Warsaw* **32** B1
Benaki Museum *Athens* **2** B2
Bendale *Toronto* **31** A3
Benefica *Rio de Janeiro* **25** B1
Benfica *Lisbon* **16** A1
Benitez Int. ✈ (SCL) *Santiago* **27** B1
Benito Juárez, Int. ✈ (MEX) *Mexico City* **18** B2
Bensonhurst *New York* **22** C2
Berchem-Ste-Agathe *Brussels* **6** A1
Berg am Laim *Munich* **21** B2
Bergenfield *New York* **22** A2
Bergham *Munich* **21** B2
Bergvliet *Cape Town* **8** B1
Beri *Barcelona* **4** A1
Berkeley *San Francisco* **26** A3
Berlin *Berlin* **5** A3
Berlin Dom *Berlin* **5** A3
Berlin Tegel ✈ (TXL) *Berlin* **5** A2
Bermondsey *London* **15** B3
Bernabeu, Estadio *Madrid* **17** B1
Bernal Heights *San Francisco* **26** B2
Berwyn *Chicago* **9** B2
Besiktas *Istanbul* **12** B2
Besòs *Barcelona* **4** A2
Besòs → *Barcelona* **4** A2
Bessie, L. *Orlando* **23** B1
Bet Horon *Jerusalem* **13** A2
Bethesda *Washington* **33** B3
Bethlehem = Bayt Lahm *Jerusalem* **13** B2
Bethnal Green *London* **15** A3
Betor *Kolkata* **14** B1
Beulah *Orlando* **23** A1
Beulah, L. *Orlando* **23** A1
Beverley Hills *Sydney* **29** B1
Beverley Park *Sydney* **29** B2
Beverly *Chicago* **9** C2
Beverly Glen *Los Angeles* **16** B2
Beverly Hills *Los Angeles* **16** B2

Beverly Hills -Morgan Park Historic District *Chicago* **9** C2
Bexley *Sydney* **29** B1
Bexley ☐ *London* **15** B4
Bexleyheath *London* **15** B4
Beykoz *Istanbul* **12** B2
Beylerbeyi *Istanbul* **12** B2
Beyoğlu *Istanbul* **12** B1
Bezons *Paris* **24** A2
Bezuidenhout Park *Johannesburg* **13** B2
Bhadrakali *Kolkata* **14** A2
Bhalswa *Delhi* **10** A2
Bhambo Khan Qarmati *Karachi* **13** B2
Bhatsala *Kolkata* **14** B1
Bhawanipur *Kolkata* **14** B2
Bhendkhal *Mumbai* **20** B2
Bhuleshwar *Mumbai* **20** B2
Bialoleka Dworska *Warsaw* **32** B2
Bicentennial Park *Los Angeles* **16** B4
Bicentennial Park *Sydney* **29** B1
Bickley *London* **15** B4
Bicutan *Manila* **17** C2
Bidhan Nagar *Kolkata* **14** B2
Bidu *Jerusalem* **13** B1
Bielany *Warsaw* **32** B1
Bielawa *Warsaw* **32** C2
Biesdorf *Berlin* **5** A4
Bièvre → *Paris* **24** B2
Bièvres *Paris* **24** B2
Big Sand Lake *Orlando* **23** B1
Bilston *Edinburgh* **11** B2
Binacayan *Manila* **17** C1
Bintaro Jaya *Jakarta* **12** B1
Bir Nabala *Jerusalem* **13** A2
Birch Cliff *Toronto* **31** A3
Birkenstein *Berlin* **5** A5
Birkholz *Berlin* **5** A4
Birkholzaue *Berlin* **5** A4
Birrarrung Park *Melbourne* **18** A2
Biscayne Park *Miami* **18** A2
Bishop Lavis *Cape Town* **8** A2
Bishopscourt *Cape Town* **8** A1
Bispebjerg *Copenhagen* **8** A3
Bissonet Plaza *New Orleans* **21** A1
Bittsevsky Forest Park *Moscow* **19** C2
Björknas *Stockholm* **29** B3
Black Cr. → *Toronto* **31** A2
Black Creek Pioneer Village *Toronto* **31** A2
Blackfen *London* **15** B4
Blackheath *London* **15** B3
Blackrock *Dublin* **10** B2
Bladensburg *Washington* **33** B4
Blair Village *Atlanta* **3** C2
Blairgowrie *Johannesburg* **13** A1
Blake House *Boston* **6** B2
Blakehurst *Sydney* **29** B1
Blakstad *Oslo* **23** A2
Blanche, L. *Orlando* **23** B2
Blankenburg *Berlin* **5** A3
Blankenfelde *Berlin* **5** A3
Bliznw *Warsaw* **32** B1
Blota *Warsaw* **32** B1
Blue Island *Chicago* **9** D2
Blue Mosque = Sultanahme Camil *Istanbul* **12** B1
Bluebell *Dublin* **10** B1
Bluff Hd. *Hong Kong* **12** B2
Bluffers Park *Toronto* **31** A3
Blumberg *Berlin* **5** A4
Blunt Pt. *San Francisco* **26** A2
Blutenberg *Munich* **21** B1
Blylaget *Oslo* **23** B3
Boa Vista, Alto do *Rio de Janeiro* **25** B1
Boardwalk *New York* **22** C3
Boavista *Lisbon* **16** A2
Bobigny *Paris* **24** A3
Bocanegra *Lima* **34** B2
Boedo *Buenos Aires* **7** B2
Bogenhausen *Munich* **21** B2
Bogorodskoye *Moscow* **19** B3
Bogota *New York* **22** A1
Bogstadvatnet *Oslo* **23** A2
Bohnsdorf *Berlin* **5** B4
Bois-Colombes *Paris* **24** A2
Bois-d'Arcy *Paris* **24** B1
Boissy-St-Léger *Paris* **24** B3
Boldinasco *Milan* **19** A1
Boler *Oslo* **23** A4
Bollate *Milan* **19** A1
Bollebek *Brussels* **6** A1
Bollensdorf *Berlin* **5** A5
Bollmora *Stockholm* **29** B3
Bolshaya Okhta *St. Petersburg* **27** B2
Bolton *Milan* **19** A1
Bom Retiro *São Paulo* **27** B2
Bombay = Mumbai *Mumbai* **20** B2
Bondi *Sydney* **29** B2
Bondy *Paris* **24** A3
Bonifacio Monument *Manila* **17** B1
Bonneuil-sur-Marne *Paris* **24** B3
Bonnington *Edinburgh* **11** B3
Bonnyrigg and Lasswade *Edinburgh* **11** B3
Bonsucesso *Rio de Janeiro* **25** B1
Bontheuwel *Cape Town* **8** A2

Boo *Stockholm* **29** A3
Booterstown *Dublin* **10** B2
Borisovo *Moscow* **19** C3
Borle *Mumbai* **20** A2
Boronia Park *Sydney* **29** A1
Bosmont *Johannesburg* **13** B1
Bosön *Stockholm* **29** A3
Bosporus = İstanbul Boğazı *Istanbul* **12** B2
Bostancı *Istanbul* **12** C2
Boston *Boston* **6** A2
Boston Common *Boston* **6** A2
Boston Logan Int. ✈ (BOS) *Boston* **6** A3
Botafogo *Rio de Janeiro* **25** B1
Botany *Sydney* **29** B2
Botany B. *Sydney* **29** B2
Botany Bay → *Sydney* **29** B2
Botič → *Prague* **25** B3
Botica Sete *Lisbon* **16** A1
Boucherville *Montreal* **20** A3
Boucherville, Îs. de *Montreal* **20** A3
Bougival *Paris* **24** A1
Boulder Pt. *Hong Kong* **12** B1
Boulogne, Bois de *Paris* **24** A2
Boulogne-Billancourt *Paris* **24** A2
Bouviers *Paris* **24** B1
Bovenkerk *Amsterdam* **2** B2
Bovenkerker Polder *Amsterdam* **2** B2
Bovisa *Milan* **19** A2
Bow *London* **15** A3
Boyacıköy *Istanbul* **12** B2
Boyd Conservation Area *Toronto* **31** A1
Boyle Heights *Los Angeles* **16** B3
Braepark *Edinburgh* **11** B2
Braid *Edinburgh* **11** B2
Bramley *Johannesburg* **13** A2
Brandeis Univ. *Boston* **6** A1
Brandenburger Tor *Berlin* **5** A3
Brani, Pulau *Singapore* **28** B3
Braník *Prague* **25** B2
Brännkyrka *Stockholm* **29** B2
Brás *São Paulo* **27** B2
Brasilândia *São Paulo* **27** A1
Brateyevo *Moscow* **19** C3
Braybrook *Melbourne* **18** A1
Brázdim *Prague* **25** A3
Breakheart Reservation *Boston* **6** A2
Brede *Copenhagen* **8** A3
Breezy Point *New York* **22** C2
Breitenlee *Vienna* **32** A3
Breña *Lima* **34** B2
Brent □ *London* **15** A2
Brent Res. *London* **15** A2
Brentford *London* **15** B2
Brentwood *Los Angeles* **16** B2
Brentwood Park *Los Angeles* **16** B2
Brera *Milan* **19** B2
Bresso *Milan* **19** A2
Brevik *Stockholm* **29** A3
Břevnov *Prague* **25** B2
Brickyard, The *Chicago* **9** B2
Bridge City *New Orleans* **21** B2
Bridgeport *Chicago* **9** B3
Bridgetown *Cape Town* **8** A2
Bridgeview *Chicago* **9** C2
Brighton *Boston* **6** A3
Brighton *Melbourne* **18** B1
Brighton Beach *New York* **22** C2
Brighton Park *Chicago* **9** C2
Brighton-Le-Sands *Sydney* **29** B1
Brightwater *Washington* **33** B3
Brigittenau *Vienna* **32** A2
Brimbank Park *Melbourne* **18** A1
Brisbane *San Francisco* **26** B2
Britz *Berlin* **5** B3
Brixton *London* **15** B3
Broadmeadows *Melbourne* **18** A1
Broadmoor *San Francisco* **26** B2
Broadview *Chicago* **9** B1
Brockley *London* **15** B3
Bródno *Warsaw* **32** B2
Bródnowski, Kanal *Warsaw* **32** B2
Broek □ *Amsterdam* **2** A2
Bromley □ *London* **15** B4
Bromley Common *London* **15** B4
Bromma *Stockholm* **29** B1
Bromma ✈ (BMA) *Stockholm* **29** B1
Brøndby Strand *Copenhagen* **8** B2
Brøndbyøster *Copenhagen* **8** B2
Brøndbyvester *Copenhagen* **8** B2
Brøndebury *London* **15** A2
Brønnøya *Oslo* **23** A2
Bronsnøj *Copenhagen* **8** A3
Bronxville *New York* **22** A2
Brookfield *Chicago* **9** C1
Brookhaven *Atlanta* **3** A2
Brookline *Boston* **6** A3
Brooklyn *New York* **22** C2
Brooklyn Heights *New York* **22** B2
Brookmont *Washington* **33** B3
Brossard *Montreal* **20** B3
Brou-sur-Chanterenne *Paris* **24** A4
Brown *Toronto* **31** A3
Broyhill Park *Washington* **33** B2
Brughério *Milan* **19** A2
Brunswick *Melbourne* **18** A1
Brussel *Brussels* **6** A2
Brussel ✈ (BRU) *Brussels* **6** A2
Brussels = Brussel *Brussels* **6** A2
Bruxelles = Brussel *Brussels* **6** A2

Bruzzano *Milan* **19** A2
Bry-sur-Marne *Paris* **24** A4
Bryan, L. *Orlando* **23** B2
Bryanston *Johannesburg* **13** A1
Bryn *Oslo* **23** A4
Brzeziny *Warsaw* **32** B2
Bubeneč *Prague* **25** B2
Buc *Paris* **24** B1
Buchenhain *Munich* **21** B1
Buchholz *Berlin* **5** A3
Buckhead *Atlanta* **3** A2
Buckingham Palace *London* **15** A3
Buckow *Berlin* **5** B3
Bucktown *New Orleans* **21** A2
Buda *Budapest* **7** B2
Buda Castle = Budavárlpalota *Budapest* **7** A2
Budafok *Budapest* **7** B2
Budaörs *Budapest* **7** B1
Budapest *Budapest* **7** A2
Budapest ✈ (BUD) *Budapest* **7** B3
Budatétény *Budapest* **7** B2
Budavárlpalota *Budapest* **7** A2
Buddinge *Copenhagen* **8** A3
Buenos Aires *Buenos Aires* **7** B2
Buenos Aires Ezeiza ✈ (EZE) *Buenos Aires* **7** C1
Bufalotta *Rome* **26** B2
Bugio *Lisbon* **16** B1
Buiksloot *Amsterdam* **2** A2
Buitenveldert *Amsterdam* **2** B2
Buizingen *Brussels* **6** B1
Bukhansan *Seoul* **27** B1
Bukit Panjang Nature Reserve *Singapore* **28** A2
Bukit Timah Nature Reserve *Singapore* **28** A2
Bukum, Pulau *Singapore* **28** B2
Bûlâq *Cairo* **7** A2
Bule *Manila* **17** C2
Bulim *Singapore* **28** A2
Bullen Park *Melbourne* **18** A2
Bund, The *Shanghai* **28** B1
Bundoora North *Melbourne* **18** A2
Bundoora Park *Melbourne* **18** A2
Bunker Hill Memorial *Boston* **6** A2
Bunker I. *Karachi* **13** B1
Bunkyō *Tokyo* **30** A3
Bunnefjorden *Oslo* **23** A3
Buona Vista Park *Singapore* **28** B2
Burbank *Chicago* **9** C2
Burbank *Los Angeles* **16** A3
Burden, L. *Orlando* **23** B1
Burlington *Boston* **6** A1
Burnham Park *Chicago* **9** C3
Burnham Park Harbor *Chicago* **9** B3
Burnhamthorpe *Toronto* **31** B1
Burnt Oak *London* **15** A2
Burtonland *Edinburgh* **11** A2
Burnwynd *Edinburgh* **11** B1
Burqa *Jerusalem* **13** A2
Burtus *Cairo* **7** A1
Burudvatn *Oslo* **23** A2
Burwood *Sydney* **29** B1
Bushwick *New York* **22** B2
Bushy Park *London* **15** B1
Butantã *São Paulo* **27** B1
Butcher I. *Mumbai* **20** B2
Butler, L. *Orlando* **23** B1
Butts Corner *Washington* **33** C2
Büyükdere *Istanbul* **12** B2
Byculla *Mumbai* **20** B2
Bygdøy *Oslo* **23** A3
Bywater *New Orleans* **21** B2

C

C.B.S. Fox Studios *Los Angeles* **16** B2
C.N.N. Center *Atlanta* **3** B2
C.N. Tower *Toronto* **31** B2
Caballito *Buenos Aires* **7** B2
Cabin John *Washington* **33** B2
Cabin John Regional Park □ *Washington* **33** A2
Cabinteely *Dublin* **10** B3
Cabra *Dublin* **10** A2
Cabuçu de Baixo → *São Paulo* **27** A1
Cabuçu de Cima → *São Paulo* **27** A2
Cachan *Paris* **24** B2
Cachoeira, Rib. da → *São Paulo* **27** A2
Cacilhas *Lisbon* **16** A2
Cahuenga Park *Los Angeles* **16** B3
Cain, L. *Orlando* **23** B1
Cairo = El Qâhira *Cairo* **7** A2
Cairo Int. ✈ (CAI) *Cairo* **7** A3
Caju *Rio de Janeiro* **25** B1
Čakovice *Prague* **25** A3
Calcutta = Kolkata *Kolkata* **14** B2
California Inst. of Tech. *Los Angeles* **16** B4
California Los Angeles, Univ. of *Los Angeles* **16** B2
California State Univ. *Los Angeles* **16** B3
Callao *Lima* **34** B2
Caloocan *Manila* **17** B1
Calumet, L. *Chicago* **9** C3
Calumet Park *Chicago* **9** C3
Calumet Sag Channel → *Chicago* **9** C2
Calvaire *Milan* **19** B2
Camarate *Lisbon* **16** A2
Camaroes *Lisbon* **16** A1

Camberwell *London* 15 B3
Camberwell *Melbourne* 18 B2
Cambridge *Boston* 6 A2
Cambuci *São Paulo* 27 B2
Camden □ *London* 15 A3
Cameron, Mt. *Wellington* 33 B2
Çamlıca *Istanbul* 12 B2
Camp Springs *Washington* 33 C4
Campamento *Madrid* 17 B1
Campbellfield *Melbourne* 18 A1
Camperdown *Sydney* 29 B2
Campo, Casa de *Madrid* 17 B1
Campo F.C. Barcelona
  Barcelona 4 A1
Campo Grande *Lisbon* 16 A2
Campo Pequeño *Lisbon* 16 A2
Campolide *Lisbon* 16 A2
Camps Bay *Cape Town* 8 A1
C'an San Joan *Barcelona* 4 A2
Cañacao B. *Manila* 17 C1
Canarsie *New York* 22 C2
Candiac *Montreal* 20 B3
Caneças *Lisbon* 16 A1
Canillas *Madrid* 17 B2
Canillejas *Madrid* 17 B2
Canning Town *London* 15 A4
Canteras de Vallecas
  Madrid 17 B2
Canterbury *Melbourne* 18 A2
Canterbury *Sydney* 29 B1
Canton = Guangzhou
  Guangzhou 11 B2
Caoheijing *Shanghai* 28 B1
Capão Redondo *São Paulo* 27 B1
Caparica *Lisbon* 16 A2
Caparica, Costa da *Lisbon* 16 B1
Cape Flats *Cape Town* 8 B2
Cape Town *Cape Town* 8 A1
Cape Town Int. ✈ *(CPT)*
  Cape Town 8 A2
Capitol Heights *Washington* 33 B4
Captain Cook Bridge
  Sydney 29 C2
Captain Cook Landing
  Place Park *Sydney* 29 C2
Capuchos *Lisbon* 16 B1
Carabanchel Alto *Madrid* 17 B1
Carabanchel Bajo *Madrid* 17 B1
Carapachay *Buenos Aires* 7 B1
Caraza *Buenos Aires* 7 C2
Caridad *Manila* 17 C1
Carmen de Huechuraba
  Santiago 27 B1
Carmen de la Legua *Lima* 14 B2
Carnaxide *Lisbon* 16 A1
Carnegie *Melbourne* 18 B2
Carnide *Lisbon* 16 A1
Carol City *Miami* 18 A1
Carrascal *Santiago* 27 B1
Carrickmines *Dublin* 10 B3
Carrières-sous-Bois *Paris* 24 A1
Carrières-sur-Seine *Paris* 24 A2
Carrigeen B. *Dublin* 10 A3
Cartierville *Montreal* 20 A1
Casa Loma *Toronto* 31 A2
Casa Verde *São Paulo* 27 B1
Casál Morena *Rome* 26 C2
Casalotti *Rome* 26 B1
Cascade Heights *Atlanta* 3 B2
Castèl di Leva *Rome* 26 C2
Castel Sant'Angelo *Rome* 26 B1
Castleknock *Dublin* 10 A1
Castleton Corners *New York* 22 C1
Cataouatche, L. *New Orleans* 21 B1
Catete *Rio de Janeiro* 25 B1
Catford *London* 15 B3
Catherine, L. *Orlando* 23 B2
Caufield *Melbourne* 18 B2
Cavite *Manila* 17 C1
Caxias *Lisbon* 16 A1
Cebecci *Istanbul* 12 B1
Cecchignola *Rome* 26 C2
Cecilienhof, Schloss *Berlin* 5 B1
Cedar Grove *Atlanta* 3 C3
Cedarvale Park *Toronto* 31 A2
Cempaka Putih *Jakarta* 12 B2
Çengelköy *Istanbul* 12 B2
Cengkareng *Jakarta* 12 A1
Centennial Olympic Park
  Atlanta 3 B2
Centennial Park *Sydney* 29 B2
Center Hill *Atlanta* 3 B2
Centocelle *Rome* 26 B2
Central, Gare *Montreal* 20 B2
Central Park *New York* 22 B2
Century City *Los Angeles* 16 B2
Cerdanyola del Vallès
  Barcelona 4 A1
Cerillos *Santiago* 27 B1
Cerro de la Estrella △
  Mexico City 18 B2
Cerro de los Ángeles *Madrid* 17 C1
Cerro Navia *Santiago* 27 B1
Cesano Boscone *Milan* 19 B1
Cesate *Milan* 19 A1
Cha Kwo Ling *Hong Kong* 12 B2
Chacarrita *Buenos Aires* 7 B2
Chadwell Heath *London* 15 A4
Chai Chee *Singapore* 28 B3
Chai Wan *Hong Kong* 12 B2
Chai Wan Kok *Hong Kong* 12 A1
Chaidari *Athens* 2 A1
Chakdaha *Kolkata* 14 C1
Chalandri *Athens* 2 A2
Chamartin *Madrid* 17 B1
Chamberi *Madrid* 17 B1
Chambourcy *Paris* 24 A1
Champigny-sur-Marne
  Paris 24 A4
Champlain, Pont *Montreal* 20 B2
Champs-sur-Marne *Paris* 24 A4
Chamrail *Kolkata* 14 B1
Chanakyapuri *Delhi* 10 B2
Chanditala *Kolkata* 14 A1
Changfeng Park *Shanghai* 28 B1
Changhai = Shanghai
  Shanghai 28 B1
Changi *Singapore* 28 A3
Changi, Singapore ✈
  (SIN) *Singapore* 28 A3
Changning *Shanghai* 28 B1
Chantereine *Paris* 24 A4
Chantian *Guangzhou* 11 A2
Chaoyang *Beijing* 4 B2
Chaoyangmen *Beijing* 4 B2
Chapelizod *Dublin* 10 A1
Chapultepec, Bosque de
  Mexico City 18 B1
Chapultepec, Castillo de
  Mexico City 18 B1
Charenton-le-Pont *Paris* 24 B3
Charleroi, Kanal de →
  Brussels 6 B1
Charles Bridge = Karlův
  most *Prague* 25 B2
Charles Gates Dawes
  House *Chicago* 9 A2

Charlestown *Boston* 6 A2
Charlottenburg *Berlin* 5 A2
Charlottenburg, Schloss
  Berlin 5 A2
Charlottenlund *Copenhagen* 8 A3
Charlton *London* 15 B4
Charneca *Lisbon* 16 A2
Charneca *Lisbon* 16 B1
Chase, L. *Orlando* 23 B1
Châteaufort *Paris* 24 B1
Châtenay-Malabry *Paris* 24 B2
Chatham *Sydney* 29 C3
Châtillon *Paris* 24 B2
Chatou *Paris* 24 A1
Chatpur *Kolkata* 14 B2
Chatswood *Sydney* 29 A2
Chatuchak *Bangkok* 3 B2
Chatuchak Park *Bangkok* 3 B2
Chauki *Karachi* 13 A1
Chavarria *Lima* 14 B2
Chaville *Paris* 24 B2
Chayang *Seoul* 27 B2
Chelles *Paris* 24 A4
Chelles, Canal de *Paris* 24 A4
Chells-le-Pin ✈ *Paris* 24 A4
Chelsea *Boston* 6 A2
Chelsea *London* 15 B2
Chembur *Mumbai* 20 A2
Chengshousi *Beijing* 4 C2
Chennevières-sur-Marne
  Paris 24 B4
Cheongdam *Seoul* 27 B2
Cheonho *Seoul* 27 B2
Cheops *Cairo* 7 B1
Chertanovka → *Moscow* 19 C2
Chertanovo *Moscow* 19 B2
Cheryomushki *Moscow* 19 B2
Chestnut Hill *Boston* 6 B1
Cheung Sha Van
  Hong Kong 12 A1
Cheverly *Washington* 33 B4
Chevilly-Larue *Paris* 24 B3
Cheviot Hills *Los Angeles* 16 B2
Chevy Chase *Washington* 33 B3
Chhatrapati Shivaji,
  Mumbai ✈ *(BOM)*
  Mumbai 20 A2
Chia Keng *Singapore* 28 A3
Chiaravalle Milanese *Milan* 19 B2
Chicago *Chicago* 9 C2
Chicago, Univ. of *Chicago* 9 C3
Chicago Harbor *Chicago* 9 B3
Chicago Lawn *Chicago* 9 C2
Chicago-Midway ✈
  (MDW) *Chicago* 9 C2
Chicago O'Hare Int. ✈
  (ORD) *Chicago* 9 B1
Chicago Ridge *Chicago* 9 C2
Chicago River, North
  Branch → *Chicago* 9 B2
Chicago Sanitary and Ship
  Canal *Chicago* 9 C2
Chicago State Univ. *Chicago* 9 C3
Chicago Zoo *Chicago* 9 B1
Chienzui *Guangzhou* 11 A1
Chik Sha *Hong Kong* 12 B2
Child's Hill *London* 15 A2
Chile, Univ. de *Santiago* 27 B2
Chilla Saroda *Delhi* 10 B2
Chillum *Washington* 33 B4
Chilly-Mazarin *Paris* 24 B2
Chinguota *Kolkata* 14 C1
Chinna Cr. → *Karachi* 13 B2
Chiquihuite, Cerro
  Mexico City 18 A2
Chislehurst *London* 15 B4
Chiswick *London* 15 B2
Chiswick House *London* 15 B2
Chitose *Tokyo* 30 B2
Chitralada Palace *Bangkok* 3 B2
Chiyoda *Tokyo* 30 A3
Choa Chu Kang *Singapore* 28 A2
Chodov u Prahy *Prague* 25 B3
Chōfu *Tokyo* 30 B2
Choisy-le-Roi *Paris* 24 B3
Cholargos *Athens* 2 A2
Cholupice *Prague* 25 C2
Chom Thong *Bangkok* 3 B1
Chong Pang *Singapore* 28 A2
Chongwen *Beijing* 4 B2
Chorrillos *Lima* 14 C2
Chowpatty Beach *Mumbai* 20 B1
Christianshavn *Copenhagen* 8 A3
Chrzanów *Warsaw* 32 B1
Chuen Lung *Hong Kong* 12 A1
Chuk Kok *Hong Kong* 12 A2
Chulalongkorn Univ.
  Bangkok 3 B2
Chūō *Tokyo* 30 A3
Church End *London* 15 A2
Church of our Lady =
  Frauenkirche *Munich* 21 B2
Churchtown *Dublin* 10 B2
Ciampino *Rome* 26 C2
Ciampino ✈ *(CIA)* *Rome* 26 C2
Cicero *Chicago* 9 B2
Cilandak *Jakarta* 12 B1
Cilincing *Jakarta* 12 A2
Ciliwung → *Jakarta* 12 B2
Čimice *Prague* 25 B2
Cinecittà *Rome* 26 B2
Ciniselo Bálsamo *Milan* 19 A2
Cinkota *Budapest* 7 A3
Cipete *Jakarta* 12 B1
Citta degli Studi *Milan* 19 B2
Città del Vaticano =
  Vatican City ■ *Rome* 26 B1
City, The *London* 15 A3
City Hall = Rådhus *Oslo* 23 A3
City Hall = Stadshuset
  Stockholm 29 B2
City of the Dead *Cairo* 7 A2
City Park *New Orleans* 21 A2
City Terrace *Los Angeles* 16 B3
Ciudad de México
  Mexico City 18 B2
Ciudad Deportiva
  Mexico City 18 B2
Ciudad Fin de Semana
  Madrid 17 B2
Ciudad General Belgrano
  Buenos Aires 7 C1
Ciudad Lineál *Madrid* 17 B2
Ciudad Satélite *Mexico City* 18 A1
Ciudad Universitaria
  Buenos Aires 7 B2
Ciudad Universitaria
  Mexico City 18 C1
Claireville Res. *Toronto* 31 A1
Clamart *Paris* 24 B2
Clapham *London* 15 B3
Clapton *London* 15 A3
Claremont *Cape Town* 8 A1
Clayhall *London* 15 A4
Clear, L. *Orlando* 23 A2
Clermiston *Edinburgh* 11 B2
Clichy *Paris* 24 A2
Clichy-sous-Bois *Paris* 24 A4
Cliffside *Toronto* 31 A3
Cliffside Park *New York* 22 B1
Clifton *Cape Town* 8 A1

Clifton *Karachi* 13 B2
Clifton *New York* 22 C1
Clifton Beach *Karachi* 13 B2
Cliftondale *Boston* 6 A2
Cloghran *Dublin* 10 A2
Clonskeagh *Dublin* 10 B2
Clontarf *Dublin* 10 A2
Clontarf *Sydney* 29 A2
Clovelly *Sydney* 29 B2
Cobras, I. das *Rio de Janeiro* 25 B2
Coburg *Melbourne* 18 A1
Cocotá *Rio de Janeiro* 25 A1
Codet *Jakarta* 12 B2
Ceuilly *Paris* 24 B4
Coina *Lisbon* 16 B2
Coker *Lagos* 14 B2
Colaba *Mumbai* 20 B1
Colaba Pt. *Mumbai* 20 B1
Colegiales *Buenos Aires* 7 B2
Colindale *London* 15 A2
Colinton *Edinburgh* 11 B2
College Park *Washington* 33 B4
College Point *New York* 22 B2
Collégien *Paris* 24 A4
Collier Row *London* 15 A4
Colliers Wood *London* 15 B3
Colma *San Francisco* 26 B2
Colney Hatch *London* 15 A3
Cologno Monzese *Milan* 19 A2
Colombes *Paris* 24 A2
Colonia Güell *Barcelona* 4 A1
Colonial Knob *Wellington* 33 A1
Colosseo *Rome* 26 B1
Colosseum = Colosseo
  Rome 26 B1
Combault *Paris* 24 A4
Comércio, Praça do *Lisbon* 16 A2
Commerce *Los Angeles* 16 B4
Conceição, I. da
  Rio de Janeiro 25 B2
Conchali *Santiago* 27 B1
Concord *Sydney* 29 B1
Concord *Toronto* 31 A2
Concorde, Place de la *Paris* 24 A2
Concorezzo *Milan* 19 A2
Condet *Jakarta* 12 B2
Coney Island *New York* 22 C2
Congonhas São Paulo ✈
  (CGH) *São Paulo* 27 B2
Conley → *Atlanta* 3 C2
Connaught Place *Delhi* 10 B2
Consolação *São Paulo* 27 B2
Constantia *Cape Town* 8 B1
Constitución *Buenos Aires* 7 B2
Constitution *Atlanta* 3 B2
Convention Center
  Los Angeles 16 B3
Conway *Orlando* 23 B2
Conway, L. *Orlando* 23 B2
Coogee *Sydney* 29 B2
Cooksville *Toronto* 31 B1
Coolock *Dublin* 10 A2
Copacabana *Rio de Janeiro* 25 B1
Copenhagen =
  København *Copenhagen* 8 A2
Coral Gables *Miami* 18 B2
Coral Hills *Washington* 33 B4
Corcovado, Cristo
  Redentar *Rio de Janeiro* 25 B1
Corduff *Dublin* 10 A1
Cormano *Milan* 19 A2
Cornaredo *Milan* 19 A1
Córsico *Milan* 19 B1
Corstorphine *Edinburgh* 11 B2
Corviale *Rome* 26 B1
Coslada *Madrid* 17 B2
Cossigny *Paris* 24 B4
Cotao *Lisbon* 16 A1
Côte-St-Luc *Montreal* 20 B2
Cotunduba, I. de
  Rio de Janeiro 25 B2
Coubron *Paris* 24 A4
Countryside *Chicago* 9 C1
County Art Museum
  Los Angeles 16 B2
Courbevoie *Paris* 24 A2
Courtry *Paris* 24 A4
Cowley *London* 15 A1
Coyoacán *Mexico City* 18 B2
Craighall Park *Johannesburg* 13 A2
Craiglockhart *Edinburgh* 11 B2
Craigmillar *Edinburgh* 11 B3
Cramond *Edinburgh* 11 B2
Cramond Bridge *Edinburgh* 11 B1
Cramond I. *Edinburgh* 11 B2
Cranford *London* 15 B1
Crawford *Cape Town* 8 A2
Crayford *London* 15 B5
Creekmouth *London* 15 A4
Crescent, L. *Orlando* 23 A1
Crescenzago *Milan* 19 A2
Cresskill *New York* 22 A2
Créteil *Paris* 24 B3
Cricklewood *London* 15 A2
Cristo Redentor,
  Corcovado *Rio de Janeiro* 25 B1
Crockenhill *London* 15 B5
Croissy-Beaubourg *Paris* 24 B4
Croissy-sur-Seine *Paris* 24 A1
Crosby *Johannesburg* 13 B1
Crosne *Paris* 24 B3
Cross I. *Mumbai* 20 B2
Crouch End *London* 15 A3
Crown Mine *Johannesburg* 13 B1
Crows Nest *Sydney* 29 B2
Croydon *London* 15 B3
Croydon Park *Sydney* 29 B1
Cruagh Mt. *Dublin* 10 B2
Crumlin *Dublin* 10 B2
Cruz de Pau *Lisbon* 16 B2
Crystal Palace *London* 15 B3
Csepel *Budapest* 7 B2
Csepelsziget *Budapest* 7 B2
Csillaghegy *Budapest* 7 A2
Csillagtelep *Budapest* 7 B2
Csömör *Budapest* 7 A3
Csömöri-patak → *Budapest* 7 A3
Cuatro Vientos *Madrid* 17 B1
Cuauhtémoc *Mexico City* 18 B2
Cuban Museum *Miami* 18 B2
Cubao *Manila* 17 B2
Çubuklu *Istanbul* 12 B2
Cudahy *Los Angeles* 16 C3
Cuicuilco, Pirámide de
  Mexico City 18 C1
Culmore *Washington* 33 B3
Culver City *Los Angeles* 16 C2
Cupecé → *São Paulo* 27 B1
Currie *Edinburgh* 11 B2
Cusago *Milan* 19 B1
Cusano Milanino *Milan* 19 A2
Cutler Park *Boston* 6 B1
Çuvuşabaşı → *Istanbul* 12 B1
Cuvei *Delhi* 4 B1
Cypress Hills *New York* 22 B2
Cypress Park *Los Angeles* 16 B3
Czernaków *Warsaw* 32 B1
Czyste *Warsaw* 32 B1

D

Da Mooca → *São Paulo* 27 B2
Ďáblice *Prague* 25 B2
Dabrowa *Warsaw* 32 B1
Dachang *Shanghai* 28 B1
Dachang ✈ *Shanghai* 28 B1
Dachau *Munich* 21 A1
Dachau-Ost *Munich* 21 A1
Dachauer Moos *Munich* 21 A1
Dadar *Mumbai* 20 A1
Daebang *Seoul* 27 B1
Daechi *Seoul* 27 B2
Dafni *Athens* 2 B2
Dagenham *London* 15 A4
Daglfing *Munich* 21 B2
Dahab, Gezîret el *Cairo* 7 B2
Daheisha *Jerusalem* 13 B2
Dahlem *Berlin* 5 B2
Dahlwitz-Hoppegarten
  Berlin 5 A5
Dahongmen *Beijing* 4 C2
Dajiaoting *Beijing* 4 B2
Dakhnoye *St. Petersburg* 27 C1
Dalejsky potok → *Prague* 25 B2
Dalkeith *Edinburgh* 11 B3
Dalkey *Dublin* 10 B3
Dalkey I. *Dublin* 10 B3
Dallgow *Berlin* 5 A1
Dalmeny *Edinburgh* 11 B1
Dalston *London* 15 A3
Daly City *San Francisco* 26 B2
Damaia *Lisbon* 16 A1
Damarakia *Athens* 2 B1
Dämeritzsee *Berlin* 5 B5
Dan Ryan Woods *Chicago* 9 C2
Danderhall *Edinburgh* 11 B3
Danderyd *Stockholm* 29 A2
Danforth *Toronto* 31 A3
Darakeh *Tehran* 31 A2
Darband *Tehran* 31 A2
Darling Point *Sydney* 29 B2
Darndale *Dublin* 10 A2
Darrüs *Tehran* 31 A2
Dartford *London* 15 B5
Dashi *Guangzhou* 11 B2
Datansha *Guangzhou* 11 B2
Datun *Beijing* 4 B2
Daulatpur *Delhi* 10 A1
Davidson, Mt. *San Francisco* 26 B2
Davidson's Mains
  Edinburgh 11 B2
Dāvūdiyeh *Tehran* 31 A2
Davydkovo *Moscow* 19 B1
Dawidy *Warsaw* 32 C1
Daxing *Beijing* 4 C2
Days Bay *Wellington* 33 B2
Decatur *Atlanta* 3 B2
Dedham *Boston* 6 B1
Degunino *Moscow* 19 A2
Deir Dibwan *Jerusalem* 13 A2
Deir Ibzi'e *Jerusalem* 13 A1
Dejvice *Prague* 25 B2
Dekabristov, Ostrov
  St. Petersburg 27 B1
Del Rey *Los Angeles* 16 C2
Delhi *Delhi* 10 B2
Delhi Indira Gandhi Int. ✈
  (DEL) *Delhi* 10 B1
Demarest *New York* 22 A2
Den IIp *Amsterdam* 2 A2
Denistone Heights *Sydney* 29 A1
Dentonia Park *Toronto* 31 A3
DePaul Univ. *Chicago* 9 B3
Deptford *London* 15 B3
Des Plaines *Chicago* 9 A1
Desert Wetlands Park
  Las Vegas 14 B2
Deutsche Oper *Berlin* 5 A2
Deutsches Museum *Munich* 21 B2
Devil's Peak *Cape Town* 8 A1
Dhakuria *Kolkata* 14 B2
Dharavi *Mumbai* 20 A2
Diadema *São Paulo* 27 C2
Diegen *Brussels* 6 A2
Diemen *Amsterdam* 2 A2
Diepkloof *Johannesburg* 13 B1
Dieprivier *Cape Town* 8 B1
Difficult Run → *Washington* 33 B2
Dilbeek *Brussels* 6 A1
Dilli = Delhi *Delhi* 10 B2
Dirnismaning *Munich* 21 A2
Disney-M.G.M. Studios
  Orlando 23 B1
Disney Studios *Los Angeles* 16 B3
District Heights *Washington* 33 B4
Djakarta = Jakarta *Jakarta* 12 A1
Djursholm *Stockholm* 29 A2
Döberitz *Berlin* 5 A1
Döbling *Vienna* 32 A2
Dobong *Seoul* 27 A2
Dobongsan *Seoul* 27 A2
Docklands *London* 15 A3
Doctor Phillips *Orlando* 23 B2
Dodder → *Dublin* 10 B2
Dodger Stadium *Los Angeles* 16 B3
Dogs, Isle of *London* 15 B3
Dolgoe Ozero *St. Petersburg* 27 A1
Dollis Hill *London* 15 A2
Dollymount *Dublin* 10 A2
Dolni *Prague* 25 B3
Dolni Chabry *Prague* 25 B2
Dolni Počernice *Prague* 25 B3
Dolphins Barn *Dublin* 10 B2
Dom Pedro II, Parque
  São Paulo 27 B2
Don Mills *Toronto* 31 A2
Don Muang Int. ✈ *(BKK)*
  Bangkok 3 A2
Donaghmede *Dublin* 10 A3
Donau-Oder Kanal *Vienna* 32 A3
Donaufeld *Vienna* 32 A2
Donaupark *Vienna* 32 A2
Donaustadt *Vienna* 32 A2
Dongan Hills *New York* 22 C1
Dongcheng *Beijing* 4 B2
Dongdaemung *Seoul* 27 B2
Donggou *Shanghai* 28 B2
Dongjiak *Seoul* 27 B1
Dongjiao *Guangzhou* 11 B2
Dongri *Mumbai* 20 B2
Dongshanhu Park
  Guangzhou 11 B2
Dongzhimen *Beijing* 4 B2
Donnybrook *Dublin* 10 B2
Doornfontein *Johannesburg* 13 B2
Dorchester *Boston* 6 B2
Dorchester B. *Boston* 6 B2
Dorchester Heights Nat.
  Historical Site → *Boston* 6 B2
Dornach *Munich* 21 B3
Dorval Int., Montréal ✈
  (YUL) *Montreal* 20 B1
Dos Morrinos → *São Paulo* 27 C2
Douglas Park *Chicago* 9 B2
Dover Heights *Sydney* 29 B2
Dowlatābād *Tehran* 31 A2
Down, L. *Orlando* 23 A1

Downey *Los Angeles* 16 C4
Downsview *Toronto* 31 A1
Dragør *Copenhagen* 8 B3
Drancy *Paris* 24 A3
Dranesville *Washington* 33 A1
Drapetsona *Athens* 2 B1
Dreilinden *Berlin* 5 B2
Drewnica *Warsaw* 32 B2
Drigh Road *Karachi* 13 A2
Drimnagh *Dublin* 10 B2
Drogenbos *Brussels* 6 B1
Druid Hills *Atlanta* 3 B2
Drumcondra *Dublin* 10 A2
Drummoyne *Sydney* 29 B1
Drylaw *Edinburgh* 11 B2
Dubeč *Prague* 25 B3
Dublin *Dublin* 10 A2
Dublin ✈ *(DUB)* *Dublin* 10 A1
Dublin B. *Dublin* 10 A3
Dublin Harbour *Dublin* 10 A2
Duddingston *Edinburgh* 11 B3
Dugnano *Milan* 19 A2
Duivendrecht *Amsterdam* 2 B2
Dülāb *Tehran* 31 A2
Dulles Int. ✈ *(IAD)*
  Washington 33 B1
Dulwich *London* 15 B3
Dum Dum *Kolkata* 14 B2
Dum Dum Int. ✈ *(CCU)*
  Kolkata 14 B2
Dumont *New York* 22 A2
Dún Laoghaire *Dublin* 10 B3
Dundrum *Dublin* 10 B2
Dunearn *Singapore* 28 B2
Dúnleary = Dún
  Laoghaire *Dublin* 10 B3
Dunn Loring *Washington* 33 B2
Dunning *Chicago* 9 B2
Dunvegan *Johannesburg* 13 A2
Duomo *Milan* 19 B2
Duque de Caxias
  Rio de Janeiro 25 A1
Duren Sawit *Jakarta* 12 B2
Dusit *Bangkok* 3 B2
Dworp *Brussels* 6 B1
Dyakovo *Moscow* 19 B2
Dyker Beach Park
  New York 22 C1
Dzerzhinskiy *Moscow* 19 B2
Dzerzhinskiy Park *Moscow* 19 B2

E

E.U.R. = Esposizione
  Universale di Roma
  Rome 26 C1
Eagle Rock *Los Angeles* 16 B3
Ealing □ *London* 15 A2
Earlsfield *London* 15 B2
Earlwood *Sydney* 29 B1
East Arlington *Boston* 6 A3
East Arlington *Washington* 33 B3
East Bedfont *London* 15 B1
East Don → *Toronto* 31 A2
East Don Parkland *Toronto* 31 A2
East Elmhurst *New York* 22 B2
East Finchley *London* 15 A2
East Flatbush *New York* 22 C2
East Ham *London* 15 A4
East Humber → *Toronto* 31 A1
East Lammas Channel
  Hong Kong 12 B1
East Las Vegas = Whitney
  Las Vegas 14 B2
East Lexington *Boston* 6 A1
East Los Angeles *Los Angeles* 16 B3
East Molesey *London* 15 B1
East New York *New York* 22 B2
East Pines *Washington* 33 B4
East Point *Atlanta* 3 B2
East Potomac Park
  Washington 33 B3
East River → *New York* 22 B2
East Rutherford *New York* 22 B1
East Sheen *London* 15 B2
East Talpiyot *Jerusalem* 13 B2
East Wickham *London* 15 B4
East York *Toronto* 31 A2
Eastbourne *Wellington* 33 B2
Eastcote *London* 15 A1
Easter Howgate *Edinburgh* 11 B2
Eastpoint Park *Toronto* 31 A4
Eastwood *Sydney* 29 A1
Eaton Canyon Park
  Los Angeles 16 B4
Ebara *Tokyo* 30 B3
Ebisu *Tokyo* 30 B3
Ebute-Ikorodu *Lagos* 14 A2
Ebute-Metta *Lagos* 14 B2
Eda → *Tokyo* 30 B2
Edendale *Johannesburg* 13 A2
Edenmore *Dublin* 10 A2
Edgars Cr. → *Melbourne* 18 A1
Edgeley *Toronto* 31 A1
Edgemar *San Francisco* 26 C2
Edgewater *New York* 22 B2
Edgewood *Orlando* 23 B2
Edinburgh *Edinburgh* 11 B2
Edinburgh ✈ *(EDI)*
  Edinburgh 11 B1
Edinburgh Castle *Edinburgh* 11 B2
Edison Park *Chicago* 9 A2
Edmonstons *Washington* 33 B4
Edmondstown *Dublin* 10 B2
Edo → *Tokyo* 30 B4
Edogawa *Tokyo* 30 A4
Edsberg *Stockholm* 29 A1
Edwards L. *Melbourne* 18 A1
Eēzonos *Athens* 2 B2
Egaleo *Athens* 2 B1
Egaleo, Oros *Athens* 2 B1
Eiche *Berlin* 5 A4
Eiche Süd *Berlin* 5 A4
Eiffel, Tour *Paris* 24 A2
Ein Arik *Jerusalem* 13 A1
Ein Naquba *Jerusalem* 13 B1
Ein Rafa *Jerusalem* 13 B1
Eizariya *Jerusalem* 13 B2
Ejby *Copenhagen* 8 A2
Ejigbo *Lagos* 14 A1
Ekeberg *Oslo* 23 A3
Eknäs *Stockholm* 29 B2
El 'Abbasiya *Cairo* 7 A2
El Agustino, Cerro *Lima* 14 B3
El Baragil *Cairo* 7 A1
El Basâlîn *Cairo* 7 B2
El Bira *Jerusalem* 13 A2
El Bosque *Santiago* 27 C2
El Carmen *Santiago* 27 B1
El Cortijo *Santiago* 27 B1
El Cristo, Vaso Regulador
  Mexico City 18 B1
El Duqqi *Cairo* 7 A2
El Encinar de los Reyes
  Madrid 17 A2
El Gezira *Cairo* 7 A2
El Ghuriya *Cairo* 7 A2
El Gîza *Cairo* 7 A2

El Khadr *Jerusalem* 13 B1
El Khalifa *Cairo* 7 A2
El Kôm el Ahmar *Cairo* 7 A2
El Ma'âdi *Cairo* 7 B2
El Matariya *Cairo* 7 A2
El Mohandessin *Cairo* 7 A2
El Monte *Los Angeles* 16 B4
El Muqattam *Cairo* 7 A2
El Mûskî *Cairo* 7 A2
El Pardo *Madrid* 17 A1
El Portal *Miami* 18 A2
El Prat de Llobregat
  Barcelona 4 B1
El Qâhira *Cairo* 7 A2
El Qubba *Cairo* 7 A2
El Reloj *Mexico City* 18 C2
El Retiro *Madrid* 17 B1
El Salto *Santiago* 27 B2
El Sereno *Los Angeles* 16 B3
El Talbiya *Cairo* 7 B1
El Vergel *Mexico City* 18 C2
El Wâhli *Cairo* 7 A2
El Zamâlik *Cairo* 7 A2
El Zeitún *Cairo* 7 A2
Eleftherios Venizelos ✈
  (ATH) *Athens* 2 B2
Elephanta Caves *Mumbai* 20 B2
Elephanta I. *Mumbai* 20 B2
Ellboda *Stockholm* 29 A3
Ellenor, L. *Orlando* 23 B2
Elliniko Olympic Complex
  Athens 2 B2
Ellis I. *New York* 22 B1
Elmers End *London* 15 B3
Elmhurst *New York* 22 B2
Elmstead *London* 15 B4
Elmwood *New Orleans* 21 B1
Elmwood Park *Chicago* 9 B2
Elmwood Park *New York* 22 A1
Elsdon *Wellington* 33 A1
Elsiesrivier *Cape Town* 8 A2
Elsternwick *Melbourne* 18 B2
Eltham *London* 15 B4
Elwood *Melbourne* 18 B1
Élysée *Paris* 24 A2
Elysian Park *Los Angeles* 16 B3
Emämzâdeh Sâleh *Tehran* 31 A2
Émerainville *Paris* 24 B4
Emeryville *San Francisco* 26 A3
Eminönü *Istanbul* 12 B1
Emirgan *Istanbul* 12 B2
Emmarentia *Johannesburg* 13 A2
Empire State Building
  New York 22 B2
Encantado *Rio de Janeiro* 25 B1
Encino *Los Angeles* 16 B2
Encino Res. *Los Angeles* 16 B1
Eneyberg *Stockholm* 29 A1
Enfield *Sydney* 29 B1
Engenho, I. do *Rio de Janeiro* 25 B2
Englewood *Chicago* 9 C3
Englewood *New York* 22 A1
Englewood Cliffs *New York* 22 A1
Enmore *Sydney* 29 B2
Enskede *Stockholm* 29 B2
Enterprise *Las Vegas* 14 B1
Entrevias *Madrid* 17 B1
Epcot *Orlando* 23 B1
Epping *Sydney* 29 A1
Erenköy *Istanbul* 12 C2
Erith *London* 15 B5
Erlaa *Vienna* 32 B1
Ermington *Sydney* 29 A1
Ermita *Manila* 17 B1
Ershatou *Guangzhou* 11 B2
Erskineville *Sydney* 29 B2
Erunkan *Lagos* 14 A2
Esenler *Istanbul* 12 B1
Esher *London* 15 B1
Eskbank *Edinburgh* 11 B3
Esplugas *Barcelona* 4 A1
Esposizione Universale di
  Roma *Rome* 26 C1
Essendon *Melbourne* 18 A1
Essendon ✈ *(MEB)*
  Melbourne 18 A1
Essingen *Stockholm* 29 B1
Essling *Vienna* 32 A3
Est, Gare de l' *Paris* 24 A3
Estado, Parque do *São Paulo* 27 B2
Estelle *New Orleans* 21 B2
Estrela, Basilica da *Lisbon* 16 A2
Etobicoke *Toronto* 31 A1
Etobicoke Cr. → *Toronto* 31 B1
Etterbeek *Brussels* 6 A2
Eung-am *Seoul* 27 B1
Eunpyeong *Seoul* 27 B1
Evanston *Chicago* 9 A2
Even Sapir *Jerusalem* 13 B1
Everett *Boston* 6 A2
Evergreen Park *Chicago* 9 C2
Evin *Tehran* 31 A2
Ewu *Lagos* 14 A1
Exhibition Place *Toronto* 31 B2
Expo 2010 *Shanghai* 28 B1
Exposições, Palácio das
  Rio de Janeiro 25 B1
Eyüp *Istanbul* 12 B1
Ezeiza ✈ *(EZE)* *Buenos Aires* 7 C1

F

Fabour, Mt. *Singapore* 28 B2
Fælledparken *Copenhagen* 8 A3
Fågelön *Stockholm* 29 B1
Fagersjö *Stockholm* 29 B2
Fairfax *Washington* 33 B2
Fairfax Station *Washington* 33 C2
Fairland *Johannesburg* 13 A1
Fairmilehead *Edinburgh* 11 B2
Fairmount Heights
  Washington 33 B4
Fairport *Toronto* 31 A4
Fairview *New York* 22 B1
Fairview, L. *Orlando* 23 A2
Falenty *Warsaw* 32 C1
Faliro *Athens* 2 B2
Faliro, Ormos *Athens* 2 B2
Falkenburg *Athens* 5 A4
Falkenhagen *Berlin* 5 A1
Falkensee *Berlin* 5 A1
Falls Church *Washington* 33 B3
Falomo *Lagos* 14 B2
False Bay *Cape Town* 8 B2
Fangcun *Guangzhou* 11 B2
Farahābād *Tehran* 31 A2
Farforovskaya *St. Petersburg* 27 B2
Farningham *London* 15 B5
Farsta *Stockholm* 29 B2
Fasanerie-Nord *Munich* 21 A2
Fasangarten *Munich* 21 B2
Fatih *Istanbul* 12 B1
Favoriten *Vienna* 32 B2
Fawkner *Melbourne* 18 A1
Fawkner Park *Melbourne* 18 B1
FedEx Field *Washington* 33 B4
Feldkirchen *Munich* 21 B3

Feldmoching *Munich* 21 A2
Feltham *London* 15 B1
Fener *Istanbul* 12 B1
Fenerbahçe *Istanbul* 12 C2
Fengtai *Beijing* 4 B1
Fengtai Stadium *Beijing* 4 B1
Ferencváros *Budapest* 7 B2
Ferihegy, Budapest ✈
  (BUD) *Budapest* 7 B3
Ferndale *Johannesburg* 13 A2
Fichtenau *Berlin* 5 B5
Field Museum of Natural
  History *Chicago* 9 C3
Fields Corner *Boston* 6 B2
Fiera Camp *Milan* 19 B1
Figino *Milan* 19 B1
Fijir *Baghdad* 3 A2
Filadélfia *Athens* 2 A2
Fili-Mazilovo *Moscow* 19 B1
Filothei *Athens* 2 A2
Finchley *London* 15 A2
Fine Arts, Museum of *Boston* 6 A2
Finglas *Dublin* 10 A2
Finsbury *London* 15 A3
Finsbury Park *London* 15 A3
Fiorito *Buenos Aires* 7 C2
Firhouse *Dublin* 10 B2
Fischerhäuser *Munich* 21 A3
Fisher Island *Miami* 18 B2
Fisherville *Toronto* 31 A1
Fisksätra *Stockholm* 29 B3
Fitzroy Gardens *Melbourne* 18 A1
Five Cowrie Cr. → *Lagos* 14 B2
Five Dock *Sydney* 29 B1
Fjellstrand *Oslo* 23 B2
Flamengo *Rio de Janeiro* 25 B1
Flamingo *Orlando* 23 B2
Flaminio *Rome* 26 B1
Flaskebekk *Oslo* 23 A2
Flatbush *New York* 22 C2
Flaten *Stockholm* 29 B2
Flatlands *New York* 22 C2
Flemington Racecourse
  Melbourne 18 A1
Flint Pk. *Los Angeles* 16 B3
Florence *Los Angeles* 16 C3
Florence Bloom Bird
  Sanctuary →
  Johannesburg 13 A2
Florentia *Johannesburg* 13 B2
Flores *Buenos Aires* 7 B2
Flores, Mercado de
  Mexico City 18 C2
Floresta *Buenos Aires* 7 B2
Florida *Buenos Aires* 7 B2
Florida *Johannesburg* 13 A1
Floridsdorf *Vienna* 32 A2
Flushing *New York* 22 B3
Flushing Meadows
  Corona Park *New York* 22 B2
Flysta *Stockholm* 29 A1
Fo Tan *Hong Kong* 12 A2
Foggy Bottom *Washington* 33 B3
Föhrenhain *Vienna* 32 A2
Fontainebleau *Johannesburg* 13 A1
Fontenay-aux-Roses *Paris* 24 B2
Fontenay-le-Fleury *Paris* 24 B1
Fontenay-sous-Bois *Paris* 24 A3
Foots Cray *London* 15 B4
Footscray *Melbourne* 18 B1
Forbidden City = Imperial
  Palace Museum *Beijing* 4 B2
Forest *Brussels* 6 B1
Forest Gate *London* 15 A4
Forest Heights *Washington* 33 C3
Forest Hill *London* 15 B3
Forest Hill *Toronto* 31 A2
Forest Hills *New York* 22 B2
Forest Park *Chicago* 9 B2
Forest Park *New York* 22 B2
Forest View *Chicago* 9 C2
Forestville *Washington* 33 B4
Fornebu *Oslo* 23 A2
Foro Romano *Rome* 26 B1
Forstenried *Munich* 21 B1
Forstenrieder Park *Munich* 21 B1
Fort Dupont Park
  Washington 33 B4
Fort Foote Village
  Washington 33 C3
Fort Lee *New York* 22 A2
Forth, Firth of *Edinburgh* 11 A3
Forth Rail Bridge *Edinburgh* 11 A1
Forth Road Bridge
  Edinburgh 11 A1
Foshan *Guangzhou* 11 B2
Fôt *Budapest* 7 A2
Fourqueux *Paris* 24 A1
Fox Studios *Sydney* 29 B2
Foxrock *Dublin* 10 B3
Franconia *Washington* 33 C3
Frank Lloyd Wright Home
  Chicago 9 B2
Frankel *Singapore* 28 B3
Franklin Park *Boston* 6 B2
Franklin Park *Chicago* 9 B1
Franklin Park *New York* 22 B2
Franklin Res. *Los Angeles* 16 B2
Franz Josef Strauss ✈
  (MUC) *Munich* 21 A3
Frauenkirche *Munich* 21 B2
Frederiksberg *Copenhagen* 8 A3
Frederiksdal *Copenhagen* 8 A3
Fredersdorf *Berlin* 5 A5
Freguesia do *Rio de Janeiro* 25 B1
Freidrichshain, Volkspark
  Berlin 5 A3
Freiham *Munich* 21 B1
Freimann *Munich* 21 A2
French Quarter *New Orleans* 21 B2
Fresh Pond *Boston* 6 A2
Fresnes *Paris* 24 B2
Freudenau *Vienna* 32 A2
Friarstown *Dublin* 10 B1
Friedenau *Berlin* 5 B3
Friedrichsfelde *Berlin* 5 A4
Friedrichshagen *Berlin* 5 B4
Friedrichshain *Berlin* 5 A3
Friedrichsfeld *Berlin* 5 A5
Friherrs *Helsinki* 11 B1
Frilufts Museum *Helsinki* 11 B2
Frontón, I. *Lima* 14 B1
Frunze *Moscow* 19 B2
Fuchū *Tokyo* 30 A1
Fuencarral *Madrid* 17 B1
Fuenlabrada *Madrid* 17 C1
Fukagawa *Tokyo* 30 B3
Fukushima *Osaka* 23 A1
Funabori *Tokyo* 30 A4
Fundão, I. do *Rio de Janeiro* 25 B2
Fünfhaus *Vienna* 32 A2
Fureso *Copenhagen* 8 A2
Fürth *Munich* 21 A2
Fuzigo-tamagawaen *Tokyo* 30 B2
Fuxing Dao *Shanghai* 28 B2
Fuxing Park *Shanghai* 28 B1
Fuxinglu *Beijing* 4 B1

G

G. Ross Lord Park *Toronto* 31 A2
Gaebong *Seoul* 27 C1
Gage Park *Chicago* 9 C2
Gagny *Paris* 24 A4
Galata *Istanbul* 12 B1
Galata Tower *Istanbul* 12 B1
Galatsi *Athens* 2 A2
Galeão, Int. de ✈ *(GIG)*
  Rio de Janeiro 25 B2
Galyanovo *Moscow* 19 B3
Gambir *Jakarta* 12 A1
Gamboa *Rio de Janeiro* 25 B1
Gambolóita *Milan* 19 A1
Gamlebyen *Oslo* 23 A3
Gangdong *Seoul* 27 B2
Gangnam *Seoul* 27 B2
Gangseo *Seoul* 27 B1
Gangtou *Guangzhou* 11 A2
Gangwei *Guangzhou* 11 B2
Ganjiakou *Beijing* 4 B1
Ganshoren *Brussels* 6 A1
Gants Hill *London* 15 A4
Gaoqiao *Shanghai* 28 A2
Garbagnate Milanese *Milan* 19 A1
Garbatella *Rome* 26 B1
Garches *Paris* 24 A2
Garching *Munich* 21 A2
Garden City *Cairo* 7 A2
Garden Reach *Kolkata* 14 B1
Garder *Oslo* 23 B2
Garfield *New York* 22 A1
Garfield Park *Chicago* 9 B2
Gargareta *Athens* 2 B2
Garibong *Seoul* 27 C1
Garvanza *Los Angeles* 16 B3
Gåshaga *Stockholm* 29 A3
Gateway → *New York* 22 C2
Gateway of India *Mumbai* 20 B2
Gatow *Berlin* 5 B1
Gävà *Barcelona* 4 B1
Gavamar *Barcelona* 4 B1
Gávea *Rio de Janeiro* 25 B1
Gávea, Pedra da
  Rio de Janeiro 25 B1
Gazdagrét *Budapest* 7 B1
Gaziosmanpaşa *Istanbul* 12 B1
Gebel el Ahmar *Cairo* 7 A2
Gebel el Muqattam *Cairo* 7 A2
Gebel el Tura *Cairo* 7 B2
Geiselgasteig *Munich* 21 B2
General San Martin
  Buenos Aires 7 B1
Gennevilliers *Paris* 24 A2
Gentilly *New Orleans* 21 A2
Gentilly *Paris* 24 B2
Gentofte *Copenhagen* 8 A3
Genval *Brussels* 6 B2
George I. *Hong Kong* 12 B1
Georges River Bridge
  Sydney 29 C1
Georgetown *Washington* 33 B3
Georgia Dome *Atlanta* 3 B2
Gerasdorf bei Wien *Vienna* 32 A2
Gerberau *Munich* 21 A1
Gerli *Buenos Aires* 7 C2
Germiston *Johannesburg* 13 B2
Gern *Munich* 21 B2
Getafe *Madrid* 17 C1
Getty Center, The
  Los Angeles 16 B2
Geva Binyamin *Jerusalem* 13 A2
Geylang Serai *Singapore* 28 B3
Gharapuri *Mumbai* 20 B2
Gharb = Shahrak-e Qods
  Tehran 31 A1
Ghatkopar *Mumbai* 20 A2
Ghazipur *Delhi* 10 B2
Ghizri *Karachi* 13 B2
Ghizri Cr. → *Karachi* 13 B2
Ghonda *Delhi* 10 A2
Ghusuri *Kolkata* 14 B2
Gianicolense *Rome* 26 B1
Giant Wheel = Riesenrad
  Vienna 32 A2
Gibraltar Pt. *Toronto* 31 B2
Gidea Park *London* 15 A5
Giesing *Munich* 21 B2
Gilmerton *Edinburgh* 11 B3
Gimmerstad *Edinburgh* 11 B3
Gimmersta *Stockholm* 29 B3
Ginza *Tokyo* 30 A3
Giv'at Ram *Jerusalem* 13 B1
Giv'at Ye'arim *Jerusalem* 13 B1
Giv'at Ze'ev *Jerusalem* 13 A2
Giv'on *Jerusalem* 13 A2
Giza = El Gîza *Cairo* 7 A2
Giza Pyramids *Cairo* 7 B1
Gjersjøen *Oslo* 23 B3
Gladesville *Sydney* 29 B1
Gladsakse *Copenhagen* 8 A2
Glasnevin *Dublin* 10 A2
Glassmanor *Washington* 33 C4
Glasthule *Dublin* 10 B3
Glen Iris *Melbourne* 18 B2
Glen Mar Park *Washington* 33 B3
Glen Rouge Park *Toronto* 31 A4
Glenanden *Washington* 33 B4
Glenasmole Reservoirs
  Dublin 10 B1
Glencorse Res. *Edinburgh* 11 B2
Glencullen *Dublin* 10 B2
Glendale *Los Angeles* 16 B3
Glendoo Mt. *Dublin* 10 B2
Glenhuntly *Melbourne* 18 B2
Glenside *Wellington* 33 B1
Glenview *Chicago* 9 A2
Glenview Countryside
  Chicago 9 A2
Glenista *Johannesburg* 13 B2
Glifada *Athens* 2 B2
Glostrup *Copenhagen* 8 B2
Gogar *Edinburgh* 11 B2
Golabki *Warsaw* 32 B1
Golabki *Warsaw* 32 B1
Gold Coast *Chicago* 9 A3
Golden Gate *San Francisco* 26 B2
Golden Gate △ *San Francisco* 26 A2
Golden Gate Bridge
  San Francisco 26 B2
Golden Gate Park
  San Francisco 26 B2
Golden Horn = Haliç
  Istanbul 12 B1
Golders Green *London* 15 A2
Golestan Palace *Tehran* 31 A2
Gollans Stream →
  Wellington 33 B2
Gonen *Jerusalem* 13 B2
Goodmáyes *London* 15 A4
Goodwood *Cape Town* 8 A2
Gopalpur *Kolkata* 14 B2
Górce *Warsaw* 32 B1
Gore Hill *Sydney* 29 B2
Gorelovo → *St. Petersburg* 27 C1
Gorgie *Edinburgh* 11 B2

Gorky Park *Moscow* 19 B2
Gosen *Berlin* 5 B5
Gosener kanal *Berlin* 5 B5
Gospel Oak *London* 15 A3
Gotanda *Tokyo* 30 B3
Goth Goli Mar *Karachi* 13 A2
Goth Sher Shah *Karachi* 13 A1
Gotha *Orlando* 23 A1
Gournay-sur-Marne *Paris* 24 A4
Governador, I. do
  Rio de Janeiro 25 A1
Governors I. *New York* 22 B1
Grabów *Warsaw* 32 C1
Grace, Mt. *Wellington* 33 B2
Gracefield *Wellington* 33 B2
Gràcia *Barcelona* 4 A1
Gräfelfing *Munich* 21 B1
Gragoatá *Rio de Janeiro* 25 B2
Grand Bazaar = Kapalı
  Carsı *Istanbul* 12 B1
Grand Central Station
  New York 22 B2
Grand Palace *Bangkok* 3 B1
Grande Place *Brussels* 6 A2
Grankulla = Kauniainen
  Helsinki 11 B1
Grant Park *Chicago* 9 B3
Granton *Edinburgh* 11 B2
Grassy Park *Cape Town* 8 B2
Gratosóglio *Milan* 19 B2
Gratzwalde *Berlin* 5 B5
Gravesend *New York* 25 A1
Grazhdanka *St. Petersburg* 27 B2
Great Falls *Washington* 33 B2
Great Falls Park *Washington* 33 B2
Great Western Forum
  Los Angeles 16 C2
Greco *Milan* 19 A2
Green I. *Hong Kong* 12 B1
Green Point *Cape Town* 8 A1
Green Point Stadium
  Cape Town 8 A1
Greenbelt *Washington* 33 A4
Greenbelt Park *Washington* 33 B4
Greenfield Park *Montreal* 20 B3
Greenford *London* 15 A1
Greenhill *London* 15 A2
Greenhills *Dublin* 10 B1
Greenwich □ *London* 15 B3
Greenwich Observatory
  London 15 B3
Greenwich Village
  New York 22 B2
Greenwood *Boston* 6 A2
Grefsen *Oslo* 23 A3
Gresham Park *Atlanta* 3 B2
Gretna *New Orleans* 21 B2
Gretna City Park
  New Orleans 21 B2
Greve Strand *Copenhagen* 8 B1
Griebnitzsee *Berlin* 5 B1
Griffith Park *Los Angeles* 16 B3
Grimbergen *Brussels* 6 A2
Grinzing *Vienna* 32 A2
Gröbenried *Munich* 21 A1
Grochów *Warsaw* 32 B2
Grodzisk *Warsaw* 32 B2
Groenendaal *Brussels* 6 B2
Grogol Petamburin *Jakarta* 12 A1
Gronsdorf *Munich* 21 B3
Grorud *Oslo* 23 A4
Gross-Glienicke *Berlin* 5 A1
Gross-Hadern *Munich* 21 B1
Gross-Lappen *Munich* 21 A2
Grosse Krampe *Berlin* 5 B5
Grosse Müggelsee *Berlin* 5 B4
Grosse Point Lighthouse
  Chicago 9 A2
Grossenzersdorf *Vienna* 32 A3
Grossenzersdorfer Arm →
  Vienna 32 A3
Grosser Biberhaufen *Vienna* 32 A2
Grosser Wannsee *Berlin* 5 B2
Grossfeld-Siedlung *Vienna* 32 A2
Grosshesselohe *Munich* 21 B2
Grossjedlersdorf *Vienna* 32 A2
Grosszieten *Berlin* 5 B3
Ground Zero *New York* 22 B1
Grove, The *Chicago* 9 A1
Grove Hall *Boston* 6 B2
Grove Park *Atlanta* 3 B2
Grove Park *London* 15 B4
Grove Park *London* 15 B4
Groveton *Washington* 33 C3
Grünau *Berlin* 5 B4
Grunewald *Berlin* 5 B2
Grünwald *Munich* 21 B2
Grünwalder Forst *Munich* 21 B2
Grymes Hill *New York* 22 C1
Guadalupe *Manila* 17 B2
Guadalupe, Basilica de
  Mexico City 18 B2
Guanabara, B. de
  Rio de Janeiro 25 B2
Guanabara, Jardim
  Rio de Janeiro 25 B2
Guanabara, Palácio da
  Rio de Janeiro 25 B2
Guang'anmen *Beijing* 4 B1
Guangqumen *Beijing* 4 B2
Guangzhou *Guangzhou* 11 B2
Guanshuo *Guangzhou* 11 B3
Gudö *Stockholm* 29 B3
Güell, Parque de *Barcelona* 4 A2
Guinardó *Barcelona* 4 A1
Gulbai *Karachi* 13 A1
Güngören *Istanbul* 12 B1
Gunnersbury *London* 15 B2
Guomao *Beijing* 4 B2
Gustavo A. Madero
  Mexico City 18 B2
Guttenberg *New York* 22 B1
Gutuyevskiy, Ostrov
  St. Petersburg 27 B2
Guyancourt *Paris* 24 B1
Gwanak *Seoul* 27 C1
Gwanaksan *Seoul* 27 C1
Gyál *Budapest* 7 B3
Gyáli-patak → *Budapest* 7 B2

H

Haaga *Helsinki* 11 B2
Haar *Munich* 21 B3
Habay *Manila* 17 B1
Hackbridge *London* 15 B3
Hackensack *New York* 22 A1
Hackensack → *New York* 22 B1
Hackney □ *London* 15 A3
Hackney Wick *London* 15 A3
Hadr. *Warräq* el *Cairo* 7 A2
Haga *Stockholm* 29 B2
Hagenbrunn *Vienna* 32 A2
Hägersten *Stockholm* 29 B1
Häggvik *Stockholm* 29 A1
Hagonoy *Manila* 17 B2
Hague Park *Toronto* 31 A3
Haidari = Chaidari *Athens* 2 B1
Haidarpur *Delhi* 10 A1
Haidhausen *Munich* 21 B2

Haidian *Beijing* 4 B1
Haight-Ashbury
  San Francisco 26 B2
Hainault *London* 15 A4
Haizhou *Guangzhou* 11 B3
Haizhu Guangchang
  Guangzhou 11 B2
Hakunila *Helsinki* 11 B3
Halandri = Chalandri *Athens* 2 A2
Halászelek *Budapest* 7 B2
Halic *Istanbul* 12 B1
Halim Perdana Kusuma
  Int. ✈ (HLP) *Jakarta* 12 B2
Halle *Brussels* 6 B1
Haltiala *Helsinki* 11 B2
Haltiavuori *Helsinki* 11 B2
Ham *London* 15 B2
Hämeenkylä *Helsinki* 11 B1
Hammarby *Stockholm* 29 B2
Hamme *Brussels* 6 A1
Hammersmith *London* 15 B2
Hampstead *London* 15 A2
Hampstead *Montreal* 20 B2
Hampstead Garden
  Suburb *London* 15 A2
Hampstead Heath *London* 15 A2
Hampton Court Palace
  London 15 B1
Hampton Wick *London* 15 B2
Hamra' *Baghdad* 3 B2
Hanala *Helsinki* 11 B3
Haneda *Tokyo* 30 B3
Haneda, Tōkyō ✈ (HND)
  Tokyo 30 B3
Hang Hau *Hong Kong* 12 B2
Hanging Gardens *Mumbai* 20 B1
Hanlon *Toronto* 31 B1
Hanwell *London* 15 A1
Hanworth *London* 15 B1
Haora *Kolkata* 14 B1
Hapeville *Atlanta* 3 C2
Happy Valley *Hong Kong* 12 B2
Har Adar *Jerusalem* 13 B1
Har Gilo *Jerusalem* 13 B2
Har Homa *Jerusalem* 13 B2
Har Nof *Jerusalem* 13 B2
Harahan *New Orleans* 21 B1
Haren *Brussels* 6 A2
Hareskovby *Copenhagen* 8 A2
Haringey □ *London* 15 A3
Harjusuo *Helsinki* 11 B3
Harlaching *Munich* 21 B2
Harlaw Res. *Edinburgh* 11 B2
Harlem *New York* 22 B2
Harlesden *London* 15 A2
Harlington *London* 15 B1
Harmaja *Helsinki* 11 C2
Harmashatar hegy *Budapest* 7 A2
Harolds Cross *Dublin* 10 B2
Háperrig Res. *Edinburgh* 11 B1
Harrow □ *London* 15 A1
Harrow on the Hill *London* 15 A1
Harrow School *London* 15 A1
Harrow Weald *London* 15 A1
Hartsfield-Atlanta Int. ✈
  (ATL) *Atlanta* 3 C2
Harumi *Tokyo* 30 B3
Harvard Univ. *Boston* 6 A2
Harvey *New Orleans* 21 B2
Harwood Heights *Chicago* 9 B2
Hasanābād *Tehran* 31 A1
Hasbrouck Heights
  New York 22 A1
Haselhorst *Berlin* 5 A2
Hasköy *Istanbul* 12 B1
Hasle *Oslo* 23 A4
Haslum *Oslo* 23 A2
Hästhagen *Stockholm* 29 B2
Hataitai *Wellington* 33 B1
Hatch End *London* 15 A1
Hatiara *Kolkata* 14 B2
Hauketo *Oslo* 23 A3
Hauz Khas *Delhi* 10 B2
Havel → *Berlin* 5 A2
Havelkanal *Berlin* 5 A1
Havering □ *London* 15 A5
Havering-atte-Bower
  London 15 A5
Haworth *New York* 22 A2
Hawthorne Racecourse
  Chicago 9 C2
Hayes *London* 15 B4
Hayes *London* 15 A1
Hayes End *London* 15 A1
Hayford *Chicago* 9 C2
Haywards *Wellington* 33 A2
Heathfield *Cape Town* 8 B1
Heathrow, London ✈
  (LHR) *London* 15 B1
Hebe Haven *Hong Kong* 12 A2
Hedong *Guangzhou* 11 B2
Heidelberg Heights
  Melbourne 18 A1
Heidelberg West *Melbourne* 18 A2
Heidemühle *Berlin* 5 B5
Heideveld *Cape Town* 8 A2
Heiligensee *Berlin* 5 A2
Heiligenstadt *Vienna* 32 A2
Heinersdorf *Berlin* 5 A3
Hélène de Champlain,
  Parc □ *Montreal* 20 A2
Helenenlund *Stockholm* 29 A1
Heliopolis = Masr el
  Gedida *Cairo* 7 A2
Hellersdorf *Berlin* 5 A4
Hellerup *Copenhagen* 8 A3
Helsingfors = Helsinki
  Helsinki 11 B2
Helsinki *Helsinki* 11 B2
Helsinki-Vantaa ✈ (HEL)
  Helsinki 11 B2
Hen and Chicken Bs. *Sydney* 29 B1
Henderson *Las Vegas* 14 B2
Hendon *London* 15 A2
Hengsha *Guangzhou* 11 B2
Hennigsdorf *Berlin* 5 A2
Henryków *Warsaw* 32 B1
Henson Cr. → *Washington* 33 C4
Henttaa *Helsinki* 11 B1
Heping Park *Shanghai* 28 B2
Hepingli *Beijing* 4 B1
Herlev *Copenhagen* 8 A2
Herman Eckstein Park
  Johannesburg 13 A2
Hermiston *Edinburgh* 11 B2
Hermitage and Winter
  Palace *St. Petersburg* 27 B2
Hermsdorf *Berlin* 5 A3
Herne Hill *London* 15 B3
Héroes de Churubusco
  Mexico City 18 B2
Herons, Î. aux *Montreal* 20 B2
Herstedøster *Copenhagen* 8 A2
Herttoniemi *Helsinki* 11 B3
Hesarak *Tehran* 31 A1
Heston *London* 15 B1
Hetzendorf *Vienna* 32 B1

Hextable *London* 15 B5
Hialeah *Miami* 18 A1
Hiawassa, L. *Orlando* 23 A2
Hickory Hills *Chicago* 9 C2
Hietaniemi *Helsinki* 11 B2
Hiekkaharju *Helsinki* 11 B3
Hietzing *Vienna* 32 A1
Higashi *Osaka* 23 A2
Higashimurayama *Tokyo* 30 A1
Higashinari *Osaka* 23 A2
Higashiosaka *Osaka* 23 A2
Higashiyodogawa *Osaka* 23 A1
High Park *Toronto* 31 B2
Highbury *London* 15 A3
Highgate *London* 15 A3
Highland Cr. → *Toronto* 31 A3
Highland Creek *Toronto* 31 A3
Highland Park *Los Angeles* 16 B3
Highlands North
  Johannesburg 13 A2
Hillcrest Heights
  Washington 33 C4
Hillend *Edinburgh* 11 A1
Hillingdon □ *London* 15 A1
Hillwood *Washington* 33 B3
Hilmîya *Cairo* 7 A2
Hin Keng *Hong Kong* 12 A2
Hirota *Osaka* 23 A1
Hirschstetten *Vienna* 32 A2
Hither Green *London* 15 B3
Hiyoshi *Tokyo* 30 B2
Hizma *Jerusalem* 13 A2
Hjortekær *Copenhagen* 8 A3
Hjortespring *Copenhagen* 8 A2
Hlubočepy *Prague* 25 B2
Ho Chung *Hong Kong* 12 A2
Hoboken *New York* 22 B1
Hobsons B. *Melbourne* 18 B1
Hochbrück *Munich* 21 A2
Hochelaga *Montreal* 20 A2
Hodgkins *Chicago* 9 C1
Hoegi *Seoul* 27 B2
Hoeilaart *Brussels* 6 B2
Hofburg *Vienna* 32 A2
Hoffman I. *New York* 22 C1
Hohenbrunn *Munich* 21 B3
Hohenschönhausen *Berlin* 5 A4
Holargos = Cholargos
  Athens 2 B2
Holborn *London* 15 A3
Holden, L. *Orlando* 23 B2
Holešovice *Prague* 25 B2
Holland Village *Singapore* 28 B2
Höllriegelskreuth *Munich* 21 B1
Hollywood *Los Angeles* 16 B3
Hollywood Bowl *Los Angeles* 16 B2
Holmenkollen *Oslo* 23 A3
Holmes Run Acres
  Washington 33 B2
Holmgård *Stockholm* 29 B3
Holmlia *Oslo* 23 A4
Holocaust Memorial
  Jerusalem 13 B2
Holyrood House, Palace of
  Edinburgh 11 B3
Holysloot *Amsterdam* 2 A3
Homerton *London* 15 A3
Hometown *Chicago* 9 C2
Hōnanchō *Tokyo* 30 A3
Honcho *Tokyo* 30 A3
Honden *Tokyo* 30 A4
Hondo, Rio → *Los Angeles* 16 B4
Hong Kong *Hong Kong* 12 B2
Hong Kong, Univ. of
  Hong Kong 12 B1
Hong Kong I. *Hong Kong* 12 B2
Hongje *Seoul* 27 B1
Hongjimun Tunnel *Seoul* 27 B1
Hongkou *Shanghai* 28 B1
Hongqiao *Shanghai* 28 B1
Honjo *Tokyo* 30 A3
Honoré Mercier, Pont
  Montreal 20 B2
Hönow *Berlin* 5 A4
Hook *London* 15 B2
Horikiri *Tokyo* 30 A4
Horn Pond *Boston* 6 A1
Hornchurch *London* 15 A5
Horni *Prague* 25 B3
Horni Počernice *Prague* 25 B3
Hornsey *London* 15 A3
Horoměřice *Prague* 25 B1
Hortaleza *Madrid* 17 B2
Hosoyama *Tokyo* 30 B2
Hostafranchs *Barcelona* 4 A1
Hostivař *Prague* 25 B3
Houbětín *Prague* 25 B3
Houghton *Johannesburg* 13 B2
Houilles *Paris* 24 A2
Hounslow □ *London* 15 B1
Hout Bay *Cape Town* 8 B1
Hove Å → *Copenhagen* 8 B2
Hovedøya *Oslo* 23 A3
Høvik *Oslo* 23 A2
Hovorčovice *Prague* 25 A3
Howard Beach *New York* 22 C2
Howrah = Haora *Kolkata* 14 B1
Howth *Dublin* 10 A3
Howth Hd. *Dublin* 10 A3
Hōya *Tokyo* 30 A2
Hradčany *Prague* 25 B2
Huanghuagang
  Mausoleum *Guangzhou* 11 B2
Huangpu *Shanghai* 28 B2
Huangpu Jiang → *Shanghai* 28 B1
Huangtugan *Beijing* 4 C1
Huascar *Lima* 14 A2
Huay Khwang *Bangkok* 3 B2
Huddinge *Stockholm* 29 B2
Huechuraba *Santiago* 27 B1
Huizingen *Brussels* 6 B1
Humayun's Tomb *Delhi* 10 B2
Humber → *Toronto* 31 A1
Humber B. *Toronto* 31 B2
Humber Bay *Toronto* 31 B2
Humber Bay Park *Toronto* 31 B2
Humber College *Toronto* 31 A1
Humber Summit *Toronto* 31 A1
Humber Valley Village
  Toronto 31 A1
Humberlea *Toronto* 31 A1
Humberwood Park *Toronto* 31 A1
Humboldt Park *Chicago* 9 B2
Humera *Madrid* 17 B1
Hunaydī *Baghdad* 3 B2
Hundige *Copenhagen* 8 B1
Hundige Strand *Copenhagen* 8 B1
Hung Hom *Hong Kong* 12 B2
Hunters Hill *Sydney* 29 B1
Hunters Pt. *San Francisco* 26 B2
Huntington *Washington* 33 C3
Huntington Park
  Los Angeles 16 C3
Huriya *Baghdad* 3 A1
Hurstville *Sydney* 29 B1
Husan *Jerusalem* 13 B1
Husby *Stockholm* 29 A1
Husum *Copenhagen* 8 A2
Hutt → *Wellington* 33 B2

Hütteldorf *Vienna* 32 A1
Hüvösvölgy *Budapest* 7 A2
Huwon Secret Garden *Seoul* 27 B1
Hvalstad *Oslo* 23 A1
Hvalstrand *Oslo* 23 A1
Hvidovre *Copenhagen* 8 B2
Hwagok *Seoul* 27 B1
Hyattsville *Washington* 33 B4
Hyde Park *Boston* 6 B2
Hyde Park *Chicago* 9 C3
Hyde Park *Johannesburg* 13 A2
Hyde Park *London* 15 A2
Hyde Park *Los Angeles* 16 C3

I

Ibese *Lagos* 14 A2
Ibirapuera *São Paulo* 27 B1
Ibirapuera, Parque do
  São Paulo 27 B2
Icaraí *Rio de Janeiro* 25 B2
İçerenköy *Istanbul* 12 C2
Ichgao *Tokyo* 30 B2
Ichigaya *Tokyo* 30 A3
Ichikawa *Tokyo* 30 A4
Ickenham *London* 15 A1
Iddo *Lagos* 14 B2
Idi-Oro *Lagos* 14 A2
Iganmu *Lagos* 14 B2
Igbobi *Lagos* 14 A2
Igbologun *Lagos* 14 B1
Igny *Paris* 24 B2
Ikebe *Tokyo* 30 B2
Ikebukuro *Tokyo* 30 A3
Ikegami *Tokyo* 30 B3
Ikeja *Lagos* 14 A2
Ikeuchi *Osaka* 23 B2
Ikoyi *Lagos* 14 B2
Ikuta *Tokyo* 30 B2
Ikuno *Osaka* 23 A2
Ikuta *Tokyo* 30 B2
Ila *Oslo* 23 A3
Ilford *London* 15 A4
Ilioupoli *Athens* 2 B2
Illinois at Chicago, Univ.
  of *Chicago* 9 B3
Illinois Institute of
  Technology *Chicago* 9 B3
Ilpendam *Amsterdam* 2 A2
Ilsos → *Athens* 2 B2
Imbâbah *Cairo* 7 A2
Imielin *Warsaw* 32 C2
Imirim *São Paulo* 27 A2
Imitos *Athens* 2 B2
Imitos, Oros *Athens* 2 B2
Imperial Palace Museum
  Beijing 4 B1
Inagi *Tokyo* 30 B2
Incheon *Seoul* 27 B2
Inchicore *Dublin* 10 B2
Inchkeith *Edinburgh* 11 A2
Inchmickery *Edinburgh* 11 A2
Incirano *Milan* 19 A1
Independencia *Lima* 14 A2
Independencia *São Paulo* 27 B2
India Gate *Delhi* 10 B2
Indian Creek Village *Miami* 18 A2
Indianópolis *São Paulo* 27 B1
Indira Gandhi Int. ✈
  (DEL) *Delhi* 10 B1
Industria *Johannesburg* 13 B1
Industrial Canal →
  New Orleans 21 B2
Ingierstrand *Oslo* 23 B3
Inglewood *Los Angeles* 16 C3
Ingliston *Edinburgh* 11 B1
Inhaúma *Rio de Janeiro* 25 B1
Inner Port Shelter
  Hong Kong 12 A2
Interlagos *São Paulo* 27 C1
Intramuros *Manila* 17 B1
Invalides *Paris* 24 A2
Inverkeithing *Edinburgh* 11 A1
Inzersdorf *Vienna* 32 B2
Ipanema *Rio de Janeiro* 25 B2
Ipiranga *São Paulo* 27 B2
Ipiranga → *São Paulo* 27 B2
Iponri *Lagos* 14 B2
Ireland's Eye *Dublin* 10 A3
Irving Park *Chicago* 9 B2
Isabel *Rio de Janeiro* 25 B1
Isagatedo *Lagos* 14 A1
Isar → *Munich* 21 B2
Ishbilīya *Baghdad* 3 A2
Ishoj Strand *Copenhagen* 8 B2
Island Bay *Wellington* 33 B1
Island Park *Toronto* 31 B2
Islev *Copenhagen* 8 A2
Isleworth *London* 15 B2
Islington *Toronto* 31 B1
Islington □ *London* 15 A3
Ismaning *Munich* 21 A3
Ismayloskiy Park *Moscow* 19 B3
Isolo *Lagos* 14 A1
Issy-les-Moulineaux *Paris* 24 B2
İstanbul *Istanbul* 12 C1
İstanbul Boğazı *Istanbul* 12 B2
İstinye *Istanbul* 12 B2
İtä Hakkila *Helsinki* 11 B3
Itaewon *Seoul* 27 B2
Itami *Osaka* 23 A1
Itanhanga *Rio de Janeiro* 25 B1
Ivanhoe *Melbourne* 18 A1
Ivry-sur-Seine *Paris* 24 B3
Ixelles *Brussels* 6 B2
Izmaylovo *Moscow* 19 B3
Iztacalco *Mexico City* 18 B2
Iztapalapa *Mexico City* 18 B2

J

Jaba *Jerusalem* 13 A2
Jacaré *Rio de Janeiro* 25 B1
Jackson Heights *New York* 22 B2
Jackson Park *Chicago* 9 C3
Jacques-Cartier *Montreal* 20 A3
Jacques-Cartier, Pont
  Montreal 20 A2
Jadavpur *Kolkata* 14 C2
Jade Buddha Temple
  Shanghai 28 B1
Jægersborg *Copenhagen* 8 A3
Jægersborg Dyrehave
  Copenhagen 8 A3
Jagadishpur *Kolkata* 14 B1
Jagatpur *Delhi* 10 A2
Jaguaré, Rib. do →
  São Paulo 27 B1
Jahangirpur *Delhi* 10 A2
Jakarta *Jakarta* 12 A1
Jakarta, Teluk *Jakarta* 12 A1
Jakarta Halim Perdana
  Kusuma Int. ✈ (HLP)
  Jakarta 12 B2
Jalan Kayu *Singapore* 28 A3

Jamaica B. *New York* 22 C3
Jamaica Plain *Boston* 6 B2
Jamakpuri *Delhi* 10 B1
Jamshīdīyeh *Tehran* 31 A2
Jamsil *Seoul* 27 B2
Jamwon *Seoul* 27 B2
Janki *Warsaw* 32 C1
Jaraguá *São Paulo* 27 B1
Jaraguá, Pico de *São Paulo* 27 A1
Jardim Paulista *São Paulo* 27 B1
Järvafältet *Stockholm* 29 A1
Jaskhar *Mumbai* 20 B2
Jatinegara *Jakarta* 12 B2
Jāvādīyeh *Tehran* 31 B1
Jaworowa *Warsaw* 32 C1
Jean Lafitte Nat. Historical
  Park □ *New Orleans* 21 B1
Jedlesee *Vienna* 32 A2
Jefferson *New Orleans* 21 B2
Jefferson Memorial
  Washington 33 B3
Jefferson Park *Chicago* 9 B2
Jefferson Park *Los Angeles* 16 B3
Jegi *Seoul* 27 B2
Jelambar *Jakarta* 12 A1
Jelonki *Warsaw* 32 B1
Jerónimos, Mosteiro dos
  Lisbon 16 A1
Jersey City *New York* 22 B1
Jerusalem *Jerusalem* 13 B2
Jessamine, L. *Orlando* 23 B2
Jesús, I. *Montreal* 20 A1
Jésus Maria *Lima* 14 B2
Jette *Brussels* 6 A1
Jey *Tehran* 31 B2
Jianggao *Guangzhou* 11 B2
Jiangwan *Shanghai* 28 B1
Jib *Jerusalem* 13 A2
Jihād *Baghdad* 3 B1
Jingan *Shanghai* 28 B1
Jinočany *Prague* 25 B1
Jinonice *Prague* 25 B2
Jiulong = Kowloon
  Hong Kong 12 B2
Jiyūgaoka *Tokyo* 30 B3
Jizā'ir *Baghdad* 3 B2
Jizīra *Baghdad* 3 A2
Joglo *Jakarta* 12 B1
Johannesburg *Johannesburg* 13 B2
Johannesburg, Univ. of
  Johannesburg 13 B2
Johanneskirchen *Munich* 21 A2
Johannesstift *Berlin* 5 A2
Johannisthal *Berlin* 5 B4
John F. Kennedy Nat.
  Historic Site □ *Boston* 6 A2
John McLaren Park
  San Francisco 26 B2
Johnsonville *Wellington* 33 B1
Joinville-le-Pont *Paris* 24 B3
Joli-Bois *Brussels* 6 B2
Jollas *Helsinki* 11 C3
Jongmyo Royal Shrine
  Seoul 27 B1
Jongno *Seoul* 27 B1
Jonstrup *Copenhagen* 8 A2
Joppa *Edinburgh* 11 B3
Jorge Chavez, Int. ✈ (LIM)
  Lima 14 B2
Jorge Newbery ✈ (AEP)
  Buenos Aires 7 B2
Josefa Piłsudskiego Park
  Warsaw 32 B1
Jōtō *Osaka* 23 A2
Jouy-en-Josas *Paris* 24 B2
Juan Anchorena
  Buenos Aires 7 B2
Juan González Romero
  Mexico City 18 A2
Juárez Int. ✈ (MEX)
  Mexico City 18 B2
Judeira *Jerusalem* 13 A2
Juhdum *Jerusalem* 13 B2
Juhu *Mumbai* 20 A2
Jūjā *Tokyo* 30 A3
Jukskeirivier →
  Johannesburg 13 A2
Julianów *Warsaw* 32 B1
Jung *Seoul* 27 B1
Jungfernheide, Volkspark
  Berlin 5 A2
Jungfernsee *Berlin* 5 B1
Junggwa *Seoul* 27 B2
Jungnang *Seoul* 27 B2
Jungnangcheon → *Seoul* 27 B2
Juniper Green *Edinburgh* 11 B2
Junk B. *Hong Kong* 12 B2
Jurong *Singapore* 28 B2
Jurong, Selat *Singapore* 28 B2
Jurong Industrial Estate
  Singapore 28 B2
Jurujuba, Enseada de
  Rio de Janeiro 25 B2
Jūsō *Osaka* 23 A1
Justice *Chicago* 9 C2
Jwalahari *Delhi* 10 B1

K

Kaapstad = Cape Town
  Cape Town 8 A1
Kabaty *Warsaw* 32 C2
Kadıköy *Istanbul* 12 C2
Kadoma *Osaka* 23 A2
Kafr 'Aqab *Jerusalem* 13 A2
Kâğıthane *Istanbul* 12 B1
Kâğıthane → *Istanbul* 12 B1
Kagran *Vienna* 32 A2
Kahnawake *Montreal* 20 B1
Kaimes *Edinburgh* 11 B2
Kaiserebersdorf *Vienna* 32 B2
Kaivoksela *Helsinki* 11 B2
Kalamaki *Athens* 2 B2
Kalbadevi *Mumbai* 20 B1
Kalipur *Kolkata* 14 A1
Kalithea *Athens* 2 B2
Kalkaji *Delhi* 10 B2
Kalkulorn *Bangkok* 3 B2
Kalveboderne *Copenhagen* 8 B3
Kalvebod Fælled *Copenhagen* 8 B3
Kamarhati *Kolkata* 14 A2
Kamata *Tokyo* 30 B3
Kameari *Tokyo* 30 A4
Kameido *Tokyo* 30 A4
Kamikitazawa *Tokyo* 30 B2
Kamitsuruma *Tokyo* 30 B1
Kamoshida *Tokyo* 30 B2
Kampong Bali *Singapore* 28 B2
Kampong Landang
  Singapore 28 A2
Kampong Tanjong
  Penjuru *Singapore* 28 B2
Kampung Bali *Jakarta* 12 B1
Kamppi *Helsinki* 11 B2
Kanda *Tokyo* 30 A3
Kandilli *Istanbul* 12 B2
Kankurgachi *Kolkata* 14 B2
Kanonerskiy, Ostrov
  St. Petersburg 27 B1
Kanō Athens* 2 B2
Kısıklı *Istanbul* 12 B2

Kansai Int. ✈ (KIX) *Osaka* 23 B1
Kanzaki → *Osaka* 23 A1
Kapalı Carsı *Istanbul* 10 B1
Kapellerfeld *Vienna* 32 A2
Kápostásmegyer *Budapest* 7 A2
Kapotnya *Moscow* 19 C3
Käppala *Stockholm* 29 A3
Kapuk *Jakarta* 12 A1
Kāpylä *Helsinki* 11 B2
Karachi *Karachi* 13 A2
Karachi Int. ✈ (KHI)
  Karachi 13 A2
Karkh *Baghdad* 3 A2
Karlfeld *Prague* 25 B2
Karlhorst *Berlin* 5 B4
Karlõv most *Prague* 25 B2
Karol Bagh *Delhi* 10 B2
Karolinenhof *Berlin* 5 B4
Karori *Wellington* 33 B1
Karow *Berlin* 5 A3
Karrädah *Baghdad* 3 B2
Kärson *Stockholm* 29 B1
Kasai *Tokyo* 30 A4
Kasipur *Kolkata* 14 B2
Kastrup *Copenhagen* 8 B3
Kastrup, København ✈
  (CPH) *Copenhagen* 8 B3
Kasuga *Tokyo* 30 A2
Kasuge *Tokyo* 30 A3
Kasumigaseki *Tokyo* 30 B3
Katong *Singapore* 28 B3
Katsushika *Tokyo* 30 A4
Kau Pai Chau *Hong Kong* 12 B2
Kau Yi Chau *Hong Kong* 12 B1
Kaulsdorf *Berlin* 5 A4
Kauniainen *Helsinki* 11 B1
Kawasaki *Tokyo* 30 B3
Kawawa *Tokyo* 30 B2
Kawęczyn *Warsaw* 32 B2
Kayu Putih *Jakarta* 12 B2
Kbely *Prague* 25 B3
Kebayoran Baru *Jakarta* 12 B2
Kebayoran Lama *Jakarta* 12 B1
Kebon Jeruk *Jakarta* 12 B1
Kedar *Jerusalem* 13 B2
Kedoya *Jakarta* 12 B1
Keilor *Melbourne* 18 A1
Keilor North *Melbourne* 18 A1
Keimola *Helsinki* 11 A1
Kelapa Gading *Jakarta* 12 A2
Kelenföld *Budapest* 7 B2
Kelvin *Johannesburg* 13 A2
Kemang *Jakarta* 12 B2
Kemayoran *Jakarta* 12 A2
Kemerburgaz *Istanbul* 12 B1
Kempton Park Races
  London 15 B1
Kenilworth *Cape Town* 8 B1
Kennedy Town *Hong Kong* 12 B1
Kenner *New Orleans* 21 B1
Kensal Green *London* 15 A2
Kensington *Johannesburg* 13 B2
Kensington *London* 15 B2
Kensington *New York* 22 C2
Kensington *Sydney* 29 B2
Kensington Palace *London* 15 A2
Kent Village *Washington* 33 B4
Kenton *London* 15 A2
Kenwood House *London* 15 A3
Kepa *Warsaw* 32 B2
Keppel Harbour *Singapore* 28 B2
Kesariani *Athens* 2 B2
Kettering *Washington* 33 B5
Kew *London* 15 B2
Kew *Melbourne* 18 A2
Kew Gardens *London* 15 B2
Kew Gardens *Toronto* 31 A3
Key Biscayne *Miami* 18 B2
Khalīj *Baghdad* 3 B2
Khandallah *Wellington* 33 B1
Khansā' *Baghdad* 3 A2
Kharavli *Mumbai* 20 B2
Khefren *Cairo* 7 B1
Khichripur *Delhi* 10 B2
Khidirpur *Kolkata* 14 B1
Khimki-Khovrino *Moscow* 19 A2
Khirbet Batin Abu Lihyah
  Jerusalem 13 A2
Khirbet el-Misbah *Jerusalem* 13 A1
Khirbet Jub e-Rum
  Jerusalem 13 A2
Khlong San *Bangkok* 3 B2
Khlong Toey *Bangkok* 3 B2
Khorel *Kolkata* 14 A1
Khorosovo *Moscow* 19 B1
Kiamari *Karachi* 13 A2
Kierling *Vienna* 32 A1
Kierlingbach → *Vienna* 32 A1
Kifisos → *Athens* 2 B2
Kikuna *Tokyo* 30 B2
Kilbarrack *Dublin* 10 A3
Kilbirnie *Wellington* 33 B1
Kilby *Dublin* 10 A2
Kilbride *Dublin* 10 A2
Kilcock *Dublin* 10 A1
Kilimainham *Dublin* 10 B2
Kilmainham Gaol *Dublin* 10 B2
Kilmashogue Mt. *Dublin* 10 B2
Kilo *Helsinki* 11 B1
Kilokri *Delhi* 10 B2
Kiltiernan *Dublin* 10 B2
Kimmage *Dublin* 10 B2
Kindi *Baghdad* 3 B2
Kinghorn *Edinburgh* 11 A2
Kings Domain *Melbourne* 18 A1
Kings Forest =
  Kongelunden *Copenhagen* 8 C3
Kings Park *Washington* 33 C2
Kings Park West
  Washington 33 C2
Kingsbury *London* 15 A2
Kingsbury *Melbourne* 18 A2
Kingsford Smith,
  Sydney ✈ (SYD) *Sydney* 29 B2
Kingsland *Dublin* 10 A2
Kingsway *Toronto* 31 B1
Kingston-upon-Thames □
  London 15 B2
Kingston Vale *London* 15 B2
Kinsale *Dublin* 10 A1
Kipling Heights *Toronto* 31 A1
Kipseli *Athens* 2 B2
Kirchstockbach *Munich* 21 B3
Kirchtruderung *Munich* 21 B3
Kirikiri *Lagos* 14 B2
Kirke Værløse *Copenhagen* 8 A1
Kirkhill *Edinburgh* 11 B3
Kirkliston *Edinburgh* 11 B1
Kirknewton *Edinburgh* 11 B1
Kirov Palace of Culture
  St. Petersburg 27 B1
Kiryat Anavim *Jerusalem* 13 B1
Kiryat Ha Yovel *Jerusalem* 13 B2
Kıbıkı *Istanbul* 12 B2
Kıştkı *Istanbul* 12 B1

Kispest *Budapest* 7 B2
Kista *Stockholm* 29 A1
Kita *Osaka* 23 A2
Kita *Tokyo* 30 A3
Kitazawa *Tokyo* 30 B3
Kiu Tsiu *Hong Kong* 12 A2
Kivistö *Helsinki* 11 B2
Kizuri *Osaka* 23 B2
Kjelsås *Oslo* 23 A3
Kladow *Berlin* 5 B1
Klampenborg *Copenhagen* 8 A3
Klečany *Prague* 25 A2
Kledering *Vienna* 32 B2
Klein Jukskei →
  Johannesburg 13 A1
Kleinmachnow *Berlin* 5 B2
Kleinschönebeck *Berlin* 5 B5
Klemetsrud *Oslo* 23 A4
Klender *Jakarta* 12 B2
Kličany *Prague* 25 A2
Klipriviersberg Nature
  Reserve *Johannesburg* 13 B2
Klosterneuburg *Vienna* 32 A1
Kōbánya *Budapest* 7 B2
Kobbegem *Brussels* 6 A1
København *Copenhagen* 8 A2
København ✈ (CPH)
  Copenhagen 8 B3
Kobylisy *Prague* 25 B2
Kobyłka *Warsaw* 32 A3
Kodaira *Tokyo* 30 A1
Kodanaka *Tokyo* 30 B2
Koganei *Tokyo* 30 A2
Kogarah *Sydney* 29 B1
Koivupää *Helsinki* 11 B2
Koja *Jakarta* 12 A2
Koja Utara *Jakarta* 12 A2
Kokhav Ya'akov *Jerusalem* 13 A2
Kokobunji *Tokyo* 30 A1
Kokobunji-Temple *Tokyo* 30 A1
Kolaringsen *Stockholm* 29 B3
Kolbotn *Oslo* 23 B3
Kolkata *Kolkata* 14 B2
Kolkata Dum Dum Int. ✈
  (CCU) *Kolkata* 14 A2
Kolkata Maidan *Kolkata* 14 B1
Kolo *Warsaw* 32 B1
Kolokinthou *Athens* 2 B2
Kolomyagi *St. Petersburg* 27 A1
Kolonos *Athens* 2 B2
Kolsås *Oslo* 23 A2
Komae *Tokyo* 30 B2
Komagome *Tokyo* 30 A3
Komazawa *Tokyo* 30 B3
Kona *Kolkata* 14 B1
Konala *Helsinki* 11 B2
Kondli *Delhi* 10 B2
Kongelunden *Copenhagen* 8 B3
Kongens Lyngby *Copenhagen* 8 A3
Kongo *Helsinki* 11 B2
Konnagar *Kolkata* 14 A2
Konohana *Osaka* 23 A1
Konradshöhe *Berlin* 5 A2
Kopanina *Prague* 25 B1
Koparkhairna *Mumbai* 20 A2
Köpenick *Berlin* 5 B4
Korangi *Karachi* 13 B2
Koremasa *Tokyo* 30 B1
Koridalos *Athens* 2 B1
Korokoro *Wellington* 33 B2
Korokoro Stream →
  Wellington 33 B2
Kosino *Moscow* 19 B4
Kosugi *Tokyo* 30 B2
Kota *Jakarta* 12 A1
Kōtō *Tokyo* 30 A4
Kotrung *Kolkata* 14 A2
Kouponia *Athens* 2 B2
Kowloon *Hong Kong* 12 B2
Kowloon Peak *Hong Kong* 12 A2
Kowloon Res. *Hong Kong* 12 A2
Kowloon Tong *Hong Kong* 12 A2
Kraainem *Brussels* 6 A2
Krailling *Munich* 21 B1
Krampnitz *Berlin* 5 B1
Krampnitzsee *Berlin* 5 B1
Kranji, Sungei → *Singapore* 28 A2
Kranji Industrial Estate
  Singapore 28 A2
Krasno-Presnenskaya
  Moscow 19 B2
Krč *Prague* 25 B2
Kremlin *Moscow* 19 B2
Krestovskiye, Ostrov
  St. Petersburg 27 B1
Kreuzberg *Berlin* 5 A3
Kreizford *Vienna* 32 A1
Krumme Lanke *Berlin* 5 B2
Krummensee *Berlin* 5 A5
Krung Thep = Bangkok
  Bangkok 3 B2
Krusboda *Stockholm* 29 B3
Kuangchou = Guangzhou
  Guangzhou 11 B2
Küçükköy *Istanbul* 12 B1
Küçükkuyu *Istanbul* 12 C2
Kudrovo *St. Petersburg* 27 B3
Kulosaari *Helsinki* 11 B3
Kumla *Stockholm* 29 B3
Kungens kurva *Stockholm* 29 B1
Kungliga Slottet *Stockholm* 29 B2
Kungshatt *Stockholm* 29 B2
Kungsholmen *Stockholm* 29 A2
Kuningan *Jakarta* 12 B2
Kunitachi *Tokyo* 30 A1
Kunming Hu *Beijing* 4 B1
Kunratice *Prague* 25 B3
Kupchino *St. Petersburg* 27 C2
Kuramo Waters *Lagos* 14 B2
Kurbağalı → *Istanbul* 12 C2
Kurihara *Tokyo* 30 A3
Kurla *Mumbai* 20 A2
Kurmuri *Mumbai* 20 A2
Kurume *Tokyo* 30 A2
Kuryanovo *Moscow* 19 C3
Kusković *Moscow* 19 B3
Kustia *Kolkata* 14 B2
Kuzguncuk *Istanbul* 12 B2
Kuzminki *Moscow* 19 B3
Kwai Chung *Hong Kong* 12 A1
Kwangbok *Seoul* 27 B1
Kwangchow =
  Guangzhou *Guangzhou* 11 B2
Kwun Tong *Hong Kong* 12 B2
Kyje *Prague* 25 B3
Kyūhōji *Osaka* 23 B2

L

La Barceloneta *Barcelona* 4 A1
La Blanca *Santiago* 27 C2
La Boca *Buenos Aires* 7 B2
La Bretèche *Paris* 24 A1
La Campiña *Lima* 14 C2
La Celle-St-Cloud *Paris* 24 A1
La Cisterna *Santiago* 27 C2
La Courneuve *Paris* 24 A3
La Dehesa *Santiago* 27 B2
La Encantada *Lima* 14 C2

La Estación *Madrid* 17 B1
La Floresta *Barcelona* 4 A1
La Florida *Santiago* 27 C2
La Fortuna *Madrid* 17 B1
La França *Barcelona* 4 A1
La Garenne-Colombes *Paris* 24 A2
La Giustiniana *Rome* 26 B1
La Grange *Chicago* 9 C1
La Grange Park *Chicago* 9 C1
La Granja *Santiago* 27 C2
La Guardia, New York ✈
  (LGA) *New York* 22 B2
La Hulpe *Brussels* 6 B2
La Llacuna *Barcelona* 4 A1
La Loma *Mexico City* 18 B1
La Lucila *Buenos Aires* 7 B2
La Maladrerie *Paris* 24 A1
La Milla, Cerro *Lima* 14 B2
La Monachina *Rome* 26 B1
La Moraleja *Madrid* 17 B2
La Nopalera *Mexico City* 18 C2
La Paternal *Buenos Aires* 7 B2
La Perla *Lima* 14 B2
La Perouse *Sydney* 29 B2
La Pisana *Rome* 26 B1
La Prairie *Montreal* 20 B3
La Punta *Lima* 14 B2
La Puntigala *Barcelona* 4 A1
La Queue-en-Brie *Paris* 24 B4
La Reina *Santiago* 27 B2
La Ribera *Barcelona* 4 A1
La Sagrera *Barcelona* 4 A1
La Salada *Buenos Aires* 7 C2
La Scala *Milan* 19 B2
La Storta *Rome* 26 A1
La Taxonera *Barcelona* 4 A1
La Victoria *Lima* 14 B2
Laajalahti *Helsinki* 11 B1
Laaksolahti *Helsinki* 11 B1
Labagou National Forest
  Park *Beijing* 4 B2
Lábāba, W. el → *Cairo* 7 A2
Lachine *Montreal* 20 B2
Lachine, Canal de *Montreal* 20 B2
Lad Phrao *Bangkok* 3 B2
Ladera Heights *Los Angeles* 16 C2
Làdvi *Prague* 25 B2
Lady *Warsaw* 32 C1
Lafontaine, Parc *Montreal* 20 A2
Lagoa *Rio de Janeiro* 25 B1
Lagos *Lagos* 14 B2
Lagos Harbour *Lagos* 14 B2
Lagos-Ikeja ✈ (LOS) *Lagos* 14 A1
Lagos Island *Lagos* 14 B2
Lagos Lagoon *Lagos* 14 B2
Laguna de B. *Manila* 17 C2
Laim *Munich* 21 B2
Lainate *Milan* 19 A1
Lainz *Vienna* 32 A1
Lake Nona Vista *Orlando* 23 B2
Lake Cain Hills *Orlando* 23 B2
Lake Fairfax Park
  Washington 33 B2
Lakemba *Sydney* 29 B1
Lakeside *Cape Town* 8 B1
Lakeside *Johannesburg* 13 A2
Lakeview *Chicago* 9 B3
Lakeview *New Orleans* 21 A2
Lakewood Park *Chicago* 9 A2
Lakhtinskiy *St. Petersburg* 27 B1
Lakhtinskiy Razliv, Oz.
  St. Petersburg 27 B1
Lakshmanpur *Kolkata* 14 B1
Laksi *Bangkok* 3 B1
Lal Qila *Delhi* 10 B2
Lam Tin *Hong Kong* 12 B2
Lambert *Oslo* 23 A3
Lambeth □ *London* 15 B3
Lambrate *Milan* 19 B2
Lambro, Parco *Milan* 19 B2
Lambton Mills *Toronto* 31 B1
Lamma I. *Hong Kong* 12 B1
Landianchang *Beijing* 4 B1
Landover Hills *Washington* 33 B4
Landsmeer *Amsterdam* 2 A2
Landstrasse *Vienna* 32 A2
Landwehr kanal *Berlin* 5 B3
Lane Cove *Sydney* 29 A1
Lane Cove Nat. Park △
  Sydney 29 A1
Langa *Cape Town* 8 A2
Langenzersdorf *Vienna* 32 A2
Langer See *Berlin* 5 B4
Langley *Washington* 33 B3
Langley Park *Washington* 33 B4
Langwald *Munich* 21 A3
Lanham *Washington* 33 B4
Lankwitz *Berlin* 5 B3
L'Annunziatella *Rome* 26 C2
Lansdowne *Cape Town* 8 B2
Lansing *Toronto* 31 A2
Lanus *Buenos Aires* 7 C2
Lapa *Rio de Janeiro* 25 B1
Laranjeiras *Rio de Janeiro* 25 B1
Las *Warsaw* 32 B2
Las Corts *Barcelona* 4 A1
Las Kabacki *Warsaw* 32 C2
Las Pinas *Manila* 17 C1
Las Rejas *Santiago* 27 B1
Las Vegas *Las Vegas* 14 B2
Las Vegas McCarran
  Int. ✈ (LAS) *Las Vegas* 14 B2
LaSalle *Montreal* 20 B2
LaSalle Street Station
  Chicago 9 B3
Lasek Bielański *Warsaw* 32 B1
Lasek Na Kole *Warsaw* 32 B1
Latina *Madrid* 17 B1
Lauttasaari *Helsinki* 11 B2
Laval-des-Rapides *Montreal* 20 A1
Lavižan *Tehran* 31 A2
Lavradio *Lisbon* 16 A2
Lawndale *Chicago* 9 B2
Lawne L. *Orlando* 23 A2
Lawrence Heights *Toronto* 31 A2
Layari *Karachi* 13 A2
Layari → *Karachi* 13 A2
Łazienkowski Park *Warsaw* 32 B2
Le Blanc-Mesnil *Paris* 24 A3
Le Bourget *Paris* 24 A3
Le Chenoi *Brussels* 6 B2
Le Christ de Saclay *Paris* 24 B1
Le Mesnil-le-Roi *Paris* 24 A1
Le Pecq *Paris* 24 A1
Le Perreux *Paris* 24 A4
Le Pin *Paris* 24 A4
Le Plessis-Robinson *Paris* 24 B2
Le Plessis-Trévise *Paris* 24 B4
Le Port-Marly *Paris* 24 A1
Le Pré-St-Gervais *Paris* 24 A3
Le Raincy *Paris* 24 A4
Le Vésinet *Paris* 24 A1
Lea Bridge *London* 15 A3
Leaside *Toronto* 31 A2
Leblon *Rio de Janeiro* 25 B1
Lee *London* 15 B3
Leganés *Madrid* 17 C1
Legazpi *Madrid* 17 B1

Lehtisaari *Helsinki* 11 B2
Lei Yue Mun *Hong Kong* 12 B2
Leião *Lisbon* 16 A1
Leichhardt *Sydney* 29 B1
Leith *Edinburgh* 11 B3
Lekki *Lagos* 14 B2
Leme *Rio de Janeiro* 25 B1
Lemoyne *Montreal* 20 B3
Lenin *Moscow* 19 B2
Lenino *Moscow* 19 C2
Leninskiye Gory *Moscow* 19 B2
Lennox *Los Angeles* 16 C2
Leonia *New York* 22 A2
Leopardstown *Dublin* 10 B2
Leopoldau *Vienna* 32 A2
Leopoldsdorf *Vienna* 32 B2
Leopoldstadt *Vienna* 32 A2
Leportovo *Moscow* 19 B3
Leppävaara *Helsinki* 11 B1
Les Lilas *Paris* 24 A3
Les Loges-en-Josas *Paris* 24 B1
Lésigny *Paris* 24 B4
Lesnozavodskaya
  St. Petersburg 27 B2
Lester B. Pearson Int.,
  Toronto ✈ (YYZ) *Toronto* 31 A1
L'Étang-la-Ville *Paris* 24 A1
Letňany *Prague* 25 B2
Letopolis = Ausim *Cairo* 7 A1
Levallois-Perret *Paris* 24 A2
Levent *Istanbul* 12 B2
Lewisdale *Washington* 33 B4
Lewisham □ *London* 15 B3
Lexington *Boston* 6 A1
Leyton *London* 15 A3
Leytonstone *London* 15 A4
L'Haÿ-les-Roses *Paris* 24 B3
L'Hospitalet de Llobregat
  Barcelona 4 A1
Lhotka *Prague* 25 B2
Liangshui He ➟ *Beijing* 4 C2
Lianhua Chi *Beijing* 4 B1
Lianhua He ➟ *Beijing* 4 B1
Libčice nad Vltavou *Prague* 25 A2
Libeň *Prague* 25 B2
Libeznice *Prague* 25 A2
Libuš *Prague* 25 B2
Lichiao *Guangzhou* 11 B2
Lichtenburg *Berlin* 5 A4
Lichterfelde *Berlin* 5 B3
Lidingö *Stockholm* 29 A2
Lieshi Lingyuan *Guangzhou* 11 B2
Liesing *Vienna* 32 B1
Liesing = *Vienna* 32 B2
Ligovo 51 *St. Petersburg* 27 C1
Lijordet *Oslo* 23 A2
Likhoborka ➟ *Moscow* 19 A2
Lilla Värtan *Stockholm* 29 A3
Lille Værløse *Copenhagen* 8 A2
Liluah *Kolkata* 14 B1
Lim Chu Kang *Singapore* 28 A2
Lima *Lima* 15 B2
Lima Jorge Chavez, Int. ✈
  (LIM) *Lima* 15 B2
Limbiate *Milan* 19 A1
Limehouse *London* 15 A3
Limhamn-Bronmarks *Paris* 24 B3
Linate, Milano ✈ (LIN)
  Milan 19 B2
Linbropark *Johannesburg* 13 A2
Lincoln Center for
  Performing Arts
  New York 22 B2
Lincoln Heights *Los Angeles* 16 B3
Lincoln Memorial
  Washington 33 B3
Lincoln Park *Chicago* 9 B3
Lincoln Park *New York* 22 B1
Lincoln Park *San Francisco* 26 B1
Lincoln Park Zoo *Chicago* 9 B3
Lincolnwood *Chicago* 9 B2
Linda-a-Pastora *Lisbon* 16 A1
Linden *Johannesburg* 13 A2
Linden *Wellington* 33 A1
Lindenberg *Berlin* 5 A4
Lindoya *Oslo* 23 A3
Liniers *Buenos Aires* 7 B1
Linkebeek *Brussels* 6 B2
Linksfield *Johannesburg* 13 A2
Linmeyer *Johannesburg* 13 B2
Linna *Helsinki* 11 A2
Lintuvaara *Helsinki* 11 B1
Lion Rock Country
  Park ➟ *Hong Kong* 12 A2
Lion's Head *Cape Town* 8 A1
Lioumi *Athens* 2 B2
Lisboa *Lisbon* 16 A2
Lisboa ✈ (LIS) *Lisbon* 16 A2
Lisbon = *Lisbon* 16 A2
Lishui *Guangzhou* 11 A1
Little B. *Sydney* 29 B2
Little Calumet ➟ *Chicago* 9 D3
Little Ferry *New York* 22 A1
Little Lake Conway *Orlando* 23 B2
Little Red School House
  Nature Center *Chicago* 9 C1
Little Rouge ➟ *Toronto* 31 A4
Liuhang *Shanghai* 28 B1
Liurong Temple *Guangzhou* 11 B2
Live Oak Manor
  New Orleans 21 A1
Livry-Gargan *Paris* 24 A4
Liwan *Guangzhou* 11 B2
Ljan *Oslo* 23 A3
Llano de Can Gineu
  Barcelona 4 A2
Lo Aranguiz *Santiago* 27 B2
Lo Boza *Santiago* 27 B1
Lo Chau *Hong Kong* 12 B2
Lo Chau Pak Mai
  Hong Kong 12 B2
Lo Espejo *Santiago* 27 C1
Lo Hermida *Santiago* 27 B2
Lo Prado *Santiago* 27 B1
Lo So Shing *Hong Kong* 12 B1
Lo Wai *Hong Kong* 12 A2
Loanhead *Edinburgh* 11 B3
Lobau *Vienna* 32 A3
Lobos, Pt. *San Francisco* 26 B1
Locham *Munich* 21 B1
Lochkov *Prague* 25 B2
Lockhausen *Munich* 21 A1
Lodi *New York* 22 A1
Lodi Estate *Delhi* 10 B2
Logan Int. *Boston* ✈
  (BOS) *Boston* 6 A2
Logan Square *Chicago* 9 B2
Lognes-Émerainville ✈
  (XLG) *Paris* 24 B4
Löhme *Berlin* 5 A5
Lokomotiv ➟ *St. Petersburg* 27 B2
Lomas Chapultepec
  Mexico City 18 B1

Lomas de San Angel Inn
  Mexico City 18 B1
Lombardy East *Johannesburg* 13 A2
Lomianki *Warsaw* 32 A1
Lomus Reforma *Mexico City* 18 B1
London *London* 15 B3
London Avenue Canal
  New Orleans 21 A2
London City ✈ (LCY)
  London 15 A4
London Heathrow ✈
  (LHR) *London* 15 B1
London Zoo *London* 15 A3
Long B. *Sydney* 29 B2
Long Branch *Toronto* 31 B1
Long Brook ➟ *Washington* 33 C2
Long Ditton *London* 15 B2
Long Island City *New York* 22 B2
Longchamp, Hippodrome
  de *Paris* 24 A2
Longhua Pagoda *Shanghai* 28 B1
Longhua Park *Shanghai* 28 B1
Longjohn Slough *Chicago* 9 C1
Longtan Hu ➟ *Beijing* 4 B2
Longue-Pointe *Montreal* 20 A2
Longueuil *Montreal* 20 A3
Loni *Delhi* 10 A2
Loop, The *Chicago* 9 B3
Lord's Cricket Ground
  London 15 A2
Loreto *Milan* 19 B2
Los Angeles *Los Angeles* 16 B3
Los Angeles Int. ✈ (LAX)
  Los Angeles 16 C2
Los Cerrillos ✈ (ULC)
  Santiago 27 B2
Los Nietos *Los Angeles* 16 C4
Los Olivos *Lima* 14 A2
Los Remedios 🛦 *Mexico City* 18 B1
Los Reyes *Mexico City* 18 B2
Losiny Ostrov 🛦 *Moscow* 19 A3
Lot *Brussels* 6 B1
Lotus River *Cape Town* 8 B2
Lotus Temple *Delhi* 10 B2
Loughlinstown *Dublin* 10 B3
Louis Armstrong New
  Orleans Int. ✈ (MSY)
  New Orleans 21 A1
Louise, L. *Orlando* 23 A2
Louisiana Superdome
  New Orleans 21 B2
Loures *Lisbon* 16 A1
Louveciennes *Paris* 24 A1
Louvre, Musée du *Paris* 24 A3
Lower B. *New York* 22 C1
Lower Hutt *Wellington* 33 B2
Lower New York B. ➟
  New York 22 C1
Lower Shing Mun Res.
  Hong Kong 12 A1
Lowry Bay *Wellington* 33 B2
Loyola Univ. *Chicago* 9 B3
Lu Xun, Tomb of *Shanghai* 28 B1
Lu Xun Park *Shanghai* 28 B1
Lübars *Berlin* 5 A3
Lucy, L. *Orlando* 23 A2
Ludwigsfeld *Munich* 21 A1
Luhu *Guangzhou* 11 B2
Lumiar *Lisbon* 16 A2
Lundtofte *Copenhagen* 8 A3
Lung Mei *Hong Kong* 12 A2
Luojiang *Guangzhou* 11 B2
Lustheim *Munich* 21 A2
Luwan *Shanghai* 28 B1
Luzhniki Sports Centre
  Moscow 19 B2
Lyndhurst *New York* 22 B1
Lynn Woods Res. *Boston* 6 A2
Lyon, Gare de *Paris* 24 A3
Lyons *Chicago* 9 C2
Lysaker *Oslo* 23 A2
Lysakerselva ➟ *Oslo* 23 A2
Lysolaje *Prague* 25 B2
Lyublino *Moscow* 19 B3

M

Ma Nam Wat *Hong Kong* 12 A2
Ma On Shan Country
  Park ➟ *Hong Kong* 12 A2
Ma'ale Adumin *Jerusalem* 13 B2
Ma'ale Ha Khamisha
  Jerusalem 13 B1
Ma'ale Mikhmas *Jerusalem* 13 A2
Maantiekylä *Helsinki* 11 A3
Maarifa *Baghdad* 3 B2
Mabato Pt. *Manila* 17 C2
Mabel, L. *Orlando* 23 A2
Macacos, Morro do
  Rio de Janeiro 25 B1
McCarran Int., Las
  Vegas ✈ (LAS) *Las Vegas* 14 B2
McCook *Chicago* 9 C2
McGill Univ. *Montreal* 20 A2
Machelen *Brussels* 6 A2
Machida *Tokyo* 30 B1
Maciołki *Warsaw* 32 B1
McKerrow, Mt. *Wellington* 33 B2
McKinley Park *Chicago* 9 C2
McLean *Washington* 33 B2
Macopocho ➟ *Santiago* 27 B1
MacRitchie Res. *Singapore* 28 A2
Macul *Santiago* 27 B2
Madhudaha *Kolkata* 14 B2
Madhyamgram *Kolkata* 14 A2
Madin *Mexico City* 18 A1
Madin, L. *Mexico City* 18 A1
Madinah Al Mansūr
  Baghdad 3 B2
Madinat Nasr *Cairo* 7 A2
Madrid *Madrid* 17 B1
Madrid Barajas ✈ (MAD)
  Madrid 17 B2
Madrona *Barcelona* 4 A1
Maesawa *Tokyo* 30 A2
Magdalena *Lima* 14 B2
Magdalena Contreras
  Mexico City 18 C1
Maghreb *Baghdad* 3 A2
Maginu *Tokyo* 30 B2
Magliana *Rome* 26 B1
Magny-les-Hameaux *Paris* 24 B1
Maheshtala *Kolkata* 14 C1
Mahim *Mumbai* 20 A2
Mahim B. *Mumbai* 20 A2
Mahlsdorf *Berlin* 5 A4
Mahmoodabad *Karachi* 13 A2
Mahrauli *Delhi* 10 B2
Mahul *Mumbai* 20 A2
Maida Vale *London* 15 A2
Maidstone *Melbourne* 18 A1
Maipú *Santiago* 27 C1
Maisonneuve, Parc
  Montreal 20 A2
Maisons-Alfort *Paris* 24 B3
Maisons-Laffitte *Paris* 24 A1
Maissonette *Montreal* 20 A2
Maitland *Cape Town* 8 A1
Makasar *Jakarta* 12 B2
Makati *Manila* 17 B2
Méier *Rio de Janeiro* 25 B1

Mäkiniitty *Helsinki* 11 A2
Malá Strana *Prague* 25 B2
Malabar *Sydney* 29 B2
Malabar Hill *Mumbai* 20 B1
Malabar Pt. *Mumbai* 20 B1
Malabon *Manila* 17 B1
Malacañang Palace *Manila* 17 B1
Malakoff *Helsinki* 11 A3
Malakoff *Paris* 24 B2
Malahide *Dublin* 10 A3
Malakoff *Paris* 24 B2
Malate *Montreal* 20 A2
Malaya Neva ➟ *St. Petersburg* 27 B1
Malaya Okhta
  St. Petersburg 27 B1
Malchow *Berlin* 5 A3
Malden *Boston* 6 A1
Malden *London* 15 B2
Maleizen *Brussels* 6 B3
Malir ➟ *Karachi* 13 B2
Malleny Mills *Edinburgh* 11 B2
Malmi *Helsinki* 11 B2
Malmoya *Oslo* 23 A3
Malton *Toronto* 31 A1
Malvern *Johannesburg* 13 B2
Malvern *Melbourne* 18 B2
Malvern *Toronto* 31 A3
Mampang Prapatan *Jakarta* 12 B1
Mampukuji *Tokyo* 30 B2
Man Budrukh *Mumbai* 20 A2
Man Khurd *Mumbai* 20 A2
Manakhat *Jerusalem* 13 B2
Mandaluyong *Manila* 17 B2
Mandaoli *Delhi* 10 B2
Mandaqui ➟ *São Paulo* 27 A2
Mandoli *Delhi* 10 A2
Mandvi *Mumbai* 20 B2
Manenberg *Cape Town* 8 A2
Mang Kung Uk *Hong Kong* 12 B2
Mang-won *Seoul* 27 B1
Mangolpuri *Delhi* 10 A1
Manguinhos ✈
  Rio de Janeiro 25 B1
Manhattan *New York* 22 B2
Manhattan Beach
  New York 22 C1
Manila *Manila* 17 B1
Manila Ninoy Aquino
  Int. ✈ (MNL) *Manila* 17 B2
Mankkaa *Helsinki* 11 B1
Manly *Sydney* 29 A2
Mann, L. *Orlando* 23 A2
Mann's Chinese Theatre
  Los Angeles 16 B2
Mannswörth *Vienna* 32 B3
Manor Park *London* 15 A4
Manor Park *Wellington* 33 A2
Manora *Karachi* 13 B1
Manora Pt. *Karachi* 13 B1
Manquehue, Cerro *Santiago* 27 B2
Manzanares, Canal de
  Madrid 17 C2
Mapo *Seoul* 27 B1
Mar Vista *Los Angeles* 16 B2
Maracaná *Rio de Janeiro* 25 B1
Maraoli *Mumbai* 20 A2
Marcelin *Warsaw* 32 B1
Mareil-Marly *Paris* 24 A1
Margareten *Vienna* 32 A2
Maria *Vienna* 32 A2
Maridalen *Oslo* 23 A3
Maridalsvatnet *Oslo* 23 A3
Mariendorf *Berlin* 5 B3
Marienfelde *Berlin* 5 B3
Marikina *Manila* 17 B2
Marikina ➟ *Manila* 17 B2
Marin City *San Francisco* 26 A1
Marin Pen. *San Francisco* 26 A1
Marina del Rey *Los Angeles* 16 C2
Marino *Dublin* 10 A2
Marisco, Ponta do
  Rio de Janeiro 25 C1
Markham *New York* 22 C1
Marki *Warsaw* 32 B2
Markland Wood *Toronto* 31 B1
Marly, Forêt de *Paris* 24 A1
Marly-le-Roi *Paris* 24 A1
Marne-la-Vallée *Paris* 24 A4
Marolles-en-Brie *Paris* 24 B4
Maroubra *Sydney* 29 B2
Marquette Park *Chicago* 9 C2
Marrero *New Orleans* 21 B2
Marrickville *Sydney* 29 B1
Marsfield *Sydney* 29 A1
Marsha, L. *Orlando* 23 B2
Marte, Campo de São Paulo 27 B2
Martesana, Naviglio della
  Milan 19 A2
Martin Luther King Nat.
  Historic Site 🛦 *Atlanta* 3 B2
Martinez *Buenos Aires* 7 A1
Martinkylä *Helsinki* 11 A2
Martinsried *Munich* 21 B1
Maruko *Tokyo* 30 B3
Maryino *Moscow* 19 B3
Maryland *Singapore* 28 B2
Marymont *Warsaw* 32 B1
Marysin Wawerski *Warsaw* 32 B2
Marzahn *Berlin* 5 A4
Mascot *Sydney* 29 B1
Masmo *Stockholm* 29 B1
Maspeth *New York* 22 B2
Masr el Gedida *Cairo* 7 A2
Masr el Qadîma *Cairo* 7 A2
Massachusetts Inst. of
  Tech. *Boston* 6 A2
Massamá *Lisbon* 16 A1
Massey ➟ *Toronto* 31 A3
Massy *Paris* 24 B2
Mata *Jerusalem* 13 B1
Matinha *Lisbon* 16 A2
Matramam *Jakarta* 12 B2
Matsubara *Osaka* 23 B2
Mattapan *Boston* 6 B1
Mátyásföld *Budapest* 7 A3
Mau Tso Ngam *Hong Kong* 12 A2
Mauer *Vienna* 32 B1
Mauripur *Karachi* 13 A1
Maxhof *Munich* 21 B1
Mayfair *Johannesburg* 13 B2
Maywood *Chicago* 9 B1
Maywood *Los Angeles* 16 C3
Maywood *New York* 22 A1
Maywood Park Race
  Track *Chicago* 9 B1
Mazagaon *Mumbai* 20 B2
Meadowbank Park *Sydney* 29 A1
Mech
olupy *Prague* 25 B2
Měcice *Prague* 25 A2
Mecidiyeköy *Istanbul* 12 B2
Medford *Boston* 6 A1
Mediodia *Madrid* 17 B2
Meguro *Tokyo* 30 B3
Meguro ➟ *Tokyo* 30 B3
Mehrábád (TBR) *Tehran* 31 A1
Mehrápalpur *Delhi* 10 B2
Mehran Nagar *Delhi* 10 B2
Mehrow *Berlin* 5 A4
Meidling *Vienna* 32 B1

Meiji Shrine *Tokyo* 30 A3
Meise *Brussels* 6 A1
Mejiro *Tokyo* 30 A3
Melbourne *Melbourne* 18 A1
Melbourne ✈ (MEL)
  Melbourne 18 A1
Melkki *Helsinki* 11 B2
Mellunkylä *Helsinki* 11 B3
Mellunmäki *Helsinki* 11 B3
Melrose *Boston* 6 A1
Melrose *New York* 22 B2
Melrose Park *Chicago* 9 B1
Melsbroek *Brussels* 6 A2
Melville *Johannesburg* 13 B2
Menteng *Jakarta* 12 B1
Mérantaise ➟ *Paris* 24 B1
Mercamadrid *Madrid* 17 B2
Merced, L. *San Francisco* 26 B2
Meredale *Johannesburg* 13 B1
Merlimau, Pulau *Singapore* 28 B2
Merri Cr. ➟ *Melbourne* 18 A1
Merrion *Dublin* 10 B2
Merrionette Park *Chicago* 9 C2
Merton □ *London* 15 B2
Mesgarābād *Tehran* 31 B3
Messe *Vienna* 32 A2
Metairie *New Orleans* 21 A2
Metanópoli *Milan* 19 B2
Metro-Dade Cultural
  Centre *Miami* 18 B2
Metro Toronto Zoo *Toronto* 31 A3
Metropolitan Museum of
  Art *New York* 22 B2
Meudon *Paris* 24 B2
Mevaseret Tsiyon *Jerusalem* 13 B1
Mevo Beitar *Jerusalem* 13 B1
México *Mexico City* 18 B1
México, Ciudad de
  Mexico City 18 B1
Mexico City Int. ✈ (MEX)
  Mexico City 18 B2
Meyersdal *Johannesburg* 13 B2
Mezzate *Milan* 19 B2
Miadong *Seoul* 27 B2
Miami *Miami* 18 B2
Miami Beach *Miami* 18 B2
Miami Canal *Miami* 18 A1
Miami ✈ (MIA) *Miami* 18 B1
Miami Shores *Miami* 18 A2
Miami Springs *Miami* 18 B1
Miasto *Warsaw* 32 B2
Michalowice *Warsaw* 32 B1
Michle *Prague* 25 B2
Mid-City *Los Angeles* 16 B2
Mid City *New Orleans* 21 A2
Middle Harbour *Sydney* 29 A2
Middle Hd. *Sydney* 29 A2
Middle Park *Melbourne* 18 B1
Middle Village *New York* 22 B2
Middlesex Fells
  Reservation *Boston* 6 A2
Midland Beach *New York* 22 C1
Midrand *Johannesburg* 13 A2
Midwood *New York* 22 C2
Miedeszyn *Warsaw* 32 B2
Międzylesie *Warsaw* 32 B2
Miessaari *Helsinki* 11 C1
Miguel Hidalgo *Mexico City* 18 B1
Milan = *Milan* 19 B1
Milanese, Parco
  Regionale ➟ *Milan* 19 A1
Milano *Milan* 19 B1
Milano Due *Milan* 19 B2
Milano Linate ✈ (LIN)
  Milan 19 B2
Milano San Felice *Milan* 19 B2
Milbertshofen *Munich* 21 A2
Mill Hill *London* 15 A2
Millennium Dome *London* 15 A4
Miller Meadow *Chicago* 9 B1
Millerhill *Edinburgh* 11 B3
Milltown *Dublin* 10 A2
Millwood *Washington* 33 B4
Milnerton *Cape Town* 8 A1
Milon-la-Chapelle *Paris* 24 B1
Milton *Boston* 6 B1
Milton Bridge *Edinburgh* 11 B2
Mimico *Toronto* 31 B2
Mimico Creek ➟ *Toronto* 31 B1
Minami *Osaka* 23 B2
Minamitsunashima *Tokyo* 30 B2
Minato *Osaka* 23 B1
Minato *Tokyo* 30 B3
Minshât el Bekkarî *Cairo* 7 A1
Miraflores *Lima* 14 B2
Miramar *Wellington* 33 B2
Misericordia, Sa. da
  Rio de Janeiro 25 B1
Mission *San Francisco* 26 B2
Mississauga *Toronto* 31 B1
Mitaka *Tokyo* 30 A2
Mitcham *London* 15 B2
Mitcham Common *London* 15 B3
Mitchell Museum of the
  American Indian *Chicago* 9 A2
Mitchell's Plain *Cape Town* 8 B2
Mitte *Berlin* 5 A3
Mittel Isarkanal ➟ *Munich* 21 A3
Mixcoac *Mexico City* 18 B1
Miyakojima *Osaka* 23 A2
Mizonokuchi *Tokyo* 30 B2
Mizue *Tokyo* 30 A4
Mlocinski Park *Warsaw* 32 B1
Mlociny *Warsaw* 32 B1
Mnevniki *Moscow* 19 B1
Moba *Lagos* 14 B2
Moczydlo *Warsaw* 32 B1
Modderfontein *Johannesburg* 13 A2
Modřany *Prague* 25 B2
Mogyoród *Budapest* 7 A3
Moinho Velho, Cor. ➟
  São Paulo 27 B2
Mok *Seoul* 27 B1
Mokotów *Warsaw* 32 B1
Molenbeek-St-Jean *Brussels* 6 A1
Molino de Rosas
  Mexico City 18 B1
Mollem *Brussels* 6 A1
Mollins de Rey *Barcelona* 4 A1
Mondeor *Johannesburg* 13 B2
Moneda, Palacio de la
  Santiago 27 B2
Moneró *Rio de Janeiro* 25 A1
Mong Kok *Hong Kong* 12 B2
Monkstown *Dublin* 10 B2
Monnickendam *Amsterdam* 2 A3
Monrovia *Los Angeles* 16 B4
Monsanto *Lisbon* 16 A1
Monsanto, Parque
  Florestal de *Lisbon* 16 A1
Mont-Royal *Montreal* 20 A2
Mont-Royal, Parc *Montreal* 20 A2
Montana de Montjuïc
  Barcelona 4 A2
Montcada i Reixac *Barcelona* 4 A2
Monte Chingolo *Buenos Aires* 7 C2
Monte Pulciano *Rome* 26 B1
Monteamaro *Rome* 26 B2
Monterey Hills *Los Angeles* 16 B3
Monterey Park *Los Angeles* 16 B4
Montespaccato *Rome* 26 B1
Montesson *Paris* 24 A1

Monteverde Nuovo *Rome* 26 B1
Montfermeil *Paris* 24 A4
Montigny-le-Bretonneux
  Paris 24 B1
Montjay-la-Tour *Paris* 24 A4
Montjuïc *Barcelona* 4 A1
Montparnasse, Gare *Paris* 24 A3
Montréal *Montreal* 20 A2
Montréal, Î. de *Montreal* 20 A2
Montréal Est *Montreal* 20 A3
Montréal, Univ. de *Montreal* 20 B2
Montréal-Nord *Montreal* 20 A2
Montréal-Ouest *Montreal* 20 B2
Montréal Trudeau Int. ✈
  (YUL) *Montreal* 20 B1
Montreuil *Paris* 24 A3
Montrouge *Paris* 24 B2
Montserrat *Buenos Aires* 7 B2
Monza *Milan* 19 A2
Monzoro *Milan* 19 B1
Móoca *São Paulo* 27 B2
Moonachie *New York* 22 B1
Moonee Ponds *Melbourne* 18 A1
Moonee Valley
  Racecourse *Melbourne* 18 A1
Moosach *Munich* 21 A2
Mora *Mumbai* 20 B2
Moratalaz *Madrid* 17 B2
Mörby *Stockholm* 29 A2
Morden *London* 15 B2
Morée ➟ *Paris* 24 A3
Morgan Park *Chicago* 9 C3
Moriguchi *Osaka* 23 A2
Morivione *Milan* 19 B2
Morningside *Edinburgh* 11 B2
Morningside *Johannesburg* 13 A2
Morningside *Washington* 33 C4
Morningside Park *Orlando* 23 B2
Morro Solar, Cerro *Lima* 14 C2
Mortlake *London* 15 B2
Mortlake *Sydney* 29 B1
Morton Grove *Chicago* 9 A2
Morumbi *São Paulo* 27 B2
Moscavide *Lisbon* 16 A2
Moschato *Athens* 2 B2
Moscow = *Moscow* 19 B2
Moskva *Moscow* 19 B2
Moskvoretskiy *Moscow* 19 B2
Mosman *Sydney* 29 A2
Moti Bagh *Delhi* 10 B2
Motol *Prague* 25 B2
Motsa *Jerusalem* 13 B1
Motsa Ilit *Jerusalem* 13 B1
Mottingham *London* 15 B4
Mount Dennis *Toronto* 31 A2
Mount Greenwood *Chicago* 9 C2
Mount Hood Memorial
  Park 🛦 *Boston* 6 A2
Mount Merrion *Dublin* 10 B2
Mount Olympus *Los Angeles* 16 B2
Mount Rainier *Washington* 33 B4
Mount Vernon *New York* 22 A3
Mouquet Farm *Paris* 24 A3
Müggelberge *Berlin* 5 B4
Müggelheim *Berlin* 5 B5
Muggiò *Milan* 19 A2
Mühleiten *Vienna* 32 A3
Mühlenfliess ➟ *Berlin* 5 A5
Muiden *Amsterdam* 2 A3
Muizenberg *Cape Town* 8 B2
Mujahidpur *Delhi* 10 B2
Mukandpur *Delhi* 10 A2
Mukhmas *Jerusalem* 13 A2
Muko ➟ *Osaka* 23 A1
Mukojima *Tokyo* 30 A3
Mulbarton *Johannesburg* 13 B2
Mullach Ide = Malahide
  Dublin 10 A3
Mumbai *Mumbai* 20 A2
Mumbai Chhatrapati
  Shivaji Int. ✈ (BOM)
  Mumbai 20 A2
Mumbai Harbour *Mumbai* 20 B2
Munch-museum *Oslo* 23 A3
Münchehofe *Berlin* 5 B5
München *Munich* 21 B2
München Franz Josef
  Strauss Int. ✈ (MUC)
  Munich 21 A2
Munich = München
  Munich 21 B2
Munkkiniemi *Helsinki* 11 B2
Munro *Buenos Aires* 7 B1
Muntinlupa *Manila* 17 C2
Murai Res. *Singapore* 28 A1
Muranów *Warsaw* 32 B1
Murino *St. Petersburg* 27 A2
Murrayfield *Edinburgh* 11 B2
Murtala Mohammed
  International ✈ (LOS)
  Lagos 14 A1
Musashino *Tokyo* 30 A2
Museu Nacional
  Rio de Janeiro 25 B1
Mushin *Lagos* 14 A2
Musocco *Milan* 19 B1
Mustansiriya *Baghdad* 3 A2
Musturud *Cairo* 7 A2
Muswell Hill *London* 15 A3
Mutanabi *Baghdad* 3 B2
Muthana *Baghdad* 3 B2
Mykerinos *Cairo* 7 B1
Myllypuro *Helsinki* 11 B3
Mystic ➟ *Boston* 6 A2

N

Nacka *Stockholm* 29 B3
Naenae *Wellington* 33 B2
Nærsnes *Oslo* 23 B1
Nagatsuta *Tokyo* 30 B2
Nagytétény *Budapest* 7 B1
Nahalin *Jerusalem* 13 B1
Najafgarh Drain ➟ *Delhi* 10 B1
Nakahara *Tokyo* 30 B3
Nakano *Tokyo* 30 A2
Namsan Park *Seoul* 27 B1
Namyeong *Seoul* 27 B1
Nanbiancun *Guangzhou* 11 B1
Nanchang He ➟ *Beijing* 4 B1
Nandang *Guangzhou* 11 B2
Nangal Dewat *Delhi* 10 B1
Naniwa *Osaka* 23 B1
Nanole *Mumbai* 20 A2
Nanpu Bridge *Shanghai* 28 B2
Nanshi *Shanghai* 28 B1
Nanterre *Paris* 24 A2
Napier Mole *Karachi* 13 B1
Naraina *Delhi* 10 B2
Nariman Point *Mumbai* 20 B1
Nariman Pt. *Mumbai* 20 B1
Naruo *Osaka* 23 A1
Naruto *Osaka* 23 A1
Nacogatino *Rome* 26 B2
Nangi *Kolkata* 14 B1
National Arboretum
  Washington 33 B4
National Zoological Park
  Washington 33 B3

Nationals Park *Washington* 33 B3
Nativity, Basilica of
  Jerusalem 13 B2
Natolin *Warsaw* 32 C2
Naucalpan de Juárez
  Mexico City 18 B1
Naupada *Mumbai* 20 A2
Navi Mumbai *Mumbai* 20 A2
Naviglio di Pavia *Milan* 19 B1
Naviglio Grande *Milan* 19 B1
Navotas *Manila* 17 B1
Navy Pier *Chicago* 9 B3
Nazal Hikmat Beg *Baghdad* 3 A2
Nazimabad *Karachi* 13 A2
Nazlet el Sisi *Cairo* 7 B1
Nea Alexandria *Athens* 2 A1
Nea Ionia *Athens* 2 A2
Nea Liosia *Athens* 2 A2
Nea Smirni *Athens* 2 B2
Neapoli *Athens* 2 B2
Near North *Chicago* 9 B3
Nebušice *Prague* 25 B1
Nederhorst *Amsterdam* 2 B3
Nedlitz *Berlin* 5 B1
Nee Soon *Singapore* 28 A2
Needham *Boston* 6 B1
Needham Heights *Boston* 6 B1
Nellis Air Force Base ✈
  (LSV) *Las Vegas* 14 A2
N'emätäbäd *Tehran* 31 B2
Nerima *Tokyo* 30 A3
Nesodden *Oslo* 23 B3
Nesoddtangen *Oslo* 23 B3
Nesoya *Oslo* 23 A2
Neu Aubing *Munich* 21 B1
Neu Buch *Berlin* 5 A4
Neu Buchhorst *Berlin* 5 B5
Neu Fahrland *Berlin* 5 B1
Neu Lindenberg *Berlin* 5 A4
Neubberg *Munich* 21 B3
Neuenhagen *Berlin* 5 A4
Neuessling *Vienna* 32 A3
Neuhausen *Munich* 21 B2
Neuherberg *Munich* 21 A2
Neuhönow *Berlin* 5 A5
Neuilly-Plaisance *Paris* 24 A4
Neuilly-sur-Marne *Paris* 24 A4
Neuilly-sur-Seine *Paris* 24 A2
Neukagran *Vienna* 32 A3
Neukettenhof *Vienna* 32 B2
Neukölln *Berlin* 5 B3
Neuperlach *Munich* 21 B2
Neuried *Munich* 21 B1
Neustift am Walde *Vienna* 32 A2
Neusüssenbrunn *Vienna* 32 A2
Neuwaldegg *Vienna* 32 A1
Neve Ya'akov *Jerusalem* 13 B2
Neves *Rio de Janeiro* 25 B2
Newberg *Baghdad* 3 A2
New Barakpur *Kolkata* 14 A2
New Brighton *New York* 22 B1
New Canada *Johannesburg* 13 B1
New Carrollton *Washington* 33 B4
New Cross *London* 15 B3
New Delhi *Delhi* 10 B2
New Dorp *New York* 22 C1
New Dorp Beach *New York* 22 C1
New Malden *London* 15 B2
New Milford *New York* 22 A1
New Mumbai = Navi
  Mumbai *Mumbai* 20 A2
New Orleans *New Orleans* 21 B2
New Orleans Int. ✈ (MSY)
  New Orleans 21 A1
New Territories *Hong Kong* 12 A1
New Toronto *Toronto* 31 B1
New Utrecht *New York* 22 C2
New York La Guardia ✈
  (LGA) *New York* 22 B2
Newark B. *New York* 22 B1
Newbattle *Edinburgh* 11 B3
Newbury Park *London* 15 A4
Newcraighall *Edinburgh* 11 B3
Newham □ *London* 15 A4
Newhaven *Edinburgh* 11 B2
Newington *Edinburgh* 11 B2
Newlands *Johannesburg* 13 B1
Newlands *Wellington* 33 B1
Newport *Melbourne* 18 B1
Newton *Boston* 6 A1
Newtonbrook *Toronto* 31 A2
Newtongrange *Edinburgh* 11 B3
Newtonville *Boston* 6 A1
Newtown *Sydney* 29 B2
Ngaio *Wellington* 33 B1
Ngau Chi Wan *Hong Kong* 12 A2
Ngau Tau Kok *Hong Kong* 12 B2
Ngauranga *Wellington* 33 B1
Ngong Shuen Chau
  Hong Kong 12 B1
Ngua Kok Wan *Hong Kong* 12 A1
Nhava Sheva *Mumbai* 20 B2
Niävarän *Tehran* 31 A2
Nibra *Kolkata* 14 B1
Nidäl *Baghdad* 3 A2
Niddrie *Edinburgh* 11 B3
Niddrie *Melbourne* 18 A1
Nieder Neuendorf *Berlin* 5 A2
Niederschönhausen *Berlin* 5 A3
Niederschönhausen *Berlin* 5 A3
Niemeyer *Rio de Janeiro* 25 B1
Nieuwendam *Amsterdam* 2 A2
Nihonbashi *Tokyo* 30 A3
Nippori *Helsinki* 11 B1
Nikea *Athens* 2 B1
Nikolassee *Berlin* 5 B2
Nikolskiy *Moscow* 19 B1
Niles *Chicago* 9 B2
Nimta *Kolkata* 14 A2
Ninoy Aquino Int. ✈
  (MNL) *Manila* 17 B2
Nippa *Tokyo* 30 B2
Nippori *Tokyo* 30 A3
Nishi *Osaka* 23 B1
Nishinari *Osaka* 23 B1
Nishinomiya *Osaka* 23 A1
Nishiyodogawa *Osaka* 23 B1
Niterói *Rio de Janeiro* 25 B2
Nockeby *Stockholm* 29 B1
Noel Park *London* 15 A3
Nogatino *Moscow* 19 B3
Nogent-sur-Marne *Paris* 24 A4
Noida *Delhi* 10 B2
Noiseau *Paris* 24 B4
Noisiel *Paris* 24 A4
Noisy-le-Grand *Paris* 24 A4
Noisy-le-Roi *Paris* 24 A1
Noisy-le-Sec *Paris* 24 A3
Nokkala *Helsinki* 11 C1
Nomentano *Rome* 26 B2
Nonakashimbo *Osaka* 23 A1
Nongminyundong
  Jiangxisuo *Guangzhou* 11 B2
Nonhyeon *Seoul* 27 B2
Noordhaburi *Sapan* 4 A1
Noorderpark *Amsterdam* 2 A2
Noordgezig *Johannesburg* 13 B1
Noordzeekanaal *Amsterdam* 2 A1
Nord, Gare du *Paris* 24 A3

Nordmarka *Oslo* 23 A3
Nordrand-Siedlung *Vienna* 32 A2
Nordstrand *Oslo* 23 A3
Normandale *Wellington* 33 B2
Norridge *Chicago* 9 B2
Norrmalm *Stockholm* 29 A2
North Arlington *New York* 22 B1
North Bay Village *Miami* 18 A2
North Bergen *New York* 22 B1
North Bull I. *Dublin* 10 A3
North Cheam *London* 15 B4
North Cray *London* 15 B4
North Decatur *Atlanta* 3 B3
North Druid Hills *Atlanta* 3 B3
North Esk ➟ *Edinburgh* 11 B2
North Gyle *Edinburgh* 11 B2
North Hackensack
  New York 22 A1
North Harbor *Manila* 17 B1
North Hd. *Sydney* 29 A2
North Hollywood
  Los Angeles 16 B2
North Las Vegas *Las Vegas* 14 A1
North Las Vegas ✈ (VGT)
  Las Vegas 14 A1
North Lexington *Boston* 6 A1
North Miami *Miami* 18 A2
North Miami Beach *Miami* 18 A2
North Nazimabad *Karachi* 13 A2
North Pt. *Hong Kong* 12 B2
North Queensferry
  Edinburgh 11 A1
North Quincy *Boston* 6 B2
North Riverside *Chicago* 9 B2
North Saugus *Boston* 6 A2
North York *Toronto* 31 A2
Northbridge *Sydney* 29 A2
Northbridge Park *Sydney* 29 A2
Northchild *Johannesburg* 13 A1
Northcote *Melbourne* 18 A1
Northeastern Univ. *Boston* 6 A2
Northern Virginia
  Regional Park 🛦
  Washington 33 B3
Northlake *Chicago* 9 B1
Northmount *Toronto* 31 A2
Northolt *London* 15 A1
Northumberland Heath
  London 15 B5
Northwestern Station
  Chicago 9 B3
Northwestern Univ. *Chicago* 9 A2
Northwood *Chicago* 15 A1
Northwood Park *Toronto* 31 A1
Norwood *Johannesburg* 13 A2
Norwood Park *Chicago* 9 B2
Noryangjin *Seoul* 27 B1
Nossa Senhora do Ó
  São Paulo 27 B2
Nossegem *Brussels* 6 A2
Notre-Dame *Paris* 24 A3
Notre-Dame, Basilique
  Montreal 20 B2
Notre-Dame, Bois *Paris* 24 B4
Notre-Dame-de-Grace
  Montreal 20 B2
Notting Hill *London* 15 A2
Nova Milanese *Milan* 19 A2
Novate Milanese *Milan* 19 A1
Novaya Derevnya
  St. Petersburg 27 A1
Nové Město *Prague* 25 B2
Novodeksandrovskoye
  St. Petersburg 27 B2
Novodevichy Convent
  Moscow 19 B2
Novogireyevo *Moscow* 19 B3
Novosaratovka
  St. Petersburg 27 B2
Nowe-Babice *Warsaw* 32 B1
Nöykkiö *Helsinki* 11 B1
Nueva Atzacoalco
  Mexico City 18 B2
Nueva Pompeya *Buenos Aires* 7 C2
Nueva Tenochtitlán
  Mexico City 18 B2
Nuijala *Helsinki* 11 B1
Numabukuro *Tokyo* 30 A2
Núñez *Buenos Aires* 7 B2
Nunhead *London* 15 B3
Ñuñoa *Santiago* 27 B2
Nusle *Prague* 25 B2
Nussdorf *Vienna* 32 A2
Nyanga *Cape Town* 8 A2
Nymphenburg *Munich* 21 B2
Nymphenburg, Schloss
  Munich 21 B2

O

O.R. Tambo Int. ✈ (JNB)
  Johannesburg 13 B2
Oak Grove *Atlanta* 3 A3
Oak Hill *Boston* 6 B1
Oak Lawn *Chicago* 9 C2
Oak Park *Chicago* 9 B2
Oak View *Washington* 33 A4
Oakdale *Atlanta* 3 A2
Oakland *San Francisco* 26 B3
Oakland *Washington* 33 C4
Oakleigh *Melbourne* 18 B2
Oakton *Chicago* 9 A2
Oakwood Beach *New York* 22 C1
Oatley *Sydney* 29 B1
Oba's Palace *Lagos* 14 B2
Oberföhring *Munich* 21 B2
Oberhaching *Munich* 21 B2
Oberlaa *Vienna* 32 B2
Oberlisse *Vienna* 32 A2
Obermenzing *Munich* 21 A1
Obermoos Schwaige
  Munich 21 A1
Oberschleissheim *Munich* 21 A2
Oberschöneweide *Berlin* 5 B4
Observatory *Johannesburg* 13 B2
Obuda *Budapest* 7 A2
Obukhovo *St. Petersburg* 27 B2
Obvodnyy Kanal ➟
  St. Petersburg 27 B1
Ocean Park *Hong Kong* 12 B2
Ochota *Warsaw* 32 B1
Ocoee *Orlando* 23 A1
Ōdana *Tokyo* 30 B2
Oden-Stockach *Munich* 21 B3
Odivelas *Lisbon* 16 A1
Odolany *Warsaw* 32 B1
Odori Park *Tokyo* 30 A3
Ofin *Lagos* 14 A2
Ogawa *Tokyo* 30 A1

Ogden Park *Chicago* 9 C2
Ogikubo *Tokyo* 30 A2
Ogogoro *Lagos* 14 B2
Ogoyo *Lagos* 14 B2
Ogudu *Lagos* 14 A2
O'Hare Int., Chicago ✈
  (ORD) *Chicago* 9 B1
Ohariu Stream ➟
  Wellington 33 B1
O'Higgins, Parque *Santiago* 27 B2
Ōimachi *Tokyo* 30 B3
Ojota *Lagos* 14 A2
Oke-Ira *Lagos* 14 A2
Okęcie *Warsaw* 32 B1
Okęcie, Warszawa ✈
  (WAW) *Warsaw* 32 B1
Okeogbe *Lagos* 14 B2
Okhla *Delhi* 10 B2
Okhta ➟ *St. Petersburg* 27 B2
Okkervil ➟ *St. Petersburg* 27 B2
Okrzeszyn *Warsaw* 32 C2
Oksval *Oslo* 23 A3
Oktyabrskiy *Moscow* 19 B2
Okubo *Tokyo* 30 A2
Ōkura *Tokyo* 30 B1
Olari *Helsinki* 11 B1
Olaria *Rio de Janeiro* 25 B1
Old Admiralty *St. Petersburg* 27 B1
Old City *Jerusalem* 13 B2
Old City *Shanghai* 28 B1
Old Fort York *Toronto* 31 B2
Old Harbor *Boston* 6 B2
Old Town = Stare Miasto
  Warsaw 32 B2
Old Town *Chicago* 9 B3
Old Town Hall = Altes
  Rathaus *Munich* 21 B2
Oldbawn *Dublin* 10 B1
Olgino *St. Petersburg* 27 A1
Olimpico, Estadio
  Mexico City 18 C1
Olivais *Lisbon* 16 A2
Olivar de los Padres
  Mexico City 18 B1
Olivar del Conde
  Mexico City 18 B1
Olives, Mt. of *Jerusalem* 13 B2
Olivia, L. *Orlando* 23 A2
Olivos *Buenos Aires* 7 B2
Olona ➟ *Milan* 19 B1
Olympia, L. *Orlando* 23 A1
Olympic Green *Beijing* 4 B2
Olympic Stadium =
  Turner Field *Atlanta* 3 B2
Olympic Stadium *Beijing* 4 B2
Olympic Stadium *Helsinki* 11 B2
Olympique, Stade *Montreal* 20 A2
Ōmori *Tokyo* 30 B3
Onisigun *Lagos* 14 A2
Ontario Science Centre
  Toronto 31 A2
Ōokayama *Tokyo* 30 B3
Oostzaan Tuindorp
  Amsterdam 2 A2
Opa-Locka *Miami* 18 A1
Opa-Locka ✈ (OPF) *Miami* 18 A1
Opacz *Warsaw* 32 B1
Ophirton *Johannesburg* 13 B2
Oppegård *Oslo* 23 B3
Oppem *Brussels* 6 A1
Oppsal *Oslo* 23 A3
Ora *Jerusalem* 13 B1
Oradell *New York* 22 A1
Oradell Res. *New York* 22 A1
Orange Bowl Stadium
  Miami 18 B2
Orangi *Karachi* 13 A2
Ordrup *Copenhagen* 8 A3
Orech *Prague* 25 B1
Orestad *Copenhagen* 8 B3
Orient Heights *Boston* 6 A3
Orlando *Orlando* 23 A2
Orlando Dam *Johannesburg* 13 B1
Orlando East *Johannesburg* 13 B1
Orlando Executive ✈
  (ORL) *Orlando* 23 B2
Orlando Int. ✈ (MCO)
  Orlando 23 B2
Orlovista *Orlando* 23 A2
Orly *Paris* 24 B3
Orly, Paris ✈ (ORY) *Paris* 24 B3
Ormesson-sur-Marne *Paris* 24 B4
Ormond *Melbourne* 18 B2
Ormoya *Oslo* 23 A3
Orpington *London* 15 B4
Ortaköy *Istanbul* 12 B2
Ortica *Milan* 19 B2
Oruba *Lagos* 14 B2
Ōsaka *Osaka* 23 B2
Ōsaka Castle *Osaka* 23 A2
Ōsaka Harbour *Osaka* 23 B1
Ōsaka Itami Int. ✈ (ITM)
  Osaka 23 A2
Ōsaka Kansai Int. ✈ (KIX)
  Osaka 23 B2
Ōsaki *Tokyo* 30 B3
Osasco *São Paulo* 27 B1
Osdorf *Berlin* 5 B2
Osdorp *Amsterdam* 2 A1
Oshodi *Lagos* 14 A2
Oslo *Oslo* 23 A3
Oslo ✈ (OSL) *Oslo* 23 A4
Osone *Tokyo* 30 B2
Osorun *Lagos* 14 A2
Ospiate *Milan* 19 A1
Ostankino *Moscow* 19 A2
Osterley *London* 15 B1
Osterley Park *London* 15 B1
Österskär *Stockholm* 29 A2
Östersker *Stockholm* 29 A2
Ostia Malpasso *Rome* 26 C1
Ostiense *Rome* 26 B1
Ostmarkkapellet *Oslo* 23 A3
Ostoya *Oslo* 23 A2
Østre Aker *Oslo* 23 A3
Ōta *Tokyo* 30 B3
Otaniemi *Helsinki* 11 B1
Otari Open Air Museum
  Wellington 33 B1
Otsuka *Tokyo* 30 A3
Ottakring *Vienna* 32 A1
Ottávia *Rome* 26 B1
Ottery *Cape Town* 8 B2
Ouderkerk *Amsterdam* 2 B2
Oulunkylä *Helsinki* 11 B2
Ourcq, Canal de l' *Paris* 24 A3
Outer Mission *San Francisco* 26 C2
Outremont *Montreal* 20 A2
Overijse *Brussels* 6 B3
Owhiro Bay *Wellington* 33 C1
Oworonski *Lagos* 14 A2
Oxgangs *Edinburgh* 11 B2
Oxon Hill *Washington* 33 C4
Oyster Rock *Mumbai* 20 B1
Oyster Rocks *Karachi* 13 B2
Ozoir-la-Ferrière *Paris* 24 B4
Ozone Park *New York* 22 B2

P

Pacific Heights
 San Francisco 26 B2
Pacific Manor San Francisco 26 C2
Pacific Palisades Los Angeles 16 B1
Pacifica San Francisco 26 C2
Paco Manila 17 B1
Paco de Arcos Lisbon 16 A1
Paddington London 15 A2
Paddington Sydney 29 A1
Paderno Milan 19 A1
Pagewood Sydney 29 B2
Pagote Mumbai 20 B2
Pai. I. do Rio de Janeiro 25 B2
Pak Kok Hong Kong 12 A2
Pak Kong Hong Kong 12 A2
Pakila Helsinki 11 B2
Palacio Real Madrid 17 B1
Palaiseau Paris 24 B2
Palazzolo Milan 19 A1
Paleo Faliro Athens 2 B2
Palermo Buenos Aires 7 B2
Palhais Lisbon 16 B2
Palisades Park New York 22 A1
Palmer Park Washington 33 B4
Palmerston Dublin 10 A1
Palms Los Angeles 16 B2
Palohenia Helsinki 11 B2
Palomeras Madrid 17 B2
Palos Heights Chicago 9 D2
Palos Hills Chicago 9 C1
Palos Hills Forest Chicago 9 C1
Palos Park Chicago 9 C1
Palpara Kolkata 14 B2
Panchur Kolkata 14 B1
Pandacan Manila 17 B2
Pandan, Selat Singapore 28 B2
Pandan Res. Singapore 28 B2
Pangrati Athens 2 B2
Pangsua, Sungei →
 Singapore 28 A2
Panihati Kolkata 14 A1
Panjang, Bukit Singapore 28 A2
Panke → Berlin 5 A3
Pankow Berlin 5 A3
Pantheon Rome 26 B1
Panthersville Atlanta 3 B3
Pantin Paris 24 A3
Pantitlán Mexico City 18 B2
Panyu Guangzhou 11 B2
Paparangi Wellington 33 B1
Papiol Barcelona 4 A1
Paradise Las Vegas 14 B2
Paramount Studios
 Los Angeles 16 B3
Paramus New York 22 A1
Paranaque Manila 17 B1
Paray-Vieille-Poste Paris 24 B3
Pardisän Nature Park
 Tehran 31 A2
Parel Mumbai 20 B1
Pari São Paulo 27 B2
Parioli Rome 26 B1
Paris Paris 24 A3
Paris Orly ✈ (ORY) Paris 24 B3
Parje Mumbai 20 B2
Pärk-e Äzädegän Tehran 31 B2
Pärk-e Mellat Tehran 31 A2
Park Ridge Chicago 9 A1
Park Royal London 15 A2
Parkchester New York 22 B2
Parkdale Toronto 31 B1
Parkhurst Johannesburg 13 A2
Parklawn Washington 33 B3
Parkmore Johannesburg 13 B3
Parkside San Francisco 26 B2
Parktown Johannesburg 13 B2
Parkview Johannesburg 13 A2
Parkville New York 22 C2
Parkwood Cape Town 8 B1
Parkwood Cape Town 8 B1
Parow Cape Town 8 A2
Parque Chacabuco
 Buenos Aires 7 B2
Parque Patricios Buenos Aires 7 B2
Parramatta → Sydney 29 A1
Paşabahçe Istanbul 12 B2
Pasadena Los Angeles 16 B4
Pasar Minggu Jakarta 12 B2
Pasay Manila 17 B1
Pascoe Vale Melbourne 18 A1
Pasig Manila 17 B2
Pasig → Manila 17 B2
Pasila Helsinki 11 B2
Pasing Munich 21 B1
Pasir Panjang Singapore 28 B2
Pasir Ris Singapore 28 A3
Passaic New York 22 A1
Passaic → New York 22 A1
Passirana Milan 19 A1
Patel Nagar Delhi 10 B1
Pateros Manila 17 B2
Pathumwan Bangkok 3 B2
Patipukur Kolkata 14 B2
Patisia Athens 2 A2
Paulo E. Virginia, Gruta
 Rio de Janeiro 25 B1
Paulshof Berlin 5 A5
Paya Lebar Singapore 28 A3
Peakhurst Sydney 29 B1
Peania Athens 2 B3
Pearson Int. Toronto ✈
 (YYZ) Toronto 31 A1
Peckham London 15 B3
Pederstrup Copenhagen 8 A2
Pedralbes Barcelona 4 A1
Pedregal de San Angel,
 Jardines del Mexico City 18 C1
Peip'ing = Beijing Beijing 4 B1
Peking = Beijing Beijing 4 B1
Pelcowizna Warsaw 32 B2
Peñalolén Santiago 27 B2
Pencarrow Hd. Wellington 33 C2
Peng Siang → Singapore 28 A2
Penge London 15 B3
Penha Rio de Janeiro 25 B2
Penicuik Edinburgh 11 B2
Penjaringan Jakarta 12 A1
Pentagon Washington 33 B3
Penzing Vienna 32 A1
People's Park Shanghai 28 B1
People's Square Shanghai 28 B1
Perales del Rio Madrid 17 C2
Perchtoldsdorf Vienna 32 B1
Perdizes São Paulo 27 B2
Peristeri Athens 2 A2
Perivale London 15 A2
Perk Brussels 6 A2
Perlach Munich 21 B2
Perlacher Forst Munich 21 B2
Pero Milan 19 A1
Peropok, Bukit Singapore 28 A2
Perovo Moscow 19 B3
Pertusella Milan 19 A1
Pesagot Jerusalem 13 A2
Pesanggrahan, Kali →
 Jakarta 12 B1
Peschiera Borromeo Milan 19 B2

Pest Budapest 7 B2
Pesterzsébet Budapest 7 B2
Pesthidegkút Budapest 7 A1
Pestimre Budapest 7 B3
Pestlőrinc Budapest 7 B2
Pestújhely Budapest 7 A2
Petas Helsinki 11 B3
Petone Wellington 33 B2
Petrogradskaya Storona
 St. Petersburg 27 B1
Petroupoli Athens 2 A2
Petrovice Prague 25 B3
Petrovsky Park Moscow 19 B2
Petrovsko-Razumovskoye
 Moscow 19 B2
Pettycur Edinburgh 11 A2
Peutie Brussels 6 A2
Pfaueninsel Berlin 5 B2
Phaya Thai Bangkok 3 B2
Phihai Karachi 13 A2
Phillip B. Sydney 29 B2
Phoenix Park Dublin 10 A2
Phra Khanong Bangkok 3 B2
Phra Nakhon Bangkok 3 B2
Phra Pradaeng Bangkok 3 C2
Phranakhon Bangkok 3 B1
Pico Rivera Los Angeles 16 C4
Piedade Lisbon 16 A1
Piedade Rio de Janeiro 25 B1
Piedade, Cova da Lisbon 16 A2
Piedmont Park Atlanta 3 B2
Pierre Elliott Trudeau ✈
 (YUL) Montreal 20 B1
Pietralata Rome 26 B2
Pihlajamäki Helsinki 11 B2
Pihlajasaari Helsinki 11 C2
Pilares Rio de Janeiro 25 B1
Pilton Edinburgh 11 B2
Pinmit Hills Washington 33 B2
Pine Castle Orlando 23 B2
Pine Grove Toronto 31 A1
Pine Hills Orlando 23 B1
Pinewood Park Miami 18 A2
Piney Run → Washington 33 B2
Pingzhou Guangzhou 11 B2
Pinheiros → São Paulo 27 B1
Pinjrapur Karachi 13 A2
Pinner London 15 A1
Pinner Green London 15 A1
Piottello Milan 19 A2
Pipinui Pt. Wellington 33 A1
Piraeus = Pireas Athens 2 B1
Piraiévs = Pireas Athens 2 B1
Pirajuçara → São Paulo 27 B1
Pireas Athens 2 B1
Pirinçci Istanbul 12 B1
Pirituba São Paulo 27 A1
Pirkkola Helsinki 11 B2
Pisgat O'mer Jerusalem 13 B2
Pisgat Ze'ev Jerusalem 13 B2
Pisnice Prague 25 C2
Pitampura Delhi 10 B2
Pitäjänmäki Helsinki 11 B1
Planegg Munich 21 B1
Plaza Mayor Madrid 17 B1
Pleasure Island Orlando 23 B1
Plumstead Cape Town 8 B1
Plumstead London 15 B4
Plyushchevo Moscow 19 B3
Po Toi Hong Kong 12 B2
Po Toi O Hong Kong 12 B2
Poasco Milan 19 B2
Podbaba Prague 25 B2
Podoli Prague 25 B2
Pohick Creek →
 Washington 33 C3
Pointe-Aux-Trembles
 Montreal 20 A2
Poissy Paris 24 A1
Pok Fu Lam Hong Kong 12 B1
Pokcheong Seoul 27 C2
Polton Edinburgh 11 B3
Polvoranca, Parque de
 Madrid 17 C1
Polyustrovo St. Petersburg 27 B2
Pomprap Bangkok 3 B2
Pondok Gede Jakarta 12 A2
Pondok Indah Jakarta 12 B1
Pont-Viau Montreal 20 A1
Pontault-Combault Paris 24 B4
Pontinha Lisbon 16 A1
Poplar London 15 A3
Poppintree Dublin 10 A2
Porirua Wellington 33 A2
Porirua East Wellington 33 A2
Porr Jerusalem 13 A2
Pórt Meárnóg =
 Portmarnock Dublin 10 A3
Port Melbourne Melbourne 18 B1
Port Nicholson Wellington 33 B2
Port Richmond New York 22 C1
Port Shelter Hong Kong 12 A2
Port Union Toronto 31 A4
Portage Park Chicago 9 B2
Portela, Lisboa ✈ (LIS)
 Lisbon 16 A2
Porter, I. Orlando 23 A3
Portmarnock Dublin 10 A3
Pôrto Brandão Lisbon 16 A1
Pôrto Novo Rio de Janeiro 25 A2
Porto Novo Cr. → Lagos 14 B2
Portobello Edinburgh 11 B3
Portreros San Francisco 26 B2
Potomac Washington 33 A2
Potrero Pt. San Francisco 26 B2
Potsdam Berlin 5 B1
Potzham Munich 21 B2
Pötzleinsdorf Vienna 32 A1
Póvoa de Santo Adraio
 Lisbon 16 A2
Powązki Warsaw 32 B1
Powisle Warsaw 32 C2
Powsin Warsaw 32 C2
Powsinek Warsaw 32 C2
Poyan Res. Singapore 28 A2
Pozuelo de Alarcón Madrid 17 B1
Prado, Museo del Madrid 17 B1
Prado Churubusco
 Mexico City 18 B2
Praga Warsaw 32 B2
Prague = Praha Prague 25 B2
Praha Prague 25 B2
Praha ✈ (PRG) Prague 25 B2
Praires, R. des → Montreal 20 A2
Prater Vienna 32 A2
Precotto Milan 19 A2
Prenestino Labicano Rome 26 B2
Prenzlauerberg Berlin 5 A3
Preston Melbourne 18 A1
Pretos Forros, Sa. dos
 Rio de Janeiro 25 B1
Préville Montreal 20 B3
Prezletice Prague 25 B3
Prima Porta Rome 26 B1
Primorskaya Wellington 33 B1
Primrose Johannesburg 13 B2
Primrose Johannesburg 13 B2
Pho Bangkok 3 B1
Recleta Buenos Aires 7 B2
Progreso Nacional
 Mexico City 18 A2
Prosek Prague 25 B3
Prospect Hill Park Boston 6 A1
Providencia Santiago 27 B2

Prühonice Prague 25 C3
Psichiko Athens 2 A2
Pudong New Area Shanghai 28 B2
Pueblo Libre Lima 14 B2
Pueblo Nuevo Barcelona 4 A2
Pueblo Nuevo Madrid 17 B2
Puerto Madero Buenos Aires 7 B2
Puhuangyu Beijing 4 B2
Puistola Helsinki 11 B3
Pukinmäki Helsinki 11 B2
Pulkovo Int. ✈ (LED)
 St. Petersburg 27 B1
Pullach Munich 21 B1
Pullman Historic District
 Chicago 9 C3
Pulo Gadung Jakarta 12 B2
Pünak Tehran 31 A2
Punchbowl Sydney 29 B1
Punde Mumbai 20 B2
Punggol Singapore 28 A3
Punggol, Sungei →
 Singapore 28 A3
Punggol Pt. Singapore 28 A3
Punjabi Bagh Delhi 10 B1
Puotila Helsinki 11 B3
Puteaux Paris 24 A2
Putney London 15 B2
Putuo Shanghai 28 B1
Putxet Barcelona 4 A1
Puxi Shanghai 28 B1
Pyramids Cairo 7 B1
Pyry Warsaw 32 C1

Q

Qalandiya Jerusalem 13 A2
Qal'eh Morghi Tehran 31 B2
Qanā el ismā'iliya Cairo 7 A2
Qäsembäbäd Tehran 31 A3
Qasr-e Firüzeh Tehran 31 A3
Qatane Jerusalem 13 B1
Qianmen Beijing 4 B2
Qinghuayuan Beijing 4 B1
Qingningsi Shanghai 28 B2
Qolhak Tehran 31 A2
Quadraro Rome 26 B2
Quaid-i-Azam Karachi 13 A1
Quartiere Zingone Milan 19 B1
Qubeiba Jerusalem 13 B1
Quds Baghdad 3 A2
Queen Mary Res. London 15 B1
Queen Victoria Market
 Melbourne 18 A1
Queensbury London 15 A2
Queenscliffe Sydney 29 A2
Queensferry Edinburgh 11 B1
Queenstown Singapore 28 B2
Quellerina Johannesburg 13 A1
Quezon City Manila 17 B2
Quilicura Santiago 27 B1
Quincy Boston 6 B3
Quincy B. Boston 6 B3
Quinta Normal Santiago 27 B1
Quinto de Stampi Milan 19 B2
Quinto Romano Milan 19 B1
Quirinale Rome 26 B1

R

R.F.K. Memorial Stadium
 Washington 33 B4
Raasdorf Vienna 32 A3
Radcliffe College Boston 6 A2
Rådhus Oslo 23 A3
Radlice Prague 25 B2
Radosé Warsaw 32 B3
Radotin Prague 25 C2
Rafat Jerusalem 13 A2
Raffles Park Singapore 28 B2
Raheny Dublin 10 A3
Rahnsdorf Berlin 5 B5
Rajakylä Helsinki 11 B3
Rajpura Delhi 10 A2
Rákos-patak → Budapest 7 A3
Rákoshegy Budapest 7 B3
Rákoskeresztúr Budapest 7 B3
Rákoskert Budapest 7 B3
Rákosliget Budapest 7 B3
Rákospalota Budapest 7 A2
Rákosszentmihály Budapest 7 A2
Raków Warsaw 32 B1
Rām Allāh Jerusalem 13 A2
Ramadān Baghdad 3 B2
Ramakrishna Puram Delhi 10 B1
Rāmallāh = Rām Allāh
 Jerusalem 13 A2
Ramanathpur Kolkata 14 A1
Ramat Allon Jerusalem 13 A1
Ramat Eshkol Jerusalem 13 B2
Ramat Razi'el Jerusalem 13 B1
Ramat Shafet Jerusalem 13 B2
Rambler Channel
 Hong Kong 12 A1
Ramenki Moscow 19 B2
Ramersdorf Munich 21 B2
Rameses Station Cairo 7 A2
Ramos Rio de Janeiro 25 B1
Ramos Mejía Buenos Aires 7 B1
Ramot Jerusalem 13 B2
Rampur Delhi 10 A2
Ramsgate Sydney 29 B1
Rancho Park Los Angeles 16 B2
Rand (QRA) Johannesburg 13 A2
Randalls I. New York 22 B2
Randburg Johannesburg 13 A1
Randpark Johannesburg 13 A1
Randpark Ridge
 Johannesburg 13 A1
Randwick Sydney 29 B2
Ranelagh Dublin 10 A2
Rangpuri Delhi 10 B1
Rannersdorf Vienna 32 B2
Ransbèche Brussels 6 B2
Ransdorp Amsterdam 2 A2
Ranvad Mumbai 20 B2
Raposo Lisbon 16 A1
Rastaala Helsinki 11 B1
Rastila Helsinki 11 B3
Raszyn Warsaw 32 C1
Rathfarnham Dublin 10 B2
Ratho Edinburgh 11 B2
Ratho Station Edinburgh 11 B1
Rato Lisbon 16 A2
Ravelston Edinburgh 11 B2
Rawamangun Jakarta 12 B2
Rayners Lane London 15 A1
Raynes Park London 15 B2
Raypur Kolkata 14 B2
Real Felipe, Fuerte Lima 14 B2
Reams, L. Orlando 23 B1
Reclining Buddha = Wat
 Pho Bangkok 3 B1
Recoleta Buenos Aires 7 B2
Recoleta Santiago 27 B2
Red Fort = Lal Qila Delhi 10 B2
Red Square Moscow 19 B3
Redbridge □ London 15 A4

Redfern Sydney 29 B2
Redwood Wellington 33 B1
Refshaleøen Copenhagen 8 A3
Regents Park Johannesburg 13 B2
Regent's Park London 15 A3
Rego Park New York 22 B2
Reinickendorf Berlin 5 A3
Rekola Helsinki 11 B3
Rembertów Warsaw 32 B2
Rembrandtpark Amsterdam 2 A2
Remedios de Escalada
 Buenos Aires 7 C2
Rémola, Estany del Barcelona 4 B1
Renca Santiago 27 B1
Rennemoulin Paris 24 A1
Répvorje Prague 25 B1
Repulse Bay Hong Kong 12 B2
Repy Prague 25 B1
Residenz Munich 21 B2
Reston Washington 33 B2
Retiro Buenos Aires 7 B2
Retiro Madrid 17 B1
Retiro, Puerto Buenos Aires 7 B2
Retreat Cape Town 8 B1
Reutov Moscow 19 B4
Réveillon → Paris 24 B4
Revere Boston 6 A2
Rexdale Toronto 31 A1
Reynosa Tamaulipas
 Mexico City 18 A1
Rho Milan 19 A1
Rhodes Sydney 29 A1
Rhodon Paris 24 B1
Rhodon → Paris 24 B1
Rialto Towers Melbourne 18 A1
Ribeira Rio de Janeiro 25 B1
Ricarda, Estany de la
 Barcelona 4 B1
Richmond Melbourne 18 A1
Richmond San Francisco 26 B2
Richmond Hill New York 22 B2
Richmond Park London 15 B2
Richmond-upon-
 Thames □ London 15 B2
Ridge, The Delhi 10 B2
Ridgefield New York 22 B1
Ridgefield Park New York 22 A1
Ridgewood New York 22 B2
Riem Munich 21 B3
Riesenrad Vienna 32 A2
Rijksmuseum Amsterdam 2 A2
Rikers I. New York 22 B2
Rimac Lima 14 B2
Ringsend Dublin 10 A2
Rinkeby Stockholm 29 A1
Rio Compride Rio de Janeiro 25 B1
Rio de Janeiro Rio de Janeiro 25 B1
Rio de Janeiro Galeão ✈
 (GIG) Rio de Janeiro 25 A1
Rio de Mouro Lisbon 16 A1
Ripollet Barcelona 4 A1
Ris Oslo 23 A3
Risby Copenhagen 8 A1
Rishra Kolkata 14 A2
Ritchie Washington 33 B4
Rithala Delhi 10 A1
Rive Sud, Canal de la
 Montreal 20 B3
River Edge New York 22 A1
River Forest Chicago 9 B2
River Grove Chicago 9 B1
River Ridge New Orleans 21 B1
Riverdale New York 22 A2
Riverdale Washington 33 B4
Riverdale Park Toronto 31 A2
Riverlea Johannesburg 13 B1
Riverside Chicago 9 C2
Riverwood Sydney 29 B1
Rivière-des-Prairies
 Montreal 20 A2
Rixensart Brussels 6 B3
Riyad Baghdad 3 B2
Rizal Park Manila 17 B1
Rizal Stadium Manila 17 B1
Røa Oslo 23 A2
Robbins Chicago 9 C2
Robertsham Johannesburg 13 B2
Rochelle Park New York 22 A1
Rock Cr. → Washington 33 B3
Rock Creek Park
 Washington 33 B3
Rock Pt. Wellington 33 A1
Rockaway Beach New York 22 C3
Rockaway Pt. New York 22 C2
Rockdale Sydney 29 B1
Rockefeller Center
 New York 22 B2
Rocky Run → Washington 33 B2
Roda, Gezîret el Cairo 7 A2
Roda ⊾ = Roda, Gezîret el
 Cairo 7 A2
Rodaon Vienna 32 B1
Rødovre Copenhagen 8 A2
Rodrigo de Freitas, L.
 Rio de Janeiro 25 B2
Roehampton London 15 B2
Rogers Park Chicago 9 B2
Roihuvuori Helsinki 11 B3
Roissy-en-Brie Paris 24 B4
Rokytka → Prague 25 B3
Roma Rome 26 B1
Roma Urbe ✈ Rome 26 B2
Romai-Fürdö Budapest 7 A2
Romainville Paris 24 A3
Roman Forum = Foro
 Romano Rome 26 B1
Romano Banco Milan 19 B1
Rome = Roma Rome 26 B1
Romema Jerusalem 13 B2
Romford London 15 A5
Ronald Reagan Nat.
 Washington ✈ (DCA)
 Washington 33 B3
Rondebosch Cape Town 8 A1
Roppongi Tokyo 30 B3
Rose, L. Orlando 23 A4
Rose Bowl Los Angeles 16 B3
Rose Hill Washington 33 C3
Rosebank Johannesburg 13 A2
Rosebank New York 22 C1
Rosebery Sydney 29 B2
Rosedal La Candelaria
 Mexico City 18 B2
Roseland Chicago 9 C3
Rosemead Los Angeles 16 B4
Rosemont Chicago 9 B1
Rosemont Montreal 20 A2
Rosenberg Slot Copenhagen 8 A3
Rosenthal Berlin 5 A3
Rosettenville Johannesburg 13 B2
Rosewell Edinburgh 11 B3
Rosherville Dam
 Johannesburg 13 B2
Rösjön Stockholm 29 A2
Roslags-Näsby Stockholm 29 A2
Roslindale Boston 6 B3
Rosny-sous-Bois Paris 24 A4
Rosslyn Washington 33 B3
Rosyth Edinburgh 11 A1
Rotherhithe London 15 B3

Rothneusiedl Vienna 32 B2
Rothschmaige Munich 21 A1
Rouge Hill Toronto 31 A4
Round I. Hong Kong 12 B2
Roxbury Boston 6 A2
Roxeth London 15 A1
Royal Botanic Gardens
 Edinburgh 11 B2
Royal Observatory
 Edinburgh 11 B3
Royal Palace = Kungliga
 Slottet Stockholm 29 B2
Royal Palace = Palacio
 Real Madrid 17 B1
Royal Park Melbourne 18 A1
Roztoky Prague 25 B2
Rozzano Milan 19 B1
Rubi → Barcelona 4 A1
Rudolfsheim Vienna 32 A1
Rudolfshöhe Berlin 5 A5
Rudow Berlin 5 B3
Rueil-Malmaison Paris 24 A2
Ruisbroek Brussels 6 B1
Ruislip London 15 A1
Rumelihisari Istanbul 12 B2
Rungis Paris 24 B3
Rusáfa Baghdad 3 B2
Rush Green London 15 A5
Russa Kolkata 14 B2
Rutherford New York 22 B1
Ruzynė Prague 25 B1
Ruzyne, Praha ✈ (PRG)
 Prague 25 B1
Rybatskaya St. Petersburg 27 B2
Rydboholm Stockholm 29 A3
Ryde Sydney 29 A1
Ryogoku Tokyo 30 A3
Rzhevka St. Petersburg 27 B3

S

Sa'ädatäbäd Tehran 31 A2
Saadün Baghdad 3 B2
Saavedra Buenos Aires 7 B2
Saboli Delhi 10 A2
Sabugo Lisbon 16 A1
Sabzî Mand Delhi 10 A2
Sacavém Lisbon 16 A2
Saclay Paris 24 B2
Saclay, Étang de Paris 24 B2
Sacomã São Paulo 27 B2
Sacré Cœur Paris 24 A3
Sacrow Berlin 5 B1
Sacrower See Berlin 5 B1
Sadang Seoul 27 B1
Saddle Brook New York 22 A1
Saddle → New York 22 A1
Sadr Karachi 13 A2
Sadr City Baghdad 3 A2
Sadyba Warsaw 32 B2
Safdar Jang's Tomb Delhi 10 B2
Saft el Laban Cairo 7 A2
Saganashkee Slough Chicago 9 C1
Sagene Oslo 23 A3
Sagrada Familia, Templo
 de Barcelona 4 A2
Sahar, Mumbai ✈ (BOM)
 Mumbai 20 A2
Sai Kung Hong Kong 12 A2
Sai Wan Ho Hong Kong 12 B2
Sai Ying Pun Hong Kong 12 B1
St-Aubin Paris 24 B2
St-Cloud Paris 24 A2
St-Cyr-l'École Paris 24 B1
St-Cyr-l'École ✈ Paris 24 B1
St-Denis Paris 24 A3
St-Germain, Forêt de Paris 24 A1
St-Germain-en-Laye Paris 24 A1
St-Gilles Brussels 6 B2
St. Helier London 15 B2
St-Hubert Montreal 20 B3
St. Isaac's Cathedral
 St. Petersburg 27 B1
St-Jacques → Montreal 20 B3
St-Joost-Ten-Node Brussels 6 A2
St. Kilda Melbourne 18 B1
St-Lambert Montreal 20 A3
St-Lambert Paris 24 B1
St-Laurent Montreal 20 A1
St-Léonard Montreal 20 A2
St. Magelungen Stockholm 29 B2
St-Mandé Paris 24 A3
St. Margaret's Dublin 10 A2
St-Martin, Bois Paris 24 B4
St. Mary Cray London 15 B4
St-Maur-des-Fossés Paris 24 A3
St-Maurice Paris 24 A3
St-Michel Montreal 20 A2
St. Nikolaus-Kirken Prague 25 B2
St-Ouen Paris 24 A3
St. Paul's Cray London 15 B4
St. Peters Sydney 29 B2
St. Peter's Square = San
 Pietro, Piazza di Rome 26 B1
St. Petersburg = Sankt-
 Peterburg St. Petersburg 27 B2
St. Petersburg Pulkovo
 Int. ✈ (LED) St. Petersburg 27 C1
St-Pierre Montreal 20 B2
St-Pieters Leew Brussels 6 B1
St-Quentin, Étang de Paris 24 B1
St. Stephens Cathedral =
 Stephansdom Vienna 32 A2
St-Stevens-Woluwe Brussels 6 A2
St-Vincent-de-Paul
 Montreal 20 A2
St. Xavier Univ. Chicago 9 C2
Ste-Catherine Montreal 20 B2
Ste-Hélène, Î. Montreal 20 A2
Saiwai Tokyo 30 B3
Sakai Osaka 23 B2
Sakai Harbour Osaka 23 B1
Sakra, Pulau Singapore 28 B2
Salam Baghdad 3 B2
Salamanca Madrid 17 B1
Sallynoggin Dublin 10 B3
Salmannsdorf Vienna 32 A1
Salmedina Madrid 17 C2
Salomea Warsaw 32 B1
Salsette I. Mumbai 20 A2
Salt Lake City = Bidhan
 Nagar Kolkata 14 B2
Salt River Cape Town 8 A1
Salt Water I. Mumbai 20 A2
Saltsjö-Duvnäs Stockholm 29 B3
Samatya Istanbul 12 C1
Sampaloc Manila 17 B1
Samphan Thawong Bangkok 3 B2
Samseon Seoul 27 B2
Samuel Smith Park Toronto 31 B1
Samut Prakan Bangkok 3 B2
San Andrés Mexico City 18 C1
San Angel Mexico City 18 B1
San Basilio Rome 26 B2
San Borja Lima 14 B3

Sarandi Buenos Aires 7 C2
Saraswati → Kolkata 14 A1
Sarecky potok → Prague 25 B2
Sarimbun Res. Singapore 28 A2
Sarimbun Res. Singapore 28 A2
Sariyer Istanbul 12 B2
Sarriá Barcelona 4 A1
Sartrouville Paris 24 A2
Sasad Budapest 7 B2
Sashalom Budapest 7 A3
Saska Warsaw 32 B2
Satpukur Kolkata 14 B2
Satra Stockholm 29 B1
Saúde São Paulo 27 B2
Saugus Boston 6 A2
Saugus → Boston 6 A2
Sault-au-Récollet Montreal 20 A2
Sausalito San Francisco 26 A2
Sawah Besar Jakarta 12 A1
Sawtelle Los Angeles 16 B2
Scald Law Edinburgh 11 B2
Scarborough Toronto 31 A3
Scarborough Bluffs Toronto 31 A3
Sceaux Paris 24 B2
Schaerbeek Brussels 6 A2
Scharfenberg Berlin 5 A2
Schiller Park Chicago 9 B1
Schiller Woods Chicago 9 B1
Schinkel Berlin 5 A1
Schiphol, Amsterdam ✈
 (AMS) Amsterdam 2 B1
Schlachtensee Berlin 5 B2
Schlossgarten Berlin 5 A2
Schmargendorf Berlin 5 B2
Schöneberg Berlin 5 B3
Schönblick Berlin 5 B5
Schönbrunn Vienna 32 A1
Schöneberg Berlin 5 B3
Schönefeld Berlin 5 B4
Schöneiche Berlin 5 B5
Schönwalde Berlin 5 A1
Schulzendorf Berlin 5 A2
Schwabing Munich 21 B2
Schwanebeck Berlin 5 A4
Schwanenwerder Berlin 5 B2
Schwarzackenau Vienna 32 A2
Schwechat Vienna 32 B2
Schwechat, Wien ✈ (VIE)
 Vienna 32 B3
Science and Industry,
 Museum of Chicago 9 C3
Scitrek Museum Atlanta 3 B2
Scopus, Mt. Jerusalem 13 B2
Scottdale Atlanta 3 B3
Sea Point Cape Town 8 A1
Seabrook Washington 33 B5
Seaburn Berlin 5 A1
Seacliff San Francisco 26 B2
Seaforth Sydney 29 A2
Seagate New York 22 C1
Seat Pleasant Washington 33 B4
Seaview Wellington 33 B2
SeaWorld Orlando 23 B2
Secaucus New York 22 B1
Seddinsee Berlin 5 B5
Seeberg Berlin 5 A5
Seeburg Berlin 5 A1
Seefeld Berlin 5 A5
Seehof Berlin 5 B1
Segeltorp Stockholm 29 B1
Segrate Milan 19 B2
Seguro Milan 19 B1
Seixal Lisbon 16 B2
Selby Johannesburg 13 B2
Seletar, Pulau Singapore 28 A3
Seletar Hills Singapore 28 A3
Seletar Res. Singapore 28 A2
Selhurst London 15 B3
Sembawang Singapore 28 A2
Senago Milan 19 A1
Sendling Munich 21 B2
Senju Tokyo 30 A3
Senriyama Osaka 23 A2
Sentosa Singapore 28 B2
Seobinggo Seoul 27 B1
Seocho Seoul 27 C1
Seodaemun Seoul 27 B1
Seokkwan Seoul 27 B2
Seongbuk Seoul 27 B2
Seongsu Seoul 27 B2
Seoul Nat. Univ. Seoul 27 C1
Seoul Tower Seoul 27 B1
Sepolia Athens 2 A2
Sepulveda Dam Rec.
 Area Los Angeles 16 A2
Serangoon Singapore 28 A3
Serangoon, Pulau Singapore 28 A3
Serangoon, Sungei →
 Singapore 28 A3
Serangoon Harbour
 Singapore 28 A3
Seraya, Pulau Singapore 28 B2
Serebryanka → Moscow 19 B3
Serramonte San Francisco 26 C2
Sesto San Giovanni Milan 19 A2
Sesto Ulteriano Milan 19 B2
Setagaya Tokyo 30 B3
Seter Oslo 23 A3
Setia Budi Jakarta 12 B2
Setebagni Rome 26 A2
Settecamini Rome 26 B2
Séttimo Milanese Milan 19 B1
Seutula Helsinki 11 A2
Seven Corners Washington 33 B3
Seven Kings London 15 A4
Seventeenth Street Canal
 New Orleans 21 A2
Sévesco → Milan 19 A1
Sevran Paris 24 A4
Sewri Mumbai 20 B2
Sforzesso, Castello Milan 19 B2
Sha Kok Mei Hong Kong 12 A2
Sha Tin Hong Kong 12 A2
Sha'ar Binyamin Jerusalem 13 A2
Shabrämant Cairo 7 B1
Shah Mosque Tehran 31 A2
Shahdara Delhi 10 A2
Shahe Guangzhou 11 B2
Shahr-e Rey Tehran 31 B2
Shahrak-e Golshahr Tehran 31 A2
Shahrak-e Qods Tehran 31 A2
Shaikh Aomar Baghdad 3 B2
Shakurbasti Delhi 10 A1
Shalkiya Kolkata 14 B2
Sham Shui Po Hong Kong 12 A1
Shamian Guangzhou 11 B2
Sham Mei Hong Kong 12 A2
Shanghai Shanghai 28 B1
Shanghai Hongqiao ✈
 (SHA) Shanghai 28 B1
Shanghai Pudong ✈
 (PVG) Shanghai 28 B2
Shankill Dublin 10 B3
Sharp I. Hong Kong 12 A2

Shastrinagar Delhi 10 A2
Shau Kei Wan Hong Kong 12 B2
Shawocun Beijing 4 B1
Shayuan Guangzhou 11 B2
Sheen, L. Edinburgh 11 B2
Sheepshead Bay New York 22 C2
Shek O Hong Kong 12 B2
Shelter I. Hong Kong 12 B2
Shepherds Bush London 15 A2
Shepperton London 15 B1
Sheremetyevo ✈ (SVO)
 Moscow 19 B2
Sherman Oaks Los Angeles 16 B2
Sherman Park Chicago 9 C2
Sherwood, L. Orlando 23 B3
Shet Bandar Mumbai 20 A2
Sheung Fa Shan Hong Kong 12 A1
Sheung Lau Wan
 Hong Kong 12 B2
Sheung Wan Hong Kong 12 B1
Sheva Mumbai 20 B2
Sheva Nhava Mumbai 20 B2
Shiba Tokyo 30 B3
Shibpur Kolkata 14 B1
Shibuya Tokyo 30 B3
Shilihe Beijing 4 B2
Shimogawara Tokyo 30 A4
Shimosalo Tokyo 30 A4
Shimoshakuiji Tokyo 30 A2
Shinagawa Tokyo 30 B3
Shing Mun Res. Hong Kong 12 A1
Shinjuku Tokyo 30 A3
Shinjuku Nat. Garden
 Tokyo 30 A3
Shinkoiwa Tokyo 30 A4
Shinnakano Tokyo 30 A3
Shipai Guangzhou 11 B3
Shirinashi → Osaka 23 B1
Shirogane Tokyo 30 B3
Shitennoji Temple Osaka 23 B2
Shiweitang Guangzhou 11 B2
Shogunle Lagos 14 B2
Shomolu Lagos 14 B2
Shooters Hill London 15 B4
Shoreditch London 15 A3
Shortlands London 15 B4
Shu'afat Jerusalem 13 B2
Shubrâ Cairo 7 A2
Shubrâ el Kheima Cairo 7 A2
Shuikuo Guangzhou 11 A2
Sidcup London 15 B4
Siebenhirten Vienna 32 B1
Siedlung Berlin 5 A1
Siekierki Warsaw 32 B2
Sielce Warsaw 32 B2
Siemensstadt Berlin 5 A2
Sierra Madre Los Angeles 16 B5
Sievering Vienna 32 A2
Sighthill Edinburgh 11 B2
Signal Hill Cape Town 8 A1
Siheung Seoul 27 C1
Sikátorpuszta Budapest 7 A3
Silampur Delhi 10 B2
Silver, L. Orlando 23 A2
Silver, L. Orlando 23 A3
Silver Hill Washington 33 C4
Silver Lake Los Angeles 16 B3
Silver Spring Washington 33 B3
Silvermine Nature
 Reserve Cape Town 8 B1
Silvolantekojärvi Helsinki 11 B2
Simei Singapore 28 A3
Simla Kolkata 14 B2
Simmering Vienna 32 A2
Simmering Heide Vienna 32 A2
Simonkylä Helsinki 11 B3
Sinchon Seoul 27 B1
Sindang Seoul 27 B2
Singapore ■ Singapore 28 A2
Singapore, Univ. of
 Singapore 28 B2
Singapore Changi ✈ (SIN)
 Singapore 28 A3
Sinki, Selat Singapore 28 B2
Sinsa Seoul 27 B2
Sint-Genesius-Rode Brussels 6 B2
Sion Mumbai 20 A2
Sipson London 15 B1
Sişli Istanbul 12 B1
Skansen Stockholm 29 B2
Skärholmen Stockholm 29 B1
Skarpäng Stockholm 29 A2
Skarpnäck Stockholm 29 B2
Skaryszewski, Park
 Warsaw 32 B2
Skokie Chicago 9 A2
Skokie → Chicago 9 A2
Skokie Heritage Museum
 Chicago 9 A2
Skoklefall Chicago 9 A2
Sköndal Stockholm 29 B2
Skovlunde Copenhagen 8 A2
Skovshoved Copenhagen 8 A3
Skuru Stockholm 29 B3
Sky Lake Orlando 23 B2
Skyland Atlanta 3 A3
Slade Green London 15 B5
Slependen Oslo 23 A2
Slipi Jakarta 12 B1
Slivenec Prague 25 B2
Sloten Amsterdam 2 A1
Sloterdijk Amsterdam 2 A1
Sloterpark Amsterdam 2 A1
Sluhy Prague 25 B2
Służew Warsaw 32 B2
Służewiec Warsaw 32 B2
Smíchov Prague 25 B2
Smith Forest Preserve
 Chicago 9 B1
Smolny St. Petersburg 27 B2
Smolny Cathedral
 St. Petersburg 27 B2
Snake Creek Canal Miami 18 A2
Snakeden Branch →
 Washington 33 B1
Snarøya Oslo 23 A2
Snättringe Stockholm 29 B1
Søborg Copenhagen 8 A2
Sobreda Lisbon 16 B1
Söderby Stockholm 29 A2
Södermalm Stockholm 29 B2
Sodpur Kolkata 14 A2
Soeurs, Î. des Montreal 20 B2
Sognsvatn Oslo 23 A3
Soignes, Forêt de Brussels 6 B2
Sok Kwu Wan Hong Kong 12 B1
Sokolniki Moscow 19 B3
Sokolniki Park Moscow 19 B3
Sokołów Warsaw 32 C1
Solalinden Munich 21 B3
Sollentuna Stockholm 29 A1
Solln Munich 21 B2
Solna Stockholm 29 A1
Somerset Washington 33 B3
Somerville Boston 6 A3
Somes I. Wellington 33 B2
Sonari Mumbai 20 B2
Sønderso Copenhagen 8 A2
Songnei Guangzhou 11 A2
Sony Picture Studio
 Los Angeles 16 B2

Sord = Swords Dublin 10 A2
Soroksár Budapest 7 B2
Soroksari Duna → Budapest 7 B2
Sosenka → Moscow 19 B3
Sosnovka St. Petersburg 27 B2
Sŏul = Seoul Seoul 27 B2
Soundview New York 22 B2
South Beach New York 22 C1
South Bend Park Atlanta 3 B2
South Boston Boston 6 B2
South Decatur Atlanta 3 B3
South Deering Chicago 9 C3
South El Monte Los Angeles 16 B4
South Gate Los Angeles 16 C3
South Harbor Manila 17 B1
South Harrow London 15 A1
South Hd. Sydney 29 B2
South Hills Johannesburg 13 B2
South Lawn Washington 33 C3
South Miami Miami 18 B1
South Norwood London 15 B3
South of Market
San Francisco 26 B2
South Ozone Park
New York 22 B3
South Pasadena Los Angeles 16 B4
South Res. Boston 6 A2
South Ruislip London 15 A1
South San Francisco
San Francisco 26 C2
South San Gabriel
Los Angeles 16 B4
South Shore Chicago 9 C3
Southall London 15 A1
Southborough London 15 B4
Southend London 15 B3
Southern California, Univ.
of Los Angeles 16 B3
Southfields London 15 B2
Southport New Orleans 21 B2
Southwark □ London 15 B3
Southwest Museum
Los Angeles 16 B3
Søvang Copenhagen 8 B3
Soweto Johannesburg 13 B1
Sowhānak Tehran 31 A3
Soya Tokyo 30 A4
Spandau Berlin 5 A1
Spånga Stockholm 29 A1
Spanish Monastery Miami 18 A2
Spectacle I. Boston 6 A3
Speicher-See Munich 21 A3
Speising Vienna 32 B1
Sphinx Cairo 7 B1
Spinaceto Rome 26 C1
Spit Junction Sydney 29 A2
Spořilov Prague 25 B3
Spot Pond Boston 6 A2
Spotswood Melbourne 18 B1
Spring Valley Las Vegas 14 B1
Springeberg Berlin 5 B5
Springfield Washington 33 C2
Squantum Boston 6 B2
Srednaya Rogatka
St. Petersburg 27 C2
Środmieście Warsaw 32 B2
Staaken Berlin 5 A1
Stabekk Oslo 23 A2
Stadlau Vienna 32 A2
Stadshuset Stockholm 29 B2
Stains Paris 24 A3
Stamford Hill London 15 A3
Stammersdorf Vienna 32 A2
Stanley Hong Kong 12 B2
Stanley Pen. Hong Kong 12 B2
Stanmore London 15 A2
Stapleton New York 22 C1
Staraya Derevnya
St. Petersburg 27 B1
Staré Město Prague 25 B2
Stare Miasto Warsaw 32 B2
Starke, L. Orlando 23 A1
Staten Island Zoo New York 22 C1
Staten Islands Ferry
Terminal New York 22 C1
Statenice Prague 25 B1
Stedelijk Museum
Amsterdam 2 A2
Steele Creek Melbourne 18 A1
Steenokkerzeel Brussels 6 A2
Steer, L. Orlando 23 A2
Steglitz Berlin 5 B3
Stepaside Dublin 10 B2
Stephansdom Vienna 32 A2
Stepney London 15 A3
Sterling Park San Francisco 26 B2
Stickling udde Stockholm 29 A2
Stickney Chicago 9 C2
Stillorgan Dublin 10 B2
Stockholm Stockholm 29 B2
Stockholm Arlanda ✈
(ARN) Stockholm 29 A1
Stocksund Stockholm 29 A2
Stodůlky Prague 25 B1
Stoke Newington London 15 A3
Stokes Valley Wellington 33 B2
Stone Canyon Res.
Los Angeles 16 B2
Stone Park Chicago 9 B1
Stonebridge London 15 A2
Stoneham Boston 6 A2
Stony Brook Res. Boston 6 B2
Stony Creek → Chicago 9 C2
Stora Värtan Stockholm 29 A2
Store Hareskov Copenhagen 8 A2
Store Magleby Copenhagen 8 B3
Storholmen Stockholm 29 A2
Stoyka St. Petersburg 27 B2
Straiton Edinburgh 11 B3
Strandfontein Cape Town 8 B2
Strašnice Prague 25 B2
Strasstrudering Munich 21 B3
Stratford London 15 A4
Strathfield Sydney 29 B1
Streatham London 15 B3
Streatham Vale London 15 B3
Strebersdorf Vienna 32 A2
Střešovice Prague 25 B2
Strip, The Las Vegas 14 B2
Střížkov Prague 25 B2
Strombeek-Bever Brussels 6 A2
Stromovka Prague 25 B2
Studio City Los Angeles 16 B2
Stureby Stockholm 29 B2
Stuvsta Stockholm 29 B2
Subhepur Delhi 10 A2
Suburban Canal
New Orleans 21 B1
Sucat Manila 17 C2
Suchdol Prague 25 B2
Sucy-en-Brie Paris 24 B4
Sue, L. Orlando 23 A2
Sugamo Tokyo 30 A3
Sugar Loaf Mt. = Açúcar,
Pão de Rio de Janeiro 25 B2
Suge Tokyo 30 B2
Suginami Tokyo 30 A2
Sugō Tokyo 30 B2
Sui Sai Wan Hong Kong 12 B1
Suita Osaka 23 A2
Suitland Washington 33 B4
Sukchar Kolkata 14 A2
Sultanahme Camil Istanbul 12 B1
Sumida Tokyo 30 A3
Sumida → Tokyo 30 A3
Sumiyoshi Osaka 23 B2
Sumiyoshi Shrine Osaka 23 B1
Summerville Toronto 31 B1
Summit Chicago 9 C2
Sunamachi Tokyo 30 A4
Sunbury-on-Thames
London 15 B1
Sundbyberg Stockholm 29 A1
Sundbyerne Copenhagen 8 B3
Sung Kong Hong Kong 12 B2
Sungei Kadut Industrial
Estate Singapore 28 A2
Sungei Selatar Res.
Singapore 28 A3
Sunrise Manor Las Vegas 14 A2
Sunrise Mountain Natural
Area Las Vegas 14 A2
Sunset Park Las Vegas 14 B2
Sunset Park New York 22 B2
Sunter Jakarta 12 A2
Sunter, Kali → Jakarta 12 B2
Suomenlinna Helsinki 11 C2
Sur Bahr Jerusalem 13 B2
Sura Kolkata 14 B2
Suraksan Seoul 27 A2
Suresnes Paris 24 A2
Surfside Miami 18 A2
Surquillo Lima 14 B2
Surrey Hills Sydney 29 B2
Susaek Seoul 27 B1
Süssenbrunn Vienna 32 A2
Sutton Dublin 10 A3
Sutton London 15 B2
Suyu Seoul 27 B2
Suzukishinden Tokyo 30 A2
Svanemøllen Copenhagen 8 A3
Sveaborg = Suomenlinna
Helsinki 11 C2
Sverdlov Moscow 19 B2
Svestad Oslo 23 B2
Svinö Helsinki 11 C1
Swanley London 15 B4
Swansea Toronto 31 B2
Swinburne I. New York 22 C1
Swords Dublin 10 A2
Sydenham Johannesburg 13 A2
Sydney Sydney 29 B2
Sydney, Univ. of Sydney 29 B2
Sydney Harbour △ Sydney 29 B2
Sydney Harbour Bridge
Sydney 29 B2
Sydney Kingsford Smith ✈
(SYD) Sydney 29 B2
Sydstranden Copenhagen 8 B3
Sylvania Sydney 29 C1
Syon Park London 15 B2
Szczęśliwice Warsaw 32 B1
Széchnenyi-hegy Budapest 7 B1
Széphalom Budapest 7 A1

T

Taastrup Copenhagen 8 B1
Tabata Tokyo 30 A3
Tablada Buenos Aires 7 C1
Table B. Cape Town 8 A1
Table Mountain △
Cape Town 8 A1
Table Mt. Cape Town 8 A1
Taboão da Serra São Paulo 27 B1
Täby Stockholm 29 A2
Tacuba Mexico City 18 B1
Tacubaya Mexico City 18 B1
Tafelbaai = Table B.
Cape Town 8 A1
Taft Orlando 23 B2
Tagig → Manila 17 B2
Taguig Manila 17 B2
Tai Lo Shan Hong Kong 12 A2
Tai Po Tsai Hong Kong 12 A2
Tai Seng Singapore 28 A3
Tai Shui Hang Hong Kong 12 A2
Tai Tam B. Hong Kong 12 B2
Tai Tam Tuk Res.
Hong Kong 12 B2
Tai Wai Hong Kong 12 A2
Tai Wan Tau Hong Kong 12 B2
Tai Wo Hau Hong Kong 12 A1
Tainaka Osaka 23 B2
Taishō Osaka 23 B1
Taita Wellington 33 B2
Tajrish Tehran 31 A2
Takaido Tokyo 30 A2
Takaishi Tokyo 30 B2
Takarazuka Osaka 23 A1
Takasago Tokyo 30 A4
Takatsu Tokyo 30 B2
Takeshita Tokyo 30 B2
Takinegawa Tokyo 30 A3
Takoma Park Washington 33 B3
Taksim Istanbul 12 B1
Talaide Lisbon 16 A1
Taliganga Kolkata 14 B2
Talipapa Manila 17 A2
Tallaght Dublin 10 B1
Tallkrogen Stockholm 29 B2
Tama Tokyo 30 B1
Tama → Tokyo 30 B2
Tama Kyūryō Tokyo 30 B2
Tamaden Tokyo 30 B2
Tamagawa-josui → Tokyo 30 A1
Taman Sari Jakarta 12 A1
Tamanduateí → São Paulo 27 B2
Tamboerskloof Cape Town 8 A1
Tambora Jakarta 12 A1
Tammisalo Helsinki 11 B3
Tammūh Cairo 7 B2
Tampines Singapore 28 A3
Tanah Abang Jakarta 12 B1
Tanah Kusir Jakarta 12 B1
Tangelo Park Orlando 23 B2
Tanjung Duren Jakarta 12 B1
Tanjung Priok Jakarta 12 A2
Tanum Oslo 23 A1
Tapada Lisbon 16 A1
Tapanila Helsinki 11 B3
Tapiales Buenos Aires 7 C1
Tapiola Helsinki 11 B1
Tapsia Kolkata 14 B2
Tara Mumbai 20 A1
Tarabya Istanbul 12 B2
Tårbæk Copenhagen 8 A3
Tarchomin Warsaw 32 B1
Tardeo Mumbai 20 B1
Targówek Warsaw 32 B2
Tårnby Copenhagen 8 B3
Tarqua Bay Lagos 14 B2
Tathong Channel
Hong Kong 12 B2
Tathong Pt. Hong Kong 12 B2
Tatuapé São Paulo 27 B2
Taufkirchen Munich 21 B2
Tavares, I. dos Rio de Janeiro 25 A2
Tavros Athens 2 B2
Tawa Wellington 33 A1
Te Papa Museum
Wellington 33 B1
Teaneck New York 22 A1
Tebet Jakarta 12 B2
Tecamachalco Mexico City 18 B1
Ted Williams Tunnel Boston 6 A2
Teddington London 15 B1
Tegel Berlin 5 A2
Tegel, Berlin ✈ (TXL) Berlin 5 A2
Tegeler See Berlin 5 A2
Tegelort Berlin 5 A2
Teheran = Tehrān Tehran 31 A2
Tehrān Tehran 31 A2
Tehrān Mehrābād ✈
(THR) Tehran 31 A1
Tehrān Pārs Tehran 31 A3
Tei Tong Tsui Hong Kong 12 B2
Tejo, Rio → Lisbon 16 A2
Tekstilyshchik Moscow 19 B3
Telhal Lisbon 16 A1
Telok Blangah Singapore 28 B2
Teltow Berlin 5 B2
Teltow kanal Berlin 5 B3
Tempelhof Berlin 5 B3
Temple City Los Angeles 16 B4
Temple Hills Washington 33 C4
Temple of Heaven Beijing 4 B2
Templeogue Dublin 10 B2
Temppeliaukio Church
Helsinki 11 B2
Tenafly New York 22 A2
Tenayuca, Piramide de
Mexico City 18 A1
Tengah → Singapore 28 A2
Tennoji Osaka 23 B2
Tepalcates Mexico City 18 B2
Tepeyac △ Mexico City 18 B2
Terrazzano Milan 19 A1
Terre des Hommes Montreal 20 A2
Terrugem Lisbon 16 A1
Terrytown New Orleans 21 B2
Tervuren Brussels 6 B3
Tervuren, Park van Brussels 6 B3
Tetuán Madrid 17 B1
Teufelsberg Berlin 5 B2
Thalkirchen Munich 21 B2
Thames Ditton London 15 B1
Thamesmead London 15 A4
Thana Cr. → Mumbai 20 A2
Thiais Paris 24 B3
Thisio Athens 2 B2
Thistletown Toronto 31 A1
Thomastown Melbourne 18 A2
Thompson I. Boston 6 B3
Thon Buri Bangkok 3 B1
Thornbury Melbourne 18 A2
Thorncliffe Toronto 31 A2
Thornhill Toronto 31 A2
Thornton Cape Town 8 A2
Thornton Heath London 15 B3
Threipmuir Res. Edinburgh 11 B2
Throgs Neck New York 22 B3
Tiancun Beijing 4 B1
Tianhe Guangzhou 11 B3
Tibet, L. Orlando 23 B1
Tibidabo Barcelona 4 A1
Tibradden Mt. Dublin 10 B2
Tiburon San Francisco 26 A2
Tiburtino Rome 26 B2
Ticomán Mexico City 18 A2
Tiefersee Berlin 5 B1
Tiergarten Berlin 5 A3
Tijgerhof Cape Town 8 A2
Tijuca Rio de Janeiro 25 B1
Tijuca, Pico da Rio de Janeiro 25 B1
Tijuca △ Rio de Janeiro 25 B1
Tikkurila Helsinki 11 B3
Tilak Nagar Delhi 10 B1
Tilanqiao Shanghai 28 B1
Timah, Bukit Singapore 28 A2
Timiryazev Park Moscow 19 B2
Tin Can I. Lagos 14 B2
Ting Kau Hong Kong 12 A1
Tira Jerusalem 13 A1
Tirsa Cairo 7 B2
Tishrīyaa Baghdad 3 B2
Tiu Keng Leng Hong Kong 12 B2
Tizapán Mexico City 18 C1
Tlalnepantla → Mexico City 18 A1
Tlalpan Mexico City 18 C2
To Kwai Wan Hong Kong 12 B2
Toa Payoh Singapore 28 A3
Točná Prague 25 C2
Toco Hills Atlanta 3 B2
Todt Hill New York 22 C1
Tōkagi Tokyo 30 A4
Tokai Plantation Cape Town 8 B1
Tōkaichiba Tokyo 30 B2
Tōkyō Tokyo 30 B3
Tōkyō B. = Tōkyō-Wan
Tokyo 30 B4
Tōkyō Disneyland Tokyo 30 B4
Tōkyō Haneda ✈ (HND)
Tokyo 30 B3
Tōkyō Harbour Tokyo 30 B3
Tōkyō-Wan Tokyo 30 B4
Tolka → Dublin 10 A1
Tollygunge = Taliganga
Kolkata 14 B2
Tolworth London 15 B2
Tomba di Nerone Rome 26 B1
Tommy Thompson Park
Toronto 31 B3
Tondo Manila 17 B1
Tongbinggo Seoul 27 B1
Tongqiao Shanghai 28 A1
Toorak Melbourne 18 B2
Topanga State Park ⌂
Los Angeles 16 B1
Topkapı Istanbul 12 B1
Topkapı Palaca Istanbul 12 B1
Tor di Quinto Rome 26 B1
Tor Pignattara Rome 26 B2
Tor Sapienza Rome 26 B2
Torcy Paris 24 A4
Toronto Toronto 31 B2
Toronto, Univ. of Toronto 31 B2
Toronto City Centre ✈
(YTZ) Toronto 31 B2
Toronto Harbour Toronto 31 B2
Toronto I. Toronto 31 B2
Toronto Lester B. Pearson
Int. ✈ (YYZ) Toronto 31 A1
Torre Lupara Rome 26 B2
Torre Nova Rome 26 B2
Torrellas → Barcelona 4 A1
Torrevècchia Rome 26 B1
Toshima Tokyo 30 A3
Toshimaen Tokyo 30 A2
Tottenham London 15 A3
Tottenham Melbourne 18 A1
Toussus-le-Noble Paris 24 B1
Toussus-le-Noble ✈ (TNF)
Paris 24 B1
Towchāl Cable Car Tehran 31 A2
Tower Hamlets □ London 15 A3
Tower of London London 15 A3
Towra Pt. Sydney 29 C2
Tøyen Oslo 23 A3
Toyonaka Osaka 23 A1
Trafaria Lisbon 16 A1
Traição, Cor. → São Paulo 27 B2
Tranegilde Copenhagen 8 B2
Trångsund Stockholm 29 B2
Trappenfelde Berlin 5 A4
Trastévere Rome 26 B1
Treasure I. San Francisco 26 B2
Třeboradice Prague 25 B3
Třebotov Prague 25 C1
Tremblay-en-France Paris 24 A4
Tremembe → São Paulo 27 A2
Tremont New York 22 A2
Trenno Milan 19 B1
Treptow Berlin 5 B3
Três Rios, Sa. dos
Rio de Janeiro 25 B1
Trevi, Fontana di Rome 26 B1
Trezzano sul Navíglio Milan 19 B1
Trieste Rome 26 B2
Trinidad Washington 33 B4
Trinity Edinburgh 11 B2
Trinity College Dublin 10 A2
Trionfale Rome 26 B1
Triulzo Milan 19 B2
Troja Prague 25 B2
Trollbäcken Stockholm 29 B3
Trombay Mumbai 20 A2
Troparevo Moscow 19 C1
Trudeau, Montréal ✈
(YUL) Montreal 20 B1
Trudyashchikhsya,
Ostrov St. Petersburg 27 B1
Tryvasshøgda Oslo 23 A3
Tseng Lan Shue Hong Kong 12 A2
Tseung Kwan Hong Kong 12 B2
Tsim Sha Tsui Hong Kong 12 B2
Tsing Yi Hong Kong 12 A1
Tsova Jerusalem 13 B1
Tsuen Wan Hong Kong 12 A1
Tsur Hadassa Jerusalem 13 B1
Tsurumi → Tokyo 30 B3
Tsz Wan Shan Hong Kong 12 A2
Tuas Singapore 28 B1
Tuchoměřice Prague 25 B1
Tuckahoe New York 22 A3
Tucuruvi São Paulo 27 A2
Tufello Rome 26 B2
Tufnell Park London 15 A3
Tufts Univ. Boston 6 A2
Tughlakabad Delhi 10 B2
Tullamarine Melbourne 18 A1
Tulse Hill London 15 B3
Tung Lung Chau Hong Kong 12 B2
Tung O Hong Kong 12 B1
Tunis Baghdad 3 A2
Tuomarila Helsinki 11 B1
Tureberg Stockholm 29 A1
Turffontein Johannesburg 13 B2
Turkey L. Orlando 23 B1
Turkey Lake Park Orlando 23 A2
Turner Field Atlanta 3 B2
Turnham Green London 15 B2
Turnhouse Edinburgh 11 B1
Tuscolana, Via Rome 26 B2
Twelve Apostles Cape Town 8 A1
Twentieth Century Fox
Studios Los Angeles 16 B2
Twickenham London 15 B1
Twickenham Rugby
Ground London 15 B1
Twin Peaks San Francisco 26 B2
Two Rock Mt. Dublin 10 B2
Tymon North Dublin 10 B1
Tysons Corner Washington 33 B2

U

U.S. Capitol Washington 33 B3
U.S. Cellular Field Chicago 9 C3
Ubeidiya Jerusalem 13 B2
Uberaba → São Paulo 27 B2
Ubin, Pulau Singapore 28 A3
Uccle Brussels 6 B2
Udelnaya St. Petersburg 27 A2
Udelnoe St. Petersburg 27 B1
Udlding Munich 21 A1
Ueno Tokyo 30 A3
Úholičky Prague 25 B1
Uhříněves Prague 25 B3
Uithoorn Amsterdam 2 B1
Ujazdów Warsaw 32 B2
Újpalota Budapest 7 A2
Újpest Budapest 7 A2
Ukita Tokyo 30 A4
Ullerup Copenhagen 8 B3
Ullevål Oslo 23 A3
Ulriksdal Stockholm 29 A1
Ulyanka St. Petersburg 27 B1
Um Al-Khanazir Island
Baghdad 3 B2
Umeda Osaka 23 A1
Ümraniye Istanbul 12 B2
Underground Atlanta
Atlanta 3 B2
Underhill, L. Orlando 23 A3
Unětický potok → Prague 25 B2
Unhos Lisbon 16 A2
Unidad Santa Fe
Mexico City 18 B1
Union City New York 22 B1
Union Port New York 22 B2
Union Station Toronto 31 B2
United Center Chicago 9 B2
United Nations
Headquarters New York 22 B2
Universal Studios
Los Angeles 16 B2
Universal Studios Orlando 23 B2
Universidad Madrid 17 B1
University Park Washington 33 B4
Unterbiberg Munich 21 B2
Unterföhring Munich 21 A3
Unterhaching Munich 21 B2
Unterlaa Vienna 32 B2
Untermenzing Munich 21 A1
Upper B. New York 22 B1
Upper Elmers End London 15 B3
Upper New York B. =
Upper B. New York 22 C1
Upper Norwood London 15 B3
Upper Peirce Res. Singapore 28 A2
Upper Sydenham London 15 B3
Upper Tooting London 15 B3
Upton London 15 A4
Uptown Chicago 9 B2
Uran Mumbai 20 B2
Urayasu Tokyo 30 B4
Urbe ✈ Rome 26 B2
Urca Rio de Janeiro 25 B2
Uritsk St. Petersburg 27 C1
Úrōm Budapest 7 A2
Ursus Warsaw 32 B1
Ursvik Stockholm 29 A1
Usera Madrid 17 B1
Ushigome Tokyo 30 A3
Usina Rio de Janeiro 25 B1
Üsküdar Istanbul 12 B2
Ust-Slavyanka
St. Petersburg 27 C3
Uteke Stockholm 29 A3
Utrata Warsaw 32 B2
Uttarpara Kolkata 14 B1
Utterslev Mose Copenhagen 8 A2

V

Vaclavské náměstí Prague 25 B2
Vadaul Mumbai 20 A2
Vaires-sur-Marne Paris 24 A4
Valby Copenhagen 8 B2
Valcannuta Rome 26 B1
Valdelatas Madrid 17 A1
Vale Washington 33 B1
Valenton Paris 24 B3
Valera Milan 19 A1
Vallcarca Barcelona 4 A1
Valldoreix Barcelona 4 A1
Vallecas Madrid 17 B2
Vallecas, Cumbres de
Madrid 17 B2
Vallensbæk Copenhagen 8 B2
Vallensbæk Strand
Copenhagen 8 B2
Vallentunasjön Stockholm 29 A2
Valleranello Rome 26 C1
Vallisaari Helsinki 11 C3
Valvidrera Barcelona 4 A1
Valvidrera → Barcelona 4 A1
Van Gogh Museum
Amsterdam 2 A2
Vanak Tehran 31 A2
Vanda = Vantaa Helsinki 11 B2
Vangede Copenhagen 8 A3
Vaniköy Istanbul 12 B2
Vanløse Copenhagen 8 A2
Vantaa Helsinki 11 B2
Vantaankoski Helsinki 11 B2
Vantaanpuisto Helsinki 11 B2
Vanves Paris 24 B2
Varedo Milan 19 A1
Varkiza Athens 2 C2
Vartiokylä Helsinki 11 B3
Vartiosaari Helsinki 11 B3
Vasamuseet Stockholm 29 B2
Vasco Cape Town 8 A2
Vasfanārd Tehran 31 B2
Vashi Mumbai 20 A2
Vasilyevskiy, Ostrov
St. Petersburg 27 B1
Vatican City ■ Rome 26 B1
Vaucluse Sydney 29 B2
Vaucluse House Sydney 29 B2
Vaucresson Paris 24 A1
Vaughan Toronto 31 A1
Vauhallan Paris 24 B2
Vaujours Paris 24 A4
Vauxhall London 15 B3
Vecsés Budapest 7 B3
Veleň Prague 25 A3
Veleslavín Prague 25 B2
Vélizy-Villacoublay Paris 24 B2
Velka-Chuchle Prague 25 B2
Velké Přílepy Prague 25 B1
Venda Seca Lisbon 16 A1
Venetian Islands Miami 18 B2
Venice Los Angeles 16 C2
Ventas Madrid 17 B1
Ventorro del Cano Madrid 17 B1
Venustiano Carranza
Mexico City 18 B2
Verde → São Paulo 27 A1
Verdi Athens 2 A2
Verdugo Mts. Los Angeles 16 A2
Verdun Montreal 20 B2
Verhalom Budapest 7 A2
Vermelho → São Paulo 27 B1
Vermont Knolls Los Angeles 16 C3
Vernon Los Angeles 16 B3
Verrières-le-Buisson Paris 24 B2
Versailles Buenos Aires 7 B1
Versailles Paris 24 B1
Veshnyaki Moscow 19 B3
Vesolyy Posolok
St. Petersburg 27 B2
Vestra Helsinki 11 B1
Vestskoven Copenhagen 8 A2
Vicálvaro Madrid 17 B2
Vicente Lopez Buenos Aires 7 B2
Victoria Hong Kong 12 B2
Victoria, Mt. Wellington 33 B1
Victoria, Pont Montreal 20 B2
Victoria and Alfred
Waterfront Cape Town 8 A1
Victoria Gardens Mumbai 20 B2
Victoria Harbour Hong Kong 12 B1
Victoria Island Lagos 14 B2
Victoria L. Johannesburg 13 B2
Victoria Lawn Tennis
Courts Melbourne 18 B2
Victoria Park Singapore 28 B2
Victoria Peak Hong Kong 12 B1
Vienna = Wien Vienna 32 A2
Vienna Washington 33 B2
Vietnam Veterans
Memorial Washington 33 B3
Vietnam War Museum
Chicago 9 B3
Vieux Carré = French
Quarter New Orleans 21 B2
View Park Los Angeles 16 B3
Vigário Geral Rio de Janeiro 25 A1
Vigentino Milan 19 B2
Viggbyholm Stockholm 29 A2
Vighignolo Milan 19 B1
Viikki Helsinki 11 B3
Vikhroli Mumbai 20 A2
Vila Guilherme São Paulo 27 B2
Vila Isabel Rio de Janeiro 25 B1
Vila Jaguára São Paulo 27 B1
Vila Madalena São Paulo 27 B1
Vila Maria São Paulo 27 B2
Vila Mariana São Paulo 27 B2
Vila Prudente São Paulo 27 B2
Viladecans Barcelona 4 B1
Vile Parle Mumbai 20 A2
Villa Adelina Buenos Aires 7 B1
Villa Ballester Buenos Aires 7 B1
Villa Barilari Buenos Aires 7 C2
Villa Bosch Buenos Aires 7 B1
Villa C. Colon Buenos Aires 7 C2
Villa Ciudadela Buenos Aires 7 B1
Villa de Guadalupe
Mexico City 18 B2
Villa Devoto Buenos Aires 7 B1
Villa Diamante Buenos Aires 7 C2
Villa Dominico Buenos Aires 7 C3
Villa Lugano Buenos Aires 7 C2
Villa Lynch Buenos Aires 7 B1
Villa Madero Buenos Aires 7 C1
Villa Sáenz Pena
Buenos Aires 7 B1
Villa Urquiza Buenos Aires 7 B2
Villaverde Madrid 17 B1
Villaverde Bajo Madrid 17 B1
Ville-d'Avray Paris 24 B2
Villecresnes Paris 24 B4
Villejuif Paris 24 B3
Villemomble Paris 24 A4
Villeneuve-la-Garenne
Paris 24 A2
Villeneuve-le-Roi Paris 24 B3
Villeneuve-St-Georges Paris 24 B3
Villeparisis Paris 24 A4
Villevaudé Paris 24 A4
Villiers-le-Bâcle Paris 24 B1
Villiers-sur-Marne Paris 24 B4
Villinki Helsinki 11 C3
Villoresi, Canale Milan 19 A1
Vilvoorde Brussels 6 A2
Vimodrone Milan 19 A2
Vimont Montreal 20 A1
Vincennes Paris 24 A3
Vincennes, Bois de Paris 24 B3
Vineland Orlando 23 B1
Vinings Atlanta 3 A2
Vinohrady Prague 25 B2
Vinoř Prague 25 B3
Violet Hill Hong Kong 12 B2
Virányos Budapest 7 A2
Virginia, L. Orlando 23 A2
Virginia Gardens Miami 18 B1
Virginia Key Miami 18 B2
Viroflay Paris 24 B2
Vironas Athens 2 B2
Virum Copenhagen 8 A2
Visitacion Valley
San Francisco 26 B2
Vista Alegre Lima 14 B3
Vista Alegre Santiago 27 C1
Vista Grove Atlanta 3 A3
Vitacura Santiago 27 B2
Vitinia Rome 26 C1
Vitry-sur-Seine Paris 24 B3
Vizcaya Museum and
Gardens Miami 18 B2
Vladykino Moscow 19 A2
Vokovice Prague 25 B2
Volgelsdorf Berlin 5 B5
Volkhonka-Zil Moscow 19 C2
Vollen Oslo 23 B1
Volodarskoye St. Petersburg 27 B2
Volynkina-Derevnya
St. Petersburg 27 B1
Vondelpark Amsterdam 2 A2
Vösendorf Vienna 32 B2
Voula Athens 2 C2
Vouliagmeni Athens 2 C2
Vredehoek Cape Town 8 A1
Vršovice Prague 25 B2
Vyborgskaya Storona
St. Petersburg 27 B2
Vykhino Moscow 19 B3
Vyšehrad Prague 25 B2

W

Wachterhof Munich 21 B3
Wadala Mumbai 20 A2
Wadestown Wellington 33 B1
Wadi al-Arayis Jerusalem 13 B2
Wadi Fukin Jerusalem 13 B1
Waduk Pluit Jakarta 12 A1
Waggaman New Orleans 21 B1
Wah Fu Hong Kong 12 B1
Wahda Baghdad 3 B2
Wahring Vienna 32 A2
Waidmannslust Berlin 5 A3
Wainuiomata Wellington 33 B2
Wainuiomata →
Wellington 33 B2
Wakefield Boston 6 A2
Waldesruh Berlin 5 B4
Waldperlach Munich 21 B3
Waldtrudering Munich 21 B3
Walkinstown Dublin 10 B1
Wall Street New York 22 B1
Walt Disney World Orlando 23 B1
Walter D. Stone Memorial
Zoo Boston 6 A2
Waltham Boston 6 A1
Waltham Forest □ London 15 A3
Walthamstow London 15 A3
Walton-on-Thames London 15 B1
Wambeek Brussels 6 A3
Wan Chai Hong Kong 12 B2
Wandle → London 15 B2
Wandsworth □ London 15 B2
Wangjing Beijing 4 B2
Wannsee Berlin 5 B1
Wansdorf Berlin 5 A1
Wanstead London 15 A4
Wapping London 15 A3
Ward I. Wellington 33 B2
Wards I. New York 22 B2
Warnberg Munich 21 B2
Warner Brothers Studios
Los Angeles 16 B2
Warrâq el 'Arab Cairo 7 A2
Warringal Park Melbourne 18 A2
Warriston Edinburgh 11 B2
Warsaw = Warszawa
Warsaw 32 B2
Warszawa Warsaw 32 B2
Warszawa ✈ (WAW)
Warsaw 32 B1
Wartenberg Berlin 5 A4
Washington Washington 33 B3
Washington Dulles Int. ✈
(IAD) Washington 33 B1
Washington Heights
New York 22 A2
Washington Park Chicago 9 C3
Washington Ronald
Reagan Nat. ✈ (DCA)
Washington 33 B3
Wat Pho Bangkok 3 B1
Water of Leith → Edinburgh 11 B1
Watergraafsmeer Amsterdam 2 A2
Waterland Amsterdam 2 A2
Waterloo Brussels 6 B2
Waterloo Wellington 33 B2
Watermael-Boitsfort Brussels 6 B2
Watertown Boston 6 A1
Watsonia Melbourne 18 A2
Waverley Boston 6 A1
Waverley Johannesburg 13 A2
Waverley Sydney 29 B2
Wawer Warsaw 32 B2
Wawrzyszew Warsaw 32 B1
Wazirabad Delhi 10 A2
Wazīrīya Baghdad 3 A2
Wazirpur Delhi 10 A2
Wealdstone London 15 A1
Wedding Berlin 5 A3
Weehawken New York 22 B1
Weesp Amsterdam 2 B3
Weidling Vienna 32 A1
Weidlingbach Vienna 32 A1
Weissensee Berlin 5 A3
Wellesley Hills Boston 6 B1
Welling London 15 B4
Wellington Boston 6 A2
Wellington Wellington 33 B1
Wellington Int. ✈ (WLE)
Wellington 33 B1
Weltevreden Park
Johannesburg 13 A1
Wembley London 15 A2
Wemmel Brussels 6 A1
Wemmer Pan Johannesburg 13 B2
Wenceslas Square =
Vaclavské náměstí
Prague 25 B2
Wendenschloss Berlin 5 B4
Wennington London 15 A5
Wernerhöhe Berlin 5 A5
West Don → Toronto 31 A2
West Drayton London 15 A1
West Ham London 15 A4
West Harrow London 15 A1
West Heath London 15 B4
West Hill Toronto 31 A3
West Hollywood Los Angeles 16 B2
West Lamma Channel
Hong Kong 12 B1
West Los Angeles, Univ. of
Los Angeles 16 C2
West Medford Boston 6 A2
West Miami Miami 18 B1
West Molesey London 15 B1
West New York New York 22 B1
West of Twin Peaks
San Francisco 26 B2
West Park Johannesburg 13 A1
West Rouge Toronto 31 A4
West Roxbury Boston 6 B2
West Springfield
Washington 33 C2
West Town Chicago 9 B2
West Wharf Karachi 13 B1
Westchester Chicago 9 B1
Westchester Los Angeles 16 C2
Westchester New York 22 A2
Westcliff Johannesburg 13 B2
Westdene Johannesburg 13 B1
Westend Helsinki 11 C1
Wester Hailes Edinburgh 11 B2
Westerham Munich 21 B2
Western Addition
San Francisco 26 B2
Westgate New Orleans 21 A1
Westgate Washington 33 B3
Westlake Cape Town 8 B1
Westlake Los Angeles 16 B3
Westlake San Francisco 26 B2
Westminster London 15 A3
Westmount Montreal 20 B2
Weston Toronto 31 A1
Westwego New Orleans 21 B2
Westwood Village
Los Angeles 16 B2
Westzaan Amsterdam 2 A1
Wetton Cape Town 8 B2
Wexford Toronto 31 A3
Weybridge London 15 B1
Wezembeek-Oppem Brussels 6 A2
White Cloud Hill = Baiyun
Hill Guangzhou 11 B2
White House, The
Washington 33 B3
Whitechapel London 15 A3
Whitehall Dublin 10 A2
Whitney Las Vegas 14 B2
Whittier Los Angeles 16 C4
Whitton London 15 B1
Wieden Vienna 32 A2
Wien Vienna 32 A2
Wien-Schwechat ✈ (VIE)
Vienna 32 B3
Wienerberg Vienna 32 B2
Wierzbno Warsaw 32 B2
Wijde Wormer Amsterdam 2 A2
Wilanów Warsaw 32 B2
Wilanówka → Warsaw 32 C2
Wilds, The Johannesburg 13 B2
Wilhelmshagen Berlin 5 B5
Wilket Creek Park Toronto 31 A2
Wilkieston Edinburgh 11 B1
Will Rogers State
Historical Park ⌂
Los Angeles 16 B1
Willbrook Dublin 10 B2
Willesden London 15 A2
Willesden Green London 15 A2
Williamsbridge New York 22 A2
Williamsburg New York 22 B2
Williamsburg Orlando 23 B2
Williamstown Melbourne 18 B1
Willis, L. Orlando 23 B2
Willoughby Sydney 29 A2
Willow Springs Chicago 9 C1
Willowdale New Orleans 21 A1
Willowdale Toronto 31 A2
Wilmersdorf Berlin 5 B2
Wilmette Chicago 9 A2
Wilmington London 15 B5
Wimbledon London 15 B2
Wimbledon Common
London 15 B2
Wimbledon Park London 15 B2
Wimbledon Tennis
Ground London 15 B2
Winchester Boston 6 A2
Winchester Las Vegas 14 B2
Windermere Cape Town 8 A2
Windermere Orlando 23 B1
Windsor Johannesburg 13 A1
Windsor, Gare Montreal 20 B2
Windsor Hills Los Angeles 16 C2
Windy Arbour Dublin 10 B2
Winning Munich 21 B2
Wissous Paris 24 B2
Wittenau Berlin 5 A2
Witwatersrand, Univ. of
Johannesburg 13 B2
Włochy Warsaw 32 B1
Wo Mei Hong Kong 12 A2
Wo Yi Hop Hong Kong 12 A1
Woburn Boston 6 A2
Woburn Toronto 31 A3
Wola Warsaw 32 B1
Wolf Trap Farm Park
Washington 33 B2
Wolgok Seoul 27 B2
Wolica Warsaw 32 C2
Wolica Warsaw 32 C1
Wollaston Boston 6 B2
Woltersdorf Berlin 5 B5
Woluwe-St-Lambert Brussels 6 A2
Woluwe-St-Pierre Brussels 6 A2
Wong Chuk Hang
Hong Kong 12 B2
Wong Chuk Wan
Hong Kong 12 A2
Wong Chuk Yeung
Hong Kong 12 A2
Wood Green London 15 A3
Wood Ridge New York 22 A1
Woodbine Race Track
Toronto 31 A1
Woodbridge Toronto 31 A1
Woodford London 15 A4
Woodford Bridge London 15 A4
Woodford Green London 15 A4
Woodhaven New York 22 B2
Woodhouselee Edinburgh 11 B2
Woodlands Singapore 28 A2
Woodmont Washington 33 B3
Woodside London 15 B3
Woodside New York 22 B2
Woodstock Cape Town 8 A1
Woollahra Sydney 29 B2
Woolooware B. Sydney 29 C1
Woolwich London 15 B4
Worker's Stadium Beijing 4 B2
World Financial Centre
Shanghai 28 B2
World Trade Center, Site
of former = Ground
Zero New York 22 B1
Worli Mumbai 20 A1
Worth Chicago 9 C2
Wren's Nest Atlanta 3 B2
Wrigley Field Chicago 9 B3
Wuhlgarten Berlin 5 A4
Wujiaochang Shanghai 28 B2
Würm → Munich 21 B1
Würm-kanal Munich 21 A1
Wusong Shanghai 28 A1
Wyczółki Warsaw 32 C1
Wygoda Warsaw 32 B2
Wynberg Cape Town 8 B1

X

Xabregas Lisbon 16 A2
Xiaogang Park Guangzhou 11 B2
Xiaoping Guangzhou 11 A2
Xiasha chong Guangzhou 11 B1
Xichang Guangzhou 11 B2
Xicheng Beijing 4 B1
Xidan Beijing 4 B2
Xizhimen Beijing 4 B1
Xochimilco, Parque
Ecológico Mexico City 18 C2
Xuanwu Beijing 4 B1
Xuhui Shanghai 28 B1

Y

Yaba Lagos 14 A2
Yaftābād Tehran 31 B1
Yahara Tokyo 30 A2
Yaho Tokyo 30 A1
Yakire Tokyo 30 A4
Yaksu Seoul 27 B2
Yamada Osaka 23 A2
Yamada Tokyo 30 B2
Yamato → Osaka 23 B1
Yan Kit Singapore 28 A3
Yanbu Guangzhou 11 B1
Yangcheon Seoul 27 B1
Yanghuayuan Beijing 4 C1
Yangjae Seoul 27 C2
Yangjiazhuang Shanghai 28 A1
Yangjing Shanghai 28 B2
Yangpu Shanghai 28 B2
Yangpu Park Shanghai 28 B2
Yannawa Bangkok 3 B2
Yarmūk Baghdad 3 B1
Yarra Bend Park Melbourne 18 A2
Yarraville Melbourne 18 A1
Yauza → Moscow 19 B4
Yeading London 15 A1
Yedikule Istanbul 12 C1
Yenikapı Istanbul 12 B1
Yeniköy Istanbul 12 B2
Yeongdeungpo Seoul 27 B1
Yeongdong Seoul 27 B2
Yeouido Seoul 27 B1
Yerba Buena I.
San Francisco 26 B2
Yerres Paris 24 B4
Yerushalayim =
Jerusalem Jerusalem 13 B2
Yiexiu Guangzhou 11 B2
Yiheyuan Beijing 4 B1
Yıldız Park Istanbul 12 B2
Yinhangzhen Shanghai 28 A2
Yishun Singapore 28 A3
Ylästö Helsinki 11 B2
Yodo → Osaka 23 A2
Yongdingman Beijing 4 B2
Yongfucun Guangzhou 11 B2
Yongsan Seoul 27 B1
Yonkers New York 22 A2
York Toronto 31 A2
York Mills Toronto 31 A2
York Univ. Toronto 31 A1
You'anmen Beijing 4 B1
Youngsfield Cape Town 8 B1
Yuanmingyuan Park Beijing 4 A1
Yuanxiatian Guangzhou 11 A2
Yuexiu Park Guangzhou 11 B2
Yugo-Zarad Moscow 19 B2
Yuhalixqui, Volcan
Mexico City 18 C2
Yung Shue Wan Hong Kong 12 B1
Yūsofābād Tehran 31 A2

Z

Zaandam Amsterdam 2 A1
Zaandijk Amsterdam 2 A1
Zaanstad Amsterdam 2 A1
Zāběhlice Prague 25 B2
Zabki Warsaw 32 B2
Żacisze Warsaw 32 B2
Zahrā Baghdad 3 A1
Žalov Prague 25 B2
Załuski Warsaw 32 C1
Zamdorf Munich 21 B2
Zanevka St. Petersburg 27 B3
Zapote Manila 17 C1
Zaventem Brussels 6 A2
Zawady Warsaw 32 B2
Zāwiyet Abû Musallam
Cairo 7 B1
Zawrā' Park Baghdad 3 B2
Zbraslav Prague 25 C2
Zbuzany Prague 25 B1
Zdiby Prague 25 B2
Zeekoevlei Cape Town 8 B2
Zehlendorf Berlin 5 B2
Zenne → Brussels 6 A2
Zephyr Field New Orleans 21 B1
Żerań Warsaw 32 B2
Zerzeń Warsaw 32 B2
Zeytinburnu Istanbul 12 C1
Zhabei Shanghai 28 B1
Zhdanov Moscow 19 B3
Zhenru Shanghai 28 B1
Zhernovka St. Petersburg 27 B2
Zhicun Guangzhou 11 B2
Zhongguancun Beijing 4 B1
Zhongshan Park Shanghai 28 B1
Zhoucun Guangzhou 11 A2
Zhoujiadu Shanghai 28 B1
Zhoujiazhen Shanghai 28 B2
Zhouzhuangzi Beijing 4 B1
Zhulebino Moscow 19 B4
Zhushadi Guangzhou 11 A3
Zielona Warsaw 32 B3
Zielonka Warsaw 32 B2
Zizhuyuan Park Beijing 4 B1
Žižkov Prague 25 B2
Zličín Prague 25 B1
Zografou Athens 2 B2
Żoliborz Warsaw 32 B1
Zonnebloem Cape Town 8 A1
Zugliget Budapest 7 B1
Zugló Budapest 7 A2
Zuiderwoude Amsterdam 2 A3
Zumbi Rio de Janeiro 25 A1
Zunderdorp Amsterdam 2 A2
Zuvuvu → São Paulo 27 C1
Zwanenburg Amsterdam 2 A1
Zwölfaxing Vienna 32 B2

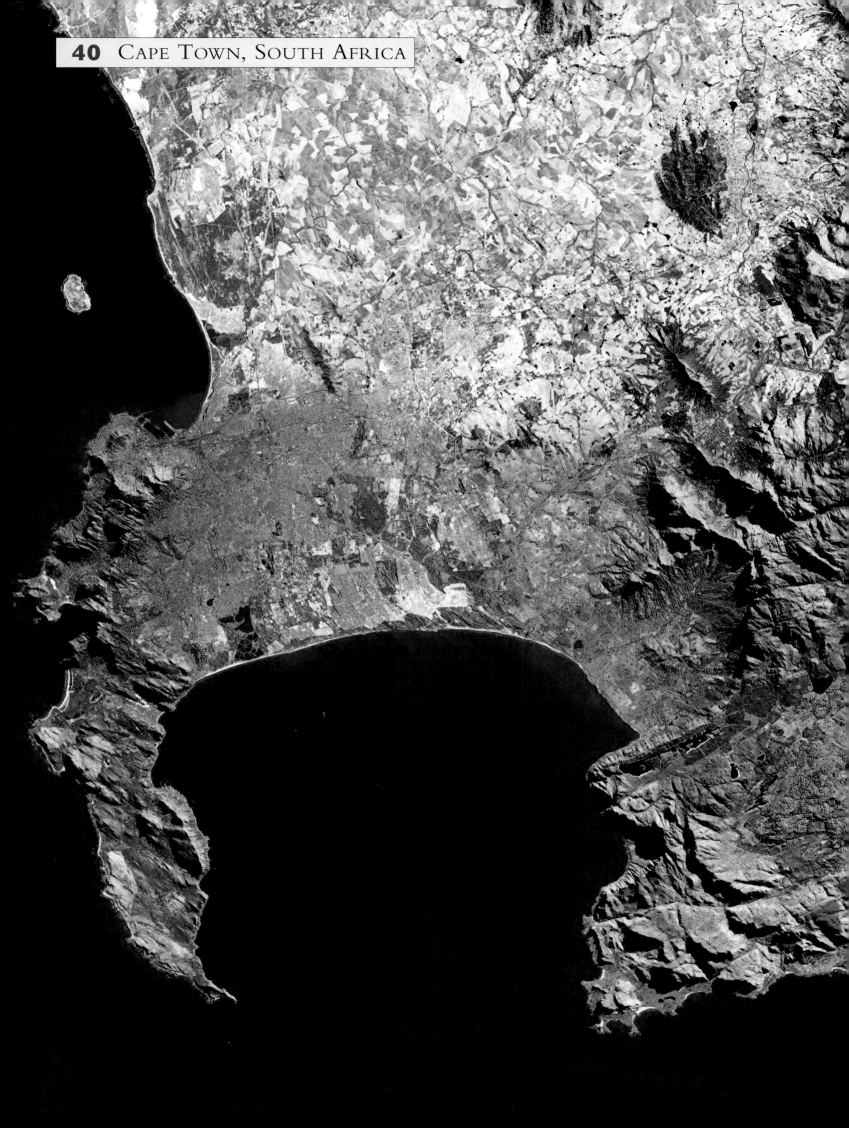

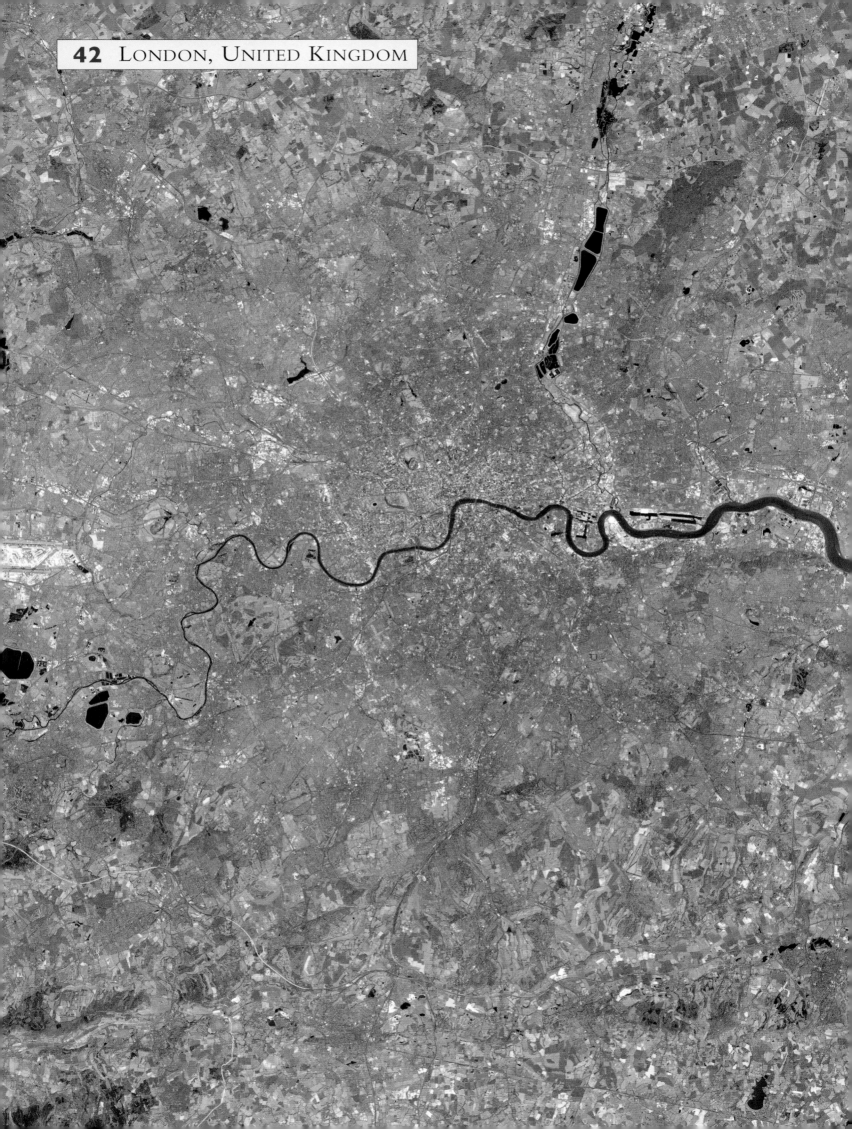

WORLD MAPS

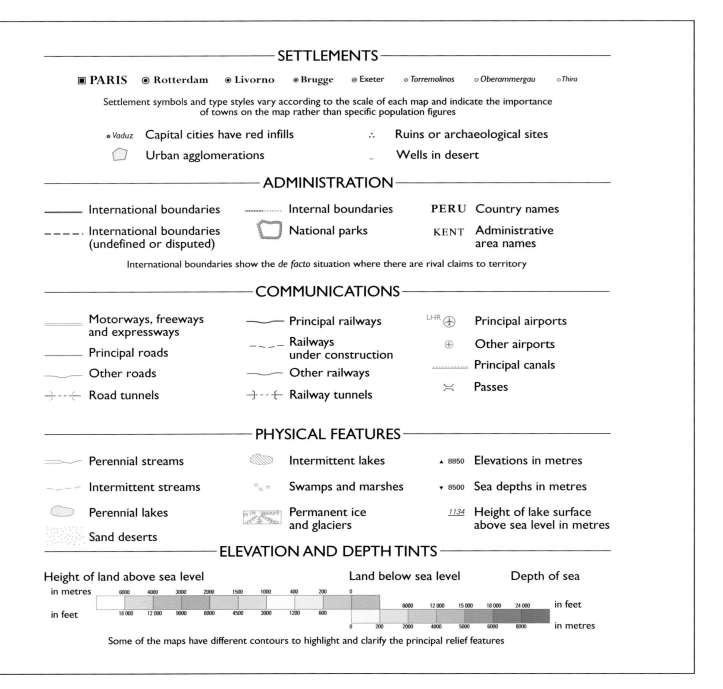

SETTLEMENTS

■ PARIS　　◉ Rotterdam　　◉ Livorno　　◉ Brugge　　◉ Exeter　　◦ Torremolinos　　◦ Oberammergau　　◦ Thira

Settlement symbols and type styles vary according to the scale of each map and indicate the importance of towns on the map rather than specific population figures

● Vaduz　Capital cities have red infills

∴　Ruins or archaeological sites

⬠　Urban agglomerations

˽　Wells in desert

ADMINISTRATION

———— International boundaries

┈┈┈ Internal boundaries

PERU Country names

– – – · International boundaries (undefined or disputed)

⬡ National parks

KENT Administrative area names

International boundaries show the *de facto* situation where there are rival claims to territory

COMMUNICATIONS

═══ Motorways, freeways and expressways

——— Principal railways

ᴸᴴᴿ ✈ Principal airports

——— Principal roads

– – – Railways under construction

⊕ Other airports

——— Other roads

——— Other railways

┈┈┈ Principal canals

+–·–+ Road tunnels

+–·–+ Railway tunnels

⋈ Passes

PHYSICAL FEATURES

⌇ Perennial streams

Intermittent lakes

▲ 8850 Elevations in metres

– – – Intermittent streams

Swamps and marshes

▼ 8500 Sea depths in metres

Perennial lakes

Permanent ice and glaciers

1134 Height of lake surface above sea level in metres

Sand deserts

ELEVATION AND DEPTH TINTS

Height of land above sea level

Land below sea level

Depth of sea

in metres　6000　4000　3000　2000　1500　1000　400　200　0

6000　12 000　15 000　18 000　24 000　in feet

in feet　18 000　12 000　9000　6000　4500　3000　1200　600

0　200　2000　4000　5000　6000　8000　in metres

Some of the maps have different contours to highlight and clarify the principal relief features

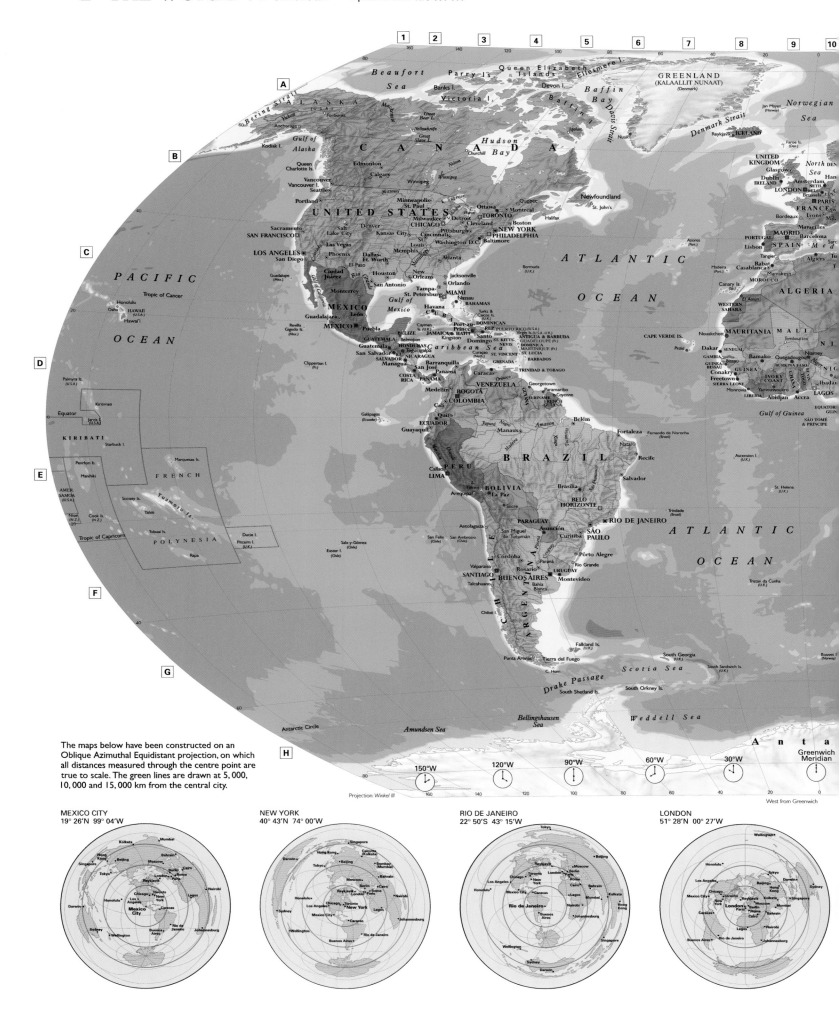

The maps below have been constructed on an Oblique Azimuthal Equidistant projection, on which all distances measured through the centre point are true to scale. The green lines are drawn at 5,000, 10,000 and 15,000 km from the central city.

Projection: Winkel III

West from Greenwich

MEXICO CITY
19° 26'N 99° 04'W

NEW YORK
40° 43'N 74° 00'W

RIO DE JANEIRO
22° 50'S 43° 15'W

LONDON
51° 28'N 00° 27'W

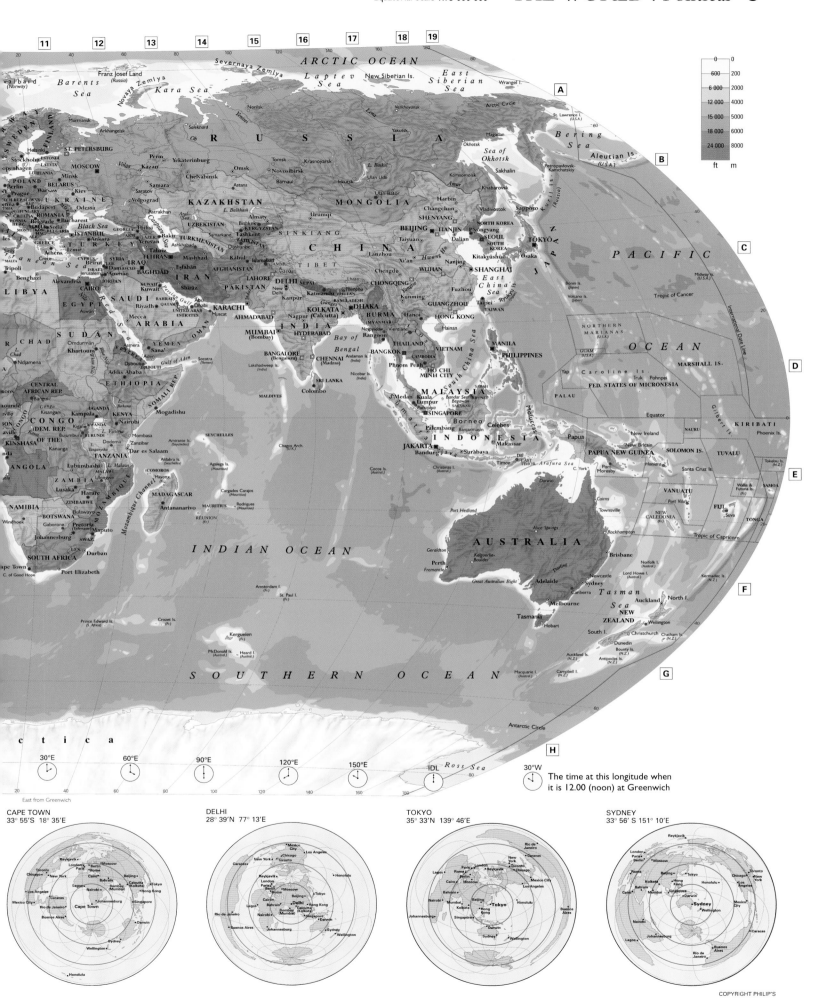

4 ARCTIC OCEAN

100 0   200   400   600   800   1000   1200   1400 km
100 0   200   400   600   800   1000 miles

1:35 000 000

18 **17** **16** **15**

JAPAN

PACIFIC OCEAN

Tufts Abyssal Plain

Gilbert Seamounts

Aleutian Trench
Aleutian Islands (U.S.A.)

Bowers Ridge
Bowers Basin

Near Is. (U.S.A.)

Kurilskiye Ostrova (Russia)
La Perouse Str.
Kuril Str.
Hokkaido
SAPPORO

Mys Lopatka

Komandorskiye Ostrova
Petropavlovsk-Kamchatskiy
Gora 4750
Klyuchevskaya
Ust-Kamchatsk
Ostrov Karaginskiy

Yuzhno-Sakhalinsk
Sakhalin (Russia) 1609
Vanino

1

Dutch Harbor
Unimak I. 2857

Bering Sea

Aleutian Basin

Pribilof Is. (U.S.A.)

International Date Line

Mys Olyutorski

Poluostrov Kamchatka

Sea of Okhotsk

Nikolayevsk
Amur
Komsomolsk-na-Amur
Khabarovsk

14

G. of Alaska

Kodiak I. 1362

Bristol Bay

Seward
Prince William Sd.
Anchorage Mt. McKinley 6194
Cordova

ALASKA

St. Matthew (U.S.A.)

Nunivak

St. Lawrence I. (U.S.A.)

Nome
Bering Str.
Providentiya Zaliv
Mys Dezhneva

Anadyrskiy Zaliv
Anadyr

Penzhinskaya G.
Gizhiginskaya Guba

Tauiskaya Guba
Magadan

2453

Okhotsk

Stanovoy Khrebet

Udskaya Guba

Queen Charlotte Is.
Alexander Arch. 44
Prince Rupert

Mt. St. Elias 5489
4949
Skagway Mt. Logan 5959
Juneau
Whitehorse
4019

Fairbanks

Yukon
Kuskokwim

Norton Sd.

Kotzebue Sd.
Pt. Hope
C. Lisburne

Chukchi Sea

C

Chukotskoye Nagorye

Pevek
Nizhne Kolymsk
Srednekolymsk

Kolyma
Omolon
Kolymskoye Nagorye

3147

Verkhoyansk

Yana
Kazachye

Indigirka

Yakutsk
Lena
Aldan

Stanovoy Khrebet

Olekma

13

Rocky Mountains

Dawson Creek
2782

Fort Nelson
Fort Simpson

Dawson
Stewart
Fort Yukon
Fort McPherson

Peel
Mackenzie

Herschel I.

Prudhoe Bay 2761
C. Halkett
Harrison Bay
Pt. Barrow

Ostrov Vrangelya (Russia) 1096

Proliv Longa

B

East Siberian Sea

46

Chaunskaya

3147

Verkhoyansk
Verkhoyanskiy Khrebet
2295

Bulun
Zhigansk

Tiksi

Lena

Olenek

North America

Fort Vermilion
Peace
Fort Good Hope

Tulita

Great Bear Lake

Mackenzie
Fort Good Hope

Tuktoyaktuk
C. Bathurst

Mackenzie Bay 2882

Beaufort Sea

Canada Abyssal Plain

Novosibirskiye Ostrova

O. Delonga

374
Kotelnyy

Lyakhovskiye Ostrova

2

Athabasca Lake

Yellowknife
Great Slave Lake

Coppermine
Kugluktuk

Dolphin & Union Str.
Coronation Gulf

Banks I.
C. Kellett

Prince Albert Pen.
C. Prince Alfred 371

Prince Patrick I.

Canada Basin

ARCTIC

Chukchi Plateau
3327

Mendeleyev Ridge

Laptev Sea

OCEAN

Anabar

Nizhnyaya Tunguska

13

America

NUNAVUT

Churchill

Chesterfield Inlet
Back

King William I.

Victoria Island

M'Clintock Chan.
Viscount Melville Sd.

M'Clure Str.

Queen Melville I.

Parry Is.
Borden I.

3700
North Magnetic Pole 2007

3546

3849
Ostrova Petra

Nordvik

Kheta

Khatanga

Ozero Taymyr

Gory Putorana

3

Hudson Bay

Southampton I.
Coats I.

Mansel I.

Melville Pen.
Rae Welcome Sd.

Boothia Pen.
Somerset

Prince of Wales I.
Resolute

Prince of Bathurst
Elizabeth Islands

Axel Heiberg I.

Ellef Ringnes I.
Sverdrup Is.

Alpha Ridge

2104

Nansen Sd.

Makarov Basin

Lomonosov Ridge

NORTH POLE

Amundsen Basin

4346

Arctic Mid-Ocean Ridge
4484
4100

Nansen Basin

Severnaya Zemlya
Ostrov Komsomolets
Oktyabrskoy Revolyutsii
965

O. Ushakova

O. Uedineniya

O. Vise

Poluostrov Taymyr
Mys Chelyuskin

Dikson

Dudinka
Norilsk

Pyasina

Igarka

Yenisey

Gydanskiy Poluostrov
Taz

12

Labrador

Foxe Basin
Foxe Chan.
Fury & Hecla Str.

Prince Charles I.

Gulf of Boothia
Prince Regent Inlet

Lancaster Sd.

Devon
Jones Sound

Ellesmere I. (Canada) 2616
C. Columbia

Lincoln Sea

Peary Land

3741

3910

Zemlya Frantsa Iosifa (Russia)

O. Greem-Bell
Z. Vilcheka

O. Belyy

Novyy Urengoy
Novyy Port
Nadym
Nizhnevartovsk

Surgut

Nefteyugansk

11

ft m
12 000 4000

6000 2000

4500 1500

3000 1000

1200 400

600 200

0 0

500 1500

1000 3000

2000 6000

3000 9000

4000 12 000

5000 15 000

m ft

Chatham Str.
C. Wolstenholme
C. Feuilles

Hudson Str.

Frobisher Bay
Ungava Bay

Iqaluit
2147

Baffin Island

Nettilling L.
2469

Baffin Bay

Uummannaq
K. York

Knud Rasmussen Land
Kronprins Frederik Land

Kong Frederik VIII.s Land

Semersooq

K. Morris Jesup

Kronprins Frederik Land 2170

Independence Fjord

McKinley Sea

A

Nordkapp

90

Kara Sea

Poluostrov Yamal

Baydaratskaya Guba

Poluostrov Yamal

1547

Novaya

Zemlya

Vorkuta
Amderma

Belushya Guba
O. Kolguyev

11

Labrador Sea

C. Chidley

Resolution I.

Davis Str.

Cumberland Sd.

Qikiqtarjuaq
C. Dyer

Upernavik

Uummannaq
Qeqertarsuaq

Qeqertat

Kong Frederik IX.s Land

GREENLAND
(KALAALLIT NUNAAT)
(Denmark)

Kong Christian X.s Land

Kejser Franz Joseph Fd.
Kong Oscar Fjord

Ittoqqortoormiit

2571

Nordaustlandet

Vestspitsbergen
Longyearbyen 1717
Svalbard (Norway)
Edgeøya

Zemlya

Nordkapp

Barents Sea

Belushya Guba

Mys Kanin Nos

1894
Narodnaya

Naryan-Mar

Pechora

Ukhta

Uralskie Gory

YEKATERINBURG

4

2276

Nuuk

Paamiut

Kong Frederik VI.s Kyst

Mt. Forel 3238
Kong Christian IX.s Land
Mt. Forel 3360

3700
Gunnbjørn Fjeld
Kangikajik

Kong Frederik VI.s Kyst 2850

Northwest Mid-Ocean Canyon

Greenland Sea

Jan Mayen (Norway) 2277

Mohns Ridge

480

Bjørnøya (Norway)

Vardø

Nordkapp
Hammerfest
Kirkenes
Tromsø

Murmansk
Kolskiy Poluostrov
Kandalaksha

Arkhangelsk
Sev. Dvina
Severodvinsk

Mezen
Mezen

Onega

Syktyvkar

PERM

UFA

10

Qaqortoq
Alluitsup Paa

Nunap Isua (Kap Farvel)

Hamilton Inlet

Labrador

Atlantic Mid-Ocean Ridge

Tasiilaq

Icelandic Plateau

Denmark Str.

Horn
Breiðafjörður
Fontur

Iceland
Snæfellsjökull 1446

Öræfajökull 2119

Arctic Circle

Norwegian Basin

Norwegian Sea

C

Lofoten
Narvik

Trondheim

Oslo
STOCKHOLM

Oulu
Tornio

SWEDEN

NORWAY

Gulf of Bothnia

FINLAND

Helsinki
Tallinn
EST.

Onezhskoye Ozero
Ladozhskoye Ozero

ST. PETERBURG

Chudskoye Ozero

MOSKVA

RUSSIA

Volga

SAMARA

NIZHNIY NOVGOROD

Saratov

VOLGOGRAD

10

5

4563

North Atlantic Ridge

ATLANTIC

Charlie Gibbs Fracture Zone

Iceland Basin

Reykjavik
ICELAND

2469

3800

Føroyar (Den.)

Shetland Is. (U.K.)

Bergen

North Sea

Skagerrak
København
DENMARK

Baltic Sea

Gulf of Finland

Rīga
LAT.
LITH.
Vilnius
Kaliningrad (Russia)

BELARUS

KYYIV

KHARKIV

ROSTOV

DONETSK

Rockall (U.K.)

Hebrides (U.K.)

Orkney Is. (U.K.)

D

King's Trough

Rockall Trough

UNITED KINGDOM
SCOTLAND
Edinburgh
GLASGOW
Belfast
IRELAND
DUBLIN

North Sea

NETH.
AMSTERDAM

HAMBURG
BERLIN
GERMANY

POLAND
WARSZAWA

Kraków

Wisła
Elbe

PRAHA

LONDON

UKRAINE

MOLDOVA
ROMANIA
ODESA

Sea of Azov

Black Sea

OCEAN

C. Clear

ENGLAND

Legend:
- Maximum extent of sea ice
- Minimum extent of sea ice (September 2007)
- Ice caps and permanent ice shelf

Projection : Zenithal Equidistant

20   West from Greenwich 0 East from Greenwich   20

COPYRIGHT PHILIP'S

6   **7**   **8**   **9**

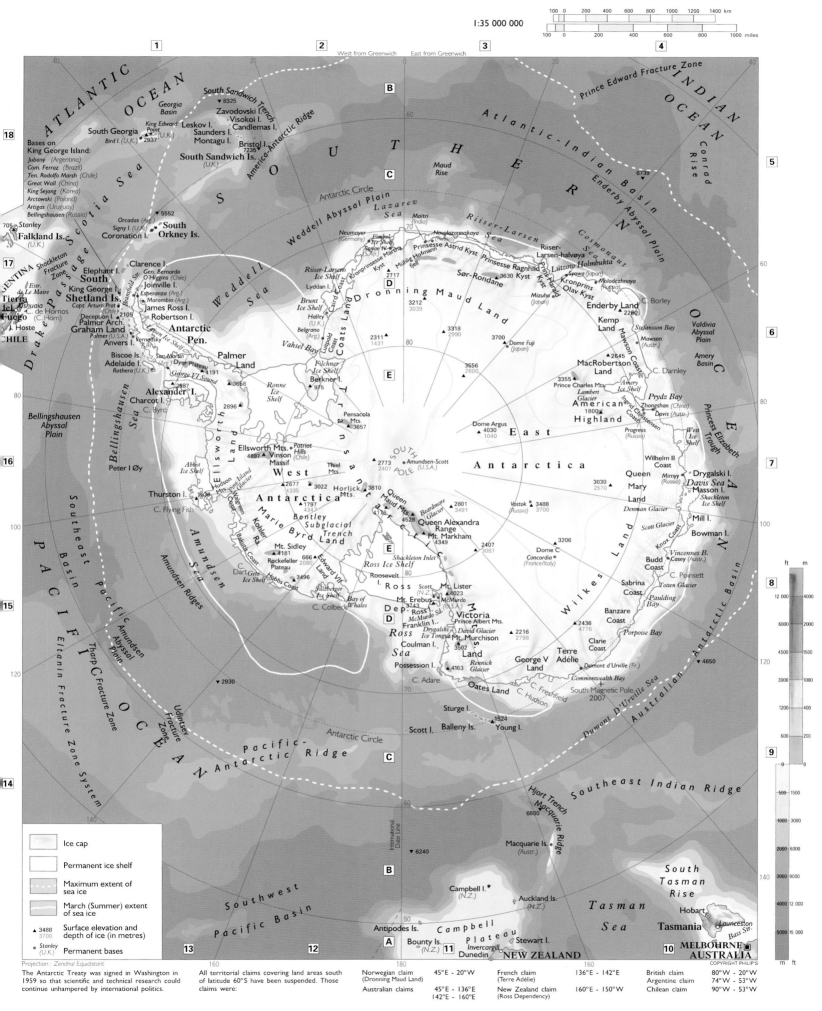

1:35 000 000

| 100 | 0 | 200 | 400 | 600 | 800 | 1000 | 1200 | 1400 km |

| 100 | 0 | 200 | 400 | 600 | 800 | 1000 miles |

ft | m

12 000 | 4000

6000 | 2000

4500 | 1500

3000 | 1000

1200 | 400

600 | 200

0 | 0

500 | 1500

1000 | 3000

2000 | 6000

3000 | 9000

4000 | 12 000

5000 | 15 000

m | ft

Legend:

- Ice cap
- Permanent ice shelf
- Maximum extent of sea ice
- March (Summer) extent of sea ice
- ▲ 3488 / 3700 Surface elevation and depth of ice (in metres)
- • Stanley (U.K.) Permanent bases

Projection: Zenithal Equidistant

COPYRIGHT PHILIP'S

The Antarctic Treaty was signed in Washington in 1959 so that scientific and technical research could continue unhampered by international politics.

All territorial claims covering land areas south of latitude 60°S have been suspended. Those claims were:

Norwegian claim (Dronning Maud Land)	45°E – 20°W	French claim (Terre Adélie)	136°E – 142°E	British claim	80°W – 20°W
Australian claims	45°E – 136°E 142°E – 160°E	New Zealand claim (Ross Dependency)	160°E – 150°W	Argentine claim	74°W – 53°W
				Chilean claim	90°W – 53°W

Bases on King George Island:
Jubany (Argentina)
Com. Ferraz (Brazil)
Ten. Rodolfo Marsh (Chile)
Great Wall (China)
King Sejong (Korea)
Arctowski (Poland)
Artigas (Uruguay)
Bellingshausen (Russia)

1:20 000 000

1:20 000 000

100 0 100 200 300 400 500 600 700 800 km
100 0 100 200 300 400 500 miles

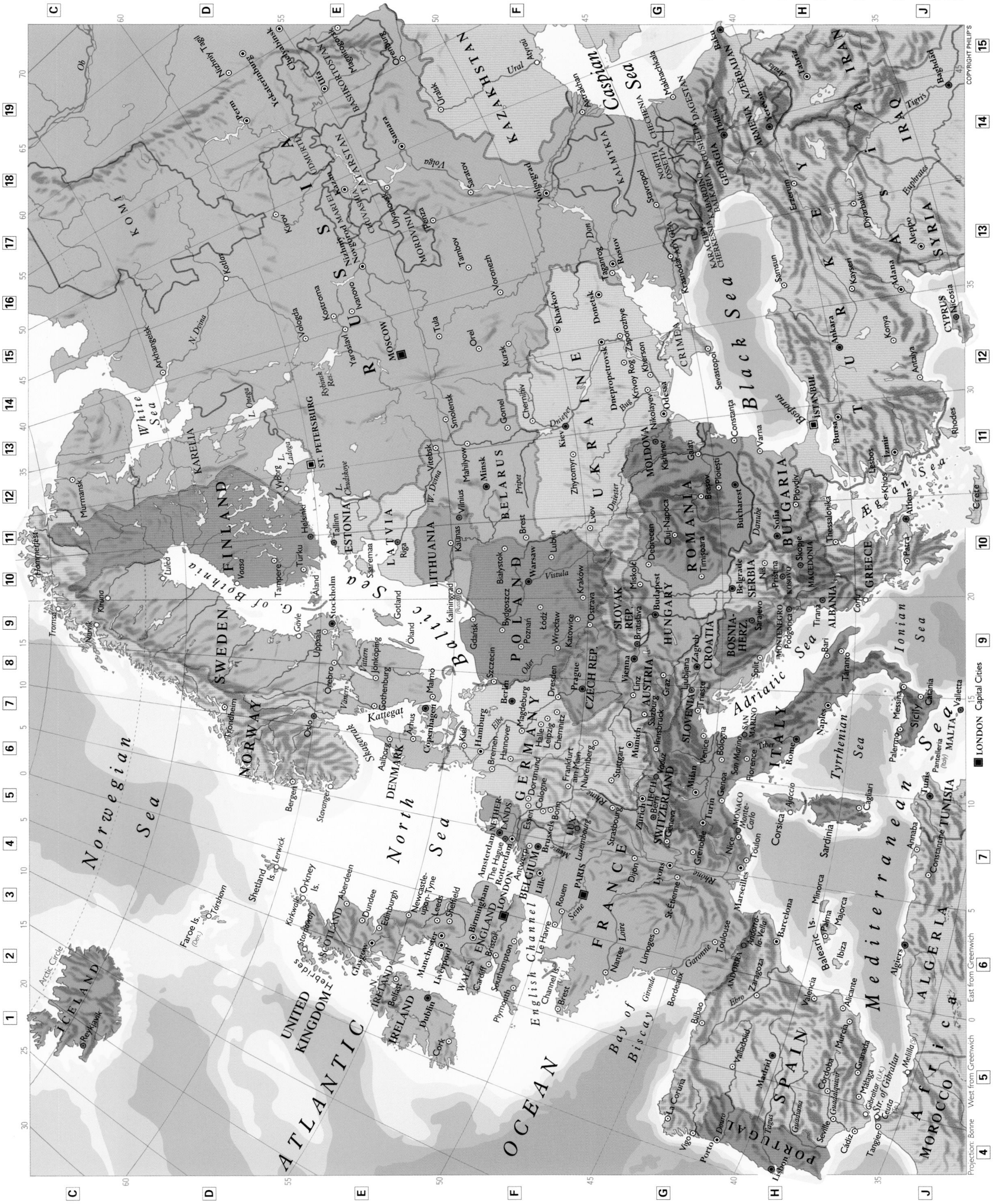

COPYRIGHT PHILIP'S

Projection: Bonne

West from Greenwich | East from Greenwich

■ LONDON Capital Cities

ICELAND
Reykjavik

NORWEGIAN SEA

ATLANTIC OCEAN

NORWAY
SWEDEN
FINLAND
DENMARK

UNITED KINGDOM
IRELAND
ENGLAND
SCOTLAND
WALES

NETHERLANDS
BELGIUM
LUX.
FRANCE
GERMANY
SWITZERLAND
AUSTRIA
ITALY
SPAIN
PORTUGAL
MOROCCO
ALGERIA
TUNISIA
MALTA

POLAND
CZECH REP.
SLOVAK REP.
HUNGARY
SLOVENIA
CROATIA
BOSNIA-HERZ.
SERBIA
MONTENEGRO
ALBANIA
MACEDONIA
ROMANIA
MOLDOVA
BULGARIA
GREECE

ESTONIA
LATVIA
LITHUANIA
BELARUS
UKRAINE
RUSSIA

KAZAKHSTAN

TURKEY
GEORGIA
ARMENIA
AZERBAIJAN
IRAN
IRAQ
SYRIA
CYPRUS

White Sea
Baltic Sea
North Sea
Mediterranean Sea
Black Sea
Caspian Sea
Adriatic Sea
Aegean Sea
Ionian Sea
Tyrrhenian Sea
Bay of Biscay
English Channel
Gulf of Bothnia

MOSCOW
ST. PETERSBURG
LONDON
PARIS
Berlin
Madrid
Rome
Warsaw
Bucharest
Sofia
Athens
Ankara
Baghdad

Arctic Circle

Africa

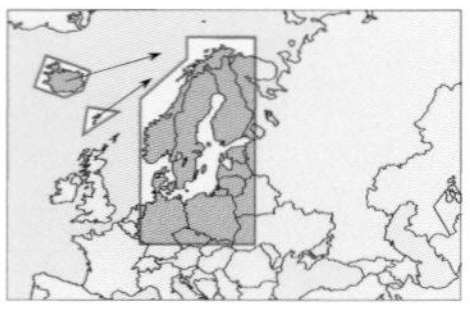

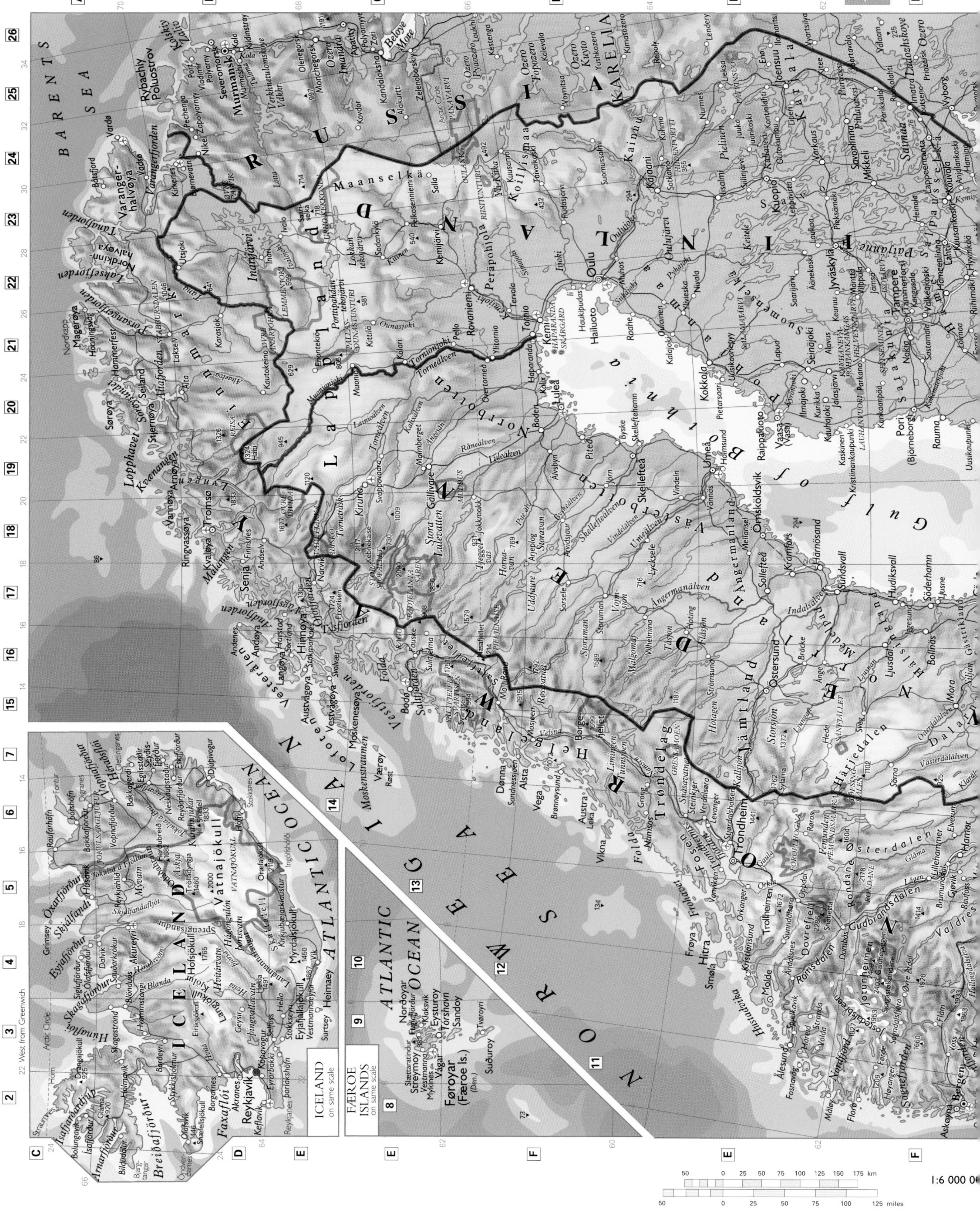

18

BARENTS SEA

RUSSIA

KARELIA

FINLAND

Lappland

NORWAY

SWEDEN

ICELAND
on same scale

FAROE ISLANDS
on same scale

ATLANTIC OCEAN

NORWEGIAN SEA

Gulf of Bothnia

Murmansk

Oulu

Tampere

Trondheim

Reykjavik

Tórshavn

Føroyar (Færoe Is.) (Den.)

Vatnajökull

ICELAND

1:6 000 000

| 50 | | 0 | 25 | 50 | 75 | 100 | 125 | 150 | 175 km |

| 50 | | 0 | 25 | 50 | 75 | 100 | 125 miles |

22 West from Greenwich

Arctic Circle

1:2 000 000

Projection: Lambert's Conformal Conic

West from Greenwich

SCOTLAND
Kintyre
Brodick
Arran
Campbeltown
Firth of Clyde
Mull of Kintyre
Ailsa Craig
L. Ryan
Stranraer
Portpatrick

NORTH CHANNEL

Giants Causeway
Fair Hd.
Rathlin I.
Ballycastle
Cushendall
Garron Pt.
GLENARIFF
Cushendun
Carnlough
Larne
Carrickfergus
Cairnryan

Malin Hd.
Malin
Inishtrahull
Trawbreaga B.
Carndonagh
Moville
Inishowen Pen.
Buncrana
L. Foyle
Coleraine
Limavady
Ballymoney
Portrush
Portstewart
Mts. of Antrim
ANTRIM
Ballymena
Antrim
Randalstown Ballyclare
Newtownabbey
Lough Neagh
Belfast
BELFAST
Bangor
Donaghadee
Newtownards
Comber
Ards Pen.
Strangford L.
Portaferry
Ballyquintin Pt.

Tory I.
Horn Hd.
Sheep Haven
Mulroy B.
Lough Swilly
Fanad Hd.
Dunfanaghy
Rathmullen
Letterkenny
Lifford
Strabane
Sion Mills
Newtownstewart
Omagh
Cookstown
Magherafelt
Moneymore
Coalisland
Dungannon
Londonderry
LONDONDERRY
Sawel Mt.
Sperrin Mts.
TYRONE
NORTHERN IRELAND
Craigavon
Lurgan
Portadown
Lagan
Lisburn
DOWN
Banbridge
Tandragee
Ballynahinch
Downpatrick
Dundrum
St. John's Pt.
Dundrum B.

Bloody Foreland
Gweedore
Errigal
Derryveagh Mts.
GLENVEAGH
The Rosses
Dungloe
Crohy Hd.
Aran I.
Inishfree B.
Gweebarra B.
Dawros Hd.
Loughros More B.
Rossan Pt.
DONEGAL
Glenties
Ardara
Glencolumbkille
Lavagh More
Glen?
Stranorlar
Castlederg
Derg
L. Derg
Irvinestown
Dromore
Ballygawley
Aughnacloy
Monaghan
MONAGHAN
Castleblaney
Clones
Cootehill
Keady
Middletown
Armagh
ARMAGH
Newry
Mourne Mts.
Slieve Donard
Warrenpoint
Rostrevor
Kilkeel
Greenore
Carlingford L.
Dundalk

Slieve League
St. John's Pt.
Killybegs
Donegal
Donegal Bay
Ballyshannon
Bundoran
Erne
Lough Melvin
Lower L. Erne
Upper L. Erne
Enniskillen
FERMANAGH
ULSTER
Lisnaskea
Beltubet
Cavan
CAVAN
Carrickmacross
Crossmaglen
Dundalk Bay
LOUTH
Ardee
Dunleer
Clogher Hd.

ATLANTIC OCEAN

Erris Hd.
Portacloy
Downpatrick Hd.
Broad Haven
Mullet Pen.
Belmullet
Inishkea North
Inishkea South
Blacksod Bay
Achill Hd.
Achill I.
Clare I.
Inishturk
Inishbofin
Inishshark
Killary Harbour
Slyne Hd.
Roundstone
Bertraghboy B.
Clifden
CONNEMARA
Slieve More
Ballycroy
Nephin Beg Range
Crossmolina
Ballina
Killala
Killala B.
Lenadoon Pt.
Dromore West
Sligo Bay
Sligo
SLIGO
Inishmurray I.
Manorhamilton
Lackagh Hills
Drumkeeran
L. Allen
LEITRIM
Leitrim
Carrick-on-Shannon
L. Key
L. Arrow
Collooney
Ballymote
Boyle
L. Oughter
Annalee
L. Gowna
L. Sheelin
Kingscourt
Oldcastle
Ceanannus Mor (Kells)
Nobber
Slane
Drogheda
Balbriggan
Skerries

Nephin
Foxford
Swinford
Charlestown
Knock
Ballaghaderreen
Castlerea
ROSCOMMON
Strokestown
Longford
LONGFORD
Granard
Castlepollard
MEATH
An Uaimh (Navan)
Trim
Dunshaughlin
Balbriggan
Rush
Lambay I.

MAYO
Castlebar
Newport
Westport
Clew Bay
Louisburgh
Croagh Patrick
Mweelrea
Partry Mts.
L. Cara
L. Mask
Ballinrobe
Ballyhaunis
Claremorris
Glennamaddy
Tuam
Connacht
Lough Corrib
Oughterard
Galway
GALWAY
Galway Bay
Spiddle
Aran Is.
Inishmore
Inishmaan
Inisheer
Black Hd.
Burren
Lisdoonvarna
Cliffs of Moher
Hags Hd.
Ennistimon
Liscannor Bay
Mal Bay
Mutton I.
Milltown Malbay
CLARE
Ennis
Kilkee
Kilrush
Loop Hd.
Kilbaha
Tarbert
Foynes
Glin
Ballybunion

Mount Bellew
Bridge
Athenry
Aughrim
Loughrea
Ballinasloe
Shannonbridge
Portumna
Slieve Aughty
Gort
Kinvara
Lough Ree
Athlone
Moate
WESTMEATH
Mullingar
Kilbeggan
Clara
Tullamore
OFFALY
Edenderry
Daingean
Bog of Allen
Rathangan
Monasterevin
Portarlington
Mountmellick
Birr
Roscrea
Borrisokane
Nenagh
Lough Derg
Killaloe
Silvermine Mts.
Keeper Hill
Feakle
Tulla
Crusheen
Sixmilebridge
Limerick
LIMERICK
Rathkeale
Newcastle West
Abbeyfeale
Listowel
Feale

Royal Canal
Grand Canal
Liffey
KILDARE
Kildare
Naas
Droichead Nua
Clane
Maynooth
Celbridge
Clondalkin
DUBLIN
DUB.
Howth Hd.
Malahide
Swords
Dun Laoghaire
Killiney
Bray
Greystones
WICKLOW
Wicklow Mts.
Poulaphouca Res.
Blessington
Baltinglass
Lugnaquilla
Rathdrum
Wicklow
Wicklow Hd.
Arklow
Mizen Hd.
IRISH SEA

IRELAND
Leinster
LAOIS
Port Laoise
Arderin
Slieve Bloom
Mountrath
Durrow
Abbeyleix
Donaghmore
Templemore
Thurles
Johnstown
Carlow
CARLOW
Muine Bheag
Tullow
Shillelagh
Gorey
Ballycanew
Courtown

TIPPERARY
Tipperary
Golden Vale
Cashel
Cahir
Clonmel
Carrick-on-Suir
KILKENNY
Kilkenny
Callan
Thomastown
New Ross
Enniscorthy
WEXFORD
Wexford
Wexford Harbour
Rosslare
Rosslare Harbour
Greenore Pt.
Carnsore Pt.
Saltee Is.

MUNSTER
Tralee B.
Brandon B.
Smerwick Harbour
Brandon Mt.
Slieve Mish
Dingle
Dingle Bay
Great Blasket I.
Inishvickillane
Dunmore Hd.
KERRY
Castlegregory
Tralee
Killorglin
Killarney
Macgillycuddy's Reeks
Carrauntoohil
Valencia I.
Cahersiveen
Puffin I.
Great Skellig
Ballinskelligs B.
Scariff I.
Dursey I.
Crow Hd.
Bear I.
Castletownbearhaven
Kenmare River
Sneem
Kenmare
Caha Mts.
Glengarriff
Bantry
Bantry Bay
Whiddy I.
Dunmanway
Dunmanus B.
Long I.
Skull
Baltimore
Sherkin I.
Clear I.
C. Clear
Fastnet Rock
Mizen Hd.

Newmarket
Kanturk
Mallow
Buttevant
Mitchelstown
Galty Mts.
Galtymore
Knockmealdown Mts.
Comeragh Mts.
Slievenamon
Fermoy
Nagles Mts.
CORK
Macroom
Blarney
Cork
CORK
Cork Harbour
Cobh
Crosshaven
Kinsale
Old Head of Kinsale
Clonakilty
Clonakilty B.
Galley Hd.
Skibbereen
Ballydehob
Timoleague

Blackwater
Lismore
Dungarvan
Dungarvan Harbour
WATERFORD
Waterford
Tramore
Tramore B.
Passage East
Waterford Harbour
Hook Hd.
Dunmore East
Kilmore Quay

ST. GEORGE'S CHANNEL

St. David's Hd.
St. David's
St. Brides Bay
WALES

CELTIC SEA

ft m
1500 500
600 200
300 100
0 0
50 150
100 300
200 600
500 1500
1000 3000
2000 6000
m ft

COPYRIGHT PHILIP'S

1:2 000 000

10 0 10 20 30 40 50 60 70 80 km
10 0 10 20 30 40 50 miles

Key to Scottish unitary authorities on map
1 CITY OF ABERDEEN
2 DUNDEE CITY
3 WEST DUNBARTONSHIRE
4 EAST DUNBARTONSHIRE
5 CITY OF GLASGOW
6 INVERCLYDE
7 RENFREWSHIRE
8 EAST RENFREWSHIRE
9 NORTH LANARKSHIRE
10 FALKIRK
11 CLACKMANNANSHIRE
12 WEST LOTHIAN
13 CITY OF EDINBURGH
14 MIDLOTHIAN

ORKNEY IS.
on same scale

ORKNEY

SHETLAND IS.
on same scale

Projection : Lambert's Conformal Conic

West from Greenwich

COPYRIGHT PHILIP'S

12 ENGLAND AND WALES

1:2 000 000

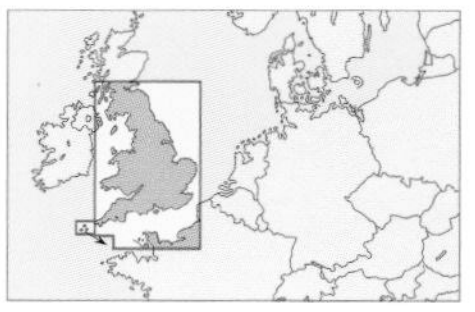

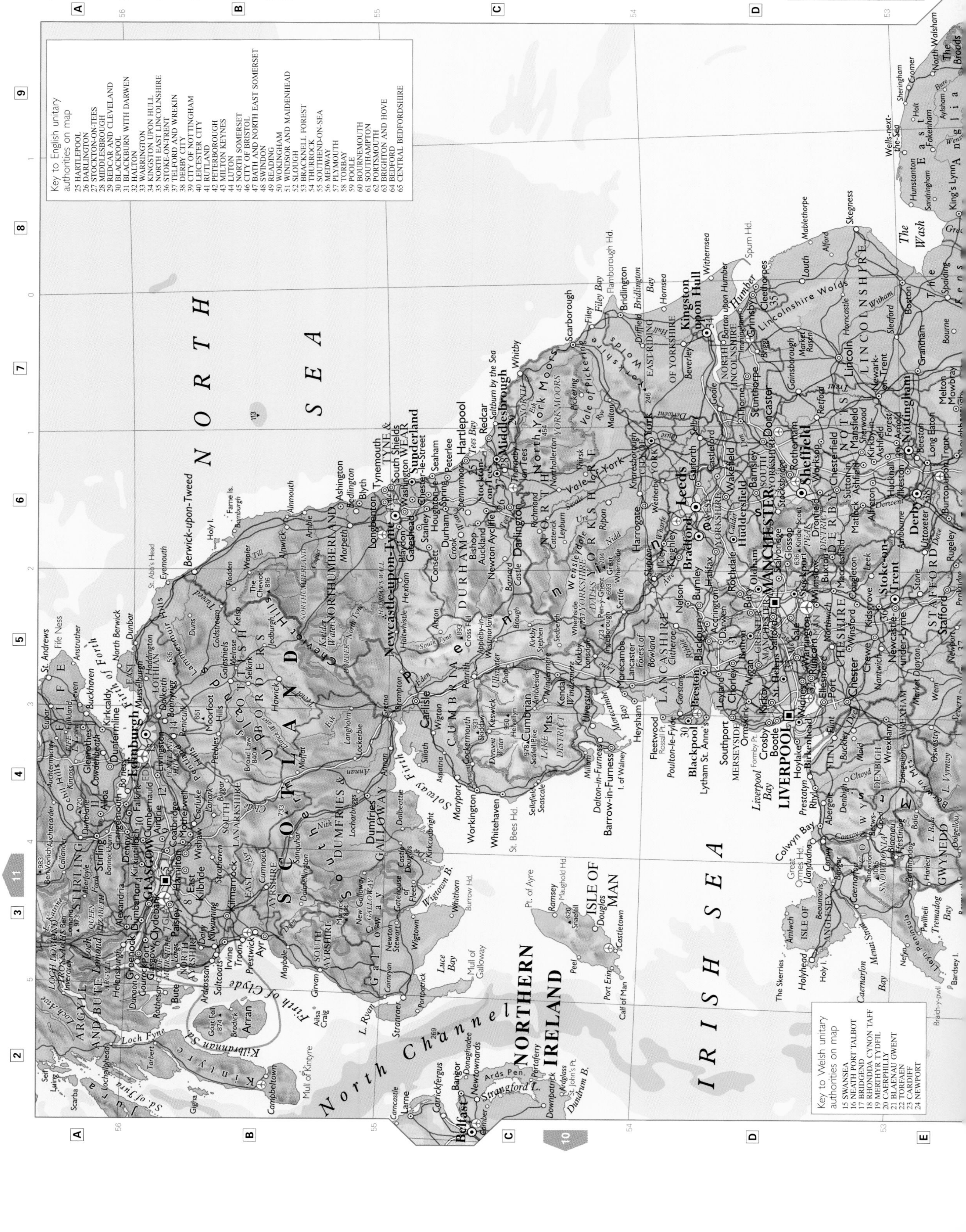

10 0 10 20 30 40 50 60 70 80 km
10 0 10 20 30 40 50 miles

Key to English unitary authorities on map
25 HARTLEPOOL
26 DARLINGTON
27 STOCKTON-ON-TEES
28 MIDDLESBROUGH
29 REDCAR AND CLEVELAND
30 BLACKPOOL
31 BLACKBURN WITH DARWEN
32 HALTON
33 WARRINGTON
34 KINGSTON UPON HULL
35 NORTH EAST LINCOLNSHIRE
36 STOKE-ON-TRENT
37 TELFORD AND WREKIN
38 DERBY CITY
39 CITY OF NOTTINGHAM
40 LEICESTER CITY
41 RUTLAND
42 PETERBOROUGH
43 MILTON KEYNES
44 LUTON
45 NORTH SOMERSET
46 CITY OF BRISTOL
47 BATH AND NORTH EAST SOMERSET
48 SWINDON
49 READING
50 WOKINGHAM
51 WINDSOR AND MAIDENHEAD
52 SLOUGH
53 BRACKNELL FOREST
54 THURROCK
55 SOUTHEND-ON-SEA
56 MEDWAY
57 TORBAY
58 POOLE
59 POOLE
60 BOURNEMOUTH
61 SOUTHAMPTON
62 PORTSMOUTH
63 BRIGHTON AND HOVE
64 BEDFORD
65 CENTRAL BEDFORDSHIRE

Key to Welsh unitary authorities on map
15 SWANSEA
16 NEATH PORT TALBOT
17 BRIDGEND
18 RHONDDA CYNON TAFF
19 MERTHYR TYDFIL
20 CAERPHILLY
21 BLAENAU GWENT
22 TORFAEN
23 CARDIFF
24 NEWPORT

NORTH SEA
IRISH SEA
North Channel
NORTHERN IRELAND
SCOTLAND
ENGLAND
WALES
ISLE OF MAN

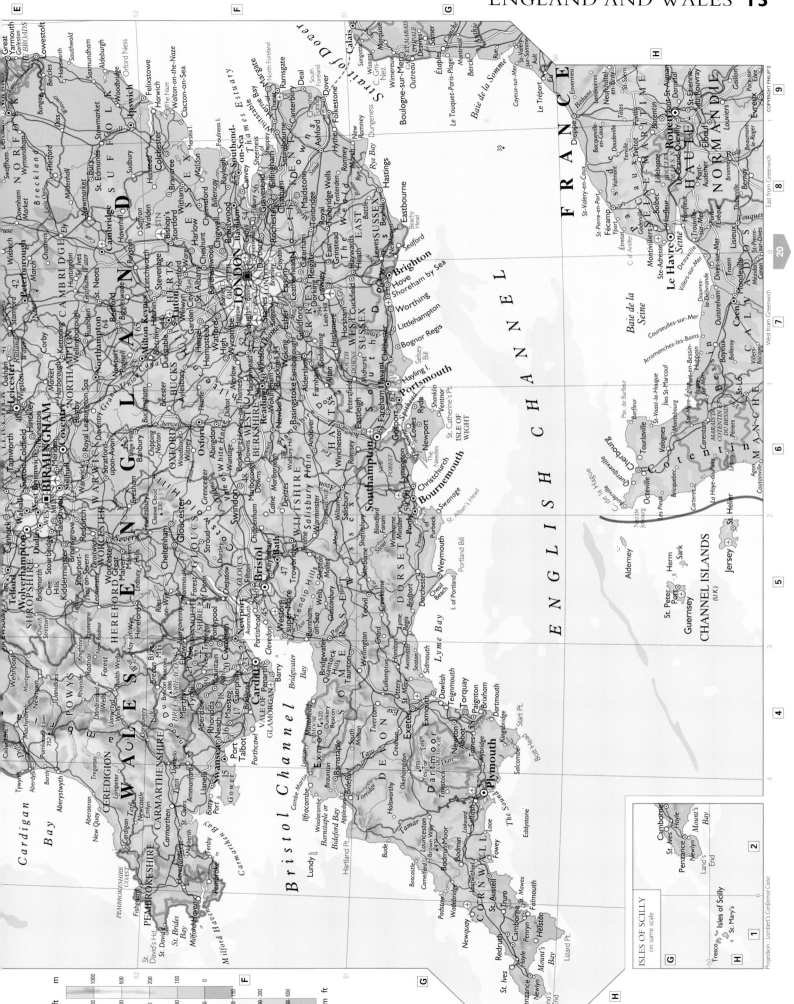

Projection : Lambert's Conformal Conic

50 0 25 50 75 100 125 150 175 km
50 0 25 50 75 100 125 miles

1:5 000 000

1 2 3 4 5 6 7 8 9

ft m
3000 1000
1500 500
600 200
0 0
50 150
100 300
200 600
500 1500
1000 3000
2000 6000
m ft

ATLANTIC OCEAN

NORTH SEA

NORWAY
Bergen
Osøyro
Stord
Bømlo Leirvi
Haugesund
Kopervik
Åkrahamn
Boknafj
Stavanger
Sandnes Bryne
Nærbø

Shetland Is. (U.K.)
Yell Unst
Fetlar
Foula
Mainland
Lerwick
Fair Isle

Orkney Is.
Westray Sanday
Stronsay
Mainland Kirkwall
Hoy South Ronaldsay

1224

316

Pentland Firth
C. Wrath
Thurso
Wick
Helmsdale

Lewis
Stornoway
North Minch
Outer Hebrides
St. Kilda (U.K.)
Harris
789
North Uist
Benbecula
South Uist
Barra

Ullapool
Lairg
Golspie
Tain
Invergordon
Dingwall
Inverness
Nairn Elgin Buckie Banff
Moray Firth
Fraserburgh
Peterhead
Huntly Inverurie
CAIRNGORMS
1311
Aberdeen
Stonehaven

North West Highlands
Skye
1182
Glen More
L. Ness
Aviemore
Portree
Rhum
Eigg
Fort William
1342
Ben Nevis
Coll
Tobermory
Mull
Tiree
Oban
Colonsay
L. Awe
L. Fyne
Jura
Islay
Campbeltown
Arran

SCOTLAND
Grampian Mts.
1214
Dee
Ballater
Forfar
Montrose
Arbroath
L. Earn
L. Tay
L. Lomond
973
Perth
Dundee
St. Andrews
Stirling
Dunfermline
Kirkcaldy
Glenrothes
Dumbarton
Greenock
Paisley
GLASGOW
Edinburgh
Dunbar
East Kilbride
Hamilton
Motherwell
Berwick-upon-Tweed
Irvine
Kilmarnock
Ayr
Galashiels
Girvan
Jedburgh
Hawick
840
Alnwick
816
Cheviot Hills
Southern Uplands

Inner Hebrides
Sea of the Hebrides
Firth of Clyde
North Channel

Malin Hd.
Buncrana
Aran I.
Letterkenny
Coleraine
Ballymena
Larne
GLENVEAGH
Londonderry
Antrim
Bangor
Donegal
Omagh
NORTHERN IRELAND
Lough Neagh
Lisburn
Belfast
Bundoran
Ulster
Lower L.
Enniskillen
Armagh
Lurgan
Portadown
Newry
Mull of Galloway
Stranraer
Kirkcudbright
Dumfries
Annan
Workington
Whitehaven
Carlisle
Hexham
978
893
Cumbrian Mts.
LAKE DISTRICT
Newcastle-upon-Tyne
South Shields
Sunderland
Gateshead
Durham
Hartlepool
Redcar
Darlington
Middlesbrough
Stockton-on-Tees
N. YORK MOORS
Scarborough

Ballina
L. Conn
Castlebar
Sligo
Leitrim
Cavan
Castleblaney
Dundalk
Drogheda
Douglas
I. of Man
Barrow-in-Furness
Lancaster
Harrogate
Bridlington
YORKSHIRE DALES
Beverley
York
Kingston upon Hull

UNITED KINGDOM

Achill I.
Lough Mask
Connemara
Westport
Roscommon
Athlone
Ballinasloe
Longford
Mullingar
Ceanannus Mor
Boyne
Blackpool
Burnley
Keighley
Leeds
Bradford
Halifax
Huddersfield
Barnsley
Doncaster
Grimsby
Scunthorpe
Preston
Blackburn
Bolton
Oldham
MANCHESTER
Stockport
Rotherham
Sheffield
Lincoln
Louth
Skegness

Galway B.
Galway
Aran Is.
BURREN
Lough Corrib
Lough Ree
Tullamore
Birr
Portlaoise
Athy
Carlow
926
Wicklow Mts.
DUBLIN
Dun Laoghaire
Bray
Holyhead
Anglesey
Bangor
Colwyn Bay
Chester
Crewe
Warrington
LIVERPOOL
Wrexham
Stoke on Trent
Chesterfield
Mansfield
PEAK DISTRICT
630
Derby
Nottingham
Boston
The Wash
Cromer

IRELAND
IRISH SEA
Lough Derg
Nenagh
Limerick
Thurles
Clonmel
Kilkenny
Carrick-on-Suir
Wexford
Rosslare
953
Dingle
Tralee
Listowel
Killarney
Carrantoohill
1041
Macgillycuddy's Reeks
Valencia
Mallow
Blackwater
Cork
Bandon
Kinsale
Cobh
Youghal
Dungarvan
Waterford
Tipperary

SNOWDONIA
1085
Snowdon
Cambrian Mts.
Welshpool
Shrewsbury
Telford
Stafford
Grantham
Trent
Leicester
Corby
Peterborough
Ely
Thetford
THE BROADS
Great Yarmouth
Lowestoft
Norwich
King's Lynn

Cardigan Bay
Aberystwyth
WALES
Wolverhampton
BIRMINGHAM
Redditch
Royal Leamington Spa
Coventry
Rugby
Northampton
Bedford
Milton Keynes
Cambridge
Bury St. Edmunds
Ipswich
Felixstowe
Harwich
Colchester

St. George's Channel
Fishguard
Haverfordwest
Milford Haven
Pembroke
PEMBROKESHIRE COAST
Carmarthen
886
Merthyr Tydfil
BRECON BEACONS
Brecon
Hereford
Worcester
Gloucester
Cheltenham
COTSWOLD HILLS
Oxford
High Wycombe
Hemel Hempstead
Luton
Stevenage
Harlow
Chelmsford
Southend-on-Sea
Margate

Llanelli
Neath
Port Talbot
Rhondda
Newport
Cardiff
Barry
Bristol
Bath
Swindon
Newbury
Reading
Slough
LONDON
Thames
Chatham
Canterbury
Dover
Folkestone
Maidstone

99

ENGLAND

Bristol Channel
EXMOOR
Barnstaple
Exmoor
Weston-super-Mare
Bridgwater
Taunton
Yeovil
Salisbury
Basingstoke
Guildford
Reigate
Crawley
Ashford
Hastings
Eastbourne

CELTIC SEA

Bude
618
DARTMOOR
Dartmoor
Exeter
Exmouth
NEW FOREST
Bournemouth
Poole
Weymouth
Isle of Wight
Newport
Portsmouth
Worthing
Brighton
Southampton
Fareham
Havant
Winchester

Newquay
Truro
St. Austell
Plymouth
Torbay
Land's End
Penzance
Falmouth
Isles of Scilly

English Channel

Str. of Dover
Gris-Nez
Calais
Boulogne-sur-Mer
Le Touquet-Paris-Plage
33
C. de la Hague
Pte. de Barfleur
Cherbourg
Alderney
St. Peter Port
Guernsey
Sark
Channel Is. (U.K.)
Jersey
St. Helier
Valognes
Bayeux
Caen
Trouville-sur-Mer
Lisieux
Elbeuf
Seine
Bolbec
Le Havre
Fécamp
Dieppe
Le Tréport
Abbeville
Amiens
FRANCE
Rouen
Pays de Caux
Picardie
St. Quentin
Cambrai
Laon

NETHERLANDS
's-Gravenhage (Den Haag)
Hoek van Holland
ROTTERDAM
Dordrecht
Haarlem
Alkma
Den Helde
Texe

BELGIUM
Antwerpe
Brugge
Gent
Mechel
BRUSSEL (Bruxelles)
Oostende
Zeebrugge
Vlissingen
Dunkerque
St-Omer
Béthune
Bruay-la-Buissière
LILLE
Tourcoing
Roubaix
Villeneuve d'Ascq
Tournai
Valenciennes

238

16

36

20

Projection: Conical with two standard parallels

East from Greenwich
West from Greenwich
COPYRIGHT PHILIP'S

Underlined towns give their name to the administrative area in which they stand.

CENTRAL EUROPE

1:5 000 000

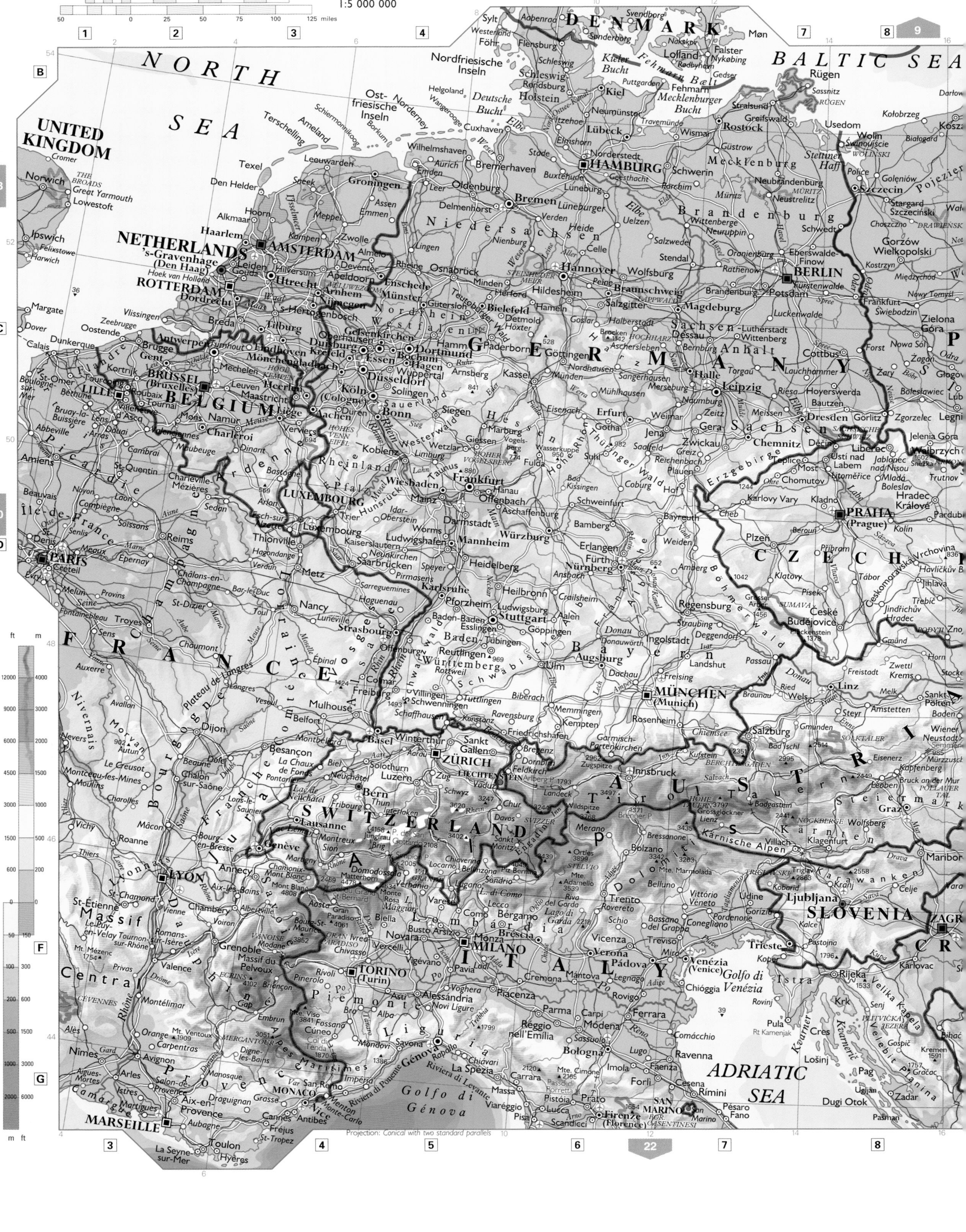

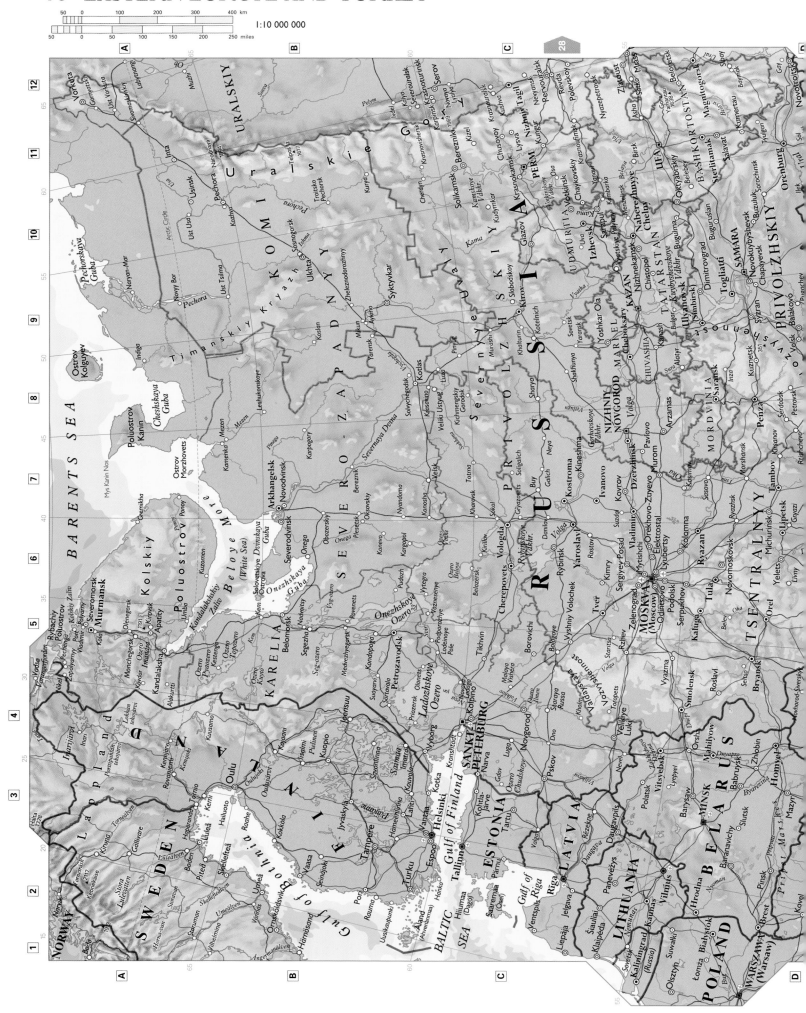

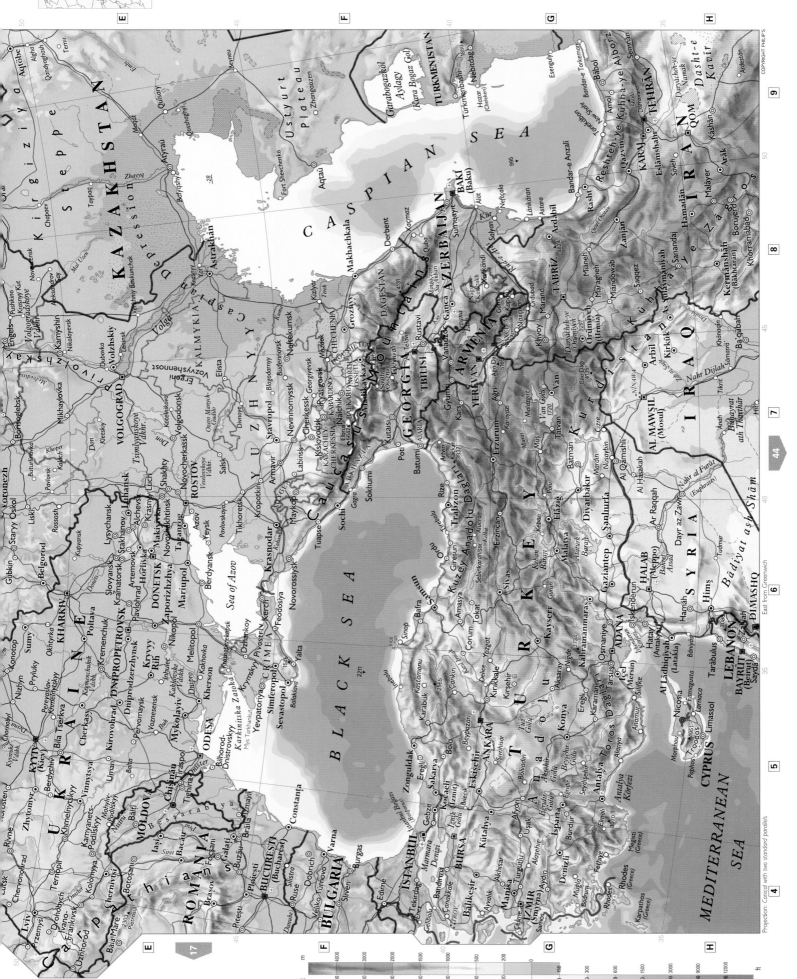

CASPIAN SEA

BLACK SEA

MEDITERRANEAN SEA

Sea of Azov

KAZAKHSTAN

TURKMENISTAN

IRAN

IRAQ

SYRIA

LEBANON

CYPRUS

TURKEY

AZERBAIJAN

ARMENIA

GEORGIA

UKRAINE

ROMANIA

BULGARIA

MOLDOVA

Projection: Conical with two standard parallels

East from Greenwich

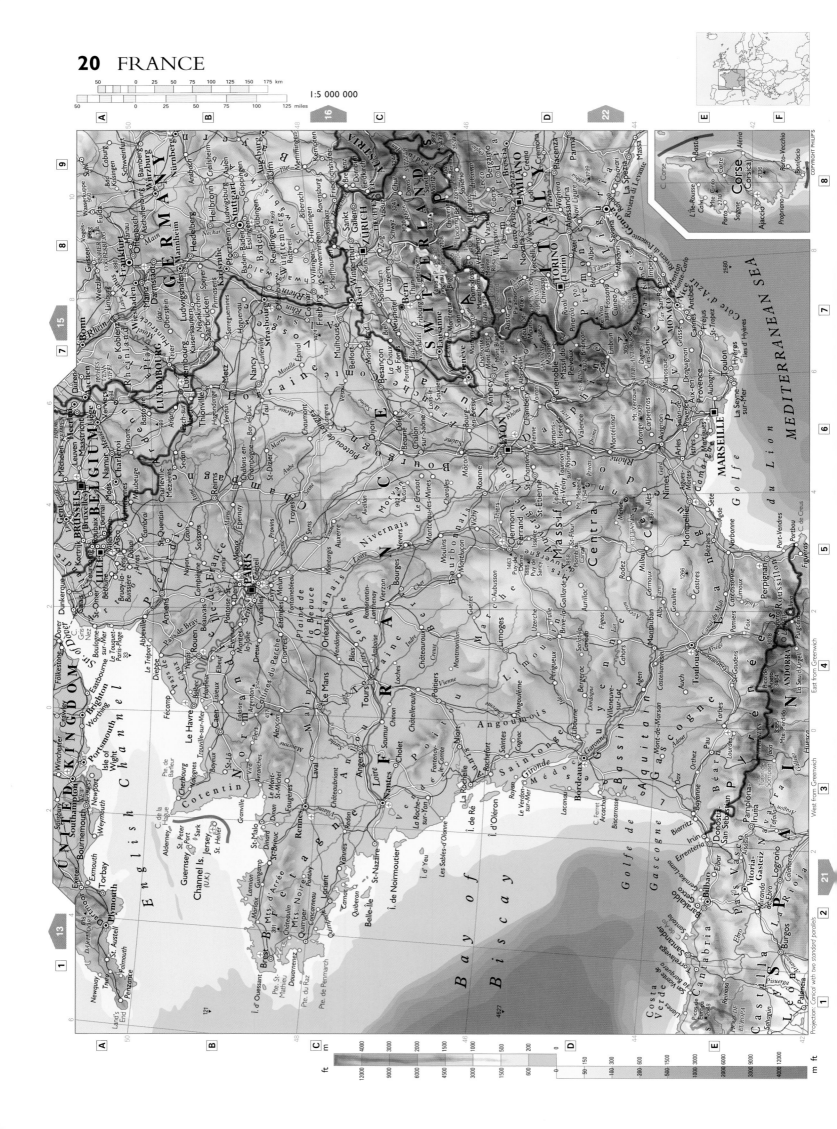

1:5 000 000

Projection: Conical with two standard parallels

COPYRIGHT PHILIP'S

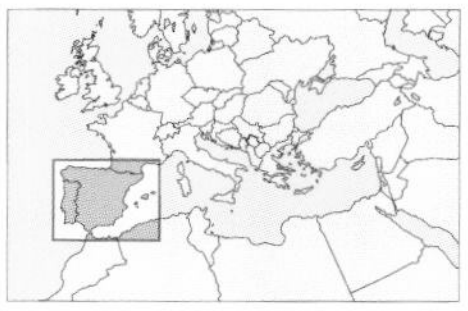

1:5 000 000

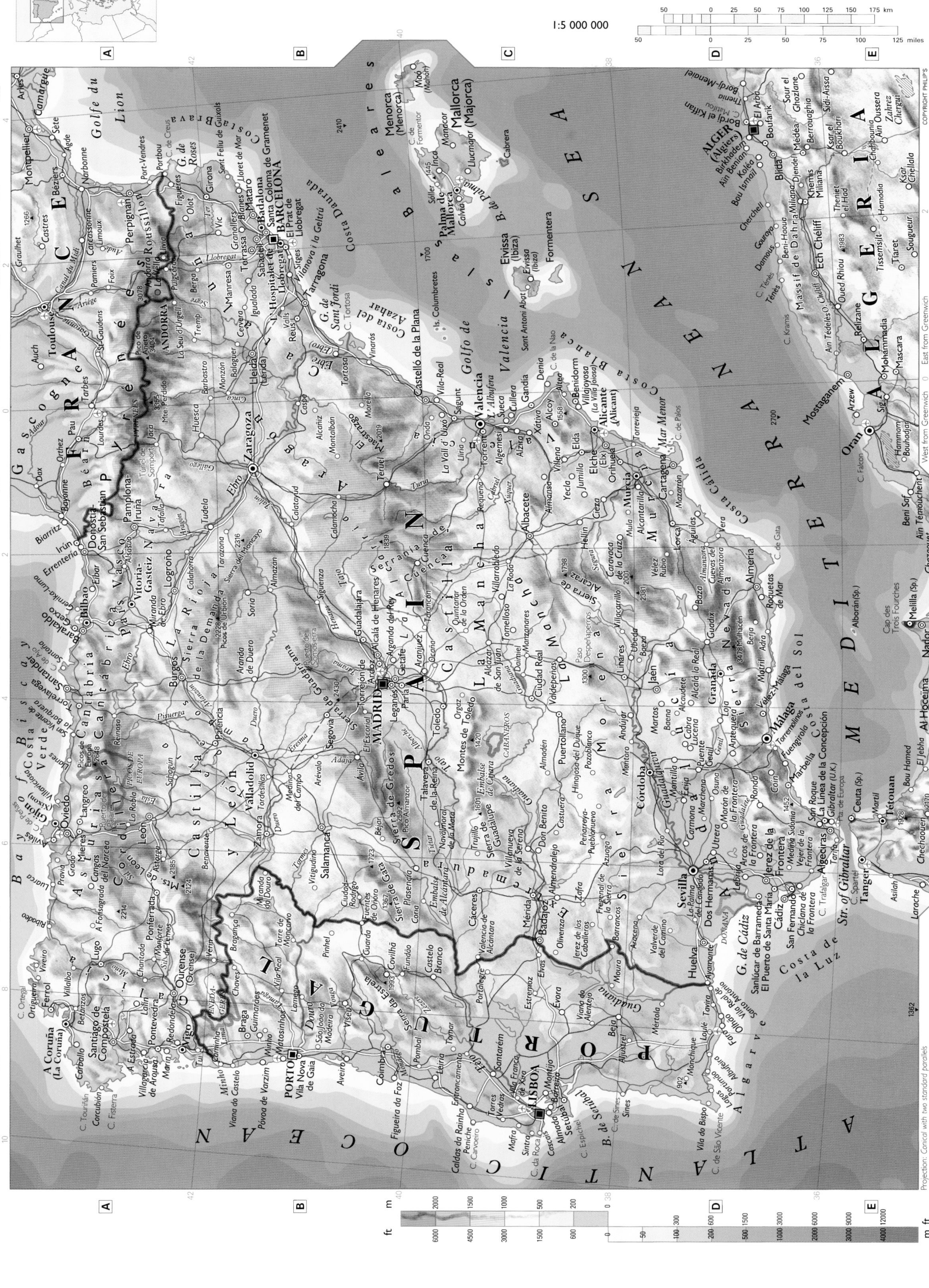

50 0 25 50 75 100 125 150 175 km

50 0 25 50 75 100 125 miles

COPYRIGHT PHILIP'S

East from Greenwich

West from Greenwich

Projection: Conical with two standard parallels

ft m
6000 2000
4500 1500
3000 1000
1500 500
600 200
0
0
-50 -100
-200 -300
-500 -600
-1500 -1500
-3000 -3000
-6000 -6000
-9000 -12000 -4000 m ft

HUNGARY

Szekszárd Kalocsa Kiskőrös Kiskunhalas Orosháza Hódmezővásárhely Makó Arad Muntii Bihor 1848 Odorheiu Secuiesc Miercurea Ciuc Oneşti Siret Bârlad Cădâr-Lunga Tatarbunary

UKRAINE

Pécs Szeged Subotica Sânnicolau Mare Crişul Alb Brad Alba-Iulia Aiud Târnăveni Sighişoara Sfântu Gheorghe Focşani Tecuci Bolhrad Ozero Sasyk Kiliya

Mohács Baja Sombor Senta Kikinda Lugoj Simeria Sibiu Fāgāraş Braşov 1783 Vulcaneşti Izmayil Vylkove Sulina

ROMANIA

Osijek Vukovar Novi Sad Zrenjanin Reşiţa Deva Hunedoara Petroşani Câmpulung Vf. Omul 2507 Câmpina Buzău Râmnicu Sărat Galaţi Brăila Reni Tulcea

SERBIA

Beograd (Belgrade) Pančevo Smederevo Drobeta-Turnu Severin Craiova Slatina Piteşti Bucureşti (Bucharest) Feteşti Constanţa

MONTENEGRO

Podgorica Kotor Peje Pristina Kosovo Niš Sofiya

BULGARIA

Pleven Varna

BLACK SEA

ALBANIA

MACEDONIA

Skopje Tetovo

GREECE

Thessaloniki (Salonica)

TURKEY

Istanbul İzmir (Smyrna)

Athina (Athens)

AEGEAN SEA

Crete (Kriti)

MEDITERRANEAN SEA

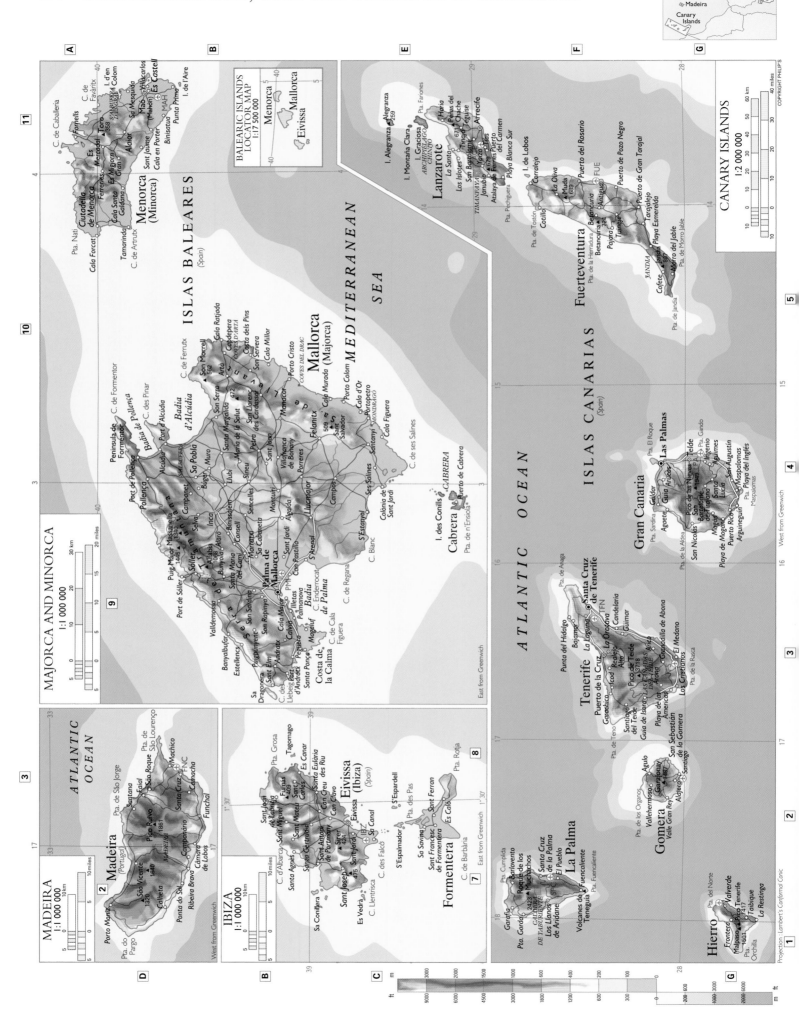

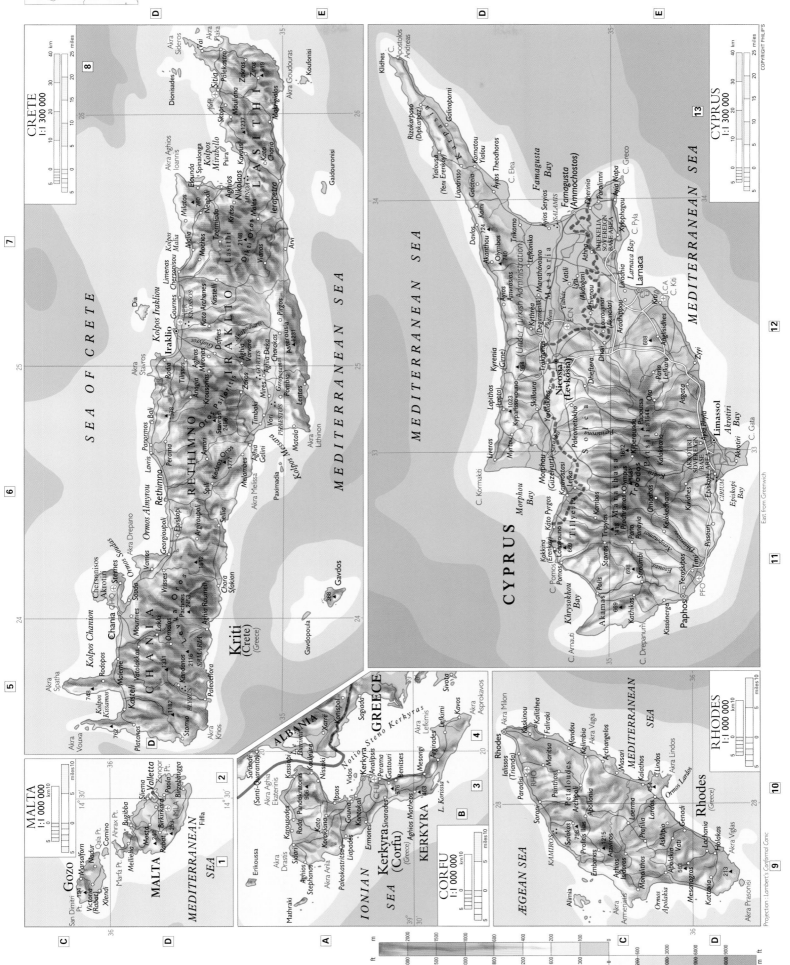

100 0 200 400 600 800 1000 1200 1400 km

1:47 000 000

100 0 200 400 600 800 1000 miles

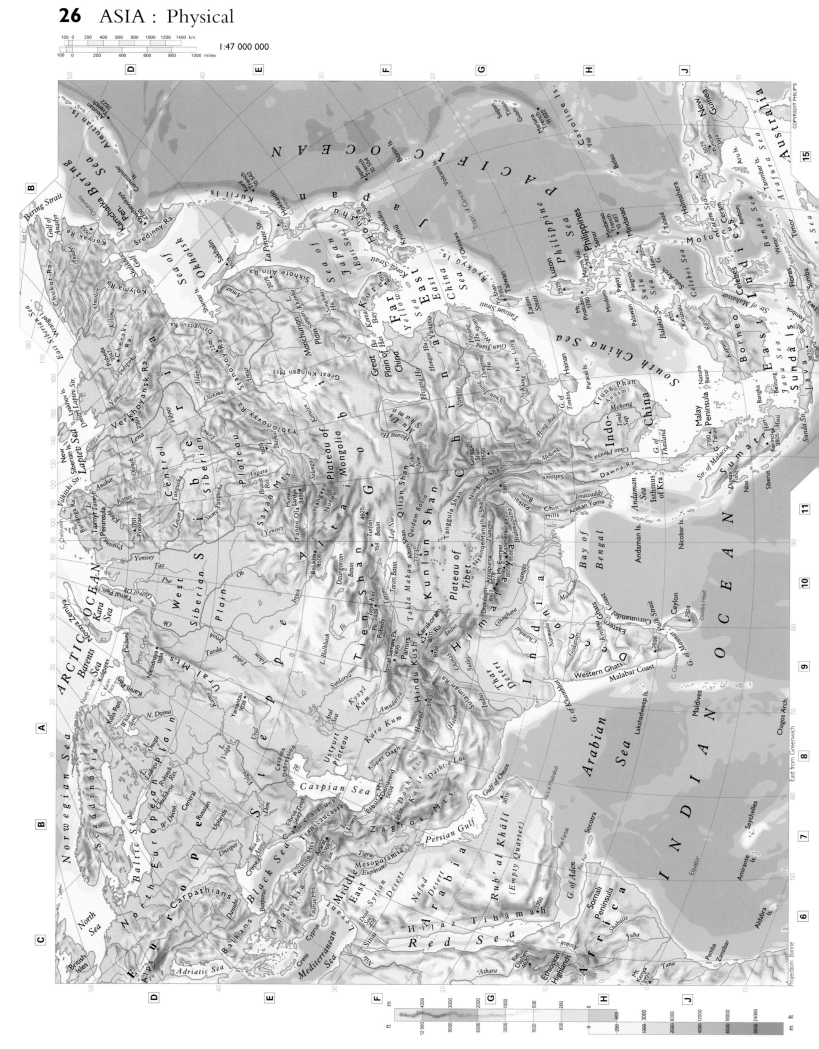

Projection: Bonne

m
ft

1:47 000 000

Projection: Bonne

100 0 100 200 300 400 500 600 700 800 km

1:20 000 000

100 0 100 200 300 400 500 miles

	RUSSIA
1	Adygea
2	Karachey-Cherkessia
3	Kabardino-Balkaria
4	North Ossetia
5	Ingushetia
6	Chechenia
7	Dagestan
8	Mordvinia
9	Chuvashia
10	Mari El
11	Tatarstan
12	Udmurtia
13	Khakassia

AZERBAIJAN
14 Naxçivan

GEORGIA   UKRAINE
15 Ajaria   17 Crimea
16 Abkhazia

Projection: Conical Orthomorphic with two standard parallels

East from Greenwich

45   32

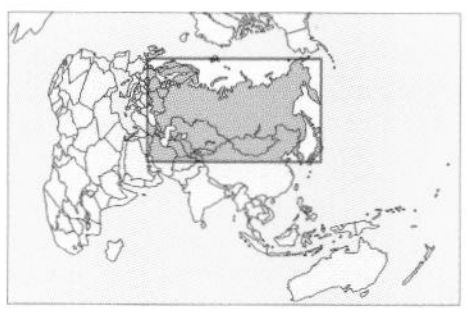

A 4 B 18 C

Chukchi Sea
Mys Dezhneva (East C.)
Uelen
Bering Str.
St. Lawrence I. (U.S.A.)
International Date Line
Mys Navarin

OCEAN
Ostrov Shmidta
Mys Arkticheskiy
Ostrov Komsomolets
Ostrov Pioner
Ostrov Ushakova
Ostrov Oktyabrskoy Revolyutsii
Severnaya Zemlya
Ostrov Bolshevik
Ostrova Sergeya Kirova
Ostrov Russkiy
Proliv Vilkitskogo
Mys Chelyuskin
Ostrova Petra

Laptev Sea
Novosibirskiye Ostrova
Ostrova Delonga
Ostrov Bennetta
Ostrov Genriyetty
Ostrov Zhinnetty
Ostrov Zhokhova
Ostrov Faddeyevskiy
Novaya Sibir
Ostrov Belkovskiy
Ostrov Kotelnyy
Ostrov Bolshoy Lyakhovskiy
Ostrov Malyy Lyakhovskiy
Lyakhovskiye Ostrova
Ostrov Stolbovoy

East Siberian Sea
Ostrov Vrangelya
Ostrov Medvezhi

Chaunskaya Guba
Mys Shmidta

Bering Sea

Poluostrov Gory Byrranga Taymyr
Oz. Taymyr
Nordvik
Ostrov Bolshoy Begichev
Mys Buorkhaya

Chukotskoye Nagorye
Koryakskoye Nagorye
Sredinnyy Khrebet
Poluostrov Kamchatka

Volochanka
Kheta
Khatanga
Novorybnoye
Saskylakh
Tiksi
Tit-Ary
Ust Olenek
Bulun
Kyusyur
Verkhoyansk
Batagay

Norilsk
Talnakh
Gory Putorana
Noginsk
Yessey
Zhilinda
Olenek
Zhigansk
Verkhoyanskiy Khrebet
Khrebet Cherskogo

Tura
Chernysheyskiy
Udachnyy
Aykhal
Vilyuysk
Verkhnevilyuysk
Nyurba
Suntar
Mirnyy
Yakutsk
Nizhniy Bestyakh
Pokrovsk
Sinsk
Olekminsk
Tommot
Aldan

Yerbogachen
Lensk
Vitim
Ust-Maya

Sea of Okhotsk
Sakhalin
Yuzhno-Sakhalinsk
Kurilskiye Ostrova

Krasnoyarsk
Bratsk
Ust-Ilimsk
Ust-Kut
Severobaykalsk
Tynda
Skovorodino
Neryungri
Stanovoy Khrebet

Irkutsk
Ulan Ude
Ozero Baykal
Chita
Komsomolsk-na-Amure
Khabarovsk
Sikhote Alin

Angarsk
Ulaanbaatar

MONGOLIA
Gobi

Hangayn Nuruu

Hentiyn Nuruu

Vladivostok
Hokkaidō
SAPPORO
Hakodate

Honshū

Sea of Japan (East Sea)

QIQIHAR
DAQING
HARBIN
JIAMUSI
JIXI
MUDANJIANG
JILIN
CHANGCHUN
FUYU
Dongbei (Manchuria)
Da Hinggan Ling
Dahei

CHIFENG
FUSHUN
SHENYANG
ANSHAN
NORTH KOREA
PYONGYANG
Hamhŭng
Wŏnsan

CHINA
BAOTOU
HOHHOT
ZHANGJIAKOU
BEIJING
Tangshan
DALIAN
SEOUL
INCHEON
SOUTH KOREA
DAEJEON
DAEGU
BUSAN
GWANGJU

JAPAN KYOTO
KOBE
OSAKA

10 11 33 12 13 14

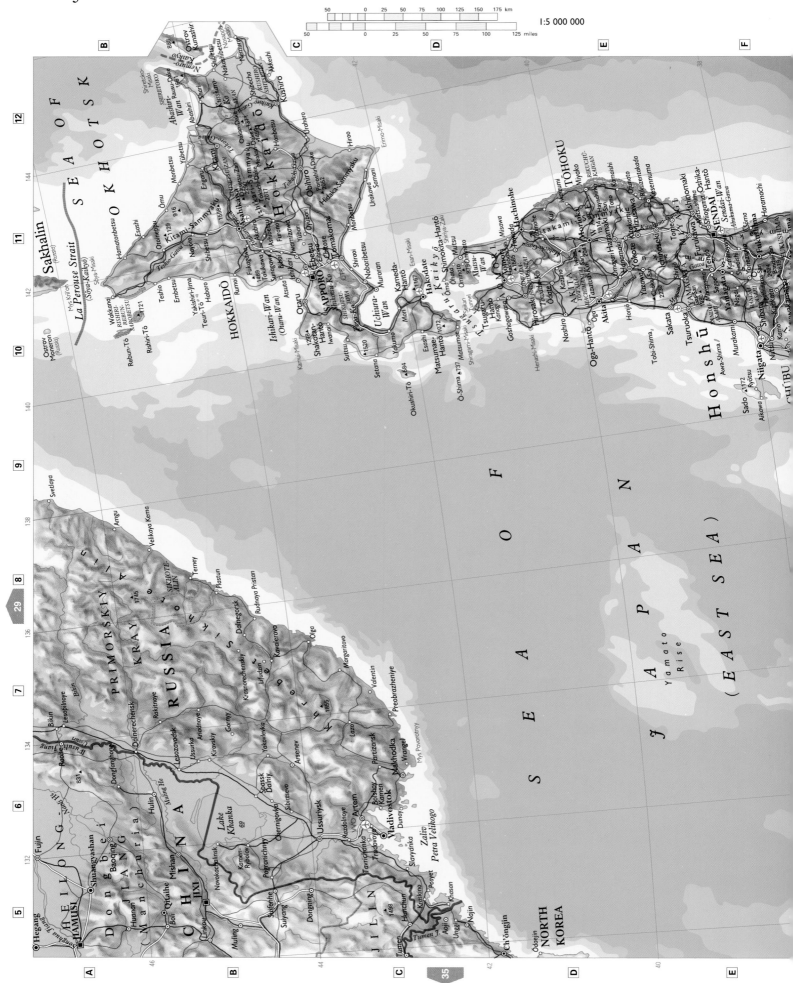

1:5 000 000

| 50 | | 0 | 25 | 50 | 75 | 100 | 125 | 150 | 175 km |
| 50 | | | 0 | | 25 | 50 | | 75 | 100 | 125 miles |

SEA OF OKHOTSK

Sakhalin

La Perouse Strait
(Sōya-Kaikyō)

Ostrov Moneron (Russia)

HOKKAIDŌ

SAPPORO

Ishikari-Wan
(Otaru-Wan)

Shakotan-Hantō

Uchiura-Wan

Kameda-Hantō

Hakodate

Matsumae-Hantō

Okushiri-Tō

TŌHOKU

Honshū

Sado

Niigata

CHIBU

SENDAI

Sendai-Wan

SEA

OF

JAPAN

(EAST SEA)

Yamato Rise

Svetlaya

Amgu

Velikaya Kema

Terney

Plastun

Rudnaya Pristan

Dalnegorsk

Kavalerovo

PRIMORSKIY

KRAY

RUSSIA

SIKHOTE-ALIN

Olga

Margaritovo

Valentin

Preobrazheniye

Bikin

Lesozplinoye

Dalnerechensk

Rakovoye

Letozavodsk

Ussurka

Kirovskiy

Anadnoye

Gorny

Yakovlevka

Krasnorechenskiy

Lifudzin

Lazo

Partizansk

Arsenev

Spassk Dalniy

Sibirtsevo

Chernigovka

Ussuriysk

Razdolnoye

Artem

Vladivostok

Nakhodka

Wrangel

Partizansk

Mys Povorotny

Zaliv Petra Velikogo

Fujin

Shuangyashan

Boli

Mishan

HEILONGJIANG

Dongbei

Manchuria

Hulin

CHINA

Lake Khanka

JILIN

NORTH KOREA

Ch'ŏngjin

Najin

Tumen J.

HAMUSI

Hegang

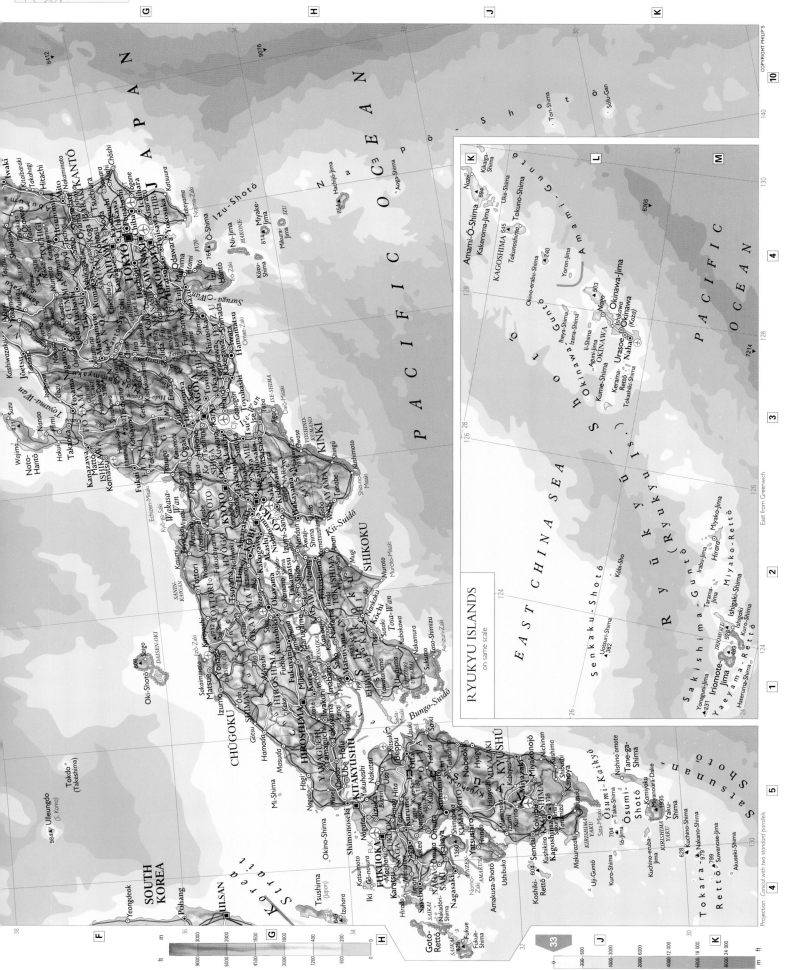

1:15 000 000

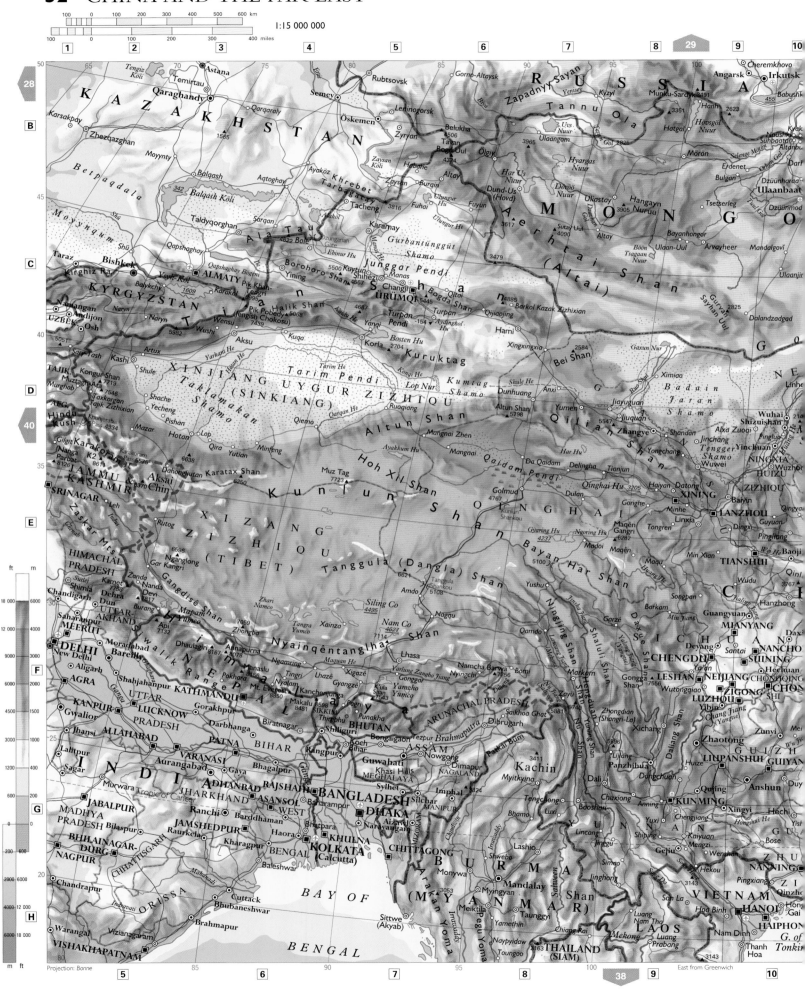

Projection: Bonne

East from Greenwich

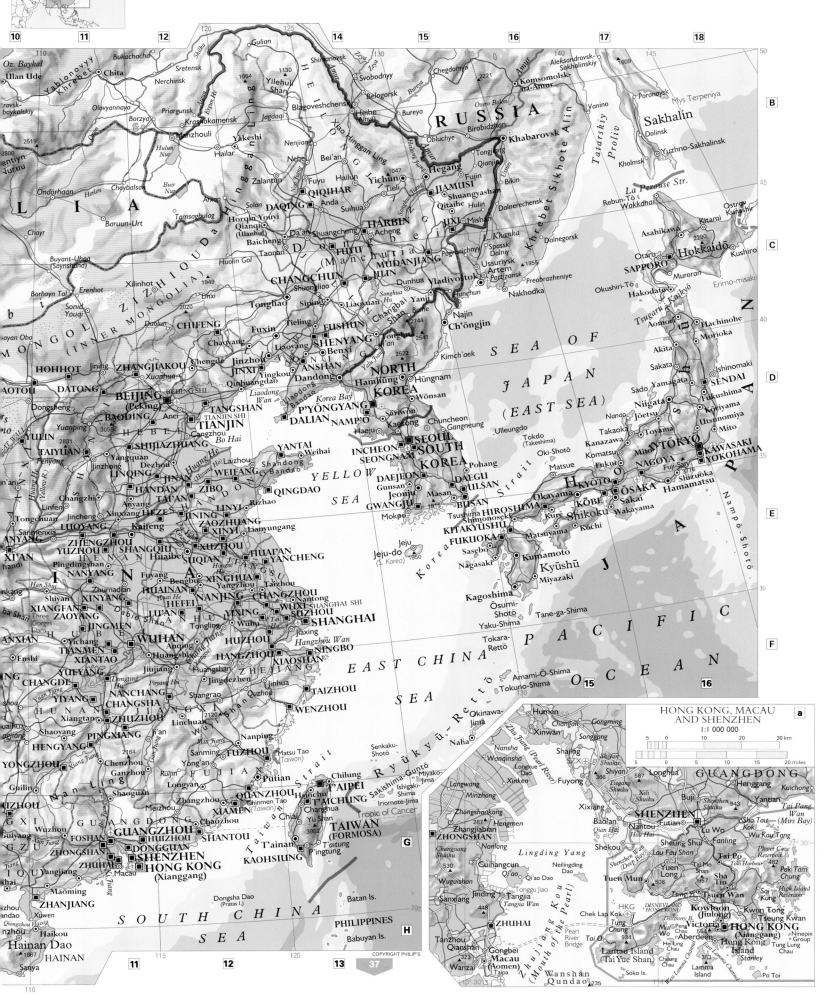

10 11 12 14 15 16 17 18

Oz. Baykal
Ulan Ude
110
Bukachacha
Chita
Yablonovyy Khrebet
Sretensk
Nerchinsk
Olovyannaya
Borzya
rovsk-baykalskiy
Manzhouli
Krasnokamensk
2519
Priargunsk
Yakeshi
2800
Hailar
Hulun Nur
Hailun
Ondorhaan
Herlen
Choyr
Buir Nur
Buyant-Uhaa (Saynshand)
b
Borhoyn Tal
Erenhot
Sonid Youqi
Xilinhot
Duolun
ayan Obo
CHIFENG
MONGOL
(INNER MONGOLIA)
AOTOU
HOHHOT
Jining
Xuanhua
ZHANGJIAKOU
no
DATONG
Dongsheng
Yuanping
YULIN
2831
TAIYUAN
GREAT WALL
Yangquan
n'an
Jinzhong
N
HUANG HE (Yellow R.)
Han Shui
XI'AN
handi
LUOYANG
ZHENGZHOU
YUZHOU
NANYANG
Pingdingshan
ba Shan
Shiyan
XIANGFAN
ZAOYANG
JINGMEN
ANXIAN
TIANMEN
XIANTAO
Enshi
Yichang
Three Gorges Dam
WUHAN
Huangshi
Anqing
YUEYANG
Dongting Hu
CHANGDE
YIYANG
NANCHANG
CHANGSHA
ZHUZHOU
JIANGXI
HUNAN
Xiangtan
Xiang Jiang
2120
Wuyi Shan
Shaoyang
PINGXIANG
HENGYANG
Linchuan
YONGZHOU
Xiang Jiang
Guilin
ngjiang
IZHOU
Nan Ling
Liuzhou
GXI
Wuzhou
GUANGDONG
GUANGZHOU
FOSHAN
Guiyang
Xun Jiang
GZ
ZHONGSHAN
Yangjiang
DONGGUAN
SHENZHEN
HONG KONG (Xianggang)
ZHUHAI
Macau
thai
ndao
ZHANJIANG
Maoming
Xuwen
Qiongzhou Haixia
nzhou
Haikou
Hainan Dao
HAINAN
1867
Sanya
110

Gulian
Shilka
120
Yilehuli Shan
1054
Shimanovsk
1130
Zeya
125
130
Amur
Svobodnyy
Chegdomyn
2221
140
Aleksandrovsk-Sakhalinskiy
1609
Komsomolsk-na-Amur
Poronaysk
Mys Terpeniya
50
B
Sakhalin
Dolinsk
45
Yuzhno-Sakhalinsk
La Perouse Str.
C
Hokkaidō
SAPPORO
Otaru
Muroran
2290
Asahikawa
Kitami
Ostrov Kunashir
N
Kushiro
Hakodate
Okushiri-Tō
Erimo-misaki
40
Aomori
Hachinohe
Morioka
Akita
Ishinomaki
Yamagata
SENDAI
D
Niigata
Fukushima
Nagaoka
Koriyama
Jōetsu
Mito
Utsunomiya
35
Toyama
Takaoka
Kanazawa
Komatsu
Fukui
NAGOYA
TŌKYŌ
KAWASAKI
YOKOHAMA
Fuji-San 3776
Shizuoka
KYŌTO
ŌSAKA
Sakai
KŌBE
Okayama
Hamamatsu
E
HIROSHIMA
Kure
Shikoku
Wakayama
Kōchi
Matsuyama
Nampō-Shotō
Nerchinsk
Shilka
Ergun He
Argun
Heihe
Aihui
HEILONGJIANG
Xiao Hinggan Ling
Nenjiang
Bei'an
Belogorsk
Bureya
Birobidzhan
RUSSIA
Obluchye
Amur
Khabarovsk
Tongjiang
Qianjin
Ussuri
Bikin
Khrebet Sikhote Alin
Tatarskiy Proliv
Rebun-Tō
Wakkanai
SEA OF
JAPAN
(EAST SEA)
Ulleungdo
Tokdo (Takeshima)
Oki-Shotō
Matsue
Tsugaru Kaikyō
Kholmsk
Vanino
Dalnegorsk
Sado
Yamagata

Ulan Ude
Borzya

SOUTH CHINA
SEA
PHILIPPINES
Babuyan Is.
Batan Is.

EAST CHINA
SEA
Senkaku-Shotō
Okinawa-Jima
Naha
Ryūkyū-Rettō
Sakishima-Guntō
Miyako-Jima
Ishigaki-Jima
Iriomote-Jima
Tropic of Cancer
TAIWAN
(FORMOSA)
T'AIPEI
CHILUNG
T'AICHUNG
Changhua
Chiai
Yu Shan
3952
T'ainan
P'ingtung
T'aitung
KAOHSIUNG
Taiwan Strait
Matsu Tao (Taiwan)
Chinmen Tao
QUANZHOU
XIAMEN
Chaozhou
SHANTOU
HUIZHOU
Meizhou
FUJIAN
Longyan
Shaoguan
FUZHOU
Putian
Sanming
Nanping
Yong'an
2164
Ruijin
Ganzhou
Chenzhou
Dongsha Dao (Pratas I.)

G
H

COPYRIGHT PHILIP'S
11 12 13 37

HONG KONG, MACAU AND SHENZHEN
1:1 000 000
a
5 0 10 20 30 km
5 0 5 10 15 20 miles

Humen
Changan
Gongming
Xinwan
Songgang
Nansha
Shajing
SZX
Shiyan Shuiku
GUANGDONG
Longhua
Henggang
Kuichong
Wanqinsha
Shiyan
Longxue
Xinken
Fuyong
366
Tiegang Shuiku
587
Buji
Shenchen Shuiku
943
Yantian
Langwang
Minzhong
Zhongshankou
Xixiang
Baolong
287
Xili Shuiku
SHENZHEN
Futian
Tai Pang Wan (Mirs Bay)
Zhangjiabian
Hengmen
Qian Hai
Nantou
Lu Wo
Sha Tau Kok
ZHONGSHAN
Nanlang
Shenchen Wan (Deep Bay)
Shekou
Lau Fau Shan
Sheung Shui
Wu Kau Tang
Fanling
Changjiang Shuiku
530
Cuihangcun
Qi'ao Dao
Neilingding Dao
Plover Cove Reservoir
462
Yuen Long
Tai Po
Tai Mo Shan
957
Pak Tam Chung
Sanxiang
Jinding
Tonggu Jiao
Tangjia
Lingding Yang
Shenchen Wan
506
Tai Lam Chung
Tuen Mun
High Island Reservoir
Sai Kung
Zhuhai
448
Tangjia
Tangna Wan
Tsing Yi
Tsuen Wan
Kwun Tong
Tseung Kwan
Zhuhai
Tanzhou
Qianshan
323
Gongbei
Macau (Aomen)
Taipa
HKG
DISNEYLAND HONG KONG
Chek Lap Kok
Tung Chung
Tai O
934
Lantau Island (Tai Yue Shan)
Kowloon (Jiulong)
Victoria
Hong Kong Island
Aberdeen
Mui Wo
Hei Ling Chau
Cheung Chau
Ninepin Group
Tung Lung
353
HONG KONG (Xianggang)
Stanley
Wanzai
Soko Is.
Lamma Island
235
Po Toi
Wanshan Qundao

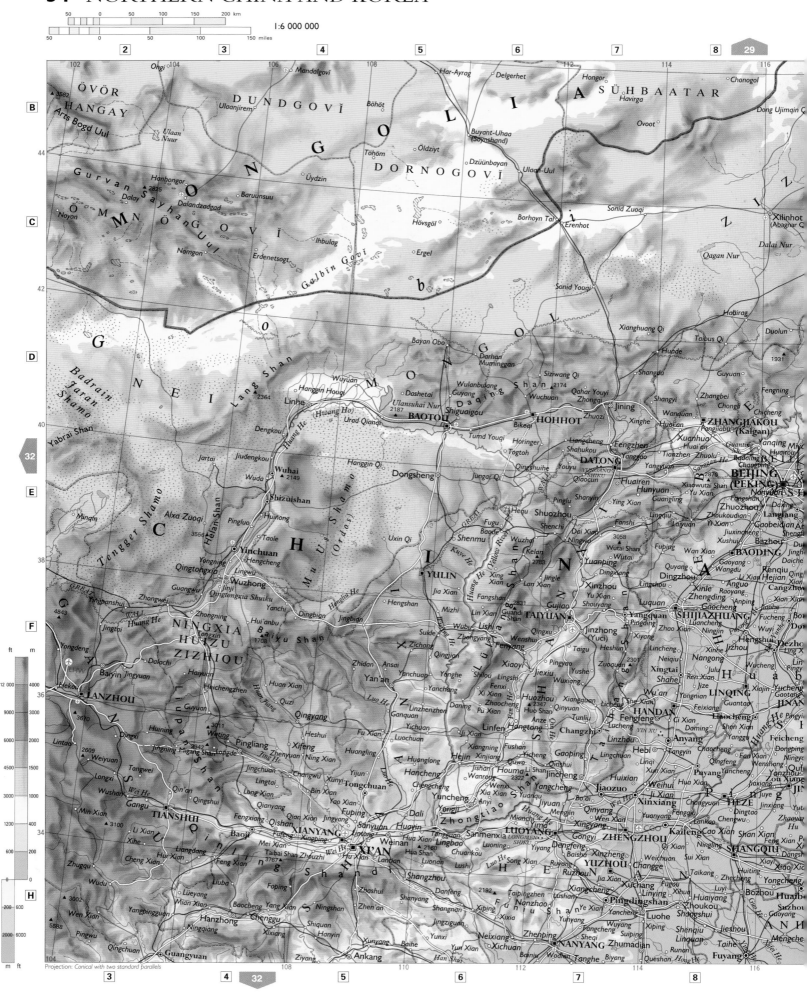

1:6 000 000

Projection: Conical with two standard parallels

B

118 120 126 128 130 132

Horqin Youyi Qianqi
(Ulanhot)
HARBIN   Bin Xian
HRB
Zhenlai   Maoxing Zhaoyuan Shuangcheng Acheng   Yanshou
Da'an   Changchunling   Lalin Yimianpo   Linkou   HXI
Baicheng   Taonan   Anguang   Qiqan Qian Gorlos Beitaolaizhai Sanchahe   Wuchang Shangzhi   Muling   Novokachalinsk 69
Tuquan   FUYU   Kaoshan Shenjingzi   Yushu   Shanhetun   Hengdaohezi Maqiaohe   Lake
Shenjingzi   Dehui   Gangyao   Suiyang Sufenhe Khanka

HEILONGJIANG   Xiaobezezi
44

Huolin Gol   Tongyu   Zhanyu   Beizhengzhen Taipingchuan   Nong'an Wulajie   Hailin   Muling Ning'an   Dongning   Ussuriya
Jarud Qi   Horqin Zuoyi   Zhongqi   Changling   Huaidezhen   Jiutai   Gangyao   Dongjingcheng Luozigou   RUSSIA

Xi Ujimqin Qi   1949   Xebert   Xinkai He   Maolin   CHANGCHUN   JILIN   Jiaohe   Emu   Jingpo   Wangqing   Shixian   Vladivostok
Bairin   Xinkai He   Huaidezhen   Fanjiatun   Yongji   Songhua Hu   Hu 1690   Dongningcheng   Slavyanka
Zuoqi   Linxi   Zhanyu   Dongliao He   Lishu   Shuangyang   Yitong   Yantongshan   Dunhua   Daxinggou   Hunchun Kraskino

C
MANCHURIA

42

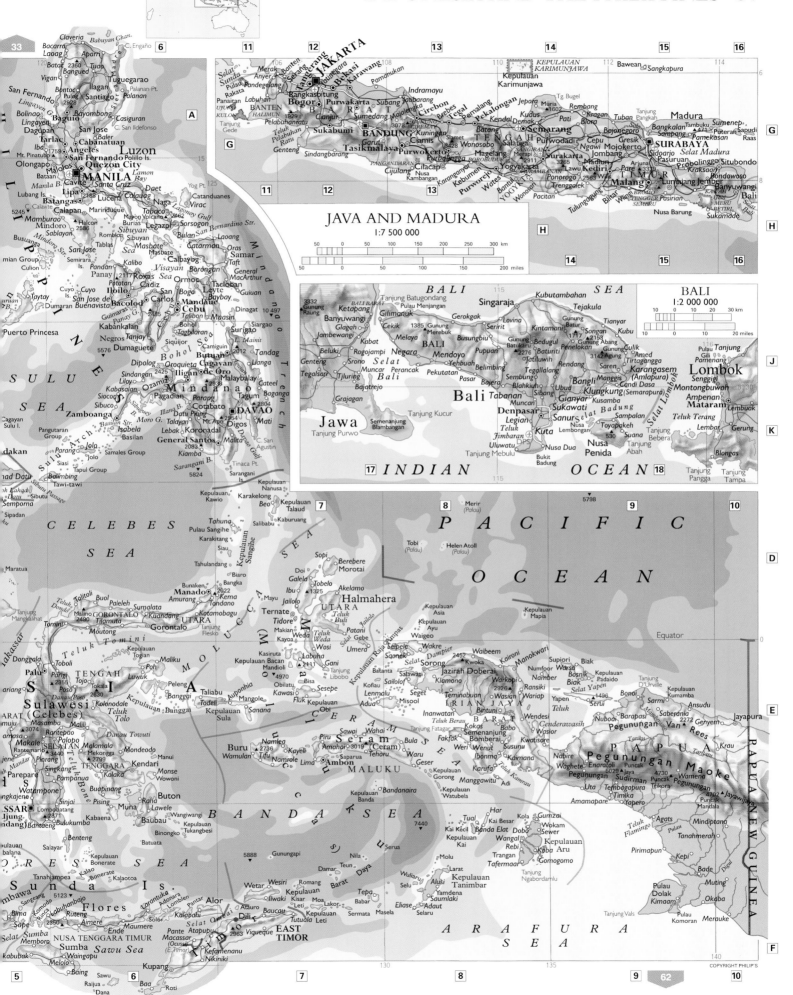

JAVA AND MADURA
1:7 500 000

BALI
1:2 000 000

1:6 000 000

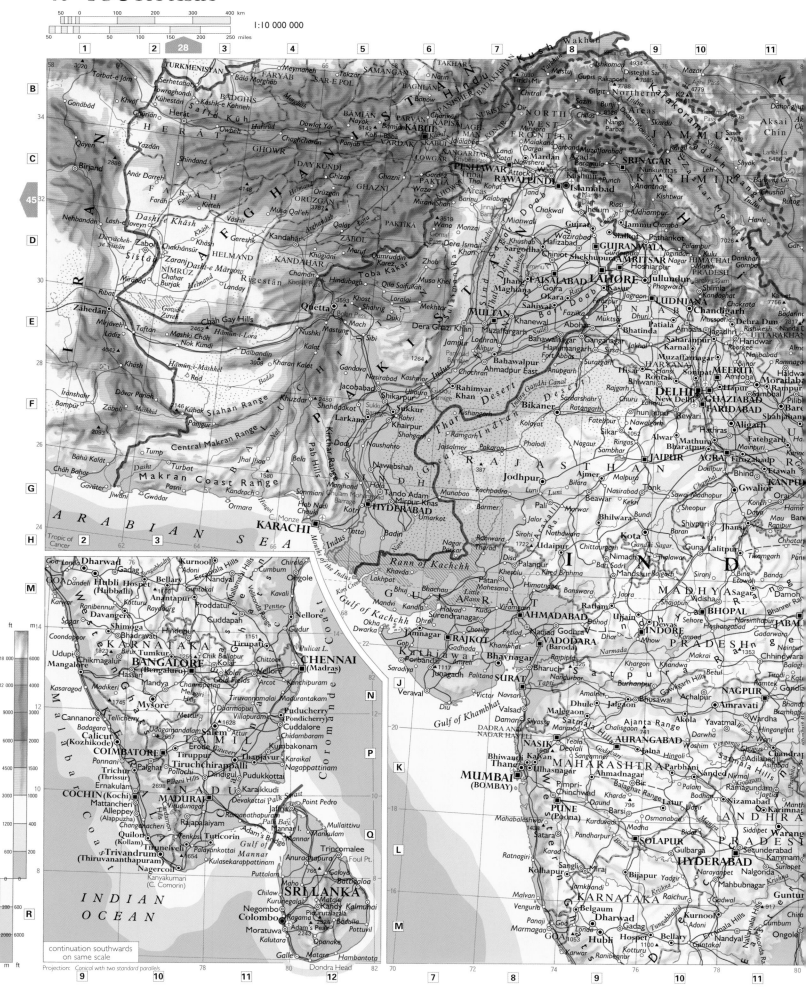

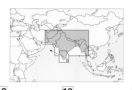

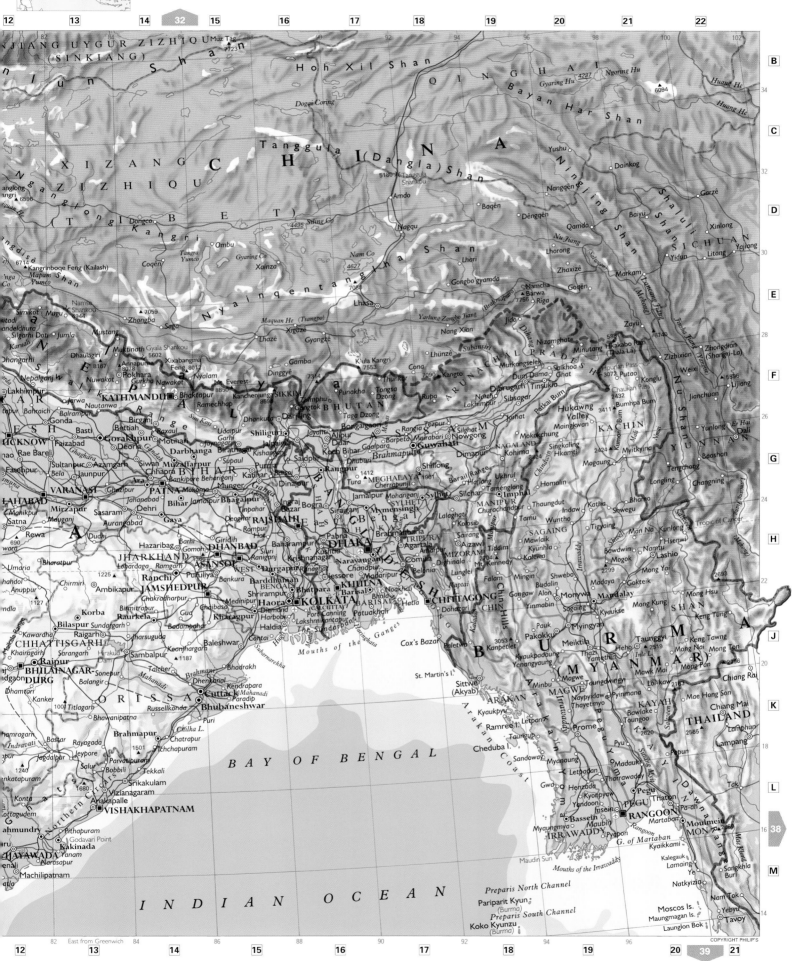

JAMMU AND KASHMIR
on same scale

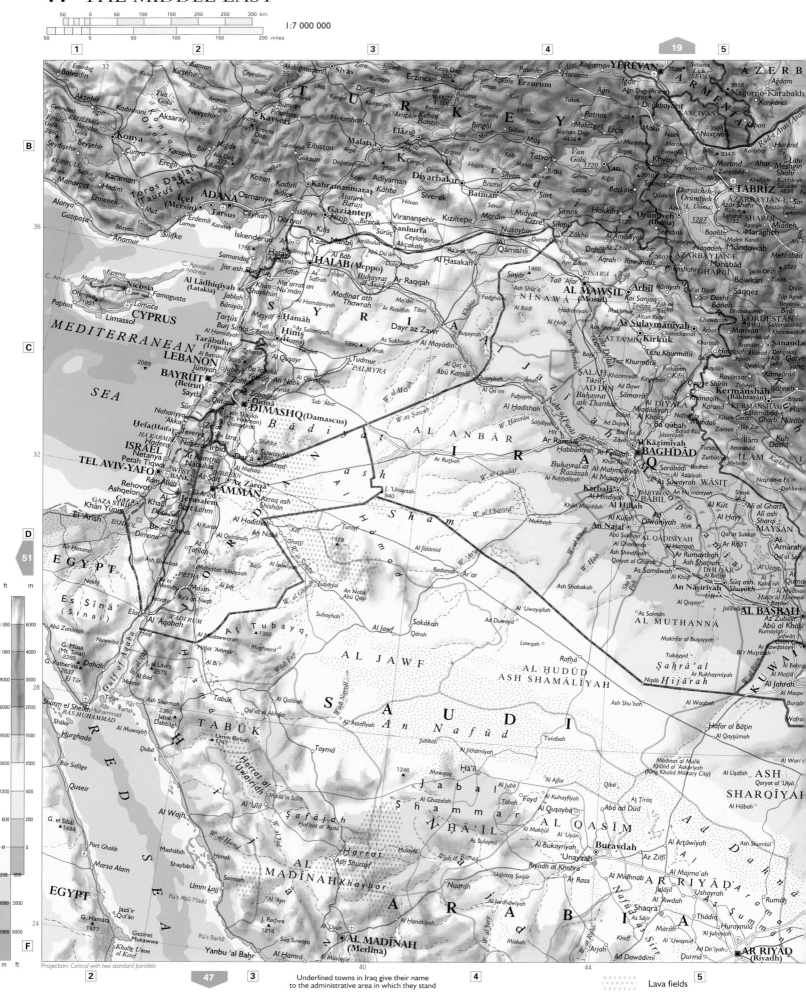

Projection: Conical with two standard parallels

Underlined towns in Iraq give their name
to the administrative area in which they stand

Lava fields

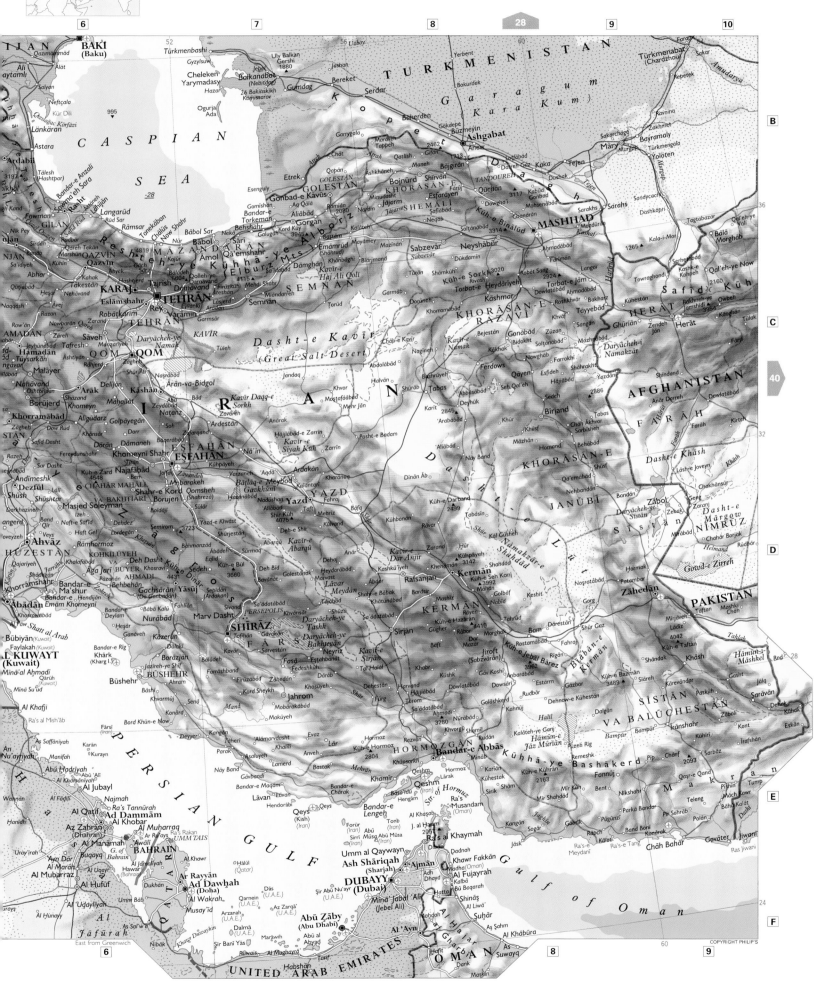

B

40

C

40

D

E

F

TURKMENISTAN

Garagum (Kara Kum)

Ashgabat

MASHHAD

HERĀT

AFGHANISTAN

FARĀH

KHORĀSĀN-E JANŪBĪ

NIMRŪZ

Zābol

Zāhedān

PAKISTAN

SĪSTĀN VA BALŪCHESTĀN

CASPIAN SEA

BAKÍ (Baku)

GILĀN

MĀZANDARĀN

GOLESTĀN

KHORĀSĀN-E SHEMĀLĪ

KHORĀSĀN-E RAZAVĪ

QAZVIN

KARAJ

TEHRĀN

QOM

SEMNĀN

I R A N

YAZD

KERMĀN

ESFAHĀN

CHAHĀR MAHĀLL VA BAKHTĪĀRĪ

FĀRS

SHIRĀZ

PERSEPOLIS

KOHKILŪYEH VA BUYER AHMADĪ

AHVĀZ

HUZESTĀN

Dezful

Ābādān

Khorramshahr

AL KUWAYT (Kuwait)

Dasht-e Kavīr (Great Salt Desert)

Dasht-e Lūt

HORMOZGĀN

Bandar-e ʿAbbās

Kūhhā-ye Bashākerd

MAKRĀN

Chāh Bahār

PERSIAN GULF

Gulf of Oman

BAHRAIN

Al Manāmah

Ad Dammām

Al Khobar

QATAR

Ad Dawḥah (Doha)

DUBAYY (Dubai)

Abū Ẓaby (Abu Dhabi)

Ash Shāriqah (Sharjah)

Ajmān

Al Fujayrah

Ra's al Khaymah

UNITED ARAB EMIRATES

OMAN

East from Greenwich

COPYRIGHT PHILIP'S

6　　7　　8　　9

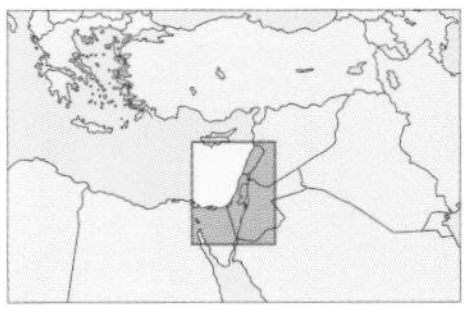

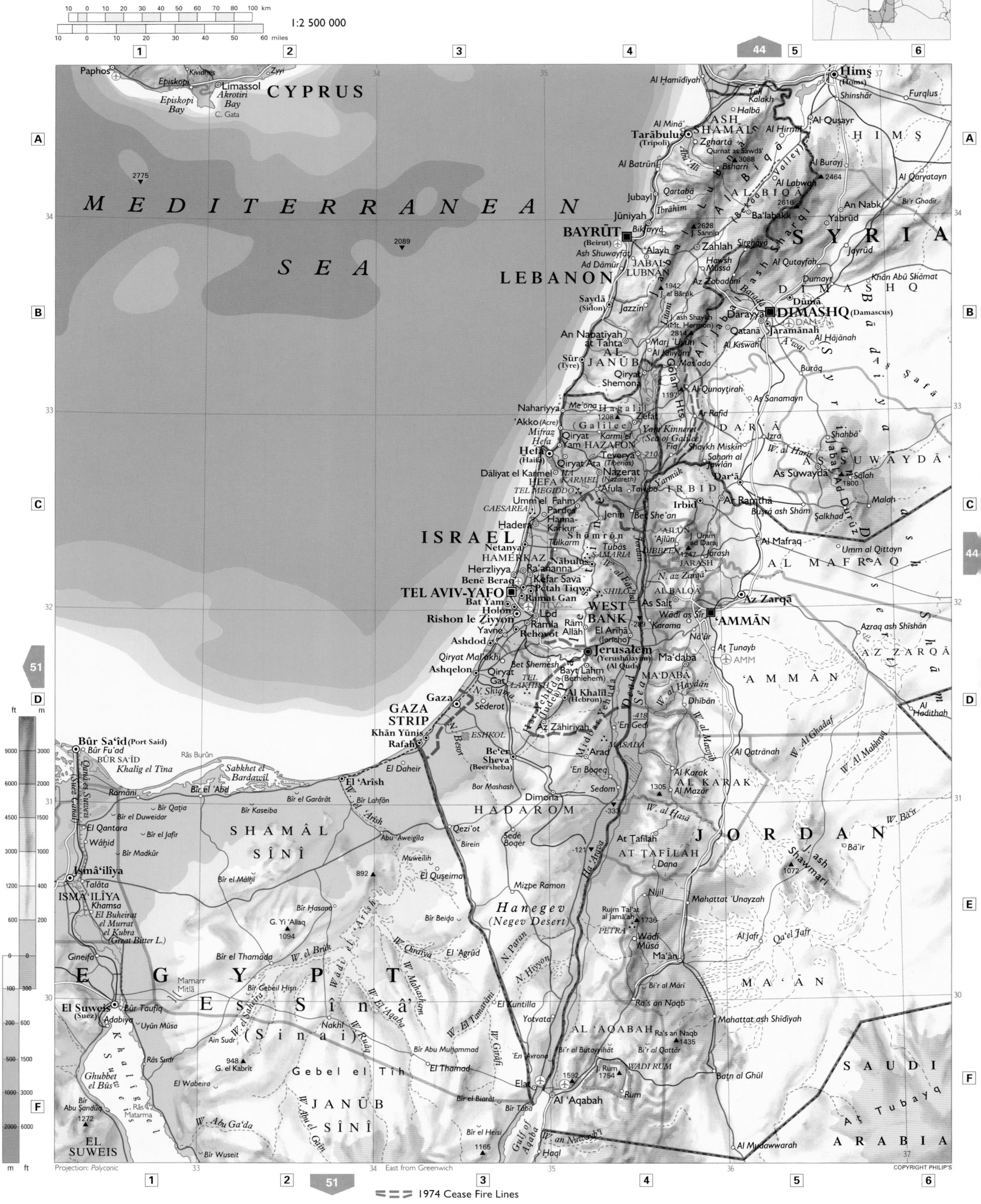

1:2 500 000

10 0 10 20 30 40 50 60 70 80 100 km
10 0 10 20 30 40 50 60 miles

1 **2** **3** **4** 44 **5** **6**

CYPRUS

Paphos
Episkopi
Kivides
Zyyi
Limassol
Akrotiri Bay
Episkopi Bay
C. Gata

Al Ḥamīdīyah
Hims (Homs)
Tall Kalakh
Shinshār
Furqlus

ASH SHAMĀL
Al Minā'
Tarābulus (Tripoli)
Zgharta
Halbā
Al Ḥirmil
Al Quşayr
Qurnat as Sawdā' 3088

HIMŞ

Al Batrūn
Bsharrī
Al Burayj
2464
Al Qaryatayn

Jubayl
Qartabā
Al Labwah
2616

Jūniyah
Ibrāhīm
Ba'labakk
Yabrūd
An Nabk
Bi'r Ghadīr

BAYRŪT (Beirut)
Biljayyā
J. Sannīn 2628
Ash Shuwayfāt
'Alayh
Zaḥlah
Sirghāyā

SYRIA

Ad Dāmūr
JABAL LUBNĀN
Hawsh Mūssā
Az Zabadānī
Al Qutayfah

LEBANON

Saydā (Sidon)
1942 al Bārūk
Ash Shaykh (Mt. Hermon) 2814
DIMASHQ (Damascus)
Dūma

Jazzīn
Darayyā
Jaramānah
Al Hājānah

An Nabaţīyah at Tahta
AL JANŪB
Marj 'Uyūn
Al Khiyām
Qatanā
Al Kiswah
Burāq

DIMASHQ

Şūr (Tyre)
Qiryat Shemona
Mas'ada
Buşrā

MEDITERRANEAN SEA

Al Qunayţirah
As Sanamayn
Şafā

Nahariyya
Me'ona
Hagalil
Ar Rafid
W. al Harir
Shahbā
SUWAYDĀ

'Akko (Acre)
Zefat
Yam Kinneret (Sea of Galilee)
Fiq
Shaykh Miskin
Izra

Mifraz Hefa
Qiryat
(Galilee)
Yam HAZAFON
Teverya (Tiberias) -210
Saham al Jawlān
Dar'ā
As Suwaydā
1800
Jabal ad Durūz

Hefa (Haifa)
Qiryat Ata
Shaykh Miskin
Malah
Salkhad

Dāliyat el Karmel
HA KARMEL
Nazerat (Nazareth)
IRBID
Buşrā ash Shām
Şalkhad

TEL MEGIDDO
Afula
Ţayba
Al Mafraq
Umm al Qittayn

Umm el Fahm
CAESAREA
Jenin
Bet She'an
AJLŪN
Ajlūn
Umm ad Daraj

Hadera
Pardes Hanna-Karkur
Shōmrōn
SAMARIA
Jarash
JARASH
AL MAFRAQ

ISRAEL

Netanya
Tulkarm
Nābulus
N. az Zarqā

HAMERKAZ
Ra'ananna
Tūbas

Herzliyya
Kefar Sava
Petah Tiqwa
SHILOA
As Salt
Az Zarqā

Benē Beraq
Ramat Gan
WEST BANK
AL BALQA
AMMĀN

TEL AVIV-YAFO
Bat Yam
Lod
Karama

Holon
Ramla
Ram Allāh
Wādī as Sīr

Rishon le Ziyyon
Rehovot
El Arīhā (Jericho)
Na'ūr

Yavne
Ashdod
Jerusalem (Yerushalayim) (Al Quds)
Ma'daba
AMM
Azraq ash Shīshān

Ashqelon
Qiryat Mal'akhi
Bet Shemesh
MA'DABA
AZ ZARQĀ

Qiryat Gat
Bayt Laḥm (Bethlehem)
'AMMĀN

GAZA STRIP
Gaza
Sederot
TEL LAKHISH
Al Khalīl (Hebron)
W. al Mawjib
Dhībān

Khān Yūnis
Be'er Sheva (Beersheba)
Az Zāhiriyah
'En Gedi
-418

Rafah
El Daheir
Arad
MASADA

Būr Sa'īd (Port Said)
Būr Fu'ād
BŪR SA'ID
Sabkhet el Bardawīl
El 'Arīsh
Bor Mashash
-333
Al Karak
AL KARAK

Râs Burûn
Dimona
Sedom
1305
Al Mazār

Ramāni
Bir el 'Abd
W. al Hasā
JORDAN

El Qantara
Bir Qaţia
Bir Kaseiba
HADAROM
At Ţafīlah

Wâhid
Bir el Duweidar
Bir el Jafir
Bir el Garārāt
W. al 'Arīsh
Qezi'ot
Sedé Boqér
AT TAFILAH
Dana

Bir Madkûr
Bir el Mālḥi
Abu-Aweigila
Birein
1072
ash Shawmarī

Ismâ'ilîya
Ţalâta
SHAMĀL SĪNÎ
Muweilih
Mizpe Ramon
Nijil

ISMĀ'ILĪYA
Khamsa
892
El Quşeima
Mahattat 'Unayzah

El Buheirat el Murrat el Kubra (Great Bitter L.)
G. Yi 'Allaq 1094
Bir Beida
Hanegev (Negev Desert)
Rujm Tal'at al Jamā'ah 1736

W. el Bruk
N. Paran
PETRA
Al Jafr
Qa'el Jafr

Gineifa
Bir el Thamâda
W. Ghraiya
El 'Agrûd
N. Hiyyon
Wādī Mūsā
Ma'ān

EGYPT
Mamarr Mitlā
W. Mahashim
MA'ĀN

EL SUWEIS
G. Gebeil Hişn
N. Hiyyon

El Suweis (Suez)
Nakhl
Yotvata
Bi'r al Mārī

Adabiya
ES SĪNÂ (Sinai)
El Kuntilla
Ra's an Naqb
1435

'Uyûn Mûsa
Ain Sudr
Bir Abu Muḥammad
'En 'Avrona
Bi'r al Buţayḥāt
Bi'r al Qaţţar

Râs Sudr
948 G. el Kabrit
El Thamad
1592 Rum 1754
WADI RUM
Baţn al Ghūl

SAUDI

Khalig el Suweis
El Wabeira
Gebel el Tih
AL 'AQABA
Elat

Ghubbet el Bûs
JANÛB SĪNÎ
Bi'r el Biarât
Al 'Aqabah
Gulf of Aqaba
Al Mudawwarah

Abu Shandûa 1272
Râs Matarma
W. Abu Ga'da
W. Abu el Gefin
Bîr el Heisi
1165
Haql
Aş Tubayq

EL SUWEIS
Bîr Wuseit
ARABIA

Projection: Polyconic
East from Greenwich
COPYRIGHT PHILIP'S

1 **2** 51 **3** **4** **5** **6**

▬ ▬ ▬ 1974 Cease Fire Lines

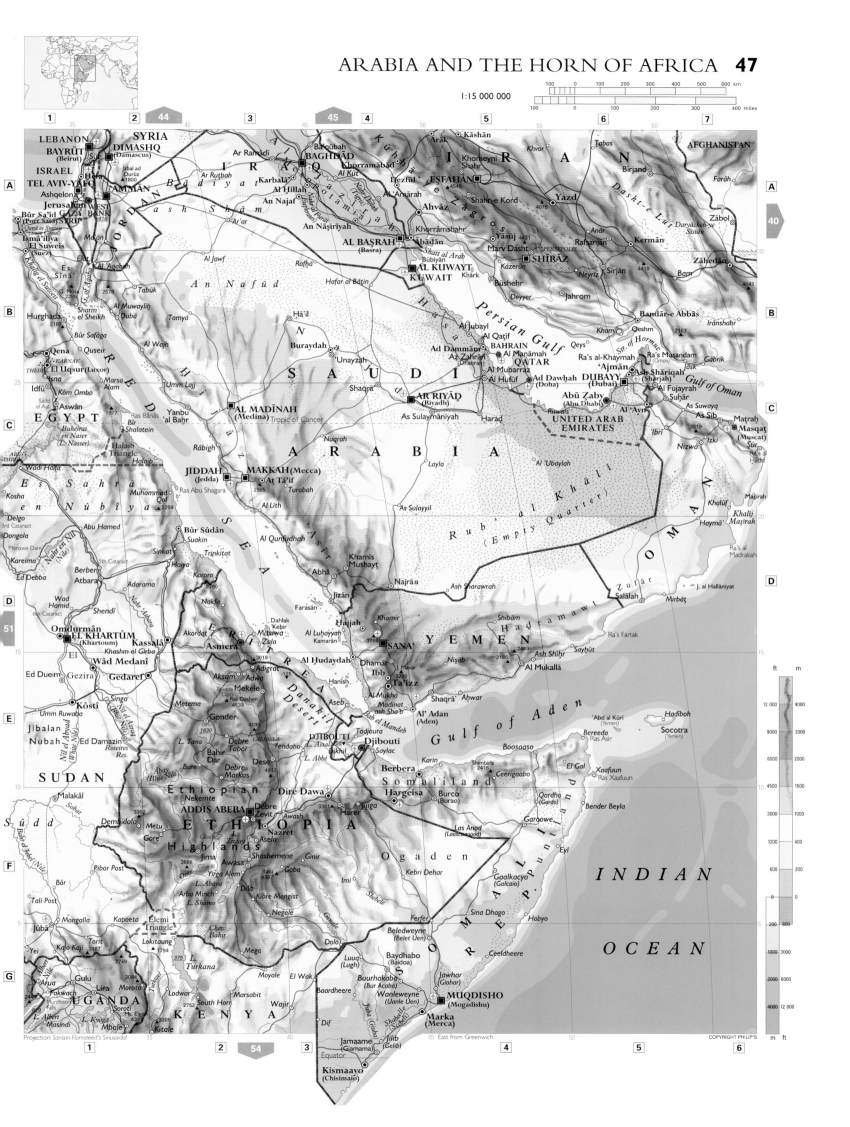

1:15 000 000

| 100 | 0 | 100 | 200 | 300 | 400 | 500 | 600 km |
| 100 | 0 | 100 | 200 | 300 | 400 miles |

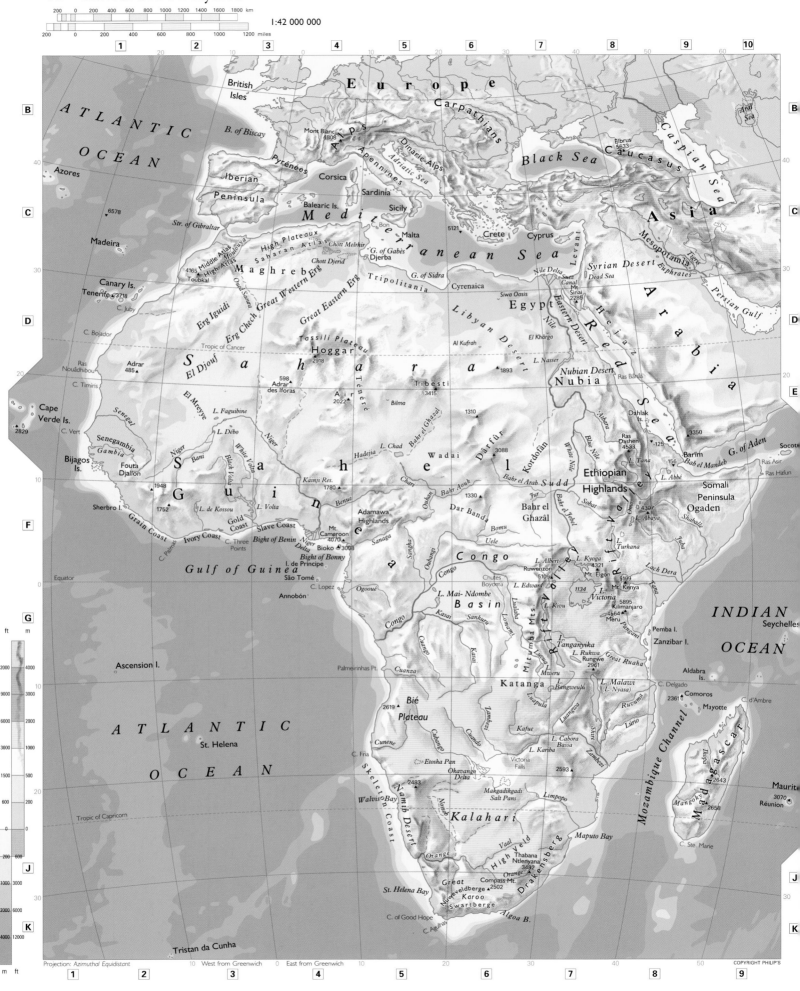

1:42 000 000

Projection: Azimuthal Equidistant

COPYRIGHT PHILIP'S

1:42 000 000

● Dakar Capital Cities

Projection: Azimuthal Equidistant   West from Greenwich   East from Greenwich   COPYRIGHT PHILIP'S

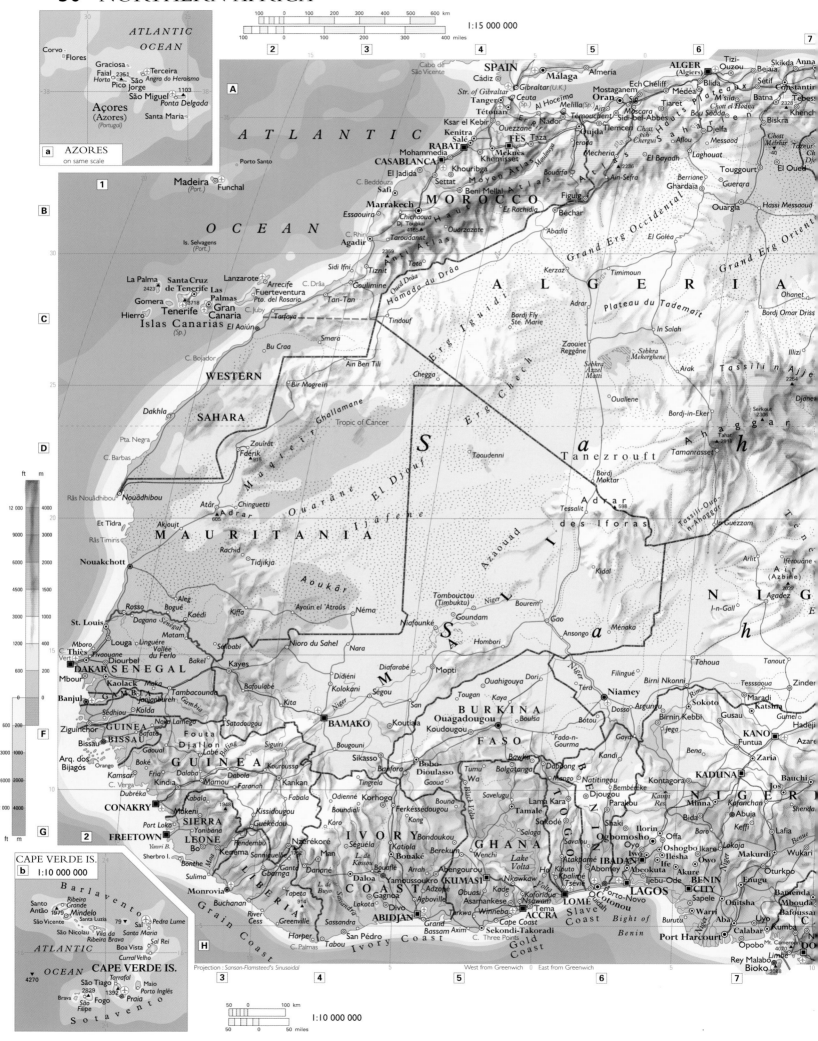

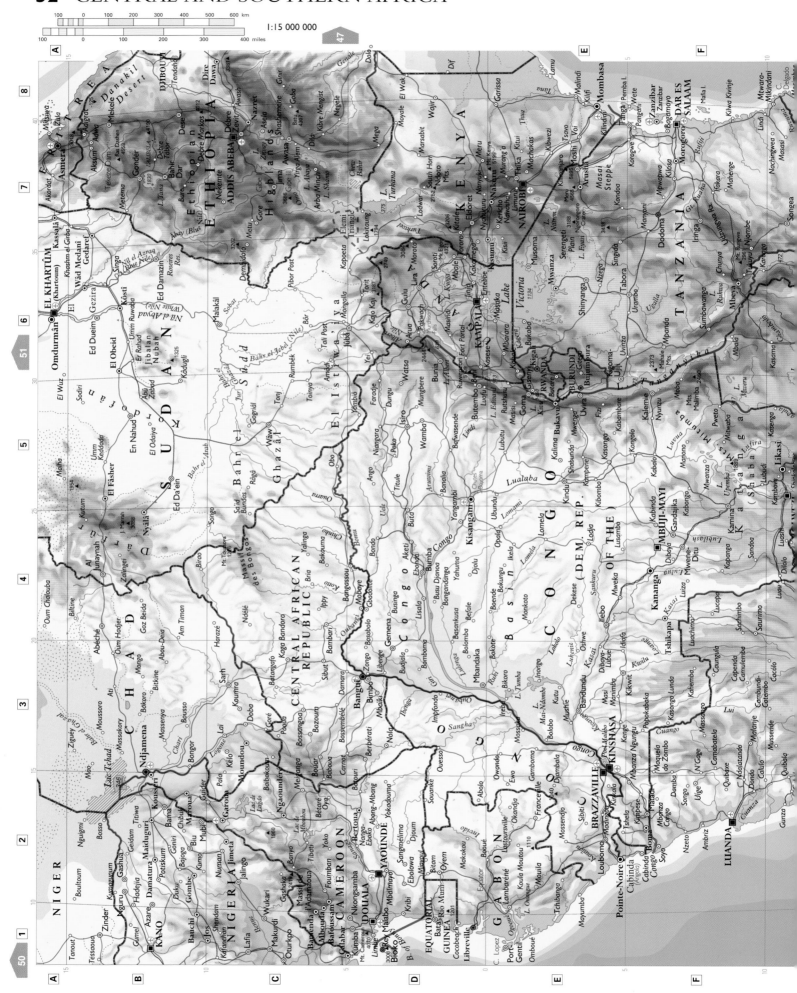

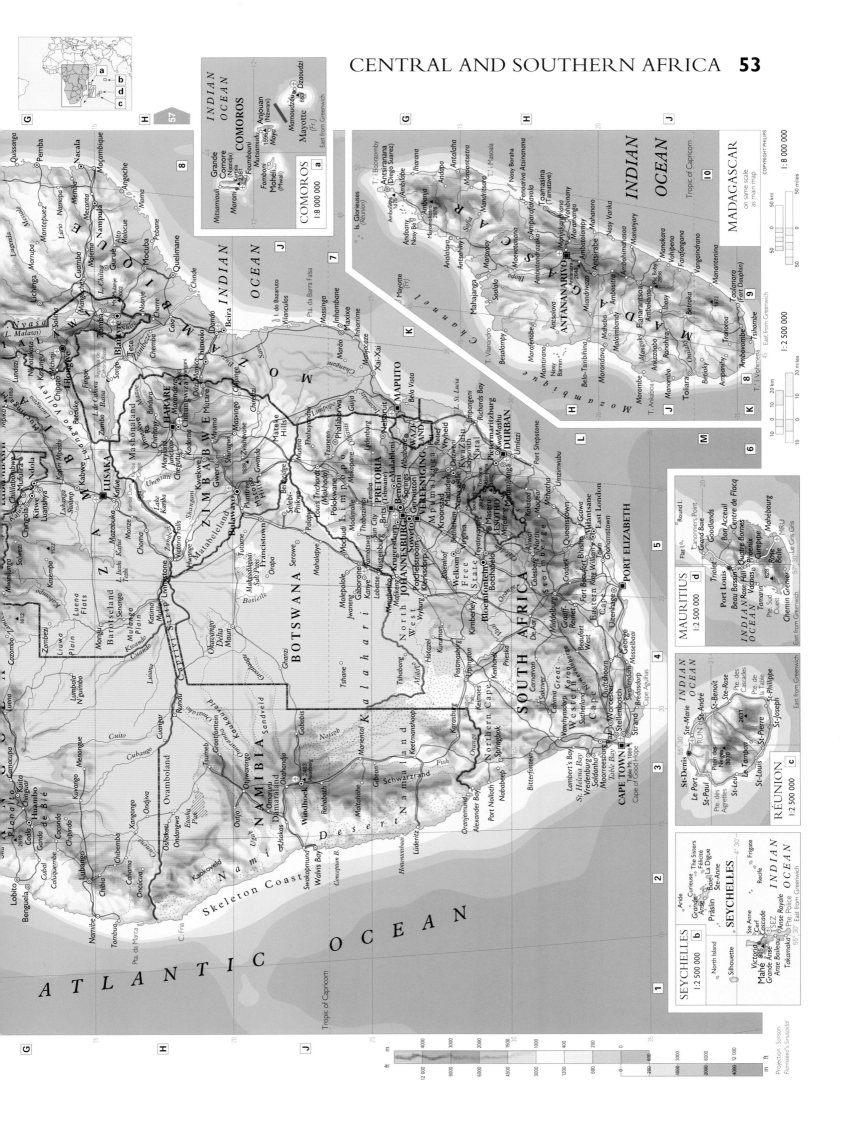

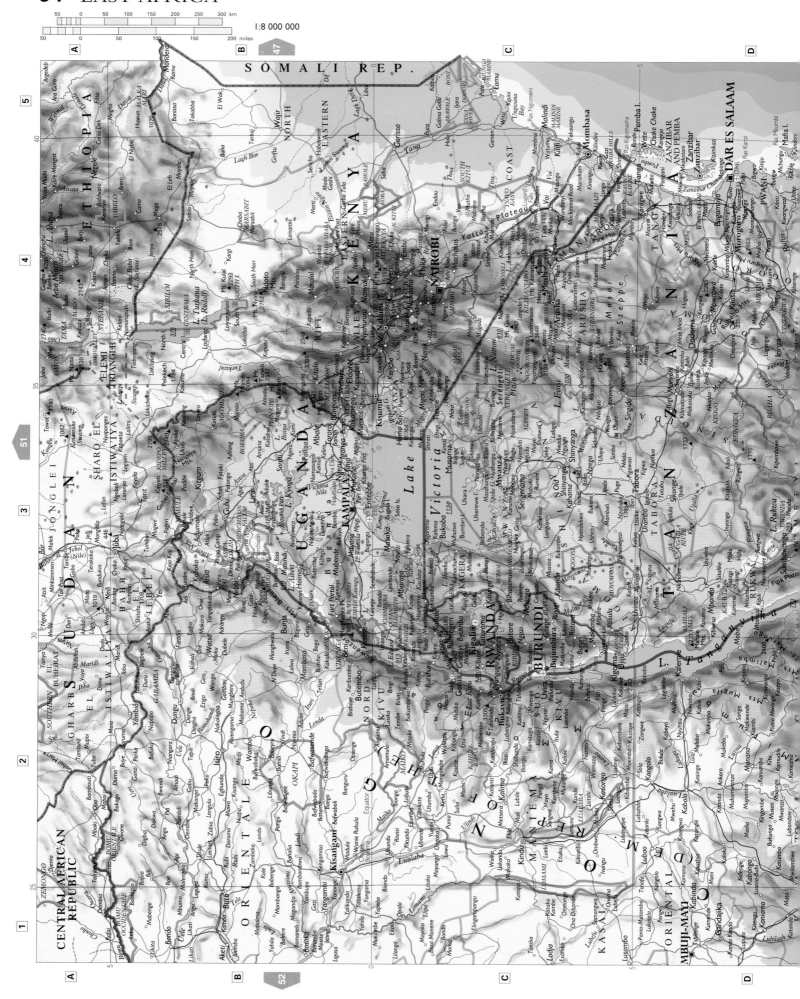

1:8 000 000

Projection: Lambert's Equivalent Azimuthal

East from Greenwich

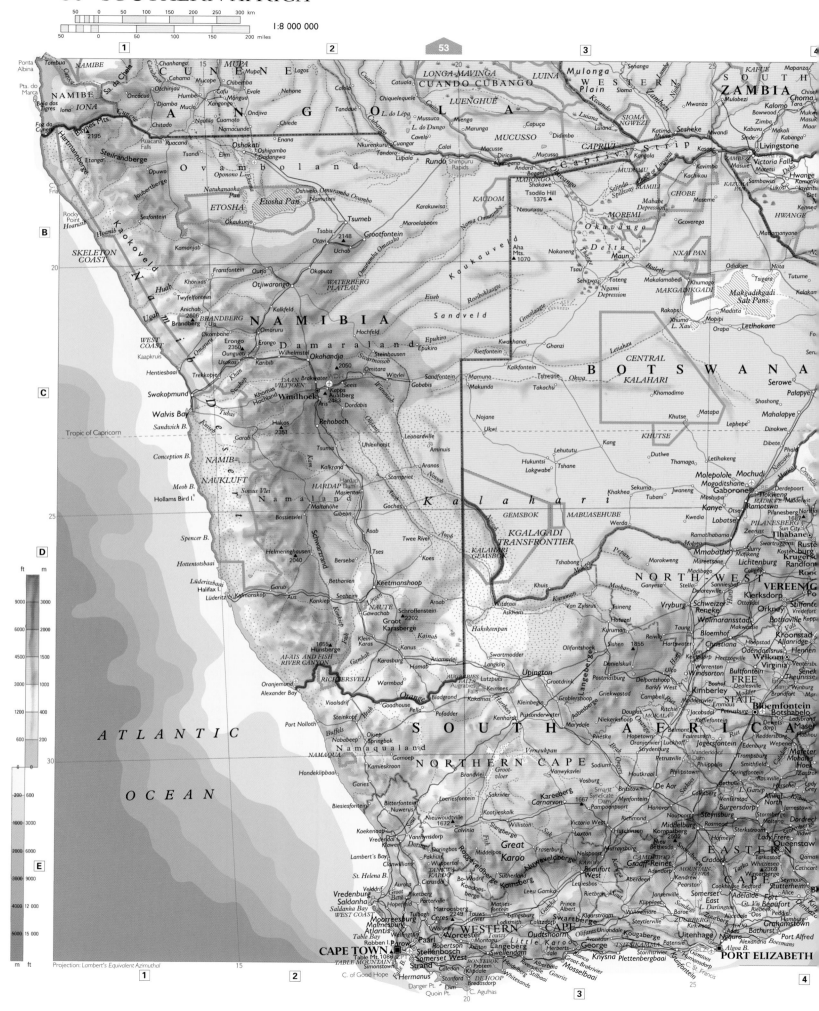

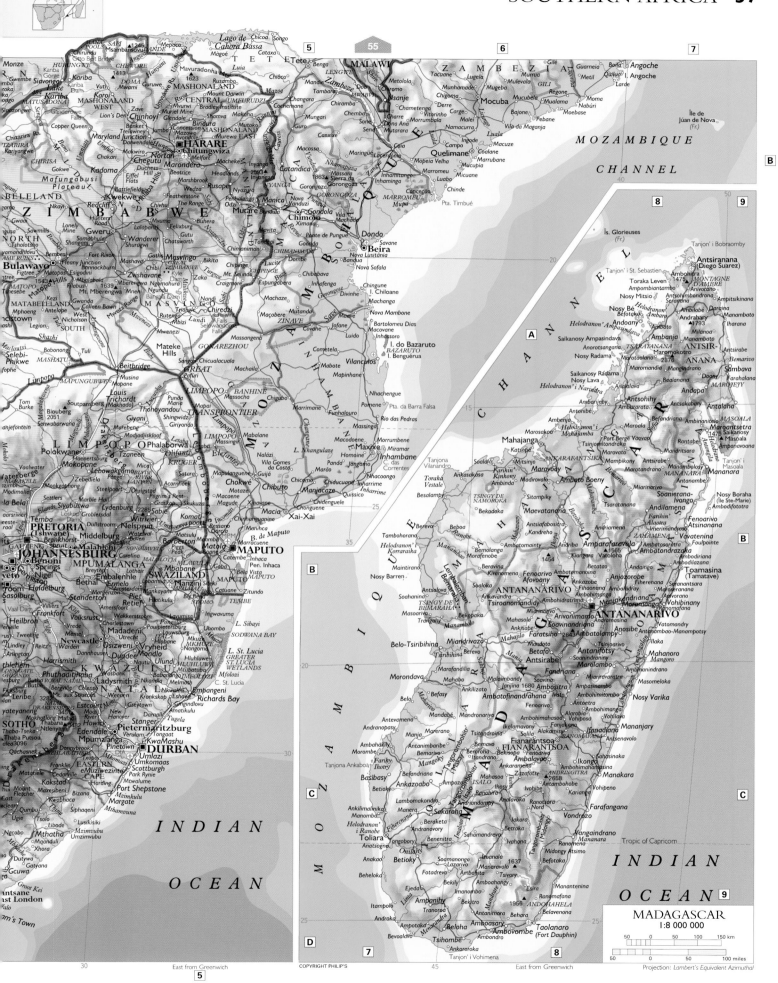

MOZAMBIQUE CHANNEL

INDIAN OCEAN

INDIAN OCEAN

MADAGASCAR
1:8 000 000

East from Greenwich

East from Greenwich

Projection: Lambert's Equivalent Azimuthal

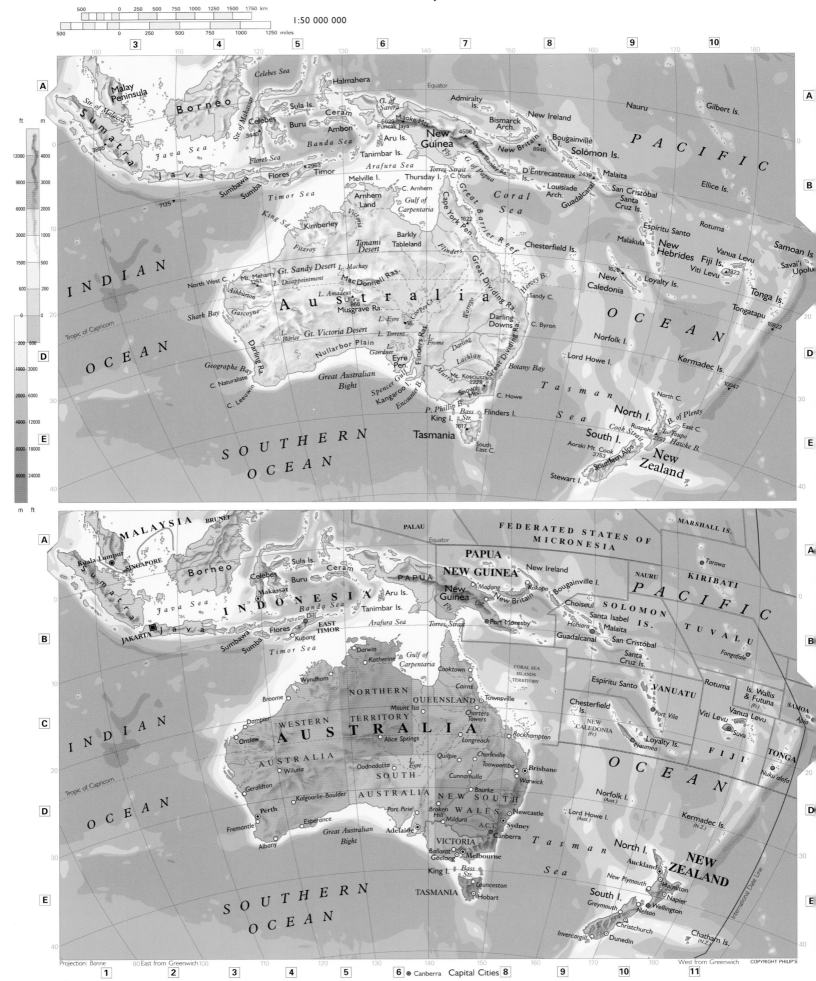

1:50 000 000

Physical map labels:

Malay Peninsula, Str. of Malacca, Sumatra, Borneo, Celebes Sea, Halmahera, Admiralty Is., Equator, Nauru, Gilbert Is., PACIFIC, Java Sea, Str. of Makassar, Celebes, Sula Is., Ceram, Buru, Ambon, Banda Sea, Maoke Mts., Puncak Jaya 5029, New Guinea 4508, Bismarck Arch., New Ireland, New Britain 8940, Bougainville I., Solomon Is., Owen Stanley Ra., 3440, 3895, Aru Is., Tanimbar Is., Arafura Sea, G. of Papua, Torres Strait, C. York, D'Entrecasteaux 2439, Malaita, San Cristobal, Santa Cruz Is., Ellice Is., Java, Sumbawa, Flores, Timor 2963, Melville I., Thursday I., C. Arnhem, Cape York Pen. 1622, Great Barrier Reef, Coral Sea, Louisiade Arch., Guadalcanal, Rotuma, Espíritu Santo, Sumba, Timor Sea, Arnhem Land, Gulf of Carpentaria, Victoria, Great Dividing Ra., Chesterfield Is., Malakula, New Hebrides, Vanua Levu, Fiji Is., Viti Levu 1323, Samoan Is., 7125, King Sd., Kimberley, Barkly Tableland, Flinders, Harvey B., New Caledonia, 1628, Loyalty Is., Savai'i, Upolu, Fitzroy, Tanami Desert, Musgrave Ra., Gt. Sandy Desert, L. Mackay, MacDonnell Ras., Sandy C., Tonga Is., INDIAN, North West C., Mt. Meharry 1251, L. Disappointment, Australia, Cooper Cr., Warrego, C. Byron, Norfolk I., Tongatapu 10822, Ashburton, Uluru 868, Musgrave Ra., L. Amadeus, Darling Downs, Gascoyne, Shark Bay, L. Eyre, 36, Darling, OCEAN, Tropic of Capricorn, Darling Ra., L. Barlee, Gt. Victoria Desert, L. Torrens, Lachlan, Lord Howe I., Kermadec Is., OCEAN, Geographe Bay, Nullarbor Plain, Gairdner, Flinders Ras., Frome, Murray, Botany Bay, 10047, C. Naturaliste, Eyre Pen., Spencer Gulf, Mt. Kosciuszko 2228, C. Leeuwin, Great Australian Bight, Kangaroo I., Encounter B., Snowy Mts., C. Howe, Tasman Sea, North C., C. Leeuwin, P. Phillip B., Bass Str., Flinders I., North I., B. of Plenty, King I. 1617, East C., Ruapehu 2797, Taupo, Hawke B., Tasmania, South East C., Aoraki Mt. Cook 3753, Cook Strait, South I., Southern Alps, SOUTHERN OCEAN, Stewart I., New Zealand

Political map labels:

MALAYSIA, BRUNEI, PALAU, FEDERATED STATES OF MICRONESIA, Equator, MARSHALL IS., Kuala Lumpur, SINGAPORE, Borneo, Celebes, Sula Is., Ceram, PAPUA, PAPUA NEW GUINEA, New Ireland, Tarawa, NAURU, KIRIBATI, Sumatra, Makassar, Buru, INDONESIA, Madang, Kokopo, New Britain, Bougainville I., PACIFIC, Java, Banda Sea, Tanimbar Is., Aru Is., New Guinea, Lae, Fly, Choiseul, SOLOMON IS., Santa Isabel, TUVALU, JAKARTA, Java, Flores, Dili, EAST TIMOR, Kupang, Arafura Sea, Torres Strait, Port Moresby, Honiara, Malaita, Guadalcanal, San Cristóbal, Fongafale, Sumbawa, Sumba, Timor Sea, Darwin, Katherine, Gulf of Carpentaria, Santa Cruz Is., Rotuma, VANUATU, SAMOA, Apia, Wyndham, Cooktown, CORAL SEA ISLANDS TERRITORY, Espíritu Santo, Broome, NORTHERN TERRITORY, Cairns, Townsville, QUEENSLAND, Mount Isa, Charters Towers, Chesterfield Is., NEW CALEDONIA (Fr), Port Vila, Is. Wallis & Futuna (Fr), Viti Levu, Vanua Levu, Dampier, WESTERN TERRITORY, Alice Springs, Longreach, Rockhampton, Port Vila, Suva, FIJI, Onslow, AUSTRALIA, Quilpie, Charleville, Toowoomba, Noumea, Loyalty Is., TONGA, Wiluna, SOUTH AUSTRALIA, Oodnadatta, L. Eyre, Cunnamulla, Brisbane, Norfolk I. (Aust), Nuku'alofa, Geraldton, Bourke, Warwick, Kalgoorlie-Boulder, NEW SOUTH WALES, Newcastle, Lord Howe I. (Aust), Kermadec Is. (N.Z.), Perth, Port Pirie, Broken Hill, Mildura, Sydney, Fremantle, Esperance, Adelaide, A.C.T., Canberra, Tasman Sea, North I., Albany, Great Australian Bight, VICTORIA, Ballarat, Geelong, Melbourne, Auckland, NEW ZEALAND, King I., Bass Str., New Plymouth, Hamilton, Launceston, South I., Napier, INDIAN OCEAN, TASMANIA, Hobart, Greymouth, Wellington, Nelson, SOUTHERN OCEAN, Invercargill, Christchurch, Dunedin, Chatham Is. (N.Z.)

Projection: Bonne   90 East from Greenwich 100   West from Greenwich   COPYRIGHT PHILIP'S

Canberra ● Capital Cities

1:6 000 000

50   0   50   100   150   200 km
50   0   50   100   150 miles

4   64   **5**   **6**   **7**

FIJI [a]
on same scale

Great Sea Reef   Kia   Udu Pt.   Ringgold Is.

PACIFIC OCEAN

Yaqaga   Labasa   Rabi
Yasawa   Yadua   Bua   **Vanua Levu** 1031   Qamea
Yasawa Group   Nabouwalu   Savusavu   Savusavu Bay   Somosomo   Naitaba
Naviti   Nacula   Namenalala   **Taveuni**   Naitaba
Waya   Vomo   Tavua   Rakiraki   Nasau   Koro   Kanacea   Vanua Balavu
Viwa   Lautoka   Tomanni 1323   Lawaki   **Ovalau**   Wakaya   Mago   Lomaloma
Mamanuca Group   Malolo   Nadi   Keiyasi   **Viti Levu**   Vunidawa   Korovou   **Levuka**   Batiki   Cicia   Tuvuca   Northern Lau Group
Sigatoka   Korolevu   Navua   **Suva**   Nausori   Nairai   Gau   Nayau   Lakeba Passage
Yanuca   Beqa   **FIJI**   Moala   Lakeba   Tubou   Oneata
Vatulele   Kadavu Passage   Southern Lau Group   Moce   Namuka-i-Lau
Kadavu   Ono   Matuku   Totoya   Fulaga   Ogea   Yagasa Cluster
Tavuki   Yunisea   Kabara   Ogea Driki   Levu

KORO SEA

East from Greenwich   West from Greenwich

SAMOA
Asau   Safune   1858   Pu'apu'a
Savai'i   Salelologa   Manono   Falefa
Taga   Mulifanua   **Apia**   Falefa
Falelatai   Siumu   Amaile
OLE PUPŪ PUŌ   Safata Bay   **Upolu**

PACIFIC OCEAN

AMERICAN SAMOA (U.S.A.)
Tutuila   Pago Pago   Ofu Olosega   Ta'ū
Leone   Vaitogi   Aunu'u   Luma   Manu'a Is.   AMERICAN SAMOA

West from Greenwich

SAMOAN ISLANDS [b]
on same scale

TONGA [c]
on same scale

PACIFIC OCEAN

Fonualei   Toku
Late   Vava'u   Neiafu
Vava'u Group
Home Reef
Disney Reef
Ofolanga   Ha'ano
Tofua   Kao   Foa   Ha'apai   Lifuka Group
Kotu Group   Uiha
Fonuafo'ou   Nomuka   Mango   Oto Tolu Group
Hunga Ha'apai   Nomuka Group   Tonumea

TONGA
Nuku'alofa   **Tongatapu**   Eua
Tongatapu Group

West from Greenwich

TASMAN SEA

NORTH ISLAND

C. Reinga   North C.
C. Maria van Diemen   Rangaunu B.
Houhora Heads   Mongonui   Whangaroa Harb.
Ahipara B.   Kaitaia   Mangonui
Tauroa Pt.   Okaihau   B. of Islands   C. Brett
Rawene   Kaikohe   Opua
Hokianga Harbour   Kerikeri   **Hikurangi**
Waipoua Forest   Waipu   **Whangarei**   Whangarei Harb.   Bream Hd.   Bream B.
Dargaville   Bream Hd.   Little Barrier I.
Kaipara Harbour   Warkworth   C. Rodney   Great Barrier I.
Helensville   C. Colville   Cuvier I.
Takapuna   Hauraki Gulf   Coromandel   Whitianga
□ **AUCKLAND**   Whangamata   Mayor I.
Manukau   Papakura   Thames   Waihi
Waiuku   Pukekohe   Mercer   Te Aroha   Tauranga Harb.
Huntly   Paeroa   **Tauranga**   Te Puke   Whakatane   **Whakaari (White I.)**
Hamilton   Morrinsville   Mount Maunganui   Bay of Plenty   Runaway
Raglan   Cambridge   Whakatane   Opotiki   East C.
Kawhia   Te Awamutu   Matata   Kawerau   **UREWERA**   Raukumara Ra.   Hikurangi 1753
Kawhia Harbour   Otorohanga   **Rotorua**   Te Teko   Taneatua   Waipiro
Waitomo Caves   Te Kuiti   Kinleith   L. Rotorua   Murupara   Motu   Tolaga Bay
Mokau   Mangakino   Wairakei   L. Tarawera   **Gisborne**
North Taranaki Bight   Mokau   Ongarue   Taupo   L. Taupo   Waikaremoana   Nuhaka   Poverty Bay
Inglewood   Taumarunui   Turangi   Tarawera   Wairoa   Mahia Pen.
New Plymouth   Mt. Taranaki or Mt. Egmont   **WHANGANUI**   Targwera   Waikokopu
Mt. Taranaki or Mt. Egmont   C. Egmont   Whangamomona   **TONGARIRO** 2797   Ruapehu   Bay View   Hawke Bay
Opunake   Stratford   Ohakune   **EGMONT** 2518   Waiouru   **Napier**
Kaponga   Eltham   Raetihi   Ruahine Ra.   C. Kidnappers
Hawera   Waverley   Taihape   **Hastings**
South Taranaki Bight   Patea   **Wanganui**   Mangaweka   Hunterville   Waipawa
Bulls   Marton   Halcombe   Dannevirke   Waipukurau
Palmerston North   Feilding   Woodville
Foxton   Shannon   Pahiatua   C. Turnagain
Paraparaumu   Levin   Eketahuna
Kapiti I.   Otaki   Masterton
Upper Hutt   Featherston   Carterton   Greytown
Petone   **Lower Hutt**   Martinborough
Wellington   Eastbourne   Wairarapa
Cook Strait

C. Farewell
Golden B.   D'Urville I.
Collingwood   Takaka   ABEL TASMAN
KAHURANGI   **Tasman Mts.**   Tasman B.   Motueka   Pelorus Sd.
Karamea   Motueka   Havelock   Picton
Karamea Bight   Matiri Ra.   **Nelson**   Richmond   Wakefield
Seddonville   Tadmor   **Blenheim**
Granity   Lyell   Murchison   **NELSON LAKES**   Seddon   Ward
Westport   Inangahua   L. Rotoroa   2885 Tapuae-o-Uenuku
PAPAROA   Mt. Travers 2337   **Spenser Mts.**   Kaikoura
Punakaiki   Reefton   Lewis Pass   Clarence
Blackball   Runanga   Maruia   Hanmer Springs
Greymouth   Kumara   Stillwater   Waiau   Kaikoura
L. Brunner   Jacksons   Culverden
Hokitika   **ARTHUR'S PASS**   Waikari   Waipara
Ross   Arthur's Pass   Hurunui   Amberley
Abut Hd.   Oxford   Waimate North   Rangiora   Pegasus Bay
WESTLAND   Coleridge   Springfield   Kaiapoi   New Brighton
Westland   Aoraki Mt. Cook 3753   Whitecliffs   Darfield   **Christchurch**
Mount Cook   Methven   Lincoln   Riccarton   Lyttelton
Okuru   Haast   Staveley   L. Ellesmere   Banks Pen.   Akaroa
Jackson Bay   Little River

SOUTH ISLAND
Westland Bight

MOUNT ASPIRING   Mt. Aspiring 3033   Fairlie   Canterbury Plains
Southern Alps / Tiritiri-o-te-Moana   L. Tekapo   Pleasant Pt.   **Timaru**
Milford Sd.   Earnslaw 2819   L. Wanaka   L. Pukaki   Pareora
Sutherland Falls   Milford Sound   **Wanaka**   Ohau   L. Ohau   St. Andrews
Bligh Sound   **Arrowtown**   Cromwell   Omarama   Waimate
George Sound   **Queenstown**   **Clyde**   **Oamaru**   Canterbury Bight
Secretary I.   Anau   Kingston   **Alexandra**   Naseby   Maheno
Doubtful Sd.   Te Anau   Wakatipu   Kakanui Mts.   Hampden
FIORDLAND   L. Manapouri   Mossburn   Roxburgh   Dunback   Palmerston
Breaksea Sd.   Manapouri   **Lumsden**   **Eyre Mts.**   **Otago**   Waikouaiti   Port Chalmers
Resolution I.   Dusky Sd.   Ohai   Nightcaps   Garvie Mts.   Tapanui   Otago Harbour   C. Saunders
Chalky Inlet   Clifden   Tuatapere   Winton   Umbrella Mts.   **Lawrence**   Milton   Mosgiel   **Dunedin**
Preservation Inlet   Te Waewae Bay   Orepuki   **Gore**   Edievale   Kelso   Waihola
Hedgehope   Mataura   Clinton   Balclutha
Solander I.   Riverton   **Invercargill**   Wyndham   Kaitangata   Nugget Pt.
Bluff   Invercargill   Tokanui   Tahakopa
Ruapuke I.   Foveaux Str.
Halfmoon Bay
Stewart I. (Rakiura)   **RAKIURA**   Port Pegasus
South West C.

Projection : Conical with two standard parallels

East from Greenwich

PACIFIC OCEAN

TAHITI & MOOREA [d]
1:1 000 000

Pte. Aroa
B. de Matavai   Pte. Vénus
Papetoai   Paopao   Mahina
Papeete   Arue   Papenoo
Mt. Tohiea 1207   Pirae   Tiarei
Moorea (France)   Faaa   **Tahiti** (France)
Haapiti   Afareaitu   Hitiaa
Pte. Nuupere   Mt. Aorai 2060   Mt. Orohena 2241   Faaone
PACIFIC OCEAN   Punaauia   Mt. Terufera 1799   Lac Vaihiria
Paea   Isthme de Taravao
Maraa   Papara   Taravao   Afaahiti   Pte. Tatutua
Atimaono   Mataiea   Pueu
Vairao   Mt. Rooniu 1332   Tautira
Teahupoo   **Presqu'île de Taiarapu**

West from Greenwich

COPYRIGHT PHILIP'S

10   0   10 km
10   0   10 miles
1:1 000 000

ft   m
9000   3000
6000   2000
3000   1000
1200   400
600   200
0   0
200   600
2000   6000
4000   12 000
6000   18 000
m   ft

COPYRIGHT PHILIP'S

E   63   F   G

Projection: Bonne

East from Greenwich   3

Aboriginal lands

1. NGALIIPURRU / NUNGALI   5. RODNA
2. WANIMYN   6. NTARIA
3. WAMBARDI   7. ROULPMAULPMA
4. LIIALALTUMA   8. URUNA

WESTERN AUSTRALIA

NORTHERN TERRITORY

SOUTH AUSTRALIA

INDIAN OCEAN

SOUTHERN OCEAN

OCEAN

Great Australian Bight

Nullarbor Plain

Hampton Tableland

Nullarbor

Great Victoria Desert

Central Desert

Petermann Ranges

Musgrave Ranges

Uluru / Kata Tjuta

Kata Tjuta (The Olgas) 868
Uluru (Ayers Rock) 1069

Mann Ranges

Everard Ranges

SPINIFEX

Gibson Desert

Warburton

NGAANYATJARRA

Shark Bay

Geraldton

Kalbarri

PERTH
Fremantle
Rockingham
Mandurah
Bunbury
Busselton

Albany

Esperance

Kalgoorlie-Boulder

Norseman

Carnarvon

Meekatharra

Mount Magnet

Wiluna

Laverton

Leonora

Coolgardie

TRANS-AUSTRALIAN HWY

EYRE HWY

GREAT NORTHERN HWY

m   ft
1000   3000
400   1200
200   600
0   0
         -200   600
         1000   3000
         2000   6000
         4000   12 000
         6000   18 000
m   ft

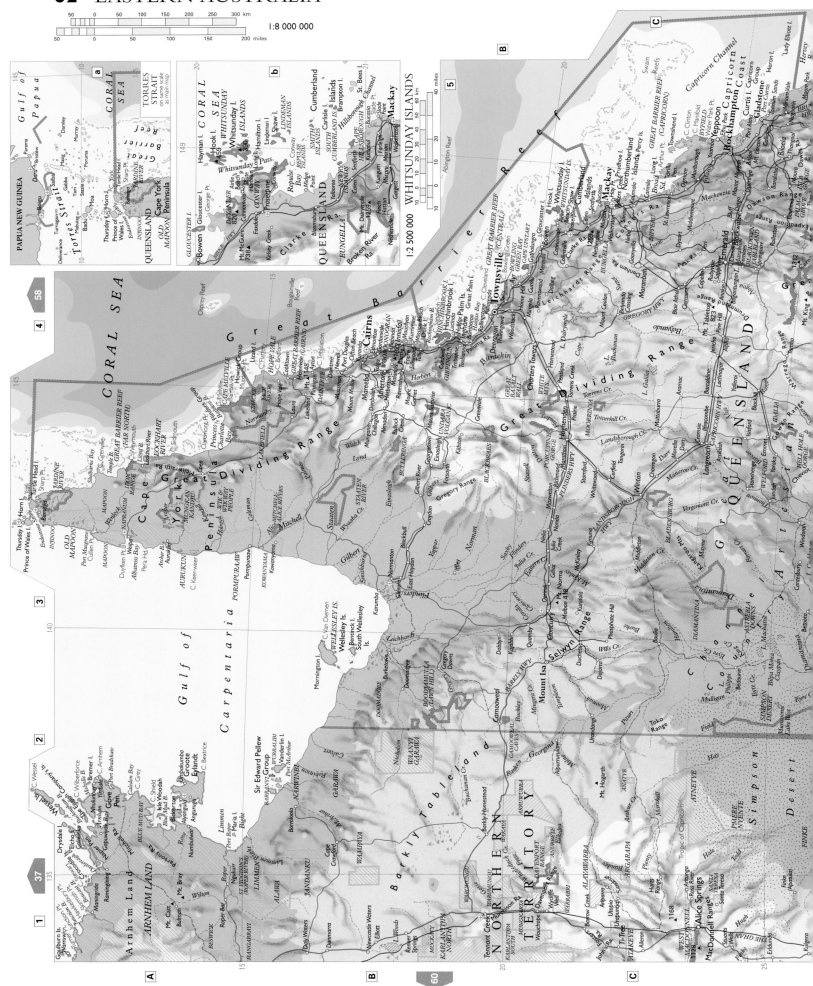

1:8 000 000

WHITSUNDAY ISLANDS

1:2 500 000

TORRES STRAIT
on same scale
as main map

PAPUA NEW GUINEA

Gulf of Papua

C O R A L   S E A

Torres Strait

QUEENSLAND

OLD MAPOON

Cape York Peninsula

C O R A L   S E A

QUEENSLAND

Great Barrier Reef

Cairns

Townsville

Mackay

Rockhampton

Capricorn Coast

Gladstone

GREAT BARRIER REEF

Gulf of Carpentaria

Arnhem Land

NORTHERN TERRITORY

Barkly Tableland

Mount Isa

Selwyn Range

G r e a t   D i v i d i n g   R a n g e

Q U E E N S L A N D

Channel Country

Simpson Desert

Alice Springs

MacDonnell Ranges

T A S M A N   S E A

NEW SOUTH WALES

SOUTH AUSTRALIA

BRISBANE
SYDNEY
Canberra
MELBOURNE
ADELAIDE
Newcastle
Wollongong
Broken Hill
TASMANIA
Hobart

Bass Strait

COPYRIGHT PHILIP'S

East from Greenwich

Aboriginal lands

on same scale

Projection: Bonne

61

m
ft

Yekaterinburg
Moskva
Volga
Astana (Aqmola)
Semey
Tomsk
Novosibirsk
Ob'
Irkutsk
Lena
Chita
R U S S I A
Okhotsk
Sea of Okhotsk
Poluostrov Kamchatka
Shirshov Ridge
Aleutian Basin
Beri Sea
Komandorskiye Ostrova (Russia)
Near Is. (U.S.A.)
Andreanof Is. (U.S.A.)
Aleutia
Aleutian Trench
Ozero Baykal
Blagoveshchensk
Amur
Khabarovsk
Petropavlovsk-Kamchatskiy
7822
KAZAKHSTAN
Aral Sea
Balqash Köl
Altai
Ulaanbaatar
MONGOLIA
Harbin
Sakhalin
Kurilskiye Ostrova (Russia)
La Perouse Str.
Kuril-Kamchatka Trench
10,542
Emperor Trough
Northwest
Chinook Trou
Almaty
Ürümqi
Changchun
Shenyang
Vladivostok
Sapporo
Hakodate
NORTH KOREA
Sea of Japan
Emperor Seamount Chain
Toshkent
KYRGYZSTAN
Beijing
Tianjin
Taiyuan
Huang He
Dalian
Seoul
SOUTH KOREA
Nagoya
Kyoto
Sendai
Tokyo
Yokohama
JAPAN
Shatsky Rise
Pacific
TAJIKISTAN
CHINA
Lanzhou
Xi'an
Qingdao
Kyushu Shikoku
Osaka
Fuji-San 3776
Basin
AFGHANISTAN
Kabul
Srinagar
Kunlun Shan
XIZANG
Nanjing
Wuhan
Yellow Sea
Okinawa
Japan Trench
10,554
Midway Is. (U.S.A.)
Howa
PAKISTAN
Lahore
Delhi
Himalaya
Lhasa
Chongqing
Hangzhou
Shanghai
East China Sea
Kazan-Retto (Japan)
Lisianski I. (U.S.A.)
Kanpur
NEPAL
Mt. Everest 8850
Changsha
Fuzhou
Ryukyu-retto (Japan)
Minami-Tori-Shima (Japan)
Ogasawara Gunto (Japan)
INDIA
Ganga
Brahmaputra
Kunming
Guangzhou
Taipei
TAIWAN
Iwo-Jima (Japan)
Kyushu-Palau Ridge
Strito-Ozima Ridge
Mid-Pacific Mount
Kolkata (Calcutta)
Dhaka
BANGLADESH
Irrawaddy
Mandalay
BURMA
Macau
Hong Kong
Philippine Sea
Wake I. (U.S.A.)
International Date Line
PA
Hyderabad
Bay of Bengal
Rangoon
Salween
LAOS
Hanoi
Hainan
C. Engano
Luzon
West Mariana Basin
NORTHERN MARIANAS (U.S.A.)
East Mariana Basin
Chennai (Madras)
Andaman Is. (India)
THAILAND
Bangkok
Mekong
VIETNAM
Paracel Is.
Manila
Philippine Basin
Tinian
Saipan
MARSHALL IS.
SRI LANKA
Nicobar Is. (India)
Phnom Penh
CAMBODIA
G. of Thailand
South China Sea
Mindoro
Palawan
Samar
PHILIPPINES
GUAM (U.S.A.)
Challenger 11,022 Deep
Yap
Mariana Trench
Micro
Eneweta Atoll
Bikini Atoll
Ralik Chain
Ratak Chain
Kwajalein
Majuro
Colombo
Thanh Pho Ho Chi Minh
Sulu Sea
Mindanao
Davao
10,497
Mindanao Trench
Melekeok
Caroline Is.
FED. STATES OF MICRONESIA
Chuuk
Pohnpei Palikir
Jaluit I.
Ce
MALAYSIA
4101
BRUNEI SABAH
Celebes Sea
PALAU
West Caroline Basin
Eauripik Rise
M
East Caroline Basin
Mela
Solomon Rise
Melanesian Basin
Butaritari
Howland I Baker I.
Pacifi
Kuala Lumpur
Singapore
Borneo
SARAWAK
Halmahera
Sulawesi
Buru
Seram
Puncak Jaya 5029
PAPUA
New Guinea
Admiralty Is.
Bismarck Arch.
New Ireland
PAPUA NEW GUINEA
NAURU
Tarawa
Banaba
Gilbert Is.
Phoenix Is.
Abariringa Enderbury
O
Sumatera
INDONESIA
Palembang
Makassar
Banda Sea
7440
New Britain
Kokopo
8940
Bougainville
SOLOMON IS.
Fongafale
TUVALU
KI
Selat Sunda
Jakarta
Jawa
Surabaya
Flores Sea
Flores
Dili
EAST TIMOR
Lae
Port Moresby
Honiara
Guadalcanal
Santa Cruz I.
9165
Rotuma
Is. Wallis & Futuna (Fr.)
SAMOA
Apia
Java Trench
Bali
Sumbawa
Sumba
Timor
Arafura Sea
Torres Strait
C. York
Louisiade Arch.
Coral Sea Basin
Espíritu Santo
VANUATU
Port Vila
NEW
West Fiji Basin
Vanua Levu
Viti Levu
FIJI
Suva
Cocos Is. (Austral.)
Christmas I. (Austral.)
North Australian Basin
C. Arnhem
Darwin
Gulf of Carpentaria
Cairns
Coral Sea
Is. Chesterfield
7570
South Fiji Basin
Nuku'alofa
TONGA
INDIAN
Wharton Basin
Exmouth Plateau
North West C.
Broome
Mount Isa
Great Barrier Reef
Townsville
Rockhampton
NEW CALEDONIA (Fr.)
Nouméa
Is. Loyauté
10,822
Tonga Trench
OCEAN
Broken Ridge
Perth Basin
Geraldton
AUSTRALIA
Alice Springs
L. Eyre
Darling
Brisbane
Middleton Basin
Lord Howe Rise
Norfolk I. (Austral.)
Norfolk Ridge
South Fiji Basin
Tonga Trench
Lou
Naturaliste Plateau
Perth
Albany
Great Australian Bight
Murray
Adelaide
Canberra
Sydney
Mt. Kosciuszko 2228
Lord Howe I. (Austral.)
Kermadec Is. (N.Z.)
Kermadec Trench 10,047
NEW ZEALAND
Mid
Indian
Ridge
South Australian Basin
Melbourne
Bass Str.
Tasmania
Hobart
East Tasman Plateau
Tasman Sea
Aoraki Mt. Cook 3753
Auckland
Cook Strait
Wellington
Christchurch
Chatham Rise
Chatham Is. (N.Z.)
Nouvelle Amsterdam (Fr.)
I. St. Paul (Fr.)
SOUTHERN
OCEAN
South Tasman Rise
South Tasman Basin
Dunedin
Invercargill
Bounty Trough
Bounty Is. (N.Z.)
Is. Crozet (Fr.)
Macquarie I. (Austral.)
Auckland Is. (N.Z.)
Campbell (N.Z.) Plateau
Antipodes Is. (N.Z.)
Kerguelen (Fr.)
Campbell I. (N.Z.)
Heard I. (Austral.)

ft m
12 000 4000
9000 3000
6000 2000
3000 1000
1500 500
600 200
0 0
200 600
1000 3000
2000 6000
4000 12 000
6000 18 000
8000 24 000
m ft

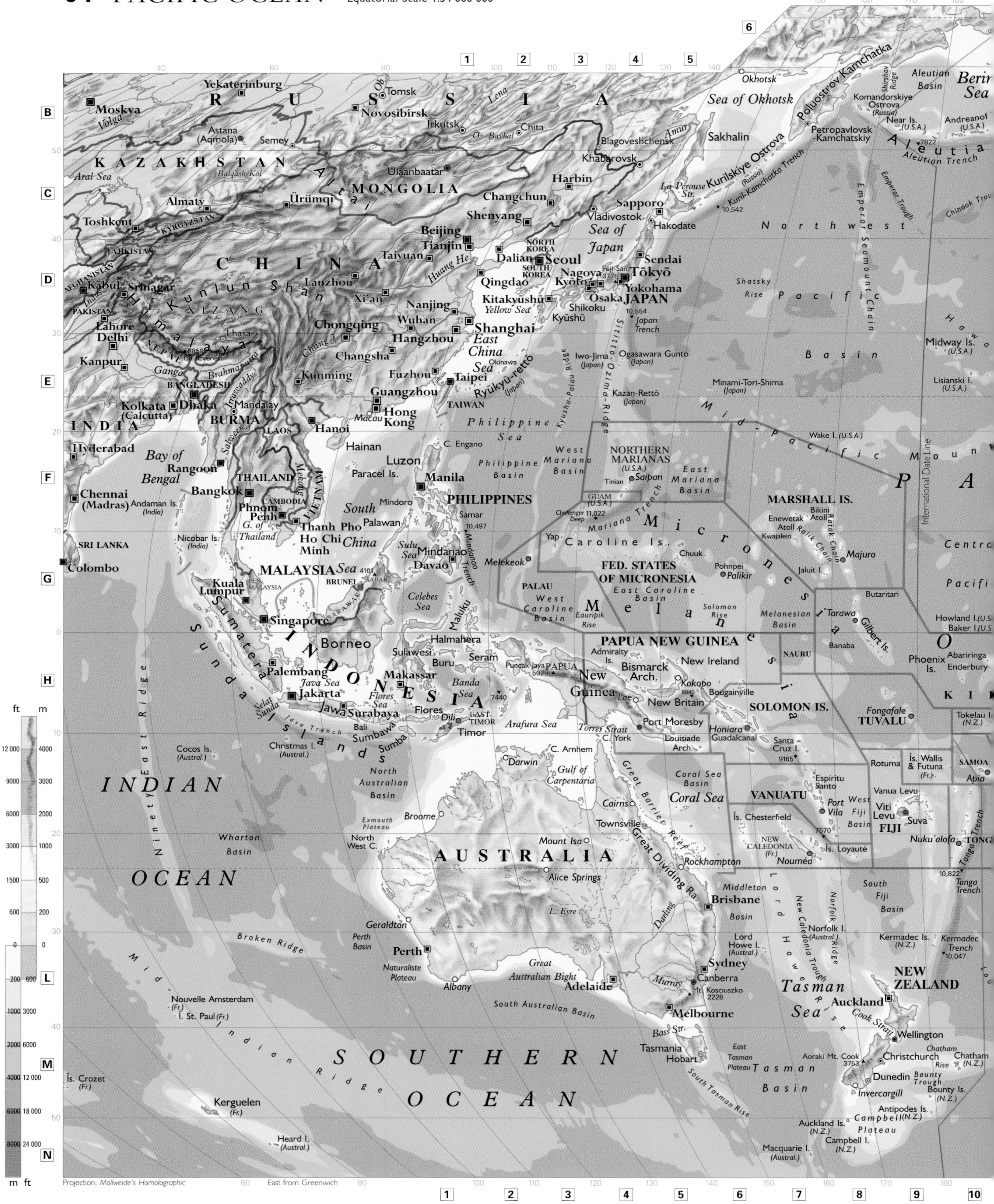

11 12 13 14

15

16 17 18 19 20

Arctic Circle

ALASKA
(U.S.A.)
Anchorage
5959

Bristol Bay
Gulf of Alaska
Juneau

R O C K Y

Prince of Wales I.
(U.S.A.) Prince Rupert
Queen Charlotte Is.
(Canada)

Is. (U.S.A.)

C A N A D A

Edmonton
Calgary
Regina
Winnipeg
L. Winnipeg
Newfoundland

Tufts
Abyssal
Plain

Vancouver
Vancouver I.
Victoria
Seattle
Portland
Boise

Snake

Québec
Montréal
Ottawa
St. Lawrence
St. John's

L. Superior
Minneapolis
Missouri
L. Michigan
L. Huron
Toronto
Detroit
L. Ontario
Buffalo
L. Erie
Boston
New York
Philadelphia
Baltimore
Washington D.C.

C

Northeast

Mendocino Fracture Zone C. Mendocino

Sacramento
San Francisco

6741

Salt Lake
City
5610

Denver

Kansas City

Chicago

Pittsburgh

Cincinnati

St. Louis

A T L A N T I C

D

Pacific

Murray Fracture Zone

4418

Colorado

UNITED STATES

Los Angeles
San Diego

Phoenix

Oklahoma City
Memphis

Dallas

Atlanta

Appalachian Mts.

C. Hatteras

Bermuda
(U.K.)

Guadalupe
(Mex.)

Molokai Fracture Zone

Ciudad
Juárez

Baja California

Houston
San Antonio

Mississippi

New
Orleans

Jacksonville

Sargasso Sea

Tropic of Cancer

Basin

C. San Lucas

Golfo de California

Monterrey

Gulf of Mexico

Tampa
Miami

La Habana

Florida Str.

BAHAMAS

CUBA

West Indies

O C E A N

E

Ridge

Honolulu
Kauai Oahu
HAWAIIAN IS.
Maui (U.S.A.)
4205
Hilo
Hawaii

Clarion Fracture Zone

Is. Revilla Gigedo
(Mex.)

Guadalajara

Acapulco

Mexico
Puebla

MEXICO

Mérida

Canal de Yucatan

9200

HAITI

DOMINICAN REP.

Leeward

JAMAICA

Kingston

PUERTO
RICO
(U.S.A.)

Johnston I.
U.S.A.

C I F I C

Palmyra Is.
(U.S.A.)

BELIZE

7680

GUATEMALA
6662

HONDURAS
Guatemala

Middle America Trench

Î. Clipperton
(Fr.)

Clipperton Fracture Zone

San Salvador
EL SALVADOR
NICARAGUA
Managua

Guatemala
Basin

Caribbean Sea

BARBADOS

Windward Is.

F

Teraina
Tabuaeran
Kiritimati

Cooper Ridge

COSTA
RICA

Cocos Ridge

Panama
Basin

Barranquilla

San José
Colón
PANAMA

I. del Coco
(Costa Rica)

Panamá

Maracaibo

Caracas

VENEZUELA

Medellín

I. de Malpelo
(Colombia)

Orinoco

Cali
Bogotá

COLOMBIA

G

Jarvis I.
(U.S.A.)

E A N

B A T I

Line Islands

Malden I.

Starbuck I.

Vostok I.

Caroline I.
(Millennium I.)

Flint I.

Equator

Galápagos Fracture Zone

Galápagos
(Ecuador)

Carnegie Ridge

Quito
ECUADOR

Guayaquil

Iquitos

Amazonas

BRAZIL

H

Penrhyn
(Tongareva)

Manihiki
Pukapuka
Manihiki

Plateau

Suwarrow Is.

Îs. de la
Société

Nuku Hiva
Îs. Marquises
Hiva Oa

Marquesas Fracture Zone

East Pacific Ridge

Yupanqui
Basin

Galápagos Fracture Zone

C. Palinas

Trujillo

6369

PERU

J

Cook Is.
(N.Z.)

Aitutaki

Rarotonga

Mangaia

Bora Bora
Huahine
Raiatea
Papeete
Tahiti

Rangiroa

Îs. Tuamotu

Austral Seamount Chain

Îs. Tubuai

Îs. Gambier

Mururoa

FRENCH POLYNESIA

Peru Basin

Mendaña Fracture Zone

Nazca Ridge

6866
Peru-
Chile

Lima

Cusco

Arequipa
6886

Arica

Iquique
Chile

L. Titicaca

Nevado Ancohuma
6550

La Paz
BOLIVIA

J

Tropic of Capricorn

East Pacific Ridge

Oeno I.
Henderson I.
Pitcairn I.
(U.K.)
Ducie I.

Rapa

Easter Fracture Zone

Sala-y-Gómez

I. de Pascua
(Chile)

Sala y Gómez Ridge

San Felix
(Chile)

San Ambrosio
(Chile)

Antofagasta

8050
Trench

PARAGUAY

Asunción

San Miguel
de Tucumán

Porto
Alegre

K

Pacific-Antarctic East Pacific Ridge

Roggeveen
Basin

Arch. de
Juan Fernández
(Chile)

Challenger Fracture Zone

Chile Rise

Aconcagua
6962
Córdoba
Rosario

Valparaíso
Santiago

Concepción

Buenos
Aires

URUGUAY
Montevideo

Río de la Plata

L

Southwest

Pacific

Nazca Ridge

ARGENTINA

Patagonian

ATLANTIC

M

Basin

Menard Fracture Zone

6212

OCEAN

Southeast
Pacific Basin

Punta Arenas
C. de Hornos

Est. de Magallanes
Tierra del Fuego

Drake Passage

Falkland Is.
(U.K.)

South Georgia
(U.K.)

N

West from Greenwich

100 0 200 400 600 800 1000 1200 1400 km
100 0 200 400 600 800 1000 miles

1:35 000 000

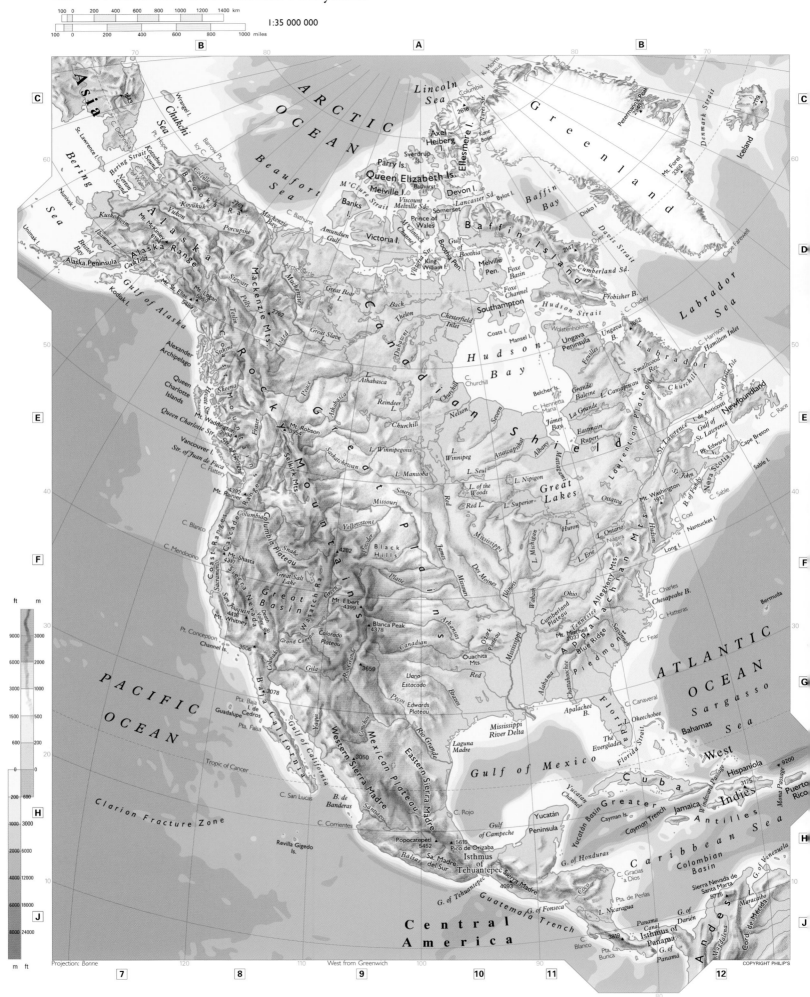

ft m
9000 3000
6000 2000
3000 1000
1500 500
600 200
0 0
200 600
1000 3000
2000 6000
4000 12000
6000 18000
8000 24000
m ft

Projection: Bonne

A S I A

Asia

A R C T I C

O C E A N

Lincoln
Sea

G r e e n l a n d

Iceland

Denmark Strait

Chukchi
Sea

Bering
Sea

Beaufort
Sea

Queen Elizabeth Is.

Baffin
Bay

Baffin Island

Labrador
Sea

A l a s k a
R a n g e

Gulf of Alaska

R o c k y   M o u n t a i n s

C a n a d i a n   S h i e l d

Hudson
Bay

Labrador

Newfoundland

P A C I F I C

O C E A N

G r e a t   P l a i n s

Great
Lakes

A T L A N T I C

O C E A N

Sargasso
Sea

G r e a t
B a s i n

Tropic of Cancer

Gulf of Mexico

West
Indies

Cuba
Hispaniola
Puerto Rico

Greater   Antilles

Bermuda

Bahamas

C a r i b b e a n   S e a
Colombian
Basin

Clarion Fracture Zone

Revilla Gigedo
Is.

M e x i c a n   P l a t e a u

West from Greenwich

C e n t r a l
A m e r i c a

Isthmus of
Panama

A n d e s

COPYRIGHT PHILIP'S

1:35 000 000

100 0 200 400 600 800 1000 1200 1400 km
100 0 200 400 600 800 1000 miles

B **A** **B**

C RUSSIA
Asia
St. Lawrence I.
Bering Strait
Bering
Sea

ARCTIC OCEAN

GREENLAND
(Denmark)

ICELAND
Denmark Strait
Reykjavík
C

Queen Elizabeth Is.
Ellesmere I.

Beaufort
Sea

Baffin
Bay

D ALASKA
(U.S.A.)
Yukon
Porcupine
Anchorage
Fairbanks
Kodiak I.
Gulf of Alaska
YUKON
TERRITORY
Arctic Circle
Victoria I.

NORTHWEST

NUNAVUT

Baffin Island
Iqaluit

Davis Strait

Nuuk
D

Whitehorse
Juneau
Whitehorse

Great Bear L.
Mackenzie

Hudson Strait

E BRITISH
COLUMBIA
Skeena
Peace
Fraser
Yellowknife
TERRITORIES
Liard
Great Slave L.
Athabasca
ALBERTA
Athabasca
Edmonton
Calgary
Saskatchewan

C A N A D A

Back
Churchill
MANITOBA
Nelson

Hudson
Bay

Eastmain

QUÉBEC

St. Lawrence

NEWFOUNDLAND &
LABRADOR

St. John's
St-Pierre
et Miquelon (Fr.)
PRINCE
EDWARD I.
Charlottetown
NEW
BRUNSWICK
NOVA
SCOTIA
Halifax
E

Vancouver
Victoria
WASHINGTON
Olympia
Seattle
SASKATCHEWAN
Regina
L. Winnipeg
Winnipeg

ONTARIO

Québec
Fredericton
MAINE
Augusta

F Portland
Salem
OREGON
Columbia
MONTANA
Helena
Missouri
IDAHO
Boise
Snake
WYOMING
NORTH
DAKOTA
Bismarck
SOUTH
DAKOTA

MINNESOTA
Minneapolis-
St. Paul
WISCONSIN
Madison
IOWA
Milwaukee
L. Superior
L. Michigan
L. Huron
MICHIGAN
Lansing
Toledo
CHICAGO
ILLINOIS
INDIANA
Indianapolis
L. Ontario
L. Erie
TORONTO
Detroit
Cleveland
Buffalo
Pittsburgh
OHIO
Columbus
Cincinnati

Ottawa
Montréal
VER.
N.H.
Concord
MASS.
Boston
Providence
R.I.
Hartford
CONN.
NEW YORK
NEW YORK
PHILADELPHIA
PA.
N.J.
Baltimore
MD.
DEL.
Washington
D.C.
W.VA.
Richmond
F

G Sacramento
San Francisco
San Jose
CALIFORNIA
Carson
City
NEVADA
Salt Lake
City
UTAH
Colorado
NEBRASKA
Lincoln
Denver
COLORADO
UNITED STATES
KANSAS
Topeka
Kansas City
Springfield
St. Louis
MISSOURI
Nashville
KENTUCKY
TENNESSEE
Memphis
VIRGINIA
NORTH
CAROLINA
Raleigh
Charlotte
Columbia
SOUTH
CAROLINA
Charleston

Bermuda
(U.K.)
ATLANTIC
OCEAN
G

Las Vegas
LOS ANGELES
San Diego
Tijuana
Mexicali
ARIZONA
Phoenix
Tucson
NEW MEXICO
Santa Fe
Albuquerque
El Paso
OKLAHOMA
Oklahoma
City
Little Rock
ARKANSAS
Mississippi
Birmingham
ALABAMA
GEORGIA
Atlanta
Montgomery
Jackson
MISSISSIPPI

PACIFIC
OCEAN
Guadalupe
(Mex.)

Ciudad Juárez
Hermosillo
Rio Grande
TEXAS
Dallas-
Ft. Worth
Austin
Houston
San Antonio
LOUISIANA
Baton
Rouge
New
Orleans
Jacksonville
FLORIDA
Tallahassee
Tampa-
St. Petersburg
Orlando
MIAMI

H Tropic of Cancer
Revilla Gigedo Is.
(Mex.)
Culiacán
Monterrey
Torreón
San Luis Potosí
M E X I C O
León
Guadalajara
MÉXICO
Toluca
Puebla
Acapulco
Mérida

Gulf of Mexico

Havana
CUBA
Nassau
BAHAMAS
Florida Str.
Cayman Is.
(U.K.)
JAMAICA
Kingston

Turks & Caicos Is.
(U.K.)

HAITI
Port-au-
Prince
DOMINICAN
REP.
Santo
Domingo
PUERTO
RICO
(U.S.A.)
San Juan
H

Caribbean Sea

J Belmopan
BELIZE
GUATEMALA
Guatemala
San Salvador
EL SALVADOR
HONDURAS
Tegucigalpa
NICARAGUA
Managua
L. Nicaragua
COSTA
RICA
San José
PANAMA
COLOMBIA
Maracaibo
VENEZUELA
Barranquilla
Medellín
South
America
J

Projection: *Bonne*
120   110   West from Greenwich   100   90

7 ■ MÉXICO Capital Cities **8**   **9**   **10**   **11**   **12**

COPYRIGHT PHILIP'S

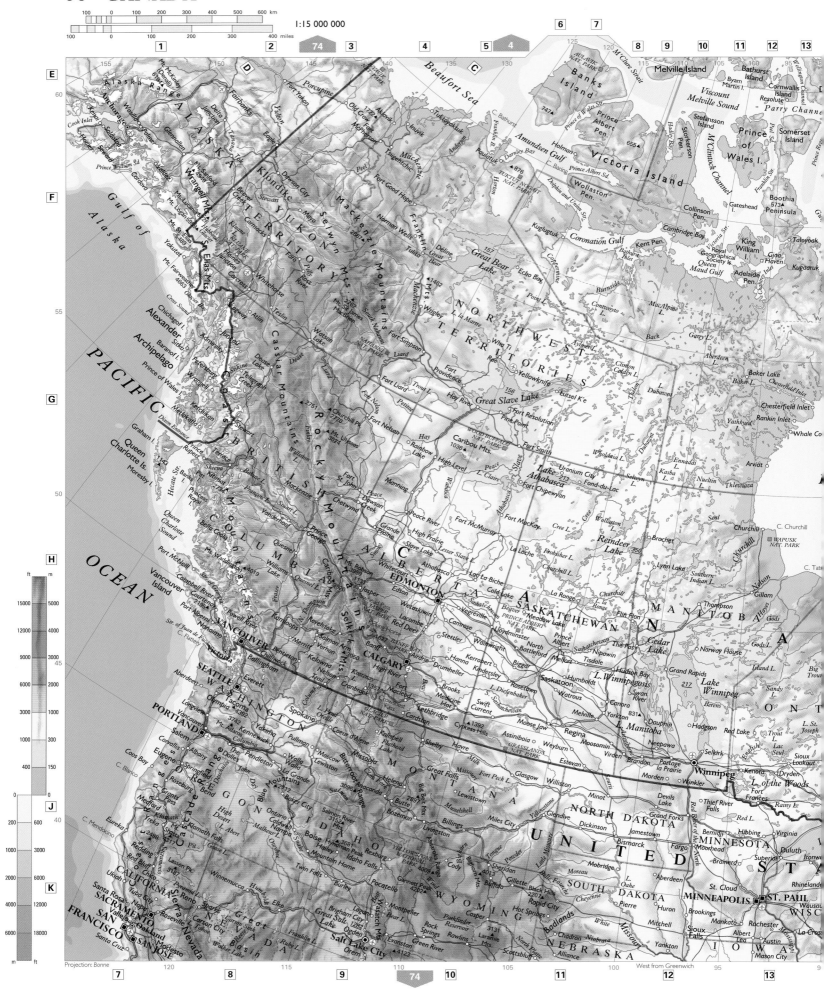

100 0 100 200 300 400 500 600 km

1:15 000 000

100 0 100 200 300 400 miles

Projection: Bonne

West from Greenwich

4

NORTHERN CANADA
continuation northwards on same scale as main map

ARCTIC OCEAN

GREENLAND (KALAALLIT NUNAAT)

Kronprins Frederik Land

North Magnetic Pole 2007

Queen Elizabeth Islands

NUNAVUT

N.W.T.

Parry Islands

Melville Island

Devon Island

Baffin Bay

Prince of Wales I.

Somerset Island

Lancaster Sound

Baffin Bay

Baffin Island

Davis Strait

Foxe Basin

Cumberland Peninsula

NUNAVUT

Hudson Strait

Hudson Bay

James Bay

Labrador Sea

ATLANTIC OCEAN

Labrador

NEWFOUNDLAND & LABRADOR

Ungava Bay

Péninsule d'Ungava

QUÉBEC

Newfoundland

Gulf of St. Lawrence

PRINCE EDWARD I.

NEW BRUNSWICK

NOVA SCOTIA

MAINE

QUÉBEC

MONTRÉAL

OTTAWA

Québec

TORONTO

Lake Huron

L. Ontario

BOSTON

NEW YORK

DETROIT

CLEVELAND

MILWAUKEE

Grand Rapids

COPYRIGHT PHILIP'S

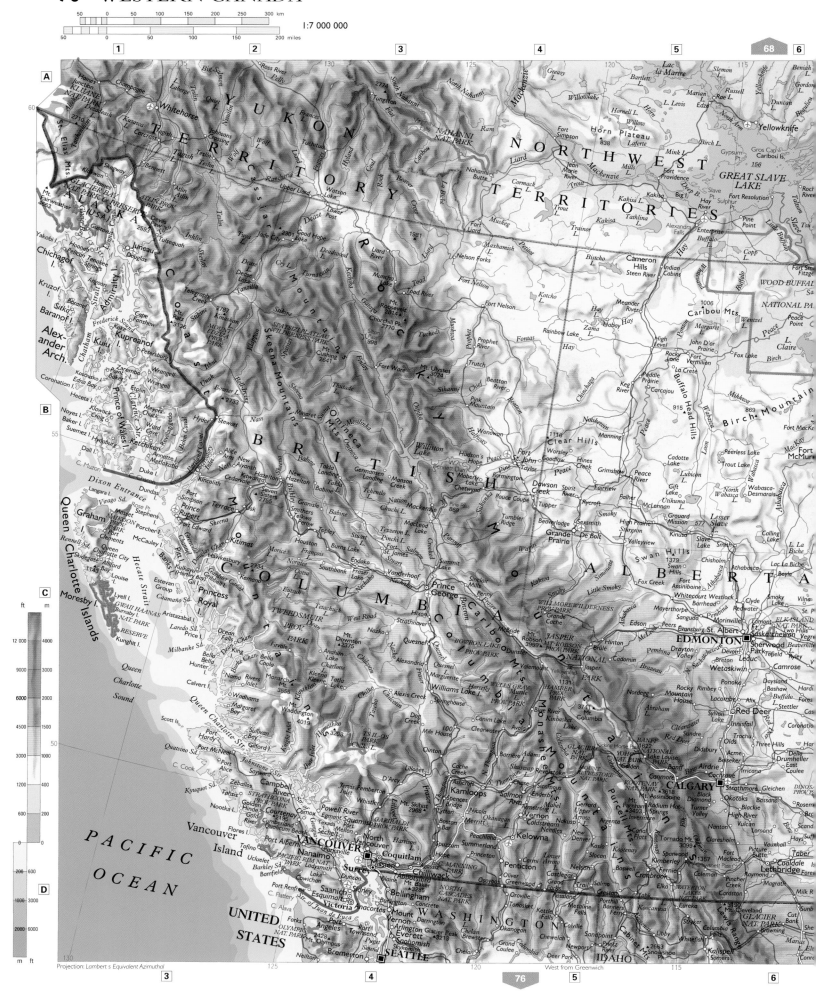

50 0 50 100 150 200 250 300 km

50 0 50 100 150 200 miles

1:7 000 000

ft m

12 000 4000

9000 3000

6000 2000

4500 1500

3000 1000

1200 400

600 200

0 0

200 600

1000 3000

2000 6000

m ft

Projection: Lambert's Equivalent Azimuthal

PACIFIC OCEAN

YUKON TERRITORY

NORTHWEST TERRITORIES

ALASKA

BRITISH COLUMBIA

ALBERTA

UNITED STATES

WASHINGTON

IDAHO

GREAT SLAVE LAKE

WOOD BUFFALO NATIONAL PARK

Yellowknife

Whitehorse

Juneau

EDMONTON

CALGARY

VANCOUVER

Victoria

SEATTLE

Red Deer

Prince George

Kamloops

Kelowna

Vancouver Island

Queen Charlotte Islands

Queen Charlotte Sound

Dixon Entrance

Hecate Strait

Prince Rupert

Kitimat

Williams Lake

West from Greenwich

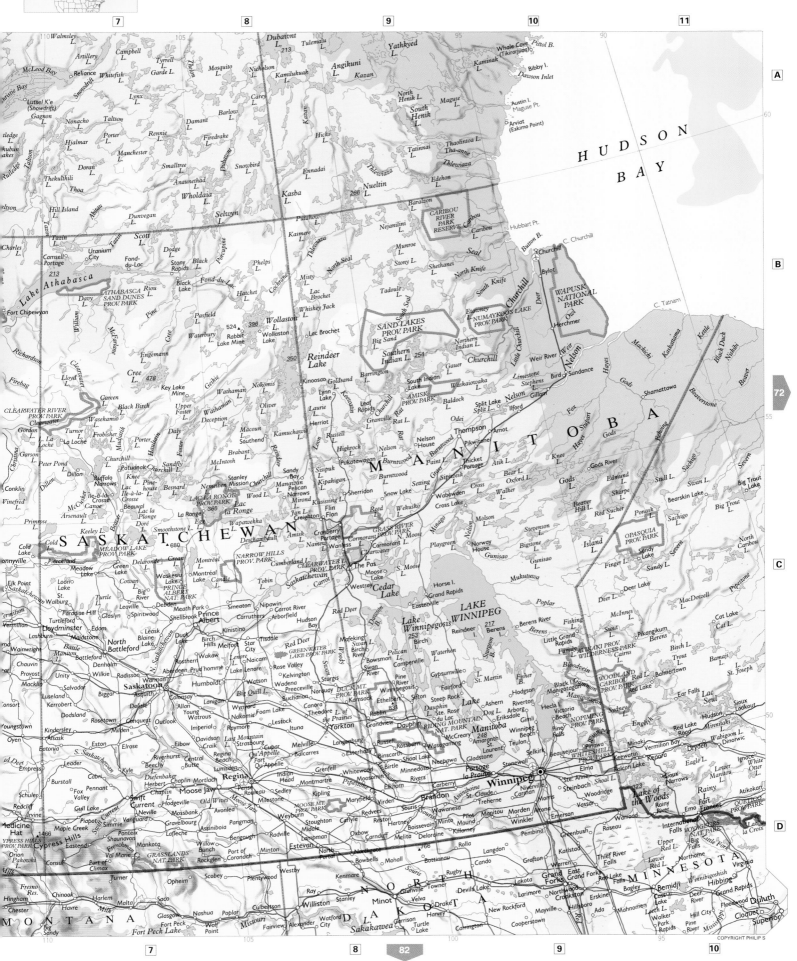

50 0 50 100 150 200 250 300 km

1:7 000 000

50 0 50 100 150 200 miles

Projection: Lambert's Equivalent Azimuthal

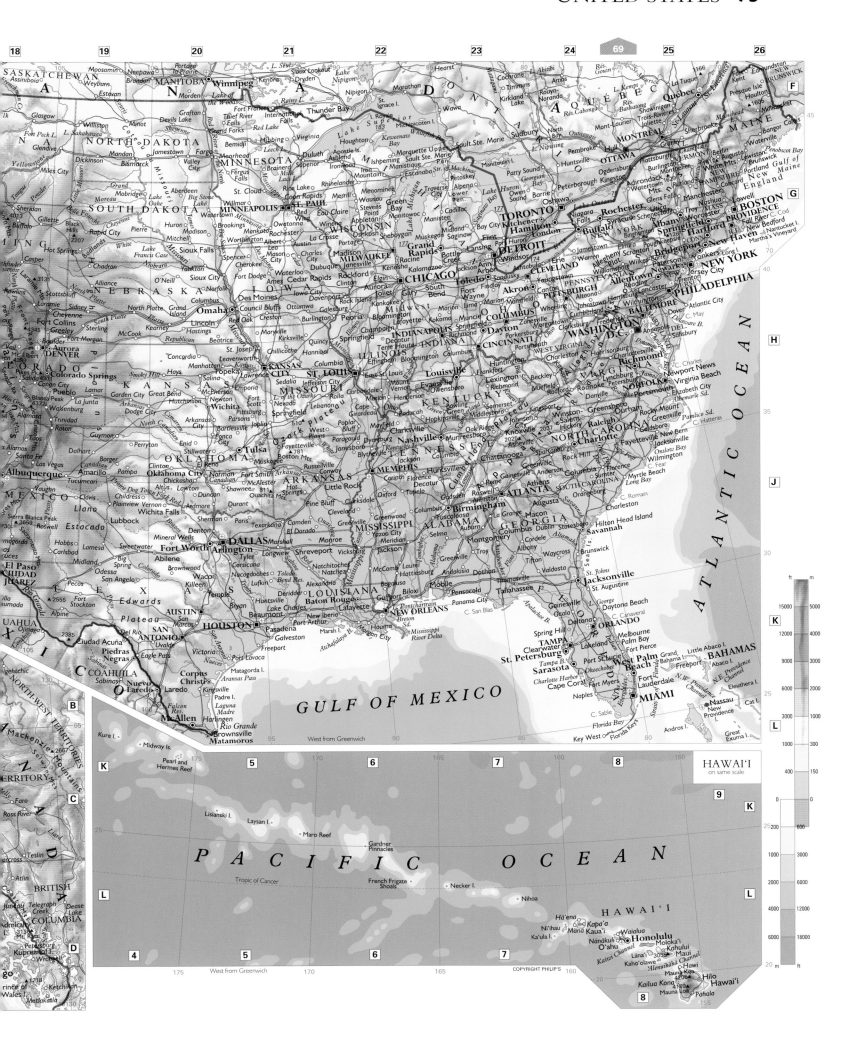

GULF OF MEXICO

ATLANTIC OCEAN

PACIFIC OCEAN

HAWAI'I
on same scale

West from Greenwich

COPYRIGHT PHILIP'S

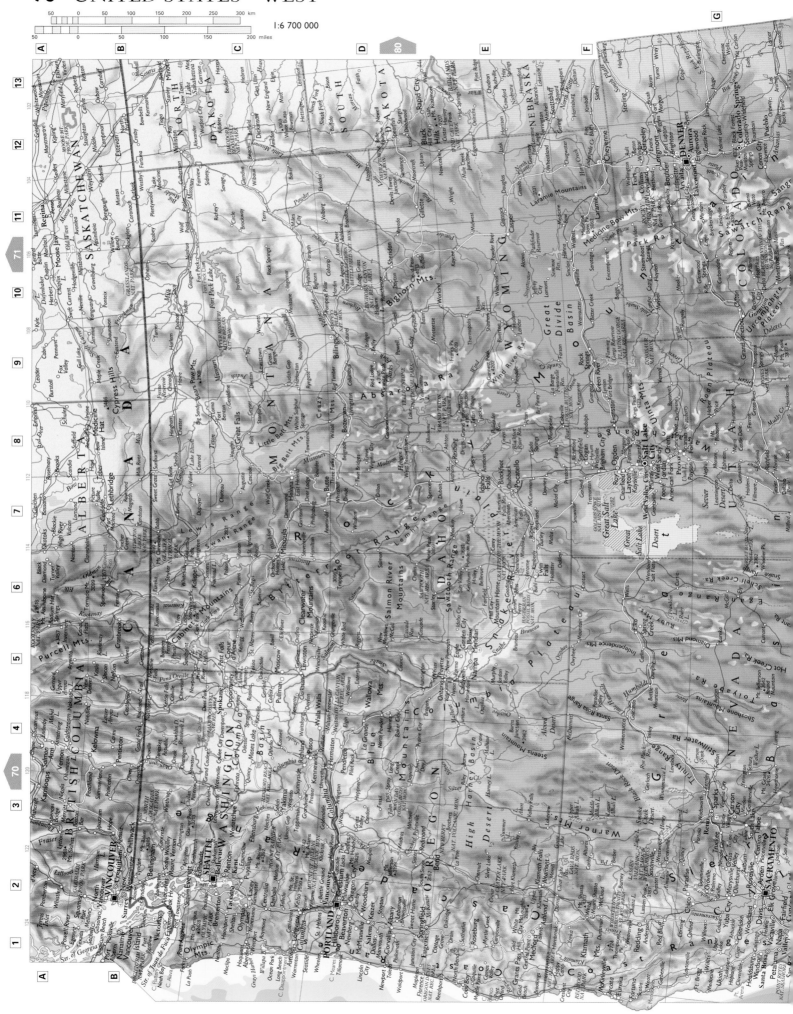

PACIFIC

OCEAN

Golfo de California

BAJA CALIFORNIA

BAJA CALIFORNIA SUR

M E X I C O

S O N O R A

C H I H U A H U A

T E X A S

N E W   M E X I C O

A R I Z O N A

C A L I F O R N I A

LOS ANGELES

SAN DIEGO

TIJUANA

PHOENIX

Tucson

Nogales

CIUDAD JUÁREZ

El Paso

Albuquerque

Santa Fe

LAS VEGAS

SAN FRANCISCO

Fresno

Bakersfield

Chihuahua

Hermosillo

Ciudad Obregón

Los Mochis

Lava fields

Projection: Albers' Equal Area with two standard parallels

West from Greenwich

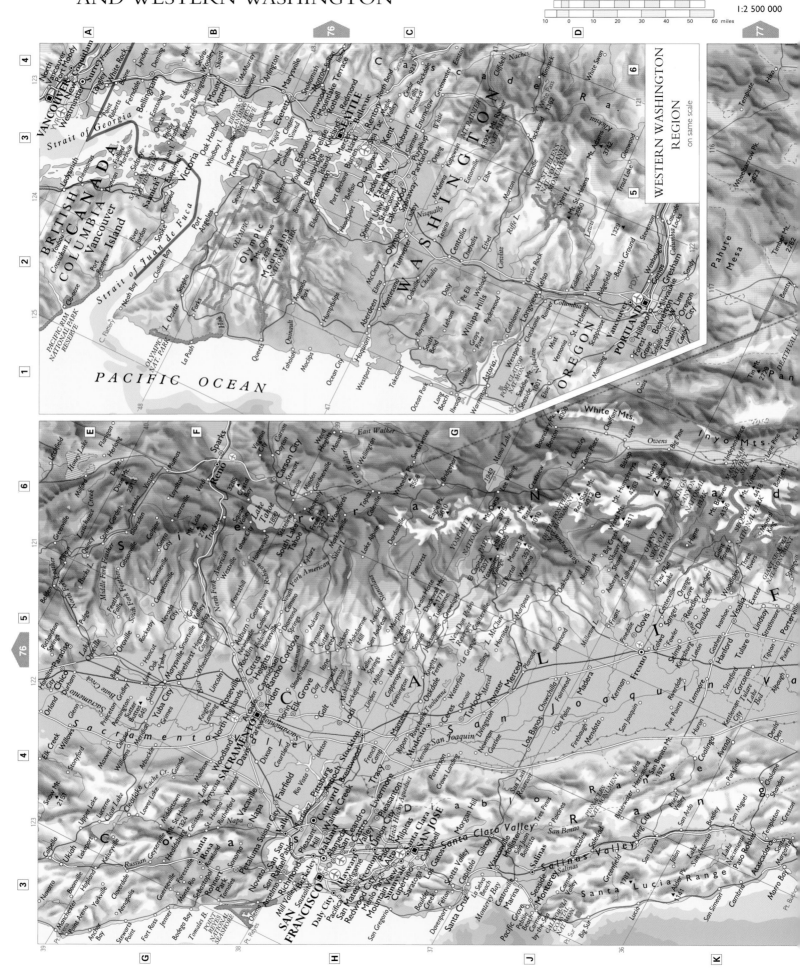

1:2 500 000

WESTERN WASHINGTON
REGION
on same scale

PACIFIC OCEAN

BRITISH COLUMBIA

CANADA

WASHINGTON

OREGON

PORTLAND

Strait of Georgia

Vancouver Island

Strait of Juan de Fuca

OLYMPIC Mountains NATIONAL PARK

Puget Sound

SEATTLE

VANCOUVER

Victoria

CALIFORNIA

NEVADA

Sierra Nevada

SACRAMENTO

SAN FRANCISCO

SAN JOSE

Sacramento Valley

San Joaquin Valley

Fresno

YOSEMITE NATIONAL PARK

KINGS CANYON NAT. PARK

SEQUOIA NAT. PARK

Inyo Mts.

White Mts.

Santa Clara Valley

Salinas Valley

Santa Lucia Range

Monterey

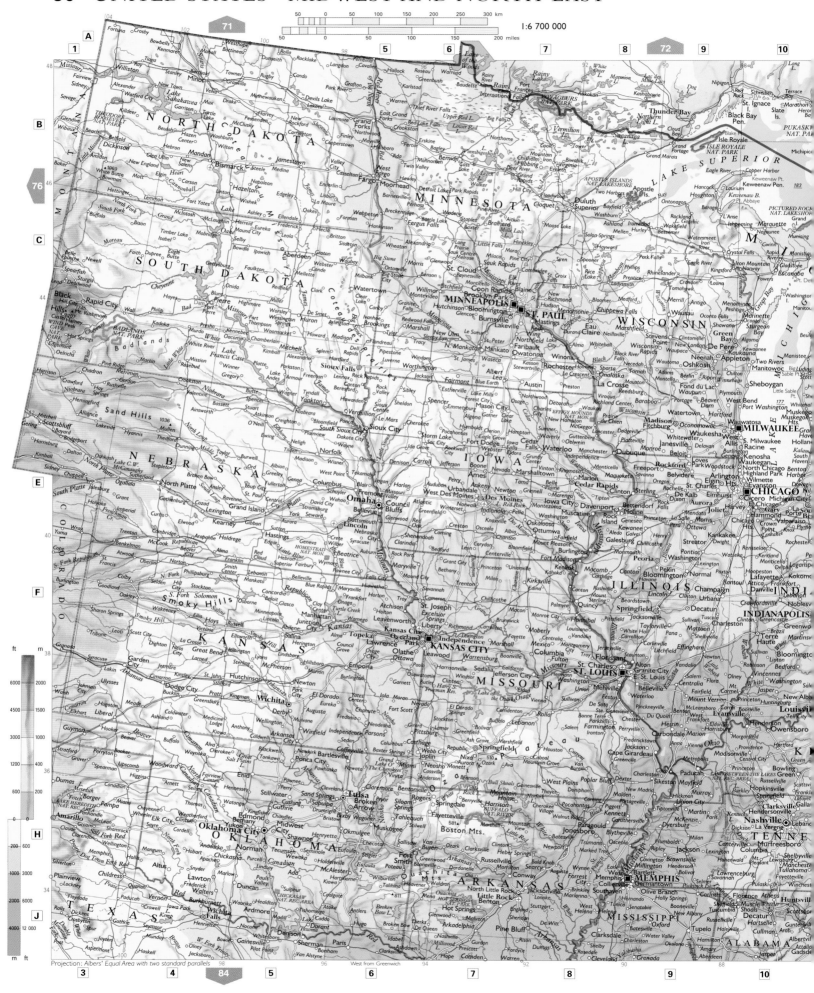

1:6 700 000

Projection: Albers' Equal Area with two standard parallels

West from Greenwich

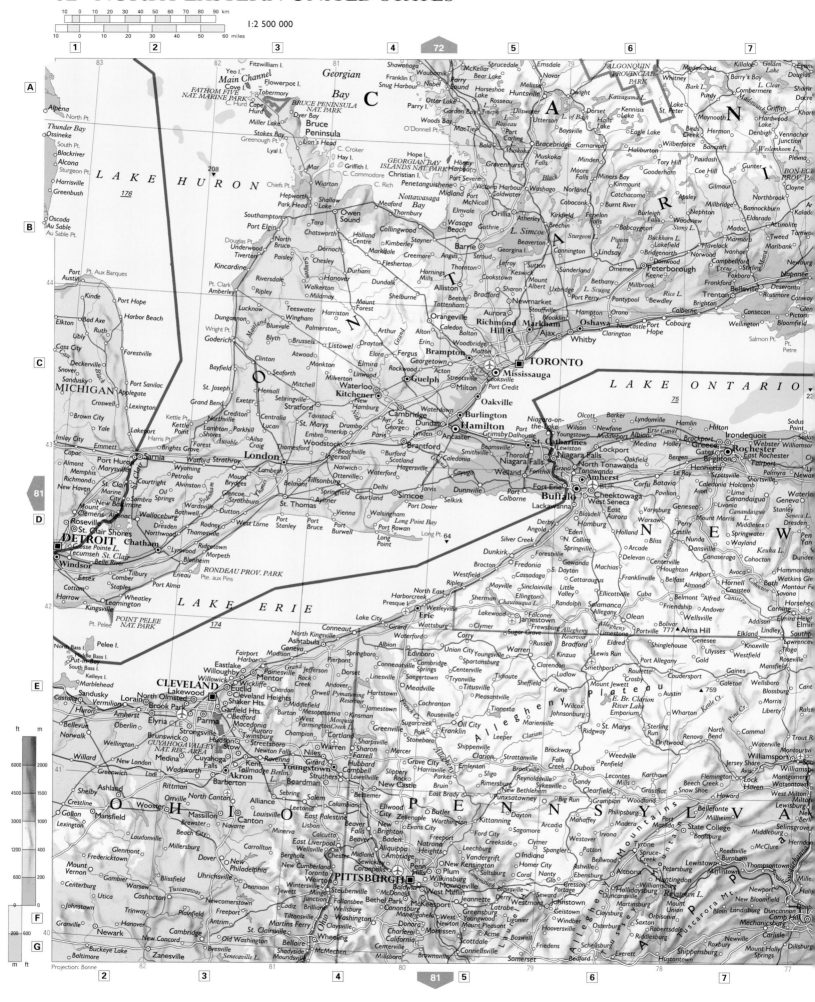

1:2 500 000

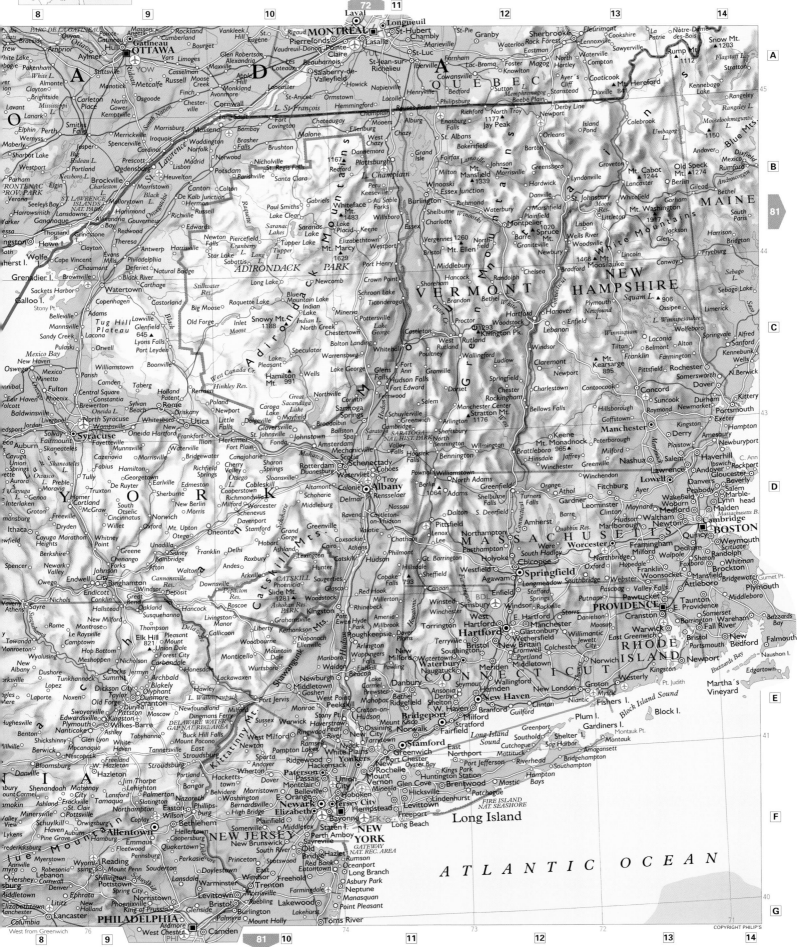

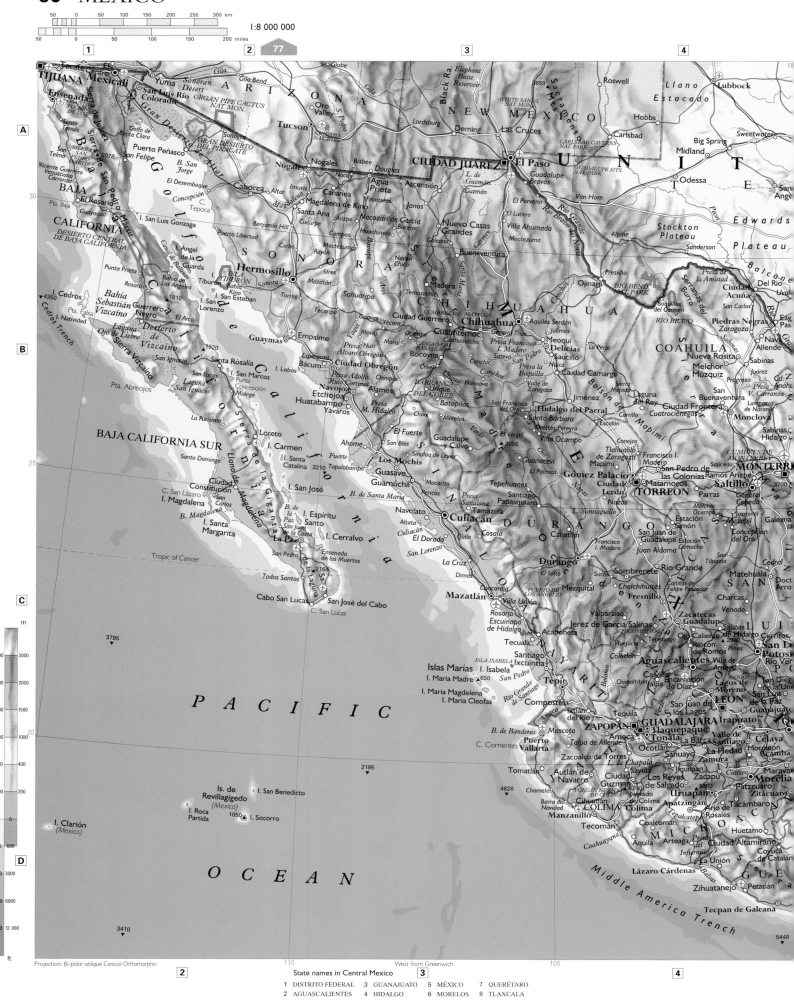

50 0 50 100 150 200 250 300 km
1:8 000 000
50 0 50 100 150 200 miles

77

1 | 2 | 3 | 4

ft m
9000 3000
6000 2000
4500 1500
3000 1000
1200 400
600 200
0 0
200 600
1000 3000
2000 6000
4000 12 000
m ft

Projection: Bi-polar oblique Conical Orthomorphic

West from Greenwich

State names in Central Mexico

1 DISTRITO FEDERAL   3 GUANAJUATO   5 MÉXICO   7 QUERÉTARO
2 AGUASCALIENTES   4 HIDALGO   6 MORELOS   8 TLAXCALA

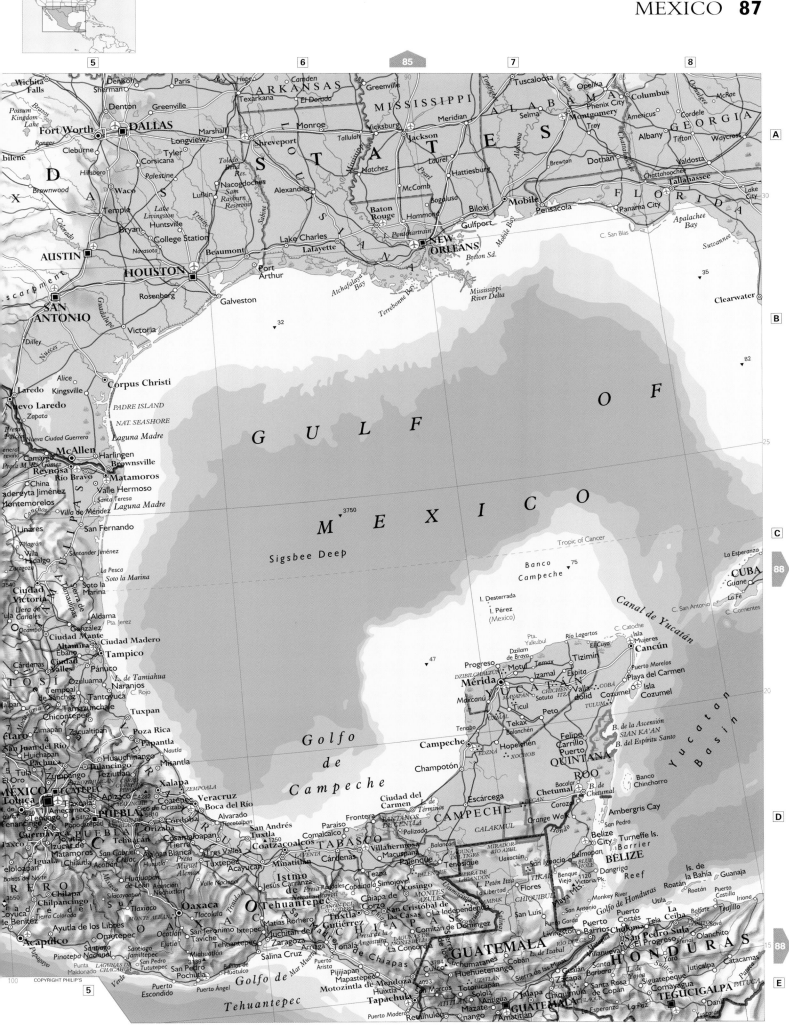

5   6   7   8

Wichita
Falls
Denison
Paris
Red
Camden
ARKANSAS
Greenville
Tuscaloosa
Copia
Opelika
Columbus
McRae
Dominise
Sherman
Hope
El Dorado
Monroe
MISSISSIPPI
Meridian
Selma
Phenix City
Americus
Cordele
Possum
Kingdom
Lake
Denton
Marshall
Texarkana
Vicksburg
Jackson
Montgomery
Troy
A L A B A M A
GEORGIA
Fort Worth
DALLAS
Longview
Tallulah
Natchez
Laurel
Hattiesburg
Brewton
Dothan
Tifton
Waycross
Albany
Cleburne
Tyler
Shreveport
McComb
Bogalusa
Panama City
Valdosta
Ranger
Hillsboro
Corsicana
Palestine
Nacogdoches
Alexandria
Baton
Rouge
Hammond
Biloxi
Mobile
Pensacola
F L O R I D A

Abilene
Waco
Temple
Lufkin
Sam
Rayburn
Reservoir
Lake
Livingston
Lake Charles
Lafayette
L. Pontchartrain
**NEW
ORLEANS**
Gulfport
Mobile Bay
Apalachee
Bay
Lake
City
30

Brownwood
Bryan
Huntsville
Beaumont
Breton Sd.
C. San Blas

Ranger
College Station
Port
Arthur
Atchafalaya
Bay
Terrebonne Bay
Clearwater

AUSTIN
HOUSTON
Rosenberg
Galveston
Mississippi
River Delta
35

**SAN
ANTONIO**
Victoria
G U L F   O F

Dilley
Alice
Corpus Christi

Laredo
Kingsville
PADRE ISLAND
NAT. SEASHORE
G   U   L   F
O   F

Nuevo Laredo
Zapata
McAllen
Harlingen
Brownsville
Laguna Madre
25

China
Rio Bravo
Matamoros
Reynosa

Montemorelos
Valle Hermoso
M   E   X   I   C   O

Linares
San Fernando
3750

Villagrán
Santander Jiménez
La Pesca
Soto la Marina
Sigsbee Deep
Tropic of Cancer
CUBA
88

Ciudad
Victoria
Banco
Campeche
75
La Esperanza

I. Desterrada
Guane

I. Pérez
(Mexico)
Canal de Yucatán
La Fé

Ciudad Madero
Pta.
Yalkubul
Río Lagartos
C. San Antonio
C. Corrientes

Tampico
47
Progreso
Dzilam
de Bravo
El Cuyo
C. Catoche
Isla
Mujeres
Cancún
Puerto Morelos

Mérida
Motul
Temax
Espita
Tizimín
Playa del Carmen
Isla
Cozumel
20

Poza Rica
Papantla
Golfo
Valla-
dolid
Cozumel

Huauchinango
de
Tekax
Felipe,
B. de la Ascensión
SIAN KA'AN

MEXICO
Xalapa
Veracruz
Campeche
Champotón
QUINTANA
ROO
Yucatan
Basin

PUEBLA
Orizaba
Ciudad del
Carmen
Escárcega
Chetumal
Banco
Chinchorro

Cuernavaca
Tehuacán
San Andrés
Tuxtla
Frontera
Orange Walk
Belize
City
Turneffe Is.

Oaxaca
TABASCO
Villahermosa
Palenque
BELIZE
Belmopan
BELIZE

GUATEMALA
HONDURAS
TEGUCIGALPA

Acapulco
Golfo de
Tehuantepec
Tapachula
GUATEMALA

COPYRIGHT PHILIP'S
100

PUERTO RICO
1:3 000 000

VIRGIN ISLANDS
1:2 000 000

ST. LUCIA
1:1 000 000

BARBADOS
1:1 000 000

ATLANTIC OCEAN

PUERTO RICO (U.S.A.)

Aguadilla · Arecibo · Barceloneta · Vega Baja · Manati · San Juan · Rio Grande · Carolina · Fajardo · Dewey
Mayagüez · San Sebastian · Adjuntas · Utuado · Cordillera Central · Caguas · Humacao · Naguabo · Vieques · Esperanza
San German · Mts. de Uroyan · Yauco · Cayey · Coamo · Yabucoa
Pta. Aguila · Guanica · Ponce · Guayama · I. Caja de Muertos

Virgin Islands (U.K.)
Virgin Is. (U.S.A.)
Jost Van Dyke I. · Great Camanoe · Ruffing Pt. · The Settlement · Anegada · East Pt. · Virgin Gorda
Hans Lollik I. · Guana I. · Beef · Spanish Town
Charlotte Amalie · St. Thomas I. · Tortola · Road Town · Peter I.
Cruz Bay · St. John I.

ST. LUCIA
Cap Point · Pte. Hardy · Esperance Bay
Gros Islet · Marquis
Castries · Girard
Anse la Raye · Canaries · Millet · Dennery
Soufrière · Mt. Gimie 950 · Trou Gras Pt.
Soufrière Bay 750 · Petit Piton · Micoud
Gros Piton Pt. · 796 Gros Piton · Vierge Pt.
Choiseul · Laborie · Vieux Fort · C. Moule à Chique

BARBADOS
Crab Hill · North Point · Spring Hall · Boscobelle
Fustic · Portland · 249 · Belleplaine
Speightstown · Westmoreland · Bathsheba 340 · BARBADOS · Hillcrest
Alleynes Bay · Mt. Hillaby · Martin's Bay
Holetown · Jackson · Bridgefield · Massiah Street · Ragged Pt.
Black Rock · Ellerton · Six Cross Roads · The Crane
Bridgetown · Ivy · Edey · St. Martins
Carlisle Bay · Worthing · Oistins · Chancery Lane
Oistins Bay · South Point · BGI

Main map

ATLANTIC OCEAN

Tropic of Cancer

BAHAMAS
New Bight · Cat I. · San Salvador I. · Conception I. · Rum Cay · Long I. · Clarence Town · Samana Cay · Crooked I. · Plana Cays · Mayaguana I. · Albert Town · Snug Corner · Acklins I. · Mira por vos Cay · Hogsty Reef · Little Inagua I. · Cockburn Town · Turks Is. · Great Inagua I. · Lake Rose · Matthew Town

Crooked I. Passage · Caicos Passage · Turks & Caicos Is. (U.K.) · Turks Island Passage · Silver Bank Passage · Mouchoir Bank · Silver Bank · Navidad Bank

HAITI · PORT-AU-PRINCE · Jérémie · Dame Marie · Les Cayes · Aquin · Jacmel · Massif de la Hotte · 2680 · Pointe-à-Gravois · Î. à Vache · Pedernales · Barahona · Sierra de Bahoruco

DOMINICAN REP. · SANTO DOMINGO · San Pedro de Macoris · La Romana · Higüey · C. Engaño · Isla Saona · B. de Yuma · San Cristóbal · Baní · Azua de Compostela · Cord. Central · Pico Duarte 3175 · La Vega · Santiago de los Caballeros · San Francisco de Macoris · Nagua · Sánchez · Sabana de la Mar · Hato Mayor · Samaná

GUANTANAMO BAY (U.S.A) · Baracoa · Maisi · Pta. de Maisi · Î. de la Tortue · Cap-Haïtien · Monte Cristi · LA ISABELA · Puerto Plata · Port-de-Paix · Jean Rabel · Fort Liberté · Gonaïves · St-Marc · Hinche · ARMANDO BERMÚDEZ · Î. de la Gonâve · G. de la Gonâve · Cap-à-Foux

Hispaniola · Antilles · Beata Ridge · I. Beata · C. Beata

Milwaukee Deep 9200 · Puerto Rico Trench

PUERTO RICO (U.S.A.) · Aguadilla · Arecibo · Bayamón · SAN JUAN · Carolina · Fajardo · Culebra · Vieques · Mayagüez · 1338 · Ponce · Caguas · Guayama · Isla Mona (U.S.A.) · Mona Passage

Virgin Gorda · Anegada · Virgin Is. (U.K.) · Tortola · Road Town · Virgin Is. (U.S.A.) · St. Thomas · Charlotte Amalie · St. Croix · Christiansted · Frederiksted · Sombrero (U.K.) · Anguilla (U.K.) · St-Martin · St-Barthélemy (Fr.) · Saba (Neth.) · St. Maarten (Neth.) · St. Eustatius (Neth.) · Barbuda · ANTIGUA & BARBUDA · St. John's · Antigua · Redonda · ST. KITTS & NEVIS · Basseterre · Nevis 1156 · Mt. Liamuiga

CARIBBEAN SEA · Venezuelan Basin · Colombian Basin · I. de Aves (Venezuela)

Aves Ridge

Leeward Islands · Lesser Antilles · Windward Islands

Montserrat (U.K.) · Soufrière Hills 914 · Brades · Guadeloupe Passage · GUADELOUPE (Fr.) · Ste-Rose · Le Moule · La Désirade · Pointe-à-Pitre · Marie-Galante (Fr.) · Grand-Bourg · Basse-Terre · 1467 · I. des Saintes (Fr.) · Dominica Passage · Portsmouth · Morne Diablotin 1419 · DOMINICA · Roseau · MORNE TROIS PITONS · Martinique Passage · Ste-Marie · Mt. Pelée 1397 · Le François · Fort-de-France · Rivière-Pilote · MARTINIQUE · St. Lucia Channel (Fr.) · Castries 950 · ST. LUCIA · Soufrière · St. Vincent Passage · Soufrière 1234 · St. Vincent · Speightstown 340 · Kingstown · Bridgetown · BARBADOS · Bequia · ST. VINCENT & THE GRENADINES · The Grenadines · Canouan · Carriacou · 840 · GRENADA · St. George's

ABC · Lesser · Islands · Aruba (Neth.) · Oranjestad · Curaçao (Neth.) · Willemstad · Bonaire (Neth.) · ARC. LOS ROQUES · I. Orchila (Ven.) · I. Blanquilla (Ven.) · Is. Los Hermanos (Ven.) · Is. Los Testigos (Ven.) · Tobago · Scarborough · Galera Point · Port of Spain · Arima · Rio Claro · San Fernando · TRINIDAD & TOBAGO · Serpent's Mouth · MARIUSA DELTA · Tucupita · AMACURO

COLOMBIA · Santa Marta · Riohacha · Uribia · Pen. de la Guajira · Pta. Gallinas · C. San Román · Pta. Espada · GUAJIRA · Ciénaga · SA. NEVADA DEL · Barranquilla · Soledad · Sabanalarga · ISLA DE SALAMANCA · Valledupar · CÉSAR · Ocaña · Cúcuta · TÁCHIRA

VENEZUELA · MARACAIBO · Lago de Maracaibo · ZULIA · Cabimas · Santa Rita · La Concepción · Mene Grande · Machiques · Mérida · Barinas · BARINAS · San Fernando de Apure · San Cristóbal · FALCÓN · Coro · Pta. Cardón · Punto Fijo · Paraguaná · MÉDANOS DE CORO · Puerto Cumarebo · La Vela · Puerto Cabello · Maracay · CARACAS · La Guaira · Valencia · VALENCIA · BARQUISIMETO · LARA · Carora · YARACUY · CARABOBO · MIRANDA · Los Teques · Ocumare del Tuy · Barcelona · Cumaná · Carúpano · Güiria · SUCRE · Pen. de Paria · NUEVA ESPARTA · I. de Margarita · La Asunción · Porlamar · GUÁRICO · Calabozo · San Juan de los Morros · ANZOÁTEGUI · El Tigre · MONAGAS · Maturín · Anaco · Cantaura · Ciudad Guayana · BOLÍVAR · Ciudad Bolívar · Soledad · El Pao · Upata · El Callao · Tumeremo · Embalse de Guri · Guasipati

COPYRIGHT PHILIP'S

Scale (elevation legend)
ft: 24 000 · 18 000 · 12 000 · 6000 · 600 · 0
m: 8000 · 6000 · 4000 · 2000 · 1000 · 400 · 200 · 0

4000 · 3000 · 2000 · 1500 · 1000 · 400 · 200
12 000 · 9000 · 6000 · 4500 · 3000 · 1200 · 600

West from Greenwich

100 0   200   400   600   800 1000 1200 1400 km

100   0   200   400   600   800   1000 miles

1:35 000 000

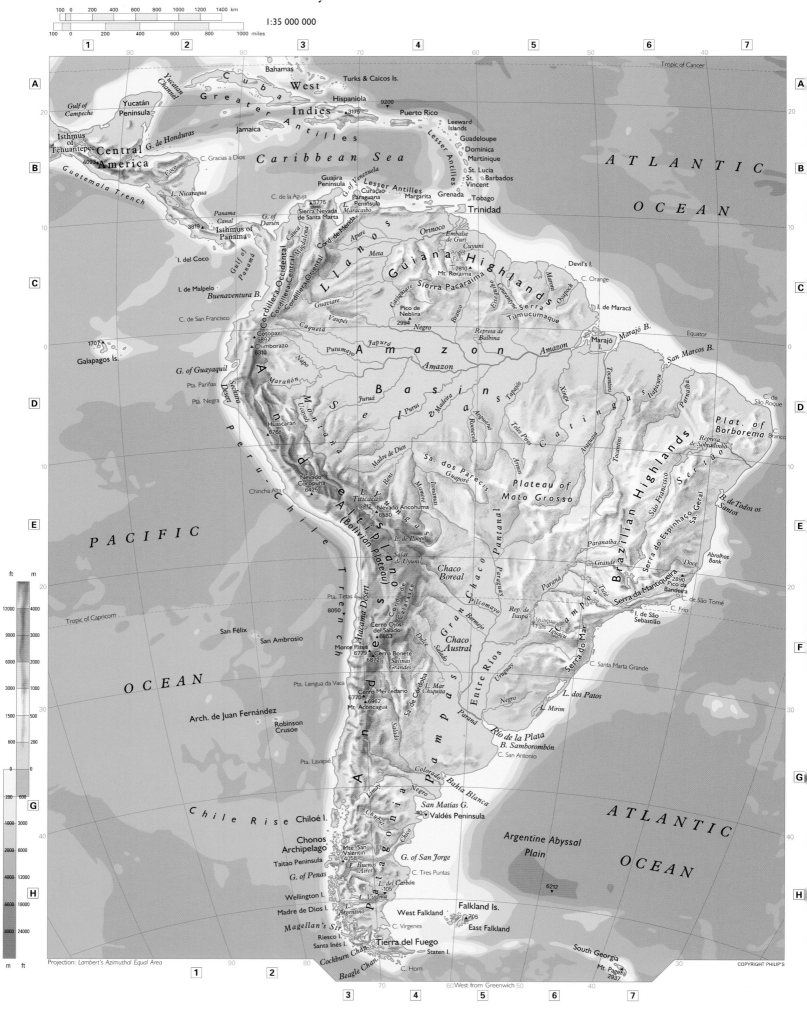

Projection: *Lambert's Azimuthal Equal Area*

COPYRIGHT PHILIP'S

1:35 000 000

100 0 200 400 600 800 1000 1200 1400 km

100 0 200 400 600 800 1000 miles

Projection: Lambert's Azimuthal Equal Area

COPYRIGHT PHILIP'S

■ LIMA Capital Cities

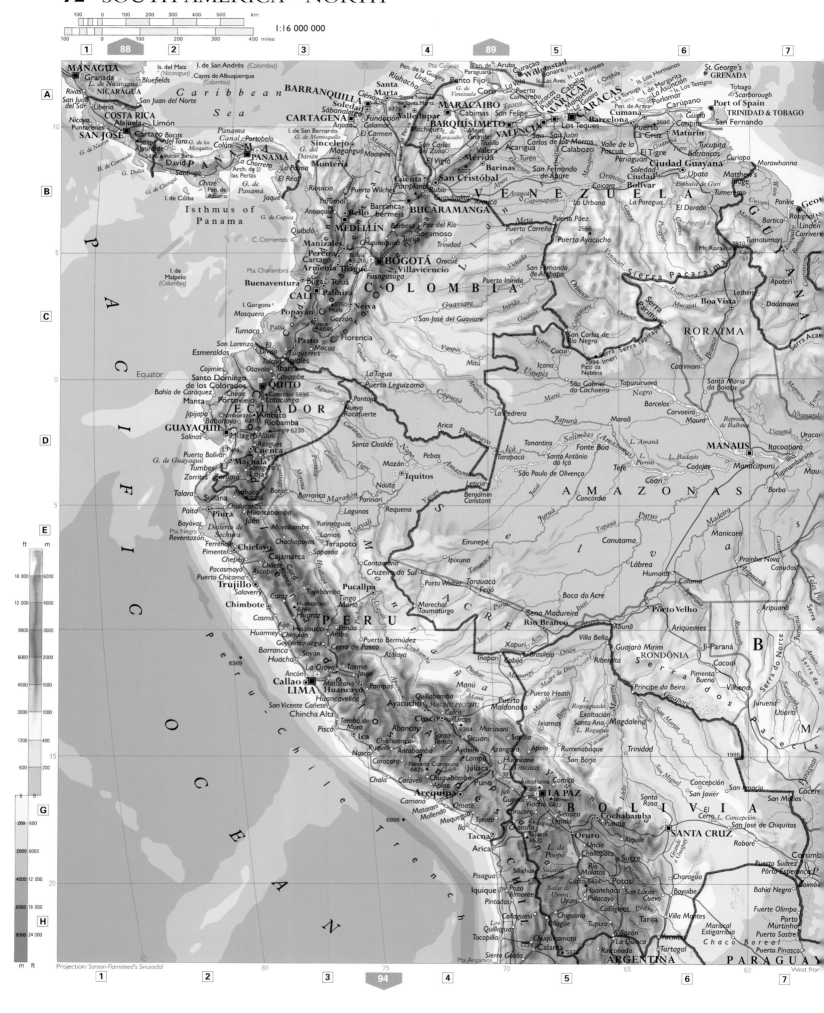

TRINIDAD AND TOBAGO
1:2 500 000

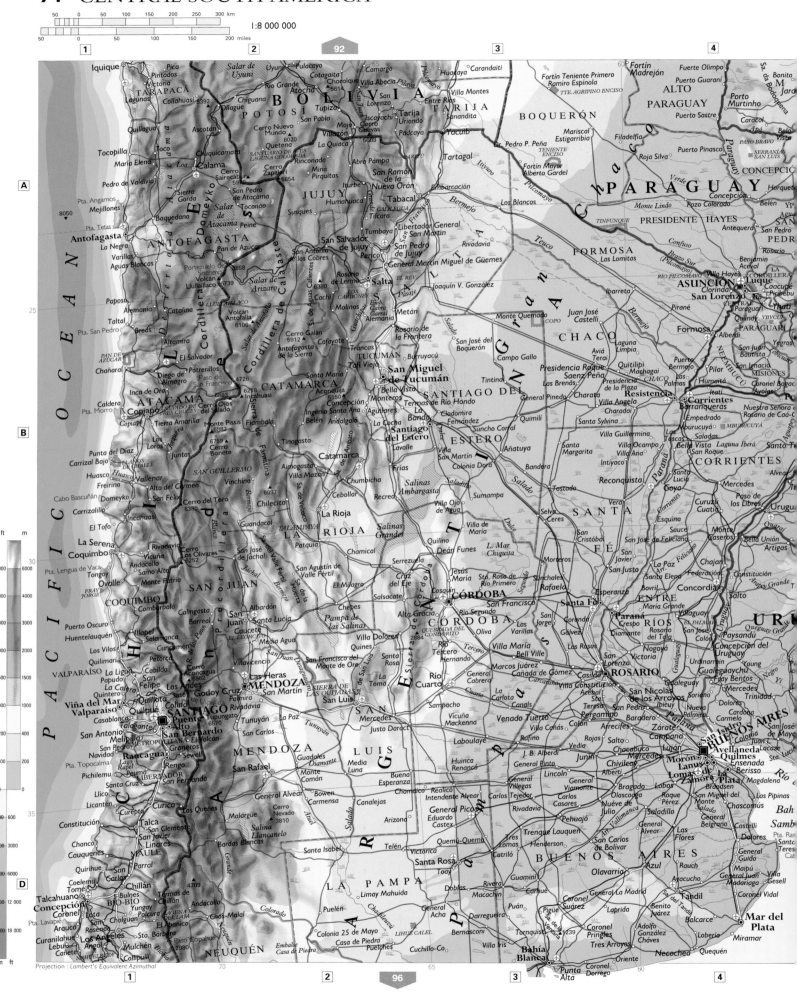

1:8 000 000

Projection : Lambert's Equivalent Azimuthal

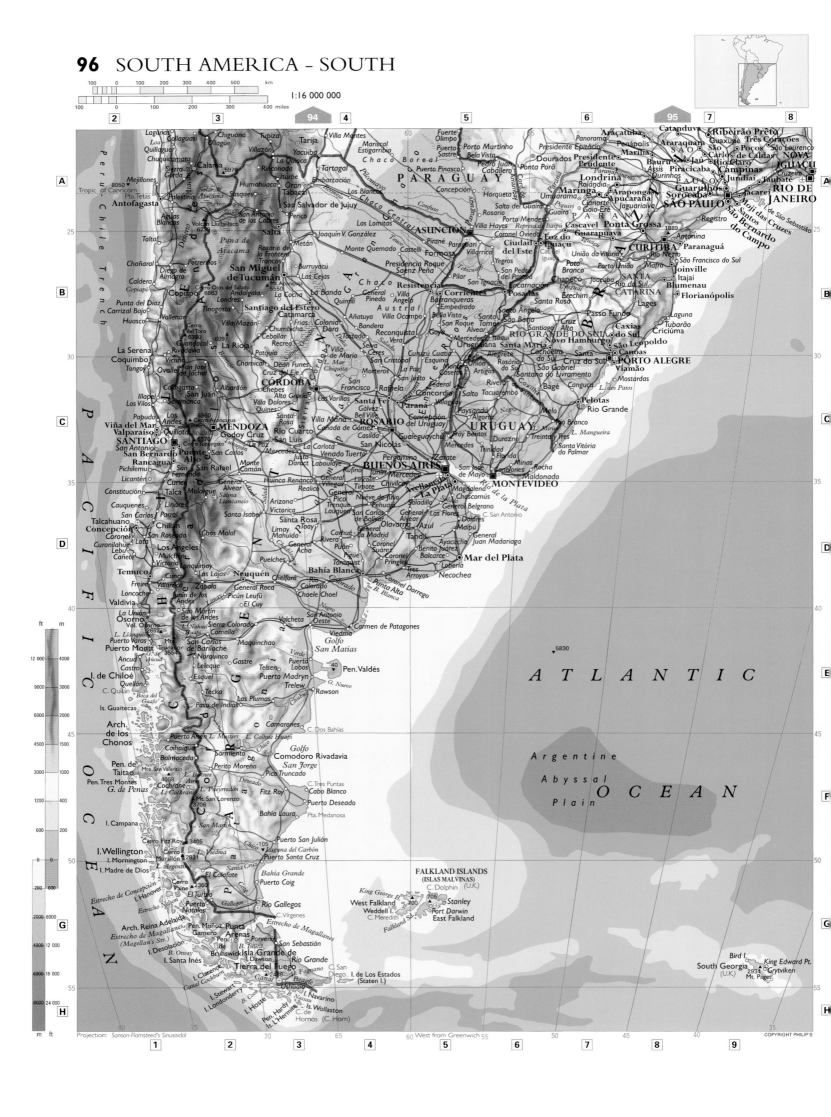

INDEX TO WORLD MAPS

The index contains the names of all the principal places and features shown on the World Maps. Each name is followed by an additional entry in italics giving the country or region within which it is located. The alphabetical order of names composed of two or more words is governed primarily by the first word, then by the second, and then by the country or region name that follows. This is an example of the rule:

Mīr Kūh *Iran*	26°22N 58°55E	**45** E8	
Mīr Shahdād *Iran*	26°15N 58°29E	**45** E8	
Mira *Italy*	45°26N 12°8E	**22** B5	
Mira por vos Cay *Bahamas*	22°9N 74°30W	**89** B5	

Physical features composed of a proper name (Erie) and a description (Lake) are positioned alphabetically by the proper name. The description is positioned after the proper name and is usually abbreviated:

Erie, L. *N. Amer.*	42°15N 81°0W	**82** D4

Where a description forms part of a settlement or administrative name, however, it is always written in full and put in its true alphabetical position:

Mount Morris *U.S.A.*	42°44N 77°52W	**82** D7

Names beginning with M' and Mc are indexed as if they were spelled Mac. Names beginning St. are alphabetized under Saint, but Sankt, Sint, Sant', Santa and San are all spelt in full and are alphabetized accordingly. If the same place name occurs two or more times in the index and all are in the same country, each is followed by the name of the administrative subdivision in which it is located.

The geographical co-ordinates which follow each name in the index give the latitude and longitude of each place. The first co-ordinate indicates latitude – the distance north or south of the Equator. The second co-ordinate indicates longitude – the distance east or west of the Greenwich Meridian. Both latitude and longitude are measured in degrees and minutes (there are 60 minutes in a degree).

The latitude is followed by N(orth) or S(outh) and the longitude by E(ast) or W(est).

The number in bold type which follows the geographical co-ordinates refers to the number of the map page where that feature or place will be found. This is usually the largest scale at which the place or feature appears.

The letter and figure that are immediately after the page number give the grid square on the map page, within which the feature is situated. The letter represents the latitude and the figure the longitude. A lower-case letter immediately after the page number refers to an inset map on that page.

In some cases the feature itself may fall within the specified square, while the name is outside. This is usually the case only with features that are larger than a grid square.

Rivers are indexed to their mouths or confluences, and carry the symbol ➜ after their names. The following symbols are also used in the index: ■ country, ☑ overseas territory or dependency, □ first-order administrative area, △ national park, ⌂ other park (provincial park, nature reserve or game reserve), ✖ (LHR) principal airport (and location identifier), ⚙ Australian aboriginal land.

Abbreviations used in the index

A.C.T. – Australian Capital Territory
A.R. – Autonomous Region
Afghan. – Afghanistan
Afr. – Africa
Ala. – Alabama
Alta. – Alberta
Amer. – America(n)
Ant. – Antilles
Arch. – Archipelago
Ariz. – Arizona
Ark. – Arkansas
Atl. Oc. – Atlantic Ocean
B. – Baie, Bahía, Bay, Bucht, Bugt
B.C. – British Columbia
Bangla. – Bangladesh
Barr. – Barrage
Bos.-H. – Bosnia-Herzegovina
C. – Cabo, Cap, Cape, Coast
C.A.R. – Central African Republic
C. Prov. – Cape Province
Calif. – California
Cat. – Catarata
Cent. – Central
Chan. – Channel
Colo. – Colorado
Conn. – Connecticut
Cord. – Cordillera
Cr. – Creek
Czech. – Czech Republic
D.C. – District of Columbia
Del. – Delaware
Dem. – Democratic
Dep. – Dependency
Des. – Desert
Dét. – Détroit
Dist. – District
Dj. – Djebel
Dom. Rep. – Dominican Republic

E. – East
El Salv. – El Salvador
Eq. Guin. – Equatorial Guinea
Est. – Estrecho
Falk. Is. – Falkland Is.
Fd. – Fjord
Fla. – Florida
Fr. – French
G. – Golfe, Golfo, Gulf, Guba, Gebel
Ga. – Georgia
Gt. – Great, Greater
Guinea-Biss. – Guinea-Bissau
H.K. – Hong Kong
H.P. – Himachal Pradesh
Hants. – Hampshire
Harb. – Harbor, Harbour
Hd. – Head
Hts. – Heights
I.(s). – Île, Ilha, Insel, Isla, Island, Isle
Ill. – Illinois
Ind. – Indiana
Ind. Oc. – Indian Ocean
Ivory C. – Ivory Coast
J. – Jabal, Jebel
Jaz. – Jazīrah
Junc. – Junction
K. – Kap, Kapp
Kans. – Kansas
Kep. – Kepulauan
Ky. – Kentucky
L. – Lac, Lacul, Lago, Lagoa, Lake, Limni, Loch, Lough
La. – Louisiana
Ld. – Land
Liech. – Liechtenstein
Lux. – Luxembourg
Mad. P. – Madhya Pradesh
Madag. – Madagascar
Man. – Manitoba
Mass. – Massachusetts

Md. – Maryland
Me. – Maine
Medit. S. – Mediterranean Sea
Mich. – Michigan
Minn. – Minnesota
Miss. – Mississippi
Mo. – Missouri
Mont. – Montana
Mozam. – Mozambique
Mt.(s) – Mont, Montaña, Mountain
Mte. – Monte
Mti. – Monti
N. – Nord, Norte, North, Northern, Nouveau, Nahal, Nahr
N.B. – New Brunswick
N.C. – North Carolina
N. Cal. – New Caledonia
N. Dak. – North Dakota
N.H. – New Hampshire
N.I. – North Island
N.J. – New Jersey
N. Mex. – New Mexico
N.S. – Nova Scotia
N.S.W. – New South Wales
N.W.T. – North West Territory
N.Y. – New York
N.Z. – New Zealand
Nac. – Nacional
Nat. – National
Nebr. – Nebraska
Neths. – Netherlands
Nev. – Nevada
Nfld & L. – Newfoundland and Labrador
Nic. – Nicaragua
O. – Oued, Ouadi
Occ. – Occidentale
Okla. – Oklahoma
Ont. – Ontario
Or. – Orientale

Oreg. – Oregon
Os. – Ostrov
Oz. – Ozero
P. – Pass, Passo, Pasul, Pulau
P.E.I. – Prince Edward Island
Pa. – Pennsylvania
Pac. Oc. – Pacific Ocean
Papua N.G. – Papua New Guinea
Pass. – Passage
Peg. – Pegunungan
Pen. – Peninsula, Péninsule
Phil. – Philippines
Pk. – Peak
Plat. – Plateau
Prov. – Province, Provincial
Pt. – Point
Pta. – Ponta, Punta
Pte. – Pointe
Qué. – Québec
Queens. – Queensland
R. – Rio, River
R.I. – Rhode Island
Ra. – Range
Raj. – Rajasthan
Recr. – Recreational, Récréatif
Reg. – Region
Rep. – Republic
Res. – Reserve, Reservoir
Rhld-Pfz. – Rheinland-Pfalz
S. – South, Southern, Sur
Si. Arabia – Saudi Arabia
S.C. – South Carolina
S. Dak. – South Dakota
S.I. – South Island
S. Leone – Sierra Leone
Sa. – Serra, Sierra
Sask. – Saskatchewan
Scot. – Scotland
Sd. – Sound
Sev. – Severnaya
Sib. – Siberia

Sprs. – Springs
St. – Saint
Sta. – Santa
Ste. – Sainte
Sto. – Santo
Str. – Strait, Stretto
Switz. – Switzerland
Tas. – Tasmania
Tenn. – Tennessee
Terr. – Territory, Territoire
Tex. – Texas
Tg. – Tanjung
Trin. & Tob. – Trinidad & Tobago
U.A.E. – United Arab Emirates
U.K. – United Kingdom
U.S.A. – United States of America
Ut. P. – Uttar Pradesh
Va. – Virginia
Vdkhr. – Vodokhranilishche
Vdskh. – Vodoskhovyshche
Vf. – Vírful
Vic. – Victoria
Vol. – Volcano
Vt. – Vermont
W. – Wadi, West
W. Va. – West Virginia
Wall. & F. Is. – Wallis and Futuna Is.
Wash. – Washington
Wis. – Wisconsin
Wlkp. – Wielkopolski
Wyo. – Wyoming
Yorks. – Yorkshire

A

A Coruña Spain 43°20N 8°25W 21 A1
A Estrada Spain 42°43N 8°27W 21 A1
A Fonsagrada Spain 43°8N 7°4W 21 A2
A Shau Vietnam 16°6N 107°22E 38 D6
Aabenraa Denmark 55°3N 9°25E 9 J13
Aachen Germany 50°45N 6°6E 16 C4
Aalborg Denmark 57°2N 9°54E 9 H13
Aalen Germany 48°51N 10°6E 16 D6
Aalst Belgium 50°56N 4°2E 15 D4
Aalten Neths. 51°56N 6°35E 15 C6
Aalter Belgium 51°5N 3°28E 15 C3
Äänekoski Finland 62°36N 25°44E 8 E21
Aarau Switz. 47°23N 8°4E 20 C8
Aare → Switz. 47°33N 8°14E 20 C8
Aarhus = Århus Denmark 56°8N 10°11E 9 H14
Aarschot Belgium 50°59N 4°49E 15 D4
Aba Dem. Rep. of the Congo 3°58N 30°17E 54 B3
Aba Nigeria 5°10N 7°19E 50 G7
Abaco I. Bahamas 26°25N 77°10W 88 A4
Ābādān Iran 30°22N 48°20E 45 D6
Ābādeh Iran 31°8N 52°40E 45 D7
Abadla Algeria 31°2N 2°45W 50 B5
Abaetetuba Brazil 1°40S 48°50W 93 D9
Abagnar Qi = Xilinhot China 43°52N 116°2E 34 C9
Abah, Tanjung Indonesia 8°46S 115°38E 37 K18
Abai Paraguay 25°58S 55°54W 95 B4
Abakan Russia 53°40N 91°10E 29 D10
Abancay Peru 13°35S 72°55W 92 F4
Abang, Gunung Indonesia 8°16S 115°25E 37 J18
Abariringa Kiribati 2°50S 171°40W 64 H10
Abarqū Iran 31°10N 53°20E 45 D7
Abashiri Japan 44°0N 144°15E 30 B12
Abashiri-Wan Japan 44°0N 144°30E 30 C12
Ābay = Nîl el Azraq → Sudan 15°38N 32°31E 51 E12
Abay Kazakhstan 49°38N 72°53E 28 E8
Abaya, L. Ethiopia 6°30N 37°50E 47 F2
Abaza Russia 52°39N 90°6E 28 D10
'Abbāsābād Iran 33°34N 58°23E 45 C8
Abbay = Nîl el Azraq → Sudan 15°38N 32°31E 51 E12
Abbaye, Pt. U.S.A. 46°58N 88°8W 80 B9
Abbé, L. Ethiopia 11°8N 41°47E 47 E3
Abbeville France 50°6N 1°49E 20 A4
Abbeville Ala., U.S.A. 31°34N 85°15W 85 F12
Abbeville La., U.S.A. 29°58N 92°8W 84 G8
Abbeville S.C., U.S.A. 34°11N 82°23W 85 D13
Abbeyfeale Ireland 52°23N 9°18W 10 D2
Abbot Ice Shelf Antarctica 73°0S 92°0W 5 D16
Abbotsford Canada 49°5N 122°20W 70 D4
Abbottabad Pakistan 34°10N 73°15E 42 B5
ABC Islands W. Indies 12°15N 69°0W 89 D6
Abd al Kūrī Yemen 12°5N 52°20E 47 E5
Ābdar Iran 30°16N 55°19E 45 D7
'Abdolābād Iran 34°12N 56°30E 45 C8
Abdulpur Bangla. 24°15N 88°59E 43 G13
Abéché Chad 13°50N 20°35E 51 F10
Abel Tasman △ N.Z. 40°59S 173°3E 59 D4
Abengourou Ivory C. 6°42N 3°27W 50 G5
Åbenrå = Aabenraa Denmark 55°3N 9°25E 9 J13
Abeokuta Nigeria 7°3N 3°19E 50 G6
Aberaeron U.K. 52°15N 4°15W 13 E3
Aberayron = Aberaeron U.K. 52°15N 4°15W 13 E3
Aberchirder U.K. 57°34N 2°37W 11 D6
Abercorn Australia 25°12S 151°5E 63 D5
Aberdare U.K. 51°43N 3°27W 13 F4
Aberdare △ Kenya 0°22S 36°44E 54 C4
Aberdare Ra. Kenya 0°15S 36°50E 54 C4
Aberdeen Australia 32°9S 150°56E 63 E5
Aberdeen Canada 52°20N 106°8W 71 C7
Aberdeen China 22°14N 114°8E 33 a
Aberdeen S. Africa 32°28S 24°2E 56 E3
Aberdeen U.K. 57°9N 2°5W 11 D6
Aberdeen Idaho, U.S.A. 42°57N 112°50W 76 E7
Aberdeen Md., U.S.A. 39°31N 76°10W 81 F15
Aberdeen Miss., U.S.A. 33°49N 88°33W 85 E10
Aberdeen S. Dak., U.S.A. 45°28N 98°29W 80 C4
Aberdeen Wash., U.S.A. 46°59N 123°50W 78 D3
Aberdeen, City of □ U.K. 57°10N 2°10W 11 D6
Aberdeen L. Canada 64°30N 99°0W 68 E12
Aberdeenshire □ U.K. 57°17N 2°36W 11 D6
Aberdovey = Aberdyfi U.K. 52°33N 4°3W 13 E3
Aberdyfi U.K. 52°33N 4°3W 13 E3
Aberfeldy U.K. 56°37N 3°51W 11 E5
Aberfoyle U.K. 56°11N 4°23W 11 E4
Abergavenny U.K. 51°49N 3°1W 13 F4
Abergele U.K. 53°17N 3°35W 12 D4
Abernathy U.S.A. 33°50N 101°51W 84 E4
Abert, L. U.S.A. 42°38N 120°14W 76 E3
Aberystwyth U.K. 52°25N 4°5W 13 E3
Abhā Si. Arabia 18°0N 42°34E 47 D3
Abhar Iran 36°9N 49°13E 45 B6
Abhayapuri India 26°24N 90°38E 43 F14
Abidjan Ivory C. 5°26N 3°58W 50 G5
Abilene Kans., U.S.A. 38°55N 97°13W 80 F5
Abilene Tex., U.S.A. 32°28N 99°43W 84 E5
Abingdon U.K. 51°40N 1°17W 13 F6
Abingdon U.S.A. 36°43N 81°59W 81 G13
Abington Reef Australia 18°0S 149°35E 62 B4
Abitau → Canada 59°53N 109°3W 71 B7
Abitibi → Canada 51°3N 80°55W 72 B3
Abitibi, L. Canada 48°40N 79°40W 72 C4
Abkhaz Republic = Abkhazia □ Georgia 43°12N 41°5E 19 F7
Abkhazia □ Georgia 43°12N 41°5E 19 F7
Abminga Australia 26°8S 134°51E 63 D1
Åbo = Turku Finland 60°30N 22°19E 9 F20
Abohar India 30°10N 74°10E 42 D6
Abomey Benin 7°10N 2°5E 50 G6
Abong-Mbang Cameroon 4°0N 13°8E 52 D2
Abou-Deïa Chad 11°20N 19°20E 51 F9
Aboyne U.K. 57°4N 2°47W 11 D6
Abra Pampa Argentina 22°43S 65°42W 94 A2
Abraham L. Canada 52°15N 116°35W 70 C5
Abreojos, Pta. Mexico 26°50N 113°40W 86 B2
Abrolhos, Banco dos Brazil 18°0S 38°0W 90 E7
Abrud Romania 46°19N 23°5E 17 E12
Absaroka Range U.S.A. 44°45N 109°50W 76 D9
Abu India 24°41N 72°50E 42 G5
Abū al Abyad U.A.E. 24°11N 53°50E 45 E7
Abū al Khaşīb Iraq 30°25N 48°0E 44 D5
Abū 'Alī Si. Arabia 27°20N 49°27E 45 E6
Abū 'Alī → Lebanon 34°25N 35°50E 46 A4
Abu Dhabi = Abū Ẓāby U.A.E. 24°28N 54°22E 45 E7
Abū Du'ān Syria 36°25N 38°15E 44 B3
Abu el Gaīn, W. → Egypt 29°35N 33°30E 46 F2
Abu Ga'da, W. → Egypt 29°15N 32°53E 46 F1
Abū Ḩadrīyah Si. Arabia 27°20N 48°58E 45 E6
Abu Hamed Sudan 19°32N 33°13E 51 E12
Abū Kamāl Syria 34°30N 41°0E 44 C4
Abū Madd, Ra's Si. Arabia 24°50N 37°7E 44 E3
Abū Mūsā U.A.E. 25°52N 55°3E 45 E7
Abū Qaşr Si. Arabia 30°21N 38°34E 44 D3
Abu Shagara, Ras Sudan 21°4N 37°19E 51 D13
Abu Simbel Egypt 22°18N 31°40E 51 D12
Abū Şukhayr Iraq 31°54N 44°30E 44 D5
Abu Zabad Sudan 12°25N 29°10E 51 F11
Abū Ẓāby U.A.E. 24°28N 54°22E 45 E7
Abū Zeydābād Iran 33°54N 51°45E 45 C6
Abuja Nigeria 9°5N 7°32E 50 G7
Abukuma-Gawa → Japan 38°6N 140°52E 30 E10
Abukuma-Sammyaku Japan 37°30N 140°45E 30 F10
Abunã Brazil 9°40S 65°20W 92 E5
Abunã → Brazil 9°41S 65°20W 92 E5
Aburo Dem. Rep. of the Congo 2°4N 30°53E 54 B3
Abut Hd. N.Z. 43°7S 170°15E 59 E3
Ābyek Iran 36°4N 50°33E 45 B6
Acadia △ U.S.A. 44°20N 68°13W 81 C19
Açailândia Brazil 4°57S 47°0W 93 D9
Acajutla El Salv. 13°36N 89°50W 88 D2
Acámbaro Mexico 20°2N 100°44W 86 D4
Acaponeta Mexico 22°30N 105°22W 86 C3
Acapulco Mexico 16°51N 99°55W 87 D5
Acaraí, Serra Brazil 1°50N 57°50W 92 C7
Acarigua Venezuela 9°33N 69°12W 92 B5
Acatlán Mexico 18°12N 98°3W 87 D5
Acayucán Mexico 17°57N 94°55W 87 D6
Accomac U.S.A. 37°43N 75°40W 81 G16
Accra Ghana 5°35N 0°6W 50 G5
Accrington U.K. 53°45N 2°22W 12 D5
Acebal Argentina 33°20S 60°50W 94 C3
Aceh □ Indonesia 4°15N 97°30E 36 D1
Achalpur India 21°22N 77°32E 40 J10
Acharnes Greece 38°5N 23°44E 23 E10
Acheloos → Greece 38°19N 21°7E 23 E9
Acheng China 45°30N 126°58E 35 B14
Acher India 23°10N 72°32E 42 H5
Achill Hd. Ireland 53°58N 10°15W 10 C1
Achill I. Ireland 53°58N 10°1W 10 C1
Achinsk Russia 56°20N 90°20E 29 D10
Acireale Italy 37°37N 15°10E 22 F6
Ackerman U.S.A. 33°19N 89°11W 85 E10
Acklins I. Bahamas 22°30N 74°0W 89 B5
Acme Canada 51°33N 113°30W 70 C6
Acme U.S.A. 40°8N 79°26W 82 F5
Aconcagua, Cerro Argentina 32°39S 70°0W 94 C2
Aconquija, Mt. Argentina 27°0S 66°0W 94 B2
Açores, Is. dos Atl. Oc. 38°0N 27°0W 50 a
Acornhoek S. Africa 24°37S 31°2E 57 C5
Acraman, L. Australia 32°2S 135°23E 63 E2
Acre = 'Akko Israel 32°55N 35°4E 46 C4
Acre □ Brazil 9°1S 71°0W 92 E4
Acre → Brazil 8°45S 67°22W 92 E5
Actinolite Canada 44°32N 77°19W 82 B7
Acton Canada 43°38N 80°3W 82 C4
Ad Dammām Si. Arabia 26°20N 50°5E 45 E6
Ad Dāmūr Lebanon 33°43N 35°27E 46 B4
Ad Dawādimī Si. Arabia 24°35N 44°15E 44 E5
Ad Dawḩah Qatar 25°15N 51°35E 45 E6
Ad Dawr Iraq 34°27N 43°47E 44 C4
Ad Dir'īyah Si. Arabia 24°44N 46°35E 44 E5
Ad Dīwānīyah Iraq 32°0N 45°0E 44 D5
Ad Dujayl Iraq 33°51N 44°14E 44 C5
Ad Duwayd Si. Arabia 30°15N 42°17E 44 D4
Ada Minn., U.S.A. 47°18N 96°31W 80 B5
Ada Okla., U.S.A. 34°46N 96°41W 84 D6
Adabiya Egypt 29°53N 32°28E 46 F1
Adair, C. Canada 71°30N 71°34W 69 C17
Adaja → Spain 41°32N 4°52W 21 B3
Adak U.S.A. 51°45N 176°45W 74 E4
Adak I. U.S.A. 51°45N 176°45W 74 E4
Adamaoua, Massif de l' Cameroon 7°20N 12°20E 51 G8
Adamawa Highlands = Adamaoua, Massif de l' Cameroon 7°20N 12°20E 51 G8
Adamello, Mte. Italy 46°9N 10°30E 20 C9
Adaminaby Australia 36°0S 148°45E 63 F4
Adams Mass., U.S.A. 42°38N 73°7W 83 D11
Adams N.Y., U.S.A. 43°49N 76°1W 83 C8
Adams Wis., U.S.A. 43°57N 89°49W 80 D9
Adams, Mt. U.S.A. 46°12N 121°30W 78 D5
Adam's Bridge Sri Lanka 9°15N 79°40E 40 Q11
Adams L. Canada 51°10N 119°40W 70 C5
Adam's Peak Sri Lanka 6°48N 80°30E 40 R12
Adana Turkey 37°0N 35°16E 44 B2
Adang, Ko Thailand 6°33N 99°18E 39 J2
Adapazarı = Sakarya Turkey 40°48N 30°25E 19 F5
Adarama Sudan 17°10N 34°52E 51 E12
Adare, C. Antarctica 71°0S 171°0E 5 D11
Adaut Indonesia 8°8S 131°7E 37 F8
Adavale Australia 25°52S 144°32E 63 D3
Adda → Italy 45°8N 9°53E 20 D8
Addis Ababa = Addis Abeba Ethiopia 9°2N 38°42E 47 F2
Addis Abeba Ethiopia 9°2N 38°42E 47 F2
Addison U.S.A. 42°1N 77°14W 82 D7
Addo S. Africa 33°32S 25°45E 56 E4
Addo △ S. Africa 33°30S 25°50E 56 E4
Ādeh Iran 37°42N 45°11E 44 B5
Adel U.S.A. 31°8N 83°25W 85 F13
Adelaide Australia 34°52S 138°30E 63 E2
Adelaide S. Africa 32°42S 26°20E 56 E4
Adelaide I. Antarctica 67°15S 68°30W 5 C17
Adelaide Pen. Canada 68°15N 97°30W 68 D12
Adelaide River Australia 13°15S 131°7E 60 B5
Adelaide Village Bahamas 25°0N 77°31W 88 A4
Adelanto U.S.A. 34°35N 117°22W 79 L9
Adele I. Australia 15°32S 123°9E 60 C3
Adélie, Terre Antarctica 68°0S 140°0E 5 C10
Adelie Land = Adélie, Terre Antarctica 68°0S 140°0E 5 C10
Aden = Al 'Adan Yemen 12°45N 45°0E 47 E4
Aden, G. of Ind. Oc. 12°30N 47°30E 47 E4
Adendorp S. Africa 32°15S 24°30E 56 E3
Adh Dhayd U.A.E. 25°17N 55°53E 45 E7
Adhoi India 23°26N 70°32E 42 H4
Adi Indonesia 4°15S 133°30E 37 E8
Adieu, C. Australia 32°0S 132°10E 61 F5
Adieu Pt. Australia 15°14S 124°35E 60 C3
Adige → Italy 45°9N 12°20E 22 B5
Adigrat Ethiopia 14°20N 39°26E 47 E2
Adilabad India 19°33N 78°20E 40 K11
Adirondack ⌓ U.S.A. 44°0N 74°20W 83 C10
Adirondack Mts. U.S.A. 44°0N 74°0W 83 C10
Adis Abeba = Addis Abeba Ethiopia 9°2N 38°42E 47 F2
Adjumani Uganda 3°20N 31°50E 54 B3
Adjuntas Puerto Rico 18°10N 66°43W 89 d
Adlavik Is. Canada 55°0N 58°40W 73 B8
Admiralty G. Australia 14°20S 125°55E 60 B4
Admiralty Gulf ✪ Australia 14°16S 125°52E 60 B4
Admiralty I. U.S.A. 57°30N 134°30W 70 B2
Admiralty Inlet Canada 72°30N 86°0W 69 C14
Admiralty Is. Papua N. G. 2°0S 147°0E 58 B7
Adolfo González Chaves Argentina 38°2S 60°5W 94 D3
Adolfo Ruiz Cortines, Presa Mexico 27°15N 109°6W 86 B3
Adonara Indonesia 8°15S 123°5E 37 F6
Adoni India 15°33N 77°18E 40 M10
Adour → France 43°32N 1°32W 20 E3
Adra India 23°30N 86°42E 43 H12
Adra Spain 36°43N 3°3W 21 D4
Adrano Italy 37°40N 14°50E 22 F6
Adrar Algeria 27°51N 0°11E 50 C6
Adrar Mauritania 20°30N 7°30W 50 D3
Adrar des Iforas Africa 19°40N 1°40E 50 E6
Adrian Mich., U.S.A. 41°54N 84°2W 81 E11
Adrian Tex., U.S.A. 35°16N 102°40W 84 D3
Adriatic Sea Medit. S. 43°0N 16°0E 22 C6
Adua Indonesia 1°45S 129°50E 37 E7
Adwa Ethiopia 14°15N 38°52E 47 E2
Adygea □ Russia 45°0N 40°0E 19 F7
Adzhar Republic = Ajaria □ Georgia 41°30N 42°0E 19 F7
Adzopé Ivory C. 6°7N 3°49W 50 G5
Ægean Sea Medit. S. 38°30N 25°0E 23 E11
Aerhtai Shan Mongolia 46°40N 92°45E 32 B7
Afaahiti Tahiti 17°45S 149°17W 59 d
'Afak Iraq 32°4N 45°15E 44 C5
Afandou Greece 36°18N 28°12E 25 C10
Afareaitu Moorea 17°33S 149°47W 59 d
Afghanistan ■ Asia 33°0N 65°0E 40 C4
Aflou Algeria 34°7N 2°3E 50 B6
Afognak I. U.S.A. 58°15N 152°30W 74 D9
Africa 10°0N 20°0E 48 E6
'Afrīn Syria 36°32N 36°50E 44 B3
Afton N.Y., U.S.A. 42°14N 75°32W 83 D9
Afton Wyo., U.S.A. 42°44N 110°56W 76 E8
Afuá Brazil 0°15S 50°20W 93 D8
'Afula Israel 32°37N 35°17E 46 C4
Afyon Turkey 38°45N 30°33E 19 G5
Afyonkarahisar = Afyon Turkey 38°45N 30°33E 19 G5
Āgā Jarī Iran 30°42N 49°50E 45 D6
Agadés = Agadez Niger 16°58N 7°59E 50 E7
Agadez Niger 16°58N 7°59E 50 E7
Agadir Morocco 30°28N 9°55W 50 B4
Agaete Canary Is. 28°6N 15°43W 24 F4
Agalega Is. Mauritius 11°0S 57°0E 3 E12
Agar India 23°40N 76°2E 42 H7
Agartala India 23°50N 91°23E 41 H17
Agassiz Canada 49°14N 121°46W 70 D4
Agassiz Icecap Canada 80°15N 76°0W 69 A16
Agats Indonesia 5°33S 138°0E 37 F9
Agattu I. U.S.A. 52°25N 173°35E 74 E2
Agawam U.S.A. 42°5N 72°37W 83 D12
Agboville Ivory C. 5°55N 4°15W 50 G5
Ağdam Azerbaijan 40°0N 46°58E 44 B5
Agde France 43°19N 3°28E 20 E5
Agen France 44°12N 0°38E 20 D4
Āgh Kand Iran 37°15N 48°4E 45 B6
Aghia Deka Greece 35°3N 24°58E 25 D6
Aghia Ekaterinis, Akra Greece 39°50N 19°50E 25 A3
Aghia Galini Greece 35°6N 24°41E 25 D6
Aghia Varvara Greece 35°8N 25°1E 25 D7
Aghios Efstratios Greece 39°34N 24°58E 23 E11
Aghios Ioannis, Akra Greece 35°20N 25°40E 25 D7
Aghios Isidoros Greece 36°9N 27°51E 25 C9
Aghios Matheos Greece 39°30N 19°47E 25 B3
Aghios Nikolaos Greece 35°11N 25°41E 25 D7
Aghios Stephanos Greece 39°46N 19°39E 25 A3
Aghiou Orous, Kolpos Greece 40°6N 24°0E 23 D11
Aginskoye Russia 51°6N 114°32E 29 D12
Agnew Australia 28°1S 120°31E 61 E3
Agori India 24°33N 82°57E 43 G10
Agra India 27°17N 77°58E 42 F7
Ağri Turkey 39°44N 43°3E 19 G7
Agri → Italy 40°13N 16°44E 22 D7
Ağrı Dağı Turkey 39°50N 44°15E 44 B5
Ağri Karakose = Ağri Turkey 39°44N 43°3E 19 G7
Agrigento Italy 37°19N 13°34E 22 F5
Agrinio Greece 38°37N 21°27E 23 E9
Agua Caliente Mexico 32°29N 116°59W 79 N10
Agua Caliente Springs U.S.A. 32°56N 116°19W 79 N10
Água Clara Brazil 20°25S 52°45W 93 H8
Agua Fria ⌓ U.S.A. 34°14N 112°0W 77 J8
Agua Hechicera Mexico 32°28N 116°15W 79 N10
Agua Prieta Mexico 31°18N 109°34W 86 A3
Aguadilla Puerto Rico 18°26N 67°10W 89 d
Aguadulce Panama 8°15N 80°32W 88 E3
Aguanga U.S.A. 33°27N 116°51W 79 M10
Aguanish Canada 50°14N 62°2W 73 B7
Aguanish → Canada 50°13N 62°5W 73 B7
Aguapey → Argentina 29°7S 56°36W 94 B4
Aguaray Guazú → Paraguay 24°47S 57°19W 94 A4
Aguarico → Ecuador 0°59S 75°11W 92 D3
Aguaro-Guariquito △ Venezuela 8°20N 66°35W 89 E6
Aguas Blancas Chile 24°15S 69°55W 94 A2
Aguas Calientes, Sierra de Argentina 25°26S 66°40W 94 B2
Aguascalientes Mexico 21°53N 102°18W 86 C4
Aguascalientes □ Mexico 22°0N 102°20W 86 C4
Aguila, Punta Puerto Rico 17°57N 67°13W 89 d
Aguilares Argentina 27°26S 65°35W 94 B2
Águilas Spain 37°23N 1°35W 21 D5
Agüimes Canary Is. 27°58N 15°27W 24 G4
Aguja, C. de la Colombia 11°18N 74°12W 90 B3
Agujereada, Pta. Puerto Rico 18°30N 67°8W 89 d
Agulhas, C. S. Africa 34°52S 20°0E 56 E3
Agulo Canary Is. 28°11N 17°12W 24 F2
Agung, Gunung Indonesia 8°20S 115°28E 37 J18
Aguni-Jima Japan 26°30N 127°10E 31 L3
Agur Uganda 2°28N 32°55E 54 B3
Agusan → Phil. 9°0N 125°30E 37 C7
Aha Mts. Botswana 19°45S 21°0E 56 B3
Ahaggar Algeria 23°0N 6°30E 50 D7
Ahar Iran 38°35N 47°0E 44 B5
Ahipara B. N.Z. 35°5S 173°5E 59 A4
Ahiri India 19°30N 80°0E 40 K12
Ahmad Wal Pakistan 29°18N 65°58E 42 E1
Ahmadabad India 23°0N 72°40E 42 H5
Aḩmadābād Khorāsān, Iran 35°3N 60°50E 45 C9
Aḩmadābād Khorāsān, Iran 35°49N 59°42E 45 C8
Aḩmadī Iran 27°56N 56°42E 45 E8
Ahmadnagar India 19°7N 74°46E 40 K9
Ahmadpur East Pakistan 29°12N 71°10E 42 E4
Ahmadpur Lamma Pakistan 28°19N 70°3E 42 E4
Ahmedabad = Ahmadabad India 23°0N 72°40E 42 H5
Ahmednagar = Ahmadnagar India 19°7N 74°46E 40 K9
Ahome Mexico 25°55N 109°11W 86 B3
Ahoskie U.S.A. 36°17N 76°59W 85 C16
Ahram Iran 28°52N 51°16E 45 D6
Ahrax Pt. Malta 36°0N 14°22E 25 D1
Ahuachapán El Salv. 13°54N 89°52W 88 D2
Ahvāz Iran 31°20N 48°40E 45 D6
Ahvenanmaa = Åland Finland 60°15N 20°0E 9 F19
Aḩwar Yemen 13°30N 46°40E 47 E4
Ai → India 26°26N 90°44E 43 F14
Ai-Ais Namibia 27°54S 17°59E 56 D2
Ai-Ais and Fish River Canyon △ Namibia 24°45S 17°15E 56 C2
Aichi □ Japan 35°0N 137°15E 31 G8
Aigrettes, Pte. des Réunion 21°3S 55°13E 53 c
Aiguá Uruguay 34°13S 54°46W 95 C5
Aigues-Mortes France 43°35N 4°12E 20 E6
Aihui = Heihe China 50°10N 127°30E 33 A14
Aija Peru 9°50S 77°45W 92 E3
Aikawa Japan 38°2N 138°15E 30 E9
Aiken U.S.A. 33°34N 81°43W 85 E14
Aileron Australia 22°39S 133°20E 62 C1
Aillik Canada 55°11N 59°18W 73 A8
Ailsa Craig Canada 43°8N 81°33W 82 C3
Ailsa Craig U.K. 55°15N 5°6W 11 F3
Aim Russia 59°0N 133°55E 29 D14
Aimere Indonesia 8°45S 121°3E 37 F6
Aimogasta Argentina 28°33S 66°50W 94 B2
Aïn Ben Tili Mauritania 25°59N 9°27W 50 C4
Aïn-Sefra Algeria 32°47N 0°37W 50 B5
Ain Sudr Egypt 29°50N 33°6E 46 F2
Aïn Témouchent Algeria 35°16N 1°8W 50 A5
Ainaži Latvia 57°50N 24°24E 9 H21
Ainsworth U.S.A. 42°33N 99°52W 80 D4
Aiquile Bolivia 18°10S 65°10W 92 G5
Aïr Niger 18°30N 8°0E 50 E7
Air Force I. Canada 67°58N 74°5W 69 D17
Air Hitam Malaysia 1°55N 103°11E 39 M4
Airdrie Canada 51°18N 114°2W 70 C6
Airdrie U.K. 55°52N 3°57W 11 F5
Aire → U.K. 53°43N 0°55W 12 D7
Aire, I. de l' Spain 39°48N 4°16E 24 B11
Airlie Beach Australia 20°16S 148°43E 62 b
Aisne → France 49°26N 2°50E 20 B5
Ait India 25°54N 79°14E 43 G8
Aitkin U.S.A. 46°32N 93°42W 80 B7
Aitutaki Cook Is. 18°52S 159°45W 65 J12
Aiud Romania 46°19N 23°44E 17 E12
Aix-en-Provence France 43°32N 5°27E 20 E6
Aix-la-Chapelle = Aachen Germany 50°45N 6°6E 16 C4
Aix-les-Bains France 45°41N 5°53E 20 D6
Aizawl India 23°40N 92°44E 41 H18
Aizkraukle Latvia 56°36N 25°11E 9 H21
Aizpute Latvia 56°43N 21°40E 9 H19
Aizuwakamatsu Japan 37°30N 139°56E 30 F9
Ajaccio France 41°55N 8°40E 20 F8
Ajai ⌓ Uganda 2°52N 31°16E 54 B3
Ajaigarh India 24°52N 80°16E 43 G9
Ajalpan Mexico 18°22N 97°15W 87 D5
Ajanta Ra. India 20°28N 75°50E 40 J9
Ajari Rep. = Ajaria □ Georgia 41°30N 42°0E 19 F7
Ajaria □ Georgia 41°30N 42°0E 19 F7
Ajax Canada 43°50N 79°1W 82 C5
Ajdābiyā Libya 30°54N 20°4E 51 B10
Ajka Hungary 47°4N 17°31E 17 E9
'Ajlūn Jordan 32°18N 35°47E 46 C4
'Ajlūn □ Jordan 32°18N 35°47E 46 C4
'Ajmān U.A.E. 25°25N 55°30E 45 E7
Ajmer India 26°28N 74°37E 42 F6
Ajnala India 31°50N 74°48E 42 D6
Ajo U.S.A. 32°22N 112°52W 77 K7
Ajo, C. de Spain 43°31N 3°35W 21 A4
Akabira Japan 43°33N 142°5E 30 C11
Akagera △ Rwanda 1°31S 30°33E 54 C3
Akamas Cyprus 35°3N 32°18E 25 D11
Akan △ Japan 43°20N 144°20E 30 C12
Akanthou Cyprus 35°22N 33°45E 25 D12
Akaroa N.Z. 43°49S 172°59E 59 E4
Akashi Japan 34°45N 134°58E 31 G7
Akbarpur Bihar, India 24°39N 83°58E 43 G10
Akbarpur Ut. P., India 26°25N 82°32E 43 F10
Akçakale Turkey 36°41N 38°56E 44 B3
Akdoğan = Lysi Cyprus 35°6N 33°41E 25 D12
Akelamo Indonesia 1°35N 129°40E 37 D7
Aketi Dem. Rep. of the Congo 2°38N 23°47E 52 D4
Akhisar Turkey 38°56N 27°48E 23 E12
Akhnur India 32°52N 74°45E 43 C6
Akhtyrka = Okhtyrka Ukraine 50°25N 35°0E 19 D5
Aki Japan 33°30N 133°54E 31 H6
Akimiski I. Canada 52°50N 81°30W 72 B3
Akincilar = Louroujina Cyprus 35°0N 33°28E 25 E12
Akita Japan 39°45N 140°7E 30 E10
Akita □ Japan 39°40N 140°30E 30 E10
Akjoujt Mauritania 19°45N 14°15W 50 E3
Akkeshi Japan 43°2N 144°51E 30 C12
'Akko Israel 32°55N 35°4E 46 C4
Aklavik Canada 68°12N 135°0W 68 D4
Aklera India 24°26N 76°32E 42 G7
Akō Japan 34°45N 134°24E 31 G7
Akola India 20°42N 77°2E 40 J10
Akordat Eritrea 15°30N 37°40E 47 D2
Akpatok I. Canada 60°25N 68°8W 69 E18
Åkrahamn Norway 59°15N 5°10E 9 G11
Akranes Iceland 64°19N 22°5W 8 D2
Akron Colo., U.S.A. 40°10N 103°13W 76 F12
Akron Ohio, U.S.A. 41°5N 81°31W 82 E3
Akrotiri Cyprus 34°36N 32°57E 25 E11
Akrotiri Bay Cyprus 34°35N 33°10E 25 E12
Aksai Chin China 35°15N 79°55E 43 B8
Aksaray Turkey 38°25N 34°2E 44 B2
Aksay = Aqsay Kazakhstan 51°11N 53°0E 19 D9
Akşehir Turkey 38°18N 31°30E 44 B1
Akşehir Gölü Turkey 38°30N 31°25E 19 G5
Aksu China 41°5N 80°10E 32 C5
Aksum Ethiopia 14°5N 38°40E 47 E2
Aktsyabrski Belarus 52°38N 28°53E 17 B15
Aktyubinsk = Aqtöbe Kazakhstan 50°17N 57°10E 19 D10
Akure Nigeria 7°15N 5°5E 50 G7
Akureyri Iceland 65°40N 18°6W 8 D4
Akuseki-Shima Japan 29°27N 129°37E 31 K4
Akyab = Sittwe Burma 20°18N 92°45E 41 J18
Al 'Adan Yemen 12°45N 45°0E 47 E4
Al Aḩsā = Hasa Si. Arabia 25°50N 49°0E 45 E6
Al Ajfar Si. Arabia 27°26N 43°0E 44 E4
Al Amādīyah Iraq 37°5N 43°30E 44 B4
Al 'Amārah Iraq 31°55N 47°15E 44 D5
Al Anbār □ Iraq 33°25N 42°0E 44 C4
Al 'Aqabah Jordan 29°31N 35°0E 46 F4
Al 'Aqabah □ Jordan 29°30N 35°0E 46 F4
Al Arak Syria 34°38N 38°35E 44 C3
Al 'Aramah Si. Arabia 25°30N 46°0E 44 E5
Al 'Artāwīyah Si. Arabia 26°31N 45°20E 44 E5
Al 'Āşimah = 'Ammān □ Jordan 31°40N 36°30E 46 D5
Al 'Assāfīyah Si. Arabia 28°17N 38°59E 44 D3
Al 'Awdah Si. Arabia 25°32N 45°41E 44 E5
Al 'Ayn Si. Arabia 25°4N 38°6E 44 E3
Al 'Ayn U.A.E. 24°15N 55°45E 45 E7
Al 'Azīzīyah Iraq 32°54N 45°4E 44 C5
Al Bāb Syria 36°23N 37°29E 44 B3
Al Bad' Si. Arabia 28°28N 35°1E 44 D2
Al Bādī Iraq 35°56N 41°32E 44 C4
Al Baḩrah Kuwait 29°40N 47°52E 44 D5
Al Baḩral Mayyit = Dead Sea Asia 31°30N 35°30E 46 D4
Al Balqā' □ Jordan 32°5N 35°45E 46 C4
Al Bārūk, J. Lebanon 33°39N 35°40E 46 B4
Al Başrah Iraq 30°30N 47°50E 44 D5
Al Baṭḩā Iraq 31°6N 45°53E 44 D5
Al Batrūn Lebanon 34°15N 35°40E 46 A4
Al Bayḑā Libya 32°50N 21°44E 51 B10
Al Biqā Lebanon 34°10N 36°10E 46 A5
Al Bi'r Si. Arabia 28°51N 36°16E 44 D3
Al Bukayrīyah Si. Arabia 26°9N 43°40E 44 E4
Al Burayj Syria 34°15N 36°46E 46 A5
Al Faḑilī Si. Arabia 26°58N 49°10E 45 E6
Al Fallūjah Iraq 33°20N 43°55E 44 C4
Al Fāw Iraq 30°0N 48°30E 45 D6
Al Fujayrah U.A.E. 25°7N 56°18E 45 E8
Al Ghadaf, W. → Jordan 31°26N 36°43E 46 D5
Al Ghammās Iraq 31°45N 44°37E 44 D5
Al Ghazālah Si. Arabia 26°48N 41°19E 44 E4
Al Ḩadīthah Iraq 34°0N 41°13E 44 C4
Al Ḩadīthah Si. Arabia 31°28N 37°8E 46 D6
Al Ḩaḑr Iraq 35°35N 42°44E 44 C4
Al Ḩājānah Syria 33°20N 36°33E 46 B5

Al Ḥajar al Gharbī *Oman* 24°10N 56°15E **45** E8
Al Ḥāmad *Si. Arabia* 31°30N 39°30E **44** D3
Al Ḥamdānīyah *Syria* 35°25N 36°50E **44** C3
Al Ḥamīdīyah *Syria* 34°42N 35°57E **46** A4
Al Ḥammār *Iraq* 30°57N 46°51E **44** D5
Al Ḥamrāʾ *Si. Arabia* 24°2N 38°55E **44** E3
Al Ḥamzah *Iraq* 31°43N 44°58E **44** D5
Al Ḥanākīyah *Si. Arabia* 24°51N 40°31E **44** E4
Al Ḥarūj al Aswad *Libya* 27°0N 17°10E **51** C9
Al Ḥasakah *Syria* 36°35N 40°45E **44** B4
Al Ḥayy *Iraq* 32°5N 46°5E **44** C5
Al Ḥijarah *Asia* 30°0N 44°0E **44** D4
Al Ḥillah *Iraq* 32°30N 44°25E **44** C5
Al Ḥindīyah *Iraq* 32°30N 44°10E **44** C5
Al Ḥirmil *Lebanon* 34°26N 36°24E **46** A5
Al Hoceïma *Morocco* 35°8N 3°58W **50** A5
Al Ḥudaydah *Yemen* 14°50N 43°0E **47** E3
Al Ḥudūd ash Shamālīyah □
  Si. Arabia 29°10N 42°30E **44** D4
Al Ḥufūf *Si. Arabia* 25°25N 49°45E **45** E6
Al Ḥumaydah *Si. Arabia* 29°14N 34°56E **44** D2
Al Ḥunayy *Si. Arabia* 25°58N 48°45E **45** E6
Al Īsāwīyah *Si. Arabia* 30°43N 37°59E **44** D3
Al Jafr *Jordan* 30°18N 36°14E **46** E5
Al Jāfūrah *Si. Arabia* 25°0N 50°15E **45** E7
Al Jaghbūb *Libya* 29°42N 24°38E **51** C10
Al Jahrah *Kuwait* 29°25N 47°40E **44** D5
Al Jalāmīd *Si. Arabia* 31°20N 40°6E **44** D3
Al Jamalīyah *Qatar* 25°37N 51°5E **45** E6
Al Janūb □ *Lebanon* 33°20N 35°20E **46** B4
Al Jawf *Libya* 24°10N 23°24E **51** D10
Al Jawf *Si. Arabia* 29°55N 39°40E **44** D3
Al Jawf □ *Si. Arabia* 29°30N 39°30E **44** D3
Al Jazair = Algeria ■
  Africa 28°30N 2°0E **50** C6
Al Jazirah *Iraq* 33°30N 44°0E **44** C5
Al Jithāmīyah *Si. Arabia* 27°41N 41°43E **44** E4
Al Jubayl *Si. Arabia* 27°0N 49°50E **45** E6
Al Jubaylah *Si. Arabia* 24°55N 46°25E **44** E5
Al Jubb *Si. Arabia* 27°11N 42°17E **44** E4
Al Junaynah *Sudan* 13°27N 22°45E **51** F10
Al Kabaʾish *Iraq* 30°58N 47°0E **44** D5
Al Karak *Jordan* 31°11N 35°42E **46** D4
Al Karak □ *Jordan* 31°0N 36°0E **46** E5
Al Kāẓimīyah *Iraq* 33°22N 44°18E **44** C5
Al Khābūrah *Oman* 23°57N 57°5E **45** F8
Al Khafji *Si. Arabia* 28°24N 48°29E **45** E6
Al Khalīl *West Bank* 31°32N 35°6E **46** D4
Al Khāliṣ *Iraq* 33°49N 44°32E **44** C5
Al Kharsānīyah
  Si. Arabia 27°13N 49°18E **45** E6
Al Khaṣab *Oman* 26°14N 56°15E **45** E8
Al Khawr *Qatar* 25°41N 51°30E **45** E6
Al Khiḍr *Iraq* 31°12N 45°33E **44** D5
Al Khiyām *Lebanon* 33°20N 35°36E **46** B4
Al Khobar *Si. Arabia* 26°17N 50°12E **45** E6
Al Khums *Libya* 32°40N 14°17E **51** B8
Al Kiswah *Syria* 33°23N 36°14E **46** B5
Al Kūfah *Iraq* 32°2N 44°24E **44** C5
Al Kufrah *Libya* 24°17N 23°15E **51** D10
Al Kuhayfiyah *Si. Arabia* 27°12N 43°3E **44** E4
Al Kūt *Iraq* 32°30N 46°0E **44** C5
Al Kuwayt *Kuwait* 29°30N 48°0E **44** D5
Al Labwah *Lebanon* 34°11N 36°20E **46** A5
Al Lādhiqīyah *Syria* 35°30N 35°45E **44** C2
Al Līth *Si. Arabia* 20°9N 40°15E **47** C3
Al Liwāʾ *Oman* 24°31N 56°36E **45** E8
Al Luḥayyah *Yemen* 15°45N 42°40E **47** D3
Al Madīnah *Iraq* 30°57N 47°16E **44** D5
Al Madīnah *Si. Arabia* 24°35N 39°52E **44** E3
Al Mafraq *Jordan* 32°17N 36°14E **46** C5
Al Mafraq □ *Jordan* 32°17N 36°15E **46** C5
Al Maghreb = Morocco ■
  N. Afr. 32°0N 5°50W **50** B4
Al Maḥmūdīyah *Iraq* 32°3N 44°21E **44** C5
Al Majmaʿah *Si. Arabia* 25°57N 45°22E **44** E5
Al Makhruq, W. ➤
  Jordan 31°28N 37°0E **46** D6
Al Makhūl *Si. Arabia* 26°37N 42°39E **44** E4
Al Manāmah *Bahrain* 26°10N 50°30E **45** E6
Al Maqwaʿ *Kuwait* 29°10N 47°59E **44** D5
Al Marāb *Si. Arabia* 25°35N 49°35E **45** E6
Al Marj *Libya* 32°25N 20°30E **51** B10
Al Maṭlā *Kuwait* 29°24N 47°40E **44** D5
Al Mawṣil *Iraq* 36°15N 43°5E **44** B4
Al Mayādin *Syria* 35°1N 40°27E **44** C4
Al Mazār *Jordan* 31°4N 35°41E **46** D4
Al Midhnab *Si. Arabia* 25°50N 44°18E **44** E5
Al Mināʾ *Lebanon* 34°24N 35°49E **46** A4
Al Miqdādīyah *Iraq* 34°0N 45°0E **44** C5
Al Mubarraz *Si. Arabia* 25°30N 49°40E **45** E6
Al Mudawwarah *Jordan* 29°19N 36°0E **46** F5
Al Mughayrāʾ *U.A.E.* 24°5N 53°32E **45** E7
Al Muharraq *Bahrain* 26°15N 50°40E **45** E6
Al Mukallā *Yemen* 14°33N 49°2E **47** E4
Al Mukhā *Yemen* 13°18N 43°15E **47** E3
Al Musayjīd *Si. Arabia* 24°5N 39°5E **44** E3
Al Musayyib *Iraq* 32°49N 44°20E **44** C5
Al Muthannā □ *Iraq* 30°30N 45°15E **44** D5
Al Muwaylih *Si. Arabia* 27°40N 35°30E **44** E2
Al Qādisīyah □ *Iraq* 30°0N 45°0E **44** D5
Al Qāʾim *Iraq* 34°21N 41°7E **44** C4
Al Qalībah *Si. Arabia* 28°24N 37°42E **44** D3
Al Qāmishlī *Syria* 37°2N 41°14E **44** B4
Al Qaryatayn *Syria* 34°12N 37°13E **46** A6
Al Qaṣīm □ *Si. Arabia* 26°0N 43°0E **44** E4
Al Qaṭʿā *Syria* 34°40N 40°48E **44** C4
Al Qaṭīf *Si. Arabia* 26°35N 50°0E **45** E6
Al Qaṭrānah *Jordan* 31°12N 36°6E **46** D5
Al Qaṭrūn *Libya* 24°56N 15°3E **51** D9
Al Qayṣūmah *Si. Arabia* 28°20N 46°7E **44** D5
Al Quds = Jerusalem
  Israel/West Bank 31°47N 35°10E **46** D4
Al Qunayṭirah *Syria* 35°5N 35°45E **46** B4
Al Qunfudhah *Si. Arabia* 19°3N 41°4E **47** D3
Al Quṣayr *Iraq* 30°39N 45°50E **44** D5
Al Quṣayr *Syria* 34°31N 36°34E **46** A5
Al Quṭayfah *Syria* 33°44N 36°36E **46** B5
Al ʿUbaylah *Si. Arabia* 21°59N 50°57E **47** C5

Al ʿUdaylīyah *Si. Arabia* 25°8N 49°18E **45** E6
Al ʿUlā *Si. Arabia* 26°35N 38°0E **44** E3
Al ʿUqayr *Si. Arabia* 25°40N 50°15E **45** E6
Al ʿUwaynid *Si. Arabia* 24°50N 46°0E **44** E5
Al ʿUwayqīlah *Si. Arabia* 30°30N 42°10E **44** D4
Al ʿUyūn *Ḥijāz, Si. Arabia* 24°33N 39°35E **44** E3
Al ʿUyūn *Najd, Si. Arabia* 26°30N 43°50E **44** E4
Al ʿUzayr *Iraq* 31°19N 47°25E **44** D5
Al Wajh *Si. Arabia* 26°10N 36°30E **44** E3
Al Wakrah *Qatar* 25°10N 51°40E **45** E6
Al Waqbah *Si. Arabia* 28°48N 45°33E **44** D5
Al Wariʿah *Si. Arabia* 27°51N 47°25E **44** E5
Al Yaman = Yemen ■
  Asia 15°0N 44°0E **47** E3
Ala Dağ *Turkey* 37°44N 35°9E **44** B2
Ala Tau *Asia* 45°30N 80°40E **32** B5
Ala Tau Shankou = Dzungarian
  Gate *Asia* 45°10N 82°0E **32** B5
Alabama □ *U.S.A.* 33°0N 87°0W **85** E11
Alabama ➤ *U.S.A.* 31°8N 87°57W **85** F11
Alabaster *U.S.A.* 33°15N 86°49W **85** E11
Alaçam Dağları *Turkey* 38°9N 28°49E **23** E13
Alacant = Alicante *Spain* 38°23N 0°30W **21** C5
Alachua *U.S.A.* 29°47N 82°30W **85** G13
Alagoa Grande *Brazil* 7°3S 35°35W **93** E11
Alagoas □ *Brazil* 9°0S 36°0W **93** E11
Alagoinhas *Brazil* 12°7S 38°20W **93** F11
Alaheaieatnu = Altaelva ➤
  Norway 69°54N 23°17E **8** B20
Alaior *Spain* 39°57N 4°8E **24** B11
Alajero *Canary Is.* 28°3N 17°13W **24** F2
Alajuela *Costa Rica* 10°2N 84°8W **88** D3
Alakamisy *Madag.* 21°19S 47°14E **57** C8
Alaknanda ➤ *India* 30°8N 78°36E **43** D8
Alakurtti *Russia* 66°58N 30°25E **8** C24
Alamarvdasht *Iran* 27°37N 52°59E **45** E7
Alameda *Calif., U.S.A.* 37°46N 122°15W **78** H4
Alameda *N. Mex.,*
  U.S.A. 35°11N 106°37W **77** J10
Alamo *U.S.A.* 37°22N 115°10W **79** H11
Alamogordo *U.S.A.* 32°54N 105°57W **77** K11
Alamos *Mexico* 27°1N 108°56W **86** B3
Alamosa *U.S.A.* 37°28N 105°52W **77** H11
Åland *Finland* 60°15N 20°0E **9** F19
Ålands hav *Europe* 60°0N 19°30E **9** G18
Alania = North Ossetia □
  Russia 43°30N 44°30E **19** F7
Alanya *Turkey* 36°38N 32°0E **44** B1
Alaotra, Farihin' *Madag.* 17°30S 48°30E **57** B8
Alapayevsk *Russia* 57°52N 61°42E **28** D7
Alappuzha = Alleppey
  India 9°30N 76°28E **40** Q10
Alaró *Spain* 39°42N 2°47E **24** B9
Alarobia-Vohiposa
  Madag. 20°59S 47°9E **57** C8
Alaşehir *Turkey* 38°23N 28°30E **23** E13
Alaska □ *U.S.A.* 64°0N 154°0W **74** C9
Alaska, G. of *Pac. Oc.* 58°0N 145°0W **68** F3
Alaska Peninsula *U.S.A.* 56°0N 159°0W **74** D8
Alaska Range *U.S.A.* 62°50N 151°0W **68** E1
Älät *Azerbaijan* 39°58N 49°25E **45** B6
Alatau Shan = Ala Tau
  Asia 45°30N 80°40E **32** B5
Alatyr *Russia* 54°55N 46°35E **18** D8
Alausi *Ecuador* 2°0S 78°50W **92** D3
Alava, C. *U.S.A.* 48°10N 124°44W **76** B1
Alavo = Alavus *Finland* 62°35N 23°36E **8** E20
Alavus *Finland* 62°35N 23°36E **8** E20
Alawa ◊ *Australia* 15°42S 134°39E **62** B1
Alawoona *Australia* 34°45S 140°30E **63** E3
Alayawarra ◊ *Australia* 22°0S 134°30E **62** C1
'Alayh *Lebanon* 33°46N 35°33E **46** B4
Alba *Italy* 44°42N 8°2E **20** D8
Alba-Iulia *Romania* 46°8N 23°39E **17** E12
Albacete *Spain* 39°0N 1°50W **21** C5
Albacutya, L. *Australia* 35°45S 141°58E **63** F3
Albanel, L. *Canada* 50°55N 73°12W **72** B5
Albania ■ *Europe* 41°0N 20°0E **23** D9
Albany *Australia* 35°1S 117°58E **61** G2
Albany *Ga., U.S.A.* 31°35N 84°10W **85** F12
Albany *N.Y., U.S.A.* 42°39N 73°45W **83** D11
Albany *Oreg., U.S.A.* 44°38N 123°6W **76** D2
Albany *Tex., U.S.A.* 32°44N 99°18W **84** E5
Albany ➤ *Canada* 52°17N 81°31W **72** B3
Albarca, C. d' *Spain* 39°4N 1°22E **24** B7
Albardón *Argentina* 31°20S 68°30W **94** C2
Albatross B. *Australia* 12°45S 141°30E **62** A3
Albemarle *U.S.A.* 35°21N 80°12W **85** D14
Albemarle Sd. *U.S.A.* 36°5N 76°0W **85** C16
Alberche ➤ *Spain* 39°58N 4°46W **21** C3
Alberdi *Paraguay* 26°14S 58°20W **94** B4
Alberga ➤ *Australia* 27°6S 135°33E **63** D2
Albert, L. *Africa* 1°30N 31°0E **54** B3
Albert, L. *Australia* 35°30S 139°10E **63** F2
Albert Edward Ra.
  Australia 18°17S 127°57E **60** C4
Albert Lea *U.S.A.* 43°39N 93°22W **80** D7
Albert Nile ➤ *Uganda* 3°36N 32°2E **54** B3
Albert Town *Bahamas* 22°37N 74°33W **89** B5
Alberta □ *Canada* 54°40N 115°0W **70** C6
Alberti *Argentina* 35°1S 60°16W **94** D3
Albertinia *S. Africa* 34°11S 21°34E **56** E3
Alberton *Canada* 46°50N 64°0W **73** C7
Albertville *France* 45°40N 6°22E **20** D7
Albertville *U.S.A.* 34°16N 86°13W **85** D11
Albi *France* 43°56N 2°9E **20** E5
Albia *U.S.A.* 41°2N 92°48W **80** E7
Albina *Suriname* 5°37N 54°15W **93** B8
Albina, Ponta *Angola* 15°52S 11°44E **56** B1
Albion *Mich., U.S.A.* 42°15N 84°45W **81** D11
Albion *Nebr., U.S.A.* 41°42N 98°0W **80** E4
Albion *Pa., U.S.A.* 41°53N 80°22W **82** E4
Alborán *Medit. S.* 35°57N 3°0W **21** E4
Ålborg = Aalborg *Denmark* 57°2N 9°54E **9** H13
Alborz, Reshteh-ye Kūhhā-ye
  Iran 36°0N 52°0E **45** C7
Albufeira *Portugal* 37°5N 8°15W **21** D1
Albuquerque *U.S.A.* 35°5N 106°39W **77** J10
Albuquerque, Cayos de
  Caribbean 12°10N 81°50W **88** D3

Alburg *U.S.A.* 44°59N 73°18W **83** B11
Albury *Australia* 36°3S 146°56E **63** F4
Alcalá de Henares *Spain* 40°28N 3°22W **21** B4
Alcalá la Real *Spain* 37°27N 3°57W **21** D4
Álcamo *Italy* 37°59N 12°55E **22** F5
Alcañiz *Spain* 41°2N 0°8W **21** B5
Alcântara *Brazil* 2°20S 44°30W **93** D10
Alcántara, Embalse de
  Spain 39°44N 6°50W **21** C2
Alcantarilla *Spain* 37°59N 1°12W **21** D5
Alcaraz, Sierra de *Spain* 38°40N 2°20W **21** C4
Alcaudete *Spain* 37°35N 4°5W **21** D3
Alcázar de San Juan
  Spain 39°24N 3°12W **21** C4
Alchevsk *Ukraine* 48°30N 38°45E **19** E6
Alcira = Alzira *Spain* 39°9N 0°30W **21** C5
Alcova *U.S.A.* 42°34N 106°43W **76** E10
Alcoy *Spain* 38°43N 0°30W **21** C5
Alcúdia *Spain* 39°51N 3°7E **24** B10
Alcúdia, B. d' *Spain* 39°47N 3°15E **24** B10
Aldabra Is. *Seychelles* 9°22S 46°28E **49** G8
Aldama *Mexico* 22°55N 98°4W **87** C5
Aldan *Russia* 58°40N 125°30E **29** D13
Aldan ➤ *Russia* 63°28N 129°35E **29** C13
Aldea, Pta. de la
  Canary Is. 28°0N 15°50W **24** G4
Aldeburgh *U.K.* 52°10N 1°37E **13** E9
Alder Pk. *U.S.A.* 35°53N 121°22W **78** K5
Alderney *U.K.* 49°42N 2°11W **13** H5
Aldershot *U.K.* 51°15N 0°44W **13** F7
Aledo *U.S.A.* 41°12N 90°45W **80** E8
Aleg *Mauritania* 17°3N 13°55W **50** E3
Alegranza *Canary Is.* 29°23N 13°32W **24** E6
Alegranza, I. *Canary Is.* 29°23N 13°32W **24** E6
Alegre *Brazil* 20°50S 41°30W **95** A7
Alegrete *Brazil* 29°40S 56°0W **95** B4
Aleksandriya = Oleksandriya
  Ukraine 50°37N 26°19E **17** C14
Aleksandrov Gay *Russia* 50°9N 48°34E **19** D8
Aleksandrovsk-Sakhalinskiy
  Russia 50°50N 142°20E **33** A17
Aleksandry, Zemlya
  Russia 80°25N 48°0E **28** A5
Além Paraíba *Brazil* 21°52S 42°41W **95** A7
Alemania *Argentina* 25°40S 65°30W **94** B2
Alemania *Chile* 25°10S 69°55W **94** B2
Alençon *France* 48°27N 0°4E **20** B4
Alenquer *Brazil* 1°56S 54°46W **93** D8
'Alenuihāhā Channel
  U.S.A. 20°30N 156°0W **75** L8
Aleppo = Ḥalab *Syria* 36°10N 37°15E **44** B3
Aléria *France* 42°5N 9°26E **20** E9
Alert *Canada* 83°2N 60°0W **69** A20
Alès *France* 44°9N 4°5E **20** D6
Alessándria *Italy* 44°54N 8°37E **20** D8
Ålesund *Norway* 62°28N 6°12E **8** E12
Aleutian Basin *Pac. Oc.* 57°0N 177°0E **64** B9
Aleutian Is. *Pac. Oc.* 52°0N 175°0W **64** B10
Aleutian Range *U.S.A.* 60°0N 154°0W **74** D9
Aleutian Trench *Pac. Oc.* 48°0N 180°0E **4** D17
Alexander *U.S.A.* 47°51N 103°39W **80** B2
Alexander, Mt.
  Australia 28°58S 120°16E **61** E3
Alexander Arch. *U.S.A.* 56°0N 136°0W **74** D6
Alexander Bay *S. Africa* 28°40S 16°30E **56** D2
Alexander City *U.S.A.* 32°56N 85°58W **85** E12
Alexander I. *Antarctica* 69°0S 70°0W **5** C17
Alexandra *Australia* 37°8S 145°40E **63** F4
Alexandra *N.Z.* 45°14S 169°25E **59** F2
Alexandra Falls *Canada* 60°29N 116°18W **70** A5
Alexandria = El Iskandarîya
  Egypt 31°13N 29°58E **51** B11
Alexandria *B.C.,*
  Canada 52°35N 122°27W **70** C4
Alexandria *Ont.,*
  Canada 45°19N 74°38W **83** A10
Alexandria *Romania* 43°57N 25°24E **17** G13
Alexandria *S. Africa* 33°38S 26°28E **56** E4
Alexandria *U.K.* 55°59N 4°35W **11** F4
Alexandria *La., U.S.A.* 31°18N 92°27W **84** F8
Alexandria *Minn.,*
  U.S.A. 45°53N 95°22W **80** C6
Alexandria *S. Dak.,*
  U.S.A. 43°39N 97°47W **80** D5
Alexandria *Va., U.S.A.* 38°49N 77°5W **81** F15
Alexandria Bay *U.S.A.* 44°20N 75°55W **83** B9
Alexandrina, L.
  Australia 35°25S 139°10E **63** F2
Alexandroupoli *Greece* 40°50N 25°54E **23** D11
Alexis ➤ *Canada* 52°33N 56°8W **73** B8
Alexis Creek *Canada* 52°10N 123°20W **70** C4
Aleysk *Russia* 52°40N 83°0E **28** D9
Alfabia *Spain* 39°44N 2°44E **24** B9
Alfenas *Brazil* 21°20S 46°10W **95** A6
Alford *Aberds., U.K.* 57°14N 2°41W **11** D6
Alford *Lincs., U.K.* 53°15N 0°10E **12** D8
Alfred *Maine, U.S.A.* 43°29N 70°43W **83** C14
Alfred *N.Y., U.S.A.* 42°16N 77°48W **82** D7
Alfreton *U.K.* 53°6N 1°24W **12** D6
Algaida *Spain* 39°33N 2°53E **24** B9
Ålgård *Norway* 58°46N 5°53E **9** G11
Algarve *Portugal* 36°58N 8°20W **21** E1
Algeciras *Spain* 36°9N 5°28W **21** D3
Algemesí *Spain* 39°11N 0°27W **21** C5
Alger *Algeria* 36°42N 3°8E **50** A6
Algeria ■ *Africa* 28°30N 2°0E **50** C6
Algha *Kazakhstan* 49°53N 57°20E **19** E10
Alghero *Italy* 40°33N 8°19E **22** D3
Algiers = Alger *Algeria* 36°42N 3°8E **50** A6
Algoa B. *S. Africa* 33°50S 25°45E **56** E4
Algoma *U.S.A.* 44°36N 87°26W **80** C10
Algona *U.S.A.* 43°4N 94°14W **80** D6
Algonac *U.S.A.* 42°37N 82°32W **82** D2
Algorta *Uruguay* 32°25S 57°23W **94** C5
Alhambra *U.S.A.* 34°5N 118°7W **79** L8
Alhucemas = Al Hoceïma
  Morocco 35°8N 3°58W **50** A5
'Alī al Gharbī *Iraq* 32°30N 46°45E **44** C5
'Alī ash Sharqī *Iraq* 32°7N 46°44E **44** C5

Äli Bayramlı *Azerbaijan* 39°59N 48°52E **45** B6
'Alī Khēl *Afghan.* 33°57N 69°43E **42** C3
Alī Shāh *Iran* 38°9N 45°50E **44** B5
'Alīābād *Golestān, Iran* 36°40N 54°33E **45** B7
'Alīābād *Khorāsān, Iran* 32°30N 57°30E **45** C8
'Alīābād *Kordestān, Iran* 35°4N 46°58E **44** C5
'Alīābād *Yazd, Iran* 31°41N 53°49E **45** D7
Aliağa *Turkey* 38°47N 26°59E **23** E12
Aliakmonas ➤ *Greece* 40°30N 22°36E **23** D10
Alicante *Spain* 38°23N 0°30W **21** C5
Alice *S. Africa* 32°48S 26°55E **56** E4
Alice *U.S.A.* 27°45N 98°5W **84** H5
Alice ➤ *Queens.,*
  Australia 24°2S 144°50E **62** C3
Alice ➤ *Queens.,*
  Australia 15°35S 142°20E **62** B3
Alice Arm *Canada* 55°29N 129°31W **70** B3
Alice Springs *Australia* 23°40S 133°50E **62** C1
Alicedale *S. Africa* 33°15S 26°4E **56** E4
Aliceville *U.S.A.* 33°8N 88°9W **85** E10
Aliganj *India* 27°30N 79°10E **43** F8
Aligarh *Raj., India* 25°55N 76°15E **42** G7
Aligarh *Ut. P., India* 27°55N 78°10E **42** F8
Alīgūdarz *Iran* 33°25N 49°45E **45** C6
Alimia *Greece* 36°16N 27°43E **25** C9
Alingsås *Sweden* 57°56N 12°31E **9** H15
Alipur *Pakistan* 29°25N 70°55E **42** E4
Alipur Duar *India* 26°30N 89°35E **41** F16
Aliquippa *U.S.A.* 40°37N 80°15W **82** F4
Aliwal North *S. Africa* 30°45S 26°45E **56** E4
Alix *Canada* 52°24N 113°11W **70** C6
Aljustrel *Portugal* 37°55N 8°10W **21** D1
Alkmaar *Neths.* 52°37N 4°45E **15** B4
All American Canal
  U.S.A. 32°45N 115°15W **77** K6
Allagash ➤ *U.S.A.* 47°5N 69°3W **81** B19
Allah Dad *Pakistan* 25°38N 67°34E **42** G2
Allahabad *India* 25°25N 81°58E **43** G9
Allan *Canada* 51°53N 106°4W **71** C7
Allanridge *S. Africa* 27°45S 26°40E **56** D4
Allegany *U.S.A.* 42°6N 78°30W **82** D6
Allegheny ➤ *U.S.A.* 40°27N 80°1W **82** F5
Allegheny Mts. *U.S.A.* 38°15N 80°10W **81** F13
Allegheny Plateau
  U.S.A. 41°30N 78°30W **81** E14
Allegheny Res. *U.S.A.* 41°50N 79°0W **82** E6
Allègre, Pte. *Guadeloupe* 16°22N 61°46W **88** b
Allen, Bog of *Ireland* 53°15N 7°0W **10** C5
Allen, L. *Ireland* 54°8N 8°4W **10** B3
Allendale *U.S.A.* 33°1N 81°18W **85** E14
Allende *Mexico* 28°20N 100°51W **86** B4
Allentown *U.S.A.* 40°37N 75°29W **83** F9
Alleppey *India* 9°30N 76°28E **40** Q10
Aller ➤ *Germany* 52°56N 9°12E **16** B5
Alleynes B. *Barbados* 13°13N 59°39W **89** g
Alliance *Nebr., U.S.A.* 42°6N 102°52W **80** D2
Alliance *Ohio, U.S.A.* 40°55N 81°6W **82** F3
Allier ➤ *France* 46°57N 3°4E **20** C5
Alliford Bay *Canada* 53°12N 131°58W **70** C2
Alligator Pond *Jamaica* 17°52N 77°34W **88** a
Alliston *Canada* 44°9N 79°52W **82** B5
Alloa *U.K.* 56°7N 3°47W **11** E5
Allora *Australia* 28°2S 152°0E **63** D5
Alluitsup Paa *Greenland* 60°30N 45°35W **4** C5
Alma *Canada* 48°35N 71°40W **73** C5
Alma *Ga., U.S.A.* 31°33N 82°28W **85** F13
Alma *Kans., U.S.A.* 39°1N 96°17W **80** F5
Alma *Mich., U.S.A.* 43°23N 84°39W **81** D11
Alma *Nebr., U.S.A.* 40°6N 99°22W **80** E4
Alma *Wis., U.S.A.* 44°20N 91°55W **80** C8
Alma Ata = Almaty
  Kazakhstan 43°15N 76°57E **32** C4
Alma Hill *U.S.A.* 42°2N 78°0W **82** D6
Almada *Portugal* 38°41N 9°8W **21** C1
Almadén *Australia* 17°22S 144°40E **62** B3
Almadén *Spain* 38°49N 4°52W **21** C3
Almalyk = Olmaliq
  Uzbekistan 40°50N 69°35E **28** E7
Almanor, L. *U.S.A.* 40°14N 121°9W **76** F3
Almansa *Spain* 38°51N 1°5W **21** C5
Almanzor, Pico *Spain* 40°15N 5°18W **21** B3
Almanzora ➤ *Spain* 37°14N 1°46W **21** D5
Almaty *Kazakhstan* 43°15N 76°57E **32** C4
Almazán *Spain* 41°30N 2°30W **21** B4
Almeirim *Brazil* 1°30S 52°34W **93** D8
Almelo *Neths.* 52°22N 6°42E **15** B6
Almendralejo *Spain* 38°41N 6°26W **21** C2
Almere-Stad *Neths.* 52°20N 5°15E **15** B5
Almería *Spain* 36°52N 2°27W **21** D4
Almirante *Panama* 9°10N 82°30W **88** E3
Almond *U.S.A.* 42°19N 77°44W **82** D7
Almont *U.S.A.* 42°55N 83°3W **82** D1
Almonte *Canada* 45°14N 76°12W **83** A8
Almora *India* 29°38N 79°40E **43** E8
Almyrou, Ormos *Greece* 35°23N 24°20E **25** D6
Alness *U.K.* 57°41N 4°16W **11** D4
Alnmouth *U.K.* 55°24N 1°37W **12** B6
Alnwick *U.K.* 55°24N 1°42W **12** B6
Aloi *Uganda* 2°16N 33°10E **54** B3
Alon *Burma* 22°12N 95°5E **41** H19
Alor *Indonesia* 8°15S 124°30E **37** F6
Alor Setar *Malaysia* 6°7N 100°22E **39** J3
Alot *India* 23°56N 75°40E **42** H6
Aloysius, Mt. *Australia* 26°0S 128°38E **61** E4
Alpaugh *U.S.A.* 35°53N 119°29W **78** K7
Alpena *U.S.A.* 45°4N 83°27W **81** C12
Alpha *Australia* 23°39S 146°37E **62** C4
Alpha Ridge *Arctic* 84°0N 118°0W **4** A2
Alphen aan den Rijn
  Neths. 52°7N 4°40E **15** B4
Alpine *Ariz., U.S.A.* 33°51N 109°9W **77** K9
Alpine *Calif., U.S.A.* 32°50N 116°46W **79** N10
Alpine *Tex., U.S.A.* 30°22N 103°40W **84** F3
Alps *Europe* 46°30N 9°30E **20** C8
Alpurrulam *Australia* 20°59S 137°50E **62** C2
Alsace □ *France* 48°15N 7°25E **20** B7
Alsask *Canada* 51°21N 109°59W **71** C7
Alsasua *Spain* 42°54N 2°10W **21** A4
Alsek ➤ *U.S.A.* 59°10N 138°12W **70** B1

Alsta *Norway* 65°58N 12°40E **8** D15
Alston *U.K.* 54°49N 2°25W **12** C5
Alta *Norway* 69°57N 23°10E **8** B20
Alta Gracia *Argentina* 31°40S 64°30W **94** C3
Alta Sierra *U.S.A.* 35°42N 118°33W **79** K8
Altaelva ➤ *Norway* 69°54N 23°17E **8** B20
Altafjorden *Norway* 70°5N 23°5E **8** A20
Altai = Aerhtai Shan
  Mongolia 46°40N 92°45E **32** B7
Altai = Gorno-Altay □
  Russia 51°0N 86°0E **28** D9
Altamaha ➤ *U.S.A.* 31°20N 81°20W **85** F14
Altamira *Brazil* 3°12S 52°10W **93** D8
Altamira *Chile* 25°47S 69°51W **94** B2
Altamira *Mexico* 22°24N 97°55W **87** C5
Altamont *U.S.A.* 42°42N 74°3W **83** D10
Altamura *Italy* 40°49N 16°33E **22** D7
Altanbulag *Mongolia* 50°16N 106°30E **32** A10
Altar *Mexico* 30°43N 111°44W **86** A2
Altar, Gran Desierto de
  Mexico 31°50N 114°10W **86** D2
Altata *Mexico* 24°40N 107°55W **86** C3
Altavista *U.S.A.* 37°6N 79°17W **81** G14
Altay *China* 47°48N 88°10E **32** B6
Altay *Mongolia* 46°22N 96°15E **32** B8
Altea *Spain* 38°38N 0°2W **21** C5
Altiplano *Bolivia* 17°0S 68°0W **92** G5
Alto Araguaia *Brazil* 17°15S 53°20W **93** G8
Alto Cuchumatanes =
  Cuchumatanes, Sierra de los
  Guatemala 15°35N 91°25W **88** C1
Alto del Carmen *Chile* 28°46S 70°30W **94** B1
Alto Ligonha *Mozam.* 15°30S 38°11E **55** F4
Alto Molocue *Mozam.* 15°50S 37°35E **55** F4
Alto Paraguay □
  Paraguay 21°0S 58°30W **94** A4
Alto Paraná □ *Paraguay* 25°30S 54°50W **95** B5
Alton *Canada* 43°54N 80°5W **82** C4
Alton *U.K.* 51°9N 0°59W **13** F7
Alton *Ill., U.S.A.* 38°53N 90°11W **80** F8
Alton *N.H., U.S.A.* 43°27N 71°13W **83** C13
Altona *Canada* 49°6N 97°33W **71** D9
Altoona *U.S.A.* 40°31N 78°24W **82** F6
Altun Kupri *Iraq* 35°45N 44°9E **44** C5
Altun Shan *Xinjiang Uygur,*
  China 39°18N 93°42E **32** D7
Altun Shan *Xinjiang Uygur,*
  China 38°30N 88°0E **32** D6
Alturas *U.S.A.* 41°29N 120°32W **76** F3
Altus *U.S.A.* 34°38N 99°20W **84** D5
Alucra *Turkey* 40°22N 38°47E **19** F6
Alūksne *Latvia* 57°24N 27°3E **9** H22
Alunite *U.S.A.* 35°59N 114°55W **79** K12
Alusi *Indonesia* 7°35S 131°40E **37** F8
Alva *U.S.A.* 36°48N 98°40W **84** C5
Alvarado *Mexico* 18°46N 95°46W **87** D5
Alvarado *U.S.A.* 32°24N 97°13W **84** E6
Alvaro Obregón, Presa
  Mexico 27°52N 109°52W **86** B3
Alvear *Argentina* 29°5S 56°30W **94** B4
Alvesta *Sweden* 56°54N 14°35E **9** H16
Alvin *U.S.A.* 29°26N 95°15W **84** G7
Alvinston *Canada* 42°49N 81°52W **82** D3
Älvkarleby *Sweden* 60°34N 17°26E **9** F17
Alvord Desert *U.S.A.* 42°30N 118°25W **76** E4
Älvsbyn *Sweden* 65°40N 21°0E **8** D19
Alwar *India* 27°38N 76°34E **42** F7
Alxa Zuoqi *China* 38°50N 105°40E **34** E3
Alyangula *Australia* 13°55S 136°30E **62** A2
Alyata = Älät *Azerbaijan* 39°58N 49°25E **45** B6
Alyth *U.K.* 56°38N 3°13W **11** E5
Alytus *Lithuania* 54°24N 24°3E **9** J21
Alzada *U.S.A.* 45°2N 104°25W **76** D11
Alzamay *Russia* 55°33N 98°39E **29** D10
Alzira *Spain* 39°9N 0°30W **21** C5
Am Timan *Chad* 11°0N 20°10E **51** F10
Amadeus, L. *Australia* 24°54S 131°0E **61** D5
Amadi
  Dem. Rep. of the Congo 3°40N 26°40E **54** B2
Âmâdi *Sudan* 5°29N 30°25E **51** G12
Amadjuak L. *Canada* 65°0N 71°8W **69** E17
Amagansett *U.S.A.* 40°59N 72°9W **83** F12
Amagasaki *Japan* 34°42N 135°23E **31** G7
Amagi *Japan* 33°25N 130°39E **31** H5
Amahai *Indonesia* 3°20S 128°55E **37** E7
Amaile *Samoa* 13°59S 171°22W **59** b
Amakusa-Shotō *Japan* 32°15N 130°10E **31** H5
Åmål *Sweden* 59°3N 12°42E **9** G15
Amaliada *Greece* 37°47N 21°22E **23** F9
Amalner *India* 21°5N 75°5E **40** J9
Amamapare *Indonesia* 4°53S 136°38E **37** E9
Amambaí *Brazil* 23°5S 55°13W **95** A4
Amambaí ➤ *Brazil* 23°22S 53°56W **95** A5
Amambay □ *Paraguay* 23°0S 56°0W **95** A4
Amambay, Cordillera de
  S. Amer. 23°0S 55°45W **95** A4
Amami-Guntō *Japan* 27°16N 129°21E **31** L4
Amami-Ō-Shima *Japan* 28°16N 129°21E **31** K4
Aman, Pulau *Malaysia* 5°16N 100°24E **39** c
Amaná, L. *Brazil* 2°35S 64°40W **92** D6
Amanat ➤ *India* 24°7N 84°4E **43** G11
Amanda Park *U.S.A.* 47°28N 123°55W **78** C3
Amankeldi *Kazakhstan* 50°10N 65°10E **28** D7
Amapá *Brazil* 2°5N 50°50W **93** C8
Amapá □ *Brazil* 1°40N 52°0W **93** C8
Amarante *Brazil* 6°14S 42°50W **93** E10
Amaranth *Canada* 50°36N 98°43W **71** C9
Amargosa Desert
  U.S.A. 36°40N 116°30W **79** J10
Amargosa Range
  U.S.A. 36°20N 116°45W **79** J10
Amari *Greece* 35°13N 24°40E **25** D6
Amarillo *U.S.A.* 35°13N 101°50W **84** D4
Amarkantak *India* 22°40N 81°45E **43** H9
Amaro, Mte. *Italy* 42°5N 14°5E **22** C6
Amarpur *India* 25°5N 87°0E **43** G12
Amarwara *India* 22°18N 79°10E **43** H8
Amasya *Turkey* 40°40N 35°50E **19** F5
Amata *Australia* 26°9S 131°9E **61** E5

Amatikulu *S. Africa* 29°3S 31°33E **57** D5
Amatitlán *Guatemala* 14°29N 90°38W **88** D1
Amay *Belgium* 50°33N 5°19E **15** D5
Amazon = Amazonas →
S. Amer. 0°5S 50°0W **93** D8
Amazonas □ *Brazil* 5°0S 65°0W **92** E6
Amazonas → *S. Amer.* 0°5S 50°0W **93** D8
Ambah *India* 26°43N 78°13E **42** F8
Ambahakily *Madag.* 21°36S 43°41E **57** C7
Ambahita *Madag.* 24°1S 45°16E **57** C8
Ambala *India* 30°23N 76°56E **42** D7
Ambalavao *Madag.* 21°50S 46°56E **57** C8
Ambanja *Madag.* 13°40S 48°27E **57** A8
Ambararata *Madag.* 15°3S 48°33E **57** B8
Ambarchik *Russia* 69°40N 162°20E **29** C17
Ambarijeby *Madag.* 14°56S 47°41E **57** A8
Ambaro, Helodranon'
Madag. 13°23S 48°38E **57** A8
Ambato *Ecuador* 1°5S 78°42W **92** D3
Ambato *Madag.* 13°24S 48°29E **57** A8
Ambato, Sierra de
Argentina 28°25S 66°10W **94** B2
Ambato Boeny *Madag.* 16°28S 46°43E **57** B8
Ambatofinandrahana
Madag. 20°33S 46°48E **57** C8
Ambatolampy *Madag.* 19°20S 47°35E **57** B8
Ambatomainty *Madag.* 17°41S 45°40E **57** B8
Ambatomanoina *Madag.* 18°18S 47°37E **57** B8
Ambatondrazaka
Madag. 17°55S 48°28E **57** B8
Ambatosoratra *Madag.* 17°37S 48°31E **57** B8
Ambenja *Madag.* 15°17S 46°58E **57** B8
Amberg *Germany* 49°26N 11°52E **16** D6
Ambergris Cay *Belize* 18°0N 87°55W **87** D7
Amberley *Canada* 44°2N 81°42W **82** B3
Amberley *N.Z.* 43°9S 172°44E **59** E4
Ambikapur *India* 23°15N 83°15E **43** H10
Ambilobé *Madag.* 13°10S 49°3E **57** A8
Ambinanindrano *Madag.* 20°5S 48°23E **57** C8
Ambinanitelo *Madag.* 15°21S 49°35E **57** B8
Ambinda *Madag.* 16°25S 45°52E **57** B8
Amble *U.K.* 55°20N 1°36W **12** B6
Ambleside *U.K.* 54°26N 2°58W **12** C5
Ambo *Peru* 10°5S 76°10W **92** F3
Amboahangy *Madag.* 24°15S 46°22E **57** C8
Ambodifototra *Madag.* 16°59S 49°52E **57** B8
Ambodilazana *Madag.* 18°6S 49°10E **57** B8
Ambodiriana *Madag.* 17°55S 49°18E **57** B8
Ambohidratrimo *Madag.* 18°50S 47°26E **57** B8
Ambohidray *Madag.* 18°36S 48°18E **57** B8
Ambohimahamasina
Madag. 21°56S 47°11E **57** C8
Ambohimahasoa *Madag.* 21°7S 47°13E **57** C8
Ambohimanga *Madag.* 20°52S 47°36E **57** C8
Ambohimitombo *Madag.* 20°43S 47°26E **57** C8
Ambohitra *Madag.* 12°30S 49°10E **57** A8
Amboise *France* 47°24N 1°2E **20** C4
Ambon *Indonesia* 3°43S 128°12E **37** E7
Ambondro *Madag.* 25°13S 45°44E **57** D8
Amboseli, L. *Kenya* 2°40S 37°10E **54** C4
Amboseli △ *Kenya* 2°37S 37°13E **54** C4
Ambositra *Madag.* 20°31S 47°25E **57** C8
Ambovombe *Madag.* 25°11S 46°5E **57** D8
Amboy *U.S.A.* 34°33N 115°45W **79** L11
Amboyna Cay
S. China Sea 7°50N 112°50E **36** C4
Ambridge *U.S.A.* 40°36N 80°14W **82** F4
Ambriz *Angola* 7°48S 13°8E **52** F2
Amchitka I. *U.S.A.* 51°32N 179°0E **74** E3
Amderma *Russia* 69°45N 61°30E **28** C7
Amdhi *India* 23°51N 81°27E **43** H9
Amdo *China* 32°20N 91°40E **32** E7
Ameca *Mexico* 20°33N 104°2W **86** C4
Ameca → *Mexico* 20°41N 105°18W **86** C3
Amecameca de Juárez
Mexico 19°8N 98°46W **87** D5
Amed *Indonesia* 8°19S 115°39E **37** J18
Ameland *Neths.* 53°27N 5°45E **15** A5
Amenia *U.S.A.* 41°51N 73°33W **83** E11
America-Antarctica Ridge
S. Ocean 59°0S 16°0W **5** B2
American Falls *U.S.A.* 42°47N 112°51W **76** E7
American Falls Res.
U.S.A. 42°47N 112°52W **76** E7
American Fork *U.S.A.* 40°23N 111°48W **76** F8
American Highland
Antarctica 73°0S 75°0E **5** D6
American Samoa ☒
Pac. Oc. 14°20S 170°0W **59** b
American Samoa △
Amer. Samoa 14°15S 170°28W **59** b
Americana *Brazil* 22°45S 47°20W **95** A6
Americus *U.S.A.* 32°4N 84°14W **85** E12
Amersfoort *Neths.* 52°9N 5°23E **15** B5
Amersfoort *S. Africa* 26°59S 29°53E **57** D4
Amery Basin *S. Ocean* 68°15S 74°30E **5** C6
Amery Ice Shelf *Antarctica* 69°30S 72°0E **5** C6
Ames *U.S.A.* 42°2N 93°37W **80** D7
Amesbury *U.S.A.* 42°51N 70°56W **83** D14
Amet *India* 25°18N 73°56E **42** G5
Amga *Russia* 60°50N 132°0E **29** C14
Amga → *Russia* 62°38N 134°32E **29** C14
Amgu *Russia* 45°45N 137°15E **30** B8
Amgun → *Russia* 52°56N 139°38E **29** D14
Amherst *Canada* 45°48N 64°8W **73** C7
Amherst *Mass., U.S.A.* 42°23N 72°31W **83** D12
Amherst *N.Y., U.S.A.* 42°59N 78°48W **82** D6
Amherst *Ohio, U.S.A.* 41°24N 82°14W **82** E2
Amherst I. *Canada* 44°8N 76°43W **83** B8
Amherstburg *Canada* 42°6N 83°6W **72** D3
Amiata, Mte. *Italy* 42°53N 11°37E **22** C4
Amidon *U.S.A.* 46°29N 103°19W **80** B2
Amiens *France* 49°54N 2°16E **20** B5
Aminuis *Namibia* 23°43S 19°21E **56** C2
Amīrābād *Iran* 33°20N 46°16E **44** C5
Amirante Is. *Seychelles* 6°0S 53°0E **26** J7
Amisk ⌂ *Canada* 56°43N 98°0W **71** B9
Amisk L. *Canada* 54°35N 102°15W **71** C8
Amistad, Presa de la
Mexico 29°26N 101°3W **86** B4
Amistad ⌂ *U.S.A.* 29°32N 101°12W **84** G4
Amite *U.S.A.* 30°44N 90°30W **85** F9
Amla *India* 21°56N 78°7E **42** J8
Amlapura *Indonesia* 8°27S 115°37E **37** J18
Amlia I. *U.S.A.* 52°4N 173°30W **74** E5
Amlwch *U.K.* 53°24N 4°20W **12** D3
'Ammān *Jordan* 31°57N 35°52E **46** D4
'Ammān □ *Jordan* 31°40N 36°30E **46** D5
'Ammān ✈ (AMM)
Jordan 31°45N 36°2E **46** D5
Ammanford *U.K.* 51°48N 3°59W **13** F4
Ammassalik = Tasiilaq
Greenland 65°40N 37°20W **4** C6
Ammochostos = Famagusta
Cyprus 35°8N 33°55E **25** D12
Ammon *U.S.A.* 43°28N 111°58W **76** E8
Amnat Charoen
Thailand 15°51N 104°38E **38** E5
Amnura *Bangla.* 24°37N 88°25E **43** G13
Āmol *Iran* 36°23N 52°20E **45** B7
Amorgos *Greece* 36°50N 25°57E **23** F11
Amory *U.S.A.* 33°59N 88°29W **85** E10
Amos *Canada* 48°35N 78°5W **72** C4
Åmot *Norway* 59°57N 9°54E **9** G13
Amoy = Xiamen *China* 24°25N 118°4E **33** G12
Ampanavoana *Madag.* 15°41S 50°22E **57** B9
Ampang *Malaysia* 3°8N 101°45E **39** L3
Ampangalana, Lakandranon'
Madag. 22°48S 47°50E **57** C8
Ampanihy *Madag.* 24°40S 44°45E **57** C7
Amparafaravola *Madag.* 17°35S 48°13E **57** B8
Ampasinambo *Madag.* 20°31S 48°0E **57** C8
Ampasindava, Helodranon'
Madag. 13°40S 48°15E **57** A8
Ampasindava, Saikanosy
Madag. 13°42S 47°55E **57** A8
Ampenan *Indonesia* 8°34S 116°4E **37** K18
Amper → *Germany* 48°29N 11°55E **16** D6
Amphoe Kathu *Thailand* 7°55N 98°21E **39** a
Amphoe Thalang *Thailand* 8°1N 98°20E **39** a
Ampitsikinana *Madag.* 12°57S 49°49E **57** A8
Ampombiantambo
Madag. 12°42S 48°57E **57** A8
Ampotaka *Madag.* 25°3S 44°41E **57** D7
Ampoza *Madag.* 22°20S 44°44E **57** C7
Amqui *Canada* 48°28N 67°27W **73** C6
Amravati *India* 20°55N 77°45E **40** J10
Amreli *India* 21°35N 71°17E **42** J4
Amritsar *India* 31°35N 74°57E **42** D6
Amroha *India* 28°53N 78°30E **43** E8
Amsterdam *Neths.* 52°23N 4°54E **15** B4
Amsterdam *U.S.A.* 42°56N 74°11W **83** D10
Amsterdam ✈ (AMS)
Neths. 52°18N 4°45E **15** B4
Amsterdam, I. = Nouvelle
Amsterdam, Î. *Ind. Oc.* 38°30S 77°30E **3** F13
Amstetten *Austria* 48°7N 14°51E **16** D8
Amudarya → *Uzbekistan* 43°58N 59°34E **28** E6
Amund Ringnes I.
Canada 78°20N 96°25W **69** B12
Amundsen Abyssal Plain
S. Ocean 65°0S 125°0W **5** C14
Amundsen Basin *Arctic* 87°30N 80°0E **4** A
Amundsen Gulf *Canada* 71°0N 124°0W **68** C7
Amundsen Ridges
S. Ocean 69°15S 123°0W **5** C14
Amundsen-Scott *Antarctica* 90°0S 166°0E **5** E
Amundsen Sea *Antarctica* 72°0S 115°0W **5** D15
Amuntai *Indonesia* 2°28S 115°25E **36** E5
Amur → *Russia* 52°56N 141°10E **29** D15
Amurang *Indonesia* 1°5N 124°40E **37** D6
Amursk *Russia* 50°14N 136°54E **29** D14
Amyderya = Amudarya →
Uzbekistan 43°58N 59°34E **28** E6
An Bien *Vietnam* 9°45N 105°0E **39** H5
An Cabhán = Cavan
Ireland 54°0N 7°22W **10** B4
An Cóbh = Cóbh *Ireland* 51°51N 8°17W **10** E3
An Daingean = Dingle
Ireland 52°9N 10°17W **10** D1
An Hoa *Vietnam* 15°40N 108°5E **38** E7
An Khe *Vietnam* 13°57N 108°51E **38** F7
An Longfort = Longford
Ireland 53°43N 7°49W **10** C4
An Muileann gCearr = Mullingar
Ireland 53°31N 7°21W **10** C4
An Nabatīyah at Tahta
Lebanon 33°23N 35°27E **46** B4
An Nabk *Si. Arabia* 31°20N 37°20E **44** D3
An Nabk *Syria* 34°2N 36°44E **46** A5
An Nafūd *Si. Arabia* 28°15N 41°0E **44** D4
An Najaf *Iraq* 32°3N 44°15E **44** C5
An Nás = Naas *Ireland* 53°12N 6°40W **10** C5
An Nāşirīyah *Iraq* 31°0N 46°15E **44** D5
An Nhon = Binh Dinh
Vietnam 13°55N 109°7E **38** F7
An Nu'ayrīyah *Si. Arabia* 27°30N 48°30E **45** E6
An Nu'mānīyah *Iraq* 32°32N 45°25E **44** C5
An Ros = Rush *Ireland* 53°31N 6°6W **10** C5
An tAonach = Nenagh
Ireland 52°52N 8°11W **10** D3
An Thoi, Quan Dao
Vietnam 9°58N 104°0E **39** H5
An tInbhear Mór = Arklow
Ireland 52°48N 6°10W **10** D5
An Uaimh *Ireland* 53°39N 6°41W **10** C5
Anabar → *Russia* 73°8N 113°36E **29** B12
Anaconda *U.S.A.* 46°8N 112°57W **76** C7
Anacortes *U.S.A.* 48°30N 122°37W **78** B4
Anadarko *U.S.A.* 35°4N 98°15W **84** D5
Anadolu *Turkey* 39°0N 30°0E **19** G5
Anadyr *Russia* 64°35N 177°20E **29** C18
Anadyr → *Russia* 64°55N 176°5E **29** C18
Anadyrskiy Zaliv *Russia* 64°0N 180°0E **29** C19
Anaga, Pta. de *Canary Is.* 28°34N 16°9W **24** F3
'Ānah *Iraq* 34°25N 42°0E **44** C4
Anaheim *U.S.A.* 33°50N 117°55W **79** M9
Anahim Lake *Canada* 52°28N 125°18W **70** C3
Anakapalle *India* 17°42N 83°6E **41** L13
Anakie *Australia* 23°32S 147°45E **62** C4
Analalava *Madag.* 14°35S 48°0E **57** A8
Analavoka *Madag.* 22°23S 46°30E **57** C8
Analipsis *Greece* 39°36N 19°55E **25** A3
Anambar → *Pakistan* 30°15N 68°50E **42** D3
Anambas, Kepulauan
Indonesia 3°20N 106°30E **36** D3
Anambas Is. = Anambas,
Kepulauan *Indonesia* 3°20N 106°30E **36** D3
Anamosa *U.S.A.* 42°7N 91°17W **80** D8
Anamur *Turkey* 36°8N 32°58E **44** B2
Anan *Japan* 33°54N 134°40E **31** H7
Anand *India* 22°32N 72°59E **42** H5
Anangu Pitjantjatjara ☼
Australia 27°0S 132°0E **61** E5
Anantapur *India* 14°39N 77°42E **40** M10
Anantnag *India* 33°45N 75°10E **43** C6
Ananyiv *Ukraine* 47°44N 29°58E **17** E15
Anapodiaris → *Greece* 34°59N 25°20E **25** E7
Anápolis *Brazil* 16°15S 48°50W **93** G9
Anapu → *Brazil* 1°53S 50°53W **93** D8
Anār *Iran* 30°55N 55°13E **45** D7
Anārak *Iran* 33°25N 53°40E **45** C7
Anas → *India* 23°26N 74°0E **42** H5
Anatolia = Anadolu
Turkey 39°0N 30°0E **19** G5
Anatsogno *Madag.* 23°33S 43°46E **57** C7
Añatuya *Argentina* 28°20S 62°50W **94** B3
Anatye ☼ *Australia* 22°29S 137°3E **62** C2
Anaunethad L. *Canada* 60°55N 104°25W **71** A8
Anbyŏn *N. Korea* 39°1N 127°35E **35** E14
Ancaster *Canada* 43°13N 79°59W **82** C5
Anchor Bay *U.S.A.* 38°48N 123°34W **78** G3
Anchorage *U.S.A.* 61°13N 149°54W **68** E2
Anci *China* 39°20N 116°40E **34** E9
Ancohuma, Nevado
Bolivia 16°0S 68°50W **92** G5
Ancón *Peru* 11°50S 77°10W **92** F3
Ancona *Italy* 43°38N 13°30E **22** C5
Ancud *Chile* 42°0S 73°50W **96** E2
Ancud, G. de *Chile* 42°0S 73°0W **96** E2
Anda *China* 46°24N 125°19E **33** B14
Andacollo *Argentina* 37°10S 70°42W **94** D1
Andacollo *Chile* 30°14S 71°6W **94** C1
Andaingo *Madag.* 18°12S 48°17E **57** B8
Andalgalá *Argentina* 27°40S 66°30W **94** B2
Åndalsnes *Norway* 62°35N 7°43E **8** E12
Andalucía □ *Spain* 37°35N 5°0W **21** D3
Andalusia = Andalucía □
Spain 37°35N 5°0W **21** D3
Andalusia *U.S.A.* 31°18N 86°29W **85** F11
Andaman Is. *Ind. Oc.* 12°30N 92°45E **27** G11
Andaman Sea *Ind. Oc.* 13°0N 96°0E **36** B1
Andamooka *Australia* 30°27S 137°9E **63** E2
Andapa *Madag.* 14°39S 49°39E **57** A8
Andara *Namibia* 18°2S 21°9E **56** B3
Andenes *Norway* 69°19N 16°18E **8** B17
Andenne *Belgium* 50°28N 5°5E **15** D5
Anderson *Alaska,*
U.S.A. 64°25N 149°15W **74** C10
Anderson *Calif., U.S.A.* 40°27N 122°18W **76** F2
Anderson *Ind., U.S.A.* 40°10N 85°41W **81** E11
Anderson *Mo., U.S.A.* 36°39N 94°27W **80** G6
Anderson *S.C., U.S.A.* 34°31N 82°39W **85** D13
Anderson → *Canada* 69°42N 129°0W **68** D6
Andes *U.S.A.* 42°12N 74°47W **83** D10
Andes, Cord. de los
S. Amer. 20°0S 68°0W **92** H5
Andfjorden *Norway* 69°10N 16°20E **8** B17
Andhra Pradesh □ *India* 18°0N 79°0E **40** L11
Andijon *Uzbekistan* 41°10N 72°15E **32** C3
Andikíthira = Antikythira
Greece 35°52N 23°15E **23** G10
Andilamena *Madag.* 17°1S 48°35E **57** B8
Andīmeshk *Iran* 32°27N 48°21E **45** C6
Andizhan = Andijon
Uzbekistan 41°10N 72°15E **32** C3
Andoany *Madag.* 13°25S 48°16E **57** A8
Andohahela ⌂ *Madag.* 24°4S 46°44E **57** C8
Andong *S. Korea* 36°40N 128°43E **35** F15
Andorra ■ *Europe* 42°30N 1°30E **20** E4
Andorra La Vella *Andorra* 42°31N 1°32E **20** E4
Andover *U.K.* 51°12N 1°29W **13** F6
Andover *Maine, U.S.A.* 44°38N 70°45W **83** B14
Andover *Mass., U.S.A.* 42°40N 71°8W **83** D13
Andover *N.J., U.S.A.* 40°59N 74°45W **83** F10
Andover *N.Y., U.S.A.* 42°10N 77°48W **82** D7
Andover *Ohio, U.S.A.* 41°36N 80°34W **82** E4
Andøya *Norway* 69°10N 15°50E **8** B16
Andradina *Brazil* 20°54S 51°23W **93** H8
Andrahary *Madag.* 13°37S 49°17E **57** A8
Andramasina *Madag.* 19°11S 47°35E **57** B8
Andranopasy *Madag.* 21°17S 43°44E **57** C7
Andranovory *Madag.* 23°8S 44°10E **57** C7
Andratx *Spain* 39°39N 2°25E **24** B9
Andreanof Is. *U.S.A.* 51°30N 176°0W **74** E4
Andrews *S.C., U.S.A.* 33°27N 79°34W **85** E15
Andrews *Tex., U.S.A.* 32°19N 102°33W **84** E3
Ándria *Italy* 41°13N 16°17E **22** D7
Andriamena *Madag.* 17°26S 47°30E **57** B8
Andriandampy *Madag.* 22°45S 45°41E **57** C8
Andriba *Madag.* 17°30S 46°58E **57** B8
Andringitra ⌂ *Madag.* 22°13S 46°5E **57** C8
Androka *Madag.* 24°58S 44°2E **57** C7
Andros *Greece* 37°50N 24°57E **23** F11
Andros I. *Bahamas* 24°30N 78°0W **88** B4
Andros Town *Bahamas* 24°43N 77°47W **88** B4
Androscoggin →
U.S.A. 43°58N 69°52W **83** C14
Andselv *Norway* 69°4N 18°34E **8** B18
Andújar *Spain* 38°3N 4°5W **21** C3
Andulo *Angola* 11°25S 16°45E **52** G3
Anegada *Br. Virgin Is.* 18°45N 64°20W **89** e
Anegada Passage
W. Indies 18°15N 63°45W **89** C7
Aneto, Pico de *Spain* 42°37N 0°40E **21** A6
Ang Mo Kio *Singapore* 1°23N 103°50E **39** d
Ang Thong *Thailand* 14°35N 100°31E **38** E3
Ang Thong, Ko *Thailand* 9°37N 99°41E **39** b
Ang Thong, Mu Ko △
Thailand 9°40N 99°43E **39** H2
Angamos, Punta *Chile* 23°1S 70°32W **94** A1
Angara → *Russia* 58°5N 94°20E **29** D10
Angarsk *Russia* 52°30N 104°0E **32** A9
Angas Hills *Australia* 23°0S 127°50E **60** D4
Angaston *Australia* 34°30S 139°8E **63** E2
Ånge *Sweden* 62°31N 15°35E **8** E16
Ángel, Salto = Angel Falls
Venezuela 5°57N 62°30W **92** B6
Ángel de la Guarda, I.
Mexico 29°20N 113°25W **86** B2
Angel Falls *Venezuela* 5°57N 62°30W **92** B6
Angeles *Phil.* 15°9N 120°33E **37** A6
Ängelholm *Sweden* 56°15N 12°50E **9** H15
Angels Camp *U.S.A.* 38°4N 120°32W **78** G6
Ångermanälven →
Sweden 64°0N 17°20E **8** E17
Ångermanland *Sweden* 63°36N 17°45E **8** E17
Angers *Canada* 45°31N 75°29W **83** A9
Angers *France* 47°30N 0°35W **20** C3
Ängesån → *Sweden* 66°16N 22°47E **8** C20
Angikuni L. *Canada* 62°12N 99°59W **71** A9
Angkor *Cambodia* 13°22N 103°50E **38** F4
Angledool *Australia* 29°5S 147°55E **63** D4
Anglesey *U.K.* 53°17N 4°20W **12** D3
Anglesey, Isle of □ *U.K.* 53°16N 4°18W **12** D3
Angleton *U.S.A.* 29°10N 95°26W **84** G7
Anglisidhes *Cyprus* 34°51N 33°27E **25** E12
Angmagssalik = Tasiilaq
Greenland 65°40N 37°20W **4** C6
Ango *Dem. Rep. of the Congo* 4°10N 26°5E **54** B2
Angoche *Mozam.* 16°8S 39°55E **55** F4
Angoche, I. *Mozam.* 16°20S 39°50E **55** F4
Angol *Chile* 37°56S 72°45W **94** D1
Angola *Ind., U.S.A.* 41°38N 85°0W **81** E11
Angola *N.Y., U.S.A.* 42°38N 79°2W **82** D5
Angola ■ *Africa* 12°0S 18°0E **53** G3
Angoulême *France* 45°39N 0°10E **20** D4
Angoumois *France* 45°50N 0°25E **20** D3
Angra do Heroismo
Azores 38°39N 27°13W **50** a
Angra dos Reis *Brazil* 23°0S 44°10W **95** A7
Angtassom *Cambodia* 11°1N 104°41E **39** G5
Angu
Dem. Rep. of the Congo 3°23N 24°30E **54** B1
Anguang *China* 45°15N 123°45E **35** B12
Anguilla ☒ *W. Indies* 18°14N 63°5W **89** C7
Anguo *China* 38°28N 115°15E **34** E8
Angurugu *Australia* 14°0S 136°25E **62** A2
Angus *Canada* 44°19N 79°53W **82** B5
Angus □ *U.K.* 56°46N 2°56W **11** E6
Angwa → *Zimbabwe* 16°0S 30°23E **57** B5
Anhanduí → *Brazil* 21°46S 52°9W **95** A5
Anholt *Denmark* 56°42N 11°33E **9** H14
Anhui □ *China* 32°0N 117°0E **33** E12
Anhwei = Anhui □
China 32°0N 117°0E **33** E12
Anichab *Namibia* 21°0S 14°46E **56** C1
Animas → *U.S.A.* 36°43N 108°13W **77** H9
Anin *Burma* 15°36N 97°50E **38** E1
Anivorano *Madag.* 18°44S 48°58E **57** B8
Anjalankoski *Finland* 60°45N 26°51E **8** F22
Anjar *India* 23°6N 70°10E **42** H4
Anjou *France* 47°20N 0°15W **20** C3
Anjouan *Comoros Is.* 12°15S 44°20E **53** a
Anjozorobe *Madag.* 18°22S 47°52E **57** B8
Anju *N. Korea* 39°36N 125°40E **35** E13
Ankaboa, Tanjona
Madag. 21°58S 43°20E **57** C7
Ankang *China* 32°40N 109°1E **34** H5
Ankara *Turkey* 39°57N 32°54E **19** G5
Ankarafantsika ⌂ *Madag.* 16°8S 47°5E **57** B8
Ankaramena *Madag.* 21°57S 46°39E **57** C8
Ankaratra *Madag.* 19°25S 47°12E **53** H9
Ankasakasa *Madag.* 16°21S 44°52E **57** B7
Ankavandra *Madag.* 18°46S 45°18E **57** B8
Ankazoabo *Madag.* 22°18S 44°31E **57** C7
Ankazobe *Madag.* 18°20S 47°10E **57** B8
Ankeny *U.S.A.* 41°44N 93°36W **80** E7
Ankilimalinika *Madag.* 22°58S 43°45E **57** C7
Ankilizato *Madag.* 20°25S 45°1E **57** C8
Ankisabe *Madag.* 19°17S 46°29E **57** B8
Ankoro
Dem. Rep. of the Congo 6°45S 26°55E **54** D2
Ankororoka *Madag.* 25°30S 45°11E **57** D8
Anlong Veng *Cambodia* 14°14N 104°5E **38** E5
Anmyeondo *S. Korea* 36°25N 126°25E **35** F14
Ann, C. *U.S.A.* 42°38N 70°35W **83** D14
Ann Arbor *U.S.A.* 42°17N 83°45W **81** D12
Anna *U.S.A.* 37°28N 89°15W **80** G9
Annaba *Algeria* 36°50N 7°46E **50** A7
Annalee → *Ireland* 54°2N 7°24W **10** B4
Annam = Trung-Phan
Vietnam 17°0N 109°0E **38** D6
Annamitique, Chaîne
Asia 17°0N 106°0E **38** D6
Annan *U.K.* 54°59N 3°16W **11** G5
Annan → *U.K.* 54°58N 3°16W **11** G5
Annapolis *U.S.A.* 38°59N 76°30W **81** F15
Annapolis Royal *Canada* 44°44N 65°32W **73** D6
Annapurna *Nepal* 28°34N 83°50E **43** E10
Annean, L. *Australia* 26°54S 118°14E **61** E2
Annecy *France* 45°55N 6°8E **20** D7
Annette I. *U.S.A.* 55°9N 131°28W **70** B2
Anning *China* 24°55N 102°26E **32** G9
Anniston *U.S.A.* 33°39N 85°50W **85** E12
Annobón *Atl. Oc.* 1°25S 5°36E **49** G4
Annotto B. *Jamaica* 18°17N 76°45W **88** a
Annville *U.S.A.* 40°20N 76°31W **83** F8
Anogia *Greece* 35°16N 24°52E **25** D6
Anorotsangana *Madag.* 13°56S 47°55E **57** A8
Anosibe *Madag.* 19°26S 48°13E **57** B8
Anping *Hebei, China* 38°15N 115°30E **34** E8
Anping *Liaoning, China* 41°5N 123°30E **35** D12
Anqing *China* 30°30N 117°3E **33** E12
Anqiu *China* 36°25N 119°10E **35** F10
Ansai *China* 36°50N 109°20E **34** F5
Ansan *S. Korea* 37°21N 126°52E **35** F14
Ansbach *Germany* 49°28N 10°34E **16** D6
Anse Boileau *Seychelles* 4°43S 55°29E **53** b
Anse Royale *Seychelles* 4°44S 55°31E **53** b
Anshan *China* 41°5N 122°58E **35** D12
Anshun *China* 26°18N 105°57E **32** F10
Ansley *U.S.A.* 41°18N 99°23W **80** E4
Anson *U.S.A.* 32°45N 99°54W **84** E5
Anson B. *Australia* 13°20S 130°6E **60** B5
Ansongo *Mali* 15°25N 0°35E **50** E6
Ansonia *U.S.A.* 41°21N 73°5W **83** E11
Anstruther *U.K.* 56°14N 2°41W **11** E6
Ansudu *Indonesia* 2°11S 139°22E **37** E9
Antabamba *Peru* 14°40S 73°0W **92** F4
Antakya = Hatay *Turkey* 36°14N 36°10E **44** B3
Antalaha *Madag.* 14°57S 50°20E **57** A9
Antalya *Turkey* 36°52N 30°45E **19** G5
Antalya Körfezi *Turkey* 36°15N 31°30E **19** G5
Antambohobe *Madag.* 22°20S 46°47E **57** C8
Antanambao-Manampotsy
Madag. 19°29S 48°34E **57** B8
Antanambe *Madag.* 16°26S 49°52E **57** B8
Antananarivo *Madag.* 18°55S 47°31E **57** B8
Antananarivo □ *Madag.* 19°0S 47°0E **57** B8
Antanifotsy *Madag.* 19°39S 47°19E **57** B8
Antanimbaribe *Madag.* 21°30S 44°48E **57** C7
Antanimora *Madag.* 24°49S 45°40E **57** C8
Antarctic Pen. *Antarctica* 67°0S 60°0W **5** C18
Antarctica 90°0S 0°0 **5** E3
Antelope *Zimbabwe* 21°2S 28°31E **55** G2
Antequera *Paraguay* 24°8S 57°7W **94** A4
Antequera *Spain* 37°5N 4°33W **21** D3
Antero, Mt. *U.S.A.* 38°41N 106°15W **76** G10
Antevamena *Madag.* 21°2S 44°8E **57** C7
Anthony *Kans., U.S.A.* 37°9N 98°2W **80** G4
Anthony *N. Mex.,*
U.S.A. 32°0N 106°36W **77** K10
Anti Atlas *Morocco* 30°0N 8°30W **50** C4
Anti-Lebanon = Sharqi, Al Jabal
ash *Lebanon* 33°40N 36°10E **46** B5
Antibes *France* 43°34N 7°6E **20** E7
Anticosti, Î. d' *Canada* 49°30N 63°0W **73** C7
Antigo *U.S.A.* 45°9N 89°9W **80** C9
Antigonish *Canada* 45°38N 61°58W **73** C7
Antigua *Canary Is.* 28°24N 14°1W **24** F5
Antigua *Guatemala* 14°34N 90°41W **88** D1
Antigua *W. Indies* 17°0N 61°50W **89** C7
Antigua & Barbuda ■
W. Indies 17°20N 61°48W **89** C7
Antikythira *Greece* 35°52N 23°15E **23** G10
Antilla *Cuba* 20°40N 75°50W **88** B4
Antilles = West Indies
Cent. Amer. 15°0N 65°0W **89** D7
Antioch *U.S.A.* 38°1N 121°48W **78** G5
Antioquia *Colombia* 6°40N 75°55W **92** B3
Antipodes Is. *Pac. Oc.* 49°45S 178°40E **64** M9
Antlers *U.S.A.* 34°14N 95°37W **84** D7
Antoetra *Madag.* 20°46S 47°20E **57** C8
Antofagasta *Chile* 23°50S 70°30W **94** A1
Antofagasta □ *Chile* 24°0S 69°0W **94** A2
Antofagasta de la Sierra
Argentina 26°5S 67°20W **94** B2
Antofalla *Argentina* 25°30S 68°5W **94** B2
Antofalla, Salar de
Argentina 25°40S 67°45W **94** B2
Anton *U.S.A.* 33°49N 102°10W **84** E3
Antongila, Helodrano
Madag. 15°30S 49°50E **57** B8
Antonibé *Madag.* 15°7S 47°24E **57** B8
Antonibé, Presqu'île d'
Madag. 14°55S 47°20E **57** A8
Antonina *Brazil* 25°26S 48°42W **95** B6
Antrim *U.K.* 54°43N 6°14W **10** B5
Antrim *U.S.A.* 40°7N 81°21W **82** F3
Antrim □ *U.K.* 54°56N 6°25W **10** B5
Antrim, Mts. of *U.K.* 55°3N 6°14W **10** A5
Antrim Plateau *Australia* 18°8S 128°20E **60** C4
Antsakabary *Madag.* 15°3S 48°56E **57** B8
Antsalova *Madag.* 18°40S 44°37E **57** B7
Antsenavolo *Madag.* 21°24S 48°3E **57** C8
Antsiafabositra *Madag.* 17°18S 46°57E **57** B8
Antsirabe *Antananarivo,*
Madag. 19°55S 47°2E **57** B8
Antsirabe *Antsiranana,*
Madag. 14°0S 49°59E **57** A8
Antsirabe *Mahajanga,*
Madag. 15°57S 48°58E **57** B8
Antsiranana *Madag.* 12°25S 49°20E **57** A8
Antsiranana □ *Madag.* 12°16S 49°17E **57** A8
Antsohihy *Madag.* 14°50S 47°59E **57** A8
Antsohimbondrona Seranana
Madag. 13°7S 48°48E **57** A8
Antu *China* 42°30N 128°20E **35** C15
Antwerp = Antwerpen
Belgium 51°13N 4°25E **15** C4
Antwerp *U.S.A.* 44°12N 75°37W **83** B9
Antwerpen *Belgium* 51°13N 4°25E **15** C4
Antwerpen □ *Belgium* 51°15N 4°40E **15** C4
Anupgarh *India* 29°10N 73°10E **42** E5
Anuppur *India* 23°6N 81°41E **43** H9
Anuradhapura *Sri Lanka* 8°22N 80°28E **40** Q12
Anurrete ☼ *Australia* 20°50S 135°38E **62** C2
Anveh *Iran* 27°23N 54°11E **45** E7
Anvers = Antwerpen
Belgium 51°13N 4°25E **15** C4
Anvers I. *Antarctica* 64°30S 63°40W **5** C17
Anxi *China* 40°30N 95°43E **32** C8
Anxious B. *Australia* 33°24S 134°45E **63** E1
Anyang *China* 36°5N 114°21E **34** F8
Anyang *S. Korea* 37°23N 126°55E **35** F14
Anyer *Indonesia* 6°4S 105°53E **37** G11
Anyi *China* 35°2N 111°2E **34** G6
Anza *U.S.A.* 33°35N 116°39W **79** M10
Anze *China* 36°10N 112°12E **34** F7
Anzhero-Sudzhensk
Russia 56°10N 86°0E **28** D9
Ánzio *Italy* 41°27N 12°37E **22** D5
Ao Makham *Thailand* 7°50N 98°24E **39** a
Ao Phangnga △ *Thailand* 8°10N 98°32E **39** a
Aoga-Shima *Japan* 32°28N 139°46E **31** H9
Aohan Qi *China* 43°18N 119°43E **35** C10
Aoji *N. Korea* 42°31N 130°23E **35** C16
Aomen = Macau *China* 22°12N 113°33E **33** a
Aomori *Japan* 40°45N 140°45E **30** D10

Aomori □ Japan 40°45N 140°40E 30 D10
Aonla India 28°16N 79°11E 43 E8
Aorai, Mt. Tahiti 17°34S 149°30W 59 d
Aoraki Mount Cook
  N.Z. 43°36S 170°9E 59 E3
Aoral, Phnum Cambodia 12°0N 104°15E 39 G5
Aosta Italy 45°45N 7°20E 20 D7
Aotearoa = New Zealand ■
  Oceania 40°0S 176°0E 59 D6
Aoukâr Mauritania 17°40N 10°0W 50 E3
Aozou, Couloir d' Chad 22°0N 19°0E 51 D9
Apá → S. Amer. 22°6S 58°2W 94 A4
Apache U.S.A. 34°54N 98°22W 84 D5
Apache Junction
  U.S.A. 33°25N 111°33W 77 K8
Apalachee B. U.S.A. 30°0N 84°0W 85 G13
Apalachicola U.S.A. 29°43N 84°59W 85 G12
Apalachicola →
  U.S.A. 29°43N 84°58W 85 G12
Apaporis → Colombia 1°23S 69°25W 92 D5
Aparados da Serra △
  Brazil 29°10S 50°8W 95 B5
Aparri Phil. 18°22N 121°38E 37 A6
Apatity Russia 67°34N 33°22E 8 C25
Apatula = Finke
  Australia 25°34S 134°35E 62 D1
Apatzingán Mexico 19°5N 102°21W 86 D4
Apeldoorn Neths. 52°13N 5°57E 15 B5
Apennines = Appennini
  Italy 44°30N 10°0E 22 B4
Api Nepal 30°0N 80°57E 32 F5
Apia Samoa 13°50S 171°50W 59 b
Apiacás, Serra dos Brazil 9°50S 57°0W 92 E7
Apies → S. Africa 25°15S 28°8E 57 D4
Apizaco Mexico 19°25N 98°8W 87 D5
Aplao Peru 16°0S 72°40W 92 G4
Apo, Mt. Phil. 6°53N 125°14E 37 C7
Apolakia Greece 36°5N 27°48E 25 C9
Apolakia, Ormos Greece 36°5N 27°45E 25 C9
Apollonia = Marsá Súsah
  Libya 32°52N 21°59E 51 B10
Apollonia Greece 36°15N 27°58E 25 D9
Apolo Bolivia 14°30S 68°30W 92 F5
Apopa El Salv. 13°48N 89°10W 88 D2
Aporé → Brazil 19°27S 50°57W 93 G8
Apostle Is. U.S.A. 47°0N 90°40W 80 B8
Apostle Islands △ U.S.A. 46°55N 91°0W 80 B8
Apóstoles Argentina 28°0S 56°0W 95 B4
Apostolos Andreas, C.
  Cyprus 35°42N 34°35E 25 D13
Apoteri Guyana 4°2N 58°32W 92 C7
Appalachian Mts. U.S.A. 38°0N 80°0W 81 G14
Appennini Italy 44°30N 10°0E 22 B4
Apple Hill Canada 45°13N 74°46W 83 A10
Apple Valley U.S.A. 34°32N 117°14W 79 L9
Appleby-in-Westmorland
  U.K. 54°35N 2°29W 12 C5
Appledore U.K. 51°3N 4°13F 13 F3
Appleton U.S.A. 44°16N 88°25W 80 C9
Approuague →
  Fr. Guiana 4°30N 51°57W 93 C8
Aprília Italy 41°36N 12°39E 22 D5
Apsley Canada 44°45N 78°6W 82 B6
Apucarana Brazil 23°55S 51°33W 95 A5
Apure → Venezuela 7°37N 66°25W 92 B5
Apurimac → Peru 12°17S 73°56W 92 F4
Āq Qālā Iran 37°10N 54°30E 45 B7
Aqaba = Al 'Aqabah
  Jordan 29°31N 35°0E 46 F4
'Aqaba, G. of Red Sea 29°0N 34°40E 44 D2
'Aqabah, Khalīj al = Aqaba, G. of
  Red Sea 29°0N 34°40E 44 D2
'Aqdā Iran 32°26N 53°37E 45 C7
'Aqrah Iraq 36°46N 43°45E 44 B4
Aqsay Kazakhstan 51°11N 53°0E 19 D9
Aqtaū Kazakhstan 43°39N 51°12E 19 F9
Aqtöbe Kazakhstan 50°17N 57°10E 19 D10
Aqtogay Kazakhstan 46°57N 79°40E 28 E8
Aquidauana Brazil 20°30S 55°50W 93 H7
Aquila Mexico 18°36N 103°30W 86 D4
Aquiles Serdán Mexico 28°36N 105°53W 86 B3
Aquin Haiti 18°16N 73°24W 89 C5
Aquitain, Bassin France 44°0N 0°30W 20 D3
Ar Horqin Qi China 43°45N 120°0E 35 C11
Ar Rafid Syria 32°57N 35°52E 46 C4
Ar Raḥḥālīyah Iraq 32°44N 43°23E 44 C4
Ar Ramādī Iraq 33°25N 43°20E 44 C4
Ar Ramtha Jordan 32°34N 36°0E 46 C5
Ar Raqqah Syria 35°59N 39°8E 44 C3
Ar Rashidiya = Er Rachidia
  Morocco 31°58N 4°20W 50 B5
Ar Rass Si. Arabia 25°50N 43°40E 44 E4
Ar Rayyan Qatar 25°17N 51°25E 45 E6
Ar Rifā'ī Iraq 31°50N 46°10E 44 D5
Ar Riyāḍ Si. Arabia 24°41N 46°42E 44 E5
Ar Ru'ays Qatar 26°8N 51°12E 45 E6
Ar Rukhaymīyah Iraq 29°22N 45°38E 44 D5
Ar Rumaythah Iraq 31°31N 45°12E 44 D5
Ar Ruṣāfah Syria 35°45N 38°49E 44 C3
Ar Ruṭbah Iraq 33°0N 40°15E 44 C4
Ara India 25°35N 84°32E 43 G11
Arab U.S.A. 34°19N 86°30W 85 D11
'Arab, Bahr el → Sudan 9°0N 29°30E 51 G11
'Arab, Shatt al → Asia 29°57N 48°34E 45 D6
'Arabābād Iran 33°2N 57°41E 45 C8
Arabia Asia 25°0N 45°0E 26 F6
Arabian Desert = Es Sahrâ' Esh
  Sharqîya Egypt 27°30N 32°30E 51 C12
Arabian Gulf = Persian Gulf
  Asia 27°0N 50°0E 45 E6
Arabian Sea Ind. Oc. 16°0N 65°0E 26 G8
Aracaju Brazil 10°55S 37°4W 93 F11
Aracati Brazil 4°30S 37°44W 93 D11
Araçatuba Brazil 21°10S 50°30W 95 A5
Aracena Spain 37°53N 6°38W 21 D2
Araçuaí Brazil 16°52S 42°4W 93 G10
'Arad Israel 31°15N 35°12E 46 D4
Arad Romania 46°10N 21°20E 17 E11
Arādān Iran 35°21N 52°30E 45 C7
Aradhippou Cyprus 34°57N 33°36E 25 E12

Arafura Sea E. Indies 9°0S 135°0E 58 B6
Aragón □ Spain 41°25N 0°40W 21 B5
Aragón → Spain 42°13N 1°44W 21 A5
Araguacema Brazil 8°50S 49°20W 93 E9
Araguaia → Brazil 5°21S 48°41W 93 E9
Araguaína Brazil 7°12S 48°12W 93 E9
Araguari Brazil 18°38S 48°11W 93 G9
Araguari → Brazil 1°15N 49°55W 93 C9
Arain India 26°27N 75°2E 42 F6
Arak Algeria 25°20N 3°45E 50 C6
Arāk Iran 34°0N 49°40E 45 C6
Arakan Coast Burma 19°0N 94°0E 41 K19
Arakan Yoma Burma 20°0N 94°40E 41 K19
Araks = Aras, Rūd-e →
  Asia 40°5N 48°29E 44 B5
Aral Kazakhstan 46°41N 61°45E 28 E7
Aral Sea Asia 44°30N 60°0E 28 E7
Aral Tengizi = Aral Sea
  Asia 44°30N 60°0E 28 E7
Aralsk = Aral Kazakhstan 46°41N 61°45E 28 E7
Aralskoye More = Aral Sea
  Asia 44°30N 60°0E 28 E7
Aramac Australia 22°58S 145°14E 62 C4
Aran I. Ireland 55°0N 8°30W 10 A3
Aran Is. Ireland 53°6N 9°38W 10 C2
Aranda de Duero Spain 41°39N 3°42W 21 B4
Arandán Iran 35°23N 46°55E 44 C5
Aranjuez Spain 40°1N 3°40W 21 B4
Aranos Namibia 24°9S 19°7E 56 C2
Aransas Pass U.S.A. 27°55N 97°9W 84 H6
Aranyaprathet Thailand 13°41N 102°30E 38 F4
Arapahoe U.S.A. 40°18N 99°54W 80 E4
Arapey Grande →
  Uruguay 30°55S 57°49W 94 C4
Arapgir Turkey 39°5N 38°30E 44 B3
Arapiraca Brazil 9°45S 36°39W 93 E11
Arapongas Brazil 23°29S 51°28W 95 A5
Ar'ar Si. Arabia 30°59N 41°2E 44 D4
Araranguá Brazil 29°0S 49°30W 95 B6
Araraquara Brazil 21°50S 48°0W 93 H9
Ararás, Serra das Brazil 25°0S 53°10W 95 B5
Ararat Australia 37°16S 142°58E 63 F3
Ararat, Mt. = Ağrı Dağı
  Turkey 39°50N 44°15E 44 B5
Araria India 26°9N 87°33E 43 F12
Araripe, Chapada do
  Brazil 7°20S 40°0W 93 E11
Araruama, L. de Brazil 22°53S 42°12W 95 A7
Aras, Rūd-e → Asia 40°5N 48°29E 44 B5
Arauca Colombia 7°0N 70°40W 92 B4
Arauca → Venezuela 7°24N 66°35W 92 B5
Arauco Chile 37°16S 73°25W 94 D1
Aravalli Range India 25°0N 73°30E 42 G5
Arawale → Kenya 1°24S 40°9E 54 C5
Araxá Brazil 19°35S 46°55W 93 G9
Araya, Pen. de Venezuela 10°40N 64°0W 92 A6
Arba Minch Ethiopia 6°0N 37°30E 47 F2
Arbat Iraq 35°25N 45°35E 44 C5
Arbatax Italy 39°56N 9°42E 22 E3
Arbīl Iraq 36°15N 44°5E 44 B5
Arborfield Canada 53°6N 103°39W 71 C8
Arborg Canada 50°54N 97°13W 71 C9
Arbroath U.K. 56°34N 2°35W 11 E6
Arbuckle U.S.A. 39°1N 122°3W 78 F4
Arcachon France 44°40N 1°10W 20 D3
Arcade U.S.A. 42°32N 78°25W 82 D6
Arcadia Fla., U.S.A. 27°13N 81°52W 85 H14
Arcadia La., U.S.A. 32°33N 92°55W 84 E8
Arcadia Pa., U.S.A. 40°47N 78°51W 82 F6
Arcata U.S.A. 40°52N 124°5W 76 F1
Archangel = Arkhangelsk
  Russia 64°38N 40°36E 18 B7
Archangelos Greece 36°13N 28°7E 25 C10
Archbald U.S.A. 41°30N 75°32W 83 E9
Archer → Australia 13°28S 141°41E 62 A3
Archer B. Australia 13°20S 141°30E 62 A3
Archer Bend = Mungkan
  Kandju △ Australia 13°35S 142°52E 62 A3
Archers Post Kenya 0°35N 37°35E 54 B4
Arches △ U.S.A. 38°45N 109°25W 76 G9
Archipel-de-Mingan △
  Canada 50°13N 63°10W 73 B7
Archipiélago Chinijo △
  Canary Is. 29°20N 13°30W 24 E6
Archipiélago Los Roques △
  Venezuela 11°50N 66°44W 89 D6
Arckaringa Cr. →
  Australia 28°10S 135°22E 63 D2
Arco U.S.A. 43°38N 113°18W 76 E7
Arcos de la Frontera
  Spain 36°45N 5°49W 21 D3
Arcot India 12°53N 79°20E 40 N11
Arctic Bay Canada 73°1N 85°7W 69 C14
Arctic Mid-Ocean Ridge
  Arctic 87°0N 90°0E 4 A
Arctic Ocean Arctic 78°0N 160°0W 4 B18
Arctic Red River = Tsiigehtchic
  Canada 67°15N 134°0W 68 D5
Arctowski Antarctica 62°30S 58°0W 5 C18
Arda → Bulgaria 41°40N 26°30E 23 D12
Ardabīl Iran 38°15N 48°18E 45 B6
Ardabīl □ Iran 38°15N 48°18E 45 B6
Ardakān = Sepīdān Iran 30°20N 52°5E 45 D7
Ardakān Iran 32°19N 53°59E 45 C7
Ardara Ireland 54°46N 8°25W 10 B3
Ardee Ireland 53°52N 6°33W 10 C5
Arden Canada 44°43N 76°56W 82 B8
Arden Calif., U.S.A. 38°36N 121°33W 78 G5
Arden Nev., U.S.A. 36°1N 115°14W 79 J11
Ardenne Belgium 49°50N 5°5E 15 E5
Ardennes = Ardenne
  Belgium 49°50N 5°5E 15 E5
Arderin Ireland 53°2N 7°39W 10 C4
Ardestān Iran 33°20N 52°25E 45 C7
Ardfert Ireland 52°20N 9°47W 10 D2
Ardglass U.K. 54°16N 5°36W 10 B6
Ardivachar Pt. U.K. 57°23N 7°26W 11 D1
Ardlethan Australia 34°22S 146°53E 63 E4
Ardmore Okla., U.S.A. 34°10N 97°8W 84 D6
Ardmore Pa., U.S.A. 40°2N 75°17W 83 F9

Ardnamurchan, Pt. of
  U.K. 56°43N 6°14W 11 E2
Ardnave Pt. U.K. 55°53N 6°20W 11 F2
Ardrossan Australia 34°26S 137°53E 63 E2
Ardrossan U.K. 55°39N 4°49W 11 F4
Arecibo Puerto Rico 18°29N 66°43W 89 d
Areia Branca Brazil 5°0S 37°0W 93 E11
Arena, Pt. U.S.A. 38°57N 123°44W 78 G3
Arenal Honduras 15°21N 86°50W 88 C2
Arendal Norway 58°28N 8°46E 9 G13
Arequipa Peru 16°20S 71°30W 92 G4
Arévalo Spain 41°3N 4°43W 21 B3
Arezzo Italy 43°25N 11°53E 22 C4
Arga Turkey 38°21N 37°59E 44 B3
Arganda del Rey Spain 40°19N 3°26W 21 B4
Argarapa ◌ Australia 22°20S 134°58E 62 C1
Argenta Canada 50°11N 116°56W 70 C5
Argentan France 48°45N 0°1W 20 B3
Argentário, Mte. Italy 42°24N 11°9E 22 C4
Argentia Canada 47°18N 53°58W 73 C9
Argentina ■ S. Amer. 35°0S 66°0W 96 D3
Argentine Basin Atl. Oc. 45°0S 45°0W 96 F6
Argentino, L. Argentina 50°10S 73°0W 96 G2
Argeş → Romania 44°5N 26°38E 17 F14
Arghandab → Afghan. 31°30N 64°15E 42 D1
Argirades Greece 39°27N 19°58E 25 B3
Argiroupoli Greece 35°17N 24°20E 25 D6
Argolikos Kolpos Greece 37°20N 22°52E 23 F10
Argos Greece 37°40N 22°43E 23 F10
Argostoli Greece 38°11N 20°29E 23 E9
Arguello, Pt. U.S.A. 34°35N 120°39W 79 L6
Arguineguín Canary Is. 27°46N 15°41W 24 G4
Argun → Russia 53°20N 121°28E 33 A13
Argungu Nigeria 12°40N 4°31E 50 F6
Argus Pk. U.S.A. 35°52N 117°26W 79 K9
Argyle, L. Australia 16°20S 128°40E 60 C4
Argyle U.S.A. 56°6N 5°10W 11 E3
Argyll △ U.K. 56°13N 5°28W 11 E3
Argyll & Bute □ U.K. 56°13N 5°28W 11 E3
Århus Denmark 56°8N 10°11E 9 H14
Ariadnoye Russia 45°8N 134°25E 30 B7
Ariamsvlei Namibia 28°9S 19°51E 56 D2
Ariana Tunisia 36°52N 10°12E 51 A8
Arica Chile 18°32S 70°20W 92 G4
Arica Colombia 2°0S 71°50W 92 D4
Arico Canary Is. 28°9N 16°29W 24 F3
Arid, C. Australia 34°1S 123°10E 61 F3
Arida Japan 34°5N 135°8E 31 G7
Aride Seychelles 4°13S 55°40E 53 b
Ariège → France 43°30N 1°25E 20 E4
Arila, Akra Greece 39°43N 19°39E 25 A3
Arima Trin. & Tob. 10°38N 61°17W 93 K15
Arinos → Brazil 10°25S 58°20W 92 F7
Ario de Rosales Mexico 19°12N 101°43W 86 D4
Aripo, Mt. Trin. & Tob. 10°45N 61°15W 93 K15
Aripuanã Brazil 9°25S 60°30W 92 E6
Aripuanã → Brazil 5°7S 60°25W 92 E6
Ariquemes Brazil 9°55S 63°6W 92 E6
Arisaig U.K. 56°55N 5°51W 11 E3
Aristazabal I. Canada 52°40N 129°10W 70 C3
Arivonimamo Madag. 19°1S 47°11E 57 B8
Arizaro, Salar de
  Argentina 24°40S 67°50W 94 A2
Arizona Argentina 35°45S 65°25W 94 D2
Arizona □ U.S.A. 34°0N 112°0W 77 J8
Arizpe Mexico 30°20N 110°10W 86 A2
'Arjah Si. Arabia 24°43N 44°17E 44 E5
Arjeplog Sweden 66°3N 17°54E 8 C17
Arjepluovve = Arjeplog
  Sweden 66°3N 17°54E 8 C17
Arjona Colombia 10°14N 75°22W 92 A3
Arjuna Indonesia 7°49S 112°34E 37 G15
Arka Russia 60°15N 142°0E 29 C15
Arkadelphia U.S.A. 34°7N 93°4W 84 D8
Arkaig, L. U.K. 56°59N 5°10W 11 E3
Arkalyk = Arqalyk
  Kazakhstan 50°13N 66°50E 28 D7
Arkansas □ U.S.A. 35°0N 92°30W 84 D8
Arkansas → U.S.A. 33°47N 91°4W 84 E9
Arkansas City U.S.A. 37°4N 97°2W 80 G5
Arkaroola Australia 30°20S 139°22E 63 E2
Arkhangelsk Russia 64°38N 40°36E 18 B7
Arki India 31°9N 76°58E 42 D7
Arklow Ireland 52°48N 6°10W 10 D5
Arkport U.S.A. 42°24N 77°42W 82 D7
Arkticheskiy, Mys
  Russia 81°10N 95°0E 29 A10
Arkville U.S.A. 42°9N 74°37W 83 D10
Arlanzón → Spain 42°3N 4°17W 21 A3
Arlbergpass Austria 47°9N 10°12E 16 E6
Arlbergtunnel Austria 47°9N 10°12E 16 E6
Arles France 43°41N 4°40E 20 E6
Arlington S. Africa 28°1S 27°53E 57 D4
Arlington N.Y., U.S.A. 41°42N 73°54W 83 E11
Arlington Oreg., U.S.A. 45°43N 120°12W 76 D3
Arlington S. Dak., U.S.A. 44°22N 97°8W 80 C5
Arlington Tex., U.S.A. 32°44N 97°6W 84 E6
Arlington Va., U.S.A. 38°53N 77°7W 81 F15
Arlington Vt., U.S.A. 43°5N 73°9W 83 C11
Arlington Wash., U.S.A. 48°12N 122°8W 78 B4
Arlington Heights
  U.S.A. 42°5N 87°59W 80 D10
Arlit Niger 19°0N 7°38E 50 E7
Arlon Belgium 49°42N 5°49E 15 E5
Arlparra Australia 22°11S 134°30E 62 C1
Arltunga Australia 23°26S 134°41E 62 C1
Armadale Australia 32°9S 116°0E 61 F2
Armagh U.K. 54°21N 6°39W 10 B5
Armagh □ U.K. 54°18N 6°37W 10 B5
Armando Bermudez △
  Dom. Rep. 19°3N 71°0W 89 C5
Armavir Russia 45°2N 41°7E 19 E7
Armenia Colombia 4°35N 75°45W 92 C3
Armenia ■ Asia 40°20N 45°0E 19 F7
Armenistis, Akra Greece 36°8N 27°42E 25 C9
Armidale Australia 30°30S 151°40E 63 E5
Armour U.S.A. 43°19N 98°21W 80 D4
Armstrong B.C.,
  Canada 50°25N 119°10W 70 C5
Armstrong Ont., Canada 50°18N 89°4W 72 B2

Arnarfjörður Iceland 65°48N 23°40W 8 D2
Arnaud → Canada 59°59N 69°46W 69 F18
Arnauti, C. Cyprus 35°6N 32°17E 25 D11
Arnett U.S.A. 36°8N 99°46W 84 C5
Arnhem Neths. 51°58N 5°55E 15 C5
Arnhem, C. Australia 12°20S 137°30E 62 A2
Arnhem B. Australia 12°20S 136°10E 62 A2
Arnhem Land Australia 13°10S 134°30E 62 A1
Arnhem Land ◌
  Australia 12°50S 134°50E 62 A1
Arno → Italy 43°41N 10°17E 22 C4
Arno Bay Australia 33°54S 136°34E 63 E2
Arnold U.K. 53°1N 1°7W 12 D6
Arnold U.S.A. 38°15N 120°21W 78 G6
Arnot Canada 55°56N 96°41W 71 B9
Arnøya Norway 70°9N 20°40E 8 A19
Arnprior Canada 45°26N 76°21W 83 A8
Arnsberg Germany 51°24N 8°5E 16 C5
Aroa, Pte. Moorea 17°28S 149°46W 59 d
Aroab Namibia 26°41S 19°39E 56 D2
Aron India 25°57N 77°56E 42 G6
Arona Canary Is. 28°6N 16°40W 24 F3
Aros → Mexico 29°9N 107°57W 86 B3
Arqalyk Kazakhstan 50°13N 66°50E 28 D7
Arrah = Ara India 25°35N 84°32E 43 G11
Arrah Ivory C. 6°40N 3°58W 50 G5
Arran U.K. 55°34N 5°12W 11 F3
Arras France 50°17N 2°46E 20 A5
Arrecife Canary Is. 28°57N 13°37W 24 F6
Arrecifes Argentina 34°6S 60°9W 94 C3
Arrée, Mts. d' France 48°26N 3°55W 20 B2
Arriaga Mexico 16°14N 93°54W 87 D6
Arrilalah Australia 23°43S 143°54E 62 C3
Arrino Australia 29°30S 115°40E 61 E2
Arrow, L. Ireland 54°3N 8°19W 10 B3
Arrowtown N.Z. 44°57S 168°50E 59 F2
Arroyo Grande U.S.A. 35°7N 120°35W 79 K6
Ars Iran 37°9N 47°46E 44 B5
Arsenault L. Canada 55°6N 108°32W 71 B7
Arsenev Russia 44°10N 133°15E 30 B6
Arta Greece 39°8N 21°2E 23 E9
Artà Spain 39°41N 3°21E 24 B10
Artà, Coves d' Spain 39°40N 3°24E 24 B10
Arteaga Mexico 18°28N 102°25W 86 D4
Artem Russia 43°22N 132°13E 30 C6
Artemovsk Russia 54°45N 93°35E 29 D10
Artemovsk Ukraine 48°35N 38°0E 19 E6
Artesia U.S.A. 32°51N 104°24W 77 K11
Arthur Canada 43°50N 80°32W 82 C4
Arthur → Australia 41°2S 144°40E 63 G3
Arthur Cr. → Australia 22°30S 136°25E 62 C2
Arthur Pt. Australia 22°7S 150°3E 62 C5
Arthur River Australia 33°20S 117°2E 61 F2
Arthur's Pass N.Z. 42°54S 171°35E 59 E3
Arthur's Pass △ N.Z. 42°53S 171°42E 59 E3
Arthur's Town Bahamas 24°38N 75°42W 89 B4
Artigas Antarctica 62°30S 58°0W 5 C18
Artigas Uruguay 30°20S 56°30W 94 C4
Artillery L. Canada 63°9N 107°52W 71 A7
Artois France 50°20N 2°30E 20 A5
Artrutx, C. de Spain 39°55N 3°49E 24 B10
Arts Bogd Uul Mongolia 44°40N 102°20E 34 B2
Artsyz Ukraine 46°4N 29°26E 17 E15
Artux China 39°40N 76°10E 32 C4
Artvin Turkey 41°14N 41°44E 19 F7
Artyk Russia 64°12N 145°6E 29 C15
Aru, Kepulauan Indonesia 6°0S 134°30E 37 F8
Aru Is. = Aru, Kepulauan
  Indonesia 6°0S 134°30E 37 F8
Arua Uganda 3°1N 30°58E 54 B3
Aruanã Brazil 14°54S 51°10W 93 F8
Aruba ☑ W. Indies 12°30N 70°0W 89 D6
Arucas Canary Is. 28°7N 15°32W 24 F4
Arué Tahiti 17°31S 149°30W 59 d
Arun → Nepal 26°55N 87°10E 43 F12
Arun → U.K. 50°49N 0°33W 13 G7
Arunachal Pradesh □
  India 28°0N 95°0E 41 F19
Arusha Tanzania 3°20S 36°40E 54 C4
Arusha □ Tanzania 4°0S 36°30E 54 C4
Arusha △ Tanzania 3°16S 36°47E 54 C4
Arusha Chini Tanzania 3°32S 37°20E 54 C4
Aruwimi →
  Dem. Rep. of the Congo 1°13N 23°36E 54 B1
Arvada Colo., U.S.A. 39°48N 105°5W 76 G11
Arvada Wyo., U.S.A. 44°39N 106°8W 76 D10
Arvayheer Mongolia 46°15N 102°48E 32 B9
Arvi Greece 34°59S 25°28E 25 E7
Arviat Canada 61°6N 93°59W 71 A10
Arvidsjaur Sweden 65°35N 19°10E 8 D18
Arvika Sweden 59°40N 12°36E 9 G15
Arvin U.S.A. 35°12N 118°50W 79 K8
Arwal India 25°15N 84°41E 43 G11
Arxan China 47°11N 119°57E 33 B12
Arys Kazakhstan 42°26N 68°48E 28 E7
Arzamas Russia 55°27N 43°55E 18 C7
Arzanah U.A.E. 24°47N 52°34E 45 E7
Aş Şafā Syria 33°10N 37°0E 46 B6
As Saffānīyah Si. Arabia 27°55N 48°50E 45 E6
Aş Şafirah Syria 36°5N 37°21E 44 B3
As Salamīyah Syria 35°1N 37°2E 44 C3
As Salmān Iraq 30°30N 44°32E 44 D5
Aş Şalt Jordan 32°2N 35°43E 46 C4
Aş Sal'w'a Qatar 24°23N 50°50E 45 E6
As Samāwah Iraq 31°15N 45°15E 44 D5
As Sanamayn Syria 33°3N 36°10E 46 B5
As Sohar = Şuḥār Oman 24°20N 56°40E 45 E8
As Sukhnah Syria 34°52N 38°52E 44 C3
As Sulaymānīyah Iraq 35°35N 45°29E 44 C5
As Sulaymī Si. Arabia 26°17N 41°21E 44 E4
As Sulayyil Si. Arabia 20°27N 45°34E 47 C4
As Summān Si. Arabia 25°0N 47°0E 44 E5
As Suwaydā' Syria 32°40N 36°30E 46 C5
As Suwaydā' □ Syria 32°45N 36°45E 46 C5
As Suwayq Oman 23°51N 57°26E 45 F8
Aş Şuwayrah Iraq 32°55N 45°0E 44 C5
Asab Namibia 25°30S 18°0E 56 D2
Asad, Buḥayrat al Syria 36°0N 38°15E 44 C3

Asahi Japan 35°43N 140°39E 31 E10
Asahi-Gawa → Japan 34°36N 133°58E 31 G6
Asahigawa = Asahikawa
  Japan 43°46N 142°22E 30 C11
Asahikawa Japan 43°46N 142°22E 30 C11
Asaluyeh Iran 27°29N 52°37E 45 E7
Asamankese Ghana 5°50N 0°40W 50 G5
Asan → India 26°37N 78°24E 43 F8
Asansol India 23°40N 87°1E 43 H12
Asau Samoa 13°27S 172°33W 59 b
Asbesberge S. Africa 29°0S 23°0E 56 D3
Asbestos Canada 45°47N 71°58W 73 C5
Asbury Park U.S.A. 40°13N 74°1W 83 F10
Ascensión Mexico 31°6N 107°59W 86 A3
Ascensión, B. de la
  Mexico 19°40N 87°30W 87 D7
Ascension I. Atl. Oc. 7°57S 14°23W 49 G2
Aschaffenburg Germany 49°58N 9°6E 16 D5
Aschersleben Germany 51°45N 11°29E 16 C6
Áscoli Piceno Italy 42°51N 13°34E 22 C5
Ascope Peru 7°46S 79°8W 92 E3
Ascotán Chile 21°45S 68°17W 94 A2
Aseb Eritrea 13°0N 42°40E 47 E3
Asela Ethiopia 8°0N 39°0E 47 F2
Asenovgrad Bulgaria 42°1N 24°51E 23 C11
Aşgabat = Ashgabat
  Turkmenistan 38°0N 57°50E 45 B8
Asgata Cyprus 34°46N 33°15E 25 E12
Ash Fork U.S.A. 35°13N 112°29W 77 J7
Ash Grove U.S.A. 37°19N 93°35W 80 G7
Ash Shabakah Iraq 30°49N 43°39E 44 D4
Ash Shamal □ Lebanon 34°25N 36°0E 46 A5
Ash Shāmīyah Iraq 31°55N 44°35E 44 D5
Ash Shāriqah U.A.E. 25°23N 55°26E 45 E7
Ash Sharmah Si. Arabia 28°1N 35°16E 44 D2
Ash Sharqāt Iraq 35°27N 43°16E 44 C4
Ash Shaṭrah Iraq 31°30N 46°10E 44 D5
Ash Shawbak Jordan 30°32N 35°34E 44 D2
Ash Shiḥr Yemen 14°45N 49°36E 47 E4
Ash Shinafīyah Iraq 31°35N 44°39E 44 D5
Ash Shumlūl Si. Arabia 26°31N 47°20E 44 E5
Ash Shūr'ab Si. Arabia 28°54N 44°44E 44 D5
Ash Shur'a Iraq 35°58N 43°13E 44 C4
Ash Shurayf Si. Arabia 25°43N 39°14E 44 E3
Ash Shuwayfāt Lebanon 33°45N 35°30E 46 B4
Asha Russia 55°0N 57°16E 18 D10
Ashbourne U.K. 53°2N 1°43W 12 D6
Ashburn U.S.A. 31°43N 83°39W 85 F13
Ashburton N.Z. 43°53S 171°48E 59 E3
Ashburton → Australia 21°40S 114°56E 60 D1
Ashcroft Canada 50°40N 121°20W 70 C4
Ashdod Israel 31°49N 34°35E 46 D3
Ashdown U.S.A. 33°40N 94°8W 84 E7
Asheboro U.S.A. 35°43N 79°49W 85 D15
Ashern Canada 51°11N 98°21W 71 C9
Asherton U.S.A. 28°27N 99°46W 84 G5
Asheville U.S.A. 35°36N 82°33W 85 D13
Ashewat Pakistan 31°22N 68°32E 42 D3
Asheweig → Canada 54°17N 87°12W 72 B2
Ashford Australia 29°15S 151°3E 63 D5
Ashford U.K. 51°8N 0°53E 13 F8
Ashgabat Turkmenistan 38°0N 57°50E 45 B8
Ashibetsu Japan 43°31N 142°11E 30 C11
Ashikaga Japan 36°28N 139°29E 31 F9
Ashington U.K. 55°11N 1°33W 12 B6
Ashizuri-Uwakai △
  Japan 32°56N 132°32E 31 H6
Ashizuri-Zaki Japan 32°44N 133°0E 31 H6
Ashkarkot Afghan. 33°3N 67°58E 42 C2
Ashkhabad = Ashgabat
  Turkmenistan 38°0N 57°50E 45 B8
Äshkhäneh Iran 37°26N 56°55E 45 B8
Ashland Kans., U.S.A. 37°11N 99°46W 80 G4
Ashland Ky., U.S.A. 38°28N 82°38W 81 F12
Ashland Maine, U.S.A. 46°38N 68°24W 81 B19
Ashland Mont., U.S.A. 45°36N 106°16W 76 D10
Ashland Ohio, U.S.A. 40°52N 82°19W 82 F2
Ashland Oreg., U.S.A. 42°12N 122°43W 76 E2
Ashland Pa., U.S.A. 40°45N 76°22W 83 F8
Ashland Va., U.S.A. 37°46N 77°29W 81 G15
Ashland Wis., U.S.A. 46°35N 90°53W 80 B8
Ashley N. Dak., U.S.A. 46°2N 99°22W 80 B4
Ashley Pa., U.S.A. 41°12N 75°55W 83 E9
Ashmore and Cartier Is.
  Ind. Oc. 12°15S 123°0E 60 B3
Ashmore Reef Australia 12°14S 123°5E 60 B3
Ashmyany Belarus 54°26N 25°52E 17 A13
Ashokan Res. U.S.A. 41°56N 74°13W 83 E10
Ashoknagar India 24°34N 77°43E 42 G7
Ashqelon Israel 31°42N 34°35E 46 D3
Ashta India 23°1N 76°43E 42 H7
Ashtabula U.S.A. 41°52N 80°47W 82 E4
Äshtiyän Iran 34°31N 50°0E 45 C6
Ashton S. Africa 33°50S 20°5E 56 E3
Ashton U.S.A. 44°4N 111°27W 76 D8
Ashuanipi, L. Canada 52°45N 66°15W 73 B6
Ashville U.S.A. 40°34N 78°33W 82 F6
Asia 45°0N 75°0E 26 E9
Asia, Kepulauan
  Indonesia 1°0N 131°13E 37 D8
Asifabad India 19°20N 79°24E 40 K11
Asinara Italy 41°4N 8°16E 22 D3
Asinara, G. dell' Italy 41°0N 8°30E 22 D3
Asino Russia 57°0N 86°0E 28 D9
Asipovichy Belarus 53°19N 28°33E 17 B15
'Asīr □ Si. Arabia 18°40N 42°30E 47 D3
'Asir, Ras Somali Rep. 11°55N 51°10E 47 E5
Askham S. Africa 26°59S 20°47E 56 D3
Askim Norway 59°35N 11°10E 9 G14
Askja Iceland 65°3N 16°48W 8 D5
Asklipio Greece 36°4N 27°56E 25 C9
Askoyna Norway 60°29N 5°10E 8 F11
Asmara = Asmera
  Eritrea 15°19N 38°55E 47 D2
Asmera Eritrea 15°19N 38°55E 47 D2
Åsnen Sweden 56°37N 14°45E 9 H16
Aso Kujū △ Japan 32°53N 131°6E 31 H5
Aspatria U.K. 54°47N 3°19W 12 C4

Aspen *U.S.A.* 39°11N 106°49W **76** G10
Aspermont *U.S.A.* 33°8N 100°14W **84** E4
Aspiring, Mt. *N.Z.* 44°23S 168°46E **59** F2
Asprokavos, Akra *Greece* 39°21N 20°6E **25** B4
Aspur *India* 23°58N 74°7E **42** H6
Asquith *Canada* 52°8N 107°13W **71** C7
Assab = Aseb *Eritrea* 13°0N 42°40E **47** E3
Assal, L. *Djibouti* 11°40N 42°26E **47** E3
Assam □ *India* 26°0N 93°0E **41** G18
Assateague Island △
  U.S.A. 38°15N 75°10W **81** F16
Asse *Belgium* 50°24N 4°10E **15** D4
Assen *Neths.* 53°0N 6°35E **15** A6
Assiniboia *Canada* 49°40N 105°59W **71** D7
Assiniboine → *Canada* 49°53N 97°8W **71** D9
Assiniboine, Mt.
  Canada 50°52N 115°39W **70** C5
Assis *Brazil* 22°40S 50°20W **95** A5
Assisi *Italy* 43°4N 12°37E **22** C5
Assynt, L. *U.K.* 58°10N 5°3W **11** C3
Astana *Kazakhstan* 51°10N 71°30E **32** A3
Āstāneh *Iran* 37°17N 49°59E **45** B6
Astara *Azerbaijan* 38°30N 48°50E **45** B6
Astarabad = Gorgān
  Iran 36°55N 54°30E **45** B7
Asterousia *Greece* 34°59N 25°3E **25** E7
Asti *Italy* 44°54N 8°12E **20** D8
Astipalea *Greece* 36°32N 26°22E **23** F12
Astorga *Spain* 42°29N 6°8W **21** A2
Astoria *U.S.A.* 46°11N 123°50W **78** D3
Astrakhan *Russia* 46°25N 48°5E **19** E8
Astrebla Downs
  Australia 24°12S 140°34E **62** C3
Asturias □ *Spain* 43°15N 6°0W **21** A3
Asunción *Paraguay* 25°10S 57°30W **94** B4
Asunción Nochixtlán
  Mexico 17°28N 97°14W **87** D5
Aswa → *Uganda* 3°43N 31°55E **54** B3
Aswa-Lolim △ *Uganda* 2°43N 31°35E **54** B3
Aswân *Egypt* 24°4N 32°57E **51** D12
Aswan High Dam = Sadd el Aali
  Egypt 23°54N 32°54E **51** D12
Asyût *Egypt* 27°11N 31°4E **51** C12
At Ţafilah *Jordan* 30°45N 35°30E **46** E4
Aţ Ţafilah □ *Jordan* 30°45N 35°30E **46** E4
Aţ Tā'if *Si. Arabia* 21°5N 40°27E **47** C3
Aţ Ta'mīm □ *Iraq* 35°30N 44°20E **44** C5
Aţ Ţirāq *Si. Arabia* 27°19N 44°33E **44** E5
Aţ Tubayq *Si. Arabia* 29°30N 37°0E **44** D3
Aţ Ţunayb *Jordan* 31°48N 35°57E **46** D4
Atacama □ *Chile* 27°30S 70°0W **94** B2
Atacama, Desierto de
  Chile 24°0S 69°20W **94** A2
Atacama, Salar de *Chile* 23°30S 68°20W **94** A2
Atakeye ☼ *Australia* 22°30S 133°45E **60** D5
Atakpamé *Togo* 7°31N 1°13E **50** G6
Atalaya *Peru* 10°45S 73°50W **92** F4
Atalaya de Femes
  Canary Is. 28°56N 13°47W **24** F6
Atami *Japan* 35°5N 139°4E **31** G9
Atamyrat *Turkmenistan* 37°50N 65°12E **28** F7
Atapupu *Indonesia* 9°0S 124°51E **37** F6
Atâr *Mauritania* 20°30N 13°5W **50** D3
Atari *Pakistan* 30°56N 74°2E **42** D6
Atascadero *U.S.A.* 35°29N 120°40W **78** K6
Atasū *Kazakhstan* 48°30N 71°0E **28** E8
Atatürk Barajı *Turkey* 37°28N 38°30E **19** G6
Atauro *E. Timor* 8°10S 125°30E **37** F7
Ataviros *Greece* 36°12N 27°50E **25** C9
Atbara *Sudan* 17°42N 33°59E **51** E12
'Atbara, Nahr → *Sudan* 17°40N 33°56E **51** E12
Atbasar *Kazakhstan* 51°48N 68°20E **28** D7
Atchafalaya B. *U.S.A.* 29°25N 91°25W **84** G9
Atchison *U.S.A.* 39°34N 95°7W **80** F6
Āteshān *Iran* 35°35N 52°37E **45** C7
Ath *Belgium* 50°38N 3°47E **15** D3
Athabasca *Canada* 54°45N 113°20W **70** C6
Athabasca → *Canada* 58°40N 110°50W **71** B6
Athabasca, L. *Canada* 59°15N 109°15W **71** B7
Athabasca Sand Dunes △
  Canada 59°4N 108°43W **71** B7
Athboy *Ireland* 53°37N 6°56W **10** C5
Athenry *Ireland* 53°18N 8°44W **10** C3
Athens = Athina *Greece* 37°58N 23°43E **23** F10
Athens *Ala., U.S.A.* 34°48N 86°58W **85** D11
Athens *Ga., U.S.A.* 33°57N 83°23W **85** E13
Athens *N.Y., U.S.A.* 42°16N 73°49W **83** D11
Athens *Ohio, U.S.A.* 39°20N 82°6W **81** F12
Athens *Tenn., U.S.A.* 35°27N 84°36W **85** D12
Athens *Tex., U.S.A.* 32°12N 95°51W **84** E7
Atherley *Canada* 44°37N 79°20W **82** B5
Atherton *Australia* 17°17S 145°30E **62** B4
Athi River *Kenya* 1°28S 36°58E **54** C4
Athienou *Cyprus* 35°3N 33°32E **25** D12
Athina *Greece* 37°58N 23°43E **23** F10
Athínai = Athina
  Greece 37°58N 23°43E **23** F10
Athlone *Ireland* 53°25N 7°56W **10** C4
Athna *Cyprus* 35°3N 33°47E **25** D12
Athol *U.S.A.* 42°36N 72°14W **83** D12
Atholl, Forest of *U.K.* 56°51N 3°50W **11** E5
Atholville *Canada* 47°59N 66°43W **73** C6
Athos *Greece* 40°9N 24°22E **23** D11
Athy *Ireland* 53°0N 7°0W **10** C5
Ati *Chad* 13°13N 18°20E **51** F9
Atiak *Uganda* 3°12N 32°2E **54** B3
Atik L. *Canada* 55°15N 96°0W **71** B9
Atikaki △ *Canada* 51°30N 95°31W **71** C9
Atikameg → *Canada* 52°30N 82°46W **72** B3
Atikokan *Canada* 48°45N 91°37W **72** C1
Atikonak L. *Canada* 52°40N 64°32W **73** B7
Atimaono *Tahiti* 17°46S 149°28W **59** d
Atitlán △ *Cent. Amer.* 14°38N 91°10W **87** E6
Atiu *Cook Is.* 20°0S 158°10W **65** J12
Atka *Russia* 60°50N 151°48E **29** C16
Atka I. *U.S.A.* 52°7N 174°30W **74** E5
Atkinson *U.S.A.* 42°32N 98°59W **80** D4
Atlanta *Ga., U.S.A.* 33°45N 84°23W **85** E12
Atlanta *Tex., U.S.A.* 33°7N 94°10W **84** E7

Atlantic *U.S.A.* 41°24N 95°1W **80** E6
Atlantic City *U.S.A.* 39°21N 74°27W **81** F16
Atlantic-Indian Basin
  Antarctica 60°0S 30°0E **5** B4
Atlantic Ocean 0°0 20°0W **2** D8
Atlas Mts. = Haut Atlas
  Morocco 32°30N 5°0W **50** B4
Atlin *Canada* 59°31N 133°41W **70** B2
Atlin, L. *Canada* 59°26N 133°45W **70** B2
Atlin △ *Canada* 59°10N 134°30W **70** B2
Atmore *U.S.A.* 31°2N 87°29W **85** F11
Atoka *U.S.A.* 34°23N 96°8W **84** D6
Atolia *U.S.A.* 35°19N 117°37W **79** K9
Atmore → *Bangla.* 24°7N 89°22E **43** G13
Atrak = Atrek →
  Turkmenistan 37°35N 53°58E **45** B8
Atrauli *India* 28°2N 78°20E **42** E8
Atrek → *Turkmenistan* 37°35N 53°58E **45** B8
Atsuta *Japan* 43°24N 141°26E **30** C10
Attalla *U.S.A.* 34°1N 86°6W **85** D11
Attapeu *Laos* 14°48N 106°50E **38** E6
Attawapiskat *Canada* 52°56N 82°24W **72** B3
Attawapiskat →
  Canada 52°57N 82°18W **72** B3
Attawapiskat L. *Canada* 52°18N 87°54W **72** B2
Attica *Ind., U.S.A.* 40°18N 87°15W **80** E10
Attica *Ohio, U.S.A.* 41°4N 82°53W **82** E2
Attikamagen L. *Canada* 55°0N 66°30W **73** B6
Attleboro *U.S.A.* 41°57N 71°17W **83** E13
Attock *Pakistan* 33°52N 72°20E **42** C5
Attopu = Attapeu *Laos* 14°48N 106°50E **38** E6
Attu I. *U.S.A.* 52°55N 172°55E **74** E2
Attur *India* 11°35N 78°30E **40** P11
Atuel → *Argentina* 36°17S 66°50W **94** D2
Atura *Uganda* 2°7N 32°20E **54** B3
Åtvidaberg *Sweden* 58°12N 16°0E **9** G17
Atwater *U.S.A.* 37°21N 120°37W **78** H6
Atwood *Canada* 43°40N 81°1W **82** C3
Atwood *U.S.A.* 39°48N 101°3W **80** F3
Atyraū *Kazakhstan* 47°5N 52°0E **19** E9
Au Sable *U.S.A.* 44°25N 83°20W **81** C12
Au Sable → *U.S.A.* 44°25N 83°20W **81** C12
Au Sable Forks *U.S.A.* 44°27N 73°41W **83** B11
Au Sable Pt. *U.S.A.* 44°20N 83°20W **81** C12
Auas *Honduras* 15°29N 84°20W **88** C3
Auasberg *Namibia* 22°37S 17°13E **56** C2
Aubagne *France* 43°17N 5°37E **20** E6
Aube → *France* 48°34N 3°43E **20** B5
Auberry *U.S.A.* 37°7N 119°29W **78** H7
Auburn *Ala., U.S.A.* 32°36N 85°29W **85** E12
Auburn *Calif., U.S.A.* 38°54N 121°4W **78** G5
Auburn *Ind., U.S.A.* 41°22N 85°4W **81** E11
Auburn *Maine, U.S.A.* 44°6N 70°14W **81** C18
Auburn *N.Y., U.S.A.* 42°56N 76°34W **83** D8
Auburn *Nebr., U.S.A.* 40°23N 95°51W **80** E6
Auburn *Pa., U.S.A.* 40°36N 76°6W **83** F8
Auburn *Wash., U.S.A.* 47°18N 122°14W **78** C4
Auburn Ra. *Australia* 25°15S 150°30E **63** D5
Auburndale *U.S.A.* 28°4N 81°48W **85** G14
Aubusson *France* 45°57N 2°11E **20** D5
Auch *France* 43°39N 0°36E **20** E4
Auchterarder *U.K.* 56°18N 3°41W **11** E5
Auchtermuchty *U.K.* 56°18N 3°13W **11** E5
Auckland *N.Z.* 36°52S 174°46E **59** B5
Auckland Is. *Pac. Oc.* 50°40S 166°5E **64** N8
Aude → *France* 43°13N 3°14E **20** E5
Auden *Canada* 50°14N 87°53W **72** B2
Audubon *U.S.A.* 41°43N 94°56W **80** E6
Augathella *Australia* 25°48S 146°35E **63** D4
Aughnacloy *U.K.* 54°25N 6°59W **10** B5
Aughrim *Ireland* 53°18N 8°19W **10** C3
Augrabies Falls *S. Africa* 28°35S 20°20E **56** D3
Augrabies Falls △
  S. Africa 28°40S 20°22E **56** D3
Augsburg *Germany* 48°25N 10°52E **16** D6
Augusta *Australia* 34°19S 115°9E **61** F2
Augusta *Italy* 37°13N 15°13E **22** F6
Augusta *Ark., U.S.A.* 35°17N 91°22W **84** D9
Augusta *Ga., U.S.A.* 33°28N 81°58W **85** E14
Augusta *Kans., U.S.A.* 37°41N 96°59W **80** G5
Augusta *Maine, U.S.A.* 44°19N 69°47W **81** C19
Augusta *Mont., U.S.A.* 47°30N 112°24W **76** C7
Augustów *Poland* 53°51N 23°0E **17** B12
Augustus, Mt. *Australia* 24°20S 116°50E **61** D2
Augustus I. *Australia* 15°20S 124°30E **60** C3
Aujuittuq = Grise Fiord
  Canada 76°25N 82°57W **69** B15
Aukštaitija △ *Lithuania* 55°15N 26°0E **9** J22
Aukum *U.S.A.* 38°34N 120°43W **78** G6
Aulavik △ *Canada* 73°42N 119°55W **68** C8
Auld, L. *Australia* 22°25S 123°50E **60** D3
Ault *U.S.A.* 40°35N 104°44W **76** F11
Aunis *France* 46°5N 0°50W **20** C3
Aunu'u *Amer. Samoa* 14°20S 170°31W **59** b
Auponhia *Indonesia* 1°58S 125°27E **37** E7
Aur, Pulau *Malaysia* 2°35N 104°10E **39** L5
Auraiya *India* 26°28N 79°33E **43** F8
Aurangabad *Bihar,*
  India 24°45N 84°18E **43** G11
Aurangabad *Maharashtra,*
  India 19°50N 75°23E **40** K9
Aurich *Germany* 53°28N 7°28E **16** B4
Aurillac *France* 44°55N 2°26E **20** D5
Aurora *Canada* 44°0N 79°28W **82** C5
Aurora *S. Africa* 32°40S 18°29E **56** E2
Aurora *Colo., U.S.A.* 39°43N 104°49W **76** G11
Aurora *Ill., U.S.A.* 41°45N 88°19W **80** E9
Aurora *Mo., U.S.A.* 36°58N 93°43W **80** G7
Aurora *N.Y., U.S.A.* 42°45N 76°42W **83** D8
Aurora *Nebr., U.S.A.* 40°52N 98°0W **80** E5
Aurora *Ohio, U.S.A.* 41°21N 81°20W **82** E3
Aurukun *Australia* 13°20S 141°45E **62** A3
Aurukun ◎ *Australia* 13°35S 141°48E **62** A3
Aus *Namibia* 26°35S 16°12E **56** D2
Ausable → *Canada* 43°19N 81°46W **82** C3
Auschwitz = Oświęcim
  Poland 50°2N 19°11E **17** C10
Auski Roadhouse
  Australia 22°22S 118°41E **60** D2

Austin *Minn., U.S.A.* 43°40N 92°58W **80** D7
Austin *Nev., U.S.A.* 39°30N 117°4W **76** G5
Austin *Pa., U.S.A.* 41°38N 78°6W **82** E6
Austin *Tex., U.S.A.* 30°17N 97°45W **84** F6
Austin, L. *Australia* 27°40S 118°0E **61** E2
Austin I. *Canada* 61°10N 94°0W **71** A10
Austra *Norway* 65°8N 11°55E **8** D14
Austral Is. = Tubuaï, Îs.
  French Polynesia 25°0S 150°0W **65** K13
Austral Seamount Chain
  Pac. Oc. 24°0S 150°0W **65** K13
Australia ■ *Oceania* 23°0S 135°0E **58** D6
Australian-Antarctic Basin
  S. Ocean 60°0S 120°0E **5** C9
Australian Capital Territory □
  Australia 35°30S 149°0E **63** F4
Australind *Australia* 33°17S 115°42E **61** F2
Austria ■ *Europe* 47°0N 14°0E **16** E8
Austvågøya *Norway* 68°20N 14°40E **8** B16
Autlán de Navarro
  Mexico 19°46N 104°22W **86** D4
Autun *France* 46°58N 4°17E **20** C6
Auvergne □ *France* 45°20N 3°15E **20** D5
Auvergne, Mts. d' *France* 45°20N 2°55E **20** D5
Auxerre *France* 47°48N 3°32E **20** C5
Auyuittuq △ *Canada* 67°30N 66°0W **69** D18
Av-Dovurak *Russia* 51°17N 91°35E **29** D10
Ava *U.S.A.* 36°57N 92°40W **80** G7
Avallon *France* 47°30N 3°53E **20** C5
Avalon *U.S.A.* 33°21N 118°20W **79** M8
Avalon Pen. *Canada* 47°30N 53°20W **73** C9
Avanos *Turkey* 38°43N 34°51E **44** B6
Avaré *Brazil* 23°4S 48°58W **95** A6
Avawatz Mts. *U.S.A.* 35°40N 116°30W **79** K10
Aveiro *Brazil* 3°10S 55°5W **93** D7
Aveiro *Portugal* 40°37N 8°38W **21** B1
Āvej *Iran* 35°40N 49°15E **45** C6
Avellaneda *Argentina* 34°40S 58°22W **94** C4
Avellino *Italy* 40°54N 14°47E **22** D6
Avenal *U.S.A.* 36°0N 120°8W **78** K6
Aversa *Italy* 40°58N 14°12E **22** D6
Avery *U.S.A.* 47°15N 115°49W **76** C6
Aves, I. de *W. Indies* 15°45N 63°55W **89** C7
Aves, Is. las *Venezuela* 12°0N 67°30W **89** D6
Avesta *Sweden* 60°9N 16°10E **9** F17
Aveyron → *France* 44°5N 1°16E **20** D4
Avezzano *Italy* 42°2N 13°25E **22** C5
Aviá Terai *Argentina* 26°45S 60°50W **94** B3
Aviemore *U.K.* 57°12N 3°50W **11** D5
Avignon *France* 43°57N 4°50E **20** E6
Ávila *Spain* 40°39N 4°43W **21** B3
Avila Beach *U.S.A.* 35°11N 120°44W **79** K6
Avilés *Spain* 43°35N 5°57W **21** A3
Avis *U.S.A.* 41°11N 77°19W **82** E7
Avoca *U.S.A.* 42°25N 77°25W **82** D7
Avoca → *Australia* 35°40S 143°43E **63** F3
Avoca → *Ireland* 52°48N 6°10W **10** D5
Avola *Canada* 51°45N 119°19W **70** C5
Avola *Italy* 36°56N 15°7E **22** F6
Avon *U.S.A.* 42°55N 77°45W **82** D7
Avon → *Australia* 31°40S 116°7E **61** F2
Avon → *Bristol, U.K.* 51°29N 2°41W **13** F5
Avon → *Dorset, U.K.* 50°44N 1°46W **13** G6
Avon → *Warks., U.K.* 52°0N 2°8W **13** E5
Avon Park *U.S.A.* 27°36N 81°31W **85** H14
Avondale *Zimbabwe* 17°43S 30°58E **55** F3
Avonlea *Canada* 50°0N 105°0W **71** D8
Avonmore *Canada* 45°10N 74°58W **83** A10
Avonmouth *U.K.* 51°30N 2°42W **13** F5
Avranches *France* 48°40N 1°20E **20** B3
Awa-Shima *Japan* 38°27N 139°14E **30** E9
A'waj → *Syria* 33°23N 36°20E **46** B5
Awaji-Shima *Japan* 34°30N 134°50E **31** G7
'Awālī *Bahrain* 26°0N 50°30E **45** E6
Awantipur *India* 33°55N 75°3E **43** C6
Awasa *Ethiopia* 7°2N 38°28E **47** F2
Awash *Ethiopia* 9°1N 40°10E **47** F3
Awatere → *N.Z.* 41°37S 174°10E **59** D5
Awbārī *Libya* 26°46N 12°57E **51** C8
Awbārī, Idehan *Libya* 27°10N 11°30E **51** C8
Awe, L. *U.K.* 56°17N 5°16W **11** E3
Awjilah *Libya* 29°8N 21°7E **51** C10
Axe → *U.K.* 50°42N 3°4W **13** G4
Axel Heiberg I. *Canada* 80°0N 90°0W **69** B14
Axim *Ghana* 4°51N 2°15W **50** H5
Axios → *Greece* 40°57N 22°35E **23** D10
Axminster *U.K.* 50°46N 3°0W **13** G4
Ayabaca *Peru* 4°40S 79°53W **92** D3
Ayabe *Japan* 35°20N 135°20E **31** G7
Ayacucho *Argentina* 37°5S 58°20W **94** D4
Ayacucho *Peru* 13°0S 74°0W **92** F4
Ayaguz = Ayaköz
  Kazakhstan 48°10N 80°10E **32** B5
Ayakkum Hu *China* 37°30N 89°20E **32** D6
Ayaköz *Kazakhstan* 48°10N 80°10E **32** B5
Ayamonte *Spain* 37°12N 7°24W **21** D2
Ayan *Russia* 56°30N 138°16E **29** D14
Ayaviri *Peru* 14°50S 70°35W **92** F4
Aydın *Turkey* 37°51N 27°51E **23** F12
Aydıngkol Hu *China* 42°40N 89°15E **32** C6
Ayer *U.S.A.* 42°34N 71°35W **83** D13
Ayer Hitam *Malaysia* 5°24N 100°16E **39** c
Ayer's Cliff *Canada* 45°10N 72°3W **83** A12
Ayers Rock = Uluru
  Australia 25°23S 131°5E **61** E5
Ayeyarwady = Irrawaddy →
  Burma 15°50N 95°6E **41** M19
Áyia Napa *Cyprus* 34°59N 34°0E **25** E13
Áyia Phyla *Cyprus* 34°43N 33°1E **25** E12
Áyios Amvrósios
  Cyprus 35°20N 33°35E **25** D12
Áyios Seryios *Cyprus* 35°12N 33°53E **25** D12
Áyios Theodhoros
  Cyprus 35°22N 34°1E **25** D13
Aykhal *Russia* 66°0N 111°30E **29** C12
Aykino *Russia* 62°15N 49°56E **18** B8
Aylesbury *U.K.* 51°49N 0°49W **13** F7
Aylmer *Canada* 42°46N 80°59W **82** D4
Aylmer, L. *Canada* 64°5N 108°30W **68** E10

Ayn Dār *Si. Arabia* 25°55N 49°10E **45** E7
Ayn Zālah *Iraq* 36°45N 42°35E **44** B4
Ayolas *Paraguay* 27°10S 56°59W **94** B4
Ayon, Ostrov *Russia* 69°50N 169°0E **29** C17
'Ayoûn el 'Atroûs
  Mauritania 16°38N 9°37W **50** E4
Ayr *Australia* 19°35S 147°25E **62** B4
Ayr *Canada* 43°17N 80°27W **82** C4
Ayr *U.K.* 55°28N 4°38W **11** F4
Ayr → *U.K.* 55°28N 4°38W **11** F4
Ayre, Pt. of *I. of Man* 54°25N 4°21W **12** C3
Ayton *Australia* 15°56S 145°22E **62** B4
Aytos *Bulgaria* 42°42N 27°16E **23** C12
Ayu, Kepulauan
  Indonesia 0°35N 131°5E **37** D8
Ayutla *Guatemala* 14°40N 92°10W **88** D1
Ayutla de los Libres
  Mexico 16°54N 99°13W **87** D5
Ayvacık *Turkey* 39°36N 26°24E **23** E12
Ayvalık *Turkey* 39°20N 26°46E **23** E12
Az Zabadānī *Syria* 33°43N 36°5E **46** B5
Aẕ Ẕāhirīyah *West Bank* 31°25N 34°58E **46** D3
Aẕ Ẕahrān *Si. Arabia* 26°10N 50°7E **45** E6
Az Zarqā *Jordan* 32°5N 36°4E **46** C5
Az Zarqā' *U.A.E.* 24°53N 53°4E **45** E7
Az Zarqā' □ *Jordan* 32°5N 36°4E **46** C5
Az Zāwiyah *Libya* 32°52N 12°56E **51** B8
Az Zībār *Iraq* 36°52N 44°4E **44** B5
Az Zilfī *Si. Arabia* 26°12N 44°52E **44** E5
Az Zubayr *Iraq* 30°26N 47°40E **44** D5
Azad Kashmir □
  Pakistan 33°50N 73°50E **43** C5
Azamgarh *India* 26°5N 83°13E **43** F10
Azángaro *Peru* 14°55S 70°13W **92** F4
Azaouad *Mali* 19°0N 3°0W **50** E5
Āzār Shahr *Iran* 37°45N 45°59E **44** B5
Azarān *Iran* 37°25N 47°16E **44** B5
Āzarbāyjān = Azerbaijan ■
  Asia 40°20N 48°0E **19** F8
Āzarbāyjān-e Gharbī □
  Iran 37°0N 44°30E **44** B5
Āzarbāyjān-e Sharqī □
  Iran 37°20N 47°0E **44** B5
Azare *Nigeria* 11°55N 10°10E **50** F8
A'zāz *Syria* 36°36N 37°4E **44** B3
Azbine = Aïr *Niger* 18°30N 8°0E **50** E7
Azerbaijan ■ *Asia* 40°20N 48°0E **19** F8
Azimganj *India* 24°14N 88°16E **43** G13
Azogues *Ecuador* 2°35S 78°0W **92** D3
Azores = Açores, Is. dos
  Atl. Oc. 38°0N 27°0W **50** a
Azov *Russia* 47°3N 39°25E **19** E6
Azov, Sea of *Europe* 46°0N 36°30E **19** E6
Azovskoye More = Azov, Sea of
  Europe 46°0N 36°30E **19** E6
Azraq ash Shīshān
  Jordan 31°50N 36°49E **46** D5
Aztec *U.S.A.* 36°49N 107°59W **77** H10
Azúa de Compostela
  Dom. Rep. 18°25N 70°44W **89** C5
Azuaga *Spain* 38°16N 5°39W **21** C3
Azuero, Pen. de *Panama* 7°30N 80°30W **88** E3
Azul *Argentina* 36°42S 59°43W **94** D4
Azumino *Japan* 36°20N 137°50E **31** F8
Azusa *U.S.A.* 34°8N 117°52W **79** L9
Azzel Matti, Sebkra
  Algeria 26°10N 0°43E **50** C6

B

Ba Be △ *Vietnam* 22°25N 105°37E **38** A5
Ba Don *Vietnam* 17°45N 106°26E **38** D6
Ba Dong *Vietnam* 9°40N 106°33E **39** H6
Ba Ngoi *Vietnam* 11°54N 109°10E **39** G7
Ba Ria *Vietnam* 10°30N 107°10E **39** G6
Ba Tri *Vietnam* 10°2N 106°36E **39** G6
Ba Vi *Vietnam* 21°1N 105°22E **38** B5
Ba Xian = Bazhou *China* 39°8N 116°22E **34** E9
Baa *Indonesia* 10°50S 123°0E **60** B3
Baardheere *Somali Rep.* 2°20N 42°27E **47** G3
Baarle-Nassau *Belgium* 51°27N 4°56E **15** C4
Baarle-Nassau *Belgium* 51°27N 4°56E **15** C4
Bāb el Mandeb *Red Sea* 12°35N 43°25E **47** E3
Bābā, Koh-i- *Afghan.* 34°30N 67°0E **40** B5
Baba Burnu *Turkey* 39°29N 26°2E **23** E12
Baba Kalū *Iran* 30°7N 50°49E **45** D6
Babadag *Romania* 44°53N 28°44E **17** F15
Babaeski *Turkey* 41°26N 27°6E **23** D12
Babahoyo *Ecuador* 1°40S 79°30W **92** D3
Babai = Sarju → *India* 27°21N 81°23E **43** F9
Babar *Indonesia* 8°0S 129°30E **37** F7
Babar *Pakistan* 31°7N 69°32E **42** D3
Babarkach *Pakistan* 29°45N 68°0E **42** E3
Babb *U.S.A.* 48°51N 113°27W **76** B7
Baberu *India* 25°33N 80°43E **43** G9
Babi Besar, Pulau
  Malaysia 2°25N 103°59E **39** L4
Bābil □ *Iraq* 32°34N 44°22E **44** C5
Babinda *Australia* 17°20S 145°56E **62** B4
Babine *Canada* 55°22N 126°37E **70** B3
Babine → *Canada* 55°45N 127°44W **70** B3
Babine L. *Canada* 54°48N 126°0W **70** C3
Babo *Indonesia* 2°30S 133°30E **37** E8
Bābol *Iran* 36°40N 52°50E **45** B7
Bābol Sar *Iran* 36°45N 52°45E **45** B7
Baboua *C.A.R.* 5°49N 14°58E **52** C2
Babruysk *Belarus* 53°10N 29°15E **17** B15
Babuhri *India* 26°49N 71°45E **42** F3
Babusar Pass *Pakistan* 35°12N 73°59E **43** B5
Babuyan Chan. *Phil.* 18°40N 121°30E **37** A6
Babylon *Iraq* 32°34N 44°22E **44** C5
Bac Can *Vietnam* 22°8N 105°49E **38** A5
Bac Giang *Vietnam* 21°16N 106°11E **38** B6
Bac Lieu *Vietnam* 9°17N 105°43E **39** H5
Bac Ninh *Vietnam* 21°13N 106°4E **38** B6
Bac Phan *Vietnam* 22°0N 105°0E **38** B5
Bacabal *Brazil* 4°15S 44°45W **93** D10
Bacalar *Mexico* 18°43N 88°27W **87** D7
Bacan, Kepulauan
  Indonesia 0°35S 127°30E **37** E7

Bacarra *Phil.* 18°15N 120°37E **37** A6
Bacău *Romania* 46°35N 26°55E **17** E14
Bacerac *Mexico* 30°18N 108°50W **86** A3
Bach Long Vi. Dao
  Vietnam 20°10N 107°40E **38** B6
Bach Ma △ *Vietnam* 16°11N 107°49E **38** D6
Bachhwara *India* 25°35N 85°54E **43** G11
Back → *Canada* 65°10N 104°0W **68** D11
Bacolod *Phil.* 10°40N 122°57E **37** B6
Bácum *Mexico* 27°33N 110°5W **86** B2
Bād *Iran* 33°41N 52°1E **45** C7
Bad → *U.S.A.* 44°21N 100°22W **80** C3
Bad Axe *U.S.A.* 43°48N 83°0W **82** C2
Bad Ischl *Austria* 47°44N 13°38E **16** E7
Bad Kissingen *Germany* 50°11N 10°4E **16** C6
Bada Barabil *India* 22°7N 85°24E **43** H11
Badagara *India* 11°35N 75°40E **40** P9
Badain Jaran Shamo
  China 40°23N 102°0E **32** C9
Badajós, L. *Brazil* 3°15S 62°50W **92** D6
Badajoz *Spain* 38°50N 6°59W **21** C2
Badakhshān □ *Afghan.* 36°30N 71°0E **40** A7
Badaling *China* 40°20N 116°0E **34** D8
Badalona *Spain* 41°26N 2°15E **21** B7
Badalzai *Afghan.* 29°50N 65°35E **42** E1
Badampahar *India* 22°10N 86°10E **41** H15
Badanah *Si. Arabia* 30°58N 41°30E **44** D4
Badarinath *India* 30°45N 79°30E **43** D8
Badas, Kepulauan
  Indonesia 0°45N 107°5E **36** D3
Baddo → *Pakistan* 28°0N 64°20E **40** F4
Bade *Indonesia* 7°10S 139°35E **37** F9
Baden *Austria* 48°1N 16°13E **16** D9
Baden *U.S.A.* 40°38N 80°14W **82** F4
Baden-Baden *Germany* 48°44N 8°13E **16** D5
Baden-Württemberg □
  Germany 48°20N 8°40E **16** D5
Badgam *India* 34°1N 74°45E **43** B6
Badgastein *Austria* 47°7N 13°9E **16** E7
Badger *Canada* 49°0N 56°4W **73** C8
Badger *U.S.A.* 36°38N 119°1W **78** J7
Bādghīs □ *Afghan.* 35°0N 63°0E **40** B3
Badgingarra △
  Australia 30°23S 115°22E **61** F2
Badin *Pakistan* 24°38N 68°54E **42** G3
Badlands *U.S.A.* 43°55N 102°30W **80** D2
Badlands △ *U.S.A.* 43°38N 102°56W **80** D2
Badrah *Iraq* 33°6N 45°58E **44** C5
Badrain Jaran Shamo
  China 40°40N 103°0E **34** D2
Badrinath *India* 30°44N 79°29E **43** D8
Badu *Australia* 10°5S 142°11E **62** a
Badulla *Sri Lanka* 7°1N 81°7E **40** R12
Badung, Bukit *Indonesia* 8°49S 115°10E **37** K18
Badung, Selat *Indonesia* 8°40S 115°22E **37** K18
Baena *Spain* 37°37N 4°20W **21** D3
Baengnyeongdo
  S. Korea 37°57N 124°40E **35** F13
Baeza *Spain* 37°57N 3°25W **21** D4
Bafatá *Guinea-Biss.* 12°8N 14°40W **50** F3
Baffin B. *N. Amer.* 72°0N 64°0W **66** B13
Baffin I. *Canada* 68°0N 75°0W **69** D17
Bafing → *Mali* 13°49N 10°50W **50** F3
Bafliyūn *Syria* 36°37N 36°59E **44** B3
Bafoulabé *Mali* 13°50N 10°55W **50** F3
Bafoussam *Cameroon* 5°28N 10°25E **52** C2
Bāfq *Iran* 31°40N 55°25E **45** D7
Bafra *Turkey* 41°34N 35°54E **19** F6
Bāft *Iran* 29°15N 56°38E **45** D8
Bafwasende
  Dem. Rep. of the Congo 1°3N 27°5E **54** B2
Bagaha *India* 27°6N 84°5E **43** F11
Bagamoyo *Tanzania* 6°28S 38°55E **54** D4
Bagan Datoh *Malaysia* 3°59N 100°47E **39** L3
Bagan Serai *Malaysia* 5°1N 100°32E **39** K3
Baganga *Phil.* 7°34N 126°33E **37** C7
Bagani *Namibia* 18°7S 21°41E **56** B3
Bagansiapiapi *Indonesia* 2°12N 100°50E **36** D2
Bagasra *India* 21°30N 71°0E **42** J4
Bagaud *India* 22°19N 75°53E **42** H6
Bagdad *U.S.A.* 34°35N 115°53W **79** L11
Bagdarin *Russia* 54°26N 113°36E **29** D12
Bagé *Brazil* 31°20S 54°15W **95** C5
Bagenalstown = Muine Bheag
  Ireland 52°42N 6°58W **10** D5
Baggs *U.S.A.* 41°2N 107°39W **76** F10
Bagh *Pakistan* 33°59N 73°45E **43** C5
Baghain → *India* 25°32N 81°1E **43** G9
Baghdād *Iraq* 33°20N 44°23E **44** C5
Bagheria *Italy* 38°5N 13°30E **22** E5
Baghlān *Afghan.* 32°12N 68°46E **40** A6
Baghlān □ *Afghan.* 36°0N 68°30E **40** B6
Bagley *U.S.A.* 47°32N 95°24W **80** B6
Bago = Pegu *Burma* 17°20N 96°29E **41** L20
Bagodar *India* 24°5N 85°52E **43** G11
Bagrationovsk *Russia* 54°23N 20°39E **9** J19
Baguio *Phil.* 16°26N 120°34E **37** A6
Bah *India* 26°53N 78°36E **43** F8
Bahadurganj *India* 26°16N 87°49E **43** F12
Bahadurgarh *India* 28°40N 76°57E **42** E7
Bahama, Canal Viejo de
  W. Indies 22°10N 77°30W **88** B4
Bahamas ■ *N. Amer.* 24°0N 75°0W **89** B5
Bahār *Iran* 34°54N 48°26E **45** C6
Baharampur *India* 24°2N 88°27E **43** G13
Baharu Pandan = Pandan
  Malaysia 1°32N 103°46E **39** d
Bahawalnagar *Pakistan* 30°0N 73°15E **42** E5
Bahawalpur *Pakistan* 29°24N 71°40E **42** E4
Bäherden *Turkmenistan* 38°25N 57°26E **45** B8
Baheri *India* 28°45N 79°34E **43** E8
Bahgul → *India* 27°45N 79°36E **43** F8
Bahi *Tanzania* 5°58S 35°21E **54** D4
Bahi Swamp *Tanzania* 6°10S 35°0E **54** D4
Bahia = Salvador *Brazil* 13°0S 38°30W **93** F11
Bahia □ *Brazil* 12°0S 42°0W **93** F10
Bahia, Is. de la *Honduras* 16°45N 86°15W **88** C2
Bahía Blanca *Argentina* 38°35S 62°13W **94** D3
Bahía de Caráquez
  Ecuador 0°40S 80°27W **92** D2

Bahía Kino Mexico 28°47N 111°58W 86 B2
Bahía Laura Argentina 48°10S 66°30W 96 F3
Bahía Negra Paraguay 20°5S 58°5W 92 H7
Bahir Dar Ethiopia 11°37N 37°10E 47 E2
Bahmanzād Iran 31°15N 51°47E 45 D6
Bahraich India 27°38N 81°37E 43 F9
Bahrain ■ Asia 26°0N 50°35E 45 E6
Bahror India 27°51N 76°20E 42 F7
Bāhū Kalāt Iran 25°43N 61°25E 45 E9
Bai Bung, Mui = Ca Mau, Mui
Vietnam 8°38N 104°44E 39 H5
Bai Thuong Vietnam 19°54N 105°23E 38 C5
Baia Mare Romania 47°40N 23°35E 17 E12
Baião Brazil 2°40S 49°40W 93 D9
Baïbokoum Chad 7°46N 15°43E 51 G9
Baicheng China 45°38N 122°42E 35 B12
Baidoa = Baydhabo
Somali Rep. 3°8N 43°30E 47 G3
Baie-Comeau Canada 49°12N 68°10W 73 C6
Baie-St-Paul Canada 47°28N 70°32W 73 C5
Baie Ste-Anne Seychelles 4°18S 55°45E 53 b
Baie-Trinité Canada 49°25N 67°20W 73 C6
Baie Verte Canada 49°55N 56°12W 73 C8
Baihar India 22°6N 80°33E 43 H9
Baihe Hubei, China 32°50N 110°5E 34 H6
Baihe Jilin, China 42°27N 128°9E 35 C15
Ba'ījī Iraq 35°0N 43°30E 44 C4
Baijnath India 29°55N 79°37E 43 E8
Baikal, L. = Baykal, Oz.
Russia 53°0N 108°0E 29 D11
Baikonur = Bayqongyr
Kazakhstan 45°40N 63°20E 28 E7
Baikunthpur India 23°15N 82°33E 43 H10
Baile Átha Cliath = Dublin
Ireland 53°21N 6°15W 10 C5
Baile Átha Fhirdhia = Ardee
Ireland 53°52N 6°33W 10 C5
Baile Átha I = Athy Ireland 53°0N 7°0W 10 C5
Baile Átha Luain = Athlone
Ireland 53°25N 7°56W 10 C4
Baile Átha Troim = Trim
Ireland 53°33N 6°48W 10 C5
Baile Brigín = Balbriggan
Ireland 53°37N 6°11W 10 C5
Băileşti Romania 44°1N 23°20E 17 F12
Bainbridge Ga., U.S.A. 30°55N 84°35W 85 F12
Bainbridge N.Y., U.S.A. 42°18N 75°29W 83 D9
Bainbridge Island
U.S.A. 47°38N 122°32W 78 C4
Baine China 42°0N 128°0E 33 C14
Baing Indonesia 10°14S 120°34E 37 F6
Bainiu China 32°50N 112°15E 34 H7
Bā'ir Jordan 30°45N 36°55E 46 E5
Baird Mts. U.S.A. 67°0N 160°0W 74 B8
Bairiki = Tarawa Kiribati 1°30N 173°0E 64 G9
Bairin Youqi China 43°30N 118°35E 35 C10
Bairin Zuoqi China 43°58N 119°15E 35 C10
Bairnsdale Australia 37°48S 147°36E 63 F4
Baisha China 34°20N 112°32E 34 G7
Baisha Li China 19°12N 109°20E 38 C7
Baishan China 42°43N 127°14E 35 C14
Baitadi Nepal 29°35N 80°25E 43 E9
Baiyin China 36°45N 104°14E 34 F3
Baiyu Shan China 37°15N 107°30E 34 F4
Baj Baj India 22°30N 88°5E 43 H13
Baja Hungary 46°12N 18°59E 17 E10
Baja, Pta. Mexico 29°58N 115°49W 86 B1
Baja California Mexico 31°10N 115°12W 86 A1
Baja California □ Mexico 30°0N 115°0W 86 B2
Baja California Sur □
Mexico 25°50N 111°50W 86 B2
Bajag India 22°40N 81°21E 43 H9
Bajamar Canary Is. 28°33N 16°20W 24 F3
Bajana India 23°7N 71°49E 42 H4
Bajatrejo Indonesia 8°29S 114°19E 37 J17
Bajera Indonesia 8°31S 115°2E 37 J18
Bājgīrān Iran 37°36N 58°24E 45 B8
Bajimba, Mt. Australia 29°17S 152°6E 63 D5
Bajo Boquete Panama 8°46N 82°27W 88 E3
Bajo Nuevo Caribbean 15°40N 78°50W 88 C4
Bajoga Nigeria 10°57N 11°20E 51 F8
Bajool Australia 23°40S 150°35E 62 C5
Bakel Senegal 14°56N 12°20W 50 F3
Baker Calif., U.S.A. 35°16N 116°4W 79 K10
Baker Mont., U.S.A. 46°22N 104°17W 76 C11
Baker, L. Canada 64°0N 96°0W 68 E12
Baker, Mt. U.S.A. 48°50N 121°49W 76 B3
Baker City U.S.A. 44°47N 117°50W 76 D5
Baker I. Pac. Oc. 0°10N 176°35W 64 G10
Baker I. U.S.A. 55°20N 133°40W 70 B2
Baker L. Australia 26°54S 126°5E 61 E4
Baker Lake Canada 64°20N 96°3W 68 E12
Bakers Creek Australia 21°13S 149°7E 62 C4
Bakers Dozen Is. Canada 56°45N 78°45W 72 A4
Bakersfield Calif., U.S.A. 35°23N 119°1W 79 K8
Bakersfield Vt., U.S.A. 44°45N 72°48W 83 B12
Bakharden = Bäherden
Turkmenistan 38°25N 57°26E 45 B8
Bākhtarān = Kermānshāh
Iran 34°23N 47°0E 44 C5
Bākhtarān = Kermānshāh □
Iran 34°0N 46°30E 44 C5
Bakı Azerbaijan 40°29N 49°56E 45 A6
Bakkafjörður Iceland 66°2N 14°48W 8 C6
Bakkagerði Iceland 65°31N 13°49W 8 D7
Bakony Hungary 47°10N 17°30E 17 E9
Bakony Forest = Bakony
Hungary 47°10N 17°30E 17 E9
Bakouma C.A.R. 5°40N 22°56E 52 C4
Bakswaho India 24°15N 79°18E 43 G8
Baku = Bakı Azerbaijan 40°29N 49°56E 45 A6
Bakutis Coast Antarctica 74°0S 120°0W 5 D15
Baky = Bakı Azerbaijan 40°29N 49°56E 45 A6
Bala Canada 45°1N 79°37W 82 A5
Bala U.K. 52°54N 3°36W 12 E4
Bala, L. U.K. 52°53N 3°37W 12 E4
Balabac I. Phil. 8°0N 117°0E 36 C5
Balabac Str. E. Indies 7°53N 117°5E 36 C5
Balabagh Afghan. 34°25N 70°12E 42 B4
Ba'labakk Lebanon 34°0N 36°10E 46 B5
Balabalangan, Kepulauan
Indonesia 2°20S 117°30E 36 E5
Balad Iraq 34°0N 44°9E 44 C5
Balad Rūz Iraq 33°42N 45°5E 44 C5
Bālādeh Fārs, Iran 29°17N 51°56E 45 D6
Bālādeh Māzandaran, Iran 36°12N 51°48E 45 B6
Balaghat India 21°49N 80°12E 40 J12
Balaghat Ra. India 18°50N 76°30E 40 K10
Balaguer Spain 41°50N 0°50E 21 B6
Balaklava Ukraine 44°30N 33°30E 19 F5
Balakovo Russia 52°4N 47°55E 18 D8
Balamau India 27°10N 80°21E 43 F9
Balancán Mexico 17°48N 91°32W 87 D6
Balashov Russia 51°30N 43°10E 19 D7
Balasinor India 22°57N 73°23E 42 H5
Balasore = Baleshwar
India 21°35N 87°3E 41 J15
Balaton Hungary 46°50N 17°40E 17 E9
Balbina, Represa de Brazil 2°0S 59°30W 92 D7
Balboa Panama 8°57N 79°34W 88 E4
Balbriggan Ireland 53°37N 6°11W 10 C5
Balcarce Argentina 38°0S 58°10W 94 D4
Balcarres Canada 50°50N 103°35W 71 C8
Balchik Bulgaria 43°28N 28°11E 23 C13
Balclutha N.Z. 46°15S 169°45E 59 G2
Balcones Escarpment
U.S.A. 29°30N 99°15W 84 G5
Bald I. Australia 34°57S 118°27E 61 F2
Bald Knob U.S.A. 35°19N 91°34W 84 D9
Baldock L. Canada 56°33N 97°57W 71 B9
Baldwin Mich., U.S.A. 43°54N 85°51W 81 D11
Baldwin Pa., U.S.A. 40°21N 79°58W 82 F5
Baldwinsville U.S.A. 43°10N 76°20W 83 C8
Baldy Peak U.S.A. 33°54N 109°34W 77 K9
Baleares, Is. Spain 39°30N 3°0E 24 B10
Balearic Is. = Baleares, Is.
Spain 39°30N 3°0E 24 B10
Baleine → Canada 58°15N 67°40W 73 A6
Baleine, Petite R. de la →
Canada 56°0N 76°45W 72 A4
Baler Phil. 15°46N 121°34E 37 A6
Baleshare U.K. 57°31N 7°22W 11 D1
Baleshwar India 21°35N 87°3E 41 J15
Baley Russia 51°36N 116°37E 29 D12
Balfate Honduras 15°48N 86°25W 88 C2
Balgo Australia 20°9S 127°58E 60 D4
Bali Greece 35°25N 24°47E 25 D6
Bali India 25°11N 73°17E 42 G5
Bali Indonesia 8°20S 115°0E 37 J18
Bali □ Indonesia 8°20S 115°0E 37 J17
Bali, Selat Indonesia 8°18S 114°25E 37 J17
Bali Barat △ Indonesia 8°12S 114°35E 37 J17
Bali Sea Indonesia 8°0S 115°0E 37 J17
Baliapal India 21°40N 87°17E 43 J12
Balik Pulau Malaysia 5°21N 100°14E 39 c
Balıkeşir Turkey 39°39N 27°53E 23 E12
Balikpapan Indonesia 1°10S 116°55E 36 E5
Balimbing Phil. 5°5N 119°58E 37 C5
Baling Malaysia 5°41N 100°55E 39 K3
Balkan Mts. = Stara Planina
Bulgaria 43°15N 23°0E 23 C10
Balkanabat Turkmenistan 39°30N 54°22E 45 B7
Balkhash = Balqash
Kazakhstan 46°50N 74°50E 28 E8
Balkhash, Ozero = Balqash Köli
Kazakhstan 46°0N 74°50E 32 B3
Ballachulish U.K. 56°41N 5°8W 11 E3
Balladonia Australia 32°27S 123°51E 61 F3
Ballaghaderreen Ireland 53°55N 8°34W 10 C3
Ballarat Australia 37°33S 143°50E 63 F3
Ballard, L. Australia 29°20S 120°40E 61 E3
Ballater U.K. 57°3N 3°3W 11 D5
Ballenas, Canal de
Mexico 29°10N 113°29W 86 B2
Balleny Is. Antarctica 66°30S 163°0E 5 C11
Ballia India 25°46N 84°12E 43 G11
Ballina Australia 28°50S 153°31E 63 D5
Ballina Ireland 54°7N 9°9W 10 B2
Ballinasloe Ireland 53°20N 8°13W 10 C3
Ballinger U.S.A. 31°45N 99°57W 84 F5
Ballinrobe Ireland 53°38N 9°13W 10 C2
Ballinskelligs B. Ireland 51°48N 10°13W 10 E1
Ballston Spa U.S.A. 43°0N 73°51W 83 D11
Ballyboghil Ireland 53°32N 6°16W 10 C5
Ballybunion Ireland 52°31N 9°40W 10 D2
Ballycanew Ireland 52°37N 6°19W 10 D5
Ballycastle U.K. 55°12N 6°15W 10 A5
Ballyclare U.K. 54°46N 6°0W 10 B5
Ballydehob Ireland 51°34N 9°28W 10 E2
Ballygawley U.K. 54°27N 7°2W 10 B4
Ballyhaunis Ireland 53°46N 8°46W 10 C3
Ballyheige Ireland 52°23N 9°49W 10 D2
Ballymena U.K. 54°52N 6°17W 10 B5
Ballymoney U.K. 55°5N 6°31W 10 A5
Ballymote Ireland 54°5N 8°31W 10 B3
Ballynahinch U.K. 54°24N 5°54W 10 B6
Ballyquintin Pt. U.K. 54°20N 5°30W 10 B6
Ballyshannon Ireland 54°30N 8°11W 10 B3
Balmaceda Chile 46°0S 71°50W 96 F2
Balmertown Canada 51°4N 93°41W 71 C10
Balmoral Australia 37°15S 141°48E 63 F3
Balmorhea U.S.A. 30°59N 103°45W 84 F3
Balochistan = Baluchistan □
Pakistan 27°30N 65°0E 40 F4
Balonne → Australia 28°47S 147°56E 63 D4
Balotra India 25°50N 72°14E 42 G5
Balqash Kazakhstan 46°50N 74°50E 28 E8
Balqash Köli Kazakhstan 46°0N 74°50E 32 B3
Balrampur India 27°30N 82°20E 43 F10
Balranald Australia 34°38S 143°33E 63 E3
Balsas → Brazil 7°15S 44°35W 93 E9
Balsas → Mexico 17°55N 102°10W 86 D4
Balsas del Norte Mexico 18°0N 99°46W 87 D5
Balta Ukraine 47°56N 29°45E 17 D15
Bălţi Moldova 47°48N 27°58E 17 E14
Baltic Sea Europe 57°0N 19°0E 9 H18
Baltimore Ireland 51°29N 9°22W 10 E2
Baltimore Md., U.S.A. 39°17N 76°36W 81 F15
Baltimore Ohio, U.S.A. 39°51N 82°36W 82 G2
Baltinglass Ireland 52°56N 6°43W 10 D5
Baltit Pakistan 36°15N 74°40E 43 A6
Baltiysk Russia 54°41N 19°58E 9 J18
Baluchistan □ Pakistan 27°30N 65°0E 40 F4
Balurghat India 25°15N 88°44E 43 G13
Balvi Latvia 57°8N 27°15E 9 H22
Balya Turkey 39°44N 27°35E 23 E12
Balykchy Kyrgyzstan 42°26N 76°12E 32 C4
Balyqshy Kazakhstan 47°4N 51°52E 19 E9
Bam Iran 29°7N 58°14E 45 D8
Bama Nigeria 11°33N 13°41E 51 F8
Bamaga Australia 10°50S 142°25E 62 A3
Bamaji L. Canada 51°9N 91°25W 72 B1
Bamako Mali 12°34N 7°55W 50 F4
Bambari C.A.R. 5°40N 20°35E 52 C4
Bambaroo Australia 18°50S 146°10E 62 B4
Bamberg Germany 49°54N 10°54E 16 D6
Bamberg U.S.A. 33°18N 81°2W 85 E14
Bambili
Dem. Rep. of the Congo 3°40N 26°0E 54 B2
Bamburgh U.K. 55°37N 1°43W 12 B6
Bamenda Cameroon 5°57N 10°11E 52 C2
Bamfield Canada 48°45N 125°10W 70 D3
Bāmīān □ Afghan. 35°0N 67°0E 40 B5
Bamiancheng China 43°15N 124°2E 35 C13
Bampūr Iran 27°15N 60°21E 45 E9
Bampūr → Iran 27°24N 59°0E 45 E8
Ban Ao Tu Khun Thailand 8°9N 98°20E 39 a
Ban Ban Laos 19°31N 103°30E 38 C4
Ban Bang Hin Thailand 9°32N 98°35E 39 H2
Ban Bang Khu Thailand 7°57N 98°23E 39 a
Ban Bang Rong Thailand 8°3N 98°25E 39 a
Ban Bo Phut Thailand 9°33N 100°2E 39 b
Ban Chaweng Thailand 9°32N 100°3E 39 b
Ban Chiang Thailand 17°30N 103°10E 38 D4
Ban Chiang Klang
Thailand 19°25N 100°55E 38 C3
Ban Choho Thailand 15°2N 102°9E 38 E4
Ban Dan Lan Hoi Thailand 17°0N 99°35E 38 D2
Ban Don = Surat Thani
Thailand 9°6N 99°20E 39 H2
Ban Don Vietnam 12°53N 107°48E 38 F6
Ban Don, Ao → Thailand 9°20N 99°25E 39 H2
Ban Dong Thailand 19°30N 100°59E 38 C3
Ban Hong Thailand 18°18N 98°50E 38 C2
Ban Hua Thanon Thailand 9°26N 100°1E 39 b
Ban Kantang Thailand 7°25N 99°31E 39 J2
Ban Karon Thailand 7°51N 98°18E 39 a
Ban Kata Thailand 7°50N 98°18E 39 a
Ban Keun Laos 18°22N 102°35E 38 C4
Ban Khai Thailand 12°46N 101°18E 38 F3
Ban Kheun Laos 20°13N 101°7E 38 B3
Ban Khlong Khian
Thailand 8°10N 98°26E 39 a
Ban Khlong Kua Thailand 6°57N 100°8E 39 J3
Ban Khuan Thailand 8°20N 98°25E 39 a
Ban Ko Yai Chim
Thailand 11°17N 99°26E 39 G2
Ban Laem Thailand 13°13N 99°59E 38 F2
Ban Lamai Thailand 9°28N 100°3E 39 b
Ban Lao Ngam Laos 15°28N 106°10E 38 E6
Ban Le Kathe Thailand 15°49N 98°53E 38 E2
Ban Lo Po Noi Thailand 8°1N 98°34E 39 a
Ban Mae Chedi Thailand 19°11N 99°31E 38 C2
Ban Mae Nam Thailand 9°34N 100°0E 39 b
Ban Mae Sariang
Thailand 18°10N 97°56E 38 C1
Ban Mê Thuôt = Buon Ma Thuot
Vietnam 12°40N 108°3E 38 F7
Ban Mi Thailand 15°3N 100°32E 38 E3
Ban Muang Mo Laos 19°4N 103°58E 38 C4
Ban Na Bo Thailand 9°19N 99°41E 39 b
Ban Na San Thailand 8°53N 99°52E 39 H2
Ban Na Tong Laos 20°56N 101°47E 38 B3
Ban Nam Bac Laos 20°38N 102°20E 38 B4
Ban Nammi Laos 17°7N 105°40E 38 D5
Ban Nong Bok Laos 17°5N 104°48E 38 D5
Ban Nong Pling
Thailand 15°40N 100°10E 38 E3
Ban Pak Chan Thailand 10°32N 98°51E 39 G2
Ban Patong Thailand 7°54N 98°18E 39 a
Ban Phai Thailand 16°4N 102°44E 38 D4
Ban Phak Chit Thailand 8°0N 98°24E 39 a
Ban Pong Thailand 13°50N 99°55E 38 F2
Ban Rawai Thailand 7°47N 98°20E 39 a
Ban Ron Phibun Thailand 8°9N 99°51E 39 H2
Ban Sakhu Thailand 8°4N 98°18E 39 a
Ban Sanam Chai
Thailand 7°33N 100°25E 39 J3
Ban Tak Thailand 17°2N 99°4E 38 D2
Ban Tako Thailand 14°5N 102°40E 38 E4
Ban Tha Nun Thailand 8°12N 98°18E 39 a
Ban Tha Rua Thailand 7°59N 98°22E 39 a
Ban Tha Yu Thailand 8°17N 98°22E 39 a
Ban Thong Krut Thailand 9°25N 99°57E 39 b
Ban Xien Kok Laos 20°54N 100°39E 38 B3
Ban Yen Nhan Vietnam 20°57N 106°2E 38 B6
Banaba Kiribati 0°45S 169°50E 64 H8
Banalia
Dem. Rep. of the Congo 1°32N 25°5E 54 B2
Banam Cambodia 11°20N 105°17E 39 G5
Bananal, I. do Brazil 11°30S 50°30W 93 F8
Banaras = Varanasi
India 25°22N 83°0E 43 G10
Banas → Gujarat, India 23°45N 71°25E 42 H4
Banas → Mad. P., India 24°15N 81°30E 43 G9
Bânâs, Ras Egypt 23°57N 35°59E 51 D13
Banbridge U.K. 54°22N 6°16W 10 B5
Banbury U.K. 52°4N 1°20W 13 E6
Banchory U.K. 57°3N 2°29W 11 D6
Bancroft Canada 45°3N 77°51W 82 A7
Band Bonī Iran 25°30N 59°33E 45 E8
Band Qīr Iran 31°39N 48°53E 45 D6
Banda Mad. P., India 24°3N 78°57E 43 G8
Banda Ut. P., India 25°30N 80°26E 43 G9
Banda, Kepulauan
Indonesia 4°37S 129°50E 37 E7
Banda Aceh Indonesia 5°35N 95°20E 36 C1
Banda Banda, Mt.
Australia 31°10S 152°28E 63 E5
Banda Elat Indonesia 5°40S 133°5E 37 F8
Banda Is. = Banda, Kepulauan
Indonesia 4°37S 129°50E 37 E7
Banda Sea Indonesia 6°0S 130°0E 37 F8
Bandai-Asahi △ Japan 37°38N 140°5E 30 F10
Bandai-San Japan 37°36N 140°4E 30 F10
Bandān Iran 31°23N 60°44E 45 D9
Bandanaira Indonesia 4°32S 129°54E 37 E7
Bandanwara India 26°9N 74°38E 42 F6
Bandar = Machilipatnam
India 16°12N 81°8E 41 L12
Bandar-e Abbās Iran 27°15N 56°15E 45 E8
Bandar-e Anzalī Iran 37°30N 49°30E 45 B6
Bandar-e Bushehr = Būshehr
Iran 28°55N 50°55E 45 D6
Bandar-e Chārak Iran 26°45N 54°20E 45 E7
Bandar-e Deylam Iran 30°5N 50°10E 45 D6
Bandar-e Emām Khomeynī
Iran 30°30N 49°5E 45 D6
Bandar-e Lengeh Iran 26°35N 54°58E 45 E7
Bandar-e Maqām Iran 26°56N 53°29E 45 E7
Bandar-e Ma'shur Iran 30°35N 49°10E 45 D6
Bandar-e Rīg Iran 29°29N 50°38E 45 D6
Bandar-e Torkeman Iran 37°0N 54°10E 45 B7
Bandar Labuan Malaysia 5°20N 115°14E 36 C5
Bandar Lampung
Indonesia 5°20S 105°10E 36 F3
Bandar Maharani = Muar
Malaysia 2°3N 102°34E 39 L4
Bandar Penggaram = Batu Pahat
Malaysia 1°50N 102°56E 39 M4
Bandar Seri Begawan
Brunei 4°52N 115°0E 36 D5
Bandar Sri Aman
Malaysia 1°15N 111°32E 36 D4
Bandawe Malawi 11°58S 34°5E 55 E3
Bandeira, Pico da Brazil 20°26S 41°47W 95 A7
Bandera Argentina 28°55S 62°20W 94 B3
Banderas, B. de Mexico 20°40N 105°25W 86 C3
Bandhavgarh India 23°40N 81°2E 43 H9
Bandi → India 26°12N 75°47E 42 F6
Bandikui India 27°3N 76°34E 42 F7
Bandırma Turkey 40°20N 28°0E 23 D13
Bandjarmasin = Banjarmasin
Indonesia 3°20S 114°35E 36 E4
Bandon Ireland 51°44N 8°44W 10 E3
Bandon → Ireland 51°43N 8°37W 10 E3
Bandula Mozam. 19°0S 33°7E 55 F3
Bandundu
Dem. Rep. of the Congo 3°15S 17°22E 52 E3
Bandung Indonesia 6°54S 107°36E 37 G12
Bāneh Iran 35°59N 45°53E 44 C5
Banes Cuba 21°0N 75°42W 89 B4
Banff Canada 51°10N 115°34W 70 C5
Banff U.K. 57°40N 2°33W 11 D6
Banff △ Canada 51°30N 116°15W 70 C5
Bang Fai → Laos 16°57N 104°45E 38 D5
Bang Hieng → Laos 16°10N 105°10E 38 D5
Bang Krathum Thailand 16°34N 100°18E 38 D3
Bang Lamung Thailand 13°3N 100°56E 38 F3
Bang Lang △ Thailand 5°58N 101°19E 39 K3
Bang Lang Res. Thailand 6°6N 101°17E 39 J3
Bang Mun Nak Thailand 16°2N 100°23E 38 D3
Bang Pa In Thailand 14°14N 100°35E 38 E3
Bang Rakam Thailand 16°45N 100°7E 38 D3
Bang Saphan Thailand 11°14N 99°28E 39 G2
Bang Thao Thailand 7°59N 98°18E 39 a
Bangaduni I. India 21°34N 88°52E 43 J13
Bangala Dam Zimbabwe 21°7S 31°25E 55 G3
Bangalore India 12°59N 77°40E 40 N10
Banganga → India 27°6N 77°25E 42 F6
Bangaon India 23°0N 88°47E 43 H13
Bangassou C.A.R. 4°55N 23°7E 52 D4
Banggai Indonesia 1°34S 123°30E 37 E6
Banggai, Kepulauan
Indonesia 1°40S 123°30E 37 E6
Banggai Arch. = Banggai,
Kepulauan Indonesia 1°40S 123°30E 37 E6
Banggi, Pulau Malaysia 7°17N 117°12E 36 C5
Banghāzī Libya 32°11N 20°3E 51 B10
Bangka Sulawesi, Indonesia 1°50N 125°5E 37 D7
Bangka Sumatera,
Indonesia 2°0S 105°50E 36 E3
Bangka, Selat Indonesia 2°30S 105°30E 36 E3
Bangka-Belitung □
Indonesia 2°30S 107°0E 36 E3
Bangkalan Indonesia 7°2S 112°46E 37 G15
Bangkinang Indonesia 0°18N 101°5E 36 D2
Bangko Indonesia 2°5S 102°9E 36 E2
Bangkok Thailand 13°45N 100°35E 38 F3
Bangkok, Bight of
Thailand 12°55N 100°30E 38 F3
Bangla = West Bengal □
India 23°0N 88°0E 43 H13
Bangladesh ■ Asia 24°0N 90°0E 41 H17
Bangli Indonesia 8°27S 115°21E 37 J18
Bangong Co China 33°45N 78°43E 43 C8
Bangor Down, U.K. 54°40N 5°40W 10 B6
Bangor Gwynedd, U.K. 53°14N 4°8W 12 D3
Bangor Maine, U.S.A. 44°48N 68°46W 81 C19
Bangor Pa., U.S.A. 40°52N 75°13W 83 F9
Bangued Phil. 17°40N 120°37E 37 A6
Bangui C.A.R. 4°23N 18°35E 52 D3
Banguru
Dem. Rep. of the Congo 0°30N 27°10E 54 B2
Bangweulu, L. Zambia 11°0S 30°0E 55 E3
Bangweulu Swamp
Zambia 11°20S 30°15E 55 E3
Banhine △ Mozam. 22°49S 32°55E 57 C5
Baní Dom. Rep. 18°16N 70°22W 89 C5
Banī Sa'd Iraq 33°34N 44°32E 44 C5
Banihal Pass India 33°30N 75°12E 43 C6
Banissa Kenya 3°55N 40°19E 54 B4
Bāniyās Syria 35°10N 36°0E 44 C3
Banja Luka Bos.-H. 44°49N 17°11E 22 B7
Banjar India 31°38N 77°21E 42 D7
Banjar → India 22°36N 80°22E 43 H9
Banjarmasin Indonesia 3°20S 114°35E 36 E4
Banjul Gambia 13°28N 16°40W 50 F2
Banka India 24°53N 86°55E 43 G12
Banket Zimbabwe 17°27S 30°19E 55 F3
Bankipore India 25°35N 85°10E 41 G14
Banks I. = Moa Australia 10°11S 142°16E 62 a
Banks I. B.C., Canada 53°20N 130°0W 70 C3
Banks I. N.W.T., Canada 73°15N 121°30W 68 C7
Banks Pen. N.Z. 43°45S 173°15E 59 E4
Banks Str. Australia 40°40S 148°10E 63 G4
Bankura India 23°11N 87°18E 43 H12
Banmankhi India 25°53N 87°11E 43 G12
Bann → Armagh, U.K. 54°30N 6°31W 10 B5
Bann → L'derry., U.K. 55°8N 6°41W 10 A5
Bannang Sata Thailand 6°16N 101°16E 39 J3
Banning U.S.A. 33°56N 116°53W 79 M10
Bannockburn Canada 44°39N 77°33W 82 B7
Bannockburn U.K. 56°5N 3°55W 11 E5
Bannockburn Zimbabwe 20°17S 29°48E 55 G2
Bannu Pakistan 33°0N 70°18E 40 C7
Bano India 22°40N 84°55E 43 H11
Bansgaon India 26°33N 83°21E 43 F10
Banská Bystrica
Slovak Rep. 48°46N 19°14E 17 D10
Banswara India 23°32N 74°24E 42 H6
Bantaeng Indonesia 5°32S 119°56E 37 F5
Banteay Prei Nokor
Cambodia 11°56N 105°40E 39 G5
Banten □ Indonesia 6°30S 106°0E 37 G11
Bantry Ireland 51°41N 9°27W 10 E2
Bantry B. Ireland 51°37N 9°44W 10 E2
Bantva India 21°29N 70°12E 42 J4
Banyak, Kepulauan
Indonesia 2°10N 97°10E 36 D1
Banyalbufar Spain 39°42N 2°31E 24 B9
Banyo Cameroon 6°52N 11°45E 52 C2
Banyuwangi Indonesia 8°13S 114°21E 37 J17
Banzare Coast Antarctica 68°0S 125°0E 5 C9
Bao Ha Vietnam 22°11N 104°21E 38 A5
Bao Lac Vietnam 22°57N 105°40E 38 A5
Bao Loc Vietnam 11°32N 107°48E 39 G6
Bao'an China 22°34N 113°52E 33 a
Baocheng China 33°12N 106°56E 34 H4
Baode China 39°1N 111°5E 34 E6
Baodi China 39°38N 117°20E 35 E9
Baoding China 38°50N 115°28E 34 E8
Baoji China 34°20N 107°5E 34 G4
Baoshan China 25°10N 99°5E 32 F8
Baotou China 40°32N 110°2E 34 D6
Baoying China 33°17N 119°20E 35 H10
Baoyou = Ledong China 18°41N 109°5E 38 C7
Bap India 27°23N 72°18E 42 F5
Bapatla India 15°55N 80°30E 41 M12
Bāqerābād Iran 33°2N 51°58E 45 C6
Ba'qūbah Iraq 33°45N 44°50E 44 C5
Baquedano Chile 23°20S 69°52W 94 A2
Bar Montenegro 42°8N 19°6E 23 C8
Bar Ukraine 49°4N 27°40E 17 D14
Bar Bigha India 25°21N 85°47E 43 G11
Bar Harbor U.S.A. 44°23N 68°13W 81 C19
Bar-le-Duc France 48°47N 5°10E 20 B6
Bara India 25°16N 81°43E 43 G9
Bara Banki India 26°55N 81°12E 43 F9
Barabai Indonesia 2°32S 115°34E 36 E5
Baraboo U.S.A. 43°28N 89°45W 80 D9
Baracoa Cuba 20°20N 74°30W 89 B5
Baradā → Syria 33°33N 36°34E 46 B5
Baradero Argentina 33°52S 59°29W 94 C4
Baraga U.S.A. 46°47N 88°30W 80 B9
Baragoi Kenya 1°47N 36°47E 54 B4
Barah → India 27°42N 77°5E 42 F6
Barahona Dom. Rep. 18°13N 71°7W 89 C5
Barail Range India 25°15N 93°20E 41 G18
Barakaldo Spain 43°18N 2°59W 21 A4
Barakar → India 24°7N 86°14E 43 G12
Barakot India 21°33N 84°59E 43 J11
Barakpur India 22°47N 88°21E 43 H13
Baralaba Australia 24°13S 149°50E 62 C4
Baralzon L. Canada 60°0N 98°3W 71 B9
Baramula India 34°15N 74°20E 43 B6
Baran India 25°9N 76°40E 42 G7
Baran → Pakistan 25°13N 68°17E 42 G3
Baranavichy Belarus 53°10N 26°0E 17 B14
Baranof U.S.A. 57°5N 134°50W 70 B2
Baranof I. U.S.A. 57°0N 135°0W 68 F4
Barapasi Indonesia 2°15S 137°5E 37 E9
Barasat India 22°46N 88°31E 43 H13
Barat Daya, Kepulauan
Indonesia 7°30S 128°0E 37 F7
Barataria B. U.S.A. 29°20N 89°55W 85 G10
Barauda India 23°33N 75°15E 42 H6
Baraut India 29°13N 77°7E 42 E7
Barbacena Brazil 21°15S 43°56W 95 A7
Barbados ■ W. Indies 13°10N 59°30W 89 g
Barbària, C. de Spain 38°39N 1°24E 24 C7
Barbas, C. W. Sahara 22°20N 16°42W 50 D2
Barbastro Spain 42°2N 0°5E 21 A6
Barbeau Pk. Canada 81°54N 75°1W 69 A16
Barberton S. Africa 25°42S 31°2E 57 D5
Barberton U.S.A. 41°1N 81°39W 82 E3
Barbosa Colombia 5°57N 73°37W 92 B4
Barbourville U.S.A. 36°52N 83°53W 81 G12
Barbuda W. Indies 17°30N 61°40W 89 C7
Barcaldine Australia 23°43S 145°6E 62 C4
Barcellona Pozzo di Gotto
Italy 38°9N 15°13E 22 E6
Barcelona Spain 41°22N 2°10E 21 B7
Barcelona Venezuela 10°10N 64°40W 92 A6
Barceloneta Puerto Rico 18°27N 66°32W 89 d
Barcelos Brazil 1°0S 63°0W 92 D6
Barcoo → Australia 25°30S 142°50E 62 D3
Bardaï Chad 21°25N 17°0E 51 D9
Bardas Blancas
Argentina 35°49S 69°45W 94 D2
Bardawīl, Sabkhet el
Egypt 31°10N 33°15E 46 D2
Barddhaman India 23°14N 87°39E 43 H12
Bardejov Slovak Rep. 49°18N 21°15E 17 D11
Bardera = Baardheere
Somali Rep. 2°20N 42°27E 47 G3
Bardīyah Libya 31°45N 25°5E 51 B10
Bardsey I. U.K. 52°45N 4°47W 12 E3
Bardstown U.S.A. 37°49N 85°28W 81 G11
Bareilly India 28°22N 79°27E 43 E8

Barela India 23°6N 80°3E 43 H9
Barents Sea Arctic 73°0N 39°0E 4 B9
Barfleur, Pte. de France 49°42N 1°16W 20 B3
Bargara Australia 24°50S 152°25E 62 C5
Bargi Dam India 22°59N 80°0E 43 H9
Barguzin Russia 53°37N 109°37E 29 D11
Barh India 25°29N 85°46E 43 G11
Barhaj India 26°18N 83°44E 43 F10
Barharwa India 24°52N 87°47E 43 G12
Barhi India 24°15N 85°25E 43 G11
Bari India 26°39N 77°39E 42 F7
Bari Italy 41°8N 16°51E 22 D7
Bari Doab Pakistan 30°20N 73°0E 42 D5
Bari Sadri India 24°28N 74°30E 42 G6
Barīdī, Ra's Si. Arabia 24°17N 37°31E 44 E3
Barīm Yemen 12°39N 43°25E 48 E8
Barinas Venezuela 8°36N 70°15W 92 B4
Baring, C. Canada 70°0N 117°30W 68 D8
Baringo, L. Kenya 0°47N 36°16E 54 B4
Barisal Bangla. 22°45N 90°20E 41 H17
Barisal □ Bangla. 22°45N 90°20E 41 H17
Barisan, Pegunungan
Indonesia 3°30S 102°15E 36 E2
Barito → Indonesia 4°0S 114°50E 36 E4
Baritú △ Argentina 23°43S 64°40W 94 A3
Barjūj, Wadi → Libya 25°26N 12°12E 51 C8
Bark L. Canada 45°27N 77°51W 82 A7
Barkakana India 23°37N 85°29E 43 H11
Barkam China 31°51N 102°28E 32 E9
Barker U.S.A. 43°20N 78°33W 82 C6
Barkley, L. U.S.A. 37°1N 88°14W 85 C10
Barkley Sound Canada 48°50N 125°10W 70 D3
Barkly East S. Africa 30°58S 27°33E 56 E4
Barkly Homestead
Australia 19°52S 135°50E 62 B2
Barkly Tableland
Australia 17°50S 136°40E 62 B2
Barkly West S. Africa 28°5S 24°31E 56 D3
Barkol Kazak Zizhixian
China 43°37N 93°2E 32 C7
Bârlad Romania 46°15N 27°38E 17 E14
Bârlad → Romania 45°38N 27°32E 17 F14
Barlee, L. Australia 29°15S 119°30E 61 E2
Barlee, Mt. Australia 24°38S 128°13E 61 D4
Barletta Italy 41°19N 16°17E 22 D7
Barlovento Canary Is. 28°48N 17°48W 24 F2
Barlovento C. Verde Is. 17°0N 25°0W 50 b
Barlow L. Canada 62°0N 103°0W 71 A8
Barmedman Australia 34°9S 147°21E 63 E4
Barmer India 25°45N 71°20E 42 G4
Barmera Australia 34°15S 140°28E 63 E3
Barmouth U.K. 52°44N 4°4W 12 E3
Barna → India 25°21N 83°3E 43 G10
Barnagar India 23°7N 75°19E 42 H6
Barnala India 30°23N 75°33E 42 D6
Barnard Castle U.K. 54°33N 1°55W 12 C6
Barnaul Russia 53°20N 83°40E 28 D9
Barnesville Ga., U.S.A. 33°3N 84°9W 85 E12
Barnesville Minn.,
U.S.A. 46°43N 96°28W 80 B5
Barnet □ U.K. 51°38N 0°9W 13 F7
Barneveld Neths. 52°7N 5°36E 15 B5
Barnhart U.S.A. 31°8N 101°10W 84 F4
Barnsley U.K. 53°34N 1°27W 12 D6
Barnstable U.S.A. 41°42N 70°18W 81 E18
Barnstaple U.K. 51°5N 4°4W 13 F3
Barnstaple Bay = Bideford Bay
U.K. 51°5N 4°20W 13 F3
Barnwell U.S.A. 33°15N 81°23W 85 E14
Baro Nigeria 8°35N 6°18E 50 G7
Baroda = Vadodara
India 22°20N 73°10E 42 H5
Baroda India 25°29N 76°35E 42 G7
Baroe S. Africa 33°13S 24°33E 56 E3
Baron Ra. Australia 23°30S 127°45E 60 D4
Barotseland Zambia 15°0S 24°0E 53 H4
Barpeta India 26°20N 91°10E 41 F17
Barqa Libya 27°0N 23°0E 51 C10
Barques, Pt. Aux U.S.A. 44°4N 82°58W 82 B2
Barquísimeto Venezuela 10°4N 69°19W 92 A5
Barr Smith Range
Australia 27°4S 120°20E 61 E3
Barra Brazil 11°5S 43°10W 93 F10
Barra U.K. 57°0N 7°29W 11 E1
Barra, Sd. of U.K. 57°4N 7°25W 11 D1
Barra de Navidad
Mexico 19°12N 104°41W 86 D4
Barra do Corda Brazil 5°30S 45°10W 93 E9
Barra do Garças Brazil 15°54S 52°16W 93 G8
Barra do Piraí Brazil 22°30S 43°50W 95 A7
Barra Falsa, Pta. da
Mozam. 22°58S 35°37E 57 C6
Barra Hd. U.K. 56°47N 7°40W 11 E1
Barra Mansa Brazil 22°35S 44°12W 95 A7
Barraba Australia 30°21S 150°35E 63 E5
Barrackpur = Barakpur
India 22°47N 88°21E 43 H13
Barraigh = Barra U.K. 57°0N 7°29W 11 E1
Barranca Lima, Peru 10°45S 77°50W 92 F3
Barranca Loreto, Peru 4°50S 76°50W 92 D3
Barranca del Cobre ⌂
Mexico 27°18N 107°40W 86 B3
Barrancabermeja
Colombia 7°0N 73°50W 92 B4
Barrancas Venezuela 8°55N 62°5W 92 B6
Barrancos Portugal 38°10N 6°58W 21 C2
Barranqueras Argentina 27°30S 59°0W 94 B4
Barranquilla Colombia 11°0N 74°50W 92 A4
Barraute Canada 48°26N 77°38W 72 C4
Barre Mass., U.S.A. 42°25N 72°6W 83 D12
Barre Vt., U.S.A. 44°12N 72°30W 83 B12
Barreal Argentina 31°33S 69°28W 94 C2
Barreiras Brazil 12°8S 45°0W 93 F10
Barreirinhas Brazil 2°30S 42°50W 93 D10
Barreiro Portugal 38°39N 9°5W 21 C1
Barren, Nosy Madag. 18°25S 43°40E 57 B7
Barretos Brazil 20°30S 48°35W 93 H9
Barrhead Canada 54°10N 114°24W 70 C6
Barrie Canada 44°24N 79°40W 82 B5
Barrier Ra. Australia 31°0S 141°30E 63 E3
Barrier Reef Belize 17°9N 88°3W 87 D7
Barrière Canada 51°12N 120°7W 70 C4
Barrington U.S.A. 41°44N 71°18W 83 E13
Barrington L. Canada 56°55N 100°15W 71 B8
Barrington Tops
Australia 32°6S 151°28E 63 E5
Barringun Australia 29°1S 145°41E 63 D4
Barron U.S.A. 45°24N 91°51W 80 C8
Barrow U.S.A. 71°18N 156°47W 74 A8
Barrow → Ireland 52°25N 6°58W 10 D5
Barrow, Pt. U.S.A. 71°23N 156°29W 74 A8
Barrow Creek Australia 21°30S 133°55E 62 C1
Barrow I. Australia 20°45S 115°20E 60 D2
Barrow-in-Furness U.K. 54°7N 3°14W 12 C4
Barrow Pt. Australia 14°20S 144°40E 62 A3
Barrow Ra. Australia 26°0S 127°40E 61 E4
Barrow Str. Canada 74°20N 95°0W 4 B3
Barry U.K. 51°24N 3°16W 13 F4
Barry's Bay Canada 45°29N 77°41W 82 A7
Barsat Pakistan 36°10N 72°45E 43 A5
Barsi India 18°10N 75°50E 40 K9
Barsoi India 25°48N 87°57E 41 G15
Barstow U.S.A. 34°54N 117°1W 79 L9
Bartica Guyana 6°25N 58°40W 92 B7
Bartle Frere Australia 17°27S 145°50E 62 B4
Bartlesville U.S.A. 36°45N 95°59W 84 C7
Bartlett Calif., U.S.A. 36°29N 118°2W 78 J8
Bartlett Tenn., U.S.A. 35°12N 89°52W 85 D10
Bartlett, L. Canada 63°5N 118°20W 70 A5
Bartolomeu Dias Mozam. 21°10S 35°8E 55 G4
Barton U.S.A. 44°45N 72°11W 83 B12
Barton upon Humber
U.K. 53°41N 0°25W 12 D7
Bartow U.S.A. 27°54N 81°50W 85 H14
Barú, Volcan Panama 8°55N 82°35W 88 E3
Barumba
Dem. Rep. of the Congo 1°3N 23°37E 54 B1
Barung, Nusa Indonesia 8°30S 113°30E 37 H15
Baruun Urt Mongolia 46°46N 113°15E 33 B11
Baruunsuu Mongolia 43°43N 105°35E 34 C3
Barwani India 22°2N 74°57E 42 H6
Barysaw Belarus 54°17N 28°28E 17 A15
Barzān Iraq 36°55N 44°3E 44 B5
Bāsa'idū Iran 26°35N 55°20E 45 E7
Basal Pakistan 33°33N 72°13E 42 C5
Basankusa
Dem. Rep. of the Congo 1°5N 19°50E 52 D3
Basarabeasca Moldova 46°21N 28°58E 17 E15
Basarabia = Bessarabiya
Moldova 47°0N 28°10E 17 E15
Basawa Afghan. 34°15N 70°50E 42 B4
Bascuñán, C. Chile 28°52S 71°35W 94 B1
Basel Switz. 47°35N 7°35E 20 C7
Bashākerd, Kūhhā-ye
Iran 26°42N 58°35E 45 E8
Bashaw Canada 52°35N 112°58W 70 C6
Bāshī Iran 28°41N 51°4E 45 D6
Bashkir Republic =
Bashkortostan □
Russia 54°0N 57°0E 18 D10
Bashkortostan □ Russia 54°0N 57°0E 18 D10
Basibasy Madag. 22°10S 43°40E 57 C7
Basilan I. Phil. 6°35N 122°0E 37 C6
Basilan Str. Phil. 6°50N 122°0E 37 C6
Basildon U.K. 51°34N 0°28E 13 F8
Basim = Washim India 20°3N 77°0E 40 J10
Basin U.S.A. 44°23N 108°2W 76 D9
Basingstoke U.K. 51°15N 1°5W 13 F6
Baskatong, Rés. Canada 46°46N 75°50W 72 C4
Basle = Basel Switz. 47°35N 7°35E 20 C7
Basoda India 23°52N 77°54E 42 H7
Basoko
Dem. Rep. of the Congo 1°16N 23°40E 54 B1
Basque Provinces = País Vasco □
Spain 42°50N 2°45W 21 A4
Basra = Al Başrah Iraq 30°30N 47°50E 44 D5
Bass Str. Australia 39°15S 146°30E 63 F4
Bassano Canada 50°48N 112°20W 70 C6
Bassano del Grappa Italy 45°46N 11°44E 22 B4
Bassas da India Ind. Oc. 22°0S 39°0E 55 G4
Basse-Pointe Martinique 14°52N 61°8W 88 c
Basse-Terre Guadeloupe 16°0N 61°44W 88 b
Basse Terre Trin. & Tob. 10°7N 61°19W 93 K15
Bassein Burma 16°45N 94°30E 41 L19
Basses, Pte. des
Guadeloupe 15°52N 61°17W 88 b
Basseterre
St. Kitts & Nevis 17°17N 62°43W 89 C7
Bassett U.S.A. 42°35N 99°32W 80 D4
Bassi India 30°44N 76°21E 42 D7
Bastak Iran 27°15N 54°25E 45 E7
Baştām Iran 36°29N 55°4E 45 B7
Bastar India 19°15N 81°40E 41 K12
Basti India 26°52N 82°55E 43 F10
Bastia France 42°40N 9°30E 20 E8
Bastogne Belgium 50°1N 5°43E 15 D5
Bastrop La., U.S.A. 32°47N 91°55W 84 E9
Bastrop Tex., U.S.A. 30°7N 97°19W 84 F6
Basuo = Dongfang
China 18°50N 108°33E 38 C7
Bat Yam Israel 32°2N 34°44E 46 C3
Bata Eq. Guin. 1°57N 9°50E 52 D1
Bataan □ Phil. 14°40N 120°25E 37 B6
Batabanó Cuba 22°41N 82°18W 88 B3
Batabanó, G. de Cuba 22°30N 82°30W 88 B3
Batac Phil. 18°3N 120°34E 37 A6
Batagai Russia 67°38N 134°38E 29 C14
Batala India 31°48N 75°12E 42 D6
Batama
Dem. Rep. of the Congo 0°58N 26°33E 54 B2
Batamay Russia 63°30N 129°15E 29 C13
Batang Indonesia 6°55S 109°45E 37 G13
Batangafo C.A.R. 7°25N 18°20E 52 C3
Batangas Phil. 13°35N 121°10E 37 B6
Batanta Indonesia 0°55S 130°40E 37 E8
Batatais Brazil 20°54S 47°37W 95 A6
Batavia U.S.A. 43°0N 78°11W 82 D6
Batchelor Australia 13°4S 131°1E 60 B5
Batdambang Cambodia 13°7N 103°12E 38 F4
Batemans B. Australia 35°40S 150°12E 63 F5
Batemans Bay Australia 35°44S 150°11E 63 F5
Batesburg-Leesville
U.S.A. 33°54N 81°33W 85 E14
Batesville Ark., U.S.A. 35°46N 91°39W 84 D9
Batesville Miss., U.S.A. 34°19N 89°57W 85 D10
Batesville Tex., U.S.A. 28°58N 99°37W 84 G5
Bath Canada 44°11N 76°47W 83 B8
Bath U.K. 51°23N 2°22W 13 F5
Bath Maine, U.S.A. 43°55N 69°49W 81 D19
Bath N.Y., U.S.A. 42°20N 77°19W 82 D7
Bath & North East Somerset □
U.K. 51°21N 2°27W 13 F5
Batheay Cambodia 11°59N 104°57E 39 G5
Bathsheba Barbados 13°13N 59°32W 89 g
Bathurst Australia 33°25S 149°31E 63 E4
Bathurst Canada 47°37N 65°43W 73 C6
Bathurst S. Africa 33°30S 26°50E 56 E4
Bathurst, C. Canada 70°34N 128°0W 68 C6
Bathurst B. Australia 14°16S 144°25E 62 A3
Bathurst Harb.
Australia 43°15S 146°10E 63 G4
Bathurst I. Australia 11°30S 130°10E 60 B5
Bathurst I. Canada 76°0N 100°30W 69 B11
Bathurst Inlet Canada 66°50N 108°1W 68 D10
Batiki Fiji 17°48S 179°10E 59 a
Batlow Australia 35°31S 148°9E 63 F4
Batman Turkey 37°55N 41°5E 44 B4
Baţn al Ghūl Jordan 29°36N 35°56E 46 F4
Batna Algeria 35°34N 6°15E 50 A7
Batoka Zambia 16°45S 27°15E 55 F2
Baton Rouge U.S.A. 30°27N 91°11W 84 F9
Batong, Ko Thailand 6°32N 99°12E 39 J2
Batopilas Mexico 27°1N 107°44W 86 B3
Batouri Cameroon 4°30N 14°25E 52 D2
Båtsfjord Norway 70°38N 29°39E 8 A23
Battambang = Batdambang
Cambodia 13°7N 103°12E 38 F4
Batticaloa Sri Lanka 7°43N 81°45E 40 R12
Battipáglia Italy 40°37N 14°58E 22 D6
Battle U.K. 50°55N 0°30E 13 G8
Battle → Canada 52°43N 108°15W 71 C7
Battle Creek U.S.A. 42°19N 85°11W 81 D11
Battle Ground U.S.A. 45°47N 122°32W 78 E4
Battle Harbour Canada 52°16N 55°35W 73 B8
Battle Lake U.S.A. 46°17N 95°43W 80 B6
Battle Mountain
U.S.A. 40°38N 116°56W 76 F5
Battlefields Zimbabwe 18°37S 29°47E 55 F2
Battleford Canada 52°45N 108°15W 71 C7
Batu Ethiopia 6°55N 39°45E 47 F2
Batu Malaysia 3°15N 101°40E 39 L3
Batu, Kepulauan
Indonesia 0°30S 98°25E 36 E1
Batu Ferringhi Malaysia 5°28N 100°15E 39 c
Batu Gajah Malaysia 4°28N 101°3E 39 K3
Batu Is. = Batu, Kepulauan
Indonesia 0°30S 98°25E 36 E1
Batu Pahat Malaysia 1°50N 102°56E 39 M4
Batu Puteh, Gunung
Malaysia 4°15N 101°31E 39 K3
Batuata Indonesia 6°12S 122°42E 37 F6
Batugondang, Tanjung
Indonesia 8°6S 114°29E 37 J17
Batukaru, Gunung
Indonesia 8°20S 115°5E 37 J18
Batumi Georgia 41°39N 41°44E 19 F7
Batur, Gunung
Indonesia 8°14S 115°23E 37 J18
Batura Sar Pakistan 36°30N 74°31E 43 A6
Baturaja Indonesia 4°11S 104°15E 36 E2
Baturité Brazil 4°28S 38°45W 93 D11
Baturiti Indonesia 8°19S 115°11E 37 J18
Bau Malaysia 1°25N 110°9E 36 D4
Baubau Indonesia 5°25S 122°38E 37 F6
Baucau E. Timor 8°27S 126°27E 37 F7
Bauchi Nigeria 10°22N 9°48E 50 F7
Baudette U.S.A. 48°43N 94°36W 80 A6
Bauer, C. Australia 32°44S 134°4E 63 E1
Bauhinia Australia 24°35S 149°18E 62 C4
Baukau = Baucau
E. Timor 8°27S 126°27E 37 F7
Bauld, C. Canada 51°38N 55°26W 69 G20
Bauru Brazil 22°10S 49°0W 95 A6
Bausi India 24°48N 87°1E 43 G12
Bauska Latvia 56°24N 24°15E 9 H21
Bautzen Germany 51°10N 14°26E 16 C8
Bavānāt Iran 30°28N 53°27E 45 D7
Bavaria = Bayern □
Germany 48°50N 12°0E 16 D6
Bavispe → Mexico 29°15N 109°11W 86 B3
Bawdwin Burma 23°5N 97°20E 41 H20
Bawean Indonesia 5°46S 112°35E 36 F4
Bawku Ghana 11°3N 0°19W 50 F5
Bawlake Burma 19°11N 97°21E 41 K20
Baxley U.S.A. 31°47N 82°21W 85 F13
Baxter U.S.A. 46°21N 94°17W 80 B6
Baxter Springs U.S.A. 37°2N 94°44W 80 G6
Baxter State ⌂ U.S.A. 46°5N 68°57W 81 B19
Bay City Mich., U.S.A. 43°36N 83°54W 81 D12
Bay City Tex., U.S.A. 28°59N 95°58W 84 G7
Bay Minette U.S.A. 30°53N 87°46W 85 F11
Bay Roberts Canada 47°36N 53°16W 73 C9
Bay St. Louis U.S.A. 30°19N 89°20W 85 F10
Bay Springs U.S.A. 31°59N 89°17W 85 F10
Bay View N.Z. 39°25S 176°50E 59 C6
Baya
Dem. Rep. of the Congo 11°53S 27°25E 55 E2
Bayamo Cuba 20°20N 76°40W 88 B4
Bayamón Puerto Rico 18°24N 66°9W 89 d
Bayan Har Shan China 34°0N 98°0E 32 E8
Bayan Hot = Alxa Zuoqi
China 38°50N 105°40E 34 E3
Bayan Lepas Malaysia 5°17N 100°16E 39 c
Bayan Obo China 41°52N 109°59E 34 D5
Bayan-Ovoo = Erdenetsogt
Mongolia 42°55N 106°5E 34 C4
Bayana India 26°55N 77°18E 42 F7
Bayanaūyl Kazakhstan 50°45N 75°45E 28 D8
Bayanhongor Mongolia 46°8N 102°43E 32 B9
Bayard N. Mex., U.S.A. 32°46N 108°9W 77 K9
Bayard Nebr., U.S.A. 41°45N 103°20W 80 E2
Baybay Phil. 10°40N 124°55E 37 B6
Baydaratskaya Guba
Russia 69°0N 67°30E 28 C7
Baydhabo Somali Rep. 3°8N 43°30E 47 G3
Bayern □ Germany 48°50N 12°0E 16 D6
Bayeux France 49°17N 0°42W 20 B3
Bayfield Canada 43°34N 81°42W 82 C3
Bayfield U.S.A. 46°49N 90°49W 80 B8
Bayındır Turkey 38°13N 27°39E 23 E12
Baykal, Oz. Russia 53°0N 108°0E 29 D11
Baykan Turkey 38°7N 41°44E 44 B4
Baymak Russia 52°36N 58°19E 18 D10
Baynes Mts. Namibia 17°15S 13°0E 56 B1
Bayombong Phil. 16°30N 121°10E 37 A6
Bayonne France 43°30N 1°28W 20 E3
Bayonne U.S.A. 40°40N 74°6W 83 F10
Bayovar Peru 5°50S 81°0W 92 E2
Bayqongyr Kazakhstan 45°40N 63°20E 28 E7
Bayram-Ali = Baýramaly
Turkmenistan 37°37N 62°10E 45 B9
Baýramaly Turkmenistan 37°37N 62°10E 45 B9
Bayramiç Turkey 39°48N 26°36E 23 E12
Bayreuth Germany 49°56N 11°35E 16 D6
Bayrūt Lebanon 33°53N 35°31E 46 B4
Bays, L. of Canada 45°15N 79°4W 82 A5
Baysville Canada 45°9N 79°7W 82 A5
Bayt Lahm West Bank 31°43N 35°12E 46 D4
Baytown U.S.A. 29°43N 94°59W 84 G7
Baza Spain 37°30N 2°47W 21 D4
Bazaruto, I. do Mozam. 21°40S 35°28E 57 C6
Bazaruto △ Mozam. 21°42S 35°26E 57 C6
Bazhou China 39°8N 116°22E 34 E9
Bazmān, Kūh-e Iran 28°4N 60°1E 45 D9
Beach U.S.A. 46°58N 104°0W 80 B2
Beach City U.S.A. 40°39N 81°35W 82 F3
Beachport Australia 37°29S 140°0E 63 F3
Beachville Canada 43°5N 80°49W 82 C4
Beachy Hd. U.K. 50°44N 0°15E 13 G8
Beacon Australia 30°26S 117°52E 61 F2
Beacon U.S.A. 41°30N 73°58W 83 E11
Beaconsfield Australia 41°11S 146°48E 63 G4
Beagle, Canal S. Amer. 55°0S 68°30W 96 H3
Beagle Bay Australia 16°58S 122°40E 60 C3
Beagle Bay ✪ Australia 16°53S 122°40E 60 C3
Beagle G. Australia 12°15S 130°25E 60 B5
Béal an Átha = Ballina
Ireland 54°7N 9°9W 10 B2
Béal Átha na Sluaighe =
Ballinasloe Ireland 53°20N 8°13W 10 C3
Bealanana Madag. 14°33S 48°44E 57 A8
Beals Cr. → U.S.A. 32°10N 100°51W 84 E4
Beamsville Canada 43°12N 79°28W 82 C5
Bear → Calif., U.S.A. 38°56N 121°36W 78 G5
Bear → Utah, U.S.A. 41°30N 112°8W 74 G17
Bear I. Ireland 51°38N 9°50W 10 E2
Bear L. Canada 55°8N 96°0W 71 B9
Bear L. U.S.A. 41°59N 111°21W 76 F8
Bear Lake Canada 45°27N 79°35W 82 A5
Beardmore Canada 49°36N 87°57W 72 C2
Beardmore Glacier
Antarctica 84°30S 170°0E 5 E11
Beardstown U.S.A. 40°1N 90°26W 80 E8
Bearma → India 24°20N 79°51E 43 G8
Béarn France 43°20N 0°30W 20 E3
Bearpaw Mts. U.S.A. 48°12N 109°30W 76 B9
Bearskin Lake Canada 53°58N 91°2W 72 B1
Beas → India 31°10N 74°59E 42 D6
Beata, C. Dom. Rep. 17°40N 71°30W 89 C5
Beata, I. Dom. Rep. 17°34N 71°31W 89 C5
Beatrice U.S.A. 40°16N 96°45W 80 E5
Beatrice Zimbabwe 18°15S 30°55E 55 F3
Beatrice, C. Australia 14°20S 136°55E 62 A2
Beatton → Canada 56°15N 120°45W 70 B4
Beatton River Canada 57°26N 121°20W 70 B4
Beatty U.S.A. 36°54N 116°46W 78 J10
Beau Bassin Mauritius 20°13S 57°27E 53 d
Beauce, Plaine de la
France 48°10N 1°45E 20 B4
Beauceville Canada 46°13N 70°46W 73 C5
Beaudesert Australia 27°59S 153°0E 63 D5
Beaufort Malaysia 5°30N 115°40E 36 C5
Beaufort N.C., U.S.A. 34°43N 76°40W 85 D16
Beaufort S.C., U.S.A. 32°26N 80°40W 85 E14
Beaufort Sea Arctic 72°0N 140°0W 66 B5
Beaufort West S. Africa 32°18S 22°36E 56 E3
Beauharnois Canada 45°20N 73°52W 83 A11
Beaulieu → Canada 62°3N 113°11W 70 A6
Beauly U.K. 57°30N 4°28W 11 D4
Beauly → U.K. 57°29N 4°27W 11 D4
Beaumaris U.K. 53°16N 4°6W 12 D3
Beaumont Belgium 50°15N 4°14E 15 D4
Beaumont U.S.A. 30°5N 94°6W 84 F7
Beaune France 47°2N 4°50E 20 C6
Beaupré Canada 47°3N 70°54W 73 C5
Beauraing Belgium 50°7N 4°57E 15 D4
Beausejour Canada 50°5N 96°35W 71 C9
Beauvais France 49°25N 2°8E 20 B5
Beauval Canada 55°9N 107°37W 71 B7
Beaver Okla., U.S.A. 36°49N 100°31W 84 C4
Beaver Pa., U.S.A. 40°42N 80°19W 82 F4
Beaver Utah, U.S.A. 38°17N 112°38W 76 G7
Beaver → B.C., Canada 59°52N 124°20W 70 B4
Beaver → Ont., Canada 55°55N 87°48W 72 A2
Beaver → Sask., Canada 55°26N 107°45W 71 B7
Beaver → U.S.A. 36°35N 99°30W 84 C5
Beaver City U.S.A. 40°8N 99°50W 80 E4
Beaver Creek Canada 63°0N 141°0W 68 E3
Beaver Dam U.S.A. 43°28N 88°50W 80 D9
Beaver Falls U.S.A. 40°46N 80°20W 82 F4
Beaver Hill L. Canada 54°5N 94°50W 71 C10
Beaver I. U.S.A. 45°40N 85°33W 81 C11
Beavercreek U.S.A. 39°43N 84°11W 81 F11
Beaverhill L. Canada 53°27N 112°32W 70 C6
Beaverlodge Canada 55°11N 119°29W 70 B5
Beaverstone → Canada 54°59N 89°25W 72 B2
Beaverton Canada 44°26N 79°9W 82 B5
Beaverton U.S.A. 45°29N 122°48W 78 E4
Beawar India 26°3N 74°18E 42 F6
Bebedouro Brazil 21°0S 48°25W 95 A6
Bebera, Tanjung
Indonesia 8°44S 115°51E 37 K18
Beboa Madag. 17°22S 44°33E 57 B7
Becán Mexico 18°34N 89°31W 87 D7
Bécancour Canada 46°20N 72°26W 81 B17
Beccles U.K. 52°27N 1°35E 13 E9
Bečej Serbia 45°36N 20°3E 23 B9
Béchar Algeria 31°38N 2°18W 50 B5
Becharof L. U.S.A. 57°56N 156°23W 74 D8
Beckley U.S.A. 37°47N 81°11W 81 G13
Beddouza, C. Morocco 32°33N 9°9W 50 B4
Bedford Canada 45°7N 72°59W 83 A12
Bedford S. Africa 32°40S 26°10E 56 E4
Bedford U.K. 52°8N 0°28W 13 E7
Bedford Ind., U.S.A. 38°52N 86°29W 80 F10
Bedford Iowa, U.S.A. 40°40N 94°44W 80 E6
Bedford Ohio, U.S.A. 41°23N 81°32W 82 E3
Bedford Pa., U.S.A. 40°1N 78°30W 82 F6
Bedford Va., U.S.A. 37°20N 79°31W 81 G14
Bedford □ U.K. 52°4N 0°28W 13 E7
Bedford, C. Australia 15°14S 145°21E 62 B4
Bedok Singapore 1°19N 103°56E 39 d
Bedourie Australia 24°30S 139°30E 62 C2
Bedugul Indonesia 8°17S 115°10E 37 J18
Bedum Neths. 53°18N 6°36E 15 A6
Beebe Plain Canada 45°1N 72°9W 83 A12
Beech Creek U.S.A. 41°5N 77°36W 82 E7
Beechy Canada 50°53N 107°24W 71 C7
Beed = Bir India 19°4N 75°46E 40 K9
Beef I. Br. Virgin Is. 18°26N 64°30W 89 e
Beenleigh Australia 27°43S 153°10E 63 D5
Be'er Menuḥa Israel 30°19N 35°8E 44 D2
Be'er Sheva Israel 31°15N 34°48E 46 D3
Beersheba = Be'er Sheva
Israel 31°15N 34°48E 46 D3
Beestekraal S. Africa 25°23S 27°38E 57 D4
Beeston U.K. 52°56N 1°14W 12 E6
Beeton Canada 44°5N 79°47W 82 B5
Beeville U.S.A. 28°24N 97°45W 84 G6
Befale
Dem. Rep. of the Congo 0°25N 20°45E 52 D4
Befandriana Mahajanga,
Madag. 15°16S 48°32E 57 B8
Befandriana Toliara,
Madag. 21°55S 44°0E 57 C7
Befasy Madag. 20°33S 44°23E 57 C7
Befotaka Antsiranana,
Madag. 13°15S 48°16E 57 A8
Befotaka Fianarantsoa,
Madag. 23°49S 47°0E 57 C8
Bega Australia 36°41S 149°51E 63 F4
Begusarai India 25°24N 86°9E 43 G12
Behābād Iran 32°24N 59°47E 45 C8
Behala India 22°30N 88°18E 43 H13
Behara Madag. 24°55S 46°20E 57 C8
Behbehān Iran 30°30N 50°15E 45 D6
Behm Canal U.S.A. 55°10N 131°0W 70 B2
Behshahr Iran 36°45N 53°35E 45 B7
Bei Jiang → China 23°2N 112°58E 33 G11
Bei Shan China 41°30N 96°0E 32 C8
Bei'an China 48°10N 126°20E 33 B14
Beihai China 21°28N 109°6E 33 G10
Beijing China 39°53N 116°21E 34 E9
Beijing □ China 39°55N 116°20E 34 E9
Beilen Neths. 52°52N 6°27E 15 B6
Beilpajah Australia 32°54S 143°52E 63 E3
Beinn na Faoghla = Benbecula
U.K. 57°26N 7°21W 11 D1
Beipiao China 41°52N 120°32E 35 D11
Beira Mozam. 19°50S 34°52E 55 F3
Beirut = Bayrūt Lebanon 33°53N 35°31E 46 B4
Beiseker Canada 51°23N 113°32W 70 C6
Beit Lekhem = Bayt Lahm
West Bank 31°43N 35°12E 46 D4
Beitaolaizhao China 44°58N 125°58E 35 B13
Beitbridge Zimbabwe 22°12S 30°0E 55 G3
Beizhen = Binzhou
China 37°20N 118°2E 35 F10
Beizhen China 41°38N 121°54E 35 D11
Beizhengzhen China 44°31N 123°30E 35 B12
Beja Portugal 38°2N 7°53W 21 C2
Béja Tunisia 36°43N 9°12E 51 A7
Bejaïa Algeria 36°42N 5°2E 50 A7
Béjar Spain 40°23N 5°46W 21 B3
Bejestān Iran 34°30N 58°5E 45 C8
Bekaa Valley = Al Biqā
Lebanon 34°10N 36°10E 46 A5
Bekasi Indonesia 6°14S 106°59E 37 G12
Békéscsaba Hungary 46°40N 21°5E 17 E11
Bekily Madag. 24°13S 45°19E 57 C8
Bekisopa Madag. 21°40S 45°54E 57 C8
Bekitro Madag. 24°33S 45°18E 57 C8
Bekodoka Madag. 16°58S 45°7E 57 B8
Bekok Malaysia 2°20N 103°7E 39 L4
Bekopaka Madag. 19°9S 44°48E 57 B7
Bela India 25°50N 82°0E 43 G10
Bela Pakistan 26°12N 66°20E 42 F2
Bela Bela S. Africa 24°51S 28°19E 57 C4
Bela Crkva Serbia 44°55N 21°27E 23 B9
Bela Vista Brazil 22°12S 56°20W 94 A4
Bela Vista Mozam. 26°10S 32°44E 57 D5
Belan → India 24°2N 81°45E 43 G9
Belarus ■ Europe 53°30N 27°0E 17 B14
Belau = Palau ■ Palau 7°30N 134°30E 58 A6
Belavenona Madag. 24°50S 47°4E 57 C8
Belawan Indonesia 3°33N 98°32E 36 D1
Belaya → Russia 54°40N 56°0E 18 C9
Belaya Tserkov = Bila Tserkva
Ukraine 49°45N 30°10E 17 D16
Belaya Zemlya, Ostrova
Russia 81°36N 62°18E 28 A7
Belcher Is. Canada 56°15N 78°45W 72 A3
Belden U.S.A. 40°2N 121°17W 78 E5
Belebey Russia 54°7N 54°7E 18 D9
Beledweyne Somali Rep. 4°30N 45°5E 47 G4
Belém Brazil 1°20S 48°30W 93 D9
Belén Argentina 27°40S 67°5W 94 B2
Belén Paraguay 23°30S 57°6W 94 A4
Belen U.S.A. 34°40N 106°46W 77 J10
Belet Uen = Beledweyne
Somali Rep. 4°30N 45°5E 47 G4

Belev *Russia* 53°50N 36°5E **18** D6
Belfair *U.S.A.* 47°27N 122°50W **78** C4
Belfast *S. Africa* 25°42S 30°2E **57** D5
Belfast *U.K.* 54°37N 5°56W **10** B6
Belfast *Maine, U.S.A.* 44°26N 69°1W **81** C19
Belfast *N.Y., U.S.A.* 42°21N 78°7W **82** D6
Belfast L. *U.K.* 54°40N 5°50W **10** B6
Belfield *U.S.A.* 46°53N 103°12W **80** B2
Belfort *France* 47°38N 6°50E **20** C7
Belfry *U.S.A.* 45°9N 109°1W **76** D9
Belgaum *India* 15°55N 74°35E **40** M9
Belgavi = Belgaum *India* 15°55N 74°35E **40** M9
Belgium ■ *Europe* 50°30N 5°0E **15** D4
Belgorod *Russia* 50°35N 36°35E **19** D6
Belgorod-Dnestrovskiy =
  Bilhorod-Dnistrovskyy
  Ukraine 46°11N 30°23E **19** E5
Belgrade = Beograd
  Serbia 44°50N 20°37E **23** B9
Belgrade *U.S.A.* 45°47N 111°11W **76** D8
Belgrano *Antarctica* 77°52S 34°37W **5** D1
Belhaven *U.S.A.* 35°33N 76°37W **85** D16
Beli Drim → *Europe* 42°6N 20°25E **23** C9
Belimbing *Indonesia* 8°24S 115°2E **37** J18
Belinyu *Indonesia* 1°35S 105°50E **36** E3
Beliton Is. = Belitung
  Indonesia 3°10S 107°50E **36** E3
Belitung *Indonesia* 3°10S 107°50E **36** E3
Belize ■ *Cent. Amer.* 17°0N 88°30W **87** D7
Belize City *Belize* 17°25N 88°10W **87** D7
Belkovskiy, Ostrov
  Russia 75°32N 135°44E **29** B14
Bell → *Canada* 49°48N 77°38W **72** C4
Bell I. *Canada* 50°46N 55°35W **73** B8
Bell-Irving → *Canada* 56°12N 129°5W **70** B3
Bell Peninsula *Canada* 63°50N 82°0W **69** E15
Bell Ville *Argentina* 32°40S 62°40W **94** C3
Bella Bella *Canada* 52°10N 128°10W **70** C3
Bella Coola *Canada* 52°25N 126°40W **70** C3
Bella Unión *Uruguay* 30°15S 57°40W **94** C4
Bella Vista *Corrientes,
  Argentina* 28°33S 59°0W **94** B4
Bella Vista *Tucuman,
  Argentina* 27°10S 65°25W **94** B2
Bellaire *U.S.A.* 40°1N 80°45W **82** F4
Bellary *India* 15°10N 76°56E **40** M10
Bellata *Australia* 29°53S 149°46E **63** D4
Belle Fourche *U.S.A.* 44°40N 103°51W **80** C2
Belle Fourche →
  U.S.A. 44°26N 102°18W **75** G19
Belle Glade *U.S.A.* 26°41N 80°40W **85** H14
Belle-Île *France* 47°20N 3°10W **20** C2
Belle Isle *Canada* 51°57N 55°25W **73** B8
Belle Isle, Str. of *Canada* 51°30N 56°30W **73** B8
Belle Plaine *U.S.A.* 41°54N 92°17W **80** E7
Belle River *Canada* 42°18N 82°43W **82** D2
Bellefontaine *U.S.A.* 40°22N 83°46W **81** E12
Bellefonte *U.S.A.* 40°55N 77°47W **82** F7
Belleoram *Canada* 47°31N 55°25W **73** C8
Belleplaine *Barbados* 13°15N 59°34W **89** g
Belleville *Canada* 44°10N 77°23W **82** B7
Belleville *Ill., U.S.A.* 38°31N 89°59W **80** F9
Belleville *Kans., U.S.A.* 39°50N 97°38W **80** F5
Belleville *N.J., U.S.A.* 40°47N 74°9W **83** F10
Belleville *N.Y., U.S.A.* 43°46N 76°10W **83** C8
Bellevue *Idaho, U.S.A.* 43°28N 114°16W **76** E6
Bellevue *Nebr., U.S.A.* 41°9N 95°54W **80** E6
Bellevue *Ohio, U.S.A.* 41°17N 82°51W **82** E2
Bellevue *Wash., U.S.A.* 47°37N 122°12W **78** C4
Bellin = Kangirsuk
  Canada 60°0N 70°0W **69** F18
Bellingen *Australia* 30°25S 152°50E **63** E5
Bellingham *U.S.A.* 48°46N 122°29W **78** B4
Bellingshausen Abyssal Plain
  S. Ocean 64°0S 90°0W **5** C16
Bellingshausen Sea
  Antarctica 66°0S 80°0W **5** C17
Bellinzona *Switz.* 46°11N 9°1E **20** C8
Bello *Colombia* 6°20N 75°33W **92** B3
Bellows Falls *U.S.A.* 43°8N 72°27W **83** C12
Bellpat *Pakistan* 29°0N 68°5E **42** E3
Belluno *Italy* 46°9N 12°13E **22** A5
Bellwood *U.S.A.* 40°36N 78°20W **82** F6
Belmont *Canada* 42°53N 81°5W **82** D3
Belmont *S. Africa* 29°28S 24°22E **56** D3
Belmont *U.S.A.* 42°14N 78°2W **82** D6
Belmonte *Brazil* 16°0S 39°0W **93** G11
Belmopan *Belize* 17°18N 88°30W **87** D7
Belmullet *Ireland* 54°14N 9°58W **10** B2
Belo Horizonte *Brazil* 19°55S 43°56W **93** G10
Belo-Tsiribihina *Madag.* 19°40S 44°30E **57** B7
Belogorsk *Russia* 51°0N 128°20E **29** D13
Beloha *Madag.* 25°10S 45°3E **57** D8
Beloit *Kans., U.S.A.* 39°28N 98°6W **80** F4
Beloit *Wis., U.S.A.* 42°31N 89°2W **80** D9
Belokorovichi *Ukraine* 51°7N 28°2E **17** C15
Belomorsk *Russia* 64°35N 34°54E **18** B5
Belonia *India* 23°15N 91°30E **41** H17
Beloretsk *Russia* 53°58N 58°24E **18** D10
Belorussia = Belarus ■
  Europe 53°30N 27°0E **17** B14
Belovo *Russia* 54°30N 86°0E **28** D9
Beloyarskiy *Russia* 63°42N 66°40E **28** C7
Beloye, Ozero *Russia* 60°10N 37°35E **18** B6
Beloye More *Russia* 66°30N 38°0E **18** A6
Belozersk *Russia* 60°1N 37°40E **18** B6
Belpre *U.S.A.* 39°17N 81°34W **81** F13
Belrain *India* 28°24N 80°55E **43** E9
Belt *U.S.A.* 47°23N 110°55W **76** C8
Beltana *Australia* 30°48S 138°25E **63** E2
Belterra *Brazil* 2°45S 55°0W **93** D8
Belton *U.S.A.* 31°3N 97°28W **84** F6
Belton L. *U.S.A.* 31°6N 97°28W **84** F6
Beltsy = Bălți *Moldova* 47°48N 27°58E **17** E14
Belturbet *Ireland* 54°6N 7°26W **10** B4
Belukha *Russia* 49°50N 86°50E **32** B6
Beluran *Malaysia* 5°48N 117°35E **36** C5
Belushya Guba *Russia* 71°30N 54°31E **28** B6
Belvidere *Ill., U.S.A.* 42°15N 88°50W **80** D9
Belvidere *N.J., U.S.A.* 40°50N 75°5W **83** F9

Belyando → *Australia* 21°38S 146°50E **62** C4
Belyando Crossing
  Australia 21°32S 146°51E **62** C4
Belyuen *Australia* 12°34S 130°42E **60** B5
Belyy, Ostrov *Russia* 73°30N 71°0E **28** B8
Belyy Yar *Russia* 58°26N 84°39E **28** D9
Belzoni *U.S.A.* 33°11N 90°29W **85** E9
Bemaraha, Lembalemban' i
  Madag. 18°40S 44°45E **57** B7
Bemarivo *Madag.* 21°45S 44°45E **57** C7
Bemarivo → *Antsiranana,
  Madag.* 14°9S 50°9E **57** A9
Bemarivo → *Mahajanga,
  Madag.* 15°27S 47°40E **57** B8
Bemavo *Madag.* 21°33S 45°25E **57** C8
Bembéréke *Benin* 10°11N 2°43E **50** F6
Bembesi *Zimbabwe* 20°0S 28°58E **55** G2
Bembesi → *Zimbabwe* 18°57S 27°47E **55** F2
Bemetara *India* 21°42N 81°32E **43** J9
Bemidji *U.S.A.* 47°28N 94°53W **80** B6
Bemolanga *Madag.* 17°44S 45°6E **57** B8
Ben *Iran* 32°32N 50°45E **45** C6
Ben Cruachan *U.K.* 56°26N 5°8W **11** E3
Ben Dearg *U.K.* 57°47N 4°56W **11** D4
Ben En △ *Vietnam* 19°37N 105°30E **38** C5
Ben Gardane *Tunisia* 33°11N 11°11E **51** B8
Ben Hope *U.K.* 58°25N 4°36W **11** C4
Ben Lawers *U.K.* 56°32N 4°14W **11** E4
Ben Lomond *N.S.W.,
  Australia* 30°1S 151°43E **63** E5
Ben Lomond *Tas.,
  Australia* 41°38S 147°42E **63** G4
Ben Lomond *U.K.* 56°11N 4°38W **11** E4
Ben Lomond △
  Australia 41°33S 147°39E **63** G4
Ben Luc *Vietnam* 10°39N 106°29E **39** G6
Ben Macdhui *U.K.* 57°4N 3°40W **11** D5
Ben Mhor *U.K.* 57°15N 7°18W **11** D1
Ben More *Argyll & Bute,
  U.K.* 56°26N 6°1W **11** E2
Ben More *Stirling, U.K.* 56°23N 4°32W **11** E4
Ben More Assynt *U.K.* 58°8N 4°52W **11** C4
Ben Nevis *U.K.* 56°48N 5°1W **11** E3
Ben Quang *Vietnam* 17°3N 106°55E **38** D6
Ben Tre *Vietnam* 10°14N 106°23E **39** G6
Ben Vorlich *U.K.* 56°21N 4°14W **11** E4
Ben Wyvis *U.K.* 57°40N 4°35W **11** D4
Bena *Nigeria* 11°20N 5°50E **50** F7
Benalla *Australia* 36°30S 146°0E **63** F4
Benares = Varanasi
  India 25°22N 83°0E **43** G10
Benavente *Spain* 42°2N 5°43W **21** A3
Benavides *U.S.A.* 27°36N 98°25W **84** H5
Benbecula *U.K.* 57°26N 7°21W **11** D1
Benbonyathe Hill
  Australia 30°25S 139°11E **63** E2
Bend *U.S.A.* 44°4N 121°19W **76** D3
Bender Beyla *Somali Rep.* 9°30N 50°48E **47** F5
Bendery = Tighina
  Moldova 46°50N 29°30E **17** E15
Bendigo *Australia* 36°40S 144°15E **63** F3
Benē Beraq *Israel* 32°6N 34°51E **46** C3
Benenitra *Madag.* 23°27S 45°5E **57** C8
Benevento *Italy* 41°8N 14°45E **22** D6
Beng Mealea *Cambodia* 13°28N 104°14E **38** F5
Benga *Mozam.* 16°11S 33°40E **55** F3
Bengal, Bay of *Ind. Oc.* 15°0N 90°0E **41** M17
Bengaluru = Bangalore
  India 12°59N 77°40E **40** N10
Bengbu *China* 32°58N 117°20E **35** H9
Benghazi = Banghāzī
  Libya 32°11N 20°3E **51** B10
Bengkalis *Indonesia* 1°30N 102°10E **39** M4
Bengkulu *Indonesia* 3°50S 102°12E **36** E2
Bengkulu □ *Indonesia* 3°48S 102°16E **36** E2
Bengough *Canada* 49°25N 105°10W **71** D7
Benguela *Angola* 12°37S 13°25E **53** G2
Benguérua, I. *Mozam.* 21°58S 35°28E **57** C6
Beni *Dem. Rep. of the Congo* 0°30N 29°27E **54** B2
Beni → *Bolivia* 10°23S 65°24W **92** F5
Beni Mellal *Morocco* 32°21N 6°21W **50** B4
Beni Suef *Egypt* 29°5N 31°6E **51** C12
Beniah L. *Canada* 63°23N 112°17W **70** A6
Benidorm *Spain* 38°33N 0°9W **21** C5
Benin ■ *Africa* 10°0N 2°0E **50** G6
Benin, Bight of *W. Afr.* 5°0N 3°0E **50** H6
Benin City *Nigeria* 6°20N 5°31E **50** G7
Benito Juárez *Argentina* 37°40S 59°43W **94** D4
Benitses *Greece* 39°32N 19°55E **25** A3
Benjamin Aceval
  Paraguay 24°58S 57°34W **94** A4
Benjamin Constant
  Brazil 4°40S 70°15W **92** D4
Benjamin Hill *Mexico* 30°9N 111°7W **86** A2
Benkelman *U.S.A.* 40°3N 101°32W **80** E3
Bennett *Canada* 59°51N 135°0W **70** B2
Bennett, L. *Australia* 22°50S 131°2E **60** D5
Bennetta, Ostrov
  Russia 76°21N 148°56E **29** B15
Bennettsville *U.S.A.* 34°37N 79°41W **85** D15
Bennington *N.H., U.S.A.* 43°0N 71°55W **83** D11
Bennington *Vt., U.S.A.* 42°53N 73°12W **83** D11
Benom *Malaysia* 3°50N 102°6E **39** L4
Benoni *S. Africa* 26°11S 28°18E **57** D4
Benque Viejo *Belize* 17°5N 89°8W **87** D7
Benson *Ariz., U.S.A.* 31°58N 110°18W **77** L8
Benson *Minn., U.S.A.* 45°19N 95°36W **80** C6
Bent *Iran* 26°20N 59°31E **45** E8
Benteng *Indonesia* 6°10S 120°30E **37** F6
Bentinck I. *Australia* 17°3S 139°35E **62** B2
Bentinck I. *Burma* 11°45N 98°3E **39** G2
Bentley Subglacial Trench
  Antarctica 80°0S 115°0W **5** E15
Bento Gonçalves *Brazil* 29°10S 51°31W **95** B5
Benton *Ark., U.S.A.* 34°34N 92°35W **84** D8
Benton *Calif., U.S.A.* 37°48N 118°32W **78** H8
Benton *Ill., U.S.A.* 38°0N 88°55W **80** F9
Benton *Pa., U.S.A.* 41°12N 76°23W **83** E8
Benton Harbor *U.S.A.* 42°6N 86°27W **80** D10
Bentong *Malaysia* 3°31N 101°55E **39** L3

Bentonville *U.S.A.* 36°22N 94°13W **84** C7
Benue → *Nigeria* 7°48N 6°46E **50** G7
Benxi *China* 41°20N 123°48E **35** D12
Beo *Indonesia* 4°25N 126°50E **37** D7
Beograd *Serbia* 44°50N 20°37E **23** B9
Beolgyo *S. Korea* 34°51N 127°21E **35** G14
Beppu *Japan* 33°15N 131°30E **31** H5
Beqa *Fiji* 18°23S 178°8E **59** a
Beqaa Valley = Al Biqâ
  Lebanon 34°10N 36°10E **46** A5
Ber Mota *India* 23°27N 68°34E **42** H3
Bera, Tasik *Malaysia* 3°5N 102°38E **39** L4
Berach → *India* 25°15N 75°2E **42** G6
Beraketa *Madag.* 23°7S 44°25E **57** C7
Berastagi *Indonesia* 3°11N 98°31E **39** L2
Berat *Albania* 40°43N 19°59E **23** D8
Berau → *Tanjungredeb
  Indonesia* 2°9N 117°29E **36** D5
Berau, Teluk *Indonesia* 2°30S 132°30E **37** E8
Beravina *Madag.* 18°10S 45°14E **57** B8
Berber *Sudan* 18°0N 34°0E **51** E12
Berbera *Somali Rep.* 10°30N 45°2E **47** E4
Berbérati *C.A.R.* 4°15N 15°40E **52** D3
Berbice → *Guyana* 6°20N 57°32W **92** B7
Berdichev = Berdychiv
  Ukraine 49°57N 28°30E **17** D15
Berdsk *Russia* 54°47N 83°2E **28** D9
Berdyansk *Ukraine* 46°45N 36°50E **19** E6
Berdychiv *Ukraine* 49°57N 28°30E **17** D15
Berea *U.S.A.* 37°34N 84°17W **81** G11
Berebere *Indonesia* 2°25N 128°45E **37** D7
Bereeda *Somali Rep.* 11°45N 51°0E **47** E5
Berehove *Ukraine* 48°15N 22°35E **17** D12
Bereket *Turkmenistan* 39°16N 55°32E **45** B7
Berekum *Ghana* 7°29N 2°34W **50** G5
Berens → *Canada* 52°25N 97°2W **71** C9
Berens I. *Canada* 52°18N 97°18W **71** C9
Berens River *Canada* 52°25N 97°0W **71** C9
Beresford *U.S.A.* 43°5N 96°47W **80** D5
Berestechko *Ukraine* 50°22N 25°5E **17** C13
Berevo *Mahajanga,
  Madag.* 17°14S 44°17E **57** B7
Berevo *Toliara, Madag.* 19°44S 44°58E **57** B7
Bereza = Byaroza
  Belarus 52°31N 24°51E **17** B13
Berezhany *Ukraine* 49°26N 24°58E **17** D13
Berezina = Byarezina →
  Belarus 52°33N 30°14E **17** B16
Bereznik *Russia* 62°51N 42°40E **18** B7
Berezniki *Russia* 59°24N 56°46E **18** C10
Berezovo *Russia* 64°0N 65°0E **28** C7
Berga *Spain* 42°6N 1°48E **21** A6
Bergama *Turkey* 39°8N 27°11E **23** E12
Bérgamo *Italy* 45°41N 9°43E **20** D8
Bergen *Neths.* 52°40N 4°43E **15** B4
Bergen *Norway* 60°20N 5°20E **8** F11
Bergen *U.S.A.* 43°5N 77°57W **82** C7
Bergen op Zoom *Neths.* 51°28N 4°18E **15** C4
Bergerac *France* 44°51N 0°30E **20** D4
Bergholz *U.S.A.* 40°31N 80°53W **82** F4
Bergisch Gladbach
  Germany 50°59N 7°8E **15** D7
Bergville *S. Africa* 28°52S 29°18E **57** D4
Berhala, Selat *Indonesia* 1°0S 104°15E **36** E2
Berhampore = Baharampur
  India 24°2N 88°27E **43** G13
Berhampur = Brahmapur
  India 19°15N 84°54E **41** K14
Bering Glacier *U.S.A.* 60°20N 143°30W **74** C11
Bering Sea *Pac. Oc.* 58°0N 171°0W **66** D2
Bering Strait *Pac. Oc.* 65°30N 169°0W **74** B6
Beringovskiy *Russia* 63°3N 179°19E **29** C18
Berisso *Argentina* 34°56S 57°50W **94** C4
Berja *Spain* 36°50N 2°56W **21** D4
Berkeley *U.S.A.* 37°51N 122°16W **78** H4
Berkner I. *Antarctica* 79°30S 50°0W **5** D18
Berkshire □ *U.K.* 51°33N 1°29W **13** F6
Berkshire Downs *U.K.* 51°33N 1°29W **13** F6
Berlin *Germany* 52°31N 13°23E **16** B7
Berlin *Md., U.S.A.* 38°20N 75°13W **81** F16
Berlin *N.H., U.S.A.* 44°28N 71°11W **83** B13
Berlin *N.Y., U.S.A.* 42°42N 73°23W **83** D11
Berlin *Wis., U.S.A.* 43°58N 88°57W **80** D9
Berlin L. *U.S.A.* 41°3N 81°0W **82** E4
Bermejo → *Formosa,
  Argentina* 26°51S 58°23W **94** B4
Bermejo → *San Juan,
  Argentina* 32°30S 67°30W **94** C2
Bermejo, Paso = Uspallata, P. de
  Argentina 32°37S 69°22W **94** C2
Bermen, L. *Canada* 53°35N 68°55W **73** B6
Bermuda ☑ *Atl. Oc.* 32°18N 64°45W **67** F13
Bern *Switz.* 46°57N 7°28E **20** C7
Bernalillo *U.S.A.* 35°18N 106°33W **77** J10
Bernardo de Irigoyen
  Argentina 26°15S 53°40W **95** B5
Bernardsville *U.S.A.* 40°43N 74°34W **83** F10
Bernasconi *Argentina* 37°55S 63°44W **94** D3
Bernburg *Germany* 51°47N 11°44E **16** C6
Berne = Bern *Switz.* 46°57N 7°28E **20** C7
Berneray *U.K.* 57°43N 7°11W **11** D1
Bernier I. *Australia* 24°50S 113°12E **61** D1
Bernina, Piz *Switz.* 46°20N 9°54E **20** C8
Beroroha *Madag.* 21°40S 45°10E **57** C8
Beroun *Czech Rep.* 49°57N 14°5E **16** D8
Berri *Australia* 34°14S 140°35E **63** E3
Berriane *Algeria* 32°50N 3°46E **50** B6
Berry *Australia* 34°46S 150°43E **63** E5
Berry *France* 46°50N 2°0E **20** C5
Berry Is. *Bahamas* 25°40N 77°50W **88** A4
Berryessa, L. *U.S.A.* 38°31N 122°6W **78** G4
Berryville *U.S.A.* 36°22N 93°34W **84** C8
Berseba *Namibia* 26°0S 17°46E **56** D2
Bershad *Ukraine* 48°22N 29°31E **17** D15
Berthold *U.S.A.* 48°19N 101°44W **80** A3
Berthoud *U.S.A.* 40°19N 105°5W **76** F11
Bertoua *Cameroon* 4°30N 13°45E **52** D2
Bertraghboy B. *Ireland* 53°22N 9°54W **10** C2
Berwick *U.S.A.* 41°3N 76°14W **83** E8
Berwick-upon-Tweed
  U.K. 55°46N 2°0W **12** B6

Berwyn Mts. *U.K.* 52°54N 3°26W **12** E4
Besal *Pakistan* 35°4N 73°56E **43** B5
Besalampy *Madag.* 16°43S 44°29E **57** B7
Besançon *France* 47°15N 6°2E **20** C7
Besar *Indonesia* 2°40S 116°0E **36** E5
Besnard L. *Canada* 55°25N 106°0W **71** B7
Besni *Turkey* 37°41N 37°52E **44** B3
Besor, N. → *Egypt* 31°28N 34°22E **46** D3
Bessarabia = Basarabeasca
  Moldova 46°21N 28°58E **17** E15
Bessarabka = Basarabeasca
  Moldova 46°21N 28°58E **17** E15
Bessemer *Ala., U.S.A.* 33°24N 86°58W **85** E11
Bessemer *Mich., U.S.A.* 46°29N 90°3W **80** B8
Bessemer *Pa., U.S.A.* 40°59N 80°30W **82** F4
Beswick *Australia* 14°34S 132°53E **60** B5
Beswick ◎ *Australia* 14°31S 132°51E **60** B5
Bet She'an *Israel* 32°30N 35°30E **46** C4
Bet Shemesh *Israel* 31°44N 35°0E **46** D4
Betafo *Madag.* 19°50S 46°51E **57** B8
Betancuria *Canary Is.* 28°25N 14°3W **24** F5
Betanzos *Spain* 43°15N 8°12W **21** A1
Bétaré Oya *Cameroon* 5°40N 14°5E **52** C2
Betatao *Madag.* 18°11S 47°52E **57** B8
Bethal *S. Africa* 26°27S 29°28E **57** D4
Bethanien *Namibia* 26°31S 17°8E **56** D2
Bethany *Canada* 44°11N 78°34W **82** B6
Bethany *Mo., U.S.A.* 40°16N 94°2W **80** E6
Bethany *Okla., U.S.A.* 35°31N 97°38W **84** D6
Bethel *Alaska, U.S.A.* 60°48N 161°45W **74** C7
Bethel *Conn., U.S.A.* 41°22N 73°25W **83** E11
Bethel *Maine, U.S.A.* 44°25N 70°47W **83** B14
Bethel *Vt., U.S.A.* 43°50N 72°38W **83** C12
Bethel Park *U.S.A.* 40°19N 80°2W **82** F4
Bethlehem = Bayt Laḥm
  West Bank 31°43N 35°12E **46** D4
Bethlehem *S. Africa* 28°14S 28°18E **57** D4
Bethlehem *U.S.A.* 40°37N 75°23W **83** F9
Bethulie *S. Africa* 30°30S 25°59E **56** E4
Béthune *France* 50°30N 2°38E **20** A5
Betioky *Madag.* 23°48S 44°20E **57** C7
Betong *Malaysia* 1°24N 111°31E **36** D4
Betong *Thailand* 5°45N 101°5E **39** K3
Betoota *Australia* 25°45S 140°42E **62** D3
Betpaqdala *Kazakhstan* 45°45N 70°30E **32** B8
Betroka *Madag.* 23°16S 46°0E **57** C8
Betsiamites *Canada* 48°56N 68°40W **73** C6
Betsiamites → *Canada* 48°56N 68°38W **73** C6
Betsiboka → *Madag.* 16°3S 46°36E **57** B8
Bettendorf *U.S.A.* 41°32N 90°30W **80** E8
Bettiah *India* 26°48N 84°33E **43** F11
Betul *India* 21°58N 77°59E **40** J10
Betws-y-Coed *U.K.* 53°5N 3°48W **12** D4
Beulah *Mich., U.S.A.* 44°38N 86°6W **80** C10
Beulah *N. Dak., U.S.A.* 47°16N 101°47W **80** B3
Beveren *Belgium* 51°12N 4°16E **15** C4
Beverley *Australia* 32°9S 116°56E **61** F2
Beverley *U.K.* 53°51N 0°26W **12** D7
Beverly *U.S.A.* 42°33N 70°53W **83** D14
Beverly Hills *Calif.,
  U.S.A.* 34°5N 118°24W **79** L8
Beverly Hills *Fla.,
  U.S.A.* 28°55N 82°28W **85** G13
Bevoalavo *Madag.* 25°13S 44°26E **57** D7
Bewas → *India* 23°59N 79°21E **43** H8
Bewdley *Canada* 44°5N 78°19W **82** B6
Bexhill *U.K.* 50°51N 0°29E **13** G8
Beyānlū *Iran* 36°0N 47°51E **44** C5
Beyneu *Kazakhstan* 45°18N 55°9E **19** E10
Beypazarı *Turkey* 40°10N 31°56E **19** F5
Beyşehir Gölü *Turkey* 37°41N 31°33E **44** B1
Béziers *France* 43°20N 3°12E **20** E5
Bezwada = Vijayawada
  India 16°31N 80°39E **41** L12
Bhabua *India* 25°3N 83°37E **43** G10
Bhachau *India* 23°20N 70°16E **42** H4
Bhadar → *Gujarat, India* 22°17N 72°20E **42** H5
Bhadar → *Gujarat, India* 21°27N 69°47E **42** J3
Bhadarwah *India* 32°58N 75°46E **43** C6
Bhadgaon = Bhaktapur
  Nepal 27°38N 85°24E **43** F11
Bhadohi *India* 25°25N 82°34E **43** G10
Bhadra *India* 29°8N 75°14E **42** E6
Bhadrakh *India* 21°10N 86°30E **41** J15
Bhadran *India* 22°19N 72°6E **42** H5
Bhadravati *India* 13°49N 75°40E **40** N9
Bhag *Pakistan* 29°2N 67°49E **42** E2
Bhagalpur *India* 25°10N 87°0E **43** G12
Bhagirathi → *Uttarakhand,
  India* 30°8N 78°35E **43** D8
Bhagirathi → *W. Bengal,
  India* 23°25N 88°23E **43** H13
Bhakkar *Pakistan* 31°40N 71°5E **42** D4
Bhakra Dam *India* 31°30N 76°45E **42** D7
Bhaktapur *Nepal* 27°38N 85°24E **43** F11
Bhamo *Burma* 24°15N 97°15E **41** G20
Bhandara *India* 21°5N 79°42E **40** J11
Bhanpura *India* 24°31N 75°44E **42** G6
Bhanrer Ra. *India* 23°40N 79°45E **43** H8
Bhaptiahi *India* 26°19N 86°44E **43** F12
Bharat = India ■ *Asia* 20°0N 78°0E **40** K11
Bharatpur *Chhattisgarh,
  India* 23°44N 81°46E **43** H9
Bharatpur *Raj., India* 27°15N 77°30E **42** F7
Bharatpur *Nepal* 27°34N 84°10E **43** F11
Bharno *India* 23°14N 84°53E **43** H11
Bharuch *India* 21°47N 73°0E **40** J8
Bhatinda *India* 30°15N 74°57E **42** D6
Bhatpara *India* 22°50N 88°25E **43** H13
Bhattu *India* 29°36N 75°19E **42** E6
Bhaun *Pakistan* 32°55N 72°40E **42** C5
Bhaunagar = Bhavnagar
  India 21°45N 72°10E **40** J8
Bhavnagar *India* 21°45N 72°10E **40** J8
Bhawari *India* 25°42N 73°4E **42** G5
Bhayavadar *India* 21°51N 70°15E **42** J4
Bhera *Pakistan* 32°29N 72°57E **42** C5
Bhikangaon *India* 21°52N 75°57E **42** J6
Bhilai = Bhilainagar-Durg
  India 21°13N 81°26E **41** J12
Bhilainagar-Durg *India* 21°13N 81°26E **41** J12

Bhilsa = Vidisha *India* 23°28N 77°53E **42** H7
Bhilwara *India* 25°25N 74°38E **42** G6
Bhima → *India* 16°25N 77°17E **40** L10
Bhimbar *Pakistan* 32°59N 74°3E **43** C6
Bhind *India* 26°30N 78°46E **43** F8
Bhinga *India* 27°43N 81°56E **43** F9
Bhinmal *India* 25°0N 72°15E **42** G5
Bhisho *S. Africa* 32°50S 27°23E **56** E4
Bhiwandi *India* 19°20N 73°0E **40** K8
Bhiwani *India* 28°50N 76°9E **42** E7
Bhogava → *India* 22°26N 72°20E **42** H5
Bhola *Bangla.* 22°45N 90°35E **41** H17
Bholari *Pakistan* 25°19N 68°13E **42** G3
Bhopal *India* 23°20N 77°30E **42** H7
Bhubaneshwar *India* 20°15N 85°50E **41** J14
Bhusawal *India* 21°3N 75°46E **40** J9
Bhutan ■ *Asia* 27°25N 90°30E **41** F17
Biafra, B. of = Bonny, Bight of
  Africa 3°30N 9°20E **52** D1
Biak *Indonesia* 1°10S 136°6E **37** E9
Biała Podlaska *Poland* 52°4N 23°6E **17** B12
Białogard *Poland* 54°2N 15°58E **16** A8
Białystok *Poland* 53°10N 23°10E **17** B12
Biaora *India* 23°56N 76°56E **42** H7
Biärjmand *Iran* 36°6N 55°53E **45** B7
Biaro *Indonesia* 2°5N 125°26E **37** D7
Biarritz *France* 43°29N 1°33W **20** E3
Bibai *Japan* 43°19N 141°52E **30** C10
Bibby I. *Canada* 61°55N 93°0W **71** A10
Biberach *Germany* 48°5N 9°47E **16** D5
Bibungwa
  Dem. Rep. of the Congo 2°40S 28°15E **54** C2
Bicester *U.K.* 51°54N 1°9W **13** F6
Bicheno *Australia* 41°52S 148°18E **63** G4
Bichia *India* 22°27N 80°42E **43** H9
Bickerton I. *Australia* 13°45S 136°10E **62** A2
Bid = Bir *India* 19°4N 75°46E **40** K9
Bida *Nigeria* 9°3N 5°58E **50** G7
Bidar *India* 17°55N 77°35E **40** L10
Biddeford *U.S.A.* 43°30N 70°28W **81** D18
Bideford *U.K.* 51°1N 4°13W **13** F3
Bideford Bay *U.K.* 51°5N 4°20W **13** F3
Bidhuna *India* 26°49N 79°31E **43** F8
Bīdokht *Iran* 34°20N 58°46E **45** C8
Bidor *Malaysia* 4°6N 101°15E **39** K3
Bidyadanga *Australia* 18°45S 121°43E **60** C3
Bié, Planalto de *Angola* 12°0S 16°0E **53** G3
Bieber *U.S.A.* 41°7N 121°8W **76** F3
Biel *Switz.* 47°8N 7°14E **20** C7
Bielefeld *Germany* 52°1N 8°33E **16** B5
Biella *Italy* 45°34N 8°3E **20** D8
Bielsk Podlaski *Poland* 52°47N 23°12E **17** B12
Bielsko-Biała *Poland* 49°50N 19°2E **17** D10
Bien Hoa *Vietnam* 10°57N 106°49E **39** G6
Bienne = Biel *Switz.* 47°8N 7°14E **20** C7
Bienville, L. *Canada* 55°5N 72°40W **72** A5
Biesiesfontein *S. Africa* 30°57S 17°58E **56** E2
Big → *Canada* 54°50N 58°55W **73** B8
Big B. *Canada* 55°43N 60°35W **73** A7
Big Bear City *U.S.A.* 34°16N 116°51W **79** L10
Big Bear Lake *U.S.A.* 34°15N 116°56W **79** L10
Big Belt Mts. *U.S.A.* 46°30N 111°25W **76** C8
Big Bend *Swaziland* 26°50S 31°58E **57** D5
Big Bend △ *U.S.A.* 29°20N 103°5W **84** G3
Big Black → *U.S.A.* 32°3N 91°4W **85** F9
Big Blue → *U.S.A.* 39°35N 96°34W **80** F5
Big Creek *U.S.A.* 37°11N 119°14W **78** H7
Big Cypress △ *U.S.A.* 26°0N 81°10W **85** H14
Big Desert *Australia* 35°45S 141°10E **63** F3
Big Falls *U.S.A.* 48°12N 93°48W **80** A7
Big Fork → *U.S.A.* 48°31N 93°43W **80** A7
Big Horn Mts. = Bighorn Mts.
  U.S.A. 44°25N 107°0W **76** D10
Big I. *Canada* 61°7N 116°45W **70** A5
Big Lake *U.S.A.* 31°12N 101°28W **84** F4
Big Moose *U.S.A.* 43°49N 74°58W **83** C10
Big Muddy Cr. →
  U.S.A. 48°8N 104°36W **76** B11
Big Pine *U.S.A.* 37°10N 118°17W **78** H8
Big Piney *U.S.A.* 42°32N 110°7W **76** E8
Big Quill L. *Canada* 51°55N 104°30W **71** C8
Big Rapids *U.S.A.* 43°42N 85°29W **81** D11
Big Rideau L. *Canada* 44°40N 76°15W **83** B8
Big River *Canada* 53°50N 107°0W **71** C7
Big Run *U.S.A.* 40°57N 78°55W **82** F6
Big Sable Pt. *U.S.A.* 44°3N 86°1W **80** C10
Big Salmon → *Canada* 61°52N 134°55W **70** A2
Big Sand L. *Canada* 57°45N 99°45W **71** B9
Big Sandy *U.S.A.* 48°11N 110°7W **76** B8
Big Sandy → *U.S.A.* 38°25N 82°36W **81** F12
Big Sandy Cr. = Sandy Cr. →
  U.S.A. 41°51N 109°47W **76** F9
Big Sandy Cr. →
  U.S.A. 38°7N 102°29W **76** G12
Big Sioux → *U.S.A.* 42°29N 96°27W **80** D5
Big South Fork △
  U.S.A. 36°27N 84°47W **85** C12
Big Spring *U.S.A.* 32°15N 101°28W **84** E4
Big Stone City *U.S.A.* 45°18N 96°28W **80** C5
Big Stone Gap *U.S.A.* 36°52N 82°47W **81** G12
Big Stone L. *U.S.A.* 45°18N 96°27W **80** C5
Big Sur *U.S.A.* 36°15N 121°48W **78** J5
Big Timber *U.S.A.* 45°50N 109°57W **76** D9
Big Trout L. *Canada* 53°40N 90°0W **72** B2
Big Trout Lake *Canada* 53°45N 90°0W **72** B1
Biga *Turkey* 40°13N 27°14E **23** D12
Bigadiç *Turkey* 39°22N 28°7E **23** E13
Biggar *Canada* 52°4N 108°0W **71** C7
Biggar *U.K.* 55°38N 3°32W **11** F5
Bigge I. *Australia* 14°35S 125°10E **60** B4
Biggenden *Australia* 25°31S 152°4E **63** D5
Biggleswade *U.K.* 52°5N 0°14W **13** E7
Biggs *U.S.A.* 39°25N 121°43W **78** F5
Bighorn *U.S.A.* 46°10N 107°27W **76** C10
Bighorn → *U.S.A.* 46°10N 107°28W **76** C10
Bighorn Canyon △
  U.S.A. 45°10N 108°0W **76** D10
Bighorn L. *U.S.A.* 44°55N 108°15W **76** D9

Bighorn Mts. *U.S.A.* 44°25N 107°0W **76** D10
Bigstone L. *Canada* 53°42N 95°44W **71** C9
Bigwa *Tanzania* 7°10S 39°10E **54** D4
Bihać *Bos.-H.* 44°49N 15°57E **16** F8
Bihar *India* 25°5N 85°40E **43** G11
Bihar □ *India* 25°0N 86°0E **43** G12
Biharamulo *Tanzania* 2°25S 31°25E **54** C3
Biharamulo △ *Tanzania* 2°24S 31°26E **54** C3
Bihariganj *India* 25°44N 86°59E **43** G12
Bihor, Munţii *Romania* 46°29N 22°47E **17** E12
Bijagós, Arquipélago dos *Guinea-Biss.* 11°15N 16°10W **50** F2
Bijaipur *India* 26°2N 77°20E **42** F7
Bijapur *Chhattisgarh, India* 18°50N 80°50E **41** K12
Bijapur *Karnataka, India* 16°50N 75°55E **40** L9
Bījār *Iran* 35°52N 47°35E **44** C5
Bijawar *India* 24°38N 79°30E **43** G8
Bijeljina *Bos.-H.* 44°46N 19°14E **23** B8
Bijnor *India* 29°27N 78°11E **42** E8
Bikaner *India* 28°2N 73°18E **42** E5
Bikapur *India* 26°30N 82°7E **43** F10
Bikeqi *China* 40°43N 111°20E **34** D6
Bikfayyā *Lebanon* 33°55N 35°41E **46** B4
Bikin *Russia* 46°50N 134°20E **30** A7
Bikin → *Russia* 46°51N 134°2E **30** A7
Bikini Atoll *Marshall Is.* 12°0N 167°30E **64** F8
Bikita *Zimbabwe* 20°6S 31°41E **57** C5
Bikkū Bīttī *Libya* 22°0N 19°12E **51** D9
Bila Tserkva *Ukraine* 49°45N 30°10E **17** D16
Bilara *India* 26°14N 73°53E **42** F5
Bilaspur *Chhattisgarh, India* 22°2N 82°15E **43** H10
Bilaspur *Punjab, India* 31°19N 76°50E **42** D7
Bilauk Taungdan *Thailand* 13°0N 99°0E **38** F2
Bilbao *Spain* 43°16N 2°56W **21** A4
Bilbo = Bilbao *Spain* 43°16N 2°56W **21** A4
Bildudalur *Iceland* 65°41N 23°36W **8** D2
Bílé Karpaty *Europe* 49°5N 18°0E **17** D9
Bilecik *Turkey* 40°5N 30°5E **19** F5
Bilgram *India* 27°11N 80°2E **43** F9
Bilhaur *India* 26°51N 80°5E **43** F9
Bilhorod-Dnistrovskyy *Ukraine* 46°11N 30°23E **19** E5
Bilibino *Russia* 68°3N 166°20E **29** C17
Bilibiza *Mozam.* 12°30S 40°20E **55** E5
Billiluna *Australia* 19°37S 127°41E **60** C4
Billings *U.S.A.* 45°47N 108°30W **76** D9
Billiton Is. = Belitung *Indonesia* 3°10S 107°50E **36** E3
Bilma *Niger* 18°50N 13°30E **51** E8
Biloela *Australia* 24°24S 150°31E **62** C5
Biloxi *U.S.A.* 30°24N 88°53W **85** F10
Bilpa Morea Claypan *Australia* 25°0S 140°0E **62** D3
Biltine *Chad* 14°40N 20°50E **51** F10
Bim Son *Vietnam* 20°4N 105°51E **38** B5
Bima *Indonesia* 8°22S 118°49E **37** F5
Bimbo *C.A.R.* 4°15N 18°33E **52** D3
Bimini Is. *Bahamas* 25°42N 79°25W **88** A4
Bin Xian *Heilongjiang, China* 45°42N 127°32E **35** B14
Bin Xian *Shaanxi, China* 35°2N 108°4E **34** G5
Bina-Etawah *India* 24°13N 78°14E **42** G8
Binalong *Australia* 34°40S 148°39E **63** E4
Bīnālūd, Kūh-e *Iran* 36°30N 58°30E **45** B8
Binatang = Bintangau *Malaysia* 2°10N 111°40E **36** D4
Binche *Belgium* 50°26N 4°10E **15** D4
Bindki *India* 26°2N 80°36E **43** F9
Bindura *Zimbabwe* 17°18S 31°18E **55** F3
Bingara *Australia* 29°52S 150°36E **63** D5
Bingham *U.S.A.* 45°3N 69°53W **81** C19
Binghamton *U.S.A.* 42°6N 75°55W **83** D9
Bingöl *Turkey* 38°53N 40°29E **44** B4
Binh Dinh *Vietnam* 13°55N 109°7E **38** F7
Binh Son *Vietnam* 15°20N 108°40E **38** E7
Binhai *China* 34°2N 119°49E **35** G10
Binisatua *Spain* 39°50N 4°11E **24** B11
Binissalem *Spain* 39°41N 2°50E **24** B9
Binjai *Indonesia* 3°20N 98°30E **36** D3
Binnaway *Australia* 31°28S 149°24E **63** E4
Binongko *Indonesia* 5°57S 124°2E **37** F6
Binscarth *Canada* 50°37N 101°17W **71** C8
Bintan *Indonesia* 1°0N 104°0E **36** D2
Bintangau *Malaysia* 2°10N 111°40E **36** D4
Bintulu *Malaysia* 3°10N 113°0E **36** D4
Bintuni *Indonesia* 2°7S 133°32E **37** E8
Binzert = Bizerte *Tunisia* 37°15N 9°50E **51** A7
Binzhou *China* 37°20N 118°2E **35** F10
Bío Bío □ *Chile* 37°35S 72°0W **94** D1
Biobío → *Chile* 36°49S 73°10W **94** D1
Bioko *Eq. Guin.* 3°30N 8°40E **52** D1
Bir *India* 19°4N 75°46E **40** K9
Bîr Abu Muḥammad *Egypt* 29°44N 34°14E **46** F3
Bi'r al Butayyihāt *Jordan* 29°47N 35°20E **46** F4
Bi'r al Mārī *Jordan* 30°4N 35°33E **46** E4
Bi'r al Qattār *Jordan* 29°47N 35°32E **46** F4
Bîr Atrun *Sudan* 18°15N 26°40E **51** E11
Bîr Beiḍa *Egypt* 30°25N 34°29E **46** E3
Bîr el 'Abd *Egypt* 31°2N 33°0E **46** D2
Bîr el Biarât *Egypt* 29°30N 34°43E **46** F3
Bîr el Duweidar *Egypt* 30°56N 32°32E **46** E1
Bîr el Garârât *Egypt* 31°3N 33°34E **46** D2
Bîr el Heisi *Egypt* 29°22N 34°36E **46** F3
Bîr el Jafir *Egypt* 30°50N 32°41E **46** E1
Bîr el Mâlḥi *Egypt* 30°38N 33°19E **46** E2
Bîr el Thamâda *Egypt* 30°12N 33°27E **46** E2
Bîr Gebeil Ḥiṣn *Egypt* 30°2N 33°18E **46** E2
Bi'r Ghadīr *Syria* 34°6N 37°3E **46** A6
Bîr Ḥasana *Egypt* 30°29N 33°46E **46** E2
Bîr Kaseiba *Egypt* 31°0N 33°17E **46** E2
Bîr Lahfân *Egypt* 31°0N 33°51E **46** E2
Bîr Madkûr *Egypt* 30°44N 32°33E **46** E1
Bîr Mogreïn *Mauritania* 25°10N 11°25W **50** C3
Bi'r Muṭribah *Kuwait* 29°54N 47°17E **44** D5
Bîr Qaṭia *Egypt* 30°58N 32°45E **46** E1
Bîr Shalatein *Egypt* 23°5N 35°25E **51** D13
Birāk *Libya* 27°31N 14°20E **51** C8
Biratnagar *Nepal* 26°27N 87°17E **43** F12
Birawa *Dem. Rep. of the Congo* 2°20S 28°48E **54** C2
Birch → *Canada* 58°28N 112°17W **70** B6
Birch Hills *Canada* 52°59N 105°25W **71** C7
Birch I. *Canada* 52°26N 99°54W **71** C9
Birch L. *N.W.T., Canada* 62°4N 116°33W **70** A5
Birch L. *Ont., Canada* 51°23N 92°18W **72** B1
Birch Mts. *Canada* 57°30N 113°10W **70** B6
Birch River *Canada* 52°24N 101°6W **71** C8
Birchip *Australia* 35°56S 142°55E **63** F3
Bird *Canada* 56°30N 94°13W **71** B10
Bird I. = Aves, I. de *W. Indies* 15°45N 63°55W **89** C7
Bird I. *S. Georgia* 54°0S 38°3W **96** G9
Birds Creek *Canada* 45°6N 77°52W **82** A7
Birdsville *Australia* 25°51S 139°20E **62** D2
Birdum Cr. → *Australia* 15°14S 133°0E **60** C5
Birecik *Turkey* 37°2N 38°0E **44** B3
Birein *Israel* 30°50N 34°28E **46** E3
Bireuen *Indonesia* 5°14N 96°39E **36** C1
Birganj *Nepal* 27°1N 84°52E **43** F11
Birigüi *Brazil* 21°18S 50°16W **95** A5
Bīrjand *Iran* 32°53N 59°13E **45** C8
Birkenhead *U.K.* 53°23N 3°2W **12** D4
Bîrlad = Bârlad *Romania* 46°15N 27°38E **17** E14
Birmingham *U.K.* 52°29N 1°52W **13** E6
Birmingham *U.S.A.* 33°31N 86°48W **85** E11
Birmingham Int. ✈ (BHX) *U.K.* 52°26N 1°45W **13** E6
Birmitrapur *India* 22°24N 84°46E **41** H14
Birni Nkonni *Niger* 13°55N 5°15E **50** F7
Birnin Kebbi *Nigeria* 12°32N 4°12E **50** F6
Birobidzhan *Russia* 48°50N 132°50E **33** B15
Birr *Ireland* 53°6N 7°54W **10** C4
Birrie → *Australia* 29°43S 146°37E **63** D4
Birsilpur *India* 28°11N 72°15E **42** E5
Birsk *Russia* 55°25N 55°30E **18** C10
Birtle *Canada* 50°30N 101°5W **71** C8
Birur *India* 13°30N 75°55E **40** N9
Biržai *Lithuania* 56°11N 24°45E **9** H21
Birżebbugga *Malta* 35°50N 14°32E **25** D2
Bisa *Indonesia* 1°15S 127°28E **37** E7
Bisalpur *India* 28°14N 79°48E **43** E8
Bisbee *U.S.A.* 31°27N 109°55W **77** L9
Biscarrosse *France* 44°22N 1°20W **20** D3
Biscay, B. of *Atl. Oc.* 45°0N 2°0W **20** D1
Biscayne B. *U.S.A.* 25°40N 80°12W **85** J14
Biscoe Is. *Antarctica* 66°0S 67°0W **5** C17
Biscotasing *Canada* 47°18N 82°9W **72** C3
Bishkek *Kyrgyzstan* 42°54N 74°46E **32** C3
Bishnupur *India* 23°8N 87°20E **43** H12
Bisho = Bhisho *S. Africa* 32°50S 27°23E **56** E4
Bishop *Calif., U.S.A.* 37°22N 118°24W **78** H8
Bishop *Tex., U.S.A.* 27°35N 97°48W **84** H6
Bishop Auckland *U.K.* 54°39N 1°40W **12** C6
Bishop's Falls *Canada* 49°2N 55°30W **73** C8
Bishop's Stortford *U.K.* 51°52N 0°10E **13** F8
Bisina, L. *Uganda* 1°38N 33°56E **54** B3
Biskra *Algeria* 34°50N 5°44E **50** B7
Bismarck *U.S.A.* 46°48N 100°47W **80** B3
Bismarck Arch. *Papua N. G.* 2°30S 150°0E **58** B7
Biso *Uganda* 1°44N 31°26E **54** B3
Bison *U.S.A.* 45°31N 102°28W **80** C2
Bīsotūn *Iran* 34°23N 47°26E **44** C5
Bissagos = Bijagós, Arquipélago dos *Guinea-Biss.* 11°15N 16°10W **50** F2
Bissau *Guinea-Biss.* 11°45N 15°45W **50** F2
Bistcho L. *Canada* 59°45N 118°50W **70** B5
Bistriţa *Romania* 47°9N 24°35E **17** E13
Bistriţa → *Romania* 46°30N 26°57E **17** E14
Biswan *India* 27°29N 81°2E **43** F9
Bitam *Gabon* 2°5N 11°25E **52** D2
Bitkine *Chad* 11°59N 18°13E **51** F9
Bitlis *Turkey* 38°20N 42°3E **44** B4
Bitola *Macedonia* 41°1N 21°20E **23** D9
Bitolj = Bitola *Macedonia* 41°1N 21°20E **23** D9
Bitter Creek *U.S.A.* 41°33N 108°33W **76** F9
Bitterfontein *S. Africa* 31°1S 18°32E **56** E2
Bitterroot → *U.S.A.* 46°52N 114°7W **76** C6
Bitterroot Range *U.S.A.* 46°0N 114°20W **76** C6
Bitterwater *U.S.A.* 36°23N 121°0W **78** J6
Biu *Nigeria* 10°40N 12°3E **51** F8
Biwa-Ko *Japan* 35°15N 136°10E **31** G8
Biwabik *U.S.A.* 47°32N 92°21W **80** B7
Bixby *U.S.A.* 35°57N 95°53W **84** D7
Biyang *China* 32°38N 113°21E **34** H7
Biysk *Russia* 52°40N 85°0E **28** D9
Bizana *S. Africa* 30°50S 29°52E **57** E4
Bizen *Japan* 34°43N 134°8E **31** G7
Bizerte *Tunisia* 37°15N 9°50E **51** A7
Bjargtangar *Iceland* 65°30N 24°30W **8** D1
Bjelovar *Croatia* 45°56N 16°49E **22** B7
Björneborg = Pori *Finland* 61°29N 21°48E **8** F19
Bjørnevatn *Norway* 69°40N 30°0E **8** B24
Bjørnøya *Arctic* 74°30N 19°0E **4** B8
Black = Da → *Vietnam* 21°15N 105°20E **38** B5
Black → *Canada* 44°42N 79°19W **82** B5
Black → *Ariz., U.S.A.* 33°44N 110°13W **77** K8
Black → *Ark., U.S.A.* 35°38N 91°20W **84** D9
Black → *La., U.S.A.* 31°16N 91°50W **84** F9
Black → *Mich., U.S.A.* 42°59N 82°27W **82** D2
Black → *N.Y., U.S.A.* 43°59N 76°4W **83** C8
Black → *Wis., U.S.A.* 43°57N 91°22W **80** D8
Black Bay Pen. *Canada* 48°38N 88°21W **72** C2
Black Birch L. *Canada* 56°53N 107°45W **71** B7
Black Canyon of the Gunnison △ *U.S.A.* 38°40N 107°35W **76** G10
Black Diamond *Canada* 50°45N 114°14W **70** C6
Black Duck → *Canada* 56°51N 89°2W **72** A2
Black Forest = Schwarzwald *Germany* 48°30N 8°20E **16** D5
Black Forest *U.S.A.* 39°0N 104°43W **76** G11
Black Hd. *Ireland* 53°9N 9°16W **10** C2
Black Hills *U.S.A.* 44°0N 103°45W **80** D2
Black I. *Canada* 51°12N 96°30W **71** C9
Black L. *Canada* 59°12N 105°15W **71** B7
Black L. *Mich., U.S.A.* 45°28N 84°16W **81** C11
Black L. *N.Y., U.S.A.* 44°31N 75°36W **83** B9
Black Lake *Canada* 59°11N 105°20W **71** B7
Black Mesa *U.S.A.* 36°58N 102°58W **84** C3
Black Mt. = Mynydd Du *U.K.* 51°52N 3°50W **13** F4
Black Mts. *U.K.* 51°55N 3°7W **13** F4
Black Range *U.S.A.* 33°15N 107°50W **77** K10
Black River *Jamaica* 18°0N 77°50W **88** a
Black River *U.S.A.* 44°0N 75°47W **83** C9
Black River Falls *U.S.A.* 44°18N 90°51W **80** C8
Black Rock *Barbados* 13°7N 59°37W **89** g
Black Rock Desert *U.S.A.* 41°10N 118°50W **76** F4
Black Sea *Eurasia* 43°30N 35°0E **19** F6
Black Tickle *Canada* 53°28N 55°45W **73** B8
Black Volta → *Africa* 8°41N 1°33W **50** G5
Black Warrior → *U.S.A.* 32°32N 87°51W **85** E11
Blackall *Australia* 24°25S 145°45E **62** C4
Blackball *N.Z.* 42°22S 171°26E **59** E3
Blackbraes △ *Australia* 19°10S 144°10E **62** B3
Blackbull *Australia* 17°55S 141°45E **62** B3
Blackburn *U.K.* 53°45N 2°29W **12** D5
Blackburn, Mt. *U.S.A.* 61°44N 143°26W **74** C11
Blackburn with Darwen □ *U.K.* 53°45N 2°29W **12** D5
Blackdown Tableland △ *Australia* 23°52S 149°8E **62** C4
Blackfoot *U.S.A.* 43°11N 112°21W **76** E7
Blackfoot → *U.S.A.* 46°52N 113°53W **76** C7
Blackfoot Res. *U.S.A.* 42°55N 111°39W **76** E8
Blackpool *U.K.* 53°49N 3°3W **12** D4
Blackpool □ *U.K.* 53°49N 3°3W **12** D4
Blackriver *U.S.A.* 44°46N 83°17W **82** B1
Blacks Harbour *Canada* 45°3N 66°49W **73** C6
Blacksburg *U.S.A.* 37°14N 80°25W **81** G13
Blacksod B. *Ireland* 54°6N 10°0W **10** B1
Blackstairs Mt. *Ireland* 52°33N 6°48W **10** D5
Blackstone *U.S.A.* 37°5N 78°0W **81** G14
Blackstone Ra. *Australia* 26°0S 128°30E **61** E4
Blackwater = West Road → *Canada* 53°18N 122°53W **70** C4
Blackwater *Australia* 23°35S 148°53E **62** C4
Blackwater → *Meath, Ireland* 53°39N 6°41W **10** C4
Blackwater → *Waterford, Ireland* 52°4N 7°52W **10** D4
Blackwater → *U.K.* 54°31N 6°35W **10** B5
Blackwell *U.S.A.* 36°48N 97°17W **84** C6
Blackwells Corner *U.S.A.* 35°37N 119°47W **79** K7
Bladensburg △ *Australia* 22°30S 142°59E **62** C3
Blaenau Ffestiniog *U.K.* 53°0N 3°56W **12** E4
Blaenau Gwent □ *U.K.* 51°48N 3°12W **13** F4
Blagodarnoye = Blagodarnyy *Russia* 45°7N 43°37E **19** E7
Blagodarnyy *Russia* 45°7N 43°37E **19** E7
Blagoevgrad *Bulgaria* 42°2N 23°5E **23** C10
Blagoveshchensk *Russia* 50°20N 127°30E **33** A14
Blahkiuh *Indonesia* 8°31S 115°12E **37** J18
Blain *U.S.A.* 40°20N 77°31W **82** F7
Blaine *Minn., U.S.A.* 45°10N 93°13W **80** C7
Blaine *Wash., U.S.A.* 48°59N 122°45W **78** B4
Blaine Lake *Canada* 52°51N 106°52W **71** C7
Blair *U.S.A.* 41°33N 96°8W **80** E5
Blair Athol *Australia* 22°42S 147°31E **62** C4
Blair Atholl *U.K.* 56°46N 3°50W **11** E5
Blairgowrie *U.K.* 56°35N 3°21W **11** E5
Blairsden *U.S.A.* 39°47N 120°37W **78** F6
Blairsville *U.S.A.* 40°26N 79°16W **82** F5
Blakang Mati, Pulau *Singapore* 1°15N 103°50E **39** d
Blake Pt. *U.S.A.* 48°11N 88°25W **80** A9
Blakely *Ga., U.S.A.* 31°23N 84°56W **85** F12
Blakely *Pa., U.S.A.* 41°28N 75°37W **83** E9
Blambangan, Semenanjung *Indonesia* 8°42S 114°29E **37** K17
Blanc, C. *Spain* 39°21N 2°51E **24** B9
Blanc, Mont *Europe* 45°48N 6°50E **20** D7
Blanca, B. *Argentina* 39°10S 61°30W **96** D4
Blanca, Cord. *Peru* 9°10S 77°35W **92** E3
Blanca Peak *U.S.A.* 37°35N 105°29W **77** H11
Blanche, C. *Australia* 33°1S 134°9E **63** E1
Blanche, L. *S. Austral., Australia* 29°15S 139°40E **63** D2
Blanche, L. *W. Austral., Australia* 22°25S 123°17E **60** D3
Blanchisseuse *Trin. & Tob.* 10°48N 61°18W **93** K15
Blanco *S. Africa* 33°55S 22°23E **56** E3
Blanco *U.S.A.* 30°6N 98°25W **84** F5
Blanco → *Argentina* 30°20S 68°42W **94** C2
Blanco, C. *Costa Rica* 9°34N 85°8W **88** E2
Blanco, C. *U.S.A.* 42°51N 124°34W **76** E1
Blanda → *Iceland* 65°37N 20°9W **8** D3
Blandford Forum *U.K.* 50°51N 2°9W **13** G5
Blanding *U.S.A.* 37°37N 109°29W **77** H9
Blanes *Spain* 41°40N 2°48E **21** B7
Blankenberge *Belgium* 51°20N 3°9E **15** C3
Blanquilla *Venezuela* 11°51N 64°37W **89** D7
Blanquillo *Uruguay* 32°53S 55°37W **95** C4
Blantyre *Malawi* 15°45S 35°0E **55** F4
Blarney *Ireland* 51°56N 8°33W **10** E3
Blasdell *U.S.A.* 42°48N 78°50W **82** D6
Blåvands Huk *Denmark* 55°33N 8°4E **9** J13
Blaydon *U.K.* 54°58N 1°42W **12** C6
Blayney *Australia* 33°32S 149°14E **63** E4
Blaze, Pt. *Australia* 12°56S 130°11E **60** B5
Blekinge *Sweden* 56°25N 15°20E **9** H16
Blenheim *Canada* 42°20N 82°0W **82** D3
Blenheim *N.Z.* 41°38S 173°57E **59** D4
Bletchley *U.K.* 51°59N 0°44W **13** F7
Bleus, Monts *Dem. Rep. of the Congo* 1°30N 30°30E **54** B3
Blida *Algeria* 36°30N 2°49E **50** A6
Bligh Sound *N.Z.* 44°47S 167°32E **59** F1
Bligh Water *Fiji* 17°0S 178°0E **59** a
Blind River *Canada* 46°10N 82°58W **72** C3
Bliss *Idaho, U.S.A.* 42°56N 114°57W **76** E6
Bliss *N.Y., U.S.A.* 42°34N 78°15W **82** D6
Blissfield *U.S.A.* 40°24N 81°58W **82** F3
Blitar *Indonesia* 8°5S 112°11E **37** H15
Block I. *U.S.A.* 41°11N 71°35W **83** E13
Block Island Sd. *U.S.A.* 41°15N 71°40W **83** E13
Bloemfontein *S. Africa* 29°6S 26°7E **56** D4
Bloemhof *S. Africa* 27°38S 25°32E **56** D4
Blois *France* 47°35N 1°20E **20** C4
Blönduós *Iceland* 65°40N 20°12W **8** D3
Blongas *Indonesia* 8°53S 116°2E **37** K19
Bloodvein → *Canada* 51°47N 96°43W **71** C9
Bloody Foreland *Ireland* 55°10N 8°17W **10** A3
Bloomer *U.S.A.* 45°6N 91°29W **80** C8
Bloomfield *Canada* 43°59N 77°14W **82** C7
Bloomfield *Iowa, U.S.A.* 40°45N 92°25W **80** E7
Bloomfield *N. Mex., U.S.A.* 36°43N 107°59W **77** H10
Bloomfield *Nebr., U.S.A.* 42°36N 97°39W **80** D5
Bloomington *Ill., U.S.A.* 40°28N 89°0W **80** E9
Bloomington *Ind., U.S.A.* 39°10N 86°32W **80** F10
Bloomington *Minn., U.S.A.* 44°50N 93°17W **80** C7
Bloomsburg *U.S.A.* 41°0N 76°27W **83** F8
Bloomsbury *Australia* 20°48S 148°38E **62** b
Blora *Indonesia* 6°57S 111°25E **37** G14
Blossburg *U.S.A.* 41°41N 77°4W **82** E7
Blouberg *S. Africa* 23°8S 28°59E **57** C4
Blountstown *U.S.A.* 30°27N 85°3W **85** F12
Blue Earth *U.S.A.* 43°38N 94°6W **80** D6
Blue Hole △ *Belize* 17°24N 88°30W **88** C2
Blue Lagoon △ *Zambia* 15°28S 27°26E **55** F2
Blue Mesa Res. *U.S.A.* 38°28N 107°20W **76** G10
Blue Mountain Lake *U.S.A.* 43°51N 74°27W **83** C10
Blue Mountain Pk. *Jamaica* 18°3N 76°36W **88** a
Blue Mt. *U.S.A.* 40°30N 76°30W **83** F8
Blue Mts. *Jamaica* 18°3N 76°36W **88** a
Blue Mts. *Maine, U.S.A.* 44°50N 70°35W **83** B14
Blue Mts. *Oreg., U.S.A.* 45°0N 118°20W **76** D4
Blue Mud B. *Australia* 13°30S 136°0E **62** A2
Blue Mud Bay ✪ *Australia* 13°25S 136°2E **62** A2
Blue Nile = Nîl el Azraq → *Sudan* 15°38N 32°31E **51** E12
Blue Rapids *U.S.A.* 39°41N 96°39W **80** F5
Blue Ridge *U.S.A.* 36°40N 80°50W **81** G13
Blue River *Canada* 52°6N 119°18W **70** C5
Bluefield *U.S.A.* 37°15N 81°17W **81** G13
Bluefields *Nic.* 12°20N 83°50W **88** D3
Bluevale *Canada* 43°51N 81°15W **82** C3
Bluff *Australia* 23°35S 149°4E **62** C4
Bluff *N.Z.* 46°37S 168°20E **59** G2
Bluff *U.S.A.* 37°17N 109°33W **77** H9
Bluff Knoll *Australia* 34°24S 118°15E **61** F2
Bluff Pt. *Australia* 27°50S 114°5E **61** E1
Bluffton *U.S.A.* 40°44N 85°11W **81** E11
Blumenau *Brazil* 27°0S 49°0W **95** B6
Blunt *U.S.A.* 44°31N 99°59W **80** C4
Bly *U.S.A.* 42°24N 121°3W **76** E3
Blyde River Canyon △ *S. Africa* 24°37S 31°2E **57** C5
Blyth *Canada* 43°44N 81°26W **82** C3
Blyth *U.K.* 55°8N 1°31W **12** B6
Blythe *U.S.A.* 33°37N 114°36W **79** M12
Blytheville *U.S.A.* 35°56N 89°55W **85** D10
Bo *S. Leone* 7°55N 11°50W **50** G3
Bo Duc *Vietnam* 11°58N 106°50E **39** G6
Bo Hai *China* 39°0N 119°0E **35** E10
Bo Hai Haixia *Asia* 38°25N 121°10E **35** E11
Bo Xian = Bozhou *China* 33°55N 115°41E **34** H8
Boa Vista *Brazil* 2°48N 60°30W **92** C6
Boa Vista *C. Verde Is.* 16°0N 22°49W **50** b
Boaco *Nic.* 12°29N 85°35W **88** D2
Bo'ai *China* 35°10N 113°3E **34** G7
Boalsburg *U.S.A.* 40°47N 77°49W **82** F7
Boane *Mozam.* 26°6S 32°19E **57** D5
Boao *China* 19°8N 110°34E **38** C8
Boardman *U.S.A.* 41°2N 80°40W **82** E4
Bobadah *Australia* 32°19S 146°41E **63** E4
Bobbili *India* 18°35N 83°30E **41** K13
Bobcaygeon *Canada* 44°33N 78°33W **82** B6
Bobo-Dioulasso *Burkina Faso* 11°8N 4°13W **50** F5
Bobonong *Botswana* 21°58S 28°20E **55** G2
Bóbr → *Poland* 52°4N 15°4E **16** B8
Bobraomby, Tanjon' i *Madag.* 12°40S 49°10E **57** A8
Bobruysk = Babruysk *Belarus* 53°10N 29°15E **17** B15
Boby, Pic *Madag.* 22°12S 46°55E **53** J9
Boca del Río *Mexico* 19°5N 96°4W **87** D5
Boca do Acre *Brazil* 8°50S 67°27W **92** E5
Boca Raton *U.S.A.* 26°21N 80°5W **85** H14
Bocas del Dragón = Dragon's Mouths *Venezuela* 11°0N 61°50W **93** K15
Bocas del Toro *Panama* 9°15N 82°20W **88** E3
Bochnia *Poland* 49°58N 20°27E **17** D11
Bochum *Germany* 51°28N 7°13E **16** C4
Bocoyna *Mexico* 27°52N 107°35W **86** B3
Bodaybo *Russia* 57°50N 114°0E **29** D12
Boddam *U.K.* 59°56N 1°17W **11** B7
Boddington *Australia* 32°50S 116°30E **61** F2
Bodega Bay *U.S.A.* 38°20N 123°3W **78** G3
Boden *Sweden* 65°50N 21°42E **8** D19
Bodensee *Europe* 47°35N 9°25E **20** C8
Bodhan *India* 18°40N 77°44E **40** K10
Bodmin *U.K.* 50°28N 4°43W **13** G3
Bodmin Moor *U.K.* 50°33N 4°36W **13** G3
Bodø *Norway* 67°17N 14°24E **8** C16
Bodrog → *Hungary* 48°11N 21°22E **17** D11
Bodrum *Turkey* 37°3N 27°30E **23** F12
Boende *Dem. Rep. of the Congo* 0°24S 21°12E **52** E4
Boerne *U.S.A.* 29°47N 98°44W **84** G5
Boesmans → *S. Africa* 33°42S 26°39E **56** E4
Bogalusa *U.S.A.* 30°47N 89°52W **85** F10
Bogan → *Australia* 30°20S 146°55E **63** D4
Bogan Gate *Australia* 33°7S 147°49E **63** E4
Bogantungan *Australia* 23°41S 147°17E **62** C4
Bogata *U.S.A.* 33°28N 95°13W **84** E7
Bogda Shan *China* 43°35N 89°40E **32** C6
Boggabilla *Australia* 28°36S 150°24E **63** D5
Boggabri *Australia* 30°45S 150°5E **63** E5
Boggeragh Mts. *Ireland* 52°2N 8°55W **10** D3
Boglan = Solhan *Turkey* 38°57N 41°3E **44** B4
Bognor Regis *U.K.* 50°47N 0°40W **13** G7
Bogo *Phil.* 11°3N 124°0E **37** B6
Bogong, Mt. *Australia* 36°47S 147°17E **63** F4
Bogor *Indonesia* 6°36S 106°48E **37** G12
Bogotá *Colombia* 4°34N 74°0W **92** C4
Bogotol *Russia* 56°15N 89°50E **28** D9
Bogra *Bangla.* 24°51N 89°22E **41** G16
Boguchany *Russia* 58°40N 97°30E **29** D10
Bogué *Mauritania* 16°45N 14°10W **50** E3
Bohemian Forest = Böhmerwald *Germany* 49°8N 13°14E **16** D7
Böhmerwald *Germany* 49°8N 13°14E **16** D7
Bohol □ *Phil.* 9°50N 124°10E **37** C6
Bohol Sea *Phil.* 9°0N 124°0E **37** C6
Bohorok *Indonesia* 3°30N 98°12E **39** L2
Böhöt *Mongolia* 45°13N 108°16E **34** B5
Bohuslän *Sweden* 58°25N 12°0E **9** G15
Boi, Pta. do *Brazil* 23°55S 45°15W **95** A6
Boiaçu *Brazil* 0°27S 61°46W **92** D6
Boigu *Australia* 9°16S 142°13E **62** a
Boileau, C. *Australia* 17°40S 122°7E **60** C3
Boise *U.S.A.* 43°37N 116°13W **76** E5
Boise City *U.S.A.* 36°44N 102°31W **84** C3
Boissevain *Canada* 49°15N 100°5W **71** D8
Bojador, C. *W. Sahara* 26°0N 14°30W **50** C3
Bojana → *Albania* 41°52N 19°22E **23** D8
Bojnūrd *Iran* 37°30N 57°20E **45** B8
Bojonegoro *Indonesia* 7°11S 111°54E **37** G14
Bokaro *India* 23°46N 85°55E **43** H11
Boké *Guinea* 10°56N 14°17W **50** F3
Bokhara → *Australia* 29°55S 146°42E **63** D4
Boknafjorden *Norway* 59°14N 5°40E **9** G11
Bokor △ *Cambodia* 10°50N 104°1E **39** G5
Bokora △ *Uganda* 2°12N 31°32E **54** B3
Bokoro *Chad* 12°25N 17°14E **51** F9
Bokpyin *Burma* 11°18N 98°42E **39** G2
Bokungu *Dem. Rep. of the Congo* 0°35S 22°50E **52** E4
Bolan → *Pakistan* 28°38N 67°42E **42** E2
Bolan Pass *Pakistan* 29°50N 67°20E **40** E5
Bolaños → *Mexico* 21°12N 104°5W **86** C4
Bolbec *France* 49°30N 0°30E **20** B4
Boldājī *Iran* 31°56N 51°3E **45** D6
Bole *China* 44°55N 81°37E **32** C5
Bolekhiv *Ukraine* 49°0N 23°57E **17** D12
Bolesławiec *Poland* 51°17N 15°37E **16** C8
Bolgatanga *Ghana* 10°44N 0°53W **50** F5
Bolgrad = Bolhrad *Ukraine* 45°40N 28°32E **17** F15
Bolhrad *Ukraine* 45°40N 28°32E **17** F15
Bolinao *Phil.* 16°23N 119°54E **37** A5
Bolivar *Mo., U.S.A.* 37°37N 93°25W **80** G7
Bolivar *N.Y., U.S.A.* 42°4N 78°10W **82** D6
Bolivar *Tenn., U.S.A.* 35°12N 89°0W **85** D10
Bolivia ■ *S. Amer.* 17°6S 64°0W **92** G6
Bolivian Plateau = Altiplano *Bolivia* 17°0S 68°0W **92** G5
Bollnäs *Sweden* 61°21N 16°24E **8** F17
Bollon *Australia* 28°2S 147°29E **63** D4
Bolmen *Sweden* 56°55N 13°40E **9** H15
Bolobo *Dem. Rep. of the Congo* 2°6S 16°20E **52** E3
Bologna *Italy* 44°29N 11°20E **22** B4
Bologoye *Russia* 57°55N 34°5E **18** C5
Bolomba *Dem. Rep. of the Congo* 0°35N 19°0E **52** D3
Bolonchén *Mexico* 20°1N 89°45W **87** D7
Boloven, Cao Nguyen *Laos* 15°10N 106°30E **38** E6
Bolpur *India* 23°40N 87°45E **43** H12
Bolsena, L. di *Italy* 42°36N 11°56E **22** C4
Bolshevik, Ostrov *Russia* 78°30N 102°0E **29** B11
Bolshoy Anyuy → *Russia* 68°30N 160°49E **29** C17
Bolshoy Begichev, Ostrov *Russia* 74°20N 112°30E **29** B12
Bolshoy Kamen *Russia* 43°7N 132°19E **30** C6
Bolshoy Kavkas = Caucasus Mountains *Eurasia* 42°50N 44°0E **19** F7
Bolshoy Lyakhovskiy, Ostrov *Russia* 73°35N 142°0E **29** B15
Bolshoy Tyuters, Ostrov *Russia* 59°51N 27°13E **9** G22
Bolsward *Neths.* 53°3N 5°32E **15** A5
Bolt Head *U.K.* 50°12N 3°48W **13** G4
Bolton *Canada* 43°54N 79°45W **82** C5
Bolton *U.K.* 53°35N 2°26W **12** D5
Bolton Landing *U.S.A.* 43°32N 73°35W **83** C11
Bolu *Turkey* 40°45N 31°35E **19** F5
Bolungavík *Iceland* 66°9N 23°15W **8** C2
Bolvadin *Turkey* 38°45N 31°4E **44** B1
Bolzano *Italy* 46°31N 11°22E **22** A4
Bom Jesus da Lapa *Brazil* 13°15S 43°25W **93** F10
Boma *Dem. Rep. of the Congo* 5°50S 13°4E **52** F2
Bombala *Australia* 36°56S 149°15E **63** F4
Bombay = Mumbai *India* 18°56N 72°50E **40** K8
Bombay *U.S.A.* 44°56N 74°34W **83** B10
Bombedor, Pta. *Venezuela* 9°53N 61°37W **93** L15
Bomberai, Semenanjung *Indonesia* 3°0S 133°0E **37** E8
Bomboma *Dem. Rep. of the Congo* 2°25N 18°55E **52** D3
Bombombwa *Dem. Rep. of the Congo* 1°40N 25°40E **54** B2
Bomi *China* 29°50N 95°45E **32** F8
Bomili *Dem. Rep. of the Congo* 1°45N 27°5E **54** B2

Bømlo Norway 59°37N 5°13E 9 G11
Bomokandi → Dem. Rep. of the Congo 3°39N 26°8E 54 B2
Bomu → C.A.R. 4°40N 22°30E 52 D4
Bon, C. = Ra's aṭ Tib Tunisia 37°1N 11°2E 22 F4
Bon Acceuil Mauritius 20°10S 57°39E 53 d
Bon Echo △ Canada 44°55N 77°16W 82 B7
Bon Sar Pa Vietnam 12°24N 107°35E 38 F6
Bonāb Iran 36°35N 48°41E 45 B6
Bonaigarh India 21°50N 84°57E 43 J11
Bonaire W. Indies 12°10N 68°15W 89 D6
Bonampak Mexico 16°44N 91°5W 87 D6
Bonang Australia 37°11S 148°41E 63 F4
Bonanza Nic. 13°54N 84°35W 88 D3
Bonaparte Arch. Australia 14°0S 124°30E 60 B3
Bonar Bridge U.K. 57°54N 4°20W 11 D4
Bonasse Trin. & Tob. 10°5N 61°54W 93 K15
Bonaventure Canada 48°5N 65°32W 73 C6
Bonavista Canada 48°40N 53°5W 73 C9
Bonavista, C. Canada 48°42N 53°5W 73 C9
Bonavista B. Canada 48°45N 53°25W 73 C9
Bondo Dem. Rep. of the Congo 3°55N 23°53E 54 B1
Bondoukou Ivory C. 8°2N 2°47W 50 G5
Bondowoso Indonesia 7°55S 113°49E 37 G15
Bone, Teluk Indonesia 4°10S 120°50E 37 E6
Bonerate Indonesia 7°25S 121°5E 37 F6
Bonerate, Kepulauan Indonesia 6°30S 121°10E 37 F6
Bo'ness U.K. 56°1N 3°37W 11 E5
Bonete, Cerro Argentina 27°55S 68°40W 94 B2
Bong Son = Hoai Nhon Vietnam 14°28N 109°1E 38 E7
Bongaigaon India 26°28N 90°34E 32 F7
Bongandanga Dem. Rep. of the Congo 1°24N 21°3E 52 D4
Bongor Chad 10°35N 15°20E 51 F9
Bongos, Massif des C.A.R. 8°40N 22°25E 52 C4
Bonham U.S.A. 33°35N 96°11W 84 E6
Boni △ Kenya 1°35S 41°18E 54 C5
Bonifacio France 41°24N 9°10E 20 F8
Bonifacio, Bouches de Medit. S. 41°12N 9°15E 22 D3
Bonin Is. = Ogasawara Gunto Pac. Oc. 27°0N 142°0E 27 F16
Bonn Germany 50°46N 7°6E 16 C4
Bonne Terre U.S.A. 37°55N 90°33W 80 G8
Bonners Ferry U.S.A. 48°42N 116°19W 76 B5
Bonney, L. Australia 37°50S 140°20E 63 F3
Bonnie Rock Australia 30°29S 118°22E 61 F2
Bonny, Bight of Africa 3°30N 9°20E 52 D1
Bonnyrigg U.K. 55°53N 3°6W 11 F5
Bonnyville Canada 54°20N 110°45W 71 C6
Bonoi Indonesia 1°45S 137°41E 37 E9
Bonsall U.S.A. 33°16N 117°14W 79 M9
Bontang Indonesia 0°10N 117°30E 36 D5
Bontebok △ S. Africa 34°5S 20°28E 56 E3
Bonthe S. Leone 7°30N 12°33W 50 G3
Bontoc Phil. 17°7N 120°58E 37 A6
Bonython Ra. Australia 23°40S 128°45E 60 D4
Boodjamulla △ Australia 18°15S 138°6E 62 B2
Bookabie Australia 31°50S 132°41E 61 F5
Booker U.S.A. 36°27N 100°32W 84 C4
Booligal Australia 33°58S 144°53E 63 E3
Böön Tsagaan Nuur Mongolia 45°35N 99°9E 32 B8
Boonah Australia 27°58S 152°41E 63 D5
Boone Iowa, U.S.A. 42°4N 93°53W 80 D7
Boone N.C., U.S.A. 36°13N 81°41W 85 C14
Booneville Ark., U.S.A. 35°8N 93°55W 84 D8
Booneville Miss., U.S.A. 34°39N 88°34W 85 D10
Boonville Calif., U.S.A. 39°1N 123°22W 78 F3
Boonville Ind., U.S.A. 38°3N 87°16W 80 F10
Boonville Mo., U.S.A. 38°58N 92°44W 80 F7
Boonville N.Y., U.S.A. 43°29N 75°20W 83 C9
Boorabbin △ Australia 31°30S 120°10E 61 F3
Boorindal Australia 30°22S 146°11E 63 E4
Boorowa Australia 34°28S 148°44E 63 E4
Boosaaso Somali Rep. 11°12N 49°18E 47 E4
Boothia, Gulf of Canada 71°0N 90°0W 68 C14
Boothia Pen. Canada 71°0N 94°0W 68 C13
Bootle U.K. 53°28N 3°1W 12 D4
Booué Gabon 0°5S 11°55E 52 E2
Boquilla, Presa de la Mexico 27°31N 105°30W 86 B3
Boquillas del Carmen Mexico 29°11N 102°58W 86 B4
Bor Serbia 44°5N 22°7E 23 C10
Bôr Sudan 6°10N 31°40E 51 G12
Bor Mashash Israel 31°7N 34°50E 46 D3
Bora Bora French Polynesia 16°30S 151°45W 65 J12
Borah Peak U.S.A. 44°8N 113°47W 76 D7
Borås Sweden 57°43N 12°56E 9 H15
Borāzjān Iran 29°22N 51°10E 45 D6
Borba Brazil 4°12S 59°34W 92 D7
Borborema, Planalto da Brazil 7°0S 37°0W 90 D7
Bord Khūn-e Now Iran 28°3N 51°28E 45 D6
Borda, C. Australia 35°45S 136°34E 63 F2
Bordeaux France 44°50N 0°36W 20 D3
Borden Australia 34°3S 118°12E 61 F2
Borden-Carleton Canada 46°18N 63°47W 73 C7
Borden I. Canada 78°30N 111°30W 69 B9
Borden Pen. Canada 73°0N 83°0W 69 C15
Border Ranges △ Australia 28°24S 152°56E 63 D5
Borders = Scottish Borders □ U.K. 55°35N 2°50W 11 F6
Bordertown Australia 36°19S 140°45E 63 F3
Borðeyri Iceland 65°12N 21°6W 8 D3
Bordj Fly Ste. Marie Algeria 27°19N 2°32W 50 C5
Bordj-in-Eker Algeria 24°9N 5°3E 50 D7
Bordj Mokhtar Algeria 21°20N 0°56E 50 D6
Bordj Omar Driss Algeria 28°10N 6°40E 50 C7
Borehamwood U.K. 51°40N 0°15W 13 F7
Borgarnes Iceland 64°32N 21°55W 8 D3
Børgefjellet Norway 65°20N 13°45E 8 D15
Borger Neths. 52°54N 6°44E 15 B6
Borger U.S.A. 35°39N 101°24W 84 D4
Borgholm Sweden 56°52N 16°39E 9 H17
Borhoyn Tal Mongolia 43°50N 111°58E 34 C6
Borikhane Laos 18°33N 103°43E 38 C4
Borisoglebsk Russia 51°27N 42°5E 19 D7
Borisov = Barysaw Belarus 54°17N 28°28E 17 A15
Borja Peru 4°20S 77°40W 92 D3
Borkou Chad 18°15N 18°50E 51 E9
Borkum Germany 53°34N 6°40E 16 B4
Borlänge Sweden 60°29N 15°26E 9 F16
Borley, C. Antarctica 66°15S 52°30E 5 C5
Borneo E. Indies 1°0N 115°0E 36 D5
Bornholm Denmark 55°10N 15°0E 9 J16
Borobudur △ Indonesia 7°36S 110°12E 37 G14
Borogontsy Russia 62°42N 131°8E 29 C14
Borohoro Shan China 44°6N 83°10E 32 C5
Boron U.S.A. 35°0N 117°39W 79 L9
Borongan Phil. 11°37N 125°26E 37 B7
Borovichi Russia 58°25N 33°55E 18 C5
Borrego Springs U.S.A. 33°15N 116°23W 79 M10
Borrisokane Ireland 53°0N 8°7W 10 D3
Borroloola Australia 16°4S 136°17E 62 B2
Borşa Romania 47°41N 24°50E 17 E13
Borsad India 22°25N 72°54E 42 H5
Borth U.K. 52°29N 4°2W 13 E3
Borūjerd Iran 33°55N 48°50E 45 C6
Boryeong S. Korea 36°21N 126°36E 35 F14
Boryslav Ukraine 49°18N 23°28E 17 D12
Borzya Russia 50°24N 116°31E 33 A12
Bosa Italy 40°18N 8°30E 22 D3
Bosanska Gradiška Bos.-H. 45°10N 17°15E 22 B7
Boscastle U.K. 50°41N 4°42W 13 G3
Boscobelle Barbados 13°17N 59°35W 89 g
Bose China 23°53N 106°35E 32 G10
Boseong S. Korea 34°46N 127°5E 35 G14
Boshan China 36°28N 117°49E 35 F9
Boshof S. Africa 28°31S 25°13E 56 D4
Boshrūyeh Iran 33°50N 57°30E 45 C8
Bosna → Bos.-H. 45°4N 18°29E 23 B8
Bosna i Hercegovina = Bosnia-Herzegovina ■ Europe 44°0N 18°0E 22 B7
Bosnia-Herzegovina ■ Europe 44°0N 18°0E 22 B7
Bosnik Indonesia 1°5S 136°10E 37 E9
Bosobolo Dem. Rep. of the Congo 4°15N 19°50E 52 D3
Bosporus = İstanbul Boğazı Turkey 41°5N 29°3E 23 D13
Bosque Farms U.S.A. 35°51N 106°42W 77 J10
Bossangoa C.A.R. 6°35N 17°30E 52 C3
Bossier City U.S.A. 32°31N 93°44W 84 E8
Bosso Niger 13°43N 13°19E 51 F8
Bostan Pakistan 30°26N 67°2E 42 D2
Bostānābād Iran 37°50N 46°50E 44 B5
Bosten Hu China 41°55N 87°40E 32 C6
Boston U.K. 52°59N 0°2W 12 E7
Boston U.S.A. 42°22N 71°3W 83 D13
Boston Bar Canada 49°52N 121°30W 70 D4
Boston Mts. U.S.A. 35°42N 93°15W 84 D8
Boswell Canada 49°28N 116°45W 70 D5
Boswell U.S.A. 40°10N 79°2W 82 F5
Botad India 22°15N 71°40E 42 H4
Botany B. Australia 33°58S 151°11E 58 E8
Botene Laos 17°35N 101°12E 38 D3
Bothaville S. Africa 27°23S 26°34E 56 D4
Bothnia, G. of Europe 62°0N 20°0E 8 F19
Bothwell Australia 42°20S 147°1E 63 G4
Bothwell Canada 42°38N 81°52W 82 D3
Botletle → Botswana 20°10S 23°15E 56 C3
Botoşani Romania 47°42N 26°41E 17 E14
Botou Burkina Faso 12°42N 1°59E 50 F6
Botou China 38°4N 116°34E 34 E9
Botshabelo S. Africa 29°14S 26°44E 56 D4
Botswana ■ Africa 22°0S 24°0E 56 C3
Bottineau U.S.A. 48°50N 100°27W 80 A3
Bottrop Germany 51°31N 6°58E 15 C6
Botucatu Brazil 22°55S 48°30W 95 A6
Botum Sakor △ Cambodia 11°5N 103°15E 39 G4
Botwood Canada 49°6N 55°23W 73 C8
Bou Saâda Algeria 35°11N 4°9E 50 A6
Bouaflé Ivory C. 7°1N 5°47W 50 G4
Bouaké Ivory C. 7°40N 5°2W 50 G4
Bouar C.A.R. 6°0N 15°40E 52 C3
Bouârfa Morocco 32°32N 1°58W 50 B5
Boucaut B. Australia 12°0S 134°25E 62 A1
Bouctouche Canada 46°30N 64°45W 73 C7
Bougainville, C. Australia 13°57S 126°4E 60 B4
Bougainville I. Papua N. G. 6°0S 155°0E 58 B8
Bougainville Reef Australia 15°30S 147°5E 62 B4
Bougie = Bejaïa Algeria 36°42N 5°2E 50 A7
Bougouni Mali 11°30N 7°20W 50 F4
Bouillon Belgium 49°44N 5°3E 15 E5
Boulder Colo., U.S.A. 40°1N 105°17W 76 F11
Boulder Mont., U.S.A. 46°14N 112°7W 76 C7
Boulder City U.S.A. 35°58N 114°49W 79 K12
Boulder Creek U.S.A. 37°7N 122°7W 78 H4
Boulder Dam = Hoover Dam U.S.A. 36°1N 114°44W 79 K12
Boulia Australia 22°52S 139°51E 62 C2
Boulogne-sur-Mer France 50°42N 1°36E 20 A4
Boulsa Burkina Faso 12°39N 0°34W 50 F5
Boultoum Niger 14°45N 10°25E 51 F8
Bouma △ Fiji 16°50S 179°52E 59 a
Boun Neua Laos 21°38N 101°54E 38 B3
Boun Tai Laos 21°23N 101°58E 38 B3
Bouna Ivory C. 9°10N 3°0W 50 G5
Boundary Peak U.S.A. 37°51N 118°21W 78 H8
Boundiali Ivory C. 9°30N 6°20W 50 G4
Bountiful U.S.A. 40°53N 111°52W 76 F8
Bounty Is. Pac. Oc. 48°0S 178°30E 64 M9
Bounty Trough Pac. Oc. 46°0S 178°0E 64 M9
Bourbonnais France 46°28N 3°0E 20 C5
Bourdel L. Canada 56°43N 74°10W 72 A5
Bourem Mali 17°0N 0°24W 50 E5
Bourg-en-Bresse France 46°13N 5°12E 20 C6
Bourg-St-Maurice France 45°35N 6°46E 20 D7
Bourgas = Burgas Bulgaria 42°33N 27°29E 23 C12
Bourges France 47°9N 2°25E 20 C5
Bourget Canada 45°26N 75°9W 83 A9
Bourgogne □ France 47°0N 4°50E 20 C6
Bourke Australia 30°8S 145°55E 63 E4
Bourne U.K. 52°47N 0°22W 12 E7
Bournemouth U.K. 50°43N 1°52W 13 G6
Bournemouth □ U.K. 50°43N 1°52W 13 G6
Bouse U.S.A. 33°56N 114°0W 79 M13
Bousso Chad 10°34N 16°52E 51 F9
Bouvet I. = Bouvetøya Antarctica 54°26S 3°24E 2 G10
Bouvetøya Antarctica 54°26S 3°24E 2 G10
Bovill U.S.A. 46°51N 116°24W 76 C5
Bovril Argentina 31°21S 59°26W 94 C4
Bow → Canada 49°57N 111°41W 70 C6
Bow Island Canada 49°50N 111°23W 76 B8
Bowbells U.S.A. 48°48N 102°15W 80 A2
Bowdle U.S.A. 45°27N 99°39W 80 C4
Bowelling Australia 33°25S 116°30E 61 F2
Bowen Argentina 35°0S 67°31W 94 D2
Bowen Australia 20°0S 148°16E 62 J6
Bowen Mts. Australia 37°0S 147°50E 63 F4
Bowers Basin Pac. Oc. 53°45N 176°0E 4 D16
Bowers Ridge Pac. Oc. 54°0N 180°0E 4 D17
Bowie Ariz., U.S.A. 32°19N 109°29W 77 K9
Bowie Tex., U.S.A. 33°34N 97°51W 84 E6
Bowkān Iran 36°31N 46°12E 44 B5
Bowland, Forest of U.K. 54°0N 2°30W 12 D5
Bowling Green Ky., U.S.A. 36°59N 86°27W 80 G10
Bowling Green Ohio, U.S.A. 41°23N 83°39W 81 E12
Bowling Green, C. Australia 19°19S 147°25E 62 B4
Bowling Green Bay △ Australia 19°26S 146°57E 62 B4
Bowman U.S.A. 46°11N 103°24W 80 B2
Bowman I. Antarctica 65°0S 104°0E 5 C8
Bowmanville = Clarington Canada 43°55N 78°41W 82 C6
Bowmore U.K. 55°45N 6°17W 11 F2
Bowral Australia 34°26S 150°27E 63 E5
Bowraville Australia 30°37S 152°52E 63 E5
Bowron → Canada 54°3N 121°50W 70 C4
Bowron Lake △ Canada 53°10N 121°5W 70 C4
Bowser L. Canada 56°30N 129°30W 70 B3
Bowsman Canada 52°14N 101°12W 71 C8
Bowwood Zambia 17°5S 26°20E 55 F2
Box Cr. → Australia 34°10S 143°50E 63 E3
Boxmeer Neths. 51°38N 5°56E 15 C5
Boxtel Neths. 51°36N 5°20E 15 C5
Boyce U.S.A. 31°23N 92°40W 84 F8
Boyd L. Canada 52°46N 76°42W 72 B4
Boyle Canada 54°35N 112°49W 70 C6
Boyle Ireland 53°59N 8°18W 10 C3
Boyne → Ireland 53°43N 6°15W 10 C5
Boyne City U.S.A. 45°13N 85°1W 81 C11
Boynton Beach U.S.A. 26°32N 80°4W 85 H14
Boyoma, Chutes Dem. Rep. of the Congo 0°35N 25°23E 54 B2
Boysen Res. U.S.A. 43°25N 108°11W 76 E9
Boyuibe Bolivia 20°25S 63°17W 92 G6
Boyup Brook Australia 33°50S 116°23E 61 F2
Boz Dağları Turkey 38°20N 28°0E 23 E13
Bozburun Turkey 36°43N 28°4E 23 F13
Bozcaada Turkey 39°49N 26°3E 23 E12
Bozdoğan Turkey 37°40N 28°17E 23 F13
Bozeman U.S.A. 45°41N 111°2W 76 D8
Bozen = Bolzano Italy 46°31N 11°22E 22 A4
Bozhou China 33°55N 115°41E 34 H8
Bozoum C.A.R. 6°25N 16°35E 52 C3
Bozyazı Turkey 36°6N 33°0E 44 B2
Bra Italy 44°42N 7°51E 20 D7
Brabant □ Belgium 50°46N 4°30E 15 D4
Brabant L. Canada 55°58N 103°43W 71 B8
Brač Croatia 43°20N 16°40E 22 C7
Bracadale, L. U.K. 57°20N 6°30W 11 D2
Bracciano, L. di Italy 42°7N 12°14E 22 C5
Bracebridge Canada 45°2N 79°19W 82 A5
Bräcke Sweden 62°45N 15°26E 8 E16
Brackettville U.S.A. 29°19N 100°25W 84 G4
Bracknell U.K. 51°25N 0°43W 13 F7
Bracknell Forest □ U.K. 51°25N 0°44W 13 F7
Brad Romania 46°10N 22°50E 17 E12
Bradenton U.S.A. 27°30N 82°34W 85 H13
Bradford Canada 44°7N 79°34W 82 B5
Bradford U.K. 53°47N 1°45W 12 D6
Bradford Pa., U.S.A. 41°58N 78°38W 82 E6
Bradford Vt., U.S.A. 43°59N 72°9W 83 C12
Bradley Ark., U.S.A. 33°6N 93°39W 84 E8
Bradley Calif., U.S.A. 35°52N 120°48W 78 K6
Bradley Institute Zimbabwe 17°7S 31°25E 55 F3
Brady U.S.A. 31°9N 99°20W 84 F5
Braeside Canada 45°28N 76°24W 83 A8
Braga Portugal 41°35N 8°25W 21 B1
Bragado Argentina 35°2S 60°27W 94 D3
Bragança Brazil 1°0S 47°2W 93 D9
Bragança Portugal 41°48N 6°50W 21 B2
Bragança Paulista Brazil 22°55S 46°32W 95 A6
Brahestad = Raahe Finland 64°40N 24°28E 8 D21
Brahmanbaria Bangla. 23°58N 91°15E 41 H17
Brahmani → India 20°39N 86°46E 41 J15
Brahmapur India 19°15N 84°54E 41 K14
Brahmaputra → Asia 23°40N 90°35E 43 H13
Braich-y-pwll U.K. 52°47N 4°46W 12 E3
Braidwood Australia 35°27S 149°49E 63 F4
Brăila Romania 45°19N 27°59E 17 F14
Brainerd U.S.A. 46°22N 94°12W 80 B6
Braintree U.K. 51°53N 0°34E 13 F8
Braintree U.S.A. 42°13N 71°0W 83 D14
Brak → S. Africa 29°35S 22°55E 56 D3
Brakwater Namibia 22°28S 17°3E 56 C2
Brampton Canada 43°45N 79°45W 82 C5
Brampton U.K. 54°57N 2°44W 12 C5
Brampton I. Australia 20°49S 149°16E 62 b
Branco → Brazil 1°20S 61°50W 92 D6
Branco, C. Brazil 7°9S 34°47W 90 D7
Brandberg Namibia 21°10S 14°33E 56 C1
Brandberg △ Namibia 21°10S 14°30E 56 C1
Brandenburg = Neubrandenburg Germany 53°33N 13°15E 16 B7
Brandenburg Germany 52°25N 12°33E 16 B7
Brandenburg □ Germany 52°50N 13°0E 16 B6
Brandfort S. Africa 28°40S 26°30E 56 D4
Brandon Canada 49°50N 99°57W 71 D9
Brandon U.S.A. 43°48N 73°6W 83 C11
Brandon B. Ireland 52°17N 10°8W 10 D1
Brandon Mt. Ireland 52°15N 10°15W 10 D1
Brandsen Argentina 35°10S 58°15W 94 D4
Brandvlei S. Africa 30°25S 20°30E 56 E3
Branford U.S.A. 41°17N 72°49W 83 E12
Braniewo Poland 54°25N 19°50E 17 A10
Bransfield Str. Antarctica 63°0S 59°0W 5 C18
Branson U.S.A. 36°39N 93°13W 80 G7
Brantford Canada 43°10N 80°15W 82 C4
Bras d'Or L. Canada 45°50N 60°50W 73 C7
Brasher Falls U.S.A. 44°49N 74°47W 83 B10
Brasil = Brazil ■ S. Amer. 12°0S 50°0W 93 F9
Brasil, Planalto Brazil 18°0S 46°30W 90 E6
Brasiléia Brazil 11°0S 68°45W 92 F5
Brasília Brazil 15°47S 47°55W 93 G9
Brasília Legal Brazil 3°49S 55°36W 93 D7
Braslaw Belarus 55°38N 27°0E 9 J22
Braşov Romania 45°38N 25°35E 17 F13
Brasschaat Belgium 51°19N 4°27E 15 C4
Brassey, Banjaran Malaysia 5°0N 117°15E 36 D5
Brassey Ra. Australia 25°8S 122°15E 61 E3
Brasstown Bald U.S.A. 34°53N 83°49W 85 D13
Brastad Sweden 58°23N 11°30E 9 G14
Bratislava Slovak Rep. 48°10N 17°7E 17 D9
Bratsk Russia 56°10N 101°30E 29 D11
Brattleboro U.S.A. 42°51N 72°34W 83 D12
Braunau Austria 48°15N 13°3E 16 D7
Braunschweig Germany 52°15N 10°31E 16 B6
Braunton U.K. 51°7N 4°10W 13 F3
Brava C. Verde Is. 15°0N 24°40W 50 b
Bravo del Norte, Rio = Grande, Rio → N. Amer. 25°58N 97°9W 84 J6
Brawley U.S.A. 32°59N 115°31W 79 N11
Bray Ireland 53°13N 6°7W 10 C5
Bray, Mt. Australia 14°0S 134°30E 62 A1
Bray, Pays de France 49°46N 1°26E 20 B4
Brazeau → Canada 52°55N 115°14W 70 C5
Brazil U.S.A. 39°32N 87°8W 80 F10
Brazil ■ S. Amer. 12°0S 50°0W 93 F9
Brazilian Highlands = Brasil, Planalto Brazil 18°0S 46°30W 90 E6
Brazo Sur → S. Amer. 25°21S 57°42W 94 B4
Brazos → U.S.A. 28°53N 95°23W 84 G7
Brazzaville Congo 4°9S 15°12E 52 E3
Brčko Bos.-H. 44°54N 18°46E 23 B8
Bré = Bray Ireland 53°13N 6°7W 10 C5
Breaden, L. Australia 25°51S 125°28E 61 E4
Breaksea Sd. N.Z. 45°35S 166°35E 59 F1
Bream B. N.Z. 35°56S 174°28E 59 A5
Bream Hd. N.Z. 35°51S 174°36E 59 A5
Breas Chile 25°29S 70°24W 94 B1
Brebes Indonesia 6°52S 109°3E 37 G13
Brechin Canada 44°32N 79°10W 82 B5
Brechin U.K. 56°44N 2°39W 11 E6
Brecht Belgium 51°21N 4°38E 15 C4
Breckenridge Colo., U.S.A. 39°29N 106°3W 76 G10
Breckenridge Minn., U.S.A. 46°16N 96°35W 80 B5
Breckenridge Tex., U.S.A. 32°45N 98°54W 84 E5
Breckland U.K. 52°30N 0°40E 13 E8
Brecon U.K. 51°57N 3°23W 13 F4
Brecon Beacons U.K. 51°53N 3°26W 13 F4
Brecon Beacons △ U.K. 51°50N 3°30W 13 F4
Breda Neths. 51°35N 4°45E 15 C4
Bredasdorp S. Africa 34°33S 20°2E 56 E3
Bree Belgium 51°8N 5°35E 15 C5
Bregenz Austria 47°30N 9°45E 16 E5
Breiðafjörður Iceland 65°15N 23°15W 8 D2
Brejo Brazil 3°41S 42°47W 93 D10
Bremen Germany 53°4N 8°47E 16 B5
Bremer Bay Australia 34°21S 119°20E 61 F2
Bremer I. Australia 12°5S 136°45E 62 A2
Bremerhaven Germany 53°33N 8°36E 16 B5
Bremerton U.S.A. 47°34N 122°37W 78 C4
Brenham U.S.A. 30°10N 96°24W 84 F6
Brennerpass Austria 47°2N 11°30E 16 E6
Brent U.S.A. 32°56N 87°10W 85 E11
Brentwood U.K. 51°37N 0°19E 13 F8
Brentwood Calif., U.S.A. 37°56N 121°42W 78 H5
Brentwood N.Y., U.S.A. 40°47N 73°15W 83 F11
Bréscia Italy 45°33N 10°15E 20 D9
Breskens Neths. 51°23N 3°33E 15 C3
Breslau = Wrocław Poland 51°5N 17°5E 17 C9
Bressanone Italy 46°43N 11°39E 22 A4
Bressay U.K. 60°9N 1°6W 11 A7
Brest Belarus 52°10N 23°40E 17 B12
Brest France 48°24N 4°31W 20 B1
Brest □ Belarus 52°30N 26°10E 17 B13
Brest-Litovsk = Brest Belarus 52°10N 23°40E 17 B12
Bretagne □ France 48°10N 3°0W 20 B2
Breton Canada 53°7N 114°28W 70 C6
Breton Sd. U.S.A. 29°35N 89°15W 85 G10
Brett, C. N.Z. 35°10S 174°20E 59 A5
Brevard U.S.A. 35°14N 82°44W 85 D13
Breves Brazil 1°40S 50°29W 93 D8
Brewarrina Australia 30°0S 146°51E 63 E4
Brewer U.S.A. 44°48N 68°46W 81 C19
Brewer, Mt. U.S.A. 36°44N 118°28W 78 J8
Brewster N.Y., U.S.A. 41°24N 73°36W 83 E11
Brewster Ohio, U.S.A. 40°43N 81°36W 82 F3
Brewster Wash., U.S.A. 48°6N 119°47W 76 B4
Brewster, Kap = Kangikajik Greenland 70°7N 22°0W 4 B6
Brewton U.S.A. 31°7N 87°4W 85 F11
Breyten S. Africa 26°16S 30°0E 57 D5
Bria C.A.R. 6°30N 21°58E 52 C4
Briançon France 44°54N 6°39E 20 D7
Bribie I. Australia 27°0S 153°10E 63 D5
Bribri Costa Rica 9°38N 82°50W 88 E3
Bridgefield Barbados 13°9N 59°36W 89 g
Bridgehampton U.S.A. 40°56N 72°19W 83 F12
Bridgend U.K. 51°30N 3°34W 13 F4
Bridgend □ U.K. 51°36N 3°36W 13 F4
Bridgenorth Canada 44°23N 78°23W 82 B6
Bridgeport Calif., U.S.A. 38°15N 119°14W 78 G7
Bridgeport Conn., U.S.A. 41°11N 73°12W 83 E11
Bridgeport N.Y., U.S.A. 43°9N 75°58W 83 C9
Bridgeport Nebr., U.S.A. 41°40N 103°6W 80 E2
Bridgeport Tex., U.S.A. 33°13N 97°45W 84 E6
Bridger U.S.A. 45°18N 108°55W 76 D9
Bridgeton U.S.A. 39°26N 75°14W 81 F16
Bridgetown Australia 33°58S 116°7E 61 F2
Bridgetown Barbados 13°6N 59°37W 89 g
Bridgetown Canada 44°55N 65°18W 73 D6
Bridgewater Australia 42°44S 147°14E 63 G4
Bridgewater Canada 44°25N 64°31W 73 D7
Bridgewater Mass., U.S.A. 41°59N 70°58W 83 E14
Bridgewater N.Y., U.S.A. 42°53N 75°15W 83 D9
Bridgewater, C. Australia 38°23S 141°23E 63 F3
Bridgnorth U.K. 52°32N 2°25W 13 E5
Bridgton U.S.A. 44°3N 70°42W 83 B14
Bridgwater U.K. 51°8N 2°59W 13 F5
Bridgwater B. U.K. 51°15N 3°15W 13 F4
Bridlington U.K. 54°5N 0°12W 12 C7
Bridlington B. U.K. 54°4N 0°10W 12 C7
Bridport Australia 40°59S 147°23E 63 G4
Bridport U.K. 50°44N 2°45W 13 G5
Brig Switz. 46°18N 7°59E 20 C7
Brigg U.K. 53°34N 0°28W 12 D7
Brigham City U.S.A. 41°31N 112°1W 76 F7
Bright Australia 36°42S 146°56E 63 F4
Brighton Australia 35°5S 138°30E 63 F2
Brighton Canada 44°2N 77°44W 82 B7
Brighton Trin. & Tob. 10°13N 61°39W 93 K15
Brighton U.K. 50°49N 0°7W 13 G7
Brighton U.S.A. 43°8N 77°34W 82 C7
Brightside Canada 45°7N 76°29W 83 A8
Brilliant U.S.A. 40°15N 80°39W 82 F4
Brindisi Italy 40°39N 17°55E 23 D7
Brinkley U.S.A. 34°53N 91°12W 84 D9
Brinnon U.S.A. 47°41N 122°54W 78 C4
Brion, Î. Canada 47°46N 61°26W 73 C7
Brisay Canada 54°26N 70°31W 73 B5
Brisbane Australia 27°25S 153°2E 63 D5
Brisbane → Australia 27°24S 153°9E 63 D5
Bristol U.K. 51°26N 2°35W 13 F5
Bristol Conn., U.S.A. 41°40N 72°57W 83 E12
Bristol Pa., U.S.A. 40°6N 74°51W 83 F10
Bristol R.I., U.S.A. 41°40N 71°16W 83 E13
Bristol Tenn., U.S.A. 36°36N 82°11W 85 C13
Bristol Vt., U.S.A. 44°8N 73°4W 83 B11
Bristol, City of □ U.K. 51°27N 2°36W 13 F5
Bristol B. U.S.A. 58°0N 160°0W 74 D8
Bristol Channel U.K. 51°18N 4°30W 13 F3
Bristol I. Antarctica 58°45S 28°0W 5 B1
Bristol L. U.S.A. 34°28N 115°41W 77 J6
Bristow U.S.A. 35°50N 96°23W 84 D6
Britain = Great Britain Europe 54°0N 2°15W 6 E5
British Columbia □ Canada 55°0N 125°15W 70 C3
British Indian Ocean Terr. = Chagos Arch. ☑ Ind. Oc. 6°0S 72°0E 27 J9
British Isles Europe 54°0N 4°0W 14 D5
British Mts. N. Amer. 68°50N 140°0W 74 B12
British Virgin Is. ☑ W. Indies 18°30N 64°30W 89 e
Brits S. Africa 25°37S 27°48E 57 D4
Britstown S. Africa 30°37S 23°30E 56 E3
Britt Canada 45°46N 80°34W 72 C3
Brittany = Bretagne □ France 48°10N 3°0W 20 B2
Britton U.S.A. 45°48N 97°45W 80 C5
Brive-la-Gaillarde France 45°10N 1°32E 20 D4
Brixen = Bressanone Italy 46°43N 11°39E 22 A4
Brixham U.K. 50°23N 3°31W 13 G4
Brno Czech Rep. 49°10N 16°35E 17 D9
Broach = Bharuch India 21°47N 73°0E 40 J8
Broad → U.S.A. 34°1N 81°4W 85 D14
Broad Arrow Australia 30°23S 121°15E 61 F3
Broad B. U.K. 58°14N 6°18W 11 C2
Broad Haven Ireland 54°20N 9°55W 10 B2
Broad Law U.K. 55°30N 3°21W 11 F5
Broad Pk. = Faichan Kangri India 35°48N 76°34E 43 B7
Broad Sd. Australia 22°0S 149°45E 62 C4
Broadalbin U.S.A. 43°4N 74°12W 83 C10
Broadback → Canada 51°21N 78°52W 72 B4
Broadhurst Ra. Australia 22°30S 122°30E 60 D3
Broads, The U.K. 52°45N 1°30E 12 E9
Broadus U.S.A. 45°27N 105°25W 76 D11
Brochet Canada 57°53N 101°40W 71 B8
Brochet, L. Canada 58°36N 101°35W 71 B8
Brock I. Canada 77°52N 114°19W 69 B9
Brocken Germany 51°47N 10°37E 16 C6
Brockport U.S.A. 43°13N 77°56W 82 C7
Brockton U.S.A. 42°5N 71°1W 83 D13
Brockville Canada 44°35N 75°41W 83 B9
Brockway Mont., U.S.A. 47°18N 105°45W 76 C11
Brockway Pa., U.S.A. 41°15N 78°47W 82 E6
Brocton U.S.A. 42°23N 79°26W 82 D5
Brodeur Pen. Canada 72°30N 88°10W 69 C14
Brodick U.K. 55°35N 5°9W 11 F3
Brodnica Poland 53°15N 19°25E 17 B10

Brody *Ukraine* 50°5N 25°10E 17 C13
Brogan *U.S.A.* 44°15N 117°31W 76 D5
Broken Arrow *U.S.A.* 36°3N 95°48W 84 C7
Broken Bow *Nebr., U.S.A.* 41°24N 99°38W 80 E4
Broken Bow *Okla., U.S.A.* 34°2N 94°44W 84 D7
Broken Bow Lake *U.S.A.* 34°9N 94°40W 84 D7
Broken Hill *Australia* 31°58S 141°29E 63 E3
Broken Ridge *Ind. Oc.* 30°0S 94°0E 64 L1
Broken River Ra. *Australia* 21°0S 148°22E 62 b
Bromley □ *U.K.* 51°24N 0°2E 13 F8
Bromo Tengger Semeru △ *Indonesia* 7°56S 112°57E 37 H15
Bromsgrove *U.K.* 52°21N 2°2W 13 E5
Brønderslev *Denmark* 57°16N 9°57E 9 H13
Bronkhorstspruit *S. Africa* 25°46S 28°45E 57 D4
Brønnøysund *Norway* 65°28N 12°14E 8 D15
Brook Park *U.S.A.* 41°23N 81°48W 82 E4
Brookhaven *U.S.A.* 31°35N 90°26W 85 F9
Brookings *Oreg., U.S.A.* 42°3N 124°17W 76 E1
Brookings *S. Dak., U.S.A.* 44°19N 96°48W 80 C5
Brooklin *Canada* 43°55N 78°55W 82 C6
Brooklyn Park *U.S.A.* 45°6N 93°23W 80 C7
Brooks *Canada* 50°35N 111°55W 70 C6
Brooks Range *U.S.A.* 68°0N 152°0W 74 B9
Brooksville *U.S.A.* 28°33N 82°23W 85 G13
Brookton *Australia* 32°22S 117°0E 61 F2
Brookville *U.S.A.* 41°10N 79°5W 82 E5
Broom, L. *U.K.* 57°55N 5°15W 11 D3
Broome *Australia* 18°0S 122°15E 60 C3
Brora *U.K.* 58°0N 3°52W 11 C5
Brora → *U.K.* 58°0N 3°51W 11 C5
Brosna → *Ireland* 53°14N 7°58W 10 C4
Brothers *U.S.A.* 43°49N 120°36W 76 E3
Brough *U.K.* 54°32N 2°18W 12 C5
Brough Hd. *U.K.* 59°8N 3°20W 11 B5
Broughton Island = Qikiqtarjuaq *Canada* 67°33N 63°0W 69 D19
Brown, L. *Australia* 31°5S 118°15E 61 F2
Brown, Pt. *Australia* 32°32S 133°50E 63 E1
Brown City *U.S.A.* 43°13N 82°59W 82 C2
Brown Willy *U.K.* 50°35N 4°37W 13 G3
Brownfield *U.S.A.* 33°11N 102°17W 84 E3
Browning *U.S.A.* 48°34N 113°1W 76 B7
Brownsville *Oreg., U.S.A.* 44°24N 122°59W 76 D2
Brownsville *Pa., U.S.A.* 40°1N 79°53W 82 F5
Brownsville *Tenn., U.S.A.* 35°36N 89°16W 85 D10
Brownsville *Tex., U.S.A.* 25°54N 97°30W 84 J6
Brownville *U.S.A.* 44°0N 75°59W 83 C9
Brownwood *U.S.A.* 31°43N 98°59W 84 F5
Browse I. *Australia* 14°7S 123°33E 60 B3
Bruas *Malaysia* 4°30N 100°47E 39 K3
Bruay-la-Buissière *France* 50°29N 2°33E 20 A5
Bruce, Mt. *Australia* 22°37S 118°8E 60 D2
Bruce Pen. *Canada* 45°0N 81°30W 82 B3
Bruce Peninsula △ *Canada* 45°14N 81°36W 82 A3
Bruce Rock *Australia* 31°52S 118°8E 61 F2
Bruck an der Leitha *Austria* 48°1N 16°47E 17 D9
Bruck an der Mur *Austria* 47°24N 15°16E 16 E8
Brue → *U.K.* 51°13N 2°59W 13 F5
Bruges = Brugge *Belgium* 51°13N 3°13E 15 C3
Brugge *Belgium* 51°13N 3°13E 15 C3
Bruin *U.S.A.* 41°3N 79°43W 82 E5
Brûk, W. el → *Egypt* 30°15N 33°50E 46 E2
Brûlé *Canada* 53°15N 117°58W 70 C5
Brûlé, L. *Canada* 53°35N 64°4W 73 B7
Brumado *Brazil* 14°14S 41°40W 93 F10
Brumunddal *Norway* 60°53N 10°56E 8 F14
Bruneau *U.S.A.* 42°53N 115°48W 76 E6
Bruneau → *U.S.A.* 42°56N 115°57W 76 E6
Brunei = Bandar Seri Begawan *Brunei* 4°52N 115°0E 36 D5
Brunei ■ *Asia* 4°50N 115°0E 36 D5
Brunner, L. *N.Z.* 42°37S 171°27E 59 E3
Brunssum *Neths.* 50°57N 5°59E 15 D5
Brunswick = Braunschweig *Germany* 52°15N 10°31E 16 B6
Brunswick *Ga., U.S.A.* 31°10N 81°30W 85 F14
Brunswick *Maine, U.S.A.* 43°55N 69°58W 81 D19
Brunswick *Md., U.S.A.* 39°19N 77°38W 81 F15
Brunswick *Mo., U.S.A.* 39°26N 93°8W 80 F7
Brunswick *Ohio, U.S.A.* 41°14N 81°51W 82 E3
Brunswick, Pen. de *Chile* 53°30S 71°30W 96 G2
Brunswick B. *Australia* 15°15S 124°50E 60 C3
Brunswick Junction *Australia* 33°15S 115°50E 61 F2
Brunt Ice Shelf *Antarctica* 75°30S 25°0W 5 D2
Brus Laguna *Honduras* 15°47N 84°35W 88 C3
Brush *U.S.A.* 40°15N 103°37W 76 F12
Brushton *U.S.A.* 44°50N 74°31W 83 B10
Brusque *Brazil* 27°5S 49°0W 95 B6
Brussel *Belgium* 50°51N 4°21E 15 D4
Brussel ✕ (BRU) *Belgium* 50°54N 4°29E 15 D5
Brussels = Brussel *Belgium* 50°51N 4°21E 15 D4
Brussels *Canada* 43°44N 81°15W 82 C3
Bruthen *Australia* 37°42S 147°50E 63 F4
Bruxelles = Brussel *Belgium* 50°51N 4°21E 15 D4
Bryan *Ohio, U.S.A.* 41°28N 84°33W 81 E11
Bryan *Tex., U.S.A.* 30°40N 96°22W 84 F6
Bryan, Mt. *Australia* 33°30S 139°5E 63 E2
Bryansk *Russia* 53°13N 34°25E 18 D4
Bryce Canyon △ *U.S.A.* 37°30N 112°10W 77 H7
Bryne *Norway* 58°44N 5°38E 9 G11
Bryson City *U.S.A.* 35°26N 83°27W 85 D13
Bsharri *Lebanon* 34°15N 36°0E 46 A5
Bū Baqarah *U.A.E.* 25°35N 56°25E 45 E8
Bu Craa *W. Sahara* 26°45N 12°50W 50 C3
Bū Ḩasā *U.A.E.* 23°30N 53°20E 45 F7
Bua *Fiji* 16°48S 178°37E 59 a
Bua → *Malaysia* 12°45S 34°16E 55 E3
Bua Yai *Thailand* 15°33N 102°26E 38 E4
Buan *S. Korea* 35°44N 126°44E 35 G14
Buapinang *Indonesia* 4°40S 121°30E 37 E6
Bubanza *Burundi* 3°6S 29°23E 54 C2
Bubi → *Zimbabwe* 22°20S 31°7E 55 G3
Būbiyān *Kuwait* 29°45N 48°15E 45 D6
Buca *Fiji* 16°38S 179°52E 59 a
Bucaramanga *Colombia* 7°0N 73°0W 92 B4
Bucasia *Australia* 21°2S 149°10E 62 b
Buccaneer Arch. *Australia* 16°7S 123°20E 60 C3
Buccoo Reef *Trin. & Tob.* 11°10N 60°51W 93 J16
Buchach *Ukraine* 49°5N 25°25E 17 D13
Buchan *U.K.* 57°32N 2°21W 11 D6
Buchan Ness *U.K.* 57°29N 1°46W 11 D7
Buchanan *Canada* 51°40N 102°45W 71 C8
Buchanan *Liberia* 5°57N 10°2W 50 G3
Buchanan, L. *Queens., Australia* 21°35S 145°52E 62 C4
Buchanan, L. *W. Austral., Australia* 25°33S 123°2E 61 E3
Buchanan, L. *U.S.A.* 30°45N 98°25W 84 F5
Buchanan Cr. → *Australia* 19°13S 136°33E 62 B2
Buchans *Canada* 48°50N 56°52W 73 C8
Bucharest = Bucureşti *Romania* 44°27N 26°10E 17 F14
Bucheon *S. Korea* 37°28N 126°45E 35 F14
Buchon, Pt. *U.S.A.* 35°15N 120°54W 78 K6
Buck Hill Falls *U.S.A.* 41°11N 75°16W 83 E9
Buckeye Lake *U.S.A.* 39°55N 82°29W 82 G2
Buckhannon *U.S.A.* 39°0N 80°8W 81 F13
Buckhaven *U.K.* 56°11N 3°3W 11 E5
Buckhorn L. *Canada* 44°29N 78°23W 82 B6
Buckie *U.K.* 57°41N 2°58W 11 D6
Buckingham *Canada* 45°37N 75°24W 72 C4
Buckingham *U.K.* 51°59N 0°57W 13 F7
Buckingham B. *Australia* 12°10S 135°40E 62 A2
Buckinghamshire □ *U.K.* 51°53N 0°55W 13 F7
Buckle Hd. *Australia* 14°26S 127°52E 60 B4
Buckleboo *Australia* 32°54S 136°12E 63 E2
Buckley *U.K.* 53°10N 3°5W 12 D4
Buckley → *Australia* 20°10S 138°49E 62 C2
Bucklin *U.S.A.* 37°33N 99°38W 80 G4
Bucks L. *U.S.A.* 39°54N 121°12W 78 F5
Bucureşti *Romania* 44°27N 26°10E 17 F14
Bucyrus *U.S.A.* 40°48N 82°59W 81 E12
Budalin *Burma* 22°20N 95°10E 41 H19
Budapest *Hungary* 47°29N 19°3E 17 E10
Budaun *India* 28°5N 79°10E 43 E8
Budd Coast *Antarctica* 68°0S 112°0E 5 C8
Bude *U.K.* 50°49N 4°34W 13 G3
Budennovsk *Russia* 44°50N 44°10E 19 F7
Budge Budge = Baj Baj *India* 22°30N 88°5E 43 H13
Budgewoi *Australia* 33°13S 151°34E 63 E5
Budjala *Dem. Rep. of the Congo* 2°50N 19°40E 52 D3
Budo-Sungai Padi △ *Thailand* 6°19N 101°42E 39 J3
Buellton *U.S.A.* 34°37N 120°12W 79 L6
Buena Esperanza *Argentina* 34°45S 65°15W 94 C2
Buena Park *U.S.A.* 33°52N 117°59W 79 M9
Buena Vista *Colo., U.S.A.* 38°51N 106°8W 76 G10
Buena Vista *Va., U.S.A.* 37°44N 79°21W 81 G14
Buena Vista Lake Bed *U.S.A.* 35°12N 119°18W 79 K7
Buenaventura *Colombia* 3°53N 77°4W 92 C3
Buenaventura *Mexico* 29°51N 107°29W 86 B3
Buenos Aires *Argentina* 34°36S 58°22W 94 C4
Buenos Aires *Costa Rica* 9°10N 83°20W 88 E3
Buenos Aires □ *Argentina* 36°30S 60°0W 94 D4
Buenos Aires, L. *Argentina* 46°35S 72°30W 96 F2
Buffalo *Mo., U.S.A.* 37°39N 93°6W 80 G7
Buffalo *N.Y., U.S.A.* 42°53N 78°53W 82 D6
Buffalo *Okla., U.S.A.* 36°50N 99°38W 84 C5
Buffalo *S. Dak., U.S.A.* 45°35N 103°33W 80 C2
Buffalo *Wyo., U.S.A.* 44°21N 106°42W 76 D10
Buffalo → *Canada* 60°5N 115°5W 70 A5
Buffalo → *S. Africa* 28°43S 30°37E 57 D5
Buffalo ⌂ *U.S.A.* 36°14N 92°36W 84 C8
Buffalo Head Hills *Canada* 57°25N 115°55W 70 B5
Buffalo L. *Alta., Canada* 52°27N 112°54W 70 C6
Buffalo L. *N.W.T., Canada* 60°12N 115°25W 70 A5
Buffalo Narrows *Canada* 55°51N 108°29W 71 B7
Buffalo Springs ⌂ *Kenya* 0°32N 37°35E 54 B4
Buffels → *S. Africa* 29°36S 17°3E 56 D2
Buford *U.S.A.* 34°10N 84°0W 85 D12
Bug = Buh → *Ukraine* 46°59N 31°58E 19 E5
Bug → *Poland* 52°31N 21°5E 17 B11
Buga *Colombia* 4°0N 76°15W 92 C3
Bugala I. *Uganda* 0°40S 32°20E 54 C3
Buganda *Uganda* 0°0 31°30E 54 C3
Buganga *Uganda* 0°3S 32°0E 54 C3
Bugel, Tanjung *Indonesia* 6°26S 111°3E 37 G14
Búger *Spain* 39°45N 2°59E 24 B9
Bugibba *Malta* 35°57N 14°25E 25 D1
Bugsuk I. *Phil.* 8°12N 117°18E 36 C5
Bugulma *Russia* 54°33N 52°48E 18 D9
Bugungu ⌂ *Uganda* 2°17N 31°50E 54 B3
Buguruslan *Russia* 53°39N 52°26E 18 D9
Buh → *Ukraine* 46°59N 31°58E 19 E5
Buhera *Zimbabwe* 19°18S 31°29E 57 B5
Buhl *U.S.A.* 42°36N 114°46W 76 E6
Builth Wells *U.K.* 52°9N 3°25W 13 E4
Buir Nur *Mongolia* 47°50N 117°42E 33 B12
Buji *China* 22°37N 114°5E 33 a
Bujumbura *Burundi* 3°16S 29°18E 54 C2
Bukachacha *Russia* 52°55N 116°50E 29 D12
Bukama *Dem. Rep. of the Congo* 9°10S 25°50E 55 D2
Bukavu *Dem. Rep. of the Congo* 2°20S 28°52E 54 C2
Bukene *Tanzania* 4°15S 32°48E 54 C3
Bukhara = Buxoro *Uzbekistan* 39°48N 64°25E 28 F7
Bukhoro = Buxoro *Uzbekistan* 39°48N 64°25E 28 F7
Bukhtarma Res. = Zaysan Köli *Kazakhstan* 48°0N 83°0E 28 E9
Bukima *Tanzania* 1°50S 33°25E 54 C3
Bukit Bendera *Malaysia* 5°25N 100°15E 39 c
Bukit Mertajam *Malaysia* 5°22N 100°28E 39 c
Bukit Nil *Malaysia* 1°22N 104°12E 39 d
Bukit Panjang *Singapore* 1°23N 103°46E 39 d
Bukit Tengah *Malaysia* 5°22N 100°25E 39 c
Bukittinggi *Indonesia* 0°20S 100°20E 36 E2
Bukoba *Tanzania* 1°20S 31°49E 54 C3
Bukum, Pulau *Singapore* 1°14N 103°46E 39 d
Bukuya *Uganda* 0°40N 31°52E 54 B3
Būl, Kuh-e *Iran* 30°48N 52°45E 45 D7
Bula *Indonesia* 3°6S 130°30E 37 E8
Bulahdelah *Australia* 32°23S 152°13E 63 E5
Bulan *Phil.* 12°40N 123°52E 37 B6
Bulandshahr *India* 28°28N 77°51E 42 E7
Bulawayo *Zimbabwe* 20°7S 28°32E 55 G2
Buldan *Turkey* 38°2N 28°50E 23 E13
Buldir I. *U.S.A.* 52°21N 175°56E 74 E3
Bulgan *Mongolia* 48°45N 103°34E 32 B9
Bulgar *Russia* 54°57N 49°4E 18 D8
Bulgaria ■ *Europe* 42°35N 25°30E 23 C11
Buli, Teluk *Indonesia* 0°48N 128°25E 37 D7
Buliluyan, C. *Phil.* 8°20N 117°15E 36 C5
Bulim *Singapore* 1°22N 103°43E 39 d
Bulkley → *Canada* 55°15N 127°40W 70 B3
Bull Shoals L. *U.S.A.* 36°22N 92°35W 84 C8
Bulleringa △ *Australia* 17°39S 143°56E 62 B3
Bullhead City *U.S.A.* 35°8N 114°32W 79 K12
Büllingen *Belgium* 50°25N 6°16E 15 D6
Bullock Creek *Australia* 17°43S 144°31E 62 B3
Bulloo → *Australia* 28°43S 142°30E 63 D3
Bulloo L. *Australia* 28°43S 142°25E 63 D3
Bulls *N.Z.* 40°10S 175°24E 59 D5
Bulman *Australia* 13°39S 134°20E 62 A1
Bulnes *Chile* 36°42S 72°19W 94 D1
Bulsar = Valsad *India* 20°40N 72°58E 40 J8
Bultfontein *S. Africa* 28°18S 26°10E 56 D4
Bulukumba *Indonesia* 5°33S 120°11E 37 F6
Bulun *Russia* 70°37N 127°30E 29 B13
Bumba *Dem. Rep. of the Congo* 2°13N 22°30E 52 D4
Bumbah, Khalīj *Libya* 32°20N 23°15E 51 B10
Bumbiri I. *Tanzania* 1°40S 31°55E 54 C3
Bumhpa Bum *Burma* 26°51N 97°14E 41 F20
Bumi → *Zimbabwe* 17°0S 28°20E 55 F2
Buna *Kenya* 2°58N 39°30E 54 B4
Bunaken *Indonesia* 1°37N 124°46E 37 D6
Bunazi *Tanzania* 1°3S 31°23E 54 C3
Bunbury *Australia* 33°20S 115°35E 61 F2
Bunclody *Ireland* 52°39N 6°40W 10 D5
Buncrana *Ireland* 55°8N 7°27W 10 A4
Bundaberg *Australia* 24°54S 152°22E 63 C5
Bundey → *Australia* 21°46S 135°37E 62 C2
Bundi *India* 25°30N 75°35E 42 G6
Bundjalung △ *Australia* 29°16S 153°21E 63 D5
Bundoran *Ireland* 54°28N 8°16W 10 B3
Bung Kan *Thailand* 18°23N 103°37E 38 C4
Bungay *U.K.* 52°27N 1°28E 13 E9
Bungil Cr. → *Australia* 27°5S 149°5E 63 D4
Bungle Bungle = Purnululu △ *Australia* 17°20S 128°20E 60 C4
Bungo-Suidō *Japan* 33°0N 132°15E 31 H6
Bungoma *Kenya* 0°34N 34°34E 54 B3
Bungotakada *Japan* 33°35N 131°25E 31 H5
Bungu *Tanzania* 7°35S 39°0E 54 D4
Bunia *Dem. Rep. of the Congo* 1°35N 30°20E 54 B3
Bunji *Pakistan* 35°45N 74°40E 43 B6
Bunkie *U.S.A.* 30°57N 92°11W 84 F8
Bunnell *U.S.A.* 29°28N 81°16W 85 G14
Buntok *Indonesia* 1°40S 114°58E 36 E4
Bunya Mts. △ *Australia* 26°51S 151°34E 63 D5
Bunyola *Spain* 39°41N 2°42E 24 B9
Bunyu *Indonesia* 3°35N 117°50E 36 D5
Buol *Indonesia* 1°15N 121°32E 37 D6
Buon Brieng *Vietnam* 13°9N 108°12E 38 F7
Buon Ho *Vietnam* 12°57N 108°18E 38 F7
Buon Ma Thuot *Vietnam* 12°40N 108°3E 38 F7
Buong Long *Cambodia* 13°44N 106°59E 38 F6
Buorkhaya, Mys *Russia* 71°50N 132°40E 29 B14
Buqayq *Si. Arabia* 26°0N 49°45E 45 E6
Bur Acaba = Buurhakaba *Somali Rep.* 3°12N 44°20E 47 G3
Bûr Safâga *Egypt* 26°43N 33°57E 44 E2
Bûr Sa'îd *Egypt* 31°16N 32°18E 51 B12
Bûr Sûdân *Sudan* 19°32N 37°9E 51 E13
Bura *Kenya* 1°4S 39°58E 54 C4
Burakin *Australia* 30°31S 117°10E 61 F2
Burang *China* 30°15N 81°10E 32 E5
Burao = Burco *Somali Rep.* 9°32N 45°32E 47 F4
Burāq *Syria* 33°11N 36°29E 46 B5
Buraydah *Si. Arabia* 26°20N 43°59E 44 E4
Burbank *U.S.A.* 34°12N 118°18W 79 L8
Burco *Somali Rep.* 9°32N 45°32E 47 F4
Burda *India* 25°50N 77°35E 42 G7
Burdekin → *Australia* 19°38S 147°25E 62 B4
Burdur *Turkey* 37°45N 30°17E 19 G5
Burdwan = Barddhaman *India* 23°14N 87°39E 43 H12
Bure *Ethiopia* 10°40N 37°4E 47 E2
Bure → *U.K.* 52°38N 1°43E 12 E9
Bureya → *Russia* 49°27N 129°30E 29 E13
Burford *Canada* 43°7N 80°27W 82 C4
Burgas *Bulgaria* 42°33N 27°29E 23 C12
Burgeo *Canada* 47°37N 57°38W 73 C8
Burgersdorp *S. Africa* 31°0S 26°20E 56 E4
Burgess, Mt. *Australia* 30°50S 121°5E 61 F3
Burghead *U.K.* 57°43N 3°30W 11 D5
Burgos *Spain* 42°21N 3°41W 21 A4
Burgsvik *Sweden* 57°3N 18°19E 9 H18
Burgundy = Bourgogne □ *France* 47°0N 4°50E 20 C6
Burhaniye *Turkey* 39°30N 26°58E 23 E12
Burhanpur *India* 21°18N 76°14E 40 J10
Burhi Gandak → *India* 25°20N 86°37E 43 G12
Burhner → *India* 22°43N 80°31E 43 H9
Burias I. *Phil.* 12°55N 123°5E 37 B6
Burica, Pta. *Costa Rica* 8°3N 82°51W 88 E3
Burien *U.S.A.* 47°28N 122°20W 78 C4
Burigi, L. *Tanzania* 2°2S 31°22E 54 C3
Burigi ⌂ *Tanzania* 2°20S 31°6E 54 C3
Burin *Canada* 47°1N 55°14W 73 C8
Buriram *Thailand* 15°0N 103°0E 38 E4
Burkburnett *U.S.A.* 34°6N 98°34W 84 D5
Burke → *Australia* 23°12S 139°33E 62 C2
Burke Chan. *Canada* 52°10N 127°30W 70 C3
Burketown *Australia* 17°45S 139°33E 62 B2
Burkina Faso ■ *Africa* 12°0N 1°0W 50 F5
Burk's Falls *Canada* 45°37N 79°24W 72 C4
Burleigh Falls *Canada* 44°33N 78°12W 82 B6
Burley *U.S.A.* 42°32N 113°48W 76 E7
Burlingame *U.S.A.* 37°35N 122°21W 78 H4
Burlington *Canada* 43°18N 79°45W 82 C5
Burlington *Colo., U.S.A.* 39°18N 102°16W 76 G12
Burlington *Iowa, U.S.A.* 40°49N 91°14W 80 E8
Burlington *Kans., U.S.A.* 38°12N 95°45W 80 F6
Burlington *N.C., U.S.A.* 36°6N 79°26W 85 C15
Burlington *N.J., U.S.A.* 40°4N 74°51W 83 F10
Burlington *Vt., U.S.A.* 44°29N 73°12W 83 B11
Burlington *Wash., U.S.A.* 48°28N 122°20W 78 B4
Burlington *Wis., U.S.A.* 42°41N 88°17W 80 D9
Burma ■ *Asia* 21°0N 96°30E 41 J20
Burnaby I. *Canada* 52°25N 131°19W 70 C2
Burnet *U.S.A.* 30°45N 98°14W 84 F5
Burney *U.S.A.* 40°53N 121°40W 76 F3
Burnham *U.S.A.* 40°38N 77°34W 82 F7
Burnham-on-Sea *U.K.* 51°14N 3°0W 13 F5
Burnie *Australia* 41°4S 145°56E 63 G4
Burnley *U.K.* 53°47N 2°14W 12 D5
Burns *U.S.A.* 43°35N 119°3W 76 E4
Burns Junction *U.S.A.* 42°47N 117°51W 76 E5
Burns Lake *Canada* 54°14N 125°45W 70 C3
Burnside → *Canada* 66°51N 108°4W 68 D10
Burnside, L. *Australia* 25°22S 123°0E 61 E3
Burnsville *U.S.A.* 44°47N 93°17W 80 C7
Burnt River *Canada* 44°41N 78°42W 82 B6
Burntwood → *Canada* 56°8N 96°34W 71 B9
Burntwood L. *Canada* 55°22N 100°26W 71 B8
Burqān *Kuwait* 29°0N 47°57E 44 D5
Burqin *China* 47°43N 87°0E 32 B6
Burra *Australia* 33°40S 138°55E 63 E2
Burray *U.K.* 58°51N 2°54W 11 C6
Burren *Ireland* 53°9N 9°5W 10 C2
Burren △ *Ireland* 53°1N 8°58W 10 C3
Burren Junction *Australia* 30°7S 148°58E 63 E4
Burrinjuck, L. *Australia* 35°0S 148°36E 63 F4
Burro, Serranías del *Mexico* 28°56N 102°5W 86 B4
Burrow Hd. *U.K.* 54°41N 4°24W 11 G4
Burrum Coast △ *Australia* 25°13S 152°36E 63 D5
Burruyacú *Argentina* 26°30S 64°40W 94 B3
Burry Port *U.K.* 51°41N 4°15W 13 F3
Bursa *Turkey* 40°15N 29°5E 23 D13
Burstall *Canada* 50°39N 109°54W 71 C7
Burton *Ohio, U.S.A.* 41°28N 81°8W 82 E3
Burton *S.C., U.S.A.* 32°26N 80°43W 85 E14
Burton, L. *Canada* 54°45N 78°20W 72 B4
Burton upon Trent *U.K.* 52°48N 1°38W 12 E6
Buru *Indonesia* 3°30S 126°30E 37 E7
Burûn, Râs *Egypt* 31°14N 33°7E 46 D2
Burundi ■ *Africa* 3°15S 30°0E 54 C3
Bururi *Burundi* 3°57S 29°37E 54 C2
Burutu *Nigeria* 5°20N 5°29E 50 G7
Burwell *U.S.A.* 41°47N 99°8W 80 E4
Burwick *U.K.* 58°45N 2°58W 11 C5
Bury *U.K.* 53°35N 2°17W 12 D5
Bury St. Edmunds *U.K.* 52°15N 0°43E 13 E8
Buryatia □ *Russia* 53°0N 110°0E 29 D12
Busan *S. Korea* 35°5N 129°0E 35 G15
Busango Swamp *Zambia* 14°15S 25°45E 55 E2
Busaso = Boosaaso *Somali Rep.* 11°12N 49°18E 47 E4
Buşayrah *Syria* 35°9N 40°26E 44 C4
Būshehr *Iran* 28°55N 50°55E 45 D6
Būshehr □ *Iran* 28°20N 51°45E 45 D6
Bushenyi *Uganda* 0°35S 30°10E 54 C3
Bushire = Būshehr *Iran* 28°55N 50°55E 45 D6
Businga *Dem. Rep. of the Congo* 3°16N 20°59E 52 D4
Buşra ash Shām *Syria* 32°30N 36°25E 46 C5
Busselton *Australia* 33°42S 115°15E 61 F2
Bussum *Neths.* 52°16N 5°10E 15 B5
Busto Arsízio *Italy* 45°37N 8°51E 20 D8
Busu Djanoa *Dem. Rep. of the Congo* 1°43N 21°23E 52 D4
Busuanga I. *Phil.* 12°10N 120°0E 37 B6
Busungbiu *Indonesia* 8°16S 114°58E 37 J17
Buta *Dem. Rep. of the Congo* 2°50N 24°53E 54 B1
Butare *Rwanda* 2°31S 29°52E 54 C2
Butaritari *Kiribati* 3°30N 174°0E 64 G9
Bute *U.K.* 55°48N 5°2W 11 F3
Bute Inlet *Canada* 50°40N 124°53W 70 C4
Butemba *Uganda* 1°9N 31°37E 54 B3
Butembo *Dem. Rep. of the Congo* 0°9N 29°18E 54 B2
Butere *Kenya* 0°13N 34°30E 54 B3
Butha Qi *China* 48°0N 122°32E 33 B13
Butiaba *Uganda* 1°50N 31°20E 54 B3
Butler *Mo., U.S.A.* 38°16N 94°20W 80 F6
Butler *Pa., U.S.A.* 40°52N 79°54W 82 F5
Buton *Indonesia* 5°0S 122°45E 37 E6
Butte *Mont., U.S.A.* 46°0N 112°32W 76 C7
Butte *Nebr., U.S.A.* 42°58N 98°51W 80 D4
Butte Creek → *U.S.A.* 39°12N 121°56W 78 F5
Butterworth = Gcuwa *S. Africa* 32°20S 28°11E 57 E4
Butterworth *Malaysia* 5°24N 100°23E 39 c
Buttevant *Ireland* 52°14N 8°40W 10 D3
Buttfield, Mt. *Australia* 24°45S 128°9E 61 D4
Button B. *Canada* 58°45N 94°23W 71 B10
Buttonwillow *U.S.A.* 35°24N 119°28W 79 K7
Butty Hd. *Australia* 33°54S 121°39E 61 F3
Butuan *Phil.* 8°57N 125°33E 37 C7
Butung = Buton *Indonesia* 5°0S 122°45E 37 E6
Buturlinovka *Russia* 50°50N 40°35E 19 D7
Butwal *Nepal* 27°33N 83°31E 43 F10
Buurhakaba *Somali Rep.* 3°12N 44°20E 47 G3
Buxa Duar *India* 27°45N 89°35E 43 F13
Buxar *India* 25°34N 83°58E 43 G10
Buxoro *Uzbekistan* 39°48N 64°25E 28 F7
Buxtehude *Germany* 53°28N 9°39E 16 B5
Buxton *U.K.* 53°16N 1°54W 12 D6
Buy *Russia* 58°28N 41°28E 18 C7
Buyant-Uhaa *Mongolia* 44°55N 110°11E 34 B6
Buyo, L. de *Ivory C.* 6°16N 7°10W 50 G4
Büyük Menderes → *Turkey* 37°28N 27°11E 23 F12
Büyükçekmece *Turkey* 41°2N 28°35E 23 D13
Buyun Shan *China* 40°4N 122°43E 35 D12
Buzău *Romania* 45°10N 26°50E 17 F14
Buzău → *Romania* 45°26N 27°44E 17 F14
Buzen *Japan* 33°35N 131°5E 31 H5
Buzi → *Mozam.* 19°50S 34°43E 55 F3
Büzmeýin *Turkmenistan* 38°3N 58°12E 45 B8
Buzuluk *Russia* 52°48N 52°12E 18 D9
Buzzards Bay *U.S.A.* 41°45N 70°37W 83 E14
Bwana Mkubwa *Zambia* 13°8S 28°38E 55 E2
Bwindi △ *Uganda* 1°2S 29°42E 54 C2
Byam Martin I. *Canada* 75°15N 104°15W 69 B11
Byarezina → *Belarus* 52°33N 30°14E 17 B16
Byaroza *Belarus* 52°31N 24°51E 17 B13
Bydgoszcz *Poland* 53°10N 18°0E 17 B9
Byelorussia = Belarus ■ *Europe* 53°30N 27°0E 17 B14
Byers *U.S.A.* 39°43N 104°14W 76 G11
Byesville *U.S.A.* 39°58N 81°32W 82 G3
Byfield △ *Australia* 22°52S 150°45E 62 C5
Bykhaw *Belarus* 53°31N 30°14E 17 B16
Bykhov = Bykhaw *Belarus* 53°31N 30°14E 17 B16
Bylas *U.S.A.* 33°8N 110°7W 77 K8
Bylot *Canada* 58°25N 94°8W 71 B10
Bylot I. *Canada* 73°13N 78°34W 69 C16
Byrd, C. *Antarctica* 69°38S 76°7W 5 C17
Byrock *Australia* 30°40S 146°27E 63 E4
Byron, C. *Australia* 28°43S 153°38E 63 D5
Byron Bay *Australia* 28°43S 153°37E 63 D5
Byrranga, Gory *Russia* 75°0N 100°0E 29 B11
Byrranga Mts. = Byrranga, Gory *Russia* 75°0N 100°0E 29 B11
Byske *Sweden* 64°57N 21°11E 8 D19
Byskeälven → *Sweden* 64°57N 21°13E 8 D19
Bytom *Poland* 50°25N 18°54E 17 C10
Bytów *Poland* 54°10N 17°30E 17 A9
Byumba *Rwanda* 1°35S 30°4E 54 C3

C

C.W. McConaughy, L. *U.S.A.* 41°14N 101°40W 80 E3
Ca → *Vietnam* 18°45N 105°45E 38 C5
Ca Mau *Vietnam* 9°7N 105°8E 39 H5
Ca Mau, Mui *Vietnam* 8°38N 104°44E 39 H5
Ca Na *Vietnam* 11°20N 108°54E 39 G7
Caacupé *Paraguay* 25°23S 57°5W 94 B4
Caaguazú △ *Paraguay* 26°5S 55°31W 95 B4
Caála *Angola* 12°46S 15°30E 53 G3
Caamaño Sd. *Canada* 52°55N 129°25W 70 C3
Caazapá *Paraguay* 26°8S 56°19W 94 B4
Caazapá □ *Paraguay* 26°10S 56°0W 95 B4
Caballeria, C. de *Spain* 40°5N 4°5E 24 A11
Cabanatuan *Phil.* 15°30N 120°58E 37 A6
Cabano *Canada* 47°40N 68°56W 73 C6
Cabazon *U.S.A.* 33°55N 116°47W 79 M10
Cabedelo *Brazil* 7°0S 34°50W 93 E12
Cabildo *Chile* 32°30S 71°5W 94 C1
Cabimas *Venezuela* 10°23N 71°25W 92 A4
Cabinda *Angola* 5°33S 12°11E 52 F2
Cabinda □ *Angola* 5°0S 12°30E 52 F2
Cabinet Mts. *U.S.A.* 48°10N 115°50W 76 B6
Cabo Blanco *Argentina* 47°15S 65°47W 96 F3
Cabo Frio *Brazil* 22°51S 42°3W 95 A7
Cabo Pantoja *Peru* 1°0S 75°10W 92 D3
Cabo San Lucas *Mexico* 22°53N 109°54W 86 C3
Cabo Verde = Cape Verde Is. ■ *Atl. Oc.* 16°0N 24°0W 50 b
Cabonga, Réservoir *Canada* 47°20N 76°40W 72 C4
Cabool *U.S.A.* 37°7N 92°6W 80 G7
Caboolture *Australia* 27°5S 152°58E 63 D5
Cabora Bassa Dam = Cahora Bassa, Lago de *Mozam.* 15°20S 32°50E 55 F3
Caborca *Mexico* 30°37N 112°6W 86 A2
Cabot, Mt. *U.S.A.* 44°30N 71°25W 83 B13
Cabot Hd. *Canada* 45°14N 81°17W 82 A3
Cabot Str. *Canada* 47°15N 59°40W 73 C8
Cabra *Spain* 37°30N 4°28W 21 D3
Cabrera *Spain* 39°8N 2°57E 24 B9
Cabri *Canada* 50°35N 108°25W 71 C7
Cabriel → *Spain* 39°14N 1°3W 21 C5
Caçador *Brazil* 26°47S 51°0W 95 B5
Čačak *Serbia* 43°54N 20°20E 23 C9
Caçapava do Sul *Brazil* 30°30S 53°30W 95 C5
Cáceres *Brazil* 16°5S 57°40W 92 G7
Cáceres *Spain* 39°26N 6°23W 21 C2
Cache Bay *Canada* 46°22N 80°0W 72 C4
Cache Cr. → *U.S.A.* 38°42N 121°42W 78 G5
Cache Creek *Canada* 50°48N 121°19W 70 C4
Cachi *Argentina* 25°5S 66°10W 94 B2
Cachimbo, Serra do *Brazil* 9°30S 55°30W 93 E7

Cachinal de la Sierra
  Chile 24°58S 69°32W 94 A2
Cachoeira Brazil 12°30S 39°0W 93 F11
Cachoeira do Sul Brazil 30°3S 52°53W 95 C5
Cachoeiro de Itapemirim
  Brazil 20°51S 41°7W 95 A7
Cacoal Brazil 11°32S 61°18W 92 F6
Cacólo Angola 10°9S 19°21E 52 G3
Caconda Angola 13°48S 15°8E 53 G3
Caddo U.S.A. 34°7N 96°16W 84 D6
Cader Idris U.K. 52°42N 3°53W 13 E4
Cadereyta de Jiménez
  Mexico 25°36N 100°0W 86 B5
Cadibarrawirracanna, L.
  Australia 28°52S 135°27E 63 D2
Cadillac U.S.A. 44°15N 85°24W 81 C11
Cadiz Phil. 10°57N 123°15E 37 B6
Cádiz Spain 36°30N 6°20W 21 D2
Cadiz Calif., U.S.A. 34°30N 115°28W 79 L11
Cadiz Ohio, U.S.A. 40°22N 81°0W 82 F4
Cádiz, G. de Spain 36°40N 7°0W 21 D2
Cadiz L. U.S.A. 34°18N 115°24W 77 J6
Cadney Park Australia 27°55S 134°3E 63 D1
Cadomin Canada 53°2N 117°20W 70 C5
Cadotte Lake Canada 56°26N 116°23W 70 B5
Cadoux Australia 30°46S 117°7E 61 F2
Caen France 49°10N 0°22W 20 B3
Caernarfon U.K. 53°8N 4°16W 12 D3
Caernarfon B. U.K. 53°4N 4°40W 12 D3
Caernarvon = Caernarfon
  U.K. 53°8N 4°16W 12 D3
Caerphilly U.K. 51°35N 3°13W 13 F4
Caerphilly □ U.K. 51°37N 3°12W 13 F4
Caesarea Israel 32°30N 34°53E 46 C3
Caetité Brazil 13°50S 42°32W 93 F10
Cafayate Argentina 26°2S 66°0W 94 B2
Cafu Angola 16°30S 15°8E 56 B2
Cagayan de Oro Phil. 8°30N 124°40E 37 C6
Cágliari Italy 39°13N 9°7E 22 E3
Cágliari, G. di Italy 39°8N 9°11E 22 E3
Caguán → Colombia 0°8S 74°18W 92 D4
Caguas Puerto Rico 18°14N 66°2W 89 d
Caha Mts. Ireland 51°45N 9°40W 10 E2
Cahama Angola 16°17S 14°19E 56 B1
Caher Ireland 52°22N 7°56W 10 D4
Cahersiveen Ireland 51°56N 10°14W 10 E1
Cahora Bassa, Lago de
  Mozam. 15°20S 32°50E 55 F3
Cahore Pt. Ireland 52°33N 6°12W 10 D5
Cahors France 44°27N 1°27E 20 D4
Cahul Moldova 45°50N 28°15E 17 F15
Cai Bau, Dao Vietnam 21°10N 107°27E 38 B6
Cai Be Vietnam 10°20N 106°2E 39 G6
Cai Nuoc Vietnam 8°56N 105°1E 39 H5
Caia Mozam. 17°51S 35°24E 55 F4
Caianda Angola 11°2S 23°31E 55 E1
Caibarién Cuba 22°30N 79°30W 88 B4
Caicara Venezuela 7°38N 66°10W 92 B5
Caicó Brazil 6°20S 37°0W 93 E11
Caicos Is. Turks & Caicos 21°40N 71°40W 89 B5
Caicos Passage W. Indies 22°45N 72°45W 89 B5
Caiguna Australia 32°16S 125°29E 61 F4
Caird Coast Antarctica 75°0S 25°0W 5 D1
Cairn Gorm U.K. 57°7N 3°39W 11 D5
Cairngorm Mts. U.K. 57°6N 3°42W 11 D5
Cairngorms △ U.K. 57°10N 3°50W 11 D5
Cairnryan U.K. 54°59N 5°1W 11 G3
Cairns Australia 16°57S 145°45E 62 B4
Cairns L. Canada 51°42N 94°30W 71 C10
Cairo = El Qâhira Egypt 30°2N 31°13E 51 B12
Cairo Ga., U.S.A. 30°52N 84°13W 85 F12
Cairo Ill., U.S.A. 37°0N 89°11W 80 G9
Cairo N.Y., U.S.A. 42°18N 74°0W 83 D10
Caiseal = Cashel Ireland 52°30N 7°53W 10 D4
Caisleán an Bharraigh = Castlebar
  Ireland 53°52N 9°18W 10 C2
Caithness U.K. 58°25N 3°35W 11 C5
Caithness, Ord of U.K. 58°8N 3°36W 11 C5
Caja de Muertos, I.
  Puerto Rico 17°54N 66°32W 89 d
Cajamarca Peru 7°5S 78°28W 92 E3
Cajazeiras Brazil 6°52S 38°30W 93 E11
Cala d'Or Spain 39°23N 3°14E 24 B10
Cala en Porter Spain 39°52N 4°8E 24 B11
Cala Figuera Spain 39°20N 3°10E 24 B10
Cala Figuera, C. de Spain 39°27N 2°31E 24 B9
Cala Forcat Spain 40°0N 3°47E 24 B10
Cala Major Spain 39°33N 2°37E 24 B9
Cala Mezquida = Sa Mesquida
  Spain 39°55N 4°16E 24 B11
Cala Millor Spain 39°35N 3°22E 24 B10
Cala Murada Spain 39°27N 3°17E 24 B10
Cala Ratjada Spain 39°43N 3°27E 24 B10
Cala Santa Galdana
  Spain 39°56N 3°58E 24 B10
Calabar Nigeria 4°57N 8°20E 50 H7
Calabogie Canada 45°18N 76°43W 83 A8
Calabozo Venezuela 9°0N 67°28W 92 B5
Calábria □ Italy 39°0N 16°30E 22 E7
Calahorra Spain 42°18N 1°59W 21 A5
Calais France 50°57N 1°56E 20 A4
Calais U.S.A. 45°11N 67°17W 81 C20
Calakmul △ Mexico 18°14N 89°48W 87 D7
Calalaste, Cord. de
  Argentina 25°0S 67°0W 94 B2
Calama Brazil 8°0S 62°50W 92 E6
Calama Chile 22°30S 68°55W 94 A2
Calamar Colombia 10°15N 74°55W 92 A4
Calamian Group Phil. 11°50N 119°55E 37 B5
Calamocha Spain 40°50N 1°17W 21 B5
Calang Indonesia 4°37N 95°37E 36 D1
Calanscio, Sarīr Libya 27°30N 21°30E 51 C10
Calapan Phil. 13°25N 121°7E 37 B6
Călăraşi Romania 44°12N 27°20E 17 F14
Calatayud Spain 41°20N 1°40W 21 B5
Calauag Phil. 13°55N 122°15E 37 B6
Calavite, C. Phil. 13°26N 120°20E 37 B6
Calbayog Phil. 12°4N 124°38E 37 B6
Calca Peru 13°22S 72°0W 92 F4
Calcasieu L. U.S.A. 29°55N 93°18W 84 G8

Calcium U.S.A. 44°1N 75°50W 83 B9
Calcutta = Kolkata
  India 22°34N 88°21E 43 H13
Calcutta U.S.A. 40°40N 80°34W 82 F4
Caldas da Rainha Portugal 39°24N 9°8W 21 C1
Calder → U.K. 53°44N 1°22W 12 D6
Caldera Chile 27°5S 70°55W 94 B1
Caldera de Taburiente △
  Canary Is. 28°43N 17°52W 24 F2
Caldwell Idaho, U.S.A. 43°40N 116°41W 76 E5
Caldwell Kans., U.S.A. 37°2N 97°37W 80 G5
Caldwell Tex., U.S.A. 30°32N 96°42W 84 F6
Caledon Canada 43°51N 79°51W 82 C5
Caledon S. Africa 34°14S 19°26E 56 E2
Caledon → S. Africa 30°31S 26°5E 56 E4
Caledon B. Australia 12°45S 137°0E 62 A2
Caledonia Canada 43°7N 79°58W 82 C5
Caledonia U.S.A. 42°58N 77°51W 82 D7
Calemba Angola 16°0S 15°44E 56 B2
Calen Australia 20°56S 148°48E 62 b
Calexico U.S.A. 32°40N 115°30W 79 N11
Calf of Man I. of Man 54°3N 4°48W 12 C3
Calgary Canada 51°0N 114°10W 70 C6
Calheta Madeira 32°44N 17°11W 24 D2
Calhoun U.S.A. 34°30N 84°57W 85 D12
Cali Colombia 3°25N 76°35W 92 C3
Calicut India 11°15N 75°43E 40 P9
Caliente U.S.A. 37°37N 114°31W 77 H6
California Mo., U.S.A. 38°38N 92°34W 80 F7
California Pa., U.S.A. 40°4N 79°54W 82 F5
California □ U.S.A. 37°30N 119°30W 78 H7
California, Baja, T.N. = Baja
  California □ Mexico 30°0N 115°0W 86 B2
California, Baja, T.S. = Baja
  California Sur □
  Mexico 25°50N 111°50W 86 B2
California, G. de Mexico 27°0N 111°0W 86 B2
California City U.S.A. 35°10N 117°55W 79 K9
California Hot Springs
  U.S.A. 35°51N 118°41W 79 K8
Calilegua △ Argentina 25°36S 64°50W 94 B3
Calingasta Argentina 31°15S 69°30W 94 C2
Calipatria U.S.A. 33°8N 115°31W 79 M11
Calistoga U.S.A. 38°35N 122°35W 78 G4
Calitzdorp S. Africa 33°33S 21°42E 56 E3
Callabonna, L. Australia 29°40S 140°5E 63 D3
Callan Ireland 52°32N 7°24W 10 D4
Callander U.K. 56°15N 4°13W 11 E4
Callao Peru 12°3S 77°8W 92 F3
Callicoon U.S.A. 41°46N 75°3W 83 E9
Calling Lake Canada 55°15N 113°12W 70 B6
Calliope Australia 24°0S 151°16E 62 C5
Calma, Costa de la Spain 39°28N 2°26E 24 B9
Calobre Panama 8°20N 80°50W 88 E3
Calola Angola 16°25S 17°48E 56 B2
Caloundra Australia 26°45S 153°10E 63 D5
Calpella U.S.A. 39°14N 123°12W 78 F3
Calpine U.S.A. 39°40N 120°27W 78 F6
Calstock Canada 49°47N 84°9W 72 C3
Caltagirone Italy 37°14N 14°31E 22 F6
Caltanissetta Italy 37°29N 14°4E 22 F6
Calulo Angola 10°1S 14°56E 52 G2
Calvert → Australia 16°17S 137°44E 62 B2
Calvert I. Canada 51°30N 128°0W 70 C3
Calvert Ra. Australia 24°0S 122°30E 60 D3
Calvi France 42°34N 8°45E 20 E8
Calvià Spain 39°34N 2°31E 24 B9
Calvillo Mexico 21°51N 102°43W 86 C4
Calvinia S. Africa 31°28S 19°45E 56 E2
Calwa U.S.A. 36°42N 119°46W 78 J7
Cam → U.K. 52°21N 0°16E 13 E8
Cam Lam = Ba Ngoi
  Vietnam 11°54N 109°10E 39 G7
Cam Pha Vietnam 21°7N 107°18E 38 B6
Cam Ranh Vietnam 11°54N 109°12E 39 G7
Cam Xuyen Vietnam 18°15N 106°0E 38 C6
Camabatela Angola 8°20S 15°26E 52 F3
Camacha Madeira 32°41N 16°49W 24 D3
Camacupa Angola 11°58S 17°22E 53 G3
Camagüey Cuba 21°20N 77°55W 88 B4
Camaná Peru 16°30S 72°50W 92 G4
Camanche Res. U.S.A. 38°14N 121°1W 78 G6
Camaquã Brazil 30°51S 51°49W 95 C5
Camaquã → Brazil 31°17S 51°47W 95 C5
Câmara de Lobos
  Madeira 32°39N 16°59W 24 D3
Camargo Mexico 26°19N 98°50W 87 B5
Camarillo U.S.A. 34°13N 119°2W 79 L7
Camarón, C. Honduras 16°0N 85°5W 88 C2
Camarones Argentina 44°50S 65°40W 96 E3
Camas U.S.A. 45°35N 122°24W 78 E4
Camas Valley U.S.A. 43°2N 123°40W 76 E2
Camballin Australia 17°59S 124°12E 60 C3
Cambará Brazil 23°2S 50°5W 95 A5
Cambay = Khambhat
  India 22°23N 72°33E 42 H5
Cambay, G. of = Khambhat, G. of
  India 20°45N 72°30E 40 J8
Cambodia ■ Asia 12°15N 105°0E 38 F5
Camborne U.K. 50°12N 5°19W 13 G2
Cambrai France 50°11N 3°14E 20 A5
Cambria U.S.A. 35°34N 121°5W 78 K5
Cambrian Mts. U.K. 52°3N 3°57W 13 E4
Cambridge Canada 43°23N 80°15W 82 C4
Cambridge Jamaica 18°18N 77°54W 88 a
Cambridge N.Z. 37°54S 175°29E 59 B5
Cambridge U.K. 52°12N 0°8E 13 E8
Cambridge Mass., U.S.A. 42°23N 71°7W 83 D13
Cambridge Minn., U.S.A. 45°34N 93°13W 80 C7
Cambridge N.Y., U.S.A. 43°2N 73°23W 83 C11
Cambridge Nebr.,
  U.S.A. 40°17N 100°10W 80 E4
Cambridge Ohio, U.S.A. 40°2N 81°35W 82 F3
Cambridge Bay Canada 69°10N 105°0W 68 D11
Cambridge G. Australia 14°55S 128°15E 60 B4
Cambridge Springs
  U.S.A. 41°48N 80°4W 82 E4
Cambridgeshire □ U.K. 52°25N 0°7W 13 E7
Cambuci Brazil 21°35S 41°55W 95 A7

Cambundi-Catembo
  Angola 10°10S 17°35E 52 G3
Camden Australia 34°1S 150°43E 63 B5
Camden Ala., U.S.A. 31°59N 87°17W 85 F11
Camden Ark., U.S.A. 33°35N 92°50W 84 E8
Camden Maine, U.S.A. 44°13N 69°4W 81 C19
Camden N.J., U.S.A. 39°55N 75°7W 83 G9
Camden N.Y., U.S.A. 43°20N 75°45W 83 C9
Camden S.C., U.S.A. 34°16N 80°36W 85 D14
Camden Sd. Australia 15°27S 124°25E 60 C3
Camdenton U.S.A. 38°1N 92°45W 80 F7
Camelford U.K. 50°37N 4°42W 13 G3
Cameron Ariz., U.S.A. 35°53N 111°25W 77 J8
Cameron La., U.S.A. 29°48N 93°20W 84 G8
Cameron Mo., U.S.A. 39°44N 94°14W 80 F6
Cameron Tex., U.S.A. 30°51N 96°59W 84 F6
Cameron Highlands
  Malaysia 4°27N 101°22E 39 K3
Cameron Hills Canada 59°48N 118°0W 70 B5
Cameroon ■ Africa 6°0N 12°30E 51 G7
Cameroun, Mt. Cameroon 4°13N 9°10E 52 D1
Cametá Brazil 2°12S 49°30W 93 D9
Camilla U.S.A. 31°14N 84°12W 85 F12
Caminha Portugal 41°50N 8°50W 21 B1
Camino U.S.A. 38°44N 120°41W 78 G6
Cammal U.S.A. 41°24N 77°28W 82 E7
Camocim Brazil 2°55S 40°50W 93 D10
Camooweal Australia 19°56S 138°7E 62 B2
Camooweal Caves △
  Australia 20°1S 138°11E 62 C2
Camopi Fr. Guiana 3°12N 52°17W 93 C8
Camp Hill U.S.A. 40°14N 76°55W 82 F8
Camp Nelson U.S.A. 36°8N 118°39W 79 J8
Camp Pendleton
  U.S.A. 33°13N 117°24W 79 M9
Camp Verde U.S.A. 34°34N 111°51W 77 J8
Camp Wood U.S.A. 29°40N 100°1W 84 G4
Campana Argentina 34°10S 58°55W 94 C4
Campana, I. Chile 48°20S 75°20W 96 F1
Campanário Madeira 32°39N 17°2W 24 D2
Campanet Spain 39°46N 2°58E 24 B9
Campánia □ Italy 41°0N 14°30E 22 D6
Campbell S. Africa 28°48S 23°44E 56 D3
Campbell Calif., U.S.A. 37°17N 121°57W 78 H5
Campbell Ohio, U.S.A. 41°5N 80°37W 82 E4
Campbell I. Pac. Oc. 52°30S 169°0E 64 N8
Campbell L. Canada 63°14N 106°55W 71 A7
Campbell Plateau S. Ocean 55°0S 170°0E 5 A11
Campbell River Canada 50°5N 125°20W 70 C3
Campbellford Canada 44°18N 77°48W 82 B7
Campbellpur Pakistan 33°46N 72°26E 42 C5
Campbellsville U.S.A. 37°21N 85°20W 81 G11
Campbellton Canada 47°57N 66°43W 73 C6
Campbelltown Australia 34°4S 150°49E 63 B5
Campbeltown U.K. 55°26N 5°36W 11 F3
Campeche Mexico 19°51N 90°32W 87 D6
Campeche □ Mexico 19°0N 90°30W 87 D6
Campeche, Golfo de
  Mexico 19°30N 93°0W 87 D6
Camperdown Australia 38°14S 143°9E 63 F3
Camperville Canada 51°59N 100°9W 71 C8
Câmpina Romania 45°10N 25°45E 17 F13
Campina Grande Brazil 7°20S 35°47W 93 E11
Campinas Brazil 22°50S 47°0W 95 A6
Campo Grande Brazil 20°25S 54°40W 93 H8
Campo Maior Brazil 4°50S 42°12W 93 D10
Campo Mourão Brazil 24°3S 52°22W 95 A5
Campobasso Italy 41°34N 14°39E 22 D6
Campos Brazil 21°50S 41°20W 95 A7
Campos Belos Brazil 13°10S 47°3W 93 F9
Campos Novos Brazil 27°21S 51°50W 95 B5
Camptonville U.S.A. 39°27N 121°3W 78 F5
Camptown U.S.A. 41°44N 76°14W 83 E8
Câmpulung Romania 45°17N 25°3E 17 F13
Camrose Canada 53°0N 112°50W 70 C6
Camsell Portage
  Canada 59°37N 109°15W 71 B7
Çan Turkey 40°2N 27°3E 23 D12
Can Clavo Spain 38°57N 1°27E 24 C7
Can Creu Spain 38°58N 1°28E 24 C7
Can Gio Vietnam 10°25N 106°58E 39 G6
Can Pastilla Spain 39°32N 2°42E 24 B9
Can Tho Vietnam 10°2N 105°46E 39 G5
Canaan U.S.A. 42°2N 73°20W 83 D11
Canada ■ N. Amer. 60°0N 100°0W 68 G11
Canada Abyssal Plain
  Arctic 80°0N 140°0W 4 B18
Canada Basin Arctic 80°0N 145°0W 4 B18
Cañada de Gómez
  Argentina 32°40S 61°30W 94 C3
Canadian U.S.A. 35°55N 100°23W 84 D4
Canadian → U.S.A. 35°28N 95°3W 84 D7
Canadian Shield Canada 53°0N 75°0W 66 C10
Canajoharie U.S.A. 42°54N 74°35W 83 D10
Canakkale Turkey 40°8N 26°24E 23 D12
Çanakkale Boğazı
  Turkey 40°17N 26°32E 23 D12
Canal Flats Canada 50°10N 115°48W 70 C5
Canalejas Argentina 35°15S 66°34W 94 D2
Canals Argentina 33°35S 62°53W 94 C3
Canandaigua U.S.A. 42°54N 77°17W 82 D7
Canandaigua L. U.S.A. 42°47N 77°19W 82 D7
Cananea Mexico 31°0N 110°18W 86 A2
Canarias, Is. Atl. Oc. 28°30N 16°0W 24 F4
Canaries St. Lucia 13°55N 61°4W 89 f
Canarreos, Arch. de los
  Cuba 21°35N 81°40W 88 B3
Canary Is. = Canarias, Is.
  Atl. Oc. 28°30N 16°0W 24 F4
Canaseraga U.S.A. 42°27N 77°45W 82 D7
Canatlán Mexico 24°31N 104°47W 86 C4
Canaveral, C. U.S.A. 28°27N 80°32W 85 G14
Canaveral △ U.S.A. 28°28N 80°34W 85 G14
Canavieiras Brazil 15°39S 39°0W 93 G11
Canberra Australia 35°15S 149°8E 63 F4
Canby Calif., U.S.A. 41°27N 120°52W 76 F3
Canby Minn., U.S.A. 44°43N 96°16W 80 C5
Canby Oreg., U.S.A. 45°16N 122°42W 78 E4
Cancún Mexico 21°8N 86°44W 87 C7

Candelaria Argentina 27°29S 55°44W 95 B4
Candelaria Canary Is. 28°22N 16°22W 24 F3
Candelo Australia 36°47S 149°43E 63 F4
Candi Dasa Indonesia 8°30S 115°34E 37 J18
Candia = Iraklio Greece 35°20N 25°12E 25 D7
Candle L. Canada 53°50N 105°18W 71 C7
Candlemas I. Antarctica 57°3S 26°40W 5 B1
Cando U.S.A. 48°32N 99°12W 80 A4
Canea = Chania Greece 35°30N 24°4E 25 D6
Canelones Uruguay 34°32S 56°17W 95 C4
Cañete Chile 37°50S 73°30W 94 D1
Cangas del Narcea Spain 43°10N 6°32W 21 A2
Cangshan China 34°50N 118°2E 35 G10
Canguaretama Brazil 6°20S 35°5E 93 E11
Canguçu Brazil 31°22S 52°43W 95 C5
Canguçu, Serra do
  Brazil 31°20S 52°40W 95 C5
Cangzhou China 38°19N 116°52E 34 E9
Caniapiscau → Canada 56°40N 69°30W 73 A6
Caniapiscau, L. Canada 54°10N 69°55W 73 B6
Canicattì Italy 37°21N 13°51E 22 F5
Canim Lake Canada 51°47N 120°54W 70 C4
Canindeyu □ Paraguay 24°10S 55°0W 95 A5
Canisteo U.S.A. 42°16N 77°36W 82 D7
Canisteo → U.S.A. 42°7N 77°8W 82 D7
Cañitas de Felipe Pescador
  Mexico 23°36N 102°43W 86 C4
Çankırı Turkey 40°40N 33°37E 19 F5
Cankuzo Burundi 3°10S 30°31E 54 C3
Canmore Canada 51°7N 115°18W 70 C5
Cann River Australia 37°35S 149°7E 63 F4
Canna U.K. 57°3N 6°33W 11 D2
Cannanore India 11°53N 75°27E 40 P9
Cannes France 43°32N 7°1E 20 E7
Canning Town = Port Canning
  India 22°23N 88°40E 43 H13
Cannington Canada 44°20N 79°2W 82 B5
Cannock U.K. 52°41N 2°1W 13 E5
Cannonball → U.S.A. 46°26N 100°35W 80 B3
Cannondale Mt.
  Australia 25°13S 148°57E 62 D4
Cannonsville Res. U.S.A. 42°4N 75°22W 83 D9
Cannonvale Australia 20°17S 148°43E 62 b
Canoas Brazil 29°56S 51°11W 95 B5
Canoe L. Canada 55°10N 108°15W 71 B7
Cañon City U.S.A. 38°27N 105°14W 76 G11
Cañón de Río Blanco △
  Mexico 18°43N 97°15W 87 D5
Cañón del Sumidero △
  Mexico 19°22N 96°24W 87 D5
Canonniers Pt. Mauritius 20°2S 57°32E 53 d
Canora Canada 51°40N 102°30W 71 C8
Canowindra Australia 33°35S 148°38E 63 E4
Canso Canada 45°20N 61°0W 73 C7
Cantabria □ Spain 43°10N 4°0W 21 A4
Cantabrian Mts. = Cantábrica,
  Cordillera Spain 43°0N 5°10W 21 A3
Cantábrica, Cordillera
  Spain 43°0N 5°10W 21 A3
Cantal, Plomb du France 45°3N 2°45E 20 D5
Canterbury Australia 38°14S 141°53E 62 D3
Canterbury U.K. 51°16N 1°6E 13 F9
Canterbury Bight N.Z. 44°16S 171°55E 59 F3
Canterbury Plains N.Z. 43°55S 171°22E 59 E3
Cantil U.S.A. 35°18N 117°58W 79 K9
Canton = Guangzhou
  China 23°6N 113°13E 33 G11
Canton Ga., U.S.A. 34°14N 84°29W 85 D12
Canton Ill., U.S.A. 40°33N 90°2W 80 E8
Canton Miss., U.S.A. 32°37N 90°2W 85 E9
Canton Mo., U.S.A. 40°8N 91°32W 80 E8
Canton N.Y., U.S.A. 44°36N 75°10W 83 B9
Canton Ohio, U.S.A. 40°48N 81°23W 82 F3
Canton Pa., U.S.A. 41°39N 76°51W 83 E8
Canton S. Dak., U.S.A. 43°18N 96°35W 80 D5
Canton L. U.S.A. 36°6N 98°35W 84 C5
Canudos Brazil 7°13S 58°5W 92 E7
Canumã → Brazil 3°55S 59°10W 92 D7
Canutama Brazil 6°30S 64°20W 92 E6
Canutillo U.S.A. 31°55N 106°36W 84 F1
Canvey U.K. 51°31N 0°37E 13 F8
Canyon U.S.A. 34°59N 101°55W 84 D4
Canyon De Chelly △
  U.S.A. 36°10N 109°20W 77 H9
Canyonlands △ U.S.A. 38°15N 110°0W 77 G9
Canyons of the Ancients △
  U.S.A. 37°30N 108°55W 77 H9
Canyonville U.S.A. 42°56N 123°17W 76 E2
Cao Bang Vietnam 22°40N 106°15E 38 A6
Cao He → China 40°10N 124°32E 35 D13
Cao Lanh Vietnam 10°27N 105°38E 39 G5
Cao Xian China 34°50N 115°35E 34 G8
Cap-aux-Meules Canada 47°23N 61°52W 73 C7
Cap-Chat Canada 49°6N 66°40W 73 C6
Cap-de-la-Madeleine
  Canada 46°22N 72°31W 72 C5
Cap-Haïtien Haiti 19°40N 72°20W 89 C5
Cap Pt. St. Lucia 14°7N 60°57W 89 f
Capac U.S.A. 43°1N 82°56W 82 D2
Capanaparo → Venezuela 7°1N 67°7W 92 B5
Cape → Australia 20°59S 146°51E 62 C4
Cape Arid △ Australia 33°58S 123°13E 61 F3
Cape Barren I. Australia 40°25S 148°15E 63 G4
Cape Breton Highlands △
  Canada 46°50N 60°40W 73 C7
Cape Breton I. Canada 46°0N 60°30W 73 C7
Cape Charles U.S.A. 37°16N 76°1W 81 G15
Cape Coast Ghana 5°5N 1°15W 50 G5
Cape Cod △ U.S.A. 41°56N 70°6W 81 E18
Cape Coral U.S.A. 26°33N 81°57W 85 H14
Cape Crawford Australia 16°41S 135°43E 62 B2
Cape Dorset = Kinngait
  Canada 64°14N 76°32W 69 E16
Cape Fear → U.S.A. 33°53N 78°1W 85 D15
Cape Girardeau U.S.A. 37°19N 89°32W 80 G9
Cape Hatteras △
  U.S.A. 35°30N 75°28W 85 D17
Cape Hillsborough △
  Australia 20°54S 149°2E 62 b
Cape Le Grand △
  Australia 33°54S 122°26E 61 F3

Cape Lookout △
  U.S.A. 35°45N 76°25W 85 D16
Cape May U.S.A. 38°56N 74°56W 81 F16
Cape May Point U.S.A. 38°56N 74°58W 81 F16
Cape Melville △
  Australia 14°26S 144°28E 62 A3
Cape Range △ Australia 22°3S 114°0E 60 D1
Cape St. George Canada 48°28N 59°14W 73 C8
Cape Tormentine Canada 46°8N 63°47W 73 C7
Cape Town S. Africa 33°55S 18°22E 56 E2
Cape Upstart △
  Australia 19°45S 147°48E 62 B4
Cape Verde Is. ■ Atl. Oc. 16°0N 24°0W 50 b
Cape Vincent U.S.A. 44°8N 76°20W 83 B8
Cape York Peninsula
  Australia 12°0S 142°30E 62 A3
Capela Brazil 10°30S 37°0W 93 F11
Capella Australia 23°2S 148°1E 62 C4
Capesterre-Belle-Eau
  Guadeloupe 16°4N 61°36W 88 b
Capesterre-de-Marie-Galante
  Guadeloupe 15°53N 61°14W 88 b
Capim → Brazil 1°40S 47°47W 93 D9
Capitan U.S.A. 33°35N 105°35W 77 K11
Capitán Arturo Prat
  Antarctica 63°0S 61°0W 5 C17
Capitol Reef △ U.S.A. 38°15N 111°10W 77 G8
Capitola U.S.A. 36°59N 121°57W 78 J5
Capoche → Mozam. 15°35S 33°0E 55 F3
Capraia Italy 43°2N 9°50E 20 E8
Capri Italy 40°33N 14°14E 22 D6
Capricorn Coast
  Australia 23°16S 150°49E 62 C5
Capricorn Group
  Australia 23°30S 151°55E 62 C5
Capricorn Ra. Australia 23°20S 116°50E 60 D2
Caprivi □ Namibia 17°55S 22°37E 56 B3
Caprivi Strip Namibia 18°0S 23°0E 56 B3
Captains Flat Australia 35°35S 149°27E 63 F4
Capulin Volcano △
  U.S.A. 36°47N 103°58W 84 C3
Caquetá → Colombia 1°15S 69°15W 92 D5
Caracal Romania 44°8N 24°22E 17 F13
Caracas Venezuela 10°30N 66°55W 92 A5
Caracol Belize 16°45N 89°6W 88 C2
Caracol Mato Grosso do Sul,
  Brazil 22°18S 57°1W 94 A4
Caracol Piauí, Brazil 9°15S 43°22W 93 E10
Carajas Brazil 6°5S 50°23W 93 E8
Carajás, Serra dos Brazil 6°0S 51°30W 93 E8
Carangola Brazil 20°44S 42°5W 95 A7
Caransebeş Romania 45°28N 22°18E 17 F12
Caraquet Canada 47°48N 64°57W 73 C6
Caratasca, L. de
  Honduras 15°20N 83°40W 88 C3
Caratinga Brazil 19°50S 42°10W 93 G10
Caraúbas Brazil 5°43S 37°33W 93 E11
Caravaca de la Cruz Spain 38°8N 1°52W 21 C5
Caravelas Brazil 17°45S 39°15W 93 G11
Caraveli Peru 15°45S 73°25W 92 G4
Caravelle, Presqu'île de la
  Martinique 14°46N 60°48W 88 c
Caraz Peru 9°3S 77°47W 92 E3
Carazinho Brazil 28°16S 52°46W 95 B5
Carballo Spain 43°13N 8°41W 21 A1
Carberry Canada 49°50N 99°25W 71 D9
Carbó Mexico 29°42N 110°58W 86 B2
Carbón, L. del Argentina 49°35S 68°21W 96 G3
Carbonara, C. Italy 39°6N 9°31E 22 E3
Carbondale Colo.,
  U.S.A. 39°24N 107°13W 76 G10
Carbondale Ill., U.S.A. 37°44N 89°13W 80 G9
Carbondale Pa., U.S.A. 41°35N 75°30W 83 E9
Carbonear Canada 47°42N 53°13W 73 C9
Carbónia Italy 39°10N 8°30E 22 E3
Carcajou Canada 57°47N 117°6W 70 B5
Carcarana → Argentina 32°27S 60°48W 94 C3
Carcasse, C. Haiti 18°30N 74°28W 89 C5
Carcassonne France 43°13N 2°20E 20 E5
Carcross Canada 60°13N 134°45W 70 A2
Cardamon Hills India 9°30N 77°15E 40 Q10
Cardamon Mts. = Kravanh,
  Chuor Phnum
  Cambodia 12°0N 103°32E 39 G4
Cárdenas Cuba 23°0N 81°30W 88 B3
Cárdenas San Luis Potosí,
  Mexico 22°0N 99°38W 87 C5
Cárdenas Tabasco,
  Mexico 17°59N 93°22W 87 D6
Cardiff U.K. 51°29N 3°10W 13 F4
Cardiff □ U.K. 51°31N 3°12W 13 F4
Cardiff-by-the-Sea
  U.S.A. 33°1N 117°17W 79 M9
Cardigan U.K. 52°5N 4°40W 13 E3
Cardigan B. U.K. 52°30N 4°30W 13 E3
Cardinal Canada 44°47N 75°23W 83 B9
Cardona Uruguay 33°53S 57°18W 94 C4
Cardoso, Ilha do Brazil 25°8S 47°58W 95 B5
Cardston Canada 49°15N 113°20W 70 D6
Cardwell Australia 18°14S 146°2E 62 B4
Careen L. Canada 57°0N 108°11W 71 B7
Carei Romania 47°40N 22°29E 17 E12
Carey U.S.A. 43°19N 113°57W 76 E7
Carey, L. Australia 29°0S 122°15E 61 E3
Carey L. Canada 62°12N 102°55W 71 A8
Carhué Argentina 37°10S 62°50W 94 D3
Caria Turkey 37°20N 28°10E 23 F13
Cariacica Brazil 20°16S 40°25W 93 H10
Caribbean Sea W. Indies 15°0N 75°0W 89 D5
Cariboo Mts. Canada 53°0N 121°0W 70 C4
Caribou U.S.A. 46°52N 68°1W 81 B19
Caribou → Man.,
  Canada 59°20N 94°44W 71 B10
Caribou → N.W.T.,
  Canada 61°27N 125°45W 70 A3
Caribou I. Canada 47°22N 85°49W 72 C2
Caribou Is. Canada 61°55N 113°15W 70 A6
Caribou L. Man., Canada 59°21N 96°10W 71 B9
Caribou L. Ont., Canada 50°25N 89°5W 72 B2
Caribou Mts. Canada 59°12N 115°40W 70 B5

Caribou River ⌂ Canada 59°35N 96°35W 71 B9
Carichíc Mexico 27°56N 107°3W 86 B3
Carinda Australia 30°28S 147°41E 63 E4
Carinhanha Brazil 14°15S 44°46W 93 F10
Carinhanha → Brazil 14°20S 43°47W 93 F10
Carinthia = Kärnten □ Austria 46°52N 13°30E 16 E8
Caripito Venezuela 10°8N 63°6W 92 A6
Carleton, Mt. Canada 47°23N 66°53W 73 C6
Carleton Place Canada 45°8N 76°9W 83 A8
Carlin U.S.A. 40°43N 116°7W 76 F5
Carlingford L. U.K. 54°3N 6°9W 10 B5
Carlinville U.S.A. 39°17N 89°53W 80 F9
Carlisle U.K. 54°54N 2°56W 12 C5
Carlisle U.S.A. 40°12N 77°12W 82 F7
Carlisle B. Barbados 13°5N 59°37W 89 g
Carlisle I. Australia 20°49S 149°18E 62 b
Carlos Casares Argentina 35°32S 61°20W 94 D3
Carlos Tejedor Argentina 35°25S 62°25W 94 D3
Carlow Ireland 52°50N 6°56W 10 D5
Carlow □ Ireland 52°43N 6°50W 10 D5
Carlsbad Calif., U.S.A. 33°10N 117°21W 79 M9
Carlsbad N. Mex., U.S.A. 32°25N 104°14W 77 K11
Carlsbad Caverns △ U.S.A. 32°10N 104°35W 77 K11
Carluke U.K. 55°45N 3°50W 11 F5
Carlyle Canada 49°40N 102°20W 71 D8
Carmacks Canada 62°5N 136°16W 68 E4
Carman Canada 49°30N 98°0W 71 D9
Carmarthen U.K. 51°52N 4°19W 13 F3
Carmarthen B. U.K. 51°40N 4°30W 13 F3
Carmarthenshire □ U.K. 51°55N 4°13W 13 F3
Carmaux France 44°3N 2°10E 20 D5
Carmel U.S.A. 41°26N 73°41W 83 E11
Carmel-by-the-Sea U.S.A. 36°33N 121°55W 78 J5
Carmel Valley U.S.A. 36°29N 121°43W 78 J5
Carmelo Uruguay 34°0S 58°20W 94 C4
Carmen Paraguay 27°13S 56°12W 95 B4
Carmen → Mexico 30°42N 106°29W 86 A3
Carmen, I. Mexico 25°57N 111°12W 86 B2
Carmen de Patagones Argentina 40°50S 63°0W 96 E4
Carmensa Argentina 35°15S 67°40W 94 D2
Carmi Canada 49°36N 119°8W 70 D5
Carmi U.S.A. 38°5N 88°10W 80 F9
Carmichael U.S.A. 38°38N 121°19W 78 G5
Carmila Australia 21°55S 149°24E 62 C4
Carmona Costa Rica 10°0N 85°15W 88 E2
Carmona Spain 37°28N 5°42W 21 D3
Carn Ban U.K. 57°7N 4°15W 11 D4
Carn Eige U.K. 57°17N 5°8W 11 D3
Carnamah Australia 29°41S 115°53E 61 E2
Carnarvon U.S.A. 24°51S 113°42E 61 D1
Carnarvon Canada 45°3N 78°41W 82 A6
Carnarvon S. Africa 30°56S 22°8E 56 E3
Carnarvon △ Australia 24°54S 148°2E 62 C4
Carnarvon Ra. Queens., Australia 25°15S 148°30E 62 D4
Carnarvon Ra. W. Austral., Australia 25°20S 120°45E 61 E3
Carnation U.S.A. 47°39N 121°55W 78 C5
Carncastle U.K. 54°54N 5°53W 10 B6
Carndonagh Ireland 55°16N 7°15W 10 A4
Carnduff Canada 49°10N 101°50W 71 D8
Carnegie U.S.A. 40°24N 80°5W 82 F4
Carnegie, L. Australia 26°5S 122°30E 61 E3
Carnegie Ridge Pac. Oc. 1°0S 87°0W 65 H19
Carnic Alps = Karnische Alpen Europe 46°36N 13°0E 16 E7
Carniche Alpi = Karnische Alpen Europe 46°36N 13°0E 16 E7
Carnot C.A.R. 4°59N 15°56E 52 D3
Carnot, C. Australia 34°57S 135°38E 63 E2
Carnoustie U.K. 56°30N 2°42W 11 E6
Carnsore Pt. Ireland 52°10N 6°22W 10 D5
Caro U.S.A. 43°29N 83°24W 81 D12
Caroga Lake U.S.A. 43°8N 74°28W 83 C10
Carol City U.S.A. 25°56N 80°14W 85 J14
Carolina Brazil 7°10S 47°30W 93 E9
Carolina Puerto Rico 18°23N 65°58W 89 d
Carolina S. Africa 26°5S 30°6E 57 D5
Caroline I. Kiribati 9°58S 150°13W 65 H12
Caroline Is. Micronesia 8°0N 150°0E 64 G6
Caroni Trin. & Tob. 10°34N 61°23W 93 K15
Caroní → Venezuela 8°21N 62°43W 92 B6
Caronie = Nébrodi, Monti Italy 37°54N 14°35E 22 F6
Caroona Australia 31°24S 150°26E 63 E5
Carpathians Europe 49°30N 21°0E 17 D11
Carpaţii Meridionali Romania 45°30N 25°0E 17 F13
Carpentaria, G. of Australia 14°0S 139°0E 62 A2
Carpentras France 44°3N 5°2E 20 D6
Carpi Italy 44°47N 10°53E 22 B4
Carpinteria U.S.A. 34°24N 119°31W 79 L7
Carr Boyd Ra. Australia 16°15S 128°35E 60 C4
Carra, L. Ireland 53°41N 9°14W 10 C2
Carrabelle U.S.A. 29°51N 84°40W 85 G12
Carraig Mhachaire Rois = Carrickmacross Ireland 53°59N 6°43W 10 C5
Carraig na Siúire = Carrick-on-Suir Ireland 52°21N 7°24W 10 D4
Carranya ◎ Australia 19°13S 127°46E 60 C4
Carranza, Presa V. Mexico 27°20N 100°50W 86 B4
Carrara Italy 44°5N 10°6E 20 D9
Carrauntoohill Ireland 52°0N 9°45W 10 D2
Carrick-on-Shannon Ireland 53°57N 8°5W 10 C3
Carrick-on-Suir Ireland 52°21N 7°24W 10 D4
Carrickfergus U.K. 54°43N 5°49W 10 B6
Carrickmacross Ireland 53°59N 6°43W 10 C5
Carrieton Australia 32°25S 138°31E 63 E2
Carrillo Mexico 26°54N 103°55W 86 B4
Carrington U.S.A. 47°27N 99°8W 80 B4

Carrizal Bajo Chile 28°5S 71°20W 94 B1
Carrizalillo Chile 29°5S 71°30W 94 B1
Carrizo Cr. → U.S.A. 36°55N 103°55W 77 H12
Carrizo Plain △ U.S.A. 35°11N 119°47W 78 K7
Carrizo Springs U.S.A. 28°31N 99°52W 84 G5
Carrizozo U.S.A. 33°38N 105°53W 77 K11
Carroll U.S.A. 42°4N 94°52W 80 D6
Carrollton Ga., U.S.A. 33°35N 85°5W 85 E12
Carrollton Ill., U.S.A. 39°18N 90°24W 80 F8
Carrollton Ky., U.S.A. 38°41N 85°11W 81 F11
Carrollton Mo., U.S.A. 39°22N 93°30W 80 F7
Carrollton Ohio, U.S.A. 40°34N 81°5W 82 F3
Carron → U.K. 57°53N 4°22W 11 D4
Carron, L. U.K. 57°22N 5°35W 11 D3
Carrot → Canada 53°50N 101°17W 71 C8
Carrot River Canada 53°17N 103°35W 71 C8
Carruthers Canada 52°52N 109°16W 71 C7
Carson Calif., U.S.A. 33°49N 118°16W 79 M8
Carson N. Dak., U.S.A. 46°25N 101°34W 80 B3
Carson → U.S.A. 39°45N 118°40W 78 F8
Carson City U.S.A. 39°10N 119°46W 78 F7
Carson Sink U.S.A. 39°50N 118°25W 76 G4
Cartagena Colombia 10°25N 75°33W 92 A3
Cartagena Spain 37°38N 0°59W 21 D5
Cartago Colombia 4°45N 75°55W 92 C3
Cartago Costa Rica 9°50N 83°55W 88 E3
Cartersville U.S.A. 34°10N 84°48W 85 D12
Carterton N.Z. 41°2S 175°31E 59 D5
Carthage Tunisia 36°52N 10°20E 22 F4
Carthage Ill., U.S.A. 40°25N 91°8W 80 E8
Carthage Mo., U.S.A. 37°11N 94°19W 80 G6
Carthage N.Y., U.S.A. 43°59N 75°37W 81 D16
Carthage Tex., U.S.A. 32°9N 94°20W 84 E7
Cartier I. Australia 12°31S 123°29E 60 B3
Cartwright Canada 53°41N 56°58W 73 B8
Caruaru Brazil 8°15S 35°55W 93 E11
Carúpano Venezuela 10°39N 63°15W 92 A6
Caruthersville U.S.A. 36°11N 89°39W 80 G9
Carvoeiro Brazil 1°30S 61°59W 92 D6
Carvoeiro, C. Portugal 39°21N 9°24W 21 C1
Cary U.S.A. 35°47N 78°46W 85 D15
Casa de Piedra Argentina 38°5S 67°32W 94 D2
Casa de Piedra, Embalse Argentina 38°5S 67°32W 94 D2
Casa Grande U.S.A. 32°53N 111°45W 77 K8
Casa Nova Brazil 9°25S 41°5W 93 E10
Casablanca Chile 33°20S 71°25W 94 C1
Casablanca Morocco 33°36N 7°36W 50 B4
Cascada de Basaseachic △ Mexico 28°9N 108°15W 86 B3
Cascade Seychelles 4°39S 55°29E 53 b
Cascade Idaho, U.S.A. 44°31N 116°2W 76 D5
Cascade Mont., U.S.A. 47°16N 111°42W 76 C8
Cascade Locks U.S.A. 45°40N 121°54W 78 E5
Cascade Ra. U.S.A. 47°0N 121°30W 78 D5
Cascade Res. U.S.A. 44°32N 116°3W 76 D5
Cascades, Pte. des Réunion 21°9S 55°51E 53 c
Cascais Portugal 38°41N 9°25W 21 C1
Cascavel Brazil 24°57S 53°28W 95 A5
Cáscina Italy 43°41N 10°33E 22 C4
Casco B. U.S.A. 43°45N 70°0W 81 D18
Caserta Italy 41°4N 14°20E 22 D6
Casey Antarctica 66°0S 76°0E 5 C8
Caseyr, Raas = Asir, Ras Somali Rep. 11°55N 51°10E 47 E5
Cashel Ireland 52°30N 7°53W 10 D4
Casiguran Phil. 16°22N 122°7E 37 A6
Casilda Argentina 33°10S 61°10W 94 C3
Casino Australia 28°52S 153°3E 63 D5
Casiquiare → Venezuela 2°1N 67°7W 92 C5
Casma Peru 9°30S 78°20W 92 E3
Casmalia U.S.A. 34°50N 120°32W 79 L6
Caspe Spain 41°14N 0°1W 21 B5
Casper U.S.A. 42°51N 106°19W 76 E10
Caspian Depression Eurasia 47°0N 48°0E 19 E8
Caspian Sea Eurasia 43°0N 50°0E 19 F9
Cass City U.S.A. 43°36N 83°10W 82 C1
Cass Lake U.S.A. 47°23N 94°37W 80 B6
Cassadaga U.S.A. 42°20N 79°19W 82 D5
Casselman Canada 45°19N 75°5W 83 A9
Casselton U.S.A. 46°54N 97°13W 80 B5
Cassiar Mts. Canada 59°30N 130°30W 70 B2
Cassino Italy 41°30N 13°49E 22 D5
Cassville U.S.A. 36°41N 93°52W 80 G7
Castaic U.S.A. 34°30N 118°38W 79 L8
Castalia U.S.A. 41°24N 82°49W 82 E2
Castanhal Brazil 1°18S 47°55W 93 D9
Castara Trin. & Tob. 11°17N 60°42W 93 J16
Castellammare di Stábia Italy 40°42N 14°29E 22 D6
Castelli Argentina 36°7S 57°47W 94 D4
Castelló de la Plana Spain 39°58N 0°3W 21 C5
Castelo Brazil 20°33S 41°14W 95 A7
Castelo Branco Portugal 39°50N 7°31W 21 C2
Castelsarrasin France 44°2N 1°7E 20 E4
Castelvetrano Italy 37°41N 12°47E 22 F5
Casterton Australia 37°30S 141°30E 63 F3
Castile U.S.A. 42°38N 78°3W 82 D6
Castilla-La Mancha □ Spain 39°30N 3°30W 21 C4
Castilla y Leon □ Spain 42°0N 5°0W 21 B3
Castillos Uruguay 34°12S 53°52W 95 C5
Castle Dale U.S.A. 39°13N 111°1W 76 G8
Castle Douglas U.K. 54°56N 3°56W 11 G5
Castle Rock Colo., U.S.A. 39°22N 104°51W 76 G11
Castle Rock Wash., U.S.A. 46°17N 122°54W 78 D4
Castlebar Ireland 53°52N 9°18W 10 C2
Castlebay U.K. 56°57N 7°31W 11 E1
Castleblaney Ireland 54°7N 6°44W 10 B5
Castlederg U.K. 54°42N 7°35W 10 B4
Castleford U.K. 53°43N 1°21W 12 D6
Castlegar Canada 49°20N 117°40W 70 D5
Castlemaine Australia 37°2S 144°12E 63 F3
Castlemaine Ireland 52°10N 9°42W 10 D2
Castlepollard Ireland 53°41N 7°19W 10 C4
Castlerea Ireland 53°46N 8°29W 10 C3
Castlereagh → Australia 30°12S 147°32E 63 E4

Castlereagh B. Australia 12°10S 135°10E 62 A2
Castleton U.S.A. 43°37N 73°11W 83 C11
Castleton-on-Hudson U.S.A. 42°31N 73°45W 83 D11
Castletown I. of Man 54°5N 4°38W 12 C3
Castletown Bearhaven Ireland 51°39N 9°55W 10 E2
Castor Canada 52°15N 111°50W 70 C6
Castor → Canada 53°24N 78°58W 72 B4
Castorland U.S.A. 43°53N 75°31W 83 C9
Castres France 43°37N 2°13E 20 E5
Castricum Neths. 52°33N 4°40E 15 B4
Castries St. Lucia 14°2N 60°58W 89 f
Castro Brazil 24°45S 50°0W 95 A6
Castro Chile 42°30S 73°50W 96 E2
Castro Alves Brazil 12°46S 39°33W 93 F11
Castro Valley U.S.A. 37°41N 122°5W 78 H4
Castroville U.S.A. 36°46N 121°45W 78 J5
Castuera Spain 38°43N 5°37W 21 C3
Cat Ba, Dao Vietnam 20°50N 107°0E 38 B6
Cat Ba △ Vietnam 20°47N 107°3E 38 B6
Cat I. Bahamas 24°30N 75°30W 89 B4
Cat L. Canada 51°40N 91°50W 72 B1
Cat Lake Canada 51°40N 91°50W 72 B1
Cat Tien △ Vietnam 11°25N 107°17E 39 G6
Catacamas Honduras 14°54N 85°56W 88 D2
Cataguases Brazil 21°23S 42°39W 95 A7
Cataló Brazil 18°10S 47°57W 93 G9
Çatalca Turkey 41°8N 28°27E 23 D13
Catalina Canada 48°31N 53°4W 73 C9
Catalina Chile 25°13S 69°43W 94 B2
Catalina U.S.A. 32°30N 110°50W 77 K8
Catalonia = Cataluña □ Spain 41°40N 1°15E 21 B6
Cataluña □ Spain 41°40N 1°15E 21 B6
Catamarca Argentina 28°30S 65°50W 94 B2
Catamarca □ Argentina 27°0S 65°50W 94 B2
Catanduanes □ Phil. 13°50N 124°20E 37 B6
Catanduva Brazil 21°5S 48°58W 95 A6
Catánia Italy 37°30N 15°6E 22 F6
Catanzaro Italy 38°54N 16°35E 22 E7
Cataman Phil. 12°28N 124°35E 37 B6
Catatumbo-Bari △ Colombia 9°3N 73°12W 89 E5
Catchacoma Canada 44°44N 78°19W 82 B6
Cateel Phil. 7°47N 126°24E 37 C7
Catembe Mozam. 26°0S 32°33E 57 D5
Caterham U.K. 51°15N 0°4W 13 F7
Cathair na Mart = Westport Ireland 53°48N 9°31W 10 C2
Cathair Saidhbhín = Cahersiveen Ireland 51°56N 10°14W 10 E1
Cathart S. Africa 32°18S 27°10E 56 E4
Cathedral City U.S.A. 33°47N 116°28W 79 M10
Cathlamet U.S.A. 46°12N 123°23W 78 D3
Catlettsburg U.S.A. 38°25N 82°36W 81 F12
Catoche, C. Mexico 21°35N 87°5W 87 C7
Catriló Argentina 36°26S 63°24W 94 D3
Catrimani Brazil 0°27N 61°41W 92 C6
Catrimani → Brazil 0°28N 61°44W 92 C6
Catskill U.S.A. 42°14N 73°52W 83 D11
Catskill Mts. U.S.A. 42°10N 74°25W 83 D10
Catt, Mt. Australia 13°49S 134°23E 62 A1
Cattaraugus U.S.A. 42°20N 78°52W 82 D6
Catterick U.K. 54°23N 1°37W 12 C6
Catuala Angola 16°25S 19°2E 56 B2
Catuane Mozam. 26°48S 32°18E 57 D5
Catur Mozam. 13°45S 35°30E 55 E4
Caubvick, Mt. = Iberville, Mt. d' Canada 58°50N 63°50W 69 F19
Cauca → Colombia 8°54N 74°28W 92 B4
Caucaia Brazil 3°40S 38°35W 93 D11
Caucasus Mountains Eurasia 42°50N 44°0E 19 F7
Caucete Argentina 31°38S 68°20W 94 C2
Cauese Mts. Mozam. 15°14S 30°33E 55 F3
Caungula Angola 8°26S 18°38E 52 F3
Cauquenes Chile 36°0S 72°22W 94 D1
Caura → Venezuela 7°38N 64°53W 92 B6
Cauresi → Mozam. 17°8S 33°0E 55 F3
Causapscal Canada 48°19N 67°12W 73 C6
Cauvery → India 11°9N 78°52E 40 P11
Caux, Pays de France 49°38N 0°35E 20 B4
Cavalier U.S.A. 48°48N 97°37W 80 A5
Cavan Ireland 54°0N 7°22W 10 B4
Cavan □ Ireland 54°1N 7°16W 10 C4
Cave Creek U.S.A. 33°50N 111°57W 77 K8
Cavenagh Ra. Australia 26°12S 127°55E 61 E4
Cavendish Australia 37°31S 142°2E 63 F3
Caviana, I. Brazil 0°10N 50°10W 93 C8
Cavite Phil. 14°29N 120°54E 37 B6
Cawndilla L. Australia 32°30S 142°15E 63 E3
Cawnpore = Kanpur India 26°28N 80°20E 43 F9
Caxias Brazil 4°55S 43°20W 93 D10
Caxias do Sul Brazil 29°10S 51°10W 95 B5
Cay Sal Bank Bahamas 23°45N 80°0W 88 B4
Cayambe Ecuador 0°3N 78°8W 92 C3
Cayenne Fr. Guiana 5°5N 52°18W 93 B8
Cayey Puerto Rico 18°7N 66°10W 89 d
Cayman Brac Cayman Is. 19°43N 79°49W 88 C4
Cayman Is. ☑ W. Indies 19°40N 80°30W 88 C3
Cayman Trench Caribbean 17°0N 83°0W 66 H11
Cayuga Canada 42°59N 79°50W 82 D5
Cayuga U.S.A. 42°27N 76°44W 83 D8
Cayuga Heights U.S.A. 42°27N 76°29W 83 D8
Cayuga L. U.S.A. 42°41N 76°41W 83 D8
Cazenovia U.S.A. 42°56N 75°51W 83 D9
Cazombo Angola 11°54S 22°56E 53 G4
Ceanannus Mor Ireland 53°44N 6°53W 10 C5
Ceará = Fortaleza Brazil 3°45S 38°35W 93 D11
Ceará □ Brazil 5°0S 40°0W 93 E11
Ceará-Mirim Brazil 5°38S 35°25W 93 E11
Ceatharlach = Carlow Ireland 52°50N 6°56W 10 D5
Cébaco, I. de Panama 7°33N 81°9W 88 E3
Cebollar Argentina 29°10S 66°35W 94 B2

Cebu Phil. 10°18N 123°54E 37 B6
Cecil Plains Australia 27°30S 151°11E 63 D5
Cedar → U.S.A. 41°17N 91°21W 80 E8
Cedar City U.S.A. 37°41N 113°4W 77 H7
Cedar Creek Res. U.S.A. 32°11N 96°4W 84 E6
Cedar Falls Iowa, U.S.A. 42°32N 92°27W 80 D7
Cedar Falls Wash., U.S.A. 47°25N 121°45W 78 C5
Cedar Key U.S.A. 29°8N 83°2W 85 G13
Cedar L. Canada 53°10N 100°0W 71 C9
Cedar Park U.S.A. 30°30N 97°49W 84 F6
Cedar Rapids U.S.A. 41°59N 91°40W 80 E8
Cedartown U.S.A. 34°1N 85°15W 85 D12
Cedarvale Canada 55°1N 128°22W 70 B3
Cedarville S. Africa 30°23S 29°3E 57 E4
Cedarville U.S.A. 41°32N 120°10W 76 F3
Cedral Mexico 23°50N 100°45W 86 C4
Cedro Brazil 6°34S 39°3W 93 E11
Cedros, I. Mexico 28°12N 115°15W 86 B1
Cedros B. Trin. & Tob. 10°16N 61°54W 93 K15
Ceduna Australia 32°7S 133°46E 63 E1
Ceel Gaal Somali Rep. 10°58N 50°20E 47 E5
Ceel Waaq Kenya 2°49N 40°56E 52 D8
Ceelbuur Somali Rep. 4°35N 46°39E 47 G4
Ceerigaabo Somali Rep. 10°35N 47°20E 47 E4
Cefalù Italy 38°2N 14°1E 22 E6
Cegléd Hungary 47°11N 19°47E 17 E10
Cekik Indonesia 8°12S 114°27E 37 J17
Celaque △ Honduras 14°30N 88°43W 88 D2
Celaya Mexico 20°31N 100°37W 86 C4
Celebes = Sulawesi Indonesia 2°0S 120°0E 37 E6
Celebes Sea Indonesia 3°0N 123°0E 37 D6
Celina U.S.A. 40°33N 84°35W 81 E11
Celje Slovenia 46°16N 15°18E 16 E8
Celle Germany 52°37N 10°4E 16 B6
Celtic Sea Atl. Oc. 50°9N 9°34W 14 F2
Cenderwasih, Teluk Indonesia 3°0S 135°20E 37 E9
Center N. Dak., U.S.A. 47°7N 101°18W 80 B3
Center Tex., U.S.A. 31°48N 94°11W 84 F7
Centerburg U.S.A. 40°18N 82°42W 82 F2
Centerville Calif., U.S.A. 36°44N 119°30W 78 J7
Centerville Iowa, U.S.A. 40°44N 92°52W 80 E7
Centerville Pa., U.S.A. 40°3N 79°59W 82 F5
Centerville Tenn., U.S.A. 35°47N 87°28W 85 D11
Centerville Tex., U.S.A. 31°16N 95°59W 84 F7
Central = Tsentralnyy □ Russia 52°0N 40°0E 28 D4
Central □ Kenya 0°30S 37°30E 54 C4
Central □ Malawi 13°30S 33°30E 55 E3
Central □ Zambia 14°25S 28°50E 55 E2
Central, Cordillera Colombia 5°0N 75°0W 92 C4
Central, Cordillera Costa Rica 10°10N 84°5W 88 D3
Central, Cordillera Dom. Rep. 19°15N 71°0W 89 C5
Central, Cordillera Puerto Rico 18°8N 66°35W 89 d
Central African Rep. ■ Africa 7°0N 20°0E 51 G9
Central America America 12°0N 85°0W 66 H11
Central Australia ◎ Australia 22°30S 128°30E 60 D4
Central Bedfordshire □ U.K. 52°5N 0°20W 13 E7
Central Butte Canada 50°48N 106°31W 71 C7
Central City Colo., U.S.A. 39°48N 105°31W 76 G11
Central City Ky., U.S.A. 37°18N 87°7W 80 G10
Central City Nebr., U.S.A. 41°7N 98°0W 80 E4
Central Desert ◎ Australia 19°56S 130°46E 60 C5
Central I. Kenya 3°30N 36°0E 54 B4
Central Island △ Kenya 2°33N 36°1E 54 B4
Central Kalahari ⌂ Botswana 22°36S 23°58E 56 C3
Central Makran Range Pakistan 26°30N 64°15E 40 F4
Central Pacific Basin Pac. Oc. 8°0N 175°0W 64 G10
Central Patricia Canada 51°30N 90°9W 72 B1
Central Point U.S.A. 42°23N 122°55W 76 E2
Central Russian Uplands Europe 54°0N 36°0E 6 E13
Central Siberian Plateau Russia 65°0N 105°0E 26 B12
Central Square U.S.A. 43°17N 76°9W 83 C8
Centralia Canada 43°17N 81°28W 82 C3
Centralia Ill., U.S.A. 38°32N 89°8W 80 F9
Centralia Mo., U.S.A. 39°13N 92°8W 80 F7
Centralia Wash., U.S.A. 46°43N 122°58W 78 D4
Centre de Flacq Mauritius 20°12S 57°43E 53 d
Centreville N.Y., U.S.A. 42°28N 78°14W 82 D6
Centreville Pa., U.S.A. 41°44N 79°45W 82 E5
Cephalonia = Kefalonia Greece 38°15N 20°30E 23 E9
Cepu Indonesia 7°9S 111°35E 37 G14
Ceram = Seram Indonesia 3°10S 129°0E 37 E7
Ceram Sea = Seram Sea Indonesia 2°30S 128°30E 37 E7
Ceredigion □ U.K. 52°16N 4°15W 13 E3
Ceres Argentina 29°55S 61°55W 94 B3
Ceres S. Africa 33°21S 19°18E 56 E2
Ceres U.S.A. 37°35N 120°57W 78 H6
Cerf Seychelles 4°38S 55°40E 53 b
Cerignola Italy 41°17N 15°53E 22 D6
Cerigo = Kythira Greece 36°8N 23°0E 23 F10
Çerkezköy Turkey 41°17N 28°0E 23 D12
Cerralvo, I. Mexico 24°15N 109°55W 86 C3
Cerritos Mexico 22°25N 100°16W 86 C4
Cerro Chato Uruguay 33°6S 55°8W 95 C4
Cerro Cofre de Perote △ Mexico 19°29N 97°8W 87 D5
Cerro Corá □ Paraguay 22°35S 56°5W 95 A4
Cerro de Pasco Peru 10°45S 76°10W 92 F3
Cerro el Copey △ Venezuela 10°59N 63°53W 89 D7
Cerro Hoya △ Panama 7°7N 80°45W 88 E3

Cerro Saroche △ Venezuela 10°8N 69°38W 89 D6
Cerventes Australia 30°31S 115°3E 61 F2
Cervera Spain 41°40N 1°16E 21 B6
Cesena Italy 44°8N 12°15E 22 B5
Cēsis Latvia 57°18N 25°15E 9 H21
Česká Rep. = Czech Rep. ■ Europe 50°0N 15°0E 16 D8
České Budějovice Czech Rep. 48°55N 14°25E 16 D8
Českomoravská Vrchovina Czech Rep. 49°30N 15°40E 16 D8
Çeşme Turkey 38°20N 26°23E 23 E12
Cessnock Australia 32°50S 151°21E 63 E5
Cetinje Montenegro 42°23N 18°59E 23 C8
Cetraro Italy 39°31N 15°55E 22 E6
Ceuta N. Afr. 35°52N 5°18W 21 E3
Cévennes France 44°10N 3°50E 20 D5
Ceyhan Turkey 37°4N 35°47E 44 B2
Ceylanpınar Turkey 36°50N 40°2E 44 B4
Ceylon = Sri Lanka ■ Asia 7°30N 80°50E 40 R12
Cha-am Thailand 12°48N 99°58E 38 F2
Chacabuco Argentina 34°40S 60°27W 94 C3
Chachapoyas Peru 6°15S 77°50W 92 E3
Chachoengsao Thailand 13°42N 101°5E 38 F3
Chachran Pakistan 28°55N 70°30E 42 E4
Chachro Pakistan 25°5N 70°15E 42 G4
Chaco □ Argentina 26°30S 61°0W 94 B3
Chaco □ Paraguay 26°0S 60°0W 94 B3
Chaco → U.S.A. 36°46N 108°39W 77 H9
Chaco Austral S. Amer. 27°0S 61°30W 96 B4
Chaco Boreal S. Amer. 22°0S 60°0W 92 H6
Chaco Central S. Amer. 24°0S 61°0W 96 A4
Chaco Culture △ U.S.A. 36°3N 107°58W 77 H10
Chacon, C. U.S.A. 54°42N 132°0W 70 C2
Chad ■ Africa 15°0N 17°15E 51 F8
Chad, L. = Tchad, L. Chad 13°30N 14°30E 51 F8
Chadileuvú → Argentina 37°46S 66°0W 94 D2
Chadiza Zambia 14°45S 32°27E 55 E3
Chadron U.S.A. 42°50N 103°0W 80 D2
Chadyr-Lunga = Ciadâr-Lunga Moldova 46°3N 28°51E 17 E15
Chae Hom Thailand 18°43N 99°35E 38 C2
Chae Son △ Thailand 18°42N 99°20E 38 C2
Chaem → Thailand 18°11N 98°38E 38 C2
Chaeryŏng N. Korea 38°24N 125°36E 35 E13
Chagai Hills = Chāh Gay Hills Afghan. 29°30N 64°0E 40 E3
Chagda Russia 58°45N 130°38E 29 D14
Chaghcharān Afghan. 34°31N 65°15E 40 B4
Chagos Arch. ☑ Ind. Oc. 6°0S 72°0E 27 J9
Chagres △ Panama 9°33N 79°37W 88 E4
Chaguanas Trin. & Tob. 10°30N 61°26W 93 K15
Chāh Ākhvor Iran 32°41N 59°40E 45 C8
Chāh Bahar Iran 25°20N 60°40E 45 E9
Chāh-e Kavīr Iran 34°29N 56°52E 45 C8
Chāh Gay Hills Afghan. 29°30N 64°0E 40 E3
Chāhār Borjak Afghan. 30°17N 62°3E 40 D3
Chahār Mahāll va Bakhtiārī □ Iran 32°0N 49°0E 45 C6
Chai Badan Thailand 15°12N 101°8E 38 E3
Chaibasa India 22°42N 85°49E 43 H11
Chainat Thailand 15°11N 100°8E 38 E3
Chaiya Thailand 9°23N 99°14E 39 H2
Chaiyaphum Thailand 15°48N 102°2E 38 E4
Chaj Doab Pakistan 32°15N 73°0E 42 C5
Chajari Argentina 30°42S 58°0W 94 C4
Chak Amru Pakistan 32°22N 75°11E 42 C6
Chakar → Pakistan 29°29N 68°2E 42 E3
Chakari Zimbabwe 18°5S 29°51E 57 B4
Chake Chake Tanzania 5°15S 39°45E 54 D4
Chakhānsūr Afghan. 31°10N 62°0E 40 D3
Chakradharpur India 22°45N 85°40E 43 H11
Chakrata India 30°42N 77°51E 42 D7
Chakwal Pakistan 32°56N 72°53E 42 C5
Chala Peru 15°48S 74°20W 92 G4
Chalchihuites Mexico 23°29N 103°53W 86 C4
Chalcis = Chalkida Greece 38°27N 23°42E 23 E10
Chaleur B. Canada 47°55N 65°30W 73 C6
Chalfant U.S.A. 37°32N 118°21W 78 H8
Chalhuanca Peru 14°15S 73°15W 92 F4
Chalisgaon India 20°30N 75°10E 40 J9
Chalk River Canada 46°1N 77°27W 72 C4
Chalkida Greece 38°27N 23°42E 23 E10
Chalky Inlet N.Z. 46°3S 166°31E 59 G1
Challapata Bolivia 18°53S 66°50W 92 G5
Challenger Deep Pac. Oc. 11°30N 142°0E 64 F6
Challenger Fracture Zone Pac. Oc. 35°0S 105°0W 65 L17
Challis U.S.A. 44°30N 114°14W 76 D6
Chalmette U.S.A. 29°56N 89°57W 85 G10
Chaloem Rattanakosin △ Thailand 14°40N 99°17E 38 E2
Chalon-sur-Saône France 46°48N 4°50E 20 C6
Chalong Thailand 7°50N 98°22E 39 a
Châlons-en-Champagne France 48°58N 4°20E 20 B6
Chálten, Cerro = Fitz Roy, Cerro Argentina 49°17S 73°5W 96 F2
Chālūs Iran 36°38N 51°26E 45 B6
Cham, Cu Lao Vietnam 15°57N 108°30E 38 E7
Chamaicó Argentina 35°3S 64°58W 94 D3
Chaman Pakistan 30°58N 66°25E 40 D5
Chamba India 32°35N 76°10E 42 C7
Chamba Tanzania 11°37S 37°0E 55 E4
Chambal → India 26°29N 79°15E 43 F8
Chamberlain Australia 15°30S 127°54E 60 C4
Chamberlain U.S.A. 43°49N 99°20W 80 D4
Chamberlain L. U.S.A. 46°14N 69°19W 81 B19
Chambersburg U.S.A. 39°56N 77°40W 81 F15
Chambéry France 45°34N 5°55E 20 D6

Chambeshi → Zambia 11°53S 29°48E 52 G6
Chambly Canada 45°27N 73°17W 83 A11
Chambord Canada 48°25N 72°6W 73 C5
Chamchamal Iraq 35°32N 44°50E 44 C5
Chamela Mexico 19°32N 105°5W 86 D3
Chamical Argentina 30°22S 66°27W 94 C2
Chamkar Luong
  Cambodia 11°0N 103°45E 39 G4
Chamoli India 30°24N 79°21E 43 D8
Chamonix-Mont Blanc
  France 45°55N 6°51E 20 D7
Chamouchouane =
  Ashuapmushuan →
  Canada 48°37N 72°20W 72 C5
Champa India 22°2N 82°43E 43 H10
Champagne Canada 60°49N 136°30W 70 A1
Champagne France 48°40N 4°20E 20 B6
Champaign U.S.A. 40°7N 88°15W 80 E9
Champassak Laos 14°53N 105°52E 38 E5
Champawat India 29°20N 80°6E 43 E9
Champdoré, L. Canada 55°55N 65°49W 73 A6
Champion U.S.A. 41°19N 80°51W 82 E4
Champlain U.S.A. 44°59N 73°27W 83 B11
Champlain, L. U.S.A. 44°40N 73°20W 83 B11
Champotón Mexico 19°21N 90°43W 87 D6
Champua India 22°5N 85°40E 43 H11
Chana Thailand 6°55N 100°44E 39 J3
Chañaral Chile 26°23S 70°40W 94 B1
Chanārān Iran 36°39N 59°6E 45 B8
Chanasma India 23°44N 72°5E 42 H5
Chancery Lane Barbados 13°3N 59°30W 89 g
Chanco Chile 35°44S 72°32W 94 D1
Chand India 21°57N 79°7E 43 J8
Chandan India 24°38N 86°40E 43 G12
Chandan Chauki India 28°33N 80°47E 43 E9
Chandannagar India 22°52N 88°24E 43 H13
Chandausi India 28°27N 78°49E 43 E8
Chandeleur Is. U.S.A. 29°55N 88°57W 85 G10
Chandeleur Sd. U.S.A. 29°55N 89°0W 85 G10
Chandigarh India 30°43N 76°47E 42 D7
Chandil India 22°58N 86°3E 43 H12
Chandler Australia 27°0S 133°19E 63 D1
Chandler Canada 48°18N 64°46W 73 C7
Chandler Ariz., U.S.A. 33°18N 111°50W 77 K8
Chandler Okla., U.S.A. 35°42N 96°53W 84 D6
Chandod India 21°59N 73°28E 42 J5
Chandpur Bangla. 23°8N 90°45E 41 H17
Chandrapur India 19°57N 79°25E 40 K11
Chānf Iran 26°38N 60°29E 45 E9
Chang Pakistan 26°59N 68°30E 42 F3
Chang, Ko Thailand 12°0N 102°23E 39 G4
Chang, Ko Thailand 9°50N 98°27E 39 H2
Ch'ang Chiang = Chang Jiang →
  China 31°48N 121°10E 33 E13
Chang Jiang → China 31°48N 121°10E 33 E13
Chang-won S. Korea 35°16N 128°37E 35 G15
Changan China 22°48N 113°48E 33 a
Changanacheri India 9°25N 76°31E 40 Q10
Changanassery = Changanacheri
  India 9°25N 76°31E 40 Q10
Changane → Mozam. 24°30S 33°30E 57 C5
Changbai China 41°25N 128°5E 35 D15
Changbai Shan China 42°20N 129°0E 35 C15
Changchiak'ou = Zhangjiakou
  China 40°48N 114°55E 34 D8
Ch'angchou = Changzhou
  China 31°47N 119°58E 33 E12
Changchun China 43°57N 125°17E 35 C13
Changchunling China 45°18N 125°27E 35 B13
Changde China 29°4N 111°35E 33 F11
Changdo-ri N. Korea 38°30N 127°40E 35 E14
Changge China 34°13N 113°46E 34 G7
Changhai = Shanghai
  China 31°15N 121°26E 33 E13
Changhua Taiwan 24°2N 120°30E 33 G13
Changhŭngni
  N. Korea 40°24N 128°19E 35 D15
Changi Singapore 1°23N 103°59E 39 d
Changi, Singapore ✈ (SIN)
  Singapore 1°23N 103°59E 39 M4
Changji China 44°1N 87°19E 32 C6
Changjiang China 19°20N 108°55E 38 C7
Changjiang Shuiku
  China 22°29N 113°27E 33 a
Changjin N. Korea 40°23N 127°15E 35 D14
Changjin-ho N. Korea 40°30N 127°15E 35 D14
Changli China 39°40N 119°13E 35 E10
Changling China 44°20N 123°58E 35 B12
Changlun Malaysia 6°25N 100°26E 39 J3
Changping China 40°14N 116°12E 34 D9
Changsha China 28°12N 113°0E 33 F11
Changshan Qundao
  China 39°11N 122°32E 35 E12
Changtu China 42°46N 124°6E 35 C13
Changuinola Panama 9°26N 82°31W 88 E3
Changwu China 35°10N 107°45E 34 G4
Changyi China 36°40N 119°30E 35 F10
Changyŏn N. Korea 38°15N 125°6E 35 E13
Changyuan China 35°15N 114°42E 34 G8
Changzhi China 36°10N 113°6E 34 F7
Changzhou China 31°47N 119°58E 33 E12
Chanhanga Angola 16°0S 14°8E 56 B1
Chania Greece 35°30N 24°4E 25 D6
Chania □ Greece 35°30N 24°0E 25 D6
Chanion, Kolpos Greece 35°33N 23°55E 25 D5
Channapatna India 12°40N 77°15E 40 N10
Channel Is. U.K. 49°19N 2°24W 13 H5
Channel Is. U.S.A. 33°40N 119°15W 79 M7
Channel Islands △
  U.S.A. 34°0N 119°24W 79 L7
Channel-Port aux Basques
  Canada 47°30N 59°9W 73 C8
Channel Tunnel Europe 51°0N 1°30E 13 F9
Channing U.S.A. 35°41N 102°20W 84 D3
Chantada Spain 42°36N 7°46W 21 A2
Chanthaburi Thailand 12°38N 102°12E 38 F4
Chantrey Inlet Canada 67°48N 96°20W 68 D12
Chao Phraya →
  Thailand 13°40N 100°31E 38 F3

Chao Phraya Lowlands
  Thailand 15°30N 100°0E 38 E3
Chaocheng China 36°4N 115°37E 34 F8
Chaoyang China 41°35N 120°22E 35 D11
Chaozhou China 23°42N 116°32E 33 G12
Chapaev Kazakhstan 50°25N 51°10E 19 D9
Chapais Canada 49°47N 74°51W 72 C5
Chapala Mozam. 15°50S 37°35E 55 F4
Chapala, L. de Mexico 20°15N 103°0W 86 C4
Chapayev =
  Kazakhstan 50°25N 51°10E 19 D9
Chapayevsk Russia 53°0N 49°40E 18 D8
Chapecó Brazil 27°14S 52°41W 95 B5
Chapel Hill U.S.A. 35°55N 79°4W 85 D15
Chapleau Canada 47°50N 83°24W 72 C3
Chaplin Canada 50°28N 106°40W 71 C7
Chaplin L. Canada 50°22N 106°36W 71 C7
Chappell U.S.A. 41°6N 102°28W 80 E2
Chapra = Chhapra
  India 25°48N 84°44E 43 G11
Chara Russia 56°54N 118°20E 29 D12
Charadai Argentina 27°35S 59°55W 94 B4
Charagua Bolivia 19°45S 63°10W 92 G6
Charakas Greece 35°1N 25°7E 25 D7
Charambirá, Punta
  Colombia 4°16N 77°32W 92 C3
Charaña Bolivia 17°30S 69°25W 92 G5
Charanwala India 27°51N 72°10E 42 F5
Charata Argentina 27°13S 61°14W 94 B3
Charcas Mexico 23°8N 101°7W 86 C4
Charcot I. Antarctica 70°0S 70°0W 5 C17
Chard U.K. 50°52N 2°58W 13 G5
Chardon U.S.A. 41°35N 81°12W 82 E3
Chardzhou = Türkmenabat
  Turkmenistan 39°6N 63°34E 45 B9
Charente → France 45°57N 1°5W 20 D3
Chari → Chad 12°58N 14°31E 51 F8
Chārīkār Afghan. 35°0N 69°10E 40 B6
Chariton U.S.A. 41°1N 93°19W 80 E7
Chariton → U.S.A. 39°19N 92°58W 80 F7
Chärjew = Türkmenabat
  Turkmenistan 39°6N 63°34E 45 B9
Charkhari India 25°24N 79°45E 43 G8
Charkhi Dadri India 28°37N 76°17E 42 E7
Charleroi Belgium 50°24N 4°27E 15 D4
Charleroi U.S.A. 40°9N 79°57W 82 F5
Charles, C. U.S.A. 37°7N 75°58W 81 G16
Charles, Peak Australia 32°52S 121°11E 61 F3
Charles City U.S.A. 43°4N 92°41W 80 D7
Charles L. Canada 62°39N 74°15W 69 E17
Charles L. Canada 59°50N 110°33W 71 B6
Charles Town U.S.A. 39°17N 77°52W 81 F15
Charlesbourg Canada 46°51N 71°16W 81 B18
Charleston Ill., U.S.A. 39°30N 88°10W 80 F9
Charleston Miss., U.S.A. 34°1N 90°4W 85 D9
Charleston Mo., U.S.A. 36°55N 89°21W 80 G9
Charleston S.C., U.S.A. 32°46N 79°56W 85 E15
Charleston W. Va.,
  U.S.A. 38°21N 81°38W 81 F13
Charleston L. Canada 44°32N 76°0W 83 B9
Charleston Peak
  U.S.A. 36°16N 115°42W 79 J11
Charlestown Ireland 53°58N 8°48W 10 C3
Charlestown S. Africa 27°26S 29°53E 57 D4
Charlestown Ind.,
  U.S.A. 38°27N 85°40W 81 F11
Charlestown N.H.,
  U.S.A. 43°14N 72°25W 83 C12
Charlestown of Aberlour
  U.K. 57°28N 3°14W 11 D5
Charleville = Rath Luirc
  Ireland 52°21N 8°40W 10 D3
Charleville Australia 26°24S 146°15E 63 D4
Charleville-Mézières
  France 49°44N 4°40E 20 B6
Charlevoix U.S.A. 45°19N 85°16W 81 C11
Charlotte Mich., U.S.A. 42°34N 84°50W 81 D11
Charlotte N.C., U.S.A. 35°13N 80°50W 85 D14
Charlotte Vt., U.S.A. 44°19N 73°16W 83 B11
Charlotte Amalie
  U.S. Virgin Is. 18°21N 64°56W 89 e
Charlotte Harbor U.S.A. 26°57N 82°4W 85 H13
Charlotte L. Canada 52°12N 125°19W 70 C3
Charlottesville U.S.A. 38°2N 78°30W 81 F14
Charlottetown Nfld. & L.,
  Canada 52°46N 56°7W 73 B8
Charlottetown P.E.I.,
  Canada 46°14N 63°8W 73 C7
Charlotteville
  Trin. & Tob. 11°20N 60°33W 93 J16
Charlton Australia 36°16S 143°24E 63 F3
Charlton I. Canada 52°0N 79°20W 72 B4
Charny Canada 46°43N 71°15W 73 C5
Charolles France 46°27N 4°16E 20 C6
Charre Mozam. 17°13S 35°10E 55 F4
Charsadda Pakistan 34°7N 71°45E 42 B4
Charters Towers
  Australia 20°5S 146°13E 62 C4
Chartres France 48°29N 1°30E 20 B4
Chascomús Argentina 35°30S 58°0W 94 D4
Chase Canada 50°50N 119°41W 70 C5
Chasefu Zambia 11°55S 33°8E 55 E3
Chashma Barrage
  Pakistan 32°27N 71°20E 42 C4
Chât Iran 37°59N 55°16E 45 B7
Châteaubriant France 47°43N 1°23W 20 C3
Chateaugay U.S.A. 44°56N 74°5W 83 B10
Chateauguay, L. Canada 56°26N 70°3W 73 A5
Châteaulin France 48°11N 4°8W 20 B1
Châteauroux France 46°50N 1°40E 20 C4
Châteaux, Pte. des
  Guadeloupe 16°15N 61°10W 88 b
Châtellerault France 46°50N 0°30E 20 C4
Chatham = Miramichi
  Canada 47°2N 65°28W 73 C6
Chatham Canada 42°24N 82°11W 82 D2
Chatham U.K. 51°22N 0°32E 13 F8
Chatham, U.S.A. 42°21N 73°36W 83 D11
Chatham Is. Pac. Oc. 44°0S 176°40W 64 M10
Chatham Rise Pac. Oc. 43°30S 180°0E 64 M10

Chatmohar Bangla. 24°15N 89°15E 43 G13
Chatra India 24°12N 84°56E 43 G11
Chatrapur India 19°22N 85°2E 41 K14
Chats, L. des Canada 45°30N 76°20W 83 A8
Chatsu India 26°36N 75°57E 42 F6
Chatsworth Canada 44°27N 80°54W 82 B4
Chatsworth Zimbabwe 19°38S 31°13E 55 F3
Chāttagām = Chittagong
  Bangla. 22°19N 91°48E 41 H17
Chattahoochee U.S.A. 30°42N 84°51W 85 F12
Chattahoochee →
  U.S.A. 30°54N 84°57W 85 F12
Chattanooga U.S.A. 35°3N 85°19W 85 D12
Chatteris U.K. 52°28N 0°2E 13 E8
Chatturat Thailand 15°40N 101°51E 38 E3
Chau Doc Vietnam 10°42N 105°7E 39 G5
Chaukan Pass Burma 27°8N 97°10E 41 F20
Chaumont France 48°7N 5°8E 20 B6
Chaumont U.S.A. 44°4N 76°8W 83 B8
Chaunskaya G. Russia 69°0N 169°0E 29 C17
Chautauqua L. U.S.A. 42°10N 79°24W 82 D5
Chauvin Canada 52°45N 110°10W 71 C6
Chaves Brazil 0°15S 49°55W 93 D9
Chaves Portugal 41°45N 7°32W 21 B2
Chawang Thailand 8°25N 99°30E 39 H2
Chaykovskiy Russia 56°47N 54°9E 18 C9
Chazy U.S.A. 44°53N 73°26W 83 B11
Cheb Czech Rep. 50°9N 12°28E 16 C7
Cheboksary Russia 56°8N 47°12E 18 C8
Cheboygan U.S.A. 45°39N 84°29W 81 C11
Chech, Erg Africa 25°0N 2°15W 50 D5
Chechenia □ Russia 43°30N 45°29E 19 F8
Checheno-Ingush Republic =
  Chechenia □ Russia 43°30N 45°29E 19 F8
Chechnya = Chechenia □
  Russia 43°30N 45°29E 19 F8
Checotah U.S.A. 35°28N 95°31W 84 D7
Chedabucto B. Canada 45°25N 61°8W 73 C7
Cheduba I. Burma 18°45N 93°40E 41 K18
Cheektowaga U.S.A. 42°54N 78°45W 82 D6
Cheepie Australia 26°33S 145°0E 63 D4
Chegdomyn Russia 51°7N 133°1E 29 D14
Chegga Mauritania 25°27N 5°40W 50 C4
Chegutu Zimbabwe 18°10S 30°14E 55 F3
Chehalis U.S.A. 46°40N 122°58W 78 D4
Chehalis → U.S.A. 46°57N 123°50W 78 D3
Cheju = Jeju S. Korea 33°31N 126°32E 35 H14
Cheju-do = Jeju-do
  S. Korea 33°29N 126°34E 35 H14
Chek Lap Kok China 22°18N 113°56E 33 a
Chekiang = Zhejiang □
  China 29°0N 120°0E 33 F13
Chela, Sa. da Angola 16°20S 13°20E 56 B1
Chelan U.S.A. 47°51N 120°1W 76 C3
Chelan, L. U.S.A. 48°11N 120°30W 76 B3
Cheleken = Hazar
  Turkmenistan 39°34N 53°16E 19 G9
Cheleken Yarymadasy
  Turkmenistan 39°30N 53°15E 45 B7
Chelforó Argentina 39°0S 66°33W 96 D3
Chelkar = Shalqar
  Kazakhstan 47°48N 59°39E 28 E6
Chelm Poland 51°8N 23°30E 17 C12
Chelmno Poland 53°20N 18°30E 17 B10
Chelmsford U.K. 51°44N 0°29E 13 F8
Chelsea Australia 38°5S 145°8E 63 F4
Chelsea U.S.A. 43°59N 72°27W 83 C12
Cheltenham U.K. 51°54N 2°4W 13 F5
Chelyabinsk Russia 55°10N 61°24E 28 D7
Chelyuskin, C. = Chelyuskin, Mys
  Russia 77°30N 103°0E 29 B11
Chelyuskin, Mys Russia 77°30N 103°0E 29 B11
Chemainus Canada 48°55N 123°42W 78 B3
Chemba Mozam. 17°9S 34°53E 53 H6
Chemin Grenier Mauritius 20°29S 57°28E 53 d
Chemnitz Germany 50°51N 12°54E 16 C7
Chemult U.S.A. 43°14N 121°47W 76 E3
Chen, Gora Russia 65°16N 141°50E 29 C15
Chenab → Pakistan 30°23N 71°2E 42 D4
Chenab Nagar Pakistan 31°45N 72°55E 42 D5
Chenango Forks U.S.A. 42°15N 75°51W 83 D9
Cheney U.S.A. 47°30N 117°35W 76 C5
Cheng Xian China 33°43N 105°42E 34 H3
Chengcheng China 35°8N 109°56E 34 G5
Chengchou = Zhengzhou
  China 34°45N 113°34E 34 G7
Chengde China 40°59N 117°58E 35 D9
Chengdu China 30°38N 104°2E 32 E9
Chenggu China 33°10N 107°21E 34 H4
Chengjiang China 24°39N 103°0E 32 D5
Chengmai China 19°50N 109°58E 38 C7
Chengshan Jiao China 37°25N 122°44E 35 F12
Ch'engtu = Chengdu
  China 30°38N 104°2E 32 E9
Chengwu China 34°58N 115°50E 34 G8
Chengyang China 36°18N 120°21E 35 F11
Chenjiagang China 34°23N 119°47E 35 G10
Chennai India 13°8N 80°19E 40 N12
Chenzhou China 25°47N 113°1E 33 F11
Cheò, Eilean a' = Skye
  U.K. 57°15N 6°10W 11 D2
Cheo Reo Vietnam 13°20N 108°25E 38 F7
Cheom Ksan Cambodia 14°13N 104°56E 38 E5
Cheonan S. Korea 36°48N 127°9E 35 F14
Cheongdo S. Korea 35°38N 128°42E 35 G15
Cheongju S. Korea 36°39N 127°27E 35 F14
Cheorwon S. Korea 38°15N 127°10E 35 E14
Chepén Peru 7°15S 79°23W 92 E3
Chepes Argentina 31°20S 66°35W 94 C2
Chepo Panama 9°10N 79°6W 88 E4
Chepstow U.K. 51°38N 2°41W 13 F5
Chequamegon B. U.S.A. 46°39N 90°51W 80 B8
Cher → France 47°21N 0°29E 20 C4
Cheraw U.S.A. 34°42N 79°53W 85 D15
Cherbourg France 49°39N 1°40W 20 B3
Cherdyn Russia 60°24N 56°29E 18 B10
Cheremkhovo Russia 53°8N 103°1E 32 A9
Cherepovets Russia 59°5N 37°55E 18 C6
Chergui, Chott ech
  Algeria 34°21N 0°25E 50 B6

Cherikov = Cherykaw
  Belarus 53°32N 31°20E 17 B16
Cherkasy Ukraine 49°27N 32°4E 19 E5
Cherkessk Russia 44°15N 42°5E 19 F7
Cherlak Russia 54°15N 74°55E 28 D8
Chernaya Russia 70°30N 89°10E 29 B9
Chernigov = Chernihiv
  Ukraine 51°28N 31°20E 18 D5
Chernigovka Russia 44°19N 132°34E 30 B6
Chernihiv Ukraine 51°28N 31°20E 18 D5
Chernivtsi Ukraine 48°15N 25°52E 17 D13
Chernobyl = Chornobyl
  Ukraine 51°20N 30°15E 17 C16
Chernogorsk Russia 53°49N 91°18E 29 D10
Chernovtsy = Chernivtsi
  Ukraine 48°15N 25°52E 17 D13
Chernyakhovsk Russia 54°36N 21°48E 9 J19
Chernysheyskiy Russia 63°0N 112°30E 29 C12
Cherokee Iowa, U.S.A. 42°45N 95°33W 80 D6
Cherokee Okla., U.S.A. 36°45N 98°21W 84 C5
Cherokee Village U.S.A. 36°18N 91°31W 84 C9
Cherokees, Grand Lake O' The
  U.S.A. 36°28N 94°55W 84 C7
Cherrapunji India 25°17N 91°47E 41 G17
Cherry Valley U.S.A. 42°48N 74°45W 83 D10
Cherskiy Russia 68°45N 161°18E 29 C17
Cherskogo Khrebet
  Russia 65°0N 143°0E 29 C15
Chersonisos Greece 35°18N 25°22E 25 D7
Chersonisos Akrotiri
  Greece 35°30N 24°10E 25 D6
Cherven Belarus 53°45N 28°28E 17 B15
Chervonohrad Ukraine 50°25N 24°10E 17 C13
Cherwell → U.K. 51°44N 1°14W 13 F6
Cherykaw Belarus 53°32N 31°20E 17 B16
Chesapeake U.S.A. 36°49N 76°16W 81 G15
Chesapeake B. U.S.A. 38°0N 76°10W 81 F14
Cheshire □ U.K. 53°14N 2°30W 12 D5
Cheshskaya Guba Russia 67°20N 47°0E 18 A8
Cheshunt U.K. 51°43N 0°1W 13 F7
Chesil Beach U.K. 50°37N 2°33W 13 G5
Chesley Canada 44°17N 81°5W 82 B3
Chester U.K. 53°12N 2°53W 12 D5
Chester Calif., U.S.A. 40°19N 121°14W 76 F3
Chester Ill., U.S.A. 37°55N 89°49W 80 G9
Chester Mont., U.S.A. 48°31N 110°58W 76 B8
Chester Pa., U.S.A. 39°51N 75°22W 81 F16
Chester S.C., U.S.A. 34°43N 81°12W 85 D14
Chester W. Va., U.S.A. 40°37N 80°34W 82 F4
Chester-le-Street U.K. 54°51N 1°34W 12 C6
Chesterfield U.K. 53°15N 1°25W 12 D6
Chesterfield, Îs. N. Cal. 19°52S 158°15E 58 C8
Chesterfield Inlet
  Canada 63°30N 90°45W 68 E13
Chesterton Ra.
  Australia 25°30S 147°27E 63 D4
Chesterton Range △
  Australia 26°16S 147°22E 63 D4
Chestertown U.S.A. 43°40N 73°48W 83 C11
Chesterville Canada 45°6N 75°14W 83 A9
Chesuncook L. U.S.A. 46°0N 69°21W 81 C19
Chéticamp Canada 46°37N 60°59W 73 C7
Chetumal Mexico 18°30N 88°20W 87 D7
Chetumal, B. de
  Cent. Amer. 18°40N 88°10W 87 D7
Chetwynd Canada 55°45N 121°36W 70 B4
Cheung Chau China 22°13N 114°1E 33 a
Cheviot, The U.K. 55°29N 2°9W 12 B5
Cheviot Hills U.K. 55°20N 2°30W 12 B5
Cheviot Ra. Australia 25°20S 143°45E 62 D3
Chew Bahir Ethiopia 4°40N 36°50E 47 G2
Chewelah U.S.A. 48°17N 117°43W 76 B5
Chewore △ Zimbabwe 16°0S 29°52E 55 F2
Cheyenne Okla., U.S.A. 35°37N 99°40W 84 D5
Cheyenne Wyo., U.S.A. 41°8N 104°49W 76 F11
Cheyenne → U.S.A. 44°41N 101°18W 80 C3
Cheyenne Wells
  U.S.A. 38°49N 102°21W 76 G12
Cheyne B. Australia 34°35S 118°50E 61 F2
Chhabra India 24°40N 76°54E 42 G7
Chhaktala India 22°6N 74°11E 42 H6
Chhapra India 25°48N 84°44E 43 G11
Chhata India 27°42N 77°30E 42 F7
Chhatarpur Jharkhand,
  India 24°23N 84°11E 43 G11
Chhatarpur Mad. P.,
  India 24°55N 79°35E 43 G8
Chhattisgarh □ India 22°0N 82°0E 43 J10
Chhep Cambodia 13°45N 105°24E 38 F5
Chhindwara Mad. P.,
  India 23°3N 79°29E 43 H8
Chhindwara Mad. P.,
  India 22°2N 78°59E 43 H8
Chhlong Cambodia 12°15N 105°58E 38 F5
Chhota Tawa → India 22°14N 76°36E 42 H7
Chhoti Kali Sindh →
  India 24°2N 75°31E 42 G6
Chhuikhadan India 21°32N 80°59E 43 J9
Chhuk Cambodia 10°46N 104°28E 39 G5
Chi → Thailand 15°11N 104°43E 38 E5
Chi Thanh Vietnam 13°17N 109°16E 38 F7
Chiai Taiwan 23°29N 120°25E 33 G13
Chiang Dao Thailand 19°22N 98°58E 38 C2
Chiang Dao, Doi
  Thailand 19°23N 98°54E 38 C2
Chiang Kham Thailand 19°32N 100°18E 38 C3
Chiang Khan Thailand 17°52N 101°36E 38 D3
Chiang Khong Thailand 20°17N 100°24E 38 B3
Chiang Mai Thailand 18°47N 98°59E 38 C2
Chiang Rai Thailand 19°52N 99°50E 38 C2
Chiang Saen Thailand 20°16N 100°5E 38 B3
Chiapa → Mexico 16°42N 93°0W 87 D6
Chiapa de Corzo Mexico 16°42N 93°0W 87 D6
Chiapas □ Mexico 16°30N 92°30W 87 D6
Chiapas, Sa. Madre de
  Mexico 15°40N 93°0W 87 D6
Chiautla de Tapia
  Mexico 18°18N 98°36W 87 D5
Chiávari Italy 44°19N 9°19E 20 D8

Chiavenna Italy 46°19N 9°24E 20 C8
Chiba Japan 35°30N 140°7E 31 G10
Chiba □ Japan 35°30N 140°20E 31 G10
Chibabava Mozam. 20°17S 33°35E 57 C5
Chibemba Cunene, Angola 15°48S 14°8E 53 H2
Chibemba Huíla, Angola 16°20S 15°20E 56 B2
Chibi Zimbabwe 20°18S 30°25E 57 C5
Chibia Angola 15°10S 13°42E 53 H2
Chibougamau Canada 49°56N 74°24W 72 C5
Chibougamau, L.
  Canada 49°50N 74°20W 72 C5
Chibuk Nigeria 10°52N 12°50E 51 F8
Chibuto Mozam. 24°40S 33°33E 57 C5
Chic-Chocs, Mts. Canada 48°55N 66°0W 73 C6
Chicacole = Srikakulam
  India 18°14N 83°58E 41 K13
Chicago U.S.A. 41°52N 87°38W 80 E9
Chicago Heights U.S.A. 41°30N 87°38W 80 E10
Chichagof I. U.S.A. 57°30N 135°30W 68 F4
Chichaoua Morocco 31°32N 8°44W 50 B4
Chichawatni Pakistan 30°32N 72°42E 42 D5
Chichén-Itzá Mexico 20°37N 88°35W 87 C7
Chicheng China 40°55N 115°55E 34 D8
Chichester U.K. 50°50N 0°47W 13 G7
Chichester Ra. Australia 22°12S 119°15E 60 D2
Chichibu Japan 35°59N 139°10E 31 F9
Chichibu-Tama-Kai △
  Japan 35°52N 138°42E 31 G9
Ch'ich'ihaerh = Qiqihar
  China 47°26N 124°0E 33 B13
Chicholi India 22°1N 77°40E 42 H8
Chickasaw △ U.S.A. 34°26N 97°0W 84 D6
Chickasha U.S.A. 35°3N 97°58W 84 D6
Chiclana de la Frontera
  Spain 36°26N 6°9W 21 D2
Chiclayo Peru 6°42S 79°50W 92 E3
Chico U.S.A. 39°44N 121°50W 78 F5
Chico → Chubut, Argentina 44°0S 67°0W 96 E3
Chico → Santa Cruz,
  Argentina 50°0S 68°30W 96 G3
Chicoa Mozam. 15°36S 32°20E 55 F3
Chicomo Mozam. 24°31S 34°6E 57 C5
Chicomostoc Mexico 22°28N 102°46W 86 C4
Chicontepec Mexico 20°58N 98°10W 87 C5
Chicopee U.S.A. 42°9N 72°37W 83 D12
Chicoutimi Canada 48°28N 71°5W 73 C5
Chicualacuala Mozam. 22°6S 31°42E 57 C5
Chidambaram India 11°20N 79°45E 40 P11
Chidenguele Mozam. 24°55S 34°11E 57 C5
Chidley, C. Canada 60°23N 64°26W 69 E19
Chiducuane Mozam. 24°35S 34°25E 57 C5
Chiede Angola 17°15S 16°22E 56 B2
Chiefs Pt. Canada 44°41N 81°18W 82 B3
Chiem Hoa Vietnam 22°12N 105°17E 38 A5
Chiemsee Germany 47°53N 12°28E 16 E7
Chiengi Zambia 8°45S 29°10E 55 D2
Chiengmai = Chiang Mai
  Thailand 18°47N 98°59E 38 C2
Chiese → Italy 45°8N 10°25E 20 D9
Chieti Italy 42°21N 14°10E 22 C6
Chifeng China 42°18N 118°58E 35 C10
Chignecto B. Canada 45°30N 64°40W 73 C7
Chiguana Bolivia 21°0S 67°58W 94 A2
Chigwell U.K. 51°37N 0°6E 13 F8
Chihli, G. of = Bo Hai
  China 39°0N 119°0E 35 E10
Chihuahua Mexico 28°38N 106°5W 86 B3
Chihuahua □ Mexico 28°30N 106°0W 86 B3
Chiili = Shieli Kazakhstan 44°20N 66°15E 28 E7
Chik Bollapur India 13°25N 77°45E 40 N10
Chikmagalur India 13°15N 75°45E 40 N9
Chikwawa Malawi 16°2S 34°50E 55 F3
Chilanga Zambia 15°33S 28°16E 55 F2
Chilapa Mexico 17°36N 99°10W 87 D5
Chilas Pakistan 35°25N 74°5E 43 B6
Chilaw Sri Lanka 7°30N 79°50E 40 R11
Chilcotin → Canada 51°44N 122°23W 70 C4
Childers Australia 25°15S 152°17E 63 D5
Childress U.S.A. 34°25N 100°13W 84 D4
Chile ■ S. Amer. 35°0S 72°0W 96 D2
Chile Rise Pac. Oc. 38°0S 92°0W 65 L18
Chilecito Argentina 29°10S 67°30W 94 B2
Chilete Peru 7°10S 78°50W 92 E3
Chililabombwe Zambia 12°18S 27°43E 55 E2
Chilim Pakistan 35°5N 75°5E 43 B6
Chilin = Jilin China 43°44N 126°30E 35 C14
Chilka L. India 19°40N 85°25E 41 K14
Chilko → Canada 52°0N 123°40W 70 C4
Chilko L. Canada 51°20N 124°10W 70 C4
Chillagoe Australia 17°7S 144°33E 62 B3
Chillán Chile 36°40S 72°10W 94 D1
Chillicothe Ill., U.S.A. 40°55N 89°29W 80 E9
Chillicothe Mo., U.S.A. 39°48N 93°33W 80 F7
Chillicothe Ohio, U.S.A. 39°20N 82°59W 81 F12
Chilliwack Canada 49°10N 121°54W 70 D4
Chilo India 27°25N 73°32E 42 F5
Chiloane, I. Mozam. 20°40S 34°55E 57 C5
Chiloé, I. de Chile 42°30S 73°50W 96 E2
Chilpancingo Mexico 17°33N 99°30W 87 D5
Chiltern Hills U.K. 51°40N 0°53W 13 F7
Chilton U.S.A. 44°2N 88°10W 80 C9
Chilubi Zambia 11°5S 29°58E 55 E2
Chilubula Zambia 10°14S 30°51E 55 E3
Chilumba Malawi 10°28S 34°12E 55 E3
Chilung Taiwan 25°3N 121°45E 33 F13
Chilwa, L. Malawi 15°15S 35°40E 55 F4
Chimaltitán Mexico 21°35N 103°50W 86 C4
Chimán Panama 8°45N 78°40E 88 E4
Chimanimani Zimbabwe 19°48S 32°52E 57 B5
Chimay Belgium 50°3N 4°20E 15 D4
Chimayo U.S.A. 36°0N 105°56W 77 J11
Chimba Zambia 9°54S 31°28E 55 D3
Chimborazo Ecuador 1°29S 78°55W 92 D3
Chimbote Peru 9°0S 78°35W 92 E3
Chimboy Uzbekistan 42°57N 59°47E 28 E6
Chimkent = Shymkent
  Kazakhstan 42°18N 69°36E 28 E7
Chimoio Mozam. 19°4S 33°30E 55 F3
Chimpembe Zambia 9°31S 29°33E 55 D2
Chin □ Burma 22°0N 93°0E 41 J18

Chin Hills *Burma* 22°30N 93°30E **41** H18
Chin Ling Shan = Qinling Shandi
  China 33°50N 108°10E **34** H5
China *Mexico* 25°42N 99°14W **87** B5
China ■ *Asia* 30°0N 110°0E **33** E11
China, Great Plain of
  Asia 35°0N 115°0E **26** E13
China Lake *U.S.A.* 35°44N 117°37W **79** K9
Chinan = Jinan *China* 36°38N 117°1E **34** F9
Chinandega *Nic.* 12°35N 87°12W **88** D2
Chinati Peak *U.S.A.* 29°57N 104°29W **84** G2
Chincha Alta *Peru* 13°25S 76°7W **92** F3
Chinchaga → *Canada* 58°53N 118°20W **70** B5
Chinchilla *Australia* 26°45S 150°38E **63** D5
Chinchorro, Banco
  Mexico 18°35N 87°22W **87** D7
Chinchou = Jinzhou
  China 41°5N 121°3E **35** D11
Chincoteague *U.S.A.* 37°56N 75°23W **81** G16
Chinde *Mozam.* 18°35S 36°30E **55** F4
Chindwin → *Burma* 21°26N 95°15E **41** J19
Chineni *India* 33°2N 75°15E **43** C6
Chingola *Zambia* 12°31S 27°53E **55** E2
Chingole *Malawi* 13°4S 34°17E **55** E3
Ch'ingtao = Qingdao
  China 36°5N 120°20E **35** F11
Chinguetti *Mauritania* 20°25N 12°24W **50** D3
Chingune *Mozam.* 20°33S 34°58E **57** C5
Chinhanguanine
  Mozam. 25°21S 32°30E **57** D5
Chinhoyi *Zimbabwe* 17°20S 30°8E **55** F3
Chini *India* 31°32N 78°15E **42** D8
Chiniot *Pakistan* 31°45N 73°0E **42** D5
Chínipas *Mexico* 27°23N 108°32W **86** B3
Chinji *Pakistan* 32°42N 72°22E **42** C5
Chinju = Jinju *S. Korea* 35°12N 128°2E **35** G15
Chinko → *C.A.R.* 4°50N 23°53E **52** D4
Chinle *U.S.A.* 36°9N 109°33W **77** H9
Chinmen Tao *Taiwan* 24°26N 118°22E **33** G12
Chinnampo = Namp'o
  N. Korea 38°52N 125°10E **35** E13
Chino *Japan* 35°59N 138°9E **31** G9
Chino *U.S.A.* 34°1N 117°41W **79** L9
Chino Valley *U.S.A.* 34°45N 112°27W **77** J7
Chinon *France* 47°10N 0°15E **20** C4
Chinook *U.S.A.* 48°35N 109°14W **76** B9
Chinook Trough
  Pac. Oc. 44°0N 175°0W **64** C10
Chinsali *Zambia* 10°30S 32°2E **55** E3
Chinsura = Chunchura
  India 22°53N 88°27E **43** H13
Chióggia *Italy* 45°13N 12°17E **22** B5
Chios *Greece* 38°27N 26°9E **23** E12
Chipata *Zambia* 13°38S 32°28E **55** E3
Chipindo *Angola* 13°49S 15°48E **53** G3
Chipinge *Zimbabwe* 20°13S 32°28E **55** G3
Chipinge △ *Zimbabwe* 20°14S 33°0E **55** G3
Chipley *U.S.A.* 30°47N 85°32W **85** F12
Chipman *Canada* 46°6N 65°53W **73** C6
Chipoka *Malawi* 13°57S 34°28E **55** E3
Chippenham *U.K.* 51°27N 2°6W **13** F5
Chippewa → *U.S.A.* 44°25N 92°5W **80** C7
Chippewa Falls *U.S.A.* 44°56N 91°24W **80** C8
Chipping Norton *U.K.* 51°56N 1°32W **13** F6
Chiputneticook Lakes
  N. Amer. 45°35N 67°35W **81** C20
Chiquián *Peru* 10°10S 77°0W **92** F3
Chiquibul △ *Belize* 16°49N 88°52W **88** C2
Chiquimula *Guatemala* 14°51N 89°37W **88** D2
Chiquinquira *Colombia* 5°37N 73°50W **92** B4
Chirala *India* 15°50N 80°26E **40** M12
Chiramba *Mozam.* 16°55S 34°39E **55** F3
Chirawa *India* 28°14N 75°42E **42** E6
Chirchiq *Uzbekistan* 41°29N 69°35E **28** E7
Chiredzi *Zimbabwe* 21°0S 31°38E **57** C5
Chiricahua △ *U.S.A.* 32°0N 109°20W **77** K9
Chiricahua Peak
  U.S.A. 31°51N 109°18W **77** L9
Chirikof I. *U.S.A.* 55°50N 155°40W **74** D8
Chiriquí, G. de *Panama* 8°0N 82°10W **88** E3
Chiriquí, L. de *Panama* 9°10N 82°0W **88** E3
Chirisa △ *Zimbabwe* 17°53S 28°15E **55** F2
Chirivira Falls *Zimbabwe* 21°10S 32°12E **55** G3
Chirmiri *India* 23°15N 82°20E **43** H10
Chirripó Grande, Cerro
  Costa Rica 9°29N 83°29W **88** E3
Chirundu *Zimbabwe* 16°3S 28°50E **57** B4
Chisamba *Zambia* 14°55S 28°20E **55** E2
Chisapani *Nepal* 28°37N 81°16E **43** E9
Chisasibi *Canada* 53°50N 79°0W **72** B4
Chisholm *Canada* 54°55N 114°10W **70** C6
Chisholm *U.S.A.* 47°29N 92°53W **80** B7
Chishtian Mandi
  Pakistan 29°50N 72°55E **42** E5
Chisimaio = Kismaayo
  Somali Rep. 0°22S 42°32E **47** H3
Chisimba Falls *Zambia* 10°12S 30°56E **55** E3
Chişinău *Moldova* 47°2N 28°50E **17** E15
Chisos Mts. *U.S.A.* 29°5N 103°15W **84** G3
Chistopol *Russia* 55°25N 50°38E **18** C9
Chita *Russia* 52°0N 113°35E **33** A11
Chitipa *Malawi* 9°41S 33°19E **55** D3
Chitose *Japan* 42°49N 141°39E **30** C10
Chitral *Pakistan* 35°50N 71°56E **40** B7
Chitré *Panama* 7°59N 80°27W **88** E3
Chittagong *Bangla.* 22°19N 91°48E **41** H17
Chittagong □ *Bangla.* 24°5N 91°0E **41** G17
Chittaurgarh *India* 24°52N 74°38E **42** G6
Chittoor *India* 13°15N 79°5E **40** N11
Chitungwiza *Zimbabwe* 18°0S 31°6E **55** F3
Chiusi *Italy* 43°1N 11°57E **22** C4
Chivasso *Italy* 45°11N 7°53E **20** D7
Chivhu *Zimbabwe* 19°2S 30°52E **55** F3
Chivilcoy *Argentina* 34°55S 60°0W **94** C4
Chiwanda *Tanzania* 11°23S 34°55E **55** E3
Chizarira *Zimbabwe* 17°36S 27°45E **55** F2
Chizarira △ *Zimbabwe* 17°44S 27°52E **55** F2
Chizela *Zimbabwe* 13°8S 25°0E **55** E2
Chkalov = Orenburg
  Russia 51°45N 55°6E **18** D10

Chloride *U.S.A.* 35°25N 114°12W **79** K12
Cho-do *N. Korea* 38°30N 124°40E **35** E13
Cho Phuoc Hai *Vietnam* 10°26N 107°18E **39** G6
Choa Chu Kang *Singapore* 1°22N 103°41E **39** d
Chobe △ *Botswana* 18°37S 24°23E **56** B4
Chocolate Mts.
  U.S.A. 33°15N 115°15W **79** M11
Choctawhatchee →
  U.S.A. 30°25N 86°8W **85** F11
Choele Choel *Argentina* 39°11S 65°40W **96** D3
Choiseul *St. Lucia* 13°47N 61°3W **89** f
Choiseul *Solomon Is.* 7°0S 156°40E **58** B8
Choix *Mexico* 26°43N 108°17W **86** B3
Chojnice *Poland* 53°42N 17°32E **17** B9
Chok Chai *Thailand* 14°44N 102°10E **38** E4
Chōkai-San *Japan* 39°6N 140°3E **30** E10
Choke Canyon Res.
  U.S.A. 28°30N 98°20W **84** G5
Chokurdakh *Russia* 70°38N 147°55E **29** B15
Cholame *U.S.A.* 35°44N 120°18W **78** K6
Cholet *France* 47°4N 0°52W **20** C3
Cholguan *Chile* 37°10S 72°3W **94** D1
Choloma *Honduras* 15°37N 87°57W **88** C2
Choluteca *Honduras* 13°20N 87°14W **88** D2
Choluteca → *Honduras* 13°0N 87°20W **88** D2
Chom Bung *Thailand* 13°37N 99°36E **38** F2
Chom Thong *Thailand* 18°25N 98°41E **38** C2
Choma *Zambia* 16°48S 26°59E **55** F2
Chomolungma = Everest, Mt.
  Nepal 28°5N 86°58E **43** E12
Chomun *India* 27°15N 75°40E **42** F6
Chomutov *Czech Rep.* 50°28N 13°23E **16** C7
Chon Buri *Thailand* 13°21N 101°1E **38** F3
Chon Thanh *Vietnam* 11°24N 106°36E **39** G6
Chone *Ecuador* 0°40S 80°0W **92** D3
Chong Kai *Cambodia* 13°57N 103°35E **38** F4
Chong Mek *Thailand* 15°10N 105°27E **38** E5
Chong Phangan *Thailand* 9°39N 100°0E **39** b
Chong Samui *Thailand* 9°21N 99°50E **39** b
Ch'ŏngjin *N. Korea* 41°47N 129°50E **35** D15
Chŏngju *N. Korea* 39°40N 125°5E **35** E13
Chongli *China* 40°58N 115°15E **34** D8
Chŏngp'yŏng *N. Korea* 39°47N 127°23E **35** E14
Chongqing *China* 29°35N 106°25E **32** F10
Chongqing Shi □ *China* 30°0N 108°0E **32** F10
Chonguene *Mozam.* 25°3S 33°49E **57** C5
Chongwe *Zambia* 15°21S 28°42E **55** F2
Chonogol *Mongolia* 45°54N 115°22E **34** B8
Chonos, Arch. de los *Chile* 45°0S 75°0W **96** F2
Chop *Ukraine* 48°26N 22°12E **17** D12
Chopim → *Brazil* 25°35S 53°5W **95** B5
Chor *Pakistan* 25°31N 69°46E **42** G3
Chora Sfakion *Greece* 35°15N 24°9E **25** D6
Chorbat La *India* 34°42N 76°37E **43** B7
Chorley *U.K.* 53°39N 2°38W **12** D5
Chornobyl *Ukraine* 51°20N 30°15E **17** C16
Chorolque, Cerro *Bolivia* 20°59S 66°5W **94** A2
Chorregon *Australia* 22°40S 143°32E **62** C3
Chorro el Indio △
  Venezuela 7°43N 72°9W **89** E5
Chortkiv *Ukraine* 49°2N 25°46E **17** D13
Chorzów *Poland* 50°18N 18°57E **17** C10
Chos-Malal *Argentina* 37°20S 70°15W **94** D1
Ch'osan *N. Korea* 40°50N 125°47E **35** D13
Choszczno *Poland* 53°7N 15°25E **16** B8
Choteau *U.S.A.* 47°49N 112°11W **76** C7
Chotila *India* 22°23N 71°15E **42** H4
Chotta Udepur *India* 22°19N 74°1E **42** H6
Chowchilla *U.S.A.* 37°7N 120°16W **78** H6
Choybalsan *Mongolia* 48°4N 114°30E **33** B11
Choyr *Mongolia* 46°24N 108°30E **33** B10
Christchurch *N.Z.* 43°33S 172°47E **59** E4
Christchurch *U.K.* 50°44N 1°47W **13** G6
Christian I. *Canada* 44°50N 80°12W **82** B4
Christian Sd. *U.S.A.* 55°56N 134°40W **75** D13
Christiana *S. Africa* 27°52S 25°8E **56** D4
Christiansted
  U.S. Virgin Is. 17°45N 64°42W **89** C7
Christie B. *Canada* 62°32N 111°10W **71** A6
Christina → *Canada* 56°40N 111°3W **71** B6
Christmas Cr. →
  Australia 18°29S 125°23E **60** C4
Christmas I. = Kiritimati
  Kiribati 1°58N 157°27W **65** G12
Christmas I. *Ind. Oc.* 10°30S 105°40E **64** J2
Christopher, L.
  Australia 24°49S 127°42E **61** D4
Chtimba *Malawi* 10°35S 34°13E **55** E3
Chū = Shū *Kazakhstan* 43°36N 73°42E **28** E8
Chu → *Vietnam* 19°53N 105°45E **38** C5
Chu Lai *Vietnam* 15°28N 108°45E **38** E7
Chu Mom Ray △
  Vietnam 14°29N 107°38E **38** E6
Chu Se *Vietnam* 13°40N 108°8E **38** F7
Chuadanga *Bangla.* 23°38N 88°51E **43** H13
Chuak, Ko *Thailand* 9°28N 99°41E **39** b
Ch'uanchou = Quanzhou
  China 24°55N 118°34E **33** G12
Chuankou *China* 24°20N 110°59E **34** G6
Chubbuck *U.S.A.* 42°55N 112°28W **76** E7
Chūbu □ *Japan* 36°45N 137°30E **31** F8
Chūbu-Sangaku △
  Japan 36°30N 137°40E **31** F8
Chubut → *Argentina* 43°20S 65°5W **96** E3
Chuchi L. *Canada* 55°12N 124°30W **70** B4
Chuda *India* 22°29N 71°41E **42** H4
Chudskoye, Ozero
  Russia 58°13N 27°30E **9** G22
Chugach Mts. *U.S.A.* 60°45N 147°0W **74** C10
Chūgoku □ *Japan* 35°0N 133°0E **31** G6
Chūgoku-Sanchi *Japan* 35°0N 133°0E **31** G6
Chugwater *U.S.A.* 41°46N 104°50W **76** F11
Chuka *Kenya* 0°20S 37°39E **54** C4
Chukchi Plateau *Arctic* 78°0N 165°0W **4** B17
Chukchi Sea *Russia* 68°0N 175°0W **29** C19
Chukotskiy Mys *Russia* 64°14N 173°8W **74** C5
Chukotskiy Poluostrov
  Russia 66°0N 174°0W **74** B5
Chukotskoye Nagorye
  Russia 68°0N 175°0E **29** C18

Chula Vista *U.S.A.* 32°38N 117°5W **79** N9
Chulucanas *Peru* 5°8S 80°10W **92** E2
Chulym → *Russia* 57°43N 83°51E **28** D9
Chum Phae *Thailand* 16°40N 102°6E **38** D4
Chum Saeng *Thailand* 15°55N 100°15E **38** E3
Chumar *India* 32°40N 78°35E **43** C8
Chumbicha *Argentina* 29°0S 66°10W **94** B2
Chumikan *Russia* 54°40N 135°10E **29** D14
Chumphon *Thailand* 10°35N 99°14E **39** G2
Chumuare *Mozam.* 14°31S 31°50E **55** E3
Chuna → *Russia* 57°47N 94°37E **29** D10
Chuncheon *S. Korea* 37°58N 127°44E **35** F14
Chunchura *India* 22°53N 88°27E **43** H13
Chunga *Zambia* 15°0S 26°2E **55** F2
Chunggang-ŭp
  N. Korea 41°48N 126°48E **35** D14
Chunghwa *N. Korea* 38°52N 125°47E **35** E13
Chungju *S. Korea* 36°58N 127°58E **35** F14
Chungking = Chongqing
  China 29°35N 106°25E **32** F10
Chungt'iaoshan = Zhongtiao
  Shan *China* 35°0N 111°10E **34** G6
Chunian *Pakistan* 30°57N 74°0E **42** D6
Chunya *Tanzania* 8°30S 33°27E **55** D3
Chunyang *China* 43°38N 129°23E **35** C15
Chupara Pt.
  Trin. & Tob. 10°49N 61°22W **93** K15
Chuquibamba *Peru* 15°47S 72°44W **92** G4
Chuquicamata *Chile* 22°15S 69°0W **94** A2
Chur *Switz.* 46°52N 9°32E **20** C8
Churachandpur *India* 24°20N 93°40E **41** G18
Church Stretton *U.K.* 52°32N 2°48W **13** E5
Churchill *Canada* 58°47N 94°11W **71** B10
Churchill → *Man.,
  Canada* 58°47N 94°12W **71** B10
Churchill → *Nfld. & L.,
  Canada* 53°19N 60°10W **73** B7
Churchill, C. *Canada* 58°46N 93°12W **71** B10
Churchill Falls *Canada* 53°36N 64°19W **73** B7
Churchill L. *Canada* 55°55N 108°20W **71** B7
Churchill Pk. *Canada* 58°10N 125°10W **70** B3
Churki *India* 23°50N 83°12E **43** H10
Churu *India* 28°20N 74°50E **42** E6
Churún Merú = Angel Falls
  Venezuela 5°57N 62°30W **92** B6
Chushal *India* 33°40N 78°40E **43** C8
Chuska Mts. *U.S.A.* 36°15N 108°50W **77** H9
Chusovoy *Russia* 58°22N 57°50E **18** C10
Chute-aux-Outardes
  Canada 49°7N 68°24W **73** C6
Chuuk = Truk
  Micronesia 7°25N 151°46E **64** G7
Chuvash Republic = Chuvashia □
  Russia 55°30N 47°0E **18** C8
Chuvashia □ *Russia* 55°30N 47°0E **18** C8
Chuwärtah *Iraq* 35°43N 45°34E **44** C5
Chuxiong *China* 25°2N 101°28E **32** F9
Chuy *Uruguay* 33°41S 53°27W **95** C5
Ci Xian *China* 36°28N 114°25E **34** F8
Ciadâr-Lunga *Moldova* 46°3N 28°51E **17** E15
Ciamis *Indonesia* 7°20S 108°21E **37** G13
Cianjur *Indonesia* 6°49S 107°8E **37** G12
Cianorte *Brazil* 23°37S 52°37W **95** A5
Cibola *U.S.A.* 33°17N 114°42W **79** M12
Cicero *U.S.A.* 41°51N 87°44W **80** E2
Cicia *Fiji* 17°45S 179°18W **59** a
Ciéagas del Cataumbo △
  Venezuela 9°25N 71°54W **89** E5
Ciechanów *Poland* 52°52N 20°38E **17** B11
Ciego de Ávila *Cuba* 21°50N 78°50W **88** B4
Ciénaga *Colombia* 11°1N 74°15W **92** A4
Cienfuegos *Cuba* 22°10N 80°30W **88** B3
Cieszyn *Poland* 49°45N 18°35E **17** D10
Cieza *Spain* 38°17N 1°23W **21** C5
Cihuatlán *Mexico* 19°14N 104°35W **86** D4
Cijara, Embalse de *Spain* 39°18N 4°52W **21** C3
Cijulang *Indonesia* 7°42S 108°27E **37** G13
Cilacap *Indonesia* 7°43S 109°0E **37** G13
Cill Airne = Killarney
  Ireland 52°4N 9°30W **10** D2
Cill Chainnigh = Kilkenny
  Ireland 52°39N 7°15W **10** D4
Cill Dara = Kildare *Ireland* 53°9N 6°55W **10** C5
Cill Mhantáin = Wicklow
  Ireland 52°59N 6°3W **10** D5
Cilo Dağı *Turkey* 37°28N 43°55E **19** G7
Cima *U.S.A.* 35°14N 115°30W **79** K11
Cimarron *Kans., U.S.A.* 37°48N 100°21W **80** G3
Cimarron *N. Mex.,
  U.S.A.* 36°31N 104°55W **77** H11
Cimarron → *U.S.A.* 36°10N 96°16W **84** C6
Cimişlia *Moldova* 46°34N 28°44E **17** E15
Cimone, Mte. *Italy* 44°12N 10°42E **22** B4
Cinca → *Spain* 41°26N 0°21E **21** B6
Cincar *Bos.-H.* 43°55N 17°5E **22** C7
Cincinnati *U.S.A.* 39°9N 84°27W **81** F11
Cincinnatus *U.S.A.* 42°33N 75°54W **83** D9
Çine *Turkey* 37°37N 28°2E **23** F13
Ciney *Belgium* 50°18N 5°5E **15** D5
Cinto, Mte. *France* 42°24N 8°54E **20** E8
Circle *Alaska, U.S.A.* 65°50N 144°4W **74** B11
Circle *Mont., U.S.A.* 47°25N 105°35W **76** C11
Circleville *U.S.A.* 39°36N 82°57W **81** F12
Cirebon *Indonesia* 6°45S 108°32E **37** G13
Cirencester *U.K.* 51°43N 1°57W **13** F6
Cirium *Cyprus* 34°40N 32°53E **25** E11
Cisco *U.S.A.* 32°23N 98°59W **84** E5
Citlaltépetl = Orizaba, Pico de
  Mexico 18°58N 97°15W **87** D5
Citrus Heights *U.S.A.* 38°42N 121°17W **78** G5
Citrusdal *S. Africa* 32°35S 19°0E **56** E2
Città del Vaticano = Vatican
  City ■ *Europe* 41°54N 12°27E **22** D5
Città di Castello *Italy* 43°27N 12°14E **22** C5
Ciudad Acuña *Mexico* 29°18N 100°55W **86** B4
Ciudad Altamirano
  Mexico 18°20N 100°40W **86** D4
Ciudad Anáhuac
  Mexico 27°14N 100°7W **86** B4
Ciudad Bolívar *Venezuela* 8°5N 63°36W **92** B6

Ciudad Camargo
  Mexico 27°40N 105°10W **86** B3
Ciudad Cortés *Costa Rica* 8°55N 84°0W **88** E3
Ciudad de México *Mexico* 19°24N 99°9W **87** D5
Ciudad de Valles *Mexico* 22°0N 99°0W **87** C5
Ciudad del Carmen
  Mexico 18°38N 91°50W **87** D6
Ciudad del Este *Paraguay* 25°30S 54°50W **95** B5
Ciudad Delicias = Delicias
  Mexico 28°13N 105°28W **86** B3
Ciudad Frontera
  Mexico 26°56N 101°27W **86** B4
Ciudad Guayana
  Venezuela 8°0N 62°30W **92** B6
Ciudad Guerrero
  Mexico 28°33N 107°30W **86** B3
Ciudad Guzmán
  Mexico 19°41N 103°29W **86** D4
Ciudad Juárez *Mexico* 31°44N 106°29W **86** A3
Ciudad Lerdo *Mexico* 25°33N 103°32W **86** B4
Ciudad Madero *Mexico* 22°19N 97°50W **87** C5
Ciudad Mante *Mexico* 22°44N 98°59W **87** C5
Ciudad Obregón
  Mexico 27°29N 109°56W **86** B3
Ciudad Real *Spain* 38°59N 3°55W **21** C4
Ciudad Rodrigo *Spain* 40°35N 6°32W **21** B2
Ciudad Victoria *Mexico* 23°44N 99°8W **87** C5
Ciudadela *Spain* 40°0N 3°50E **24** B10
Civitanova Marche *Italy* 43°18N 13°44E **22** C5
Civitavécchia *Italy* 42°6N 11°48E **22** C4
Cizre *Turkey* 37°19N 42°10E **44** B4
Clackmannanshire □
  U.K. 56°10N 3°43W **11** E5
Clacton-on-Sea *U.K.* 51°47N 1°11E **13** F9
Claire, L. *Canada* 58°35N 112°5W **70** B6
Clairton *U.S.A.* 40°18N 79°53W **82** F5
Clallam Bay *U.S.A.* 48°15N 124°16W **78** B2
Clanton *U.S.A.* 32°51N 86°38W **85** E11
Clanwilliam *S. Africa* 32°11S 18°52E **56** E2
Clara *Ireland* 53°21N 7°37W **10** C4
Claraville *U.S.A.* 35°24N 118°20W **79** K8
Clare *Australia* 33°50S 138°37E **63** E2
Clare □ *Ireland* 52°45N 9°0W **10** D3
Clare → *Ireland* 53°20N 9°2W **10** C2
Clare I. *Ireland* 53°49N 10°0W **10** C1
Claremont *Calif., U.S.A.* 34°6N 117°43W **79** L9
Claremont *N.H., U.S.A.* 43°23N 72°20W **83** C12
Claremont Pt. *Australia* 14°1S 143°41E **62** A3
Claremore *U.S.A.* 36°19N 95°36W **84** C7
Claremorris *Ireland* 53°45N 9°0W **10** C3
Clarence → *Australia* 29°25S 153°22E **63** D5
Clarence → *N.Z.* 42°10S 173°56E **59** E4
Clarence, I. *Chile* 54°0S 72°0W **96** G2
Clarence I. *Antarctica* 61°10S 54°0W **5** C18
Clarence Str. *Australia* 12°0S 131°0E **60** B5
Clarence Town *Bahamas* 23°6N 74°59W **89** B5
Clarendon *Pa., U.S.A.* 41°47N 79°6W **82** E5
Clarendon *Tex., U.S.A.* 34°56N 100°53W **84** D4
Clarenville *Canada* 48°10N 54°1W **73** C9
Claresholm *Canada* 50°0N 113°33W **70** D6
Clarie Coast *Antarctica* 68°0S 135°0E **5** C9
Clarinda *U.S.A.* 40°44N 95°2W **80** E6
Clarington *Canada* 43°55N 78°41W **82** C6
Clarion *Iowa, U.S.A.* 42°44N 93°44W **80** D7
Clarion *Pa., U.S.A.* 41°13N 79°23W **82** E5
Clarion → *U.S.A.* 41°7N 79°41W **82** E5
Clarion Fracture Zone
  Pac. Oc. 20°0N 120°0W **66** H7
Clark *U.S.A.* 44°53N 97°44W **80** C5
Clark, Pt. *Canada* 44°4N 81°45W **82** B3
Clark Fork *U.S.A.* 48°9N 116°11W **76** B5
Clark Fork → *U.S.A.* 48°9N 116°15W **76** B5
Clarkdale *U.S.A.* 34°46N 112°3W **77** J7
Clarke City *Canada* 50°12N 66°38W **73** B6
Clarke I. *Australia* 40°32S 148°10E **63** G4
Clarke Ra. *Australia* 20°40S 148°30E **62** b
Clarks Fork Yellowstone →
  U.S.A. 45°39N 108°43W **76** D9
Clark's Harbour *Canada* 43°25N 65°38W **73** D6
Clarks Hill L. = J. Strom
  Thurmond L. *U.S.A.* 33°40N 82°12W **85** E13
Clarks Summit *U.S.A.* 41°30N 75°42W **83** E9
Clarksburg *U.S.A.* 39°17N 80°30W **81** F13
Clarksdale *U.S.A.* 34°12N 90°35W **85** D9
Clarkston *U.S.A.* 46°25N 117°3W **76** C5
Clarksville *Ark., U.S.A.* 35°28N 93°28W **84** D8
Clarksville *Tenn.,
  U.S.A.* 36°32N 87°21W **85** C11
Clarksville *Tex., U.S.A.* 33°37N 95°3W **84** E7
Clatskanie *U.S.A.* 46°6N 123°12W **78** D3
Claude *U.S.A.* 35°7N 101°22W **84** D4
Claveria *Phil.* 18°37N 121°4E **37** A6
Clay *U.S.A.* 38°17N 121°10W **78** G5
Clay Center *U.S.A.* 39°23N 97°8W **80** F5
Claypool *U.S.A.* 33°25N 110°51W **77** K8
Claysburg *U.S.A.* 40°17N 78°27W **82** F6
Claysville *U.S.A.* 40°7N 80°25W **82** F4
Clayton *Canada* 45°11N 76°19W **83** A8
Clayton *N. Mex.,
  U.S.A.* 36°27N 103°11W **77** H12
Clayton *N.Y., U.S.A.* 44°14N 76°5W **83** B8
Clear, C. *Ireland* 51°25N 9°32W **10** E2
Clear, L. *Canada* 45°26N 77°12W **82** A7
Clear Hills *Canada* 56°40N 119°30W **70** B5
Clear I. *Ireland* 51°26N 9°30W **10** E2
Clear Lake *Iowa, U.S.A.* 43°8N 93°23W **80** D7
Clear Lake *S. Dak.,
  U.S.A.* 44°45N 96°41W **80** C5
Clear Lake Res. *U.S.A.* 41°56N 121°5W **76** F3
Clearfield *Pa., U.S.A.* 41°2N 78°27W **82** E6
Clearfield *Utah, U.S.A.* 41°7N 112°2W **76** F7
Clearlake *U.S.A.* 38°57N 122°38W **78** G4
Clearwater *Canada* 51°38N 120°2W **70** C4
Clearwater *U.S.A.* 27°59N 82°48W **85** H13
Clearwater → *Alta.,
  Canada* 52°22N 114°57W **70** C6
Clearwater → *Alta.,
  Canada* 56°44N 111°23W **71** B6

Clearwater L. *Canada* 53°34N 99°49W **71** C9
Clearwater Lake △
  Canada 54°0N 101°0W **71** C8
Clearwater Mts. *U.S.A.* 46°5N 115°20W **76** C6
Clearwater River △
  Canada 56°55N 109°10W **71** B7
Cleburne *U.S.A.* 32°21N 97°23W **84** E6
Clee Hills *U.K.* 52°26N 2°35W **13** E5
Cleethorpes *U.K.* 53°33N 0°3W **12** D7
Cleeve Cloud *U.K.* 51°56N 2°0W **13** F6
Clemson *U.S.A.* 34°41N 82°50W **85** D13
Clerke Reef *Australia* 17°22S 119°20E **60** C2
Clermont *Australia* 22°49S 147°39E **62** C4
Clermont *U.S.A.* 28°33N 81°46W **85** G14
Clermont-Ferrand *France* 45°46N 3°4E **20** D5
Clervaux *Lux.* 50°4N 6°2E **15** D6
Clevedon *U.K.* 51°26N 2°52W **13** F5
Cleveland *Miss., U.S.A.* 33°45N 90°43W **85** E9
Cleveland *Ohio, U.S.A.* 41°29N 81°41W **82** E3
Cleveland *Okla., U.S.A.* 36°19N 96°28W **84** C6
Cleveland *Tenn., U.S.A.* 35°10N 84°53W **85** D12
Cleveland *Tex., U.S.A.* 30°21N 95°5W **84** F7
Cleveland, C. *Australia* 19°11S 147°1E **62** B4
Cleveland, Mt. *U.S.A.* 48°56N 113°51W **76** B7
Cleveland Heights
  U.S.A. 41°31N 81°33W **82** E3
Clevelândia *Brazil* 26°24S 52°23W **95** B5
Clew B. *Ireland* 53°50N 9°49W **10** C2
Clewiston *U.S.A.* 26°45N 80°56W **85** H14
Clifden *Ireland* 53°29N 10°1W **10** C1
Clifden *N.Z.* 46°1S 167°42E **59** G1
Cliffdell *U.S.A.* 46°56N 121°5W **78** D5
Cliffy Hd. *Australia* 35°1S 116°29E **61** G2
Clifton *Australia* 27°59S 151°53E **63** D5
Clifton *Ariz., U.S.A.* 33°3N 109°18W **77** K9
Clifton *Colo., U.S.A.* 39°7N 108°25W **76** G9
Clifton *Tex., U.S.A.* 31°47N 97°35W **84** F6
Clifton Beach *Australia* 16°46S 145°39E **62** B4
Clinch → *U.S.A.* 35°53N 84°29W **85** D12
Clingmans Dome
  U.S.A. 35°34N 83°30W **85** D13
Clint *U.S.A.* 31°35N 106°14W **84** F1
Clinton *B.C., Canada* 51°6N 121°35W **70** C4
Clinton *Ont., Canada* 43°37N 81°32W **82** C3
Clinton *N.Z.* 46°12S 169°23E **59** G2
Clinton *Ark., U.S.A.* 35°36N 92°28W **84** D8
Clinton *Conn., U.S.A.* 41°17N 72°32W **83** E12
Clinton *Ill., U.S.A.* 40°9N 88°57W **80** E9
Clinton *Ind., U.S.A.* 39°40N 87°24W **80** F10
Clinton *Iowa, U.S.A.* 41°51N 90°12W **80** E8
Clinton *Mass., U.S.A.* 42°25N 71°41W **83** D13
Clinton *Miss., U.S.A.* 32°20N 90°20W **85** E9
Clinton *Mo., U.S.A.* 38°22N 93°46W **80** F7
Clinton *N.C., U.S.A.* 35°0N 78°22W **85** D15
Clinton *Okla., U.S.A.* 35°31N 98°58W **84** D5
Clinton *S.C., U.S.A.* 34°29N 81°53W **85** D14
Clinton *Tenn., U.S.A.* 36°6N 84°8W **85** C12
Clinton *Wash., U.S.A.* 47°59N 122°21W **78** C4
Clinton, C. *Australia* 22°30S 150°45E **62** C5
Clinton Colden L.
  Canada 63°58N 107°27W **68** E10
Clintonville *U.S.A.* 44°37N 88°46W **80** C9
Clipperton, Î. *Pac. Oc.* 10°18N 109°13W **65** F17
Clipperton Fracture Zone
  Pac. Oc. 19°0N 122°0W **65** G16
Clisham *U.K.* 57°58N 6°49W **11** D2
Clitheroe *U.K.* 53°53N 2°22W **12** D5
Clo-oose *Canada* 48°39N 124°49W **78** B2
Cloates, Pt. *Australia* 22°43S 113°40E **60** D1
Clocolan *S. Africa* 28°55S 27°34E **57** D4
Clodomira *Argentina* 27°35S 64°14W **94** B3
Clogher Hd. *Ireland* 53°48N 6°14W **10** C5
Clonakilty *Ireland* 51°37N 8°53W **10** E3
Clonakilty B. *Ireland* 51°35N 8°51W **10** E3
Cloncurry *Australia* 20°40S 140°28E **62** C3
Cloncurry *Ireland* 53°26N 6°48W **10** C5
Cloncurry → *Australia* 18°37S 140°40E **62** B3
Clondalkin *Ireland* 53°19N 6°25W **10** C5
Clones *Ireland* 54°11N 7°15W **10** B4
Clonmel *Ireland* 52°21N 7°42W **10** D4
Cloquet *U.S.A.* 46°43N 92°28W **80** B7
Clorinda *Argentina* 25°16S 57°45W **94** B4
Cloud Peak *U.S.A.* 44°23N 107°11W **76** D10
Cloudcroft *U.S.A.* 32°58N 105°45W **77** K11
Cloverdale *U.S.A.* 38°48N 123°1W **78** G4
Clovis *Calif., U.S.A.* 36°49N 119°42W **78** J7
Clovis *N. Mex., U.S.A.* 34°24N 103°12W **77** J12
Cloyne *Canada* 44°49N 77°11W **82** B7
Cluain Meala = Clonmel
  Ireland 52°21N 7°42W **10** D4
Cluj-Napoca *Romania* 46°47N 23°38E **17** E12
Clunes *Australia* 37°20S 143°45E **63** F3
Clutha → *N.Z.* 46°20S 169°49E **59** G2
Clwyd □ *U.K.* 53°19N 3°31W **12** D4
Clwyd → *U.K.* 53°19N 3°30W **12** D4
Clyde *Canada* 54°9N 113°39W **70** C6
Clyde *N.Z.* 45°12S 169°20E **59** F2
Clyde *U.S.A.* 43°5N 76°52W **82** C8
Clyde → *U.K.* 55°55N 4°30W **11** F4
Clyde, Firth of *U.K.* 55°22N 5°1W **11** F3
Clyde Muirshiel △ *U.K.* 55°50N 4°44W **11** F4
Clyde River *Canada* 70°30N 68°30W **69** C18
Clydebank *U.K.* 55°54N 4°23W **11** F4
Clymer *N.Y., U.S.A.* 42°1N 79°37W **82** D5
Clymer *Pa., U.S.A.* 40°40N 79°1W **82** D5
Coachella *U.S.A.* 33°41N 116°10W **79** M10
Coachella Canal
  U.S.A. 32°43N 114°57W **79** N12
Coahoma *U.S.A.* 32°18N 101°18W **84** E4
Coahuayana →
  Mexico 18°41N 103°45W **86** D4
Coahuila □ *Mexico* 27°0N 102°0W **86** B4
Coal → *Canada* 59°39N 126°57W **70** B3
Coalane *Mozam.* 17°48S 37°2E **55** F4
Coalcomán *Mexico* 18°47N 103°9W **86** D4
Coaldale *Canada* 49°45N 112°35W **70** D6
Coalgate *U.S.A.* 34°32N 96°13W **84** D6
Coalinga *U.S.A.* 36°9N 120°21W **78** J6
Coalisland *U.K.* 54°33N 6°42W **10** B5
Coalville *U.K.* 52°44N 1°23W **12** E6
Coalville *U.S.A.* 40°55N 111°24W **76** F8

Coamo *Puerto Rico* 18°5N 66°22W **89 d**
Coari *Brazil* 4°8S 63°7W **92 D6**
Coast □ *Kenya* 2°40S 39°45E **54 C4**
Coast Mts. *Canada* 55°0N 129°20W **70 C3**
Coast Ranges *U.S.A.* 39°0N 123°0W **78 G4**
Coatbridge *U.K.* 55°52N 4°6W **11 F4**
Coatepec *Mexico* 19°27N 96°58W **87 D5**
Coatepeque *Guatemala* 14°46N 91°55W **88 D1**
Coatesville *U.S.A.* 39°59N 75°50W **81 F10**
Coaticook *Canada* 45°10N 71°46W **83 A13**
Coats I. *Canada* 62°30N 83°0W **69 E15**
Coats Land *Antarctica* 77°0S 25°0W **5 D1**
Coatzacoalcos *Mexico* 18°7N 94°25W **87 D6**
Cobá *Mexico* 20°31N 87°42W **87 C7**
Cobalt *Canada* 47°25N 79°42W **72 C4**
Cobán *Guatemala* 15°30N 90°21W **88 C1**
Cobar *Australia* 31°27S 145°48E **63 E4**
Cóbh *Ireland* 51°51N 8°17W **10 E3**
Cobija *Bolivia* 11°0S 68°50W **92 F5**
Cobleskill *U.S.A.* 42°41N 74°29W **83 D10**
Coboconk *Canada* 44°39N 78°48W **82 B6**
Cobourg *Canada* 43°58N 78°10W **82 C6**
Cobourg Pen. *Australia* 11°20S 132°15E **60 B5**
Cobram *Australia* 35°54S 145°40E **63 F4**
Cóbué *Mozam.* 12°0S 34°58E **55 E3**
Coburg *Germany* 50°15N 10°58E **16 C6**
Coburg I. *Canada* 75°57N 79°26W **69 B16**

Cocanada = Kakinada
  India 16°57N 82°11E **41 L13**
Cochabamba *Bolivia* 17°26S 66°10W **92 G5**
Cochemane *Mozam.* 17°0S 32°54E **55 F3**
Cochin *India* 9°58N 76°20E **40 Q10**
Cochin China = Nam-Phan
  Vietnam 10°30N 106°0E **39 G6**
Cochran *U.S.A.* 32°23N 83°21W **85 E13**
Cochrane *Alta., Canada* 51°11N 114°30W **70 C6**
Cochrane *Ont., Canada* 49°0N 81°0W **72 C3**
Cochrane *Chile* 47°15S 72°33W **96 F2**
Cochrane → *Canada* 59°0N 103°40W **71 B8**
Cochrane, L. *Chile* 47°10S 72°0W **96 F2**
Cochranton *U.S.A.* 41°31N 80°3W **82 E4**
Cockburn *Australia* 32°5S 141°0E **63 E3**
Cockburn, Canal *Chile* 54°30S 72°0W **96 G2**
Cockburn I. *Canada* 45°55N 83°22W **72 C3**
Cockburn Ra. *Australia* 15°46S 128°0E **60 C4**
Cockermouth *U.K.* 54°40N 3°22W **12 C4**
Cocklebiddy *Australia* 32°0S 126°3E **61 F4**

Cockpit Country, The
  Jamaica 18°15N 77°45W **88 a**
Coco → *Cent. Amer.* 15°0N 83°8W **88 D3**
Coco, I. del *Pac. Oc.* 5°25N 87°55W **65 G19**
Cocoa *U.S.A.* 28°21N 80°44W **85 G14**
Cocobeach *Gabon* 0°59N 9°34E **52 D1**
Cocos B. *Trin. & Tob.* 10°25N 61°2W **93 K15**
Cocos Is. *Ind. Oc.* 12°10S 96°55E **64 J1**
Cocos Ridge *Pac. Oc.* 4°0N 88°0W **65 G19**
Cod, C. *U.S.A.* 42°5N 70°10W **81 D18**
Codajás *Brazil* 3°55S 62°0W **92 D6**
Codó *Brazil* 4°30S 43°55W **93 D10**
Cody *U.S.A.* 44°32N 109°3W **76 D9**
Coe Hill *Canada* 44°52N 77°50W **82 B7**
Coelemu *Chile* 36°30S 72°48W **94 D1**
Coen *Australia* 13°52S 143°12E **62 A3**

Coeur d'Alene *U.S.A.* 47°41N 116°46W **76 C5**
Coeur d'Alene L.
  U.S.A. 47°32N 116°49W **76 C5**
Coevorden *Neths.* 52°40N 6°44E **15 B6**
Cofete *Canary Is.* 28°6N 14°23W **24 F5**
Coffeyville *U.S.A.* 37°2N 95°37W **80 G6**
Coffin B. *Australia* 34°38S 135°28E **63 E2**
Coffin Bay *Australia* 34°37S 135°29E **63 E2**
Coffin Bay → *Australia* 34°34S 135°19E **63 E2**
Coffin Bay Peninsula
  Australia 34°32S 135°15E **63 E2**
Coffs Harbour *Australia* 30°16S 153°5E **63 E5**
Cognac *France* 45°41N 0°20W **20 D3**
Cohocton *U.S.A.* 42°30N 77°30W **82 D7**
Cohocton → *U.S.A.* 42°9N 77°6W **82 D7**
Cohoes *U.S.A.* 42°46N 73°42W **83 D11**
Cohuna *Australia* 35°45S 144°15E **63 F3**
Coiba, I. de *Panama* 7°30N 81°40W **88 E3**
Coig → *Argentina* 51°0S 69°10W **96 G3**
Coigeach, Rubha *U.K.* 58°6N 5°26W **11 C3**
Coihaique *Chile* 45°30S 71°45W **96 F2**
Coimbatore *India* 11°2N 76°59E **40 P10**
Coimbra *Brazil* 19°55S 57°48W **92 G7**
Coimbra *Portugal* 40°15N 8°27W **21 B1**
Coín *Spain* 36°40N 4°48W **21 D3**
Coipasa, Salar de *Bolivia* 19°26S 68°9W **92 G5**
Cojimies *Ecuador* 0°20N 80°0W **92 C3**
Cojutepequé *El Salv.* 13°41N 88°54W **88 D2**
Cokeville *U.S.A.* 42°5N 110°57W **76 E8**
Colac *Australia* 38°21S 143°35E **63 F3**
Colatina *Brazil* 19°32S 40°37W **93 G10**
Colbeck, C. *Antarctica* 77°6S 157°48W **5 D13**
Colborne *Canada* 44°0N 77°53W **82 C7**
Colby *U.S.A.* 39°24N 101°3W **80 F3**
Colca → *Peru* 15°5S 72°43W **92 G4**
Colchester *U.K.* 51°54N 0°55E **13 F8**
Colchester *U.S.A.* 41°35N 72°20W **83 E12**
Cold L. *Canada* 54°33N 110°5W **71 C7**
Cold Lake *Canada* 54°27N 110°10W **71 C6**
Coldstream *Canada* 50°13N 119°11W **70 C5**
Coldstream *U.K.* 55°39N 2°15W **11 F6**
Coldwater *Canada* 44°42N 79°40W **82 B5**
Coldwater *Kans., U.S.A.* 37°16N 99°20W **80 G4**
Coldwater *Mich., U.S.A.* 41°57N 85°0W **81 E11**
Colebrook *U.S.A.* 44°54N 71°30W **83 B13**
Coleman *Canada* 49°40N 114°30W **70 D6**
Coleman *U.S.A.* 31°50N 99°26W **84 F5**
Coleman → *Australia* 15°6S 141°38E **62 B3**
Colenso *S. Africa* 28°44S 29°50E **57 D4**
Coleraine *Australia* 37°36S 141°40E **63 F3**
Coleraine *U.K.* 55°8N 6°41W **10 A5**
Coleridge, L. *N.Z.* 43°17S 171°30E **59 E3**
Colesberg *S. Africa* 30°45S 25°5E **56 E4**
Coleville *U.S.A.* 38°34N 119°30W **78 G7**
Colfax *Calif., U.S.A.* 39°6N 120°57W **78 F6**
Colfax *La., U.S.A.* 31°31N 92°42W **84 F8**
Colfax *Wash., U.S.A.* 46°53N 117°22W **76 C5**

Colhué Huapi, L.
  Argentina 45°30S 69°0W **96 F3**
Coligny *S. Africa* 26°17S 26°15E **56 D4**
Colima *Mexico* 19°14N 103°43W **86 D4**
Colima □ *Mexico* 19°10N 104°0W **86 D4**
Colima, Nevado de
  Mexico 19°33N 103°38W **86 D4**
Colina *Chile* 33°13S 70°45W **94 C1**
Colinas *Brazil* 6°0S 44°10W **93 E10**
Coll *U.K.* 56°39N 6°34W **11 E2**
Collaguasi *Chile* 21°5S 68°45W **94 A2**
Collarenebri *Australia* 29°33S 148°34E **63 D4**
College *U.S.A.* 64°52N 147°49W **74 C10**
College Park *U.S.A.* 33°39N 84°27W **85 E12**
College Station *U.S.A.* 30°37N 96°21W **84 F6**
Collie *Australia* 33°22S 116°8E **61 F2**
Collier B. *Australia* 16°10S 124°15E **60 C3**
Collier Ra. *Australia* 24°45S 119°10E **61 D2**
Collier Range △
  Australia 24°39S 119°7E **61 D2**
Collierville *U.S.A.* 35°3N 89°40W **85 D10**
Collina, Passo di *Italy* 44°2N 10°56E **22 B4**
Collingwood *Canada* 44°29N 80°13W **82 B4**
Collingwood *N.Z.* 40°41S 172°40E **59 D4**
Collins *Canada* 50°17N 89°27W **72 B2**
Collins Bay *Canada* 44°14N 76°36W **83 B8**
Collinson Pen. *Canada* 69°58N 101°24W **68 D11**
Collinsville *Australia* 20°30S 147°56E **62 C4**
Collipulli *Chile* 37°55S 72°30W **94 D1**
Collooney *Ireland* 54°11N 8°29W **10 B3**
Colmar *France* 48°5N 7°20E **20 B7**
Colo → *Australia* 33°25S 150°52E **63 E5**
Cologne = Köln *Germany* 50°56N 6°57E **16 C4**
Colom, I. d'en *Spain* 39°58N 4°16E **24 B11**
Coloma *U.S.A.* 38°48N 120°53W **78 G6**
Colomb-Béchar = Béchar
  Algeria 31°38N 2°18W **50 B5**
Colombia ■ *S. Amer.* 3°45N 73°0W **92 C4**
Colombian Basin
  Caribbean 14°0N 76°0W **88 D4**
Colombo *Sri Lanka* 6°56N 79°58E **40 R11**
Colón *B. Aires, Argentina* 33°53S 61°7W **94 C3**
Colón *Entre Ríos,
  Argentina* 32°12S 58°10W **94 C4**
Colón *Cuba* 22°42N 80°54W **88 B3**
Colón *Panama* 9°20N 79°54W **88 E4**
Colón, Arch. de *Ecuador* 0°0 91°0W **90 D1**
Colònia de Sant Jordi
  Spain 39°19N 2°59E **24 B9**
Colonia del Sacramento
  Uruguay 34°25S 57°50W **94 C4**
Colonia Dora *Argentina* 28°34S 62°59W **94 B3**
Colonial Beach *U.S.A.* 38°15N 76°58W **81 F15**
Colonie *U.S.A.* 42°43N 73°50W **83 D11**
Colonsay *Canada* 51°59N 105°52W **71 C7**
Colonsay *U.K.* 56°5N 6°12W **11 E2**
Colorado □ *U.S.A.* 39°30N 105°30W **76 G11**
Colorado → *Argentina* 39°50S 62°8W **96 D4**
Colorado → *N. Amer.* 31°45N 114°40W **77 L6**
Colorado → *U.S.A.* 28°36N 95°59W **84 G7**
Colorado City *U.S.A.* 32°24N 100°52W **84 E4**
Colorado Plateau *U.S.A.* 37°0N 111°0W **77 H8**
Colorado River Aqueduct
  U.S.A. 33°50N 117°23W **79 L12**
Colorado Springs
  U.S.A. 38°50N 104°49W **76 G11**
Colotlán *Mexico* 22°6N 103°16W **86 C4**
Colstrip *U.S.A.* 45°53N 106°38W **76 D10**
Colton *U.S.A.* 44°33N 74°56W **83 B10**
Columbia *Ky., U.S.A.* 37°6N 85°18W **81 G11**
Columbia *La., U.S.A.* 32°6N 92°5W **84 E8**
Columbia *Miss., U.S.A.* 31°15N 89°50W **85 F10**
Columbia *Mo., U.S.A.* 38°57N 92°20W **80 F7**
Columbia *Pa., U.S.A.* 40°2N 76°30W **83 F8**
Columbia *S.C., U.S.A.* 34°0N 81°2W **85 D14**
Columbia *Tenn., U.S.A.* 35°37N 87°2W **85 D11**
Columbia → *N. Amer.* 46°15N 124°5W **78 D2**
Columbia, C. *Canada* 83°6N 69°57W **69 A18**
Columbia, District of □
  U.S.A. 38°55N 77°0W **81 F15**
Columbia, Mt. *Canada* 52°8N 117°20W **70 C5**
Columbia Basin *U.S.A.* 46°45N 119°5W **76 C4**
Columbia Falls *U.S.A.* 48°23N 114°11W **76 B6**
Columbia Mts. *Canada* 52°0N 119°0W **70 C5**
Columbia Plateau
  U.S.A. 44°0N 117°30W **76 D5**
Columbiana *U.S.A.* 40°53N 80°42W **82 F4**
Columbretes, Is. *Spain* 39°50N 0°0E **21 C6**
Columbus *Ga., U.S.A.* 32°28N 84°59W **85 E12**
Columbus *Ind., U.S.A.* 39°13N 85°55W **81 F11**
Columbus *Kans., U.S.A.* 37°10N 94°50W **80 G6**
Columbus *Miss., U.S.A.* 33°30N 88°25W **85 E10**
Columbus *Mont.,
  U.S.A.* 45°38N 109°15W **76 D9**
Columbus *N. Mex.,
  U.S.A.* 31°50N 107°38W **77 L10**
Columbus *Nebr., U.S.A.* 41°26N 97°22W **80 E5**
Columbus *Ohio, U.S.A.* 39°58N 83°0W **81 F12**
Columbus *Tex., U.S.A.* 29°42N 96°33W **84 G6**
Colusa *U.S.A.* 39°13N 122°1W **78 F4**
Colville *U.S.A.* 48°33N 117°54W **76 B5**
Colville → *U.S.A.* 70°25N 150°30W **74 A9**
Colville, C. *N.Z.* 36°29S 175°21E **59 B5**
Colwood *Canada* 48°26N 123°29W **78 B3**
Colwyn Bay *U.K.* 53°18N 3°44W **12 D4**
Comácchio *Italy* 44°42N 12°11E **22 B5**
Comalcalco *Mexico* 18°16N 93°13W **87 D6**
Comallo *Argentina* 41°0S 70°5W **96 E2**
Comanche *U.S.A.* 31°54N 98°36W **84 F5**
Comandante Ferraz
  Antarctica 62°30S 58°0W **5 C18**
Comayagua *Honduras* 14°25N 87°37W **88 D2**
Combahee → *U.S.A.* 32°31N 80°31W **85 E14**
Combarbalá *Chile* 31°11S 71°2W **94 C1**
Combe Martin *U.K.* 51°12N 4°3W **13 F3**
Comber *Canada* 42°14N 82°33W **82 D2**
Comber *U.K.* 54°33N 5°45W **10 B6**
Combermere *Canada* 45°22N 77°37W **82 A7**
Comblain-au-Pont
  Belgium 50°29N 5°35E **15 D5**

Comeragh Mts. *Ireland* 52°18N 7°34W **10 D4**
Comet *Australia* 23°36S 148°38E **62 C4**
Comilla *Bangla.* 23°28N 91°10E **41 H17**
Comino *Malta* 36°1N 14°20E **25 C1**
Comino, C. *Italy* 40°32N 9°49E **22 D3**
Comitán de Domínguez
  Mexico 16°15N 92°8W **87 D6**
Commerce *Ga., U.S.A.* 34°12N 83°28W **85 D13**
Commerce *Tex., U.S.A.* 33°15N 95°54W **84 E7**
Committee B. *Canada* 68°30N 86°30W **69 D14**
Commodore, C. *Canada* 44°47N 80°54W **82 B4**
Commonwealth B.
  Antarctica 67°0S 144°0E **5 C10**
Commoron Cr. →
  Australia 28°22S 150°8E **63 D5**
Communism Pk. = imeni Ismail
  Samani, Pik *Tajikistan* 39°0N 72°2E **28 F8**
Como *Italy* 45°47N 9°5E **20 D8**
Como, Lago di *Italy* 46°0N 9°11E **20 D8**
Comodoro Rivadavia
  Argentina 45°50S 67°40W **96 F3**
Comorin, C. = Kanniyakumari
  India 8°3N 77°40E **40 Q10**
Comoros ■ *Ind. Oc.* 12°10S 44°15E **53 a**
Comox *Canada* 49°42N 124°55W **70 D4**
Compiègne *France* 49°24N 2°50E **20 B5**
Compostela *Mexico* 21°14N 104°55W **86 C4**
Comprida, I. *Brazil* 24°50S 47°42W **95 A6**
Compton *Canada* 45°14N 71°49W **83 A13**
Compton *U.S.A.* 33°53N 118°13W **79 M8**
Comrat *Moldova* 46°18N 28°40E **17 E15**
Con Cuong *Vietnam* 19°2N 104°54E **38 C5**
Con Dao △ *Vietnam* 8°42N 106°35E **39 H6**
Con Son, Dao *Vietnam* 8°41N 106°37E **39 H6**
Conakry *Guinea* 9°29N 13°49W **50 G3**
Conara *Australia* 41°50S 147°26E **63 G4**
Concarneau *France* 47°52N 3°56W **20 C2**
Conceição *Mozam.* 18°47S 36°7E **55 F4**
Conceição da Barra
  Brazil 18°35S 39°45W **93 G11**
Conceição do Araguaia
  Brazil 8°0S 49°2W **93 E9**
Concepción *Argentina* 27°20S 65°35W **94 B2**
Concepción *Bolivia* 16°15S 62°8W **92 G6**
Concepción *Chile* 36°50S 73°0W **94 D1**
Concepción *Mexico* 18°15N 90°5W **87 D6**
Concepción *Paraguay* 23°22S 57°26W **94 A4**
Concepción □ *Chile* 37°0S 72°30W **94 D1**
Concepción → *Mexico* 30°32N 113°2W **86 A2**
Concepción, Est. de
  Chile 50°30S 74°55W **96 G2**
Concepción, L. *Bolivia* 17°20S 61°20W **92 G6**
Concepción, Pta.
  Mexico 26°53N 111°50W **86 B2**
Concepción del Oro
  Mexico 24°38N 101°25W **86 C4**
Concepción del Uruguay
  Argentina 32°35S 58°20W **94 C4**
Conception, Pt. *U.S.A.* 34°27N 120°28W **79 L6**
Conception B. *Canada* 47°45N 53°0W **73 C9**
Conception B. *Namibia* 23°55S 14°22E **56 C1**
Conception I. *Bahamas* 23°52N 75°9W **89 B4**
Concession *Zimbabwe* 17°27S 30°56E **55 F3**
Conchas Dam *U.S.A.* 35°22N 104°11W **77 J11**
Concho *U.S.A.* 34°28N 109°36W **77 J9**
Concho → *U.S.A.* 31°34N 99°43W **84 F5**
Conchos → *Chihuahua,
  Mexico* 29°35N 104°25W **86 B4**
Conchos → *Chihuahua,
  Mexico* 27°29N 106°45W **86 B3**
Conchos → *Tamaulipas,
  Mexico* 24°55N 97°38W **87 B5**
Concord *Calif., U.S.A.* 37°59N 122°2W **78 H4**
Concord *N.C., U.S.A.* 35°25N 80°35W **85 D14**
Concord *N.H., U.S.A.* 43°12N 71°32W **83 C13**
Concordia *Antarctica* 75°6S 123°23E **5 D9**
Concordia *Argentina* 31°20S 58°2W **94 C4**
Concórdia *Amazonas,
  Brazil* 4°36S 66°36W **92 D5**
Concórdia *Sta. Catarina,
  Brazil* 27°14S 52°1W **95 B5**
Concordia *Mexico* 23°17N 106°4W **86 C3**
Concordia *U.S.A.* 39°34N 97°40W **80 F5**
Concrete *U.S.A.* 48°32N 121°45W **76 B3**
Condamine *Australia* 26°56S 150°9E **63 D5**
Conde *U.S.A.* 45°9N 98°6W **80 C4**
Condeúba *Brazil* 14°52S 42°0W **93 F10**
Condobolin *Australia* 33°4S 147°6E **63 E4**
Condon *U.S.A.* 45°14N 120°11W **76 D3**
Conegliano *Italy* 45°53N 12°18E **22 B5**
Conejera, I. = Conills, I. des
  Spain 39°11N 2°58E **24 B9**
Conejos *Mexico* 26°14N 103°53W **86 B4**
Conemaugh → *U.S.A.* 40°28N 79°19W **82 F5**
Confuso → *Paraguay* 25°9S 57°34W **94 B4**
Congleton *U.K.* 53°10N 2°13W **12 D5**
Congo (Brazzaville) = Congo ■
  Africa 1°0S 16°0E **52 E3**
Congo (Kinshasa) = Congo, Dem.
  Rep. of the ■ *Africa* 3°0S 23°0E **52 E4**
Congo ■ *Africa* 1°0S 16°0E **52 E3**
Congo → *Africa* 6°4S 12°24E **52 F2**
Congo, Dem. Rep. of the ■
  Africa 3°0S 23°0E **52 E4**
Congo Basin *Africa* 0°10S 24°30E **52 E4**
Congonhas *Brazil* 20°30S 43°52W **95 A7**
Congress *U.S.A.* 34°9N 112°51W **77 J7**
Conills, I. des *Spain* 39°11N 2°58E **24 B9**
Coniston *Canada* 46°29N 80°51W **72 C3**
Conjeeveram = Kanchipuram
  India 12°52N 79°45E **40 N11**
Conklin *Canada* 55°38N 111°5W **71 B6**
Conklin *U.S.A.* 42°2N 75°49W **83 D9**
Conn, L. *Ireland* 54°3N 9°15W **10 B2**
Connacht □ *Ireland* 53°43N 9°12W **10 C2**
Conneaut *U.S.A.* 41°57N 80°34W **82 E4**
Conneautville *U.S.A.* 41°45N 80°22W **82 E4**
Connecticut □ *U.S.A.* 41°30N 72°45W **83 E12**
Connecticut → *U.S.A.* 41°16N 72°20W **83 E12**
Connell *U.S.A.* 46°40N 118°52W **76 C4**

Connellsville *U.S.A.* 40°1N 79°35W **82 F5**
Connemara *Ireland* 53°29N 9°45W **10 C2**
Connemara △ *Ireland* 53°32N 9°52W **10 C2**
Connersville *U.S.A.* 39°39N 85°8W **81 F11**
Connors Ra. *Australia* 21°40S 149°10E **62 C4**
Conquest *Canada* 51°32N 107°14W **71 C7**
Conrad *U.S.A.* 48°10N 111°57W **76 B8**
Conrad Rise *S. Ocean* 53°0S 41°0E **5 B5**
Conran, C. *Australia* 37°49S 148°44E **63 F4**
Conroe *U.S.A.* 30°19N 95°27W **84 F7**
Consecon *Canada* 44°0N 77°31W **82 C7**
Conselheiro Lafaiete
  Brazil 20°40S 43°48W **95 A7**
Consell *Spain* 39°40N 2°49E **24 B9**
Consett *U.K.* 54°51N 1°50W **12 C6**
Consort *Canada* 52°1N 110°46W **71 C6**
Constance = Konstanz
  Germany 47°40N 9°10E **16 E5**
Constance, L. = Bodensee
  Europe 47°35N 9°25E **20 C8**
Constanța *Romania* 44°14N 28°38E **17 F15**
Constantine *Algeria* 36°25N 6°42E **50 A7**
Constitución *Chile* 35°20S 72°30W **94 D1**
Constitución *Uruguay* 31°0S 57°50W **94 C4**
Constitución de 1857 △
  Mexico 32°4N 115°55W **86 A1**
Consul *Canada* 49°20N 109°30W **71 D7**
Contact *U.S.A.* 41°46N 114°45W **76 F6**
Contai *India* 21°54N 87°46E **43 J12**
Contamana *Peru* 7°19S 74°55W **92 E4**
Contas → *Brazil* 14°17S 39°1W **93 F11**
Contoocook *U.S.A.* 43°13N 71°45W **83 C13**
Contwoyto L. *Canada* 65°42N 110°50W **68 D9**
Conway = Conwy *U.K.* 53°17N 3°50W **12 D4**
Conway = Conwy →
  U.K. 53°17N 3°50W **12 D4**
Conway *Australia* 20°24S 148°41E **62 b**
Conway *Canada* 44°6N 76°54W **82 B8**
Conway *Ark., U.S.A.* 35°5N 92°26W **84 D8**
Conway *N.H., U.S.A.* 43°59N 71°7W **83 C13**
Conway *S.C., U.S.A.* 33°51N 79°3W **85 E15**
Conway, C. *Australia* 20°34S 148°46E **62 b**
Conway, L. *Australia* 28°17S 135°35E **63 D2**
Conwy *U.K.* 53°17N 3°50W **12 D4**
Conwy □ *U.K.* 53°10N 3°44W **12 D4**
Conwy → *U.K.* 53°17N 3°50W **12 D4**
Coober Pedy *Australia* 29°1S 134°43E **63 D1**
Cooch Behar = Koch Bihar
  India 26°22N 89°29E **41 F16**
Cooinda *Australia* 13°15S 130°5E **60 B5**
Cook *Australia* 30°37S 130°25E **61 F5**
Cook, B. *Chile* 55°10S 70°0W **96 H3**
Cook, C. *Canada* 50°8N 127°55W **70 C3**
Cook, Mt. = Aoraki Mount Cook
  N.Z. 43°36S 170°9E **59 E3**
Cook Inlet *U.S.A.* 60°0N 152°0W **68 F1**
Cook Is. ☒ *Pac. Oc.* 17°0S 160°0W **65 J12**
Cook Strait *N.Z.* 41°15S 174°29E **59 D5**
Cookeville *U.S.A.* 36°10N 85°30W **85 C12**
Cookhouse *S. Africa* 32°44S 25°47E **56 E4**
Cooks Harbour *Canada* 51°36N 55°52W **73 B8**
Cookshire *Canada* 45°25N 71°38W **83 A13**
Cookstown *Canada* 44°11N 79°42W **82 B5**
Cookstown *U.K.* 54°39N 6°45W **10 B5**
Cooksville *Canada* 43°35N 79°38W **82 C5**
Cooktown *Australia* 15°30S 145°16E **62 B4**
Coolabah *Australia* 31°1S 146°43E **63 E4**
Cooladdi *Australia* 26°37S 145°23E **63 D4**
Coolah *Australia* 31°48S 149°41E **63 E4**
Coolamon *Australia* 34°46S 147°8E **63 E4**
Coolgardie *Australia* 30°55S 121°8E **61 F3**
Coolidge *U.S.A.* 32°59N 111°31W **77 K8**
Coolidge Dam *U.S.A.* 33°10N 110°32W **77 K8**
Cooma *Australia* 36°12S 149°8E **63 F4**
Coon Rapids *U.S.A.* 45°9N 93°19W **80 C7**
Coonabarabran
  Australia 31°14S 149°18E **63 E4**
Coonamble *Australia* 30°56S 148°27E **63 E4**
Coonana *Australia* 31°0S 123°0E **61 F3**
Coonana ⊙ *Australia* 30°51S 122°53E **61 F3**
Coondapoor *India* 13°42N 74°40E **40 N9**
Cooninnie, L. *Australia* 26°4S 139°59E **63 D2**
Cooper *U.S.A.* 33°23N 95°42W **84 E7**
Cooper Cr. → *Australia* 28°29S 137°46E **63 D2**
Cooper Ridge *Pac. Oc.* 10°0N 150°30W **65 G12**
Coopersburg *U.S.A.* 40°30N 75°23W **83 F9**
Cooperstown *N. Dak.,
  U.S.A.* 47°27N 98°8W **80 B4**
Cooperstown *N.Y.,
  U.S.A.* 42°42N 74°56W **83 D10**
Coorabie *Australia* 31°54S 132°18E **61 F5**
Coorong, The *Australia* 35°50S 139°20E **63 F2**
Coorow *Australia* 29°53S 116°2E **61 E2**
Cooroy *Australia* 26°22S 152°54E **63 D5**
Coos Bay *U.S.A.* 43°22N 124°13W **76 E1**
Coosa → *U.S.A.* 32°30N 86°16W **85 E11**
Cootamundra *Australia* 34°36S 148°1E **63 E4**
Cootehill *Ireland* 54°4N 7°5W **10 B4**
Copahue Paso *Argentina* 37°49S 71°8W **94 D1**
Copainalá *Mexico* 17°4N 93°18W **87 D6**
Copake *U.S.A.* 42°7N 73°31W **83 D11**
Copán *Honduras* 14°50N 89°9W **88 D2**
Cope *U.S.A.* 39°40N 102°51W **76 G12**
Copenhagen = København
  Denmark 55°40N 12°26E **9 J15**
Copenhagen *U.S.A.* 43°54N 75°41W **83 C9**
Copiapó *Chile* 27°30S 70°20W **94 B1**
Copiapó → *Chile* 27°19S 70°56W **94 B1**
Coplay *U.S.A.* 40°44N 75°29W **83 F9**
Copo △ *Argentina* 25°53S 61°41W **94 B3**
Copp L. *Canada* 60°14N 114°40W **70 A6**
Coppename → *Suriname* 5°48N 55°55W **93 B7**
Copper Canyon = Barranca del
  Cobre △ *Mexico* 27°18N 107°40W **86 B3**
Copper Center *U.S.A.* 61°58N 145°18W **74 C10**
Copper Harbor *U.S.A.* 47°28N 87°53W **80 B10**
Copper Queen *Zimbabwe* 17°29S 29°18E **55 F2**
Copperas Cove *U.S.A.* 31°8N 97°54W **84 F6**
Copperbelt □ *Zambia* 13°15S 27°30E **55 E2**
Coppermine = Kugluktuk
  Canada 67°50N 115°5W **68 D8**

Coppermine → *Canada* 67°49N 116°4W **68 D8**
Copperopolis *U.S.A.* 37°58N 120°38W **78 H6**
Coquet → *U.K.* 55°20N 1°32W **12 B6**
Coquille *U.S.A.* 43°11N 124°11W **76 E1**
Coquimbo *Chile* 30°0S 71°20W **94 C1**
Coquimbo □ *Chile* 31°0S 71°0W **94 C1**
Coquitlam *Canada* 49°17N 122°45W **70 D4**
Corabia *Romania* 43°48N 24°30E **17 G13**
Coracora *Peru* 15°5S 73°45W **92 G4**
Coraki *Australia* 28°59S 153°17E **63 D5**
Coral *U.S.A.* 40°29N 79°10W **82 F5**
Coral Bay *Australia* 23°8S 113°46E **60 D1**
Coral Gables *U.S.A.* 25°43N 80°16W **85 J14**
Coral Harbour *Canada* 64°8N 83°10W **69 E15**
Coral Sea *Pac. Oc.* 15°0S 150°0E **58 C8**
Coral Sea Basin *Pac. Oc.* 14°0S 152°0E **64 J7**
Coral Sea Islands Terr. □
  Australia 20°0S 155°0E **58 C8**
Coral Springs *U.S.A.* 26°16N 80°16W **85 H14**
Coraopolis *U.S.A.* 40°31N 80°10W **82 F4**
Corato *Italy* 41°9N 16°25E **22 D7**
Corbett △ *India* 29°20N 79°0E **43 E8**
Corbin *U.S.A.* 36°57N 84°6W **81 G11**
Corby *U.K.* 52°30N 0°41W **13 E7**
Corcaigh = Cork *Ireland* 51°54N 8°29W **10 E3**
Corcoran *U.S.A.* 36°6N 119°33W **78 J7**
Corcovado △ *Costa Rica* 8°33N 83°35W **88 E3**
Corcubión *Spain* 42°56N 9°12W **21 A1**
Cordele *U.S.A.* 31°58N 83°47W **85 F13**
Cordell *U.S.A.* 35°17N 98°59W **84 D5**
Córdoba *Argentina* 31°20S 64°10W **94 C3**
Córdoba *Mexico* 18°53N 96°56W **87 D5**
Córdoba *Spain* 37°50N 4°50W **21 D3**
Córdoba □ *Argentina* 31°22S 64°15W **94 C3**
Córdoba, Sierra de
  Argentina 31°10S 64°25W **94 C3**
Cordova *U.S.A.* 60°33N 145°45W **68 E2**
Corella → *Australia* 19°34S 140°47E **62 C3**
Corfield *Australia* 21°40S 143°21E **62 C3**
Corfu = Kerkyra *Greece* 39°38N 19°50E **25 A3**
Corfu *U.S.A.* 42°57N 78°24W **82 D6**
Corfu, Str. of = Kerkyras, Notio
  Steno *Greece* 39°34N 20°0E **25 A4**
Coria *Spain* 39°58N 6°33E **21 C2**
Corigliano Cálabro *Italy* 39°36N 16°31E **22 E7**
Coringa Is. *Australia* 16°58S 149°58E **62 B4**
Corinth = Korinthos
  Greece 37°56N 22°55E **23 F10**
Corinth *Miss., U.S.A.* 34°56N 88°31W **85 D10**
Corinth *N.Y., U.S.A.* 43°15N 73°49W **83 C11**
Corinth, G. of = Korinthiakos
  Kolpos *Greece* 38°16N 22°30E **23 E10**
Corinto *Brazil* 18°20S 44°30W **93 G10**
Corinto *Nic.* 12°30N 87°10W **88 D2**
Cork *Ireland* 51°54N 8°29W **10 E3**
Cork □ *Ireland* 51°57N 8°40W **10 E3**
Cork Harbour *Ireland* 51°47N 8°16W **10 E3**
Çorlu *Turkey* 41°11N 27°49E **23 D12**
Cormack L. *Canada* 60°56N 121°37W **70 A4**
Cormorant *Canada* 54°14N 100°35W **71 C8**
Cormorant L. *Canada* 54°15N 100°50W **71 C8**
Corn Is. = Maíz, Is. del
  Nic. 12°15N 83°4W **88 D3**
Cornélio Procópio *Brazil* 23°7S 50°40W **95 A5**
Corner Brook *Canada* 48°57N 57°58W **73 C8**
Cornești *Moldova* 47°21N 28°1E **17 E15**
Corning *Ark., U.S.A.* 36°25N 90°35W **85 C9**
Corning *Calif., U.S.A.* 39°56N 122°11W **76 G2**
Corning *Iowa, U.S.A.* 40°59N 94°44W **80 E6**
Corning *N.Y., U.S.A.* 42°9N 77°3W **82 D7**
Cornwall *Canada* 45°2N 74°44W **83 A10**
Cornwall *U.S.A.* 40°17N 76°25W **83 F8**
Cornwall □ *U.K.* 50°26N 4°40W **13 G3**
Cornwall I. *Canada* 77°37N 94°38W **69 B13**
Cornwallis I. *Canada* 75°8N 95°0W **69 B13**
Corny Pt. *Australia* 34°55S 137°0E **63 E2**
Coro *Venezuela* 11°25N 69°41W **92 A5**
Coroatá *Brazil* 4°8S 44°0W **93 D10**
Corocoro *Bolivia* 17°15S 68°28W **92 G5**
Coroico *Bolivia* 16°0S 67°50W **92 G5**
Coromandel *N.Z.* 36°45S 175°31E **59 B5**
Coromandel Coast *India* 12°30N 81°0E **40 N12**
Corona *Calif., U.S.A.* 33°53N 117°34W **79 M9**
Corona *N. Mex., U.S.A.* 34°15N 105°36W **77 J11**
Coronado *U.S.A.* 32°41N 117°10W **79 N9**
Coronado, B. de *Costa Rica* 9°0N 83°40W **88 E3**
Coronados, Is. Los
  Mexico 32°26N 117°19W **79 N9**
Coronation *Canada* 52°5N 111°27W **70 C6**
Coronation Gulf
  Canada 68°25N 110°0W **68 D10**
Coronation I. *Antarctica* 60°45S 46°0W **5 C18**
Coronation Is. *Australia* 14°57S 124°55E **60 B3**
Coronda *Argentina* 31°58S 60°56W **94 C3**
Coronel *Chile* 37°0S 73°10W **94 D1**
Coronel Bogado
  Paraguay 27°11S 56°18W **94 B4**
Coronel Dorrego
  Argentina 38°40S 61°10W **94 D3**
Coronel Oviedo
  Paraguay 25°24S 56°30W **94 B4**
Coronel Pringles
  Argentina 38°0S 61°30W **94 D3**
Coronel Suárez
  Argentina 37°30S 61°52W **94 D3**
Coronel Vidal *Argentina* 37°28S 57°45W **94 D4**
Coropuna, Nevado *Peru* 15°30S 72°41W **92 G4**
Corowa *Australia* 35°58S 146°21E **63 F4**
Corozal □ *Belize* 18°23N 88°23W **87 D7**
Corozal Pt. *Trin. & Tob.* 10°45N 61°37W **93 K15**
Corpus *Argentina* 27°10S 55°30W **95 B4**
Corpus Christi *U.S.A.* 27°47N 97°24W **84 H6**
Corpus Christi, L. *U.S.A.* 28°2N 97°52W **84 G6**
Corralejo *Canary Is.* 28°43N 13°53W **24 F6**
Corraun Pen. *Ireland* 53°54N 9°54W **10 C2**
Correntes, C. das *Mozam.* 24°6S 35°34E **57 C6**
Corrib, L. *Ireland* 53°27N 9°16W **10 C2**
Corrientes *Argentina* 27°30S 58°45W **94 B4**
Corrientes □ *Argentina* 28°0S 57°0W **94 B4**
Corrientes → *Argentina* 30°42S 59°38W **94 C4**

Corrientes → *Peru* 3°43S 74°35W **92** D4
Corrientes, C. *Colombia* 5°30N 77°34W **92** B3
Corrientes, C. *Cuba* 21°43N 84°30W **88** B3
Corrientes, C. *Mexico* 20°25N 105°42W **86** C3
Corrigan *U.S.A.* 31°0N 94°52W **84** F7
Corrigin *Australia* 32°20S 117°53E **61** F2
Corriverton *Guyana* 5°55N 57°20W **92** B7
Corry *U.S.A.* 41°55N 79°39W **82** E5
Corse □ *France* 42°0N 9°0E **20** F8
Corse, C. *France* 43°1N 9°25E **20** E8
Corsica = Corse □ *France* 42°0N 9°0E **20** F8
Corsicana *U.S.A.* 32°6N 96°28W **84** E6
Corte *France* 42°19N 9°11E **20** E8
Cortés, Mar de = California, G. de
Mexico 27°0N 111°0W **86** B2
Cortez *U.S.A.* 37°21N 108°35W **77** H9
Cortland *N.Y., U.S.A.* 42°36N 76°11W **83** D8
Cortland *Ohio, U.S.A.* 41°20N 80°44W **82** E4
Çorum *Turkey* 40°30N 34°57E **19** F5
Corumbá *Brazil* 19°0S 57°30W **92** G7
Corunna = A Coruña
Spain 43°20N 8°25W **21** A1
Corvallis *U.S.A.* 44°34N 123°16W **76** D2
Corvette, L. de la *Canada* 53°25N 74°3W **72** B5
Corvo *Azores* 39°43N 31°8W **50** a
Corydon *U.S.A.* 40°46N 93°19W **80** E7
Cosalá *Mexico* 24°23N 106°41W **86** C3
Cosamaloapan de Carpio
Mexico 18°22N 95°48W **87** D5
Cosenza *Italy* 39°18N 16°15E **22** E7
Coshocton *U.S.A.* 40°16N 81°51W **82** F3
Cosmo Newberry
Australia 28°0S 122°54E **61** E3
Cosmo Newberry ⊚
Australia 27°59S 122°53E **61** E3
Cosmonaut Sea *S. Ocean* 66°30S 40°0E **5** C5
Coso Junction *U.S.A.* 36°3N 117°57W **79** J9
Coso Pk. *U.S.A.* 36°13N 117°44W **79** J9
Cosquín *Argentina* 31°15S 64°30W **94** C3
Costa Blanca *Spain* 38°25N 0°10W **21** C5
Costa Brava *Spain* 41°30N 3°0E **21** B7
Costa Cálida *Spain* 37°30N 1°30W **21** D5
Costa Daurada *Spain* 41°12N 1°15E **21** B6
Costa de la Luz *Spain* 36°15N 5°58W **21** D2
Costa del Azahar *Spain* 39°30N 0°13W **21** B6
Costa del Sol *Spain* 36°30N 4°30W **21** D3
Costa dels Pins *Spain* 39°38N 3°26E **24** B10
Costa Mesa *U.S.A.* 33°38N 117°55W **79** M9
Costa Rica ■ *Cent. Amer.* 10°0N 84°0W **88** E3
Costa Smeralda *Italy* 41°5N 9°35E **22** D3
Costa Verde *Spain* 43°22N 4°14W **21** A3
Cosumnes → *U.S.A.* 38°16N 121°26W **78** G5
Cotabato *Phil.* 7°14N 124°15E **37** C6
Cotagaita *Bolivia* 20°45S 65°40W **94** A2
Côte d'Azur *France* 43°25N 7°10E **20** E7
Côte-d'Ivoire = Ivory Coast ■
Africa 7°30N 5°0W **50** G4
Coteau des Prairies
U.S.A. 45°20N 97°50W **80** C5
Coteau du Missouri
U.S.A. 47°0N 100°0W **80** B4
Cotentin *France* 49°15N 1°30W **20** B3
Cotillo *Canary Is.* 28°41N 14°1W **24** F5
Cotonou *Benin* 6°20N 2°25E **50** G6
Cotopaxi *Ecuador* 0°40S 78°30W **92** D3
Cotswold Hills *U.K.* 51°42N 2°10W **13** F5
Cottage Grove *U.S.A.* 43°48N 123°3W **76** E2
Cottam *Canada* 42°8N 82°45W **82** D2
Cottbus *Germany* 51°45N 14°20E **16** C8
Cottonwood *U.S.A.* 34°45N 112°1W **77** J7
Cotulla *U.S.A.* 28°26N 99°14W **84** G5
Coudersport *U.S.A.* 41°46N 78°1W **82** E6
Couedic, C. du *Australia* 36°5S 136°40E **63** F2
Coulee City *U.S.A.* 47°37N 119°17W **76** C4
Coulee Dam Nat. Recr. Area =
Lake Roosevelt △
U.S.A. 48°5N 118°14W **76** B4
Coulman I. *Antarctica* 73°35S 170°0E **5** D11
Coulonge → *Canada* 45°52N 76°46W **72** C4
Coulterville *U.S.A.* 37°43N 120°12W **78** H6
Council *Alaska, U.S.A.* 64°53N 163°41W **74** C7
Council *Idaho, U.S.A.* 44°44N 116°26W **76** D5
Council Bluffs *U.S.A.* 41°16N 95°52W **80** E6
Council Grove *U.S.A.* 38°40N 96°29W **80** F6
Coupeville *U.S.A.* 48°13N 122°41W **78** B4
Courantyne → *S. Amer.* 5°55N 57°5W **92** B7
Courcelles *Belgium* 50°28N 4°22E **15** D4
Courtenay *Canada* 49°45N 125°0W **70** D4
Courtland *Canada* 42°51N 80°38W **82** D4
Courtland *U.S.A.* 38°20N 121°34W **78** G5
Courtrai = Kortrijk
Belgium 50°50N 3°17E **15** D3
Courtright *Canada* 42°49N 82°28W **82** D2
Coushatta *U.S.A.* 32°1N 93°21W **84** E8
Coutts Crossing
Australia 29°49S 152°55E **63** D5
Couva *Trin. & Tob.* 10°25N 61°27W **93** K15
Couvin *Belgium* 50°3N 4°29E **15** D4
Cove I. *Canada* 45°17N 81°44W **82** A3
Coventry *U.K.* 52°25N 1°28W **13** E6
Covilhã *Portugal* 40°17N 7°31W **21** B2
Covington *Ga., U.S.A.* 33°36N 83°51W **85** E13
Covington *Ky., U.S.A.* 39°5N 84°30W **81** F11
Covington *Tenn., U.S.A.* 35°34N 89°39W **85** D10
Covington *Va., U.S.A.* 37°47N 79°59W **81** G14
Cowal, L. *Australia* 33°40S 147°25E **63** E4
Cowan, L. *Australia* 31°45S 121°45E **61** F3
Cowan L. *Canada* 54°0N 107°15W **71** C7
Cowangie *Australia* 35°12S 141°26E **63** F3
Cowansville *Canada* 45°14N 72°46W **83** A12
Coward Springs
Australia 29°24S 136°49E **63** D2
Cowcowing Lakes
Australia 30°55S 117°20E **61** F2
Cowdenbeath *U.K.* 56°7N 3°21W **11** E5
Cowell *Australia* 33°39S 136°56E **63** E2
Cowes *U.K.* 50°45N 1°18W **13** G6
Cowichan L. *Canada* 48°53N 124°17W **78** B2
Cowlitz → *U.S.A.* 46°6N 122°55W **78** D4
Cowra *Australia* 33°49S 148°42E **63** E4

Coxilha Grande *Brazil* 28°18S 51°30W **95** B5
Coxim *Brazil* 18°30S 54°55W **93** G8
Cox's Bazar *Bangla.* 21°26N 91°59E **41** J17
Coyote Wells *U.S.A.* 32°44N 115°58W **79** N11
Coyuca de Benitez
Mexico 17°2N 100°4W **87** D4
Coyuca de Catalán
Mexico 18°20N 100°39W **86** D4
Cozad *U.S.A.* 40°52N 99°59W **80** E4
Cozumel *Mexico* 20°31N 86°55W **87** C7
Cozumel, Isla *Mexico* 20°30N 86°40W **87** C7
Crab Hill *Barbados* 13°19N 59°38W **89** g
Cracow = Kraków
Poland 50°4N 19°57E **17** C10
Cracow *Australia* 25°17S 150°17E **63** D5
Cradle Mt.-Lake St. Clair △
Australia 41°49S 147°56E **63** G4
Cradock *Australia* 32°6S 138°31E **63** E2
Cradock *S. Africa* 32°8S 25°36E **56** E4
Craig *U.S.A.* 40°31N 107°33W **76** F10
Craigavon *U.K.* 54°27N 6°23W **10** B5
Craigmore *Zimbabwe* 20°28S 32°50E **55** G3
Craik *Canada* 51°3N 105°49W **71** C7
Crailsheim *Germany* 49°8N 10°5E **16** D6
Craiova *Romania* 44°21N 23°48E **17** F12
Cramsie *Australia* 23°20S 144°15E **62** C3
Cranberry L. *U.S.A.* 44°11N 74°50W **83** B10
Cranberry Portage
Canada 54°35N 101°23W **71** C8
Cranbrook *Australia* 34°18S 117°33E **61** F2
Cranbrook *Canada* 49°30N 115°46W **70** D5
Crandon *U.S.A.* 45°34N 88°54W **80** C9
Crane *Oreg., U.S.A.* 43°25N 118°35W **76** E4
Crane *Tex., U.S.A.* 31°24N 102°21W **84** F3
Crane, The *Barbados* 13°6N 59°27W **89** g
Cranston *U.S.A.* 41°47N 71°26W **83** E13
Crater L. *U.S.A.* 42°56N 122°6W **76** E2
Crater Lake △ *U.S.A.* 42°55N 122°10W **76** E2
Craters of the Moon ☐
U.S.A. 43°25N 113°30W **76** E7
Crateús *Brazil* 5°10S 40°39W **93** E11
Crato *Brazil* 7°10S 39°25W **93** E11
Craven, L. *Canada* 54°20N 76°56W **72** B4
Crawford *U.S.A.* 42°41N 103°25W **80** D2
Crawfordsville *U.S.A.* 40°2N 86°54W **80** E10
Crawley *U.K.* 51°7N 0°11W **13** F7
Crazy Mts. *U.S.A.* 46°12N 110°20W **76** C8
Crean L. *Canada* 54°5N 106°9W **71** C7
Crediton *Canada* 43°17N 81°33W **82** C3
Crediton *U.K.* 50°47N 3°40W **13** G4
Cree → *Canada* 58°57N 105°47W **71** B7
Cree → *U.K.* 54°55N 4°25W **11** G4
Cree L. *Canada* 57°30N 106°30W **71** B7
Creede *U.S.A.* 37°51N 106°56W **77** H10
Creekside *U.S.A.* 40°40N 79°11W **82** F5
Creel *Mexico* 27°45N 107°38W **86** B3
Creemore *Canada* 44°19N 80°6W **82** B4
Creighton *Canada* 54°45N 101°54W **71** C8
Creighton *U.S.A.* 42°28N 97°54W **80** D5
Crema *Italy* 45°22N 9°41E **20** D8
Cremona *Italy* 45°7N 10°2E **20** D9
Cres *Croatia* 44°58N 14°25E **16** F8
Crescent City *U.S.A.* 41°45N 124°12W **76** F1
Crespo *Argentina* 32°2S 60°19W **94** C3
Cresson *U.S.A.* 40°28N 78°36W **82** F6
Crestline *Calif., U.S.A.* 34°14N 117°18W **79** L9
Crestline *Ohio, U.S.A.* 40°47N 82°44W **82** F2
Creston *Canada* 49°10N 116°31W **70** D5
Creston *Calif., U.S.A.* 35°32N 120°33W **78** K6
Creston *Iowa, U.S.A.* 41°4N 94°22W **80** E6
Crestview *Calif., U.S.A.* 37°46N 118°58W **78** H8
Crestview *Fla., U.S.A.* 30°46N 86°34W **85** F11
Crete = Kriti *Greece* 35°15N 25°0E **25** D7
Crete *U.S.A.* 40°38N 96°58W **80** E5
Créteil *France* 48°47N 2°27E **20** B5
Creus, C. de *Spain* 42°20N 3°19E **21** A7
Creuse → *France* 47°0N 0°34E **20** C4
Crewe *U.K.* 53°6N 2°26W **12** D5
Crewkerne *U.K.* 50°53N 2°48W **13** G5
Crianlarich *U.K.* 56°24N 4°37W **11** E4
Criciúma *Brazil* 28°40S 49°23W **95** B6
Crieff *U.K.* 56°22N 3°50W **11** E5
Crimean Pen. = Krymskyy
Pivostriv *Ukraine* 45°0N 34°0E **19** F5
Crimea ☐ *Ukraine* 45°30N 33°10E **19** E5
Crișul Alb → *Romania* 46°42N 21°17E **17** E11
Crișul Negru →
Romania 46°42N 21°16E **17** E11
Crna → *Macedonia* 41°33N 21°59E **23** D9
Crna Gora = Montenegro ■
Europe 42°40N 19°20E **23** C8
Crna Gora *Macedonia* 42°10N 21°30E **23** C9
Crna Reka = Crna →
Macedonia 41°33N 21°59E **23** D9
Croagh Patrick *Ireland* 53°46N 9°40W **10** C2
Croatia ■ *Europe* 45°20N 16°0E **16** F9
Crocker, Banjaran
Malaysia 5°40N 116°30E **36** C5
Crockett *U.S.A.* 31°19N 95°27W **84** F7
Crocodile = Umgwenya →
Mozam. 25°14S 32°18E **57** D5
Crocodile Is. *Australia* 12°3S 134°58E **62** A1
Crohy Hd. *Ireland* 54°55N 8°26W **10** B3
Croix, L. la *Canada* 48°20N 92°15W **72** C1
Croker, C. *Australia* 10°58S 132°35E **60** B5
Croker, C. *Canada* 44°58N 80°59W **82** B4
Croker I. *Australia* 11°12S 132°32E **60** B5
Croker Islands Seas ⊚
Australia 11°20S 132°30E **60** B5
Cromarty *U.K.* 57°40N 4°2W **11** D4
Cromer *U.K.* 52°56N 1°17E **12** E9
Cromwell *N.Z.* 45°3S 169°14E **59** F2
Cromwell *U.S.A.* 41°36N 72°39W **83** E12
Crook *U.K.* 54°43N 1°45W **12** C6
Crooked → *Canada* 54°50N 122°54W **70** C4
Crooked → *U.S.A.* 44°32N 121°16W **76** D3
Crooked I. *Bahamas* 22°50N 74°10W **89** B5
Crooked Island Passage
Bahamas 22°55N 74°35W **89** B5
Crookston *Minn., U.S.A.* 47°47N 96°37W **80** B5

Crookston *Nebr., U.S.A.* 42°56N 100°45W **80** D3
Crookwell *Australia* 34°28S 149°24E **63** E4
Crosby *U.K.* 53°30N 3°3W **12** D4
Crosby *N. Dak., U.S.A.* 48°55N 103°18W **80** A2
Crosby *Pa., U.S.A.* 41°45N 78°23W **82** E6
Crosbyton *U.S.A.* 33°40N 101°14W **84** E4
Cross City *U.S.A.* 29°38N 83°7W **85** G13
Cross Fell *U.K.* 54°43N 2°28W **12** C5
Cross L. *Canada* 54°45N 97°30W **71** C9
Cross Lake *Canada* 54°37N 97°47W **71** C9
Cross Sound *U.S.A.* 58°0N 135°0W **68** F4
Crossett *U.S.A.* 33°8N 91°58W **84** E9
Crosshaven *Ireland* 51°47N 8°17W **10** E3
Crossmaglen *U.K.* 54°5N 6°36W **10** B5
Crossmolina *Ireland* 54°6N 9°20W **10** B2
Crossville *U.S.A.* 35°57N 85°2W **85** D12
Croswell *U.S.A.* 43°16N 82°37W **82** C2
Croton-on-Hudson
U.S.A. 41°12N 73°55W **83** E11
Crotone *Italy* 39°5N 17°8E **22** E7
Crow → *Canada* 59°41N 124°20W **70** B4
Crow Agency *U.S.A.* 45°36N 107°28W **76** D10
Crow Hd. *Ireland* 51°35N 10°9W **10** E1
Crowell *U.S.A.* 33°59N 99°43W **84** E5
Crowley *U.S.A.* 30°13N 92°22W **84** F8
Crowley, L. *U.S.A.* 37°35N 118°42W **78** H8
Crown Point *Ind.,*
U.S.A. 41°25N 87°22W **80** E10
Crown Point *N.Y.,*
U.S.A. 43°57N 73°26W **83** C11
Crown Pt. *Trin. & Tob.* 11°18N 60°51W **93** J16
Crownpoint *U.S.A.* 35°41N 108°9W **77** J9
Crows Landing *U.S.A.* 37°23N 121°6W **78** H5
Crows Nest *Australia* 27°16S 152°4E **63** D5
Crowsnest Pass *Canada* 49°40N 114°40W **70** D6
Croydon *Australia* 18°13S 142°14E **62** B3
Croydon □ *U.K.* 51°22N 0°5W **13** F7
Crozet, Îs. *Ind. Oc.* 46°27S 52°0E **3** G12
Crozet, Îs. *Ind. Oc.* 46°27S 52°0E **3** G12
Crusheen *Ireland* 52°57N 8°53W **10** D3
Cruz, C. *Cuba* 19°50N 77°50W **88** C4
Cruz Alta *Brazil* 28°45S 53°40W **95** B5
Cruz Bay *U.S. Virgin Is.* 18°20N 64°48W **89** e
Cruz del Eje *Argentina* 30°45S 64°50W **94** C3
Cruzeiro *Brazil* 22°33S 45°0W **95** A7
Cruzeiro do Oeste *Brazil* 23°46S 53°4W **95** A5
Cruzeiro do Sul *Brazil* 7°35S 72°35W **92** E4
Cry L. *Canada* 58°45N 129°0W **70** B3
Crystal Bay *U.S.A.* 39°15N 120°0W **78** F7
Crystal Brook *Australia* 33°21S 138°12E **63** E2
Crystal City *U.S.A.* 28°41N 99°50W **84** G5
Crystal Falls *U.S.A.* 46°5N 88°20W **80** B9
Crystal River *U.S.A.* 28°54N 82°35W **85** G13
Crystal Springs *U.S.A.* 31°59N 90°21W **85** F9
Csongrád *Hungary* 46°43N 20°12E **17** E11
Cu Lao Hon *Vietnam* 10°54N 108°18E **39** G7
Cua Rao *Vietnam* 19°16N 104°27E **38** C5
Cuácua → *Mozam.* 17°54S 37°0E **55** F4
Cuamato *Angola* 17°2S 15°7E **56** B2
Cuamba *Mozam.* 14°45S 36°22E **55** E4
Cuando → *Angola* 17°30S 23°15E **53** H4
Cuando Cubango ☐
Angola 16°25S 20°0E **56** B3
Cuangar *Angola* 17°36S 18°39E **56** B2
Cuango = Kwango →
Dem. Rep. of the Congo 3°14S 17°22E **52** E3
Cuanza → *Angola* 9°21S 13°9E **52** F2
Cuarto → *Argentina* 33°25S 63°2W **94** C3
Cuatrociénegas *Mexico* 26°59N 102°5W **86** B4
Cuauhtémoc *Mexico* 28°25N 106°52W **86** B3
Cuba *N. Mex., U.S.A.* 36°1N 107°4W **77** H10
Cuba *N.Y., U.S.A.* 42°13N 78°17W **82** D6
Cuba ■ *W. Indies* 22°0N 79°0W **88** B4
Cubango → *Africa* 18°50S 22°25E **56** B3
Cuchumatanes, Sierra de los
Guatemala 15°35N 91°25W **88** C1
Cuckfield *U.K.* 51°1N 0°8W **13** F7
Cucuí *Brazil* 1°12N 66°50W **92** C5
Cucurpé *Mexico* 30°20N 110°43W **86** A2
Cúcuta *Colombia* 7°54N 72°31W **92** B4
Cuddalore *India* 11°46N 79°45E **40** P11
Cuddapah *India* 14°30N 78°47E **40** M11
Cuddapan, L. *Australia* 25°45S 141°26E **62** D3
Cue *Australia* 27°25S 117°54E **61** E2
Cuenca *Ecuador* 2°50S 79°9W **92** D3
Cuenca *Spain* 40°5N 2°10W **21** B4
Cuenca, Serranía de
Spain 39°55N 1°50W **21** C5
Cuernavaca *Mexico* 18°55N 99°15W **87** D5
Cuero *U.S.A.* 29°6N 97°17W **84** G6
Cueva de la Quebrada del Toro △
Venezuela 10°46N 69°3W **89** D6
Cuevas del Almanzora
Spain 37°18N 1°58W **21** D5
Cuevo *Bolivia* 20°15S 63°30W **92** H6
Cuiabá *Brazil* 15°30S 56°0W **93** G7
Cuiabá → *Brazil* 17°5S 56°36W **93** G7
Cuihangcun *China* 22°27N 113°32E **33** a
Cuijk *Neths.* 51°44N 5°50E **15** C5
Cuilco *Guatemala* 15°24N 91°58W **88** C1
Cuillin Hills *U.K.* 57°13N 6°15W **11** D2
Cuillin Sd. *U.K.* 57°4N 6°20W **11** D2
Cuilo → Kwilu →
Dem. Rep. of the Congo 3°22S 17°22E **52** E3
Cuito → *Angola* 18°1S 20°48E **56** B3
Cuitzeo, L. de *Mexico* 19°55N 101°5W **86** D4
Cukai *Malaysia* 4°13N 103°25E **39** K4
Culbertson *U.S.A.* 48°9N 104°31W **76** B11
Culcairn *Australia* 35°41S 147°3E **63** F4
Culebra *Puerto Rico* 18°19N 65°18W **89** d
Culgoa → *Australia* 29°56S 146°20E **63** D4
Culgoa Flood Plain △
Australia 28°58S 147°5E **63** D4
Culiacán *Mexico* 24°50N 107°23W **86** C3
Culiacán → *Mexico* 24°30N 107°42W **86** C3
Culik *Indonesia* 8°21S 115°37E **37** J18
Culion *Phil.* 11°54N 119°58E **37** B6
Cullarin Ra. *Australia* 34°30S 149°30E **63** E4
Cullera *Spain* 39°9N 0°17W **21** C5
Cullman *U.S.A.* 34°11N 86°51W **85** D11
Cullompton *U.K.* 50°51N 3°24W **13** G4
Culpeper *U.S.A.* 38°30N 78°0W **81** F14
Culuene → *Brazil* 12°56S 52°51W **93** F8
Culver, Pt. *Australia* 32°54S 124°43E **61** F3
Culverden *N.Z.* 42°47S 172°49E **59** E4
Cumaná *Venezuela* 10°30N 64°5W **92** A6
Cumberland *B.C.,*
Canada 49°40N 125°0W **70** D4
Cumberland *Ont.,*
Canada 45°29N 75°24W **83** A9
Cumberland *U.S.A.* 39°39N 78°46W **81** F14
Cumberland → *U.S.A.* 37°9N 88°25W **80** G9
Cumberland, L. *U.S.A.* 36°52N 85°9W **81** G11
Cumberland Gap △
U.S.A. 36°36N 83°40W **81** G12
Cumberland I. *U.S.A.* 30°50N 81°25W **85** F14
Cumberland Is. *Australia* 20°35S 149°10E **62** b
Cumberland Island △
U.S.A. 30°12N 81°24W **85** F14
Cumberland L. *Canada* 54°3N 102°18W **71** C8
Cumberland Pen. *Canada* 67°0N 64°0W **69** D19
Cumberland Plateau
U.S.A. 36°0N 85°0W **85** D12
Cumberland Sd. *Canada* 65°30N 66°0W **69** D18
Cumbernauld *U.K.* 55°57N 3°58W **11** F5
Cumborah *Australia* 29°40S 147°45E **63** D4
Cumbria □ *U.K.* 54°42N 2°52W **12** C5
Cumbrian Mts. *U.K.* 54°30N 3°0W **12** C5
Cumbum *India* 15°40N 79°10E **40** M11
Cuminá → *Brazil* 1°30S 56°0W **93** D7
Cummings Mt. *U.S.A.* 35°2N 118°34W **79** K8
Cummins *Australia* 34°16S 135°43E **63** E2
Cumnock *Australia* 32°59S 148°46E **63** E4
Cumnock *U.K.* 55°28N 4°17W **11** F4
Cumpas *Mexico* 30°2N 109°48W **86** B3
Cumplida, Pta.
Canary Is. 28°50N 17°48W **24** F2
Cunco *Chile* 38°55S 72°2W **96** D2
Cuncumén *Chile* 31°53S 70°38W **94** C1
Cundeelee ⊚ *Australia* 30°43S 123°25E **61** F3
Cunderdin *Australia* 31°37S 117°12E **61** F2
Cunene → *Angola* 17°20S 11°50E **56** B1
Cúneo *Italy* 44°23N 7°32E **20** D7
Cung Son *Vietnam* 13°2N 108°58E **38** F7
Çüngüş *Turkey* 38°13N 39°17E **44** B3
Cunillera, I. = Sa Conillera
Spain 38°59N 1°13E **24** C7
Cunnamulla *Australia* 28°2S 145°38E **63** D4
Cupar *Canada* 50°57N 104°10W **71** C8
Cupar *U.K.* 56°19N 3°1W **11** E5
Cupertino *U.S.A.* 37°19N 122°2W **78** H4
Cupica, G. de *Colombia* 6°25N 77°30W **92** B3
Curaçao *W. Indies* 12°10N 69°0W **89** D6
Curanilahue *Chile* 37°29S 73°28W **94** D1
Curaray → *Peru* 2°20S 74°5W **92** D4
Curepipe *Mauritius* 20°19S 57°31E **53** d
Curepto *Chile* 35°8S 72°1W **94** D1
Curiapo *Venezuela* 8°33N 61°5W **92** B6
Curicó *Chile* 34°55S 71°20W **94** C1
Curitiba *Brazil* 25°20S 49°10W **95** B6
Curitibanos *Brazil* 27°18S 50°36W **95** B5
Currabubula *Australia* 31°16S 150°44E **63** E5
Currais Novos *Brazil* 6°13S 36°30W **93** E11
Curral Velho *C. Verde Is.* 16°8N 22°48W **50** b
Curralinho *Brazil* 1°45S 49°46W **93** D9
Currane, L. *Ireland* 51°49N 10°4W **10** E1
Currant *U.S.A.* 38°44N 115°28W **76** G6
Currawinya △ *Australia* 28°25S 144°27E **63** D3
Current → *U.S.A.* 36°15N 90°55W **84** C9
Currie *Australia* 39°56S 143°53E **63** F3
Currie *U.S.A.* 40°16N 114°45W **76** F6
Curtea de Argeş
Romania 45°12N 24°42E **17** F13
Curtin Springs *Australia* 25°20S 131°45E **61** E5
Curtis *U.S.A.* 40°38N 100°31W **80** E3
Curtis Group *Australia* 39°30S 146°37E **63** F4
Curtis I. *Australia* 23°35S 151°10E **62** C5
Curuápanema → *Brazil* 2°25S 55°2W **93** D7
Curuçá *Brazil* 0°43S 47°50W **93** D9
Curuguaty *Paraguay* 24°31S 55°42W **95** A4
Çürüksu Çayı = Büyük
Menderes → *Turkey* 37°28N 27°11E **23** F12
Curup *Indonesia* 3°26S 102°13E **36** E2
Cururupu *Brazil* 1°50S 44°50W **93** D10
Curuzú Cuatiá *Argentina* 29°50S 58°5W **94** B4
Curvelo *Brazil* 18°45S 44°27W **93** G10
Cusco *Peru* 13°32S 72°0W **92** F4
Cushendall *U.K.* 55°6N 6°4W **10** A5
Cushing *U.S.A.* 35°59N 96°46W **84** D6
Cushing, Mt. *Canada* 57°35N 126°57W **70** B3
Cusihuiriáchic *Mexico* 28°14N 106°50W **86** B3
Custer *U.S.A.* 43°46N 103°36W **80** D2
Cut Bank *U.S.A.* 48°38N 112°20W **76** B7
Cutchogue *U.S.A.* 41°1N 72°30W **83** E12
Cuthbert *U.S.A.* 31°46N 84°48W **85** F12
Cutler *U.S.A.* 36°31N 119°17W **78** J7
Cuttaburra → *Australia* 29°43S 144°22E **63** D3
Cuttack *India* 20°25N 85°57E **41** J14
Cuvier, C. *Australia* 23°14S 113°22E **61** D1
Cuvier I. *N.Z.* 36°27S 175°50E **59** B5
Cuxhaven *Germany* 53°51N 8°41E **16** B5
Cuyahoga Falls *U.S.A.* 41°8N 81°29W **82** E3
Cuyahoga Valley △
U.S.A. 41°24N 81°33W **82** E3
Cuyo *Phil.* 10°51N 121°2E **37** B6
Cuyuni → *Guyana* 6°23N 58°41W **92** B7
Cuzco = Cusco *Peru* 13°32S 72°0W **92** F4
Cuzco *Bolivia* 20°0S 66°50W **92** H5
Cwmbran *U.K.* 51°39N 3°2W **13** F4
Cyangugu *Rwanda* 2°29S 28°54E **54** C2
Cyclades *Greece* 37°0N 24°30E **23** F11
Cygnet *Australia* 43°8S 147°1E **63** G4
Cynthiana *U.S.A.* 38°23N 84°18W **81** F11

Cullera *Spain* 39°9N 0°17W **21** C5
Cypress Hills *Canada* 49°40N 109°30W **71** D7
Cypress Hills △ *Canada* 49°40N 109°30W **71** D7
Cyprus ■ *Asia* 35°0N 33°0E **25** E12
Cyrenaica = Barqa *Libya* 27°0N 23°0E **51** C10
Cyrene *Libya* 32°55N 21°52E **51** B10
Czar *Canada* 52°27N 110°50W **71** C6
Czech Rep. ■ *Europe* 50°0N 15°0E **16** D8
Częstochowa *Poland* 50°49N 19°7E **17** C10

D

Da → *Vietnam* 21°15N 105°20E **38** B5
Da Hinggan Ling *China* 48°0N 121°0E **33** B13
Da Lat *Vietnam* 11°56N 108°25E **39** G7
Da Nang *Vietnam* 16°4N 108°13E **38** D7
Da Qaidam *China* 37°50N 95°15E **32** C4
Da Yunhe → *Hopei,*
China 39°10N 117°10E **35** E9
Da Yunhe → *Jiangsu,*
China 34°25N 120°5E **35** G11
Da'an *China* 45°30N 124°7E **35** B13
Daan Viljoen △ *Namibia* 22°2S 16°45E **56** C2
Daba Shan *China* 32°0N 109°0E **33** C10
Dabbagh, Jabal *Si. Arabia* 27°52N 35°45E **44** E2
Dabhoi *India* 22°10N 73°20E **42** H5
Dabie Shan *China* 31°20N 115°20E **33** C11
Dabola *Guinea* 10°50N 11°5W **50** F3
Dabung *Malaysia* 5°23N 102°1E **39** K4
Dacca = Dhaka *Bangla.* 23°43N 90°26E **43** H14
Dacca = Dhaka □
Bangla. 24°25N 90°25E **43** G14
Dachau *Germany* 48°15N 11°26E **16** D6
Dachigam △ *India* 34°10N 75°0E **42** B6
Dacre *Canada* 45°22N 76°57W **82** A8
Dadanawa *Guyana* 2°50N 59°30W **92** C7
Dade City *U.S.A.* 28°22N 82°11W **85** G13
Dadhar *Pakistan* 29°28N 67°39E **42** E2
Dadnah *U.A.E.* 25°32N 56°22E **45** E8
Dadra & Nagar Haveli □
India 20°5N 73°0E **40** J8
Dadri = Charkhi Dadri
India 28°37N 76°17E **42** E7
Dadu *Pakistan* 26°45N 67°45E **42** F2
Daegu *S. Korea* 35°50N 128°37E **35** G15
Daejeon *S. Korea* 36°20N 127°28E **35** F14
Daejeong *S. Korea* 33°8N 126°17E **35** H14
Daet *Phil.* 14°2N 122°55E **37** B6
Dafeng *China* 33°3N 120°45E **35** H11
Dafnes *Greece* 35°13N 25°3E **25** D7
Dagana *Senegal* 16°30N 15°35W **50** E2
Dagestan □ *Russia* 42°30N 47°0E **19** F8
Daggett *U.S.A.* 34°52N 116°52W **79** L10
Daghestan Republic =
Dagestan □ *Russia* 42°30N 47°0E **19** F8
Dağlıq Qarabağ =
Nagorno-Karabakh □
Azerbaijan 39°55N 46°45E **44** B5
Dagö = Hiiumaa *Estonia* 58°50N 22°45E **9** G20
Dagu *China* 38°59N 117°40E **35** E9
Dagupan *Phil.* 16°3N 120°20E **37** A6
Daguragu *Australia* 17°33S 130°30E **60** C5
Daguragu ⊚ *Australia* 17°24S 130°48E **60** C5
Dahab *Egypt* 28°31N 34°31E **44** D2
Dahlak Kebir *Eritrea* 15°50N 40°10E **47** D3
Dahlonega *U.S.A.* 34°32N 83°59W **85** D13
Dahod *India* 22°50N 74°15E **42** H6
Dahongliutan *China* 35°45N 79°20E **43** B8
Dahra *Libya* 29°30N 17°50E **51** C9
Dahūk *Iraq* 36°50N 43°1E **44** B3
Dai Hao *Vietnam* 18°1N 106°25E **38** C6
Dai-Sen *Japan* 35°22N 133°32E **31** G6
Dai Xian *China* 39°4N 112°58E **34** E7
Daicheng *China* 38°42N 116°38E **34** E9
Daikondi = Day Kundī □
Afghan. 34°0N 66°0E **40** C5
Daingean *Ireland* 53°18N 7°17W **10** C4
Daintree *Australia* 16°20S 145°20E **62** B4
Daintree *Australia* 16°8S 145°2E **62** B4
Daiō-Misaki *Japan* 34°15N 136°45E **31** G8
Daisen-Oki △ *Japan* 35°23N 133°34E **31** G6
Daisetsu-Zan *Japan* 43°30N 142°57E **30** C11
Daisetsu-Zan △ *Japan* 43°30N 142°52E **30** C11
Dajarra *Australia* 21°42S 139°30E **62** C2
Dajiawa *China* 37°9N 119°0E **35** F10
Dak Dam *Cambodia* 12°20N 107°21E **38** F6
Dak Nhe *Vietnam* 15°28N 107°48E **38** E6
Dak Pek *Vietnam* 15°4N 107°44E **38** E6
Dak Song *Vietnam* 12°19N 107°35E **39** F6
Dak Sui *Vietnam* 14°55N 107°43E **38** E6
Dakar *Senegal* 14°34N 17°29W **50** F2
Dakhla *W. Sahara* 23°50N 15°53W **50** D2
Dakhla, El Wâhât el
Egypt 25°30N 28°50E **51** C11
Dakhovskaya *Russia* 44°13N 40°13E **19** F7
Dakor *India* 22°45N 73°11E **42** H5
Dakota City *U.S.A.* 42°25N 96°25W **80** D5
Đakovica *Kosovo* 42°22N 20°26E **23** C9
Dalachi *China* 36°48N 105°0E **34** F3
Dalai Nur *China* 43°20N 116°45E **34** C9
Đălakī *Iran* 29°26N 51°17E **45** D6
Dālälven → *Sweden* 60°12N 16°43E **9** F17
Dalaman *Turkey* 36°41N 28°43E **23** F13
Dalandzadgad *Mongolia* 43°27N 104°30E **34** C3
Dalap-Uliga-Darrit = Majuro
Marshall Is. 7°9N 171°12E **64** G9
Dalarna *Sweden* 61°0N 14°0E **9** F16
Dalay *Mongolia* 43°20N 103°50E **34** C2
Dālbandīn *Pakistan* 29°0N 64°23E **40** E4
Dalbeattie *U.K.* 54°56N 3°50W **11** G5
Dalbeg *Australia* 20°16S 147°18E **62** C4
Dalby *Australia* 27°10S 151°17E **63** D5
Dale City *U.S.A.* 38°38N 77°19W **81** F15
Dale Hollow L. *U.S.A.* 36°32N 85°27W **85** C12
Dalgān *Iran* 27°31N 59°19E **45** E8
Dalhart *U.S.A.* 36°4N 102°31W **84** C3
Dalhousie *Canada* 48°5N 66°26W **73** C6
Dalhousie *India* 32°38N 75°58E **42** C6
Dali *Shaanxi, China* 34°48N 109°58E **34** G5
Dali *Yunnan, China* 25°40N 100°10E **41** G22
Dalian *China* 38°50N 121°40E **35** E11

Daliang Shan China 28°0N 102°45E 32 F9
Daling He → China 40°55N 121°40E 35 D11
Dāliyat el Karmel Israel 32°43N 35°2E 46 C4
Dalkeith U.K. 55°54N 3°4W 11 F5
Dallas Oreg., U.S.A. 44°55N 123°19W 76 D2
Dallas Tex., U.S.A. 32°47N 96°48W 84 E6
Dalles, The U.S.A. 45°36N 121°10W 76 D3
Dalmā U.A.E. 24°30N 52°20E 45 E7
Dalmacija Croatia 43°20N 17°0E 22 C7
Dalmas, L. Canada 53°30N 71°50W 73 B5
Dalmatia = Dalmacija
Croatia 43°20N 17°0E 22 C7
Dalmau India 26°4N 81°2E 43 F9
Dalmellington U.K. 55°19N 4°23W 11 F4
Dalnegorsk Russia 44°32N 135°33E 30 B7
Dalnerechensk Russia 45°50N 133°40E 30 B6
Dalnevostochnyy □
Russia 67°0N 140°0E 29 C14
Daloa Ivory C. 7°0N 6°30W 50 G4
Dalry U.K. 55°42N 4°43W 11 F4
Dalrymple, L. Australia 20°40S 147°0E 62 C4
Dalrymple, Mt. Australia 21°1S 148°39E 62 b
Dalsland Sweden 58°50N 12°15E 9 G15
Daltenganj India 24°0N 84°4E 43 H11
Dalton Ga., U.S.A. 34°46N 84°58W 85 D12
Dalton Mass., U.S.A. 42°28N 73°11W 83 D11
Dalton Nebr., U.S.A. 41°25N 102°58W 80 E2
Dalton-in-Furness U.K. 54°10N 3°11W 12 C4
Dalvík Iceland 65°58N 18°32W 8 D4
Dálvvadis = Jokkmokk
Sweden 66°35N 19°50E 8 C18
Dalwallinu Australia 30°17S 116°40E 61 F2
Daly → Australia 13°35S 130°19E 60 B5
Daly City U.S.A. 37°42N 122°27W 78 H4
Daly L. Canada 56°32N 105°39W 71 B7
Daly River Australia 13°46S 130°42E 60 B5
Daly River-Port Keats ☼
Australia 14°13S 129°36E 60 B4
Daly Waters Australia 16°15S 133°24E 62 B1
Dam Doi Vietnam 8°50N 105°12E 39 H5
Dam Ha Vietnam 21°21N 107°36E 38 B6
Daman India 20°25N 72°57E 40 J8
Dāmaneh Iran 33°1N 50°29E 45 C6
Damanhûr Egypt 31°0N 30°30E 51 B12
Damant L. Canada 61°45N 105°5W 71 A7
Damar Indonesia 7°7S 128°40E 37 F7
Damara C.A.R. 4°58N 18°42E 52 D3
Damaraland Namibia 20°0S 15°0E 56 C2
Damascus = Dimashq
Syria 33°30N 36°18E 46 B5
Damatura Nigeria 11°45N 11°55E 52 B2
Damāvand Iran 35°47N 52°0E 45 C7
Damāvand, Qolleh-ye
Iran 35°56N 52°10E 45 C7
Damba Angola 6°44S 15°20E 52 F3
Dâmboviţa → Romania 44°12N 26°26E 17 F14
Dame Marie Haiti 18°36N 74°26W 89 C5
Dāmghān Iran 36°10N 54°17E 45 B7
Damiel Spain 39°4N 3°37W 21 C4
Damietta = Dumyât
Egypt 31°24N 31°48E 51 B12
Daming China 36°15N 115°6E 34 F8
Damīr Qābū Syria 36°58N 41°51E 44 B4
Dammam = Ad Dammām
Si. Arabia 26°20N 50°5E 45 E6
Damodar → India 23°17N 87°35E 43 H12
Damoh India 23°50N 79°28E 43 H8
Dampier Australia 20°41S 116°42E 60 D2
Dampier, Selat Indonesia 0°40S 131°0E 37 E8
Dampier Arch.
Australia 20°38S 116°32E 60 D2
Damrei, Chuor Phnum
Cambodia 11°30N 103°0E 39 G4
Damyang S. Korea 35°19N 126°59E 35 G14
Dana Indonesia 11°0S 121°15E 37 F6
Dana Jordan 30°41N 35°37E 46 E4
Dana, L. Canada 50°53N 77°20W 72 B4
Dana, Mt. U.S.A. 37°54N 119°12W 78 H7
Danakil Desert Ethiopia 12°45N 41°0E 47 E3
Danané Ivory C. 7°16N 8°9W 50 G4
Danbury U.S.A. 41°24N 73°28W 83 E11
Danby L. U.S.A. 34°13N 115°5W 77 J6
Dand Afghan. 31°28N 65°32E 42 D1
Dande ⌂ Zimbabwe 15°56S 30°16E 55 F3
Dandeldhura Nepal 29°20N 80°35E 43 E9
Dandeli India 15°5N 74°30E 40 M9
Dandenong Australia 38°0S 145°15E 63 F4
Dandong China 40°10N 124°20E 35 D13
Danfeng China 33°45N 110°25E 34 H6
Danger Is. = Pukapuka
Cook Is. 10°53S 165°49W 65 J11
Danger Pt. S. Africa 34°40S 19°17E 56 E2
Dangla Shan = Tanggula Shan
China 32°40N 92°10E 32 E7
Dangrek, Mts. = Dangrek, Phnom
Thailand 14°20N 104°0E 38 E5
Dangrek, Phnom
Thailand 14°20N 104°0E 38 E5
Dangriga Belize 17°0N 88°13W 87 D7
Dangshan China 34°27N 116°22E 34 G9
Daniel U.S.A. 42°52N 110°4W 76 E8
Daniel's Harbour
Canada 50°13N 57°35W 73 B8
Danielskuil S. Africa 28°11S 23°33E 56 D3
Danielson U.S.A. 41°48N 71°53W 83 E13
Danilov Russia 58°16N 40°13E 18 C7
Daning China 36°28N 110°45E 34 F6
Ḍank Oman 23°33N 56°16E 45 F8
Dankhar Gompa India 32°10N 78°10E 42 C8
Danlí Honduras 14°4N 86°35W 88 D2
Danmark = Denmark ■
Europe 55°45N 10°0E 9 J14
Dannemora U.S.A. 44°43N 73°44W 83 B11
Dannevirke N.Z. 40°12S 176°8E 59 D6
Dannhauser S. Africa 28°0S 30°3E 57 D5
Dansville U.S.A. 42°34N 77°42W 82 D7
Danta India 24°11N 72°46E 42 G5
Dantan India 21°57N 87°20E 43 J12
Dante = Xaafuun
Somali Rep. 10°25N 51°16E 47 E5
Danube = Dunărea →
Europe 45°20N 29°40E 17 F15
Danvers U.S.A. 42°34N 70°56W 83 D14
Danville Ill., U.S.A. 40°8N 87°37W 80 E10
Danville Ky., U.S.A. 37°39N 84°46W 81 G11
Danville Pa., U.S.A. 40°58N 76°37W 83 F8
Danville Va., U.S.A. 36°36N 79°23W 81 G14
Danville Vt., U.S.A. 44°25N 72°9W 83 B12
Danzhou China 19°31N 109°33E 38 C7
Danzig = Gdańsk
Poland 54°22N 18°40E 17 A10
Dapaong Togo 10°55N 0°16E 50 F6
Daqing China 46°35N 125°0E 33 B13
Daqing Shan China 40°40N 111°0E 34 D6
Daqq-e Sorkh, Kavīr
Iran 33°45N 52°50E 45 C7
Dar Banda Africa 8°0N 23°0E 48 F6
Dar el Beida = Casablanca
Morocco 33°36N 7°36W 50 B4
Dar es Salaam Tanzania 6°50S 39°12E 54 D4
Dar Mazār Iran 29°14N 57°20E 45 D8
Dar'ā Syria 32°36N 36°7E 46 C5
Dar'ā □ Syria 32°55N 36°10E 46 C5
Dārāb Iran 28°50N 54°30E 45 D7
Daraban Pakistan 31°44N 70°20E 42 D4
Daraina Madag. 13°12S 49°40E 57 A8
Daraj Libya 30°10N 10°28E 51 B8
Dārān Iran 32°59N 50°24E 45 C6
Dārayyā Syria 33°28N 36°15E 46 B5
Darband Pakistan 34°20N 72°50E 42 B5
Darband, Kūh-e Iran 31°34N 57°8E 45 D8
Darbhanga India 26°15N 85°55E 43 F11
D'Arcy Canada 50°33N 122°29W 70 C4
Dardanelle Ark., U.S.A. 35°13N 93°9W 84 D8
Dardanelle Calif.,
U.S.A. 38°20N 119°50W 78 G7
Dardanelles = Çanakkale Boğazı
Turkey 40°17N 26°32E 23 D12
Dārestān Iran 29°9N 58°42E 45 D8
Dârfûr Sudan 13°40N 24°0E 51 F10
Dargai Pakistan 34°25N 71°55E 42 B4
Dargaville N.Z. 35°57S 173°52E 59 A4
Darhan Mongolia 49°37N 106°21E 32 B10
Darhan Muminggan
China 41°40N 110°28E 34 D6
Darıca Turkey 40°45N 29°23E 23 D13
Darién, G. del Colombia 9°0N 77°0W 92 B3
Darién △ Panama 7°36N 77°57W 88 E4
Dariganga = Ovoot
Mongolia 45°21N 113°45E 34 B7
Darjeeling = Darjiling
India 27°3N 88°18E 43 F13
Darjiling India 27°3N 88°18E 43 F13
Darkan Australia 33°20S 116°43E 61 F2
Darkhana Pakistan 30°39N 72°11E 42 D5
Darkhazīneh Iran 31°54N 48°39E 45 D6
Darkot Pass Pakistan 36°45N 73°26E 43 A5
Darling → Australia 34°4S 141°54E 63 E3
Darling Downs
Australia 27°30S 150°30E 63 D5
Darling Ra. Australia 32°30S 116°20E 61 F2
Darlington U.K. 54°32N 1°33W 12 C6
Darlington U.S.A. 34°18N 79°52W 85 D15
Darlington □ U.K. 54°32N 1°33W 12 C6
Darlington, L. S. Africa 33°10S 25°9E 56 E4
Darlot, L. Australia 27°48S 121°35E 61 E3
Darłowo Poland 54°25N 16°25E 16 A9
Darmstadt Germany 49°51N 8°39E 16 D5
Darnah Libya 32°45N 22°45E 51 B10
Darnall S. Africa 29°23S 31°18E 57 D5
Darnley Australia 9°35S 143°46E 62 a
Darnley, C. Antarctica 68°0S 69°0E 5 C6
Darnley B. Canada 69°30N 123°30W 68 D7
Darr → Australia 23°39S 143°50E 62 C3
Darra Pezu Pakistan 32°19N 70°44E 42 C4
Darrequeira Argentina 37°42S 63°10W 94 D3
Darrington U.S.A. 48°15N 121°36W 76 B3
Dart → U.K. 50°24N 3°39W 13 G4
Dart, C. Antarctica 73°6S 126°20W 5 D14
Dartford U.K. 51°26N 0°13E 13 F8
Dartmoor U.K. 50°38N 3°57W 13 G4
Dartmoor △ U.K. 50°37N 3°59W 13 G4
Dartmouth Canada 44°40N 63°30W 73 D7
Dartmouth U.K. 50°21N 3°36W 13 G4
Dartmouth Res.
Australia 26°4S 145°18E 63 D4
Dartuch, C. = Artrutx, C. de
Spain 39°55N 3°49E 24 B10
Darvel, Teluk = Lahad Datu,
Telok Malaysia 4°50N 118°20E 37 D5
Darwen U.K. 53°42N 2°29W 12 D5
Darwendale Zimbabwe 17°41S 30°33E 57 B5
Darwha India 20°15N 77°45E 40 J10
Darwin Australia 12°25S 130°51E 60 B5
Darwin U.S.A. 36°15N 117°35W 79 J9
Darya Khan Pakistan 31°48N 71°6E 42 D4
Daryācheh-ye Bakhtegān
Iran 29°40N 53°50E 45 D7
Daryoi Amu = Amudarya →
Uzbekistan 43°58N 59°34E 28 E6
Dās U.A.E. 25°20N 53°30E 45 E7
Dashen, Ras Ethiopia 13°8N 38°26E 47 E2
Dashetai China 41°0N 109°5E 34 D5
Dashiqiao China 40°38N 122°30E 35 D12
Dashköpri Turkmenistan 36°16N 62°8E 45 B9
Dashoguz Turkmenistan 41°49N 59°58E 28 E6
Dasht → Pakistan 25°10N 61°40E 40 G2
Daska Pakistan 32°20N 74°20E 42 C6
Dasuya India 31°49N 75°38E 42 D6
Datça Turkey 36°46N 27°40E 23 F12
Datia India 25°39N 78°27E 43 G8
Datong Qinghai, China 36°20N 102°50E 32 D9
Datong Shanxi, China 40°6N 113°18E 34 D7
Dattakhel Pakistan 32°54N 69°46E 42 C3
Datu, Tanjung Indonesia 2°5N 109°39E 36 D3
Datu Piang Phil. 7°2N 124°30E 37 C6
Datuk, Tanjong = Datu, Tanjung
Indonesia 2°5N 109°39E 36 D3
Daud Khel Pakistan 32°53N 71°34E 42 C4
Daudnagar India 25°2N 84°24E 43 G11
Daugava → Latvia 57°4N 24°3E 9 H21
Daugavpils Latvia 55°53N 26°32E 9 J22
Daulpur India 26°45N 77°59E 42 F7
Daung Kyun Burma 12°13N 98°4E 39 F1
Dauphin Canada 51°9N 100°5W 71 C8
Dauphin U.S.A. 40°22N 76°56W 82 F8
Dauphin L. Canada 51°20N 99°45W 71 C9
Dauphiné France 45°15N 5°25E 20 D6
Dausa India 26°52N 76°20E 42 F7
Davangere India 14°25N 75°55E 40 M9
Davao Phil. 7°0N 125°40E 37 C7
Davao G. Phil. 6°30N 125°48E 37 C7
Dāvar Panāh = Sarāvān
Iran 27°25N 62°15E 45 E9
Davenport Calif., U.S.A. 37°1N 122°12W 78 H4
Davenport Iowa, U.S.A. 41°32N 90°35W 80 E8
Davenport Wash., U.S.A. 47°39N 118°9W 76 C4
Davenport Ra. Australia 20°28S 134°0E 62 C1
Davenport Range △
Australia 20°36S 134°22E 62 C1
Daventry U.K. 52°16N 1°10W 13 E6
David Panama 8°30N 82°30W 88 E3
David City U.S.A. 41°15N 97°8W 80 E5
David Glacier Antarctica 75°20S 162°0E 5 D11
David Gorodok = Davyd Haradok
Belarus 52°4N 27°8E 17 B14
Davidson Canada 51°16N 105°59W 71 C7
Davidson Mts. U.S.A. 68°41N 142°22W 74 B11
Davis Antarctica 68°34S 77°55E 5 C6
Davis U.S.A. 38°33N 121°44W 78 G5
Davis Dam U.S.A. 35°12N 114°34W 79 K12
Davis Inlet Canada 55°50N 60°59W 73 A7
Davis Mts. U.S.A. 30°50N 103°55W 84 F3
Davis Sea Antarctica 66°0S 92°0E 5 C7
Davis Str. N. Amer. 65°0N 58°0W 69 D19
Davlos Cyprus 35°25N 33°54E 25 D12
Davos Switz. 46°48N 9°49E 20 C8
Davy L. Canada 58°53N 108°18W 71 B7
Davyd Haradok Belarus 52°4N 27°8E 17 B14
Dawei = Tavoy Burma 14°2N 98°12E 38 E2
Dawes Ra. Australia 24°40S 150°40E 62 C5
Dawlish U.K. 50°35N 3°28W 13 G4
Dawna Ra. Burma 16°30N 98°30E 38 D2
Dawros Hd. Ireland 54°50N 8°33W 10 B3
Dawson U.S.A. 31°46N 84°27W 85 F12
Dawson, I. Chile 53°50S 70°50W 96 G2
Dawson B. Canada 52°53N 100°49W 71 C8
Dawson City Canada 64°10N 139°30W 68 E4
Dawson Creek Canada 55°45N 120°15W 70 B4
Dawson Inlet Canada 61°50N 93°25W 71 A10
Dawson Ra. Australia 24°30S 149°48E 62 C4
Dax France 43°44N 1°3W 20 E3
Daxian China 31°15N 107°23E 32 E10
Daxindian China 37°30N 120°50E 35 F11
Daxing China 39°47N 116°24E 34 E9
Daxinggou China 43°25N 129°40E 35 C15
Daxue Shan China 30°30N 101°30E 32 E9
Day Kundī □ Afghan. 34°0N 66°0E 40 C5
Daylesford Australia 37°21S 144°9E 63 F3
Dayr az Zawr Syria 35°20N 40°5E 44 C4
Daysland Canada 52°50N 112°20W 70 C6
Dayton Nev., U.S.A. 39°14N 119°36W 78 F7
Dayton Ohio, U.S.A. 39°45N 84°12W 81 F11
Dayton Pa., U.S.A. 40°53N 79°15W 82 F5
Dayton Tenn., U.S.A. 35°30N 85°1W 85 D12
Dayton Wash., U.S.A. 46°19N 117°59W 76 C5
Dayton Wyo., U.S.A. 44°53N 107°16W 76 D10
Daytona Beach U.S.A. 29°13N 81°1W 85 G14
Dayville U.S.A. 44°28N 119°32W 76 D4
De Aar S. Africa 30°39S 24°0E 56 E3
De Biesbosch △ Neths. 51°45N 4°48E 15 C4
De Funiak Springs
U.S.A. 30°43N 86°7W 85 F11
De Grey → Australia 20°12S 119°13E 60 D2
De Haan Belgium 51°16N 3°2E 15 C3
De Hoge Veluwe △ Neths. 52°5N 5°46E 15 B5
De Hoop ⌂ S. Africa 34°30S 20°28E 56 E3
De Kalb Junction U.S.A. 44°30N 75°16W 83 B9
De Kennemerduinen △
Neths. 52°27N 4°33E 15 B4
De Land U.S.A. 29°2N 81°18W 85 G14
De Leon U.S.A. 32°7N 98°32W 84 E5
De Long Mts. U.S.A. 68°10N 163°30W 74 B7
De Panne Belgium 51°6N 2°34E 15 C2
De Pere U.S.A. 44°27N 88°4W 80 C9
De Queen U.S.A. 34°2N 94°21W 84 D7
De Quincy U.S.A. 30°27N 93°26W 84 F8
De Ruyters U.S.A. 42°45N 75°53W 83 D9
De Smet U.S.A. 44°23N 97°33W 80 C5
De Soto U.S.A. 38°8N 90°34W 80 F8
De Tour Village U.S.A. 46°0N 83°56W 81 B12
De Witt U.S.A. 34°18N 91°20W 84 D9
Dead Sea Asia 31°30N 35°30E 46 D4
Deadwood U.S.A. 44°23N 103°44W 80 C2
Deadwood L. Canada 59°10N 128°30W 70 B3
Deal U.K. 51°13N 1°25E 13 F9
Deal I. Australia 39°30S 147°20E 63 F4
Dealesville S. Africa 28°41S 25°44E 56 D4
Dean → Canada 52°49N 126°58W 70 C3
Dean, Forest of U.K. 51°45N 2°33W 13 F5
Dean Chan. Canada 52°30N 127°15W 70 C3
Deán Funes Argentina 30°20S 64°20W 94 C3
Dease → Canada 59°56N 128°32W 70 B3
Dease L. Canada 58°40N 130°5W 70 B2
Dease Lake Canada 58°25N 130°6W 70 B2
Death Valley U.S.A. 36°15N 116°50W 79 J10
Death Valley △ U.S.A. 36°29N 117°6W 79 J9
Death Valley Junction
U.S.A. 36°20N 116°25W 79 J10
Deatnu = Tana →
Norway 70°30N 28°14E 8 A23
Debagram India 23°51N 90°33E 43 H14
Debar Macedonia 41°31N 20°30E 23 D9
Debden Canada 53°30N 106°50W 71 C7
Dębica Poland 50°2N 21°25E 17 C11
DeBolt Canada 55°12N 118°1W 70 B5
Deborah East, L.
Australia 30°45S 119°30E 61 F2
Deborah West, L.
Australia 30°45S 119°5E 61 F2
Debre Markos Ethiopia 10°20N 37°40E 47 E2
Debre Tabor Ethiopia 11°50N 38°26E 47 E2
Debre Zebit Ethiopia 11°48N 38°30E 47 F2
Debrecen Hungary 47°33N 21°42E 17 E11
Decatur Ala., U.S.A. 34°36N 86°59W 85 D11
Decatur Ga., U.S.A. 33°46N 84°16W 85 E12
Decatur Ill., U.S.A. 39°51N 88°57W 80 F9
Decatur Ind., U.S.A. 40°50N 84°56W 81 E11
Decatur Tex., U.S.A. 33°14N 97°35W 84 E6
Deccan India 18°0N 79°0E 40 L11
Deception Bay Australia 27°10S 153°5E 63 D5
Deception I. Antarctica 63°0S 60°15W 5 C17
Deception L. Canada 56°33N 104°13W 71 B8
Dechhu India 26°46N 72°20E 42 F5
Děčín Czech Rep. 50°47N 14°12E 16 C8
Deckerville U.S.A. 43°32N 82°44W 82 C2
Decorah U.S.A. 43°18N 91°48W 80 D8
Dedéagach = Alexandroupoli
Greece 40°50N 25°54E 23 D11
Dedham U.S.A. 42°15N 71°10W 83 D13
Dedza Malawi 14°20S 34°20E 55 E3
Dee → Aberds., U.K. 57°9N 2°5W 11 D6
Dee → Dumf. & Gall., U.K. 54°51N 4°3W 11 G4
Dee → Wales, U.K. 53°22N 3°17W 12 D4
Deep B. Canada 61°15N 116°35W 70 A5
Deep Bay = Shenzhen Wan
China 22°27N 113°55E 33 a
Deepwater Australia 29°25S 151°51E 63 D5
Deer → Canada 58°23N 94°13W 71 B10
Deer L. Canada 52°40N 94°20W 71 C10
Deer Lake Nfld. & L.,
Canada 49°11N 57°27W 73 C8
Deer Lake Ont., Canada 52°36N 94°20W 71 C10
Deer Lodge U.S.A. 46°24N 112°44W 76 C7
Deer Park U.S.A. 47°57N 117°28W 76 C5
Deer River U.S.A. 47°20N 93°48W 80 B7
Deeragun Australia 19°16S 146°33E 62 B4
Defiance U.S.A. 41°17N 84°22W 81 E11
Degana India 26°50N 74°20E 42 F6
Dégelis Canada 47°30N 68°35W 73 C6
Deggendorf Germany 48°50N 12°57E 16 D7
Degh → Pakistan 31°3N 73°21E 42 D5
Değirmenlik = Kythréa
Cyprus 35°15N 33°29E 25 D12
Deh Bīd Iran 30°39N 53°11E 45 D7
Deh Dasht Iran 30°47N 50°33E 45 D6
Deh-e Shīr Iran 31°29N 53°45E 45 D7
Dehaj Iran 30°42N 54°53E 45 D7
Dehak Iran 27°11N 62°37E 45 E9
Dehdez Iran 31°43N 50°17E 45 D6
Dehej India 21°44N 72°40E 42 J5
Dehestān Iran 28°30N 55°35E 45 D7
Dehgolān Iran 35°17N 47°25E 44 C5
Dehibat Tunisia 32°0N 10°47E 51 B8
Dehlorān Iran 32°41N 47°16E 44 C5
Dehnow-e Kūhestān
Iran 27°58N 58°32E 45 E8
Dehra Dun India 30°20N 78°4E 42 D8
Dehri India 24°50N 84°15E 43 G11
Dehui China 44°30N 125°40E 35 B13
Deinze Belgium 50°59N 3°32E 15 D3
Dej Romania 47°10N 23°52E 17 E12
Deka → Zimbabwe 18°4S 26°42E 56 B4
DeKalb U.S.A. 41°56N 88°46W 80 E9
Dekese
Dem. Rep. of the Congo 3°24S 21°24E 52 E4
Del Mar U.S.A. 32°58N 117°16W 79 N9
Del Norte U.S.A. 37°41N 106°21W 77 H10
Del Rio U.S.A. 29°22N 100°54W 84 G4
Delambre I. Australia 20°26S 117°5E 60 D2
Delano U.S.A. 35°46N 119°15W 79 K7
Delano Peak U.S.A. 38°22N 112°22W 76 G7
Delareyville S. Africa 26°41S 25°26E 56 D4
Delaronde L. Canada 54°3N 107°3W 71 C7
Delavan U.S.A. 42°38N 88°39W 80 D9
Delaware U.S.A. 40°18N 83°4W 81 E12
Delaware □ U.S.A. 39°0N 75°20W 81 F16
Delaware → U.S.A. 39°15N 75°20W 83 G9
Delaware B. U.S.A. 39°0N 75°10W 81 F16
Delaware Water Gap ⌂
U.S.A. 41°10N 74°55W 83 E10
Delay → Canada 56°56N 71°28W 73 A5
Delegate Australia 37°4S 148°56E 63 F4
Delevan U.S.A. 42°29N 78°29W 82 D6
Delft Neths. 52°1N 4°22E 15 B4
Delfzijl Neths. 53°20N 6°55E 15 A6
Delgado, C. Mozam. 10°45S 40°40E 55 E5
Delgerhet Mongolia 45°50N 110°30E 34 B6
Delgo Sudan 20°6N 30°40E 51 D12
Delhi Canada 42°51N 80°30W 82 D4
Delhi India 28°39N 77°13E 42 E7
Delhi La., U.S.A. 32°28N 91°30W 84 E9
Delhi N.Y., U.S.A. 42°17N 74°55W 83 D10
Delia Canada 51°38N 112°23W 70 C6
Delice Turkey 39°54N 34°2E 19 G5
Delicias Mexico 28°13N 105°28W 86 B3
Delījān Iran 33°59N 50°40E 45 C6
Déline Canada 65°11N 123°25W 68 D7
Delingha China 37°23N 97°23E 32 D8
Delisle Canada 51°55N 107°8W 71 C7
Deliverance I. Australia 9°31S 141°34E 62 a
Dell City U.S.A. 31°56N 105°12W 84 F2
Dell Rapids U.S.A. 43°50N 96°43W 80 D5
Delmar U.S.A. 42°37N 73°47W 83 D11
Delmenhorst Germany 53°3N 8°37E 16 B5
Delonga, Ostrova
Russia 76°40N 149°20E 29 B15
Deloraine Australia 41°30S 146°40E 63 G4
Deloraine Canada 49°15N 100°29W 71 D8
Delphi U.S.A. 40°36N 86°41W 80 E10
Delphos U.S.A. 40°51N 84°21W 81 E11
Delportshoop S. Africa 28°22S 24°20E 56 D3
Delray Beach U.S.A. 26°28N 80°4W 85 H14
Delta Colo., U.S.A. 38°44N 108°4W 76 G9
Delta Utah, U.S.A. 39°21N 112°35W 76 G7
Delta Dunărea ⌂
Romania 45°15N 29°25E 17 F15
Delta Junction U.S.A. 64°2N 145°44W 68 E2
Deltona U.S.A. 28°54N 81°16W 85 G14
Delungra Australia 29°39S 150°51E 63 D5
Delvada India 20°46N 71°2E 42 J4
Delvinë Albania 39°59N 20°6E 23 E9
Demak Indonesia 6°53S 110°38E 37 G14
Demanda, Sierra de la
Spain 42°15N 3°0W 21 A4
Demavend = Damāvand,
Qolleh-ye Iran 35°56N 52°10E 45 C7
Dembia C.A.R. 4°56N 23°53E 54 B1
Dembia
Dem. Rep. of the Congo 3°33N 25°48E 54 B2
Dembidolo Ethiopia 8°34N 34°50E 47 F1
Demchok India 32°42N 79°29E 43 C8
Demer → Belgium 50°57N 4°42E 15 D4
Deming N. Mex.,
U.S.A. 32°16N 107°46W 77 K10
Deming Wash., U.S.A. 48°50N 122°13W 78 B4
Demini → Brazil 0°46S 62°56W 92 D6
Demirci Turkey 39°2N 28°38E 23 E13
Demirköy Turkey 41°49N 27°45E 23 D12
Demopolis U.S.A. 32°31N 87°50W 85 E11
Dempo Indonesia 4°2S 103°15E 36 E2
Den Bosch = 's-Hertogenbosch
Neths. 51°42N 5°17E 15 C5
Den Burg Neths. 53°3N 4°47E 15 A4
Den Chai Thailand 17°59N 100°4E 38 D3
Den Haag = 's-Gravenhage
Neths. 52°7N 4°17E 15 B4
Den Helder Neths. 52°57N 4°45E 15 B4
Den Oever Neths. 52°56N 5°2E 15 B5
Denair U.S.A. 37°32N 120°48W 78 H6
Denali = McKinley, Mt.
U.S.A. 63°4N 151°0W 68 E1
Denau Uzbekistan 38°16N 67°54E 28 F7
Denbigh Canada 45°8N 77°15W 82 A7
Denbigh U.K. 53°12N 3°25W 12 D4
Denbighshire □ U.K. 53°8N 3°22W 12 D4
Dendang Indonesia 3°7S 107°56E 36 E3
Dendermonde Belgium 51°2N 4°5E 15 C4
Dengfeng China 34°25N 113°2E 34 G7
Dengkou China 40°18N 106°55E 34 D4
Denham Australia 25°56S 113°31E 61 E1
Denham, Mt. Jamaica 18°13N 77°32W 88 a
Denham Ra. Australia 21°55S 147°46E 62 C4
Denham Sd. Australia 25°45S 113°15E 61 E1
Denholm Canada 52°39N 108°1W 71 C7
Denia Spain 38°49N 0°8E 21 C6
Denial B. Australia 32°14S 133°32E 63 E1
Deniliquin Australia 35°30S 144°58E 63 F3
Denimoo = Fort Resolution
Canada 61°10N 113°40W 70 A6
Denison Iowa, U.S.A. 42°1N 95°21W 80 D6
Denison Tex., U.S.A. 33°45N 96°33W 84 E6
Denison Plains Australia 18°35S 128°0E 60 C4
Denizli Turkey 37°42N 29°2E 19 G4
Denman Glacier
Antarctica 66°45S 100°0E 5 C8
Denmark Australia 34°59S 117°25E 61 F2
Denmark ■ Europe 55°45N 10°0E 9 J14
Denmark Str. Atl. Oc. 66°0N 30°0W 66 C17
Dennery St. Lucia 13°55N 60°54W 89 f
Dennison U.S.A. 40°24N 81°19W 82 F3
Denny U.K. 56°1N 3°55W 11 E5
Denpasar Indonesia 8°39S 115°13E 37 K18
Denpasar ✈ (DPS)
Indonesia 8°44S 115°10E 37 K18
Denton Mont., U.S.A. 47°19N 109°57W 76 C9
Denton Tex., U.S.A. 33°13N 97°8W 84 E6
D'Entrecasteaux, Pt.
Australia 34°50S 115°57E 61 F2
D'Entrecasteaux △
Australia 34°20S 115°33E 61 F2
D'Entrecasteaux Is.
Papua N. G. 9°0S 151°0E 58 B8
Denver Colo., U.S.A. 39°42N 104°59W 76 G11
Denver Pa., U.S.A. 40°14N 76°8W 83 F8
Denver City U.S.A. 32°58N 102°50W 84 E3
Deoband India 29°42N 77°43E 42 E7
Deogarh India 25°32N 73°54E 42 G5
Deoghar India 24°30N 86°42E 43 G12
Deolali India 19°58N 73°50E 40 K8
Deoli = Devli India 25°50N 75°20E 42 G6
Deora India 26°22N 70°55E 42 F4
Deori India 23°24N 79°1E 43 H8
Deoria India 26°31N 83°48E 43 F10
Deosai Mts. Pakistan 35°40N 75°0E 43 B6
Deosri India 26°46N 90°29E 43 F14
Depalpur India 22°51N 75°33E 42 H6
Deposit U.S.A. 42°4N 75°25W 83 D9
Depuch I. Australia 20°37S 117°44E 60 D2
Deputatskiy Russia 69°18N 139°54E 29 C14
Dera Ghazi Khan
Pakistan 30°5N 70°43E 42 D4
Dera Ismail Khan
Pakistan 31°50N 70°50E 42 D4
Derabugti Pakistan 29°2N 69°9E 42 E3
Derawar Fort Pakistan 28°46N 71°20E 42 E4
Derbent Russia 42°5N 48°15E 19 F8
Derby Australia 17°18S 123°38E 60 C3
Derby U.K. 52°56N 1°28W 12 E6
Derby Conn., U.S.A. 41°19N 73°5W 83 E11
Derby Kans., U.S.A. 37°33N 97°16W 80 G5
Derby N.Y., U.S.A. 42°41N 78°58W 82 D6
Derby City □ U.K. 52°56N 1°28W 12 E6
Derby Line U.S.A. 45°0N 72°6W 83 B12
Derbyshire □ U.K. 53°11N 1°38W 12 D6
Derdepoort S. Africa 24°38S 26°24E 56 C4
Dereham U.K. 52°41N 0°57E 13 E8
Derg → U.K. 54°44N 7°26W 10 B4
Derg, L. Ireland 53°0N 8°20W 10 D3
Deridder U.S.A. 30°51N 93°17W 84 F8
Dermott U.S.A. 33°32N 91°26W 84 E9
Derry = Londonderry
U.K. 55°0N 7°20W 10 B4
Derry = Londonderry □
U.K. 55°0N 7°20W 10 B4
Derry N.H., U.S.A. 42°53N 71°19W 83 D13
Derry Pa., U.S.A. 40°20N 79°18W 82 F5
Derryveagh Mts. Ireland 54°56N 8°11W 10 B3
Derwent → Cumb., U.K. 54°39N 3°33W 12 C4
Derwent → Derby, U.K. 52°57N 1°28W 12 E6

Derwent → N. Yorks., U.K. 53°45N 0°58W 12 D7
Derwent Water U.K. 54°35N 3°9W 12 C4
Des Moines Iowa, U.S.A. 41°35N 93°37W 80 E7
Des Moines N. Mex., U.S.A. 36°46N 103°50W 77 H12
Des Moines Wash., U.S.A. 47°24N 122°19W 78 C4
Des Moines → U.S.A. 40°23N 91°25W 80 E8
Desaguadero → Argentina 34°30S 66°46W 94 C2
Desaguadero → Bolivia 16°35S 69°5W 92 G5
Desaru Malaysia 1°31N 104°17E 39 d
Descanso, Pta. Mexico 32°21N 117°3W 79 N9
Deschaillons-sur-St-Laurent Canada 46°32N 72°7W 73 C5
Deschambault L. Canada 54°50N 103°30W 71 C8
Deschutes → U.S.A. 45°38N 120°55W 76 D3
Dese Ethiopia 11°5N 39°40E 47 E2
Deseado → Argentina 47°45S 65°54W 96 F3
Deseronto Canada 44°12N 77°3W 82 B7
Desert Center U.S.A. 33°43N 115°24W 79 M11
Desert Hot Springs U.S.A. 33°58N 116°30W 79 M10
Deshnok India 27°48N 73°21E 42 F5
Desierto Central de Baja California ⌓ Mexico 29°40N 114°50W 86 B2
Desna → Ukraine 50°33N 30°32E 17 C16
Desolación, I. Chile 53°0S 74°0W 96 G2
Despeñaperros, Paso Spain 38°24N 3°30W 21 C4
Dessau Germany 51°51N 12°14E 16 C7
Dessye = Dese Ethiopia 11°5N 39°40E 47 E2
D'Estrees B. Australia 35°55S 137°45E 63 F2
Desuri India 25°18N 73°35E 42 G5
Det Udom Thailand 14°54N 105°5E 38 E5
Dete Zimbabwe 18°38S 26°50E 56 B4
Detmold Germany 51°56N 8°52E 16 C5
Detour, Pt. U.S.A. 45°40N 86°40W 80 C10
Detroit U.S.A. 42°19N 83°12W 82 D1
Detroit Lakes U.S.A. 46°49N 95°51W 80 B6
Deua △ Australia 35°32S 149°46E 63 F4
Deurne Neths. 51°27N 5°49E 15 C5
Deutsche Bucht Germany 54°15N 8°0E 16 A5
Deutschland = Germany ■ Europe 51°0N 10°0E 16 C6
Deva Romania 45°53N 22°55E 17 F12
Devakottai India 9°55N 78°45E 40 Q11
Devaprayag India 30°13N 78°35E 43 D8
Deventer Neths. 52°15N 6°10E 15 B6
Deveron → U.K. 57°41N 2°32W 11 D6
Devgadh Bariya India 22°40N 73°55E 42 H5
Devikot India 26°42N 71°12E 42 F4
Devils Den U.S.A. 35°46N 119°58W 78 K7
Devils Hole = Death Valley △ U.S.A. 36°29N 117°6W 79 J9
Devils Lake U.S.A. 48°7N 98°52W 80 A4
Devils Paw Canada 58°47N 134°0W 70 B2
Devils Postpile △ U.S.A. 37°37N 119°5W 78 H7
Devils Tower U.S.A. 44°35N 104°42W 76 D11
Devils Tower △ U.S.A. 44°48N 104°55W 76 D11
Devine U.S.A. 29°8N 98°54W 84 G5
Devizes U.K. 51°22N 1°58W 13 F6
Devli India 25°50N 75°20E 42 G6
Devon Canada 53°24N 113°44W 70 C6
Devon □ U.K. 50°50N 3°40W 13 G4
Devon I. Canada 75°10N 85°0W 69 B15
Devonport Australia 41°10S 146°22E 63 G4
Devonport N.Z. 36°49S 174°49E 59 B5
Dewas India 22°59N 76°3E 42 H7
Dewetsdorp S. Africa 29°33S 26°39E 56 D4
Dewey Puerto Rico 18°18N 65°18W 89 d
Dexter Maine, U.S.A. 45°1N 69°18W 81 C19
Dexter Mo., U.S.A. 36°48N 89°57W 80 G9
Dexter N. Mex., U.S.A. 33°12N 104°22W 77 K11
Dey-Dey, L. Australia 29°12S 131°4E 61 E5
Deyang China 31°3N 104°27E 32 E9
Deyhūk Iran 33°15N 57°30E 45 C8
Deyyer Iran 27°55N 51°55E 45 E6
Dez → Iran 31°39N 48°52E 45 D6
Dezadeash L. Canada 60°28N 136°58W 70 A1
Dezfūl Iran 32°20N 48°30E 45 C6
Dezhneva, Mys Russia 66°5N 169°40W 29 C19
Dezhou China 37°26N 116°18E 34 F9
Dhadhar → India 24°56N 85°24E 43 G11
Dhahiriya = Az Ẓāhirīyah West Bank 31°25N 34°58E 46 D3
Dhahran = Az Ẓahrān Si. Arabia 26°10N 50°7E 45 E6
Dhak Pakistan 32°25N 72°33E 42 C5
Dhaka Bangla. 23°43N 90°26E 43 H14
Dhaka □ Bangla. 24°25N 90°25E 43 G14
Dhali Cyprus 35°1N 33°25E 25 D12
Dhamār Yemen 14°30N 44°20E 47 E3
Dhampur India 29°19N 78°33E 43 E8
Dhamtari India 20°42N 81°35E 41 J12
Dhanbad India 23°50N 86°30E 43 H12
Dhangarhi Nepal 28°55N 80°40E 43 E9
Dhankuta Nepal 26°55N 87°40E 43 F12
Dhanpuri India 23°13N 81°30E 43 H9
Dhar India 22°35N 75°26E 42 H6
Dharampur India 22°13N 75°18E 42 H6
Dharamsala = Dharmsala India 32°16N 76°23E 42 C7
Dharan Nepal 26°49N 87°17E 43 F12
Dhariwal India 31°57N 75°19E 42 D6
Dharla → Bangla. 25°46N 89°42E 43 G13
Dharmapuri India 12°10N 78°10E 40 N11
Dharmjaygarh India 22°28N 83°13E 43 H10
Dharmsala India 32°16N 76°23E 42 C7
Dharni India 21°33N 76°53E 42 J7
Dharwad India 15°30N 75°4E 40 M9
Dhasan → India 25°48N 79°24E 43 G8
Dhaulagiri Nepal 28°39N 83°28E 43 E10
Dhebar, L. India 24°10N 74°0E 42 G6
Dheftera Cyprus 35°5N 33°16E 25 D12
Dhenkanal India 20°45N 85°35E 41 J14
Dherinia Cyprus 35°3N 33°57E 25 D12
Dhī Qār □ Iraq 31°0N 46°15E 44 D5
Dhiarrizos → Cyprus 34°41N 32°34E 25 E11
Dhībān Jordan 31°30N 35°46E 46 D4
Dhilwan India 31°31N 75°21E 42 D6
Dhimarkhera India 23°28N 80°22E 43 H9
Dhodhekánisos = Dodecanese Greece 36°35N 27°0E 23 F12
Dholka India 22°44N 72°29E 42 H5
Dhoraji India 21°45N 70°37E 42 J4
Dhrangadhra India 22°59N 71°31E 42 H4
Dhrol India 22°33N 70°25E 42 H4
Dhuburi India 26°2N 89°59E 41 F16
Dhule India 20°58N 74°50E 40 J9
Di Linh Vietnam 11°35N 108°4E 39 G7
Di Linh, Cao Nguyen Vietnam 11°30N 108°0E 39 G7
Dia Greece 35°28N 25°14E 25 D7
Diablo Range U.S.A. 37°20N 121°25W 78 J5
Diafarabé Mali 14°9N 4°57W 50 F5
Diamante Argentina 32°5S 60°40W 94 C3
Diamante → Argentina 34°30S 66°46W 94 C2
Diamantina Brazil 18°17S 43°40W 93 G10
Diamantina → Australia 26°45S 139°10E 63 D2
Diamantina △ Australia 23°33S 141°23E 62 C3
Diamantino Brazil 14°30S 56°30W 93 F7
Diamond Bar U.S.A. 34°1N 117°48W 79 L9
Diamond Harbour India 22°11N 88°14E 43 H13
Diamond Is. Australia 17°25S 151°5E 62 B5
Diamond Mts. U.S.A. 39°40N 115°50W 76 G6
Diamond Springs U.S.A. 38°42N 120°49W 78 G6
Diaoyu Dao = Senkaku-Shotō E. China Sea 25°45N 123°30E 31 M1
Diaoyu Tai = Senkaku-Shotō E. China Sea 25°45N 123°30E 31 M1
Dībā U.A.E. 25°45N 56°16E 45 E8
Dibai India 28°13N 78°15E 42 E8
Dibaya Dem. Rep. of the Congo 6°30S 22°57E 52 F4
Dibaya-Lubue Dem. Rep. of the Congo 4°12S 19°54E 52 E3
Dibbeen △ Jordan 32°20N 35°45E 46 C4
D'Iberville, Lac Canada 55°55N 73°15W 72 A5
Dibete Botswana 23°45S 26°32E 56 C4
Dibrugarh India 27°29N 94°55E 41 F19
Dickens U.S.A. 33°37N 100°50W 84 E4
Dickinson U.S.A. 46°53N 102°47W 80 B2
Dickson U.S.A. 36°5N 87°23W 85 C11
Dickson City U.S.A. 41°28N 75°36W 83 E9
Diéméni Mali 13°53N 8°6W 50 F4
Didsbury Canada 51°35N 114°10W 70 C6
Didwana India 27°23N 74°36E 42 F6
Diefenbaker, L. Canada 51°0N 106°55W 71 C7
Diego de Almagro Chile 26°22S 70°3W 94 B1
Diego Suarez = Antsiranana Madag. 12°25S 49°20E 57 A8
Diekirch Lux. 49°52N 6°10E 15 E6
Dien Ban Vietnam 15°53N 108°16E 38 E7
Dien Bien Phu Vietnam 21°20N 103°0E 38 B4
Dien Chau, Vinh Vietnam 19°0N 105°55E 38 C5
Dien Khanh Vietnam 12°15N 109°6E 39 F7
Dieppe France 49°54N 1°4E 20 B4
Dierks U.S.A. 34°7N 94°1W 84 D7
Diest Belgium 50°58N 5°4E 15 D5
Dif Somali Rep. 0°59N 40°58E 47 G3
Differdange Lux. 49°31N 5°54E 15 E5
Dig India 27°28N 77°20E 42 F7
Digba Dem. Rep. of the Congo 4°25N 25°48E 54 B2
Digby Canada 44°38N 65°50W 73 D6
Digges Is. Canada 62°40N 77°50W 69 E16
Diggi India 26°22N 75°26E 42 F6
Dighinala Bangla. 23°15N 92°5E 41 H18
Dighton U.S.A. 38°29N 100°28W 80 F3
Digne-les-Bains France 44°5N 6°12E 20 D7
Digos Phil. 6°45N 125°20E 37 C7
Digranes Iceland 66°4N 14°44W 8 C6
Digul → Indonesia 7°7S 138°42E 37 F9
Dihang = Brahmaputra → Asia 23°40N 90°35E 43 H13
Dijlah, Nahr → Asia 31°0N 47°25E 44 D5
Dijon France 47°20N 5°3E 20 C6
Dikhil Djibouti 11°8N 42°20E 47 E3
Dikkil = Dikhil Djibouti 11°8N 42°20E 47 E3
Diksmuide Belgium 51°2N 2°52E 15 C2
Dikson Russia 73°40N 80°5E 28 B9
Dikti Oros Greece 35°8N 25°30E 25 D7
Dila Ethiopia 6°21N 38°22E 47 F2
Dili E. Timor 8°39S 125°34E 37 F7
Dilley U.S.A. 28°40N 99°10W 84 G5
Dilli = Delhi India 28°39N 77°13E 42 E7
Dillingham U.S.A. 59°3N 158°28W 74 D8
Dillon Canada 55°56N 108°35W 71 B7
Dillon Mont., U.S.A. 45°13N 112°38W 76 D7
Dillon S.C., U.S.A. 34°25N 79°22W 85 D15
Dillon → Canada 55°56N 108°56W 71 B7
Dillsburg U.S.A. 40°7N 77°2W 82 F7
Dilolo Dem. Rep. of the Congo 10°28S 22°18E 52 G4
Dimapur India 25°54N 93°45E 32 F7
Dimas Mexico 23°43N 106°47W 86 C3
Dimashq Syria 33°30N 36°18E 46 B5
Dimashq □ Syria 33°30N 36°30E 46 B5
Dimbaza S. Africa 32°50S 27°14E 56 E4
Dimboola Australia 36°28S 142°7E 63 F3
Dîmboviţa = Dâmboviţa → Romania 44°12N 26°26E 17 F14
Dimbulah Australia 17°8S 145°4E 62 B4
Dimitrovgrad Bulgaria 42°5N 25°35E 23 C11
Dimitrovgrad Russia 54°14N 49°39E 18 D8
Dimitrovo = Pernik Bulgaria 42°35N 23°2E 23 C10
Dimmitt U.S.A. 34°33N 102°19W 84 D3
Dimona Israel 31°2N 35°1E 46 D4
Dinagat I. Phil. 10°10N 125°40E 37 B7
Dinajpur Bangla. 25°33N 88°43E 41 G16
Dinan France 48°28N 2°2W 20 B2
Dīnān Āb Iran 32°4N 56°49E 45 C8
Dinant Belgium 50°16N 4°55E 15 D4
Dinapur India 25°38N 85°5E 43 G11
Dīnār, Kūh-e Iran 30°42N 51°46E 45 D6
Dinara Planina Croatia 44°0N 16°30E 22 C7
Dinard France 48°38N 2°6W 20 B2
Dinaric Alps = Dinara Planina Croatia 44°0N 16°30E 22 C7
Dindigul India 10°25N 78°0E 40 P11
Dindori India 22°57N 81°5E 43 H9
Ding Xian = Dingzhou China 38°30N 114°59E 34 E8
Dinga Pakistan 25°26N 67°10E 42 G2
Ding'an China 19°42N 110°19E 38 C8
Dingbian China 37°35N 107°32E 34 F4
Dingle Ireland 52°9N 10°17W 10 D1
Dingle B. Ireland 52°3N 10°20W 10 D1
Dingmans Ferry U.S.A. 41°13N 74°55W 83 E10
Dingo Australia 23°38S 149°19E 62 C4
Dingtao China 35°5N 115°35E 34 G8
Dingwall U.K. 57°36N 4°26W 11 D4
Dingxi China 35°30N 104°33E 34 G3
Dingxiang China 38°30N 112°58E 34 E7
Dingzhou China 38°30N 114°59E 34 E8
Dinh, Mui Vietnam 11°22N 109°1E 39 G7
Dinh Lap Vietnam 21°33N 107°6E 38 B6
Dinin → Ireland 52°43N 7°18W 10 D4
Dinira △ Venezuela 9°57N 70°6W 89 E6
Dinokwe Botswana 23°29S 26°37E 56 C4
Dinorwic Canada 49°41N 92°30W 71 D10
Dinosaur ⌓ Canada 50°47N 111°30W 70 C6
Dinosaur ⌓ U.S.A. 40°30N 108°45W 76 F9
Dinuba U.S.A. 36°32N 119°23W 78 J7
Dionisades Greece 35°20N 26°10E 25 D8
Diourbel Senegal 14°39N 16°12W 50 F2
Dipalpur Pakistan 30°40N 73°39E 42 D5
Dipkarpaz = Rizokarpaso Cyprus 35°36N 34°23E 25 D13
Diplo Pakistan 24°35N 69°35E 42 G3
Dipolog Phil. 8°36N 123°20E 37 C6
Dipperu △ Australia 21°56S 148°42E 62 C4
Dir Pakistan 35°8N 71°59E 40 B7
Dire Dawa Ethiopia 9°35N 41°45E 47 F3
Dirfis Oros Greece 38°40N 23°54E 23 E10
Diriamba Nic. 11°51N 86°19W 88 D2
Dirk Hartog I. Australia 25°50S 113°5E 61 E1
Dirranbandi Australia 28°33S 148°17E 63 D4
Disa India 24°18N 72°10E 42 G5
Disappointment, C. U.S.A. 46°18N 124°5W 76 C1
Disappointment, L. Australia 23°20S 122°40E 60 D3
Disaster B. Australia 37°15S 149°58E 63 F4
Discovery B. Australia 38°10S 140°40E 63 F3
Discovery B. China 22°18N 114°1E 33 a
Disko = Qeqertarsuaq Greenland 69°45N 53°30W 4 C5
Disney Reef Tonga 19°17S 174°7W 59 c
Disneyland Hong Kong China 22°18N 114°2E 33 a
Diss U.K. 52°23N 1°7E 13 E9
Disteghil Sar Pakistan 36°20N 75°12E 43 A6
District of Columbia □ U.S.A. 38°55N 77°0W 81 F15
Distrito Federal □ Brazil 15°45S 47°45W 93 G9
Distrito Federal □ Mexico 19°15N 99°10W 87 D5
Diu India 20°45N 70°58E 42 J4
Dīvāndarreh Iran 35°55N 47°2E 44 C5
Divide U.S.A. 45°45N 112°45W 76 D7
Dividing Ra. Australia 27°45S 116°0E 61 E2
Divinópolis Brazil 20°10S 44°54W 93 H10
Divnoye Russia 45°55N 43°21E 19 E7
Divo Ivory C. 5°48N 5°15W 50 G4
Dīwāl Kol Afghan. 34°23N 67°52E 42 B2
Dixie Mt. U.S.A. 39°55N 120°16W 78 F6
Dixon Calif., U.S.A. 38°27N 121°49W 78 G5
Dixon Ill., U.S.A. 41°50N 89°29W 80 E9
Dixon Entrance U.S.A. 54°30N 132°0W 68 G5
Dixville Canada 45°4N 71°46W 83 A13
Diyālā □ Iraq 33°45N 44°50E 44 C5
Diyālā → Iraq 33°13N 44°30E 44 C5
Diyarbakır Turkey 37°55N 40°18E 44 B4
Diyodar India 24°8N 71°50E 42 G4
Djakarta = Jakarta Indonesia 6°9S 106°52E 37 G12
Djamba Angola 16°45S 13°58E 56 B1
Djambala Congo 2°32S 14°30E 52 E2
Djanet Algeria 24°35N 9°32E 50 D7
Djawa = Jawa Indonesia 7°0S 110°0E 36 F3
Djelfa Algeria 34°40N 3°15E 50 B6
Djema C.A.R. 6°3N 25°15E 54 A2
Djerba, Î. de Tunisia 33°50N 10°48E 51 B8
Djerid, Chott Tunisia 33°42N 8°30E 50 B7
Djibouti Djibouti 11°30N 43°5E 47 E3
Djibouti ■ Africa 12°0N 43°0E 47 E3
Djolu Dem. Rep. of the Congo 0°35N 22°5E 52 D4
Djougou Benin 9°40N 1°45E 50 G6
Djoum Cameroon 2°41N 12°35E 52 D2
Djourab, Erg du Chad 16°40N 18°50E 51 E9
Djugu Dem. Rep. of the Congo 1°55N 30°35E 54 B3
Djukbinj △ Australia 12°11S 131°2E 60 B5
Djúpivogur Iceland 64°39N 14°17W 8 D6
Dmitriya Lapteva, Proliv Russia 73°0N 140°0E 29 B15
Dnepr = Dnipro → Ukraine 46°30N 32°18E 19 E5
Dneprodzerzhinsk = Dniprodzerzhynsk Ukraine 48°32N 34°37E 19 E5
Dnepropetrovsk = Dnipropetrovsk Ukraine 48°30N 35°0E 19 E6
Dnestr = Dnister → Europe 46°18N 30°17E 17 E16
Dnieper = Dnipro → Ukraine 46°30N 32°18E 19 E5
Dniester = Dnister → Europe 46°18N 30°17E 17 E16
Dnipro → Ukraine 46°30N 32°18E 19 E5
Dniprodzerzhynsk Ukraine 48°32N 34°37E 19 E5
Dnipropetrovsk Ukraine 48°30N 35°0E 19 E6
Dnister → Europe 46°18N 30°17E 17 E16
Dno Russia 57°50N 29°58E 9 H23
Dnyapro = Dnipro → Ukraine 46°30N 32°18E 19 E5
Do Gonbadān = Gachsārān Iran 30°15N 50°45E 45 D6
Doaktown Canada 46°33N 66°8W 73 C6
Doan Hung Vietnam 21°30N 105°10E 38 B5
Doany Madag. 14°21S 49°30E 57 A8
Doba Chad 8°40N 16°50E 51 G9
Dobandi Pakistan 31°13N 66°50E 42 D2
Dobbyn Australia 19°44S 140°2E 62 B3
Dobele Latvia 56°37N 23°16E 9 H20
Doberai, Jazirah Indonesia 1°25S 133°0E 37 E8
Doblas Argentina 37°5S 64°0W 94 D3
Dobo Indonesia 5°45S 134°15E 37 F8
Doboj Bos.-H. 44°46N 18°4E 23 B8
Dobrich Bulgaria 43°37N 27°49E 23 C12
Dobruja Europe 44°30N 28°15E 17 F15
Dobrush Belarus 52°25N 31°22E 17 B16
Doc, Mui Vietnam 17°58N 106°30E 38 D6
Docker River = Kaltukatjara Australia 24°52S 129°5E 61 D4
Doctor Arroyo Mexico 23°40N 100°11W 86 C4
Doctor Pedro P. Peña Paraguay 22°27S 62°21W 94 A3
Doda India 33°10N 75°34E 43 C6
Doda, L. Canada 49°25N 75°13W 72 C4
Dodecanese Greece 36°35N 27°0E 23 F12
Dodekanisa = Dodecanese Greece 36°35N 27°0E 23 F12
Dodge City U.S.A. 37°45N 100°1W 80 G3
Dodge L. Canada 59°50N 105°36W 71 B7
Dodgeville U.S.A. 42°58N 90°8W 80 D8
Dodoma Tanzania 6°8S 35°45E 54 D4
Dodoma □ Tanzania 6°0S 36°0E 54 D4
Dodori ⌓ Kenya 1°55S 41°7E 54 C5
Dodsland Canada 51°50N 108°45W 71 C7
Dodson U.S.A. 48°24N 108°15W 76 B9
Doesburg Neths. 52°1N 6°9E 15 B6
Doetinchem Neths. 51°59N 6°18E 15 C6
Dog Creek Canada 51°35N 122°14W 70 C4
Dog L. Man., Canada 51°2N 98°31W 71 C9
Dog L. Ont., Canada 48°48N 89°30W 72 C2
Dogran Pakistan 31°48N 73°35E 42 D5
Doğubayazıt Turkey 39°31N 44°5E 44 B5
Doha = Ad Dawḩah Qatar 25°15N 51°35E 45 E6
Dohazari Bangla. 22°10N 92°5E 41 H18
Dohrighat India 26°16N 83°31E 43 F10
Doi Indonesia 2°14N 127°49E 37 D7
Doi Inthanon Thailand 18°35N 98°29E 38 C2
Doi Inthanon △ Thailand 18°33N 98°34E 38 C2
Doi Khuntan △ Thailand 18°33N 99°14E 38 C2
Doi Luang Thailand 18°30N 101°0E 38 C3
Doi Luang △ Thailand 19°22N 99°35E 38 C2
Doi Phukha △ Thailand 19°8N 101°9E 38 C3
Doi Saket Thailand 18°52N 99°9E 38 C2
Doi Suthep Pui △ Thailand 18°49N 98°53E 38 C2
Doi Toa Thailand 17°55N 98°30E 38 D2
Dois Irmãos, Sa. Brazil 9°0S 42°30W 93 E10
Dokkum Neths. 53°20N 5°59E 15 A5
Dokri Pakistan 27°25N 68°7E 42 F3
Dolak, Pulau Indonesia 8°0S 138°30E 37 F9
Dolbeau-Mistassini Canada 48°53N 72°14W 73 C5
Dole France 47°7N 5°31E 20 C6
Dolgellau U.K. 52°45N 3°53W 12 E4
Dolgelley = Dolgellau U.K. 52°45N 3°53W 12 E4
Dolinsk Russia 47°21N 142°48E 29 E15
Dollard Neths. 53°20N 7°10E 15 A7
Dolo Ethiopia 4°11N 42°3E 47 G3
Dolomites = Dolomiti Italy 46°23N 11°51E 22 A4
Dolomiti Italy 46°23N 11°51E 22 A4
Dolores Argentina 36°20S 57°40W 94 D4
Dolores Uruguay 33°34S 58°15W 94 C4
Dolores U.S.A. 37°28N 108°30W 77 H9
Dolores → U.S.A. 38°49N 109°17W 76 G9
Dolphin, C. Falk. Is. 51°10S 59°0W 96 G5
Dolphin and Union Str. Canada 69°5N 114°45W 68 D9
Dom Pedrito Brazil 31°0S 54°40W 95 C5
Doma ⌓ Zimbabwe 16°28S 30°12E 55 F3
Domariaganj → India 26°17N 83°44E 43 F10
Domasi Malawi 15°15S 35°22E 55 F4
Dombarovskiy Russia 50°46N 59°32E 28 D6
Dombås Norway 62°4N 9°8E 8 E13
Dome Argus Antarctica 80°50S 76°30E 5 E6
Dome C. Antarctica 75°12S 123°37E 5 D9
Dome Fuji Antarctica 77°20S 39°45E 5 D5
Domel I. = Letsôk-aw Kyun Burma 11°30N 98°25E 39 G2
Domeyko Chile 29°0S 71°0W 94 B1
Domeyko, Cordillera Chile 24°30S 69°0W 94 A2
Dominador Chile 24°21S 69°20W 94 A2
Dominica ■ W. Indies 15°20N 61°20W 89 C7
Dominica Passage W. Indies 15°10N 61°20W 89 C7
Dominican Rep. ■ W. Indies 19°0N 70°30W 89 C5
Domodóssola Italy 46°7N 8°17E 20 C8
Domville, Mt. Australia 28°1S 151°15E 63 D5
Don → Russia 47°4N 39°18E 19 E6
Don → Aberds., U.K. 57°11N 2°5W 11 D6
Don → S. Yorks., U.K. 53°41N 0°52W 12 D7
Don, C. Australia 11°18S 131°46E 60 B5
Don Benito Spain 38°53N 5°51W 21 C3
Don Figuerero Mts. Jamaica 18°5N 77°36W 88 a
Don Sak Thailand 9°18N 99°41E 39 b
Dona Ana = Nhamaabué Mozam. 17°25S 35°5E 55 F4
Donaghadee U.K. 54°39N 5°33W 10 B6
Donaghmore Ireland 52°52N 7°36W 10 D4
Donald Australia 36°23S 143°0E 63 F3
Donaldsonville U.S.A. 30°6N 90°59W 84 F9
Donalsonville U.S.A. 31°3N 84°53W 85 F12
Donau = Dunărea → Europe 45°20N 29°40E 17 F15
Donauwörth Germany 48°43N 10°47E 16 D6
Doncaster U.K. 53°32N 1°6W 12 D6
Dondo Angola 9°45S 14°25E 52 F2
Dondo Mozam. 19°33S 34°46E 55 F3
Dondo, Teluk Indonesia 0°50N 120°30E 37 D6
Dondra Head Sri Lanka 5°55N 80°40E 40 S12
Donegal Ireland 54°39N 8°5W 10 B3
Donegal □ Ireland 54°53N 8°0W 10 B4
Donegal B. Ireland 54°31N 8°49W 10 B3
Donets → Russia 47°33N 40°55E 19 E7
Donets Basin Ukraine 49°0N 38°0E 6 F13
Donetsk Ukraine 48°0N 37°45E 19 E6
Dong Ba Thin Vietnam 12°8N 109°13E 39 F7
Dong Dang Vietnam 21°54N 106°42E 38 B6
Dong Giang Vietnam 19°25N 105°31E 38 C5
Dong Ha Vietnam 16°55N 107°8E 38 D6
Dong Hene Laos 16°40N 105°18E 38 D5
Dong Hoi Vietnam 17°29N 106°36E 38 D6
Dong Khe Vietnam 22°26N 106°27E 38 A6
Dong Phrayayen Thailand 14°20N 101°22E 38 E3
Dong Ujimqin Qi China 45°32N 116°55E 34 B9
Dong Van Vietnam 23°16N 105°22E 38 A5
Dong Xoai Vietnam 11°32N 106°55E 39 G6
Dongara Australia 29°14S 114°57E 61 E1
Dongbei China 45°0N 125°0E 35 D13
Dongchuan China 26°8N 103°1E 32 F9
Dongfang China 18°50N 108°33E 38 C7
Dongfeng China 42°40N 125°34E 35 C13
Donggala Indonesia 0°30S 119°40E 37 E5
Donggang China 39°52N 124°10E 35 E13
Dongguan China 22°58N 113°44E 33 G11
Dongguang China 37°50N 116°30E 34 F9
Donghae S. Korea 37°29N 129°7E 35 F15
Dongjingcheng China 44°5N 129°10E 35 B15
Dongliao He → China 42°58N 123°32E 35 C12
Dongnae S. Korea 35°12N 129°5E 35 G15
Dongning China 44°2N 131°5E 35 B16
Dongola Sudan 19°9N 30°22E 51 E12
Dongping China 35°55N 116°20E 34 G9
Dongsha Dao S. China Sea 20°45N 116°43E 33 G12
Dongsheng China 39°50N 110°0E 34 E6
Dongtai China 32°51N 120°21E 35 H11
Dongting Hu China 29°18N 112°45E 33 F11
Dongying China 37°37N 118°37E 35 F10
Dongyinggang China 37°55N 118°58E 35 F10
Donington, C. Australia 34°45S 136°0E 63 E2
Doniphan U.S.A. 36°37N 90°50W 80 G8
Dønna Norway 66°6N 12°30E 8 C15
Donna U.S.A. 26°9N 98°4W 84 H5
Donnacona Canada 46°41N 71°41W 73 C5
Donnelly's Crossing N.Z. 35°42S 173°38E 59 A4
Donnybrook Australia 33°34S 115°48E 61 F2
Donnybrook S. Africa 29°59S 29°48E 57 D4
Donora U.S.A. 40°11N 79°52W 82 F5
Donostia = Donostia-San Sebastián Spain 43°17N 1°58W 21 A5
Donostia-San Sebastián Spain 43°17N 1°58W 21 A5
Donwood Canada 44°19N 78°16W 82 B6
Doomadgee Australia 17°56S 138°49E 62 B2
Doomadgee ❂ Australia 17°56S 138°49E 62 B2
Doon → U.K. 55°27N 4°39W 11 F4
Doon Doon ❂ Australia 16°18S 128°14E 60 C4
Dora, L. Australia 22°0S 123°0E 60 D3
Dora Báltea → Italy 45°11N 8°3E 20 D8
Doran L. Canada 61°13N 108°6W 71 A7
Dorchester U.K. 50°42N 2°27W 13 G5
Dorchester, C. Canada 65°27N 77°27W 69 D16
Dordabis Namibia 22°52S 17°38E 56 C2
Dordogne → France 45°2N 0°36W 20 D3
Dordrecht Neths. 51°48N 4°39E 15 C4
Dordrecht S. Africa 31°20S 27°3E 56 E4
Doré L. Canada 54°46N 107°17W 71 C7
Dori Burkina Faso 14°3N 0°2W 50 F5
Doring → S. Africa 31°54S 18°39E 56 E2
Doringbos S. Africa 31°59S 19°16E 56 E2
Dorking U.K. 51°14N 0°19W 13 F7
Dornbirn Austria 47°25N 9°45E 16 E5
Dornie U.K. 57°17N 5°31W 11 D3
Dornoch Canada 44°18N 80°51W 82 B4
Dornoch U.K. 57°53N 4°2W 11 D4
Dornoch Firth U.K. 57°51N 4°4W 11 D4
Dornogovĭ □ Mongolia 44°0N 110°0E 34 C6
Doro, Kavo Greece 38°9N 24°38E 23 E11
Dorohoi Romania 47°56N 26°23E 17 E14
Döröö Nuur Mongolia 48°0N 93°0E 32 B7
Dorr Iran 33°17N 50°38E 45 C6
Dorre I. Australia 25°13S 113°12E 61 E1
Dorrigo Australia 30°20S 152°44E 63 E5
Dorris U.S.A. 41°58N 121°55W 76 F3
Dorset Canada 45°14N 78°54W 82 A6
Dorset Ohio, U.S.A. 41°40N 80°40W 82 E4
Dorset Vt., U.S.A. 43°15N 73°5W 83 C11
Dorset □ U.K. 50°45N 2°26W 13 G5
Dortmund Germany 51°30N 7°28E 16 C4
Dörtyol Turkey 36°50N 36°13E 44 B3
Doruma Dem. Rep. of the Congo 4°42N 27°33E 54 B2
Dorūneh Iran 35°10N 57°18E 45 C8
Dos Bahías, C. Argentina 44°58S 65°32W 96 E3
Dos Hermanas Spain 37°16N 5°55W 21 D3
Dos Palos U.S.A. 36°59N 120°37W 78 J6
Dosso Niger 13°0N 3°13E 50 F6
Dothan U.S.A. 31°13N 85°24W 85 F12
Doty U.S.A. 46°38N 123°17W 78 D3
Douai France 50°21N 3°4E 20 A5
Douala Cameroon 4°0N 9°45E 52 D1
Douarnenez France 48°6N 4°21W 20 B1
Double Island Pt. Australia 25°56S 153°11E 63 D5

Double Mountain Fork →
 U.S.A. 33°16N 100°0W **84 E4**
Doubs → France 46°53N 5°1E **20 C6**
Doubtful Sd. N.Z. 45°20S 166°49E **59 F1**
Doubtless B. N.Z. 34°55S 173°26E **59 A4**
Douglas Canada 45°31N 76°56W **82 A8**
Douglas I. of Man 54°10N 4°28W **12 C3**
Douglas S. Africa 29°4S 23°46E **56 D3**
Douglas Ariz., U.S.A. 31°21N 109°33W **77 L9**
Douglas Ga., U.S.A. 31°31N 82°51W **85 F13**
Douglas Wyo., U.S.A. 42°45N 105°24W **76 E11**
Douglas Apsley △
 Australia 41°45S 148°11E **63 G4**
Douglas Chan. Canada 53°40N 129°20W **70 C3**
Douglas Pt. Canada 44°19N 81°37W **82 B3**
Douglasville U.S.A. 33°45N 84°45W **85 E12**
Dounreay U.K. 58°35N 3°44W **11 C5**
Dourada, Serra Brazil 13°10S 48°45W **93 F9**
Dourados Brazil 22°9S 54°50W **95 A5**
Dourados → Brazil 21°58S 54°18W **95 A5**
Dourados, Serra dos
 Brazil 23°30S 53°30W **95 A5**
Douro → Europe 41°8N 8°40W **21 B1**
Dove → U.K. 52°51N 1°36W **12 E6**
Dove Creek U.S.A. 37°46N 108°54W **77 H9**
Dover Australia 43°18S 147°2E **63 G4**
Dover U.K. 51°7N 1°19E **13 F9**
Dover Del., U.S.A. 39°10N 75°32W **81 F16**
Dover N.H., U.S.A. 43°12N 70°56W **83 C14**
Dover N.J., U.S.A. 40°53N 74°34W **83 F10**
Dover Ohio, U.S.A. 40°32N 81°29W **82 F3**
Dover, Pt. Australia 32°32S 125°32E **61 F4**
Dover, Str. of Europe 51°0N 1°30E **13 G9**
Dover-Foxcroft U.S.A. 45°11N 69°13W **81 C19**
Dover Plains U.S.A. 41°43N 73°35W **83 E11**
Dovey = Dyfi → U.K. 52°32N 4°3W **13 E3**
Dovrefjell Norway 62°15N 9°33E **8 E13**
Dow Rūd Iran 33°28N 49°4E **45 C6**
Dowa Malawi 13°38S 33°58E **55 E3**
Dowagiac U.S.A. 41°59N 86°6W **80 E10**
Dowerin Australia 31°12S 117°2E **61 F2**
Dowgha'i Iran 36°54N 58°32E **45 B8**
Dowlatābād Kermān,
 Iran 28°20N 56°40E **45 D8**
Dowlatābād Khorāsān,
 Iran 35°16N 59°29E **45 C8**
Down □ U.K. 54°23N 6°2W **10 B5**
Downey Calif., U.S.A. 33°56N 118°9W **79 M8**
Downey Idaho, U.S.A. 42°26N 112°7W **76 E7**
Downham Market U.K. 52°37N 0°23E **13 E8**
Downieville U.S.A. 39°34N 120°50W **78 F6**
Downpatrick U.K. 54°20N 5°43W **10 B6**
Downpatrick Hd. Ireland 54°20N 9°21W **10 B2**
Downsville U.S.A. 42°5N 75°0W **83 D10**
Downton, Mt. Canada 52°42N 124°52W **70 C4**
Dowsāri Iran 28°25N 57°59E **45 D8**
Doyle U.S.A. 40°2N 120°6W **78 E6**
Doylestown U.S.A. 40°21N 75°10W **83 F9**
Dozois, Rés. Canada 47°30N 77°5W **72 C4**
Dra Khel Pakistan 27°58N 66°45E **42 F2**
Drâa, C. Morocco 28°47N 11°0W **50 C3**
Drâa, Hamada du Algeria 28°0N 7°0W **50 C4**
Drâa, Oued → Morocco 28°40N 11°10W **50 C3**
Drac, Coves del Spain 39°31N 3°19E **24 B10**
Drachten Neths. 53°7N 6°5E **15 A6**
Drăgăşani Romania 44°39N 24°17E **17 F13**
Dragichyn Belarus 52°15N 25°8E **17 B13**
Dragoman, Prokhod
 Bulgaria 42°58N 22°53E **23 C10**
Dragon's Mouths
 Venezuela 11°0N 61°50W **93 K15**
Draguignan France 43°32N 6°27E **20 E7**
Drain U.S.A. 43°40N 123°19W **76 E2**
Drake U.S.A. 47°55N 100°23W **80 B3**
Drake Passage S. Ocean 58°0S 68°0W **5 B17**
Drakensberg S. Africa 31°0S 28°0E **57 D4**
Drama Greece 41°9N 24°10E **23 D11**
Drammen Norway 59°42N 10°12E **9 G14**
Drangajökull Iceland 66°9N 22°15W **8 C2**
Dras India 34°25N 75°48E **43 B6**
Drastis, Akra Greece 39°48N 19°40E **25 A3**
Drau = Drava →
 Croatia 45°33N 18°55E **23 B8**
Drava → Croatia 45°33N 18°55E **23 B8**
Drayton Canada 43°46N 80°40W **82 C4**
Drayton Valley Canada 53°12N 114°58W **70 C6**
Drenthe □ Neths. 52°52N 6°40E **15 B6**
Drepano, Akra Greece 35°28N 24°14E **25 D6**
Drepanum, C. Cyprus 34°54N 32°19E **25 E11**
Dresden Canada 42°35N 82°11W **82 D2**
Dresden Germany 51°3N 13°44E **16 C7**
Dreux France 48°44N 1°23E **20 B4**
Driffield U.K. 54°0N 0°26W **12 C7**
Driftwood U.S.A. 41°20N 78°8W **82 E6**
Driggs U.S.A. 43°44N 111°6W **76 E8**
Drin → Albania 42°1N 19°38E **23 C8**
Drina → Bos.-H. 44°53N 19°21E **23 B8**
Drøbak Norway 59°39N 10°39E **9 G14**
Drobeta-Turnu Severin
 Romania 44°39N 22°41E **17 F12**
Drochia Moldova 48°2N 27°48E **17 D14**
Drogheda Ireland 53°43N 6°22W **10 C5**
Drogichin = Dragichyn
 Belarus 52°15N 25°8E **17 B13**
Drogobych = Drohobych
 Ukraine 49°20N 23°30E **17 D12**
Drohobych Ukraine 49°20N 23°30E **17 D12**
Droichead Atha = Drogheda
 Ireland 53°43N 6°22W **10 C5**
Droichead na Bandan = Bandon
 Ireland 51°44N 8°44W **10 E3**
Droichead Nua Ireland 53°11N 6°48W **10 C5**
Droitwich U.K. 52°16N 2°8W **13 E5**
Drôme → France 44°46N 4°46E **20 D6**
Dromedary, C. Australia 36°17S 150°10E **63 F5**
Dromore U.K. 54°31N 7°28W **10 B4**
Dromore West Ireland 54°15N 8°52W **10 B3**
Dronfield U.K. 53°19N 1°27W **12 D6**
Dronning Maud Land
 Antarctica 72°30S 12°0E **5 D3**

Dronten Neths. 52°32N 5°43E **15 B5**
Druk Yul = Bhutan ■
 Asia 27°25N 90°30E **41 F17**
Drumbo Canada 43°16N 80°35W **82 C4**
Drumcliff Ireland 54°20N 8°29W **10 B3**
Drumheller Canada 51°25N 112°40W **70 C6**
Drummond U.S.A. 46°40N 113°9W **76 C7**
Drummond I. U.S.A. 46°1N 83°39W **81 B12**
Drummond Pt. Australia 34°9S 135°16E **63 E2**
Drummond Ra.
 Australia 23°45S 147°10E **62 C4**
Drummondville Canada 45°55N 72°25W **72 C5**
Drumright U.S.A. 35°59N 96°36W **84 D6**
Druskininkai Lithuania 54°3N 23°58E **9 J20**
Drut → Belarus 53°8N 30°5E **17 B16**
Dry Harbour Mts.
 Jamaica 18°19N 77°24W **88 a**
Dry Tortugas U.S.A. 24°38N 82°55W **85 F13**
Dryander △ Australia 20°13S 148°34E **62 b**
Dryden Canada 49°47N 92°50W **71 D10**
Dryden U.S.A. 42°30N 76°18W **83 D8**
Drygalski I. Antarctica 66°0S 92°0E **5 C7**
Drygalski Ice Tongue
 Antarctica 75°24S 163°30E **5 D11**
Drysdale → Australia 13°59S 126°51E **60 B4**
Drysdale I. Australia 11°41S 136°0E **62 A2**
Drysdale River △
 Australia 14°56S 127°2E **60 B4**
Du Gué → Canada 57°21N 70°45W **72 A5**
Du Quoin U.S.A. 38°1N 89°14W **80 F9**
Duanesburg U.S.A. 42°45N 74°11W **83 D10**
Duaringa Australia 23°42S 149°42E **62 C4**
Duarte, Pico Dom. Rep. 19°2N 70°59W **89 C5**
Dubai = Dubayy U.A.E. 25°18N 55°20E **45 E7**
Dubāsari Moldova 47°15N 29°10E **17 E15**
Dubāsari Vdkhr.
 Moldova 47°30N 29°0E **17 E15**
Dubawnt → Canada 64°33N 100°6W **71 A8**
Dubawnt L. Canada 63°8N 101°28W **71 A8**
Dubayy U.A.E. 25°18N 55°20E **45 E7**
Dubbo Australia 32°11S 148°35E **63 E4**
Dubele
 Dem. Rep. of the Congo 2°56N 29°35E **54 B2**
Dublin Ireland 53°21N 6°15W **10 C5**
Dublin Ga., U.S.A. 32°32N 82°54W **85 E13**
Dublin Tex., U.S.A. 32°5N 98°21W **84 E5**
Dublin □ Ireland 53°24N 6°20W **10 C5**
Dublin ✈ (DUB) Ireland 53°26N 6°15W **10 C5**
Dubno Ukraine 50°25N 25°45E **17 C13**
Dubois Idaho, U.S.A. 44°10N 112°14W **76 D7**
DuBois Pa., U.S.A. 41°7N 78°46W **82 E6**
Dubossary = Dubāsari
 Moldova 47°15N 29°10E **17 E15**
Dubossary Vdkhr. = Dubāsari
 Vdkhr. Moldova 47°30N 29°0E **17 E15**
Dubovka Russia 49°5N 44°50E **19 E7**
Dubrajpur India 23°48N 87°25E **43 H12**
Dubréka Guinea 9°46N 13°31W **50 G3**
Dubrovitsa = Dubrovytsya
 Ukraine 51°31N 26°35E **17 C14**
Dubrovnik Croatia 42°39N 18°6E **23 C8**
Dubrovytsya Ukraine 51°31N 26°35E **17 C14**
Dubuque U.S.A. 42°30N 90°41W **80 D8**
Duc Tho Vietnam 18°32N 105°35E **38 C5**
Duchesne U.S.A. 40°10N 110°24W **76 F8**
Duchess Australia 21°20S 139°50E **62 C2**
Ducie I. Pac. Oc. 24°40S 124°48W **65 K15**
Duck → U.S.A. 36°2N 87°52W **85 C11**
Duck Cr. → Australia 22°37S 116°53E **60 D2**
Duck Lake Canada 52°50N 106°16W **71 C7**
Duck Mountain △
 Canada 51°45N 101°0W **71 C8**
Duckwall, Mt. U.S.A. 37°58N 120°7W **78 H6**
Dudhi India 24°15N 83°10E **43 G10**
Dudinka Russia 69°30N 86°13E **29 C9**
Dudley U.K. 52°31N 2°5W **13 E5**
Dudwa India · 28°30N 80°41E **43 E9**
Dudwa △ India 28°30N 80°40E **43 E9**
Duero = Douro → Europe 41°8N 8°40W **21 B1**
Dufftown U.K. 57°27N 3°8W **11 D5**
Dugi Otok Croatia 44°0N 15°3E **16 G8**
Duisburg Germany 51°26N 6°45E **16 C4**
Duiwelskloof = Modjadjskloof
 S. Africa 23°42S 30°10E **57 C5**
Dūkdamīn Iran 35°59N 57°43E **45 C8**
Dukelský Průsmyk
 Slovak Rep. 49°25N 21°42E **17 D11**
Dukhān Qatar 25°25N 50°50E **45 E6**
Duki Pakistan 30°14N 68°25E **40 D6**
Duku Nigeria 10°43N 10°43E **51 F8**
Dulan China 36°0N 97°11E **32 D8**
Dulce U.S.A. 36°56N 107°0W **77 H10**
Dulce → Argentina 30°32S 62°33W **94 C3**
Dulce, G. Costa Rica 8°40N 83°20W **88 E3**
Dulf Iraq 35°7N 45°51E **44 C5**
Duliu China 39°2N 116°55E **34 E9**
Dullewala Pakistan 31°50N 71°25E **42 D4**
Dullstroom S. Africa 25°27S 30°7E **57 D5**
Dulq Maghār Syria 36°22N 38°39E **44 B3**
Duluth U.S.A. 46°47N 92°6W **80 B7**
Dum Dum India 22°39N 88°26E **43 H13**
Dum Duma India 27°40N 95°40E **41 F19**
Dūmā Syria 33°34N 36°24E **46 B5**
Dumaguete Phil. 9°17N 123°15E **37 C6**
Dumai Indonesia 1°35N 101°28E **36 D2**
Dumaran Phil. 10°33N 119°50E **37 B5**
Dumas Ark., U.S.A. 33°53N 91°29W **84 E9**
Dumas Tex., U.S.A. 35°52N 101°58W **84 D4**
Dumayr Syria 33°39N 36°42E **46 B5**
Dumbarton U.K. 55°57N 4°33W **11 F4**
Dumbleyung Australia 33°17S 117°42E **61 F2**
Dumfries U.K. 55°4N 3°37W **11 F5**
Dumfries & Galloway □
 U.K. 55°9N 3°58W **11 F5**
Dumka India 24°12N 87°15E **43 G12**
Dumoine → Canada 46°13N 77°51W **72 C4**
Dumoine, L. Canada 46°55N 77°55W **72 C4**
Dumont d'Urville
 Antarctica 66°40S 140°0E **5 C10**

Dumont d'Urville Sea
 S. Ocean 63°30S 138°0E **5 C9**
Dumraon India 25°33N 84°8E **43 G11**
Dumyât Egypt 31°24N 31°48E **51 B12**
Dún Dealgan = Dundalk
 Ireland 54°1N 6°24W **10 B5**
Dún Garbhán = Dungarvan
 Ireland 52°5N 7°37W **10 D4**
Dún Laoghaire Ireland 53°17N 6°8W **10 C5**
Duna = Dunārea →
 Europe 45°20N 29°40E **17 F15**
Dunagiri India 30°31N 79°52E **43 D8**
Dunaj = Dunārea →
 Europe 45°20N 29°40E **17 F15**
Dunakeszi Hungary 47°37N 19°8E **17 E10**
Dunārea → Europe 45°20N 29°40E **17 F15**
Dunaújváros Hungary 46°58N 18°57E **17 E10**
Dunav = Dunārea →
 Europe 45°20N 29°40E **17 F15**
Dunay Russia 42°52N 132°22E **30 C6**
Dunback N.Z. 45°23S 170°36E **59 F3**
Dunbar U.K. 56°0N 2°31W **11 E6**
Dunblane U.K. 56°11N 3°58W **11 E5**
Duncan Canada 48°45N 123°40W **78 B3**
Duncan Ariz., U.S.A. 32°43N 109°6W **77 K9**
Duncan Okla., U.S.A. 34°30N 97°57W **84 D6**
Duncan, L. Canada 53°29N 77°58W **72 B4**
Duncan L. Canada 62°51N 113°58W **70 A6**
Duncan Town Bahamas 22°15N 75°45W **88 B4**
Duncannon U.S.A. 40°23N 77°2W **82 F7**
Duncansby Head U.K. 58°38N 3°1W **11 C5**
Duncansville U.S.A. 40°25N 78°26W **82 F6**
Dund-Us Mongolia 48°1N 91°38E **32 B7**
Dundalk Canada 44°10N 80°24W **82 B4**
Dundalk Ireland 54°1N 6°24W **10 B5**
Dundalk U.S.A. 39°15N 76°31W **81 F15**
Dundalk Bay Ireland 53°55N 6°15W **10 C5**
Dundas = Uummannaq
 Greenland 77°33N 68°52W **69 B18**
Dundas Canada 43°17N 79°59W **82 C5**
Dundas, L. Australia 32°35S 121°50E **61 F3**
Dundas I. Canada 54°30N 130°50W **70 C2**
Dundas Str. Australia 11°15S 131°35E **60 B5**
Dundee S. Africa 28°11S 30°15E **57 D5**
Dundee U.K. 56°28N 2°59W **11 E6**
Dundee U.S.A. 42°32N 76°58W **82 D8**
Dundee City □ U.K. 56°30N 2°58W **11 E6**
Dundgovĭ □ Mongolia 45°10N 106°0E **34 B4**
Dundrum U.K. 54°16N 5°52W **10 B6**
Dundrum B. U.K. 54°13N 5°47W **10 B6**
Dunedin N.Z. 45°50S 170°33E **59 F3**
Dunedin U.S.A. 28°1N 82°46W **85 G13**
Dunfanaghy Ireland 55°11N 7°58W **10 A4**
Dunfermline U.K. 56°5N 3°27W **11 E5**
Dungannon Canada 43°51N 81°36W **82 C3**
Dungannon U.K. 54°31N 6°46W **10 B5**
Dungarpur India 23°52N 73°45E **42 H5**
Dungarvan Ireland 52°5N 7°37W **10 D4**
Dungarvan Harbour
 Ireland 52°4N 7°35W **10 D4**
Dungeness U.K. 50°54N 0°59E **13 G8**
Dunglow Ireland 54°57N 8°21W **10 B3**
Dungo, L. do Angola 17°15S 19°0E **56 B2**
Dungog Australia 32°22S 151°46E **63 E5**
Dungu
 Dem. Rep. of the Congo 3°40N 28°32E **54 B2**
Dungun Malaysia 4°45N 103°25E **39 K4**
Dunhua China 43°20N 128°14E **35 C15**
Dunhuang China 40°8N 94°36E **32 C7**
Dunk I. Australia 17°59S 146°29E **62 B4**
Dunkeld Australia 33°25S 149°29E **63 E4**
Dunkeld U.K. 56°34N 3°35W **11 E5**
Dunkerque France 51°2N 2°20E **20 A5**
Dunkery Beacon U.K. 51°9N 3°36W **13 F4**
Dunkirk = Dunkerque
 France 51°2N 2°20E **20 A5**
Dunkirk U.S.A. 42°29N 79°20W **82 D5**
Dúnleary = Dún Laoghaire
 Ireland 53°17N 6°8W **10 C5**
Dunleer Ireland 53°50N 6°24W **10 C5**
Dunmanus B. Ireland 51°31N 9°50W **10 E2**
Dunmanway Ireland 51°43N 9°6W **10 E2**
Dunmarra Australia 16°42S 133°25E **62 B1**
Dunmore U.S.A. 41°25N 75°38W **83 E9**
Dunmore East Ireland 52°9N 7°0W **10 D5**
Dunmore Hd. Ireland 52°10N 10°35W **10 D1**
Dunmore Town
 Bahamas 25°30N 76°39W **88 A4**
Dunn U.S.A. 35°19N 78°37W **85 D15**
Dunnellon U.S.A. 29°3N 82°28W **85 G13**
Dunnet Hd. U.K. 58°40N 3°21W **11 C5**
Dunning U.S.A. 41°50N 100°6W **80 E3**
Dunnville Canada 42°54N 79°36W **82 D5**
Dunolly Australia 36°51S 143°44E **63 F3**
Dunoon U.K. 55°57N 4°56W **11 F4**
Duns U.K. 55°47N 2°20W **11 F6**
Dunseith U.S.A. 48°50N 100°3W **80 A3**
Dunshaughlin Ireland 53°31N 6°33W **10 C5**
Dunsmuir U.S.A. 41°13N 122°16W **76 F2**
Dunstable U.K. 51°53N 0°32W **13 F7**
Dunstan Mts. N.Z. 44°53S 169°35E **59 F2**
Dunster Canada 53°8N 119°50W **70 C5**
Dunvegan U.K. 57°27N 6°35W **11 D2**
Dunvegan L. Canada 60°8N 107°10W **71 A7**
Duolun China 42°12N 116°28E **34 C9**
Duong Dong Vietnam 10°13N 103°58E **39 G4**
Dupree U.S.A. 45°4N 101°35W **80 C3**
Dupuyer U.S.A. 48°13N 112°30W **76 B7**
Duque de Caxias Brazil 22°46S 43°18W **95 A7**
Durack → Australia 15°33S 127°52E **60 C4**
Durack Ra. Australia 16°50S 127°40E **60 C4**
Durack River Australia 15°32S 127°39E **60 C4**
Durance → France 43°55N 4°45E **20 E6**
Durand U.S.A. 44°38N 91°58W **80 C8**
Durango Mexico 24°3N 104°39W **86 C4**
Durango U.S.A. 37°16N 107°53W **77 H10**
Durango □ Mexico 25°0N 105°20W **86 C4**
Durant Miss., U.S.A. 33°4N 89°51W **85 E10**
Durant Okla., U.S.A. 33°59N 96°25W **84 E6**
Durazno Uruguay 33°25S 56°31W **94 C4**

Durazzo = Durrës
 Albania 41°19N 19°28E **23 D8**
Durban S. Africa 29°49S 31°1E **57 D5**
Durbuy Belgium 50°21N 5°28E **15 D5**
Düren Germany 50°48N 6°29E **16 C4**
Durg = Bhilainagar-Durg
 India 21°13N 81°26E **41 J12**
Durgapur India 23°30N 87°20E **43 H12**
Durham Canada 44°10N 80°49W **82 B4**
Durham U.K. 54°47N 1°34W **12 C6**
Durham Calif., U.S.A. 39°39N 121°48W **78 F5**
Durham N.C., U.S.A. 35°59N 78°54W **85 D15**
Durham N.H., U.S.A. 43°8N 70°56W **83 C14**
Durham □ U.K. 54°42N 1°45W **12 C6**
Durlas = Thurles Ireland 52°41N 7°49W **10 D4**
Durmā Si. Arabia 24°37N 46°8E **44 E5**
Durmitor Montenegro 43°10N 19°0E **23 C8**
Durness U.K. 58°34N 4°45W **11 C4**
Durrës Albania 41°19N 19°28E **23 D8**
Durrow Ireland 52°51N 7°24W **10 D4**
Dursey I. Ireland 51°36N 10°12W **10 E1**
Dursley U.K. 51°40N 2°21W **13 F5**
Dursunbey Turkey 39°35N 28°37E **23 E13**
Duru
 Dem. Rep. of the Congo 4°14N 28°50E **54 B2**
Durūz, Jabal ad Jordan 32°35N 36°40E **46 C5**
D'Urville, Tanjung
 Indonesia 1°28S 137°54E **37 E9**
D'Urville I. N.Z. 40°50S 173°55E **59 D4**
Duryea U.S.A. 41°20N 75°45W **83 E9**
Dushak Turkmenistan 37°13N 60°1E **45 B9**
Dushanbe Tajikistan 38°33N 68°48E **28 F7**
Dushore U.S.A. 41°31N 76°24W **83 E8**
Dusky Sd. N.Z. 45°47S 166°30E **59 F1**
Dussejour, C. Australia 14°45S 128°13E **60 B4**
Düsseldorf Germany 51°14N 6°47E **16 C4**
Dutch Harbor U.S.A. 53°53N 166°32W **74 E6**
Dutlwe Botswana 23°58S 23°46E **56 C3**
Dutton Canada 42°39N 81°30W **82 D3**
Dutton → Australia 20°44S 143°10E **62 C3**
Dutywa S. Africa 32°8S 28°18E **57 E4**
Duwayhin, Khawr
 U.A.E. 24°20N 51°25E **45 E6**
Duyfken Pt. Australia 12°33S 141°38E **62 A3**
Duyun China 26°18N 107°29E **32 F10**
Dvina, Severnaya →
 Russia 64°32N 40°30E **18 B7**
Dvinsk = Daugavpils
 Latvia 55°53N 26°32E **9 J22**
Dvinskaya Guba Russia 65°0N 39°0E **18 B6**
Dwarka India 22°18N 69°8E **42 H3**
Dwellingup Australia 32°43S 116°4E **61 F2**
Dwight U.S.A. 41°5N 88°26W **80 E9**
Dyatkovo Russia
 Belarus 53°28N 25°28E **17 B13**
Dyce U.K. 57°13N 2°12W **11 D6**
Dyer, C. Canada 66°37N 61°16W **69 D19**
Dyer Bay Canada 45°10N 81°20W **82 A3**
Dyer Plateau Antarctica 70°45S 65°30W **5 D17**
Dyersburg U.S.A. 36°3N 89°23W **85 C10**
Dyfi → U.K. 52°32N 4°3W **13 E3**
Dymer Ukraine 50°47N 30°18E **17 C16**
Dysart Australia 22°32S 148°23E **62 C4**
Dzaoudzi Mayotte 12°47S 45°16E **53 a**
Dzavhan Gol →
 Mongolia 48°54N 93°23E **32 B7**
Dzerzhinsk Russia 56°14N 43°30E **18 C7**
Dzhalinda Russia 53°26N 124°0E **29 D13**
Dzhambul = Taraz
 Kazakhstan 42°54N 71°22E **32 C3**
Dzhankoy Ukraine 45°40N 34°20E **19 E5**
Dzhezkazgan = Zhezqazghan
 Kazakhstan 47°44N 67°40E **28 E7**
Dzhizak = Jizzax
 Uzbekistan 40°6N 67°50E **28 E7**
Dzhugdzur, Khrebet
 Russia 57°30N 138°0E **29 D14**
Dzhungarskiye Vorota =
 Dzungarian Gate Asia 45°10N 82°0E **32 B5**
Działdowo Poland 53°15N 20°15E **17 B11**
Dzibilchaltún Mexico 21°10N 89°35W **87 C7**
Dzierżoniów Poland 50°45N 16°39E **17 C9**
Dzilam de Bravo Mexico 21°24N 88°53W **87 C7**
Dzūkija △ Lithuania 54°10N 24°30E **9 J21**
Dzungarian Basin = Junggar
 Pendi China 44°30N 86°0E **32 C6**
Dzungarian Gate Asia 45°10N 82°0E **32 B5**
Dzüünbayan Mongolia 44°29N 110°2E **34 B6**
Dzüünharaa Mongolia 48°52N 106°28E **32 B10**
Dzüünmod Mongolia 47°45N 106°58E **32 B10**
Dzyarzhynsk Belarus 53°40N 27°1E **17 B14**
Dzyatlava Belarus 53°28N 25°28E **17 B13**

E

E.C. Manning △ Canada 49°5N 120°45W **70 D4**
Eabamet L. Canada 51°30N 87°46W **72 B2**
Eabametoong Canada 51°30N 88°0W **72 B2**
Éadan Doire = Edenderry
 Ireland 53°21N 7°4W **10 C4**
Eads U.S.A. 38°29N 102°47W **76 G12**
Eagar U.S.A. 34°6N 109°17W **77 J9**
Eagle Alaska, U.S.A. 64°47N 141°12W **74 C11**
Eagle Colo., U.S.A. 39°39N 106°50W **76 G10**
Eagle → Canada 53°36N 57°26W **73 B8**
Eagle Butte U.S.A. 45°0N 101°10W **80 C3**
Eagle L. Canada 49°42N 93°13E **71 D10**
Eagle L. Calif., U.S.A. 40°39N 120°45W **76 F3**
Eagle L. Maine, U.S.A. 46°20N 69°22W **81 B19**
Eagle Lake Maine, U.S.A. 47°3N 68°36W **81 B19**
Eagle Lake Tex., U.S.A. 29°35N 96°20W **84 G6**
Eagle Mountain
 U.S.A. 33°49N 115°27W **79 M11**
Eagle Nest U.S.A. 36°33N 105°16W **77 H11**
Eagle Pass U.S.A. 28°43N 100°30W **84 G4**
Eagle Pk. U.S.A. 38°10N 119°25W **78 G7**

Eagle Pt. Australia 16°11S 124°23E **60 C3**
Eagle River Mich., U.S.A. 47°25N 88°18W **80 B9**
Eagle River Wis., U.S.A. 45°55N 89°15W **80 C9**
Eaglehawk Australia 36°44S 144°15E **63 F3**
Eagles Mere U.S.A. 41°25N 76°33W **83 E8**
Ealing □ U.K. 51°31N 0°20W **13 F7**
Ear Falls Canada 50°38N 93°13E **71 C10**
Earle U.S.A. 35°16N 90°28W **85 D9**
Earlimart U.S.A. 35°53N 119°16W **79 K7**
Earlville U.S.A. 42°44N 75°32W **83 D9**
Earn → U.K. 56°21N 3°18W **11 E5**
Earn, L. U.K. 56°23N 4°13W **11 E4**
Earnslaw, Mt. N.Z. 44°32S 168°27E **59 F2**
Earth U.S.A. 34°14N 102°24W **84 D3**
Easley U.S.A. 34°50N 82°36W **85 D13**
East Anglia U.K. 52°30N 1°0E **12 E9**
East Angus Canada 45°30N 71°40W **73 C5**
East Antarctica Antarctica 80°0S 90°0E **5 D7**
East Aurora U.S.A. 42°46N 78°37W **82 D6**
East Ayrshire □ U.K. 55°26N 4°11W **11 F4**
East Bengal Bangla. 24°0N 90°0E **41 G17**
East Beskids = Vychodné Beskydy
 Europe 49°20N 22°0E **17 D11**
East Brady U.S.A. 40°59N 79°37W **82 F5**
East Branch Clarion River L.
 U.S.A. 41°35N 78°35W **82 E6**
East C. = Dezhneva, Mys
 Russia 66°5N 169°40W **29 C19**
East C. N.Z. 37°42S 178°35E **59 B7**
East Caroline Basin
 Pac. Oc. 4°0N 146°45E **64 G6**
East Chicago U.S.A. 41°38N 87°27W **80 E10**
East China Sea Asia 30°0N 126°0E **33 F14**
East Coulee Canada 51°23N 112°27W **70 C6**
East Dereham = Dereham
 U.K. 52°41N 0°57E **13 E8**
East Dunbartonshire □
 U.K. 55°57N 4°13W **11 F4**
East Falkland Falk. Is. 51°30S 58°30W **96 G5**
East Grand Forks U.S.A. 47°56N 97°1W **80 B6**
East Greenwich U.S.A. 41°40N 71°27W **83 E13**
East Grinstead U.K. 51°7N 0°0 **13 F8**
East Hartford U.S.A. 41°46N 72°39W **83 E12**
East Haydon Australia 18°0S 141°30E **62 B3**
East Helena U.S.A. 46°35N 111°56W **76 C8**
East Indies Asia 0°0 120°0E **26 J14**
East Kilbride U.K. 55°47N 4°11W **11 F4**
East Lamma Channel
 China 22°14N 114°9E **33 a**
East Lansing U.S.A. 42°44N 84°29W **81 D11**
East Liverpool U.S.A. 40°37N 80°35W **82 F4**
East London S. Africa 33°0S 27°55E **57 E4**
East Lothian □ U.K. 55°58N 2°44W **11 F6**
East Main = Eastmain
 Canada 52°10N 78°30W **72 B4**
East Mariana Basin
 Pac. Oc. 12°0N 153°0E **64 F7**
East Northport U.S.A. 40°53N 73°20W **83 F11**
East Orange U.S.A. 40°46N 74°12W **83 F10**
East Pacific Rise Pac. Oc. 15°0S 110°0W **65 J17**
East Palestine U.S.A. 40°50N 80°33W **82 F4**
East Pine Canada 55°48N 120°12W **70 B4**
East Point U.S.A. 33°41N 84°25W **85 E12**
East Providence U.S.A. 41°49N 71°23W **83 E13**
East Pt. Br. Virgin Is. 18°40N 64°18W **89 e**
East Pt. Canada 46°27N 61°58W **73 C7**
East Renfrewshire □
 U.K. 55°46N 4°21W **11 F4**
East Retford = Retford
 U.K. 53°19N 0°56W **12 D7**
East Riding of Yorkshire □
 U.K. 53°55N 0°30W **12 D7**
East Rochester U.S.A. 43°7N 77°29W **82 C7**
East St. Louis U.S.A. 38°37N 90°9W **80 F8**
East Schelde = Oosterschelde →
 Neths. 51°33N 4°0E **15 C4**
East Sea = Japan, Sea of
 Asia 40°0N 135°0E **30 E7**
East Siberian Sea Russia 73°0N 160°0E **29 B17**
East Stroudsburg U.S.A. 41°1N 75°11W **83 E9**
East Sussex □ U.K. 50°56N 0°19E **13 G8**
East Tasman Plateau
 Pac. Oc. 43°30S 152°0E **64 M7**
East Tawas U.S.A. 44°17N 83°29W **81 C12**
East Timor ■ Asia 8°50S 126°0E **37 F7**
East Toorale Australia 30°27S 145°28E **63 E4**
East Walker → U.S.A. 38°52N 119°10W **78 G7**
East Windsor U.S.A. 40°17N 74°34W **83 F10**
Eastbourne N.Z. 41°19S 174°55E **59 D5**
Eastbourne U.K. 50°46N 0°18E **13 G8**
Eastend Canada 49°32N 108°50W **71 D7**
Easter Fracture Zone
 Pac. Oc. 25°0S 115°0W **65 K16**
Easter I. = Pascua, I. de
 Chile 27°7S 109°23W **65 K17**
Eastern □ Kenya 0°0 38°30E **54 C4**
Eastern Cape □ S. Africa 32°0S 26°0E **56 E4**
Eastern Cr. → Australia 20°40S 141°35E **62 C3**
Eastern Desert = Es Sahrâ' Esh
 Sharqîya Egypt 27°30N 32°30E **51 C12**
Eastern Ghats India 14°0N 78°50E **40 N11**
Eastern Group = Lau Group
 Fiji 17°0S 178°30W **59 a**
Eastern Group Australia 33°30S 124°30E **61 F3**
Eastern Guruma □
 Australia 22°0S 117°0E **60 D2**
Eastern Transvaal =
 Mpumalanga □
 S. Africa 26°0S 30°0E **57 D5**
Easterville Canada 53°8N 99°49W **71 C9**
Easthampton U.S.A. 42°16N 72°40W **83 D12**
Eastlake U.S.A. 41°40N 81°26W **82 E3**
Eastland U.S.A. 32°24N 98°49W **84 E5**
Eastleigh U.K. 50°58N 1°21W **13 G6**
Eastmain Canada 52°10N 78°30W **72 B4**
Eastmain → Canada 52°27N 78°26W **72 B4**
Eastman Canada 45°18N 72°19W **83 A12**
Eastman U.S.A. 32°12N 83°11W **85 E13**
Easton Md., U.S.A. 38°47N 76°5W **81 F15**
Easton Pa., U.S.A. 40°41N 75°13W **83 F9**

Easton *Wash., U.S.A.*   47°14N 121°11W **78** C5
Eastport *U.S.A.*   44°56N 67°00W **81** D20
Eastsound *U.S.A.*   48°42N 122°55W **78** B4
Eaton *U.S.A.*   40°32N 104°42W **76** F11
Eatonia *Canada*   51°13N 109°25W **71** C7
Eatonton *U.S.A.*   33°20N 83°23W **85** E13
Eatontown *U.S.A.*   40°19N 74°4W **83** F10
Eatonville *U.S.A.*   46°52N 122°16W **78** D4
Eau Claire *U.S.A.*   44°49N 91°30W **80** C8
Eau Claire, L. à l' *Canada*   56°10N 74°25W **72** A5
Eauripik Rise *Pac. Oc.*   2°0N 142°0E **64** G6
Ebano *Mexico*   22°13N 98°24W **87** C5
Ebbw Vale *U.K.*   51°46N 3°12W **13** F4
Ebeltoft *Denmark*   56°12N 10°41E **9** H14
Ebensburg *U.S.A.*   40°29N 78°44W **82** F6
Eberswalde-Finow
    Germany   52°50N 13°49E **16** B7
Ebetsu *Japan*   43°7N 141°34E **30** C10
Ebey's Landing △
    U.S.A.   48°12N 122°41W **78** B4
Ebinur Hu *China*   44°55N 82°55E **32** C5
Ebolowa *Cameroon*   2°55N 11°10E **52** D2
Ebonda
    Dem. Rep. of the Congo   2°12N 22°21E **52** D4
Ebre = Ebro → *Spain*   40°43N 0°54E **21** B6
Ebro → *Spain*   40°43N 0°54E **21** B6
Ecatepec de Morelos
    Mexico   19°36N 99°3W **87** D5
Ecbatana = Hamadān
    Iran   34°52N 48°32E **45** C6
Eceabat *Turkey*   40°11N 26°21E **23** D12
Ech Chélif *Algeria*   36°10N 1°20E **50** A6
Echigo-Sammyaku
    Japan   36°50N 139°50E **31** F9
Echizen-Misaki *Japan*   35°59N 135°57E **31** G7
Echo Bay *N.W.T., Canada*   66°5N 117°55W **68** D8
Echo Bay *Ont., Canada*   46°29N 84°4W **72** C3
Echoing → *Canada*   55°51N 92°5W **72** B1
Echternach *Lux.*   49°49N 6°25E **15** E6
Echuca *Australia*   36°10S 144°45E **63** F3
Écija *Spain*   37°30N 5°10W **21** D3
Eclipse I. *Australia*   35°5S 117°58E **61** G2
Eclipse Is. *Australia*   13°54S 126°19E **60** B4
Eclipse Sd. *Canada*   72°38N 79°0W **69** C16
Ecuador ■ *S. Amer.*   2°0S 78°0W **92** D3
Ed *Eritrea*   14°0N 41°38E **49** E3
Ed Da'ein *Sudan*   11°26N 26°9E **52** B5
Ed Damazin *Sudan*   11°46N 34°21E **51** F12
Ed Dâmer *Sudan*   17°27N 34°0E **51** E12
Ed Dar el Beida = Casablanca
    Morocco   33°36N 7°36W **50** B4
Ed Debba *Sudan*   18°0N 30°51E **51** E12
Ed Déffa *Egypt*   30°40N 26°30E **51** B11
Ed Dueim *Sudan*   14°0N 32°10E **51** F12
Edam *Canada*   53°11N 108°46W **71** C7
Edam *Neths.*   52°31N 5°3E **15** B5
Eday *U.K.*   59°11N 2°47W **11** B6
Eddrachillis B. *U.K.*   58°17N 5°14W **11** C3
Eddystone *U.K.*   50°11N 4°16W **13** G3
Eddystone Pt. *Australia*   40°59S 148°20E **63** G4
Ede *Neths.*   52°4N 5°40E **15** B5
Edehon L. *Canada*   60°25N 97°15W **71** A9
Eden *Australia*   37°3S 149°55E **63** F4
Eden *N.C., U.S.A.*   36°29N 79°53W **85** C15
Eden *N.Y., U.S.A.*   42°39N 78°55W **82** D6
Eden *Tex., U.S.A.*   31°13N 99°51W **84** F5
Eden → *U.K.*   54°57N 3°1W **12** C4
Edenburg *S. Africa*   29°43S 25°58E **56** D4
Edendale *S. Africa*   29°39S 30°18E **57** D5
Edenderry *Ireland*   53°21N 7°4W **10** C4
Edenton *U.S.A.*   36°4N 76°39W **85** C16
Edenville *S. Africa*   27°37S 27°34E **57** D4
Eder → *Germany*   51°12N 9°28E **16** C5
Edessa *Greece*   40°48N 22°5E **23** D10
Edfu = Idfû *Egypt*   24°55N 32°49E **51** D12
Edgar *U.S.A.*   40°22N 97°58W **80** E5
Edgartown *U.S.A.*   41°23N 70°31W **83** E14
Edge Hill *U.K.*   52°8N 1°26W **13** E6
Edgefield *U.S.A.*   33°47N 81°56W **85** E14
Edgeley *U.S.A.*   46°22N 98°43W **80** B4
Edgemont *U.S.A.*   43°18N 103°50W **80** D2
Edgeøya *Svalbard*   77°45N 22°30E **4** B9
Édhessa = Édessa *Greece*   40°48N 22°5E **23** D10
Edievale *N.Z.*   45°49S 169°22E **59** F2
Edina *U.S.A.*   40°10N 92°11W **80** E7
Edinboro *U.S.A.*   41°52N 80°8W **82** E4
Edinburg *U.S.A.*   26°18N 98°10W **84** H5
Edinburgh *U.K.*   55°57N 3°13W **11** F5
Edinburgh ✈ (EDI) *U.K.*   55°54N 3°22W **11** F5
Edinburgh, City of □
    U.K.   55°57N 3°17W **11** F5
Edineț *Moldova*   48°9N 27°18E **17** D14
Edirne *Turkey*   41°40N 26°34E **23** D12
Edison *U.S.A.*   48°33N 122°27W **78** B4
Edithburgh *Australia*   35°5S 137°43E **63** F2
Edmeston *U.S.A.*   42°42N 75°15W **83** D9
Edmond *U.S.A.*   35°39N 97°29W **84** D6
Edmonds *U.S.A.*   47°48N 122°22W **78** C4
Edmonton *Australia*   17°2S 145°46E **62** B4
Edmonton *Canada*   53°30N 113°30W **70** C6
Edmund L. *Canada*   54°45N 93°17W **72** B1
Edmundston *Canada*   47°23N 68°20W **73** C6
Edna *U.S.A.*   28°59N 96°39W **84** G6
Edremit *Turkey*   39°34N 27°0E **23** E12
Edremit Körfezi *Turkey*   39°30N 26°45E **23** E12
Edson *Canada*   53°35N 116°28W **70** C5
Eduardo Castex
    Argentina   35°50S 64°18W **94** D3
Edward → *Australia*   35°5S 143°30E **63** F3
Edward, L. *Africa*   0°25S 29°40E **54** C2
Edward VII Land
    Antarctica   80°0S 150°0W **5** E13
Edwards *Calif., U.S.A.*   34°50N 117°40W **79** L9
Edwards *N.Y., U.S.A.*   44°20N 75°15W **83** B9
Edwards Plateau
    U.S.A.   30°45N 101°20W **84** F4
Edwardsville *U.S.A.*   41°15N 75°56W **83** E9
Edzná *Mexico*   19°39N 90°19W **87** D6
Edzo *Canada*   62°49N 116°4W **70** A5
Eeklo *Belgium*   51°11N 3°33E **15** C3
Eesti = Estonia ■ *Europe*   58°30N 25°30E **9** G21

Effigy Mounds △ *U.S.A.*   43°5N 91°11W **80** D8
Effingham *U.S.A.*   39°7N 88°33W **80** F9
Égadi, Ísole *Italy*   37°55N 12°16E **22** F5
Egan Range *U.S.A.*   39°35N 114°55W **76** G6
Eganville *Canada*   45°32N 77°5W **82** A7
Eger = Cheb *Czech Rep.*   50°9N 12°28E **16** C7
Eger *Hungary*   47°53N 20°27E **17** E11
Egersund *Norway*   58°26N 6°1E **9** G12
Egg L. *Canada*   55°5N 105°30W **71** B7
Éghezée *Belgium*   50°35N 4°55E **15** D4
Egilsstaðir *Iceland*   65°16N 14°25W **8** D6
Egio *Greece*   38°15N 22°5E **23** E10
Eglinton I. *Canada*   75°48N 118°30W **69** B8
Egmont *Canada*   49°45N 123°56W **78** D5
Egmont, C. *N.Z.*   39°16S 173°45E **59** C4
Egmont, Mt. = Taranaki, Mt.
    N.Z.   39°17S 174°5E **59** C5
Egmont △ *N.Z.*   39°17S 174°4E **59** C5
Egra *India*   21°54N 87°32E **43** J12
Eğridir *Turkey*   37°52N 30°51E **19** G5
Eğridir Gölü *Turkey*   37°53N 30°50E **44** B1
Egvekinot *Russia*   66°19N 179°50W **29** C19
Ehime □ *Japan*   33°30N 132°40E **31** H6
Ehrenberg *U.S.A.*   33°36N 114°31W **79** M12
Eibar *Spain*   43°11N 2°28W **21** A4
Eidsvold *Australia*   25°25S 151°12E **63** D5
Eidsvoll *Norway*   60°19N 11°14E **9** F14
Eielson *U.S.A.*   64°40N 147°4W **74** C10
Eifel *Germany*   50°15N 6°50E **16** C4
Eiffel Flats *Zimbabwe*   18°20S 30°0E **55** F3
Eigg *U.K.*   56°54N 6°10W **11** E2
Eighty Mile Beach
    Australia   19°30S 120°40E **60** C3
Eil, L. *U.K.*   56°51N 5°16W **11** E3
Eildon, L. *Australia*   37°10S 146°0E **63** F4
Eilean Sar = Western Isles □
    U.K.   57°30N 7°10W **11** D1
Einasleigh *Australia*   18°32S 144°5E **62** B3
Einasleigh → *Australia*   17°30S 142°17E **62** B3
Eindhoven *Neths.*   51°26N 5°28E **15** C5
Eire = Ireland ■ *Europe*   53°50N 7°52W **10** C4
Eiríksjökull *Iceland*   64°46N 20°24W **8** D3
Eirunepé *Brazil*   6°35S 69°53W **92** E5
Eiseb → *Namibia*   20°33S 20°59E **56** C2
Eisenach *Germany*   50°58N 10°19E **16** C6
Eisenerz *Austria*   47°32N 14°54E **16** E8
Eivissa *Spain*   38°54N 1°26E **24** C7
Ejeda *Madag.*   24°20S 44°31E **57** C7
Ejutla *Mexico*   16°34N 96°44W **87** D5
Ekalaka *U.S.A.*   45°53N 104°33W **76** D11
Ekaterinburg = Yekaterinburg
    Russia   56°50N 60°30E **28** D7
Ekenäs = Raasepori
    Finland   60°0N 23°26E **9** G20
Eketahuna *N.Z.*   40°38S 175°43E **59** D5
Ekibastuz *Kazakhstan*   51°50N 75°10E **28** D8
Ekoli *Dem. Rep. of the Congo*   0°23S 24°13E **54** C1
Eksjö *Sweden*   57°40N 14°58E **9** H16
Ekuma → *Namibia*   18°40S 16°2E **56** B2
Ekwan → *Canada*   53°12N 82°15W **72** B3
Ekwan Pt. *Canada*   53°16N 82°7W **72** B3
El Aaiún *W. Sahara*   27°9N 13°12W **50** C3
El Abanico *Chile*   37°20S 71°31W **94** D1
El 'Agrûd *Egypt*   30°14N 34°24E **46** E3
El Alamein *Egypt*   30°48N 28°58E **51** B11
El 'Aqaba, W. → *Egypt*   30°7N 33°54E **46** E2
El Arīḥā *West Bank*   31°52N 35°27E **46** D4
El 'Arîsh *Egypt*   31°8N 33°50E **46** D2
El 'Arîsh, W. → *Egypt*   31°8N 33°47E **46** D2
El Asnam = Ech Chélif
    Algeria   36°10N 1°20E **50** A6
El Bayadh *Algeria*   33°40N 1°1E **50** B6
El Bluff *Nic.*   11°59N 83°40W **88** D3
El Cajon *U.S.A.*   32°48N 116°58W **79** N10
El Calafate *Argentina*   50°19S 72°15W **96** G2
El Campo *U.S.A.*   29°12N 96°16W **84** G6
El Capitan *U.S.A.*   37°44N 119°38E **78** H7
El Carbón *Honduras*   15°25N 85°32W **88** C2
El Carmen *Colombia*   9°43N 75°8W **92** B3
El Centro *U.S.A.*   32°48N 115°34W **79** N11
El Cerro *Bolivia*   17°30S 61°40W **92** G6
El Compadre *Mexico*   32°20N 116°14W **79** N10
El Cuy *Argentina*   39°55S 68°25W **96** D3
El Cuyo *Mexico*   21°31N 87°41W **87** C7
El Daheir *Egypt*   31°13N 34°10E **46** D3
El Descanso *Mexico*   32°12N 116°58W **79** N10
El Desemboque *Mexico*   30°33N 113°1W **86** A2
El Diviso *Colombia*   1°22N 78°14W **92** C3
El Djouf *Mauritania*   20°0N 9°0W **50** D4
El Dorado *Mexico*   24°17N 107°21W **86** C3
El Dorado *Ark., U.S.A.*   33°12N 92°40W **84** E8
El Dorado *Kans., U.S.A.*   37°49N 96°52W **80** G5
El Dorado *Venezuela*   6°55N 61°37W **92** B6
El Dorado Springs *U.S.A.*   37°52N 94°1W **80** G6
El Escorial *Spain*   40°35N 4°7W **21** B3
El Faiyûm *Egypt*   29°19N 30°50E **51** C12
El Fâsher *Sudan*   13°33N 25°26E **51** F11
El Ferrol = Ferrol *Spain*   43°29N 8°15W **21** A1
El Fuerte *Mexico*   26°25N 108°39W **86** B3
El Geneina = Al Junaynah
    Sudan   13°27N 22°45E **51** F10
El Gezira □ *Sudan*   15°0N 33°0E **51** F12
El Giza *Egypt*   30°0N 31°12E **51** C12
El Gogorrón △ *Mexico*   21°49N 100°57W **86** C4
El Goléa *Algeria*   30°30N 2°50E **50** B6
El Golfo de Santa Clara
    Mexico   31°42N 114°30W **86** A2
El Guácharo △ *Venezuela*   10°8N 63°21W **89** D7
El Guache △ *Venezuela*   9°45N 69°30W **89** E6
El Iskandarîya *Egypt*   31°13N 29°58E **51** B11
El Istiwa'iya *Sudan*   5°0N 28°0E **51** G11
El Jadida *Morocco*   33°11N 8°17W **50** B4
El Jardal *Honduras*   14°54N 88°50W **88** D2
El Kef □ *Tunisia*   36°0N 9°0E **51** A7
El Khârga *Egypt*   25°30N 30°33E **51** C12
El Khartûm *Sudan*   15°31N 32°35E **51** E12
El Khartûm Bahrî
    Sudan   15°40N 32°31E **51** E12
El Kuntilla *Egypt*   30°1N 34°45E **46** E3

El Leoncito △ *Argentina*   31°58S 69°10W **94** C2
El Lucero *Mexico*   30°37N 106°31W **86** A3
El Maestrazgo *Spain*   40°30N 0°25W **21** B5
El Mahalla el Kubra
    Egypt   31°0N 31°0E **51** B12
El Malpais △ *U.S.A.*   34°53N 108°0W **77** J10
El Mansûra *Egypt*   31°0N 31°19E **51** B12
El Medano *Canary Is.*   28°3N 16°32W **24** F3
El Ménia = El Goléa
    Algeria   30°30N 2°50E **50** B6
El Milagro *Argentina*   30°59S 65°59W **94** C2
El Minyâ *Egypt*   ·28°7N 30°33E **51** C12
El Monte *U.S.A.*   34°4N 118°1W **79** L8
El Obeid *Sudan*   13°8N 30°10E **51** F12
El Odaiya *Sudan*   12°8N 28°12E **51** F11
El Oro *Mexico*   19°51N 100°7W **87** D4
El Oued *Algeria*   33°20N 6°58E **50** B7
El Palmar △ *Argentina*   32°1S 58°31W **94** C4
El Palmito, Presa
    Mexico   25°40N 105°30W **86** B3
El Paso *U.S.A.*   31°45N 106°29W **84** F1
El Pinacate y Gran Desierto de
    Altar = Gran Desierto del
    Pinacate △ *Mexico*   31°51N 113°32W **86** A2
El Portal *U.S.A.*   37°41N 119°47W **78** H7
El Porvenir *Mexico*   31°15N 105°51W **86** A3
El Prat de Llobregat *Spain*   41°19N 2°5E **21** B7
El Progreso *Honduras*   15°26N 87°51W **88** C2
El Pueblito *Mexico*   29°6N 105°7W **86** B3
El Pueblo *Canary Is.*   28°36N 17°47W **24** F2
El Puerto de Santa María
    Spain   36°36N 6°13W **21** D2
El Qâhira *Egypt*   30°2N 31°13E **51** B12
El Qantara *Egypt*   30°51N 32°20E **46** E1
El Queseima *Egypt*   30°51N 34°40E **46** E3
El Real de Santa María
    Panama   8°0N 77°40W **92** B3
El Reno *U.S.A.*   35°32N 97°57W **75** H20
El Rey △ *Argentina*   24°40S 64°34W **94** A3
El Río *U.S.A.*   34°14N 119°10W **79** L7
El Roque, Pta. *Canary Is.*   28°10N 15°25W **24** F4
El Rosarito *Mexico*   28°38N 114°4W **86** B2
El Salvador ■ *Cent. Amer.*   13°50N 89°0W **88** D2
El Sauce *Nic.*   13°0N 86°40W **88** D2
El Sueco *Mexico*   29°54N 106°24W **86** B3
El Suweis *Egypt*   29°58N 32°31E **51** C12
El Tamarâni, W. → *Egypt*   30°7N 34°43E **46** E3
El Thamad *Egypt*   29°40N 34°28E **46** F3
El Tigre *Venezuela*   8°44N 64°15W **92** B6
El Tîh, Gebel *Egypt*   29°40N 33°50E **46** F2
El Tofo *Chile*   29°22S 71°18W **94** B1
El Tránsito *Chile*   28°52S 70°17W **94** B1
El Tûr *Egypt*   28°14N 33°36E **44** D2
El Turbio *Argentina*   51°45S 72°5W **96** G2
El Uqsur *Egypt*   25°41N 32°38E **51** C12
El Vergel *Mexico*   26°28N 106°22W **86** B3
El Vigía *Venezuela*   8°38N 71°39W **92** B4
El Wabeira *Egypt*   29°34N 33°6E **46** F2
El Wuz *Sudan*   15°0N 30°7E **51** E12
Elat *Israel*   29°30N 34°56E **46** F3
Elâzığ *Turkey*   38°37N 39°14E **44** B3
Elba *Italy*   42°46N 10°17E **22** C4
Elba *U.S.A.*   31°25N 86°4W **85** F11
Elbasan *Albania*   41°9N 20°9E **23** D9
Elbe → *Europe*   53°50N 9°0E **16** B5
Elbert, Mt. *U.S.A.*   39°7N 106°27W **76** G10
Elberton *U.S.A.*   34°7N 82°52W **85** D13
Elbeuf *France*   49°17N 1°2E **20** B4
Elbing = Elbląg *Poland*   54°10N 19°25E **17** A10
Elbistan *Turkey*   38°13N 37°15E **44** B3
Elbląg *Poland*   54°10N 19°25E **17** A10
Elbow *Canada*   51°7N 106°35W **71** C7
Elbrus *Russia*   43°21N 42°30E **19** F7
Elburz Mts. = Alborz, Reshteh-ye
    Kühhā-ye *Iran*   36°0N 52°0E **45** C7
Elche *Spain*   38°15N 0°42W **21** C5
Elcho I. *Australia*   11°55S 135°45E **62** A2
Elda *Spain*   38°29N 0°47W **21** C5
Eldama Ravine *Kenya*   0°3N 35°43E **54** B4
Elde → *Germany*   53°7N 11°15E **16** B6
Eldon *Mo., U.S.A.*   38°21N 92°35W **80** F7
Eldon *Wash., U.S.A.*   47°33N 123°3W **78** C3
Eldora *U.S.A.*   42°22N 93°5W **80** D7
Eldorado *Argentina*   26°28S 54°43W **95** B5
Eldorado *Canada*   44°35N 77°31W **82** B7
Eldorado *Ill., U.S.A.*   37°49N 88°26W **80** G9
Eldorado *Tex., U.S.A.*   30°52N 100°36W **84** F4
Eldoret *Kenya*   0°30N 35°17E **54** B4
Eldred *U.S.A.*   41°58N 78°23W **82** E6
Elea, C. *Cyprus*   35°19N 34°4E **25** D13
Eleanora, Pk. *Australia*   32°57S 121°9E **61** F3
Elefantes → *Africa*   24°10S 32°40E **57** C5
Elektrostal *Russia*   55°41N 38°32E **18** C6
Elemi Triangle *Africa*   5°0N 35°20E **54** B4
Elephant Butte Res.
    U.S.A.   33°9N 107°11W **77** K10
Elephant I. *Antarctica*   61°0S 55°0W **5** C18
Eleuthera *Bahamas*   25°0N 76°20W **88** B4
Elgin *Canada*   44°36N 76°13W **83** B8
Elgin *U.K.*   57°39N 3°19W **11** D5
Elgin *Ill., U.S.A.*   42°2N 88°17W **80** D9
Elgin *N. Dak., U.S.A.*   46°24N 101°51W **80** B3
Elgin *Nev., U.S.A.*   37°21N 114°32W **77** H6
Elgin *Tex., U.S.A.*   30°21N 97°22W **84** F6
Elgon, Mt. *Africa*   1°10N 34°30E **54** B3
Eliase *Indonesia*   8°21S 130°48E **37** F8
Elim *Namibia*   17°48S 15°31E **56** B2
Elim *S. Africa*   34°35S 19°45E **56** E2
Elista *Russia*   46°16N 44°14E **19** E7
Elizabeth *Australia*   34°42S 138°41E **63** E2
Elizabeth *U.S.A.*   40°39N 74°12W **83** F10
Elizabeth City *U.S.A.*   36°18N 76°14W **85** C16
Elizabethton *U.S.A.*   36°21N 82°13W **85** C13
Elizabethtown *Ky.,
    U.S.A.*   37°42N 85°52W **81** G11
Elizabethtown *N.Y.,
    U.S.A.*   44°13N 73°36W **83** B11
Elizabethtown *Pa., U.S.A.*   40°9N 76°36W **83** F8

Elk *Poland*   53°50N 22°21E **17** B12
Elk → *U.S.A.*   49°11N 115°14W **70** D5
Elk → *U.S.A.*   34°46N 87°16W **85** D11
Elk City *U.S.A.*   35°25N 99°25W **84** D5
Elk Creek *U.S.A.*   39°36N 122°32W **78** F4
Elk Grove *U.S.A.*   38°25N 121°22W **78** G5
Elk Island △ *Canada*   53°35N 112°59W **70** C6
Elk Lake *Canada*   47°40N 80°25W **72** C3
Elk Point *Canada*   53°54N 110°55W **71** C6
Elk River *Idaho, U.S.A.*   46°47N 116°11W **76** C5
Elk River *Minn., U.S.A.*   45°18N 93°35W **80** C7
Elkedra → *Australia*   21°8S 136°22E **62** C2
Elkhart *Ind., U.S.A.*   41°41N 85°58W **81** E11
Elkhart *Kans., U.S.A.*   37°0N 101°54W **80** G3
Elkhorn *Canada*   49°59N 101°14W **71** D8
Elkhorn → *U.S.A.*   41°8N 96°19W **80** E5
Elkhovo *Bulgaria*   42°10N 26°35E **23** C12
Elkin *U.S.A.*   36°15N 80°51W **85** C14
Elkins *U.S.A.*   38°55N 79°51W **81** F14
Elkland *U.S.A.*   41°59N 77°19W **82** E7
Elko *Canada*   49°20N 115°10W **70** D5
Elko *U.S.A.*   40°50N 115°46W **76** F6
Elkton *U.S.A.*   43°49N 83°11W **82** C1
Ellas = Greece ■ *Europe*   40°0N 23°0E **23** E9
Ellef Ringnes I. *Canada*   78°30N 102°2W **69** B11
Ellen, Mt. *U.S.A.*   44°9N 72°56W **83** B12
Ellenburg *U.S.A.*   44°54N 73°48W **83** B11
Ellensburg *U.S.A.*   46°59N 120°34W **76** C3
Ellenville *U.S.A.*   41°43N 74°24W **83** E10
Ellerton *Barbados*   13°7N 59°33W **89** g
Ellery, Mt. *Australia*   37°28S 148°47E **63** F4
Ellesmere, L. *N.Z.*   43°47S 172°28E **59** G4
Ellesmere I. *Canada*   79°30N 80°0W **69** B16
Ellesmere Island = Quttinirpaaq △
    Canada   82°13N 72°13W **69** A17
Ellesmere Port *U.K.*   53°17N 2°54W **12** D5
Ellice Is. = Tuvalu ■
    Pac. Oc.   8°0S 178°0E **58** B10
Ellicottville *U.S.A.*   42°17N 78°40W **82** D6
Ellington *U.S.A.*   42°13N 79°6W **82** D5
Elliot *Australia*   17°33S 133°32E **62** B1
Elliot *S. Africa*   31°22S 27°48E **57** E4
Elliot Lake *Canada*   46°25N 82°35W **72** C3
Elliotdale = Xhora
    S. Africa   31°55S 28°38E **57** E4
Ellis *U.S.A.*   38°56N 99°34W **80** F4
Elliston *Australia*   33°39S 134°53E **63** E1
Ellisville *U.S.A.*   31°36N 89°12W **85** F10
Ellon *U.K.*   57°22N 2°4W **11** D6
Ellore = Eluru *India*   16°48N 81°8E **41** L12
Ellsworth *Kans., U.S.A.*   38°44N 98°14W **80** F4
Ellsworth *Maine, U.S.A.*   44°33N 68°25W **81** C19
Ellsworth Land *Antarctica*   76°0S 89°0W **5** D16
Ellsworth Mts. *Antarctica*   78°30S 85°0W **5** D16
Elma *Canada*   49°52N 95°55W **71** D9
Elma *U.S.A.*   47°0N 123°25W **78** D3
Elmalı *Turkey*   36°44N 29°56E **19** G4
Elmhurst *U.S.A.*   41°53N 87°56W **80** E10
Elmira *Canada*   43°36N 80°33W **82** C4
Elmira *U.S.A.*   42°6N 76°48W **82** D8
Elmira Heights *U.S.A.*   42°8N 76°50W **82** D8
Elmore *Australia*   36°30S 144°37E **63** F3
Elmshorn *Germany*   53°43N 9°40E **16** B5
Elmvale *Canada*   44°35N 79°52W **82** B5
Elora *Canada*   43°41N 80°26W **82** C4
Elounda *Greece*   35°16N 25°42E **25** D7
Eloy *U.S.A.*   32°45N 111°33W **77** K8
Elphin *Canada*   44°55N 76°37W **83** B8
Elrose *Canada*   51°12N 108°0W **71** C7
Elsby △ *Australia*   14°55S 133°10E **60** B5
Elsie *U.S.A.*   45°52N 123°36E **78** E3
Elsinore = Helsingør
    Denmark   56°2N 12°35E **9** H15
Eltanin Fracture Zone System
    S. Ocean   54°0S 130°0W **5** B14
Eltham *N.Z.*   39°26S 174°19E **59** C5
Eluru *India*   16°48N 81°8E **41** L12
Elvas *Portugal*   38°50N 7°10W **21** C2
Elverum *Norway*   60°53N 11°34E **8** F14
Elvire → *Australia*   17°51S 128°11E **60** C4
Elvire, Mt. *Australia*   29°13N 116°36E **61** E2
Elwell, L. = Tiber Res.
    U.S.A.   48°19N 111°6W **76** B8
Elwood *Ind., U.S.A.*   40°17N 85°50W **81** E11
Elwood *Nebr., U.S.A.*   40°36N 99°52W **80** E4
Elx = Elche *Spain*   38°15N 0°42W **21** C5
Ely *U.K.*   52°24N 0°16E **13** E8
Ely *Minn., U.S.A.*   47°55N 91°51W **80** B8
Ely *Nev., U.S.A.*   39°15N 114°54W **76** G6
Elyria *U.S.A.*   41°22N 82°7W **82** E2
eMalahleni *S. Africa*   25°51S 29°14E **57** D4
Emāmrūd *Iran*   36°30N 55°0E **45** B7
Embarcación *Argentina*   23°10S 64°0W **94** A3
Embetsu *Japan*   44°44N 141°47E **30** B10
Embi *Kazakhstan*   48°50N 58°8E **28** E6
Embi → *Kazakhstan*   46°55N 53°28E **19** E9
Embonas *Greece*   36°13N 27°51E **25** C9
Embro *Canada*   43°9N 80°54W **82** C4
Embrun *France*   44°34N 6°30E **20** D7
Embu *Kenya*   0°32S 37°38E **54** C4
Emden *Germany*   53°21N 7°12E **16** B4
Emerald *Australia*   23°32S 148°10E **62** C4
Emerald I. *Canada*   76°48N 114°10W **69** B9
Emerson *Canada*   49°0N 97°10W **71** D9
Emet *Turkey*   39°20N 29°15E **23** E13
Emi Koussi *Chad*   19°45N 18°55E **51** E9
Eminabad *Pakistan*   32°2N 74°8E **42** C6
Emine, Nos *Bulgaria*   42°40N 27°56E **23** C12
Emissi, Tarso *Chad*   21°27N 18°36E **51** D9
Emlenton *U.S.A.*   41°11N 79°43W **82** E5
Emmaus *S. Africa*   29°2S 25°15E **56** D4
Emmaus *U.S.A.*   40°32N 75°30W **83** F9
Emmeloord *Neths.*   52°44N 5°46E **15** B5
Emmen *Neths.*   52°48N 6°57E **15** B6
Emmet *Australia*   24°45S 144°30E **62** C3
Emmetsburg *U.S.A.*   43°7N 94°41W **80** D7
Emmett *Idaho, U.S.A.*   43°52N 116°30W **76** E5
Emmett *Mich., U.S.A.*   42°59N 82°46W **82** D2

Emmonak *U.S.A.*   62°47N 164°31W **74** C7
Emo *Canada*   48°38N 93°50W **71** D10
Empalme *Mexico*   27°58N 110°51W **86** B2
Empangeni *S. Africa*   28°50S 31°52E **57** D5
Empedrado *Argentina*   28°0S 58°46W **94** B4
Emperor Seamount Chain
    Pac. Oc.   40°0N 170°0E **64** D9
Emperor Trough *Pac. Oc.*   43°0N 175°30E **64** C9
Emporia *Kans., U.S.A.*   38°25N 96°11W **80** F5
Emporia *Va., U.S.A.*   36°42N 77°32W **81** G15
Emporium *U.S.A.*   41°31N 78°14W **82** E6
Empress *Canada*   50°57N 110°0W **71** C6
Empty Quarter = Rub' al Khālī
    Si. Arabia   19°0N 48°0E **47** D4
Ems → *Germany*   53°20N 7°12E **16** B4
Emsdale *Canada*   45°32N 79°19W **82** A5
Emu *China*   43°40N 128°6E **35** C15
Emu Park *Australia*   23°13S 150°50E **62** C5
eMuziwezinto *S. Africa*   30°15S 30°45E **57** E5
'En 'Avrona *Israel*   29°43N 35°0E **46** F4
'En Boqeq *Israel*   31°12N 35°21E **45** D4
'En Gedi *Israel*   31°28N 35°25E **46** D4
En Nahud *Sudan*   12°45N 28°25E **51** F11
Ena *Japan*   35°25N 137°25E **31** G8
Enana *Namibia*   17°30S 16°23E **56** B2
Enard B. *U.K.*   58°5N 5°20W **11** C3
Enare träsk = Inarijärvi
    Finland   69°0N 28°0E **8** B23
Enarotali *Indonesia*   3°55S 136°21E **37** E9
Encampment *U.S.A.*   41°12N 106°47W **76** F10
Encantadas, Serra *Brazil*   30°40S 53°0W **95** C5
Encarnación de Díaz
    Mexico   21°31N 102°14W **86** C4
Encinitas *U.S.A.*   33°3N 117°17W **79** M9
Encino *U.S.A.*   34°39N 105°28W **77** J11
Encounter B. *Australia*   35°45S 138°45E **63** F2
Endako *Canada*   54°6N 125°2W **70** C3
Endau *Kenya*   1°18S 38°31E **54** C4
Endau Rompin △
    Malaysia   2°27N 103°45E **39** L4
Ende *Indonesia*   8°45S 121°40E **37** F6
Endeavour Str. *Australia*   10°45S 142°0E **62** A3
Enderbury *Kiribati*   3°8S 171°5W **64** H10
Enderby *Canada*   50°35N 119°10W **70** C5
Enderby Abyssal Plain
    S. Ocean   60°0S 40°0E **5** C5
Enderby I. *Australia*   20°35S 116°30E **60** D2
Enderby Land *Antarctica*   66°0S 53°0E **5** C5
Enderlin *U.S.A.*   46°38N 97°36W **80** B5
Enderrocat, C. *Spain*   39°28N 2°43E **24** B9
Endicott *U.S.A.*   42°6N 76°4W **83** D8
Endicott Mts. *U.S.A.*   68°0N 152°0W **74** B9
Endwell *U.S.A.*   42°6N 76°2W **83** D8
Endyalgout I. *Australia*   11°40S 132°35E **60** B5
Eneabba *Australia*   29°49S 115°16E **61** E2
Enewetak Atoll
    Marshall Is.   11°30N 162°15E **64** F8
Enez *Turkey*   40°45N 26°5E **23** D12
Enfer, Pte. d' *Martinique*   14°22N 60°54W **88** c
Enfield *Canada*   44°56N 63°32W **73** D7
Enfield *Conn., U.S.A.*   41°58N 72°36W **83** E12
Enfield *N.C., U.S.A.*   36°11N 77°41W **85** C16
Enfield *N.H., U.S.A.*   43°39N 72°9W **83** C12
Engadin *Switz.*   46°45N 10°10E **20** C9
Engaño, C. *Dom. Rep.*   18°30N 68°20W **89** C6
Engaño, C. *Phil.*   18°35N 122°23E **37** A6
Engaru *Japan*   44°3N 143°31E **30** B11
Engcobo = Ngcobo
    S. Africa   31°37S 28°0E **57** E4
Engels *Russia*   51°28N 46°6E **19** D8
Engemann L. *Canada*   58°0N 106°55W **71** B7
Enggano *Indonesia*   5°20S 102°40E **36** F2
England ■ *U.S.A.*   34°33N 91°58W **84** D9
England □ *U.K.*   53°0N 2°0W **13** E5
Englee *Canada*   50°45N 56°5W **73** B8
Englehart *Canada*   47°49N 79°52W **72** C4
Englewood *U.S.A.*   39°38N 104°59W **76** G11
English Bazar = Ingraj Bazar
    India   24°58N 88°10E **43** G13
English Channel *Europe*   50°0N 2°0W **13** G6
English Company's Is., The
    Australia   11°50S 136°32E **62** A2
English River *Canada*   49°14N 91°0W **72** C1
Enid *U.S.A.*   36°24N 97°53W **84** C6
Eniwa *Japan*   43°0N 141°30E **30** C10
Enkhuizen *Neths.*   52°42N 5°17E **15** B5
Enna *Italy*   37°34N 14°16E **22** F6
Ennadai L. *Canada*   60°58N 101°20W **71** A8
Ennedi *Chad*   17°15N 22°0E **51** E10
Enngonia *Australia*   29°21S 145°50E **63** D4
Ennis *Ireland*   52°51N 8°59W **10** D3
Ennis *Mont., U.S.A.*   45°21N 111°44W **76** D8
Ennis *Tex., U.S.A.*   32°20N 96°38W **84** E6
Enniscorthy *Ireland*   52°30N 6°34W **10** D5
Enniskillen *U.K.*   54°21N 7°39W **10** B4
Ennistimon *Ireland*   52°57N 9°17W **10** D2
Enns → *Austria*   48°14N 14°32E **16** D8
Eno *Finland*   62°47N 30°10E **8** E24
Enontekiö *Finland*   68°23N 23°37E **8** B20
Enosburg Falls *U.S.A.*   44°55N 72°48W **83** B12
Enriquillo, L. *Dom. Rep.*   18°20N 72°5W **89** C5
Enschede *Neths.*   52°13N 6°53E **15** B6
Ensenada *Argentina*   34°55S 57°55W **94** C4
Ensenada *Mexico*   31°52N 116°37W **86** A1
Ensenada de los Muertos
    Mexico   23°59N 109°51W **86** C2
Enshi *China*   30°18N 109°29E **34** B7
Ensiola, Pta. de n' *Spain*   39°7N 2°55E **24** B9
Entebbe *Uganda*   0°4N 32°28E **54** B3
Enterprise *Canada*   60°47N 115°45W **70** A5
Enterprise *Ala., U.S.A.*   31°19N 85°51W **85** F12
Enterprise *Oreg., U.S.A.*   45°25N 117°17W **76** D5
Entre Ríos *Bolivia*   21°30S 64°25W **94** A3
Entre Ríos □ *Argentina*   30°30S 58°30W **94** C4
Entroncamento *Portugal*   39°28N 8°28W **21** C1
Enugu *Nigeria*   6°30N 7°30E **50** G7
Enumclaw *U.S.A.*   47°12N 121°59W **78** C5
Eochail = Youghal
    Ireland   51°56N 7°52W **10** E4

Eólie, Ís. Italy 38°30N 14°57E 22 E6
Epe Neths. 52°21N 5°59E 15 B5
Épernay France 49°3N 3°56E 20 B5
Ephesus Turkey 37°55N 27°22E 23 F12
Ephraim U.S.A. 39°22N 111°35W 76 G8
Ephrata Pa., U.S.A. 40°11N 76°11W 83 F8
Ephrata Wash., U.S.A. 47°19N 119°33W 76 C4
Épinal France 48°10N 6°27E 20 B7
Episkopi Cyprus 34°40N 32°54E 25 E11
Episkopi Greece 35°20N 24°20E 25 D6
Episkopi Bay Cyprus 34°35N 32°50E 25 E11
Epsom U.K. 51°19N 0°16W 13 F7
Epukiro Namibia 21°40S 19°9E 56 C2
Equatoria = El Istiwa'iya Sudan 5°0N 28°0E 51 G11
Equatorial Guinea ■ Africa 2°0N 8°0E 52 D1
Er Hai China 25°48N 100°11E 41 G22
Er Rachidia Morocco 31°58N 4°20W 50 B5
Er Rahad Sudan 12°45N 30°32E 51 F12
Er Rif Morocco 35°1N 4°1W 50 A5
Erāwadī Myit = Irrawaddy → Burma 15°50N 95°6E 41 M19
Erāwadī Myitwanya = Irrawaddy, Mouths of the Burma 15°30N 95°0E 41 M19
Erawan ▲ Thailand 14°25N 98°58E 38 E2
Erbil = Arbīl Iraq 36°15N 44°5E 44 B5
Erçek Turkey 38°39N 43°36E 44 B4
Erciyaş Dağı Turkey 38°30N 35°30E 44 B2
Érd Hungary 47°22N 18°56E 17 E10
Erdao Jiang → China 42°37N 128°0E 35 C14
Erdek Turkey 40°23N 27°47E 23 D12
Erdene = Ulaan-Uul Mongolia 46°4N 100°49E 34 B6
Erdenet Mongolia 49°2N 104°5E 32 B9
Erdenetsogt Mongolia 42°55N 106°5E 34 C4
Erebus, Mt. Antarctica 77°35S 167°0E 5 D11
Erechim Brazil 27°35S 52°15W 95 B5
Ereğli Konya, Turkey 37°31N 34°4E 44 B2
Ereğli Zonguldak, Turkey 41°15N 31°24E 19 F5
Erenhot China 43°48N 112°2E 34 C7
Eresma → Spain 41°26N 4°45W 21 B3
Erfenisdam S. Africa 28°30S 26°50E 56 D4
Erfurt Germany 50°58N 11°2E 16 C6
Ergani Turkey 38°17N 39°49E 44 B3
Ergel Mongolia 43°8N 109°5E 34 C5
Ergeni Vozvyshennost Russia 47°0N 44°0E 19 E7
Ērgli Latvia 56°54N 25°38E 9 H21
Eriboll, L. U.K. 58°30N 4°42W 11 C4
Érice Italy 38°2N 12°35E 22 E5
Erie U.S.A. 42°8N 80°5W 82 D4
Erie, L. N. Amer. 42°15N 81°0W 82 D4
Erie Canal U.S.A. 43°5N 78°43W 82 C7
Erieau Canada 42°16N 81°57W 82 D3
Erigavo = Ceerigaabo Somali Rep. 10°35N 47°20E 47 E4
Erikoussa Greece 39°53N 19°34E 25 A3
Eriksdale Canada 50°52N 98°7W 71 C9
Erimanthos Greece 37°57N 21°50E 23 F9
Erimo-misaki Japan 41°50N 143°15E 30 D11
Erin Canada 43°45N 80°7W 82 C4
Erin Pt. Trin. & Tob. 10°3N 61°39W 93 K15
Erinpura India 25°9N 73°3E 42 G5
Eriskay U.K. 57°4N 7°18W 11 D1
Eritrea ■ Africa 14°0N 38°30E 47 D2
Erlangen Germany 49°36N 11°0E 16 D6
Erldunda Australia 25°14S 133°12E 62 D1
Ermelo Neths. 52°18N 5°35E 15 B5
Ermelo S. Africa 26°31S 29°59E 57 D4
Ermenek Turkey 36°38N 33°0E 44 B2
Ermones Greece 39°37N 19°46E 25 A3
Ermoupoli Greece 37°28N 24°57E 23 F11
Ernakulam India 9°59N 76°22E 40 Q10
Erne → Ireland 54°30N 8°16W 10 B3
Erne, Lower L. U.K. 54°28N 7°47W 10 B4
Erne, Upper L. U.K. 54°14N 7°32W 10 B4
Ernest Giles Ra. Australia 27°0S 123°45E 61 E3
Erode India 11°24N 77°45E 40 P10
Eromanga Australia 26°40S 143°11E 63 D3
Erongo Namibia 21°39S 15°58E 56 C2
Erramala Hills India 15°30N 78°15E 40 M11
Errentería Spain 43°19N 1°54W 21 A5
Errigal Ireland 55°2N 8°6W 10 A3
Errinundra ▲ Australia 37°20S 148°47E 63 F4
Erris Hd. Ireland 54°19N 10°0W 10 B1
Erskine U.S.A. 47°40N 96°0W 80 B6
Ertis = Irtysh → Russia 61°4N 68°52E 28 C7
Erwin U.S.A. 36°9N 82°25W 85 C13
Erzgebirge Germany 50°27N 12°55E 16 C7
Erzin Russia 50°15N 95°10E 29 D10
Erzincan Turkey 39°46N 39°30E 44 B3
Erzurum Turkey 39°57N 41°15E 44 B4
Es Caló Spain 38°40N 1°30E 24 C8
Es Canar Spain 39°2N 1°36E 24 B8
Es Mercadal Spain 39°59N 4°5E 24 B11
Es Migjorn Gran Spain 39°57N 4°3E 24 B11
Es Sahrâ' Esh Sharqîya Egypt 27°30N 32°30E 51 C12
Es Sînâ' Egypt 29°0N 34°0E 46 F2
Es Vedrà Spain 38°52N 1°12E 24 C7
Esambo Dem. Rep. of the Congo 3°48S 23°30E 54 C1
Esan-Misaki Japan 41°40N 141°10E 30 D10
Esashi Hokkaidō, Japan 44°56N 142°35E 30 B11
Esashi Hokkaidō, Japan 41°52N 140°7E 30 D10
Esbjerg Denmark 55°29N 8°29E 9 J13
Esbo = Espoo Finland 60°12N 24°40E 9 F21
Escalante U.S.A. 37°47N 111°36W 77 H8
Escalante → U.S.A. 37°24N 110°57W 77 H8
Escalón Mexico 26°45N 104°20W 86 B4
Escambia → U.S.A. 30°32N 87°11W 85 F11
Escanaba U.S.A. 45°45N 87°4W 80 C10
Esch-sur-Alzette Lux. 49°32N 6°0E 15 E6
Escondido U.S.A. 33°7N 117°5W 79 M9
Escuinapa de Hidalgo Mexico 22°50N 105°50W 86 C3
Escuintla Guatemala 14°20N 90°48W 88 D1
Esenguly Turkmenistan 37°37N 53°59E 28 F6
Eşfahān Iran 32°39N 51°43E 45 C6
Eşfahān □ Iran 32°50N 51°50E 45 C6
Esfarāyen Iran 37°4N 57°30E 45 B8
Esfideh Iran 33°39N 59°46E 45 C8
Esh Sham = Dimashq Syria 33°30N 36°18E 46 B5
Esha Ness U.K. 60°29N 1°38W 11 A7
Esher U.K. 51°21N 0°20W 13 F7
Eshkol ▲ Israel 31°20N 34°30E 46 D3
Eshowe S. Africa 28°50S 31°30E 57 D5
Esigodini Zimbabwe 20°18S 28°56E 57 C4
Esil = Ishim → Russia 57°45N 71°10E 28 D8
Esira Madag. 24°20S 46°42E 57 C8
Esk → Dumf. & Gall., U.K. 54°58N 3°2W 11 G5
Esk → N. Yorks., U.K. 54°30N 0°37W 12 C7
Eskān Iran 26°48N 63°9E 45 E9
Esker Siding Canada 53°53N 66°25W 73 B6
Eskifjörður Iceland 65°3N 13°55W 8 D7
Eskilstuna Sweden 59°22N 16°32E 9 G17
Eskimo Point = Arviat Canada 61°6N 93°59W 71 A10
Eskişehir Turkey 39°50N 30°30E 19 G5
Esla → Spain 41°29N 6°3W 21 B2
Eslāmābād-e Gharb Iran 34°10N 46°30E 44 C5
Eslāmshahr Iran 35°40N 51°10E 45 C6
Eşme Turkey 38°23N 28°58E 23 E13
Esmeraldas Ecuador 1°0N 79°40W 92 C3
Esna = Isna Egypt 25°17N 32°30E 51 C12
Esnagi L. Canada 48°36N 84°33W 72 C3
España = Spain ■ Europe 39°0N 4°0W 21 B4
Espanola Canada 46°15N 81°46W 72 C3
Espanola U.S.A. 35°59N 106°5W 77 J10
Esparza Costa Rica 9°59N 84°40W 88 E3
Esperance Australia 33°45S 121°55E 61 F3
Esperance B. Australia 33°48S 121°55E 61 F3
Esperance Harbour St. Lucia 14°4N 60°55W 89 f
Esperanza Antarctica 65°0S 55°0W 5 C18
Esperanza Argentina 31°29S 61°3W 94 C3
Esperanza Puerto Rico 18°6N 65°28W 89 d
Espichel, C. Portugal 38°22N 9°16W 21 C1
Espigão, Serra do Brazil 26°35S 50°30W 95 B5
Espinazo, Sierra del = Espinhaço, Serra do Brazil 17°30S 43°30W 93 G10
Espinhaço, Serra do Brazil 17°30S 43°30W 93 G10
Espinilho, Serra do Brazil 28°30S 55°0W 95 B5
Espírito Santo □ Brazil 20°0S 40°45W 93 H10
Espirito Santo do Pinhal Brazil 22°10S 46°46W 95 A6
Espíritu Santo Vanuatu 15°15S 166°50E 58 C9
Espíritu Santo, B. del Mexico 19°20N 87°35W 87 D7
Espíritu Santo, I. Mexico 24°30N 110°22W 86 C2
Espita Mexico 21°1N 88°19W 87 C7
Espoo Finland 60°12N 24°40E 9 F21
Espungabera Mozam. 20°29S 32°45E 57 C5
Esquel Argentina 42°55S 71°20W 96 E2
Esquimalt Canada 48°26N 123°25W 78 B3
Esquina Argentina 30°0S 59°30W 94 C4
Essaouira Morocco 31°32N 9°42W 50 B4
Essen Belgium 51°28N 4°28E 15 C4
Essen Germany 51°28N 7°2E 16 C4
Essendon, Mt. Australia 25°0S 120°29E 61 E3
Essequibo → Guyana 6°50N 58°30W 92 B7
Essex Canada 42°10N 82°49W 82 D2
Essex Calif., U.S.A. 34°44N 115°15W 79 L11
Essex N.Y., U.S.A. 44°19N 73°21W 83 B11
Essex □ U.K. 51°54N 0°27E 13 F8
Essex Junction U.S.A. 44°29N 73°7W 83 B11
Esslingen Germany 48°44N 9°18E 16 D5
Estación Camacho Mexico 24°25N 102°18W 86 C4
Estación Simón Mexico 24°42N 102°35W 86 C4
Estados, I. de Los Argentina 54°40S 64°30W 96 G4
Eştahbānāt Iran 29°8N 54°4E 45 D7
Estância Brazil 11°16S 37°26W 93 F11
Estancia U.S.A. 34°46N 106°4W 77 J10
Estārm Iran 28°21N 58°21E 45 D8
Estcourt S. Africa 29°0S 29°53E 57 D4
Este ▲ Dom. Rep. 18°14N 68°42W 89 C6
Estelí Nic. 13°9N 86°22W 88 D2
Estellencs Spain 39°39N 2°29E 24 B9
Esterhazy Canada 50°37N 102°5W 71 C8
Estevan Canada 49°10N 102°59W 71 D8
Estevan Group Canada 53°3N 129°38W 70 C3
Estherville U.S.A. 43°24N 94°50W 80 D6
Eston Canada 51°8N 108°40W 71 C7
Estonia ■ Europe 58°30N 25°30E 9 G21
Estreito Brazil 6°32S 47°25W 93 E9
Estrela, Serra da Portugal 40°10N 7°45W 21 B2
Estremoz Portugal 38°51N 7°39W 21 C2
Estrondo, Serra do Brazil 7°20S 48°0W 93 E9
Esztergom Hungary 47°47N 18°44E 17 E10
Et Tîdra Mauritania 19°45N 16°20W 50 E2
Etah India 27°35N 78°40E 43 F8
Étampes France 48°26N 2°10E 20 B5
Etanga Namibia 17°55S 13°0E 56 B1
Etawah India 26°48N 79°6E 43 F8
Etawney L. Canada 57°50N 96°50W 71 B9
Etchojoa Mexico 26°55N 109°38W 86 B3
eThekwini = Durban S. Africa 29°49S 31°1E 57 D5
Ethel U.S.A. 46°32N 122°46W 78 D4
Ethelbert Canada 51°32N 100°25W 71 C8
Ethiopia ■ Africa 8°0N 40°0E 47 F3
Ethiopian Highlands Ethiopia 10°0N 37°0E 47 F2
Etive, L. U.K. 56°29N 5°10W 11 E3
Etna Italy 37°50N 14°55E 22 F6
Etoile Dem. Rep. of the Congo 11°33S 27°30E 55 E2
Etolin Strait U.S.A. 60°20N 165°15W 74 C6
Etosha ▲ Namibia 19°0S 16°0E 56 B2
Etosha Pan Namibia 18°40S 16°30E 56 B2
Etowah U.S.A. 35°20N 84°32W 85 D12
Etrek Turkmenistan 37°36N 54°46E 45 B7
Ettelbruck Lux. 49°51N 6°5E 15 E6
Ettrick Water → U.K. 55°31N 2°55W 11 F6
Etuku Dem. Rep. of the Congo 3°42S 25°45E 54 C2
Etzná-Tixmucuy = Edzná Mexico 19°39N 90°19W 87 D6
Eua Tonga 21°22S 174°56W 59 c
Euboea = Evia Greece 38°30N 24°0E 23 E11
Eucla Australia 31°41S 128°52E 61 F4
Euclid U.S.A. 41°34N 81°32W 82 E3
Eucumbene, L. Australia 36°2S 148°40E 63 F4
Eudora U.S.A. 33°7N 91°16W 84 E9
Eufaula Ala., U.S.A. 31°54N 85°9W 85 F12
Eufaula Okla., U.S.A. 35°17N 95°35W 84 D7
Eufaula L. U.S.A. 35°18N 95°21W 84 D7
Eugene U.S.A. 44°5N 123°4W 76 D2
Eugowra Australia 33°22S 148°24E 63 E4
Eulo Australia 28°10S 145°3E 63 D4
Eungella ▲ Australia 20°57S 148°40E 62 b
Eunice La., U.S.A. 30°30N 92°25W 84 F8
Eunice N. Mex., U.S.A. 32°26N 103°10W 77 K12
Eupen Belgium 50°37N 6°3E 15 D6
Euphrates = Furāt, Nahr al → Asia 31°0N 47°25E 44 D5
Eureka Canada 80°0N 85°56W 69 B14
Eureka Calif., U.S.A. 40°47N 124°9W 76 F1
Eureka Kans., U.S.A. 37°49N 96°17W 80 G5
Eureka Mont., U.S.A. 48°53N 115°3W 76 B6
Eureka Nev., U.S.A. 39°31N 115°58W 76 G6
Eureka S. Dak., U.S.A. 45°46N 99°38W 80 C4
Eureka, Mt. Australia 26°35S 121°35E 61 E3
Eureka Sd. Canada 79°0N 85°0W 69 B15
Euroa Australia 36°44S 145°35E 63 F4
Europa, Picos de Spain 43°10N 4°49W 21 A3
Europa, Pt. Gib. 36°3N 5°21W 21 D3
Europe 50°0N 20°0E 6 E10
Europoort Neths. 51°57N 4°10E 15 C4
Eustis U.S.A. 28°51N 81°41W 85 G14
Eutsuk L. Canada 53°20N 126°45W 70 C3
Evale Angola 16°33S 15°44E 56 B2
Evans U.S.A. 40°23N 104°41W 76 F11
Evans, L. Canada 50°50N 77°0W 72 B4
Evans City U.S.A. 40°46N 80°4W 82 F4
Evans Head Australia 29°7S 153°27E 63 D5
Evansburg Canada 53°36N 114°59W 70 C5
Evanston Ill., U.S.A. 42°3N 87°40W 80 D10
Evanston Wyo., U.S.A. 41°16N 110°58W 76 F8
Evansville U.S.A. 37°58N 87°35W 80 G10
Evaz Iran 27°46N 53°59E 45 E7
Eveleth U.S.A. 47°28N 92°32W 80 B7
Evensk Russia 62°12N 159°30E 29 C16
Everard, L. Australia 31°30S 135°0E 63 E2
Everard Ranges Australia 27°5S 132°28E 61 E5
Everest, Mt. Nepal 28°5N 86°58E 43 E12
Everett Pa., U.S.A. 40°1N 78°23W 82 F6
Everett Wash., U.S.A. 47°59N 122°12W 78 C4
Everglades, The U.S.A. 25°50N 81°0W 85 J14
Everglades ▲ U.S.A. 25°30N 81°0W 85 J14
Everglades City U.S.A. 25°52N 81°23W 85 J14
Evergreen Ala., U.S.A. 31°26N 86°57W 85 F11
Evergreen Mont., U.S.A. 48°14N 114°17W 76 B6
Evesham U.K. 52°6N 1°56W 13 E6
Evia Greece 38°30N 24°0E 23 E11
Evje Norway 58°36N 7°51E 9 G12
Évora Portugal 38°33N 7°57W 21 C2
Evowghlī Iran 38°43N 45°13E 44 B5
Évreux France 49°3N 1°8E 20 B4
Evros → Greece 41°40N 26°34E 23 D12
Évry France 48°38N 2°27E 20 B5
Évvoia = Evia Greece 38°30N 24°0E 23 E11
Ewe, L. U.K. 57°49N 5°38W 11 D3
Ewing U.S.A. 42°16N 98°21W 80 D4
Ewo Congo 0°48S 14°45E 52 E2
Exaltación Bolivia 13°10S 65°20W 92 F5
Excelsior Springs U.S.A. 39°20N 94°13W 80 F6
Exe → U.K. 50°41N 3°29W 13 G4
Exeter Canada 43°21N 81°29W 82 C3
Exeter U.K. 50°43N 3°31W 13 G4
Exeter Calif., U.S.A. 36°18N 119°9W 78 J7
Exeter N.H., U.S.A. 42°59N 70°57W 83 D14
Exmoor U.K. 51°12N 3°45W 13 F4
Exmoor ▲ U.K. 51°8N 3°42W 13 F4
Exmouth Australia 21°54S 114°10E 60 D1
Exmouth U.K. 50°37N 3°25W 13 G4
Exmouth G. Australia 22°15S 114°15E 60 D1
Exmouth Plateau Ind. Oc. 19°0S 114°0E 64 J3
Expedition ▲ Australia 25°41S 149°7E 63 D4
Expedition Ra. Australia 24°30S 149°12E 62 C4
Extremadura □ Spain 39°30N 6°5W 21 C2
Exuma Sound Bahamas 24°30N 76°20W 88 B4
Eyasi, L. Tanzania 3°30S 35°0E 54 C4
Eye Pen. U.K. 58°13N 6°10W 11 C2
Eyemouth U.K. 55°52N 2°5W 11 F6
Eyjafjallajökull Iceland 63°38N 19°36W 8 E4
Eyjafjörður Iceland 66°15N 18°30W 8 C4
Eyl Somali Rep. 8°0N 49°50E 47 F4
Eyre (North), L. Australia 28°30S 137°20E 63 D2
Eyre (South), L. Australia 29°18S 137°25E 63 D2
Eyre, L. Australia 29°30S 137°26E 58 D6
Eyre Mts. N.Z. 45°25S 168°25E 59 F2
Eyre Pen. Australia 33°30S 136°17E 63 E2
Eysturoy Færoe Is. 62°13N 6°54W 8 E9
Eyvān = Jūy Zar Iran 33°50N 46°18E 44 C5
Eyvānkī Iran 35°24N 51°56E 45 C6
Ezine Turkey 39°48N 26°20E 23 E12
Ezouza → Cyprus 34°44N 32°27E 25 E11

F

F.Y.R.O.M. = Macedonia ■ Europe 41°53N 21°40E 23 D9
Faaa Tahiti 17°34S 149°35W 59 d
Faaone Tahiti 17°40S 149°21W 59 d
Fabala Guinea 9°44N 9°5W 50 G4
Fabens U.S.A. 31°30N 106°10W 84 F1
Fabius U.S.A. 42°50N 75°59W 83 D9
Fabriano Italy 43°20N 12°54E 22 C5
Fachi Niger 18°6N 11°34E 51 E8
Fada Chad 17°13N 21°34E 51 E10
Fada-n-Gourma Burkina Faso 12°10N 0°30E 50 F6
Faddeyevskiy, Ostrov Russia 76°0N 144°0E 29 B15
Fadghāmī Syria 35°53N 40°52E 44 C4
Faenza Italy 44°17N 11°53E 22 B4
Færoe Is. = Føroyar ⊿ Atl. Oc. 62°0N 7°0W 8 F9
Făgăras Romania 45°48N 24°58E 17 F13
Fagersta Sweden 60°1N 15°46E 9 F16
Fagnano, L. Argentina 54°30S 68°0W 96 G3
Fahlīān Iran 30°11N 51°28E 45 D6
Fahraj Kermān, Iran 29°0N 59°0E 45 D8
Fahraj Yazd, Iran 31°46N 54°36E 45 D7
Faial Azores 38°34N 28°42W 50 a
Faial Madeira 32°47N 16°53W 24 D3
Faichan Kangri India 35°48N 76°34E 43 B7
Fair Haven N.Y., U.S.A. 43°18N 76°42W 83 C8
Fair Haven Vt., U.S.A. 43°36N 73°16W 81 D17
Fair Hd. U.K. 55°14N 6°9W 10 A5
Fair Isle U.K. 59°32N 1°38W 14 B6
Fair Oaks U.S.A. 38°39N 121°16W 78 G5
Fairbanks U.S.A. 64°51N 147°43W 68 E2
Fairbury U.S.A. 40°8N 97°11W 80 E5
Fairfax U.S.A. 44°40N 73°1W 83 B11
Fairfield Ala., U.S.A. 33°29N 86°55W 85 E11
Fairfield Calif., U.S.A. 38°15N 122°3W 78 G4
Fairfield Conn., U.S.A. 41°9N 73°16W 83 E11
Fairfield Idaho, U.S.A. 43°21N 114°44W 76 E6
Fairfield Ill., U.S.A. 38°23N 88°22W 80 F9
Fairfield Iowa, U.S.A. 40°56N 91°57W 80 E8
Fairfield Tex., U.S.A. 31°44N 96°10W 84 F6
Fairford Canada 51°37N 98°38W 71 C9
Fairhope U.S.A. 30°31N 87°54W 85 F11
Fairlie N.Z. 44°5S 170°49E 59 F3
Fairmead U.S.A. 37°5N 120°10W 78 H6
Fairmont Minn., U.S.A. 43°39N 94°28W 80 D6
Fairmont W. Va., U.S.A. 39°29N 80°9W 81 F13
Fairmount Calif., U.S.A. 34°45N 118°26W 79 L8
Fairmount N.Y., U.S.A. 43°5N 76°12W 83 C8
Fairplay U.S.A. 39°15N 106°2W 76 G10
Fairport U.S.A. 43°6N 77°27W 82 C7
Fairport Harbor U.S.A. 41°45N 81°17W 82 E3
Fairview Canada 56°5N 118°25W 70 B5
Fairview Mont., U.S.A. 47°51N 104°3W 76 C11
Fairview Okla., U.S.A. 36°16N 98°29W 84 C5
Fairweather, Mt. U.S.A. 58°55N 137°32W 70 B1
Faisalabad Pakistan 31°30N 73°5E 42 D5
Faith U.S.A. 45°2N 102°2W 80 C2
Faizabad India 26°45N 82°10E 43 F10
Fajardo Puerto Rico 18°20N 65°39W 89 d
Fajr, W. → Si. Arabia 29°10N 38°10E 44 D3
Fakenham U.K. 52°51N 0°51E 12 E8
Fakfak Indonesia 2°55S 132°18E 37 E8
Faku China 42°32N 123°21E 35 C12
Falaise France 48°54N 0°12W 20 B3
Falam Burma 23°0N 93°45E 41 H18
Falcó, C. des Spain 38°50N 1°23E 24 C7
Falcón, Presa Mexico 26°35N 99°10W 87 B5
Falcon Lake Canada 49°42N 95°15W 71 D9
Falcon Res. U.S.A. 26°34N 99°10W 84 H5
Falconara Marittima Italy 43°37N 13°24E 22 C5
Falcone, C. del Italy 40°58N 8°12E 22 D3
Falconer U.S.A. 42°7N 79°12W 82 D5
Falefa Samoa 13°54S 171°31W 59 b
Falelatai Samoa 13°55S 171°59W 59 b
Falelima Samoa 13°32S 172°41W 59 b
Faleshty = Făleşti Moldova 47°32N 27°44E 17 E14
Făleşti Moldova 47°32N 27°44E 17 E14
Falfurrias U.S.A. 27°14N 98°9W 84 H5
Falher Canada 55°44N 117°15W 70 B5
Faliraki Greece 36°22N 28°12E 25 C10
Falkenberg Sweden 56°54N 12°30E 9 H15
Falkirk U.K. 56°0N 3°47W 11 F5
Falkirk □ U.K. 55°58N 3°49W 11 F5
Falkland U.K. 56°16N 3°12W 11 E5
Falkland Is. ⊿ Atl. Oc. 51°30S 59°0W 96 G5
Falkland Sd. Falk. Is. 52°0S 60°0W 96 G5
Fall River U.S.A. 41°43N 71°10W 83 E13
Fallbrook U.S.A. 33°23N 117°15W 79 M9
Fallon U.S.A. 39°28N 118°47W 76 G4
Falls City U.S.A. 40°3N 95°36W 80 E6
Falls Creek U.S.A. 41°9N 78°48W 82 E6
Falmouth Jamaica 18°30N 77°40W 88 a
Falmouth U.K. 50°9N 5°5W 13 G2
Falmouth U.S.A. 41°33N 70°37W 83 E14
Falsa, Pta. Mexico 27°51N 115°3W 86 B1
False B. S. Africa 34°15S 18°40E 56 E2
Falso, C. Honduras 15°12N 83°21W 88 C3
Falster Denmark 54°45N 11°55E 9 J14
Fălticeni Romania 47°21N 26°20E 17 E14
Falun Sweden 60°37N 15°37E 8 F16
Famagusta Cyprus 35°8N 33°55E 25 D12
Famagusta Bay Cyprus 35°15N 34°0E 25 D13
Famatina, Sierra de Argentina 27°30S 68°0W 94 B2
Family L. Canada 51°54N 95°27W 71 C9
Famoso U.S.A. 35°37N 119°12W 79 K7
Fan Xian China 35°55N 115°38E 34 G8
Fanad Hd. Ireland 55°17N 7°38W 10 A4
Fandriana Madag. 20°14S 47°21E 57 C8
Fang Thailand 19°55N 99°13E 38 C2
Fangcheng China 33°18N 112°59E 34 H7
Fangshan Beijing, China 39°41N 116°0E 34 E9
Fangshan Shanxi, China 38°3N 111°25E 34 E6
Fangzi China 36°33N 119°10E 35 F10
Fanjakana Madag. 21°10S 46°53E 57 C8
Fanjiatun China 43°40N 125°15E 35 C13
Fanling China 22°30N 114°8E 33 a
Fannich, L. U.K. 57°38N 4°59W 11 D4
Fannūj Iran 26°35N 59°38E 45 E8
Fanø Denmark 55°25N 8°25E 9 J13
Fano Italy 43°50N 13°1E 22 C5
Fanshi China 39°12N 113°20E 34 E7
Fao = Al Fāw Iraq 30°0N 48°30E 45 D6
Faqirwali Pakistan 29°27N 73°0E 42 E5
Far East = Dalnevostochnyy □ Russia 67°0N 140°0E 29 C14
Far East Asia 40°0N 130°0E 26 E14
Faradje Dem. Rep. of the Congo 3°50N 29°45E 54 B2
Farafangana Madag. 22°49S 47°50E 57 C8
Farāh Afghan. 32°20N 62°7E 40 C3
Farāh □ Afghan. 32°25N 62°10E 40 C3
Farahalana Madag. 14°26S 50°10E 57 A9
Faranah Guinea 10°3N 10°45W 50 F3
Farasān, Jazā'ir Si. Arabia 16°45N 41°55E 47 D3
Farasan Is. = Farasān, Jazā'ir Si. Arabia 16°45N 41°55E 47 D3
Faratsiho Madag. 19°24S 46°57E 57 B8
Fareham U.K. 50°51N 1°11W 13 G6
Farewell, C. N.Z. 40°29S 172°43E 59 D4
Farewell C. = Nunap Isua Greenland 59°48N 43°55W 66 D15
Farghona Uzbekistan 40°23N 71°19E 28 E8
Fargo U.S.A. 46°53N 96°48W 80 B5
Fār'iah, W. al → West Bank 32°12N 35°27E 46 C4
Faribault U.S.A. 44°18N 93°16W 80 C7
Faridabad India 28°26N 77°19E 42 E6
Faridkot India 30°44N 74°45E 42 D6
Faridpur Bangla. 23°15N 89°55E 43 H13
Faridpur India 28°13N 79°33E 43 E8
Farīmān Iran 35°40N 59°49E 45 C8
Fariones, Pta. Canary Is. 29°13N 13°28W 24 E6
Farleigh Australia 21°4S 149°8E 62 b
Farmerville U.S.A. 32°47N 92°24W 84 E8
Farmingdale U.S.A. 40°12N 74°10W 83 F10
Farmington Canada 55°54N 120°30W 70 B4
Farmington Calif., U.S.A. 37°55N 120°59W 78 H6
Farmington Maine, U.S.A. 44°40N 70°9W 81 C18
Farmington Mo., U.S.A. 37°47N 90°25W 80 G8
Farmington N.H., U.S.A. 43°24N 71°4W 83 C13
Farmington N. Mex., U.S.A. 36°44N 108°12W 77 H9
Farmington Utah, U.S.A. 40°59N 111°53W 76 F8
Farmington → U.S.A. 41°51N 72°38W 83 E12
Farmville U.S.A. 37°18N 78°24W 81 G14
Farne Is. U.K. 55°38N 1°37W 12 B6
Farnham Canada 45°17N 72°59W 83 A12
Farnham, Mt. Canada 50°29N 116°30W 70 C5
Faro Brazil 2°10S 56°39W 93 D7
Faro Canada 62°11N 133°22W 68 E5
Faro Portugal 37°2N 7°55W 21 D2
Fårö Sweden 57°55N 19°5E 9 H18
Farquhar, C. Australia 23°50S 113°36E 61 D1
Farrars Cr. → Australia 25°35S 140°43E 62 D3
Farrāshband Iran 28°57N 52°5E 45 D7
Farrell U.S.A. 41°13N 80°30W 82 E4
Farrokhī Iran 33°50N 59°31E 45 C8
Farruch, C. = Ferrutx, C. de Spain 39°47N 3°21E 24 B10
Farrukhabad India 27°24N 79°34E 43 F8
Fārs □ Iran 29°30N 55°0E 45 D7
Farsala Greece 39°17N 22°23E 23 E10
Fārsī Iran 27°58N 50°11E 45 E6
Farson U.S.A. 42°7N 109°26W 76 E9
Farsund Norway 58°5N 6°55E 9 G12
Fartak, Râs Si. Arabia 28°5N 34°34E 44 D2
Fartak, Ra's Yemen 15°38N 52°15E 47 D5
Fartura, Serra da Brazil 26°21S 52°52W 95 B5
Fārūj Iran 37°14N 58°14E 45 B8
Farvel, Kap = Nunap Isua Greenland 59°48N 43°55W 66 D15
Farwell U.S.A. 34°23N 103°2W 84 D3
Fāryāb □ Afghan. 36°0N 65°0E 40 B4
Fasā Iran 29°0N 53°39E 45 D7
Fasano Italy 40°50N 17°22E 22 D7
Fastiv Ukraine 50°7N 29°57E 17 C15
Fastnet Rock Ireland 51°22N 9°37W 10 E2
Fastov = Fastiv Ukraine 50°7N 29°57E 17 C15
Fatagar, Tanjung Indonesia 2°46S 131°57E 37 E8
Fatehabad Haryana, India 29°31N 75°27E 42 E6
Fatehabad Ut. P., India 27°1N 78°19E 42 F8
Fatehgarh India 27°25N 79°35E 43 F8
Fatehpur Bihar, India 24°38N 85°14E 43 G11
Fatehpur Raj., India 28°0N 74°40E 42 F6
Fatehpur Ut. P., India 25°56N 81°13E 43 G9
Fatehpur Ut. P., India 27°10N 81°13E 43 F9
Fatehpur Sikri India 27°6N 77°40E 42 F6
Fathom Five ▲ Canada 45°17N 81°40W 82 A3
Fatima Canada 47°24N 61°53W 73 C7
Faulkton U.S.A. 45°2N 99°8W 80 C4
Faure I. Australia 25°52S 113°50E 61 E1
Fauresmith S. Africa 29°44S 25°17E 56 D4
Fauske Norway 67°17N 15°25E 8 C16
Favara Italy 37°19N 13°39E 22 F5
Favàritx, C. de Spain 40°0N 4°15E 24 B11
Favignana Italy 37°56N 12°20E 22 F5
Fawcett, Pt. Australia 11°46S 130°2E 60 B5
Fawn → Canada 55°20N 87°35W 72 A2
Fawnskin U.S.A. 34°16N 116°56W 79 L10
Faxaflói Iceland 64°29N 23°0W 8 D2
Faya-Largeau Chad 17°58N 19°6E 51 E9
Fayd Si. Arabia 27°1N 42°52E 44 E4
Fayette Ala., U.S.A. 33°41N 87°50W 85 E11
Fayette Mo., U.S.A. 39°9N 92°41W 80 F7
Fayette N.Y., U.S.A. 42°48N 76°48W 83 D8
Fayetteville Ark., U.S.A. 36°4N 94°10W 84 C7
Fayetteville N.C., U.S.A. 35°3N 78°53W 85 D15
Fayetteville N.Y., U.S.A. 43°1N 76°0W 83 C9
Fayetteville Tenn., U.S.A. 35°9N 86°34W 85 D11
Faylakah Kuwait 29°27N 48°20E 45 D6
Fazilka India 30°27N 74°2E 42 D6
Fazilpur Pakistan 29°18N 70°29E 42 E4
Fdérik Mauritania 22°40N 12°45W 50 D3
Feakle Ireland 52°56N 8°40W 10 D3
Feale → Ireland 52°27N 9°37W 10 D2
Fear, C. U.S.A. 33°50N 77°58W 85 E16
Feather → U.S.A. 38°47N 121°36W 76 G3
Feather Falls U.S.A. 39°36N 121°16W 78 F5
Featherston N.Z. 41°6S 175°20E 59 D5
Featherstone Zimbabwe 18°42S 30°55E 55 F3
Fécamp France 49°45N 0°22E 20 B4

Fedala = Mohammedia
  Morocco 33°44N 7°21W **50** B4
Federación Argentina 31°0S 57°55W **94** C4
Féderal Argentina 30°57S 58°48W **96** D5
Federal Way U.S.A. 47°18N 122°19W **78** C4
Fedeshkūh Iran 28°49N 53°50E **45** D7
Fehmarn Germany 54°27N 11°7E **16** A6
Fehmarn Bælt Europe 54°35N 11°20E **9** J14
Fehmarn Belt = Fehmarn Bælt
  Europe 54°35N 11°20E **9** J14
Fei Xian China 35°18N 117°59E **35** G9
Feicheng China 36°14N 116°45E **34** F9
Feijó Brazil 8°9S 70°21W **92** E4
Feilding N.Z. 40°13S 175°35E **59** D5
Feira de Santana Brazil 12°15S 38°57W **93** F11
Feixiang China 36°30N 114°45E **34** F8
Felanitx Spain 39°28N 3°9E **24** B10
Feldkirch Austria 47°15N 9°37E **16** E5
Félicité Seychelles 4°19S 55°52E **53** b
Felipe Carrillo Puerto
  Mexico 19°38N 88°3W **87** D7
Felixburg Zimbabwe 19°29S 30°51E **57** B5
Felixstowe U.K. 51°58N 1°23E **13** F9
Felton U.S.A. 37°3N 122°4W **78** H4
Femer Bælt = Fehmarn Bælt
  Europe 54°35N 11°20E **9** J14
Femunden Norway 62°10N 11°53E **8** E14
Fen He → China 35°36N 110°42E **34** G6
Fenelon Falls Canada 44°32N 78°45W **82** B6
Feng Xian Jiangsu, China 34°43N 116°35E **34** G9
Feng Xian Shaanxi,
  China 33°54N 106°40E **34** H4
Fengcheng China 40°28N 124°5E **35** D13
Fengfeng China 36°28N 114°8E **34** F8
Fengning China 41°10N 116°33E **34** D9
Fengqiu China 35°2N 114°25E **34** G8
Fengrun China 39°48N 118°8E **35** E10
Fengxiang China 34°29N 107°25E **34** G4
Fengyang China 32°51N 117°29E **35** H9
Fengzhen China 40°25N 113°2E **34** D7
Fenoarivo Fianarantsoa,
  Madag. 21°43S 46°24E **57** C8
Fenoarivo Fianarantsoa,
  Madag. 20°52S 46°53E **57** C8
Fenoarivo Afovoany
  Madag. 18°26S 46°34E **57** B8
Fenoarivo Atsinanana
  Madag. 17°22S 49°25E **57** B8
Fens, The U.K. 52°38N 0°2W **12** E7
Fenton U.S.A. 42°48N 83°42W **81** D12
Fenxi China 36°40N 111°31E **34** F6
Fenyang China 37°18N 111°48E **34** F6
Feodosiya Ukraine 45°2N 35°16E **19** E6
Ferbane Ireland 53°16N 7°50W **10** C4
Ferdows Iran 33°58N 58°2E **45** C8
Ferfer Somali Rep. 5°4N 45°9E **47** F4
Fergana = Farghona
  Uzbekistan 40°23N 71°19E **28** E8
Fergus Canada 43°43N 80°24W **82** C4
Fergus Falls U.S.A. 46°17N 96°4W **80** B5
Ferizaj = Uroševac
  Kosovo 42°23N 21°10E **23** C9
Ferkéssédougou Ivory C. 9°35N 5°6W **50** G4
Ferland Canada 50°19N 88°27W **72** B2
Ferlo, Vallée du Senegal 15°15N 14°15W **50** E2
Fermanagh □ U.K. 54°21N 7°40W **10** B4
Fermo Italy 43°9N 13°43E **22** C5
Fermont Canada 52°47N 67°5W **73** B6
Fermoy Ireland 52°9N 8°16W **10** D3
Fernández Argentina 27°55S 63°50W **94** B3
Fernandina Beach
  U.S.A. 30°40N 81°27W **85** F14
Fernando de Noronha
  Brazil 4°0S 33°10W **93** D12
Fernando Póo = Bioko
  Eq. Guin. 3°30N 8°40E **52** D1
Ferndale Canada 44°58N 81°17W **82** B3
Ferndale U.S.A. 48°51N 122°36W **78** B4
Fernie Canada 49°30N 115°5W **70** D5
Fernlees Australia 23°51S 148°7E **62** C4
Fernley U.S.A. 39°36N 119°15W **76** G4
Fernwood U.S.A. 43°16N 73°38W **83** C11
Ferozepore = Firozpur
  India 30°55N 74°40E **42** D6
Ferrara Italy 44°50N 11°35E **22** B4
Ferreñafe Peru 6°42S 79°50W **92** E3
Ferrerías Spain 39°59N 4°1E **24** B11
Ferret, C. France 44°38N 1°15W **20** D3
Ferriday U.S.A. 31°38N 91°33W **84** F9
Ferrol Spain 43°29N 8°15W **21** A1
Ferron U.S.A. 39°5N 111°8W **76** G8
Ferrutx, C. de Spain 39°47N 3°21E **24** B10
Ferryland Canada 47°2N 52°53W **73** C9
Fertile U.S.A. 47°32N 96°17W **80** B5
Fès Morocco 34°0N 5°0W **50** B5
Fessenden U.S.A. 47°39N 99°38W **80** B4
Festus U.S.A. 38°13N 90°24W **80** F9
Fetești Romania 44°22N 27°51E **17** F14
Fethiye Turkey 36°36N 29°6E **19** G4
Fetlar U.K. 60°36N 0°52W **11** A8
Feuilles → Canada 58°47N 70°4W **69** F17
Fez = Fès Morocco 34°0N 5°0W **50** B5
Fezzan Libya 27°0N 13°0E **51** C8
Fiambalá Argentina 27°45S 67°37W **94** B2
Fianarantsoa Madag. 21°26S 47°5E **57** C8
Fianarantsoa □ Madag. 22°30S 47°0E **57** C8
Ficksburg S. Africa 28°51S 27°53E **57** D4
Field → Australia 23°48S 138°0E **62** C2
Field I. Australia 12°5S 132°23E **60** B5
Fier Albania 40°43N 19°33E **23** D8
Fife □ U.K. 56°16N 3°1W **11** E5
Fife Ness U.K. 56°17N 2°35W **11** E6
Fifth Cataract Sudan 18°22N 33°50E **51** E12
Figeac France 44°37N 2°2E **20** D5
Figtree Zimbabwe 20°22S 28°20E **55** G2
Figueira da Foz Portugal 40°7N 8°54W **21** B1
Figueres Spain 42°18N 2°58E **21** A7
Figuig Morocco 32°5N 1°11W **50** B5
Fihaonana Madag. 18°36S 47°12E **57** B8

Fiherenana Madag. 18°29S 48°24E **57** B8
Fiherenana → Madag. 23°19S 43°37E **57** C7
Fiji ■ Pac. Oc. 17°20S 179°0E **59** a
Filabus Zimbabwe 20°34S 29°20E **57** C4
Filadelfia Paraguay 22°21S 60°2W **94** A3
Filchner Ice Shelf Antarctica 79°0S 40°0W **5** D1
Filey U.K. 54°12N 0°18W **12** C7
Filey B. U.K. 54°12N 0°15W **12** C7
Filfla Malta 35°47N 14°24E **25** D1
Filiatra Greece 37°9N 21°35E **23** F9
Filingué Niger 14°21N 3°22E **50** F6
Filipstad Sweden 59°43N 14°9E **9** G16
Fillmore Calif., U.S.A. 34°24N 118°55W **79** L8
Fillmore Utah, U.S.A. 38°58N 112°20W **76** G7
Finch Canada 45°11N 75°7W **83** A9
Finch Hatton Australia 20°25S 148°39E **62** b
Findhorn → U.K. 57°38N 3°38W **11** D5
Findlay U.S.A. 41°2N 83°39W **81** E12
Fine U.S.A. 44°14N 75°8W **83** B9
Finger L. Canada 53°33N 93°30W **72** B1
Finger Lakes U.S.A. 42°40N 76°30W **83** D8
Fingoè Mozam. 15°55S 31°50E **55** F3
Finisterre, C. = Fisterra, C.
  Spain 42°50N 9°19W **21** A1
Finke Australia 25°34S 134°35E **62** D1
Finke Gorge △ Australia 24°8S 132°49E **60** D5
Finland ■ Europe 63°0N 27°0E **8** E22
Finland, G. of Europe 60°0N 26°0E **9** G22
Finlay → Canada 57°0N 125°10W **70** B3
Finley Australia 35°38S 145°35E **63** F4
Finley U.S.A. 47°31N 97°50W **80** B5
Finn → Ireland 54°51N 7°28W **10** B4
Finnigan, Mt. Australia 15°49S 145°17E **62** B4
Finniss, C. Australia 33°8S 134°51E **63** E1
Finnmark Norway 69°37N 23°57E **8** B20
Finnsnes Norway 69°14N 18°0E **8** B18
Finspång Sweden 58°43N 15°47E **9** G16
Fiora → Italy 42°20N 11°34E **22** C4
Fiordland △ N.Z. 45°46S 167°0E **59** F1
Fiq Syria 32°46N 35°41E **46** C4
Firat = Furāt, Nahr al →
  Asia 31°0N 47°25E **44** D5
Fire Island △ U.S.A. 40°38N 73°8W **83** F11
Firebag → Canada 57°45N 111°21W **71** B6
Firebaugh U.S.A. 36°52N 120°27W **78** J6
Firedrake L. Canada 61°25N 104°30W **71** A8
Firenze Italy 43°46N 11°15E **22** C4
Firk, Sha'ib → Iraq 30°59N 44°34E **44** D5
Firozabad India 27°10N 78°25E **43** F8
Firozpur India 30°55N 74°40E **42** D6
Firozpur-Jhirka India 27°48N 76°57E **42** F7
Fīrūzābād Iran 28°52N 52°35E **45** D7
Fīrūzkūh Iran 35°50N 52°50E **45** C7
Firvale Canada 52°27N 126°13W **70** C3
Fish → Namibia 28°7S 17°10E **56** D2
Fish → S. Africa 31°30S 20°16E **56** E3
Fish River Canyon
  Namibia 27°40S 17°35E **56** D2
Fisher B. Canada 51°35N 97°13W **71** C9
Fishers I. U.S.A. 41°15N 72°0W **83** E13
Fishguard U.K. 52°0N 4°58W **13** E3
Fishing L. Canada 52°10N 95°24W **71** C9
Fishkill U.S.A. 41°32N 73°54W **83** E11
Fisterra, C. Spain 42°50N 9°19W **21** A1
Fitchburg Mass., U.S.A. 42°35N 71°48W **83** D13
Fitchburg Wis., U.S.A. 42°58N 89°28W **80** D9
Fitz Roy Argentina 47°0S 67°0W **96** F3
Fitz Roy, Cerro Argentina 49°17S 73°5W **96** F2
Fitzgerald Canada 59°51N 111°36W **70** B6
Fitzgerald U.S.A. 31°43N 83°15W **85** F13
Fitzgerald River △
  Australia 33°53S 119°55E **61** F3
Fitzmaurice → Australia 14°45S 130°5E **60** B5
Fitzroy → Queens.,
  Australia 23°32S 150°52E **62** C5
Fitzroy → W. Austral.,
  Australia 17°31S 123°35E **60** C3
Fitzroy Crossing
  Australia 18°9S 125°38E **60** C4
Fitzwilliam I. Canada 45°30N 81°45W **82** A3
Fiume = Rijeka Croatia 45°20N 14°21E **16** F8
Five Points U.S.A. 36°26N 120°6W **78** J6
Fizi Dem. Rep. of the Congo 4°17S 28°55E **54** C2
Flagstaff U.S.A. 35°12N 111°39W **77** J8
Flagstaff L. U.S.A. 45°12N 70°18W **83** A14
Flaherty I. Canada 56°15N 79°15W **72** A4
Flåm Norway 60°50N 7°7E **8** F12
Flambeau → U.S.A. 45°18N 91°14W **80** C8
Flamborough Hd. U.K. 54°7N 0°5W **12** C7
Flaming Gorge △
  U.S.A. 41°10N 109°25W **76** F9
Flaming Gorge Res.
  U.S.A. 41°10N 109°25W **76** F9
Flamingo, Teluk Indonesia 5°30S 138°0E **37** F9
Flanders = Flandre
  Europe 50°50N 2°30E **15** B9
Flandre Europe 50°50N 2°30E **15** B9
Flandre-Occidentale = West-
  Vlaanderen □ Belgium 51°0N 3°0E **15** D2
Flandre-Orientale = Oost-
  Vlaanderen □ Belgium 51°5N 3°50E **15** C3
Flandreau U.S.A. 44°3N 96°36W **80** C5
Flanigan U.S.A. 40°10N 119°53W **78** E7
Flannan Is. U.K. 58°9N 7°52W **11** C1
Flåsjön Sweden 64°5N 15°40E **8** D16
Flat → Canada 61°33N 125°18W **70** A3
Flat I. Mauritius 19°53S 57°35E **53** d
Flathead L. U.S.A. 47°51N 114°8W **76** C6
Flattery, C. Australia 14°58S 145°21E **62** A4
Flattery, C. U.S.A. 48°23N 124°29W **78** B2
Flatwoods U.S.A. 38°31N 82°43W **81** F12
Fleetwood U.K. 53°55N 3°1W **12** D4
Fleetwood U.S.A. 40°27N 75°49W **83** F9
Flekkefjord Norway 58°18N 6°39E **9** G12
Flemington U.S.A. 41°7N 77°28W **82** F7
Flensburg Germany 54°47N 9°27E **16** A5
Flers France 48°47N 0°33W **20** B3
Flesherton Canada 44°16N 80°33W **82** B4
Flesko, Tanjung
  Indonesia 0°29N 124°30E **37** D6

Fleurieu Pen. Australia 35°40S 138°5E **63** F2
Flevoland □ Neths. 52°30N 5°30E **15** B5
Flin Flon Canada 54°46N 101°53W **71** C8
Flinders → Australia 17°36S 140°36E **62** B3
Flinders B. Australia 34°19S 115°19E **61** F2
Flinders Group Australia 14°11S 144°15E **62** A3
Flinders I. S. Austral.,
  Australia 33°44S 134°41E **63** E1
Flinders I. Tas., Australia 40°0S 148°0E **63** G4
Flinders Ranges
  Australia 31°30S 138°30E **63** E2
Flinders Reefs Australia 17°37S 148°31E **62** B4
Flint U.K. 53°15N 3°8W **12** D4
Flint U.S.A. 43°1N 83°41W **81** D12
Flint → U.S.A. 30°57N 84°34W **85** F12
Flint I. Kiribati 11°26S 151°48W **65** J12
Flintshire □ U.K. 53°17N 3°17W **12** D4
Flodden U.K. 55°37N 2°8W **12** B5
Floodwood U.S.A. 46°56N 92°55W **80** B7
Flora U.S.A. 38°40N 88°29W **80** F9
Florala U.S.A. 31°0N 86°20W **85** F11
Florence = Firenze Italy 43°46N 11°15E **22** C4
Florence Ala., U.S.A. 34°48N 87°41W **85** D11
Florence Ariz., U.S.A. 33°2N 111°23W **77** K8
Florence Colo., U.S.A. 38°23N 105°8W **76** G11
Florence Oreg., U.S.A. 43°58N 124°7W **76** D1
Florence S.C., U.S.A. 34°12N 79°46W **85** D15
Florence, L. Australia 28°53S 138°9E **63** D2
Florencia Colombia 1°36N 75°36W **92** C3
Florennes Belgium 50°15N 4°35E **15** D4
Florenville Belgium 49°40N 5°19E **15** E5
Flores Argentina 39°26N 31°13W **50** a
Flores Guatemala 16°59N 89°50W **88** C2
Flores Indonesia 8°35S 121°0E **37** F6
Flores I. Canada 49°20N 126°10W **70** D3
Flores Sea Indonesia 6°30S 120°0E **37** F6
Floreşti Moldova 47°53N 28°17E **17** E15
Floresville U.S.A. 29°8N 98°10W **84** G5
Floriano Brazil 6°50S 43°0W **93** E10
Florianópolis Brazil 27°30S 48°30W **95** B6
Florida Cuba 21°32N 78°14W **88** B4
Florida Uruguay 34°7S 56°10W **95** C4
Florida □ U.S.A. 28°0N 82°0W **85** G14
Florida, Straits of U.S.A. 25°0N 80°0W **88** B3
Florida B. U.S.A. 25°0N 80°45W **88** B3
Florida Keys U.S.A. 24°40N 81°0W **85** J14
Florin U.S.A. 38°30N 121°24W **78** G5
Florina Greece 40°48N 21°26E **23** D9
Florissant U.S.A. 38°47N 90°19W **80** F8
Florø Norway 61°35N 5°1E **8** F11
Flower Station Canada 45°10N 76°41W **83** A8
Flowerpot I. Canada 45°18N 81°38W **82** A3
Floydada U.S.A. 33°59N 101°20W **84** E4
Fluk Indonesia 1°42S 127°44E **37** E7
Flushing = Vlissingen
  Neths. 51°26N 3°34E **15** C3
Fly → Papua N. G. 8°25S 143°0E **58** B7
Flying Fish, C. Antarctica 72°6S 102°29W **5** D15
Foa Tonga 19°45S 174°18W **59** c
Foam Lake Canada 51°40N 103°32W **71** C8
Foça Turkey 38°39N 26°46E **23** E12
Fochabers U.K. 57°37N 3°6W **11** D5
Focşani Romania 45°41N 27°15E **17** F14
Fóggia Italy 41°27N 15°34E **22** D6
Fogo Canada 49°43N 54°17W **73** C9
Fogo C. Verde Is. 15°5N 24°20W **50** b
Fogo I. Canada 49°40N 54°5W **73** C9
Föhr Germany 54°43N 8°30E **16** A5
Foix France 42°58N 1°38E **20** E4
Folda Nord-Trøndelag,
  Norway 64°32N 10°30E **8** D14
Folda Nordland, Norway 67°38N 14°50E **8** C16
Foley Botswana 21°34S 27°21E **56** C4
Foley U.S.A. 30°24N 87°41W **85** F11
Foleyet Canada 48°15N 82°25W **72** C3
Folgefonna Norway 60°3N 6°23E **9** F12
Foligno Italy 42°57N 12°42E **22** C5
Folkestone U.K. 51°5N 1°12E **13** F9
Folkston U.S.A. 30°50N 82°0W **85** F13
Follansbee U.S.A. 40°19N 80°35W **82** F4
Folsom L. U.S.A. 38°42N 121°9W **78** G5
Fomboni Comoros Is. 12°18S 43°46E **53** a
Fond-du-Lac Canada 59°19N 107°12W **71** B7
Fond du Lac U.S.A. 43°47N 88°27W **80** D9
Fond-du-Lac → Canada 59°17N 106°0W **71** B7
Fondi Italy 41°21N 13°25E **22** D5
Fongafale Tuvalu 8°31S 179°13E **58** B10
Fonsagrada = A Fonsagrada
  Spain 43°8N 7°4W **21** A2
Fonseca, G. de
  Cent. Amer. 13°10N 87°40W **88** D2
Fontainebleau France 48°24N 2°40E **20** B5
Fontana U.S.A. 34°6N 117°26W **79** L9
Fontas → Canada 58°14N 121°48W **70** B4
Fonte Boa Brazil 2°33S 66°0W **92** D5
Fontenay-le-Comte
  France 46°28N 0°48W **20** C3
Fontenelle Res. U.S.A. 42°1N 110°3W **76** E8
Fontur Iceland 66°23N 14°32W **8** C6
Fonuafo'ou Tonga 20°19S 175°25W **59** c
Fonualei Tonga 18°1S 174°19W **59** c
Foochow = Fuzhou
  China 26°5N 119°16E **33** F12
Foping China 33°41N 108°0E **34** H5
Foraker, Mt. U.S.A. 62°58N 151°24W **74** C9
Forbes Australia 33°22S 148°5E **63** E4
Forbesganj India 26°17N 87°18E **43** F12
Ford City Calif., U.S.A. 35°9N 119°27W **79** K7
Ford City Pa., U.S.A. 40°46N 79°32W **82** F5
Førde Norway 61°27N 5°53E **8** F11
Fords Bridge Australia 29°41S 145°29E **63** D4
Fordyce U.S.A. 33°49N 92°25W **84** E8
Forel, Mt. Greenland 66°52N 36°55W **4** C6
Foremost Canada 49°26N 111°34W **70** D6
Forest Canada 43°6N 82°0W **82** C3
Forest U.S.A. 32°22N 89°29W **85** E10
Forest City Iowa, U.S.A. 43°16N 93°39W **80** D7
Forest City N.C., U.S.A. 35°20N 81°52W **85** D14
Forest City Pa., U.S.A. 41°39N 75°28W **83** E9

Forest Grove U.S.A. 45°31N 123°7W **78** E3
Forestburg Canada 52°35N 112°1W **70** C6
Foresthill U.S.A. 39°1N 120°49W **78** F6
Forestier Pen. Australia 43°0S 148°0E **63** G4
Forestville Canada 48°48N 69°2W **73** C6
Forestville Calif., U.S.A. 38°28N 122°54W **78** G4
Forestville N.Y., U.S.A. 42°28N 79°10W **82** D5
Forfar U.K. 56°39N 2°53W **11** E6
Forillon △ Canada 48°46N 64°12W **73** C7
Forks U.S.A. 47°57N 124°23W **78** C2
Forksville U.S.A. 41°29N 76°35W **83** E8
Forlì Italy 44°13N 12°3E **22** B5
Forman U.S.A. 46°7N 97°38W **80** B5
Formby Pt. U.K. 53°33N 3°6W **12** D4
Formentera Spain 38°43N 1°27E **24** C7
Formentor, C. de Spain 39°58N 3°13E **24** B10
Formentor, Pen. de
  Spain 39°56N 3°11E **24** B10
Former Yugoslav Republic of
  Macedonia = Macedonia ■
  Europe 41°53N 21°40E **23** D9
Fórmia Italy 41°15N 13°37E **22** D5
Formosa = Taiwan ■
  Asia 23°30N 121°0E **33** G13
Formosa Argentina 26°15S 58°10W **94** B4
Formosa Brazil 15°32S 47°20W **93** G9
Formosa □ Argentina 25°0S 60°0W **94** B4
Formosa, Serra Brazil 12°0S 55°0W **93** F8
Formosa B. = Ungwana B.
  Kenya 2°45S 40°20E **54** C5
Fornells Spain 40°3N 4°7E **24** A11
Føroyar ☑ Atl. Oc. 62°0N 7°0W **8** F9
Forres U.K. 57°37N 3°37W **11** D5
Forrest Australia 30°51S 128°6E **61** F4
Forrest, Mt. Australia 24°48S 127°45E **61** D4
Forrest City U.S.A. 35°1N 90°47W **85** D9
Forsayth Australia 18°33S 143°34E **62** B3
Forssa Finland 60°49N 23°38E **8** F20
Forst Germany 51°45N 14°37E **16** C8
Forster Australia 32°12S 152°31E **63** E5
Forsyth U.S.A. 46°16N 106°41W **76** C10
Fort Abbas Pakistan 29°12N 72°52E **42** E5
Fort Albany Canada 52°15N 81°35W **72** B3
Fort Assiniboine
  Canada 54°20N 114°45W **70** C6
Fort Augustus U.K. 57°9N 4°42W **11** D4
Fort Beaufort S. Africa 32°46S 26°40E **56** E4
Fort Benton U.S.A. 47°49N 110°40W **76** C8
Fort Bragg U.S.A. 39°26N 123°48W **76** G2
Fort Bridger U.S.A. 41°19N 110°23W **76** F8
Fort Chipewyan Canada 58°42N 111°8W **71** B6
Fort Clatsop = Lewis and Clark △
  U.S.A. 46°8N 123°53W **78** D3
Fort Collins U.S.A. 40°35N 105°5W **76** F11
Fort-Coulonge Canada 45°50N 76°45E **72** C4
Fort Covington U.S.A. 44°59N 74°29W **83** B10
Fort Dauphin = Taolanaro
  Madag. 25°2S 47°0E **57** D8
Fort Davis U.S.A. 30°35N 103°54W **84** F3
Fort-de-France Martinique 14°36N 61°2W **88** d
Fort Defiance U.S.A. 35°45N 109°5W **77** J9
Fort Dodge U.S.A. 42°30N 94°11W **80** D6
Fort Edward U.S.A. 43°16N 73°35W **83** C11
Fort Erie Canada 42°54N 78°56W **82** D6
Fort Fairfield U.S.A. 46°46N 67°50W **81** B20
Fort Frances Canada 48°36N 93°24W **71** D10
Fort Franklin = Déline
  Canada 65°11N 123°25W **68** D7
Fort Garland U.S.A. 37°26N 105°26W **77** H11
Fort George = Chisasibi
  Canada 53°50N 79°0W **72** B4
Fort Good Hope Canada 66°14N 128°40W **68** C6
Fort Hancock U.S.A. 31°18N 105°51W **84** F2
Fort Hope = Eabametoong
  Canada 51°30N 88°0W **72** B2
Fort Irwin U.S.A. 35°16N 116°41W **79** K10
Fort Kent U.S.A. 47°15N 68°36W **81** B19
Fort Klamath U.S.A. 42°42N 122°0W **76** D3
Fort Laramie U.S.A. 42°13N 104°31W **76** E11
Fort Lauderdale U.S.A. 26°7N 80°8W **85** H14
Fort Liard Canada 60°14N 123°30W **70** A4
Fort Liberté Haiti 19°42N 71°51W **89** C5
Fort Lupton U.S.A. 40°5N 104°49W **76** F11
Fort MacKay Canada 57°12N 111°41W **70** B6
Fort Macleod Canada 49°45N 113°30W **70** D6
Fort McMurray Canada 56°44N 111°7W **70** B6
Fort McPherson
  Canada 67°30N 134°55W **68** D5
Fort Madison U.S.A. 40°38N 91°27W **80** E8
Fort Meade U.S.A. 27°45N 81°48W **85** H14
Fort Morgan U.S.A. 40°15N 103°48W **76** F12
Fort Myers U.S.A. 26°39N 81°52W **85** H14
Fort Nelson Canada 58°50N 122°44W **70** B4
Fort Nelson → Canada 59°32N 124°0W **70** B4
Fort Norman = Tulita
  Canada 64°57N 125°30W **68** E6
Fort Payne U.S.A. 34°26N 85°43W **85** D12
Fort Peck U.S.A. 48°1N 106°27W **76** B10
Fort Peck Dam U.S.A. 48°0N 106°26W **76** C10
Fort Peck L. U.S.A. 48°0N 106°26W **76** C10
Fort Pierce U.S.A. 27°27N 80°20W **85** H14
Fort Pierre U.S.A. 44°21N 100°22W **80** C3
Fort Plain U.S.A. 42°56N 74°37W **83** D10
Fort Portal Uganda 0°40N 30°20E **54** B3
Fort Providence Canada 61°3N 117°40W **70** A5
Fort Qu'Appelle
  Canada 50°45N 103°50W **71** C8
Fort Resolution Canada 61°10N 113°40W **70** A6
Fort Rixon Zimbabwe 20°2S 29°17E **55** G2
Fort Ross U.S.A. 38°32N 123°13W **78** G3
Fort Rupert = Waskaganish
  Canada 51°30N 78°40W **72** B4
Fort St. James Canada 54°30N 124°10W **70** C4
Fort St. John Canada 56°15N 120°50W **70** B4
Fort Saskatchewan
  Canada 53°40N 113°15W **70** C6
Fort Scott U.S.A. 37°50N 94°42W **80** G6
Fort Severn Canada 56°0N 87°40W **72** A2
Fort Shevchenko
  Kazakhstan 44°35N 50°23E **19** F9

Fort Simpson Canada 61°45N 121°15W **70** A4
Fort Smith Canada 60°0N 111°51W **70** B6
Fort Smith U.S.A. 35°23N 94°25W **84** D7
Fort Stockton U.S.A. 30°53N 102°53W **84** F3
Fort Sumner U.S.A. 34°28N 104°15W **77** J11
Fort Thompson U.S.A. 44°3N 99°26W **80** C4
Fort Union △ U.S.A. 35°54N 105°1W **77** J11
Fort Valley U.S.A. 32°33N 83°53W **85** E13
Fort Vermilion Canada 58°24N 116°0W **70** B5
Fort Walton Beach
  U.S.A. 30°25N 86°36W **85** F11
Fort Ware Canada 57°26N 125°41W **70** B3
Fort Wayne U.S.A. 41°4N 85°9W **81** E11
Fort William U.K. 56°49N 5°7W **11** E3
Fort Worth U.S.A. 32°43N 97°19W **84** E6
Fort Yates U.S.A. 46°5N 100°38W **80** B3
Fort Yukon U.S.A. 66°34N 145°16W **68** D2
Fortaleza Brazil 3°45S 38°35W **93** D11
Forteau Canada 51°28N 56°58W **73** B8
Fortescue → Australia 21°0S 116°4E **60** D2
Fortescue River Roadhouse
  Australia 21°17S 116°8E **60** D2
Forth → U.K. 56°9N 3°50W **11** E5
Forth, Firth of U.K. 56°5N 2°55W **11** E6
Fortrose U.K. 57°35N 4°9W **11** D4
Fortuna Calif., U.S.A. 40°36N 124°9W **76** F1
Fortuna N. Dak., U.S.A. 48°55N 103°47W **80** A2
Fortune Canada 47°4N 55°50W **73** C8
Fortune B. Canada 47°30N 55°22W **73** C8
Forūr Iran 26°17N 54°32E **45** E7
Fosen Norway 63°50N 10°20E **8** E14
Foshan China 23°6N 113°9E **33** G11
Fosnavåg Norway 62°22N 5°38E **8** E11
Fossano Italy 44°33N 7°43E **20** D7
Fossil U.S.A. 45°0N 120°9W **76** D3
Fossil Butte △ U.S.A. 41°50N 110°27W **76** F8
Foster Canada 45°17N 72°30W **83** A12
Foster → Canada 55°47N 105°49W **71** B7
Fosters Ra. Australia 21°35S 133°48E **62** C1
Fostoria U.S.A. 41°10N 83°25W **81** E12
Fotadrevo Madag. 24°3S 45°1E **57** C8
Fougères France 48°21N 1°14W **20** B3
Foul Pt. Sri Lanka 8°35N 81°18E **40** Q12
Foula U.K. 60°10N 2°5W **11** A6
Foulness I. U.K. 51°36N 0°55E **13** F8
Foulpointe Madag. 17°41S 49°31E **57** B8
Fouman Cameroon 5°45N 10°50E **52** C2
Foumbouni Comoros Is. 11°51S 43°29E **53** a
Fountain U.S.A. 38°41N 104°42W **76** G11
Fountain Hills U.S.A. 33°37N 111°43W **77** K8
Fountain Springs
  U.S.A. 35°54N 118°51W **79** K8
Four Mountains, Is. of
  U.S.A. 53°0N 170°0W **74** E5
Fouriesburg S. Africa 28°38S 28°14E **57** D4
Fourni Greece 37°36N 26°32E **23** F12
Fouta Djalon Guinea 11°20N 12°10W **50** F3
Foux, Cap-à- Haiti 19°43N 73°27W **89** C5
Foveaux Str. N.Z. 46°42S 168°10E **59** G2
Fowey U.K. 50°20N 4°39W **13** G3
Fowler Calif., U.S.A. 36°38N 119°41W **78** J7
Fowler Colo., U.S.A. 38°8N 104°2W **76** G11
Fowler, Pt. Australia 32°2S 132°3E **61** F5
Fowlers B. Australia 31°59S 132°34E **61** F5
Fowman Iran 37°13N 49°19E **45** B6
Fox → Canada 56°3N 93°18W **71** B10
Fox Creek Canada 54°24N 116°48W **70** C5
Fox Is. U.S.A. 53°0N 168°0W **74** E4
Fox Lake Canada 58°28N 114°31W **70** B6
Fox Valley Canada 50°30N 109°25W **71** C7
Foxboro Canada 44°14N 77°26W **82** B7
Foxboro U.S.A. 42°4N 71°16W **83** D13
Foxdale Australia 20°22S 148°35E **62** b
Foxe Basin Canada 66°0N 77°0W **69** D16
Foxe Chan. Canada 65°0N 80°0W **69** E16
Foxe Pen. Canada 65°0N 76°0W **69** E16
Foxford Ireland 53°59N 9°7W **10** C2
Foxton N.Z. 40°29S 175°18E **59** D5
Foyle, Lough U.K. 55°7N 7°4W **10** A4
Foynes Ireland 52°37N 9°7W **10** D2
Foz do Cunene Angola 17°15S 11°48E **56** B1
Foz do Iguaçu Brazil 25°30S 54°30W **95** B5
Frackville U.S.A. 40°47N 76°14W **83** F8
Fraile Muerto Uruguay 32°31S 54°32W **95** C5
Framingham U.S.A. 42°18N 71°24W **83** D13
Franca Brazil 20°33S 47°30W **93** H9
Francavilla Fontana
  Italy 40°32N 17°35E **23** D7
France ■ Europe 47°0N 3°0E **20** C5
Frances Australia 36°41S 140°55E **63** F3
Frances → Canada 60°16N 129°10W **70** A3
Frances L. Canada 61°23N 129°30W **70** A3
Franceville Gabon 1°40S 13°32E **52** E2
Franche-Comté □ France 46°50N 5°55E **20** C6
Francis Case, L. U.S.A. 43°4N 98°34W **80** D4
Francisco Beltrão Brazil 26°5S 53°4W **95** B5
Francisco Ignacio Madero
  Coahuila, Mexico 25°48N 103°18W **86** B4
Francisco Ignacio Madero Durango,
  Mexico 24°26N 104°18W **86** C4
Francisco Ignacio Madero, Presa
  Mexico 28°10N 105°37W **86** B3
Francistown Botswana 21°7S 27°33E **57** C4
François Canada 47°35N 56°45W **73** C8
François L. Canada 54°0N 125°30W **70** C3
François Peron △
  Australia 25°42S 113°33E **61** E1
Franks Pk. U.S.A. 43°58N 109°20W **76** E9
Franeker Neths. 53°12N 5°33E **15** A5
Frank Hann △ Australia 32°52S 120°19E **61** F3
Frankford Canada 44°12N 77°36W **82** B7
Frankfort S. Africa 27°17S 28°30E **57** D4
Frankfort Ind., U.S.A. 40°17N 86°31W **81** E10
Frankfort Kans., U.S.A. 39°42N 96°25W **80** F5
Frankfort Ky., U.S.A. 38°12N 84°52W **81** F11
Frankfort N.Y., U.S.A. 43°2N 75°4W **83** C9
Frankfurt Brandenburg,
  Germany 52°20N 14°32E **16** B8
Frankfurt Hessen, Germany 50°7N 8°41E **16** C5
Fränkische Alb Germany 49°10N 11°23E **16** D6

Frankland → Australia 35°0S 116°48E 61 G2
Franklin Ky., U.S.A. 36°43N 86°35W 80 G10
Franklin La., U.S.A. 29°48N 91°30W 84 G9
Franklin Mass., U.S.A. 42°5N 71°24W 83 D13
Franklin N.H., U.S.A. 43°27N 71°39W 83 C13
Franklin N.Y., U.S.A. 42°20N 75°9W 83 D9
Franklin Nebr., U.S.A. 40°6N 98°57W 80 E4
Franklin Pa., U.S.A. 41°24N 79°50W 82 E5
Franklin Va., U.S.A. 36°41N 76°56W 81 G15
Franklin W. Va., U.S.A. 38°39N 79°20W 81 F14
Franklin B. Canada 69°45N 126°0W 68 D6
Franklin D. Roosevelt L. U.S.A. 48°18N 118°9W 76 B4
Franklin-Gordon Wild Rivers △ Australia 42°19S 145°51E 63 G4
Franklin I. Antarctica 76°10S 168°30E 5 D11
Franklin I. Canada 45°24N 80°20W 82 A4
Franklin L. U.S.A. 40°25N 115°22W 76 F6
Franklin Mts. Canada 65°0N 125°0W 68 D6
Franklin Str. Canada 72°0N 96°0W 68 C12
Franklinton U.S.A. 30°51N 90°9W 85 F9
Franklinville U.S.A. 42°20N 78°27W 82 D6
Frankston Australia 38°8S 145°8E 63 F4
Fransfontein Namibia 20°12S 15°1E 56 C2
Frantsa Iosifa, Zemlya Russia 82°0N 55°0E 28 A6
Franz Canada 48°25N 84°30W 72 C3
Franz Josef Land = Frantsa Iosifa, Zemlya Russia 82°0N 55°0E 28 A6
Fraser U.S.A. 42°32N 82°57W 82 D2
Fraser → B.C., Canada 49°7N 123°11W 78 A3
Fraser → Nfld. & L., Canada 56°39N 62°10W 73 A7
Fraser, Mt. Australia 25°35S 118°20E 61 E2
Fraser I. Australia 25°15S 153°10E 63 D5
Fraser Lake Canada 54°0N 124°50W 70 C4
Fraserburg S. Africa 31°55S 21°30E 56 E3
Fraserburgh U.K. 57°42N 2°1W 11 D6
Fraserdale Canada 49°55N 81°37W 72 C3
Fray Bentos Uruguay 33°10S 58°15W 94 C4
Fray Jorge △ Chile 30°42S 71°40W 94 C1
Frazier Downs ❂ Australia 18°48S 121°42E 60 C3
Fredericia Denmark 55°34N 9°45E 9 J13
Frederick Md., U.S.A. 39°25N 77°25W 81 F15
Frederick Okla., U.S.A. 34°23N 99°1W 84 D5
Frederick S. Dak., U.S.A. 45°50N 98°31W 80 C4
Fredericksburg Pa., U.S.A. 40°27N 76°26W 83 F8
Fredericksburg Tex., U.S.A. 30°16N 98°52W 84 F5
Fredericksburg Va., U.S.A. 38°18N 77°28W 81 F15
Fredericktown Mo., U.S.A. 37°34N 90°18W 80 G8
Fredericktown Ohio, U.S.A. 40°29N 82°33W 82 F2
Frederico Westphalen Brazil 27°22S 53°24W 95 B5
Fredericton Canada 45°57N 66°40W 73 C6
Fredericton Junction Canada 45°41N 66°40W 73 C6
Frederikshåb = Paamiut Greenland 62°0N 49°43W 4 C5
Frederikshamn = Hamina Finland 60°34N 27°12E 8 F22
Frederikshavn Denmark 57°28N 10°31E 9 H14
Frederiksted U.S. Virgin Is. 17°43N 64°53W 89 C7
Fredonia Ariz., U.S.A. 36°57N 112°32W 77 H7
Fredonia Kans., U.S.A. 37°32N 95°49W 80 G6
Fredonia N.Y., U.S.A. 42°26N 79°20W 82 D5
Fredrikstad Norway 59°13N 10°57E 9 G14
Free State ☐ S. Africa 28°30S 27°0E 56 D4
Freehold U.S.A. 40°16N 74°17W 83 F10
Freeland U.S.A. 41°1N 75°54W 83 E9
Freels, C. Nfld. & L., Canada 49°15N 53°30W 73 C9
Freels, C. Nfld. & L., Canada 46°37N 53°32W 73 C9
Freeman Calif., U.S.A. 35°35N 117°53W 79 K9
Freeman S. Dak., U.S.A. 43°21N 97°26W 80 D5
Freeport Bahamas 26°30N 78°47W 88 A4
Freeport Ill., U.S.A. 42°17N 89°36W 80 D9
Freeport N.Y., U.S.A. 40°39N 73°35W 83 F11
Freeport Ohio, U.S.A. 40°12N 81°15W 82 F3
Freeport Pa., U.S.A. 40°41N 79°41W 82 F5
Freeport Tex., U.S.A. 28°57N 95°21W 84 G7
Freetown S. Leone 8°30N 13°17W 50 G3
Freeville U.S.A. 42°30N 76°20W 83 D8
Frégate, L. de la Canada 53°15N 74°45W 72 B5
Fregenal de la Sierra Spain 38°10N 6°39W 21 C2
Fregon Australia 26°45S 132°1E 61 E5
Freibourg = Fribourg Switz. 46°49N 7°9E 20 C7
Freiburg Germany 47°59N 7°51E 16 E4
Freire Chile 38°54S 72°38W 96 D2
Freirina Chile 28°30S 71°10W 94 B1
Freising Germany 48°24N 11°45E 16 D6
Freistadt Austria 48°30N 14°30E 16 D8
Fréjus France 43°25N 6°44E 20 E7
Fremantle Australia 32°7S 115°47E 61 F2
Fremont Calif., U.S.A. 37°32N 121°57W 78 H4
Fremont Mich., U.S.A. 43°28N 85°57W 81 D11
Fremont Nebr., U.S.A. 41°26N 96°30W 80 E5
Fremont Ohio, U.S.A. 41°21N 83°7W 81 E12
Fremont → U.S.A. 38°24N 110°42W 76 G8
French Camp U.S.A. 37°53N 121°16W 78 H5
French Cays = Plana Cays Bahamas 22°38N 73°30W 89 B5
French Creek → U.S.A. 41°24N 79°50W 82 E5
French Frigate Shoals U.S.A. 23°45N 166°10W 75 L6
French Guiana ⊠ S. Amer. 4°0N 53°0W 93 C8
French Polynesia ⊠ Pac. Oc. 20°0S 145°0W 65 J13
French Riviera = Côte d'Azur France 43°25N 7°10E 20 E7
Frenchman Cr. → N. Amer. 48°31N 107°10W 76 B10
Frenchman Cr. → U.S.A. 40°14N 100°50W 80 E3
Fresco → Brazil 7°15S 51°30W 93 E8
Freshfield, C. Antarctica 68°25S 151°10E 5 C10
Fresnillo Mexico 23°10N 102°53W 86 C4
Fresno U.S.A. 36°44N 119°47W 78 J7
Fresno Res. U.S.A. 48°36N 109°57W 76 B9
Frew → Australia 20°0S 135°38E 62 C2
Frewsburg U.S.A. 42°3N 79°10W 82 D5
Freycinet △ Australia 42°11S 148°19E 63 G4
Freycinet Pen. Australia 42°10S 148°25E 63 G4
Fria Guinea 10°27N 13°38W 50 F3
Fria, C. Namibia 18°0S 12°0E 56 B1
Friant U.S.A. 36°59N 119°43W 78 J7
Frías Argentina 28°40S 65°5W 94 B2
Fribourg Switz. 46°49N 7°9E 20 C7
Friday Harbor U.S.A. 48°32N 123°1W 78 B3
Friedens U.S.A. 40°3N 78°59W 82 F6
Friedrichshafen Germany 47°39N 9°30E 16 E5
Friendship U.S.A. 42°12N 78°8W 82 D6
Friesland ☐ Neths. 53°5N 5°50E 15 A5
Frigate Seychelles 4°35S 55°56E 53 b
Frio → U.S.A. 28°26N 98°11W 84 G5
Frio, C. Brazil 22°50S 41°50W 90 F6
Friona U.S.A. 34°38N 102°43W 84 D3
Fritch U.S.A. 35°38N 101°36W 84 D4
Frobisher B. Canada 62°30N 66°0W 69 E18
Frobisher Bay = Iqaluit Canada 63°44N 68°31W 69 E18
Frobisher L. Canada 56°20N 108°15W 71 B7
Frohavet Norway 64°0N 9°30E 8 E13
Frome U.K. 51°14N 2°19W 13 F5
Frome → U.K. 50°41N 2°6W 13 G5
Frome, L. Australia 30°45S 139°45E 63 E2
Front Range U.S.A. 40°25N 105°45W 75 G18
Front Royal U.S.A. 38°55N 78°12W 81 F14
Frontenac ⌂ Canada 44°32N 76°30W 83 B8
Frontera Canary Is. 27°47N 17°59W 24 G2
Frontera Mexico 18°32N 92°38W 87 D6
Fronteras Mexico 30°56N 109°31W 86 A3
Frosinone Italy 41°38N 13°19E 22 D5
Frostburg U.S.A. 39°39N 78°56W 81 F14
Frostisen Norway 68°14N 17°10E 8 B17
Frøya Norway 63°43N 8°40E 8 E13
Frunze = Bishkek Kyrgyzstan 42°54N 74°46E 32 C3
Frutal Brazil 20°0S 49°0W 93 H9
Frýdek-Místek Czech Rep. 49°40N 18°20E 17 D10
Fryeburg U.S.A. 44°1N 70°59W 83 B14
Fu Xian = Wafangdian China 39°38N 121°58E 35 E11
Fu Xian China 36°0N 109°20E 34 G5
Fucheng China 37°50N 116°10E 34 F9
Fuchou = Fuzhou China 26°5N 119°16E 33 F12
Fuchū Japan 34°34N 133°14E 31 G6
Fuencaliente Canary Is. 28°28N 17°50W 24 F2
Fuencaliente, Pta. Canary Is. 28°27N 17°51W 24 F2
Fuengirola Spain 36°32N 4°41W 21 D3
Fuentes de Oñoro Spain 40°33N 6°52W 21 B2
Fuerte → Mexico 25°54N 109°22W 86 B3
Fuerte Olimpo Paraguay 21°0S 57°51W 94 A4
Fuerteventura Canary Is. 28°30N 14°0W 24 F6
Fuerteventura ✈ (FUE) Canary Is. 28°24N 13°52W 24 F6
Fufeng China 34°22N 108°0E 34 G5
Fugou China 34°3N 114°25E 34 G8
Fugu China 39°2N 111°3E 34 E6
Fuhai China 47°2N 87°25E 32 B6
Fuḩaymī Iraq 34°16N 42°10E 44 C4
Fuji Japan 35°9N 138°39E 31 G9
Fuji-Hakone-Izu △ Japan 35°15N 138°45E 31 G9
Fuji-San Japan 35°22N 138°44E 31 G9
Fuji-Yoshida Japan 35°30N 138°46E 31 G9
Fujian ☐ China 26°0N 118°0E 33 F12
Fujin China 47°16N 132°1E 33 B15
Fujinomiya Japan 35°10N 138°40E 31 G9
Fujisawa Japan 35°22N 139°29E 31 G9
Fujiyama, Mt. = Fuji-San Japan 35°22N 138°44E 31 G9
Fukagawa Japan 43°43N 142°2E 30 C11
Fukien = Fujian ☐ China 26°0N 118°0E 33 F12
Fukuchiyama Japan 35°19N 135°9E 31 G7
Fukue-Shima Japan 32°40N 128°45E 31 H4
Fukui Japan 36°5N 136°10E 31 F8
Fukui ☐ Japan 36°0N 136°12E 31 G8
Fukuoka Japan 33°39N 130°21E 31 H5
Fukuoka ☐ Japan 33°30N 131°0E 31 H5
Fukushima Japan 37°44N 140°28E 30 F10
Fukushima ☐ Japan 37°30N 140°15E 30 F10
Fukuyama Japan 34°35N 133°20E 31 G6
Fulaga Fiji 19°8S 178°33W 59 a
Fulda Germany 50°32N 9°40E 16 C5
Fulda → Germany 51°25N 9°39E 16 C5
Fulford Harbour Canada 48°47N 123°27W 78 B3
Fullerton Calif., U.S.A. 33°53N 117°56W 79 M9
Fullerton Nebr., U.S.A. 41°22N 97°58W 80 E5
Fulongquan China 44°20N 124°42E 35 B13
Fulton Mo., U.S.A. 38°52N 91°57W 80 F8
Fulton N.Y., U.S.A. 43°19N 76°25W 83 C8
Funabashi Japan 35°45N 140°0E 31 G10
Funafuti = Fongafale Tuvalu 8°31S 179°13E 58 B10
Funchal Madeira 32°38N 16°54W 24 D3
Funchal ✈ (FNC) Madeira 32°42N 16°45W 24 D3
Fundación Colombia 10°31N 74°11W 92 A4
Fundão Portugal 40°8N 7°30W 21 B2
Fundy, B. of Canada 45°0N 66°0W 73 D6
Fundy △ Canada 45°35N 65°10W 73 C6
Funhalouro Mozam. 23°3S 34°25E 57 C5
Funing Hebei, China 39°53N 119°12E 35 E10
Funing Jiangsu, China 33°45N 119°50E 35 H10
Funiu Shan China 33°30N 112°20E 34 H7
Funtua Nigeria 11°30N 7°18E 50 F7
Fuping Hebei, China 38°48N 114°12E 34 E8
Fuping Shaanxi, China 34°42N 109°10E 34 G5
Furano Japan 43°21N 142°23E 30 C11
Furāt, Nahr al → Asia 31°0N 47°25E 44 D5
Fūrg Iran 28°18N 55°13E 45 D7
Furnás Spain 39°3N 1°32E 24 B8
Furnas, Represa de Brazil 20°50S 45°30W 95 A6
Furneaux Group Australia 40°10S 147°50E 63 G4
Furqlus Syria 34°36N 37°8E 46 A6
Fürstenwalde Germany 52°22N 14°3E 16 B8
Fürth Germany 49°28N 10°59E 16 D6
Furukawa Japan 38°34N 140°58E 30 E10
Fury and Hecla Str. Canada 69°56N 84°0W 69 D15
Fusagasugá Colombia 4°21N 74°22W 92 C4
Fushan Shandong, China 37°30N 121°15E 35 F11
Fushan Shanxi, China 35°58N 111°51E 34 G6
Fushun China 41°50N 123°56E 35 D12
Fusong China 42°20N 127°15E 35 C14
Fustic Barbados 13°16N 59°38W 89 g
Futian China 22°32N 114°4E 33 a
Fuxin China 42°5N 121°48E 35 C11
Fuyang China 33°0N 115°48E 34 H8
Fuyang He → China 38°12N 117°0E 34 E9
Fuyong China 22°40N 113°49E 33 a
Fuyu Heilongjiang, China 47°49N 124°27E 33 B13
Fuyu Jilin, China 45°12N 124°43E 35 B13
Fuyun China 47°0N 89°28E 32 B6
Fuzhou = Linchuan China 27°57N 116°15E 33 F12
Fuzhou China 26°5N 119°16E 33 F12
Fyn Denmark 55°20N 10°30E 9 J14
Fyne, L. U.K. 55°59N 5°23W 11 F3

G

Gaalkacyo Somali Rep. 6°30N 47°30E 47 F4
Gabba Australia 9°45S 142°38E 62 a
Gabela Angola 11°0S 14°24E 52 G2
Gabès Tunisia 33°53N 10°2E 51 B8
Gabès, G. de Tunisia 34°0N 10°30E 51 B8
Gabon ■ Africa 0°10S 10°0E 52 E2
Gaborone Botswana 24°45S 25°57E 56 C4
Gabriels U.S.A. 44°26N 74°12W 83 B10
Gābrīk Iran 25°44N 58°28E 45 E8
Gabrovo Bulgaria 42°52N 25°19E 23 C11
Gāch Sār Iran 36°7N 51°19E 45 B6
Gachsārān Iran 30°15N 50°45E 45 D6
Gadag India 15°30N 75°45E 40 M9
Gadap Pakistan 25°5N 67°28E 42 G2
Gadarwara India 22°50N 78°50E 43 H8
Gadhada India 22°0N 71°35E 42 J4
Gadra Pakistan 25°40N 70°38E 42 G4
Gadsden U.S.A. 34°1N 86°1W 85 D11
Gadwal India 16°10N 77°50E 40 L10
Gaffney U.S.A. 35°5N 81°39W 85 D14
Gafsa Tunisia 34°24N 8°43E 51 B7
Gagaria India 25°43N 70°46E 42 G4
Găgăuzia ☐ Moldova 46°10N 28°40E 17 E15
Gagnoa Ivory C. 6°56N 5°16W 50 G4
Gagnon Canada 51°50N 68°5W 73 B6
Gagnon, L. Canada 62°3N 110°27W 71 A6
Gahini Rwanda 1°50S 30°30E 54 C3
Gahmar India 25°27N 83°49E 43 G10
Gai Xian = Gaizhou China 40°22N 122°20E 35 D12
Gaidouronisi Greece 34°53N 25°41E 25 E7
Gail U.S.A. 32°46N 101°27W 84 E4
Gaillimh = Galway Ireland 53°17N 9°3W 10 C2
Gaines U.S.A. 41°46N 77°35W 82 E7
Gainesville Fla., U.S.A. 29°40N 82°20W 85 G13
Gainesville Ga., U.S.A. 34°18N 83°50W 85 D13
Gainesville Mo., U.S.A. 36°36N 92°26W 80 G7
Gainesville Tex., U.S.A. 33°38N 97°8W 84 E6
Gainsborough U.K. 53°24N 0°46W 12 D7
Gairdner, L. Australia 31°30S 136°0E 63 E2
Gairloch U.K. 57°43N 5°41W 11 D3
Gairloch, L. U.K. 57°43N 5°45W 11 D3
Gaizhou China 40°22N 122°20E 35 D12
Gaj → Pakistan 26°26N 67°21E 42 F2
Gakuch Pakistan 36°7N 73°45E 43 A5
Galán, Cerro Argentina 25°55S 66°52W 94 B2
Galana → Kenya 3°9S 40°8E 54 C5
Galápagos = Colón, Arch. de Ecuador 0°0 91°0W 90 D1
Galapagos Fracture Zone Pac. Oc. 3°0N 110°0W 65 G17
Galapagos Rise Pac. Oc. 15°0S 95°0W 65 J18
Galashiels U.K. 55°37N 2°49W 11 F6
Galateia Cyprus 35°25N 34°4E 25 D13
Galaţi Romania 45°27N 28°2E 17 F15
Galatina Italy 40°10N 18°10E 23 D8
Galax U.S.A. 36°40N 80°56W 81 G13
Galbīn Govī Mongolia 43°0N 107°0E 34 C4
Galcaio = Gaalkacyo Somali Rep. 6°30N 47°30E 47 F4
Galdhøpiggen Norway 61°38N 8°18E 8 F13
Galeana Chihuahua, Mexico 30°7N 107°38W 86 A3
Galeana Nuevo León, Mexico 24°50N 100°4W 86 A3
Galela Indonesia 1°50N 127°49E 37 D7
Galeota Pt. Trin. & Tob. 10°8N 60°59W 93 K16
Galera Pt. Trin. & Tob. 10°49N 60°54W 93 K16
Galesburg U.S.A. 40°57N 90°22W 80 E8
Galestan △ Iran 37°30N 56°0E 45 B8
Galeton U.S.A. 41°44N 77°39W 82 E7
Galich Russia 58°22N 42°24E 18 C7
Galicia ☐ Spain 42°43N 7°45W 21 A2
Galilee = Hagalil Israel 32°53N 35°18E 46 C4
Galilee, L. Australia 22°20S 145°50E 62 C4
Galilee, Sea of = Yam Kinneret Israel 32°45N 35°35E 46 C4
Galina Pt. Jamaica 18°24N 76°58W 88 a
Galinoporni Cyprus 35°31N 34°18E 25 D13
Galion U.S.A. 40°44N 82°47W 82 F2
Galiuro Mts. U.S.A. 32°30N 110°20W 77 K8
Galiwinku Australia 12°2S 135°34E 62 A2
Gallan Hd. U.K. 58°15N 7°2W 11 C1
Gallatin U.S.A. 36°24N 86°27W 85 C11
Galle Sri Lanka 6°5N 80°10E 40 R12
Gállego → Spain 41°39N 0°51W 21 B5
Gallegos → Argentina 51°35S 69°0W 96 G3
Galley Hd. Ireland 51°32N 8°55W 10 E3
Gallinas, Pta. Colombia 12°28N 71°40W 92 A4
Gallipoli = Gelibolu Turkey 40°28N 26°43E 23 D12
Gallipoli Italy 40°3N 17°58E 23 D8
Gallipolis U.S.A. 38°49N 82°12W 81 F12
Gällivare Sweden 67°9N 20°40E 8 C19
Galloo I. U.S.A. 43°55N 76°25W 83 C8
Galloway U.K. 55°1N 4°29W 11 F4
Galloway, Mull of U.K. 54°39N 4°52W 11 G4
Galloway ⌂ U.K. 55°3N 4°20W 11 F4
Gallup U.S.A. 35°32N 108°45W 77 J9
Galoya Sri Lanka 8°10N 80°55E 40 Q12
Galt U.S.A. 38°15N 121°18W 78 G5
Galty Mts. Ireland 52°22N 8°10W 10 D3
Galtymore Ireland 52°21N 8°11W 10 D3
Galugāh Iran 36°43N 53°48E 45 B7
Galva U.S.A. 41°10N 90°3W 80 E8
Galveston U.S.A. 29°18N 94°48W 84 G7
Galveston B. U.S.A. 29°36N 94°50W 84 G7
Gálvez Argentina 32°0S 61°14W 94 C3
Galway Ireland 53°17N 9°3W 10 C2
Galway ☐ Ireland 53°22N 9°1W 10 C2
Galway B. Ireland 53°13N 9°10W 10 C2
Gam → Vietnam 21°55N 105°12E 38 B5
Gamagōri Japan 34°50N 137°14E 31 G8
Gambat Pakistan 27°17N 68°26E 42 F3
Gambhir → India 26°58N 77°27E 42 F6
Gambia ■ W. Afr. 13°25N 16°0W 50 F2
Gambia → W. Afr. 13°28N 16°34W 50 F2
Gambier U.S.A. 40°22N 82°23W 82 F2
Gambier, C. Australia 11°56S 130°57E 60 B5
Gambier, Îs. French Polynesia 23°8S 134°58W 65 K14
Gambier Is. Australia 35°3S 136°30E 63 F2
Gambo Canada 48°47N 54°13W 73 C9
Gamboli Pakistan 29°53N 68°24E 42 E3
Gamboma Congo 1°55S 15°52E 52 E3
Gamka → S. Africa 33°18S 21°39E 56 E3
Gamkab → Namibia 28°4S 17°54E 56 D2
Gamlakarleby = Kokkola Finland 63°50N 23°8E 8 E20
Gammon → Canada 51°24N 95°44W 71 C9
Gammon Ranges △ Australia 30°38S 139°8E 63 E2
Gamtoos → S. Africa 33°58S 25°1E 56 E4
Gan Jiang → China 29°15N 116°0E 33 F12
Ganado U.S.A. 35°43N 109°33W 77 J9
Gananoque Canada 44°20N 76°10W 83 B8
Ganāveh Iran 29°35N 50°35E 45 D6
Gäncä Azerbaijan 40°45N 46°20E 19 F8
Gancheng China 18°51N 108°37E 38 C7
Gand = Gent Belgium 51°2N 3°42E 15 C3
Ganda Angola 13°3S 14°35E 53 G2
Gandajika Dem. Rep. of the Congo 6°46S 23°58E 52 F4
Gandak → India 25°39N 85°13E 43 G11
Gandava Pakistan 28°32N 67°32E 42 E2
Gander Canada 48°58N 54°35W 73 C9
Gander L. Canada 48°58N 54°35W 73 C9
Ganderowe Falls Zimbabwe 17°20S 29°10E 55 F2
Gandhi Sagar India 24°40N 75°40E 42 G6
Gandhinagar India 23°15N 72°45E 42 H5
Gandia Spain 38°58N 0°9W 21 C5
Gando, Pta. Canary Is. 27°55N 15°22W 24 G4
Ganedidalem = Gani Indonesia 0°48S 128°14E 37 E7
Ganga → India 23°20N 90°30E 43 H14
Ganga Sagar India 21°38N 88°5E 43 J13
Gangan → India 28°38N 78°58E 43 E8
Ganganagar India 29°56N 73°56E 42 E5
Gangapur India 26°32N 76°49E 42 F7
Gangaw Burma 22°5N 94°5E 41 H19
Gangdisê Shan China 31°20N 81°0E 43 D9
Ganges = Ganga → India 23°20N 90°30E 43 H14
Ganges Canada 48°51N 123°31W 70 D4
Ganges, Mouths of the India 21°30N 90°0E 43 J14
Ganggyeong S. Korea 36°10N 127°0E 35 F14
Gangneung S. Korea 37°45N 128°54E 35 F15
Gangoh India 29°46N 77°18E 42 E7
Gangotri India 30°50N 79°10E 43 D8
Gangotri △ India 30°50N 79°10E 43 D8
Gangseong S. Korea 38°24N 128°30E 35 E15
Gangtok India 27°20N 88°37E 41 F16
Gangu China 34°40N 105°15E 34 G3
Gangyao China 44°12N 126°37E 35 B14
Gani Indonesia 0°48S 128°14E 37 E7
Ganj India 27°45N 78°57E 43 F8
Gannett Peak U.S.A. 43°11N 109°39W 76 E9
Ganquan China 36°20N 109°20E 34 F5
Gansu ☐ China 36°0N 104°0E 34 G3
Ganta Liberia 7°15N 8°59W 50 G4
Gantheaume, C. Australia 36°4S 137°32E 63 F2
Gantheaume B. Australia 27°40S 114°10E 61 E1
Gantsevichi = Hantsavichy Belarus 52°49N 26°30E 17 B14
Ganyem = Genyem Indonesia 2°46S 140°12E 37 E10
Ganyu China 34°50N 119°8E 35 G10
Ganzhou China 25°51N 114°56E 33 F11
Gao Mali 16°15N 0°5W 50 E5
Gaobeidian China 39°19N 115°51E 34 E8
Gaocheng China 38°2N 114°49E 34 E8
Gaomi China 36°20N 119°42E 35 F10
Gaoping China 35°45N 112°55E 34 G7
Gaotang China 36°50N 116°15E 34 F9
Gaoua Burkina Faso 10°20N 3°8W 50 F5
Gaoual Guinea 11°45N 13°25W 50 F3
Gaoxiong = Kaohsiung Taiwan 22°35N 120°16E 33 G13
Gaoyang China 38°40N 115°45E 34 E8
Gaoyou Hu China 32°45N 119°20E 35 H10
Gaoyuan China 37°8N 117°58E 35 F9
Gap France 44°33N 6°5E 20 D7
Gapat → India 24°30N 82°28E 43 G10
Gapuwiyak Australia 12°25S 135°43E 62 A2
Gar China 32°10N 79°58E 32 E4
Gara, L. Ireland 53°57N 8°26W 10 C3
Garabogazköl Aylagy Turkmenistan 41°0N 53°30E 19 F9
Garachico Canary Is. 28°22N 16°46W 24 F3
Garachiné Panama 8°0N 78°12W 88 E4
Garafia Canary Is. 28°48N 17°57W 24 F2
Garagum Turkmenistan 39°30N 60°0E 45 B8
Garah Australia 29°5S 149°38E 63 D4
Garajonay Canary Is. 28°7N 17°14W 24 F2
Garamba △ Dem. Rep. of the Congo 4°10N 29°40E 54 B2
Garanhuns Brazil 8°50S 36°30W 93 E11
Garautha India 25°34N 79°18E 43 G8
Garawa ❂ Australia 16°43S 136°51E 62 B2
Garba Tula Kenya 0°30N 38°32E 54 B4
Garberville U.S.A. 40°6N 123°48W 76 F2
Garbiyang India 30°8N 80°54E 43 D9
Gard → France 43°51N 4°37E 20 E6
Garda, L. di Italy 45°40N 10°41E 22 B4
Garde L. Canada 62°50N 106°13W 71 A7
Garden City Ga., U.S.A. 32°6N 81°9W 85 E14
Garden City Kans., U.S.A. 37°58N 100°53W 80 G3
Garden City Tex., U.S.A. 31°52N 101°29W 84 F4
Garden Grove U.S.A. 33°47N 117°55W 79 M9
Gardēz Afghan. 33°37N 69°9E 42 C3
Gardiner Maine, U.S.A. 44°14N 69°47W 81 C19
Gardiner Mont., U.S.A. 45°2N 110°22W 76 D8
Gardiners I. U.S.A. 41°6N 72°6W 83 E12
Gardner U.S.A. 42°34N 71°59W 83 D13
Gardner Canal Canada 53°27N 128°8W 70 C3
Gardner Pinnacles U.S.A. 25°0N 167°55W 75 L6
Gardnerville U.S.A. 38°56N 119°45W 78 G7
Gardo = Qardho Somali Rep. 9°30N 49°6E 47 F4
Garey U.S.A. 34°53N 120°19W 79 L6
Garfield U.S.A. 47°1N 117°9W 76 C5
Garforth U.K. 53°47N 1°24W 12 D6
Gargantua, C. Canada 47°36N 85°2W 81 B11
Gargett Australia 21°9S 148°46E 62 b
Garibaldi ⌂ Canada 49°50N 122°40W 70 D4
Gariep, L. S. Africa 30°40S 25°40E 56 E4
Garies S. Africa 30°32S 17°59E 56 E2
Garig Gunak Barlu △ Australia 11°26S 131°58E 60 B5
Garigliano → Italy 41°13N 13°45E 22 D5
Garissa Kenya 0°25S 39°40E 54 C4
Garland Tex., U.S.A. 32°54N 96°38W 84 E6
Garland Utah, U.S.A. 41°45N 112°10W 76 F7
Garmāb Iran 35°25N 56°45E 45 C8
Garmisch-Partenkirchen Germany 47°30N 11°6E 16 E6
Garmsār Iran 35°20N 52°25E 45 C7
Garner U.S.A. 43°6N 93°36W 80 D7
Garnett U.S.A. 38°17N 95°14W 80 F6
Garo Hills India 25°30N 90°30E 43 G14
Garoe = Garoowe Somali Rep. 8°25N 48°33E 47 F4
Garonne → France 45°2N 0°36W 20 D3
Garoowe Somali Rep. 8°25N 48°33E 47 F4
Garot India 24°19N 75°41E 42 G6
Garoua Cameroon 9°19N 13°21E 51 G8
Garrauli India 25°5N 79°22E 43 G8
Garrison Mont., U.S.A. 46°31N 112°49W 76 C7
Garrison N. Dak., U.S.A. 47°40N 101°25W 80 B3
Garrison Res. = Sakakawea, L. U.S.A. 47°30N 101°25W 80 B3
Garron Pt. U.K. 55°3N 5°59W 10 A6
Garry → U.K. 56°44N 3°47W 11 E5
Garry, L. Canada 65°58N 100°18W 68 D11
Garrygala Turkmenistan 38°31N 56°29E 45 B8
Garsen Kenya 2°20S 40°5E 54 C5
Garson L. Canada 56°19N 110°2W 71 B6
Garstang U.K. 53°55N 2°46W 12 D5
Garu India 23°40N 84°14E 43 H11
Garub Namibia 26°37S 16°0E 56 D2
Garut Indonesia 7°14S 107°53E 37 G12
Garvie Mts. N.Z. 45°30S 168°50E 59 F2
Garwa = Garoua Cameroon 9°19N 13°21E 51 G8
Garwa India 24°11N 83°47E 43 G10
Gary U.S.A. 41°36N 87°20W 80 E10
Garzê China 31°38N 100°1E 32 E9
Garzón Colombia 2°10N 75°40W 92 C3
Gas-San Japan 38°32N 140°1E 30 E10
Gasan Kuli = Esenguly Turkmenistan 37°37N 53°59E 28 F6
Gascogne France 43°45N 0°20E 20 E4
Gascogne, G. de Europe 44°0N 2°0W 20 D2
Gascony = Gascogne France 43°45N 0°20E 20 E4
Gascoyne → Australia 24°52S 113°37E 61 D1
Gascoyne Junction Australia 25°2S 115°17E 61 E2
Gashaka Nigeria 7°20N 11°29E 51 G8
Gasherbrum Pakistan 35°40N 76°40E 43 B7
Gashua Nigeria 12°54N 11°0E 51 F8
Gasparillo Trin. & Tob. 10°18N 61°26W 93 K15
Gaspé Canada 48°52N 64°30W 73 C7
Gaspé, C. de Canada 48°48N 64°7W 73 C7
Gaspé Pen. = Gaspésie, Pén. de la Canada 48°45N 65°40W 73 C6
Gaspésie, Pén. de la Canada 48°45N 65°40W 73 C6
Gaspésie ⌂ Canada 48°55N 66°10W 73 C6
Gasteiz = Vitoria-Gasteiz Spain 42°50N 2°41W 21 A4
Gastonia U.S.A. 35°16N 81°11W 85 D14
Gastre Argentina 42°20S 69°15W 96 E3

Gata, C. *Cyprus* 34°34N 33°2E **25** E12
Gata, C. de *Spain* 36°41N 2°13W **21** D4
Gata, Sierra de *Spain* 40°20N 6°45W **21** B2
Gataga → *Canada* 58°35N 126°59W **70** B3
Gatchina *Russia* 59°35N 30°9E **9** G24
Gatehouse of Fleet *U.K.* 54°53N 4°12W **11** G4
Gates *U.S.A.* 43°9N 77°42W **82** C7
Gateshead I. *Canada* 70°36N 100°26W **68** C11
Gateshead *U.K.* 54°57N 1°35W **12** C6
Gatesville *U.S.A.* 31°26N 97°45W **84** F6
Gateway △ *U.S.A.* 40°38N 73°51W **83** F11
Gaths *Zimbabwe* 20°2S 30°32E **55** G3
Gatineau *Canada* 45°29N 75°39W **83** A9
Gatineau → *Canada* 45°27N 75°42W **72** C4
Gatineau △ *Canada* 45°40N 76°0W **72** C4
Gatton *Australia* 27°32S 152°17E **63** D5
Gatún, L. *Panama* 9°7N 79°56W **88** E4
Gatwick, London ✈ (LGW)
   U.K. 51°10N 0°11W **13** F7
Gatyana *S. Africa* 32°16S 28°31E **57** E4
Gau *Fiji* 18°2S 179°18E **59** a
Gauer L. *Canada* 57°0N 97°50W **71** B9
Gauhati = Guwahati
   India 26°10N 91°45E **41** F17
Gauja → *Latvia* 57°10N 24°16E **9** H21
Gaujas → *Latvia* 57°10N 24°50E **9** H21
Gaula → *Norway* 63°21N 10°14E **8** E14
Gaustatoppen *Norway* 59°48N 8°40E **9** G13
Gauteng □ *S. Africa* 26°0S 28°0E **57** D4
Gāv Koshī *Iran* 28°38N 57°12E **45** D8
Gāvakān *Iran* 29°37N 53°10E **45** D7
Gavāter *Iran* 25°10N 61°31E **45** E9
Gāvbandī *Iran* 27°12N 53°4E **45** E7
Gavdopoula *Greece* 34°56N 24°0E **25** E6
Gavdos *Greece* 34°50N 24°5E **25** E6
Gaviota *U.S.A.* 34°29N 120°13W **79** L6
Gävle *Sweden* 60°40N 17°9E **8** F17
Gawachab *Namibia* 27°4S 17°55E **56** D2
Gawilgarh Hills *India* 21°15N 76°45E **40** J10
Gawler *Australia* 34°30S 138°42E **63** E2
Gawler Ranges
   Australia 32°30S 135°45E **63** E2
Gaxun Nur *China* 42°22N 100°30E **32** C9
Gay *Russia* 51°27N 58°27E **18** D10
Gaya *India* 24°47N 85°4E **43** G11
Gaya *Niger* 11°52N 3°28E **50** F6
Gaylord *U.S.A.* 45°2N 84°41W **81** C11
Gayndah *Australia* 25°35S 151°32E **63** D5
Gaysin = Haysyn
   Ukraine 48°57N 29°25E **17** D15
Gayvoron = Hayvoron
   Ukraine 48°22N 29°52E **17** D15
Gaza *Gaza Strip* 31°30N 34°28E **46** D3
Gaza □ *Mozam.* 23°10S 32°45E **57** C5
Gaza Strip ■ *Asia* 31°29N 34°25E **46** D3
Gazanjyk = Bereket
   Turkmenistan 39°16N 55°32E **45** B7
Gāzbor *Iran* 28°5N 58°51E **45** D8
Gazi *Dem. Rep. of the Congo* 1°3N 24°30E **54** B1
Gaziantep *Turkey* 37°6N 37°23E **44** B3
Gazimağusa = Famagusta
   Cyprus 35°8N 33°55E **25** D12
Gbadolite
   Dem. Rep. of the Congo 4°17N 21°1E **52** G4
Gbarnga *Liberia* 7°19N 9°13W **50** G4
Gcoverega *Botswana* 19°8S 24°18E **56** B3
Gcuwa *S. Africa* 32°20S 28°11E **57** E4
Gdańsk *Poland* 54°22N 18°40E **17** A10
Gdańsk, Zatoka
   Poland 54°30N 19°20E **17** A10
Gdov *Russia* 58°48N 27°55E **9** G22
Gdynia *Poland* 54°35N 18°33E **17** A10
Gebe *Indonesia* 0°5N 129°25E **37** D7
Gebze *Turkey* 40°47N 29°25E **23** D13
Gedaref *Sudan* 14°2N 35°28E **51** F13
Gede, Tanjung *Indonesia* 6°46S 105°12E **37** G11
Gediz → *Turkey* 38°35N 26°48E **23** E12
Gedser *Denmark* 54°35N 11°55E **9** J14
Gedung, Pulau *Malaysia* 5°17N 100°23E **39** c
Geegully Cr. →
   Australia 18°32S 123°41E **60** C3
Geel *Belgium* 51°10N 4°59E **15** C4
Geelong *Australia* 38°10S 144°22E **63** F3
Geelvink B. = Cenderwasih, Teluk
   Indonesia 3°0S 135°20E **37** E9
Geelvink Chan. *Australia* 28°30S 114°0E **61** E1
Geesthacht *Germany* 53°26N 10°22E **16** B6
Geidam *Nigeria* 12°57N 11°57E **51** F8
Geikie → *Canada* 57°45N 103°52W **71** B8
Geikie Gorge △ *Australia* 18°3S 125°41E **60** C4
Geistown *U.S.A.* 40°18N 78°52W **82** F6
Geita *Tanzania* 2°48S 32°12E **54** C3
Gejiu *China* 23°20N 103°10E **32** G9
Gel, Meydān-e *Iran* 29°4N 54°50E **45** D7
Gela *Italy* 37°4N 14°15E **22** F6
Gelang Patah *Malaysia* 1°27N 103°35E **39** d
Gelderland □ *Neths.* 52°5N 6°10E **15** B6
Geldrop *Neths.* 51°25N 5°32E **15** C5
Geleen *Neths.* 50°57N 5°49E **15** D5
Gelib = Jilib *Somali Rep.* 0°29N 42°46E **47** G3
Gelibolu *Turkey* 40°28N 26°43E **23** D12
Gelsenkirchen *Germany* 51°32N 7°6E **16** C4
Gelugur *Malaysia* 5°22N 100°18E **39** c
Gemas *Malaysia* 2°37N 102°36E **39** L4
Gembloux *Belgium* 50°34N 4°43E **15** D4
Gemena
   Dem. Rep. of the Congo 3°13N 19°48E **52** D3
Gemerek *Turkey* 39°15N 36°10E **44** B3
Gemlik *Turkey* 40°26N 29°9E **23** D13
Gemsbok △ *Botswana* 25°5S 21°1E **56** D3
Genadi *Greece* 36°2N 27°56E **25** C9
Genale → *Ethiopia* 6°2N 39°1E **47** F2
General Acha *Argentina* 37°20S 64°38W **94** D3
General Alvear *B. Aires,
   Argentina* 36°0S 60°0W **94** D4
General Alvear *Mendoza,
   Argentina* 35°0S 67°40W **94** D2
General Artigas
   Paraguay 26°52S 56°16W **94** B4

General Belgrano
   Argentina 36°35S 58°47W **94** D4
General Bernardo O'Higgins
   Antarctica 63°0S 58°3W **5** C18
General Cabrera
   Argentina 32°53S 63°52W **94** C3
General Cepeda *Mexico* 25°21N 101°22W **86** B4
General Guido *Argentina* 36°40S 57°50W **94** D4
General Juan Madariaga
   Argentina 37°0S 57°0W **94** D4
General La Madrid
   Argentina 37°17S 61°20W **94** D3
General MacArthur
   Phil. 11°18N 125°28E **37** B7
General Martín Miguel de Güemes
   Argentina 24°50S 65°0W **94** A3
General Pico *Argentina* 35°45S 63°50W **94** D3
General Pinedo
   Argentina 27°15S 61°20W **94** B3
General Pinto *Argentina* 34°45S 61°50W **94** C3
General Roca *Argentina* 39°2S 67°35W **96** D3
General Santos *Phil.* 6°5N 125°14E **37** C7
General Treviño *Mexico* 26°14N 99°29W **87** B5
General Trías *Mexico* 28°21N 106°22W **86** B3
General Viamonte
   Argentina 35°1S 61°3W **94** D3
General Villegas *Argentina* 35°5S 63°0W **94** D3
Genesee *Idaho, U.S.A.* 46°33N 116°56W **76** C5
Genesee *Pa., U.S.A.* 41°59N 77°54W **82** E7
Genesee → *U.S.A.* 43°16N 77°36W **82** C7
Geneseo *Ill., U.S.A.* 41°27N 90°9W **80** E8
Geneseo *N.Y., U.S.A.* 42°48N 77°49W **82** D7
Geneva = Genève *Switz.* 46°12N 6°9E **20** C7
Geneva *Ala., U.S.A.* 31°2N 85°52W **85** F12
Geneva *N.Y., U.S.A.* 42°52N 76°59W **82** D8
Geneva *Nebr., U.S.A.* 40°32N 97°36W **80** E5
Geneva *Ohio, U.S.A.* 41°48N 80°57W **82** E4
Geneva, L. = Léman, L.
   Europe 46°26N 6°30E **20** C7
Genève *Switz.* 46°12N 6°9E **20** C7
Genil → *Spain* 37°42N 5°19W **21** D3
Genk *Belgium* 50°58N 5°32E **15** D5
Gennargentu, Mti. del
   Italy 40°1N 9°19E **22** D3
Genoa = Génova *Italy* 44°25N 8°57E **20** D8
Genoa *Australia* 37°29S 149°35E **63** F4
Genoa *N.Y., U.S.A.* 42°40N 76°32W **83** D8
Genoa *Nebr., U.S.A.* 41°27N 97°44W **80** E5
Genoa *Nev., U.S.A.* 39°2N 119°50W **78** F7
Génova *Italy* 44°25N 8°57E **20** D8
Génova, G. di *Italy* 44°0N 9°0E **22** C3
Genriyetty, Ostrov
   Russia 77°6N 156°30E **29** B16
Gent *Belgium* 51°2N 3°42E **15** C3
Genteng *Jawa Barat,
   Indonesia* 7°22S 106°24E **37** G12
Genteng *Jawa Timur,
   Indonesia* 8°22S 114°9E **37** J17
Genyem *Indonesia* 2°46S 140°12E **37** E10
Geochang *S. Korea* 35°41N 127°55E **35** G14
Geographe B. *Australia* 33°30S 115°15E **61** F2
Geographe Chan.
   Australia 24°30S 113°0E **61** D1
Georga, Zemlya *Russia* 80°30N 49°0E **28** A5
George *S. Africa* 33°58S 22°29E **56** E3
George → *Canada* 58°49N 66°10W **73** A6
George, L. *N.S.W.,
   Australia* 35°10S 149°25E **63** F4
George, L. *S. Austral.,
   Australia* 37°25S 140°0E **63** F3
George, L. *W. Austral.,
   Australia* 22°45S 123°40E **60** D3
George, L. *Uganda* 0°5N 30°10E **54** B3
George, L. *Fla., U.S.A.* 29°17N 81°36W **85** G14
George, L. *N.Y., U.S.A.* 43°37N 73°33W **83** C11
George Gill Ra.
   Australia 24°22S 131°45E **60** D5
George Pt. *Australia* 20°6S 148°36E **62** b
George River = Kangiqsualujjuaq
   Canada 58°30N 65°59W **69** F18
George Sound *N.Z.* 44°52S 167°25E **59** F1
George Town *Australia* 41°6S 146°49E **63** G4
George Town *Bahamas* 23°33N 75°47W **88** B4
George Town *Cayman Is.* 19°20N 81°24W **88** c
George Town *Malaysia* 5°25N 100°20E **39** c
George V Land *Antarctica* 69°0S 148°0E **5** C10
George VI Sound
   Antarctica 71°0S 68°0W **5** D17
George West *U.S.A.* 28°20N 98°7W **84** G5
Georgetown = Janjanbureh
   Gambia 13°14N 14°47W **50** F3
Georgetown *Australia* 18°17S 143°33E **62** B3
Georgetown *Ont.,
   Canada* 43°40N 79°56W **82** C5
Georgetown *P.E.I.,
   Canada* 46°13N 62°24W **73** C7
Georgetown *Guyana* 6°50N 58°12W **92** B7
Georgetown *Calif.,
   U.S.A.* 38°54N 120°50W **78** G6
Georgetown *Colo.,
   U.S.A.* 39°42N 105°42W **76** G11
Georgetown *Ky., U.S.A.* 38°13N 84°33W **81** F11
Georgetown *N.Y.,
   U.S.A.* 42°46N 75°44W **83** D9
Georgetown *Ohio,
   U.S.A.* 38°52N 83°54W **81** F12
Georgetown *S.C.,
   U.S.A.* 33°23N 79°17W **85** E15
Georgetown *Tex., U.S.A.* 30°38N 97°41W **84** F6
Georgia □ *U.S.A.* 32°50N 83°15W **85** E13
Georgia ■ *Asia* 42°0N 43°0E **19** F7
Georgia, Str. of *N. Amer.* 49°25N 124°0W **78** A3
Georgia Basin *S. Ocean* 50°45S 35°30W **5** B1
Georgian B. *Canada* 45°15N 81°0W **82** A4
Georgian Bay Islands △
   Canada 44°53N 79°52W **82** B5
Georgievka *Kazakhstan* 49°19N 84°34E **28** E9
Georgina → *Australia* 23°30S 139°47E **62** C2
Georgina I. *Canada* 44°22N 79°17W **82** B5
Georgioupoli *Greece* 35°20N 24°15E **25** D6

Georgiyevsk *Russia* 44°12N 43°28E **19** F7
Gera *Germany* 50°53N 12°4E **16** C7
Geraardsbergen *Belgium* 50°45N 3°53E **15** D3
Geral, Serra *Brazil* 26°25S 50°0W **95** B6
Geral de Goiás, Serra
   Brazil 12°0S 46°0W **93** F9
Geraldine *U.S.A.* 47°36N 110°16W **76** C8
Geraldton *Australia* 28°48S 114°32E **61** E1
Geraldton *Canada* 49°44N 86°59W **72** C2
Gerdine, Mt. *U.S.A.* 61°35N 152°27W **74** C9
Gereshk *Afghan.* 31°47N 64°35E **40** D4
Gerik *Malaysia* 5°50N 101°15E **39** K3
Gering *U.S.A.* 41°50N 103°40W **80** E2
Gerlach *U.S.A.* 40°39N 119°21W **76** F4
German Bight = Deutsche Bucht
   Germany 54°15N 8°0E **16** A5
Germansen Landing
   Canada 55°43N 124°40W **70** B4
Germantown *U.S.A.* 35°5N 89°49W **85** D10
Germany ■ *Europe* 51°0N 10°0E **16** C6
Germí *Iran* 39°1N 48°3E **45** B6
Germiston *S. Africa* 26°13S 28°10E **57** D4
Gernika-Lumo *Spain* 43°19N 2°40W **21** A4
Gero *Japan* 35°48N 137°14E **31** G8
Gerokgak *Indonesia* 8°11S 114°27E **37** J17
Gerona = Girona *Spain* 41°58N 2°46E **21** B7
Geropotamos → *Greece* 35°3N 24°50E **25** D6
Gerrard *Canada* 50°30N 117°17W **70** C5
Gertak Sanggul *Malaysia* 5°17N 100°12E **39** c
Gertak Sanggul, Tanjung
   Malaysia 5°16N 100°11E **39** c
Gerung *Indonesia* 8°43S 116°7E **37** K19
Geser *Indonesia* 3°50S 130°54E **37** E8
Getafe *Spain* 40°18N 3°43W **21** B4
Gettysburg *Pa., U.S.A.* 39°50N 77°14W **81** F15
Gettysburg *S. Dak., U.S.A.* 45°1N 99°57W **80** C4
Getxo *Spain* 43°21N 2°59W **21** A4
Getz Ice Shelf *Antarctica* 75°0S 130°0W **5** D14
Geyser *U.S.A.* 47°16N 110°30W **76** C8
Geyserville *U.S.A.* 38°42N 122°54W **78** G4
Ghadāf, W. al → *Iraq* 32°56N 43°30E **44** C4
Ghadāmis *Libya* 30°11N 9°29E **51** B8
Ghaggar → *India* 29°30N 74°53E **42** E6
Ghaghara → *India* 25°45N 84°40E **43** G11
Ghaghat → *Bangla.* 25°19N 89°38E **43** G13
Ghagra *India* 23°17N 84°33E **43** H11
Ghagra → *India* 27°29N 81°9E **43** F9
Ghallamane *Mauritania* 23°15N 10°0W **50** D4
Ghana ■ *W. Afr.* 8°0N 1°0W **50** G5
Ghansor *India* 22°39N 80°1E **43** H9
Ghanzi *Botswana* 21°50S 21°34E **56** C3
Gharb Bahr el Ghazāl □
   Sudan 7°30N 27°30E **48** F6
Ghardaïa *Algeria* 32°20N 3°37E **50** B6
Gharm *Tajikistan* 39°0N 70°20E **28** F8
Gharyān *Libya* 32°10N 13°0E **51** B8
Ghāt *Libya* 24°59N 10°11E **51** D8
Ghatal *India* 22°40N 87°46E **43** H12
Ghatampur *India* 26°8N 80°13E **43** F9
Ghats, Eastern *India* 14°0N 78°50E **40** N11
Ghats, Western *India* 14°0N 75°0E **40** N9
Ghatsila *India* 22°36N 86°29E **43** H12
Ghaṭṭī *Si. Arabia* 31°16N 37°31E **44** D3
Ghawdex = Gozo *Malta* 36°3N 14°15E **25** C1
Ghazal, Bahr el → *Chad* 13°0N 15°47E **51** F9
Ghazāl, Bahr el →
   Sudan 9°31N 30°25E **51** G12
Ghaziabad *India* 28°42N 77°26E **42** E7
Ghazipur *India* 25°38N 83°35E **43** G10
Ghaznī *Afghan.* 33°30N 68°28E **42** C3
Ghaznī □ *Afghan.* 32°10N 68°20E **40** C6
Ghent = Gent *Belgium* 51°2N 3°42E **15** C3
Gheorghe Gheorghiu-Dej = Onești
   Romania 46°17N 26°47E **17** E14
Ghīnah, Wādī al →
   Si. Arabia 30°27N 38°14E **44** D3
Ghizar → *Pakistan* 36°15N 73°43E **43** A5
Ghotaru *India* 27°20N 70°1E **42** F4
Ghotki *Pakistan* 28°5N 69°21E **42** E3
Ghowr □ *Afghan.* 34°0N 64°20E **40** C4
Ghughri *India* 22°39N 80°41E **43** H9
Ghugus *India* 19°58N 79°12E **40** K11
Ghulam Mohammad Barrage
   Pakistan 25°30N 68°20E **42** G3
Ghūrīān *Afghan.* 34°17N 61°25E **40** B2
Gia Dinh *Vietnam* 10°49N 106°42E **39** G6
Gia Lai = Plei Ku
   Vietnam 13°57N 108°0E **38** F7
Gia Nghia *Vietnam* 11°58N 107°42E **39** G6
Gia Ngoc *Vietnam* 14°50N 108°58E **38** E7
Gia Vuc *Vietnam* 14°42N 108°34E **38** E7
Giamama = Jamaame
   Somali Rep. 0°4N 42°44E **47** G3
Gianitsa *Greece* 40°46N 22°24E **23** D10
Giant Forest *U.S.A.* 36°36N 118°43W **78** J8
Giant Sequoia △
   U.S.A. 36°10N 118°35W **78** K8
Giants Causeway *U.K.* 55°16N 6°29W **10** A5
Gianyar *Indonesia* 8°32S 115°20E **37** K18
Giarabub = Al Jaghbūb
   Libya 29°42N 24°38E **51** C10
Giarre *Italy* 37°43N 15°11E **22** F6
Gibara *Cuba* 21°9N 76°11W **88** B4
Gibbon *U.S.A.* 40°45N 98°51W **80** E4
Gibe II *Ethiopia* 8°0N 37°30E **47** F2
Gibe III *Ethiopia* 7°0N 37°30E **47** F2
Gibeon *Namibia* 25°9S 17°43E **56** D2
Gibraltar ■ *Europe* 36°7N 5°22W **21** D3
Gibraltar, Str. of *Medit.* 35°55N 5°40W **21** E3
Gibraltar Range △
   Australia 29°31S 152°19E **63** D5
Gibson Desert *Australia* 24°0S 126°0E **60** D4
Gibsons *Canada* 49°24N 123°32W **70** D4
Gibsonville *U.S.A.* 39°46N 120°54W **78** F6
Giddings *U.S.A.* 30°11N 96°56W **84** F6
Giebnegáisi = Kebnekaise
   Sweden 67°53N 18°33E **8** C18
Giessen *Germany* 50°34N 8°41E **16** C5
Gīfān *Iran* 37°54N 57°28E **45** B8
Gift Lake *Canada* 55°53N 115°49W **70** B5

Gifu *Japan* 35°30N 136°45E **31** G8
Gifu □ *Japan* 35°40N 137°0E **31** G8
Giganta, Sa. de la
   Mexico 26°0N 111°39W **86** B2
Gíghia *U.K.* 55°42N 5°44W **11** F3
Gíglio *Italy* 42°20N 10°52E **22** C4
Gijón *Spain* 43°32N 5°42W **21** A3
Gikongoro *Rwanda* 2°28S 29°34E **54** C2
Gil I. *Canada* 53°12N 129°15W **70** C3
Gila → *U.S.A.* 32°43N 114°33W **77** K6
Gila Bend *U.S.A.* 32°57N 112°43W **77** K7
Gila Bend Mts. *U.S.A.* 33°10N 113°0W **77** K7
Gila Cliff Dwellings △
   U.S.A. 33°12N 108°16W **77** K9
Gīlān □ *Iran* 37°0N 50°0E **45** B6
Gilbert → *Australia* 16°35S 141°15E **62** B3
Gilbert Is. *Kiribati* 1°0N 172°0E **58** A10
Gilbert River *Australia* 18°9S 142°52E **62** B3
Gilbert Seamounts
   Pac. Oc. 52°50N 150°10W **4** D18
Gilead *U.S.A.* 44°24N 70°59W **83** B14
Gilf el Kebīr, Hadabat el
   Egypt 23°50N 25°50E **51** D11
Gilford I. *Canada* 50°40N 126°30W **70** C3
Gilgandra *Australia* 31°43S 148°39E **63** E4
Gilgil *Kenya* 0°30S 36°20E **54** C4
Gilgit *India* 35°50N 74°15E **43** B6
Gilgit → *Pakistan* 35°44N 74°37E **43** B6
Gili *Mozam.* 16°39S 38°27E **55** F4
Gilimanuk *Indonesia* 8°10S 114°26E **37** J17
Gillam *Canada* 56°20N 94°40W **71** B10
Gillen, L. *Australia* 26°11S 124°38E **61** E3
Gilles, L. *Australia* 32°50S 136°45E **63** E2
Gillette *U.S.A.* 44°18N 105°30W **76** D11
Gilliat *Australia* 20°40S 141°28E **62** C3
Gillingham *U.K.* 51°23N 0°33E **13** F8
Gilmer *U.S.A.* 32°44N 94°57W **84** E7
Gilmore, L. *Australia* 32°29S 121°37E **61** F3
Gilmour *Canada* 44°48N 77°37W **82** B7
Gilroy *U.S.A.* 37°1N 121°34W **78** H5
Gimcheon *S. Korea* 36°11N 128°4E **35** F15
Gimhae *S. Korea* 35°14N 128°53E **35** G15
Gimhwa *S. Korea* 38°17N 127°28E **35** E14
Gimie, Mt. *St. Lucia* 13°54N 61°0W **89** f
Gimje *S. Korea* 35°48N 126°45E **35** G14
Gimli *Canada* 50°40N 97°0W **71** C9
Gin Gin *Australia* 25°0S 151°58E **63** D5
Gingin *Australia* 31°22S 115°54E **61** F2
Gingindlovu *S. Africa* 29°2S 31°30E **57** D5
Ginir *Ethiopia* 7°6N 40°40E **47** F3
Giofyros → *Greece* 35°20N 25°6E **25** D7
Giohar = Jawhar
   Somali Rep. 2°48N 45°30E **47** G4
Giona, Oros *Greece* 38°38N 22°14E **23** E10
Gir → *India* 21°0N 71°0E **42** J4
Gir Hills *India* 21°0N 71°0E **42** J4
Girab *India* 26°2N 70°38E **42** F4
Girâfi, W. → *Egypt* 29°58N 34°39E **46** F3
Girard *St. Lucia* 13°59N 60°57W **89** D7
Girard *Kans., U.S.A.* 37°31N 94°51W **80** G6
Girard *Ohio, U.S.A.* 41°9N 80°42W **82** E4
Girard *Pa., U.S.A.* 42°0N 80°19W **82** E4
Girdle Ness *U.K.* 57°9N 2°3W **11** D6
Giresun *Turkey* 40°55N 38°30E **19** F6
Girga *Egypt* 26°17N 31°55E **51** C12
Giri → *India* 30°28N 77°41E **42** D7
Giridih *India* 24°10N 86°21E **43** G12
Girifu *Kenya* 1°59N 39°46E **54** B4
Girilambone *Australia* 31°16S 146°57E **63** E4
Giriyondo *S. Africa* 23°15S 31°40E **57** C5
Girna → *India* 21°0N 74°15E **40** J9
Girne = Kyrenia *Cyprus* 35°20N 33°20E **25** D12
Giron = Kiruna *Sweden* 67°52N 20°15E **8** C19
Girona *Spain* 41°58N 2°46E **21** B7
Gironde → *France* 45°32N 1°7W **20** D3
Girraween △ *Australia* 28°46S 151°54E **63** D5
Girringun △ *Australia* 18°15S 145°32E **62** B4
Giru *Australia* 19°30S 147°5E **62** B4
Girvan *U.K.* 55°14N 4°51W **11** F4
Gisborne *N.Z.* 38°39S 178°5E **59** C7
Gisenyi *Rwanda* 1°41S 29°15E **54** C2
Gislaved *Sweden* 57°19N 13°32E **9** H15
Gitarama *Rwanda* 2°4S 29°45E **54** C2
Gitega *Burundi* 3°26S 29°56E **54** C2
Githio *Greece* 36°46N 22°34E **23** F10
Giuba = Juba →
   Somali Rep. 1°30N 42°35E **47** G3
Giurgiu *Romania* 43°52N 25°57E **17** G13
Giza = El Gîza *Egypt* 30°0N 31°12E **51** C12
Giza Pyramids *Egypt* 29°58N 31°9E **51** C12
Gizab *Afghan.* 33°22N 66°17E **42** C1
Gizhiga *Russia* 62°3N 160°30E **29** C17
Gizhiginskaya Guba
   Russia 61°0N 158°0E **29** C16
Giżycko *Poland* 54°2N 21°48E **17** A11
Gjakovë = Dakovica
   Kosovo 42°22N 20°26E **23** C9
Gjirokastër *Albania* 40°7N 20°10E **23** D9
Gjoa Haven *Canada* 68°38N 95°53W **68** D12
Gjøvik *Norway* 60°47N 10°43E **8** F14
Glace Bay *Canada* 46°11N 59°58W **73** C8
Glacier *U.S.A.* 51°15N 117°30W **78** B5
Glacier △ *U.S.A.* 48°42N 113°48W **76** B7
Glacier Bay *U.S.A.* 58°40N 136°0W **68** F4
Glacier Bay △ *U.S.A.* 58°30N 136°0W **70** B1
Glacier Peak *U.S.A.* 48°7N 121°7W **76** B3
Gladewater *U.S.A.* 32°33N 94°56W **84** E7
Gladstone *Queens.,
   Australia* 23°52S 151°16E **62** C5
Gladstone *S. Austral.,
   Australia* 33°15S 138°22E **63** E2
Gladstone *Canada* 50°13N 98°57W **71** C9
Gladstone *U.S.A.* 45°51N 87°1W **80** C10
Gladwin *U.S.A.* 43°59N 84°29W **81** D11
Glagah *Indonesia* 8°13S 114°18E **37** J17
Glåma = Glomma →
   Norway 59°12N 10°57E **9** G14
Glåma *Iceland* 65°48N 23°0W **8** D2
Glamis *U.S.A.* 32°55N 115°5W **79** N11
Glamorgan, Vale of □
   U.K. 51°28N 3°25W **13** F4

Glasco *N.Y., U.S.A.* 42°3N 73°57W **83** D11
Glasgow *U.K.* 55°51N 4°15W **11** F4
Glasgow *Ky., U.S.A.* 37°0N 85°55W **81** G11
Glasgow *Mont., U.S.A.* 48°12N 106°38W **76** B10
Glasgow, City of □ *U.K.* 55°51N 4°12W **11** F4
Glasgow Int. ✈ (GLA)
   U.K. 55°51N 4°21W **11** F4
Glaslyn *Canada* 53°22N 108°21W **71** C7
Glastonbury *U.K.* 51°9N 2°43W **13** F5
Glastonbury *U.S.A.* 41°43N 72°37W **83** E12
Glazov *Russia* 58°9N 52°40E **18** C9
Gleichen *Canada* 50°52N 113°3W **70** C6
Gleiwitz = Gliwice
   Poland 50°22N 18°41E **17** C10
Glen *U.S.A.* 44°7N 71°11W **83** B13
Glen Affric *U.K.* 57°17N 5°1W **11** D3
Glen Canyon △ *U.S.A.* 37°15N 111°0W **77** H8
Glen Canyon Dam
   U.S.A. 36°57N 111°29W **77** H8
Glen Coe *U.K.* 56°40N 5°0W **11** E3
Glen Cove *U.S.A.* 40°51N 73°38W **83** F11
Glen Garry *U.K.* 57°3N 5°7W **11** D3
Glen Innes *Australia* 29°44S 151°44E **63** D5
Glen Lyon *U.S.A.* 41°10N 76°5W **83** E8
Glen Mor *U.K.* 57°9N 4°37W **11** D4
Glen More *U.K.* 57°8N 3°40W **11** D5
Glen Moriston *U.K.* 57°11N 4°52W **11** D4
Glen Robertson *Canada* 45°22N 74°30W **83** A10
Glen Spean *U.K.* 56°53N 4°40W **11** E4
Glen Ullin *U.S.A.* 46°49N 101°50W **80** B3
Glenariff △ *Ireland* 55°2N 6°10W **10** A5
Glenbeigh *Ireland* 52°3N 9°58W **10** D2
Glencoe *Canada* 42°45N 81°43W **82** D3
Glencoe *S. Africa* 28°11S 30°11E **57** D5
Glencoe *U.S.A.* 44°46N 94°9W **80** C6
Glencolumbkille *Ireland* 54°43N 8°42W **10** B3
Glendale *Ariz., U.S.A.* 33°32N 112°11W **77** K7
Glendale *Calif., U.S.A.* 34°9N 118°15W **79** L8
Glendale *Zimbabwe* 17°22S 31°5E **55** F3
Glendive *U.S.A.* 47°7N 104°43W **76** C11
Glendo *U.S.A.* 42°30N 105°2W **76** E11
Glenelg → *Australia* 38°4S 140°59E **63** F3
Glenfield *U.S.A.* 43°43N 75°24W **83** C9
Glengad Hd. *Ireland* 55°20N 7°10W **10** A4
Glengarriff *Ireland* 51°45N 9°34W **10** E2
Glenmont *U.S.A.* 40°31N 82°6W **82** F2
Glenmorgan *Australia* 27°14S 149°42E **63** D4
Glenn *U.S.A.* 39°31N 122°1W **78** F4
Glennallen *U.S.A.* 62°7N 145°33W **68** E2
Glennamaddy *Ireland* 53°37N 8°33W **10** C3
Glenns Ferry *U.S.A.* 42°57N 115°18W **76** E6
Glenora *Canada* 47°7N 77°39W **82** B7
Glenorchy *Australia* 42°49S 147°18E **63** G4
Glenore *Australia* 17°50S 141°12E **62** B3
Glenreagh *Australia* 30°2S 153°1E **63** E5
Glenrock *U.S.A.* 42°52N 105°52W **76** E11
Glenrothes *U.K.* 56°12N 3°10W **11** E5
Glens Falls *U.S.A.* 43°19N 73°39W **83** C11
Glenside *U.S.A.* 40°6N 75°9W **83** F9
Glenties *Ireland* 54°49N 8°16W **10** B3
Glenveagh △ *Ireland* 55°3N 8°1W **10** A3
Glenville *U.S.A.* 38°56N 80°50W **81** F13
Glenwood *Canada* 49°0N 54°58W **73** C9
Glenwood *Ark., U.S.A.* 34°20N 93°33W **84** D8
Glenwood *Iowa, U.S.A.* 41°3N 95°45W **80** E6
Glenwood *Minn., U.S.A.* 45°39N 95°23W **80** C6
Glenwood *Wash., U.S.A.* 46°1N 121°17W **78** D5
Glenwood Springs
   U.S.A. 39°33N 107°19W **76** G10
Glettinganes *Iceland* 65°30N 13°37W **8** D7
Glin *Ireland* 52°34N 9°17W **10** D2
Gliwice *Poland* 50°22N 18°41E **17** C10
Globe *U.S.A.* 33°24N 110°47W **77** K8
Głogów *Poland* 51°37N 16°5E **16** C9
Glomma → *Norway* 59°12N 10°57E **9** G14
Glorieuses, Îs. *Ind. Oc.* 11°30S 47°20E **57** A8
Glossop *U.K.* 53°27N 1°56E **12** D6
Gloucester *Australia* 32°0S 151°59E **63** E5
Gloucester *U.K.* 51°53N 2°15W **13** F5
Gloucester *U.S.A.* 42°37N 70°40W **83** D14
Gloucester I. *Australia* 20°0S 148°30E **62** b
Gloucester Island △
   Australia 20°2S 148°30E **62** b
Gloucester Point
   U.S.A. 37°15N 76°30W **81** G15
Gloucestershire □ *U.K.* 51°46N 2°15W **13** F5
Gloversville *U.S.A.* 43°3N 74°21W **83** C10
Glovertown *Canada* 48°40N 54°3W **73** C9
Glusk *Belarus* 52°53N 28°41E **17** B15
Gmünd *Austria* 48°45N 15°0E **16** D8
Gmunden *Austria* 47°55N 13°48E **16** E7
Gniezno *Poland* 52°30N 17°35E **17** B9
Gnowangerup *Australia* 33°58S 117°59E **61** F2
Go Cong *Vietnam* 10°22N 106°40E **39** G6
Gô-no-ura *Japan* 33°44N 129°40E **31** H4
Goa *India* 15°33N 73°59E **40** M8
Goa □ *India* 15°33N 73°59E **40** M8
Goalen Hd. *Australia* 36°33S 150°4E **63** F5
Goalpara *India* 26°10N 90°40E **41** F17
Goaltor *India* 22°43N 87°10E **43** H12
Goalundo Ghat *Bangla.* 23°50N 89°47E **43** H13
Goat Fell *U.K.* 55°38N 5°11W **11** F3
Goba *Ethiopia* 7°1N 39°59E **47** F2
Goba *Mozam.* 26°15S 32°13E **57** D5
Gobabis *Namibia* 22°30S 19°0E **56** C2
Gobi *Asia* 44°0N 110°0E **34** C6
Gobō *Japan* 33°53N 135°10E **31** H7
Gochas *Namibia* 24°59S 18°55E **56** C2
Godalming *U.K.* 51°11N 0°36W **13** F7
Godavari → *India* 16°25N 82°18E **41** L13
Godavari Pt. *India* 17°0N 82°20E **41** L13
Godbout *Canada* 49°20N 67°38W **73** C6
Godda *India* 24°50N 87°13E **43** G12
Goderich *Canada* 43°45N 81°41W **82** C3
Godfrey Ra. *Australia* 24°0S 117°0E **61** D2
Godhavn = Qeqertarsuaq
   Greenland 69°15N 53°38W **4** C5
Godhra *India* 22°49N 73°40E **42** H5
Godoy Cruz *Argentina* 32°56S 68°52W **94** C2
Gods → *Canada* 56°22N 92°51W **72** A1

Gods L. *Canada* 54°40N 94°15W **72** B1
Gods River *Canada* 54°50N 94°5W **71** C10
Godthåb = Nuuk
  Greenland 64°10N 51°35W **67** C14
Goeie Hoop, Kaap die = Good
  Hope, C. of *S. Africa* 34°24S 18°30E **56** E2
Goéland, L. au *Canada* 49°47N 76°48W **72** C4
Goélands, L. aux *Canada* 55°27N 64°17W **73** A7
Goeree *Neths.* 51°50N 4°0E **15** C3
Goes *Neths.* 51°30N 3°55E **15** C3
Goffstown *U.S.A.* 43°1N 71°36W **83** C13
Gogama *Canada* 47°35N 81°43W **72** C3
Gogebic, L. *U.S.A.* 46°30N 89°35W **80** B9
Gogra = Ghaghara →
  India 25°45N 84°40E **43** G11
Gogriâl *Sudan* 8°30N 28°8E **51** G11
Gohana *India* 29°8N 76°42E **42** E7
Goharganj *India* 23°1N 77°41E **42** H7
Goi → *India* 22°4N 74°46E **42** H6
Goiânia *Brazil* 16°43S 49°20W **93** G9
Goiás *Brazil* 15°55S 50°10W **93** G8
Goiás □ *Brazil* 12°10S 48°0W **93** F9
Goio-Erê *Brazil* 24°12S 53°1W **95** A5
Gojō *Japan* 34°21N 135°42E **31** G7
Gojra *Pakistan* 31°10N 72°40E **42** D5
Gökçeada *Turkey* 40°10N 25°50E **23** D11
Gökova Körfezi *Turkey* 36°55N 27°50E **23** F12
Göksu → *Turkey* 36°19N 34°5E **44** B2
Gokteik *Burma* 22°26N 97°0E **41** H20
Gokurt *Pakistan* 29°40N 67°26E **42** E2
Gokwe *Zimbabwe* 18°7S 28°58E **57** B4
Gola *India* 28°3N 80°32E **43** E9
Golakganj *India* 26°8N 89°52E **43** F13
Golan Heights = Hagolan
  Syria 33°0N 35°45E **46** C4
Golāshkerd *Iran* 27°59N 57°16E **45** E8
Golconda *U.S.A.* 40°58N 117°30W **76** F5
Gold *U.S.A.* 41°52N 77°50W **82** E7
Gold Beach *U.S.A.* 42°25N 124°25W **76** E1
Gold Coast *W. Afr.* 4°0N 1°40W **50** H5
Gold Hill *U.S.A.* 42°26N 123°3W **76** E2
Gold River *Canada* 49°46N 126°3W **70** D3
Golden *Canada* 51°20N 116°59W **70** C5
Golden B. *N.Z.* 40°40S 172°50E **59** D4
Golden Gate *U.S.A.* 37°48N 122°29W **77** H2
Golden Gate Highlands △
  S. Africa 28°40S 28°40E **57** D4
Golden Hinde *Canada* 49°40N 125°44W **70** D3
Golden Lake *Canada* 45°34N 77°21W **82** A7
Golden Spike △ *U.S.A.* 41°37N 112°33W **76** F7
Golden Vale *Ireland* 52°33N 8°17W **10** D3
Goldendale *U.S.A.* 45°49N 120°50W **76** D3
Goldfield *U.S.A.* 37°42N 117°14W **77** H5
Goldsand L. *Canada* 57°2N 101°8W **71** B8
Goldsboro *U.S.A.* 35°23N 77°59W **85** D16
Goldsmith *U.S.A.* 31°59N 102°37W **84** F3
Goldthwaite *U.S.A.* 31°27N 98°34W **84** F5
Goleniów *Poland* 53°35N 14°50E **16** B8
Golestān □ *Iran* 37°20N 55°25E **45** B7
Golestānak *Iran* 30°36N 54°14E **45** D7
Goleta *U.S.A.* 34°27N 119°50W **79** L7
Golfito *Costa Rica* 8°41N 83°5W **88** E3
Golfo Aranci *Italy* 40°59N 9°38E **22** D3
Goliad *U.S.A.* 28°40N 97°23W **84** G6
Golmud *China* 36°25N 94°53E **32** D7
Golpāyegān *Iran* 33°27N 50°18E **45** C6
Golra *Pakistan* 33°37N 72°56E **42** C5
Golspie *U.K.* 57°58N 3°59W **11** D5
Goma
  Dem. Rep. of the Congo 1°37S 29°10E **54** C2
Gomal Pass *Pakistan* 31°56N 69°20E **42** D3
Gomati → *India* 25°32N 83°11E **43** G10
Gombari
  Dem. Rep. of the Congo 2°45N 29°3E **54** B2
Gombe *Nigeria* 10°19N 11°2E **51** F8
Gombe → *Tanzania* 4°38S 31°40E **54** C3
Gombe Stream △
  Tanzania 4°42S 29°37E **54** C2
Gomel = Homyel *Belarus* 52°28N 31°0E **17** B16
Gomera *Canary Is.* 28°7N 17°14W **24** F2
Gómez Palacio *Mexico* 25°34N 103°30W **86** B4
Gomīshān *Iran* 37°4N 54°6E **45** B7
Gomogomo *Indonesia* 6°39S 134°43E **37** F8
Gomoh *India* 23°52N 86°10E **43** H12
Gompa = Ganta *Liberia* 7°15N 8°59W **50** G4
Gonābād *Iran* 34°15N 58°45E **45** C8
Gonaïves *Haiti* 19°20N 72°42W **89** C5
Gonarezhou △ *Zimbabwe* 21°32S 31°55E **55** G3
Gonâve, G. de la *Haiti* 19°29N 72°42W **89** C5
Gonâve, Île de la *Haiti* 18°51N 73°3W **89** C5
Gonbad-e Kāvūs *Iran* 37°20N 55°25E **45** B7
Gonda *India* 27°9N 81°58E **43** F9
Gondal *India* 21°58N 70°52E **42** J4
Gonder *Ethiopia* 12°39N 37°30E **47** E2
Gondia *India* 21°23N 80°10E **40** J12
Gondola *Mozam.* 19°10S 33°37E **55** F3
Gönen *Turkey* 40°6N 27°39E **23** D12
Gongbei *China* 22°12N 113°32E **33** a
Gongchangling *China* 41°7N 123°27E **35** D12
Gongga Shan *China* 29°40N 101°55E **32** F9
Gonggar *China* 29°23N 91°7E **32** F7
Gonghe *China* 36°18N 100°32E **32** D9
Gongju *S. Korea* 36°27N 127°17E **35** F14
Gongming *China* 22°47N 113°53E **33** a
Gongolgon *Australia* 30°21S 146°54E **63** E4
Gongyi *China* 34°45N 113°0E **34** G7
Gongzhuling *China* 43°30N 124°40E **35** C13
Goniri *Nigeria* 11°30N 12°15E **51** F8
Gonzales *Calif., U.S.A.* 36°30N 121°26W **78** J5
Gonzales *Tex., U.S.A.* 29°30N 97°27W **84** G6
González *Mexico* 22°48N 98°25W **87** C5
Good Hope, C. of *S. Africa* 34°24S 18°30E **56** E2
Good Hope Lake
  Canada 59°16N 129°18W **70** B3
Gooderham *Canada* 44°54N 78°21W **82** B6
Goodhouse *S. Africa* 28°5S 18°13E **56** D2
Gooding *U.S.A.* 42°56N 114°43W **76** E6
Goodland *U.S.A.* 39°21N 101°43W **80** F3
Goodlands *Mauritius* 20°2S 57°39E **53** d
Goodlow *Canada* 56°20N 120°8W **70** B4

Goodooga *Australia* 29°3S 147°28E **63** D4
Goodsprings *U.S.A.* 35°49N 115°27W **79** K11
Goole *U.K.* 53°42N 0°53W **12** D7
Goolgowi *Australia* 33°58S 145°41E **63** E4
Goomalling *Australia* 31°15S 116°49E **61** F2
Goomeri *Australia* 26°12S 152°6E **63** D5
Goonda *Mozam.* 19°48S 33°57E **55** F3
Goondiwindi *Australia* 28°30S 150°21E **63** D5
Goongarrie, L. *Australia* 30°2S 121°9E **61** F3
Goongarrie △ *Australia* 30°7S 121°30E **61** F3
Goonyella *Australia* 21°47S 147°58E **62** C4
Goose → *Canada* 53°20N 60°35W **73** B7
Goose Creek *U.S.A.* 32°59N 80°2W **85** E14
Goose L. *U.S.A.* 41°56N 120°26W **76** F3
Gop *India* 22°5N 69°50E **42** H3
Gopalganj *India* 26°28N 84°30E **43** F11
Göppingen *Germany* 48°42N 9°39E **16** D5
Gorakhpur *India* 26°47N 83°23E **43** F10
Goražde *Bos.-H.* 43°38N 18°58E **23** C8
Gorda, Pta. *Canary Is.* 28°45N 18°0W **24** F2
Gorda, Pta. *Nic.* 14°20N 83°10W **88** D3
Gordan B. *Australia* 11°35S 130°10E **60** B5
Gordon *U.S.A.* 42°48N 102°12W **80** D2
Gordon → *Australia* 42°27S 145°30E **63** G4
Gordon Bay *Canada* 45°12N 79°47W **82** A5
Gordon L. *Alta., Canada* 56°30N 110°25W **71** B6
Gordon L. *N.W.T.,*
  Canada 63°5N 113°11W **70** A6
Gordonvale *Australia* 17°5S 145°50E **62** B4
Goré *Chad* 7°59N 16°31E **51** G9
Gore *Ethiopia* 8°12N 35°32E **47** F2
Gore *N.Z.* 46°5S 168°58E **59** G2
Gore Bay *Canada* 45°57N 82°28W **72** C3
Gorey *Ireland* 52°41N 6°18W **10** D5
Gorg *Iran* 29°29N 59°43E **45** D8
Gorgān *Iran* 36°55N 54°30E **45** B7
Gorgona, I. *Colombia* 3°0N 78°10W **92** C3
Gorham *U.S.A.* 44°23N 71°10W **83** B13
Goriganga → *India* 29°45N 80°23E **43** E9
Gorinchem *Neths.* 51°50N 4°59E **15** C4
Gorizia *Italy* 45°56N 13°37E **22** B5
Gorkiy = Nizhniy Novgorod
  Russia 56°20N 44°0E **18** C7
Gorkovskoye Vdkhr.
  Russia 57°2N 43°4E **18** C7
Gorleston *U.K.* 52°35N 1°44E **13** E9
Görlitz *Germany* 51°9N 14°58E **16** C8
Gorlovka = Horlivka
  Ukraine 48°19N 38°5E **19** E6
Gorman *U.S.A.* 34°47N 118°51W **79** L8
Gorna Dzhumaya = Blagoevgrad
  Bulgaria 42°2N 23°5E **23** C10
Gorna Oryakhovitsa
  Bulgaria 43°7N 25°40E **23** C11
Gorno-Altay □ *Russia* 51°0N 86°0E **28** D9
Gorno-Altaysk *Russia* 51°50N 86°5E **28** D9
Gornozavodsk *Russia* 46°33N 141°50E **29** E15
Gornyatski *Russia* 67°32N 64°3E **18** A11
Gornyy *Russia* 44°57N 133°59E **30** B6
Gorodenka = Horodenka
  Ukraine 48°41N 25°29E **17** D13
Gorodok = Horodok
  Ukraine 49°46N 23°32E **17** D12
Gorokhov = Horokhiv
  Ukraine 50°30N 24°45E **17** C13
Goromonzi *Zimbabwe* 17°52S 31°22E **55** F3
Gorong, Kepulauan
  Indonesia 3°59S 131°25E **37** E8
Gorongose → *Mozam.* 20°30S 34°40E **57** C5
Gorongoza *Mozam.* 18°44S 34°2E **55** F3
Gorongoza, Sa. da *Mozam.* 18°27S 34°2E **55** F3
Gorongoza △ *Mozam.* 18°50S 34°29E **57** B5
Gorontalo *Indonesia* 0°35N 123°5E **37** D6
Gorontalo □ *Indonesia* 0°50N 122°30E **37** D6
Gort *Ireland* 53°3N 8°49W **10** C3
Gortis *Greece* 35°4N 24°58E **25** D6
Goryeong *S. Korea* 35°44N 128°15E **35** G15
Gorzów Wielkopolski
  Poland 52°43N 15°15E **16** B8
Gosford *Australia* 33°23S 151°18E **63** E5
Goshen *Calif., U.S.A.* 36°21N 119°25W **78** J7
Goshen *Ind., U.S.A.* 41°35N 85°50W **81** E11
Goshen *N.Y., U.S.A.* 41°24N 74°20W **83** E10
Goshogawara *Japan* 40°48N 140°27E **30** D10
Goslar *Germany* 51°54N 10°25E **16** C6
Gospić *Croatia* 44°35N 15°23E **16** F8
Gosport *U.K.* 50°48N 1°9W **13** G6
Gosse → *Australia* 19°32S 134°37E **62** B1
Göta älv → *Sweden* 57°42N 11°54E **9** H14
Göta kanal *Sweden* 58°30N 15°58E **9** G16
Götaland *Sweden* 57°30N 14°30E **9** H16
Göteborg *Sweden* 57°43N 11°59E **9** H14
Gotha *Germany* 50°56N 10°42E **16** C6
Gothenburg = Göteborg
  Sweden 57°43N 11°59E **9** H14
Gothenburg *U.S.A.* 40°56N 100°10W **80** E3
Gotland *Sweden* 57°30N 18°33E **9** H18
Gotō-Rettō *Japan* 32°55N 129°5E **31** H4
Gotska Sandön *Sweden* 58°24N 19°15E **9** G18
Gōtsu *Japan* 35°0N 132°14E **31** G6
Göttingen *Germany* 51°31N 9°55E **16** C5
Gottwaldov = Zlín
  Czech Rep. 49°14N 17°40E **17** D9
Goubangzi *China* 41°20N 121°52E **35** D11
Gouda *Neths.* 52°1N 4°42E **15** B4
Goudoúras, Ákra *Greece* 34°59N 26°6E **25** E8
Gouin, Rés. *Canada* 48°35N 74°40W **72** C5
Goulburn *Australia* 34°44S 149°44E **63** E4
Goulburn Is. *Australia* 11°40S 133°20E **62** A1
Goulimine *Morocco* 28°56N 10°0W **50** C3
Goundam *Mali* 16°27N 3°40W **50** E5
Gourits → *S. Africa* 34°21S 21°52E **56** E3
Gournes *Greece* 35°19N 25°16E **25** D7
Gourock *U.K.* 55°57N 4°49W **11** F4
Gouverneur *U.S.A.* 44°20N 75°28W **83** B9
Gouvia *Greece* 39°39N 19°50E **25** A3
Gove Peninsula
  Australia 12°17S 136°49E **62** A2
Governador Valadares
  Brazil 18°15S 41°57W **93** G10

Governor's Harbour
  Bahamas 25°10N 76°14W **88** A4
Govindgarh *India* 24°23N 81°18E **43** G9
Gowan Ra. *Australia* 25°0S 145°0E **62** D4
Gowanda *U.S.A.* 42°28N 78°56W **82** D6
Gower *U.K.* 51°35N 4°10W **13** F3
Gowna, L. *Ireland* 53°51N 7°34W **10** C4
Goya *Argentina* 29°10S 59°10W **94** B4
Goyang *S. Korea* 37°39N 126°52E **35** F14
Goyder Lagoon *Australia* 27°3S 138°58E **63** D2
Goyllarisquizga *Peru* 10°31S 76°24W **92** F3
Goz Beïda *Chad* 12°10N 21°20E **51** F10
Gozo *Malta* 36°3N 14°15E **25** C1
Graaff-Reinet *S. Africa* 32°13S 24°32E **56** E3
Gračac *Croatia* 44°18N 15°57E **16** F8
Gracias a Dios, C.
  Honduras 15°0N 83°10W **88** D3
Graciosa *Azores* 39°4N 28°0W **50** a
Graciosa, I. *Canary Is.* 29°15N 13°32W **24** E6
Grado *Spain* 43°23N 6°4W **21** A2
Grady *U.S.A.* 34°49N 103°19W **77** J12
Grafham Water *U.K.* 52°19N 0°18W **13** E7
Grafton *Australia* 29°38S 152°58E **63** D5
Grafton *N. Dak., U.S.A.* 48°25N 97°25W **80** A6
Grafton *W. Va., U.S.A.* 39°21N 80°2W **81** F13
Graham *Canada* 49°20N 90°30W **72** C1
Graham *U.S.A.* 33°6N 98°35W **84** E5
Graham, Mt. *U.S.A.* 32°42N 109°52W **77** K9
Graham Bell, Ostrov = Greem-
  Bell, Ostrov *Russia* 81°0N 62°0E **28** A7
Graham I. *B.C., Canada* 53°40N 132°30W **70** C2
Graham I. *Nunavut,*
  Canada 77°25N 90°30W **69** B13
Graham Land *Antarctica* 65°0S 64°0W **5** C17
Grahamstown *S. Africa* 33°19S 26°31E **56** E4
Grahamsville *U.S.A.* 41°51N 74°33W **83** E10
Grain Coast *W. Afr.* 4°20N 10°0W **50** H3
Grajagan *Indonesia* 8°35S 114°13E **37** K17
Grajaú *Brazil* 5°50S 46°4W **93** E9
Grajaú → *Brazil* 3°41S 44°48W **93** D10
Grampian *U.S.A.* 40°58N 78°37W **82** F6
Grampian Highlands = Grampian
  Mts. *U.K.* 56°50N 4°0W **11** E5
Grampian Mts. *U.K.* 56°50N 4°0W **11** E5
Grampians, The
  Australia 37°15S 142°20E **63** F3
Gran Canaria *Canary Is.* 27°55N 15°35W **24** G4
Gran Chaco *S. Amer.* 25°0S 61°0W **94** B3
Gran Desierto del Pinacate △
  Mexico 31°51N 113°32W **86** A2
Gran Paradiso *Italy* 45°33N 7°17E **20** D7
Gran Sasso d'Itália *Italy* 42°27N 13°42E **22** C5
Granada *Nic.* 11°58N 86°0W **88** D2
Granada *Spain* 37°10N 3°35W **21** D4
Granada *U.S.A.* 38°4N 102°19W **76** G12
Granadilla de Abona
  Canary Is. 28°7N 16°33W **24** F3
Granard *Ireland* 53°47N 7°30W **10** C4
Granbury *U.S.A.* 32°27N 97°47W **84** E6
Granby *Canada* 45°25N 72°45W **83** A12
Granby *U.S.A.* 40°5N 105°56W **76** F11
Grand → *Canada* 42°51N 79°34W **82** D5
Grand → *Mo., U.S.A.* 39°23N 93°7W **80** F7
Grand → *S. Dak.,*
  U.S.A. 45°40N 100°45W **80** C3
Grand Bahama I.
  Bahamas 26°40N 78°30W **88** A4
Grand Baie *Mauritius* 20°0S 57°35E **53** d
Grand Bank *Canada* 47°6N 55°48W **73** C8
Grand Bassam *Ivory C.* 5°10N 3°49W **50** G5
Grand Bend *Canada* 43°18N 81°45W **82** C3
Grand-Bourg *Guadeloupe* 15°53N 61°19W **88** b
Grand Canal = Da Yunhe
  China 39°10N 117°10E **35** E9
Grand Canyon *U.S.A.* 36°3N 112°9W **77** H7
Grand Canyon △
  U.S.A. 36°15N 112°30W **77** H7
Grand Canyon-Parashant △
  U.S.A. 36°30N 113°45W **77** H7
Grand Cayman
  Cayman Is. 19°20N 81°20W **88** C3
Grand Coulee *U.S.A.* 47°57N 119°0W **76** C4
Grand Coulee Dam
  U.S.A. 47°57N 118°59W **76** C4
Grand Erg de Bilma *Niger* 18°30N 14°0E **51** E8
Grand Falls *Canada* 47°3N 67°44W **73** C6
Grand Falls-Windsor
  Canada 48°56N 55°40W **73** C8
Grand Forks *Canada* 49°0N 118°30W **70** D5
Grand Forks *U.S.A.* 47°55N 97°3W **80** B5
Grand Gorge *U.S.A.* 42°21N 74°29W **83** D10
Grand Haven *U.S.A.* 43°4N 86°13W **80** D10
Grand I. *Mich., U.S.A.* 46°31N 86°40W **80** B10
Grand I. *N.Y., U.S.A.* 43°0N 78°58W **82** D6
Grand Island *U.S.A.* 40°55N 98°21W **80** E4
Grand Isle *La., U.S.A.* 29°14N 90°0W **85** G9
Grand Isle *Vt., U.S.A.* 44°43N 73°18W **83** B11
Grand Junction *U.S.A.* 39°4N 108°33W **76** G9
Grand L. *N.B., Canada* 45°57N 66°7W **73** C6
Grand L. *Nfld. & L.,*
  Canada 49°0N 57°30W **73** C8
Grand L. *Nfld. & L.,*
  Canada 53°40N 60°30W **73** B7
Grand L. *U.S.A.* 29°55N 92°47W **84** G8
Grand Manan I. *Canada* 44°45N 66°52W **73** C6
Grand Marais *Mich.,*
  U.S.A. 46°40N 85°59W **81** B11
Grand Marais *Minn.,*
  U.S.A. 47°45N 90°25W **72** C1
Grand-Mère *Canada* 46°36N 72°40W **72** C5
Grand Portage *U.S.A.* 47°58N 89°41W **80** B9
Grand Prairie *U.S.A.* 32°44N 96°59W **84** E6
Grand Rapids *Canada* 53°12N 99°19W **71** C9
Grand Rapids *Mich.,*
  U.S.A. 42°58N 85°40W **81** D11
Grand Rapids *Minn.,*
  U.S.A. 47°14N 93°31W **80** B7
Grand St-Bernard, Col du
  Europe 45°50N 7°10E **20** D7

Grand Staircase-Escalante △
  U.S.A. 37°25N 111°33W **77** H8
Grand Teton *U.S.A.* 43°54N 110°50W **76** E8
Grand Teton △ *U.S.A.* 43°50N 110°50W **76** E8
Grand Union Canal *U.K.* 52°7N 0°53W **13** E7
Grande → *Jujuy,*
  Argentina 24°20S 65°2W **94** A2
Grande → *Mendoza,*
  Argentina 36°52S 69°45W **94** D2
Grande → *Bolivia* 15°51S 64°39W **92** G6
Grande → *Bahia, Brazil* 11°30S 44°30W **93** F10
Grande → *Minas Gerais,*
  Brazil 20°6S 51°4W **93** H8
Grande, B. *Argentina* 50°30S 68°20W **96** G3
Grande, Rio → *N. Amer.* 25°58N 97°9W **84** J6
Grande Anse *Seychelles* 4°18S 55°45E **53** b
Grande Baleine →
  Canada 55°16N 77°47W **72** A4
Grande Cache *Canada* 53°53N 119°8W **70** C5
Grande Comore
  Comoros Is. 11°35S 43°20E **53** a
Grande-Entrée *Canada* 47°30N 61°40W **73** C7
Grande Prairie *Canada* 55°10N 118°50W **70** B5
Grande-Rivière *Canada* 48°26N 64°30W **73** C7
Grande-Terre *Guadeloupe* 16°20N 61°25W **88** b
Grande-Vallée *Canada* 49°14N 65°8W **73** C6
Grande Vigie, Pte. de la
  Guadeloupe 16°32N 61°27W **88** b
Grandfalls *U.S.A.* 31°20N 102°51W **84** F3
Grands-Jardins △
  Canada 47°41N 70°51W **73** C5
Grandview *Canada* 51°10N 100°42W **71** C8
Grandview *U.S.A.* 46°15N 119°54W **76** C4
Graneros *Chile* 34°5S 70°45W **94** C1
Grangemouth *U.K.* 56°1N 3°42W **11** E5
Granger *U.S.A.* 41°3N 109°58W **76** F9
Grangeville *U.S.A.* 45°56N 116°7W **76** D5
Granisle *Canada* 54°53N 126°13W **70** C3
Granite City *U.S.A.* 38°42N 90°8W **80** F8
Granite Falls *U.S.A.* 44°49N 95°33W **80** C6
Granite L. *Canada* 48°8N 57°5W **73** C8
Granite Mtn. *U.S.A.* 33°5N 116°28W **79** M10
Granite Pk. *U.S.A.* 45°10N 109°48W **76** D9
Graniteville *U.S.A.* 44°8N 72°29W **83** B12
Granity *N.Z.* 41°39S 171°51E **59** D3
Granja *Brazil* 3°7S 40°50W **93** D10
Granollers *Spain* 41°39N 2°18E **21** B7
Grant *U.S.A.* 40°50N 101°43W **80** E3
Grant, Mt. *U.S.A.* 38°34N 118°48W **76** G4
Grant City *U.S.A.* 40°29N 94°25W **80** E6
Grant I. *Australia* 11°10S 132°52E **60** B5
Grant Range *U.S.A.* 38°30N 115°25W **76** G6
Grantham *U.K.* 52°55N 0°38W **12** E7
Grantown-on-Spey *U.K.* 57°20N 3°36W **11** D5
Grants *U.S.A.* 35°9N 107°52W **77** J10
Grants Pass *U.S.A.* 42°26N 123°19W **76** E2
Grantsville *U.S.A.* 40°36N 112°28W **76** F7
Granville *France* 48°50N 1°35W **20** B3
Granville *N. Dak.,*
  U.S.A. 48°16N 100°47W **80** A3
Granville *N.Y., U.S.A.* 43°24N 73°16W **83** C11
Granville *Ohio, U.S.A.* 40°4N 82°31W **82** F2
Granville L. *Canada* 56°18N 100°30W **71** B8
Graskop *S. Africa* 24°56S 30°49E **57** C5
Grass → *Canada* 56°3N 96°33W **71** B9
Grass Range *U.S.A.* 47°2N 108°48W **76** C9
Grass River △ *Canada* 54°40N 100°50W **71** C8
Grass Valley *Calif.,*
  U.S.A. 39°13N 121°4W **78** F6
Grass Valley *Oreg.,*
  U.S.A. 45°22N 120°47W **76** D3
Grasse *France* 43°38N 6°56E **20** E7
Grassflat *U.S.A.* 41°0N 78°6W **82** E6
Grasslands △ *Canada* 49°11N 107°38W **71** D7
Grassy *Australia* 40°3S 144°5E **63** G3
Graulhet *France* 43°45N 1°59E **20** E4
Gravelbourg *Canada* 49°50N 106°35W **71** D7
's-Gravenhage *Neths.* 52°7N 4°17E **15** B4
Gravenhurst *Canada* 44°52N 79°20W **82** B5
Gravesend *Australia* 29°35S 150°20E **63** D5
Gravesend *U.K.* 51°26N 0°22E **13** F8
Gravois, Pointe-à- *Haiti* 16°15N 73°56W **89** C5
Grayling *U.S.A.* 44°40N 84°43W **81** C11
Grays *U.K.* 51°28N 0°21E **13** F8
Grays Harbor *U.S.A.* 46°59N 124°1W **76** C1
Grays L. *U.S.A.* 43°4N 111°26W **76** E8
Grays River *U.S.A.* 46°21N 123°37W **78** D3
Graz *Austria* 47°4N 15°27E **16** E8
Greasy L. *Canada* 62°55N 122°12W **70** A4
Great Abaco I. = Abaco I.
  Bahamas 26°25N 77°10W **88** A4
Great Artesian Basin
  Australia 23°0S 144°0E **62** C3
Great Australian Bight
  Australia 33°30S 130°0E **61** F5
Great Bahama Bank
  Bahamas 23°15N 78°0W **88** B4
Great Barrier I. *N.Z.* 36°11S 175°25E **59** B5
Great Barrier Reef
  Australia 18°0S 146°50E **62** B4
Great Barrier Reef △
  Australia 20°0S 150°0E **62** B4
Great Barrington
  U.S.A. 42°12N 73°22W **83** D11
Great Basalt Wall △
  Australia 19°52S 145°43E **62** B4
Great Basin *U.S.A.* 40°0N 117°0W **76** G5
Great Basin △ *U.S.A.* 38°56N 114°15W **76** G6
Great Bear → *Canada* 65°0N 126°0W **68** E7
Great Bear L. *Canada* 65°30N 120°0W **68** D8
Great Belt = Store Bælt
  Denmark 55°20N 11°0E **9** J14
Great Bend *Kans., U.S.A.* 38°22N 98°46W **80** F4
Great Bend *Pa., U.S.A.* 41°58N 75°45W **83** E9
Great Blasket I. *Ireland* 52°6N 10°32W **10** D1
Great Britain *Europe* 54°0N 2°15W **6** E5
Great Camanoe
  Br. Virgin Is. 18°30N 64°35W **89** e
Great Coco I. = Koko Kyunzu
  Burma 14°7N 93°22E **41** M18

Great Codroy *Canada* 47°51N 59°16W **73** C8
Great Divide, The = Great
  Dividing Ra. *Australia* 23°0S 146°0E **62** C4
Great Divide Basin
  U.S.A. 42°0N 108°0W **76** E9
Great Dividing Ra.
  Australia 23°0S 146°0E **62** C4
Great Driffield = Driffield
  U.K. 54°0N 0°26W **12** C7
Great Exuma I. *Bahamas* 23°30N 75°50W **88** B4
Great Falls *U.S.A.* 47°30N 111°17W **76** C8
Great Fish = Groot-Vis →
  S. Africa 33°28S 27°5E **56** E4
Great Guana Cay
  Bahamas 24°0N 76°20W **88** B4
Great Himalayan △
  India 31°30N 77°30E **42** D7
Great Inagua I. *Bahamas* 21°0N 73°20W **89** B5
Great Indian Desert = Thar Desert
  India 28°0N 72°0E **42** F5
Great Karoo *S. Africa* 31°55S 21°0E **56** E3
Great Khingan Mts. = Da
  Hinggan Ling *China* 48°0N 121°0E **33** B13
Great Lake *Australia* 41°50S 146°40E **63** G4
Great Lakes *N. Amer.* 46°0N 84°0W **66** E11
Great Limpopo Transfrontier △
  Africa 23°0S 31°45E **57** C5
Great Malvern *U.K.* 52°7N 2°18W **13** E5
Great Miami → *U.S.A.* 39°7N 84°49W **81** F11
Great Ormes Head *U.K.* 53°20N 3°52W **12** D4
Great Ouse → *U.K.* 52°48N 0°21E **12** E8
Great Palm I. *Australia* 18°45S 146°40E **62** B4
Great Pedro Bluff *Jamaica* 17°51N 77°44W **88** a
Great Pee Dee →
  U.S.A. 33°21N 79°10W **85** E15
Great Plains *N. Amer.* 47°0N 105°0W **66** E9
Great Ruaha → *Tanzania* 7°56S 37°52E **54** D4
Great Sacandaga L.
  U.S.A. 43°6N 74°16W **83** C10
Great Saint Bernard Pass = Grand
  St-Bernard, Col du
  Europe 45°50N 7°10E **20** D7
Great Salt Desert = Kavīr, Dasht-e
  Iran 34°30N 55°0E **45** C7
Great Salt L. *U.S.A.* 41°15N 112°40W **76** F7
Great Salt Lake Desert
  U.S.A. 40°50N 113°30W **76** F7
Great Salt Plains L.
  U.S.A. 36°45N 98°8W **84** C5
Great Sand Dunes △
  U.S.A. 37°48N 105°45W **77** H11
Great Sandy △ *Australia* 26°13S 153°2E **63** D5
Great Sandy Desert
  Australia 21°0S 124°0E **60** D3
Great Sangi = Sangihe, Pulau
  Indonesia 3°35N 125°30E **37** D7
Great Sea Reef *Fiji* 16°15S 179°0E **59** a
Great Sitkin I. *U.S.A.* 52°3N 176°6W **74** E4
Great Skellig *Ireland* 51°47N 10°33W **10** E1
Great Slave L. *Canada* 61°23N 115°38W **70** A5
Great Smoky Mts. △
  U.S.A. 35°40N 83°40W **85** D13
Great Stour = Stour →
  U.K. 51°18N 1°22E **13** F9
Great Victoria Desert
  Australia 29°30S 126°30E **61** E4
Great Wall *Antarctica* 62°30S 58°0W **5** C18
Great Wall *China* 38°30N 109°30E **34** E5
Great Whernside *U.K.* 54°10N 1°58W **12** C6
Great Yarmouth *U.K.* 52°37N 1°44E **13** E9
Great Zab = Zāb al Kabīr →
  Iraq 36°1N 43°24E **44** B4
Great Zimbabwe
  Zimbabwe 20°16S 30°54E **55** G3
Greater Antilles *W. Indies* 17°40N 74°0W **89** C5
Greater London □ *U.K.* 51°31N 0°6W **13** F7
Greater Manchester □
  U.K. 53°30N 2°15W **12** D5
Greater St. Lucia Wetlands △
  S. Africa 28°6S 32°27E **57** D5
Greater Sudbury = Sudbury
  Canada 46°30N 81°0W **72** C3
Greater Sunda Is. *Indonesia* 7°0S 112°0E **36** F4
Greco, C. *Cyprus* 34°57N 34°5E **25** E13
Gredos, Sierra de *Spain* 40°20N 5°0W **21** B3
Greece *U.S.A.* 43°13N 77°41W **82** C7
Greece ■ *Europe* 40°0N 23°0E **23** E9
Greeley *Colo., U.S.A.* 40°25N 104°42W **76** F11
Greeley *Nebr., U.S.A.* 41°33N 98°32W **80** E4
Greely Fd. *Canada* 80°30N 85°0W **69** A15
Greem-Bell, Ostrov *Russia* 81°0N 62°0E **28** A7
Green → *Ky., U.S.A.* 37°54N 87°30W **80** G10
Green → *Utah, U.S.A.* 38°11N 109°53W **76** G9
Green B. *U.S.A.* 45°0N 87°30W **80** C10
Green Bay *U.S.A.* 44°31N 88°0W **80** C9
Green C. *Australia* 37°13S 150°1E **63** F5
Green Cove Springs
  U.S.A. 29°59N 81°42W **85** G14
Green Lake *Canada* 54°17N 107°47W **71** C7
Green Mts. *U.S.A.* 43°45N 72°45W **83** C12
Green River *Utah,*
  U.S.A. 38°59N 110°10W **76** G8
Green River *Wyo.,*
  U.S.A. 41°32N 109°28W **76** F9
Green Valley *U.S.A.* 31°52N 110°56W **77** L8
Greenbank *U.S.A.* 48°6N 122°34W **78** B4
Greenbush *Mich., U.S.A.* 44°35N 83°19W **82** B1
Greenbush *Minn., U.S.A.* 48°42N 96°11W **80** A5
Greencastle *U.S.A.* 39°38N 86°52W **80** F10
Greene *U.S.A.* 42°20N 75°46W **83** D9
Greeneville *U.S.A.* 36°10N 82°50W **85** C13
Greenfield *Calif., U.S.A.* 36°19N 121°15W **78** J5
Greenfield *Calif., U.S.A.* 35°15N 119°0W **79** K8
Greenfield *Ind., U.S.A.* 39°47N 85°46W **81** F11
Greenfield *Iowa, U.S.A.* 41°18N 94°28W **80** E6
Greenfield *Mass.,*
  U.S.A. 42°35N 72°36W **83** D12
Greenfield *Mo., U.S.A.* 37°25N 93°51W **80** G7
Greenfield Park *Canada* 45°29N 73°29W **83** A11
Greenland ☑ *N. Amer.* 66°0N 45°0W **67** C15

124 Greenland Sea INDEX TO WORLD MAPS

Greenland Sea *Arctic* 73°0N 10°0W **4** B7
Greenock *U.K.* 55°57N 4°46W **11** F4
Greenore *Ireland* 54°2N 6°8W **10** B5
Greenore Pt. *Ireland* 52°14N 6°19W **10** D5
Greenough *Australia* 28°58S 114°43E **61** E1
Greenough → *Australia* 28°51S 114°38E **61** E1
Greenough Pt. *Canada* 44°58N 81°26W **82** B3
Greenport *U.S.A.* 41°6N 72°22W **83** E12
Greensboro *Ga., U.S.A.* 33°35N 83°11W **85** E13
Greensboro *N.C., U.S.A.* 36°4N 79°48W **85** C15
Greensboro *Vt., U.S.A.* 44°36N 72°18W **83** B12
Greensburg *Ind., U.S.A.* 39°20N 85°29W **81** F11
Greensburg *Kans., U.S.A.* 37°36N 99°18W **80** G4
Greensburg *Pa., U.S.A.* 40°18N 79°33W **82** F5
Greenstone = Geraldton *Canada* 49°44N 87°10W **72** C2
Greenstone Pt. *U.K.* 57°55N 5°37W **11** D3
Greenvale *Australia* 18°59S 145°7E **62** B4
Greenville *Liberia* 5°1N 9°6W **50** G4
Greenville *Ala., U.S.A.* 31°50N 86°38W **85** F11
Greenville *Calif., U.S.A.* 40°8N 120°57W **78** E6
Greenville *Maine, U.S.A.* 45°28N 69°35W **81** C19
Greenville *Mich., U.S.A.* 43°11N 85°15W **81** D11
Greenville *Miss., U.S.A.* 33°24N 91°4W **85** E9
Greenville *Mo., U.S.A.* 37°8N 90°27W **80** G8
Greenville *N.C., U.S.A.* 35°37N 77°23W **85** D16
Greenville *N.H., U.S.A.* 42°46N 71°49W **83** D13
Greenville *N.Y., U.S.A.* 42°25N 74°1W **83** D10
Greenville *Ohio, U.S.A.* 40°6N 84°38W **81** E11
Greenville *Pa., U.S.A.* 41°24N 80°23W **82** E4
Greenville *S.C., U.S.A.* 34°51N 82°24W **85** D13
Greenville *Tex., U.S.A.* 33°8N 96°7W **84** E6
Greenwater Lake ⌓ *Canada* 52°32N 103°30W **71** C8
Greenwich *Conn., U.S.A.* 41°2N 73°38W **83** E11
Greenwich *N.Y., U.S.A.* 43°5N 73°30W **83** C11
Greenwich *Ohio, U.S.A.* 41°2N 82°31W **82** E2
Greenwich □ *U.K.* 51°29N 0°1E **13** F8
Greenwood *Canada* 49°10N 118°40W **70** D5
Greenwood *Ark., U.S.A.* 35°13N 94°16W **84** D7
Greenwood *Ind., U.S.A.* 39°37N 86°7W **80** F10
Greenwood *Miss., U.S.A.* 33°31N 90°11W **85** E9
Greenwood *S.C., U.S.A.* 34°12N 82°10W **85** D13
Greenwood, Mt. *Australia* 13°48S 130°4E **60** B5
Gregory *U.S.A.* 43°14N 99°26W **80** D4
Gregory → *Australia* 17°53S 139°17E **62** B2
Gregory, L. *S. Austral., Australia* 28°55S 139°0E **63** D2
Gregory, L. *W. Austral., Australia* 20°0S 127°40E **60** D4
Gregory, L. *W. Austral., Australia* 25°38S 119°58E **61** E2
Gregory △ *Australia* 15°38S 131°15E **60** C5
Gregory Downs *Australia* 18°35S 138°45E **62** B2
Gregory Ra. *Queens., Australia* 19°30S 143°40E **62** B3
Gregory Ra. *W. Austral., Australia* 21°20S 121°12E **60** D3
Greifswald *Germany* 54°5N 13°23E **16** A7
Greiz *Germany* 50°39N 12°10E **16** C7
Gremikha *Russia* 67°59N 39°47E **18** A6
Grenaa *Denmark* 56°25N 10°53E **9** H14
Grenada *U.S.A.* 33°47N 89°49W **85** E10
Grenada ■ *W. Indies* 12°10N 61°40W **89** D7
Grenadier I. *U.S.A.* 44°3N 76°22W **83** B8
Grenadines, The *St. Vincent* 12°40N 61°20W **89** D7
Grenen *Denmark* 57°44N 10°40E **9** H14
Grenfell *Australia* 33°52S 148°8E **63** E4
Grenfell *Canada* 50°30N 102°56W **71** C8
Grenoble *France* 45°12N 5°42E **20** D6
Grenville, C. *Australia* 12°0S 143°13E **62** A3
Grenville Chan. *Canada* 53°40N 129°46W **70** C3
Gresham *U.S.A.* 45°30N 122°25W **78** E4
Gresik *Indonesia* 7°13S 112°38E **37** G15
Gretna *U.K.* 55°0N 3°3W **11** F5
Gretna *U.S.A.* 29°54N 90°3W **85** G9
Grevenmacher *Lux.* 49°41N 6°26E **15** E6
Grey → *Canada* 47°34N 57°6W **73** C8
Grey → *N.Z.* 42°27S 171°12E **59** E3
Grey, C. *Australia* 13°0S 136°35E **62** A2
Grey Is. *Canada* 50°50N 55°35W **69** G20
Grey Ra. *Australia* 27°0S 143°30E **63** D3
Greybull *U.S.A.* 44°30N 108°3W **76** D9
Greymouth *N.Z.* 42°29S 171°13E **59** E3
Greystones *Ireland* 53°9N 6°5W **10** C5
Greytown *N.Z.* 41°5S 175°29E **59** D5
Greytown *S. Africa* 29°1S 30°36E **57** D5
Gribbell I. *Canada* 53°23N 129°0W **70** C3
Gridley *U.S.A.* 39°22N 121°42W **78** F5
Griekwastad *S. Africa* 28°49S 23°15E **56** D3
Griffin *U.S.A.* 33°15N 84°16W **85** E12
Griffith *Australia* 34°18S 146°2E **63** E4
Griffith *Canada* 45°15N 77°10W **82** A7
Griffith I. *Canada* 44°50N 80°55W **82** B4
Grimaylov = Hrymayliv *Ukraine* 49°20N 26°5E **17** D14
Grimes *U.S.A.* 39°4N 121°54W **78** F5
Grimsay *U.K.* 57°29N 7°14W **11** D1
Grimsby *Canada* 43°12N 79°34W **82** C5
Grimsby *U.K.* 53°34N 0°5W **12** D7
Grímsey *Iceland* 66°33N 17°58W **8** C5
Grimshaw *Canada* 56°10N 117°40W **70** B5
Grimstad *Norway* 58°20N 8°35E **9** G13
Grindstone I. *U.S.A.* 44°17N 76°27W **83** B8
Grinnell *U.S.A.* 41°45N 92°43W **80** E7
Grinnell Pen. *Canada* 76°40N 95°0W **69** B13
Gris-Nez, C. *France* 50°52N 1°35E **20** A4
Grise Fiord *Canada* 76°25N 82°57W **69** B15
Groais I. *Canada* 50°55N 55°35W **73** B8
Groblersdal *S. Africa* 25°15S 29°25E **57** D4
Grodno = Hrodna *Belarus* 53°42N 23°52E **17** B12
Grodzyanka = Hrodzyanka *Belarus* 53°31N 28°42E **17** B15
Groesbeck *U.S.A.* 31°31N 96°32W **84** F6
Grójec *Poland* 51°50N 20°58E **17** C11
Grong *Norway* 64°25N 12°8E **8** D15
Groningen *Neths.* 53°15N 6°35E **15** A6
Groningen □ *Neths.* 53°16N 6°40E **15** A6
Groom *U.S.A.* 35°12N 101°6W **84** D4
Groot → *S. Africa* 33°45S 24°36E **56** E3
Groot-Berg → *S. Africa* 32°47S 18°8E **56** E2
Groot-Brakrivier *S. Africa* 34°2S 22°18E **56** E3
Groot Karasberge *Namibia* 27°20S 18°40E **56** D2
Groot Kei → *S. Africa* 32°41S 28°22E **57** E4
Groot-Vis → *S. Africa* 33°28S 27°5E **56** E4
Grootdrink *S. Africa* 28°33S 21°42E **56** D3
Groote Eylandt *Australia* 14°0S 136°40E **62** A2
Grootfontein *Namibia* 19°31S 18°6E **56** B2
Grootlaagte → *Africa* 20°55S 21°27E **56** C3
Grootvloer → *S. Africa* 30°0S 20°40E **56** E3
Gros C. *Canada* 61°59N 113°32W **70** A6
Gros Islet *St. Lucia* 14°5N 60°58W **89** f
Gros Morne △ *Canada* 49°40N 57°50W **73** C8
Gros Piton *St. Lucia* 13°49N 61°5W **89** f
Gros Piton Pt. *St. Lucia* 13°49N 61°5W **89** f
Grossa, Pta. *Spain* 39°6N 1°36E **24** B8
Grosse Point *U.S.A.* 42°23N 82°54W **82** D2
Grosser Arber *Germany* 49°6N 13°8E **16** D7
Grosseto *Italy* 42°46N 11°8E **22** C4
Grossglockner *Austria* 47°5N 12°40E **16** E7
Groswater B. *Canada* 54°20N 57°40W **73** B8
Groton *Conn., U.S.A.* 41°21N 72°5W **83** E12
Groton *N.Y., U.S.A.* 42°36N 76°22W **83** D8
Groton *S. Dak., U.S.A.* 45°27N 98°6W **80** C4
Grouard Mission *Canada* 55°33N 116°9W **70** B5
Groundhog → *Canada* 48°45N 82°58W **72** C3
Grouw *Neths.* 53°5N 5°51E **15** A5
Grove City *U.S.A.* 41°10N 80°5W **82** E4
Grove Hill *U.S.A.* 31°42N 87°47W **85** F11
Groveland *U.S.A.* 37°50N 120°14W **78** H6
Grover Beach *U.S.A.* 35°7N 120°37W **79** K6
Groves *U.S.A.* 29°57N 93°54W **84** G8
Groveton *U.S.A.* 44°36N 71°31W **83** B13
Groznyy *Russia* 43°20N 45°45E **19** F8
Grudziądz *Poland* 53°30N 18°47E **17** B10
Gruinard B. *U.K.* 57°56N 5°35W **11** D3
Grundy Center *U.S.A.* 42°22N 92°47W **80** D7
Gruver *U.S.A.* 36°16N 101°24W **84** C4
Gryazi *Russia* 52°30N 39°58E **18** D6
Gryazovets *Russia* 58°50N 40°10E **18** C7
Grytviken *S. Georgia* 54°19S 36°33W **96** G9
Gua *India* 22°18N 85°20E **43** H11
Gua Musang *Malaysia* 4°53N 101°58E **39** K3
Guacanayabo, G. de *Cuba* 20°40N 77°20W **88** B4
Guachípas → *Argentina* 25°40S 65°30W **94** B2
Guadalajara *Mexico* 20°40N 103°20W **86** C4
Guadalajara *Spain* 40°37N 3°12W **21** B4
Guadalcanal *Solomon Is.* 9°32S 160°12E **58** B9
Guadales *Argentina* 34°30S 67°55W **94** C2
Guadalete → *Spain* 36°35N 6°13W **21** D2
Guadalquivir → *Spain* 36°47N 6°22W **21** D2
Guadalupe = Guadeloupe ☒ *W. Indies* 16°20N 61°40W **88** b
Guadalupe *Mexico* 22°45N 102°31W **86** C4
Guadalupe *U.S.A.* 34°58N 120°34W **79** L6
Guadalupe → *U.S.A.* 28°27N 96°47W **84** G6
Guadalupe, Sierra de *Spain* 39°28N 5°30W **21** C3
Guadalupe Bravos *Mexico* 31°20N 106°10W **86** A3
Guadalupe I. *Pac. Oc.* 29°0N 118°50W **66** G8
Guadalupe Mts. △ *U.S.A.* 31°40N 104°30W **84** F2
Guadalupe Peak *U.S.A.* 31°50N 104°52W **84** F2
Guadalupe y Calvo *Mexico* 26°6N 106°58W **86** B3
Guadarrama, Sierra de *Spain* 41°0N 4°0W **21** B4
Guadeloupe ☒ *W. Indies* 16°20N 61°40W **88** b
Guadeloupe △ *Guadeloupe* 16°10N 61°40W **88** b
Guadeloupe Passage *W. Indies* 16°50N 62°15W **89** C7
Guadiana → *Portugal* 37°14N 7°22W **21** D2
Guadix *Spain* 37°18N 3°11W **21** D4
Guafo, Boca del *Chile* 43°35S 74°0W **96** E2
Guaico *Trin. & Tob.* 10°35N 61°9W **93** K15
Guainía → *Colombia* 2°1N 67°7W **92** C5
Guaíra *Brazil* 24°5S 54°10W **95** A5
Guaíra □ *Paraguay* 25°45S 56°30W **94** B4
Guaire = Gorey *Ireland* 52°41N 6°18W **10** D5
Guaitecas, Is. *Chile* 44°0S 74°30W **96** E2
Guajará-Mirim *Brazil* 10°50S 65°20W **92** F5
Guajira, Pen. de la *Colombia* 12°0N 72°0W **92** A4
Gualán *Guatemala* 15°8N 89°22W **88** C2
Gualeguay *Argentina* 33°10S 59°14W **94** C4
Gualeguaychú *Argentina* 33°3S 59°31W **94** C4
Gualequay → *Argentina* 33°19S 59°39W **94** C4
Guam ☒ *Pac. Oc.* 13°27N 144°45E **64** F6
Guaminí *Argentina* 37°1S 62°28W **94** D3
Guamúchil *Mexico* 25°28N 108°6W **86** B3
Guana I. *Br. Virgin Is.* 18°30N 64°30W **89** e
Guanabacoa *Cuba* 23°8N 82°18W **88** B3
Guanacaste, Cordillera de *Costa Rica* 10°40N 85°4W **88** D2
Guanacaste △ *Costa Rica* 10°57N 85°30W **88** D2
Guanaceví *Mexico* 25°56N 105°57W **86** B3
Guanahani = San Salvador I. *Bahamas* 24°0N 74°40W **89** B5
Guanaja *Honduras* 16°30N 85°55W **88** C2
Guanajay *Cuba* 22°56N 82°42W **88** B3
Guanajuato *Mexico* 21°1N 101°15W **86** C4
Guanajuato □ *Mexico* 21°0N 101°0W **86** C4
Guandacol *Argentina* 29°30S 68°40W **94** B2
Guandi Shan *China* 37°53N 111°29E **34** F6
Guane *Cuba* 22°10N 84°7W **88** B3
Guangdong □ *China* 23°0N 113°0E **33** G11
Guangling *China* 39°47N 114°22E **34** E8
Guangrao *China* 37°5N 118°25E **35** F10
Guangwu *China* 37°48N 105°57E **34** F3
Guangxi Zhuangzu Zizhiqu □ *China* 24°0N 109°0E **33** G10
Guangyuan *China* 32°26N 105°51E **34** H3
Guangzhou *China* 23°6N 113°13E **33** G11
Guanica *Puerto Rico* 17°58N 66°55W **89** d
Guanipa → *Venezuela* 9°56N 62°26W **92** B6
Guannan *China* 34°8N 119°21E **35** G10
Guantánamo *Cuba* 20°10N 75°14W **89** B4
Guantánamo B. *Cuba* 19°59N 75°10W **89** C4
Guantao *China* 36°42N 115°25E **34** F8
Guanting Shuiku *China* 40°14N 115°35E **34** D8
Guanyun *China* 34°20N 119°18E **35** G10
Guapay = Grande → *Bolivia* 15°51S 64°39W **92** G6
Guápiles *Costa Rica* 10°10N 83°46W **88** D3
Guapo B. *Trin. & Tob.* 10°12N 61°41W **93** K15
Guaporé *Brazil* 28°51S 51°54W **95** B5
Guaporé → *Brazil* 11°55S 65°4W **92** F5
Guaqui *Bolivia* 16°41S 68°54W **92** G5
Guaramacal △ *Venezuela* 9°13N 70°12W **89** E5
Guarapari *Brazil* 20°40S 40°30W **95** A7
Guarapuava *Brazil* 25°20S 51°30W **95** B5
Guaratinguetá *Brazil* 22°49S 45°9W **95** A6
Guaratuba *Brazil* 25°53S 48°38W **95** B6
Guarda *Portugal* 40°32N 7°20W **21** B2
Guardafui, C. = Asir, Ras *Somali Rep.* 11°55N 51°10E **47** E5
Guárico □ *Venezuela* 8°40N 66°35W **92** B5
Guarujá *Brazil* 24°2S 46°25W **95** A6
Guarulhos *Brazil* 23°29S 46°33W **95** A6
Guasave *Mexico* 25°34N 108°27W **86** B3
Guasdualito *Venezuela* 7°15N 70°44W **92** B4
Guatemala *Guatemala* 14°40N 90°22W **88** D1
Guatemala ■ *Cent. Amer.* 15°40N 90°30W **88** C1
Guatemala Basin *Pac. Oc.* 11°0N 95°0W **65** F18
Guatemala Trench *Pac. Oc.* 14°0N 95°0W **66** H10
Guatopo △ *Venezuela* 10°5N 66°30W **89** D6
Guatuaro Pt. *Trin. & Tob.* 10°19N 60°59W **93** K16
Guaviare → *Colombia* 4°3N 67°44W **92** C5
Guaxupé *Brazil* 21°10S 47°5W **95** A6
Guayaguayare *Trin. & Tob.* 10°8N 61°2W **93** K15
Guayama *Puerto Rico* 17°59N 66°7W **89** d
Guayaquil *Ecuador* 2°15S 79°52W **92** D3
Guayaquil *Mexico* 29°59N 115°4W **86** B1
Guayaquil, G. de *Ecuador* 3°10S 81°0W **92** D2
Guaymas *Mexico* 27°56N 110°54W **86** B2
Guba *Dem. Rep. of the Congo* 10°38S 26°27E **55** E2
Gubkin *Russia* 51°17N 37°32E **19** D6
Gubkinskiy *Russia* 64°27N 76°36E **28** C8
Gudbrandsdalen *Norway* 61°33N 10°10E **8** F14
Guddu Barrage *Pakistan* 28°30N 69°50E **42** E3
Gudur *India* 14°12N 79°55E **40** M11
Guecho = Getxo *Spain* 43°21N 2°59W **21** A4
Guékédou *Guinea* 8°40N 10°5W **50** G3
Guelmine = Goulimine *Morocco* 28°56N 10°0W **50** C3
Guelph *Canada* 43°35N 80°20W **82** C4
Guerara *Algeria* 32°51N 4°22E **50** B6
Guéret *France* 46°11N 1°51E **20** C4
Guerneville *U.S.A.* 38°30N 123°0W **78** G4
Guernica = Gernika-Lumo *Spain* 43°19N 2°40W **21** A4
Guernsey *U.K.* 49°26N 2°35W **13** H5
Guernsey *U.S.A.* 42°16N 104°45W **76** E11
Guerrero □ *Mexico* 17°40N 100°0W **87** D5
Gügher *Iran* 29°28N 56°27E **45** D8
Guia *Canary Is.* 28°8N 15°38W **24** F4
Guia de Isora *Canary Is.* 28°12N 16°46W **24** F3
Guia Lopes da Laguna *Brazil* 21°26S 56°7W **95** A4
Guiana Highlands *S. Amer.* 5°10N 60°40W **90** C4
Guidónia-Montecélio *Italy* 42°1N 12°45E **22** C5
Guigang *China* 23°8N 109°35E **33** G10
Guijá *Mozam.* 24°27S 33°0E **57** C5
Guildford *U.K.* 51°14N 0°34W **13** F7
Guilford *U.S.A.* 41°17N 72°41W **83** E12
Guilin *China* 25°18N 110°15E **33** F11
Guillaume-Delisle, L. *Canada* 56°15N 76°17W **72** A4
Güimar *Canary Is.* 28°18N 16°24W **24** F3
Guimarães *Portugal* 41°28N 8°24W **21** B1
Guimaras □ *Phil.* 10°35N 122°37E **37** B6
Guinda *U.S.A.* 38°50N 122°12W **78** G4
Guinea *Africa* 8°0N 8°0E **48** F4
Guinea ■ *W. Afr.* 10°20N 11°30W **50** F3
Guinea, Gulf of *Atl. Oc.* 3°0N 2°30E **49** F4
Guinea-Bissau ■ *Africa* 12°0N 15°0W **50** F3
Güines *Cuba* 22°50N 82°0W **88** B3
Guingamp *France* 48°34N 3°10W **20** B2
Güiria *Venezuela* 10°32N 62°18W **93** K14
Guiuan *Phil.* 11°5N 125°55E **37** B7
Guiyang *China* 26°32N 106°40E **32** F10
Guizhou □ *China* 27°0N 107°0E **32** F10
Gujar Khan *Pakistan* 33°16N 73°19E **42** C5
Gujarat □ *India* 23°20N 71°0E **42** H4
Gujiao *China* 37°54N 112°8E **34** F7
Gujranwala *Pakistan* 32°10N 74°12E **42** C6
Gujrat *Pakistan* 32°40N 74°2E **42** C6
Gulbarga *India* 17°20N 76°50E **40** L10
Gulbene *Latvia* 57°8N 26°52E **9** H22
Gulf, The = Persian Gulf *Asia* 27°0N 50°0E **45** E6
Gulf Islands ⌓ *U.S.A.* 30°10N 87°10W **85** F11
Gulfport *U.S.A.* 30°22N 89°6W **85** F10
Gulgong *Australia* 32°20S 149°49E **63** E4
Gulian *China* 52°56N 122°21E **33** A13
Gulistan *Pakistan* 30°30N 66°35E **42** D2
Gulja = Yining *China* 43°58N 81°10E **32** C5
Gull Lake *Canada* 50°10N 108°29W **71** C7
Güllük *Turkey* 37°14N 27°35E **23** F12
Gulmarg *India* 34°3N 74°25E **43** B6
Gülshat *Kazakhstan* 46°38N 74°21E **28** C8
Gulu *Uganda* 2°48N 32°17E **54** B3
Gulwe *Tanzania* 6°30S 36°25E **54** D4
Gumal → *Pakistan* 31°40N 71°50E **42** D4
Gumbaz *Pakistan* 30°2N 69°0E **42** D3
Gumel *Nigeria* 12°39N 9°22E **50** F7
Gumi *S. Korea* 36°10N 128°12E **35** F15
Gumla *India* 23°3N 84°33E **43** H11
Gumlu *Australia* 19°53S 147°41E **62** B4
Gumma □ *Japan* 36°30N 138°20E **31** F9
Gumzai *Indonesia* 5°28S 134°42E **37** F8
Guna *India* 24°40N 77°19E **42** G7
Gunbalanya *Australia* 12°20S 133°4E **60** B5
Gundabooka △ *Australia* 30°30S 145°20E **63** E4
Gunisao → *Canada* 53°56N 97°53W **71** C9
Gunisao L. *Canada* 53°33N 96°15W **71** C9
Gunjyal *Pakistan* 32°20N 71°55E **42** C4
Gunnbjørn Fjeld *Greenland* 68°55N 29°47W **4** C6
Gunnedah *Australia* 30°59S 150°15E **63** E5
Gunnewin *Australia* 25°59S 148°33E **63** D4
Gunningbar Cr. → *Australia* 31°14S 147°6E **63** E4
Gunnison *Colo., U.S.A.* 38°33N 106°56W **76** G10
Gunnison *Utah, U.S.A.* 39°9N 111°49W **76** G8
Gunnison → *U.S.A.* 39°4N 108°35W **76** G9
Gunsan *S. Korea* 35°59N 126°45E **35** G14
Guntakal *India* 15°11N 77°27E **40** M10
Gunter *Canada* 44°52N 77°32W **82** B7
Guntersville *U.S.A.* 34°21N 86°18W **85** D11
Guntong *Malaysia* 4°36N 101°3E **39** K3
Guntur *India* 16°23N 80°30E **41** L12
Gunung Ciremay △ *Indonesia* 6°53S 108°24E **37** G13
Gunungapi *Indonesia* 6°45S 126°30E **37** F7
Gunungsitoli *Indonesia* 1°15N 97°30E **36** D1
Gunza *Angola* 10°50S 13°50E **52** G2
Guo He → *China* 32°59N 117°10E **35** H9
Guoyang *China* 33°32N 116°12E **34** H9
Gupis *Pakistan* 36°15N 73°20E **43** A5
Gurbantünggüt Shamo *China* 45°8N 87°20E **32** B6
Gurdaspur *India* 32°5N 75°31E **42** C6
Gurdon *U.S.A.* 33°55N 93°9W **84** E8
Gurgaon *India* 28°27N 77°1E **42** E7
Gurgueia → *Brazil* 6°50S 43°24W **93** E10
Gurha *India* 25°12N 71°39E **42** G4
Guri, Embalse de *Venezuela* 7°50N 62°52W **92** B6
Gurkha *Nepal* 28°5N 84°40E **43** E11
Gurla Mandhata = Naimona'nyi Feng *Nepal* 30°26N 81°18E **43** D9
Gurley *Australia* 29°45S 149°48E **63** D4
Gurnet Point *U.S.A.* 42°1N 70°34W **83** D14
Guro *Mozam.* 17°26S 32°30E **55** F3
Gurué *Mozam.* 15°25S 36°58E **55** F4
Gurun *Malaysia* 5°49N 100°27E **39** K3
Gürün *Turkey* 38°43N 37°15E **19** G6
Gurupá *Brazil* 1°25S 51°35W **93** D8
Gurupá, I. Grande de *Brazil* 1°25S 51°45W **93** D8
Gurupi *Brazil* 11°43S 49°4W **93** F9
Gurupi → *Brazil* 1°13S 46°6W **93** D9
Guruwe *Zimbabwe* 16°40S 30°42E **57** B5
Gurvan Sayhan Uul *Mongolia* 43°50N 104°0E **34** C3
Guryev = Atyraū *Kazakhstan* 47°5N 52°0E **19** E9
Gusau *Nigeria* 12°12N 6°40E **50** F7
Gushan *China* 39°50N 123°35E **35** E12
Gushgy = Serhetabat *Turkmenistan* 35°20N 62°18E **45** C9
Gusinoozersk *Russia* 51°16N 106°27E **29** D11
Gustavus *U.S.A.* 58°25N 135°44W **70** B1
Gustine *U.S.A.* 37°16N 121°0W **78** H6
Güstrow *Germany* 53°47N 12°10E **16** B7
Gütersloh *Germany* 51°54N 8°24E **16** C5
Gutha *Australia* 28°58S 115°55E **61** E2
Guthalungra *Australia* 19°52S 147°50E **62** B4
Guthrie *Canada* 44°28N 79°32W **82** B5
Guthrie *Okla., U.S.A.* 35°53N 97°25W **84** D6
Guthrie *Tex., U.S.A.* 33°37N 100°19W **84** E4
Guttenberg *U.S.A.* 42°47N 91°6W **80** D8
Gutu *Zimbabwe* 19°41S 31°9E **57** B5
Guwahati *India* 26°10N 91°45E **41** F17
Guy Fawkes River △ *Australia* 30°0S 152°20E **63** D5
Guyana ■ *S. Amer.* 5°0N 59°0W **92** C7
Guyane française = French Guiana ☒ *S. Amer.* 4°0N 53°0W **93** C8
Guyang *China* 41°0N 110°5E **34** D6
Guyenne *France* 44°30N 0°40E **20** D4
Guymon *U.S.A.* 36°41N 101°29W **84** C4
Guyra *Australia* 30°15S 151°40E **63** E5
Guyuan *Hebei, China* 41°37N 115°40E **34** D8
Guyuan *Ningxia Huizu, China* 36°0N 106°20E **34** F4
Güzelyurt = Morphou *Cyprus* 35°12N 32°59E **25** D11
Guzhen *China* 33°22N 117°18E **35** H9
Guzmán, L. de *Mexico* 31°20N 107°30W **86** A3
Gwa *Burma* 17°36N 94°34E **41** L19
Gwaai *Zimbabwe* 19°15S 27°45E **55** F2
Gwaai → *Zimbabwe* 17°59S 26°52E **55** F2
Gwabegar *Australia* 30°37S 148°59E **63** E4
Gwādar *Pakistan* 25°10N 62°18E **40** G3
Gwaii Haanas △ *Canada* 52°21N 131°26W **70** C2
Gwalior *India* 26°12N 78°10E **42** F8
Gwanda *Zimbabwe* 20°55S 29°0E **55** G2
Gwane *Dem. Rep. of the Congo* 4°45N 25°48E **54** B2
Gwangju *S. Korea* 35°9N 126°54E **35** G14
Gwanju = Gwangju *S. Korea* 35°9N 126°54E **35** G14
Gweebarra B. *Ireland* 54°51N 8°23W **10** B3
Gweedore *Ireland* 55°3N 8°13W **10** A3
Gweru *Zimbabwe* 19°28S 29°45E **55** F2
Gwinn *U.S.A.* 46°19N 87°27W **80** B10
Gwydir → *Australia* 29°27S 149°48E **63** D4
Gwynedd □ *U.K.* 52°52N 4°10W **12** E3
Gyandzha = Gäncä *Azerbaijan* 40°45N 46°20E **19** F8
Gyangzê *China* 29°5N 89°47E **32** F6
Gyaring Hu *China* 34°50N 97°40E **32** E8
Gydanskiy Poluostrov *Russia* 70°0N 78°0E **28** C8
Gyeongju *S. Korea* 35°51N 129°14E **35** G15
Gympie *Australia* 26°11S 152°38E **63** D5
Gyöngyös *Hungary* 47°48N 19°56E **17** E10
Győr *Hungary* 47°41N 17°40E **17** E9
Gypsum Pt. *Canada* 61°53N 114°35W **70** A6
Gypsumville *Canada* 51°45N 98°40W **71** C9
Gyula *Hungary* 46°38N 21°17E **17** E11
Gyumri *Armenia* 40°47N 43°50E **19** F7
Gyzylarbat = Serdar *Turkmenistan* 39°4N 56°23E **45** B8
Gyzyletrek = Etrek *Turkmenistan* 37°36N 54°46E **45** B7

H

Ha 'Arava → *Israel* 30°50N 35°20E **46** E4
Ha Coi *Vietnam* 21°26N 107°46E **38** B6
Ha Dong *Vietnam* 20°58N 105°46E **38** B5
Ha Giang *Vietnam* 22°50N 104°59E **38** A5
Ha Karmel △ *Israel* 32°45N 35°5E **46** C4
Ha Long = Hong Gai *Vietnam* 20°57N 107°5E **38** B6
Ha Long, Vinh *Vietnam* 20°56N 107°3E **38** B6
Ha Tien *Vietnam* 10°23N 104°29E **39** G5
Ha Tinh *Vietnam* 18°20N 105°54E **38** C5
Ha Trung *Vietnam* 19°58N 105°50E **38** C5
Haaksbergen *Neths.* 52°9N 6°45E **15** B6
Ha'ano *Tonga* 19°41S 174°18W **59** c
Ha'apai Group *Tonga* 19°47S 174°27W **59** c
Haapiti *Moorea* 17°34S 149°52W **59** d
Haapsalu *Estonia* 58°56N 23°30E **9** G20
Haarlem *Neths.* 52°23N 4°39E **15** B4
Haast → *N.Z.* 43°50S 169°2E **59** E2
Haasts Bluff *Australia* 23°22S 132°0E **60** D5
Haasts Bluff ✪ *Australia* 23°39S 130°34E **60** D5
Hab → *Pakistan* 24°53N 66°41E **42** G3
Hab Nadi Chauki *Pakistan* 25°0N 66°50E **42** G2
Habahe *China* 48°3N 86°23E **32** B6
Habaswein *Kenya* 1°2N 39°30E **54** B4
Habay *Canada* 58°50N 118°44W **70** B5
Ḩabbānīyah *Iraq* 33°17N 43°29E **44** C4
Habirag *China* 42°17N 115°42E **34** C8
Haboro *Japan* 44°22N 141°42E **30** B10
Ḩabshān *U.A.E.* 23°50N 53°37E **45** F7
Hachijō-Jima *Japan* 33°5N 139°45E **31** H9
Hachiman *Japan* 35°45N 136°57E **31** G8
Hachinohe *Japan* 40°30N 141°29E **30** D10
Hachiōji *Japan* 35°40N 139°20E **31** G9
Hackensack *U.S.A.* 40°52N 74°4W **83** F10
Hackettstown *U.S.A.* 40°51N 74°50W **83** F10
Hadali *Pakistan* 32°16N 72°11E **42** C5
Hadarba, Ras *Sudan* 22°4N 36°51E **51** D13
Hadarom □ *Israel* 31°0N 35°0E **46** E4
Ḩadd, Ra's al *Oman* 22°35N 59°50E **47** C6
Haddington *U.K.* 55°57N 2°47W **11** F6
Hadejia *Nigeria* 12°30N 10°5E **50** F7
Ḩadera *Israel* 32°27N 34°55E **46** C3
Ḩadera, N. → *Israel* 32°28N 34°52E **46** C3
Haderslev *Denmark* 55°15N 9°30E **9** J13
Hadhramaut = Ḩaḑramawt *Yemen* 15°30N 49°30E **47** D4
Hadībоh *Yemen* 12°39N 54°2E **47** E5
Hadley B. *Canada* 72°31N 108°12W **68** C10
Hadong *S. Korea* 35°5N 127°44E **35** G14
Ḩaḑramawt *Yemen* 15°30N 49°30E **47** D4
Ḩadrānīyah *Iraq* 35°38N 43°14E **44** C4
Hadrian's Wall *U.K.* 55°0N 2°30W **12** B5
Hae, Ko *Thailand* 7°44N 98°22E **39** a
Haeju *N. Korea* 38°3N 125°45E **35** E13
Hä'ena *U.S.A.* 22°14N 159°34W **75** L8
Haenam *S. Korea* 34°34N 126°35E **35** G14
Haenertsburg *S. Africa* 24°0S 29°50E **57** C4
Haerhpin = Harbin *China* 45°48N 126°40E **35** B14
Hafar al Bāţin *Si. Arabia* 28°32N 45°52E **44** D5
Ḩafirat al 'Aydā *Si. Arabia* 26°26N 39°12E **44** E3
Ḩafit *Oman* 23°59N 55°49E **45** F7
Hafizabad *Pakistan* 32°5N 73°40E **42** C5
Haflong *India* 25°10N 93°5E **41** G18
Haft Gel *Iran* 31°30N 49°32E **45** D6
Hagalil *Israel* 32°53N 35°18E **46** C4
Hagemeister I. *U.S.A.* 58°39N 160°54W **74** D7
Hagen *Germany* 51°21N 7°27E **16** C4
Hagerman *U.S.A.* 33°7N 104°20W **77** K11
Hagerman Fossil Beds ⌓ *U.S.A.* 42°48N 114°57W **76** E6
Hagerstown *U.S.A.* 39°39N 77°43W **81** F15
Hagersville *Canada* 42°58N 80°3W **82** D4
Hagfors *Sweden* 60°3N 13°45E **9** F15
Hagi *Japan* 34°30N 131°22E **31** G5
Hagolan *Syria* 33°0N 35°45E **46** C4
Hagondange *France* 49°16N 6°11E **20** B7
Hags Hd. *Ireland* 52°57N 9°28W **10** D2
Hague, C. de la *France* 49°44N 1°56W **20** B3
Hague, The = 's-Gravenhage *Neths.* 52°7N 4°17E **15** B4
Haguenau *France* 48°49N 7°47E **20** B7
Hai Duong *Vietnam* 20°56N 106°19E **38** B6
Haicheng *China* 40°50N 122°45E **35** D12
Haidar Khel *Afghan.* 33°58N 68°38E **42** C3
Haidarâbâd = Hyderabad *India* 17°22N 78°29E **40** L11
Haidargarh *India* 26°37N 81°22E **43** F9
Haifa = Ḩefa *Israel* 32°46N 35°0E **46** C4
Haikou *China* 20°1N 110°16E **38** B8
Ḩā'il *Si. Arabia* 27°28N 41°45E **44** E4
Ḩā'il □ *Si. Arabia* 26°40N 41°40E **44** E4
Hailar *China* 49°10N 119°38E **33** B12
Hailey *U.S.A.* 43°31N 114°19W **76** E6
Haileybury *Canada* 47°30N 79°38W **72** C4
Hailin *China* 44°37N 129°30E **35** B15
Hailun *China* 47°28N 126°50E **33** B14
Hailuoto *Finland* 65°3N 24°45E **8** D21

Hainan □ *China* 19°0N 109°30E **38** C7
Hainan Dao *China* 19°0N 109°30E **38** C7
Hainan Str. = Qiongzhou Haixia *China* 20°10N 110°15E **38** B8
Hainaut □ *Belgium* 50°30N 4°0E **15** D4
Haines *Alaska, U.S.A.* 59°14N 135°26W **70** B1
Haines *Oreg., U.S.A.* 44°55N 117°56W **76** D5
Haines City *U.S.A.* 28°7N 81°38W **85** G14
Haines Junction *Canada* 60°45N 137°30W **70** A1
Haiphong *Vietnam* 20°47N 106°41E **38** B6
Haiti ■ *W. Indies* 19°0N 72°30W **89** C5
Haiya *Sudan* 18°20N 36°21E **51** E13
Haiyan *China* 36°53N 100°59E **32** D9
Haiyang *China* 36°47N 121°9E **35** F11
Haiyuan *China* 36°35N 105°52E **34** F3
Haizhou *China* 34°37N 119°7E **35** G10
Haizhou Wan *China* 34°50N 119°20E **35** G10
Haj Ali Qoli, Kavīr *Iran* 35°55N 54°50E **45** C7
Hajdúböszörmény *Hungary* 47°40N 21°30E **17** E11
Haji Ibrahim *Iraq* 36°40N 44°30E **44** B5
Hājjābād *Iran* 33°37N 60°0E **45** C9
Hajipur *India* 25°45N 85°13E **43** G11
Ḩajjah *Yemen* 15°42N 43°36E **47** D3
Ḩājjīābād *Iran* 28°19N 55°55E **45** D7
Ḩājjīābād-e Zarrīn *Iran* 33°9N 54°51E **45** C7
Hajnówka *Poland* 52°47N 23°35E **17** B12
Hakansson, Mts. *Dem. Rep. of the Congo* 8°40S 25°45E **55** D2
Hakkâri *Turkey* 37°34N 43°44E **44** B4
Hakken-Zan *Japan* 34°10N 135°54E **31** G7
Hakkōda San *Japan* 40°50N 141°0E **30** D10
Hakodate *Japan* 41°45N 140°44E **30** D10
Hakos *Namibia* 23°13S 16°21E **56** C2
Haku-San *Japan* 36°9N 136°46E **31** F8
Haku-San △ *Japan* 36°15N 136°45E **31** F8
Hakui *Japan* 36°53N 136°47E **31** F8
Hala *Pakistan* 25°43N 68°20E **40** G6
Ḩalab *Syria* 36°10N 37°15E **44** B3
Ḩalabjah *Iraq* 35°10N 45°58E **44** C5
Halaib *Sudan* 22°12N 36°30E **51** D13
Halaib Triangle *Africa* 22°30N 35°20E **51** D13
Hālat 'Ammār *Si. Arabia* 29°10N 36°4E **44** D3
Halbā *Lebanon* 34°34N 36°6E **46** A5
Halberstadt *Germany* 51°54N 11°3E **16** C6
Halcombe *N.Z.* 40°8S 175°30E **59** D5
Halcon, Mt. *Phil.* 13°16N 121°0E **37** B6
Halde Fjäll = Haltiatunturi *Finland* 69°17N 21°18E **8** B19
Halden *Norway* 59°9N 11°23E **9** G14
Haldia *Bangla.* 22°1N 88°3E **43** H13
Haldwani *India* 29°31N 79°30E **43** E8
Hale → *Australia* 24°56S 135°53E **62** C2
Halesowen *U.K.* 52°27N 2°3W **13** E5
Halesworth *U.K.* 52°20N 1°31E **13** E9
Haleyville *U.S.A.* 34°14N 87°37W **85** D11
Half Dome *U.S.A.* 37°44N 119°32E **78** H7
Halfmoon Bay *N.Z.* 46°50S 168°5E **59** G2
Halfway → *Canada* 56°12N 121°32W **70** B4
Halia *India* 24°50N 82°19E **43** G10
Haliburton *Canada* 45°3N 78°30W **82** A6
Halifax *Australia* 18°32S 146°22E **62** B4
Halifax *Canada* 44°38N 63°35W **73** D7
Halifax *U.K.* 53°43N 1°52W **12** D6
Halifax *U.S.A.* 40°25N 76°55W **82** F8
Halifax B. *Australia* 18°50S 147°0E **62** B4
Halifax I. *Namibia* 26°38S 15°4E **56** D2
Halik Shan *China* 42°20N 81°22E **32** C5
Halīl → *Iran* 27°40N 58°30E **45** E8
Halimun △ *Indonesia* 6°42S 106°26E **37** G11
Halkida = Chalkida *Greece* 38°27N 23°42E **23** E10
Halkirk *U.K.* 58°30N 3°29W **11** C5
Hall Beach *Canada* 68°46N 81°12W **69** D15
Hall Pen. *Canada* 63°30N 66°0W **69** E18
Hall Pt. *Australia* 15°40S 124°23E **60** C3
Halland *Sweden* 57°8N 12°47E **9** H15
Hallāniyat, Jazā'ir al *Oman* 17°30N 55°58E **47** D6
Hallasan *S. Korea* 33°22N 126°32E **35** H14
Halle *Belgium* 50°44N 4°13E **15** D4
Halle *Germany* 51°30N 11°56E **16** C6
Hällefors *Sweden* 59°47N 14°31E **9** G16
Hallett *Australia* 33°25S 138°55E **63** E2
Hallettsville *U.S.A.* 29°27N 96°57W **84** G6
Halley *Antarctica* 75°35S 26°39W **5** D1
Hallim *S. Korea* 33°24N 126°15E **35** H14
Hallingdalselva → *Norway* 60°23N 9°35E **8** F13
Hallock *U.S.A.* 48°47N 96°57W **80** A5
Halls Creek *Australia* 18°16S 127°38E **60** C4
Halls Gap *Australia* 37°8S 142°34E **63** F3
Halls Lake *Canada* 45°7N 78°45W **82** A6
Hallsberg *Sweden* 59°5N 15°7E **9** G16
Hallstead *U.S.A.* 41°58N 75°45W **83** E9
Halmahera *Indonesia* 0°40N 128°0E **37** D7
Halmstad *Sweden* 56°41N 12°52E **9** H15
Hälsingborg = Helsingborg *Sweden* 56°3N 12°42E **9** H15
Hälsingland *Sweden* 61°40N 16°5E **8** F17
Halstead *U.K.* 51°57N 0°40E **13** F8
Haltiatunturi *Finland* 69°17N 21°18E **8** B19
Halton □ *U.K.* 53°22N 2°45W **12** D5
Haltwhistle *U.K.* 54°58N 2°26W **12** C5
Ḩālūl *Qatar* 25°40N 52°40E **45** E7
Halvad *India* 23°1N 71°11E **42** H4
Ḩalvān *Iran* 33°57N 56°15E **45** C8
Hamab *Namibia* 28°7S 19°16E **56** D2
Hamada *Japan* 34°56N 132°4E **31** G6
Hamadān *Iran* 34°52N 48°32E **45** C6
Hamadān □ *Iran* 35°0N 49°0E **45** C6
Ḩamāh *Syria* 35°5N 36°40E **44** C3
Hamamatsu *Japan* 34°45N 137°45E **31** G8
Hamar *Norway* 60°48N 11°7E **8** F14
Hamâta, Gebel *Egypt* 24°17N 35°0E **44** E2
Hamatonbetsu *Japan* 45°10N 142°20E **30** B11
Hambantota *Sri Lanka* 6°10N 81°10E **40** R12
Hamber ⌓ *Canada* 52°20N 118°0W **70** C5
Hamburg *Germany* 53°33N 9°59E **16** B5
Hamburg *Ark., U.S.A.* 33°14N 91°48W **84** E9
Hamburg *N.Y., U.S.A.* 42°43N 78°50W **82** D6
Hamburg *Pa., U.S.A.* 40°33N 75°59W **83** F9
Ḩamḑ, W. al → *Si. Arabia* 24°55N 36°20E **44** E3
Hamden *U.S.A.* 41°23N 72°54W **83** E12
Häme *Finland* 61°38N 25°10E **8** F21
Hämeenlinna *Finland* 61°0N 24°28E **8** F21
Hamelin Pool *Australia* 26°22S 114°20E **61** E1
Hameln *Germany* 52°6N 9°21E **16** B5
Hamerkaz □ *Israel* 32°15N 34°55E **46** C3
Hamersley Ra. *Australia* 22°0S 117°45E **60** D2
Hamhŭng *N. Korea* 39°54N 127°30E **35** E14
Hami *China* 42°55N 93°25E **32** C7
Hamilton *Australia* 37°45S 142°2E **63** F3
Hamilton *Canada* 43°15N 79°50W **82** C5
Hamilton *N.Z.* 37°47S 175°19E **59** B5
Hamilton *U.K.* 55°46N 4°2W **11** F4
Hamilton *Ala., U.S.A.* 34°9N 87°59W **85** D11
Hamilton *Mont., U.S.A.* 46°15N 114°10W **76** C6
Hamilton *N.Y., U.S.A.* 42°50N 75°33W **83** D9
Hamilton *Ohio, U.S.A.* 39°24N 84°34W **81** F11
Hamilton *Tex., U.S.A.* 31°42N 98°7W **84** F5
Hamilton → *Queens., Australia* 23°30S 139°47E **62** C2
Hamilton → *S. Austral., Australia* 26°40S 135°19E **63** D2
Hamilton City *U.S.A.* 39°45N 122°1W **78** F4
Hamilton I. *Australia* 20°21S 148°56E **62** b
Hamilton Inlet *Canada* 54°0N 57°30W **73** B8
Hamilton Mt. *U.S.A.* 43°25N 74°22W **83** C10
Hamina *Finland* 60°34N 27°12E **8** F22
Hamirpur *H.P., India* 31°41N 76°31E **42** D7
Hamirpur *Ut. P., India* 25°57N 80°9E **43** G9
Hamlet *U.S.A.* 34°53N 79°42W **85** D15
Hamley Bridge *Australia* 34°17S 138°35E **63** E2
Hamlin = Hameln *Germany* 52°6N 9°21E **16** B5
Hamlin *N.Y., U.S.A.* 43°17N 77°55W **82** C7
Hamlin *Tex., U.S.A.* 32°53N 100°8W **84** E4
Hamm *Germany* 51°40N 7°50E **16** C4
Ḩammār, Hawr al *Iraq* 30°50N 47°10E **44** D5
Hammerfest *Norway* 70°39N 23°41E **8** A20
Hammond *Ind., U.S.A.* 41°38N 87°30W **80** E10
Hammond *La., U.S.A.* 30°30N 90°28W **85** F9
Hammond *N.Y., U.S.A.* 44°27N 75°42W **83** B9
Hammondsport *U.S.A.* 42°25N 77°13W **82** D7
Hammonton *U.S.A.* 39°39N 74°48W **81** F16
Hampden *N.Z.* 45°18S 170°50E **59** F3
Hampshire □ *U.K.* 51°7N 1°23W **13** F6
Hampshire Downs *U.K.* 51°15N 1°10W **13** F6
Hampton *N.B., Canada* 45°32N 65°51W **73** C6
Hampton *Ont., Canada* 43°58N 78°45W **82** C6
Hampton *Ark., U.S.A.* 33°32N 92°28W **84** E8
Hampton *Iowa, U.S.A.* 42°45N 93°13W **80** D7
Hampton *N.H., U.S.A.* 42°57N 70°50W **83** D14
Hampton *S.C., U.S.A.* 32°52N 81°7W **85** E14
Hampton *Va., U.S.A.* 37°2N 76°21W **81** G15
Hampton Bays *U.S.A.* 40°53N 72°30W **83** F12
Hampton Tableland *Australia* 32°0S 127°0E **61** F4
Hamyang *S. Korea* 35°32N 127°42E **35** G14
Han Pijesak *Bos.-H.* 44°5N 18°57E **23** B8
Han Shui → *China* 30°34N 114°17E **33** E11
Hanak *Si. Arabia* 25°32N 37°0E **44** E3
Hanamaki *Japan* 39°23N 141°7E **30** E10
Hanang *Tanzania* 4°30S 35°25E **54** C4
Hanau *Germany* 50°7N 8°56E **16** C5
Hanbogd = Ihbulag *Mongolia* 43°11N 107°10E **34** C4
Hancheng *China* 35°31N 110°25E **34** G6
Hancock *Mich., U.S.A.* 47°8N 88°35W **80** B9
Hancock *N.Y., U.S.A.* 41°57N 75°17W **83** E9
Hancock *Vt., U.S.A.* 43°55N 72°50W **83** C12
Handa *Japan* 34°53N 136°55E **31** G8
Handa I. *U.K.* 58°23N 5°11W **11** C3
Handan *China* 36°35N 114°28E **34** F8
Handeni *Tanzania* 5°25S 38°2E **54** D4
Handwara *India* 34°21N 74°20E **43** B6
Hanegev *Israel* 30°50N 35°0E **46** E4
Hanford *U.S.A.* 36°20N 119°39W **78** J7
Hanford Reach ⌓ *U.S.A.* 46°40N 119°30W **76** C4
Hang Chat *Thailand* 18°20N 99°21E **38** C2
Hangang → *S. Korea* 37°50N 126°30E **35** F14
Hangayn Nuruu *Mongolia* 47°30N 99°0E **32** B8
Hangchou = Hangzhou *China* 30°18N 120°11E **33** E13
Hanggin Houqi *China* 40°58N 107°4E **34** D4
Hanggin Qi *China* 39°52N 108°50E **34** E5
Hangu *China* 39°18N 117°53E **35** E9
Hangzhou *China* 30°18N 120°11E **33** E13
Hangzhou Wan *China* 30°15N 120°45E **33** E13
Hanh *Mongolia* 51°32N 100°35E **32** A9
Hanhongor *Mongolia* 43°55N 104°28E **34** C3
Hania = Chania *Greece* 35°30N 24°4E **25** D6
Ḩanīdh *Si. Arabia* 26°35N 48°38E **45** E6
Ḩanīsh *Yemen* 13°45N 42°46E **47** E3
Hankinson *U.S.A.* 46°4N 96°54W **80** B5
Hankö *Finland* 59°50N 22°57E **9** G20
Hanksville *U.S.A.* 38°22N 110°43W **76** G8
Hanle *India* 32°42N 79°4E **43** C8
Hanmer Springs *N.Z.* 42°32S 172°50E **59** E4
Hann → *Australia* 17°26S 126°17E **60** C4
Hann, Mt. *Australia* 15°45S 126°0E **60** C4
Hanna *Canada* 51°40N 111°54W **70** C6
Hanna *U.S.A.* 41°52N 106°34W **76** F10
Hannah B. *Canada* 51°40N 80°0W **72** B4
Hannibal *Mo., U.S.A.* 39°42N 91°22W **80** F8
Hannibal *N.Y., U.S.A.* 43°19N 76°35W **83** C8
Hannover *Germany* 52°22N 9°46E **16** B5
Hanoi *Vietnam* 21°5N 105°55E **38** B5
Hanover = Hannover *Germany* 52°22N 9°46E **16** B5
Hanover *Canada* 44°9N 81°2W **82** B3
Hanover *S. Africa* 31°4S 24°29E **56** E3
Hanover *N.H., U.S.A.* 43°42N 72°17W **83** C12
Hanover *Ohio, U.S.A.* 40°4N 82°16W **82** F2
Hanover *Pa., U.S.A.* 39°48N 76°59W **81** F15
Hanover, I. *Chile* 51°0S 74°50W **96** G2
Hans Lollik I. *U.S. Virgin Is.* 18°24N 64°53W **89** e
Hansdiha *India* 24°36N 87°5E **43** G12
Hansi *H.P., India* 32°27N 77°50E **42** C7
Hansi *Haryana, India* 29°10N 75°57E **42** E6
Hanson, L. *Australia* 31°0S 136°15E **63** E2
Hanting *China* 36°46N 119°12E **35** F10
Hantsavichy *Belarus* 52°49N 26°30E **17** B14
Hanumangarh *India* 29°35N 74°19E **42** E6
Hanyin *China* 32°54N 108°28E **34** H5
Hanzhong *China* 33°10N 107°1E **34** H4
Hanzhuang *China* 34°33N 117°23E **35** G9
Haora *India* 22°34N 88°18E **43** H13
Haparanda *Sweden* 65°52N 24°8E **8** D21
Happy *U.S.A.* 34°45N 101°52W **84** D4
Happy Camp *U.S.A.* 41°48N 123°23W **76** F2
Happy Valley-Goose Bay *Canada* 53°15N 60°20W **73** B7
Hapsu *N. Korea* 41°13N 128°51E **35** D15
Hapur *India* 28°45N 77°45E **42** E7
Ḩaql *Si. Arabia* 29°10N 34°58E **46** F3
Har *Indonesia* 5°16S 133°14E **37** F8
Har-Ayrag *Mongolia* 45°47N 109°16E **34** B5
Har Hu *China* 38°20N 97°38E **32** D8
Har Us Nuur *Mongolia* 48°0N 92°0E **32** B7
Har Yehuda *Israel* 31°35N 34°57E **46** D3
Ḩaraḑ *Si. Arabia* 24°22N 49°0E **47** C4
Haramosh *Pakistan* 35°50N 74°54E **43** B6
Haranomachi *Japan* 37°38N 140°58E **30** F10
Harare *Zimbabwe* 17°43S 31°2E **55** F3
Harazé *Chad* 9°57N 20°48E **51** G10
Harbin *China* 45°48N 126°40E **35** B14
Harbor Beach *U.S.A.* 43°51N 82°39W **82** C2
Harborcreek *U.S.A.* 42°9N 79°57W **82** D5
Harbour Breton *Canada* 47°29N 55°50W **73** C8
Harbour Deep *Canada* 50°25N 56°32W **73** B8
Harda *India* 22°27N 77°5E **42** H7
Hardangerfjorden *Norway* 60°5N 6°0E **9** F12
Hardangervidda *Norway* 60°7N 7°20E **8** F12
Hardap ⌓ *Namibia* 24°29S 17°45E **56** C2
Hardap Dam *Namibia* 24°32S 17°50E **56** C2
Hardenberg *Neths.* 52°34N 6°37E **15** B6
Harderwijk *Neths.* 52°21N 5°38E **15** B5
Hardey → *Australia* 22°45S 116°8E **60** D2
Hardin *U.S.A.* 45°44N 107°37W **76** D10
Harding *S. Africa* 30°35S 29°55E **57** E4
Harding Ra. *Australia* 16°17S 124°55E **60** C3
Hardisty *Canada* 52°40N 111°18W **70** C6
Hardoi *India* 27°26N 80°6E **43** F9
Hardwar = Haridwar *India* 29°58N 78°9E **42** E8
Hardwick *U.S.A.* 44°30N 72°22W **83** B12
Hardwood Lake *Canada* 45°12N 77°26W **82** A7
Hardy, Pen. *Chile* 55°30S 68°20W **96** H3
Hardy, Pte. *St. Lucia* 14°6N 60°56W **89** f
Hare B. *Canada* 51°15N 55°45W **73** B8
Hareid *Norway* 62°22N 6°1E **8** E12
Harer *Ethiopia* 9°20N 42°8E **47** F3
Hargeisa *Somali Rep.* 9°30N 44°2E **47** F3
Hari → *Indonesia* 1°16S 104°5E **36** E2
Haria *Canary Is.* 29°8N 13°32W **24** E6
Haridwar *India* 29°58N 78°9E **42** E8
Harim, Jabal al *Oman* 25°58N 56°14E **45** E8
Haringhata → *Bangla.* 22°0N 89°58E **41** J16
Harīr, W. al → *Syria* 32°44N 35°59E **46** C4
Harīrūd → *Asia* 37°24N 60°38E **45** B9
Härjedalen *Sweden* 62°22N 13°5E **8** E15
Harlan *Iowa, U.S.A.* 41°39N 95°19W **80** E6
Harlan *Ky., U.S.A.* 36°51N 83°19W **81** G12
Harlech *U.K.* 52°52N 4°6W **12** E3
Harlem *U.S.A.* 48°32N 108°47W **76** B9
Harlingen *Neths.* 53°11N 5°25E **15** A5
Harlingen *U.S.A.* 26°12N 97°42W **84** H6
Harlow *U.K.* 51°46N 0°8E **13** F8
Harlowton *U.S.A.* 46°26N 109°50W **76** C9
Harnai *Pakistan* 30°6N 67°56E **42** D2
Harney Basin *U.S.A.* 43°0N 119°30W **76** E4
Harney L. *U.S.A.* 43°14N 119°8W **76** E4
Harney Peak *U.S.A.* 43°52N 103°32W **80** D2
Härnösand *Sweden* 62°38N 17°55E **8** E17
Haroldswick *U.K.* 60°48N 0°50W **11** A8
Harp L. *Canada* 55°5N 61°50W **73** A7
Harper *Liberia* 4°25N 7°43W **50** H4
Harper, Mt. *U.S.A.* 64°14N 143°51W **74** C11
Harrai *India* 22°37N 79°13E **43** H8
Harrand *Pakistan* 29°28N 70°3E **42** E4
Harricana → *Canada* 50°56N 79°32W **72** B4
Harriman *U.S.A.* 35°56N 84°33W **85** D12
Harrington Harbour *Canada* 50°31N 59°30W **73** B8
Harris *U.K.* 57°50N 6°55W **11** D2
Harris, L. *Australia* 31°10S 135°10E **63** E2
Harris, Sd. of *U.K.* 57°44N 7°6W **11** D1
Harris Pt. *Canada* 43°6N 82°9W **82** C2
Harrisburg *Ill., U.S.A.* 37°44N 88°32W **80** G9
Harrisburg *Nebr., U.S.A.* 41°33N 103°44W **80** E2
Harrisburg *Pa., U.S.A.* 40°16N 76°53W **82** F8
Harrismith *S. Africa* 28°15S 29°8E **57** D4
Harrison *Ark., U.S.A.* 36°14N 93°7W **84** C8
Harrison *Maine, U.S.A.* 44°7N 70°39W **83** B14
Harrison *Nebr., U.S.A.* 42°41N 103°53W **80** D2
Harrison, C. *Canada* 54°55N 57°55W **73** B8
Harrison Bay *U.S.A.* 70°40N 151°0W **74** A9
Harrison L. *Canada* 49°33N 121°50W **70** D4
Harrisonburg *U.S.A.* 38°27N 78°52W **81** F14
Harrisonville *U.S.A.* 38°39N 94°21W **80** F6
Harriston *Canada* 43°57N 80°53W **82** C4
Harrisville *Mich., U.S.A.* 44°39N 83°17W **82** B1
Harrisville *N.Y., U.S.A.* 44°9N 75°19W **83** B9
Harrisville *Pa., U.S.A.* 41°8N 80°0W **82** E5
Harrodsburg *U.S.A.* 37°46N 84°51W **81** G11
Harrogate *U.K.* 54°0N 1°33W **12** C6
Harrow *Canada* 42°2N 82°55W **82** D2
Harrow □ *U.K.* 51°35N 0°21W **13** F7
Harrowsmith *Canada* 44°24N 76°40W **83** B8
Harry S. Truman Res. *U.S.A.* 38°16N 93°24W **80** F7
Harsīn *Iran* 34°18N 47°33E **44** C5
Harstad *Norway* 68°48N 16°30E **8** B17
Harsud *India* 22°6N 76°44E **42** H7
Hart *U.S.A.* 43°42N 86°22W **80** D10
Hart, L. *Australia* 31°10S 136°25E **63** E2
Hartbees → *S. Africa* 28°45S 20°32E **56** D3
Hartford *Conn., U.S.A.* 41°46N 72°41W **83** E12
Hartford *Ky., U.S.A.* 37°27N 86°55W **80** G10
Hartford *S. Dak., U.S.A.* 43°38N 96°57W **80** D5
Hartford *Vt., U.S.A.* 43°40N 72°20W **83** C12
Hartford *Wis., U.S.A.* 43°19N 88°22W **80** D9
Hartford City *U.S.A.* 40°27N 85°22W **81** E11
Hartland *Canada* 46°20N 67°32W **73** C6
Hartland Pt. *U.K.* 51°1N 4°32W **13** F3
Hartlepool *U.K.* 54°42N 1°13W **12** C6
Hartlepool □ *U.K.* 54°42N 1°17W **12** C6
Hartley Bay *Canada* 53°25N 129°15W **70** C3
Hartmannberge *Namibia* 17°0S 13°0E **56** B1
Hartney *Canada* 49°30N 100°35W **71** D8
Harts → *S. Africa* 28°24S 24°17E **56** D3
Harts Range *Australia* 23°6S 134°55E **62** C1
Hartselle *U.S.A.* 34°27N 86°56W **85** D11
Hartshorne *U.S.A.* 34°51N 95°34W **84** D7
Hartstown *U.S.A.* 41°33N 80°23W **82** E4
Hartsville *U.S.A.* 34°23N 80°4W **85** D14
Hartswater *S. Africa* 27°34S 24°43E **56** D3
Hartwell *U.S.A.* 34°21N 82°56W **85** D13
Harunabad *Pakistan* 29°35N 73°8E **42** E5
Harvand *Iran* 28°25N 55°43E **45** D7
Harvey *Australia* 33°5S 115°54E **61** F2
Harvey *Ill., U.S.A.* 41°36N 87°50W **80** E10
Harvey *N. Dak., U.S.A.* 47°47N 99°56W **80** B4
Harwich *U.K.* 51°56N 1°17E **13** F9
Haryana □ *India* 29°0N 76°10E **42** E7
Haryn → *Belarus* 52°7N 27°17E **17** B14
Harz *Germany* 51°38N 10°44E **16** C6
Hasa *Si. Arabia* 25°50N 49°0E **45** E6
Ḩasā, W. al → *Jordan* 31°4N 35°29E **46** D4
Ḩasanābād *Iran* 32°8N 52°44E **45** C7
Ḩasb, W. → *Iraq* 31°45N 44°17E **44** D5
Hasdo → *India* 21°44N 82°44E **43** J10
Hashimoto *Japan* 34°19N 135°37E **31** G7
Hashtjerd *Iran* 35°52N 50°40E **45** C6
Hashtpur = Tālesh *Iran* 37°58N 48°58E **45** B6
Haskell *U.S.A.* 33°10N 99°44W **84** E5
Haskovo = Khaskovo *Bulgaria* 41°56N 25°30E **23** D11
Haslemere *U.K.* 51°5N 0°43W **13** F7
Hasselt *Belgium* 50°56N 5°21E **15** D5
Hassi Messaoud *Algeria* 31°51N 6°1E **50** B7
Hässleholm *Sweden* 56°10N 13°46E **9** H15
Hastings *N.Z.* 39°39S 176°52E **59** C6
Hastings *U.K.* 50°51N 0°35E **13** G8
Hastings *Mich., U.S.A.* 42°39N 85°17W **81** D11
Hastings *Minn., U.S.A.* 44°44N 92°51W **80** C7
Hastings *Nebr., U.S.A.* 40°35N 98°23W **80** E4
Hastings Ra. *Australia* 31°15S 152°14E **63** E5
Hat Lot *Vietnam* 21°15N 104°7E **38** B5
Hat Yai *Thailand* 7°1N 100°27E **39** J3
Hatanbulag = Ergel *Mongolia* 43°8N 109°5E **34** C5
Hatay *Turkey* 36°14N 36°10E **44** B3
Hatch *U.S.A.* 32°40N 107°9W **77** K10
Hatchet L. *Canada* 58°36N 103°40W **71** B8
Hateruma-Shima *Japan* 24°3N 123°47E **31** M1
Hatfield *Australia* 33°54S 143°49E **63** E3
Hatgal *Mongolia* 50°26N 100°9E **32** A9
Hathras *India* 27°36N 78°6E **42** F8
Hatia *Bangla.* 22°30N 91°5E **41** H17
Hato Mayor *Dom. Rep.* 18°46N 69°15W **89** C6
Hatta *India* 24°7N 79°36E **43** G8
Hatta *U.A.E.* 24°45N 56°4E **45** E8
Hattah *Australia* 34°48S 142°17E **63** E3
Hattah Kulkyne △ *Australia* 34°16S 142°33E **63** E3
Hatteras, C. *U.S.A.* 35°14N 75°32W **85** D17
Hattiesburg *U.S.A.* 31°20N 89°17W **85** F10
Hatvan *Hungary* 47°40N 19°45E **17** E10
Hau → *Vietnam* 9°30N 106°13E **39** H6
Haugesund *Norway* 59°23N 5°13E **9** G11
Haukipudas *Finland* 65°12N 25°20E **8** D21
Haultain → *Canada* 55°51N 106°46W **71** B7
Hauraki G. *N.Z.* 36°35S 175°5E **59** B5
Haut Atlas *Morocco* 32°30N 5°0W **50** B4
Hautes Fagnes = Hohes Venn *Belgium* 50°30N 6°5E **15** D6
Hauts Plateaux *Algeria* 35°0N 1°0E **50** B6
Havana = La Habana *Cuba* 23°8N 82°22W **88** B3
Havana *U.S.A.* 40°18N 90°4W **80** E8
Havant *U.K.* 50°51N 0°58W **13** G7
Havasor = Kığzı *Turkey* 38°18N 43°25E **44** B4
Havasu, L. *U.S.A.* 34°18N 114°28W **79** L12
Havel → *Germany* 52°50N 12°3E **16** B7
Havelian *Pakistan* 34°2N 73°10E **42** B5
Havelock *Canada* 44°26N 77°53W **82** B7
Havelock *N.Z.* 41°17S 173°48E **59** D4
Havelock *U.S.A.* 34°53N 76°54W **85** D16
Haverfordwest *U.K.* 51°48N 4°58W **13** F3
Haverhill *U.K.* 52°5N 0°28E **13** E8
Haverhill *U.S.A.* 42°47N 71°5W **83** D13
Haverstraw *U.S.A.* 41°12N 73°58W **83** E11
Havirga *Mongolia* 45°41N 113°5E **34** B7
Havířov *Czech Rep.* 49°46N 18°20E **17** D10
Havlíčkův Brod *Czech Rep.* 49°36N 15°33E **16** D8
Havre *U.S.A.* 48°33N 109°41W **76** B9
Havre-Aubert *Canada* 47°12N 61°56W **73** C7
Havre-St.-Pierre *Canada* 50°18N 63°33W **73** B7
Haw → *U.S.A.* 35°36N 79°3W **85** D15
Hawai'i *U.S.A.* 19°30N 155°30W **75** M8
Hawai'i □ *U.S.A.* 19°30N 156°30W **75** M8
Hawaiian Is. *Pac. Oc.* 20°30N 156°0W **65** E12
Hawaiian Ridge *Pac. Oc.* 24°0N 165°0W **65** E11
Hawarden *U.S.A.* 43°0N 96°29W **80** D5
Hawea, L. *N.Z.* 44°28S 169°19E **59** F2
Hawera *N.Z.* 39°35S 174°19E **59** C5
Hawi *U.S.A.* 20°14N 155°50W **75** L8
Hawick *U.K.* 55°26N 2°47W **11** F6
Hawk Junction *Canada* 48°5N 84°38W **72** C3
Hawke B. *N.Z.* 39°25S 177°20E **59** C6
Hawker *Australia* 31°59S 138°22E **63** E2
Hawke's Bay *Canada* 50°36N 57°10W **73** B8
Hawkesbury *Canada* 45°37N 74°37W **72** C5
Hawkesbury I. *Canada* 53°37N 129°3W **70** C3
Hawkesbury Pt. *Australia* 11°55S 134°5E **62** A1
Hawkinsville *U.S.A.* 32°17N 83°28W **85** E13
Hawley *Minn., U.S.A.* 46°53N 96°19W **80** B5
Hawley *Pa., U.S.A.* 41°28N 75°11W **83** E9
Ḩawrān, W. → *Iraq* 33°58N 42°34E **44** C4
Hawsh Mūssá *Lebanon* 33°45N 35°55E **46** B4
Hawthorne *U.S.A.* 38°32N 118°38W **76** G4
Hay *Australia* 34°30S 144°51E **63** E3
Hay → *Australia* 24°50S 138°0E **62** C2
Hay → *Canada* 60°50N 116°26W **70** A5
Hay, C. *Australia* 14°5S 129°29E **60** B4
Hay I. *Canada* 44°53N 80°58W **82** B4
Hay L. *Canada* 58°50N 118°50W **70** B5
Hay-on-Wye *U.K.* 52°5N 3°8W **13** E4
Hay Point *Australia* 21°18S 149°17E **62** C4
Hay River *Canada* 60°51N 115°44W **70** A5
Hay Springs *U.S.A.* 42°41N 102°41W **80** D2
Haya = Tehoru *Indonesia* 3°23S 129°30E **37** E7
Hayachine-San *Japan* 39°34N 141°29E **30** E10
Hayastan = Armenia ■ *Asia* 40°20N 45°0E **19** F7
Haydān, W. al → *Jordan* 31°29N 35°34E **46** D4
Hayden *U.S.A.* 40°30N 107°16W **76** F10
Hayes *U.S.A.* 44°23N 101°1W **80** C3
Hayes → *Canada* 57°3N 92°12W **72** A1
Hayes, Mt. *U.S.A.* 63°37N 146°43W **74** C10
Hayes Creek *Australia* 13°43S 131°22E **60** B5
Hayle *U.K.* 50°11N 5°26W **13** G2
Hayling I. *U.K.* 50°48N 0°59W **13** G7
Hayman I. *Australia* 20°4S 148°53E **62** b
Hayrabolu *Turkey* 41°12N 27°5E **23** D12
Hays *Canada* 50°6N 111°48W **70** C6
Hays *U.S.A.* 38°53N 99°20W **80** F4
Haysyn *Ukraine* 48°57N 29°25E **17** D15
Hayvoron *Ukraine* 48°22N 29°52E **17** D15
Hayward *Calif., U.S.A.* 37°40N 122°4W **78** H4
Hayward *Wis., U.S.A.* 46°1N 91°29W **80** B8
Haywards Heath *U.K.* 51°0N 0°5W **13** G7
Hazafon □ *Israel* 32°40N 35°20E **46** C4
Hazar *Turkmenistan* 39°34N 53°16E **19** G9
Hazārān, Kūh-e *Iran* 29°35N 57°20E **45** D8
Hazard *U.S.A.* 37°15N 83°12W **81** G12
Hazaribag *India* 23°58N 85°26E **43** H11
Hazaribag Road *India* 24°12N 85°57E **43** G11
Hazelton *Canada* 55°20N 127°42W **70** B3
Hazelton *U.S.A.* 46°29N 100°17W **80** B3
Hazen *U.S.A.* 47°18N 101°38W **80** B3
Hazen, L. *Canada* 81°47N 71°1W **69** A17
Hazlehurst *Ga., U.S.A.* 31°52N 82°36W **85** F13
Hazlehurst *Miss., U.S.A.* 31°52N 90°24W **85** F9
Hazlet *U.S.A.* 40°25N 74°12W **83** F10
Hazleton *U.S.A.* 40°57N 75°59W **83** F9
Hazlett, L. *Australia* 21°30S 128°48E **60** D4
Hazro *Turkey* 38°15N 40°47E **44** B4
Head of Bight *Australia* 31°30S 131°25E **61** F5
Headlands *Zimbabwe* 18°15S 32°2E **55** F3
Healdsburg *U.S.A.* 38°37N 122°52W **78** G4
Healdton *U.S.A.* 34°14N 97°29W **84** D6
Healesville *Australia* 37°35S 145°30E **63** F4
Healy *U.S.A.* 63°52N 148°58W **74** C10
Heany Junction *Zimbabwe* 20°6S 28°54E **57** C4
Heard I. *Ind. Oc.* 53°6S 72°36E **3** G13
Hearne *U.S.A.* 30°53N 96°36W **84** F6
Hearst *Canada* 49°40N 83°41W **72** C3
Heart → *U.S.A.* 46°46N 100°50W **80** B3
Heart's Content *Canada* 47°54N 53°27W **73** C9
Heath, Pte. *Canada* 49°8N 61°40W **73** C7
Heathrow, London ✈ **(LHR)** *U.K.* 51°28N 0°27W **13** F7
Heavener *U.S.A.* 34°53N 94°36W **84** D7
Hebbronville *U.S.A.* 27°18N 98°41W **84** H5
Hebei □ *China* 39°0N 116°0E **34** E9
Hebel *Australia* 28°58S 147°47E **63** D4
Heber *U.S.A.* 32°44N 115°32W **79** N11
Heber Springs *U.S.A.* 35°30N 92°2W **84** D8
Hebgen L. *U.S.A.* 44°52N 111°20W **76** D8
Hebi *China* 35°57N 114°7E **34** G8
Hebrides *U.K.* 57°30N 7°0W **6** D4
Hebrides, Sea of the *U.K.* 57°5N 7°0W **11** D2
Hebron = Al Khalīl *West Bank* 31°32N 35°6E **46** D4
Hebron *Canada* 58°5N 62°30W **69** F19
Hebron *N. Dak., U.S.A.* 46°54N 102°3W **80** B2
Hebron *Nebr., U.S.A.* 40°10N 97°35W **80** E5
Hecate Str. *Canada* 53°10N 130°30W **70** C2
Heceta I. *U.S.A.* 55°46N 133°40W **70** B2
Hechi *China* 24°40N 108°2E **32** G10
Hechuan *China* 30°2N 106°12E **32** E10
Hecla *U.S.A.* 45°53N 98°9W **80** C4
Hecla I. *Canada* 51°10N 96°43W **71** C9
Hede *Sweden* 62°23N 13°30E **8** E15
Hedemora *Sweden* 60°18N 15°58E **9** F16
Heerde *Neths.* 52°24N 6°2E **15** B6
Heerenveen *Neths.* 52°57N 5°55E **15** B5
Heerhugowaard *Neths.* 52°40N 4°51E **15** B4
Heerlen *Neths.* 50°55N 5°58E **15** D5
Ḩefa *Israel* 32°46N 35°0E **46** C4
Ḩefa □ *Israel* 32°40N 35°0E **46** C4
Hefei *China* 31°52N 117°18E **33** E12
Hegang *China* 47°20N 130°19E **33** B15
Hei Ling Chau *China* 22°15N 114°2E **33** a
Heichengzhen *China* 36°24N 106°3E **34** F4
Heidelberg *Germany* 49°24N 8°42E **16** D5
Heidelberg *S. Africa* 34°6S 20°59E **56** E3
Heihe *China* 50°10N 127°30E **33** A14
Heilbron *S. Africa* 27°16S 27°59E **57** D4
Heilbronn *Germany* 49°9N 9°13E **16** D5
Heilongjiang □ *China* 48°0N 126°0E **33** B14
Heilunkiang = Heilongjiang □ *China* 48°0N 126°0E **33** B14
Heimaey *Iceland* 63°26N 20°17W **8** E3
Heinola *Finland* 61°13N 26°2E **8** F22
Heinze Chaung *Burma* 14°42N 97°52E **38** E1
Heinze Kyun *Burma* 14°25N 97°45E **38** E1
Heishan *China* 41°40N 122°5E **35** D12
Heishui *China* 42°8N 119°30E **35** C10

Hejaz = Ḥijāz *Si. Arabia* 24°0N 40°0E **44** E3
Hejian *China* 38°25N 116°5E **34** E9
Hejin *China* 35°35N 110°42E **34** G6
Hekimhan *Turkey* 38°50N 37°55E **44** B3
Hekla *Iceland* 63°56N 19°35W **8** E4
Hekou *Gansu, China* 36°10N 103°26E **34** F2
Hekou *Yunnan, China* 22°30N 103°59E **32** G9
Helan Shan *China* 38°30N 105°55E **34** E3
Helen Atoll *Palau* 2°40N 132°0E **37** D8
Helena *Ark., U.S.A.* 34°32N 90°36W **85** D9
Helena *Mont., U.S.A.* 46°36N 112°2W **76** C7
Helendale *U.S.A.* 34°44N 117°19W **79** L9
Helensburgh *U.K.* 56°1N 4°43W **11** E4
Helensville *N.Z.* 36°41S 174°29E **59** B5
Helenvale *Australia* 15°43S 145°14E **62** B4
Helgeland *Norway* 66°7N 13°29E **8** C15
Helgoland *Germany* 54°10N 7°53E **16** A4
Heligoland = Helgoland
Germany 54°10N 7°53E **16** A4
Heligoland B. = Deutsche Bucht
Germany 54°15N 8°0E **16** A5
Hell Hole Gorge △
Australia 25°31S 144°12E **62** D3
Hella *Iceland* 63°50N 20°24W **8** E3
Hellertown *U.S.A.* 40°35N 75°21W **83** F9
Hellespont = Çanakkale Boğazı
Turkey 40°17N 26°32E **23** D12
Hellevoetsluis *Neths.* 51°50N 4°8E **15** C4
Hellín *Spain* 38°31N 1°40W **21** C5
Hells Canyon *U.S.A.* 45°30N 117°45W **76** D5
Hell's Gate △ *Kenya* 0°54S 36°19E **54** C4
Helmand □ *Afghan.* 31°20N 64°0E **40** D4
Helmand → *Afghan.* 31°12N 61°34E **40** D2
Helmeringhausen
Namibia 25°54S 16°57E **56** D2
Helmond *Neths.* 51°29N 5°41E **15** C5
Helmsdale *U.K.* 58°7N 3°39W **11** C5
Helmsdale → *U.K.* 58°8N 3°43W **11** C5
Helong *China* 42°40N 129°0E **35** C15
Helper *U.S.A.* 39°41N 110°51W **76** G8
Helsingborg *Sweden* 56°3N 12°42E **9** H15
Helsingfors = Helsinki
Finland 60°10N 24°55E **9** F21
Helsingør *Denmark* 56°2N 12°35E **9** H15
Helsinki *Finland* 60°10N 24°55E **9** F21
Helston *U.K.* 50°6N 5°17W **13** G2
Helvellyn *U.K.* 54°32N 3°1W **12** C4
Helwân *Egypt* 29°50N 31°20E **51** C12
Hemel Hempstead *U.K.* 51°44N 0°28W **13** F7
Hemet *U.S.A.* 33°45N 116°58W **79** M10
Hemingford *U.S.A.* 42°19N 103°4W **80** D3
Hemis △ *India* 34°10N 77°15E **42** B7
Hemmingford *Canada* 45°3N 73°35W **83** A11
Hempstead *N.Y., U.S.A.* 40°42N 73°37W **83** F11
Hempstead *Tex., U.S.A.* 30°6N 96°5W **84** F6
Hemse *Sweden* 57°15N 18°22E **9** H18
Henan □ *China* 34°0N 114°0E **34** H8
Henares → *Spain* 40°24N 3°30W **21** B4
Henashi-Misaki *Japan* 40°37N 139°51E **30** D9
Henderson *Argentina* 36°18S 61°43W **94** D3
Henderson *Ky., U.S.A.* 37°50N 87°35W **80** G10
Henderson *N.C., U.S.A.* 36°20N 78°25W **85** C15
Henderson *N.Y., U.S.A.* 43°50N 76°10W **83** C8
Henderson *Nev., U.S.A.* 36°2N 114°58W **79** J12
Henderson *Tenn.,
U.S.A.* 35°26N 88°38W **85** D10
Henderson *Tex., U.S.A.* 32°9N 94°48W **84** E7
Henderson I. *Pac. Oc.* 24°22S 128°19W **65** K15
Hendersonville *N.C.,
U.S.A.* 35°19N 82°28W **85** D13
Hendersonville *Tenn.,
U.S.A.* 36°18N 86°37W **85** C11
Hendijān *Iran* 30°14N 49°43E **45** D6
Hendorābī *Iran* 26°40N 53°37E **45** E7
Hengcheng *China* 38°18N 106°28E **34** E4
Hengdaohezi *China* 44°52N 129°0E **35** B15
Hengduan Shan *China* 28°30N 98°50E **32** F8
Hengelo *Neths.* 52°16N 6°48E **15** B6
Henggang *China* 22°39N 114°12E **33** a
Hengshan *China* 22°33N 113°35E **33** a
Hengshui *China* 37°41N 115°40E **34** F8
Hengyang *China* 26°59N 112°22E **33** F11
Henley-on-Thames *U.K.* 51°32N 0°54W **13** F7
Henlopen, C. *U.S.A.* 38°48N 75°6W **81** F16
Hennenman *S. Africa* 27°59S 27°1E **56** D4
Hennessey *U.S.A.* 36°6N 97°54W **84** C6
Henri Pittier △
Venezuela 10°26N 67°37W **89** D6
Henrietta *N.Y., U.S.A.* 43°4N 77°37W **82** C7
Henrietta *Tex., U.S.A.* 33°49N 98°12W **84** E5
Henrietta, Ostrov = Genriyetty,
Ostrov *Russia* 77°6N 156°30E **29** B16
Henrietta Maria, C.
Canada 55°9N 82°20W **72** A3
Henry *U.S.A.* 41°7N 89°22W **80** E9
Henryetta *U.S.A.* 35°27N 95°59W **84** D7
Henryville *Canada* 45°8N 73°11W **83** A11
Hensall *Canada* 43°26N 81°30W **82** C3
Hentiesbaai *Namibia* 22°8S 14°18E **56** C1
Hentiyn Nuruu
Mongolia 48°30N 108°30E **33** B10
Henty *Australia* 35°30S 147°3E **63** F4
Henzada *Burma* 17°38N 95°26E **41** L19
Heppner *U.S.A.* 45°21N 119°33W **76** D4
Hepworth *Canada* 44°37N 81°9W **82** B3
Hequ *China* 39°20N 111°15E **34** E6
Héraðsflói *Iceland* 65°42N 14°12W **8** D6
Héraðsvötn → *Iceland* 65°45N 19°25W **8** D4
Heraklion = Iraklio
Greece 35°20N 25°12E **25** D7
Herald Cays *Australia* 16°58S 149°9E **62** B4
Herāt *Afghan.* 34°20N 62°7E **40** B3
Herāt □ *Afghan.* 35°0N 62°0E **40** B3
Herbert → *Australia* 18°31S 146°17E **62** B4
Herberton *Australia* 17°20S 145°25E **62** B4
Herbertsdale *S. Africa* 34°1S 21°46E **56** E3
Herceg-Novi *Montenegro* 42°30N 18°33E **23** C8

Herchmer *Canada* 57°22N 94°10W **71** B10
Herðubreið *Iceland* 65°11N 16°21W **8** D5
Hereford *U.K.* 52°4N 2°43W **13** E5
Hereford *U.S.A.* 34°49N 102°24W **84** D3
Herefordshire □ *U.K.* 52°8N 2°40W **13** E5
Herentals *Belgium* 51°12N 4°51E **15** C4
Herford *Germany* 52°7N 8°39E **16** B5
Herington *U.S.A.* 38°40N 96°57W **80** F5
Herkimer *U.S.A.* 43°2N 74°59W **83** D10
Herlong *U.S.A.* 40°8N 120°8W **78** E6
Herm *U.K.* 49°30N 2°28W **13** H5
Hermann *U.S.A.* 38°42N 91°27W **80** F8
Hermannsburg
Australia 23°57S 132°45E **60** D5
Hermanus *S. Africa* 34°27S 19°12E **56** E2
Hermidale *Australia* 31°30S 146°42E **63** E4
Hermiston *U.S.A.* 45°51N 119°17W **76** D4
Hermon *Canada* 45°6N 77°37W **82** A7
Hermon *U.S.A.* 44°28N 75°14W **83** B9
Hermon, Mt. = Shaykh, J. ash
Lebanon 33°25N 35°50E **46** B4
Hermosillo *Mexico* 29°10N 111°0W **86** B2
Hernád → *Hungary* 47°56N 21°8E **17** D11
Hernandarias *Paraguay* 25°20S 54°40W **95** B5
Hernandez *U.S.A.* 36°24N 120°46W **78** J6
Hernando *Argentina* 32°28S 63°40W **94** C3
Hernando *U.S.A.* 34°50N 90°0W **85** D10
Herndon *U.S.A.* 40°43N 76°51W **83** F8
Herne *Germany* 51°32N 7°14E **15** C7
Herne Bay *U.K.* 51°21N 1°8E **13** F9
Herning *Denmark* 56°8N 8°58E **9** H13
Heroica Caborca = Caborca
Mexico 30°37N 112°6W **86** A2
Heroica Nogales = Nogales
Mexico 31°19N 110°56W **86** A2
Heron Bay *Canada* 48°40N 86°25W **72** C2
Heron I. *Australia* 23°27S 151°55E **62** C5
Herradura, Pta. de la
Canary Is. 28°26N 14°8W **24** F5
Herreid *U.S.A.* 45°50N 100°4W **80** C3
Herrin *U.S.A.* 37°48N 89°2W **80** G9
Herriot *Canada* 56°22N 101°16W **71** B8
Herschel I. *Canada* 69°35N 139°5W **4** C1
Hershey *U.S.A.* 40°17N 76°39W **83** F8
Herstal *Belgium* 50°40N 5°38E **15** D5
Hertford *U.K.* 51°48N 0°4W **13** F7
Hertfordshire □ *U.K.* 51°51N 0°5W **13** F7
's-Hertogenbosch *Neths.* 51°42N 5°17E **15** C5
Hertzogville *S. Africa* 28°9S 25°30E **56** D4
Hervey B. *Australia* 25°0S 152°52E **62** C5
Herzliyya *Israel* 32°10N 34°50E **46** C3
Heşār *Fārs, Iran* 29°52N 50°16E **45** D6
Heşār *Markazī, Iran* 35°50N 49°12E **45** C6
Heshui *China* 35°48N 108°0E **34** G5
Heshun *China* 37°22N 113°32E **34** F7
Hesperia *U.S.A.* 34°25N 117°18W **79** L9
Hesse = Hessen □
Germany 50°30N 9°0E **16** C5
Hessen □ *Germany* 50°30N 9°0E **16** C5
Hetauda *Nepal* 27°25N 85°2E **43** F11
Hetch Hetchy Aqueduct
U.S.A. 37°29N 122°19W **78** H5
Hettinger *U.S.A.* 46°0N 102°42W **80** B2
Heuksando *S. Korea* 34°40N 125°30E **35** G13
Heunghae *S. Korea* 36°12N 129°21E **35** F15
Heuvelton *U.S.A.* 44°37N 75°25W **83** B9
Hewitt *U.S.A.* 31°28N 97°12W **84** F6
Hexham *U.K.* 54°58N 2°4W **12** C5
Hexigten Qi *China* 43°18N 117°30E **35** C9
Heysham *U.K.* 54°3N 2°53W **12** C5
Heywood *Australia* 38°8S 141°37E **63** F3
Heze *China* 35°14N 115°20E **34** G8
Hi Vista *U.S.A.* 34°45N 117°46W **79** L9
Hialeah *U.S.A.* 25°51N 80°16W **85** J14
Hiawatha *U.S.A.* 39°51N 95°32W **80** F6
Hibbing *U.S.A.* 47°25N 92°56W **80** B7
Hibernia Reef *Australia* 12°0S 123°23E **60** B3
Hickman *U.S.A.* 36°34N 89°11W **80** G9
Hickory *U.S.A.* 35°44N 81°21W **85** D14
Hicks, Pt. *Australia* 37°49S 149°17E **63** F4
Hicks L. *Canada* 61°25N 100°0W **71** A9
Hicksville *U.S.A.* 40°46N 73°32W **83** F11
Hida-Gawa → *Japan* 35°26N 137°3E **31** G8
Hida-Sammyaku *Japan* 36°30N 137°40E **31** F8
Hidaka-Sammyaku
Japan 42°35N 142°45E **30** C11
Hidalgo □ *Mexico* 20°30N 99°0W **87** C5
Hidalgo, Presa M.
Mexico 26°30N 108°35W **86** B3
Hidalgo del Parral
Mexico 26°56N 105°40W **86** B3
Hierro *Canary Is.* 27°44N 18°0W **24** G1
Higashiajima-San
Japan 37°40N 140°10E **30** F10
Higashiōsaka *Japan* 34°39N 135°37E **31** G7
Higgins *U.S.A.* 36°7N 100°2W **84** C4
Higgins Corner *U.S.A.* 39°2N 121°5W **78** F5
High Bridge *U.S.A.* 40°40N 74°54W **83** F10
High Desert *U.S.A.* 43°40N 120°20W **76** E3
High Island Res. *China* 22°22N 114°21E **33** a
High Level *Canada* 58°31N 117°8W **70** B5
High Point *U.S.A.* 35°57N 80°0W **85** D15
High Prairie *Canada* 55°30N 116°30W **70** B5
High River *Canada* 50°30N 113°50W **70** C6
High Tatra = Tatry
Slovak Rep. 49°20N 20°0E **17** D11
High Veld *Africa* 27°0S 27°0E **48** J6
High Wycombe *U.K.* 51°37N 0°45W **13** F7
Highland □ *U.K.* 57°17N 4°21W **11** D4
Highland Park *U.S.A.* 42°11N 87°48W **80** D10
Highmore *U.S.A.* 44°31N 99°27W **80** C4
Highrock L. *Canada* 55°45N 100°30W **71** B8
Higüey *Dom. Rep.* 18°37N 68°42W **89** C6
Hiiumaa *Estonia* 58°50N 22°45E **9** G20
Ḥijārah, Şaḥrā' al *Iraq* 30°25N 44°30E **44** D5
Ḥijāz *Si. Arabia* 24°0N 40°0E **44** E3
Hijo = Tagum *Phil.* 7°33N 125°53E **37** C7
Hikari *Japan* 33°58N 131°58E **31** H5

Hiko *U.S.A.* 37°32N 115°14W **78** H11
Hikone *Japan* 35°15N 136°10E **31** G8
Hikurangi *Gisborne, N.Z.* 37°55S 178°4E **59** C6
Hikurangi *Northland,
N.Z.* 35°36S 174°17E **59** A5
Hildesheim *Germany* 52°9N 9°56E **16** B5
Hill → *Australia* 30°23S 115°3E **61** F2
Hill City *Idaho, U.S.A.* 43°18N 115°3W **76** E6
Hill City *Kans., U.S.A.* 39°22N 99°51W **80** F4
Hill City *Minn., U.S.A.* 46°59N 93°36W **80** B7
Hill City *S. Dak., U.S.A.* 43°56N 103°35W **80** D2
Hill Island L. *Canada* 60°30N 109°50W **71** A7
Hillaby, Mt. *Barbados* 13°12N 59°35W **89** g
Hillcrest *Barbados* 13°13N 59°31W **89** g
Hillcrest Center *U.S.A.* 35°23N 118°57W **79** K8
Hillegom *Neths.* 52°18N 4°35E **15** B4
Hillsboro *Kans., U.S.A.* 38°21N 97°12W **80** F5
Hillsboro *N. Dak., U.S.A.* 47°26N 97°3W **80** B5
Hillsboro *Ohio, U.S.A.* 39°12N 83°37W **81** F12
Hillsboro *Oreg., U.S.A.* 45°31N 122°59W **78** E4
Hillsboro *Tex., U.S.A.* 32°1N 97°8W **84** E6
Hillsborough *Grenada* 12°28N 61°28W **89** D7
Hillsborough *U.S.A.* 43°7N 71°54W **83** C13
Hillsborough Channel
Australia 20°56S 149°15E **62** b
Hillsdale *Mich., U.S.A.* 41°56N 84°38W **81** E11
Hillsdale *N.Y., U.S.A.* 42°11N 73°32W **83** D11
Hillsport *Canada* 49°27N 85°34W **72** C2
Hillston *Australia* 33°30S 145°31E **63** E4
Hilo *U.S.A.* 19°44N 155°5W **75** M8
Hilton *U.S.A.* 43°17N 77°48W **82** C7
Hilton Head Island
U.S.A. 32°13N 80°45W **85** E14
Hilversum *Neths.* 52°14N 5°10E **15** B5
Himachal Pradesh □
India 31°30N 77°0E **42** D7
Himalaya *Asia* 29°0N 84°0E **43** E11
Himalchuli *Nepal* 28°27N 84°38E **43** E11
Himatnagar *India* 23°37N 72°57E **42** H5
Himeji *Japan* 34°50N 134°40E **31** G7
Himi *Japan* 36°50N 136°55E **31** F8
Ḥimş *Syria* 34°40N 36°45E **46** A5
Ḥimş □ *Syria* 34°30N 37°0E **46** A6
Hinche *Haiti* 19°9N 72°1W **89** C5
Hinchinbrook I.
Australia 18°20S 146°15E **62** B4
Hinchinbrook Island △
Australia 18°14S 146°6E **62** B4
Hinckley *U.K.* 52°33N 1°22W **13** E6
Hinckley *U.S.A.* 46°1N 92°56W **80** B7
Hindaun *India* 26°44N 77°5E **42** F7
Hindmarsh, L. *Australia* 36°5S 141°55E **63** F3
Hindu Bagh *Pakistan* 30°56N 67°50E **42** D2
Hindu Kush *Asia* 36°0N 71°0E **40** B7
Hindupur *India* 13°49N 77°32E **40** N10
Hines Creek *Canada* 56°20N 118°40W **70** B5
Hinesville *U.S.A.* 31°51N 81°36W **85** F14
Hinganghat *India* 20°30N 78°52E **40** J11
Hingham *U.S.A.* 48°33N 110°25W **76** B8
Hingir *India* 21°57N 83°41E **43** J10
Hingoli *India* 19°41N 77°15E **40** K10
Hinna = Imi *Ethiopia* 6°28N 42°10E **47** F3
Hinnøya *Norway* 68°35N 15°50E **8** B16
Hinojosa del Duque *Spain* 38°30N 5°9W **21** C3
Hinsdale *U.S.A.* 42°47N 72°29W **83** D12
Hinthada = Henzada
Burma 17°38N 95°26E **41** L19
Hinton *Canada* 53°26N 117°34W **70** C5
Hinton *U.S.A.* 37°40N 80°54W **81** G13
Hios = Chios *Greece* 38°27N 26°9E **23** E12
Hirado *Japan* 33°22N 129°33E **31** H4
Hirakud Dam *India* 21°32N 83°45E **41** J13
Hiran → *India* 23°6N 79°21E **43** H8
Hirapur *India* 24°22N 79°13E **43** G8
Hirara *Japan* 24°48N 125°17E **31** M2
Hiratsuka *Japan* 35°19N 139°21E **31** G9
Hiroo *Japan* 42°17N 143°19E **30** C11
Hirosaki *Japan* 40°34N 140°28E **30** D10
Hiroshima *Japan* 34°24N 132°30E **31** G6
Hiroshima □ *Japan* 34°50N 133°0E **31** G6
Hisar *India* 29°12N 75°45E **42** E6
Hisb, Sha'ib → Ḥasb, W. →
Iraq 31°45N 44°17E **44** D5
Ḥismā *Si. Arabia* 28°30N 36°0E **44** D3
Hispaniola *W. Indies* 19°0N 71°0W **89** C5
Hīt *Iraq* 33°38N 42°49E **44** C4
Hita *Japan* 33°20N 130°58E **31** H5
Hitachi *Japan* 36°36N 140°39E **31** F10
Hitchin *U.K.* 51°58N 0°16W **13** F7
Hitiaa *Tahiti* 17°36S 149°18W **59** d
Hitoyoshi *Japan* 32°13N 130°45E **31** H5
Hitra *Norway* 63°30N 8°45E **8** E13
Hiva Oa *French Polynesia* 9°45S 139°0W **65** H14
Hixon *Canada* 53°25N 122°35W **70** C4
Ḥiyyon, N. → *Israel* 30°25N 35°10E **46** E4
Hjalmar L. *Canada* 61°33N 109°25W **71** A7
Hjälmaren *Sweden* 59°18N 15°40E **9** G16
Hjørring *Denmark* 57°29N 9°59E **9** H13
Hkakabo Razi *Burma* 28°25N 97°23E **41** E20
Hkamti = Singkaling Hkamti
Burma 26°0N 95°39E **41** G19
Hlobane *S. Africa* 27°42S 31°0E **57** D5
Hluhluwe *S. Africa* 28°1S 32°15E **57** D5
Hluhluwe → *S. Africa* 28°1S 32°16E **57** D5
Hlyboka *Ukraine* 48°5S 25°56E **17** D13
Ho *Ghana* 6°37N 0°27E **50** G6
Ho Chi Minh City = Thanh Pho
Ho Chi Minh *Vietnam* 10°58N 106°40E **39** G6
Ho Hoa Binh *Vietnam* 20°50N 105°0E **38** B5
Ho Thac Ba *Vietnam* 21°42N 105°1E **38** A5
Ho Thuong *Vietnam* 19°32N 105°48E **38** C5
Hoa Binh *Vietnam* 20°50N 105°20E **38** B5
Hoa Hiep *Vietnam* 11°34N 105°51E **39** G5
Hoai Nhon *Vietnam* 14°28N 109°1E **38** E7
Hoang Lien △ *Vietnam* 21°30N 103°32E **38** A4
Hoang Lien Son *Vietnam* 22°0N 104°0E **38** A4
Hoanib → *Namibia* 19°27S 12°46E **56** B1
Hoare B. *Canada* 65°17N 62°30W **69** D19
Hoarusib → *Namibia* 19°3S 12°36E **56** B2

Honcut *U.S.A.* 39°20N 121°32W **78** F5
Honda, Bahía *Cuba* 22°54N 83°10W **88** B3
Hondeklipbaai *S. Africa* 30°19S 17°17E **56** E2
Hondo *Japan* 32°27N 130°12E **31** H5
Hondo *U.S.A.* 29°21N 99°9W **84** G5
Hondo, Río → *Belize* 18°25N 88°21W **87** D7
Honduras ■ *Cent. Amer.* 14°40N 86°30W **88** D2
Honduras, G. de
Caribbean 16°50N 87°0W **88** C2
Honefoss *Norway* 60°10N 10°18E **9** F14
Honesdale *U.S.A.* 41°34N 75°16W **83** E9
Honey Harbour *Canada* 44°52N 79°49W **82** B5
Honey L. *U.S.A.* 40°15N 120°19W **78** E6
Honfleur *France* 49°25N 0°13E **20** B4
Hong → *Vietnam* 20°16N 106°34E **38** B6
Hong He → *China* 32°25N 115°35E **34** H8
Hong Kong □ *China* 22°11N 114°14E **33** a
Hong Gai *Vietnam* 20°57N 107°5E **38** B6
Hong Kong Int. ✈ (HKG)
China 22°19N 113°57E **33** a
Hongcheon *S. Korea* 37°44N 127°53E **35** F14
Hongjiang *China* 27°7N 109°59E **33** F10
Honglu He → *China* 38°0N 109°50E **34** F5
Hongseong *S. Korea* 36°37N 126°38E **35** F14
Hongshan *China* 36°16N 111°40E **34** F6
Hongshui He → *China* 23°48N 109°30E **33** G10
Hongtong *China* 36°16N 111°40E **34** F6
Honguedo, Détroit d'
Canada 49°15N 64°0W **73** C7
Hongwon *N. Korea* 40°0N 127°56E **35** E14
Hongze Hu *China* 33°15N 118°35E **35** H10
Honiara *Solomon Is.* 9°27S 159°57E **58** B8
Honiton *U.K.* 50°47N 3°11W **13** G4
Honjō *Japan* 39°23N 140°3E **30** E10
Honningsvåg *Norway* 70°59N 25°59E **8** A21
Honolulu *U.S.A.* 21°19N 157°52W **75** L8
Honshū *Japan* 36°0N 138°0E **30** F9
Hood, Mt. *U.S.A.* 45°23N 121°42W **76** D3
Hood, Pt. *Australia* 34°23S 119°34E **61** F2
Hood River *U.S.A.* 45°43N 121°31W **76** D3
Hoodsport *U.S.A.* 47°24N 123°9W **78** C3
Hoogeveen *Neths.* 52°44N 6°28E **15** B6
Hoogezand-Sappemeer
Neths. 53°9N 6°45E **15** A6
Hooghly = Hugli →
India 21°56N 88°4E **43** J13
Hooghly-Chinsura = Chunchura
India 22°53N 88°27E **43** H13
Hook Hd. *Ireland* 52°7N 6°56W **10** D5
Hook I. *Australia* 20°4S 149°0E **62** b
Hook of Holland = Hoek van
Holland *Neths.* 52°0N 4°7E **15** C4
Hooker *U.S.A.* 36°52N 101°13W **84** C4
Hooker Creek = Lajamanu
Australia 18°23S 130°38E **60** C5
Hooker Creek ◌
Australia 18°6S 130°23E **60** C5
Hoonah *U.S.A.* 58°7N 135°27W **70** B1
Hooper Bay *U.S.A.* 61°32N 166°6W **74** C6
Hoopeston *U.S.A.* 40°28N 87°40W **80** E10
Hoopstad *S. Africa* 27°50S 25°55E **56** D4
Hoorn *Neths.* 52°38N 5°4E **15** B5
Hoover *U.S.A.* 33°24N 86°49W **85** E11
Hoover Dam *U.S.A.* 36°1N 114°44W **79** K12
Hooversville *U.S.A.* 40°9N 78°55W **82** F6
Hop Bottom *U.S.A.* 41°42N 75°46W **83** E9
Hope *Canada* 49°25N 121°25W **70** D4
Hope *Ariz., U.S.A.* 33°43N 113°42W **79** M13
Hope *Ark., U.S.A.* 33°40N 93°36W **84** E8
Hope, L. *S. Austral.,
Australia* 28°24S 139°18E **63** D2
Hope, L. *W. Austral.,
Australia* 32°35S 120°15E **61** F3
Hope, Pt. *U.S.A.* 68°21N 166°47W **66** C3
Hope I. *Canada* 44°55N 80°11W **82** B4
Hope Town *Bahamas* 26°35N 76°57W **88** A4
Hope Vale *Australia* 15°16S 145°20E **62** B4
Hope Vale ◌ *Australia* 15°8S 145°6E **62** B4
Hopedale *Canada* 55°28N 60°13W **73** A7
Hopedale *U.S.A.* 42°8N 71°33W **83** D13
Hopefield *S. Africa* 33°3S 18°22E **56** E2
Hopei = Hebei □ *China* 39°0N 116°0E **34** E9
Hopelchén *Mexico* 19°46N 89°51W **87** D7
Hopetoun *Vic., Australia* 35°42S 142°22E **63** F3
Hopetoun *W. Austral.,
Australia* 33°57S 120°7E **61** F3
Hopetown *S. Africa* 29°34S 24°3E **56** D3
Hopewell *U.S.A.* 37°18N 77°17W **81** G15
Hopkins, L. *Australia* 24°15S 128°35E **60** D4
Hopkinsville *U.S.A.* 36°52N 87°29W **80** G10
Hopland *U.S.A.* 38°58N 123°7W **78** G3
Hoquiam *U.S.A.* 46°59N 123°53W **78** D3
Hordern Hills *Australia* 20°15S 130°0E **60** D5
Horinger *China* 40°28N 111°48E **34** D6
Horizontina *Brazil* 27°35S 54°19W **95** B5
Horlick Mts. *Antarctica* 84°0S 102°0W **5** E15
Horlivka *Ukraine* 48°19N 38°5E **19** E6
Hormak *Iran* 29°58N 60°51E **45** D9
Hormoz *Iran* 27°35N 55°0E **45** E7
Hormoz, Jaz-ye *Iran* 27°8N 56°28E **45** E8
Hormozgān □ *Iran* 27°30N 56°0E **45** E8
Hormuz, Kūh-e *Iran* 27°27N 55°10E **45** E7
Hormuz, Str. of *The Gulf* 26°30N 56°30E **45** E8
Horn *Austria* 48°39N 15°40E **16** D8
Horn → *Canada* 61°30N 118°1W **70** A5
Horn, Cape = Hornos, C. de
Chile 55°50S 67°30W **96** H3
Horn Head *Ireland* 55°14N 8°0W **10** A3
Horn I. *Australia* 10°37S 142°17E **62** A3
Horn Plateau *Canada* 62°15N 119°15W **70** A5
Hornavan *Sweden* 66°15N 17°30E **8** C17
Hornbeck *U.S.A.* 31°20N 93°24W **84** F8
Hornbrook *U.S.A.* 41°55N 122°33W **76** F2
Horncastle *U.K.* 53°13N 0°7W **12** D7
Hornell *U.S.A.* 42°20N 77°40W **82** D7
Hornell L. *Canada* 62°20N 119°25W **70** A5
Hornepayne *Canada* 49°14N 84°48W **72** C3
Hornings Mills *Canada* 44°9N 80°12W **82** B4

Hornitos *U.S.A.* 37°30N 120°14W **78 H6**
Hornos, C. de *Chile* 55°50S 67°30W **96 H3**
Hornsby *Australia* 33°42S 151°2E **63 B5**
Hornsea *U.K.* 53°55N 0°11W **12 D7**
Horobetsu = Noboribetsu
  Japan 42°24N 141°6E **30 C10**
Horodenka *Ukraine* 48°41N 25°29E **17 D13**
Horodok *Khmelnytskyy,*
  Ukraine 49°10N 26°34E **17 D14**
Horodok *Lviv, Ukraine* 49°46N 23°32E **17 D12**
Horokhiv *Ukraine* 50°30N 24°45E **17 C13**
Horqin Youyi Qianqi
  China 46°5N 122°3E **35 A12**
Horqin Zuoyi Zhongqi
  China 44°8N 123°18E **35 B12**
Horqueta *Paraguay* 23°15S 56°55W **94 A4**
Horse Cr. → *U.S.A.* 41°57N 103°58W **76 F12**
Horse I. *Canada* 53°20N 99°6W **71 C9**
Horse Is. *Canada* 50°15N 55°50W **73 B8**
Horsefly L. *Canada* 52°25N 121°0W **70 C4**
Horseheads *U.S.A.* 42°10N 76°49W **82 D7**
Horsens *Denmark* 55°52N 9°51E **9 J13**
Horseshoe Lake *Canada* 45°17N 79°51W **82 A5**
Horsham *Australia* 36°44S 142°13E **63 F3**
Horsham *U.K.* 51°4N 0°20W **13 F7**
Horta *Azores* 38°32N 28°38W **50 a**
Horten *Norway* 59°25N 10°32E **9 G14**
Horton *U.S.A.* 39°40N 95°32W **80 F6**
Horton → *Canada* 69°56N 126°52W **68 D6**
Horwood L. *Canada* 48°5N 82°20W **72 C3**
Hosapete = Hospet
  India 15°15N 76°20E **40 M10**
Ḥoseynābād *Khuzestan,*
  Iran 32°45N 48°20E **45 C6**
Ḥoseynābād *Kordestan,*
  Iran 35°33N 47°8E **44 C5**
Hoshangabad *India* 22°45N 77°45E **42 H7**
Hoshiarpur *India* 31°30N 75°58E **42 D6**
Hospet *India* 15°15N 76°20E **40 M10**
Hoste, I. *Chile* 55°0S 69°0W **96 H3**
Hot *Thailand* 18°8N 98°29E **38 C2**
Hot Creek Range
  U.S.A. 38°40N 116°20W **76 G5**
Hot Springs *Ark., U.S.A.* 34°31N 93°3W **84 D8**
Hot Springs *S. Dak.,*
  U.S.A. 43°26N 103°29W **80 D2**
Hot Springs → *U.S.A.* 34°31N 93°3W **84 D8**
Hotagen *Sweden* 63°59N 14°12E **8 E16**
Hotan *China* 37°25N 79°55E **32 D4**
Hotan He → *China* 40°22N 80°56E **32 C5**
Hotazel *S. Africa* 27°17S 22°58E **56 D3**
Hotchkiss *U.S.A.* 38°48N 107°43W **76 G10**
Hotham, C. *Australia* 12°2S 131°18E **60 B5**
Hoting *Sweden* 64°8N 16°15E **8 D17**
Hotte, Massif de la *Haiti* 18°30N 73°45W **89 C5**
Hottentotsbaai *Namibia* 26°8S 14°59E **56 D1**
Hou Hai *China* 22°32N 113°56E **33 a**
Houei Sai *Laos* 20°18N 100°26E **38 B3**
Houffalize *Belgium* 50°8N 5°48E **15 D5**
Houghton *Mich., U.S.A.* 47°7N 88°34W **80 B9**
Houghton *N.Y., U.S.A.* 42°25N 78°10W **82 D6**
Houghton L. *U.S.A.* 44°21N 84°44W **81 C11**
Houghton-le-Spring
  U.K. 54°51N 1°28W **12 C6**
Houhora Heads *N.Z.* 34°49S 173°9E **59 A4**
Houlton *U.S.A.* 46°8N 67°51W **81 B20**
Houma *China* 35°36N 111°20E **34 G6**
Houma *U.S.A.* 29°36N 90°43W **85 G9**
Housatonic → *U.S.A.* 41°10N 73°7W **83 E11**
Houston *Canada* 54°25N 126°39W **70 C3**
Houston *Mo., U.S.A.* 37°22N 91°58W **80 G8**
Houston *Tex., U.S.A.* 29°45N 95°21W **84 G7**
Hout = Mogwadi →
  S. Africa 23°4S 29°36E **57 C4**
Houtkraal *S. Africa* 30°23S 24°5E **56 E3**
Houtman Abrolhos
  Australia 28°43S 113°48E **61 E1**
Hovd = Dund-Us
  Mongolia 48°1N 91°38E **32 B7**
Hove *U.K.* 50°50N 0°10W **13 G7**
Hovenweep △ *U.S.A.* 37°20N 109°0W **77 H9**
Hoveyzeh *Iran* 31°27N 48°4E **45 D6**
Hövsgöl *Mongolia* 43°37N 109°39E **34 C5**
Hövsgöl Nuur *Mongolia* 51°0N 100°30E **32 A9**
Howar, Wadi → *Sudan* 17°30N 27°8E **51 E11**
Howard *Australia* 25°16S 152°32E **63 D5**
Howard *Pa., U.S.A.* 41°1N 77°40W **82 F7**
Howard *S. Dak., U.S.A.* 44°1N 97°32W **80 C7**
Howe *U.S.A.* 43°48N 113°0W **76 E7**
Howe, C. *Australia* 37°30S 150°0E **63 F5**
Howe, West Cape
  Australia 35°8S 117°36E **61 G2**
Howe I. *Canada* 44°16N 76°17W **83 B8**
Howell *U.S.A.* 42°36N 83°56W **81 D12**
Howick *Canada* 45°11N 73°51W **83 A11**
Howick *S. Africa* 29°28S 30°14E **57 D5**
Howick Group *Australia* 14°20S 145°30E **62 A4**
Howitt, L. *Australia* 27°40S 138°40E **63 D2**
Howland I. *Pac. Oc.* 0°48N 176°38W **64 G10**
Howrah = Haora *India* 22°34N 88°18E **43 H13**
Howth *Ireland* 53°23N 6°6W **10 C5**
Howth Hd. *Ireland* 53°22N 6°4W **10 C5**
Höxter *Germany* 51°46N 9°22E **16 C5**
Hoy *U.K.* 58°50N 3°15W **11 C5**
Hoyanger *Norway* 61°13N 6°4E **8 F12**
Hoyerswerda *Germany* 51°26N 14°14E **16 C8**
Hoylake *U.K.* 53°24N 3°10W **12 D4**
Hpa-an = Pa-an *Burma* 16°51N 97°40E **41 L20**
Hpunan Pass *Burma* 27°30N 96°55E **41 F20**
Hradec Králové
  Czech Rep. 50°15N 15°50E **16 C8**
Hrodna *Belarus* 53°42N 23°52E **17 B12**
Hrodzyanka *Belarus* 53°31N 28°42E **17 B15**
Hron → *Slovak Rep.* 47°49N 18°45E **17 E10**
Hrvatska = Croatia ■
  Europe 45°20N 16°0E **16 F9**
Hrymayliv *Ukraine* 49°20N 26°5E **17 D14**
Hsenwi *Burma* 23°22N 97°55E **41 H20**
Hsiamen = Xiamen
  China 24°25N 118°4E **33 G12**

Hsian = Xi'an *China* 34°15N 109°0E **34 G5**
Hsinchu *Taiwan* 24°48N 120°58E **33 G13**
Hsinhailien = Lianyungang
  China 34°40N 119°11E **35 G10**
Hsüchou = Xuzhou
  China 34°18N 117°10E **35 G9**
Hu Xian *China* 34°8N 108°42E **34 G5**
Hua Hin *Thailand* 12°34N 99°58E **38 F2**
Hua Muang *Laos* 20°13N 103°52E **38 B4**
Hua Shan *China* 34°28N 110°4E **34 G6**
Hua Xian *Henan, China* 35°30N 114°30E **34 G8**
Hua Xian *Shaanxi, China* 34°30N 109°48E **34 G5**
Huab → *Namibia* 20°52S 13°25E **56 B2**
Huachinera *Mexico* 30°9N 108°55W **86 A3**
Huacho *Peru* 11°10S 77°35W **92 F3**
Huade *China* 41°55N 113°59E **34 D7**
Huadian *China* 43°0N 126°40E **35 C14**
Huahine, Î.
  French Polynesia 16°46S 150°58W **65 J12**
Huai Hat △ *Thailand* 16°52N 104°17E **38 D5**
Huai He → *China* 33°0N 118°30E **33 E12**
Huai Kha Khaeng △
  Thailand 15°48N 99°7E **38 E2**
Huai Nam Dang △
  Thailand 19°30N 98°30E **38 C2**
Huai Yot *Thailand* 7°45N 99°37E **39 J2**
Huai'an *Hebei, China* 40°30N 114°20E **34 D8**
Huai'an *Jiangsu, China* 33°30N 119°10E **35 H10**
Huaibei *China* 34°0N 116°48E **34 G9**
Huaide = Gongzhuling
  China 43°30N 124°40E **35 C13**
Huaidezhen *China* 43°48N 124°50E **35 C13**
Huaihua *China* 27°32N 109°57E **33 F10**
Huainan *China* 32°38N 116°58E **33 E12**
Huairen *China* 39°48N 113°20E **34 E7**
Huairou *China* 40°20N 116°35E **34 D9**
Huaiyang *China* 33°40N 114°52E **34 H8**
Huaiyin *China* 33°30N 119°2E **35 H10**
Huaiyuan *China* 32°55N 117°10E **35 H9**
Huajuapán de León
  Mexico 17°48N 97°46W **87 D5**
Hualapai Peak *U.S.A.* 35°5N 113°54W **77 J7**
Huallaga → *Peru* 5°15S 75°30W **92 E3**
Huambo *Angola* 12°42S 15°54E **53 G3**
Huan Jiang → *China* 34°28N 109°0E **34 G5**
Huan Xian *China* 36°33N 107°7E **34 F4**
Huancabamba *Peru* 5°10S 79°15W **92 E3**
Huancane *Peru* 15°10S 69°44W **92 G5**
Huancavelica *Peru* 12°50S 75°5W **92 F3**
Huancayo *Peru* 12°5S 75°12W **92 F3**
Huanchaca *Bolivia* 20°15S 66°40W **92 H5**
Huang Hai = Yellow Sea
  China 35°0N 123°0E **35 G12**
Huang He → *China* 37°55N 118°50E **35 F10**
Huang Xian *China* 37°38N 120°30E **35 F11**
Huangdao *China* 36°0N 120°7E **35 G11**
Huanghua *China* 38°22N 117°20E **35 E9**
Huanghuagang *China* 38°20N 117°54E **35 E9**
Huangling *China* 35°34N 109°15E **34 G5**
Huanglong *China* 35°30N 109°59E **34 G5**
Huangshan *China* 29°42N 118°25E **33 F12**
Huangshi *China* 30°10N 115°3E **33 F12**
Huangsongdian *China* 43°45N 127°25E **35 C14**
Huanren *China* 41°23N 125°20E **35 D13**
Huantai *China* 36°58N 117°56E **35 F9**
Huánuco *Peru* 9°55S 76°15W **92 E3**
Huaraz *Peru* 9°30S 77°32W **92 E3**
Huarmey *Peru* 10°5S 78°5W **92 F3**
Huascarán, Nevado *Peru* 9°7S 77°37W **92 E3**
Huasco *Chile* 28°30S 71°15W **94 B1**
Huasco → *Chile* 28°27S 71°13W **94 B1**
Huasna *U.S.A.* 35°6N 120°24W **79 K6**
Huatabampo *Mexico* 26°50N 109°38W **86 B3**
Huauchinango *Mexico* 20°12N 98°3W **87 C5**
Huautla de Jiménez
  Mexico 18°8N 96°51W **87 D5**
Huayin *China* 34°35N 110°5E **34 G6**
Hubballi = Hubli *India* 15°22N 75°15E **40 M9**
Hubbard *Ohio, U.S.A.* 41°9N 80°34W **82 E4**
Hubbard *Tex., U.S.A.* 31°51N 96°48W **84 F6**
Hubbard Glacier
  Canada 60°18N 139°22W **68 E4**
Hubbart Pt. *Canada* 59°21N 94°41W **71 B10**
Hubei □ *China* 31°0N 112°0E **33 E11**
Hubli *India* 15°22N 75°15E **40 M9**
Huch'ang *N. Korea* 41°25N 127°2E **35 D14**
Hucknall *U.K.* 53°3N 1°13W **12 D6**
Huddersfield *U.K.* 53°39N 1°47W **12 D6**
Hudiksvall *Sweden* 61°43N 17°10E **8 F17**
Hudson *Canada* 50°6N 92°9W **72 B1**
Hudson *Mass., U.S.A.* 42°23N 71°34W **83 D13**
Hudson *N.Y., U.S.A.* 42°15N 73°46W **83 D11**
Hudson *Wis., U.S.A.* 44°58N 92°45W **80 C7**
Hudson *Wyo., U.S.A.* 42°54N 108°35W **76 E9**
Hudson → *U.S.A.* 40°42N 74°2W **83 F10**
Hudson, C. *Antarctica* 68°21S 153°45E **5 C10**
Hudson Bay *Nunavut,*
  Canada 60°0N 86°0W **69 F14**
Hudson Bay *Sask.,*
  Canada 52°51N 102°23W **71 C8**
Hudson Falls *U.S.A.* 43°18N 73°35W **83 C11**
Hudson Mts. *Antarctica* 74°32S 99°20W **5 D16**
Hudson Str. *Canada* 62°0N 70°0W **69 E18**
Hudson's Hope *Canada* 56°0N 121°54W **70 B4**
Huehuetenango
  Guatemala 15°20N 91°28W **88 C1**
Huejúcar *Mexico* 22°21N 103°13W **86 C4**
Huelva *Spain* 37°18N 6°57W **21 D2**
Huentelauquén *Chile* 31°38S 71°33W **94 C1**
Huerta, Sa. de la
  Argentina 31°10S 67°30W **94 C2**
Huesca *Spain* 42°8N 0°25W **21 A5**
Huetamo *Mexico* 18°35N 100°53W **86 D4**
Hugh → *Australia* 25°1S 134°1E **62 D1**
Hughenden *Australia* 20°52S 144°10E **62 C3**
Hughesville *U.S.A.* 41°14N 76°44W **83 E8**
Hugli → *India* 21°56N 88°4E **43 J13**
Hugo *Colo., U.S.A.* 39°8N 103°28W **76 G12**
Hugo *Okla., U.S.A.* 34°1N 95°31W **84 D7**

Hugoton *U.S.A.* 37°11N 101°21W **80 G3**
Hui Xian = Huixian
  China 35°27N 113°12E **34 G7**
Hui Xian *China* 33°50N 106°4E **34 H4**
Hui'anbu *China* 37°28N 106°38E **34 F4**
Huichapan *Mexico* 20°23N 99°39W **87 C5**
Huichon *N. Korea* 40°10N 126°16E **35 D14**
Huifa He → *China* 43°0N 127°50E **35 C14**
Huila, Nevado del *Colombia* 3°0N 76°0W **92 C3**
Huimin *China* 37°27N 117°28E **35 F9**
Huinan *China* 42°40N 126°2E **35 C14**
Huinca Renancó
  Argentina 34°51S 64°22W **94 C3**
Huining *China* 35°38N 105°0E **34 G3**
Huinong *China* 39°5N 106°35E **34 E4**
Huiting *China* 34°5N 116°5E **34 G9**
Huixian *China* 35°27N 113°12E **34 G7**
Huixtla *Mexico* 15°9N 92°28W **87 D6**
Huize *China* 26°24N 103°15E **32 F9**
Huizhou *China* 23°0N 114°23E **33 G11**
Hukawng Valley
  Burma 26°30N 96°30E **41 F20**
Hukuntsi *Botswana* 23°58S 21°45E **56 C3**
Ḥulayfā' *Si. Arabia* 25°58N 40°45E **44 E4**
Hulin *China* 45°48N 132°59E **33 B15**
Hulin He → *China* 45°0N 122°10E **35 B12**
Hull = Kingston upon Hull
  U.K. 53°45N 0°21W **12 D7**
Hull *Canada* 45°26N 75°43W **83 A9**
Hull → *U.K.* 53°44N 0°20W **12 D7**
Hulst *Neths.* 51°17N 4°2E **15 C4**
Huludao *China* 40°45N 120°50E **35 D11**
Hulun Nur *China* 49°0N 117°30E **33 B12**
Huma, Tanjung *Malaysia* 5°29N 100°16E **39 c**
Humacao *Puerto Rico* 18°9N 65°50W **89 d**
Humahuaca *Argentina* 23°10S 65°25W **94 A2**
Humaitá *Brazil* 7°35S 63°1W **92 E6**
Humaitá *Paraguay* 27°2S 58°31W **94 B4**
Humansdorp *S. Africa* 34°2S 24°46E **56 E3**
Humbe *Angola* 16°40S 14°55E **56 B1**
Humber → *U.K.* 53°42N 0°27W **12 D7**
Humboldt *Canada* 52°15N 105°9W **71 C7**
Humboldt *Iowa, U.S.A.* 42°44N 94°13W **80 D6**
Humboldt *Tenn., U.S.A.* 35°50N 88°55W **85 D10**
Humboldt → *U.S.A.* 39°59N 118°36W **76 G4**
Humboldt Gletscher =
  Sermersuaq *Greenland* 79°30N 62°0W **69 B19**
Hume, L. *Australia* 36°0S 147°5E **63 F4**
Humen *China* 22°50N 113°40E **33 a**
Humenné *Slovak Rep.* 48°55N 21°50E **17 D11**
Humphreys, Mt.
  U.S.A. 37°17N 118°40W **78 H8**
Humphreys Peak
  U.S.A. 35°21N 111°41W **77 J8**
Humptulips *U.S.A.* 47°14N 123°57W **78 C3**
Hūn *Libya* 29°2N 16°0E **51 C9**
Hun Jiang → *China* 40°50N 125°38E **35 D13**
Húnaflói *Iceland* 65°50N 20°50W **8 D3**
Hunan □ *China* 27°30N 112°0E **33 F11**
Hunchun *China* 42°52N 130°28E **35 C16**
Hundewali *Pakistan* 31°55N 72°38E **42 D5**
Hundred Mile House
  Canada 51°38N 121°18W **70 C4**
Hunedoara *Romania* 45°40N 22°50E **17 F12**
Hung Yen *Vietnam* 20°39N 106°4E **38 B6**
Hunga Ha'apai *Tonga* 20°41S 175°7W **59 c**
Hungary ■ *Europe* 47°20N 19°20E **17 E10**
Hungary, Plain of *Europe* 47°0N 20°0E **6 F10**
Hungerford *Australia* 28°58S 144°24E **63 D3**
Hŭngnam *N. Korea* 39°49N 127°45E **35 E14**
Hunjiang *China* 41°54N 126°26E **35 D14**
Hunsberge *Namibia* 27°45S 17°12E **56 D2**
Hunsrück *Germany* 49°56N 7°27E **16 D4**
Hunstanton *U.K.* 52°56N 0°29E **12 E8**
Hunter *U.S.A.* 42°13N 74°13W **83 D10**
Hunter I. *Australia* 40°30S 144°45E **63 G3**
Hunter I. *Canada* 51°55N 128°0W **70 C3**
Hunter Ra. *Australia* 32°45S 150°15E **63 E5**
Hunters Road *Zimbabwe* 19°9S 29°49E **55 F2**
Hunterville *N.Z.* 39°56S 175°35E **59 C5**
Huntingburg *U.S.A.* 38°18N 86°57W **80 F10**
Huntingdon *U.K.* 52°20N 0°11W **13 E7**
Huntingdon *U.S.A.* 40°30N 78°1W **82 F6**
Huntington *Ind., U.S.A.* 40°53N 85°30W **81 E11**
Huntington *N.Y.,*
  U.S.A. 40°52N 73°26W **83 F11**
Huntington *Oreg.,*
  U.S.A. 44°21N 117°16W **76 D5**
Huntington *Utah,*
  U.S.A. 39°20N 110°58W **76 G8**
Huntington *W. Va.,*
  U.S.A. 38°25N 82°27W **81 F12**
Huntington Beach
  U.S.A. 33°40N 118°5W **79 M9**
Huntly *N.Z.* 37°34S 175°11E **59 B5**
Huntly *U.K.* 57°27N 2°47W **11 D6**
Huntsville *Canada* 45°20N 79°14W **82 A5**
Huntsville *Ala., U.S.A.* 34°44N 86°35W **85 D11**
Huntsville *Tex., U.S.A.* 30°43N 95°33W **84 F7**
Hunyani → *Zimbabwe* 15°57S 30°39E **55 F3**
Hunyuan *China* 39°42N 113°42E **34 E7**
Hunza → *India* 35°54N 74°20E **43 B6**
Huo Shan *China* 36°26N 111°52E **34 F6**
Huo Xian = Huozhou
  China 36°36N 111°42E **34 F6**
Huolin Gol *China* 45°32N 119°38E **35 B10**
Huong Khe *Vietnam* 18°13N 105°41E **38 C5**
Huonville *Australia* 43°0S 147°5E **63 G4**
Hupeh = Hubei □ *China* 31°0N 112°0E **33 E11**
Ḥūr *Iran* 30°50N 57°7E **45 D8**
Hurānd *Iran* 38°51N 47°22E **44 B5**
Hurd, C. *Canada* 45°13N 81°44W **82 A3**
Hure Qi *China* 42°45N 121°45E **35 C11**
Hurghada *Egypt* 27°15N 33°50E **51 C12**
Hurley *N. Mex., U.S.A.* 32°42N 108°8W **77 K9**
Hurley *Wis., U.S.A.* 46°27N 90°11W **80 B8**
Huron *Calif., U.S.A.* 36°12N 120°6W **78 J6**

Huron *Ohio, U.S.A.* 41°24N 82°33W **82 E2**
Huron *S. Dak., U.S.A.* 44°22N 98°13W **80 C4**
Huron, L. *U.S.A.* 44°30N 82°40W **82 B2**
Huron East *Canada* 43°37N 81°18W **82 C3**
Hurricane *U.S.A.* 37°11N 113°17W **77 H7**
Hurungwe △ *Zimbabwe* 16°7S 29°5E **55 F2**
Hurunui → *N.Z.* 42°54S 173°18E **59 E4**
Húsavík *Iceland* 66°3N 17°21W **8 C5**
Huşi *Romania* 46°41N 28°7E **17 E15**
Hustadvika *Norway* 63°0N 7°0E **8 E12**
Hustontown *U.S.A.* 40°3N 78°2W **82 F6**
Hutchinson *Kans., U.S.A.* 38°5N 97°56W **80 F5**
Hutchinson *Minn.,*
  U.S.A. 44°54N 94°22W **80 C6**
Hutte Sauvage, L. de la
  Canada 56°15N 64°45W **73 A7**
Hutton, Mt. *Australia* 25°51S 148°20E **63 D4**
Huy *Belgium* 50°31N 5°15E **15 D5**
Huzhou *China* 30°51N 120°8E **33 E13**
Hvammstangi *Iceland* 65°24N 20°57W **8 D3**
Hvar *Croatia* 43°11N 16°28E **22 C7**
Hvítá → *Iceland* 64°30N 21°58W **8 D3**
Hwachon-Cheosuji
  S. Korea 38°5N 127°50E **35 E14**
Hwang Ho = Huang He →
  China 37°55N 118°50E **35 F10**
Hwange *Zimbabwe* 18°18S 26°30E **55 F2**
Hwange △ *Zimbabwe* 19°0S 26°30E **56 B4**
Hyannis *Mass., U.S.A.* 41°39N 70°17W **81 E18**
Hyannis *Nebr., U.S.A.* 42°0N 101°46W **80 E3**
Hyargas Nuur *Mongolia* 49°0N 93°0E **32 B7**
Hydaburg *U.S.A.* 55°15N 132°50W **70 B2**
Hyde Park *U.S.A.* 41°47N 73°56W **83 E11**
Hyden *Australia* 32°24S 118°53E **61 F2**
Hyder *U.S.A.* 55°55N 130°5W **70 B2**
Hyderabad *India* 17°22N 78°29E **40 L11**
Hyderabad *Pakistan* 25°23N 68°24E **42 G3**
Hydra *Greece* 37°20N 23°28E **23 F10**
Hyères *France* 43°8N 6°9E **20 E7**
Hyères, Îs. d' *France* 43°0N 6°20E **20 E7**
Hyesan *N. Korea* 41°20N 128°10E **35 D15**
Hyland → *Canada* 59°52N 128°12W **70 B3**
Hyndman Peak *U.S.A.* 43°45N 114°8W **76 E6**
Hyōgo □ *Japan* 35°15N 134°50E **31 G7**
Hyrum *U.S.A.* 41°38N 111°51W **76 F8**
Hysham *U.S.A.* 46°18N 107°14W **76 C10**
Hythe *U.K.* 51°4N 1°5E **13 F9**
Hyūga *Japan* 32°25N 131°35E **31 H5**
Hyvinge = Hyvinkää
  Finland 60°38N 24°50E **8 F21**
Hyvinkää *Finland* 60°38N 24°50E **8 F21**

I

I-n-Gall *Niger* 16°51N 7°1E **50 E7**
Iaco → *Brazil* 9°3S 68°34W **92 E5**
Iakora *Madag.* 23°6S 46°40E **57 C8**
Ialissos *Greece* 36°24N 28°10E **25 C10**
Ialomița → *Romania* 44°42N 27°51E **17 F14**
Iași *Romania* 47°10N 27°40E **17 E14**
Ib → *India* 21°34N 83°48E **43 J10**
Iba *Phil.* 15°22N 120°0E **37 A6**
Ibadan *Nigeria* 7°22N 3°58E **50 G6**
Ibagué *Colombia* 4°20N 75°20W **92 C3**
Ibar → *Serbia* 43°43N 20°45E **23 C9**
Ibaraki □ *Japan* 36°10N 140°10E **31 F10**
Ibarra *Ecuador* 0°21N 78°7W **92 C3**
Ibb *Yemen* 14°2N 44°10E **47 E3**
Ibembo
  Dem. Rep. of the Congo 2°35N 23°35E **54 B1**
Ibenga → *Congo* 2°19N 18°9E **52 D3**
Ibera, L. *Argentina* 28°30S 57°9W **94 B4**
Iberian Peninsula *Europe* 40°0N 5°0W **6 H5**
Iberville *Canada* 45°19N 73°17W **83 A11**
Iberville, Mt. d' *Canada* 58°50N 63°50W **69 F19**
Ibiá *Brazil* 19°30S 46°30W **93 G9**
Ibiapaba, Sa. da *Brazil* 4°0S 41°30W **93 D10**
Ibicuí → *Brazil* 29°25S 56°47W **95 B4**
Ibicuy *Argentina* 33°55S 59°10W **94 C4**
Ibiza = Eivissa *Spain* 38°54N 1°26E **24 C7**
Ibo *Mozam.* 12°22S 40°40E **55 E5**
Ibonma *Indonesia* 3°29S 133°31E **37 E8**
Ibotirama *Brazil* 12°13S 43°12W **93 F10**
Ibrāhīm → *Lebanon* 34°4N 35°38E **46 A4**
'Ibrī *Oman* 23°14N 56°30E **45 F8**
Ibu *Indonesia* 1°35N 127°33E **37 D7**
Ibusuki *Japan* 31°12N 130°40E **31 J5**
Ica *Peru* 14°0S 75°48W **92 F3**
Iça → *Brazil* 2°55S 67°58W **92 D5**
Icacos Pt. *Trin. & Tob.* 10°3N 61°57W **93 K15**
Içana *Brazil* 0°21N 67°19W **92 C5**
Içana → *Brazil* 0°26N 67°19W **92 C5**
İçel *Turkey* 36°51N 34°36E **44 B2**
Iceland ■ *Europe* 64°45N 19°0W **8 D4**
Iceland Basin *Atl. Oc.* 61°0N 19°0W **4 C7**
Icelandic Plateau *Arctic* 64°0N 10°0W **4 C7**
Ich'ang = Yichang
  China 30°40N 111°20E **33 E11**
Ichchapuram *India* 19°10N 84°40E **41 K14**
Ichhawar *India* 23°1N 77°1E **42 H7**
Ichihara *Japan* 35°28N 140°5E **31 G10**
Ichikawa *Japan* 35°43N 139°54E **31 G9**
Ichilo → *Bolivia* 15°57S 64°50W **92 G6**
Ichinohe *Japan* 40°13N 141°17E **30 D10**
Ichinomiya *Japan* 35°18N 136°48E **31 G8**
Ichinoseki *Japan* 38°55N 141°8E **30 E10**
Icod *Canary Is.* 28°22N 16°43W **24 F3**
Içoguz *Turkmenistan* 40°11N 58°24E **28 E6**
Icy C. *U.S.A.* 70°20N 161°52W **66 B3**
Ida Grove *U.S.A.* 42°21N 95°28W **80 D6**
Idabel *U.S.A.* 33°54N 94°50W **84 E7**
Idaho □ *U.S.A.* 45°0N 115°0W **76 D7**
Idaho City *U.S.A.* 43°50N 115°50W **76 E6**
Idaho Falls *U.S.A.* 43°30N 112°2W **76 E7**
Idalia △ *Australia* 24°49S 144°36E **62 C3**
Idar-Oberstein *Germany* 49°43N 7°16E **16 D4**
Idensalmi = Iisalmi
  Finland 63°32N 27°10E **8 E22**
Idfû *Egypt* 24°55N 32°49E **51 D12**

Ídhra = Hydra *Greece* 37°20N 23°28E **23 F10**
Idi *Indonesia* 5°2N 97°37E **36 C1**
Idi, Oros = Psiloritis, Oros
  Greece 35°15N 24°45E **25 D6**
Idiofa
  Dem. Rep. of the Congo 4°55S 19°42E **52 E3**
Idlib *Syria* 35°55N 36°36E **44 C3**
Idria *U.S.A.* 36°25N 120°41W **78 J6**
Idutywa = Dutywa
  S. Africa 32°8S 28°18E **57 E4**
Ieper *Belgium* 50°51N 2°53E **15 D2**
Ierapetra *Greece* 35°1N 25°44E **25 E7**
Iesi *Italy* 43°31N 13°14E **22 C5**
Ifakara *Tanzania* 8°8S 36°41E **52 F7**
'Ifāl, W. al → *Si. Arabia* 28°7N 35°3E **44 D2**
Ifanadiana *Madag.* 21°19S 47°39E **57 C8**
Ife *Nigeria* 7°30N 4°31E **50 G6**
Iffley *Australia* 18°53S 141°12E **62 B3**
Iforas, Adrar des *Africa* 19°40N 1°40E **50 E6**
Ifould, L. *Australia* 30°52S 132°6E **61 F5**
Iganga *Uganda* 0°37N 33°28E **54 B3**
Igarapava *Brazil* 20°3S 47°47W **93 H9**
Igarka *Russia* 67°30N 86°33E **28 C9**
Iggesund *Sweden* 61°39N 17°10E **8 F17**
Iglésias *Italy* 39°19N 8°32E **22 E3**
Igloolik = Iglulik
  Canada 69°20N 81°49W **69 D15**
Igluligaarjuk = Chesterfield Inlet
  Canada 63°30N 90°45W **68 E13**
Iglulik *Canada* 69°20N 81°49W **69 D15**
Ignace *Canada* 49°30N 91°40W **72 C1**
İğneada Burnu *Turkey* 41°53N 28°2E **23 D13**
Igoumenitsa *Greece* 39°32N 20°18E **23 E9**
Igrim *Russia* 63°12N 64°30E **28 C7**
Iguaçu → *Brazil* 25°36S 54°36W **95 B5**
Iguaçu, Cat. del *Brazil* 25°41S 54°26W **95 B5**
Iguaçu △ *Brazil* 25°30S 54°0W **95 B5**
Iguaçu Falls = Iguaçu, Cat. del
  Brazil 25°41S 54°26W **95 B5**
Iguala *Mexico* 18°21N 99°32W **87 D5**
Igualada *Spain* 41°37N 1°37E **21 B6**
Iguassu = Iguaçu →
  Brazil 25°36S 54°36W **95 B5**
Iguatu *Brazil* 6°20S 39°18W **93 E11**
Iguazú △ *Argentina* 25°42S 54°22W **95 B5**
Iguidi, Erg *Africa* 27°0N 7°0W **50 C4**
Iharana *Madag.* 13°25S 50°0E **57 A9**
Ihbulag *Mongolia* 43°11N 107°10E **34 C4**
Iheya-Shima *Japan* 27°4N 127°58E **31 L3**
Ihosy *Madag.* 22°24S 46°8E **57 C8**
Ihotry, Farihy *Madag.* 21°56S 43°41E **57 C7**
Ii *Finland* 65°19N 25°22E **8 D21**
Ii → *Finland* 65°19N 25°22E **8 D21**
Iida *Japan* 35°35N 137°50E **31 G8**
Iijoki → *Finland* 65°20N 25°20E **8 D21**
Iisalmi *Finland* 63°32N 27°10E **8 E22**
Iiyama *Japan* 36°51N 138°22E **31 F9**
Iizuka *Japan* 33°38N 130°42E **31 H5**
Ijâfene *Mauritania* 20°40N 8°0W **50 D4**
Ijebu-Ode *Nigeria* 6°47N 3°58E **50 G6**
IJmuiden *Neths.* 52°28N 4°35E **15 B4**
Ijo älv = Iijoki →
  Finland 65°20N 25°20E **8 D21**
IJssel → *Neths.* 52°35N 5°50E **15 B5**
IJsselmeer *Neths.* 52°45N 5°20E **15 B5**
Ijuí *Brazil* 28°23S 53°55W **95 B5**
Ijuí → *Brazil* 27°58S 55°20W **95 B4**
Ikalamavony *Madag.* 21°9S 46°35E **57 C8**
Ikanga *Kenya* 1°42S 38°4E **54 C4**
Ikare *Nigeria* 7°32N 5°40E **50 G7**
Ikaria *Greece* 37°35N 26°10E **23 F12**
Ikeda *Japan* 34°1N 133°48E **31 G6**
Ikela *Dem. Rep. of the Congo* 1°6S 23°6E **52 E4**
Iki *Japan* 33°45N 129°42E **31 H4**
Ikimba L. *Tanzania* 1°30S 31°20E **54 C3**
Ikopa → *Madag.* 16°45S 46°40E **57 B8**
Ikongo *Tanzania* 1°50S 34°53E **54 C3**
Ikparjuk = Arctic Bay
  Canada 73°1N 85°7W **69 C14**
Iksan *S. Korea* 35°59N 127°0E **35 G14**
Ikungu *Tanzania* 1°33S 33°42E **54 C3**
Ikuntji = Haasts Bluff
  Australia 23°22S 132°0E **60 D5**
Ilagan *Phil.* 17°7N 121°53E **37 A6**
Ilaka *Madag.* 19°33S 48°52E **57 B8**
'Ilām *Iran* 33°36N 46°36E **44 C5**
Ilam *Nepal* 26°58N 87°58E **43 F12**
Ilām □ *Iran* 33°0N 47°0E **44 C5**
Ilanskiy *Russia* 56°14N 96°3E **29 D10**
Iława *Poland* 53°36N 19°34E **17 B10**
Île → *Kazakhstan* 45°53N 77°10E **28 E8**
Île-à-la-Crosse *Canada* 55°27N 107°53W **71 B7**
Île-à-la-Crosse, Lac
  Canada 55°40N 107°45W **71 B7**
Île-de-France □ *France* 49°0N 2°20E **20 B5**
Ilebo *Dem. Rep. of the Congo* 4°17S 20°55E **52 E4**
Ilek *Russia* 51°32N 53°21E **28 D6**
Ilek → *Russia* 51°30N 53°22E **18 D9**
Ilesha *Nigeria* 7°37N 4°40E **50 G6**
Ilford *Canada* 56°4N 95°35W **71 B9**
Ilfracombe *Australia* 23°30S 144°30E **62 C3**
Ilfracombe *U.K.* 51°12N 4°8W **13 F3**
Ilha Grande, Represa
  Brazil 23°10S 53°5W **95 A5**
Ilha Grande △ *Brazil* 23°10S 53°20W **95 A5**
Ilhéus *Brazil* 14°49S 39°2W **93 F11**
Ili = Ile → *Kazakhstan* 45°53N 77°10E **28 E8**
Iliamna L. *U.S.A.* 59°30N 155°0W **74 D8**
Ilias, Profitis *Greece* 36°17N 27°56E **25 C9**
Iligan *Phil.* 8°12N 124°13E **37 C6**
Ilion *U.S.A.* 43°1N 75°2W **83 D9**
Ilkeston *U.K.* 52°58N 1°19W **12 E6**
Ilkley *U.K.* 53°56N 1°48W **12 D6**
Illampu = Ancohuma, Nevado
  Bolivia 16°0S 68°50W **92 G5**
Illana B. *Phil.* 7°35N 123°45E **37 C6**
Illapel *Chile* 32°0S 71°10W **94 C1**
Iller → *Germany* 48°23N 9°58E **16 D6**
Illetas *Spain* 39°32N 2°35E **24 B9**

128 Illimani, Nevado INDEX TO WORLD MAPS

Illimani, Nevado Bolivia 16°30S 67°50W 92 G5
Illinois □ U.S.A. 40°15N 89°30W 80 E9
Illinois → U.S.A. 38°58N 90°28W 80 F8
Illizi Algeria 26°31N 8°32E 50 C7
Ilma, L. Australia 29°13S 127°46E 61 E4
Ilmajoki Finland 62°44N 22°34E 8 E20
Ilmen, Ozero Russia 58°15N 31°10E 18 C5
Ilo Peru 17°40S 71°20W 92 G4
Iloilo Phil. 10°45N 122°33E 37 B6
Ilomantsi Finland 62°38N 30°57E 8 E24
Ilorin Nigeria 8°30N 4°35E 50 G6
Ilwaco U.S.A. 46°19N 124°3W 78 D2
Ilwaki Indonesia 7°55S 126°30E 37 F7
Imabari Japan 34°4N 133°0E 31 G6
Imaloto → Madag. 23°27S 45°13E 57 C8
Imandra, Ozero Russia 67°30N 33°0E 8 C25
Imanombo Madag. 24°26S 45°49E 57 C8
Imari Japan 33°15N 129°52E 31 H4
Imatra Finland 61°12N 28°48E 8 F23
imeni 26 Bakinskikh Komissarov = Neftçala Azerbaijan 39°19N 49°12E 45 B6
imeni 26 Bakinskikh Komissarov Turkmenistan 39°22N 54°10E 45 B7
imeni Ismail Samani, Pik Tajikistan 39°0N 72°2E 28 F8
Imeri, Serra Brazil 0°50N 65°25W 92 C5
Imerimandroso Madag. 17°26S 48°35E 57 B8
Imfolozi ⌂ S. Africa 28°18S 31°50E 57 D5
Imi Ethiopia 6°28N 42°10E 47 F3
Imlay U.S.A. 40°40N 118°9W 76 F4
Imlay City U.S.A. 43°2N 83°5W 82 D1
Immingham U.K. 53°37N 0°13W 12 D7
Immokalee U.S.A. 26°25N 81°25W 85 H14
Ímola Italy 44°20N 11°42E 22 B4
Imperatriz Brazil 5°30S 47°29W 93 E9
Impéria Italy 43°53N 8°3E 20 E8
Imperial Canada 51°21N 105°28W 71 C7
Imperial Calif., U.S.A. 32°51N 115°34W 79 N11
Imperial Nebr., U.S.A. 40°31N 101°39W 80 E3
Imperial Beach U.S.A. 32°35N 117°6W 79 N9
Imperial Dam U.S.A. 32°55N 114°25W 79 N12
Imperial Res. U.S.A. 32°53N 114°28W 79 N12
Imperial Valley U.S.A. 33°0N 115°30W 79 N11
Imperieuse Reef Australia 17°36S 118°50E 60 C2
Impfondo Congo 1°40N 18°0E 52 D3
Imphal India 24°48N 93°56E 41 G18
İmroz = Gökçeada Turkey 40°10N 25°50E 23 D11
Imuris Mexico 30°47N 110°52W 86 A2
Imuruan B. Phil. 10°40N 119°10E 37 B5
In Guezzam Algeria 19°37N 5°52E 50 E7
In Salah Algeria 27°10N 2°32E 50 C6
Ina Japan 35°50N 137°55E 31 G8
Inagua △ Bahamas 21°5N 73°24W 89 B5
Inangahua N.Z. 41°52S 171°59E 59 D3
Inanwatan Indonesia 2°8S 132°10E 37 E8
Iñapari Peru 11°0S 69°40W 92 F5
Inari Finland 68°54N 27°1E 8 B22
Inarijärvi Finland 69°0N 28°0E 8 B23
Inawashiro-Ko Japan 37°29N 140°6E 30 F10
Inca Spain 39°43N 2°54E 24 B9
Inca de Oro Chile 26°45S 69°54W 94 B2
Incahuasi Argentina 27°2S 68°18W 94 B2
Incahuasi Chile 29°12S 71°5W 94 B1
İnce Burun Turkey 42°7N 34°56E 19 F5
İncesu Turkey 38°38N 35°11E 44 B2
Incheon S. Korea 37°27N 126°40E 35 F14
İncirliova Turkey 37°50N 27°41E 23 F12
Incline Village U.S.A. 39°10N 119°58W 76 G4
Incomáti → Mozam. 25°46S 32°43E 57 D5
Indalsälven → Sweden 62°36N 17°30E 8 E17
Indaw Burma 24°15N 96°5E 41 G20
Independence Calif., U.S.A. 36°48N 118°12W 78 J8
Independence Iowa, U.S.A. 42°28N 91°54W 80 D8
Independence Kans., U.S.A. 37°14N 95°42W 80 G6
Independence Ky., U.S.A. 38°57N 84°33W 81 F11
Independence Mo., U.S.A. 39°6N 94°25W 80 F6
Independence Fjord Greenland 82°10N 29°0W 4 A6
Independence Mts. U.S.A. 41°20N 116°0W 76 F5
Index U.S.A. 47°50N 121°33W 78 C5
India ■ Asia 20°0N 78°0E 40 K11
Indian → U.S.A. 27°59N 80°34W 85 H14
Indian Cabins Canada 59°52N 117°40W 70 B5
Indian Harbour Canada 54°27N 57°13W 73 B8
Indian Head Canada 50°30N 103°41W 71 C8
Indian L. U.S.A. 43°46N 74°16W 83 C10
Indian Lake U.S.A. 43°47N 74°16W 83 C10
Indian Springs U.S.A. 36°35N 115°40W 79 J11
Indiana U.S.A. 40°37N 79°9W 82 F5
Indiana □ U.S.A. 40°0N 86°0W 81 F11
Indianapolis U.S.A. 39°46N 86°9W 80 F10
Indianola Iowa, U.S.A. 41°22N 93°34W 80 E7
Indianola Miss., U.S.A. 33°27N 90°39W 85 E9
Indiga Russia 67°38N 49°9E 18 A8
Indigirka → Russia 70°48N 148°54E 29 B15
Indio U.S.A. 33°43N 116°13W 79 M10
Indira Gandhi Canal India 28°0N 72°0E 42 F5
Indira Sagar India 22°15N 76°40E 42 H7
Indo-China Asia 15°0N 102°0E 26 G12
Indonesia ■ Asia 5°0S 115°0E 36 F5
Indore India 22°42N 75°53E 42 H6
Indramayu Indonesia 6°20S 108°19E 37 G13
Indravati → India 19°20N 80°20E 41 K12
Indre → France 47°16N 0°11E 20 C4
Indulkana Australia 26°58S 133°5E 63 D1
Indus → Pakistan 24°20N 67°47E 42 G2
Indus, Mouths of the Pakistan 24°0N 68°0E 42 H3
İnebolu Turkey 41°55N 33°40E 19 F5
Infiernillo, Presa del Mexico 18°35N 101°50W 86 D4
Ingenio Canary Is. 27°55N 15°26W 24 G4
Ingenio Santa Ana Argentina 27°25S 65°40W 94 B2
Ingersoll Canada 43°4N 80°55W 82 C4
Ingham Australia 18°43S 146°10E 62 B4
Ingleborough U.K. 54°10N 2°22W 12 C5
Inglewood Queens., Australia 28°25S 151°2E 63 D5
Inglewood Vic., Australia 36°29S 143°53E 63 F3
Inglewood N.Z. 39°9S 174°14E 59 C5
Inglewood U.S.A. 33°58N 118°21W 79 M8
Ingólfshöfði Iceland 63°48N 16°39W 8 E5
Ingolstadt Germany 48°46N 11°26E 16 D6
Ingomar U.S.A. 46°35N 107°23W 76 C10
Ingonish Canada 46°42N 60°18W 73 C7
Ingraj Bazar India 24°58N 88°10E 43 G13
Ingrid Christensen Coast Antarctica 69°30S 76°0E 5 C6
Ingulec = Inhulec Ukraine 47°42N 33°14E 19 E5
Ingushetia □ Russia 43°20N 44°50E 19 F8
Ingwavuma S. Africa 27°9S 31°59E 57 D5
Inhaca Mozam. 26°1S 32°57E 57 D5
Inhafenga Mozam. 20°36S 33°53E 57 C5
Inhambane Mozam. 23°54S 35°30E 57 C6
Inhambane □ Mozam. 22°30S 34°20E 57 C5
Inhaminga Mozam. 18°26S 35°0E 55 F4
Inharrime Mozam. 24°30S 35°0E 57 C6
Inharrime → Mozam. 24°30S 35°0E 57 C6
Inhulec Ukraine 47°42N 33°14E 19 E5
Ining = Yining China 43°58N 81°10E 32 C5
Inírida → Colombia 3°55N 67°52W 92 C5
Inis = Ennis Ireland 52°51N 8°59W 10 D3
Inis Córthaidh = Enniscorthy Ireland 52°30N 6°34W 10 D5
Inishbofin Ireland 53°37N 10°13W 10 C1
Inisheer Ireland 53°3N 9°32W 10 C2
Inishfree B. Ireland 55°4N 8°23W 10 A3
Inishkea North Ireland 54°9N 10°11W 10 B1
Inishkea South Ireland 54°7N 10°12W 10 B1
Inishmaan Ireland 53°5N 9°35W 10 C2
Inishmore Ireland 53°8N 9°45W 10 C2
Inishmurray I. Ireland 54°26N 8°39W 10 B3
Inishowen Pen. Ireland 55°14N 7°15W 10 A4
Inishshark Ireland 53°37N 10°16W 10 C1
Inishturk Ireland 53°42N 10°7W 10 C1
Inishvickillane Ireland 52°3N 10°37W 10 D1
Injinoo ❂ Australia 10°56S 142°15E 62 A3
Injune Australia 25°53S 148°32E 63 D4
Inklin → N. Amer. 58°50N 133°10W 70 B2
Inland Kaikoura Ra. N.Z. 41°59S 173°41E 59 D4
Inland Sea = Setonaikai Japan 34°20N 133°30E 31 G6
Inle L. Burma 20°30N 96°58E 41 J20
Inlet U.S.A. 43°45N 74°48W 83 C10
Inn → Austria 48°35N 13°28E 16 D7
Innamincka Australia 27°44S 140°46E 63 D3
Inner Hebrides U.K. 57°0N 6°30W 11 E2
Inner Mongolia = Nei Mongol Zizhiqu □ China 42°0N 112°0E 34 D7
Inner Sound U.K. 57°30N 5°55W 11 D3
Innerkip Canada 43°13N 80°42W 82 C4
Innetalling I. Canada 56°0N 79°0W 72 A4
Innisfail Australia 17°33S 146°5E 62 B4
Innisfail Canada 52°2N 113°57W 70 C6
In'noshima Japan 34°19N 133°10E 31 G6
Innsbruck Austria 47°16N 11°23E 16 E6
Inny → Ireland 53°30N 7°50W 10 C4
Inongo Dem. Rep. of the Congo 1°55S 18°30E 52 E3
Inoucdjouac = Inukjuak Canada 58°25N 78°15W 69 F16
Inowrocław Poland 52°50N 18°12E 17 B10
Inscription, C. Australia 25°29S 112°59E 61 E1
Insein Burma 16°50N 96°5E 41 L20
Inta Russia 66°5N 60°8E 18 A11
Intendente Alvear Argentina 35°12S 63°32W 94 D3
Interlaken Switz. 46°41N 7°50E 20 C7
Interlaken U.S.A. 42°37N 76°44W 83 D8
International Falls U.S.A. 48°36N 93°25W 80 A7
Intiyaco Argentina 28°43S 60°5W 94 B3
Inukjuak Canada 58°25N 78°15W 69 F16
Inútil, B. Chile 53°30S 70°15W 96 G2
Inuvik Canada 68°16N 133°40W 68 D5
Inveraray U.K. 56°14N 5°5W 11 E3
Inverbervie U.K. 56°51N 2°17W 11 E6
Invercargill N.Z. 46°24S 168°24E 59 G2
Inverclyde □ U.K. 55°55N 4°49W 11 F4
Inverell Australia 29°45S 151°8E 63 D5
Invergordon U.K. 57°41N 4°10W 11 D4
Inverloch Australia 38°38S 145°45E 63 F4
Invermere Canada 50°30N 116°2W 70 C5
Inverness Canada 46°15N 61°19W 73 C7
Inverness U.K. 57°29N 4°13W 11 D4
Inverness U.S.A. 28°50N 82°20W 85 G13
Inverurie U.K. 57°17N 2°23W 11 D6
Investigator Group Australia 34°45S 134°20E 63 E1
Investigator Str. Australia 35°30S 137°0E 63 F2
Inya Russia 50°28N 86°37E 28 D9
Inyanga Zimbabwe 18°12S 32°40E 55 F3
Inyangani Zimbabwe 18°5S 32°50E 55 F3
Inyantue Zimbabwe 18°33S 26°39E 56 B4
Inyo Mts. U.S.A. 36°40N 118°0W 78 J9
Inyokern U.S.A. 35°39N 117°49W 79 K9
Inyonga Tanzania 6°45S 32°5E 54 D3
Inza Russia 53°55N 46°25E 18 D8
Iō-Jima Japan 30°48N 130°18E 31 J5
Ioannina Greece 39°42N 20°47E 23 E9
Iola U.S.A. 37°55N 95°24W 80 G6
Iona U.K. 56°20N 6°25W 11 E2
Ione U.S.A. 38°21N 120°56W 78 G6
Ionia U.S.A. 42°59N 85°4W 81 D11
Ionian Is. = Ionioi Nisoi Greece 38°40N 20°0E 23 E9
Ionian Sea Medit. S. 37°30N 17°30E 23 E7
Ionioi Nisoi Greece 38°40N 20°0E 23 E9
Ios Greece 36°41N 25°20E 23 F11
Iowa □ U.S.A. 42°18N 93°30W 80 D7
Iowa → U.S.A. 41°10N 91°1W 80 E8
Iowa City U.S.A. 41°40N 91°32W 80 E8
Iowa Falls U.S.A. 42°31N 93°16W 80 D7
Iowa Park U.S.A. 33°57N 98°40W 84 E5
Ipala Tanzania 4°30S 32°52E 54 C3
Ipameri Brazil 17°44S 48°9W 93 G9
Ipatinga Brazil 19°32S 42°30W 93 G10
Ipiales Colombia 0°50N 77°37W 92 C3
Ipin = Yibin China 28°45N 104°32E 32 F9
Ipixuna Brazil 7°0S 71°40W 92 E4
Ipoh Malaysia 4°35N 101°5E 39 K3
Ippy C.A.R. 6°5N 21°7E 52 C4
İpsala Turkey 40°55N 26°23E 23 D12
Ipswich Australia 27°35S 152°40E 63 D5
Ipswich U.K. 52°4N 1°10E 13 E9
Ipswich Mass., U.S.A. 42°41N 70°50W 83 D14
Ipswich S. Dak., U.S.A. 45°27N 99°2W 80 C4
Ipu Brazil 4°23S 40°44W 93 D10
Iqaluit Canada 63°44N 68°31W 69 E18
Iqaluktuutiaq = Cambridge Bay Canada 69°10N 105°0W 68 D11
Iquique Chile 20°19S 70°5W 92 H4
Iquitos Peru 3°45S 73°10W 92 D4
Irabu-Jima Japan 24°50N 125°10E 31 M2
Iracoubo Fr. Guiana 5°30N 53°10W 93 B8
Īrafshān Iran 26°42N 61°56E 45 E9
Iraklio Greece 35°20N 25°12E 25 D7
Iraklio □ Greece 35°10N 25°10E 25 D7
Iráklion = Iraklio Greece 35°20N 25°12E 25 D7
Irakliou, Kolpos Greece 35°23N 25°8E 25 D7
Irala Paraguay 25°55S 54°35W 95 B5
Iran ■ Asia 33°0N 53°0E 45 C7
Iran, Pegunungan Malaysia 2°20N 114°50E 36 D4
Iran Ra. = Iran, Pegunungan Malaysia 2°20N 114°50E 36 D4
Īrānshahr Iran 27°15N 60°40E 45 E9
Irapuato Mexico 20°41N 101°28W 86 C4
Iraq ■ Asia 33°0N 44°0E 44 C5
Irati Brazil 25°25S 50°38W 95 B5
Irbid Jordan 32°35N 35°48E 46 C4
Irbid □ Jordan 32°30N 35°50E 46 C5
Irebu Dem. Rep. of the Congo 0°40S 17°46E 52 E3
Ireland ■ Europe 53°50N 7°52W 10 C4
Iri = Iksan S. Korea 35°59N 127°0E 35 G14
Irian Jaya = Papua □ Indonesia 4°0S 137°0E 37 E9
Irian Jaya Barat □ Indonesia 2°5S 132°50E 37 E8
Iringa Tanzania 7°48S 35°43E 54 D4
Iringa □ Tanzania 7°48S 35°43E 54 D4
Iriomote △ Japan 24°29N 123°53E 31 M1
Iriomote-Jima Japan 24°19N 123°48E 31 M1
Iriona Honduras 15°57N 85°11W 88 C2
Iriri → Brazil 3°52S 52°37W 93 D8
Irish Republic ■ Europe 53°50N 7°52W 10 C4
Irish Sea Europe 53°38N 4°48W 12 D3
Irkutsk Russia 52°18N 104°20E 32 A9
Irma Canada 52°55N 111°14W 71 C6
Irō-Zaki Japan 34°36N 138°51E 31 G9
Iron Baron Australia 32°58S 137°11E 63 E2
Iron Gate = Portile de Fier Europe 44°44N 22°30E 17 F12
Iron Knob Australia 32°46S 137°8E 63 E2
Iron Mountain U.S.A. 45°49N 88°4W 80 C9
Iron Range △ Australia 12°34S 143°18E 62 A3
Iron River U.S.A. 46°6N 88°39W 80 B9
Irondequoit U.S.A. 43°13N 77°35W 82 C7
Ironton Mo., U.S.A. 37°36N 90°38W 80 G8
Ironton Ohio, U.S.A. 38°32N 82°41W 81 F12
Ironwood U.S.A. 46°27N 90°9W 80 B8
Ironwood Forest ⌂ U.S.A. 32°32N 111°28W 77 K8
Iroquois Canada 44°51N 75°19W 83 B9
Iroquois Falls Canada 48°46N 80°41W 72 C3
Irpin Ukraine 50°30N 30°15E 17 C16
Irrara Cr. → Australia 29°35S 145°31E 63 D4
Irrawaddy □ Burma 17°0N 95°0E 41 L19
Irrawaddy → Burma 15°50N 95°6E 41 M19
Irrawaddy, Mouths of the Burma 15°30N 95°0E 41 M19
Irricana Canada 51°19N 113°37W 70 C6
Irrunytju Australia 26°3S 128°56E 61 E4
Irtysh → Russia 61°4N 68°52E 28 C7
Irumu Dem. Rep. of the Congo 1°32N 29°53E 54 B2
Irún Spain 43°20N 1°52W 21 A5
Irunea = Pamplona-Iruña Spain 42°48N 1°38W 21 A5
Irvine Canada 49°57N 110°16W 71 D6
Irvine U.K. 55°37N 4°41W 11 F4
Irvine Calif., U.S.A. 33°41N 117°46W 79 M9
Irvine Ky., U.S.A. 37°42N 83°58W 81 G12
Irvinestown U.K. 54°28N 7°39W 10 B4
Irving U.S.A. 32°48N 96°56W 84 E6
Irvona U.S.A. 40°46N 78°33W 82 F6
Irwin → Australia 29°15S 114°54E 61 E1
Irymple Australia 34°14S 142°8E 63 E3
Isa Khel Pakistan 32°41N 71°17E 42 C4
Isaac → Australia 22°55S 149°20E 62 C4
Isabel U.S.A. 45°24N 101°26W 80 C3
Isabel, I. Mexico 21°51N 105°55W 86 C3
Isabela Phil. 6°40N 121°59E 37 C6
Isabela Puerto Rico 18°30N 67°2W 89 d
Isabella, Cord. Nic. 13°30N 85°25W 88 D2
Isabella Ra. Australia 21°0S 121°4E 60 D3
Isachsen, C. Canada 79°20N 105°28W 69 B10
Ísafjarðardjúp Iceland 66°10N 23°0W 8 C2
Ísafjörður Iceland 66°5N 23°9W 8 C2
Isagarh India 24°48N 77°51E 42 G7
Isahaya Japan 32°52N 130°2E 31 H5
Isaka Tanzania 3°56S 32°59E 54 C3
Isalo △ Madag. 22°23S 45°16E 57 C8
Isan → India 26°51N 80°7E 43 F9
Isana = Içana → Brazil 0°26N 67°19W 92 C5
Isangano △ Zambia 11°8S 30°35E 55 E3
Isar → Germany 48°48N 12°57E 16 D7
Íschia Italy 40°44N 13°57E 22 D5
Isdell → Australia 16°27S 124°51E 60 C3
Ise Japan 34°25N 136°45E 31 G8
Ise-Shima △ Japan 34°25N 136°48E 31 G8
Ise-Wan Japan 34°43N 136°43E 31 G8
Iseramagazi Tanzania 4°37S 32°10E 54 C3
Isère → France 44°59N 4°51E 20 D6
Isérnia Italy 41°36N 14°14E 22 D6
Isfahan = Eşfahān Iran 32°39N 51°43E 45 C6
Ishigaki Japan 24°26N 124°10E 31 M2
Ishigaki-Shima Japan 24°20N 124°10E 31 M2
Ishikari Japan 43°20N 141°15E 30 C10
Ishikari-Gawa → Japan 43°15N 141°23E 30 C10
Ishikari-Sammyaku Japan 43°30N 143°0E 30 C11
Ishikari-Wan Japan 43°25N 141°1E 30 C10
Ishikawa Japan 26°25N 127°49E 31 L3
Ishikawa □ Japan 36°30N 136°30E 31 F8
Ishim Russia 56°10N 69°30E 28 D7
Ishim → Russia 57°45N 71°10E 28 D8
Ishinomaki Japan 38°32N 141°20E 30 E10
Ishioka Japan 36°11N 140°16E 31 F10
Ishkoman Pakistan 36°30N 73°50E 43 A5
Ishpeming U.S.A. 46°29N 87°40W 80 B10
Isil Kul Russia 54°55N 71°16E 28 D8
Isiolo Kenya 0°24N 37°33E 54 B4
Isiro Dem. Rep. of the Congo 2°53N 27°40E 54 B2
Isisford Australia 24°15S 144°21E 62 C3
İskenderun Turkey 36°32N 36°10E 44 B3
İskenderun Körfezi Turkey 36°40N 35°50E 19 G6
Iskŭr → Bulgaria 43°45N 24°25E 23 C11
Iskut → Canada 56°45N 131°49W 70 B2
Isla → U.K. 56°32N 3°20W 11 E5
Isla Coiba △ Panama 7°33N 81°36W 88 E3
Isla de Salamanca △ Colombia 10°59N 74°40W 89 D5
Isla Gorge △ Australia 25°10S 149°57E 62 D4
Isla Isabel △ Mexico 21°54N 105°58W 86 C3
Isla Tiburón y San Esteban ⌂ Mexico 29°0N 112°27W 86 B2
Isla Vista U.S.A. 34°25N 119°53W 79 L7
Islam Headworks Pakistan 29°49N 72°33E 42 E5
Islamabad Pakistan 33°40N 73°10E 42 C5
Islamgarh Pakistan 27°51N 70°48E 42 F4
Islamkot Pakistan 24°42N 70°13E 42 G4
Islampur Bihar, India 25°9N 85°12E 43 G11
Islampur W. Bengal, India 26°16N 88°12E 43 F13
Island = Iceland ■ Europe 64°45N 19°0W 8 D4
Island L. Canada 53°47N 94°25W 71 C10
Island Lagoon Australia 31°30S 136°40E 63 E2
Island Pond U.S.A. 44°49N 71°53W 83 B13
Islands, B. of Canada 49°11N 58°15W 73 C8
Islands, B. of N.Z. 35°15S 174°6E 59 A5
Islay U.K. 55°46N 6°10W 11 F2
Isle → France 44°55N 0°15W 20 D3
Isle aux Morts Canada 47°35N 59°0W 73 C8
Isle of Wight □ U.K. 50°41N 1°17W 13 G6
Isle Royale △ U.S.A. 48°0N 88°55W 80 B9
Isleton U.S.A. 38°10N 121°37W 78 G5
Ismail = Izmayil Ukraine 45°22N 28°46E 17 F15
Ismâ'ilîya Egypt 30°37N 32°18E 51 B12
Isna Egypt 25°17N 32°30E 51 C12
Isoanala Madag. 23°50S 45°44E 57 C8
Isparta Turkey 37°47N 30°30E 19 G5
Íspica Italy 36°47N 14°55E 22 F6
Israel ■ Asia 32°0N 34°50E 46 D3
Issoire France 45°32N 3°15E 20 D5
Issyk-Kul = Balykchy Kyrgyzstan 42°26N 76°12E 32 C4
Issyk-Kul, Ozero = Ysyk-Köl Kyrgyzstan 42°25N 77°15E 28 E8
İstanbul Turkey 41°0N 28°58E 23 D13
İstanbul Boğazı Turkey 41°5N 29°3E 23 D13
Istiea Greece 38°57N 23°9E 23 E10
Isto, Mt. U.S.A. 69°12N 143°48W 74 B11
Istokpoga, L. U.S.A. 27°23N 81°17W 85 H14
Istra Croatia 45°10N 14°0E 16 F7
Istres France 43°31N 4°59E 20 E6
Istria = Istra Croatia 45°10N 14°0E 16 F7
Itá Paraguay 25°29S 57°21W 94 B4
Itaberaba Brazil 12°32S 40°18W 93 F10
Itabira Brazil 19°37S 43°13W 93 G10
Itabirito Brazil 20°15S 43°48W 95 A7
Itabuna Brazil 14°48S 39°16W 93 F11
Itacaunas → Brazil 5°21S 49°8W 93 E9
Itacoatiara Brazil 3°8S 58°25W 92 D7
Itaipú, Represa de Brazil 25°30S 54°30W 95 B5
Itaituba Brazil 4°10S 55°50W 93 D7
Itajaí Brazil 27°50S 48°39W 95 B6
Itajubá Brazil 22°24S 45°30W 95 A6
Itaka Tanzania 8°50S 32°49E 55 D3
Itala ⌂ S. Africa 27°30S 31°7E 57 D5
Italy ■ Europe 42°0N 13°0E 22 C5
Itamaraju Brazil 17°4S 39°32W 93 G11
Itampolo Madag. 24°41S 43°57E 57 C7
Itandrano Madag. 21°47S 45°17E 57 C8
Itapecuru Mirim Brazil 3°24S 44°20W 93 D10
Itaperuna Brazil 21°10S 41°54W 95 A7
Itapetininga Brazil 23°36S 48°7W 95 A6
Itapeva Brazil 23°59S 48°59W 95 A6
Itapicuru → Bahia, Brazil 11°47S 37°32W 93 F11
Itapicuru → Maranhão, Brazil 2°52S 44°12W 93 D10
Itapipoca Brazil 3°30S 39°35W 93 D11
Itapuá □ Paraguay 26°40S 55°40W 95 B4
Itaquí Brazil 29°8S 56°30W 94 B4
Itararé Brazil 24°6S 49°23W 95 A6
Itarsi India 22°36N 77°51E 42 H7
Itatí Argentina 27°16S 58°15W 94 B4
Itatiaia △ Brazil 22°22S 44°38W 95 A7
Itchen → U.K. 50°55N 1°22W 13 G6
Itezhi Tezhi, L. Zambia 15°30S 25°30E 55 F2
Ithaca = Ithaki Greece 38°25N 20°40E 23 E9
Ithaca U.S.A. 42°27N 76°30W 83 D8
Ithaki Greece 38°25N 20°40E 23 E9
Itiquira → Brazil 17°18S 56°44W 93 G7
Itiyuro → Argentina 22°40S 63°50W 94 A3
Itō Japan 34°58N 139°5E 31 G9
Itoigawa Japan 37°2N 137°51E 31 F8
Itonamas → Bolivia 12°28S 64°24W 92 F6
Ittoqqortoormiit Greenland 70°20N 23°0W 4 B6
Itu Brazil 23°17S 47°15W 95 A6
Itu Aba I. S. China Sea 10°23N 114°21E 36 B4
Ituiutaba Brazil 19°0S 49°25W 93 G9
Itumbiara Brazil 18°20S 49°10W 93 G9
Ituna Canada 51°10N 103°24W 71 C8
Itunge Port Tanzania 9°40S 33°55E 55 D3
Iturbe Argentina 23°0S 65°25W 94 A2
Ituri → Dem. Rep. of the Congo 1°40N 27°1E 54 B2
Iturup, Ostrov Russia 45°0N 148°0E 29 E15
Ituxi → Brazil 7°18S 64°51W 92 E6
Itzehoe Germany 53°55N 9°31E 16 B5
Ivahona Madag. 23°27S 46°10E 57 C8
Ivaí → Brazil 23°18S 53°42W 95 A5
Ivalo Finland 68°38N 27°35E 8 B22
Ivalojoki → Finland 68°40N 27°40E 8 B22
Ivanava Belarus 52°7N 25°29E 17 B13
Ivanhoe Australia 32°56S 144°20E 63 E3
Ivanhoe Canada 44°23N 77°28W 82 B7
Ivanhoe Calif., U.S.A. 36°23N 119°13W 78 J7
Ivanhoe Minn., U.S.A. 44°28N 96°15W 80 C5
Ivano-Frankivsk Ukraine 48°40N 24°40E 17 D13
Ivanovo = Ivanava Belarus 52°7N 25°29E 17 B13
Ivanovo Russia 57°5N 41°0E 18 C7
Ivato Madag. 20°37S 47°10E 57 C8
Ivatsevichy Belarus 52°43N 25°21E 17 B13
Ivdel Russia 60°42N 60°24E 18 B11
Ivinheima → Brazil 23°14S 53°42W 95 A5
Ivinhema Brazil 22°10S 53°37W 95 A5
Ivohibe Madag. 22°31S 46°57E 57 C8
Ivory Coast W. Afr. 4°20N 5°0W 50 H4
Ivory Coast ■ Africa 7°30N 5°0W 50 G4
Ivrea Italy 45°28N 7°52E 20 D7
Ivujivik Canada 62°24N 77°55W 69 E16
Ivvavik △ Canada 69°6N 139°30W 68 D4
Ivybridge U.K. 50°23N 3°56W 13 G4
Iwaizumi Japan 39°50N 141°45E 30 E10
Iwaki Japan 37°3N 140°55E 31 F10
Iwakuni Japan 34°15N 132°8E 31 G6
Iwamizawa Japan 43°12N 141°46E 30 C10
Iwanai Japan 42°58N 140°30E 30 C10
Iwata Japan 34°42N 137°51E 31 G8
Iwate □ Japan 39°30N 141°30E 30 E10
Iwate-San Japan 39°51N 141°0E 30 E10
Iwo Nigeria 7°39N 4°9E 50 G6
Iwŏn N. Korea 40°19N 128°39E 35 D15
Ixiamas Bolivia 13°50S 68°5W 92 F5
Ixopo S. Africa 30°11S 30°5E 57 E5
Ixtepec Mexico 16°34N 95°6W 87 D5
Ixtlán del Río Mexico 21°2N 104°22W 86 C4
Iyo Japan 33°45N 132°45E 31 H6
Izabal, L. de Guatemala 15°30N 89°10W 88 C2
Izamal Mexico 20°56N 89°1W 87 C7
Izena-Shima Japan 26°56N 127°56E 31 L3
Izhevsk Russia 56°51N 53°14E 18 C9
Izhma → Russia 65°19N 52°54E 18 A9
Izmayil Ukraine 45°22N 28°46E 17 F15
İzmir Turkey 38°25N 27°8E 23 E12
İzmit = Kocaeli Turkey 40°45N 29°50E 19 F4
İznik Gölü Turkey 40°27N 29°30E 23 D13
Izra Syria 32°51N 36°15E 46 C5
Izu-Hantō Japan 34°45N 139°0E 31 G9
Izu-Shotō Japan 34°30N 140°0E 31 G10
Izúcar de Matamoros Mexico 18°36N 98°28W 87 D5
Izumi Japan 32°5N 130°22E 31 H5
Izumi-Sano Japan 34°23N 135°18E 31 G7
Izumo Japan 35°20N 132°46E 31 G6
Izyaslav Ukraine 50°5N 26°50E 17 C14

J

J.F.K. Int. ✈ (JFK) U.S.A. 40°38N 73°47W 83 F11
J. Strom Thurmond L. U.S.A. 33°40N 82°12W 85 E13
Jabalpur India 23°9N 79°58E 43 H8
Jabbūl Syria 36°4N 37°30E 44 B3
Jabiru Australia 12°40S 132°53E 60 B5
Jablah Syria 35°20N 36°0E 44 C3
Jablonec nad Nisou Czech Rep. 50°43N 15°10E 16 C8
Jaboatão Brazil 8°7S 35°1W 93 E11
Jaboticabal Brazil 21°15S 48°17W 95 A6
Jaca Spain 42°35N 0°33W 21 A5
Jacareí Brazil 23°20S 46°0W 95 A6
Jacarèzinho Brazil 23°5S 49°58W 95 A6
Jack River ⌂ Australia 14°58S 144°19E 62 A3
Jackman U.S.A. 45°37N 70°15W 81 C18
Jacksboro U.S.A. 33°13N 98°10W 84 E5
Jackson Barbados 13°7N 59°36W 89 g
Jackson Ala., U.S.A. 31°31N 87°53W 85 F11
Jackson Calif., U.S.A. 38°21N 120°46W 78 G6
Jackson Ky., U.S.A. 37°33N 83°23W 81 G12
Jackson Mich., U.S.A. 42°15N 84°24W 81 D11
Jackson Minn., U.S.A. 43°37N 95°1W 80 D6
Jackson Miss., U.S.A. 32°18N 90°12W 85 E9
Jackson Mo., U.S.A. 37°23N 89°40W 80 G9
Jackson N.H., U.S.A. 44°10N 71°11W 83 B13
Jackson Ohio, U.S.A. 39°3N 82°39W 81 F12
Jackson Tenn., U.S.A. 35°37N 88°49W 85 D10
Jackson Wyo., U.S.A. 43°29N 110°46W 76 E8
Jackson B. N.Z. 43°58S 168°42E 59 E2
Jackson L. U.S.A. 43°52N 110°36W 76 E8
Jacksons N.Z. 42°46S 171°32E 59 E3
Jackson's Arm Canada 49°52N 56°47W 73 C8
Jacksonville Ala., U.S.A. 33°49N 85°46W 85 E12
Jacksonville Ark., U.S.A. 34°52N 92°7W 84 D8
Jacksonville Calif., U.S.A. 37°52N 120°24W 78 H6
Jacksonville Fla., U.S.A. 30°20N 81°39W 85 F14

Jacksonville *Ill., U.S.A.* 39°44N 90°14W **80** F8
Jacksonville *N.C.,*
  U.S.A. 34°45N 77°26W **85** D16
Jacksonville *Tex., U.S.A.* 31°58N 95°17W **84** F7
Jacksonville Beach
  U.S.A. 30°17N 81°24W **85** F14
Jacmel *Haiti* 18°14N 72°32W **89** C5
Jacob Lake *U.S.A.* 36°43N 112°13W **77** H7
Jacobabad *Pakistan* 28°20N 68°29E **42** E3
Jacobina *Brazil* 11°11S 40°30W **93** F10
Jacques-Cartier, Dét. de
  Canada 50°0N 63°30W **73** C7
Jacques-Cartier, Mt.
  Canada 48°57N 66°0W **73** C6
Jacques-Cartier △
  Canada 47°15N 71°33W **73** C5
Jacuí → *Brazil* 30°2S 51°15W **95** C5
Jacumba *U.S.A.* 32°37N 116°11W **79** N10
Jacundá → *Brazil* 1°57S 50°26W **93** D8
Jade City *Canada* 59°15N 129°37W **70** B3
Jade Mt. = Yü Shan
  Taiwan 23°25N 120°52E **33** G13
Jaén *Peru* 5°25S 78°40W **92** E3
Jaén *Spain* 37°44N 3°43W **21** D4
Jafarabad *India* 20°52N 71°22E **42** J4
Jaffa = Tel Aviv-Yafo
  Israel 32°4N 34°48E **46** C3
Jaffa, C. *Australia* 36°58S 139°40E **63** F2
Jaffna *Sri Lanka* 9°45N 80°2E **40** Q12
Jaffrey *U.S.A.* 42°49N 72°2W **83** D12
Jagadhri *India* 30°10N 77°20E **42** D7
Jagadishpur *India* 25°30N 84°21E **43** G11
Jagdalpur *India* 19°3N 82°0E **41** K13
Jagdaqi *India* 50°25N 124°7E **33** A13
Jagersfontein *S. Africa* 29°44S 25°27E **56** D4
Jaghīn → *Iran* 27°17N 57°13E **45** E8
Jagodina *Serbia* 44°5N 21°15E **23** C9
Jagraon *India* 30°50N 75°25E **42** D6
Jagtial *India* 18°50N 79°0E **40** K11
Jaguariaíva *Brazil* 24°10S 49°50W **95** A6
Jaguaribe → *Brazil* 4°25S 37°45W **93** D11
Jagüey Grande *Cuba* 22°35N 81°7W **88** B3
Jahanabad *India* 25°13N 84°59E **43** G11
Jahazpur *India* 25°37N 75°17E **42** G6
Jahrom *Iran* 28°30N 53°31E **45** D7
Jaijon *India* 31°21N 76°9E **42** D7
Jailolo *Indonesia* 1°5N 127°30E **37** D7
Jailolo, Selat *Indonesia* 0°5N 129°5E **37** D7
Jaipur *India* 27°0N 75°50E **42** F6
Jais *India* 26°15N 81°32E **43** F9
Jaisalmer *India* 26°55N 70°54E **42** F4
Jaisinghnagar *India* 23°38N 78°34E **43** H8
Jaitaran *India* 26°12N 73°56E **42** F5
Jaithari *India* 23°14N 78°37E **43** H8
Jājarm *Iran* 36°58N 56°27E **45** B8
Jakam → *India* 23°54N 74°13E **42** H6
Jakarta *Indonesia* 6°9S 106°52E **37** G12
Jakhal *India* 29°48N 75°50E **42** E6
Jakhau *India* 23°13N 68°43E **42** H3
Jakobstad = Pietarsaari
  Finland 63°40N 22°43E **8** E20
Jal *U.S.A.* 32°7N 103°12W **77** K12
Jalājil *Si. Arabia* 25°40N 45°27E **44** E5
Jalālābād *Afghan.* 34°30N 70°29E **42** B4
Jalalabad *India* 27°41N 79°42E **43** F8
Jalalpur Jattan *Pakistan* 32°38N 74°11E **42** C6
Jalama *U.S.A.* 34°29N 120°29W **79** L6
Jalandhar = Jullundur
  India 31°20N 75°40E **42** D6
Jalapa *Guatemala* 14°39N 89°59W **88** D2
Jalapa Enriquez = Xalapa
  Mexico 19°32N 96°55W **87** D5
Jalasjärvi *Finland* 62°29N 22°47E **8** E20
Jalaun *India* 26°8N 79°25E **43** F8
Jaldhaka → *Bangla.* 26°16N 89°16E **43** F13
Jalesar *India* 27°29N 78°19E **42** F8
Jaleswar *Nepal* 26°38N 85°48E **43** F11
Jalgaon *India* 21°0N 75°42E **40** J9
Jalībah *Iraq* 30°35N 46°32E **44** D5
Jalingo *Nigeria* 8°55N 11°25E **51** G8
Jalisco □ *Mexico* 20°20N 103°40W **86** D4
Jalkot *Pakistan* 35°14N 73°24E **43** B5
Jalna *India* 19°48N 75°38E **40** K9
Jalón → *Spain* 41°47N 1°4W **21** B5
Jalor *India* 25°21N 72°37E **42** G5
Jalpa *Mexico* 21°38N 102°58W **86** C4
Jalpaiguri *India* 26°32N 88°46E **41** F16
Jalpan *Mexico* 21°14N 99°29W **87** C5
Jaluit I. *Marshall Is.* 6°0N 169°30E **64** G8
Jalūlā *Iraq* 34°16N 45°10E **44** C5
Jamaame *Somali Rep.* 0°4N 42°44E **47** G3
Jamaica ■ *W. Indies* 18°10N 77°30W **88** a
Jamalpur *Bangla.* 24°52N 89°56E **41** G16
Jamalpur *India* 25°18N 86°28E **43** G12
Jamalpurganj *India* 23°2N 87°59E **43** H12
Jamanxim → *Brazil* 4°43S 56°18W **93** D7
Jambewangi *Indonesia* 8°17S 114°7E **37** J17
Jambi *Indonesia* 1°38S 103°30E **36** E2
Jambi □ *Indonesia* 1°30S 102°30E **36** E2
Jambongan, Pulau
  Malaysia 6°45N 117°20E **36** C5
Jambusar *India* 22°3N 72°51E **42** H5
James → *S. Dak., U.S.A.* 42°52N 97°18W **80** D6
James → *Va., U.S.A.* 36°56N 76°27W **81** G15
James B. *Canada* 54°0N 80°0W **72** B3
James Ranges *Australia* 24°10S 132°30E **60** D5
James Ross I. *Antarctica* 63°58S 57°50W **5** C18
Jamesabad *Pakistan* 25°17N 69°15E **42** G3
Jamestown *Australia* 33°10S 138°32E **63** E2
Jamestown *S. Africa* 31°6S 26°45E **56** E4
Jamestown *N. Dak.,*
  U.S.A. 46°54N 98°42W **80** B4
Jamestown *N.Y., U.S.A.* 42°6N 79°14W **82** D5
Jamestown *Pa., U.S.A.* 41°29N 80°27W **82** E4
Jamīlābād *Iran* 34°24N 48°28E **45** C6
Jamira → *India* 21°35N 88°28E **43** J13
Jamkhandi *India* 16°30N 75°15E **40** L9
Jammu *India* 32°43N 74°54E **42** C6
Jammu & Kashmir □
  India 34°25N 77°0E **43** B7

Jamnagar *India* 22°30N 70°6E **42** H4
Jamni → *India* 25°13N 78°35E **43** G8
Jampur *Pakistan* 29°39N 70°40E **42** E4
Jamrud *Pakistan* 33°59N 71°24E **42** C4
Jämsä *Finland* 61°53N 25°10E **8** F21
Jamshedpur *India* 22°44N 86°12E **43** H12
Jamtara *India* 23°59N 86°49E **43** H12
Jämtland *Sweden* 63°31N 14°0E **8** E16
Jan L. *Canada* 54°56N 102°55W **71** C8
Jan Mayen *Arctic* 71°0N 9°0W **4** B7
Janakpur *Nepal* 26°42N 85°55E **43** F11
Janaúba *Brazil* 15°48S 43°19W **93** G10
Jand *Pakistan* 33°30N 72°6E **42** C5
Jandanku ◎ *Australia* 16°20S 135°45E **62** B2
Jandia *Canary Is.* 28°6N 14°21W **24** F5
Jandía, Pta. de *Canary Is.* 28°3N 14°31W **24** F5
Jandia △ *Canary Is.* 28°4N 14°19W **24** F5
Jandola *Pakistan* 32°20N 70°9E **42** C4
Jandowae *Australia* 26°45S 151°7E **63** D5
Janesville *U.S.A.* 42°41N 89°1W **80** D9
Jangamo *Mozam.* 24°6S 35°21E **57** C6
Janghai *India* 25°33N 82°19E **43** G10
Jangheung *S. Korea* 34°41N 126°52E **35** G14
Janin → *India* 13°30N 14°47W **50** F3
Janjgir *India* 22°1N 82°34E **43** J10
Janjina *Madag.* 20°30S 45°50E **57** C8
Janos *Mexico* 30°54N 108°10W **86** A3
Januária *Brazil* 15°25S 44°25W **93** G10
Janūb Sīnī □ *Egypt* 29°30N 33°50E **46** F2
Janubio *Canary Is.* 28°56N 13°50W **24** F6
Jaora *India* 23°40N 75°10E **42** H6
Japan ■ *Asia* 36°0N 136°0E **31** G8
Japan, Sea of *Asia* 40°0N 135°0E **30** D7
Japan Trench *Pac. Oc.* 32°0N 142°0E **64** D6
Japen = Yapen *Indonesia* 1°50S 136°0E **37** E9
Japla *India* 24°33N 84°1E **43** G11
Japurá → *Brazil* 3°8S 65°46W **92** D5
Jaquarão *Brazil* 32°34S 53°23W **95** C5
Jaqué *Panama* 7°27N 78°8W **88** E4
Jarābulus *Syria* 36°49N 38°1E **44** B3
Jarama → *Spain* 40°24N 3°32W **21** B4
Jaranwala *Pakistan* 31°15N 73°26E **42** D5
Jarash *Jordan* 32°17N 35°54E **46** C4
Jarash → *Jordan* 32°17N 35°54E **46** C4
Jardim *Brazil* 21°28S 56°2W **94** A4
Jardín América *Argentina* 27°3S 55°14W **95** B4
Jardine River △ *Australia* 11°9S 142°21E **62** A3
Jardines de la Reina, Arch. de los
  Cuba 20°50N 78°50W **88** B4
Jargalang *China* 43°5N 122°55E **35** C12
Jari → *Brazil* 1°9S 51°54W **93** D8
Jarīr, W. al → *Si. Arabia* 25°38N 42°30E **44** E4
Jarosław *Poland* 50°2N 22°42E **17** C12
Jarrahdale *Australia* 32°24S 116°5E **61** F2
Jarrahi → *Iran* 30°49N 48°48E **45** D6
Jartai *China* 39°45N 105°48E **34** E3
Jarud Qi *China* 44°28N 120°50E **35** B11
Järvenpää *Finland* 60°29N 25°5E **8** F21
Jarvis *Canada* 42°53N 80°6W **82** D4
Jarvis I. *Pac. Oc.* 0°15S 160°5W **65** H11
Jarwa *India* 27°38N 82°30E **43** F10
Jasdan *India* 22°2N 71°12E **42** H4
Jashpurnagar *India* 22°54N 84°9E **43** H11
Jasidih *India* 24°31N 86°39E **43** G12
Jāsimīyah *Iraq* 33°45N 44°41E **44** C5
Jasin *Malaysia* 2°20N 102°26E **39** L4
Jāsk *Iran* 25°38N 57°45E **45** E8
Jasło *Poland* 49°45N 21°30E **17** D11
Jaso *India* 24°30N 80°29E **43** G9
Jasper *Alta., Canada* 52°55N 118°5W **70** C5
Jasper *Ont., Canada* 44°52N 75°57W **83** B9
Jasper *Ala., U.S.A.* 33°50N 87°17W **85** E11
Jasper *Fla., U.S.A.* 30°31N 82°57W **85** F13
Jasper *Ind., U.S.A.* 38°24N 86°56W **80** F10
Jasper *Tex., U.S.A.* 30°56N 94°1W **84** F7
Jasper △ *Canada* 52°50N 118°8W **70** C5
Jasrasar *India* 27°43N 73°49E **42** F5
Jászberény *Hungary* 47°30N 19°55E **17** E10
Jataí *Brazil* 17°58S 51°48W **93** G8
Jati *Pakistan* 24°20N 68°19E **42** G3
Jatibarang *Indonesia* 6°28S 108°18E **37** G13
Jatiluwih *Indonesia* 8°23S 115°8E **37** J18
Jatinegara *Indonesia* 6°13S 106°52E **37** G12
Játiva = Xàtiva *Spain* 38°59N 0°32W **21** C5
Jaú *Brazil* 22°10S 48°30W **95** A6
Jauja *Peru* 11°45S 75°15W **92** F3
Jaunpur *India* 25°46N 82°44E **43** G10
Java = Jawa *Indonesia* 7°0S 110°0E **36** F3
Java Sea *Indonesia* 4°35S 107°15E **36** E3
Java Trench *Ind. Oc.* 9°0S 105°0E **36** F3
Jawa *Indonesia* 7°0S 110°0E **36** F3
Jawa Barat □ *Indonesia* 7°0S 107°0E **37** G12
Jawa Tengah □ *Indonesia* 7°0S 110°0E **37** G14
Jawa Timur □ *Indonesia* 8°0S 113°0E **37** G15
Jawad *India* 24°36N 74°51E **42** G6
Jawhar *Somali Rep.* 2°48N 45°30E **47** G4
Jawoyn ◎ *Australia* 14°16S 132°28E **60** B5
Jaya, Puncak *Indonesia* 3°57S 137°17E **37** E9
Jayanti *India* 26°45N 89°40E **41** F16
Jayapura *Indonesia* 2°28S 140°38E **37** E10
Jayawijaya, Pegunungan
  Indonesia 5°0S 139°0E **37** F9
Jaynagar *India* 26°43N 86°9E **43** F12
Jaypur = Jeypore *India* 18°50N 82°38E **41** K13
Jayrūd *Syria* 33°49N 36°44E **44** C3
Jayton *U.S.A.* 33°15N 100°34W **84** E4
Jāz Mūrīān, Hāmūn-e
  Iran 27°20N 58°55E **45** E8
Jazīreh-ye Shīf *Iran* 29°4N 50°54E **45** D6
Jazminal *Mexico* 24°52N 101°24W **86** C4
Jazzīn *Lebanon* 33°31N 35°35E **46** B4
Jean *U.S.A.* 35°47N 115°20W **79** K11
Jean Marie River
  Canada 61°32N 120°38W **70** A4
Jean-Rabel *Haiti* 19°50N 73°5W **89** C5
Jeanerette *U.S.A.* 29°55N 91°40W **84** G9
Jeanette, Ostrov = Zhannetty,
  Ostrov *Russia* 76°43N 158°0E **29** B16

Jeannette *U.S.A.* 40°20N 79°36W **82** F5
Jebäl Bārez, Kūh-e *Iran* 28°30N 58°20E **45** D8
Jebel, Bahr el → *Sudan* 9°30N 30°25E **51** G12
Jebel Ali = Minā' Jabal 'Alī
  U.A.E. 25°2N 55°8E **45** E7
Jecheon *S. Korea* 37°8N 128°12E **35** F15
Jedburgh *U.K.* 55°29N 2°33W **11** F6
Jedda = Jiddah *Si. Arabia* 21°29N 39°10E **47** C2
Jędrzejów *Poland* 50°35N 20°15E **17** C11
Jefferson *Iowa, U.S.A.* 42°1N 94°23W **80** D6
Jefferson *Ohio, U.S.A.* 41°44N 80°46W **82** E4
Jefferson *Tex., U.S.A.* 32°46N 94°21W **84** E7
Jefferson, Mt. *Nev.,*
  U.S.A. 38°47N 116°56W **76** G5
Jefferson, Mt. *Oreg.,*
  U.S.A. 44°41N 121°48W **76** D3
Jefferson City *Mo.,*
  U.S.A. 38°34N 92°10W **80** F7
Jefferson City *Tenn.,*
  U.S.A. 36°7N 83°30W **85** C13
Jeffersontown *U.S.A.* 38°12N 85°35W **81** F11
Jeffersonville *U.S.A.* 38°17N 85°44W **81** F11
Jeffrey City *U.S.A.* 42°30N 107°49W **76** E10
Jega *Nigeria* 12°15N 4°23E **50** F6
Jeju *S. Korea* 33°31N 126°32E **35** H14
Jeju-do *S. Korea* 33°29N 126°34E **35** H14
Jēkabpils *Latvia* 56°29N 25°57E **9** H21
Jekyll I. *U.S.A.* 31°4N 81°25W **85** F14
Jelenia Góra *Poland* 50°50N 15°45E **16** C8
Jelgava *Latvia* 56°41N 23°49E **9** H20
Jemaluang *Malaysia* 2°16N 103°52E **39** L4
Jember *Indonesia* 8°11S 113°41E **37** H15
Jena *Germany* 50°54N 11°35E **16** C6
Jena *U.S.A.* 31°41N 92°8W **84** F8
Jengish Chokoso = Pobedy, Pik
  Kyrgyzstan 42°0N 79°58E **32** C4
Jenkins *U.S.A.* 37°10N 82°38W **81** G12
Jenner *U.S.A.* 38°27N 123°7W **78** G3
Jennings *U.S.A.* 30°13N 92°40W **84** F8
Jeong-eup *S. Korea* 35°35N 126°50E **35** G14
Jeongseon *S. Korea* 37°20N 128°45E **35** F15
Jeonju *S. Korea* 35°50N 127°4E **35** G14
Jepara *Indonesia* 7°40S 109°14E **37** G14
Jeparit *Australia* 36°8S 142°1E **63** F3
Jequié *Brazil* 13°51S 40°5W **93** F10
Jequitinhonha *Brazil* 16°30S 41°0W **93** G10
Jequitinhonha →
  Brazil 15°51S 38°53W **93** G11
Jerada *Morocco* 34°17N 2°10W **50** B5
Jerantut *Malaysia* 3°56N 102°22E **39** L4
Jerejak, Pulau *Malaysia* 5°19N 100°19E **39** c
Jérémie *Haiti* 18°40N 74°10W **89** C5
Jerez, Pta. *Mexico* 22°58N 97°40W **87** C5
Jerez de García Salinas
  Mexico 22°39N 103°0W **86** C4
Jerez de la Frontera *Spain* 36°41N 6°7W **21** D2
Jerez de los Caballeros
  Spain 38°20N 6°45W **21** C2
Jericho = El Arīḥā
  West Bank 31°52N 35°27E **46** D4
Jericho *Australia* 23°38S 146°6E **62** C4
Jerid, Chott el = Djerid, Chott
  Tunisia 33°42N 8°30E **50** B7
Jerilderie *Australia* 35°20S 145°41E **63** F4
Jermyn *U.S.A.* 41°32N 75°33W **83** E9
Jerome *U.S.A.* 42°44N 114°31W **76** E6
Jerramungup *Australia* 33°55S 118°55E **61** F2
Jersey *U.K.* 49°11N 2°7W **13** H5
Jersey City *U.S.A.* 40°42N 74°4W **83** F10
Jersey Shore *U.S.A.* 41°12N 77°15W **82** E7
Jerseyville *U.S.A.* 39°7N 90°20W **80** F8
Jerusalem
  Israel/West Bank 31°47N 35°10E **46** D4
Jervis B. *Australia* 35°8S 150°46E **63** F5
Jervis Inlet *Canada* 50°0N 123°57W **70** C4
Jesi = Iesi *Italy* 43°31N 13°14E **22** C5
Jessore *Bangla.* 23°10N 89°10E **41** H16
Jesup *U.S.A.* 31°36N 81°53W **85** F14
Jesús Carranza *Mexico* 17°26N 95°2W **87** D5
Jesús María *Argentina* 30°59S 64°5W **94** C3
Jetmore *U.S.A.* 38°4N 99°54W **80** F4
Jetpur *India* 21°45N 70°10E **42** J4
Jevnaker *Norway* 60°15N 10°26E **9** F14
Jewett *U.S.A.* 40°22N 81°2W **82** F3
Jewett City *U.S.A.* 41°36N 71°59W **83** E13
Jeyḥūnābād *Iran* 34°58N 48°59E **45** C6
Jeypore *India* 18°50N 82°38E **41** K13
Jha Jha *India* 24°46N 86°22E **43** G12
Jhaarkand = Jharkhand □
  India 24°0N 85°50E **43** H11
Jhabua *India* 22°46N 74°36E **42** H6
Jhajjar *India* 28°37N 76°42E **42** E7
Jhal *Pakistan* 28°17N 67°27E **42** E2
Jhal Jhao *Pakistan* 26°20N 65°35E **40** F4
Jhalawar *India* 24°40N 76°10E **42** G7
Jhalida *India* 23°22N 85°58E **43** H11
Jhalrapatan *India* 24°33N 76°10E **42** G7
Jhang Maghiana
  Pakistan 31°15N 72°22E **42** D5
Jhansi *India* 25°30N 78°36E **43** G8
Jhargram *India* 22°27N 86°59E **43** H12
Jharia *India* 23°45N 86°26E **43** H12
Jharkhand □ *India* 24°0N 85°50E **43** H11
Jharsuguda *India* 21°56N 84°5E **41** J14
Jhelum *Pakistan* 33°0N 73°45E **42** C5
Jhelum → *Pakistan* 31°20N 72°10E **42** D5
Jhilmilli *India* 23°24N 82°51E **43** H10
Jhudo *Pakistan* 24°58N 69°18E **42** G3
Jhunjhunu *India* 28°10N 75°30E **42** E6
Ji-Paraná *Brazil* 10°52S 62°57W **92** F6
Jia Xian *Henan, China* 33°59N 113°12E **34** H7
Jia Xian *Shaanxi, China* 38°12N 110°28E **34** E6
Jiamusi *China* 46°40N 130°26E **33** B15
Jian *China* 27°6S 55°14W **35** E11
Ji'an *Jilin, China* 41°5N 126°10E **35** D14
Jianchang *China* 40°55N 120°35E **35** D11

Jiangsu □ *China* 33°0N 120°0E **35** H11
Jiangxi □ *China* 27°30N 116°0E **33** F12
Jiangyuan *China* 42°2N 126°34E **35** C14
Jiangyuan *China* 41°53N 119°42E **35** D10
Jiao Xian = Jiaozhou
  China 36°18N 120°1E **35** F11
Jiaohe *Hebei, China* 38°2N 116°20E **34** E9
Jiaohe *Jilin, China* 43°40N 127°22E **35** C14
Jiaonan *China* 35°52N 119°58E **35** G10
Jiaozhou *China* 36°18N 120°1E **35** F11
Jiaozhou Wan *China* 36°5N 120°10E **35** F11
Jiaozuo *China* 35°16N 113°12E **34** G7
Jiawang *China* 34°28N 117°26E **35** G9
Jiaxiang *China* 35°25N 116°20E **34** G9
Jiaxing *China* 30°49N 120°45E **33** E13
Jiayi = Chiai *Taiwan* 23°29N 120°25E **33** F13
Jiayuguan *China* 39°49N 98°18E **32** D8
Jibuti = Djibouti ■ *Africa* 12°0N 43°0E **47** E3
Jicarón, I. *Panama* 7°10N 81°50W **88** E3
Jiddah *Si. Arabia* 21°29N 39°10E **47** C2
Jido *India* 29°2N 94°58E **41** E19
Jieshou *China* 33°18N 115°22E **34** H8
Jiexiu *China* 37°2N 111°55E **34** F6
Jigalong *Australia* 23°21S 120°47E **60** D3
Jigalong ◎ *Australia* 23°21S 120°46E **60** D3
Jigni *India* 25°45N 79°25E **43** G8
Jihlava *Czech Rep.* 49°28N 15°35E **16** D8
Jihlava → *Czech Rep.* 48°55N 16°36E **17** D9
Jijiga *Ethiopia* 9°20N 42°50E **47** F3
Jilib *Somali Rep.* 0°29N 42°46E **47** G3
Jilin *China* 43°44N 126°30E **35** C14
Jilin □ *China* 44°0N 127°0E **35** C14
Jilong = Chilung *Taiwan* 25°3N 121°45E **33** F13
Jima *Ethiopia* 7°40N 36°47E **47** F2
Jimbaran, Teluk
  Indonesia 8°46S 115°9E **37** K18
Jiménez *Mexico* 27°8N 104°54W **86** B4
Jimeta *Nigeria* 9°17N 12°28E **52** C2
Jimo *China* 36°23N 120°30E **35** F11
Jin Xian = Jinzhou
  China 38°55N 121°42E **35** E11
Jinan *China* 36°38N 117°1E **34** F9
Jinchang *China* 38°30N 102°10E **32** D9
Jincheng *China* 35°29N 112°50E **34** G7
Jind *India* 29°19N 76°22E **42** E7
Jindabyne *Australia* 36°25S 148°35E **63** F4
Jinding *China* 22°22N 113°33E **33** a
Jindo *S. Korea* 34°28N 126°15E **35** G14
Jindřichův Hradec
  Czech Rep. 49°10N 15°2E **16** D8
Jing He → *China* 34°27N 109°4E **34** G5
Jingbian *China* 37°20N 108°30E **34** F5
Jingchuan *China* 35°20N 107°20E **34** G4
Jingdezhen *China* 29°20N 117°11E **33** F12
Jinggu *China* 23°35N 100°41E **32** G9
Jinghai *China* 38°55N 116°55E **34** E9
Jinghong *China* 22°0N 100°45E **32** G9
Jingle *China* 38°20N 111°55E **34** E6
Jingmen *China* 31°0N 112°10E **33** E11
Jingning *China* 35°30N 105°43E **34** G3
Jingpo Hu *China* 43°55N 128°55E **35** C15
Jingtai *China* 37°10N 104°6E **34** F3
Jingtanggang *China* 39°10N 119°5E **35** E10
Jingyang *China* 34°30N 108°50E **34** G5
Jingyu *China* 42°25N 126°45E **35** C14
Jingyuan *China* 36°30N 104°40E **34** F3
Jingziguan *China* 33°15N 111°0E **34** H6
Jinhua *China* 29°8N 119°38E **33** F12
Jining *Nei Monggol Zizhiqu,*
  China 41°5N 113°0E **34** D7
Jining *Shandong, China* 35°22N 116°34E **34** G9
Jinja *Uganda* 0°25N 33°12E **54** B3
Jinjang *Malaysia* 3°13N 101°39E **39** L3
Jinji *China* 37°58N 106°8E **34** F4
Jinju *S. Korea* 35°12N 128°2E **35** G15
Jinmu Jiao *China* 18°9N 109°34E **38** C7
Jinnah Barrage *Pakistan* 32°58N 71°33E **42** C4
Jinotega *Nic.* 13°6N 85°59W **88** D2
Jinotepe *Nic.* 11°50N 86°10W **88** D2
Jinsha Jiang → *China* 28°50N 104°36E **32** F9
Jinxi *China* 40°52N 120°50E **35** D11
Jinxiang *China* 35°5N 116°22E **34** G9
Jinzhong *China* 37°42N 112°46E **34** F7
Jinzhou *Liaoning, China* 38°55N 121°42E **35** E11
Jinzhou *Liaoning, China* 41°5N 121°3E **35** D11
Jiparaná → *Brazil* 8°3S 62°52W **92** E6
Jipijapa *Ecuador* 1°0S 80°40W **92** D2
Jiquilpan *Mexico* 19°59N 102°43W **86** D4
Jirisan *S. Korea* 35°20N 127°44E **35** G14
Jiroft *Iran* 28°45N 57°50E **45** D8
Jishan *China* 35°34N 110°58E **34** G6
Jishou *China* 28°21N 109°43E **33** F10
Jisr ash Shughūr *Syria* 35°49N 36°18E **44** C3
Jitarning *Australia* 32°48S 117°57E **61** F2
Jitra *Malaysia* 6°16N 100°25E **39** J3
Jiu → *Romania* 43°47N 23°48E **17** F12
Jiudengkou *China* 39°56N 106°40E **34** E4
Jiujiang *China* 29°42N 115°58E **33** F12
Jiulong = Kowloon
  China 22°19N 114°11E **33** G11
Jiuquan *China* 39°50N 98°20E **32** D8
Jiutai *China* 44°10N 125°50E **35** B13
Jiuxincheng *China* 39°17N 115°59E **34** E8
Jiwani *Pakistan* 25°1N 61°44E **40** G2
Jixi *China* 45°20N 130°50E **35** B16
Jiyang *China* 37°0N 117°12E **34** F9
Jiyuan *China* 35°7N 112°57E **34** G7
Jīzān *Si. Arabia* 17°0N 42°20E **47** D3
Jize *China* 36°54N 114°56E **34** F8
Jizhou *China* 37°35N 115°30E **34** F8
Jizl, Wādī al → *Si. Arabia* 25°39N 38°25E **44** E3
Jizō-Zaki *Japan* 35°34N 133°20E **31** G6
Joaçaba *Brazil* 27°5S 51°31W **95** B5
João Pessoa *Brazil* 7°10S 34°52W **93** E12
Joaquín V. González
  Argentina 25°10S 64°0W **94** B3
Jobat *India* 22°25N 74°34E **42** H6
Jodhpur *India* 26°23N 73°8E **42** F5

Jodiya *India* 22°42N 70°18E **42** H4
Joensuu *Finland* 62°37N 29°49E **8** E23
Jōetsu *Japan* 37°12N 138°10E **31** F9
Jofane *Mozam.* 21°15S 34°18E **57** C5
Jogbani *India* 26°25N 87°15E **43** F12
Jõgeva *Estonia* 58°45N 26°24E **9** G22
Jogjakarta = Yogyakarta
  Indonesia 7°49S 110°22E **37** G14
Johannesburg *S. Africa* 26°11S 28°2E **57** D4
Johannesburg *U.S.A.* 35°22N 117°38W **79** K9
Johilla → *India* 23°37N 81°14E **43** H9
John Crow Mts. *Jamaica* 18°5N 76°25W **88** a
John Day *U.S.A.* 44°25N 118°57W **76** D4
John Day → *U.S.A.* 45°44N 120°39W **76** D3
John Day Fossil Beds △
  U.S.A. 44°33N 119°38W **76** D4
John D'or Prairie
  Canada 58°30N 115°8W **70** B5
John H. Kerr Res.
  U.S.A. 36°36N 78°18W **85** C15
John o' Groats *U.K.* 58°38N 3°4W **11** C5
Johnnie *U.S.A.* 36°25N 116°5W **79** J10
Johnson *U.S.A.* 44°38N 72°41W **83** B12
Johnson City *Kans.,*
  U.S.A. 37°34N 101°45W **80** G3
Johnson City *N.Y., U.S.A.* 42°7N 75°58W **83** D9
Johnson City *Tenn.,*
  U.S.A. 36°19N 82°21W **85** C13
Johnson City *Tex., U.S.A.* 30°17N 98°25W **84** F5
Johnsonburg *U.S.A.* 41°29N 78°41W **82** E6
Johnsondale *U.S.A.* 35°58N 118°32W **79** K8
Johnsons Crossing
  Canada 60°29N 133°18W **70** A2
Johnston, L. *Australia* 32°25S 120°30E **61** F3
Johnston Falls = Mambilima Falls
  Zambia 10°31S 28°45E **55** E2
Johnston I. *Pac. Oc.* 17°10N 169°8W **65** F11
Johnstone Str. *Canada* 50°28N 126°0W **70** C3
Johnstone Ireland 52°45N 7°33W **10** D4
Johnstown *N.Y., U.S.A.* 43°0N 74°22W **83** C10
Johnstown *Ohio, U.S.A.* 40°9N 82°41W **82** F2
Johnstown *Pa., U.S.A.* 40°20N 78°55W **82** F6
Johor □ *Malaysia* 2°5N 103°20E **39** M4
Johor, Selat *Asia* 1°28N 103°47E **39** d
Johor Bahru *Malaysia* 1°28N 103°46E **39** d
Jõhvi *Estonia* 59°22N 27°27E **9** G22
Joinville *Brazil* 26°15S 48°55W **95** B6
Joinville I. *Antarctica* 65°0S 55°30W **5** C18
Jojutla *Mexico* 18°37N 99°11W **87** D5
Jokkmokk *Sweden* 66°35N 19°50E **8** C18
Jökulsá á Bru → *Iceland* 65°40N 14°16W **8** D6
Jökulsá á Fjöllum →
  Iceland 66°10N 16°30E **8** D5
Jökulsárgljúfur △ *Iceland* 65°56N 16°31W **8** D5
Jolfā *Āzarbājān-e Sharqī,*
  Iran 38°57N 45°38E **44** B5
Jolfā *Esfahan, Iran* 32°58N 51°37E **45** C6
Joliet *U.S.A.* 41°32N 88°5W **80** E9
Joliette *Canada* 46°3N 73°24W **72** C5
Jolo *Phil.* 6°0N 121°0E **37** C6
Jolon *U.S.A.* 35°58N 121°9W **78** K5
Jombang *Indonesia* 7°33S 112°14E **37** G15
Jonava *Lithuania* 55°8N 24°12E **9** J21
Jones Sound *Canada* 76°0N 85°0W **69** B15
Jonesboro *Ark., U.S.A.* 35°50N 90°42W **85** D9
Jonesboro *La., U.S.A.* 32°15N 92°43W **84** E8
Joniškis *Lithuania* 56°13N 23°35E **9** H20
Jönköping *Sweden* 57°45N 14°8E **9** H16
Jonquière *Canada* 48°27N 71°14W **73** C5
Joplin *U.S.A.* 37°6N 94°31W **80** G6
Jora *India* 26°20N 77°49E **42** F6
Jordan *Mont., U.S.A.* 47°19N 106°55W **76** C10
Jordan *N.Y., U.S.A.* 43°4N 76°29W **83** C8
Jordan ■ *Asia* 31°0N 36°0E **46** E5
Jordan → *Asia* 31°48N 35°32E **46** D4
Jordan Valley *U.S.A.* 42°59N 117°3W **76** E5
Jorhat *India* 26°45N 94°12E **41** F19
Jörn *Sweden* 65°4N 20°1E **8** D19
Jorong *Indonesia* 3°58S 114°56E **36** E4
Jørpeland *Norway* 59°3N 6°1E **9** G12
Jorquera → *Chile* 28°3S 69°58W **94** B2
Jos *Nigeria* 9°53N 8°51E **50** G7
José Batlle y Ordóñez
  Uruguay 33°20S 55°10W **95** C4
Joseph, L. *Canada* 45°10N 79°44W **82** A5
Joseph Bonaparte G.
  Australia 14°35S 128°50E **60** B4
Joseph L. *Canada* 52°45N 65°18W **73** B6
Joshinath *India* 30°34N 79°34E **43** D8
Joshinetsu-Kōgen △
  Japan 36°42N 138°32E **31** F9
Joshua Tree *U.S.A.* 34°8N 116°19W **79** L10
Joshua Tree △ *U.S.A.* 33°55N 116°0W **79** M10
Jost Van Dyke I.
  Br. Virgin Is. 18°29N 64°47W **89** e
Jostedalsbreen *Norway* 61°40N 6°59E **8** F12
Jotunheimen *Norway* 61°35N 8°25E **8** F13
Joubertberge *Namibia* 18°30S 14°0E **56** B1
Jourdanton *U.S.A.* 28°55N 98°33W **84** G5
Jovellanos *Cuba* 22°40N 81°10W **88** B3
Ju Xian *China* 36°35N 118°20E **35** F10
Juan Aldama *Mexico* 24°19N 103°21W **86** C4
Juan Bautista Alberdi
  Argentina 34°26S 61°48W **94** C3
Juan de Fuca, Str. of.
  N. Amer. 48°15N 124°0W **78** B3
Juán de Nova *Ind. Oc.* 17°3S 43°45E **57** B7
Juan Fernández, Arch. de
  Pac. Oc. 33°50S 80°0W **90** G2
Juan José Castelli
  Argentina 25°27S 60°57W **94** B3
Juan L. Lacaze *Uruguay* 34°26S 57°25W **94** C4
Juankoski *Finland* 63°3N 28°19E **8** E23
Juárez *Mexico* 27°37N 100°44W **86** B4
Juárez, Sierra de *Mexico* 32°0N 116°0W **86** A1
Juàzeiro *Brazil* 9°30S 40°30W **93** E10
Juàzeiro do Norte *Brazil* 7°10S 39°18W **93** E11
Jūbā *Sudan* 4°50N 31°35E **51** H12
Juba → *Somali Rep.* 1°30N 42°35E **47** G3

Jubany Antarctica 62°30S 58°0W 5 C18
Jubayl Lebanon 34°5N 35°39E 46 A4
Jubbah Si. Arabia 28°2N 40°56E 44 D4
Jubbal India 31°5N 77°40E 42 D7
Jubbulpore = Jabalpur
India 23°9N 79°58E 43 H8
Jubilee L. Australia 29°0S 126°50E 61 E4
Juby, C. Morocco 28°0N 12°59W 50 C3
Júcar = Xúquer → Spain 39°5N 0°10W 21 C5
Júcaro Cuba 21°37N 78°51W 88 B4
Juchitán de Zaragoza
Mexico 16°26N 95°1W 87 D5
Judea = Har Yehuda
Israel 31°35N 34°57E 46 D3
Judith → U.S.A. 47°44N 109°39W 76 C9
Judith, Pt. U.S.A. 41°22N 71°29W 83 E13
Judith Gap U.S.A. 46°41N 109°45W 76 C9
Juigalpa Nic. 12°6N 85°26W 88 D2
Juiz de Fora Brazil 21°43S 43°19W 95 A7
Jujuy □ Argentina 23°20S 65°40W 94 A2
Julesburg U.S.A. 40°59N 102°16W 76 F12
Juli Peru 16°10S 69°25W 92 G5
Julia Cr. → Australia 20°0S 141°11E 62 C3
Julia Creek Australia 20°39S 141°44E 62 C3
Juliaca Peru 15°25S 70°10W 92 G4
Julian U.S.A. 33°4N 116°38W 79 M10
Julian, L. Canada 54°25N 77°57W 72 B4
Julianatop Suriname 3°40N 56°30W 93 C7
Julianehåb = Qaqortoq
Greenland 60°43N 46°0W 4 C5
Julimes Mexico 28°25N 105°27W 86 B3
Jullundur India 31°20N 75°40E 42 D6
Julu China 37°15N 115°2E 34 F8
Jumbo Zimbabwe 17°30S 30°58E 55 F3
Jumbo Pk. U.S.A. 36°12N 114°11W 79 J12
Jumentos Cays Bahamas 23°0N 75°40W 88 B4
Jumilla Spain 38°28N 1°19W 21 C5
Jumla Nepal 29°15N 82°13E 43 E10
Jumna = Yamuna →
India 25°30N 81°53E 43 G9
Jumunjin S. Korea 37°55N 128°54E 35 F15
Junagadh India 21°30N 70°30E 42 J4
Junan China 35°12N 118°53E 35 G10
Junction Tex., U.S.A. 30°29N 99°46W 84 F5
Junction Utah, U.S.A. 38°14N 112°13W 77 G7
Junction B. Australia 11°52S 133°55E 62 A1
Junction City Kans.,
U.S.A. 39°2N 96°50W 80 F5
Junction City Oreg.,
U.S.A. 44°13N 123°12W 76 D2
Junction Pt. Australia 11°45S 133°50E 62 A1
Jundah Australia 24°46S 143°2E 62 C3
Jundiaí Brazil 24°30S 47°0W 95 A6
Juneau U.S.A. 58°18N 134°25W 70 B2
Junee Australia 34°53S 147°35E 63 E4
Jungar Qi China 39°49N 110°57E 34 E6
Jungfrau Switz. 46°32N 7°58E 20 C7
Junggar Pendi China 44°30N 86°0E 32 C6
Jungshahi Pakistan 24°52N 67°44E 42 G2
Juniata → U.S.A. 40°24N 77°1W 82 F7
Junín Argentina 34°33S 60°57W 94 C3
Junín de los Andes
Argentina 39°45S 71°0W 96 D2
Juniyah Lebanon 33°59N 35°38E 46 B4
Juntas Chile 28°24S 69°58W 94 B2
Juntura U.S.A. 43°45N 118°5W 76 E4
Jur, Nahr el → Sudan 8°45N 29°15E 51 G11
Jura = Jura, Mts. du
Europe 46°40N 6°5E 20 C7
Jura = Schwäbische Alb
Germany 48°20N 9°30E 16 D5
Jura U.K. 56°0N 5°50W 11 F3
Jura, Mts. du Europe 46°40N 6°5E 20 C7
Jura, Sd. of U.K. 55°57N 5°45W 11 F3
Jurbarkas Lithuania 55°4N 22°46E 9 J20
Jurien Bay Australia 30°18S 115°2E 61 F2
Jūrmala Latvia 56°58N 23°34E 9 H20
Jurong Singapore 1°19N 103°42E 39 d
Juruá → Brazil 2°37S 65°44W 92 D5
Juruena Brazil 13°0S 58°10W 92 F7
Juruena → Brazil 7°20S 58°3W 92 E7
Juruti Brazil 2°9S 56°4W 93 D7
Justo Daract Argentina 33°52S 65°12W 94 C2
Jutaí → Brazil 2°43S 66°57W 92 D5
Juticalpa Honduras 14°40N 86°12W 88 D2
Jutland = Jylland
Denmark 56°25N 9°30E 9 H13
Juuka Finland 63°13N 29°17E 8 E23
Juventud, I. de la Cuba 21°40N 82°40W 88 B3
Jüy Zar Iran 33°50N 46°18E 44 C5
Juye China 35°22N 116°5E 34 G9
Jwaneng Botswana 24°45S 24°50E 53 J4
Jylland Denmark 56°25N 9°30E 9 H13
Jyväskylä Finland 62°14N 25°50E 8 E21

K

K2 Pakistan 35°58N 76°32E 43 B7
Kaakha = Kaka
Turkmenistan 37°21N 59°36E 45 B8
Kaapkruis Namibia 21°55S 13°57E 56 C1
Kaapstad = Cape Town
S. Africa 33°55S 18°22E 56 E2
Kabaena Indonesia 5°15S 122°0E 37 F6
Kabala S. Leone 9°38N 11°37W 50 G3
Kabale Uganda 1°15S 30°0E 54 C3
Kabalo Dem. Rep. of the Congo 6°0S 27°0E 54 D2
Kabambare
Dem. Rep. of the Congo 4°41S 27°39E 54 C2
Kabango
Dem. Rep. of the Congo 8°35S 28°30E 55 D2
Kabanjahe Indonesia 3°6N 98°30E 36 D1
Kabankalan Phil. 9°59N 122°49E 37 C6
Kabara Fiji 18°59S 178°56W 59 a
Kabardino-Balkaria □
Russia 43°30N 43°30E 19 F7
Kabarega Falls = Murchison Falls
Uganda 2°15N 31°30E 54 B3
Kabarnet Kenya 0°30N 35°45E 54 B4

Kabasalan Phil. 7°47N 122°44E 37 C6
Kabat Indonesia 8°16S 114°19E 37 J17
Kabin Buri Thailand 13°57N 101°43E 38 F3
Kabinakagami L.
Canada 48°54N 84°25W 72 C3
Kabinda
Dem. Rep. of the Congo 6°19S 24°20E 52 F4
Kabompo Zambia 13°36S 24°14E 55 E1
Kabompo → Zambia 14°11S 23°11E 53 G4
Kabondo
Dem. Rep. of the Congo 8°58S 25°40E 55 D2
Kabongo
Dem. Rep. of the Congo 7°22S 25°33E 54 D2
Kabrît, G. el Egypt 29°42N 33°16E 46 F2
Kābul Afghan. 34°28N 69°11E 42 B6
Kābul □ Afghan. 34°30N 69°0E 40 B6
Kābul → Pakistan 33°55N 72°14E 42 C5
Kabunga
Dem. Rep. of the Congo 1°38S 28°3E 54 C2
Kaburuang Indonesia 3°50N 126°30E 37 D7
Kabwe Zambia 14°30S 28°29E 55 E2
Kachchh, Gulf of India 22°50N 69°15E 42 H3
Kachchh, Rann of India 24°0N 70°0E 42 H4
Kachchhidhana India 21°44N 78°46E 43 J8
Kachebera Zambia 13°50S 32°50E 55 E3
Kachikau Botswana 18°8S 24°26E 56 B3
Kachin □ Burma 26°0N 97°30E 41 G20
Kachira, L. Uganda 0°40S 31°7E 54 C3
Kachīry Kazakhstan 53°10N 75°50E 28 D8
Kachnara India 23°50N 75°6E 42 H6
Kachot Cambodia 11°30N 103°3E 39 G4
Kadanai → Afghan. 31°22N 65°45E 42 D1
Kadavu Fiji 19°0S 178°15E 59 a
Kadavu Passage Fiji 18°45S 178°0E 59 a
Kade Ghana 6°7N 0°56W 50 G5
Kadhimain = Al Kāẓimīyah
Iraq 33°22N 44°18E 44 C5
Kadi India 23°18N 72°23E 42 H5
Kadina Australia 33°55S 137°43E 63 E2
Kadipur India 26°10N 82°23E 43 F10
Kadirli Turkey 37°23N 36°5E 44 B3
Kadiyevka = Stakhanov
Ukraine 48°35N 38°40E 19 E6
Kadoka U.S.A. 43°50N 101°31W 80 D3
Kadoma Zimbabwe 18°20S 29°52E 55 F2
Kâdugli Sudan 11°0N 29°45E 51 F11
Kaduna Nigeria 10°30N 7°21E 50 F7
Kaédi Mauritania 16°9N 13°28W 50 E3
Kaeng Khoi Thailand 14°35N 101°0E 38 E3
Kaeng Krachan △
Thailand 12°57N 99°23E 38 F2
Kaeng Krung △ Thailand 9°30N 98°50E 39 H2
Kaeng Tana △ Thailand 15°25N 105°32E 38 E6
Kaesŏng N. Korea 37°58N 126°35E 35 F14
Kāf Si. Arabia 31°25N 37°29E 44 D3
Kafan = Kapan Armenia 39°18N 46°27E 44 B5
Kafanchan Nigeria 9°40N 8°20E 50 G7
Kafinda Zambia 12°32S 30°20E 55 E3
Kafue Zambia 15°46S 28°9E 55 F2
Kafue → Zambia 15°30S 29°0E 53 H5
Kafue △ Zambia 15°12S 25°38E 55 F2
Kafue Flats Zambia 15°40S 27°25E 55 F2
Kafulwe Zambia 9°0S 29°1E 55 D2
Kaga Afghan. 34°14N 70°10E 42 B4
Kaga Bandoro C.A.R. 7°0N 19°10E 52 C3
Kagawa □ Japan 34°15N 134°0E 31 G7
Kagera □ Tanzania 2°0S 31°30E 54 C3
Kagera → Tanzania 0°57S 31°47E 54 C3
Kağızman Turkey 40°5N 43°10E 44 B4
Kagoshima Japan 31°35N 130°33E 31 J5
Kagoshima □ Japan 31°30N 130°30E 31 J5
Kagul = Cahul Moldova 45°50N 28°15E 17 F15
Kahak Iran 36°6N 49°46E 45 B6
Kahama Tanzania 4°8S 32°30E 54 C3
Kahan Pakistan 29°18N 68°54E 42 E3
Kahang Malaysia 2°12N 103°32E 39 L4
Kahayan → Indonesia 3°40S 114°0E 36 E4
Kahe Tanzania 3°30S 37°25E 54 C4
Kahemba
Dem. Rep. of the Congo 7°18S 18°55E 52 F3
Kahnūj Iran 27°55N 57°40E 45 E8
Kahoka U.S.A. 40°25N 91°44W 80 E8
Kaho'olawe U.S.A. 20°33N 156°37W 75 L8
Kahramanmaraş Turkey 37°37N 36°53E 44 B3
Kâhta Turkey 37°46N 38°36E 44 B3
Kahului U.S.A. 20°54N 156°28W 75 L8
Kahurangi △ N.Z. 41°10S 172°32E 59 D4
Kahuta Pakistan 33°35N 73°24E 42 C5
Kahuzi-Biega △
Dem. Rep. of the Congo 1°50S 27°55E 54 C2
Kai, Kepulauan Indonesia 5°55S 132°45E 37 F8
Kai Besar Indonesia 5°55S 133°0E 37 F8
Kai Is. = Kai, Kepulauan
Indonesia 5°55S 132°45E 37 F8
Kai Kecil Indonesia 5°45S 132°40E 37 F8
Kaiapoi N.Z. 43°24S 172°40E 59 E4
Kaidu He → China 41°46N 86°31E 32 C6
Kaieteur Falls Guyana 5°1N 59°10W 92 B7
Kaifeng China 34°48N 114°21E 34 G8
Kaikohe N.Z. 35°25S 173°49E 59 A4
Kaikoura N.Z. 42°25S 173°43E 59 E4
Kailash = Kangrinboqe Feng
China 31°0N 81°25E 43 D9
Kailu China 43°38N 121°18E 35 C11
Kailua Kona U.S.A. 19°39N 155°59W 75 M8
Kaimana Indonesia 3°39S 133°45E 37 E8
Kaimanawa Mts. N.Z. 39°15S 175°56E 59 C5
Kaimganj India 27°33N 79°24E 43 F8
Kaimur Hills India 24°30N 82°0E 43 G10
Kainab → Namibia 28°32S 19°34E 56 D2
Kainji Res. Nigeria 10°1N 4°40E 50 F6
Kainuu Finland 64°30N 29°7E 8 D23
Kaipara Harbour N.Z. 36°25S 174°14E 59 B5
Kaipokok B. Canada 54°54N 59°47W 73 B8
Kaira India 22°45N 72°50E 42 H5
Kairana India 29°24N 77°15E 42 E7

Kaironi Indonesia 0°47S 133°40E 37 E8
Kairouan Tunisia 35°45N 10°5E 51 A8
Kaiserslautern Germany 49°26N 7°45E 16 D4
Kaitaia N.Z. 35°8S 173°17E 59 A4
Kaitangata N.Z. 46°17S 169°51E 59 G2
Kaithal India 29°48N 76°26E 42 E7
Kaitu → Pakistan 33°10N 70°30E 42 C4
Kaiwi Channel U.S.A. 21°15N 157°30W 75 L8
Kaiyuan Liaoning, China 42°28N 124°1E 35 C13
Kaiyuan Yunnan, China 23°40N 103°12E 32 G9
Kaiyuh Mts. U.S.A. 64°30N 158°0W 74 C8
Kajaani Finland 64°17N 27°46E 8 D22
Kajabbi Australia 20°0S 140°1E 62 C3
Kajana = Kajaani
Finland 64°17N 27°46E 8 D22
Kajang Malaysia 2°59N 101°48E 39 L3
Kajiado Kenya 1°53S 36°48E 54 C4
Kajo Kaji Sudan 3°58N 31°40E 51 H12
Kaka Turkmenistan 37°21N 59°36E 45 B8
Kakabeka Falls Canada 48°24N 89°37W 72 C2
Kakadu △ Australia 12°0S 132°3E 60 B5
Kakamas S. Africa 28°45S 20°33E 56 D3
Kakamega Kenya 0°20N 34°46E 54 B3
Kakanui Mts. N.Z. 45°10S 170°30E 59 F3
Kakdwip India 21°53N 88°11E 43 J13
Kake Japan 34°36N 132°19E 31 G6
Kake U.S.A. 56°59N 133°57W 70 D2
Kakegawa Japan 34°45N 138°1E 31 G9
Kakeroma-Jima Japan 28°8N 129°14E 31 K4
Kākhak Iran 34°9N 58°38E 45 C8
Kakhovka Ukraine 46°45N 33°30E 19 E5
Kakhovske Vdskh.
Ukraine 47°5N 34°0E 19 E5
Kakinada India 16°57N 82°11E 41 L13
Kakisa Canada 60°56N 117°25W 70 A5
Kakisa → Canada 61°3N 118°10W 70 A5
Kakisa L. Canada 60°56N 117°43W 70 A5
Kakogawa Japan 34°46N 134°51E 31 G7
Kakuma Kenya 3°43N 34°52E 54 B3
Kakwa → Canada 54°37N 118°28W 70 C5
Kāl Gūsheh Iran 30°59N 58°12E 45 D8
Kal Sefīd Iran 34°52N 47°23E 44 C5
Kalaallit Nunaat = Greenland ☑
N. Amer. 66°0N 45°0W 67 C15
Kalabagh Pakistan 33°0N 71°28E 42 C4
Kalabahi Indonesia 8°13S 124°31E 37 F6
Kalach Russia 50°22N 41°0E 19 D7
Kaladan → Burma 20°20N 93°5E 41 J18
Kaladar Canada 44°37N 77°5W 82 B7
Kalahari Africa 24°0S 21°30E 56 C3
Kalahari Gemsbok △
S. Africa 25°30S 20°30E 56 D3
Kalajoki Finland 64°12N 24°10E 8 D21
Kalakamati Botswana 20°40S 27°25E 57 C4
Kalakan Russia 55°15N 116°45E 29 D12
K'alak'unlun Shank'ou =
Karakoram Pass Asia 35°33N 77°50E 43 B7
Kalam Pakistan 35°34N 72°30E 43 B5
Kalama
Dem. Rep. of the Congo 2°52S 28°35E 54 C2
Kalama U.S.A. 46°1N 122°51W 78 E4
Kalamata Greece 37°3N 22°10E 23 F10
Kalamazoo U.S.A. 42°17N 85°35W 81 D11
Kalamazoo → U.S.A. 42°40N 86°10W 80 D10
Kalambo Falls Tanzania 8°37S 31°35E 55 D3
Kalan Turkey 39°7N 39°32E 44 B3
Kalannie Australia 30°22S 117°5E 61 F2
Kalāntarī Iran 32°10N 54°8E 45 C7
Kalao Indonesia 7°21S 121°0E 37 F6
Kalaotoa Indonesia 7°20S 121°50E 37 F6
Kalasin Thailand 16°26N 103°30E 38 D4
Kalāt Iran 25°29N 59°22E 45 E8
Kalat Pakistan 29°8N 66°31E 40 E5
Kalāteh Iran 36°33N 55°41E 45 B7
Kalāteh-ye Ganj Iran 27°31N 57°55E 45 E8
Kalbā U.A.E. 25°5N 56°22E 45 E8
Kalbarri Australia 27°40S 114°10E 61 E1
Kalbarri △ Australia 27°51S 114°10E 61 E1
Kalburgi = Gulbarga
India 17°20N 76°50E 40 L10
Kalce Slovenia 45°54N 14°13E 16 F8
Kale Turkey 37°26N 28°49E 23 F13
Kalegauk Kyun Burma 15°33N 97°35E 38 E1
Kalehe
Dem. Rep. of the Congo 2°6S 28°50E 54 C2
Kalema Tanzania 1°12S 31°55E 54 C3
Kalemie
Dem. Rep. of the Congo 5°55S 29°9E 54 D2
Kalewa Burma 23°10N 94°15E 41 H19
Kaleybar Iran 38°47N 47°2E 44 B5
Kalgoorlie-Boulder
Australia 30°40S 121°22E 61 F3
Kali → India 27°6N 79°55E 43 F8
Kali Sindh → India 25°32N 76°17E 42 G6
Kaliakra, Nos Bulgaria 43°21N 28°30E 23 C13
Kalianda Indonesia 5°50S 105°45E 36 F3
Kalibo Phil. 11°43N 122°22E 37 B6
Kalima
Dem. Rep. of the Congo 2°33S 26°32E 54 C2
Kalimantan Indonesia 0°0 114°0E 36 E4
Kalimantan Barat □
Indonesia 0°0 110°30E 36 E4
Kalimantan Selatan □
Indonesia 2°30S 115°30E 36 E5
Kalimantan Tengah □
Indonesia 2°0S 113°30E 36 E4
Kalimantan Timur □
Indonesia 1°30N 116°30E 36 D5
Kálimnos Greece 37°0N 27°0E 23 F12
Kalimpong India 27°4N 88°35E 43 F13
Kaliningrad Russia 54°42N 20°32E 9 J19
Kalinkavichy Belarus 52°12N 29°20E 17 B15
Kalinkovichi = Kalinkavichy
Belarus 52°12N 29°20E 17 B15
Kaliro Uganda 0°56N 33°30E 54 B3
Kalispell U.S.A. 48°12N 114°19W 76 B6
Kalisz Poland 51°45N 18°8E 17 C10
Kaliua Tanzania 5°5S 31°48E 54 D3
Kalix = Kalixälven →
Sweden 65°50N 23°11E 8 D20

Kalix Sweden 65°53N 23°12E 8 D20
Kalixälven → Sweden 65°50N 23°11E 8 D20
Kalka India 30°46N 76°57E 42 D7
Kalkarindji Australia 17°30S 130°47E 60 C5
Kalkaska U.S.A. 44°44N 85°11W 81 C11
Kalkfeld Namibia 20°57S 16°14E 56 C2
Kalkfontein Botswana 22°4S 20°57E 56 C3
Kalkrand Namibia 24°1S 17°35E 56 C2
Kallavesi Finland 62°58N 27°30E 8 E22
Kallsjön Sweden 63°38N 13°0E 8 E15
Kalmar Sweden 56°40N 16°20E 9 H17
Kalmykia □ Russia 46°5N 46°1E 19 E8
Kalna India 23°13N 88°25E 43 H13
Kalnai India 22°46N 83°30E 43 H10
Kalocsa Hungary 46°32N 19°0E 17 E10
Kalokhorio Cyprus 34°51N 33°2E 25 E12
Kaloko
Dem. Rep. of the Congo 6°47S 25°48E 54 D2
Kalol Gujarat, India 22°37N 73°31E 42 H5
Kalol Gujarat, India 23°15N 72°33E 42 H5
Kalomo Zambia 17°0S 26°30E 55 F2
Kalpi India 26°8N 79°47E 43 F8
Kaltag U.S.A. 64°20N 158°43W 74 C8
Kaltukatjara Australia 24°52S 129°5E 61 D4
Kalu Pakistan 25°5N 67°39E 42 G2
Kaluga Russia 54°35N 36°10E 18 D6
Kalulushi Zambia 12°50S 28°3E 55 E2
Kalumburu Australia 13°55S 126°35E 60 B4
Kalumburu ◉ Australia 14°17S 126°38E 60 B4
Kalush Ukraine 49°3N 24°23E 17 D13
Kalutara Sri Lanka 6°35N 80°0E 40 R12
Kalya Russia 60°15N 59°59E 18 B10
Kalyan India 19°15N 73°9E 40 K8
Kama Dem. Rep. of the Congo 3°30S 27°5E 54 C2
Kama → Russia 55°45N 52°0E 18 C9
Kamachumu Tanzania 1°37S 31°37E 54 C3
Kamaishi Japan 39°16N 141°53E 30 E10
Kamalia Pakistan 30°44N 72°42E 42 D5
Kaman India 27°39N 77°16E 42 F6
Kamanjab Namibia 19°35S 14°51E 56 B2
Kamapanda Zambia 12°5S 24°0E 55 E1
Kamarán Yemen 15°21N 42°35E 47 D3
Kamativi Zimbabwe 18°20S 27°6E 56 B4
Kambalda West
Australia 31°10S 121°37E 61 F3
Kambangan, Nusa
Indonesia 7°40S 108°10E 37 G13
Kambar Pakistan 27°37N 68°1E 42 F3
Kambarka Russia 56°15N 54°11E 18 C9
Kambolé Zambia 8°47S 30°48E 55 D3
Kambos Cyprus 35°2N 32°44E 25 D11
Kambove
Dem. Rep. of the Congo 10°51S 26°33E 55 E2
Kamchatka, Poluostrov
Russia 57°0N 160°0E 29 D17
Kamchatka Pen. = Kamchatka,
Poluostrov Russia 57°0N 160°0E 29 D17
Kamchiya → Bulgaria 43°4N 27°44E 23 C12
Kame Ruins Zimbabwe 20°7S 28°25E 55 G2
Kameda-Hantō Japan 41°50N 141°0E 30 D10
Kamen Russia 53°50N 81°30E 28 D9
Kamen-Rybolov Russia 44°46N 132°2E 30 B5
Kamenjak, Rt Croatia 44°47N 13°55E 16 F7
Kamenka Russia 65°58N 44°0E 18 A7
Kamenka Bugskaya =
Kamyanka-Buzka
Ukraine 50°8N 24°16E 17 C13
Kamensk Uralskiy Russia 56°25N 62°2E 28 D7
Kamenskoye Russia 62°45N 165°30E 29 C17
Kameoka Japan 35°0N 135°35E 31 G7
Kamet India 30°55N 79°35E 43 D8
Kamiah U.S.A. 46°14N 116°2W 76 C5
Kamieskroon S. Africa 30°9S 17°56E 56 E2
Kamilukuak L. Canada 62°22N 101°40W 71 A8
Kamin-Kashyrskyy
Ukraine 51°39N 24°56E 17 C13
Kamina
Dem. Rep. of the Congo 8°45S 25°0E 55 D2
Kaminak L. Canada 62°10N 95°0W 71 A10
Kaminoyama Japan 38°9N 140°17E 30 E10
Kamiros Greece 36°20N 27°56E 25 C9
Kamituga
Dem. Rep. of the Congo 3°2S 28°10E 54 C2
Kamla → India 25°35N 86°36E 43 G12
Kamloops Canada 50°40N 120°20W 70 C4
Kamo Japan 37°39N 139°3E 30 F9
Kamoke Pakistan 32°4N 74°4E 42 C6
Kampala Uganda 0°20N 32°30E 54 B3
Kampar Malaysia 4°18N 101°9E 39 K3
Kampar → Indonesia 0°30N 103°8E 36 D2
Kampen Neths. 52°33N 5°53E 15 B5
Kampene
Dem. Rep. of the Congo 3°36S 26°40E 52 E5
Kamphaeng Phet
Thailand 16°28N 99°30E 38 D2
Kampolombo, L. Zambia 11°37S 29°42E 55 E2
Kampong Cham
Cambodia 12°0N 105°30E 39 G5
Kampong Chhnang
Cambodia 12°20N 104°35E 39 G5
Kampong Pengerang
Malaysia 1°22N 104°7E 39 d
Kampong Punggai
Malaysia 1°27N 104°18E 39 d
Kampong Saom
Cambodia 10°38N 103°30E 39 G4
Kampong Saom, Chaak
Cambodia 10°50N 103°32E 39 G4
Kampong Tanjong Langsat
Malaysia 1°30N 104°1E 39 d
Kampong Telok Ramunia
Malaysia 1°22N 104°15E 39 d
Kampot Cambodia 10°36N 104°10E 39 G5
Kampuchea = Cambodia ■
Asia 12°15N 105°0E 38 F5
Kampung Air Putih
Malaysia 4°15N 103°10E 39 K4
Kampung Jerangau
Malaysia 4°50N 103°10E 39 K4
Kampung Raja Malaysia 5°45N 102°35E 39 K4

Kampungbaru = Tolitoli
Indonesia 1°5N 120°50E 37 D6
Kamrau, Teluk Indonesia 3°30S 133°36E 37 E8
Kamsack Canada 51°34N 101°54W 71 C8
Kamsar Guinea 10°40N 14°36W 50 F3
Kamskoye Vdkhr.
Russia 58°41N 56°7E 18 C10
Kamuchawie L.
Canada 56°18N 101°59W 71 B8
Kamui-Misaki Japan 43°20N 140°21E 30 C10
Kamyanets-Podilskyy
Ukraine 48°45N 26°40E 17 D14
Kamyanka-Buzka
Ukraine 50°8N 24°16E 17 C13
Kāmyārān Iran 34°47N 46°56E 44 C5
Kamyshin Russia 50°10N 45°24E 19 D8
Kanaaupscow → Canada 54°2N 76°30W 72 B4
Kanab U.S.A. 37°3N 112°32W 77 H7
Kanab → U.S.A. 36°24N 112°38W 77 H7
Kanacea Lau Group, Fiji 17°15S 179°6W 59 a
Kanacea Taveuni, Fiji 16°59S 179°56E 59 a
Kanaga I. U.S.A. 51°45N 177°22W 74 E4
Kanagi Japan 40°54N 140°27E 30 D10
Kanairiktok → Canada 55°2N 60°18W 73 A7
Kananga
Dem. Rep. of the Congo 5°55S 22°18E 52 F4
Kanash Russia 55°30N 47°32E 18 C8
Kanaskat U.S.A. 47°19N 121°54W 78 C5
Kanastraíon, Ákra = Paliouri,
Akra Greece 39°57N 23°45E 23 E10
Kanawha → U.S.A. 38°50N 82°9W 81 F12
Kanazawa Japan 36°30N 136°38E 31 F8
Kanchanaburi Thailand 14°2N 99°31E 38 E2
Kanchenjunga Nepal 27°50N 88°10E 43 F13
Kanchipuram India 12°52N 79°45E 40 N11
Kandaghat India 30°59N 77°7E 42 D7
Kandahār India 31°32N 65°43E 40 D4
Kandahār □ Afghan. 31°0N 65°0E 40 D4
Kandalaksha Russia 67°9N 32°30E 8 C25
Kandalakshskiy Zaliv
Russia 66°0N 35°0E 18 A6
Kandangan Indonesia 2°50S 115°20E 36 E5
Kandanos Greece 35°19N 23°44E 25 D5
Kandavu = Kadavu Fiji 19°0S 178°15E 59 a
Kandavu Passage = Kadavu
Passage Fiji 18°45S 178°0E 59 a
Kandhkot Pakistan 28°16N 69°8E 42 E3
Kandhla India 29°18N 77°19E 42 E7
Kandi Benin 11°7N 2°55E 50 F6
Kandi India 23°58N 88°5E 43 H13
Kandiaro Pakistan 27°4N 68°13E 42 F3
Kandla India 23°0N 70°10E 42 H4
Kandos Australia 32°45S 149°58E 63 E4
Kandreho Madag. 17°29S 46°6E 57 B8
Kandy Sri Lanka 7°18N 80°43E 40 R12
Kane U.S.A. 41°40N 78°49W 82 E6
Kane Basin Greenland 79°1N 70°0W 69 B18
Kang Botswana 23°41S 22°50E 56 C3
Kangān Fārs, Iran 27°50N 52°3E 45 E7
Kangān Hormozgān, Iran 25°48N 57°28E 45 E8
Kangar Malaysia 6°27N 100°12E 39 J3
Kangaroo I. Australia 35°45S 137°0E 63 F2
Kangaroo Mts.
Australia 23°29S 141°51E 62 C3
Kangasala Finland 61°28N 24°4E 8 F21
Kangāvar Iran 34°40N 48°0E 45 C6
Kangdong N. Korea 39°9N 126°5E 35 E14
Kangean, Kepulauan
Indonesia 6°55S 115°23E 36 F5
Kangean Is. = Kangean,
Kepulauan Indonesia 6°55S 115°23E 36 F5
Kanggye N. Korea 41°0N 126°35E 35 D14
Kangikajik Greenland 70°7N 22°0W 4 B6
Kangiqcliniq = Rankin Inlet
Canada 62°30N 93°0W 68 E13
Kangiqsualujjuaq
Canada 58°30N 65°59W 69 F18
Kangiqsujuaq Canada 61°30N 72°0W 69 E17
Kangiqtugaapik = Clyde River
Canada 70°30N 68°30W 69 C18
Kangirsuk Canada 60°0N 70°0W 69 F18
Kangkar Chemaran
Malaysia 1°34N 104°12E 39 d
Kangkar Sungai Tiram
Malaysia 1°35N 103°55E 39 d
Kangkar Teberau
Malaysia 1°32N 103°51E 39 d
Kangping China 42°43N 123°18E 35 C12
Kangra India 32°6N 76°16E 42 C7
Kangrinboqe Feng China 31°0N 81°25E 43 D9
Kangto China 27°50N 92°35E 41 F18
Kanha △ India 22°15N 80°40E 43 H9
Kanhar → India 24°28N 83°8E 43 G10
Kaniama
Dem. Rep. of the Congo 7°30S 24°12E 54 D1
Kaniapiskau = Caniapiscau →
Canada 56°40N 69°30W 73 A6
Kaniapiskau, L. = Caniapiscau, L.
Canada 54°10N 69°55W 73 B6
Kanin, Poluostrov Russia 68°0N 45°0E 18 A8
Kanin Nos, Mys Russia 68°39N 43°32E 18 A7
Kanin Pen. = Kanin, Poluostrov
Russia 68°0N 45°0E 18 A8
Kaniva Australia 36°22S 141°18E 63 F3
Kanjut Sar Pakistan 36°7N 75°25E 43 A6
Kankaanpää Finland 61°44N 22°50E 8 F20
Kankakee U.S.A. 41°7N 87°52W 80 E2
Kankakee → U.S.A. 41°23N 88°15W 80 E1
Kankan Guinea 10°23N 9°15W 50 F4
Kankendy = Xankändi
Azerbaijan 39°52N 46°49E 44 B5
Kanker India 20°10N 81°40E 41 J12
Kankroli India 25°4N 73°53E 42 G5
Kanmaw Kyun Burma 11°40N 98°28E 39 G2
Kannapolis U.S.A. 35°30N 80°37W 85 D14
Kannauj India 27°3N 79°56E 43 F8
Kannod India 22°45N 76°40E 40 H10
Kannur = Cannanore
India 11°53N 75°27E 40 P9
Kannyakumari India 8°3N 77°40E 40 Q10

Kano Nigeria 12°2N 8°30E 50 F7
Kan'onji Japan 34°7N 133°39E 31 G6
Kanowit Malaysia 2°14N 112°20E 36 D4
Kanoya Japan 31°25N 130°50E 31 J5
Kanpetlet Burma 21°10N 93°59E 41 J18
Kanpur India 26°28N 80°20E 43 F9
Kansas □ U.S.A. 38°30N 99°0W 80 F4
Kansas → U.S.A. 39°7N 94°37W 80 F6
Kansas City Kans., U.S.A. 39°7N 94°38W 80 F6
Kansas City Mo., U.S.A. 39°6N 94°35W 80 F6
Kansenia Dem. Rep. of the Congo 10°20S 26°0E 55 E2
Kansk Russia 56°20N 95°37E 29 D10
Kansu = Gansu □ China 36°0N 104°0E 34 G9
Kantaphor India 22°35N 76°34E 42 H7
Kantharalak Thailand 14°39N 104°39E 38 E5
Kanthi = Contai India 21°54N 87°46E 43 J12
Kantli → India 28°20N 79°50E 42 E6
Kantō □ Japan 36°15N 139°30E 31 F9
Kantō-Sanchi Japan 35°59N 138°50E 31 G9
Kanturk Ireland 52°11N 8°54W 10 D3
Kanuma Japan 36°34N 139°42E 31 F9
Kanus Namibia 27°50S 18°39E 56 D2
Kanye Botswana 24°55S 25°28E 56 C4
Kanzenze
Dem. Rep. of the Congo 10°30S 25°12E 55 E2
Kanzi, Ras Tanzania 7°1S 39°33E 54 D4
Kao Tonga 19°40S 175°1W 59 c
Kao Phara Thailand 8°3N 98°22E 39 a
Kaohsiung Taiwan 22°35N 120°16E 33 G13
Kaokoveld Namibia 19°15S 14°30E 56 B1
Kaolack Senegal 14°5N 16°8W 50 F2
Kaoshan China 44°38N 124°50E 35 B13
Kapa'a U.S.A. 22°5N 159°19W 75 L8
Kapadvanj India 23°5N 73°0E 42 H5
Kapan Armenia 39°18N 46°27E 44 B5
Kapanga
Dem. Rep. of the Congo 8°30S 22°40E 52 F4
Kapchagai = Qapshaghay
Kazakhstan 43°51N 77°14E 28 E8
Kapedo Kenya 1°10N 36°6E 54 B4
Kapela = Velika Kapela
Croatia 45°10N 15°5E 16 F8
Kapema
Dem. Rep. of the Congo 10°45S 28°22E 55 E2
Kapenguria Kenya 1°14N 35°7E 54 B4
Kapfenberg Austria 47°26N 15°18E 16 E8
Kapiri Mposhi Zambia 13°59S 28°43E 55 E2
Kāpīsā □ Afghan. 35°0N 69°20E 40 B6
Kapiskau → Canada 52°47N 81°55W 72 B3
Kapit Malaysia 2°0N 112°55E 36 D4
Kapiti I. N.Z. 40°50S 174°56E 59 D5
Kaplan U.S.A. 30°0N 92°17W 84 F8
Kapoe Thailand 9°34N 98°32E 39 H2
Kapoeta Thailand 4°50N 33°35E 51 H12
Kaposvár Hungary 46°25N 17°47E 17 E9
Kapowsin U.S.A. 46°59N 122°13W 78 D4
Kapps Namibia 22°32S 17°18E 56 C2
Kapsabet Kenya 0°12N 35°6E 54 B4
Kapsan N. Korea 41°4N 128°19E 35 D15
Kapsukas = Marijampolè
Lithuania 54°33N 23°19E 9 J20
Kaptai L. Bangla. 22°40N 92°20E 41 H18
Kapuas → Indonesia 0°25S 109°20E 36 E3
Kapuas Hulu, Pegunungan
Malaysia 1°30N 113°30E 36 D4
Kapuas Hulu Ra. = Kapuas Hulu,
Pegunungan Malaysia 1°30N 113°30E 36 D4
Kapulo
Dem. Rep. of the Congo 8°18S 29°15E 55 D2
Kapunda Australia 34°20S 138°56E 63 E2
Kapuni N.Z. 39°29S 174°8E 59 C5
Kapurthala India 31°23N 75°25E 42 D6
Kapuskasing Canada 49°25N 82°30W 72 C3
Kapuskasing → Canada 49°49N 82°0W 72 C3
Kaputar, Mt. Australia 30°15S 150°10E 63 E5
Kaputir Kenya 2°5N 35°28E 54 B4
Kara Russia 69°10N 65°0E 28 C7
Kara Bogaz Gol, Zaliv =
Garabogazköl Aylagy
Turkmenistan 41°0N 53°30E 19 F9
Kara-Kala = Garrygala
Turkmenistan 38°31N 56°29E 45 B8
Kara Kalpak Republic =
Qoraqalpoghistan □
Uzbekistan 43°0N 58°0E 28 E6
Kara Kum = Garagum
Turkmenistan 39°30N 60°0E 45 B8
Kara Sea Russia 75°0N 70°0E 28 B8
Karabiğa Turkey 40°23N 27°17E 23 D12
Karabük Turkey 41°12N 32°37E 19 F5
Karaburun Turkey 38°41N 26°28E 23 E12
Karabutak = Qarabutaq
Kazakhstan 50°0N 60°14E 28 E7
Karacabey Turkey 40°12N 28°21E 23 D13
Karacasu Turkey 37°43N 28°35E 23 F13
Karachey-Cherkessia □
Russia 43°40N 41°30E 19 F7
Karachi Pakistan 24°50N 67°0E 42 G2
Karad India 17°15N 74°10E 40 L9
Karaganda = Qaraghandy
Kazakhstan 49°50N 73°10E 32 B3
Karagayly = Qaraghayly
Kazakhstan 49°26N 76°0E 28 E8
Karaginskiy, Ostrov
Russia 58°45N 164°0E 29 D17
Karagiye, Vpadina Kazakhstan 43°27N 51°45E 19 F9
Karagiye Depression = Karagiye,
Vpadina Kazakhstan 43°27N 51°45E 19 F9
Karagola Road India 25°29N 87°23E 43 G12
Karaikal India 10°59N 79°50E 40 P11
Karaikkudi India 10°5N 78°45E 40 P11
Karaj Iran 35°48N 51°0E 45 C6
Karajarri ⊚ Australia 19°0S 122°30E 60 C3
Karak Malaysia 3°25N 102°2E 39 L4
Karakalpakstan =
Qoraqalpoghistan □
Uzbekistan 43°0N 58°0E 28 E6
Karakelong Indonesia 4°35N 126°50E 37 D7

Karakitang Indonesia 3°14N 125°28E 37 D7
Karakol Kyrgyzstan 42°30N 78°20E 32 C4
Karakoram Pass Asia 35°33N 77°50E 43 B7
Karakoram Ra. Pakistan 35°30N 77°0E 43 B7
Karakuwisa Namibia 18°56S 19°40E 56 B2
Karalon Russia 57°5N 115°50E 29 D12
Karama Jordan 31°57N 35°35E 46 D4
Karaman Turkey 37°14N 33°13E 44 B2
Karamay China 45°30N 84°58E 32 B5
Karambu Indonesia 3°53S 116°6E 36 E5
Karamea Bight N.Z. 41°22S 171°40E 59 D3
Karamnasa → India 25°31N 83°52E 43 G10
Karān Si. Arabia 27°43N 49°49E 45 E6
Karand Iran 34°16N 46°15E 44 C5
Karanganyar Indonesia 7°38S 109°37E 37 G13
Karangasem = Amlapura
Indonesia 8°27S 115°37E 37 J18
Karanjia India 21°47N 85°58E 43 J11
Karasburg Namibia 28°0S 18°44E 56 D2
Karasino Russia 66°50N 86°50E 28 C9
Karasjok Norway 69°27N 25°30E 8 B21
Karasuk Russia 53°44N 78°2E 28 D8
Karasuyama Japan 36°39N 140°9E 31 F10
Karatau, Khrebet = Qarataū
Kazakhstan 43°30N 69°30E 28 E7
Karatax Shan China 35°57N 81°0E 32 D5
Karatsu Japan 33°26N 129°58E 31 H5
Karaul Russia 70°6N 82°15E 28 B9
Karauli India 26°30N 77°4E 42 F7
Karavostasi Cyprus 35°8N 32°50E 25 D11
Karawang Indonesia 6°30S 107°15E 37 G12
Karawanken Europe 46°30N 14°40E 16 E8
Karayazı Turkey 39°41N 42°9E 19 G7
Karazhal = Qarazhal
Kazakhstan 48°2N 70°49E 28 E8
Karcag Hungary 47°19N 20°57E 17 E11
Karcha → Pakistan 34°45N 76°10E 43 B7
Karchana India 25°17N 81°56E 43 G9
Karditsa Greece 39°23N 21°54E 23 E9
Kärdla Estonia 59°0N 22°45E 9 G20
Kardzhali = Kürdzhali
Bulgaria 41°38N 25°21E 23 D11
Kareeberge S. Africa 30°59S 21°50E 56 E3
Kareha → India 25°44N 86°21E 43 G12
Kareima Sudan 18°30N 31°49E 51 E12
Karelia □ Russia 65°30N 32°30E 18 A5
Karelian Republic = Karelia □
Russia 65°30N 32°30E 18 A5
Karera India 25°32N 78°9E 42 G8
Kārevāndar Iran 27°53N 60°44E 45 E9
Kargasok Russia 59°3N 80°53E 28 D9
Kargat Russia 55°10N 80°15E 28 D9
Kargi Kenya 2°31N 37°34E 54 B4
Kargil India 34°32N 76°12E 43 B7
Kargopol Russia 61°30N 38°58E 18 B6
Karhal India 27°1N 78°57E 43 F8
Kariān Iran 26°57N 57°14E 45 E8
Karianga Madag. 22°25S 47°22E 57 C8
Kariba Zimbabwe 16°28S 28°50E 55 F2
Kariba, L. Zimbabwe 16°40S 28°25E 55 F2
Kariba Dam Zimbabwe 16°30S 28°35E 55 F2
Kariba Gorge Zambia 16°30S 28°50E 55 F2
Karibib Namibia 22°0S 15°56E 56 C2
Karijini △ Australia 23°8S 118°15E 60 D2
Karimata, Kepulauan
Indonesia 1°25S 109°0E 36 E3
Karimata, Selat Indonesia 2°0S 108°40E 36 E3
Karimata Is. = Karimata,
Kepulauan Indonesia 1°25S 109°0E 36 E3
Karimnagar India 18°26N 79°10E 40 K11
Karimun, Pulau Indonesia 1°3N 103°22E 39 d
Karimun Kecil, Pulau
Indonesia 1°8N 103°22E 39 d
Karimunjawa, Kepulauan
Indonesia 5°50S 110°30E 36 F4
Karin Somali Rep. 10°50N 45°52E 47 E4
Karīt Iran 33°29N 56°55E 45 C8
Kariya Japan 34°58N 137°1E 31 G8
Kariyangwe Zimbabwe 18°0S 27°38E 57 B4
Karjala Finland 62°0N 30°25E 8 F24
Karkaralinsk = Qarqaraly
Kazakhstan 49°26N 75°30E 32 B4
Karkheh → Iran 31°2N 47°29E 44 D5
Karkinitska Zatoka
Ukraine 45°56N 33°0E 19 E5
Karkinitskiy Zaliv = Karkinitska
Zatoka Ukraine 45°56N 33°0E 19 E5
Karkuk = Kirkūk Iraq 35°30N 44°21E 44 C5
Karlantijpa North ⊚
Australia 19°27S 133°33E 60 C5
Karlantijpa South ⊚
Australia 20°31S 133°9E 60 D5
Karleby = Kokkola
Finland 63°50N 23°8E 8 E20
Karlovac Croatia 45°31N 15°36E 16 F8
Karlovo Bulgaria 42°38N 24°47E 23 C11
Karlovy Vary Czech Rep. 50°13N 12°51E 16 C7
Karlsbad = Karlovy Vary
Czech Rep. 50°13N 12°51E 16 C7
Karlsena, Mys Russia 77°0N 67°42E 28 B7
Karlshamn Sweden 56°10N 14°51E 9 H16
Karlskoga Sweden 59°28N 14°33E 9 G16
Karlskrona Sweden 56°10N 15°35E 9 H16
Karlsruhe Germany 49°0N 8°23E 16 D5
Karlstad Sweden 59°23N 13°30E 9 G15
Karlstad U.S.A. 48°35N 96°31W 80 A5
Karmi'el Israel 32°55N 35°18E 46 C4
Karnak Egypt 25°43N 32°39E 51 C12
Karnal India 29°42N 77°2E 42 E7
Karnali → Nepal 28°45N 81°16E 43 E9
Karnaphuli Res. = Kaptai L.
Bangla. 22°40N 92°20E 41 H18
Karnaprayag India 30°16N 79°15E 43 D8
Karnataka □ India 13°15N 77°0E 40 N10
Karnes City U.S.A. 28°53N 97°54W 84 G6
Karnische Alpen Europe 46°36N 13°0E 16 E7
Kärnten □ Austria 46°52N 13°30E 16 E8
Karoi Zimbabwe 16°48S 29°45E 55 F2
Karon, Ao Thailand 7°51N 98°17E 39 a

Karonga Malawi 9°57S 33°55E 55 D3
Karoo △ S. Africa 32°18S 22°27E 56 E3
Karoonda Australia 35°1S 139°59E 63 F2
Karor Pakistan 31°15N 70°59E 42 D4
Karora Sudan 17°44N 38°15E 51 E13
Karpasia Cyprus 35°32N 34°15E 25 D13
Karpathos Greece 35°37N 27°10E 23 G12
Karpinsk Russia 59°45N 60°1E 18 C11
Karpogory Russia 64°0N 44°27E 18 B7
Karpuz Burnu = Apostolos
Andreas, C. Cyprus 35°42N 34°35E 25 D13
Karratha Australia 20°44S 116°52E 60 D2
Kars Turkey 40°40N 43°5E 19 F7
Karsakpay Kazakhstan 47°55N 66°40E 28 E7
Karshi = Qarshi
Uzbekistan 38°53N 65°48E 28 F7
Karsiyang India 26°56N 88°18E 43 F13
Karsog India 31°23N 77°12E 42 D7
Kartala Comoros Is. 11°45S 43°21E 53 a
Kartaly Russia 53°3N 60°40E 28 D7
Kartapur India 31°27N 75°32E 42 D6
Karthaus U.S.A. 41°8N 78°9W 82 E6
Karufa Indonesia 3°50S 133°20E 37 E8
Karuma △ Uganda 2°5N 32°15E 54 B3
Karumba Australia 17°31S 140°50E 62 B3
Karumo Tanzania 2°25S 32°50E 54 C3
Karumwa Tanzania 3°12S 32°38E 54 C3
Kārūn → Iran 30°26N 48°10E 45 D6
Karungu Kenya 0°50S 34°10E 54 C3
Karviná Czech Rep. 49°53N 18°31E 17 D10
Karwan → India 27°26N 78°4E 42 F8
Karwar India 14°55N 74°13E 40 M9
Karwi India 25°12N 80°57E 43 G9
Karymskoye Russia 51°36N 114°21E 29 D12
Kasache Malawi 13°25S 34°20E 55 E3
Kasai →
Dem. Rep. of the Congo 3°30S 16°10E 52 E3
Kasai-Oriental □
Dem. Rep. of the Congo 5°0S 24°30E 54 D1
Kasaji
Dem. Rep. of the Congo 10°25S 23°27E 55 E1
Kasama Zambia 10°16S 31°9E 55 E3
Kasan-dong N. Korea 41°18N 126°55E 35 D14
Kasandra Kolpos Greece 40°5N 23°30E 23 D10
Kasane Namibia 17°34S 24°50E 56 B3
Kasanga Tanzania 8°30S 31°10E 55 D3
Kasanka △ Zambia 11°34S 30°15E 55 E3
Kasaragod India 12°30N 74°58E 40 N9
Kasba L. Canada 60°20N 102°10W 71 A8
Kāseh Garān Iran 34°5N 46°2E 44 C5
Kasempa Zambia 13°30S 25°44E 55 E2
Kasenga
Dem. Rep. of the Congo 10°20S 28°45E 55 E2
Kasese Uganda 0°13N 30°3E 54 B3
Kasganj India 27°48N 78°42E 43 F8
Kashabowie Canada 48°40N 90°26W 72 C1
Kashaf → Iran 35°58N 61°7E 45 C9
Kāshān Iran 34°5N 51°30E 45 C6
Kashechewan Canada 52°18N 81°37W 72 B3
Kashgar = Kashi China 39°30N 76°2E 32 D4
Kashi China 39°30N 76°2E 32 D4
Kashimbo
Dem. Rep. of the Congo 11°12S 26°19E 55 E2
Kashipur India 29°15N 79°0E 43 E8
Kashiwazaki Japan 37°22N 138°33E 31 F9
Kashk-e Kohneh
Afghan. 34°55N 62°30E 40 B3
Kashkūʼīyeh Iran 30°31N 55°40E 45 D7
Kāshmar Iran 35°16N 58°26E 45 C8
Kashmir Asia 34°0N 76°0E 43 C7
Kashmor Pakistan 28°28N 69°32E 42 E3
Kashun Noerh = Gaxun Nur
China 42°22N 100°30E 32 C9
Kasiari India 22°8N 87°14E 43 H12
Kasimov Russia 54°55N 41°20E 18 D7
Kasinge
Dem. Rep. of the Congo 6°15S 26°58E 54 D2
Kasiruta Indonesia 0°25S 127°12E 37 E7
Kaskaskia → U.S.A. 37°58N 89°57W 80 G9
Kaskattama → Canada 57°3N 90°4W 71 B10
Kaskinen Finland 62°22N 21°15E 8 E19
Kaskö = Kaskinen
Finland 62°22N 21°15E 8 E19
Kaslo Canada 49°55N 116°55W 70 D5
Kasmere L. Canada 59°34N 101°10W 71 B8
Kasongo
Dem. Rep. of the Congo 4°30S 26°33E 54 C2
Kasongo Lunda
Dem. Rep. of the Congo 6°35S 16°49E 52 F3
Kasos Greece 35°20N 26°55E 23 G12
Kassalâ Sudan 15°30N 36°0E 51 E13
Kassel Germany 51°18N 9°26E 16 C5
Kassiopi Greece 39°48N 19°53E 25 A3
Kasson U.S.A. 44°2N 92°45W 80 C7
Kastamonu Turkey 41°25N 33°43E 19 F5
Kasteli Greece 35°29N 23°38E 25 D5
Kastelli Greece 35°12N 25°20E 25 D7
Kasterlee Belgium 51°15N 4°59E 15 C4
Kastoria Greece 40°30N 21°19E 23 D9
Kasulu Tanzania 4°37S 30°5E 54 C3
Kasumi Japan 35°38N 134°38E 31 G7
Kasungu Malawi 13°0S 33°29E 55 E3
Kasungu △ Malawi 12°53S 33°9E 55 E3
Kasur Pakistan 31°5N 74°25E 42 D6
Kata, Ao Thailand 7°48N 98°18E 39 a
Kata Archanes Greece 35°15N 25°10E 25 D7
Kata Tjuta Australia 25°20S 130°50E 61 E5
Kataba Zambia 16°5S 25°10E 55 F2
Katahdin, Mt. U.S.A. 45°54N 68°56W 81 C19
Kataka = Cuttack India 20°25N 85°57E 41 J14
Katako Kombe
Dem. Rep. of the Congo 3°25S 24°20E 54 C1
Katale Tanzania 4°52S 31°7E 54 C3
Katanda Katanga,
Dem. Rep. of the Congo 7°52S 24°13E 54 D1
Katanda Nord-Kivu,
Dem. Rep. of the Congo 0°55S 29°21E 54 C2
Katanga □
Dem. Rep. of the Congo 8°0S 25°0E 54 D2
Katangi India 21°56N 79°50E 40 J11

Katanning Australia 33°40S 117°33E 61 F2
Katavi △ Tanzania 6°51S 31°3E 54 D3
Katavi Swamp Tanzania 6°50S 31°10E 54 D3
Katerini Greece 40°18N 22°37E 23 D10
Katghora India 22°30N 82°33E 43 H10
Katha Burma 24°10N 96°30E 41 G20
Katherîna, Gebel Egypt 28°30N 33°57E 44 D2
Katherine Australia 14°27S 132°20E 60 B5
Katherine Gorge = Nitmiluk △
Australia 14°9S 132°15E 60 B5
Kathi India 21°47N 74°3E 42 J6
Kathiawar India 22°20N 71°0E 42 H4
Kathikas Cyprus 34°55N 32°25E 25 E11
Kathmandu Nepal 27°45N 85°20E 43 F11
Kathua India 32°23N 75°34E 42 C6
Katihar India 25°34N 87°36E 43 G12
Katima Mulilo Namibia 17°28S 24°13E 56 B3
Katimbira Malawi 12°40S 34°0E 55 E3
Katingan = Mendawai →
Indonesia 3°30S 113°0E 36 E4
Katiola Ivory C. 8°10N 5°10W 50 G4
Katitii ⊚ Australia 25°1S 131°11E 61 E5
Katmandu = Kathmandu
Nepal 27°45N 85°20E 43 F11
Katni = Murwara India 23°46N 80°28E 43 H9
Katni India 23°51N 80°24E 43 H9
Kato Chorio Greece 35°3N 25°47E 25 D7
Kato Korakiana Greece 39°42N 19°45E 25 A3
Káto Pyrgos Cyprus 35°11N 32°41E 25 D11
Katompe
Dem. Rep. of the Congo 6°2S 26°23E 54 D2
Katong Singapore 1°18N 103°53E 39 d
Katonga → Uganda 0°34N 31°50E 54 B3
Katoomba Australia 33°41S 150°19E 63 E5
Katowice Poland 50°17N 19°5E 17 C10
Katrine, L. U.K. 56°15N 4°30W 11 E4
Katrineholm Sweden 59°9N 16°12E 9 G17
Katsepe Madag. 15°45S 46°15E 57 B8
Katsina Nigeria 13°0N 7°32E 50 F7
Katsumoto Japan 33°51N 129°42E 31 H4
Katsuura Japan 35°10N 140°20E 31 G10
Katsuyama Japan 36°3N 136°30E 31 F8
Kattavia Greece 35°57N 27°46E 25 D9
Kattegat Denmark 56°40N 11°20E 9 H14
Katumba
Dem. Rep. of the Congo 7°40S 25°17E 54 D2
Katwa India 23°30N 88°5E 43 H13
Katwijk Neths. 52°12N 4°24E 15 B4
Kau-Ye Kyun Burma 11°1N 98°32E 39 G2
Kaua'i U.S.A. 22°3N 159°30W 75 L8
Kaudom △ Namibia 18°45S 20°51E 56 B3
Kaufman U.S.A. 32°35N 96°19W 84 E6
Kauhajoki Finland 62°25N 22°10E 8 E20
Kaukauna U.S.A. 44°17N 88°17W 80 C9
Kaukauveld Namibia 20°0S 20°15E 56 C3
Ka'ula I. U.S.A. 21°40N 160°33W 75 L7
Kaunas Lithuania 54°54N 23°54E 9 J20
Kaunia Bangla. 25°46N 89°26E 43 G13
Kautokeino Norway 69°0N 23°4E 8 B20
Kauwapur India 27°31N 82°18E 43 F10
Kavacha Russia 60°16N 169°51E 29 C17
Kavala Greece 40°57N 24°28E 23 D11
Kavalerovo Russia 44°15N 135°4E 30 B7
Kavali India 14°55N 80°1E 40 M12
Kavār Iran 29°11N 52°44E 45 D7
Kavi India 22°12N 72°38E 42 H5
Kavimba Botswana 18°2S 24°38E 56 B3
Kavīr, Dasht-e Iran 34°30N 55°0E 45 C7
Kavīr △ Iran 34°40N 52°0E 45 C7
Kavos Greece 39°23N 20°3E 25 B4
Kaw Fr. Guiana 4°30N 52°15W 93 C8
Kawagama L. Canada 45°18N 78°45W 82 A6
Kawagoe Japan 35°55N 139°29E 31 G9
Kawaguchi Japan 35°52N 139°45E 31 G9
Kawah Ijen △ Indonesia 8°3S 114°14E 37 H15
Kawambwa Zambia 9°48S 29°3E 55 D2
Kawanoe Japan 34°1N 133°34E 31 G6
Kawardha India 22°0N 81°17E 43 J9
Kawasaki Japan 35°31N 139°43E 31 G9
Kawasi Indonesia 1°38S 127°28E 37 E7
Kawawachikamach
Canada 54°48N 66°50W 73 B6
Kawerau N.Z. 38°7S 176°42E 59 C6
Kawhia N.Z. 38°4S 174°49E 59 C5
Kawhia Harbour N.Z. 38°5S 174°51E 59 C5
Kawio, Kepulauan
Indonesia 4°30N 125°30E 37 D7
Kawthaung Burma 10°5N 98°36E 39 H2
Kawthoolei = Kayin □
Burma 18°0N 97°30E 41 L20
Kawthule = Kayin □
Burma 18°0N 97°30E 41 L20
Kaya Burkina Faso 13°4N 1°10W 50 F5
Kayah □ Burma 19°15N 97°15E 41 K20
Kayak I. U.S.A. 59°56N 144°23W 74 D11
Kayan → Indonesia 2°55N 117°35E 36 D5
Kaycee U.S.A. 43°43N 106°38W 76 E10
Kayeli Indonesia 3°20S 127°10E 37 E7
Kayenta U.S.A. 36°44N 110°15W 77 H8
Kayes Mali 14°25N 11°30W 50 F3
Kayin □ Burma 18°0N 97°30E 41 L20
Kayoa Indonesia 0°1N 127°28E 37 D7
Kayomba Zambia 13°11S 24°2E 55 E1
Kayseri Turkey 38°45N 35°30E 44 B2
Kaysville U.S.A. 41°2N 111°56W 76 F8
Kazachye Russia 70°52N 135°58E 29 B14
Kazakhstan ■ Asia 50°0N 70°0E 28 E8
Kazan → Canada 64°2N 95°29W 71 A9
Kazan Russia 55°50N 49°10E 18 C8
Kazan-Rettō Pac. Oc. 25°0N 141°0E 64 E6
Kazanlük Bulgaria 42°38N 25°20E 23 C11
Kazatin = Kozyatyn
Ukraine 49°45N 28°50E 17 D15
Kāzerūn Iran 29°38N 51°40E 45 D6
Kazi Magomed = Qazimämmäd
Azerbaijan 40°3N 49°0E 45 A6
Kazuma Pan △
Zimbabwe 18°20S 25°48E 55 F2
Kazuno Japan 40°10N 140°45E 30 D10
Kazym → Russia 63°54N 65°50E 28 C7

Kea Greece 37°35N 24°22E 23 F11
Keady U.K. 54°15N 6°42W 10 B5
Kearney U.S.A. 40°42N 99°5W 80 E4
Kearney ⊚ Australia 20°10S 128°18E 60 D4
Kearny U.S.A. 33°3N 110°55W 77 K8
Kearsarge, Mt. U.S.A. 43°22N 71°50W 83 C13
Keban Turkey 38°50N 38°50E 19 G6
Keban Barajı Turkey 38°41N 38°33E 44 B3
Kebnekaise Sweden 67°53N 18°33E 8 C18
Kebri Dehar Ethiopia 6°45N 44°17E 47 F3
Kebumen Indonesia 7°42S 109°40E 37 G13
Kechika → Canada 59°41N 127°12W 70 B3
Kecskemét Hungary 46°57N 19°42E 17 E10
Kedah □ Malaysia 5°50N 100°40E 39 K3
Kėdainiai Lithuania 55°15N 24°2E 9 J21
Kedarnath India 30°44N 79°4E 43 D8
Kedgwick Canada 47°40N 67°20W 73 C6
Kediri Indonesia 7°51S 112°1E 37 G15
Kedros Oros Greece 35°11N 24°37E 25 D6
Keeler U.S.A. 36°29N 117°52W 78 J9
Keeley L. Canada 54°54N 108°8W 71 C7
Keeling Is. = Cocos Is.
Ind. Oc. 12°10S 96°55E 64 J1
Keelung = Chilung
Taiwan 25°3N 121°45E 33 F13
Keene Canada 44°15N 78°10W 82 B6
Keene Calif., U.S.A. 35°13N 118°33W 79 K8
Keene N.H., U.S.A. 42°56N 72°17W 83 D12
Keene N.Y., U.S.A. 44°16N 73°46W 83 B11
Keep River △ Australia 15°49S 129°8E 60 C4
Keeper Hill Ireland 52°45N 8°16W 10 D3
Keerweer, C. Australia 14°0S 141°32E 62 A3
Keeseville U.S.A. 44°29N 73°30W 83 B11
Keetmanshoop Namibia 26°35S 18°8E 56 D2
Keewatin Canada 49°46N 94°34W 71 D10
Keewatin → Canada 56°29N 100°46W 71 B8
Kefalonia Greece 38°15N 20°30E 23 E9
Kefamenanu Indonesia 9°28S 124°29E 37 F6
Kefar Sava Israel 32°11N 34°54E 46 C3
Keffi Nigeria 8°55N 7°43E 50 G7
Keflavik Iceland 64°2N 22°35W 8 D2
Keg River Canada 57°54N 117°55W 70 B5
Kegaska Canada 50°9N 61°18W 73 B7
Kehancha Kenya 1°11S 34°37E 54 C3
Keighley U.K. 53°52N 1°54W 12 D6
Keila Estonia 59°18N 24°25E 9 G21
Keimoes S. Africa 28°41S 20°59E 56 D3
Keitele Finland 63°10N 26°20E 8 E22
Keith Australia 36°6S 140°20E 63 F3
Keith U.K. 57°32N 2°57W 11 D6
Keiyasi Fiji 17°53S 177°46E 59 a
Keizer U.S.A. 44°57N 123°1W 76 D2
Kejimkujik △ Canada 44°25N 65°25W 73 D6
Kejserr Franz Joseph Fd.
Greenland 73°30N 24°30W 4 B6
Kekri India 26°0N 75°10E 42 G6
Kelan China 38°43N 111°31E 34 E6
Kelang = Klang Malaysia 3°2N 101°26E 39 L3
Kelantan □ Malaysia 5°10N 102°0E 39 K3
Kelantan → Malaysia 6°13N 102°14E 39 J4
Kelkit → Turkey 40°45N 36°32E 19 F6
Kellerberrin Australia 31°36S 117°38E 61 F2
Kellett, C. Canada 72°0N 126°0W 4 B1
Kelleys I. U.S.A. 41°36N 82°42W 82 E2
Kellogg U.S.A. 47°32N 116°7W 76 C5
Kells = Ceanannus Mor
Ireland 53°44N 6°53W 10 C5
Kélo Chad 9°10N 15°45E 51 G9
Kelokedhara Cyprus 34°48N 32°39E 25 E11
Kelowna Canada 49°50N 119°25W 70 D5
Kelsey Creek Australia 20°26S 148°31E 62 b
Kelseyville U.S.A. 38°59N 122°50W 78 G4
Kelso N.Z. 45°54S 169°15E 59 F2
Kelso U.K. 55°36N 2°26W 11 F6
Kelso U.S.A. 46°9N 122°54W 78 D4
Keluang = Kluang
Malaysia 2°3N 103°18E 39 L4
Kelvington Canada 52°10N 103°30W 71 C8
Kem Russia 65°0N 34°38E 18 B5
Kem → Russia 64°57N 34°41E 18 B5
Kema Indonesia 1°22N 125°8E 37 D7
Kemah Turkey 39°32N 39°5E 44 B3
Kemaman Malaysia 4°12N 103°18E 39 K4
Kemano Canada 53°35N 128°0W 70 C3
Kemasik Malaysia 4°25N 103°27E 39 K4
Kemerovo Russia 55°20N 86°5E 28 D9
Kemi Finland 65°44N 24°34E 8 D21
Kemi älv = Kemijoki →
Finland 65°47N 24°32E 8 D21
Kemi träsk = Kemijärvi
Finland 66°43N 27°22E 8 C22
Kemijärvi Finland 66°43N 27°22E 8 C22
Kemijoki → Finland 65°47N 24°32E 8 D21
Kemmerer U.S.A. 41°48N 110°32W 76 F8
Kemmuna = Comino
Malta 36°1N 14°20E 25 C1
Kemp, L. U.S.A. 33°46N 99°9W 84 E5
Kemp Land Antarctica 69°0S 55°0E 5 C5
Kempas Malaysia 1°33N 103°42E 39 d
Kempsey Australia 31°1S 152°50E 63 E5
Kempt, L. Canada 47°25N 74°22W 72 C5
Kempten Germany 47°45N 10°17E 16 E6
Kempton Australia 42°31S 147°12E 63 G4
Kemptville Canada 45°0N 75°38W 83 B9
Ken → India 25°13N 80°27E 43 G9
Kenai U.S.A. 60°33N 151°16W 68 E1
Kenai Mts. U.S.A. 60°0N 150°0W 74 D9
Kenamuke Swamp Sudan 5°55N 33°48E 54 A3
Kendai India 22°45N 82°37E 43 H10
Kendal Indonesia 6°56S 110°14E 37 G14
Kendal U.K. 54°20N 2°44W 12 C5
Kendall Australia 31°35S 152°44E 63 E5
Kendall → Australia 14°4S 141°35E 62 A3
Kendallville U.S.A. 41°27N 85°16W 81 E11
Kendari Indonesia 3°50S 122°30E 37 E6
Kendawangan Indonesia 2°32S 110°17E 36 E4
Kendi, Pulau Malaysia 5°13N 100°11E 39 c
Kendrapara India 20°35N 86°30E 41 J15
Kendrew S. Africa 32°32S 24°30E 56 E3

Kene Thao *Laos*	17°44N 101°10E	38 D3	
Kenedy *U.S.A.*	28°49N 97°51W	84 G6	
Kenema *S. Leone*	7°50N 11°14W	50 G3	
Keng Kok *Laos*	16°26N 105°12E	38 D5	
Keng Tawng *Burma*	20°45N 98°18E	41 J21	
Keng Tung *Burma*	21°18N 99°39E	38 B2	
Kengeja *Tanzania*	5°26S 39°45E	54 D4	
Kenhardt *S. Africa*	29°19S 21°12E	56 D3	
Kenitra *Morocco*	34°15N 6°40W	50 B4	
Kenli *China*	37°30N 118°20E	35 F10	
Kenmare *Ireland*	51°53N 9°36W	10 E2	
Kenmare *U.S.A.*	48°41N 102°5W	80 A2	
Kenmare River *Ireland*	51°48N 9°51W	10 E2	
Kennebago Lake *U.S.A.*	45°4N 70°40W	83 A14	
Kennebec *U.S.A.*	43°54N 99°52W	80 D4	
Kennebec → *U.S.A.*	43°45N 69°46W	81 D19	
Kennebunk *U.S.A.*	43°23N 70°33W	83 C14	
Kennedy *Zimbabwe*	18°52S 27°10E	56 B4	
Kennedy Channel			
Arctic	80°50N 66°0W	69 A18	
Kennedy Ra. *Australia*	24°45S 115°10E	61 D2	
Kennedy Range △			
Australia	24°34S 115°2E	61 D2	
Kenner *U.S.A.*	29°59N 90°14W	85 G9	
Kennet → *U.K.*	51°27N 0°57W	13 F7	
Kenneth Ra. *Australia*	23°50S 117°8E	61 D2	
Kennett *U.S.A.*	36°14N 90°3W	80 G8	
Kennewick *U.S.A.*	46°12N 119°7W	76 C4	
Kennisis Lake *Canada*	45°13N 78°36W	82 A6	
Kenogami → *Canada*	51°6N 84°28W	72 B3	
Kenora *Canada*	49°47N 94°29W	71 D10	
Kenosha *U.S.A.*	42°35N 87°49W	80 D10	
Kensington *Canada*	46°28N 63°34W	73 C7	
Kent *Ohio, U.S.A.*	41°9N 81°22W	82 E3	
Kent *Tex., U.S.A.*	31°4N 104°13W	84 F2	
Kent *Wash., U.S.A.*	47°22N 122°14W	78 C4	
Kent □ *U.K.*	51°12N 0°40E	13 F8	
Kent Group *Australia*	39°30S 147°20E	63 F4	
Kent Pen. *Canada*	68°30N 107°0W	68 D10	
Kentaū *Kazakhstan*	43°32N 68°36E	28 E7	
Kentland *U.S.A.*	40°46N 87°27W	80 E10	
Kenton *U.S.A.*	40°39N 83°37W	81 E12	
Kentucky □ *U.S.A.*	37°0N 84°0W	81 G11	
Kentucky → *U.S.A.*	38°41N 85°11W	81 F11	
Kentucky L. *U.S.A.*	37°1N 88°16W	80 G9	
Kentville *Canada*	45°6N 64°29W	73 C7	
Kentwood *U.S.A.*	30°56N 90°31W	85 F9	
Kenya ■ *Africa*	1°0N 38°0E	54 B4	
Kenya, Mt. *Kenya*	0°10S 37°18E	54 C4	
Kenyir, Tasik *Malaysia*	5°1N 102°54E	39 K4	
Keo Neua, Deo *Vietnam*	18°23N 105°10E	38 C5	
Keokuk *U.S.A.*	40°24N 91°24W	80 E8	
Keoladeo △ *India*	27°0N 77°20E	42 F7	
Keonjhargarh *India*	21°28N 85°35E	43 J11	
Kep *Cambodia*	10°29N 104°19E	39 G5	
Kep *Vietnam*	21°24N 106°16E	38 B6	
Kep △ *Cambodia*	10°30N 104°18E	39 G5	
Kepala Batas *Malaysia*	5°31N 100°26E	39 c	
Kepi *Indonesia*	6°32S 139°19E	37 F9	
Kerala □ *India*	11°0N 76°15E	40 P10	
Kerama-Rettō *Japan*	26°5N 127°15E	31 L3	
Keran *Pakistan*	34°35N 73°59E	43 B5	
Kerang *Australia*	35°40S 143°55E	63 F3	
Keraudren, C. *Australia*	19°58S 119°45E	60 C2	
Kerch *Ukraine*	45°20N 36°20E	19 E6	
Kerguelen *Ind. Oc.*	49°15S 69°10E	3 G13	
Kerian, Kuala *Malaysia*	5°10N 100°25E	39 c	
Kericho *Kenya*	0°22S 35°15E	54 C4	
Kerinci *Indonesia*	1°40S 101°15E	36 E2	
Kerki = Atamyrat			
Turkmenistan	37°50N 65°12E	28 F7	
Kerkrade *Neths.*	50°53N 6°4E	15 D6	
Kerkyra *Greece*	39°38N 19°50E	25 A3	
Kerkyras, Notio Steno			
Greece	39°34N 20°0E	25 A4	
Kermadec Is. *Pac. Oc.*	30°0S 178°15W	58 E11	
Kermadec Trench			
Pac. Oc.	30°30S 176°0W	64 L10	
Kermān *Iran*	30°15N 57°1E	45 D8	
Kerman *U.S.A.*	36°43N 120°4W	78 J6	
Kermān □ *Iran*	30°0N 57°0E	45 D8	
Kermān, Bīābān-e *Iran*	28°45N 59°45E	45 D8	
Kermānī *Iran*	34°23N 47°0E	44 C5	
Kermānshāh □ *Iran*	34°0N 46°30E	44 C5	
Kermit *U.S.A.*	31°52N 103°6W	84 F3	
Kern → *U.S.A.*	35°16N 119°18W	79 K7	
Kernow = Cornwall □			
U.K.	50°26N 4°40W	13 G3	
Kernville *U.S.A.*	35°45N 118°26W	79 K8	
Keroh *Malaysia*	5°43N 101°1E	39 K3	
Kerrera *U.K.*	56°24N 5°33W	11 E3	
Kerrobert *Canada*	51°56N 109°8W	71 C7	
Kerrville *U.S.A.*	30°3N 99°8W	84 F5	
Kerry □ *Ireland*	52°7N 9°35W	10 D2	
Kerry Hd. *Ireland*	52°25N 9°56W	10 D2	
Kerulen = Herlen →			
Asia	48°48N 117°0E	33 B12	
Kerzaz *Algeria*	29°29N 1°37W	50 C5	
Kesagami → *Canada*	51°40N 79°45W	72 B4	
Kesagami L. *Canada*	50°23N 80°15W	72 B3	
Keşan *Turkey*	40°49N 26°38E	23 D12	
Kesennuma *Japan*	38°54N 141°35E	30 E10	
Keshit *Iran*	29°43N 58°17E	45 D8	
Kestell *S. Africa*	28°17S 28°42E	57 D4	
Kestenga *Russia*	65°50N 31°45E	8 D24	
Keswick *U.K.*	54°36N 3°8W	12 C4	
Ket → *Russia*	58°55N 81°32E	28 D9	
Ketapang *Jawa Timur,*			
Indonesia	8°9S 114°23E	37 J17	
Ketapang *Kalimantan Barat,*			
Indonesia	1°55S 110°0E	36 E4	
Ketchikan *U.S.A.*	55°21N 131°39W	70 B2	
Ketchum *U.S.A.*	43°41N 114°22W	76 E6	
Ketef, Khalīg Umm el			
Egypt	23°40N 35°35E	44 F2	
Keti Bandar *Pakistan*	24°8N 67°27E	42 G2	
Ketri *India*	28°1N 75°50E	42 E6	
Kętrzyn *Poland*	54°7N 21°22E	17 A11	
Kettering *U.K.*	52°24N 0°43W	13 E7	
Kettering *U.S.A.*	39°41N 84°10W	81 F11	
Kettle → *Canada*	56°40N 89°34W	71 B11	
Kettle Falls *U.S.A.*	48°37N 118°3W	76 B4	
Kettle Point *Canada*	43°10N 82°1W	82 C2	
Kettle Pt. *Canada*	43°13N 82°1W	82 C2	
Kettleman City *U.S.A.*	36°1N 119°58W	78 J7	
Keuka L. *U.S.A.*	42°30N 77°9W	82 D7	
Keuruu *Finland*	62°16N 24°41E	8 E21	
Kewanee *U.S.A.*	41°14N 89°56W	80 E9	
Kewaunee *U.S.A.*	44°27N 87°31W	80 C10	
Keweenaw B. *U.S.A.*	47°0N 88°15W	80 B9	
Keweenaw Pen. *U.S.A.*	47°15N 88°15W	80 B9	
Keweenaw Pt. *U.S.A.*	47°25N 87°43W	80 B10	
Key, L. *Ireland*	54°0N 8°15W	10 C3	
Key Lake Mine *Canada*	57°25N 105°32W	71 B7	
Key Largo *U.S.A.*	25°5N 80°27W	85 J14	
Key West *U.S.A.*	24°33N 81°48W	88 B3	
Keynsham *U.K.*	51°24N 2°29W	13 F5	
Keyser *U.S.A.*	39°26N 78°59W	81 F14	
Kezhma *Russia*	58°59N 101°9E	29 D11	
Kezi *Zimbabwe*	20°58S 28°32E	57 C4	
Kgalagadi Transfrontier △			
Africa	25°10S 21°0E	56 D3	
Khabarovsk *Russia*	48°30N 135°5E	33 B16	
Khabr *Iran*	28°51N 56°22E	45 D8	
Khābūr → *Syria*	35°17N 40°35E	44 C4	
Khachmas = Xaçmaz			
Azerbaijan	41°31N 48°42E	19 F8	
Khachrod *India*	23°25N 75°20E	42 H6	
Khadro *Pakistan*	26°11N 68°50E	42 F3	
Khadzhilyangar = Dahongliutan			
China	35°45N 79°20E	43 B8	
Khaga *India*	25°47N 81°7E	43 G9	
Khagaria *India*	25°30N 86°32E	43 G12	
Khaipur *Pakistan*	29°34N 72°17E	42 E5	
Khair *India*	27°57N 77°46E	42 F7	
Khairabad *India*	27°33N 80°47E	43 F9	
Khairagarh *India*	21°27N 81°2E	43 J9	
Khairpur *Pakistan*	27°32N 68°49E	42 F3	
Khairpur Nathan Shah			
Pakistan	27°6N 67°44E	42 F2	
Khairwara *India*	23°58N 73°38E	42 H5	
Khaisor → *Pakistan*	31°17N 68°59E	42 D3	
Khajuri Kach *Pakistan*	32°4N 69°51E	42 C3	
Khakassia □ *Russia*	53°0N 90°0E	28 D9	
Khakhea *Botswana*	24°48S 23°22E	56 C3	
Khalafābād *Iran*	30°54N 49°24E	45 D6	
Khalilabad *India*	26°48N 83°5E	43 F10	
Khalīlī *Iran*	27°38N 53°17E	45 E7	
Khalkhāl *Iran*	37°37N 48°32E	45 B6	
Khalkis = Chalkida			
Greece	38°27N 23°42E	23 E10	
Khalmer Yu *Russia*	67°58N 65°1E	28 C7	
Khalturin *Russia*	58°40N 48°50E	18 C8	
Khalūf *Oman*	20°30N 58°13E	47 C6	
Kham Keut *Laos*	18°15N 104°43E	38 C5	
Khamaria *India*	23°5N 80°48E	43 H9	
Khambhaliya *India*	22°14N 69°41E	42 H3	
Khambhat *India*	22°23N 72°33E	42 H5	
Khambhat, G. of *India*	20°45N 72°30E	40 J8	
Khamīr *Iran*	26°57N 55°36E	45 E7	
Khamir *Yemen*	16°2N 44°0E	47 D3	
Khamis Mushayt			
Si. Arabia	18°18N 42°44E	47 D3	
Khamsa *Egypt*	30°27N 32°23E	46 E1	
Khan → *Namibia*	22°37S 14°56E	56 C1	
Khān Abū Shāmat *Syria*	33°39N 36°53E	46 B5	
Khān Azād *Iraq*	33°7N 44°22E	44 C4	
Khān Mujiddah *Iraq*	32°1N 43°48E	44 C4	
Khān Shaykhūn *Syria*	35°26N 36°38E	44 C3	
Khan Tengri, Pik *Asia*	42°12N 80°10E	32 C5	
Khān Yūnis *Gaza Strip*	31°21N 34°18E	46 D3	
Khanai *Pakistan*	30°30N 67°8E	42 D2	
Khānaqīn *Iraq*	34°23N 45°25E	44 C5	
Khānbāghī *Iran*	36°10N 55°25E	45 B7	
Khandwa *India*	21°49N 76°22E	40 J10	
Khandyga *Russia*	62°42N 135°35E	29 C14	
Khanewal *Pakistan*	30°20N 71°55E	42 D4	
Khangah Dogran			
Pakistan	31°50N 73°37E	42 D5	
Khanh Duong *Vietnam*	12°44N 108°44E	38 F7	
Khaniá = Chania *Greece*	35°30N 24°4E	25 D6	
Khaniadhana *India*	25°1N 78°8E	42 G8	
Khanka, L. *Asia*	45°0N 132°24E	30 B6	
Khankendy = Xankändi			
Azerbaijan	39°52N 46°49E	44 B5	
Khanna *India*	30°42N 76°16E	42 D7	
Khanozai *Pakistan*	30°37N 67°19E	42 D2	
Khanpur *Pakistan*	28°42N 70°35E	42 E4	
Khanty-Mansiysk *Russia*	61°0N 69°0E	28 C7	
Khao Khitchakut △			
Thailand	12°50N 102°10E	38 F4	
Khao Laem △ *Thailand*	14°56N 98°31E	38 E2	
Khao Laem Res. *Thailand*	14°50N 98°31E	38 E2	
Khao Lak △ *Malaysia*	8°38N 98°18E	39 H2	
Khao Luang △ *Thailand*	8°34N 99°42E	39 H2	
Khao Nam Khang △			
Thailand	6°32N 100°35E	39 J3	
Khao Phlu *Thailand*	9°29N 99°59E	39 b	
Khao Pu-Khao Ya △			
Thailand	7°26N 99°57E	39 J2	
Khao Sam Roi Yot △			
Thailand	12°13N 99°57E	39 F2	
Khao Sok △ *Thailand*	8°55N 98°38E	39 H2	
Khao Yai △ *Thailand*	14°21N 101°29E	38 E3	
Khaoen Si Nakarin △			
Thailand	14°47N 99°0E	38 E2	
Khapalu *Pakistan*	35°10N 76°20E	43 B7	
Khapcheranga *Russia*	49°42N 112°24E	29 E12	
Khaptao △ *Nepal*	29°20N 81°10E	43 E9	
Kharaghoda *India*	23°11N 71°46E	42 H4	
Kharagpur *India*	22°20N 87°25E	43 H12	
Kharan Kalat *Pakistan*	28°34N 65°21E	40 E4	
Kharānaq *Iran*	32°20N 54°45E	45 C7	
Kharda *India*	18°40N 75°34E	40 K9	
Khardung La *India*	34°20N 77°43E	43 B7	
Kharg = Khārk, Jazīreh-ye			
Iran	29°15N 50°28E	45 D6	
Khârga, El Wâhât el			
Egypt	25°10N 30°35E	51 C12	
Khargon *India*	21°45N 75°40E	40 J9	
Khari → *India*	25°54N 74°31E	42 G6	
Kharian *Pakistan*	32°49N 73°52E	42 C5	
Khārk, Jazīreh-ye *Iran*	29°15N 50°28E	45 D6	
Kharkiv *Ukraine*	49°58N 36°20E	19 E6	
Kharkov = Kharkiv			
Ukraine	49°58N 36°20E	19 E6	
Kharovsk *Russia*	59°56N 40°13E	18 C7	
Kharsawangarh *India*	22°48N 85°50E	43 H11	
Kharta *Turkey*	40°55N 29°7E	23 D13	
Khartoum = El Khartûm			
Sudan	15°31N 32°35E	51 E12	
Khartum *Canada*	45°15N 77°5W	82 A7	
Khasan *Russia*	42°25N 130°40E	30 C5	
Khāsh *Iran*	28°15N 61°15E	45 D9	
Khashm el Girba *Sudan*	14°59N 35°58E	51 F13	
Khaskovo *Bulgaria*	41°56N 25°30E	23 D11	
Khatanga *Russia*	72°0N 102°20E	29 B11	
Khatanga → *Russia*	72°55N 106°0E	29 B11	
Khatauli *India*	29°17N 77°43E	42 E7	
Khatra *India*	22°59N 86°51E	43 H12	
Khatyrka *Russia*	62°3N 175°15E	29 C18	
Khavda *India*	23°51N 69°43E	42 H3	
Khawr Fakkān *U.A.E.*	25°21N 56°22E	45 E8	
Khaybar, Harrat			
Si. Arabia	25°30N 39°45E	44 E4	
Khāzimiyah *Iraq*	34°46N 43°37E	44 C4	
Khe Bo *Vietnam*	19°8N 104°41E	38 C5	
Khe Long *Vietnam*	21°29N 104°46E	38 B5	
Khe Sanh *Vietnam*	16°37N 106°45E	38 D6	
Khed Brahma *India*	24°7N 73°5E	42 G5	
Khekra *India*	28°52N 77°20E	42 E7	
Khemarak Phouminville = Krong			
Kaoh Kong *Cambodia*	11°37N 102°59E	39 G4	
Khemisset *Morocco*	33°50N 6°1W	50 B4	
Khemmarat *Thailand*	16°10N 105°15E	38 D5	
Khenāmān *Iran*	30°27N 56°29E	45 D8	
Khenchela *Algeria*	35°28N 7°11E	50 A7	
Khersān → *Iran*	31°33N 50°22E	45 D6	
Kherson *Ukraine*	46°35N 32°35E	19 E5	
Kheta → *Russia*	71°54N 102°6E	29 B11	
Khewari *Pakistan*	26°36N 68°52E	42 F3	
Khilchipur *India*	24°2N 76°34E	42 G7	
Khilok *Russia*	51°30N 110°45E	29 D12	
Khíos = Chios *Greece*	38°27N 26°9E	23 E12	
Khirsadoh *India*	22°11N 78°47E	43 H8	
Khiuma = Hiiumaa			
Estonia	58°50N 22°45E	9 G20	
Khiva *Uzbekistan*	41°30N 60°18E	28 E7	
Khlong Khlung *Thailand*	16°12N 99°43E	38 D2	
Khlong Lan △ *Thailand*	16°12N 99°13E	38 D2	
Khlong Phanom △			
Thailand	8°45N 98°38E	39 H2	
Khmelnik *Ukraine*	49°33N 27°58E	17 D14	
Khmelnytskyy *Ukraine*	49°23N 27°0E	17 D14	
Khmelnytskyy □			
Ukraine	50°0N 26°40E	17 D14	
Khmer Rep. = Cambodia ■			
Asia	12°15N 105°0E	38 F5	
Khoai, Hon *Vietnam*	8°26N 104°50E	39 H5	
Khodoriv *Ukraine*	49°24N 24°19E	17 D13	
Khodzent = Khŭjand			
Tajikistan	40°17N 69°37E	28 E7	
Khojak Pass *Afghan.*	30°51N 66°34E	42 D2	
Khok Kloi *Thailand*	8°17N 98°19E	39 a	
Khok Pho *Thailand*	6°43N 101°6E	39 J3	
Khok Samrong *Thailand*	15°3N 100°43E	38 E3	
Kholm *Russia*	57°10N 31°15E	18 C5	
Kholmsk *Russia*	47°40N 142°5E	29 E15	
Khomas Hochland			
Namibia	22°40S 16°0E	56 C2	
Khomeyn *Iran*	33°40N 50°7E	45 C6	
Khomeynī Shahr *Iran*	32°41N 51°31E	45 C6	
Khomodino *Botswana*	22°46S 23°52E	56 C3	
Khon Kaen *Thailand*	16°30N 102°47E	38 D4	
Khong → *Cambodia*	13°32N 105°58E	38 F5	
Khong Sedone *Laos*	15°34N 105°49E	38 E5	
Khonuu *Russia*	66°30N 143°12E	29 C15	
Khoper → *Russia*	49°30N 42°20E	19 D6	
Khorāsān-e Janūb □ *Iran*	32°0N 59°0E	45 C8	
Khorāsān-e Razavī □ *Iran*	35°0N 59°0E	45 C8	
Khorāsān-e Shemālī □			
Iran	37°0N 57°0E	45 B8	
Khorat = Nakhon Ratchasima			
Thailand	14°59N 102°12E	38 E4	
Khorat, Cao Nguyen			
Thailand	15°30N 102°50E	38 E4	
Khorixas *Namibia*	20°16S 14°59E	56 C1	
Khorramābād *Khorāsān,*			
Iran	35°6N 57°57E	45 C8	
Khorramābād *Lorestān,*			
Iran	33°30N 48°25E	45 C6	
Khorramshahr *Iran*	30°29N 48°15E	45 D6	
Khorugh *Tajikistan*	37°30N 71°36E	28 F8	
Khosravi *Iran*	30°48N 51°28E	45 D6	
Khosrowābād *Khuzestān,*			
Iran	30°10N 48°25E	45 D6	
Khosrowābād *Kordestān,*			
Iran	35°31N 47°38E	44 C5	
Khost *Pakistan*	30°13N 67°35E	42 D2	
Khosūyeh *Iran*	28°32N 54°26E	45 D7	
Khotyn *Ukraine*	48°31N 26°27E	17 D14	
Khouribga *Morocco*	32°58N 6°57W	50 B4	
Khowst *Afghan.*	33°22N 69°58E	40 C6	
Khoynki *Belarus*	51°54N 29°55E	17 C15	
Khoyniki = Khoynki			
Belarus	51°54N 29°55E	17 C15	
Khram, Ko *Thailand*	12°42N 100°47E	38 F3	
Khrysokhou B. *Cyprus*	35°6N 32°25E	25 D11	
Khu Khan *Thailand*	14°42N 104°12E	38 E5	
Khudzhand = Khŭjand			
Tajikistan	40°17N 69°37E	28 E7	
Khuff *Si. Arabia*	24°55N 44°53E	44 E5	
Khūgīānī *Afghan.*	31°34N 66°32E	42 D1	
Khuis *Botswana*	26°40S 21°49E	56 D3	
Khuiyala *India*	27°9N 70°25E	42 F4	
Khŭjand *Tajikistan*	40°17N 69°37E	28 E7	
Khujner *India*	23°47N 76°36E	42 H7	
Khukhan *Thailand*	14°42N 104°12E	38 E5	
Khulna *Bangla.*	22°45N 89°34E	41 H16	
Khulna □ *Bangla.*	22°25N 89°35E	41 H16	
Khumago *Botswana*	20°26S 24°32E	56 C3	
Khunjerab △ *Pakistan*	36°40N 75°30E	43 A6	
Khunjerab Pass = Kinjirap Daban			
Asia	36°40N 75°25E	40 A9	
Khunti *India*	23°5N 85°17E	43 H11	
Khūr *Iran*	32°55N 58°18E	45 C8	
Khurai *India*	24°3N 78°23E	42 G8	
Khurayş *Si. Arabia*	25°6N 48°2E	45 E6	
Khurja *India*	28°15N 77°58E	42 E7	
Khūrmāl *Iraq*	35°18N 46°2E	44 C5	
Khurr, Wādī al *Iraq*	32°3N 43°52E	44 C4	
Khūsf *Iran*	32°46N 58°53E	45 C8	
Khushab *Pakistan*	32°20N 72°20E	42 C5	
Khust *Ukraine*	48°10N 23°18E	17 D12	
Khutse △ *Botswana*	23°31S 24°12E	56 C3	
Khuzdar *Pakistan*	27°52N 66°30E	42 F2	
Khūzestān □ *Iran*	31°0N 49°0E	45 D6	
Khvāf *Iran*	34°33N 60°8E	45 C9	
Khvājeh *Iran*	38°9N 46°35E	44 B5	
Khvānsār *Iran*	29°56N 54°8E	45 D7	
Khvor *Iran*	33°45N 55°0E	45 C7	
Khvorgū *Iran*	27°34N 56°27E	45 E8	
Khvormūj *Iran*	28°40N 51°30E	45 D6	
Khvoy *Iran*	38°35N 45°0E	44 B5	
Khwae Noi → *Thailand*	14°1N 99°32E	38 E2	
Khyber Pass *Afghan.*	34°10N 71°8E	42 B4	
Kia *Fiji*	16°15S 179°8E	59 a	
Kiabukwa			
Dem. Rep. of the Congo	8°40S 24°48E	55 D1	
Kiama *Australia*	34°40S 150°50E	63 E5	
Kiamba *Phil.*	6°2N 124°46E	37 C6	
Kiambi			
Dem. Rep. of the Congo	7°15S 28°0E	54 D2	
Kiambu *Kenya*	1°8S 36°50E	54 C4	
Kiangara *Madag.*	17°58S 47°2E	57 B8	
Kiangsi = Jiangxi □			
China	27°30N 116°0E	33 F12	
Kiangsu = Jiangsu □			
China	33°0N 120°0E	35 H11	
Kibale △ *Uganda*	0°16N 30°18E	54 B3	
Kibanga Port *Uganda*	0°10N 32°58E	54 B3	
Kibara *Tanzania*	2°8S 33°30E	54 C3	
Kibare, Mts.			
Dem. Rep. of the Congo	8°25S 27°10E	54 D2	
Kibira △ *Burundi*	3°6S 30°24E	54 C2	
Kiboga *Uganda*	0°58N 31°45E	54 B3	
Kibombo			
Dem. Rep. of the Congo	3°57S 25°53E	54 C2	
Kibondo *Tanzania*	3°35S 30°45E	54 C3	
Kibre Mengist *Ethiopia*	5°54N 38°59E	47 F2	
Kíbrıs = Cyprus ■ *Asia*	35°0N 33°0E	25 E12	
Kibumbu *Burundi*	3°32S 29°45E	54 C2	
Kibungo *Rwanda*	2°10S 30°32E	54 C3	
Kibuye *Burundi*	3°39S 29°59E	54 C2	
Kibuye *Rwanda*	2°3S 29°21E	54 C2	
Kibwesa *Tanzania*	6°30S 29°58E	54 D2	
Kibwezi *Kenya*	2°27S 37°57E	54 C4	
Kichha *India*	28°53N 79°30E	43 E8	
Kichha → *India*	28°41N 79°18E	43 E8	
Kichmengskiy Gorodok			
Russia	59°59N 45°48E	18 B8	
Kicking Horse Pass			
Canada	51°28N 116°16W	70 C5	
Kidal *Mali*	18°26N 1°22E	50 E6	
Kidderminster *U.K.*	52°24N 2°15W	13 E5	
Kidepo Valley △ *Uganda*	3°52N 33°50E	54 B3	
Kidete *Tanzania*	6°25S 37°17E	54 D4	
Kidnappers, C. *N.Z.*	39°38S 177°5E	59 C6	
Kidsgrove *U.K.*	53°5N 2°14W	12 D5	
Kidston *Australia*	18°52S 144°8E	62 B3	
Kidugallo *Tanzania*	6°49S 38°15E	54 D4	
Kiel *Germany*	54°19N 10°8E	16 A6	
Kiel Canal = Nord-Ostsee-Kanal			
Germany	54°12N 9°32E	16 A5	
Kielce *Poland*	50°52N 20°42E	17 C11	
Kielder Water *U.K.*	55°11N 2°31W	12 B5	
Kieler Bucht *Germany*	54°35N 10°25E	16 A6	
Kienge			
Dem. Rep. of the Congo	10°30S 27°30E	55 E2	
Kiev = Kyyiv *Ukraine*	50°30N 30°28E	17 C16	
Kiffa *Mauritania*	16°37N 11°24W	50 E3	
Kifrī *Iraq*	34°45N 45°0E	44 C5	
Kigali *Rwanda*	1°59S 30°4E	54 C3	
Kigarama *Tanzania*	1°1S 31°50E	54 C3	
Kigezi □ *Uganda*	0°34S 29°55E	54 C2	
Kigoma □ *Tanzania*	5°0S 30°0E	54 D2	
Kigoma-Ujiji *Tanzania*	4°55S 29°36E	54 C2	
Kigomasha, Ras *Tanzania*	4°58S 38°58E	54 C4	
Kigosi □ *Tanzania*	4°10S 31°45E	54 C3	
Kiğzı *Turkey*	38°18N 43°25E	44 B4	
Kihnu *Estonia*	58°9N 24°1E	9 G21	
Kii-Sanchi *Japan*	34°20N 136°0E	31 G8	
Kii-Suidō *Japan*	33°40N 134°45E	31 H7	
Kiira Dam *Uganda*	0°25N 33°0E	54 B3	
Kikaiga-Shima *Japan*	28°19N 129°59E	31 K4	
Kikiak = Rigolet *Canada*	54°10N 58°23W	73 B8	
Kikinda *Serbia*	45°50N 20°30E	23 B9	
Kikládhes = Cyclades			
Greece	37°0N 24°30E	23 F11	
Kikuchi *Japan*	32°59N 130°47E	31 H5	
Kikwit			
Dem. Rep. of the Congo	5°0S 18°45E	52 F3	
Kilar *India*	33°6N 76°25E	42 C7	
Kilbrannan Sd. *U.K.*	55°37N 5°26W	11 F3	
Kilbuck Mts. *U.S.A.*	60°36N 159°53W	74 C8	
Kilchu *N. Korea*	40°57N 129°25E	35 D15	
Kilcoy *Australia*	26°59S 152°30E	63 D5	
Kildare *Ireland*	53°9N 6°55W	10 C5	
Kildare □ *Ireland*	53°10N 6°50W	10 C5	
Kildinstroy *Russia*	68°48N 33°6E	8 B25	
Kilfinnane *Ireland*	52°21N 8°28W	10 D3	
Kilgarvan *Ireland*	51°54N 9°27W	10 E2	
Kilgore *U.S.A.*	32°23N 94°53W	84 E7	
Kilgoris *Kenya*	1°0S 34°50E	54 C3	
Kilifi *Kenya*	3°40S 39°48E	54 C4	
Kilimanjaro *Tanzania*	3°7S 37°20E	54 C4	
Kilimanjaro □ *Tanzania*	4°0S 38°0E	54 C4	
Kilimanjaro △ *Tanzania*	3°2S 37°19E	54 C4	
Kilindini *Kenya*	4°4S 39°40E	54 C4	
Kilis *Turkey*	36°42N 37°6E	44 B3	
Kiliya *Ukraine*	45°28N 29°16E	17 F15	
Kilkee *Ireland*	52°41N 9°39W	10 D2	
Kilkeel *U.K.*	54°4N 6°0W	10 B5	
Kilkenny *Ireland*	52°39N 7°15W	10 D4	
Kilkenny □ *Ireland*	52°35N 7°15W	10 D4	
Kilkieran B. *Ireland*	53°20N 9°41W	10 C2	
Kilkis *Greece*	40°58N 22°57E	23 D10	
Killala *Ireland*	54°13N 9°12W	10 B2	
Killala B. *Ireland*	54°16N 9°8W	10 B2	
Killaloe *Canada*	45°33N 77°25W	82 A7	
Killaloe *Ireland*	52°48N 8°28W	10 D3	
Killarney *Australia*	28°20S 152°18E	63 D5	
Killarney *Canada*	49°10N 99°40W	71 D9	
Killarney *Ireland*	52°4N 9°30W	10 D2	
Killary Harbour *Ireland*	53°38N 9°52W	10 C2	
Killdeer *U.S.A.*	47°22N 102°45W	80 B2	
Killeen *U.S.A.*	31°7N 97°44W	84 F6	
Killin *U.K.*	56°28N 4°19W	11 E4	
Killiney *Ireland*	53°15N 6°7W	10 C5	
Killington Pk. *U.S.A.*	43°36N 72°49W	83 C12	
Killini *Greece*	37°54N 22°25E	23 F10	
Killorglin *Ireland*	52°6N 9°47W	10 D2	
Killybegs *Ireland*	54°38N 8°26W	10 B3	
Kilmarnock *U.K.*	55°37N 4°29W	11 F4	
Kilmore *Australia*	37°25S 144°53E	63 F3	
Kilmore Quay *Ireland*	52°10N 6°36W	10 D5	
Kilondo *Tanzania*	9°45S 34°20E	55 D3	
Kilosa *Tanzania*	6°48S 37°0E	54 D4	
Kilrush *Ireland*	52°38N 9°29W	10 D2	
Kilwa Kisiwani *Tanzania*	8°58S 39°32E	55 D4	
Kilwa Kivinje *Tanzania*	8°45S 39°25E	55 D4	
Kilwa Masoko *Tanzania*	8°55S 39°30E	55 D4	
Kilwinning *U.K.*	55°39N 4°43W	11 F4	
Kim *U.S.A.*	37°15N 103°21W	77 H12	
Kimaam *Indonesia*	7°58S 138°53E	37 F9	
Kimamba *Tanzania*	6°45S 37°10E	54 D4	
Kimba *Australia*	33°8S 136°23E	63 E2	
Kimball *Nebr., U.S.A.*	41°14N 103°40W	80 E2	
Kimball *S. Dak., U.S.A.*	43°45N 98°57W	80 D4	
Kimberley *Australia*	16°20S 127°0E	60 C4	
Kimberley *B.C., Canada*	49°40N 115°59W	70 D5	
Kimberley *Ont., Canada*	44°23N 80°32W	82 B4	
Kimberley *S. Africa*	28°43S 24°46E	56 D3	
Kimberly *U.S.A.*	42°32N 114°22W	76 E6	
Kimch'aek *N. Korea*	40°40N 129°10E	35 D15	
Kimhae = Gimhae			
S. Korea	35°14N 128°53E	35 G15	
Kimmirut *Canada*	62°50N 69°50W	69 E18	
Kimpese			
Dem. Rep. of the Congo	5°35S 14°26E	52 F2	
Kimry *Russia*	56°55N 37°15E	18 C6	
Kinabalu, Gunung			
Malaysia	6°3N 116°14E	36 C5	
Kinango *Kenya*	4°8S 39°19E	54 C4	
Kinaskan L. *Canada*	57°38N 130°8W	70 B2	
Kinbasket L. *Canada*	52°0N 118°10W	70 C5	
Kincardine *Canada*	44°10N 81°40W	82 B3	
Kincolith *Canada*	55°0N 129°57W	70 B3	
Kinda *Dem. Rep. of the Congo*	9°18S 25°4E	55 D2	
Kinde *U.S.A.*	43°56N 83°0W	82 C2	
Kinder Scout *U.K.*	53°24N 1°52W	12 D6	
Kindersley *Canada*	51°30N 109°10W	71 C7	
Kindia *Guinea*	10°0N 12°52W	50 F3	
Kindu			
Dem. Rep. of the Congo	2°55S 25°50E	54 C2	
Kineshma *Russia*	57°30N 42°5E	18 C7	
Kinesi *Tanzania*	1°25S 33°50E	54 C3	
King, L. *Australia*	33°10S 119°35E	61 F2	
King, Mt. *Australia*	25°10S 147°30E	62 D4	
King Christian I.			
Canada	77°48N 101°40W	69 B11	
King City *U.S.A.*	36°13N 121°8W	78 J5	
King Cr. → *Australia*	24°35S 139°30E	62 C2	
King Edward →			
Australia	14°14S 126°35E	60 B4	
King Edward Point			
S. Georgia	54°17S 36°30W	96 G9	
King Frederick VI Land = Kong			
Frederik VI.s Kyst			
Greenland	63°0N 43°0W	4 C5	
King George B. *Falk. Is.*	51°30S 60°30W	96 G4	
King George I. *Antarctica*	60°0S 60°0W	5 C18	
King George Is. *Canada*	57°20N 80°30W	69 F15	
King George Sd. *Australia*	35°5S 118°0E	61 G2	
King I. = Kadan Kyun			
Burma	12°30N 98°20E	38 F2	
King I. *Australia*	39°50S 144°0E	63 F3	
King I. *Canada*	52°10N 127°40W	70 C3	
King Khalid Military City =			
Madinat al Malik Khālid al			
Askarīyah *Si. Arabia*	27°54N 45°31E	44 E5	
King Leopold Ranges			
Australia	17°30S 125°45E	60 C4	
King of Prussia *U.S.A.*	40°5N 75°23W	83 F9	
King Sd. *Australia*	16°50S 123°20E	60 C3	
King Sejong *Antarctica*	62°30S 58°0W	5 C18	
King William I. *Canada*	69°10N 97°25W	68 D12	
King William's Town			
S. Africa	32°51S 27°22E	56 E4	
Kingaok = Bathurst Inlet			
Canada	66°50N 108°1W	68 D10	
Kingaroy *Australia*	26°32S 151°51E	63 D5	
Kingfisher *U.S.A.*	35°52N 97°56W	84 D6	
Kingirbān *Iraq*	34°40N 44°54E	44 C5	
Kingisepp = Kuressaare			
Estonia	58°15N 22°30E	9 G20	
Kingisepp *Russia*	59°25N 28°40E	9 G23	
Kingman *Ariz., U.S.A.*	35°12N 114°4W	79 K12	
Kingman *Kans., U.S.A.*	37°39N 98°7W	80 G4	
Kingoonya *Australia*	30°55S 135°19E	63 E2	
Kingri *Pakistan*	30°27N 69°49E	42 D3	
Kings → *U.S.A.*	36°3N 119°50W	78 J7	
Kings Canyon *Australia*	24°15S 131°34E	60 D5	
Kings Canyon △			
U.S.A.	36°50N 118°40W	78 J8	
King's Lynn *U.K.*	52°45N 0°24E	12 E8	
Kings Park *U.S.A.*	40°53N 73°16W	83 F11	

Kings Peak *U.S.A.* 40°46N 110°23W **76** F8
Kingsbridge *U.K.* 50°17N 3°47W **13** G4
Kingsburg *U.S.A.* 36°31N 119°33W **78** J7
Kingscote *Australia* 35°40S 137°38E **63** F2
Kingscourt *Ireland* 53°55N 6°48W **10** C5
Kingsford *U.S.A.* 45°48N 88°4W **80** C9
Kingsland *U.S.A.* 30°48N 81°41W **85** F14
Kingsport *U.S.A.* 36°33N 82°33W **85** C13
Kingston *Canada* 44°14N 76°30W **83** B8
Kingston *Jamaica* 18°0N 76°50W **88** a
Kingston *N.Z.* 45°20S 168°43E **59** F2
Kingston *N.H., U.S.A.* 42°56N 71°3W **83** D13
Kingston *N.Y., U.S.A.* 41°56N 73°59W **83** E11
Kingston *Pa., U.S.A.* 41°16N 75°54W **83** E9
Kingston *R.I., U.S.A.* 41°29N 71°30W **83** E13
Kingston Pk. *U.S.A.* 35°44N 115°55W **79** K11
Kingston South East
  Australia 36°51S 139°55E **63** F2
Kingston upon Hull *U.K.* 53°45N 0°21W **12** D7
Kingston upon Hull □
  U.K. 53°45N 0°21W **12** D7
Kingston-upon-Thames □
  U.K. 51°24N 0°17W **13** F7
Kingstown *St. Vincent* 13°10N 61°10W **89** D7
Kingstree *U.S.A.* 33°40N 79°50W **85** E15
Kingsville *Canada* 42°2N 82°45W **82** D2
Kingsville *U.S.A.* 27°31N 97°52W **84** H6
Kingussie *U.K.* 57°6N 4°2W **11** D4
Kingwood *U.S.A.* 30°2N 95°16W **84** F7
Kınık *Turkey* 39°6N 27°24E **23** E12
Kinistino *Canada* 52°57N 105°2W **71** C7
Kinjirap Daban *Asia* 36°40N 75°25E **40** A9
Kinkala *Congo* 4°18S 14°49E **52** E2
Kinki □ *Japan* 33°45N 136°0E **31** H8
Kinleith *N.Z.* 38°20S 175°56E **59** C5
Kinlochleven *U.K.* 56°43N 5°0W **11** E4
Kinmount *Canada* 44°48N 78°45W **82** B6
Kinna *Sweden* 57°32N 12°42E **9** H15
Kinnairds Hd. *U.K.* 57°43N 2°1W **11** D6
Kinngait *Canada* 64°14N 76°32W **69** C16
Kino Nuevo *Mexico* 28°52N 112°3W **86** B2
Kinoje → *Canada* 52°8N 81°25W **72** B3
Kinomoto *Japan* 35°30N 136°13E **31** G8
Kinoni *Uganda* 0°41S 30°28E **54** C3
Kinoosao *Canada* 57°5N 102°1W **71** B8
Kinross *U.K.* 56°13N 3°25W **11** E5
Kinsale *Ireland* 51°42N 8°31W **10** E3
Kinsale, Old Hd. of
  Ireland 51°37N 8°33W **10** E3
Kinsha = Chang Jiang →
  China 31°48N 121°10E **33** E13
Kinshasa
  Dem. Rep. of the Congo 4°20S 15°15E **52** E3
Kinsley *U.S.A.* 37°55N 99°25W **80** G4
Kinsman *U.S.A.* 41°26N 80°35W **82** E4
Kinston *U.S.A.* 35°16N 77°35W **85** D16
Kintampo *Ghana* 8°14S 115°19E **37** J18
Kintore *U.K.* 57°14N 2°20W **11** D6
Kintore Ra. *Australia* 23°15S 128°47E **60** D4
Kintyre *U.K.* 55°30N 5°35W **11** F3
Kintyre, Mull of *U.K.* 55°17N 5°47W **11** F3
Kinushseo → *Canada* 55°15N 83°45W **72** A3
Kinuso *Canada* 55°20N 115°25W **70** B5
Kinvarra *Ireland* 53°8N 8°56W **10** C3
Kinyangiri *Tanzania* 4°25S 34°37E **54** C3
Kinyeti *Sudan* 3°57N 32°54E **54** B3
Kinzua *U.S.A.* 41°52N 78°58W **82** E6
Kiosk *Canada* 46°6N 78°53W **72** C4
Kiowa *Kans., U.S.A.* 37°1N 98°29W **80** G4
Kiowa *Okla., U.S.A.* 34°43N 95°54W **84** D7
Kipahigan L. *Canada* 55°20N 101°55W **71** B8
Kipanga *Tanzania* 6°15S 35°20E **54** D4
Kiparissia *Greece* 37°15N 21°40E **23** F9
Kiparissiakos Kolpos
  Greece 37°25N 21°25E **23** F9
Kipawa, L. *Canada* 46°50N 79°0W **72** C4
Kipembawe *Tanzania* 7°38S 33°27E **54** D3
Kipengere Ra. *Tanzania* 9°12S 34°15E **55** D3
Kipili *Tanzania* 7°28S 30°32E **54** D3
Kipini *Kenya* 2°30S 40°32E **54** C5
Kipling *Canada* 50°6N 102°38W **71** C8
Kippure *Ireland* 53°11N 6°21W **10** C5
Kipushi
  Dem. Rep. of the Congo 11°48S 27°12E **55** E2
Kiranomena *Madag.* 18°17S 46°2E **57** B8
Kirensk *Russia* 57°50N 107°55E **29** D11
Kirghiz Range *Asia* 42°40N 73°40E **32** C3
Kirghizia = Kyrgyzstan ■
  Asia 42°0N 75°0E **28** E8
Kirgiziya Steppe *Eurasia* 50°0N 55°0E **19** E10
Kiribati ■ *Pac. Oc.* 3°0S 180°0E **58** B10
Kırıkkale *Turkey* 39°51N 33°32E **19** G5
Kirillov *Russia* 59°49N 38°24E **18** B6
Kirin = Jilin *China* 43°44N 126°30E **35** C14
Kirinyaga = Kenya, Mt.
  Kenya 0°10S 37°18E **54** C4
Kirirom △ *Cambodia* 11°18N 104°5E **39** G5
Kirishima Yaku △
  Japan 31°24N 130°50E **31** J5
Kiritimati *Kiribati* 1°58N 157°27W **65** G12
Kirkby *U.K.* 53°30N 2°54W **12** D5
Kirkby-in-Ashfield *U.K.* 53°6N 1°14W **12** D6
Kirkby Lonsdale *U.K.* 54°12N 2°36W **12** C5
Kirkby Stephen *U.K.* 54°29N 2°21W **12** C5
Kirkcaldy *U.K.* 56°7N 3°9W **11** E5
Kirkcudbright *U.K.* 54°50N 4°2W **11** G4
Kirkenes *Norway* 69°40N 30°5E **8** B24
Kirkfield *Canada* 44°34N 78°59W **82** B6
Kirkintilloch *U.K.* 55°56N 4°8W **11** F4
Kirkjubæjarklaustur
  Iceland 63°47N 18°4W **8** E4
Kirkkonummi *Finland* 60°8N 24°26E **9** F21
Kirkland *U.S.A.* 47°40N 122°12W **78** C4
Kirkland Lake *Canada* 48°9N 80°2W **72** C3
Kirksville *U.S.A.* 40°12N 92°35W **80** E7
Kirkūk *Iraq* 35°30N 44°21E **44** C5
Kirkwall *U.K.* 58°59N 2°58W **11** C6
Kirkwood *S. Africa* 33°22S 25°15E **56** E4
Kirov *Russia* 58°35N 49°40E **18** C8

Kirovabad = Gäncä
  Azerbaijan 40°45N 46°20E **19** F8
Kirovograd = Kirovohrad
  Ukraine 48°35N 32°20E **19** E5
Kirovohrad *Ukraine* 48°35N 32°20E **19** E5
Kirovsk *Russia* 67°32N 33°41E **18** A5
Kirovskiy *Kamchatka,*
  Russia 54°27N 155°42E **29** D16
Kirovskiy *Primorsk,*
  Russia 45°7N 133°30E **30** B6
Kirriemuir *U.K.* 56°41N 3°1W **11** E5
Kirsanov *Russia* 52°35N 42°40E **18** D7
Kırşehir *Turkey* 39°14N 34°5E **44** B2
Kirthar △ *Pakistan* 27°0N 67°30E **42** F2
Kirthar Range *Pakistan* 27°0N 67°0E **42** F2
Kirtland *U.S.A.* 36°44N 108°21W **77** H9
Kiruna *Sweden* 67°52N 20°15E **8** C19
Kirundu
  Dem. Rep. of the Congo 0°50S 25°35E **54** C2
Kiryū *Japan* 36°24N 139°20E **31** F9
Kisaga *Tanzania* 4°30S 34°23E **54** C3
Kisanga
  Dem. Rep. of the Congo 2°30N 26°35E **54** B2
Kisangani
  Dem. Rep. of the Congo 0°35N 25°15E **54** B2
Kisar *Indonesia* 8°5S 127°10E **37** F7
Kisarawe *Tanzania* 6°53S 39°0E **54** D4
Kisarazu *Japan* 35°23N 139°55E **31** G9
Kiselevsk *Russia* 54°5N 86°39E **28** D9
Kish = Qeys *Iran* 26°32N 53°58E **45** E7
Kishanganga →
  Pakistan 34°18N 73°28E **43** B5
Kishanganj *India* 26°3N 88°14E **43** F13
Kishangarh *Raj., India* 26°34N 74°52E **42** F6
Kishangarh *Raj., India* 27°50N 70°30E **42** F4
Kishinev = Chişinău
  Moldova 47°2N 28°50E **17** E15
Kishiwada *Japan* 34°28N 135°22E **31** G7
Kishtwar *India* 33°20N 75°48E **42** C6
Kisigo → *Tanzania* 6°27S 34°17E **54** D3
Kisii *Kenya* 0°40S 34°45E **54** C3
Kisiju *Tanzania* 7°23S 39°19E **54** D4
Kisizi *Uganda* 1°0S 29°58E **54** C2
Kiska I. *U.S.A.* 51°59N 177°30E **74** E3
Kiskőrös *Hungary* 46°37N 19°20E **17** E10
Kiskunfélegyháza
  Hungary 46°42N 19°53E **17** E10
Kiskunhalas *Hungary* 46°28N 19°37E **17** E10
Kislovodsk *Russia* 43°50N 42°45E **19** F7
Kismaayo *Somali Rep.* 0°22S 42°32E **47** H3
Kiso-Gawa → *Japan* 35°20N 136°45E **31** G8
Kiso-Sammyaku *Japan* 35°45N 137°45E **31** G8
Kisofukushima *Japan* 35°52N 137°43E **31** G8
Kisoro *Uganda* 1°17S 29°48E **54** C2
Kissamos = Kasteli
  Greece 35°29N 23°38E **25** D5
Kissamos, Kolpos *Greece* 35°30N 23°38E **25** D5
Kissidougou *Guinea* 9°5N 10°5W **50** G3
Kissimmee *U.S.A.* 28°18N 81°24W **85** G14
Kissimmee → *U.S.A.* 27°9N 80°52W **85** H14
Kississing L. *Canada* 55°10N 101°20W **71** B8
Kissónerga *Cyprus* 34°49N 32°24E **25** E11
Kisumu *Kenya* 0°3S 34°45E **54** C3
Kiswani *Tanzania* 4°5S 37°57E **54** C4
Kiswere *Tanzania* 9°27S 39°30E **55** D4
Kit Carson *U.S.A.* 38°46N 102°48W **76** G12
Kita *Mali* 13°5N 9°25W **50** F3
Kitaibaraki *Japan* 36°50N 140°45E **31** F10
Kitakami *Japan* 39°20N 141°10E **30** E10
Kitakami-Gawa →
  Japan 38°25N 141°19E **30** E10
Kitakami-Sammyaku
  Japan 39°30N 141°30E **30** E10
Kitakata *Japan* 37°39N 139°52E **30** F9
Kitakyūshū *Japan* 33°50N 130°50E **31** H5
Kitale *Kenya* 1°0N 35°0E **54** B4
Kitami *Japan* 43°48N 143°54E **30** C11
Kitami-Sammyaku
  Japan 44°22N 142°43E **30** B11
Kitangiri, L. *Tanzania* 4°5S 34°20E **54** C3
Kitaya *Tanzania* 10°38S 40°8E **55** E5
Kitchener *Canada* 43°27N 80°29W **82** C4
Kitee *Finland* 62°5N 30°8E **8** E24
Kitega = Gitega *Burundi* 3°26S 29°56E **54** C2
Kitengo
  Dem. Rep. of the Congo 7°26S 24°8E **54** D1
Kitgum *Uganda* 3°17N 32°52E **54** B3
Kíthira = Kythira *Greece* 36°8N 23°0E **23** F10
Kithnos *Greece* 37°26N 24°27E **23** F11
Kiti *Cyprus* 34°50N 33°34E **25** E12
Kiti, C. *Cyprus* 34°48N 33°36E **25** E12
Kitimat *Canada* 54°3N 128°38W **70** C3
Kitinen → *Finland* 67°14N 27°27E **8** C22
Kitsuki *Japan* 33°25N 131°37E **31** H5
Kittakittaooloo, L.
  Australia 28°3S 138°14E **63** D2
Kittanning *U.S.A.* 40°49N 79°31W **82** F5
Kittatinny Mt. *U.S.A.* 41°19N 74°39W **83** F10
Kittery *U.S.A.* 43°5N 70°45W **83** C14
Kittilä *Finland* 67°40N 24°51E **8** C21
Kitui *Kenya* 1°17S 38°0E **54** C4
Kitwanga *Canada* 55°6N 128°4W **70** B3
Kitwe *Zambia* 12°54S 28°13E **55** E2
Kiunga Marine △ *Kenya* 2°1S 41°14E **54** C5
Kivarli *India* 24°33N 72°46E **42** G5
Kivertsi *Ukraine* 50°50N 25°28E **17** C13
Kividhes *Cyprus* 34°46N 32°51E **25** E11
Kivu, L.
  Dem. Rep. of the Congo 1°48S 29°0E **54** C2
Kiwirrkurra *Australia* 22°49S 127°45E **60** D4
Kiwirrkurra ◊
  Australia 22°49S 127°45E **60** D4
Kiyev = Kyyiv *Ukraine* 50°30N 30°28E **17** C16
Kiyevskoye Vdkhr. = Kyyivske
  Vdskh. *Ukraine* 51°0N 30°25E **17** C16
Kizel *Russia* 59°3N 57°40E **18** C10
Kiziba-Baluba ◊ *Congo* 11°50S 28°0E **55** E2
Kizigura *Rwanda* 1°46S 30°23E **54** C3
Kızıl Irmak → *Turkey* 41°44N 35°58E **19** F6
Kizil Jilga *China* 35°26N 78°50E **43** B8

Kızıldağ △ *Turkey* 38°5N 31°20E **44** B1
Kızıltepe *Turkey* 37°12N 40°35E **44** B4
Kizimkazi *Tanzania* 6°28S 39°30E **54** D4
Kizlyar *Russia* 43°51N 46°40E **19** F8
Kizyl-Arvat = Serdar
  Turkmenistan 39°4N 56°23E **45** B8
Kjölur *Iceland* 64°50N 19°25E **8** D4
Kjøur *Iran* 36°23N 51°43E **45** B6
Klaeng *Thailand* 12°47N 101°39E **38** F3
Klagenfurt *Austria* 46°38N 14°20E **16** E8
Klaipėda *Lithuania* 55°43N 21°10E **9** J19
Klaksvík *Færoe Is.* 62°14N 6°35W **8** E9
Klamath → *U.S.A.* 41°33N 124°5W **76** F1
Klamath Falls *U.S.A.* 42°13N 121°46W **76** E3
Klamath Mts. *U.S.A.* 41°50N 123°0W **76** F2
Klamono *Indonesia* 1°8S 131°30E **37** E8
Klang *Malaysia* 3°2N 101°26E **39** L3
Klappan → *Canada* 58°0N 129°43W **70** B3
Klarälven → *Sweden* 59°23N 13°32E **9** G15
Klatovy *Czech Rep.* 49°23N 13°18E **16** D7
Klawer *S. Africa* 31°44S 18°36E **56** E2
Klazienaveen *Neths.* 52°44N 7°0E **15** B6
Kleena Kleene *Canada* 52°0N 124°59W **70** C4
Klein-Karas *Namibia* 27°33S 18°7E **56** D2
Klerksdorp *S. Africa* 26°53S 26°38E **56** D4
Kletsk = Klyetsk *Belarus* 53°5N 26°45E **17** B14
Kletskiy *Russia* 49°16N 43°11E **19** E7
Klickitat *U.S.A.* 45°49N 121°9W **76** D3
Klickitat → *U.S.A.* 45°42N 121°17W **78** E5
Klidhes *Cyprus* 35°42N 34°36E **25** D13
Klip → *S. Africa* 27°3S 29°3E **57** D4
Klipdale *S. Africa* 34°19S 19°57E **56** E2
Klipplaat *S. Africa* 33°1S 24°22E **56** E3
Kłodzko *Poland* 50°28N 16°38E **17** C9
Klondike *Canada* 64°0N 139°26W **68** E4
Klong Wang Chao △
  Thailand 16°20N 99°9E **38** D2
Klouto *Togo* 6°57N 0°44E **50** G6
Kluane △ *Canada* 60°45N 139°30W **70** A1
Kluane L. *Canada* 61°15N 138°40W **68** E4
Kluang *Malaysia* 2°3N 103°18E **39** L4
Kluczbork *Poland* 50°58N 18°12E **17** C10
Klukwan *U.S.A.* 59°24N 135°54W **70** B1
Klungkung *Indonesia* 8°32S 115°24E **37** K18
Klyetsk *Belarus* 53°5N 26°45E **17** B14
Klyuchevskaya, Gora
  Russia 55°50N 160°30E **29** D17
Klyuchi *Russia* 56°18N 160°51E **29** D17
Knaresborough *U.K.* 54°1N 1°28W **12** C6
Knee L. *Man., Canada* 55°3N 94°45W **72** A1
Knee L. *Sask., Canada* 55°51N 107°0W **71** B7
Knight Inlet *Canada* 50°45N 125°40W **70** C3
Knighton *U.K.* 52°21N 3°3W **13** E4
Knights Ferry *U.S.A.* 37°50N 120°40W **78** H6
Knights Landing
  U.S.A. 38°48N 121°43W **78** G5
Knob, C. *Australia* 34°32S 119°16E **61** F2
Knock *Ireland* 53°48N 8°55W **10** C3
Knockmealdown Mts.
  Ireland 52°14N 7°56W **10** D4
Knokke-Heist *Belgium* 51°21N 3°17E **15** C3
Knossós *Greece* 35°16N 25°10E **25** D7
Knowlton *Canada* 45°13N 72°31W **83** A12
Knox *U.S.A.* 41°18N 86°37W **80** E10
Knox Coast *Antarctica* 66°30S 108°0E **5** C8
Knoxville *Iowa, U.S.A.* 41°19N 93°6W **80** E7
Knoxville *Pa., U.S.A.* 41°57N 77°27W **82** E7
Knoxville *Tenn., U.S.A.* 35°58N 83°55W **85** D13
Knud Rasmussen Land
  Greenland 78°0N 60°0W **69** B20
Knysna *S. Africa* 34°2S 23°2E **56** E3
Ko Kha *Thailand* 18°11N 99°24E **38** C2
Ko Tarutao △ *Thailand* 6°31N 99°26E **39** J2
Ko Yao *Thailand* 8°7N 98°35E **39** a
Koartac = Quaqtaq
  Canada 60°55N 69°40W **69** E18
Koba *Indonesia* 6°37S 134°37E **37** F8
Kobarid *Slovenia* 46°15N 13°30E **16** E7
Kobayashi *Japan* 31°56N 130°59E **31** J5
Kōbe *Japan* 34°41N 135°13E **31** G7
København *Denmark* 55°40N 12°26E **9** J15
Kōbi-Sho *Japan* 25°56N 123°41E **31** M1
Koblenz *Germany* 50°21N 7°36E **16** C4
Kobryn *Belarus* 52°15N 24°22E **17** B13
Kobuk → *U.S.A.* 66°54N 160°38W **74** B7
Kocaeli *Turkey* 40°45N 29°50E **19** F4
Kočani *Macedonia* 41°55N 22°25E **23** D10
Kochas *India* 25°15N 83°56E **43** G10
Kochi = Cochin *India* 9°58N 76°20E **40** Q10
Kōchi *Japan* 33°30N 133°35E **31** H6
Kōchi □ *Japan* 33°40N 133°30E **31** H6
Kochiu = Gejiu *China* 23°20N 103°10E **32** G9
Kodarma *India* 24°28N 85°36E **43** G11
Kodi *Indonesia* 9°33S 119°0E **60** A2
Kodiak *U.S.A.* 57°47N 152°24W **74** D9
Kodiak I. *U.S.A.* 57°30N 152°45W **74** D9
Kodinar *India* 20°46N 70°46E **42** J4
Kodinsk *Russia* 58°30N 99°10E **29** D10
Koedoesberge *S. Africa* 32°40S 20°11E **56** E3
Koes *Namibia* 26°0S 19°15E **56** D2
Koffiefontein *S. Africa* 29°30S 25°0E **56** D4
Kofiau *Indonesia* 1°11S 129°50E **37** E7
Koforidua *Ghana* 6°3N 0°17W **50** G5
Kōfu *Japan* 35°40N 138°30E **31** G9
Koga *Japan* 36°11N 139°43E **31** F9
Kogaluc → *Canada* 56°12N 61°44E **73** A6
Køge *Denmark* 55°27N 12°11E **9** J15
Kogon *Indonesia* 39°43N 64°33E **28** F7
Koh-i-Khurd *Afghan.* 33°30N 65°59E **42** C1
Koh-i-Maran *Pakistan* 29°18N 66°50E **42** E2
Koh Ker *Cambodia* 13°48N 105°14E **38** F5
Koh Wai *Thailand* 11°54N 102°25E **39** H4
Kohat *Pakistan* 33°40N 71°5E **42** C4
Kohima *India* 25°35N 94°10E **41** G19
Kohkīlūyeh va Būyer Aḥmadī □
  Iran 31°30N 50°30E **45** D6
Kohler Ra. *Antarctica* 77°0S 110°0W **5** D15
Kohlu *Pakistan* 29°54N 69°15E **42** E3

Kohtla-Järve *Estonia* 59°20N 27°20E **9** G22
Koi Sanjaq *Iraq* 36°5N 44°38E **44** B5
Koillismaa *Finland* 65°44N 28°36E **8** D23
Koin *N. Korea* 40°28N 126°18E **35** D14
Kojō *N. Korea* 38°58N 127°58E **35** E14
Kojonup *Australia* 33°48S 117°10E **61** F2
Kojūr *Iran* 36°23N 51°43E **45** B6
Kokand = Qŭqon
  Uzbekistan 40°31N 70°56E **28** E8
Kokas *Indonesia* 2°42S 132°26E **37** E8
Kokchetav = Kökshetaū
  Kazakhstan 53°20N 69°25E **28** D7
Kokemäenjoki →
  Finland 61°32N 21°44E **8** F19
Kokkola *Finland* 63°50N 23°8E **8** E20
Koko Kyunzu *Burma* 14°7N 93°22E **41** M18
Kokomo *U.S.A.* 40°29N 86°8W **80** E10
Kokopo *Papua N. G.* 4°22S 152°19E **64** H7
Koksan *N. Korea* 38°46N 126°40E **35** E14
Kökshetaū *Kazakhstan* 53°20N 69°25E **28** D7
Koksoak → *Canada* 58°30N 68°10W **69** F18
Kokstad *S. Africa* 30°32S 29°29E **57** E4
Kokubu *Japan* 31°44N 130°46E **31** J5
Kola *Indonesia* 5°35S 134°30E **37** F8
Kola *Russia* 68°45N 33°8E **8** B25
Kola Pen. = Kolskiy Poluostrov
  Russia 67°30N 38°0E **18** A6
Kolachi → *Pakistan* 27°8N 67°2E **42** F2
Kolahoi *India* 34°12N 75°22E **43** B6
Kolaka *Indonesia* 4°3S 121°46E **37** E6
Kolar *India* 13°12N 78°15E **40** N11
Kolar Gold Fields *India* 12°58N 78°16E **40** N11
Kolaras *India* 25°14N 77°36E **42** G6
Kolari *Finland* 67°20N 23°48E **8** C20
Kolayat *India* 27°50N 72°50E **42** F5
Kolda *Senegal* 12°55N 14°57W **50** F3
Kolding *Denmark* 55°30N 9°29E **9** J13
Kolepom = Dolak, Pulau
  Indonesia 8°0S 138°30E **37** F9
Kolguyev, Ostrov *Russia* 69°20N 48°30E **18** A8
Kolhapur *India* 16°43N 74°15E **40** L9
Kolímbia *Greece* 36°15N 28°10E **25** C10
Kolín *Czech Rep.* 50°2N 15°9E **16** C8
Kolkas rags *Latvia* 57°46N 22°37E **9** H20
Kolkata *India* 22°34N 88°21E **43** H13
Kollam = Quilon *India* 8°50N 76°38E **40** Q10
Kollum *Neths.* 53°17N 6°10E **15** A6
Kolmanskop *Namibia* 26°45S 15°14E **56** D2
Köln *Germany* 50°56N 6°57E **16** C4
Kolo *Poland* 52°14N 18°40E **17** B10
Kołobrzeg *Poland* 54°10N 15°35E **16** A8
Kolokani *Mali* 13°35N 7°45W **50** F4
Kolomna *Russia* 55°8N 38°45E **18** C6
Kolomyya *Ukraine* 48°31N 25°2E **17** D13
Kolonodale *Indonesia* 2°0S 121°19E **37** E6
Kolosib *India* 24°15N 92°45E **41** G18
Kolpashevo *Russia* 58°20N 83°5E **28** D9
Kolpino *Russia* 59°44N 30°39E **18** C5
Kolskiy Poluostrov
  Russia 67°30N 38°0E **18** A6
Kolskiy Zaliv *Russia* 69°23N 34°0E **8** B26
Kolwezi
  Dem. Rep. of the Congo 10°40S 25°25E **55** E2
Kolyma → *Russia* 69°30N 161°0E **29** C17
Kolymskoye Nagorye
  Russia 63°0N 157°0E **29** C16
Kôm Ombo *Egypt* 24°25N 32°52E **51** D12
Komandorskiye Is. =
  Komandorskiye Ostrova
  Russia 55°0N 167°0E **29** D17
Komandorskiye Ostrova
  Russia 55°0N 167°0E **29** D17
Komárno *Slovak Rep.* 47°49N 18°5E **17** E10
Komatipoort *S. Africa* 25°25S 31°55E **57** D5
Komatou Yialou *Cyprus* 35°25N 34°8E **25** D13
Komatsu *Japan* 36°25N 136°30E **31** F8
Komatsushima *Japan* 34°0N 134°35E **31** H7
Kome Channel *Uganda* 0°10S 32°35E **54** C3
Komi □ *Cyprus* 35°24N 34°0E **25** D13
Komi □ *Russia* 64°0N 55°0E **18** B10
Kommunarsk = Alchevsk
  Ukraine 48°30N 38°45E **19** E6
Kommunizma, Pik = imeni Ismail
  Samani, Pik *Tajikistan* 39°0N 72°2E **28** F8
Komodo *Indonesia* 8°37S 119°20E **37** F5
Komoran, Pulau
  Indonesia 8°18S 138°45E **37** F9
Komoro *Japan* 36°19N 138°26E **31** F9
Komotini *Greece* 41°9N 25°26E **23** D11
Kompasberg *S. Africa* 31°45S 24°32E **56** E3
Kompong Chhnang = Kampong
  Chhnang *Cambodia* 12°20N 104°35E **39** F5
Kompong Chikreng
  Cambodia 13°5N 104°18E **38** F5
Kompong Kleang
  Cambodia 13°6N 104°8E **38** F5
Kompong Luong
  Cambodia 11°49N 104°48E **39** G5
Kompong Pranak
  Cambodia 13°35N 104°55E **38** F5
Kompong Som = Kampong Saom
  Cambodia 10°38N 103°30E **39** G4
Kompong Som, Chhung =
  Kampong Saom, Chaak
  Cambodia 10°50N 103°32E **39** G4
Kompong Speu
  Cambodia 11°26N 104°32E **39** G5
Kompong Sralau
  Cambodia 14°5N 105°46E **38** E5
Kompong Thom
  Cambodia 12°35N 104°51E **38** F5
Kompong Trabeck
  Cambodia 13°6N 105°14E **38** F5
Kompong Trach
  Cambodia 11°25N 105°48E **39** G5
Kompong Tralach
  Cambodia 11°54N 104°47E **39** G5
Komrat = Comrat
  Moldova 46°18N 28°40E **17** E15
Komsberg *S. Africa* 32°40S 20°45E **56** E3

Komsomolets, Ostrov
  Russia 80°30N 95°0E **29** A10
Komsomolsk-na-Amur
  Russia 50°30N 137°0E **33** A16
Kon Ka Kinh △
  Vietnam 14°19N 107°23E **38** E6
Kon Tum *Vietnam* 14°24N 108°0E **38** E7
Kon Tum, Plateau du
  Vietnam 14°30N 108°30E **38** E7
Konar □ *Afghan.* 34°30N 71°3E **40** B7
Konārī *Iran* 28°13N 51°36E **45** D6
Konch *India* 26°0N 79°10E **43** G8
Konde *Tanzania* 4°57S 39°45E **54** C4
Kondinin *Australia* 32°34S 118°8E **61** F2
Kondoa *Tanzania* 4°55S 35°50E **54** C4
Kondopoga *Russia* 62°12N 34°17E **18** B5
Kondratyevo *Russia* 57°22N 98°15E **29** D10
Köneürgench
  Turkmenistan 42°19N 59°10E **28** E6
Konevo *Russia* 62°8N 39°20E **18** B6
Kong = Khong →
  Cambodia 13°32N 105°58E **38** F5
Kong *Ivory C.* 8°54N 4°36W **50** G5
Kong, Koh *Cambodia* 11°20N 103°0E **39** G4
Kong Christian IX.s Land
  Greenland 68°0N 36°0W **4** C6
Kong Christian X.s Land
  Greenland 74°0N 29°0W **4** B6
Kong Frederik IX.s Land
  Greenland 67°0N 52°0W **4** C5
Kong Frederik VI.s Kyst
  Greenland 63°0N 43°0W **4** C5
Kong Frederik VIII.s Land
  Greenland 78°30N 26°0W **4** B6
Kong Oscar Fjord
  Greenland 72°20N 24°0W **4** B6
Konglu *Burma* 27°13N 97°57E **41** F20
Kongola *Namibia* 17°45S 23°20E **56** B3
Kongolo *Kasai-Or.,*
  Dem. Rep. of the Congo 5°26S 24°49E **54** D1
Kongolo *Katanga,*
  Dem. Rep. of the Congo 5°22S 27°0E **54** D2
Kongsberg *Norway* 59°39N 9°39E **9** G13
Kongsvinger *Norway* 60°12N 12°2E **9** F15
Kongur Shan *China* 38°34N 75°18E **32** D4
Kongwa *Tanzania* 6°11S 36°26E **54** D4
Koni
  Dem. Rep. of the Congo 10°40S 27°11E **55** E2
Konin *Poland* 52°12N 18°15E **17** B10
Konjic *Bos.-H.* 43°42N 17°58E **23** C7
Konkiep *Namibia* 26°49S 17°15E **56** D2
Konosha *Russia* 61°0N 40°5E **18** B7
Kōnosu *Japan* 36°3N 139°31E **31** F9
Konotop *Ukraine* 51°12N 33°7E **19** D5
Konqi He → *China* 40°45N 90°10E **32** B3
Końskie *Poland* 51°15N 20°23E **17** C11
Konstanz *Germany* 47°40N 9°10E **16** E5
Kont *Iran* 26°55N 61°50E **45** E9
Kontagora *Nigeria* 10°23N 5°27E **50** F7
Kontiolahti *Finland* 62°46N 29°50E **8** E23
Kontokali *Greece* 39°38N 19°51E **25** A3
Konya *Turkey* 37°52N 32°35E **44** B2
Konza *Kenya* 1°45S 37°7E **54** C4
Koocanusa, L. *Canada* 49°20N 115°15W **76** B6
Kookynie *Australia* 29°17S 121°22E **61** E3
Koolyanobbing
  Australia 30°48S 119°36E **61** F2
Koonibba *Australia* 31°54S 133°25E **63** E1
Koorawatha *Australia* 34°2S 148°33E **63** E4
Koorda *Australia* 30°48S 117°35E **61** F2
Kooskia *U.S.A.* 46°9N 115°59W **76** C6
Kootenay △ *Canada* 49°19N 117°39W **70** D5
Kootenay → *Canada* 51°0N 116°0W **70** C5
Kootenay L. *Canada* 49°45N 116°50W **76** B5
Kootjieskolk *S. Africa* 31°15S 20°21E **56** E3
Kopaonik *Serbia* 43°10N 20°50E **23** C9
Kópavogur *Iceland* 64°6N 21°55W **8** D3
Kopervik *Norway* 59°17N 5°17E **9** G11
Kopet Dagh *Asia* 38°0N 58°0E **45** B8
Kopi *Australia* 33°24S 135°40E **63** E2
Köping *Sweden* 59°31N 16°3E **9** G17
Koppeh Dāgh = Kopet Dagh
  Asia 38°0N 58°0E **45** B8
Koppies *S. Africa* 27°20S 27°30E **57** D4
Koprivnica *Croatia* 46°12N 16°45E **22** A7
Köprülü △ *Turkey* 37°20N 31°5E **44** B1
Kopychyntsi *Ukraine* 49°7N 25°58E **17** D13
Kora △ *Kenya* 0°14S 38°44E **54** C4
Korab *Macedonia* 41°44N 20°40E **23** D9
Koral *India* 21°50N 73°12E **42** J5
Korba *India* 22°20N 82°45E **43** H10
Korbu, Gunung
  Malaysia 4°41N 101°18E **39** K3
Korçë *Albania* 40°37N 20°50E **23** D9
Korčula *Croatia* 42°56N 16°57E **22** C7
Kord Kūy *Iran* 36°48N 54°7E **45** B7
Kord Sheykh *Iran* 28°31N 52°53E **45** D7
Kordestān □ *Iran* 36°0N 47°0E **44** C5
Kordofān □ *Sudan* 13°0N 29°0E **51** F11
Korea, North ■ *Asia* 40°0N 127°0E **35** E14
Korea, South ■ *Asia* 36°0N 128°0E **35** G15
Korea Bay *Korea* 39°0N 124°0E **35** E13
Korea Strait *Asia* 34°0N 129°30E **35** H15
Korets *Ukraine* 50°40N 27°5E **17** C14
Korhogo *Ivory C.* 9°29N 5°28W **50** G4
Korinthiakos Kolpos
  Greece 38°16N 22°30E **23** E10
Korinthos *Greece* 37°56N 22°55E **23** F10
Korissia, L. *Greece* 39°27N 19°53E **25** B3
Kōriyama *Japan* 37°24N 140°23E **30** F10
Korla *China* 41°45N 86°4E **32** C6
Kormakiti, C. *Cyprus* 35°23N 32°56E **25** D11
Korneshty = Corneşti
  Moldova 47°21N 28°1E **17** E15
Koro *Fiji* 17°19S 179°23E **59** a
Koro *Ivory C.* 8°32N 7°30W **50** G4
Koro Sea *Fiji* 17°30S 179°45W **59** a
Korogwe *Tanzania* 5°5S 38°25E **54** D4
Korolevu *Fiji* 18°12S 177°46E **59** a

Koronadal Phil. 6°12N 124°51E 37 C6
Körös → Hungary 46°43N 20°12E 17 E11
Korosten Ukraine 50°54N 28°36E 17 C15
Korostyshev Ukraine 50°19N 29°4E 17 C15
Korovou Fiji 17°47S 178°32E 59 a
Koroyanitu △ Fiji 17°40S 177°35E 59 a
Korraraika, Helodranon' i
Madag. 17°45S 43°57E 57 B7
Korsakov Russia 46°36N 142°42E 29 E15
Korshunovo Russia 58°37N 110°10E 29 D12
Korsør Denmark 55°20N 11°9E 9 J14
Kortrijk Belgium 50°50N 3°17E 15 D3
Korwai India 24°7N 78°5E 42 G8
Koryakskoye Nagorye
Russia 61°0N 171°0E 29 C18
Kos Greece 36°50N 27°15E 23 F12
Kosan N. Korea 38°52N 127°25E 35 E14
Kościan Poland 52°5N 16°40E 17 B9
Kosciusko U.S.A. 33°4N 89°35W 85 E10
Kosciuszko, Mt.
Australia 36°27S 148°16E 63 F4
Kosha Sudan 20°50N 30°30E 51 D12
K'oshih = Kashi China 39°30N 76°2E 32 D4
Koshiki-Rettō Japan 31°45N 129°49E 31 J4
Kosi India 27°48N 77°29E 42 F7
Kosi → India 28°41N 78°57E 43 E8
Košice Slovak Rep. 48°42N 21°15E 17 D11
Koskinou Greece 36°23N 28°13E 25 C10
Koslan Russia 63°34N 49°14E 18 B8
Kosŏng N. Korea 38°40N 128°22E 35 E15
Kosovo ■ Europe 42°30N 21°0E 23 C9
Kosovska Mitrovica
Kosovo 42°54N 20°52E 23 C9
Kossou, L. de Ivory C. 6°59N 5°31W 50 G4
Koster S. Africa 25°52S 26°54E 56 D4
Kôstî Sudan 13°8N 32°43E 51 F12
Kostopil Ukraine 50°51N 26°22E 17 C14
Kostroma Russia 57°50N 40°58E 18 C7
Kostrzyn Poland 52°35N 14°39E 16 B8
Koszalin Poland 54°11N 16°8E 16 A9
Kot Addu Pakistan 30°30N 71°0E 42 D4
Kot Kapura India 30°35N 74°50E 42 D6
Kot Moman Pakistan 32°13N 73°0E 42 C5
Kot Sultan Pakistan 30°46N 70°56E 42 D4
Kota India 25°14N 75°49E 42 G6
Kota Barrage India 25°6N 75°51E 42 G6
Kota Belud Malaysia 6°21N 116°26E 36 C5
Kota Bharu Malaysia 6°7N 102°14E 39 J4
Kota Kinabalu Malaysia 6°0N 116°4E 36 C5
Kota Tinggi Malaysia 1°44N 103°53E 39 M4
Kotaagung Indonesia 5°38S 104°29E 36 F2
Kotabaru Indonesia 3°20S 116°20E 36 E5
Kotabumi Indonesia 4°49S 104°54E 36 E2
Kotamobagu Indonesia 0°57N 124°31E 37 D6
Kotapinang Indonesia 1°53N 100°5E 39 M3
Kotcho L. Canada 59°7N 121°12W 70 B4
Kotdwara India 29°45N 78°32E 43 E8
Kotelnich Russia 58°22N 48°24E 18 C8
Kotelnikovo Russia 47°38N 43°8E 19 E7
Kotelnyy, Ostrov
Russia 75°10N 139°0E 29 B14
Kothari → India 25°20N 75°4E 42 G6
Kothi Chhattisgarh, India 23°21N 82°3E 43 H10
Kothi Mad. P., India 24°45N 80°40E 43 G9
Kotiro Pakistan 26°17N 67°13E 42 F2
Kotka Finland 60°28N 26°58E 8 F22
Kotlas Russia 61°17N 46°43E 18 B8
Kotli Pakistan 33°30N 73°55E 42 C5
Kotlik U.S.A. 63°2N 163°33W 74 C7
Kotma India 23°12N 81°58E 43 H9
Kotor Montenegro 42°25N 18°47E 23 C8
Kotovsk Ukraine 47°45N 29°35E 17 E15
Kotputli India 27°43N 76°12E 42 F7
Kotri Pakistan 25°22N 68°22E 42 G3
Kotto → C.A.R. 4°14N 22°2E 52 D4
Kotturu India 14°45N 76°10E 40 M10
Kotu Group Tonga 20°0S 174°45W 59 c
Kotuy → Russia 71°54N 102°6E 29 B11
Kotzebue U.S.A. 66°53N 162°39W 74 B7
Kotzebue Sound U.S.A. 66°20N 163°0W 74 B7
Kouchibouguac △
Canada 46°50N 65°0W 73 C6
Koudougou Burkina Faso 12°10N 2°20W 50 F5
Koufonisi Greece 34°56N 26°8E 25 E8
Kougaberge S. Africa 33°48S 23°50E 56 E3
Kouilou → Congo 4°10S 12°5E 52 E2
Koukdjuak → Canada 66°43N 73°0W 69 D17
Koula Moutou Gabon 1°15S 12°25E 52 E2
Koulen = Kulen
Cambodia 13°50N 104°40E 38 F5
Kouloura Greece 39°42N 19°54E 25 A3
Koumala Australia 21°38S 149°15E 62 C4
Koumra Chad 8°50N 17°35E 51 G9
Kountze U.S.A. 30°22N 94°19W 84 F7
Kouris → Cyprus 34°38N 32°54E 25 E11
Kourou Fr. Guiana 5°9N 52°39W 93 B8
Kouroussa Guinea 10°45N 9°45W 50 F4
Kousseri Cameroon 12°0N 14°55E 51 F8
Koutiala Mali 12°25N 5°23W 50 F4
Kouvola Finland 60°52N 26°43E 8 F22
Kovdor Russia 67°34N 30°24E 8 C24
Kovel Ukraine 51°11N 24°38E 17 C13
Kovrov Russia 56°25N 41°25E 18 C7
Kowanyama Australia 15°29S 141°44E 62 B3
Kowanyama ✪
Australia 15°20S 141°47E 62 B3
Kowloon China 22°19N 114°11E 33 G11
Kowŏn N. Korea 39°26N 127°14E 35 E14
Koyampattur = Coimbatore
India 11°2N 76°59E 40 P10
Köyceğiz Turkey 36°57N 28°40E 23 F13
Koyukuk → U.S.A. 64°55N 157°32W 74 C8
Koza = Okinawa Japan 26°19N 127°46E 31 L3
Kozan Turkey 37°26N 35°50E 44 B2
Kozani Greece 40°19N 21°47E 23 D9
Kozhikode = Calicut
India 11°15N 75°43E 40 P9
Kozhva Russia 65°10N 57°0E 18 A10
Kōzu-Shima Japan 34°13N 139°10E 31 G9
Kozyatyn Ukraine 49°45N 28°50E 17 D15
Kozyrevsk Russia 56°3N 159°51E 29 D16
Kpalimé Togo 6°57N 0°44E 50 G6
Kra, Isthmus of = Kra, Kho Khot
Thailand 10°15N 99°30E 39 G2
Kra, Kho Khot Thailand 10°15N 99°30E 39 G2
Kra Buri Thailand 10°22N 98°46E 39 G2
Kraai → S. Africa 30°40S 26°45E 56 E4
Krabi Thailand 8°4N 98°55E 39 H2
Kracheh = Kratie
Cambodia 12°32N 106°10E 38 F6
Kragan Indonesia 6°43S 111°38E 37 G14
Kragerø Norway 58°52N 9°25E 9 G13
Kragujevac Serbia 44°2N 20°56E 23 B9
Krakatau = Rakata, Pulau
Indonesia 6°10S 105°20E 37 G11
Krakatoa = Rakata, Pulau
Indonesia 6°10S 105°20E 37 G11
Krakor Cambodia 12°32N 104°12E 38 F5
Kraków Poland 50°4N 19°57E 17 C10
Kraksaan Indonesia 7°43S 113°23E 37 G16
Kralanh Cambodia 13°35N 103°25E 38 F4
Kraljevo Serbia 43°44N 20°41E 23 C9
Kramatorsk Ukraine 48°50N 37°30E 19 E6
Kramfors Sweden 62°55N 17°48E 8 E17
Kranj Slovenia 46°16N 14°22E 16 E8
Krankskop S. Africa 28°0S 30°47E 57 D5
Krasavino Russia 60°58N 46°29E 18 B8
Krasieo Res. Thailand 14°49N 99°30E 38 E2
Kraskino Russia 42°44N 130°48E 30 C5
Kraśnik Poland 50°55N 22°15E 17 C12
Krasnoarmeysk Russia 51°0N 45°42E 28 D5
Krasnodar Russia 45°5N 39°0E 19 E6
Krasnokamensk Russia 50°3N 118°0E 29 D12
Krasnokamsk Russia 58°4N 55°48E 18 C10
Krasnoperekopsk Ukraine 46°0N 33°54E 19 E5
Krasnorechenskiy
Russia 44°41N 135°14E 30 B7
Krasnoselkup Russia 65°20N 82°10E 28 C9
Krasnoturinsk Russia 59°46N 60°12E 18 C11
Krasnoufimsk Russia 56°36N 57°38E 18 C10
Krasnouralsk Russia 58°21N 60°3E 18 C11
Krasnovishersk Russia 60°23N 57°3E 18 B10
Krasnoyarsk Russia 56°8N 93°0E 29 D10
Krasnyy Kut Russia 50°50N 47°0E 19 D8
Krasnyy Luch Ukraine 48°13N 39°0E 19 E6
Krasnyy Yar Russia 46°43N 48°23E 19 E8
Kratie Cambodia 12°32N 106°10E 38 F6
Krau Indonesia 3°19S 140°5E 37 E10
Kravanh, Chuor Phnum
Cambodia 12°0N 103°32E 39 G4
Krefeld Germany 51°20N 6°33E 16 C4
Kremen Croatia 44°28N 15°53E 16 F8
Kremenchuk Ukraine 49°5N 33°25E 19 E5
Kremenchuksk Vdskh.
Ukraine 49°20N 32°30E 19 E5
Kremenets Ukraine 50°8N 25°43E 17 C13
Kremmling U.S.A. 40°4N 106°24W 76 F10
Krems Austria 48°25N 15°36E 16 D8
Kretinga Lithuania 55°53N 21°15E 9 J19
Kribi Cameroon 2°57N 9°56E 52 D1
Krichev = Krychaw
Belarus 53°40N 31°41E 17 B16
Kril'on, Mys Russia 45°53N 142°5E 30 B11
Krios, Akra Greece 35°13N 23°34E 25 D5
Krishna → India 15°57N 80°59E 41 M12
Krishnanagar India 23°24N 88°33E 43 H13
Kristiansand Norway 58°8N 8°1E 9 G13
Kristianstad Sweden 56°2N 14°9E 9 H16
Kristiansund Norway 63°7N 7°45E 8 E12
Kristiinankaupunki
Finland 62°16N 21°21E 8 E19
Kristinehamn Sweden 59°18N 14°7E 9 G16
Kristinestad =
Kristiinankaupunki
Finland 62°16N 21°21E 8 E19
Kriti Greece 35°15N 25°0E 25 D7
Kritsa Greece 35°10N 25°41E 25 D7
Krivoy Rog = Kryvyy Rih
Ukraine 47°51N 33°20E 19 E5
Krk Croatia 45°8N 14°40E 16 F8
Krokodil = Umgwenya →
Mozam. 25°14S 32°18E 57 D5
Krong Kaoh Kong
Cambodia 11°37N 102°59E 39 G4
Kronprins Frederik Land
Greenland 81°0N 45°0W 4 B5
Kronprins Olav Kyst
Antarctica 69°0S 42°0E 5 C5
Kronprinsesse Märtha Kyst
Antarctica 73°30S 10°0W 5 D2
Kronshtadt Russia 59°57N 29°51E 18 B4
Kroonstad S. Africa 27°43S 27°19E 56 D4
Kropotkin Russia 45°28N 40°28E 19 E7
Krosno Poland 49°42N 21°46E 17 D11
Krotoszyn Poland 51°42N 17°23E 17 C9
Krousonas Greece 35°13N 24°59E 25 D6
Kruger △ S. Africa 24°50S 26°10E 57 C5
Krugersdorp S. Africa 26°5S 27°46E 57 D4
Kruisfontein S. Africa 33°59S 24°43E 56 E3
Krung Thep = Bangkok
Thailand 13°45N 100°35E 38 F3
Krupki Belarus 54°19N 29°8E 17 A15
Kruševac Serbia 43°35N 21°28E 23 C9
Krychaw Belarus 53°40N 31°41E 17 B16
Krymskiy Poluostrov = Krymskyy
Pivostriv Ukraine 45°0N 34°0E 19 F5
Krymskyy Pivostriv
Ukraine 45°0N 34°0E 19 F5
Kryvyy Rih Ukraine 47°51N 33°20E 19 E5
Ksar el Kebir Morocco 35°0N 6°0W 50 B4
Ksar es Souk = Er Rachidia
Morocco 31°58N 4°20W 50 B5
Kuah Malaysia 6°19N 99°51E 39 J2
Kuala Belait Malaysia 4°35N 114°11E 36 D4
Kuala Berang Malaysia 5°5N 103°1E 39 K4
Kuala Dungun = Dungun
Malaysia 4°45N 103°25E 39 K4
Kuala Kangsar Malaysia 4°46N 100°56E 39 K3
Kuala Kelawang Malaysia 2°56N 102°5E 39 L4
Kuala Kerai Malaysia 5°30N 102°12E 39 K4
Kuala Kubu Bharu
Malaysia 3°34N 101°39E 39 L3
Kuala Lipis Malaysia 4°10N 102°3E 39 K4
Kuala Lumpur Malaysia 3°9N 101°41E 39 L3
Kuala Nerang Malaysia 6°16N 100°37E 39 J3
Kuala Pilah Malaysia 2°45N 102°15E 39 L4
Kuala Rompin Malaysia 2°49N 103°29E 39 L4
Kuala Selangor Malaysia 3°20N 101°15E 39 L3
Kuala Sepetang
Malaysia 4°49N 100°28E 39 K3
Kuala Terengganu
Malaysia 5°20N 103°8E 39 K4
Kualajelai Indonesia 2°58S 110°46E 36 E4
Kualakapuas Indonesia 2°55S 114°20E 36 E4
Kualakurun Indonesia 1°10S 113°50E 36 E4
Kualapembuang
Indonesia 3°14S 112°38E 36 E4
Kualasimpang Indonesia 4°17N 98°3E 36 D1
Kuancheng China 40°37N 118°30E 35 D10
Kuandang Indonesia 0°56N 123°1E 37 D6
Kuandian China 40°45N 124°45E 35 D13
Kuangchou = Guangzhou
China 23°6N 113°13E 33 G11
Kuantan Malaysia 3°49N 103°20E 39 L4
Kuba = Quba Azerbaijan 41°21N 48°32E 19 F8
Kuban → Russia 45°20N 37°30E 19 E6
Kubokawa Japan 33°12N 133°8E 31 H6
Kubu Indonesia 8°16S 115°35E 37 J18
Kubutambahan
Indonesia 8°5S 115°10E 37 J18
Kucar, Tanjung
Indonesia 8°39S 114°34E 37 K18
Kuchaman India 27°13N 74°47E 42 F6
Kuchinda India 21°44N 84°21E 43 J11
Kuching Malaysia 1°33N 110°25E 36 D4
Kuchino-eruba-Jima
Japan 30°28N 130°12E 31 J5
Kuchino-Shima Japan 29°57N 129°55E 31 K4
Kuchinotsu Japan 32°36N 130°11E 31 H5
Kucing = Kuching
Malaysia 1°33N 110°25E 36 D4
Kud → Pakistan 26°5N 66°20E 42 F2
Kuda India 23°10N 71°15E 42 H4
Kudat Malaysia 6°55N 116°55E 36 C5
Kudus Indonesia 6°48S 110°51E 37 G14
Kudymkar Russia 59°1N 54°39E 18 C9
Kueiyang = Guiyang
China 26°32N 106°40E 32 F10
Kufra Oasis = Al Kufrah
Libya 24°17N 23°15E 51 D10
Kufstein Austria 47°35N 12°11E 16 E7
Kugaaruk = Pelly Bay
Canada 68°38N 89°50W 69 D14
Kugluktuk Canada 67°50N 115°5W 68 D8
Kugong I. Canada 56°18N 79°50W 72 A4
Kūh Dasht Iran 33°32N 47°36E 44 C5
Kūh-e-Jebāl Bārez Iran 29°0N 58°0E 45 D8
Kūhak Iran 27°12N 63°10E 45 E9
Kuhan Pakistan 28°19N 67°14E 42 E2
Kūhbonān Iran 31°23N 56°19E 45 D8
Kūhestak Iran 26°47N 57°2E 45 E8
Kuhin Iran 36°22N 49°40E 45 B6
Kūhīrī Iran 26°55N 61°2E 45 E9
Kuhmo Finland 64°7N 29°31E 8 D23
Kuhn Chae △ Thailand 19°8N 99°24E 38 C2
Kūhpāyeh Eşfahan, Iran 32°44N 52°20E 45 C7
Kūhpāyeh Kermān, Iran 30°35N 57°15E 45 D8
Kūhrān, Kūh-e Iran 26°46N 58°12E 45 E8
Kui Buri Thailand 12°3N 99°52E 39 F2
Kuiburi △ Thailand 12°10N 99°37E 39 F2
Kuichong China 22°38N 114°25E 33 a
Kuiseb → Namibia 22°59S 14°31E 56 C1
Kuito Angola 12°22S 16°55E 53 G3
Kuiu I. U.S.A. 57°45N 134°10W 70 B2
Kujang N. Korea 39°57N 126°1E 35 E14
Kuji Japan 40°11N 141°46E 30 D10
Kujū-San Japan 33°5N 131°15E 31 H5
Kukës Albania 42°5N 20°27E 23 C9
Kukup Malaysia 1°20N 103°27E 39 d
Kukup, Pulau Malaysia 1°18N 103°25E 39 d
Kula Turkey 38°32N 28°40E 23 E13
K'ula Shan Bhutan 28°14N 90°36E 32 F7
Kulachi Pakistan 31°56N 70°27E 42 D4
Kulai Malaysia 1°44N 103°35E 39 M4
Kulasekarappattinam
India 8°20N 78°5E 40 Q11
Kuldīga Latvia 56°58N 21°59E 9 H19
Kulen Cambodia 13°50N 104°40E 38 F5
Kulgam India 33°36N 75°2E 43 C6
Kulgera Australia 25°50S 133°18E 62 D1
Kulim Malaysia 5°22N 100°34E 39 K3
Kulin Australia 32°40S 118°2E 61 F2
Kulkayu = Hartley Bay
Canada 53°25N 129°15W 70 C3
Kullu India 31°58N 77°6E 42 D7
Kŭlob Tajikistan 37°55N 69°50E 28 F7
Kulsary = Qulsary
Kazakhstan 46°59N 54°1E 19 E9
Kulti India 23°43N 86°50E 43 H12
Kulunda Russia 52°35N 78°57E 28 D8
Kulungar Afghan. 34°0N 69°2E 42 C3
Kūlvand Iran 31°21N 54°35E 45 D7
Kulwin Australia 35°2S 142°42E 63 F3
Kulyab = Kŭlob
Tajikistan 37°55N 69°50E 28 F7
Kuma → Russia 44°55N 47°0E 19 F8
Kumaganum Nigeria 13°8N 10°38E 51 F8
Kumagaya Japan 36°9N 139°22E 31 F9
Kumai Indonesia 2°44S 111°43E 36 E4
Kumamba, Kepulauan
Indonesia 1°36S 138°45E 37 E9
Kumamoto Japan 32°45N 130°45E 31 H5
Kumamoto □ Japan 32°55N 130°55E 31 H5
Kumanovo Macedonia 42°9N 21°42E 23 C9
Kumara N.Z. 42°37S 171°12E 59 E3
Kumarina Roadhouse
Australia 24°41S 119°32E 61 D2
Kumasi Ghana 6°41N 1°38W 50 G5
Kumba Cameroon 4°36N 9°24E 52 D1
Kumbakonam India 10°58N 79°25E 40 P11
Kumbarilla Australia 27°15S 150°55E 63 D5
Kumbhraj India 24°22N 77°3E 42 G7
Kumbia Australia 26°41S 151°39E 63 D5
Kŭmch'on N. Korea 38°10N 126°29E 35 E14
Kume-Shima Japan 26°20N 126°47E 31 L3
Kumertau Russia 52°45N 55°57E 18 D10
Kumharsain India 31°19N 77°27E 42 D7
Kumi Uganda 1°30N 33°58E 54 B3
Kumo Nigeria 10°1N 11°12E 51 F8
Kumo älv = Kokemäenjoki →
Finland 61°32N 21°44E 8 F19
Kumon Bum Burma 26°30N 97°15E 41 F20
Kumtag Shamo China 39°40N 92°0E 32 D7
Kunashir, Ostrov Russia 44°0N 146°0E 29 E15
Kunda Estonia 59°30N 26°34E 9 G22
Kunda India 25°43N 81°31E 43 G9
Kundar → Pakistan 31°56N 69°19E 42 D3
Kundelungu △
Dem. Rep. of the Congo 10°30S 27°40E 55 E2
Kundelungu Ouest △
Dem. Rep. of the Congo 9°55S 27°17E 55 D2
Kundian Pakistan 32°27N 71°28E 42 C4
Kundla India 21°21N 71°25E 42 J4
Kung, Ao Thailand 8°5N 98°24E 39 a
Kunga → Bangla. 21°46N 89°30E 43 J13
Kunghit I. Canada 52°6N 131°3W 70 C2
Kungrad = Qŭnghirot
Uzbekistan 43°2N 58°50E 28 E6
Kungsbacka Sweden 57°30N 12°5E 9 H15
Kungur Russia 57°25N 56°57E 18 C10
Kungurri Australia 21°4S 148°45E 62 b
Kunhar → Pakistan 34°20N 73°30E 43 B5
Kuningan Indonesia 6°59S 108°29E 37 G13
Kunlong Burma 23°20N 98°50E 41 H21
Kunlun Shan Asia 36°0N 86°30E 32 D6
Kunlun Shankou China 35°38N 94°4E 32 D7
Kunming China 25°1N 102°41E 32 F9
Kunmunya ✪ Australia 15°26S 124°42E 60 C3
Kununurra Australia 15°40S 128°50E 60 C4
Kunwari → India 26°26N 79°11E 43 F8
Kunya-Urgench = Köneürgench
Turkmenistan 42°19N 59°10E 28 E6
Kuopio Finland 62°53N 27°35E 8 E22
Kupa → Croatia 45°28N 16°24E 16 F9
Kupang Indonesia 10°19S 123°39E 37 F6
Kupreanof I. U.S.A. 56°50N 133°30W 70 B2
Kupyansk-Uzlovoi
Ukraine 49°40N 37°43E 19 E6
Kuqa China 41°35N 82°30E 32 C5
Kür → Azerbaijan 39°29N 49°15E 19 G8
Kür Dili Azerbaijan 39°3N 49°13E 45 B6
Kura = Kür →
Azerbaijan 39°29N 49°15E 19 G8
Kuranda Australia 16°48S 145°35E 62 B4
Kuranga India 22°4N 69°10E 42 H3
Kurashiki Japan 34°40N 133°50E 31 G6
Kurayn Si. Arabia 27°39N 49°50E 45 E6
Kurayoshi Japan 35°26N 133°50E 31 G6
Kŭrchatov Kazakhstan 50°45N 78°32E 28 D8
Kŭrdzhali Bulgaria 41°38N 25°21E 23 D11
Kure Japan 34°14N 132°32E 31 G6
Kure I. U.S.A. 28°25N 178°25W 75 K4
Kuressaare Estonia 58°15N 22°30E 9 G20
Kurgan Russia 55°26N 65°18E 28 D7
Kuri India 26°37N 70°43E 42 F4
Kuria Maria Is. = Ḥallāniyat,
Jazā'ir al Oman 17°30N 55°58E 47 D6
Kuridala Australia 21°16S 140°29E 62 C3
Kurigram Bangla. 25°49N 89°39E 41 G16
Kurikka Finland 62°36N 22°24E 8 E20
Kuril Basin Pac. Oc. 47°0N 150°0E 4 E15
Kuril Is. = Kurilskiye Ostrova
Russia 45°0N 150°0E 29 E16
Kuril-Kamchatka Trench
Pac. Oc. 44°0N 153°0E 64 C7
Kurilsk Russia 45°14N 147°53E 29 E15
Kurilskiye Ostrova
Russia 45°0N 150°0E 29 E16
Kurino Japan 31°57N 130°43E 31 J5
Kurinskaya Kosa = Kür Dili
Azerbaijan 39°3N 49°13E 45 B6
Kurlkuta ✪ Australia 24°0S 127°5E 60 D4
Kurnool India 15°45N 78°0E 40 M11
Kuro-Shima Kagoshima,
Japan 30°50N 129°57E 31 J4
Kuro-Shima Okinawa,
Japan 24°14N 124°1E 31 M2
Kurow N.Z. 44°44S 170°29E 59 F3
Kurram → Pakistan 32°36N 71°20E 42 C4
Kurri Kurri Australia 32°50S 151°28E 63 E5
Kurrimine Australia 17°47S 146°6E 62 B4
Kurseong = Karsiyang
India 26°56N 88°18E 43 F13
Kurshskiy Zaliv Russia 55°9N 21°6E 9 J19
Kursk Russia 51°42N 36°11E 18 D6
Kuruçay Turkey 39°39N 38°29E 44 B3
Kurukshetra = Thanesar
India 30°1N 76°52E 42 D7
Kuruktag China 41°0N 89°0E 32 C6
Kuruman S. Africa 27°28S 23°28E 56 D3
Kuruman → S. Africa 26°56S 20°39E 56 D3
Kurume Japan 33°15N 130°30E 31 H5
Kurunegala Sri Lanka 7°30N 80°23E 40 R12
Kurya Russia 61°42N 57°9E 18 B10
Kus Gölü Turkey 40°10N 27°55E 23 D12
Kuşadası Turkey 37°52N 27°15E 23 F12
Kusamba Indonesia 8°34S 115°27E 37 K18
Kusatsu Japan 36°37N 138°36E 31 F9
Kusawa L. Canada 60°20N 136°13W 70 A1
Kushalgarh India 23°10N 74°27E 42 H6
Kushikino Japan 31°44N 130°16E 31 J5
Kushima Japan 31°29N 131°14E 31 J5
Kushimoto Japan 33°28N 135°47E 31 H7
Kushiro Japan 43°0N 144°25E 30 C12
Kushiro-Gawa →
Japan 42°59N 144°23E 30 C12
Kushiro Shitsugen △
Japan 43°9N 144°26E 30 C12
Kūshk Iran 28°46N 56°51E 45 D8
Kushka = Serhetabat
Turkmenistan 35°20N 62°18E 45 C9
Kushol India 33°40N 76°36E 43 C7
Kushtia Bangla. 23°55N 89°5E 41 H16
Kushva Russia 58°18N 59°45E 18 C10
Kuskokwim → U.S.A. 60°5N 162°25W 74 C7
Kuskokwim B. U.S.A. 59°45N 162°25W 74 D7
Kuskokwim Mts.
U.S.A. 62°30N 156°0W 74 C8
Kusmi India 23°17N 83°55E 43 H10
Kusŏng N. Korea 39°59N 125°15E 35 E13
Kussharo-Ko Japan 43°38N 144°21E 30 C12
Kustanay = Qostanay
Kazakhstan 53°10N 63°35E 28 D7
Kut, Ko Thailand 11°40N 102°35E 39 G4
Kuta Indonesia 8°43S 115°11E 37 K18
Kütahya Turkey 39°30N 30°2E 19 G5
Kutaisi Georgia 42°19N 42°40E 19 F7
Kutaraja = Banda Aceh
Indonesia 5°35N 95°20E 36 C1
Kutch, Gulf of = Kachchh, Gulf of
India 22°50N 69°15E 42 H3
Kutch, Rann of = Kachchh, Rann
of India 24°0N 70°0E 42 H4
Kutiyana India 21°36N 70°2E 42 J4
Kutno Poland 52°15N 19°23E 17 B10
Kuttabul Australia 21°1S 148°54E 62 b
Kutu Dem. Rep. of the Congo 2°40S 18°11E 52 E3
Kutum Sudan 14°10N 24°40E 51 F10
Kuujjuaq Canada 58°6N 68°15W 69 F18
Kuujjuarapik Canada 55°20N 77°35W 72 A4
Kuusamo Finland 65°57N 29°8E 8 D23
Kuusankoski Finland 60°55N 26°38E 8 F22
Kuwait = Al Kuwayt
Kuwait 29°30N 48°0E 44 D5
Kuwait ■ Asia 29°30N 47°30E 44 D5
Kuwana Japan 35°5N 136°43E 31 G8
Kuwana → India 26°25N 83°15E 43 F10
Kuybyshev = Samara
Russia 53°8N 50°6E 18 D9
Kuybyshev Russia 55°27N 78°19E 28 D8
Kuybyshevskoye Vdkhr.
Russia 55°2N 49°30E 18 C8
Kuye He → China 38°23N 110°46E 34 E6
Kūyeh Iran 38°45N 47°57E 44 B5
Kuyto, Ozero Russia 65°6N 31°20E 8 D24
Kuytun China 44°25N 85°0E 32 C6
Kuyumba Russia 60°58N 96°59E 29 C10
Kuzey Anadolu Dağları
Turkey 41°0N 36°45E 19 F6
Kuznetsk Russia 53°12N 46°40E 18 D8
Kuzomen Russia 66°22N 36°50E 18 A6
Kvænangen Norway 70°5N 21°15E 8 A19
Kvaløya Norway 69°40N 18°30E 8 B18
Kvarner Croatia 44°50N 14°10E 16 F8
Kvarnerič Croatia 44°43N 14°37E 16 F8
Kwabhaca S. Africa 30°51S 29°0E 57 E4
Kwai = Khwae Noi →
Thailand 14°1N 99°32E 38 E2
Kwajalein Marshall Is. 9°5N 167°20E 64 G8
Kwakhanai Botswana 21°39S 21°16E 56 C3
Kwakoegron Suriname 5°12N 55°25W 93 B7
Kwale Kenya 4°15S 39°31E 54 C4
KwaMashu S. Africa 29°45S 30°58E 57 D5
Kwando → Africa 18°27S 23°32E 56 B3
Kwangchow = Guangzhou
China 23°6N 113°13E 33 G11
Kwangdaeri N. Korea 40°34N 127°33E 35 D14
Kwango →
Dem. Rep. of the Congo 3°14S 17°22E 52 E3
Kwangsi-Chuang = Guangxi
Zhuangzu Zizhiqu □
China 24°0N 109°0E 33 G10
Kwangtung = Guangdong □
China 23°0N 113°0E 33 G11
Kwataboahegan →
Canada 51°9N 80°50W 72 B3
Kwatisore Indonesia 3°18S 134°50E 37 E8
KwaZulu Natal □ S. Africa 29°0S 30°0E 57 D5
Kweichow = Guizhou □
China 27°0N 107°0E 32 F10
Kwekwe Zimbabwe 18°58S 29°48E 55 F2
Kwidzyn Poland 53°44N 18°55E 17 B10
Kwilu →
Dem. Rep. of the Congo 3°22S 17°22E 52 E3
Kwinana Australia 32°15S 115°47E 61 F2
Kwoka Indonesia 0°31S 132°27E 37 E8
Kwun Tong China 22°19N 114°13E 33 a
Kyabra Cr. → Australia 25°36S 142°55E 63 D3
Kyabram Australia 36°19S 145°4E 63 F4
Kyaikto Burma 17°20N 97°3E 38 D1
Kyaing Tong = Keng Tung
Burma 21°18N 99°39E 38 B2
Kyakhta Russia 50°30N 106°25E 29 D11
Kyambura △ Uganda 0°7S 30°9E 54 C3
Kyancutta Australia 33°8S 135°33E 63 E2
Kyaukpadaung Burma 20°52N 95°8E 41 J19
Kyaukpyu Burma 19°28N 93°30E 41 K18
Kyaukse Burma 21°36N 96°10E 41 J20
Kyburz U.S.A. 38°47N 120°18W 78 G6
Kyelang India 32°35N 77°2E 42 C7
Kyenjojo Uganda 0°40N 30°37E 54 B3
Kyle Canada 50°50N 108°2W 71 C7
Kyle Dam Zimbabwe 20°15S 31°0E 55 G3
Kyle of Lochalsh U.K. 57°17N 5°44W 11 D3
Kymijoki → Finland 60°30N 26°55E 8 F22
Kymmene älv = Kymijoki →
Finland 60°30N 26°55E 8 F22
Kyneton Australia 37°10S 144°29E 63 F3
Kynuna Australia 21°37S 141°55E 62 C3
Kyō-ga-Saki Japan 35°45N 135°15E 31 G7
Kyoga, L. Uganda 1°35N 33°0E 54 B3
Kyogle Australia 28°40S 153°0E 63 D5
Kyŏngju = Gyeongju
S. Korea 35°51N 129°14E 35 G15
Kyongpyaw Burma 17°12N 95°10E 41 L19
Kyŏngsŏng N. Korea 41°35N 129°36E 35 D15
Kyōto Japan 35°0N 135°45E 31 G7
Kyōto □ Japan 35°15N 135°45E 31 G7
Kyparissovouno Cyprus 35°19N 33°10E 25 D12
Kyperounda Cyprus 34°56N 32°58E 25 E11
Kypros = Cyprus ■ Asia 35°0N 33°0E 25 E12

Kyrenia Cyprus 35°20N 33°20E 25 D12
Kyrgyzstan ■ Asia 42°00N 75°0E 28 E8
Kyro älv = Kyrönjoki →
  Finland 63°14N 21°45E 8 E19
Kyrönjoki → Finland 63°14N 21°45E 8 E19
Kystatyam Russia 67°20N 123°10E 29 C13
Kythira Greece 36°8N 23°0E 23 F10
Kythréa Cyprus 35°15N 33°29E 25 D12
Kyunhla Burma 23°25N 95°15E 41 H19
Kyuquot Sound Canada 50°2N 127°22W 70 D3
Kyūshū Japan 33°0N 131°0E 31 H5
Kyūshū □ Japan 33°0N 131°0E 31 H5
Kyushu-Palau Ridge
  Pac. Oc. 20°0N 136°0E 64 E5
Kyūshū-Sanchi Japan 32°35N 131°17E 31 H5
Kyustendil Bulgaria 42°16N 22°41E 23 C10
Kyusyur Russia 70°19N 127°30E 29 B13
Kyyiv Ukraine 50°30N 30°28E 17 C16
Kyyivske Vdskh.
  Ukraine 51°0N 30°25E 17 C16
Kyzyl Russia 51°50N 94°30E 32 A7
Kyzyl Kum Uzbekistan 42°30N 65°0E 28 E7
Kyzyl Kyya Kyrgyzstan 40°16N 72°8E 28 E8
Kyzyl Orda = Qyzylorda
  Kazakhstan 44°48N 65°28E 28 E7

L

La Alcarria Spain 40°31N 2°45W 21 B4
La Amistad △ Cent. Amer. 9°28N 83°18W 88 E3
La Asunción Venezuela 11°2N 63°53W 92 A6
La Baie Canada 48°19N 70°53W 73 C5
La Banda Argentina 27°45S 64°10W 94 B3
La Barca Mexico 20°17N 102°34W 86 C4
La Barge U.S.A. 42°16N 110°12W 76 E8
La Barra Nic. 12°54N 83°33W 88 D3
La Belle U.S.A. 26°46N 81°26W 85 H14
La Biche → Canada 59°57N 123°50W 70 B4
La Biche, L. Canada 54°50N 112°3W 70 C6
La Brea Trin. & Tob. 10°15N 61°37W 93 K15
La Calera Chile 32°50S 71°10W 94 C1
La Campana △ Chile 32°58S 71°14W 94 C1
La Canal = Sa Canal
  Spain 38°51N 1°23E 24 C7
La Carlota Argentina 33°30S 63°20W 94 C3
La Ceiba Honduras 15°40N 86°50W 88 C2
La Chaux-de-Fonds Switz. 47°7N 6°50E 20 C7
La Chorrera Panama 8°53N 79°47W 88 E4
La Cocha Argentina 27°50S 65°40W 94 B2
La Concepción Panama 8°31N 82°37W 88 E3
La Concordia Mexico 16°5N 92°38W 87 D6
La Coruña = A Coruña
  Spain 43°20N 8°25W 21 A1
La Crescent U.S.A. 43°50N 91°18W 80 D8
La Crete Canada 58°11N 116°24W 70 B5
La Crosse Kans., U.S.A. 38°32N 99°18W 80 F4
La Crosse Wis., U.S.A. 43°48N 91°15W 80 D8
La Cruz Costa Rica 11°4N 85°39W 88 D2
La Cruz Mexico 23°55N 106°54W 86 C3
La Désirade Guadeloupe 16°18N 61°3W 88 b
La Digue Seychelles 4°20S 55°51E 53 b
La Esperanza Cuba 22°46N 83°44W 88 B3
La Esperanza Honduras 14°15N 88°10W 88 D2
La Estrada = A Estrada
  Spain 42°43N 8°27W 21 A1
La Fayette U.S.A. 34°42N 85°17W 85 D12
La Fé Cuba 22°2N 84°15W 88 B3
La Follette U.S.A. 36°23N 84°7W 85 C12
La Gi Vietnam 10°40N 107°45E 39 G6
La Grande → Canada 45°20N 118°5W 76 D4
La Grande → Canada 53°50N 79°0W 72 B5
La Grande 3, Rés.
  Canada 53°40N 75°10W 72 B4
La Grande 4, Rés. Canada 54°0N 73°15W 72 B5
La Grange Calif., U.S.A. 37°42N 120°27W 78 H6
La Grange Ga., U.S.A. 33°2N 85°2W 85 E12
La Grange Ky., U.S.A. 38°24N 85°22W 81 F11
La Grange Tex., U.S.A. 29°54N 96°52W 84 G6
La Guaira Venezuela 10°36N 66°56W 92 A5
La Habana Cuba 23°8N 82°22W 88 B3
La Independencia Mexico 16°15N 92°1W 87 D6
La Isabela Dom. Rep. 19°58N 71°2W 89 C5
La Junta U.S.A. 37°59N 103°33W 76 H12
La Laguna Canary Is. 28°28N 16°18W 24 F3
La Libertad = Puerto Libertad
  Mexico 29°55N 112°43W 86 B2
La Libertad Guatemala 16°47N 90°7W 88 C1
La Ligua Chile 32°30S 71°16W 94 C1
La Línea de la Concepción
  Spain 36°15N 5°23W 21 D3
La Loche Canada 56°29N 109°26W 71 B7
La Louvière Belgium 50°27N 4°10E 15 D4
La Lune Trin. & Tob. 10°3N 61°22W 93 K15
La Malbaie Canada 47°40N 70°10W 73 C5
La Malinche △ Mexico 19°15N 98°3W 87 D5
La Mancha Spain 39°10N 2°54W 21 C4
La Martre, L. Canada 63°15N 117°55W 70 A5
La Mesa Mexico 32°30N 116°57W 79 N10
La Mesa U.S.A. 32°46N 117°1W 79 N9
La Mesilla U.S.A. 32°16N 106°48W 77 K10
La Misión Mexico 32°6N 116°53W 86 A1
La Moure U.S.A. 46°21N 98°18W 80 B4
La Negra Chile 23°46S 70°18W 94 A1
La Oliva Canary Is. 28°36N 13°57W 24 F6
La Orotava Canary Is. 28°22N 16°31W 24 F3
La Oroya Peru 11°32S 75°54W 92 F3
La Palma Panama 8°15N 78°0W 88 E4
La Palma Canary Is. 28°40N 17°50W 24 F2
La Palma del Condado
  Spain 37°21N 6°38W 21 D2
La Paloma Chile 30°35S 71°0W 94 C1
La Pampa □ Argentina 36°50S 66°0W 94 D2
La Paragua Venezuela 6°50N 63°20W 92 B6
La Paz Entre Ríos,
  Argentina 30°50S 59°45W 94 C4
La Paz San Luis,
  Argentina 33°30S 67°20W 94 C2
La Paz Bolivia 16°20S 68°10W 92 G5
La Paz Honduras 14°20N 87°47W 88 D2

La Paz Mexico 24°10N 110°18W 86 C2
La Paz Centro Nic. 12°20N 86°41W 88 D2
La Pedrera Colombia 1°18S 69°43W 92 D5
La Pérade Canada 46°35N 72°12W 73 C5
La Perla Mexico 28°18N 104°32W 86 B4
La Perouse Str. Asia 45°40N 142°0E 30 B11
La Pesca Mexico 23°46N 97°47W 87 C5
La Piedad Mexico 20°21N 102°0W 86 C4
La Pine U.S.A. 43°40N 121°30W 76 E3
La Plata Argentina 35°0S 57°55W 94 C4
La Pocatière Canada 47°22N 70°2W 73 C5
La Porte U.S.A. 29°40N 95°1W 84 G7
La Purísima Mexico 26°10N 112°4W 86 B2
La Push U.S.A. 47°55N 124°38W 78 C2
La Quiaca Argentina 22°5S 65°35W 94 A2
La Restinga Canary Is. 27°38N 17°59W 24 G2
La Rioja Argentina 29°20S 67°0W 94 B2
La Rioja □ Argentina 29°30S 67°0W 94 B2
La Rioja □ Spain 42°20N 2°20W 21 A4
La Robla Spain 42°50N 5°41W 21 A3
La Roche-en-Ardenne
  Belgium 50°11N 5°35E 15 D5
La Roche-sur-Yon France 46°40N 1°25W 20 C3
La Rochelle France 46°10N 1°9W 20 C3
La Roda Spain 39°13N 2°15W 21 C4
La Romaine Canada 50°13N 60°40W 73 B7
La Romana Dom. Rep. 18°27N 68°57W 89 C6
La Ronge Canada 55°5N 105°20W 71 B7
La Rumorosa Mexico 32°34N 116°6W 79 N10
La Sabina = Sa Savina
  Spain 38°44N 1°25E 24 C7
La Salle U.S.A. 41°20N 89°6W 80 E9
La Santa Canary Is. 29°5N 13°40W 24 E6
La Sarre Canada 48°45N 79°15W 72 C4
La Scie Canada 49°57N 55°36W 73 C8
La Selva Beach U.S.A. 36°56N 121°51W 78 J5
La Serena Chile 29°55S 71°10W 94 B1
La Seu d'Urgell Spain 42°22N 1°23E 21 A6
La Seyne-sur-Mer France 43°7N 5°52E 20 E6
La Soufrière St. Vincent 13°20N 61°11W 89 D7
La Spézia Italy 44°7N 9°50E 20 D8
La Tagua Colombia 0°3N 74°40W 92 C4
La Tortuga Venezuela 11°0N 65°22W 89 D6
La Trinité Martinique 14°45N 60°58W 88 c
La Tuque Canada 47°30N 72°50W 73 C5
La Unión Chile 40°10S 73°0W 96 E2
La Unión El Salv. 13°20N 87°50W 88 D2
La Unión Mexico 17°58N 101°49W 86 D4
La Urbana Venezuela 7°8N 66°56W 92 B5
La Vache Pt.
  Trin. & Tob. 10°47N 61°28W 93 K15
La Vall d'Uixó Spain 39°49N 0°15W 21 C5
La Vega Dom. Rep. 19°20N 70°30W 89 C5
La Vela de Coro
  Venezuela 11°27N 69°34W 92 A5
La Venta Mexico 18°5N 94°3W 87 D6
La Vergne U.S.A. 36°1N 86°35W 85 C11
La Villa Joiosa = Villajoyosa
  Spain 38°30N 0°12W 21 C5
Laascaanood = Las Anod
  Somali Rep. 8°26N 47°19E 47 F4
Labasa Fiji 16°30S 179°27E 59 a
Labdah = Leptis Magna
  Libya 32°40N 14°12E 51 B8
Labe = Elbe → Europe 53°50N 9°0E 16 B5
Labé Guinea 11°24N 12°16W 50 F3
Laberge, L. Canada 61°11N 135°12W 70 A1
Labinsk Russia 44°40N 40°48E 19 F7
Labis Malaysia 2°22N 103°2E 39 L4
Laborie St. Lucia 13°45N 61°2W 89 f
Laboulaye Argentina 34°10S 63°30W 94 C3
Labrador Canada 53°20N 61°0W 73 B7
Labrador City Canada 52°57N 66°55W 73 B6
Labrador Sea Atl. Oc. 57°0N 54°0W 69 F21
Lábrea Brazil 7°15S 64°51W 92 E6
Labuan □ Malaysia 5°20N 115°12E 36 C4
Labuha Indonesia 0°30S 127°30E 37 E7
Labuhan Indonesia 6°22S 105°50E 37 G11
Labuhanbajo Indonesia 8°28S 119°54E 37 F6
Labuhanbilik Indonesia 2°31N 100°10E 39 L3
Labuk, Telok Malaysia 6°10N 117°50E 36 C5
Labyrinth, L. Australia 30°40S 135°11E 63 E2
Labytnangi Russia 66°39N 66°21E 18 A12
Lac-Bouchette Canada 48°16N 72°11W 73 C5
Lac Édouard Canada 47°40N 72°16W 72 C5
Lac La Biche Canada 54°45N 111°58W 70 C6
Lac la Martre = Wha Ti
  Canada 63°8N 117°16W 68 E8
Lac La Ronge △ Canada 55°9N 104°41W 71 B7
Lac-Mégantic Canada 45°35N 70°53W 73 C5
Lac Thien Vietnam 12°25N 108°11E 38 F7
Lacanau France 44°58N 1°5W 20 D3
Lacantún → Mexico 16°36N 90°39W 87 D6
Laccadive Is. = Lakshadweep Is.
  India 10°0N 72°30E 3 D13
Lacepede B. Australia 36°40S 139°40E 63 F2
Lacepede Is. Australia 16°55S 122°0E 60 C3
Lacerdónia Mozam. 18°3S 35°35E 55 F4
Lacey U.S.A. 47°7N 122°49W 78 C4
Lachania Greece 35°58N 27°54E 25 D9
Lachhmangarh India 27°50N 75°4E 42 F6
Lachi Pakistan 33°25N 71°20E 42 C4
Lachine Canada 45°26N 73°42W 72 C5
Lachlan → Australia 34°22S 143°55E 63 E3
Lachute Canada 45°39N 74°21W 72 C5
Lackagh Hills Ireland 54°16N 8°10W 10 B3
Lackawanna U.S.A. 42°50N 78°50W 82 D6
Lackawaxen U.S.A. 41°29N 74°59W 83 E10
Lacolle Canada 45°5N 73°22W 83 A11
Lacombe Canada 52°30N 113°44W 70 C6
Lacona U.S.A. 43°39N 76°10W 83 C8
Laconia U.S.A. 43°32N 71°28W 83 C13
Ladakh Ra. India 34°0N 78°0E 43 C8
Ladismith S. Africa 33°28S 21°15E 56 E3
Lādīz Iran 28°55N 61°15E 45 D9
Ladnun India 27°38N 74°25E 42 F6
Ladoga, L. = Ladozhskoye Ozero
  Russia 61°15N 30°30E 8 F24
Ladozhskoye Ozero
  Russia 61°15N 30°30E 8 F24

Lady Elliott I. Australia 24°7S 152°42E 62 C5
Lady Grey S. Africa 30°43S 27°13E 56 E4
Ladybrand S. Africa 29°9S 27°29E 56 D4
Ladysmith Canada 49°0N 123°49W 78 B3
Ladysmith S. Africa 28°32S 29°46E 57 D4
Ladysmith U.S.A. 45°28N 91°12W 80 C8
Lae Papua N. G. 6°40S 147°2E 58 B7
Laem Hin Khom Thailand 9°25N 99°56E 39 b
Laem Khat Thailand 8°6N 98°26E 39 a
Laem Nga Thailand 7°55N 98°27E 39 a
Laem Ngop Thailand 12°10N 102°26E 39 F4
Laem Phan Wa Thailand 7°47N 98°25E 39 a
Laem Pho Thailand 6°55N 101°19E 39 J3
Laem Phrom Thep Thailand 7°45N 98°19E 39 a
Laem Riang Thailand 8°7N 98°21E 39 a
Laem Sam Rong Thailand 9°35N 100°4E 39 b
Laem Son Thailand 7°59N 98°16E 39 a
Laem Son △ Thailand 9°29N 98°24E 39 H2
Laem Yamu Thailand 7°59N 98°26E 39 a
Laerma Greece 36°9N 27°57E 25 C9
Læsø Denmark 57°15N 11°5E 9 H14
Lafayette Ind., U.S.A. 40°25N 86°54W 80 E10
Lafayette La., U.S.A. 30°14N 92°1W 84 F8
Lafayette Tenn., U.S.A. 36°31N 86°2W 85 C11
Laferte → Canada 61°53N 117°44W 70 A5
Lafia Nigeria 8°30N 8°34E 50 G7
Lafleche Canada 49°45N 106°40W 71 D7
Lagan → U.K. 54°36N 5°55W 10 B6
Lagarfljót → Iceland 65°40N 14°18W 8 D6
Lagdo, L. de Cameroon 8°40N 14°0E 51 G8
Lågen → Oppland, Norway 61°8N 10°25E 8 F14
Lågen → Vestfold, Norway 59°3N 10°3E 9 G14
Lages Brazil 27°48S 50°20W 95 B5
Laghouat Algeria 33°50N 2°59E 50 B6
Lagoa do Peixe △ Brazil 31°12S 50°55W 95 C5
Lagoa Vermelha Brazil 28°13S 51°32W 95 B5
Lagonoy G. Phil. 13°35N 123°50E 37 B6
Lagos Nigeria 6°25N 3°27E 50 G6
Lagos Portugal 37°5N 8°41W 21 D1
Lagos de Moreno
  Mexico 21°21N 101°55W 86 C4
Lagrange = Bidyadanga
  Australia 18°45S 121°43E 60 C3
Lagrange B. Australia 18°38S 121°42E 60 C3
Laguna Brazil 28°30S 48°50W 95 B6
Laguna U.S.A. 35°2N 107°25W 77 J10
Laguna, Sa. de la
  Mexico 23°35N 109°55W 86 C3
Laguna Beach U.S.A. 33°33N 117°47W 79 M9
Laguna de la Restinga △
  Venezuela 10°58N 64°0W 89 D6
Laguna de Lachuá △
  Guatemala 15°55N 90°40W 88 C1
Laguna del Laja △ Chile 37°27S 71°20W 94 D1
Laguna del Tigre △
  Guatemala 17°32N 90°56W 88 C1
Laguna Limpia
  Argentina 26°32S 59°45W 94 B4
Lagunas Chile 21°0S 69°45W 94 A2
Lagunas Peru 5°10S 75°35W 92 E3
Lagunas de Chacahua △
  Mexico 16°0N 97°43W 87 D5
Lagunas de Montebello △
  Mexico 16°4N 91°42W 87 D6
Lahad Datu Malaysia 5°0N 118°20E 37 D5
Lahad Datu, Telok
  Malaysia 4°50N 118°20E 37 D5
Lahan Sai Thailand 14°25N 102°52E 38 E4
Lahanam Laos 16°16N 105°16E 38 D5
Lahar India 26°12N 78°57E 43 F8
Laharpur India 27°43N 80°56E 43 F9
Lahat Indonesia 3°45S 103°30E 36 E2
Lahewa Indonesia 1°22N 97°12E 36 D1
Lāhījān Iran 37°10N 50°6E 45 B6
Lahn → Germany 50°19N 7°37E 16 C4
Laholm Sweden 56°30N 13°2E 9 H15
Lahore Pakistan 31°32N 74°22E 42 D6
Lahri Pakistan 29°11N 68°13E 42 E3
Lāhrūd Iran 38°30N 47°52E 44 B5
Lahti Finland 60°58N 25°40E 8 F21
Lahtis = Lahti Finland 60°58N 25°40E 8 F21
Laï Chad 9°25N 16°18E 51 G9
Lai Chau Vietnam 22°5N 103°3E 38 A4
Laila = Layla Si. Arabia 22°10N 46°40E 47 C4
Laingsburg S. Africa 33°9S 20°52E 56 E3
Lainioälven → Sweden 67°35N 22°40E 8 C20
Lairg U.K. 58°2N 4°24W 11 C4
Laisamis Kenya 1°36N 37°48E 54 B4
Laiwu China 36°15N 117°40E 35 F9
Laixi China 36°50N 120°31E 35 F11
Laiyang China 36°59N 120°45E 35 F11
Laiyuan China 39°20N 114°40E 34 E8
Laizhou China 37°8N 119°57E 35 F10
Laizhou Wan China 37°30N 119°30E 35 F10
Laja → Mexico 20°55N 100°46W 86 C4
Lajamanu Australia 18°23S 130°38E 60 C5
Lak Sao Laos 18°11N 104°59E 38 C5
Lakaband Pakistan 31°2N 69°15E 42 D3
Lake → U.S.A. 44°33N 110°24W 76 D8
Lake Alpine U.S.A. 38°29N 120°0W 78 G7
Lake Andes U.S.A. 43°9N 98°32W 80 D4
Lake Arthur U.S.A. 30°5N 92°41W 84 F8
Lake Bindegolly △
  Australia 28°0S 144°0E 63 D3
Lake Cargelligo
  Australia 33°15S 146°22E 63 E4
Lake Charles U.S.A. 30°14N 93°13W 84 F8
Lake City Colo., U.S.A. 38°2N 107°19W 77 G10
Lake City Fla., U.S.A. 30°11N 82°38W 85 F13
Lake City Mich., U.S.A. 44°20N 85°13W 81 C11
Lake City Minn., U.S.A. 44°27N 92°16W 80 C7
Lake City Pa., U.S.A. 42°1N 80°21W 82 D4
Lake City S.C., U.S.A. 33°52N 79°45W 85 E15
Lake Cowichan Canada 48°49N 124°3W 70 D4
Lake District △ U.K. 54°30N 3°21W 12 C4
Lake Elsinore U.S.A. 33°38N 117°20W 79 M9
Lake Eyre △ Australia 28°40S 137°31E 63 D2
Lake Gairdner △
  Australia 31°41S 135°51E 63 E2
Lake George U.S.A. 43°26N 73°43W 83 C11

Lake Grace Australia 33°7S 118°28E 61 F2
Lake Gregory ○
  Australia 20°12S 127°27E 60 D4
Lake Harbour = Kimmirut
  Canada 62°50N 69°50W 69 E18
Lake Havasu City
  U.S.A. 34°27N 114°22W 79 L12
Lake Hughes U.S.A. 34°41N 118°26W 79 L8
Lake Isabella U.S.A. 35°38N 118°28W 79 K8
Lake Jackson U.S.A. 29°3N 95°27W 84 G7
Lake King Australia 33°5S 119°45E 61 F2
Lake Lenore Canada 52°24N 104°59W 71 C8
Lake Louise Canada 51°30N 116°10W 70 C5
Lake Mackay ○
  Australia 22°30S 129°0E 60 D4
Lake Mburo △ Uganda 0°33S 30°56E 54 C3
Lake Mead △ U.S.A. 36°30N 114°22W 79 K12
Lake Meredith △
  U.S.A. 35°50N 101°50W 84 D4
Lake Mills U.S.A. 43°25N 93°32W 80 D7
Lake Nakuru △ Kenya 0°21S 36°8E 54 C4
Lake Placid U.S.A. 44°17N 73°59W 83 B11
Lake Pleasant U.S.A. 43°28N 74°25W 83 C10
Lake Providence U.S.A. 32°48N 91°10W 84 E9
Lake Roosevelt △
  U.S.A. 48°5N 118°14W 76 B4
Lake St. Peter Canada 45°18N 78°2W 82 A6
Lake Superior △ Canada 47°45N 84°45W 72 C3
Lake Torrens △
  Australia 30°55S 137°40E 63 E2
Lake Village U.S.A. 33°20N 91°17W 84 E9
Lake Wales U.S.A. 27°54N 81°35W 85 H14
Lake Worth U.S.A. 26°37N 80°3W 85 H14
Lakeba Fiji 18°13S 178°47W 59 a
Lakeba Passage Fiji 18°0S 178°45W 59 a
Lakefield Canada 44°25N 78°16W 82 B6
Lakefield △ Australia 15°24S 144°26E 62 B3
Lakehurst U.S.A. 40°1N 74°19W 83 F10
Lakeland Australia 15°49S 144°57E 62 B3
Lakeland U.S.A. 28°3N 81°57W 85 G14
Lakemba = Lakeba Fiji 18°13S 178°47W 59 a
Lakeport Calif., U.S.A. 39°3N 122°55W 78 F4
Lakeport Mich., U.S.A. 43°7N 82°30W 82 C2
Lakes Entrance Australia 37°50S 148°0E 63 F4
Lakeside Calif., U.S.A. 32°52N 116°55W 79 N10
Lakeside Nebr., U.S.A. 42°3N 102°26W 80 D2
Lakeview U.S.A. 42°11N 120°21W 76 E3
Lakeville U.S.A. 44°39N 93°14W 80 C7
Lakewood Colo., U.S.A. 39°42N 105°4W 76 G11
Lakewood N.J., U.S.A. 40°6N 74°13W 83 F10
Lakewood N.Y., U.S.A. 42°6N 79°19W 82 D5
Lakewood Ohio, U.S.A. 41°28N 81°47W 82 E3
Lakewood Wash.,
  U.S.A. 47°11N 122°32W 78 C4
Lakha India 26°9N 70°54E 42 F4
Lakhimpur India 27°57N 80°46E 43 F9
Lakhisarai India 25°11N 86°5E 43 G12
Lakhnadon India 22°36N 79°36E 43 H8
Lakhnau = Lucknow
  India 26°50N 81°0E 43 F9
Lakhonpheng Laos 15°54N 105°34E 38 E5
Lakhpat India 23°48N 68°47E 42 H3
Lakin U.S.A. 37°57N 101°15W 80 G3
Lakitusaki → Canada 54°21N 82°25W 72 B3
Lakki Greece 35°24N 23°57E 25 D5
Lakki Pakistan 32°36N 70°55E 42 C4
Lakonikos Kolpos
  Greece 36°40N 22°40E 23 F10
Lakor Indonesia 8°15S 128°17E 37 F7
Lakota Ivory C. 5°50N 5°30W 50 G4
Lakota U.S.A. 48°2N 98°21W 80 A4
Laksar India 29°46N 78°3E 42 E8
Laksefjorden Norway 70°45N 26°50E 8 A22
Lakselv Norway 70°2N 25°0E 8 A21
Lakshadweep Is. India 10°0N 72°30E 3 D13
Lakshmanpur India 22°58N 83°3E 43 H10
Lakshmikantapur India 22°5N 88°20E 43 H13
Lala Musa Pakistan 32°40N 73°57E 42 C5
Lalaghat India 24°30N 92°40E 41 G18
Lalago Tanzania 3°28S 33°58E 54 C3
Lalapanzi Zimbabwe 19°20S 30°15E 55 F3
L'Albufera Spain 39°20N 0°27W 21 C5
Lalganj India 25°52N 85°13E 43 G11
Lalgola India 24°25N 88°15E 43 G13
Lālī Iran 32°21N 49°6E 45 C6
Lalin China 45°12N 127°0E 35 B14
Lalín Spain 42°40N 8°5W 21 A1
Lalin He → China 45°32N 125°40E 35 B13
Lalitapur Nepal 27°40N 85°20E 43 F11
Lalitpur India 24°42N 78°28E 43 G8
Lalkua India 29°5N 79°31E 43 E8
Lalsot India 26°34N 76°20E 42 F7
Lam Nam Nan △
  Thailand 17°55N 100°28E 38 D3
Lam Pao Res. Thailand 16°50N 103°15E 38 D4
Lama Kara Togo 9°30N 1°15E 50 G6
Lamae Thailand 9°51N 99°5E 39 H2
Lamaing Burma 15°25N 97°53E 38 E1
Lamar Colo., U.S.A. 38°5N 102°37W 76 G12
Lamar Mo., U.S.A. 37°30N 94°16W 80 G6
Lamas Peru 6°28S 76°31W 92 E3
Lamayuru India 34°25N 76°56E 43 C7
Lambaréné Gabon 0°41S 10°12E 52 E2
Lambasa = Labasa Fiji 16°30S 179°27E 59 a
Lambay I. Ireland 53°29N 6°1W 10 C5
Lambert's Bay S. Africa 32°5S 18°17E 56 E2
Lambeth Canada 42°54N 81°18W 82 D3
Lambomakondro
  Madag. 22°41S 44°44E 57 C7
Lame Deer U.S.A. 45°37N 106°40W 76 D10
Lamego Portugal 41°5N 7°52W 21 B2
Lamèque Canada 47°45N 64°38W 73 C7
Lameroo Australia 35°19S 140°33E 63 F3
Lamesa U.S.A. 32°44N 101°58W 84 E4
Lamia Greece 38°55N 22°26E 23 E10
Lamington △ Australia 28°13S 153°12E 63 D5
Lamma I. China 22°12N 114°7E 33 a
Lammermuir Hills U.K. 55°50N 2°40W 11 F6
Lamoille → U.S.A. 44°38N 73°13W 83 B11

Lamon B. Phil. 14°30N 122°20E 37 B6
Lamont Canada 53°46N 112°50W 70 C6
Lamont Calif., U.S.A. 35°15N 118°55W 79 K8
Lamont Wyo., U.S.A. 42°13N 107°29W 76 E10
Lampa Peru 15°22S 70°22W 92 G4
Lampang Thailand 18°16N 99°32E 38 C2
Lampasas U.S.A. 31°4N 98°11W 84 F5
Lampazos de Naranjo
  Mexico 27°1N 100°31W 86 B4
Lampedusa Medit. S. 35°36N 12°40E 22 G5
Lampeter U.K. 52°7N 4°4W 13 E3
Lamphun Thailand 18°40N 99°2E 38 C2
Lampione Medit. S. 35°33N 12°20E 22 G5
Lampman Canada 49°25N 102°50W 71 D8
Lampung □ Indonesia 5°30S 104°30E 36 F2
Lamta India 22°8N 80°7E 43 H9
Lamu Kenya 2°16S 40°55E 54 C5
Lamy U.S.A. 35°29N 105°53W 77 J11
Lan Xian China 38°15N 111°35E 34 E6
Läna'i U.S.A. 20°50N 156°55W 75 L8
Lanak La China 34°27N 79°32E 43 B8
Lanak'o Shank'ou = Lanak La
  China 34°27N 79°32E 43 B8
Lanark Canada 45°1N 76°22W 83 A8
Lanark U.K. 55°40N 3°47W 11 F5
Lanbi Kyun Burma 10°50N 98°20E 39 G2
Lancang Jiang →
  China 21°40N 101°10E 32 G9
Lancashire □ U.K. 53°50N 2°48W 12 D5
Lancaster Canada 45°10N 74°30W 83 A10
Lancaster U.K. 54°3N 2°48W 12 C5
Lancaster Calif., U.S.A. 34°42N 118°8W 79 L8
Lancaster Ky., U.S.A. 37°37N 84°35W 81 G11
Lancaster N.H., U.S.A. 44°29N 71°34W 83 B13
Lancaster Ohio, U.S.A. 39°43N 82°36W 81 F12
Lancaster Pa., U.S.A. 40°2N 76°19W 83 F8
Lancaster S.C., U.S.A. 34°43N 80°46W 85 D14
Lancaster Wis., U.S.A. 42°51N 90°43W 80 D8
Lancaster Sd. Canada 74°13N 84°0W 69 C15
Lancelin Australia 31°0S 115°18E 61 F2
Lanchow = Lanzhou
  China 36°1N 103°52E 34 F2
Lanciano Italy 42°14N 14°23E 22 C6
Lancun China 36°25N 120°10E 35 F11
Land Between the Lakes △
  U.S.A. 36°25N 88°0W 85 C11
Landeck Austria 47°9N 10°34E 16 E6
Lander U.S.A. 42°50N 108°44W 76 E9
Lander → Australia 22°0S 132°0E 60 D5
Landes France 44°0N 1°0W 20 D3
Landi Kotal Pakistan 34°7N 71°6E 42 B4
Landisburg U.S.A. 40°21N 77°19W 82 F7
Land's End U.K. 50°4N 5°44W 13 G2
Landsborough Cr. →
  Australia 22°28S 144°35E 62 C3
Landshut Germany 48°34N 12°8E 16 D7
Lanesboro U.S.A. 41°57N 75°34W 83 E9
Lanett U.S.A. 32°52N 85°12W 85 E12
Lang Shan China 41°0N 106°30E 34 D4
Lang Son Vietnam 21°52N 106°42E 38 B6
Lang Suan Thailand 9°57N 99°4E 39 H2
La'nga Co China 30°45N 81°15E 43 D9
Langar Iran 35°23N 60°25E 45 C9
Langara I. Canada 54°14N 133°1W 70 C2
Langdon U.S.A. 48°45N 98°22W 80 A4
Langeberg S. Africa 33°55S 21°0E 56 E3
Langeberge S. Africa 28°15S 22°33E 56 D3
Langeland Denmark 54°56N 10°48E 9 J14
Langenburg Canada 50°51N 101°43W 71 C8
Langfang China 39°30N 116°41E 34 E9
Langholm U.K. 55°9N 3°0W 11 F5
Langjökull Iceland 64°39N 20°12W 8 D3
Langkawi, Pulau
  Malaysia 6°25N 99°45E 39 J2
Langklip S. Africa 28°12S 20°20E 56 D3
Langkon Malaysia 6°30N 116°40E 36 C5
Langley Canada 49°7N 122°39W 78 A4
Langøya Norway 68°45N 14°50E 8 B16
Langreo Spain 43°18N 5°40W 21 A3
Langres France 47°52N 5°20E 20 C6
Langres, Plateau de France 47°45N 5°3E 20 C6
Langsa Indonesia 4°30N 97°57E 36 D1
Langtang △ Nepal 28°30N 85°30E 43 E11
Langtou China 40°1N 124°19E 35 D13
Langtry U.S.A. 29°49N 101°34W 84 G4
Langu Thailand 6°53N 99°47E 39 J2
Languedoc France 43°58N 3°55E 20 E5
Langwang China 22°38N 113°27E 33 a
Langxiang Canada 51°51N 105°2W 71 C7
Lankao China 34°48N 114°50E 34 G8
Länkäran Azerbaijan 38°48N 48°52E 45 B6
Lannion France 48°46N 3°29W 20 B2
L'Annonciation Canada 46°25N 74°55W 72 C5
Lansang △ Thailand 16°45N 99°0E 38 D2
Lansdale U.S.A. 40°14N 75°17W 83 F9
Lansdowne Australia 31°48S 152°30E 63 E5
Lansdowne Canada 44°24N 76°1W 83 B8
Lansdowne India 29°50N 78°41E 43 E8
Lansdowne House = Neskantaga
  Canada 52°14N 87°53W 72 B2
L'Anse U.S.A. 46°45N 88°27W 80 B9
L'Anse au Loup Canada 51°32N 56°50W 73 B8
L'Anse aux Meadows
  Canada 51°36N 55°32W 73 B8
L'Anse la Raye St. Lucia 13°55N 61°3W 89 f
Lansford U.S.A. 40°50N 75°53W 83 F9
Lanshantou China 35°5N 119°20E 35 G10
Länsi-Turunmaa Finland 60°18N 22°18E 9 F20
Lansing U.S.A. 42°44N 84°33W 81 D11
Lanta, Ko Thailand 7°35N 99°3E 39 J2
Lantau I. China 22°15N 113°56E 33 a
Lantian China 34°11N 109°20E 34 G5
Lanús Argentina 34°42S 58°23W 94 C4
Lanusei Italy 39°52N 9°34E 22 E3
Lanzarote Canary Is. 29°0N 13°40W 24 F6
Lanzarote ✈ (ACE)
  Canary Is. 28°57N 13°40W 24 F6
Lanzhou China 36°1N 103°52E 34 F2

Lao Cai *Vietnam* 22°30N 103°57E **38** A4
Laoag *Phil.* 18°7N 120°34E **37** A6
Laoang *Phil.* 12°32N 125°8E **37** B7
Laoha He → *China* 43°25N 120°35E **35** C11
Laois □ *Ireland* 52°57N 7°36W **10** D4
Laon *France* 49°33N 3°35E **20** B5
Laona *U.S.A.* 45°34N 88°40W **80** C9
Laos ■ *Asia* 17°45N 105°0E **38** D5
Lapa *Brazil* 25°46S 49°44W **95** B6
Lapeer *U.S.A.* 43°3N 83°19W **81** D12
Lapithos *Cyprus* 35°21N 33°11E **25** D12
Lapland = Lappland
  Europe 68°7N 24°0E **8** B21
LaPorte *Ind., U.S.A.* 41°36N 86°43W **80** E10
Laporte *Pa., U.S.A.* 41°25N 76°30W **83** E8
Lappeenranta *Finland* 61°3N 28°12E **8** F23
Lappland *Europe* 68°7N 24°0E **8** B21
Lappo = Lapua *Finland* 62°58N 23°0E **8** E20
Laprida *Argentina* 37°34S 60°45W **94** D3
Lâpseki *Turkey* 40°20N 26°41E **23** D12
Laptev Sea *Russia* 76°0N 125°0E **29** B13
Lapua *Finland* 62°58N 23°0E **8** E20
L'Aquila *Italy* 42°22N 13°22E **22** C5
Lār *Iran* 27°40N 54°14E **45** E7
Laramie *U.S.A.* 41°19N 105°35W **76** F11
Laramie Mts. *U.S.A.* 42°0N 105°30W **76** F11
Laranjeiras do Sul *Brazil* 25°23S 52°23W **95** B5
Larantuka *Indonesia* 8°21S 122°55E **37** F6
Larat *Indonesia* 7°0S 132°0E **37** F8
Larde *Mozam.* 16°28S 39°43E **55** F4
Larder Lake *Canada* 48°5N 79°40W **72** C4
Lardos *Greece* 36°6N 28°1E **25** C10
Lardos, Akra = Lindos, Akra
  Greece 36°4N 28°10E **25** C10
Lardos, Ormos *Greece* 36°4N 28°2E **25** C10
Lare *Kenya* 0°2N 37°56E **54** C4
Laredo *U.S.A.* 27°30N 99°30W **84** H5
Laredo Sd. *Canada* 52°30N 128°53W **70** C3
Largo *U.S.A.* 27°54N 82°47W **85** H13
Largs *U.K.* 55°47N 4°52W **11** F4
Lariang *Indonesia* 1°26S 119°17E **37** E5
Larimore *U.S.A.* 47°54N 97°38W **80** B5
Larisa *Greece* 39°36N 22°27E **23** E10
Larkana *Pakistan* 27°32N 68°18E **42** F3
Larnaca *Cyprus* 34°55N 33°38E **25** E12
Larnaca Bay *Cyprus* 34°53N 33°45E **25** E12
Larne *U.K.* 54°51N 5°51W **10** B6
Larned *U.S.A.* 38°11N 99°6W **80** F4
Larose *U.S.A.* 29°34N 90°23W **85** G9
Larrimah *Australia* 15°35S 133°12E **60** C5
Larsen Ice Shelf *Antarctica* 67°0S 62°0W **5** C17
Larvik *Norway* 59°4N 10°2E **9** G14
Las Animas *U.S.A.* 38°4N 103°13W **76** G12
Las Anod *Somali Rep.* 8°26N 47°19E **47** F4
Las Brenãs *Argentina* 27°5S 61°7W **94** B3
Las Cañadas del Teide △
  Canary Is. 28°15N 16°37W **24** F3
Las Cejas *Argentina* 26°53S 64°44W **96** B4
Las Chimeneas *Mexico* 32°8N 116°5W **79** N10
Las Cruces *U.S.A.* 32°19N 106°47W **77** K10
Las Flores *Argentina* 36°10S 59°7W **94** D4
Las Heras *Argentina* 32°51S 68°49W **94** C2
Las Lajas *Argentina* 38°30S 70°25W **96** D2
Las Lomitas *Argentina* 24°43S 60°35W **94** A3
Las Palmas *Argentina* 27°8S 58°45W **94** B4
Las Palmas *Canary Is.* 28°7N 15°26W **24** F4
Las Palmas → *Mexico* 32°31N 116°58W **79** N10
Las Palmas ✈ (LPA)
  Canary Is. 27°55N 15°25W **24** G4
Las Piedras *Uruguay* 34°44S 56°14W **95** C4
Las Pipinas *Argentina* 35°30S 57°19W **94** D4
Las Plumas *Argentina* 43°40S 67°15W **96** E3
Las Rosas *Argentina* 32°30S 61°35W **94** C3
Las Tablas *Panama* 7°49N 80°14W **88** E3
Las Toscas *Argentina* 28°21S 59°18W **94** B4
Las Truchas *Mexico* 17°57N 102°13W **86** D4
Las Tunas *Cuba* 20°58N 76°59W **88** B4
Las Varillas *Argentina* 31°50S 62°50W **94** C3
Las Vegas *N. Mex.,*
  U.S.A. 35°36N 105°13W **77** J11
Las Vegas *Nev., U.S.A.* 36°10N 115°8W **79** J11
Las Vegas McCarran Int. ✈ (LAS)
  U.S.A. 36°5N 115°9W **79** J11
Lascano *Uruguay* 33°35S 54°12W **95** C5
Lash-e Joveyn *Afghan.* 31°45N 61°30E **40** D2
Lashburn *Canada* 53°10N 109°40W **71** C7
Lashio *Burma* 22°56N 97°45E **41** H20
Lashkar *India* 26°10N 78°10E **42** F8
Lasithi *Greece* 35°11N 25°31E **25** D7
Lasithi □ *Greece* 35°5N 25°50E **25** D7
Lāsjerd *Iran* 35°24N 53°4E **45** C7
Lassen Pk. *U.S.A.* 40°29N 121°30W **76** F3
Lassen Volcanic △
  U.S.A. 40°30N 121°20W **76** F3
Last Mountain L.
  Canada 51°5N 105°14W **71** C7
Lastchance Cr. →
  U.S.A. 40°2N 121°15W **78** E5
Lastoursville *Gabon* 0°55S 12°38E **52** E2
Lastovo *Croatia* 42°46N 16°55E **22** C7
Lat Yao *Thailand* 15°45N 99°48E **38** E2
Latacunga *Ecuador* 0°50S 78°35W **92** D3
Latakia = Al Lādhiqīyah
  Syria 35°30N 35°45E **44** C2
Latchford *Canada* 47°20N 79°50W **72** C4
Late *Tonga* 18°48S 174°39W **59** c
Latehar *India* 23°45N 84°30E **43** H11
Latham *Australia* 29°44S 116°20E **61** E2
Lathi *India* 27°43N 71°23E **42** F4
Lathrop Wells *U.S.A.* 36°39N 116°24W **79** J10
Latina *Italy* 41°28N 12°52E **22** D5
Latium = Lazio □ *Italy* 42°10N 12°30E **22** C5
Laton *U.S.A.* 36°26N 119°41W **78** J7
Latouche Treville, C.
  Australia 18°27S 121°49E **60** C3
Latrobe *Australia* 41°14S 146°30E **63** G4
Latrobe *U.S.A.* 40°19N 79°23W **82** F5
Latvia ■ *Europe* 56°50N 24°0E **9** H21
Lau Fau Shan *China* 22°28N 113°59E **33** a
Lau Group *Fiji* 17°0S 178°30W **59** a

Lauchhammer *Germany* 51°29N 13°47E **16** C7
Lauge Koch Kyst
  Greenland 75°45N 57°45W **69** B20
Laughlin *U.S.A.* 35°10N 114°34W **79** K12
Laukaa *Finland* 62°24N 25°56E **8** E21
Launceston *Australia* 41°24S 147°8E **63** G4
Launceston *U.K.* 50°38N 4°22W **13** G3
Launglon Bok *Burma* 13°50N 97°54E **38** F1
Laura *Australia* 15°32S 144°32E **62** B3
Laurel *Miss., U.S.A.* 31°41N 89°8W **85** F10
Laurel *Mont., U.S.A.* 45°40N 108°46W **76** D9
Laurel Hill *U.S.A.* 40°14N 79°6W **82** F5
Laurencekirk *U.K.* 56°50N 2°28W **11** E6
Laurens *U.S.A.* 34°30N 82°1W **85** D13
Laurentian Plateau
  Canada 52°0N 70°0W **73** B6
Lauria *Italy* 40°2N 15°50E **22** E6
Laurie L. *Canada* 56°35N 101°57W **71** B8
Laurinburg *U.S.A.* 34°47N 79°28W **85** D15
Laurium *U.S.A.* 47°14N 88°27W **80** B9
Lausanne *Switz.* 46°32N 6°38E **20** C7
Laut *Indonesia* 4°45N 108°0E **36** D3
Laut, Pulau *Indonesia* 3°40S 116°10E **36** E5
Laut Kecil, Kepulauan
  Indonesia 4°45S 115°40E **36** E5
Lautoka *Fiji* 17°37S 177°27E **59** a
Lava Beds △ *U.S.A.* 41°40N 121°30W **76** F3
Lavagh More *Ireland* 54°46N 8°6W **10** B3
Laval *France* 48°4N 0°48W **20** B3
Laval-des-Rapides
  Canada 45°33N 73°42W **72** C5
Lavalle *Argentina* 28°15S 65°15W **94** B2
Lāvān *Iran* 26°48N 53°22E **45** E7
Lavant *Canada* 45°3N 76°42W **83** A8
Lāvar Meydān *Iran* 30°20N 54°30E **45** D7
Laverton *Australia* 28°44S 122°29E **61** E3
Lavras *Brazil* 21°20S 45°0W **95** A7
Lavrio *Greece* 37°40N 24°4E **23** F11
Lavris *Greece* 35°25N 24°40E **25** D6
Lavumisa *Swaziland* 27°20S 31°55E **57** D5
Lavushi Manda △ *Zambia* 12°46S 31°10E **55** E3
Lawaki *Fiji* 17°40S 178°35E **59** a
Lawas *Malaysia* 4°55N 115°25E **36** D5
Lawele *Indonesia* 5°13S 122°57E **37** F6
Lawn Hill = Boodjamulla △
  Australia 18°15S 138°6E **62** B2
Lawqah *Si. Arabia* 29°49N 42°45E **44** D4
Lawrence *N.Z.* 45°55S 169°41E **59** F2
Lawrence *Ind., U.S.A.* 39°50N 86°2W **80** F10
Lawrence *Kans., U.S.A.* 38°58N 95°14W **80** F6
Lawrence *Mass., U.S.A.* 42°43N 71°10W **83** D13
Lawrenceburg *Ind.,*
  U.S.A. 39°6N 84°52W **81** F11
Lawrenceburg *Tenn.,*
  U.S.A. 35°14N 87°20W **85** D11
Lawrenceville *Ga.,*
  U.S.A. 33°57N 83°59W **85** E13
Lawrenceville *Pa., U.S.A.* 41°59N 77°8W **82** E7
Laws *U.S.A.* 37°24N 118°20W **78** H8
Lawton *U.S.A.* 34°37N 98°25W **84** H5
Lawu *Indonesia* 7°40S 111°13E **37** G14
Laxford, L. *U.K.* 58°24N 5°6W **11** C3
Layla *Si. Arabia* 22°10N 46°40E **47** C4
Laylān *Iraq* 35°18N 44°31E **44** C5
Laysan I. *U.S.A.* 25°50N 171°50W **75** K5
Layton *U.S.A.* 41°4N 111°58W **76** F8
Laytonville *U.S.A.* 39°41N 123°29W **76** G2
Lazarev *Russia* 52°13N 141°30E **29** D15
Lazarev Sea *S. Ocean* 67°30S 3°0W **5** C2
Lazarivo *Madag.* 23°54S 44°59W **57** C8
Lázaro Cárdenas
  Mexico 17°55N 102°11W **86** D4
Lazio □ *Italy* 42°10N 12°30E **22** C5
Lazo *Russia* 43°25N 133°55E **30** C6
Le Bic *Canada* 48°20N 68°41W **73** C6
Le Creusot *France* 46°48N 4°24E **20** C6
Le François *Martinique* 14°38N 60°57W **88** c
Le Gosier *Guadeloupe* 16°14N 61°29W **88** b
Le Gris Gris *Mauritius* 20°31S 57°32E **53** d
Le Havre *France* 49°30N 0°5E **20** B4
Le Lamentin *Martinique* 14°35N 61°2W **88** c
Le Mans *France* 48°0N 0°10E **20** C4
Le Marin *Martinique* 14°27N 60°55W **88** c
Le Mars *U.S.A.* 42°47N 96°10W **80** D5
Le Mont-St-Michel
  France 48°40N 1°30W **20** B3
Le Moule *Guadeloupe* 16°20N 61°22W **88** b
Le Moyne, L. *Canada* 56°45N 68°47W **73** A6
Le Port *Réunion* 20°56S 55°18E **53** c
Le Prêcheur *Martinique* 14°50N 61°12W **88** c
Le Puy-en-Velay *France* 45°3N 3°52E **20** D5
Le Raysville *U.S.A.* 41°50N 76°10W **83** E8
Le Robert *Martinique* 14°40N 60°56W **88** c
Le Roy *U.S.A.* 42°58N 77°59W **82** D7
Le St-Esprit *Martinique* 14°34N 60°56W **88** c
Le Sueur *U.S.A.* 44°28N 93°55W **80** C7
Le Tampon *Réunion* 21°16S 55°32E **53** c
Le Thuy *Vietnam* 17°14N 106°49E **38** D6
Le Touquet-Paris-Plage
  France 50°30N 1°36E **20** A4
Le Tréport *France* 50°3N 1°20E **20** A4
Le Verdon-sur-Mer *France* 45°33N 1°4W **20** D3
Lea → *U.K.* 51°31N 0°1E **13** F8
Leach *Cambodia* 12°21N 103°46E **39** F4
Lead *U.S.A.* 44°21N 103°46W **80** C2
Leaf → *U.S.A.* 30°59N 88°44W **85** F10
Leaf Rapids *Canada* 56°30N 99°59W **71** B9
Leamington *Canada* 42°3N 82°36W **82** D2
Leamington *U.S.A.* 39°32N 112°17W **76** G7
Leamington Spa = Royal
  Leamington Spa *U.K.* 52°18N 1°31W **13** E6
Leandro Norte Alem
  Argentina 27°34S 55°15W **95** B4
Leane, L. *Ireland* 52°2N 9°32W **10** D2
Learmonth *Australia* 22°13S 114°10E **60** D1
Leask *Canada* 53°5N 106°45W **71** C7
Leatherhead *U.K.* 51°18N 0°20W **13** F7

Leavdnja = Lakselv
  Norway 70°2N 25°0E **8** A21
Leavenworth *Kans.,*
  U.S.A. 39°19N 94°55W **80** F6
Leavenworth *Wash.,*
  U.S.A. 47°36N 120°40W **76** C3
Leawood *U.S.A.* 38°58N 94°37W **80** F6
Lebak *Phil.* 6°32N 124°5E **37** C6
Lebam *U.S.A.* 46°34N 123°33W **78** D3
Lebanon *Ind., U.S.A.* 40°3N 86°28W **80** E10
Lebanon *Kans., U.S.A.* 39°49N 98°33W **80** F4
Lebanon *Ky., U.S.A.* 37°34N 85°15W **81** G11
Lebanon *Mo., U.S.A.* 37°41N 92°40W **80** G7
Lebanon *N.H., U.S.A.* 43°39N 72°15W **83** C12
Lebanon *Oreg., U.S.A.* 44°32N 122°55W **76** D2
Lebanon *Pa., U.S.A.* 40°20N 76°26W **83** F8
Lebanon *Tenn., U.S.A.* 36°12N 86°18W **85** C11
Lebanon ■ *Asia* 34°0N 36°0E **46** B5
Lebec *U.S.A.* 34°51N 118°52W **79** L8
Lebel-sur-Quévillon
  Canada 49°3N 76°59W **72** C4
Lebomboberge *S. Africa* 24°30S 32°0E **57** C5
Lebork *Poland* 54°33N 17°46E **17** A9
Lebrija *Spain* 36°53N 6°5W **21** D2
Lebu *Chile* 37°40S 73°47W **94** D1
Lecce *Italy* 40°23N 18°11E **23** D8
Lecco *Italy* 45°51N 9°23E **20** D8
Lech → *Germany* 48°43N 10°56E **16** D6
Lecontes Mills *U.S.A.* 41°5N 78°17W **82** E6
Łęczyca *Poland* 52°5N 19°15E **17** B10
Ledang, Gunung
  Malaysia 2°22N 102°37E **39** L4
Ledong *China* 18°41N 109°5E **38** C7
Leduc *Canada* 53°15N 113°30W **70** C6
Lee *U.S.A.* 42°19N 73°15W **83** D11
Lee → *Ireland* 51°53N 8°56W **10** E3
Lee Vining *U.S.A.* 37°58N 119°7W **78** H7
Leech L. *U.S.A.* 47°10N 94°24W **80** B6
Leechburg *U.S.A.* 40°37N 79°36W **82** F5
Leeds *U.K.* 53°48N 1°33W **12** D6
Leeds *U.S.A.* 33°33N 86°33W **85** E11
Leek *Neths.* 53°10N 6°24E **15** A6
Leek *U.K.* 53°7N 2°1W **12** D5
Leeman *Australia* 29°57S 114°58E **61** E1
Leeper *U.S.A.* 41°22N 79°18W **82** E5
Leer *Germany* 53°13N 7°26E **16** B4
Leesburg *U.S.A.* 28°49N 81°53W **85** G14
Leeton *Australia* 34°33S 146°23E **63** E4
Leetonia *U.S.A.* 40°53N 80°45W **82** F4
Leeu Gamka *S. Africa* 32°47S 21°59E **56** E3
Leeuwarden *Neths.* 53°15N 5°48E **15** A5
Leeuwin, C. *Australia* 34°20S 115°9E **61** F2
Leeuwin Naturaliste △
  Australia 34°6S 115°3E **61** F2
Leeward Is. *Atl. Oc.* 16°30N 63°30W **89** C7
Lefka *Cyprus* 35°6N 32°51E **25** D11
Lefkada *Greece* 38°40N 20°43E **23** E9
Lefkimi *Greece* 39°25N 20°3E **25** B4
Lefkimis, Akra *Greece* 39°29N 20°4E **25** B4
Lefkoniko *Cyprus* 35°18N 33°44E **25** D12
Lefroy *Canada* 44°16N 79°34W **82** B5
Lefroy, L. *Australia* 31°21S 121°40E **61** F3
Legazpi *Phil.* 13°10N 123°45E **37** B6
Legendre I. *Australia* 20°22S 116°55E **60** D2
Leghorn = Livorno *Italy* 43°33N 10°19E **22** C4
Legian *Indonesia* 8°42S 115°10E **37** K18
Legionowo *Poland* 52°25N 20°50E **17** B11
Legnago *Italy* 45°11N 11°18E **22** B4
Legnica *Poland* 51°12N 16°10E **16** C9
Leh *India* 34°9N 77°35E **43** B7
Lehigh Acres *U.S.A.* 26°36N 81°39W **85** H14
Lehighton *U.S.A.* 40°50N 75°43W **83** F9
Lehutu *Botswana* 23°54S 21°55E **56** C3
Leiah *Pakistan* 30°58N 70°58E **42** D4
Leicester *U.K.* 52°38N 1°8W **13** E6
Leicester City □ *U.K.* 52°38N 1°9W **13** E6
Leicestershire □ *U.K.* 52°41N 1°17W **13** E6
Leichhardt → *Australia* 17°35S 139°48E **62** B2
Leichhardt Ra. *Australia* 20°46S 147°40E **62** C4
Leiden *Neths.* 52°9N 4°30E **15** B4
Leie → *Belgium* 51°2N 3°45E **15** C3
Leimus *Nic.* 14°40N 84°3W **88** D3
Leine → *Germany* 52°43N 9°36E **16** B5
Leinster *Australia* 27°51S 120°36E **61** E3
Leinster □ *Ireland* 53°3N 7°8W **10** C4
Leinster, Mt. *Ireland* 52°37N 6°46W **10** D5
Leipzig *Germany* 51°18N 12°22E **16** C7
Leiria *Portugal* 39°46N 8°53W **21** C1
Leirvik *Norway* 59°47N 5°28E **9** G11
Leisler, Mt. *Australia* 23°23S 129°20E **60** D4
Leith *U.K.* 55°59N 3°11W **11** F5
Leith Hill *U.K.* 51°11N 0°22W **13** F7
Leitir Ceanainn = Letterkenny
  Ireland 54°57N 7°45W **10** B4
Leitrim *Ireland* 54°0N 8°5W **10** B3
Leitrim □ *Ireland* 54°8N 8°0W **10** B4
Leizhou Bandao *China* 21°0N 110°0E **33** G11
Lek → *Neths.* 51°54N 4°35E **15** C4
Leka *Norway* 65°5N 11°35E **8** D14
Leland *Mich., U.S.A.* 45°1N 85°45W **81** C11
Leland *Miss., U.S.A.* 33°24N 90°54W **85** E9
Leleque *Argentina* 42°28S 71°0W **96** E2
Leling *China* 37°44N 117°13E **35** F9
Lelystad *Neths.* 52°30N 5°25E **15** B5
Léman, L. *Europe* 46°26N 6°30E **20** C7
Lembar *Indonesia* 8°45S 116°4E **37** K19
Lembongan, Nusa
  Indonesia 8°40S 115°27E **37** K18
Lembuak *Indonesia* 8°36S 116°11E **37** K19
Lemera
  Dem. Rep. of the Congo 3°0S 28°55E **54** C2
Lemhi Ra. *U.S.A.* 44°0N 113°0W **76** D7
Lemmer *Neths.* 52°51N 5°43E **15** B5
Lemmon *U.S.A.* 45°57N 102°10W **80** C2
Lemon Grove *U.S.A.* 32°44N 117°1W **79** N9
Lemoore *U.S.A.* 36°18N 119°46W **78** J7
Lemvig *Denmark* 56°33N 8°20E **9** H13
Lena → *Russia* 72°52N 126°40E **29** B13

Lenadoon Pt. *Ireland* 54°18N 9°3W **10** B2
Lenggong *Malaysia* 5°6N 100°58E **39** K3
Lengua de Vaca, Pta.
  Chile 30°14S 71°38W **94** C1
Lengwe △ *Malawi* 16°14S 34°45E **55** F3
Leninogorsk *Kazakhstan* 50°20N 83°30E **28** D9
Leninsk *Russia* 48°40N 45°15E **19** E8
Leninsk-Kuznetskiy
  Russia 54°44N 86°10E **28** D9
Lenkoran = Länkäran
  Azerbaijan 38°48N 48°52E **45** B6
Lenmalu *Indonesia* 1°45S 130°15E **37** E8
Lennox *U.S.A.* 43°21N 96°53W **80** D6
Lennoxville *Canada* 45°22N 71°51W **83** A13
Lenoir *U.S.A.* 35°55N 81°32W **85** D14
Lenoir City *U.S.A.* 35°48N 84°16W **85** D12
Lenore L. *Canada* 52°30N 104°59W **71** C8
Lenox *U.S.A.* 42°22N 73°17W **83** D11
Lens *France* 50°26N 2°50E **20** A5
Lensk *Russia* 60°48N 114°55E **29** C12
Lentas *Greece* 34°56N 24°56E **25** E6
Lentini *Italy* 37°17N 15°0E **22** F6
Lenwood *U.S.A.* 34°53N 117°7W **79** L9
Lenya *Burma* 11°33N 98°57E **39** G2
Leoben *Austria* 47°22N 15°5E **16** E8
Leodhas = Lewis *U.K.* 58°9N 6°40W **11** C2
Leola *U.S.A.* 45°43N 98°56W **80** C4
Leominster *U.K.* 52°14N 2°43W **13** E5
Leominster *U.S.A.* 42°32N 71°46W **83** D13
León *Mexico* 21°6N 101°41W **86** C4
León *Nic.* 12°27N 86°51W **88** D2
León *Spain* 42°38N 5°34W **21** A3
León □ *Spain* 40°44N 93°45W **80** E7
León → *U.S.A.* 31°14N 97°28W **84** F6
León, Montes de *Spain* 42°30N 6°18W **21** A2
Leonardtown *U.S.A.* 38°17N 76°38W **81** F15
Leonardville *Namibia* 23°29S 18°49E **56** C2
Leone, Amer. Samoa *Amer. Samoa* 14°23S 170°48W **59** b
Leongatha *Australia* 38°30S 145°58E **63** F4
Leonora *Australia* 28°49S 121°19E **61** E3
Leopoldina *Brazil* 21°28S 42°40W **95** A7
Leopoldsburg *Belgium* 51°7N 5°13E **15** C5
Leoti *U.S.A.* 38°29N 101°21W **80** F3
Leova *Moldova* 46°28N 28°15E **17** E15
Leoville *Canada* 53°39N 107°33W **71** C7
Lepel = Lyepyel *Belarus* 54°50N 28°40E **9** J23
Lépo, L. do *Angola* 17°0S 19°0E **56** B2
Leppävirta *Finland* 62°29N 27°46E **8** E22
Leptis Magna *Libya* 32°40N 14°12E **51** B8
Lercara Friddi *Italy* 37°44N 13°36E *ILLEGIBLE*
Léré *Chad* 9°39N 14°13E **51** G8
Leribe *Lesotho* 28°51S 28°3E **57** D4
Lérida = Lleida *Spain* 41°37N 0°39E **21** B6
Lerwick *U.K.* 60°9N 1°9W **11** A7
Les Cayes *Haiti* 18°15N 73°46W **89** C5
Les Coteaux *Canada* 45°15N 74°13W **83** A10
Les Escoumins *Canada* 48°21N 69°24W **73** C6
Les Sables-d'Olonne
  France 46°30N 1°45W **20** C3
Lesbos *Greece* 39°10N 26°20E **23** E12
Leshan *China* 29°33N 103°41E **32** D5
Leshukonskoye *Russia* 64°54N 45°46E **18** B8
Leshwe △
  Dem. Rep. of the Congo 12°45S 29°30E **55** E2
Leskov I. *Antarctica* 56°0S 28°0W **5** B1
Leskovac *Serbia* 43°0N 21°58E **23** C9
Lesopilnoye *Russia* 46°44N 134°20E **30** A7
Lesozavodsk *Russia* 45°30N 133°29E **30** B6
Lesse → *Belgium* 50°15N 4°54E **15** D4
Lesse et Lomme = Lomme
  Belgium 50°8N 5°9E **15** D5
Lesser Antilles *W. Indies* 15°0N 61°0W **89** D7
Lesser Slave L. *Canada* 55°30N 115°25W **70** B5
Lesser Sunda Is. *Indonesia* 8°0S 120°0E **37** F6
Lessines *Belgium* 50°42N 3°50E **15** D3
Lester B. Pearson Int., Toronto ✈
  (YYZ) *Canada* 43°46N 79°35W **82** C5
Lestock *Canada* 51°19N 103°59W **71** C8
Lesueur I. *Australia* 13°50S 127°17E **60** B4
Lesueur △ *Australia* 30°11S 115°10E **61** F2
Lésvos = Lesbos *Greece* 39°10N 26°20E **23** E12
Leszno *Poland* 51°50N 16°30E **17** C9
Letaba *S. Africa* 23°59S 31°50E **57** C5
Letchworth *U.K.* 51°59N 0°13W **13** F7
Lethbridge *Canada* 49°45N 112°45W **70** D6
Lethem *Guyana* 3°20N 59°50W **92** C7
Leti, Kepulauan *Indonesia* 8°10S 128°0E **37** F7
Leti Is. = Leti, Kepulauan
  Indonesia 8°10S 128°0E **37** F7
Letiahau → *Botswana* 21°16S 24°0E **56** C3
Leticia *Colombia* 4°9S 70°0W **92** D5
Leting *China* 39°23N 118°55E **35** E10
Letjiesbos *S. Africa* 32°34S 22°16E **56** E3
Letlhakane *Botswana* 21°27S 25°30E **56** C4
Letlhakeng *Botswana* 24°0S 24°59E **56** C3
Letpadan *Burma* 17°45N 95°45E **41** L19
Letpan *Burma* 19°28N 94°10E **41** K19
Letsôk-aw Kyun *Burma* 11°30N 98°25E **39** G2
Letterkenny *Ireland* 54°57N 7°45W **10** B4
Leucadia *U.S.A.* 33°4N 117°18W **79** M9
Leuchars *U.K.* 56°24N 2°53W **11** E6
Leuser, Gunung *Indonesia* 3°46N 97°12E **36** D1
Leuven *Belgium* 50°52N 4°42E **15** D4
Leuze-en-Hainaut
  Belgium 50°36N 3°37E **15** D3
Levanger *Norway* 63°45N 11°19E **8** E14
Levelland *U.S.A.* 33°35N 102°23W **84** E3
Leven *U.K.* 56°12N 3°0W **11** E6
Leven, L. *U.K.* 56°12N 3°22W **11** E5
Leven, Toraka *Madag.* 12°30S 47°45E **57** A8
Leveque C. *Australia* 16°20S 123°0E **60** C3
Levice *Slovak Rep.* 48°13N 18°35E **17** D10
Levin *N.Z.* 40°37S 175°18E **59** D5
Lévis *Canada* 46°48N 71°9W **73** C5
Levis, L. *Canada* 62°37N 117°58W **70** A5
Levittown *N.Y., U.S.A.* 40°44N 73°31W **83** F11
Levittown *Pa., U.S.A.* 40°9N 74°51W **83** F10
Levka Oros *Greece* 35°18N 24°3E **25** D6
Levkás = Lefkada *Greece* 38°40N 20°43E **23** E9
Levkôsia = Nicosia
  Cyprus 35°10N 33°25E **25** D12
Levskigrad = Karlovo
  Bulgaria 42°38N 24°47E **23** C11

Levuka *Fiji* 17°34S 179°0E **59** a
Lewes *U.K.* 50°52N 0°1E **13** G8
Lewes *U.S.A.* 38°46N 75°9W **81** F16
Lewis *U.K.* 58°9N 6°40W **11** C2
Lewis → *U.S.A.* 45°51N 122°48W **78** E4
Lewis, Butt of *U.K.* 58°31N 6°16W **11** C2
Lewis and Clark △
  U.S.A. 46°8N 123°53W **78** D3
Lewis Ra. *Australia* 20°3S 128°50E **60** D4
Lewis Range *U.S.A.* 48°5N 113°5W **76** B7
Lewis Run *U.S.A.* 41°52N 78°40W **82** E6
Lewisburg *Pa., U.S.A.* 40°58N 76°54W **82** F8
Lewisburg *Tenn., U.S.A.* 35°27N 86°48W **85** D11
Lewisburg *W. Va.,*
  U.S.A. 37°48N 80°27W **81** G13
Lewisporte *Canada* 49°15N 55°3W **73** C8
Lewiston *Idaho, U.S.A.* 46°25N 117°1W **76** C5
Lewiston *Maine, U.S.A.* 44°6N 70°13W **81** C18
Lewiston *N.Y., U.S.A.* 43°11N 79°3W **82** C5
Lewistown *Mont., U.S.A.* 47°4N 109°26W **76** C9
Lewistown *Pa., U.S.A.* 40°36N 77°34W **82** F7
Lexington *Ill., U.S.A.* 40°39N 88°47W **80** E9
Lexington *Ky., U.S.A.* 38°3N 84°30W **81** F11
Lexington *Mich., U.S.A.* 43°16N 82°32W **82** C2
Lexington *Mo., U.S.A.* 39°11N 93°52W **80** F7
Lexington *N.C., U.S.A.* 35°49N 80°15W **85** D14
Lexington *N.Y., U.S.A.* 42°15N 74°22W **83** D10
Lexington *Nebr., U.S.A.* 40°47N 99°45W **80** E5
Lexington *Ohio, U.S.A.* 40°41N 82°35W **82** F2
Lexington *Tenn., U.S.A.* 35°39N 88°24W **85** D10
Lexington *Va., U.S.A.* 37°47N 79°27W **81** G14
Lexington Park *U.S.A.* 38°16N 76°27W **81** F15
Leyburn *U.K.* 54°19N 1°48W **12** C6
Leyland *U.K.* 53°42N 2°43W **12** D5
Leyte □ *Phil.* 11°0N 125°0E **37** B7
Lezhë *Albania* 41°47N 19°39E **23** D8
Lhasa *China* 29°25N 90°58E **32** F7
Lhazê *China* 29°5N 87°38E **32** F6
L'Hermite, I. *Chile* 55°50S 68°0W **96** H3
Lhokkruet *Indonesia* 4°55N 95°24E **36** D1
Lhokseumawe *Indonesia* 5°10N 97°10E **36** C1
L'Hospitalet de Llobregat
  Spain 41°21N 2°6E **21** B7
Li *Thailand* 17°48N 98°57E **38** D2
Li Shan *China* 35°30N 111°56E **34** G6
Li Xian *Gansu, China* 34°10N 105°5E **34** G3
Li Xian *Hebei, China* 38°30N 115°35E **34** E8
Liancourt Rocks = Tokdo
  Asia 37°15N 131°52E **31** F5
Lianga *Phil.* 8°38N 126°6E **37** C7
Liangcheng *Nei Monggol Zizhiqu,*
  China 40°28N 112°25E **34** D7
Liangcheng *Shandong,*
  China 35°32N 119°37E **35** G10
Liangdang *China* 33°56N 106°18E **34** H4
Liangpran *Indonesia* 1°4N 114°23E **36** D4
Lianshanguan *China* 40°53N 123°43E **35** D12
Lianshui *China* 33°42N 119°20E **35** H10
Lianyungang *China* 34°40N 119°11E **35** G10
Liao He → *China* 41°0N 121°50E **35** D11
Liaocheng *China* 36°28N 115°58E **34** F8
Liaodong Bandao *China* 40°0N 122°30E **35** E12
Liaodong Wan *China* 40°20N 121°10E **35** D11
Liaoning □ *China* 41°40N 122°30E **35** D12
Liaotung, G. of = Liaodong Wan
  China 40°20N 121°10E **35** D11
Liaoyang *China* 41°15N 122°58E **35** D12
Liaoyuan *China* 42°58N 125°2E **35** C13
Liaozhong *China* 41°23N 122°50E **35** D12
Liapades *Greece* 39°42N 19°40E **25** A3
Liard → *Canada* 61°51N 121°18W **70** A4
Liard River *Canada* 59°25N 126°5W **70** B3
Liari *Pakistan* 25°37N 66°30E **42** G2
Libau = Liepāja *Latvia* 56°30N 21°0E **9** H19
Libby *U.S.A.* 48°23N 115°33W **76** B6
Libenge
  Dem. Rep. of the Congo 3°40N 18°55E **52** D3
Liberal *U.S.A.* 37°3N 100°55W **80** G4
Liberec *Czech Rep.* 50°47N 15°7E **16** C8
Liberia *Costa Rica* 10°40N 85°30W **88** D2
Liberia ■ *W. Afr.* 6°30N 9°30W **50** G4
Libertador □ *Chile* 34°15S 70°45W **94** C1
Liberty *Mo., U.S.A.* 39°15N 94°25W **80** F7
Liberty *N.Y., U.S.A.* 41°48N 74°45W **83** E10
Liberty *Pa., U.S.A.* 41°34N 77°6W **82** E7
Liberty *Tex., U.S.A.* 30°3N 94°48W **84** F7
Liberty-Newark Int. ✈ (EWR)
  U.S.A. 40°42N 74°10W **83** F10
Lībîya, Sahrâ' *Africa* 25°0N 25°0E **51** C10
Libobo, Tanjung
  Indonesia 0°54S 128°28E **37** E7
Libode *S. Africa* 31°33S 29°2E **57** E4
Libong, Ko *Thailand* 7°15N 99°23E **39** J2
Libourne *France* 44°55N 0°14W **20** D3
Libramont *Belgium* 49°55N 5°23E **15** E5
Libreville *Gabon* 0°25N 9°26E **52** D1
Libya ■ *N. Afr.* 27°0N 17°0E **51** C9
Libyan Desert = Lībîya, Sahrâ'
  Africa 25°0N 25°0E **51** C10
Libyan Plateau = Ed Déffa
  Egypt 30°40N 26°30E **51** B11
Licantén *Chile* 35°55S 72°0W **94** D1
Licata *Italy* 37°6N 13°56E **22** F5
Licheng *China* 36°28N 113°20E **34** F7
Lichfield *U.K.* 52°41N 1°49W **13** E6
Lichinga *Mozam.* 13°13S 35°11E **55** E4
Lichtenburg *S. Africa* 26°8S 26°8E **56** D4
Licking → *U.S.A.* 39°6N 84°30W **81** F11
Licungo → *Mozam.* 17°40S 37°15E **55** F4
Lida *Belarus* 53°53N 25°15E **17** B13
Lidköping *Sweden* 58°31N 13°7E **9** G15
Liebig, Mt. *Australia* 23°18S 131°22E **60** D5
Liechtenstein ■ *Europe* 47°8N 9°35E **20** C8
Liège *Belgium* 50°38N 5°35E **15** D5
Liège □ *Belgium* 50°32N 5°35E **15** D5
Liegnitz = Legnica
  Poland 51°12N 16°10E **16** C9
Lieksa *Finland* 63°18N 30°2E **8** E24
Lienart
  Dem. Rep. of the Congo 3°3N 25°31E **54** B2

Lienyünchiangshih =
  Lianyungang China 34°40N 119°11E 35 G10
Lienz Austria 46°50N 12°46E 16 E7
Liepāja Latvia 56°30N 21°0E 9 H19
Lier Belgium 51°7N 4°34E 15 C4
Lietuva = Lithuania ■
  Europe 55°30N 24°0E 9 J21
Lièvre → Canada 45°31N 75°26W 72 C4
Liffey → Ireland 53°21N 6°13W 10 C5
Lifford Ireland 54°51N 7°29W 10 B4
Lifudzin Russia 44°21N 134°58E 30 B7
Lightning Ridge
  Australia 29°22S 148°0E 63 D4
Ligonha → Mozam. 16°54S 39°9E 55 F4
Ligonier U.S.A. 40°15N 79°14W 82 F5
Liguria □ Italy 44°30N 8°50E 20 D8
Ligurian Sea Medit. S. 43°20N 9°0E 22 C3
Lihou Reefs and Cays
  Australia 17°25S 151°40E 62 B5
Lihué Calel △ Argentina 38°0S 65°10W 94 D2
Lijiang China 26°55N 100°20E 32 F9
Lik → Laos 18°31N 102°30E 38 C4
Likasi
  Dem. Rep. of the Congo 10°55S 26°48E 55 E2
Likoma I. Malawi 12°3S 34°45E 55 E3
Likumburu Tanzania 9°43S 35°8E 55 D4
L'Île-Rousse France 42°38N 8°57E 20 E8
Lille France 50°38N 3°3E 20 A5
Lille Bælt Denmark 55°20N 9°45E 9 J13
Lillehammer Norway 61°8N 10°30E 8 F14
Lillesand Norway 58°15N 8°23E 9 G13
Lillian Pt. Australia 27°40S 126°6E 61 E4
Lillooet Canada 50°44N 121°57W 70 C4
Lillooet → Canada 49°15N 121°57W 70 D4
Lilongwe Malawi 14°0S 33°48E 55 E3
Liloy Phil. 8°4N 122°39E 37 C6
Lim → Europe 43°45N 19°15E 23 C8
Lim Chu Kang Singapore 1°26N 103°43E 39 d
Lima Indonesia 3°39S 127°58E 37 E7
Lima Peru 12°3S 77°2W 92 F3
Lima Mont., U.S.A. 44°38N 112°36W 76 D7
Lima N.Y., U.S.A. 42°54N 77°36W 82 D7
Lima Ohio, U.S.A. 40°44N 84°6W 81 E11
Lima → Portugal 41°41N 8°50W 21 B1
Limassol Cyprus 34°42N 33°1E 25 E12
Limavady U.K. 55°3N 6°56W 10 A5
Limay → Argentina 39°0S 68°0W 96 D3
Limay Mahuida
  Argentina 37°10S 66°45W 94 D2
Limbang Malaysia 4°42N 115°6E 36 D5
Limbaži Latvia 57°31N 24°42E 9 H21
Limbdi India 22°34N 71°51E 42 H4
Limbe Cameroon 4°1N 9°10E 52 D1
Limburg Germany 50°22N 8°4E 16 C5
Limburg □ Belgium 51°2N 5°25E 15 C5
Limburg □ Neths. 51°20N 5°55E 15 C5
Limeira Brazil 22°35S 47°28W 95 A6
Limerick Ireland 52°40N 8°37W 10 D3
Limerick U.S.A. 43°41N 70°48W 83 C14
Limerick □ Ireland 52°30N 8°50W 10 D3
Limestone U.S.A. 42°2N 78°38W 82 D6
Limestone → Canada 56°31N 94°7W 71 B10
Limfjorden Denmark 56°55N 9°0E 9 H13
Limia = Lima → Portugal 41°41N 8°50W 21 B1
Limingen Norway 64°48N 13°35E 8 D15
Limmen ◊ Australia 15°15S 135°30E 62 B2
Limmen Bight Australia 14°40S 135°35E 62 A2
Limmen Bight →
  Australia 15°7S 135°44E 62 B2
Limnos Greece 39°50N 25°5E 23 E11
Limoges Canada 45°20N 75°16W 83 A9
Limoges France 45°50N 1°15E 20 D4
Limón Costa Rica 10°0N 83°2W 88 E3
Limon U.S.A. 39°16N 103°41W 76 G12
Limousin □ France 45°30N 1°30E 20 D4
Limoux France 43°4N 2°12E 20 E5
Limpopo □ S. Africa 24°5S 29°0E 57 C4
Limpopo → Africa 25°5S 33°30E 57 D5
Limuru Kenya 1°2S 36°35E 54 C4
Lin Xian China 37°57N 110°58E 34 F6
Linares Chile 35°50S 71°40W 94 D1
Linares Mexico 24°52N 99°34W 87 C5
Linares Spain 38°10N 3°40W 21 C4
Lincang China 23°58N 100°1E 32 G9
Lincheng China 37°25N 114°30E 34 F8
Linchuan China 27°57N 116°15E 33 F12
Lincoln = Beamsville
  Canada 43°12N 79°28W 82 C5
Lincoln Argentina 34°55S 61°30W 94 C3
Lincoln N.Z. 43°38S 172°30E 59 E4
Lincoln U.K. 53°14N 0°32W 12 D7
Lincoln Calif., U.S.A. 38°54N 121°17W 78 G5
Lincoln Ill., U.S.A. 40°9N 89°22W 80 E9
Lincoln Kans., U.S.A. 39°3N 98°9W 80 F4
Lincoln Maine, U.S.A. 45°22N 68°30W 81 C19
Lincoln N.H., U.S.A. 44°3N 71°40W 83 B13
Lincoln N. Mex.,
  U.S.A. 33°30N 105°23W 77 K11
Lincoln Nebr., U.S.A. 40°49N 96°41W 80 E5
Lincoln City U.S.A. 44°57N 124°1W 76 D1
Lincoln Hav = Lincoln Sea
  Arctic 84°0N 55°0W 69 A21
Lincoln Sea Arctic 84°0N 55°0W 69 A21
Lincolnshire □ U.K. 53°14N 0°32W 12 D7
Lincolnshire Wolds U.K. 53°26N 0°13W 12 D7
Lincolnton U.S.A. 35°29N 81°16W 85 D14
Lind U.S.A. 46°58N 118°37W 76 C4
Linda U.S.A. 39°8N 121°34W 78 F5
Lindeman I. Australia 20°27S 149°3E 62 b
Lindeman Islands △
  Australia 20°28S 149°5E 62 b
Linden Guyana 6°0N 58°10W 92 B7
Linden Ala., U.S.A. 32°18N 87°48W 85 E11
Linden Calif., U.S.A. 38°1N 121°5W 78 G5
Linden Tex., U.S.A. 33°1N 94°22W 84 E7
Lindenhurst U.S.A. 40°41N 73°23W 83 F11
Lindesnes Norway 57°58N 7°3E 9 H12
Lindi Tanzania 9°58S 39°38E 55 D4
Lindi → Tanzania 9°40S 38°30E 55 D4
Lindi →
  Dem. Rep. of the Congo 0°33N 25°5E 54 B2

Lindley U.S.A. 42°1N 77°8W 82 D7
Lindos Greece 36°6N 28°4E 25 C10
Lindos, Akra Greece 36°4N 28°10E 25 C10
Lindsay Canada 44°22N 78°43W 82 B6
Lindsay Calif., U.S.A. 36°12N 119°5W 78 J7
Lindsay Okla., U.S.A. 34°50N 97°38W 84 H6
Lindsborg U.S.A. 38°35N 97°40W 80 F5
Line Islands Pac. Oc. 7°0N 160°0W 65 H12
Linesville U.S.A. 41°39N 80°26W 82 E4
Linfen China 36°3N 111°30E 34 F6
Ling Xian China 37°22N 116°30E 34 F9
Lingao China 19°56N 109°42E 38 C7
Lingayen Phil. 16°1N 120°14E 37 A6
Lingayen G. Phil. 16°10N 120°15E 37 A6
Lingbao China 34°31N 110°51E 34 G6
Lingbi China 33°33N 117°33E 35 H9
Lingchuan China 35°45N 113°12E 34 G7
Lingding Yang China 22°25N 113°44E 33 a
Lingen Germany 52°31N 7°19E 16 B4
Lingga Indonesia 0°12S 104°37E 36 E2
Lingga, Kepulauan
  Indonesia 0°10S 104°30E 36 E2
Lingga Arch. = Lingga,
  Kepulauan Indonesia 0°10S 104°30E 36 E2
Lingle U.S.A. 42°8N 104°21W 76 E11
Lingqiu China 39°28N 114°22E 34 E8
Lingshi China 36°48N 111°48E 34 F6
Lingshou China 38°20N 114°20E 34 E8
Lingshui China 18°27N 110°0E 38 C8
Lingtai China 35°0N 107°40E 34 G4
Linguère Senegal 15°25N 15°5W 50 E2
Lingwu China 38°6N 106°20E 34 E4
Lingyuan China 41°10N 119°15E 35 D10
Linhares Brazil 19°25S 40°4W 93 G10
Linhe China 40°48N 107°20E 34 D4
Linjiang China 41°50N 127°0E 35 D14
Linköping Sweden 58°28N 15°36E 9 G16
Linkou China 45°15N 130°18E 35 B16
Linnhe, L. U.K. 56°36N 5°25W 11 E3
Linosa Medit. S. 35°51N 12°50E 22 G5
Linqi China 35°45N 113°52E 34 G7
Linqing China 36°50N 115°42E 34 F8
Linqu China 36°25N 118°30E 35 F10
Linquan China 33°5N 115°17E 34 H8
Lins Brazil 21°40S 49°44W 95 A6
Linshu China 34°53N 118°38E 35 G10
Linstead Jamaica 18°8N 77°2W 88 a
Linta → Madag. 25°2S 44°5E 57 D7
Lintao China 35°26N 103°58E 34 G2
Linton Ind., U.S.A. 39°2N 87°10W 80 F10
Linton N. Dak., U.S.A. 46°16N 100°14W 80 B3
Lintong China 34°20N 109°10E 34 G5
Linwood Canada 43°35N 80°43W 82 C4
Linwood U.S.A. 42°15N 78°48W 82 D6
Linxi Hebei, China 39°42N 118°26E 35 E10
Linxi Liaoning, China 43°36N 118°2E 35 C10
Linxia China 35°36N 103°10E 32 D9
Linyanti → Africa 17°50S 25°5E 56 B4
Linyi Shandong, China 37°13N 116°54E 34 F9
Linyi Shandong, China 35°5N 118°21E 35 G10
Linying China 33°48N 113°56E 34 H7
Linz Austria 48°18N 14°18E 16 D8
Linzhenzhen China 36°30N 109°59E 34 F5
Linzhou China 36°4N 113°49E 34 F7
Linzi China 36°50N 118°20E 35 F10
Lion, G. du France 43°10N 4°0E 20 E6
Lionárisso Cyprus 35°28N 34°8E 25 D13
Lions, G. of = Lion, G. du
  France 43°10N 4°0E 20 E6
Lion's Den Zimbabwe 17°15S 30°5E 55 F3
Lion's Head Canada 44°58N 81°15W 82 B3
Lipa Phil. 13°57N 121°10E 37 B6
Lipali Mozam. 15°50S 35°50E 55 F4
Lípari Italy 38°26N 14°58E 22 E6
Lípari, Is. = Eólie, Ís.
  Italy 38°30N 14°57E 22 E6
Lipcani Moldova 48°14N 26°48E 17 D14
Liperi Finland 62°31N 29°24E 8 E23
Lipetsk Russia 52°37N 39°35E 18 D6
Lipkany = Lipcani
  Moldova 48°14N 26°48E 17 D14
Lipovets Ukraine 49°12N 29°1E 17 D15
Lippe → Germany 51°39N 6°36E 16 C4
Lipscomb U.S.A. 36°14N 100°16W 84 C4
Liptrap, C. Australia 38°50S 145°55E 63 F4
Lira Uganda 2°17N 32°57E 54 B3
Liria = Lliria Spain 39°37N 0°35W 21 C5
Lisala
  Dem. Rep. of the Congo 2°12N 21°38E 52 D4
Lisboa Portugal 38°42N 9°8W 21 C1
Lisbon = Lisboa Portugal 38°42N 9°8W 21 C1
Lisbon N. Dak., U.S.A. 46°27N 97°41W 80 B5
Lisbon N.H., U.S.A. 44°13N 71°55W 83 B13
Lisbon N.Y., U.S.A. 44°43N 75°19W 83 B9
Lisbon Ohio, U.S.A. 40°46N 80°46W 82 F4
Lisbon Falls U.S.A. 44°0N 70°4W 81 D18
Lisburn U.K. 54°31N 6°3W 10 B5
Lisburne, C. U.S.A. 68°53N 166°13W 74 B6
Liscannor B. Ireland 52°55N 9°24W 10 D2
Lisdoonvarna Ireland 53°2N 9°18W 10 C2
Lishi China 37°31N 111°8E 34 F6
Lishu China 43°20N 124°18E 35 C13
Lisianski I. U.S.A. 26°2N 174°0W 75 K5
Lisichansk = Lysychansk
  Ukraine 48°55N 38°30E 19 E6
Lisieux France 49°10N 0°12E 20 B4
Liski Russia 51°3N 39°30E 19 D6
Lismore Australia 28°44S 153°21E 63 D5
Lismore Ireland 52°8N 7°55W 10 D4
Lista Norway 58°7N 6°39E 9 G12
Lister, Mt. Antarctica 78°0S 162°0E 5 D11
Liston Australia 28°39S 152°6E 63 D5
Listowel Canada 43°44N 80°58W 82 C4
Listowel Ireland 52°27N 9°29W 10 D2
Litani → Lebanon 33°20N 35°15E 46 B4
Litchfield Calif., U.S.A. 40°24N 120°23W 78 E6
Litchfield Conn., U.S.A. 41°45N 73°11W 83 E11
Litchfield Ill., U.S.A. 39°11N 89°39W 80 F9
Litchfield Minn., U.S.A. 45°8N 94°32W 80 C6
Litchfield △ Australia 13°14S 131°1E 60 B5
Lithgow Australia 33°25S 150°8E 63 E5

Lithino, Akra Greece 34°55N 24°44E 25 E6
Lithuania ■ Europe 55°30N 24°0E 9 J21
Lititz U.S.A. 40°9N 76°18W 83 F8
Litoměřice Czech Rep. 50°33N 14°10E 16 C8
Little Abaco Bahamas 26°50N 77°30W 88 A4
Little Barrier I. N.Z. 36°12S 175°8E 59 B5
Little Belt Mts. U.S.A. 46°40N 110°45W 76 C8
Little Bighorn Battlefield △
  U.S.A. 45°34N 107°25W 76 D10
Little Blue → U.S.A. 39°42N 96°41W 80 F5
Little Buffalo → Canada 61°0N 113°46W 70 A6
Little Cayman Cayman Is. 19°41N 80°3W 88 C3
Little Churchill →
  Canada 57°30N 95°22W 71 B9
Little Colorado →
  U.S.A. 36°12N 111°48W 77 H8
Little Current Canada 45°55N 82°0W 72 C3
Little Current → Canada 50°57N 84°36W 72 B3
Little Diomede I.
  U.S.A. 65°45N 168°56W 74 B6
Little Falls Minn., U.S.A. 45°59N 94°22W 80 C6
Little Falls N.Y., U.S.A. 43°3N 74°51W 83 C10
Little Fork → U.S.A. 48°31N 93°35W 80 A7
Little Grand Rapids
  Canada 52°0N 95°29W 71 C9
Little Humboldt →
  U.S.A. 41°1N 117°43W 76 F5
Little Inagua I. Bahamas 21°40N 73°50W 89 B5
Little Karoo S. Africa 33°45S 21°0E 56 E3
Little Khingan Mts. = Xiao
  Hinggan Ling China 49°0N 127°0E 33 B14
Little Lake U.S.A. 35°56N 117°55W 79 K9
Little Laut Is. = Laut Kecil,
  Kepulauan Indonesia 4°45S 115°40E 36 E5
Little Mecatina = Petit-
  Mécatina → Canada 50°40N 59°30W 73 B8
Little Minch U.K. 57°35N 6°45W 11 D2
Little Missouri →
  U.S.A. 47°36N 102°25W 80 B2
Little Ouse → U.K. 52°22N 1°12E 13 E9
Little Rann India 23°25N 71°25E 42 H4
Little Red → U.S.A. 35°11N 91°27W 84 D9
Little River N.Z. 43°45S 172°49E 59 E4
Little Rock U.S.A. 34°45N 92°17W 84 D8
Little Ruaha → Tanzania 7°57S 37°53E 54 D4
Little Sable Pt. U.S.A. 43°38N 86°33W 80 D10
Little Sioux → U.S.A. 41°48N 96°4W 80 E5
Little Smoky →
  Canada 54°44N 117°11W 70 C5
Little Snake → U.S.A. 40°27N 108°26W 76 F9
Little Tobago
  Trin. & Tob. 11°18N 60°30W 93 J16
Little Valley U.S.A. 42°15N 78°48W 82 D6
Little Wabash → U.S.A. 37°54N 88°5W 80 G9
Little White → U.S.A. 43°40N 100°40W 80 D3
Little Zab = Zāb aş Şaghīr →
  Iraq 35°17N 43°29E 44 C4
Littlefield U.S.A. 33°55N 102°20W 84 E3
Littlehampton U.K. 50°49N 0°32W 13 G7
Littleton U.S.A. 44°18N 71°46W 83 B13
Liu He → China 40°55N 121°35E 35 D11
Liuba China 33°38N 106°55E 34 H4
Liugou China 40°57N 118°15E 35 D10
Liuhe China 42°17N 125°43E 35 C13
Liukang Tenggaja = Sabalana,
  Kepulauan Indonesia 6°45S 118°50E 37 F5
Liuli Tanzania 11°3S 34°38E 55 E3
Liupan Shan China 35°39N 106°12E 34 G4
Liupanshui China 26°38N 104°48E 32 D5
Liuwa Plain Zambia 14°20S 22°30E 53 G4
Liuzhou China 24°22N 109°22E 33 G10
Liuzhuang China 33°12N 120°18E 35 H11
Livadhia Cyprus 34°57N 33°38E 25 E12
Livadia Greece 38°27N 22°54E 23 E10
Live Oak Calif., U.S.A. 39°17N 121°40W 78 F5
Live Oak Fla., U.S.A. 30°18N 82°59W 85 F13
Lively Canada 46°26N 81°9W 81 B13
Liveras Cyprus 35°23N 32°57E 25 D11
Livermore U.S.A. 37°41N 121°47W 78 H5
Livermore, Mt. U.S.A. 30°38N 104°11W 84 F2
Livermore Falls U.S.A. 44°29N 70°11W 81 C18
Liverpool Australia 33°54S 150°58E 63 B5
Liverpool Canada 44°5N 64°41W 73 D7
Liverpool U.K. 53°25N 3°0W 12 D4
Liverpool U.S.A. 43°6N 76°13W 83 C8
Liverpool Bay U.K. 53°30N 3°20W 12 D4
Liverpool Ra. Australia 31°50S 150°30E 63 E5
Livingston Guatemala 15°50N 88°50W 88 C2
Livingston U.K. 55°54N 3°30W 11 F5
Livingston Ala., U.S.A. 32°35N 88°11W 85 E10
Livingston Calif., U.S.A. 37°23N 120°43W 78 H6
Livingston Mont.,
  U.S.A. 45°40N 110°34W 76 D8
Livingston S.C., U.S.A. 33°38N 81°7W 85 E14
Livingston Tenn.,
  U.S.A. 36°23N 85°19W 85 C12
Livingston Tex., U.S.A. 30°43N 94°56W 84 F7
Livingston, L. U.S.A. 30°50N 95°10W 84 F7
Livingston Manor
  U.S.A. 41°54N 74°50W 83 E10
Livingstone Zambia 17°46S 25°52E 55 F2
Livingstone Mts. Tanzania 9°40S 34°20E 55 D3
Livingstonia Malawi 10°38S 34°5E 55 E3
Livny Russia 52°30N 37°30E 18 D6
Livonia Mich., U.S.A. 42°23N 83°23W 81 D12
Livonia N.Y., U.S.A. 42°49N 77°40W 82 D7
Livorno Italy 43°33N 10°19E 22 C4
Livramento Brazil 30°55S 55°30W 95 C4
Liwale Tanzania 9°48S 37°58E 55 D4
Liwonde Malawi 15°4S 35°13E 55 F4
Liwonde △ Malawi 14°42S 145°30E 62 A4
Lizard I. Australia 14°42S 145°30E 62 A4
Lizard Pt. U.K. 49°57N 5°13W 13 H2
Ljubljana Slovenia 46°4N 14°33E 16 E8
Ljungan → Sweden 62°18N 17°23E 8 E17
Ljungby Sweden 56°49N 13°55E 9 H15
Ljusdal Sweden 61°46N 16°3E 8 F17
Ljusnan → Sweden 61°12N 17°8E 8 F17
Ljusne Sweden 61°13N 17°7E 8 F17
Llancanelo, Salina
  Argentina 35°40S 69°8W 94 D2

Llandeilo U.K. 51°53N 3°59W 13 F4
Llandovery U.K. 51°59N 3°48W 13 F4
Llandrindod Wells U.K. 52°14N 3°22W 13 E4
Llandudno U.K. 53°19N 3°50W 12 D4
Llanelli U.K. 51°41N 4°10W 13 F3
Llanes Spain 43°25N 4°50W 21 A3
Llangollen U.K. 52°58N 3°11W 12 E4
Llanidloes U.K. 52°27N 3°31W 13 E4
Llano U.S.A. 30°45N 98°41W 84 F5
Llano → U.S.A. 30°39N 98°26W 84 F5
Llano Estacado U.S.A. 33°30N 103°0W 84 E3
Llanos S. Amer. 5°0N 71°35W 92 C4
Llanos de Challe △ Chile 28°8S 71°1W 94 B1
Llanquihue, L. Chile 41°10S 72°50W 96 E1
Llanwrtyd Wells U.K. 52°7N 3°38W 13 E4
Llebeig, C. des Spain 39°33N 2°18E 24 B9
Lleida Spain 41°37N 0°39E 21 B6
Llentrisca, C. Spain 38°52N 1°15E 24 C7
Llera de Canales Mexico 23°19N 99°1W 87 C5
Lleyn Peninsula U.K. 52°51N 4°36W 12 E3
Llico Chile 34°46S 72°5W 94 C1
Lliria Spain 39°37N 0°35W 21 C5
Llobregat → Spain 41°19N 2°5E 21 B7
Lloret de Mar Spain 41°41N 2°53E 21 B7
Lloseta Spain 39°43N 2°52E 24 B9
Lloyd B. Australia 12°45S 143°27E 62 A3
Lloyd L. Canada 57°22N 108°57W 71 B7
Lloydminster Canada 53°17N 110°0W 71 C7
Llubí Spain 39°42N 3°0E 24 B10
Llucmajor Spain 39°29N 2°53E 24 B9
Llullaillaco, Volcán
  S. Amer. 24°43S 68°30W 94 A2
Llullaillaco △ Chile 24°50S 68°51W 94 A2
Lo → Vietnam 21°18N 105°25E 38 B5
Loa U.S.A. 38°24N 111°39W 76 G8
Loa → Chile 21°26S 70°41W 94 A1
Loaita I. S. China Sea 10°41N 114°25E 36 B4
Loange →
  Dem. Rep. of the Congo 4°17S 20°2E 52 E4
Lobatse Botswana 25°12S 25°40E 56 D4
Lobería Argentina 38°10S 58°40W 94 D4
Lobito Angola 12°18S 13°35E 53 G2
Lobos Argentina 35°10S 59°0W 94 D4
Lobos, I. Mexico 27°20N 110°36W 86 B2
Lobos, I. de Canary Is. 28°45N 13°50W 24 F6
Loc Binh Vietnam 21°46N 106°54E 38 B6
Loc Ninh Vietnam 11°50N 106°34E 39 G6
Locarno Switz. 46°10N 8°47E 20 C8
Loch Baghasdail = Lochboisdale
  U.K. 57°9N 7°20W 11 D1
Loch Garman = Wexford
  Ireland 52°20N 6°28W 10 D5
Loch Lomond and the
  Trossachs △ U.K. 56°10N 4°40W 11 E4
Loch Nam Madadh = Lochmaddy
  U.K. 57°36N 7°10W 11 D1
Lochaber U.K. 56°59N 5°1W 11 E3
Locharbriggs U.K. 55°7N 3°35W 11 F5
Lochboisdale U.K. 57°9N 7°20W 11 D1
Loche, L. La Canada 56°30N 109°30W 71 B7
Lochem Neths. 52°9N 6°26E 15 B6
Loches France 47°7N 1°0E 20 C4
Lochgilphead U.K. 56°2N 5°26W 11 E3
Lochinvar △ Zambia 15°55S 27°15E 55 F2
Lochinver U.K. 58°9N 5°14W 11 C3
Lochmaddy U.K. 57°36N 7°10W 11 D1
Lochnagar Australia 23°33S 145°38E 62 C4
Lochnagar U.K. 56°57N 3°15W 11 E5
Lochy, L. U.K. 57°0N 4°53W 11 E4
Lock Australia 33°34S 135°46E 63 E2
Lock Haven U.S.A. 41°8N 77°28W 82 E7
Lockeford U.S.A. 38°10N 121°9W 78 G5
Lockeport Canada 43°47N 65°4W 73 D6
Lockerbie U.K. 55°7N 3°21W 11 F5
Lockhart U.S.A. 29°53N 97°40W 84 G6
Lockhart, L. Australia 33°15S 119°3E 61 F2
Lockhart River
  Australia 12°58S 143°30E 62 A3
Lockhart River ◊
  Australia 12°47S 143°20E 62 A3
Lockney U.S.A. 34°7N 101°27W 84 D4
Lockport U.S.A. 43°10N 78°42W 82 C6
Lod Israel 31°57N 34°54E 46 D3
Lodeinoye Pole Russia 60°44N 33°33E 18 B5
Lodge Bay Canada 52°14N 55°51W 73 B8
Lodge Grass U.S.A. 45°19N 107°22W 76 D10
Lodhran Pakistan 29°32N 71°30E 42 E4
Lodi Italy 45°19N 9°30E 20 D8
Lodi Calif., U.S.A. 38°8N 121°16W 78 G5
Lodi Ohio, U.S.A. 41°2N 82°1W 82 E3
Lodja
  Dem. Rep. of the Congo 3°30S 23°23E 54 C1
Lodwar Kenya 3°7N 35°36E 54 B4
Łódź Poland 51°45N 19°27E 17 C10
Loei Thailand 17°29N 101°35E 38 D3
Loengo
  Dem. Rep. of the Congo 4°48S 26°30E 54 C2
Loeriesfontein S. Africa 31°0S 19°26E 56 E2
Lofoten Norway 68°30N 13°59E 8 B16
Logan Iowa, U.S.A. 41°39N 95°47W 80 E6
Logan Ohio, U.S.A. 39°32N 82°25W 81 F12
Logan Utah, U.S.A. 41°44N 111°50W 76 F8
Logan W. Va., U.S.A. 37°51N 81°59W 81 G13
Logan, Mt. Canada 60°34N 140°23W 68 C4
Logansport Ind., U.S.A. 40°45N 86°22W 80 E10
Logansport La., U.S.A. 31°58N 94°0W 84 F8
Logone → Chad 12°6N 15°2E 51 F8
Logroño Spain 42°28N 2°27W 21 A4
Lohardaga India 23°27N 84°45E 43 H11
Loharia India 23°45N 74°14E 42 H6
Loharu India 28°27N 75°49E 42 E6
Lohri Wah → Pakistan 27°27N 67°37E 42 F2
Loi-kaw Burma 19°40N 97°17E 41 K20
Loimaa Finland 60°50N 23°5E 8 F20
Loir → France 47°33N 0°32W 20 C3
Loire → France 47°16N 2°10W 20 C2
Loja Ecuador 3°59S 79°16W 92 D3
Loja Spain 37°10N 4°10W 21 D3
Loji = Kawasi Indonesia 1°38S 127°28E 37 E7

Lokandu
  Dem. Rep. of the Congo 2°30S 25°45E 54 C2
Lokeren Belgium 51°6N 3°59E 15 C3
Lokgwabe Botswana 24°10S 21°50E 56 C3
Lokichar Kenya 2°23N 35°39E 54 B4
Lokichokio Kenya 4°19N 34°13E 54 B3
Lokitaung Kenya 4°12N 35°48E 54 B4
Lokkan tekojärvi
  Finland 67°55N 27°35E 8 C22
Lokoja Nigeria 7°47N 6°45E 50 G7
Lokolo →
  Dem. Rep. of the Congo 1°43S 18°23E 52 E3
Lokoro →
  Dem. Rep. of the Congo 1°43S 18°23E 52 E3
Lola, Mt. U.S.A. 39°26N 120°22W 78 F6
Lolgorien Kenya 1°14S 34°48E 54 C3
Loliondo Tanzania 2°2S 35°39E 54 C4
Lolland Denmark 54°45N 11°30E 9 J14
Lolo U.S.A. 46°45N 114°5W 76 C6
Lom Bulgaria 43°48N 23°12E 23 C10
Lom Kao Thailand 16°53N 101°14E 38 D3
Lom Sak Thailand 16°47N 101°15E 38 D3
Loma U.S.A. 47°56N 110°30W 76 C8
Loma Linda U.S.A. 34°3N 117°16W 79 L9
Lomaloma Fiji 17°17S 178°59W 59 a
Lomami →
  Dem. Rep. of the Congo 0°46N 24°16E 54 B1
Lomas de Zamora
  Argentina 34°45S 58°24W 94 C4
Lombadina Australia 16°31S 122°54E 60 C3
Lombárdia □ Italy 45°40N 9°30E 20 D8
Lombardy = Lombárdia □
  Italy 45°40N 9°30E 20 D8
Lomblen Indonesia 8°30S 123°32E 37 F6
Lombok Indonesia 8°45S 116°30E 37 F5
Lombok, Selat Indonesia 8°30S 115°50E 37 K18
Lomé Togo 6°9N 1°20E 50 G6
Lomela
  Dem. Rep. of the Congo 2°19S 23°15E 52 E4
Lomela →
  Dem. Rep. of the Congo 0°15S 20°40E 52 E4
Lommel Belgium 51°14N 5°19E 15 C5
Lomond Canada 50°24N 112°36W 70 C6
Lomond, L. U.K. 56°8N 4°38W 11 E4
Lomonosov Ridge Arctic 88°0N 140°0E 4 A
Lomphat Cambodia 13°30N 106°59E 38 F6
Lompobatang Indonesia 5°24S 119°56E 37 F5
Lompoc U.S.A. 34°38N 120°28W 79 L6
Łomża Poland 53°10N 22°2E 17 B12
Lon, Ko Thailand 7°47N 98°23E 39 a
Loncoche Chile 39°20S 72°50W 96 D2
Londa India 15°30N 74°30E 40 M9
Londiani Kenya 0°10S 35°33E 54 C4
London Canada 42°59N 81°15W 82 D3
London U.K. 51°30N 0°3W 13 F7
London Ky., U.S.A. 37°8N 84°5W 81 G11
London Ohio, U.S.A. 39°53N 83°27W 81 F12
London, Greater □ U.K. 51°36N 0°5W 13 F7
London Gatwick ✈ (LGW)
  U.K. 51°10N 0°11W 13 F7
London Heathrow ✈ (LHR)
  U.K. 51°28N 0°27W 13 F7
London Stansted ✈ (STN)
  U.K. 51°54N 0°14E 13 F8
Londonderry U.K. 55°0N 7°20W 10 B4
Londonderry □ U.K. 55°0N 7°20W 10 B4
Londonderry, C.
  Australia 13°45S 126°55E 60 B4
Londonderry, I. Chile 55°0S 71°0W 96 H2
Londres Argentina 27°43S 67°7W 94 B2
Londrina Brazil 23°18S 51°10W 95 A5
Lone Pine U.S.A. 36°36N 118°4W 78 J8
Lonely Mine Zimbabwe 19°30S 28°49E 57 B4
Long B. U.S.A. 33°35N 78°45W 85 E15
Long Beach Calif.,
  U.S.A. 33°46N 118°11W 79 M8
Long Beach N.Y.,
  U.S.A. 40°35N 73°39W 83 F11
Long Beach Wash.,
  U.S.A. 46°21N 124°3W 78 D2
Long Branch U.S.A. 40°18N 74°0W 83 F11
Long Creek U.S.A. 44°43N 119°6W 76 D4
Long Eaton U.K. 52°53N 1°15W 12 E6
Long I. Australia 20°22S 148°51E 62 b
Long I. Bahamas 23°20N 75°10W 89 B4
Long I. Canada 54°50N 79°20W 72 B4
Long I. Ireland 51°30N 9°34W 10 E2
Long I. U.S.A. 40°45N 73°30W 83 F11
Long Island Sd. U.S.A. 41°10N 73°0W 83 E12
Long L. Canada 49°30N 86°50W 72 C2
Long Lake U.S.A. 43°58N 74°25W 83 C10
Long Point Canada 42°34N 80°25W 82 D4
Long Point B. Canada 42°40N 80°10W 82 D4
Long Prairie U.S.A. 45°59N 94°52W 80 C6
Long Prairie → U.S.A. 46°20N 94°36W 80 B6
Long Pt., Ont., Canada 42°35N 80°2W 82 D4
Long Pt., Ont., Canada 43°56N 76°53W 83 C8
Long Range Mts.
  Canada 49°30N 57°30W 73 C8
Long Reef Australia 14°1S 125°48E 60 B4
Long Sault Canada 45°2N 74°53W 83 A10
Long Str. = Longa, Proliv
  Russia 70°0N 175°0E 29 C18
Long Thanh Vietnam 10°47N 106°57E 39 G6
Long Xian China 34°55N 106°55E 34 G4
Long Xuyen Vietnam 10°19N 105°28E 39 G5
Longa, Proliv Russia 70°0N 175°0E 29 C18
Longbenton U.K. 55°1N 1°31W 12 B6
Longboat Key U.S.A. 27°23N 82°39W 85 H13
Longde China 35°30N 106°20E 34 G4
Longford Australia 41°32S 147°3E 63 G4
Longford Ireland 53°43N 7°49W 10 C4
Longford □ Ireland 53°42N 7°45W 10 C4
Longhua Guangdong, China 22°39N 114°0E 33 a
Longhua Hebei, China 41°18N 117°45E 35 D9
Longido Tanzania 2°43S 36°42E 54 C4
Longiram Indonesia 0°5S 115°45E 36 E5
Longjing China 42°46N 129°25E 35 C15
Longmeadow U.S.A. 42°3N 72°34W 83 D12
Longmen Shiku China 34°34N 112°10E 34 G7

Longmont *U.S.A.* 40°10N 105°6W **76** F11
Longnawan *Indonesia* 1°51N 114°55E **36** D4
Longreach *Australia* 23°28S 144°14E **62** C3
Longueuil *Canada* 45°31N 73°29W **83** A11
Longview *Tex., U.S.A.* 32°30N 94°44W **84** E7
Longview *Wash., U.S.A.* 46°8N 122°57W **78** C2
Longxi *China* 34°53N 104°40E **34** G3
Longyan *China* 25°10N 117°0E **33** F12
Longyearbyen *Svalbard* 78°13N 15°40E **4** B8
Lonoke *U.S.A.* 34°47N 91°54W **84** D9
Lonquimay *Chile* 38°26S 71°14W **96** D2
Lons-le-Saunier *France* 46°40N 5°31E **20** C6
Looe *U.K.* 50°22N 4°28E **13** G3
Lookout, C. *Canada* 55°18N 83°56W **72** A3
Lookout, C. *U.S.A.* 34°35N 76°32W **85** D16
Loolmalasin *Tanzania* 3°0S 35°53E **54** C4
Loon → *Alta., Canada* 57°8N 115°3W **70** B5
Loon → *Man., Canada* 55°53N 101°59W **71** B8
Loon Lake *Canada* 54°2N 109°10W **71** C7
Loongana *Australia* 30°52S 127°5E **61** F4
Loop Hd. *Ireland* 52°34N 9°56W **10** D2
Lop *China* 37°3N 80°11E **32** D5
Lop Nor = Lop Nur
   China 40°20N 90°10E **32** C7
Lop Nur *China* 40°20N 90°10E **32** C7
Lopatina, Gora *Russia* 50°47N 143°10E **29** D15
Lopatka, Mys *Russia* 50°52N 156°40E **29** D16
Lopburi *Thailand* 14°48N 100°37E **38** E3
Lopez *U.S.A.* 41°27N 76°20W **83** E8
Lopez, C. *Gabon* 0°47S 8°40E **52** E1
Lopphavet *Norway* 70°27N 21°15E **8** A19
Lora → *Afghan.* 31°35N 66°32E **40** D4
Lora, Hāmūn-i- *Pakistan* 29°38N 64°58E **40** E4
Lora Cr. → *Australia* 28°10S 135°22E **63** D2
Lora del Río *Spain* 37°39N 5°33W **21** D3
Lorain *U.S.A.* 41°28N 82°11W **82** E2
Loralai *Pakistan* 30°20N 68°41E **42** D3
Lorca *Spain* 37°41N 1°42W **21** D5
Lord Howe I. *Pac. Oc.* 31°33S 159°6E **58** E8
Lord Howe Rise *Pac. Oc.* 30°0S 162°30E **64** L8
Lord Loughborough I.
   Burma 10°25N 97°54E **39** G1
Lordsburg *U.S.A.* 32°21N 108°43W **77** K9
Lorestān □ *Iran* 33°30N 48°40E **45** C6
Loreto *Brazil* 7°5S 45°10W **93** E9
Loreto *Mexico* 26°0N 111°21W **86** B2
Lorient *France* 47°45N 3°23W **20** C2
Lormi *India* 22°17N 81°41E **43** H9
Lorn *U.K.* 56°26N 5°10W **11** E3
Lorn, Firth of *U.K.* 56°20N 5°40W **11** E3
Lorne *Australia* 38°33S 143°59E **63** F3
Lorovouno *Cyprus* 35°8N 32°36E **25** D11
Lorraine □ *France* 48°53N 6°0E **20** B7
Los Alamos *Calif.,
   U.S.A.* 34°44N 120°17W **79** L6
Los Alamos *N. Mex.,
   U.S.A.* 35°53N 106°19W **77** J10
Los Altos *U.S.A.* 37°23N 122°7W **78** H4
Los Andes *Chile* 32°50S 70°40W **94** C1
Los Angeles *Chile* 37°28S 72°23W **94** D1
Los Angeles *U.S.A.* 34°4N 118°15W **79** M8
Los Angeles, Bahia de
   Mexico 28°56N 113°34W **86** B2
Los Angeles Aqueduct
   U.S.A. 35°22N 118°5W **79** K9
Los Angeles Int. ✈ (LAX)
   U.S.A. 33°57N 118°25W **79** M8
Los Banos *U.S.A.* 37°4N 120°51W **78** H6
Los Blancos *Argentina* 23°40S 62°30W **94** A3
Los Cardones △ *Argentina* 25°8S 65°55W **94** B2
Los Chiles *Costa Rica* 11°2N 84°43W **88** D3
Los Cristianos *Canary Is.* 28°3N 16°42W **24** F3
Los Gatos *U.S.A.* 37°14N 121°59W **78** H5
Los Haïtises △ *Dom. Rep.* 19°4N 69°36W **89** C6
Los Hermanos Is.
   Venezuela 11°45N 64°25W **89** D7
Los Islotes *Canary Is.* 29°4N 13°44W **24** E6
Los Llanos de Aridane
   Canary Is. 28°38N 17°54W **24** F2
Los Loros *Chile* 27°50S 70°6W **94** B1
Los Lunas *U.S.A.* 34°48N 106°44W **77** J10
Los Mochis *Mexico* 25°45N 108°57W **86** B3
Los Olivos *U.S.A.* 34°40N 120°7W **79** L6
Los Palacios *Cuba* 22°35N 83°15W **88** B3
Los Queñes *Chile* 35°1S 70°48W **94** D1
Los Reyes de Salgado
   Mexico 19°35N 102°29W **86** D4
Los Roques Is. *Venezuela* 11°50N 66°45W **89** D6
Los Teques *Venezuela* 10°21N 67°2W **92** A5
Los Testigos, Is. *Venezuela* 11°23N 63°6W **92** A6
Los Vilos *Chile* 32°10S 71°30W **94** C1
Losap *Micronesia* 6°35N 152°40E ?
Lošinj *Croatia* 44°30N 14°30E **16** F8
Loskop Dam *S. Africa* 25°23S 29°20E **57** D4
Lossiemouth *U.K.* 57°42N 3°17W **11** D5
Lostwithiel *U.K.* 50°24N 4°41W **13** G3
Lot → *France* 44°18N 0°20E **20** D4
Lota *Chile* 37°5S 73°10W **94** D1
Lotfābād *Iran* 37°32N 59°20E **45** B8
Lothair *S. Africa* 26°22S 30°27E **57** D5
Lotta → *Europe* 68°42N 31°6E **8** B24
Loubomo *Congo* 4°9S 12°47E **52** E2
Loudonville *U.S.A.* 40°38N 82°14W **82** F2
Louga *Senegal* 15°45N 16°5W **50** E2
Loughborough *U.K.* 52°47N 1°11W **12** E6
Lougheed I. *Canada* 77°26N 105°6W **69** B10
Loughrea *Ireland* 53°12N 8°33W **10** C3
Loughros More B. *Ireland* 54°48N 8°32W **10** B3
Louis Trichardt *S. Africa* 23°1S 29°43E **57** C4
Louis XIV, Pte. *Canada* 54°37N 79°45W **72** B4
Louisa *U.S.A.* 38°7N 82°36W **81** F12
Louisbourg *Canada* 45°55N 60°0W **73** C8
Louisburgh *Ireland* 53°46N 9°49W **10** C1
Louise I. *Canada* 52°55N 131°50W **70** C2
Louiseville *Canada* 46°20N 72°56W **72** C5
Louisiade Arch.
   Papua N. G. 11°10S 153°0E **58** C8
Louisiana *U.S.A.* 39°27N 91°3W **80** F9
Louisiana □ *U.S.A.* 30°50N 92°0W **84** F9
Louisville *Ky., U.S.A.* 38°15N 85°46W **81** F11

Louisville *Miss., U.S.A.* 33°7N 89°3W **85** E10
Louisville *Ohio, U.S.A.* 40°50N 81°16W **82** F3
Louisville Ridge
   Pac. Oc. 31°0S 172°30W **64** L10
Loulé *Portugal* 37°9N 8°0W **21** D1
Loup City *U.S.A.* 41°17N 98°58W **80** E4
Loups Marins, Lacs des
   Canada 56°30N 73°45W **72** A5
Lourdes *France* 43°6N 0°3W **20** E3
Lourdes-de-Blanc-Sablon
   Canada 51°24N 57°12W **73** B8
Louroujina *Cyprus* 35°0N 33°28E **25** E12
Louth *Australia* 30°30S 145°8E **63** E4
Louth *Ireland* 53°58N 6°32W **10** C5
Louth *U.K.* 53°22N 0°1W **12** D7
Louth □ *Ireland* 53°56N 6°34W **10** C5
Louvain = Leuven
   Belgium 50°52N 4°42E **15** D4
Louwsburg *S. Africa* 27°37S 31°7E **57** D5
Lovech *Bulgaria* 43°8N 24°42E **23** C11
Loveland *U.S.A.* 40°24N 105°5W **76** F11
Lovell *U.S.A.* 44°50N 108°24W **76** D9
Lovelock *U.S.A.* 40°11N 118°28W **76** F4
Loviisa *Finland* 60°28N 26°12E **8** F22
Lovina *Indonesia* 8°9S 115°1E **37** J18
Loving *U.S.A.* 32°17N 104°6W **77** K11
Lovington *U.S.A.* 32°57N 103°21W **77** K12
Lovisa = Loviisa *Finland* 60°28N 26°12E **8** F22
Low, L. *Canada* 52°29N 76°17W **72** B4
Low Pt. *Australia* 32°25S 127°25E **61** F4
Low Tatra = Nízké Tatry
   Slovak Rep. 48°55N 19°30E **17** D10
Lowa
   Dem. Rep. of the Congo 1°25S 25°47E **54** C2
Lowa →
   Dem. Rep. of the Congo 1°24S 25°51E **54** C2
Lowell *U.S.A.* 42°38N 71°19W **83** D13
Lowellville *U.S.A.* 41°2N 80°32W **82** E4
Löwen → *Namibia* 26°51S 18°17E **56** D2
Lower Alkali L. *U.S.A.* 41°16N 120°2W **76** F3
Lower Arrow L. *Canada* 49°40N 118°5W **70** D5
Lower California = Baja California
   Mexico 31°0N 115°12W **86** A1
Lower Hutt *N.Z.* 41°10S 174°55E **59** D5
Lower Lake *U.S.A.* 38°55N 122°37W **78** G4
Lower Manitou L.
   Canada 49°15N 93°0W **71** D10
Lower Post *Canada* 59°58N 128°30W **70** B3
Lower Red L. *U.S.A.* 47°58N 95°0W **80** B7
Lower Saxony = Niedersachsen □
   Germany 52°50N 9°0E **16** B5
Lower Tunguska = Tunguska,
   Nizhnyaya → *Russia* 65°48N 88°4E **29** C9
Lower Zambezi △ *Zambia* 15°25S 29°40E **55** F2
Lowestoft *U.K.* 52°29N 1°45E **13** E9
Lowgar □ *Afghan.* 34°0N 69°0E **40** B6
Łowicz *Poland* 52°6N 19°55E **17** B10
Lowther I. *Canada* 74°33N 97°30W **69** C12
Lowville *U.S.A.* 43°47N 75°29W **83** C9
Loxton *Australia* 34°28S 140°31E **63** E3
Loxton *S. Africa* 31°30S 22°22E **56** E3
Loyalton *U.S.A.* 39°41N 120°14W **78** F6
Loyalty Is. = Loyauté, Îs.
   N. Cal. 20°50S 166°30E **58** D9
Loyang = Luoyang
   China 34°40N 112°26E **34** G7
Loyauté, Îs. *N. Cal.* 20°50S 166°30E **58** D9
Loyev = Loyew *Belarus* 51°56N 30°46E **17** C16
Loyew *Belarus* 51°56N 30°46E **17** C16
Loyoro *Uganda* 3°22N 34°14E **54** B3
Ltaltaltuma ۞ *Australia* 23°57S 132°25E **60** D5
Lu Wo *China* 22°33N 114°6E **33** a
Luachimo *Angola* 7°23S 20°48E **52** F4
Luajan → *India* 24°44N 85°1E **43** G11
Lualaba →
   Dem. Rep. of the Congo 0°26N 25°20E **54** B2
Luambe △ *Zambia* 12°30S 32°15E **55** E3
Luampa *Zambia* 15°4S 24°20E **55** F1
Lu'an *China* 31°45N 116°29E **33** E12
Luan Chau *Vietnam* 21°38N 103°24E **38** B4
Luan He → *China* 39°20N 119°5E **35** E10
Luan Xian *China* 39°40N 118°40E **35** E10
Luancheng *China* 37°53N 114°40E **34** F8
Luanda *Angola* 8°50S 13°15E **52** F2
Luang, Doi *Thailand* 18°30N 101°15E **38** C3
Luang, Thale *Thailand* 7°30N 100°15E **39** J3
Luang Nam Tha *Laos* 20°58N 101°30E **38** B3
Luang Prabang *Laos* 19°52N 102°10E **38** C4
Luangwa *Zambia* 15°35S 30°16E **55** F3
Luangwa → *Zambia* 14°25S 30°25E **55** E3
Luangwa Valley *Zambia* 13°30S 31°30E **55** E3
Luanne *China* 40°55N 117°40E **35** D9
Luanping *China* 40°53N 117°23E **35** D9
Luanshya *Zambia* 13°3S 28°28E **55** E2
Luapula □ *Zambia* 11°0S 29°0E **55** E2
Luapula → *Africa* 9°26S 28°33E **55** D2
Luarca *Spain* 43°32N 6°32W **21** A2
Luashi
   Dem. Rep. of the Congo 10°50S 23°36E **55** E1
Luau *Angola* 10°40S 22°10E **52** G4
Lubana, Ozero = Lubānas Ezers
   Latvia 56°45N 27°0E **9** H22
Lubānas Ezers *Latvia* 56°45N 27°0E **9** H22
Lubang Is. *Phil.* 13°50N 120°12E **37** B6
Lubao
   Dem. Rep. of the Congo 5°17S 25°42E **54** D2
Lubbock *U.S.A.* 33°35N 101°51W **84** E4
Lübeck *Germany* 53°52N 10°40E **16** B6
Lubefu
   Dem. Rep. of the Congo 4°47S 24°27E **54** C1
Lubefu →
   Dem. Rep. of the Congo 4°10S 23°0E **54** C1
Lubero = Luofu
   Dem. Rep. of the Congo 0°1S 29°15E **54** C2
Lubicon L. *Canada* 56°23N 115°56W **70** B5
Lubilash →
   Dem. Rep. of the Congo 6°2S 23°45E **54** F4

Lubin *Poland* 51°24N 16°11E **16** C9
Lublin *Poland* 51°12N 22°38E **17** C12
Lubnān = Lebanon ■ *Asia* 34°0N 36°0E **46** B5
Lubnān, Jabal *Lebanon* 33°45N 35°40E **46** B4
Lubny *Ukraine* 50°3N 32°58E **28** D4
Lubongola
   Dem. Rep. of the Congo 2°35S 27°50E **54** C2
Lubudi *Dem. Rep. of the Congo* 9°57S 25°58E **52** F5
Lubudi →
   Dem. Rep. of the Congo 9°0S 25°35E **55** D2
Lubuklinggau *Indonesia* 3°15S 102°55E **36** E2
Lubuksikaping *Indonesia* 0°10N 100°15E **36** D2
Lubumbashi
   Dem. Rep. of the Congo 11°40S 27°28E **55** E2
Lubunda
   Dem. Rep. of the Congo 5°12S 26°41E **54** D2
Lubungu *Zambia* 14°35S 26°24E **55** E2
Lubutu
   Dem. Rep. of the Congo 0°45S 26°30E **54** C2
Lucan *Canada* 43°11N 81°24W **82** C3
Lucania, Mt. *Canada* 61°1N 140°27W **68** E3
Lucas Channel = Main Channel
   Canada 45°21N 81°45W **82** A3
Lucca *Italy* 43°50N 10°29E **22** C4
Luce Bay *U.K.* 54°45N 4°48W **11** G4
Lucea *Jamaica* 18°27N 78°10W **88** a
Lucedale *U.S.A.* 30°56N 88°35W **85** F10
Lucena *Phil.* 13°56N 121°37E **37** B6
Lucena *Spain* 37°27N 4°31W **21** D3
Lučenec *Slovak Rep.* 48°18N 19°42E **17** D10
Lucerne = Luzern *Switz.* 47°3N 8°18E **20** C8
Lucerne *U.S.A.* 39°6N 122°48W **78** F4
Lucerne Valley *U.S.A.* 34°27N 116°57W **79** L10
Lucero *Mexico* 30°49N 106°30W **86** A3
Lucheng *China* 36°20N 113°11E **34** F7
Lucheringo → *Mozam.* 11°43S 36°17E **55** E4
Lucia *U.S.A.* 36°2N 121°33W **78** J5
Lucinda *Australia* 18°32S 146°20E **62** B4
Luckenwalde *Germany* 52°5N 13°10E **16** B7
Luckhoff *S. Africa* 29°44S 24°43E **56** D3
Lucknow *Canada* 43°57N 81°31W **82** C3
Lucknow *India* 26°50N 81°0E **43** F9
Lüda = Dalian *China* 38°50N 121°40E **35** E11
Lüderitz *Namibia* 26°41S 15°8E **56** D2
Lüderitzbaai *Namibia* 26°36S 15°8E **56** D2
Ludhiana *India* 30°57N 75°56E **42** D6
Ludington *U.S.A.* 43°57N 86°27W **80** D10
Ludlow *U.K.* 52°22N 2°42E **13** E5
Ludlow *Calif., U.S.A.* 34°43N 116°10W **79** L10
Ludlow *Pa., U.S.A.* 41°43N 78°56W **82** E6
Ludlow *Vt., U.S.A.* 43°24N 72°42W **83** C12
Ludvika *Sweden* 60°8N 15°14E **9** F16
Ludwigsburg *Germany* 48°53N 9°11E **16** D5
Ludwigshafen *Germany* 49°29N 8°26E **16** D5
Lueki
   Dem. Rep. of the Congo 3°20S 25°48E **54** C2
Luena
   Dem. Rep. of the Congo 9°28S 25°43E **55** D2
Luena *Zambia* 10°40S 30°25E **55** E3
Luena Flats *Zambia* 14°47S 23°17E **53** G4
Luenha = Ruenya →
   Africa 16°24S 33°48E **55** F3
Lüeyang *China* 33°22N 106°10E **34** H4
Lufira →
   Dem. Rep. of the Congo 9°30S 27°0E **55** D2
Lufkin *U.S.A.* 31°21N 94°44W **84** F7
Lufupa
   Dem. Rep. of the Congo 10°37S 24°56E **55** E1
Luga *Russia* 58°40N 29°55E **9** G23
Lugano *Switz.* 46°1N 8°57E **20** C8
Lugansk = Luhansk
   Ukraine 48°38N 39°15E **19** E6
Lugard's Falls *Kenya* 3°6S 38°41E **54** C4
Lugela *Mozam.* 16°25S 36°43E **55** F4
Lugenda →
   Mozam. 11°25S 38°33E **55** E4
Lugh = Luuq *Somali Rep.* 3°48N 42°34E **47** G3
Lugnaquillia *Ireland* 52°58N 6°28W **10** D5
Lugo *Italy* 44°25N 11°54E **22** B4
Lugo *Spain* 43°2N 7°35W **21** A2
Lugoj *Romania* 45°42N 21°57E **17** F11

Lumberton *U.S.A.* 34°37N 79°0W **85** D15
Lumsden *Canada* 50°39N 104°52W **71** C8
Lumsden *N.Z.* 45°44S 168°27E **59** F2
Lumut *Malaysia* 4°13N 100°37E **39** K3
Lumut, Tanjung
   Indonesia 3°50S 105°58E **36** E3
Luna *India* 23°43N 69°16E **42** H3
Lunavada *India* 23°8N 73°37E **42** H5
Lund *Sweden* 55°44N 13°12E **9** J15
Lundazi *Zambia* 12°20S 33°7E **55** E3
Lundi → *Zimbabwe* 21°43S 32°34E **55** G3
Lundu *Malaysia* 1°40N 109°50E **36** D3
Lundy *U.K.* 51°10N 4°41W **13** F3
Lune → *U.K.* 54°0N 2°51W **12** C5
Lüneburg *Germany* 53°15N 10°24E **16** B6
Lüneburg Heath = Lüneburger
   Heide *Germany* 53°10N 10°12E **16** B6
Lüneburger Heide
   Germany 53°10N 10°12E **16** B6
Lunenburg *Canada* 44°22N 64°18W **73** D7
Lunéville *France* 48°36N 6°30E **20** B7
Lunga → *Zambia* 14°34S 26°25E **55** E2
Lunga Lunga *Kenya* 4°33S 39°7E **54** C4
Lunglei *India* 22°55N 92°45E **41** H18
Luni *India* 26°0N 73°6E **42** G5
Luni → *India* 24°41N 71°14E **42** G4
Luninets = Luninyets
   Belarus 52°15N 26°50E **17** B14
Luning *U.S.A.* 38°30N 118°11W **76** G4
Luninyets *Belarus* 52°15N 26°50E **17** B14
Lunkaransar *India* 28°29N 73°44E **42** E5
Lunsemfwa → *Zambia* 14°54S 30°12E **55** E3
Lunsemfwa Falls *Zambia* 14°30S 29°6E **55** E2
Luo He → *China* 34°35N 110°20E **34** G6
Luochuan *China* 35°45N 109°26E **34** G5
Luofu
   Dem. Rep. of the Congo 0°10S 29°15E **54** C2
Luohe *China* 33°32N 114°2E **34** H8
Luonan *China* 34°5N 110°10E **34** G6
Luoning *China* 34°35N 111°40E **34** G6
Luoyang *China* 34°40N 112°26E **34** G7
Luozigou *China* 43°42N 130°18E **35** C16
Lupilichi *Mozam.* 11°47S 35°13E **55** E4
Luqa *Malta* 35°50N 14°29E ?
Luquan *China* 38°4N 114°17E **34** E8
Luque *Paraguay* 25°19S 57°25W **94** B4
Luquillo, Sierra de
   Puerto Rico 18°20N 65°47W **89** d
Luray *U.S.A.* 38°40N 78°28W **81** F14
Lurgan *U.K.* 54°28N 6°19W **10** B5
Lúrio *Mozam.* 13°32S 40°30E **55** E5
Lusaka *Zambia* 15°28S 28°16E **55** F2
Lusaka □ *Zambia* 15°30S 29°0E **55** F2
Lusambo
   Dem. Rep. of the Congo 4°58S 23°28E **54** C1
Lusangaye
   Dem. Rep. of the Congo 4°54S 26°0E **54** C2
Luseland *Canada* 52°5N 109°24W **71** C7
Lusenga Plain △ *Zambia* 9°22S 29°14E **55** D2
Lushan *China* 33°45N 112°55E **34** H7
Lushi *China* 34°3N 111°3E **34** G6
Lushnjë *Albania* 40°55N 19°41E **23** D8
Lushoto *Tanzania* 4°47S 38°20E **54** C4
Lüshün *China* 38°45N 121°15E **35** E11
Lusk *U.S.A.* 42°46N 104°27W **76** E11
Lūt, Dasht-e *Iran* 31°30N 58°0E **45** D8
Luta = Dalian *China* 38°50N 121°40E **35** E11
Lutherstadt Wittenberg
   Germany 51°53N 12°39E **16** C7
Luton *U.K.* 51°53N 0°24W **13** F7
Luton □ *U.K.* 51°53N 0°24W **13** F7
Lutsel K'e *Canada* 62°24N 110°44W **71** A6
Lutsk *Ukraine* 50°50N 25°15E **17** C13
Lutto = Lotta → *Europe* 68°42N 31°6E **8** B24
Lützow Holmbukta
   Antarctica 69°10S 37°30E **5** C4
Lutzputs *S. Africa* 28°3S 20°40E **56** D3
Luuq *Somali Rep.* 3°48N 42°34E **47** G3
Luverne *Ala., U.S.A.* 31°43N 86°16W **85** F11
Luverne *Minn., U.S.A.* 43°39N 96°13W **80** D5
Luvua
   Dem. Rep. of the Congo 8°48S 25°17E **55** D2
Luvua →
   Dem. Rep. of the Congo 6°50S 27°30E **54** D2
Luvuvhu → *S. Africa* 22°25S 31°18E **57** C5
Luwegu → *Tanzania* 8°31S 37°23E **55** D4
Luwuk *Indonesia* 0°56S 122°47E **37** E6
Luxembourg *Lux.* 49°37N 6°9E **15** E6
Luxembourg □ *Belgium* 49°58N 5°30E **15** E5
Luxembourg ■ *Europe* 49°45N 6°0E **15** E5
Luxembourg ✈ (LUX)
   Lux. 49°37N 6°10E **15** E6
Luxi *China* 24°27N 98°36E **32** G8
Luxor = El Uqsur *Egypt* 25°41N 32°38E **51** C12
Luyi *China* 33°50N 115°35E **34** H8
Luza *Russia* 60°39N 47°10E **18** B8
Luzern *Switz.* 47°3N 8°18E **20** C8
Luzhou *China* 28°52N 105°20E **32** F10
Luziânia *Brazil* 16°20S 48°0W **93** G9
Luzon *Phil.* 16°0N 121°0E **37** A6
Lviv *Ukraine* 49°50N 24°0E **17** D13
Lviv □ *Ukraine* 49°30N 23°45E **17** D12
Lvov = Lviv *Ukraine* 49°50N 24°0E **17** D13
Lyakhavichy *Belarus* 53°2N 26°32E **17** B14
Lyakhovskiye, Ostrova
   Russia 73°40N 141°0E **29** B15
Lyal I. *Canada* 44°57N 81°24W **82** B3
Lyallpur = Faisalabad
   Pakistan 31°30N 73°5E **42** D5
Lyantonde *Uganda* 0°22S 31°9W **54** C3
Lyakhovskiye ✈?
Lyallpur ?

Lymington *U.K.* 50°45N 1°32W **13** G6
Łyna → *Poland* 54°37N 21°14E **17** A11
Lynchburg *U.S.A.* 37°25N 79°9W **81** G14
Lynd → *Australia* 16°28S 143°18E **62** B3
Lynd Ra. *Australia* 25°30S 149°20E **63** D4
Lynden *Canada* 43°14N 80°9W **82** C4
Lynden *U.S.A.* 48°57N 122°27W **78** B4
Lyndhurst *Australia* 30°15S 138°18E **63** E2
Lyndon → *Australia* 23°29S 114°6E **61** D1
Lyndonville *N.Y., U.S.A.* 43°20N 78°23W **82** C6
Lyndonville *Vt., U.S.A.* 44°31N 72°1W **83** B12
Lyngen *Norway* 69°45N 20°30E **8** B19
Lynher Reef *Australia* 15°27S 121°55E **60** C3
Lynn *U.S.A.* 42°28N 70°57W **83** D14
Lynn Canal *U.S.A.* 58°50N 135°15W **74** D22
Lynn Haven *U.S.A.* 30°15N 85°39W **85** F12
Lynn Lake *Canada* 56°51N 101°3W **71** B8
Lynnwood *U.S.A.* 47°49N 122°18W **78** C4
Lynton *U.K.* 51°13N 3°50W **13** F4
Lyntupy *Belarus* 55°4N 26°23E **9** J22
Lynx L. *Canada* 62°25N 106°15W **71** A7
Lyon *France* 45°46N 4°50E **20** D6
Lyonnais *France* 45°45N 4°15E **20** D6
Lyons = Lyon *France* 45°46N 4°50E **20** D6
Lyons *Ga., U.S.A.* 32°12N 82°19W **85** E13
Lyons *Kans., U.S.A.* 38°21N 98°12W **80** F4
Lyons *N.Y., U.S.A.* 43°5N 77°0W **82** C8
Lyons → *Australia* 25°2S 115°9E **61** E2
Lyons Falls *U.S.A.* 43°37N 75°22W **83** C9
Lys = Leie → *Belgium* 51°2N 3°45E **15** C3
Lysí *Cyprus* 35°6N 33°41E **25** D12
Lysva *Russia* 58°7N 57°49E **18** C10
Lysychansk *Ukraine* 48°55N 38°30E **19** E6
Lytham St. Anne's *U.K.* 53°45N 3°0W **12** D4
Lyttelton *N.Z.* 43°35S 172°44E **59** E4
Lytton *Canada* 50°13N 121°31W **70** C4
Lyubertsy *Russia* 55°40N 37°51E **18** C6
Lyuboml *Ukraine* 51°11N 24°4E **17** C13

M

Ma → *Vietnam* 19°47N 105°56E **38** C5
Ma'adaba *Jordan* 31°43N 35°47E **46** D4
Maamba *Zambia* 17°17S 26°28E **56** B4
Ma'ān *Jordan* 30°12N 35°44E **46** E4
Ma'ān □ *Jordan* 30°0N 36°0E **46** F5
Maanselkä *Finland* 63°52N 28°32E **8** E23
Maarianhamina = Mariehamn
   Finland 60°5N 19°55E **9** F18
Ma'arrat an Nu'mān
   Syria 35°43N 36°43E **44** C3
Maas → *Neths.* 51°45N 4°32E **15** C4
Maaseik *Belgium* 51°6N 5°45E **15** C5
Maasin *Phil.* 10°8N 124°50E **37** B6
Maastricht *Neths.* 50°50N 5°40E **15** D5
Maave *Mozam.* 21°4S 34°47E **57** C5
Mababe Depression
   Botswana 18°50S 24°15E **56** B3
Mabalane *Mozam.* 23°37S 32°31E **57** C5
Mabel L. *Canada* 50°35N 118°43W **70** C5
Mabenge
   Dem. Rep. of the Congo 4°15N 24°12E **54** B1
Maberly *Canada* 44°50N 76°32W **83** B8
Mablethorpe *U.K.* 53°20N 0°15E **12** D8
Maboma
   Dem. Rep. of the Congo 2°30N 28°10E **54** B2
Mabuasehube △
   Botswana 25°5S 21°10E **56** D3
Mabuiag *Australia* 9°57S 142°11E **62** a
Mac Bac *Vietnam* 9°46N 106°7E **39** H6
Macachin *Argentina* 37°10S 63°43W **94** D3
Macaé *Brazil* 22°20S 41°43W **95** A7
McAlester *U.S.A.* 34°56N 95°46W **84** D7
McAllen *U.S.A.* 26°12N 98°14W **84** H5
MacAlpine L. *Canada* 66°32N 102°45W **68** D11
Macamic *Canada* 48°45N 79°0W **72** C4
Macao = Macau *China* 22°12N 113°33E **33** a
Macapá *Brazil* 0°5N 51°4W **93** C8
Macaroa → *Venezuela* 10°22N 67°7W **89** D6
McArthur → *Australia* 15°54S 136°40E **62** B2
McArthur, Port *Australia* 16°4S 136°23E **62** B2
Macau *Brazil* 5°15S 36°40W **93** E11
Macau *China* 22°12N 113°33E **33** a
McBride *Canada* 53°20N 120°19W **70** C4
McCall *U.S.A.* 44°55N 116°6W **76** D5
McCamey *U.S.A.* 31°8N 102°14W **84** F3
McCammon *U.S.A.* 42°39N 112°12W **76** E7
McCarran Int., Las Vegas ✈ (LAS)
   U.S.A. 36°5N 115°9W **79** J11
McCauley I. *Canada* 53°40N 130°15W **70** C2
McCleary *U.S.A.* 47°3N 123°16W **78** C3
Macclenny *U.S.A.* 30°17N 82°7W **85** F13
Macclesfield *U.K.* 53°15N 2°8W **12** D5
M'Clintock Chan.
   Canada 72°0N 102°0W **68** C11
McClintock Ra.
   Australia 18°44S 127°38E **60** C4
McCloud *U.S.A.* 41°15N 122°8W **76** F2
McCluer I. *Australia* 11°5S 133°0E **60** B5
McClure *U.S.A.* 40°42N 77°19W **82** F7
McClure, L. *U.S.A.* 37°35N 120°16W **78** H6
M'Clure Str. *Canada* 75°0N 119°0W **69** C8
McClusky *U.S.A.* 47°29N 100°27W **80** B3
McComb *U.S.A.* 31°15N 90°27W **85** F9
McCook *U.S.A.* 40°12N 100°38W **80** E3
McCreary *Canada* 50°47N 99°29W **71** C9
McCullough Mt.
   U.S.A. 35°35N 115°13W **79** K11
McCusker → *Canada* 55°32N 108°39W **71** B7
McDermitt *U.S.A.* 41°59N 117°43W **76** F5
McDonald *U.S.A.* 40°22N 80°14W **82** F4
Macdonald, L. *Australia* 23°30S 129°0E **60** D4
McDonald Is. *Ind. Oc.* 53°0S 73°0E **3** G13
MacDonnell Ranges
   Australia 23°40S 133°0E **60** D5
MacDowell L. *Canada* 52°15N 92°45W **72** B1
Macduff *U.K.* 57°40N 2°31W **11** D6
Macedonia = Macedonia □
   Greece 40°39N 22°0E **23** D10
Macedonia □ *Greece* 40°39N 22°0E **23** D10

Macedonia ■ *Europe* 41°53N 21°40E **23** D9
Maceió *Brazil* 9°40S 35°41W **93** E11
Macerata *Italy* 43°18N 13°27E **22** C5
McFarland *U.S.A.* 35°41N 119°14W **78** K7
McFarlane □ *Canada* 59°12N 107°58W **71** B7
Macfarlane, L. *Australia* 32°0S 136°40E **63** E2
McGehee *U.S.A.* 33°38N 91°24W **84** E9
McGill *U.S.A.* 39°23N 114°47W **76** G6
Macgillycuddy's Reeks
　Ireland 51°58N 9°45W **10** E2
McGraw *U.S.A.* 42°36N 76°8W **83** D8
McGregor *U.S.A.* 43°1N 91°11W **80** D8
McGregor Ra. *Australia* 27°0S 142°45E **63** D3
McGuire, Mt. *Australia* 20°18S 148°23E **62** b
Mach *Pakistan* 29°50N 67°20E **42** E2
Māch Kowr *Iran* 25°48N 61°28E **45** E9
Machado = Jiparaná →
　Brazil 8°3S 62°52W **92** E6
Machagai *Argentina* 26°56S 60°2W **94** B3
Machakos *Kenya* 1°30S 37°15E **54** C4
Machala *Ecuador* 3°20S 79°57W **92** D3
Machanga *Mozam.* 20°59S 35°0E **57** C6
Machattie, L. *Australia* 24°50S 139°48E **62** C2
Macheke *Zimbabwe* 18°5S 31°51E **57** B5
Machu = *India* 23°6N 70°46E **42** H4
Machiara △ *Pakistan* 34°40N 73°30E **42** B5
Machias *Maine, U.S.A.* 44°43N 67°28W **81** C20
Machias *N.Y., U.S.A.* 42°25N 78°29W **82** D6
Machichi → *Canada* 57°3N 92°6W **71** B10
Machico *Madeira* 32°43N 16°44W **24** D3
Machilipatnam *India* 16°12N 81°8E **41** L12
Machiques *Venezuela* 10°4N 72°34W **92** A4
Machu Picchu *Peru* 13°8S 72°30W **92** F4
Machynlleth *U.K.* 52°35N 3°50W **13** E4
Macia *Mozam.* 25°2S 33°8E **57** D5
McIlwraith Ra.
　Australia 13°50S 143°20E **62** A3
McInnes L. *Canada* 52°13N 93°45W **71** C10
McIntosh *U.S.A.* 45°55N 101°21W **80** C3
McIntosh L. *Canada* 55°45N 105°0W **71** B8
Macintyre → *Australia* 28°37S 150°47E **63** D5
Mackay *Australia* 21°8S 149°11E **62** K7
Mackay *U.S.A.* 43°55N 113°37W **76** E7
MacKay → *Canada* 57°10N 111°38W **70** B6
Mackay, L. *Australia* 22°30S 129°0E **60** D4
McKay Ra. *Australia* 23°0S 122°30E **60** D3
McKeesport *U.S.A.* 40°20N 79°51W **82** F5
McKellar *Canada* 45°30N 79°55W **82** A5
McKenna *U.S.A.* 46°56N 122°33W **78** D4
Mackenzie *Canada* 55°20N 123°5W **70** B4
McKenzie *U.S.A.* 36°8N 88°31W **85** C10
Mackenzie → *Australia* 23°38S 149°46E **62** C4
Mackenzie → *Canada* 69°10N 134°20W **68** D5
McKenzie → *U.S.A.* 44°7N 123°6W **76** D2
Mackenzie Bay *Canada* 69°0N 137°30W **66** C6
Mackenzie City = Linden
　Guyana 6°0N 58°10W **92** B7
Mackenzie King I.
　Canada 77°45N 111°0W **69** B9
Mackenzie Mts. *Canada* 64°0N 130°0W **66** C6
Mackinac, Straits of
　U.S.A. 45°50N 84°40W **75** F23
Mackinaw City *U.S.A.* 45°47N 84°44W **81** C11
McKinlay *Australia* 21°16S 141°18E **62** C3
McKinlay → *Australia* 20°50S 141°28E **62** C3
McKinley, Mt. *U.S.A.* 63°4N 151°0W **68** E1
McKinley Sea *Arctic* 82°0N 0°0 **4** A7
McKinney *U.S.A.* 33°12N 96°37W **84** E6
Mackinnon Road *Kenya* 3°40S 39°1E **54** C4
McKittrick *U.S.A.* 35°18N 119°37W **79** K7
Macklin *Canada* 52°20N 109°56W **71** C7
Macksville *Australia* 30°40S 152°56E **63** E5
McLaughlin *U.S.A.* 45°49N 100°49W **80** C3
Maclean *Australia* 29°26S 153°16E **63** D5
McLean *U.S.A.* 35°14N 100°36W **84** D4
McLeansboro *U.S.A.* 38°6N 88°32W **80** F9
Maclear *S. Africa* 31°2S 28°23E **57** E4
Maclear, C. *Malawi* 13°58S 34°49E **55** E3
Macleay → *Australia* 30°56S 153°0E **63** E5
McLennan *Canada* 55°42N 116°50W **70** B5
McLeod → *Canada* 54°9N 115°44W **70** C5
MacLeod, L. *Australia* 24°9S 113°47E **61** D1
MacLeod B. *Canada* 62°53N 110°0W **71** A7
MacLeod Lake *Canada* 54°58N 123°0W **70** C4
McLoughlin, Mt.
　U.S.A. 42°27N 122°19W **76** E2
McMechen *U.S.A.* 39°57N 80°44W **82** G4
McMinnville *Oreg.,*
　U.S.A. 45°13N 123°12W **76** D2
McMinnville *Tenn.,*
　U.S.A. 35°41N 85°46W **85** D12
McMurdo *Antarctica* 77°51S 166°37E **5** D11
McMurdo Sd. *Antarctica* 77°0S 170°0E **5** D11
McMurray = Fort McMurray
　Canada 56°44N 111°7W **70** B6
McMurray *U.S.A.* 48°19N 122°14W **78** B4
Maçobere *Mozam.* 21°13S 32°47E **55** G3
Macodoene *Mozam.* 23°32S 35°5E **57** C6
Macomb *U.S.A.* 40°27N 90°40W **80** E8
Mâcon *France* 46°19N 4°50E **20** C6
Macon *Ga., U.S.A.* 32°51N 83°38W **85** E13
Macon *Miss., U.S.A.* 33°7N 88°34W **85** E10
Macon *Mo., U.S.A.* 39°44N 92°28W **80** F7
Macossa *Mozam.* 17°55S 33°56E **55** F3
Macoun L. *Canada* 56°32N 103°40W **71** B8
Macovane *Mozam.* 21°30S 35°2E **57** C6
McPherson *U.S.A.* 38°22N 97°40W **80** F6
McPherson Pk. *U.S.A.* 34°53N 119°53W **79** L7
McPherson Ra.
　Australia 28°15S 153°15E **63** D5
Macquarie → *Australia* 30°7S 147°24E **63** E4
Macquarie Harbour
　Australia 42°15S 145°23E **63** G4
Macquarie I. *Pac. Oc.* 54°36S 158°55E **64** N7
Macquarie Ridge *S. Ocean* 57°0S 159°0E **5** B10
MacRobertson Land
　Antarctica 71°0S 64°0E **5** D6
Macroom *Ireland* 51°54N 8°57W **10** E3
MacTier *Canada* 45°8N 79°47W **82** A5

Macubela *Mozam.* 16°53S 37°49E **55** F4
Macuira △ *Colombia* 12°9N 71°21W **89** D5
Macumba → *Australia* 27°52S 137°12E **63** D2
Macuro *Venezuela* 10°42N 61°55W **93** K15
Macusani *Peru* 14°4S 70°29W **92** F4
Macuspana *Mexico* 17°46N 92°36W **87** D6
Macusse *Angola* 17°48S 20°23E **56** B3
Ma'dabā □ *Jordan* 31°43N 35°47E **46** D4
Madadeni *S. Africa* 27°43S 30°3E **57** D5
Madagascar ■ *Africa* 20°0S 47°0E **57** C8
Madā'in Sālih *Si. Arabia* 22°0N 13°40E **51** D8
Madama *Niger* 22°0N 13°40E **51** D8
Madame, I. *Canada* 45°30N 60°58W **73** C7
Madang *Papua N. G.* 5°12S 145°49E **58** B7
Madaripur *Bangla.* 23°19N 90°15E **41** H17
Madauk *Burma* 17°56N 96°52E **41** L20
Madawaska *Canada* 45°30N 78°0W **82** A7
Madawaska → *Canada* 45°27N 76°21W **82** A7
Madaya *Burma* 22°12N 96°10E **41** H20
Maddalena *Italy* 41°16N 9°23E **22** D3
Madeira *Atl. Oc.* 32°50N 17°0W **24** D3
Madeira → *Brazil* 3°22S 58°45W **92** D7
Madeleine, Îs. de la
　Canada 47°30N 61°40W **73** C7
Madera *Mexico* 29°12N 108°7W **86** B3
Madera *Calif., U.S.A.* 36°57N 120°3W **78** J6
Madera *Pa., U.S.A.* 40°49N 78°26W **82** F6
Madha *India* 18°0N 75°30E **40** L9
Madhavpur *India* 21°15N 69°58E **42** J3
Madhepura *India* 26°11N 86°23E **43** F12
Madhubani *India* 26°21N 86°7E **43** F12
Madhupur *India* 24°16N 86°39E **43** G12
Madhya Pradesh □ *India* 22°50N 78°0E **42** J8
Madidi → *Bolivia* 12°32S 66°52W **92** F5
Madikeri *India* 12°30N 75°45E **40** N9
Madikwe → *S. Africa* 27°38S 32°15E **57** D5
Madill *U.S.A.* 34°6N 96°46W **84** D6
Madimba
　Dem. Rep. of the Congo 4°58S 15°5E **52** E3
Ma'din *Syria* 35°45N 39°36E **44** C3
Madinat al Malik Khālid al
　Askarīyah *Si. Arabia* 27°54N 45°31E **44** E5
Madingou *Congo* 4°10S 13°33E **52** E2
Madirovalo *Madag.* 16°26S 46°32E **57** B8
Madison *Calif., U.S.A.* 38°41N 121°59W **78** G5
Madison *Fla., U.S.A.* 30°28N 83°25W **85** F13
Madison *Ind., U.S.A.* 38°44N 85°23W **81** F11
Madison *Nebr., U.S.A.* 41°50N 97°27W **80** E5
Madison *Ohio, U.S.A.* 41°46N 81°3W **82** E3
Madison *S. Dak., U.S.A.* 44°0N 97°7W **80** C5
Madison *Wis., U.S.A.* 43°4N 89°24W **80** D9
Madison → *U.S.A.* 45°56N 111°31W **76** D8
Madison Heights *U.S.A.* 37°25N 79°8W **81** G14
Madisonville *Ky.,*
　U.S.A. 37°20N 87°30W **80** G10
Madisonville *Tex.,*
　U.S.A. 30°57N 95°55W **84** F7
Madista *Botswana* 21°15S 25°6E **56** C4
Madiun *Indonesia* 7°38S 111°32E **37** G14
Mado Gashi *Kenya* 0°44N 39°10E **54** B4
Madoc *Canada* 44°30N 77°28W **82** B7
Madoi *China* 34°46N 98°18E **32** E8
Madona *Latvia* 56°53N 26°5E **9** H22
Madrakah, Ra's al *Oman* 19°0N 57°50E **47** D6
Madras = Chennai *India* 13°8N 80°19E **40** N12
Madras = Tamil Nadu □
　India 11°0N 77°0E **40** P10
Madras *U.S.A.* 44°38N 121°8W **76** D3
Madre, L. *U.S.A.* 25°15N 97°30W **84** H6
Madre, Sierra *Phil.* 17°0N 122°0E **37** A6
Madre de Dios → *Bolivia* 10°59S 66°8W **92** F5
Madre de Dios, I. *Chile* 50°20S 75°10W **96** G1
Madre del Sur, Sierra
　Mexico 17°30N 100°0W **87** D5
Madre Occidental, Sierra
　Mexico 27°0N 107°0W **86** B3
Madre Oriental, Sierra
　Mexico 25°0N 100°0W **86** C5
Madula
　Dem. Rep. of the Congo 0°27N 25°22E **54** B2
Madura *Australia* 31°55S 127°0E **61** F4
Madura *Indonesia* 7°30S 114°0E **37** G15
Madura, Selat *Indonesia* 7°30S 113°20E **37** G15
Madurai *India* 9°55N 78°10E **40** Q11
Madurantakam *India* 12°30N 79°50E **40** N11
Mae Chan *Thailand* 20°9N 99°52E **38** B2
Mae Charim △ *Thailand* 18°17N 100°59E **38** C3
Mae Hong Son *Thailand* 19°16N 97°56E **38** C2
Mae Khlong → *Thailand* 13°24N 100°0E **38** F3
Mae Moei △ *Thailand* 17°26N 98°7E **38** D2
Mae Phang △ *Thailand* 19°7N 99°13E **38** C2
Mae Phrik *Thailand* 17°27N 99°7E **38** D2
Mae Ping △ *Thailand* 17°37N 98°51E **38** D2
Mae Ramat *Thailand* 16°58N 98°31E **38** D2
Mae Rim *Thailand* 18°54N 98°57E **38** C2
Mae Sai *Thailand* 20°20N 99°55E **38** B2
Mae Sot *Thailand* 16°43N 98°34E **38** D2
Mae Suai *Thailand* 19°39N 99°33E **38** C2
Mae Tha *Thailand* 18°28N 99°8E **38** C2
Mae Tup Res. *Thailand* 17°52N 98°45E **38** D2
Mae Wa △ *Thailand* 17°30N 99°16E **38** D2
Mae Wong △ *Thailand* 15°54N 99°12E **38** E2
Mae Yom △ *Thailand* 18°43N 100°15E **38** C3
Maebaru *Japan* 33°33N 130°12E **31** H5
Maebashi *Japan* 36°24N 139°4E **31** F9
Maelpaeg L. *Canada* 48°20N 56°30W **73** C8
Maesteg *U.K.* 51°36N 3°40W **13** F4
Maestra, Sierra *Cuba* 20°15N 77°0W **88** B4
Maevatanana *Madag.* 16°56S 46°49E **57** B8
Mafeking = Mafikeng
　S. Africa 25°50S 25°38E **56** D4
Mafeking *Canada* 52°40N 101°10W **71** C8
Mafeteng *Lesotho* 29°51S 27°15E **56** D4
Maffra *Australia* 37°53S 146°58E **63** F4
Mafia I. *Tanzania* 7°45S 39°50E **54** D4
Mafikeng *S. Africa* 25°50S 25°38E **56** D4

Mafra *Brazil* 26°10S 49°55W **95** B6
Mafra *Portugal* 38°55N 9°20W **21** C1
Mafungabusi Plateau
　Zimbabwe 18°30S 29°8E **55** F2
Magadan *Russia* 59°38N 150°50E **29** D16
Magadi *Kenya* 1°54S 36°19E **54** C4
Magadi, L. *Kenya* 1°54S 36°19E **54** C4
Magallanes, Estrecho de
　Chile 52°30S 75°0W **96** G2
Magangué *Colombia* 9°14N 74°45W **92** B4
Magdagachi *Russia* 53°27N 125°48E **29** D13
Magdalen Is. = Madeleine, Îs. de la
　Canada 47°30N 61°40W **73** C7
Magdalena *Argentina* 35°5S 57°30W **94** D4
Magdalena *Bolivia* 13°13S 63°57W **92** F6
Magdalena *U.S.A.* 34°7N 107°15W **77** J10
Magdalena → *Colombia* 11°6N 74°51W **92** A4
Magdalena → *Mexico* 30°40N 112°25W **86** A2
Magdalena, B. *Mexico* 24°35N 112°0W **86** C2
Magdalena, I. *Mexico* 24°40N 112°15W **86** C2
Magdalena, Llano de
　Mexico 25°0N 111°25W **86** C2
Magdalena de Kino
　Mexico 30°38N 110°57W **86** A2
Magdeburg *Germany* 52°7N 11°38E **16** B6
Magdelaine Cays
　Australia 16°33S 150°18E **62** B5
Magee *U.S.A.* 31°52N 89°44W **85** F10
Magelang *Indonesia* 7°29S 110°13E **37** G14
Magellan's Str. = Magallanes,
　Estrecho de *Chile* 52°30S 75°0W **96** G2
Magenta, L. *Australia* 33°30S 119°2E **61** F2
Magerøya *Norway* 71°3N 25°40E **8** A21
Maggiore, Lago *Italy* 45°57N 8°39E **20** D8
Maggotty *Jamaica* 18°9N 77°46W **88** a
Maghâgha *Egypt* 28°38N 30°50E **51** C12
Magherafelt *U.K.* 54°45N 6°37W **10** B5
Maghreb *N. Afr.* 32°0N 4°0W **48** C3
Magistralnyy *Russia* 56°16N 107°36E **29** D11
Magnetic Pole (North)
　Arctic 82°42N 114°24W **4** A1
Magnetic Pole (South)
　Antarctica 64°8S 138°8E **5** C9
Magnitogorsk *Russia* 53°27N 59°4E **18** D10
Magnolia *Ark., U.S.A.* 33°16N 93°14W **84** E8
Magnolia *Miss., U.S.A.* 31°9N 90°28W **85** F9
Mago *Fiji* 17°26S 179°8W **59** a
Magog *Canada* 45°18N 72°9W **83** A12
Magoro *Uganda* 1°45N 34°12E **54** B3
Magosa = Famagusta
　Cyprus 35°8N 33°55E **25** D12
Magoulades *Greece* 39°45N 19°42E **25** A3
Magoye *Zambia* 16°1S 27°30E **55** F2
Magpie, L. *Canada* 51°0N 64°41W **73** B7
Magrath *Canada* 49°25N 112°50W **70** D6
Magu *Tanzania* 2°30S 33°30E **54** C3
Maguarinho, C. *Brazil* 0°15S 48°30W **93** D9
Magude *Mozam.* 25°2S 32°40E **57** D5
Maǧusa = Famagusta
　Cyprus 35°8N 33°55E **25** D12
Maguse L. *Canada* 61°37N 95°10W **71** A9
Maguse Pt. *Canada* 61°20N 93°50W **71** A10
Magvana *India* 23°13N 69°22E **42** H3
Magwe *Burma* 20°10N 95°0E **41** J19
Magyarorszag = Hungary ■
　Europe 47°20N 19°20E **17** E10
Maha Sarakham
　Thailand 16°12N 103°16E **38** D4
Mahābād *Iran* 36°50N 45°45E **44** B5
Mahabharat Lekh *Nepal* 28°30N 82°0E **43** E10
Mahabo *Madag.* 20°23S 44°40E **57** C7
Mahadeo Hills *India* 22°20N 78°30E **43** H8
Mahaffey *U.S.A.* 40°53N 78°44W **82** F6
Mahagi
　Dem. Rep. of the Congo 2°20N 31°0E **54** B3
Mahajamba → *Madag.* 15°33S 47°8E **57** B8
Mahajanga, Helodranon' i
　Madag. 15°24S 47°5E **57** B8
Mahajan *India* 28°48N 73°56E **42** E5
Mahajanga *Madag.* 15°40S 46°25E **57** B8
Mahajilo → *Madag.* 19°42S 45°22E **57** B8
Mahakam → *Indonesia* 0°35S 117°17E **36** E5
Mahalapye *Botswana* 23°1S 26°51E **56** C4
Mahale Mts. *Tanzania* 6°20S 30°0E **54** D3
Mahale Mts. △ *Tanzania* 6°10S 29°50E **54** D2
Mahallāt *Iran* 33°55N 50°30E **45** C6
Mahān *Iran* 30°5N 57°18E **45** D8
Mahan → *India* 23°30N 82°50E **43** H10
Mahanadi → *India* 20°20N 86°25E **41** J15
Mahananda → *India* 25°12N 87°52E **43** G12
Mahanoro *Madag.* 19°54S 48°48E **57** B8
Mahanoy City *U.S.A.* 40°49N 76°9W **83** F8
Maharashtra □ *India* 20°30N 75°30E **40** J9
Mahasham, W. →
　Egypt 30°15N 34°10E **46** E3
Mahasoa *Madag.* 22°12S 46°6E **57** C8
Mahasolo *Madag.* 19°7S 46°22E **57** B8
Mahattat ash Shīdīyah
　Jordan 29°55N 35°55E **46** F4
Mahattat 'Unayzah
　Jordan 30°30N 35°47E **46** E4
Mahavavy → *Madag.* 15°57S 45°54E **57** B8
Mahaxay *Laos* 17°22N 105°12E **38** D5
Mahbubnagar *India* 16°45N 77°59E **40** L10
Mahda *U.A.E.* 25°20N 56°15E **45** E8
Mahdah *Oman* 24°24N 55°59E **45** E7
Mahdia *Tunisia* 35°28N 11°0E **51** A8
Mahe *India* 33°10N 78°32E **43** C8
Mahé *Seychelles* 5°0S 55°30E **53** b
Mahé ✈ (SEZ) *Seychelles* 4°40S 55°31E **53** b
Mahébourg *Mauritius* 20°24S 57°42E **53** d
Mahendranagar *Nepal* 28°17N 80°20E **43** E9
Mahenge *Tanzania* 8°45S 36°41E **55** D4
Maheno *N.Z.* 45°10S 170°50E **59** F3
Mahesana *India* 23°39N 72°26E **42** H5
Maheshwar *India* 22°11N 75°35E **42** H6
Mahgawan *India* 26°29N 78°37E **43** F8
Mahi → *India* 22°15N 72°55E **42** H5

Mahia Pen. *N.Z.* 39°9S 177°55E **59** C6
Mahilyow *Belarus* 53°55N 30°18E **17** B16
Mahina *Tahiti* 17°30S 149°27W **59** d
Mahinerangi, L. *N.Z.* 45°50S 169°56E **59** F2
Mahmud Kot *Pakistan* 30°16N 71°0E **42** D4
Mahnomen *U.S.A.* 47°19N 95°58W **80** B6
Mahoba *India* 25°15N 79°55E **43** G8
Mahón = Maó *Spain* 39°53N 4°16E **24** B11
Mahone Bay *Canada* 44°27N 64°23W **73** D7
Mahopac *U.S.A.* 41°22N 73°45W **83** E11
Mahuva *India* 21°5N 71°48E **42** J4
Mai-Ndombe, L.
　Dem. Rep. of the Congo 2°0S 18°20E **52** E3
Mai Thon, Ko *Thailand* 7°40N 98°28E **39** a
Maicuru → *Brazil* 2°14S 54°17W **93** D8
Maidan Khula *Afghan.* 33°36N 69°50E **42** C3
Maidenhead *U.K.* 51°31N 0°42W **13** F7
Maidstone *Canada* 53°5N 109°20W **71** C7
Maidstone *U.K.* 51°16N 0°32E **13** F8
Maiduguri *Nigeria* 12°0N 13°20E **51** F8
Maigh Nuad = Maynooth
　Ireland 53°23N 6°34W **10** C5
Maihar *India* 24°16N 80°45E **43** G9
Maikala Ra. *India* 22°0N 81°0E **41** J12
Maiko △
　Dem. Rep. of the Congo 0°30S 27°50E **54** C2
Mailani *India* 28°17N 80°21E **43** E9
Mailsi *Pakistan* 29°48N 72°15E **42** E5
Main → *Germany* 50°0N 8°18E **16** C5
Main → *U.K.* 54°48N 6°18W **10** B5
Main Channel *Canada* 45°21N 81°45W **82** A3
Main Range △
　Australia 28°11S 152°27E **63** D5
Main Ridge *Trin. & Tob.* 11°16N 60°40W **93** J16
Maine *France* 48°20N 0°15W **20** C3
Maine □ *U.S.A.* 45°20N 69°0W **81** C19
Maine → *Ireland* 52°9N 9°45W **10** D2
Maine, G. of *U.S.A.* 43°0N 68°30W **81** D19
Maingkwan *Burma* 26°15N 96°37E **41** F20
Mainistir an Corann = Midleton
　Ireland 51°55N 8°10W **10** E3
Mainit, L. *Phil.* 9°31N 125°30E **37** C7
Mainland *Orkney, U.K.* 58°59N 3°8W **11** C5
Mainland *Shet., U.K.* 60°15N 1°22W **11** A7
Mainpuri *India* 27°18N 79°4E **43** F8
Maintirano *Madag.* 18°3S 44°1E **57** B7
Mainz *Germany* 50°1N 8°14E **16** C5
Maio *C. Verde Is.* 15°10N 23°10W **50** b
Maipú *Argentina* 36°52S 57°50W **94** D4
Maiquetía *Venezuela* 10°36N 66°57W **92** A5
Mairabari *India* 26°30N 92°22E **41** F18
Maisí *Cuba* 20°17N 74°9W **89** B5
Maisí, Pta. de *Cuba* 20°10N 74°10W **89** B5
Maitland *N.S.W.,*
　Australia 32°33S 151°36E **63** E5
Maitland *S. Austral.,*
　Australia 34°23S 137°40E **63** E2
Maitland → *Canada* 43°45N 81°43W **82** C3
Maitri *Antarctica* 70°0S 3°0W **5** D3
Maiz, Is. del *Nic.* 12°15N 83°4W **88** D3
Maizuru *Japan* 35°25N 135°22E **31** G7
Majalengka *Indonesia* 6°50S 108°13E **37** G13
Majanji *Uganda* 0°16N 34°0E **54** B3
Majene *Indonesia* 3°38S 118°57E **37** E5
Majete △ *Malawi* 15°54S 34°34E **55** F3
Majorca = Mallorca
　Spain 39°30N 3°0E **24** B10
Majuro *Marshall Is.* 7°9N 171°12E **64** G9
Mak, Ko *Thailand* 11°49N 102°29E **39** G4
Maka *Senegal* 13°40N 14°10W **50** F3
Makaha *Zimbabwe* 17°20S 32°39E **57** B5
Makalamabedi *Botswana* 20°19S 23°51E **56** C3
Makale *Indonesia* 3°6S 119°51E **37** E5
Makalu *Asia* 27°55N 87°8E **43** F12
Makalu-Barun △ *Nepal* 27°45N 87°10E **43** F12
Makamba *Burundi* 4°8S 29°49E **54** C2
Makarikari = Makgadikgadi Salt
　Pans *Botswana* 20°40S 25°45E **56** C4
Makarov Basin *Arctic* 87°0N 150°0W **4** A
Makarovo *Russia* 57°40N 107°45E **29** D11
Makassar *Indonesia* 5°10S 119°20E **37** F5
Makassar, Selat *Indonesia* 1°0S 118°20E **37** E5
Makassar, Str. of = Makassar,
　Selat *Indonesia* 1°0S 118°20E **37** E5
Makat = Maqat
　Kazakhstan 47°39N 53°19E **19** E9
Makedonija = Macedonia ■
　Europe 41°53N 21°40E **23** D9
Makeni *S. Leone* 8°55N 12°5W **50** G3
Makeyevka = Makiyivka
　Ukraine 48°0N 38°0E **19** E6
Makgadikgadi △
　Botswana 20°27S 24°47E **56** C3
Makgadikgadi Salt Pans
　Botswana 20°40S 25°45E **56** C4
Makhachkala *Russia* 43°0N 47°30E **19** F8
Makhado = Louis Trichardt
　S. Africa 23°1S 29°43E **57** C4
Makham, Ao *Thailand* 7°51N 98°25E **39** a
Makhfar al Buşayyah
　Iraq 30°0N 46°10E **44** D5
Makhmūr *Iraq* 35°46N 43°35E **44** C4
Makian *Indonesia* 0°20N 127°20E **37** D7
Makindu *Kenya* 2°18S 37°50E **54** C4
Makīnsk *Kazakhstan* 52°37N 70°26E **28** D8
Makira = San Cristóbal
　Solomon Is. 10°30S 161°0E **58** C9
Makiyivka *Ukraine* 48°0N 38°0E **19** E6
Makkah *Si. Arabia* 21°30N 39°54E **47** C2
Makkovik *Canada* 55°10N 59°10W **73** A8
Makó *Hungary* 46°14N 20°33E **17** E11
Makokou *Gabon* 0°40N 12°50E **52** D2
Makongo
　Dem. Rep. of the Congo 3°25N 26°17E **54** B2
Makoro
　Dem. Rep. of the Congo 3°10N 29°59E **54** B2
Makrai *India* 22°2N 77°0E **42** H7
Makran Coast Range
　Pakistan 25°40N 64°0E **40** G4

Makrana *India* 27°2N 74°46E **42** F6
Makrigialos *Greece* 35°2N 25°59E **25** D7
Mākū *Iran* 39°15N 44°31E **44** B5
Makunda *Botswana* 22°30S 20°7E **56** C3
Makurazaki *Japan* 31°15N 130°20E **31** J5
Makurdi *Nigeria* 7°43N 8°35E **50** G7
Makushin Volcano
　U.S.A. 53°53N 166°55W **74** E6
Makũyeh *Iran* 28°7N 53°9E **45** D7
Makwassie *S. Africa* 27°17S 26°0E **56** D4
Makwiro *Zimbabwe* 17°58S 30°25E **57** B5
Mal B. *Ireland* 52°50N 9°30W **10** D2
Mala = Mallow *Ireland* 52°8N 8°39W **10** D3
Mala ☼ *Australia* 21°39S 130°45E **60** D5
Mala, Pta. *Panama* 7°28N 80°2W **88** E3
Malabar Coast *India* 11°0N 75°0E **40** P9
Malacca, Straits of
　Indonesia 3°0N 101°0E **39** L3
Malad City *U.S.A.* 42°12N 112°15W **76** E7
Maladzyechna *Belarus* 54°20N 26°50E **17** A14
Málaga *Spain* 36°43N 4°23W **21** D3
Malagarasi *Tanzania* 5°5S 30°50E **54** D3
Malagarasi → *Tanzania* 5°12S 29°47E **54** D2
Malagasy Rep. = Madagascar ■
　Africa 20°0S 47°0E **57** C8
Malahide *Ireland* 53°26N 6°9W **10** C5
Malaimbandy *Madag.* 20°20S 45°36E **57** C8
Malaita *Solomon Is.* 9°0S 161°0E **58** B9
Malakâl *Sudan* 9°33N 31°40E **51** G12
Malakand *Pakistan* 34°40N 71°55E **42** B4
Malakula *Vanuatu* 16°15S 167°30E **58** C9
Malakwal *Pakistan* 32°34N 73°13E **42** C5
Malamala *Indonesia* 3°21S 120°55E **37** E6
Malanda *Australia* 17°22S 145°35E **62** B4
Malang *Indonesia* 7°59S 112°45E **37** G15
Malanga *Mozam.* 13°28S 36°7E **55** E4
Malangen *Norway* 69°24N 18°37E **8** B18
Malanje *Angola* 9°36S 16°17E **52** F3
Mälaren *Sweden* 59°30N 17°10E **9** G17
Malargüe *Argentina* 35°32S 69°30W **94** D2
Malartic *Canada* 48°9N 78°9W **72** C4
Malaryta *Belarus* 51°50N 24°3E **17** C13
Malaspina Glacier
　U.S.A. 59°50N 140°30W **74** D11
Malatya *Turkey* 38°25N 38°20E **44** B3
Malawi ■ *Africa* 11°55S 34°0E **55** E3
Malawi, L. *Africa* 12°30S 34°30E **55** E3
Malay Pen. *Asia* 7°25N 100°0E **39** J3
Malaya Vishera *Russia* 58°55N 32°25E **18** C5
Malaybalay *Phil.* 8°5N 125°7E **37** C7
Malãyer *Iran* 34°19N 48°51E **45** C6
Malaysia ■ *Asia* 5°0N 110°0E **39** K4
Malazgirt *Turkey* 39°10N 42°33E **44** B4
Malbon *Australia* 21°5S 140°17E **62** C3
Malbooma *Australia* 30°41S 134°11E **63** E1
Malbork *Poland* 54°3N 19°1E **17** B10
Malcolm *Australia* 28°51S 121°25E **61** E3
Malcolm, Pt. *Australia* 33°48S 123°45E **61** F3
Maldah *India* 25°2N 88°9E **43** G13
Maldegem *Belgium* 51°14N 3°26E **15** C3
Malden *Mass., U.S.A.* 42°26N 71°3W **83** D13
Malden *Mo., U.S.A.* 36°34N 89°57W **80** G9
Malden I. *Kiribati* 4°3S 155°1W **65** H12
Maldives ■ *Ind. Oc.* 5°0N 73°0E **27** H9
Maldon *U.K.* 51°44N 0°42E **13** F8
Maldonado *Uruguay* 34°59S 55°0W **95** C5
Maldonado, Pta. *Mexico* 16°20N 98°33W **87** D5
Malé Karpaty *Slovak Rep.* 48°30N 17°0E **17** D9
Maleas, Ákra *Greece* 36°28N 23°7E **23** F10
Malebo, Pool *Africa* 4°17S 15°20E **52** E3
Malegaon *India* 20°30N 74°38E **40** J9
Malei *Mozam.* 17°12S 36°58E **55** F4
Malek Kandī *Iran* 37°9N 46°6E **44** B5
Malela
　Dem. Rep. of the Congo 4°22S 26°8E **54** C2
Malema *Mozam.* 14°57S 37°20E **55** E4
Maleme *Greece* 35°31N 23°49E **25** D5
Malerkotla *India* 30°32N 75°58E **42** D6
Males *Greece* 35°6N 25°35E **25** D7
Malgomaj *Sweden* 64°40N 16°30E **8** D17
Malha *Sudan* 15°8N 25°10E **51** E11
Malhargarh *India* 24°17N 74°59E **42** G6
Malheur → *U.S.A.* 44°4N 116°59W **76** D5
Malheur L. *U.S.A.* 43°20N 118°48W **76** E4
Mali ■ *Africa* 17°0N 3°0W **50** E5
Mali → *Burma* 25°42N 97°30E **41** G20
Mali Kyun *Burma* 13°0N 98°20E **38** F2
Malia *Greece* 35°17N 25°32E **25** D7
Malia, Kolpos *Greece* 35°19N 25°27E **25** D7
Malibu *U.S.A.* 34°2N 118°41W **79** L8
Maliku *Indonesia* 0°39S 123°16E **37** E6
Malili *Indonesia* 2°42S 121°6E **37** E6
Malimba, Mts.
　Dem. Rep. of the Congo 7°30S 29°30E **54** D2
Malin Hd. *Ireland* 55°23N 7°23W **10** A4
Malin Pen. *Ireland* 55°20N 7°17W **10** A4
Malindi *Kenya* 3°12S 40°5E **54** C5
Malindi Marine △ *Kenya* 3°15S 40°7E **54** C5
Malines = Mechelen
　Belgium 51°2N 4°29E **15** C4
Malino *Indonesia* 1°0N 121°0E **37** D6
Malinyi *Tanzania* 8°56S 36°0E **55** D4
Malita *Phil.* 6°19N 125°39E **37** C7
Maliwun *Burma* 10°17N 98°40E **39** G2
Maliya *India* 23°5N 70°46E **42** H4
Malka Mari △ *Kenya* 4°1N 40°46E **54** B5
Malkara *Turkey* 40°53N 26°53E **23** D12
Mallacoota Inlet
　Australia 37°34S 149°40E **63** F4
Mallaig *U.K.* 57°0N 5°50W **11** D3
Mallawan *India* 27°4N 80°12E **43** F9
Mallawi *Egypt* 27°44N 30°44E **51** C12
Mallicolo = Malakula
　Vanuatu 16°15S 167°30E **58** C9
Mallorca *Spain* 39°30N 3°0E **24** B10
Mallorytown *Canada* 44°29N 75°53W **83** B9
Mallow *Ireland* 52°8N 8°39W **10** D3
Malmberget *Sweden* 67°11N 20°40E **8** C19
Malmédy *Belgium* 50°25N 6°2E **15** D6
Malmesbury *S. Africa* 33°28S 18°41E **56** E2

Malmivaara = Malmberget
  Sweden 67°11N 20°40E **8** C19
Malmö Sweden 55°36N 12°59E **9** J15
Malolo Fiji 17°45S 177°11E **59** a
Malolos Phil. 14°50N 120°49E **37** B6
Malolotja △ Swaziland 26°4S 31°6E **57** D5
Malombe L. Malawi 14°40S 35°15E **55** E4
Malone U.S.A. 44°51N 74°18W **83** B10
Måløy Norway 61°57N 5°6E **8** F11
Malpaso Canary Is. 27°43N 18°3W **24** G1
Malpaso, Presa =
  Netzahualcóyotl, Presa
  Mexico 17°8N 93°35W **87** D6
Malpelo, I. de Colombia 4°3N 81°35W **92** C2
Malpur India 23°21N 73°27E **42** H5
Malpura India 26°17N 75°23E **42** F6
Malta Idaho, U.S.A. 42°18N 113°22W **76** E7
Malta Mont., U.S.A. 48°21N 107°52W **76** B10
Malta ■ Europe 35°55N 14°26E **25** D2
Maltahöhe Namibia 24°55S 17°0E **56** C2
Malton Canada 43°42N 79°38W **82** C5
Malton U.K. 54°8N 0°49W **12** C7
Maluku Indonesia 1°0S 127°0E **37** E7
Maluku □ Indonesia 3°0S 128°0E **37** E7
Maluku Sea = Molucca Sea
  Indonesia 0°0 125°0E **37** E6
Malvan India 16°2N 73°30E **40** L8
Malvern U.S.A. 34°22N 92°49W **84** H8
Malvern Hills U.K. 52°0N 2°19W **13** E5
Malvinas, Is. = Falkland Is. ⧄
  Atl. Oc. 51°30S 59°0W **96** G5
Malya Tanzania 3°5S 33°38E **54** C3
Malyn Ukraine 50°46N 29°3E **17** C15
Malyy Lyakhovskiy, Ostrov
  Russia 74°7N 140°36E **29** B15
Malyy Taymyr, Ostrov
  Russia 78°6N 107°15E **29** B11
Mama Russia 58°18N 112°54E **29** D12
Mamanguape Brazil 6°50S 35°4W **93** E11
Mamanuca Group Fiji 17°35S 177°5E **59** a
Mamarr Mitlâ Egypt 30°2N 32°54E **46** E1
Mamasa Indonesia 2°55S 119°20E **37** E5
Mambasa
  Dem. Rep. of the Congo 1°22N 29°3E **54** B2
Mamberamo → Indonesia 2°0S 137°50E **37** E9
Mambilima Falls Zambia 10°31S 28°45E **55** E2
Mambirima
  Dem. Rep. of the Congo 11°25S 27°33E **55** E2
Mambo Tanzania 4°52S 38°22E **54** C4
Mambrui Kenya 3°5S 40°5E **54** C5
Mamburao Phil. 13°13N 120°39E **37** B6
Mameigwess L. Canada 52°35N 87°50W **72** B2
Mammoth U.S.A. 32°43N 110°39W **77** K8
Mammoth Cave △
  U.S.A. 37°8N 86°13W **80** G10
Mamoré → Bolivia 10°23S 65°53W **92** F5
Mamou Guinea 10°15N 12°0W **50** F3
Mamoudzou Mayotte 12°48S 45°14E **53** a
Mampikony Madag. 16°6S 47°38E **57** B8
Mamuju Indonesia 2°41S 118°50E **37** E5
Mamuno Botswana 22°16S 20°1E **56** C3
Man Ivory C. 7°30N 7°40W **50** G4
Man, I. of U.K. 54°15N 4°30W **12** C3
Man-Bazar India 23°4N 86°39E **43** H12
Man Na Burma 23°27N 97°19E **41** H20
Mänä U.S.A. 22°2N 159°47W **75** L8
Mana → Fr. Guiana 5°45N 53°55W **93** B8
Mana Pools △ Zimbabwe 15°56S 29°25E **55** F2
Manaar, G. of = Mannar, G. of
  Asia 8°30N 79°0E **40** Q11
Manacapuru Brazil 3°16S 60°37W **92** D6
Manacor Spain 39°34N 3°13E **24** B10
Manado Indonesia 1°29N 124°51E **37** D6
Managua Nic. 12°6N 86°20W **88** D2
Managua, L. de Nic. 12°20N 86°30W **88** D2
Manakara Madag. 22°8S 48°1E **57** C8
Manali India 32°16N 77°10E **42** C7
Manama = Al Manāmah
  Bahrain 26°10N 50°30E **45** E6
Manambao → Madag. 17°35S 44°0E **57** B7
Manambato Madag. 13°43S 49°7E **57** A8
Manambolo → Madag. 19°18S 44°22E **57** B7
Manambolosy Madag. 16°2S 49°40E **57** B8
Mananara Madag. 16°10S 49°46E **57** B8
Mananara → Madag. 23°21S 47°42E **57** C8
Mananara △ Madag. 16°14S 49°45E **57** B8
Mananjary Madag. 21°13S 48°20E **57** C8
Manantenina Madag. 24°17S 47°19E **57** C8
Manaos = Manaus Brazil 3°0S 60°0W **92** D7
Manapire → Venezuela 7°42N 66°7W **92** B5
Manapouri N.Z. 45°34S 167°39E **59** F1
Manapouri, L. N.Z. 45°32S 167°32E **59** F1
Manār, Jabal Yemen 14°2N 44°17E **47** E3
Manaravolo Madag. 23°59S 45°39E **57** C8
Manas China 44°17N 86°10E **32** C6
Manas → India 26°12N 90°40E **41** F17
Manas He → China 45°38N 85°12E **32** B6
Manaslu Nepal 28°33N 84°33E **43** E11
Manasquan U.S.A. 40°8N 74°3W **83** F10
Manassa U.S.A. 37°11N 105°56W **77** H11
Manatí Puerto Rico 18°26N 66°29W **89** d
Manaung Burma 18°45N 93°40E **41** K18
Manaus Brazil 3°0S 60°0W **92** D7
Manawan L. Canada 55°24N 103°14W **71** B8
Manbij Syria 36°31N 37°57E **44** B3
Manchegorsk Russia 67°54N 32°58E **28** C4
Manchester U.K. 53°29N 2°12W **12** D5
Manchester Calif.,
  U.S.A. 38°58N 123°41W **78** G3
Manchester Conn.,
  U.S.A. 41°47N 72°31W **83** E12
Manchester Ga., U.S.A. 32°51N 84°37W **85** E12
Manchester Iowa, U.S.A. 42°29N 91°27W **80** D8
Manchester Ky., U.S.A. 37°9N 83°46W **81** G12
Manchester N.H.,
  U.S.A. 42°59N 71°28W **83** D13
Manchester N.Y., U.S.A. 42°56N 77°16W **82** D7
Manchester Tenn.,
  U.S.A. 35°29N 86°5W **85** D11

Manchester Vt., U.S.A. 43°10N 73°5W **83** C11
Manchester Int. ✈ (MAN)
  U.K. 53°21N 2°17W **12** D5
Manchester L. Canada 61°28N 107°29W **71** A7
Manchuria = Dongbei
  China 45°0N 125°0E **35** D13
Manchurian Plain China 47°0N 124°0E **26** D14
Mand → India 21°42N 83°15E **43** J10
Mand → Iran 28°20N 52°30E **45** D7
Manda Ludewa, Tanzania 10°30S 34°40E **55** E3
Manda Mbeya, Tanzania 7°58S 32°29E **54** D3
Manda Mbeya, Tanzania 8°30S 32°49E **55** D3
Mandabé Madag. 21°0S 44°55E **57** C7
Mandaguari Brazil 23°32S 51°42W **95** A5
Mandah = Töhöm
  Mongolia 44°27N 108°2E **34** B5
Mandal Norway 58°2N 7°25E **9** G12
Mandala, Puncak
  Indonesia 4°44S 140°20E **37** E10
Mandalay Burma 22°0N 96°4E **41** J20
Mandale = Mandalay
  Burma 22°0N 96°4E **41** J20
Mandalgarh India 25°12N 75°6E **42** G6
Mandalgovĭ Mongolia 45°45N 106°10E **34** B4
Mandalī Iraq 33°43N 45°28E **44** C5
Mandan U.S.A. 46°50N 100°54W **80** B3
Mandar, Teluk Indonesia 3°32S 119°21E **37** E5
Mandaue Phil. 10°20N 123°56E **37** B6
Mandera Kenya 3°55N 41°53E **54** B5
Mandeville Jamaica 18°2N 77°31W **88** a
Mandi India 31°39N 76°58E **42** D7
Mandi Burewala Pakistan 30°9N 72°41E **42** D5
Mandi Dabwali India 29°58N 74°42E **42** E6
Mandimba Mozam. 14°20S 35°40E **55** E4
Mandioli Indonesia 0°40S 127°20E **37** E7
Mandla India 22°39N 80°30E **43** H9
Mandorah Australia 12°32S 130°42E **60** B5
Mandoto Madag. 19°34S 46°17E **57** B8
Mandra Pakistan 33°23N 73°12E **42** C5
Mandrare → Madag. 25°10S 46°30E **57** D8
Mandritsara Madag. 15°50S 48°49E **57** B8
Mandronarivo Madag. 21°7S 45°38E **57** C8
Mandsaur India 24°3N 75°8E **42** G6
Mandurah Australia 32°36S 115°48E **61** F2
Mandvi India 22°51N 69°22E **42** H3
Mandya India 12°30N 77°0E **40** N10
Mandzai Pakistan 30°55N 67°6E **42** D2
Maneh Iran 37°39N 57°7E **45** B8
Manera Madag. 22°55S 44°20E **57** C7
Maneroo Cr. →
  Australia 23°21S 143°53E **62** C3
Manfalût Egypt 27°20N 30°52E **51** C12
Manfredónia Italy 41°38N 15°55E **22** D6
Mangabeiras, Chapada das
  Brazil 10°0S 46°30W **93** F9
Mangaia Cook Is. 21°55S 157°55W **65** K12
Mangalia Romania 43°50N 28°35E **17** G15
Mangalore India 12°55N 74°47E **40** N9
Mangaluru = Mangalore
  India 12°55N 74°47E **40** N9
Mangan India 27°31N 88°32E **43** F13
Mangawan India 24°41N 81°33E **43** G9
Mangaweka N.Z. 39°48S 175°47E **59** C5
Manggar Indonesia 2°50S 108°10E **36** E3
Manggawitu Indonesia 4°8S 133°32E **37** E8
Mangghystaū Tübegi
  Kazakhstan 44°30N 52°30E **28** E6
Manggis Indonesia 8°29S 115°31E **37** J18
Mangindrano Madag. 14°17S 48°58E **57** A8
Mangkalihat, Tanjung
  Indonesia 1°2N 118°59E **37** D5
Mangkururrpa ♦
  Australia 20°35S 129°43E **60** D4
Mangla Pakistan 33°7N 73°39E **42** C5
Mangla Dam Pakistan 33°9N 73°44E **43** C5
Manglaur India 29°44N 77°49E **42** E7
Mangnai China 37°52N 91°43E **32** D7
Mangnai Zhen China 38°24N 90°14E **32** D7
Mango Togo 10°20N 0°30E **50** F6
Mango Tonga 20°17S 174°29W **59** c
Mangoche Malawi 14°25S 35°16E **55** E4
Mangoky → Madag. 21°29S 43°41E **57** C7
Mangole Indonesia 1°50S 125°55E **37** E6
Mangombe
  Dem. Rep. of the Congo 1°20S 26°48E **54** C2
Mangonui N.Z. 35°1S 173°32E **59** A4
Mangoro → Madag. 20°0S 48°45E **57** B8
Mangrol Mad. P., India 21°7N 70°7E **42** J4
Mangrol Raj., India 25°20N 76°31E **42** G6
Mangueira, L. da Brazil 33°0S 52°50W **95** C5
Mangum U.S.A. 34°53N 99°30W **84** D5
Manguri Australia 28°58S 134°22E **63** A1
Mangyshlak, Poluostrov =
  Mangghystaū Tübegi
  Kazakhstan 44°30N 52°30E **28** E6
Manhattan U.S.A. 39°11N 96°35W **80** F5
Manhiça Mozam. 25°23S 32°49E **57** D5
Mania → Madag. 19°42S 45°22E **57** B8
Mania Mozam. 18°58S 32°59E **57** B5
Manica □ Mozam. 19°10S 33°45E **57** B5
Manicaland □ Zimbabwe 19°0S 32°30E **55** F3
Manicoré Brazil 5°48S 61°16W **92** E6
Manicouagan →
  Canada 49°30N 68°30W **73** B6
Manicouagan, Rés.
  Canada 51°5N 68°40W **73** B6
Maniema □
  Dem. Rep. of the Congo 3°0S 26°0E **54** C2
Manifah Si. Arabia 27°44N 49°0E **45** E6
Manifold, C. Australia 22°41S 150°50E **62** C5
Manigotagan Canada 51°6N 96°18W **71** C9
Manigotagan → Canada 51°7N 96°20W **71** C9
Manihari India 25°21N 87°38E **43** G12
Manihiki Cook Is. 10°24S 161°1W **65** J11
Manihiki Plateau
  Pac. Oc. 11°0S 164°0W **65** J11
Manika, Plateau de la
  Dem. Rep. of the Congo 10°0S 25°5E **55** E2
Manikpur India 25°4N 81°7E **43** G9

Manila Phil. 14°35N 120°58E **37** B6
Manila U.S.A. 40°59N 109°43W **76** F9
Manila B. Phil. 14°40N 120°35E **37** B6
Manilla Australia 30°45S 150°43E **63** E5
Maningrida Australia 12°3S 134°13E **62** A1
Manipur □ India 25°0N 94°0E **41** G19
Manipur → Burma 23°45N 94°20E **41** H19
Manisa Turkey 38°38N 27°30E **23** E12
Manistee U.S.A. 44°15N 86°19W **80** C10
Manistee → U.S.A. 44°15N 86°21W **80** C10
Manistique U.S.A. 45°57N 86°15W **80** C10
Manitoba □ Canada 53°30N 97°0W **71** B9
Manitoba, L. Canada 51°0N 98°45W **71** C9
Manitou Canada 49°15N 98°32W **71** D9
Manitou → Canada 50°55N 65°17W **73** B6
Manitou Is. U.S.A. 45°8N 86°0W **80** C10
Manitou L. Canada 45°55N 82°0W **80** C10
Manitou Springs
  U.S.A. 38°52N 104°55W **76** G11
Manitoulin I. Canada 45°40N 82°30W **72** C3
Manitouwadge Canada 49°8N 85°48W **72** C2
Manitowoc U.S.A. 44°5N 87°40W **80** C2
Manizales Colombia 5°5N 75°32W **92** B3
Manja Madag. 21°26S 44°20E **57** C7
Manjacaze Mozam. 24°45S 34°0E **57** C5
Manjakandriana Madag. 18°55S 47°47E **57** B8
Manjhand Pakistan 25°50N 68°10E **42** G3
Manjimup Australia 34°15S 116°6E **61** F2
Manjra → India 18°49N 77°52E **40** K10
Mankato Kans., U.S.A. 39°47N 98°13W **80** F4
Mankato Minn., U.S.A. 44°10N 94°0W **80** C6
Mankayane Swaziland 26°40S 31°4E **57** D5
Mankera Pakistan 31°23N 71°26E **42** D4
Mankota Canada 49°25N 107°5W **71** D7
Manlay = Üydzin
  Mongolia 44°9N 107°0E **34** B4
Manmad India 20°18N 74°28E **40** J9
Mann Ranges Australia 26°6S 130°5E **61** E5
Manna Indonesia 4°25S 102°55E **36** E2
Mannahill Australia 32°25S 140°0E **63** E3
Mannar Sri Lanka 9°1N 79°54E **40** Q11
Mannar, G. of Asia 8°30N 79°0E **40** Q11
Mannar I. Sri Lanka 9°5N 79°45E **40** Q11
Mannheim Germany 49°29N 8°29E **16** D5
Manning Oreg., U.S.A. 45°45N 123°13W **78** B5
Manning S.C., U.S.A. 33°42N 80°13W **85** E14
Mannum Australia 34°50S 139°20E **63** E2
Manoharpur India 22°23N 85°12E **43** H11
Manokwari Indonesia 0°54S 134°0E **37** E8
Manombo Madag. 22°57S 43°28E **57** C7
Manono
  Dem. Rep. of the Congo 7°15S 27°25E **54** D2
Manono Samoa 13°50S 172°5W **59** b
Manorhamilton Ireland 54°18N 8°9W **10** B3
Manosque France 43°49N 5°47E **20** E6
Manotick Canada 45°13N 75°41W **83** A9
Manouane → Canada 49°30N 71°10W **73** C5
Manouane, L. Canada 50°45N 70°45W **73** B5
Manp'o N. Korea 41°6N 126°24E **35** D14
Manpojin = Manp'o
  N. Korea 41°6N 126°24E **35** D14
Manpur Chhattisgarh,
  India 23°17N 83°35E **43** H10
Manpur Mad. P., India 22°26N 75°37E **42** H6
Manresa Spain 41°48N 1°50E **21** B6
Mansa Gujarat, India 23°27N 72°45E **42** H5
Mansa Punjab, India 30°0N 75°27E **42** E6
Mansa Zambia 11°13S 28°55E **55** E2
Mansehra Pakistan 34°20N 73°15E **42** B5
Mansel I. Canada 62°0N 80°0W **69** E15
Mansfield Australia 37°4S 146°6E **63** F4
Mansfield U.K. 53°9N 1°11W **12** D6
Mansfield La., U.S.A. 32°2N 93°43W **84** E8
Mansfield Mass., U.S.A. 42°2N 71°13W **83** D13
Mansfield Ohio, U.S.A. 40°45N 82°31W **82** F2
Mansfield Pa., U.S.A. 41°48N 77°5W **82** E7
Mansfield Tex., U.S.A. 32°33N 97°8W **84** E6
Mansfield, Mt. U.S.A. 44°33N 72°49W **83** B12
Manson Creek Canada 55°37N 124°32W **70** B4
Manta Ecuador 1°0S 80°40W **92** D2
Mantadia △ Madag. 18°54S 48°21E **57** B8
Mantalingajan, Mt.
  Phil. 8°55N 117°45E **36** C5
Mantare Tanzania 2°42S 33°13E **54** C3
Manteca U.S.A. 37°48N 121°13W **78** H5
Manteo U.S.A. 35°55N 75°40W **85** D17
Mantes-la-Jolie France 48°58N 1°41E **20** B4
Manthani India 18°40N 79°35E **40** K11
Manti U.S.A. 39°16N 111°38W **76** G8
Mantiqueira, Serra da
  Brazil 22°0S 44°0W **95** A7
Manton U.S.A. 44°25N 85°24W **81** C11
Mántova Italy 45°9N 10°48E **22** B4
Mänttä Vilppula Finland 62°3N 24°40E **8** E21
Mantua = Mántova Italy 45°9N 10°48E **22** B4
Manú Peru 12°10S 70°51W **92** F4
Manú → Peru 12°16S 70°55W **92** F4
Manu'a Is. Amer. Samoa 14°13S 169°35W **59** b
Manuel Alves → Brazil 11°19S 48°28W **93** F9
Manui Indonesia 3°35S 123°5E **37** E6
Manukau N.Z. 37°0S 174°52E **59** B5
Manuripi → Bolivia 11°6S 67°36W **92** F5
Many U.S.A. 31°34N 93°29W **84** F8
Manyallaluk ♦
  Australia 14°16S 132°49E **60** B5
Manyani Kenya 3°5S 38°30E **54** C4
Manyara △ Tanzania 3°35S 35°50E **54** C4
Manych-Gudilo, Ozero
  Russia 46°24N 42°38E **19** E7
Manyonga → Tanzania 4°10S 34°15E **54** C3
Manyoni Tanzania 5°45S 34°55E **54** D3
Manzai Pakistan 32°12N 70°15E **42** C4
Manzanar △ U.S.A. 36°44N 118°9W **78** J7
Manzanares Spain 39°2N 3°22E **21** C4
Manzanillo Cuba 20°20N 77°31W **88** B4
Manzanillo Mexico 19°3N 104°20W **86** D4
Manzanillo, Pta. Panama 9°30N 79°40W **88** E4
Manzano Mts. U.S.A. 34°40N 106°20W **77** J10

Manzarīyeh Iran 34°53N 50°50E **45** C6
Manzhouli China 49°35N 117°25E **33** B12
Manzini Swaziland 26°30S 31°25E **57** D5
Manzouli = Manzhouli
  China 49°35N 117°25E **33** B12
Manzur Vadisi △ Turkey 39°10N 39°30E **44** B3
Mao Chad 14°4N 15°19E **51** F9
Maó Spain 39°53N 4°16E **24** B11
Maoke, Pegunungan
  Indonesia 3°40S 137°30E **37** E9
Maolin China 43°58N 123°30E **35** C12
Maoming China 21°50N 110°54E **33** D6
Maoxing China 45°28N 124°40E **35** B13
Mapam Yumco China 30°45N 81°28E **43** D9
Mapastepec Mexico 15°26N 92°54W **87** D6
Maphrao, Ko Thailand 7°56N 98°26E **39** a
Mapia, Kepulauan
  Indonesia 0°50N 134°20E **37** D8
Mapimí Mexico 25°49N 103°51W **86** B4
Mapimí, Bolsón de
  Mexico 27°0N 104°15W **86** B4
Maping Tanzania 6°40S 39°12E **54** D4
Mapinhane Mozam. 22°20S 35°0E **57** C6
Maple Creek Canada 49°55N 109°29W **71** D7
Maple Valley U.S.A. 47°25N 122°3W **78** C4
Mapleton U.S.A. 44°2N 123°52W **76** D2
Mapoon ♦ Australia 11°4S 142°8E **62** A3
Mapuera → Brazil 1°5S 57°2W **92** D7
Mapulanguene Mozam. 24°29S 32°6E **57** C5
Mapungubwe △
  S. Africa 22°12S 29°22E **55** G2
Maputo Mozam. 25°58S 32°32E **57** D5
Maputo □ Mozam. 26°0S 32°25E **57** D5
Maputo, B. de Mozam. 25°50S 32°45E **48** J7
Maputo → Mozam. 26°23S 32°48E **57** D5
Maqat Kazakhstan 47°39N 53°19E **19** E9
Maqên China 34°24N 100°6E **32** E9
Maqên Gangri China 34°55N 99°18E **32** E8
Maqiaohe China 44°40N 130°30E **35** B16
Maqnā Si. Arabia 28°25N 34°50E **44** D2
Maqteïr Mauritania 21°50N 11°40W **50** D3
Maqu China 34°9N 102°45E **32** E9
Maquan He = Brahmaputra →
  Asia 23°40N 90°35E **43** H13
Maquela do Zombo Angola 6°0S 15°15E **52** F3
Maquinchao Argentina 41°15S 68°50W **96** E3
Maquoketa U.S.A. 42°4N 90°40W **80** D8
Mar Canada 44°49N 81°12W **82** B3
Mar, Serra do Brazil 25°30S 49°0W **95** B6
Mar Chiquita, L.
  Argentina 30°40S 62°50W **94** C3
Mar del Plata Argentina 38°0S 57°30W **94** D4
Mar Menor Spain 37°40N 0°45W **21** D5
Mara Tanzania 1°30S 34°32E **54** C3
Mara □ Tanzania 1°45S 34°20E **54** C3
Maraã Brazil 1°52S 65°25W **92** D5
Maraa Tahiti 17°46S 149°34W **59** d
Marabá Brazil 5°20S 49°5W **93** E9
Maraboon, L. Australia 23°41S 148°0E **62** C4
Maracá, I. de Brazil 2°10N 50°30W **93** C8
Maracaibo Venezuela 10°40N 71°37W **92** A4
Maracaibo, L. de
  Venezuela 9°40N 71°30W **92** B4
Maracaju Brazil 21°38S 55°9W **95** A4
Maracas Bay Village
  Trin. & Tob. 10°46N 61°28W **93** K15
Maracay Venezuela 10°15N 67°28W **92** A5
Marādah Libya 29°15N 19°15E **51** C9
Maradi Niger 13°29N 7°20E **50** F7
Marāgheh Iran 37°30N 46°12E **44** B5
Marāh Si. Arabia 25°0N 45°35E **44** E5
Marajo, I. de Brazil 1°0S 49°30W **93** D9
Marākand Iran 38°51N 45°16E **44** B5
Marakele △ S. Africa 24°30S 25°30E **57** C4
Maralal Kenya 1°0N 36°38E **54** B4
Maralinga Australia 30°13S 131°32E **61** F5
Maralinga Tjarutja ♦
  Australia 29°30S 131°0E **61** E5
Marambio Antarctica 64°0S 56°0W **5** C18
Maran Malaysia 3°35N 102°45E **39** L4
Marana U.S.A. 32°27N 111°13W **77** K8
Maranboy Australia 14°40S 132°39E **60** B5
Marand Iran 38°30N 45°45E **44** B5
Marang Malaysia 5°12N 103°13E **39** K4
Maranguape Brazil 3°55S 38°50W **93** D11
Maranhão = São Luís
  Brazil 2°39S 44°15W **93** D10
Maranhão □ Brazil 5°0S 46°0W **93** E9
Maranoa → Australia 27°50S 148°37E **63** D4
Marañón → Peru 4°30S 73°35W **92** D4
Marão Mozam. 24°18S 34°2E **57** C5
Maraş = Kahramanmaraş
  Turkey 37°37N 36°53E **44** B3
Marathasa Cyprus 34°59N 32°51E **25** E11
Marathon Australia 20°51S 143°32E **62** C3
Marathon Canada 48°44N 86°23W **72** C2
Marathon N.Y., U.S.A. 42°27N 76°2W **83** D8
Marathon Tex., U.S.A. 30°12N 103°15W **84** F3
Maratua Indonesia 2°10N 118°35E **37** D5
Maraval Trin. & Tob. 10°42N 61°31W **93** K15
Maravatío Mexico 19°54N 100°27W **86** D4
Marāwih U.A.E. 24°18N 53°18E **45** E7
Marawi Somali Rep. 1°48N 44°50E **47** G3
Marbella Spain 36°30N 4°57W **21** D3
Marble Bar Australia 21°9S 119°44E **60** D2
Marble Falls U.S.A. 30°35N 98°16W **84** F5
Marblehead Mass.,
  U.S.A. 42°30N 70°51W **83** D14
Marblehead Ohio, U.S.A. 41°32N 82°44W **82** E2
Marburg Germany 50°47N 8°46E **16** C5
Marca, Pta. do Angola 16°31S 11°43E **53** H2
March U.K. 52°33N 0°5E **13** E8
Marche □ Italy 43°20N 13°10E **22** C5
Marche France 46°5N 1°20E **20** C4
Marche-en-Famenne
  Belgium 50°14N 5°19E **15** D5
Marchena Spain 37°18N 5°23W **21** D3
Marco Island U.S.A. 25°58N 81°44W **85** J14
Marcos Juárez Argentina 32°42S 62°5W **94** C3
Marcus Baker, Mt.
  U.S.A. 61°26N 147°45W **74** C10

Marcus I. = Minami-Tori-Shima
  Pac. Oc. 24°20N 153°58E **64** E7
Marcy, Mt. U.S.A. 44°7N 73°56W **83** B11
Mardan Pakistan 34°20N 72°0E **42** B5
Mardie Australia 21°12S 115°59E **60** D2
Mardin Turkey 37°20N 40°43E **44** B4
Maree, L. U.K. 57°40N 5°26W **11** D3
Mareeba Australia 16°59S 145°28E **62** B4
Mareetsane S. Africa 26°9S 25°25E **56** D4
Marek = Stanke Dimitrov
  Bulgaria 42°17N 23°9E **23** C10
Marengo U.S.A. 41°48N 92°4W **80** E7
Marerano Madag. 21°23S 44°52E **57** C7
Marfa U.S.A. 30°19N 104°1W **84** F2
Marfa Pt. Malta 35°59N 14°19E **25** C1
Margaret → Australia 18°9S 125°41E **60** C4
Margaret Bay Canada 51°20N 127°35W **70** C3
Margaret L. Canada 58°56N 115°25W **70** B5
Margaret River Australia 33°57S 115°6E **61** F2
Margarita, I. de Venezuela 11°0N 64°0W **92** A6
Margaritovo Russia 43°25N 134°45E **30** C7
Margate S. Africa 30°50S 30°20E **57** E5
Margate U.K. 51°23N 1°23E **13** F9
Marghilon Uzbekistan 40°27N 71°42E **28** E8
Märgow, Dasht-e
  Afghan. 30°40N 62°30E **40** D3
Marguerite Canada 52°30N 122°25W **70** C4
Mari El □ Russia 56°30N 48°0E **18** C8
Mari Indus Pakistan 32°57N 71°34E **42** C4
Mari Republic = Mari El □
  Russia 56°30N 48°0E **18** C8
María de la Salut Spain 39°40N 3°5E **24** B10
María Elena Chile 22°18S 69°40W **94** A2
María Grande Argentina 31°45S 59°55W **94** C4
Maria I. N. Terr.,
  Australia 14°52S 135°45E **62** A2
Maria I. Tas., Australia 42°35S 148°0E **63** G4
Maria Island △ Australia 42°38S 148°5E **63** G4
Maria van Diemen, C.
  N.Z. 34°29S 172°40E **59** A4
Mariakani Kenya 3°50S 39°27E **54** C4
Mariala △ Australia 25°57S 145°2E **63** D4
Marian Australia 21°9S 148°57E **62** b
Marian L. Canada 63°0N 116°15W **70** A5
Mariana Trench Pac. Oc. 13°0N 145°0E **64** F6
Marianao Cuba 23°8N 82°24W **88** B3
Marianna Ark., U.S.A. 34°46N 90°46W **85** D9
Marianna Fla., U.S.A. 30°46N 85°14W **85** F12
Marias → U.S.A. 47°56N 110°30W **76** C8
Marias, Is. Mexico 21°25N 106°28W **86** C3
Mariato, Punta Panama 7°12N 80°52W **88** E3
Maribor Slovenia 46°36N 15°40E **16** E8
Marico → Africa 23°35S 26°57E **56** C4
Maricopa Ariz., U.S.A. 33°4N 112°3W **77** K7
Maricopa Calif., U.S.A. 35°4N 119°24W **79** K7
Marié → Brazil 0°27S 66°26W **92** D5
Marie Byrd Land
  Antarctica 79°30S 125°0W **5** D14
Marie-Galante
  Guadeloupe 15°56N 61°16W **88** b
Mariecourt = Kangiqsujuaq
  Canada 61°30N 72°0W **69** E17
Mariehamn Finland 60°5N 19°55E **9** F18
Mariembourg Belgium 50°6N 4°31E **15** D4
Mariental Namibia 24°36S 18°0E **56** C2
Marienville U.S.A. 41°28N 79°8W **82** E5
Mariestad Sweden 58°43N 13°50E **9** G15
Marietta Ga., U.S.A. 33°57N 84°33W **85** E12
Marietta Ohio, U.S.A. 39°25N 81°27W **81** F13
Marieville Canada 45°26N 73°10W **83** A11
Mariinsk Russia 56°10N 87°20E **28** D9
Marijampolė Lithuania 54°33N 23°19E **9** J20
Marília Brazil 22°13S 50°0W **95** A6
Marín Spain 42°23N 8°42W **21** A1
Marina U.S.A. 36°41N 121°48W **78** J5
Marine City U.S.A. 42°43N 82°30W **82** D2
Marinette U.S.A. 45°6N 87°38W **80** C2
Maringá Brazil 23°26S 52°2W **95** A5
Marion Ala., U.S.A. 32°38N 87°19W **85** E11
Marion Ill., U.S.A. 37°44N 88°56W **80** G9
Marion Ind., U.S.A. 40°32N 85°40W **81** E11
Marion Iowa, U.S.A. 42°2N 91°36W **80** D8
Marion Kans., U.S.A. 38°21N 97°1W **80** F5
Marion N.C., U.S.A. 35°41N 82°1W **85** D13
Marion Ohio, U.S.A. 40°35N 83°8W **81** E12
Marion S.C., U.S.A. 34°11N 79°24W **85** D15
Marion Va., U.S.A. 36°50N 81°31W **81** G13
Marion, L. U.S.A. 33°28N 80°10W **85** E14
Mariposa U.S.A. 37°29N 119°58W **78** H7
Mariscal Estigarribia
  Paraguay 22°3S 60°40W **94** A3
Maritime Alps = Maritimes, Alpes
  Europe 44°10N 7°10E **20** D7
Maritimes, Alpes Europe 44°10N 7°10E **20** D7
Maritsa = Evros →
  Greece 41°40N 26°34E **23** D12
Maritsa Greece 36°22N 28°8E **25** C10
Mariupol Ukraine 47°5N 37°31E **19** E6
Mariusa → Venezuela 9°24N 61°27W **89** E7
Marīvān Iran 35°30N 46°25E **44** C5
Marj 'Uyūn Lebanon 33°21N 35°34E **46** B4
Marka Somali Rep. 1°48N 44°50E **47** G3
Markam China 29°42N 98°38E **41** E21
Markdale Canada 44°19N 80°39W **82** B4
Marked Tree U.S.A. 35°32N 90°25W **85** D9
Market Drayton U.K. 52°54N 2°29W **12** E5
Market Harborough
  U.K. 52°29N 0°55W **13** E7
Market Rasen U.K. 53°24N 0°20W **12** D7
Markham Canada 43°52N 79°16W **82** C5
Markham, Mt. Antarctica 83°0S 164°0E **5** E11
Markleeville U.S.A. 38°42N 119°47W **78** G7
Markovo Russia 64°40N 170°24E **29** C17
Marks Russia 51°45N 46°50E **18** D8
Marksville U.S.A. 31°8N 92°4W **84** F8
Marla Australia 27°19S 133°33E **63** D1
Marlbank Canada 44°26N 77°6W **82** B7
Marlboro Mass., U.S.A. 42°21N 71°33W **83** D13
Marlborough Australia 22°46S 149°52E **62** C4

Marlborough *U.K.* 51°25N 1°43W **13** F6
Marlborough *U.S.A.* 42°21N 71°33W **83** D13
Marlborough Downs *U.K.* 51°27N 1°53W **13** F6
Marlin *U.S.A.* 31°18N 96°54W **84** F6
Marlow *U.K.* 51°34N 0°46W **13** F7
Marlow *U.S.A.* 34°39N 97°58W **84** D6
Marmagao *India* 15°25N 73°56E **40** M8
Marmara *Turkey* 40°35N 27°34E **23** D12
Marmara, Sea of = Marmara Denizi *Turkey* 40°45N 28°15E **23** D13
Marmara Denizi *Turkey* 40°45N 28°15E **23** D13
Marmaris *Turkey* 36°50N 28°14E **23** F13
Marmion, Mt. *Australia* 29°16S 119°50E **61** E2
Marmion L. *Canada* 48°55N 91°20W **72** C1
Marmolada, Mte. *Italy* 46°26N 11°51E **22** A4
Marmora *Canada* 44°28N 77°41W **82** B7
Marmugao = Marmagao *India* 15°25N 73°56E **40** M8
Marne → *France* 48°47N 2°29E **20** B5
Maro Reef *U.S.A.* 25°25N 170°35W **75** K5
Maroala *Madag.* 15°23S 47°59E **57** B8
Maroantsetra *Madag.* 15°26S 49°44E **57** B8
Maroelaboom *Namibia* 19°15S 18°53E **56** B2
Marofandilia *Madag.* 20°7S 44°34E **57** C7
Marojejy ⌂ *Madag.* 14°26S 49°21E **57** A8
Marolambo *Madag.* 20°2S 48°7E **57** C8
Maromandia *Madag.* 14°13S 48°5E **57** A8
Maromokotro *Madag.* 14°0S 49°0E **57** A8
Marondera *Zimbabwe* 18°5S 31°42E **55** F3
Maroni → *Fr. Guiana* 5°30N 54°0W **93** B8
Maroochydore *Australia* 26°29S 153°5E **63** D5
Maroona *Australia* 37°27S 142°54E **63** F3
Marosakoa *Madag.* 15°26S 46°38E **57** B8
Maroseranana *Madag.* 18°32S 48°51E **57** B8
Marotandrano *Madag.* 16°10S 48°50E **57** B8
Marotaolano *Madag.* 12°47S 49°15E **57** A8
Maroua *Cameroon* 10°40N 14°20E **51** F8
Marovato *Madag.* 15°48S 48°5E **57** B8
Marovoay *Madag.* 16°6S 46°39E **57** B8
Marquard *S. Africa* 28°40S 27°28E **56** D4
Marquesas Fracture Zone *Pac. Oc.* 9°0S 125°0W **65** H15
Marquesas Is. = Marquises, Îs. *French Polynesia* 9°30S 140°0W **65** H14
Marquette *U.S.A.* 46°33N 87°24W **80** B10
Marquis *St. Lucia* 14°2N 60°54W **89** f
Marquises, Îs. *French Polynesia* 9°30S 140°0W **65** H14
Marra, Djebel *Sudan* 13°10N 24°22E **51** F10
Marracuene *Mozam.* 25°45S 32°35E **57** D5
Marrakech *Morocco* 31°9N 8°0W **50** B4
Marrawah *Australia* 40°55S 144°42E **63** G3
Marree *Australia* 29°39S 138°1E **63** D2
Marrero *U.S.A.* 29°53N 90°6W **85** G9
Marrimane *Mozam.* 22°58S 33°34E **57** C5
Marromeu *Mozam.* 18°15S 36°25E **57** B6
Marromeu ⌂ *Mozam.* 19°0S 36°0E **57** B6
Marrowie Cr. → *Australia* 33°23S 145°40E **63** E4
Marrubane *Mozam.* 18°0S 37°0E **55** F4
Marrupa *Mozam.* 13°8S 37°30E **55** E4
Mars Hill *U.S.A.* 46°31N 67°52W **81** B20
Marsá 'Alam *Egypt* 25°5N 34°54E **47** B1
Marsá Matrûh *Egypt* 31°19N 27°9E **51** B11
Marsā Sūsah *Libya* 32°52N 21°59E **51** B10
Marsabit *Kenya* 2°18N 38°0E **54** B4
Marsabit △ *Kenya* 2°23N 37°56E **54** B4
Marsala *Italy* 37°48N 12°26E **22** F5
Marsalforn *Malta* 36°4N 14°16E **25** C1
Marsden *Australia* 33°47S 147°32E **63** E4
Marseille *France* 43°18N 5°23E **20** E6
Marseilles = Marseille *France* 43°18N 5°23E **20** E6
Marsh I. *U.S.A.* 29°34N 91°53W **84** G9
Marshall *Ark., U.S.A.* 35°55N 92°38W **84** D8
Marshall *Mich., U.S.A.* 42°16N 84°58W **81** D11
Marshall *Minn., U.S.A.* 44°27N 95°47W **80** C6
Marshall *Mo., U.S.A.* 39°7N 93°12W **80** F7
Marshall *Tex., U.S.A.* 32°33N 94°23W **84** E7
Marshall → *Australia* 22°59S 136°59E **62** C2
Marshall Is. ■ *Pac. Oc.* 9°0N 171°0E **58** A10
Marshalltown *U.S.A.* 42°3N 92°55W **80** D7
Marshbrook *Zimbabwe* 18°33S 31°9E **57** B5
Marshfield *Mo., U.S.A.* 37°15N 92°54W **80** G7
Marshfield *Vt., U.S.A.* 44°20N 72°20W **83** B12
Marshfield *Wis., U.S.A.* 44°40N 90°10W **80** C8
Marshūn *Iran* 36°19N 49°23E **45** B6
Märsta *Sweden* 59°37N 17°52E **9** G17
Mart *U.S.A.* 31°33N 96°50W **84** F6
Martaban *Burma* 16°30N 97°35E **41** L20
Martaban, G. of *Burma* 16°5N 96°30E **41** L20
Martapura *Kalimantan Selatan, Indonesia* 3°22S 114°47E **36** E4
Martapura *Sumatera Selatan, Indonesia* 4°19S 104°22E **36** E2
Marte R. Gómez, Presa *Mexico* 26°10N 99°0W **87** B5
Martelange *Belgium* 49°49N 5°43E **15** E5
Martha's Vineyard *U.S.A.* 41°25N 70°38W **83** E14
Martigny *Switz.* 46°6N 7°3E **20** C7
Martigues *France* 43°24N 5°4E **20** E6
Martin *Slovak Rep.* 49°6N 18°58E **17** D10
Martin *S. Dak., U.S.A.* 43°11N 101°44W **80** D3
Martin *Tenn., U.S.A.* 36°21N 88°51W **85** C10
Martin L. *U.S.A.* 32°41N 85°55W **85** E12
Martina Franca *Italy* 40°42N 17°20E **22** D7
Martinborough *N.Z.* 41°14S 175°29E **59** D5
Martinez *Calif., U.S.A.* 38°1N 122°8W **78** G4
Martinez *Ga., U.S.A.* 33°31N 82°5W **85** E13
Martinique ☒ *W. Indies* 14°40N 61°0W **88** c
Martinique Passage *W. Indies* 15°15N 61°0W **89** C7
Martinópolis *Brazil* 22°11S 51°12W **95** A5
Martin's Bay *Barbados* 13°12N 59°29W **89** g
Martins Ferry *U.S.A.* 40°6N 80°44W **82** F4
Martinsburg *Pa., U.S.A.* 40°19N 78°20W **82** F6
Martinsburg *W. Va., U.S.A.* 39°27N 77°58W **81** F15
Martinsville *Ind., U.S.A.* 39°26N 86°25W **80** F10
Martinsville *Va., U.S.A.* 36°41N 79°52W **81** G14
Marton *N.Z.* 40°4S 175°23E **59** D5
Martos *Spain* 37°44N 3°58W **21** D4
Martu ✪ *Australia* 22°30S 122°30E **60** D3
Marudi *Malaysia* 4°11N 114°19E **36** D4
Maruf *Afghan.* 31°30N 67°6E **40** D5
Marugame *Japan* 34°15N 133°40E **31** G6
Marunga *Angola* 17°28S 20°2E **56** B3
Marungu, Mts. *Dem. Rep. of the Congo* 7°30S 30°0E **54** D3
Maruwa ✪ *Australia* 22°30S 127°30E **60** D4
Marv Dasht *Iran* 29°50N 52°40E **45** D7
Marvast *Iran* 30°30N 54°15E **45** D7
Marvel Loch *Australia* 31°28S 119°29E **61** F2
Marwar *India* 25°43N 73°45E **42** G5
Mary *Turkmenistan* 37°40N 61°50E **45** B9
Maryborough = Port Laoise *Ireland* 53°2N 7°18W **10** C4
Maryborough *Queens., Australia* 25°31S 152°37E **63** D5
Maryborough *Vic., Australia* 37°3S 143°44E **63** F3
Maryfield *Canada* 49°50N 101°35W **71** D8
Maryland □ *U.S.A.* 39°0N 76°30W **81** F15
Maryland Junction *Zimbabwe* 17°45S 30°31E **55** F3
Maryport *U.K.* 54°44N 3°28W **12** C4
Mary's Harbour *Canada* 52°18N 55°51W **73** B8
Marystown *Canada* 47°10N 55°10W **73** C8
Marysville *Calif., U.S.A.* 39°9N 121°35W **78** F5
Marysville *Kans., U.S.A.* 39°51N 96°39W **80** F5
Marysville *Mich., U.S.A.* 42°54N 82°29W **82** D2
Marysville *Ohio, U.S.A.* 40°14N 83°22W **81** E12
Marysville *Wash., U.S.A.* 48°3N 122°11W **78** B4
Maryville *Mo., U.S.A.* 40°21N 94°52W **80** E6
Maryville *Tenn., U.S.A.* 35°46N 83°58W **85** D13
Marzūq *Libya* 25°53N 13°57E **51** C8
Marzūq, Idehān *Libya* 24°50N 13°51E **51** D8
Masada *Israel* 31°15N 35°20E **46** D4
Masahunga *Tanzania* 2°6S 33°18E **54** C3
Masai *Malaysia* 1°29N 103°55E **39** d
Masai Mara △ *Kenya* 1°25S 35°5E **54** C4
Masai Steppe *Tanzania* 4°30S 36°30E **54** C4
Masaka *Uganda* 0°21S 31°45E **54** C3
Masalembo, Kepulauan *Indonesia* 5°35S 114°30E **36** F4
Masalima, Kepulauan *Indonesia* 5°4S 117°5E **36** F5
Masamba *Indonesia* 2°30S 120°15E **37** E6
Masan *S. Korea* 35°11N 128°32E **35** G15
Masandam, Ra's *Oman* 26°30N 56°30E **45** E8
Masasi *Tanzania* 10°45S 38°52E **55** E4
Masaya *Nic.* 12°0N 86°7W **88** D2
Masbate *Phil.* 12°21N 123°36E **37** B6
Mascara *Algeria* 35°26N 0°6E **50** A6
Mascarene Is. *Ind. Oc.* 22°0S 55°0E **48** J9
Mascota *Mexico* 20°32N 104°49W **86** C4
Masela *Indonesia* 8°9S 129°51E **37** F7
Maseru *Lesotho* 29°18S 27°30E **56** D4
Mashaba *Zimbabwe* 20°2S 30°29E **55** G3
Mashābih *Si. Arabia* 25°35N 36°30E **44** E3
Mashang *China* 36°48N 117°57E **35** F9
Mashatu ⌂ *Botswana* 22°45S 29°5E **57** C4
Masherbrum *Pakistan* 35°38N 76°18E **43** B7
Mashhad *Iran* 36°20N 59°35E **45** B8
Mashīz *Iran* 29°56N 56°37E **45** D8
Māshkel, Hāmūn-i- *Pakistan* 28°20N 62°56E **45** D9
Mashki Chāh *Pakistan* 29°5N 62°30E **40** E3
Mashonaland *Zimbabwe* 16°30S 31°0E **53** H6
Mashonaland Central □ *Zimbabwe* 17°30S 31°0E **57** B5
Mashonaland East □ *Zimbabwe* 18°0S 32°0E **57** B5
Mashonaland West □ *Zimbabwe* 17°30S 29°30E **57** B4
Mashrakh *India* 26°7N 84°48E **43** F11
Masi Manimba *Dem. Rep. of the Congo* 4°40S 17°54E **52** E3
Masig *Australia* 9°45S 143°24E **62** a
Masindi *Uganda* 1°40N 31°43E **54** B3
Masindi Port *Uganda* 1°43N 32°2E **54** B3
Masinga Res. *Kenya* 0°58S 37°38E **54** C4
Maṣīrah, Jazīrat *Oman* 21°0N 58°50E **47** C6
Maṣīrah, Khalīj *Oman* 20°10N 58°10E **47** C6
Masisi *Dem. Rep. of the Congo* 1°23S 28°49E **54** C2
Masjed Soleyman *Iran* 31°55N 49°18E **45** D6
Mask, L. *Ireland* 53°36N 9°22W **10** C2
Maskin *Oman* 23°44N 56°52E **45** F8
Masoala, Tanjon' i *Madag.* 15°59S 50°13E **57** B9
Masoala △ *Madag.* 15°30S 50°12E **57** B9
Masoarivo *Madag.* 19°3S 44°19E **57** B7
Masohi = Amahai *Indonesia* 3°20S 128°55E **37** E7
Masomeloka *Madag.* 20°17S 48°37E **57** C8
Mason *Nev., U.S.A.* 38°56N 119°8W **78** G7
Mason *Tex., U.S.A.* 30°45N 99°14W **84** F5
Mason City *U.S.A.* 43°9N 93°12W **80** D7
Maspalomas *Canary Is.* 27°46N 15°35W **24** G4
Maspalomas, Pta. *Canary Is.* 27°43N 15°36W **24** G4
Masqat *Oman* 23°37N 58°36E **47** C6
Massa *Italy* 44°1N 10°9E **20** D9
Massachusetts □ *U.S.A.* 42°30N 72°0W **83** D13
Massachusetts B. *U.S.A.* 42°25N 70°50W **83** D14
Massakory *Chad* 13°0N 15°49E **51** F9
Massamba *Mozam.* 15°58S 33°31E **55** F3
Massanella *Spain* 39°48N 2°51E **24** B9
Massangena *Mozam.* 21°34S 33°0E **57** C5
Massango *Angola* 8°2S 16°21E **52** F3
Massawa = Mitsiwa *Eritrea* 15°35N 39°25E **47** D2
Massena *U.S.A.* 44°56N 74°54W **83** B10
Massenya *Chad* 11°21N 16°9E **51** F9
Masset *Canada* 54°2N 132°10W **70** C2
Massiah Street *Barbados* 13°9N 59°29W **89** g
Massif Central *France* 44°55N 3°0E **20** D5
Massillon *U.S.A.* 40°48N 81°32W **82** F3
Massinga *Mozam.* 23°15S 35°22E **57** C6
Massingir *Mozam.* 23°51S 32°4E **57** C5
Masson-Angers *Canada* 45°32N 75°25W **83** A9
Masson I. *Antarctica* 66°10S 93°20E **5** C7
Mastanli = Momchilgrad *Bulgaria* 41°33N 25°23E **23** D11
Masterton *N.Z.* 40°56S 175°39E **59** D5
Mastic *U.S.A.* 40°47N 72°54W **83** F12
Mastuj *Pakistan* 36°20N 72°36E **43** A5
Mastung *Pakistan* 29°50N 66°56E **40** E5
Masty *Belarus* 53°27N 24°38E **17** B13
Masuda *Japan* 34°40N 131°51E **31** G5
Masuku = Franceville *Gabon* 1°40S 13°32E **52** E2
Masurian Lakes = Mazurski, Pojezierze *Poland* 53°50N 21°0E **17** B11
Masvingo *Zimbabwe* 20°8S 30°49E **55** G3
Masvingo □ *Zimbabwe* 21°0S 31°30E **55** G3
Maswa ⌂ *Tanzania* 2°58S 34°19E **54** C3
Maṣyāf *Syria* 35°4N 36°20E **44** C3
Mata-au = Clutha → *N.Z.* 46°20S 169°49E **59** G2
Matabeleland *Zimbabwe* 18°0S 27°0E **53** H5
Matabeleland North □ *Zimbabwe* 19°0S 28°0E **55** F2
Matabeleland South □ *Zimbabwe* 21°0S 29°0E **55** G2
Matachewan *Canada* 47°56N 80°39W **72** C3
Matadi *Dem. Rep. of the Congo* 5°52S 13°31E **52** F2
Matagalpa *Nic.* 13°0N 85°58W **88** D2
Matagami *Canada* 49°45N 77°34W **72** C4
Matagami, L. *Canada* 49°50N 77°40W **72** C4
Matagorda B. *U.S.A.* 28°40N 96°12W **84** G6
Matagorda I. *U.S.A.* 28°15N 96°30W **84** G6
Mataiea *Tahiti* 17°46S 149°25W **59** d
Matak *Indonesia* 3°18N 106°16E **36** D3
Matala *Greece* 34°59N 24°45E **25** E6
Matam *Senegal* 15°34N 13°17W **50** E3
Matamoros *Campeche, Mexico* 18°50N 90°50W **87** D6
Matamoros *Coahuila, Mexico* 25°32N 103°15W **86** B4
Matamoros *Tamaulipas, Mexico* 25°53N 97°30W **87** B5
Ma'ṭan as Sarra *Libya* 21°45N 22°0E **51** D10
Matandu → *Tanzania* 8°45S 34°19E **55** D3
Matane *Canada* 48°50N 67°33W **73** C6
Matanomadh *India* 23°33N 68°57E **42** H3
Matanzas *Cuba* 23°0N 81°40W **88** B3
Matapa *Botswana* 23°11S 24°39E **56** C3
Matapan, C. = Tenaro, Akra *Greece* 36°22N 22°27E **23** F10
Matapédia *Canada* 48°0N 66°59W **73** C6
Matapo △ *Zimbabwe* 20°30S 29°40E **55** G2
Matara *Sri Lanka* 5°58N 80°30E **40** S12
Mataram *Indonesia* 8°35S 116°7E **37** K19
Matarani *Peru* 17°0S 72°10W **92** G4
Mataranka *Australia* 14°55S 133°4E **60** B5
Matarma, Râs *Egypt* 30°27N 32°44E **46** E1
Mataró *Spain* 41°32N 2°29E **21** B7
Matatiele *S. Africa* 30°20S 28°49E **57** E4
Mataura *N.Z.* 46°11S 168°51E **59** G2
Matavai, B. de *Tahiti* 17°30S 149°23W **59** d
Matehuala *Mexico* 23°39N 100°39W **86** C4
Mateke Hills *Zimbabwe* 21°48S 31°0E **55** G3
Matelot *Trin. & Tob.* 10°50N 61°7W **93** K15
Matera *Italy* 40°40N 16°36E **22** D7
Matetsi *Zimbabwe* 18°12S 26°0E **55** F2
Matheniko ⌂ *Uganda* 2°49N 34°27E **54** B3
Mathis *U.S.A.* 28°6N 97°50W **84** G6
Mathraki *Greece* 39°48N 19°31E **25** A3
Mathura *India* 27°30N 77°40E **42** F7
Mati *Phil.* 6°55N 126°15E **37** C7
Matiali *India* 26°56N 88°49E **43** F13
Matías Romero *Mexico* 16°53N 95°2W **87** D5
Matibane *Mozam.* 14°49S 40°45E **55** E5
Matiri Ra. *N.Z.* 41°38S 172°20E **59** D4
Matjiesfontein *S. Africa* 33°14S 20°35E **56** E3
Matla → *India* 21°40N 88°40E **43** J13
Matlamanyane *Botswana* 19°33S 25°57E **56** B4
Matli *Pakistan* 25°2N 68°39E **42** G3
Matlock *U.K.* 53°9N 1°33W **12** D6
Mato Grosso □ *Brazil* 14°0S 55°0W **93** F8
Mato Grosso, Planalto do *Brazil* 15°0S 55°0W **93** G8
Mato Grosso do Sul □ *Brazil* 18°0S 55°0W **93** G8
Matobo = Matapo △ *Zimbabwe* 20°30S 29°40E **55** G2
Matochkin Shar, Proliv *Russia* 73°23N 55°12E **28** B6
Matopo Hills *Zimbabwe* 20°36S 28°20E **55** G2
Matopos *Zimbabwe* 20°20S 28°29E **55** G2
Matosinhos *Portugal* 41°11N 8°42W **21** B1
Matroosberg *S. Africa* 33°23S 19°40E **56** E2
Maṭruḥ *Oman* 23°37N 58°30E **47** C6
Matsu Tao *Taiwan* 26°8N 119°56E **33** F12
Matsue *Japan* 35°25N 133°10E **31** G6
Matsum, Ko *Thailand* 9°22N 99°59E **39** b
Matsumae *Japan* 41°26N 140°7E **30** D10
Matsumae-Hantō *Japan* 41°30N 140°15E **30** D10
Matsumoto *Japan* 36°15N 138°0E **31** F9
Matsusaka *Japan* 34°34N 136°32E **31** G8
Matsushima *Japan* 38°20N 141°10E **30** E10
Matsuura *Japan* 33°20N 129°49E **31** H4
Matsuyama *Japan* 33°45N 132°45E **31** H6
Mattagami → *Canada* 50°43N 81°29W **72** B3
Mattancheri *India* 9°50N 76°15E **40** Q10
Mattawa *Canada* 46°20N 78°45W **72** C4
Matterhorn *Switz.* 45°58N 7°39E **20** D7
Matthew Town *Bahamas* 20°57N 73°40W **89** B5
Matthews Ridge *Guyana* 7°37N 60°10W **92** B6
Mattice *Canada* 49°40N 83°20W **72** C3
Mattituck *U.S.A.* 40°59N 72°32W **83** F12
Mattō *Japan* 36°31N 136°34E **31** F8
Mattoon *U.S.A.* 39°29N 88°23W **80** F9
Matucana *Peru* 11°55S 76°25W **92** F3
Matuku *Fiji* 19°10S 179°44E **59** a
Matūn = Khowst *Afghan.* 33°22N 69°58E **42** C3
Matura B. *Trin. & Tob.* 10°39N 61°1W **93** K15
Maturín *Venezuela* 9°45N 63°11W **92** B6
Matusadona △ *Zimbabwe* 16°58S 28°42E **55** F2
Mau *Mad. P., India* 26°17N 78°41E **43** F8
Mau *Ut. P., India* 25°56N 83°33E **43** G10
Mau *Ut. P., India* 25°17N 81°23E **43** G9
Mau Escarpment *Kenya* 0°40S 36°0E **54** C4
Mau Ranipur *India* 25°16N 79°8E **43** G8
Maua *Kenya* 0°14N 37°56E **54** C4
Maua *Mozam.* 13°53S 37°10E **55** E4
Maubeuge *France* 50°17N 3°57E **20** A6
Maubin *Burma* 16°44N 95°39E **41** L19
Maud, Pt. *Australia* 23°6S 113°45E **60** D1
Maud Rise *S. Ocean* 66°0S 3°0E **5** C3
Maude *Australia* 34°29S 144°18E **63** E3
Maudin Sun *Burma* 16°0N 94°30E **41** M19
Maués *Brazil* 3°20S 57°45W **92** D7
Mauganj *India* 24°50N 81°55E **43** G9
Maughold Hd. *I. of Man* 54°18N 4°18W **12** C3
Maui *U.S.A.* 20°48N 156°20W **75** L8
Maulamyaing = Moulmein *Burma* 16°30N 97°40E **41** L20
Maule □ *Chile* 36°5S 72°30W **94** D1
Maumee *U.S.A.* 41°34N 83°39W **81** E12
Maumee → *U.S.A.* 41°42N 83°28W **81** E12
Maumere *Indonesia* 8°38S 122°13E **37** F6
Maun *Botswana* 20°0S 23°26E **56** C3
Mauna Kea *U.S.A.* 19°50N 155°28W **75** M8
Mauna Loa *U.S.A.* 19°30N 155°35W **75** M8
Maunath Bhanjan = Mau *India* 25°56N 83°33E **43** G10
Maungmagan Kyunzu *Burma* 14°0N 97°48E **38** E1
Maungu *Kenya* 3°33S 38°45E **54** C4
Maupin *U.S.A.* 45°11N 121°5W **76** D3
Maurepas, L. *U.S.A.* 30°15N 90°30W **85** F9
Maurice, L. *Australia* 29°30S 131°0E **61** E5
Mauricie △ *Canada* 46°45N 73°0W **72** C5
Mauritania ■ *Africa* 20°50N 10°0W **50** E3
Mauritius ■ *Ind. Oc.* 20°0S 57°0E **53** d
Mauston *U.S.A.* 43°48N 90°5W **80** D8
Mavli *India* 24°45N 73°55E **42** G5
Mavuradonha Mts. *Zimbabwe* 16°30S 31°30E **55** F3
Mawa *Dem. Rep. of the Congo* 2°45N 26°40E **54** B2
Mawai *India* 22°30N 81°4E **43** H9
Mawana *India* 29°6N 77°58E **42** E7
Mawand *Pakistan* 29°33N 68°38E **42** E3
Mawjib, W. al → *Jordan* 31°28N 35°36E **46** D4
Mawk Mai *Burma* 20°14N 97°37E **41** J20
Mawlaik *Burma* 23°40N 94°26E **41** H19
Mawlamyine = Moulmein *Burma* 16°30N 97°40E **41** L20
Mawqaq *Si. Arabia* 27°25N 41°8E **44** E4
Mawson *Antarctica* 67°30S 62°53E **5** C6
Mawson Coast *Antarctica* 68°30S 63°0E **5** C6
Max *U.S.A.* 47°49N 101°18W **80** B3
Maxcanú *Mexico* 20°35N 90°0W **87** C6
Maxesibeni *S. Africa* 30°49S 29°23E **57** E4
Maxhamish L. *Canada* 59°50N 123°17W **70** B4
Maxixe *Mozam.* 23°54S 35°17E **57** C6
Maxville *Canada* 45°17N 74°51W **83** A10
Maxwell *U.S.A.* 39°17N 122°11W **78** F4
Maxwelton *Australia* 20°43S 142°41E **62** C3
May, C. *U.S.A.* 38°56N 74°58W **81** F16
May Pen *Jamaica* 17°58N 77°15W **88** a
Maya → *Russia* 60°28N 134°28E **29** D14
Maya Mts. *Belize* 16°30N 89°0W **87** D7
Mayaguana *Bahamas* 22°30N 72°44W **89** B5
Mayagüez *Puerto Rico* 18°12N 67°9W **89** d
Mayāmey *Iran* 36°24N 55°42E **45** B7
Mayanup *Australia* 33°57S 116°27E **61** F2
Mayapán *Mexico* 20°29N 89°11W **87** C7
Mayarí *Cuba* 20°40N 75°41W **89** B4
Mayaro B. *Trin. & Tob.* 10°14N 60°59W **93** K16
Maybell *U.S.A.* 40°31N 108°5W **76** F9
Maybole *U.K.* 55°21N 4°42W **11** F4
Maydān *Iraq* 34°55N 45°37E **44** C5
Mayenne → *France* 47°30N 0°32W **20** C3
Mayer *U.S.A.* 34°24N 112°14W **77** J7
Mayerthorpe *Canada* 53°57N 115°8W **70** C5
Mayfield *Ky., U.S.A.* 36°44N 88°38W **80** G9
Mayfield *N.Y., U.S.A.* 43°6N 74°16W **83** C10
Mayhill *U.S.A.* 32°53N 105°29W **77** K11
Maykop *Russia* 44°35N 40°10E **19** F7
Maymyo *Burma* 22°2N 96°28E **38** A1
Maynard *Mass., U.S.A.* 42°26N 71°27W **83** D13
Maynard *Wash., U.S.A.* 47°59N 122°55W **78** C4
Maynard Hills *Australia* 28°28S 119°49E **61** E2
Mayne → *Australia* 23°40S 141°55E **62** C3
Maynooth *Canada* 45°13N 77°56W **82** A7
Maynooth *Ireland* 53°23N 6°34W **10** C5
Mayo *Canada* 63°38N 135°57W **68** E4
Mayo □ *Ireland* 53°53N 9°3W **10** C2
Mayon Volcano *Phil.* 13°15N 123°41E **37** B6
Mayor I. *N.Z.* 37°16S 176°17E **59** B6
Mayotte ☒ *Ind. Oc.* 12°50S 45°10E **53** a
Maysān □ *Iraq* 31°55N 47°15E **44** D5
Maysville *U.S.A.* 38°39N 83°46W **81** F12
Mayu *Indonesia* 1°30N 126°30E **37** D7
Mayville *N. Dak., U.S.A.* 47°30N 97°20W **80** B5
Mayville *N.Y., U.S.A.* 42°15N 79°30W **82** D5
Mazabuka *Zambia* 15°52S 27°44E **55** F2
Mazagán = El Jadida *Morocco* 33°11N 8°17W **50** B4
Mazagão *Brazil* 0°7S 51°16W **93** D8
Mazán *Peru* 3°30S 73°0W **92** D4
Māzandarān □ *Iran* 36°30N 52°0E **45** B7
Mazapil *Mexico* 24°39N 101°34W **86** C4
Mazar *China* 36°32N 77°1E **32** D4
Mazara del Vallo *Italy* 37°39N 12°35E **22** F5
Mazarrón *Spain* 37°38N 1°19W **21** D5
Mazaruni → *Guyana* 6°25N 58°35W **92** B7
Mazatán *Mexico* 29°0N 110°8W **86** B2
Mazatenango *Guatemala* 14°35N 91°30W **88** D1
Mazatlán *Mexico* 23°13N 106°25W **86** C3
Mažeikiai *Lithuania* 56°20N 22°20E **9** H20
Māzhān *Iran* 32°30N 59°0E **45** C8
Mazīnān *Iran* 36°19N 56°56E **45** B8
Mazoe *Mozam.* 16°42S 33°7E **55** F3
Mazoe → *Mozam.* 16°20S 33°30E **55** F3
Mazowe *Zimbabwe* 17°28S 30°58E **55** F3
Mazurski, Pojezierze *Poland* 53°50N 21°0E **17** B11
Mazyr *Belarus* 51°59N 29°15E **17** B15
Mba *Fiji* 17°33S 177°41E **59** a
Mbabane *Swaziland* 26°18S 31°6E **57** D5
Mbaïki *C.A.R.* 3°53N 18°1E **52** D3
Mbala *Zambia* 8°46S 31°24E **55** D3
Mbalabala *Zimbabwe* 20°27S 29°3E **57** C4
Mbale *Uganda* 1°8N 34°12E **54** B3
Mbalmayo *Cameroon* 3°33N 11°33E **52** D2
Mbamba Bay *Tanzania* 11°13S 34°49E **55** E3
Mbandaka *Dem. Rep. of the Congo* 0°1N 18°18E **52** D3
Mbanza Congo *Angola* 6°18S 14°16E **52** F2
Mbanza Ngungu *Dem. Rep. of the Congo* 5°12S 14°53E **52** F2
Mbarangandu *Tanzania* 10°11S 36°48E **55** D4
Mbarara *Uganda* 0°35S 30°40E **54** C3
Mbengga = Beqa *Fiji* 18°23S 178°8E **59** a
Mbenkuru → *Tanzania* 9°25S 39°50E **55** D4
Mberengwa *Zimbabwe* 20°29S 29°57E **55** G2
Mberengwa, Mt. *Zimbabwe* 20°37S 29°55E **55** G2
Mbesuma *Zambia* 10°0S 32°2E **55** E3
Mbeya *Tanzania* 8°54S 33°29E **55** D3
Mbeya □ *Tanzania* 8°15S 33°30E **54** D3
Mbhashe → *S. Africa* 32°15S 28°54E **57** E4
Mbinga *Tanzania* 10°50S 35°0E **55** E4
Mbini = Río Muni □ *Eq. Guin.* 1°30N 10°0E **52** D2
Mbizi *Zimbabwe* 21°23S 31°1E **55** G3
Mbouda *Cameroon* 5°38N 10°15E **50** G8
M'boukou, L. de *Cameroon* 6°23N 12°50E **52** C2
Mbour *Senegal* 14°22N 16°54W **50** F2
Mbuji-Mayi *Dem. Rep. of the Congo* 6°9S 23°40E **54** D1
Mbulu *Tanzania* 3°45S 35°30E **54** C4
Mburucuyá *Argentina* 28°1S 58°14W **94** B4
Mburucuyá △ *Argentina* 28°1S 58°12W **94** B4
Mchinga *Tanzania* 9°44S 39°45E **55** D4
Mchinji *Malawi* 13°47S 32°58E **55** E3
Mdantsane *S. Africa* 32°56S 27°46E **57** E4
Mead, L. *U.S.A.* 36°0N 114°44W **79** J12
Meade *U.S.A.* 37°17N 100°20W **80** G3
Meade River = Atqasuk *U.S.A.* 70°28N 157°24W **74** A8
Meadow Lake *Canada* 54°10N 108°26W **71** C7
Meadow Lake ⌂ *Canada* 54°27N 109°0W **71** C7
Meadow Valley Wash → *U.S.A.* 36°40N 114°34W **79** J12
Meadville *U.S.A.* 41°39N 80°9W **82** E4
Meaford *Canada* 44°36N 80°35W **82** B4
Meakan Dake *Japan* 45°15N 144°0E **30** C11
Mealy Mts. *Canada* 53°10N 58°0W **73** B8
Meander River *Canada* 59°2N 117°42W **70** B5
Meares, C. *U.S.A.* 45°37N 124°0W **76** D1
Mearim → *Brazil* 3°4S 44°35W **93** D10
Meath □ *Ireland* 53°40N 6°57W **10** C5
Meath Park *Canada* 53°27N 105°22W **71** C7
Meaux *France* 48°58N 2°50E **20** B5
Mebechi-Gawa → *Japan* 40°31N 141°31E **30** D10
Mebulu, Tanjung *Indonesia* 8°50S 115°5E **37** K18
Mecanhelas *Mozam.* 15°12S 35°54E **55** F4
Mecca = Makkah *Si. Arabia* 21°30N 39°54E **47** C2
Mecca *U.S.A.* 33°34N 116°5W **79** M10
Mechanicsburg *U.S.A.* 40°13N 77°1W **82** F8
Mechanicville *U.S.A.* 42°54N 73°41W **83** D11
Mechelen *Belgium* 51°2N 4°29E **15** C4
Mecheria *Algeria* 33°35N 0°18W **50** B5
Mecklenburg *Germany* 53°33N 11°40E **16** B7
Mecklenburger Bucht *Germany* 54°20N 11°40E **16** A6
Meconta *Mozam.* 14°59S 39°50E **55** E4
Mecubúri *Mozam.* 14°39S 38°54E **55** E4
Mecubúri → *Mozam.* 14°10S 40°30E **55** E5
Mecúfi *Mozam.* 13°20S 40°32E **55** E5
Medan *Indonesia* 3°40N 98°38E **36** D1
Médanos de Coro △ *Venezuela* 11°35N 69°44W **89** D6
Medanosa, Pta. *Argentina* 48°8S 66°0W **96** F3
Médéa *Algeria* 36°12N 2°50E **50** A6
Medellín *Colombia* 6°15N 75°35W **92** B3
Medelpad *Sweden* 62°33N 16°30E **8** E17
Medemblik *Neths.* 52°46N 5°8E **15** B5
Medford *Mass., U.S.A.* 42°25N 71°7W **83** D13
Medford *Oreg., U.S.A.* 42°19N 122°52W **76** E2
Medford *Wis., U.S.A.* 45°9N 90°20W **80** C8
Medgidia *Romania* 44°15N 28°19E **17** F15
Media Agua *Argentina* 31°58S 68°25W **94** C2
Media Luna *Argentina* 34°45S 66°44W **94** C2
Medianeira *Brazil* 25°17S 54°5W **95** B5
Mediaş *Romania* 46°9N 24°22E **17** E13
Medicine Bow *U.S.A.* 41°54N 106°12W **76** F10
Medicine Bow Mts. *U.S.A.* 40°40N 106°0W **76** F10
Medicine Bow Pk. *U.S.A.* 41°21N 106°19W **76** F10
Medicine Hat *Canada* 50°0N 110°45W **71** D6
Medicine Lake *U.S.A.* 48°30N 104°30W **76** B11
Medicine Lodge *U.S.A.* 37°17N 98°35W **80** G4
Medina = Al Madīnah *Si. Arabia* 24°35N 39°52E **44** E3
Medina *N. Dak., U.S.A.* 46°54N 99°18W **80** B4
Medina *N.Y., U.S.A.* 43°13N 78°23W **82** C6
Medina *Ohio, U.S.A.* 41°8N 81°52W **82** E3
Medina → *U.S.A.* 29°16N 98°29W **84** G5

Medina del Campo Spain 41°18N 4°55W 21 B3
Medina L. U.S.A. 29°32N 98°56W 84 G5
Medina Sidonia Spain 36°28N 5°57W 21 D3
Medinipur India 22°25N 87°21E 43 H12
Mediterranean Sea Europe 35°0N 15°0E 6 H7
Médoc France 45°10N 0°50W 20 D3
Medveditsa → Russia 49°35N 42°41E 19 E7
Medvezhi, Ostrava
  Russia 71°0N 161°0E 29 B17
Medvezhyegorsk Russia 63°0N 34°25E 18 B5
Medway □ U.K. 51°25N 0°32E 13 F8
Medway → U.K. 51°27N 0°46E 13 F8
Meekatharra Australia 26°32S 118°29E 61 E2
Meeker U.S.A. 40°2N 107°55W 76 F10
Meerut India 29°1N 77°42E 42 E7
Meeteetse U.S.A. 44°9N 108°52W 76 D9
Mega Ethiopia 3°57N 38°19E 47 G2
Megara Greece 37°58N 23°22E 23 F10
Megasini India 21°38N 86°21E 43 J12
Meghalaya □ India 25°50N 91°0E 41 G17
Meghna → Bangla. 22°50N 90°50E 41 H17
Megion Russia 61°3N 76°6E 28 C8
Mégiscane, L. Canada 48°35N 75°55W 72 C4
Meharry, Mt. Australia 22°59S 118°35E 60 D2
Mehlville U.S.A. 38°31N 90°19W 80 F8
Mehndawal India 26°58N 83°5E 43 F10
Mehr Jān Iran 33°50N 55°6E 45 C7
Mehrābād Iran 36°53N 47°55E 44 B5
Mehrān Iran 33°7N 46°10E 44 C5
Mehrān → Iran 26°45N 55°26E 45 E7
Mehrgarh Pakistan 29°30N 67°30E 42 E2
Mehrīz Iran 31°35N 54°28E 45 D7
Mei Xian China 34°18N 107°55E 34 G4
Meighen I. Canada 80°0N 99°30W 69 B12
Meihekou China 42°32N 125°40E 35 C13
Meiktila Burma 20°53N 95°54E 41 J19
Meissen Germany 51°9N 13°29E 16 C7
Meitan China 27°45N 107°29E 32 F10
Meizhou China 24°16N 116°6E 33 G12
Meja India 25°9N 82°7E 43 G10
Mejillones Chile 23°10S 70°30W 94 A1
Mekele Ethiopia 13°33N 39°30E 47 E2
Mekerghene, Sebkra
  Algeria 26°21N 1°30E 50 C6
Mekhtar Pakistan 30°30N 69°15E 40 D6
Meknès Morocco 33°57N 5°33W 50 B4
Mekong → Asia 9°30N 106°15E 39 H6
Mekongga Indonesia 3°39S 121°15E 37 E6
Mekvari = Kür →
  Azerbaijan 39°29N 49°15E 19 G8
Melagiri Hills India 12°20N 77°30E 40 N10
Melaka Malaysia 2°15N 102°15E 39 L4
Melaka □ Malaysia 2°15N 102°15E 39 L4
Melambes Greece 35°8N 24°40E 25 D6
Melanesia Pac. Oc. 4°0S 155°0E 64 H7
Melanesian Basin Pac. Oc. 0°5N 160°35E 64 G8
Melaya Indonesia 8°17S 114°30E 37 J17
Melbourne Australia 37°48S 144°58E 63 F4
Melbourne U.S.A. 28°5N 80°37W 85 G14
Melchor Múzquiz
  Mexico 27°53N 101°31W 86 B4
Melchor Ocampo
  Mexico 24°51N 101°39W 86 C4
Melekeok Palau 7°27N 134°38E 64 G5
Mélèzes → Canada 57°40N 69°29W 72 A5
Melfort Canada 52°50N 104°37W 71 C8
Melfort Zimbabwe 18°0S 31°25E 55 F3
Melhus Norway 63°17N 10°18E 8 E14
Melilla N. Afr. 35°21N 2°57W 21 E4
Melipilla Chile 33°42S 71°15W 94 C1
Melissa Canada 45°24N 79°14W 82 A5
Melissa, Akra Greece 35°6N 24°33E 25 D6
Melita Canada 49°15N 101°0W 71 D8
Melitopol Ukraine 46°50N 35°22E 19 E6
Melk Austria 48°13N 15°20E 16 D8
Mellansel Sweden 63°26N 18°19E 8 E18
Mellen U.S.A. 46°20N 90°40W 80 B8
Mellerud Sweden 58°41N 12°28E 9 G15
Mellette U.S.A. 45°9N 98°30W 80 C4
Mellieha Malta 35°57N 14°22E 25 D1
Melo Uruguay 32°20S 54°10W 95 C5
Melolo Indonesia 9°53S 120°40E 37 F6
Melouprey Cambodia 13°48N 105°16E 38 F5
Melrhir, Chott Algeria 34°13N 6°30E 50 B7
Melrose Australia 32°42S 146°57E 63 E4
Melrose U.K. 55°36N 2°43W 11 F6
Melrose Minn., U.S.A. 45°40N 94°49W 80 C6
Melrose N. Mex.,
  U.S.A. 34°26N 103°38W 77 J12
Melstone U.S.A. 46°36N 107°52W 76 C10
Melton Mowbray U.K. 52°47N 0°54W 12 E7
Melun France 48°32N 2°39E 20 B5
Melville Canada 50°55N 102°50W 71 C8
Melville, C. Australia 14°11S 144°30E 62 A3
Melville, L. Canada 53°30N 60°0W 73 B8
Melville B. Australia 12°0S 136°45E 62 A2
Melville B. Greenland 75°30N 63°0W 69 B19
Melville I. Australia 11°30S 131°0E 60 B5
Melville I. Canada 75°30N 112°0W 69 B9
Melville Pen. Canada 68°0N 84°0W 69 D15
Melvin, Lough Ireland 54°26N 8°10W 10 B3
Memba Mozam. 14°11S 40°30E 55 E5
Memboro Indonesia 9°30S 119°30E 60 A2
Memel = Klaipėda
  Lithuania 55°43N 21°10E 9 J19
Memel S. Africa 27°38S 29°36E 57 D4
Memmingen Germany 47°58N 10°10E 16 E6
Mempawah Indonesia 0°30N 109°5E 36 D3
Memphis Mich., U.S.A. 42°54N 82°46W 82 D2
Memphis Tenn., U.S.A. 35°8N 90°2W 85 D9
Memphis Tex., U.S.A. 34°44N 100°33W 84 D4
Memphrémagog, L.
  N. Amer. 45°8N 72°17W 83 B12
Mena U.S.A. 34°35N 94°15W 84 D7
Menado = Manado
  Indonesia 1°29N 124°51E 37 D6
Menai Strait U.K. 53°11N 4°13W 12 D3
Ménaka Mali 15°59N 2°18E 50 E6
Menan = Chao Phraya →
  Thailand 13°40N 100°31E 38 F3

Menarandra → Madag. 25°17S 44°30E 57 D7
Menard U.S.A. 30°55N 99°47W 84 F5
Menard Fracture Zone
  Pac. Oc.
Mendaña Fracture Zone
  Pac. Oc. 16°0S 91°0W 65 J18
Mendawai → Indonesia 3°30S 113°0E 36 E4
Mende France 44°31N 3°30E 20 D5
Mendeleyev Ridge Arctic 80°0N 178°0W 4 B17
Mendhar India 33°35N 74°10E 43 C6
Mendip Hills U.K. 51°17N 2°40W 13 F5
Mendocino U.S.A. 39°19N 123°48W 76 G2
Mendocino, C. U.S.A. 40°26N 124°25W 76 F1
Mendocino Fracture Zone
  Pac. Oc. 40°0N 142°0W 65 D13
Mendota Calif., U.S.A. 36°45N 120°23W 78 J6
Mendota Ill., U.S.A. 41°33N 89°7W 80 E9
Mendoyo Indonesia 8°23S 114°42E 37 J17
Mendoza Argentina 32°50S 68°52W 94 C2
Mendoza □ Argentina 33°0S 69°0W 94 C2
Mene Grande Venezuela 9°49N 70°56W 92 B4
Menemen Turkey 38°34N 27°3E 23 E12
Mengcheng China 33°12N 116°36E 34 H9
Menggala Indonesia 4°30S 105°15E 36 E3
Mengjin China 34°55N 112°45E 34 G7
Mengyin China 35°40N 117°58E 35 G9
Mengzi China 23°20N 103°22E 32 G9
Menihek Canada 54°28N 56°36W 73 B6
Menihek L. Canada 54°0N 67°0W 73 B6
Menin = Menen Belgium 50°47N 3°7E 15 D3
Menindee Australia 32°20S 142°25E 63 E3
Menindee L. Australia 32°20S 142°25E 63 E3
Meningie Australia 35°50S 139°18E 63 F2
Menjangan, Pulau
  Indonesia 8°7S 114°31E 37 J17
Menlo Park U.S.A. 37°27N 122°12W 78 H4
Menngen ⓒ Australia 15°21S 131°16E 60 C5
Menominee U.S.A. 45°6N 87°37W 80 C10
Menominee → U.S.A. 45°6N 87°35W 80 C10
Menomonie U.S.A. 44°53N 91°55W 80 C8
Menongue Angola 14°48S 17°52E 53 G3
Menorca Spain 40°0N 4°0E 24 B11
Mentakab Malaysia 3°29N 102°21E 39 L4
Mentawai, Kepulauan
  Indonesia 2°0S 99°0E 36 E1
Menton France 43°50N 7°29E 20 E7
Mentor U.S.A. 41°40N 81°21W 82 E3
Menzelinsk Russia 55°47N 53°11E 18 C9
Menzies Australia 29°40S 121°2E 61 E3
Meob B. Namibia 24°25S 14°34E 56 C1
Me'ona Israel 33°1N 35°15E 46 B4
Meoqui Mexico 28°17N 105°29W 86 B3
Meppel Neths. 52°42N 6°12E 15 B6
Merak Indonesia 6°10N 106°26E 37 F12
Meramangye, L.
  Australia 28°25S 132°13E 61 E5
Meran = Merano Italy 46°40N 11°9E 22 A4
Merano Italy 46°40N 11°9E 22 A4
Merauke Indonesia 8°29S 140°24E 37 F10
Merbein Australia 34°10S 142°2E 63 E3
Merca = Marka
  Somali Rep. 1°48N 44°50E 47 G3
Merced U.S.A. 37°18N 120°29W 78 H6
Merced → U.S.A. 37°21N 120°59W 78 H6
Merced Pk. U.S.A. 37°36N 119°24W 78 H7
Mercedes B. Aires,
  Argentina 34°40S 59°30W 94 C4
Mercedes Corrientes,
  Argentina 29°10S 58°5W 94 B4
Mercedes San Luis,
  Argentina 33°40S 65°21W 94 C2
Mercedes Uruguay 33°12S 58°0W 94 C4
Merceditas Chile 28°20S 70°35W 94 B1
Mercer N.Z. 37°16S 175°5E 59 B5
Mercer U.S.A. 41°14N 80°15W 82 E4
Mercer Island U.S.A. 47°34N 122°13W 78 C4
Mercury U.S.A. 36°40N 115°59W 79 J11
Mercy, C. Canada 65°0N 63°30W 69 E19
Mere U.K. 51°6N 2°16W 13 F5
Merebuk, Gunung
  Indonesia 8°13S 114°39E 37 J17
Meredith, C. Falk. Is. 52°15S 60°40W 96 G4
Meredith, L. U.S.A. 35°43N 101°33W 84 D4
Mergui Burma 12°26N 98°34E 38 F2
Mergui Arch. = Myeik Kyunzu
  Burma 11°30N 97°30E 39 G1
Mérida Mexico 20°58N 89°37W 87 C7
Mérida Spain 38°55N 6°25W 21 C2
Mérida Venezuela 8°24N 71°8W 92 B4
Mérida, Cord. de Venezuela 9°0N 71°0W 92 B4
Meriden U.K. 52°26N 1°38W 13 E6
Meriden U.S.A. 41°32N 72°48W 83 E12
Meridian Calif., U.S.A. 39°9N 121°55W 78 F5
Meridian Idaho, U.S.A. 43°37N 116°24W 76 E5
Meridian Miss., U.S.A. 32°22N 88°42W 85 E10
Merinda Australia 20°2S 148°11E 62 C4
Merir Palau 4°10N 132°30E 37 D8
Merirumã Brazil 1°15N 54°50W 93 C8
Merkel U.S.A. 32°28N 100°1W 84 E4
Merksem Belgium 51°16N 4°25E 15 C4
Merowe Dam Sudan 18°35N 31°56E 51 E12
Merredin Australia 31°28S 118°18E 61 F2
Merrick U.K. 55°8N 4°28W 11 F4
Merrickville Canada 44°55N 75°50W 83 B9
Merrill Oreg., U.S.A. 42°1N 121°36W 76 E3
Merrill Wis., U.S.A. 45°11N 89°41W 80 C9
Merrimack → U.S.A. 42°49N 70°49W 83 D14
Merriman U.S.A. 42°55N 101°42W 80 D3
Merritt Canada 50°10N 120°45W 70 C4
Merritt Island U.S.A. 28°21N 80°42W 85 G14
Merriwa Australia 32°6S 150°22E 63 E5
Merry I. Canada 55°29N 77°31W 72 A4
Merryville U.S.A. 30°45N 93°33W 84 F8
Mersch Lux. 49°44N 6°7E 15 E6
Mersea I. U.K. 51°47N 0°58E 13 F8
Merseburg Germany 51°22N 11°59E 16 C6
Mersey → U.K. 53°25N 3°1W 12 D4
Merseyside □ U.K. 53°31N 3°2W 12 D4

Mersin = İçel Turkey 36°51N 34°36E 44 B2
Mersing Malaysia 2°25N 103°50E 39 L4
Merta India 26°39N 74°4E 42 F6
Merta Road India 26°43N 73°55E 42 F5
Merthyr Tydfil U.K. 51°45N 3°22W 13 F4
Merthyr Tydfil □ U.K. 51°46N 3°21W 13 F4
Merti Kenya 1°4N 38°40E 54 B4
Mértola Portugal 37°40N 7°40W 21 D2
Mertzon U.S.A. 31°16N 100°49W 84 F4
Meru Kenya 0°3N 37°40E 54 B4
Meru Tanzania 3°15S 36°46E 54 C4
Meru → Kenya 0°5N 38°10E 54 B4
Meru Betiri △ Indonesia 8°27S 113°51E 37 H15
Mesa U.S.A. 33°25N 111°50W 77 K8
Mesa Verde △ U.S.A. 37°11N 108°29W 77 H9
Mesanagros Greece 36°1N 27°49E 25 C9
Mesaoria Cyprus 35°12N 33°14E 25 D12
Mesgouez, L. Canada 51°20N 75°0W 72 B5
Meshed = Mashhad Iran 36°20N 59°35E 45 B8
Meshgīn Shahr Iran 38°30N 47°45E 44 B5
Meshoppen U.S.A. 41°36N 76°3W 83 E8
Mesilinka → Canada 56°6N 124°30W 70 B4
Mesologi Greece 38°21N 21°28E 23 E9
Mesongi Greece 39°29N 19°56E 25 B3
Mesopotamia = Al Jazirah
  Iraq 33°30N 44°0E 44 C5
Mesopotamia U.S.A. 41°27N 80°57W 82 E4
Mesquite U.S.A. 36°48N 114°4W 77 H6
Messaad Algeria 34°8N 3°30E 50 B6
Messalo → Mozam. 12°25S 39°15E 54 E4
Messara, Kolpos Greece 35°6N 24°47E 25 D6
Messina
  S. Africa 22°20S 30°5E 57 C5
Messina Italy 38°11N 15°34E 22 E6
Messina, Str. di Italy 38°15N 15°35E 22 E6
Messini Greece 37°4N 22°1E 23 F10
Messiniakos Kolpos
  Greece 36°45N 22°5E 23 F10
Mesta = Nestos →
  Europe 40°54N 24°49E 23 D11
Meta → S. Amer. 6°12N 67°28W 92 B5
Meta Incognita Pen.
  Canada 62°45N 68°30W 69 E18
Metabetchouan Canada 48°26N 71°52W 73 C5
Metairie U.S.A. 29°59N 90°9W 85 G9
Metaline Falls U.S.A. 48°52N 117°22W 76 B5
Metán Argentina 25°30S 65°0W 94 B3
Metangula Mozam. 12°40S 34°50E 55 E3
Metcalfe Canada 45°14N 75°28W 83 A9
Metema Ethiopia 12°56N 36°12E 47 E2
Metengobalame Mozam. 14°49S 34°30E 55 E3
Methven N.Z. 43°38S 171°40E 59 E3
Metil Mozam. 16°24S 39°0E 55 F4
Metlakatla U.S.A. 55°8N 131°35W 68 F5
Metropolis U.S.A. 37°9N 88°44W 80 G9
Metropolitana □ Chile 33°30S 70°50W 94 C1
Metu Ethiopia 8°18N 35°35E 47 F2
Metz France 49°8N 6°10E 20 B7
Meulaboh Indonesia 4°11N 96°3E 36 D1
Meureudu Indonesia 5°19N 96°10E 36 C1
Meuse → Europe 50°45N 5°41E 15 D5
Mexia U.S.A. 31°41N 96°29W 84 F6
Mexiana, I. Brazil 0°0 49°30W 93 D9
Mexicali Mexico 32°40N 115°30W 79 N11
Mexican Plateau Mexico 25°0N 104°0W 66 G9
Mexican Water U.S.A. 36°57N 109°32W 77 H9
México Mexico 19°24N 99°9W 87 D5
Mexico Maine, U.S.A. 44°34N 70°33W 83 B14
Mexico Mo., U.S.A. 39°10N 91°53W 80 F8
Mexico N.Y., U.S.A. 43°28N 76°14W 83 C8
México □ Mexico 19°20N 99°30W 87 D5
Mexico ■ Cent. Amer. 25°0N 105°0W 86 C4
México, Ciudad de
  Mexico 19°24N 99°9W 87 D5
Mexico, G. of Cent. Amer. 25°0N 90°0W 87 C7
Mexico B. U.S.A. 43°35N 76°20W 83 C8
Meydân-e Naftûn Iran 31°56N 49°18E 45 D6
Meydani, Ra's-e Iran 25°24N 59°6E 45 E8
Meyers Chuck U.S.A. 55°45N 132°15W 70 B2
Meymaneh Afghan. 35°53N 64°38E 40 B4
Mezen Russia 65°50N 44°20E 18 A7
Mezen → Russia 65°44N 44°22E 18 A7
Mézenc, Mt. France 44°54N 4°11E 20 D6
Mezhdurechensk Russia 53°41N 88°3E 28 D9
Mezhdurechenskiy
  Russia 59°36N 65°56E 28 D7
Mezőkövesd Hungary 47°49N 20°35E 17 E11
Mezőtúr Hungary 47°1N 20°41E 17 E11
Mezquital Mexico 23°29N 104°23W 86 C4
Miajadas Spain 39°9N 5°54W 21 C3
Miami Fla., U.S.A. 25°46N 80°11W 85 J14
Miami Okla., U.S.A. 36°53N 94°53W 84 C7
Miami Tex., U.S.A. 35°42N 100°38W 84 D4
Miami Beach U.S.A. 25°47N 80°7W 85 J14
Mian Xian China 33°10N 106°32E 34 H4
Mianchi China 34°48N 111°48E 34 G6
Miāndarreh Iran 35°37N 53°39E 45 C7
Miāndowāb Iran 37°0N 46°5E 44 B5
Miandrivazo Madag. 19°31S 45°29E 57 B8
Miāneh Iran 37°30N 47°40E 44 B5
Mianwali Pakistan 32°38N 71°28E 42 C4
Mianyang China 31°22N 104°47E 32 E9
Miaodao Qundao
  China 38°10N 120°45E 35 E11

Michoacán □ Mexico 19°10N 101°50W 86 D4
Michurin Bulgaria 42°9N 27°51E 23 C12
Michurinsk Russia 52°58N 40°27E 18 D7
Micoud St. Lucia 13°49N 60°54W 89 f
Micronesia Pac. Oc. 11°0N 160°0E 64 G7
Micronesia, Federated States of ■
  Pac. Oc. 9°0N 150°0E 58 A8
Mid-Indian Ridge Ind. Oc. 30°0S 75°0E 64 M1
Mid-Oceanic Ridge
  Ind. Oc. 42°0S 90°0E 64 M1
Mid-Pacific Seamounts
  Pac. Oc. 18°0N 177°0W 64 F10
Midai Indonesia 3°0N 107°47E 36 D3
Midale Canada 49°25N 103°20W 71 D8
Middelburg Neths. 51°30N 3°36E 15 C3
Middelburg Eastern Cape,
  S. Africa 31°30S 25°0E 56 E4
Middelburg Mpumalanga,
  S. Africa 25°49S 29°28E 57 D4
Middelpos S. Africa 31°55S 20°13E 56 E3
Middelwit S. Africa 24°51S 27°3E 56 C4
Middle Alkali L. U.S.A. 41°27N 120°5W 76 F3
Middle America Trench =
  Guatemala Trench
  Pac. Oc. 14°0N 95°0W 66 H10
Middle Bass I. U.S.A. 41°41N 82°48W 82 E2
Middle East Asia 35°0N 40°0E 26 C5
Middle Fork Feather →
  U.S.A. 38°33N 121°30W 78 F5
Middle I. Australia 34°6S 123°11E 61 F3
Middle Loup → U.S.A. 41°17N 98°24W 80 E4
Middleboro U.S.A. 41°54N 70°55W 83 E14
Middleburg Fla., U.S.A. 30°4N 81°52W 85 F14
Middleburg Pa., U.S.A. 40°47N 77°3W 82 F7
Middleburgh U.S.A. 42°36N 74°20W 83 D10
Middlebury U.S.A. 44°1N 73°10W 83 B11
Middlefield U.S.A. 41°27N 81°4W 82 E3
Middlemount Australia 22°50S 148°40E 62 C4
Middleport N.Y., U.S.A. 43°13N 78°29W 82 C6
Middleport Ohio, U.S.A. 39°0N 82°3W 81 F12
Middlesboro U.S.A. 36°36N 83°43W 81 G12
Middlesbrough U.K. 54°35N 1°13W 12 C6
Middlesbrough □ U.K. 54°28N 1°13W 12 C6
Middlesex Belize 17°2N 88°31W 88 C2
Middlesex N.J., U.S.A. 40°36N 74°30W 83 F10
Middlesex N.Y., U.S.A. 42°42N 77°16W 82 D7
Middleton Australia 22°22S 141°32E 62 C3
Middleton Canada 44°57N 65°4W 73 D6
Middleton Cr. →
  Australia 22°35S 141°51E 62 C3
Middleton I. U.S.A. 59°26N 146°20W 74 D10
Middletown U.K. 54°17N 6°51W 10 B5
Middletown Calif.,
  U.S.A. 38°45N 122°37W 78 G4
Middletown Conn.,
  U.S.A. 41°34N 72°39W 83 E12
Middletown N.Y.,
  U.S.A. 41°27N 74°25W 83 E10
Middletown Ohio,
  U.S.A. 39°31N 84°24W 81 F11
Middletown Pa., U.S.A. 40°12N 76°44W 83 F8
Midge Point Australia 20°39S 148°43E 62 b
Midhurst Canada 44°26N 79°43W 82 B5
Midhurst U.K. 50°59N 0°44W 13 G7
Midi, Canal du → France 43°45N 1°21E 20 E4
Midland Canada 44°45N 79°50W 82 B5
Midland Calif., U.S.A. 33°52N 114°48W 79 M12
Midland Mich., U.S.A. 43°37N 84°14W 81 D11
Midland Pa., U.S.A. 40°39N 80°27W 82 F4
Midland Tex., U.S.A. 32°0N 102°3W 84 F3
Midlands □ Zimbabwe 19°40S 29°0E 55 F2
Midleton Ireland 51°55N 8°10W 10 E3
Midlothian U.S.A. 32°30N 97°0W 84 E6
Midlothian □ U.K. 55°51N 3°5W 11 F5
Midnapore = Medinipur
  India 22°25N 87°21E 43 H12
Midongy, Tangorombohitr' i
  Madag. 23°30S 47°0E 57 C8
Midongy Atsimo Madag. 23°35S 47°1E 57 C8
Midway Is. Pac. Oc. 28°13N 177°22W 75 K4
Midway Wells U.S.A. 32°41N 115°7W 79 N11
Midwest U.S.A. 42°0N 90°0W 75 G22
Midwest Wyo., U.S.A. 43°25N 106°16W 76 E10
Midwest City U.S.A. 35°27N 97°24W 84 D6
Midyat Turkey 37°25N 41°23E 44 B4
Midzŏr Bulgaria 43°24N 22°40E 23 C10
Mie □ Japan 34°30N 136°10E 31 G8
Międzychód Poland 52°35N 15°53E 16 B8
Międzyrzec Podlaski
  Poland 51°58N 22°45E 17 C12
Mielec Poland 50°15N 21°25E 17 C11
Mienga Angola 17°12S 19°48E 56 B2
Miercurea-Ciuc
  Romania 46°21N 25°48E 17 E13
Mieres Spain 43°18N 5°48W 21 A3
Mifflintown U.S.A. 40°34N 77°24W 82 F7
Mifraz Ḥefa Israel 32°52N 35°0E 46 C4
Migang Shan China 35°32N 106°13E 34 G4
Migori Kenya 1°4S 34°28E 54 C3
Miguasha, Parc de ⌂
  Canada 48°5N 66°19W 73 C6
Miguel Alemán, Presa
  Mexico 18°15N 96°32W 87 D5
Mihara Japan 34°24N 133°5E 31 G6
Mikese Tanzania 6°48S 37°55E 54 D4
Mikhaylovgrad = Montana
  Bulgaria 43°27N 23°16E 23 C10
Mikhaylovka Russia 50°3N 43°5E 19 D7
Mikines Greece 37°43N 22°46E 23 F10
Mikkeli Finland 61°43N 27°15E 8 F22
Mikkwa → Canada 58°25N 114°46W 70 B6
Míkonos = Mykonos
  Greece 37°30N 25°25E 23 F11
Mikumi Tanzania 7°26S 37°0E 54 D4
Mikumi △ Tanzania 7°35S 37°15E 54 D4
Mikun Russia 62°20N 50°0E 18 B9
Milaca U.S.A. 45°45N 93°39W 80 C7
Milagro Ecuador 2°11S 79°36W 92 D3
Milan = Milano Italy 45°28N 9°10E 20 D8
Milan Mo., U.S.A. 40°12N 93°7W 80 E7

Milan Tenn., U.S.A. 35°55N 88°46W 85 D10
Milange Mozam. 16°3S 35°45E 55 F4
Milano Italy 45°28N 9°10E 20 D8
Milanoa Madag. 13°35S 49°47E 57 A8
Milâs Turkey 37°20N 27°50E 23 F12
Milatos Greece 35°18N 25°34E 25 D7
Milazzo Italy 38°13N 15°15E 22 E6
Milbank U.S.A. 45°13N 96°38W 80 C5
Milbanke Sd. Canada 52°15N 128°33W 70 C3
Milden Canada 51°29N 107°32W 71 C7
Mildenhall U.K. 52°21N 0°32E 13 E8
Mildmay Canada 44°3N 81°7W 82 B3
Mildura Australia 34°13S 142°9E 63 E3
Miles Australia 26°40S 150°9E 63 D5
Miles City U.S.A. 46°25N 105°51W 76 C11
Milestone Canada 49°59N 104°31W 71 D8
Miletus Turkey 37°30N 27°18E 23 F12
Milford Calif., U.S.A. 40°10N 120°22W 78 E6
Milford Conn., U.S.A. 41°14N 73°3W 83 E11
Milford Del., U.S.A. 38°55N 75°26W 81 F16
Milford Mass., U.S.A. 42°8N 71°31W 83 D13
Milford N.H., U.S.A. 42°50N 71°39W 83 D13
Milford N.Y., U.S.A. 42°35N 74°56W 83 D10
Milford Pa., U.S.A. 41°19N 74°48W 83 E10
Milford Utah, U.S.A. 38°24N 113°1W 76 G7
Milford Haven U.K. 51°42N 5°7W 13 F2
Milford Sd. N.Z. 44°41S 167°47E 59 F1
Milford Sound N.Z. 44°41S 167°55E 59 F1
Milḥ, Baḥr al = Razāzah,
  Buḥayrat ar Iraq 32°40N 43°35E 44 C4
Milikapiti Australia 11°26S 130°40E 60 B5
Miling Australia 30°30S 116°17E 61 F2
Milk River Canada 49°10N 112°5W 70 D6
Mill → U.S.A. 42°57N 83°23W 82 D1
Mill I. Antarctica 66°0S 101°30E 5 C8
Mill I. Canada 63°58N 77°47W 69 E16
Mill Valley U.S.A. 37°54N 122°32W 78 H4
Millau France 44°8N 3°4E 20 D5
Millbridge Canada 44°41N 77°36W 82 B7
Millbrook Canada 44°10N 78°29W 82 B6
Millbrook Ala., U.S.A. 32°29N 86°22W 85 E11
Mille Lacs, L. des Canada 48°45N 90°35W 72 C1
Mille Lacs L. U.S.A. 46°15N 93°39W 80 B7
Milledgeville U.S.A. 33°5N 83°14W 85 E13
Millen U.S.A. 32°48N 81°57W 85 E14
Millennium I. = Caroline I.
  Kiribati 9°58S 150°13W 65 H12
Miller U.S.A. 44°31N 98°59W 80 C4
Miller Lake Canada 45°6N 81°26W 82 A3
Millersburg Ohio, U.S.A. 40°33N 81°55W 82 F3
Millersburg Pa., U.S.A. 40°32N 76°58W 82 F8
Millerton U.S.A. 41°57N 73°31W 83 E11
Millerton L. U.S.A. 37°1N 119°41W 78 J7
Millet St. Lucia 13°55N 60°59W 89 f
Millheim U.S.A. 40°54N 77°29W 82 F7
Millicent Australia 37°34S 140°21E 63 F3
Millington U.S.A. 35°20N 89°53W 85 D10
Millinocket U.S.A. 45°39N 68°43W 81 C19
Millmerran Australia 27°53S 151°16E 63 D5
Mills L. Canada 61°30N 118°20W 70 A5
Millstream Chichester △
  Australia 21°35S 117°6E 60 D2
Millstreet Ireland 52°4N 9°4W 10 D2
Milltown Malbay Ireland 52°52N 9°24W 10 D2
Millville N.J., U.S.A. 39°24N 75°2W 81 F16
Millville Pa., U.S.A. 41°7N 76°32W 83 E8
Millwood L. U.S.A. 33°42N 93°58W 84 E8
Milne → Australia 21°10S 137°33E 62 C2
Milo U.S.A. 45°15N 68°59W 81 C19
Milon, Akra Greece 36°46N 28°11E 25 C10
Milos Greece 36°44N 24°25E 23 F11
Milparinka Australia 29°46S 141°57E 63 D3
Milpitas U.S.A. 37°26N 121°55W 78 H5
Milton N.S., Canada 44°4N 64°45W 73 D7
Milton Ont., Canada 43°31N 79°53W 82 C5
Milton N.Z. 46°7S 169°59E 59 G2
Milton Calif., U.S.A. 38°3N 120°51W 78 G6
Milton Fla., U.S.A. 30°38N 87°3W 85 F11
Milton Pa., U.S.A. 41°1N 76°51W 82 F8
Milton Vt., U.S.A. 44°38N 73°7W 83 B11
Milton-Freewater
  U.S.A. 45°56N 118°23W 76 D4
Milton Keynes U.K. 52°1N 0°44W 13 E7
Milton Keynes □ U.K. 52°1N 0°44W 13 E7
Milverton Canada 43°34N 80°55W 82 C4
Milwaukee U.S.A. 43°2N 87°54W 80 D10
Milwaukee Deep Atl. Oc. 19°50N 68°0W 89 C6
Milwaukie U.S.A. 45°27N 122°38W 78 E4
Mimili Australia 27°0S 132°42E 61 E5
Min Jiang → Fujian,
  China 26°0N 119°35E 33 F12
Min Jiang → Sichuan,
  China 28°45N 104°40E 32 F9
Min Xian China 34°25N 104°5E 34 G3
Minâ' Jabal 'Alī U.A.E. 25°2N 55°8E 45 E7
Mina Pirquitas
  Argentina 22°40S 66°30W 94 A2
Minâ Su'ud Si. Arabia 28°45N 48°28E 45 D6
Minâ'al Aḥmadī Kuwait 29°5N 48°10E 45 D6
Minago → Canada 54°33N 98°59W 71 C9
Minaki Canada 49°59N 94°40W 71 D10
Minamata Japan 32°10N 130°30E 31 H5
Minami-Arapusa △
  Japan 35°30N 138°9E 31 G9
Minami-Tori-Shima
  Pac. Oc. 24°20N 153°58E 64 E7
Minas Uruguay 34°20S 55°10W 95 C4
Minas, Sierra de las
  Guatemala 15°9N 89°31W 88 C2
Minas Basin Canada 45°20N 64°12W 73 C7
Minas Gerais □ Brazil 18°50S 46°0W 93 G9
Minatitlán Mexico 17°59N 94°31W 87 D6
Minbu Burma 20°10N 94°52E 41 J19
Minchinabad Pakistan 30°10N 73°34E 42 D5
Mindanao Phil. 8°0N 125°0E 37 C7
Mindanao Sea = Bohol Sea
  Phil. 9°0N 124°0E 37 C6

Mindanao Trench *Pac. Oc.* 12°0N 126°6E **37** B7
Mindelo *C. Verde Is.* 16°24N 25°0W **50** b
Minden *Canada* 44°55N 78°43W **82** B6
Minden *Germany* 52°17N 8°55E **16** B5
Minden *La., U.S.A.* 32°37N 93°17W **84** E8
Minden *Nev., U.S.A.* 38°57N 119°46W **78** G7
Mindibungu = Billiluna *Australia* 19°37S 127°41E **60** C4
Mindiptana *Indonesia* 5°55S 140°22E **37** F10
Mindoro *Phil.* 13°0N 121°0E **37** B6
Mindoro Str. *Phil.* 12°30N 120°30E **37** B6
Mine *Japan* 34°12N 131°7E **31** G5
Minehead *U.K.* 51°12N 3°29W **13** F4
Mineola *N.Y., U.S.A.* 40°44N 73°38W **83** F11
Mineola *Tex., U.S.A.* 32°40N 95°29W **84** E7
Mineral King *U.S.A.* 36°27N 118°36W **78** J8
Mineral Wells *U.S.A.* 32°48N 98°7W **84** E5
Miners Bay *Canada* 44°49N 78°46W **82** B6
Minersville *U.S.A.* 40°41N 76°16W **83** F8
Minerva *N.Y., U.S.A.* 43°47N 73°59W **83** C11
Minerva *Ohio, U.S.A.* 40°44N 81°6W **82** F3
Minetto *U.S.A.* 43°24N 76°28W **83** C8
Minfeng *China* 37°4N 82°46E **32** D5
Mingäçevir Su Anbarı *Azerbaijan* 40°57N 46°50E **19** F8
Mingan *Canada* 50°20N 64°0W **73** B7
Mingechaurskoye Vdkhr. = Mingäçevir Su Anbarı *Azerbaijan* 40°57N 46°50E **19** F8
Mingela *Australia* 19°52S 146°38E **62** B4
Mingenew *Australia* 29°12S 115°21E **61** E2
Mingera Cr. → *Australia* 20°38S 137°45E **62** C2
Mingin *Burma* 22°50N 94°30E **41** H19
Mingo Junction *U.S.A.* 40°19N 80°37W **82** F4
Mingora *Pakistan* 34°48N 72°22E **43** B5
Mingteke Daban = Mintaka Pass *Pakistan* 37°0N 74°58E **43** A6
Mingyuegue *China* 43°2N 128°50E **35** C15
Minhe *China* 36°9N 102°45E **32** D9
Minho = Miño → *Spain* 41°52N 8°40W **21** A2
Minho *Portugal* 41°25N 8°20W **21** B1
Minidoka *U.S.A.* 42°45N 113°29W **76** E7
Minigwal, L. *Australia* 29°31S 123°14E **61** E3
Minilya → *Australia* 23°45S 114°0E **61** D1
Minilya Roadhouse *Australia* 23°55S 114°0E **61** D1
Minipi L. *Canada* 52°25N 60°45W **73** B7
Minjilang *Australia* 11°8S 132°33E **60** B5
Mink L. *Canada* 61°54N 117°40W **70** A5
Minna *Nigeria* 9°37N 6°30E **50** G7
Minneapolis *Kans., U.S.A.* 39°8N 97°42W **80** F5
Minneapolis *Minn., U.S.A.* 44°57N 93°16W **80** C7
Minnedosa *Canada* 50°14N 99°50W **71** C9
Minnesota □ *U.S.A.* 46°0N 94°15W **80** B6
Minnesota → *U.S.A.* 44°54N 93°9W **80** C7
Minnewaukan *U.S.A.* 48°4N 99°15W **80** A4
Minnipa *Australia* 32°51S 135°9E **63** E2
Minnitaki L. *Canada* 49°57N 92°10W **72** C1
Mino *Japan* 35°32N 136°55E **31** G8
Miño → *Spain* 41°52N 8°40W **21** A2
Minorca = Menorca *Spain* 40°0N 4°0E **24** B11
Minot *U.S.A.* 48°14N 101°18W **80** A3
Minqin *China* 38°38N 103°20E **34** E2
Minsk *Belarus* 53°52N 27°30E **17** B14
Mińsk Mazowiecki *Poland* 52°10N 21°33E **17** B11
Mintabie *Australia* 27°15S 133°7E **63** D1
Mintaka Pass *Pakistan* 37°0N 74°58E **43** A6
Minto *Canada* 46°5N 66°5W **73** C6
Minto, L. *Canada* 57°13N 75°0W **72** A5
Minton *Canada* 49°10N 104°35W **71** D8
Minturn *U.S.A.* 39°35N 106°26W **76** G10
Minudasht *Iran* 37°17N 56°7E **45** B8
Minusinsk *Russia* 53°43N 91°20E **29** D10
Minutang *India* 28°15N 96°30E **41** E20
Minvoul *Gabon* 2°9N 12°8E **52** D2
Minya Konka = Gongga Shan *China* 29°40N 101°55E **32** F9
Minzhong *China* 22°37N 113°30E **33** a
Miquelon *Canada* 49°25N 76°27W **72** C4
Miquelon *St-P. & M.* 47°8N 56°22W **73** C8
Mīr Kūh *Iran* 26°22N 58°55E **45** E8
Mīr Shahdād *Iran* 26°15N 58°29E **45** E8
Mira *Italy* 45°26N 12°8E **22** B5
Mira por vos Cay *Bahamas* 22°9N 74°30W **89** B5
Mirabello, Kolpos *Greece* 35°10N 25°50E **25** D7
Mirador-Río Azul △ *Guatemala* 17°45N 89°50W **88** C2
Miraj *India* 16°50N 74°45E **40** L9
Miram Shah *Pakistan* 33°0N 70°2E **42** C4
Miramar *Argentina* 38°15S 57°50W **94** D4
Miramar *Mozam.* 23°50S 35°35E **57** C6
Miramichi *Canada* 47°2N 65°28W **73** C6
Miramichi B. *Canada* 47°15N 65°0W **73** C7
Miranda *Brazil* 20°10S 56°15W **93** H7
Miranda → *Brazil* 19°25S 57°20W **92** G7
Miranda de Ebro *Spain* 42°41N 2°57W **21** A4
Miranda do Douro *Portugal* 41°30N 6°16W **21** B2
Mirandópolis *Brazil* 21°9S 51°6W **95** A5
Mirango *Malawi* 13°32S 34°58E **55** E3
Mirani *Australia* 21°8S 148°53E **62** b
Mirassol *Brazil* 20°46S 49°28W **95** A6
Mirbāṭ *Oman* 17°0N 54°45E **47** D5
Mires *Greece* 35°4N 24°56E **25** D6
Miri *Malaysia* 4°23N 113°59E **36** D4
Miriam Vale *Australia* 24°20S 151°33E **62** C5
Mirim, L. *S. Amer.* 32°45S 52°50W **95** C5
Miriuwung Gajerrong ⚙ *Australia* 15°0S 128°45E **60** C4
Mirjāveh *Iran* 29°1N 61°30E **45** D9
Mirnyy *Antarctica* 66°50S 92°30E **5** C14
Mirnyy *Russia* 62°33N 113°53E **29** C12
Mirokhan *Pakistan* 27°46N 68°6E **42** F3
Mirond L. *Canada* 55°6N 102°47W **71** B8
Mirpur *Pakistan* 33°32N 73°56E **43** C5
Mirpur Batoro *Pakistan* 24°44N 68°16E **42** G3
Mirpur Bibiwari *Pakistan* 28°33N 67°44E **42** E2
Mirpur Khas *Pakistan* 25°30N 69°0E **42** G3
Mirpur Sakro *Pakistan* 24°33N 67°41E **42** G2
Mirs Bay = Tai Pang Wan *China* 22°33N 114°24E **33** a
Mirtağ *Turkey* 38°23N 41°56E **44** B4
Mirtoo Sea *Greece* 37°0N 23°20E **23** F10
Miryang *S. Korea* 35°31N 128°44E **35** G15
Mirzapur *India* 25°10N 82°34E **43** G10
Mirzapur-cum-Vindhyachal = Mirzapur *India* 25°10N 82°34E **43** G10
Misantla *Mexico* 19°56N 96°50W **87** D5
Misawa *Japan* 40°41N 141°24E **30** D10
Miscou I. *Canada* 47°57N 64°31W **73** C7
Mish'āb, Ra's al *Si. Arabia* 28°15N 48°43E **45** D6
Mishamo *Tanzania* 5°41S 30°41E **54** D3
Mishan *China* 45°37N 131°48E **30** B5
Mishawaka *U.S.A.* 41°40N 86°11W **80** E10
Mishima *Japan* 35°10N 138°52E **31** G9
Misión *Mexico* 32°6N 116°53W **79** N10
Misiones □ *Argentina* 27°0S 55°0W **95** B5
Misiones □ *Paraguay* 27°0S 56°0W **94** B4
Miskah *Si. Arabia* 24°49N 42°56E **44** E4
Miskitos, Cayos *Nic.* 14°26N 82°50W **88** D3
Miskolc *Hungary* 48°7N 20°50E **17** D11
Misoke *Dem. Rep. of the Congo* 0°42S 28°2E **54** C2
Misool *Indonesia* 1°52S 130°10E **37** E8
Mişr = Egypt ■ *Africa* 28°0N 31°0E **51** C12
Mişrātah *Libya* 32°24N 15°3E **51** B9
Missanabie *Canada* 48°20N 84°6W **72** C3
Missinaibi → *Canada* 50°43N 81°29W **72** B3
Missinaibi L. *Canada* 48°23N 83°40W **72** C3
Mission *Canada* 49°10N 122°15W **70** D4
Mission *S. Dak., U.S.A.* 43°18N 100°39W **80** D3
Mission *Tex., U.S.A.* 26°13N 98°20W **84** H5
Mission Beach *Australia* 17°53S 146°6E **62** B4
Mission Viejo *U.S.A.* 33°36N 117°40W **79** M9
Missisa L. *Canada* 52°20N 85°7W **72** B2
Missisicabi → *Canada* 51°14N 79°31W **72** B4
Mississagi → *Canada* 46°15N 83°9W **72** C3
Mississauga *Canada* 43°32N 79°35W **82** C5
Mississippi □ *U.S.A.* 33°0N 90°0W **85** E10
Mississippi → *U.S.A.* 29°9N 89°15W **85** G10
Mississippi L. *Canada* 45°5N 76°10W **83** A8
Mississippi River Delta *U.S.A.* 29°10N 89°15W **85** G10
Mississippi Sd. *U.S.A.* 30°20N 89°0W **85** F10
Missoula *U.S.A.* 46°52N 114°1W **76** C6
Missouri □ *U.S.A.* 38°25N 92°30W **80** F7
Missouri → *U.S.A.* 38°49N 90°7W **80** F8
Missouri City *U.S.A.* 29°37N 95°32W **84** G7
Missouri Valley *U.S.A.* 41°34N 95°53W **80** E6
Mist *U.S.A.* 45°59N 123°15W **78** E3
Mistassibi → *Canada* 48°53N 72°13W **73** B5
Mistassini *Canada* 48°53N 72°12W **73** C5
Mistassini → *Canada* 48°42N 72°20W **73** C5
Mistassini, L. *Canada* 51°0N 73°30W **72** B5
Mistastin L. *Canada* 55°57N 63°20W **73** A7
Mistinibi, L. *Canada* 55°56N 64°17W **73** A7
Mistissini *Canada* 48°53N 72°12W **73** C5
Misty L. *Canada* 58°53N 101°40W **71** B8
Misurata = Mişrātah *Libya* 32°24N 15°3E **51** B9
Mitande *Mozam.* 14°6S 35°58E **55** E4
Mitchell *Australia* 26°29S 147°58E **63** D4
Mitchell *Canada* 43°28N 81°12W **82** C3
Mitchell *Nebr., U.S.A.* 41°57N 103°49W **80** E2
Mitchell *Oreg., U.S.A.* 44°34N 120°9W **76** D3
Mitchell *S. Dak., U.S.A.* 43°43N 98°2W **80** D4
Mitchell → *Australia* 15°12S 141°35E **62** B3
Mitchell, Mt. *U.S.A.* 35°46N 82°16W **85** D13
Mitchell-Alice Rivers △ *Australia* 15°28S 142°5E **62** B3
Mitchell Ra. *Australia* 12°49S 135°36E **62** A2
Mitchelstown *Ireland* 52°15N 8°16W **10** D3
Mitha Tiwana *Pakistan* 32°13N 72°6E **42** C5
Mithi *Pakistan* 24°44N 69°48E **42** G3
Mithrao *Pakistan* 27°28N 69°40E **42** F3
Mitilini *Greece* 39°6N 26°35E **23** E12
Mitla Pass = Mamarr Mitlā *Egypt* 30°2N 32°54E **46** E1
Mito *Japan* 36°20N 140°30E **31** F10
Mitrovica = Kosovska Mitrovica *Kosovo* 42°54N 20°52E **23** C9
Mitsamiouli *Comoros Is.* 11°20S 43°16E **53** a
Mitsinjo *Madag.* 16°1S 45°52E **57** B8
Mitsiwa *Eritrea* 15°35N 39°25E **47** D2
Mitsukaidō *Japan* 36°1N 139°59E **31** F9
Mittagong *Australia* 34°28S 150°29E **63** E5
Mittimatalik = Pond Inlet *Canada* 72°40N 77°0W **69** C16
Mitú *Colombia* 1°15N 70°13W **92** C4
Mitumba *Tanzania* 7°8S 31°2E **54** D3
Mitumba, Mts. *Dem. Rep. of the Congo* 7°0S 27°30E **54** D2
Mitwaba *Dem. Rep. of the Congo* 8°2S 27°17E **55** D2
Mityana *Uganda* 0°23N 32°2E **54** B3
Mixteco → *Mexico* 18°11N 98°30W **87** D5
Miyagi □ *Japan* 38°15N 140°45E **30** E10
Miyāh, W. el → *Syria* 34°44N 39°57E **44** C3
Miyake-Jima *Japan* 34°5N 139°30E **31** G9
Miyako *Japan* 39°40N 141°59E **30** E10
Miyako-Jima *Japan* 24°45N 125°20E **31** M2
Miyako-Rettō *Japan* 24°24N 125°0E **31** M2
Miyakonojō *Japan* 31°40N 131°5E **31** J5
Miyani *India* 21°50N 69°26E **42** J3
Miyanoura-Dake *Japan* 30°20N 130°31E **31** J5
Miyazaki *Japan* 31°56N 131°30E **31** J5
Miyazaki □ *Japan* 32°30N 131°30E **31** H5
Miyazu *Japan* 35°35N 135°10E **31** G7
Miyet, Bahr el = Dead Sea *Asia* 31°30N 35°30E **46** D4
Miyoshi *Japan* 34°48N 132°51E **31** G6
Miyun *China* 40°28N 116°50E **34** D9
Miyun Shuiku *China* 40°30N 117°0E **35** D9
Mizdah *Libya* 31°30N 13°0E **51** B8
Mizen Hd. *Cork, Ireland* 51°27N 9°50W **10** E2
Mizen Hd. *Wicklow, Ireland* 52°51N 6°4W **10** D5
Mizhi *China* 37°47N 110°12E **34** F6
Mizoram □ *India* 23°30N 92°40E **41** H18
Mizpe Ramon *Israel* 30°34N 34°49E **46** E3
Mizuho *Antarctica* 70°30S 41°0E **5** D5
Mizusawa *Japan* 39°8N 141°8E **30** E10
Mjölby *Sweden* 58°20N 15°10E **9** G16
Mjøsa *Norway* 60°40N 11°0E **8** F14
Mkata *Tanzania* 5°45S 38°20E **54** D4
Mkhaya ⌓ *Swaziland* 26°34S 31°45E **57** D5
Mkhuze ⌓ *S. Africa* 29°27S 29°30E **57** D4
Mkokotoni *Tanzania* 5°55S 39°15E **54** D4
Mkomazi *Tanzania* 4°40S 38°7E **54** C4
Mkomazi → *S. Africa* 30°12S 30°50E **57** E5
Mkomazi ⌓ *Tanzania* 4°4S 30°2E **54** C3
Mkulwe *Tanzania* 8°37S 32°20E **55** D3
Mkumbi, Ras *Tanzania* 7°38S 39°55E **54** D4
Mkushi *Zambia* 14°25S 29°15E **55** E2
Mkushi River *Zambia* 13°32S 29°45E **55** E2
Mkuze *S. Africa* 27°10S 32°0E **57** D5
Mladá Boleslav *Czech Rep.* 50°27N 14°53E **16** C8
Mlala Hills *Tanzania* 6°50S 31°40E **54** D3
Mlange = Mulanje, Mt. *Malawi* 16°2S 35°33E **55** F4
Mława *Poland* 53°9N 20°25E **17** B11
Mlawula ⌓ *Swaziland* 26°12S 32°2E **57** D5
Mljet *Croatia* 42°43N 17°30E **22** C7
Mmabatho *S. Africa* 25°49S 25°30E **56** D4
Mo i Rana *Norway* 66°20N 14°7E **8** C16
Moa *Australia* 10°11S 142°16E **62** a
Moa *Cuba* 20°40N 74°56W **89** B4
Moa *Indonesia* 8°0S 128°0E **37** F7
Moa → *S. Leone* 6°59N 11°36W **50** G3
Moab *U.S.A.* 38°35N 109°33W **76** G9
Moala *Fiji* 18°36S 179°53E **59** a
Moama *Australia* 36°7S 144°46E **63** F3
Moamba *Mozam.* 25°36S 32°15E **57** D5
Moapa *U.S.A.* 36°40N 114°37W **79** J12
Moate *Ireland* 53°24N 7°44W **10** C4
Moba *Dem. Rep. of the Congo* 7°0S 29°48E **54** D2
Mobārakābād *Iran* 28°24N 53°20E **45** D7
Mobaye *C.A.R.* 4°25N 21°5E **52** D4
Moberly *U.S.A.* 39°25N 92°26W **80** F7
Moberly Lake *Canada* 55°50N 121°44W **70** B4
Mobile *U.S.A.* 30°41N 88°3W **85** F10
Mobile B. *U.S.A.* 30°30N 88°0W **85** F11
Mobridge *U.S.A.* 45°32N 100°26W **80** C3
Moc Chau *Vietnam* 20°50N 104°38E **38** B5
Moc Hoa *Vietnam* 10°46N 105°56E **39** G5
Mocabe Kasari *Dem. Rep. of the Congo* 9°58S 26°12E **55** D2
Moçambique = Mozambique ■ *Africa* 19°0S 35°0E **55** F4
Moçambique *Mozam.* 15°3S 40°42E **55** F5
Mocanaqua *U.S.A.* 41°9N 76°8W **83** E8
Moce *Fiji* 18°40S 178°29W **59** a
Mochima △ *Venezuela* 10°30N 64°5W **89** D7
Mochos *Greece* 35°16N 25°27E **25** D7
Mochudi *Botswana* 24°27S 26°7E **56** C4
Mocimboa da Praia *Mozam.* 11°25S 40°20E **55** E5
Moclips *U.S.A.* 47°14N 124°13W **78** C2
Mocoa *Colombia* 1°7N 76°35W **92** C3
Mococa *Brazil* 21°28S 47°0W **95** A6
Mocorito *Mexico* 25°29N 107°55W **86** B3
Moctezuma *Mexico* 29°48N 109°42W **86** B3
Moctezuma → *Mexico* 21°59N 98°34W **87** C5
Mocuba *Mozam.* 16°54S 36°57E **55** F4
Modane *France* 45°12N 6°40E **20** D7
Modasa *India* 23°30N 73°21E **42** H5
Modder → *S. Africa* 29°2S 24°37E **56** D3
Modderrivier *S. Africa* 29°2S 24°38E **56** D3
Módena *Italy* 44°40N 10°55E **22** B4
Modena *U.S.A.* 37°48N 113°56W **77** H7
Modesto *U.S.A.* 37°39N 121°0W **78** H6
Módica *Italy* 36°52N 14°46E **22** F6
Modimolle *S. Africa* 24°42S 28°22E **57** C4
Modjadjiskloof *S. Africa* 23°42S 30°10E **57** C5
Moe *Australia* 38°12S 146°19E **63** F4
Moebase *Mozam.* 17°3S 38°41E **55** F4
Moengo *Suriname* 5°45N 54°20W **93** B8
Moffat *U.K.* 55°21N 3°27W **11** F5
Moga *India* 30°48N 75°8E **42** D6
Mogadishu = Muqdisho *Somali Rep.* 2°2N 45°25E **47** G4
Mogador = Essaouira *Morocco* 31°32N 9°42W **50** B4
Mogalakwena → *S. Africa* 22°38S 28°40E **57** C4
Mogami-Gawa → *Japan* 38°45N 140°0E **30** E10
Mogán *Canary Is.* 27°53N 15°43W **24** G4
Mogaung *Burma* 25°20N 97°0E **41** G20
Mogi-Mirim *Brazil* 22°29S 47°0W **93** H9
Mogilev = Mahilyow *Belarus* 53°55N 30°18E **17** B16
Mogilev-Podolskiy = Mohyliv-Podilskyy *Ukraine* 48°26N 27°48E **17** D14
Mogincual *Mozam.* 15°35S 40°25E **55** F5
Mogocha *Russia* 53°40N 119°50E **29** D12
Mogok *Burma* 23°0N 96°40E **41** H20
Mogollon Rim *U.S.A.* 34°10N 110°50W **77** J8
Mogumber *Australia* 31°2S 116°3E **61** F2
Mogwadi → *S. Africa* 23°4S 29°36E **57** C4
Mohács *Hungary* 45°58N 18°41E **17** F10
Mohales Hoek *Lesotho* 30°7S 27°26E **56** E4
Mohall *U.S.A.* 48°46N 101°31W **80** A3
Moḩammadābād *Iran* 37°52N 59°5E **45** B8
Mohammedia *Morocco* 33°44N 7°21W **50** B4
Mohana → *India* 24°43N 85°0E **43** G11
Mohanlalganj *India* 26°41N 80°58E **43** F9
Mohave, L. *U.S.A.* 35°12N 114°34W **79** K12
Mohawk → *U.S.A.* 42°47N 73°41W **83** D11
Mohéli *Comoros Is.* 12°20S 43°40E **53** a
Mohenjodaro *Pakistan* 27°19N 68°7E **42** F3
Moher, Cliffs of *Ireland* 52°58N 9°27W **10** D2
Mohicanville Res. *U.S.A.* 40°45N 82°9W **82** F2
Mohns Ridge *Arctic* 72°30N 5°0W **4** B7
Mohoro *Tanzania* 8°6S 39°8E **54** D4
Mohsenābād *Iran* 36°40N 59°35E **45** B8
Mohyliv-Podilskyy *Ukraine* 48°26N 27°48E **17** D14
Moidart, L. *U.K.* 56°47N 5°52W **11** E3
Moira → *Canada* 44°21N 77°24W **82** B7
Moisaküla *Estonia* 58°3N 25°12E **9** G21
Moisie *Canada* 50°12N 66°1W **73** B6
Moisie → *Canada* 50°14N 66°5W **73** B6
Mojave *U.S.A.* 35°3N 118°10W **79** K8
Mojave ⌓ *U.S.A.* 35°7N 115°32W **79** K11
Mojave Desert *U.S.A.* 35°0N 116°30W **79** L10
Moji das Cruzes *Brazil* 23°31S 46°11W **95** A6
Moji-Guaçu → *Brazil* 20°53S 48°10W **95** A6
Mojo *Bolivia* 21°48S 65°33W **94** A2
Mojokerto *Indonesia* 7°28S 112°26E **37** G15
Mokai *N.Z.* 38°32S 175°56E **59** C5
Mokambo *Dem. Rep. of the Congo* 12°25S 28°20E **55** E2
Mokameh *India* 25°24N 85°55E **43** G11
Mokau *N.Z.* 38°42S 174°39E **59** C5
Mokelumne → *U.S.A.* 38°13N 121°28W **78** G5
Mokelumne Hill *U.S.A.* 38°18N 120°43W **78** G6
Mokhotlong *Lesotho* 29°22S 29°2E **57** D4
Mokoan, L. *Australia* 36°27S 146°5E **63** C4
Mokokchung *India* 26°15N 94°30E **41** F19
Mokolo → *S. Africa* 23°14S 27°43E **57** C4
Mokopane *S. Africa* 24°10S 28°55E **57** C4
Mokpo *S. Korea* 34°50N 126°25E **35** G14
Mokra Gora *Europe* 42°50N 20°30E **23** C9
Mol *Belgium* 51°11N 5°5E **15** C5
Molchanovo *Russia* 57°40N 83°50E **28** D9
Mold *U.K.* 53°9N 3°8W **12** D4
Moldavia = Moldova ■ *Europe* 47°0N 28°0E **17** E15
Moldavia *Romania* 46°30N 27°0E **17** E14
Molde *Norway* 62°45N 7°9E **8** E12
Moldova ■ *Europe* 47°0N 28°0E **17** E15
Moldoveanu, Vf. *Romania* 45°36N 24°45E **17** F13
Mole → *U.K.* 51°24N 0°21W **13** F7
Molepolole *Botswana* 24°28S 25°28E **56** C4
Molfetta *Italy* 41°12N 16°36E **22** D7
Moline *U.S.A.* 41°30N 90°31W **80** E8
Molinos *Argentina* 25°28S 66°15W **94** B2
Moliro *Dem. Rep. of the Congo* 8°12S 30°30E **54** D3
Mollendo *Peru* 17°0S 72°0W **92** G4
Mollerin, L. *Australia* 30°30S 117°35E **61** F2
Molo *Kenya* 0°15S 35°44E **54** C4
Molodechno = Maladzyechna *Belarus* 54°20N 26°50E **17** A14
Molodezhnaya *Antarctica* 67°40S 45°51E **5** C9
Moloka'i *U.S.A.* 21°8N 157°0W **75** L8
Molokai Fracture Zone *Pac. Oc.* 28°0N 125°0W **65** E15
Molong *Australia* 33°5S 148°54E **63** E4
Molopo → *Africa* 28°30S 20°12E **56** D3
Molson L. *Canada* 54°22N 96°40W **71** C9
Molteno *S. Africa* 31°22S 26°22E **56** E4
Molu *Indonesia* 6°45S 131°40E **37** F8
Molucca Sea *Indonesia* 0°0 125°0E **37** E6
Moluccas = Maluku *Indonesia* 1°0S 127°0E **37** E7
Moma *Dem. Rep. of the Congo* 1°35S 23°52E **54** C1
Moma *Mozam.* 16°47S 39°4E **55** F4
Mombasa *Kenya* 4°3S 39°40E **54** C4
Mombetsu *Japan* 44°21N 143°22E **30** B11
Momchilgrad *Bulgaria* 41°33N 25°23E **23** D11
Momi *Dem. Rep. of the Congo* 1°42S 27°0E **54** C2
Mompós *Colombia* 9°14N 74°26W **92** B4
Møn *Denmark* 54°57N 12°20E **9** J15
Mon □ *Burma* 16°0N 97°30E **41** L20
Mona, Canal de la = Mona Passage *W. Indies* 18°30N 67°45W **89** C6
Mona, Isla *Puerto Rico* 18°5N 67°54W **89** C6
Mona, Pta. *Costa Rica* 9°37N 82°36W **88** E3
Mona Passage *W. Indies* 18°30N 67°45W **89** C6
Monaca *U.S.A.* 40°41N 80°17W **82** F4
Monaco ■ *Europe* 43°46N 7°23E **20** E7
Monadhliath Mts. *U.K.* 57°10N 4°4W **11** D4
Monadnock, Mt. *U.S.A.* 42°52N 72°7W **83** D12
Monaghan *Ireland* 54°15N 6°57W **10** B5
Monaghan □ *Ireland* 54°11N 6°56W **10** B5
Monahans *U.S.A.* 31°36N 102°54W **84** F3
Monapo *Mozam.* 14°56S 40°19E **55** E5
Monar, L. *U.K.* 57°26N 5°8W **11** D3
Monarch Mt. *Canada* 51°55N 125°57W **70** C3
Monashee Mts. *Canada* 51°0N 118°43W **70** C5
Monasterevin *Ireland* 53°8N 7°4W **10** C4
Monastir = Bitola *Macedonia* 41°1N 21°20E **23** D9
Monastir *Tunisia* 35°50N 10°49E **51** A8
Monbetsu *Japan* 42°30N 142°10E **30** C11
Moncayo, Sierra del *Spain* 41°48N 1°50W **21** B5
Monchegorsk *Russia* 67°54N 32°58E **8** C25
Mönchengladbach *Germany* 51°11N 6°27E **16** C4
Monchique *Portugal* 37°19N 8°38W **21** D1
Moncks Corner *U.S.A.* 33°12N 80°1W **85** E14
Monclova *Mexico* 26°54N 101°25W **86** B4
Moncton *Canada* 46°7N 64°51W **73** C7
Mondego → *Portugal* 40°9N 8°52W **21** B1
Mondeodo *Indonesia* 3°34S 122°9E **37** E6
Mondovì *Italy* 44°23N 7°49E **20** D7
Mondrain I. *Australia* 34°9S 122°14E **61** F3
Moneague *Jamaica* 18°16N 77°7W **88** a
Moneron, Ostrov *Russia* 46°15N 141°16E **30** A10
Monessen *U.S.A.* 40°9N 79°54W **82** F5
Monett *U.S.A.* 36°55N 93°55W **80** G7
Moneymore *U.K.* 54°41N 6°40W **10** B5
Monforte de Lemos *Spain* 42°31N 7°33W **21** A2
Mong Hpayak *Burma* 20°52N 99°55E **38** B2
Mong Hsat *Burma* 20°31N 99°15E **38** B2
Mong Hsu *Burma* 21°54N 98°30E **41** J21
Mong Kung *Burma* 21°35N 97°35E **41** J20
Mong Nai *Burma* 20°32N 97°46E **41** J20
Mong Ton *Burma* 20°17N 98°45E **41** J21
Mong Yai *Burma* 22°21N 98°3E **41** H21
Mong Yang *Burma* 21°50N 99°41E **38** B2
Mongalla *Sudan* 5°8N 31°42E **51** G12
Mongers, L. *Australia* 29°25S 117°5E **61** E2
Monghyr = Munger *India* 25°23N 86°30E **43** G12
Mongibello = Etna *Italy* 37°50N 14°55E **22** F6
Mongo *Chad* 12°14N 18°43E **51** F9
Mongolia ■ *Asia* 47°0N 103°0E **32** B9
Mongolia, Plateau of *Asia* 45°0N 105°0E **26** D12
Mongu *Zambia* 15°16S 23°12E **53** H4
Môngua *Angola* 16°43S 15°20E **56** B2
Monifieth *U.K.* 56°30N 2°48W **11** E6
Monkey Bay *Malawi* 14°7S 35°1E **55** E4
Monkey Mia *Australia* 25°48S 113°43E **61** E1
Monkey River *Belize* 16°22N 88°29W **87** D7
Monkland *Canada* 45°11N 74°52W **83** A10
Monkoto *Dem. Rep. of the Congo* 1°38S 20°35E **52** E4
Monkton *Canada* 43°35N 81°5W **82** C3
Monmouth *U.K.* 51°48N 2°42W **13** F5
Monmouth *Ill., U.S.A.* 40°55N 90°39W **80** E8
Monmouth *Oreg., U.S.A.* 44°51N 123°14W **76** D2
Monmouthshire □ *U.K.* 51°48N 2°54W **13** F5
Mono, Pta. *Nic.* 12°0N 83°30W **88** D3
Mono L. *U.S.A.* 38°1N 119°1W **78** H7
Monolith *U.S.A.* 35°7N 118°22W **79** K8
Monolithos *Greece* 36°7N 27°45E **25** C9
Monongahela *U.S.A.* 40°12N 79°56W **82** F5
Monópoli *Italy* 40°57N 17°18E **22** D7
Monos I. *Trin. & Tob.* 10°42N 61°44W **93** K15
Monroe *Ga., U.S.A.* 33°47N 83°43W **85** E13
Monroe *La., U.S.A.* 32°30N 92°7W **84** E8
Monroe *Mich., U.S.A.* 41°55N 83°24W **81** E12
Monroe *N.C., U.S.A.* 34°59N 80°33W **85** D14
Monroe *N.Y., U.S.A.* 41°20N 74°11W **83** E10
Monroe *Utah, U.S.A.* 38°38N 112°7W **76** G7
Monroe *Wash., U.S.A.* 47°51N 121°58W **78** C5
Monroe *Wis., U.S.A.* 42°36N 89°38W **80** D9
Monroe City *U.S.A.* 39°39N 91°44W **80** F8
Monroeton *U.S.A.* 41°43N 76°29W **83** E8
Monroeville *Ala., U.S.A.* 31°31N 87°20W **85** F11
Monroeville *Pa., U.S.A.* 40°26N 79°45W **82** F5
Monrovia *Liberia* 6°18N 10°47W **50** G3
Mons *Belgium* 50°27N 3°58E **15** D3
Monse *Indonesia* 4°7S 123°15E **37** E6
Mont-de-Marsan *France* 43°54N 0°31W **20** E3
Mont-Joli *Canada* 48°37N 68°10W **73** C6
Mont-Laurier *Canada* 46°35N 75°30W **72** C4
Mont-Louis *Canada* 49°15N 65°44W **73** C6
Mont-St-Michel, Le *France* 48°40N 1°30W **20** B3
Mont-Tremblant ⌓ *Canada* 46°30N 74°30W **72** C5
Montagne d'Ambre △ *Madag.* 12°37S 49°8E **57** A8
Montagu *S. Africa* 33°45S 20°8E **56** E3
Montagu I. *Antarctica* 58°25S 26°20W **5** B1
Montague *Canada* 46°10N 62°39W **73** C7
Montague, I. *Mexico* 31°45N 114°48W **86** A2
Montague I. *U.S.A.* 60°0N 147°30W **74** D10
Montague Ra. *Australia* 27°15S 119°30E **61** E2
Montague Sd. *Australia* 14°28S 125°20E **60** B4
Montalbán *Spain* 40°50N 0°45W **21** B5
Montalvo *U.S.A.* 34°15N 119°12W **79** L7
Montana *Bulgaria* 43°27N 23°16E **23** C10
Montaña *Peru* 6°0S 73°0W **92** E4
Montana □ *U.S.A.* 47°0N 110°0W **76** C9
Montaña Clara, I. *Canary Is.* 29°17N 13°33W **24** E6
Montargis *France* 47°59N 2°43E **20** C5
Montauban *France* 44°2N 1°21E **20** D4
Montauk *U.S.A.* 41°3N 71°57W **83** E13
Montauk Pt. *U.S.A.* 41°4N 71°51W **83** E13
Montbéliard *France* 47°31N 6°48E **20** C7
Montceau-les-Mines *France* 46°40N 4°23E **20** C6
Montclair *U.S.A.* 40°49N 74°12W **83** F10
Monte Albán *Mexico* 17°2N 96°46W **87** D5
Monte Alegre *Brazil* 2°0S 54°0W **93** D8
Monte Azul *Brazil* 15°9S 42°53W **93** G10
Monte-Carlo *Monaco* 43°44N 7°25E **20** E7
Monte Caseros *Argentina* 30°10S 57°50W **94** C4
Monte Comán *Argentina* 34°40S 67°53W **94** C2
Monte Cristi *Dom. Rep.* 19°52N 71°39W **89** C5
Monte Lindo → *Paraguay* 23°56S 57°12W **94** A4
Monte Patria *Chile* 30°42S 70°58W **94** C1
Monte Quemado *Argentina* 25°53S 62°41W **94** B3
Monte Rio *U.S.A.* 38°28N 123°0W **78** G4
Monte Santu, C. di *Italy* 40°5N 9°44E **22** D3
Monte Vista *U.S.A.* 37°35N 106°9W **77** H10
Monteagudo *Argentina* 27°14S 54°8W **95** B5
Montebello *Canada* 45°40N 74°55W **72** C5
Montebello Is. *Australia* 20°30S 115°45E **60** D2
Montecarlo *Argentina* 26°34S 54°47W **95** B5
Montecito *U.S.A.* 34°26N 119°40W **79** L7
Montecristo *Italy* 42°20N 10°19E **22** C4
Montego Bay *Jamaica* 18°28N 77°55W **88** a
Montélimar *France* 44°33N 4°45E **20** D6
Montello *U.S.A.* 43°48N 89°20W **80** D9
Montemorelos *Mexico* 25°12N 99°49W **87** B5
Montenegro *Brazil* 29°39S 51°29W **95** B5
Montenegro ■ *Europe* 42°40N 19°20E **23** C8
Montepuez *Mozam.* 13°8S 38°59E **55** E4
Montepuez → *Mozam.* 12°32S 40°27E **55** E5
Monterey *U.S.A.* 36°37N 121°55W **78** J5
Monterey B. *U.S.A.* 36°45N 122°0W **78** J5
Montería *Colombia* 8°46N 75°53W **92** B3
Monteros *Argentina* 27°11S 65°30W **94** B2
Monterrey *Mexico* 25°40N 100°19W **86** B4
Montes Azules ⌓ *Mexico* 16°21N 91°3W **87** D6
Montes Claros *Brazil* 16°30S 43°50W **93** G10

Montesano U.S.A. 46°59N 123°36W 78 D3
Montesilvano Italy 42°29N 14°8E 22 C6
Montevideo Uruguay 34°50S 56°11W 95 C4
Montevideo U.S.A. 44°57N 95°43W 80 C6
Montezuma U.S.A. 41°35N 92°32W 80 E7
Montezuma Castle ⌂ U.S.A. 34°39N 111°45W 77 J8
Montgomery U.K. 52°34N 3°8W 13 E4
Montgomery Ala., U.S.A. 32°23N 86°19W 85 E11
Montgomery Pa., U.S.A. 41°10N 76°53W 82 E8
Montgomery W. Va., U.S.A. 38°11N 81°19W 81 F13
Montgomery City U.S.A. 38°59N 91°30W 80 F8
Monticello Ark., U.S.A. 33°38N 91°47W 84 E9
Monticello Fla., U.S.A. 30°33N 83°52W 85 F13
Monticello Ind., U.S.A. 40°45N 86°46W 80 E10
Monticello Iowa, U.S.A. 42°15N 91°12W 80 D8
Monticello Ky., U.S.A. 36°50N 84°51W 81 G11
Monticello Minn., U.S.A. 45°18N 93°48W 80 C7
Monticello Miss., U.S.A. 31°33N 90°7W 85 F9
Monticello N.Y., U.S.A. 41°39N 74°42W 83 E10
Monticello Utah, U.S.A. 37°52N 109°21W 77 H9
Montijo Portugal 38°41N 8°54W 21 C1
Montilla Spain 37°36N 4°40W 21 D3
Montluçon France 46°22N 2°36E 20 C5
Montmagny Canada 46°58N 70°34W 73 C5
Montmartre Canada 50°14N 103°27W 71 C8
Montmorillon France 46°26N 0°50E 20 C4
Monto Australia 24°52S 151°6E 62 C5
Montongbuwoh Indonesia 8°33S 116°4E 37 K19
Montoro Spain 38°1N 4°27W 21 C3
Montour Falls U.S.A. 42°21N 76°51W 82 D8
Montoursville U.S.A. 41°15N 76°55W 82 E8
Montpelier Idaho, U.S.A. 42°19N 111°18W 76 E8
Montpelier Vt., U.S.A. 44°16N 72°35W 83 B12
Montpellier France 43°37N 3°52E 20 E5
Montréal Canada 45°30N 73°33W 83 A11
Montreal → Canada 47°14N 84°39W 72 C3
Montréal L. Canada 54°20N 105°45W 71 C7
Montreal Lake Canada 54°3N 105°46W 71 C7
Montreux Switz. 46°26N 6°55E 20 C7
Montrose U.K. 56°44N 2°27W 11 E6
Montrose Colo., U.S.A. 38°29N 107°53W 76 G10
Montrose Pa., U.S.A. 41°50N 75°53W 83 E9
Monts, Pte. des Canada 49°20N 67°12W 73 C6
Montserrat ⊠ W. Indies 16°40N 62°10W 89 C7
Montuiri Spain 39°34N 2°59E 24 B9
Monywa Burma 22°7N 95°11E 41 H19
Monza Italy 45°35N 9°16E 20 D8
Monze Zambia 16°17S 27°29E 55 F2
Monze, C. Pakistan 24°47N 66°37E 42 G2
Monzón Spain 41°52N 0°10E 21 B6
Mooers U.S.A. 44°58N 73°35W 83 B11
Mooi → S. Africa 28°45S 30°34E 57 D5
Mooi River S. Africa 29°13S 29°50E 57 D4
Moomba Australia 28°6S 140°12E 63 A3
Moonah → Australia 22°3S 138°33E 62 C2
Moonda, L. Australia 25°52S 140°25E 62 D3
Moonie Australia 27°46S 150°20E 63 D5
Moonie → Australia 29°19S 148°43E 63 D4
Moonta Australia 34°6S 137°32E 63 E2
Moora Australia 30°37S 115°58E 61 F2
Moorcroft U.S.A. 44°16N 104°57W 76 D11
Moore → Australia 31°22S 115°30E 61 F2
Moore, L. Australia 29°50S 117°35E 61 E2
Moore Falls Canada 44°48N 78°48W 82 B6
Moore Park Australia 24°43S 152°17E 62 C5
Moore Res. U.S.A. 44°20N 71°53W 83 B13
Moore River △ Australia 31°7S 115°39E 61 F2
Moorea French Polynesia 17°30S 149°50W 59 d
Moorefield U.S.A. 39°4N 78°58W 81 F14
Moorfoot Hills U.K. 55°44N 3°8W 11 F5
Moorhead U.S.A. 46°53N 96°45W 80 B5
Moorpark U.S.A. 34°17N 118°53W 79 L8
Moorreesburg S. Africa 33°6S 18°38E 56 E2
Moorrinya △ Australia 21°42S 144°58E 62 C3
Moose → Canada 51°20N 80°25W 72 B3
Moose → U.S.A. 43°38N 75°24W 83 C9
Moose Creek Canada 45°15N 74°58W 83 A10
Moose Factory Canada 51°16N 80°32W 72 B3
Moose Jaw Canada 50°24N 105°30W 71 C7
Moose Jaw → Canada 50°34N 105°18W 71 C7
Moose Lake Canada 53°46N 100°8W 71 C8
Moose Lake U.S.A. 46°27N 92°46W 80 B7
Moose Mountain ⌂ Canada 49°48N 102°25W 71 D8
Moosehead L. U.S.A. 45°38N 69°40W 81 C19
Mooselookmeguntic L. U.S.A. 44°55N 70°49W 83 B14
Moosilauke, Mt. U.S.A. 44°3N 71°40W 83 B13
Moosomin Canada 50°9N 101°40W 71 C8
Moosonee Canada 51°17N 80°39W 72 B3
Moosup U.S.A. 41°43N 71°53W 83 E13
Mopane S. Africa 22°37S 29°52E 57 C4
Mopeia Velha Mozam. 17°30S 35°40E 55 F4
Mopipi Botswana 21°6S 24°55E 56 C3
Mopoi C.A.R. 5°6N 26°54E 54 A2
Mopti Mali 14°30N 4°0W 50 F5
Moqor Afghan. 32°50N 67°42E 42 C2
Moquegua Peru 17°15S 70°46W 92 G4
Mora Sweden 61°2N 14°38E 8 F16
Mora Minn., U.S.A. 45°53N 93°18W 80 C7
Mora N. Mex., U.S.A. 35°58N 105°20W 77 J11
Moradabad India 28°50N 78°50E 43 E8
Morafenobe Madag. 17°50S 44°53E 57 B7
Moramanga Madag. 18°56S 48°12E 57 B8
Moran Kans., U.S.A. 37°55N 95°10W 80 G6
Moran Wyo., U.S.A. 43°50N 110°31W 76 E8
Moranbah Australia 22°1S 148°6E 62 C4
Morang = Biratnagar Nepal 26°27N 87°17E 43 F12
Morant Bay Jamaica 17°53N 76°25W 88 a
Morant Cays Jamaica 17°22N 76°0W 88 C4
Morant Pt. Jamaica 17°55N 76°12W 88 a
Morar India 26°14N 78°14E 42 F8
Morar, L. U.K. 56°57N 5°40W 11 E3
Moratuwa Sri Lanka 6°45N 79°55E 40 R11
Morava → Serbia 44°36N 21°4E 23 B9
Morava → Slovak Rep. 48°10N 16°59E 17 D9
Moravia U.S.A. 42°43N 76°25W 83 D8
Moravian Hts. = Českomoravská Vrchovina Czech Rep. 49°30N 15°40E 16 D8
Morawa Australia 29°13S 116°0E 61 E2
Morawhanna Guyana 8°30N 59°40W 92 B7
Moray □ U.K. 57°31N 3°18W 11 D5
Moray Firth U.K. 57°40N 3°52W 11 D5
Morbi India 22°50N 70°42E 42 H4
Morden Canada 49°15N 98°10W 71 D9
Mordovian Republic = Mordvinia □ Russia 54°20N 44°30E 18 D7
Mordvinia □ Russia 54°20N 44°30E 18 D7
Moreau → U.S.A. 45°18N 100°43W 80 C3
Morebeng S. Africa 23°30S 29°55E 57 C4
Morecambe U.K. 54°5N 2°52W 12 C5
Morecambe B. U.K. 54°7N 3°0W 12 C5
Moree Australia 29°28S 149°54E 63 D4
Morehead U.S.A. 38°11N 83°26W 81 F12
Morehead City U.S.A. 34°43N 76°43W 85 D16
Morel → India 26°13N 76°36E 42 F7
Morelia Mexico 19°42N 101°7W 86 D4
Morella Australia 23°0S 143°52E 62 C3
Morella Spain 40°35N 0°5W 21 B5
Morelos Mexico 26°42N 107°40W 86 B3
Morelos □ Mexico 18°45N 99°0W 87 D5
Moremi ⌂ Botswana 19°18S 23°10E 56 B3
Morena India 26°30N 78°4E 42 F8
Morena, Sierra Spain 38°20N 4°0W 21 C3
Moreno Valley U.S.A. 33°56N 117°14W 79 M10
Moresby I. Canada 52°30N 131°40W 70 C2
Moreton I. Australia 27°10S 153°25E 63 D5
Moreton Island △ Australia 27°2S 153°24E 63 D5
Morgan Australia 34°2S 139°35E 63 E2
Morgan U.S.A. 41°2N 111°41W 76 F8
Morgan City U.S.A. 29°42N 91°12W 84 G9
Morgan Hill U.S.A. 37°8N 121°39W 78 H5
Morganfield U.S.A. 37°41N 87°55W 80 G10
Morganton U.S.A. 35°45N 81°41W 85 D14
Morgantown U.S.A. 39°38N 79°57W 81 F14
Morgenzon S. Africa 26°45S 29°36E 57 D4
Morghak Iran 29°7N 57°54E 45 D8
Morhar → India 25°29N 85°11E 43 G11
Mori Japan 42°6N 140°35E 30 C10
Moriarty U.S.A. 34°59N 106°3W 77 J10
Morice L. Canada 53°50N 127°40W 70 C3
Morinville Canada 53°49N 113°41W 70 C6
Morioka Japan 39°45N 141°8E 30 E10
Moris Mexico 28°10N 108°32W 86 B3
Morlaix France 48°36N 3°52W 20 B2
Mornington Australia 38°15S 145°5E 63 F4
Mornington, I. Chile 49°50S 75°30W 96 F1
Mornington I. Australia 16°30S 139°30E 62 B2
Moro Pakistan 26°40N 68°0E 42 F2
Moro → Pakistan 29°42N 67°22E 42 E2
Moro G. Phil. 6°30N 123°0E 37 C6
Morocco ■ N. Afr. 32°0N 5°50W 50 B4
Morogoro Tanzania 6°50S 37°40E 54 D4
Morogoro □ Tanzania 8°0S 37°0E 54 D4
Moroleón Mexico 20°8N 101°12W 86 C4
Morombe Madag. 21°45S 43°22E 57 C7
Moron Argentina 34°39S 58°37W 94 C4
Morón Cuba 22°8N 78°39W 88 B4
Mörön Mongolia 49°38N 100°9E 32 B9
Morón de la Frontera Spain 37°6N 5°28W 21 D3
Morona → Peru 4°40S 77°10W 92 D3
Morondava Madag. 20°17S 44°17E 57 C7
Morongo Valley U.S.A. 34°3N 116°37W 79 L10
Moroni Comoros Is. 11°40S 43°16E 53 a
Moroni U.S.A. 39°32N 111°35W 76 G8
Morotai Indonesia 2°10N 128°30E 37 D7
Moroto Uganda 2°28N 34°42E 54 B3
Moroto, Mt. Uganda 2°30N 34°43E 54 B3
Morpeth Canada 42°23N 81°50W 82 D3
Morpeth U.K. 55°10N 1°41W 12 B6
Morphou Cyprus 35°12N 32°59E 25 D11
Morphou Bay Cyprus 35°15N 32°50E 25 D11
Morrilton U.S.A. 35°9N 92°44W 84 D8
Morrinhos Brazil 17°45S 49°10W 93 G9
Morrinsville N.Z. 37°40S 175°32E 59 B5
Morris Canada 49°25N 97°22W 71 D9
Morris Ill., U.S.A. 41°22N 88°26W 80 E9
Morris Minn., U.S.A. 45°35N 95°55W 80 C6
Morris N.Y., U.S.A. 42°33N 75°15W 83 D9
Morris Pa., U.S.A. 41°35N 77°17W 82 E7
Morris, Mt. Australia 26°9S 131°4E 61 E5
Morris Jesup, Kap Greenland 83°40N 34°0W 66 A16
Morrisburg Canada 44°55N 75°7W 83 B9
Morristown Ariz., U.S.A. 33°51N 112°37W 77 K7
Morristown N.J., U.S.A. 40°48N 74°29W 83 F10
Morristown N.Y., U.S.A. 44°35N 75°39W 83 B9
Morristown Tenn., U.S.A. 36°13N 83°18W 85 C13
Morrisville N.Y., U.S.A. 42°53N 75°35W 83 D9
Morrisville Pa., U.S.A. 40°13N 74°47W 83 F10
Morrisville Vt., U.S.A. 44°34N 72°36W 83 B12
Morro, Pta. Chile 27°6S 71°0W 94 B1
Morro Bay U.S.A. 35°22N 120°51W 78 K6
Morro del Jable Canary Is. 28°3N 14°23W 24 F5
Morro Jable, Pta. de Canary Is. 28°2N 14°20W 24 F5
Morrocoy △ Venezuela 10°48N 68°13W 89 D6
Morrosquillo, G. de Colombia 9°35N 75°40W 88 E4
Morrumbene Mozam. 23°31S 35°16E 57 C6
Morshansk Russia 53°28N 41°50E 18 D7
Morteros Argentina 30°50S 62°0W 94 C3
Mortlach Canada 50°27N 106°4W 71 C7
Mortlake Australia 38°5S 142°50E 63 F3
Morton Tex., U.S.A. 33°44N 102°46W 84 E3
Morton Wash., U.S.A. 46°34N 122°17W 78 D4
Moruga Trin. & Tob. 10°4N 61°16W 93 K15
Morundah Australia 34°57S 146°19E 63 E4
Moruya Australia 35°58S 150°3E 63 F5
Morvan France 47°5N 4°3E 20 C6
Morven Australia 26°22S 147°5E 63 D4
Morvern U.K. 56°38N 5°44W 11 E3
Morwell Australia 38°10S 146°22E 63 F4
Morzhovets, Ostrov Russia 66°44N 42°35E 18 A7
Mosakahiken = Moose Lake Canada 53°46N 100°8W 71 C8
Moscos Is. Burma 14°0N 97°30E 38 F1
Moscow = Moskva Russia 55°45N 37°37E 18 C6
Moscow Idaho, U.S.A. 46°44N 117°0W 76 C5
Moscow Pa., U.S.A. 41°20N 75°31W 83 E9
Mosel → Europe 50°22N 7°36E 20 A7
Moselle = Mosel → Europe 50°22N 7°36E 20 A7
Moses Lake U.S.A. 47°8N 119°17W 76 C4
Mosgiel N.Z. 45°53S 170°21E 59 F3
Moshaweng → S. Africa 26°35S 22°50E 56 D3
Moshchnyy, Ostrov Russia 60°1N 27°50E 9 F22
Moshi Tanzania 3°22S 37°18E 54 C4
Moshupa Botswana 24°46S 25°29E 56 C4
Mosjøen Norway 65°51N 13°12E 8 D15
Moskenesøya Norway 67°58N 13°0E 8 C15
Moskenstraumen Norway 67°47N 12°45E 8 C15
Moskva Russia 55°45N 37°37E 18 C6
Mosonmagyaróvár Hungary 47°52N 17°18E 17 E9
Mosquera Colombia 2°35N 78°24W 92 C3
Mosquero U.S.A. 35°47N 103°58W 77 J12
Mosquitia Honduras 15°20N 84°10W 88 C3
Mosquito Coast = Mosquitia Honduras 15°20N 84°10W 88 C3
Mosquito Creek L. U.S.A. 41°18N 80°46W 82 E4
Mosquito L. Canada 62°35N 103°20W 71 A8
Mosquitos, G. de los Panama 9°15N 81°10W 88 E3
Moss Norway 59°27N 10°40E 9 G14
Moss Vale Australia 34°32S 150°25E 63 E5
Mossaka Congo 1°15S 16°45E 52 E3
Mossbank Canada 49°56N 105°56W 71 D7
Mossburn N.Z. 45°41S 168°15E 59 F2
Mosselbaai S. Africa 34°11S 22°8E 56 E3
Mossendjo Congo 2°55S 12°42E 52 E2
Mossgiel Australia 33°15S 144°5E 63 E3
Mossman Australia 16°21S 145°15E 62 B4
Mossoró Brazil 5°10S 37°15W 93 E11
Mossuril Mozam. 14°58S 40°42E 55 E5
Most Czech Rep. 50°31N 13°38E 16 C7
Mosta Malta 35°55N 14°26E 25 D1
Mostaganem Algeria 35°54N 0°5E 50 A6
Mostar Bos.-H. 43°22N 17°50E 23 C7
Mostardas Brazil 31°2S 50°51W 95 C5
Mostiska = Mostyska Ukraine 49°48N 23°4E 17 D12
Mosty = Masty Belarus 53°27N 24°38E 17 B13
Mostyska Ukraine 49°48N 23°4E 17 D12
Mosul = Al Mawşil Iraq 36°15N 43°5E 44 B4
Motagua → Guatemala 15°44N 88°14W 88 C2
Motala Sweden 58°32N 15°1E 9 G16
Motaze Mozam. 24°48S 32°52E 57 C5
Moth India 25°43N 78°57E 43 G8
Motherwell U.K. 55°47N 3°58W 11 F5
Motihari India 26°30N 84°55E 43 F11
Motozintla de Mendoza Mexico 15°22N 92°14W 87 D6
Motril Spain 36°31N 3°37W 21 D4
Mott U.S.A. 46°23N 102°20W 80 B2
Motueka N.Z. 41°7S 173°1E 59 D4
Motueka → N.Z. 41°5S 173°1E 59 D4
Motul Mexico 21°6N 89°17W 87 C7
Mouchalagane → Canada 50°56N 68°41W 73 B6
Moudros Greece 39°50N 25°18E 23 E11
Mouhoun = Black Volta → Africa 8°41N 1°33W 50 G5
Mouila Gabon 1°50S 11°0E 52 E2
Moulamein Australia 35°3S 144°1E 63 F3
Moule à Chique, C. St. Lucia 13°43N 60°57W 89 f
Mouliana Greece 35°10N 25°59E 25 D7
Moulins France 46°35N 3°19E 20 C5
Moulmein Burma 16°30N 97°40E 41 L20
Moulouya, O. → Morocco 35°5N 2°25W 50 B5
Moultrie U.S.A. 31°11N 83°47W 85 F13
Moultrie, L. U.S.A. 33°20N 80°5W 85 E14
Mound City Mo., U.S.A. 40°7N 95°14W 80 E6
Mound City S. Dak., U.S.A. 45°44N 100°4W 80 C3
Moundou Chad 8°40N 16°10E 51 G9
Moundsville U.S.A. 39°55N 80°44W 82 G4
Moung Cambodia 12°46N 103°27E 38 F4
Mount Airy U.S.A. 36°31N 80°37W 85 C14
Mount Albert Canada 44°8N 79°19W 82 B5
Mount Aspiring △ N.Z. 44°19S 168°47E 59 F2
Mount Barker S. Austral., Australia 35°5S 138°52E 63 F2
Mount Barker W. Austral., Australia 34°38S 117°40E 61 F2
Mount Barnett Roadhouse Australia 16°39S 125°57E 60 C4
Mount Bellew Bridge Ireland 53°28N 8°31W 10 C3
Mount Brydges Canada 42°54N 81°29W 82 D3
Mount Burr Australia 37°34S 140°26E 63 F3
Mount Carmel = Ha Karmel △ Israel 32°45N 35°5E 46 C4
Mount Carmel Ill., U.S.A. 38°25N 87°46W 80 F10
Mount Carmel Pa., U.S.A. 40°47N 76°26W 83 F8
Mount Clemens U.S.A. 42°35N 82°53W 82 D2
Mount Coolon Australia 21°25S 147°25E 62 C4
Mount Darwin Zimbabwe 16°47S 31°38E 55 F3
Mount Desert I. U.S.A. 44°21N 68°20W 81 C19
Mount Dora U.S.A. 28°48N 81°38W 85 G14
Mount Ebenezer Australia 25°6S 132°34E 61 E5
Mount Edziza ⌂ Canada 57°30N 130°45W 70 B2
Mount Elgon △ E. Afr. 1°4N 34°42E 54 B3
Mount Field △ Australia 42°39S 146°35E 63 G4
Mount Fletcher S. Africa 30°40S 28°30E 57 E4
Mount Forest Canada 43°59N 80°43W 82 C4
Mount Frankland △ Australia 31°47S 116°37E 61 F2
Mount Frederick ✪ Australia 19°39S 129°18E 60 C4
Mount Gambier Australia 37°50S 140°46E 63 F3
Mount Garnet Australia 17°37S 145°6E 62 B4
Mount Holly U.S.A. 39°59N 74°47W 83 G10
Mount Holly Springs U.S.A. 40°7N 77°12W 82 F7
Mount Hope N.S.W., Australia 32°51S 145°51E 63 E4
Mount Hope S. Austral., Australia 34°7S 135°23E 63 E2
Mount Isa Australia 20°42S 139°26E 62 C2
Mount James ✪ Australia 24°51S 116°54E 61 D2
Mount Jewett U.S.A. 41°44N 78°39W 82 E6
Mount Kaputar △ Australia 30°16S 150°10E 63 E5
Mount Kenya △ Kenya 0°7S 37°21E 54 C4
Mount Kisco U.S.A. 41°12N 73°44W 83 E11
Mount Laguna U.S.A. 32°52N 116°25W 79 N10
Mount Larcom Australia 23°48S 150°59E 62 C5
Mount Lofty Ranges Australia 34°35S 139°5E 63 E2
Mount Magnet Australia 28°2S 117°47E 61 E2
Mount Maunganui N.Z. 37°40S 176°14E 59 B6
Mount Molloy Australia 16°42S 145°20E 62 B4
Mount Morgan Australia 23°40S 150°25E 62 C5
Mount Morris U.S.A. 42°44N 77°52W 82 D7
Mount Pearl Canada 47°31N 52°47W 73 C9
Mount Penn U.S.A. 40°20N 75°54W 83 F9
Mount Perry Australia 25°13S 151°42E 63 D5
Mount Pleasant Iowa, U.S.A. 40°58N 91°33W 80 E8
Mount Pleasant Mich., U.S.A. 43°36N 84°46W 81 D11
Mount Pleasant Pa., U.S.A. 40°9N 79°33W 82 F5
Mount Pleasant S.C., U.S.A. 32°47N 79°52W 85 E15
Mount Pleasant Tenn., U.S.A. 35°32N 87°12W 85 D11
Mount Pleasant Tex., U.S.A. 33°9N 94°58W 84 E7
Mount Pleasant Utah, U.S.A. 39°33N 111°27W 76 G8
Mount Pocono U.S.A. 41°7N 75°22W 83 E9
Mount Rainier △ U.S.A. 46°55N 121°50W 78 D5
Mount Revelstoke △ Canada 51°5N 118°30W 70 C5
Mount Robson ⌂ Canada 53°0N 119°0W 70 C5
Mount St. Helens ⌂ U.S.A. 46°14N 122°11W 78 D4
Mount Selinda Zimbabwe 20°24S 32°43E 57 C5
Mount Shasta U.S.A. 41°19N 122°19W 76 F2
Mount Signal U.S.A. 32°39N 115°37W 79 N11
Mount Sterling Ill., U.S.A. 39°59N 90°45W 80 F8
Mount Sterling Ky., U.S.A. 38°4N 83°56W 81 F12
Mount Surprise Australia 18°10S 144°17E 62 B3
Mount Union U.S.A. 40°23N 77°53W 82 F7
Mount Upton U.S.A. 42°26N 75°23W 83 D9
Mount Vernon Ill., U.S.A. 38°19N 88°55W 80 F9
Mount Vernon Ind., U.S.A. 37°56N 87°54W 80 G10
Mount Vernon N.Y., U.S.A. 40°54N 73°49W 83 F11
Mount Vernon Ohio, U.S.A. 40°23N 82°29W 82 F2
Mount Vernon Wash., U.S.A. 48°25N 122°20W 78 B4
Mount William △ Australia 40°56S 148°14E 63 G4
Mountain Ash U.K. 51°40N 3°23W 13 F4
Mountain Center U.S.A. 33°42N 116°44W 79 M10
Mountain City Nev., U.S.A. 41°50N 115°58W 76 F6
Mountain City Tenn., U.S.A. 36°29N 81°48W 85 C14
Mountain Dale U.S.A. 41°41N 74°32W 83 E10
Mountain Grove U.S.A. 37°8N 92°16W 80 G7
Mountain Home Ark., U.S.A. 36°20N 92°23W 84 C8
Mountain Home Idaho, U.S.A. 43°8N 115°41W 76 E6
Mountain Iron U.S.A. 47°32N 92°37W 80 B7
Mountain Pass U.S.A. 35°29N 115°35W 79 K11
Mountain View Ark., U.S.A. 35°52N 92°7W 84 D8
Mountain View Calif., U.S.A. 37°23N 122°5W 78 H4
Mountain Zebra △ S. Africa 32°14S 25°27E 56 E4
Mountainair U.S.A. 34°31N 106°15W 77 J10
Mountlake Terrace U.S.A. 47°47N 122°18W 78 C4
Mountmellick Ireland 53°7N 7°20W 10 C4
Mountrath Ireland 53°0N 7°28W 10 D4
Moura Australia 24°35S 149°58E 62 C4
Moura Brazil 1°32S 61°38W 92 D6
Moura Portugal 38°7N 7°30W 21 C2
Mourdi, Dépression du Chad 18°10N 23°0E 51 E10
Mourilyan Australia 17°35S 146°3E 62 B4
Mourne → U.K. 54°52N 7°26W 10 B4
Mourne Mts. U.K. 54°10N 6°0W 10 B5
Mournies Greece 35°29N 24°1E 25 D6
Mouscron Belgium 50°45N 3°12E 15 D3
Moussoro Chad 13°41N 16°35E 51 F9
Moutong Indonesia 0°28N 121°13E 37 D6
Movas Mexico 28°10N 109°25W 86 B3
Moville Ireland 55°11N 7°3W 10 A4
Mowandjum Australia 17°22S 123°40E 60 C3
Moy → Ireland 54°8N 9°8W 10 B2
Moya Comoros Is. 12°18S 44°18E 53 a
Moyale Ethiopia 3°34N 39°5E 54 B4
Moyale Kenya 3°30N 39°4E 54 B4
Moyen Atlas Morocco 33°0N 5°0W 50 B4
Moyo Indonesia 8°10S 117°40E 36 F5
Moyobamba Peru 6°0S 77°0W 92 E3
Moyowosi ⌂ Tanzania 3°50S 31°0E 54 C3
Moyyero → Russia 68°44N 103°42E 29 C11
Moyynqum Kazakhstan 44°12N 71°0E 32 C3
Moyynty Kazakhstan 47°10N 73°18E 28 E8
Mozambique = Moçambique Mozam. 15°3S 40°42E 55 F5
Mozambique ■ Africa 19°0S 35°0E 55 F4
Mozambique Chan. Africa 17°30S 42°30E 57 B7
Mozdok Russia 43°45N 44°48E 19 F7
Mozdūrān Iran 36°9N 60°35E 45 B9
Mozhnābād Iran 34°7N 60°6E 45 C9
Mozyr = Mazyr Belarus 51°59N 29°15E 17 B15
Mpanda Tanzania 6°23S 31°1E 54 D3
Mphoeng Zimbabwe 21°10S 27°51E 55 G2
Mpika Zambia 11°51S 31°25E 55 E3
Mpulungu Zambia 8°51S 31°5E 55 D3
Mpumalanga S. Africa 29°50S 30°33E 57 D5
Mpumalanga □ S. Africa 26°0S 30°0E 57 D5
Mpwapwa Tanzania 6°23S 36°30E 54 D4
Mqanduli S. Africa 31°49S 28°45E 57 E4
Msaken Tunisia 35°49N 10°33E 51 A8
Msambansovu Zimbabwe 15°50S 30°3E 55 F3
M'sila Algeria 35°46N 4°30E 50 A6
Msoro Zambia 13°35S 31°50E 55 E3
Mstislavl = Mstsislaw Belarus 54°0N 31°50E 17 A16
Mstsislaw Belarus 54°0N 31°50E 17 A16
Mtama Tanzania 10°17S 39°21E 55 E4
Mtamvuna = Mthamvuna → S. Africa 31°6S 30°12E 57 E5
Mthamvuna → S. Africa 31°6S 30°12E 57 E5
Mthatha S. Africa 31°36S 28°49E 57 E4
Mtilikwe → Zimbabwe 21°9S 31°30E 55 G3
Mtito Andei Kenya 2°41S 38°10E 54 C4
Mtubatuba S. Africa 28°30S 32°8E 57 D5
Mtwalume S. Africa 30°30S 30°38E 57 E5
Mtwara-Mikindani Tanzania 10°20S 40°20E 55 E5
Mu Gia, Deo Vietnam 17°40N 105°47E 38 D5
Mu Ko Chang △ Thailand 11°59N 102°22E 39 G4
Mu Ko Surin Thailand 9°30N 97°55E 39 H1
Mu Us Shamo China 39°0N 109°0E 34 E5
Muang Beng Laos 20°23N 101°46E 38 B3
Muang Chiang Rai = Chiang Rai Thailand 19°52N 99°50E 38 C2
Muang Et Laos 20°49N 104°1E 38 B5
Muang Hiam Laos 20°5N 103°22E 38 B4
Muang Hongsa Laos 19°43N 101°20E 38 C3
Muang Houn Laos 20°8N 101°23E 38 B3
Muang Kau Laos 15°6N 105°47E 38 E5
Muang Khao Laos 19°38N 103°32E 38 C4
Muang Khong Laos 14°7N 105°51E 38 E5
Muang Khoua Laos 21°5N 102°31E 38 B4
Muang Liap Laos 18°29N 101°40E 38 C3
Muang Mai Thailand 8°5N 98°21E 39 a
Muang May Laos 14°49N 106°56E 38 E6
Muang Ngeun Laos 20°36N 101°3E 38 B3
Muang Ngoi Laos 20°43N 102°41E 38 B4
Muang Nong Laos 16°22N 106°30E 38 D6
Muang Ou Neua Laos 22°18N 101°48E 38 A3
Muang Ou Tay Laos 22°7N 101°48E 38 A3
Muang Pak Beng Laos 19°54N 101°8E 38 C3
Muang Phalane Laos 16°39N 105°34E 38 D5
Muang Phiang Laos 19°6N 101°32E 38 C3
Muang Phine Laos 16°32N 106°2E 38 D6
Muang Saiapoun Laos 18°24N 101°31E 38 C3
Muang Sing Laos 21°11N 101°9E 38 B3
Muang Son Laos 20°27N 103°19E 38 B4
Muang Soui Laos 19°33N 102°52E 38 C4
Muang Va Laos 18°18N 101°20E 38 C3
Muang Va Laos 21°53N 102°19E 38 B4
Muang Xai Laos 20°42N 101°59E 38 B3
Muang Xamteu Laos 19°59N 104°38E 38 C5
Muar Malaysia 2°3N 102°34E 39 L4
Muarabungo Indonesia 1°28S 102°52E 36 E2
Muaraenim Indonesia 3°40S 103°50E 36 E2
Muarajuloi Indonesia 0°12S 114°3E 36 E4
Muarakaman Indonesia 0°2S 116°45E 36 E5
Muaratebo Indonesia 1°30S 102°26E 36 E2
Muaratembesi Indonesia 1°42S 103°8E 36 E2
Muarateweh Indonesia 0°58S 114°52E 36 E4
Mubarakpur India 26°6N 83°18E 43 F10
Mubarraz = Al Mubarraz Si. Arabia 25°30N 49°40E 45 E6
Mubende Uganda 0°33N 31°22E 54 B3
Mubi Nigeria 10°18N 13°16E 51 F8
Mucajaí → Brazil 2°25N 60°52W 92 C6
Muchachos, Roque de los Canary Is. 28°44N 17°52W 24 F2
Muchinga Mts. Zambia 11°30S 31°30E 55 E3
Muck U.K. 56°50N 6°15W 11 E2
Muckadilla Australia 26°35S 148°23E 63 D4
Muckaty ✪ Australia 18°37S 133°52E 62 B1
Muckle Flugga U.K. 60°51N 0°54W 11 A8
Mucuri Brazil 18°0S 39°36W 93 G11
Mucusso Angola 18°1S 21°25E 56 B3
Muda Canary Is. 28°34N 13°57W 24 F6
Mudanjiang China 44°38N 129°30E 35 B15
Mudanya Turkey 40°25N 28°50E 23 D13
Muddy Cr. → U.S.A. 38°24N 110°42W 76 G8
Mudgee Australia 32°32S 149°31E 63 E4
Mudjatik → Canada 56°1N 107°36W 71 B7

Muecate *Mozam.* 14°55S 39°40E **55 E4**
Mueda *Mozam.* 11°36S 39°28E **55 E4**
Mueller Ranges
  Australia 18°18S 126°46E **60 C4**
Muende *Mozam.* 14°28S 33°0E **55 E3**
Muerto, Mar *Mexico* 16°10N 94°10W **87 D6**
Mufulira *Zambia* 12°32S 28°15E **55 E2**
Mufumbiro Range *Africa* 1°25S 29°30E **54 C2**
Mughal Sarai *India* 25°18N 83°7E **43 G10**
Mughayrā *Si. Arabia* 29°17N 37°41E **44 D3**
Mugi *Japan* 33°40N 134°25E **31 H7**
Muğla *Turkey* 37°15N 28°22E **23 F13**
Mugu *Nepal* 29°45N 82°30E **43 E10**
Muhala *Congo* 5°40S 28°43E **54 D2**
Muhammad, Râs *Egypt* 27°44N 34°16E **44 E2**
Muhammad Qol *Sudan* 20°53N 37°9E **51 D13**
Muhammadabad *India* 26°4N 83°25E **43 F10**
Muhesi → *Tanzania* 7°0S 35°20E **54 D4**
Mühlhausen *Germany* 51°12N 10°27E **16 C6**
Mühlig Hofmann fjell
  Antarctica 72°30S 5°0E **5 D3**
Muhos *Finland* 64°47N 25°59E **8 D21**
Muhu *Estonia* 58°36N 23°11E **9 G20**
Muhutwe *Tanzania* 1°35S 31°45E **54 C3**
Mui Wo *China* 22°16N 113°59E **33 a**
Muika *Japan* 37°5N 138°50E **31 F9**
Muine Bheag *Ireland* 52°42N 6°58W **10 D5**
Muir, L. *Australia* 34°30S 116°40E **61 F2**
Muir of Ord *U.K.* 57°32N 4°28W **11 D4**
Mujeres, I. *Mexico* 21°13N 86°43W **88 B2**
Mujnak = Muynak
  Uzbekistan 43°44N 59°10E **28 E6**
Muka, Tanjung *Malaysia* 5°28N 100°11E **39 c**
Mukacheve *Ukraine* 48°27N 22°45E **17 D12**
Mukachevo = Mukacheve
  Ukraine 48°27N 22°45E **17 D12**
Mukah *Malaysia* 2°55N 112°5E **36 D4**
Mukandwara *India* 24°49N 75°59E **42 G6**
Mukawwa, Geziret
  Egypt 23°55N 35°53E **44 F2**
Mukdahan *Thailand* 16°32N 104°43E **38 D5**
Mukdahan △ *Thailand* 16°26N 104°45E **38 D5**
Mukden = Shenyang
  China 41°48N 123°27E **35 D12**
Mukerian *India* 31°57N 75°37E **42 D6**
Mukinbudin *Australia* 30°55S 118°5E **61 F2**
Mukishi
  Dem. Rep. of the Congo 8°30S 24°44E **55 D1**
Muko Phetra △ *Thailand* 6°57N 99°33E **39 J2**
Mukomuko *Indonesia* 2°30S 101°10E **36 E2**
Mukomwenze
  Dem. Rep. of the Congo 6°49S 27°15E **54 D2**
Mukono *Uganda* 0°21N 32°45E **54 B3**
Muktsar *India* 30°30N 74°30E **42 D6**
Mukur = Moqor *Afghan.* 32°50N 67°42E **42 C2**
Mukutuwa → *Canada* 53°10N 97°24W **71 C9**
Mukwela *Zambia* 17°0S 26°40E **55 F2**
Mula *Spain* 38°3N 1°33W **21 C5**
Mula → *Pakistan* 27°57N 67°36E **42 E2**
Mulange
  Dem. Rep. of the Congo 3°40S 27°10E **54 C2**
Mulanje, Mt. *Malawi* 16°2S 35°33E **55 F4**
Mulchatna → *U.S.A.* 59°40N 157°7W **74 D8**
Mulchén *Chile* 37°45S 72°20W **94 D1**
Mulde → *Germany* 51°53N 12°15E **16 C7**
Mule Creek Junction
  U.S.A. 43°23N 104°13W **76 E11**
Muleba *Tanzania* 1°50S 31°37E **54 C3**
Mulegé *Mexico* 26°53N 111°59W **86 B2**
Muleshoe *U.S.A.* 34°13N 102°43W **84 D3**
Mulgrave *Canada* 45°38N 61°31W **73 C7**
Mulgrave I. = Badu
  Australia 10°7S 142°11E **62 a**
Mulhacén *Spain* 37°4N 3°20W **21 D4**
Mulhouse *France* 47°40N 7°20E **20 C7**
Muling *China* 44°35N 130°10E **35 B16**
Mull *U.K.* 56°25N 5°56W **11 E3**
Mull, Sound of *U.K.* 56°30N 5°50W **11 E3**
Mullach Íde = Malahide
  Ireland 53°26N 6°9W **10 C5**
Mullaittivu *Sri Lanka* 9°15N 80°49E **40 Q12**
Mullen *U.S.A.* 42°3N 101°1W **80 D3**
Mullengudgery
  Australia 31°43S 147°23E **63 B4**
Mullens *U.S.A.* 37°35N 81°23W **81 G13**
Muller, Pegunungan
  Indonesia 0°30N 113°30E **36 D4**
Mullet Pen. *Ireland* 54°13N 10°2W **10 B1**
Mullewa *Australia* 28°29S 115°30E **61 E2**
Mulligan → *Australia* 25°0S 139°0E **62 D2**
Mullingar *Ireland* 53°31N 7°21W **10 C4**
Mullins *U.S.A.* 34°12N 79°15W **85 D15**
Mullumbimby *Australia* 28°30S 153°30E **63 D5**
Mulobezi *Zambia* 16°45S 25°7E **55 F2**
Mulonga Plain *Zambia* 16°20S 22°40E **53 H4**
Mulroy B. *Ireland* 55°15N 7°46W **10 A4**
Multan *Pakistan* 30°15N 71°36E **42 D4**
Mulumbe, Mts.
  Dem. Rep. of the Congo 8°40S 27°30E **55 D2**
Mulungushi Dam
  Zambia 14°48S 28°48E **55 E2**
Mulvane *U.S.A.* 37°29N 97°15W **80 G5**
Mulwala, L. *Australia* 35°59S 146°1E **63 C4**
Mumbai *India* 18°56N 72°50E **40 K8**
Mumbwa *Zambia* 15°0S 27°0E **55 F2**
Mumias *Kenya* 0°20N 34°29E **54 C4**
Mun → *Thailand* 15°19N 105°30E **38 E5**
Muna *Indonesia* 5°0S 122°30E **37 F6**
Munabao *India* 25°45N 70°17E **42 G4**
Munamagi *Estonia* 57°43N 27°4E **9 H22**
Muncan *Indonesia* 8°34S 115°11E **37 K18**
Muncar *Indonesia* 8°26S 114°20E **37 J17**
München *Germany* 48°8N 11°34E **16 D6**

Muncho Lake *Canada* 59°0N 125°50W **70 B3**
Munch'ön *N. Korea* 39°14N 127°19E **35 E14**
Muncie *U.S.A.* 40°12N 85°23W **81 E11**
Muncoonie L. West
  Australia 25°12S 138°40E **62 D2**
Mundabbera *Australia* 25°36S 151°18E **63 D5**
Munday *U.S.A.* 33°27N 99°38W **84 E5**
Münden *Germany* 51°25N 9°38E **16 C5**
Mundiwindi *Australia* 23°47S 120°9E **60 D3**
Mundo Novo *Brazil* 11°50S 40°29W **93 F10**
Mundra *India* 22°54N 69°48E **42 H3**
Mundrabilla *Australia* 31°52S 127°51E **61 F4**
Mundra → *Mozam.* 18°58S 35°54E **55 F4**
Mungallala *Australia* 26°28S 147°34E **63 D4**
Mungallala Cr. →
  Australia 28°53S 147°5E **63 D4**
Mungana *Australia* 17°8S 144°27E **62 B3**
Mungaoli *India* 24°24N 78°7E **42 G8**
Mungari *Mozam.* 17°12S 33°30E **55 F3**
Mungbere
  Dem. Rep. of the Congo 2°36N 28°28E **54 B2**
Mungeli *India* 22°4N 81°41E **43 H9**
Munger *India* 25°23N 86°30E **43 G12**
Mungerannie *Australia* 28°1S 138°39E **63 A2**
Mungilli △ *Australia* 25°14S 124°17E **61 E3**
Mungkan Kandju △
  Australia 13°35S 142°52E **62 A3**
Mungkarta ◉ *Australia* 20°25S 134°2E **62 C1**
Munich = München
  Germany 48°8N 11°34E **16 D6**
Munising *U.S.A.* 46°25N 86°40W **80 B10**
Munku-Sardyk *Russia* 51°45N 100°20E **29 D11**
Munnsville *U.S.A.* 42°58N 75°35W **83 D9**
Muñoz Gamero, Pen.
  Chile 52°30S 73°5W **96 G2**
Munroe L. *Canada* 59°13N 98°35W **71 B9**
Munsan *S. Korea* 37°51N 126°48E **35 F14**
Münster *Germany* 51°58N 7°37E **16 C4**
Münster □ *Ireland* 52°18N 8°44W **10 D3**
Muntadgin *Australia* 31°45S 118°33E **61 F2**
Muntok *Indonesia* 2°5S 105°10E **36 E3**
Muong Nhie *Vietnam* 22°12N 102°28E **38 A4**
Muong Sen *Vietnam* 19°24N 104°8E **38 C5**
Muong Te *Vietnam* 22°24N 102°49E **38 A4**
Muong Xia *Vietnam* 20°19N 104°50E **38 B5**
Muonio *Finland* 67°57N 23°40E **8 C20**
Muonio älv = Muonionjoki →
  Finland 67°11N 23°34E **8 C20**
Muonioälven = Muonionjoki →
  Finland 67°11N 23°34E **8 C20**
Muonionjoki → *Finland* 67°11N 23°34E **8 C20**
Mupa → *Mozam.* 18°58S 35°54E **55 F4**
Muping *China* 37°22N 121°36E **35 F11**
Muqdisho *Somali Rep.* 2°2N 45°25E **47 G4**
Mur → *Austria* 46°18N 16°52E **17 E9**
Murakami *Japan* 38°14N 139°29E **30 E9**
Muralag = Prince of Wales I.
  Australia 10°40S 142°10E **62 A3**
Murallón, Cerro *Chile* 49°48S 73°30W **96 F2**
Muranda *Rwanda* 1°52S 29°20E **54 C2**
Murang'a *Kenya* 0°45S 37°9E **54 C4**
Murashi *Russia* 59°30N 49°0E **18 C8**
Murat → *Turkey* 38°46N 40°0E **19 G7**
Muratlı *Turkey* 41°10N 27°29E **23 D12**
Murayama *Japan* 38°30N 140°25E **30 E10**
Murchison → *Australia* 27°45S 114°0E **61 E1**
Murchison, Mt.
  Antarctica 73°25S 166°20E **5 D11**
Murchison Falls *Uganda* 2°15N 31°30E **54 B3**
Murchison Falls △
  Uganda 2°17N 31°48E **54 B3**
Murchison Ra. *Australia* 20°0S 134°10E **62 C1**
Murchison Rapids
  Malawi 15°55S 34°35E **55 F3**
Murchison Roadhouse
  Australia 27°39S 116°14E **61 E2**
Murcia *Spain* 38°5N 1°10W **21 D5**
Murcia □ *Spain* 37°50N 1°30W **21 D5**
Murdo *U.S.A.* 43°53N 100°43W **80 D3**
Murdoch Pt. *Australia* 14°37S 144°55E **62 A3**
Mureş → *Romania* 46°15N 20°13E **17 E11**
Mureşul = Mureş →
  Romania 46°15N 20°13E **17 E11**
Murewa *Zimbabwe* 17°39S 31°47E **57 B5**
Murfreesboro *N.C.,*
  U.S.A. 36°27N 77°6W **85 C16**
Murfreesboro *Tenn.,*
  U.S.A. 35°51N 86°24W **85 D11**
Murgab = Murghob
  Tajikistan 38°10N 74°2E **28 F8**
Murgap → *Turkmenistan* 38°18N 61°12E **45 B9**
Murgenella *Australia* 11°34S 132°56E **60 B5**
Murgha Kibzai *Pakistan* 30°44N 69°25E **42 D3**
Murghob = Murgap
  Tajikistan 38°10N 74°2E **28 F8**
Murgon *Australia* 26°15S 151°54E **63 D5**
Muri *India* 23°22N 85°52E **43 H11**
Muria *Indonesia* 6°36S 110°53E **37 G14**
Muriaé *Brazil* 21°8S 42°23W **95 A7**
Muriel Mine *Zimbabwe* 17°14S 30°40E **55 F3**
Müritz *Germany* 53°25N 12°42E **16 B7**
Murliganj *India* 25°54N 86°59E **43 G12**
Murmansk *Russia* 68°57N 33°10E **8 B25**
Murmashi *Russia* 68°47N 32°42E **8 B25**
Muro *Spain* 39°44N 3°3E **24 B10**
Murom *Russia* 55°35N 42°3E **18 C7**
Muroran *Japan* 42°25N 141°0E **30 C10**
Muroto *Japan* 33°18N 134°9E **31 H7**
Muroto-Misaki *Japan* 33°15N 134°10E **31 H7**
Murphy *U.S.A.* 43°13N 116°33W **76 E5**
Murphys *U.S.A.* 38°8N 120°28W **78 G6**
Murray *Australia* 9°56S 144°2E **62 a**
Murray *Ky., U.S.A.* 36°37N 88°19W **80 G9**
Murray *Utah, U.S.A.* 40°40N 111°53W **76 F8**
Murray → *Australia* 35°20S 139°22E **63 F2**
Murray, L. *U.S.A.* 34°3N 81°13W **85 D14**
Murray Bridge *Australia* 35°6S 139°14E **63 F2**
Murray Harbour *Canada* 46°0N 62°28W **73 C7**
Murray Fracture Zone
  Pac. Oc. 35°0N 130°0W **65 D14**
Murray River △
  Australia 34°23S 140°32E **63 E3**

Murraysburg *S. Africa* 31°58S 23°47E **56 E3**
Murree *Pakistan* 33°56N 73°28E **42 C5**
Murrieta *U.S.A.* 33°33N 117°13W **79 M9**
Murrumbidgee →
  Australia 34°43S 143°12E **63 E3**
Murrumburrah
  Australia 34°32S 148°22E **63 E4**
Murrurundi *Australia* 31°42S 150°51E **63 E5**
Murshidabad *India* 24°11N 88°19E **43 G13**
Murtle L. *Canada* 52°8N 119°38W **70 C5**
Murtoa *Australia* 36°35S 142°28E **63 F3**
Murungu *Tanzania* 4°12S 31°10E **54 C3**
Mururoa
  French Polynesia 21°52S 138°55W **65 K14**
Murwara *India* 23°46N 80°28E **43 H9**
Murwillumbah
  Australia 28°18S 153°27E **63 D5**
Mürzzuschlag *Austria* 47°36N 15°41E **16 E8**
Muş *Turkey* 38°45N 41°30E **44 B4**
Mûsa, Gebel *Egypt* 28°33N 33°59E **44 D2**
Musa Khel *Pakistan* 30°59N 69°52E **42 D3**
Musa Qal'eh *Afghan.* 32°20N 64°50E **40 C4**
Musafirkhana *India* 26°22N 81°48E **43 F9**
Musala *Bulgaria* 42°13N 23°37E **23 C10**
Musala *Indonesia* 1°41N 98°28E **36 D1**
Musan *N. Korea* 42°12N 129°12E **35 C15**
Musangu
  Dem. Rep. of the Congo 10°28S 23°55E **55 E1**
Musasa *Tanzania* 3°25S 31°30E **54 C3**
Musay'īd *Qatar* 25°0N 51°33E **45 E6**
Muscat = Masqat *Oman* 23°37N 58°36E **47 C6**
Muscatine *U.S.A.* 41°25N 91°3W **80 E8**
Muscle Shoals *U.S.A.* 34°45N 87°40W **85 D11**
Musengezi = Unsengedsi →
  Zimbabwe 15°43S 31°14E **55 F3**
Musgrave Harbour
  Canada 49°27N 53°58W **73 C9**
Musgrave Ranges
  Australia 26°0S 132°0E **61 E5**
Mushie
  Dem. Rep. of the Congo 2°56S 16°55E **52 E3**
Musi → *Indonesia* 2°20S 104°56E **36 E2**
Musina *S. Africa* 22°20S 30°5E **57 C5**
Muskeg → *Canada* 60°20N 123°20W **70 A4**
Muskegon *U.S.A.* 43°14N 86°16W **80 D10**
Muskegon → *U.S.A.* 43°14N 86°21W **80 D10**
Muskegon Heights
  U.S.A. 43°12N 86°16W **80 D10**
Muskogee *U.S.A.* 35°45N 95°22W **84 D7**
Muskoka, L. *Canada* 45°0N 79°25W **82 B5**
Muskoka Falls *Canada* 44°59N 79°17W **82 B5**
Muskwa → *Canada* 58°47N 122°48W **70 B4**
Muslīmiyah *Syria* 36°19N 37°12E **44 B3**
Musofu *Zambia* 13°30S 29°0E **55 E2**
Musoma *Tanzania* 1°30S 33°48E **54 C3**
Musquaro, L. *Canada* 50°38N 61°5W **73 B7**
Musquodoboit Harbour
  Canada 44°50N 63°9W **73 D7**
Musselburgh *U.K.* 55°57N 3°2W **11 F5**
Musselshell → *U.S.A.* 47°21N 107°57W **76 C10**
Mussende *Angola* 10°32S 16°5E **52 G3**
Mussoorie *India* 30°27N 78°6E **42 D8**
Mussuco *Angola* 17°2S 19°3E **56 B2**
Mustafakemalpaşa
  Turkey 40°2N 28°24E **23 D13**
Mustang *Nepal* 29°10N 83°55E **43 E10**
Musters, L. *Argentina* 45°20S 69°25W **96 F3**
Musudan *N. Korea* 40°50N 129°43E **35 D15**
Muswellbrook *Australia* 32°16S 150°56E **63 E5**
Mût *Egypt* 25°28N 28°58E **51 C11**
Mut *Turkey* 36°40N 33°28E **44 B2**
Mutanda *Mozam.* 21°0S 33°34E **57 C5**
Mutanda *Zambia* 12°24S 26°13E **55 E2**
Mutare *Zimbabwe* 18°58S 32°38E **55 F3**
Mutawintji △ *Australia* 31°10S 142°30E **63 E3**
Mutha *Kenya* 1°48S 38°26E **54 C4**
Muting *Indonesia* 7°23S 140°20E **37 F10**
Mutki = Mirtağ *Turkey* 38°23N 41°56E **44 B4**
Mutoko *Zimbabwe* 17°24S 32°13E **57 B5**
Mutomo *Kenya* 1°51S 38°12E **54 C4**
Mutoray *Russia* 60°56N 101°0E **29 C11**
Mutsamudu *Comoros Is.* 12°10S 44°25E **53 a**
Mutsu *Japan* 41°5N 140°55E **30 D10**
Mutsu-Wan *Japan* 41°5N 140°55E **30 D10**
Muttaburra *Australia* 22°38S 144°29E **62 C3**
Mutton I. *Ireland* 52°49N 9°32W **10 D2**
Mutuáli *Mozam.* 14°55S 37°0E **55 E4**
Mutumba *Burundi* 3°25S 29°21E **54 C2**
Muweilih *Egypt* 30°42N 34°19E **46 E3**
Muy Muy *Nic.* 12°39N 85°36W **88 D2**
Muyinga *Burundi* 3°14S 30°33E **54 C3**
Muynak *Uzbekistan* 43°44N 59°10E **28 E6**
Muyunkum, Peski = Moyynqum
  Kazakhstan 44°12N 71°0E **32 C3**
Muz Tag *China* 36°25N 87°25E **32 D6**
Muzaffarabad *Pakistan* 34°25N 73°30E **43 B5**
Muzaffargarh *Pakistan* 30°5N 71°14E **42 D4**
Muzaffarnagar *India* 29°26N 77°40E **42 E7**
Muzaffarpur *Pakistan* 26°23N 83°23E **43 F11**
Muzaffirpur *Pakistan* 30°58N 69°9E **42 D3**
Muzhi *Russia* 65°25N 64°40E **18 A11**
Muztagh-Ata *China* 38°17N 75°7E **32 D4**
Mvuma *Zimbabwe* 19°16S 30°30E **55 F3**
Mvurwi *Zimbabwe* 17°0S 30°57E **55 F3**
Mwabvi △ *Malawi* 16°42S 35°0E **55 F3**
Mwadui *Tanzania* 3°26S 33°32E **54 C3**
Mwali = Mohéli
  Comoros Is. 12°20S 43°40E **53 a**
Mwambo *Tanzania* 10°30S 40°22E **55 E5**
Mwandi *Zambia* 17°30S 24°51E **55 F1**
Mwanza
  Dem. Rep. of the Congo 7°55S 26°43E **54 D2**
Mwanza *Tanzania* 2°30S 32°58E **54 C3**
Mwanza *Zambia* 16°58S 24°28E **55 F1**
Mwanza □ *Tanzania* 2°0S 33°0E **54 C3**
Mwaya *Tanzania* 9°32S 33°55E **55 D3**
Mweelrea *Ireland* 53°39N 9°49W **10 C2**
Mweka
  Dem. Rep. of the Congo 4°50S 21°34E **52 E4**

Mwene-Ditu
  Dem. Rep. of the Congo 6°35S 22°27E **52 F4**
Mwenezi *Zimbabwe* 21°15S 30°48E **55 G3**
Mwenezi → *Mozam.* 22°40S 31°50E **55 G3**
Mwenga
  Dem. Rep. of the Congo 3°1S 28°28E **54 C2**
Mweru, L. *Zambia* 9°0S 28°40E **55 D2**
Mweru Wantipa △
  Zambia 8°39S 29°25E **55 D2**
Mweza Range *Zimbabwe* 21°0S 30°0E **55 G3**
Mwilambwe
  Dem. Rep. of the Congo 8°7S 25°5E **54 D2**
Mwimbi *Tanzania* 8°38S 31°39E **55 D3**
Mwingi *Kenya* 0°56S 38°4E **54 C4**
Mwinilunga *Zambia* 11°43S 24°25E **55 E1**
My Son *Vietnam* 15°48N 108°7E **38 E7**
My Tho *Vietnam* 10°29N 106°23E **39 G6**
Myajlar *India* 26°15N 70°20E **42 F4**
Myanaung *Burma* 18°18N 95°22E **41 K19**
Myanmar = Burma ■
  Asia 21°0N 96°30E **41 J20**
Myaungmya *Burma* 16°30N 94°40E **41 L19**
Mycenæ = Mikines
  Greece 37°43N 22°46E **23 F10**
Myeik = Mergui *Burma* 12°26N 98°34E **38 F2**
Myeik Kyunzu *Burma* 11°30N 97°30E **39 G1**
Myerstown *U.S.A.* 40°22N 76°19W **83 F8**
Myingyan *Burma* 21°30N 95°20E **41 J19**
Myitkyina *Burma* 25°24N 97°26E **41 G20**
Mykines *Færoe Is.* 62°7N 7°35W **8 E9**
Mykolayiv *Ukraine* 46°58N 32°0E **19 E5**
Mykonos *Greece* 37°30N 25°25E **23 F11**
Mymensingh *Bangla.* 24°45N 90°24E **41 G17**
Mynydd Du *U.K.* 51°52N 3°50W **13 F4**
Myrdalsjökull *Iceland* 63°40N 19°6W **8 E4**
Myrtle Beach *U.S.A.* 33°42N 78°53W **85 E15**
Myrtle Creek *U.S.A.* 43°1N 123°17W **76 E2**
Myrtle Point *U.S.A.* 43°4N 124°8W **76 E1**
Myrtou *Cyprus* 35°18N 33°4E **25 D12**
Mysia *Turkey* 39°50N 27°0E **23 E12**
Mysore = Karnataka □
  India 13°15N 77°0E **40 N10**
Mysore *India* 12°17N 76°41E **40 N10**
Mystic *U.S.A.* 41°21N 71°58W **83 E13**
Mysuru = Mysore *India* 12°17N 76°41E **40 N10**
Myszków *Poland* 50°45N 19°22E **17 C10**
Mytishchi *Russia* 55°50N 37°50E **18 C6**
Mývatn *Iceland* 65°36N 17°0W **8 D5**
Mzimba *Malawi* 11°55S 33°39E **55 E3**
Mzimkulu → *S. Africa* 30°44S 30°28E **57 E5**
Mzimvubu → *S. Africa* 31°38S 29°33E **57 E4**
Mzuzu *Malawi* 11°30S 33°55E **55 E3**

N

Na Clocha Liatha = Greystones
  Ireland 53°9N 6°5W **10 C5**
Na Haeo △ *Thailand* 17°31N 100°58E **38 D3**
Na Hearadh = Harris
  U.K. 57°50N 6°55W **11 D2**
Na Noi *Thailand* 18°19N 100°43E **38 C3**
Na Phao *Laos* 17°35N 105°44E **38 D5**
Na Sam *Vietnam* 22°3N 106°37E **38 A6**
Na Thon *Thailand* 9°32N 99°56E **39 b**
Naab → *Germany* 49°1N 12°2E **16 D6**
Naantali *Finland* 60°29N 22°2E **9 F20**
Naas *Ireland* 53°12N 6°40W **10 C5**
Nababeep *S. Africa* 29°36S 17°46E **56 D2**
Nabadwip = Navadwip
  India 23°34N 88°20E **43 H13**
Nabawa *Australia* 28°30S 114°48E **61 E1**
Nabberu, L. *Australia* 25°50S 120°30E **61 E3**
Naberezhnyye Chelny
  Russia 55°42N 52°19E **18 C9**
Nabeul *Tunisia* 36°30N 10°44E **51 A8**
Nabha *India* 30°26N 76°14E **42 D7**
Nabīd *Iran* 29°40N 57°38E **45 D8**
Nabire *Indonesia* 3°15S 135°26E **37 E9**
Nabisar *Pakistan* 25°8N 69°40E **42 G3**
Nabisipi → *Canada* 50°14N 62°13W **73 B7**
Nabiswera *Uganda* 1°27N 32°15E **54 B3**
Nāblus = Nābulus
  West Bank 32°14N 35°15E **46 C4**
Nabouwalu *Fiji* 17°0S 178°45E **59 a**
Nābulus *West Bank* 32°14N 35°15E **46 C4**
Nacala *Mozam.* 14°32S 40°34E **55 E5**
Nacaome *Honduras* 13°31N 87°30W **88 D2**
Nacaroa *Mozam.* 14°22S 39°56E **55 E4**
Naches *U.S.A.* 46°44N 120°42W **76 C3**
Naches → *U.S.A.* 46°38N 120°31W **78 D6**
Nachicapau, L. *Canada* 56°40N 68°5W **73 A6**
Nachingwea *Tanzania* 10°23S 38°49E **55 E4**
Nachna *India* 27°34N 71°41E **42 F4**
Nacimiento, L. *U.S.A.* 35°46N 120°53W **78 K6**
Naco *Mexico* 31°19N 109°56W **86 A3**
Nacogdoches *U.S.A.* 31°36N 94°39W **84 F7**
Nácori Chico *Mexico* 29°40N 108°57W **86 B3**
Nacozari de García
  Mexico 30°25N 109°38W **86 A3**
Nacula *Fiji* 16°54S 177°27E **59 a**
Nada = Danzhou *China* 19°31N 109°33E **38 C7**
Nådendal = Naantali
  Finland 60°29N 22°2E **9 F20**
Nadi *Fiji* 17°42S 177°20E **59 a**
Nadiad *India* 22°41N 72°56E **42 H5**
Nador *Morocco* 35°14N 2°58E **50 B5**
Nadur *Malta* 36°2N 14°18E **25 C1**
Nadūshan *Iran* 32°2N 53°35E **45 C7**
Nadvirna *Ukraine* 48°37N 24°30E **17 D13**
Nadvoitsy *Russia* 63°52N 34°14E **18 B5**
Nadvornaya = Nadvirna
  Ukraine 48°37N 24°30E **17 D13**
Nadym *Russia* 65°35N 72°42E **28 C8**
Nadym → *Russia* 66°12N 72°0E **28 C8**
Nærbø *Norway* 58°40N 5°39E **9 G11**
Næstved *Denmark* 55°13N 11°44E **9 J14**
Nafarroa = Navarra □ *Spain* 42°40N 1°40W **21 A5**
Nafpaktos *Greece* 38°24N 21°50E **23 E9**
Nafplio *Greece* 37°33N 22°50E **23 F10**
Naft-e Safid *Iran* 31°40N 49°17E **45 D6**

Naftshahr *Iran* 34°0N 45°30E **44 C5**
Nafud Desert = An Nafūd
  Si. Arabia 28°15N 41°0E **44 D4**
Naga *Phil.* 13°38N 123°15E **37 B6**
Nagagami *Canada* 50°23N 84°20W **72 B3**
Nagahama *Japan* 35°23N 136°16E **31 G8**
Nagai *Japan* 38°6N 140°2E **30 E10**
Nagaland □ *India* 26°0N 94°30E **41 G19**
Nagano *Japan* 36°40N 138°10E **31 F9**
Nagano □ *Japan* 36°15N 138°0E **31 F9**
Nagaoka *Japan* 37°27N 138°51E **31 F9**
Nagaon = Nowgong
  India 26°20N 92°50E **41 F18**
Nagappattinam *India* 10°46N 79°51E **40 P11**
Nagar → *Bangla.* 24°27N 89°12E **43 G13**
Nagar Parkar *Pakistan* 24°28N 70°46E **42 G4**
Nagasaki *Japan* 32°47N 129°50E **31 H4**
Nagasaki □ *Japan* 32°50N 129°40E **31 H4**
Nagato *Japan* 34°19N 131°5E **31 G5**
Nagaur *India* 27°15N 73°45E **42 F5**
Nagda *India* 23°27N 75°25E **42 H6**
Nagercoil *India* 8°12N 77°26E **40 Q10**
Nagina *India* 29°30N 78°30E **43 E8**
Naghīneh *Iran* 34°20N 57°15E **45 C8**
Nagir *Pakistan* 36°12N 74°42E **43 A6**
Nagles Mts. *Ireland* 52°8N 8°30W **10 D3**
Nagod *India* 24°34N 80°36E **43 G9**
Nagoorin *Australia* 24°17S 151°15E **62 C5**
Nagorno-Karabakh □
  Azerbaijan 39°55N 46°45E **44 B5**
Nagornyy *Russia* 55°58N 124°57E **29 D13**
Nagoya *Japan* 35°10N 136°50E **31 G8**
Nagpur *India* 21°8N 79°10E **40 J11**
Nagqu *China* 31°29N 92°3E **32 F7**
Nagua *Dom. Rep.* 19°23N 69°50W **89 C6**
Naguabo *Puerto Rico* 18°13N 65°44W **89 d**
Nagurunguru ◉
  Australia 16°45S 129°45E **60 C4**
Nagykanizsa *Hungary* 46°28N 17°0E **17 E9**
Nagykőrös *Hungary* 47°5N 19°48E **17 E10**
Naha *Japan* 26°13N 127°42E **31 L3**
Nahan *India* 30°33N 77°18E **42 D7**
Nahanni △ *Canada* 61°36N 125°41W **70 A4**
Nahanni Butte *Canada* 61°2N 123°31W **70 A4**
Nahargarh *Mad. P., India* 24°10N 75°14E **42 G6**
Nahargarh *Raj., India* 24°55N 76°50E **42 G7**
Nahariyya *Israel* 33°1N 35°5E **46 C4**
Nahāvand *Iran* 34°10N 48°22E **45 C6**
Nahuel Huapi, L.
  Argentina 41°0S 71°32W **96 E2**
Nahuelbuta △ *Chile* 37°44S 72°57W **94 D1**
Nai Yong *Thailand* 8°14N 98°22E **39 a**
Naicá *Mexico* 27°53N 105°31W **86 B3**
Naicam *Canada* 52°30N 104°30W **71 C8**
Naikoon ◌ *Canada* 53°55N 131°55W **70 C2**
Naimisharanya *India* 27°21N 80°30E **43 F9**
Naimona'nyi Feng *Nepal* 30°26N 81°18E **43 D9**
Nain *Canada* 56°34N 61°40W **73 A7**
Nā'īn *Iran* 32°54N 53°0E **45 C7**
Naini Tal *India* 29°30N 79°30E **43 E8**
Nainpur *India* 22°30N 80°10E **43 H9**
Nainwa *India* 25°46N 75°51E **42 G6**
Nairai *Fiji* 17°49S 179°15E **59 a**
Nairn *U.K.* 57°35N 3°53W **11 D5**
Nairobi *Kenya* 1°17S 36°48E **54 C4**
Nairobi □ *Kenya* 1°22S 36°50E **54 C4**
Naissaar *Estonia* 59°34N 24°29E **9 G21**
Naitaba *Fiji* 17°0S 179°16W **59 a**
Naivasha *Kenya* 0°40S 36°30E **54 C4**
Naivasha, L. *Kenya* 0°48S 36°20E **54 C4**
Najaf = An Najaf *Iraq* 32°3N 44°15E **44 C5**
Najafābād *Iran* 32°40N 51°15E **45 C6**
Najd *Si. Arabia* 26°30N 42°0E **47 B3**
Najibabad *India* 29°40N 78°20E **42 E8**
Najin *N. Korea* 42°12N 130°15E **35 C16**
Najmah *Si. Arabia* 26°42N 50°6E **45 E6**
Najrān *Si. Arabia* 17°34N 44°18E **47 D3**
Naju *S. Korea* 35°3N 126°43E **35 G14**
Nakadōri-Shima *Japan* 32°57N 129°4E **31 H4**
Nakalagba
  Dem. Rep. of the Congo 2°50N 27°58E **54 B2**
Nakaminato *Japan* 36°21N 140°36E **31 F10**
Nakamura *Japan* 32°59N 132°56E **31 H6**
Nakano *Japan* 36°45N 138°22E **31 F9**
Nakano-Shima *Japan* 29°51N 129°52E **31 K4**
Nakashibetsu *Japan* 43°33N 144°59E **30 C12**
Nakfa *Eritrea* 16°40N 38°32E **47 D2**
Nakha Yai, Ko *Thailand* 8°3N 98°28E **39 a**
Nakhichevan = Naxçıvan
  Azerbaijan 39°12N 45°15E **44 B5**
Nakhichevan Rep. = Naxçıvan □
  Azerbaijan 39°25N 45°26E **44 B5**
Nakhl *Egypt* 29°55N 33°43E **46 F2**
Nakhl-e Taqī *Iran* 27°28N 52°36E **45 E7**
Nakhodka *Russia* 42°53N 132°54E **30 C6**
Nakhon Nayok
  Thailand 14°12N 101°13E **38 E3**
Nakhon Pathom
  Thailand 13°49N 100°3E **38 F3**
Nakhon Phanom
  Thailand 17°23N 104°43E **38 D5**
Nakhon Ratchasima
  Thailand 14°59N 102°12E **38 E4**
Nakhon Sawan
  Thailand 15°35N 100°10E **38 E3**
Nakhon Si Thammarat
  Thailand 8°29N 100°0E **39 H3**
Nakhon Thai *Thailand* 17°5N 100°44E **38 D3**
Nakhtarana *India* 23°20N 69°15E **42 H3**
Nakina *Canada* 50°10N 86°40W **72 B2**
Nakodar *India* 31°8N 75°31E **42 D6**
Naktong → *S. Korea* 35°7N 128°57E **35 G15**
Nakuru *Kenya* 0°15S 36°4E **54 C4**
Nakuru, L. *Kenya* 0°23S 36°5E **54 C4**
Nakusp *Canada* 50°20N 117°45W **70 C5**
Nal *Pakistan* 27°40N 66°12E **42 F2**
Nal → *Pakistan* 25°20N 65°30E **42 G1**
Nalázi *Mozam.* 24°3S 33°20E **57 C5**
Nalchik *Russia* 43°30N 43°33E **19 F7**
Nalgonda *India* 17°6N 79°15E **40 L11**

Nalhati India 24°17N 87°52E 43 G12
Naliya India 23°16N 68°50E 42 H3
Nallamalai Hills India 15°30N 78°50E 40 M11
Nalubaale Dam Uganda 0°30N 33°5E 54 B3
Nam Can Vietnam 8°46N 104°59E 39 H5
Nam-ch'on N. Korea 38°15N 126°26E 35 E14
Nam Co China 30°30N 90°45E 32 E7
Nam Dinh Vietnam 20°25N 106°5E 38 B6
Nam Du, Quan Dao Vietnam 9°41N 104°21E 39 H5
Nam Loi → Burma 21°3N 98°27E 38 B2
Nam Nao △ Thailand 16°44N 101°32E 38 D3
Nam Ngum Res. Laos 18°35N 102°34E 38 C4
Nam-Phan Vietnam 10°30N 106°0E 39 G6
Nam Phong Thailand 16°42N 102°52E 38 D4
Nam Theun Res. Laos 17°51N 105°3E 38 D5
Nam Tok Thailand 14°21N 99°4E 38 E2
Nam Un Res. Thailand 17°13N 103°44E 38 D4
Namacunde Angola 17°18S 15°50E 56 B2
Namacurra Mozam. 17°30S 36°50E 57 B6
Namak, Daryācheh-ye Iran 34°30N 52°0E 45 C7
Namak, Kavir-e Iran 34°30N 57°30E 45 C8
Namakzār, Daryācheh-ye Iran 34°0N 60°30E 45 C9
Namaland Namibia 26°0S 17°0E 56 C2
Namanga Kenya 2°33S 36°47E 54 C4
Namangan Uzbekistan 41°0N 71°40E 32 C3
Namapa Mozam. 13°43S 39°50E 55 E4
Namaqualand S. Africa 30°0S 17°25E 56 E2
Namasagali Uganda 1°2N 33°0E 54 B3
Namber Indonesia 1°2S 134°49E 37 E8
Nambour Australia 26°32S 152°58E 63 D5
Nambouwalu = Nabouwalu Fiji 17°0S 178°45E 59 a
Nambucca Heads Australia 30°37S 153°0E 63 E5
Nambung △ Australia 30°30S 115°5E 61 F2
Namcha Barwa China 29°40N 95°10E 32 F8
Namche Bazar Nepal 27°51N 86°47E 43 F12
Namchonjŏm = Nam-ch'on N. Korea 38°15N 126°26E 35 E14
Namecunda Mozam. 14°54S 37°37E 55 E4
Namenalala Fiji 17°8S 179°9E 59 a
Nameponda Mozam. 15°50S 39°50E 55 F4
Nametil Mozam. 15°40S 39°21E 55 F4
Namew L. Canada 54°14N 101°56W 71 C8
Namgia India 31°48N 78°40E 43 D8
Namialo Mozam. 14°55S 39°59E 55 E4
Namib Desert Namibia 22°30S 15°0E 56 C2
Namib-Naukluft ⌂ Namibia 24°40S 15°16E 56 C2
Namibe Angola 15°7S 12°11E 53 H2
Namibe □ Angola 16°35S 12°30E 56 B1
Namibia ■ Africa 22°0S 18°9E 56 C2
Namibwoestyn = Namib Desert Namibia 22°30S 15°0E 56 C2
Namjeju S. Korea 33°14N 126°33E 35 H14
Namlea Indonesia 3°18S 127°5E 37 E7
Namoi → Australia 30°12S 149°30E 63 E4
Nampa U.S.A. 43°34N 116°34W 76 E5
Namp'o N. Korea 38°52N 125°10E 35 E13
Nampō-Shotō Japan 32°0N 140°0E 31 J10
Nampula Mozam. 15°6S 39°15E 55 F4
Namrole Indonesia 3°46S 126°46E 37 E7
Namse Shankou China 30°0N 82°25E 43 E10
Namsen → Norway 64°28N 11°37E 8 D14
Namsos Norway 64°29N 11°30E 8 D14
Namtok Chat Trakan △ Thailand 17°17N 100°40E 38 D3
Namtok Huay Yang △ Thailand 11°35N 99°30E 39 G2
Namtok Mae Surin △ Thailand 18°55N 98°2E 38 C2
Namtok Ngao △ Thailand 9°58N 98°46E 39 H2
Namtok Phlew △ Thailand 12°32N 102°13E 38 F4
Namtok Yong △ Thailand 8°15N 98°45E 39 H2
Namtsy Russia 62°43N 129°37E 29 C13
Namtu Burma 23°5N 97°28E 41 H20
Namtumbo Tanzania 10°30S 36°4E 55 E4
Namu Canada 51°52N 127°50W 70 C3
Namuka-i-Lau Fiji 18°53S 178°37W 59 a
Namur Belgium 50°27N 4°52E 15 D4
Namur □ Belgium 50°17N 5°0E 15 D4
Namuruputh Kenya 4°34N 35°57E 54 B4
Namutoni Namibia 18°49S 16°55E 56 B2
Namwala Zambia 15°44S 26°30E 55 F2
Namwon S. Korea 35°23N 127°23E 35 G14
Namyang N. Korea 42°57N 129°52E 35 C15
Nan Thailand 18°48N 100°46E 38 C3
Nan → Thailand 15°42N 100°9E 38 E3
Nan-ch'ang = Nanchang China 28°42N 115°55E 33 F12
Nan Ling China 25°0N 112°30E 33 F11
Nanaimo Canada 49°10N 124°0W 70 D4
Nānākuli U.S.A. 21°24N 158°9W 75 L8
Nanam N. Korea 41°44N 129°40E 35 D15
Nanango Australia 26°40S 152°0E 63 D5
Nanao Japan 37°0N 137°0E 31 F8
Nanchang China 28°42N 115°55E 33 F12
Nanching = Nanjing China 32°2N 118°47E 33 E12
Nanchong China 30°43N 106°2E 32 E10
Nancy France 48°42N 6°12E 20 B7
Nanda Devi India 30°23N 79°59E 43 D8
Nanda Devi △ India 30°30N 79°50E 43 D8
Nanda Kot India 30°17N 80°5E 43 D9
Nandan Japan 34°10N 134°42E 31 G7
Nanded India 19°10N 77°20E 40 K10
Nandewar Ra. Australia 30°15S 150°35E 63 E5
Nandi = Nadi Fiji 17°42S 177°20E 59 a
Nandi Zimbabwe 20°58S 31°44E 55 G3
Nandigram India 22°1N 87°58E 43 H12
Nandurbar India 21°20N 74°15E 40 J9
Nandyal India 15°30N 78°30E 40 M11
Nang Rong Thailand 14°38N 102°48E 38 E4
Nanga-Eboko Cameroon 4°41N 12°22E 52 D2
Nanga Parbat Pakistan 35°10N 74°35E 43 B6
Nangade Mozam. 11°5S 39°36E 55 E4
Nangapinoh Indonesia 0°20S 111°44E 36 E4
Nangarhār □ Afghan. 34°20N 70°0E 40 B7
Nangatayap Indonesia 1°32S 110°34E 36 E4
Nangeya Mts. Uganda 3°30N 33°30E 54 B3
Nangong China 37°23N 115°22E 34 F8
Nanhuang China 36°58N 121°48E 35 F11
Nanisivik Canada 73°2N 84°33W 69 C15
Nanjing China 32°2N 118°47E 33 E12
Nanjirinji Tanzania 9°41S 39°5E 55 D4
Nankana Sahib Pakistan 31°27N 73°38E 42 D5
Nanking = Nanjing China 32°2N 118°47E 33 E12
Nankoku Japan 33°39N 133°44E 31 H6
Nanlang China 22°30N 113°32E 33 a
Nanning China 22°48N 108°20E 32 G10
Nannup Australia 33°59S 115°48E 61 F2
Nanpara India 27°52N 81°33E 43 F9
Nanping China 26°38N 118°10E 33 F12
Nansei-Shotō = Ryūkyū-Rettō Japan 26°0N 126°0E 31 M3
Nansen Basin Arctic 84°0N 50°0E 4 A10
Nansen Sd. Canada 81°0N 91°0W 69 A13
Nansha China 22°45N 113°34E 33 a
Nanshan China 18°19N 109°10E 38 C7
Nanshan I. S. China Sea 10°45N 115°49E 36 B5
Nansio Tanzania 2°3S 33°4E 54 C3
Nantawarrinna ☼ Australia 30°49S 138°58E 63 B2
Nantes France 47°12N 1°33W 20 C3
Nanticoke U.S.A. 41°12N 76°0W 83 E8
Nanton Canada 50°21N 113°46W 70 C6
Nantong China 32°1N 120°52E 33 E13
Nantou China 22°32N 113°55E 33 a
Nantucket U.S.A. 41°17N 70°6W 81 E18
Nantucket I. U.S.A. 41°16N 70°5W 81 E18
Nantulo Mozam. 12°32S 38°45E 55 E4
Nantwich U.K. 53°4N 2°31W 12 D5
Nanty Glo U.S.A. 40°28N 78°50W 82 F6
Nanuku Passage Fiji 16°45S 179°15W 59 a
Nanuque Brazil 17°50S 40°21W 93 G10
Nanusa, Kepulauan Indonesia 4°45N 127°1E 37 D7
Nanutarra Roadhouse Australia 22°32S 115°30E 60 D2
Nanyang China 33°11N 112°30E 34 H7
Nanyuan China 39°47N 116°24E 34 E9
Nanyuki Kenya 0°2N 37°4E 54 B4
Nanzhao China 33°30N 112°20E 34 H7
Nao, C. de la Spain 38°44N 0°14E 21 C6
Naococane, L. Canada 52°50N 70°45W 73 B5
Napa U.S.A. 38°18N 122°17W 78 G4
Napa → U.S.A. 38°10N 122°19W 78 G4
Napanee Canada 44°15N 77°0W 82 B8
Napanoch U.S.A. 41°44N 74°22W 83 E10
Nape Laos 18°18N 105°6E 38 C5
Nape Pass = Keo Neua, Deo Vietnam 18°23N 105°10E 38 C5
Napier N.Z. 39°30S 176°56E 59 C6
Napier Broome B. Australia 14°2S 126°37E 60 B4
Napier Pen. Australia 12°4S 135°43E 62 A2
Napierville Canada 45°11N 73°25W 83 A11
Naples = Nápoli Italy 40°50N 14°15E 22 D6
Naples U.S.A. 26°8N 81°48W 85 H14
Napo → Peru 3°20S 72°40W 92 D4
Napoleon N. Dak., U.S.A. 46°30N 99°46W 80 B4
Napoleon Ohio, U.S.A. 41°23N 84°8W 81 E11
Nápoli Italy 40°50N 14°15E 22 D6
Napopo Dem. Rep. of the Congo 4°15N 28°0E 54 B2
Naqadeh Iran 36°57N 45°23E 44 B5
Naqb, Ra's an Jordan 29°48N 35°44E 46 F4
Naqqāsh Iran 35°40N 49°6E 45 C6
Nara Japan 34°40N 135°49E 31 G7
Nara Mali 15°10N 7°20W 50 E4
Nara □ Japan 34°30N 136°0E 31 G8
Nara Canal Pakistan 24°30N 69°20E 42 G3
Nara Visa U.S.A. 35°37N 103°6W 77 J12
Naracoorte Australia 36°58S 140°45E 63 F3
Naradhan Australia 33°34S 146°17E 63 E4
Naraini India 25°11N 80°29E 43 G9
Naranjos Mexico 21°21N 97°41W 87 C5
Narasapur India 16°26N 81°40E 41 L12
Narathiwat Thailand 6°30N 101°48E 39 J3
Narayangadh = Bharatpur Nepal 27°34N 84°10E 43 F11
Narayanganj Bangla. 23°40N 90°33E 41 H17
Narayanpet India 16°45N 77°30E 40 L10
Narberth U.K. 51°47N 4°44W 13 F3
Narbonne France 43°11N 3°0E 20 E5
Nardīn Iran 37°3N 55°59E 45 B7
Nardò Italy 40°11N 18°2E 23 D8
Narembeen Australia 32°7S 118°24E 61 F2
Narendranagar India 30°10N 78°18E 42 D8
Nares Str. Arctic 80°0N 70°0W 69 B18
Naretha Australia 31°0S 124°45E 61 F3
Narew → Poland 52°26N 20°41E 17 B11
Nari → Pakistan 28°0N 67°40E 42 F2
Narin Afghan. 36°5N 69°0E 40 A6
Narindra, Helodranon' i Madag. 14°55S 47°30E 57 A8
Narita Japan 35°47N 140°19E 31 G10
Nariva Swamp Trin. & Tob. 10°26N 61°4W 93 K15
Narmada → India 21°38N 72°36E 42 J5
Narnaul India 28°5N 76°11E 42 E7
Narodnaya Russia 65°5N 59°58E 18 A10
Narok Kenya 1°55S 35°52E 54 C4
Narooma Australia 36°14S 150°4E 63 F5
Narowal Pakistan 32°6N 74°52E 42 C6
Narrabri Australia 30°19S 149°46E 63 E4
Narran → Australia 28°37S 148°12E 63 D4
Narrandera Australia 34°42S 146°31E 63 E4
Narrogin Australia 32°58S 117°14E 61 F2
Narromine Australia 32°12S 148°12E 63 E4
Narrow Hills ⌂ Canada 54°0N 104°37W 71 C8
Narsimhapur India 22°54N 79°14E 43 H8
Narsinghgarh India 23°45N 76°40E 42 H7
Naruto Japan 34°11N 134°37E 31 G7
Narva Estonia 59°23N 28°12E 18 C4
Narva → Russia 59°27N 28°2E 9 G23
Narva Bay = Narva Laht Estonia 59°35N 27°35E 9 G22
Narva Laht Estonia 59°35N 27°35E 9 G22
Narvik Norway 68°28N 17°26E 8 B17
Narwana India 29°39N 76°6E 42 E7
Narwinbi ☼ Australia 16°7S 136°17E 62 B2
Naryan-Mar Russia 67°42N 53°12E 18 A9
Narym Russia 59°0N 81°30E 28 D9
Naryn Kyrgyzstan 41°26N 75°58E 32 C4
Naryn Qum Kazakhstan 47°30N 49°0E 28 E5
Nasa Norway 66°29N 15°23E 8 C16
Nasau Fiji 17°19S 179°27E 59 a
Nasca Peru 14°50S 74°57W 92 F4
Nasca Ridge Pac. Oc. 20°0S 80°0W 65 K19
Naseby N.Z. 45°1S 170°10E 59 F3
Naselle U.S.A. 46°22N 123°49W 78 D3
Naser, Buheirat en Egypt 23°0N 32°30E 51 D12
Nashik = Nasik India 19°58N 73°50E 40 K8
Nashua Mont., U.S.A. 48°8N 106°22W 76 B10
Nashua N.H., U.S.A. 42°45N 71°28W 83 D13
Nashville Ark., U.S.A. 33°57N 93°51W 84 E8
Nashville Ga., U.S.A. 31°12N 83°15W 85 F13
Nashville Tenn., U.S.A. 36°10N 86°47W 85 C11
Nasik India 19°58N 73°50E 40 K8
Nasirabad India 26°15N 74°45E 42 F6
Nasirabad Pakistan 28°23N 68°24E 42 E3
Nasiri = Ahvāz Iran 31°20N 48°40E 45 D6
Nasiriyah = An Nāşirīyah Iraq 31°0N 46°15E 44 D5
Naskaupi → Canada 53°47N 60°51W 73 B7
Naşrābād Iran 34°8N 51°26E 45 C6
Naşriān-e Pā'īn Iran 32°52N 46°52E 44 C5
Nass → Canada 55°0N 129°40W 70 C3
Nassau Bahamas 25°5N 77°20W 88 A4
Nassau U.S.A. 42°31N 73°37W 83 D11
Nassau, B. Chile 55°20S 68°0W 96 H3
Nasser, L. = Naser, Buheirat en Egypt 23°0N 32°30E 51 D12
Nässjö Sweden 57°39N 14°42E 9 H16
Nastapoka → Canada 56°55N 76°33W 72 A4
Nastapoka, Is. Canada 56°55N 76°50W 72 A4
Nata Botswana 20°12S 26°12E 56 C4
Nata → Botswana 20°14S 26°10E 56 C4
Natal Brazil 5°47S 35°13W 93 E11
Natal Indonesia 0°35N 99°7E 36 D1
Natal Drakensberg ⌂ S. Africa 29°27S 29°30E 57 D4
Naţanz Iran 33°30N 51°55E 45 C6
Natashquan Canada 50°14N 61°46W 73 B7
Natashquan → Canada 50°7N 61°50W 73 B7
Natchez U.S.A. 31°34N 91°24W 84 F9
Natchitoches U.S.A. 31°46N 93°5W 84 F8
Natewa B. Fiji 16°35S 179°40E 59 a
Nathalia Australia 36°1S 145°13E 63 F4
Nathdwara India 24°55N 73°50E 42 G5
Nati, Pta. Spain 40°3N 3°50E 24 A10
Natimuk Australia 36°42S 142°0E 63 F3
Nation → Canada 55°30N 123°32W 70 B4
National City U.S.A. 32°40N 117°5W 79 N9
Natitingou Benin 10°20N 1°26E 50 F6
Natividad, I. Mexico 27°52N 115°11W 86 B1
Natkyizin Burma 14°57N 97°59E 38 E1
Natron, L. Tanzania 2°20S 36°0E 54 C4
Natrona Heights U.S.A. 40°37N 79°44W 82 F5
Natukanaoka Pan Namibia 18°40S 15°45E 56 B2
Natuna Besar, Kepulauan Indonesia 4°0N 108°15E 36 D3
Natuna Is. = Natuna Besar, Kepulauan Indonesia 4°0N 108°15E 36 D3
Natuna Selatan, Kepulauan Indonesia 2°45N 109°0E 36 D3
Natural Bridge U.S.A. 44°5N 75°30W 83 B9
Natural Bridges ⌂ U.S.A. 37°36N 110°0W 77 H9
Naturaliste, C. Tas., Australia 40°50S 148°15E 63 G4
Naturaliste, C. W. Austral., Australia 33°32S 115°0E 61 F2
Naturaliste Plateau Ind. Oc. 34°0S 112°0E 64 L3
Nau Qala Afghan. 34°5N 68°5E 42 B3
Naugatuck U.S.A. 41°30N 73°3W 83 E11
Naujaat = Repulse Bay Canada 66°30N 86°30W 69 D14
Naumburg Germany 51°9N 11°47E 16 C6
Nauru ■ Pac. Oc. 1°0S 166°0E 58 B9
Naushahra = Nowshera Pakistan 34°0N 72°0E 40 C8
Naushahro Pakistan 26°50N 68°7E 42 F3
Naushon I. U.S.A. 41°29N 70°45W 83 E14
Nausori Fiji 18°2S 178°32E 59 a
Nauta Peru 4°31S 73°35W 92 D4
Nautanwa India 27°20N 83°25E 43 F10
Naute ⌂ Namibia 26°55S 17°57E 56 D2
Nautla Mexico 20°13N 96°47W 87 C5
Nava Mexico 28°25N 100°45W 86 B4
Navadwip India 23°34N 88°20E 43 H13
Navahrudak Belarus 53°40N 25°50E 17 B13
Navajo Res. U.S.A. 36°48N 107°36W 77 H10
Navalmoral de la Mata Spain 39°52N 5°33W 21 C3
Navan = An Uaimh Ireland 53°39N 6°41W 10 C5
Navarin, Mys Russia 62°15N 179°5E 29 C18
Navarino, I. Chile 55°0S 67°40W 96 H3
Navarra □ Spain 42°40N 1°40W 21 A5
Navarre U.S.A. 40°43N 81°31W 82 F3
Navarro → U.S.A. 39°11N 123°45W 78 F3
Navasota U.S.A. 30°23N 96°5W 84 F6
Navassa I. W. Indies 18°30N 75°0W 89 C5
Naver → U.K. 58°32N 4°14W 11 C4
Navibandar India 21°26N 69°48E 42 J3
Navidad Chile 33°57S 71°50W 94 C1
Naviraí Brazil 23°8S 54°13W 95 A5
Naviti Fiji 17°7S 177°15E 59 a
Navlakhi India 22°58N 70°28E 42 H4
Năvodari Romania 44°19N 28°36E 17 F15
Navoi Uzbekistan 40°9N 65°22E 28 E7
Navojoa Mexico 27°6N 109°26W 86 B3
Navolato Mexico 24°47N 107°42W 86 C3
Navsari India 20°57N 72°59E 40 J8
Navua Fiji 18°12S 178°11E 59 a
Nawa Kot Pakistan 28°21N 71°24E 42 E4
Nawab Khan Pakistan 30°17N 69°12E 42 D3
Nawabganj Ut. P., India 26°56N 81°14E 43 F9
Nawabganj Ut. P., India 28°32N 79°40E 43 E8
Nawabshah Pakistan 26°15N 68°25E 42 F3
Nawada India 24°50N 85°33E 43 G11
Nawakot Nepal 27°55N 85°10E 43 F11
Nawalgarh India 27°50N 75°15E 42 F6
Nawanshahr India 32°33N 74°48E 43 C6
Nawar, Dasht-i- Afghan. 33°52N 68°0E 42 C3
Nawoiy = Navoi Uzbekistan 40°9N 65°22E 28 E7
Naxçıvan Azerbaijan 39°12N 45°15E 44 B5
Naxçıvan □ Azerbaijan 39°25N 45°26E 44 B5
Naxos Greece 37°8N 25°25E 23 F11
Nay, Mui Vietnam 12°54N 109°26E 38 F7
Nāy Band Būshehr, Iran 27°20N 52°40E 45 E7
Nāy Band Khorāsān, Iran 32°20N 57°34E 45 C8
Nayakhan Russia 61°56N 159°0E 29 C16
Nayarit □ Mexico 22°0N 105°0W 86 C4
Nayau Fiji 18°6S 178°10E 59 a
Nayoro Japan 44°21N 142°28E 30 B11
Naypyidaw Burma 19°44N 96°12E 38 C1
Nayyāl, W. → Si. Arabia 28°35N 39°4E 44 D3
Nazaré Brazil 13°2S 39°0W 93 F11
Nazareth = Nazerat Israel 32°42N 35°17E 46 C4
Nazareth U.S.A. 40°44N 75°19W 83 F9
Nazarovo Russia 57°2N 90°40E 29 D10
Nazas Mexico 25°14N 104°8W 86 B4
Nazas → Mexico 25°12N 104°12W 86 B4
Nazca = Nasca Peru 14°50S 74°57W 92 F4
Naze Japan 28°22N 129°27E 31 K4
Naze, The U.K. 51°53N 1°18E 13 F9
Nazerat Israel 32°42N 35°17E 46 C4
Nāzīk Iran 39°1N 45°4E 44 B5
Nazilli Turkey 37°55N 28°15E 23 F13
Nazko Canada 53°1N 123°37W 70 C4
Nazko → Canada 53°7N 123°34W 70 C4
Nazret Ethiopia 8°32N 39°22E 47 F2
Nchanga Zambia 12°30S 27°49E 55 E2
Ncheu Malawi 14°50S 34°47E 55 E3
Ndala Tanzania 4°45S 33°15E 54 C3
Ndalatando Angola 9°12S 14°48E 52 F2
Ndareda Tanzania 4°12S 35°30E 54 C4
Ndélé C.A.R. 8°25N 20°36E 52 C4
Ndjamena Chad 12°10N 15°0E 51 F8
Ndola Zambia 13°0S 28°34E 55 E2
Ndomo ⌂ S. Africa 26°52S 32°15E 57 D5
Ndoto Mts. Kenya 2°0N 37°0E 54 B4
Nduguti Tanzania 4°18S 34°41E 54 C3
Neagh, Lough U.K. 54°37N 6°25W 10 B5
Neah Bay U.S.A. 48°22N 124°37W 78 B2
Neale, L. Australia 24°15S 130°0E 60 D5
Neales → Australia 28°8S 136°47E 63 D2
Neapoli Greece 35°15N 25°37E 25 D7
Near Is. U.S.A. 52°30N 174°0E 74 E2
Neath U.K. 51°39N 3°48W 13 F4
Neath Port Talbot □ U.K. 51°42N 3°45W 13 F4
Nebbi Uganda 2°28N 31°6E 54 B3
Nebine Cr. → Australia 29°27S 146°56E 63 D4
Nebitdag = Balkanabat Turkmenistan 39°30N 54°22E 45 B7
Nebo Australia 21°42S 148°42E 62 C4
Nebraska □ U.S.A. 41°30N 99°30W 80 E4
Nebraska City U.S.A. 40°41N 95°52W 80 E6
Nébrodi, Monti Italy 37°54N 14°35E 22 F6
Necedah U.S.A. 44°2N 90°4W 80 C8
Nechako → Canada 53°55N 122°42W 70 C4
Neches → U.S.A. 29°58N 93°51W 84 G8
Neckar → Germany 49°27N 8°29E 16 D5
Necker I. U.S.A. 23°35N 164°42W 75 L7
Necochea Argentina 38°30S 58°50W 94 D4
Nederland = Netherlands ■ Europe 52°0N 5°30E 15 C5
Needles Canada 49°53N 118°7W 70 D5
Needles U.S.A. 34°51N 114°37W 79 L12
Needles, The U.K. 50°39N 1°35W 13 G6
Neembucú □ Paraguay 27°0S 58°0W 94 B4
Neemuch = Nimach India 24°30N 74°56E 42 G6
Neenah U.S.A. 44°11N 88°28W 80 C9
Neepawa Canada 50°15N 99°30W 71 C9
Neftçala Azerbaijan 39°19N 49°12E 45 B6
Neftegorsk Russia 53°1N 142°58E 29 D15
Neftekumsk Russia 44°46N 44°50E 19 F7
Nefteyugansk Russia 61°5N 72°42E 28 C8
Nefyn U.K. 52°56N 4°31W 12 E3
Negapatam = Nagappattinam India 10°46N 79°51E 40 P11
Negara Indonesia 8°22S 114°37E 37 J17
Negaunee U.S.A. 46°30N 87°36W 80 B10
Negele Ethiopia 5°20N 39°36E 47 F2
Negeri Sembilan □ Malaysia 2°45N 102°10E 39 L4
Negev Desert = Hanegev Israel 30°50N 35°0E 46 E4
Negombo Sri Lanka 7°12N 79°50E 40 R11
Negotin Serbia 44°16N 22°37E 23 B10
Negra, Pta. Mauritania 22°54N 16°18W 50 D2
Negra, Pta. Peru 6°6S 81°10W 92 E2
Negrais, C. = Maudin Sun Burma 16°0N 94°30E 41 M19
Negril Jamaica 18°22N 78°20W 88 a
Negro → Argentina 41°2S 62°47W 96 E4
Negro → Brazil 3°0S 60°0W 92 D7
Negro → Uruguay 33°24S 58°22W 94 C4
Negros Phil. 9°30N 122°40E 37 C6
Neguac Canada 47°15N 65°5W 73 C6
Nehalem → U.S.A. 45°40N 123°56W 78 E3
Nehāvand Iran 35°56N 49°31E 45 C6
Nehbandān Iran 31°35N 60°5E 45 D9
Nehe China 48°29N 124°50E 33 B13
Nei Mongol Zizhiqu □ China 42°0N 112°0E 34 D7
Neiafu Tonga 18°39S 173°59W 59 c
Neiges, Piton des Réunion 21°5S 55°29E 53 c
Neijiang China 29°35N 104°55E 32 F9
Neilingding Dao China 22°25N 113°48E 33 a
Neillsville U.S.A. 44°34N 90°36W 80 C8
Neilton U.S.A. 47°25N 123°53W 76 C2
Neiqiu China 37°15N 114°30E 34 F8
Neiva Colombia 2°56N 75°18W 92 C3
Neixiang China 33°10N 111°52E 34 H6
Nejanilini L. Canada 59°33N 97°48W 71 B9
Nejd = Najd Si. Arabia 26°30N 42°0E 47 B3
Nekā Iran 36°39N 53°19E 45 B7
Nekemte Ethiopia 9°4N 36°30E 47 F2
Neksø Denmark 55°4N 15°8E 9 J16
Nelia Australia 20°39S 142°12E 62 C3
Neligh U.S.A. 42°8N 98°2W 80 D4
Nelkan Russia 57°40N 136°4E 29 D14
Nellore India 14°27N 79°59E 40 M11
Nelson Canada 49°30N 117°20W 70 D5
Nelson N.Z. 41°18S 173°16E 59 D4
Nelson U.K. 53°50N 2°13W 12 D5
Nelson Ariz., U.S.A. 35°31N 113°19W 77 J7
Nelson Nev., U.S.A. 35°42N 114°49W 79 K12
Nelson → Canada 54°33N 98°2W 71 C9
Nelson, C. Australia 38°26S 141°32E 63 F3
Nelson, Estrecho Chile 51°30S 75°0W 96 G2
Nelson Forks Canada 59°30N 124°0W 70 B4
Nelson House Canada 55°47N 98°51W 71 B9
Nelson L. Canada 55°48N 100°7W 71 B8
Nelson Lakes △ N.Z. 41°55S 172°44E 59 D4
Nelspoort S. Africa 32°7S 23°0E 56 E3
Nelspruit S. Africa 25°29S 30°59E 57 D5
Néma Mauritania 16°40N 7°15W 50 E4
Neman = Nemunas → Lithuania 55°25N 21°10E 9 J19
Nembrala Indonesia 10°53S 122°50E 60 B3
Nemeiben L. Canada 55°20N 105°20W 71 B7
Nemiscau Canada 51°18N 76°54W 72 B4
Nemiscau, L. Canada 51°25N 76°40W 72 B4
Nemunas → Lithuania 55°25N 21°10E 9 J19
Nemuro Japan 43°20N 145°35E 30 C12
Nemuro-Kaikyō Japan 43°30N 145°30E 30 C12
Nen Jiang → China 45°28N 124°30E 35 B13
Nenagh Ireland 52°52N 8°11W 10 D3
Nenana U.S.A. 64°34N 149°5W 74 C10
Nenasi Malaysia 3°9N 103°23E 39 L4
Nene → U.K. 52°49N 0°11E 13 E8
Nenjiang China 49°10N 125°10E 33 B14
Neno Malawi 15°25S 34°40E 55 F3
Neodesha U.S.A. 37°25N 95°41W 80 G6
Neora Valley △ India 27°0N 88°45E 43 F13
Neosho U.S.A. 36°52N 94°22W 80 G6
Neosho → U.S.A. 36°48N 95°18W 84 C7
Nepal ■ Asia 28°0N 84°30E 43 F11
Nepalganj Nepal 28°5N 81°40E 43 E9
Nepalganj Road India 28°1N 81°41E 43 E9
Nephi U.S.A. 39°43N 111°50W 76 G8
Nephin Ireland 54°1N 9°22W 10 B2
Nephin Beg Range Ireland 54°0N 9°40W 10 C2
Neptune U.S.A. 40°13N 74°2W 83 F10
Neqāb Iran 36°42N 57°25E 45 B8
Nerang Australia 27°58S 153°20E 63 D5
Nerchinsk Russia 52°0N 116°39E 29 D12
Néret, L. Canada 54°45N 70°44W 73 B5
Neretva → Croatia 43°1N 17°27E 23 C7
Neringa Lithuania 55°20N 21°5E 9 J19
Neris → Lithuania 55°8N 24°16E 9 J21
Neryungri Russia 57°38N 124°28E 29 D13
Nescopeck U.S.A. 41°3N 76°12W 83 E8
Neskantaga Canada 52°14N 87°53W 72 B2
Neskaupstaður Iceland 65°9N 13°42W 8 D7
Ness, L. U.K. 57°15N 4°32W 11 D4
Ness City U.S.A. 38°27N 99°54W 80 F4
Nesterov = Zhovkva Ukraine 50°4N 23°58E 17 C12
Nestos → Europe 40°54N 24°49E 23 D11
Nesvizh = Nyasvizh Belarus 53°14N 26°38E 17 B14
Netanya Israel 32°20N 34°51E 46 C3
Netarhat India 23°29N 84°16E 43 H11
Nete → Belgium 51°7N 4°14E 15 C4
Netherdale Australia 21°10S 148°33E 62 b
Netherlands ■ Europe 52°0N 5°30E 15 C5
Netherlands Antilles = ABC Islands W. Indies 12°15N 69°0W 89 D6
Netrang India 21°39N 73°21E 42 J5
Nettilling L. Canada 66°30N 71°0W 69 D17
Netzahualcóyotl, Presa Mexico 17°8N 93°35W 87 D6
Neubrandenburg Germany 53°33N 13°15E 16 B7
Neuchâtel Switz. 47°0N 6°55E 20 C7
Neuchâtel, Lac de Switz. 46°53N 6°50E 20 C7
Neufchâteau Belgium 49°50N 5°25E 15 E5
Neumayer Antarctica 71°0S 68°30W 5 D17
Neumünster Germany 54°4N 9°58E 16 A5
Neunkirchen Germany 49°20N 7°9E 16 D4
Neuquén Argentina 38°55S 68°0W 96 D3
Neuquén □ Argentina 38°0S 69°50W 94 D2
Neuruppin Germany 52°55N 12°48E 16 B7
Neuse → U.S.A. 35°6N 76°29W 85 D16
Neusiedler See Austria 47°50N 16°47E 17 E9
Neustrelitz Germany 53°21N 13°4E 16 B7
Neva → Russia 59°56N 30°20E 18 C5
Nevada Iowa, U.S.A. 42°1N 93°27W 80 D7
Nevada Mo., U.S.A. 37°51N 94°22W 80 G6
Nevada □ U.S.A. 39°0N 117°0W 76 G5
Nevada City U.S.A. 39°16N 121°1W 78 F6
Nevado, Cerro Argentina 35°30S 68°32W 94 D2
Nevado de Colima = Volcán de Colima △ Mexico 19°30N 103°40W 86 D4
Nevado de Tres Cruces △ Chile 27°13S 69°5W 94 B2
Nevel Russia 56°0N 29°55E 18 C4
Nevelsk Russia 46°40N 141°51E 29 E15
Nevers France 47°0N 3°9E 20 C5
Nevertire Australia 31°50S 147°44E 63 E4
Neville Canada 49°58N 107°39W 71 D7
Nevinnomyssk Russia 44°40N 42°0E 19 F7
Nevis St. Kitts & Nevis 17°0N 62°30W 89 C7

Nevşehir Turkey 38°33N 34°40E **44** B2
Nevyansk Russia 57°30N 60°13E **18** C11
New → U.S.A. 38°10N 81°12W **81** F13
New Aiyansh Canada 55°12N 129°4W **70** B3
New Albany Ind., U.S.A. 38°18N 85°49W **81** F11
New Albany Miss., U.S.A. 34°29N 89°0W **85** D10
New Albany Pa., U.S.A. 41°36N 76°27W **83** E8
New Amsterdam Guyana 6°15N 57°36W **92** B7
New Baltimore U.S.A. 42°41N 82°44W **82** D2
New Bedford U.S.A. 41°38N 70°56W **83** E14
New Berlin N.Y., U.S.A. 42°37N 75°20W **83** D9
New Berlin Pa., U.S.A. 40°50N 76°57W **82** F8
New Bern U.S.A. 35°7N 77°3W **85** D16
New Bethlehem U.S.A. 41°0N 79°20W **82** F5
New Bight Bahamas 24°19N 75°24W **89** B4
New Bloomfield U.S.A. 40°25N 77°11W **82** F7
New Boston U.S.A. 33°28N 94°25W **84** F7
New Braunfels U.S.A. 29°42N 98°8W **84** G5
New Brighton N.Z. 43°29S 172°43E **59** E4
New Brighton U.S.A. 40°42N 80°19W **82** F4
New Britain Papua N. G. 5°50S 150°20E **58** B8
New Britain U.S.A. 41°40N 72°47W **83** E12
New Brunswick U.S.A. 40°30N 74°27W **83** F10
New Brunswick □ Canada 46°50N 66°30W **73** C6
New Caledonia ☑ Pac. Oc. 21°0S 165°0E **58** D9
New Caledonia Trough Pac. Oc. 30°0S 165°0E **64** L8
New Castile = Castilla-La Mancha □ Spain 39°30N 3°30W **21** C4
New Castle Ind., U.S.A. 39°55N 85°22W **81** F11
New Castle Pa., U.S.A. 41°0N 80°21W **82** F4
New City U.S.A. 41°9N 73°59N **83** E11
New Concord U.S.A. 39°59N 81°54W **82** G3
New Cumberland U.S.A. 40°30N 80°36W **82** F4
New Cuyama U.S.A. 34°57N 119°38W **79** L7
New Delhi India 28°36N 77°11E **42** E7
New Denver Canada 50°0N 117°25W **70** D5
New Don Pedro Res. U.S.A. 37°43N 120°24W **78** H6
New England U.S.A. 43°0N 71°0W **75** G25
New England N. Dak., U.S.A. 46°32N 102°52W **80** B2
New England Ra. Australia 30°20S 151°45E **63** E5
New Forest △ U.K. 50°53N 1°34W **13** G6
New Galloway U.K. 55°5N 4°9W **11** F4
New Glasgow Canada 45°35N 62°36W **73** C7
New Guinea Oceania 4°0S 136°0E **58** B6
New Hamburg Canada 43°23N 80°42W **82** C4
New Hampshire □ U.S.A. 44°0N 71°30W **83** C13
New Hampton U.S.A. 43°3N 92°19W **80** D7
New Hanover S. Africa 29°22S 30°31E **57** D5
New Hartford U.S.A. 43°4N 75°18W **83** D9
New Haven Conn., U.S.A. 41°18N 72°55W **83** E12
New Haven Mich., U.S.A. 42°44N 82°48W **82** D2
New Haven N.Y., U.S.A. 43°28N 76°18W **83** C8
New Hazelton Canada 55°20N 127°30W **70** B3
New Hebrides = Vanuatu ■ Pac. Oc. 15°0S 168°0E **58** C9
New Holland U.S.A. 40°6N 76°5W **83** F8
New Iberia U.S.A. 30°1N 91°49W **84** F9
New Ireland Papua N. G. 3°20S 151°50E **58** B8
New Jersey □ U.S.A. 40°0N 74°30W **81** F16
New Kensington U.S.A. 40°34N 79°46W **82** F5
New Lexington U.S.A. 39°43N 82°13W **81** F12
New Liskeard Canada 47°31N 79°41W **72** C4
New London Conn., U.S.A. 41°22N 72°6W **83** E12
New London Ohio, U.S.A. 41°5N 82°24W **82** E2
New London Wis., U.S.A. 44°23N 88°45W **80** C9
New Madrid U.S.A. 36°36N 89°32W **80** G9
New Martinsville U.S.A. 39°39N 80°52W **81** F13
New Meadows U.S.A. 44°58N 116°18W **76** D5
New Melones L. U.S.A. 37°57N 120°31W **78** H6
New Mexico □ U.S.A. 34°30N 106°0W **77** J11
New Milford Conn., U.S.A. 41°35N 73°25W **83** E11
New Milford Pa., U.S.A. 41°52N 75°44W **83** E9
New Norcia Australia 30°57S 116°13E **61** F2
New Norfolk Australia 42°46S 147°2E **63** G4
New Orleans U.S.A. 29°57N 90°4W **85** G9
New Philadelphia U.S.A. 40°30N 81°27W **82** F3
New Plymouth N.Z. 39°4S 174°5E **59** C5
New Plymouth U.S.A. 43°58N 116°49W **76** E5
New Port Richey U.S.A. 28°16N 82°43W **85** G13
New Providence Bahamas 25°25N 78°35W **88** A4
New Quay U.K. 52°13N 4°21N **13** E3
New Radnor U.K. 52°15N 3°9W **13** E4
New Richmond Canada 48°15N 65°45W **73** C6
New Richmond U.S.A. 45°7N 92°32W **80** C7
New River Gorge △ U.S.A. 37°53N 81°6W **81** G13
New Roads U.S.A. 30°42N 91°26W **84** F9
New Rochelle U.S.A. 40°55N 73°46W **83** F11
New Rockford U.S.A. 47°41N 99°8W **80** B4
New Romney U.K. 50°59N 0°57E **13** G8
New Ross Ireland 52°23N 6°57W **10** D5
New Salem U.S.A. 46°51N 101°25W **80** B3
New Scone = Scone U.K. 56°25N 3°24W **11** E5
New Siberian I. = Novaya Sibir, Ostrov Russia 75°10N 150°0E **29** B16
New Siberian Is. = Novosibirskiye Ostrova Russia 75°0N 142°0E **29** B15
New Smyrna Beach U.S.A. 29°1N 80°56W **85** G14
New South Wales □ Australia 33°0S 146°0E **63** E4
New Tecumseth = Alliston Canada 44°9N 79°52W **82** B5

New Town U.S.A. 47°59N 102°30W **80** B2
New Tredegar U.K. 51°44N 3°16W **13** F4
New Ulm U.S.A. 44°19N 94°28W **80** C6
New Waterford Canada 46°13N 60°4W **73** C7
New Westminster Canada 49°13N 122°55W **78** A4
New York U.S.A. 40°43N 74°0W **83** F11
New York □ U.S.A. 43°0N 75°0W **83** D9
New York J.F. Kennedy Int. ✈ (JFK) U.S.A. 40°38N 73°47W **83** F11
New Zealand ■ Oceania 40°0S 176°0E **59** D6
Newaj → India 24°24N 76°49E **42** G7
Newala Tanzania 10°58S 39°18E **55** E4
Newark Del., U.S.A. 39°41N 75°46W **81** F16
Newark N.J., U.S.A. 40°44N 74°10W **83** F10
Newark N.Y., U.S.A. 43°3N 77°6W **82** C7
Newark Ohio, U.S.A. 40°3N 82°24W **82** F2
Newark Liberty Int. ✈ (EWR) U.S.A. 40°42N 74°10W **83** F10
Newark-on-Trent U.K. 53°5N 0°48W **12** D7
Newark Valley U.S.A. 42°14N 76°11W **83** D8
Newberg U.S.A. 45°18N 122°58W **76** D2
Newberry Mich., U.S.A. 46°21N 85°30W **81** B11
Newberry S.C., U.S.A. 34°17N 81°37W **85** D14
Newberry Springs U.S.A. 34°50N 116°41W **79** L10
Newboro L. Canada 44°38N 76°20W **83** B8
Newbridge = Droichead Nua Ireland 53°11N 6°48W **10** C5
Newburgh Canada 44°19N 76°52W **82** B8
Newburgh U.S.A. 41°30N 74°1W **83** E10
Newbury U.K. 51°24N 1°20W **13** F6
Newbury N.H., U.S.A. 43°19N 72°3W **83** B12
Newbury Vt., U.S.A. 44°5N 72°4W **83** B12
Newburyport U.S.A. 42°49N 70°53W **83** D14
Newcastle Australia 33°0S 151°46E **63** E5
Newcastle N.B. Canada 47°1N 65°38W **73** C6
Newcastle Ont. Canada 43°55N 78°35W **72** D4
Newcastle S. Africa 27°45S 29°58E **57** D4
Newcastle U.K. 54°13N 5°54W **10** B6
Newcastle Calif., U.S.A. 38°53N 121°8W **78** G5
Newcastle Wyo., U.S.A. 43°50N 104°11W **76** E11
Newcastle Emlyn U.K. 52°2N 4°28W **13** E3
Newcastle Ra. Australia 15°45S 130°15E **60** C5
Newcastle-under-Lyme U.K. 53°1N 2°14W **12** D5
Newcastle-upon-Tyne U.K. 54°58N 1°36W **12** C6
Newcastle Waters Australia 17°30S 133°28E **62** B1
Newcastle West Ireland 52°27N 9°3W **10** D2
Newcomb U.S.A. 43°58N 74°10W **83** C10
Newcomerstown U.S.A. 40°16N 81°36W **82** F3
Newdegate Australia 33°6S 119°0E **61** F2
Newell Australia 16°20S 145°16E **62** B4
Newell U.S.A. 44°43N 103°25W **80** C2
Newenham, C. U.S.A. 58°39N 162°11W **74** D7
Newfane U.S.A. 43°17N 78°43W **82** C6
Newfield U.S.A. 42°18N 76°33W **83** D8
Newfound L. U.S.A. 43°40N 71°47W **83** C13
Newfoundland Canada 49°0N 55°0W **73** C8
Newfoundland U.S.A. 41°18N 75°19W **83** E9
Newfoundland & Labrador □ Canada 53°0N 58°0W **73** B8
Newhaven U.K. 50°47N 0°3E **13** G8
Newkirk U.S.A. 36°53N 97°3W **84** C6
Newlyn U.K. 50°6N 5°34W **13** G2
Newman Australia 23°18S 119°45E **60** D2
Newman U.S.A. 37°19N 121°1W **78** H5
Newmarket Canada 44°3N 79°28W **82** B5
Newmarket Ireland 52°13N 9°0W **10** D2
Newmarket U.K. 52°15N 0°25E **13** E8
Newmarket U.S.A. 43°5N 70°56W **83** C14
Newnan U.S.A. 33°23N 84°48W **85** E12
Newport Ireland 53°53N 9°33W **10** C2
Newport I. of W., U.K. 50°42N 1°17W **13** G6
Newport Newport, U.K. 51°35N 3°0W **13** F5
Newport Ark., U.S.A. 35°37N 91°16W **84** D9
Newport Ky., U.S.A. 39°5N 84°29W **81** F11
Newport N.H., U.S.A. 43°22N 72°10W **83** C12
Newport N.Y., U.S.A. 43°11N 75°1W **83** C9
Newport Oreg., U.S.A. 44°39N 124°3W **76** D1
Newport Pa., U.S.A. 40°29N 77°8W **82** F7
Newport R.I., U.S.A. 41°29N 71°19W **83** E13
Newport Tenn., U.S.A. 35°58N 83°11W **85** D13
Newport Vt., U.S.A. 44°56N 72°13W **83** B12
Newport Wash., U.S.A. 48°11N 117°3W **76** B5
Newport □ U.K. 51°33N 3°1W **13** F4
Newport Beach U.S.A. 33°37N 117°56W **79** M9
Newport News U.S.A. 36°58N 76°25W **81** G15
Newport Pagnell U.K. 52°5N 0°43W **13** E7
Newquay U.K. 50°25N 5°6W **13** G2
Newry U.K. 54°11N 6°21W **10** B5
Newry Islands △ Australia 20°51S 148°56E **62** b
Newton Ill., U.S.A. 38°59N 88°10W **80** F9
Newton Iowa, U.S.A. 41°42N 93°3W **80** E7
Newton Kans., U.S.A. 38°3N 97°21W **80** F5
Newton Mass., U.S.A. 42°21N 71°12W **83** D13
Newton Miss., U.S.A. 32°19N 89°10W **85** E10
Newton N.C., U.S.A. 35°40N 81°13W **85** D14
Newton N.J., U.S.A. 41°3N 74°45W **83** E10
Newton Tex., U.S.A. 30°51N 93°46W **84** F8
Newton Abbot U.K. 50°32N 3°37W **13** G4
Newton Aycliffe U.K. 54°37N 1°34W **12** C6
Newton Falls N.Y., U.S.A. 44°12N 74°59W **83** B10
Newton Falls Ohio, U.S.A. 41°11N 80°59W **82** E4
Newton Stewart U.K. 54°57N 4°30W **11** G4
Newtonmore U.K. 57°4N 4°8W **11** D4
Newtown U.K. 52°31N 3°19W **13** E4
Newtownabbey U.K. 54°40N 5°56W **10** B6
Newtownards U.K. 54°36N 5°42W **10** B6
Newtownbarry = Bunclody Ireland 52°39N 6°40W **10** D5
Newtownstewart U.K. 54°43N 7°23W **10** B4
Newville U.S.A. 40°10N 77°24W **82** F7
Neya Russia 58°21N 43°49E **18** C7

Neyrīz Iran 29°15N 54°19E **45** D7
Neyshābūr Iran 36°10N 58°50E **45** B8
Nezperce U.S.A. 46°14N 116°14W **76** C5
Ngaanyatjarra ◇ Australia 22°40S 127°0E **60** D4
Ngabang Indonesia 0°23N 109°55E **36** D3
Ngabordamlu, Tanjung Indonesia 6°56S 134°11E **37** F8
Ngalia Indonesia 3°55N 133°16E **31** H6
N'Gage Angola 7°46S 15°15E **52** F3
Ngaliwurru Nungali ◇ Australia 15°42S 130°4E **60** C5
Ngalurrtju ◇ Australia 22°44S 132°5E **60** D5
Ngami Depression Botswana 20°30S 22°46E **56** C3
Ngamo Zimbabwe 19°3S 27°32E **55** F2
Nganglong Kangri China 33°0N 81°0E **43** C9
Ngao Thailand 18°46N 99°59E **38** C2
Ngaoundéré Cameroon 7°15N 13°35E **52** C2
Ngapara N.Z. 44°57S 170°46E **59** F3
Ngara Tanzania 2°29S 30°40E **54** C3
Ngarluma ◇ Australia 21°30S 118°30E **60** D2
Ngawi Indonesia 7°24S 111°26E **37** G14
Ngcobo S. Africa 31°37S 28°0E **57** E4
Ngeru Uganda 0°27N 33°10E **54** B3
Nghia Lo Vietnam 21°33N 104°28E **38** B5
Ngoma Malawi 13°8S 33°45E **55** E3
Ngomahura Zimbabwe 20°26S 30°43E **55** G3
Ngomba Tanzania 8°20S 32°53E **55** D3
Ngomeni, Ras Kenya 2°59S 40°14E **54** C5
Ngong Kenya 1°22S 36°39E **54** C4
Ngoring Hu China 34°55N 97°5E **32** E8
Ngorongoro Tanzania 3°11S 35°32E **54** C4
Ngorongoro △ Tanzania 2°40S 35°30E **54** C4
Ngozi Burundi 2°54S 29°50E **54** C2
Ngudu Tanzania 2°58S 33°25E **54** C3
Nguigmi Niger 14°20N 13°20E **51** F8
Nguiu Australia 11°46S 130°38E **60** B5
Ngukurr Australia 14°44S 134°44E **62** A1
Ngum → Laos 18°31N 102°32E **38** C4
Ngundu Zimbabwe 18°11S 31°15E **55** F3
Ngunga Tanzania 3°37S 33°37E **54** C3
Nguru Nigeria 12°56N 10°29E **51** F8
Nguru Mts. Tanzania 6°0S 37°30E **54** D4
Ngusi Malawi 14°0S 34°50E **55** E3
Nguyen Binh Vietnam 22°39N 105°56E **38** A5
Nha Bang Vietnam 10°37N 105°0E **39** G5
Nha Trang Vietnam 12°16N 109°10E **39** F7
Nhacoongo Mozam. 24°18S 35°14E **57** C6
Nhamaabué Mozam. 17°25S 35°5E **55** F4
Nhamundá → Brazil 2°12S 56°41W **93** D7
Nhangulaze, L. Mozam. 24°0S 34°30E **57** C5
Nharnuwangga, Wajarri and Ngarlawangga ◇ Australia 24°40S 118°0E **61** D2
Nhill Australia 36°18S 141°40E **63** F3
Nho Quan Vietnam 20°18N 105°45E **38** B5
Nhulunbuy Australia 12°10S 137°20E **62** A2
Nia-nia Dem. Rep. of the Congo 1°30N 27°40E **54** B2
Niafounké Mali 16°0N 4°5W **50** E5
Niagara Falls Canada 43°7N 79°5W **82** C5
Niagara Falls U.S.A. 43°5N 79°4W **82** C6
Niagara-on-the-Lake Canada 43°15N 79°4W **82** C5
Niah Malaysia 3°58N 113°46E **36** D4
Niamey Niger 13°27N 2°6E **50** F6
Niangara Dem. Rep. of the Congo 3°42N 27°50E **54** B2
Niantic U.S.A. 41°20N 72°11W **83** E12
Nias Indonesia 1°0N 97°30E **36** D1
Niassa □ Mozam. 13°30S 36°0E **55** E4
Niassa △ Mozam. 12°45S 36°57E **55** E4
Nibāk Si. Arabia 24°25N 50°50E **45** E7
Nicaragua ■ Cent. Amer. 11°40N 85°30W **88** D2
Nicaragua, L. de Nic. 12°0N 85°30W **88** D2
Nicastro Italy 38°59N 16°19E **22** E7
Nice France 43°42N 7°14E **20** E7
Niceville U.S.A. 30°31N 86°30W **85** F11
Nichicun, L. Canada 53°5N 71°0W **73** B5
Nichinan Japan 31°38N 131°23E **31** J5
Nicholás, Canal W. Indies 23°30N 80°5W **88** B3
Nicholasville U.S.A. 37°53N 84°34W **81** G11
Nichols U.S.A. 42°1N 76°22W **83** D8
Nicholson Australia 18°2S 128°54E **60** C4
Nicholson U.S.A. 41°37N 75°47W **83** E9
Nicholson → Australia 17°31S 139°36E **62** B2
Nicholson L. Canada 62°40N 102°40W **71** A8
Nicholson Ra. Australia 27°15S 116°45E **61** E2
Nicholville U.S.A. 44°41N 74°39W **83** B10
Nicobar Is. Ind. Oc. 8°0N 93°30E **27** H11
Nicola Canada 50°12N 120°40W **70** C4
Nicolls Town Bahamas 25°8N 78°0W **88** A4
Nicosia Cyprus 35°10N 33°25E **25** D12
Nicoya Costa Rica 10°9N 85°27W **88** D2
Nicoya, G. de Costa Rica 10°0N 85°0W **88** E3
Nicoya, Pen. de Costa Rica 9°45N 85°40W **88** E2
Nidd → U.K. 53°59N 1°23W **12** D6
Niedersachsen □ Germany 52°50N 9°0E **16** B5
Niekerkshoop S. Africa 29°19S 22°51E **56** D3
Niemba Dem. Rep. of the Congo 5°58S 28°24E **54** D2
Niemen = Nemunas → Lithuania 55°25N 21°10E **9** J19
Nienburg Germany 52°39N 9°13E **16** B5
Nieu Bethesda S. Africa 31°51S 24°34E **56** E3
Nieuw Amsterdam Suriname 5°53N 55°5W **93** B7
Nieuw Nickerie Suriname 6°0N 56°59W **93** B7
Nieuwoudtville S. Africa 31°23S 19°7E **56** E2
Nieuwpoort Belgium 51°8N 2°45E **15** C2
Nieves, Pico de las Canary Is. 27°57N 15°35W **24** G4
Niğde Turkey 37°58N 34°40E **44** B2
Nigel S. Africa 26°27S 28°25E **57** D4
Niger ■ W. Afr. 17°30N 10°0E **50** E7
Niger → W. Afr. 5°33N 6°33E **50** G7

Nigeria ■ W. Afr. 8°30N 8°0E **50** G7
Nighasin India 28°14N 80°52E **43** E9
Nightcaps N.Z. 45°57S 168°2E **59** F2
Nihoa U.S.A. 23°6N 161°58W **75** L7
Nihon = Japan ■ Asia 36°0N 136°0E **31** G8
Nii-Jima Japan 34°20N 139°15E **31** G9
Niigata Japan 37°58N 139°0E **30** F9
Niigata □ Japan 37°15N 138°45E **31** F9
Niihama Japan 33°55N 133°16E **31** H6
Ni'ihau U.S.A. 21°54N 160°9W **75** L7
Niimi Japan 34°59N 133°28E **31** G6
Niitsu Japan 37°48N 139°7E **30** F9
Nijil Jordan 30°32N 35°33E **46** E4
Nijkerk Neths. 52°13N 5°30E **15** B5
Nijmegen Neths. 51°50N 5°52E **15** C5
Nijverdal Neths. 52°22N 6°28E **15** B6
Nīk Pey Iran 36°50N 48°10E **45** B6
Nikel Russia 69°24N 30°13E **8** B24
Nikiniki Indonesia 9°49S 124°30E **60** A3
Nikkō Japan 36°45N 139°35E **31** F9
Nikkō △ Japan 36°56N 139°37E **31** F9
Nikolayev = Mykolayiv Ukraine 46°58N 32°0E **19** E5
Nikolayevsk Russia 50°0N 45°35E **19** E8
Nikolayevsk-na-Amur Russia 53°8N 140°44E **29** D15
Nikolskoye Russia 55°12N 166°0E **29** D17
Nikopol Ukraine 47°35N 34°25E **19** E5
Nikshahr Iran 26°15N 60°10E **45** E9
Nikšić Montenegro 42°50N 18°57E **23** C8
Nīl, Nahr en → Africa 30°10N 31°6E **51** B12
Nīl el Abyad → Sudan 15°38N 32°31E **51** E12
Nīl el Azraq → Sudan 15°38N 32°31E **51** E12
Nila Indonesia 6°44S 129°31E **37** F7
Niland U.S.A. 33°14N 115°31W **79** M11
Nile = Nīl, Nahr en → Africa 30°10N 31°6E **51** B12
Niles Mich., U.S.A. 41°50N 86°15W **80** E10
Niles Ohio, U.S.A. 41°11N 80°46W **82** E4
Nim Ka Thana India 27°44N 75°48E **42** F6
Nimach India 24°30N 74°56E **42** G6
Nimbahera India 24°37N 74°45E **42** G6
Nîmes France 43°50N 4°23E **20** E6
Nimfaíon, Ákra = Pines, Akra Greece 40°5N 24°20E **23** D11
Nimmitabel Australia 36°29S 149°15E **63** F4
Nīnawá Iraq 36°25N 43°10E **44** B4
Nīnawá □ Iraq 36°15N 43°0E **44** B4
Nindigully Australia 28°21S 148°50E **63** D4
Ninepin Group China 22°16N 114°21E **33** a
Nineveh = Nīnawā Iraq 36°25N 43°10E **44** B4
Ning Xian China 35°30N 107°58E **34** G4
Ningaloo Marine △ Australia 22°23S 113°32E **60** D1
Ning'an China 44°22N 129°20E **35** B15
Ningbo China 29°51N 121°28E **33** F13
Ningcheng China 41°32N 119°53E **35** D10
Ningjin China 37°35N 114°57E **34** F8
Ningjing Shan China 31°0N 98°20E **41** E21
Ningling China 34°25N 115°22E **34** G8
Ningpo = Ningbo China 29°51N 121°28E **33** F13
Ningqiang China 32°47N 106°15E **34** H4
Ningshan China 33°21N 108°21E **34** H5
Ningsia Hui A.R. = Ningxia Huizu Zizhiqu □ China 38°0N 106°0E **34** F4
Ningwu China 39°0N 112°18E **34** E7
Ningxia Huizu Zizhiqu □ China 38°0N 106°0E **34** F4
Ningyang China 35°47N 116°45E **34** G9
Ninh Binh Vietnam 20°15N 105°55E **38** B5
Ninh Giang Vietnam 20°44N 106°24E **38** B6
Ninh Hoa Vietnam 12°30N 109°7E **38** F7
Ninh Ma Vietnam 12°48N 109°21E **38** F7
Ninove Belgium 50°51N 4°2E **15** D4
Nioaque Brazil 21°5S 55°50W **95** A4
Niobrara U.S.A. 42°45N 98°2W **80** D4
Niobrara → U.S.A. 42°46N 98°3W **80** D4
Nioro du Sahel Mali 15°15N 9°30W **50** E4
Niort France 46°19N 0°29W **20** C3
Nipawin Canada 53°20N 104°0W **71** C8
Nipigon Canada 49°0N 88°17W **72** C2
Nipigon, L. Canada 49°50N 88°30W **72** C2
Nipishish L. Canada 54°12N 60°45W **73** B7
Nipissing, L. Canada 46°20N 80°0W **72** C4
Nipomo U.S.A. 35°3N 120°29W **79** K6
Nippon = Japan ■ Asia 36°0N 136°0E **31** G8
Nipton U.S.A. 35°28N 115°16W **79** K11
Niquelândia Brazil 14°33S 48°23W **93** F9
Nīr Iran 38°2N 47°59E **44** B5
Nirasaki Japan 35°42N 138°27E **31** G9
Nirmal India 19°3N 78°20E **40** K11
Nirmali India 26°20N 86°35E **43** F12
Niš Serbia 43°19N 21°58E **23** C9
Nişāb Si. Arabia 29°11N 44°43E **44** D5
Nişāb Yemen 14°25N 46°29E **47** E4
Nishinomiya Japan 34°45N 135°20E **31** G7
Nishino'omote Japan 30°43N 130°59E **31** J5
Nishiwaki Japan 34°59N 134°58E **31** G7
Niskibi → Canada 56°29N 88°9W **72** A2
Nisqually → U.S.A. 47°7N 122°42W **78** C4
Nissaki Greece 39°43N 19°52E **25** A3
Nissum Bredning Denmark 56°40N 8°20E **9** H13
Nistru = Dnister → Europe 46°18N 30°17E **17** E16
Nisutlin → Canada 60°14N 132°34W **70** A2
Nitchequon Canada 53°10N 70°58W **73** B5
Niterói Brazil 22°53S 43°7W **95** A7
Nith → Canada 43°12N 80°23W **82** C4
Nith → U.K. 55°14N 3°33W **11** F5
Nitmiluk △ Australia 14°6S 132°15E **60** B5
Nitra Slovak Rep. 48°19N 18°4E **17** D10
Nitra → Slovak Rep. 47°46N 18°10E **17** E10
Niue ☑ Pac. Oc. 19°2S 169°54W **65** J11
Niut Indonesia 0°55N 109°54E **36** D4
Niuzhuang China 40°58N 122°28E **35** D12
Nivala Finland 63°56N 24°57E **8** E21
Nivelles Belgium 50°35N 4°20E **15** D4
Nivernais France 47°15N 3°30E **20** C5

Niverville Canada 49°36N 97°3W **71** D9
Niwas India 23°3N 80°26E **43** H9
Nixa U.S.A. 37°3N 93°18W **80** G7
Nixon U.S.A. 29°16N 97°46W **84** G6
Nizamabad India 18°45N 78°7E **40** K11
Nizamghat India 28°20N 95°45E **41** E19
Nizhne Kolymsk Russia 68°34N 160°55E **29** C17
Nizhnekamsk Russia 55°38N 51°49E **18** C9
Nizhneudinsk Russia 54°54N 99°3E **29** D10
Nizhnevartovsk Russia 60°56N 76°38E **28** C8
Nizhniy Bestyakh Russia 61°57N 129°54E **29** C13
Nizhniy Novgorod Russia 56°20N 44°0E **18** C7
Nizhniy Tagil Russia 57°55N 59°57E **18** C10
Nizhyn Ukraine 51°5N 31°55E **19** D5
Nizip Turkey 37°5N 37°50E **44** B3
Nízké Tatry Slovak Rep. 48°55N 19°30E **17** D10
Nizwá Oman 22°56N 57°32E **47** C6
Njakwa Malawi 11°1S 33°56E **55** E3
Njanji Zambia 14°25S 31°46E **55** E3
Njazidja = Grande Comore Comoros Is. 11°35S 43°20E **53** a
Njinjo Tanzania 8°48S 38°54E **55** D4
Njombe Tanzania 9°20S 34°50E **55** D3
Njombe → Tanzania 6°56S 35°6E **54** D4
Nkana Zambia 12°50S 28°8E **55** E2
Nkandla S. Africa 28°37S 31°5E **57** D5
Nkawkaw Ghana 6°36N 0°49W **50** G5
Nkayi Zimbabwe 19°41S 29°20E **55** F2
Nkhotakota Malawi 12°56S 34°15E **55** E3
Nkhotakota △ Malawi 12°50S 34°0E **55** E3
Nkondwe Tanzania 5°51S 30°51E **54** D3
Nkongsamba Cameroon 4°55N 9°55E **52** D1
Nkurenkuru Namibia 17°42S 18°32E **56** B2
Nmai → Burma 25°30N 97°25E **41** G20
Noakhali Bangla. 22°48N 91°10E **41** H17
Nobel Canada 45°25N 80°6W **82** A4
Nobeoka Japan 32°36N 131°41E **31** H5
Noblesville U.S.A. 40°3N 86°1W **80** E10
Noboribetsu Japan 42°24N 141°6E **30** C10
Noccundra Australia 27°50S 142°36E **63** D3
Nocera Inferiore Italy 40°44N 14°38E **22** D6
Nocona U.S.A. 33°47N 97°44W **84** E6
Noda U.S.A. 35°56N 139°52E **31** G9
Nogales Mexico 31°19N 110°56W **86** A2
Nogales U.S.A. 31°21N 110°56W **77** L8
Nōgata Japan 33°48N 130°44E **31** H5
Noggerup Australia 33°32S 116°5E **61** F2
Noginsk Russia 64°30N 90°50E **29** C10
Nogliki Russia 51°50N 143°10E **29** D15
Nogoa → Australia 23°40S 147°55E **62** C4
Nogoyá Argentina 32°24S 59°48W **94** C4
Nohar India 29°11N 74°49E **42** E6
Nohta India 23°40N 79°34E **43** H8
Noires, Mts. France 48°11N 3°40W **20** B2
Noirmoutier, Î. de France 46°58N 2°10W **20** C2
Nojane Botswana 23°15S 20°14E **56** C3
Nojima-Zaki Japan 34°54N 139°53E **31** G9
Nok Kundi Pakistan 28°50N 62°45E **40** E3
Nok Ta Phao, Ko Thailand 9°23N 99°40E **39** b
Nokaneng Botswana 19°40S 22°17E **56** B3
Nokia Finland 61°30N 23°30E **8** F20
Nokomis Canada 51°35N 105°0W **71** C8
Nokomis L. Canada 57°0N 103°0W **71** B8
Nola C.A.R. 3°35N 16°4E **52** D3
Noma Omuramba → Namibia 18°52S 20°53E **56** B3
Nombre de Dios Panama 9°34N 79°28W **88** E4
Nome U.S.A. 64°30N 165°25W **74** C6
Nomgon Mongolia 42°50N 105°8E **34** C3
Nomo-Zaki Japan 32°35N 129°44E **31** H4
Nomuka Tonga 20°17S 174°48W **59** c
Nomuka Group Tonga 20°20S 174°48W **59** c
Nonacho L. Canada 61°42N 109°40W **71** A7
Nonda Australia 20°40S 142°28E **62** C3
Nong Chang Thailand 15°23N 99°51E **38** E2
Nong Han Res. Thailand 17°11N 104°9E **38** D5
Nong Het Laos 19°29N 103°59E **38** C4
Nong Khai Thailand 17°50N 102°46E **38** D4
Nong'an China 44°25N 125°5E **35** B13
Nongoma S. Africa 27°58S 31°35E **57** D5
Nongsa Indonesia 1°11N 104°8E **39** d
Nonoava Mexico 27°28N 106°44W **86** B3
Nonsan S. Korea 36°12N 127°5E **35** F14
Nonthaburi Thailand 13°50N 100°29E **38** F3
Noonamah Australia 12°40S 131°4E **60** B5
Noondie, L. Australia 28°30S 119°30E **61** E2
Noonkanbah ◇ Australia 18°30S 124°50E **60** C3
Noord Brabant □ Neths. 51°40N 5°0E **15** C5
Noord Holland □ Neths. 52°30N 4°45E **15** B4
Noordbeveland Neths. 51°35N 3°50E **15** C3
Noordoostpolder Neths. 52°45N 5°45E **15** B5
Noordwijk Neths. 52°14N 4°26E **15** B4
Noosa Heads Australia 26°25S 153°6E **63** D5
Nootka I. Canada 49°32N 126°42W **70** D3
Nopiming △ Canada 50°30N 95°37W **71** C9
Noralee Canada 53°59N 126°26W **70** C3
Noranda = Rouyn-Noranda Canada 48°20N 79°0W **72** C4
Norco U.S.A. 33°56N 117°33W **79** M9
Nord-Kivu □ Dem. Rep. of the Congo 1°0S 29°0E **54** C2
Nord-Ostsee-Kanal Germany 54°12N 9°32E **16** A5
Nordaustlandet Svalbard 79°14N 23°0E **4** B9
Norddeich Germany 52°29N 7°9E **16** B4
Norderney Germany 53°42N 7°9E **16** B4
Norderstedt Germany 53°42N 10°1E **16** B5
Nordfjord Norway 61°55N 5°30E **8** F11
Nordfriesische Inseln Germany 54°40N 8°20E **16** A5
Nordhausen Germany 51°30N 10°47E **16** C6
Norðoyar Faroe Is. 62°17N 6°35W **8** E9
Nordkapp Norway 71°10N 25°50E **8** A21
Nordkapp Svalbard 80°31N 20°0E **4** A9
Nordkinnhalvøya Norway 70°55N 27°40E **8** A22
Nordrhein-Westfalen □ Germany 51°45N 7°30E **16** C4

Nordvik *Russia* 74°2N 111°32E **29** B12
Nore → *Ireland* 52°25N 6°58W **10** D4
Noreland *Canada* 44°43N 78°48W **82** B6
Norfolk = Simcoe
Canada 42°50N 80°23W **82** D4
Norfolk *N.Y., U.S.A.* 44°48N 74°59W **83** B10
Norfolk *Nebr., U.S.A.* 42°2N 97°25W **80** D5
Norfolk *Va., U.S.A.* 36°50N 76°17W **81** G15
Norfolk □ *U.K.* 52°39N 0°54E **13** E8
Norfolk Broads △ *U.K.* 52°45N 1°30E **13** E9
Norfolk I. *Pac. Oc.* 28°58S 168°3E **58** D9
Norfolk Ridge *Pac. Oc.* 29°0S 168°0E **64** K8
Norfork L. *U.S.A.* 36°15N 92°14W **84** C8
Norge = Norway ■ *Europe* 63°0N 11°0E **8** E14
Norilsk *Russia* 69°20N 88°6E **29** C9
Norma, Mt. *Australia* 20°55S 140°42E **62** C3
Normal *U.S.A.* 40°31N 88°59W **80** E9
Norman *U.S.A.* 35°13N 97°26W **84** D6
Norman → *Australia* 19°18S 141°51E **62** B3
Norman Wells *Canada* 65°17N 126°51W **68** D6
Normanby → *Australia* 14°23S 144°10E **62** A3
Normandie *France* 48°45N 0°10E **20** B4
Normandin *Canada* 48°49N 72°31W **72** C5
Normandy = Normandie
France 48°45N 0°10E **20** B4
Normanhurst, Mt.
Australia 25°4S 122°30E **61** E3
Normanton *Australia* 17°40S 141°10E **62** B3
Normétal *Canada* 49°0N 79°22W **72** C4
Norquay *Canada* 51°53N 102°5W **71** C8
Norquinco *Argentina* 41°51S 70°55W **96** E2
Norrbottens län □
Sweden 66°50N 20°0E **8** C19
Norris Point *Canada* 49°31N 57°53W **73** C8
Norristown *U.S.A.* 40°7N 75°21W **83** F9
Norrköping *Sweden* 58°37N 16°11E **9** G17
Norrland *Sweden* 62°15N 15°45E **8** E16
Norrtälje *Sweden* 59°46N 18°42E **9** G18
Norseman *Australia* 32°8S 121°43E **61** F3
Norsk *Russia* 52°30N 130°5E **29** D14
Norte, Pta. del *Canary Is.* 27°51N 17°57W **24** G2
Norte, Serra do *Brazil* 11°20S 59°0W **92** F7
North, C. *Canada* 47°2N 60°20W **73** C7
North Adams *U.S.A.* 42°42N 73°7W **83** D11
North America 40°0N 100°0W **66** F10
North Arm *Canada* 62°0N 114°30W **70** A5
North Augusta *U.S.A.* 33°30N 81°59W **85** E14
North Australian Basin
Ind. Oc. 14°30S 116°30E **64** J3
North Ayrshire □ *U.K.* 55°45N 4°44W **11** F4
North Bass I. *U.S.A.* 41°40N 82°56W **82** E2
North Battleford
Canada 52°50N 108°17W **71** C7
North Bay *Canada* 46°20N 79°30W **72** C4
North Belcher Is. *Canada* 56°50N 79°50W **72** A4
North Bend *Oreg.,*
U.S.A. 43°24N 124°14W **76** E1
North Bend *Pa., U.S.A.* 41°20N 77°42W **82** E7
North Bend *Wash.,*
U.S.A. 47°30N 121°47W **78** C5
North Bennington
U.S.A. 42°56N 73°15W **83** D11
North Berwick *U.K.* 56°4N 2°42W **11** E6
North Berwick *U.S.A.* 43°18N 70°44W **83** C14
North Bruce *Canada* 44°22N 81°26W **82** B3
North C. *Canada* 47°5N 64°0W **73** C7
North C. *N.Z.* 34°23S 173°4E **59** A4
North Canadian →
U.S.A. 35°22N 95°37W **84** D7
North Canton *U.S.A.* 40°53N 81°24W **82** F3
North Cape = Nordkapp
Norway 71°10N 25°50E **8** A21
North Caribou L.
Canada 52°50N 90°40W **72** B1
North Carolina □
U.S.A. 35°30N 80°0W **85** D15
North Cascades △
U.S.A. 48°45N 121°10W **76** B3
North Channel *Canada* 46°0N 83°0W **72** C3
North Channel *U.K.* 55°13N 5°52W **11** F3
North Charleston
U.S.A. 32°53N 79°58W **85** E15
North Chicago *U.S.A.* 42°19N 87°51W **80** D10
North Collins *U.S.A.* 42°35N 78°56W **82** D6
North Creek *U.S.A.* 43°42N 73°59W **83** C11
North Dakota □
U.S.A. 47°30N 100°15W **80** B3
North Downs *U.K.* 51°19N 0°21E **13** F8
North East *U.S.A.* 42°13N 79°50W **82** D5
North East Frontier Agency =
Arunachal Pradesh □
India 28°0N 95°0E **41** F19
North East Lincolnshire □
U.K. 53°34N 0°2W **12** D7
North Eastern □ *Kenya* 1°30N 40°0E **54** B5
North Esk → *U.K.* 56°46N 2°24W **11** E6
North European Plain
Europe 55°0N 25°0E **6** E10
North Foreland *U.K.* 51°22N 1°28E **13** F9
North Fork *U.S.A.* 37°14N 119°21W **78** H7
North Fork American →
U.S.A. 38°57N 120°59W **78** G5
North Fork Feather →
U.S.A. 38°33N 121°30W **78** F5
North Fork Grand →
U.S.A. 45°47N 102°16W **80** C2
North Fork Red →
U.S.A. 34°24N 99°14W **84** D5
North Frisian Is. = Nordfriesische
Inseln *Germany* 54°40N 8°20E **16** A5
North Gower *Canada* 45°8N 75°43W **83** A9
North Hd. *Australia* 30°14S 114°59E **61** F1
North Henik L. *Canada* 61°45N 97°40W **71** A9
North Highlands
U.S.A. 38°40N 121°23W **78** G5
North Horr *Kenya* 3°20N 37°8E **54** B4
North I. *Kenya* 4°5N 36°5E **54** B4
North I. *N.Z.* 38°0S 175°0E **59** C5
North I. *Seychelles* 4°25S 55°13E **53** b
North Kingsville *U.S.A.* 41°54N 80°42W **82** E4
North Kitui ⌓ *Kenya* 0°15S 38°29E **54** C4
North Knife → *Canada* 58°53N 94°45W **71** B10
North Koel → *India* 24°45N 83°50E **43** G10
North Korea ■ *Asia* 40°0N 127°0E **35** E14
North Lakhimpur *India* 27°14N 94°7E **41** F19
North Lanarkshire □
U.K. 55°52N 3°56W **11** F5
North Las Vegas *U.S.A.* 36°11N 115°7W **79** J11
North Lincolnshire □
U.K. 53°36N 0°30W **12** D7
North Little Rock
U.S.A. 34°45N 92°16W **84** D8
North Loup → *U.S.A.* 41°17N 98°24W **80** E4
North Luangwa △ *Zambia* 11°49S 32°9E **55** E3
North Magnetic Pole
Arctic 82°42N 114°24W **4** A1
North Mankato *U.S.A.* 44°10N 94°2W **80** C6
North Minch *U.K.* 58°5N 5°55W **11** C3
North Moose L. *Canada* 54°4N 100°12W **71** C8
North Myrtle Beach
U.S.A. 33°48N 78°42W **85** E15
North Nahanni →
Canada 62°15N 123°20W **70** A4
North Olmsted *U.S.A.* 41°25N 81°56W **82** E3
North Ossetia □ *Russia* 43°30N 44°30E **19** F7
North Pagai, I. = Pagai Utara,
Pulau *Indonesia* 2°35S 100°0E **36** E2
North Palisade *U.S.A.* 37°6N 118°31W **78** H8
North Platte *U.S.A.* 41°8N 100°46W **80** E3
North Platte → *U.S.A.* 41°7N 100°42W **80** E3
North Pole *Arctic* 90°0N 0°0 **4** A
North Portal *Canada* 49°0N 102°33W **71** D8
North Powder *U.S.A.* 45°2N 117°55W **76** D5
North Pt. *Barbados* 13°20N 59°37W **89** g
North Pt. *Trin. & Tob.* 11°21N 60°31W **93** J16
North Pt. *U.S.A.* 45°2N 83°16W **82** A1
North Rhine Westphalia =
Nordrhein-Westfalen □
Germany 51°45N 7°30E **16** C4
North River *Canada* 53°49N 57°6W **73** B8
North Ronaldsay *U.K.* 59°22N 2°26W **11** B6
North Saskatchewan →
Canada 53°15N 105°5W **71** C7
North Sea *Europe* 56°0N 4°0E **6** D6
North Seal → *Canada* 58°50N 98°7W **71** B9
North Slope ☆ *U.S.A.* 69°15N 152°0W **74** B9
North Somerset □ *U.K.* 51°24N 2°45W **13** F5
North Sydney *Canada* 46°12N 60°15W **73** C7
North Syracuse *U.S.A.* 43°8N 76°7W **83** C8
North Taranaki Bight
N.Z. 38°50S 174°15E **59** C5
North Thompson →
Canada 50°40N 120°20W **70** C4
North Tonawanda
U.S.A. 43°2N 78°53W **82** C6
North Troy *U.S.A.* 45°0N 72°24W **83** B12
North Twin I. *Canada* 53°20N 80°0W **72** B4
North Tyne → *U.K.* 55°0N 2°8W **12** B5
North Uist *U.K.* 57°40N 7°15W **11** D1
North Vancouver
Canada 49°19N 123°4W **78** A3
North Vernon *U.S.A.* 39°0N 85°38W **81** F11
North Wabasca L.
Canada 56°0N 113°55W **70** B6
North Walsham *U.K.* 52°50N 1°22E **12** E9
North West = Severo-Zapadnyy □
Russia 65°0N 40°0E **28** C4
North-West □ *S. Africa* 27°0S 25°0E **56** D4
North West C. *Australia* 21°45S 114°9E **60** D1
North West Christmas I. Ridge
Pac. Oc. 6°30N 165°0W **65** F11
North West Frontier □
Pakistan 34°0N 72°0E **42** C4
North West Highlands
U.K. 57°33N 4°58W **11** D4
North West River
Canada 53°30N 60°10W **73** B7
North Western □ *Zambia* 13°30S 25°30E **55** E2
North Wildwood *U.S.A.* 39°0N 74°48W **81** F16
North York Moors *U.K.* 54°23N 0°53W **12** C7
North York Moors △
U.K. 54°27N 0°51W **12** C7
North Yorkshire □ *U.K.* 54°15N 1°25W **12** C6
Northallerton *U.K.* 54°20N 1°26W **12** C6
Northam *Australia* 31°35S 116°42E **61** F2
Northam *S. Africa* 24°56S 27°18E **56** C4
Northampton *Australia* 28°27S 114°33E **61** E1
Northampton *U.K.* 52°15N 0°53W **13** E7
Northampton *Mass.,*
U.S.A. 42°19N 72°38W **83** D12
Northampton *Pa.,*
U.S.A. 40°41N 75°30W **83** F9
Northamptonshire □
U.K. 52°16N 0°55W **13** E7
Northbridge *U.S.A.* 42°9N 71°39W **83** D13
Northbrook *Canada* 44°44N 77°9W **82** B7
Northcliffe *Australia* 34°39S 116°7E **61** F2
Northeast Pacific Basin
Pac. Oc. 32°0N 145°0W **65** D13
Northeast Providence Chan.
W. Indies 26°0N 76°0W **88** A4
Northern = Limpopo □
S. Africa 24°5S 29°0E **57** C4
Northern □ *Malawi* 11°0S 34°0E **55** E3
Northern □ *Zambia* 10°30S 31°0E **55** E3
Northern Areas □
Pakistan 36°30N 73°0E **43** A5
Northern Cape □ *S. Africa* 30°0S 20°0E **56** D3
Northern Circars *India* 17°30N 82°30E **41** L13
Northern Indian L.
Canada 57°20N 97°20W **71** B9
Northern Ireland □ *U.K.* 54°45N 7°0W **10** B5
Northern Lau Group
Fiji 17°30S 178°59W **59** a
Northern Light L.
Canada 48°15N 90°39W **72** C1
Northern Marianas ☑
Pac. Oc. 17°0N 145°0E **64** F6
Northern Province □
S. Africa 24°0S 29°0E **57** C4
Northern Range
Trin. & Tob. 10°46N 61°15W **93** K15
Northern Sporades
Greece 39°15N 23°30E **23** E10
Northern Territory □
Australia 20°0S 133°0E **60** D5
Northfield *Minn., U.S.A.* 44°27N 93°9W **80** C7
Northfield *Vt., U.S.A.* 44°9N 72°40W **83** B12
Northgate *Canada* 49°0N 102°16W **71** D8
Northland □ *N.Z.* 35°30S 173°30E **59** A4
Northome *U.S.A.* 47°52N 94°17W **80** B6
Northport *Ala., U.S.A.* 33°14N 87°35W **85** E11
Northport *Wash.,*
U.S.A. 48°55N 117°48W **76** B5
Northumberland □ *U.K.* 55°12N 2°0W **12** B6
Northumberland, C.
Australia 38°5S 140°40E **63** F3
Northumberland Is.
Australia 21°30S 149°50E **62** C4
Northumberland Str.
Canada 46°20N 64°0W **73** C7
Northville *Canada* 43°10N 81°56W **82** C3
Northville *U.S.A.* 43°13N 74°11W **83** C10
Northwest Pacific Basin
Pac. Oc. 32°0N 165°0E **64** D8
Northwest Providence Channel
W. Indies 26°0N 78°0W **88** A4
Northwest Territories □
Canada 63°0N 118°0W **68** E8
Northwich *U.K.* 53°15N 2°31W **12** D5
Northwood *Iowa, U.S.A.* 43°27N 93°13W **80** D7
Northwood *N. Dak.,*
U.S.A. 47°44N 97°34W **80** B5
Norton *U.S.A.* 39°50N 99°53W **80** F4
Norton *Zimbabwe* 17°52S 30°40E **55** F3
Norton Sd. *U.S.A.* 63°50N 164°0W **74** C7
Norwalk *Calif., U.S.A.* 33°54N 118°4W **79** M8
Norwalk *Conn., U.S.A.* 41°7N 73°22W **83** E11
Norwalk *Iowa, U.S.A.* 41°29N 93°41W **80** E7
Norwalk *Ohio, U.S.A.* 41°15N 82°37W **82** E2
Norway *Maine, U.S.A.* 44°13N 70°32W **81** C18
Norway *Mich., U.S.A.* 45°47N 87°55W **80** C10
Norway ■ *Europe* 63°0N 11°0E **8** E14
Norway House *Canada* 53°59N 97°50W **71** C9
Norwegian B. *Canada* 77°30N 90°0W **69** B14
Norwegian Basin *Atl. Oc.* 68°0N 2°0W **4** C7
Norwegian Sea *Atl. Oc.* 66°0N 1°0E **6** B6
Norwich *Canada* 42°59N 80°36W **82** D4
Norwich *U.K.* 52°38N 1°18E **13** E9
Norwich *Conn., U.S.A.* 41°31N 72°5W **83** E12
Norwich *N.Y., U.S.A.* 42°32N 75°32W **83** D9
Norwood *Canada* 44°23N 77°59W **82** B7
Norwood *U.S.A.* 44°45N 75°0W **83** B10
Nosappu-Misaki *Japan* 45°26N 141°39E **30** C12
Noshiro *Japan* 40°12N 140°0E **30** D10
Noşratābād *Iran* 29°55N 60°0E **45** D8
Noss Hd. *U.K.* 58°28N 3°3W **11** C5
Nossob → *S. Africa* 26°55S 20°45E **56** D3
Nosy Barren *Madag.* 18°25S 43°40E **53** H8
Nosy Bé *Madag.* 13°25S 48°15E **53** G9
Nosy Boraha *Madag.* 16°50S 49°55E **57** B8
Nosy Lava *Madag.* 14°33S 47°36E **57** A8
Nosy Varika *Madag.* 20°35S 48°32E **57** C8
Noteć → *Poland* 52°44N 15°26E **16** B8
Notikewin → *Canada* 57°2N 117°38W **70** B5
Noto-Hantō *Japan* 37°15N 136°40E **31** F8
Notodden *Norway* 59°35N 9°17E **9** G13
Notre Dame B. *Canada* 49°45N 55°30W **73** C8
Notre-Dame-de-Koartac =
Quaqtaq *Canada* 60°55N 69°40W **69** E18
Notre-Dame-des-Bois
Canada 45°24N 71°4W **83** A13
Notre-Dame-d'Ivugivic = Ivujivik
Canada 62°24N 77°55W **69** E16
Notre-Dame-du-Nord
Canada 47°36N 79°30W **72** C4
Nottawasaga B. *Canada* 44°35N 80°15W **82** B4
Nottaway → *Canada* 51°22N 78°55W **72** B4
Nottingham *U.K.* 52°58N 1°10W **12** E6
Nottingham, City of □
U.K. 52°58N 1°10W **12** E6
Nottingham I. *Canada* 63°20N 77°55W **69** E16
Nottinghamshire □ *U.K.* 53°10N 1°3W **12** D6
Nottoway → *U.S.A.* 36°33N 76°55W **81** G15
Notwane → *Botswana* 23°35S 26°58E **56** C4
Nouâdhibou *Mauritania* 20°54N 17°0W **50** D2
Nouâdhibou, Râs
Mauritania 20°50N 17°0W **50** D2
Nouakchott *Mauritania* 18°9N 15°58W **50** E2
Nouméa *N. Cal.* 22°17S 166°30E **58** D9
Noupoort *S. Africa* 31°10S 24°57E **56** E3
Nouveau Comptoir = Wemindji
Canada 53°0N 78°49W **72** B4
Nouvelle Amsterdam, Î.
Ind. Oc. 38°30S 77°30E **3** F13
Nouvelle-Calédonie = New
Caledonia ☑ *Pac. Oc.* 21°0S 165°0E **58** D9
Nova Esperança *Brazil* 23°8S 52°24W **95** A5
Nova Friburgo *Brazil* 22°16S 42°30W **95** A7
Nova Iguaçu *Brazil* 22°45S 43°28W **95** A7
Nova Iorque *Brazil* 7°0S 44°5W **93** E10
Nova Lamego
Guinea-Biss. 12°19N 14°11W **50** F3
Nova Lusitânia *Mozam.* 19°50S 34°34E **55** F3
Nova Mambone *Mozam.* 21°0S 35°3E **57** C6
Nova Scotia □ *Canada* 45°10N 63°0W **73** C7
Nova Sofala *Mozam.* 20°7S 34°42E **57** C5
Nova Venécia *Brazil* 18°45S 40°24W **93** G10
Nova Zagora *Bulgaria* 42°32N 26°1E **23** C11
Novar *Canada* 45°27N 79°15W **82** A5
Novara *Italy* 45°28N 8°38E **20** D8
Novato *U.S.A.* 38°6N 122°35W **78** G4
Novaya Ladoga *Russia* 60°7N 32°16E **18** B5
Novaya Lyalya *Russia* 59°4N 60°45E **18** C11
Novaya Sibir, Ostrov
Russia 75°10N 150°0E **29** B16
Novaya Zemlya *Russia* 75°0N 56°0E **28** B6
Nové Zámky *Slovak Rep.* 48°2N 18°8E **17** D10
Novgorod *Russia* 58°30N 31°25E **18** C5
Novgorod-Severskiy = Novhorod-
Siverskyy *Ukraine* 52°2N 33°10E **18** D5
Novhorod-Siverskyy
Ukraine 52°2N 33°10E **18** D5
Novi Lígure *Italy* 44°46N 8°47E **20** D8
Novi Pazar *Serbia* 43°12N 20°28E **23** C9
Novi Sad *Serbia* 45°18N 19°52E **23** B8
Novo Hamburgo *Brazil* 29°37S 51°7W **95** B5
Novo Mesto *Slovenia* 45°47N 15°12E **22** B6
Novoaltaysk *Russia* 53°30N 84°0E **28** D9
Novocherkassk *Russia* 47°27N 40°15E **19** E7
Novodvinsk *Russia* 64°25N 40°42E **18** B7
Novogrudok = Navahrudak
Belarus 53°40N 25°50E **17** B13
Novohrad-Volynskyy
Ukraine 50°34N 27°35E **17** C14
Novokachalinsk *Russia* 45°5N 132°0E **30** B5
Novokuybyshevsk *Russia* 53°7N 49°58E **18** D8
Novokuznetsk *Russia* 53°45N 87°10E **28** D9
Novolazarevskaya
Antarctica 71°0S 12°0E **5** D3
Novomoskovsk *Russia* 54°5N 38°15E **18** D6
Novorossiysk *Russia* 44°43N 37°46E **19** F6
Novorybnoye *Russia* 72°50N 105°50E **29** B11
Novoselytsya *Ukraine* 48°14N 26°15E **17** D14
Novoshakhtinsk *Russia* 47°46N 39°58E **19** E6
Novosibirsk *Russia* 55°0N 83°5E **28** D9
Novosibirskiye Ostrova
Russia 75°0N 142°0E **29** B15
Novotroitsk *Russia* 51°10N 58°15E **18** D10
Novouzensk *Russia* 50°32N 48°17E **19** D8
Novovolynsk *Ukraine* 50°45N 24°4E **17** C13
Novska *Croatia* 45°19N 17°0E **22** B7
Novyy Bor *Russia* 66°43N 52°19E **18** A9
Novyy Port *Russia* 67°40N 72°30E **28** C8
Novyy Urengoy *Russia* 65°48N 76°52E **28** C8
Nowa Sól *Poland* 51°48N 15°44E **16** C8
Nowata *U.S.A.* 36°42N 95°38W **84** C7
Nowbarān *Iran* 35°8N 49°42E **45** C6
Nowghāb *Iran* 33°53N 59°4E **45** C8
Nowgong *Assam, India* 26°20N 92°50E **41** F18
Nowgong *Mad. P., India* 25°4N 79°27E **43** G8
Nowra *Australia* 34°53S 150°35E **63** E5
Nowshera *Pakistan* 34°0N 72°0E **40** C8
Nowy Sącz *Poland* 49°40N 20°41E **17** D11
Nowy Targ *Poland* 49°29N 20°2E **17** D11
Nowy Tomyśl *Poland* 52°19N 16°10E **16** B9
Noxen *U.S.A.* 41°25N 76°4W **83** E8
Noyabr'sk *Russia* 64°34N 76°21E **28** C8
Noyon *France* 49°34N 2°59E **20** B5
Noyon *Mongolia* 43°2N 102°4E **34** C2
Nqutu *S. Africa* 28°13S 30°32E **57** D5
Nsanje *Malawi* 16°55S 35°12E **55** F4
Nsawam *Ghana* 5°50N 0°24W **50** G5
Nseluka *Zambia* 9°58S 31°16E **55** D3
Nsomba *Zambia* 10°45S 29°51E **55** E2
Ntaria ✿ *Australia* 24°0S 132°41E **60** D5
Ntungamo *Uganda* 0°56S 30°17E **54** C3
Nu Jiang → *China* 29°58N 97°25E **32** F8
Nu Shan *China* 26°0N 99°20E **41** G21
Nuba Mts. = Nubah, Jibalan
Sudan 12°0N 31°0E **51** F12
Nubah, Jibalan *Sudan* 12°0N 31°0E **51** F12
Nubia *Africa* 21°0N 32°0E **48** D7
Nubian Desert = Nûbîya, Es Sahrâ
en *Sudan* 21°30N 33°30E **51** D12
Nûbîya, Es Sahrâ en
Sudan 21°30N 33°30E **51** D12
Nuboai *Indonesia* 2°10S 136°30E **37** E9
Nubra → *India* 34°35N 77°35E **43** B7
Nueces → *U.S.A.* 27°51N 97°30W **84** H6
Nueltin L. *Canada* 60°30N 99°30W **71** A9
Nuestra Señora del Rosario de
Caá-Catí *Argentina* 27°45S 57°36W **94** B4
Nueva Ciudad Guerrero
Mexico 26°34N 99°12W **87** B5
Nueva Gerona *Cuba* 21°53N 82°49W **88** B3
Nueva Palmira *Uruguay* 33°52S 58°20W **94** C4
Nueva Rosita *Mexico* 27°57N 101°13W **86** B4
Nueva San Salvador
El Salv. 13°40N 89°18W **88** D2
Nuéve de Julio *Argentina* 35°30S 61°0W **94** D3
Nuevitas *Cuba* 21°30N 77°20W **88** B4
Nuevo, G. *Argentina* 43°0S 64°30W **96** E4
Nuevo Casas Grandes
Mexico 30°25N 107°55W **86** A3
Nuevo Laredo *Mexico* 27°30N 99°31W **87** B5
Nuevo León □ *Mexico* 25°20N 100°0W **86** C5
Nuevo Rocafuerte
Ecuador 0°55S 75°27W **92** D3
Nugget Pt. *N.Z.* 46°27S 169°50E **59** G2
Nuhaka *N.Z.* 39°3S 177°45E **59** C6
Nukey Bluff *Australia* 32°26S 135°29E **63** E2
Nukhayb *Iraq* 32°4N 42°3E **44** C4
Nuku Hiva
French Polynesia 8°54S 140°6W **65** H13
Nuku'alofa *Tonga* 21°10S 175°12W **59** c
Nukus *Uzbekistan* 42°27N 59°41E **28** E6
Nulato *U.S.A.* 64°43N 158°6W **74** C8
Nullagine *Australia* 21°53S 120°7E **60** D3
Nullagine → *Australia* 21°20S 120°20E **60** D3
Nullarbor *Australia* 31°28S 130°55E **61** F5
Nullarbor △ *Australia* 32°39S 130°0E **61** F2
Nullarbor Plain *Australia* 31°10S 129°0E **61** F4
Numalla, L. *Australia* 28°43S 144°20E **63** D3
Numan *Nigeria* 9°29N 12°3E **51** G8
Numata *Japan* 36°45N 139°4E **31** F9
Numaykoos Lake ⌓
Canada 57°52N 95°58W **71** B9
Numazu *Japan* 35°7N 138°51E **31** G9
Numbulwar *Australia* 14°15S 135°45E **62** A2
Numfoor *Indonesia* 1°0S 134°50E **37** E8
Numurkah *Australia* 36°5S 145°26E **63** F4
Nunaksaluk I. *Canada* 55°49N 60°20W **73** A7
Nunap Isua *Greenland* 59°48N 43°55W **66** D15
Nunavik *Greenland* 71°50N 54°25W **69** C21
Nunavut □ *Canada* 66°0N 85°0W **69** D15
Nunda *U.S.A.* 42°35N 77°56W **82** D7
Nuneaton *U.K.* 52°32N 1°27W **13** E6
Nungarin *Australia* 31°12S 118°6E **61** F2
Nungo *Mozam.* 13°23S 37°43E **55** E4
Nungwe *Tanzania* 2°48S 32°2E **54** C3
Nunivak I. *U.S.A.* 60°10N 166°30W **74** C6
Nunkun *India* 33°57N 76°2E **43** C7
Nùoro *Italy* 40°20N 9°20E **22** D3
Nūr *Iran* 36°33N 52°1E **45** B7
Nūrābād *Hormozgān, Iran* 27°47N 57°12E **45** E8
Nūrābād *Lorestān, Iran* 34°4N 47°58E **44** C5
Nuremberg = Nürnberg
Germany 49°27N 11°3E **16** D6
Nuri *Mexico* 28°5N 109°22W **86** B3
Nuriootpa *Australia* 34°27S 139°0E **63** E2
Nuristān □ *Afghan.* 35°20N 71°0E **40** B7
Nurmes *Finland* 63°33N 29°10E **8** E23
Nürnberg *Germany* 49°27N 11°3E **16** D6
Nurpur *Pakistan* 31°53N 71°54E **42** D4
Nurran, L. = Terewah, L.
Australia 29°52S 147°35E **63** D4
Nurrari Lakes *Australia* 29°1S 130°5E **61** E5
Nusa Dua *Indonesia* 8°48S 115°14E **37** K18
Nusa Tenggara Barat □
Indonesia 8°50S 117°30E **36** F5
Nusa Tenggara Timur □
Indonesia 9°30S 122°0E **37** F6
Nusaybin *Turkey* 37°3N 41°10E **19** G7
Nushki *Pakistan* 29°35N 66°0E **42** E2
Nuuk *Greenland* 64°10N 51°35W **67** C14
Nuupere, Pte. *Moorea* 17°36S 149°47W **59** d
Nuwakot *Nepal* 28°10N 83°55E **43** E10
Nuwayb'ī, W. an →
Si. Arabia 29°18N 34°57E **46** F3
Nuweiba' *Egypt* 28°59N 34°39E **44** D2
Nuwerus *S. Africa* 31°8S 18°24E **56** E2
Nuweveldberge *S. Africa* 32°10S 21°45E **56** E3
Nuyts, Pt. *Australia* 35°4S 116°38E **61** G2
Nuyts Arch. *Australia* 32°35S 133°20E **63** E1
Nxai Pan △ *Botswana* 19°50S 24°46E **56** B3
Nxaunxau *Botswana* 18°57S 21°4E **56** B3
Nyabing *Australia* 33°33S 118°9E **61** F2
Nyack *U.S.A.* 41°5N 73°55W **83** E11
Nyagan *Russia* 62°30N 65°38E **28** C7
Nyahanga *Tanzania* 2°20S 33°37E **54** C3
Nyahua *Tanzania* 5°25S 33°23E **54** D3
Nyahururu *Kenya* 0°2N 36°27E **54** B4
Nyainqêntanglha Shan
China 30°0N 90°0E **32** F7
Nyakanazi *Tanzania* 3°2S 31°10E **54** C3
Nyâlâ *Sudan* 12°2N 24°58E **51** F10
Nyalam *China* 28°32N 86°4E **32** F6
Nyamandhlovu
Zimbabwe 19°55S 28°16E **55** F2
Nyambiti *Tanzania* 2°48S 33°27E **54** C3
Nyamira *Kenya* 0°36S 34°52E **54** B4
Nyamwaga *Tanzania* 1°27S 34°33E **54** C3
Nyandekwa *Tanzania* 3°57S 32°32E **54** C3
Nyandoma *Russia* 61°40N 40°12E **18** B7
Nyanga △ *Zimbabwe* 18°17S 32°46E **55** F3
Nyangana *Namibia* 18°0S 20°40E **56** B3
Nyanguge *Tanzania* 2°30S 33°12E **54** C3
Nyanji *Zambia* 14°25S 31°46E **55** E3
Nyanza *Rwanda* 2°20S 29°42E **54** C2
Nyanza □ *Kenya* 0°10S 34°15E **54** C3
Nyanza-Lac *Burundi* 4°21S 29°36E **54** C2
Nyasa, L. = Malawi, L.
Africa 12°30S 34°30E **55** E3
Nyasvizh *Belarus* 53°14N 26°38E **17** B14
Nyazepetrovsk *Russia* 56°3N 59°36E **18** C10
Nyazura *Zimbabwe* 18°40S 32°16E **55** F3
Nyazwidzi → *Zimbabwe* 20°0S 31°17E **55** G3
Nybro *Sweden* 56°44N 15°55E **9** H16
Nyda *Russia* 66°40N 72°58E **28** C8
Nyeboe Land *Greenland* 82°0N 57°0W **69** A20
Nyeri *Kenya* 0°23S 36°56E **54** C4
Nyika △ *Malawi* 10°30S 33°53E **55** E3
Nyimba *Zambia* 14°33S 30°50E **55** E3
Nyingchi *China* 29°32N 94°25E **32** F7
Nyíregyháza *Hungary* 47°58N 21°47E **17** E11
Nyiru, Mt. *Kenya* 2°8N 36°50E **54** B4
Nykarleby = Uusikaarlepyy
Finland 63°32N 22°31E **8** E20
Nykøbing *Nordjylland,*
Denmark 56°48N 8°51E **9** H13
Nykøbing *Sjælland,*
Denmark 54°56N 11°52E **9** J14
Nykøbing *Sjælland,*
Denmark 55°55N 11°40E **9** J14
Nyköping *Sweden* 58°45N 17°1E **9** G17
Nylstroom = Modimolle
S. Africa 24°42S 28°22E **57** C4
Nymagee *Australia* 32°7S 146°20E **63** E4
Nymboida △ *Australia* 29°38S 152°26E **63** D5
Nynäshamn *Sweden* 58°54N 17°57E **9** G17
Nyngan *Australia* 31°30S 147°8E **63** E4
Nyoma Rap *India* 33°10N 78°40E **43** C8
Nyoman = Nemunas →
Lithuania 55°25N 21°10E **9** J19
Nysa *Poland* 50°30N 17°22E **17** C9
Nysa → *Europe* 52°4N 14°46E **16** B8
Nyslott = Savonlinna
Finland 61°52N 28°53E **8** F23
Nyssa *U.S.A.* 43°53N 117°0W **76** E5
Nystad = Uusikaupunki
Finland 60°47N 21°25E **8** F19
Nyunzu
Dem. Rep. of the Congo 5°57S 27°58E **54** D2
Nyurba *Russia* 63°17N 118°28E **29** C12
Nzega *Tanzania* 4°10S 33°12E **54** C3
Nzérékoré *Guinea* 7°49N 8°48W **50** G4
Nzeto *Angola* 7°10S 12°52E **52** F2
Nzilo, Chutes de
Dem. Rep. of the Congo 10°18S 25°27E **55** E2
Nzubuka *Tanzania* 4°45S 32°50E **54** C3
Nzwani = Anjouan
Comoros Is. 12°15S 44°20E **53** a

O

O Le Pupū Pu'e △
Samoa 13°59S 171°43W **59** b
Ō-Shima *Hokkaidō,*
Japan 41°30N 139°22E **30** D9
Ō-Shima *Shizuoka, Japan* 34°44N 139°24E **31** G9
Oa, Mull of *U.K.* 55°35N 6°20W **11** F2

INDEX TO WORLD MAPS
Orford Ness 149

Oacoma U.S.A. 43°48N 99°24W 80 D4
Oahe, L. U.S.A. 44°27N 100°24W 80 C3
Oahe Dam U.S.A. 44°27N 100°24W 80 C3
O'ahu U.S.A. 21°28N 157°58W 75 L8
Oak Harbor U.S.A. 48°18N 122°39W 78 B4
Oak Hill U.S.A. 37°59N 81°9W 81 G13
Oak Island U.S.A. 33°55N 78°10W 85 E15
Oak Ridge U.S.A. 36°1N 84°16W 85 C12
Oak View U.S.A. 34°24N 119°18W 79 L7
Oakan-Dake Japan 43°27N 144°10E 30 C12
Oakdale Calif., U.S.A. 37°46N 120°51W 78 H6
Oakdale La., U.S.A. 30°49N 92°40W 84 F8
Oakes U.S.A. 46°8N 98°6W 80 B4
Oakesdale U.S.A. 47°8N 117°15W 76 C5
Oakey Australia 27°25S 151°43E 63 D5
Oakfield U.S.A. 43°4N 78°16W 82 C6
Oakham U.K. 52°40N 0°43W 13 E7
Oakhurst U.S.A. 37°19N 119°40W 78 H7
Oakland Calif., U.S.A. 37°48N 122°18W 78 H4
Oakland Pa., U.S.A. 41°57N 75°36W 83 E9
Oakley Idaho, U.S.A. 42°15N 113°53W 76 E7
Oakley Kans., U.S.A. 39°8N 100°51W 80 F3
Oakover → Australia 21°0S 120°40E 60 D3
Oakridge U.S.A. 43°45N 122°28W 76 E2
Oakville Canada 43°27N 79°41W 82 C5
Oakville U.S.A. 46°51N 123°14W 78 D3
Oamaru N.Z. 45°5S 170°59E 59 F3
Oasis Calif., U.S.A. 37°29N 117°55W 78 H9
Oasis Calif., U.S.A. 33°28N 116°6W 79 M10
Oates Land Antarctica 69°0S 160°0E 5 C11
Oatman U.S.A. 35°1N 114°19W 79 K12
Oaxaca Mexico 17°3N 96°43W 87 D5
Oaxaca □ Mexico 17°0N 96°30W 87 D5
Ob → Russia 66°45N 69°30E 28 C7
Oba Canada 49°4N 84°7W 72 C3
Obama Japan 35°30N 135°45E 31 G7
Oban U.K. 56°25N 5°29W 11 E3
Obbia = Hobyo Somali Rep. 5°25N 48°30E 47 F4
Oberá Argentina 27°21S 55°2W 95 B4
Oberhausen Germany 51°28N 6°51E 16 C4
Oberlin Kans., U.S.A. 39°49N 100°32W 80 F3
Oberlin La., U.S.A. 30°37N 92°46W 84 F8
Oberlin Ohio, U.S.A. 41°18N 82°13W 82 E2
Oberon Australia 33°45S 149°52E 63 E4
Obi, Kepulauan Indonesia 1°23S 127°45E 37 E7
Óbidos Brazil 1°50S 55°30W 93 D7
Obihiro Japan 42°56N 143°12E 30 C11
Obilatu Indonesia 1°25S 127°20E 37 E7
Obluchye Russia 49°1N 131°4E 29 E14
Obo C.A.R. 5°20N 26°32E 54 A2
Oboyan Russia 51°15N 36°21E 28 D4
Obozerskaya = Obozerskiy Russia 63°34N 40°21E 18 B7
Obozerskiy Russia 63°34N 40°21E 18 B7
Observatory Inlet Canada 55°10N 129°54W 70 B3
Obshchi Syrt Russia 52°0N 53°0E 6 E16
Obskaya Guba Russia 69°0N 73°0E 28 C8
Obuasi Ghana 6°17N 1°40W 50 G5
Ocala U.S.A. 29°11N 82°8W 85 G13
Ocampo Chihuahua, Mexico 28°11N 108°23W 86 B3
Ocampo Tamaulipas, Mexico 22°50N 99°20W 87 C5
Ocaña Spain 39°55N 3°30W 21 C4
Occidental, Cordillera Colombia 5°0N 76°0W 92 C3
Occidental, Grand Erg Algeria 30°20N 1°0E 50 B6
Ocean City Md., U.S.A. 38°20N 75°5W 81 F16
Ocean City N.J., U.S.A. 39°17N 74°35W 81 F16
Ocean City Wash., U.S.A. 47°4N 124°10W 78 C2
Ocean Falls Canada 52°18N 127°48W 70 C3
Ocean I. = Banaba Kiribati 0°45S 169°50E 64 H8
Ocean Park U.S.A. 46°30N 124°3W 78 D2
Oceano U.S.A. 35°6N 120°37W 79 K6
Oceanport U.S.A. 40°19N 74°3W 83 F10
Oceanside U.S.A. 33°12N 117°23W 79 M9
Ochil Hills U.K. 56°14N 3°40W 11 E5
Ocho Rios Jamaica 18°24N 77°6W 88 a
Ocilla U.S.A. 31°36N 83°15W 85 F13
Ocmulgee → U.S.A. 31°58N 82°33W 85 F13
Ocniţa Moldova 48°25N 27°30E 17 D14
Oconee → U.S.A. 31°58N 82°33W 85 F13
Oconomowoc U.S.A. 43°7N 88°30W 80 D9
Oconto U.S.A. 44°53N 87°52W 80 C10
Oconto Falls U.S.A. 44°52N 88°9W 80 C9
Ocosingo Mexico 16°53N 92°6W 87 D6
Ocotal Nic. 13°41N 86°31W 88 D2
Ocotlán Jalisco, Mexico 20°21N 102°46W 86 C4
Ocotlán Oaxaca, Mexico 16°48N 96°40W 87 D5
Ocussi = Pante Macassar E. Timor 9°30S 123°58E 37 F6
Ōda Japan 35°11N 132°30E 31 G6
Ódáðahraun Iceland 65°5N 17°0W 8 D5
Ŏdaejin N. Korea 41°34N 129°40E 30 D4
Odate Japan 40°16N 140°34E 30 D10
Odawara Japan 35°20N 139°6E 31 G9
Odda Norway 60°3N 6°35E 9 F12
Odei → Canada 56°6N 96°54W 71 B9
Ödemiş Turkey 38°15N 28°0E 23 E13
Odendaalsrus S. Africa 27°48S 26°45E 56 D4
Odense Denmark 55°22N 10°23E 9 J14
Oder → Europe 53°33N 14°38E 16 B8
Odesa Ukraine 46°30N 30°45E 19 E5
Odessa = Odesa Ukraine 46°30N 30°45E 19 E5
Odessa Canada 44°17N 76°43W 83 B8
Odessa Tex., U.S.A. 31°52N 102°23W 84 F3
Odessa Wash., U.S.A. 47°20N 118°41W 76 C4
Odiakwe Botswana 20°12S 25°17E 56 C4
Odienné Ivory C. 9°30N 7°34W 50 G4
Odintsovo Russia 55°40N 37°16E 18 C6
O'Donnell U.S.A. 32°58N 101°50W 84 E4
O'Donnell Pt. Canada 45°5N 80°5W 82 A4
Odorheiu Secuiesc Romania 46°21N 25°21E 17 E13
Odra = Oder → Europe 53°33N 14°38E 16 B8
Odzi Zimbabwe 19°0S 32°20E 57 B5
Odzi → Zimbabwe 19°45S 32°23E 57 B5
Oeiras Brazil 7°0S 42°8W 93 E10
Oelrichs U.S.A. 43°11N 103°14W 80 D2
Oelwein U.S.A. 42°41N 91°55W 80 D8
Oeno I. Pac. Oc. 24°0S 131°0W 65 K14
Oenpelli = Gunbalanya Australia 12°20S 133°4E 60 B5
Ofanto → Italy 41°22N 16°13E 22 D7
Offa Nigeria 8°13N 4°42E 50 G6
Offaly □ Ireland 53°15N 7°30W 10 C4
Offenbach Germany 50°6N 8°44E 16 C5
Offenburg Germany 48°28N 7°56E 16 D4
Officer Cr. → Australia 27°46S 132°30E 61 E5
Ofolanga Tonga 19°38S 174°27W 59 c
Ofotfjorden Norway 68°27N 17°0E 8 B17
Ofu Amer. Samoa 14°11S 169°41W 59 b
Ōfunato Japan 39°4N 141°43E 30 E10
Oga Japan 39°55N 139°50E 30 E9
Oga-Hantō Japan 39°58N 139°47E 30 E9
Ogaden Ethiopia 7°30N 45°30E 47 F3
Ōgaki Japan 35°21N 136°37E 31 G8
Ogallala U.S.A. 41°8N 101°43W 80 E3
Ogasawara Gunto Pac. Oc. 27°0N 142°0E 27 F16
Ogbomosho Nigeria 8°1N 4°11E 50 G6
Ogden U.S.A. 41°13N 111°58W 76 F8
Ogdensburg U.S.A. 44°42N 75°30W 83 B9
Ogea Driki Fiji 19°12S 178°27W 59 a
Ogea Levu Fiji 19°8S 178°24W 59 a
Ogeechee → U.S.A. 31°50N 81°3W 85 F14
Ogilby U.S.A. 32°49N 114°50W 79 N12
Óglio → Italy 45°2N 10°39E 22 B4
Ogmore Australia 22°37S 149°35E 62 C4
Ogoki Canada 51°38N 85°58W 72 B2
Ogoki → Canada 51°38N 85°57W 72 B2
Ogoki L. Canada 50°50N 87°10W 72 B2
Ogoki Res. Canada 50°45N 88°15W 72 B2
Ogooué → Gabon 1°0S 9°0E 52 E1
Ogowe = Ogooué → Gabon 1°0S 9°0E 52 E1
Ogre Latvia 56°49N 24°36E 9 H21
Ogurja Ada Turkmenistan 38°55N 53°2E 45 B7
Ohai N.Z. 45°55S 168°0E 59 F2
Ohakune N.Z. 39°24S 175°24E 59 C5
Ohata Japan 41°24N 141°10E 30 D10
Ohau, L. N.Z. 44°15S 169°53E 59 F2
Ohio □ U.S.A. 40°15N 82°45W 82 F2
Ohio → U.S.A. 36°59N 89°8W 80 G9
Ohře → Czech Rep. 50°30N 14°10E 16 C8
Ohrid Macedonia 41°8N 20°52E 23 D9
Ohridsko Jezero Macedonia 41°8N 20°52E 23 D9
Ohrigstad S. Africa 24°39S 30°36E 57 C5
Oiapoque Brazil 3°50N 51°50W 93
Oikou China 38°35N 117°42E 35 E9
Oil City U.S.A. 41°26N 79°42W 82 E5
Oil Springs Canada 42°47N 82°7W 82 D2
Oildale U.S.A. 35°25N 119°1W 79 K7
Oise → France 49°0N 2°4E 20 B5
Oistins Barbados 13°4N 59°33W 89 g
Oistins B. Barbados 13°4N 59°33W 89 g
Ōita Japan 33°14N 131°36E 31 H5
Ōita □ Japan 33°15N 131°30E 31 H5
Oiticica Brazil 5°3S 41°5W 93 E10
Ojai U.S.A. 34°27N 119°15W 79 L7
Ojinaga Mexico 29°34N 104°25W 86 B4
Ojiya Japan 37°18N 138°48E 31 F9
Ojo Caliente Mexico 21°53N 102°15W 86 C4
Ojo de Liebre, L. Mexico 27°45N 114°15W 86 B2
Ojos del Salado, Cerro Argentina 27°0S 68°40W 94 B2
Oka → Russia 56°20N 43°59E 18 C7
Okaba Indonesia 8°6S 139°42E 37 F9
Okahandja Namibia 22°0S 16°59E 56 C2
Okanagan L. Canada 50°0N 119°30W 70 D5
Okandja Gabon 0°35S 13°45E 52 E2
Okanogan U.S.A. 48°22N 119°35W 76 B4
Okanogan → U.S.A. 48°6N 119°44W 76 B4
Okanogan Range N. Amer. 49°0N 119°55W 70 D5
Okapi △ Dem. Rep. of the Congo 2°30N 27°20E 54 B2
Okaputa Namibia 20°5S 17°0E 56 C2
Okara Pakistan 30°50N 73°31E 42 D5
Okaukuejo Namibia 19°10S 16°0E 56 B2
Okavango Delta Botswana 18°45S 22°45E 56 B3
Okavango Swamp = Okavango Delta Botswana 18°45S 22°45E 56 B3
Okaya Japan 36°5N 138°10E 31 F9
Okayama Japan 34°40N 133°54E 31 G6
Okayama □ Japan 35°0N 133°50E 31 G6
Okazaki Japan 34°57N 137°10E 31 G8
Okeechobee U.S.A. 27°15N 80°50W 85 H14
Okeechobee, L. U.S.A. 27°0N 80°50W 85 H14
Okefenokee ⌓ U.S.A. 30°45N 82°18W 85 F13
Okefenokee Swamp U.S.A. 30°40N 82°20W 85 F13
Okehampton U.K. 50°44N 4°0W 13 G4
Okha India 22°27N 69°4E 42 H3
Okha Russia 53°40N 143°0E 29 D15
Okhotsk Russia 59°20N 143°10E 29 D15
Okhotsk, Sea of Asia 55°0N 145°0E 29 D15
Okhotskiy Perevoz Russia 61°52N 135°35E 29 C14
Okhtyrka Ukraine 50°25N 35°0E 19 D5
Oki-Shotō Japan 36°5N 133°15E 31 F6
Okiep S. Africa 29°39S 17°53E 56 D2
Okinawa Japan 26°19N 127°46E 31 L3
Okinawa □ Japan 26°40N 128°0E 31 L4
Okinawa-Guntō Japan 26°40N 128°0E 31 L4
Okinawa-Jima Japan 26°32N 128°0E 31 L4
Okino-erabu-Shima Japan 27°21N 128°33E 31 L4
Oklahoma □ U.S.A. 35°20N 97°30W 84 D6
Oklahoma City U.S.A. 35°30N 97°30W 84 D6
Okmulgee U.S.A. 35°37N 95°58W 84 D7
Oknitsa = Ocniţa Moldova 48°25N 27°30E 17 D14
Okolo Uganda 2°37N 31°8E 54 B3
Okolona U.S.A. 34°0N 88°45W 85 E10
Okombahe Namibia 21°23S 15°22E 56 C2
Okotoks Canada 50°43N 113°58W 70 C6
Oksovskiy Russia 62°33N 39°57E 18 B6
Oktyabrsk = Qandyaghash Kazakhstan 49°28N 57°25E 19 E10
Oktyabrskiy = Aktsyabrski Belarus 52°38N 28°53E 17 B15
Oktyabrskiy Bashkortostan, Russia 54°28N 53°28E 18 D9
Oktyabrskiy Kamchatka, Russia 52°39N 156°14E 29 D16
Oktyabrskoy Revolyutsii, Ostrov Russia 79°30N 97°0E 29 B10
Okuru N.Z. 43°55S 168°55E 59 E2
Okushiri-Tō Japan 42°15N 139°30E 30 C9
Okwa → Botswana 22°30S 23°0E 56 C3
Ola Russia 59°35N 151°17E 29 D16
Ola U.S.A. 35°2N 93°13W 84 D8
Ólafsfjörður Iceland 66°4N 18°39W 8 C4
Ólafsvík Iceland 64°53N 23°43W 8 D2
Olancha U.S.A. 36°17N 118°1W 79 J8
Olancha Pk. U.S.A. 36°16N 118°7W 79 J8
Olanchito Honduras 15°30N 86°30W 88 C2
Öland Sweden 56°45N 16°38E 9 H17
Olary Australia 32°18S 140°19E 63 E3
Olascoaga Argentina 35°15S 60°39W 94 D3
Olathe U.S.A. 38°53N 94°49W 80 F6
Olavarría Argentina 36°55S 60°20W 94 D3
Oława Poland 50°57N 17°20E 17 C9
Ólbia Italy 40°55N 9°31E 22 D3
Olcott U.S.A. 43°20N 78°42W 82 C6
Old Bahama Chan. = Bahama, Canal Viejo de W. Indies 22°10N 77°30W 88 B4
Old Baldy Pk. = San Antonio, Mt. U.S.A. 34°17N 117°38W 79 L9
Old Bridge U.S.A. 40°25N 74°22W 83 F10
Old Castile = Castilla y Leon □ Spain 42°0N 5°0W 21 B3
Old Crow Canada 67°30N 139°55W 68 D4
Old Dale U.S.A. 34°8N 115°47W 79 L11
Old Forge N.Y., U.S.A. 43°43N 74°58W 83 C10
Old Forge Pa., U.S.A. 41°22N 75°45W 83 E9
Old Mapoon ☼ Australia 11°5S 142°22E 62 A3
Old Perlican Canada 48°5N 53°1W 73 C9
Old Shinyanga Tanzania 3°33S 33°27E 54 C3
Old Speck Mt. U.S.A. 44°34N 70°57W 83 B14
Old Town U.S.A. 44°56N 68°39W 81 C19
Old Washington U.S.A. 40°2N 81°27W 82 F3
Old Wives L. Canada 50°5N 106°0W 71 C7
Oldbury U.K. 51°38N 2°33W 13 F5
Oldcastle Ireland 53°46N 7°10W 10 C4
Oldeani Tanzania 3°22S 35°35E 54 C4
Oldenburg Germany 53°9N 8°13E 16 B5
Oldenzaal Neths. 52°19N 6°53E 15 B6
Oldham U.K. 53°33N 2°7W 12 D5
Oldman → Canada 49°57N 111°42W 70 D6
Oldmeldrum U.K. 57°20N 2°19W 11 D6
Olds Canada 51°50N 114°10W 70 C6
Olduvai Gorge Tanzania 2°57S 35°23E 54 C4
Öldziyt Mongolia 44°40N 109°1E 34 B5
Olean U.S.A. 42°5N 78°26W 82 D6
Olekma → Russia 60°22N 120°42E 29 C13
Olekminsk Russia 60°25N 120°30E 29 C13
Oleksandriya Ukraine 50°37N 26°19E 17 C14
Olema U.S.A. 38°3N 122°47W 78 G4
Olenegorsk Russia 68°9N 33°18E 8 B25
Olenek Russia 68°28N 112°18E 29 C12
Olenek → Russia 73°0N 120°10E 29 B13
Oléron, Î. d' France 45°55N 1°15W 20 D3
Oleśnica Poland 51°13N 17°22E 17 C9
Olevsk Ukraine 51°12N 27°39E 17 C14
Olga, L. Canada 49°47N 77°15W 72 C4
Olgas, The = Kata Tjuta Australia 25°20S 130°50E 61 E5
Ölgiy Mongolia 48°56N 89°57E 32 B6
Olhão Portugal 37°3N 7°48W 21 D2
Olifants = Elefantes → Africa 24°10S 32°40E 57 C5
Olifants → Namibia 25°30S 19°30E 56 C2
Olifantshoek S. Africa 27°57S 22°42E 56 D3
Ólimbos, Óros = Olymbos Oros Greece 40°6N 22°23E 23 D10
Olímpia Brazil 20°44S 48°54W 95 A6
Olinda Brazil 8°1S 34°51W 93 E12
Oliva Argentina 32°0S 63°38W 94 C3
Olivares, Cerro los Argentina 30°18S 69°55W 94 C2
Olive Branch U.S.A. 34°57N 89°49W 85 D10
Olivehurst U.S.A. 39°6N 121°34W 78 F5
Olivenza Spain 38°41N 7°9W 21 C2
Oliver Canada 49°13N 119°37W 70 D5
Oliver L. Canada 56°56N 103°22W 71 B8
Ollagüe Chile 21°15S 68°10W 94 A2
Olmaliq Uzbekistan 40°50N 69°35E 28 E7
Olney Ill., U.S.A. 38°44N 88°5W 80 F9
Olney Tex., U.S.A. 33°22N 98°45W 84 E5
Oloitokitok Kenya 2°56S 37°30E 54 C4
Olomane → Canada 50°14N 60°37W 73 B7
Olomouc Czech Rep. 49°38N 17°12E 17 D9
Olonets Russia 61°0N 32°54E 18 B5
Olongapo Phil. 14°50N 120°18E 37 B6
Olosega Amer. Samoa 14°10S 169°37W 59 b
Olosenga = Swains I. Amer. Samoa 11°11S 171°4W 65 J11
Olot Spain 42°11N 2°30E 21 A7
Olovyannaya Russia 50°58N 115°35E 29 D12
Oloy → Russia 66°29N 159°29E 29 C16
Olsztyn Poland 53°48N 20°29E 17 B11
Olt → Romania 43°43N 24°51E 17 G13
Olteniţa Romania 44°7N 26°42E 17 F14
Olton U.S.A. 34°11N 102°8W 84 D3
Olymbos Cyprus 35°21N 33°45E 25 D12
Olymbos Oros Greece 40°6N 22°23E 23 D10
Olympia Greece 37°39N 21°39E 23 F9
Olympia U.S.A. 47°3N 122°53W 78 D4
Olympic △ U.S.A. 47°45N 123°43W 78 C3
Olympic Dam Australia 30°30S 136°55E 63 E2
Olympic Mts. U.S.A. 47°55N 123°45W 78 C3
Olympus Cyprus 34°56N 32°52E 25 E11
Olympus, Mt. = Olymbos Oros Greece 40°6N 22°23E 23 D10
Olympus, Mt. = Uludağ Turkey 40°4N 29°13E 23 D13
Olympus, Mt. U.S.A. 47°48N 123°43W 78 C3
Olyphant U.S.A. 41°27N 75°36W 83 E9
Olyutorskiy, Mys Russia 59°55N 170°27E 29 D18
Om → Russia 54°59N 73°22E 28 D8
Om Koi Thailand 17°48N 98°22E 38 D2
Ōma Japan 41°45N 141°5E 30 D10
Ōmachi Japan 36°30N 137°50E 31 F8
Omae-Zaki Japan 34°36N 138°14E 31 G9
Ōmagari Japan 39°27N 140°29E 30 E10
Omagh U.K. 54°36N 7°19W 10 B4
Omagh □ U.K. 54°35N 7°15W 10 B4
Omaha U.S.A. 41°17N 95°58W 80 E6
Omak U.S.A. 48°25N 119°31W 76 B4
Omalos Greece 35°19N 23°55E 25 D5
Oman ■ Asia 23°0N 58°0E 47 C6
Oman, G. of Asia 24°30N 58°30E 45 E8
Omaruru Namibia 21°26S 16°0E 56 C2
Omaruru → Namibia 22°7S 14°15E 56 C1
Omate Peru 16°45S 71°0W 92 G4
Ombai, Selat Indonesia 8°30S 124°50E 37 F6
Omboué Gabon 1°35S 9°15E 52 E1
Ombrone → Italy 42°42N 11°5E 22 C4
Omdurmân Sudan 15°40N 32°28E 51 E12
Omemee Canada 44°18N 78°33W 82 B6
Omeonga Dem. Rep. of the Congo 3°40S 24°22E 54 C1
Ometepe, I. de Nic. 11°32N 85°35W 88 D2
Ometepec Mexico 16°41N 98°25W 87 D5
Ominato Japan 41°17N 141°10E 30 D10
Omineca → Canada 56°3N 124°16W 70 B4
Omineca Mts. Canada 56°30N 125°30W 70 B3
Omitara Namibia 22°16S 18°2E 56 C2
Ōmiya = Saitama Japan 35°54N 139°38E 31 G9
Ommen Neths. 52°31N 6°26E 15 B6
Ömnögovĭ □ Mongolia 43°15N 104°0E 34 C3
Omo → Ethiopia 6°25N 36°10E 47 F2
Omodhos Cyprus 34°51N 32°48E 25 E11
Omolon → Russia 68°42N 158°36E 29 C16
Omono-Gawa → Japan 39°46N 140°3E 30 E10
Ompha Canada 45°0N 76°50W 83 B8
Omsk Russia 55°0N 73°12E 28 D8
Omsukchan Russia 62°32N 155°48E 29 C16
Ōmu Japan 44°34N 142°58E 30 B11
Omul, Vf. Romania 45°27N 25°29E 17 F13
Ōmura Japan 32°56N 129°57E 31 H4
Omuramba Omatako → Namibia 17°45S 20°25E 56 B2
Omuramba Ovambo → Namibia 18°45S 16°59E 56 B2
Ōmuta Japan 33°5N 130°26E 31 H5
Onaga U.S.A. 39°29N 96°10W 80 F5
Onalaska U.S.A. 43°53N 91°14W 80 D8
Onancock U.S.A. 37°43N 75°45W 81 G16
Onangue, L. Gabon 0°57S 10°4E 52 E2
Onaping L. Canada 47°3N 81°30W 72 C3
Onavas Mexico 28°31N 109°35W 86 B3
Onawa U.S.A. 42°2N 96°6W 80 D5
Oncócua Angola 16°30S 13°25E 56 B1
Onda Spain 39°55N 0°17W 21 C5
Ondangwa Namibia 17°57S 16°4E 56 B2
Ondjiva Angola 16°48S 15°50E 56 B2
Öndörhaan Mongolia 47°19N 110°39E 33 B11
Öndverðarnes Iceland 64°52N 24°0W 8 D2
One Arm Point Australia 16°26S 123°3E 60 C3
One Arm Point ☼ Australia 16°31S 122°53E 60 C3
One Tree Australia 34°11S 144°43E 63 E3
Oneata Fiji 18°26S 178°25W 59 a
Onega Russia 64°0N 38°10E 18 B6
Onega → Russia 63°58N 38°2E 18 B6
Onega, G. of = Onezhskaya Guba Russia 64°24N 36°38E 18 B6
Onega, L. = Onezhskoye Ozero Russia 61°44N 35°22E 18 B6
Oneida U.S.A. 43°6N 75°39W 83 C9
Oneida L. U.S.A. 43°12N 75°54W 83 C9
O'Neill U.S.A. 42°27N 98°39W 80 D4
Onekotan, Ostrov Russia 49°25N 154°45E 29 E16
Onema Dem. Rep. of the Congo 4°35S 24°30E 54 C1
Oneonta U.S.A. 42°27N 75°4W 83 D9
Oneşti Romania 46°17N 26°47E 17 E14
Onezhskaya Guba Russia 64°24N 36°38E 18 B6
Onezhskoye Ozero Russia 61°44N 35°22E 18 B6
Ongarue N.Z. 38°42S 175°19E 59 C5
Ongea Levu = Ogea Levu Fiji 19°8S 178°24W 59 a
Ongers → S. Africa 31°4S 23°13E 56 E3
Ongerup Australia 33°58S 118°28E 61 F2
Ongi Mongolia 45°27N 103°54E 34 B2
Ongjin N. Korea 37°56N 125°21E 35 F13
Ongkharak Thailand 14°8N 101°1E 38 E3
Ongniud Qi China 43°0N 118°38E 35 C10
Ongoka Dem. Rep. of the Congo 1°20S 26°0E 54 C2
Ongole India 15°33N 80°2E 40 M12
Ongon = Havirga Mongolia 45°41N 113°5E 34 B7
Onida U.S.A. 44°42N 100°4W 80 C3
Onilahy → Madag. 23°34S 43°45E 57 C7
Onitsha Nigeria 6°6N 6°42E 50 G7
Ono Fiji 18°55S 178°29E 59 a
Onoda Japan 33°59N 131°11E 31 G5
Onslow Australia 21°40S 115°12E 60 D2
Onslow B. U.S.A. 34°20N 77°15W 85 D16
Ontake-San Japan 35°53N 137°29E 31 G8
Ontario Calif., U.S.A. 34°4N 117°39W 79 L9
Ontario Oreg., U.S.A. 44°2N 116°58W 76 D5
Ontario □ Canada 48°0N 83°0W 72 B2
Ontario, L. N. Amer. 43°20N 78°0W 82 C7
Ontonagon U.S.A. 46°52N 89°19W 80 B9
Onyx U.S.A. 35°41N 118°14W 79 K8
Oodnadatta Australia 27°33S 135°30E 63 D2
Ooldea Australia 30°27S 131°50E 61 F5
Oombulgurri Australia 15°15S 127°45E 60 C4
Oombulgurri ☼ Australia 15°10S 127°50E 60 C4
Oorindi Australia 20°40S 141°1E 62 C3
Oost-Vlaanderen □ Belgium 51°5N 3°50E 15 C3
Oostende Belgium 51°15N 2°54E 15 C2
Oosterhout Neths. 51°39N 4°47E 15 C4
Oosterschelde → Neths. 51°33N 4°0E 15 C4
Oosterwolde Neths. 53°0N 6°17E 15 B6
Ootacamund = Udagamandalam India 11°30N 76°44E 40 P10
Ootsa L. Canada 53°50N 126°2W 70 C3
Ooty = Udagamandalam India 11°30N 76°44E 40 P10
Op Luang △ Thailand 18°12N 98°32E 38 C2
Opala Dem. Rep. of the Congo 0°40S 24°20E 54 C1
Opanake Sri Lanka 6°35N 80°40E 40 R12
Opasatika Canada 49°30N 82°50W 72 C3
Opasquia ⌓ Canada 53°33N 93°5W 72 B1
Opava Czech Rep. 49°57N 17°58E 17 D9
Opelika U.S.A. 32°39N 85°23W 85 E12
Opelousas U.S.A. 30°32N 92°5W 84 F8
Opémisca, L. Canada 49°56N 74°52W 72 C5
Opheim U.S.A. 48°51N 106°24W 76 B10
Ophthalmia Ra. Australia 23°15S 119°30E 60 D2
Opinaca → Canada 52°15N 78°2W 72 B4
Opinaca, Rés. Canada 52°39N 76°20W 72 B4
Opinnagau → Canada 54°12N 82°25W 72 B3
Opiscotéo, L. Canada 53°10N 68°10W 73 B6
Opobo Nigeria 4°35N 7°34E 50 H7
Opole Poland 50°42N 17°58E 17 C9
Oponono L. Namibia 18°8S 15°45E 56 B2
Oporto = Porto Portugal 41°8N 8°40W 21 B1
Opotiki N.Z. 38°1S 177°19E 59 C6
Opp U.S.A. 31°17N 86°16W 85 F11
Oppdal Norway 62°35N 9°41E 8 E13
Opportunity U.S.A. 47°39N 117°15W 76 C5
Opua N.Z. 35°19S 174°9E 59 A5
Opunake N.Z. 39°26S 173°52E 59 C4
Opuwo Namibia 18°3S 13°45E 56 B1
Ora Cyprus 34°51N 33°12E 25 E12
Oracle U.S.A. 32°37N 110°46W 77 K8
Oradea Romania 47°2N 21°58E 17 E11
Öræfajökull Iceland 64°2N 16°39W 8 D5
Orai India 25°58N 79°30E 43 G8
Oral = Zhayyq → Kazakhstan 47°0N 51°48E 19 E9
Oral Kazakhstan 51°20N 51°20E 19 D9
Oran Algeria 35°45N 0°39W 50 A5
Orange Australia 33°15S 149°7E 63 E4
Orange France 44°8N 4°47E 20 D6
Orange Calif., U.S.A. 33°47N 117°51W 79 M9
Orange Mass., U.S.A. 42°35N 72°19W 83 D12
Orange Tex., U.S.A. 30°6N 93°44W 84 F8
Orange Va., U.S.A. 38°15N 78°7W 81 F14
Orange → S. Africa 28°41S 16°28E 56 D2
Orange, C. Brazil 4°20N 51°30W 93 C8
Orange Cove U.S.A. 36°38N 119°19W 78 J7
Orange Free State = Free State □ S. Africa 28°30S 27°0E 56 D4
Orange Grove U.S.A. 27°58N 97°56W 84 H6
Orange Walk Belize 18°6N 88°33W 87 D7
Orangeburg U.S.A. 33°30N 80°52W 85 E14
Orangeville Canada 43°55N 80°5W 82 C4
Orango Guinea-Biss. 11°5N 16°0W 50 F2
Oranienburg Germany 52°45N 13°14E 16 B7
Oranje = Orange → S. Africa 28°41S 16°28E 56 D2
Oranjemund Namibia 28°38S 16°29E 56 D2
Oranjerivier S. Africa 29°40S 24°12E 56 D3
Oranjestad Aruba 12°32N 70°2W 89 D5
Orapa Botswana 21°15S 25°30E 53 J5
Oras Phil. 12°9N 125°28E 37 B7
Orbetello Italy 42°27N 11°13E 22 C4
Orbisonia U.S.A. 40°15N 77°54W 82 F7
Orbost Australia 37°40S 148°29E 63 F4
Orcadas Antarctica 60°44S 44°37W 5 C18
Orcas I. U.S.A. 48°42N 122°56W 78 B4
Orchard City U.S.A. 38°50N 107°58W 76 G10
Orchard Homes U.S.A. 46°55N 114°4W 76 C6
Orchila, I. Venezuela 11°48N 66°10W 89 D6
Orchilla, Pta. Canary Is. 27°42N 18°10W 24 G1
Orcutt U.S.A. 34°52N 120°27W 79 L6
Ord U.S.A. 41°36N 98°56W 80 E4
Ord → Australia 15°33S 128°15E 60 C4
Ord, Mt. Australia 17°20S 125°34E 60 C4
Ord Mts. U.S.A. 34°39N 116°45W 79 L10
Orderville U.S.A. 37°17N 112°38W 77 H7
Ordos = Mu Us Shamo China 39°0N 109°0E 34 E5
Ordu Turkey 40°55N 37°53E 19 F6
Ordway U.S.A. 38°13N 103°46W 76 G12
Ore Dem. Rep. of the Congo 3°17N 29°30E 54 B2
Ore Mts. = Erzgebirge Germany 50°27N 12°55E 16 C7
Örebro Sweden 59°20N 15°18E 9 G16
Oregon U.S.A. 42°1N 89°20W 80 D9
Oregon □ U.S.A. 44°0N 121°0W 76 E3
Oregon City U.S.A. 45°21N 122°36W 78 E4
Oregon Dunes ⌓ U.S.A. 43°40N 124°10W 76 E1
Orekhovo-Zuyevo Russia 55°50N 38°55E 18 C6
Orel Russia 52°57N 36°3E 18 D6
Orem U.S.A. 40°19N 111°42W 76 F8
Ören Turkey 37°3N 27°57E 23 F12
Orenburg Russia 51°45N 55°6E 18 D10
Orense = Ourense Spain 42°19N 7°55W 21 A2
Orepuki N.Z. 46°19S 167°46E 59 G1
Orestes Pereyra Mexico 26°30N 105°39W 86 B3
Orestiada Greece 41°30N 26°33E 23 D12
Orfanos Kolpos Greece 40°33N 24°0E 23 D11
Orford Ness U.K. 52°5N 1°35E 13 E9

150 Organ Pipe Cactus
INDEX TO WORLD MAPS

Organ Pipe Cactus △ U.S.A. 32°0N 112°52W 77 K7
Organos, Pta. de los Canary Is. 28°12N 17°17W 24 F2
Orgaz Spain 39°39N 3°53W 21 C4
Orgeyev = Orhei Moldova 47°24N 28°50E 17 E15
Orhaneli Turkey 39°54N 28°59E 23 E13
Orhangazi Turkey 40°29N 29°18E 23 D13
Orhei Moldova 47°24N 28°50E 17 E15
Orhon Gol → Mongolia 50°21N 106°0E 32 A10
Oriental, Cordillera Colombia 6°0N 73°0W 92 B4
Oriental, Grand Erg Algeria 30°0N 6°30E 50 B7
Orientale □ Dem. Rep. of the Congo 2°20N 26°0E 54 B2
Oriente Argentina 38°44S 60°37W 94 D3
Orihuela Spain 38°7N 0°55W 21 C5
Orillia Canada 44°40N 79°24W 82 B5
Orinoco → Venezuela 9°15N 61°30W 92 B6
Orion Canada 49°27N 110°49W 71 D6
Oriskany U.S.A. 43°10N 75°20W 83 C9
Orissa □ India 20°0N 84°0E 41 K14
Orissaare Estonia 58°34N 23°5E 9 G20
Oristano Italy 39°54N 8°36E 22 E3
Oristano, G. di Italy 39°50N 8°29E 22 E3
Orizaba Mexico 18°51N 97°6W 87 D5
Orizaba, Pico de Mexico 18°58N 97°15W 87 D5
Orkanger Norway 63°18N 9°52E 8 E13
Orkla → Norway 63°18N 9°51E 8 E13
Orkney S. Africa 26°58S 26°40E 56 D4
Orkney □ U.K. 59°2N 3°13W 11 B5
Orkney Is. U.K. 59°0N 3°0W 11 B6
Orland U.S.A. 39°45N 122°12W 78 F4
Orlando U.S.A. 28°32N 81°22W 85 G14
Orléanais France 48°0N 2°0E 20 C5
Orléans France 47°54N 1°52E 20 C4
Orleans U.S.A. 44°49N 72°12W 83 B12
Orléans, Î. d' Canada 46°54N 70°58W 73 C5
Ormara Pakistan 25°16N 64°33E 40 G4
Ormoc Phil. 11°0N 124°37E 37 B6
Ormond N.Z. 38°33S 177°56E 59 C6
Ormond Beach U.S.A. 29°17N 81°3W 85 G14
Ormskirk U.K. 53°35N 2°54W 12 D5
Ormstown Canada 45°8N 74°0W 83 A11
Örnsköldsvik Sweden 63°17N 18°40E 8 E18
Oro N. Korea 40°1N 127°27E 35 D14
Oro → Mexico 25°35N 105°2W 86 B3
Oro Grande U.S.A. 34°36N 117°20W 79 L9
Oro Valley U.S.A. 32°26N 110°58W 77 K8
Orocué Colombia 4°48N 71°20W 92 C4
Orofino U.S.A. 46°29N 116°15W 76 C5
Orohena, Mt. Tahiti 17°37S 149°28W 59 d
Orol Dengizi = Aral Sea Asia 44°30N 60°0E 28 E7
Oromocto Canada 45°54N 66°29W 73 C6
Orono Canada 43°59N 78°37W 82 C6
Orono U.S.A. 44°53N 68°40W 81 C19
Oronsay U.K. 56°1N 6°15W 11 E2
Oroquieta Phil. 8°32N 123°44E 37 C6
Orosei Italy 40°23N 9°42E 22 D3
Orosháza Hungary 46°32N 20°42E 17 E11
Orotukan Russia 62°16N 151°42E 29 C16
Oroville Calif., U.S.A. 39°31N 121°33W 78 F5
Oroville Wash., U.S.A. 48°56N 119°26W 76 B4
Oroville, L. U.S.A. 39°33N 121°29W 78 F5
Orroroo Australia 32°43S 138°38E 63 E2
Orrville U.S.A. 40°50N 81°46W 82 F3
Orsha Belarus 54°30N 30°25E 18 D5
Orsk Russia 51°12N 58°34E 28 D6
Orşova Romania 44°41N 22°25E 17 F12
Ortaca Turkey 36°49N 28°45E 23 F13
Ortegal, C. Spain 43°43N 7°52W 21 A2
Orthez France 43°29N 0°48W 20 E3
Ortigueira Spain 43°40N 7°50W 21 A2
Orting U.S.A. 47°6N 122°12W 78 C4
Ortles Italy 46°31N 10°33E 20 C9
Ortón → Bolivia 10°50S 67°0W 92 F5
Ortonville U.S.A. 45°19N 96°27W 80 C5
Orūmīyeh Iran 37°40N 45°0E 44 B5
Orūmīyeh, Daryācheh-ye Iran 37°50N 45°30E 44 B5
Oruro Bolivia 18°0S 67°9W 92 G5
Orust Sweden 58°10N 11°40E 9 G14
Oruzgān □ Afghan. 33°0N 66°0E 40 C5
Orvieto Italy 42°43N 12°7E 22 C5
Orwell N.Y., U.S.A. 43°35N 75°50W 83 C9
Orwell Ohio, U.S.A. 41°32N 80°52W 82 E4
Orwell → U.K. 51°59N 1°18E 13 F9
Orwigsburg U.S.A. 40°38N 76°6W 83 F8
Oryakhovo Bulgaria 43°40N 23°57E 23 C10
Oryol = Orel Russia 52°57N 36°3E 18 D6
Osa Russia 57°17N 55°26E 18 C10
Osa, Pen. de Costa Rica 8°0N 84°0W 88 E3
Osage U.S.A. 43°17N 92°49W 80 D7
Osage → U.S.A. 38°36N 91°57W 80 F8
Osage City U.S.A. 38°38N 95°50W 80 F6
Ōsaka Japan 34°42N 135°30E 31 G7
Osawatomie U.S.A. 38°31N 94°57W 80 F6
Osborne U.S.A. 39°26N 98°42W 80 F4
Osceola Ark., U.S.A. 35°42N 89°58W 85 D10
Osceola Iowa, U.S.A. 41°2N 93°46W 80 E7
Oscoda U.S.A. 44°26N 83°20W 82 B1
Ösel = Saaremaa Estonia 58°30N 22°30E 9 G20
Osgoode Canada 45°8N 75°36W 83 A9
Osh Kyrgyzstan 40°37N 72°49E 28 E8
Oshakati Namibia 17°45S 15°40E 53 H3
Oshawa Canada 43°50N 78°50W 82 C6
Oshigambo Namibia 17°45S 16°5E 56 B2
Oshika-Hantō Japan 38°20N 141°30E 30 E10
Oshkosh Nebr., U.S.A. 41°24N 102°21W 80 E2
Oshkosh Wis., U.S.A. 44°1N 88°33W 80 C9
Oshmyany = Ashmyany Belarus 54°26N 25°52E 17 A13
Oshnovīyeh Iran 37°2N 45°6E 44 B5
Oshogbo Nigeria 7°48N 4°37E 50 G6
Oshtorīnān Iran 34°1N 48°38E 45 C6
Oshwe Dem. Rep. of the Congo 3°25S 19°28E 52 E3
Osijek Croatia 45°34N 18°41E 23 B8
Osipovichi = Asipovichy Belarus 53°19N 28°33E 17 B15
Osiyan India 26°43N 72°55E 42 F5
Osizweni S. Africa 27°49S 30°7E 57 D5
Oskaloosa U.S.A. 41°18N 92°39W 80 E7
Oskarshamn Sweden 57°15N 16°27E 9 H17
Oskélanéo Canada 48°5N 75°15W 72 C4
Öskemen Kazakhstan 50°0N 82°36E 28 D9
Oslo Norway 59°54N 10°43E 9 G14
Oslofjorden Norway 59°20N 10°35E 9 G14
Osmanabad India 18°5N 76°10E 40 K10
Osmaniye Turkey 37°5N 36°10E 44 B3
Osnabrück Germany 52°17N 8°3E 16 B5
Osório Brazil 29°53S 50°17W 95 B5
Osorno Chile 40°25S 73°0W 96 E2
Osorno, Vol. Chile 41°0S 72°30W 96 D2
Osoyoos Canada 49°0N 119°30W 70 D5
Osøyro Norway 60°9N 5°30E 8 F11
Ospika → Canada 56°20N 124°0W 70 B4
Osprey Reef Australia 13°52S 146°36E 62 A4
Oss Neths. 51°46N 5°32E 15 C5
Ossa, Mt. Australia 41°52S 146°3E 63 G4
Ossa, Oros Greece 39°47N 22°42E 23 E10
Ossabaw I. U.S.A. 31°50N 81°5W 85 F14
Ossining U.S.A. 41°10N 73°55W 83 E11
Ossipee U.S.A. 43°41N 71°7W 83 C13
Ossokmanuan L. Canada 53°25N 65°0W 73 B7
Ossora Russia 59°20N 163°13E 29 D17
Ostend = Oostende Belgium 51°15N 2°54E 15 C2
Oster Ukraine 50°57N 30°53E 17 C16
Österbotten = Pohjanmaa Finland 62°58N 22°50E 8 E20
Osterburg U.S.A. 40°16N 78°31W 82 F6
Österdalälven → Sweden 60°30N 15°7E 8 F15
Østerdalen Norway 61°40N 10°50E 8 F14
Östermyra = Seinäjoki Finland 62°40N 22°51E 8 E20
Österreich = Austria ■ Europe 47°0N 14°0E 16 E8
Östersund Sweden 63°10N 14°38E 8 E16
Ostfriesische Inseln Germany 53°42N 7°0E 16 B4
Ostrava Czech Rep. 49°51N 18°18E 17 D10
Ostróda Poland 53°42N 19°58E 17 B10
Ostroh Ukraine 50°20N 26°30E 17 C14
Ostrołęka Poland 53°4N 21°32E 17 B11
Ostrów Mazowiecka Poland 52°50N 21°51E 17 B11
Ostrów Wielkopolski Poland 51°36N 17°44E 17 C9
Ostrowiec-Świętokrzyski Poland 50°55N 21°22E 17 C11
Ostuni Italy 40°44N 17°35E 23 D7
Ōsumi-Kaikyō Japan 30°55N 131°0E 31 J5
Ōsumi-Shotō Japan 30°30N 130°0E 31 J5
Osuna Spain 37°14N 5°8W 21 D3
Oswegatchie → U.S.A. 44°42N 75°30W 83 B9
Oswego U.S.A. 43°27N 76°31W 83 C8
Oswego → U.S.A. 43°27N 76°30W 83 C8
Oswestry U.K. 52°52N 3°3W 12 E4
Oświęcim Poland 50°2N 19°11E 17 C10
Otago □ N.Z. 45°15S 170°0E 59 F2
Otago Harbour N.Z. 45°47S 170°42E 59 F3
Otaheite B. Trin. & Tob. 10°15N 61°30W 93 K15
Ōtake Japan 34°12N 132°13E 31 G6
Otaki N.Z. 40°45S 175°10E 59 D5
Otaru Japan 43°10N 141°0E 30 C10
Otaru-Wan = Ishikari-Wan Japan 43°25N 141°1E 30 C10
Otavalo Ecuador 0°13N 78°20W 92 C3
Otavi Namibia 19°40S 17°24E 56 B2
Otawara Japan 36°50N 140°5E 31 F10
Otchinjau Angola 16°30S 13°56E 56 B1
Otego U.S.A. 42°23N 75°10W 83 D9
Otelnuk, L. Canada 56°9N 68°12W 73 A6
Othello U.S.A. 46°50N 119°10W 76 C4
Otish, Mts. Canada 52°22N 70°30W 73 B5
Otjiwarongo Namibia 20°30S 16°33E 56 C2
Oto Tolu Group Tonga 20°21S 174°32W 59 c
Otoineppu Japan 44°44N 142°16E 30 B11
Otorohanga N.Z. 38°12S 175°14E 59 C5
Otoskwin → Canada 52°13N 88°6W 72 B2
Otra → Norway 58°9N 8°1E 9 G13
Otranto Italy 40°9N 18°28E 23 D8
Otranto, C. d' Italy 40°7N 18°30E 23 D8
Otranto, Str. of Italy 40°15N 18°40E 23 D8
Otse S. Africa 25°2S 25°45E 56 D4
Otsego L. U.S.A. 42°45N 74°53W 83 D10
Ōtsu Japan 35°0N 135°50E 31 G7
Ōtsuki Japan 35°36N 138°57E 31 G9
Ottawa = Outaouais → Canada 45°27N 74°8W 72 C5
Ottawa Canada 45°26N 75°42W 83 A9
Ottawa Ill., U.S.A. 41°21N 88°51W 80 E9
Ottawa Kans., U.S.A. 38°37N 95°16W 80 F6
Ottawa Is. Canada 59°35N 80°10W 69 F15
Otter Cr. → U.S.A. 44°13N 73°17W 83 B11
Otter Lake Canada 45°17N 79°56W 82 A5
Otterville Canada 42°55N 80°36W 82 D4
Ottery St. Mary U.K. 50°44N 3°17W 13 G4
Otto Beit Bridge Zimbabwe 15°59S 28°56E 55 F2
Ottosdal S. Africa 26°46S 25°59E 56 D4
Ottumwa U.S.A. 41°1N 92°25W 80 E7
Oturkpo Nigeria 7°16N 8°8E 50 G7
Otway, B. Chile 53°30S 74°0W 96 G2
Otway, C. Australia 38°52S 143°30E 63 F3
Otwock Poland 52°5N 21°20E 17 B11
Ou → Laos 20°4N 102°13E 38 B4
Ou-Sammyaku Japan 39°20N 140°35E 30 E10
Ouachita → U.S.A. 31°38N 91°49W 84 F9
Ouachita, L. U.S.A. 34°34N 93°12W 84 D8
Ouachita Mts. U.S.A. 34°30N 94°30W 84 D7
Ouagadougou Burkina Faso 12°25N 1°30W 50 F5
Ouahigouya Burkina Faso 13°31N 2°25W 50 F5
Ouahran = Oran Algeria 35°45N 0°39W 50 A5
Ouallene Algeria 24°41N 1°11E 50 D6
Ouarâne Mauritania 21°0N 10°30W 50 D3
Ouargla Algeria 31°59N 5°16E 50 B7
Ouarra → C.A.R. 5°5N 24°26E 52 C4
Ouarzazate Morocco 30°55N 6°50W 50 B4
Oubangi → Dem. Rep. of the Congo 0°30S 17°50E 52 E3
Ouddorp Neths. 51°50N 3°57E 15 C3
Oude Rijn → Neths. 52°12N 4°24E 15 B4
Oudenaarde Belgium 50°50N 3°37E 15 D3
Oudtshoorn S. Africa 33°35S 22°14E 56 E3
Ouessant, Î. d' France 48°28N 5°6W 20 B1
Ouesso Congo 1°37N 16°5E 52 D3
Ouest, Pte. de l' Canada 49°52N 64°40W 73 C7
Ouezzane Morocco 34°51N 5°35W 50 B4
Oughter, L. Ireland 54°1N 7°28W 10 B4
Oughterard Ireland 53°26N 9°18W 10 C2
Ouidah Benin 6°25N 2°0E 50 G6
Oujda Morocco 34°41N 1°55W 50 B5
Oulainen Finland 64°17N 24°47E 8 D21
Oulu Finland 65°1N 25°29E 8 D21
Oulujärvi Finland 64°25N 27°15E 8 D22
Oulujoki → Finland 65°1N 25°30E 8 D21
Oum Chalouba Chad 15°48N 20°46E 51 E10
Oum Hadjer Chad 13°18N 19°41E 51 F9
Ounasjoki → Finland 66°31N 25°40E 8 C21
Ounguati Namibia 22°0S 15°46E 56 C2
Ounianga Kébir Chad 19°4N 20°29E 51 E10
Our → Lux. 49°55N 6°5E 15 E6
Ouray U.S.A. 38°1N 107°40W 77 G10
Ourense Spain 42°19N 7°55W 21 A2
Ouricuri Brazil 7°53S 40°5W 93 E10
Ourinhos Brazil 23°0S 49°54W 95 A6
Ouro Fino Brazil 22°16S 46°25W 95 A6
Ouro Prêto Brazil 20°20S 43°30W 95 A7
Ourthe → Belgium 50°29N 5°35E 15 D5
Ouse → E. Sussex, U.K. 50°47N 0°4E 13 G8
Ouse → N. Yorks., U.K. 53°44N 0°55W 12 D7
Outaouais → Canada 45°27N 74°8W 72 C5
Outardes → Canada 49°24N 69°30W 73 C6
Outer Hebrides U.K. 57°30N 7°40W 11 D1
Outjo Namibia 20°5S 16°7E 56 C2
Outlook Canada 51°30N 107°0W 71 C7
Outokumpu Finland 62°43N 29°1E 8 E23
Ouyen Australia 35°1S 142°22E 63 F3
Ovalau Fiji 17°40S 178°48E 59 a
Ovalle Chile 30°33S 71°18W 94 C1
Ovamboland Namibia 18°30S 16°0E 56 B2
Overflakkee Neths. 51°44N 4°10E 15 C4
Overijssel □ Neths. 52°25N 6°35E 15 B6
Overland Park U.S.A. 38°58N 94°40W 80 F6
Overlander Roadhouse Australia 26°19S 114°28E 61 E1
Overton U.S.A. 36°33N 114°27W 79 J12
Övertorneå Sweden 66°23N 23°38E 8 C20
Ovid U.S.A. 42°41N 76°49W 83 D8
Oviedo Spain 43°25N 5°50W 21 A3
Ovišrags Latvia 57°33N 21°44E 9 H19
Ovoot Mongolia 45°21N 113°45E 34 B7
Övör Hangay □ Mongolia 45°0N 102°30E 34 B2
Øvre Årdal Norway 61°19N 7°48E 8 F12
Ovruch Ukraine 51°25N 28°45E 17 C15
Owaka N.Z. 46°27S 169°40E 59 G2
Owambo = Ovamboland Namibia 18°30S 16°0E 56 B2
Owasco L. U.S.A. 42°50N 76°31W 83 D8
Owase Japan 34°7N 136°12E 31 G8
Owatonna U.S.A. 44°5N 93°14W 80 C7
Owbeh Afghan. 34°28N 63°10E 40 B3
Owego U.S.A. 42°6N 76°16W 83 D8
Owen Falls Dam = Nalubaale Dam Uganda 0°30N 33°5E 54 B3
Owen Sound Canada 44°35N 80°55W 82 B4
Owen Stanley Ra. Papua N. G. 8°30S 147°0E 58 B7
Oweniny → Ireland 54°8N 9°34W 10 B2
Owens → U.S.A. 36°32N 117°59W 78 J9
Owens L. U.S.A. 36°26N 117°57W 79 J9
Owensboro U.S.A. 37°46N 87°7W 80 G10
Owl → Canada 57°51N 92°44W 71 B10
Owo Nigeria 7°10N 5°39E 50 G7
Owosso U.S.A. 43°0N 84°10W 81 D11
Owyhee U.S.A. 41°57N 116°6W 76 F5
Owyhee → U.S.A. 43°49N 117°2W 76 E5
Owyhee, L. U.S.A. 43°38N 117°14W 76 E5
Ox Mts. = Slieve Gamph Ireland 54°6N 9°0W 10 B3
Öxarfjörður Iceland 66°15N 16°45W 8 C5
Oxbow Canada 49°14N 102°10W 71 D8
Oxelösund Sweden 58°43N 17°5E 9 G17
Oxford N.Z. 43°18S 172°11E 59 E4
Oxford U.K. 51°46N 1°15W 13 F6
Oxford Mass., U.S.A. 42°7N 71°52W 83 D13
Oxford Miss., U.S.A. 34°22N 89°31W 85 D10
Oxford N.C., U.S.A. 36°19N 78°35W 85 C15
Oxford N.Y., U.S.A. 42°27N 75°36W 83 D9
Oxford Ohio, U.S.A. 39°31N 84°45W 81 F11
Oxford L. Canada 54°51N 95°37W 71 C9
Oxfordshire □ U.K. 51°48N 1°16W 13 F6
Oxnard U.S.A. 34°12N 119°11W 79 L7
Oxus = Amudarya → Uzbekistan 43°58N 59°34E 28 E6
Oya Malaysia 2°55N 111°55E 36 D4
Oyama Japan 36°18N 139°48E 31 F9
Oyem Gabon 1°34N 11°31E 52 D2
Oyen Canada 51°22N 110°28W 71 C6
Oykel → U.K. 57°56N 4°26W 11 D4
Oymyakon Russia 63°25N 142°44E 29 C15
Oyo Nigeria 7°46N 3°56E 50 G6
Oyster Bay U.S.A. 40°52N 73°32W 83 F11
Ōyūbari Japan 43°1N 142°5E 30 C11
Ozamiz Phil. 8°15N 123°50E 37 C6
Ozark Ala., U.S.A. 31°28N 85°39W 85 F12
Ozark Ark., U.S.A. 35°29N 93°50W 84 D8
Ozark Mo., U.S.A. 37°1N 93°12W 80 G7
Ozark Plateau U.S.A. 37°20N 91°40W 80 G8
Ozarks, L. of the U.S.A. 38°12N 92°38W 80 F7
Ózd Hungary 48°14N 20°15E 17 D11
Ozernovskiy Russia 51°30N 156°31E 29 D16
Ozette, L. U.S.A. 48°6N 124°38W 78 B2
Ozieri Italy 40°35N 9°0E 22 D3
Ozona U.S.A. 30°43N 101°12W 84 F4
Ozuluama Mexico 21°40N 97°51W 87 C5

P

Pa-an Burma 16°51N 97°40E 41 L20
Pa Mong Dam Thailand 18°0N 102°22E 38 D4
Pa Sak → Thailand 15°30N 101°0E 38 E3
Paamiut Greenland 62°0N 49°43W 4 C5
Paarl S. Africa 33°45S 18°56E 56 E2
Pab Hills Pakistan 26°30N 66°45E 42 F2
Pabbay U.K. 57°46N 7°14W 11 D1
Pabianice Poland 51°40N 19°20E 17 C10
Pabna Bangla. 24°1N 89°18E 41 G16
Pabo Uganda 3°1N 32°10E 54 B3
Pacaja → Brazil 1°56S 50°50W 93 D8
Pacaraima, Sa. S. Amer. 4°0N 62°30W 92 C6
Pacasmayo Peru 7°20S 79°35W 92 E3
Pachitea → Peru 8°46S 74°33W 92 E4
Pachmarhi India 22°28N 78°26E 43 H8
Pachnes Greece 35°16N 24°4E 25 D6
Pachpadra India 25°58N 72°10E 42 G5
Pachuca Mexico 20°7N 98°44W 87 C5
Pacific Antarctic Ridge Pac. Oc. 43°0S 115°0W 5 B13
Pacific Grove U.S.A. 36°38N 121°56W 78 J5
Pacific Ocean 10°0N 140°0W 65 G14
Pacific Rim △ Canada 48°40N 124°45W 78 B2
Pacifica U.S.A. 37°37N 122°27W 78 H4
Pacitan Indonesia 8°12S 111°7E 37 H14
Packwood U.S.A. 46°36N 121°40W 78 D5
Padaido, Kepulauan Indonesia 1°15S 136°30E 37 E9
Padang Riau, Indonesia 1°30N 102°30E 39 M4
Padang Sumatera Barat, Indonesia 1°0S 100°20E 36 E2
Padang Endau Malaysia 2°40N 103°38E 39 L4
Padangpanjang Indonesia 0°40S 100°20E 36 E2
Padangsidempuan Indonesia 1°30N 99°15E 36 D1
Paddle Prairie Canada 57°57N 117°29W 70 B5
Paderborn Germany 51°42N 8°45E 16 C5
Padma India 24°12N 85°22E 43 G11
Pádova Italy 45°25N 11°53E 22 B4
Padra India 22°15N 73°7E 42 H5
Padrauna India 26°54N 83°59E 43 F10
Padre I. U.S.A. 27°10N 97°25W 84 H6
Padre Island △ U.S.A. 27°0N 97°25W 84 H6
Padstow U.K. 50°33N 4°58W 13 G3
Padua = Pádova Italy 45°25N 11°53E 22 B4
Paducah Ky., U.S.A. 37°5N 88°37W 80 G9
Paducah Tex., U.S.A. 34°1N 100°18W 84 D4
Paea Tahiti 17°41S 149°35W 59 d
Paektu-san N. Korea 41°59N 128°4E 35 D15
Paeroa N.Z. 37°23S 175°41E 59 B5
Pafúri Mozam. 22°28S 31°17E 57 C5
Pag Croatia 44°25N 15°3E 16 F8
Pagadian Phil. 7°55N 123°30E 37 C6
Pagai Selatan, Pulau Indonesia 3°0S 100°15E 36 E2
Pagai Utara, Pulau Indonesia 2°35S 100°0E 36 E2
Pagalu = Annobón Atl. Oc. 1°25S 5°36E 49 G4
Pagara India 24°22N 80°1E 43 G9
Pagastikos Kolpos Greece 39°15N 23°0E 23 E10
Pagatan Indonesia 3°33S 115°59E 36 E5
Page U.S.A. 36°57N 111°27W 77 H8
Paget, Mt. S. Georgia 54°26S 36°31W 96 G9
Pago Pago Amer. Samoa 14°16S 170°43W 59 b
Pagosa Springs U.S.A. 37°16N 107°1W 77 H10
Pagri China 27°45N 89°10E 32 F6
Pagwa River Canada 50°2N 85°14W 72 B2
Pāhala U.S.A. 19°12N 155°29W 75 M8
Pahang □ Malaysia 3°30N 102°45E 39 L4
Pahang → Malaysia 3°30N 103°9E 39 L4
Pahiatua N.Z. 40°27S 175°50E 59 D5
Pahokee U.S.A. 26°50N 80°40W 85 H14
Pahrump U.S.A. 36°12N 115°59W 79 J11
Pahute Mesa U.S.A. 37°20N 116°45W 78 H10
Pai Thailand 19°19N 98°27E 38 C2
Paicines U.S.A. 36°44N 121°17W 78 J5
Paide Estonia 58°53N 25°33E 9 G21
Paignton U.K. 50°26N 3°35W 13 G4
Päijänne Finland 61°30N 25°30E 8 F21
Pailani India 25°45N 80°26E 43 G9
Pailin Cambodia 12°46N 102°36E 38 F4
Painan Indonesia 1°21S 100°34E 36 E2
Painesville U.S.A. 41°43N 81°15W 82 E3
Paint Hills = Wemindji Canada 53°0N 78°49W 72 B4
Paint L. Canada 55°28N 97°57W 71 B9
Painted Desert U.S.A. 36°0N 111°0W 77 H8
Paintsville U.S.A. 37°49N 82°48W 81 G12
País Vasco □ Spain 42°50N 2°45W 21 A4
Paisley Canada 44°18N 81°16W 82 B3
Paisley U.K. 55°50N 4°25W 11 F4
Paisley U.S.A. 42°42N 120°32W 76 E3
Paita Peru 5°11S 81°9W 92 E2
Pajares, Puerto de Spain 42°58N 5°46W 21 A3
Pak Lay Laos 18°15N 101°27E 38 C3
Pak Ou Laos 20°3N 102°12E 38 B4
Pak Phanang Thailand 8°21N 100°12E 39 H3
Pak Sane Laos 18°22N 103°39E 38 C4
Pak Song Laos 15°11N 106°14E 38 E6
Pak Suang Laos 19°58N 102°15E 38 C4
Pak Tam Chung China 22°24N 114°19E 33 a
Pak Thong Chai Thailand 14°43N 102°1E 38 E4
Pakaur India 24°38N 87°51E 43 G12
Pakch'ŏn N. Korea 39°44N 125°35E 35 E13
Pakenham Canada 45°18N 76°18W 83 A8
Pakhuis S. Africa 32°9S 19°5E 56 E2
Pakistan ■ Asia 30°0N 70°0E 42 E4
Pakkading Laos 18°19N 103°59E 38 C4
Pakokku Burma 21°20N 95°0E 41 J19
Pakowki L. Canada 49°20N 111°0W 71 D6
Pakpattan Pakistan 30°25N 73°27E 42 D5
Paktīā □ Afghan. 33°30N 69°15E 40 C6
Paktīkā □ Afghan. 32°30N 69°0E 40 C6
Pakwach Uganda 2°28N 31°27E 54 B3
Pakxe Laos 15°5N 105°52E 38 E5
Pal Lahara India 21°27N 85°11E 43 J11
Pala Chad 9°25N 15°5E 51 G9
Pala Dem. Rep. of the Congo 6°45S 29°30E 54 D2
Pala U.S.A. 33°22N 117°5W 79 M9
Palabek Uganda 3°22N 32°33E 54 B3
Palacios U.S.A. 28°42N 96°13W 84 G6
Palagruža Croatia 42°24N 16°15E 22 C7
Palakkad = Palghat India 10°46N 76°42E 40 P10
Palam India 19°0N 77°0E 40 K10
Palampur India 32°10N 76°30E 42 C7
Palana Australia 39°45S 147°55E 63 F4
Palana Russia 59°10N 159°59E 29 D16
Palanan Phil. 17°8N 122°29E 37 A6
Palanan Pt. Phil. 17°17N 122°30E 37 A6
Palandri Pakistan 33°42N 73°40E 43 C5
Palanga Lithuania 55°58N 21°3E 9 J19
Palangkaraya Indonesia 2°16S 113°56E 36 E4
Palani Hills India 10°14N 77°33E 40 P10
Palanpur India 24°10N 72°25E 42 G5
Palapye Botswana 22°30S 27°7E 56 C4
Palas Pakistan 35°4N 73°14E 43 B5
Palasponga India 21°47N 85°34E 43 J11
Palatka Russia 60°6N 150°54E 29 C16
Palatka U.S.A. 29°39N 81°38W 85 G14
Palau ■ Palau 7°30N 134°30E 58 A6
Palauk Burma 13°10N 98°40E 38 F2
Palaw Burma 12°58N 98°39E 38 F2
Palawan Phil. 9°30N 118°30E 36 C5
Palayankottai India 8°45N 77°45E 40 Q10
Paldiski Estonia 59°23N 24°9E 9 G21
Palekastro Greece 35°12N 26°15E 25 D8
Paleleh Indonesia 1°10N 121°50E 37 D6
Palembang Indonesia 3°0S 104°50E 36 E2
Palencia Spain 42°1N 4°34W 21 A3
Palenque Mexico 17°29N 92°1W 87 D6
Paleochora Greece 35°16N 23°39E 25 D5
Paleokastritsa Greece 39°40N 19°41E 25 A3
Paleometokho Cyprus 35°7N 33°11E 25 D12
Palermo Italy 38°7N 13°22E 22 E5
Palermo U.S.A. 39°26N 121°33W 76 G3
Palestina Chile 23°50S 69°47W 96 A3
Palestine Asia 32°0N 35°0E 46 D4
Palestine U.S.A. 31°46N 95°38W 84 F7
Paletwa Burma 21°10N 92°50E 41 J18
Palghat India 10°46N 76°42E 40 P10
Palgrave, Mt. Australia 23°22S 115°58E 60 D2
Pali India 25°50N 73°20E 42 G5
Palikir Micronesia 6°55N 158°9E 64 G7
Paliouri, Akra Greece 39°57N 23°45E 23 E10
Palisades Res. U.S.A. 43°20N 111°12W 76 E8
Paliseul Belgium 49°54N 5°8E 15 E5
Palitana India 21°32N 71°49E 42 J4
Palizada Mexico 18°15N 92°5W 87 D6
Palk Bay Asia 9°30N 79°15E 40 Q11
Palk Strait Asia 10°0N 79°45E 40 Q11
Palkānah Iraq 35°49N 44°26E 44 C5
Palkot India 22°53N 84°39E 43 H11
Pallanza = Verbánia Italy 45°56N 8°33E 20 D8
Pallarenda Australia 19°12S 146°46E 62 B4
Pallinup → Australia 34°27S 118°50E 61 F2
Pallisa Uganda 1°12N 33°43E 54 B3
Pallu India 28°59N 74°14E 42 E6
Palm Bay U.S.A. 28°2N 80°35W 85 G14
Palm Beach U.S.A. 26°43N 80°2W 85 H14
Palm Coast U.S.A. 29°35N 81°12W 85 G14
Palm Desert U.S.A. 33°43N 116°22W 79 M10
Palm-Grove △ Australia 24°57S 149°21E 62 C4
Palm Is. Australia 18°40S 146°35E 62 B4
Palm Springs U.S.A. 33°50N 116°33W 79 M10
Palma Mozam. 10°46S 40°29E 55 E5
Palma, B. de Spain 39°30N 2°39E 24 B9
Palma de Mallorca Spain 39°35N 2°39E 24 B9
Palma Nova = Palmanova Spain 39°32N 2°34E 24 B9
Palma Soriano Cuba 20°15N 76°0W 88 B4
Palmanova Spain 39°32N 2°34E 24 B9
Palmares Brazil 8°41S 35°28W 93 E11
Palmas Brazil 26°29S 52°0W 95 B5
Palmas, C. Liberia 4°27N 7°46W 50 H4
Pálmas, G. di Italy 39°0N 8°30E 22 E3
Palmdale U.S.A. 34°35N 118°7W 79 L8
Palmeira das Missões Brazil 27°55S 53°17W 95 B5
Palmeira dos Índios Brazil 9°25S 36°37W 93 E11
Palmer Antarctica 64°35S 65°0W 5 C17
Palmer U.S.A. 61°36N 149°7W 68 E2
Palmer → Australia 16°0S 142°26E 62 B3
Palmer Arch. Antarctica 64°15S 65°0W 5 C17
Palmer Lake U.S.A. 39°7N 104°55W 76 G11
Palmer Land Antarctica 73°0S 63°0W 5 D18
Palmerston Australia 12°31S 130°59E 60 B5
Palmerston Canada 43°50N 80°51W 82 C4
Palmerston N.Z. 45°29S 170°43E 59 F3
Palmerston North N.Z. 40°21S 175°39E 59 D5
Palmerton U.S.A. 40°48N 75°37W 83 F9
Palmetto U.S.A. 27°31N 82°34W 85 H13
Palmi Italy 38°21N 15°51E 22 E6
Palmira Argentina 32°59S 68°34W 94 C2
Palmira Colombia 3°32N 76°16W 92 C3
Palmyra = Tudmur Syria 34°36N 38°15E 44 C3
Palmyra Mo., U.S.A. 39°48N 91°32W 80 F8
Palmyra N.J., U.S.A. 40°0N 75°1W 83 F9
Palmyra N.Y., U.S.A. 43°5N 77°18W 82 C7
Palmyra Pa., U.S.A. 40°18N 76°36W 83 F8
Palmyra Is. Pac. Oc. 5°52N 162°5W 65 G11
Palo Alto U.S.A. 37°27N 122°10W 78 H4
Palo Seco Trin. & Tob. 10°4N 61°36W 93 K15
Palo Verde U.S.A. 33°26N 114°44W 79 M12
Palo Verde △ Costa Rica 10°21N 85°21W 88 D2
Palomar Mt. U.S.A. 33°22N 116°50W 79 M10
Palopo Indonesia 3°0S 120°16E 37 E6
Palos, C. de Spain 37°38N 0°40W 21 D5
Palos Verdes, Pt. U.S.A. 33°46N 118°25W 79 M8
Palos Verdes Estates U.S.A. 33°48N 118°23W 79 M8
Palu Indonesia 1°0S 119°52E 37 E5

Palu *Turkey* 38°45N 40°0E **44** B3
Paluma Ra. *Australia* 19°9S 146°22E **62** B4
Palwal *India* 28°8N 77°19E **42** E7
Pamanukan *Indonesia* 6°16S 107°49E **37** G12
Pamekasan *Indonesia* 7°10S 113°28E **37** G15
Pamenang *Indonesia* 8°24S 116°6E **37** J19
Pamiers *France* 43°7N 1°39E **20** E4
Pamir *Tajikistan* 37°40N 73°0E **28** F8
Pamlico → *U.S.A.* 35°20N 76°28W **85** D16
Pamlico Sd. *U.S.A.* 35°20N 76°0W **85** D17
Pampa *U.S.A.* 35°32N 100°58W **84** D4
Pampa de las Salinas
  Argentina 32°1S 66°58W **94** C2
Pampanua *Indonesia* 4°16S 120°8E **37** E6
Pampas *Argentina* 35°0S 63°0W **94** D3
Pampas *Peru* 12°20S 74°50W **92** F4
Pamplona *Colombia* 7°23N 72°39W **92** B4
Pamplona-Iruña *Spain* 42°48N 1°38W **21** A5
Pampoenpoort *S. Africa* 31°3S 22°40E **56** E3
Pan de Azúcar *Chile* 24°5S 68°10W **94** A2
Pan de Azúcar *Chile* 26°0S 70°40W **94** B1
Pana *U.S.A.* 39°23N 89°5W **80** F9
Panaca *U.S.A.* 37°47N 114°23W **77** H6
Panaitan *Indonesia* 6°36S 105°12E **37** G11
Panaji *India* 15°25N 73°50E **40** M8
Panamá *Panama* 9°0N 79°25W **88** E4
Panama ■ *Cent. Amer.* 8°48N 79°55W **88** E4
Panamá, G. de *Panama* 8°4N 79°20W **88** E4
Panama, Isthmus of
  Cent. Amer. 9°0N 79°0W **88** E4
Panama Basin *Pac. Oc.* 5°0N 83°30W **65** G19
Panama Canal *Panama* 9°10N 79°37W **88** E4
Panama City *U.S.A.* 30°10N 85°40W **85** F12
Panamint Range
  U.S.A. 36°20N 117°20W **79** J9
Panamint Springs
  U.S.A. 36°20N 117°28W **79** J9
Panão *Peru* 9°55S 75°55W **92** E3
Panare *Thailand* 6°51N 101°30E **39** J3
Panay *Phil.* 11°10N 122°30E **37** B6
Panay G. *Phil.* 11°0N 122°30E **37** B6
Pančevo *Serbia* 44°52N 20°41E **23** B9
Panda *Mozam.* 24°2S 34°45E **57** C5
Pandan *Malaysia* 1°32N 103°46E **39** d
Pandan *Phil.* 11°45N 122°10E **37** B6
Pandan, Selat *Singapore* 1°15N 103°44E **39** d
Pandan Tampoi = Tampoi
  Malaysia 1°30N 103°39E **39** d
Pandegelang *Indonesia* 6°25S 106°5E **37** G12
Pandhana *India* 21°42N 76°13E **42** J7
Pandharpur *India* 17°41N 75°20E **40** L9
Pando *Uruguay* 34°44S 56°0W **95** C4
Pando, L. = Hope, L.
  Australia 28°24S 139°18E **63** D2
Pandokratoras *Greece* 39°45N 19°50E **25** A3
Pandora *Costa Rica* 9°43N 83°3W **88** E3
Panevėžys *Lithuania* 55°42N 24°25E **9** J21
Pang-Long *Burma* 23°11N 98°45E **41** H21
Pang Sida △ *Thailand* 14°5N 102°17E **38** E4
Pang-Yang *Burma* 22°7N 98°48E **41** H21
Panga
  Dem. Rep. of the Congo 1°52N 26°18E **54** B2
Pangalanes, Canal des =
  Ampangalana, Lakandranon'
  Madag. 22°48S 47°50E **57** C8
Pangandaran *Indonesia* 7°40S 108°39E **37** G13
Pangandaran △
  Indonesia 7°43S 108°42E **37** G13
Pangani *Tanzania* 5°25S 38°58E **54** D4
Pangani → *Tanzania* 5°26S 38°58E **54** D4
Pangfou = Bengbu
  China 32°58N 117°20E **35** H9
Pangga, Tanjung
  Indonesia 8°54S 116°2E **37** K19
Pangil
  Dem. Rep. of the Congo 3°10S 26°35E **54** C2
Pangjiabu *China* 40°38N 115°26E **34** D8
Pangkah, Tanjung
  Indonesia 6°51S 112°33E **37** G15
Pangkajene *Indonesia* 4°46S 119°34E **37** E5
Pangkalanbrandan
  Indonesia 4°1N 98°20E **36** D1
Pangkalanbuun
  Indonesia 2°41S 111°37E **36** E4
Pangkalpinang *Indonesia* 2°10S 106°10E **36** E3
Pangkor, Pulau
  Malaysia 4°13N 100°34E **39** K3
Pangniqtuuq = Pangnirtung
  Canada 66°8N 65°43W **69** D18
Pangnirtung *Canada* 66°8N 65°43W **69** D18
Pangody *Russia* 65°45N 74°42E **28** C8
Pangong Tso = Bangong Co
  China 35°45N 78°43E **43** C8
Panguitch *U.S.A.* 37°50N 112°26W **77** H7
Pangutaran Group *Phil.* 6°18N 120°34E **37** C6
Panhandle *U.S.A.* 35°21N 101°23W **84** D4
Pani Mines *India* 22°29N 73°50E **42** H5
Pania-Mutombo
  Dem. Rep. of the Congo 5°11S 23°51E **54** D1
Panikota I. *India* 20°46N 71°21E **42** J4
Panipat *India* 29°25N 77°2E **42** E7
Panjal Range = Pir Panjal Range
  India 32°30N 76°50E **42** C7
Panjgur *Pakistan* 27°0N 64°5E **40** F4
Panjim = Panaji *India* 15°25N 73°50E **40** M8
Panjin *China* 41°3N 122°2E **35** D12
Panjnad → *Pakistan* 28°57N 70°30E **42** E4
Panjnad Barrage
  Pakistan 29°22N 71°15E **42** E4
Panjwai *Afghan.* 31°26N 65°27E **42** D1
Panmunjŏm *N. Korea* 37°59N 126°38E **35** F14
Panna *India* 24°40N 80°15E **43** G9
Panna △ *India* 24°40N 80°0E **43** G8
Pannawonica *Australia* 21°39S 116°19E **60** D2
Pano Akil *Pakistan* 27°51N 69°7E **42** F3
Pano Lefkara *Cyprus* 34°53N 33°20E **25** E12
Pano Panayia *Cyprus* 34°55N 32°38E **25** E11
Panorama *Brazil* 21°21S 51°51W **95** A5
Panormos *Greece* 35°25N 24°41E **25** D6

Pansemal *India* 21°39N 74°42E **42** J6
Panshan = Panjin *China* 41°3N 122°2E **35** D12
Panshi *China* 42°58N 126°5E **35** C14
Pantanal *Brazil* 17°30S 57°40W **92** H7
Pantanos de Centla △
  Mexico 18°25N 92°25W **87** D6
Pantar *Indonesia* 8°28S 124°10E **37** F6
Pante Macassar *E. Timor* 9°30S 123°58E **37** F6
Pantelleria *Italy* 36°50N 11°57E **22** F4
Pánuco *Mexico* 22°3N 98°10W **87** C5
Panzhihua *China* 26°33N 101°44E **32** F9
Paola *Malta* 35°52N 14°30E **25** D2
Paola *U.S.A.* 38°35N 94°53W **80** F6
Paonia *U.S.A.* 38°52N 107°36W **76** G10
Paopao *Moorea* 17°30S 149°49W **59** d
Paoting = Baoding
  China 38°50N 115°28E **34** E8
Paot'ou = Baotou *China* 40°32N 110°2E **34** D6
Paoua *C.A.R.* 7°9N 16°20E **52** C3
Pápa *Hungary* 47°22N 17°30E **17** E9
Papa Stour *U.K.* 60°20N 1°42W **11** A7
Papa Westray *U.K.* 59°20N 2°55W **11** B6
Papagayo → *Mexico* 16°46N 99°43W **87** D5
Papagayo, G. de
  Costa Rica 10°30N 85°50W **88** D2
Papakura *N.Z.* 37°4S 174°59E **59** B5
Papantla *Mexico* 20°27N 97°19W **87** C5
Papar *Malaysia* 5°45N 116°0E **36** C5
Papara *Tahiti* 17°43S 149°31W **59** d
Paparoa △ *N.Z.* 42°7S 171°26E **59** E3
Papeete *Tahiti* 17°32S 149°34W **59** d
Papenoo *Tahiti* 17°30S 149°25W **59** d
Papenoo → *Tahiti* 17°30S 149°25W **59** d
Papetoai *Moorea* 17°29S 149°52W **59** d
Paphos *Cyprus* 34°46N 32°25E **25** E11
Paposo *Chile* 25°0S 70°30W **94** B1
Papoutsa *Cyprus* 34°54N 33°4E **25** E12
Papua □ *Indonesia* 4°0S 137°0E **37** E9
Papua, G. of *Papua N. G.* 9°0S 144°50E **58** B7
Papua New Guinea ■
  Oceania 8°0S 145°0E **58** B7
Papudo *Chile* 32°29S 71°27W **94** C1
Papun *Burma* 18°2N 97°30E **41** K20
Pará = Belém *Brazil* 1°20S 48°30W **93** D9
Pará □ *Brazil* 3°20S 52°0W **93** D8
Paraburdoo *Australia* 23°14S 117°32E **60** D2
Paracatu *Brazil* 17°10S 46°50W **93** G9
Paracel Is. *S. China Sea* 15°50N 112°0E **36** A4
Parachilna *Australia* 31°10S 138°21E **63** E2
Parachinar *Pakistan* 33°55N 70°5E **42** C4
Paradip *India* 20°15N 86°35E **41** J15
Paradise *Calif., U.S.A.* 39°46N 121°37W **78** F5
Paradise *Nev., U.S.A.* 36°5N 115°8W **79** J11
Paradise → *Canada* 53°27N 57°19W **73** B8
Paradise Hill *Canada* 53°32N 109°28W **71** C7
Paradise River *Canada* 53°27N 57°17W **73** B8
Paradise Valley *U.S.A.* 41°30N 117°32W **76** F5
Paradisi *Greece* 36°18N 28°7E **25** C10
Parado *Indonesia* 8°42S 118°30E **37** F5
Paragould *U.S.A.* 36°3N 90°29W **85** C9
Paragua → *Venezuela* 6°55N 62°55W **92** B6
Paraguaçu → *Brazil* 12°45S 38°54W **93** F11
Paraguaçu Paulista
  Brazil 22°22S 50°35W **95** A5
Paraguaná, Pen. de
  Venezuela 12°0N 70°0W **92** A5
Paraguarí *Paraguay* 25°36S 57°0W **94** B4
Paraguarí □ *Paraguay* 26°0S 57°10W **94** B4
Paraguay ■ *S. Amer.* 23°0S 57°0W **94** A4
Paraguay → *Paraguay* 27°18S 58°38W **94** B4
Paraíba = João Pessoa
  Brazil 7°10S 34°52W **93** E12
Paraíba □ *Brazil* 7°0S 36°0W **93** E11
Paraíba do Sul → *Brazil* 21°37S 41°3W **95** A7
Paraíso *Mexico* 18°24N 93°14W **87** D6
Parak *Iran* 27°38N 52°25E **45** E7
Parakou *Benin* 9°25N 2°40E **50** G6
Paralimni *Cyprus* 35°2N 33°58E **25** D12
Paramaribo *Suriname* 5°50N 55°10W **93** B7
Páramos del Batallón y La
  Negra △ *Venezuela* 8°2N 71°55W **89** E5
Paramushir, Ostrov
  Russia 50°24N 156°0E **29** D16
Paran → *Israel* 30°20N 35°10E **46** E4
Paraná *Argentina* 31°45S 60°30W **94** C3
Paraná *Brazil* 12°30S 47°48W **93** F9
Paraná □ *Brazil* 24°30S 51°0W **95** A5
Paraná → *Argentina* 33°43S 59°15W **94** C4
Paranaguá *Brazil* 25°30S 48°30W **95** B6
Paranaíba *Brazil* 19°40S 51°11W **93** G8
Paranaíba → *Brazil* 20°6S 51°4W **93** H8
Paranapanema → *Brazil* 22°40S 53°9W **95** A5
Paranapiacaba, Serra do
  Brazil 24°31S 48°35W **95** A6
Paranavaí *Brazil* 23°4S 52°56W **95** A5
Parang *Maguindanao,
  Phil.* 7°23N 124°16E **37** C6
Parang *Sulu. Phil.* 5°55N 120°54E **37** C6
Parângul Mare, Vf.
  Romania 45°20N 23°37E **17** F12
Paraparaumu *N.Z.* 40°57S 175°3E **59** D5
Parbati → *Mad. P., India* 25°50N 76°30E **42** G7
Parbati → *Raj., India* 26°54N 77°53E **42** F7
Parbhani *India* 19°8N 76°52E **40** K10
Parchim *Germany* 53°26N 11°52E **16** B6
Pardes Hanna-Karkur
  Israel 32°28N 34°57E **46** C3
Pardo → *Bahia, Brazil* 15°40S 39°0W **93** G11
Pardo → *Mato Grosso,
  Brazil* 21°46S 52°9W **95** A5
Pardoo Roadhouse
  Australia 20°6S 119°3E **60** D2
Pardubice *Czech Rep.* 50°3N 15°45E **16** C8
Pare *Indonesia* 7°43S 112°12E **37** G15
Pare Mts. *Tanzania* 4°0S 37°45E **54** C4
Parecis, Serra dos *Brazil* 13°0S 60°0W **92** F7
Paren *Russia* 62°30N 163°15E **29** C17
Parent *Canada* 47°55N 74°35W **72** C5
Parent, L. *Canada* 48°31N 77°1W **72** C4

Parepare *Indonesia* 4°0S 119°40E **37** E5
Parga *Greece* 39°15N 20°29E **23** E9
Pargas = Länsi-Turunmaa
  Finland 60°18N 22°18E **9** F20
Pargo, Pta. do *Madeira* 32°49N 17°17W **24** D2
Parham *Canada* 44°39N 76°43W **83** B8
Paria → *U.S.A.* 36°52N 111°36W **77** H8
Paria, G. de *Venezuela* 10°20N 62°0W **93** K14
Pariaguán *Venezuela* 8°51N 64°34W **92** B6
Paricutín, Cerro
  Mexico 19°28N 102°15W **86** D4
Parigi *Indonesia* 0°50S 120°5E **37** E6
Parika *Guyana* 6°50N 58°20W **92** B7
Parikkala *Finland* 61°33N 29°31E **8** F23
Parima, Serra *Brazil* 2°30N 64°0W **92** C6
Parinari *Peru* 4°35S 74°25W **92** D4
Pariñas, Pta. *Peru* 4°30S 82°0W **90** D2
Parintins *Brazil* 2°40S 56°50W **93** D7
Pariparit Kyun *Burma* 14°52N 93°41E **41** M18
Paris *Canada* 43°12N 80°25W **82** C4
Paris *France* 48°53N 2°20E **20** B5
Paris *Idaho, U.S.A.* 42°14N 111°24W **76** E8
Paris *Ky., U.S.A.* 38°13N 84°15W **81** F11
Paris *Tenn., U.S.A.* 36°18N 88°19W **85** C10
Paris *Tex., U.S.A.* 33°40N 95°33W **84** E7
Parish *U.S.A.* 43°25N 76°8W **83** C8
Parishville *U.S.A.* 44°38N 74°49W **83** B10
Pariti *Indonesia* 10°1S 123°45E **60** B3
Park *U.S.A.* 48°45N 122°18W **78** B4
Park City *U.S.A.* 37°48N 97°20W **80** G5
Park Falls *U.S.A.* 45°56N 90°27W **80** C8
Park Head *Canada* 44°36N 81°9W **82** B3
Park Hills *U.S.A.* 37°51N 90°51W **80** G8
Park Range *U.S.A.* 40°41N 106°41W **76** F10
Park Rapids *U.S.A.* 46°55N 95°4W **80** B6
Park River *U.S.A.* 48°24N 97°45W **80** A5
Park Rynie *S. Africa* 30°25S 30°45E **57** E5
Parkā Bandar *Iran* 25°55N 59°35E **45** E8
Parkano *Finland* 62°1N 23°0E **8** E20
Parker *Ariz., U.S.A.* 34°9N 114°17W **79** L12
Parker *Pa., U.S.A.* 41°5N 79°41W **82** E5
Parker Dam *U.S.A.* 34°18N 114°8W **79** L12
Parkersburg *U.S.A.* 39°16N 81°34W **81** F13
Parkes *Australia* 33°9S 148°11E **63** E4
Parkfield *U.S.A.* 35°54N 120°26W **78** K6
Parkhill *Canada* 43°15N 81°38W **82** C3
Parkland *U.S.A.* 47°9N 122°26W **78** C4
Parkston *U.S.A.* 43°24N 97°59W **80** D5
Parksville *Canada* 49°20N 124°21W **70** D4
Parkway *U.S.A.* 38°32N 121°26W **78** G5
Parla *Spain* 40°14N 3°46W **21** B4
Parma *Italy* 44°48N 10°20E **20** D9
Parma *Idaho, U.S.A.* 43°47N 116°57W **76** E5
Parma *Ohio, U.S.A.* 41°24N 81°43W **82** E3
Parnaguá *Brazil* 10°10S 44°38W **93** F10
Parnaíba *Brazil* 2°54S 41°47W **93** D10
Parnaíba → *Brazil* 3°0S 41°50W **93** D10
Parnassos *Greece* 38°35N 22°30E **23** E10
Pärnu *Estonia* 58°28N 24°33E **9** G21
Paro Dzong *Bhutan* 27°32N 89°53E **43** F13
Paroo → *Australia* 31°28S 143°32E **63** E3
Paros *Greece* 37°5N 25°12E **23** F11
Parowan *U.S.A.* 37°51N 112°50W **77** H7
Parral *Chile* 36°10S 71°52W **94** D1
Parramatta *Australia* 33°48S 151°1E **63** B5
Parras *Mexico* 25°25N 102°11W **86** B4
Parrett → *U.K.* 51°12N 3°1W **13** F4
Parris I. *U.S.A.* 32°20N 80°41W **85** E14
Parrsboro *Canada* 45°30N 64°25W **73** C7
Parry Channel *Canada* 74°15N 94°0W **69** C13
Parry I. *Canada* 45°18N 80°10W **82** A4
Parry Is. *Canada* 77°0N 110°0W **69** B10
Parry Sound *Canada* 45°20N 80°0W **82** A5
Parsaloi *Kenya* 1°16N 36°51E **54** B4
Parsnip → *Canada* 55°10N 123°2W **70** B4
Parsons *U.S.A.* 37°20N 95°16W **80** G6
Parsons Ra. *Australia* 13°30S 135°15E **62** A2
Partinico *Italy* 38°3N 13°7E **22** E5
Partizansk *Russia* 43°8N 133°9E **29** E14
Partridge I. *Canada* 55°59N 87°37W **72** A2
Partry Mts. *Ireland* 53°40N 9°28W **10** C2
Paru → *Brazil* 1°33S 52°38W **93** D8
Parvān □ *Afghan.* 35°0N 69°0E **40** B6
Parvatipuram *India* 18°50N 83°25E **41** K13
Parvatsar *India* 26°52N 74°49E **42** F6
Parys *S. Africa* 26°52S 27°29E **57** D4
Pas, Pta. des *Spain* 38°46N 1°26E **24** C7
Pas, The *Canada* 53°45N 101°15W **71** C8
Pasadena *Canada* 49°1N 57°36W **73** C8
Pasadena *Calif., U.S.A.* 34°9N 118°8W **79** L8
Pasadena *Tex., U.S.A.* 29°43N 95°13W **84** G7
Pasaje → *Argentina* 25°39S 63°56W **94** B3
Pasar *Indonesia* 8°27S 114°54E **37** J17
Pascagoula *U.S.A.* 30°21N 88°33W **85** F10
Pascagoula → *U.S.A.* 30°23N 88°37W **85** F10
Pașcani *Romania* 47°14N 26°45E **17** E14
Pasco *U.S.A.* 46°14N 119°6W **76** C4
Pasco I. *Australia* 20°57S 115°20E **60** D2
Pascoag *U.S.A.* 41°57N 71°42W **83** E13
Pascua, I. de *Chile* 27°7S 109°23W **65** K17
Pasfield L. *Canada* 58°24N 105°20W **71** B7
Pasir Mas *Malaysia* 6°2N 102°8E **39** K4
Pasir Panjang *Singapore* 1°18N 103°46E **39** d
Pasir Putih *Malaysia* 5°50N 102°24E **39** K4
Pasirian *Indonesia* 8°13S 113°8E **37** H15
Pasküh *Iran* 27°34N 61°39E **45** E9
Pasley, C. *Australia* 33°52S 123°35E **61** F3
Pašman *Croatia* 43°58N 15°20E **16** G8
Pasni *Pakistan* 25°15N 63°27E **40** G3
Paso Bravo △ *Paraguay* 22°32S 57°5W **94** A4
Paso Cantinela
  Mexico 32°33N 115°47W **79** N11
Paso de Indios *Argentina* 43°55S 69°0W **96** E3
Paso de los Libres
  Argentina 29°44S 57°10W **94** B4
Paso de los Toros
  Uruguay 32°45S 56°30W **94** C4
Paso Robles *U.S.A.* 35°38N 120°41W **78** K6
Paspébiac *Canada* 48°3N 65°17W **73** C6
Pasrur *Pakistan* 32°16N 74°43E **42** C6

Passage East *Ireland* 52°14N 7°0W **10** D5
Passage West *Ireland* 51°52N 8°21W **10** E3
Passaic *U.S.A.* 40°51N 74°7W **83** F10
Passau *Germany* 48°34N 13°28E **16** D7
Passero, C. *Italy* 36°41N 15°10E **22** F6
Passo Fundo *Brazil* 28°10S 52°20W **95** B5
Passos *Brazil* 20°45S 46°37W **93** H9
Pastavy *Belarus* 55°4N 26°50E **9** J22
Pastaza → *Peru* 4°50S 76°52W **92** D3
Pasto *Colombia* 1°13N 77°17W **92** C3
Pasuruan *Indonesia* 7°40S 112°44E **37** G15
Patagonia *Argentina* 45°0S 69°0W **96** F3
Patagonia *U.S.A.* 31°33N 110°45W **77** L8
Patambar *Iran* 29°45N 60°17E **45** D9
Patan = Lalitapur *Nepal* 27°40N 85°20E **43** F11
Patan = Somnath *India* 20°53N 70°22E **42** J4
Patan *India* 23°54N 72°14E **42** H5
Patani *Indonesia* 0°20N 128°50E **37** D7
Pataudi *India* 28°18N 76°48E **42** E7
Patchewollock *Australia* 35°22S 142°12E **63** F3
Patchogue *U.S.A.* 40°46N 73°1W **83** F11
Pate *Kenya* 2°10S 41°0E **54** C5
Patea *N.Z.* 39°45S 174°30E **59** C5
Patensie *S. Africa* 33°46S 24°49E **56** E3
Paternò *Italy* 37°34N 14°54E **22** F6
Pateros *U.S.A.* 48°3N 119°54W **76** B4
Paterson *U.S.A.* 40°54N 74°9W **83** F10
Paterson Ra. *Australia* 21°45S 122°10E **60** D3
Pathankot *India* 32°18N 75°45E **42** C6
Pathein = Bassein
  Burma 16°45N 94°30E **41** L19
Pathfinder Res. *U.S.A.* 42°28N 106°51W **76** E10
Pathiu *Thailand* 10°42N 99°19E **39** G2
Pathum Thani *Thailand* 14°1N 100°32E **38** E3
Pati *Indonesia* 6°45S 111°1E **37** G14
Patia → *Colombia* 2°13N 78°40W **92** C3
Patiala *Punjab, India* 30°23N 76°26E **42** D7
Patiala *Ut. P., India* 27°43N 79°1E **43** F8
Patkai Bum *India* 27°0N 95°30E **41** F19
Patmos *Greece* 37°21N 26°36E **23** F12
Patna *India* 25°35N 85°12E **43** G11
Pato Branco *Brazil* 26°13S 52°40W **95** B5
Patong, Ao *Thailand* 7°54N 98°17E **39** a
Patonga *Uganda* 2°45N 33°15E **54** B3
Patos *Brazil* 6°55S 37°16W **93** E11
Patos, L. dos *Brazil* 31°20S 51°0W **95** C5
Patos, Río de los →
  Argentina 31°18S 69°25W **94** C2
Patos de Minas *Brazil* 18°35S 46°32W **93** G9
Patquía *Argentina* 30°2S 66°55W **94** C2
Patra *Greece* 38°14N 21°47E **23** E9
Patraikos Kolpos *Greece* 38°17N 21°30E **23** E9
Patras = Patra *Greece* 38°14N 21°47E **23** E9
Patriot Hills *Antarctica* 82°20S 81°25W **5** E16
Patrocínio *Brazil* 18°57S 47°0W **93** G9
Pattani *Thailand* 6°48N 101°15E **39** J3
Pattaya *Thailand* 12°52N 100°55E **38** F3
Patten *U.S.A.* 46°0N 68°38W **81** B19
Patterson *Calif., U.S.A.* 37°28N 121°8W **78** H5
Patterson *La., U.S.A.* 29°42N 91°18W **84** G9
Patterson, Mt. *U.S.A.* 38°29N 119°20W **78** G7
Patti *Punjab, India* 31°17N 74°54E **42** D6
Patti *Ut. P., India* 25°55N 82°12E **43** G10
Patton *U.S.A.* 40°38N 78°39W **82** F6
Patuakhali *Bangla.* 22°20N 90°25E **41** H17
Patuanak *Canada* 55°55N 107°43W **71** B7
Patuca → *Honduras* 15°50N 84°18W **88** C3
Patuca, Punta *Honduras* 15°49N 84°14W **88** C3
Patuca △ *Honduras* 14°30N 85°30W **88** D2
Patvinsuo △ *Finland* 63°7N 30°45E **8** E24
Pátzcuaro *Mexico* 19°31N 101°38W **86** D4
Pau *France* 43°19N 0°25W **20** E3
Paudash *Canada* 44°59N 77°58W **82** B7
Pauk *Burma* 21°27N 94°30E **41** J19
Paul I. *Canada* 56°30N 61°20W **73** A7
Paul Smiths *U.S.A.* 44°26N 74°15W **83** B10
Paulatuk *Canada* 69°25N 124°0W **68** D7
Paulding Bay *S. Ocean* 66°0S 118°0E **5** C8
Paulistana *Brazil* 8°9S 41°9W **93** E10
Paulo Afonso *Brazil* 9°21S 38°15W **93** E11
Paulpietersburg *S. Africa* 27°23S 30°50E **57** D5
Pauls Valley *U.S.A.* 34°44N 97°13W **84** D6
Pauma Valley *U.S.A.* 33°16N 116°58W **79** M10
Pauri *India* 30°9N 78°47E **43** D8
Pāveh *Iran* 35°3N 46°22E **44** C5
Pavia *Italy* 45°7N 9°8E **20** D8
Pavilion *U.S.A.* 42°52N 78°1W **82** D6
Pāvilosta *Latvia* 56°53N 21°14E **9** H19
Pavlodar *Kazakhstan* 52°33N 77°0E **28** D8
Pavlograd = Pavlohrad
  Ukraine 48°30N 35°52E **19** E6
Pavlohrad *Ukraine* 48°30N 35°52E **19** E6
Pavlovo *Russia* 55°58N 43°5E **18** C7
Pavlovsk *Russia* 50°26N 40°5E **19** E7
Pavlovskaya *Russia* 46°17N 39°47E **19** E6
Pawai, Pulau *Singapore* 1°11N 103°44E **39** d
Pawayan *India* 28°4N 80°6E **43** E9
Pawhuska *U.S.A.* 36°40N 96°20W **84** C6
Pawling *U.S.A.* 41°34N 73°36W **83** E11
Pawnee *U.S.A.* 36°20N 96°48W **84** C6
Pawnee City *U.S.A.* 40°7N 96°9W **80** E6
Pawtucket *U.S.A.* 41°53N 71°23W **83** E13
Paxi *Greece* 39°14N 20°12E **23** E9
Paximadia *Greece* 35°0N 24°35E **25** E6
Paxton *U.S.A.* 40°27N 88°6W **80** E9
Payakumbuh *Indonesia* 0°20S 100°35E **36** E2
Payette *U.S.A.* 44°5N 116°56W **76** D5
Payne Bay = Kangirsuk
  Canada 60°0N 69°50W **69** F18
Payne L. *Canada* 59°30N 74°30W **69** F17
Paynes Find *Australia* 29°15S 117°42E **61** E2
Paynesville *U.S.A.* 45°23N 94°43W **80** C7
Paysandú *Uruguay* 32°19S 58°8W **94** C4
Payson *Ariz., U.S.A.* 34°14N 111°20W **77** J8
Payson *Utah, U.S.A.* 40°3N 111°44W **76** F8
Paz → *Guatemala* 13°44N 90°10W **88** D1
Paz, B. la *Mexico* 24°15N 110°25W **86** C2
Pāzanān *Iran* 30°35N 49°59E **45** D6
Pazardzhik *Bulgaria* 42°12N 24°20E **23** C11

Pe Ell *U.S.A.* 46°34N 123°18W **78** D3
Peabody *U.S.A.* 42°31N 70°56W **83** D14
Peace → *Canada* 59°0N 111°25W **70** B6
Peace Point *Canada* 59°7N 112°27W **70** B6
Peace River *Canada* 56°15N 117°18W **70** B5
Peach Springs *U.S.A.* 35°32N 113°25W **77** J7
Peachland *Canada* 49°47N 119°45W **70** D5
Peachtree City *U.S.A.* 33°25N 84°35W **85** E12
Peak, The = Kinder Scout
  U.K. 53°24N 1°52W **12** D6
Peak Charles △
  Australia 32°42S 121°10E **61** F3
Peak District △ *U.K.* 53°24N 1°46W **12** D6
Peak Hill *Australia* 32°47S 148°11E **63** E4
Peak Ra. *Australia* 22°50S 148°20E **62** C4
Peake Cr. → *Australia* 28°2S 136°7E **63** D2
Peale, Mt. *U.S.A.* 38°26N 109°14W **76** G9
Pearl → *U.S.A.* 30°11N 89°32W **85** F10
Pearl and Hermes Reef
  U.S.A. 27°55N 175°45W **75** K4
Pearl River *U.S.A.* 41°4N 74°2W **83** E10
Pearl River Bridge *China* 22°15N 113°48E **33** a
Pearsall *U.S.A.* 28°54N 99°6W **84** G5
Pearson Int. Toronto ✈ (YYZ)
  Canada 43°46N 79°35W **82** C5
Peary Land *Greenland* 82°40N 33°0W **4** A6
Pease → *U.S.A.* 34°12N 99°2W **84** D5
Peawanuck *Canada* 55°15N 85°12W **72** A2
Pebane *Mozam.* 17°10S 38°8E **55** F4
Pebas *Peru* 3°10S 71°46W **92** D4
Pebble Beach *U.S.A.* 36°34N 121°57W **78** J5
Peć *Kosovo* 42°40N 20°17E **23** C9
Pechenga *Russia* 69°29N 31°4E **8** B24
Pechenizhyn *Ukraine* 48°30N 24°48E **17** D13
Pechiguera, Pta.
  Canary Is. 28°51N 13°53W **24** F6
Pechora *Russia* 65°10N 57°11E **18** A10
Pechora → *Russia* 68°13N 54°15E **18** A9
Pechorskaya Guba *Russia* 68°40N 54°0E **18** A9
Pechory *Russia* 57°48N 27°40E **9** H22
Pecos *N. Mex., U.S.A.* 35°35N 105°41W **77** J11
Pecos *Tex., U.S.A.* 31°26N 103°30W **84** F3
Pecos → *U.S.A.* 29°42N 101°22W **84** G4
Pécs *Hungary* 46°5N 18°15E **17** E10
Pedasi *Panama* 7°32N 80°2W **88** E3
Pedder, L. *Australia* 42°55S 146°10E **63** G4
Peddie *S. Africa* 33°14S 27°7E **56** E4
Pedernales *Dom. Rep.* 18°2N 71°44W **89** C5
Pedieos → *Cyprus* 35°10N 33°54E **25** D12
Pedirka Desert *Australia* 26°47S 134°11E **63** A1
Pedra Azul *Brazil* 16°2S 41°17W **93** G10
Pedra Lume *C. Verde Is.* 16°40N 22°52W **50** b
Pedreiras *Brazil* 4°32S 44°40W **93** D10
Pedro Afonso *Brazil* 9°0S 48°10W **93** E9
Pedro Cays *Jamaica* 17°5N 77°48W **88** C4
Pedro de Valdivia *Chile* 22°55S 69°38W **94** A2
Pedro Juan Caballero
  Paraguay 22°30S 55°40W **95** A4
Pee Dee = Great Pee Dee →
  U.S.A. 33°21N 79°10W **85** E15
Peebinga *Australia* 34°52S 140°57E **63** E3
Peebles *U.K.* 55°40N 3°11W **11** F5
Peekskill *U.S.A.* 41°17N 73°55W **83** E11
Peel I. of Man* 54°13N 4°40W **12** C3
Peel → *Australia* 30°50S 150°29E **63** E5
Peel → *Canada* 67°0N 135°0W **68** D5
Peel Sd. *Canada* 73°0N 96°0W **68** C12
Peera Peera Poolanna L.
  Australia 26°30S 138°0E **63** D2
Peerless Lake *Canada* 56°37N 114°40W **70** B6
Peers *Canada* 53°40N 116°0W **70** C5
Pegasus Bay *N.Z.* 43°20S 173°10E **59** E4
Pegu *Burma* 17°20N 96°29E **41** L20
Pegu Yoma *Burma* 19°0N 96°0E **41** K20
Pehuajó *Argentina* 35°45S 62°0W **94** D3
Pei Xian *China* 34°44N 116°55E **34** G9
Peine *Chile* 23°45S 68°8W **94** A2
Peine *Germany* 52°19N 10°14E **16** B6
Peip'ing = Beijing *China* 39°53N 116°21E **34** E9
Peipus, L. = Chudskoye, Ozero
  Russia 58°13N 27°30E **9** G22
Peixe *Brazil* 12°0S 48°40W **93** F9
Peixe → *Brazil* 21°31S 51°58W **93** H8
Peje = Peć *Kosovo* 42°40N 20°17E **23** C9
Pekalongan *Indonesia* 6°53S 109°40E **37** G13
Pekan *Malaysia* 3°30N 103°25E **39** L4
Pekan Nenas *Malaysia* 1°31N 103°31E **39** d
Pekanbaru *Indonesia* 0°30N 101°15E **36** D2
Pekin *U.S.A.* 40°35N 89°40W **80** E9
Peking = Beijing *China* 39°53N 116°21E **34** E9
Pekutatan *Indonesia* 8°25S 114°49E **37** J17
Pelabuhan Ratu, Teluk
  Indonesia 7°5S 106°30E **37** G12
Pelagie, Is. *Italy* 35°39N 12°33E **22** G5
Pelaihari *Indonesia* 3°55S 114°45E **36** E4
Peleaga, Vf. *Romania* 45°22N 22°55E **17** F12
Pelée, Mt. *Martinique* 14°48N 61°10W **88** c
Pelee, Pt. *Canada* 41°54N 82°31W **82** D3
Pelee I. *Canada* 41°47N 82°40W **82** E2
Pelekech *Kenya* 3°52N 35°8E **54** B4
Peleng *Indonesia* 1°20S 123°30E **37** E6
Pelentong *Malaysia* 1°32N 103°49E **39** d
Pelican *U.S.A.* 57°58N 136°14W **70** B1
Pelican L. *Canada* 52°28N 100°20W **71** C8
Pelican Narrows
  Canada 55°10N 102°56W **71** B8
Pelješac *Croatia* 42°55N 17°25E **22** C7
Pelkosenniemi *Finland* 67°6N 27°28E **8** C22
Pella *S. Africa* 29°1S 19°6E **56** D2
Pella *U.S.A.* 41°25N 92°55W **80** E7
Pello *Finland* 66°47N 23°59E **8** C20
Pelly → *Canada* 62°47N 137°19W **70** A1
Pelly Bay *Canada* 68°38N 89°50W **69** D14
Peloponnese □ *Greece* 37°10N 22°0E **23** F10
Pelorus Sd. *N.Z.* 40°59S 173°59E **59** D4
Pelotas *Brazil* 31°42S 52°23W **95** C5
Pelotas → *Brazil* 27°28S 51°55W **95** B5
Pelvoux, Massif du
  France 44°52N 6°20E **20** D7

Pemalang *Indonesia* 6°53S 109°23E **37 G13**
Pemanggil, Pulau
  Malaysia 2°37N 104°21E **39 L5**
Pematangsiantar *Indonesia* 2°57N 99°5E **36 D1**
Pemba *Mozam.* 12°58S 40°30E **55 E5**
Pemba *Zambia* 16°30S 27°28E **55 F2**
Pemba Channel *Tanzania* 5°0S 39°37E **54 D4**
Pemba I. *Tanzania* 5°0S 39°45E **54 D4**
Pemberton *Australia* 34°30S 116°0E **61 F2**
Pemberton *Canada* 50°25N 122°50W **70 C4**
Pembina → *Canada* 54°45N 114°17W **70 C6**
Pembroke *Canada* 50°N 77°7W **72 C4**
Pembroke *U.K.* 51°41N 4°55W **13 F3**
Pembrokeshire □ *U.K.* 51°52N 4°56W **13 F3**
Pembrokeshire Coast △
  U.K. 51°50N 5°2W **13 F2**
Pen-y-Ghent *U.K.* 54°10N 2°14W **12 C5**
Penal *Trin. & Tob.* 10°9N 61°29W **93 K15**
Penang = Pinang
  Malaysia 5°25N 100°15E **39 c**
Penápolis *Brazil* 21°30S 50°0W **95 A6**
Peñarroya-Pueblonuevo
  Spain 38°19N 5°16W **21 C3**
Penarth *U.K.* 51°26N 3°11W **13 F4**
Peñas, C. de *Spain* 43°42N 5°52W **21 A3**
Peñas, G. de *Chile* 47°0S 75°0W **96 F2**
Peñas del Chache
  Canary Is. 29°6N 13°33W **24 E6**
Pench △ *India* 21°45N 79°20E **43 J8**
Pench'i = Benxi *China* 41°20N 123°48E **35 D12**
Pend Oreille → *U.S.A.* 49°4N 117°37W **76 B5**
Pend Oreille, L. *U.S.A.* 48°10N 116°21W **76 B5**
Pendembu *S. Leone* 9°7N 11°14W **50 G3**
Pender B. *Australia* 16°45S 122°42E **60 C3**
Pendleton *U.S.A.* 45°40N 118°47W **76 D4**
Pendra *India* 22°46N 81°57E **43 H9**
Penedo *Brazil* 10°15S 36°36W **93 F11**
Penelokan *Indonesia* 8°17S 115°22E **37 J18**
Penetanguishene
  Canada 44°50N 79°55W **82 B5**
Penfield *U.S.A.* 41°13N 78°35W **82 E6**
Peng Chau *China* 22°17N 114°2E **33 a**
Penge *Kasai-Or.,*
  Dem. Rep. of the Congo 5°30S 24°33E **54 D1**
Penge *Sud-Kivu,*
  Dem. Rep. of the Congo 4°27S 28°25E **54 C2**
Penglai *China* 37°48N 120°42E **35 F11**
Penguin *Australia* 41°8S 146°6E **63 G4**
Penhalonga *Zimbabwe* 18°52S 32°40E **55 F3**
Peniche *Portugal* 39°19N 9°22E **21 C1**
Penicuik *U.K.* 55°50N 3°13W **11 F5**
Penida, Nusa *Indonesia* 8°45S 115°30E **37 K18**
Peninsular Malaysia □
  Malaysia 4°0N 102°0E **39 L4**
Penitente, Serra do *Brazil* 8°45S 46°20W **93 E9**
Penkridge *U.K.* 52°44N 2°6W **12 E5**
Penmarch, Pte. de *France* 47°48N 4°22W **20 C1**
Penn Hills *U.S.A.* 40°28N 79°52W **82 F5**
Penn Yan *U.S.A.* 42°40N 77°3W **82 D7**
Pennant *Canada* 50°32N 108°14W **71 C7**
Penner → *India* 14°35N 80°10E **40 M12**
Pennines *U.K.* 54°45N 2°27W **12 C5**
Pennington *U.S.A.* 39°15N 121°47W **78 F5**
Pennsburg *U.S.A.* 40°23N 75°29W **83 F9**
Pennsylvania □ *U.S.A.* 40°45N 77°30W **81 E15**
Penny *Canada* 53°51N 121°20W **70 C4**
Penobscot → *U.S.A.* 44°30N 68°48W **81 C19**
Penobscot B. *U.S.A.* 44°30N 68°50W **81 C19**
Penola *Australia* 37°25S 140°48E **63 F3**
Penong *Australia* 31°56S 133°1E **61 F5**
Penonomé *Panama* 8°31N 80°21W **88 E3**
Penrhyn *Cook Is.* 9°0S 158°0W **65 H12**
Penrith *Australia* 33°43S 150°38E **63 E5**
Penrith *U.K.* 54°40N 2°45W **12 C5**
Penryn *U.K.* 50°9N 5°7W **13 G2**
Pensacola *U.S.A.* 30°25N 87°13W **85 F11**
Pensacola Mts. *Antarctica* 84°0S 40°0W **5 E1**
Pense *Canada* 50°25N 104°59W **71 C8**
Penshurst *Australia* 37°49S 142°20E **63 F3**
Penticton *Canada* 49°30N 119°38W **70 D5**
Pentland *Australia* 20°32S 145°25E **62 C4**
Pentland Firth *U.K.* 58°43N 3°10W **11 C5**
Pentland Hills *U.K.* 55°48N 3°25W **11 F5**
Pentland Hills △ *U.K.* 55°50N 3°20W **11 F5**
Penza *Russia* 53°15N 45°5E **18 D8**
Penzance *U.K.* 50°7N 5°33W **13 G2**
Penzhino *Russia* 63°30N 167°55E **29 C17**
Penzhinskaya Guba
  Russia 61°30N 163°0E **29 C17**
Peoria *Ariz., U.S.A.* 33°43N 112°14W **77 K7**
Peoria *Ill., U.S.A.* 40°42N 89°36W **80 E9**
Pepacton Res. *U.S.A.* 42°5N 74°58W **83 D10**
Pepani → *S. Africa* 25°49S 22°47E **56 D3**
Pera Hd. *Australia* 12°55S 141°37E **62 A3**
Perabumulih *Indonesia* 3°27S 104°15E **36 E2**
Perak □ *Malaysia* 5°0N 101°0E **39 K3**
Perak → *Malaysia* 4°0N 100°50E **39 K3**
Perama *Kerkyra, Greece* 39°34N 19°54E **25 A3**
Perama *Kriti, Greece* 35°20N 24°40E **25 D6**
Perancak *Indonesia* 8°24S 114°37E **37 J17**
Peräpohjola *Finland* 66°16N 26°10E **8 C22**
Percé *Canada* 48°31N 64°13W **73 C7**
Perche, Collines du
  France 48°30N 0°40E **20 B4**
Percival Lakes *Australia* 21°25S 125°0E **60 D4**
Percy Is. *Australia* 21°39S 150°16E **62 C5**
Perdido, Mte. *Spain* 42°40N 0°5E **21 A6**
Perdu, Mt. = Perdido, Mte.
  Spain 42°40N 0°5E **21 A6**
Pereira *Colombia* 4°49N 75°43W **92 C3**
Perenjori *Australia* 29°26S 116°16E **61 E2**
Pereyaslav-Khmelnytskyy
  Ukraine 50°3N 31°28E **19 D5**
Pérez, I. *Mexico* 22°24N 89°42W **87 C7**
Pergamino *Argentina* 33°52S 60°30W **94 C3**
Pergau → *Malaysia* 5°23N 102°2E **39 K3**
Perham *U.S.A.* 46°36N 95°34W **80 B6**

Péribonka, L. *Canada* 50°1N 71°10W **73 B5**
Péribonka, La Centrale de
  Canada 49°30N 71°10W **73 C5**
Perico *Argentina* 24°20S 65°5W **94 A2**
Pericos *Mexico* 25°3N 107°42W **86 B3**
Périgueux *France* 45°10N 0°42E **20 D4**
Perijá, Sierra de *Colombia* 9°30N 73°3W **92 B4**
Perijá △ *Venezuela* 9°30N 72°55W **89 E5**
Peringat *Malaysia* 6°2N 102°17E **39 J4**
Perkasie *U.S.A.* 40°34N 75°18W **83 F9**
Perlas, Arch. de las
  Panama 8°41N 79°7W **88 E4**
Perlas, Punta de *Nic.* 12°30N 83°30W **88 D3**
Perlis □ *Malaysia* 6°30N 100°15E **39 J2**
Perm *Russia* 58°0N 56°10E **18 C10**
Pernambuco = Recife
  Brazil 8°0S 35°0W **93 E12**
Pernambuco □ *Brazil* 8°0S 37°0W **93 E11**
Pernatty Lagoon
  Australia 31°30S 137°12E **63 E2**
Pernik *Bulgaria* 42°35N 23°2E **23 C10**
Peron Is. *Australia* 13°9S 130°4E **60 B5**
Peron Pen. *Australia* 26°0S 113°10E **61 E1**
Perow *Canada* 54°35N 126°10W **70 C3**
Perpignan *France* 42°42N 2°53E **20 E5**
Perris *U.S.A.* 33°47N 117°14W **79 M9**
Perry *Fla., U.S.A.* 30°7N 83°35W **85 F13**
Perry *Ga., U.S.A.* 32°28N 83°44W **85 E13**
Perry *Iowa, U.S.A.* 41°51N 94°6W **80 E6**
Perry *N.Y., U.S.A.* 42°42N 78°0W **82 D7**
Perry *Okla., U.S.A.* 36°17N 97°14W **84 C6**
Perryton *U.S.A.* 36°24N 100°48W **84 C4**
Perryville *U.S.A.* 37°43N 89°52W **80 G9**
Persepolis *Iran* 29°55N 52°50E **45 D7**
Pershotravensk *Ukraine* 50°13N 27°40E **17 C14**
Persia = Iran ■ *Asia* 33°0N 53°0E **45 C7**
Persian Gulf *Asia* 27°0N 50°0E **45 E6**
Perth *Australia* 31°57S 115°52E **61 F2**
Perth *Canada* 44°55N 76°15W **83 B8**
Perth *U.K.* 56°24N 3°26W **11 E5**
Perth & Kinross □ *U.K.* 56°45N 3°55W **11 E5**
Perth Amboy *U.S.A.* 40°30N 74°15W **83 F10**
Perth-Andover *Canada* 46°44N 67°42W **73 C6**
Perth Basin *Ind. Oc.* 30°0S 108°0E **64 L2**
Peru *Ind., U.S.A.* 40°45N 86°4W **80 E10**
Peru *N.Y., U.S.A.* 44°35N 73°32W **83 B11**
Peru ■ *S. Amer.* 4°0S 75°0W **92 D4**
Peru Basin *Pac. Oc.* 20°0S 95°0W **65 J18**
Peru-Chile Trench
  Pac. Oc. 20°0S 72°0W **92 G3**
Perúgia *Italy* 43°7N 12°23E **22 C5**
Pervomaysk *Ukraine* 48°10N 30°46E **19 E5**
Pervouralsk *Russia* 56°59N 59°59E **18 C10**
Pésaro *Italy* 43°54N 12°55E **22 C5**
Pescara *Italy* 42°28N 14°13E **22 C6**
Peshawar *Pakistan* 34°2N 71°37E **42 B4**
Peshkopi *Albania* 41°41N 20°25E **23 D9**
Peshtigo *U.S.A.* 45°3N 87°45W **80 C10**
Pesqueira *Brazil* 8°20S 36°42W **93 E11**
Petah Tiqwa *Israel* 32°6N 34°53E **46 C3**
Petaling Jaya *Malaysia* 3°4N 101°42E **39 L3**
Petaloudes *Greece* 36°18N 28°5E **25 C10**
Pétange *Lux.* 49°33N 5°55E **15 E5**
Petare *Venezuela* 10°31N 66°50W **89 D6**
Petatlán *Mexico* 17°31N 101°16W **86 D4**
Petauke *Zambia* 14°14S 31°20E **55 E3**
Petawawa *Canada* 45°54N 77°17W **72 C4**
Petén Itzá, L. *Guatemala* 16°58N 89°50W **88 C2**
Peter I., *Br. Virgin Is.* 18°22N 64°35W **89 e**
Peter I. Øy *Antarctica* 69°0S 91°0W **5 C16**
Peter Pond L. *Canada* 55°55N 108°44W **71 B7**
Peterbell *Canada* 48°36N 83°21W **72 C3**
Peterborough *Australia* 32°58S 138°51E **63 E2**
Peterborough *Canada* 44°20N 78°20W **82 B6**
Peterborough *U.K.* 52°35N 0°15W **13 E7**
Peterborough *U.S.A.* 42°53N 71°57W **83 D13**
Peterborough □ *U.K.* 52°35N 0°15W **13 E7**
Peterculter *U.K.* 57°6N 2°16W **11 D6**
Peterhead *U.K.* 57°31N 1°48W **11 D7**
Peterlee *U.K.* 54°47N 1°20W **12 C6**
Petermann ○ *Australia* 24°58S 130°0E **61 E4**
Petermann Gletscher
  Greenland 80°30N 60°0W **69 A20**
Petermann Ranges
  Australia 26°0S 130°30E **61 E5**
Petersburg *Alaska,*
  U.S.A. 56°48N 132°58W **68 F5**
Petersburg *Pa., U.S.A.* 40°34N 78°3W **82 F6**
Petersburg *Va., U.S.A.* 37°14N 77°24W **81 G15**
Petersburg *W. Va., U.S.A.* 39°1N 79°5W **81 F14**
Petersfield *U.K.* 51°1N 0°56W **13 F7**
Petit-Canal *Guadeloupe* 16°25N 61°31W **88 b**
Petit Goâve *Haiti* 18°27N 72°51W **89 C5**
Petit Lac Manicouagan
  Canada 51°25N 67°40W **73 B6**
Petit-Mécatina →
  Canada 50°40N 59°30W **73 B8**
Petit-Mécatina, Î. du
  Canada 50°30N 59°25W **73 B8**
Petit Piton *St. Lucia* 13°51N 61°5W **89 f**
Petit-Saguenay *Canada* 48°15N 70°4W **73 C5**
Petitcodiac *Canada* 45°57N 65°11W **73 C6**
Petite Terre, Îles de la
  Guadeloupe 16°13N 61°9W **88 b**
Petitot → *Canada* 60°14N 123°29W **70 A4**
Petitsikapau L. *Canada* 54°37N 66°25W **73 B6**
Petlad *India* 22°30N 72°45E **42 H5**
Peto *Mexico* 20°8N 88°55W **87 C7**
Petorca *Chile* 32°15S 70°56W **94 C1**
Petoskey *U.S.A.* 45°22N 84°57W **81 C11**
Petra *Jordan* 30°20N 35°22E **46 E4**
Petra *Spain* 39°37N 3°6E **24 B10**
Petra, Ostrov *Russia* 76°15N 118°30E **29 B12**
Petra Velikogo, Zaliv
  Russia 42°40N 132°0E **30 C6**
Petre, Pt. *Canada* 43°50N 77°9W **82 C7**

Petrich *Bulgaria* 41°24N 23°13E **23 D10**
Petrified Forest △ *U.S.A.* 35°0N 109°30W **77 J9**
Petrikov = Pyetrikaw
  Belarus 52°11N 28°29E **17 B15**
Petrolândia *Brazil* 9°5S 38°20W **93 E11**
Petrolia *Canada* 42°54N 82°9W **82 D2**
Petrolina *Brazil* 9°24S 40°30W **93 E10**
Petropavl *Kazakhstan* 54°53N 69°13E **28 D7**
Petropavlovsk = Petropavl
  Kazakhstan 54°53N 69°13E **28 D7**
Petropavlovsk-Kamchatskiy
  Russia 53°3N 158°43E **29 D16**
Petrópolis *Brazil* 22°33S 43°9W **95 A7**
Petroşani *Romania* 45°28N 23°20E **17 F12**
Petrovaradin *Serbia* 45°16N 19°55E **23 B8**
Petrovsk *Russia* 52°22N 45°19E **18 D8**
Petrovsk-Zabaykalskiy
  Russia 51°20N 108°55E **29 D11**
Petrozavodsk *Russia* 61°41N 34°20E **18 B5**
Petrus Steyn *S. Africa* 27°38S 28°8E **57 D4**
Petrusburg *S. Africa* 29°4S 25°26E **56 D4**
Peumo *Chile* 34°21S 71°12W **94 C1**
Peureulak *Indonesia* 4°48N 97°45E **36 D1**
Pevek *Russia* 69°41N 171°19E **29 C18**
Pforzheim *Germany* 48°52N 8°41E **16 D5**
Pha Taem △ *Thailand* 15°32N 105°30E **38 E5**
Phaestos *Greece* 35°2N 24°50E **25 D6**
Phagwara *India* 31°10N 75°40E **42 D6**
Phala *Botswana* 23°45S 26°50E **56 C4**
Phalera = Phulera *India* 26°52N 75°16E **42 F6**
Phalodi *India* 27°12N 72°24E **42 F5**
Phaluai, Ko *Thailand* 9°32N 99°41E **39 b**
Phan *Thailand* 19°28N 99°43E **38 C2**
Phan Rang-Thap Cham
  Vietnam 11°34N 109°0E **39 G7**
Phan Ri Cua *Vietnam* 11°16N 108°40E **39 G7**
Phan Si Pan *Vietnam* 22°18N 103°46E **38 A4**
Phan Thiet *Vietnam* 11°1N 108°9E **39 G7**
Phan Thiet, Vinh
  Vietnam 10°53N 108°5E **39 G7**
Phanat Nikhom
  Thailand 13°27N 101°11E **38 F3**
Phangan, Ko *Thailand* 9°45N 100°0E **39 H3**
Phangnga *Thailand* 8°28N 98°30E **39 H2**
Phangnga, Ao *Thailand* 8°16N 98°33E **39 a**
Phanom Sarakham
  Thailand 13°45N 101°21E **38 F3**
Phaphund *India* 26°36N 79°28E **43 F8**
Pharenda *India* 27°5N 83°17E **43 F10**
Pharr *U.S.A.* 26°12N 98°11W **84 H5**
Phatthalung *Thailand* 7°39N 100°6E **39 J3**
Phayam, Ko *Thailand* 9°44N 98°25E **39 H2**
Phayao *Thailand* 19°11N 99°55E **38 C2**
Phelps *U.S.A.* 42°58N 77°3W **82 D7**
Phelps L. *Canada* 59°15N 103°15W **71 B8**
Phenix City *U.S.A.* 32°28N 85°0W **85 E12**
Phet Buri = Phetchaburi
  Thailand 13°1N 99°55E **38 F2**
Phetchabun *Thailand* 16°25N 101°8E **38 D3**
Phetchabun, Thiu Khao
  Thailand 16°0N 101°20E **38 E3**
Phetchaburi *Thailand* 13°1N 99°55E **38 F2**
Phi Phi, Ko *Thailand* 7°45N 98°46E **39 J2**
Phiafay *Laos* 14°48N 106°0E **38 E6**
Phibun Mangsahan
  Thailand 15°14N 105°14E **38 E5**
Phichai *Thailand* 17°22N 100°10E **38 D3**
Phichit *Thailand* 16°26N 100°22E **38 D3**
Philadelphia *Miss.,*
  U.S.A. 32°46N 89°7W **85 E10**
Philadelphia *N.Y., U.S.A.* 44°9N 75°43W **83 B9**
Philadelphia *Pa., U.S.A.* 39°57N 75°9W **83 G9**
Philip *U.S.A.* 44°2N 101°40W **80 C3**
Philip Smith Mts. *U.S.A.* 68°0N 148°0W **74 B10**
Philippeville *Belgium* 50°12N 4°33E **15 D4**
Philippi *U.S.A.* 39°9N 80°3W **81 F13**
Philippi L. *Australia* 24°20S 138°55E **62 C2**
Philippine Basin *Pac. Oc.* 17°0N 132°0E **64 F5**
Philippine Sea *Pac. Oc.* 18°0N 125°0E **64 F4**
Philippine Trench = Mindanao
  Trench *Pac. Oc.* 12°0N 126°6E **37 B7**
Philippines ■ *Asia* 12°0N 123°0E **37 B6**
Philippolis *S. Africa* 30°15S 25°16E **56 E4**
Philippopolis = Plovdiv
  Bulgaria 42°8N 24°44E **23 C11**
Philipsburg *Canada* 45°2N 73°5W **83 A11**
Philipsburg *Mont.,*
  U.S.A. 46°20N 113°18W **76 C7**
Philipsburg *Pa., U.S.A.* 40°54N 78°13W **82 F6**
Philipstown = Daingean
  Ireland 53°18N 7°17W **10 C4**
Philipstown *S. Africa* 30°28S 24°30E **56 E3**
Phillip I. *Australia* 38°30S 145°12E **63 F4**
Phillips *U.S.A.* 45°42N 90°24W **80 C8**
Phillipsburg *Kans.,*
  U.S.A. 39°45N 99°19W **80 F4**
Phillipsburg *N.J., U.S.A.* 40°42N 75°12W **83 F9**
Philmont *U.S.A.* 42°15N 73°39W **83 D11**
Philomath *U.S.A.* 44°32N 123°22W **76 D2**
Phimai *Thailand* 15°13N 102°30E **38 E4**
Phitsanulok *Thailand* 16°50N 100°12E **38 D3**
Phnom Kulen △
  Cambodia 13°38N 104°15E **38 F5**
Phnom Penh *Cambodia* 11°33N 104°55E **39 G5**
Phnom Penh = Phnom Penh
  Cambodia 11°33N 104°55E **39 G5**
Phoenicia *U.S.A.* 42°5N 74°14W **83 D10**
Phoenix *Mauritius* 20°17S 57°30E **53 d**
Phoenix *Ariz., U.S.A.* 33°26N 112°4W **77 K7**
Phoenix *N.Y., U.S.A.* 43°14N 76°18W **83 C8**
Phoenix Is. *Kiribati* 3°30S 172°0W **64 H10**
Phoenixville *U.S.A.* 40°8N 75°31W **83 F9**
Phon *Thailand* 15°49N 102°30E **38 E4**
Phong → *Thailand* 16°23N 102°56E **38 D4**
Phong Nha -Ke Bang △
  Vietnam 17°30N 106°10E **38 D6**
Phong Saly *Laos* 21°42N 102°9E **38 A4**
Phong Tho *Vietnam* 22°32N 103°21E **38 A4**
Phonhong *Laos* 18°30N 102°25E **38 C4**
Phonsavan *Laos* 19°27N 103°10E **38 C4**

Phonum *Thailand* 8°49N 98°48E **39 H2**
Phosphate Hill *Australia* 21°53S 139°58E **62 C2**
Photharam *Thailand* 13°41N 99°51E **38 F2**
Phra Nakhon Si Ayutthaya
  Thailand 14°25N 100°30E **38 E3**
Phra Pradaeng *Thailand* 13°39N 100°33E **38 F3**
Phra Thong, Ko *Thailand* 9°5N 98°17E **39 H2**
Phrae *Thailand* 18°7N 100°9E **38 C3**
Phrom Phiram *Thailand* 17°2N 100°12E **38 D3**
Phu Bia *Laos* 19°10N 103°0E **38 C4**
Phu Chong-Na Yoi △
  Thailand 14°25N 105°30E **38 E5**
Phu Hin Rong Kla △
  Thailand 17°0N 100°59E **38 D3**
Phu Kao -Phu Phan Kham △
  Thailand 16°53N 102°31E **38 D4**
Phu Kradung △ *Thailand* 17°2N 101°44E **38 D3**
Phu Luang △ *Thailand* 17°15N 101°29E **38 D3**
Phu Ly *Vietnam* 20°35N 105°50E **38 B5**
Phu My *Vietnam* 14°15N 109°5E **38 E7**
Phu Pha Man △
  Thailand 16°44N 101°50E **38 D3**
Phu Phan △ *Thailand* 17°0N 103°56E **38 D4**
Phu Quoc, Dao *Vietnam* 10°20N 104°0E **39 G4**
Phu Sa Dok Bua △
  Thailand 16°11N 104°45E **38 D5**
Phu Sang △ *Thailand* 19°35N 100°19E **38 C3**
Phu Tho *Vietnam* 21°24N 105°13E **38 B5**
Phu Wiang △ *Thailand* 16°39N 102°23E **38 D4**
Phuc Yen *Vietnam* 21°16N 105°45E **38 B5**
Phuket *Thailand* 7°53N 98°24E **39 a**
Phuket, Ko *Thailand* 8°0N 98°22E **39 a**
Phul *India* 30°19N 75°14E **42 D6**
Phulad *India* 25°38N 73°49E **42 G5**
Phulbani *Bangla.* 25°11N 89°37E **43 G13**
Phulera *India* 26°52N 75°16E **42 F6**
Phulpur *India* 25°31N 82°49E **43 G10**
Phuntsholing *Bhutan* 26°51N 89°23E **43 F13**
Phuphrabat *Thailand* 17°40N 102°45E **38 D4**
Phunphin *Thailand* 9°7N 99°12E **39 H2**
Pia △ *Australia* 27°5S 116°23E **61 E2**
Piacenza *Italy* 45°1N 9°40E **20 B8**
Piai, Tanjung *Malaysia* 1°17N 103°30E **39 d**
Pian Cr. → *Australia* 30°2S 148°12E **63 E4**
Pian-Upe △ *Uganda* 1°44N 34°20E **54 B3**
Pianosa *Italy* 42°35N 10°5E **22 C4**
Piao'ertun *China* 41°50N 123°47E **35 D12**
Piapot *Canada* 49°59N 109°8W **71 D7**
Piatra Neamţ *Romania* 46°56N 26°21E **17 E14**
Piauí □ *Brazil* 7°0S 43°0W **93 E10**
Piauí → *Brazil* 6°38S 42°42W **93 E10**
Piave → *Italy* 45°32N 12°44E **22 B5**
Pibor Post *Sudan* 6°47N 33°3E **51 G12**
Picardie □ *France* 49°50N 3°0E **20 B5**
Picardy = Picardie □
  France 49°50N 3°0E **20 B5**
Picayune *U.S.A.* 30°32N 89°41W **85 F10**
Pichhor *India* 25°58N 78°20E **43 G8**
Pichilemu *Chile* 34°22S 72°0W **94 C1**
Pichor *India* 25°11N 78°11E **42 G8**
Pickerel L. *Canada* 48°40N 91°25W **72 C1**
Pickering *U.S.A.* 54°15N 0°46W **12 C7**
Pickering, Vale of *U.K.* 54°14N 0°45W **12 C7**
Pickle Lake *Canada* 51°30N 90°12W **72 B1**
Pickwick L. *U.S.A.* 35°4N 88°15W **85 D10**
Pico *Azores* 38°28N 28°20W **50 a**
Pico Bonito △ *Honduras* 15°34N 86°48W **88 C2**
Pico Truncado *Argentina* 46°40S 68°0W **96 F3**
Picos *Brazil* 7°5S 41°28W **93 E10**
Picton *Australia* 34°12S 150°34E **63 E5**
Picton *N.Z.* 41°18S 174°3E **59 D5**
Pictou *Canada* 45°41N 62°42W **73 C7**
Picture Butte *Canada* 49°55N 112°45W **70 D6**
Pictured Rocks △
  U.S.A. 46°30N 86°30W **80 B10**
Picún Leufú *Argentina* 39°30S 69°5W **96 D3**
Pidurutalagala *Sri Lanka* 7°10N 80°50E **40 R12**
Piedmont = Piemonte □
  Italy 45°0N 8°0E **20 D7**
Piedmont *Ala., U.S.A.* 33°55N 85°37W **85 E12**
Piedmont *S.C., U.S.A.* 34°42N 82°28W **66 F11**
Piedras Negras *Mexico* 28°42N 100°31W **86 B4**
Pieksämäki *Finland* 62°18N 27°10E **8 E22**
Pielinen *Finland* 63°15N 29°40E **8 E23**
Piemonte □ *Italy* 45°0N 8°0E **20 D7**
Pienaarsrivier *S. Africa* 25°15S 28°18E **57 D4**
Piercefield *U.S.A.* 44°13N 74°35W **83 B10**
Pierceland *Canada* 54°20N 109°46W **71 C7**
Pierpont *U.S.A.* 41°45N 80°34W **82 E4**
Pierre *U.S.A.* 44°22N 100°21W **80 C3**
Pierrefonds *Canada* 45°29N 73°51W **83 A11**
Pierreville *Trin. & Tob.* 10°16N 61°0W **93 K16**
Piet Retief *S. Africa* 27°1S 30°50E **57 D5**
Pietarsaari *Finland* 63°40N 22°43E **8 E20**
Pietermaritzburg
  S. Africa 29°35S 30°25E **57 D5**
Pietersburg = Polokwane
  S. Africa 23°54S 29°25E **57 C4**
Pietrosul, Vf. *Maramureş,*
  Romania 47°35N 24°43E **17 E13**
Pietrosul, Vf. *Suceava,*
  Romania 47°12N 25°18E **17 E13**
Pigeon L. *Canada* 44°27N 78°30W **82 B6**
Piggott *U.S.A.* 36°23N 90°11W **85 C9**
Pigüe *Argentina* 37°36S 62°25W **94 D3**
Pihani *India* 27°36N 80°15E **43 F9**
Pijijiapan *Mexico* 15°42N 93°14W **87 D6**
Pikangikum *Canada* 51°49N 94°0W **71 C10**
Pikes Peak *U.S.A.* 38°50N 105°3W **76 G2**
Piketberg *S. Africa* 32°55S 18°40E **56 E2**
Pikeville *U.S.A.* 37°29N 82°31W **81 G12**
Pikou *China* 39°18N 122°22E **35 E12**
Pikwitonei *Canada* 55°35N 97°9W **71 B9**
Pikwé *Botswana* 21°52S 27°29E **57 C4**
Piła *Poland* 53°10N 16°48E **17 B9**
Pilani *India* 28°22N 75°33E **42 E6**
Pilar *Paraguay* 26°50S 58°20W **94 B4**
Pilaya → *Bolivia* 20°55S 64°4W **92 H6**

Pilbara *Australia* 21°15S 118°16E **60 D2**
Pilcomaya → *Paraguay* 25°21S 57°42W **94 B4**
Pilgrim's Rest *S. Africa* 24°55S 30°44E **57 C5**
Pilibhit *India* 28°40N 79°50E **43 E8**
Pilica → *Poland* 51°52N 21°17E **17 C11**
Pilipinas = Philippines ■
  Asia 12°0N 123°0E **37 B6**
Pilkhawa *India* 28°43N 77°42E **42 E7**
Pilliga *Australia* 30°21S 148°54E **63 E4**
Pilos *Greece* 36°55N 21°42E **23 F9**
Pilot Mound *Canada* 49°15N 98°54W **71 D9**
Pilot Point *U.S.A.* 33°24N 96°58W **84 E6**
Pilot Rock *U.S.A.* 45°29N 118°50W **76 D4**
Pima *U.S.A.* 32°54N 109°50W **77 K9**
Pimba *Australia* 31°18S 136°46E **63 E2**
Pimenta Bueno *Brazil* 11°35S 61°10W **92 F6**
Pimentel *Peru* 6°45S 79°55W **92 E3**
Pin Valley △ *India* 31°50N 77°50E **42 D7**
Pinang *Malaysia* 5°25N 100°15E **39 c**
Pinang □ *Malaysia* 5°20N 100°20E **39 K3**
Pinar, C. des *Spain* 39°53N 3°12E **24 B10**
Pinar del Río *Cuba* 22°26N 83°40W **88 B3**
Pınarhisar *Turkey* 41°37N 27°30E **23 D12**
Pinatubo, Mt. *Phil.* 15°8N 120°21E **37 A6**
Pinawa *Canada* 50°9N 95°50W **71 C9**
Pincher Creek *Canada* 49°30N 113°57W **70 D6**
Pinchi L. *Canada* 54°38N 124°30W **70 C4**
Pinckneyville *U.S.A.* 38°5N 89°23W **80 F7**
Pińczów *Poland* 50°32N 20°32E **17 C11**
Pindar *Australia* 28°30S 115°47E **61 E2**
Pindera Downs ○
  Australia 29°24S 142°37E **63 E3**
Pindi Gheb *Pakistan* 33°14N 72°21E **42 C5**
Pindos Oros *Greece* 40°0N 21°0E **23 E9**
Pindus Mts. = Pindos Oros
  Greece 40°0N 21°0E **23 E9**
Pine → *B.C., Canada* 56°8N 120°43W **70 B4**
Pine → *Sask., Canada* 58°50N 105°38W **71 B7**
Pine Bluff *U.S.A.* 34°13N 92°1W **84 D8**
Pine Bluffs *U.S.A.* 41°11N 104°4W **76 F11**
Pine City *U.S.A.* 45°50N 92°59W **80 C7**
Pine Cr. → *U.S.A.* 41°10N 77°16W **82 E7**
Pine Creek *Australia* 13°50S 131°50E **60 B5**
Pine Falls *Canada* 50°34N 96°11W **71 C9**
Pine Flat L. *U.S.A.* 36°50N 119°20W **78 J7**
Pine Grove *U.S.A.* 40°33N 76°23W **83 F8**
Pine Island Glacier
  Antarctica 76°0S 100°0W **5 D15**
Pine Pass *Canada* 55°25N 122°42W **70 B4**
Pine Point *Canada* 60°50N 114°28W **70 A6**
Pine Ridge *U.S.A.* 43°2N 102°33W **80 D2**
Pine River *Canada* 51°45N 100°30W **71 C8**
Pine River *U.S.A.* 46°43N 94°24W **80 B6**
Pine Valley *U.S.A.* 32°50N 116°32W **79 N10**
Pinecrest *U.S.A.* 38°12N 120°1W **78 G6**
Pinedale *Calif., U.S.A.* 36°50N 119°48W **78 J7**
Pinedale *Wyo., U.S.A.* 42°52N 109°52W **76 E9**
Pinega → *Russia* 64°30N 44°19E **18 B8**
Pinehouse L. *Canada* 55°32N 106°35W **71 B7**
Pineimuta → *Canada* 52°8N 88°33W **72 B1**
Pinerolo *Italy* 44°53N 7°21E **20 D7**
Pines, Akra *Greece* 40°5N 24°20E **23 D11**
Pinetop-Lakeside *U.S.A.* 34°9N 109°58W **77 J9**
Pinetown *S. Africa* 29°48S 30°54E **57 D5**
Pineville *U.S.A.* 31°19N 92°26W **84 F8**
Ping → *Thailand* 15°42N 100°9E **38 E3**
Pingaring *Australia* 32°40S 118°32E **61 F2**
Pingding *China* 37°47N 113°38E **34 F7**
Pingdingshan *China* 33°43N 113°27E **34 H7**
Pingdu *China* 36°42N 119°59E **35 F10**
Pingelly *Australia* 32°32S 117°5E **61 F2**
Pingliang *China* 35°35N 106°31E **34 G4**
Pinglu *China* 39°31N 112°30E **34 E7**
Pingluo *China* 38°52N 106°30E **34 E4**
Pingquan *China* 41°1N 118°37E **35 D10**
Pingrup *Australia* 33°32S 118°29E **61 F2**
Pingtung *Taiwan* 22°38N 120°30E **33 G13**
Pingwu *China* 32°25N 104°30E **34 H3**
Pingxiang *Guangxi Zhuangzu,*
  China 22°6N 106°46E **32 G10**
Pingxiang *Jiangxi,*
  China 27°43N 113°48E **33 F11**
Pingyao *China* 37°12N 112°10E **34 F7**
Pingyi *China* 35°30N 117°35E **35 G9**
Pingyin *China* 36°20N 116°25E **34 F8**
Pingyuan *China* 37°10N 116°22E **34 F9**
Pinheiro *Brazil* 2°31S 45°5W **93 D9**
Pinheiro Machado
  Brazil 31°34S 53°23W **95 C5**
Pinhel *Portugal* 40°50N 7°1W **21 B2**
Pini *Indonesia* 0°10N 98°40E **36 D1**
Pinios → *Greece* 39°55N 22°41E **23 E10**
Pinjarra *Australia* 32°37S 115°52E **61 F2**
Pink Mountain *Canada* 57°3N 122°52W **70 B4**
Pinnacle Is. = Senkaku-Shotō
  E. China Sea 25°45N 123°30E **31 M1**
Pinnacles △ *U.S.A.* 36°25N 121°12W **78 J5**
Pinnaroo *Australia* 35°17S 140°53E **63 F3**
Pinon Hills *U.S.A.* 34°26N 117°39W **79 L9**
Pinos *Mexico* 22°18N 101°34W **86 C4**
Pinos, Mt. *U.S.A.* 34°49N 119°8W **79 L7**
Pinos Pt. *U.S.A.* 36°38N 121°57W **77 H3**
Pinrang *Indonesia* 3°46S 119°41E **37 E5**
Pins, Pte. aux *Canada* 42°15N 81°51W **82 D3**
Pinsk *Belarus* 52°10N 26°1E **17 B14**
Pintados *Chile* 20°35S 69°40W **92 H5**
Pinyug *Russia* 60°5N 48°0E **18 B8**
Pioche *U.S.A.* 37°56N 114°27W **77 H6**
Piombino *Italy* 42°55N 10°32E **22 C4**
Pioner, Ostrov *Russia* 79°50N 92°0E **29 B10**
Piopiotaki = Milford Sd.
  N.Z. 44°41S 167°47E **59 F1**
Piorini, L. *Brazil* 3°15S 62°35W **92 D6**
Piotrków Trybunalski
  Poland 51°23N 19°43E **17 C10**
Pip *Iran* 26°45N 60°10E **45 E9**
Pipar *India* 26°25N 73°31E **42 F5**
Pipar Road *India* 26°27N 73°27E **42 F5**
Piparia *Mad. P., India* 22°45N 78°23E **42 H8**

Piparia *Mad. P., India* 21°49N 77°37E 42 J7
Pipestone *U.S.A.* 44°0N 96°19W 80 D5
Pipestone → *Canada* 52°53N 89°23W 72 B2
Pipestone Cr. →
  Canada 49°38N 100°15W 71 D8
Piplan *Pakistan* 32°17N 71°21E 42 C4
Piploda *India* 23°37N 74°56E 42 H6
Pipmuacan, Rés. *Canada* 49°45N 70°30W 73 C5
Pippingarra *Australia* 20°27S 118°42E 60 D2
Piqua *U.S.A.* 40°9N 84°15W 81 E11
Piquiri → *Brazil* 24°3S 54°14W 95 A5
Pir Panjal Range *India* 32°30N 76°50E 42 C7
Pir Sohráb *Iran* 25°44N 60°54E 45 E9
Piracaciba *Brazil* 22°45S 47°40W 95 A6
Piracuruca *Brazil* 3°50S 41°50W 93 D10
Pirae *Tahiti* 17°31S 149°32W 59 d
Piræus = Pireas *Greece* 37°57N 23°42E 23 F10
Piraiévs = Pireas *Greece* 37°57N 23°42E 23 F10
Pirajuí *Brazil* 21°59S 49°29W 95 A6
Piram I. *India* 21°36N 72°21E 42 J5
Pirané *Argentina* 25°42S 59°6W 94 B4
Piranshahr *Iran* 36°41N 45°8E 44 B5
Pirapora *Brazil* 17°20S 44°56W 93 G10
Pirawa *India* 24°10N 76°2E 42 G7
Pireas *Greece* 37°57N 23°42E 23 F10
Pirgos *Greece* 37°40N 21°27E 23 F9
Piribebuy *Paraguay* 25°26S 57°2W 94 B4
Pirimapun *Indonesia* 6°20S 138°24E 37 F9
Pirin Planina *Bulgaria* 41°40N 23°30E 23 D10
Pirineos = Pyrénées
  Europe 42°45N 0°18E 20 E4
Piripiri *Brazil* 4°15S 41°46W 93 D10
Pirlangimpi *Australia* 11°24S 130°26E 60 B5
Pirmasens *Germany* 49°12N 7°36E 16 D4
Pirot *Serbia* 43°9N 22°33E 23 C10
Piru *Indonesia* 3°4S 128°12E 37 E7
Piru *U.S.A.* 34°25N 118°48W 79 L8
Pisa *Italy* 43°43N 10°23E 22 C4
Pisagua *Chile* 19°40S 70°15W 92 G4
Pisco *Peru* 13°50S 76°12W 92 F3
Písek *Czech Rep.* 49°19N 14°10E 16 D8
Pishan *China* 37°30N 78°33E 32 D4
Píshín *Iran* 26°6N 61°47E 45 E9
Pishin *Pakistan* 30°35N 67°0E 42 D2
Pishin Lora → *Pakistan* 29°9N 64°5E 42 E1
Pising *Indonesia* 5°8S 121°53E 37 F6
Pismo Beach *U.S.A.* 35°9N 120°38W 79 K6
Pissis, Cerro *Argentina* 27°45S 68°48W 94 B2
Pissouri *Cyprus* 34°40N 32°42E 25 E11
Pistóia *Italy* 43°55N 10°54E 22 C4
Pistol B. *Canada* 62°25N 92°37W 71 A10
Pisuerga → *Spain* 41°33N 4°52W 21 B3
Pit → *U.S.A.* 40°47N 122°6W 76 F2
Pitarpunga L. *Australia* 34°24S 143°30E 63 E3
Pitcairn I. *Pac. Oc.* 25°5S 130°5W 65 K14
Pitch L. *Trin. & Tob.* 10°12N 61°39W 93 K15
Piteå *Sweden* 65°20N 21°25E 8 D19
Piteälven → *Sweden* 65°20N 21°25E 8 D19
Pitești *Romania* 44°52N 24°54E 17 F13
Pithapuram *India* 17°10N 82°15E 41 L13
Pithara *Australia* 30°20S 116°35E 61 F2
Pithoragarh *India* 29°35N 80°13E 43 E9
Pithoro *Pakistan* 25°31N 69°23E 42 G3
Pitlochry *U.K.* 56°42N 3°44W 11 E5
Pitsilia *Cyprus* 34°55N 33°0E 25 E12
Pitt I. *Canada* 53°30N 129°50W 70 C3
Pittsburg *Calif., U.S.A.* 38°2N 121°53W 78 G5
Pittsburg *Kans., U.S.A.* 37°25N 94°42W 80 G6
Pittsburg *Tex., U.S.A.* 33°0N 94°59W 84 E7
Pittsburgh *U.S.A.* 40°26N 79°58W 82 F5
Pittsfield *Ill., U.S.A.* 39°36N 90°49W 80 F8
Pittsfield *Maine, U.S.A.* 44°47N 69°23W 81 C19
Pittsfield *Mass., U.S.A.* 42°27N 73°15W 83 D11
Pittsfield *N.H., U.S.A.* 43°18N 71°20W 83 C13
Pittston *U.S.A.* 41°19N 75°47W 83 E9
Pittsworth *Australia* 27°41S 151°37E 63 D5
Pituri → *Australia* 22°35S 138°30E 62 C2
Piura *Peru* 5°15S 80°38W 92 E2
Pixley *U.S.A.* 35°58N 119°18W 78 K7
Pizhou = Pei Xian
  China 34°44N 116°55E 34 G9
Pizhou *China* 34°18N 117°57E 35 G9
Placentia *Canada* 47°20N 54°0W 73 C9
Placentia B. *Canada* 47°0N 54°40W 73 C9
Placerville *U.S.A.* 38°44N 120°48W 78 G6
Placetas *Cuba* 22°15N 79°44W 88 B4
Plaine des Jarres *Laos* 19°27N 103°10E 38 C4
Plainfield *N.J., U.S.A.* 40°37N 74°25W 83 F10
Plainfield *Ohio, U.S.A.* 40°13N 81°43W 82 F3
Plainfield *Vt., U.S.A.* 44°17N 72°26W 83 B12
Plains *Mont., U.S.A.* 47°28N 114°53W 76 C6
Plains *Tex., U.S.A.* 33°11N 102°50W 84 E3
Plainview *Nebr., U.S.A.* 42°21N 97°47W 80 D5
Plainview *Tex., U.S.A.* 34°11N 101°43W 84 D4
Plainwell *U.S.A.* 42°27N 85°38W 81 D11
Plaistow *U.S.A.* 42°50N 71°6W 83 D13
Plaka, Ákra *Greece* 35°11N 26°19E 25 D8
Plana Cays *Bahamas* 22°38N 73°30W 89 B5
Planada *U.S.A.* 37°16N 120°19W 78 H6
Plano *U.S.A.* 33°1N 96°42W 84 E6
Plant City *U.S.A.* 28°1N 82°7W 85 G13
Plaquemine *U.S.A.* 30°17N 91°14W 84 F9
Plasencia *Spain* 40°3N 6°8W 21 B2
Plaster City *U.S.A.* 32°47N 115°51W 79 N11
Plaster Rock *Canada* 46°53N 67°22W 73 C6
Plastun *Russia* 44°45N 136°19E 30 B8
Plata, Río de la →
  S. Amer. 34°45S 57°30W 94 C4
Plátani → *Italy* 37°23N 13°16E 22 F5
Plátanos *Greece* 35°28N 23°33E 25 D5
Platte *U.S.A.* 43°23N 98°51W 80 D4
Platte → *Mo., U.S.A.* 39°16N 94°50W 80 F6
Platte → *Nebr., U.S.A.* 41°4N 95°53W 80 E6
Platteville *U.S.A.* 42°44N 90°29W 80 D9
Plattsburgh *U.S.A.* 44°42N 73°28W 83 B11
Plattsmouth *U.S.A.* 41°1N 95°53W 80 E6
Plauen *Germany* 50°30N 12°8E 16 C7
Plavinas *Latvia* 56°35N 25°46E 9 H21
Playa Blanca *Canary Is.* 28°55N 13°37W 24 F6
Playa Blanca Sur
  Canary Is. 28°51N 13°50W 24 F6

Playa de las Americas
  Canary Is. 28°5N 16°43W 24 F3
Playa de Mogán
  Canary Is. 27°48N 15°47W 24 G4
Playa del Carmen *Mexico* 20°37N 87°4W 87 C7
Playa del Inglés
  Canary Is. 27°45N 15°33W 24 G4
Playa Esmerelda
  Canary Is. 28°8N 14°16W 24 F5
Playgreen L. *Canada* 54°0N 98°15W 71 C9
Pleasant Bay *Canada* 46°51N 60°48W 73 C7
Pleasant Hill *U.S.A.* 37°57N 122°4W 78 H4
Pleasant Mount *U.S.A.* 41°44N 75°26W 83 E9
Pleasanton *Calif.,*
  U.S.A. 37°39N 121°52W 78 H5
Pleasanton *Tex., U.S.A.* 28°58N 98°29W 84 G5
Pleasantville *N.J.,*
  U.S.A. 39°24N 74°32W 81 F16
Pleasantville *Pa., U.S.A.* 41°35N 79°34W 82 E5
Plei Ku *Vietnam* 13°57N 108°0E 38 F7
Plenty → *Australia* 23°25S 136°31E 62 C2
Plenty, B. of *N.Z.* 37°45S 177°0E 59 B6
Plentywood *U.S.A.* 48°47N 104°34W 76 B11
Plesetsk *Russia* 62°43N 40°20E 18 B7
Plessisville *Canada* 46°14N 71°47W 73 C5
Plétipi, L. *Canada* 51°44N 70°6W 73 B5
Pleven *Bulgaria* 43°26N 24°37E 23 C11
Plevlja *Montenegro* 43°21N 19°21E 23 C8
Plevna *Canada* 44°58N 76°59W 82 B8
Płock *Poland* 52°32N 19°40E 17 B10
Plöckenstein *Germany* 48°46N 13°51E 16 D7
Ploieşti *Romania* 44°57N 26°5E 17 F14
Plonge, Lac la *Canada* 55°8N 107°20W 71 B7
Plovdiv *Bulgaria* 42°8N 24°44E 23 C11
Plover Cove Res. *China* 22°28N 114°15E 33 a
Plum *U.S.A.* 40°29N 79°47W 82 F5
Plum I. *U.S.A.* 41°11N 72°12W 83 E12
Plumas *U.S.A.* 39°45N 120°4W 78 F6
Plummer *U.S.A.* 47°20N 116°53W 76 C5
Plumridge Lakes
  Australia 29°26S 125°16E 61 E4
Plumtree *Zimbabwe* 20°27S 27°55E 55 G2
Plungė *Lithuania* 55°53N 21°59E 9 J19
Plymouth *Trin. & Tob.* 11°14N 60°48W 93 J16
Plymouth *U.K.* 50°22N 4°10W 13 G3
Plymouth *Calif., U.S.A.* 38°29N 120°51W 78 G6
Plymouth *Ind., U.S.A.* 41°21N 86°19W 80 E10
Plymouth *Mass., U.S.A.* 41°57N 70°40W 83 E14
Plymouth *N.C., U.S.A.* 35°52N 76°43W 85 D16
Plymouth *N.H., U.S.A.* 43°46N 71°41W 83 C13
Plymouth *Pa., U.S.A.* 41°14N 75°57W 83 E9
Plymouth *Wis., U.S.A.* 43°45N 87°59W 80 D10
Plympton-Wyoming = Wyoming
  Canada 42°57N 82°7W 82 D2
Plynlimon = Pumlumon Fawr
  U.K. 52°28N 3°46W 13 E4
Plyusa *Russia* 58°28N 29°27E 9 G23
Plzeň *Czech Rep.* 49°45N 13°22E 16 D7
Pmere Nyente ◎
  Australia 24°15S 136°10E 62 C2
Po → *Italy* 44°57N 12°4E 22 B5
Po Hai = Bo Hai *China* 39°0N 119°0E 35 E10
Po Toi *China* 22°10N 114°16E 33 a
Pobeda *Russia* 65°12N 146°12E 29 C15
Pobedy, Pik *Kyrgyzstan* 42°0N 79°58E 32 C4
Pocahontas *Ark., U.S.A.* 36°16N 90°58W 85 C9
Pocahontas *Iowa, U.S.A.* 42°44N 94°40W 80 D6
Pocatello *U.S.A.* 42°52N 112°27W 76 E7
Pocomoke City *U.S.A.* 38°5N 75°34W 81 F16
Poços de Caldas *Brazil* 21°50S 46°33W 95 A6
Podgorica *Montenegro* 42°30N 19°19E 23 C8
Podilska Vysochyna
  Ukraine 49°0N 28°0E 17 D14
Podolsk *Russia* 55°25N 37°30E 18 C6
Podporozhye *Russia* 60°55N 34°2E 18 B5
Pofadder *S. Africa* 29°10S 19°22E 56 D2
Pogranichnyy *Russia* 44°25N 131°24E 30 B5
Poh *Indonesia* 0°46S 122°51E 37 E6
Pohang *S. Korea* 36°1N 129°23E 35 F15
Pohjanmaa *Finland* 62°58N 22°50E 8 E20
Pohnpei *Micronesia* 6°55S 158°10E 64 G7
Pohri *India* 25°32N 77°22E 42 G6
Poinsett, C. *Antarctica* 65°42S 113°18E 5 C8
Point Arena *U.S.A.* 38°55N 123°41W 78 G3
Point Baker *U.S.A.* 56°21N 133°37W 70 B2
Point Fortin
  Trin. & Tob. 10°10N 61°42W 93 K15
Point Hope *U.S.A.* 68°21N 166°47W 74 B6
Point L. *Canada* 65°15N 113°4W 68 D9
Point Lisas *Trin. & Tob.* 10°24N 61°29W 93 K15
Point Pedro *Sri Lanka* 9°50N 80°15E 40 Q12
Point Pelee △ *Canada* 41°57N 82°31W 82 E2
Point Pleasant *N.J.,*
  U.S.A. 40°5N 74°4W 83 F10
Point Pleasant *W. Va.,*
  U.S.A. 38°51N 82°8W 81 F12
Point Reyes △ *U.S.A.* 38°10N 122°55W 78 G2
Pointe-à-Pitre *Guadeloupe* 16°10N 61°32W 88 b
Pointe-au-Pic = La Malbaie
  Canada 47°40N 70°10W 73 C5
Pointe-Claire *Canada* 45°26N 73°50W 83 A11
Pointe-Gatineau *Canada* 45°27N 75°41W 83 A9
Pointe-Noire *Congo* 4°48S 11°53E 52 E2
Pointe-Noire *Guadeloupe* 16°14N 61°47W 88 b
Poipet *Cambodia* 13°39N 102°33E 38 F4
Poisonbush Ra.
  Australia 22°30S 121°30E 60 D3
Poissonnier Pt.
  Australia 19°57S 119°10E 60 C2
Poitiers *France* 46°35N 0°20E 20 C4
Poitou *France* 46°40N 0°10W 20 C3
Pojoaque *U.S.A.* 35°54N 106°1W 77 J10
Pokaran *India* 27°0N 71°50E 42 F4
Pokataroo *Australia* 29°30S 148°36E 63 D4
Pokhara *Nepal* 28°14N 83°58E 43 E10
Poko *Dem. Rep. of the Congo* 3°7N 26°52E 54 B2
Pokrovsk *Russia* 61°29N 129°0E 29 C13
Pola = Pula *Croatia* 44°54N 13°57E 16 F7
Polacca *U.S.A.* 35°50N 110°23W 77 J8
Polan *Iran* 25°30N 61°10E 45 E9
Poland ■ *Europe* 52°0N 20°0E 17 C10

Poland *U.S.A.* 43°13N 75°3W 83 C9
Polar Bear △ *Canada* 55°0N 83°45W 72 A2
Polatsk *Belarus* 55°30N 28°50E 9 J23
Polcura *Chile* 37°17S 71°43W 94 D1
Polesye = Pripet Marshes
  Europe 52°10N 27°10E 17 B15
Polevskoy *Russia* 56°26N 60°11E 18 C11
Police *Poland* 53°33N 14°33E 16 B8
Police, Pte. *Seychelles* 4°51S 55°32E 53 b
Poligiros *Greece* 40°23N 23°25E 23 D10
Polillo Is. *Phil.* 14°56N 122°0E 37 B6
Polis *Cyprus* 35°2N 32°26E 25 D11
Polk *U.S.A.* 41°22N 79°56W 82 E5
Pollachi *India* 10°35N 77°0E 40 P10
Pollença *Spain* 39°54N 3°1E 24 B10
Pollença, B. de *Spain* 39°53N 3°8E 24 B10
Polnovat *Russia* 63°50N 65°54E 28 C7
Polokwane *S. Africa* 23°54S 29°25E 57 C4
Polokwane → *S. Africa* 22°25S 30°5E 57 C5
Polonne *Ukraine* 50°6N 27°30E 17 C14
Polonnoye = Polonne
  Ukraine 50°6N 27°30E 17 C14
Polson *U.S.A.* 47°41N 114°9W 76 C6
Poltava *Ukraine* 49°35N 34°35E 19 E5
Põltsamaa *Estonia* 58°39N 25°58E 9 G21
Polunochnoye *Russia* 60°52N 60°25E 28 C7
Põlva *Estonia* 58°3N 27°3E 9 G22
Polyarny *Russia* 69°8N 33°20E 8 B25
Polyarnyye Zori *Russia* 67°22N 32°30E 8 C25
Polynesia *Pac. Oc.* 10°0S 162°0W 65 F11
Polynésie française = French
  Polynesia ☑ *Pac. Oc.* 20°0S 145°0W 65 J13
Pombal *Portugal* 39°55N 8°40W 21 C1
Pombia *Greece* 35°0N 24°51E 25 D6
Pomene *Mozam.* 22°53S 35°33E 57 C6
Pomeroy *Ohio, U.S.A.* 39°2N 82°2W 81 F12
Pomeroy *Wash., U.S.A.* 46°28N 117°36W 76 C5
Pomézia *Italy* 41°40N 12°30E 22 D5
Pomona *Australia* 26°22S 152°52E 63 D5
Pomona *U.S.A.* 34°4N 117°45W 79 L9
Pomorskie, Pojezierze
  Poland 53°40N 16°37E 17 B9
Pomos *Cyprus* 35°9N 32°33E 25 D11
Pomos, C. *Cyprus* 35°10N 32°33E 25 D11
Pompano Beach *U.S.A.* 26°14N 80°7W 85 H14
Pompeys Pillar *U.S.A.* 45°59N 107°57W 76 D10
Pompeys Pillar △
  U.S.A. 46°0N 108°0W 76 D10
Pompton Lakes *U.S.A.* 41°0N 74°17W 83 F10
Ponape = Pohnpei
  Micronesia 6°55S 158°10E 64 G7
Ponask L. *Canada* 54°0N 92°41W 72 B1
Ponca *U.S.A.* 42°34N 96°43W 80 D5
Ponca City *U.S.A.* 36°42N 97°5W 84 C6
Ponce *Puerto Rico* 18°1N 66°37W 89 d
Ponchatoula *U.S.A.* 30°26N 90°26W 85 F9
Poncheville, L. *Canada* 50°10N 76°55W 72 B4
Pond *U.S.A.* 35°43N 119°20W 79 K7
Pond Inlet *Canada* 72°40N 77°0W 69 C16
Pondicherry = Puducherry
  India 11°59N 79°50E 40 P11
Ponds, I. of *Canada* 53°27N 55°52W 73 B8
Ponferrada *Spain* 42°32N 6°35W 21 A2
Ponnani *India* 10°45N 75°59E 40 P9
Ponoka *Canada* 52°42N 113°40W 70 C6
Ponorogo *Indonesia* 7°52S 111°27E 37 G14
Ponoy *Russia* 67°0N 41°13E 18 A7
Ponoy → *Russia* 66°59N 41°17E 18 A7
Ponta Delgada *Azores* 37°44N 25°40W 50 a
Ponta do Sol *Madeira* 32°42N 17°7W 24 D2
Ponta Grossa *Brazil* 25°7S 50°10W 95 B5
Ponta Porã *Brazil* 22°20S 55°35W 95 A4
Pontarlier *France* 46°54N 6°20E 20 C7
Pontchartrain, L. *U.S.A.* 30°5N 90°5W 85 F9
Ponte do Pungué
  Mozam. 19°30S 34°33E 55 F3
Ponte Nova *Brazil* 20°25S 42°54W 95 A7
Ponteix *Canada* 49°46N 107°29W 71 D7
Pontevedra *Spain* 42°26N 8°40W 21 A1
Pontiac *Ill., U.S.A.* 40°53N 88°38W 80 E9
Pontiac *Mich., U.S.A.* 42°38N 83°18W 81 D12
Pontian Kechil *Malaysia* 1°29N 103°23E 39 d
Pontianak *Indonesia* 0°3S 109°15E 36 E3
Pontine Is. = Ponziane, Ísole
  Italy 40°55N 12°57E 22 D5
Pontine Mts. = Kuzey Anadolu
  Dağları *Turkey* 41°0N 36°45E 19 F6
Pontivy *France* 48°5N 2°58W 20 B2
Pontoise *France* 49°3N 2°5E 20 B5
Ponton → *Canada* 58°27N 116°11W 70 B5
Pontypool *Canada* 44°6N 78°38W 82 B6
Pontypool *U.K.* 51°42N 3°2W 13 F4
Ponziane, Ísole *Italy* 40°55N 12°57E 22 D5
Poochera *Australia* 32°43S 134°51E 63 E1
Poole *U.K.* 50°43N 1°59W 13 G6
Poole □ *U.K.* 50°43N 1°59W 13 G6
Poona = Pune *India* 18°29N 73°57E 40 K8
Pooncarie *Australia* 33°22S 142°31E 63 E3
Poopelloe L. *Australia* 31°40S 144°0E 63 E3
Poopó, L. de *Bolivia* 18°30S 67°35W 92 G5
Popayán *Colombia* 2°27N 76°36W 92 C3
Poperinge *Belgium* 50°51N 2°42E 15 D2
Popiltah L. *Australia* 33°10S 141°42E 63 E3
Popio L. *Australia* 33°10S 141°52E 63 E3
Poplar *U.S.A.* 48°7N 105°12W 76 B11
Poplar → *Canada* 53°0N 97°19W 71 C9
Poplar Bluff *U.S.A.* 36°46N 90°24W 80 G8
Poplarville *U.S.A.* 30°51N 89°32W 85 F10
Popocatépetl, Volcán
  Mexico 19°2N 98°38W 87 D5
Popokabaka
  Dem. Rep. of the Congo 5°41S 16°40E 52 F3
Poprad *Slovak Rep.* 49°3N 20°18E 17 D11
Porali → *Pakistan* 25°58N 66°26E 42 G2
Porbandar *India* 21°44N 69°43E 42 J3
Porcher I. *Canada* 53°50N 130°30W 70 C2
Porcupine → *Canada* 59°11N 104°46W 71 B8
Porcupine → *U.S.A.* 66°34N 145°19W 68 D2
Porcupine Gorge △
  Australia 20°22S 144°26E 62 C3
Pordenone *Italy* 45°57N 12°39E 22 B5

Pori *Finland* 61°29N 21°48E 8 F19
Porkhov *Russia* 57°45N 29°38E 9 H23
Porlamar *Venezuela* 10°57N 63°51W 92 A6
Pormpuraaw *Australia* 14°59S 141°26E 62 A3
Pormpuraaw ◎
  Australia 14°55S 141°47E 62 A3
Poronaysk *Russia* 49°13N 143°0E 33 B17
Poroshiri-Dake *Japan* 42°41N 142°52E 30 C11
Poroto Mts. *Tanzania* 9°0S 33°30E 55 D3
Porpoise B. *Antarctica* 66°0S 127°0E 5 C9
Porreres *Spain* 39°31N 3°2E 24 B10
Porsangerfjorden
  Norway 70°40N 25°40E 8 A21
Porsgrunn *Norway* 59°10N 9°40E 9 G13
Port Alberni *Canada* 49°14N 124°50W 70 D4
Port Alfred *S. Africa* 33°36S 26°55E 56 E4
Port Alice *Canada* 50°20N 127°25W 70 C3
Port Allegany *U.S.A.* 41°48N 78°17W 82 E6
Port Allen *U.S.A.* 30°27N 91°12W 84 F9
Port Alma *Australia* 23°38S 150°53E 62 C5
Port Alma *Canada* 42°10N 82°14W 82 D2
Port Angeles *U.S.A.* 48°7N 123°27W 78 B3
Port Antonio *Jamaica* 18°10N 76°26W 88 a
Port Aransas *U.S.A.* 27°50N 97°4W 84 H6
Port Arthur *Australia* 43°7S 147°50E 63 G4
Port Arthur *U.S.A.* 29°54N 93°56W 84 H8
Port au Choix *Canada* 50°43N 57°22W 73 B8
Port au Port B. *Canada* 48°40N 58°50W 73 C8
Port-au-Prince *Haiti* 18°40N 72°20W 89 C5
Port Augusta *Australia* 32°30S 137°50E 63 E2
Port Austin *U.S.A.* 44°3N 83°1W 82 B2
Port Bell *Uganda* 0°18N 32°35E 54 B3
Port Bergé Vaovao
  Madag. 15°33S 47°40E 57 B8
Port Blandford *Canada* 48°20N 54°10W 73 C9
Port Bradshaw
  Australia 12°30S 137°20E 62 A2
Port Broughton
  Australia 33°37S 137°56E 63 E2
Port Bruce *Canada* 42°39N 81°0W 82 D3
Port Burwell *Canada* 42°40N 80°48W 82 D4
Port Canning *India* 22°23N 88°40E 43 H13
Port Carling *Canada* 45°7N 79°35W 82 A5
Port-Cartier *Canada* 50°2N 66°50W 73 B6
Port Chalmers *N.Z.* 45°49S 170°30E 59 F3
Port Charlotte *U.S.A.* 26°59N 82°6W 85 H13
Port Clements *Canada* 53°40N 132°10W 70 C2
Port Clinton *U.S.A.* 41°31N 82°56W 81 E12
Port Colborne *Canada* 42°50N 79°10W 82 D5
Port Coquitlam *Canada* 49°15N 122°45W 78 A4
Port Credit *Canada* 43°33N 79°35W 82 C5
Port Curtis *Australia* 23°57S 151°20E 62 C5
Port d'Alcúdia *Spain* 39°50N 3°7E 24 B10
Port Dalhousie *Canada* 43°13N 79°16W 82 C5
Port d'Andratx *Spain* 39°32N 2°23E 24 B9
Port Darwin *Australia* 12°24S 130°45E 60 B5
Port Darwin *Falk. Is.* 51°50S 59°0W 96 G5
Port Davey *Australia* 43°16S 145°55E 63 G4
Port-de-Paix *Haiti* 19°50N 72°50W 89 C5
Port de Pollença *Spain* 39°54N 3°4E 24 B10
Port de Sóller *Spain* 39°48N 2°42E 24 B9
Port Dickson *Malaysia* 2°30N 101°49E 39 L3
Port Douglas *Australia* 16°30S 145°30E 62 B4
Port Dover *Canada* 42°47N 80°12W 82 D4
Port Edward *Canada* 54°12N 130°10W 70 C2
Port Elgin *Canada* 44°25N 81°25W 82 B3
Port Elizabeth *S. Africa* 33°58S 25°40E 56 E4
Port Ellen *U.K.* 55°38N 6°11W 11 F2
Port Erin *I. of Man* 54°5N 4°45W 12 C3
Port Essington *Australia* 11°15S 132°10E 60 B5
Port Ewen *U.S.A.* 41°54N 73°59W 83 E11
Port Fairy *Australia* 38°22S 142°12E 63 F3
Port Gamble *U.S.A.* 47°51N 122°34W 78 C4
Port-Gentil *Gabon* 0°40S 8°50E 52 E1
Port Germein *Australia* 33°1S 138°1E 63 E2
Port Ghalib *Egypt* 25°20N 34°50E 44 E2
Port Gibson *U.S.A.* 31°58N 90°59W 84 F9
Port Glasgow *U.K.* 55°56N 4°41W 11 F4
Port Harcourt *Nigeria* 4°40N 7°10E 50 H7
Port Hardy *Canada* 50°41N 127°30W 70 C3
Port Harrison = Inukjuak
  Canada 58°25N 78°15W 69 F16
Port Hawkesbury
  Canada 45°36N 61°22W 73 C7
Port Hedland *Australia* 20°25S 118°35E 60 D2
Port Henry *U.S.A.* 44°3N 73°28W 83 B11
Port Hood *Canada* 46°0N 61°32W 73 C7
Port Hope *Canada* 43°56N 78°20W 82 C6
Port Hope *U.S.A.* 43°56N 82°43W 82 C2
Port Hope Simpson
  Canada 52°33N 56°18W 73 B8
Port Hueneme *U.S.A.* 34°7N 119°12W 79 L7
Port Huron *U.S.A.* 42°58N 82°26W 82 D2
Port Jefferson *U.S.A.* 40°57N 73°3W 83 F11
Port Jervis *U.S.A.* 41°22N 74°41W 83 E10
Port Kenny *Australia* 33°10S 134°41E 63 E1
Port Lairge = Waterford
  Ireland 52°15N 7°8W 10 D4
Port Laoise *Ireland* 53°2N 7°18W 10 C4
Port Lavaca *U.S.A.* 28°37N 96°38W 84 G6
Port Leyden *U.S.A.* 43°35N 75°21W 83 C9
Port Lincoln *Australia* 34°42S 135°52E 63 E2
Port Loko *S. Leone* 8°48N 12°46W 50 G3
Port-Louis *Guadeloupe* 16°28N 61°32W 88 b
Port Louis *Mauritius* 20°10S 57°30E 53 d
Port MacDonnell
  Australia 38°5S 140°48E 63 F3
Port McNeill *Canada* 50°35N 127°6W 70 C3
Port Macquarie
  Australia 31°25S 152°25E 63 E5
Port Maria *Jamaica* 18°22N 76°54W 88 a
Port Matilda *U.S.A.* 40°48N 78°3W 82 F6
Port McNicoll *Canada* 44°44N 79°48W 82 B5
Port Mellon *Canada* 49°32N 123°31W 70 D4
Port-Menier *Canada* 49°51N 64°15W 73 C7
Port Moody *Canada* 49°17N 122°51W 78 A4
Port Morant *Jamaica* 17°54N 76°19W 88 a
Port Moresby *Papua N. G.* 9°24S 147°8E 58 B7
Port Musgrave
  Australia 11°55S 141°50E 62 A3

Port Neches *U.S.A.* 30°0N 93°59W 84 G8
Port Nolloth *S. Africa* 29°17S 16°52E 56 D2
Port Nouveau-Québec =
  Kangiqsualujjuaq
  Canada 58°30N 65°59W 69 F18
Port of Climax *Canada* 49°10N 108°20W 71 D7
Port of Coronach
  Canada 49°7N 105°31W 71 D7
Port of Spain
  Trin. & Tob. 10°40N 61°31W 93 K15
Port Orange *U.S.A.* 29°9N 80°59W 85 G14
Port Orchard *U.S.A.* 47°32N 122°38W 78 C4
Port Orford *U.S.A.* 42°45N 124°30W 76 E1
Port Pegasus *N.Z.* 47°12S 167°41E 59 G1
Port Perry *Canada* 44°6N 78°56W 82 B6
Port Phillip B. *Australia* 38°10S 144°50E 63 F3
Port Pirie *Australia* 33°10S 138°1E 63 E2
Port Renfrew *Canada* 48°30N 124°20W 78 B2
Port Roper *Australia* 14°45S 135°25E 62 A2
Port Rowan *Canada* 42°40N 80°30W 82 D4
Port Safaga = Bûr Safâga
  Egypt 26°43N 33°57E 44 E2
Port Said = Bûr Sa'îd
  Egypt 31°16N 32°18E 51 B12
Port St. Joe *U.S.A.* 29°49N 85°18W 85 G12
Port St. Johns = Umzimvubu
  S. Africa 31°38S 29°33E 57 E4
Port St. Lucie *U.S.A.* 27°18N 80°21W 85 H14
Port Sanilac *U.S.A.* 43°26N 82°33W 82 C2
Port Severn *Canada* 44°48N 79°43W 82 B5
Port Shepstone *S. Africa* 30°44S 30°28E 57 E5
Port Simpson *Canada* 54°30N 130°20W 70 C2
Port Stanley = Stanley
  Falk. Is. 51°40S 59°51W 96 G5
Port Stanley *Canada* 42°40N 81°10W 82 D3
Port Sudan = Bûr Sûdân
  Sudan 19°32N 37°9E 51 E13
Port Sulphur *U.S.A.* 29°29N 89°42W 85 G10
Port Talbot *U.K.* 51°35N 3°47W 13 F4
Port Townsend *U.S.A.* 48°7N 122°45W 78 B4
Port-Vendres *France* 42°32N 3°8E 20 E5
Port Vila *Vanuatu* 17°45S 168°18E 58 C9
Port Vladimir *Russia* 69°25N 33°6E 8 B25
Port Wakefield *Australia* 34°12S 138°10E 63 E2
Port Washington
  U.S.A. 43°23N 87°53W 80 D10
Porta Orientalis *Romania* 45°6N 22°18E 17 F12
Portacloy *Ireland* 54°20N 9°46W 10 B2
Portadown *U.K.* 54°25N 6°27W 10 B5
Portaferry *U.K.* 54°23N 5°33W 10 B6
Portage *Pa., U.S.A.* 40°23N 78°41W 82 F6
Portage *Wis., U.S.A.* 43°33N 89°28W 80 D9
Portage la Prairie
  Canada 49°58N 98°18W 71 D9
Portageville *U.S.A.* 36°26N 89°42W 80 G9
Portalegre *Portugal* 39°19N 7°25W 21 C2
Portales *U.S.A.* 34°11N 103°20W 77 J12
Portarlington *Ireland* 53°9N 7°14W 10 C4
Portbou *Spain* 42°25N 3°9E 21 A7
Porter L. *N.W.T., Canada* 61°41N 108°5W 71 A7
Porter L. *Sask., Canada* 56°20N 107°20W 71 B7
Porterville *S. Africa* 33°0S 19°0E 56 E2
Porterville *U.S.A.* 36°4N 119°1W 78 J8
Porthcawl *U.K.* 51°29N 3°42W 13 F4
Porthill *U.S.A.* 48°59N 116°30W 76 B5
Porthmadog *U.K.* 52°55N 4°8E 12 E3
Portile de Fier *Europe* 44°44N 22°30E 17 F12
Portimão *Portugal* 37°8N 8°32W 21 D1
Portishead *U.K.* 51°29N 2°46W 13 F5
Portknockie *U.K.* 57°42N 2°51W 11 D6
Portland *N.S.W.,*
  Australia 33°20S 150°0E 63 E5
Portland *Vic., Australia* 38°20S 141°35E 63 F3
Portland *Canada* 44°42N 76°12W 83 B8
Portland *Conn., U.S.A.* 41°34N 72°38W 83 E12
Portland *Maine, U.S.A.* 43°39N 70°16W 81 D18
Portland *Mich., U.S.A.* 42°52N 84°54W 81 D11
Portland *Oreg., U.S.A.* 45°32N 122°37W 78 E4
Portland *Pa., U.S.A.* 40°55N 75°6W 83 F9
Portland, I. of *U.K.* 50°33N 2°26W 13 G5
Portland B. *Australia* 38°15S 141°45E 63 F3
Portland Bight *Jamaica* 17°52N 77°5W 88 a
Portland Bill *U.K.* 50°31N 2°28W 13 G5
Portland Canal *U.S.A.* 55°56N 130°0W 70 B2
Portland Int. ✈ (PDX)
  U.S.A. 45°35N 122°36W 78 E4
Portland Pt. *Jamaica* 17°42N 77°11W 88 a
Portmadoc = Porthmadog
  U.K. 52°55N 4°8W 12 E3
Portmore *Jamaica* 17°53N 76°53W 88 a
Porto *France* 42°16N 8°42E 20 E8
Porto *Portugal* 41°8N 8°40W 21 B1
Pôrto Alegre *Brazil* 30°5S 51°10W 95 C5
Porto Colom *Spain* 39°26N 3°15E 24 B10
Porto Cristo *Spain* 39°33N 3°20E 24 B10
Porto de Moz *Brazil* 1°41S 52°13W 93 D8
Porto Empédocle *Italy* 37°17N 13°32E 22 F5
Porto Esperança *Brazil* 19°37S 57°29W 92 G7
Porto Franco *Brazil* 6°20S 47°24W 93 E9
Porto Inglês *C. Verde Is.* 15°2N 23°10W 50 b
Porto Mendes *Brazil* 24°30S 54°15W 95 A5
Porto Moniz *Madeira* 32°52N 17°11W 24 D2
Porto Murtinho *Brazil* 21°45S 57°55W 92 H7
Porto Nacional *Brazil* 10°40S 48°30W 93 F9
Porto-Novo *Benin* 6°23N 2°42E 50 G6
Porto Primavera, Represa
  Brazil 22°10S 52°45W 95 A5
Porto Santo, I. de
  Madeira 33°45N 16°25W 50 B2
Pôrto São José *Brazil* 22°43S 53°10W 95 A5
Porto Seguro *Brazil* 16°26S 39°5W 93 G11
Porto Tórres *Italy* 40°50N 8°24E 22 D3
Porto União *Brazil* 26°10S 51°10W 95 B5
Porto-Vecchio *France* 41°35N 9°16E 20 F8
Pôrto Velho *Brazil* 8°46S 63°54W 92 E6
Porto Walter *Brazil* 8°15S 72°40W 92 E4
Portobelo *Panama* 9°35N 79°42W 88 E4
Portoferráio *Italy* 42°48N 10°20E 22 C4
Portola *U.S.A.* 39°49N 120°28W 78 F6
Portopetro *Spain* 39°22N 3°13E 24 B10

Portoscuso *Italy* 39°12N 8°24E **22** E3
Portoviejo *Ecuador* 1°7S 80°28W **92** D2
Portpatrick *U.K.* 54°51N 5°7W **11** G3
Portree *U.K.* 57°25N 6°12W **11** D2
Portrush *U.K.* 55°12N 6°40W **10** A5
Portsmouth *Dominica* 15°34N 61°27W **89** C7
Portsmouth *U.K.* 50°48N 1°6W **13** G6
Portsmouth *N.H., U.S.A.* 43°5N 70°45W **83** C14
Portsmouth *Ohio,*
U.S.A. 38°44N 82°57W **81** F12
Portsmouth *R.I., U.S.A.* 41°36N 71°15W **83** E13
Portsmouth *Va., U.S.A.* 36°58N 76°23W **81** G15
Portsmouth □ *U.K.* 50°48N 1°6W **13** G6
Portsoy *U.K.* 57°41N 2°41W **11** D6
Portstewart *U.K.* 55°11N 6°43W **10** A5
Porttipahdan tekojärvi
Finland 68°5N 26°40E **8** B22
Portugal ■ *Europe* 40°0N 8°0W **21** C1
Portumna *Ireland* 53°6N 8°14W **10** C3
Portville *U.S.A.* 42°3N 78°20W **82** D6
Poruma *Australia* 10°2S 143°4E **62** a
Porvenir *Chile* 53°10S 70°16W **96** G2
Porvoo *Finland* 60°24N 25°40E **9** F21
Posadas *Argentina* 27°30S 55°50W **95** B4
Posht-e Badam *Iran* 33°2N 55°23E **45** C7
Poso *Indonesia* 1°20S 120°55E **37** E6
Poso, Danau *Indonesia* 1°52S 120°35E **37** E6
Posse *Brazil* 14°4S 46°18W **93** F9
Possession I. *Antarctica* 72°4S 172°0E **5** D11
Possum Kingdom L.
U.S.A. 32°52N 98°26W **84** E5
Post *U.S.A.* 33°12N 101°23W **84** E4
Post Falls *U.S.A.* 47°43N 116°57W **76** C5
Postavy = Pastavy
Belarus 55°4N 26°50E **9** J22
Poste-de-la-Baleine =
Kuujjuarapik *Canada* 55°20N 77°35W **72** A4
Postmasburg *S. Africa* 28°18S 23°5E **56** D3
Postojna *Slovenia* 45°46N 14°12E **16** F8
Poston *U.S.A.* 34°0N 114°24W **79** M12
Postville *Canada* 54°54N 59°47W **73** B8
Posyet *Russia* 42°39N 130°48E **30** C5
Potchefstroom *S. Africa* 26°41S 27°7E **56** D4
Poteau *U.S.A.* 35°3N 94°37W **84** D7
Poteet *U.S.A.* 29°2N 98°35W **84** G5
Potenza *Italy* 40°38N 15°48E **22** D6
Poteriteri, L. *N.Z.* 46°5S 167°10E **59** G1
Potgietersrus = Mokopane
S. Africa 24°10S 28°55E **57** C4
Poti *Georgia* 42°10N 41°38E **19** F7
Potiskum *Nigeria* 11°39N 11°2E **51** F8
Potomac → *U.S.A.* 38°0N 76°23W **81** F14
Potosí *Bolivia* 19°38S 65°50W **92** G5
Potosi Mt. *U.S.A.* 35°57N 115°29W **79** K11
Pototan *Phil.* 10°54N 122°38E **37** B6
Potrerillos *Chile* 26°30S 69°30W **94** B2
Potsdam *Germany* 52°23N 13°3E **16** B7
Potsdam *U.S.A.* 44°40N 74°59W **83** B10
Pottersville *U.S.A.* 43°43N 73°50W **83** C11
Pottstown *U.S.A.* 40°15N 75°39W **83** F9
Pottsville *U.S.A.* 40°41N 76°12W **83** F8
Pottuvil *Sri Lanka* 6°55N 81°50E **40** R12
Pouce Coupé *Canada* 55°40N 120°10W **70** B4
Poughkeepsie *U.S.A.* 41°42N 73°56W **83** E11
Poulaphouca Res. *Ireland* 53°8N 6°30W **10** C5
Poulsbo *U.S.A.* 47°44N 122°38W **78** C4
Poultney *U.S.A.* 43°31N 73°14W **83** C11
Poulton-le-Fylde *U.K.* 53°51N 2°58W **12** D5
Pouso Alegre *Brazil* 22°14S 45°57W **95** A6
Pouthisat *Cambodia* 12°34N 103°50E **38** F4
Považská Bystrica
Slovak Rep. 49°8N 18°27E **17** D10
Povenets *Russia* 62°50N 34°50E **18** B5
Poverty B. *N.Z.* 38°43S 178°2E **59** C7
Póvoa de Varzim
Portugal 41°25N 8°46W **21** B1
Povorotnyy, Mys *Russia* 42°40N 133°2E **30** C6
Povungnituk = Puvirnituq
Canada 60°2N 77°10W **69** E16
Powassan *Canada* 46°5N 79°25W **72** C4
Poway *U.S.A.* 32°58N 117°2W **79** N9
Powder → *U.S.A.* 46°45N 105°26W **76** C11
Powder River *U.S.A.* 43°2N 106°59W **76** E10
Powell *U.S.A.* 44°45N 108°46W **76** D9
Powell, L. *U.S.A.* 36°57N 111°29W **77** H8
Powell River *Canada* 49°50N 124°35W **70** D4
Powers *U.S.A.* 45°41N 87°32W **80** C10
Pownal *U.S.A.* 42°45N 73°14W **83** D11
Powys □ *U.K.* 52°20N 3°20W **13** E4
Poyang Hu *China* 29°5N 116°20E **33** F12
Poyarkovo *Russia* 49°36N 128°41E **29** E13
Poza Rica *Mexico* 20°33N 97°27W **87** C5
Požarevac *Serbia* 44°35N 21°18E **23** B9
Poznań *Poland* 52°25N 16°55E **17** B9
Pozo *U.S.A.* 35°20N 120°24W **79** K6
Pozo Almonte *Chile* 20°10S 69°50W **92** H5
Pozo Colorado *Paraguay* 23°30S 58°45W **94** A4
Pozoblanco *Spain* 38°23N 4°51W **21** C3
Pozzuoli *Italy* 40°49N 14°7E **22** D6
Prachin Buri *Thailand* 14°0N 101°25E **38** E3
Prachuap Khirikhan
Thailand 11°49N 99°48E **39** G2
Prado *Brazil* 17°20S 39°13W **93** G11
Prague = Praha
Czech Rep. 50°4N 14°25E **16** C8
Praha *Czech Rep.* 50°4N 14°25E **16** C8
Praia *C. Verde Is.* 15°2N 23°34W **50** b
Prainha *Brazil* 1°45S 53°30W **93** D8
Prainha Nova *Brazil* 7°10S 60°30W **92** E6
Prairie *Australia* 20°50S 144°35E **62** C3
Prairie City *U.S.A.* 44°28N 118°43W **76** D4
Prairie Dog Town Fork Red →
U.S.A. 34°30N 99°58W **84** D5
Prairie du Chien *U.S.A.* 43°3N 91°9W **80** D8
Prairies, L. of the
Canada 51°16N 101°32W **71** C8
Prambanan △ *Indonesia* 7°45S 110°28E **37** G14
Pran Buri *Thailand* 12°23N 99°55E **38** F2
Prapat *Indonesia* 2°41N 98°58E **36** D1
Praslin *Seychelles* 4°18S 55°45E **53** b
Prasonisi, Akra *Greece* 35°42N 27°46E **25** D9
Prata *Brazil* 19°25S 48°54W **93** G9

Pratabpur *India* 23°28N 83°15E **43** H10
Pratapgarh *Raj., India* 24°2N 74°40E **42** G6
Pratapgarh *Ut. P., India* 25°56N 81°59E **43** G9
Pratas I. = Dongsha Dao
S. China Sea 20°45N 116°43E **33** G12
Prato *Italy* 43°53N 11°6E **22** C4
Pratt *U.S.A.* 37°39N 98°44W **80** G4
Prattville *U.S.A.* 32°28N 86°29W **85** E11
Praya *Indonesia* 8°39S 116°17E **36** F5
Prayag = Allahabad
India 25°25N 81°58E **43** G9
Prayagraj = Allahabad
India 25°25N 81°58E **43** G9
Preah Vihear *Cambodia* 14°23N 104°41E **38** E5
Preble *U.S.A.* 42°44N 76°8W **83** D8
Precipice △ *Australia* 25°18S 150°5E **63** D5
Precordillera *Argentina* 30°0S 69°1W **94** C2
Preeceville *Canada* 51°57N 102°40W **71** C8
Preiļi *Latvia* 56°18N 26°43E **9** H22
Premont *U.S.A.* 27°22N 98°7W **84** H5
Prentice *U.S.A.* 45°33N 90°17W **80** C8
Preobrazheniye *Russia* 42°54N 133°54E **30** C6
Preparis I. = Pariparit Kyun
Burma 14°52N 93°41E **41** M18
Preparis North Channel
Ind. Oc. 15°27N 94°5E **41** M18
Preparis South Channel
Ind. Oc. 14°33N 93°30E **41** M18
Přerov *Czech Rep.* 49°28N 17°27E **17** D9
Prescott *Canada* 44°45N 75°30W **83** B9
Prescott *Ariz., U.S.A.* 34°33N 112°28W **77** J7
Prescott *Ark., U.S.A.* 33°48N 93°23W **84** E8
Prescott Valley *U.S.A.* 34°40N 112°18W **77** J7
Preservation Inlet *N.Z.* 46°8S 166°35E **59** G1
Presho *U.S.A.* 43°54N 100°3W **80** D3
Presidencia de la Plaza
Argentina 27°0S 59°50W **94** B4
Presidencia Roque Sáenz Peña
Argentina 26°45S 60°30W **94** B3
Presidente Epitácio *Brazil* 21°56S 52°6W **93** H8
Presidente Hayes □
Paraguay 24°0S 59°0W **94** A4
Presidente Prudente
Brazil 22°5S 51°25W **95** A5
Presidio *Mexico* 29°29N 104°23W **86** B4
Presidio *U.S.A.* 29°34N 104°22W **84** G2
Prešov *Slovak Rep.* 49°0N 21°15E **17** D11
Prespa, L. = Prespansko Jezero
Macedonia 40°55N 21°0E **23** D9
Prespansko Jezero
Macedonia 40°55N 21°0E **23** D9
Presque Isle *U.S.A.* 46°41N 68°1W **81** B19
Presteigne *U.K.* 52°17N 3°0W **13** E5
Preston *Canada* 43°23N 80°21W **82** C4
Preston *U.K.* 53°46N 2°42W **12** D5
Preston *Idaho, U.S.A.* 42°6N 111°53W **76** E8
Preston *Minn., U.S.A.* 43°40N 92°5W **80** D7
Preston, C. *Australia* 20°51S 116°12E **60** D2
Prestonsburg *U.S.A.* 37°40N 82°47W **81** G12
Prestwick *U.K.* 55°29N 4°37W **11** F4
Pretoria *S. Africa* 25°44S 28°12E **57** D4
Preveza *Greece* 38°57N 20°45E **23** E9
Prey Veng *Cambodia* 11°35N 105°29E **39** G5
Pribilof Is. *U.S.A.* 57°0N 170°0W **74** D6
Příbram *Czech Rep.* 49°41N 14°2E **16** D8
Price *U.S.A.* 39°36N 110°49W **76** G8
Price I. *Canada* 52°23N 128°41W **70** C3
Prichard *U.S.A.* 30°44N 88°5W **85** F10
Priekule *Latvia* 56°26N 21°35E **9** H19
Prienai *Lithuania* 54°38N 23°57E **9** J20
Prieska *S. Africa* 29°40S 22°42E **56** D3
Priest L. *U.S.A.* 48°35N 116°52W **76** B5
Priest River *U.S.A.* 48°11N 116°55W **76** B5
Priest Valley *U.S.A.* 36°10N 120°39W **78** J6
Prievidza *Slovak Rep.* 48°46N 18°36E **17** D10
Prikaspiyskaya Nizmennost =
Caspian Depression
Eurasia 47°0N 48°0E **19** E8
Prilep *Macedonia* 41°21N 21°32E **23** D9
Priluki = Pryluky
Ukraine 50°30N 32°24E **19** D5
Prime Seal I. *Australia* 40°3S 147°43E **63** G4
Primo Tapia *Mexico* 32°16N 116°54W **79** N10
Primorskiy Kray □
Russia 45°0N 135°0E **30** B7
Primrose L. *Canada* 54°55N 109°45W **71** C7
Prince Albert *Canada* 53°15N 105°50W **71** C7
Prince Albert *S. Africa* 33°12S 22°2E **56** E3
Prince Albert △ *Canada* 54°0N 106°25W **71** C7
Prince Albert Mts.
Antarctica 76°0S 161°30E **5** D11
Prince Albert Pen.
Canada 72°30N 116°0W **68** C8
Prince Albert Sd.
Canada 70°25N 115°0W **68** C9
Prince Alfred, C. *Canada* 74°20N 124°40W **4** B1
Prince Charles I.
Canada 67°47N 76°12W **69** D16
Prince Charles Mts.
Antarctica 72°0S 67°0E **5** D6
Prince Edward Fracture Zone
Ind. Oc. 46°0S 35°0E **5** A4
Prince Edward I. □
Canada 46°20N 63°20W **73** C7
Prince Edward Is. *Ind. Oc.* 46°35S 38°0E **3** G11
Prince George *Canada* 53°55N 122°50W **70** C4
Prince of Wales, C.
U.S.A. 65°36N 168°5W **74** B6
Prince of Wales I.
Australia 10°40S 142°10E **62** A3
Prince of Wales I. *Canada* 73°0N 99°0W **68** C12
Prince of Wales I.
U.S.A. 55°47N 132°50W **68** F5
Prince of Wales Icefield
Canada 78°15N 79°0W **69** B16
Prince Patrick I. *Canada* 77°0N 120°0W **68** B8
Prince Regent Inlet
Canada 73°0N 90°0W **69** C14

Prince Rupert *Canada* 54°20N 130°20W **70** C2
Prince William Sd.
U.S.A. 60°40N 147°0W **68** E2
Princes Town
Trin. & Tob. 10°16N 61°23W **93** K15
Princess Charlotte B.
Australia 14°25S 144°0E **62** A3
Princess Elizabeth Trough
S. Ocean 64°10S 83°0E **5** C7
Princess May Ranges
Australia 15°30S 125°30E **60** C4
Princess Royal I. *Canada* 53°0N 128°40W **70** C3
Princeton *Canada* 49°27N 120°30W **70** D4
Princeton *Calif., U.S.A.* 39°24N 122°1W **78** F4
Princeton *Ill., U.S.A.* 41°23N 89°28W **80** E9
Princeton *Ind., U.S.A.* 38°21N 87°34W **80** F10
Princeton *Ky., U.S.A.* 37°7N 87°53W **80** G10
Princeton *Mo., U.S.A.* 40°24N 93°35W **80** E7
Princeton *N.J., U.S.A.* 40°21N 74°39W **83** F10
Princeton *W. Va., U.S.A.* 37°22N 81°6W **81** G13
Príncipe *São Tomé & Príncipe* 1°37N 7°25E **48** F4
Principe da Beira *Brazil* 12°20S 64°30W **92** F6
Prineville *U.S.A.* 44°18N 120°51W **76** D3
Prins Harald Kyst *Antarctica* 70°0S 35°1E **5** D4
Prinsesse Astrid Kyst
Antarctica 70°45S 12°30E **5** D3
Prinsesse Ragnhild Kyst
Antarctica 70°15S 27°30E **5** D4
Prinzapolca *Nic.* 13°20N 83°35W **88** D3
Priozersk *Russia* 61°2N 30°7E **8** F24
Pripet = Prypyat →
Europe 51°20N 30°15E **17** C16
Pripet Marshes *Europe* 52°10N 27°10E **17** B15
Pripyat Marshes = Pripet Marshes
Europe 52°10N 27°10E **17** B15
Pripyats = Prypyat →
Europe 51°20N 30°15E **17** C16
Prishtinë = Priština
Kosovo 42°40N 21°13E **23** C9
Priština *Kosovo* 42°40N 21°13E **23** C9
Privas *France* 44°45N 4°37E **20** D6
Privolzhskaya Vozvyshennost
Russia 51°0N 46°0E **19** D8
Privolzhskiy □ *Russia* 56°0N 50°0E **28** D6
Prizren *Kosovo* 42°13N 20°45E **23** C9
Probolinggo *Indonesia* 7°46S 113°13E **37** G15
Proctor *U.S.A.* 43°40N 73°2W **83** C11
Proddatur *India* 14°45N 78°30E **40** M11
Prodromos *Cyprus* 34°57N 32°50E **25** E11
Profilia *Greece* 36°5N 27°51E **25** C9
Progreso *Coahuila,*
Mexico 27°28N 100°59W **86** B4
Progreso *Yucatán,*
Mexico 21°20N 89°40W **87** C7
Progress *Antarctica* 66°22S 76°22E **5** C12
Progress *Russia* 49°45N 129°37E **29** E13
Prokopyevsk *Russia* 54°0N 86°45E **28** D9
Prokuplje *Serbia* 43°16N 21°36E **23** C9
Prome *Burma* 18°49N 95°13E **41** K19
Prophet → *Canada* 58°48N 122°40W **70** B4
Prophet River *Canada* 58°6N 122°43W **70** B4
Propriá *Brazil* 10°13S 36°51W **93** F11
Propriano *France* 41°41N 8°52E **20** F8
Proserpine *Australia* 20°21S 148°36E **62** b
Prosna → *Poland* 52°6N 17°44E **17** B9
Prospect *U.S.A.* 43°18N 75°9W **83** C9
Prosser *U.S.A.* 46°12N 119°46W **76** C4
Prostějov *Czech Rep.* 49°30N 17°9E **17** D9
Proston *Australia* 26°8S 151°32E **63** D5
Provence *France* 43°40N 5°46E **20** E6
Providence *Ky., U.S.A.* 37°24N 87°46W **80** G10
Providence *R.I., U.S.A.* 41°49N 71°24W **83** E13
Providence Bay *Canada* 45°41N 82°15W **72** C3
Providence Mts.
U.S.A. 35°10N 115°15W **79** K11
Providencia, I. de
Colombia 13°25N 81°26W **88** D3
Provideniya *Russia* 64°23N 173°18W **29** C19
Provincetown *U.S.A.* 42°3N 70°11W **81** D18
Provins *France* 48°33N 3°15E **20** B5
Provo *U.S.A.* 40°14N 111°39W **76** F8
Provost *Canada* 52°25N 110°20W **71** C6
Prudhoe Bay *U.S.A.* 70°18N 148°22W **74** A10
Prudhoe I. *Australia* 21°19S 149°41E **62** C4
Prud'homme *Canada* 52°20N 105°54W **71** C7
Pruszków *Poland* 52°9N 20°49E **17** B11
Prut → *Romania* 45°28N 28°10E **17** F15
Pruzhany *Belarus* 52°33N 24°28E **17** B13
Prydz B. *Antarctica* 69°0S 74°0E **5** C6
Pryluky *Ukraine* 50°30N 32°24E **19** D5
Pryor *U.S.A.* 36°19N 95°19W **84** C7
Prypyat → *Europe* 51°20N 30°15E **17** C16
Przemyśl *Poland* 49°50N 22°45E **17** D12
Przhevalsk = Karakol
Kyrgyzstan 42°30N 78°20E **32** C4
Psara *Greece* 38°37N 25°38E **23** E11
Psiloritis, Oros *Greece* 35°15N 24°45E **25** D6
Psira *Greece* 35°12N 25°52E **25** D7
Pskov *Russia* 57°50N 28°25E **9** H23
Ptich = Ptsich →
Belarus 52°9N 28°52E **17** B15
Ptichia = Vidos *Greece* 39°38N 19°55E **25** A3
Ptolemaida *Greece* 40°30N 21°43E **23** D9
Ptsich → *Belarus* 52°9N 28°52E **17** B15
Pu Xian *China* 36°24N 111°6E **34** F6
Pua *Thailand* 19°11N 100°55E **38** C3
Puán *Argentina* 37°30S 62°45W **94** D3
Pu'apu'a *Samoa* 13°34S 172°9W **59** b
Pucallpa *Peru* 8°25S 74°30W **92** E4
Puch'on = Bucheon
S. Korea 37°28N 126°45E **35** F14
Pudasjärvi *Finland* 65°23N 26°53E **8** D22
Pudozh *Russia* 61°48N 36°32E **18** B6
Puducherry *India* 11°59N 79°50E **40** P11
Pudukkottai *India* 10°28N 78°47E **40** P11
Puebla *Mexico* 19°3N 98°12W **87** D5
Puebla □ *Mexico* 18°50N 98°0W **87** D5
Pueblo *U.S.A.* 38°16N 104°37W **76** G11
Puelches *Argentina* 38°5S 65°51W **94** D2

Puelén *Argentina* 37°32S 67°38W **94** D2
Puente Alto *Chile* 33°32S 70°35W **94** C1
Puente-Genil *Spain* 37°22N 4°47W **21** D3
Puerca, Pta. *Puerto Rico* 18°13N 65°36W **89** d
Puerco → *U.S.A.* 34°22N 107°50W **77** J10
Puerto Aisén *Chile* 45°27S 73°0W **96** F2
Puerto Ángel *Mexico* 15°40N 96°29W **87** D5
Puerto Arista *Mexico* 15°56N 93°48W **87** D6
Puerto Armuelles
Panama 8°20N 82°51W **88** E3
Puerto Ayacucho
Venezuela 5°40N 67°35W **92** B5
Puerto Barrios
Guatemala 15°40N 88°32W **88** C2
Puerto Bermejo
Argentina 26°55S 58°34W **94** B4
Puerto Bermúdez *Peru* 10°20S 74°58W **92** F4
Puerto Bolívar *Ecuador* 3°19S 79°55W **92** D3
Puerto Cabello *Venezuela* 10°28N 68°1W **92** A5
Puerto Cabezas *Nic.* 14°0N 83°30W **88** D3
Puerto Cabo Gracias á Dios
Nic. 15°0N 83°10W **88** D3
Puerto Carreño *Colombia* 6°12N 67°22W **92** B5
Puerto Castilla *Honduras* 16°0N 86°0W **88** C2
Puerto Chicama *Peru* 7°45S 79°20W **92** E3
Puerto Coig *Argentina* 50°54S 69°15W **96** G3
Puerto Cortés *Honduras* 15°51N 88°0W **88** C2
Puerto Cumarebo
Venezuela 11°29N 69°30W **92** A5
Puerto de Alcudia = Port
d'Alcúdia *Spain* 39°50N 3°7E **24** B10
Puerto de Cabrera *Spain* 39°8N 2°56E **24** B9
Puerto de Gran Tarajal
Canary Is. 28°13N 14°1W **24** F5
Puerto de la Cruz
Canary Is. 28°24N 16°32W **24** F3
Puerto de los Angeles △
Mexico 23°50N 105°45W **86** C3
Puerto de Pozo Negro
Canary Is. 28°19N 13°55W **24** F6
Puerto de Sóller = Port de Sóller
Spain 39°48N 2°42E **24** B9
Puerto del Carmen
Canary Is. 28°55N 13°38W **24** F6
Puerto del Rosario
Canary Is. 28°30N 13°52W **24** F6
Puerto Deseado *Argentina* 47°55S 66°0W **96** F3
Puerto Escondido *Mexico* 15°50N 97°3W **87** D5
Puerto Heath *Bolivia* 12°34S 68°39W **92** F5
Puerto Inírida *Colombia* 3°53N 67°52W **92** C5
Puerto Juárez *Mexico* 21°11N 86°49W **87** C7
Puerto La Cruz
Venezuela 10°13N 64°38W **92** A6
Puerto Leguízamo
Colombia 0°12S 74°46W **92** D4
Puerto Lempira
Honduras 15°16N 83°46W **88** C3
Puerto Libertad *Mexico* 29°55N 112°43W **86** B2
Puerto Limón *Colombia* 3°23N 73°30W **92** C4
Puerto Lobos *Argentina* 42°0S 65°3W **96** E3
Puerto Madryn *Argentina* 42°48S 65°4W **96** E3
Puerto Maldonado *Peru* 12°30S 69°10W **92** F5
Puerto Manatí *Cuba* 21°22N 76°50W **88** B4
Puerto Montt *Chile* 41°28S 73°0W **96** E2
Puerto Morazán *Nic.* 12°51N 87°11W **88** D2
Puerto Morelos *Mexico* 20°50N 86°52W **87** C7
Puerto Natales *Chile* 51°45S 72°15W **96** G2
Puerto Oscuro *Chile* 31°24S 71°35W **94** C1
Puerto Padre *Cuba* 21°13N 76°35W **88** B4
Puerto Páez *Venezuela* 6°13N 67°28W **92** B5
Puerto Peñasco *Mexico* 31°20N 113°33W **86** A2
Puerto Pinasco
Paraguay 22°36S 57°50W **94** A4
Puerto Plata *Dom. Rep.* 19°48N 70°45W **89** C5
Puerto Pollensa = Port de
Pollença *Spain* 39°54N 3°4E **24** B10
Puerto Princesa *Phil.* 9°46N 118°45E **37** C5
Puerto Quepos *Costa Rica* 9°29N 84°6W **88** E3
Puerto Rico *Canary Is.* 27°47N 15°42W **24** G4
Puerto Rico ☐ *W. Indies* 18°15N 66°45W **89** d
Puerto Rico Trench
Atl. Oc. 19°50N 66°0W **89** C6
Puerto San Julián
Argentina 49°18S 67°43W **96** F3
Puerto Santa Cruz
Argentina 50°0S 68°32W **96** G3
Puerto Sastre *Paraguay* 22°2S 57°55W **94** A4
Puerto Suárez *Bolivia* 18°58S 57°52W **92** G7
Puerto Vallarta *Mexico* 20°37N 105°15W **86** C3
Puerto Varas *Chile* 41°19S 72°59W **96** E2
Puerto Wilches *Colombia* 7°21N 73°54W **92** B4
Puertollano *Spain* 38°43N 4°7W **21** C3
Pueu *Tahiti* 17°44S 149°13W **59** d
Pueyrredón, L. *Argentina* 47°20S 72°0W **96** F2
Pugachev *Russia* 52°0N 48°49E **18** D8
Pugal *India* 28°30N 72°48E **42** E5
Puge *Tanzania* 4°45S 33°11E **54** C3
Puget Sound *U.S.A.* 47°50N 122°30W **76** C2
Pugŏdong *N. Korea* 42°5N 130°0E **35** C16
Pugu *Tanzania* 6°55S 39°4E **54** D4
Pügünzi *Iran* 25°49N 59°10E **45** E8
Puig Major *Spain* 39°48N 2°47E **24** B9
Puigcerdà *Spain* 42°24N 1°50E **21** A6
Puigpunyent *Spain* 39°38N 2°32E **24** B9
Pujon-ho *N. Korea* 40°35N 127°35E **35** D14
Pukaki, L. *N.Z.* 44°4S 170°1E **59** F3
Pukapuka *Cook Is.* 10°53S 165°49W **65** J11
Pukaskwa △ *Canada* 48°20N 86°0W **72** C2
Pukatawagan *Canada* 55°45N 101°20W **71** B8
Pukchin *N. Korea* 40°12N 125°45E **35** D13
Pukch'ŏng *N. Korea* 40°14N 128°10E **35** D15
Pukekohe *N.Z.* 37°12S 174°55E **59** B5
Pukhrayan *India* 26°14N 79°51E **43** F8
Puksubaek-san
N. Korea 40°42N 127°45E **35** D14
Pula *Croatia* 44°54N 13°57E **16** F7
Pulacayo *Bolivia* 20°25S 66°41W **92** H5
Pulandian *China* 39°25N 121°58E **35** E11
Pulaski *N.Y., U.S.A.* 43°34N 76°8W **83** C8
Pulaski *Tenn., U.S.A.* 35°12N 87°2W **85** D11

Pulaski *Va., U.S.A.* 37°3N 80°47W **81** G13
Pulau → *Indonesia* 5°50S 138°15E **37** F9
Pulau Gili *Indonesia* 8°21S 116°1E **37** J19
Puławy *Poland* 51°23N 21°59E **17** C11
Pulga *U.S.A.* 39°48N 121°29W **78** F5
Pulicat L. *India* 13°40N 80°15E **40** N12
Pullman *U.S.A.* 46°44N 117°10W **76** C5
Pulog, Mt. *Phil.* 16°40N 120°50E **37** A6
Pułtusk *Poland* 52°43N 21°6E **17** B11
Pumlumon Fawr *U.K.* 52°28N 3°46W **13** E4
Puná, I. *Ecuador* 2°55S 80°5W **92** D2
Punaauia *Tahiti* 17°37S 149°34W **59** d
Punakaiki *N.Z.* 42°7S 171°20E **59** E3
Punakha Dzong *Bhutan* 27°42N 89°52E **41** F16
Punasar *India* 27°6N 73°6E **42** F5
Punata *Bolivia* 17°32S 65°50W **92** G5
Punch *India* 33°48N 74°4E **43** C6
Punda Maria *S. Africa* 22°40S 31°5E **57** C5
Pune *India* 18°29N 73°57E **40** K8
P'ungsan *N. Korea* 40°50N 128°9E **35** D15
Pungue, Ponte de *Mozam.* 19°0S 34°0E **55** F3
Punjab □ *India* 31°0N 76°0E **42** D7
Punjab □ *Pakistan* 32°0N 72°30E **42** E6
Puno *Peru* 15°55S 70°3W **92** G4
Punpun → *India* 25°31N 85°18E **43** G11
Punta, Cerro de
Puerto Rico 18°10N 66°37W **89** d
Punta Alta *Argentina* 38°53S 62°4W **96** D4
Punta Arenas *Chile* 53°10S 71°0W **96** G2
Punta del Díaz *Chile* 28°0S 70°45W **94** B1
Punta del Hidalgo
Canary Is. 28°33N 16°19W **24** F3
Punta Gorda *Belize* 16°10N 88°45W **87** D7
Punta Gorda *U.S.A.* 26°56N 82°3W **85** H13
Punta Prieta *Mexico* 28°58N 114°17W **86** B2
Punta Prima *Spain* 39°48N 4°16E **24** B11
Puntarenas *Costa Rica* 10°0N 84°50W **88** E3
Puntland *Somali Rep.* 8°0N 49°0E **47** F4
Punto Fijo *Venezuela* 11°50N 70°13W **92** A4
Punxsutawney *U.S.A.* 40°57N 78°59W **82** F6
Pupuan *Indonesia* 8°19S 115°0E **37** J18
Puqi *China* 29°40N 113°50E **33** C10
Puquio *Peru* 14°45S 74°10W **92** F4
Pur → *Russia* 67°31N 77°55E **28** C8
Puracé, Vol. *Colombia* 2°21N 76°23W **92** C3
Puralia = Puruliya
India 23°17N 86°24E **43** H12
Puranpur *India* 28°31N 80°9E **43** E9
Purbalingga *Indonesia* 7°23S 109°21E **37** G13
Purbeck, Isle of *U.K.* 50°39N 1°59W **13** G5
Purcell *U.S.A.* 35°1N 97°22W **84** D6
Purcell Mts. *Canada* 49°55N 116°15W **70** D5
Purdy *U.S.A.* 45°19N 77°44W **82** A7
Puri *India* 19°50N 85°58E **41** K14
Purmerend *Neths.* 52°32N 4°58E **15** B4
Purnia *India* 25°45N 87°31E **43** G12
Purnululu △ *Australia* 17°20S 128°20E **60** C4
Pursat = Pouthisat
Cambodia 12°34N 103°50E **38** F4
Purukcahu *Indonesia* 0°35S 114°35E **36** E4
Puruliya *India* 23°17N 86°24E **43** H12
Purus → *Brazil* 3°42S 61°28W **92** D6
Puruvesi *Finland* 61°50N 29°30E **8** F23
Purvis *U.S.A.* 31°9N 89°25W **85** F10
Purwa *India* 26°28N 80°47E **43** F9
Purwakarta *Indonesia* 6°35S 107°29E **37** G12
Purwo, Tanjung
Indonesia 8°44S 114°21E **37** K18
Purwodadi *Indonesia* 7°7S 110°55E **37** G14
Purwokerto *Indonesia* 7°25S 109°14E **37** G13
Puryŏng *N. Korea* 42°5N 129°43E **35** C15
Pusa *India* 25°59N 85°41E **43** G11
Pusan = Busan *S. Korea* 35°5N 129°0E **35** G15
Pushkin *Russia* 59°45N 30°25E **9** C6
Pushkino *Russia* 51°16N 47°0E **19** D8
Put-in-Bay *U.S.A.* 41°39N 82°49W **82** E2
Putahow L. *Canada* 59°54N 100°40W **71** B8
Putao *Burma* 27°28N 97°30E **41** F20
Putaruru *N.Z.* 38°2S 175°50E **59** C5
Puteran *Indonesia* 7°5S 114°0E **37** G15
Putian *China* 25°23N 119°0E **33** F12
Putignano *Italy* 40°51N 17°7E **22** D7
Puting, Tanjung
Indonesia 3°31S 111°46E **36** E4
Putnam *U.S.A.* 41°55N 71°55W **83** E13
Putorana, Gory *Russia* 69°0N 95°0E **29** C10
Putrajaya *Malaysia* 2°55N 101°40E **39** L3
Puttalam *Sri Lanka* 8°1N 79°55E **40** Q11
Puttgarden *Germany* 54°30N 11°10E **16** A6
Putumayo → *S. Amer.* 3°7S 67°58W **92** D5
Putussibau *Indonesia* 0°50N 112°56E **36** D4
Puvirnituq *Canada* 60°2N 77°10W **69** E16
Puy-de-Dôme *France* 45°46N 2°57E **20** D5
Puyallup *U.S.A.* 47°12N 122°18W **78** C4
Puyang *China* 35°40N 115°1E **34** G8
Pūzeh Rīg *Iran* 27°20N 58°40E **45** E8
Pwani □ *Tanzania* 7°0S 39°0E **54** D4
Pweto
Dem. Rep. of the Congo 8°25S 28°51E **54** D2
Pwllheli *U.K.* 52°53N 4°25W **12** E3
Pyaozero, Ozero *Russia* 66°5N 30°58E **8** C24
Pyapon *Burma* 16°20N 95°40E **41** L19
Pyasina → *Russia* 73°30N 87°0E **28** B9
Pyatigorsk *Russia* 44°2N 43°6E **19** F7
Pyè = Prome *Burma* 18°49N 95°13E **41** K19
Pyeongtaek *S. Korea* 37°1N 127°4E **35** F14
Pyhäjoki → *Finland* 64°28N 24°14E **8** D21
Pyhäjärvi *Finland* 63°41N 25°58E **8** E21
Pyinmana *Burma* 19°45N 96°12E **41** K20
Pyla, C. *Cyprus* 34°56N 33°51E **25** E12
Pymatuning Res. *U.S.A.* 41°30N 80°28W **82** E4
Pyŏktong *N. Korea* 40°50N 125°50E **35** D13
Pyŏnggang *N. Korea* 38°24N 127°17E **35** E14
Pyŏngsong *N. Korea* 39°14N 125°52E **35** E13
P'yŏngyang *N. Korea* 39°0N 125°30E **35** E13
Pyote *U.S.A.* 31°32N 103°8W **84** F3
Pyramid L. *U.S.A.* 40°1N 119°35W **78** G7
Pyramid Pk. *U.S.A.* 36°25N 116°37W **79** J10
Pyramids *Egypt* 29°58N 31°9E **51** C12
Pyrénées *Europe* 42°45N 0°18E **20** E4
Pyu *Burma* 18°30N 96°28E **41** K20

Q

Qaanaaq *Greenland* 77°30N 69°10W **69** B18
Qachasnek *S. Africa* 30°6S 28°42E **57** E4
Qa'el Jafr *Jordan* 30°20N 36°25E **46** E5
Qa'emābād *Iran* 31°44N 60°2E **45** D9
Qā'emshahr *Iran* 36°30N 52°53E **45** B7
Qagan Nur *Jilin, China* 45°15N 124°18E **35** B13
Qagan Nur *Nei Monggol Zizhiqu,*
  China 43°30N 114°55E **34** C8
Qahar Youyi Zhongqi
  China 41°12N 112°40E **34** D7
Qahremānshahr = Kermānshāh
  Iran 34°23N 47°0E **44** C5
Qaidam Pendi *China* 37°0N 95°0E **32** D8
Qajarīyeh *Iran* 31°1N 48°22E **45** D6
Qala, Ras il *Malta* 36°2N 14°20E **25** C1
Qala-i-Jadid = Spīn Būldak
  Afghan. 31°1N 66°25E **42** D2
Qala Point = Qala, Ras il
  Malta 36°2N 14°20E **25** C1
Qala Viala *Pakistan* 30°49N 67°17E **42** D2
Qala Yangi *Afghan.* 34°20N 66°30E **42** B2
Qal'at al Akhḍar *Si. Arabia* 28°4N 37°9E **44** E3
Qal'at Dīzah *Iraq* 36°11N 45°7E **44** B5
Qal'at Ṣāliḥ *Iraq* 31°31N 47°16E **44** D5
Qal'at Sukkar *Iraq* 31°51N 46°5E **44** D5
Qamani'tuaq = Baker Lake
  Canada 64°20N 96°3W **68** E12
Qamdo *China* 31°15N 97°6E **32** E8
Qamea *Fiji* 16°45S 179°45W **59** a
Qamruddin Karez
  Pakistan 31°45N 68°20E **42** D3
Qandahār = Kandahār
  Afghan. 31°32N 65°43E **40** D4
Qandahār = Kandahār □
  Afghan. 31°0N 65°0E **40** D4
Qandyaghash
  Kazakhstan 49°28N 57°25E **19** E10
Qapān *Iran* 37°40N 55°47E **45** B7
Qapshaghay *Kazakhstan* 43°51N 77°14E **28** E8
Qaqortoq *Greenland* 60°43N 46°0W **4** C5
Qara Qash → *China* 35°0N 78°30E **43** B8
Qarabutak *Kazakhstan* 50°0N 60°14E **28** E7
Qaraghandy *Kazakhstan* 49°50N 73°10E **32** B3
Qaraghayly *Kazakhstan* 49°26N 76°0E **28** E8
Qārah *Si. Arabia* 29°55N 40°3E **44** D4
Qaratau *Ongtüstik Qazaqstan,*
  Kazakhstan 43°30N 69°30E **28** E7
Qarataū *Zhambyl,*
  Kazakhstan 43°10N 70°28E **28** E8
Qarazhal *Kazakhstan* 48°2N 70°49E **28** E8
Qardho *Somali Rep.* 9°30N 49°6E **47** F4
Qareh → *Iran* 39°25N 47°22E **44** B5
Qareh Tekān *Iran* 36°38N 49°29E **45** B6
Qarnein *U.A.E.* 24°56N 52°52E **45** E7
Qarqan He → *China* 39°30N 88°30E **32** C6
Qarqaraly *Kazakhstan* 49°26N 75°30E **32** B4
Qarshi *Uzbekistan* 38°53N 65°48E **28** F7
Qartabā *Lebanon* 34°4N 35°50E **46** A4
Qārūh *Kuwait* 28°49N 48°46E **45** D6
Qaryat al Gharab *Iraq* 31°27N 44°48E **44** D5
Qaryat al 'Ulyā *Si. Arabia* 27°33N 47°42E **44** E5
Qasr 'Amra *Jordan* 31°48N 36°35E **44** D3
Qaṣr-e Qand *Iran* 26°15N 60°45E **45** E9
Qaṣr-e Shīrīn *Iran* 34°31N 45°35E **44** C5
Qasr Farâfra *Egypt* 27°0N 28°1E **51** C11
Qasuittuq = Resolute
  Canada 74°42N 94°54W **69** C13
Qatanā *Syria* 33°26N 36°4E **46** B5
Qatar ■ *Asia* 25°30N 51°15E **45** E6
Qatlish *Iran* 37°50N 57°19E **45** B8
Qattâra, Munkhafed el
  Egypt 29°30N 27°30E **51** C11
Qattâra Depression = Qattâra,
  Munkhafed el *Egypt* 29°30N 27°30E **51** C11
Qawām al Ḥamzah = Al Ḥamzah
  Iraq 31°43N 44°58E **44** D5
Qāyen *Iran* 33°40N 59°10E **45** C8
Qazaqstan = Kazakhstan ■
  Asia 50°0N 70°0E **28** E8
Qazimämmäd *Azerbaijan* 40°3N 49°0E **45** A6
Qazvīn *Iran* 36°15N 50°0E **45** B6
Qazvīn □ *Iran* 36°20N 50°0E **45** B6
Qena *Egypt* 26°10N 32°43E **51** C12
Qeqertarsuaq *Greenland* 69°45N 53°30W **4** C5
Qeqertarsuaq *Greenland* 69°15N 53°38W **4** C5
Qeshlāq *Iran* 34°55N 46°28E **44** C5
Qeshm *Iran* 26°55N 56°10E **45** E8
Qeys *Iran* 26°32N 53°58E **45** E7
Qezel Owzen → *Iran* 36°45N 49°22E **45** B6
Qezi'ot *Israel* 30°52N 34°26E **46** E3
Qi Xian *China* 34°40N 114°48E **34** G8
Qian Gorlos *China* 45°5N 124°42E **35** B13
Qian Hai *China* 22°32N 113°54E **33** a
Qian Xian *China* 34°31N 108°15E **34** G5
Qian'an *China* 40°0N 118°41E **35** E10
Qianjin *China* 47°34N 133°4E **33** B15
Qianshan *China* 22°15N 113°31E **33** a
Qianyang *China* 34°40N 107°8E **34** G4
Qi'ao *China* 22°25N 113°39E **33** a
Qi'ao Dao *China* 22°25N 113°38E **33** a
Qiaocun *China* 39°56N 112°55E **34** E7
Qiemo *China* 38°8N 85°32E **32** D6
Qijiaojing *China* 43°28N 91°36E **32** B4
Qikiqtarjuaq *Canada* 67°33N 63°0W **69** D19
Qila Saifullāh *Pakistan* 30°45N 68°17E **42** D3
Qilian Shan *China* 38°30N 96°0E **32** D8
Qin He → *China* 35°1N 113°22E **34** G7
Qin Ling = Qinling Shandi
  China 33°50N 108°10E **34** H5
Qin'an *China* 34°48N 105°40E **34** G3
Qing Xian *China* 38°35N 116°45E **34** E9
Qingcheng *China* 37°15N 117°40E **35** F9
Qingchuan *China* 32°36N 105°20E **34** H3
Qingdao *China* 36°5N 120°20E **35** F11
Qingfeng *China* 35°52N 115°8E **34** G8
Qinghai □ *China* 36°0N 98°0E **32** D8
Qinghai Hu *China* 36°40N 100°10E **32** D9
Qinghecheng *China* 41°28N 124°15E **35** D13
Qinghemen *China* 41°48N 121°25E **35** D11
Qingjian *China* 37°8N 110°8E **34** F6
Qingjiang = Huaiyin
  China 33°30N 119°2E **35** H10
Qingshui *China* 34°48N 106°8E **34** G4
Qingshuihe *China* 39°55N 111°35E **34** E6
Qingtongxia *China* 38°2N 106°3E **34** E4
Qingtongxia Shuiku
  China 37°50N 105°58E **34** F3
Qingxu *China* 37°34N 112°22E **34** F7
Qingyang *China* 36°2N 107°55E **34** F4
Qingyuan *China* 42°10N 124°55E **35** C13
Qingyun *China* 37°45N 117°20E **35** F9
Qinhuangdao *China* 39°56N 119°30E **35** E10
Qinshui *China* 35°40N 112°8E **34** G7
Qinyang = Jiyuan *China* 35°7N 112°57E **34** G7
Qinyang *China* 35°5N 112°56E **34** G7
Qinyuan *China* 36°29N 112°20E **34** F7
Qinzhou *China* 21°58N 108°38E **32** G10
Qionghai *China* 19°15N 110°26E **38** C8
Qiongshan *China* 19°51N 110°26E **38** C8
Qiongzhou Haixia
  China 20°10N 110°15E **38** B8
Qiqihar *China* 47°26N 124°0E **33** B13
Qira *China* 37°0N 80°48E **32** D5
Qiraîya, W. → *Egypt* 30°27N 34°0E **46** E3
Qiryat Ata *Israel* 32°47N 35°6E **46** C4
Qiryat Gat *Israel* 31°32N 34°46E **46** D3
Qiryat Mal'akhi *Israel* 31°44N 34°44E **46** D3
Qiryat Shemona *Israel* 33°13N 35°35E **46** B4
Qiryat Yam *Israel* 32°51N 35°4E **46** C4
Qishan *China* 34°25N 107°38E **34** G4
Qitai *China* 44°2N 89°35E **32** C6
Qitaihe *China* 45°48N 130°51E **30** B5
Qixia *China* 37°17N 120°52E **35** F11
Qızılağac Körfäzi
  Azerbaijan 39°9N 49°0E **45** B6
Qojūr *Iran* 36°12N 47°55E **44** B5
Qom *Iran* 34°40N 51°0E **45** C6
Qom □ *Iran* 34°40N 51°0E **45** C6
Qomolangma Feng = Everest, Mt.
  Nepal 28°5N 86°58E **43** E12
Qomsheh *Iran* 32°0N 51°55E **45** D6
Qoqek = Tacheng *China* 46°40N 82°58E **32** B5
Qoqon = Qŭqon
  Uzbekistan 40°31N 70°56E **28** E8
Qoraqalpoghistan □
  Uzbekistan 43°0N 58°0E **28** E6
Qorveh *Iran* 35°10N 47°48E **44** C5
Qosshaghyl *Kazakhstan* 46°40N 54°0E **19** E9
Qostanay *Kazakhstan* 53°10N 63°35E **28** D7
Quabbin Res. *U.S.A.* 42°20N 72°20W **83** D12
Quairading *Australia* 32°0S 117°21E **61** F2
Quakertown *U.S.A.* 40°26N 75°21W **83** F9
Qualicum Beach
  Canada 49°22N 124°26W **70** D4
Quambatook *Australia* 35°49S 143°34E **63** F3
Quambone *Australia* 30°57S 147°53E **63** E4
Quamby *Australia* 20°22S 140°17E **62** C3
Quan Long = Ca Mau
  Vietnam 9°7N 105°8E **39** H5
Quanah *U.S.A.* 34°18N 99°44W **84** D5
Quang Ngai *Vietnam* 15°13N 108°58E **38** E7
Quang Tri *Vietnam* 16°45N 107°13E **38** D6
Quang Yen *Vietnam* 20°56N 106°52E **38** B6
Quantock Hills *U.K.* 51°8N 3°10W **13** F4
Quanyang *China* 42°21N 127°32E **35** C14
Quanzhou *China* 24°55N 118°34E **33** G12
Qu'Appelle → *Canada* 50°33N 103°53W **71** C8
Quaqtaq *Canada* 60°55N 69°40W **69** E18
Quarai *Brazil* 30°15S 56°20W **94** C4
Quartu Sant'Élena *Italy* 39°15N 9°10E **22** E3
Quartzsite *U.S.A.* 33°40N 114°13W **79** M12
Quatre Bornes *Mauritius* 20°15S 57°28E **53** d
Quatsino Sd. *Canada* 50°25N 127°58W **70** C3
Quba *Azerbaijan* 41°21N 48°32E **19** F8
Qūchān *Iran* 37°10N 58°27E **45** B8
Queanbeyan *Australia* 35°17S 149°14E **63** F4
Québec *Canada* 46°52N 71°13W **73** C5
Québec □ *Canada* 48°0N 74°0W **73** B6
Quebrada del Condorito △
  Argentina 31°49S 64°40W **94** C3
Queen Alexandra Ra.
  Antarctica 85°0S 170°0E **5** E11
Queen Charlotte City
  Canada 53°15N 132°2W **70** C2
Queen Charlotte Is.
  Canada 53°20N 132°10W **70** C2
Queen Charlotte Sd.
  Canada 51°0N 128°0W **70** C3
Queen Charlotte Strait
  Canada 50°45N 127°10W **70** C3
Queen Elizabeth △ *Uganda* 0°0 30°0E **54** C3
Queen Elizabeth △ *U.K.* 56°7N 4°30W **11** E4
Queen Elizabeth Is.
  Canada 76°0N 95°0W **69** B13
Queen Mary Land
  Antarctica 70°0S 95°0E **5** D7
Queen Maud G.
  Canada 68°15N 102°30W **68** D11
Queen Maud Land = Dronning
  Maud Land *Antarctica* 72°30S 12°0E **5** D3
Queen Maud Mts.
  Antarctica 86°0S 160°0W **5** E12
Queens Channel
  Australia 15°0S 129°30E **60** C4
Queenscliff *Australia* 38°16S 144°39E **63** F3
Queensland □ *Australia* 22°0S 142°0E **62** C3
Queenstown *Australia* 42°4S 145°35E **63** G4
Queenstown *N.Z.* 45°1S 168°40E **59** F2
Queenstown *Singapore* 1°18N 103°48E **39** d
Queenstown *S. Africa* 31°52S 26°52E **56** E4
Queets *U.S.A.* 47°32N 124°19W **78** C2
Queguay Grande →
  Uruguay 32°9S 58°9W **94** C4
Queimadas *Brazil* 11°0S 39°38W **93** F11
Quelimane *Mozam.* 17°53S 36°58E **55** F4
Quellón *Chile* 43°7S 73°37W **96** E2
Quelpart = Jeju-do
  S. Korea 33°29N 126°34E **35** H14
Quemado *N. Mex.,*
  U.S.A. 34°20N 108°30W **77** J9
Quemado *Tex., U.S.A.* 28°56N 100°37W **84** G4
Quemú-Quemú
  Argentina 36°3S 63°36W **94** D3
Quequén *Argentina* 38°30S 58°30W **94** D4
Querétaro *Mexico* 20°36N 100°23W **86** C4
Querétaro □ *Mexico* 21°0N 99°55W **86** C5
Quesnel *Canada* 53°0N 122°30W **70** C4
Quesnel → *Canada* 52°58N 122°29W **70** C4
Quesnel L. *Canada* 52°30N 121°20W **70** C4
Questa *U.S.A.* 36°42N 105°36W **77** H11
Quetico △ *Canada* 48°30N 91°45W **72** C1
Quetta *Pakistan* 30°15N 66°55E **42** D2
Quezaltenango
  Guatemala 14°50N 91°30W **88** D1
Quezon City *Phil.* 14°37N 121°2E **37** B6
Qufār *Si. Arabia* 27°26N 41°37E **44** E4
Qufu *China* 35°35N 116°59E **34** G9
Qui Nhon *Vietnam* 13°40N 109°13E **38** F7
Quibala *Angola* 10°46S 14°59E **52** G2
Quibaxe *Angola* 8°24S 14°27E **52** F2
Quibdó *Colombia* 5°42N 76°40W **92** B3
Quiberon *France* 47°29N 3°9W **20** C2
Quiet L. *Canada* 61°5N 133°5W **70** A2
Quiindy *Paraguay* 25°58S 57°14W **94** B4
Quilá *Mexico* 24°23N 107°13W **86** C3
Quilán, C. *Chile* 43°15S 74°30W **96** E2
Quilcene *U.S.A.* 47°49N 122°53W **78** C4
Quilimari *Chile* 32°5S 71°30W **94** C1
Quilino *Argentina* 30°14S 64°29W **94** C3
Quillabamba *Peru* 12°50S 72°50W **92** F4
Quillagua *Chile* 21°40S 69°40W **94** A2
Quillota *Chile* 32°54S 71°16W **94** C1
Quilmes *Argentina* 34°43S 58°15W **94** C4
Quilon *India* 8°50N 76°38E **40** Q10
Quilpie *Australia* 26°35S 144°11E **63** D3
Quilpué *Chile* 33°5S 71°33W **94** C1
Quilua *Mozam.* 16°17S 39°54E **55** F4
Quimili *Argentina* 27°40S 62°30W **94** B3
Quimper *France* 48°0N 4°9W **20** B1
Quimperlé *France* 47°53N 3°33W **20** C2
Quinault → *U.S.A.* 47°21N 124°18W **78** C2
Quincy *Calif., U.S.A.* 39°56N 120°57W **78** F6
Quincy *Fla., U.S.A.* 30°35N 84°34W **85** F12
Quincy *Ill., U.S.A.* 39°56N 91°23W **80** F8
Quincy *Mass., U.S.A.* 42°14N 71°0W **83** D14
Quincy *Wash., U.S.A.* 47°14N 119°51W **76** C4
Quines *Argentina* 32°13S 65°48W **94** C2
Quinga *Mozam.* 15°49S 40°15E **55** F5
Quintana Roo □ *Mexico* 19°40N 88°30W **87** D7
Quintanar de la Orden
  Spain 39°36N 3°5W **21** C4
Quintero *Chile* 32°45S 71°30W **94** C1
Quirihue *Chile* 36°15S 72°35W **94** D1
Quirimbas △ *Mozam.* 12°30S 40°15E **55** E5
Quirindi *Australia* 31°28S 150°40E **63** E5
Quirinópolis *Brazil* 18°32S 50°30W **93** G8
Quissanga *Mozam.* 12°24S 40°28E **55** E5
Quissico *Mozam.* 24°42S 34°44E **57** C5
Quitilipi *Argentina* 26°50S 60°13W **94** B3
Quitman *U.S.A.* 30°47N 83°34W **85** F13
Quito *Ecuador* 0°15S 78°35W **92** D3
Quixadá *Brazil* 4°55S 39°0W **93** D11
Quixaxe *Mozam.* 15°17S 40°4E **55** F5
Qujing *China* 25°32N 103°41E **32** F9
Qulan *Kazakhstan* 42°55N 72°43E **28** E8
Qul'ān, Jazā'ir *Egypt* 24°22N 35°31E **44** E2
Qulsary *Kazakhstan* 46°59N 54°1E **19** E9
Qumbu *S. Africa* 31°10S 28°48E **57** E4
Qūneitra = Al Qunayṭirah
  Syria 33°5N 35°45E **46** B4
Qŭnghirot *Uzbekistan* 43°2N 58°50E **28** E6
Quoin I. *Australia* 14°54S 129°32E **60** B4
Quoin Pt. *S. Africa* 34°46S 19°37E **56** E2
Quorn *Australia* 32°25S 138°5E **63** E2
Qŭqon *Uzbekistan* 40°31N 70°56E **28** E8
Qurimbas △ *Mozam.* 12°20S 40°10E **55** E5
Qurnat as Sawdā'
  Lebanon 34°18N 36°6E **46** A5
Quṣaybā' *Si. Arabia* 26°53N 43°35E **44** E4
Qusaybah *Iraq* 34°24N 40°59E **44** C4
Quseir *Egypt* 26°7N 34°16E **44** E2
Qūshchī *Iran* 37°59N 45°3E **44** B5
Quthing *Lesotho* 30°25S 27°36E **57** E4
Qūṭīābād *Iran* 35°47N 48°30E **45** C6
Quwo *China* 35°38N 111°25E **34** G6
Quyang *China* 38°35N 114°40E **34** E8
Quynh Nhai *Vietnam* 21°49N 103°33E **38** B4
Quyon *Canada* 45°31N 76°14W **83** A8
Quzhou *China* 28°57N 118°54E **33** D12
Quzi *China* 36°20N 107°20E **34** F4
Qyzylorda *Kazakhstan* 44°48N 65°28E **28** E7

R

Ra, Ko *Thailand* 9°13N 98°16E **39** H2
Raahe *Finland* 64°40N 24°28E **8** D21
Raalte *Neths.* 52°23N 6°16E **15** B6
Raas *Indonesia* 7°8S 114°33E **37** G16
Raasay *U.K.* 57°25N 6°4W **11** D2
Raasay, Sd. of *U.K.* 57°30N 6°8W **11** D2
Raasepori *Finland* 60°0N 23°26E **9** G20
Rába → *Hungary* 47°38N 17°38E **17** E9
Rabai *Kenya* 3°50S 39°31E **54** C4
Rabat = Victoria *Malta* 36°3N 14°14E **25** C1
Rabat *Malta* 35°53N 14°24E **25** D1
Rabat *Morocco* 34°2N 6°48W **50** B4
Rabaul *Papua N. G.* 4°24S 152°18E **58** B8
Rabbit Flat *Australia* 20°11S 130°1E **60** D5
Rabbit Lake Mine *Canada* 58°4N 104°5W **71** B8
Rabi *Fiji* 16°30S 179°59W **59** a
Rābigh *Si. Arabia* 22°50N 39°5E **44** F4
Râbniţa *Moldova* 47°45N 29°0E **17** E15
Râbor *Iran* 29°17N 56°55E **45** D8
Rabwah = Chenab Nagar
  Pakistan 31°45N 72°55E **42** D5

Race, C. *Canada* 46°40N 53°5W **73** C9
Rach Gia *Vietnam* 10°5N 105°5E **39** G5
Rach Soi *Vietnam* 9°57N 105°7E **39** H5
Racha Noi, Ko *Thailand* 7°30N 98°19E **39** J2
Racha Yai, Ko *Thailand* 7°36N 98°21E **39** J2
Rachid *Mauritania* 18°45N 11°35W **50** E3
Racibórz *Poland* 50°7N 18°18E **17** C10
Racine *U.S.A.* 42°44N 87°47W **80** D10
Rackerby *U.S.A.* 39°26N 121°22W **78** F5
Radama, Nosy *Madag.* 14°0S 47°47E **57** A8
Radama, Saikanosy
  Madag. 14°16S 47°53E **57** A8
Rădăuţi *Romania* 47°50N 25°59E **17** E13
Radcliff *U.S.A.* 37°51N 85°57W **81** G11
Radekhiv *Ukraine* 50°25N 24°32E **17** C13
Radekhov = Radekhiv
  Ukraine 50°25N 24°32E **17** C13
Radford *U.S.A.* 37°8N 80°34W **81** G13
Radhanpur *India* 23°50N 71°38E **42** H4
Radhwa, Jabal *Si. Arabia* 24°34N 38°18E **44** E3
Radisson *Qué., Canada* 53°47N 77°37W **72** B4
Radisson *Sask., Canada* 52°30N 107°20W **71** C7
Radium Hot Springs
  Canada 50°35N 116°2W **70** C5
Radnor Forest *U.K.* 52°17N 3°10W **13** E4
Radom *Poland* 51°23N 21°12E **17** C11
Radomsko *Poland* 51°5N 19°28E **17** C10
Radomyshl *Ukraine* 50°30N 29°12E **17** C15
Radstock, C. *Australia* 33°12S 134°20E **63** E1
Raduzhnyy *Russia* 62°5N 77°28E **28** C8
Radviliškis *Lithuania* 55°49N 23°33E **9** J20
Radville *Canada* 49°30N 104°15W **71** D8
Rae *Canada* 62°50N 116°3W **70** A5
Rae Bareli *India* 26°18N 81°20E **43** F9
Rae Isthmus *Canada* 66°40N 87°30W **69** D14
Raeren *Belgium* 50°41N 6°7E **15** D6
Raeside, L. *Australia* 29°20S 122°0E **61** E3
Raetihi *N.Z.* 39°25S 175°17E **59** C5
Rafaela *Argentina* 31°10S 61°30W **94** C3
Rafah *Gaza Strip* 31°18N 34°14E **46** D3
Rafai *C.A.R.* 4°59N 23°58E **54** B1
Rafḥā *Si. Arabia* 29°35N 43°35E **44** D4
Rafsanjan *Iran* 30°30N 56°5E **45** D8
Raft Pt. *Australia* 16°4S 124°26E **60** C3
Râgâ *Sudan* 8°28N 25°41E **51** G11
Ragachow *Belarus* 53°8N 30°5E **17** B16
Ragama *Sri Lanka* 7°0N 79°50E **40** R11
Ragged, Mt. *Australia* 33°27S 123°25E **61** F3
Ragged Pt. *Barbados* 13°10N 59°26W **89** g
Raghunathpalli *India* 22°14N 84°48E **43** H11
Raghunathpur *India* 23°33N 86°40E **43** H12
Raglan *N.Z.* 37°55S 174°55E **59** B5
Ragusa *Italy* 36°55N 14°44E **22** F6
Raha *Indonesia* 4°55S 123°0E **37** E6
Rahaeng = Tak *Thailand* 16°52N 99°8E **38** D2
Rahatgarh *India* 23°47N 78°22E **43** H8
Rahimyar Khan *Pakistan* 28°30N 70°25E **42** E4
Rähjerd *Iran* 34°22N 50°22E **45** C6
Rahole △ *Kenya* 0°5N 38°57E **54** B4
Rahon *India* 31°3N 76°7E **42** D7
Rai, Hon *Vietnam* 9°48N 104°38E **39** H5
Raiatéa, Î.
  French Polynesia 16°50S 151°25W **65** J12
Raichur *India* 16°10N 77°20E **40** L10
Raiganj *India* 25°37N 88°10E **43** G13
Raigarh *India* 21°56N 83°25E **41** J13
Raijua *Indonesia* 10°37S 121°36E **37** F6
Raikot *India* 30°41N 75°42E **42** D6
Railton *Australia* 41°25S 146°28E **63** G4
Rainbow Bridge △
  U.S.A. 37°5N 110°58W **77** H8
Rainbow Lake *Canada* 58°30N 119°23W **70** B5
Rainier *U.S.A.* 46°53N 122°41W **78** D4
Rainier, Mt. *U.S.A.* 46°52N 121°46W **78** D5
Rainy L. *Canada* 48°42N 93°10W **71** D10
Rainy River *Canada* 48°43N 94°29W **71** D10
Raippaluoto *Finland* 63°13N 21°14E **8** E19
Raipur *India* 21°17N 81°45E **41** J12
Raisen *India* 23°20N 77°48E **42** H8
Raisio *Finland* 60°28N 22°11E **9** F20
Raj Nandgaon *India* 21°5N 81°5E **41** J12
Raj Nilgiri *India* 21°28N 86°46E **43** J12
Raja, Ujung *Indonesia* 3°40N 96°25E **36** D1
Raja Ampat, Kepulauan
  Indonesia 0°30S 130°0E **37** E8
Rajahmundry *India* 17°1N 81°48E **41** L12
Rajaji △ *India* 30°10N 78°20E **42** D8
Rajang → *Malaysia* 2°30N 112°0E **36** D4
Rajanpur *Pakistan* 29°6N 70°19E **42** E4
Rajapalaiyam *India* 9°25N 77°35E **40** Q10
Rajasthan □ *India* 26°45N 73°30E **42** F5
Rajasthan Canal = Indira Gandhi
  Canal *India* 28°0N 72°0E **42** F5
Rajauri *India* 33°25N 74°21E **43** C6
Rajgarh *Mad. P., India* 24°2N 76°45E **42** G7
Rajgarh *Raj., India* 27°14N 76°38E **42** F7
Rajgarh *Raj., India* 28°40N 75°25E **42** E6
Rajgir *India* 25°2N 85°25E **43** G11
Rajkot *India* 22°15N 70°56E **42** H4
Rajmahal Hills *India* 24°30N 87°30E **43** G12
Rajpipla *India* 21°50N 73°30E **40** J8
Rajpur *India* 22°18N 74°21E **42** H6
Rajpura *India* 30°25N 76°32E **42** D7
Rajsamand = Kankroli
  India 25°4N 73°53E **42** G5
Rajshahi *Bangla.* 24°22N 88°39E **41** G16
Rajshahi □ *Bangla.* 25°0N 89°0E **43** G13
Rajula *India* 21°3N 71°26E **42** J4
Rakaia *N.Z.* 43°45S 172°1E **59** E4
Rakaia → *N.Z.* 43°36S 172°15E **59** E4
Rakan, Ra's *Qatar* 26°10N 51°20E **45** E6
Rakaposhi *Pakistan* 36°10N 74°25E **43** A6
Rakata, Pulau *Indonesia* 6°10S 105°20E **37** G11
Rakhiv *Ukraine* 48°3N 24°12E **17** D13
Rakhni *Pakistan* 30°4N 69°56E **42** D3
Rakhni → *Pakistan* 29°31N 69°36E **42** E3
Rakitnoye *Russia* 45°36N 134°17E **30** B7
Rakiura = Stewart I.
  N.Z. 46°58S 167°54E **59** G1

Rakiura △ *N.Z.* 47°0S 167°50E **59** G1
Rakops *Botswana* 21°1S 24°28E **56** C3
Rakvere *Estonia* 59°20N 26°25E **9** G22
Raleigh *U.S.A.* 35°47N 78°39W **85** D15
Ralik Chain *Pac. Oc.* 8°0N 168°0E **64** G8
Ralls *U.S.A.* 33°41N 101°24W **84** E4
Ralston *U.S.A.* 41°30N 76°57W **82** E8
Ram → *Canada* 62°1N 123°41W **70** A4
Rām Allāh *West Bank* 31°55N 35°10E **46** D4
Rama *Nic.* 12°9N 84°15W **88** D3
Ramakona *India* 21°43N 78°50E **43** J8
Rāmallāh = Rām Allāh
  West Bank 31°55N 35°10E **46** D4
Raman *Thailand* 6°29N 101°18E **39** J3
Ramanathapuram *India* 9°25N 78°55E **40** Q11
Ramanujganj *India* 23°48N 83°42E **43** H10
Ramat Gan *Israel* 32°4N 34°48E **46** C3
Ramatlhabama *S. Africa* 25°37S 25°33E **56** D4
Ramban *India* 33°14N 75°12E **43** C6
Rambi = Rabi *Fiji* 16°30S 179°59W **59** a
Rambipuji *Indonesia* 8°12S 113°37E **37** H15
Rame Hd. *Australia* 37°47S 149°30E **63** F4
Ramechhap *Nepal* 27°25N 86°10E **43** F12
Ramganga → *India* 27°5N 79°58E **43** F8
Ramgarh *Jharkhand,*
  India 23°40N 85°35E **43** H11
Ramgarh *Raj., India* 27°16N 75°14E **42** F6
Ramgarh *Raj., India* 27°30N 70°36E **42** F4
Rämhormoz *Iran* 31°15N 49°35E **45** D6
Ramian *Iran* 37°3N 55°16E **45** B7
Ramingining *Australia* 12°19S 135°3E **62** A2
Ramla *Israel* 31°55N 34°52E **46** D3
Ramm = Rum *Jordan* 29°39N 35°26E **46** F4
Ramm, Jabal *Jordan* 29°35N 35°24E **46** F4
Ramnad = Ramanathapuram
  India 9°25N 78°55E **40** Q11
Ramnagar *Jammu & Kashmir,*
  India 32°47N 75°18E **43** C6
Ramnagar *Uttarakhand,*
  India 29°24N 79°7E **43** E8
Râmnicu Sărat *Romania* 45°26N 27°3E **17** F14
Râmnicu Vâlcea
  Romania 45°9N 24°21E **17** F13
Ramona *U.S.A.* 33°2N 116°52W **79** M10
Ramore *Canada* 48°30N 80°25W **72** C3
Ramotswa *Botswana* 24°50S 25°52E **56** C4
Rampur *H.P., India* 31°26N 77°43E **42** D7
Rampur *Mad. P., India* 23°25N 73°53E **42** H5
Rampur *U.P., India* 28°50N 79°5E **43** E8
Rampur Hat *India* 24°10N 87°50E **43** G12
Rampura *India* 24°30N 75°27E **42** G6
Ramrama Tola *India* 21°52N 79°55E **43** J8
Ramree I. *Burma* 19°0N 93°40E **41** K19
Rämsar *Iran* 36°53N 50°41E **45** B6
Ramsey *I. of Man* 54°20N 4°22W **12** C3
Ramsey *U.S.A.* 41°4N 74°9W **83** E10
Ramsey L. *Canada* 47°13N 82°15W **72** C3
Ramsgate *U.K.* 51°20N 1°25E **13** F9
Ramtek *India* 21°20N 79°15E **40** J11
Ramu *Kenya* 3°55N 41°10E **54** B5
Rana Pratap Sagar Dam
  India 24°58N 75°38E **42** G6
Ranaghat *India* 23°15N 88°35E **43** H13
Ranahu *Pakistan* 25°55N 69°45E **42** G3
Ranau *Malaysia* 6°2N 116°40E **36** C5
Rancagua *Chile* 34°10S 70°50W **94** C1
Rancheria → *Canada* 60°13N 129°7W **70** A3
Ranchester *U.S.A.* 44°54N 107°10W **76** D10
Ranchi *India* 23°19N 85°27E **43** H11
Rancho Cordova
  U.S.A. 38°36N 121°18W **78** G5
Rancho Cucamonga
  U.S.A. 34°10N 117°30W **79** L9
Randalstown *U.K.* 54°45N 6°19W **10** B5
Randers *Denmark* 56°29N 10°1E **9** H14
Randfontein *S. Africa* 26°8S 27°45E **57** D4
Randle *U.S.A.* 46°32N 121°57W **78** D5
Randolph *Mass., U.S.A.* 42°10N 71°2W **83** D13
Randolph *N.Y., U.S.A.* 42°10N 78°59W **82** D6
Randolph *Utah, U.S.A.* 41°40N 111°11W **76** F8
Randolph *Vt., U.S.A.* 43°55N 72°40W **83** C12
Randsburg *U.S.A.* 35°22N 117°39W **79** K9
Råneälven → *Sweden* 65°50N 22°20E **8** D20
Rangae *Thailand* 6°19N 101°44E **39** J3
Rangaunu B. *N.Z.* 34°51S 173°15E **59** A4
Range, The *Zimbabwe* 19°2S 31°2E **55** F3
Rangeley *U.S.A.* 44°58N 70°39W **83** B14
Rangeley L. *U.S.A.* 44°55N 70°43W **83** B14
Rangely *U.S.A.* 40°5N 108°48W **76** F9
Ranger *U.S.A.* 32°28N 98°41W **84** E5
Rangia *India* 26°28N 91°38E **41** F17
Rangiora *N.Z.* 43°19S 172°36E **59** E4
Rangitaiki → *N.Z.* 37°54S 176°49E **59** B6
Rangitata → *N.Z.* 43°45S 171°15E **59** E3
Rangitoto ke te tonga = D'Urville
  I. *N.Z.* 40°50S 173°55E **59** D4
Rangkasbitung
  Indonesia 6°21S 106°15E **37** G12
Rangoon *Burma* 16°45N 96°20E **41** L20
Rangoon → *Burma* 16°28N 96°40E **41** L20
Rangpur *Bangla.* 25°42N 89°22E **41** G16
Rangsang *Indonesia* 1°20N 103°5E **39** M4
Ranibennur *India* 14°35N 75°30E **40** M9
Raniganj *Ut. P., India* 27°3N 82°13E **43** F9
Raniganj *W. Bengal, India* 23°40N 87°5E **41** H15
Ranikhet *India* 29°39N 79°25E **43** E8
Raniwara *India* 24°50N 72°10E **42** G5
Rāniyah *Iraq* 36°15N 44°53E **44** B5
Ranka *India* 23°59N 83°47E **43** H10
Ranken → *Australia* 20°31S 137°36E **62** C2
Rankin *U.S.A.* 31°13N 101°56W **84** F4
Rankin Inlet *Canada* 62°30N 93°0W **68** E13
Rankins Springs
  Australia 33°49S 146°14E **63** E4
Rannoch, L. *U.K.* 56°41N 4°20W **11** E4
Rannoch Moor *U.K.* 56°38N 4°48W **11** E4
Ranobe, Helodranon' i
  Madag. 23°3S 43°33E **57** C7
Ranohira *Madag.* 22°29S 45°24E **57** C8
Ranomafana *Toamasina,*
  Madag. 18°57S 48°50E **57** B8

Ranomafana Toliara, Madag. 24°34S 47°0E 57 C8
Ranomafana △ Madag. 21°16S 47°25E 57 C8
Ranomena Madag. 23°25S 47°17E 57 C8
Ranong Thailand 9°56N 98°40E 39 H2
Ranotsara Nord Madag. 22°48S 46°36E 57 C8
Rānsa Iran 33°39N 48°18E 45 C6
Ransiki Indonesia 1°30S 134°10E 37 E8
Rantabe Madag. 15°42S 49°39E 57 B8
Rantau Abang Malaysia 4°52N 103°24E 39 K4
Rantauprapat Indonesia 2°15N 99°50E 36 D1
Rantemario Indonesia 3°15S 119°57E 37 E5
Ranthambore △ India 26°10N 76°30E 42 F7
Rantoul U.S.A. 40°19N 88°9W 80 E9
Raohe China 46°47N 134°0E 30 A7
Raoyang China 38°15N 115°45E 34 E8
Rap, Ko Thailand 9°19N 99°58E 39 b
Rapa French Polynesia 27°35S 144°20W 65 K13
Rapa Nui = Pascua, I. de Chile 27°7S 109°23W 65 K17
Rapallo Italy 44°21N 9°14E 20 D8
Rapar India 23°34N 70°38E 42 H4
Rāpch Iran 25°40N 59°15E 45 E8
Rapel, Lago Chile 34°20S 71°14W 94 C1
Raper, C. Canada 69°44N 67°6W 69 D18
Rapid City U.S.A. 44°5N 103°14W 80 C2
Rapid River U.S.A. 45°55N 86°58W 80 C10
Rapla Estonia 59°1N 24°52E 9 G21
Rapti → India 26°18N 83°41E 43 F10
Raquette → U.S.A. 45°0N 74°42W 83 B10
Raquette Lake U.S.A. 43°49N 74°40W 83 C10
Rara △ Nepal 29°30N 82°10E 43 E10
Rarotonga Cook Is. 21°30S 160°0W 65 K12
Ra's al 'Ayn Syria 36°45N 40°12E 44 B4
Ra's al Khaymah U.A.E. 25°50N 55°59E 45 E7
Ra's aț Tib Tunisia 37°1N 11°2E 22 F4
Rasa, Pta. Argentina 36°20S 56°41W 94 D4
Rasca, Pta. de la Canary Is. 27°59N 16°41W 24 G3
Raseiniai Lithuania 55°25N 23°5E 9 J20
Rashmi India 25°4N 74°22E 42 G6
Rasht Iran 37°20N 49°40E 45 B6
Rasi Salai Thailand 15°20N 104°9E 38 E5
Rason L. Australia 28°45S 124°25E 61 E3
Rasra India 25°50N 83°50E 43 G10
Rasul Pakistan 32°42N 73°34E 42 C5
Rat → Canada 49°35N 97°10W 71 D9
Rat Buri = Ratchaburi Thailand 13°30N 99°54E 38 F2
Rat Islands U.S.A. 52°0N 178°0E 74 E3
Rat L. Canada 56°10N 99°40W 71 B9
Ratak Chain Pac. Oc. 1°0N 170°0E 64 G8
Ratangarh India 28°5N 74°35E 42 E6
Raţāwī Iraq 30°38N 47°13E 44 D5
Ratchaburi Thailand 13°30N 99°54E 38 F2
Rath India 25°36N 79°37E 43 G8
Rath Luirc Ireland 52°21N 8°40W 10 D3
Rathangan Ireland 53°13N 7°1W 10 C4
Rathdrum Ireland 52°56N 6°14W 10 D5
Rathenow Germany 52°37N 12°19E 16 B7
Rathkeale Ireland 52°32N 8°56W 10 D3
Rathlin I. U.K. 55°18N 6°14W 10 A5
Rathmelton Ireland 55°2N 7°38W 10 A4
Ratibor = Racibórz Poland 50°7N 18°18E 17 C10
Ratlam India 23°20N 75°0E 42 H6
Ratmanova Ostrov Russia 65°46N 169°6W 74 B6
Ratnagiri India 16°57N 73°18E 40 L8
Ratodero Pakistan 27°48N 68°18E 42 F3
Raton U.S.A. 36°54N 104°24W 77 H11
Rattaphum Thailand 7°8N 100°16E 39 J3
Rattray Hd. U.K. 57°38N 1°50W 11 D7
Ratz, Mt. Canada 57°23N 132°12W 70 B2
Raub Malaysia 3°47N 101°52E 39 L3
Rauch Argentina 36°45S 59°5W 94 D4
Raudales Mexico 17°27N 93°39W 87 D6
Raufarhöfn Iceland 66°27N 15°57W 8 C6
Raufoss Norway 60°44N 10°37E 8 F14
Raukumara Ra. N.Z. 38°5S 177°55E 59 C6
Rauma Finland 61°10N 21°30E 8 F19
Raumo = Rauma Finland 61°10N 21°30E 8 F19
Raung, Gunung Indonesia 8°8S 114°3E 37 J17
Raurkela India 22°14N 84°50E 43 H11
Rausu-Dake Japan 44°4N 145°7E 30 B12
Rava-Ruska Ukraine 50°15N 23°42E 17 C12
Rava Russkaya = Rava-Ruska Ukraine 50°15N 23°42E 17 C12
Ravalli U.S.A. 47°17N 114°11W 76 C6
Ravānsar Iran 34°43N 46°40E 44 C5
Rāvar Iran 31°20N 56°51E 45 D8
Ravena U.S.A. 42°28N 73°49W 83 D11
Ravenna Italy 44°25N 12°12E 22 B5
Ravenna Nebr., U.S.A. 41°1N 98°55W 80 E4
Ravenna Ohio, U.S.A. 41°9N 81°15W 82 E3
Ravensburg Germany 47°46N 9°36E 16 E5
Ravenshoe Australia 17°37S 145°29E 62 B4
Ravensthorpe Australia 33°35S 120°2E 61 F3
Ravenswood Australia 20°6S 146°54E 62 C4
Ravenswood U.S.A. 38°57N 81°46W 81 F13
Ravi → Pakistan 30°35N 71°49E 42 D4
Rawalpindi Pakistan 33°38N 73°8E 42 C5
Rawang Malaysia 3°20N 101°35E 39 L3
Rawene N.Z. 35°25S 173°32E 59 A4
Rawi, Ko Thailand 6°33N 99°14E 39 J2
Rawlinna Australia 30°58S 125°28E 61 F4
Rawlins U.S.A. 41°47N 107°14W 76 F10
Rawlinson Ra. Australia 24°40S 128°30E 61 D4
Rawson Argentina 43°15S 65°5W 96 E3
Raxaul India 26°59N 84°51E 43 F11
Ray U.S.A. 48°21N 103°10W 80 A2
Ray, C. Canada 47°33N 59°15W 73 C8
Ray Mts. U.S.A. 66°0N 152°0W 74 B9
Raya Ring, Ko Thailand 8°18N 98°29E 39 a
Rayadurg India 14°40N 76°50E 40 M10
Rayagada India 19°15N 83°20E 41 K13
Raychikhinsk Russia 49°46N 129°25E 29 E13
Rāyen Iran 29°34N 57°26E 45 D8
Rayleigh U.K. 51°36N 0°37E 13 F8
Raymond Canada 49°30N 112°35W 70 D6
Raymond Calif., U.S.A. 37°13N 119°54W 78 H7
Raymond N.H., U.S.A. 43°2N 71°11W 83 C13
Raymond Wash., U.S.A. 46°41N 123°44W 78 D3
Raymondville U.S.A. 26°29N 97°47W 84 H6
Raymore Canada 51°25N 104°31W 71 C8
Rayón Mexico 29°43N 110°35W 86 B2
Rayong Thailand 12°40N 101°20E 38 F3
Raystown L. U.S.A. 40°25N 78°5W 82 F6
Rayville U.S.A. 32°29N 91°46W 84 E9
Raz, Pte. du France 48°2N 4°47W 20 C1
Razan Iran 35°23N 49°2E 45 C6
Razāzah, Buḩayrat ar Iraq 32°40N 43°35E 44 C4
Razazah, L. = Razāzah, Buḩayrat ar Iraq 32°40N 43°35E 44 C4
Razdel'naya = Rozdilna Ukraine 46°50N 30°2E 17 E16
Razdolnoye Russia 43°30N 131°52E 30 C5
Razeh Iran 32°47N 48°9E 45 C6
Razgrad Bulgaria 43°33N 26°34E 23 C12
Razim, Lacul Romania 44°50N 29°0E 17 F15
Razmak Pakistan 32°45N 69°50E 42 C3
Re, Cu Lao Vietnam 15°22N 109°8E 38 E7
Ré, Î. de France 46°12N 1°30W 20 C3
Reading U.K. 51°27N 0°58W 13 F7
Reading U.S.A. 40°20N 75°56W 83 F9
Reading □ U.K. 51°27N 0°58W 13 F7
Realicó Argentina 35°0S 64°15W 94 D3
Ream Cambodia 10°34N 103°39E 39 G4
Ream △ Cambodia 10°30N 103°45E 39 G4
Reay Forest U.K. 58°22N 4°55W 11 C4
Rebecca, L. Australia 30°0S 122°15E 61 F3
Rebi Indonesia 6°23S 134°7E 37 F8
Rebiana, Sahrâ' Libya 24°30N 21°0E 51 D10
Reboly Russia 63°49N 30°47E 8 E24
Rebun-Tō Japan 45°23N 141°2E 30 B10
Recherche, Arch. of the Australia 34°15S 122°50E 61 F3
Rechna Doab Pakistan 31°35N 73°30E 42 D5
Rechytsa Belarus 52°21N 30°24E 17 B16
Recife Brazil 8°0S 35°0W 93 E12
Recife Seychelles 4°36S 55°42E 53 b
Recklinghausen Germany 51°37N 7°12E 15 C7
Reconquista Argentina 29°10S 59°45W 94 B4
Recreo Argentina 29°25S 65°10W 94 B2
Red = Hong → Vietnam 20°16N 106°34E 38 B5
Red → U.S.A. 31°1N 91°45W 84 F9
Red Bank U.S.A. 40°21N 74°5W 83 F10
Red Bay Canada 51°44N 56°25W 73 B8
Red Bluff U.S.A. 40°11N 122°15W 76 F2
Red Bluff Res. U.S.A. 31°54N 103°55W 77 L12
Red Cliffs Australia 34°19S 142°11E 63 E3
Red Cloud U.S.A. 40°5N 98°32W 80 E4
Red Creek U.S.A. 43°14N 76°45W 83 C8
Red Deer Canada 52°20N 113°50W 70 C6
Red Deer → Alta., Canada 50°58N 110°0W 71 C7
Red Deer → Man., Canada 52°53N 101°1W 71 C8
Red Deer L. Canada 52°55N 101°20W 71 C8
Red Hook U.S.A. 41°55N 73°53W 83 E11
Red Indian L. Canada 48°35N 57°0W 73 C8
Red L. Canada 51°3N 93°49W 71 C10
Red Lake Canada 51°3N 93°49W 71 C10
Red Lake Falls U.S.A. 47°53N 96°16W 80 B5
Red Lake Road Canada 49°59N 93°25W 71 C10
Red Lodge U.S.A. 45°11N 109°15W 76 D9
Red Mountain U.S.A. 35°37N 117°38W 79 K9
Red Oak U.S.A. 41°1N 95°14W 80 E6
Red River of the North → N. Amer. 49°0N 97°15W 80 A5
Red Rock Canada 48°55N 88°15W 72 C2
Red Rock, L. U.S.A. 41°22N 92°59W 80 E7
Red Rocks Pt. Australia 32°13S 127°32E 61 F4
Red Sea Asia 25°0N 36°0E 47 C2
Red Slate Mt. U.S.A. 37°31N 118°52W 78 H8
Red Sucker L. Canada 54°9N 93°40W 72 B1
Red Tower Pass = Turnu Roşu, P. Romania 45°33N 24°17E 17 F13
Red Wing U.S.A. 44°34N 92°31W 80 C7
Redang, Pulau Malaysia 5°49N 103°2E 39 K4
Redange Lux. 49°46N 5°52E 15 E5
Redcar U.K. 54°37N 1°4W 12 C6
Redcar & Cleveland □ U.K. 54°29N 1°0W 12 C7
Redcliff Canada 50°10N 110°50W 76 A8
Redcliffe Australia 27°12S 153°6E 63 D5
Redcliffe, Mt. Australia 28°30S 121°30E 61 E3
Reddersburg S. Africa 29°41S 26°10E 56 D4
Redding U.S.A. 40°35N 122°24W 76 F2
Redditch U.K. 52°18N 1°55W 13 E6
Redfield U.S.A. 44°53N 98°31W 80 C4
Redford U.S.A. 44°38N 73°48W 83 B11
Redhead Trin. & Tob. 10°44N 60°58W 93 K16
Redlands U.S.A. 34°4N 117°11W 79 M9
Redmond Oreg., U.S.A. 44°17N 121°11W 76 D3
Redmond Wash., U.S.A. 47°40N 122°7W 78 C4
Redon France 47°40N 2°6W 20 C2
Redonda Antigua & B. 16°58N 62°19W 89 C7
Redondela Spain 42°15N 8°38W 21 A1
Redondo Beach U.S.A. 33°50N 118°23W 79 M8
Redoubt Volcano U.S.A. 60°29N 152°45W 74 C9
Redruth U.K. 50°14N 5°14W 13 G2
Redvers Canada 49°35N 101°40W 71 D8
Redwater Canada 53°55N 113°6W 70 C6
Redwood U.S.A. 44°18N 75°48W 83 B9
Redwood △ U.S.A. 41°40N 124°5W 76 F1
Redwood City U.S.A. 37°30N 122°15W 78 H4
Redwood Falls U.S.A. 44°32N 95°7W 80 C6
Ree, L. Ireland 53°35N 8°0W 10 C3
Reed City U.S.A. 43°53N 85°31W 81 D11
Reed L. Canada 54°38N 100°30W 71 C8
Reedley U.S.A. 36°36N 119°27W 78 J7
Reedsburg U.S.A. 43°32N 90°0W 80 D8
Reedsport U.S.A. 43°42N 124°6W 76 E1
Reedsville U.S.A. 40°39N 77°35W 82 F7
Reefton N.Z. 42°6S 171°51E 59 E3
Reese → U.S.A. 40°48N 117°4W 76 F5
Refugio U.S.A. 28°18N 97°17W 84 G6
Regana, C. de Spain 39°25N 2°43E 24 B9
Regensburg Germany 49°1N 12°6E 16 D7
Reggâne = Zaouiet Reggâne Algeria 26°32N 0°3E 50 C6
Réggio di Calábria Italy 38°6N 15°39E 22 E6
Réggio nell'Emília Italy 44°43N 10°36E 22 B4
Reghin Romania 46°46N 24°42E 17 E13
Regina Canada 50°27N 104°35W 71 C8
Regina Beach Canada 50°47N 105°0W 71 C8
Registro Brazil 24°29S 47°49W 95 A6
Rehar → India 23°55N 82°40E 43 H10
Rehli India 23°38N 79°5E 43 H8
Rehoboth Namibia 23°15S 17°4E 56 C2
Rehovot Israel 31°54N 34°48E 46 D3
Reichenbach Germany 50°37N 12°17E 16 C7
Reid Australia 30°49S 128°26E 61 F4
Reidsville U.S.A. 36°21N 79°40W 85 C15
Reigate U.K. 51°14N 0°12W 13 F7
Reims France 49°15N 4°1E 20 B6
Reina Adelaida, Arch. Chile 52°20S 74°0W 96 G2
Reina Sofía, Tenerife ✈ (TFS) Canary Is. 28°3N 16°33W 24 F3
Reindeer → Canada 55°36N 103°11W 71 B8
Reindeer I. Canada 52°30N 98°0W 71 C9
Reindeer L. Canada 57°15N 102°15W 71 B8
Reinga, C. N.Z. 34°25S 172°43E 59 A4
Reinosa Spain 43°2N 4°15W 21 A3
Reitz S. Africa 27°48S 28°29E 57 D4
Reivilo S. Africa 27°36S 24°8E 56 D3
Reliance Canada 63°0N 109°20W 71 A7
Remanso Brazil 9°41S 42°4W 93 E10
Remarkable, Mt. Australia 32°48S 138°10E 63 E2
Rembang Indonesia 6°42S 111°21E 37 G14
Remedios Panama 8°15N 81°50W 88 E3
Remeshk Iran 26°55N 58°50E 45 E8
Remich Lux. 49°32N 6°22E 15 E6
Remscheid Germany 51°11N 7°12E 15 C7
Ren Xian China 37°8N 114°40E 34 F8
Rendang Indonesia 8°26S 115°25E 37 J18
Rendsburg Germany 54°17N 9°39E 16 A5
Renfrew Canada 45°30N 76°40W 83 A8
Renfrewshire □ U.K. 55°49N 4°38W 11 F4
Rengat Indonesia 0°30S 102°45E 36 E2
Rengo Chile 34°24S 70°50W 94 C1
Reni = Taranagar India 28°43N 74°50E 42 E6
Reni Ukraine 45°28N 28°15E 17 F15
Renmark Australia 34°11S 140°43E 63 E3
Rennell Sd. Canada 53°23N 132°35W 70 C2
Renner Springs Australia 18°20S 133°47E 62 B1
Rennes France 48°7N 1°41W 20 B3
Rennick Glacier Antarctica 70°30S 161°45E 5 D11
Rennie L. Canada 61°32N 105°35W 71 A7
Reno U.S.A. 39°31N 119°48W 78 F7
Reno → Italy 44°38N 12°16E 22 B5
Renovo U.S.A. 41°20N 77°45W 82 E7
Renqiu China 38°43N 116°5E 34 E9
Rensselaer Ind., U.S.A. 40°57N 87°9W 80 E10
Rensselaer N.Y., U.S.A. 42°38N 73°45W 83 D11
Renton U.S.A. 47°28N 122°12W 78 C4
Renukoot India 24°12N 83°2E 43 G10
Reotipur India 25°33N 83°45E 43 G10
Republic Mo., U.S.A. 37°7N 93°29W 80 G7
Republic Wash., U.S.A. 48°39N 118°44W 76 B4
Republican → U.S.A. 39°4N 96°48W 80 F5
Repulse B. Australia 20°35S 148°46E 62 b
Repulse Bay Canada 66°30N 86°30W 69 D14
Requena Peru 5°5S 73°52W 92 E4
Requena Spain 39°30N 1°4W 21 C5
Reserve U.S.A. 33°43N 108°45W 77 K9
Resht = Rasht Iran 37°20N 49°40E 45 B6
Resistencia Argentina 27°30S 59°0W 94 B4
Reşiţa Romania 45°18N 21°53E 17 F11
Reso = Raisio Finland 60°28N 22°11E 9 F20
Resolute Canada 74°42N 94°54W 69 C13
Resolution I. Canada 61°30N 65°0W 69 E19
Resolution I. N.Z. 45°40S 166°40E 59 F1
Ressano Garcia Mozam. 25°25S 32°0E 57 D5
Reston Canada 49°33N 101°6W 71 D8
Retalhuleu Guatemala 14°33N 91°46W 88 D1
Retenue, L. de Dem. Rep. of the Congo 11°0S 27°0E 55 E2
Retford U.K. 53°19N 0°56W 12 D7
Rethimno Greece 35°18N 24°30E 25 D6
Rethimno □ Greece 35°23N 24°28E 25 D6
Reti Pakistan 28°5N 69°48E 42 E3
Réunion ☑ Ind. Oc. 21°0S 56°0E 53 c
Reus Spain 41°10N 1°5E 21 B6
Reutlingen Germany 48°29N 9°12E 16 D5
Reval = Tallinn Estonia 59°22N 24°48E 9 G21
Revda Russia 56°48N 59°57E 18 C10
Revelganj India 25°50N 84°40E 43 G11
Revelstoke Canada 51°0N 118°10W 70 C5
Reventazón Peru 6°10S 80°58W 92 E2
Revillagigedo, Is. de Pac. Oc. 18°40N 112°0W 86 D2
Revuè → Mozam. 19°50S 34°0E 55 F3
Rewa India 24°33N 81°25E 43 G9
Rewari India 28°15N 76°40E 42 E7
Rexburg U.S.A. 43°49N 111°47W 76 E8
Rey Iran 35°35N 51°25E 45 C6
Rey, I. del Panama 8°20N 78°30W 88 E4
Rey, L. del Mexico 27°1N 103°26W 86 B4
Rey Malabo Eq. Guin. 3°45N 8°50E 52 D1
Reyðarfjörður Iceland 65°2N 14°13W 8 D6
Reyes, Pt. U.S.A. 38°0N 123°0W 78 H3
Reykjahlíð Iceland 65°40N 16°55W 8 D5
Reykjanes Iceland 63°48N 22°40W 8 E2
Reykjavík Iceland 64°10N 21°57W 8 D3
Reynolds Ra. Australia 22°30S 133°0E 60 D5
Reynoldsville U.S.A. 41°6N 78°53W 82 E6
Reynosa Mexico 26°7N 98°18W 87 B5
Rēzekne Latvia 56°30N 27°17E 9 H22
Rezvān Iran 27°34N 56°6E 45 E8
Rhayader U.K. 52°18N 3°29W 13 E4
Rhein → Europe 51°52N 6°2E 15 C6
Rhein-Main-Donau-Kanal Germany 49°1N 11°27E 16 D6
Rheine Germany 52°17N 7°26E 16 B4
Rheinland-Pfalz □ Germany 50°0N 7°0E 16 C4
Rhin = Rhein → Europe 51°52N 6°2E 15 C6
Rhine = Rhein → Europe 51°52N 6°2E 15 C6
Rhinebeck U.S.A. 41°56N 73°55W 83 E11
Rhineland-Palatinate = Rheinland-Pfalz □ Germany 50°0N 7°0E 16 C4
Rhinelander U.S.A. 45°38N 89°25W 80 C9
Rhinns Pt. U.K. 55°40N 6°29W 11 F2
Rhino Camp Uganda 3°0N 31°22E 54 B3
Rhir, Cap Morocco 30°38N 9°54W 50 B4
Rhode Island □ U.S.A. 41°40N 71°30W 83 E13
Rhodes Greece 36°15N 28°10E 25 C10
Rhodope Mts. = Rhodopi Planina Bulgaria 41°40N 24°20E 23 D11
Rhodopi Planina Bulgaria 41°40N 24°20E 23 D11
Rhön Germany 50°24N 9°58E 16 C5
Rhondda U.K. 51°39N 3°31W 13 F4
Rhondda Cynon Taff □ U.K. 51°42N 3°27W 13 F4
Rhône → France 43°28N 4°42E 20 E6
Rhum U.K. 57°0N 6°20W 11 E2
Rhyl U.K. 53°20N 3°29W 12 D4
Riachão Brazil 7°20S 46°37W 93 E9
Riasi India 33°10N 74°50E 43 C6
Riau □ Indonesia 0°0 102°35E 36 E2
Riau, Kepulauan □ Indonesia 0°30N 104°20E 36 D2
Riau Arch. = Riau, Kepulauan □ Indonesia 0°30N 104°20E 36 D2
Ribadeo Spain 43°35N 7°5W 21 A2
Ribas do Rio Pardo Brazil 20°27S 53°46W 93 H8
Ribauè Mozam. 14°57S 38°17E 55 E4
Ribble → U.K. 53°52N 2°25W 12 D5
Ribe Denmark 55°19N 8°44E 9 J13
Ribeira Brava Madeira 32°41N 17°4W 24 D2
Ribeira Grande C. Verde Is. 17°0N 25°4W 50 b
Ribeirão Prêto Brazil 21°10S 47°50W 95 A6
Riberalta Bolivia 11°0S 66°0W 92 F5
Riccarton N.Z. 43°32S 172°37E 59 E4
Rice U.S.A. 34°5N 114°51W 79 L12
Rice L. Canada 44°12N 78°10W 82 B6
Rice Lake U.S.A. 45°30N 91°44W 80 C8
Rich, C. Canada 44°43N 80°38W 82 B4
Richards Bay S. Africa 28°48S 32°6E 57 D5
Richardson → Canada 58°25N 111°14W 71 B6
Richardson Lakes U.S.A. 44°46N 70°58W 81 C18
Richardson Springs U.S.A. 39°51N 121°46W 78 F5
Riche, C. Australia 34°36S 118°47E 61 F2
Richey U.S.A. 47°39N 105°4W 76 C11
Richfield U.S.A. 38°46N 112°5W 76 G7
Richfield Springs U.S.A. 42°51N 74°59W 83 D10
Richford U.S.A. 45°0N 72°40W 83 B12
Richibucto Canada 46°42N 64°54W 73 C7
Richland Ga., U.S.A. 32°5N 84°40W 85 E12
Richland Wash., U.S.A. 46°17N 119°18W 76 C4
Richland Center U.S.A. 43°21N 90°23W 80 D8
Richlands U.S.A. 37°6N 81°48W 81 G13
Richmond Australia 20°43S 143°8E 62 C3
Richmond N.Z. 41°20S 173°12E 59 D4
Richmond U.K. 54°25N 1°43W 12 C6
Richmond Calif., U.S.A. 37°56N 122°21W 78 H4
Richmond Ind., U.S.A. 39°50N 84°53W 81 F11
Richmond Ky., U.S.A. 37°45N 84°18W 81 G11
Richmond Mich., U.S.A. 42°49N 82°45W 82 D2
Richmond Mo., U.S.A. 39°17N 93°58W 80 F7
Richmond Tex., U.S.A. 29°35N 95°46W 84 G7
Richmond Utah, U.S.A. 41°56N 111°48W 76 F8
Richmond Va., U.S.A. 37°33N 77°27W 81 G15
Richmond Vt., U.S.A. 44°24N 72°59W 83 B12
Richmond Hill Canada 43°52N 79°27W 82 C5
Richmond Ra. Australia 29°0S 152°45E 63 D5
Richmondville U.S.A. 42°38N 74°33W 83 D10
Richtersveld △ S. Africa 28°15S 17°10E 56 D2
Richville U.S.A. 44°25N 75°23W 83 B9
Richwood U.S.A. 38°14N 80°32W 81 F13
Ridder = Leninogorsk Kazakhstan 50°20N 83°30E 28 D9
Riddlesburg U.S.A. 40°9N 78°15W 82 F6
Ridgecrest U.S.A. 35°38N 117°40W 79 K9
Ridgefield Conn., U.S.A. 41°17N 73°30W 83 E11
Ridgefield Wash., U.S.A. 45°49N 122°45W 78 E4
Ridgeland Miss., U.S.A. 32°26N 90°8W 85 E9
Ridgeland S.C., U.S.A. 32°29N 80°59W 85 E14
Ridgetown Canada 42°26N 81°52W 82 D3
Ridgewood U.S.A. 40°59N 74°7W 83 F10
Ridgway U.S.A. 41°25N 78°44W 82 E6
Riding Mountain △ Canada 50°50N 100°0W 71 C9
Ridley, Mt. Australia 33°12S 122°7E 61 F3
Riebeek-Oos S. Africa 33°10S 26°10E 56 E4
Ried Austria 48°14N 13°30E 16 D7
Riesa Germany 51°17N 13°17E 16 C7
Riet → S. Africa 29°0S 23°54E 56 D3
Rietbron S. Africa 32°54S 23°10E 56 E3
Rietfontein Namibia 21°58S 20°58E 56 C3
Rieti Italy 42°24N 12°51E 22 C5
Rif = Er Rif Morocco 35°1N 4°1W 50 A5
Riffe L. U.S.A. 46°32N 122°26W 78 D4
Rifle U.S.A. 39°32N 107°47W 76 G10
Rift Valley Africa 7°0N 30°0E 48 G7
Rift Valley □ Kenya 0°20N 36°0E 54 B4
Rīga Latvia 56°53N 24°8E 9 H21
Riga, G. of Latvia 57°40N 23°45E 9 H20
Rīgān Iran 28°37N 58°58E 45 D8
Rīgas Jūras Līcis = Riga, G. of Latvia 57°40N 23°45E 9 H20
Rigaud Canada 45°29N 74°18W 83 A10
Rigby U.S.A. 43°40N 111°55W 76 E8
Rīgestān Afghan. 30°15N 65°0E 40 D4
Riggins U.S.A. 45°25N 116°19W 76 D5
Rigolet Canada 54°10N 58°23W 73 B8
Rihand Dam India 24°9N 83°2E 43 G10
Riihimäki Finland 60°45N 24°48E 8 F21
Riiser-Larsen-halvøya Antarctica 68°0S 35°0E 5 C4
Riiser-Larsen Ice Shelf S. Ocean 74°0S 19°0W 5 D2
Riiser-Larsen Sea S. Ocean 67°30S 22°0E 5 C4
Rijeka Croatia 45°20N 14°21E 16 F8
Rijssen Neths. 52°19N 6°31E 15 B6
Rikuchū-Kaigan △ Japan 39°20N 142°0E 30 E11
Rikuzentakada Japan 39°0N 141°40E 30 E10
Riley U.S.A. 43°32N 119°28W 76 E4
Rima → Nigeria 13°4N 5°10E 50 F7
Rimah, Wadi ar → Si. Arabia 26°5N 41°30E 44 E4
Rimau, Pulau Malaysia 5°15N 100°16E 39 c
Rimbey Canada 52°35N 114°15W 70 C6
Rimersburg U.S.A. 41°3N 79°30W 82 E5
Rímini Italy 44°3N 12°33E 22 B5
Rimouski Canada 48°27N 68°30W 73 C6
Rimrock U.S.A. 46°40N 121°7W 78 D5
Rinca Indonesia 8°45S 119°35E 37 F5
Rincón de Romos Mexico 22°14N 102°18W 86 C4
Rinconada Argentina 22°26S 66°10W 94 A2
Rind → India 25°53N 80°33E 43 G9
Ringas India 27°21N 75°34E 42 F6
Ringgold Is. Fiji 16°15S 179°25W 59 a
Ringkøbing Denmark 56°5N 8°15E 9 H13
Ringvassøya Norway 69°56N 19°15E 8 B18
Ringwood U.S.A. 41°7N 74°15W 83 E10
Rinjani, Gunung Indonesia 8°24S 116°28E 36 F5
Rio Branco Brazil 9°58S 67°49W 92 E5
Río Branco Uruguay 32°40S 53°40W 95 C5
Río Bravo Mexico 25°59N 98°6W 87 B5
Río Bravo ⌒ N. Amer. 29°2N 102°45W 86 B4
Río Bravo del Norte → Mexico 25°57N 97°9W 87 B5
Rio Brilhante Brazil 21°48S 54°33W 95 A5
Rio Claro Brazil 22°19S 47°35W 95 A6
Rio Claro Trin. & Tob. 10°20N 61°25W 93 K15
Río Colorado Argentina 39°0S 64°0W 96 D4
Río Cuarto Argentina 33°10S 64°25W 94 C3
Rio das Pedras Mozam. 23°8S 35°28E 57 C6
Rio de Janeiro Brazil 22°54S 43°12W 95 A7
Rio de Janeiro □ Brazil 22°50S 43°0W 95 A7
Rio do Sul Brazil 27°13S 49°37W 95 B6
Río Dulce △ Guatemala 15°43N 88°50W 88 C2
Río Gallegos Argentina 51°35S 69°15W 96 G3
Río Grande Argentina 53°50S 67°45W 96 G3
Rio Grande Brazil 32°0S 52°20W 95 C5
Río Grande Mexico 23°50N 103°2W 86 C4
Río Grande Puerto Rico 18°23N 65°50W 89 d
Rio Grande → N. Amer. 25°58N 97°9W 84 J6
Rio Grande City U.S.A. 26°23N 98°49W 84 H5
Río Grande de Santiago → Mexico 21°36N 105°26W 86 C3
Rio Grande do Norte □ Brazil 5°40S 36°0W 93 E11
Rio Grande do Sul □ Brazil 30°0S 53°0W 95 C5
Río Hato Panama 8°22N 80°10W 88 E3
Río Lagartos Mexico 21°36N 88°10W 87 C7
Rio Largo Brazil 9°28S 35°50W 93 E11
Río Mulatos Bolivia 19°40S 66°50W 92 G5
Río Muni □ Eq. Guin. 1°30N 10°0E 52 D2
Rio Negro Brazil 26°0S 49°55W 95 B6
Rio Pardo Brazil 30°0S 52°30W 95 C5
Río Pilcomayo △ Argentina 25°5S 58°5W 94 B4
Río Platano ⌒ Honduras 15°45N 85°0W 88 C3
Rio Rancho U.S.A. 35°14N 106°41W 77 J10
Río Segundo Argentina 31°40S 63°59W 94 C3
Río Tercero Argentina 32°15S 64°8W 94 C3
Rio Verde Brazil 17°50S 51°0W 93 G8
Río Verde Mexico 21°56N 99°59W 87 C5
Rio Vista U.S.A. 38°10N 121°42W 78 G5
Riobamba Ecuador 1°50S 78°45W 92 D3
Riohacha Colombia 11°33N 72°55W 92 A4
Riosucio Colombia 7°27N 77°7W 92 B3
Riou L. Canada 59°7N 106°25W 71 B7
Ripley Canada 44°4N 81°35W 82 B3
Ripley Calif., U.S.A. 33°32N 114°39W 79 M12
Ripley N.Y., U.S.A. 42°16N 79°43W 82 D5
Ripley Tenn., U.S.A. 35°45N 89°32W 85 D10
Ripley W. Va., U.S.A. 38°49N 81°43W 81 F13
Ripon U.K. 54°9N 1°31W 12 C6
Ripon Calif., U.S.A. 37°44N 121°7W 78 H5
Ripon Wis., U.S.A. 43°51N 88°50W 80 D9
Rishā', W. ar → Si. Arabia 25°33N 44°5E 44 E5
Rishiri-Rebun-Sarobetsu △ Japan 45°26N 141°30E 30 B10
Rishiri-Tō Japan 45°11N 141°15E 30 B10
Rishon le Ẕiyyon Israel 31°58N 34°48E 46 D3
Rison U.S.A. 33°58N 92°11W 84 E8
Risør Norway 58°43N 9°13E 9 G13
Rita Blanca Cr. → U.S.A. 35°40N 102°29W 84 D3
Ritter, Mt. U.S.A. 37°41N 119°12W 78 H7
Rittman U.S.A. 40°58N 81°47W 82 F3
Ritzville U.S.A. 47°8N 118°23W 76 C4
Riva del Garda Italy 45°53N 10°50E 22 B4
Rivadavia B. Aires, Argentina 35°29S 62°59W 94 D3
Rivadavia Mendoza, Argentina 33°13S 68°30W 94 C2
Rivadavia Salta, Argentina 24°5S 62°54W 94 A3
Rivadavia Chile 29°57S 70°35W 94 B1
Rivas Nic. 11°30N 85°50W 88 D2
Rivash Iran 35°28N 58°26E 45 C8
River Cess Liberia 5°30N 9°32W 50 G4
River Jordan Canada 48°26N 124°3W 78 B2
Rivera Argentina 37°12S 63°14W 94 D3
Rivera Uruguay 31°0S 55°50W 95 C4
Riverbank U.S.A. 37°44N 120°56W 78 H6
Riverdale U.S.A. 36°26N 119°52W 78 J7

Riverhead *U.S.A.* 40°55N 72°40W **83** F12
Riverhurst *Canada* 50°55N 106°50W **71** C7
Rivers *Canada* 50°2N 100°14W **71** C8
Rivers Inlet *Canada* 51°42N 127°15W **70** C3
Riversdale *S. Africa* 34°7S 21°15E **56** E3
Riverside *U.S.A.* 33°59N 117°22W **79** M9
Riverton *Canada* 51°1N 97°0W **71** C9
Riverton *Australia* 34°10S 138°46E **63** E2
Riverton *N.Z.* 46°21S 168°0E **59** G2
Riverton *U.S.A.* 43°2N 108°23W **76** E9
Riviera = Côte d'Azur
  France 43°25N 7°10E **20** E7
Riviera *U.S.A.* 35°4N 114°35W **79** K12
Riviera di Levante *Italy* 44°15N 9°30E **20** D8
Riviera di Ponente *Italy* 44°10N 8°20E **20** D8
Rivière-au-Renard
  Canada 48°59N 64°23W **73** C7
Rivière-du-Loup *Canada* 47°50N 69°30W **73** C6
Rivière-Pentecôte *Canada* 49°57N 67°1W **73** C6
Rivière-Pilote *Martinique* 14°26N 60°53W **88** c
Rivière St-Paul *Canada* 51°28N 57°45W **73** B8
Rivière-Salée *Martinique* 14°31N 61°0W **88** c
Rivne *Ukraine* 50°40N 26°10E **17** C14
Rivne □ *Ukraine* 51°15N 26°30E **17** C14
Rívoli *Italy* 45°3N 7°31E **20** D7
Rivoli B. *Australia* 37°32S 140°3E **63** F3
Riyadh = Ar Riyāḍ
  Si. Arabia 24°41N 46°42E **44** E5
Riyadh al Khabrā'
  Si. Arabia 26°2N 43°33E **44** E4
Rize *Turkey* 41°0N 40°30E **19** F7
Rizhao *China* 35°25N 119°30E **35** G10
Rizokarpaso *Cyprus* 35°36N 34°23E **25** D13
Rizzuto, C. *Italy* 38°53N 17°5E **22** E7
Rjukan *Norway* 59°54N 8°33E **9** G13
Road Town *Br. Virgin Is.* 18°27N 64°37W **89** e
Roan Plateau *U.S.A.* 39°20N 109°20W **76** G9
Roanne *France* 46°3N 4°4E **20** C6
Roanoke *Ala., U.S.A.* 33°9N 85°22W **85** E12
Roanoke *Va., U.S.A.* 37°16N 79°56W **81** G14
Roanoke → *U.S.A.* 35°57N 76°42W **85** D16
Roanoke I. *U.S.A.* 35°53N 75°39W **85** D17
Roanoke Rapids *U.S.A.* 36°28N 77°40W **85** C16
Roatán *Honduras* 16°18N 86°35W **88** C2
Robāt Sang *Iran* 35°35N 59°10E **45** C8
Robāṭkarīm *Iran* 35°25N 50°59E **45** C6
Robbins I. *Australia* 40°42S 145°0E **63** G4
Robe → *Australia* 21°42S 116°15E **60** D2
Robert Bourassa, Rés.
  Canada 53°40N 76°55W **72** B4
Robert Lee *U.S.A.* 31°54N 100°29W **84** F4
Robertsdale *U.S.A.* 40°11N 78°6W **82** F6
Robertsganj *India* 24°44N 83°4E **43** G10
Robertson *S. Africa* 33°46S 19°50E **56** E2
Robertson I. *Antarctica* 65°15S 59°30W **5** C18
Robertson Ra. *Australia* 23°15S 121°0E **60** D3
Robertstown *Australia* 33°58S 139°5E **63** E2
Roberval *Canada* 48°32N 72°15W **73** C5
Robeson Chan. *N. Amer.* 82°0N 61°30W **69** A19
Robesonia *U.S.A.* 40°21N 76°8W **83** F8
Robinson *U.S.A.* 39°0N 87°44W **80** F10
Robinson → *Australia* 16°3S 137°16E **62** B2
Robinson Crusoe I.
  Pac. Oc. 33°38S 78°52W **90** F2
Robinson Ra. *Australia* 25°40S 119°0E **61** E2
Robinvale *Australia* 34°40S 142°45E **63** E3
Roblin *Canada* 51°14N 101°21W **71** C8
Roboré *Bolivia* 18°10S 59°45W **92** G7
Robson, Mt. *Canada* 53°10N 119°10W **70** C5
Robstown *U.S.A.* 27°47N 97°40W **84** H6
Roca, C. da *Portugal* 38°40N 9°31W **21** C1
Roca Partida, I. *Mexico* 19°1N 112°2W **86** D2
Rocas, Atol das *Brazil* 34°1N 33°41W **93** D12
Rocha *Uruguay* 34°30S 54°25W **95** C5
Rochdale *U.K.* 53°38N 2°9W **12** D5
Rochefort *Belgium* 50°9N 5°12E **15** D5
Rochefort *France* 45°56N 0°57W **20** D3
Rochelle *U.S.A.* 41°56N 89°4W **80** E9
Rocher River *Canada* 61°23N 112°44W **70** A6
Rochester *U.K.* 51°23N 0°31E **13** F8
Rochester *Ind., U.S.A.* 41°4N 86°13W **80** E10
Rochester *Minn., U.S.A.* 44°1N 92°28W **80** C7
Rochester *N.H., U.S.A.* 43°18N 70°59W **83** C14
Rochester *N.Y., U.S.A.* 43°10N 77°37W **82** C7
Rock → *U.S.A.* 60°7N 127°7W **70** A3
Rock, The *Australia* 35°15S 147°2E **63** F4
Rock Creek *U.S.A.* 41°40N 80°52W **82** E4
Rock Falls *U.S.A.* 41°47N 89°41W **80** E9
Rock Hill *U.S.A.* 34°56N 81°1W **85** D14
Rock Island *U.S.A.* 41°30N 90°34W **80** E8
Rock Port *U.S.A.* 40°25N 95°31W **80** E6
Rock Rapids *U.S.A.* 43°26N 96°10W **80** D5
Rock Sound *Bahamas* 24°54N 76°12W **88** B4
Rock Springs *Mont.,*
  U.S.A. 46°49N 106°15W **76** C10
Rock Springs *Wyo.,*
  U.S.A. 41°35N 109°14W **76** F9
Rock Valley *U.S.A.* 43°12N 96°18W **80** D5
Rockall *Atl. Oc.* 57°37N 13°42W **6** D3
Rockdale *Tex., U.S.A.* 30°39N 97°0W **84** F6
Rockdale *Wash., U.S.A.* 47°22N 121°28W **78** C5
Rockeby = Mungkan Kandju ○
  Australia 13°35S 142°52E **62** A3
Rockefeller Plateau
  Antarctica 76°0S 130°0W **5** E14
Rockford *U.S.A.* 42°16N 89°6W **80** D9
Rockglen *Canada* 49°11N 105°57W **71** D7
Rockhampton *Australia* 23°22S 150°32E **62** C5
Rockingham *Australia* 32°15S 115°38E **61** F2
Rockingham *N.C.,*
  U.S.A. 34°57N 79°46W **85** D15
Rockingham *Vt.,*
  U.S.A. 43°11N 72°29W **83** C12
Rockingham B. *Australia* 18°5S 146°10E **62** B4
Rocklake *U.S.A.* 48°47N 99°5W **80** A4
Rockland *Canada* 45°33N 75°17W **83** A9
Rockland *Idaho, U.S.A.* 42°34N 112°53W **76** E7
Rockland *Maine, U.S.A.* 44°6N 69°7W **81** C19
Rockland *Mich., U.S.A.* 46°44N 89°11W **80** B9

Rocklin *U.S.A.* 38°48N 121°14W **78** G5
Rockly B. *Trin. & Tob.* 11°9N 60°46W **93** J16
Rockmart *U.S.A.* 34°0N 85°3W **85** D12
Rockport *Mass., U.S.A.* 42°39N 70°37W **83** D14
Rockport *Tex., U.S.A.* 28°2N 97°3W **84** G6
Rockville *Conn., U.S.A.* 41°52N 72°28W **83** E12
Rockville *Md., U.S.A.* 39°5N 77°9W **81** F15
Rockwall *U.S.A.* 32°56N 96°28W **84** E6
Rockwell City *U.S.A.* 42°24N 94°38W **80** D6
Rockwood *Canada* 43°37N 80°8W **82** C4
Rockwood *Maine,*
  U.S.A. 45°41N 69°45W **81** C19
Rockwood *Tenn.,*
  U.S.A. 35°52N 84°41W **85** D12
Rocky Ford *U.S.A.* 38°3N 103°43W **76** G12
Rocky Gully *Australia* 34°30S 116°57E **61** F2
Rocky Harbour *Canada* 49°36N 57°55W **73** C8
Rocky Island L. *Canada* 46°55N 83°0W **72** C3
Rocky Lane *Canada* 58°31N 116°22W **70** B5
Rocky Mount *U.S.A.* 35°57N 77°48W **85** D16
Rocky Mountain △
  U.S.A. 40°25N 105°45W **76** F11
Rocky Mountain House
  Canada 52°22N 114°55W **70** C6
Rocky Mts. *N. Amer.* 49°0N 115°0W **76** B6
Rocky Point *Namibia* 19°3S 12°30E **56** B2
Rod *Pakistan* 28°10N 63°5E **40** E3
Roda *Greece* 39°48N 19°46E **25** A3
Rødbyhavn *Denmark* 54°39N 11°22E **9** J14
Roddickton *Canada* 50°51N 56°8W **73** B8
Rodez *France* 44°21N 2°33E **20** D5
Ródhos = Rhodes
  Greece 36°15N 28°10E **25** C10
Rodia *Greece* 35°22N 25°1E **25** D7
Rodna ○ *Australia* 23°45S 132°4E **60** D5
Rodney, C. *Australia* 42°34N 81°41W **82** D3
Rodney, C., *N.Z.* 36°17S 174°50E **59** B5
Rodrigues *Ind. Oc.* 19°45S 63°20E **3** E13
Roe → *U.K.* 55°6N 6°59W **10** A5
Roebling *U.S.A.* 40°7N 74°47W **83** F10
Roebourne *Australia* 20°44S 117°9E **60** D2
Roebuck B. *Australia* 18°5S 122°20E **60** C3
Roebuck Roadhouse
  Australia 17°59S 122°36E **60** C3
Roermond *Neths.* 51°12N 6°0E **15** C6
Roes Welcome Sd.
  Canada 65°0N 87°0W **69** E14
Roeselare *Belgium* 50°57N 3°7E **15** D3
Rogachev = Ragachow
  Belarus 53°8N 30°5E **17** B16
Rogagua, L. *Bolivia* 13°43S 66°50W **92** F5
Rogatyn *Ukraine* 49°24N 24°36E **17** D13
Rogers *U.S.A.* 36°20N 94°7W **84** C7
Rogers City *U.S.A.* 45°25N 83°49W **81** C12
Rogersville *Canada* 46°44N 65°26W **73** C6
Roggan → *Canada* 54°24N 79°25W **72** B4
Roggan L. *Canada* 54°8N 77°50W **72** B4
Roggeveen Basin
  Pac. Oc. 31°30S 95°30W **65** L18
Roggeveldberge *S. Africa* 32°10S 20°10E **56** E3
Rogoaguado, L. *Bolivia* 13°0S 65°30W **92** F5
Rogojampi *Indonesia* 8°19S 114°17E **37** J17
Rogue → *U.S.A.* 42°26N 124°26W **76** E1
Rohnert Park *U.S.A.* 38°16N 122°40W **78** G4
Rohri *Pakistan* 27°45N 68°51E **42** F3
Rohri Canal *Pakistan* 26°15N 68°27E **42** F3
Rohtak *India* 28°55N 76°43E **42** E7
Roi Et *Thailand* 16°4N 103°40E **38** D4
Roja *Latvia* 57°29N 22°43E **9** H20
Rojas *Argentina* 34°10S 60°45W **94** C3
Rojo, C. *Mexico* 21°33N 97°20W **87** C5
Rokan → *Indonesia* 2°0N 100°50E **36** D2
Rokiškis *Lithuania* 55°55N 25°35E **9** J21
Rolândia *Brazil* 23°18S 51°23W **95** A5
Rolla *Mo., U.S.A.* 37°57N 91°46W **80** G8
Rolla *N. Dak., U.S.A.* 48°52N 99°37W **80** A4
Rolleston *Australia* 24°28S 148°35E **62** C4
Rollingstone *Australia* 19°2S 146°24E **62** B4
Roma *Australia* 26°32S 148°49E **63** D4
Roma *Italy* 41°54N 12°28E **22** D5
Roma *Sweden* 57°32N 18°26E **9** H18
Roma-Los Saenz *U.S.A.* 26°24N 99°1W **84** H5
Romain, C. *U.S.A.* 33°0N 79°22W **85** E15
Romaine → *Canada* 50°18N 63°47W **73** B7
Roman *Romania* 46°57N 26°55E **17** E14
Romang *Indonesia* 7°30S 127°20E **37** F7
Români *Egypt* 30°59N 32°38E **46** E1
Romania ■ *Europe* 46°0N 25°0E **17** F12
Romano, Cayo *Cuba* 22°0N 77°30W **88** B4
Romans-sur-Isère *France* 45°3N 5°3E **20** D6
Romanzof C. *U.S.A.* 61°49N 166°6W **74** C6
Romblon *Phil.* 12°33N 122°17E **37** B6
Rome = Roma *Italy* 41°54N 12°28E **22** D5
Rome *Ga., U.S.A.* 34°15N 85°10W **85** D12
Rome *N.Y., U.S.A.* 43°13N 75°27W **83** C9
Rome *Pa., U.S.A.* 41°51N 76°21W **83** E8
Romney *U.S.A.* 39°21N 78°45W **81** F14
Romney Marsh *U.K.* 51°2N 0°54E **13** F8
Rømø *Denmark* 55°10N 8°30E **9** J13
Romorantin-Lanthenay
  France 47°21N 1°45E **20** C4
Rompin → *Malaysia* 2°49N 103°29E **39** L4
Romsdalen *Norway* 62°25N 7°52E **8** E12
Romsey *U.K.* 51°0N 1°29W **13** G6
Ron *Vietnam* 17°53N 106°27E **38** D6
Rona *U.K.* 57°34N 5°59W **11** D3
Ronan *U.S.A.* 47°32N 114°6W **76** C6
Roncador, Cayos
  Colombia 13°32N 80°4W **88** D3
Roncador, Serra do
  Brazil 12°30S 52°30W **93** F8
Ronda *Spain* 36°46N 5°12W **21** D3
Rondane *Norway* 61°57N 9°50E **8** F13
Rondônia □ *Brazil* 11°0S 63°0W **92** F6
Rondonópolis *Brazil* 16°28S 54°38W **93** G8
Rondu *Pakistan* 35°32N 75°10E **43** B6
Rong, Koh *Cambodia* 10°45N 103°15E **39** G4
Rongcheng *China* 37°9N 122°23E **35** F12

Ronge, L. la *Canada* 55°6N 105°17W **71** B7
Rønne *Denmark* 55°6N 14°43E **9** J16
Ronne Ice Shelf
  Antarctica 77°30S 60°0W **5** D18
Ronsard, C. *Australia* 24°46S 113°10E **61** D1
Ronse *Belgium* 50°45N 3°35E **15** D3
Roodepoort *S. Africa* 26°11S 27°54E **57** D4
Roof Butte *U.S.A.* 36°28N 109°5W **77** H9
Rooiboklaagte →
  Namibia 20°50S 21°0E **56** C3
Rooniu, Mt. *Tahiti* 17°49S 149°12W **59** d
Roorkee *India* 29°52N 77°59E **42** E7
Roosendaal *Neths.* 51°32N 4°29E **15** C4
Roosevelt *U.S.A.* 40°18N 109°59W **76** F9
Roosevelt → *Brazil* 7°35S 60°20W **92** E6
Roosevelt, Mt. *Canada* 58°26N 125°20W **70** B3
Roosevelt I. *Antarctica* 79°30S 162°0W **5** D12
Roper → *Australia* 14°43S 135°27E **62** A2
Roper Bar *Australia* 14°44S 134°44E **62** A1
Roper River = St. Vidgeon's ○
  Australia 14°47S 134°53E **62** A1
Roque Pérez *Argentina* 35°25S 59°24W **94** D4
Roquetas de Mar *Spain* 36°46N 2°36W **21** D4
Roraima □ *Brazil* 2°0N 61°30W **92** C6
Roraima, Mt. *Venezuela* 5°10N 60°40W **92** B6
Røros *Norway* 62°35N 11°23E **8** E14
Ros Comáin = Roscommon
  Ireland 53°38N 8°11W **10** C3
Rosa *Zambia* 9°33S 31°15E **55** D3
Rosa, Monte *Europe* 45°57N 7°53E **20** D7
Rosalia *U.S.A.* 47°14N 117°22W **76** C5
Rosamond *U.S.A.* 34°52N 118°10W **79** L8
Rosario *Argentina* 33°0S 60°40W **94** C3
Rosário *Brazil* 3°0S 44°15W **93** D10
Rosario *Baja Calif.,*
  Mexico 30°0N 115°50W **86** B1
Rosario *Sinaloa, Mexico* 22°58N 105°53W **86** C3
Rosario *Paraguay* 24°30S 57°35W **94** A4
Rosario de la Frontera
  Argentina 25°50S 65°0W **94** B3
Rosario de Lerma
  Argentina 24°59S 65°35W **94** A2
Rosario del Tala
  Argentina 32°20S 59°10W **94** C4
Rosário do Sul *Brazil* 30°15S 54°55W **95** C5
Rosarito *Mexico* 32°20N 117°2W **79** N9
Roscoe *U.S.A.* 41°56N 74°55W **83** E10
Roscommon *Ireland* 53°38N 8°11W **10** C3
Roscommon □ *Ireland* 53°49N 8°23W **10** C3
Roscrea *Ireland* 52°57N 7°49W **10** D4
Rose → *Australia* 14°16S 135°45E **62** A2
Rose, L. *Bahamas* 21°0N 73°30W **89** B5
Rose Belle *Mauritius* 20°24S 57°36E **53** d
Rose Blanche *Canada* 47°38N 58°45W **73** C8
Rose Hill *Mauritius* 20°14S 57°27E **53** d
Rose Pt. *Canada* 54°11N 131°39W **70** C2
Rose Valley *Canada* 52°19N 103°49W **71** C8
Roseau *Dominica* 15°17N 61°24W **89** C7
Roseau *U.S.A.* 48°51N 95°46W **80** A6
Rosebery *Australia* 41°46S 145°33E **63** G4
Rosebud *S. Dak., U.S.A.* 43°14N 100°51W **80** D3
Rosebud *Tex., U.S.A.* 31°4N 96°59W **84** F6
Roseburg *U.S.A.* 43°13N 123°20W **76** E2
Rosedale *U.S.A.* 33°51N 91°2W **85** E9
Rosehearty *U.K.* 57°42N 2°7W **11** D6
Roseires Res. *Sudan* 11°51N 34°23E **51** F12
Roseland *U.S.A.* 38°25N 122°43W **78** G4
Rosemary *Canada* 50°46N 112°5W **70** C6
Rosenberg *U.S.A.* 29°34N 95°49W **84** G7
Rosenheim *Germany* 47°51N 12°7E **16** E7
Roses, G. de *Spain* 42°10N 3°15E **21** A7
Rosetown *Canada* 51°35N 107°59W **71** C7
Roseville *Calif., U.S.A.* 38°45N 121°17W **78** G5
Roseville *Mich., U.S.A.* 42°30N 82°56W **82** D2
Roseville *Pa., U.S.A.* 41°51N 76°57W **83** E8
Rosewood *Australia* 27°38S 152°36E **63** D5
Roshkhvār *Iran* 34°58N 59°37E **45** C8
Rosignano Maríttimo
  Italy 43°24N 10°28E **22** C4
Rosignol *Guyana* 6°15N 57°30W **92** B7
Roșiori de Vede *Romania* 44°9N 25°0E **17** F13
Roskilde *Denmark* 55°38N 12°3E **9** J15
Roslavl *Russia* 53°57N 32°55E **18** D5
Rosmead *S. Africa* 31°29S 25°8E **56** E4
Ross *Australia* 42°2S 147°30E **63** G4
Ross *N.Z.* 42°53S 170°49E **59** E3
Ross Dependency
  Antarctica 76°0S 170°0W **5** D12
Ross I. *Antarctica* 77°30S 168°0E **5** D11
Ross Ice Shelf *Antarctica* 80°0S 180°0E **5** E12
Ross L. *U.S.A.* 48°44N 121°4W **76** B3
Ross Mhic Thriúin = New Ross
  Ireland 52°23N 6°57W **10** D5
Ross-on-Wye *U.K.* 51°54N 2°34W **13** F5
Ross River *Australia* 23°44S 134°30E **62** C1
Ross River *Canada* 62°30N 131°30W **70** A2
Ross Sea *Antarctica* 74°0S 178°0E **5** D11
Rossall Pt. *U.K.* 53°55N 3°3W **12** D4
Rossan Pt. *Ireland* 54°42N 8°47W **10** B3
Rossano *Italy* 39°36N 16°39E **22** E7
Rossburn *Canada* 50°40N 100°49W **71** C8
Rosseau *Canada* 45°16N 79°39W **82** A5
Rosseau, L. *Canada* 45°10N 79°35W **82** A5
Rosses, The *Ireland* 55°2N 8°20W **10** A3
Rossignol, L. *Canada* 52°43N 73°40W **72** B5
Rossignol L. *Canada* 44°12N 65°10W **73** D6
Rossiya = Russia ■
  Eurasia 62°0N 105°0E **29** C11
Rossland *Canada* 49°6N 117°50W **70** D5
Rosslare *Ireland* 52°17N 6°24W **10** D5
Rosslare Harbour *Ireland* 52°15N 6°20W **10** D5
Rossmore *Canada* 44°8N 77°23W **82** B7
Rosso *Mauritania* 16°40N 15°45W **50** E2
Rossosh *Russia* 50°15N 39°28E **19** D6
Røssvatnet *Norway* 65°45N 14°5E **8** D16
Røst *Norway* 67°32N 12°0E **8** C15
Rosthern *Canada* 52°40N 106°20W **71** C7
Rostock *Germany* 54°5N 12°8E **16** A7
Rostov *Don, Russia* 47°15N 39°45E **19** E6
Rostov *Yaroslavl, Russia* 57°14N 39°25E **18** C6

Roswell *Ga., U.S.A.* 34°2N 84°22W **85** D12
Roswell *N. Mex.,*
  U.S.A. 33°24N 104°32W **77** K11
Rotan *U.S.A.* 32°51N 100°28W **84** E4
Rother → *U.K.* 50°59N 0°45E **13** G8
Rothera *Antarctica* 67°34S 68°8W **5** C17
Rotherham *U.K.* 53°26N 1°20W **12** D6
Rothes *U.K.* 57°32N 3°13W **11** D5
Rothesay *Canada* 45°23N 66°0W **73** C6
Rothesay *U.K.* 55°50N 5°3W **11** F3
Roti *Indonesia* 10°50S 123°0E **37** F6
Roto *Australia* 33°0S 145°30E **63** E4
Rotondo, Mte. *France* 42°14N 9°8E **20** E8
Rotoroa, L. *N.Z.* 41°55S 172°39E **59** D4
Rotorua *N.Z.* 38°9S 176°16E **59** C6
Rotorua, L. *N.Z.* 38°5S 176°18E **59** C6
Rotterdam *Neths.* 51°55N 4°30E **15** C4
Rotterdam *U.S.A.* 42°48N 74°1W **83** D10
Rottnest I. *Australia* 32°0S 115°27E **61** F2
Rottumeroog *Neths.* 53°33N 6°34E **15** A6
Rottweil *Germany* 48°9N 8°37E **16** D5
Rotuma *Fiji* 12°25S 177°5E **58** C10
Roubaix *France* 50°40N 3°10E **20** A5
Rouen *France* 49°27N 1°4E **20** B4
Rouleau *Canada* 50°10N 104°56W **71** C8
Roulpmaulpma ○
  Australia 23°52S 133°0E **60** D5
Round I. *Mauritius* 19°51S 57°45E **53** d
Round Mountain
  U.S.A. 38°43N 117°4W **76** G5
Round Mt. *Australia* 30°26S 152°16E **63** E5
Round Rock *U.S.A.* 30°31N 97°41W **84** F6
Roundup *U.S.A.* 46°27N 108°33W **76** C9
Rousay *U.K.* 59°10N 3°2W **11** B5
Rouses Point *U.S.A.* 44°59N 73°22W **83** B11
Rouseville *U.S.A.* 41°28N 79°42W **82** E5
Rousse = Ruse *Bulgaria* 43°48N 25°59E **23** C12
Roussillon *France* 42°30N 2°35E **20** E5
Rouxville *S. Africa* 30°25S 26°50E **56** E4
Rouyn-Noranda *Canada* 48°20N 79°0W **72** C4
Rovaniemi *Finland* 66°29N 25°41E **8** C21
Rovereto *Italy* 45°53N 11°3E **22** B4
Rovigo *Italy* 45°4N 11°47E **22** B4
Rovinj *Croatia* 45°5N 13°40E **16** F7
Rovno = Rivne *Ukraine* 50°40N 26°10E **17** C14
Rovuma = Ruvuma →
  Tanzania 10°29S 40°28E **55** E5
Row'ān *Iran* 35°8N 48°51E **45** C6
Rowena *Australia* 29°48S 148°55E **63** D4
Rowley I. *Canada* 69°6N 77°52W **69** D16
Rowley Shoals *Australia* 17°30S 119°0E **60** C2
Roxas *Phil.* 11°36N 122°49E **37** B6
Roxboro *U.S.A.* 36°24N 78°59W **85** C15
Roxborough
  Trin. & Tob. 11°15N 60°35W **93** J16
Roxburgh *N.Z.* 45°33S 169°19E **59** F2
Roxbury *N.Y., U.S.A.* 42°17N 74°33W **83** D10
Roxbury *Pa., U.S.A.* 40°6N 77°39W **82** F7
Roxby Downs *Australia* 30°43S 136°46E **63** E2
Roy *Mont., U.S.A.* 47°20N 108°58W **76** C9
Roy *N. Mex., U.S.A.* 35°57N 104°12W **77** J11
Roy *Utah, U.S.A.* 41°10N 112°2W **76** F7
Royal Bardia △ *Nepal* 28°20N 81°20E **43** E9
Royal Canal *Ireland* 53°30N 7°13W **10** C4
Royal Chitawan △
  Nepal 26°30N 84°30E **43** F11
Royal Geographical Society Is.
  Canada 68°56N 100°15W **68** D11
Royal Leamington Spa
  U.K. 52°18N 1°31W **13** E6
Royal Natal △ *S. Africa* 28°43S 28°51E **57** D4
Royal Tunbridge Wells
  U.K. 51°7N 0°16E **13** F8
Royale, Isle *U.S.A.* 48°0N 88°54W **80** B9
Royan *France* 45°37N 1°2W **20** D3
Royston *U.K.* 52°3N 0°0 **13** E7
Rozdilna *Ukraine* 46°50N 30°2E **17** E16
Rozhyshche *Ukraine* 50°54N 25°15E **17** C13
Rtishchevo *Russia* 52°18N 43°46E **18** D7
Ruacaná *Namibia* 17°27S 14°21E **56** B1
Ruaha △ *Tanzania* 7°41S 34°30E **54** D3
Ruahine Ra. *N.Z.* 39°55S 176°2E **59** C6
Ruapehu *N.Z.* 39°17S 175°35E **59** C5
Ruapuke I. *N.Z.* 46°46S 168°31E **59** G2
Ruāq, W. → *Egypt* 30°0N 33°49E **46** F2
Rub' al Khālī *Si. Arabia* 19°0N 48°0E **47** D4
Rubeho Mts. *Tanzania* 6°50S 36°25E **54** D4
Rubh a' Mhail *U.K.* 55°56N 6°8W **11** F2
Rubha Hunish *U.K.* 57°42N 6°20W **11** D2
Rubha Robhanais = Lewis, Butt of
  U.K. 58°31N 6°16W **11** C2
Rubicon → *U.S.A.* 38°53N 121°4W **78** G5
Rubio *Venezuela* 7°43N 72°22W **92** B4
Rubondo △ *Tanzania* 2°18S 31°58E **54** C3
Rubtsovsk *Russia* 51°30N 81°10E **32** A5
Ruby L. *U.S.A.* 40°10N 115°28W **76** F6
Ruby Mts. *U.S.A.* 40°30N 115°20W **76** F6
Rubyvale *Australia* 23°25S 147°42E **62** C4
Rūd Sar *Iran* 37°8N 50°18E **45** B6
Rudall *Australia* 33°43S 136°17E **63** E2
Rudall → *Australia* 22°34S 122°13E **60** D3
Rudall River △
  Australia 22°38S 122°30E **60** D3
Rudbar *Iran* 36°48N 49°23E **45** B6
Rudnya *Russia* 54°55N 31°15E **18** D5
Rudnyy *Kazakhstan* 52°57N 63°7E **28** D7
Rudolfa, Ostrov *Russia* 81°45N 58°30E **28** A6
Rudyard *U.S.A.* 46°14N 84°36W **81** B11
Ruenya → *Africa* 16°24S 33°48E **55** F3
Ruffling Pt. *Br. Virgin Is.* 18°44N 64°27W **89** e
Rufiji → *Tanzania* 7°50S 39°15E **54** D4
Rufino *Argentina* 34°20S 62°50W **94** C3
Rufunsa *Zambia* 15°4S 29°34E **55** F2
Rugby *U.K.* 52°23N 1°16W **13** E6
Rugby *U.S.A.* 48°22N 100°0W **80** A4
Rügen *Germany* 54°22N 13°24E **16** A7
Ruhengeri *Rwanda* 1°30S 29°36E **54** C2
Ruhnu *Estonia* 57°48N 23°15E **9** H20
Ruhr → *Germany* 51°27N 6°43E **16** C4
Ruhuhu → *Tanzania* 10°31S 34°34E **55** E3

Ruidoso *U.S.A.* 33°20N 105°41W **77** K11
Ruijin *China* 25°48N 116°0E **33** F12
Ruivo, Pico *Madeira* 32°45N 16°56W **24** D3
Rujm Tal'at al Jamā'ah
  Jordan 30°24N 35°30E **46** E4
Ruk *Pakistan* 27°50N 68°42E **42** F3
Rukhla *Pakistan* 32°27N 71°57E **42** C4
Ruki →
  Dem. Rep. of the Congo 0°5N 18°17E **52** E3
Rukwa □ *Tanzania* 7°0S 31°30E **54** D3
Rukwa, L. *Tanzania* 8°0S 32°20E **54** D3
Rulenge *Burundi* 2°43S 30°37E **54** C3
Rulhieres, C. *Australia* 13°56S 127°22E **60** B4
Rum = Rhum □ *U.K.* 57°0N 6°20W **11** E2
Rum *Jordan* 29°39N 35°26E **46** F4
Rum Cay *Bahamas* 23°40N 74°58W **89** B5
Rum Jungle *Australia* 13°0S 130°59E **60** B5
Ruma △ *Kenya* 0°39S 34°18E **54** C3
Rumāḥ *Si. Arabia* 25°29N 47°10E **44** E5
Rumania = Romania ■
  Europe 46°0N 25°0E **17** F12
Rumaylah *Iraq* 30°47N 47°37E **44** D5
Rumbêk *Sudan* 6°54N 29°37E **51** G11
Rumford *U.S.A.* 44°33N 70°33W **83** B14
Rumia *Poland* 54°37N 18°25E **17** A10
Rumoi *Japan* 43°56N 141°39E **30** C10
Rumonge *Burundi* 3°59S 29°26E **54** C2
Rumphi *Malawi* 11°1S 33°52E **55** E3
Rumson *U.S.A.* 40°23N 74°0W **83** F11
Rumuruti *Kenya* 0°17N 36°32E **54** B4
Runan *China* 33°0N 114°30E **34** H8
Runanga *N.Z.* 42°25S 171°15E **59** E3
Runaway, C. *N.Z.* 37°32S 177°59E **59** B6
Runaway Bay *Jamaica* 18°27N 77°20W **88** a
Runcorn *U.K.* 53°21N 2°44W **12** D5
Rundu *Namibia* 17°52S 19°43E **56** B2
Rungwa *Tanzania* 6°55S 33°32E **54** D3
Rungwa → *Tanzania* 7°36S 31°50E **54** D3
Rungwa → *Tanzania* 6°53S 34°2E **54** D3
Rungwe *Tanzania* 9°11S 33°32E **55** D3
Rungwe, Mt. *Tanzania* 9°8S 33°40E **52** F6
Runton Ra. *Australia* 23°31S 123°6E **60** D3
Ruo Shui → *China* 41°0N 100°16E **32** C9
Ruokolahti *Finland* 61°17N 28°50E **8** F23
Ruoqiang *China* 38°55N 88°10E **32** D6
Rupa *India* 27°15N 92°21E **41** F18
Rupar *India* 31°2N 76°38E **42** D7
Rupat *Indonesia* 1°45N 101°40E **36** D2
Rupen → *India* 23°28N 71°31E **42** H4
Rupert *U.S.A.* 42°37N 113°41W **76** E7
Rupert → *Canada* 51°29N 78°45W **72** B4
Rupert B. *Canada* 51°35N 79°0W **72** B4
Rupert House = Waskaganish
  Canada 51°30N 78°40W **72** B4
Rupsa *India* 21°37N 87°1E **43** J12
Rurrenabaque *Bolivia* 14°30S 67°32W **92** F5
Rusambo *Zimbabwe* 16°30S 32°4E **55** F3
Rusape *Zimbabwe* 18°35S 32°8E **55** F3
Ruschuk = Ruse
  Bulgaria 43°48N 25°59E **23** C12
Ruse *Bulgaria* 43°48N 25°59E **23** C12
Rush *Ireland* 53°31N 6°6W **10** C5
Rushan *China* 36°56N 121°30E **35** F11
Rushden *U.K.* 52°18N 0°35W **13** E7
Rushmore, Mt. *U.S.A.* 43°53N 103°28W **80** D2
Rushville *Ill., U.S.A.* 40°7N 90°34W **80** E8
Rushville *Ind., U.S.A.* 39°37N 85°27W **81** F11
Rushville *Nebr., U.S.A.* 42°43N 102°28W **80** D2
Russas *Brazil* 4°55S 37°50W **93** D11
Russell *Canada* 50°50N 101°20W **71** C8
Russell *Kans., U.S.A.* 38°54N 98°52W **80** F4
Russell *N.Y., U.S.A.* 44°27N 75°9W **83** B9
Russell *Pa., U.S.A.* 41°56N 79°8W **82** E5
Russell Cave △ *U.S.A.* 34°59N 85°49W **85** D12
Russell L. *Man., Canada* 56°15N 101°30W **71** B8
Russell L. *N.W.T.,*
  Canada 63°5N 115°44W **70** A5
Russellkonda *India* 19°57N 84°42E **41** K14
Russellville *Ala., U.S.A.* 34°30N 87°44W **85** D11
Russellville *Ark., U.S.A.* 35°17N 93°8W **84** D8
Russellville *Ky., U.S.A.* 36°51N 86°53W **80** G10
Russia ■ *Eurasia* 62°0N 105°0E **29** C11
Russian → *U.S.A.* 38°27N 123°8W **78** G3
Rustam Shahr *Pakistan* 26°58N 66°6E **42** F2
Rustavi *Georgia* 41°30N 45°0E **19** F8
Rustenburg *S. Africa* 25°41S 27°14E **56** D4
Ruston *U.S.A.* 32°32N 92°38W **84** E8
Rutana *Burundi* 3°55S 30°0E **54** C3
Ruteng *Indonesia* 8°35S 120°30E **37** F6
Rutenga *Zimbabwe* 21°15S 30°44E **55** G3
Ruth *U.S.A.* 43°42N 82°45W **82** C2
Rutherford *U.S.A.* 38°26N 122°24W **78** G4
Rutland *U.S.A.* 43°37N 72°58W **83** C12
Rutland □ *U.K.* 52°38N 0°40W **13** E7
Rutland Water *U.K.* 52°39N 0°38W **13** E7
Rutledge → *Canada* 61°4N 112°0W **71** A6
Rutledge L. *Canada* 61°33N 110°47W **71** A6
Rutog *China* 33°27N 79°42E **32** E4
Rutshuru
  Dem. Rep. of the Congo 1°13S 29°25E **54** C2
Ruvu *Tanzania* 6°49S 38°43E **54** D4
Ruvu → *Tanzania* 6°23S 38°52E **54** D4
Ruvuba △ *Burundi* 3°3S 29°33E **54** C2
Ruvuma □ *Tanzania* 10°20S 36°0E **55** E4
Ruvuma → *Tanzania* 10°29S 40°28E **55** E5
Ruwais *U.A.E.* 24°5N 52°50E **45** E7
Ruwenzori *Africa* 0°30N 29°55E **54** B2
Ruwenzori △ *Uganda* 0°30N 30°0E **54** B2
Ruya → *Zimbabwe* 16°27S 32°5E **55** F3
Ruyang *China* 34°9N 112°27E **34** G7
Ruyigi *Burundi* 3°29S 30°15E **54** C3
Rizhou *China* 34°11N 112°52E **34** G7
Ružomberok *Slovak Rep.* 49°3N 19°17E **17** D10
Rwanda ■ *Africa* 2°0S 30°0E **54** C3
Ryan, L. *U.K.* 55°0N 5°2W **11** G3
Ryazan *Russia* 54°40N 39°40E **18** D6
Ryazhsk *Russia* 53°45N 40°3E **18** D7
Rybachiy Poluostrov
  Russia 69°43N 32°0E **8** B25
Rybachye = Balykchy
  Kyrgyzstan 42°26N 76°12E **32** C4

Rybinsk Russia 58°5N 38°50E 18 C6
Rybinskoye Vdkhr. Russia 58°30N 38°25E 18 C6
Rybnitsa = Râbniţa Moldova 47°45N 29°0E 17 E15
Rycroft Canada 55°45N 118°40W 70 B5
Ryde U.K. 50°43N 1°9W 13 G6
Ryderwood U.S.A. 46°23N 123°3W 78 D3
Rye U.K. 50°57N 0°45E 13 G8
Rye → U.K. 54°11N 0°44W 12 C7
Rye Bay U.K. 50°52N 0°49E 13 G8
Rye Patch Res. U.S.A. 40°28N 118°19W 76 F4
Ryegate U.S.A. 46°18N 109°15W 76 C9
Ryley Canada 53°17N 112°26W 70 C6
Rylstone Australia 32°46S 149°58E 63 E4
Ryn Peski = Naryn Qum Kazakhstan 47°30N 49°0E 28 E5
Ryōtsu Japan 38°5N 138°26E 30 E9
Rypin Poland 53°3N 19°25E 17 B10
Ryūgasaki Japan 35°54N 140°11E 31 G10
Ryukyu Is. = Ryūkyū-Rettō Japan 26°0N 126°0E 31 M3
Ryūkyū-Rettō Japan 26°0N 126°0E 31 M3
Rzeszów Poland 50°5N 21°58E 17 C11
Rzhev Russia 56°20N 34°20E 18 C5

S

Sa Cabaneta Spain 39°37N 2°45E 24 B9
Sa Canal Spain 38°51N 1°23E 24 C7
Sa Conillera Spain 38°59N 1°13E 24 C7
Sa Dec Vietnam 10°20N 105°46E 39 G5
Sa Dragonera Spain 39°35N 2°19E 24 B9
Sa Kaeo Thailand 13°49N 102°4E 38 F4
Sa Mesquida Spain 39°55N 4°16E 24 B11
Sa Pa Vietnam 22°20N 103°47E 38 A4
Sa Savina Spain 38°44N 1°25E 24 C7
Sa'ādatābād Fārs, Iran 30°10N 53°5E 45 D7
Sa'ādatābād Hormozgān, Iran 28°3N 55°53E 45 D7
Sa'ādatābād Kermān, Iran 29°40N 55°51E 45 D7
Saale → Germany 51°56N 11°54E 16 C6
Saalfeld Germany 50°38N 11°21E 16 C6
Saanich Canada 48°29N 123°26W 78 B3
Saar → Europe 49°41N 6°32E 15 E6
Saarbrücken Germany 49°14N 6°59E 16 D4
Saaremaa Estonia 58°30N 22°30E 9 G20
Saarijärvi Finland 62°43N 25°16E 8 E21
Sab 'Âbar Syria 33°46N 37°41E 44 C3
Saba W. Indies 17°38N 63°14W 89 C7
Šabac Serbia 44°48N 19°42E 23 B8
Sabadell Spain 41°28N 2°7E 21 B7
Sabah □ Malaysia 6°0N 117°0E 36 C5
Sabak Bernam Malaysia 3°46N 100°58E 39 L3
Sabalān, Kūhhā-ye Iran 38°15N 47°45E 44 B5
Sabalana, Kepulauan Indonesia 6°45S 118°50E 37 F5
Sábana de la Mar Dom. Rep. 19°7N 69°24W 89 C6
Sábanalarga Colombia 10°38N 74°55W 92 A4
Sabang Indonesia 5°50N 95°15E 36 C1
Sabarmati → India 22°18N 72°22E 42 H5
Sabattis U.S.A. 44°6N 74°40W 83 B10
Saberania Indonesia 2°5S 138°18E 37 E9
Sabhā Libya 27°9N 14°29E 51 C8
Sabi → India 28°29N 76°44E 42 E7
Sabie S. Africa 25°10S 30°48E 57 D5
Sabinal Mexico 30°57N 107°30W 86 A3
Sabinal U.S.A. 29°19N 99°28W 84 G5
Sabinas Mexico 27°51N 101°7W 86 B4
Sabinas → Mexico 27°37N 100°42W 86 B4
Sabinas Hidalgo Mexico 26°30N 100°10W 86 B4
Sabine → U.S.A. 29°59N 93°47W 84 G8
Sabine L. U.S.A. 29°53N 93°51W 84 G8
Sabine Pass U.S.A. 29°44N 93°54W 84 G8
Sablayan Phil. 12°50N 120°50E 37 B6
Sable Canada 55°30N 68°21W 73 A6
Sable, C. Canada 43°29N 65°38W 73 D6
Sable, C. U.S.A. 25°9N 81°8W 88 A3
Sable I. Canada 44°0N 60°0W 73 D8
Sabrina Coast Antarctica 68°0S 120°0E 5 C9
Sabulubek Indonesia 1°36S 98°40E 36 E1
Sabzevār Iran 36°15N 57°40E 45 B8
Sabzvārān = Jiroft Iran 28°45N 57°50E 45 D8
Sac City U.S.A. 42°25N 95°0W 80 D6
Săcele Romania 45°37N 25°41E 17 F13
Sacheon S. Korea 35°0N 128°6E 35 G15
Sachigo → Canada 55°6N 88°58W 72 A2
Sachigo, L. Canada 53°50N 92°12W 72 B1
Sachimbo Angola 9°14S 20°16E 52 F4
Sachsen □ Germany 50°55N 13°10E 16 C7
Sachsen-Anhalt □ Germany 52°0N 12°0E 16 C7
Sackets Harbor U.S.A. 43°57N 76°7W 83 C8
Sackville Canada 45°54N 64°22W 73 C7
Saco Maine, U.S.A. 43°30N 70°27W 83 C14
Saco Mont., U.S.A. 48°28N 107°21W 76 B10
Sacramento U.S.A. 38°35N 121°29W 78 G5
Sacramento → U.S.A. 38°3N 121°56W 78 G5
Sacramento Mts. U.S.A. 32°30N 105°30W 77 K11
Sacramento Valley U.S.A. 39°30N 122°0W 78 G5
Sada-Misaki Japan 33°20N 132°5E 31 H6
Sadabad India 27°27N 78°3E 42 F8
Sadani Tanzania 5°58S 38°35E 54 D4
Sadani ⌂ Tanzania 6°3S 38°47E 54 D4
Sadao Thailand 6°38N 100°26E 39 J3
Sadd el Aali Egypt 23°54N 32°54E 51 D12
Saddle Mt. U.S.A. 45°58N 123°41W 78 E3
Sadimi Dem. Rep. of the Congo 9°25S 23°32E 55 D1
Sado Japan 38°0N 138°25E 30 F9
Sadra India 23°21N 72°43E 42 H5
Sadri India 25°11N 73°26E 42 G5
Sæby Denmark 57°21N 10°30E 9 H14
Saegertown U.S.A. 41°43N 80°9W 82 E4
Şafājah Si. Arabia 26°25N 39°0E 44 E3
Safata B. Samoa 14°0S 171°50W 59 b
Säffle Sweden 59°8N 12°55E 9 G15
Safford U.S.A. 32°50N 109°43W 77 K9
Saffron Walden U.K. 52°1N 0°16E 13 E8
Safi Morocco 32°18N 9°20W 50 B4
Şafiābād Iran 36°45N 57°58E 45 B8
Safid Dasht Iran 33°27N 48°11E 45 C6
Safid Kūh Afghan. 34°45N 63°0E 40 B3
Safid Rūd → Iran 37°23N 50°11E 45 B6
Safipur India 26°44N 80°21E 43 F9
Şāfītā Syria 34°48N 36°7E 44 C3
Safune Samoa 13°25S 172°21W 59 b
Şafwān Iraq 30°7N 47°43E 44 D5
Sag Harbor U.S.A. 41°0N 72°18W 83 F12
Saga Japan 33°15N 130°16E 31 H5
Saga □ Japan 33°15N 130°20E 31 H5
Sagae Japan 38°22N 140°17E 30 E10
Sagaing Burma 21°52N 95°59E 41 J19
Sagamore U.S.A. 40°46N 79°14W 82 F5
Saganaga L. Canada 48°14N 90°52W 80 A8
Saganthit Kyun Burma 11°56N 98°29E 39 G2
Sagar Karnataka, India 14°14N 75°6E 40 M9
Sagar Mad. P., India 23°50N 78°44E 43 H8
Sagara, L. Tanzania 5°20S 31°0E 54 D3
Sagarmatha = Everest, Mt. Nepal 28°5N 86°58E 43 E12
Sagarmatha △ Nepal 27°55N 86°45E 43 F12
Saginaw U.S.A. 43°26N 83°56W 81 D12
Saginaw B. U.S.A. 43°50N 83°40W 81 D12
Saglouc = Salluit Canada 62°14N 75°38W 69 E16
Sagone France 42°7N 8°42E 20 E8
Sagua la Grande Cuba 22°50N 80°10W 88 B3
Saguache U.S.A. 38°5N 106°8W 76 G10
Saguaro △ U.S.A. 32°12N 110°38W 77 K8
Saguenay → Canada 48°22N 71°0W 73 C5
Sagunt Spain 39°42N 0°18W 21 C5
Sagunto = Sagunt Spain 39°42N 0°18W 21 C5
Sagwara India 23°41N 74°1E 42 H6
Sahagún Spain 42°18N 5°2W 21 A3
Saḥam al Jawlān Syria 32°45N 35°55E 46 C4
Sahamandrevo Madag. 23°15S 45°35E 57 C8
Sahand, Kūh-e Iran 37°44N 46°27E 44 B5
Sahara Africa 23°0N 5°0E 50 D6
Saharan Atlas = Saharien, Atlas Algeria 33°30N 1°0E 50 B6
Saharanpur India 29°58N 77°33E 42 E7
Saharien, Atlas Algeria 33°30N 1°0E 50 B6
Saharsa India 25°53N 86°36E 43 G12
Sahasinaka Madag. 21°49S 47°49E 57 C8
Sahaswan India 28°5N 78°45E 43 E8
Saheira, W. el → Egypt 30°5N 33°25E 46 E2
Sahel Africa 16°0N 5°0E 50 E5
Sahibganj India 25°12N 87°40E 43 G12
Sāḥiliyah Iraq 33°43N 42°42E 44 C4
Sahiwal Pakistan 30°45N 73°8E 42 D5
Şahneh Iran 34°29N 47°41E 44 C5
Sahrawi = Western Sahara ■ Africa 25°0N 13°0W 50 D3
Sahuaripa Mexico 29°3N 109°14W 86 B3
Sahuarita U.S.A. 31°57N 110°58W 77 L8
Sahuayo de Díaz Mexico 20°4N 102°43W 86 C4
Sai → India 25°39N 82°47E 43 G10
Sai Buri Thailand 6°43N 101°45E 39 J3
Sai Kung China 22°23N 114°16E 33 a
Sai Thong △ Thailand 15°56N 101°10E 38 E3
Sai Yok △ Thailand 14°25N 98°40E 38 E2
Saibai I. Australia 9°25S 142°40E 62 a
Sa'id Bundâs Sudan 8°24N 24°48E 51 G10
Sa'īdābād = Sīrjān Iran 29°30N 55°45E 45 D7
Sa'īdābād Iran 36°8N 54°11E 45 B7
Sa'īdīyeh Iran 36°20N 48°55E 45 B6
Saidpur Bangla. 25°48N 89°0E 41 G16
Saidpur India 25°33N 83°11E 43 G10
Saidu Sharif Pakistan 34°43N 72°24E 43 B5
Saigō Japan 36°12N 133°20E 31 F6
Saigon = Thanh Pho Ho Chi Minh Vietnam 10°58N 106°40E 39 G6
Saijō Japan 33°55N 133°11E 31 H6
Saikai △ Japan 33°12N 129°36E 31 H4
Saikanosy Masoala Madag. 15°45S 50°10E 57 B9
Saikhoa Ghat India 27°50N 95°40E 41 F19
Saiki Japan 32°58N 131°51E 31 H5
Sailana India 23°28N 74°55E 42 H6
Sailolof Indonesia 1°15S 130°46E 37 E8
Saimaa Finland 61°15N 28°15E 8 F23
Saimen = Saimaa Finland 61°15N 28°15E 8 F23
Şa'in Dezh Iran 36°40N 46°25E 44 B5
St. Abb's Head U.K. 55°55N 2°8W 11 F6
St. Alban's Canada 47°51N 55°50W 73 C8
St. Albans U.K. 51°45N 0°19W 13 F7
St. Albans Vt., U.S.A. 44°49N 73°5W 83 B11
St. Albans W. Va., U.S.A. 38°23N 81°50W 81 F13
St. Alban's Head U.K. 50°34N 2°4W 13 G5
St. Albert Canada 53°37N 113°32W 70 C6
St-André Réunion 20°57S 55°39E 53 c
St. Andrew's Canada 47°45N 59°15W 73 C8
St. Andrews U.K. 56°20N 2°47W 11 E6
St-Anicet Canada 45°8N 74°22W 83 A10
St. Annes Canada 49°40N 96°39W 71 D9
St. Anns B. Canada 46°22N 60°25W 73 C7
St. Ann's Bay Jamaica 18°26N 77°12W 88 a
St. Anthony Canada 51°22N 55°35W 73 B8
St. Anthony U.S.A. 43°58N 111°41W 76 E8
St-Antoine Canada 46°22N 64°45W 73 C7
St. Arnaud Australia 36°40S 143°16E 63 F3
St-Augustin Canada 51°13N 58°38W 73 B8
St-Augustin → Canada 51°16N 58°40W 73 B8
St. Augustine U.S.A. 29°54N 81°19W 85 G14
St. Austell U.K. 50°20N 4°47W 13 G3
St. Barbe Canada 51°12N 56°46W 73 B8
St-Barthélemy W. Indies 17°50N 62°50W 89 C7
St. Bees Hd. U.K. 54°31N 3°38W 12 C4
St. Bees I. Australia 20°56S 149°26E 62 b
St-Benoît Réunion 21°2S 55°43E 53 c
St. Bride's Canada 46°56N 54°10W 73 C9
St. Brides B. U.K. 51°49N 5°9W 13 F2
St-Brieuc France 48°30N 2°46W 20 B2
St. Catharines Canada 43°10N 79°15W 82 C5
St. Catherines I. U.S.A. 31°40N 81°10W 85 F14
St. Catherine's Pt. U.K. 50°34N 1°18W 13 G6
St-Chamond France 45°28N 4°31E 20 D6
St. Charles Ill., U.S.A. 41°54N 88°19W 80 E9
St. Charles Md., U.S.A. 38°36N 76°56W 81 F15
St. Charles Mo., U.S.A. 38°47N 90°29W 80 F8
St. Charles Va., U.S.A. 36°48N 83°4W 81 G12
St. Christopher-Nevis = St. Kitts & Nevis ■ W. Indies 17°20N 62°40W 89 C7
St. Clair Mich., U.S.A. 42°50N 82°30W 82 D2
St. Clair Pa., U.S.A. 40°43N 76°12W 83 F8
St. Clair → U.S.A. 42°38N 82°31W 82 D2
St. Clair, L. N. Amer. 42°27N 82°39W 82 D2
St. Clairsville U.S.A. 40°5N 80°54W 82 F4
St. Claude Canada 49°40N 98°20W 71 D9
St. Clears U.K. 51°49N 4°31W 13 F3
St-Clet Canada 45°21N 74°13W 83 A10
St. Cloud Fla., U.S.A. 28°15N 81°17W 85 G14
St. Cloud Minn., U.S.A. 45°34N 94°10W 80 C6
St. Cricq, C. Australia 25°17S 113°6E 61 E1
St. Croix U.S. Virgin Is. 17°45N 64°45W 89 C7
St. Croix → U.S.A. 44°45N 92°48W 80 C7
St. Croix Falls U.S.A. 45°24N 92°38W 80 C7
St. David's Canada 48°12N 58°52W 73 C8
St. David's U.K. 51°53N 5°16W 13 F2
St. David's Head U.K. 51°54N 5°19W 13 F2
St-Denis France 48°56N 2°20E 20 B5
St-Denis Réunion 20°52S 55°27E 53 c
St-Denis ✕ (RUN) Réunion 20°53S 55°32E 53 c
St-Dizier France 48°38N 4°56E 20 B6
St. Elias, Mt. U.S.A. 60°18N 140°56W 68 E3
St. Elias Mts. N. Amer. 60°33N 139°28W 70 A1
St-Étienne France 45°27N 4°22E 20 D6
St. Eugène Canada 45°30N 74°28W 83 A10
St. Eustatius W. Indies 17°20N 63°0W 89 C7
St-Félicien Canada 48°40N 72°25W 72 C5
St-Flour France 45°2N 3°6E 20 D5
St. Francis U.S.A. 39°47N 101°48W 80 F3
St. Francis → U.S.A. 34°38N 90°36W 85 D9
St. Francis, C. S. Africa 34°14S 24°49E 56 E3
St. Francisville U.S.A. 30°47N 91°23W 84 F9
St-François, L. Canada 45°10N 74°22W 83 A10
St-Gabriel Canada 46°17N 73°24W 72 C5
St. Gallen = Sankt Gallen Switz. 47°26N 9°22E 20 C8
St-Gaudens France 43°6N 0°44E 20 E4
St. George Australia 28°1S 148°30E 63 D4
St. George N.B., Canada 45°11N 66°50W 73 C6
St. George Ont., Canada 43°15N 80°15W 82 C4
St. George S.C., U.S.A. 33°11N 80°35W 85 E14
St. George Utah, U.S.A. 37°6N 113°35W 77 H7
St. George, C. Canada 48°30N 59°16W 73 C8
St. George, C. U.S.A. 29°40N 85°5W 85 G12
St. George I. U.S.A. 56°35N 169°35W 74 D6
St. George Ra. Australia 18°40S 125°0E 60 C4
St. George's Canada 48°26N 58°31W 73 C8
St-Georges Canada 46°8N 70°40W 73 C5
St. George's Grenada 12°5N 61°43W 89 D7
St. George's B. Canada 48°24N 58°53W 73 C8
St. Georges Basin N.S.W., Australia 35°7S 150°36E 63 F5
St. Georges Basin W. Austral., Australia 15°23S 125°2E 60 C4
St. George's Channel Europe 52°0N 6°0W 10 E6
St. Georges Hd. Australia 35°12S 150°42E 63 F5
St. Gotthard P. = San Gottardo, P. del Switz. 46°33N 8°33E 20 C8
St. Helena Atl. Oc. 15°58S 5°42W 48 H3
St. Helena U.S.A. 38°30N 122°28W 76 G2
St. Helena, Mt. U.S.A. 38°40N 122°36W 78 G4
St. Helena B. S. Africa 32°40S 18°10E 56 E2
St. Helens Australia 41°20S 148°15E 63 G4
St. Helens U.K. 53°27N 2°44W 12 D5
St. Helens U.S.A. 45°52N 122°48W 78 E4
St. Helens, Mt. U.S.A. 46°12N 122°12W 78 D4
St. Helier U.K. 49°10N 2°7W 13 H5
St-Hubert Belgium 50°2N 5°23E 15 D5
St-Hubert Canada 45°29N 73°25W 83 A11
St-Hyacinthe Canada 45°40N 72°58W 72 C5
St. Ignace U.S.A. 45°52N 84°44W 81 C11
St. Ignace I. Canada 48°45N 88°0W 72 C2
St. Ignatius U.S.A. 47°19N 114°6W 76 C6
St. Ives Cambs., U.K. 52°20N 0°4W 13 E7
St. Ives Corn., U.K. 50°12N 5°30W 13 G2
St. James U.S.A. 43°59N 94°38W 80 D6
St-Jean → Canada 50°17N 64°20W 73 B7
St-Jean, L. Canada 48°40N 72°0W 73 C5
St-Jean-Port-Joli Canada 47°15N 70°13W 73 C5
St-Jean-sur-Richelieu Canada 45°20N 73°20W 83 A11
St-Jérôme Canada 45°47N 74°0W 72 C5
St. John Canada 45°20N 66°8W 73 C6
St. John U.S.A. 38°0N 98°46W 80 F4
St. John → N. Amer. 45°12N 66°5W 81 C20
St. John, C. Canada 50°0N 55°32W 73 C8
St. John I. U.S. Virgin Is. 18°20N 64°42W 89 e
St. John's Antigua & B. 17°6N 61°51W 89 C7
St. John's Canada 47°35N 52°40W 73 C9
St. Johns Ariz., U.S.A. 34°30N 109°22W 77 J9
St. Johns Mich., U.S.A. 43°0N 84°33W 81 D11
St. Johns → U.S.A. 30°24N 81°24W 85 F14
St. John's Pt. Ireland 54°34N 8°27W 10 B3
St. Johnsbury U.S.A. 44°25N 72°1W 83 B12
St. Johnsville U.S.A. 43°0N 74°43W 83 C10
St. Joseph Canada 43°24N 81°42W 82 C3
St-Joseph Martinique 14°39N 61°4W 88 c
St-Joseph Réunion 21°22S 55°37E 53 c
St. Joseph La., U.S.A. 31°55N 91°14W 84 F9
St. Joseph Mo., U.S.A. 39°46N 94°50W 80 F6
St. Joseph → U.S.A. 42°7N 86°29W 80 D10
St. Joseph, I. Canada 46°12N 83°58W 72 C3
St. Joseph, L. Canada 51°10N 90°35W 72 B1
St. Kilda U.K. 57°49N 8°34W 14 C2
St. Kitts & Nevis ■ W. Indies 17°20N 62°40W 89 C7
St. Laurent Canada 50°25N 97°58W 71 C9
St. Lawrence Australia 22°16S 149°31E 62 C4
St. Lawrence Canada 46°54N 55°23W 73 C8
St. Lawrence → Canada 49°30N 66°0W 73 C6
St. Lawrence, Gulf of Canada 48°25N 62°0W 73 C7
St. Lawrence I. U.S.A. 63°30N 170°30W 74 C5
St. Lawrence Islands △ Canada 44°27N 75°52W 83 B9
St. Léonard Canada 47°12N 67°58W 73 C6
St-Leu Réunion 21°9S 55°18E 53 c
St. Lewis → Canada 52°26N 56°11W 73 B8
St-Lô France 49°7N 1°5W 20 B3
St-Louis Guadeloupe 15°56N 61°19W 88 b
St-Louis Réunion 21°16S 55°25E 53 c
St. Louis Senegal 16°8N 16°27W 50 E2
St. Louis U.S.A. 38°37N 90°11W 80 F8
St. Louis → U.S.A. 46°44N 92°9W 80 B7
St-Luc Canada 45°22N 73°18W 83 A11
St. Lucia ■ W. Indies 14°0N 60°57W 89 f
St. Lucia, L. S. Africa 28°5S 32°30E 57 D5
St. Lucia Channel W. Indies 14°15N 61°0W 89 D7
St. Maarten ☒ W. Indies 18°0N 63°5W 89 C7
St. Magnus B. U.K. 60°25N 1°35W 11 A7
St-Malo France 48°39N 2°1W 20 B2
St-Marc Haiti 19°10N 72°41W 89 C5
St. Maries U.S.A. 47°19N 116°35W 76 C5
St-Martin ☒ W. Indies 18°0N 63°0W 89 C7
St-Martin, C. Martinique 14°52N 61°14W 88 c
St. Martin, L. Canada 51°40N 98°30W 71 C9
St. Martins Barbados 13°5N 59°28W 89 g
St. Mary Pk. Australia 31°32S 138°34E 63 E2
St. Marys Australia 41°35S 148°11E 63 G4
St. Marys Canada 43°20N 81°10W 82 C3
St. Mary's Corn., U.K. 49°55N 6°18W 13 H1
St. Mary's Orkney, U.K. 58°54N 2°54W 11 C6
St. Marys Ga., U.S.A. 30°44N 81°33W 85 F14
St. Marys Pa., U.S.A. 41°26N 78°34W 82 E6
St. Mary's, C. Canada 46°50N 54°12W 73 C9
St. Mary's B. Canada 46°50N 53°50W 73 C9
St. Mary's Bay Canada 44°25N 66°10W 73 D6
St-Mathieu, Pte. France 48°20N 4°45W 20 B1
St. Matthew I. U.S.A. 60°24N 172°42W 74 C5
St-Maurice → Canada 46°21N 72°31W 72 C5
St. Mawes U.K. 50°10N 5°2W 13 G2
St-Nazaire France 47°17N 2°12W 20 C2
St. Neots U.K. 52°14N 0°15W 13 E7
St-Niklaas Belgium 51°10N 4°8E 15 C4
St-Omer France 50°45N 2°15E 20 A5
St-Pamphile Canada 46°58N 69°48W 73 C6
St-Pascal Canada 47°32N 69°48W 73 C6
St. Paul Canada 54°0N 111°17W 70 C6
St-Paul Réunion 20°59S 55°17E 53 c
St. Paul Minn., U.S.A. 44°56N 93°5W 80 C7
St. Paul Nebr., U.S.A. 41°13N 98°27W 80 E4
St-Paul → Canada 51°27N 57°42W 73 B8
St. Paul, Î. Ind. Oc. 38°55S 77°34E 3 F13
St. Paul I. Canada 47°12N 60°9W 73 C7
St. Paul I. U.S.A. 57°10N 170°15W 74 D5
St. Peter U.S.A. 44°20N 93°57W 80 C7
St. Peter Port U.K. 49°26N 2°33W 13 H5
St. Peters N.S., Canada 45°40N 60°53W 73 C7
St. Peters P.E.I., Canada 46°25N 62°35W 73 C7
St. Petersburg = Sankt-Peterburg Russia 59°55N 30°20E 9 G24
St. Petersburg U.S.A. 27°46N 82°40W 85 H13
St-Phillippe Réunion 21°21S 55°44E 53 c
St-Pie Canada 45°30N 72°54W 83 A12
St-Pierre Martinique 14°45N 61°10W 88 c
St-Pierre Réunion 21°19S 55°28E 53 c
St-Pierre St-P. & M. 46°46N 56°12W 73 C8
St-Pierre, L. Canada 46°12N 72°52W 72 C5
St-Pierre-et-Miquelon ☒ N. Amer. 46°55N 56°10W 73 C8
St-Quentin Canada 47°30N 67°23W 73 C6
St-Quentin France 49°50N 3°16E 20 B5
St. Regis U.S.A. 47°18N 115°6W 76 C6
St. Regis Falls U.S.A. 44°40N 74°32W 83 B10
St. Sebastien, Tanjon' i Madag. 12°26S 48°44E 57 A8
St-Siméon Canada 47°51N 69°54W 73 C6
St. Simons I. U.S.A. 31°12N 81°15W 85 F14
St. Simons Island U.S.A. 31°9N 81°22W 85 F14
St. Stephen Canada 45°16N 67°17W 73 C6
St. Thomas Canada 42°45N 81°10W 82 D3
St. Thomas I. U.S. Virgin Is. 18°20N 64°55W 89 e
St-Tite Canada 46°45N 72°34W 72 C5
St-Tropez France 43°17N 6°38E 20 E7
St-Troud = St. Truiden Belgium 50°48N 5°10E 15 D5
St. Truiden Belgium 50°48N 5°10E 15 D5
St. Vidgeon's ☼ Australia 14°47S 134°53E 62 A1
St. Vincent = São Vicente C. Verde Is. 17°0N 25°0W 50 b
St. Vincent, G. Australia 35°0S 138°0E 63 F2
St. Vincent & the Grenadines ■ W. Indies 13°0N 61°10W 89 D7
St. Vincent Passage W. Indies 13°30N 61°0W 89 D7
St-Vith Belgium 50°17N 6°9E 15 D6
St. Walburg Canada 53°39N 109°12W 71 C7
Ste-Agathe-des-Monts Canada 46°3N 74°17W 72 C5
Ste-Anne Guadeloupe 16°13N 61°24W 88 b
Ste-Anne Seychelles 4°36S 55°31E 53 b
Ste-Anne, L. Canada 50°0N 67°42W 73 B6
Ste-Anne-des-Monts Canada 49°8N 66°30W 73 C6
Ste. Genevieve U.S.A. 37°59N 90°2W 80 G8
Ste-Marguerite → Canada 50°9N 66°36W 73 B6
Ste-Marie Canada 46°26N 71°0W 73 C5
Ste-Marie Martinique 14°48N 61°1W 88 c
Ste-Marie Réunion 20°53S 55°33E 53 c
Ste-Marie, Ile = Nosy Boraha Madag. 16°50S 49°55E 57 B8
Ste-Rose Guadeloupe 16°20N 61°45W 88 b
Ste-Rose Réunion 21°8S 55°45E 53 c
Ste. Rose du Lac Canada 51°4N 99°30W 71 C9
Saintes France 45°45N 0°37W 20 D3
Saintes, Îs. des Guadeloupe 15°50N 61°35W 88 b
Saintfield U.K. 54°28N 5°49W 10 B6
Saintonge France 45°40N 0°50W 20 D3
Saipan N. Marianas 15°12N 145°45E 64 F6
Sairang India 23°50N 92°45E 41 H18
Sairecábur, Cerro Bolivia 22°43S 67°54W 94 A2
Saitama Japan 35°54N 139°38E 31 G9
Saitama □ Japan 36°25N 139°30E 31 F9
Saiyid Pakistan 33°7N 73°2E 42 C5
Sajama Bolivia 18°7S 69°0W 92 G5
Sajószentpéter Hungary 48°12N 20°44E 17 D11
Sajum India 33°20N 79°0E 43 C8
Sak → S. Africa 30°52S 20°25E 56 E3
Saka Kenya 0°9S 39°20E 54 B4
Sakai Japan 34°34N 135°27E 31 G7
Sakaide Japan 34°19N 133°50E 31 G6
Sakaiminato Japan 35°38N 133°11E 31 G6
Sakākah Si. Arabia 30°0N 40°8E 44 D4
Sakakawea, L. U.S.A. 47°30N 101°25W 80 B3
Sakami → Canada 53°40N 76°40W 72 B4
Sakami, L. Canada 53°15N 77°0W 72 B4
Sakania Dem. Rep. of the Congo 12°43S 28°30E 55 E2
Sakaraha Madag. 22°55S 44°32E 57 C7
Sakartvelo = Georgia ■ Asia 42°0N 43°0E 19 F7
Sakarya Turkey 40°48N 30°25E 19 F5
Sakashima-Guntō Japan 24°46N 124°0E 31 M2
Sakata Japan 38°55N 139°50E 30 E9
Sakchu N. Korea 40°23N 125°2E 35 D13
Sakeny → Madag. 20°0S 45°25E 57 C8
Sakha □ Russia 66°0N 130°0E 29 C14
Sakhalin Russia 51°0N 143°0E 29 D15
Sakhalinskiy Zaliv Russia 54°0N 141°0E 29 D15
Šakiai Lithuania 54°59N 23°2E 9 J20
Sakon Nakhon Thailand 17°10N 104°9E 38 D5
Sakrand Pakistan 26°10N 68°15E 42 F3
Sakri India 26°13N 86°5E 43 F12
Sakrivier S. Africa 30°54S 20°28E 56 E3
Sakti India 22°2N 82°58E 43 H10
Sakuma Japan 35°3N 137°49E 31 G8
Sakurai Japan 34°30N 135°51E 31 G7
Sal C. Verde Is. 16°45N 22°55W 50 b
Sal Rei C. Verde Is. 16°11N 22°53W 50 b
Sala Sweden 59°58N 16°35E 9 G17
Sala Consilina Italy 40°23N 15°36E 22 D6
Sala-y-Gómez Pac. Oc. 26°28S 105°28W 65 K17
Sala y Gómez Ridge Pac. Oc. 25°0S 98°0W 65 K18
Salaberry-de-Valleyfield Canada 45°15N 74°8W 83 A10
Salada, L. Mexico 32°20N 115°40W 77 K6
Saladas Argentina 28°15S 58°40W 94 B4
Saladillo Argentina 35°40S 59°55W 94 D4
Salado → B. Aires, Argentina 35°44S 57°22W 94 D4
Salado → La Pampa, Argentina 37°30S 67°0W 96 D3
Salado → Santa Fe, Argentina 31°40S 60°41W 94 C3
Salado → Mexico 26°52N 99°19W 84 H5
Salaga Ghana 8°31N 0°31W 50 G5
Sālah Syria 32°40N 36°45E 46 C5
Şalāḥ ad Dīn □ Iraq 34°35N 43°35E 44 C4
Salakos Greece 36°17N 27°57E 25 C9
Salālah Oman 16°56N 53°59E 47 D5
Salamanca Chile 31°46S 70°59W 94 C1
Salamanca Spain 40°58N 5°39W 21 B3
Salamanca U.S.A. 42°10N 78°43W 82 D6
Salāmatābād Iran 35°39N 47°50E 44 C5
Salamina Greece 37°56N 23°30E 23 F10
Salamis Cyprus 35°11N 33°54E 25 D12
Salar de Atacama Chile 23°30S 68°25W 94 A2
Salar de Uyuni Bolivia 20°30S 67°45W 92 H5
Salatiga Indonesia 7°19S 110°30E 37 G14
Salavat Russia 53°21N 55°55E 18 D10
Salaverry Peru 8°15S 79°0W 92 E3
Salawati Indonesia 1°7S 130°52E 37 E8
Salawin △ Thailand 18°18N 97°40E 38 C1
Salaya India 22°19N 69°35E 42 H3
Salayar Indonesia 6°7S 120°30E 37 F6
S'Albufera Spain 39°47N 3°7E 24 B10
Salcombe U.K. 50°14N 3°47W 13 G4
Saldanha S. Africa 33°0S 17°58E 56 E2
Saldanha B. S. Africa 33°6S 18°0E 56 E2
Saldus Latvia 56°38N 22°30E 9 H20
Sale Australia 38°6S 147°6E 63 F4
Salé Morocco 34°3N 6°48W 50 B4
Sale U.K. 53°26N 2°19W 12 D5
Salekhard Russia 66°30N 66°35E 28 C7
Salelologa Samoa 13°41S 172°11W 59 b
Salem India 11°40N 78°11E 40 P11
Salem Ill., U.S.A. 38°38N 88°57W 80 F9
Salem Ind., U.S.A. 38°36N 86°6W 80 F10
Salem Mass., U.S.A. 42°31N 70°53W 83 D14
Salem Mo., U.S.A. 37°39N 91°32W 80 G8
Salem N.H., U.S.A. 42°45N 71°12W 83 D13
Salem N.J., U.S.A. 39°34N 75°28W 81 F16
Salem N.Y., U.S.A. 43°10N 73°20W 83 C11
Salem Ohio, U.S.A. 40°54N 80°52W 82 F4
Salem Oreg., U.S.A. 44°56N 123°2W 76 D2
Salem S. Dak., U.S.A. 43°44N 97°23W 80 D5
Salem Va., U.S.A. 37°18N 80°3W 81 G13
Salerno Italy 40°41N 14°47E 22 D6
Salford U.K. 53°30N 2°18W 12 D5
Salgótarján Hungary 48°5N 19°47E 17 D10
Salgueiro Brazil 8°4S 39°6W 93 E11
Salibabu Indonesia 3°51N 126°40E 37 D7
Salibea = Salybia Trin. & Tob. 10°43N 61°2W 93 K15
Salida U.S.A. 38°32N 106°0W 75 H18
Salihli Turkey 38°28N 28°8E 23 E13
Salihorsk Belarus 52°51N 27°27E 17 B14
Salima Malawi 13°47S 34°28E 53 G6
Salina Italy 38°34N 14°50E 22 E6

Salina *Kans., U.S.A.* 38°50N 97°37W **80 F5**
Salina *Utah, U.S.A.* 38°58N 111°51W **76 G8**
Salina Cruz *Mexico* 16°10N 95°12W **87 D5**
Salinas *Brazil* 16°10S 42°10W **93 G10**
Salinas *Ecuador* 2°10S 80°58W **92 D2**
Salinas *U.S.A.* 36°40N 121°39W **78 J5**
Salinas → *Guatemala* 16°28N 90°31W **87 D6**
Salinas → *U.S.A.* 36°45N 121°48W **78 J5**
Salinas, B. de *Nic.* 11°4N 85°45W **88 D2**
Salinas, Pampa de las
  Argentina 31°58S 66°42W **94 C2**
Salinas Ambargasta
  Argentina 29°0S 65°0W **94 B3**
Salinas de Hidalgo
  Mexico 22°38N 101°43W **86 C4**
Salinas Grandes *Argentina* 30°0S 65°0W **94 C3**
Salinas Pueblo Missions △
  U.S.A. 34°6N 106°4W **77 J10**
Salinas Valley *U.S.A.* 36°15N 121°15W **78 J5**
Saline → *Ark., U.S.A.* 33°10N 92°8W **84 E8**
Saline → *Kans., U.S.A.* 38°52N 97°30W **80 F5**
Salines, C. de ses *Spain* 39°16N 3°4E **24 B10**
Salinópolis *Brazil* 0°40S 47°20W **93 D9**
Salisbury *Australia* 34°46S 138°38E **63 E2**
Salisbury *U.K.* 51°4N 1°47W **13 F6**
Salisbury *Md., U.S.A.* 38°22N 75°36W **81 F16**
Salisbury *N.C., U.S.A.* 35°40N 80°29W **85 D14**
Salisbury I. *Canada* 63°30N 77°0W **69 E16**
Salisbury Plain *U.K.* 51°14N 1°55W **13 F6**
Şalkhad *Syria* 32°29N 36°43E **46 C5**
Salla *Finland* 66°50N 28°49E **8 C23**
Salliq = Coral Harbour
  Canada 64°8N 83°10W **69 E15**
Sallisaw *U.S.A.* 35°28N 94°47W **84 D7**
Salluit *Canada* 62°14N 75°38W **69 E16**
Salmās *Iran* 38°11N 44°47E **44 B5**
Salmo *Canada* 49°10N 117°20W **70 D5**
Salmon *U.S.A.* 45°11N 113°54W **76 D7**
Salmon → *Canada* 54°3N 122°40W **70 C4**
Salmon → *U.S.A.* 45°51N 116°47W **76 D5**
Salmon Arm *Canada* 50°40N 119°15W **70 C5**
Salmon Gums *Australia* 32°59S 121°38E **61 F3**
Salmon Pt. *Canada* 43°52N 77°15W **82 C7**
Salmon River Mts.
  U.S.A. 44°50N 115°30W **76 D6**
Salmon River Res.
  U.S.A. 43°32N 75°55W **83 C9**
Salo *Finland* 60°22N 23°10E **9 F20**
Salome *U.S.A.* 33°47N 113°37W **79 M13**
Salon *India* 26°2N 81°27E **43 F9**
Salon-de-Provence *France* 43°39N 5°6E **20 E6**
Salonica = Thessaloniki
  Greece 40°38N 22°58E **23 D10**
Salonta *Romania* 46°49N 21°42E **17 E11**
Salpausselkä *Finland* 61°3N 26°15E **8 F22**
Salsacate *Argentina* 31°20S 65°5W **94 C2**
Salsk *Russia* 46°28N 41°30E **19 E7**
Salso → *Italy* 37°6N 13°57E **22 F5**
Salt → *Canada* 60°0N 112°25W **70 B6**
Salt → *U.S.A.* 33°23N 112°19W **77 K7**
Salt Fork Red → *U.S.A.* 34°27N 99°21W **84 D5**
Salt I. *Australia* 30°6S 142°8E **63 E3**
Salt Lake City *U.S.A.* 40°45N 111°53W **76 F8**
Salt Range *Pakistan* 32°30N 72°25E **42 C5**
Salta *Argentina* 24°57S 65°25W **94 A2**
Salta □ *Argentina* 24°48S 65°30W **94 A2**
Saltash *U.K.* 50°24N 4°14W **13 G3**
Saltburn by the Sea *U.K.* 54°35N 0°58W **12 C7**
Saltcoats *U.K.* 55°38N 4°47W **11 F4**
Saltee Is. *Ireland* 52°7N 6°37W **10 D5**
Saltfjellet *Norway* 66°40N 15°15E **8 C16**
Saltfjorden *Norway* 67°15N 14°10E **8 C16**
Saltillo *Mexico* 25°25N 101°0W **86 B4**
Salto *Argentina* 34°20S 60°15W **94 C3**
Salto *Uruguay* 31°27S 57°50W **94 C4**
Salto → *Italy* 42°26N 12°25E **22 C5**
Salto del Guairá *Paraguay* 24°3S 54°17W **95 A5**
Salton City *U.S.A.* 33°18N 115°57W **79 M11**
Salton Sea *U.S.A.* 33°15N 115°45W **79 M11**
Saltsburg *U.S.A.* 40°29N 79°27W **82 F5**
Saluda → *U.S.A.* 34°1N 81°4W **85 D14**
Salûm *Egypt* 31°31N 25°7E **51 B11**
Salur *India* 18°27N 83°18E **41 K13**
Salvador *Brazil* 13°0S 38°30W **93 F11**
Salvador *Canada* 52°10N 109°32W **71 C7**
Salvador, El ■
  Cent. Amer. 13°50N 89°0W **88 D2**
Salvador, L. *U.S.A.* 29°43N 90°15W **85 G9**
Salween → *Burma* 16°31N 97°37E **41 L20**
Salyan *Azerbaijan* 39°33N 48°59E **46 B6**
Salybia *Trin. & Tob.* 10°43N 61°2W **93 K15**
Salzach → *Austria* 48°12N 12°56E **16 D7**
Salzburg *Austria* 47°48N 13°2E **16 E7**
Salzgitter *Germany* 52°9N 10°19E **16 B6**
Salzwedel *Germany* 52°52N 11°10E **16 B6**
Sam *India* 26°50N 70°31E **42 F4**
Sam Neua *Laos* 20°29N 104°5E **38 B5**
Sam Ngao *Thailand* 17°18N 99°0E **38 D2**
Sam Rayburn Res. *U.S.A.* 31°4N 94°5W **84 F7**
Sam Son *Vietnam* 19°44N 105°54E **38 C5**
Sama de Langreo = Langreo
  Spain 43°18N 5°40W **21 A3**
Samagaltay *Russia* 50°36N 95°3E **29 D10**
Samales Group *Phil.* 6°0N 122°0E **37 C6**
Samana *India* 30°10N 76°13E **42 D7**
Samana Cay *Bahamas* 23°3N 73°45W **89 B5**
Samanga *Tanzania* 8°20S 39°13E **55 D4**
Samangān □ *Afghan.* 36°15N 68°3E **40 B5**
Samangwa
  Dem. Rep. of the Congo 4°23S 24°10E **54 C1**
Samani *Japan* 42°7N 142°56E **30 C11**
Samar *Phil.* 12°0N 125°0E **37 B7**
Samara *Russia* 53°8N 50°6E **18 D9**
Samaria = Shōmron
  West Bank 32°15N 35°13E **46 C4**
Samariá △ *Greece* 35°17N 23°58E **25 D5**
Samarinda *Indonesia* 0°30S 117°9E **36 E5**
Samarkand = Samarqand
  Uzbekistan 39°40N 66°55E **28 F7**
Samarqand *Uzbekistan* 39°40N 66°55E **28 F7**

Sāmarrā' *Iraq* 34°12N 43°52E **44 C4**
Samastipur *India* 25°50N 85°50E **43 G11**
Samba
  Dem. Rep. of the Congo 4°38S 26°22E **54 C2**
Samba *India* 32°32N 75°10E **43 C6**
Sambalpur *India* 21°28N 84°4E **41 J14**
Sambar, Tanjung
  Indonesia 2°59S 110°19E **36 E4**
Sambas *Indonesia* 1°20N 109°20E **36 D3**
Sambava *Madag.* 14°16S 50°10E **57 A9**
Sambawizi *Zimbabwe* 18°24S 26°13E **55 F2**
Sambhajinagar = Aurangabad
  India 19°50N 75°23E **40 K9**
Sambhal *India* 28°35N 78°37E **43 E8**
Sambhar *India* 26°52N 75°6E **42 F6**
Sambhar L. *India* 26°55N 75°12E **42 F6**
Sambiase *Italy* 38°58N 16°17E **22 E7**
Sambir *Ukraine* 49°30N 23°10E **17 D12**
Sambor *Cambodia* 12°46N 106°0E **38 F6**
Sambor Prei Kuk
  Cambodia 12°46N 105°58E **38 F5**
Samborombón, B.
  Argentina 36°5S 57°20W **94 D4**
Samburu △ *Kenya* 0°37N 37°31E **54 B4**
Samcheok *S. Korea* 37°30N 129°10E **35 F15**
Same *Tanzania* 4°2S 37°38E **54 C4**
Samet, Ko *Thailand* 12°34N 101°27E **38 F3**
Samfya *Zambia* 11°22S 29°31E **55 E2**
Samnah *Si. Arabia* 25°10N 37°15E **44 E3**
Samo Alto *Chile* 30°22S 71°0W **94 C1**
Samoa ■ *Pac. Oc.* 14°0S 172°0W **59 b**
Samoan Is. *Pac. Oc.* 14°0S 171°0W **59 b**
Samokov *Bulgaria* 42°18N 23°35E **23 C10**
Samos *Greece* 37°45N 26°50E **23 F12**
Samothráki = Mathraki
  Greece 39°48N 19°31E **25 A3**
Samothraki *Greece* 40°28N 25°28E **23 D11**
Sampacho *Argentina* 33°20S 64°50W **94 C3**
Sampalan *Indonesia* 8°41S 115°34E **37 K18**
Sampang *Indonesia* 7°11S 113°13E **37 G15**
Sampit *Indonesia* 2°34S 113°0E **36 E4**
Sampit, Teluk *Indonesia* 3°5S 113°3E **36 E4**
Samrong *Cambodia* 14°15N 103°30E **38 E4**
Samsø *Denmark* 55°50N 10°35E **9 J14**
Samsun *Turkey* 41°15N 36°22E **19 F6**
Samui, Ko *Thailand* 9°30N 100°0E **39 b**
Samusole
  Dem. Rep. of the Congo 10°2S 24°0E **55 E1**
Samut Prakan *Thailand* 13°32N 100°36E **38 F3**
Samut Sakhon *Thailand* 13°32N 100°17E **38 F3**
Samut Songkhram
  Thailand 13°24N 100°1E **38 F3**
Samwari *Pakistan* 28°30N 66°46E **42 E2**
San *Mali* 13°15N 4°57W **50 F5**
San → *Cambodia* 13°32N 105°57E **38 F5**
San → *Poland* 50°45N 21°51E **17 C11**
San Agustín, C. *Phil.* 6°20N 126°13E **37 C7**
San Agustín de Valle Fértil
  Argentina 30°35S 67°30W **94 C2**
San Ambrosio *Pac. Oc.* 26°28S 79°53W **90 F3**
San Andreas *U.S.A.* 38°12N 120°41W **78 G6**
San Andrés, I. de
  Caribbean 12°42N 81°46W **88 D3**
San Andres Mts.
  U.S.A. 33°0N 106°30W **77 K10**
San Andrés Tuxtla
  Mexico 18°27N 95°13W **87 D5**
San Angelo *U.S.A.* 31°28N 100°26W **84 F4**
San Anselmo *U.S.A.* 37°59N 122°34W **78 H4**
San Antonio *Belize* 16°15N 89°2W **87 D7**
San Antonio *Chile* 33°40S 71°40W **94 C1**
San Antonio *N. Mex.,
  U.S.A.* 33°55N 106°52W **77 K10**
San Antonio *Tex.,
  U.S.A.* 29°25N 98°29W **84 G5**
San Antonio → *U.S.A.* 28°30N 96°54W **84 G6**
San Antonio, C.
  Argentina 36°15S 56°40W **94 D4**
San Antonio, C. de *Cuba* 21°50N 84°57W **88 B3**
San Antonio, Mt.
  U.S.A. 34°17N 117°38W **79 L9**
San Antonio de los Baños
  Cuba 22°54N 82°31W **88 B3**
San Antonio de los Cobres
  Argentina 24°10S 66°17W **94 A2**
San Antonio Oeste
  Argentina 40°40S 65°0W **96 E4**
San Ardo *U.S.A.* 36°1N 120°54W **78 J6**
San Augustín *Canary Is.* 27°47N 15°32W **24 G4**
San Augustine *U.S.A.* 31°32N 94°7W **84 F7**
San Bartolomé
  Canary Is. 28°59N 13°37W **24 F6**
San Bartolomé de Tirajana
  Canary Is. 27°54N 15°34W **24 G4**
San Benedetto del Tronto
  Italy 42°57N 13°53E **22 C5**
San Benedicto, I.
  Mexico 19°18N 110°49W **86 D2**
San Benito *U.S.A.* 26°8N 97°38W **84 H6**
San Benito → *U.S.A.* 36°53N 121°34W **78 J5**
San Benito Mt. *U.S.A.* 36°22N 120°37W **78 J6**
San Bernardino *U.S.A.* 34°7N 117°19W **79 L9**
San Bernardino Mts.
  U.S.A. 34°10N 116°45W **79 L10**
San Bernardino Str.
  Phil. 12°30N 124°10E **37 B7**
San Bernardo *Chile* 33°40S 70°50W **94 C1**
San Bernardo, I. de
  Colombia 9°45N 75°50W **92 B3**
San Blas *Mexico* 26°5N 108°46W **86 B3**
San Blas, Arch. de
  Panama 9°50N 78°31W **88 E4**
San Blas, C. *U.S.A.* 29°40N 85°21W **85 G12**
San Borja *Bolivia* 14°50S 66°52W **92 F5**
San Buenaventura = Ventura
  U.S.A. 34°17N 119°18W **79 L7**
San Buenaventura
  Mexico 27°5N 101°32W **86 B4**
San Carlos = Sant Carles
  Spain 39°3N 1°34E **24 B8**

San Carlos *Argentina* 33°50S 69°0W **94 C2**
San Carlos *Chile* 36°10S 72°0W **94 D1**
San Carlos *Baja Calif. S.,
  Mexico* 24°47N 112°7W **86 C2**
San Carlos *Coahuila,
  Mexico* 29°1N 100°51W **86 B4**
San Carlos *Nic.* 11°12N 84°50W **88 D3**
San Carlos *Phil.* 10°29N 123°25E **37 B6**
San Carlos *Uruguay* 34°46S 54°58W **95 C5**
San Carlos *Venezuela* 33°21N 110°27W **77 K8**
San Carlos *Venezuela* 9°40N 68°36W **92 B5**
San Carlos de Bariloche
  Argentina 41°10S 71°25W **96 E2**
San Carlos de Bolívar
  Argentina 36°15S 61°6W **94 D3**
San Carlos del Zulia
  Venezuela 9°1N 71°55W **92 B4**
San Carlos L. *U.S.A.* 33°11N 110°32W **77 K8**
San Clemente *Chile* 35°30S 71°29W **94 D1**
San Clemente I. *U.S.A.* 32°53N 118°29W **79 N8**
San Cristóbal = Es Migjorn Gran
  Spain 39°57N 4°3E **24 B11**
San Cristóbal *Argentina* 30°20S 61°10W **94 C3**
San Cristóbal *Dom. Rep.* 18°25N 70°6W **89 C5**
San Cristóbal *Solomon Is.* 10°30S 161°0E **58 C9**
San Cristóbal *Venezuela* 7°46N 72°14W **92 B4**
San Cristóbal de las Casas
  Mexico 16°45N 92°38W **87 D6**
San Diego *Calif., U.S.A.* 32°42N 117°9W **79 N9**
San Diego *Tex., U.S.A.* 27°46N 98°14W **84 H5**
San Diego, C. *Argentina* 54°40S 65°10W **96 G3**
San Diego de la Unión
  Mexico 21°28N 100°52W **86 C4**
San Diego Int. ✈ (SAN)
  U.S.A. 32°44N 117°11W **79 N9**
San Dimitri, Ras *Malta* 36°4N 14°11E **25 C1**
San Dimitri Point = San Dimitri,
  Ras *Malta* 36°4N 14°11E **25 C1**
San Estanislao *Paraguay* 24°39S 56°26W **94 A4**
San Felipe *Chile* 32°43S 70°42W **94 C1**
San Felipe *Mexico* 31°1N 114°52W **86 A2**
San Felipe *Venezuela* 10°20N 68°44W **92 A5**
San Felipe → *U.S.A.* 33°10N 115°49W **79 M11**
San Félix *Chile* 28°56S 70°28W **94 B1**
San Félix *Pac. Oc.* 26°23S 80°0W **90 F2**
San Fernando = Sant Ferran
  Spain 38°42N 1°28E **24 C7**
San Fernando *Chile* 34°30S 71°0W **94 C1**
San Fernando *Mexico* 24°51N 98°10W **87 C5**
San Fernando *La Union,
  Phil.* 16°40N 120°23E **37 A6**
San Fernando *Pampanga,
  Phil.* 15°5N 120°37E **37 A6**
San Fernando *Spain* 36°28N 6°17W **21 D2**
San Fernando
  Trin. & Tob. 10°16N 61°28W **93 K15**
San Fernando *U.S.A.* 34°17N 118°26W **79 L8**
San Fernando de Apure
  Venezuela 7°54N 67°15W **92 B5**
San Fernando de Atabapo
  Venezuela 4°3N 67°42W **92 C5**
San Francisco *Argentina* 31°30S 62°5W **94 C3**
San Francisco *U.S.A.* 37°46N 122°23W **78 H4**
San Francisco →
  U.S.A. 32°59N 109°22W **77 K9**
San Francisco, C. de
  Colombia 6°18N 77°29W **90 C3**
San Francisco, Paso de
  S. Amer. 27°0S 68°0W **94 B2**
San Francisco de Macorís
  Dom. Rep. 19°19N 70°15W **89 C5**
San Francisco del Monte de Oro
  Argentina 32°36S 66°8W **94 C2**
San Francisco del Oro
  Mexico 26°52N 105°51W **86 B3**
San Francisco Int. ✈ (SFO)
  U.S.A. 37°37N 122°22W **78 H4**
San Francisco Javier = Sant
  Francesc de Formentera
  Spain 38°42N 1°26E **24 C7**
San Gabriel *Chile* 33°47S 70°15W **94 C1**
San Gabriel Chilac
  Mexico 18°19N 97°21W **87 D5**
San Gabriel Mts.
  U.S.A. 34°17N 117°38W **79 L9**
San Gavino Monreale
  Italy 39°33N 8°47E **22 E3**
San German *Puerto Rico* 18°4N 67°4W **89 d**
San Gorgonio Mt.
  U.S.A. 34°6N 116°50W **79 L10**
San Gottardo, P. del
  Switz. 46°33N 8°33E **20 C8**
San Gregorio *Uruguay* 32°37S 55°40W **95 C4**
San Gregorio *U.S.A.* 37°20N 122°23W **78 H4**
San Guillermo △
  Argentina 27°50S 69°45W **94 B2**
San Ignacio *Belize* 17°10N 89°5W **87 D7**
San Ignacio *Bolivia* 16°20S 60°55W **92 G6**
San Ignacio *Mexico* 27°27N 112°51W **86 B2**
San Ignacio *Paraguay* 26°52S 57°3W **94 B4**
San Ignacio, L. *Mexico* 26°54N 113°13W **86 B2**
San Ildefonso, C. *Phil.* 16°0N 122°1E **37 A6**
San Isidro *Argentina* 34°29S 58°31W **94 C4**
San Jacinto *U.S.A.* 33°47N 116°57W **79 M10**
San Jaime = Sant Jaume
  Spain 39°54N 4°4E **24 B11**
San Javier *Misiones,
  Argentina* 27°55S 55°5W **95 B4**
San Javier *Santa Fe,
  Argentina* 30°40S 59°55W **94 C4**
San Javier *Bolivia* 16°18S 62°30W **92 G6**
San Javier *Chile* 35°40S 71°45W **94 D1**
San Jerónimo Taviche
  Mexico 16°44N 96°35W **87 D5**
San Joaquin *U.S.A.* 36°36N 120°11W **78 J6**
San Joaquin → *U.S.A.* 38°4N 121°51W **78 G5**
San Joaquin Valley
  U.S.A. 37°20N 121°0W **78 J6**
San Jon *U.S.A.* 35°6N 103°20W **77 J12**

San Jordi = Sant Jordi
  Spain 39°33N 2°46E **24 B9**
San Jorge *Argentina* 31°54S 61°50W **94 C3**
San Jorge, B. *Mexico* 31°20N 113°20W **86 A2**
San Jorge, G. *Argentina* 46°0S 66°0W **96 F3**
San José = San Josep
  Spain 38°55N 1°18E **24 C7**
San José *Argentina* 32°12S 58°15W **94 C4**
San José *Costa Rica* 9°55N 84°2W **88 E3**
San José *Guatemala* 14°0N 90°50W **88 D1**
San José *Mind. Occ., Phil.* 12°27N 121°4E **37 B6**
San Jose *Nueva Ecija,
  Phil.* 15°45N 120°57E **37 A6**
San Jose *U.S.A.* 37°20N 121°53W **78 H5**
San José, C. *Argentina* 42°20N 102°42W **78 K6**
San José → *U.S.A.* 34°25N 106°45W **77 J10**
San José, I. *Mexico* 25°0N 110°38W **86 C2**
San José de Buenavista
  Phil. 10°45N 121°56E **37 B6**
San José de Chiquitos
  Bolivia 17°53S 60°50W **92 G6**
San José de Feliciano
  Argentina 30°26S 58°46W **94 C4**
San José de Jáchal
  Argentina 30°15S 68°46W **94 C2**
San José de Mayo
  Uruguay 34°27S 56°40W **94 C4**
San José del Cabo
  Mexico 23°3N 109°41W **86 C3**
San José del Guaviare
  Colombia 2°35N 72°38W **92 C4**
San Josep *Spain* 38°55N 1°18E **24 C7**
San Juan *Argentina* 31°30S 68°30W **94 C2**
San Juan *Puerto Rico* 18°28N 66°7W **89 d**
San Juan *Trin. & Tob.* 10°39N 61°29W **93 K15**
San Juan □ *Argentina* 31°9S 69°0W **94 C2**
San Juan → *Argentina* 32°20S 67°25W **94 C2**
San Juan → *Nic.* 10°56N 83°42W **88 D3**
San Juan → *U.S.A.* 37°16N 110°26W **77 H8**
San Juan Bautista = Sant Joan de
  Labritja *Spain* 39°5N 1°31E **24 B8**
San Juan Bautista
  Paraguay 26°37S 57°6W **94 B4**
San Juan Bautista
  U.S.A. 36°51N 121°32W **78 J5**
San Juan Capistrano
  U.S.A. 33°30N 117°40W **79 M9**
San Juan Cr. → *U.S.A.* 35°40N 120°22W **78 J5**
San Juan de Guadalupe
  Mexico 24°38N 102°44W **86 C4**
San Juan de la Costa
  Mexico 24°20N 110°41W **86 C2**
San Juan de los Lagos
  Mexico 21°15N 102°18W **86 C4**
San Juan de los Morros
  Venezuela 9°55N 67°21W **92 B5**
San Juan del Norte *Nic.* 10°58N 83°40W **88 D3**
San Juan del Norte, B. de
  Nic. 11°0N 83°40W **88 D3**
San Juan del Río *Mexico* 20°23N 100°0W **87 C5**
San Juan del Sur *Nic.* 11°20N 85°51W **88 D2**
San Juan I. *U.S.A.* 48°32N 123°5W **78 B3**
San Juan Island △
  U.S.A. 48°35N 123°8W **78 B4**
San Juan Mts. *U.S.A.* 37°30N 107°0W **77 H10**
San Justo *Argentina* 30°47S 60°30W **94 C3**
San Kamphaeng *Thailand* 18°45N 99°8E **38 C2**
San Lázaro, C. *Mexico* 24°50N 112°18W **86 C2**
San Leandro *U.S.A.* 37°42N 122°9W **78 H4**
San Lorenzo = Sant Llorenç des
  Cardassar *Spain* 39°37N 3°17E **24 B10**
San Lorenzo *Argentina* 32°45S 60°45W **94 C3**
San Lorenzo *Ecuador* 1°15N 78°50W **92 C3**
San Lorenzo *Paraguay* 25°20S 57°32W **94 B4**
San Lorenzo → *Mexico* 24°15N 107°24W **86 C3**
San Lorenzo, I. *Mexico* 28°38N 112°51W **86 B2**
San Lorenzo, Mte.
  Argentina 47°40S 72°20W **96 F2**
San Lucas = Cabo San Lucas
  Mexico 22°53N 109°54W **86 C3**
San Lucas *Bolivia* 20°5S 65°7W **92 H5**
San Lucas *Mexico* 27°10N 112°14W **86 B2**
San Lucas *U.S.A.* 36°8N 121°1W **78 J5**
San Lucas, C. *Mexico* 22°52N 109°53W **86 C3**
San Luis *Argentina* 33°20S 66°20W **94 C2**
San Luis *Cuba* 22°17N 83°46W **88 B3**
San Luis *Guatemala* 16°14N 89°27W **88 C2**
San Luis *Ariz., U.S.A.* 32°29N 114°47W **77 K6**
San Luis *Colo., U.S.A.* 37°12N 105°25W **77 H11**
San Luis □ *Argentina* 34°0S 66°0W **94 C2**
San Luis, I. *Mexico* 29°58N 114°26W **86 B2**
San Luis, Sierra de
  Argentina 32°30S 66°10W **94 C2**
San Luis de la Paz
  Mexico 21°18N 100°31W **86 C4**
San Luis Obispo *U.S.A.* 35°17N 120°40W **79 K6**
San Luis Potosí *Mexico* 22°9N 100°59W **86 C4**
San Luis Potosí □ *Mexico* 23°0N 101°0W **86 C4**
San Luis Res. *U.S.A.* 37°4N 121°5W **78 H5**
San Luis Río Colorado
  Mexico 32°29N 114°58W **86 A2**
San Manuel *U.S.A.* 32°36N 110°38W **77 K8**
San Marcos *Guatemala* 14°59N 91°52W **88 D1**
San Marcos *Calif.,
  U.S.A.* 33°9N 117°10W **79 M9**
San Marcos *Tex., U.S.A.* 29°53N 97°56W **84 G6**
San Marcos, I. *Mexico* 27°13N 112°6W **86 B2**
San Marino *San Marino* 43°55N 12°30E **16 G7**
San Marino ■ *Europe* 43°56N 12°25E **22 C5**
San Martín *Argentina* 33°5S 68°28W **94 C2**
San Martín → *Bolivia* 13°8S 63°43W **92 F6**
San Martín, L. *Argentina* 48°50S 72°50W **96 F2**
San Martín de los Andes
  Argentina 40°10S 71°20W **96 E2**
San Mateo = Sant Mateu
  Spain 39°3N 1°23E **24 B7**
San Mateo *U.S.A.* 37°34N 122°19W **78 H4**
San Matías *Bolivia* 16°25S 58°20W **92 G7**
San Matías, G. *Argentina* 41°30S 64°0W **96 E4**
San Miguel = Sant Miquel
  Spain 39°3N 1°26E **24 B7**

San Miguel *El Salv.* 13°30N 88°12W **88 D2**
San Miguel *Panama* 8°27N 78°55W **88 E4**
San Miguel *U.S.A.* 35°45N 120°42W **78 K6**
San Miguel → *Bolivia* 13°52S 63°56W **92 F6**
San Miguel de Tucumán
  Argentina 26°50S 65°20W **94 B2**
San Miguel del Monte
  Argentina 35°23S 58°50W **94 D4**
San Miguel I. *U.S.A.* 34°2N 120°23W **79 L6**
San Nicolás *Canary Is.* 27°58N 15°47W **24 G4**
San Nicolás de los Arroyos
  Argentina 33°25S 60°10W **94 C3**
San Nicolas I. *U.S.A.* 33°15N 119°30W **79 M7**
San Onofre *U.S.A.* 33°22N 117°34W **79 M9**
San Pablo *Bolivia* 21°43S 66°38W **94 A2**
San Pablo *U.S.A.* 37°58N 122°21W **78 H4**
San Pedro *B. Aires,
  Argentina* 33°40S 59°40W **94 C4**
San Pedro *Misiones,
  Argentina* 26°30S 54°10W **95 B5**
San Pedro *Chile* 33°54S 71°28W **94 C1**
San Pedro *Ivory C.* 4°50N 6°33W **50 H4**
San Pedro *Mexico* 23°55N 110°17W **86 C3**
San Pedro □ *Paraguay* 24°0S 57°0W **94 A4**
San Pedro → *Chihuahua,
  Mexico* 28°20N 106°10W **86 B3**
San Pedro → *Nayarit,
  Mexico* 21°45N 105°30W **86 C3**
San Pedro → *U.S.A.* 32°59N 110°47W **77 K8**
San Pedro, Pta. *Chile* 25°30S 70°38W **94 B1**
San Pedro Channel
  U.S.A. 33°30N 118°25W **79 M8**
San Pedro de Atacama
  Chile 22°55S 68°15W **94 A2**
San Pedro de Jujuy
  Argentina 24°12S 64°55W **94 A3**
San Pedro de las Colonias
  Mexico 25°45N 102°59W **86 B4**
San Pedro de Macorís
  Dom. Rep. 18°30N 69°18W **89 C6**
San Pedro del Norte *Nic.* 13°4N 84°33W **88 D3**
San Pedro del Paraná
  Paraguay 26°43S 56°13W **94 B4**
San Pedro Mártir, Sierra
  Mexico 31°0N 115°30W **86 A1**
San Pedro Mártir △
  Mexico 31°0N 115°21W **86 A1**
San Pedro Ocampo = Melchor
  Ocampo *Mexico* 24°51N 101°39W **86 C4**
San Pedro Pochutla
  Mexico 15°44N 96°28W **87 D5**
San Pedro Sula *Honduras* 15°30N 88°0W **88 C2**
San Pedro Tututepec
  Mexico 16°9N 97°38W **87 D5**
San Pietro *Italy* 39°8N 8°17E **22 E3**
San Rafael *Argentina* 34°40S 68°21W **94 C2**
San Rafael *Calif., U.S.A.* 37°58N 122°32W **78 H4**
San Rafael *N. Mex.,
  U.S.A.* 35°7N 107°53W **77 J10**
San Rafael Mt. *U.S.A.* 34°41N 119°52W **79 L7**
San Rafael Mts. *U.S.A.* 34°40N 119°50W **79 L7**
San Ramón de la Nueva Orán
  Argentina 23°10S 64°20W **94 A3**
San Remo *Italy* 43°49N 7°46E **20 E7**
San Roque *Argentina* 28°25S 58°45W **94 B4**
San Roque *Spain* 36°17N 5°21W **21 D3**
San Rosendo *Chile* 37°16S 72°43W **94 D1**
San Saba *U.S.A.* 31°12N 98°43W **84 F5**
San Salvador *El Salv.* 13°40N 89°10W **88 D2**
San Salvador de Jujuy
  Argentina 24°10S 64°48W **94 A3**
San Salvador I. *Bahamas* 24°0N 74°40W **89 B5**
San Sebastián = Donostia-San
  Sebastián *Spain* 43°17N 1°58W **21 A5**
San Sebastián *Argentina* 53°10S 68°30W **96 G3**
San Sebastián *Puerto Rico* 18°20N 66°59W **89 d**
San Sebastián de la Gomera
  Canary Is. 28°5N 17°7W **24 F2**
San Serra = Son Serra
  Spain 39°43N 3°13E **24 B10**
San Severo *Italy* 41°41N 15°23E **22 D6**
San Simeon *U.S.A.* 35°39N 121°11W **78 K5**
San Simon *U.S.A.* 32°16N 109°14W **77 K9**
San Telmo = Sant Elm
  Spain 39°35N 2°21E **24 B9**
San Telmo *Mexico* 30°58N 116°6W **86 A1**
San Tiburcio *Mexico* 24°8N 101°32W **86 C4**
San Valentin, Mte. *Chile* 46°30S 73°30W **96 F2**
San Vicente de Cañete
  Peru 13°8S 76°30W **92 F3**
San Vicente de la Barquera
  Spain 43°23N 4°29W **21 A3**
San Vito *Costa Rica* 8°50N 82°58W **88 E3**
Sana' *Yemen* 15°27N 44°12E **47 D3**
Sana → *Bos.-H.* 45°3N 16°23E **16 F9**
Sanae *Antarctica* 70°20S 9°0W **5 D2**
Sanaga → *Cameroon* 3°35N 9°38E **52 D1**
Sanak I. *U.S.A.* 54°25N 162°40W **74 E7**
Sanaloa, Presa *Mexico* 24°50N 107°20W **86 C3**
Sanana *Indonesia* 2°4S 125°58E **37 E7**
Sanand *India* 22°59N 72°25E **42 H5**
Sanandaj *Iran* 35°18N 47°1E **44 C5**
Sanandita *Bolivia* 21°40S 63°45W **94 A3**
Sanawad *India* 22°11N 76°5E **42 H7**
Sancellas = Sencelles
  Spain 39°39N 2°54E **24 B9**
Sanchahe *China* 44°50N 126°2E **35 B14**
Sánchez *Dom. Rep.* 19°15N 69°36W **89 C6**
Sanchor *India* 24°45N 71°55E **42 G4**
Sancti Spíritus *Cuba* 21°52N 79°33W **88 B4**
Sancy, Puy de *France* 45°32N 2°50E **20 D5**
Sand = Polokwane →
  S. Africa 22°25S 30°5E **57 C5**
Sand Hills *U.S.A.* 42°10N 101°30W **80 D3**
Sand Lakes △ *Canada* 57°51N 98°32W **71 B9**
Sand Springs *U.S.A.* 36°9N 96°7W **84 C6**
Sanda *Japan* 34°53N 135°14E **31 G7**
Sandakan *Malaysia* 5°53N 118°4E **36 C5**
Sandan = Sambor
  Cambodia 12°46N 106°0E **38 F6**

Sandanski *Bulgaria* 41°35N 23°16E **23 D10**
Sanday *U.K.* 59°16N 2°31W **11 B6**
Sandefjord *Norway* 59°10N 10°15E **9 G14**
Sanders *U.S.A.* 35°13N 109°20W **77 J9**
Sanderson *U.S.A.* 30°9N 102°24W **84 F3**
Sandersville *U.S.A.* 32°59N 82°48W **85 E13**
Sandfire Roadhouse
  Australia 19°45S 121°15E **60 C3**
Sandfly L. *Canada* 55°43N 106°6W **71 B7**
Sandfontein *Namibia* 23°48S 19°1E **56 C2**
Sandheads, The *India* 21°10N 88°28E **43 J13**
Sandia *Peru* 14°10S 69°30W **92 F5**
Sandila *India* 27°5N 80°31E **43 F9**
Sandnes *Norway* 58°50N 5°45E **9 G11**
Sandnessjøen *Norway* 66°2N 12°38E **8 C15**
Sandoa
  Dem. Rep. of the Congo 9°41S 23°0E **52 F4**
Sandomierz *Poland* 50°40N 21°43E **17 C11**
Sandover → *Australia* 21°43S 136°32E **62 C2**
Sandoway = Thandwe
  Burma 18°20N 94°30E **41 K19**
Sandoy *Færoe Is.* 61°52N 6°46W **8 F9**
Sandpoint *U.S.A.* 48°17N 116°33W **76 B5**
Sandray *U.K.* 56°53N 7°31W **11 E1**
Sandringham *U.K.* 52°51N 0°31E **12 E8**
Sandstone *Australia* 27°59S 119°16E **61 E2**
Sandusky *Mich., U.S.A.* 43°25N 82°50W **82 C2**
Sandusky *Ohio, U.S.A.* 41°27N 82°42W **82 E2**
Sandveld *Namibia* 21°25S 20°0E **56 C3**
Sandviken *Sweden* 60°38N 16°46E **8 F17**
Sandwich, C. *Australia* 18°14S 146°18E **62 B4**
Sandwich B. *Canada* 53°40N 57°15W **73 B8**
Sandwich B. *Namibia* 23°25S 14°20E **56 C1**
Sandy *Oreg., U.S.A.* 45°24N 122°16W **78 E4**
Sandy *Pa., U.S.A.* 41°6N 78°46W **82 E6**
Sandy *Utah, U.S.A.* 40°32N 111°50W **76 F8**
Sandy Bay *Canada* 55°31N 102°19W **71 B8**
Sandy Bight *Australia* 33°50S 123°20E **61 F3**
Sandy C. *Queens.,*
  Australia 24°42S 153°15E **62 C5**
Sandy C. *Tas., Australia* 41°25S 144°45E **63 G3**
Sandy Cay *Bahamas* 23°13N 75°18W **89 B4**
Sandy Cr. → *Australia* 31°54S 145°18E **63 B4**
Sandy Cr. → *U.S.A.* 41°51N 109°47W **76 F9**
Sandy Creek *U.S.A.* 43°38N 76°5W **83 C8**
Sandy L. *Canada* 53°2N 93°0W **72 B1**
Sandy Lake *Canada* 53°0N 93°15W **72 B1**
Sandy Valley *U.S.A.* 35°49N 115°38W **79 K11**
Sanford *Fla., U.S.A.* 28°48N 81°16W **85 G14**
Sanford *Maine, U.S.A.* 43°27N 70°47W **83 C14**
Sanford *N.C., U.S.A.* 35°29N 79°10W **85 D15**
Sanford → *Australia* 27°22S 115°53E **61 E2**
Sanford, Mt. *U.S.A.* 62°13N 144°8W **68 E3**
Sang-i-Masha *Afghan.* 33°8N 67°27E **42 C2**
Sanga *Mozam.* 12°22S 35°21E **55 E4**
Sanga → *Congo* 1°5S 17°0E **52 E3**
Sangamner *India* 19°37N 74°15E **40 K9**
Sangān *Iran* 34°23N 60°15E **45 C9**
Sangar *Afghan.* 32°56N 65°30E **42 C1**
Sangar *Russia* 64°2N 127°31E **29 C13**
Sangar Sarai *Afghan.* 34°27N 70°35E **42 B4**
Sangarh → *Pakistan* 30°43N 70°44E **42 D4**
Sangay *Ecuador* 2°0S 78°20W **92 D3**
Sange
  Dem. Rep. of the Congo 6°58S 28°21E **54 D2**
Sangeang *Indonesia* 8°12S 119°6E **37 F5**
Sanger *U.S.A.* 36°42N 119°33W **78 J7**
Sangerhausen *Germany* 51°28N 11°18E **16 C6**
Sanggan He → *China* 38°12N 117°15E **34 E9**
Sanggau *Indonesia* 0°5N 110°30E **36 D4**
Sanghar *Pakistan* 26°2N 68°57E **42 F3**
Sangihe, Kepulauan
  Indonesia 3°0N 125°30E **37 D7**
Sangihe, Pulau *Indonesia* 3°35N 125°30E **37 D7**
Sangiran △ *Indonesia* 7°27S 110°50E **37 G14**
Sangju *S. Korea* 36°25N 128°10E **35 F15**
Sangkapura *Indonesia* 5°52S 112°40E **36 F4**
Sangkhla *Thailand* 14°37N 103°52E **38 E4**
Sangkhla Buri *Thailand* 14°57N 98°28E **38 E2**
Sangkulirang *Indonesia* 0°59N 117°58E **36 D5**
Sangla *Pakistan* 31°43N 73°23E **42 D5**
Sangli *India* 16°55N 74°33E **40 L9**
Sangmélima *Cameroon* 2°57N 12°1E **52 D2**
Sango *Zimbabwe* 18°44S 31°44E **55 G3**
Sangod *India* 24°55N 76°17E **42 G7**
Sangre de Cristo Mts.
  U.S.A. 37°30N 105°20W **77 H11**
Sangre Grande
  Trin. & Tob. 10°35N 61°8W **93 K15**
Sangrur *India* 30°14N 75°50E **42 D6**
Sangudo *Canada* 53°50N 114°54W **70 C6**
Sangue → *Brazil* 11°1S 58°39W **92 F7**
Sanibel *U.S.A.* 26°27N 82°1W **85 H13**
Sanikluaq *Canada* 56°32N 79°14W **72 A4**
Sanin-Kaigan △ *Japan* 35°39N 134°37E **31 G7**
Sanirajak = Hall Beach
  Canada 68°46N 81°12W **69 D15**
Sanjawi *Pakistan* 30°17N 68°21E **42 D3**
Sanje *Uganda* 0°49S 31°30E **54 C3**
Sanjo *Japan* 37°37N 138°57E **30 F9**
Sankh → *India* 22°15N 84°48E **43 H11**
Sankt Gallen *Switz.* 47°26N 9°22E **20 C8**
Sankt Michel = Mikkeli
  Finland 61°43N 27°15E **8 F22**
Sankt Moritz *Switz.* 46°30N 9°51E **20 C8**
Sankt-Peterburg *Russia* 59°55N 30°20E **9 G24**
Sankt Pölten *Austria* 48°12N 15°38E **16 D8**
Sankuru →
  Dem. Rep. of the Congo 4°17S 20°25E **52 E4**
Sanliurfa *Turkey* 37°12N 38°50E **44 B3**
Sanlúcar de Barrameda
  Spain 36°46N 6°21W **21 D2**
Sanmenxia *China* 34°47N 111°12E **34 G6**
Sanming *China* 26°15N 117°40E **33 F12**
Sannicandro Gargánico
  Italy 41°50N 15°34E **22 D6**
Sânnicolau Mare
  Romania 46°5N 20°39E **17 E11**
Sannieshof *S. Africa* 26°30S 25°47E **56 D4**
Sannīn, J. *Lebanon* 33°57N 35°52E **46 B4**

Sanniquellie *Liberia* 7°19N 8°38W **50 G4**
Sano *Japan* 36°19N 139°35E **31 F9**
Sanok *Poland* 49°35N 22°10E **17 D12**
Sanquhar *U.K.* 55°22N 3°54W **11 F5**
Sans Souci *Trin. & Tob.* 10°50N 61°0W **93 K16**
Sant Antoni de Portmany
  Spain 38°59N 1°19E **24 C7**
Sant Carles *Spain* 39°3N 1°34E **24 B8**
Sant Elm *Spain* 39°35N 2°21E **24 B9**
Sant Feliu de Guíxols *Spain* 41°45N 3°1E **21 B7**
Sant Ferran *Spain* 38°42N 1°28E **24 C7**
Sant Francesc de Formentera
  Spain 38°42N 1°26E **24 C7**
Sant Jaume *Spain* 39°54N 4°4E **24 B11**
Sant Joan *Spain* 39°36N 3°4E **24 B10**
Sant Joan de Labritja *Spain* 39°5N 1°31E **24 B8**
Sant Jordi *Ibiza, Spain* 38°53N 1°24E **24 C7**
Sant Jordi *Mallorca, Spain* 39°33N 2°46E **24 B9**
Sant Llorenç des Cardassar
  Spain 39°37N 3°17E **24 B10**
Sant Mateu *Spain* 39°3N 1°23E **24 B7**
Sant Miquel *Spain* 39°3N 1°26E **24 B7**
Sant Salvador *Spain* 39°27N 3°11E **24 B10**
Sant Agnés *Spain* 39°3N 1°21E **24 B7**
Santa Ana *Bolivia* 13°50S 65°40W **92 F5**
Santa Ana *El Salv.* 14°0N 89°31W **88 D2**
Santa Ana *Mexico* 30°33N 111°7W **86 A2**
Santa Ana *U.S.A.* 33°46N 117°52W **79 M9**
Santa Bárbara *Chile* 37°40S 72°1W **94 D1**
Santa Bárbara *Honduras* 14°53N 88°14W **88 D2**
Santa Bárbara *Mexico* 26°48N 105°49W **86 B3**
Santa Barbara *U.S.A.* 34°25N 119°42W **79 L7**
Santa Barbara Channel
  U.S.A. 34°15N 120°0W **79 L7**
Santa Barbara I. *U.S.A.* 33°29N 119°2W **79 M7**
Santa Catalina, Gulf of
  U.S.A. 33°10N 117°50W **79 N9**
Santa Catalina, I.
  Mexico 25°40N 110°47W **86 B2**
Santa Catalina I.
  U.S.A. 33°23N 118°25W **79 M8**
Santa Catarina □ *Brazil* 27°25S 48°30W **95 B6**
Santa Catarina, I. de
  Brazil 27°30S 48°40W **95 B6**
Santa Cecília *Brazil* 26°56S 50°18W **95 B5**
Santa Clara *Cuba* 22°20N 80°0W **88 B4**
Santa Clara *Calif.,*
  U.S.A. 37°21N 121°57W **78 H5**
Santa Clara *N.Y.,*
  U.S.A. 44°38N 74°27W **83 B10**
Santa Clara *Utah, U.S.A.* 37°8N 113°39W **77 H7**
Santa Clara de Olimar
  Uruguay 32°50S 54°54W **95 C5**
Santa Clara Valley
  U.S.A. 36°50N 121°30W **78 J5**
Santa Clarita *U.S.A.* 34°24N 118°33W **79 L8**
Santa Clotilde *Peru* 2°33S 73°45W **92 D4**
Santa Coloma de Gramenet
  Spain 41°27N 2°13E **21 B7**
Santa Cruz *Bolivia* 17°43S 63°10W **92 G6**
Santa Cruz *Chile* 34°38S 71°27W **94 C1**
Santa Cruz *Costa Rica* 10°15N 85°35W **88 D2**
Santa Cruz *Madeira* 32°42N 16°46W **24 D3**
Santa Cruz *Phil.* 14°20N 121°24E **37 B6**
Santa Cruz *U.S.A.* 36°58N 122°1W **78 J4**
Santa Cruz → *Argentina* 50°10S 68°20W **96 G3**
Santa Cruz de la Palma
  Canary Is. 28°41N 17°46W **24 F2**
Santa Cruz de la Palma ✈ (SPC)
  Canary Is. 28°40N 17°45W **24 F2**
Santa Cruz de Tenerife
  Canary Is. 28°28N 16°15W **24 F3**
Santa Cruz del Norte
  Cuba 23°9N 81°55W **88 B3**
Santa Cruz del Sur *Cuba* 20°44N 78°0W **88 B4**
Santa Cruz do Rio Pardo
  Brazil 22°54S 49°37W **95 A6**
Santa Cruz do Sul *Brazil* 29°42S 52°25W **95 B5**
Santa Cruz I. *U.S.A.* 34°1N 119°43W **79 M7**
Santa Cruz Is. *Solomon Is.* 10°30S 166°0E **58 C9**
Santa Cruz Mts. *Jamaica* 17°58N 77°43W **88 a**
Santa Domingo, Cay
  Bahamas 21°25N 75°15W **88 B4**
Santa Elena *Argentina* 30°58S 59°47W **94 C4**
Santa Elena, C.
  Costa Rica 10°54N 85°56W **88 D2**
Santa Eulària des Riu
  Spain 38°59N 1°32E **24 C8**
Santa Fe *Argentina* 31°35S 60°41W **94 C3**
Santa Fe *U.S.A.* 35°41N 105°57W **77 J11**
Santa Fe □ *Argentina* 31°50S 60°55W **94 C3**
Santa Fé do Sul *Brazil* 20°13S 50°56W **93 H8**
Santa Filomena *Brazil* 9°6S 45°50W **93 E9**
Santa Gertrudis *Spain* 39°0N 1°26E **24 C7**
Santa Inês *Brazil* 13°17S 39°48W **93 F11**
Santa Inés, I. *Chile* 54°0S 73°0W **96 G2**
Santa Isabel *Argentina* 36°10S 66°54W **94 D2**
Santa Isabel do Morro
  Brazil 11°34S 50°40W **93 F8**
Santa Lucía *Corrientes,*
  Argentina 28°58S 59°5W **94 B4**
Santa Lucía *San Juan,*
  Argentina 31°30S 68°30W **94 C2**
Santa Lucía *Uruguay* 34°27S 56°24W **94 C4**
Santa Lucia Range
  U.S.A. 36°0N 121°20W **78 K5**
Santa Luzia *C. Verde Is.* 16°50N 24°35W **50 b**
Santa Margalida *Spain* 39°42N 3°6E **24 B10**
Santa Margarita
  Argentina 38°28S 61°35W **94 D3**
Santa Margarita
  U.S.A. 35°23N 120°37W **78 K6**
Santa Margarita →
  U.S.A. 33°13N 117°23W **79 M9**
Santa Margarita, I.
  Mexico 24°27N 111°50W **86 C2**
Santa María *Argentina* 26°40S 66°0W **94 B2**
Santa Maria *Azores* 36°58N 25°6W **50 a**

Santa Maria *Brazil* 29°40S 53°48W **95 B5**
Santa Maria *C. Verde Is.* 16°31N 22°53W **50 b**
Santa Maria *U.S.A.* 34°57N 120°26W **79 L6**
Santa María → *Mexico* 31°0N 107°14W **86 A3**
Santa María, B. de
  Mexico 25°4N 108°6W **86 B3**
Santa Maria da Vitória
  Brazil 13°24S 44°12W **93 F10**
Santa María del Camí
  Spain 39°38N 2°47E **24 B9**
Santa Maria di Léuca, C.
  Italy 39°47N 18°22E **23 E8**
Santa Marta *Colombia* 11°15N 74°13W **92 A4**
Santa Marta, Sierra Nevada de
  Colombia 10°55N 73°50W **92 A4**
Santa Marta Grande, C.
  Brazil 28°43S 48°50W **95 B6**
Santa Maura = Lefkada
  Greece 38°40N 20°43E **23 E9**
Santa Monica *U.S.A.* 34°1N 118°29W **79 M8**
Santa Monica Mts. △
  U.S.A. 34°4N 118°44W **79 L8**
Santa Paula *U.S.A.* 34°21N 119°4W **79 L7**
Santa Ponça *La Pampa,*
  Spain 39°30N 2°28E **24 B9**
Santa Rosa *La Pampa,*
  Argentina 36°40S 64°17W **94 D3**
Santa Rosa *San Luis,*
  Argentina 32°21S 65°10W **94 C2**
Santa Rosa *Brazil* 27°52S 54°29W **95 B5**
Santa Rosa *Calif.,*
  U.S.A. 38°26N 122°43W **78 G4**
Santa Rosa *N. Mex.,*
  U.S.A. 34°57N 104°41W **77 J11**
Santa Rosa and San Jacinto
  Mts. △ *U.S.A.* 33°28N 116°20W **79 M10**
Santa Rosa de Copán
  Honduras 14°47N 88°46W **88 D2**
Santa Rosa de Río Primero
  Argentina 31°8S 63°20W **94 C3**
Santa Rosa del Sara
  Bolivia 17°7S 63°35W **92 G6**
Santa Rosa I. *Calif.,*
  U.S.A. 33°58N 120°6W **79 M6**
Santa Rosa I. *Fla.,*
  U.S.A. 30°20N 86°50W **85 F11**
Santa Rosa Range
  U.S.A. 41°45N 117°40W **76 F5**
Santa Rosalía *Mexico* 27°19N 112°17W **86 B2**
Santa Sylvina *Argentina* 27°50S 61°10W **94 B3**
Santa Tecla = Nueva San
  Salvador *El Salv.* 13°40N 89°18W **88 D2**
Santa Teresa *Argentina* 33°25S 60°47W **94 C3**
Santa Teresa *Australia* 24°8S 134°22E **62 C1**
Santa Teresa *Mexico* 25°17N 97°51W **87 B5**
Santa Teresa △ *Uruguay* 33°57S 53°31W **95 C5**
Santa Teresita *Argentina* 36°32S 56°41W **94 D4**
Santa Vitória do Palmar
  Brazil 33°32S 53°25W **95 C5**
Santa Ynez → *U.S.A.* 34°41N 120°36W **79 L6**
Santa Ynez Mts. △ *U.S.A.* 34°30N 120°0W **79 L6**
Santa Ysabel *U.S.A.* 33°7N 116°40W **79 M10**
Santai *China* 31°5N 104°58E **32 E9**
Santana *Madeira* 32°48N 16°52W **24 D3**
Santana, Coxilha de
  Brazil 30°50S 55°35W **95 C4**
Santana do Livramento
  Brazil 30°55S 55°30W **95 C4**
Santander *Spain* 43°27N 3°51W **21 A4**
Santander Jiménez
  Mexico 24°13N 98°28W **87 C5**
Santanilla, Is. *Honduras* 17°22N 83°57W **88 C3**
Santanyí *Spain* 39°20N 3°5E **24 B10**
Santaquin *U.S.A.* 39°59N 111°47W **76 G8**
Santarém *Brazil* 2°25S 54°42W **93 D8**
Santarém *Portugal* 39°12N 8°42W **21 C1**
Santee Channel
  W. Indies 24°0N 79°30W **88 B4**
Santee *U.S.A.* 32°50N 116°58W **79 N10**
Santee → *U.S.A.* 33°7N 79°17W **85 E15**
Santiago = Río Grande de
  Santiago = São Tiago
  C. Verde Is. 15°0N 23°40W **50 b**
Santiago *Brazil* 29°11S 54°52W **95 B5**
Santiago *Canary Is.* 28°2N 17°12W **24 F2**
Santiago *Chile* 33°26S 70°40W **94 C1**
Santiago *Panama* 8°0N 81°0W **88 E3**
Santiago → *Peru* 4°27S 77°38W **92 D3**
Santiago de Compostela
  Spain 42°52N 8°37W **21 A1**
Santiago de Cuba *Cuba* 20°0N 75°49W **88 C4**
Santiago de los Caballeros
  Dom. Rep. 19°30N 70°40W **89 C5**
Santiago del Estero
  Argentina 27°50S 64°15W **94 B3**
Santiago del Estero □
  Argentina 27°40S 63°15W **94 B3**
Santiago del Teide
  Canary Is. 28°17N 16°48W **24 F3**
Santiago Ixcuintla
  Mexico 21°49N 105°13W **86 C3**
Santiago Jamiltepec
  Mexico 16°17N 97°49W **87 D5**
Santiago Papasquiaro
  Mexico 25°3N 105°25W **86 C4**
Santiago Pinotepa Nacional
  Mexico 16°19N 98°1W **87 D5**
Santiaguillo, L. de
  Mexico 24°48N 104°48W **86 C4**
Santo Amaro *Brazil* 12°30S 38°43W **93 F11**
Santo Anastácio *Brazil* 21°58S 51°39W **95 A5**
Santo André *Brazil* 23°39S 46°29W **95 A6**
Santo Ângelo *Brazil* 28°18S 54°15W **95 B5**
Santo Antão *C. Verde Is.* 16°52N 25°10W **50 b**
Santo Antônio do Içá
  Brazil 3°5S 67°57W **92 D5**
Santo Antônio do Leverger
  Brazil 15°52S 56°5W **93 G7**
Santo Domingo
  Dom. Rep. 18°30N 69°59W **89 C6**

Santo Domingo *Baja Calif.,*
  Mexico 30°43N 116°2W **86 A1**
Santo Domingo *Baja Calif. S.,*
  Mexico 25°29N 111°55W **86 B2**
Santo Domingo *Nic.* 12°14N 84°59W **88 D3**
Santo Domingo de los Colorados
  Ecuador 0°15S 79°9W **92 D3**
Santo Domingo Pueblo
  U.S.A. 35°31N 106°22W **77 J10**
Santo Tomás *Mexico* 31°33N 116°24W **86 A1**
Santo Tomás *Peru* 14°26S 72°8W **92 F4**
Santo Tomé *Argentina* 28°40S 56°5W **95 B4**
Santo Tomé de Guayana = Ciudad
  Guayana *Venezuela* 8°0N 62°30W **92 B6**
Santoña *Spain* 43°29N 3°27W **21 A4**
Santorini *Greece* 36°23N 25°27E **23 F11**
Santos *Brazil* 24°0S 46°20W **95 A6**
Santos Dumont *Brazil* 22°55S 43°10W **95 A7**
Santuario de Aves Laguna
  Colorada △ *Bolivia* 22°10S 67°45W **94 A2**
Sanur *Indonesia* 8°41S 115°15E **37 K18**
Sanwer *India* 22°59N 75°50E **42 H6**
Sanxiang *China* 22°21N 113°25E **33 a**
Sanya *China* 18°14N 109°29E **38 C7**
Sanyuan *China* 34°35N 108°58E **34 G5**
São Bernardo do Campo
  Brazil 23°45S 46°34W **95 A6**
São Borja *Brazil* 28°39S 56°0W **95 B4**
São Carlos *Brazil* 22°0S 47°50W **95 A6**
São Cristóvão *Brazil* 11°1S 37°15W **93 F11**
São Domingos *Brazil* 13°25S 46°19W **93 F9**
São Filipe *C. Verde Is.* 14°24N 24°30W **50 b**
São Francisco *Brazil* 16°0S 44°50W **93 G10**
São Francisco →
  Brazil 10°30S 36°24W **93 F11**
São Francisco do Sul
  Brazil 26°15S 48°36W **95 B6**
São Gabriel *Brazil* 30°20S 54°20W **95 C5**
São Gonçalo *Brazil* 22°48S 43°5W **95 A7**
Sao Hill *Tanzania* 8°20S 35°12E **55 D4**
São João da Boa Vista
  Brazil 22°0S 46°52W **95 A6**
São João da Madeira
  Portugal 40°54N 8°30W **21 B1**
São João del Rei *Brazil* 21°8S 44°15W **95 A7**
São João do Araguaia
  Brazil 5°23S 48°46W **93 E9**
São João do Piauí *Brazil* 8°21S 42°15W **93 E10**
São Joaquim *Brazil* 28°18S 49°56W **95 B6**
São Joaquim △ *Brazil* 28°12S 49°37W **95 B6**
São Jorge *Azores* 38°38N 28°3W **50 a**
São Jorge, Pta. de
  Madeira 32°50N 16°53W **24 D3**
São José *Brazil* 27°38S 48°39W **95 B5**
São José do Norte *Brazil* 32°1S 52°3W **95 C5**
São José do Rio Preto
  Brazil 20°50S 49°20W **95 A6**
São José dos Campos
  Brazil 23°7S 45°52W **95 A6**
São Leopoldo *Brazil* 29°50S 51°10W **95 B5**
São Lourenço *Brazil* 22°7S 45°3W **95 A6**
São Lourenço → *Brazil* 17°53S 57°27W **93 G7**
São Lourenço, Pta. de
  Madeira 32°44N 16°39W **24 D3**
São Lourenço do Sul
  Brazil 31°22S 51°58W **95 C5**
São Luís *Brazil* 2°39S 44°15W **93 D10**
São Luís Gonzaga *Brazil* 28°25S 55°0W **95 B5**
São Marcos → *Brazil* 18°15S 47°37W **93 G9**
São Marcos, B. de *Brazil* 2°0S 44°0W **93 D10**
São Mateus *Brazil* 18°44S 39°50W **93 G11**
São Mateus do Sul
  Brazil 25°52S 50°23W **95 B5**
São Miguel *Azores* 37°47N 25°30W **50 a**
São Miguel do Oeste
  Brazil 26°45S 53°34W **95 B5**
São Nicolau *C. Verde Is.* 16°20N 24°20W **50 b**
São Paulo *Brazil* 23°32S 46°38W **95 A6**
São Paulo □ *Brazil* 22°0S 49°0W **95 A6**
São Paulo de Olivença
  Brazil 3°27S 68°48W **92 D5**
São Roque *Madeira* 32°46N 16°48W **24 D3**
São Roque, C. de *Brazil* 5°30S 35°16W **93 E11**
São Sebastião, I. de
  Brazil 23°50S 45°18W **95 A6**
São Sebastião do Paraíso
  Brazil 20°54S 46°59W **95 A6**
São Tiago *C. Verde Is.* 15°0N 23°40W **50 b**
São Tomé
  São Tomé & Príncipe 0°10N 6°39E **48 F4**
São Tomé, C. de *Brazil* 22°0S 40°59W **95 A7**
São Tomé & Príncipe ■
  Africa 0°12N 6°39E **49 F4**
São Vicente *Brazil* 23°57S 46°23W **95 A6**
São Vicente *C. Verde Is.* 16°55N 25°2W **50 b**
São Vicente *Madeira* 32°48N 17°3W **24 D2**
São Vicente, C. de *Portugal* 37°0N 9°0W **21 D1**
Saona, I. *Dom. Rep.* 18°10N 68°40W **89 C6**
Saône → *France* 45°44N 4°50E **20 D6**
Saonek *Indonesia* 0°22S 130°55E **37 E8**
Sapam, Ao *Thailand* 8°0N 98°26E **39 a**
Saparua *Indonesia* 3°33S 128°40E **37 E7**
Sape *Indonesia* 8°34S 118°59E **37 F5**
Sapele *Nigeria* 5°50N 5°40E **50 G7**
Sapelo I. *U.S.A.* 31°25N 81°12W **85 F14**
Sapi △ *Zimbabwe* 15°48S 29°42E **55 F2**
Saposoa *Peru* 6°55S 76°45W **92 E3**
Sapphire *Australia* 23°28S 147°43E **62 C4**
Sappho *U.S.A.* 48°4N 124°16W **78 B2**
Sapporo *Japan* 43°0N 141°21E **30 C10**
Sapudi *Indonesia* 7°6S 114°20E **37 G16**
Sapulpa *U.S.A.* 35°59N 96°5W **84 D6**
Saqqez *Iran* 36°15N 46°20E **44 B5**
Sar Dasht *Āzarbāyjān-e Gharbī,*
  Iran 36°9N 45°28E **44 B5**
Sar Dasht *Khuzestān, Iran* 32°32N 48°52E **45 C6**
Sar-e Pol □ *Afghan.* 36°20N 65°50E **45 B9**
Sar Gachīneh = Yāsūj
  Iran 30°31N 51°31E **45 D6**
Sar Planina *Macedonia* 42°0N 21°0E **23 C9**

Sara Buri = Saraburi
  Thailand 14°30N 100°55E **38 E3**
Sarāb *Iran* 37°55N 47°40E **44 B5**
Sarābādī *Iraq* 33°1N 44°48E **44 C5**
Saraburi *Thailand* 14°30N 100°55E **38 E3**
Saradiya *India* 21°34N 70°2E **42 J4**
Saragossa = Zaragoza
  Spain 41°39N 0°53W **21 B5**
Saraguro *Ecuador* 3°35S 79°16W **92 D3**
Sarahs *Turkmenistan* 36°32N 61°13E **45 B9**
Saraikela *India* 22°42S 85°56E **43 H11**
Sarajevo *Bos.-H.* 43°52N 18°26E **23 C8**
Sarakhs = Sarahs
  Turkmenistan 36°32N 61°13E **45 B9**
Saran, Gunung *Indonesia* 0°30S 111°25E **36 E4**
Saranac Lake *U.S.A.* 44°20N 74°10W **83 B10**
Saranac Lakes *U.S.A.* 44°20N 74°28W **83 B10**
Saranda *Tanzania* 5°45S 34°59E **54 D3**
Sarandí del Yí *Uruguay* 33°18S 55°38W **95 C4**
Sarandí Grande
  Uruguay 33°44S 56°20W **94 C4**
Sarangani B. *Phil.* 6°0N 125°13E **37 C7**
Sarangani Is. *Phil.* 5°25N 125°25E **37 C7**
Sarangarh *India* 21°30N 83°5E **41 J13**
Saransk *Russia* 54°10N 45°10E **18 D8**
Sarapul *Russia* 56°28N 53°48E **18 C9**
Sarasota *U.S.A.* 27°20N 82°32W **85 H13**
Saratoga *Calif., U.S.A.* 37°16N 122°2W **78 H4**
Saratoga *Wyo., U.S.A.* 41°27N 106°49W **76 F10**
Saratoga △ *U.S.A.* 43°0N 73°38W **83 D11**
Saratoga L. *U.S.A.* 43°1N 73°44W **83 C11**
Saratoga Springs *U.S.A.* 43°5N 73°47W **83 C11**
Saratok *Malaysia* 1°55N 111°17E **36 D4**
Saratov *Russia* 51°30N 46°2E **19 D8**
Sarāvān *Iran* 27°25N 62°15E **45 E9**
Saravane *Laos* 15°43N 106°25E **38 E6**
Sarawak □ *Malaysia* 2°0N 113°0E **36 D4**
Saray *Turkey* 41°26N 27°55E **23 D12**
Sarayköy *Turkey* 37°55N 28°54E **23 F13**
Sarbāz *Iran* 26°38N 61°19E **45 E9**
Sarbīsheh *Iran* 32°30N 59°40E **45 C8**
Sarda → *India* 27°21N 81°23E **43 F9**
Sardarshahr *India* 28°30N 74°29E **42 E6**
Sardegna □ *Italy* 40°0N 9°0E **22 D3**
Sardhana *India* 29°9N 77°39E **42 E7**
Sardina, Pta. *Canary Is.* 28°9N 15°44W **24 F4**
Sardinia = Sardegna □
  Italy 40°0N 9°0E **22 D3**
Sardis *Turkey* 38°28N 27°58E **23 E12**
Sārdūīyeh = Dar Mazār
  Iran 29°14N 57°20E **45 D8**
Saren *Indonesia* 8°26S 115°34E **37 J18**
S'Arenal *Spain* 39°30N 2°45E **24 B9**
Sarera, G. of *Indonesia* 2°0S 135°0E **37 E9**
Sargasso Sea *Atl. Oc.* 27°0N 72°0W **66 G13**
Sargodha *Pakistan* 32°10N 72°40E **42 C5**
Sarh *Chad* 9°5N 18°23E **51 G9**
Sārī *Iran* 36°30N 53°4E **45 B7**
Saria *India* 21°38N 83°22E **43 J10**
Sariab *Pakistan* 30°6N 66°59E **42 D2**
Sarıgöl *Turkey* 38°14N 28°41E **23 E13**
Sarikei *Malaysia* 2°8N 111°30E **36 D4**
Sarila *India* 25°46N 79°41E **43 G8**
Sarina *Australia* 21°22S 149°13E **62 C4**
Sarita *U.S.A.* 27°13N 97°47W **84 M6**
Sariwŏn *N. Korea* 38°31N 125°46E **35 E13**
Sarju → *India* 27°21N 81°23E **43 F9**
Sark *U.K.* 49°25N 2°22W **13 H5**
Sarkari Tala *India* 27°39N 70°52E **42 F4**
Şarköy *Turkey* 40°36N 27°6E **23 D12**
Sarlat-la-Canéda *France* 44°54N 1°13E **20 D4**
Sarmi *Indonesia* 1°49S 138°44E **37 E9**
Sarmiento *Argentina* 45°35S 69°5W **96 F3**
Särna *Sweden* 61°41N 13°8E **8 F15**
Sarnia *Canada* 42°58N 82°23W **82 D2**
Sarolangun *Indonesia* 2°19S 102°42E **36 E2**
Saronikos Kolpos
  Greece 37°45N 23°45E **23 F10**
Saros Körfezi *Turkey* 40°30N 26°15E **23 D12**
Sarpsborg *Norway* 59°16N 11°7E **9 G14**
Sarqan *Kazakhstan* 45°24N 79°55E **32 B4**
Sarre = Saar → *Europe* 49°41N 6°32E **15 E6**
Sarthe □ *France* 47°33N 0°31W **20 C3**
Saruna → *Pakistan* 26°31N 67°7E **42 F2**
Sarvar *India* 26°4N 75°0E **42 F6**
Sarvestān *Iran* 29°20N 53°10E **45 D7**
Sary-Tash *Kyrgyzstan* 39°44N 73°15E **28 F8**
Saryshagan *Kazakhstan* 46°12N 73°38E **28 E8**
Sasan Gir *India* 21°10N 70°36E **42 J4**
Sasaram *India* 24°57N 84°5E **43 G11**
Sasebo *Japan* 33°10N 129°43E **31 H4**
Saser Kangri *India* 34°50N 77°50E **43 B7**
Saskatchewan □
  Canada 54°40N 106°0W **71 C7**
Saskatchewan →
  Canada 53°37N 100°40W **71 C8**
Saskatoon *Canada* 52°10N 106°38W **71 C7**
Saskylakh *Russia* 71°55N 114°1E **29 B12**
Saslaya △ *Nic.* 13°45N 85°4W **88 D2**
Sasolburg *S. Africa* 26°46S 27°49E **57 D4**
Sasovo *Russia* 54°25N 41°55E **18 D7**
Sassandra *Ivory C.* 4°55N 6°8W **50 H4**
Sassandra → *Ivory C.* 4°58N 6°5W **50 H4**
Sássari *Italy* 40°43N 8°34E **22 D3**
Sassie *Australia* 10°2S 142°51E **62 a**
Sassnitz *Germany* 54°29N 13°39E **16 A7**
Sassuolo *Italy* 44°33N 10°47E **22 B4**
Sasyk, Ozero *Ukraine* 45°45N 29°40E **17 F15**
Sata-Misaki *Japan* 31°0N 130°40E **31 J5**
Satadougou *Mali* 12°25N 11°25W **50 F3**
Satakunta *Finland* 61°45N 23°0E **8 F20**
Satakunta = Satakunta
  Finland 61°45N 23°0E **8 F20**
Satara *India* 17°44N 73°58E **40 L8**
Satara *S. Africa* 24°29S 31°47E **57 C5**
Satbarwa *India* 23°55N 84°16E **43 H11**
Satevó *Mexico* 27°57N 106°7W **86 B3**

Satilla → U.S.A. 30°59N 81°29W 85 F14
Satka Russia 55°3N 59°1E 18 C10
Satmala Hills Andhra Pradesh, India 19°45N 78°45E 40 K11
Satmala Hills Maharashtra, India 20°15N 74°40E 40 J9
Satna India 24°35N 80°50E 43 G9
Sátoraljaújhely Hungary 48°25N 21°41E 17 D11
Satpura △ India 22°40N 78°15E 42 H8
Satpura Ra. India 21°25N 76°10E 40 J10
Satsunai-Shotō Japan 30°0N 130°0E 31 K5
Sattahip Thailand 12°41N 100°54E 38 F3
Satu Mare Romania 47°46N 22°55E 17 E12
Satui Indonesia 3°50S 115°27E 36 E5
Satun Thailand 6°43N 100°2E 39 J3
Satupa'itea Samoa 13°45S 172°18W 59 b
Saturnina → Brazil 12°15S 58°10W 92 F7
Sauce Argentina 30°5S 58°46W 94 C4
Sauceda Mexico 25°46N 101°19W 86 B4
Saucillo Mexico 28°1N 105°17W 86 B3
Sauda Norway 59°40N 6°20E 9 G12
Sauðárkrókur Iceland 65°45N 19°40W 8 D4
Saudi Arabia ■ Asia 26°0N 44°0E 44 B3
Sauerland Germany 51°12N 7°59E 16 C4
Saugeen → Canada 44°30N 81°22W 82 B3
Saugerties U.S.A. 42°5N 73°57W 83 D11
Saugus U.S.A. 34°25N 118°32W 79 L8
Sauk Centre U.S.A. 45°44N 94°57W 80 C6
Sauk Rapids U.S.A. 45°35N 94°10W 80 C6
Sault Ste. Marie Canada 46°30N 84°20W 72 C3
Sault Ste. Marie U.S.A. 46°30N 84°21W 81 B11
Saumlaki Indonesia 7°55S 131°20E 37 F8
Saumur France 47°15N 0°5W 20 C3
Saunders U.S.A. 45°53S 170°45E 59 F3
Saunders I. Antarctica 57°48S 26°28W 5 B1
Saunders Pt. Australia 27°52S 125°38E 61 E4
Saurimo Angola 9°40S 20°12E 52 F4
Sausalito U.S.A. 37°51N 122°29W 78 H4
Savá Honduras 15°32N 86°15W 88 C2
Sava → Serbia 44°50N 20°26E 23 B9
Savage U.S.A. 47°27N 104°21W 76 C11
Savage I. = Niue ☑ Pac. Oc. 19°2S 169°54W 65 J11
Savage River Australia 41°31S 145°14E 63 G4
Savai'i Samoa 13°28S 172°24W 59 b
Savalou Benin 7°57N 1°58E 50 G6
Savane Mozam. 19°37S 35°8E 55 F4
Savanna U.S.A. 42°5N 90°8W 80 D8
Savanna-la-Mar Jamaica 18°10N 78°10W 88 a
Savannah Ga., U.S.A. 32°5N 81°6W 85 E14
Savannah Mo., U.S.A. 39°56N 94°50W 80 F6
Savannah Tenn., U.S.A. 35°14N 88°15W 85 D10
Savannah → U.S.A. 32°2N 80°53W 85 E14
Savannakhet Laos 16°30N 104°49E 38 D5
Savant L. Canada 50°16N 90°44W 72 B1
Savant Lake Canada 50°14N 90°40W 72 B1
Savarkundla = Kundla India 21°21N 71°25E 42 J4
Save → Mozam. 21°16S 34°0E 57 C5
Sāveh Iran 35°2N 50°20E 45 C6
Savelugu Ghana 9°38N 0°54W 50 G5
Savo Finland 62°45N 27°30E 8 E22
Savoie □ France 45°26N 6°25E 20 D7
Savolax = Savo Finland 62°45N 27°30E 8 E22
Savona Italy 44°17N 8°30E 20 D8
Savona U.S.A. 42°17N 77°13W 82 D7
Savonlinna Finland 61°52N 28°53E 8 F23
Savoy = Savoie □ France 45°26N 6°25E 20 D7
Savur Turkey 37°34N 40°53E 44 B4
Savusavu Fiji 16°34S 179°15E 59 a
Savusavu B. Fiji 16°45S 179°15E 59 a
Sawahlunto Indonesia 0°40S 100°52E 36 E2
Sawai Indonesia 3°0S 129°5E 37 E7
Sawai Madhopur India 26°0N 76°25E 42 G7
Sawaleke Fiji 17°59S 179°18E 59 a
Sawang Daen Din Thailand 17°28N 103°28E 38 D4
Sawankhalok Thailand 17°19N 99°50E 38 D2
Sawara Japan 35°55N 140°30E 31 G10
Sawatch Range U.S.A. 39°0N 106°30W 76 G10
Sawel Mt. U.K. 54°50N 7°2W 10 B4
Sawi Thailand 10°14N 99°5E 39 G2
Sawmills Zimbabwe 19°30S 28°2E 55 F2
Sawtooth △ U.S.A. 44°0N 114°50W 76 D6
Sawtooth Range U.S.A. 44°3N 114°58W 76 D6
Sawu Indonesia 10°35S 121°50E 37 F6
Sawu Sea Indonesia 9°30S 121°50E 37 F6
Saxby → Australia 18°25S 140°53E 62 B3
Saxmundham U.K. 52°13N 1°30E 13 E9
Saxony = Sachsen □ Germany 50°55N 13°10E 16 C7
Saxony, Lower = Niedersachsen □ Germany 52°50N 9°0E 16 B5
Saxton U.S.A. 40°13N 78°15W 82 F6
Sayabec Canada 48°35N 67°41W 73 C6
Sayaboury Laos 19°15N 101°45E 38 C3
Sayán Peru 11°8S 77°12W 92 F3
Sayan, Vostochnyy Russia 54°0N 96°0E 29 D10
Sayan, Zapadnyy Russia 52°30N 94°0E 32 A7
Sayanogorsk Russia 53°5N 91°23E 29 D10
Saydā Lebanon 33°35N 35°25E 46 B4
Sayhandulaan = Öldziyt Mongolia 44°40N 109°1E 34 B5
Sayhūt Yemen 15°12N 51°10E 47 D5
Saylac Somali Rep. 11°21N 43°30E 47 E3
Saynshand = Buyant-Uhaa Mongolia 44°55N 110°11E 34 B6
Sayre Okla., U.S.A. 35°18N 99°38E 84 H5
Sayre Pa., U.S.A. 41°59N 76°32W 83 E8
Sayreville U.S.A. 40°28N 74°22W 83 F10
Sayula Mexico 19°52N 103°36W 86 D4
Sayward Canada 50°21N 125°55W 70 C3
Sazanit Albania 40°30N 19°20E 23 D8
Sázava → Czech Rep. 49°53N 14°24E 16 D8
Sazin Pakistan 35°35N 73°30E 43 B5
Scafell Pike U.K. 54°27N 3°14W 12 C4
Scalloway U.K. 60°9N 1°17W 11 A7

Scalpay U.K. 57°18N 6°0W 11 D3
Scandia Canada 50°20N 112°2W 70 C6
Scandicci Italy 43°45N 11°11E 22 C4
Scandinavia Europe 64°0N 12°0E 8 E15
Scappoose U.S.A. 45°45N 122°53W 78 E4
Scarba U.K. 56°11N 5°43W 11 E3
Scarborough Trin. & Tob. 11°11N 60°42W 93 J16
Scarborough U.K. 54°17N 0°24W 12 C7
Scariff I. Ireland 51°44N 10°15W 10 E1
Scarp U.K. 58°1N 7°8W 11 C1
Scebeli = Shabeelle → Somali Rep. 2°0N 44°0E 47 G3
Schaffhausen Switz. 47°42N 8°39E 20 C8
Schagen Neths. 52°49N 4°48E 15 B4
Schaghticoke U.S.A. 42°54N 73°35W 83 D11
Schefferville Canada 54°48N 66°50W 73 B6
Schelde → Belgium 51°15N 4°16E 15 C4
Schell Creek Ra. U.S.A. 39°25N 114°40W 76 G6
Schellsburg U.S.A. 40°3N 78°39W 82 F6
Schenectady U.S.A. 42°49N 73°57W 83 D11
Schenevus U.S.A. 42°33N 74°50W 83 D10
Schiedam Neths. 51°55N 4°25E 15 C4
Schiermonnikoog Neths. 53°30N 6°15E 15 A6
Schio Italy 45°43N 11°21E 22 B4
Schiphol, Amsterdam ✈ (AMS) Neths. 52°18N 4°45E 15 B4
Schleswig Germany 54°31N 9°34E 16 A5
Schleswig-Holstein □ Germany 54°30N 9°30E 16 A5
Schœlcher Martinique 14°36N 61°7W 88 c
Schoharie U.S.A. 42°40N 74°19W 83 D10
Schoharie Cr. → U.S.A. 42°57N 74°18W 83 D10
Scholls U.S.A. 45°24N 122°56W 78 E4
Schouten I. Australia 42°20S 148°20E 63 G4
Schouten Is. = Supiori Indonesia 1°0S 136°0E 37 E9
Schouwen Neths. 51°43N 3°45E 15 C3
Schreiber Canada 48°45N 87°20W 72 C2
Schroffenstein Namibia 27°11S 18°42E 56 D2
Schroon Lake U.S.A. 43°50N 73°46W 83 C11
Schuler Canada 50°20N 110°6W 71 C6
Schumacher Canada 48°30N 81°16W 72 C3
Schurz U.S.A. 38°57N 118°49W 76 G4
Schuyler U.S.A. 41°27N 97°4W 80 E5
Schuylerville U.S.A. 43°6N 73°35W 83 C11
Schuylkill → U.S.A. 39°53N 75°12W 83 G9
Schuylkill Haven U.S.A. 40°37N 76°11W 83 F8
Schwäbische Alb Germany 48°20N 9°30E 16 D5
Schwaner, Pegunungan Indonesia 1°0S 112°30E 36 E4
Schwarzrand Namibia 25°37S 16°50E 56 D2
Schwarzwald Germany 48°30N 8°20E 16 D5
Schwatka Mts. U.S.A. 67°20N 156°30W 74 B8
Schwedt Germany 53°3N 14°16E 16 B8
Schweinfurt Germany 50°3N 10°14E 16 C6
Schweiz = Switzerland ■ Europe 46°30N 8°0E 20 C8
Schweizer-Reneke S. Africa 27°11S 25°18E 56 D4
Schwenningen = Villingen-Schwenningen Germany 48°3N 8°26E 16 D5
Schwerin Germany 53°36N 11°22E 16 B6
Schwyz Switz. 47°2N 8°39E 20 C8
Sciacca Italy 37°31N 13°3E 22 F5
Scilla Italy 38°15N 15°43E 22 E6
Scilly, Isles of U.K. 49°56N 6°22W 13 H1
Scioto → U.S.A. 38°44N 83°1W 81 F12
Scituate U.S.A. 42°12N 70°44W 83 D14
Scobey U.S.A. 48°47N 105°25W 76 B11
Scone Australia 32°5S 150°52E 63 E5
Scone U.K. 56°25N 3°24W 11 E5
Scoresbysund = Ittoqqortoormiit Greenland 70°20N 23°0W 4 B6
Scotia Calif., U.S.A. 40°29N 124°6W 76 F1
Scotia N.Y., U.S.A. 42°50N 73°58W 83 D11
Scotia Sea Antarctica 56°5S 56°0W 5 B18
Scotland Canada 43°1N 80°22W 82 C4
Scotland □ U.K. 57°0N 4°0W 11 E5
Scott Antarctica 77°0S 166°45E 5 D11
Scott, C. Australia 13°30S 129°49E 60 B4
Scott City U.S.A. 38°29N 100°54W 80 F3
Scott Glacier Antarctica 66°15S 100°5E 5 C8
Scott I. Antarctica 67°0S 179°0E 5 C11
Scott Is. Canada 50°48N 128°40W 70 C3
Scott L. Canada 59°55N 106°18W 71 B7
Scott Reef Australia 14°0S 121°50E 60 B3
Scottburgh S. Africa 30°15S 30°47E 57 E5
Scottdale U.S.A. 40°6N 79°35W 82 F5
Scottish Borders □ U.K. 55°35N 2°50W 11 F6
Scotts Valley U.S.A. 37°3N 122°1W 78 H4
Scottsbluff U.S.A. 41°52N 103°40W 80 E2
Scottsboro U.S.A. 34°40N 86°2W 85 D11
Scottsburg U.S.A. 38°41N 85°47W 81 F11
Scottsdale Australia 41°9S 147°31E 63 G4
Scottsdale U.S.A. 33°40N 111°53W 77 K8
Scottsville Ky., U.S.A. 36°45N 86°11W 80 G10
Scottsville N.Y., U.S.A. 43°2N 77°47W 82 C7
Scottville U.S.A. 43°58N 86°17W 80 D10
Scranton U.S.A. 41°25N 75°40W 83 E9
Scugog, L. Canada 44°10N 78°55W 82 B6
Scunthorpe U.K. 53°36N 0°39W 12 D7
Scutari = Shkodër Albania 42°4N 19°32E 23 C8
Sea Is. U.S.A. 31°30N 81°7W 85 F14
Seabrook, L. Australia 30°55S 119°40E 61 F2
Seaford U.K. 50°47N 0°7E 13 G8
Seaford U.S.A. 38°39N 75°37W 81 F16
Seaforth Australia 20°55S 148°57E 62 b
Seaforth Canada 43°35N 81°25W 82 C3
Seaforth, L. U.K. 57°52N 6°36W 11 D2
Seagraves U.S.A. 32°57N 102°34W 84 E3
Seaham U.K. 54°50N 1°20W 12 C6
Seal → Canada 59°4N 94°48W 71 B10
Seal L. Canada 54°20N 61°30W 73 B7
Sealy U.S.A. 29°47N 96°9W 84 G6
Searchlight U.S.A. 35°28N 114°55W 79 K12

Searcy U.S.A. 35°15N 91°44W 84 D9
Searles L. U.S.A. 35°44N 117°21W 79 K9
Seascale U.K. 54°24N 3°29W 12 C4
Seaside Calif., U.S.A. 36°37N 121°50W 78 J5
Seaside Oreg., U.S.A. 46°0N 123°56W 78 E3
Seaspray Australia 38°25S 147°15E 63 F4
Seattle U.S.A. 47°36N 122°19W 78 C4
Seattle-Tacoma Int. ✈ (SEA) U.S.A. 47°27N 122°18W 78 C4
Seba Indonesia 10°29S 121°50E 60 B3
Sebago L. U.S.A. 43°52N 70°34W 83 C14
Sebago Lake U.S.A. 43°51N 70°34W 83 C14
Sebastián Vizcaíno, B. Mexico 28°0N 114°30W 86 B2
Sebastopol = Sevastopol Ukraine 44°35N 33°30E 19 F5
Sebastopol U.S.A. 38°24N 122°49W 78 G4
Sebewaing U.S.A. 43°44N 83°27W 81 D12
Sebha = Sabhā Libya 27°9N 14°29E 51 C8
Şebinkarahisar Turkey 40°22N 38°28E 19 F6
Sebring Fla., U.S.A. 27°30N 81°27W 85 H14
Sebring Ohio, U.S.A. 40°55N 81°2W 82 F3
Sebringville Canada 43°24N 81°4W 82 C3
Sebta = Ceuta N. Afr. 35°52N 5°18W 21 E3
Sebuku Indonesia 3°30S 116°25E 36 E5
Sechelt Canada 49°25N 123°42W 70 D4
Sechura, Desierto de Peru 6°0S 80°30W 92 E2
Secretary I. N.Z. 45°15S 166°56E 59 F1
Secunderabad India 17°28N 78°30E 40 L11
Security U.S.A. 38°45N 104°45W 76 G11
Sedalia U.S.A. 38°42N 93°14W 80 F7
Sedan France 49°43N 4°57E 20 B6
Sedan U.S.A. 37°8N 96°11W 80 G5
Sedbergh U.K. 54°20N 2°31W 12 C5
Seddon N.Z. 41°40S 174°7E 59 D5
Seddonville N.Z. 41°33S 172°1E 59 D4
Sedé Boqér Israel 30°52N 34°47E 46 E3
Sedeh Fārs, Iran 30°45N 52°11E 45 D7
Sedeh Khorāsān, Iran 33°20N 59°14E 45 C8
Sederot Israel 31°32N 34°37E 46 D3
Sédhiou Senegal 12°44N 15°30W 50 F2
Sedley Canada 50°10N 104°0W 71 C8
Sedona U.S.A. 34°52N 111°46W 77 J8
Sedova, Pik Russia 73°29N 54°58E 28 B6
Sedro-Woolley U.S.A. 48°30N 122°14W 78 B4
Seeheim Namibia 26°50S 17°45E 56 D2
Seeis Namibia 22°29S 17°39E 56 C2
Seekoei → S. Africa 30°18S 25°1E 56 E4
Seeley's Bay Canada 44°29N 76°14W 83 B8
Seferihisar Turkey 38°10N 26°50E 23 E12
Sefophe Botswana 22°11S 27°58E 55 G2
Seg-ozero Russia 63°20N 33°46E 18 B5
Segamat Malaysia 2°30N 102°50E 39 L4
Segesta Italy 37°56N 12°50E 22 F5
Seget Indonesia 1°24S 130°58E 37 E8
Segezha Russia 63°44N 34°19E 18 B5
Ségou Mali 13°30N 6°16W 50 F4
Segovia = Coco → Cent. Amer. 15°0N 83°8W 88 D3
Segovia Spain 40°57N 4°10W 21 B3
Segre → Spain 41°40N 0°43E 21 B6
Seguam I. U.S.A. 52°19N 172°30W 74 E5
Segura → Spain 38°3N 0°44W 21 C5
Seh Konj, Kūh-e Iran 30°6N 57°30E 45 D8
Seh Qal'eh Iran 33°40N 58°24E 45 C8
Sehitwa Botswana 20°30S 22°30E 56 C3
Sehlabathebe △ Lesotho 29°53S 29°7E 57 D4
Sehore India 23°10N 77°5E 42 H7
Sehwan Pakistan 26°28N 67°53E 42 F2
Seikan Tunnel Japan 41°28N 140°10E 30 D10
Seil U.K. 56°18N 5°38W 11 E3
Seiland Norway 70°25N 23°15E 8 A20
Seiling U.S.A. 36°9N 98°56W 84 C5
Seinäjoki Finland 62°40N 22°51E 8 E20
Seine → France 49°26N 0°26E 20 B4
Seistan = Sīstān Asia 30°50N 61°0E 45 D9
Seistan, Daryācheh-ye = Sīstān, Daryācheh-ye Iran 31°0N 61°0E 45 D9
Sekayu Indonesia 2°51S 103°51E 36 E2
Seke Tanzania 3°20S 33°31E 54 C3
Sekenke Tanzania 4°18S 34°11E 54 C3
Sekondi-Takoradi Ghana 4°58N 1°45W 50 H5
Sekudai Malaysia 1°32N 103°39E 39 d
Sekuma Botswana 24°36S 23°50E 56 C3
Selah U.S.A. 46°39N 120°32W 76 C3
Selama Malaysia 5°12N 100°42E 39 K3
Selangor □ Malaysia 3°10N 101°30E 39 L3
Selaru Indonesia 8°9S 131°0E 37 F8
Selatan, Selat Malaysia 5°15N 100°20E 39 c
Selawik U.S.A. 66°30N 160°0W 74 B7
Selby U.K. 53°47N 1°5W 12 D6
Selby U.S.A. 45°31N 100°2W 80 C3
Selçuk Turkey 37°56N 27°22E 23 F12
Selden U.S.A. 39°33N 100°34W 80 F3
Sele → Italy 40°29N 14°56E 22 D6
Selebi-Phikwe Botswana 21°58S 27°48E 57 C4
Selemdzha → Russia 51°42N 128°53E 29 D13
Selenga = Selenge Mörön → Asia 52°16N 106°16E 32 A10
Selenge Mörön → Asia 52°16N 106°16E 32 A10
Seletan, Tanjung Indonesia 4°10S 114°40E 36 E4
Sélibabi Mauritania 15°10N 12°15W 50 E3
Seligman U.S.A. 35°20N 112°53W 77 J7
Selîma Sudan 21°22N 29°19E 51 D11
Selinda Spillway Botswana 18°35S 23°10E 56 B3
Selinsgrove U.S.A. 40°48N 76°52W 82 F8
Selkirk Man., Canada 50°10N 96°55W 71 C9
Selkirk U.K. 55°33N 2°50W 11 F6
Selkirk I. Canada 53°20N 99°6W 71 C9
Selkirk Mts. Canada 51°15N 117°40W 70 C5
Sellafield U.K. 54°25N 3°29W 12 C4
Sellia Greece 35°12N 24°23E 25 D6

Sells U.S.A. 31°55N 111°53W 77 L8
Selma Ala., U.S.A. 32°25N 87°1W 85 E11
Selma Calif., U.S.A. 36°34N 119°37W 78 J7
Selma N.C., U.S.A. 35°32N 78°17W 85 D15
Selmer U.S.A. 35°10N 88°36W 85 D10
Selous △ Tanzania 8°37S 37°42E 55 D4
Selowandoma Falls Zimbabwe 21°15S 31°50E 55 G3
Selpele Indonesia 0°1S 130°5E 37 E8
Selsey Bill U.K. 50°43N 0°47W 13 G7
Seltso Russia 53°22N 34°4E 18 D5
Selu Indonesia 7°32S 130°55E 37 F8
Selva Argentina 29°50S 62°0W 94 B3
Selva Spain 39°46N 2°54E 24 B9
Selva Lancandona = Montes Azules △ Mexico 16°21N 91°3W 87 D6
Selvagens, Ilhas Madeira 30°5N 15°55W 50 B2
Selvas Brazil 6°30S 67°0W 92 E5
Selwyn L. Canada 60°0N 104°30W 71 B8
Selwyn Mts. Canada 63°0N 130°0W 68 E5
Selwyn Ra. Australia 21°10S 140°0E 62 C3
Seman → Albania 40°47N 19°30E 23 D8
Semarang Indonesia 7°0S 110°26E 37 G14
Semarapura = Klungkung Indonesia 8°32S 115°24E 37 K18
Sembabule Uganda 0°4S 31°25E 54 C3
Sembawang Singapore 1°27N 103°50E 39 d
Sembung Indonesia 8°28S 115°11E 37 J18
Semey Kazakhstan 50°30N 80°10E 32 A5
Seminoe Res. U.S.A. 42°9N 106°55W 76 E10
Seminole Okla., U.S.A. 35°14N 96°41W 84 D6
Seminole Tex., U.S.A. 32°43N 102°39W 84 E3
Seminole Draw → U.S.A. 32°27N 102°20W 84 E3
Semipalatinsk = Semey Kazakhstan 50°30N 80°10E 32 A5
Semirara Is. Phil. 12°0N 121°20E 37 B6
Semisopochnoi I. U.S.A. 51°55N 179°36E 74 E3
Semitau Indonesia 0°29N 111°57E 36 D4
Semliki → Uganda 0°49N 30°4E 54 B3
Semmering P. Austria 47°41N 15°45E 16 E8
Semnān Iran 35°40N 53°23E 45 C7
Semnān □ Iran 36°0N 54°0E 45 C7
Semporna Malaysia 4°30N 118°33E 37 D5
Semuda Indonesia 2°51S 112°58E 36 E4
Sen → Cambodia 12°32N 104°28E 38 F5
Senā Iran 28°27N 51°36E 45 D6
Sena Mozam. 17°25S 35°0E 55 F4
Sena Madureira Brazil 9°5S 68°45W 92 E5
Senador Pompeu Brazil 5°40S 39°20W 93 E11
Senang, Pulau Singapore 1°11N 103°52E 39 d
Senanga Zambia 16°7S 23°16E 53 H4
Senatobia U.S.A. 34°37N 89°58W 85 D10
Sencelles Spain 39°39N 2°54E 24 B9
Sendai Kagoshima, Japan 31°50N 130°20E 31 J5
Sendai Miyagi, Japan 38°15N 140°53E 30 E10
Sendai-Wan Japan 38°15N 141°0E 30 E10
Sendhwa India 21°41N 75°6E 42 J6
Seneca U.S.A. 34°41N 82°57W 85 D13
Seneca Falls U.S.A. 42°55N 76°48W 83 D8
Seneca L. U.S.A. 42°40N 76°54W 82 D8
Senecaville L. U.S.A. 39°55N 81°25W 82 G3
Senegal ■ W. Afr. 14°30N 14°30W 50 F3
Sénégal → W. Afr. 15°48N 16°32W 50 E2
Senegambia Africa 12°45N 12°0W 48 E2
Senekal S. Africa 28°20S 27°36E 57 D4
Senga Hill Zambia 9°19S 31°11E 55 D3
Senge Khambab = Indus → Pakistan 24°20N 67°47E 42 G2
Sengerema Tanzania 2°42S 32°35E 54 C3
Senggigi Indonesia 8°29S 116°2E 37 J19
Sengua → Zimbabwe 17°7S 28°5E 55 F2
Senhor-do-Bonfim Brazil 10°30S 40°10W 93 F10
Senigállia Italy 43°43N 13°13E 22 C5
Senj Croatia 45°0N 14°58E 16 F8
Senja Norway 69°25N 17°30E 8 B17
Senkaku-Shotō E. China Sea 25°45N 123°30E 31 M1
Senlis France 49°13N 2°35E 20 B5
Senmonorom Cambodia 12°27N 107°12E 38 F6
Senneterre Canada 48°25N 77°15W 72 C4
Seno Laos 16°35N 104°50E 38 D5
Senqu = Orange → S. Africa 28°41S 16°28E 56 D2
Sens France 48°11N 3°15E 20 B5
Senta Serbia 45°55N 20°3E 23 B9
Sentery = Lubao Dem. Rep. of the Congo 5°17S 25°42E 54 D2
Sentinel U.S.A. 32°52N 113°13W 77 K7
Sentosa Singapore 1°16N 103°50E 39 d
Seo de Urgel = La Seu d'Urgell Spain 42°22N 1°23E 21 A6
Seogwipo S. Korea 33°13N 126°34E 35 H14
Seohara India 29°15N 78°33E 43 E8
Seonath → India 21°44N 82°28E 43 J10
Seondha India 26°9N 78°48E 43 F8
Seongnam S. Korea 37°26N 127°8E 35 F14
Seoni India 22°5N 79°30E 43 H8
Seoni Malwa India 22°27N 77°28E 42 H8
Seonsan S. Korea 36°14N 128°17E 35 F15
Seosan S. Korea 36°47N 126°27E 35 F14
Seoul S. Korea 37°31N 126°58E 35 F14
Sepīdān Iran 30°20N 52°5E 45 D7
Sepo-ri N. Korea 38°57N 127°25E 35 E14
Sepone Laos 16°45N 106°13E 38 D6
Sept-Îles Canada 50°13N 66°22W 73 B6
Sequim U.S.A. 48°5N 123°6W 78 B3
Sequoia △ U.S.A. 36°30N 118°30W 78 J8
Seraing Belgium 50°35N 5°32E 15 D5
Serakhis → Cyprus 35°13N 32°55E 25 D11
Seram Indonesia 3°10S 129°0E 37 E7
Seram Sea Indonesia 2°30S 128°30E 37 E7
Serampore = Shrirampur India 22°44N 88°21E 43 H13
Seranantsara Madag. 18°30S 49°5E 57 B8
Serang Indonesia 6°8S 106°10E 37 G12
Serangoon Singapore 1°23N 103°54E 39 d
Serasan Indonesia 2°29N 109°4E 36 D3

Serbia ■ Europe 43°20N 20°0E 23 B9
Serdar Turkmenistan 39°4N 56°23E 45 B8
Serdobsk Russia 52°28N 44°10E 18 D7
Seremban Malaysia 2°43N 101°53E 39 L3
Serengeti △ Tanzania 2°11S 35°0E 54 C3
Serengeti Plain Tanzania 2°40S 35°0E 54 C4
Serenje Zambia 13°14S 30°15E 55 E3
Sereth = Siret → Romania 45°24N 28°1E 17 F14
Sergeya Kirova, Ostrova Russia 77°30N 89°0E 29 B10
Sergino Russia 62°25N 65°12E 28 C7
Sergipe □ Brazil 10°30S 37°30W 93 F11
Sergiyev Posad Russia 56°20N 38°10E 18 C6
Serhetabat Turkmenistan 35°20N 62°18E 45 C9
Seria Brunei 4°37N 114°23E 36 D4
Serian Malaysia 1°10N 110°31E 36 D4
Sericho Kenya 1°5N 39°5E 54 B4
Serifos Greece 37°9N 24°30E 23 F11
Sérigny → Canada 56°47N 66°0W 73 A6
Seringapatam Reef Australia 13°38S 122°5E 60 B3
Seririt Indonesia 8°12S 114°56E 37 J17
Serkout Algeria 23°56N 6°47E 50 D7
Sermata Indonesia 8°15S 128°50E 37 F7
Sermersuaq Greenland 79°30N 62°0W 69 B19
Serov Russia 59°29N 60°35E 18 C11
Serowe Botswana 22°25S 26°43E 56 C4
Serpentine Lakes Australia 28°30S 129°10E 61 E4
Serpent's Mouth = Sierpe, Bocas de la Venezuela 10°0N 61°30W 93 L15
Serpukhov Russia 54°55N 37°28E 18 D6
Serra do Navio Brazil 0°59N 52°3W 93 C8
Serranía San Luís △ Paraguay 22°35S 57°22W 94 A4
Serranía San Rafael △ Paraguay 26°30S 56°0W 95 B4
Serres Greece 41°5N 23°31E 23 D10
Serrezuela Argentina 30°40S 65°20W 94 C2
Serrinha Brazil 11°39S 39°0W 93 F11
Sertanópolis Brazil 23°4S 51°2W 95 A5
Serua Indonesia 6°18S 130°1E 37 F8
Serui Indonesia 1°53S 136°10E 37 E9
Serule Botswana 21°57S 27°20E 56 C4
Ses Salines Spain 39°21N 3°3E 24 B10
Sese Is. Uganda 0°20S 32°20E 54 C3
Sesepe Indonesia 1°30S 127°59E 37 E7
Sesfontein Namibia 19°7S 13°39E 56 B1
Sesheke Zambia 17°29S 24°13E 56 B3
S'Espalmador Spain 38°47N 1°26E 24 C7
S'Espardell Spain 38°48N 1°29E 24 C7
S'Estanyol Spain 39°22N 2°54E 24 B9
Setana Japan 42°26N 139°51E 30 C9
Sète France 43°25N 3°42E 20 E5
Sete Lagoas Brazil 19°27S 44°16W 93 G10
Sétif Algeria 36°9N 5°26E 50 A7
Seto Japan 35°14N 137°6E 31 G8
Setonaikai Japan 34°20N 133°30E 31 G6
Setonaikai △ Japan 34°15N 133°15E 31 G6
Settat Morocco 33°0N 7°40W 50 B4
Setting L. Canada 55°0N 98°38W 71 C9
Settle U.K. 54°5N 2°16W 12 C5
Settlement, The Br. Virgin Is. 18°43N 64°22W 89 e
Settlers S. Africa 25°2S 28°30E 57 C4
Setúbal Portugal 38°30N 8°58W 21 C1
Setúbal, B. de Portugal 38°40N 8°56W 21 C1
Seul, Lac Canada 50°20N 92°30W 72 B1
Sevan, Ozero = Sevana Lich Armenia 40°30N 45°20E 44 A5
Sevana Lich Armenia 40°30N 45°20E 44 A5
Sevastopol Ukraine 44°35N 33°30E 19 F5
Seven Sisters Canada 54°56N 128°10W 70 C3
Severn → Canada 56°2N 87°36W 72 A2
Severn → U.K. 51°35N 2°40W 13 F5
Severnaya Zemlya Russia 79°0N 100°0E 29 B11
Severnyye Uvaly Russia 60°0N 50°0E 18 C8
Severo-Kurilsk Russia 50°40N 156°8E 29 D16
Severo-Yeniseyskiy Russia 60°22N 93°1E 29 C10
Severo-Zapadnyy □ Russia 65°0N 40°0E 28 C4
Severobaykalsk Russia 55°39N 109°19E 29 D11
Severodvinsk Russia 64°27N 39°58E 18 B6
Severomorsk Russia 69°5N 33°27E 8 B25
Severouralsk Russia 60°9N 59°57E 18 B10
Seversk Russia 56°36N 84°49E 28 D9
Sevier → U.S.A. 39°4N 113°6W 76 G7
Sevier Desert U.S.A. 39°40N 112°45W 76 G7
Sevier L. U.S.A. 38°54N 113°9W 76 G7
Sevilla Spain 37°23N 5°58W 21 D2
Seville = Sevilla Spain 37°23N 5°58W 21 D2
Sevlievo Bulgaria 43°2N 25°6E 23 C11
Sewani India 28°58N 75°39E 42 E6
Seward Alaska, U.S.A. 60°7N 149°27W 68 E2
Seward Nebr., U.S.A. 40°55N 97°6W 80 E5
Seward Pa., U.S.A. 40°25N 79°1W 82 F5
Seward Peninsula U.S.A. 65°30N 166°0W 74 B6
Sewell Chile 34°10S 70°23W 94 C1
Sewer Indonesia 5°53S 134°40E 37 F8
Sewickley U.S.A. 40°32N 80°12W 82 F4
Sexsmith Canada 55°21N 118°47W 70 B5
Seychelles ■ Ind. Oc. 5°0S 56°0E 53 b
Seyðisfjörður Iceland 65°16N 13°57W 8 D7
Seydişehir Turkey 37°25N 31°51E 19 G5
Seydvān Iran 38°34N 45°2E 44 B5
Seyhan → Turkey 36°43N 34°53E 44 B2
Seym → Ukraine 51°27N 32°34E 19 D5
Seymour Australia 37°2S 145°10E 63 F4
Seymour S. Africa 32°33S 26°46E 56 E4
Seymour Conn., U.S.A. 41°24N 73°4W 83 E11
Seymour Ind., U.S.A. 38°58N 85°53W 81 F11
Seymour Tex., U.S.A. 33°35N 99°16W 84 E5
Sfântu Gheorghe Romania 45°52N 25°48E 17 F13
Sfax Tunisia 34°49N 10°48E 51 B8
Sha Tau Kok China 22°33N 114°13E 33 a

Sha Tin China 22°23N 114°12E 33 a
Shaanxi □ China 35°0N 109°0E 34 G5
Shaba = Katanga □
  Dem. Rep. of the Congo 8°0S 25°0E 54 D2
Shaba △ Kenya 0°38N 37°48E 54 B4
Shabeelle → Somali Rep. 2°0N 44°0E 47 G3
Shabogamo L. Canada 53°15N 66°30W 73 B6
Shabunda
  Dem. Rep. of the Congo 2°40S 27°16E 54 C2
Shache China 38°20N 77°10E 32 D4
Shackleton Fracture Zone
  S. Ocean 60°0S 60°0W 5 B18
Shackleton Ice Shelf
  Antarctica 66°0S 100°0E 5 C8
Shackleton Inlet
  Antarctica 83°0S 160°0E 5 E11
Shādegān Iran 30°40N 48°38E 45 D6
Shadi India 33°24N 77°14E 43 C7
Shadrinsk Russia 56°5N 63°32E 28 D7
Shadyside U.S.A. 39°58N 80°45W 82 G4
Shafter U.S.A. 35°30N 119°16W 79 K7
Shaftesbury U.K. 51°0N 2°11W 13 F5
Shaftsbury U.S.A. 43°0N 73°11W 83 D11
Shagram Pakistan 36°24N 72°20E 43 A5
Shah Alam Malaysia 3°5N 101°32E 39 L3
Shah Alizai Pakistan 29°25N 66°33E 42 E2
Shah Bunder Pakistan 24°13N 67°56E 42 G2
Shahabad Punjab, India 30°10N 76°55E 42 D7
Shahabad Raj., India 25°15N 77°11E 42 G7
Shahabad Ut. P., India 27°36N 79°56E 43 F8
Shahabā' Syria 32°52N 36°38E 46 C5
Shahdād Iran 30°30N 57°40E 45 D8
Shahdād, Namakzār-e
  Iran 30°20N 58°20E 45 D8
Shahdadkot Pakistan 27°50N 67°55E 42 F2
Shahdol India 23°19N 81°26E 43 H9
Shahe China 37°0N 114°32E 34 F8
Shahganj India 26°3N 82°44E 43 F10
Shahgarh India 27°15N 69°50E 42 F3
Shahjahanpur India 27°54N 79°57E 43 F8
Shahpur = Salmās Iran 38°11N 44°47E 44 B5
Shahpur India 22°12N 77°58E 42 H7
Shahpur Baluchistan,
  Pakistan 28°46N 68°27E 42 E3
Shahpur Punjab, Pakistan 32°17N 72°26E 42 C5
Shahpur Chakar Pakistan 26°9N 68°39E 42 F3
Shahpura Mad. P., India 23°10N 80°45E 43 H9
Shahpura Raj., India 25°38N 74°56E 42 G6
Shahr-e Bābak Iran 30°7N 55°9E 45 D7
Shahr-e Kord Iran 32°15N 50°55E 45 C6
Shāhrakht Iran 33°38N 60°16E 45 C9
Shahrezā = Qomsheh
  Iran 32°0N 51°55E 45 D6
Shahrig Pakistan 30°15N 67°40E 42 D2
Shāhrud = Emāmrūd
  Iran 36°30N 55°0E 45 B7
Shahukou China 40°20N 112°18E 34 D7
Shaikhabad Afghan. 34°2N 68°45E 42 B3
Shajapur India 23°27N 76°21E 42 H7
Shajing China 22°44N 113°48E 33 a
Shakargarh Pakistan 32°17N 75°10E 42 C6
Shakawe Botswana 18°28S 21°49E 56 B3
Shaker Heights U.S.A. 41°28N 81°32W 82 E3
Shakhtersk Russia 49°10N 142°8E 29 E15
Shakhty Russia 47°40N 40°16E 19 E7
Shakhunya Russia 57°40N 46°46E 18 C8
Shaki Nigeria 8°41N 3°21E 50 G6
Shakotan-Hantō Japan 43°10N 140°30E 30 C10
Shaksam Valley Asia 36°0N 76°20E 43 A7
Shallow Lake Canada 44°36N 81°5W 82 B3
Shalqar Kazakhstan 47°48N 59°39E 28 E6
Shaluli Shan China 30°40N 99°55E 41 D21
Shām Iran 26°39N 57°21E 45 E8
Shām, Bādiyat ash Asia 32°0N 40°0E 44 C3
Shamāl Sīnī □ Egypt 30°0N 33°30E 46 E2
Shamattawa Canada 55°51N 92°5W 72 A1
Shamattawa → Canada 55°1N 85°23W 72 A2
Shamīl Iran 27°30N 56°55E 45 E8
Shāmkūh Iran 35°47N 57°50E 45 C8
Shamli India 29°32N 77°18E 42 E7
Shammar, Jabal Si. Arabia 27°40N 41°0E 44 E4
Shamo = Gobi Asia 44°0N 110°0E 34 C6
Shamo, L. Ethiopia 5°45N 37°30E 47 F2
Shamokin U.S.A. 40°47N 76°34W 83 F8
Shamrock Canada 45°23N 76°50W 83 A8
Shamrock U.S.A. 35°13N 100°15W 84 D4
Shamva Zimbabwe 17°20S 31°32E 55 F3
Shan □ Burma 21°30N 98°30E 41 J21
Shan Xian China 34°50N 116°5E 34 G9
Shanchengzhen China 42°20N 125°20E 35 C13
Shāndak Iran 28°28N 60°27E 45 D9
Shandan China 38°45N 101°15E 32 D9
Shandon U.S.A. 35°39N 120°23W 78 K6
Shandong □ China 36°0N 118°0E 35 G10
Shandong Bandao China 37°0N 121°0E 35 F11
Shandur Pass Pakistan 36°4N 72°31E 43 A5
Shang Xian = Shangzhou
  China 33°50N 109°58E 34 H5
Shangalowe
  Dem. Rep. of the Congo 10°50S 26°30E 55 E2
Shangani Zimbabwe 19°41S 29°20E 57 B4
Shangani → Zimbabwe 18°41S 27°10E 55 F2
Shangbancheng China 40°50N 118°1E 35 D10
Shangdu China 41°30N 113°30E 34 D7
Shanghai China 31°15N 121°26E 33 E13
Shanghe China 37°20N 117°10E 35 F9
Shangnan China 33°32N 110°50E 34 H6
Shangqiu China 34°26N 115°36E 34 G8
Shangrao China 28°25N 117°59E 33 F12
Shangri-La = Zhongdian
  China 27°48N 99°42E 32 F8
Shangshui China 33°42N 114°35E 34 H8
Shangyi China 41°4N 113°57E 34 D7
Shangzhi China 45°22N 127°56E 35 B14
Shangzhou China 33°50N 109°58E 34 H5
Shanhetun China 44°33N 127°15E 35 B14
Shanklin U.K. 50°38N 1°11W 13 G6
Shannon N.Z. 40°33S 175°25E 59 D5
Shannon → Ireland 52°35N 9°30W 10 D2

Shannon ✈ (SNN)
  Ireland 52°42N 8°57W 10 D3
Shannon, Mouth of the
  Ireland 52°30N 9°55W 10 D2
Shannon △ Australia 34°35S 116°25E 61 F2
Shannonbridge Ireland 53°17N 8°3W 10 C3
Shansi = Shanxi □ China 37°0N 112°0E 34 F7
Shantar, Ostrov Bolshoy
  Russia 55°9N 137°40E 29 D14
Shantipur India 23°17N 88°25E 43 H13
Shantou China 23°18N 116°40E 33 G12
Shantung = Shandong □
  China 36°0N 118°0E 35 G10
Shanxi □ China 37°0N 112°0E 34 F7
Shanyang China 33°31N 109°55E 34 H5
Shanyin China 39°25N 112°56E 34 E7
Shaoguan China 24°48N 113°35E 33 G11
Shaoyang China 27°14N 111°25E 33 F11
Shap U.K. 54°32N 2°40W 12 C5
Shapinsay U.K. 59°3N 2°51W 11 B6
Shaqra' Si. Arabia 25°15N 45°16E 44 E5
Shaqrā' Yemen 13°22N 45°44E 47 E4
Sharafkhāneh Iran 38°11N 45°29E 44 B5
Sharbot Lake Canada 44°46N 76°41W 83 B8
Shari Japan 43°55N 144°40E 30 C12
Sharjah = Ash Shāriqah
  U.A.E. 25°23N 55°26E 45 E7
Shark B. Australia 25°30S 113°32E 61 E1
Shark Bay △ Australia 25°30S 113°32E 61 E1
Sharm el Sheikh Egypt 27°53N 34°18E 51 C12
Sharon Canada 44°6N 79°26W 82 B5
Sharon Mass., U.S.A. 42°7N 71°11W 83 D13
Sharon Pa., U.S.A. 41°14N 80°31W 82 E4
Sharon Springs Kans.,
  U.S.A. 38°54N 101°45W 80 F3
Sharon Springs N.Y.,
  U.S.A. 42°48N 74°37W 83 D10
Sharp Pt. Australia 10°58S 142°43E 62 A3
Sharpe L. Canada 54°24N 93°40W 72 B1
Sharpsville U.S.A. 41°15N 80°29W 82 E4
Sharqi, Al Jabal ash
  Lebanon 33°40N 36°10E 46 B5
Sharya Russia 58°22N 45°20E 18 C8
Shashemene Ethiopia 7°13N 38°33E 47 F2
Shashi Botswana 21°15S 27°27E 55 C4
Shashi → Africa 21°14S 29°20E 55 G2
Shasta, Mt. U.S.A. 41°25N 122°12W 76 F2
Shasta L. U.S.A. 40°43N 122°25W 76 F2
Shatsky Rise Pac. Oc. 34°0N 157°0E 64 D7
Shatt al Arab Asia 29°57N 48°34E 45 D6
Shaunavon Canada 49°35N 108°25W 71 D7
Shaver L. U.S.A. 37°9N 119°18W 78 H7
Shaw → Australia 20°21S 119°17E 60 D2
Shaw I. Australia 20°30S 149°2E 62 b
Shawanaga Canada 45°31N 80°17W 82 A4
Shawangunk Mts.
  U.S.A. 41°35N 74°30W 83 E10
Shawano U.S.A. 44°47N 88°36W 80 C1
Shawinigan Canada 46°35N 72°50W 72 C5
Shawmari, J. ash Jordan 30°35N 36°35E 46 E5
Shawnee U.S.A. 35°20N 96°55W 84 D6
Shay Gap Australia 20°30S 120°10E 60 D3
Shaybārā Si. Arabia 25°26N 36°47E 44 E3
Shaykh Miskīn Syria 32°49N 36°9E 46 C5
Shaykh Sa'd Iraq 32°34N 46°17E 44 C5
Shāzand Iran 33°56N 49°24E 45 C6
Shchūchīnsk Kazakhstan 52°56N 70°12E 28 D8
She Xian China 36°30N 113°40E 34 F7
Shebele = Shabeelle →
  Somali Rep. 2°0N 44°0E 47 G3
Sheboygan U.S.A. 43°46N 87°45W 80 D10
Shediac Canada 46°14N 64°32W 73 C7
Sheelin, L. Ireland 53°48N 7°20W 10 C4
Sheenjek → U.S.A. 66°45N 144°33W 74 B11
Sheep Haven Ireland 55°11N 7°52W 10 A4
Sheep Range U.S.A. 36°35N 115°15W 79 J11
Sheerness U.K. 51°26N 0°47E 13 F8
Sheet Harbour Canada 44°56N 62°31W 73 D7
Sheffield U.K. 53°23N 1°28W 12 D6
Sheffield Ala., U.S.A. 34°46N 87°41W 85 D11
Sheffield Mass., U.S.A. 42°5N 73°21W 83 D11
Sheffield Pa., U.S.A. 41°42N 79°3W 82 E5
Sheho Canada 51°35N 103°13W 71 C8
Shekhupura Pakistan 31°42N 73°58E 42 D5
Shekou China 22°30N 113°55E 33 a
Shelburne N.S., Canada 43°47N 65°20W 73 D6
Shelburne Ont., Canada 44°4N 80°15W 82 B4
Shelburne U.S.A. 44°23N 73°14W 83 B11
Shelburne B. Australia 11°50S 142°50E 62 A3
Shelburne Falls U.S.A. 42°36N 72°45W 83 D12
Shelby Mich., U.S.A. 43°37N 86°22W 80 D10
Shelby Miss., U.S.A. 33°57N 90°46W 85 E9
Shelby Mont., U.S.A. 48°30N 111°51W 76 B8
Shelby N.C., U.S.A. 35°17N 81°32W 85 D14
Shelby Ohio, U.S.A. 40°53N 82°40W 82 F2
Shelbyville Ill., U.S.A. 39°24N 88°48W 80 F9
Shelbyville Ind., U.S.A. 39°31N 85°47W 81 F11
Shelbyville Ky., U.S.A. 38°13N 85°14W 81 F11
Shelbyville Tenn.,
  U.S.A. 35°29N 86°28W 85 D11
Sheldon U.S.A. 43°11N 95°51W 80 D6
Sheldrake Canada 50°20N 64°51W 73 B7
Shelikhova, Zaliv
  Russia 59°30N 157°0E 29 D16
Shelikof Strait U.S.A. 57°30N 155°0W 74 D9
Shell Lakes Australia 29°20S 127°30E 61 E4
Shellbrook Canada 53°13N 106°24W 71 C7
Shellharbour Australia 34°31S 150°51E 63 E5
Shelter I. U.S.A. 41°4N 72°20W 83 E12
Shelton Conn., U.S.A. 41°19N 73°5W 83 E11
Shelton Wash., U.S.A. 47°13N 123°6W 78 C3
Shen Xian China 36°15N 115°40E 34 F8
Shenandoah Iowa,
  U.S.A. 40°46N 95°22W 80 E6
Shenandoah Pa., U.S.A. 40°49N 76°12W 83 F8
Shenandoah Va.,
  U.S.A. 38°29N 78°37W 81 F14
Shenandoah → U.S.A. 39°19N 77°44W 81 F15
Shenandoah △ U.S.A. 38°35N 78°22W 81 F14

Shenchi China 39°8N 112°10E 34 E7
Shendam Nigeria 8°49N 9°30E 50 G7
Shendi Sudan 16°46N 33°22E 51 E12
Shengfang China 39°3N 116°42E 34 E9
Shenjingzi China 44°40N 124°30E 35 B13
Shenmu China 38°50N 110°29E 34 E6
Shenqiu China 33°25N 115°5E 34 H8
Shensi = Shaanxi □
  China 35°0N 109°0E 34 G5
Shenyang China 41°48N 123°27E 35 D12
Shenzhen China 22°32N 114°5E 33 a
Shenzhen ✈ (SZX) China 22°41N 113°49E 33 a
Shenzhen Shuiku China 22°34N 114°8E 33 a
Shenzhen Wan China 22°27N 113°55E 33 a
Sheo India 26°11N 71°15E 42 F4
Sheopur Kalan India 25°40N 76°40E 42 G7
Shepetivka Ukraine 50°10N 27°10E 17 C14
Shepparton Australia 36°23S 145°26E 63 F4
Sheppey, I. of U.K. 51°25N 0°48E 13 F8
Shepton Mallet U.K. 51°11N 2°33W 13 F5
Sheqi China 33°12N 112°57E 34 H7
Sher Qila Pakistan 36°7N 74°2E 43 A6
Sherborne U.K. 50°57N 2°31W 13 G5
Sherbro I. S. Leone 7°30N 12°40W 50 G3
Sherbrooke N.S., Canada 45°8N 61°59W 73 C7
Sherbrooke Qué.,
  Canada 45°28N 71°57W 83 A13
Sherburne U.S.A. 42°41N 75°30W 83 D9
Shergarh India 26°20N 72°18E 42 F5
Sherghati India 24°34N 84°47E 43 G11
Sheridan Ark., U.S.A. 34°19N 92°24W 84 D8
Sheridan Wyo., U.S.A. 44°48N 106°58W 76 D10
Sheringham U.K. 52°56N 1°13E 12 E9
Sherkot India 29°22N 78°35E 43 E8
Sherlovaya Gora
  Russia 50°34N 116°15E 29 D12
Sherman N.Y., U.S.A. 42°9N 79°35W 82 D5
Sherman Tex., U.S.A. 33°38N 96°36W 84 E6
Sherpur India 25°34N 83°47E 43 G10
Sherridon Canada 55°8N 101°5W 71 B8
Sherwood Forest U.K. 53°6N 1°7W 12 D6
Sherwood Park Canada 53°31N 113°19W 70 C6
Sheslay → Canada 58°48N 132°5W 70 B2
Shethanei L. Canada 58°48N 97°50W 71 B9
Shetland □ U.K. 60°30N 1°30W 11 A7
Shetland Is. U.K. 60°30N 1°30W 11 A7
Shetrunji → India 21°19N 72°7E 42 J5
Sheung Shui China 22°31N 114°7E 33 a
Shey-Phoksundo △
  Nepal 29°30N 82°45E 43 E10
Sheyang China 33°48N 120°29E 35 H11
Sheyenne → U.S.A. 47°2N 96°50W 80 B5
Shiashkotan, Ostrov
  Russia 48°49N 154°6E 29 E16
Shibām Yemen 15°59N 48°36E 47 D4
Shibata Japan 37°57N 139°20E 30 F9
Shibecha Japan 43°17N 144°36E 30 C12
Shibetsu Japan 43°30N 145°10E 30 C12
Shibetsu Japan 44°10N 142°23E 30 B11
Shibogama L. Canada 53°35N 88°15W 72 B2
Shibushi Japan 31°25N 131°8E 31 J5
Shickshinny U.S.A. 41°9N 76°9W 83 E8
Shickshock Mts. = Chic-Chocs,
  Mts. Canada 48°55N 66°0W 73 C6
Shidao China 36°50N 122°25E 35 F12
Shido Japan 34°19N 134°10E 31 G7
Shiel, L. U.K. 56°48N 5°34W 11 E3
Shieli Kazakhstan 44°20N 66°15E 28 E7
Shiga □ Japan 35°20N 136°0E 31 G8
Shiguaigou China 40°52N 110°15E 34 D6
Shihchiachuangi = Shijiazhuang
  China 38°2N 114°28E 34 E8
Shihezi China 44°15N 86°2E 32 C6
Shijiazhuang China 38°2N 114°28E 34 E8
Shikarpur India 28°17N 78°7E 42 E8
Shikarpur Pakistan 27°57N 68°39E 42 F3
Shikohabad India 27°6N 78°36E 43 F8
Shikoku □ Japan 33°30N 133°30E 31 H6
Shikoku-Sanchi Japan 33°30N 133°30E 31 H6
Shikotan, Ostrov Asia 43°47N 146°44E 29 E15
Shikotsu-Ko Japan 42°45N 141°25E 30 C10
Shikotsu-Tōya △ Japan 44°4N 145°8E 30 C10
Shiliguri India 26°45N 88°25E 41 F16
Shiliu = Changjiang
  China 19°20N 108°55E 38 C7
Shilka Russia 52°0N 115°55E 29 D12
Shilka → Russia 53°20N 121°26E 29 D13
Shillelagh Ireland 52°45N 6°32W 10 D5
Shillington U.S.A. 40°18N 75°58W 83 F9
Shillong India 25°35N 91°53E 41 G17
Shilo West Bank 32°4N 35°18E 46 C4
Shilou China 37°0N 110°48E 34 F6
Shimabara Japan 32°48N 130°20E 31 H5
Shimada Japan 34°49N 138°10E 31 G9
Shimane □ Japan 35°0N 132°30E 31 G6
Shimanovsk Russia 52°15N 127°30E 29 D13
Shimba Hills △ Kenya 4°14S 39°25E 54 C4
Shimbiris Somali Rep. 10°44N 47°14E 47 E4
Shimizu Japan 35°0N 138°30E 31 G9
Shimodate Japan 36°20N 139°55E 31 F9
Shimoga India 13°57N 75°32E 40 N9
Shimokita-Hantō Japan 41°20N 141°0E 30 D10
Shimoni Kenya 4°38S 39°20E 54 C4
Shimonoseki Japan 33°58N 130°55E 31 H5
Shimpuru Rapids
  Namibia 17°45S 19°55E 56 B2
Shin, L. U.K. 58°5N 4°30W 11 C4
Shinano-Gawa →
  Japan 36°50N 138°30E 31 F9
Shināş Oman 24°46N 56°28E 45 E8
Shīndand Afghan. 33°12N 62°8E 40 C3
Shinglehouse U.S.A. 41°58N 78°12W 82 E6
Shingū Japan 33°40N 135°55E 31 H7
Shingwidzi S. Africa 23°5S 31°25E 57 C5
Shinjō Japan 38°46N 140°18E 30 E10
Shinkolobwe
  Dem. Rep. of the Congo 11°10S 26°40E 52 G5

Shinshār Syria 34°36N 36°43E 46 A5
Shinyanga Tanzania 3°45S 33°27E 54 C3
Shinyanga □ Tanzania 3°50S 34°0E 54 C3
Shio-no-Misaki Japan 33°25N 135°45E 31 H7
Shiogama Japan 38°19N 141°1E 30 E10
Shiojiri Japan 36°6N 137°58E 31 F8
Shipchenski Prokhod
  Bulgaria 42°45N 25°15E 23 C11
Shiping China 23°45N 102°23E 32 G9
Shippagan Canada 47°45N 64°45W 73 C7
Shippensburg U.S.A. 40°3N 77°31W 82 F7
Shippenville U.S.A. 41°15N 79°28W 82 E5
Shiprock U.S.A. 36°47N 108°41W 77 H9
Shiqma, N. → Israel 31°37N 34°30E 46 D3
Shiquan China 33°5N 108°15E 34 H5
Shiquan He = Indus →
  Pakistan 24°20N 67°47E 42 G2
Shīr Kūh Iran 31°39N 54°3E 45 D7
Shiragami-Misaki
  Japan 41°24N 140°12E 30 D10
Shirakawa Fukushima,
  Japan 37°7N 140°13E 31 F10
Shirakawa Gifu, Japan 36°17N 136°56E 31 F8
Shirane-San Gumma,
  Japan 36°48N 139°22E 31 F9
Shirane-San Yamanashi,
  Japan 35°42N 138°9E 31 G9
Shiraoi Japan 42°33N 141°21E 30 C10
Shīrāz Iran 29°42N 52°30E 45 D7
Shire → Africa 17°42S 35°19E 55 F4
Shiren China 41°57N 126°34E 35 D14
Shiretoko △ Japan 44°15N 145°15E 30 B12
Shiretoko-Misaki
  Japan 44°21N 145°20E 30 B12
Shirinab → Pakistan 30°15N 66°28E 42 D2
Shiriya-Zaki Japan 41°25N 141°30E 30 D10
Shiroishi Japan 38°0N 140°37E 30 F10
Shirshov Ridge Pac. Oc. 58°0N 170°0E 64 B8
Shīrvān Iran 37°30N 57°50E 45 B8
Shirwa, L. = Chilwa, L.
  Malawi 15°15S 35°40E 55 F4
Shishaldin Volcano
  U.S.A. 54°45N 163°58W 74 E7
Shivamogga = Shimoga
  India 13°57N 75°32E 40 N9
Shivpuri India 25°26N 77°42E 42 G7
Shixian China 43°5N 129°50E 35 C15
Shiyan China 22°42N 113°33E 33 a
Shiyan Shuiku China 22°42N 113°54E 33 a
Shizuishan China 39°15N 106°50E 34 E4
Shizuoka Japan 34°57N 138°24E 31 G9
Shizuoka □ Japan 35°15N 138°40E 31 G9
Shklov = Shklow
  Belarus 54°16N 30°15E 17 A16
Shklow Belarus 54°16N 30°15E 17 A16
Shkodër Albania 42°4N 19°32E 23 C8
Shkumbini → Albania 41°2N 19°31E 23 D8
Shmidta, Ostrov Russia 81°0N 91°0E 29 A10
Shō-Gawa → Japan 36°47N 137°4E 31 F8
Shoal C. Australia 49°33N 95°1W 71 D9
Shoal Lake Canada 50°30N 100°35W 71 C8
Shōdo-Shima Japan 34°30N 134°15E 31 G7
Sholapur = Solapur
  India 17°43N 75°56E 40 L9
Shōmrōn West Bank 32°15N 35°13E 46 C4
Shoreham by Sea U.K. 50°50N 0°16W 13 G7
Shori → Pakistan 28°29N 69°44E 42 E3
Shorkot Pakistan 30°47N 72°15E 42 D5
Shorkot Road Pakistan 30°47N 72°15E 42 D5
Shoshone Calif.,
  U.S.A. 35°58N 116°16W 79 K10
Shoshone Idaho, U.S.A. 42°56N 114°25W 76 E6
Shoshone L. U.S.A. 44°22N 110°43W 76 D8
Shoshone Mts. U.S.A. 39°20N 117°25W 76 G5
Shoshong Botswana 22°56S 26°31E 56 C4
Shouguang China 37°52N 118°45E 35 F10
Shouyang China 37°54N 113°8E 34 F7
Show Low U.S.A. 34°15N 110°2W 77 J8
Shreveport U.S.A. 32°31N 93°45W 84 E8
Shrewsbury U.K. 52°43N 2°45W 13 E5
Shri Mohangarh India 27°17N 71°18E 42 F4
Shrirampur India 22°44N 88°21E 43 H13
Shropshire □ U.K. 52°36N 2°45W 13 E5
Shū Kazakhstan 43°36N 73°42E 28 E8
Shū → Kazakhstan 45°0N 67°44E 28 E7
Shuangcheng China 45°20N 126°15E 35 B14
Shuanggou China 34°2N 117°30E 35 G9
Shuangliao China 43°29N 123°30E 35 C12
Shuangshanzi China 40°20N 119°8E 35 D10
Shuangyang China 43°29N 125°40E 35 C13
Shuangyashan China 46°28N 131°5E 33 B15
Shuguri Falls Tanzania 8°33S 37°22E 54 D4
Shujalpur India 23°18N 76°46E 42 H7
Shukpa Kunzang India 34°22N 78°22E 43 B8
Shulan China 44°28N 127°0E 35 B14
Shule China 39°25N 76°3E 32 D4
Shule He → China 40°20N 92°50E 32 C7
Shumagin Is. U.S.A. 55°7N 160°30W 74 D7
Shumen Bulgaria 43°18N 26°55E 23 C12
Shumikha Russia 55°10N 63°15E 28 D7
Shungnak U.S.A. 66°52N 157°9W 74 B8
Shuo Xian = Shuozhou
  China 39°20N 112°33E 34 E7
Shuozhou China 39°20N 112°33E 34 E7
Shūr → Fārs, Iran 30°52N 57°37E 45 D8
Shūr → Kermān, Iran 30°52N 57°37E 45 D8
Shūr → Yazd, Iran 31°45N 55°15E 45 D7
Shūr Āb Iran 34°23N 51°11E 45 C6
Shūr Gaz Iran 29°10N 59°20E 45 D8
Shūrāb Iran 33°43N 56°29E 45 C8
Shūrjestān Iran 31°24N 52°25E 45 D7
Shūshtar Iran 32°0N 48°50E 45 D6
Shuswap L. Canada 50°55N 119°3W 70 C5
Shute Harbour △
  Australia 20°17S 148°47E 62 b

Shuyang China 34°10N 118°42E 35 G10
Shūzū Iran 29°52N 54°30E 45 D7
Shwebo Burma 22°30N 95°45E 41 H19
Shwegu Burma 24°15N 96°26E 41 G20
Shweli → Burma 23°45N 96°45E 41 H20
Shymkent Kazakhstan 42°18N 69°36E 28 E7
Shyok India 34°13N 78°12E 43 B8
Shyok → Pakistan 35°13N 75°53E 43 B6
Si Kiang = Xi Jiang →
  China 22°5N 113°20E 33 G11
Si Lanna △ Thailand 19°17N 99°12E 38 C2
Si Nakarin Res. Thailand 14°35N 99°0E 38 E2
Si-ngan = Xi'an China 34°15N 109°0E 34 G5
Si Phangnga △ Thailand 9°8N 98°29E 39 H2
Si Prachan Thailand 14°37N 100°9E 38 E3
Si Racha Thailand 13°10N 100°48E 38 F3
Sa Ket Thailand 15°8N 104°23E 38 E5
Siachen Glacier Asia 35°20N 77°30E 43 B7
Siahaf → Pakistan 29°3N 68°57E 42 E3
Siahan Range Pakistan 27°30N 64°40E 40 F4
Siak Sri Indrapura
  Indonesia 0°51N 102°0E 36 D2
Sialkot Pakistan 32°32N 74°30E 42 C6
Siam = Thailand ■ Asia 16°0N 102°0E 38 E4
Sian = Xi'an China 34°15N 109°0E 34 G5
Sian Ka'an △ Mexico 19°35N 87°40W 87 D7
Siantan Indonesia 3°10N 106°15E 36 D3
Siāreh Iran 28°5N 60°14E 45 D9
Siargao I. Phil. 9°52N 126°3E 37 C7
Siasi Phil. 5°34N 120°50E 37 C6
Siau Indonesia 2°50N 125°25E 37 D7
Šiauliai Lithuania 55°56N 23°15E 9 J20
Sibā̄, Gebel el Egypt 25°45N 34°10E 44 E2
Sibang Indonesia 8°34S 115°13E 37 K18
Sibay Russia 52°42N 58°39E 18 D10
Sibayi, L. S. Africa 27°20S 32°45E 57 D5
Šibenik Croatia 43°48N 15°54E 22 C6
Siberia = Sibirskiy □
  Russia 58°0N 90°0E 29 D10
Siberia Russia 60°0N 100°0E 4 D13
Siberut Indonesia 1°30S 99°0E 36 E1
Sibi Pakistan 29°30N 67°54E 42 E2
Sibiloi △ Kenya 4°0N 36°20E 54 B4
Sibirskiy □ Russia 58°0N 90°0E 29 D10
Sibirtsevo Russia 44°12N 132°26E 30 B5
Sibiti Congo 3°38S 13°19E 52 E2
Sibiu Romania 45°45N 24°9E 17 F13
Sibley U.S.A. 43°24N 95°45W 80 D6
Sibolga Indonesia 1°42N 98°45E 36 D1
Siborongborong Indonesia 2°13N 98°58E 39 L2
Sibsagar India 27°0N 94°36E 41 F19
Sibu Malaysia 2°18N 111°49E 36 D4
Sibuco Phil. 7°20N 122°10E 37 C6
Sibuguey B. Phil. 7°50N 122°45E 37 C6
Sibut C.A.R. 5°46N 19°10E 52 C3
Sibutu Phil. 4°45N 119°30E 37 D5
Sibutu Passage E. Indies 4°50N 120°0E 37 D5
Sibuyan I. Phil. 12°25N 122°40E 37 B6
Sibuyan Sea Phil. 12°30N 122°20E 37 B6
Sicamous Canada 50°49N 119°0W 70 C5
Siccus → Australia 31°55S 139°17E 63 E2
Sichon Thailand 9°0N 99°54E 39 H2
Sichuan □ China 30°30N 103°0E 32 E9
Sicilia Italy 37°30N 14°30E 22 F6
Sicily = Sicilia Italy 37°30N 14°30E 22 F6
Sicily, Str. of Medit. S. 37°35N 11°56E 22 F4
Sico → Honduras 15°58N 84°58W 88 C3
Sicuani Peru 14°21S 71°10W 92 F4
Sidári Greece 39°47N 19°41E 25 A3
Siddhapur India 23°56N 72°25E 42 H5
Siddipet India 18°5N 78°51E 40 K11
Sideros, Akra Greece 35°19N 26°19E 25 D8
Sidhauli India 27°17N 80°50E 43 F9
Sidhi India 24°25N 81°53E 43 G9
Sidi-bel-Abbès Algeria 35°13N 0°39W 50 A5
Sidi Ifni Morocco 29°29N 10°12W 50 C3
Sidikalang Indonesia 2°45N 98°19E 39 L2
Sidlaw Hills U.K. 56°32N 3°2W 11 E5
Sidley, Mt. Antarctica 77°2S 126°2W 5 D14
Sidmouth U.K. 50°40N 3°15W 13 G4
Sidmouth, C. Australia 13°25S 143°36E 62 A3
Sidney Canada 48°39N 123°24W 78 B3
Sidney Mont., U.S.A. 47°43N 104°9W 76 C11
Sidney N.Y., U.S.A. 42°19N 75°24W 83 D9
Sidney Nebr., U.S.A. 41°8N 102°59W 80 E2
Sidney Ohio, U.S.A. 40°17N 84°9W 81 E11
Sidney Lanier, L. U.S.A. 34°10N 84°4W 85 D12
Sidoarjo Indonesia 7°27S 112°43E 37 G15
Sidon = Saydā Lebanon 33°35N 35°25E 46 B4
Sidra, G. of = Surt, Khalīj
  Libya 31°40N 18°30E 51 B9
Siedlce Poland 52°10N 22°20E 17 B12
Sieg → Germany 50°46N 7°6E 16 C4
Siegen Germany 50°51N 8°0E 16 C5
Siem Pang Cambodia 14°7N 106°23E 38 E6
Siem Reap = Siemreab
  Cambodia 13°20N 103°52E 38 F4
Siemreab Cambodia 13°20N 103°52E 38 F4
Siena Italy 43°19N 11°21E 22 C4
Sieradz Poland 51°37N 18°41E 17 C10
Sierpe, Bocas de la
  Venezuela 10°0N 61°30W 93 L15
Sierra Blanca U.S.A. 31°11N 105°22W 84 F2
Sierra Blanca Peak
  U.S.A. 33°23N 105°49W 77 K11
Sierra City U.S.A. 39°34N 120°38W 78 F6
Sierra Colorada
  Argentina 40°35S 67°50W 96 E3
Sierra de Agalta △
  Honduras 15°1N 85°48W 88 C2
Sierra de Bahoruco △
  Dom. Rep. 18°10N 71°25W 89 C5
Sierra de La Culata △
  Venezuela 8°45N 71°10W 89 E5
Sierra de Lancandón △
  Guatemala 16°59N 90°23W 88 C1
Sierra de las Quijadas △
  Argentina 32°29S 67°5W 94 C2
Sierra de San Luis △
  Venezuela 11°20N 69°43W 89 D6

Sierra de San Pedro Mártir △
  Mexico   31°10N 115°30W **86** A1
Sierra Gorda *Chile* 22°50S 69°15W **94** A2
Sierra Leone ■ *W. Afr.* 9°0N 12°0W **50** G3
Sierra Madre *Mexico* 16°0N 93°0W **87** D6
Sierra Madre Occidental
  Mexico   27°0N 107°0W **86** B3
Sierra Madre Oriental
  Mexico   25°0N 100°0W **86** C5
Sierra Mojada *Mexico* 27°18N 103°41W **86** B4
Sierra Nevada *Spain* 37°3N 3°15W **21** D4
Sierra Nevada *U.S.A.* 39°0N 120°30W **78** H8
Sierra Nevada △
  Venezuela 8°0N 70°45W **89** E5
Sierra Nevada de Santa Marta △
  Colombia 10°56N 73°36W **89** D5
Sierra Vista *U.S.A.* 31°33N 110°18W **77** L8
Sierraville *U.S.A.* 39°36N 120°22W **78** F6
Sifnos *Greece* 37°0N 24°45E **23** F11
Sifton *Canada* 51°21N 100°8W **71** C8
Sifton Pass *Canada* 57°52N 126°15W **70** B3
Sig *Algeria* 35°32N 0°12W **50** A5
Sigatoka *Fiji* 18°8S 177°32E **59** a
Sighetu-Marmaţiei
  Romania 47°57N 23°52E **17** E12
Sighişoara *Romania* 46°12N 24°50E **17** E13
Sigli *Indonesia* 5°25N 96°0E **36** C1
Siglufjörður *Iceland* 66°12N 18°55W **8** C4
Signal de Botrang *Belgium* 50°29N 6°4E **15** D6
Signal Pk. *U.S.A.* 33°20N 114°2W **79** M12
Signy I. *Antarctica* 60°43S 45°36W **5** C18
Sigsig *Ecuador* 3°0S 78°50W **92** D3
Sigüenza *Spain* 41°3N 2°40W **21** B4
Siguiri *Guinea* 11°31N 9°10W **50** F4
Sigulda *Latvia* 57°10N 24°55E **9** H21
Sihong *China* 33°27N 118°16E **35** H10
Sihora *India* 23°29N 80°6E **43** H9
Siikajoki ➤ *Finland* 64°50N 24°43E **8** D21
Siilinjärvi *Finland* 63°4N 27°39E **8** E22
Sijarira Ra. = Chizarira
  Zimbabwe 17°36S 27°45E **55** F2
Sika *India* 22°26N 69°47E **42** H3
Sikanni Chief ➤
  Canada 57°47N 122°15W **70** B4
Sikao *Thailand* 7°34N 99°21E **39** J2
Sikar *India* 27°33N 75°10E **42** F6
Sikasso *Mali* 11°18N 5°35W **50** F4
Sikeston *U.S.A.* 36°53N 89°35W **80** G9
Sikhote Alin, Khrebet
  Russia 45°0N 136°0E **30** B8
Sikhote Alin Ra. = Sikhote Alin,
  Khrebet *Russia* 45°0N 136°0E **30** B8
Sikinos *Greece* 36°40N 25°8E **23** F11
Sikkim □ *India* 27°50N 88°30E **41** F16
Sil ➤ *Spain* 42°27N 7°43W **21** A2
Silacayoapan *Mexico* 17°30N 98°9W **87** D5
Silawad *India* 21°54N 74°54E **42** J6
Silchar *India* 24°49N 92°48E **41** G18
Siler City *U.S.A.* 35°44N 79°28W **85** D15
Silesia = Śląsk *Poland* 51°0N 16°30E **16** C9
Silgarhi Doti *Nepal* 29°15N 81°0E **43** E9
Silghat *India* 26°35N 93°0E **41** F18
Silhouette *Seychelles* 4°29S 55°12E **53** b
Silifke *Turkey* 36°22N 33°58E **44** B2
Siliguri = Shiliguri *India* 26°45N 88°25E **41** F16
Siling Co *China* 31°50N 89°20E **32** E6
Silistra *Bulgaria* 44°6N 27°19E **23** B12
Silivri *Turkey* 41°4N 28°14E **23** D13
Siljan *Sweden* 60°55N 14°45E **8** F16
Silkeborg *Denmark* 56°10N 9°32E **9** H13
Silkwood *Australia* 17°45S 146°2E **62** B4
Sillajhuay, Cordillera
  Chile 19°46S 68°40W **92** G5
Sillamäe *Estonia* 59°24N 27°45E **9** G22
Silloth *U.K.* 54°52N 3°23W **12** C4
Siloam Springs *U.S.A.* 36°11N 94°32W **84** C7
Silopi *Turkey* 37°15N 42°27E **44** B4
Silsbee *U.S.A.* 30°21N 94°11W **84** F7
Šilutė *Lithuania* 55°21N 21°33E **9** J19
Silvan *Turkey* 38°7N 41°2E **44** B4
Silvani *India* 23°18N 78°25E **43** H8
Silver City *U.S.A.* 32°46N 108°17W **77** K9
Silver Cr. ➤ *U.S.A.* 43°16N 119°13W **76** E4
Silver Creek *U.S.A.* 42°33N 79°10W **82** D5
Silver L. *U.S.A.* 38°39N 120°6W **78** G6
Silver Lake *Calif.,*
  U.S.A. 35°21N 116°7W **79** K10
Silver Lake *Oreg., U.S.A.* 43°8N 121°3W **76** E3
Silvermine Mts. *Ireland* 52°47N 8°15W **10** D3
Silverton *Colo., U.S.A.* 37°49N 107°40W **77** H10
Silverton *Tex., U.S.A.* 34°28N 101°19W **84** D4
Silvies ➤ *U.S.A.* 43°34N 119°2W **76** E4
Simaltala *India* 24°43N 86°33E **43** G12
Simanggang = Bandar Sri Aman
  Malaysia 1°15N 111°32E **36** D4
Simao *China* 22°47N 101°5E **32** G9
Simard, L. *Canada* 47°40N 78°40W **72** C4
Simav *Turkey* 39°4N 28°58E **23** E13
Simav ➤ *Turkey* 40°5N 27°0E **23** D12
Simba *Tanzania* 2°10S 37°36E **54** C4
Simbirsk = Ulyanovsk
  Russia 54°20N 48°25E **18** D8
Simbo *Tanzania* 4°51S 29°41E **54** C2
Simcoe *Canada* 42°50N 80°20W **82** D4
Simcoe, L. *Canada* 44°25N 79°20W **82** B5
Simdega *India* 22°37N 84°31E **43** H11
Simeria *Romania* 45°51N 23°1E **17** F12
Simeulue *Indonesia* 2°45N 95°45E **36** D1
Simferopol *Ukraine* 44°55N 34°3E **19** F5
Simi *Greece* 36°35N 27°50E **23** F12
Simi Valley *U.S.A.* 34°16N 118°47W **79** L8
Simikot *Nepal* 30°0N 81°50E **43** E9
Simla = Shimla *India* 31°2N 77°9E **42** D7
Simlipal △ *India* 21°45N 86°30E **43** J12
Simmie *Canada* 49°56N 108°6W **71** D7
Simmler *U.S.A.* 35°21N 119°59W **79** K7
Simo älv = Simojoki ➤
  Finland 65°35N 25°1E **8** D21
Simojoki ➤ *Finland* 65°35N 25°1E **8** D21
Simojovel *Mexico* 17°12N 92°38W **87** D6
Simonette ➤ *Canada* 55°9N 118°15W **70** B5

Simonstown *S. Africa* 34°14S 18°26E **56** E2
Simpang Empat *Malaysia* 5°27N 100°29E **39** c
Simplonpass *Switz.* 46°15N 8°3E **20** C8
Simpson Desert *Australia* 25°0S 137°0E **62** D2
Simpson Desert △
  Australia 24°59S 138°21E **62** C2
Simpson Pen. *Canada* 68°34N 88°45W **69** D14
Simrishamn *Sweden* 55°33N 14°22E **9** J16
Simsbury *U.S.A.* 41°53N 72°48W **83** E12
Simushir, Ostrov
  Russia 46°50N 152°30E **29** E16
Sin Cowe I. *S. China Sea* 9°53N 114°19E **36** C4
Sina Dhago *Somali Rep.* 5°50N 47°0E **47** F4
Sinabang *Indonesia* 2°30N 96°24E **36** D1
Sinai = Es Sînâ' *Egypt* 29°0N 34°0E **46** F2
Sinai, Mt. = Mûsa, Gebel
  Egypt 28°33N 33°59E **44** D2
Sinaloa □ *Mexico* 25°0N 107°30W **86** C3
Sinaloa de Leyva
  Mexico 25°50N 108°14W **86** B3
Sinarades *Greece* 39°34N 19°51E **25** A3
Sincelejo *Colombia* 9°18N 75°24W **92** B3
Sinch'ang *N. Korea* 40°7N 128°28E **35** D15
Sinch'ŏn *N. Korea* 38°17N 125°21E **35** E13
Sinclair *U.S.A.* 41°47N 107°7W **76** F10
Sinclair Mills *Canada* 54°5N 121°40W **70** C4
Sinclair's B. *U.K.* 58°31N 3°5W **11** C5
Sinclairville *U.S.A.* 42°16N 79°16W **82** D5
Sincorá, Serra do *Brazil* 13°30S 41°0W **93** F10
Sind = Sindh □ *Pakistan* 26°0N 69°0E **42** G3
Sind ➤ *Jammu & Kashmir,*
  India 34°18N 74°45E **43** B6
Sind ➤ *Mad. P., India* 26°26N 79°13E **43** F8
Sind Sagar Doab *Pakistan* 32°0N 71°30E **42** D4
Sindangan *Phil.* 8°10N 123°5E **37** C6
Sindangbarang *Indonesia* 7°27S 107°1E **37** G12
Sinde *Zambia* 17°28S 25°51E **55** F2
Sindh = Indus ➤
  Pakistan 24°20N 67°47E **42** G2
Sindh □ *Pakistan* 26°0N 69°0E **42** G3
Sindri *India* 23°45N 86°42E **43** H12
Sines *Portugal* 37°56N 8°51W **21** D1
Sines, C. de *Portugal* 37°58N 8°53W **21** D1
Sineu *Spain* 39°38N 3°1E **24** B10
Sing Buri *Thailand* 14°53N 100°25E **38** E3
Singa *Sudan* 13°10N 33°57E **51** F12
Singalila △ *India* 27°10N 88°5E **43** F13
Singapore ■ *Asia* 1°17N 103°51E **39** d
Singapore, Straits of *Asia* 1°15N 104°0E **39** d
Singapore Changi ✈ (SIN)
  Singapore 1°23N 103°59E **39** M4
Singaraja *Indonesia* 8°7S 115°6E **37** J18
Singatoka = Sigatoka *Fiji* 18°8S 177°32E **59** a
Singida *Tanzania* 4°49S 34°48E **54** C3
Singida □ *Tanzania* 6°0S 34°30E **54** D3
Singkaling Hkamti
  Burma 26°0N 95°39E **41** G19
Singkang *Indonesia* 4°8S 120°1E **37** E6
Singkawang *Indonesia* 1°0N 108°57E **36** D3
Singkep *Indonesia* 0°30S 104°25E **36** E2
Singkil *Indonesia* 2°17N 97°49E **39** L1
Singkuang *Indonesia* 1°3N 98°55E **39** L2
Singleton *Australia* 32°33S 151°10E **63** E5
Singleton, Mt. *N. Terr.,*
  Australia 22°0S 130°46E **60** D5
Singleton, Mt. *W. Austral.,*
  Australia 29°27S 117°15E **61** E2
Singoli *India* 25°0N 75°22E **42** G6
Singora = Songkhla
  Thailand 7°13N 100°37E **39** J3
Sinhŭng *N. Korea* 40°11N 127°34E **35** D14
Siniscóla *Italy* 40°34N 9°41E **22** D3
Sinjai *Indonesia* 5°7S 120°20E **37** F6
Sinjär *Iraq* 36°19N 41°52E **44** B4
Sinkat *Sudan* 18°55N 36°49E **51** E13
Sinkiang = Xinjiang Uygur
  Zizhiqu □ *China* 42°0N 86°0E **32** C6
Sinmak *N. Korea* 38°25N 126°14E **35** E14
Sinmi-do *N. Korea* 39°33N 124°53E **35** E13
Sinnamary *Fr. Guiana* 5°25N 53°0W **93** B8
Sinni ➤ *Italy* 40°8N 16°41E **22** D7
Sinop *Turkey* 42°1N 35°11E **19** F6
Sinor *India* 21°55N 73°20E **42** J5
Sinp'o *N. Korea* 40°0N 128°13E **35** E15
Sinsk *Russia* 61°8N 126°48E **29** C13
Sintang *Indonesia* 0°5S 111°35E **36** D4
Sinton *U.S.A.* 28°2N 97°31W **84** G6
Sintra *Portugal* 38°47N 9°25W **21** C1
Sinŭiju *N. Korea* 40°5N 124°24E **35** D13
Siocon *Phil.* 7°40N 122°10E **37** C6
Siófok *Hungary* 46°54N 18°3E **17** E10
Sion *Switz.* 46°14N 7°20E **20** C7
Sion Mills *U.K.* 54°48N 7°29W **10** B4
Sionainn = Shannon ➤
  Ireland 52°35N 9°30W **10** D2
Sioux Center *U.S.A.* 43°5N 96°11W **80** D5
Sioux City *U.S.A.* 42°30N 96°24W **80** D5
Sioux Falls *U.S.A.* 43°33N 96°44W **80** D5
Sioux Lookout *Canada* 50°10N 91°50W **72** B1
Sioux Narrows *Canada* 49°25N 94°10W **71** D10
Sipadan *Malaysia* 4°6N 118°38E **37** D5
Siping *China* 43°8N 124°21E **35** C13
Sipiwesk L. *Canada* 55°5N 97°35W **71** B9
Sipra ➤ *India* 23°55N 75°28E **42** H6
Sipura *Indonesia* 2°18S 99°40E **36** E1
Siquia ➤ *Nic.* 12°10N 84°20W **88** D3
Siquijor *Phil.* 9°12N 123°35E **37** C6
Siquirres *Costa Rica* 10°6N 83°30W **88** D3
Şır Abu Nu'ayr *U.A.E.* 25°20N 54°20E **45** E7
Şır Banî Yâs *U.A.E.* 24°19N 52°37E **45** E7
Sir Edward Pellew Group
  Australia 15°40S 137°10E **62** B2
Sir Graham Moore Is.
  Australia 13°53S 126°34E **60** B4
Sir James MacBrien, Mt.
  Canada 62°7N 127°41W **68** E6
Sira ➤ *Norway* 58°23N 6°34E **9** G12
Siracusa *Italy* 37°4N 15°17E **22** F6
Sirajganj *Bangla.* 24°25N 89°47E **43** G13

Sirathu *India* 25°39N 81°19E **43** G9
Sîrdän *Iran* 36°39N 49°12E **45** B6
Siren *U.S.A.* 45°47N 92°24W **80** C7
Sirer *Spain* 38°56N 1°22E **24** C7
Siret ➤ *Romania* 45°24N 28°1E **17** F14
Sirghâyâ *Syria* 33°51N 36°8E **46** B5
Sirikit Res. *Thailand* 17°45N 100°34E **38** C3
Sirinat △ *Thailand* 8°6N 98°17E **39** a
Sirjan *Iran* 29°30N 55°45E **45** D7
Sirmaur *India* 24°51N 81°23E **43** G9
Sirmilik △ *Canada* 72°50N 80°35W **69** C15
Sirohi *India* 24°52N 72°53E **42** G5
Sironj *India* 24°5N 77°39E **42** G7
Síros = Ermoupoli
  Greece 37°28N 24°57E **23** F11
Sirr, Nafud as *Si. Arabia* 25°33N 44°35E **44** E5
Sirretta Pk. *U.S.A.* 35°56N 118°19W **79** K8
Sîrrî *Iran* 25°55N 54°32E **45** E7
Sirsa ➤ *India* 29°33N 75°4E **42** E6
Sirsa ➤ *India* 26°51N 79°4E **43** F8
Sisak *Croatia* 45°30N 16°21E **16** F9
Sishen *S. Africa* 27°47S 22°59E **56** D3
Sishui *China* 35°42N 117°18E **35** G9
Sisipuk L. *Canada* 55°45N 101°50W **71** B8
Sisophon *Cambodia* 13°38N 102°59E **38** F4
Sisseton *U.S.A.* 45°40N 97°3W **80** C5
Sïstän *Asia* 30°50N 61°0W **45** D9
Sïstän, Daryächeh-ye *Iran* 31°0N 61°0E **45** D9
Sïstän va Balüchestän □
  Iran 27°0N 62°0E **45** E9
Sisters *U.S.A.* 44°18N 121°33W **76** D3
Sisters, The *Seychelles* 4°16S 55°52E **53** b
Siswa Bazar *India* 27°9N 83°46E **43** F10
Sitamarhi *India* 26°37N 85°30E **43** F11
Sitampiky *Madag.* 16°41S 46°6E **57** B8
Sitapur *India* 27°38N 80°45E **43** F9
Siteki *Swaziland* 26°32S 31°58E **57** D5
Sitges *Spain* 41°17N 1°47E **21** B6
Sitia *Greece* 35°13N 26°6E **25** D8
Sitito-Ozima Ridge
  Pac. Oc. 23°0N 143°0E **64** E6
Sitka *U.S.A.* 57°3N 135°20W **70** B1
Sittang Myit ➤ *Burma* 17°20N 96°45E **41** L20
Sittard *Neths.* 51°0N 5°52E **15** C5
Sittingbourne *U.K.* 51°21N 0°45E **13** F8
Sittoung = Sittang Myit ➤
  Burma 17°20N 96°45E **41** L20
Sittwe *Burma* 20°18N 92°45E **41** J18
Situbondo *Indonesia* 7°42S 113°56E **37** G16
Si'umu *Samoa* 14°1S 171°48W **59** b
Siuri *India* 23°50N 87°34E **43** H12
Sïvand *Iran* 30°5N 52°55E **45** D7
Sivas *Turkey* 39°43N 36°58E **44** B3
Siverek *Turkey* 37°50N 39°19E **44** B3
Sivomaskinskiy *Russia* 66°40N 62°35E **18** A11
Sivrihisar *Turkey* 39°30N 31°35E **19** G5
Sïwa *Egypt* 29°11N 25°31E **51** C11
Sïwa, El Wâhât es *Egypt* 29°10N 25°30E **48** D6
Siwa Oasis = Sïwa, El Wâhât es
  Egypt 29°10N 25°30E **48** D6
Siwalik Range *Nepal* 28°0N 83°0E **43** F10
Siwan *India* 26°13N 84°21E **43** F11
Siwana *India* 25°38N 72°25E **42** G5
Six Cross Roads *Barbados* 13°7N 59°28W **89** g
Sixian *China* 33°30N 117°50E **35** H9
Sixmilebridge *Ireland* 52°44N 8°46W **10** D3
Sixth Cataract *Sudan* 16°20N 32°42E **51** E12
Siyah Kuh, Kavïr-e *Iran* 32°55N 53°55E **45** C7
Siyang *China* 33°42N 118°40E **35** H10
Siziwang Qi *China* 41°25N 111°40E **34** D6
Sjælland *Denmark* 55°30N 11°30E **9** J14
Sjumen = Shumen
  Bulgaria 43°18N 26°55E **23** C12
Skadarsko Jezero *Europe* 42°10N 19°20E **23** C8
Skaftafell *Iceland* 64°1N 17°0W **8** D5
Skaftafell △ *Iceland* 64°0N 16°50W **8** D5
Skagafjörður *Iceland* 65°54N 19°35W **8** D4
Skagastølstindane
  Norway 61°28N 7°52E **8** F12
Skagaströnd *Iceland* 65°50N 20°19W **8** D3
Skagen *Denmark* 57°43N 10°35E **9** H14
Skagerrak *Denmark* 57°30N 9°0E **9** H13
Skagit ➤ *U.S.A.* 48°23N 122°22W **78** B4
Skagway *U.S.A.* 59°28N 135°19W **68** F4
Skala-Podilska *Ukraine* 48°50N 26°15E **17** D14
Skalat *Ukraine* 49°23N 25°55E **17** D13
Skåne *Sweden* 55°59N 13°30E **9** J15
Skaneateles *U.S.A.* 42°57N 76°26W **83** D8
Skaneateles L. *U.S.A.* 42°51N 76°22W **83** D8
Skardu *Pakistan* 35°20N 75°44E **43** B6
Skarżysko-Kamienna
  Poland 51°7N 20°52E **17** C11
Skeena ➤ *Canada* 54°9N 130°5W **70** C2
Skeena Mts. *Canada* 56°40N 128°30W **70** B3
Skegness *U.K.* 53°9N 0°20E **12** D8
Skeldon = Corriverton
  Guyana 5°55N 57°20W **92** B7
Skeleton Coast *Namibia* 20°0S 13°0E **53** J2
Skeleton Coast △ *Namibia* 20°0S 13°0E **56** C1
Skellefteå *Sweden* 64°45N 20°50E **8** D19
Skellefteälven ➤
  Sweden 64°45N 21°10E **8** D19
Skelleftehamn *Sweden* 64°40N 21°9E **8** D19
Skellig Michael = Great Skellig
  Ireland 51°47N 10°33W **10** E1
Skerries, The *U.K.* 53°25N 4°36W **12** D3
Ski *Norway* 59°43N 10°52E **9** G14
Skiathos *Greece* 39°12N 23°30E **23** E10
Skibbereen *Ireland* 51°33N 9°16W **10** E2
Skiddaw *U.K.* 54°39N 3°9W **12** C4
Skidegate *Canada* 53°15N 132°1W **70** C2
Skien *Norway* 59°12N 9°35E **9** G13
Skierniewice *Poland* 51°58N 20°10E **17** C11
Skikhist, Mt. *Canada* 50°12N 121°54W **70** C4
Skikda *Algeria* 36°50N 6°58E **50** A7
Skilloura *Cyprus* 35°14N 33°10E **25** D12
Skipton *U.K.* 53°58N 2°3W **12** D5
Skirmish Pt. *Australia* 11°59S 134°17E **62** A1
Skiros *Greece* 38°55N 24°34E **23** E11

Skive *Denmark* 56°33N 9°2E **9** H13
Skjálfandafljót ➤ *Iceland* 65°59N 17°25W **8** D5
Skjálfandi *Iceland* 66°5N 17°30W **8** C5
Skole *Ukraine* 49°3N 23°30E **17** D12
Skopelos *Greece* 39°9N 23°47E **23** E10
Skopi *Greece* 35°11N 26°2E **25** D8
Skopje *Macedonia* 42°1N 21°26E **23** C9
Skövde *Sweden* 58°24N 13°50E **9** G15
Skovorodino *Russia* 54°0N 124°0E **29** D13
Skowhegan *U.S.A.* 44°46N 69°43W **81** C19
Skull *Ireland* 51°32N 9°34W **10** E2
Skunk ➤ *U.S.A.* 40°42N 91°7W **80** E8
Skuodas *Lithuania* 56°16N 21°33E **9** H19
Skvyra *Ukraine* 49°44N 29°40E **17** D15
Skye *U.K.* 57°15N 6°10W **11** D2
Skykomish *U.S.A.* 47°42N 121°22W **76** C3
Skyros = Skiros *Greece* 38°55N 24°34E **23** E11
Slade Point *Australia* 21°4S 149°13E **62** b
Slade Pt. *Australia* 21°5S 149°13E **62** b
Slættaratindur *Færoe Is.* 62°18N 7°1W **8** E9
Slagelse *Denmark* 55°23N 11°19E **9** J14
Slamet *Indonesia* 7°16S 109°8E **37** G13
Slane *Ireland* 53°42N 6°33W **10** C5
Slaney ➤ *Ireland* 52°26N 6°33W **10** D5
Slangberge *S. Africa* 31°32S 20°48E **56** E3
Slangberge *S. Africa* 31°32S 20°48E **56** E3
Śląsk *Poland* 51°0N 16°30E **16** C9
Slate Is. *Canada* 48°40N 87°0W **72** C2
Slatina *Romania* 44°28N 24°22E **17** F13
Slatington *U.S.A.* 40°45N 75°37W **83** F9
Slaton *U.S.A.* 33°26N 101°39W **84** E4
Slave ➤ *Canada* 61°18N 113°39W **70** A6
Slave Coast *W. Afr.* 6°0N 2°30E **50** G6
Slave Lake *Canada* 55°17N 114°43W **70** B6
Slave Pt. *Canada* 61°11N 115°56W **70** A5
Slavgorod *Russia* 53°1N 78°37E **28** D8
Slavonski Brod *Croatia* 45°11N 18°1E **23** B8
Slavuta *Ukraine* 50°15N 27°2E **17** C14
Slavyanka *Russia* 42°53N 131°21E **30** C5
Slavyansk = Slovyansk
  Ukraine 48°55N 37°36E **19** E6
Slawharad *Belarus* 53°27N 31°0E **17** B16
Sleaford *U.K.* 53°0N 0°24W **12** D7
Sleaford B. *Australia* 34°55S 135°45E **63** E2
Sleat, Sd. of *U.K.* 57°5N 5°47W **11** D3
Sleeper Is. *Canada* 58°30N 81°0W **69** F15
Sleeping Bear Dunes △
  U.S.A. 44°50N 86°5W **80** C10
Sleepy Eye *U.S.A.* 44°18N 94°43W **80** C6
Slemon L. *Canada* 63°13N 116°4W **70** A5
Slide Mt. *U.S.A.* 42°0N 74°25W **83** E10
Slidell *U.S.A.* 30°17N 89°47W **85** F10
Sliema *Malta* 35°55N 14°30E **25** D2
Slieve Aughty *Ireland* 53°4N 8°30W **10** C3
Slieve Bloom *Ireland* 53°4N 7°40W **10** C4
Slieve Donard *Ireland* 54°11N 5°55W **10** B6
Slieve Gamph *Ireland* 54°6N 9°0W **10** B3
Slieve Gullion *Ireland* 54°7N 6°26W **10** B5
Slieve League *Ireland* 54°40N 8°42W **10** B3
Slieve Mish *Ireland* 52°12N 9°50W **10** D2
Slievenamon *Ireland* 52°25N 7°34W **10** D4
Sligeach = Sligo *Ireland* 54°16N 8°28W **10** B3
Sligo *Ireland* 54°16N 8°28W **10** B3
Sligo *U.S.A.* 41°6N 79°29W **82** E5
Sligo □ *Ireland* 54°8N 8°42W **10** B3
Sligo B. *Ireland* 54°18N 8°40W **10** B3
Slippery Rock *U.S.A.* 41°4N 80°3W **82** E4
Slite *Sweden* 57°42N 18°48E **9** H18
Sliven *Bulgaria* 42°42N 26°19E **23** C12
Sloan *U.S.A.* 35°57N 115°13W **79** K11
Sloansville *U.S.A.* 42°45N 74°22W **83** D10
Slobodskoy *Russia* 58°40N 50°6E **18** C9
Slobozia *Romania* 44°34N 27°23E **17** F14
Slocan *Canada* 49°48N 117°28W **70** D5
Slonim *Belarus* 53°4N 25°19E **17** B13
Slough *U.K.* 51°30N 0°36W **13** F7
Slough □ *U.K.* 51°30N 0°36W **13** F7
Sloughhouse *U.S.A.* 38°26N 121°12W **78** G5
Slovak Rep. ■ *Europe* 48°30N 20°0E **17** D10
Slovakia = Slovak Rep. ■
  Europe 48°30N 20°0E **17** D10
Slovakian Ore Mts. = Slovenské
  Rudohorie *Slovak Rep.* 48°45N 20°0E **17** D10
Slovenia ■ *Europe* 45°58N 14°30E **16** F8
Slovenija = Slovenia ■
  Europe 45°58N 14°30E **16** F8
Slovenská = Slovak Rep. ■
  Europe 48°30N 20°0E **17** D10
Slovenské Rudohorie
  Slovak Rep. 48°45N 20°0E **17** D10
Slovyansk *Ukraine* 48°55N 37°36E **19** E6
Sluch ➤ *Ukraine* 51°37N 26°38E **17** C14
Sluis *Neths.* 51°18N 3°23E **15** C3
Słupsk *Poland* 54°30N 17°3E **17** A9
Slurry *S. Africa* 25°49S 25°42E **56** D4
Slutsk *Belarus* 53°2N 27°31E **17** B14
Slyne Hd. *Ireland* 53°25N 10°10W **10** C1
Slyudyanka *Russia* 51°40N 103°40E **29** D11
Småland *Sweden* 57°15N 15°25E **9** H16
Smalltree L. *Canada* 61°0N 105°0W **71** A8
Smallwood Res. *Canada* 54°5N 64°30W **73** B7
Smarhon *Belarus* 54°20N 26°24E **17** A14
Smartt Syndicate Dam
  S. Africa 30°45S 23°10E **56** E3
Smartville *U.S.A.* 39°13N 121°18W **78** F5
Smeaton *Canada* 53°30N 104°49W **71** C8
Smederevo *Serbia* 44°40N 20°57E **23** B9
Smerwick Harbour
  Ireland 52°12N 10°23W **10** D1
Smethport *U.S.A.* 41°49N 78°27W **82** E6
Smidovich *Russia* 48°37N 133°49E **29** E14
Smith *Canada* 55°10N 114°0W **70** B6
Smith Center *U.S.A.* 39°47N 98°47W **80** F4
Smith I. *Canada* 60°45N 78°25W **69** E16
Smith Islands △ *Australia* 20°40S 149°9E **62** b
Smith River *U.S.A.* 45°51N 124°0W **76** F1
Smithburne ➤ *Australia* 17°3S 140°57E **62** B3
Smithers *Canada* 54°45N 127°10W **70** C3
Smithfield *S. Africa* 30°9S 26°30E **56** E4
Smithfield *N.C., U.S.A.* 35°31N 78°21W **85** D15
Smithfield *Utah, U.S.A.* 41°50N 111°50W **76** F8

Smiths Falls *Canada* 44°55N 76°0W **83** B9
Smithton *Australia* 40°53S 145°6E **63** G4
Smithville *Canada* 43°6N 79°33W **82** C5
Smithville *U.S.A.* 30°1N 97°10W **84** F6
Smoke Creek Desert
  U.S.A. 40°30N 119°40W **76** F4
Smoky ➤ *Canada* 56°10N 117°21W **70** B5
Smoky Bay *Australia* 32°22S 134°13E **63** E1
Smoky Hill ➤ *U.S.A.* 39°4N 96°48W **80** F5
Smoky Hills *U.S.A.* 39°15N 99°30W **80** F4
Smoky Lake *Canada* 54°10N 112°30W **70** C6
Smøla *Norway* 63°23N 8°3E **8** E13
Smolensk *Russia* 54°45N 32°5E **18** D5
Smolikas, Oros *Greece* 40°9N 20°58E **23** D9
Smolyan *Bulgaria* 41°36N 24°38E **23** D11
Smooth Rock Falls
  Canada 49°17N 81°37W **72** C3
Smoothstone L. *Canada* 54°40N 106°50W **71** C7
Smorgon = Smarhon
  Belarus 54°20N 26°24E **17** A14
Smyrna = İzmir *Turkey* 38°25N 27°8E **23** E12
Smyrna *U.S.A.* 39°18N 75°36W **81** F16
Snæfell *Iceland* 64°48N 15°34W **8** D6
Snaefell *I. of Man* 54°16N 4°27W **12** C3
Snæfellsjökull *Iceland* 64°49N 23°46W **8** D2
Snake ➤ *U.S.A.* 46°12N 119°2W **76** C4
Snake I. *Australia* 38°47S 146°33E **63** F4
Snake Range *U.S.A.* 39°0N 114°20W **76** G6
Snake River Plain
  U.S.A. 42°50N 114°0W **76** E7
Snåsavatnet *Norway* 64°12N 12°0E **8** D15
Sneek *Neths.* 53°2N 5°40E **15** A5
Sneem *Ireland* 51°50N 9°54W **10** E2
Sneeuberge *S. Africa* 31°46S 24°20E **56** E3
Snelling *U.S.A.* 37°31N 120°26W **78** H6
Snežka *Europe* 50°41N 15°50E **16** C8
Snizort, L. *U.K.* 57°33N 6°28W **11** D2
Snøhetta *Norway* 62°19N 9°16E **8** E13
Snohomish *U.S.A.* 47°55N 122°6W **78** C4
Snoqualmie Pass
  U.S.A. 47°25N 121°25W **78** C5
Snoul *Cambodia* 12°4N 106°26E **39** F6
Snover *U.S.A.* 43°27N 82°58W **82** C2
Snow Hill *U.S.A.* 38°11N 75°24W **81** F16
Snow Lake *Canada* 54°52N 100°3W **71** C8
Snow Mt. *Calif., U.S.A.* 39°23N 122°45W **78** F4
Snow Mt. *Maine, U.S.A.* 45°18N 70°48W **83** A14
Snow Shoe *U.S.A.* 41°2N 77°57W **82** E7
Snowbird L. *Canada* 60°45N 103°0W **71** A8
Snowdon *U.K.* 53°4N 4°5W **12** D3
Snowdonia △ *U.K.* 53°7N 3°59W **12** D4
Snowdrift = Łutsel K'e
  Canada 62°24N 110°44W **71** A6
Snowdrift ➤ *Canada* 62°24N 110°44W **71** A6
Snowflake *U.S.A.* 34°30N 110°5W **77** J8
Snowshoe Pk. *U.S.A.* 48°13N 115°41W **76** B6
Snowtown *Australia* 33°46S 138°14E **63** E2
Snowville *U.S.A.* 41°58N 112°43W **76** F7
Snowy ➤ *Australia* 37°46S 148°30E **63** F4
Snowy Mt. *U.S.A.* 43°42N 74°23W **83** C10
Snowy Mts. *Australia* 36°30S 148°20E **63** F4
Snug Corner *Bahamas* 22°33N 73°52W **89** B5
Snug Harbour *Canada* 45°22N 80°17W **82** A4
Snyatyn *Ukraine* 48°27N 25°38E **17** D13
Snyder *Okla., U.S.A.* 34°40N 98°57W **84** D5
Snyder *Tex., U.S.A.* 32°44N 100°55W **84** E4
Soahanina *Madag.* 18°42S 44°13E **57** B7
Soalala *Madag.* 16°6S 45°20E **57** B8
Soaloka *Madag.* 18°32S 45°15E **57** B8
Soamanonga *Madag.* 23°52S 44°47E **57** C7
Soan ➤ *Pakistan* 33°1N 71°44E **42** C4
Soanierana-Ivongo
  Madag. 16°55S 49°35E **57** B8
Soanindraniny *Madag.* 19°54S 47°14E **57** B8
Soavina *Madag.* 20°23S 46°56E **57** C8
Soavinandriana *Madag.* 19°9S 46°45E **57** B8
Sobat, Nahr ➤ *Sudan* 9°22N 31°33E **51** G12
Sobhapur *India* 22°47N 78°17E **42** H8
Sobradinho, Represa de
  Brazil 9°30S 42°0W **93** E10
Sobral *Brazil* 3°50S 40°20W **93** D10
Soc Giang *Vietnam* 22°54N 106°1E **38** A6
Soc Trang *Vietnam* 9°37N 105°50E **39** H5
Socastee *U.S.A.* 33°41N 78°59W **85** E15
Soch'e = Shache *China* 38°20N 77°10E **32** D4
Sochi *Russia* 43°35N 39°40E **19** F6
Société, Îs. de la
  French Polynesia 17°0S 151°0W **65** J12
Society Is. = Société, Îs. de la
  French Polynesia 17°0S 151°0W **65** J12
Socompa, Portezuelo de
  Chile 24°27S 68°18W **94** A2
Socorro *N. Mex., U.S.A.* 34°4N 106°54W **77** J10
Socorro *Tex., U.S.A.* 31°39N 106°18W **84** F1
Socorro, I. *Mexico* 18°45N 110°58W **86** D2
Socotra *Yemen* 12°30N 54°0E **47** E5
Soda L. *U.S.A.* 35°10N 116°4W **77** J5
Soda Plains *India* 35°30N 79°0E **43** B8
Soda Springs *U.S.A.* 42°39N 111°36W **76** E8
Sodankylä *Finland* 67°29N 26°40E **8** C22
Soddy-Daisy *U.S.A.* 35°17N 85°10W **85** D12
Söderhamn *Sweden* 61°18N 17°10E **8** F17
Söderköping *Sweden* 58°31N 16°20E **9** G17
Södermanland *Sweden* 58°56N 16°55E **9** G17
Södertälje *Sweden* 59°12N 17°39E **9** G17
Sodiri *Sudan* 14°27N 29°0E **51** F11
Sodus *U.S.A.* 43°14N 77°4W **82** C7
Sodwana Bay △ *S. Africa* 27°35S 32°43E **57** D5
Soe *Indonesia* 9°52S 124°17E **60** A3
Soekmekaar = Morebeng
  S. Africa 23°30S 29°55E **57** C4
Soest *Neths.* 52°9N 5°19E **15** B5
Sofala □ *Mozam.* 19°30S 34°30E **57** B5
Sofia □ = Sofiya *Bulgaria* 42°45N 23°20E **23** C10
Sofia ➤ *Madag.* 15°27S 47°23E **57** B8
Sofiya *Bulgaria* 42°45N 23°20E **23** C10
Sōfu-Gan *Japan* 29°49N 140°21E **31** K10
Sogamoso *Colombia* 5°43N 72°56W **92** B4
Sogār *Iran* 25°53N 58°6E **45** E8
Sogndalsfjøra *Norway* 61°14N 7°5E **8** F12

Søgne *Norway* 58°5N 7°48E **9** G12
Sognefjorden *Norway* 61°10N 5°50E **8** F11
Soh *Iran* 33°26N 51°27E **45** C6
Sohâg *Egypt* 26°33N 31°43E **51** C12
Sohagpur *India* 22°42N 78°12E **42** H8
Soignies *Belgium* 50°35N 4°5E **15** D4
Soissons *France* 49°25N 3°19E **20** B5
Sōja *Japan* 34°40N 133°45E **31** G6
Sojat *India* 25°55N 73°45E **42** G5
Sokal *Ukraine* 50°31N 24°15E **17** C13
Sokcho *S. Korea* 38°12N 128°36E **35** E11
Söke *Turkey* 37°48N 27°28E **23** F12
Sokelo
  Dem. Rep. of the Congo 9°55S 24°36E **55** D1
Sokhumi *Georgia* 43°0N 41°0E **19** F7
Soko Is. *China* 22°10N 113°54E **33** a
Sokodé *Togo* 9°0N 1°11E **50** G6
Sokol *Russia* 59°30N 40°5E **18** C7
Sokółka *Poland* 53°25N 23°30E **17** B12
Sokołów Podlaski
  Poland 52°25N 22°15E **17** B12
Sokoto *Nigeria* 13°2N 5°16E **50** F7
Sokoto → *Nigeria* 8°13S 115°24E **37** J18
Sol Iletsk *Russia* 51°10N 55°0E **18** D10
Solai *India* 0°2N 36°12E **54** B4
Solan *India* 30°55N 77°7E **42** D7
Solana Beach *U.S.A.* 32°58N 117°16W **79** N9
Solander I. *N.Z.* 46°34S 166°54E **59** G1
Solapur *India* 17°43N 75°56E **40** L9
Soldotna *U.S.A.* 60°29N 151°3W **68** E1
Soléa *Cyprus* 35°5N 33°4E **25** D12
Soledad *Colombia* 10°55N 74°46W **92** A4
Soledad *U.S.A.* 36°26N 121°20W **78** J5
Soledad *Venezuela* 8°10N 63°34W **92** B6
Solent, The *U.K.* 50°45N 1°25W **13** G6
Solfonntaggen *Norway* 60°2N 6°57E **9** F12
Solhan *Turkey* 38°57N 41°3E **44** B4
Soligalich *Russia* 59°5N 42°10E **18** C7
Soligorsk = Salihorsk
  Belarus 52°51N 27°27E **17** B14
Solihull *U.K.* 52°26N 1°47W **13** E6
Solikamsk *Russia* 59°38N 56°50E **18** C10
Solila *Madag.* 21°25S 46°37E **57** C8
Solimões = Amazonas →
  S. Amer. 0°5S 50°0W **93** D8
Solingen *Germany* 51°10N 7°5E **16** C4
Sollefteå *Sweden* 63°12N 17°20E **8** E17
Sóller *Spain* 39°46N 2°43E **24** B9
Solo → *Indonesia* 6°47S 112°22E **37** G15
Sologne *France* 47°40N 1°45E **20** C4
Solok *Indonesia* 0°45S 100°40E **36** E2
Sololá *Guatemala* 14°49N 91°10W **88** D1
Sololo *Kenya* 3°33N 38°39E **54** B4
Solomon, N. Fork →
  U.S.A. 39°29N 98°26W **80** F4
Solomon, S. Fork →
  U.S.A. 39°25N 99°12W **80** F4
Solomon Is. ■ *Pac. Oc.* 6°0S 155°0E **58** B8
Solomon Rise *Pac. Oc.* 1°0N 157°0E **64** G7
Solon *China* 46°32N 121°10E **33** B13
Solon Springs *U.S.A.* 46°22N 91°49W **80** B8
Solor *Indonesia* 8°27S 123°0E **37** F6
Solothurn *Switz.* 47°13N 7°32E **20** C7
Šolta *Croatia* 43°24N 16°15E **22** C7
Solţānābād *Khorāsān,*
  Iran 34°13N 59°58E **45** C8
Solţānābād *Khorāsān, Iran* 36°29N 58°5E **45** B8
Solunska Glava
  Macedonia 41°44N 21°31E **23** D9
Solvang *U.S.A.* 34°36N 120°8W **79** L6
Solvay *U.S.A.* 43°3N 76°13W **83** C8
Sölvesborg *Sweden* 56°5N 14°35E **9** H16
Solvychegodsk *Russia* 61°21N 46°56E **18** B8
Solway Firth *U.K.* 54°49N 3°35W **12** C4
Solwezi *Zambia* 12°11S 26°21E **55** E2
Sōma *Japan* 37°40N 140°50E **30** F10
Soma *Turkey* 39°10N 27°35E **23** E12
Somabhula *Zimbabwe* 19°42S 29°40E **57** B4
Somali Pen. *Africa* 7°0N 46°0E **48** F8
Somali Rep. ■ *Africa* 7°0N 47°0E **47** F4
Somalia = Somali Rep. ■
  Africa 7°0N 47°0E **47** F4
Somaliland □ *Somali Rep.* 9°0N 46°0E **47** F4
Sombor *Serbia* 45°46N 19°9E **23** B8
Sombra *Canada* 42°43N 82°29W **82** D2
Sombrerete *Mexico* 23°38N 103°39W **86** C4
Sombrero *Anguilla* 18°37N 63°30W **89** C7
Somdari *India* 25°47N 72°38E **42** G5
Somers *U.S.A.* 48°5N 114°13W **76** B6
Somerset *Ky., U.S.A.* 37°5N 84°36W **81** G11
Somerset *Mass., U.S.A.* 41°47N 71°8W **83** E13
Somerset *Pa., U.S.A.* 40°1N 79°5W **82** F5
Somerset □ *U.K.* 51°9N 3°0W **13** F5
Somerset East *S. Africa* 32°42S 25°35E **56** E4
Somerset I. *Canada* 73°30N 93°0W **68** C13
Somerset West *S. Africa* 34°8S 18°50E **56** E2
Somersworth *U.S.A.* 43°16N 70°52W **83** C14
Somerton *U.S.A.* 32°36N 114°43W **77** K6
Somerville *U.S.A.* 40°35N 74°38W **83** F10
Someş → *Romania* 47°49N 22°43E **17** D12
Somme → *France* 50°11N 1°38E **20** A4
Somnath *India* 20°53N 70°22E **42** J4
Somosierra, Puerto de
  Spain 41°4N 3°35W **21** B4
Somosomo *Fiji* 16°47S 179°58W **59** a
Somosomo Str. *Fiji* 16°0S 180°0E **59** a
Somoto *Nic.* 13°28N 86°37W **88** D2
Somport, Túnel de *Spain* 42°48N 0°31W **20** E3
Son → *India* 25°42N 84°52E **43** G11
Son Ha *Vietnam* 15°3N 108°34E **38** E7
Son La *Vietnam* 21°20N 103°50E **38** B4
Son Morrell *Spain* 39°44N 3°20E **24** B10
Son Rapinya *Spain* 39°35N 2°37E **24** B9
Son Sardina *Spain* 39°37N 2°40E **24** B9
Son Serra *Spain* 39°43N 3°13E **24** B10
Son Tay *Vietnam* 21°8N 105°30E **38** B5
Son Tinh *Vietnam* 15°10N 108°40E **38** E7
Soná *Panama* 8°0N 81°20W **88** E3
Sonamarg *India* 34°18N 75°21E **43** B6
Sonamukhi *India* 23°18N 87°27E **43** H12

Sonar → *India* 24°24N 79°56E **43** G8
Sŏnch'ŏn *N. Korea* 39°48N 124°55E **35** E13
Sondags → *S. Africa* 33°44S 25°51E **56** E4
Sønderborg *Denmark* 54°55N 9°49E **9** J13
Sóndrio *Italy* 46°10N 9°52E **20** C8
Sone *Mozam.* 17°23S 34°55E **55** F3
Sonepur *India* 20°55N 83°50E **41** J13
Song *Thailand* 18°28N 100°11E **38** C3
Song Cau *Vietnam* 13°27N 109°18E **38** F7
Song Ma *Vietnam* 20°56N 103°53E **38** B4
Song Xian *China* 34°12N 112°8E **34** G7
Songan *Indonesia* 8°13S 115°24E **37** J18
Songea *Tanzania* 10°40S 35°40E **55** E4
Songgang *China* 22°46N 113°50E **33** a
Songhua Hu *China* 43°35N 126°50E **35** C14
Songhua Jiang →
  China 47°45N 132°30E **33** B15
Songimvelo △ *S. Africa* 25°50S 31°2E **57** D5
Songjianghe *China* 42°10N 127°29E **35** C14
Söngjin = Kimch'aek
  N. Korea 40°40N 129°10E **35** D15
Songkhla *Thailand* 7°13N 100°37E **39** J3
Songnim *N. Korea* 38°45N 125°39E **35** E13
Songo *Mozam.* 15°34S 32°38E **55** F3
Songpan *China* 32°40N 103°30E **32** E9
Songwe
  Dem. Rep. of the Congo 3°20S 26°16E **54** C2
Songwe → *Africa* 9°44S 33°58E **55** D3
Sonhat *India* 23°29N 82°31E **43** H10
Sonid Youqi *China* 42°45N 112°48E **34** C7
Sonid Zuoqi *China* 43°50N 113°42E **34** C7
Sonipat *India* 29°0N 77°5E **42** E7
Sonkach *India* 22°59N 76°21E **42** H7
Sonmiani *Pakistan* 25°25N 66°40E **42** G2
Sonmiani B. *Pakistan* 25°15N 66°30E **42** G2
Sono → *Brazil* 9°58S 48°11W **93** E9
Sonoma *U.S.A.* 38°18N 122°28W **78** G4
Sonora *Calif., U.S.A.* 37°59N 120°23W **78** H6
Sonora *Tex., U.S.A.* 30°34N 100°39W **84** F4
Sonora □ *Mexico* 29°20N 110°40W **86** B2
Sonora → *Mexico* 29°5N 110°55W **86** B2
Sonoran Desert
  U.S.A. 33°40N 113°30W **79** L12
Sonoyta *Mexico* 31°51N 112°50W **86** A2
Sonsonate *El Salv.* 13°43N 89°44W **88** D2
Soochow = Suzhou
  China 31°19N 120°38E **33** E13
Sooke *Canada* 48°13N 123°43W **78** B3
Soomaaliya = Somali Rep. ■
  Africa 7°0N 47°0E **47** F4
Sop Hao *Laos* 20°33N 104°27E **38** B5
Sop Prap *Thailand* 17°53N 99°20E **38** D2
Sopi *Indonesia* 2°34N 128°28E **37** D7
Sopot *Poland* 54°27N 18°31E **17** A10
Sopron *Hungary* 47°45N 16°32E **17** E9
Sopur *India* 34°18N 74°27E **43** B6
Sør-Rondane *Antarctica* 72°0S 25°0E **5** D4
Sorah *Pakistan* 27°13N 68°56E **42** F3
Soraon *India* 25°37N 81°51E **43** G9
Sord = Swords *Ireland* 53°28N 6°13W **10** C5
Sorel-Tracy *Canada* 46°0N 73°10W **72** C5
Sórgono *Italy* 40°1N 9°6E **22** D3
Soria *Spain* 41°43N 2°32W **21** B4
Soriano *Uruguay* 33°24S 58°19W **94** C4
Soroca *Moldova* 48°8N 28°12E **17** D15
Sorocaba *Brazil* 23°31S 47°27W **95** A6
Sorochinsk *Russia* 52°26N 53°10E **18** D9
Soroki = Soroca *Moldova* 48°8N 28°12E **17** D15
Sorong *Indonesia* 0°55S 131°15E **37** E8
Soroni *Greece* 36°21N 28°1E **25** C10
Soroti *Uganda* 1°43N 33°35E **54** B3
Sørøya *Norway* 70°40N 22°30E **8** A20
Sørøysundet *Norway* 70°25N 23°0E **8** A20
Sorrell *Australia* 42°47S 147°34E **63** G4
Sorrento *Italy* 40°37N 14°22E **22** D6
Sorsele *Sweden* 65°31N 17°30E **8** D17
Sorsogon *Phil.* 13°0N 124°0E **37** B6
Sortavala *Russia* 61°42N 30°41E **8** F24
Sortland *Norway* 68°42N 15°25E **8** B16
Soscumica, L. *Canada* 50°15N 77°27W **72** B4
Sosnogorsk *Russia* 63°37N 53°51E **18** B9
Sosnowiec *Poland* 50°20N 19°10E **17** C10
Sossus Vlei *Namibia* 24°40S 15°23E **56** C2
Sōsura *N. Korea* 42°16N 130°36E **35** C16
Sot → *India* 27°27N 79°37E **43** F8
Sotavento *C. Verde Is.* 15°0N 25°0W **50** b
Sotik *Kenya* 0°41S 35°7E **54** C4
Soto la Marina *Mexico* 23°46N 98°13W **87** C5
Soto la Marina →
  Mexico 23°45N 97°45W **87** C5
Sotuta *Mexico* 20°36N 89°1W **87** C7
Souanké *Congo* 2°10N 14°3E **52** D2
Souda *Greece* 35°29N 24°4E **25** D6
Soudas, Ormos *Greece* 35°25N 24°10E **25** D6
Souderton *U.S.A.* 40°19N 75°19W **83** F9
Soufrière *Guadeloupe* 16°5N 61°40W **88** b
Soufrière *St. Lucia* 13°51N 61°3W **89** f
Soufrière Bay *Dominica* 15°13N 61°22W **89** f
Soukhouma *Laos* 14°38N 105°48E **38** E5
Sŏul = Seoul *S. Korea* 37°31N 126°58E **35** F14
Sound, The *U.K.* 50°20N 4°10W **13** G3
Sources, Mt. aux *Lesotho* 28°45S 28°50E **57** D4
Soure *Brazil* 0°35S 48°30W **93** D9
Souris *Man., Canada* 49°40N 100°20W **71** D8
Souris *P.E.I., Canada* 46°21N 62°15W **73** C7
Souris → *N. Amer.* 49°40N 99°34W **80** A4
Sousa *Brazil* 6°45S 38°10W **93** E11
Sousse *Tunisia* 35°50N 10°38E **51** A8
Sout → *S. Africa* 31°35S 18°24E **56** E2
South Africa ■ *Africa* 32°0S 23°0E **56** E3
South America 10°0S 60°0W **90** E5
South Aulatsivik I.
  Canada 56°45N 61°30W **73** A7
South Australia □
  Australia 32°0S 139°0E **63** E2
South Australian Basin
  Ind. Oc. 38°0S 126°0E **64** L4

South Baldy Pk. *U.S.A.* 34°6N 107°11W **77** J10
South Bass I. *U.S.A.* 41°39N 82°49W **82** E2
South Bend *Ind., U.S.A.* 41°41N 86°15W **80** E10
South Bend *Wash.,*
  U.S.A. 46°40N 123°48W **78** D3
South Boston *U.S.A.* 36°42N 78°54W **81** G14
South Branch *Canada* 47°55N 59°2W **73** C8
South Brook *Canada* 49°26N 56°5W **73** C8
South Bruny I. *Australia* 43°20S 147°15E **63** G4
South Carolina □ *U.S.A.* 34°0N 81°0W **85** E14
South Charleston
  U.S.A. 38°22N 81°44W **81** F13
South China Sea *Asia* 10°0N 113°0E **36** C4
South Cumberland Is. △
  Australia 20°42S 149°11E **62** b
South Dakota □ *U.S.A.* 44°15N 100°0W **80** C4
South Dayton *U.S.A.* 42°21N 79°3W **82** D5
South Deerfield *U.S.A.* 42°29N 72°37W **83** D12
South Downs *U.K.* 50°52N 0°25W **13** G7
South Downs △ *U.K.* 50°50N 0°50W **13** G7
South East C. *Australia* 43°40S 146°50E **63** G4
South East Is. *Australia* 34°17S 123°30E **61** F3
South Esk → *U.K.* 56°43N 2°31W **11** E6
South Fiji Basin *Pac. Oc.* 26°0S 175°0E **64** K9
South Fork American →
  U.S.A. 38°57N 120°59W **78** G5
South Fork Feather →
  U.S.A. 39°17N 121°36W **78** F5
South Fork Grand →
  U.S.A. 45°43N 102°17W **80** C2
South Fork Milk →
  U.S.A. 48°4N 106°19W **76** B10
South Fork Republican →
  U.S.A. 40°3N 101°31W **80** E3
South Georgia *Antarctica* 54°30S 37°0W **96** G9
South Gloucestershire □
  U.K. 51°32N 2°28W **13** F5
South Hadley *U.S.A.* 42°16N 72°35W **83** D12
South Haven *U.S.A.* 42°24N 86°16W **80** D10
South Henik L. *Canada* 61°30N 97°20W **71** A9
South Horr *Kenya* 2°12N 36°56E **54** B4
South I. *Kenya* 2°35N 36°35E **54** B4
South I. *N.Z.* 44°0S 170°0E **59** F3
South Indian Lake
  Canada 56°47N 98°56W **71** B9
South Invercargill *N.Z.* 46°26S 168°23E **59** G2
South Island △ *Kenya* 2°39N 36°35E **54** B4
South Kitui △ *Kenya* 1°48S 38°46E **54** C4
South Knife → *Canada* 58°55N 94°37W **71** B10
South Koel → *India* 22°32N 85°14E **43** H11
South Korea ■ *Asia* 36°0N 128°0E **35** G15
South Lake Tahoe
  U.S.A. 38°57N 119°59W **78** G6
South Lanarkshire □
  U.K. 55°37N 3°53W **11** F5
South Loup → *U.S.A.* 41°4N 98°39W **80** E4
South Luangwa △ *Zambia* 13°0S 31°20E **55** E3
South Magnetic Pole
  Antarctica 64°8S 138°8E **5** C9
South Milwaukee
  U.S.A. 42°55N 87°52W **80** D10
South Molton *U.K.* 51°1N 3°51W **13** F4
South Moose L. *Canada* 53°49N 100°1W **71** C8
South Nahanni →
  Canada 61°3N 123°21W **70** A4
South Nation → *Canada* 45°34N 75°6W **83** A9
South Natuna Is. = Natuna
  Selatan, Kepulauan
  Indonesia 2°45N 109°0E **36** D3
South Negril Pt. *Jamaica* 18°16N 78°22W **88** a
South Orkney Is.
  Antarctica 63°0S 45°0W **5** C18
South Ossetia □ *Georgia* 42°21N 44°2E **19** F7
South Otselic *U.S.A.* 42°38N 75°46W **83** D9
South Pagai, I. = Pagai Selatan,
  Pulau *Indonesia* 3°0S 100°15E **36** E2
South Paris *U.S.A.* 44°14N 70°31W **83** B14
South Pittsburg *U.S.A.* 35°1N 85°42W **85** D12
South Platte → *U.S.A.* 41°7N 100°42W **80** E4
South Pole *Antarctica* 90°0S 0°0 **5** E
South Porcupine *Canada* 48°30N 81°12W **72** C3
South Portland *U.S.A.* 43°38N 70°15W **81** D18
South Pt. *Barbados* 13°2N 59°32W **89** g
South Pt. *U.S.A.* 44°52N 83°19W **82** B1
South River *Canada* 45°52N 79°23W **72** C4
South River *U.S.A.* 40°27N 74°23W **83** F10
South Ronaldsay *U.K.* 58°48N 2°58W **11** C6
South Rukuru → *Malawi* 10°44S 34°14E **55** E3
South Sandwich Is.
  Antarctica 57°0S 27°0W **5** B1
South Sandwich Trench
  Atl. Oc. 56°0S 24°0W **5** B1
South Saskatchewan →
  Canada 53°15N 105°5W **71** C7
South Seal → *Canada* 58°48N 98°8W **71** B9
South Shetland Is.
  Antarctica 62°0S 59°0W **5** C18
South Shields *U.K.* 55°0N 1°25W **12** C6
South Sioux City *U.S.A.* 42°28N 96°24W **80** D5
South Sister *U.S.A.* 44°4N 121°51W **76** D3
South Taranaki Bight
  N.Z. 39°40S 174°5E **59** C5
South Tasman Rise
  S. Ocean 48°0S 146°0E **5** A10
South Thompson →
  Canada 50°40N 120°20W **70** C4
South Twin I. *Canada* 53°7N 79°52W **72** B4
South Tyne → *U.K.* 54°59N 2°8W **12** C5
South Uist *U.K.* 57°20N 7°15W **11** D1
South Valley *U.S.A.* 35°1N 106°41W **77** J10
South Wellesley Is.
  Australia 16°58S 139°17E **62** B2
South West C. *Australia* 43°34S 146°3E **63** G4
South West C. *N.Z.* 47°17S 167°28E **59** G1
South Williamsport
  U.S.A. 41°13N 77°0W **82** E8
South Yorkshire □ *U.K.* 53°27N 1°36W **12** D6
Southampton *Canada* 44°30N 81°25W **82** B3
Southampton *U.K.* 50°54N 1°23W **13** G6

Southampton *U.S.A.* 40°53N 72°23W **83** F12
Southampton □ *U.K.* 50°54N 1°23W **13** G6
Southampton I. *Canada* 64°30N 84°0W **69** E15
Southaven *U.S.A.* 34°59N 90°0W **85** D9
Southbank *Canada* 54°2N 125°46W **70** C3
Southbridge *N.Z.* 43°48S 172°16E **59** E4
Southbridge *U.S.A.* 42°5N 72°2W **83** D12
Southend *Canada* 56°19N 103°22W **71** B8
Southend-on-Sea *U.K.* 51°32N 0°44E **13** F8
Southend-on-Sea □ *U.K.* 51°32N 0°44E **13** F8
Southern = Yuzhnyy □
  Russia 44°0N 40°0E **28** E5
Southern □ *Malawi* 15°0S 35°0E **55** F4
Southern □ *Zambia* 16°20S 26°20E **55** F2
Southern Alps *N.Z.* 43°41S 170°11E **59** E3
Southern Cross
  Australia 31°12S 119°15E **61** F2
Southern Indian L.
  Canada 57°10N 98°30W **71** B9
Southern Lau Group
  Fiji 18°40S 178°40W **59** a
Southern Ocean *Antarctica* 62°0S 60°0E **5** C6
Southern Pines *U.S.A.* 35°11N 79°24W **85** D15
Southern Uplands *U.K.* 55°28N 3°52W **11** F5
Southington *U.S.A.* 41°36N 72°53W **83** E12
Southold *U.S.A.* 41°4N 72°26W **83** E12
Southport *Australia* 27°58S 153°25E **63** D5
Southport *U.K.* 53°39N 3°0W **12** D4
Southport *U.S.A.* 42°3N 76°49W **82** D8
Southwest △ *Australia* 43°8S 146°5E **63** G4
Southwest Pacific Basin
  Pac. Oc. 40°0S 140°0W **5** A12
Southwold *U.K.* 52°20N 1°41E **13** E9
Southwood △ *Australia* 27°48S 150°8E **63** D5
Soutpansberg *S. Africa* 23°0S 29°30E **57** C4
Sovetsk *Kaliningrad, Russia* 55°6N 21°50E **9** J19
Sovetsk *Kirov, Russia* 57°38N 48°53E **18** C8
Sovetskaya Gavan
  Russia 48°58N 140°18E **29** E15
Soweto *S. Africa* 26°14S 27°52E **57** D4
Sowma'eh Sarā *Iran* 37°17N 49°18E **45** B6
Sōya-Kaikyō = La Perouse Str.
  Asia 45°40N 142°0E **30** B11
Sōya-Misaki *Japan* 45°30N 141°55E **30** B10
Soyo *Angola* 6°13S 12°20E **52** F2
Sozh → *Belarus* 51°57N 30°48E **17** B16
Spa *Belgium* 50°29N 5°53E **15** D5
Spain ■ *Europe* 39°0N 4°0W **21** B4
Spalding *Australia* 33°30S 138°37E **63** E2
Spalding *U.K.* 52°48N 0°9W **12** E7
Spanaway *U.S.A.* 47°6N 122°26W **78** C4
Spangler *U.S.A.* 40°39N 78°48W **82** F6
Spanish *Canada* 46°12N 82°20W **72** C3
Spanish Fork *U.S.A.* 40°7N 111°39W **76** F8
Spanish Town
  Br. Virgin Is. 18°27N 64°26W **89** e
Spanish Town *Jamaica* 18°0N 76°57W **88** a
Sparks *U.S.A.* 39°32N 119°45W **78** F7
Sparta = Spárti *Greece* 37°5N 22°25E **23** F10
Sparta *Mich., U.S.A.* 43°10N 85°42W **81** D11
Sparta *N.J., U.S.A.* 41°2N 74°38W **83** E10
Sparta *Wis., U.S.A.* 43°56N 90°49W **80** D8
Spartanburg *U.S.A.* 34°56N 81°57W **85** D14
Spárti *Greece* 37°5N 22°25E **23** F10
Spartivento, C. *Calabria,*
  Italy 37°55N 16°4E **22** F7
Spartivento, C. *Sard., Italy* 38°53N 8°50E **22** E3
Sparwood *Canada* 49°44N 114°53W **70** D6
Spassk Dalniy *Russia* 44°40N 132°48E **30** B6
Spatha, Akra *Greece* 35°42N 23°43E **25** D5
Spatsizi → *Canada* 57°42N 128°7W **70** B3
Spatsizi Plateau Wilderness △
  Canada 57°40N 128°0W **70** B3
Spean → *U.K.* 56°55N 4°59W **11** E4
Spearfish *U.S.A.* 44°30N 103°52W **80** C2
Spearman *U.S.A.* 36°12N 101°12W **84** C4
Speculator *U.S.A.* 43°30N 74°22W **83** C10
Speightstown *Barbados* 13°15N 59°39W **89** g
Speke Gulf *Tanzania* 2°20S 32°50E **54** C3
Spence Bay = Taloyoak
  Canada 69°32N 93°32W **68** D12
Spencer *Idaho, U.S.A.* 44°22N 112°11W **76** D7
Spencer *Iowa, U.S.A.* 43°9N 95°9W **80** D6
Spencer *N.Y., U.S.A.* 42°13N 76°30W **83** D8
Spencer *Nebr., U.S.A.* 42°53N 98°42W **80** D4
Spencer, C. *Australia* 35°20S 136°53E **63** F2
Spencer B. *Namibia* 25°30S 14°47E **56** D1
Spencer G. *Australia* 34°0S 137°20E **63** E2
Spencerville *Canada* 44°51N 75°33W **83** B9
Spences Bridge *Canada* 50°25N 121°20W **70** C4
Spennymoor *U.K.* 54°42N 1°36W **12** C6
Spenser Mts. *N.Z.* 42°15S 172°45E **59** E4
Sperrin Mts. *U.K.* 54°50N 7°0W **10** B5
Spey → *U.K.* 57°40N 3°6W **11** D5
Speyer *Germany* 49°29N 8°25E **16** D5
Spezand *Pakistan* 29°59N 67°0E **42** E2
Spiddle *Ireland* 53°15N 9°18W **10** C2
Spili *Greece* 35°13N 24°31E **25** D6
Spin Búldak *Afghan.* 31°1N 66°25E **42** D2
Spinalonga *Greece* 35°18N 25°44E **25** D7
Spinifex ○ *Australia* 28°30S 128°30E **61** E4
Spirit Lake *U.S.A.* 46°15N 122°9W **78** D4
Spirit River *Canada* 55°45N 118°50W **70** B5
Spiritwood *Canada* 53°24N 107°33W **71** C7
Spithead *U.K.* 50°45N 1°10W **13** G6
Spitzbergen = Svalbard
  Arctic 78°0N 17°0E **4** B8
Spjelkavik *Norway* 62°28N 6°22E **8** E12
Split *Croatia* 43°31N 16°26E **22** C7
Split L. *Canada* 56°8N 96°15W **71** B9
Split Lake *Canada* 56°8N 96°15W **71** B9
Spofford *U.S.A.* 29°10N 100°25W **84** G4
Spokane *U.S.A.* 47°40N 117°24W **76** C5
Spoleto *Italy* 42°44N 12°44E **22** C5
Spooner *U.S.A.* 45°50N 91°53W **80** C8
Sporyy Navolok, Mys
  Russia 75°50N 68°40E **28** B7
Sprague *U.S.A.* 47°18N 117°59W **76** C5
Spratly I. *S. China Sea* 8°38N 111°55E **36** C4

Spratly Is. *S. China Sea* 8°20N 112°0E **36** C4
Spray *U.S.A.* 44°50N 119°48W **76** D4
Spree → *Germany* 52°32N 13°12E **16** B7
Sprengisandur *Iceland* 64°52N 18°7W **8** D4
Spring City *U.S.A.* 40°11N 75°33W **83** F9
Spring Creek *U.S.A.* 40°44N 115°35W **76** F6
Spring Garden *U.S.A.* 39°52N 120°47W **78** F6
Spring Hall *Barbados* 13°18N 59°36W **89** g
Spring Hill *U.S.A.* 28°27N 82°41W **85** G13
Spring Mts. *U.S.A.* 36°0N 115°45W **79** J11
Spring Valley *Calif.,*
  U.S.A. 32°44N 116°59W **79** N10
Spring Valley *Nev.,*
  U.S.A. 36°6N 115°14W **79** J11
Springbok *S. Africa* 29°42S 17°54E **56** D2
Springboro *U.S.A.* 41°48N 80°22W **82** E4
Springdale *Canada* 49°30N 56°6W **73** C8
Springdale *U.S.A.* 36°11N 94°8W **84** C7
Springer *U.S.A.* 36°22N 104°36W **77** H11
Springerville *U.S.A.* 34°8N 109°17W **77** J9
Springfield *Canada* 42°50N 80°56W **82** D4
Springfield *N.Z.* 43°19S 171°56E **59** E3
Springfield *Colo.,*
  U.S.A. 37°24N 102°37W **77** H12
Springfield *Ill., U.S.A.* 39°48N 89°39W **80** F9
Springfield *Mass., U.S.A.* 42°6N 72°35W **83** D12
Springfield *Mo., U.S.A.* 37°13N 93°17W **80** G7
Springfield *Ohio, U.S.A.* 39°55N 83°49W **81** F12
Springfield *Oreg., U.S.A.* 44°3N 123°1W **76** D2
Springfield *Tenn.,*
  U.S.A. 36°31N 86°53W **85** C11
Springfield *Vt., U.S.A.* 43°18N 72°29W **83** C12
Springfontein *S. Africa* 30°15S 25°40E **56** E4
Springhill *Canada* 45°40N 64°4W **73** C7
Springhill *U.S.A.* 33°0N 93°28W **84** E8
Springhouse *Canada* 51°56N 122°7W **70** C4
Springs *S. Africa* 26°13S 28°25E **57** D4
Springsure *Australia* 24°8S 148°6E **62** C4
Springvale *U.S.A.* 43°28N 70°48W **83** C14
Springville *Calif., U.S.A.* 36°8N 118°49W **78** J8
Springville *N.Y., U.S.A.* 42°31N 78°40W **82** D6
Springville *Utah, U.S.A.* 40°10N 111°37W **76** F8
Springwater *U.S.A.* 42°38N 77°35W **82** D7
Spruce-Creek *U.S.A.* 40°36N 78°9W **82** F6
Spruce Knob-Seneca Rocks △
  U.S.A. 38°50N 79°30W **81** F14
Spruce Mt. *U.S.A.* 44°12N 72°19W **83** B12
Sprucedale *Canada* 45°29N 79°28W **82** A5
Spur *U.S.A.* 33°28N 100°52W **84** E4
Spurn Hd. *U.K.* 53°35N 0°8E **12** D8
Spuzzum *Canada* 49°37N 121°23W **70** D4
Squam L. *U.S.A.* 43°45N 71°32W **83** C13
Squamish *Canada* 49°45N 123°10W **70** D4
Square Islands *Canada* 52°47N 55°47W **73** B8
Squires, Mt. *Australia* 26°14S 127°28E **61** E4
Srbija = Serbia ■ *Europe* 43°20N 20°0E **23** B9
Sre Ambel *Cambodia* 11°8N 103°46E **39** G4
Sre Khtum *Cambodia* 12°10N 106°52E **39** F6
Sre Umbell = Sre Ambel
  Cambodia 11°8N 103°46E **39** G4
Srebrenica *Bos.-H.* 44°6N 19°18E **23** B8
Sredinnyy Khrebet
  Russia 57°0N 160°0E **29** D16
Sredinnyy Ra. = Sredinnyy
  Khrebet *Russia* 57°0N 160°0E **29** D16
Srednekolymsk *Russia* 67°27N 153°40E **29** C16
Šrem *Poland* 52°6N 17°2E **17** B9
Sremska Mitrovica
  Serbia 44°59N 19°38E **23** B8
Srepok → *Cambodia* 13°33N 106°16E **38** F6
Sretensk *Russia* 52°10N 117°40E **29** D12
Sri Aman = Bandar Sri Aman
  Malaysia 1°15N 111°32E **36** D4
Sri Lanka ■ *Asia* 7°30N 80°50E **40** R12
Srikakulam *India* 18°14N 83°58E **41** K13
Srinagar *India* 34°5N 74°50E **43** B6
Srono *Indonesia* 8°24S 114°16E **37** J17
Ssese Is. = Sese Is. *Uganda* 0°20S 32°20E **54** C3
Staaten → *Australia* 16°24S 141°17E **62** B3
Staaten River △
  Australia 16°15S 142°40E **62** B3
Stade *Germany* 53°35N 9°29E **16** B5
Stadskanaal *Neths.* 53°4N 6°55E **15** A6
Staffa *U.K.* 56°27N 6°21W **11** E2
Stafford *U.K.* 52°49N 2°7E **12** E5
Stafford *U.S.A.* 37°58N 98°36W **80** G4
Stafford Springs *U.S.A.* 41°57N 72°18W **83** E12
Staffordshire □ *U.K.* 52°53N 2°10W **12** E5
Staines *U.K.* 51°26N 0°29W **13** F7
Stakhanov *Ukraine* 48°35N 38°40E **19** E6
Stalida *Greece* 35°17N 25°25E **25** D7
Stalowa Wola *Poland* 50°34N 22°3E **17** C12
Stalybridge *U.K.* 53°28N 2°3E **12** D5
Stamford *Australia* 21°15S 143°46E **62** C3
Stamford *U.K.* 52°39N 0°29W **12** E7
Stamford *Conn., U.S.A.* 41°3N 73°32W **83** E11
Stamford *N.Y., U.S.A.* 42°25N 74°38W **83** D10
Stamford *Tex., U.S.A.* 32°57N 99°48W **84** E5
Stampriet *Namibia* 24°20S 18°28E **56** C2
Stamps *U.S.A.* 33°22N 93°30W **84** E8
Stanberry *S. Africa* 26°55S 29°7E **57** D4
Standish *U.S.A.* 43°59N 83°57W **81** D12
Standerton *S. Africa* 34°6S 19°29E **56** E2
Stanford *U.S.A.* 47°9N 110°13W **76** C8
Stanger *S. Africa* 29°27S 31°14E **57** D5
Stängselåsen = Salpausselkä
  Finland 61°3N 26°15E **8** F22
Stanislaus → *U.S.A.* 37°40N 121°14W **78** H5
Stanke Dimitrov
  Bulgaria 42°17N 23°9E **23** C10
Stanley *Australia* 40°46S 145°19E **63** G4
Stanley *China* 22°13N 114°12E **33** a
Stanley *Falk. Is.* 51°40S 59°51W **96** G5
Stanley *U.K.* 54°53N 1°41W **12** C6
Stanley *Idaho, U.S.A.* 44°13N 114°56W **76** D6
Stanley *N. Dak., U.S.A.* 48°19N 102°23W **80** A2
Stanley *N.Y., U.S.A.* 42°48N 77°6W **82** D7
Stanley Mission
  Canada 55°25N 104°33W **71** B8
Stannards *U.S.A.* 42°5N 77°55W **82** D7

Stanovoy Khrebet *Russia* 55°0N 130°0E **29** D14
Stanovoy Ra. = Stanovoy Khrebet *Russia* 55°0N 130°0E **29** D14
Stansmore Ra. *Australia* 21°23S 128°33E **60** D4
Stansted, London ✈ (STN) *U.K.* 51°54N 0°14E **13** F8
Stanthorpe *Australia* 28°36S 151°59E **63** D5
Stanton *U.S.A.* 32°8N 101°48W **84** E4
Stanwood *U.S.A.* 48°15N 122°23W **78** B4
Staples *Canada* 42°10N 82°35W **82** D2
Staples *U.S.A.* 46°21N 94°48W **80** B6
Stapleton *U.S.A.* 41°29N 100°31W **80** E3
Star City *Canada* 52°50N 104°20W **71** C8
Star Lake *U.S.A.* 44°10N 75°2W **83** B9
Stara Planina *Bulgaria* 43°15N 23°0E **23** C10
Stara Zagora *Bulgaria* 42°26N 25°39E **23** C11
Staraya Russa *Russia* 57°58N 31°23E **18** C5
Starbuck I. *Kiribati* 5°37S 155°55W **65** H12
Starcke △ *Australia* 14°56S 145°2E **62** A4
Stargard Szczeciński *Poland* 53°20N 15°0E **16** B8
Staritsa *Russia* 56°33N 34°55E **18** C5
Starke *U.S.A.* 29°57N 82°7W **85** G13
Starkville *U.S.A.* 33°28N 88°49W **85** E10
Starogard Gdański *Poland* 53°59N 18°30E **17** B10
Starokonstantinov = Starokonstyantyniv *Ukraine* 49°48N 27°10E **17** D14
Starokonstyantyniv *Ukraine* 49°48N 27°10E **17** D14
Start Pt. *U.K.* 50°13N 3°39W **13** G4
Staryy Chartoriysk *Ukraine* 51°15N 25°54E **17** C13
Staryy Oskol *Russia* 51°19N 37°55E **19** D6
State College *U.S.A.* 40°48N 77°52W **82** F7
Stateline *U.S.A.* 38°57N 119°56W **78** G7
Staten, I. = Estados, I. de Los *Argentina* 54°40S 64°30W **96** G4
Staten I. *U.S.A.* 40°35N 74°9W **83** F10
Statesboro *U.S.A.* 32°27N 81°47W **85** E14
Statesville *U.S.A.* 35°47N 80°53W **85** D14
Statia = St. Eustatius *W. Indies* 17°20N 63°0W **89** C7
Stauffer *U.S.A.* 34°45N 119°3W **79** L7
Staunton *Ill., U.S.A.* 39°1N 89°47W **80** F9
Staunton *Va., U.S.A.* 38°9N 79°4W **81** F14
Stavanger *Norway* 58°57N 5°40E **9** G11
Staveley *N.Z.* 43°40S 171°32E **59** E3
Stavelot *Belgium* 50°23N 5°55E **15** D5
Stavern *Norway* 59°0N 10°1E **9** G14
Stavoren *Neths.* 52°53N 5°22E **15** B5
Stavropol *Russia* 45°5N 42°0E **19** E7
Stavros *Cyprus* 35°1N 32°38E **25** D11
Stavros *Greece* 35°12N 24°45E **25** D6
Stavros, Akra *Greece* 35°26N 24°58E **25** D6
Stawell *Australia* 37°5S 142°47E **63** F3
Stawell → *Australia* 20°20S 142°55E **62** C3
Stayner *Canada* 44°25N 80°5W **82** B4
Stayton *U.S.A.* 44°48N 122°48W **76** D2
Steamboat Springs *U.S.A.* 40°29N 106°50W **76** F10
Steele *U.S.A.* 46°51N 99°55W **80** B4
Steelton *U.S.A.* 40°14N 76°50W **82** F8
Steen River *Canada* 59°40N 117°12W **70** B5
Steens Mt. *U.S.A.* 42°35N 118°40W **76** E4
Steenwijk *Neths.* 52°47N 6°7E **15** B6
Steep Pt. *Australia* 26°8S 113°8E **61** E1
Steep Rock *Canada* 51°30N 98°48W **71** C9
Stefanie L. = Chew Bahir *Ethiopia* 4°40N 36°50E **47** G2
Stefansson Bay *Antarctica* 67°20S 59°8E **5** C5
Stefansson I. *Canada* 73°20N 105°45W **69** C10
Steiermark □ *Austria* 47°26N 15°0E **16** E8
Steilacoom *U.S.A.* 47°10N 122°36W **78** C4
Steilrandberge *Namibia* 17°45S 13°20E **56** B1
Steinbach *Canada* 49°32N 96°40W **71** D9
Steinhausen *Namibia* 21°49S 18°20E **56** C2
Steinkjer *Norway* 64°1N 11°31E **8** D14
Steinkopf *S. Africa* 29°18S 17°43E **56** D2
Stellarton *Canada* 45°32N 62°30W **73** C7
Stellenbosch *S. Africa* 33°58S 18°50E **56** E2
Stendal *Germany* 52°36N 11°53E **16** B6
Steornabhaigh = Stornoway *U.K.* 58°13N 6°23W **11** C2
Stepanakert = Xankändi *Azerbaijan* 39°52N 46°49E **44** B5
Stephens Creek *Australia* 31°50S 141°30E **63** E3
Stephens I. *Canada* 54°10N 130°45W **70** C2
Stephens L. *Canada* 56°32N 95°0W **71** B9
Stephenville *Canada* 48°31N 58°35W **73** C8
Stephenville *U.S.A.* 32°13N 98°12W **84** E5
Steppe *Asia* 50°0N 50°0E **26** C7
Sterkstroom *S. Africa* 31°32S 26°32E **56** E4
Sterling *Colo., U.S.A.* 40°37N 103°13W **76** F12
Sterling *Ill., U.S.A.* 41°48N 89°42W **80** E9
Sterling *Kans., U.S.A.* 38°13N 98°12W **80** F4
Sterling City *U.S.A.* 31°51N 101°0W **84** F4
Sterling Heights *U.S.A.* 42°35N 83°2W **81** D12
Sterling Run *U.S.A.* 41°25N 78°12W **82** E6
Sterlitamak *Russia* 53°40N 56°0E **18** D10
Sternes *Greece* 35°24N 24°9E **25** D6
Stettin = Szczecin *Poland* 53°27N 14°27E **16** B8
Stettiner Haff *Germany* 53°47N 14°15E **16** B8
Stettler *Canada* 52°19N 112°40W **70** C6
Steubenville *U.S.A.* 40°22N 80°37W **82** F4
Stevenage *U.K.* 51°55N 0°13W **13** F7
Stevens Point *U.S.A.* 44°31N 89°34W **80** C9
Stevenson *U.S.A.* 45°42N 121°53W **78** E5
Stevenson → *Australia* 27°6S 135°33E **63** D2
Stevenson L. *Canada* 53°55N 96°0W **71** C9
Stevensville *U.S.A.* 46°30N 114°5W **76** C6
Stewart *Canada* 55°56N 129°57W **70** B3
Stewart *U.S.A.* 39°5N 119°46W **78** F7
Stewart → *Canada* 63°19N 139°26W **68** B6
Stewart, C. *Australia* 11°57S 134°56E **62** A1
Stewart, I. *Chile* 54°50S 71°15W **96** G2

Stewart I. *N.Z.* 46°58S 167°54E **59** G1
Stewarts Point *U.S.A.* 38°39N 123°24W **78** G3
Stewartville *U.S.A.* 43°51N 92°29W **80** D7
Stewiacke *Canada* 45°9N 63°22W **73** C7
Steynsburg *S. Africa* 31°15S 25°49E **56** E4
Steyr *Austria* 48°3N 14°25E **16** D8
Steytlerville *S. Africa* 33°17S 24°19E **56** E3
Stigler *U.S.A.* 35°15N 95°8W **84** D7
Stikine → *Canada* 56°40N 132°30W **70** B2
Stilfontein *S. Africa* 26°51S 26°50E **56** D4
Stillwater *N.Z.* 42°27S 171°20E **59** E3
Stillwater *N.Y., U.S.A.* 42°55N 73°41W **83** D11
Stillwater *Okla., U.S.A.* 36°7N 97°4W **84** C6
Stillwater Range *U.S.A.* 39°50N 118°5W **76** G4
Stillwater Res. *U.S.A.* 43°54N 75°3W **83** C9
Stilwell *U.S.A.* 35°49N 94°38W **84** D7
Stînga Nistrului □ *Moldova* 47°20N 29°15E **17** E15
Ştip *Macedonia* 41°42N 22°10E **23** D10
Stirling *Canada* 44°18N 77°33W **82** B7
Stirling *U.K.* 56°8N 3°57W **11** E5
Stirling □ *U.K.* 56°12N 4°18W **11** E4
Stirling Ra. *Australia* 34°23S 118°0E **61** F2
Stirling Range △ *Australia* 34°26S 118°20E **61** F2
Stittsville *Canada* 45°15N 75°55W **83** A9
Stjernøya *Norway* 70°20N 22°40E **8** A20
Stjørdalshalsen *Norway* 63°29N 10°51E **8** E14
Stockerau *Austria* 48°24N 16°12E **16** D9
Stockholm *Sweden* 59°19N 18°4E **9** G18
Stockport *U.K.* 53°25N 2°9W **12** D5
Stocksbridge *U.K.* 53°29N 1°35W **12** D6
Stockton *Calif., U.S.A.* 37°58N 121°17W **78** H5
Stockton *Kans., U.S.A.* 39°26N 99°16W **80** F4
Stockton *Mo., U.S.A.* 37°42N 93°48W **80** G7
Stockton-on-Tees *U.K.* 54°35N 1°19W **12** C6
Stockton-on-Tees □ *U.K.* 54°35N 1°19W **12** C6
Stockton Plateau *U.S.A.* 30°30N 102°30W **84** F3
Stoeng Treng *Cambodia* 13°31N 105°58E **38** F5
Stoer, Pt. of *U.K.* 58°16N 5°23W **11** C3
Stoke-on-Trent *U.K.* 53°1N 2°11W **12** D5
Stoke-on-Trent □ *U.K.* 53°1N 2°11W **12** D5
Stokes △ *Australia* 33°45S 121°11E **61** F3
Stokes Bay *Canada* 45°0N 81°28W **82** B3
Stokes Pt. *Australia* 40°10S 143°56E **63** G3
Stokes Ra. *Australia* 15°50S 130°50E **60** C5
Stokksnes *Iceland* 64°14N 14°58W **8** D6
Stokmarknes *Norway* 68°34N 14°54E **8** B16
Stolac *Bos.-H.* 43°5N 17°59E **23** C7
Stolbovoy, Ostrov *Russia* 74°44N 135°14E **29** B14
Stolbtsy = Stowbtsy *Belarus* 53°30N 26°43E **17** B14
Stolin *Belarus* 51°53N 26°50E **17** C14
Stomio *Greece* 35°21N 23°32E **25** D5
Stone *U.K.* 52°55N 2°9W **12** E5
Stoneboro *U.S.A.* 41°20N 80°7W **82** E4
Stonehaven *U.K.* 56°59N 2°12W **11** E6
Stonehenge *Australia* 24°22S 143°17E **62** C3
Stonehenge *U.K.* 51°9N 1°45W **13** F6
Stonewall *Canada* 50°10N 97°19W **71** C9
Stony I. *U.S.A.* 43°53N 76°19W **83** C8
Stony L. *Man., Canada* 58°51N 98°40W **71** B9
Stony L. *Ont., Canada* 44°30N 78°5W **82** B6
Stony Point *U.S.A.* 41°14N 73°59W **83** E11
Stony Pt. *U.S.A.* 43°50N 76°18W **83** C8
Stony Rapids *Canada* 59°16N 105°50W **71** B7
Stony Tunguska = Tunguska, Podkamennaya → *Russia* 61°50N 90°13E **29** C10
Stonyford *U.S.A.* 39°23N 122°33W **78** F4
Stora Lulevatten *Sweden* 67°10N 19°30E **8** C18
Storavan *Sweden* 65°45N 18°10E **8** D18
Stord *Norway* 59°52N 5°23E **9** G11
Store Bælt *Denmark* 55°20N 11°0E **9** J14
Storkerson Pen. *Canada* 72°30N 106°30W **68** C10
Storm B. *Australia* 43°10S 147°30E **63** G4
Storm Lake *U.S.A.* 42°39N 95°13W **80** D6
Stormberge *S. Africa* 31°16S 26°17E **56** E4
Stormsrivier *S. Africa* 33°59S 23°52E **56** E3
Stornoway *U.K.* 58°13N 6°23W **11** C2
Storozhinets = Storozhynets *Ukraine* 48°14N 25°45E **17** D13
Storozhynets *Ukraine* 48°14N 25°45E **17** D13
Storrs *U.S.A.* 41°49N 72°15W **83** E12
Storsjön *Sweden* 63°9N 14°30E **8** E16
Storuman *Sweden* 65°5N 17°10E **8** D17
Storuman, L. *Sweden* 65°13N 16°50E **8** D17
Stouffville *Canada* 43°58N 79°15W **82** C5
Stoughton *Canada* 49°40N 103°0W **71** D8
Stour → *Dorset, U.K.* 50°43N 1°47W **13** G6
Stour → *Kent, U.K.* 51°18N 1°22E **13** F9
Stour → *Suffolk, U.K.* 51°57N 1°4E **13** F9
Stourbridge *U.K.* 52°28N 2°8W **13** E5
Stout L. *Canada* 52°0N 94°40W **71** C10
Stove Pipe Wells Village *U.S.A.* 36°35N 117°11W **79** J9
Stow *U.S.A.* 41°10N 81°27W **82** E3
Stowbtsy *Belarus* 53°30N 26°43E **17** B14
Stowmarket *U.K.* 52°12N 1°0E **13** E9
Strabane *U.K.* 54°50N 7°27W **10** B4
Strahan *Australia* 42°8N 145°20E **63** G4
Stralsund *Germany* 54°18N 13°4E **16** A7
Strand *S. Africa* 34°9S 18°48E **56** E2
Stranda *Møre og Romsdal, Norway* 62°19N 6°58E **8** E12
Stranda *Nord-Trøndelag, Norway* 63°33N 10°14E **8** E14
Strangford L. *U.K.* 54°30N 5°37W **10** B6
Stranorlar *Ireland* 54°48N 7°46W **10** B4
Stranraer *U.K.* 54°54N 5°1W **11** G3
Strasbourg *Canada* 51°4N 104°55W **71** C8
Strasbourg *France* 48°35N 7°42E **20** B7
Stratford *Canada* 43°23N 81°0W **82** C4
Stratford *N.Z.* 39°20S 174°19E **59** C5
Stratford *Calif., U.S.A.* 36°11N 119°49W **78** J7
Stratford *Conn., U.S.A.* 41°12N 73°8W **83** E11

Stratford *Tex., U.S.A.* 36°20N 102°4W **84** C3
Stratford-upon-Avon *U.K.* 52°12N 1°42W **13** E6
Strath Spey *U.K.* 57°9N 3°49W **11** D5
Strathalbyn *Australia* 35°13S 138°53E **63** F2
Strathaven *U.K.* 55°40N 4°5W **11** F4
Strathcona △ *Canada* 49°38N 125°40W **70** D3
Strathmore *Canada* 51°5N 113°18W **70** C6
Strathmore *U.K.* 56°37N 3°7W **11** E5
Strathmore *U.S.A.* 36°9N 119°4W **78** J7
Strathnaver *Canada* 53°20N 122°33W **70** C4
Strathpeffer *U.K.* 57°35N 4°32W **11** D4
Strathroy *Canada* 42°58N 81°38W **82** D3
Strathy Pt. *U.K.* 58°36N 4°1W **11** C4
Strattanville *U.S.A.* 41°12N 79°19W **82** E5
Stratton *U.S.A.* 45°8N 70°26W **83** A14
Stratton Mt. *U.S.A.* 43°4N 72°55W **83** C12
Straubing *Germany* 48°52N 12°34E **16** D7
Straumnes *Iceland* 66°26N 23°8W **8** C2
Strawberry → *U.S.A.* 40°10N 110°24W **76** F8
Streaky B. *Australia* 32°48S 134°13E **63** E1
Streaky Bay *Australia* 32°51S 134°18E **63** E1
Streator *U.S.A.* 41°8N 88°50W **80** E9
Streetsboro *U.S.A.* 41°14N 81°21W **82** E3
Streetsville *Canada* 43°35N 79°42W **82** C5
Streng → *Cambodia* 13°12N 103°37E **38** F4
Stresboro → *U.S.A.* 41°19N 81°50W **82** E3
Stresboro → U.S.A.
Streymoy *Færoe Is.* 62°8N 7°5W **8** E9
Strezhevoy *Russia* 60°42N 77°34E **28** C8
Strimonas → *Greece* 40°46N 23°51E **23** D10
Strokestown *Ireland* 53°46N 8°7W **10** C3
Stroma *U.K.* 58°41N 3°7W **11** C5
Strómboli *Italy* 38°47N 15°13E **22** E6
Stromeferry *U.K.* 57°21N 5°33W **11** D3
Stromness *U.K.* 58°58N 3°17W **11** C5
Stromsburg *U.S.A.* 41°7N 97°36W **80** E5
Strömstad *Sweden* 58°56N 11°10E **9** G14
Strömsund *Sweden* 63°51N 15°33E **8** E16
Strongsville *U.S.A.* 41°19N 81°50W **82** E3
Stronsay *U.K.* 59°7N 2°35W **11** B6
Stroud *U.K.* 51°45N 2°13W **13** F5
Stroud Road *Australia* 32°18S 151°57E **63** E5
Stroudsburg *U.S.A.* 40°59N 75°12W **83** F9
Stroumbi *Cyprus* 34°53N 32°29E **25** E11
Struer *Denmark* 56°30N 8°35E **9** H13
Strugi Krasnyye *Russia* 58°21N 29°1E **9** G23
Strumica *Macedonia* 41°28N 22°41E **23** D10
Struthers *Canada* 48°41N 85°51W **72** C2
Struthers *U.S.A.* 41°4N 80°39W **82** E4
Stryker *U.S.A.* 48°41N 114°46W **76** B6
Stryy *Ukraine* 49°16N 23°48E **17** D12
Strzelecki Cr. → *Australia* 29°37S 139°59E **63** D2
Strzelecki Desert *Australia* 29°30S 140°0E **63** D3
Stuart *Fla., U.S.A.* 27°12N 80°15W **85** H14
Stuart *Nebr., U.S.A.* 42°36N 99°8W **80** D4
Stuart → *Canada* 54°0N 123°35W **70** C4
Stuart Bluff Ra. *Australia* 22°50S 131°52E **60** D5
Stuart I. *U.S.A.* 63°35N 162°30W **74** C7
Stuart L. *Canada* 54°30N 124°30W **70** C4
Stuart Ra. *Australia* 29°10S 134°56E **63** D1
Stull L. *Canada* 54°24N 92°34W **72** B1
Stung Treng = Stoeng Treng *Cambodia* 13°31N 105°58E **38** F5
Stupart → *Canada* 56°0N 93°25W **72** A1
Sturge I. *Antarctica* 67°26S 164°47E **5** C11
Sturgeon B. *Canada* 52°0N 97°50W **71** C9
Sturgeon Bay *U.S.A.* 44°50N 87°23W **80** C10
Sturgeon Falls *Canada* 46°25N 79°57W **72** C4
Sturgeon L. *Alta., Canada* 55°6N 117°32W **70** B5
Sturgeon L. *Ont., Canada* 50°0N 90°45W **72** C1
Sturgeon L. *Ont., Canada* 44°28N 78°43W **82** B6
Sturgis *Canada* 51°56N 102°36W **71** C8
Sturgis *Mich., U.S.A.* 41°48N 85°25W **81** E11
Sturgis *S. Dak., U.S.A.* 44°25N 103°31W **80** C2
Sturt △ *Australia* 27°17S 141°37E **63** D3
Sturt Cr. → *Australia* 19°8S 127°50E **60** C4
Sturt Stony Desert *Australia* 28°30S 141°0E **63** D3
Stutterheim *S. Africa* 32°33S 27°28E **56** E4
Stuttgart *Germany* 48°48N 9°11E **16** D5
Stuttgart *U.S.A.* 34°30N 91°33W **84** D9
Stuyvesant *U.S.A.* 42°23N 73°45W **83** D11
Stykkishólmur *Iceland* 65°2N 22°40W **8** D2
Styria = Steiermark □ *Austria* 47°26N 15°0E **16** E8
Su Xian = Suzhou *China* 33°41N 116°59E **34** H9
Suakin *Sudan* 19°8N 37°20E **51** E13
Suan *N. Korea* 38°42N 126°22E **35** E14
Suana *Indonesia* 8°44S 115°36E **37** K18
Suar *India* 29°2N 79°3E **43** E8
Subā *Si. Arabia* 27°10N 35°40E **44** E2
Subang *Indonesia* 6°34S 107°45E **37** G12
Subansiri → *India* 26°48N 93°50E **41** F18
Subarnarekha → *India* 22°34N 87°24E **43** H12
Subayhah *Si. Arabia* 30°2N 38°50E **44** D3
Subi *Indonesia* 2°58N 108°50E **36** D3
Subotica *Serbia* 46°6N 19°39E **23** A8
Suceava *Romania* 47°38N 26°16E **17** E14
Suchan = Partizansk *Russia* 43°8N 133°9E **29** E14
Suchil *Mexico* 23°39N 103°54W **86** C4
Suchou = Suzhou *China* 31°19N 120°38E **33** E13
Süchow = Xuzhou *China* 34°18N 117°10E **35** G9
Suck → *Ireland* 53°17N 8°3W **10** C3
Sucre *Bolivia* 19°0S 65°15W **92** G5
Sucuriú → *Brazil* 20°47S 51°38W **93** H8
Sud, Pte. du *Canada* 49°3N 62°14W **73** C7
Sud-Kivu □ *Dem. Rep. of the Congo* 3°0S 28°30E **54** C2
Sud-Ouest, Pte. *Canada* 49°23N 63°36W **73** C7
Sud Ouest, Pte. *Mauritius* 20°28S 57°51E **53** d
Sudan *U.S.A.* 34°4N 102°31W **84** D3
Sudan ■ *Africa* 15°0N 30°0E **51** E11
Sudbury *Canada* 46°30N 81°0W **72** C3
Sudbury *U.K.* 52°2N 0°45E **13** E8
Sûdd *Sudan* 8°20N 30°0E **51** G12

Sudeten Mts. = Sudety *Europe* 50°20N 16°45E **17** C9
Sudety *Europe* 50°20N 16°45E **17** C9
Suðuroy *Færoe Is.* 61°32N 6°50W **8** F9
Sudi *Tanzania* 10°11S 39°57E **55** E4
Sudirman, Pegunungan *Indonesia* 4°30S 137°0E **37** E9
Sudong, Pulau *Singapore* 1°13N 103°44E **39** d
Sueca *Spain* 39°12N 0°21E **21** C5
Suemez I. *U.S.A.* 55°15N 133°20W **70** B2
Suez = El Suweis *Egypt* 29°58N 32°31E **51** C12
Suez, G. of = Suweis, Khalîg el *Egypt* 28°40N 33°0E **51** C12
Suez Canal = Suweis, Qanâ es *Egypt* 31°0N 32°20E **51** B12
Suffield *Canada* 50°12N 111°10W **70** C6
Suffolk *U.S.A.* 36°44N 76°35W **81** G15
Suffolk □ *U.K.* 52°16N 1°0E **13** E9
Sugar Grove *U.S.A.* 41°59N 79°20W **82** E5
Sugarcreek *U.S.A.* 41°25N 79°52W **82** E5
Sugarive → *India* 26°16N 86°24E **43** F12
Sugluk = Salluit *Canada* 62°14N 75°38W **69** E16
Şuḩār *Oman* 24°20N 56°40E **45** E8
Sühbaatar *Mongolia* 50°17N 106°10E **32** A10
Sühbaatar □ *Mongolia* 45°30N 114°0E **34** B8
Suhl *Germany* 50°36N 10°42E **16** C6
Sui *Pakistan* 28°37N 69°19E **42** E3
Sui Xian *China* 34°25N 115°2E **34** G8
Suide *China* 37°30N 110°12E **34** F6
Suifenhe *China* 44°25N 131°10E **35** B16
Suihua *China* 46°32N 126°55E **33** B14
Suining *Jiangsu, China* 33°56N 117°58E **35** H9
Suining *Sichuan, China* 30°26N 105°35E **32** C10
Suiping *China* 33°10N 113°59E **34** H7
Suir → *Ireland* 52°16N 7°9W **10** D4
Suisse = Switzerland ■ *Europe* 46°30N 8°0E **20** C8
Suisun City *U.S.A.* 38°15N 122°2W **78** G4
Suiyang *China* 44°30N 130°56E **35** B16
Suizhong *China* 40°21N 120°20E **35** D11
Sujangarh *India* 27°42N 74°31E **42** F6
Sujiatun *China* 41°39N 123°20E **35** D12
Sukabumi *Indonesia* 6°56S 106°50E **37** G12
Sukadana *Indonesia* 1°10S 110°0E **36** E4
Sukagawa *Japan* 37°17N 140°23E **31** F10
Sukamade *Indonesia* 8°30S 113°52E **37** H15
Sukaraja *Indonesia* 2°28S 110°25E **36** E4
Sukawati *Indonesia* 8°35S 115°17E **37** K18
Sukch'ŏn *N. Korea* 39°22N 125°35E **35** E13
Sukhona → *Russia* 61°15N 46°39E **18** C6
Sukhothai *Thailand* 17°1N 99°49E **38** D2
Sukhumi = Sokhumi *Georgia* 43°0N 41°0E **19** F7
Sukkur *Pakistan* 27°42N 68°54E **42** F3
Sukkur Barrage *Pakistan* 27°40N 68°50E **42** F3
Sukri → *India* 25°4N 71°43E **42** G4
Sukumo *Japan* 32°56N 132°44E **31** H6
Sukunka → *Canada* 55°45N 121°15W **70** B4
Sula, Kepulauan *Indonesia* 1°45S 125°0E **37** E7
Sulaco → *Honduras* 15°2N 87°44W **88** C2
Sulaiman Range *Pakistan* 30°30N 69°50E **42** D3
Sūlār *Iran* 31°53N 51°54E **45** D6
Sulawesi □ *Indonesia* 2°0S 120°0E **37** E6
Sulawesi Barat □ *Indonesia* 3°0S 119°0E **37** E5
Sulawesi Sea = Celebes Sea *Indonesia* 3°0N 123°0E **37** D6
Sulawesi Selatan □ *Indonesia* 2°30S 120°0E **37** E6
Sulawesi Tengah □ *Indonesia* 1°30S 121°0E **37** E6
Sulawesi Tenggara □ *Indonesia* 3°50S 122°0E **37** E6
Sulawesi Utara □ *Indonesia* 1°0N 124°0E **37** D6
Sulima *S. Leone* 6°58N 11°32W **50** G3
Sulina *Romania* 45°10N 29°40E **17** F15
Sulitjelma *Norway* 67°9N 16°3E **8** C17
Sullana *Peru* 4°52S 80°39W **92** D2
Sullivan *Ill., U.S.A.* 39°36N 88°37W **80** F9
Sullivan *Ind., U.S.A.* 39°6N 87°24W **80** F10
Sullivan *Mo., U.S.A.* 38°13N 91°10W **80** F8
Sullivan Bay *Canada* 50°55N 126°50W **70** C3
Sullivan I. = Lanbi Kyun *Burma* 10°50N 98°20E **39** G2
Sullom Voe *U.K.* 60°27N 1°20W **11** A7
Sulphur *La., U.S.A.* 30°14N 93°23W **84** F8
Sulphur *Okla., U.S.A.* 34°31N 96°58W **84** D6
Sulphur Pt. *Canada* 60°56N 114°48W **70** A6
Sulphur Springs *U.S.A.* 33°8N 95°36W **84** E7
Sultan *Canada* 47°36N 82°47W **72** C3
Sultan *U.S.A.* 47°52N 121°49W **78** C5
Sultan Hamud *Kenya* 2°1S 37°22E **54** C4
Sultanābād = Arāk *Iran* 34°0N 49°40E **45** C6
Sultanpur *Mad. P., India* 23°9N 77°56E **42** H8
Sultanpur *Punjab, India* 31°13N 75°11E **42** D6
Sultanpur *Ut. P., India* 26°18N 82°4E **43** F10
Sulu Arch. *Phil.* 6°0N 121°0E **37** C6
Sulu Sea *E. Indies* 8°0N 120°0E **37** C6
Sulūq *Libya* 31°44N 20°14E **51** B10
Sulzberger Ice Shelf *Antarctica* 78°0S 150°0W **5** E13
Sumalata *Indonesia* 1°0N 122°31E **37** D6
Sumampa *Argentina* 29°25S 63°29W **94** B3
Sumatera □ *Indonesia* 0°40N 100°20E **36** D2
Sumatera Barat □ *Indonesia* 1°0S 101°0E **36** E2
Sumatera Selatan □ *Indonesia* 3°0S 104°0E **36** E2
Sumatera Utara □ *Indonesia* 2°30N 98°0E **36** D1
Sumatra = Sumatera *Indonesia* 0°40N 100°20E **36** D2
Sumba *Indonesia* 9°45S 119°35E **37** F5
Sumba, Selat *Indonesia* 9°0S 118°40E **37** F5
Sumbawa *Indonesia* 8°26S 117°30E **37** F5
Sumbawa Besar *Indonesia* 8°30S 117°26E **37** F5
Sumbawanga □ *Tanzania* 8°0S 31°30E **52** F6
Sumbe *Angola* 11°10S 13°48E **52** G2

Sumbu △ *Zambia* 8°43S 30°22E **55** D3
Sumburgh Hd. *U.K.* 59°52N 1°17W **11** B7
Sumdeo *India* 31°26N 78°44E **43** D8
Sumdo *China* 35°6N 78°41E **43** B8
Sumedang *Indonesia* 6°52S 107°55E **37** G12
Šumen = Shumen *Bulgaria* 43°18N 26°55E **23** C12
Sumenep *Indonesia* 7°1S 113°52E **37** G15
Sumgait = Sumqayıt *Azerbaijan* 40°34N 49°38E **19** F8
Summer L. *U.S.A.* 42°50N 120°45W **76** E3
Summerland *Canada* 49°32N 119°41W **70** D5
Summerside *Canada* 46°24N 63°47W **73** C7
Summersville *U.S.A.* 38°17N 80°51W **81** F13
Summerville *Ga., U.S.A.* 34°29N 85°21W **85** D12
Summerville *S.C., U.S.A.* 33°1N 80°11W **85** E14
Summit Lake *Canada* 54°20N 122°40W **70** C4
Summit Peak *U.S.A.* 37°21N 106°42W **77** H10
Sumner *Iowa, U.S.A.* 42°51N 92°6W **80** D7
Sumner *Wash., U.S.A.* 47°12N 122°14W **78** C4
Sumoto *Japan* 34°21N 134°54E **31** G7
Šumperk *Czech Rep.* 49°59N 16°59E **17** D9
Sumqayıt *Azerbaijan* 40°34N 49°38E **19** F8
Sumter *U.S.A.* 33°55N 80°21W **85** E14
Sumy *Ukraine* 50°57N 34°50E **19** D5
Sun City *S. Africa* 25°17S 27°3E **56** D4
Sun City *Ariz., U.S.A.* 33°35N 112°16W **77** K7
Sun City *Calif., U.S.A.* 33°42N 117°11W **79** M9
Sun City Center *U.S.A.* 27°43N 82°21W **85** H13
Sun Lakes *U.S.A.* 33°10N 111°52W **77** K8
Sun Valley *U.S.A.* 43°42N 114°21W **76** E6
Sunagawa *Japan* 43°29N 141°55E **30** C10
Sunan *N. Korea* 39°15N 125°40E **35** E13
Sunart, L. *U.K.* 56°42N 5°43W **11** E3
Sunburst *U.S.A.* 48°53N 111°55W **76** B8
Sunbury *Australia* 37°35S 144°44E **63** F3
Sunbury *U.S.A.* 40°52N 76°48W **83** F8
Sunchales *Argentina* 30°58S 61°35W **94** C3
Suncheon *S. Korea* 34°52N 127°31E **35** G14
Suncho Corral *Argentina* 27°55S 63°27W **94** B3
Sunch'ŏn *N. Korea* 39°25N 125°56E **35** E13
Suncook *U.S.A.* 43°8N 71°27W **83** C13
Sunda, Selat *Indonesia* 6°20S 105°30E **36** F3
Sunda Is. *Indonesia* 5°0S 105°0E **64** G2
Sunda Str. = Sunda, Selat *Indonesia* 6°20S 105°30E **36** F3
Sunda Trench = Java Trench *Ind. Oc.* 9°0S 105°0E **36** F3
Sundance *Canada* 56°32N 94°4W **71** B10
Sundance *U.S.A.* 44°24N 104°23W **76** D11
Sundar Nagar *India* 31°32N 76°53E **42** D7
Sundarbans *Asia* 22°0N 89°0E **41** J16
Sundarbans △ *India* 22°0N 88°45E **43** J13
Sundargarh *India* 22°4N 84°5E **41** H14
Sundays = Sondags → *S. Africa* 33°44S 25°51E **56** E4
Sunderland *Canada* 44°16N 79°4W **82** B5
Sunderland *U.K.* 54°55N 1°23W **12** C6
Sundown △ *Australia* 28°49S 151°38E **63** D5
Sundre *Canada* 51°49N 114°38W **70** C6
Sundsvall *Sweden* 62°23N 17°17E **8** E17
Sungai Acheh *Malaysia* 5°8N 100°30E **39** c
Sungai Kolok *Thailand* 6°2N 101°58E **39** J3
Sungai Lembing *Malaysia* 3°55N 103°3E **39** L4
Sungai Petani *Malaysia* 5°37N 100°30E **39** K3
Sungaigerong *Indonesia* 2°59S 104°52E **36** E2
Sungailiat *Indonesia* 1°51S 106°8E **36** E3
Sungaipenuh *Indonesia* 2°1S 101°20E **36** E2
Sungari = Songhua Jiang → *China* 47°45N 132°30E **33** B15
Sunghua Chiang = Songhua Jiang → *China* 47°45N 132°30E **33** B15
Sunland Park *U.S.A.* 31°50N 106°40W **77** L10
Sunndalsøra *Norway* 62°40N 8°33E **8** E13
Sunnyside *U.S.A.* 46°20N 120°0W **76** C4
Sunnyvale *U.S.A.* 37°23N 122°2W **78** H4
Sunrise Manor *U.S.A.* 36°12N 115°4W **79** J11
Suntar *Russia* 62°15N 117°30E **29** C12
Suomenselkä *Finland* 62°52N 24°0E **8** E21
Suomi = Finland ■ *Europe* 63°0N 27°0E **8** E22
Suomussalmi *Finland* 64°54N 29°10E **8** D23
Suoyarvi *Russia* 62°3N 32°20E **18** B5
Supai *U.S.A.* 36°15N 112°41W **77** H7
Supaul *India* 26°10N 86°40E **43** F12
Superior *Ariz., U.S.A.* 33°18N 111°6W **77** K8
Superior *Mont., U.S.A.* 47°12N 114°53W **76** C6
Superior *Nebr., U.S.A.* 40°1N 98°4W **80** E4
Superior *Wis., U.S.A.* 46°44N 92°6W **80** B7
Superior, L. *N. Amer.* 47°0N 87°0W **72** C2
Suphan Buri *Thailand* 14°14N 100°10E **38** E3
Suphan Dağı *Turkey* 38°54N 42°48E **44** B4
Supiori *Indonesia* 1°0S 136°0E **37** E9
Supung Shuiku *China* 40°35N 124°50E **35** D13
Sūq ash Shuyūkh *Iraq* 30°53N 46°28E **44** D5
Sūq Suwayq *Si. Arabia* 24°23N 38°27E **44** E3
Suqian *China* 33°54N 118°8E **35** H10
Suqutrā = Socotra *Yemen* 12°30N 54°0E **47** E5
Şūr *Lebanon* 33°19N 35°16E **46** B4
Şūr *Oman* 22°34N 59°32E **47** C6
Sur, Pt. *U.S.A.* 36°18N 121°54W **78** J5
Sura → *Russia* 56°6N 46°0E **18** C8
Surab *Pakistan* 28°25N 66°15E **42** E2
Surabaja = Surabaya *Indonesia* 7°17S 112°45E **37** G15
Surabaya *Indonesia* 7°17S 112°45E **37** G15
Surakarta *Indonesia* 7°35S 110°48E **37** G14
Surat *Australia* 27°10S 149°6E **63** D4
Surat *India* 21°12N 72°55E **40** J8
Surat Thani *Thailand* 9°6N 99°20E **39** H2
Suratgarh *India* 29°18N 73°55E **42** E5
Şuraymilā *Si. Arabia* 25°7N 46°7E **44** E5
Surendranagar *India* 22°45N 71°40E **42** H4
Surf *U.S.A.* 34°41N 120°36W **79** L6
Surfers Paradise *Australia* 28°0S 153°25E **63** D5
Surgut *Russia* 61°14N 73°20E **28** C8
Suriapet *India* 17°10N 79°40E **40** L11
Surigao *Phil.* 9°47N 125°29E **37** C7
Surin *Thailand* 14°50N 103°34E **38** E4

Surinam = Suriname ■
S. Amer. 4°0N 56°0W 93 C7
Suriname ■ S. Amer. 4°0N 56°0W 93 C7
Suriname → Suriname 5°50N 55°15W 93 B7
Sürmaq Iran 31°3N 52°48E 45 D7
Surrey Canada 49°7N 122°45W 78 A4
Surrey □ U.K. 51°15N 0°31W 13 F7
Sursand India 26°39N 85°43E 43 F11
Sursar → India 26°14N 87°3E 43 F12
Surt Libya 31°11N 16°39E 51 B9
Surt, Khalij Libya 31°40N 18°30E 51 B9
Surtanahu Pakistan 26°22N 70°0E 42 F4
Surtsey Iceland 63°20N 20°30W 8 E3
Suruga-Wan Japan 34°45N 138°30E 31 G9
Susaki Japan 33°22N 133°17E 31 H6
Süsangerd Iran 31°35N 48°6E 45 D6
Susanville U.S.A. 40°25N 120°39W 76 F3
Susner India 23°57N 76°5E 42 H7
Susquehanna U.S.A. 41°57N 75°36W 83 E9
Susquehanna → U.S.A. 39°33N 76°5W 83 G8
Susques Argentina 23°35S 66°25W 94 A2
Sussex Canada 45°45N 65°37W 73 C6
Sussex U.S.A. 41°13N 74°37W 83 E10
Sussex, E. □ U.K. 51°0N 0°20E 13 G8
Sussex, W. □ U.K. 51°0N 0°30W 13 G7
Sustut → Canada 56°20N 127°30W 70 B3
Susuman Russia 62°47N 148°10E 29 C15
Susunu Indonesia 3°7S 133°39E 37 E8
Susurluk Turkey 39°54N 28°8E 23 E13
Sutay Uul Asia 46°35N 93°38E 32 B7
Sutherland S. Africa 32°24S 20°40E 56 E3
Sutherland U.K. 58°12N 4°50W 11 C4
Sutherland U.S.A. 41°10N 101°8W 80 E3
Sutherland Falls N.Z. 44°48S 167°46E 59 F1
Sutherlin U.S.A. 43°23N 123°19W 76 E2
Suthri India 23°3N 68°55E 42 H3
Sutlej → Pakistan 29°23N 71°3E 42 E4
Sutter U.S.A. 39°10N 121°45W 78 F5
Sutter Buttes U.S.A. 39°12N 121°49W 78 F5
Sutter Creek U.S.A. 38°24N 120°48W 78 G6
Sutton Canada 45°6N 72°37W 83 A12
Sutton Nebr., U.S.A. 40°36N 97°52W 80 E6
Sutton W. Va., U.S.A. 38°40N 80°43W 81 F13
Sutton → Canada 55°15N 83°45W 72 A3
Sutton Coldfield U.K. 52°35N 1°49W 13 E6
Sutton in Ashfield U.K. 53°8N 1°16W 12 D6
Sutton L. Canada 54°15N 84°42W 72 B3
Suttor → Australia 21°36S 147°2E 62 C4
Suttsu Japan 42°48N 140°14E 30 C10
Sutwik I. U.S.A. 56°34N 157°12W 74 D8
Suva Fiji 18°6S 178°30E 59 a
Suva Planina Serbia 43°10N 22°5E 23 C10
Suvorov Is. = Suwarrow Is.
Cook Is. 13°15S 163°5W 65 J11
Suwałki Poland 54°8N 22°59E 17 A12
Suwannaphum
Thailand 15°33N 103°47E 38 E4
Suwannee → U.S.A. 29°17N 83°10W 85 G13
Suwanose-Jima Japan 29°38N 129°43E 31 K4
Suwarrow Is. Cook Is. 13°15S 163°5W 65 J11
Suweis, Khalig el Egypt 28°40N 33°0E 51 C12
Suweis, Qanâ es Egypt 31°0N 32°20E 51 B12
Suwon S. Korea 37°17N 127°1E 35 F14
Suzdal Russia 56°29N 40°26E 18 C7
Suzhou Anhui, China 33°41N 116°59E 34 H9
Suzhou Jiangsu, China 31°19N 120°38E 33 E13
Suzu Japan 37°25N 137°17E 31 F8
Suzu-Misaki Japan 37°31N 137°21E 31 F8
Suzuka Japan 34°55N 136°36E 31 G8
Svalbard Arctic 78°0N 17°0E 4 B8
Svalbard Radio = Longyearbyen
Svalbard 78°13N 15°40E 4 B8
Svappavaara Sweden 67°40N 21°3E 8 C19
Svartisen Norway 66°40N 13°59E 8 C15
Svay Chek Cambodia 13°48N 102°58E 38 F4
Svay Rieng Cambodia 11°9N 105°45E 39 G5
Svealand Sweden 60°20N 15°0E 9 F16
Sveg Sweden 62°2N 14°21E 8 E16
Svendborg Denmark 55°4N 10°35E 9 J14
Sverdrup Chan. Canada 79°56N 96°25W 69 B12
Sverdrup Is. Canada 79°0N 97°0W 66 B10
Sverige = Sweden ■
Europe 57°0N 15°0E 9 H16
Svetlaya Russia 46°33N 138°18E 30 A9
Svetlogorsk = Svyetlahorsk
Belarus 52°38N 29°46E 17 B15
Svir → Russia 60°30N 32°48E 18 B5
Svishtov Bulgaria 43°36N 25°23E 23 C11
Svislach Belarus 53°3N 24°2E 17 B13
Svizzera = Switzerland ■
Europe 46°30N 8°0E 20 C8
Svobodnyy Russia 51°20N 128°0E 29 D13
Svolvær Norway 68°15N 14°34E 8 B16
Svyetlahorsk Belarus 52°38N 29°46E 17 B15
Swabian Alps = Schwäbische Alb
Germany 48°20N 9°30E 16 D5
Swaffham U.K. 52°39N 0°42E 13 E8
Swains I. Amer. Samoa 11°11S 171°4W 65 J11
Swainsboro U.S.A. 32°36N 82°20W 85 E13
Swakop → Namibia 22°38S 14°36E 56 C2
Swakopmund Namibia 22°37S 14°30E 56 C1
Swale → U.K. 54°5N 1°20W 12 C6
Swan → Australia 32°3S 115°45E 61 F2
Swan → Canada 52°30N 100°45W 71 C8
Swan Hill Australia 35°20S 143°33E 63 F3
Swan Hills Canada 54°43N 115°24W 70 C5
Swan Is. = Santanilla, Is.
Honduras 17°22N 83°57W 88 C3
Swan L. Man., Canada 52°30N 100°40W 71 C8
Swan L. Ont., Canada 54°16N 91°11W 72 B1
Swan Ra. U.S.A. 48°0N 113°45W 76 C7
Swan River Canada 52°10N 101°16W 71 C8
Swanage U.K. 50°36N 1°58W 13 G6
Swansea Australia 42°8S 148°4E 63 G4
Swansea Canada 43°38N 79°28W 82 C5
Swansea U.K. 51°37N 3°57W 13 F4
Swansea □ U.K. 51°38N 4°3W 13 F3
Swartberge S. Africa 33°20S 22°0E 56 E3
Swartmodder S. Africa 28°1S 20°32E 56 D3
Swartnossob → Namibia 23°8S 18°42E 56 C2

Swartruggens S. Africa 25°39S 26°42E 56 D4
Swastika Canada 48°7N 80°6W 72 C3
Swat → Pakistan 34°40N 72°5E 43 B5
Swatow = Shantou
China 23°18N 116°40E 33 G12
Swaziland ■ Africa 26°30S 31°30E 57 D5
Sweden ■ Europe 57°0N 15°0E 9 H16
Sweet Grass U.S.A. 48°59N 111°58W 76 B8
Sweet Home U.S.A. 44°24N 122°44W 76 D2
Sweetwater Nev., U.S.A. 38°27N 119°9W 78 G7
Sweetwater Tenn.,
U.S.A. 35°36N 84°28W 85 D12
Sweetwater Tex.,
U.S.A. 32°28N 100°25W 84 E4
Sweetwater → U.S.A. 42°31N 107°2W 76 E10
Swellendam S. Africa 34°1S 20°26E 56 E3
Świdnica Poland 50°50N 16°30E 17 C9
Świdnik Poland 51°13N 22°39E 17 C12
Świebodzin Poland 52°15N 15°31E 16 B8
Świecie Poland 53°25N 18°30E 17 B10
Świętokrzyskie → Poland 51°0N 21°0E 17 C11
Świdwin Poland 53°54N 14°16E 16 B8
Swinford Ireland 53°57N 8°58W 10 C3
Świnoujście Poland 53°54N 14°16E 16 B8
Switzerland ■ Europe 46°30N 8°0E 20 C8
Swords Ireland 53°28N 6°13W 10 C5
Swoyerville U.S.A. 41°18N 75°53W 83 E9
Sydenham → Canada 42°33N 82°25W 82 D2
Sydney Australia 33°52S 151°12E 63 E5
Sydney Canada 46°7N 60°7W 73 C7
Sydney L. Canada 50°41N 94°25W 71 C10
Sydney Mines Canada 46°18N 60°15W 73 C7
Sydprøven = Alluitsup Paa
Greenland 60°30N 45°35W 4 C5
Sydra, G. of = Surt, Khalij
Libya 31°40N 18°30E 51 B9
Sykesville U.S.A. 41°3N 78°50W 82 E6
Syktyvkar Russia 61°45N 50°40E 18 B9
Sylacauga U.S.A. 33°10N 86°15W 85 E11
Sylarna Sweden 63°2N 12°13E 8 E15
Sylhet Bangla. 24°54N 91°52E 41 G17
Sylhet □ Bangla. 24°50N 91°50E 41 G17
Sylt Germany 54°54N 8°22E 16 A5
Sylvan Beach U.S.A. 43°12N 75°44W 83 D9
Sylvan Lake Canada 52°20N 114°3W 70 C6
Sylvania Ga., U.S.A. 32°45N 81°38W 85 E14
Sylvania Ohio, U.S.A. 41°43N 83°42W 81 E12
Sylvester U.S.A. 31°32N 83°50W 85 F13
Sym Russia 60°20N 88°18E 28 C9
Synnot Ra. Australia 16°30S 125°20E 60 C4
Syowa Antarctica 68°50S 12°0E 5 C5
Syracuse Kans., U.S.A. 37°59N 101°45W 80 G3
Syracuse N.Y., U.S.A. 43°3N 76°9W 83 C8
Syracuse Nebr., U.S.A. 40°39N 96°11W 80 E6
Syrdarya → Kazakhstan 46°3N 61°0E 28 E7
Syria ■ Asia 35°0N 38°0E 44 C3
Syrian Desert = Shām, Bādiyat
ash Asia 32°0N 40°0E 44 C3
Syros = Ermoupoli
Greece 37°28N 24°57E 23 F11
Syzran Russia 53°12N 48°30E 18 D8
Szczecin Poland 53°27N 14°27E 16 B8
Szczecinek Poland 53°43N 16°41E 17 B9
Szczeciński, Zalew = Stettiner Haff
Germany 53°47N 14°15E 16 B8
Szczytno Poland 53°33N 21°0E 17 B11
Szechwan = Sichuan □
China 30°30N 103°0E 32 E9
Szeged Hungary 46°16N 20°10E 17 E11
Székesfehérvár Hungary 47°15N 18°25E 17 E10
Szekszárd Hungary 46°22N 18°42E 17 E10
Szentes Hungary 46°39N 20°21E 17 E11
Szolnok Hungary 47°10N 20°15E 17 E11
Szombathely Hungary 47°14N 16°38E 17 E9

T

Ta Khli Thailand 15°15N 100°21E 38 E3
Ta Lai Vietnam 11°24N 107°23E 39 G6
Ta Phraya △ Thailand 14°11N 102°49E 38 E4
Tabacal Argentina 23°15S 64°15W 94 A3
Tabaco Phil. 13°22N 123°44E 37 B6
Tabah Si. Arabia 26°55N 42°38E 44 E4
Tabas Khorāsān, Iran 32°48N 60°12E 45 C9
Tabas Yazd, Iran 33°35N 56°55E 45 C8
Tabasará, Serranía de
Panama 8°35N 81°40W 88 E3
Tabasco □ Mexico 18°0N 92°40W 87 D6
Tābask Iran 31°12N 57°54E 45 D8
Tabatinga, Serra da
Brazil 10°30S 44°0W 93 F10
Taber Canada 49°47N 112°8W 70 D6
Tablas I. Phil. 12°25N 122°2E 37 B6
Table, Pte. de la Réunion 21°14S 55°48E 53 c
Table B. Canada 53°40N 56°25W 73 B8
Table B. S. Africa 33°35S 18°25E 56 E2
Table Mountain △
S. Africa 34°0S 18°28E 56 E2
Table Mt. S. Africa 33°58S 18°26E 56 E2
Table Rock L. U.S.A. 36°36N 93°19W 80 G7
Tabletop, Mt. Australia 23°24S 147°11E 62 C4
Tábor Czech Rep. 49°25N 14°39E 16 D8
Tabora Tanzania 5°2S 32°50E 54 D3
Tabora □ Tanzania 5°0S 33°0E 54 D3
Tabou Ivory C. 4°30N 7°20W 50 H4
Tabrīz Iran 38°7N 46°20E 44 B5
Tabuaeran Kiribati 3°51N 159°22W 65 G12
Tabūk Si. Arabia 28°23N 36°15E 44 D3
Tabūk □ Si. Arabia 27°40N 36°50E 44 E3
Tacámbaro de Codallos
Mexico 19°14N 101°28W 86 D4
Tacheng China 46°40N 82°58E 32 B5

Tachilek Burma 20°26N 99°52E 38 B2
Tach'ing Shan = Daqing Shan
China 40°40N 111°0E 34 D6
Tacloban Phil. 11°15N 124°58E 37 B6
Tacna Peru 18°0S 70°20W 92 G4
Tacoma U.S.A. 47°14N 122°26W 78 C4
Tacuarembó Uruguay 31°45S 56°0W 95 C4
Tademaït, Plateau du
Algeria 28°30N 2°30E 50 C6
Tadjoura Djibouti 11°50N 42°55E 47 E3
Tadmor N.Z. 41°27S 172°45E 59 D4
Tadoule L. Canada 58°36N 98°20W 71 B9
Tadoussac Canada 48°11N 69°42W 73 C6
Tadzhikistan = Tajikistan ■
Asia 38°30N 70°0E 28 F8
Taegu = Daegu
S. Korea 35°50N 128°37E 35 G15
Taegwan N. Korea 40°13N 125°12E 35 D13
Taejon = Daejeon
S. Korea 36°20N 127°28E 35 F14
Taen, Ko Thailand 9°22N 99°57E 39 b
Tafalla Spain 42°30N 1°41W 21 A5
Tafelbaai = Table B.
S. Africa 33°35S 18°25E 56 E2
Tafermaar Indonesia 6°47S 134°10E 37 F8
Tafí Viejo Argentina 26°43S 65°17W 94 B2
Tafihān Iran 29°25N 52°39E 45 D7
Tafresh Iran 34°45N 49°57E 45 C6
Taft Iran 31°45N 54°14E 45 D7
Taft Phil. 11°57N 125°30E 37 B7
Taft U.S.A. 35°8N 119°28W 79 K7
Taftan Pakistan 29°0N 61°30E 40 E2
Taftān, Küh-e Iran 28°40N 61°0E 45 D9
Taga Uruguay 13°46S 172°28W 59 b
Taga Dzong Bhutan 27°5N 89°55E 41 F16
Taganrog Russia 47°12N 38°50E 19 E6
Tagbilaran Phil. 9°39N 123°51E 37 C6
Tagish Canada 60°19N 134°16W 70 A2
Tagish L. Canada 60°10N 134°20W 70 A2
Tagliamento → Italy 45°38N 13°6E 22 B5
Tagomago Spain 39°2N 1°39E 24 B8
Taguatinga Brazil 12°25S 46°22W 93 F10
Tagum Phil. 7°33N 125°53E 37 C7
Tagus = Tejo → Europe 38°40N 9°24E 21 C1
Tahakopa N.Z. 46°30S 169°23E 59 G2
Tahan, Gunung
Malaysia 4°34N 102°17E 39 K4
Tahat Algeria 23°18N 5°33E 50 D7
Tāherī Iran 27°43N 52°20E 45 E7
Tahiti French Polynesia 17°37S 149°27W 59 d
Tahiti, I. Tahiti 17°37S 149°27W 59 d
Tahlequah U.S.A. 35°55N 94°58W 84 D7
Tahoe, L. U.S.A. 39°6N 120°2W 78 F6
Tahoe City U.S.A. 39°10N 120°9W 78 F6
Tahoka U.S.A. 33°10N 101°48W 84 E2
Taholah U.S.A. 47°21N 124°17W 78 C2
Tahoua Niger 14°57N 5°16E 50 F7
Tahrūd Iran 29°26N 57°49E 45 D8
Tahsis Canada 49°55N 126°40W 70 D3
Tahta Egypt 26°44N 31°32E 51 C12
Tahulandang Indonesia 2°27N 125°23E 37 D7
Tahuna Indonesia 3°38N 125°30E 37 D7
Tai Hu China 31°5N 120°10E 33 E13
Tai Mo Shan China 22°25N 114°7E 33 a
Tai O China 22°15N 113°52E 33 a
Tai Pang Wan China 22°33N 114°24E 33 a
Tai Po China 22°27N 114°10E 33 a
Tai Rom Yen △ Thailand 8°45N 99°30E 39 H2
Tai Shan China 36°25N 117°20E 35 F9
Tai Yue Shan = Lantau I.
China 22°15N 113°56E 33 a
Tai'an China 36°12N 117°8E 35 F9
Taiarapu, Presqu'île de
Tahiti 17°47S 149°14W 59 d
Taibai Shan China 33°57N 107°45E 34 H4
Taibei = T'aipei Taiwan 25°4N 121°29E 33 F13
Taibique Canary Is. 27°42N 17°58W 24 G2
Taibus Qi China 41°54N 115°22E 34 D8
T'aichung Taiwan 24°9N 120°37E 33 G13
Taieri → N.Z. 46°3S 170°12E 59 G3
Taigu China 37°28N 112°30E 34 F7
Taihang Shan China 36°0N 113°30E 34 F7
Taihape N.Z. 39°41S 175°48E 59 C5
Taihe China 34°55N 115°42E 34 H8
Taikang China 34°5N 114°50E 34 G8
Tailem Bend Australia 35°12S 139°29E 63 F2
Taimyr Peninsula = Taymyr,
Poluostrov Russia 75°0N 100°0E 29 B11
Tain U.K. 57°49N 4°4W 11 D4
T'ainan Taiwan 23°0N 120°10E 33 G13
Taipa China 22°10N 113°35E 33 a
T'aipei Taiwan 25°4N 121°29E 33 F13
Taiping Malaysia 4°51N 100°44E 39 K3
Taipingchuan China 44°23N 123°11E 35 B12
Taipingzhen China 33°35N 111°42E 34 H6
Taitao, Pen. de Chile 46°30S 75°0W 96 F2
T'aitung Taiwan 22°43N 121°4E 33 G13
Taivalkoski Finland 65°33N 28°12E 8 D23
Taiwan ■ Asia 23°30N 121°0E 33 G13
Taiwan Strait Asia 24°40N 120°0E 33 G12
Taiyiba Israel 32°36N 35°27E 46 C4
Taiyuan China 37°52N 112°33E 34 F7
Taizhong = T'aichung
Taiwan 24°9N 120°37E 33 G13
Taizhou China 32°28N 119°55E 33 E12
Ta'izz Yemen 13°35N 44°2E 47 E3
Tājābād Iran 30°2N 54°24E 45 D7
Tajikistan ■ Asia 38°30N 70°0E 28 F8
Tajima Japan 37°12N 139°46E 31 F9
Tajo = Tejo → Europe 38°40N 9°24E 21 C1
Tajrīsh Iran 35°48N 51°25E 45 C6
Tak Thailand 16°52N 99°8E 38 D2
Takāb Iran 36°24N 47°7E 44 B5
Takachiho Japan 32°42N 131°18E 31 H5
Takachu Botswana 22°37S 21°58E 56 C3
Takada Japan 37°7N 138°15E 31 F9
Takahagi Japan 36°43N 140°45E 31 F10
Takaka N.Z. 40°51S 172°50E 59 D4

Takamaka Seychelles 4°50S 55°30E 53 b
Takamatsu Japan 34°20N 134°5E 31 G7
Takaoka Japan 36°47N 137°0E 31 F8
Takapuna N.Z. 36°47S 174°47E 59 B5
Takasaki Japan 36°20N 139°0E 31 F9
Takatsuki Japan 34°51N 135°37E 31 G7
Takaungu Kenya 3°38S 39°52E 54 C4
Takayama Japan 36°18N 137°11E 31 F8
Take-Shima Japan 30°49N 130°26E 31 J5
Takefu Japan 35°50N 136°10E 31 G8
Takengon Indonesia 4°45N 96°50E 36 D1
Takeo Cambodia 10°59N 104°47E 39 G5
Takeo Japan 33°12N 130°1E 31 H5
Takeshima = Tokdo
Asia 37°15N 131°52E 31 F5
Tākestān Iran 36°0N 49°40E 45 C6
Taketa Japan 32°58N 131°24E 31 H5
Takh India 33°6N 77°32E 43 C7
Takhmau Cambodia 11°29N 104°57E 39 G5
Takht-Sulaiman
Pakistan 31°40N 69°58E 42 D3
Takikawa Japan 43°33N 141°54E 30 C10
Takla L. Canada 55°15N 125°45W 70 B3
Takla Landing Canada 55°30N 125°50W 70 B3
Takla Makan China 38°0N 83°0E 32 D5
Taklamakan Shamo = Takla
Makan China 38°0N 83°0E 32 D5
Taksimo Russia 56°20N 114°52E 29 D12
Taku → Canada 58°30N 133°50W 70 B2
Takua Thung Thailand 8°24N 98°27E 39 a
Tal Halāl Iran 28°54N 55°1E 45 D7
Tala Uruguay 34°21S 55°46W 95 C4
Talagang Pakistan 32°55N 72°25E 42 C5
Talagante Chile 33°40S 70°50W 94 C1
Talamanca, Cordillera de
Cent. Amer. 9°20N 83°20W 88 E3
Talampaya △ Argentina 29°43S 67°42W 94 B2
Talara Peru 4°38S 81°18W 92 D2
Talas Kyrgyzstan 42°30N 72°13E 28 E8
Talâta Egypt 30°36N 32°20E 46 E1
Talaud, Kepulauan
Indonesia 4°30N 126°50E 37 D7
Talaud Is. = Talaud, Kepulauan
Indonesia 4°30N 126°50E 37 D7
Talavera de la Reina
Spain 39°55N 4°46W 21 C3
Talayan Phil. 6°52N 124°24E 37 C6
Talbandh India 22°3N 86°20E 43 H12
Talbot, C. Australia 13°48S 126°43E 60 B4
Talbragar → Australia 32°12S 148°37E 63 E4
Talca Chile 35°28S 71°40W 94 D1
Talcahuano Chile 36°40S 73°10W 94 D1
Talcher India 21°0N 85°18E 41 J14
Taldy Kurgan = Taldyqorghan
Kazakhstan 45°10N 78°45E 32 B4
Taldyqorghan
Kazakhstan 45°10N 78°45E 32 B4
Tālesh Iran 37°58N 48°58E 45 B6
Tālesh, Kühhā-ye Iran 37°42N 48°55E 45 B6
Tali Post Sudan 5°55N 30°44E 51 G12
Taliabu Indonesia 1°50S 125°0E 37 E6
Talibon Phil. 10°9N 124°20E 37 B6
Talihina U.S.A. 34°45N 95°3W 84 D7
Taliwang Indonesia 8°50S 116°55E 36 F5
Tall 'Afar Iraq 36°22N 42°27E 44 B4
Tall Kalakh Syria 34°41N 36°15E 46 A5
Talladega U.S.A. 33°26N 86°6W 85 E11
Tallahassee U.S.A. 30°27N 84°17W 85 F12
Tallangatta Australia 36°15S 147°19E 63 F4
Tallering Pk. Australia 28°6S 115°37E 61 E2
Talli Pakistan 29°32N 68°8E 42 E3
Tallinn Estonia 59°22N 24°48E 9 G21
Tallmadge U.S.A. 41°6N 81°27W 82 E3
Tallulah U.S.A. 32°25N 91°11W 84 E9
Talnakh Russia 69°29N 88°22E 29 C9
Taloyoak Canada 69°32N 93°32W 68 D13
Talpa de Allende
Mexico 20°23N 104°51W 86 C4
Talparo Trin. & Tob. 10°30N 61°17W 93 K15
Talsi Latvia 57°10N 22°30E 9 H20
Taltal Chile 25°23S 70°33W 94 B1
Taltson → Canada 61°24N 112°46W 70 A6
Talwood Australia 28°29S 149°29E 63 D4
Talyawalka Cr. →
Australia 32°28S 142°22E 63 E3
Tam Dao △ Vietnam 21°45N 105°45E 38 B5
Tam Ky Vietnam 15°34N 108°29E 38 E7
Tam Quan Vietnam 14°35N 109°3E 38 E7
Tama U.S.A. 41°58N 92°35W 80 E7
Tama Abu, Banjaran
Malaysia 3°50N 115°5E 36 D5
Tamale Ghana 9°22N 0°50W 50 G5
Tamano Japan 34°29N 133°59E 31 G6
Tamanrasset Algeria 22°50N 5°30E 50 D7
Tamaqua U.S.A. 40°48N 75°58W 83 F9
Tamar → U.K. 50°27N 4°15W 13 G3
Tamarin Mauritius 20°19S 57°20E 53 d
Tamarinda Spain 39°55N 3°49E 24 B10
Tamashima Japan 34°32N 133°40E 31 G6
Tamatave = Toamasina
Madag. 18°10S 49°25E 57 B8
Tamaulipas □ Mexico 24°0N 98°45W 87 C5
Tamaulipas, Sierra de
Mexico 23°30N 98°20W 87 C5
Tamazula Mexico 24°57N 106°57W 86 C3
Tamazunchale Mexico 21°16N 98°47W 87 C5
Tambacounda Senegal 13°45N 13°40W 50 F3
Tambelan, Kepulauan
Indonesia 1°0N 107°30E 36 D3
Tambellup Australia 34°4S 117°37E 61 F2
Tambo Australia 24°54S 146°14E 62 C4
Tambo de Mora Peru 13°30S 76°8W 92 F3
Tambohorano Madag. 17°30S 43°58E 57 B7
Tambora Indonesia 8°12S 118°5E 36 F5
Tamboura C.A.R. 5°10N 25°12E 54 B2
Tambov Russia 52°45N 41°28E 18 D7
Tambuku Indonesia 7°8S 113°40E 37 G15

Tâmega → Portugal 41°5N 8°21W 21 B1
Tamenglong India 25°0N 93°35E 41 G18
Tamiahua, L. de Mexico 21°35N 97°35W 87 C5
Tamil Nadu □ India 11°0N 77°0E 40 P10
Tamluk India 22°18N 87°58E 43 H12
Tammerfors = Tampere
Finland 61°30N 23°50E 8 F20
Tampa U.S.A. 27°56N 82°27W 85 H13
Tampa, Tanjung
Indonesia 8°55S 116°12E 37 K19
Tampa B. U.S.A. 27°50N 82°30W 85 H13
Tampere Finland 61°30N 23°50E 8 F20
Tampico Mexico 22°13N 97°51W 87 C5
Tampin Malaysia 2°28N 102°13E 39 L4
Tampoi Malaysia 1°30N 103°39E 39 d
Tamsagbulag
Mongolia 47°14N 117°21E 33 B6
Tamu Burma 24°13N 94°12E 41 G19
Tamworth Australia 31°7S 150°58E 63 E5
Tamworth Canada 44°29N 77°0W 82 B8
Tamworth U.K. 52°39N 1°41W 13 E6
Tan An Vietnam 10°32N 106°25E 39 G6
Tan Chau Vietnam 10°48N 105°12E 39 G5
Tan Hiep Vietnam 10°27N 106°21E 39 G6
Tan-Tan Morocco 28°29N 11°1W 50 C3
Tan Yen Vietnam 22°4N 105°3E 38 A5
Tana → Kenya 2°32S 40°31E 54 C5
Tana → Norway 70°30N 28°14E 8 A23
Tana, L. Ethiopia 13°5N 37°30E 47 E2
Tana River Primate △
Kenya 1°55S 40°7E 54 C5
Tanabe Japan 33°44N 135°22E 31 H7
Tanafjorden Norway 70°45N 28°25E 8 A23
Tanaga I. U.S.A. 51°48N 177°53W 74 E4
Tanah Merah Malaysia 5°48N 102°9E 39 K4
Tanahbala Indonesia 0°30S 98°30E 36 E1
Tanahgrogot Indonesia 1°55S 116°15E 36 E5
Tanahjampea Indonesia 7°10S 120°35E 37 F6
Tanahmasa Indonesia 0°12S 98°39E 36 E1
Tanahmerah Indonesia 6°5S 140°16E 37 F10
Tanakpur India 29°5N 80°7E 43 E9
Tanakura Japan 37°10N 140°20E 31 F10
Tanami Desert Australia 18°50S 132°0E 60 C5
Tanana U.S.A. 65°10N 152°4W 74 B9
Tanana → U.S.A. 65°10N 151°58W 68 D1
Tananarive = Antananarivo
Madag. 18°55S 47°31E 57 B8
Tánaro → Italy 44°55N 8°40E 20 D8
Tancheng China 34°25N 118°20E 35 G10
Tanch'on N. Korea 40°27N 128°54E 35 D15
Tanda Ut. P., India 26°33N 82°35E 43 F10
Tanda Ut. P., India 28°57N 78°56E 43 E8
Tandag Phil. 9°4N 126°9E 37 C7
Tandaia Tanzania 9°25S 34°15E 55 D3
Tandaué Angola 16°58S 18°5E 56 B2
Tandil Argentina 37°15S 59°6W 94 D4
Tandil, Sa. del Argentina 37°30S 59°0W 94 D4
Tandlianwala Pakistan 31°3N 73°9E 42 D5
Tando Adam Pakistan 25°45N 68°40E 42 G3
Tando Allahyar Pakistan 25°28N 68°43E 42 G3
Tando Bago Pakistan 24°47N 68°58E 42 G3
Tando Mohommed Khan
Pakistan 25°8N 68°32E 42 G3
Tandou L. Australia 32°40S 142°5E 63 E3
Tandragee U.K. 54°21N 6°24W 10 B5
Tane-ga-Shima Japan 30°30N 131°0E 31 J5
Taneatua N.Z. 38°4S 177°1E 59 C6
Tanen Tong Dan = Dawna Ra.
Burma 16°30N 98°30E 38 D2
Tanezrouft Algeria 23°9N 0°11E 50 D6
Tang, Koh Cambodia 10°16N 103°7E 39 G4
Tang, Ra's-e Iran 25°21N 59°52E 45 E8
Tang Krasang Cambodia 12°34N 105°3E 38 F5
Tanga Tanzania 5°5S 39°2E 54 D4
Tanga □ Tanzania 5°20S 38°0E 54 D4
Tanganyika, L. Africa 6°40S 30°0E 54 D2
Tanger Morocco 35°50N 5°49W 50 A4
Tangerang Indonesia 6°11S 106°37E 37 G12
Tanggu China 39°2N 117°40E 35 E9
Tanggula Shan China 32°40N 92°10E 32 E7
Tanggula Shankou
China 32°42N 92°27E 32 E7
China 32°47N 112°50E 34 H7
Tanghla Range = Tanggula Shan
China 32°40N 92°10E 32 E7
Tangier = Tanger
Morocco 35°50N 5°49W 50 A4
Tangjia China 22°22N 113°35E 33 a
Tangjia Wan China 22°21N 113°36E 33 a
Tangorin Australia 21°47S 144°12E 62 C3
Tangorombohitr'i Makay
Madag. 21°0S 45°15E 57 C8
Tangra Yumco China 31°0N 86°38E 32 E6
Tangshan China 39°38N 118°10E 35 E10
Tangtou China 35°28N 118°30E 35 G10
Tangyin China 35°54N 114°21E 34 G8
Tanimbar, Kepulauan
Indonesia 7°30S 131°30E 37 F8
Tanimbar Is. = Tanimbar,
Kepulauan Indonesia 7°30S 131°30E 37 F8
Taninthari = Tenasserim
Burma 12°6N 99°3E 39 F2
Tanjay Phil. 9°30N 123°5E 37 C6
Tanjong Pelepas Malaysia 1°21N 103°33E 39 d
Tanjore = Thanjavur
India 10°48N 79°12E 40 P11
Tanjung Kalimantan Selatan,
Indonesia 2°10S 115°25E 36 E5
Tanjung Nusa Tenggara Barat,
Indonesia 8°21S 116°9E 37 J19
Tanjung Malim Malaysia 3°42N 101°31E 39 L3
Tanjung Tokong Malaysia 5°28N 100°18E 39 c
Tanjungbalai Indonesia 2°55N 99°44E 36 D1
Tanjungbatu Indonesia 2°23N 118°3E 36 D5
Tanjungkarang Telukbetung =
Bandar Lampung
Indonesia 5°20S 105°10E 36 F3
Tanjungpandan
Indonesia 2°43S 107°38E 36 E3

Tanjungpinang *Indonesia* 1°5N 104°30E **36** D2
Tanjungredeb *Indonesia* 2°9N 117°29E **36** D5
Tanjungselor *Indonesia* 2°55N 117°25E **36** D5
Tank *Pakistan* 32°14N 70°25E **42** C4
Tankhala *India* 21°58N 73°47E **42** J5
Tankwa-Karoo △
  S. Africa 32°14S 19°50E **56** E2
Tannersville *U.S.A.* 41°3N 75°18W **83** E9
Tannu Ola *Asia* 51°0N 94°0E **29** D10
Tannum Sands
  Australia 23°57S 151°22E **62** C5
Tanout *Niger* 14°50N 8°55E **50** F7
Tanta *Egypt* 30°45N 30°57E **51** B12
Tantoyuca *Mexico* 21°21N 98°14W **87** C5
Tantung = Dandong
  China 40°10N 124°20E **35** D13
Tanunda *Australia* 34°30S 139°0E **63** E2
Tanzania ■ *Africa* 6°0S 34°0E **54** D3
Tanzhou *China* 22°16N 113°28E **33** a
Tanzilla → *Canada* 58°8N 130°43W **70** B2
Tao, Ko *Thailand* 10°5N 99°52E **39** G2
Tao'an = Taonan
  China 45°22N 122°40E **35** B12
Tao'er He → *China* 45°45N 124°5E **35** B13
Taolanaro *Madag.* 25°2S 47°0E **57** D8
Taole *China* 38°48N 106°40E **34** E4
Taonan *China* 45°22N 122°40E **35** B12
Taos *U.S.A.* 36°24N 105°35W **77** H11
Taoudenni *Mali* 22°40N 3°55W **50** D5
Tapa *Estonia* 59°15N 25°50E **9** G21
Tapa Shan = Daba Shan
  China 32°0N 109°0E **33** E10
Tapachula *Mexico* 14°54N 92°17W **87** E6
Tapah *Malaysia* 4°12N 101°15E **39** K3
Tapajós → *Brazil* 2°24S 54°41W **93** D8
Tapaktuan *Indonesia* 3°15N 97°10E **36** D1
Tapanahoni → *Suriname* 4°20N 54°25W **93** C8
Tapanui *N.Z.* 45°56S 169°18E **59** F2
Tapauá → *Brazil* 5°40S 64°21W **92** E6
Tapes *Brazil* 30°40S 51°23W **95** C5
Tapeta *Liberia* 6°29N 8°52W **50** G4
Taphan Hin *Thailand* 16°13N 100°26E **38** D3
Tapirapecó, Serra
  Venezuela 1°10N 65°0W **92** C6
Tapo-Capara △ *Venezuela* 7°55N 71°15W **89** E5
Tapti → *India* 21°8N 72°41E **40** J8
Tapuae-o-Uenuku *N.Z.* 42°0S 173°39E **59** E4
Tapul Group *Phil.* 5°35N 120°50E **37** C6
Tapurucuará *Brazil* 0°24S 65°2W **92** D5
Taqtaq *Iraq* 35°53N 44°35E **44** C5
Taquara *Brazil* 29°36S 50°46W **95** B5
Taquari → *Brazil* 19°15S 57°17W **92** G7
Tara *Australia* 27°17S 150°31E **63** D5
Tara *Canada* 44°28N 81°9W **82** B3
Tara *Russia* 56°55N 74°24E **28** D8
Tara *Zambia* 16°58S 26°45E **55** F2
Tara → *Montenegro* 43°21N 18°51E **23** C8
Tarābulus *Lebanon* 34°31N 35°50E **46** A4
Tarābulus *Libya* 32°49N 13°7E **51** B8
Tarābulus *N. Afr.* 31°0N 13°0E **51** B8
Taradehi *India* 23°18N 79°21E **43** H8
Tarajalejo *Canary Is.* 28°12N 14°7W **24** F5
Tarakan *Indonesia* 3°2S0N 117°35E **36** D5
Tarakit, Mt. *Kenya* 2°2N 35°10E **54** B4
Tarama-Jima *Japan* 24°39N 124°42E **31** M2
Taran, Mys *Russia* 54°56N 19°59E **9** J18
Taranagar *India* 28°43N 74°50E **42** E6
Taranaki □ *N.Z.* 39°25S 174°30E **59** C5
Taranaki, Mt. *N.Z.* 39°17S 174°5E **59** C5
Tarancón *Spain* 40°1N 3°1W **21** B4
Tarangire △ *Tanzania* 4°21S 36°7E **54** C4
Taransay *U.K.* 57°54N 7°0W **11** D1
Táranto *Italy* 40°28N 17°14E **22** D7
Táranto, G. di *Italy* 40°8N 17°20E **22** D7
Tarapacá *Colombia* 2°56S 69°46W **92** D5
Tarapacá □ *Chile* 20°45S 69°30W **94** A2
Tarapoto *Peru* 6°30S 76°20W **92** E3
Tararua Ra. *N.Z.* 40°45S 175°25E **59** D5
Tarashcha *Ukraine* 49°30N 30°31E **17** D16
Tarauacá *Brazil* 8°6S 70°48W **92** E4
Tarauacá → *Brazil* 6°42S 69°48W **92** E5
Taravao *Tahiti* 17°43S 149°19W **59** d
Taravao, Isthme de
  Tahiti 17°43S 149°19W **59** d
Tarawa *Kiribati* 1°30N 173°0E **64** G9
Tarawera *N.Z.* 39°2S 176°36E **59** C6
Tarawera, L. *N.Z.* 38°13S 176°27E **59** C6
Taraz *Kazakhstan* 42°54N 71°22E **32** C3
Tarazona *Spain* 41°55N 1°43W **21** B5
Tarbagatay, Khrebet
  Kazakhstan 48°0N 83°0E **32** B5
Tarbat Ness *U.K.* 57°52N 3°47W **11** D5
Tarbela Dam *Pakistan* 34°8N 72°52E **42** B5
Tarbert *Ireland* 52°34N 9°22W **10** D2
Tarbert *Argyll & Bute,*
  U.K. 55°52N 5°25W **11** F3
Tarbert *W. Isles, U.K.* 57°54N 6°49W **11** D2
Tarbes *France* 43°15N 0°3E **20** E4
Tarboro *U.S.A.* 35°54N 77°32W **85** D16
Tarcoola *Australia* 30°44S 134°36E **63** E1
Tarcoon *Australia* 30°15S 146°43E **63** E4
Taree *Australia* 31°50S 152°30E **63** E5
Tarfaya *Morocco* 27°55N 12°55W **50** C3
Târgoviște *Romania* 44°55N 25°27E **17** F13
Târgu Jiu *Romania* 45°5N 23°19E **17** F12
Târgu Mureş *Romania* 46°31N 24°38E **17** E13
Ţarif *U.A.E.* 24°3N 53°46E **45** E7
Tarifa *Spain* 36°1N 5°36W **21** D3
Tarija *Bolivia* 21°30S 64°40W **94** A3
Tarija □ *Bolivia* 21°30S 63°30W **94** A3
Tariku → *Indonesia* 2°55S 138°26E **37** E9
Tarim Basin = Tarim Pendi
  China 40°0N 84°0E **32** C5
Tarim He → *China* 39°30N 88°30E **32** D6
Tarim Pendi *China* 40°0N 84°0E **32** C5
Taritatu → *Indonesia* 2°54S 138°27E **37** E9
Tarka → *S. Africa* 32°10S 26°0E **56** E4
Tarka La *Bhutan* 27°12N 89°44E **43** F13
Tarkastad *S. Africa* 32°0S 26°16E **56** E4
Tarkhankut, Mys
  Ukraine 45°25N 32°30E **19** E5

Tarko Sale *Russia* 64°55N 77°50E **28** C8
Tarkwa *Ghana* 5°20N 2°0W **50** G5
Tarlac *Phil.* 15°29N 120°35E **37** A6
Tarma *Peru* 11°25S 75°45W **92** F3
Tarn → *France* 44°5N 1°6E **20** E4
Târnăveni *Romania* 46°19N 24°13E **17** E13
Tarnobrzeg *Poland* 50°35N 21°41E **17** C11
Tarnów *Poland* 50°3N 21°0E **17** C11
Tarnowskie Góry
  Poland 50°27N 18°54E **17** C10
Tārom *Iran* 28°11N 55°46E **45** D7
Taroom *Australia* 25°36S 149°48E **63** D4
Taroudannt *Morocco* 30°30N 8°52W **50** B4
Tarpon Springs *U.S.A.* 28°9N 82°45W **85** G13
Tarrafal *C. Verde Is.* 15°18N 23°39W **50** b
Tarragona *Spain* 41°5N 1°17E **21** B6
Tarraleah *Australia* 42°17S 146°26E **63** G4
Tarrasa = Terrassa *Spain* 41°34N 2°1E **21** B7
Tarrytown *U.S.A.* 41°4N 73°52W **83** E11
Tarshiha = Me'ona *Israel* 33°1N 35°15E **46** B4
Tarsus *Turkey* 36°58N 34°55E **44** B2
Tartagal *Argentina* 22°30S 63°50W **94** A3
Tartu *Estonia* 58°20N 26°44E **9** G22
Ţarţūs *Syria* 34°55N 35°55E **44** C2
Tarumizu *Japan* 31°29N 130°42E **31** J5
Tarutao = Ko Tarutao △
  Thailand 6°31N 99°26E **39** J2
Tarutao, Ko *Thailand* 6°33N 99°40E **39** J2
Tarutung *Indonesia* 2°0N 98°54E **36** D1
Taseko → *Canada* 52°8N 123°45W **70** C4
Tash-Kömür *Kyrgyzstan* 41°40N 72°10E **28** E8
Tash-Kumyr = Tash-Kömür
  Kyrgyzstan 41°40N 72°10E **28** E8
Tashauz = Dashoguz
  Turkmenistan 41°49N 59°58E **28** E6
Tashi Chho Dzong = Thimphu
  Bhutan 27°31N 89°45E **41** F16
Ţashk, Daryācheh-ye
  Iran 29°45N 53°35E **45** D7
Tashkent = Toshkent
  Uzbekistan 41°20N 69°10E **28** E7
Tashtagol *Russia* 52°47N 87°53E **28** D9
Tasiilaq *Greenland* 65°40N 37°20W **4** C6
Tasikmalaya *Indonesia* 7°18S 108°12E **37** G13
Tåsjön *Sweden* 64°15N 15°40E **8** D16
Taskan *Russia* 62°59N 150°20E **29** C16
Tasman B. *N.Z.* 40°59S 173°25E **59** D4
Tasman Basin *Pac. Oc.* 46°0S 158°0E **64** M7
Tasman Mts. *N.Z.* 41°3S 172°25E **59** D4
Tasman Pen. *Australia* 43°10S 148°0E **63** G4
Tasman Sea *Pac. Oc.* 36°0S 160°0E **58** E9
Tasmania □ *Australia* 42°0S 146°30E **63** G4
Tasmanian Wilderness World
  Heritage Area △
  Australia 43°0S 146°0E **63** G4
Tassili n' Ajjer *Algeria* 25°47N 8°1E **50** C7
Tassili-Oua-n-Ahaggar
  Algeria 20°41N 5°30E **50** D7
Tat Ton △ *Thailand* 15°57N 102°2E **38** E4
Tata *Morocco* 29°46N 7°56W **50** C4
Tatabánya *Hungary* 47°32N 18°25E **17** E10
Tataouine *Tunisia* 32°57N 10°29E **51** B8
Tatar Republic = Tatarstan □
  Russia 55°30N 51°30E **18** C9
Tatarbunary *Ukraine* 45°50N 29°39E **17** F15
Tatarsk *Russia* 55°14N 76°0E **28** D8
Tatarskiy Proliv *Russia* 50°0N 141°0E **29** E15
Tatarstan □ *Russia* 55°30N 51°30E **18** C9
Tatatua, Pte. *Tahiti* 17°44S 149°8W **59** d
Tateyama *Japan* 35°0N 139°50E **31** G9
Tathlina L. *Canada* 60°33N 117°39W **70** A5
Tathra *Australia* 36°44S 149°59E **63** F4
Tatinnai L. *Canada* 60°55N 97°40W **71** A9
Tatla Lake *Canada* 52°0N 124°20W **70** C4
Tatnam, C. *Canada* 57°16N 91°0W **71** B10
Tatra = Tatry *Slovak Rep.* 49°20N 20°0E **17** D11
Tatry *Slovak Rep.* 49°20N 20°0E **17** D11
Tatshenshini →
  Canada 59°28N 137°45W **70** B1
Tatsuno *Japan* 34°52N 134°33E **31** G7
Tatta *Pakistan* 24°42N 67°55E **42** G2
Tatuī *Brazil* 23°25S 47°53W **95** A6
Tatum *U.S.A.* 33°16N 103°19W **77** K12
Tat'ung = Datong *China* 40°6N 113°18E **34** D7
Tatvan *Turkey* 38°31N 42°15E **44** B4
Ta'ū *Amer. Samoa* 14°15S 169°30W **59** b
Taubaté *Brazil* 23°0S 45°36W **95** A6
Tauern *Austria* 47°15N 12°40E **16** E7
Taumarunui *N.Z.* 38°53S 175°15E **59** C5
Taumaturgo *Brazil* 8°54S 72°51W **92** E4
Taung *S. Africa* 27°33S 24°47E **56** D3
Taungdwingyi *Burma* 20°1N 95°40E **41** J19
Taunggyi *Burma* 20°50N 97°0E **41** J20
Taungup *Burma* 18°51N 94°14E **41** K19
Taunsa *Pakistan* 30°42N 70°39E **42** D4
Taunsa Barrage *Pakistan* 30°42N 70°50E **42** D4
Taunton *U.K.* 51°1N 3°5W **13** F4
Taunton *U.S.A.* 41°54N 71°6W **83** E13
Taunus *Germany* 50°13N 8°34E **16** C5
Taupo *N.Z.* 38°41S 176°7E **59** C6
Taupo, L. *N.Z.* 38°46S 175°55E **59** C5
Tauragė *Lithuania* 55°14N 22°16E **9** J20
Tauranga *N.Z.* 37°42S 176°11E **59** B6
Tauranga Harb. *N.Z.* 37°30S 176°5E **59** B6
Taureau, Rés. *Canada* 46°46N 73°50W **72** C5
Taurianova *Italy* 38°21N 16°1E **22** E7
Taurus Mts. = Toros Dağları
  Turkey 37°0N 32°30E **44** B2
Tautira *Tahiti* 17°44S 149°9W **59** d
Tauyskaya Guba
  Russia 59°20N 150°20E **29** D16
Tavan Bogd Uul
  Mongolia 49°10N 87°49E **32** B6
Tavastehus = Hämeenlinna
  Finland 61°0N 24°28E **8** F21
Tavda *Russia* 58°7N 65°8E **28** D7
Tavda → *Russia* 57°47N 67°18E **28** D7
Taverner B. *Canada* 67°12N 72°25W **69** D17
Taveta *Kenya* 3°23S 37°37E **54** C4
Taveuni *Fiji* 16°51S 179°58W **59** a

Tavira *Portugal* 37°8N 7°40W **21** D2
Tavistock *Canada* 43°19N 80°50W **82** C4
Tavistock *U.K.* 50°33N 4°9W **13** G3
Tavoy *Burma* 14°2N 98°12E **38** E2
Tavoy Pt. *Burma* 13°32N 98°10E **38** F2
Tavrichanka *Russia* 43°18N 131°59E **30** C5
Tavua *Fiji* 17°37S 177°5E **59** a
Tavuki *Fiji* 19°7S 178°8E **59** a
Taw → *U.K.* 51°4N 4°4W **13** F3
Tawa → *India* 22°48N 77°48E **42** H8
Tawas City *U.S.A.* 44°16N 83°31W **81** C12
Tawau *Malaysia* 4°20N 117°55E **36** D5
Tawi-tawi I. *Phil.* 5°10N 120°15E **37** C6
Taxco *Mexico* 18°33N 99°36W **87** D5
Taxila *Pakistan* 33°42N 72°52E **42** C5
Taxkorgan Tajik Zizhixian
  China 37°49N 75°14E **32** C4
Tay → *U.K.* 56°37N 3°38W **11** E5
Tay, Firth of *U.K.* 56°25N 3°8W **11** E5
Tay, L. *Australia* 32°55S 120°48E **61** F3
Tay, L. *U.K.* 56°32N 4°8W **11** E4
Tay △ *U.K.* 56°43N 3°59W **11** E5
Tay Ninh *Vietnam* 11°20N 106°5E **39** G6
Tayabamba *Peru* 8°15S 77°16W **92** E3
Taygetos Oros *Greece* 37°0N 22°23E **23** F10
Taylakova *Russia* 59°13N 74°0E **28** D8
Taylor *Canada* 56°13N 120°40W **70** B4
Taylor *Nebr., U.S.A.* 41°46N 99°23W **80** E4
Taylor *Pa., U.S.A.* 41°23N 75°43W **83** E9
Taylor *Tex., U.S.A.* 30°34N 97°25W **84** F6
Taylor, Mt. *U.S.A.* 35°14N 107°37W **77** J10
Taylorville *U.S.A.* 39°33N 89°18W **80** F10
Taymā *Si. Arabia* 27°35N 38°45E **44** E3
Taymyr, Oz. *Russia* 74°20N 102°0E **29** B11
Taymyr, Poluostrov
  Russia 75°0N 100°0E **29** B11
Taypaq *Kazakhstan* 49°0N 51°47E **19** E9
Tayport *U.K.* 56°27N 2°52W **11** E6
Tayrona △ *Colombia* 11°20N 74°2W **89** D5
Tayshet *Russia* 55°58N 98°1E **29** D10
Taytay *Phil.* 10°45N 119°30E **37** B5
Tāyyebād *Iran* 34°45N 60°45E **45** C9
Tāyyebād □ *Iran* 34°44N 60°44E **45** C9
Taz → *Russia* 67°32N 78°40E **28** C8
Taza *Morocco* 34°16N 4°6W **50** B5
Tāza Khurmātū *Iraq* 35°18N 44°20E **44** C5
Tazawa-Ko *Japan* 39°43N 140°40E **30** E10
Tazerbo *Libya* 25°45N 21°0E **51** C10
Tazin → *Canada* 59°48N 109°55W **71** B7
Tazin L. *Canada* 59°44N 108°42W **71** B7
Tazovskiy *Russia* 67°30N 78°44E **28** C8
Tbilisi *Georgia* 41°43N 44°50E **19** F7
Tchad = Chad ■ *Africa* 15°0N 17°15E **51** F8
Tchad, L. *Chad* 13°30N 14°30E **51** F8
Tch'eng-tou = Chengdu
  China 30°38N 104°2E **32** F9
Tchentlo L. *Canada* 55°15N 125°0W **70** B4
Tchibanga *Gabon* 2°45S 11°0E **52** E2
Tch'ong-k'ing = Chongqing
  China 29°35N 106°25E **32** F10
Tczew *Poland* 54°8N 18°50E **17** A10
Te Anau, L. *N.Z.* 45°15S 167°45E **59** F1
Te Aroha *N.Z.* 37°32S 175°44E **59** B5
Te Awamutu *N.Z.* 38°1S 175°20E **59** C5
Te Ika a Maui = North I.
  N.Z. 38°0S 175°0E **59** C5
Te Kuiti *N.Z.* 38°20S 175°11E **59** C5
Te Puke *N.Z.* 37°46S 176°22E **59** B6
Te Waewae B. *N.Z.* 46°13S 167°33E **59** G1
Te Wai Pounamu = South I.
  N.Z. 44°0S 170°0E **59** E3
Teague *U.S.A.* 31°38N 96°17W **84** F6
Teahupoo *Tahiti* 17°50S 149°16W **59** d
Teapa *Mexico* 17°33N 92°57W **87** D6
Tebakang *Malaysia* 1°6N 110°30E **36** D4
Teberau → *Malaysia* 1°30N 103°42E **39** d
Tébessa *Algeria* 35°22N 8°8E **50** A7
Tebicuary → *Paraguay* 26°36S 58°16W **94** B4
Tebingtinggi *Riau,*
  Indonesia 1°0N 102°45E **36** E2
Tebingtinggi *Sumatera Utara,*
  Indonesia 3°20N 99°9E **36** D1
Tecate *Mexico* 32°34N 116°38W **79** N10
Tecka *Argentina* 43°29S 70°48W **96** E2
Tecomán *Mexico* 18°55N 103°53W **86** D4
Tecopa *U.S.A.* 35°51N 116°13W **79** K10
Tecoripa *Mexico* 28°37N 109°57W **86** B3
Tecuala *Mexico* 22°23N 105°27W **86** C3
Tecuci *Romania* 45°51N 27°27E **17** F14
Tecumseh *Canada* 42°19N 82°54W **82** D2
Tecumseh *Mich., U.S.A.* 42°0N 83°57W **81** D12
Tecumseh *Okla., U.S.A.* 35°15N 96°56W **84** D6
Tedzhen = Tejen
  Turkmenistan 37°23N 60°31E **28** F7
Tees → *U.K.* 54°37N 1°10W **12** C6
Tees B. *U.K.* 54°40N 1°9W **12** C6
Teeswater *Canada* 43°59N 81°17W **82** C3
Tefé *Brazil* 3°25S 64°50W **92** D6
Tegal *Indonesia* 6°52S 109°8E **37** G13
Tegallalang *Indonesia* 8°27S 115°17E **37** J18
Tegalsari *Indonesia* 8°25S 114°8E **37** J17
Tegid, L. = Bala, L. *U.K.* 52°53N 3°37W **12** E4
Tegucigalpa *Honduras* 14°5N 87°14W **88** D2
Tehachapi *U.S.A.* 35°8N 118°27W **79** K8
Tehachapi Mts. *U.S.A.* 35°0N 118°30W **79** L8
Teheran = Tehrān *Iran* 35°41N 51°25E **45** C6
Tehoru *Indonesia* 3°23S 129°30E **37** E7
Tehrān *Iran* 35°41N 51°25E **45** C6
Tehrān □ *Iran* 35°30N 51°30E **45** C6
Tehuacán *Mexico* 18°27N 97°23W **87** D5
Tehuantepec *Mexico* 16°21N 95°13W **87** D5
Tehuantepec, G. de
  Mexico 15°50N 95°12W **87** D5
Tehuantepec, Istmo de
  Mexico 17°15N 94°30W **87** D6
Teide, Pico de *Canary Is.* 28°15N 16°38W **24** F3
Teifi → *U.K.* 52°5N 4°41W **13** E3
Teign → *U.K.* 50°32N 3°32W **13** G4
Teignmouth *U.K.* 50°33N 3°31W **13** G4

Tejakula *Indonesia* 8°8S 115°20E **37** J18
Tejam *India* 29°57N 80°11E **43** E9
Tejen *Turkmenistan* 37°23N 60°31E **28** F7
Tejen → *Turkmenistan* 37°24N 60°38E **45** B9
Tejo → *Europe* 38°40N 9°24W **21** C1
Tejon Pass *U.S.A.* 34°49N 118°53W **79** L8
Tekamah *U.S.A.* 41°47N 96°13W **80** E5
Tekapo, L. *N.Z.* 43°53S 170°33E **59** E3
Tekax *Mexico* 20°12N 89°17W **87** C7
Tekeli *Kazakhstan* 44°50N 79°0E **28** E8
Tekeze Dam *Ethiopia* 13°10N 38°45E **47** E2
Tekirdağ *Turkey* 40°58N 27°30E **23** D12
Tekkali *India* 18°37N 84°15E **41** K14
Tekoa *U.S.A.* 47°14N 117°4W **76** C5
Tekong Besar, Pulau
  Singapore 1°25N 104°3E **39** d
Tel Aviv ✈ (TLV) *Israel* 32°5N 34°49E **46** C3
Tel Aviv-Yafo *Israel* 32°4N 34°48E **46** C3
Tel Lakhish *Israel* 31°34N 34°51E **46** D3
Tel Megiddo *Israel* 32°35N 35°11E **46** C4
Tela *Honduras* 15°40N 87°28W **88** C2
Telanaipura = Jambi
  Indonesia 1°38S 103°30E **36** E2
Telavi *Georgia* 42°0N 45°30E **19** F8
Telde *Canary Is.* 27°59N 15°25W **24** G4
Telegraph Creek *Canada* 58°0N 131°10W **70** B2
Telekhany = Tsyelyakhany
  Belarus 52°30N 25°46E **17** B13
Telemark *Norway* 59°15N 7°40E **9** G12
Telén *Argentina* 36°15S 65°31W **94** D2
Teleng *Iran* 25°47N 61°3E **45** E9
Teles Pires → *Brazil* 7°21S 58°3W **92** E7
Telescope Pk. *U.S.A.* 36°10N 117°5W **79** J9
Telford *U.K.* 52°40N 2°27E **13** E5
Telford and Wrekin □
  U.K. 52°45N 2°27W **12** E5
Telkwa *Canada* 54°41N 127°5W **70** C3
Tell City *U.S.A.* 37°57N 86°46W **80** G10
Teller *U.S.A.* 65°16N 166°22W **74** B6
Tellicherry *India* 11°45N 75°30E **40** P9
Telluride *U.S.A.* 37°56N 107°49W **77** H10
Teloloapán *Mexico* 18°21N 99°51W **87** D5
Telpos Iz *Russia* 63°16N 59°13E **18** B10
Telsen *Argentina* 42°30S 66°50W **96** E3
Telšiai *Lithuania* 55°59N 22°14E **9** J20
Teluk Anson = Teluk Intan
  Malaysia 4°3N 101°0E **39** K3
Teluk Bahang *Malaysia* 5°28N 100°13E **39** c
Teluk Betung = Bandar Lampung
  Indonesia 5°20S 105°10E **36** F3
Teluk Intan *Malaysia* 4°3N 101°0E **39** K3
Teluk Kumbar *Malaysia* 5°18N 100°14E **39** c
Telukbutun *Indonesia* 4°13N 108°12E **36** D3
Telukdalam *Indonesia* 0°33N 97°50E **36** D1
Tema *Ghana* 5°41N 0°0 **50** G5
Temagami, L. *Canada* 47°0N 80°10W **72** C3
Temax *Mexico* 21°9N 88°56W **87** C7
Temba *S. Africa* 25°20S 28°17E **57** D4
Tembagapura *Indonesia* 4°20S 137°0E **37** E9
Tembe
  Dem. Rep. of the Congo 0°16S 28°14E **54** C2
Temblor Range *U.S.A.* 35°20N 119°50W **79** K7
Teme → *U.K.* 52°11N 2°13W **13** E5
Temecula *U.S.A.* 33°30N 117°9W **79** M9
Temengor, Tasik
  Malaysia 5°24N 101°18E **39** K3
Temerloh *Malaysia* 3°27N 102°25E **39** L4
Teminabuan *Indonesia* 1°26S 132°1E **37** E8
Temir *Kazakhstan* 49°1N 57°14E **19** E10
Temirtau *Kazakhstan* 50°5N 72°56E **32** A3
Témiscamie → *Canada* 50°59N 73°5W **73** B5
Témiscaming *Canada* 46°44N 79°5W **72** C4
Témiscamingue, L.
  Canada 47°10N 79°25W **72** C4
Temosachic *Mexico* 28°57N 107°51W **86** B3
Tempe *U.S.A.* 33°24N 111°54W **77** K8
Tempiute *U.S.A.* 37°39N 115°38W **78** H11
Temple *U.S.A.* 31°6N 97°21W **84** F6
Temple B. *Australia* 12°15S 143°3E **62** A3
Templemore *Ireland* 52°47N 7°51W **10** D4
Templeton *U.S.A.* 35°33N 120°42W **78** K6
Templeton → *Australia* 21°0S 138°40E **62** C2
Tempoal de Sánchez
  Mexico 21°31N 98°23W **87** C5
Temuco *Chile* 38°45S 72°40W **96** D2
Temuka *N.Z.* 44°14S 171°17E **59** F3
Tenabo *Mexico* 20°3N 90°14W **87** C6
Tenaha *U.S.A.* 31°57N 94°15W **84** F7
Tenakee Springs
  U.S.A. 57°47N 135°13W **70** B1
Tenali *India* 16°15N 80°35E **41** L12
Tenancingo de Degollado
  Mexico 18°58N 99°36W **87** D5
Tenango del Valle
  Mexico 19°7N 99°33W **87** D5
Tenaro, Akra *Greece* 36°22N 22°27E **23** F10
Tenasserim *Burma* 12°6N 99°3E **39** F2
Tenasserim □ *Burma* 14°0N 98°30E **38** F2
Tenasserim → *Burma* 12°24N 98°37E **38** F2
Tenby *U.K.* 51°40N 4°42W **13** F3
Tenda, Colle di *France* 44°7N 7°36E **20** D7
Tendaho *Ethiopia* 11°48N 40°54E **47** E3
Tendō *Japan* 38°20N 140°30E **30** E10
Tendukhera *India* 23°24N 79°33E **43** H8
Teneguía, Volcanes de
  Canary Is. 28°28N 17°51W **24** F2
Ténéré, Erg du *Niger* 17°35N 10°55E **51** E8
Tenerife *Canary Is.* 28°15N 16°35W **24** F3
Tenerife, Pico *Canary Is.* 27°43N 18°1W **24** G1
Tenerife Norte ✈ (TFN)
  Canary Is. 28°29N 16°19W **24** F3
Tenerife Sur ✈ (TFS)
  Canary Is. 28°3N 16°33W **24** F3
Teng Xian *China* 35°5N 117°10E **35** G9
Tengah, Kepulauan
  Indonesia 7°5S 118°15E **36** F5
Tengchong *China* 25°0N 98°28E **32** D8
Tengchowfu = Penglai
  China 37°48N 120°42E **35** F11

Tenggarong *Indonesia* 0°24S 116°58E **36** E5
Tengger Shamo *China* 38°0N 104°10E **34** F3
Tenggol, Pulau *Malaysia* 4°48N 103°41E **39** K4
Tengiz Köli *Kazakhstan* 50°30N 69°0E **32** A2
Tengzhou *China* 35°4N 117°9E **35** G9
Teniente Enciso △
  Paraguay 21°5S 61°8W **94** A3
Teniente Rodolfo Marsh
  Antarctica 62°30S 58°0W **5** C18
Tenino *U.S.A.* 46°51N 122°51W **78** D4
Tenkasi *India* 8°55N 77°20E **40** Q10
Tenke *Katanga,*
  Dem. Rep. of the Congo 11°22S 26°40E **55** E2
Tenke *Katanga,*
  Dem. Rep. of the Congo 10°32S 26°7E **55** E2
Tennant Creek
  Australia 19°30S 134°15E **62** B1
Tennessee □ *U.S.A.* 36°0N 86°30W **85** D11
Tennessee → *U.S.A.* 37°4N 88°34W **85** C10
Teno, Pta. de *Canary Is.* 28°21N 16°55W **24** F3
Tenojoki = Tana →
  Norway 70°30N 28°14E **8** A23
Tenom *Malaysia* 5°4N 115°57E **36** C5
Tenosique *Mexico* 17°29N 91°26W **87** D6
Tenryū-Gawa → *Japan* 35°39N 137°48E **31** G8
Tenterden *U.K.* 51°4N 0°42E **13** F8
Tenterfield *Australia* 29°0S 152°0E **63** D5
Teófilo Otoni *Brazil* 17°50S 41°30W **93** G10
Tepa *Indonesia* 7°52S 129°31E **37** F7
Tepalcatepec →
  Mexico 18°35N 101°59W **86** D4
Tepehuanes *Mexico* 25°21N 105°44W **86** B3
Tepetongo *Mexico* 22°28N 103°9W **86** C4
Tepic *Mexico* 21°30N 104°54W **86** C4
Teplice *Czech Rep.* 50°40N 13°48E **16** C7
Tepoca, C. *Mexico* 30°20N 112°25W **86** A2
Tequila *Mexico* 20°54N 103°47W **86** C4
Ter → *Spain* 42°2N 3°12E **21** A7
Ter Apel *Neths.* 52°53N 7°5E **15** B7
Téra *Niger* 14°0N 0°45E **50** F6
Teraina *Kiribati* 4°43N 160°25W **65** G12
Téramo *Italy* 42°39N 13°42E **22** C5
Terang *Australia* 38°15S 142°55E **63** F3
Terang, Teluk *Indonesia* 8°45S 116°0E **37** K19
Terceira *Azores* 38°43N 27°13W **50** a
Tercero → *Argentina* 32°58S 61°47W **94** C3
Terebovlya *Ukraine* 49°18N 25°44E **17** D13
Terek → *Russia* 44°0N 47°30E **19** F8
Terengganu □ *Malaysia* 4°55N 103°0E **39** K4
Terepaima △ *Venezuela* 9°58N 69°17W **89** E6
Teresina *Brazil* 5°9S 42°45W **93** E10
Terewah, L. *Australia* 29°52S 147°35E **63** D4
Teridgerie Cr. →
  Australia 30°25S 148°50E **63** E4
Termas de Río Hondo
  Argentina 27°29S 64°52W **94** B3
Termez = Termiz
  Uzbekistan 37°15N 67°15E **28** F7
Términi Imerese *Italy* 37°59N 13°42E **22** F5
Términos, L. de *Mexico* 18°37N 91°33W **87** D6
Termiz *Uzbekistan* 37°15N 67°15E **28** F7
Térmoli *Italy* 42°0N 15°0E **22** C6
Ternate *Indonesia* 0°45N 127°25E **37** D7
Terneuzen *Neths.* 51°20N 3°50E **15** C3
Terney *Russia* 45°3N 136°37E **30** B8
Terni *Italy* 42°34N 12°37E **22** C5
Ternopil *Ukraine* 49°30N 25°40E **17** D13
Ternopil □ *Ukraine* 48°10N 25°10E **17** D13
Ternopol = Ternopil
  Ukraine 49°30N 25°40E **17** D13
Terowie *Australia* 33°8S 138°55E **63** E2
Terra Bella *U.S.A.* 35°58N 119°3W **79** K7
Terra Nova △ *Canada* 48°33N 53°55W **73** C9
Terrace *Canada* 54°30N 128°35W **70** C3
Terrace Bay *Canada* 48°47N 87°5W **72** C2
Terracina *Italy* 41°17N 13°15E **22** D5
Terralba *Italy* 39°43N 8°39E **22** E3
Terrassa *Spain* 41°34N 2°1E **21** B7
Terre Haute *U.S.A.* 39°28N 87°25W **80** F10
Terrebonne B. *U.S.A.* 29°5N 90°35W **85** G9
Terrell *U.S.A.* 32°44N 96°17W **84** E6
Terrenceville *Canada* 47°40N 54°44W **73** C9
Terry *U.S.A.* 46°47N 105°19W **76** C11
Terryville *U.S.A.* 41°41N 73°3W **83** E11
Terschelling *Neths.* 53°25N 5°20E **15** A5
Teruel *Spain* 40°22N 1°8W **21** B5
Tervola *Finland* 66°6N 24°49E **8** C21
Teryaweynya L.
  Australia 32°18S 143°22E **63** E3
Teshio *Japan* 44°53N 141°44E **30** B10
Teshio-Gawa → *Japan* 44°53N 141°45E **30** B10
Tesiyn Gol → *Mongolia* 50°40N 93°20E **32** A7
Teslin *Canada* 60°10N 132°43W **70** A2
Teslin → *Canada* 61°34N 134°35W **70** A2
Teslin L. *Canada* 60°15N 132°57W **70** A2
Tessalit *Mali* 20°12N 1°0E **50** D6
Tessaoua *Niger* 13°47N 7°56E **50** F7
Test → *U.K.* 50°56N 1°29W **13** G6
Testigos, Is. Los *Venezuela* 11°23N 63°7W **89** D7
Tetachuck L. *Canada* 53°18N 125°55W **70** C3
Tetas, Pta. *Chile* 23°31S 70°38W **94** A1
Tete *Mozam.* 16°13S 33°33E **55** F3
Tete □ *Mozam.* 15°15S 32°40E **55** F3
Teterev → *Ukraine* 51°1N 30°5E **17** C16
Teteven *Bulgaria* 42°58N 24°17E **23** C11
Tethul → *Canada* 60°35N 112°12W **70** A6
Tetiyev *Ukraine* 49°22N 29°38E **17** D15
Tetlit Zheh = Fort McPherson
  Canada 67°30N 134°55W **68** D5
Teton → *U.S.A.* 47°56N 110°31W **76** C8
Tétouan *Morocco* 35°35N 5°21W **50** A4
Tetovo *Macedonia* 42°1N 20°59E **23** C9
Tetufera, Mt. *Tahiti* 17°40S 149°26W **59** d
Teuco → *Argentina* 25°35S 60°11W **94** B3
Teulon *Canada* 50°23N 97°16W **71** C9
Teun *Indonesia* 6°59S 129°8E **37** F7
Teuri-Tō *Japan* 44°26N 141°19E **30** B10
Teutoburger Wald
  Germany 52°5N 8°22E **16** B5
Tevere → *Italy* 41°44N 12°14E **22** D5

Teverya *Israel* 32°47N 35°32E **46** C4
Teviot → *U.K.* 55°29N 2°38W **11** F6
Tewantin *Australia* 26°27S 153°3E **63** D5
Tewkesbury *U.K.* 51°59N 2°9W **13** F5
Texada I. *Canada* 49°40N 124°25W **70** D4
Texarkana *Ark., U.S.A.* 33°26N 94°2W **84** E7
Texarkana *Tex., U.S.A.* 33°26N 94°3W **84** E7
Texas *Australia* 28°49S 151°9E **63** D5
Texas □ *U.S.A.* 31°40N 98°30W **84** F5
Texas City *U.S.A.* 29°24N 94°54W **84** G7
Texel *Neths.* 53°5N 4°50E **15** A4
Texline *U.S.A.* 36°23N 103°2W **84** G3
Texoma, L. *U.S.A.* 33°50N 96°34W **84** E6
Teyateyaneng *Lesotho* 29°7S 27°34E **53** K5
Tezin *Afghan.* 34°24N 69°30E **42** B3
Teziutlán *Mexico* 19°49N 97°21W **87** D5
Tezpur *India* 26°40N 92°45E **41** F18
Tezzeron L. *Canada* 54°43N 124°30W **70** C4
Tha-anne → *Canada* 60°31N 94°37W **71** A10
Tha Deua *Laos* 17°57N 102°53E **38** D4
Tha Deua *Laos* 19°26N 101°50E **38** C3
Tha Li *Thailand* 17°37N 101°25E **38** D3
Tha Pla *Thailand* 17°48N 100°32E **38** D3
Tha Rua *Thailand* 14°34N 100°44E **38** E3
Tha Sala *Thailand* 8°40N 99°56E **39** H2
Tha Song Yang *Thailand* 17°34N 97°55E **38** D1
Thaba Putsoa *Lesotho* 29°45S 28°0E **57** D4
Thabana Ntlenyana
  Lesotho 29°30S 29°16E **57** D4
Thabazimbi *S. Africa* 24°40S 27°21E **57** C4
Thādiq *Si. Arabia* 25°18N 45°52E **44** E5
Thai Binh *Vietnam* 20°35N 106°1E **38** B6
Thai Muang *Thailand* 8°24N 98°16E **39** H2
Thai Nguyen *Vietnam* 21°35N 105°55E **38** B5
Thailand ■ *Asia* 16°0N 102°0E **38** E4
Thailand, G. of *Asia* 11°30N 101°0E **39** G3
Thakhek *Laos* 17°25N 104°45E **38** D5
Thal *Pakistan* 33°28N 70°33E **42** C4
Thal Desert *Pakistan* 31°10N 71°30E **42** D4
Thala La = Hkakabo Razi
  Burma 28°25N 97°23E **41** E20
Thalabarivat *Cambodia* 13°33N 105°57E **38** F5
Thalang = Amphoe Thalang
  Thailand 8°1N 98°20E **39** a
Thalang *Thailand* 8°2N 98°20E **39** H2
Thalassery = Tellicherry
  India 11°45N 75°30E **40** P9
Thale Sap Songkhla
  Thailand 7°12N 100°28E **39** J3
Thallon *Australia* 28°39S 148°49E **63** D4
Thalu, Ko *Thailand* 9°26N 99°54E **39** b
Tham Lot *Thailand* 19°34N 98°16E **38** C2
Thames *N.Z.* 37°7S 175°34E **59** B5
Thames → *Canada* 42°20N 82°25W **82** D2
Thames → *U.K.* 51°29N 0°34E **13** F8
Thames → *U.S.A.* 41°18N 72°5W **83** E12
Thames Estuary *U.K.* 51°29N 0°52E **13** F8
Thamesford *Canada* 43°4N 81°0W **82** C4
Thamesville *Canada* 42°33N 81°59W **82** D3
Than *India* 22°34N 71°11E **42** H4
Than Kyun *Burma* 9°49N 98°4E **39** H1
Than Uyen *Vietnam* 22°0N 103°54E **38** B4
Thana Gazi *India* 27°25N 76°19E **42** F7
Thandla *India* 23°0N 74°34E **42** H6
Thandwe *Burma* 18°20N 94°30E **41** K19
Thane *India* 19°12N 72°59E **40** K8
Thanesar *India* 30°1N 76°52E **42** D7
Thanet, I. of *U.K.* 51°21N 1°20E **13** F9
Thangool *Australia* 24°38S 150°42E **62** C5
Thanh Hoa *Vietnam* 19°48N 105°46E **38** C5
Thanh Hung *Vietnam* 9°55N 105°43E **39** H5
Thanh Pho Ho Chi Minh
  Vietnam 10°58N 106°40E **39** G6
Thanh Thuy *Vietnam* 22°55N 104°51E **38** A5
Thanjavur *India* 10°48N 79°12E **40** P11
Thanlwin = Salween →
  Burma 16°31N 97°37E **41** L20
Thano Bula Khan
  Pakistan 25°22N 67°50E **42** G2
Thanya Buri *Thailand* 14°1N 100°45E **38** E3
Thaolintoa L. *Canada* 61°30N 96°25W **71** A9
Thap Lan △ *Thailand* 14°15N 102°16E **38** E4
Thap Sakae *Thailand* 11°30N 99°37E **39** G2
Thap Than *Thailand* 15°27N 99°54E **38** E2
Thar Desert *India* 28°0N 72°0E **42** F5
Tharad *India* 24°30N 71°44E **42** G4
Thargomindah
  Australia 27°58S 143°46E **63** D3
Tharp Fracture Zone
  S. Ocean 54°0S 135°0W **5** B14
Tharrawaddy *Burma* 17°38N 95°48E **41** L19
Tharthār, Buḥayrat ath
  Iraq 34°0N 43°15E **44** C4
Tharthar, L. = Tharthār,
  Buḥayrat ath *Iraq* 34°0N 43°15E **44** C4
Tharthār, W. ath → *Iraq* 34°32N 43°4E **44** C4
Thasos *Greece* 40°40N 24°40E **23** D11
That Khe *Vietnam* 22°16N 106°28E **38** A6
Thatcher *Ariz., U.S.A.* 32°51N 109°46W **77** K9
Thatcher *Colo., U.S.A.* 37°33N 104°7W **77** H11
Thaton *Burma* 16°55N 97°22E **41** L20
Thaungdut *Burma* 24°30N 94°40E **41** G19
Thayawthadangy Kyun
  Burma 12°19N 98°0E **38** F1
Thayer *U.S.A.* 36°31N 91°33W **80** G8
Thayetmyo *Burma* 19°20N 95°10E **41** K19
Thazi *Burma* 21°0N 96°5E **41** J20
Thbeng Meanchey
  Cambodia 13°49N 104°58E **38** F5
The Broads *U.K.* 52°45N 1°23E **13** E9
The Everglades *U.S.A.* 25°50N 81°0W **85** J14
The Gulf = Persian Gulf
  Asia 27°0N 50°0E **45** E6
The Hague = 's-Gravenhage
  Neths. 52°7N 4°17E **15** B4
The Pas *Canada* 53°45N 101°15W **71** C8
The Wash *U.K.* 52°58N 0°20E **12** E8
The Weald *U.K.* 51°4N 0°20E **13** F8
Thebes = Thíva *Greece* 38°19N 23°19E **23** E10
Thebes *Egypt* 25°40N 32°35E **51** C12

Thedford *U.S.A.* 41°59N 100°35W **80** E3
Theebine *Australia* 25°57S 152°34E **63** D5
Thekulthili L. *Canada* 61°3N 110°0W **71** A7
Thelon → *Canada* 64°16N 96°4W **71** A8
Theodore *Australia* 24°55S 150°3E **62** C5
Theodore *Canada* 51°26N 102°55W **71** C8
Theodore *U.S.A.* 30°33N 88°10W **85** F10
Theodore Roosevelt △
  U.S.A. 47°0N 103°25W **80** B2
Theodore Roosevelt L.
  U.S.A. 33°40N 111°10W **77** K8
Thepha *Thailand* 6°52N 100°58E **39** J3
Theresa *U.S.A.* 44°13N 75°48W **83** B9
Thermaïkos Kolpos *U.S.A.* 43°39N 108°13W **76** E9
Thermopylæ *Greece* 38°48N 22°35E **23** E10
Thessalon *Canada* 46°20N 83°30W **72** C3
Thessalonica, Gulf of =
  Thessaloníki Kolpos
  Greece 40°15N 22°45E **23** D10
Thessaloníki *Greece* 40°38N 22°58E **23** D10
Thessaloníki Kolpos
  Greece 40°15N 22°45E **23** D10
Thetford *U.K.* 52°25N 0°45E **13** E8
Thetford Mines *Canada* 46°8N 71°18W **73** C5
Theun → *Laos* 18°19N 104°0E **38** C5
Theunissen *S. Africa* 28°26S 26°43E **56** D4
Thevenard *Australia* 32°9S 133°38E **63** E1
Thibodaux *U.S.A.* 29°48N 90°49W **85** G9
Thicket Portage *Canada* 55°19N 97°42W **71** B9
Thief River Falls *U.S.A.* 48°7N 96°10W **80** A5
Thiel Mts. *Antarctica* 85°15S 91°0W **5** E16
Thiers *France* 45°52N 3°33E **20** D5
Thiès *Senegal* 14°50N 16°51W **50** F2
Thika *Kenya* 1°1S 37°5E **54** C4
Thimphu *Bhutan* 27°31N 89°45E **41** F16
Thina → *S. Africa* 31°18S 29°13E **57** E4
Thíra = Santoríni
  Greece 36°23N 25°27E **23** F11
Third Cataract *Sudan* 19°42N 30°20E **51** E12
Thirsk *U.K.* 54°14N 1°19W **12** C6
Thiruvananthapuram =
  Trivandrum *India* 8°41N 77°0E **40** Q10
Thisted *Denmark* 56°58N 8°40E **9** H13
Thistle I. *Australia* 35°0S 136°8E **63** F2
Thithia = Cicia *Fiji* 17°45S 179°18W **59** a
Thíva *Greece* 38°19N 23°19E **23** E10
Þjórsá → *Iceland* 63°47N 20°48W **8** E3
Thlewiaza → *Canada* 60°29N 94°40W **71** A10
Thmar Puok *Cambodia* 13°57N 103°4E **38** F4
Tho Chu, Dao *Vietnam* 9°20N 103°28E **39** H4
Tho Vinh *Vietnam* 19°16N 105°42E **38** C5
Thoa → *Canada* 60°31N 109°47W **71** A7
Thoen *Thailand* 17°43N 99°12E **38** D2
Thoeng *Thailand* 19°41N 100°12E **38** C3
Thohoyandou *S. Africa* 22°58S 30°29E **53** J6
Thomas, L. *Australia* 26°4S 137°58E **63** D2
Thomas Hubbard, C.
  Canada 82°0N 94°25W **69** A13
Thomaston *U.S.A.* 32°53N 84°20W **85** E12
Thomasville *Ala.,*
  U.S.A. 31°55N 87°44W **85** F11
Thomasville *Ga., U.S.A.* 30°50N 83°59W **85** F13
Thomasville *N.C., U.S.A.* 35°53N 80°5W **85** D14
Thompson *Canada* 55°45N 97°52W **71** B9
Thompson *U.S.A.* 41°52N 75°31W **83** E9
Thompson → *Canada* 50°15N 121°24W **70** C4
Thompson → *U.S.A.* 39°46N 93°37W **80** F7
Thompson Falls *U.S.A.* 47°36N 115°21W **76** C6
Thompson Pk. *U.S.A.* 41°0N 123°2W **76** F2
Thompson Springs
  U.S.A. 38°58N 109°43W **76** G9
Thompsontown *U.S.A.* 40°33N 77°14W **82** F7
Thomson *U.S.A.* 33°28N 82°30W **85** E13
Thomson → *Australia* 25°11S 142°53E **62** C3
Thon Buri *Thailand* 13°45N 100°29E **38** F3
Thong Yang *Thailand* 9°28N 99°56E **39** b
Thoothukudi = Tuticorin
  India 8°50N 78°12E **40** Q11
Þórisvatn *Iceland* 64°20N 18°55W **8** D4
Thornaby on Tees *U.K.* 54°33N 1°18W **12** C6
Thornbury *Canada* 44°34N 80°26W **82** B4
Thorne *U.K.* 53°37N 0°57W **12** D7
Thornton *Canada* 44°16N 79°43W **82** B5
Thornton *U.S.A.* 39°52N 104°58W **76** G11
Thorold *Canada* 43°7N 79°12W **82** C5
Þórshöfn *Iceland* 66°12N 15°20W **8** C6
Thouin, C. *Australia* 20°20S 118°10E **60** D2
Thousand Islands *U.S.A.* 44°20N 76°0W **83** B9
Thousand Oaks *U.S.A.* 34°10N 118°50W **79** L8
Thrace *Turkey* 41°0N 27°0E **23** D12
Three Forks *U.S.A.* 45°54N 111°33W **76** D8
Three Gorges Dam
  China 30°45N 111°15E **33** E11
Three Hills *Canada* 51°43N 113°15W **70** C6
Three Hummock I.
  Australia 40°25S 144°55E **63** G3
Three Pagodas Pass *Asia* 15°20N 98°30E **38** E2
Three Points, C. *Ghana* 4°42N 2°6W **50** H5
Three Rivers *Calif.,*
  U.S.A. 36°26N 118°54W **78** J8
Three Rivers *Tex.,*
  U.S.A. 28°28N 98°11W **84** G5
Three Springs *Australia* 29°32S 115°45E **61** E2
Thrissur = Trichur
  India 10°30N 76°18E **40** P10
Throssell, L. *Australia* 27°33S 124°10E **61** E3
Throssell Ra. *Australia* 22°3S 121°43E **60** D3
Thrushton △ *Australia* 27°47S 147°40E **63** D4
Thu Dau Mot *Vietnam* 10°58N 106°39E **39** G6
Thua → *Kenya* 1°31S 39°30E **54** C4
Thuan Hoa *Vietnam* 8°58N 105°30E **39** H5
Thubun Lakes *Canada* 61°30N 112°0W **71** A6
Thuin *Belgium* 50°20N 4°17E **15** D4
Thule = Qaanaaq
  Greenland 77°30N 69°10W **69** B18
Thule Air Base = Uummannaq
  Greenland 77°33N 68°52W **69** B18

Thun *Switz.* 46°45N 7°38E **20** C7
Thunder B. *U.S.A.* 45°0N 83°20W **82** B1
Thunder Bay *Canada* 48°20N 89°15W **72** C2
Thung Salaeng Luang △
  Thailand 16°43N 100°50E **38** D3
Thung Song *Thailand* 8°10N 99°40E **39** H2
Thungya △ *Thailand* 15°30N 98°40E **38** E2
Thunkar *Bhutan* 27°55N 91°0E **41** F17
Thuong Tra *Vietnam* 16°2N 107°42E **38** D6
Thüringer Wald *Germany* 50°35N 11°0E **16** C6
Thuringowa △
  Australia 19°18S 146°43E **62** B4
Thurles *Ireland* 52°41N 7°49W **10** D4
Thurrock □ *U.K.* 51°31N 0°23E **13** F8
Thursday I. *Australia* 10°30S 142°3E **62** A3
Thurso *Canada* 45°36N 75°15W **72** C4
Thurso *U.K.* 58°36N 3°32W **11** C5
Thurso → *U.K.* 58°36N 3°32W **11** C5
Thurston I. *Antarctica* 72°0S 100°0W **5** D16
Thutade L. *Canada* 57°0N 126°55W **70** B3
Thyolo *Malawi* 16°7S 35°5E **55** F4
Ti-Tree *Australia* 22°5S 133°22E **62** C1
Tian Shan *Asia* 40°30N 76°0E **32** C4
Tianjin *China* 39°7N 117°12E **35** E9
Tianjin Shi □ *China* 39°8N 117°12E **35** E9
Tianjun *China* 38°0N 98°30E **32** D8
Tianmen *China* 30°39N 113°9E **33** E11
Tianshifu *China* 41°17N 124°22E **35** D13
Tianshui *China* 34°32N 105°40E **34** G3
Tianya *China* 18°18N 109°20E **38** C7
Tianyar *Indonesia* 8°12S 115°30E **37** J18
Tianzhen *China* 40°24N 114°5E **34** D8
Tianzhuangtai *China* 40°43N 122°5E **35** D12
Tiarei *Tahiti* 17°32S 149°20W **59** d
Tiaret *Algeria* 35°20N 1°21E **50** A6
Tibagi *Brazil* 24°30S 50°24W **95** A5
Tibagi → *Brazil* 22°47S 51°1W **95** A5
Tibastī, Sarīr *Libya* 22°50N 18°30E **51** D9
Tiber = Tevere → *Italy* 41°44N 12°14E **22** D5
Tiber Res. *U.S.A.* 48°19N 111°6W **76** B8
Tiberias = Teverya *Israel* 32°47N 35°32E **46** C4
Tiberias, L. = Yam Kinneret
  Israel 32°45N 35°35E **46** C4
Tibesti *Chad* 21°0N 17°30E **51** D9
Tibet = Xizang Zizhiqu □
  China 32°0N 88°0E **32** E6
Tibet, Plateau of *Asia* 32°0N 86°0E **26** E10
Tibnī *Syria* 35°36N 39°50E **44** C3
Tibooburra *Australia* 29°26S 142°1E **63** D3
Tiburón, I. *Mexico* 29°0N 112°25W **86** B2
Ticino → *Italy* 45°9N 9°14E **20** D8
Ticonderoga *U.S.A.* 43°51N 73°26W **83** C11
Ticul *Mexico* 20°24N 89°32W **87** C7
Tidaholm *Sweden* 58°12N 13°58E **9** G15
Tiddim *Burma* 23°28N 93°45E **41** H18
Tidioute *U.S.A.* 41°41N 79°24W **82** E5
Tidjikja *Mauritania* 18°29N 11°35W **50** E3
Tidore *Indonesia* 0°40N 127°25E **37** D7
Tiefa *China* 42°28N 123°26E **35** C12
Tiegang Shuiku *China* 22°37N 113°53E **33** a
Tiel *Neths.* 51°53N 5°26E **15** C5
Tieli *China* 46°57N 128°3E **33** B14
Tieling *China* 42°20N 123°55E **35** C12
Tielt *Belgium* 51°0N 3°20E **15** C3
Tien Shan = Tian Shan
  Asia 40°30N 76°0E **32** C4
Tien-tsin = Tianjin
  China 39°7N 117°12E **35** E9
Tien Yen *Vietnam* 21°20N 107°24E **38** B6
T'ienching = Tianjin
  China 39°7N 117°12E **35** E9
Tienen *Belgium* 50°48N 4°57E **15** D4
Tientsin = Tianjin *China* 39°7N 117°12E **35** E9
Tieri *Australia* 23°2S 148°21E **62** C4
Tierra Amarilla *Chile* 27°28S 70°18W **94** B1
Tierra Amarilla
  U.S.A. 36°42N 106°33W **77** H10
Tierra Colorada *Mexico* 17°11N 99°32W **87** D5
Tierra de Campos *Spain* 42°10N 4°50W **21** A3
Tierra del Fuego, I. Grande de
  Argentina 54°0S 69°0W **96** G3
Tiétar → *Spain* 39°50N 6°1W **21** C3
Tietê → *Brazil* 20°40S 51°35W **95** A5
Tiffin *U.S.A.* 41°7N 83°11W **81** E12
Tifton *U.S.A.* 31°27N 83°31W **85** F13
Tifu *Indonesia* 3°39S 126°24E **37** E7
Tighina *Moldova* 46°50N 29°30E **17** E15
Tigil *Russia* 57°49N 158°40E **29** D16
Tignish *Canada* 46°58N 64°2W **73** C7
Tigre → *Peru* 4°30S 74°10W **92** D4
Tigre → *Venezuela* 9°20N 62°30W **92** B6
Tigris = Dijlah, Nahr →
  Asia 31°0N 47°25E **44** D5
Tigyaing *Burma* 23°45N 96°10E **41** H20
Tîhāmah *Asia* 15°3N 41°55E **47** D3
Tijara *India* 27°56N 76°31E **42** F7
Tijuana *Mexico* 32°32N 117°1W **79** N9
Tikal *Guatemala* 17°13N 89°24W **88** C2
Tikal △ *Guatemala* 17°23N 89°34W **88** C2
Tikamgarh *India* 24°44N 78°50E **43** G8
Tikhoretsk *Russia* 45°56N 40°5E **19** E7
Tikhvin *Russia* 59°35N 33°30E **18** C5
Tikirarjuaq = Whale Cove
  Canada 62°10N 92°34W **71** A10
Tikrīt *Iraq* 34°35N 43°37E **44** C4
Tiksi *Russia* 71°40N 128°45E **29** B13
Tilamuta *Indonesia* 0°32N 122°23E **37** D6
Tilburg *Neths.* 51°31N 5°6E **15** C5
Tilbury *Canada* 42°17N 82°23W **82** D2
Tilbury *U.K.* 51°27N 0°22E **13** F8
Tilcara *Argentina* 23°36S 65°23W **94** A2
Tilden *U.S.A.* 28°28N 98°7W **80** D5
Tilhar *India* 28°0N 79°45E **43** F8
Tilichiki *Russia* 60°27N 166°5E **29** C17
Tilissos *Greece* 35°20N 25°1E **25** D7
Till → *U.K.* 55°41N 2°13W **12** B5
Tillamook *U.S.A.* 45°27N 123°51W **76** D2
Tillsonburg *Canada* 42°53N 80°44W **82** D4

Tillyeria *Cyprus* 35°6N 32°40E **25** D11
Tilos *Greece* 36°27N 27°27E **23** F12
Tilpa *Australia* 30°57S 144°24E **63** E3
Tilt → *U.K.* 56°46N 3°51W **11** C5
Tilton *U.S.A.* 43°27N 71°36W **83** C13
Tiltonsville *U.S.A.* 40°10N 80°41W **82** F4
Timanfaya △ *Canary Is.* 29°0N 13°46W **24** F6
Timaru *N.Z.* 44°23S 171°14E **59** F3
Timau *Kenya* 0°4N 37°15E **54** B4
Timbaki *Greece* 35°4N 24°45E **25** D6
Timber Creek *Australia* 15°40S 130°29E **60** C5
Timber Lake *U.S.A.* 45°26N 101°5W **80** C3
Timber Mt. *U.S.A.* 37°6N 116°28W **79** H10
Timbué, Ponta *Mozam.* 18°47S 36°22E **55** F4
Timbuktu = Tombouctou
  Mali 16°50N 3°0W **50** E5
Timi *Cyprus* 34°44N 32°31E **25** E11
Timika *Indonesia* 4°47S 136°32E **37** E9
Timimoun *Algeria* 29°14N 0°16E **50** C6
Timiris, Râs *Mauritania* 19°21N 16°30W **50** E2
Timiskaming, L. =
  Témiscamingue, L.
  Canada 47°10N 79°25W **72** C4
Timişoara *Romania* 45°43N 21°15E **17** F11
Timmins *Canada* 48°28N 81°25W **72** C3
Timok → *Serbia* 44°10N 22°40E **23** B10
Timoleague *Ireland* 51°39N 8°46W **10** E3
Timor *Asia* 9°0S 125°0E **37** F7
Timor Leste = East Timor ■
  Asia 8°50S 126°0E **37** F7
Timor Sea *Ind. Oc.* 12°0S 127°0E **60** B4
Tin Can Bay *Australia* 25°56S 153°0E **63** D5
Tin Mt. *U.S.A.* 36°50N 117°10W **78** J9
Tina = Thina → *S. Africa* 31°18S 29°13E **57** E4
Tina, Khalîg el *Egypt* 31°10N 32°40E **46** D1
Tinaca Pt. *Phil.* 5°30N 125°25E **37** C7
Tinajo *Canary Is.* 29°4N 13°42W **24** E6
Tindal *Australia* 14°31S 132°22E **60** B5
Tindouf *Algeria* 27°42N 8°10W **50** C4
Tinfunque △ *Paraguay* 23°55S 60°17W **94** A3
Tinggi, Pulau *Malaysia* 2°18N 104°7E **39** L5
Tingo María *Peru* 9°10S 75°54W **92** E3
Tingrela *Ivory C.* 10°27N 6°25W **50** F4
Tingri *China* 28°34N 86°38E **32** F6
Tinh Bien *Vietnam* 10°36N 104°57E **39** G5
Tinian *N. Marianas* 15°0N 145°38E **64** F6
Tinnevelly = Tirunelveli
  India 8°45N 77°45E **40** Q10
Tinogasta *Argentina* 28°5S 67°32W **94** B2
Tinos *Greece* 37°33N 25°8E **23** F11
Tinpahar *India* 24°59N 87°44E **43** G12
Tintina *Argentina* 27°2S 62°45W **94** B3
Tintinara *Australia* 35°48S 140°2E **63** F3
Tiobraid Árran = Tipperary
  Ireland 52°28N 8°10W **10** D3
Tioga *N. Dak., U.S.A.* 48°24N 102°56W **80** A2
Tioga *Pa., U.S.A.* 41°55N 77°8W **82** E7
Tioman, Pulau *Malaysia* 2°50N 104°10E **39** L5
Tionesta *U.S.A.* 41°30N 79°28W **82** E5
Tipperary *Ireland* 52°28N 8°10W **10** D3
Tipperary □ *Ireland* 52°37N 7°55W **10** D4
Tipton *Calif., U.S.A.* 36°4N 119°19W **78** J7
Tipton *Iowa, U.S.A.* 41°46N 91°8W **80** E8
Tipton, Mt. *U.S.A.* 35°32N 114°12W **79** K12
Tiptonville *U.S.A.* 36°23N 89°29W **85** C10
Tīrān *Iran* 32°45N 51°8E **45** C6
Tiranë *Albania* 41°18N 19°49E **23** D8
Tirari Desert *Australia* 28°22S 138°7E **63** D2
Tiraspol *Moldova* 46°55N 29°35E **17** E15
Tire *Turkey* 38°5N 27°45E **23** E12
Tirebolu *Turkey* 40°58N 38°45E **19** F6
Tiree *U.K.* 56°31N 6°55W **11** E2
Tiree, Passage of *U.K.* 56°30N 6°30W **11** E2
Tîrgovişte = Târgovişte
  Romania 44°55N 25°27E **17** F13
Tîrgu Jiu = Târgu Jiu
  Romania 45°5N 23°19E **17** F12
Tîrgu Mureş = Târgu Mureş
  Romania 46°31N 24°38E **17** E13
Tirich Mir *Pakistan* 36°15N 71°55E **40** A7
Tiritiri o te Moana = Southern
  Alps *N.Z.* 43°41S 170°11E **59** E3
Tirnavos *Greece* 39°45N 22°18E **23** E10
Tirodi *India* 21°40N 79°44E **40** J11
Tirol □ *Austria* 47°3N 10°43E **16** E6
Tirso → *Italy* 39°53N 8°32E **22** E3
Tirtagangga *Indonesia* 8°24S 115°35E **37** J18
Tiruchchirappalli *India* 10°45N 78°45E **40** P11
Tirunelveli *India* 8°45N 77°45E **40** Q10
Tirupati *India* 13°39N 79°25E **40** N11
Tiruppur *India* 11°5N 77°22E **40** P10
Tiruvannamalai *India* 12°15N 79°5E **40** N11
Tisa *India* 32°50N 76°9E **42** C7
Tisa → *Serbia* 45°15N 20°17E **23** B9
Tisdale *Canada* 52°50N 104°0W **71** C8
Tishomingo *U.S.A.* 34°14N 96°41W **84** D6
Tisza = Tisa → *Serbia* 45°15N 20°17E **23** B9
Tit-Ary *Russia* 71°55N 127°2E **29** B13
Tithwal *Pakistan* 34°21N 73°50E **43** B5
Titicaca, L. *S. Amer.* 15°30S 69°30W **92** G5
Titiwa *Nigeria* 12°14N 12°53E **51** F8
Titule
  Dem. Rep. of the Congo 3°15N 25°31E **54** B2
Titusville *Fla., U.S.A.* 28°37N 80°49W **85** G14
Titusville *Pa., U.S.A.* 41°38N 79°41W **82** E5
Tivaouane *Senegal* 14°56N 16°45W **50** F2
Tiverton *Canada* 44°16N 81°32W **82** B3
Tiverton *U.K.* 50°54N 3°29W **13** G4
Tívoli *Italy* 41°58N 12°45E **22** D5
Tiwi ☉ *Australia* 11°33S 130°42E **60** B5
Tizi-Ouzou *Algeria* 36°42N 4°3E **50** A6
Tiznit *Morocco* 29°48N 9°45W **50** C4
Tjeggelvas = Tjeggelvas
  Sweden 66°37N 17°45E **8** C17
Tjirebon = Cirebon
  Indonesia 6°45S 108°32E **37** G13
Tjirrkarli ☉ *Australia* 26°0S 125°28E **61** E4

Tjluring *Indonesia* 8°25S 114°13E **37** J17
Tjörn *Sweden* 58°0N 11°35E **9** H14
Tjukayirla Roadhouse
  Australia 27°9S 124°34E **61** E3
Tjurabalan ☉ *Australia* 19°50S 128°0E **60** C4
Tlacotalpan *Mexico* 18°37N 95°40W **87** D5
Tlahualilo de Zaragoza
  Mexico 26°7N 103°27W **86** B4
Tlaquepaque *Mexico* 20°39N 103°19W **86** C4
Tlaxcala *Mexico* 19°19N 98°14W **87** D5
Tlaxcala □ *Mexico* 19°25N 98°10W **87** D5
Tlaxiaco *Mexico* 17°25N 97°35W **87** D5
Tlemcen *Algeria* 34°52N 1°21W **50** B5
To Bong *Vietnam* 12°45N 109°16E **38** F7
Toa Payoh *Singapore* 1°20N 103°51E **39** d
Toad → *Canada* 59°25N 124°57W **70** B4
Toad River *Canada* 58°51N 125°14W **70** B3
Toamasina *Madag.* 18°10S 49°25E **57** B8
Toamasina □ *Madag.* 18°0S 49°0E **57** B8
Toay *Argentina* 36°43S 64°38W **94** D3
Toba *Japan* 34°30N 136°51E **31** G8
Toba, Danau *Indonesia* 2°30N 98°30E **36** D1
Toba Kakar *Pakistan* 31°30N 69°0E **42** D3
Toba Tek Singh *Pakistan* 30°55N 72°25E **42** D5
Tobago *Trin. & Tob.* 11°10N 60°30W **93** J16
Tobelo *Indonesia* 1°45N 127°56E **37** D7
Tobermory *Canada* 45°12N 81°40W **82** A3
Tobermory *U.K.* 56°38N 6°5W **11** E2
Tobi *Pac. Is.* 2°40N 131°10E **37** D8
Tobi-Shima *Japan* 41°21N 139°34E **30** D9
Tobin, L. *Australia* 21°45S 125°49E **60** D4
Tobin, L. *Canada* 53°35N 103°30W **71** C8
Toboali *Indonesia* 3°0S 106°25E **36** E3
Tobol → *Russia* 58°10N 68°12E **28** D7
Toboli *Indonesia* 0°38S 120°5E **37** E6
Tobolsk *Russia* 58°15N 68°10E **28** D7
Tobruk = Tubruq *Libya* 32°7N 23°55E **51** B10
Tobyhanna *U.S.A.* 41°11N 75°25W **83** E9
Tobyl = Tobol → *Russia* 58°10N 68°12E **28** D7
Tocantinópolis *Brazil* 6°20S 47°25W **93** E9
Tocantins □ *Brazil* 10°0S 48°0W **93** F9
Tocantins → *Brazil* 1°45S 49°10W **93** D9
Toccoa *U.S.A.* 34°35N 83°19W **85** D13
Tochi → *Pakistan* 32°49N 70°41E **42** C4
Tochigi *Japan* 36°25N 139°45E **31** F9
Tochigi □ *Japan* 36°45N 139°45E **31** F9
Toco *Trin. & Tob.* 10°49N 60°57W **93** K16
Toconao *Chile* 23°11S 68°1W **94** A2
Tocopilla *Chile* 22°5S 70°10W **94** A1
Tocumwal *Australia* 35°51S 145°31E **63** F4
Tocuyo → *Venezuela* 11°3N 68°23W **92** A5
Todd → *Australia* 24°52S 135°48E **62** C2
Todeli *Indonesia* 1°40S 124°29E **37** E6
Todenyang *Kenya* 4°35N 35°56E **54** B4
Todgarh *India* 25°42N 73°58E **42** G5
Todos os Santos, B. de
  Brazil 12°48S 38°38W **93** F11
Todos Santos *Mexico* 23°26N 110°13W **86** C2
Toe Hd. *U.K.* 57°50N 7°8W **11** D1
Tofield *Canada* 53°25N 112°40W **70** C6
Tofino *Canada* 49°11N 125°55W **70** D3
Tofua *Tonga* 19°45S 175°5W **59** c
Tōgane *Japan* 35°33N 140°22E **31** G10
Togian, Kepulauan
  Indonesia 0°20S 121°50E **37** E6
Togliatti *Russia* 53°32N 49°24E **18** D9
Togo ■ *W. Afr.* 8°30N 1°35E **50** G6
Togtoh *China* 40°15N 111°10E **34** D6
Tohiea, Mt. *Moorea* 17°33S 149°49W **59** d
Tōhoku □ *Japan* 39°50N 141°45E **30** E10
Tōhōm *Mongolia* 44°27N 108°2E **34** B5
Toinya *Sudan* 6°17N 29°46E **51** G11
Toiyabe Range *U.S.A.* 39°30N 117°0W **76** G5
Tojikiston = Tajikistan ■
  Asia 38°30N 70°0E **28** F8
Tojo *Indonesia* 1°20S 121°15E **37** E6
Tōjō *Japan* 34°53N 133°16E **31** G6
Tok *U.S.A.* 63°20N 142°59W **68** E3
Tokachi-Dake *Japan* 43°17N 142°5E **30** C11
Tokachi-Gawa →
  Japan 42°44N 143°42E **30** C11
Tokala *Indonesia* 1°30S 121°40E **37** E6
Tōkamachi *Japan* 37°8N 138°43E **31** F9
Tokanui *N.Z.* 46°34S 168°56E **59** G2
Tokara-Rettō *Japan* 29°37N 129°43E **31** K4
Tokarahi *N.Z.* 44°56S 170°39E **59** F3
Tokashiki-Shima *Japan* 26°11N 127°21E **31** L3
Tokat *Turkey* 40°22N 36°35E **19** F6
Tŏkch'ŏn *N. Korea* 39°45N 126°18E **35** E14
Tokdo *Asia* 37°15N 131°52E **31** F5
Tokeland *U.S.A.* 46°42N 123°59W **78** D3
Tokelau Is. ☑ *Pac. Oc.* 9°0S 171°45W **64** H10
Tokmak *Kyrgyzstan* 42°49N 75°15E **28** E8
Toko Ra. *Australia* 23°5S 138°20E **62** C2
Tokoro-Gawa → *Japan* 44°7N 144°5E **30** B12
Toku *Tonga* 18°10S 174°11W **59** c
Tokuno-Shima *Japan* 27°56N 128°55E **31** L4
Tokushima *Japan* 34°4N 134°34E **31** G7
Tokushima □ *Japan* 33°55N 134°0E **31** H7
Tokuyama *Japan* 34°3N 131°50E **31** G5
Tōkyō *Japan* 35°43N 139°45E **31** G9
Tolaga Bay *N.Z.* 38°21S 178°20E **59** C7
Tolbukhin = Dobrich
  Bulgaria 43°37N 27°49E **23** C12
Toledo *Brazil* 24°44S 53°45W **95** A5
Toledo *Spain* 39°50N 4°2W **21** C3
Toledo *Ohio, U.S.A.* 41°39N 83°33W **81** E12
Toledo *Wash., U.S.A.* 46°26N 122°51W **78** D4
Toledo, Montes de *Spain* 39°33N 4°20W **21** C3
Toledo Bend Res. *U.S.A.* 31°11N 93°34W **84** F8
Tolga *Australia* 17°15S 145°29E **62** B4
Toliara *Madag.* 23°21S 43°40E **57** C7
Toliara □ *Madag.* 21°0S 45°0E **57** C8
Tolima *Colombia* 4°40N 75°19W **92** C3
Tolitoli *Indonesia* 1°5N 120°50E **37** D6
Tollhouse *U.S.A.* 37°1N 119°24W **78** H7
Tolmachevo *Russia* 58°56N 29°51E **9** G23
Tolo, Teluk *Indonesia* 2°20S 122°10E **37** E6
Tolo Harbour *China* 22°27N 114°12E **33** a

Toluca *Mexico* 19°17N 99°40W **87** D5
Tolyatti = Togliatti
  Russia 53°32N 49°24E **18** D8
Tom Burke *S. Africa* 23°5S 28°0E **57** C4
Tom Price *Australia* 22°40S 117°48E **60** D2
Tomah *U.S.A.* 43°59N 90°30W **80** D8
Tomahawk *U.S.A.* 45°28N 89°44W **80** C9
Tomakomai *Japan* 42°38N 141°36E **30** C10
Tomales *U.S.A.* 38°15N 122°53W **78** G4
Tomales B. *U.S.A.* 38°15N 123°58W **78** G3
Tomanivi *Fiji* 17°37S 178°1E **59** a
Tomar *Portugal* 39°36N 8°25W **21** C1
Tomaszów Mazowiecki
  Poland 51°30N 20°2E **17** C10
Tomatlán *Mexico* 19°56N 105°15W **86** D3
Tombador, Serra do *Brazil* 12°0S 58°0W **92** F7
Tombigbee → *U.S.A.* 31°8N 87°57W **85** F11
Tombouctou *Mali* 16°50N 3°0W **50** E5
Tombstone *U.S.A.* 31°43N 110°4W **77** L8
Tombua *Angola* 15°55S 11°55E **56** B1
Tomé *Chile* 36°36S 72°57W **94** D1
Tome *Japan* 38°40N 141°20E **30** E10
Tomelloso *Spain* 39°10N 3°2W **21** C4
Tomini *Indonesia* 0°30N 120°30E **37** D6
Tomini, Teluk *Indonesia* 0°10S 121°0E **37** E6
Tomintoul *U.K.* 57°15N 3°23W **11** D5
Tomkinson Ranges
  Australia 26°11S 129°5E **61** E4
Tommot *Russia* 59°4N 126°20E **29** D13
Tomnop Ta Suos
  Cambodia 11°20N 104°15E **39** G5
Tomo → *Colombia* 5°20N 67°48W **92** B5
Toms Place *U.S.A.* 37°34N 118°41W **78** H8
Toms River *U.S.A.* 39°58N 74°12W **83** G10
Tomsk *Russia* 56°30N 85°5E **28** D9
Tonalá *Chiapas, Mexico* 16°4N 93°45W **87** D6
Tonalá *Jalisco, Mexico* 20°37N 103°14W **86** C4
Tonantins *Brazil* 2°45S 67°45W **92** D5
Tonasket *U.S.A.* 48°42N 119°26W **76** B4
Tonawanda *U.S.A.* 43°1N 78°53W **82** D6
Tonb *Iran* 26°15N 55°15E **45** E7
Tonbridge *U.K.* 51°11N 0°17E **13** F8
Tondano *Indonesia* 1°35N 124°54E **37** D6
Tondoro *Namibia* 17°45S 18°50E **56** B2
Tone → *Australia* 34°25S 116°25E **61** F2
Tone-Gawa → *Japan* 35°44N 140°51E **31** F9
Tonekābon *Iran* 36°45N 51°12E **45** B6
Tong Xian *China* 39°55N 116°35E **34** E9
Tong-yeong *S. Korea* 34°50N 128°20E **35** G15
Tonga ■ *Pac. Oc.* 19°50S 174°30W **59** c
Tonga Trench *Pac. Oc.* 18°0S 173°0W **64** J10
Tongaat *S. Africa* 29°33S 31°9E **57** D5
Tongareva = Penrhyn
  Cook Is. 9°0S 158°0W **65** H12
Tongariro △ *N.Z.* 39°8S 175°33E **59** c
Tongatapu *Tonga* 21°10S 175°10W **59** c
Tongatapu Group *Tonga* 20°0S 174°0W **59** c
Tongchuan *China* 35°6N 109°3E **34** G5
Tongeren *Belgium* 50°47N 5°28E **15** D5
Tonggu Jiao *China* 22°22N 113°37E **33** a
Tonghua *China* 41°42N 125°58E **35** D13
Tongjiang *China* 47°40N 132°27E **33** B15
Tongjosŏn Man
  N. Korea 39°30N 128°0E **35** E15
Tongking, G. of = Tonkin, G. of
  Asia 20°0N 108°0E **38** C7
Tongliao *China* 43°38N 122°18E **35** C12
Tongling *China* 30°55N 117°48E **33** E12
Tongobory *Madag.* 23°32S 44°20E **57** C7
Tongoy *Chile* 30°16S 71°31W **94** C1
Tongren *China* 27°43N 109°11E **32** F10
Tongres = Tongeren
  Belgium 50°47N 5°28E **15** D5
Tongsa Dzong *Bhutan* 27°31N 90°31E **41** F17
Tongshi *China* 18°30N 109°20E **38** C7
Tongue *U.K.* 58°29N 4°25W **11** C4
Tongue → *U.S.A.* 46°25N 105°52W **76** C11
Tongwei *China* 35°0N 105°5E **34** G3
Tongxin *China* 36°59N 105°58E **34** F3
Tongyang *N. Korea* 39°9N 126°53E **35** E14
Tongyu *China* 44°45N 123°4E **35** B12
Tonj *Sudan* 7°20N 28°44E **51** G11
Tonk *India* 26°6N 75°54E **42** F6
Tonkawa *U.S.A.* 36°41N 97°18W **84** C6
Tonkin = Bac Phan
  Vietnam 22°0N 105°0E **38** B5
Tonkin, G. of *Asia* 20°0N 108°0E **38** C7
Tonlé Sap *Cambodia* 13°0N 104°0E **38** F5
Tono *Japan* 39°19N 141°32E **30** E10
Tonopah *U.S.A.* 38°4N 117°14W **77** G5
Tonosí *Panama* 7°20N 80°20W **88** E3
Tons → *Haryana, India* 30°30N 77°39E **42** D7
Tons → *Ut. P., India* 26°1N 83°33E **43** F10
Tønsberg *Norway* 59°19N 10°25E **9** G14
Tonto △ *U.S.A.* 33°39N 111°7W **77** K8
Tonumea *Tonga* 20°30S 174°30W **59** c
Toobanna *Australia* 18°42S 146°9E **62** B4
Toodyay *Australia* 31°34S 116°28E **61** F2
Tooele *U.S.A.* 40°32N 112°18W **76** F7
Toompine *Australia* 27°15S 144°19E **63** D3
Toora *Australia* 38°39S 146°23E **63** F4
Toora-Khem *Russia* 52°28N 96°17E **29** D10
Toowoomba *Australia* 27°32S 151°56E **63** D5
Top Springs *Australia* 16°37S 131°51E **60** C5
Topaz *U.S.A.* 38°41N 119°30W **78** G7
Topeka *U.S.A.* 39°3N 95°40W **80** F6
Topley *Canada* 54°49N 126°18W **70** C3
Topocalma, Pta. *Chile* 34°10S 72°2W **94** C1
Topock *U.S.A.* 34°46N 114°29W **79** L12
Topol'čany *Slovak Rep.* 48°35N 18°12E **17** D10
Topolobampo *Mexico* 25°36N 109°3W **86** B3
Topozero, Ozero *Russia* 65°35N 32°0E **8** D25
Toppenish *U.S.A.* 46°23N 120°19W **76** C3
Toraka Vestale *Madag.* 16°20S 43°58E **57** B7
Torata *Peru* 17°23S 70°1W **92** G4
Torbalı *Turkey* 38°10N 27°21E **23** E12
Torbat-e Heydārīyeh
  Iran 35°15N 59°12E **45** C8
Torbat-e Jām *Iran* 35°16N 60°35E **45** C9

Torbay *Canada* 47°40N 52°42W **73** C9
Torbay □ *U.K.* 50°26N 3°31W **13** G4
Tordesillas *Spain* 41°30N 5°0W **21** B3
Torfaen □ *U.K.* 51°43N 3°3W **13** F4
Torgau *Germany* 51°34N 13°0E **16** C7
Torhout *Belgium* 51°5N 3°7E **15** C3
Tori-Shima *Japan* 30°29N 140°19E **31** J10
Torilla Pen. *Australia* 22°29S 150°5E **62** C5
Torino *Italy* 45°3N 7°40E **20** D7
Torit *Sudan* 4°27N 32°31E **51** H12
Torkamān *Iran* 37°35N 47°23E **44** B5
Tormes → *Spain* 41°18N 6°29W **21** B2
Tornado Mt. *Canada* 49°55N 114°40W **70** D6
Torneå = Tornio *Finland* 65°50N 24°12E **8** D21
Torneälven → *Europe* 65°50N 24°12E **8** D21
Torneträsk *Sweden* 68°24N 19°15E **8** B18
Torngat Mts. *Canada* 59°0N 63°40W **69** F19
Tornio *Finland* 65°50N 24°12E **8** D21
Tornionjoki = Torneälven →
  Europe 65°50N 24°12E **8** D21
Tornquist *Argentina* 38°8S 62°15W **94** D3
Toro *Spain* 39°59N 4°8E **24** B11
Toro, Cerro del *Chile* 29°10S 69°50W **94** B2
Toro △ *Uganda* 1°5N 30°22E **54** C3
Toro Pk. *U.S.A.* 33°34N 116°24W **79** M10
Torokina *Papua N. G.* ...
Toronto *Canada* 43°39N 79°20W **82** C5
Toronto *U.S.A.* 40°28N 80°36W **82** F4
Toronto Lester B. Pearson Int. ✈
  (YYZ) *Canada* 43°46N 79°35W **82** C5
Toropets *Russia* 56°30N 31°40E **18** C5
Tororo *Uganda* 0°45N 34°12E **54** B3
Toros Dağları *Turkey* 37°0N 32°30E **44** C2
Torpa *India* 22°57N 85°6E **43** H11
Torquay *U.K.* 50°27N 3°32W **13** G4
Torrance *U.S.A.* 33°50N 118°20W **79** M8
Torre de Moncorvo
  Portugal 41°12N 7°8W **21** B2
Torre del Greco *Italy* 40°47N 14°22E **22** D6
Torrejón de Ardoz *Spain* 40°27N 3°29W **21** B4
Torrelavega *Spain* 43°20N 4°5W **21** A3
Torremolinos *Spain* 36°38N 4°30W **21** D3
Torrens, L. *Australia* 31°0S 137°50E **63** E2
Torrens Cr. → *Australia* 22°23S 145°9E **62** C4
Torrens Creek *Australia* 20°48S 145°3E **62** C4
Torrent *Spain* 39°27N 0°28W **21** C5
Torreón *Mexico* 25°33N 103°26W **86** B4
Torres *Brazil* 29°21S 49°44W **95** B5
Torres *Mexico* 28°46N 110°47W **86** B2
Torres Strait *Australia* 9°50S 142°20E **62** a
Torres Vedras *Portugal* 39°5N 9°15W **21** C1
Torrevieja *Spain* 37°59N 0°42W **21** D5
Torrey *U.S.A.* 38°18N 111°25W **76** G8
Torridge → *U.K.* 51°0N 4°13W **13** G3
Torridon, L. *U.K.* 57°35N 5°50W **11** D3
Torrington *Conn., U.S.A.* 41°48N 73°7W **83** E11
Torrington *Wyo.,*
  U.S.A. 42°4N 104°11W **76** E11
Tórshavn *Færoe Is.* 62°5N 6°56W **8** E9
Tortola *Br. Virgin Is.* 18°19N 64°45W **89** e
Tortosa *Spain* 40°49N 0°31E **21** B6
Tortosa, C. *Spain* 40°41N 0°52E **21** B6
Tortue, Î. de la *Haiti* 20°5N 72°57W **89** B5
Tortuguero △ *Costa Rica* 10°31N 83°29W **88** D3
Torūd *Iran* 35°25N 55°5E **45** C7
Toruń *Poland* 53°2N 18°39E **17** B10
Tory Hill *Canada* 44°58N 78°16W **82** B6
Tory I. *Ireland* 55°16N 8°14W **10** A3
Tosa *Japan* 33°24N 133°23E **31** H6
Tosa-Shimizu *Japan* 32°52N 132°58E **31** H6
Tosa-Wan *Japan* 33°15N 133°30E **31** H6
Toscana □ *Italy* 43°25N 11°0E **22** C4
Toshka Lakes *Egypt* 22°50N 31°0E **51** D12
Toshkent *Uzbekistan* 41°20N 69°10E **28** E7
Tostado *Argentina* 29°15S 61°50W **94** B3
Tostón, Pta. de *Canary Is.* 28°42N 14°2W **24** F5
Tosu *Japan* 33°22N 130°31E **31** H5
Toteng *Botswana* 20°22S 22°58E **56** C3
Totma *Russia* 60°0N 42°40E **18** C7
Totnes *U.K.* 50°26N 3°42W **13** G4
Totness *Suriname* 5°53N 56°19W **93** B7
Totonicapán *Guatemala* 14°58N 91°12W **88** D1
Totoya, I. *Fiji* 18°57S 179°50W **59** a
Totten Glacier *Antarctica* 66°45S 116°10E **5** C8
Tottenham *Australia* 32°14S 147°21E **63** E4
Tottenham *Canada* 44°1N 79°49W **82** B5
Tottori *Japan* 35°30N 134°15E **31** G7
Tottori □ *Japan* 35°30N 134°12E **31** G7
Toubkal, Djebel *Morocco* 31°0N 8°0W **50** B4
Tougan *Burkina Faso* 13°11N 2°58W **50** F5
Touggourt *Algeria* 33°6N 6°4E **50** B7
Toul *France* 48°40N 5°53E **20** B6
Toulon *France* 43°10N 5°55E **20** E6
Toulouse *France* 43°37N 1°27E **20** E4
Toummo *Niger* 22°45N 14°8E **51** D8
Toungoo *Burma* 19°0N 96°30E **41** K20
Touraine *France* 47°20N 0°30E **20** C4
Tourcoing *France* 50°42N 3°10E **20** A5
Touriñán, C. *Spain* 43°3N 9°18W **21** A1
Tournai *Belgium* 50°35N 3°25E **15** D3
Tournon-sur-Rhône
  France 45°4N 4°50E **20** D6
Tours *France* 47°22N 0°40E **20** C4
Toussoro, Mt. *C.A.R.* 9°7N 23°14E **52** C4
Touwsrivier *S. Africa* 33°20N 20°2E **56** E3
Towada *Japan* 40°37N 141°13E **30** D10
Towada-Hachimantai △
  Japan 40°20N 140°55E **30** D10
Towada-Ko *Japan* 40°28N 140°55E **30** D10
Towanda *U.S.A.* 41°46N 76°27W **83** E8
Tower *U.S.A.* 47°48N 92°17W **80** B7
Towerhill Cr. →
  Australia 22°28S 144°35E **62** C3
Towner *U.S.A.* 48°21N 100°25W **80** A3
Townsend *U.S.A.* 46°19N 111°31W **76** C8
Townshend I. *Australia* 22°10S 150°31E **62** C5
Townsville *Australia* 19°15S 146°45E **62** B4
Towot *Sudan* 6°12N 34°6E **54** B3
Towraghondī *Afghan.* 35°13N 62°16E **40** B3
Towson *U.S.A.* 39°24N 76°36W **81** F15

Towuti, Danau *Indonesia* 2°45S 121°32E **37** E6
Tōya-Ko *Japan* 42°35N 140°51E **30** C10
Toyama *Japan* 36°40N 137°15E **31** F8
Toyama □ *Japan* 36°45N 137°30E **31** F8
Toyama-Wan *Japan* 37°0N 137°30E **31** F8
Toyapakeh *Indonesia* 8°41S 115°29E **37** K18
Toyohashi *Japan* 34°45N 137°25E **31** G8
Toyokawa *Japan* 34°48N 137°27E **31** G8
Toyonaka *Japan* 34°46N 135°28E **31** G7
Toyooka *Japan* 35°35N 134°48E **31** G7
Toyota *Japan* 35°3N 137°7E **31** G8
Tozeur *Tunisia* 33°56N 8°8E **50** B7
Trá Lí = Tralee *Ireland* 52°16N 9°42W **10** D2
Trá Mhór = Tramore
  Ireland 52°10N 7°10W **10** D4
Tra On *Vietnam* 9°58N 105°55E **39** H5
Tra Vinh *Vietnam* 9°50N 106°15E **39** H6
Trabzon *Turkey* 41°0N 39°45E **19** F6
Tracadie *Canada* 47°30N 64°55W **73** C7
Tracy *Canada* 46°1N 73°9W **72** C5
Tracy *Calif., U.S.A.* 37°44N 121°26W **78** H5
Tracy *Minn., U.S.A.* 44°14N 95°37W **80** C6
Trafalgar, C. *Spain* 36°10N 6°2W **21** D2
Trail *Canada* 49°5N 117°40W **70** D5
Trainor L. *Canada* 60°24N 120°17W **70** A4
Trakai △ *Lithuania* 54°30N 25°10E **9** J21
Trákhonas *Cyprus* 35°12N 33°21E **25** D12
Tralee *Ireland* 52°16N 9°42W **10** D2
Tralee B. *Ireland* 52°17N 9°55W **10** D2
Tram Chim △ *Vietnam* 10°43N 105°31E **39** G5
Tramore *Ireland* 52°10N 7°10W **10** D4
Tramore B. *Ireland* 52°9N 7°10W **10** D4
Tramuntana, Serra de
  Spain 39°48N 2°54E **24** B9
Tran Ninh, Cao Nguyen
  Laos 19°30N 103°10E **38** C4
Tranås *Sweden* 58°3N 14°59E **9** G16
Trancas *Argentina* 26°11S 65°20W **94** B2
Trang *Thailand* 7°33N 99°38E **39** J2
Trangahy *Madag.* 19°7S 44°31E **57** B7
Trangan *Indonesia* 6°40S 134°20E **37** F8
Trangie *Australia* 32°4S 148°0E **63** E4
Trani *Italy* 41°17N 16°25E **22** D7
Tranoroa *Madag.* 24°42S 45°4E **57** C8
Tranqueras *Uruguay* 31°13S 55°45W **95** C4
Transantarctic Mts.
  Antarctica 85°0S 170°0W **5** E12
Transilvania *Romania* 46°30N 24°0E **17** E12
Transilvanian Alps = Carpaţii
  Meridionali *Romania* 45°30N 25°0E **17** F13
Transnistria = Stînga Nistrului □
  Moldova 47°20N 29°15E **17** E15
Transylvania = Transilvania
  Romania 46°30N 24°0E **17** E12
Trápani *Italy* 38°1N 12°29E **22** E5
Trapper Pk. *U.S.A.* 45°54N 114°18W **76** D6
Traralgon *Australia* 38°12S 146°34E **63** F4
Trasimeno, L. *Italy* 43°8N 12°6E **22** C5
Trat *Thailand* 12°14N 102°33E **39** F4
Tratani → *Pakistan* 29°19N 68°20E **42** E3
Traun *Austria* 48°14N 14°15E **16** D8
Travellers L. *Australia* 33°20S 142°0E **63** E3
Travemünde *Germany* 53°57N 10°52E **16** B6
Travers, Mt. *N.Z.* 42°1S 172°45E **59** E4
Traverse City *U.S.A.* 44°46N 85°38W **81** C11
Travis, L. *U.S.A.* 30°24N 97°55W **84** F6
Travnik *Bos.-H.* 44°17N 17°39E **23** B7
Trawbreaga B. *Ireland* 55°20N 7°25W **10** A4
Trébbia → *Italy* 45°4N 9°41E **20** D8
Třebíč *Czech Rep.* 49°14N 15°55E **16** D8
Trebinje *Bos.-H.* 42°44N 18°22E **23** C8
Trebonne *Australia* 18°37S 146°5E **62** B4
Tregaron *U.K.* 52°14N 3°56W **13** E4
Tregrosse Is. *Australia* 17°41S 150°43E **62** B5
Treherne *Canada* 49°38N 98°42W **71** D9
Treinta y Tres *Uruguay* 33°16S 54°17W **95** C5
Trelawney *Zimbabwe* 17°30S 30°30E **57** B5
Trelew *Argentina* 43°10S 65°20W **96** E3
Trelleborg *Sweden* 55°20N 13°10E **9** J15
Tremadog Bay *U.K.* 52°51N 4°18W **12** E3
Tremonton *U.S.A.* 41°43N 112°10W **76** F7
Tremp *Spain* 42°10N 0°52E **21** A6
Trenche → *Canada* 47°46N 72°53W **72** C5
Trenčín *Slovak Rep.* 48°52N 18°4E **17** D10
Trenggalek *Indonesia* 8°3S 111°43E **37** H14
Trenque Lauquen
  Argentina 36°5S 62°45W **94** D3
Trent → *Canada* 44°6N 77°34W **82** B7
Trent → *U.K.* 53°41N 0°42W **12** D7
Trento *Italy* 46°4N 11°8E **22** A4
Trenton *Canada* 44°10N 77°34W **82** B7
Trenton *Mo., U.S.A.* 40°5N 93°37W **80** E7
Trenton *N.J., U.S.A.* 40°14N 74°46W **83** F10
Trenton *Nebr., U.S.A.* 40°11N 101°1W **80** E3
Trepassey *Canada* 46°43N 53°25W **73** C9
Tres Arroyos *Argentina* 38°26S 60°20W **94** D3
Três Corações *Brazil* 21°44S 45°15W **95** A6
Três Lagoas *Brazil* 20°50S 51°43W **93** H8
Tres Lomas *Argentina* 36°27S 62°51W **94** D3
Tres Montes, C. *Chile* 46°50S 75°30W **96** F1
Tres Pinos *U.S.A.* 36°48N 121°19W **78** J5
Três Pontas *Brazil* 21°23S 45°29W **95** A6
Tres Puentes *Chile* 27°50S 70°15W **94** B1
Tres Puntas, C. *Argentina* 47°0S 66°0W **96** F3
Três Rios *Brazil* 22°20S 43°30W **95** A7
Tres Valles *Mexico* 18°15N 96°8W **87** D5
Tresco *U.K.* 49°57N 6°20W **13** H1
Treviso *Italy* 45°40N 12°15E **22** B5
Triabunna *Australia* 42°30S 147°55E **63** G4
Trianda *Greece* 36°25N 28°10E **25** C10
Triangle *Zimbabwe* 21°2S 31°28E **57** C5
Tribal Areas □ *Pakistan* 33°0N 70°0E **42** C4
Tribulation, C. *Australia* 16°5S 145°29E **62** B4
Tribune *U.S.A.* 38°28N 101°45W **80** F3
Trichinopoly = Tiruchchirappalli
  India 10°45N 78°45E **40** P11
Trichur *India* 10°30N 76°18E **40** P10
Trichy = Tiruchchirappalli
  India 10°45N 78°45E **40** P11
Trida *Australia* 33°1S 145°1E **63** E4

Trier *Germany* 49°45N 6°38E **16** D4
Trieste *Italy* 45°40N 13°46E **22** B5
Triglav *Slovenia* 46°21N 13°50E **16** E7
Trikala *Greece* 39°34N 21°47E **23** E9
Trikomo *Cyprus* 35°17N 33°52E **25** D12
Trikora, Puncak
  Indonesia 4°15S 138°45E **37** E9
Trim *Ireland* 53°33N 6°48W **10** C5
Trimmu Dam *Pakistan* 31°10N 72°8E **42** D5
Trincomalee *Sri Lanka* 8°38N 81°15E **40** Q12
Trindade *Atl. Oc.* 20°20S 29°50W **2** F8
Trindade *Brazil* 16°40S 49°30W **93** G9
Trinidad *Bolivia* 14°46S 64°50W **92** F6
Trinidad *Cuba* 21°48N 80°0W **88** B4
Trinidad *Uruguay* 33°30S 56°50W **94** C4
Trinidad *U.S.A.* 37°10N 104°31W **77** H11
Trinidad → *Mexico* 17°49N 95°9W **87** D5
Trinidad & Tobago ■
  W. Indies 10°30N 61°20W **93** K15
Trinity *Canada* 48°59N 53°55W **73** C9
Trinity *U.S.A.* 30°57N 95°22W **84** F7
Trinity → *Calif., U.S.A.* 41°11N 123°42W **76** F2
Trinity → *Tex., U.S.A.* 29°45N 94°43W **84** G7
Trinity B. *Canada* 48°20N 53°10W **73** C9
Trinity Hills *Trin. & Tob.* 10°7N 61°7W **93** K15
Trinity Is. *U.S.A.* 56°33N 154°25W **74** D9
Trinity Range *U.S.A.* 40°10N 118°40W **76** F4
Trinkitat *Sudan* 18°45N 37°51E **51** E13
Trinway *U.S.A.* 40°9N 82°1W **82** F2
Triolet *Mauritius* 20°4S 57°32E **53** d
Tripoli = Tarābulus
  Lebanon 34°31N 35°50E **46** A4
Tripoli = Tarābulus *Libya* 32°49N 13°7E **51** B8
Tripoli *Greece* 37°31N 22°25E **23** F10
Tripolitania = Tarābulus
  N. Afr. 31°0N 13°0E **51** B8
Tripura □ *India* 24°0N 92°0E **41** H18
Triplylos *Cyprus* 34°58N 32°45E **25** E11
Tristan da Cunha *Atl. Oc.* 37°6S 12°20W **49** K2
Trisul *India* 30°19N 79°47E **43** D8
Trivandrum *India* 8°41N 77°0E **40** Q10
Trnava *Slovak Rep.* 48°23N 17°35E **17** D9
Trochu *Canada* 51°50N 113°13W **70** C6
Trodely I. *Canada* 52°15N 79°26W **72** B4
Troglav *Croatia* 43°56N 16°36E **22** C7
Troilus, L. *Canada* 50°50N 74°35W **72** B5
Trois-Pistoles *Canada* 48°5N 69°10W **73** C6
Trois-Rivières *Canada* 46°25N 72°34W **72** C5
Trois-Rivières *Guadeloupe* 15°57N 61°40W **88** b
Troitsk *Russia* 54°10N 61°35E **28** D7
Troitsko Pechorsk
  Russia 62°40N 56°10E **18** B10
Trölladyngja *Iceland* 64°54N 17°16W **8** D5
Trollhättan *Sweden* 58°17N 12°20E **9** G15
Trollheimen *Norway* 62°46N 9°1E **8** E13
Trombetas → *Brazil* 1°55S 55°35W **93** D7
Tromsø *Norway* 69°40N 18°56E **8** B18
Tron *Thailand* 17°28N 100°7E **38** D3
Trona *U.S.A.* 35°46N 117°23W **79** K9
Tronador, Mte.
  Argentina 41°10S 71°50W **96** E2
Trondelag *Norway* 64°17N 11°50E **8** D14
Trondheim *Norway* 63°36N 10°25E **8** E14
Trondheimsfjorden
  Norway 63°35N 10°30E **8** E14
Troodos *Cyprus* 34°55N 32°52E **25** E11
Troon *U.K.* 55°33N 4°39W **11** F4
Tropic *U.S.A.* 37°37N 112°5W **77** H7
Trostan *U.K.* 55°3N 6°10W **10** A5
Trou Gras Pt. *St. Lucia* 13°51N 60°53W **89** f
Trout → *Canada* 61°19N 119°51W **70** A5
Trout L. *N.W.T., Canada* 60°40N 121°14W **70** A4
Trout L. *Ont., Canada* 51°20N 93°15W **71** C10
Trout Lake *Canada* 56°30N 114°32W **70** B6
Trout Lake *U.S.A.* 46°0N 121°32W **78** E5
Trout River *Canada* 49°29N 58°8W **73** C8
Trout Run *U.S.A.* 41°23N 77°3W **82** E7
Trouville-sur-Mer *France* 49°21N 0°5E **20** B4
Trowbridge *U.K.* 51°18N 2°12W **13** F5
Troy *Turkey* 39°57N 26°12E **23** E12
Troy *Ala., U.S.A.* 31°48N 85°58W **85** F12
Troy *Kans., U.S.A.* 39°47N 95°5W **80** F6
Troy *Mo., U.S.A.* 38°59N 90°59W **80** F8
Troy *Mont., U.S.A.* 48°28N 115°53W **76** B6
Troy *N.Y., U.S.A.* 42°44N 73°41W **83** D11
Troy *Ohio, U.S.A.* 40°2N 84°12W **81** E11
Troy *Pa., U.S.A.* 41°47N 76°47W **83** E8
Troyes *France* 48°19N 4°3E **20** B6
Truchas Pk. *U.S.A.* 35°58N 105°39W **77** J11
Trucial States = United Arab
  Emirates ■ *Asia* 23°50N 54°0E **45** F7
Truckee *U.S.A.* 39°20N 120°11W **78** F6
Trudovoye *Russia* 43°17N 132°5E **30** C6
Trujillo *Honduras* 16°0N 86°0W **88** C2
Trujillo *Peru* 8°6S 79°0W **92** E3
Trujillo *Spain* 39°28N 5°55E **21** C3
Trujillo *U.S.A.* 35°32N 104°42W **77** J11
Trujillo *Venezuela* 9°22N 70°38W **92** B4
Truk *Micronesia* 7°25N 151°46E **64** G7
Trumann *U.S.A.* 35°41N 90°31W **85** D9
Trumansburg *U.S.A.* 42°33N 76°40W **83** D8
Trumbull, Mt. *U.S.A.* 36°25N 113°19W **77** H7
Trundle *Australia* 32°53S 147°35E **63** E4
Trung Lon, Hon *Vietnam* 8°36N 106°3E **39** H6
Trung-Phan *Vietnam* 16°0N 108°0E **38** D6
Truro *Canada* 45°21N 63°14W **73** C7
Truro *U.K.* 50°16N 5°4W **13** G2
Truskavets *Ukraine* 49°17N 23°30E **17** D12
Trutch *Canada* 57°44N 122°57W **70** B4
Truth or Consequences
  U.S.A. 33°8N 107°15W **77** K10
Trutnov *Czech Rep.* 50°37N 15°54E **16** C8
Tryonville *U.S.A.* 41°42N 79°48W **82** E5
Tsandi *Namibia* 17°42S 14°50E **56** B1
Tsaratanana *Madag.* 16°47S 47°39E **57** B8
Tsaratanana, Mt. de =
  Maromokotro *Madag.* 14°0S 49°0E **57** A8
Tsaratanana △ *Madag.* 13°57S 48°52E **57** A8
Tsau *Botswana* 20°8S 22°22E **56** C3

Tsavo *Kenya* 2°59S 38°28E **54** C4
Tsavo East △ *Kenya* 2°44S 38°47E **54** C4
Tsavo West △ *Kenya* 3°19S 37°57E **54** C4
Tsentralnyy □ *Russia* 52°0N 40°0E **28** D4
Tses *Namibia* 25°58S 18°8E **56** D2
Tsetserleg *Mongolia* 47°36N 101°32E **32** B9
Tseung Kwan *China* 22°20N 114°15E **33** a
Tsévié *Togo* 6°25N 1°20E **50** G6
Tshabong *Botswana* 26°2S 22°29E **56** D3
Tshane *Botswana* 24°5S 21°54E **56** C3
Tshela
  Dem. Rep. of the Congo 4°57S 13°4E **52** E2
Tshesebe *Botswana* 21°51S 27°32E **57** C4
Tshibeke
  Dem. Rep. of the Congo 2°40S 28°35E **54** C2
Tshibinda
  Dem. Rep. of the Congo 2°23S 28°43E **54** C2
Tshikapa
  Dem. Rep. of the Congo 6°28S 20°48E **52** F4
Tshilenge
  Dem. Rep. of the Congo 6°17S 23°48E **54** D1
Tshinsenda
  Dem. Rep. of the Congo 12°20S 28°0E **55** E2
Tshofa
  Dem. Rep. of the Congo 5°13S 25°16E **54** D2
Tshwane = Pretoria
  S. Africa 25°44S 28°12E **57** D4
Tshwane *Botswana* 22°24S 22°1E **56** C3
Tsigara *Botswana* 20°22S 25°54E **56** C4
Tsihombe *Madag.* 25°10S 45°41E **57** D8
Tsiigehtchic *Canada* 67°15N 134°0W **68** D5
Ts'il-os △ *Canada* 51°9N 123°59W **70** C4
Tsimlyansk Res. = Tsimlyanskoye
  Vdkhr. *Russia* 48°0N 43°0E **19** E7
Tsimlyanskoye Vdkhr.
  Russia 48°0N 43°0E **19** E7
Tsinan = Jinan *China* 36°38N 117°1E **34** F9
Tsineng *S. Africa* 27°5S 23°5E **56** D3
Tsing Yi *China* 22°21N 114°6E **33** a
Tsinghai = Qinghai □
  China 36°0N 98°0E **32** D8
Tsingtao = Qingdao
  China 36°5N 120°20E **35** F11
Tsingy de Bemaraha △
  Madag. 18°35S 44°55E **57** B7
Tsingy de Namoroka △
  Madag. 16°29S 45°25E **57** B8
Tsinjoarivo *Madag.* 19°37S 47°40E **57** B8
Tsinjomitondraka *Madag.* 15°40S 47°8E **57** B8
Tsirigo = Kythira *Greece* 36°8N 23°0E **23** F10
Tsiroanomandidy *Madag.* 18°46S 46°2E **57** B8
Tsitondroina *Madag.* 21°19S 46°0E **57** C8
Tsitsikamma △ *S. Africa* 34°3S 23°40E **56** E3
Tsivory *Madag.* 24°4S 46°5E **57** C8
Tskhinvali *Georgia* 42°14N 44°1E **19** F7
Tsna → *Russia* 54°55N 41°58E **18** D7
Tso Moriri, L. *India* 32°50N 78°20E **43** C8
Tsobis *Namibia* 19°27S 17°30E **56** B2
Tsodilo Hill *Botswana* 18°49S 21°43E **56** B3
Tsogttsetsiy = Baruunsuu
  Mongolia 43°43N 105°35E **34** C3
Tsolo *S. Africa* 31°18S 28°37E **57** E4
Tsomo *S. Africa* 32°0S 27°42E **57** E4
Tsu *Japan* 34°45N 136°25E **31** G8
Tsu L. *Canada* 60°40N 111°52W **70** A6
Tsuchiura *Japan* 36°5N 140°15E **31** F10
Tsuen Wan *China* 22°22N 114°6E **33** a
Tsugaru-Hantō *Japan* 41°0N 140°30E **30** D10
Tsugaru-Kaikyō *Japan* 41°35N 141°0E **30** D10
Tsumeb *Namibia* 19°9S 17°44E **56** B2
Tsumis *Namibia* 23°39S 17°29E **56** C2
Tsuruga *Japan* 35°45N 136°2E **31** G8
Tsurugi-San *Japan* 33°51N 134°6E **31** H7
Tsuruoka *Japan* 38°44N 139°50E **30** E9
Tsushima *Gifu, Japan* 35°10N 136°43E **31** G8
Tsushima *Nagasaki,*
  Japan 34°20N 129°20E **31** G4
Tsuyama *Japan* 35°3N 134°0E **31** G7
Tsyelyakhany *Belarus* 52°30N 25°46E **17** B13
Tuaim = Tuam *Ireland* 53°31N 8°51W **10** C3
Tual *Indonesia* 5°38S 132°44E **37** F8
Tualatin *U.S.A.* 45°23N 122°45W **78** E4
Tuam *Ireland* 53°31N 8°51W **10** C3
Tuamotu, Îs.
  French Polynesia 17°0S 144°0W **65** J13
Tuamotu Arch. = Tuamotu, Îs.
  French Polynesia 17°0S 144°0W **65** J13
Tuamotu Ridge *Pac. Oc.* 20°0S 138°0W **65** K14
Tuan Giao *Vietnam* 21°35N 103°25E **38** B4
Tuao *Phil.* 17°45N 121°22E **37** A6
Tuapse *Russia* 44°5N 39°10E **19** F6
Tuas *Singapore* 1°19N 103°39E **39** d
Tuatapere *N.Z.* 46°8S 167°41E **59** G1
Tuba City *U.S.A.* 36°8N 111°14W **77** H8
Tuban *Indonesia* 6°54S 112°3E **37** G15
Tubani *Botswana* 24°46S 24°18E **56** C3
Tubarão *Brazil* 28°30S 49°0W **95** B6
Tübas *West Bank* 32°20N 35°22E **46** C4
Tubas → *Namibia* 22°54S 14°35E **56** C2
Tübingen *Germany* 48°31N 9°4E **16** D5
Tubou *Fiji* 18°13S 178°48W **59** a
Tubruq *Libya* 32°7N 23°55E **51** B10
Tubuaï, Îs.
  French Polynesia 25°0S 150°0W **65** K13
Tuc Trung *Vietnam* 11°1N 107°12E **39** G6
Tucacas *Venezuela* 10°48N 68°19W **92** A5
Tuchodi → *Canada* 58°17N 123°42W **70** B4
Tucson *U.S.A.* 32°13N 110°58W **77** K8
Tucumán □ *Argentina* 26°48S 66°2W **94** B2
Tucumcari *U.S.A.* 35°10N 103°44W **77** J12
Tucupita *Venezuela* 9°2N 62°3W **92** B6
Tucuruí *Brazil* 3°42S 49°44W **93** D9
Tucuruí, Represa de
  Brazil 4°0S 49°30W **93** D9
Tudela *Spain* 42°4N 1°39W **21** A5
Tudmur *Syria* 34°36N 38°15E **44** C3
Tudor, L. *Canada* 55°50N 65°25W **73** A6
Tuen Mun *China* 22°24N 113°59E **33** a

Tugela → *S. Africa* 29°14S 31°30E 57 D5
Tuguegarao *Phil.* 17°35N 121°42E 37 A6
Tugur *Russia* 53°44N 136°45E 29 D14
Tui *Spain* 42°3N 8°39W 21 A1
Tuineje *Canary Is.* 28°19N 14°3W 24 F5
Tukangbesi, Kepulauan *Indonesia* 6°0S 124°0E 37 F6
Tukarak I. *Canada* 56°15N 78°45W 72 A4
Tukayyid *Iraq* 29°47N 45°36E 44 D5
Tuktoyaktuk *Canada* 69°27N 133°2W 68 D5
Tuktut Nogait △ *Canada* 69°15N 122°0W 68 D7
Tukums *Latvia* 56°58N 23°10E 9 H20
Tukuyu *Tanzania* 9°17S 33°35E 55 D3
Tula *Hidalgo, Mexico* 20°3N 99°21W 87 C5
Tula *Tamaulipas, Mexico* 23°0N 99°43W 87 C5
Tula *Russia* 54°13N 37°38E 18 D6
Tulach Mhór = Tullamore *Ireland* 53°16N 7°31W 10 C4
Tulancingo *Mexico* 20°5N 98°22W 87 C5
Tulare *U.S.A.* 36°13N 119°21W 78 J7
Tulare Lake Bed *U.S.A.* 36°0N 119°48W 78 K7
Tularosa *U.S.A.* 33°5N 106°1W 77 K10
Tulbagh *S. Africa* 33°16S 19°6E 56 E2
Tulcán *Ecuador* 0°48N 77°43W 92 C3
Tulcea *Romania* 45°13N 28°46E 17 F15
Tulchyn *Ukraine* 48°41N 28°49E 17 D15
Tūleh *Iran* 34°35N 52°33E 45 C7
Tulemalu L. *Canada* 62°58N 99°25W 71 A9
Tuli *Zimbabwe* 21°58S 29°13E 55 G2
Tulia *U.S.A.* 34°32N 101°46W 84 D4
Tulita *Canada* 64°57N 125°30W 68 E6
Ţūlkarm *West Bank* 32°19N 35°2E 46 C4
Tulla *Ireland* 52°53N 8°46W 10 D3
Tullahoma *U.S.A.* 35°22N 86°13W 85 D11
Tullamore *Australia* 32°39S 147°36E 63 E4
Tullamore *Ireland* 53°16N 7°31W 10 C4
Tulle *France* 45°16N 1°46E 20 D4
Tullow *Ireland* 52°49N 6°45W 10 D5
Tully *Australia* 17°56S 145°55E 62 B4
Tully *U.S.A.* 42°48N 76°7W 83 D8
Tulsa *U.S.A.* 36°10N 95°55W 84 C7
Tulsequah *Canada* 58°39N 133°35W 70 B2
Tuluá *Colombia* 4°6N 76°11W 92 C3
Tulun *Russia* 54°32N 100°35E 29 D11
Tulungagung *Indonesia* 8°5S 111°54E 37 H14
Tuma → *Nic.* 13°6N 84°35W 88 D3
Tumacacori ⌓ *U.S.A.* 31°35N 111°6W 77 L8
Tumaco *Colombia* 1°50N 78°45W 92 C3
Tumakuru = Tumkur *India* 13°18N 77°6E 40 N10
Tumatumari *Guyana* 5°20N 58°55W 92 B7
Tumba *Sweden* 59°12N 17°48E 9 G17
Tumba, L. *Dem. Rep. of the Congo* 0°50S 18°0E 52 E3
Tumbarumba *Australia* 35°44S 148°0E 63 F4
Tumbaya *Argentina* 23°50S 65°26W 94 A2
Tumbes *Peru* 3°37S 80°27W 92 D2
Tumbler Ridge *Canada* 55°8N 121°0W 70 B4
Tumbwe *Dem. Rep. of the Congo* 11°25S 27°15E 55 E2
Tumby Bay *Australia* 34°21S 136°8E 63 E2
Tumd Youqi *China* 40°30N 110°30E 34 D6
Tumen *China* 43°0N 129°50E 30 C4
Tumen Jiang → *China* 42°20N 130°35E 35 C16
Tumeremo *Venezuela* 7°18N 61°30W 92 B6
Tumkur *India* 13°18N 77°6E 40 N10
Tump *Pakistan* 26°7N 62°16E 40 F3
Tumpat *Malaysia* 6°11N 102°10E 39 J4
Tumu *Ghana* 10°56N 1°56W 50 F5
Tumucumaque, Serra *Brazil* 2°0N 55°0W 93 C8
Tumut *Australia* 35°16S 148°13E 63 F4
Tumwater *U.S.A.* 47°1N 122°54W 78 C4
Tuna *India* 22°59N 70°5E 42 H4
Tunapuna *Trin. & Tob.* 10°38N 61°24W 93 K15
Tunas de Zaza *Cuba* 21°39N 79°34W 88 B4
Tunbridge Wells = Royal Tunbridge Wells *U.K.* 51°7N 0°16E 13 F8
Tunchang *China* 19°21N 110°5E 38 C8
Tuncurry *Australia* 32°17S 152°29E 63 E5
Tundla *India* 27°12N 78°17E 42 F8
Tunduru *Tanzania* 11°8S 37°25E 55 E4
Tundzha → *Bulgaria* 41°40N 26°35E 23 C11
Tung Chung *China* 22°17N 113°57E 33 a
Tung Lung Chau *China* 22°15N 114°17E 33 a
Tungabhadra → *India* 15°57N 78°15E 40 M11
Tungla *Nic.* 13°24N 84°21W 88 D3
Tungsha Tao = Dongsha Dao *S. China Sea* 20°45N 116°43E 33 G12
Tungsten *Canada* 61°57N 128°16W 70 A3
Tunguska, Nizhnyaya → *Russia* 65°48N 88°4E 29 C9
Tunguska, Podkamennaya → *Russia* 61°50N 90°13E 29 C10
Tunica *U.S.A.* 34°41N 90°23W 85 D9
Tunis *Tunisia* 36°50N 10°11E 51 A8
Tunisia ■ *Africa* 33°30N 9°10E 51 A7
Tunja *Colombia* 5°33N 73°25W 92 B4
Tunkhannock *U.S.A.* 41°32N 75°57W 83 E9
Tunliu *China* 36°13N 112°52E 34 F7
Tunnel Creek △ *Australia* 17°41S 125°18E 60 C4
Tunnsjøen *Norway* 64°45N 13°25E 8 D15
Tunungayualok I. *Canada* 56°0N 61°0W 73 A7
Tunuyán *Argentina* 33°35S 69°0W 94 C2
Tunuyán → *Argentina* 33°33S 67°30W 94 C2
Tuolumne *U.S.A.* 37°58N 120°15W 78 H6
Tuolumne → *U.S.A.* 37°36N 121°13W 78 H5
Tūp Āghāj *Iran* 36°3N 47°50E 44 B5
Tupã *Brazil* 21°57S 50°28W 95 A5
Tupelo *U.S.A.* 34°16N 88°43W 85 D10
Tupinambarana, I. *Brazil* 3°0S 58°0W 92 D7
Tupiza *Bolivia* 21°30S 65°40W 94 A2
Tupman *U.S.A.* 35°18N 119°21W 79 K7
Tupper *Canada* 55°32N 120°1W 70 B4
Tupper L. *U.S.A.* 44°10N 74°32W 83 B10
Tupper Lake *U.S.A.* 44°14N 74°28W 83 B10
Tupungato, Cerro *S. Amer.* 33°15S 69°50W 94 C2
Tuquan *China* 45°18N 121°38E 35 B11
Túquerres *Colombia* 1°5N 77°37W 92 C3
Tura *Russia* 64°20N 100°17E 29 C11
Turabah *Si. Arabia* 28°20N 43°15E 44 D4
Tūrān *Iran* 35°39N 56°42E 45 C8
Turan *Russia* 51°55N 94°0E 29 D10
Ţurayf *Si. Arabia* 31°41N 38°39E 44 D3
Turda *Romania* 46°34N 23°47E 17 E12
Turek *Poland* 52°3N 18°30E 17 B10
Turén *Venezuela* 9°17N 69°6W 92 B5
Turfan = Turpan *China* 43°58N 89°10E 32 C6
Turfan Basin = Turpan Pendi *China* 42°40N 89°25E 32 C6
Turfan Depression = Turpan Pendi *China* 42°40N 89°25E 32 C6
Turgeon → *Canada* 50°0N 78°56W 72 C4
Tŭrgovishte *Bulgaria* 43°17N 26°38E 23 C12
Turgutlu *Turkey* 38°30N 27°43E 23 E12
Turgwe → *Zimbabwe* 21°31S 32°15E 57 C5
Turia → *Spain* 39°27N 0°19W 21 C5
Turiaçu *Brazil* 1°40S 45°19W 93 D9
Turiaçu → *Brazil* 1°36S 45°19W 93 D9
Turin = Torino *Italy* 45°3N 7°40E 20 D7
Turkana, L. *Africa* 3°30N 36°5E 54 B4
Turkestan = Türkistan *Kazakhstan* 43°17N 68°16E 28 E7
Turkey ■ *Eurasia* 39°0N 36°0E 19 G6
Turkey Creek = Warmun *Australia* 17°2S 128°12E 60 C4
Türkistan *Kazakhstan* 43°17N 68°16E 28 E7
Türkmenabat *Turkmenistan* 39°6N 63°34E 45 B9
Türkmenbashi *Turkmenistan* 40°5N 53°5E 45 A7
Turkmenistan ■ *Asia* 39°0N 59°0E 28 F6
Turks & Caicos Is. ⊠ *W. Indies* 21°20N 71°20W 89 B5
Turks Island Passage *W. Indies* 21°30N 71°30W 89 B5
Turku *Finland* 60°30N 22°19E 9 F20
Turkwel → *Kenya* 3°6N 36°6E 54 B4
Turlock *U.S.A.* 37°30N 120°51W 78 H6
Turnagain *Australia* 9°34S 142°17E 62 a
Turnagain → *Canada* 59°12N 127°35W 70 B3
Turnagain, C. *N.Z.* 40°28S 176°38E 59 D6
Turneffe Is. *Belize* 17°20N 87°50W 87 D7
Turner *U.S.A.* 48°51N 108°24W 76 B9
Turner Pt. *Australia* 11°47S 133°32E 62 A1
Turner Valley *Canada* 50°40N 114°17W 70 C6
Turners Falls *U.S.A.* 42°36N 72°33W 83 D12
Turnhout *Belgium* 51°19N 4°57E 15 C4
Turnor L. *Canada* 56°35N 108°35W 71 B7
Tŭrnovo = Veliko Tŭrnovo *Bulgaria* 43°5N 25°41E 23 C11
Turnu Măgurele *Romania* 43°46N 24°56E 17 G13
Turnu Roşu, P. *Romania* 45°33N 24°17E 17 F13
Turpan *China* 43°58N 89°10E 32 C6
Turpan Pendi *China* 42°40N 89°25E 32 C6
Turriff *U.K.* 57°32N 2°27W 11 D6
Tursāq *Iraq* 33°27N 45°47E 44 C5
Turtle Head I. *Australia* 10°56S 142°37E 62 A3
Turtle L. *Canada* 53°36N 108°38W 71 C7
Turtle Lake *U.S.A.* 47°31N 100°53W 80 B3
Turtleford *Canada* 53°23N 108°57W 71 C7
Turuépano △ *Venezuela* 10°34N 62°43W 89 D7
Turukhansk *Russia* 65°21N 88°5E 29 C9
Tuscaloosa *U.S.A.* 33°12N 87°34W 85 E11
Tuscany = Toscana □ *Italy* 43°25N 11°0E 22 C4
Tuscarawas → *U.S.A.* 40°24N 81°25W 82 F3
Tuscarora Mt. *U.S.A.* 40°55N 77°55W 82 F7
Tuscola *Ill., U.S.A.* 39°48N 88°17W 80 F9
Tuscola *Tex., U.S.A.* 32°12N 99°48W 84 E5
Tuscumbia *U.S.A.* 34°44N 87°42W 85 D11
Tuskegee *U.S.A.* 32°25N 85°42W 85 E12
Tuticorin *India* 8°50N 78°12E 40 Q11
Tutóia *Brazil* 2°45S 42°20W 93 D10
Tutong *Brunei* 4°47N 114°40E 36 D4
Tutrakan *Bulgaria* 44°2N 26°40E 23 B12
Tuttle Creek L. *U.S.A.* 39°15N 96°36W 80 F5
Tuttlingen *Germany* 47°58N 8°48E 16 E5
Tutuala *E. Timor* 8°25S 127°15E 37 F7
Tutuila *Amer. Samoa* 14°19S 170°50W 59 b
Tutume *Botswana* 20°30S 27°5E 53 J5
Tuul Gol → *Mongolia* 48°30N 104°25E 32 B9
Tuva □ *Russia* 51°30N 95°0E 29 D10
Tuvalu ■ *Pac. Oc.* 8°0S 178°0E 58 B10
Tuvuca *Fiji* 17°40S 178°48W 59 a
Tuxpan *Mexico* 20°57N 97°24W 87 C5
Tuxtla Gutiérrez *Mexico* 16°45N 93°7W 87 D6
Tuy = Tui *Spain* 42°3N 8°39W 21 A1
Tuy Duc *Vietnam* 12°15N 107°27E 39 F6
Tuy Phong *Vietnam* 11°14N 108°43E 39 G7
Tuya L. *Canada* 59°7N 130°35W 70 B2
Tuyen Hoa *Vietnam* 17°50N 106°10E 38 D6
Tuyen Quang *Vietnam* 21°50N 105°10E 38 B5
Tūysarkān *Iran* 34°33N 48°27E 45 C6
Tuz Gölü *Turkey* 38°42N 33°18E 19 G5
Ţūz Khurmātū *Iraq* 34°56N 44°38E 44 C5
Tuzigoot △ *U.S.A.* 34°46N 112°2W 77 J7
Tuzla *Bos.-H.* 44°34N 18°41E 23 B8
Tver *Russia* 56°55N 35°59E 18 C6
Twain *U.S.A.* 40°1N 121°3W 78 E5
Twain Harte *U.S.A.* 38°2N 120°14W 78 G6
Tweed *Canada* 44°29N 77°19W 82 B7
Tweed → *U.K.* 55°45N 2°0W 11 F6
Tweed Heads *Australia* 28°10S 153°31E 63 D5
Tweedsmuir ⌓ *Canada* 53°0N 126°20W 70 C3
Twentynine Palms *U.S.A.* 34°8N 116°3W 79 L10
Twillingate *Canada* 49°42N 54°45W 73 C9
Twin Bridges *U.S.A.* 45°33N 112°20W 76 D7
Twin Falls *Canada* 53°30N 64°32W 73 B7
Twin Falls *U.S.A.* 42°34N 114°28W 76 E6
Twin Valley *U.S.A.* 47°16N 96°16W 80 B5
Twinsburg *U.S.A.* 41°19N 81°26W 82 E3
Twitchell Res. *U.S.A.* 34°59N 120°19W 79 L6
Two Harbors *U.S.A.* 47°2N 91°40W 80 B8
Two Hills *Canada* 53°43N 111°52W 70 C6
Two Rivers *U.S.A.* 44°9N 87°34W 80 C10
Two Rocks *Australia* 31°30S 115°35E 61 F2
Twofold B. *Australia* 37°8S 149°59E 63 F4
Tyachiv *Ukraine* 48°1N 23°35E 17 D12
Tychy *Poland* 50°9N 18°59E 17 C10
Tyler *Minn., U.S.A.* 44°17N 96°8W 80 C5
Tyler *Tex., U.S.A.* 32°21N 95°18W 84 E7
Tynda *Russia* 55°10N 124°43E 29 D13
Tyndall *U.S.A.* 43°0N 97°50W 80 D5
Tyne → *U.K.* 54°59N 1°32W 12 C6
Tyne & Wear □ *U.K.* 55°6N 1°17W 12 B6
Tynemouth *U.K.* 55°1N 1°26W 12 B6
Tyre = Sūr *Lebanon* 33°19N 35°16E 46 B4
Tyrifjorden *Norway* 60°2N 10°8E 9 F14
Tyrol = Tirol □ *Austria* 47°3N 10°43E 16 E6
Tyrone *U.S.A.* 40°40N 78°14W 82 F6
Tyrone □ *U.K.* 54°38N 7°11W 10 B4
Tyrrell → *Australia* 35°26S 142°51E 63 F3
Tyrrell, L. *Australia* 35°20S 142°50E 63 F3
Tyrrell L. *Canada* 63°7N 105°27W 71 A7
Tyrrhenian Sea *Medit. S.* 40°0N 12°30E 22 E5
Tysfjorden *Norway* 68°7N 16°25E 8 B17
Tyulgan *Russia* 52°22N 56°12E 18 D10
Tyumen *Russia* 57°11N 65°29E 28 D7
Tywi → *U.K.* 51°48N 4°21W 13 F3
Tywyn *U.K.* 52°35N 4°5W 13 E3
Tzaneen *S. Africa* 23°47S 30°9E 57 C5
Tzermiado *Greece* 35°12N 25°29E 25 D7
Tzukong = Zigong *China* 29°15N 104°48E 32 F9

U

U.S.A. = United States of America ■ *N. Amer.* 37°0N 96°0W 75 H20
U.S. Virgin Is. ⊠ *W. Indies* 18°20N 65°0W 89 e
Uanle Uen = Wanleweyne *Somali Rep.* 2°37N 44°54E 47 G3
Uatumã → *Brazil* 2°26S 57°37W 92 D7
Uaupés *Brazil* 0°8S 67°5W 92 D5
Uaupés → *Brazil* 0°2N 67°16W 92 C5
Uaxactún *Guatemala* 17°25N 89°29W 88 C2
Ubá *Brazil* 21°8S 43°0W 95 A7
Ubaitaba *Brazil* 14°18S 39°20W 93 F11
Ubangi = Oubangi → *Dem. Rep. of the Congo* 0°30S 17°50E 52 E3
Ubauro *Pakistan* 28°15N 69°45E 42 E3
Ubayyiḍ, W. al → *Iraq* 32°34N 43°48E 44 C4
Ube *Japan* 33°56N 131°15E 31 H5
Úbeda *Spain* 38°3N 3°23W 21 C4
Uberaba *Brazil* 19°50S 47°55W 93 G9
Uberlândia *Brazil* 19°0S 48°20W 93 G9
Ubin, Pulau *Singapore* 1°24N 103°57E 39 d
Ubly *U.S.A.* 43°42N 82°55W 82 C2
Ubolratna Res. *Thailand* 16°45N 102°30E 38 D4
Ubombo *S. Africa* 27°31S 32°4E 57 D5
Ubon Ratchathani *Thailand* 15°15N 104°50E 38 E5
Ubondo *Dem. Rep. of the Congo* 0°55S 25°42E 54 C2
Ubort → *Belarus* 52°6N 28°30E 17 B15
Ubud *Indonesia* 8°30S 115°16E 37 J18
Ubundu *Dem. Rep. of the Congo* 0°22S 25°30E 54 C2
Ucayali → *Peru* 4°30S 73°30W 92 D4
Uchab *Namibia* 19°47S 17°42E 56 B2
Uchiura-Wan *Japan* 42°25N 140°40E 30 C10
Uchquduq *Uzbekistan* 41°50N 62°50E 28 E7
Uchur → *Russia* 58°48N 130°35E 29 D14
Ucluelet *Canada* 48°57N 125°32W 70 D3
Uda → *Russia* 54°42N 135°14E 29 D14
Udachnyy *Russia* 66°25N 112°24E 29 C12
Udagamandalam *India* 11°30N 76°44E 40 P10
Udainagar *India* 22°33N 76°13E 42 H7
Udaipur *India* 24°36N 73°44E 42 G5
Udaipur Garhi *Nepal* 27°0N 86°35E 43 F12
Udala *India* 21°35N 86°34E 43 J12
Uddevalla *Sweden* 58°21N 11°55E 9 G14
Uddjaure *Sweden* 65°56N 17°49E 8 D17
Uden *Neths.* 51°40N 5°37E 15 C5
Udgir *India* 18°25N 77°5E 40 K10
Udhampur *India* 33°0N 75°5E 43 C6
Údine *Italy* 46°3N 13°14E 22 A5
Udintsev Fracture Zone *S. Ocean* 57°0S 145°0W 5 B13
Udmurtia □ *Russia* 57°30N 52°30E 18 C9
Udon Thani *Thailand* 17°29N 102°46E 38 D4
Udong *Cambodia* 11°48N 104°45E 39 G5
Udskaya Guba *Russia* 54°50N 135°45E 29 D14
Udu Pt. *Fiji* 16°9S 179°57W 59 a
Udupi *India* 13°25N 74°42E 40 N9
Udzungwa △ *Tanzania* 7°52S 36°35E 54 D4
Udzungwa Range *Tanzania* 9°30S 35°10E 55 D4
Ueda *Japan* 36°24N 138°16E 31 F9
Uedineniya, Os. *Russia* 78°0N 85°0E 4 B12
Uele → *Dem. Rep. of the Congo* 3°45N 24°45E 52 D4
Uelen *Russia* 66°10N 170°0W 29 C19
Uelzen *Germany* 52°57N 10°32E 16 B6
Ufa *Russia* 54°45N 55°55E 18 D10
Ufa → *Russia* 54°40N 56°0E 18 D10
Ugab → *Namibia* 20°55S 13°30E 56 C1
Ugalla → *Tanzania* 5°8S 30°42E 54 D3
Ugalla River ⌓ *Tanzania* 5°50S 31°54E 54 D3
Uganda ■ *Africa* 2°0N 32°0E 54 B3
Ugie *S. Africa* 31°10S 28°13E 57 E4
Uglegorsk *Russia* 49°5N 142°2E 29 E15
Ugljan *Croatia* 44°12N 15°10E 16 F8
Ugolnye Kopi *Russia* 64°44N 177°42E 29 C18
Uhlenhorst *Namibia* 23°45S 17°55E 56 C2
Uhrichsville *U.S.A.* 40°24N 81°21W 82 F3
Uibhist a Deas = South Uist *U.K.* 57°20N 7°15W 11 D1
Uibhist a Tuath = North Uist *U.K.* 57°40N 7°15W 11 D1
Uig *U.K.* 57°35N 6°21W 11 D2
Uíge *Angola* 7°30S 14°40E 52 F2
Uiha *Tonga* 19°54S 174°25W 59 c
Uijeongbu *S. Korea* 37°44N 127°2E 35 F14
Ŭiju *N. Korea* 40°15N 124°35E 35 D13
Uinta Mts. *U.S.A.* 40°45N 110°30W 76 F8
Uis *Namibia* 21°8S 14°49E 56 C1
Uiseong *S. Korea* 36°21N 128°45E 35 F15
Uitenhage *S. Africa* 33°40S 25°28E 56 E4
Uithuizen *Neths.* 53°24N 6°41E 15 A6
Ujh → *India* 32°10N 75°18E 42 C6
Ujhani *India* 28°0N 79°6E 43 F8
Uji-guntō *Japan* 31°15N 129°25E 31 J4
Ujjain *India* 23°9N 75°43E 42 H6
Ujung Kulon △ *Indonesia* 6°46S 105°19E 37 G11
Ujung Pandang = Makassar *Indonesia* 5°10S 119°20E 37 F5
Uka *Russia* 57°50N 162°0E 29 D17
Ukara I. *Tanzania* 1°50S 33°0E 54 C3
Uke-Shima *Japan* 28°2N 129°14E 31 K4
Ukerewe I. *Tanzania* 2°0S 33°0E 54 C3
Ukhrul *India* 25°10N 94°25E 41 G19
Ukhta *Russia* 63°34N 53°41E 18 B9
Ukiah *U.S.A.* 39°9N 123°13W 78 F3
Ukmergė *Lithuania* 55°15N 24°45E 9 J21
Ukraine ■ *Europe* 49°0N 32°0E 19 E5
Ukwi *Botswana* 23°29S 20°30E 56 C3
Ulaan Nuur *Mongolia* 44°30N 103°40E 34 B2
Ulaan-Uul *Mongolia* 46°4N 100°49E 34 B6
Ulaanbaatar *Mongolia* 47°55N 106°53E 32 B10
Ulaangom *Mongolia* 50°5N 92°10E 32 A7
Ulaanjirem *Mongolia* 45°5N 105°30E 34 B3
Ulak I. *U.S.A.* 51°22N 178°57W 74 E4
Ulamba *Dem. Rep. of the Congo* 9°3S 23°38E 55 D1
Ulan Bator = Ulaanbaatar *Mongolia* 47°55N 106°53E 32 B10
Ulan Ude *Russia* 51°45N 107°40E 33 A10
Ulanhad = Chifeng *China* 42°18N 118°58E 35 C10
Ulanhot = Horqin Youyi Qianqi *China* 46°5N 122°3E 35 A12
Ulansuhai Nur *China* 40°53N 108°51E 34 D5
Ulaya *Morogoro, Tanzania* 7°3S 36°55E 54 D4
Ulaya *Tabora, Tanzania* 4°25S 33°30E 54 C3
Ulcinj *Montenegro* 41°58N 19°10E 23 D8
Ulco *S. Africa* 28°21S 24°15E 56 D3
Ule älv = Oulujoki → *Finland* 65°1N 25°30E 8 D21
Ule träsk = Oulujärvi *Finland* 64°25N 27°15E 8 D22
Uleåborg = Oulu *Finland* 65°1N 25°29E 8 D21
Ulefoss *Norway* 59°17N 9°16E 9 G13
Ulhasnagar *India* 19°15N 73°10E 40 K8
Uliastay *Mongolia* 47°56N 97°28E 32 B8
Uljin *S. Korea* 36°59N 129°24E 35 F15
Ulladulla *Australia* 35°21S 150°29E 63 F5
Ullapool *U.K.* 57°54N 5°9W 11 D3
Ulleungdo *S. Korea* 37°30N 130°30E 31 F5
Ullswater *Canada* 45°12N 79°29W 82 A5
Ullswater *U.K.* 54°34N 2°52W 12 C5
Ulm *Germany* 48°23N 9°58E 16 D5
Ulmarra *Australia* 29°37S 153°4E 63 D5
Ulonguè *Mozam.* 14°37S 34°19E 55 E3
Ulricehamn *Sweden* 57°46N 13°26E 9 H15
Ulsan *S. Korea* 35°20N 129°15E 35 G15
Ulsta *U.K.* 60°30N 1°9W 11 A7
Ulster □ *U.K.* 54°35N 6°30W 10 B5
Ulubat Gölü *Turkey* 40°9N 28°35E 23 D13
Uludağ *Turkey* 40°4N 29°13E 23 D13
Uluguru Mts. *Tanzania* 7°15S 37°40E 54 D4
Ulungur He → *China* 47°1N 87°24E 32 B6
Ulungur Hu *China* 47°20N 87°10E 32 B6
Uluru *Australia* 25°23S 131°5E 61 E5
Uluru-Kata Tjuta △ *Australia* 25°19S 131°1E 61 E5
Ulutau *Kazakhstan* 48°39N 67°1E 28 E7
Uluwatu *Indonesia* 8°50S 115°5E 37 K18
Ulva *U.K.* 56°29N 6°13W 11 E2
Ulverston *U.K.* 54°13N 3°5W 12 C4
Ulverstone *Australia* 41°11S 146°11E 63 G4
Ulya *Russia* 59°10N 142°0E 29 D15
Ulyanovsk *Russia* 54°20N 48°25E 18 D8
Ulyasutay = Uliastay *Mongolia* 47°56N 97°28E 32 B8
Ulysses *Kans., U.S.A.* 37°35N 101°22W 80 G3
Ulysses *Pa., U.S.A.* 41°54N 77°46W 82 E7
Ulysses, Mt. *Canada* 57°20N 124°5W 70 B4
Umala *Bolivia* 17°25S 68°5W 92 G5
'Umān = Oman ■ *Asia* 23°0N 58°0E 47 C6
Uman *Ukraine* 48°40N 30°12E 17 D16
Umaria *India* 23°35N 80°50E 43 H9
Umarkot *Pakistan* 25°15N 69°40E 42 G3
Umarpada *India* 21°27N 73°30E 42 J5
Umatilla *U.S.A.* 45°55N 119°21W 76 D4
Umba *Russia* 66°42N 34°11E 18 A5
Umbagog L. *U.S.A.* 44°46N 71°3W 83 B13
Umbakumba *Australia* 13°47S 136°50E 62 A2
Umbrella Mts. *N.Z.* 45°35S 169°5E 59 F2
Umeå *Sweden* 63°45N 20°20E 8 E19
Umeälven → *Sweden* 63°45N 20°20E 8 E19
Umera *Indonesia* 0°12S 129°37E 37 E7
Umfuli → *Zimbabwe* 17°30S 29°23E 55 F2
Umfurudzi ⌓ *Zimbabwe* 17°6S 31°40E 55 F3
Umgusa *Zimbabwe* 19°29S 27°52E 55 F2
Umgwenya → *Mozam.* 25°14S 32°18E 57 D5
Umiujaq *Canada* 56°33N 76°33W 72 A4
Umkomaas *S. Africa* 30°13S 30°48E 57 E5
Umlazi *S. Africa* 29°59S 30°54E 53 L6
Umm ad Daraj, J. *Jordan* 32°18N 35°48E 46 C4
Umm al Qaywayn *U.A.E.* 25°30N 55°35E 45 E7
Umm al Qittayn *Jordan* 32°18N 36°40E 46 C5
Umm Bāb *Qatar* 25°12N 50°48E 45 E6
Umm Durman = Omdurmân *Sudan* 15°40N 32°28E 51 E12
Umm el Fahm *Israel* 32°31N 35°9E 46 C4
Umm Keddada *Sudan* 13°33N 26°35E 51 F11
Umm Lajj *Si. Arabia* 25°0N 37°23E 44 E3
Umm Qasr *Iraq* 30°1N 47°58E 44 D5
Umm Ruwaba *Sudan* 12°50N 31°20E 51 F12
Umnak I. *U.S.A.* 53°15N 168°20W 74 E6
Umniati → *Zimbabwe* 16°49S 28°45E 55 F2
Umpqua → *U.S.A.* 43°40N 124°12W 76 E1
Umreth *India* 22°41N 73°4E 42 H5
Umtata = Mthatha *S. Africa* 31°36S 28°49E 57 E4
Umuarama *Brazil* 23°45S 53°20W 95 A5
Umvukwe Ra. *Zimbabwe* 16°45S 30°45E 55 F3
Umzimvubu *S. Africa* 31°38S 29°33E 57 E4
Umzingwane → *Zimbabwe* 22°12S 29°56E 55 G2
Umzinto = eMuziwezinto *S. Africa* 30°15S 30°45E 57 E5
Una *India* 20°46N 71°8E 42 J4
Una → *Bos.-H.* 45°0N 16°20E 16 F9
Unadilla *U.S.A.* 42°20N 75°19W 83 D9
Unalakleet *U.S.A.* 63°52N 160°47W 74 C7
Unalaska *U.S.A.* 53°53N 166°32W 74 E6
Unalaska I. *U.S.A.* 53°35N 166°50W 74 E6
'Unayzah *Si. Arabia* 26°6N 43°58E 44 E4
'Unayzah, J. *Asia* 32°12N 39°18E 44 C3
Uncía *Bolivia* 18°25S 66°40W 92 G5
Uncompahgre Peak *U.S.A.* 38°4N 107°28W 76 G10
Uncompahgre Plateau *U.S.A.* 38°20N 108°15W 76 G9
Undara Volcanic △ *Australia* 18°14S 144°41E 62 B3
Underbool *Australia* 35°10S 141°51E 63 F3
Underwood *Canada* 44°18N 81°29W 82 B3
Ungarie *Australia* 33°38S 146°56E 63 E4
Ungarra *Australia* 34°12S 136°2E 63 E2
Ungava, Pén. d' *Canada* 60°0N 74°0W 69 F17
Ungava B. *Canada* 59°30N 67°30W 69 F18
Ungeny = Ungheni *Moldova* 47°11N 27°51E 17 E14
Unggi *N. Korea* 42°16N 130°28E 35 C16
Ungheni *Moldova* 47°11N 27°51E 17 E14
Ungwana B. *Kenya* 2°45S 40°20E 54 C5
União da Vitória *Brazil* 26°13S 51°5W 95 B5
Unimak I. *U.S.A.* 54°45N 164°0W 74 E7
Unimak Pass. *U.S.A.* 54°15N 164°30W 74 E7
Union *Miss., U.S.A.* 32°34N 89°7W 85 E10
Union *Mo., U.S.A.* 38°27N 91°0W 80 F8
Union *S.C., U.S.A.* 34°43N 81°37W 85 D14
Union City *Calif., U.S.A.* 37°36N 122°1W 78 H4
Union City *N.J., U.S.A.* 40°45N 74°2W 83 F10
Union City *Pa., U.S.A.* 41°54N 79°51W 82 E5
Union City *Tenn., U.S.A.* 36°26N 89°3W 85 C10
Union Dale *U.S.A.* 41°43N 75°29W 83 E9
Union Gap *U.S.A.* 46°33N 120°28W 76 C3
Union Springs *Ala., U.S.A.* 32°9N 85°43W 85 E12
Union Springs *N.Y., U.S.A.* 42°50N 76°41W 83 D8
Uniondale *S. Africa* 33°39S 23°7E 56 E3
Uniontown *U.S.A.* 39°54N 79°44W 81 F14
Unionville *U.S.A.* 40°29N 93°1W 80 E7
United Arab Emirates ■ *Asia* 23°50N 54°0E 45 F7
United Kingdom ■ *Europe* 53°0N 2°0W 14 E6
United States of America ■ *N. Amer.* 37°0N 96°0W 75 H20
Unity *Canada* 52°30N 109°5W 71 C7
University Park *U.S.A.* 32°17N 106°45W 77 K10
University Place *U.S.A.* 47°14N 122°33W 78 C4
Unjha *India* 23°46N 72°24E 42 H5
Unnao *India* 26°35N 80°30E 43 F9
Unsengedsi → *Zimbabwe* 15°43S 31°14E 55 F3
Unst *U.K.* 60°44N 0°53W 11 A8
Unuk → *Canada* 56°5N 131°3W 70 B2
Unzen-Amakusa △ *Japan* 32°15N 130°10E 31 H5
Uong Bi *Vietnam* 21°2N 106°47E 38 B6
Uozu *Japan* 36°48N 137°24E 31 F8
Upata *Venezuela* 8°1N 62°24W 92 B6
Upemba, L. *Dem. Rep. of the Congo* 8°30S 26°20E 55 D2
Upemba △ *Dem. Rep. of the Congo* 9°0S 26°35E 55 D2
Upernavik *Greenland* 72°49N 56°20W 4 B5
Upington *S. Africa* 28°25S 21°15E 56 D3
Upleta *India* 21°46N 70°16E 42 J4
'Upolu *Samoa* 13°58S 172°0W 59 b
Upper Alkali L. *U.S.A.* 41°47N 120°8W 76 F3
Upper Arrow L. *Canada* 50°30N 117°50W 70 C5
Upper Daly ⚙ *Australia* 14°26S 131°3E 60 B5
Upper Darby *U.S.A.* 39°55N 75°16W 81 F16
Upper Foster L. *Canada* 56°47N 105°20W 71 B7
Upper Hutt *N.Z.* 41°8S 175°5E 59 D5
Upper Klamath L. *U.S.A.* 42°25N 121°55W 76 E3
Upper Lake *U.S.A.* 39°10N 122°54W 78 F4
Upper Liard *Canada* 60°3N 128°54W 70 A3
Upper Manzanilla *Trin. & Tob.* 10°31N 61°4W 93 K15
Upper Missouri Breaks ⌓ *U.S.A.* 47°50N 109°55W 76 C9
Upper Musquodoboit *Canada* 45°10N 62°58W 73 C7
Upper Red L. *U.S.A.* 48°8N 94°45W 80 A6
Upper Sandusky *U.S.A.* 40°50N 83°17W 81 E12
Upper Volta = Burkina Faso ■ *Africa* 12°0N 1°0W 50 F5
Uppland *Sweden* 59°59N 17°48E 9 G17
Uppsala *Sweden* 59°53N 17°38E 9 G17
Upshi *India* 33°48N 77°52E 43 C7
Upton *U.S.A.* 44°6N 104°38W 76 D11
Uqsuqtuuq = Gjoa Haven *Canada* 68°38N 95°53W 68 D12
Ur *Iraq* 30°55N 46°25E 44 D5
Urad Qianqi *China* 40°40N 108°30E 34 D5
Urahoro *Japan* 42°50N 143°40E 30 C11
Urakawa *Japan* 42°9N 142°47E 30 C11
Ural = Uralskiy □ *Russia* 64°0N 70°0E 28 C7
Ural = Zhayyq → *Kazakhstan* 47°0N 51°48E 19 E9
Ural *Australia* 33°21S 146°12E 63 E4

Ural Mts. = Uralskie Gory
  Eurasia 60°N 59°0E **18** C10
Uralla *Australia* 30°37S 151°29E **63** E5
Uralsk = Oral *Kazakhstan* 51°20N 51°20E **19** D9
Uralskiy □ *Russia* 64°0N 70°0E **28** C7
Urambo *Tanzania* 5°4S 32°0E **54** D3
Urandangi *Australia* 21°32S 138°14E **62** C2
Uranium City *Canada* 59°34N 108°37W **71** B7
Urapuntja = Utopia
  Australia 22°14S 134°33E **62** C1
Uraricoera → *Brazil* 3°2N 60°30W **92** C6
Urasoe *Japan* 26°15N 127°43E **31** L3
Urawa = Saitama *Japan* 35°54N 139°38E **31** G9
Uray *Russia* 60°5N 65°15E **28** C7
'Uray'irah *Si. Arabia* 25°57N 48°53E **45** E6
Urbana *Ill., U.S.A.* 40°7N 88°12W **80** E9
Urbana *Ohio, U.S.A.* 40°7N 83°45W **81** E12
Urbandale *U.S.A.* 41°38N 93°43W **80** E7
Urbino *Italy* 43°43N 12°38E **22** C5
Urbión, Picos de *Spain* 42°1N 2°52W **21** A4
Urcos *Peru* 13°40S 71°38W **92** F4
Urdinarrain *Argentina* 32°37S 58°52W **94** C4
Ure → *U.K.* 54°5N 1°20W **12** C6
Urengoy *Russia* 65°58N 78°22E **28** C8
Ures *Mexico* 29°26N 110°24W **86** B2
Urewera △ *N.Z.* 38°29S 177°7E **59** C6
Urfa = Şanlıurfa *Turkey* 37°12N 38°50E **44** B3
Urganch *Uzbekistan* 41°40N 60°41E **28** E7
Urgench = Urganch
  Uzbekistan 41°40N 60°41E **28** E7
Ürgüp *Turkey* 38°38N 34°56E **44** B2
Uri *India* 34°8N 74°2E **43** B6
Uribia *Colombia* 11°43N 72°16W **92** A4
Uriondo *Bolivia* 21°41S 64°41W **94** A3
Urique *Mexico* 27°13N 107°55W **86** B3
Urique → *Mexico* 26°29N 107°58W **86** B3
Urk *Neths.* 52°39N 5°36E **15** B5
Urla *Turkey* 38°20N 26°47E **23** E12
Urmia = Orūmīyeh *Iran* 37°40N 45°0E **44** B5
Uroševac *Kosovo* 42°23N 21°10E **23** C9
Uroyan, Montanas de
  Puerto Rico 18°12N 67°0W **89** d
Urrampinyi Iltjiltarri ☉
  Australia 24°20S 132°10E **60** D5
Uruaçu *Brazil* 14°30S 49°10W **93** F9
Uruapan *Mexico* 19°24N 102°3W **86** D4
Urubamba → *Peru* 10°43S 73°48W **92** F4
Urucará *Brazil* 2°32S 57°45W **92** D7
Uruçuí *Brazil* 7°20S 44°28W **93** E10
Uruguai → *Brazil* 26°0S 53°30W **95** B5
Uruguaiana *Brazil* 29°50S 57°0W **94** B4
Uruguay ■ *S. Amer.* 32°30S 56°30W **94** C4
Uruguay → *S. Amer.* 34°12S 58°18W **94** C4
Urumchi = Ürümqi
  China 43°45N 87°45E **32** C6
Ürümqi *China* 43°45N 87°45E **32** C6
Uruna ☉ *Australia* 24°3S 133°1E **60** D5
Urup, Ostrov *Russia* 46°0N 151°0E **29** E16
Ürzhar *Kazakhstan* 47°5N 81°38E **28** E9
Usa → *Russia* 66°16N 59°49E **18** A10
Uşak *Turkey* 38°43N 29°28E **19** G4
Usakos *Namibia* 21°54S 15°31E **56** C2
Usedom *Germany* 53°55N 14°2E **16** B8
Useless Loop *Australia* 26°8S 113°23E **61** E1
Ushakova, Ostrov *Russia* 82°0N 80°0E **29** A8
Ushant = Ouessant, Î. d'
  France 48°28N 5°6W **20** B1
Ushashi *Tanzania* 1°59S 33°57E **54** C3
'Ushayrah *Si. Arabia* 25°35N 45°47E **44** E5
Ushibuka *Japan* 32°11N 130°1E **31** H5
Ushtöbe *Kazakhstan* 45°16N 78°0E **28** E8
Ushuaia *Argentina* 54°50S 68°23W **96** G3
Ushumun *Russia* 52°47N 126°32E **29** D13
Usinsk *Russia* 65°57N 57°27E **18** A10
Usk □ *U.K.* 51°33N 2°58W **13** F5
Uska *India* 27°12N 83°7E **43** F10
Usman *Russia* 52°5N 39°48E **18** D6
Usoke *Tanzania* 5°8S 32°24E **54** D3
Usolye-Sibirskoye
  Russia 52°48N 103°40E **29** D11
Uspallata, P. de
  Argentina 32°37S 69°22W **94** C2
Ussuriysk *Russia* 43°48N 131°59E **30** B6
Ussurka *Russia* 45°12N 133°31E **30** B6
Ust-Chaun *Russia* 68°47N 170°30E **29** C18
Ust-Ilimsk *Russia* 58°3N 102°39E **29** D11
Ust-Ishim *Russia* 57°45N 71°10E **28** D8
Ust-Kamchatsk *Russia* 56°10N 162°28E **29** D17
Ust-Kamenogorsk = Öskemen
  Kazakhstan 50°0N 82°36E **28** D9
Ust-Khayryuzovo
  Russia 57°15N 156°45E **29** D16
Ust-Kut *Russia* 56°50N 105°42E **29** D11
Ust-Kuyga *Russia* 70°1N 135°43E **29** B14
Ust-Maya *Russia* 60°30N 134°28E **29** C14
Ust-Mil *Russia* 59°40N 133°11E **29** D14
Ust-Nera *Russia* 64°35N 143°15E **29** C15
Ust-Nyukzha *Russia* 56°34N 121°37E **29** D13
Ust-Olenek *Russia* 73°0N 120°5E **29** B12
Ust-Omchug *Russia* 61°9N 149°38E **29** C15
Ust-Port *Russia* 69°40N 84°26E **28** C9
Ust-Tsilma *Russia* 65°28N 52°11E **18** A9
Ust-Urt = Ustyurt Plateau
  Asia 44°0N 55°0E **28** E6
Ust-Usa *Russia* 66°2N 56°57E **18** A10
Ust-Vorkuta *Russia* 67°24N 64°0E **18** A11
Ústí nad Labem *Czech Rep.* 50°41N 14°3E **16** C8
Ústica *Italy* 38°42N 13°11E **22** E5
Ustinov = Izhevsk
  Russia 56°51N 53°14E **18** C9
Ustyurt Plateau *Asia* 44°0N 55°0E **28** E6
Usuki *Japan* 33°8N 131°49E **31** H5
Usulután *El Salv.* 13°25N 88°28W **88** D2
Usumacinta → *Mexico* 18°24N 92°38W **87** D6
Usumbura = Bujumbura
  Burundi 3°16S 29°18E **54** C2
Usure *Tanzania* 4°40S 34°22E **54** C3
Usutuo → *Mozam.* 26°48S 32°7E **57** D5

Uta *Indonesia* 4°33S 136°0E **37** E9
Utah □ *U.S.A.* 39°20N 111°30W **76** G8
Utah L. *U.S.A.* 40°12N 111°48W **76** F8
Utara, Selat *Malaysia* 5°28N 100°20E **39** c
Utarni *India* 26°5N 71°58E **42** F4
Utatlan *Guatemala* 15°2N 91°11W **88** C1
Ute Creek → *U.S.A.* 35°21N 103°50W **77** J12
Utena *Lithuania* 55°27N 25°40E **9** J21
Utete *Tanzania* 8°0S 38°45E **54** D4
Uthai Thani *Thailand* 15°22N 100°3E **38** E3
Uthal *Pakistan* 25°44N 66°40E **42** G2
Utiariti *Brazil* 13°0S 58°10W **92** F7
Utica *N.Y., U.S.A.* 43°6N 75°14W **83** C9
Utica *Ohio, U.S.A.* 40°14N 82°27W **82** F2
Utikuma L. *Canada* 55°50N 115°30W **70** B5
Utila *Honduras* 16°6N 86°56W **88** C2
Utopia *Australia* 22°14S 134°33E **62** C1
Utraula *India* 27°19N 82°25E **43** F10
Utrecht *Neths.* 52°5N 5°8E **15** B5
Utrecht *S. Africa* 27°38S 30°20E **57** D5
Utrecht □ *Neths.* 52°6N 5°7E **15** B5
Utrera *Spain* 37°12N 5°48W **21** D3
Utsjoki → *Finland* 69°51N 26°59E **8** B22
Utsunomiya *Japan* 36°30N 139°50E **31** F9
Uttar Pradesh □ *India* 27°0N 80°0E **43** F9
Uttaradit *Thailand* 17°36N 100°5E **38** D3
Uttarakhand □ *India* 30°0N 79°30E **43** D8
Utterson *Canada* 45°12N 79°19W **82** A5
Uttoxeter *U.K.* 52°54N 1°52W **12** E6
Utuado *Puerto Rico* 18°16N 66°42W **89** d
Uummannaq *Avannaarsua,*
  Greenland 77°33N 68°52W **69** B18
Uummannaq *Kitaa,*
  Greenland 70°58N 52°17W **4** B5
Uummannarsuaq = Nunap Isua
  Greenland 59°48N 43°55W **66** D15
Uusikaarlepyy *Finland* 63°32N 22°31E **8** E20
Uusikaupunki *Finland* 60°47N 21°25E **8** F19
Uva *Russia* 56°59N 52°13E **18** C9
Uvalde *U.S.A.* 29°13N 99°47W **84** G5
Uvat *Russia* 59°5N 68°50E **28** D7
Uvinza *Tanzania* 5°5S 30°24E **54** D3
Uvira *Dem. Rep. of the Congo* 3°22S 29°3E **54** C2
Uvs Nuur *Mongolia* 50°20N 92°30E **32** A7
'Uwairidh, Ḥarrat al
  Si. Arabia 26°50N 38°0E **44** E3
Uwajima *Japan* 33°10N 132°35E **31** H6
Uwanda △ *Tanzania* 7°46S 32°0E **54** D3
Uweinat, Jebel *Sudan* 21°54N 24°58E **51** D10
Uxbridge *Canada* 44°6N 79°7W **82** B5
Uxin Qi *China* 38°50N 109°5E **34** E5
Uxmal *Mexico* 20°22N 89°46W **87** C7
Üydzin *Mongolia* 44°9N 107°0E **34** B4
Uyo *Nigeria* 5°1N 7°53E **50** G7
Uyûn Mûsa *Egypt* 29°53N 32°40E **46** F1
Uyuni *Bolivia* 20°28S 66°47W **92** H5
Uzbekistan ■ *Asia* 41°30N 65°0E **28** E7
Uzboy → *Turkmenistan* 39°30N 55°0E **45** B7
Uzen, Mal → *Kazakhstan* 49°4N 49°44E **19** E8
Uzerche *France* 45°25N 1°34E **20** D4
Uzh → *Ukraine* 51°15N 30°12E **17** C16
Uzhgorod = Uzhhorod
  Ukraine 48°36N 22°18E **17** D12
Uzhhorod *Ukraine* 48°36N 22°18E **17** D12
Užice *Serbia* 43°55N 19°50E **23** C8
Uzunköprü *Turkey* 41°16N 26°43E **23** D12

V

Vaal → *S. Africa* 29°4S 23°38E **56** D3
Vaal Dam *S. Africa* 27°0S 28°14E **57** D4
Vaalbos △ *S. Africa* 28°22S 24°20E **56** D3
Vaalwater *S. Africa* 24°15S 28°8E **57** C4
Vaasa *Finland* 63°6N 21°38E **8** E19
Vác *Hungary* 47°49N 19°10E **17** E10
Vacaria *Brazil* 28°31S 50°52W **95** B5
Vacata *Fiji* 17°15S 179°31W **59** a
Vacaville *U.S.A.* 38°21N 121°59W **78** G5
Vach = Vakh → *Russia* 60°45N 76°45E **28** C8
Vache, Î. à *Haiti* 18°2N 73°35W **89** C5
Vacoas *Mauritius* 20°18S 57°29E **53** d
Vadakara = Badagara
  India 11°35N 75°40E **40** P9
Vadnagar *India* 23°47N 72°40E **42** H5
Vadodara *India* 22°20N 73°10E **42** H5
Vadsø *Norway* 70°3N 29°50E **8** A23
Vaduz *Liech.* 47°8N 9°31E **20** C8
Værøy *Norway* 67°40N 12°40E **8** C15
Vágar *Færoe Is.* 62°5N 7°15W **8** E9
Vagia, Akra *Greece* 36°15N 28°11E **25** C10
Vågsfjorden *Norway* 68°50N 16°50E **8** B17
Váh → *Slovak Rep.* 47°43N 18°7E **17** D9
Vahsel B. *Antarctica* 75°0S 35°0W **5** D1
Váhtjer = Gällivare
  Sweden 67°9N 20°40E **8** C19
Vaï *Greece* 35°15N 26°18E **25** D8
Vaihiria, L. *Tahiti* 17°40S 149°25W **59** d
Vail *U.S.A.* 39°40N 106°20W **75** H14
Vairao *Tahiti* 17°47S 149°17W **59** d
Vaisali → *India* 26°28N 78°53E **43** F8
Vaitogi *Amer. Samoa* 14°14S 170°41W **59** b
Vakh → *Russia* 60°45N 76°45E **28** C8
Val-d'Or *Canada* 48°7N 77°47W **72** C4
Val Marie *Canada* 49°15N 107°45W **71** D7
Valaam *Russia* 61°22N 30°57E **8** F24
Valahia *Romania* 44°35N 25°0E **17** F13
Valandovo *Macedonia* 41°19N 22°34E **23** D10
Valatie *U.S.A.* 42°24N 73°40W **83** D11
Valcheta *Argentina* 40°40S 66°8W **96** E3
Valday Hills = Valdayskaya
  Vozvyshennost *Russia* 57°0N 33°30E **18** C5
Valdayskaya Vozvyshennost
  Russia 57°0N 33°30E **18** C5
Valdepeñas *Spain* 38°43N 3°25W **21** C4
Valdés, Pen. *Argentina* 42°30S 63°45W **96** E4
Valdez *U.S.A.* 61°7N 146°16W **68** E2
Valdivia *Chile* 39°50S 73°14W **96** D2
Valdivia Abyssal Plain
  S. Ocean 62°30S 70°0E **5** C6

Valdosta *U.S.A.* 30°50N 83°17W **85** F13
Valdres *Norway* 61°5N 9°5E **8** F13
Vale *U.S.A.* 43°59N 117°15W **76** E5
Vale of Glamorgan □
  U.K. 51°28N 3°25W **13** F4
Valemount *Canada* 52°50N 119°15W **70** C5
Valença *Brazil* 13°20S 39°5W **93** F11
Valença do Piauí *Brazil* 6°20S 41°45W **93** E10
Valence *France* 44°57N 4°54E **20** D6
Valencia *Spain* 39°27N 0°23W **21** C5
Valencia *Trin. & Tob.* 10°37N 61°11W **93** K15
Valencia *U.S.A.* 34°48N 106°43W **77** J10
Valencia *Venezuela* 10°11N 68°0W **92** A5
Valencia □ *Spain* 39°20N 0°40W **21** C5
Valencia, G. de *Spain* 39°30N 0°20E **21** C6
Valencia de Alcántara
  Spain 39°25N 7°14W **21** C2
Valencia I. *Ireland* 51°54N 10°22W **10** E1
Valenciennes *France* 50°20N 3°34E **20** A5
Valentim, Sa. do *Brazil* 6°0S 43°30W **93** E10
Valentin *Russia* 43°8N 134°17E **30** C7
Valentine *Nebr., U.S.A.* 42°52N 100°33W **80** D3
Valentine *Tex., U.S.A.* 30°35N 104°30W **84** F2
Valera *Venezuela* 9°19N 70°37W **92** B4
Valga *Estonia* 57°47N 26°2E **9** H22
Valier *U.S.A.* 48°18N 112°16W **76** B7
Valjevo *Serbia* 44°18N 19°53E **23** B8
Valka *Latvia* 57°46N 26°3E **9** H22
Valkeakoski *Finland* 61°16N 24°2E **8** F21
Valkenswaard *Neths.* 51°21N 5°29E **15** C5
Vall de Uxó = La Vall d'Uixó
  Spain 39°49N 0°15W **21** C5
Valladolid *Mexico* 20°41N 88°12W **87** C7
Valladolid *Spain* 41°38N 4°43W **21** B3
Valldemossa *Spain* 39°43N 2°37E **24** B9
Valle de la Pascua
  Venezuela 9°13N 66°0W **92** B5
Valle de las Palmas
  Mexico 32°20N 116°43W **79** N10
Valle de Santiago
  Mexico 20°23N 101°12W **86** C4
Valle de Zaragoza
  Mexico 27°25N 105°50W **86** B3
Valle Fértil, Sierra del
  Argentina 30°20S 68°0W **94** C2
Valle Gran Rey *Canary Is.* 28°5N 17°20W **24** F2
Valle Hermoso *Mexico* 25°35N 97°40W **87** B5
Valle Nacional *Mexico* 17°47N 96°18W **87** D5
Valledupar *Colombia* 10°29N 73°15W **92** A4
Vallehermoso *Canary Is.* 28°10N 17°15W **24** F2
Vallejo *U.S.A.* 38°7N 122°14W **78** G4
Vallenar *Chile* 28°30S 70°50W **94** B1
Valletta *Malta* 35°54N 14°31E **25** D2
Valley Center *U.S.A.* 33°13N 117°2W **79** M9
Valley City *U.S.A.* 46°55N 98°0W **80** B5
Valley Falls *Oreg.,*
  U.S.A. 42°29N 120°17W **76** E3
Valley Falls *R.I., U.S.A.* 41°54N 71°24W **83** E13
Valley of Flowers △
  India 30°50N 79°40E **43** D8
Valley Springs *U.S.A.* 38°12N 120°50W **78** G6
Valley View *U.S.A.* 40°39N 76°33W **83** F8
Valley Wells *U.S.A.* 35°27N 115°46W **79** K11
Valleyview *Canada* 55°5N 117°17W **70** B5
Vallimanca, Arroyo
  Argentina 35°40S 59°10W **94** D4
Valls *Spain* 41°18N 1°15E **21** B6
Valmiera *Latvia* 57°37N 25°29E **9** H21
Valognes *France* 49°30N 1°28W **20** B3
Valona = Vlorë *Albania* 40°32N 19°28E **23** D8
Valozhyn *Belarus* 54°3N 26°30E **17** A14
Valparaíso *Chile* 33°2S 71°40W **94** C1
Valparaíso *Mexico* 22°46N 103°34W **86** C4
Valparaíso *U.S.A.* 41°28N 87°4W **80** E10
Valparaíso □ *Chile* 33°2S 71°40W **94** C1
Vals → *S. Africa* 27°23S 26°30E **56** D4
Vals, Tanjung *Indonesia* 8°26S 137°25E **37** F9
Valsad *India* 20°40N 72°58E **40** J8
Valverde *Canary Is.* 27°48N 17°55W **24** G2
Valverde del Camino
  Spain 37°35N 6°47W **21** D2
Vamizi, I. *Mozam.* 11°2S 40°40E **55** E5
Vammala = Sastamala
  Finland 61°20N 22°54E **8** F20
Vamos *Greece* 35°24N 24°13E **25** D6
Van *Turkey* 38°30N 43°20E **44** B4
Van, L. = Van Gölü
  Turkey 38°30N 43°0E **44** B4
Van Alstyne *U.S.A.* 33°25N 96°35W **84** E6
Van Blommestein Meer
  Suriname 4°45N 55°5W **93** C7
Van Buren *Canada* 47°10N 67°55W **73** C6
Van Buren *Ark., U.S.A.* 35°26N 94°21W **84** D7
Van Buren *Maine,*
  U.S.A. 47°10N 67°58W **81** B20
Van Buren *Mo., U.S.A.* 37°0N 91°1W **80** G8
Van Canh *Vietnam* 13°37N 109°0E **38** F7
Van Diemen, C. *N. Terr.,*
  Australia 11°9S 130°24E **60** B5
Van Diemen, C. *Queens.,*
  Australia 16°30S 139°46E **62** B2
Van Diemen G. *Australia* 11°45S 132°0E **60** B5
Van Gölü *Turkey* 38°30N 43°0E **44** B4
Van Horn *U.S.A.* 31°3N 104°50W **84** F2
Van Ninh *Vietnam* 12°42N 109°14E **38** F7
Van Rees, Pegunungan
  Indonesia 2°35S 138°15E **37** E9
Van Wert *U.S.A.* 40°52N 84°35W **81** E11
Van Yen *Vietnam* 21°4N 104°42E **38** B5
Van Zylsrus *S. Africa* 26°52S 22°4E **56** D3
Vanadzor *Armenia* 40°48N 44°30E **19** F7
Vanavara *Russia* 60°22N 102°16E **29** C11
Vancouver *Canada* 49°15N 123°7W **78** A3
Vancouver *U.S.A.* 45°38N 122°40W **78** E4
Vancouver, C. *Australia* 35°2S 118°11E **61** G2
Vancouver I. *Canada* 49°50N 126°0W **70** D3
Vancouver Int. ✈ (YVR)
  Canada 49°10N 123°10W **78** A3
Vanda = Vantaa *Finland* 60°18N 24°56E **9** F21
Vandalia *Ill., U.S.A.* 38°58N 89°6W **80** F9

Vandalia *Mo., U.S.A.* 39°19N 91°29W **80** F8
Vandenberg Village
  U.S.A. 34°43N 120°28W **79** L6
Vandergrift *U.S.A.* 40°36N 79°34W **82** F5
Vanderhoof *Canada* 54°0N 124°0W **70** C4
Vanderkloof Dam
  S. Africa 30°4S 24°40E **56** E3
Vanderlin I. *Australia* 15°44S 137°2E **62** B2
Vänern *Sweden* 58°47N 13°30E **9** G15
Vänersborg *Sweden* 58°26N 12°19E **9** G15
Vang Vieng *Laos* 18°58N 102°32E **38** C4
Vanga *Kenya* 4°35S 39°12E **54** C4
Vangaindrano *Madag.* 23°21S 47°36E **57** C8
Vanguard *Canada* 49°55N 107°20W **71** D7
Vanino *Russia* 48°50N 140°5E **29** E15
Vankleek Hill *Canada* 45°32N 74°40W **83** A10
Vännäs *Sweden* 63°58N 19°48E **8** E18
Vannes *France* 47°40N 2°47W **20** C2
Vannøya *Norway* 70°6N 19°50E **8** A18
Vanrhynsdorp *S. Africa* 31°36S 18°44E **56** E2
Vansittart B. *Australia* 14°3S 126°17E **60** B4
Vansittart I. *Canada* 65°50N 84°0W **69** D15
Vantaa *Finland* 60°18N 24°56E **9** F21
Vanua Balavu *Fiji* 17°12S 178°55W **59** a
Vanua Levu *Fiji* 16°33S 179°15E **59** a
Vanua Vatu *Fiji* 18°22S 179°15W **59** a
Vanuatu ■ *Pac. Oc.* 15°0S 168°0E **58** C9
Vanwyksvlei *S. Africa* 30°18S 21°49E **56** E3
Vapnyarka *Ukraine* 48°32N 28°45E **17** D15
Var → *France* 43°39N 7°12E **20** E7
Varāmīn *Iran* 35°20N 51°39E **45** C6
Varāmīn *Iran* 35°18N 51°35E **45** B6
Varanasi *India* 25°22N 83°0E **43** G10
Varangerfjorden *Norway* 70°3N 29°25E **8** A23
Varangerhalvøya
  Norway 70°25N 29°30E **8** A23
Varaždin *Croatia* 46°20N 16°20E **16** E9
Varberg *Sweden* 57°6N 12°20E **9** H15
Vardak □ *Afghan.* 34°0N 68°0E **40** B6
Vardar = Axios →
  Greece 40°57N 22°35E **23** D10
Varde *Denmark* 55°38N 8°29E **9** J13
Vardø *Norway* 70°23N 31°5E **8** A24
Varella, Mui = Nay, Mui
  Vietnam 12°54N 109°26E **38** F7
Varēna *Lithuania* 54°12N 24°30E **9** J21
Varese *Italy* 45°48N 8°50E **20** D8
Varginha *Brazil* 21°33S 45°25W **95** A6
Varillas *Chile* 24°0S 70°10W **94** A1
Varkaus *Finland* 62°19N 27°50E **8** E22
Varna *Bulgaria* 43°13N 27°56E **23** C12
Värnamo *Sweden* 57°10N 14°3E **9** H16
Várnjárga = Varangerhalvøya
  Norway 70°25N 29°30E **8** A23
Vars *Canada* 45°21N 75°21W **83** A9
Varysburg *U.S.A.* 42°46N 78°19W **82** D6
Varzaneh *Iran* 32°25N 52°40E **45** C7
Vasa = Vaasa *Finland* 63°6N 21°38E **8** E19
Vasa Barris → *Brazil* 11°10S 37°10W **93** F11
Vascongadas = País Vasco □
  Spain 42°50N 2°45W **21** A4
Vasht = Khāsh *Iran* 28°15N 61°15E **45** D9
Vasilevichi *Belarus* 52°15N 29°50E **17** B15
Vasilkov = Vasylkiv
  Ukraine 50°7N 30°15E **17** C16
Vaslui *Romania* 46°38N 27°42E **17** E14
Vassar *Canada* 49°10N 95°55W **71** D9
Vassar *U.S.A.* 43°22N 83°35W **81** D12
Västerås *Sweden* 59°37N 16°38E **9** G17
Västerbotten *Sweden* 64°36N 20°4E **8** D19
Västerdalälven → *Sweden* 60°30N 15°7E **8** F16
Västervik *Sweden* 57°43N 16°33E **9** H17
Västmanland *Sweden* 59°45N 16°20E **9** G16
Vasto *Italy* 42°8N 14°40E **22** C6
Vasylkiv *Ukraine* 50°7N 30°15E **17** C16
Vat Phou *Laos* 14°51N 105°49E **38** E5
Vatersay *U.K.* 56°55N 7°32W **11** E1
Vati *Greece* 36°3N 27°53E **25** D9
Vatican City ■ *Europe* 41°54N 12°27E **22** D5
Vatili *Cyprus* 35°6N 33°40E **25** D12
Vatiu = Atiu *Cook Is.* 20°0S 158°10E **65** J12
Vatnajökull *Iceland* 64°30N 16°48W **8** D5
Vatolakkos *Greece* 35°27N 23°53E **25** D5
Vatoloha *Madag.* 17°52S 47°48E **57** B8
Vatomandry *Madag.* 19°20S 48°59E **57** B8
Vatra-Dornei *Romania* 47°22N 25°22E **17** E13
Vatrak → *India* 23°9N 73°2E **42** H5
Vättern *Sweden* 58°25N 14°30E **9** G16
Vatu Vara *Fiji* 17°26S 179°31W **59** a
Vatulele *Fiji* 18°33S 177°37E **59** a
Vaudreuil-Dorion
  Canada 45°23N 74°3W **83** A10
Vaughn *Mont., U.S.A.* 47°33N 111°33W **76** C8
Vaughn *N. Mex.,*
  U.S.A. 34°36N 105°13W **77** J11
Vaujours L. *Canada* 55°27N 74°15W **72** A5
Vaupés = Uaupés →
  Brazil 0°2N 67°16W **92** C5
Vaupés □ *Colombia* 1°0N 71°0W **92** C4
Vauxhall *Canada* 50°5N 112°9W **70** C6
Vav *India* 24°22N 71°31E **42** G4
Vavatenina *Madag.* 17°28S 49°12E **57** B8
Vava'u *Tonga* 18°36S 174°0W **59** c
Vava'u Group *Tonga* 18°40S 174°0W **59** c
Vawkavysk *Belarus* 53°9N 24°30E **17** B13
Växjö *Sweden* 56°52N 14°50E **9** H16
Vaygach, Ostrov *Russia* 70°0N 60°0E **28** C7
Veaikevárri = Svappavaara
  Sweden 67°40N 21°3E **8** C19
Vechte → *Neths.* 52°34N 6°6E **15** B6
Vedea → *Romania* 43°42N 25°41E **17** G13
Vedia *Argentina* 34°30S 61°31W **94** C3
Veendam *Neths.* 53°5N 6°52E **15** A6
Veenendaal *Neths.* 52°2N 5°34E **15** B5
Vefsna → *Norway* 65°48N 13°10E **8** D15
Vega *Norway* 65°40N 11°55W **8** D14
Vega *U.S.A.* 35°15N 102°26W **84** D3
Vega Baja *Puerto Rico* 18°27N 66°23W **89** d
Vegreville *Canada* 53°30N 112°5W **70** C6

Vejer de la Frontera
  Spain 36°15N 5°59W **21** D3
Vejle *Denmark* 55°43N 9°30E **9** J13
Velas, C. *Costa Rica* 10°21N 85°52W **88** D2
Velasco, Sierra de
  Argentina 29°20S 67°10W **94** B2
Velddrif *S. Africa* 32°42S 18°11E **56** E2
Velebit Planina *Croatia* 44°50N 15°20E **16** F8
Veles *Macedonia* 41°46N 21°47E **23** D9
Vélez-Málaga *Spain* 36°48N 4°5W **21** D3
Vélez Rubio *Spain* 37°41N 2°5W **21** D4
Velhas → *Brazil* 17°13S 44°49W **93** G10
Velika Kapela *Croatia* 45°10N 15°5E **16** F8
Velika → *Russia* 57°48N 28°10E **18** C4
Velikaya Kema *Russia* 45°30N 137°12E **30** B8
Velikaya → *Russia* 56°25N 30°32E **18** C5
Velikiye Luki *Russia* 56°25N 30°32E **18** C5
Veliki Ustyug *Russia* 60°47N 46°20E **18** B8
Veliko Tŭrnovo *Bulgaria* 43°5N 25°41E **23** C11
Velikonda Range *India* 14°45N 79°10E **40** M11
Velletri *Italy* 41°41N 12°47E **22** D5
Vellore *India* 12°57N 79°10E **40** N11
Velsk *Russia* 61°10N 42°5E **18** B7
Veluwezoom △ *Neths.* 52°5N 6°0E **15** B6
Velva *U.S.A.* 48°4N 100°56W **80** A3
Venado *Mexico* 22°56N 101°6W **86** C4
Venado Tuerto *Argentina* 33°50S 62°0W **94** C3
Vendée □ *France* 46°50N 1°35W **20** C3
Vendôme *France* 47°47N 1°3E **20** C4
Venézia *Italy* 45°27N 12°21E **22** B5
Venézia, G. di *Italy* 45°15N 13°0E **22** B5
Venezuela ■ *S. Amer.* 8°0N 66°0W **92** B5
Venezuela, G. de
  Venezuela 11°30N 71°0W **92** A4
Vengurla *India* 15°53N 73°45E **40** M8
Venice = Venézia *Italy* 45°27N 12°21E **22** B5
Venice *U.S.A.* 27°6N 82°27W **85** H13
Venkatapuram *India* 18°20N 80°30E **41** K12
Venlo *Neths.* 51°22N 6°11E **15** C6
Vennachar Junction
  Canada 45°5N 77°14W **82** A7
Vennesla *Norway* 58°15N 7°59E **9** G12
Venray *Neths.* 51°31N 6°0E **15** C6
Ventana, Punta de la
  Mexico 24°4N 109°48W **86** C3
Ventana, Sa. de la
  Argentina 38°0S 62°30W **94** D3
Ventersburg *S. Africa* 28°7S 27°9E **56** D4
Venterstad *S. Africa* 30°47S 25°48E **56** E4
Ventnor *U.K.* 50°36N 1°12W **13** G6
Ventotène *Italy* 40°47N 13°25E **22** D5
Ventoux, Mt. *France* 44°10N 5°17E **20** D6
Ventspils *Latvia* 57°25N 21°32E **9** H19
Ventuarí → *Venezuela* 3°58N 67°2W **92** C5
Ventucopa *U.S.A.* 34°50N 119°29W **79** L7
Ventura *U.S.A.* 34°17N 119°18W **79** L7
Vénus, Pte. *Tahiti* 17°29S 149°29W **59** d
Venus B. *Australia* 38°40S 145°42E **63** F4
Veracruz *Mexico* 19°11N 96°8W **87** D5
Veracruz □ *Mexico* 19°0N 96°15W **87** D5
Veraval *India* 20°53N 70°27E **42** J4
Verbánia *Italy* 45°56N 8°33E **20** D8
Vercelli *Italy* 45°19N 8°25E **20** D8
Verdalsøra *Norway* 63°48N 11°30E **8** E14
Verde → *Argentina* 41°56S 65°5W **96** E3
Verde → *Goiás, Brazil* 18°1S 50°14W **93** G8
Verde → *Mato Grosso do Sul,*
  Brazil 21°25S 52°20W **93** H8
Verde → *Chihuahua,*
  Mexico 26°29N 107°58W **86** B3
Verde → *Oaxaca, Mexico* 15°59N 97°50W **87** D5
Verde → *Veracruz,*
  Mexico 21°10N 102°50W **86** C4
Verde → *Paraguay* 23°9S 57°37W **94** A4
Verde → *U.S.A.* 33°33N 111°40W **74** J17
Verde, Cay *Bahamas* 23°0N 75°5W **88** B4
Verden *Germany* 52°55N 9°14E **16** B5
Verdi *U.S.A.* 39°31N 119°59W **78** F7
Verdun *France* 49°9N 5°24E **20** B6
Vereeniging *S. Africa* 26°38S 27°57E **57** D4
Verga, C. *Guinea* 10°30N 14°10W **50** F3
Vergara *Uruguay* 32°56S 53°57W **95** C5
Vergemont Cr. →
  Australia 24°16S 143°16E **62** C3
Vergennes *U.S.A.* 44°10N 73°15W **83** B11
Veria *Greece* 40°34N 22°12E **23** D10
Verín *Spain* 41°57N 7°27W **21** B2
Verkhnetulomskoye Vdkhr.
  Russia 68°36N 31°12E **8** B24
Verkhnevilyuysk
  Russia 63°27N 120°18E **29** C13
Verkhniy Baskunchak
  Russia 48°14N 46°44E **19** E8
Verkhoyansk *Russia* 67°35N 133°25E **29** C14
Verkhoyansk Ra. =
  Verkhoyanskiy Khrebet
  Russia 66°0N 129°0E **29** C13
Verkhoyanskiy Khrebet
  Russia 66°0N 129°0E **29** C13
Vermilion *Canada* 53°20N 110°50W **71** C6
Vermilion *U.S.A.* 41°25N 82°22W **82** E2
Vermilion → *Canada* 53°22N 110°51W **71** C6
Vermilion B. *U.S.A.* 29°42N 92°0W **84** G9
Vermilion L. *U.S.A.* 47°53N 92°26W **80** B7
Vermillion *U.S.A.* 42°47N 96°56W **72** D5
Vermillion → *Canada* 47°38N 72°56W **72** C5
Vermont □ *U.S.A.* 44°0N 73°0W **83** C12
Vernadsky *Antarctica* 65°0S 64°0W **5** C17
Vernal *U.S.A.* 40°27N 109°32W **76** F9
Vernalis *U.S.A.* 37°36N 121°17W **78** H5
Verner *Canada* 46°25N 80°8W **72** C3
Verneukpan *S. Africa* 30°0S 21°0E **56** E3
Vernon *Canada* 50°20N 119°15W **70** C5
Vernon *U.S.A.* 34°9N 99°17W **84** D5
Vernonia *U.S.A.* 45°52N 123°11W **78** E3
Vero Beach *U.S.A.* 27°38N 80°24W **85** H14

Véroia = Veria Greece 40°34N 22°12E 23 D10
Verona Canada 44°29N 76°42W 83 B8
Verona Italy 45°27N 10°59E 22 B4
Versailles France 48°48N 2°7E 20 B5
Vert, C. Senegal 14°45N 17°30W 50 F2
Verulam S. Africa 29°38S 31°2E 57 D5
Verviers Belgium 50°37N 5°52E 15 D5
Veselovskoye Vdkhr. Russia 46°58N 41°25E 19 E7
Vesoul France 47°40N 6°11E 20 C7
Vesterålen Norway 68°45N 15°0E 8 B16
Vestfjorden Norway 67°55N 14°0E 8 C16
Vestmannaeyjar Iceland 63°27N 20°15W 8 E3
Vestspitsbergen Svalbard 78°40N 17°0E 4 B8
Vestvågøya Norway 68°18N 13°50E 8 B15
Vesuvio Italy 40°49N 14°26E 22 D6
Vesuvius, Mt. = Vesuvio Italy 40°49N 14°26E 22 D6
Veszprém Hungary 47°8N 17°57E 17 E9
Vetlanda Sweden 57°24N 15°3E 9 H16
Vetlugu → Russia 56°36N 46°4E 18 C8
Vettore, Mte. Italy 42°49N 13°16E 22 C5
Veurne Belgium 51°5N 2°40E 15 C2
Veys Iran 31°30N 49°0E 45 D6
Vezhen Bulgaria 42°50N 24°20E 23 C11
Vi Thanh Vietnam 9°42N 105°26E 39 H5
Viacha Bolivia 16°39S 68°18W 92 G5
Viamão Brazil 30°5S 51°0W 95 C5
Viana Brazil 3°13S 44°55W 93 D10
Viana do Alentejo Portugal 38°17N 7°59W 21 C2
Viana do Castelo Portugal 41°42N 8°50W 21 B1
Vianden Lux. 49°56N 6°12E 15 E6
Viangchan = Vientiane Laos 17°58N 102°36E 38 D4
Vianópolis Brazil 16°40S 48°35W 93 G9
Vianos Greece 35°2N 25°21E 25 D7
Viaréggio Italy 43°52N 10°14E 22 C4
Vibo Valéntia Italy 38°40N 16°6E 22 E7
Viborg Denmark 56°27N 9°23E 9 H13
Vic Spain 41°58N 2°19E 21 B7
Vicenza Italy 45°33N 11°33E 22 B4
Vich = Vic Spain 41°58N 2°19E 21 B7
Vichada → Colombia 4°55N 67°50W 92 C5
Vichy France 46°9N 3°26E 20 C5
Vicksburg Ariz., U.S.A. 33°45N 113°45W 79 M13
Vicksburg Miss., U.S.A. 32°21N 90°53W 85 E9
Victor India 21°0N 71°30E 42 J4
Victor Harbor Australia 35°30S 138°37E 63 F2
Victoria Argentina 32°40S 60°10W 94 C3
Victoria Canada 48°30N 123°25W 78 B3
Victoria Chile 38°13S 72°20W 96 D2
Victoria China 22°17N 114°9E 33 a
Victoria Malta 36°3N 14°14E 25 C1
Victoria Seychelles 4°38S 55°28E 53 b
Victoria Kans., U.S.A. 38°52N 99°9W 80 F4
Victoria Tex., U.S.A. 28°48N 97°0W 84 G6
Victoria □ Australia 37°0S 144°0E 63 F3
Victoria → Australia 15°10S 129°40E 60 C4
Victoria, Grand L. Canada 47°31N 77°30W 72 C4
Victoria, L. Africa 1°0S 33°0E 54 C3
Victoria, L. Australia 33°57S 141°15E 63 E3
Victoria, Mt. Burma 21°14N 93°55E 41 J18
Victoria Beach Canada 50°40N 96°35W 71 C9
Victoria de Durango = Durango Mexico 24°3N 104°39W 86 C4
Victoria de las Tunas = Las Tunas Cuba 20°58N 76°59W 88 B4
Victoria Falls Zimbabwe 17°58S 25°52E 55 F2
Victoria Harbour Canada 44°45N 79°45W 82 B5
Victoria I. Canada 71°0N 111°0W 68 C9
Victoria L. Canada 48°20N 57°27W 73 C8
Victoria Ld. Antarctica 75°0S 160°0E 5 D11
Victoria Nile → Uganda 2°14N 31°26E 54 B3
Victoria Pk. Belize 16°48N 88°37W 87 D7
Victoria River Australia 16°25S 131°0E 60 C5
Victoria Str. Canada 69°31N 100°30W 68 D11
Victoria West S. Africa 31°25S 23°4E 56 E3
Victoriaville Canada 46°4N 71°56W 73 C5
Victorica Argentina 36°20S 65°30W 94 D2
Victorville U.S.A. 34°32N 117°18W 79 L9
Vicuña Chile 30°0S 70°50W 94 C1
Vicuña Mackenna Argentina 33°53S 64°25W 94 C3
Vidal U.S.A. 34°7N 114°31W 79 L12
Vidalia U.S.A. 32°13N 82°25W 85 E13
Viddolatno = Vindelälven → Sweden 63°55N 19°50E 8 E18
Vidin Bulgaria 43°59N 22°50E 23 C10
Vidisha India 23°28N 77°53E 42 H7
Vidos Greece 39°38N 19°55E 25 A3
Vidzy Belarus 55°23N 26°37E 9 J22
Viedma Argentina 40°50S 63°0W 96 E4
Viedma, L. Argentina 49°30S 72°30W 96 F2
Vielsalm Belgium 50°17N 5°54E 15 D5
Vieng Pou Kha Laos 20°41N 101°4E 38 B3
Vienna = Wien Austria 48°12N 16°22E 16 D9
Vienna Canada 42°41N 80°48W 82 D4
Vienna Ill., U.S.A. 37°25N 88°54W 80 G9
Vienna Mo., U.S.A. 38°11N 91°57W 80 F8
Vienne France 45°31N 4°53E 20 D6
Vienne → France 47°13N 0°5E 20 C4
Vientiane Laos 17°58N 102°36E 38 D4
Vientos, Paso de los Caribbean 20°0N 74°0W 89 C5
Vieques Puerto Rico 18°8N 65°25W 89 d
Vierge Pt. St. Lucia 13°49N 60°53W 89 f
Vierzon France 47°13N 2°5E 20 C5
Viet Quang Vietnam 22°30N 104°48E 38 A5
Viet Tri Vietnam 21°18N 105°25E 38 B5
Vietnam ■ Asia 19°0N 106°0E 38 C6
Vieux Fort St. Lucia 13°46N 60°58W 89 f
Vigan Phil. 17°35N 120°28E 37 A6
Vigévano Italy 45°19N 8°51E 20 D8
Vigia Brazil 0°50S 48°5W 93 D9
Viglas, Akra Greece 35°54N 27°51E 25 D9
Vigo Spain 42°12N 8°41W 21 A1
Vihowa Pakistan 31°8N 70°30E 42 D4
Vihowa → Pakistan 31°8N 70°41E 42 D4
Vijayawada India 16°31N 80°39E 41 L12
Vijosë → Albania 40°37N 19°24E 23 D8
Vík Iceland 63°25N 19°1W 8 E4
Vikeke = Viqueque E. Timor 8°52S 126°23E 37 F7
Viking Canada 53°7N 111°50W 70 C6
Vikna Norway 64°55N 10°58E 8 D14
Vila da Maganja Mozam. 17°18S 37°30E 55 F4
Vila da Ribeira Brava C. Verde Is. 16°32N 24°25W 50 b
Vila do Bispo Portugal 37°5N 8°53W 21 D1
Vila Franca de Xira Portugal 38°57N 8°59W 21 C1
Vila Gamito Mozam. 14°12S 33°0E 55 E3
Vila Gomes da Costa Mozam. 24°20S 33°37E 57 C5
Vila Machado Mozam. 19°15S 34°14E 55 F3
Vila Mouzinho Mozam. 14°48S 34°25E 55 E3
Vila Nova de Gaia Portugal 41°8N 8°37W 21 B1
Vila Real Portugal 41°17N 7°48W 21 B2
Vila-Real Spain 39°55N 0°3W 21 C5
Vila Real de Santo António Portugal 37°10N 7°28W 21 D2
Vila Vasco da Gama Mozam. 14°54S 32°14E 55 E3
Vila Velha Brazil 20°20S 40°17W 95 A7
Vilagarcía de Arousa Spain 42°34N 8°46W 21 A1
Vilaine → France 47°30N 2°27W 20 C2
Vilanandro, Tanjona Madag. 16°11S 44°27E 57 B7
Vilanculos Mozam. 22°1S 35°17E 57 C6
Vilanova i la Geltrú Spain 41°13N 1°40E 21 B6
Vilcheka, Ostrov Russia 80°0N 58°31E 28 B6
Vilcheka, Zemlya Russia 80°30N 60°30E 4 A11
Vileyka Belarus 54°30N 26°53E 17 A14
Vilhelmina Sweden 64°35N 16°39E 8 D17
Vilhena Brazil 12°40S 60°5W 92 F6
Viliya = Neris → Lithuania 55°8N 24°16E 9 J21
Viljandi Estonia 58°28N 25°30E 9 G21
Vilkitskogo, Proliv Russia 78°0N 103°0E 29 B11
Vilkovo = Vylkove Ukraine 45°28N 29°32E 17 F15
Villa Abecia Bolivia 21°0S 68°18W 94 A2
Villa Ana Argentina 28°28S 59°40W 94 B4
Villa Angela Argentina 27°34S 60°45W 94 B3
Villa Bella Bolivia 10°25S 65°22W 92 F5
Villa Cañás Argentina 34°0S 61°35W 94 C3
Villa Constitución Argentina 33°15S 60°20W 94 C3
Villa de Arriaga Mexico 21°56N 101°20W 86 C4
Villa de María Argentina 29°55S 63°43W 94 B3
Villa de Méndez Mexico 25°7N 98°34W 87 B5
Villa Dolores Argentina 31°58S 65°15W 94 C2
Villa Frontera Mexico 26°56N 101°27W 86 B4
Villa Gesell Argentina 37°15S 56°55W 94 D4
Villa Guillermina Argentina 28°15S 59°29W 94 B4
Villa Hayes Paraguay 25°5S 57°20W 94 B4
Villa Hidalgo Mexico 24°15N 99°26W 87 C5
Villa Iris Argentina 38°12S 63°12W 94 D3
Villa María Argentina 32°20S 63°10W 94 C3
Villa Mazán Argentina 28°40S 66°30W 94 B2
Villa Montes Bolivia 21°10S 63°30W 94 A3
Villa Ocampo Argentina 28°30S 59°20W 94 B4
Villa Ocampo Mexico 26°27N 105°31W 86 B3
Villa Ojo de Agua Argentina 29°30S 63°44W 94 B3
Villa San Martín Argentina 28°15S 64°9W 94 B3
Villa Unión Mexico 23°12N 106°14W 86 C3
Villacarlos Spain 39°53N 4°17E 24 B11
Villacarrillo Spain 38°7N 3°3W 21 C4
Villach Austria 46°37N 13°51E 16 E7
Villafranca de Bonany Spain 39°34N 3°5E 24 B10
Villagrán Mexico 24°29N 99°29W 87 C5
Villaguay Argentina 32°0S 59°0W 94 C4
Villahermosa Mexico 17°59N 92°55W 87 D6
Villajoyosa Spain 38°30N 0°12W 21 C5
Villalba Spain 43°26N 7°40W 21 A2
Villanueva U.S.A. 35°16N 105°22W 77 J11
Villanueva de la Serena Spain 38°59N 5°50W 21 C3
Villanueva y Geltrú = Vilanova i la Geltrú Spain 41°13N 1°40E 21 B6
Villarreal = Vila-Real Spain 39°55N 0°3W 21 C5
Villarrica Chile 39°15S 72°15W 96 D2
Villarrica Paraguay 25°40S 56°30W 94 B4
Villarrobledo Spain 39°18N 2°36W 21 C4
Villavicencio Argentina 32°28S 69°0W 94 C2
Villavicencio Colombia 4°9N 73°37W 92 C4
Villaviciosa Spain 43°32N 5°27W 21 A3
Villazón Bolivia 22°0S 65°35W 94 A2
Ville-Marie Canada 47°20N 79°30W 72 C4
Ville Platte U.S.A. 30°41N 92°17W 84 F8
Villena Spain 38°39N 0°52W 21 C5
Villeneuve-d'Ascq France 50°38N 3°9E 20 A5
Villeneuve-sur-Lot France 44°24N 0°42E 20 D4
Villiers S. Africa 27°2S 28°36E 57 D4
Villingen-Schwenningen Germany 48°3N 8°26E 16 D5
Villmanstrand = Lappeenranta Finland 61°3N 28°12E 8 F23
Vilna Canada 54°7N 111°55W 70 C6
Vilnius Lithuania 54°38N 25°19E 9 J21
Vilvoorde Belgium 50°56N 4°26E 15 D4
Vilyuchinsk Russia 52°55N 158°24E 29 D16
Vilyuy → Russia 64°24N 126°26E 29 C13
Vilyuysk Russia 63°40N 121°35E 29 C13
Viña del Mar Chile 33°0S 71°30W 94 C1
Vinarós Spain 40°30N 0°27E 21 B6
Vincennes U.S.A. 38°41N 87°32W 80 F10
Vincennes Bay S. Ocean 66°0S 109°0E 5 C8
Vincent U.S.A. 34°33N 118°11W 79 L8
Vinchina Argentina 28°45S 68°15W 94 B2
Vindelälven → Sweden 63°55N 19°50E 8 E18
Vindeln Sweden 64°12N 19°43E 8 D18
Vindhya Ra. India 22°50N 77°0E 42 H7
Vineland U.S.A. 39°29N 75°2W 81 F16
Vinh Vietnam 18°45N 105°38E 38 C5
Vinh Long Vietnam 10°16N 105°57E 39 G5
Vinh Moc Vietnam 21°18N 105°1E 38 B5
Vinh Yen Vietnam 21°21N 105°35E 38 B5
Vinita U.S.A. 36°39N 95°9W 84 C7
Vinkovci Croatia 45°19N 18°48E 23 B8
Vinnitsa = Vinnytsya Ukraine 49°15N 28°30E 17 D15
Vinnytsya Ukraine 49°15N 28°30E 17 D15
Vinnytsya □ Ukraine 49°20N 28°15E 17 D15
Vinson Massif Antarctica 78°35S 85°25W 5 D16
Vinton Calif., U.S.A. 39°48N 120°10W 78 F6
Vinton Iowa, U.S.A. 42°10N 92°1W 80 D7
Vinton La., U.S.A. 30°11N 93°35W 84 F8
Violet Valley ✪ Australia 17°10S 127°55E 60 C4
Viqueque E. Timor 8°52S 126°23E 37 F7
Virac Phil. 13°30N 124°20E 37 B6
Virachey Cambodia 13°59N 106°49E 38 F6
Virachey △ Cambodia 14°14N 106°55E 38 E6
Virago Sd. Canada 54°0N 132°30W 70 C2
Viramgam India 23°5N 72°0E 42 H5
Viranşehir Turkey 37°13N 39°45E 44 B3
Virawah Pakistan 24°31N 70°46E 42 G4
Virden Canada 49°50N 100°56W 71 D8
Vire France 48°50N 0°53W 20 B3
Vírgenes, C. Argentina 52°19S 68°21W 96 G3
Virgin → U.S.A. 36°28N 114°21W 77 H6
Virgin Gorda Br. Virgin Is. 18°30N 64°26W 89 e
Virgin Is. (British) ☑ W. Indies 18°30N 64°30W 89 e
Virgin Is. (U.S.) ☑ W. Indies 18°20N 65°0W 89 e
Virgin Islands △ U.S. Virgin Is. 18°21N 64°43W 89 C7
Virginia S. Africa 28°8S 26°55E 56 D4
Virginia U.S.A. 47°31N 92°32W 80 B7
Virginia □ U.S.A. 37°30N 78°45W 81 G14
Virginia Beach U.S.A. 36°49N 76°9W 81 F16
Virginia City Mont., U.S.A. 45°18N 111°56W 76 D8
Virginia City Nev., U.S.A. 39°19N 119°39W 78 F7
Virginia Falls Canada 61°38N 125°42W 70 A3
Virginiatown Canada 48°9N 79°36W 72 C4
Viroqua U.S.A. 43°34N 90°53W 80 D8
Virovitica Croatia 45°51N 17°21E 22 B7
Virpur India 21°51N 70°42E 42 J4
Virton Belgium 49°35N 5°32E 15 E5
Virudunagar India 9°30N 77°58E 40 Q10
Virunga △ Dem. Rep. of the Congo 0°5N 29°38E 54 B2
Vis Croatia 43°4N 16°10E 22 C7
Visalia U.S.A. 36°20N 119°18W 78 J7
Visayan Sea Phil. 11°30N 123°30E 37 B6
Visby Sweden 57°37N 18°18E 9 H18
Viscount Melville Sd. Canada 74°10N 108°0W 69 C10
Visé Belgium 50°44N 5°41E 15 D5
Vise, Ostrov Russia 79°33N 76°50E 28 B8
Višegrad Bos.-H. 43°47N 19°17E 23 C8
Viseu Brazil 1°10S 46°5W 93 D9
Viseu Portugal 40°40N 7°55W 21 B2
Vishakhapatnam India 17°45N 83°20E 41 L13
Visnagar India 23°45N 72°32E 42 H5
Viso, Mte. Italy 44°38N 7°5E 20 D7
Visokoi I. Antarctica 56°43S 27°15W 5 B1
Vista U.S.A. 33°12N 117°14W 79 M9
Vistula = Wisła → Poland 54°22N 18°55E 17 A10
Vitebsk = Vitsyebsk Belarus 55°10N 30°15E 18 C5
Viterbo Italy 42°25N 12°6E 22 C5
Viti Levu Fiji 17°30S 177°30E 59 a
Vitigudino Spain 41°1N 6°26W 21 B2
Vitim Russia 59°28N 112°35E 29 D12
Vitim → Russia 59°26N 112°34E 29 D12
Vitória Brazil 20°20S 40°22W 93 H10
Vitória da Conquista Brazil 14°51S 40°51W 93 F10
Vitória de Santo Antão Brazil 8°10S 35°20W 93 E11
Vitoria-Gasteiz Spain 42°50N 2°41W 21 A4
Vitsyebsk Belarus 55°10N 30°15E 18 C5
Vittória Italy 36°57N 14°32E 22 F6
Vittório Véneto Italy 45°59N 12°18E 22 B5
Viveiro Spain 43°39N 7°38W 21 A2
Vivian U.S.A. 32°53N 93°59W 84 E8
Viwa Fiji 17°10S 177°58E 59 a
Vizcaíno, Desierto de Mexico 27°30N 113°45W 86 B2
Vizcaíno, Sierra Mexico 27°30N 114°0W 86 B2
Vize Turkey 41°34N 27°45E 23 D12
Vizianagaram India 18°6N 83°30E 41 K13
Vlaardingen Neths. 51°55N 4°21E 15 C4
Vladikavkaz Russia 43°0N 44°35E 19 F7
Vladimir Russia 56°15N 40°30E 18 C7
Vladimir Volynskiy = Volodymyr-Volynskyy Ukraine 50°50N 24°18E 17 C13
Vladivostok Russia 43°10N 131°53E 30 C5
Vlieland Neths. 53°16N 4°55E 15 A4
Vlissingen Neths. 51°26N 3°34E 15 C3
Vlorë Albania 40°32N 19°28E 23 D8
Vltava → Czech Rep. 50°21N 14°30E 16 D8
Vo Dat Vietnam 11°9N 107°31E 39 G6
Voe U.K. 60°21N 1°16W 11 A7
Voëlkop = Doberai, Jazirah Indonesia 1°25S 133°0E 37 E8
Vogelsberg Germany 50°31N 9°12E 16 C5
Voghera Italy 44°59N 9°1E 20 D8
Vohibinany Madag. 18°49S 49°4E 57 B8
Vohilava Madag. 21°4S 48°0E 57 C8
Vohimarina = Iharana Madag. 13°25S 50°0E 57 A9
Vohimena, Tanjon' i Madag. 25°36S 45°8E 57 D8
Vohipeno Madag. 22°22S 47°51E 57 C8
Voi Kenya 3°25S 38°32E 54 C4
Voiron France 45°22N 5°35E 20 D6
Voisey B. Canada 56°15N 61°50W 73 A7
Vojmsjön Sweden 65°0N 16°24E 8 D17
Vojvodina □ Serbia 45°20N 20°0E 23 B9
Volborg U.S.A. 45°51N 105°41W 76 D11
Volcán de Colima △ Mexico 19°30N 103°40W 86 D4
Volcano Is. = Kazan-Rettō Pac. Oc. 25°0N 141°0E 64 E6
Volcans △ Rwanda 1°30S 29°26E 54 C2
Volda Norway 62°9N 6°5E 8 E12
Volga = Privolzhskiy □ Russia 56°0N 50°0E 28 D6
Volga → Russia 46°0N 48°30E 19 E8
Volga Hts. = Privolzhskaya Vozvyshennost Russia 51°0N 46°0E 19 D8
Volgodonsk Russia 47°33N 42°5E 19 E7
Volgograd Russia 48°40N 44°25E 19 E7
Volgogradskoye Vdkhr. Russia 50°0N 45°20E 19 D8
Volkhov → Russia 60°8N 32°20E 18 B5
Volkovysk = Vawkavysk Belarus 53°9N 24°30E 17 B13
Volksrust S. Africa 27°24S 29°53E 57 D4
Volochanka Russia 71°0N 94°28E 29 B10
Volodymyr-Volynskyy Ukraine 50°50N 24°18E 17 C13
Vologda Russia 59°10N 39°45E 18 C6
Volos Greece 39°24N 22°59E 23 E10
Volosovo Russia 59°27N 29°32E 9 G23
Volovets Ukraine 48°43N 23°11E 17 D12
Volozhin = Valozhyn Belarus 54°3N 26°30E 17 A14
Volsk Russia 52°5N 47°22E 18 D8
Volta → Ghana 5°46N 0°41E 48 F4
Volta, L. Ghana 7°30N 0°0 50 G6
Volta Redonda Brazil 22°31S 44°5W 95 A7
Voltaire, C. Australia 14°16S 125°35E 60 B4
Volterra Italy 43°24N 10°51E 22 C4
Volturno → Italy 41°1N 13°55E 22 D5
Volyn □ Ukraine 51°15N 24°30E 17 C13
Volzhskiy Russia 48°56N 44°46E 19 E7
Vomo Fiji 17°30S 177°15E 59 a
Vondrozo Madag. 22°49S 47°20E 57 C8
Vopnafjörður Iceland 65°45N 14°50W 8 D6
Vorkuta Russia 67°48N 64°20E 18 A11
Vormsi Estonia 59°1N 23°13E 9 G20
Voronezh Russia 51°40N 39°10E 19 D6
Võrts järv Estonia 58°16N 26°3E 9 G22
Võru Estonia 57°48N 26°54E 9 H22
Vosges France 48°20N 7°10E 20 B7
Voss Norway 60°38N 6°26E 8 F12
Vostok Antarctica 78°30S 106°50E 5 D8
Vostok I. Kiribati 10°5S 152°23W 65 J12
Votkinsk Russia 57°0N 53°55E 18 C9
Votkinskoye Vdkhr. Russia 57°22N 55°12E 18 C10
Votsuri-Shima Japan 25°45N 123°29E 31 M1
Vouga → Portugal 40°41N 8°40W 21 B1
Vouxa, Akra Greece 35°37N 23°32E 25 D5
Voyageurs △ U.S.A. 48°32N 93°0W 80 A7
Voynitsa Russia 65°10N 30°20E 8 D24
Voyvozh Russia 62°56N 54°56E 28 C6
Vozhe, Ozero Russia 60°45N 39°0E 18 B6
Voznesensk Ukraine 47°35N 31°21E 19 E5
Voznesenye Russia 61°0N 35°28E 18 B6
Vrangel Russia 42°43N 133°5E 30 C6
Vrangelya, Ostrov Russia 71°0N 180°0E 29 B18
Vranje Serbia 42°34N 21°54E 23 C9
Vratsa Bulgaria 43°15N 23°30E 23 C10
Vrbas → Bos.-H. 45°8N 17°29E 22 B7
Vrede S. Africa 27°24S 29°6E 57 D4
Vredefort S. Africa 27°0S 27°22E 56 D4
Vredenburg S. Africa 32°56S 18°0E 56 E2
Vredendal S. Africa 31°41S 18°35E 56 E2
Vrindavan India 27°37N 77°40E 42 F7
Vrisses Greece 35°23N 24°13E 25 D6
Vršac Serbia 45°8N 21°20E 23 B9
Vryburg S. Africa 26°55S 24°45E 56 D3
Vryheid S. Africa 27°45S 30°47E 57 D5
Vu Liet Vietnam 18°43N 105°23E 38 C5
Vukovar Croatia 45°21N 18°59E 23 B8
Vuktyl Russia 63°52N 57°20E 28 C6
Vulcan Canada 50°25N 113°15W 70 C6
Vulcan Romania 45°23N 23°17E 17 F12
Vulcaneşti Moldova 45°41N 28°18E 17 F15
Vulcano Italy 38°24N 14°58E 22 E6
Vulkaneshty = Vulcaneşti Moldova 45°41N 28°18E 17 F15
Vunduzi → Mozam. 18°56S 34°1E 55 F3
Vung Tau Vietnam 10°21N 107°4E 39 G6
Vunidawa Fiji 17°50S 178°21E 59 a
Vunisea Fiji 19°3S 178°10E 59 a
Vwaza ⌂ Malawi 10°58S 33°25E 55 E3
Vyartsilya Russia 62°8N 30°45E 8 E24
Vyatka = Kirov Russia 58°35N 49°40E 18 C8
Vyatka → Russia 55°37N 51°28E 18 C9
Vyatskiye Polyany Russia 56°14N 51°5E 18 C9
Vyazemskiy Russia 47°32N 134°45E 29 E14
Vyazma Russia 55°10N 34°15E 18 C5
Vyborg Russia 60°43N 28°47E 8 F23
Vychegda → Russia 61°18N 46°36E 18 B8
Vychodné Beskydy Europe 49°20N 22°0E 17 D11
Vyg-ozero Russia 63°47N 34°29E 18 B5
Vylkove Ukraine 45°28N 29°32E 17 F15
Vynohradiv Ukraine 48°9N 23°2E 17 D12
Vyrnwy, L. U.K. 52°48N 3°31W 12 E4
Vyshniy Volochek Russia 57°30N 34°30E 18 C5
Vyshzha = imeni 26 Bakinskikh Komissarov Turkmenistan 39°22N 54°10E 45 B7
Vyškov Czech Rep. 49°17N 17°0E 17 D9
Vytegra Russia 61°0N 36°27E 18 B6

W

W.A.C. Bennett Dam Canada 56°2N 122°6W 70 B4
Wa Ghana 10°7N 2°25W 50 F5
Waal → Neths. 51°37N 5°0E 15 C5
Waalwijk Neths. 51°42N 5°4E 15 C5
Waanyi-Garawa ✪ Australia 18°2S 137°33E 62 B2
Wabakimi △ Canada 50°43N 89°29W 72 B2
Wabana Canada 47°40N 53°0W 73 C9
Wabasca → Canada 58°22N 115°20W 70 B5
Wabasca-Desmarais Canada 55°57N 113°56W 70 B6
Wabash U.S.A. 40°48N 85°49W 81 E11
Wabash → U.S.A. 37°48N 88°2W 80 G9
Wabigoon L. Canada 49°44N 92°44W 71 D10
Wabowden Canada 54°55N 98°38W 71 C9
Wabuk Pt. Canada 55°20N 85°5W 72 A2
Wabush Canada 52°55N 66°52W 73 B6
Waco U.S.A. 31°33N 97°9W 84 F6
Waconichi, L. Canada 50°8N 74°0W 72 B5
Wad Hamid Sudan 16°30N 32°45E 51 E12
Wad Medanî Sudan 14°28N 33°30E 51 F12
Wad Thana Pakistan 27°22N 66°23E 42 F2
Wadai Africa 12°0N 19°0E 48 E5
Wadayama Japan 35°19N 134°52E 31 G7
Waddeneilanden Neths. 53°25N 5°10E 15 A5
Waddenzee Neths. 53°6N 5°10E 15 A5
Waddington U.S.A. 44°52N 75°12W 83 B9
Waddington, Mt. Canada 51°23N 125°15W 70 C3
Waddy Pt. Australia 24°58S 153°21E 63 C5
Wadebridge U.K. 50°31N 4°51W 13 G3
Wadena Canada 51°57N 103°47W 71 C8
Wadena U.S.A. 46°26N 95°8W 80 B6
Wadeye Australia 14°28S 129°52E 60 B4
Wadhams Canada 51°30N 127°30W 70 C3
Wadhwan India 22°42N 71°41E 42 H4
Wādī as Sīr Jordan 31°56N 35°49E 46 D4
Wadi Halfa Sudan 21°53N 31°19E 51 D12
Wadi Rum △ Jordan 29°30N 35°20E 46 F4
Wadsworth Nev., U.S.A. 39°38N 119°17W 76 G4
Wadsworth Ohio, U.S.A. 41°2N 81°44W 82 E3
Waegwan S. Korea 35°59N 128°23E 35 G15
Wafangdian China 39°38N 121°58E 35 E11
Wafrah Kuwait 28°33N 47°56E 44 D5
Wagait ✪ Australia 13°1S 130°5E 60 B5
Wageningen Neths. 51°58N 5°40E 15 C5
Wager B. Canada 65°26N 88°40W 69 D14
Wagga Wagga Australia 35°7S 147°24E 63 F4
Waghete Indonesia 4°10S 135°50E 37 E9
Wagin Australia 33°17S 117°25E 61 F2
Wagner U.S.A. 43°5N 98°18W 80 D4
Wagon Mound U.S.A. 36°1N 104°42W 77 H11
Wagoner U.S.A. 35°58N 95°22W 84 D7
Wah Pakistan 33°45N 72°40E 42 C5
Wahai Indonesia 2°48S 129°35E 37 E7
Wâhid Egypt 30°48N 32°21E 46 E1
Wahnai Afghan. 32°40N 65°50E 42 C1
Wahoo U.S.A. 41°13N 96°37W 80 E5
Wahpeton U.S.A. 46°16N 96°36W 80 B5
Waialua U.S.A. 21°34N 158°8W 75 L8
Waiau → N.Z. 42°47S 173°22E 59 E4
Waibeem Indonesia 0°30S 132°59E 37 E8
Waigeo Indonesia 0°20S 130°40E 37 E8
Waihi N.Z. 37°23S 175°52E 59 B5
Waihou → N.Z. 37°15S 175°40E 59 B5
Waika Dem. Rep. of the Congo 2°22S 25°42E 54 C2
Waikabubak Indonesia 9°45S 119°25E 37 F5
Waikaremoana, L. N.Z. 38°49S 177°9E 59 C6
Waikari N.Z. 42°58S 172°41E 59 E4
Waikato → N.Z. 37°23S 174°43E 59 B5
Waikelo Indonesia 9°24S 119°19E 60 A2
Waikerie Australia 34°9S 140°0E 63 E3
Waikokopu N.Z. 39°3S 177°52E 59 C6
Waikouaiti N.Z. 45°36S 170°41E 59 F3
Waimakariri → N.Z. 43°24S 172°42E 59 E4
Waimate N.Z. 44°45S 171°3E 59 F3
Wainganga → India 18°50N 79°55E 40 K11
Waingapu Indonesia 9°35S 120°11E 37 F6
Waini → Guyana 8°20N 59°50W 92 B7
Wainwright Canada 52°50N 110°50W 71 C6
Wainwright U.S.A. 70°38N 160°2W 74 A7
Waiouru N.Z. 39°28S 175°41E 59 C5
Waipara N.Z. 43°3S 172°46E 59 E4
Waipawa N.Z. 39°56S 176°38E 59 C6
Waipiro N.Z. 38°2S 178°22E 59 C7
Waipoua Forest N.Z. 35°39S 173°33E 59 A4
Waipu N.Z. 35°59S 174°29E 59 A5
Waipukurau N.Z. 40°1S 176°33E 59 D6
Wairakei N.Z. 38°37S 176°6E 59 C6
Wairarapa, L. N.Z. 41°14S 175°15E 59 D5
Wairoa N.Z. 39°3S 177°25E 59 C6
Waitaki → N.Z. 44°56S 171°7E 59 F3
Waitangi N.Z. 35°16S 174°5E 59 A5
Waitara N.Z. 38°59S 174°15E 59 C5
Waitomo Caves N.Z. 38°16S 175°7E 59 C5
Waitsburg U.S.A. 46°16N 118°9W 76 C4
Waiuku N.Z. 37°15S 174°45E 59 B5
Wajima Japan 37°30N 137°0E 31 F8
Wajir Kenya 1°42N 40°5E 54 B5
Wakasa Japan 35°20N 134°24E 31 G7
Wakasa-Wan Japan 35°40N 135°30E 31 G7
Wakatipu, L. N.Z. 45°5S 168°33E 59 F2
Wakaw Canada 52°39N 105°44W 71 C7
Wakaya Fiji 17°37S 179°0E 59 a
Wakayama Japan 34°15N 135°15E 31 G7
Wakayama □ Japan 33°50N 135°30E 31 H7
Wake Forest U.S.A. 35°59N 78°30W 85 D15
Wake I. Pac. Oc. 19°18N 166°36E 64 F8
WaKeeney U.S.A. 39°1N 99°53W 80 F4
Wakefield Jamaica 18°26N 77°42W 88 a
Wakefield N.Z. 41°24S 173°5E 59 D4
Wakefield U.K. 53°41N 1°29W 12 D6
Wakefield Mass., U.S.A. 42°30N 71°5W 83 D13
Wakefield Mich., U.S.A. 46°29N 89°56W 80 B9

Wakkanai *Japan* 45°28N 141°35E **30** B10
Wakkerstroom *S. Africa* 27°24S 30°10E **57** D5
Wakool *Australia* 35°28S 144°23E **63** F3
Wakool → *Australia* 35°5S 143°33E **63** F3
Wakre *Indonesia* 0°19S 131°5E **37** E8
Wakuach, L. *Canada* 55°34N 67°32W **73** A6
Walagunya ⊙ *Australia* 23°10S 120°50E **60** D3
Walamba *Zambia* 13°30S 28°42E **55** E2
Wałbrzych *Poland* 50°45N 16°18E **16** C9
Walbury Hill *U.K.* 51°21N 1°28W **13** F6
Walcha *Australia* 30°55S 151°31E **63** E5
Walchere *Neths.* 51°30N 3°35E **15** C3
Walcott *U.S.A.* 41°46N 106°51W **76** F10
Wałcz *Poland* 53°17N 16°27E **16** B9
Waldburg Ra. *Australia* 24°40S 117°35E **61** D2
Walden *Colo., U.S.A.* 40°44N 106°17W **76** F10
Walden *N.Y., U.S.A.* 41°34N 74°11W **83** E10
Waldport *U.S.A.* 44°26N 124°4W **76** D1
Waldron *U.S.A.* 34°54N 94°5W **84** D7
Walebing *Australia* 30°41S 116°13E **61** F2
Wales □ *U.K.* 52°19N 4°43W **13** E3
Wales I. *Canada* 68°1N 86°40W **69** D14
Walgett *Australia* 30°0S 148°5E **63** E4
Walgreen Coast
   Antarctica 75°15S 105°0W **5** D15
Walker *U.S.A.* 47°6N 94°35W **80** B6
Walker, L. *Canada* 50°20N 67°11W **73** B6
Walker L. *Canada* 54°42N 95°57W **71** C9
Walker L. *U.S.A.* 38°42N 118°43W **76** G4
Walkerston *Australia* 21°11S 149°8E **62** b
Walkerton *Canada* 44°10N 81°10W **82** B3
Wall *U.S.A.* 44°0N 102°8W **80** C2
Walla Walla *U.S.A.* 46°4N 118°20W **76** C4
Wallace *Idaho, U.S.A.* 47°28N 115°56W **76** C6
Wallace *N.C., U.S.A.* 34°44N 77°59W **85** D16
Wallaceburg *Canada* 42°34N 82°23W **82** D2
Wallachia = Valahia
   Romania 44°35N 25°0E **17** F13
Wallal *Australia* 26°32S 146°7E **63** D4
Wallam Cr. →
   Australia 28°40S 147°20E **63** D4
Wallambin, L. *Australia* 30°57S 117°35E **61** F2
Wallangarra *Australia* 28°56S 151°58E **63** D5
Wallaroo *Australia* 33°56S 137°39E **63** E2
Wallenpaupack, L.
   U.S.A. 41°25N 75°15W **83** E9
Wallingford *Conn.,*
   U.S.A. 41°27N 72°50W **83** E12
Wallingford *Vt., U.S.A.* 43°28N 72°58W **83** C12
Wallis & Futuna, Îs. □
   Pac. Oc. 13°18S 176°10W **58** C11
Wallowa *U.S.A.* 45°34N 117°32W **76** D5
Wallowa Mts. *U.S.A.* 45°20N 117°30W **76** D5
Walls *U.K.* 60°14N 1°33W **11** A7
Walls of Jerusalem △
   Australia 41°56S 146°15E **63** G4
Wallula *U.S.A.* 46°5N 118°54W **76** C4
Wallumbilla *Australia* 26°33S 149°9E **63** D4
Walmsley L. *Canada* 63°25N 108°36W **71** A7
Walney, I. of *U.K.* 54°6N 3°15W **12** C4
Walnut Canyon △
   U.S.A. 35°15N 111°20W **77** J8
Walnut Creek *U.S.A.* 37°54N 122°4W **78** H4
Walnut Ridge *U.S.A.* 36°4N 90°57W **85** C9
Walpole *Australia* 34°58S 116°44E **61** F2
Walpole *U.S.A.* 42°9N 71°15W **83** D13
Walpole-Nornalup △
   Australia 35°0S 116°45E **61** G2
Walsall *U.K.* 52°35N 1°58W **13** E6
Walsenburg *U.S.A.* 37°38N 104°47W **77** H11
Walsh *U.S.A.* 37°23N 102°17W **77** H12
Walsh → *Australia* 16°31S 143°42E **62** B3
Walsingham *Canada* 42°39N 80°22W **82** D4
Walter F. George Res.
   U.S.A. 31°38N 85°4W **85** F12
Walterboro *U.S.A.* 32°55N 80°40W **85** E14
Walters *U.S.A.* 34°22N 98°19W **84** D5
Waltham *U.S.A.* 42°23N 71°14W **83** D13
Waltman *U.S.A.* 43°4N 107°12W **76** E10
Walton *U.S.A.* 42°10N 75°8W **83** D9
Walton-on-the-Naze *U.K.* 51°51N 1°17E **13** F9
Walvis Bay *Namibia* 23°0S 14°28E **56** C1
Walvisbaai = Walvis Bay
   Namibia 23°0S 14°28E **56** C1
Wamba
   Dem. Rep. of the Congo 2°10N 27°57E **54** B2
Wamba *Kenya* 0°58N 37°19E **54** B4
Wambardi ⊙ *Australia* 16°2S 130°55E **60** C5
Wamego *U.S.A.* 39°12N 96°18W **80** F5
Wamena *Indonesia* 4°4S 138°57E **37** E9
Wampana Karlantijpa ⊙
   Australia 17°45S 132°10E **60** C5
Wampaya ⊙ *Australia* 17°20S 135°0E **62** B2
Wampsville *U.S.A.* 43°4N 75°42W **83** C9
Wamsutter *U.S.A.* 41°40N 107°58W **76** F10
Wamulan *Indonesia* 3°27S 126°7E **37** E7
Wan Xian *China* 38°47N 115°7E **34** E8
Wana *Pakistan* 32°20N 69°32E **42** C3
Wanaaring *Australia* 29°38S 144°9E **63** D3
Wanaka *N.Z.* 44°42S 169°9E **59** F2
Wanaka, L. *N.Z.* 44°33S 169°7E **59** F2
Wanapitei L. *Canada* 46°45N 80°40W **72** C3
Wandel Sea = McKinley Sea
   Arctic 82°0N 0°0 **4** A7
Wandhari *Pakistan* 27°42N 66°48E **42** F2
Wandoan *Australia* 26°5S 149°55E **63** D4
Wanfu *China* 40°8N 122°38E **35** D12
Wang → *Thailand* 17°8N 99°2E **38** D2
Wang Noi *Thailand* 14°13N 100°44E **38** E3
Wang Saphung
   Thailand 17°18N 101°46E **38** D3
Wang Thong *Thailand* 16°50N 100°26E **38** D3
Wanga
   Dem. Rep. of the Congo 2°58N 29°12E **54** B2
Wangal *Indonesia* 6°8S 134°9E **37** F8
Wanganella *Australia* 35°6S 144°49E **63** F3
Wanganui *N.Z.* 39°56S 175°3E **59** C5
Wangaratta *Australia* 36°21S 146°19E **63** F4
Wangary *Australia* 34°35S 135°29E **63** E2
Wangcun *China* 36°41N 117°41E **35** F9

Wangdu *China* 38°40N 115°7E **34** E8
Wangerooge *Germany* 53°47N 7°54E **16** B4
Wangiwangi *Indonesia* 5°22S 123°37E **37** F6
Wangqing *China* 43°12N 129°42E **35** C15
Wanimiyn ⊙ *Australia* 15°55S 130°49E **60** C5
Wanjina Wunggurr Wilinggin ⊙
   Australia 16°0S 127°0E **60** C4
Wankaner *India* 22°35N 71°0E **42** H4
Wanless *Canada* 54°11N 101°21W **71** C8
Wanleweyne *Somali Rep.* 2°37N 44°54E **47** G3
Wanneroo *Australia* 31°42S 115°46E **61** F2
Wanning *China* 18°48N 110°22E **38** C8
Wannoo Billabong Roadhouse
   Australia 27°25S 115°49E **61** E1
Wanon Niwat *Thailand* 17°38N 103°46E **38** D4
Wanqinsha *China* 22°43N 113°33E **33** a
Wanquan *China* 40°50N 114°40E **34** D8
Wanrong *China* 35°25N 110°50E **34** G6
Wanshan Qundao *China* 21°57N 113°45E **33** a
Wantage *U.K.* 51°35N 1°25W **13** F6
Wanxian *China* 30°42N 108°20E **32** E10
Wanzai *China* 22°12N 113°31E **33** a
Wapakoneta *U.S.A.* 40°34N 84°12W **81** E11
Wapawekka L. *Canada* 54°55N 104°40W **71** C8
Wapikopa L. *Canada* 52°56N 87°53W **72** B2
Wapiti → *Canada* 55°5N 118°18W **70** B5
Wappingers Falls
   U.S.A. 41°36N 73°55W **83** E11
Wapsipinicon → *U.S.A.* 41°44N 90°19W **80** E9
Wapusk △ *Canada* 57°46N 93°22W **71** B10
Warakurna *Australia* 24°55S 128°17E **61** D4
Warangal *India* 17°58N 79°35E **40** L11
Waraseoni *India* 21°45N 80°2E **43** J9
Waratah *Australia* 41°30S 145°30E **63** G4
Waratah B. *Australia* 38°54S 146°5E **63** F4
Warburton *Vic.,*
   Australia 37°47S 145°42E **63** F4
Warburton *W. Austral.,*
   Australia 26°8S 126°35E **61** E4
Warburton ⊙ *Australia* 26°7S 126°34E **61** E4
Warburton → *Australia* 28°4S 137°28E **63** D2
Warburton Groove
   Australia 28°18S 137°8E **63** A2
Warburton Ra.
   Australia 25°55S 126°28E **61** E4
Ward *N.Z.* 41°49S 174°11E **59** D5
Ward → *Australia* 26°28S 146°6E **63** D4
Ward Mt. *U.S.A.* 37°12N 118°54W **78** H8
Warden *S. Africa* 27°50S 29°0E **57** D4
Wardha *India* 20°45N 78°39E **40** J11
Wardha → *India* 19°57N 79°11E **40** K11
Wardsville *Canada* 42°39N 81°45W **82** D3
Ware *U.K.* 51°49N 0°0 **13** F8
Ware *U.S.A.* 42°16N 72°14W **83** D12
Waregem *Belgium* 50°53N 3°27E **15** D3
Wareham *U.S.A.* 41°46N 70°43W **83** E14
Waremme *Belgium* 50°43N 5°15E **15** D5
Warialda *Australia* 29°29S 150°33E **63** D5
Wariap *Indonesia* 1°30S 134°5E **37** E8
Warin Chamrap
   Thailand 15°12N 104°53E **38** E5
Warkopi *Indonesia* 1°12S 134°9E **37** E8
Warm Springs *U.S.A.* 38°10N 116°20W **77** G5
Warman *Canada* 52°19N 106°30W **71** C7
Warmbad = Bela Bela
   S. Africa 24°51S 28°19E **57** C4
Warmbad *Namibia* 28°25S 18°42E **56** D2
Warminster *U.K.* 51°12N 2°10W **13** F5
Warminster *U.S.A.* 40°12N 75°6W **83** F9
Warmun *Australia* 17°2S 128°12E **60** C4
Warner Mts. *U.S.A.* 41°40N 120°15W **76** F3
Warner Robins *U.S.A.* 32°37N 83°36W **85** E13
Waroona *Australia* 32°50S 115°58E **61** F2
Warrabri △ *Australia* 21°1S 134°19E **62** C1
Warracknabeal *Australia* 36°9S 142°26E **63** F3
Warragul *Australia* 38°10S 145°58E **63** F4
Warrego → *Australia* 30°24S 145°21E **63** E4
Warrego Ra. *Australia* 24°58S 146°0E **62** C4
Warren *Australia* 31°42S 147°51E **63** E4
Warren *Ark., U.S.A.* 33°37N 92°4W **84** E8
Warren *Mich., U.S.A.* 42°28N 83°1W **81** D12
Warren *Minn., U.S.A.* 48°12N 96°46W **80** A5
Warren *Ohio, U.S.A.* 41°14N 80°49W **82** E4
Warren *Pa., U.S.A.* 41°51N 79°9W **82** E5
Warrenpoint *U.K.* 54°6N 6°15W **10** B5
Warrensburg *Mo.,*
   U.S.A. 38°46N 93°44W **80** F7
Warrensburg *N.Y.,*
   U.S.A. 43°29N 73°46W **83** C11
Warrenton *S. Africa* 28°9S 24°47E **56** D3
Warrenton *U.S.A.* 46°10N 123°56W **78** D3
Warri *Nigeria* 5°30N 5°41E **50** G7
Warrington *U.K.* 53°24N 2°35W **12** D5
Warrington *U.S.A.* 30°23N 87°17W **85** F11
Warrington □ *U.K.* 53°24N 2°35W **12** D5
Warrnambool *Australia* 38°25S 142°30E **63** F3
Warroad *U.S.A.* 48°54N 95°19W **80** A6
Warruwi *Australia* 11°36S 133°20E **62** A1
Warsa *Indonesia* 0°47S 135°55E **37** E9
Warsak Dam *Pakistan* 34°11N 71°19E **42** B4
Warsaw = Warszawa
   Poland 52°14N 21°0E **17** B11
Warsaw *Ind., U.S.A.* 41°14N 85°51W **81** E11
Warsaw *N.Y., U.S.A.* 42°45N 78°8W **82** D6
Warsaw *Ohio, U.S.A.* 40°20N 82°0W **82** F2
Warszawa *Poland* 52°14N 21°0E **17** B11
Warta → *Poland* 52°35N 14°39E **16** B8
Warthe = Warta →
   Poland 52°35N 14°39E **16** B8
Waru *Indonesia* 3°30S 130°36E **37** E8
Warumungu ⊙
   Australia 19°15S 134°44E **62** B1
Warwick *Australia* 28°10S 152°1E **63** D5
Warwick *U.K.* 52°18N 1°35W **13** E6
Warwick *N.Y., U.S.A.* 41°16N 74°22W **83** E10
Warwick *R.I., U.S.A.* 41°42N 71°28W **83** E13
Warwickshire □ *U.K.* 52°14N 1°38W **13** E6
Wasaga Beach *Canada* 44°31N 80°1W **82** B4
Wasagaming *Canada* 50°39N 99°58W **71** C9

Wasatch Ra. *U.S.A.* 40°0N 111°30W **76** F8
Wasbank *S. Africa* 28°15S 30°9E **57** D5
Wasco *Calif., U.S.A.* 35°36N 119°20W **79** K7
Wasco *Oreg., U.S.A.* 45°36N 120°42W **76** D3
Waseca *U.S.A.* 44°5N 93°30W **80** C7
Wasekamio L. *Canada* 56°45N 108°45W **71** B7
Wash, The *U.K.* 52°58N 0°20E **12** E8
Washago *Canada* 44°45N 79°20W **82** B5
Washburn *N. Dak.,*
   U.S.A. 47°17N 101°2W **80** B3
Washburn *Wis., U.S.A.* 46°40N 90°54W **80** B8
Washim *India* 20°3N 77°0E **40** J10
Washington *U.K.* 54°55N 1°30W **12** C6
Washington *D.C., U.S.A.* 38°53N 77°2W **81** F15
Washington *Ga.,*
   U.S.A. 33°44N 82°44W **85** E13
Washington *Ind.,*
   U.S.A. 38°40N 87°10W **80** F10
Washington *Iowa,*
   U.S.A. 41°18N 91°42W **80** E8
Washington *Mo., U.S.A.* 38°33N 91°1W **80** F8
Washington *N.C.,*
   U.S.A. 35°33N 77°3W **85** D16
Washington *N.J.,*
   U.S.A. 40°46N 74°59W **83** F10
Washington *Pa., U.S.A.* 40°10N 80°15W **82** F4
Washington *Utah,*
   U.S.A. 37°8N 113°31W **77** H7
Washington □ *U.S.A.* 47°30N 120°30W **76** C3
Washington, Mt.
   U.S.A. 44°16N 71°18W **83** B13
Washington Court House
   U.S.A. 39°32N 83°26W **81** F12
Washington I. *U.S.A.* 45°23N 86°54W **80** C10
Washougal *U.S.A.* 45°35N 122°21W **78** E4
Wasian *Indonesia* 1°47S 133°19E **37** E8
Wasilla *U.S.A.* 61°35N 149°26W **68** E2
Wasior *Indonesia* 2°43S 134°30E **37** E8
Wāsiţ □ *Iraq* 32°50N 45°50E **44** C5
Waskaganish *Canada* 51°30N 78°40W **72** B4
Waskaiowaka L.
   Canada 56°33N 96°23W **71** B9
Waskesiu Lake *Canada* 53°55N 106°5W **71** C7
Wasserkuppe *Germany* 50°29N 9°55E **16** C5
Waswanipi *Canada* 49°40N 76°29W **72** C4
Waswanipi, L. *Canada* 49°35N 76°40W **72** C4
Watampone *Indonesia* 4°29S 120°25E **37** E6
Watamu *Kenya* 3°23S 40°0E **54** C5
Watarrka △ *Australia* 24°20S 131°30E **60** D5
Water Park Pt.
   Australia 22°56S 150°47E **62** C5
Water Valley *U.S.A.* 34°10N 89°38W **85** D10
Waterberg Plateau △
   Namibia 20°25S 17°18E **56** C2
Waterberge *S. Africa* 24°10S 28°0E **57** C4
Waterbury *Conn., U.S.A.* 41°33N 73°3W **83** E11
Waterbury *Vt., U.S.A.* 44°20N 72°46W **83** B12
Waterbury L. *Canada* 58°10N 104°22W **71** B8
Waterdown *Canada* 43°20N 79°53W **82** C5
Waterford *Canada* 42°56N 80°17W **82** D4
Waterford *Ireland* 52°15N 7°8W **10** D4
Waterford *Calif., U.S.A.* 37°38N 120°46W **78** H6
Waterford *Pa., U.S.A.* 41°57N 79°59W **82** E5
Waterford □ *Ireland* 52°10N 7°40W **10** D4
Waterford Harbour
   Ireland 52°8N 6°58W **10** D5
Waterhen L. *Canada* 52°10N 99°40W **71** C9
Waterloo *Belgium* 50°43N 4°25E **15** D4
Waterloo *Ont., Canada* 43°30N 80°32W **82** C4
Waterloo *Qué., Canada* 45°22N 72°32W **83** A12
Waterloo *Ill., U.S.A.* 38°20N 90°9W **80** F8
Waterloo *Iowa, U.S.A.* 42°30N 92°21W **80** D7
Waterloo *N.Y., U.S.A.* 42°54N 76°52W **82** D7
Watersmeet *U.S.A.* 46°16N 89°11W **80** B9
Waterton Lakes △
   Canada 48°45N 115°0W **70** D6
Watertown *Conn.,*
   U.S.A. 41°36N 73°7W **83** E11
Watertown *N.Y., U.S.A.* 43°59N 75°55W **83** C9
Watertown *S. Dak.,*
   U.S.A. 44°54N 97°7W **80** C5
Watertown *Wis., U.S.A.* 43°12N 88°43W **80** D9
Waterval-Boven *S. Africa* 25°40S 30°18E **57** D5
Waterville *Canada* 45°16N 71°54W **83** A13
Waterville *Maine,*
   U.S.A. 44°33N 69°38W **81** C19
Waterville *N.Y., U.S.A.* 42°56N 75°23W **83** D9
Waterville *Pa., U.S.A.* 41°19N 77°21W **82** E7
Waterville *Wash., U.S.A.* 47°39N 120°4W **76** C3
Watervliet *U.S.A.* 42°44N 73°42W **83** D11
Wates *Indonesia* 7°51S 110°10E **37** G14
Watford *Canada* 42°57N 81°53W **82** D3
Watford *U.K.* 51°40N 0°24W **13** F7
Watford City *U.S.A.* 47°48N 103°17W **80** B2
Wathaman → *Canada* 57°16N 102°59W **71** B8
Wathaman L. *Canada* 56°58N 103°44W **71** B8
Watheroo *Australia* 30°15S 116°5E **61** F2
Watheroo △ *Australia* 30°19S 115°48E **61** F2
Wating *China* 35°40N 106°38E **34** G4
Watkins Glen *U.S.A.* 42°23N 76°52W **82** D8
Watling I. = San Salvador I.
   Bahamas 24°0N 74°40W **89** B5
Watonga *U.S.A.* 35°51N 98°25W **84** D5
Watrous *Canada* 51°40N 105°25W **71** C7
Watrous *U.S.A.* 35°48N 104°59W **77** J11
Watsa
   Dem. Rep. of the Congo 3°4N 29°30E **54** B2
Watseka *U.S.A.* 40°47N 87°44W **80** E10
Watson *Canada* 52°10N 104°30W **71** C8
Watson Lake *Canada* 60°6N 128°49W **70** A3
Watsontown *U.S.A.* 41°5N 76°52W **82** E8
Watsonville *U.S.A.* 36°55N 121°45W **78** J5
Wattiwarriganna Cr. →
   Australia 28°57S 136°10E **63** D2
Watuata = Batuata
   Indonesia 6°12S 122°42E **37** F6
Watubela, Kepulauan
   Indonesia 4°28S 131°35E **37** E8

Watubela Is. = Watubela,
Kepulauan *Indonesia* 4°28S 131°35E **37** E8
Wau = Wâw *Sudan* 7°45N 28°1E **51** G11
Waubamik *Canada* 45°27N 80°1W **82** A4
Waubay *U.S.A.* 45°20N 97°18W **80** C5
Wauchope *N.S.W.,*
   Australia 31°28S 152°45E **63** E5
Wauchope *N. Terr.,*
   Australia 20°36S 134°15E **62** C1
Wauchula *U.S.A.* 27°33N 81°49W **85** H14
Waukarlycarly, L.
   Australia 21°18S 121°56E **60** D3
Waukegan *U.S.A.* 42°22N 87°50W **80** D10
Waukesha *U.S.A.* 43°1N 88°14W **80** D9
Waukon *U.S.A.* 43°16N 91°29W **80** D8
Waupaca *U.S.A.* 44°21N 89°5W **80** C9
Waupun *U.S.A.* 43°38N 88°44W **80** D9
Waurika *U.S.A.* 34°10N 98°0W **84** D6
Wausau *U.S.A.* 44°58N 89°38W **80** C9
Wautoma *U.S.A.* 44°4N 89°18W **80** C9
Wauwatosa *U.S.A.* 43°2N 88°0W **80** D9
Wave Hill = Kalkarindji
   Australia 17°30S 130°47E **60** C5
Wave Rock △ *Australia* 32°26S 118°53E **61** F2
Waveney → *U.K.* 52°35N 1°39E **13** E9
Waverley *N.Z.* 39°46S 174°37E **59** C5
Waverly *Iowa, U.S.A.* 42°44N 92°29W **80** D7
Waverly *N.Y., U.S.A.* 42°1N 76°32W **83** E8
Wavre *Belgium* 50°43N 4°38E **15** D4
Wâw *Sudan* 7°45N 28°1E **51** G11
Wawa *Canada* 47°59N 84°47W **72** C3
Wawanesa *Canada* 49°36N 99°40W **71** D9
Wawona *U.S.A.* 37°32N 119°39W **78** H7
Waxahachie *U.S.A.* 32°24N 96°51W **84** E6
Way, L. *Australia* 26°45S 120°16E **61** E3
Waya *Fiji* 17°19S 177°10E **59** a
Waycross *U.S.A.* 31°13N 82°21W **85** F13
Wayland *U.S.A.* 42°34N 77°35W **82** D7
Wayne *Nebr., U.S.A.* 42°14N 97°1W **80** D5
Wayne *W. Va., U.S.A.* 38°13N 82°27W **81** F12
Waynesboro *Ga., U.S.A.* 33°6N 82°1W **85** E13
Waynesboro *Miss.,*
   U.S.A. 31°40N 88°39W **85** F10
Waynesboro *Pa.,*
   U.S.A. 39°45N 77°35W **81** F15
Waynesboro *Va., U.S.A.* 38°4N 78°53W **81** F14
Waynesburg *U.S.A.* 39°54N 80°11W **81** F13
Waynesville *U.S.A.* 35°28N 82°58W **85** D13
Waynoka *U.S.A.* 36°35N 98°53W **84** C5
Wazirabad *Pakistan* 32°30N 74°8E **42** C6
Waziristan *Pakistan* 33°0N 70°0E **42** C4
We *Indonesia* 5°51N 95°18E **36** C1
Weald, The *U.K.* 51°4N 0°20E **13** F8
Wear → *U.K.* 54°55N 1°23W **12** C6
Weatherford *Okla.,*
   U.S.A. 35°32N 98°43W **84** D5
Weatherford *Tex., U.S.A.* 32°46N 97°48W **84** E6
Weaverville *U.S.A.* 40°44N 122°56W **76** F2
Webb City *U.S.A.* 37°9N 94°28W **80** G6
Webequie *Canada* 52°59N 87°21W **72** B2
Webster *Mass., U.S.A.* 42°3N 71°53W **83** D13
Webster *N.Y., U.S.A.* 43°13N 77°26W **82** C7
Webster *S. Dak., U.S.A.* 45°20N 97°31W **80** C5
Webster City *U.S.A.* 42°28N 93°49W **80** D7
Webster Springs *U.S.A.* 38°29N 80°25W **81** F13
Webuye *Kenya* 0°37N 34°46E **54** B3
Weda *Indonesia* 0°21N 127°50E **37** D7
Weda, Teluk *Indonesia* 0°20N 128°0E **37** D7
Weddell Abyssal Plain
   S. Ocean 65°0S 20°0W **5** C2
Weddell I. *Falk. Is.* 51°50S 61°0W **96** G4
Weddell Sea *Antarctica* 72°30S 40°0W **5** D1
Wedderburn *Australia* 36°26S 143°33E **63** F3
Wedgeport *Canada* 43°44N 65°59W **73** D6
Wedza *Zimbabwe* 18°40S 31°33E **55** F3
Wee Waa *Australia* 30°11S 149°26E **63** E4
Weed *U.S.A.* 41°25N 122°23W **76** F2
Weed Heights *U.S.A.* 38°59N 119°13W **78** G7
Weedsport *U.S.A.* 43°2N 76°33W **83** C8
Weedville *U.S.A.* 41°17N 78°30W **82** E6
Weenen *S. Africa* 28°48S 30°7E **57** D5
Weert *Neths.* 51°15N 5°43E **15** C5
Wei He → *Hebei, China* 36°10N 115°45E **34** F8
Wei He → *Shaanxi,*
   China 34°38N 110°15E **34** G6
Weichang *China* 41°58N 117°49E **35** D9
Weichuan *China* 34°20N 113°59E **34** G7
Weiden *Germany* 49°41N 12°10E **16** D7
Weifang *China* 36°44N 119°7E **35** F10
Weihai *China* 37°30N 122°6E **35** F12
Weihui *China* 35°25N 114°3E **34** G8
Weimar *Germany* 50°58N 11°19E **16** C6
Weinan *China* 34°31N 109°29E **34** G5
Weipa *Australia* 12°40S 141°50E **62** A3
Weir → *Australia* 28°20S 149°50E **63** D4
Weir → *Canada* 56°54N 93°21W **71** B10
Weir River *Canada* 56°49N 94°6W **71** B10
Weirton *U.S.A.* 40°24N 80°35W **82** F4
Weiser *U.S.A.* 44°15N 116°58W **76** D5
Weishan *China* 34°47N 117°5E **35** G9
Weishan Hu *China* 34°35N 117°14E **35** G9
Weiyuan *China* 35°7N 104°10E **34** G3
Wejherowo *Poland* 54°35N 18°12E **17** A10
Wekusko L. *Canada* 54°40N 99°50W **71** C9
Welbourn Hill *S. Africa* 37°26N 81°35W **81** G13
Welch *U.S.A.* 25°5S 143°16E **62** D3
Welford △ *Australia* 25°5S 26°46E **56** D4
Welkom *S. Africa* 43°0N 79°15W **82** D5
Welland *Canada* 43°0N 79°15W **82** D5
Welland → *U.K.* 52°51N 0°5W **13** E7
Wellesley Is. *Australia* 16°42S 139°30E **62** B2
Wellesley Islands ⊙
   Australia 16°32S 139°23E **62** B2
Wellingborough *U.K.* 52°19N 0°41W **13** E7
Wellington *Australia* 32°35S 148°59E **63** E4
Wellington *Canada* 43°57N 77°20W **82** C7
Wellington *N.Z.* 41°19S 174°46E **59** D5
Wellington *S. Africa* 33°38S 19°1E **56** E2
Wellington *Somst., U.K.* 50°58N 3°13W **13** G4
Wellington *Telford & Wrekin,*
   U.K. 52°42N 2°30W **13** E5

Wellington *Colo.,*
   U.S.A. 40°42N 105°0W **76** F11
Wellington *Kans., U.S.A.* 37°16N 97°24W **80** G5
Wellington *Nev., U.S.A.* 38°45N 119°23W **78** G7
Wellington *Ohio, U.S.A.* 41°10N 82°13W **82** E2
Wellington *Tex., U.S.A.* 34°51N 100°13W **84** D4
Wellington, I. *Chile* 49°30S 75°0W **96** F2
Wellington, L. *Australia* 38°6S 147°20E **63** F4
Wellington Chan. *Canada* 75°0N 93°0W **69** C13
Wells *U.K.* 51°13N 2°39W **13** F5
Wells *Maine, U.S.A.* 43°20N 70°35W **83** C14
Wells *N.Y., U.S.A.* 43°24N 74°17W **83** C10
Wells *Nev., U.S.A.* 41°7N 114°58W **76** F6
Wells, L. *Australia* 26°44S 123°15E **61** E3
Wells, Mt. *Australia* 17°25S 127°8E **60** C4
Wells Gray △ *Canada* 52°30N 120°15W **70** C4
Wells-next-the-Sea *U.K.* 52°57N 0°51E **12** E8
Wells River *U.S.A.* 44°9N 72°4W **83** B12
Wellsboro *U.S.A.* 41°45N 77°18W **82** E7
Wellsburg *U.S.A.* 40°16N 80°37W **82** F4
Wellsville *N.Y., U.S.A.* 42°7N 77°57W **82** D7
Wellsville *Ohio, U.S.A.* 40°36N 80°39W **82** F4
Wellsville *Utah, U.S.A.* 41°38N 111°56W **76** F8
Wellton *U.S.A.* 32°40N 114°8W **77** K6
Wels *Austria* 48°9N 14°1E **16** D8
Welshpool *U.K.* 52°39N 3°8W **13** E4
Welwyn Garden City
   U.K. 51°48N 0°12W **13** F7
Wem *U.K.* 52°52N 2°44W **12** E5
Wembere → *Tanzania* 4°10S 34°15E **54** C3
Wemindji *Canada* 53°0N 78°49W **72** B4
Wemyss *Canada* 44°52N 76°23W **83** B8
Wen Xian *Gansu, China* 32°43N 104°36E **34** H3
Wen Xian *Henan, China* 34°55N 113°5E **34** G7
Wenatchee *U.S.A.* 47°25N 120°19W **76** C3
Wenchang *China* 19°38N 110°42E **38** C8
Wenchi *Ghana* 7°46N 2°8W **50** G5
Wenchow = Wenzhou
   China 28°0N 120°38E **33** F13
Wenden *U.S.A.* 33°49N 113°33W **79** M13
Wendeng *China* 37°15N 122°5E **35** F12
Wendesi *Indonesia* 2°30S 134°17E **37** E8
Wendover *U.S.A.* 40°44N 114°2W **76** F6
Wenlock → *Australia* 12°2S 141°55E **62** A3
Wenshan *China* 23°20N 104°18E **32** G9
Wenshang *China* 35°45N 116°30E **34** G9
Wenshui *China* 37°26N 112°1E **34** F7
Wensleydale *U.K.* 54°17N 2°0W **12** C6
Wensu *China* 41°15N 80°10E **32** C5
Wensum → *U.K.* 52°40N 1°15E **12** E8
Wentworth *Australia* 34°2S 141°54E **63** E3
Wentzel L. *Canada* 59°2N 114°28W **70** B6
Wenut *Indonesia* 3°11S 133°19E **37** E8
Wenxi *China* 35°20N 111°10E **34** G6
Wenzhou *China* 28°0N 120°38E **33** F13
Weott *U.S.A.* 40°20N 123°55W **76** F2
Wepener *S. Africa* 29°42S 27°3E **56** D4
Werda *Botswana* 25°24S 23°15E **56** D3
Weri *Indonesia* 3°10S 132°38E **37** E8
Werra → *Germany* 51°24N 9°39E **16** C5
Werrimull *Australia* 34°25S 141°38E **63** E3
Werris Creek *Australia* 31°18S 150°38E **63** E5
Weser → *Germany* 53°36N 8°28E **16** B5
Wesiri *Indonesia* 7°30S 126°30E **37** F7
Weslaco *U.S.A.* 26°10N 97°58W **84** H6
Weslemkoon L. *Canada* 45°2N 77°25W **82** A7
Wesleyville *Canada* 49°9N 53°33W **73** C9
Wesleyville *U.S.A.* 42°9N 80°1W **82** D4
Wessel, C. *Australia* 10°59S 136°46E **62** A2
Wessel Is. *Australia* 11°10S 136°45E **62** A2
Wessington Springs
   U.S.A. 44°5N 98°34W **80** C4
West *U.S.A.* 31°48N 97°6W **84** F6
West → *U.S.A.* 42°52N 72°33W **83** D12
West Allis *U.S.A.* 43°1N 88°0W **80** D9
West Antarctica
   Antarctica 80°0S 90°0W **5** D15
West Baines →
   Australia 15°38S 129°59E **60** C4
West Bank ■ *Asia* 32°6N 35°13E **46** C4
West Bend *U.S.A.* 43°25N 88°11W **80** D9
West Bengal □ *India* 23°0N 88°0E **43** H13
West Berkshire □ *U.K.* 51°25N 1°17W **13** F6
West Beskids = Západné Beskydy
   Europe 49°30N 19°0E **17** D10
West Branch *U.S.A.* 44°17N 84°14W **81** C11
West Branch Susquehanna →
   U.S.A. 40°53N 76°48W **83** F8
West Bromwich *U.K.* 52°32N 1°59W **13** E6
West Burra *U.K.* 60°5N 1°21W **11** A7
West Canada Cr. →
   U.S.A. 43°1N 74°58W **83** C10
West Caroline Basin
   Pac. Oc. 4°0N 138°0E **64** G5
West Chazy *U.S.A.* 44°49N 73°28W **83** B11
West Chester *U.S.A.* 39°58N 75°36W **83** G9
West Coast △ *Namibia* 21°53S 14°14E **56** C1
West Coast △ *S. Africa* 33°13S 18°0E **56** E2
West Columbia *U.S.A.* 29°9N 95°39W **84** G7
West Covina *U.S.A.* 34°4N 117°54W **79** L9
West Des Moines *U.S.A.* 41°35N 93°43W **80** E7
West Dunbartonshire □
   U.K. 55°59N 4°30W **11** F4
West End *Bahamas* 26°41N 78°58W **88** A4
West Falkland *Falk. Is.* 51°40S 60°0W **96** G4
West Fargo *U.S.A.* 46°52N 96°54W **80** B5
West Fiji Basin *Pac. Oc.* 17°0S 173°0E **64** J9
West Fjord = Vestfjorden
   Norway 67°55N 14°0E **8** C16
West Fork Trinity →
   U.S.A. 32°48N 96°54W **84** E6
West Frankfort *U.S.A.* 37°54N 88°55W **80** G9
West Grand L. *U.S.A.* 45°14N 67°51W **81** C20
West Hartford *U.S.A.* 41°45N 72°44W **83** E12
West Haven *U.S.A.* 41°17N 72°57W **83** E12
West Hazleton *U.S.A.* 40°58N 76°0W **83** F9
West Helena *U.S.A.* 34°33N 90°38W **85** D9
West Hurley *U.S.A.* 41°59N 74°7W **83** E10
West Ice Shelf *Antarctica* 67°0S 85°0E **5** C7
West Indies *Cent. Amer.* 15°0N 65°0W **89** D7

West Jordan *U.S.A.* 40°36N 111°56W 76 F8
West Lamma Channel
  China 22°14N 114°4E 33 a
West Linn *U.S.A.* 45°21N 122°36W 78 E4
West Lorne *Canada* 42°36N 81°36W 82 D3
West Lothian □ *U.K.* 55°54N 3°36W 11 F5
West Lunga → *Zambia* 13°6S 24°39E 55 E1
West MacDonnell △
  Australia 23°38S 132°59E 60 D5
West Mariana Basin
  Pac. Oc. 15°0N 137°0E 64 F5
West Memphis *U.S.A.* 35°8N 90°10W 85 D9
West Midlands □ *U.K.* 52°26N 2°0W 13 E6
West Mifflin *U.S.A.* 40°21N 79°52W 82 F5
West Milford *U.S.A.* 41°8N 74°22W 83 E10
West Milton *U.S.A.* 41°1N 76°50W 82 E8
West Monroe *U.S.A.* 32°31N 92°9W 84 E8
West Newton *U.S.A.* 40°14N 79°46W 82 F5
West Nicholson *Zimbabwe* 21°2S 29°20E 55 G2
West Odessa *U.S.A.* 31°50N 102°30W 84 F3
West Palm Beach
  U.S.A. 26°43N 80°3W 85 H14
West Plains *U.S.A.* 36°44N 91°51W 80 G8
West Point *Miss.*,
  U.S.A. 33°36N 88°39W 85 E10
West Point *N.Y.*, *U.S.A.* 41°24N 73°58W 83 E11
West Point *Nebr.*, *U.S.A.* 41°51N 96°43W 80 E5
West Point *Va.*, *U.S.A.* 37°32N 76°48W 81 G15
West Point L. *U.S.A.* 32°48N 85°0W 85 E12
West Pt. = Ouest, Pte. de l'
  Canada 49°52N 64°40W 73 C7
West Pt. *Australia* 35°1S 135°56E 63 F2
West Road → *Canada* 53°18N 122°53W 70 C4
West Rutland *U.S.A.* 43°36N 73°3W 83 C11
West Schelde = Westerschelde →
  Neths. 51°25N 3°25E 15 C3
West Seneca *U.S.A.* 42°51N 78°48W 82 D6
West Siberian Plain *Russia* 62°0N 75°0E 26 B9
West Sussex □ *U.K.* 50°55N 0°30W 13 G7
West-Terschelling *Neths.* 53°22N 5°13E 15 A5
West Valley City *U.S.A.* 40°42N 111°58W 76 F8
West Virginia □ *U.S.A.* 38°45N 80°30W 81 F13
West-Vlaanderen □
  Belgium 51°0N 3°0E 15 D2
West Walker → *U.S.A.* 38°54N 119°9W 78 G7
West Wyalong *Australia* 33°56S 147°10E 63 E4
West Yellowstone
  U.S.A. 44°40N 111°6W 76 D8
West Yorkshire □ *U.K.* 53°45N 1°40W 12 D6
Westall, Pt. *Australia* 32°55S 134°4E 63 E1
Westbrook *U.S.A.* 43°41N 70°22W 81 D18
Westbury *Australia* 41°30S 146°51E 63 G4
Westby *U.S.A.* 48°52N 104°3W 76 B11
Westend *U.S.A.* 35°42N 117°24W 79 K9
Westerland *Germany* 54°54N 8°17E 16 A5
Westerly *U.S.A.* 41°22N 71°50W 83 E13
Western □ *Kenya* 0°30N 34°30E 54 B3
Western □ *Zambia* 15°0S 24°4E 55 F1
Western Australia □
  Australia 25°0S 118°0E 61 E2
Western Cape □ *S. Africa* 34°0S 20°0E 56 E3
Western Dvina = Daugava →
  Latvia 57°4N 24°3E 9 H21
Western Ghats *India* 14°0N 75°0E 40 N9
Western Isles □ *U.K.* 57°30N 7°10W 11 D1
Western Sahara ■ *Africa* 25°0N 13°0W 50 D3
Western Samoa = Samoa ■
  Pac. Oc. 14°0S 172°0W 59 b
Westernport *U.S.A.* 39°29N 79°3W 81 F14
Westerschelde → *Neths.* 51°25N 3°25E 15 C3
Westerwald *Germany* 50°38N 7°56E 16 C4
Westfield *Mass.*, *U.S.A.* 42°7N 72°45W 83 D12
Westfield *N.Y.*, *U.S.A.* 42°19N 79°35W 82 D5
Westfield *Pa.*, *U.S.A.* 41°55N 77°32W 82 E7
Westhill *U.K.* 57°9N 2°19W 11 D6
Westhope *U.S.A.* 48°55N 101°1W 80 A3
Westland □ *N.Z.* 43°16S 170°16E 59 E2
Westland Bight *N.Z.* 42°55S 170°5E 59 E3
Westlock *Canada* 54°9N 113°55W 70 C6
Westmar *Australia* 27°55S 149°44E 63 D4
Westmeath □ *Ireland* 53°33N 7°34W 10 C4
Westminster *Calif.*,
  U.S.A. 33°45N 118°0W 79 M8
Westminster *Colo.*,
  U.S.A. 39°50N 105°2W 76 G11
Westminster *Md.*,
  U.S.A. 39°34N 76°59W 81 F15
Westmont *U.S.A.* 40°19N 78°58W 82 F6
Westmoreland *Barbados* 13°13N 59°37W 89 g
Westmorland *U.S.A.* 33°2N 115°37W 79 M11
Weston *Oreg.*, *U.S.A.* 45°49N 118°26W 76 D4
Weston *W. Va.*, *U.S.A.* 39°2N 80°28W 81 F13
Weston I. *Canada* 52°33N 79°36W 72 B4
Weston-super-Mare *U.K.* 51°21N 2°58W 13 F5
Westover *U.S.A.* 40°45N 78°40W 82 F6
Westport *Canada* 44°40N 76°25W 83 B8
Westport *Ireland* 53°48N 9°31W 10 C2
Westport *N.Z.* 41°46S 171°37E 59 D3
Westport *N.Y.*, *U.S.A.* 44°11N 73°26W 83 B11
Westport *Oreg.*, *U.S.A.* 46°8N 123°23W 78 D3
Westport *Wash.*, *U.S.A.* 46°53N 124°6W 78 D2
Westray *Canada* 53°36N 101°24W 71 C8
Westray *U.K.* 59°18N 3°0W 11 B5
Westree *Canada* 47°26N 81°34W 72 C3
Westville *U.S.A.* 39°8N 102°42W 78 F6
Westwood *U.S.A.* 40°18N 121°0W 76 F3
Wetar *Indonesia* 7°48S 126°30E 37 F7
Wetaskiwin *Canada* 52°55N 113°24W 70 C6
Wete *Tanzania* 5°4S 39°43E 52 F7
Wetherby *U.K.* 53°56N 1°23W 12 D6
Wethersfield *U.S.A.* 41°42N 72°40W 83 E12
Wetteren *Belgium* 51°0N 3°53E 15 D3
Wetzlar *Germany* 50°32N 8°31E 16 C5
Wewoka *U.S.A.* 35°9N 96°30W 84 D6
Wexford *Ireland* 52°20N 6°28W 10 D5
Wexford □ *Ireland* 52°20N 6°25W 10 D5
Wexford Harbour *Ireland* 52°20N 6°25W 10 D5

Weyburn *Canada* 49°40N 103°50W 71 D8
Weymouth *Canada* 44°30N 66°1W 73 D6
Weymouth *U.K.* 50°37N 2°28W 13 G5
Weymouth *U.S.A.* 42°13N 70°58W 83 D14
Weymouth, C. *Australia* 12°37S 143°27E 62 A3
Wha Ti *Canada* 63°8N 117°16W 68 E8
Whakaari *N.Z.* 37°30S 177°13E 59 B6
Whakatane *N.Z.* 37°57S 177°1E 59 B6
Whale = Baleine →
  Canada 58°15N 67°40W 73 A6
Whale B. *Burma* 11°37N 98°38E 39 G2
Whale Cove *Canada* 62°10N 92°34W 71 A10
Whales, B. of *Antarctica* 78°0S 160°0W 5 D12
Whalsay *U.K.* 60°22N 0°59W 11 A8
Whangamata *N.Z.* 37°12S 175°53E 59 B5
Whangamomona *N.Z.* 39°8S 174°44E 59 C5
Whanganui → *N.Z.* 39°17S 174°53E 59 C5
Whangarei *N.Z.* 35°43S 174°21E 59 A5
Whangarei Harb. *N.Z.* 35°45S 174°28E 59 A5
Wharekauri = Chatham Is.
  Pac. Oc. 44°0S 176°40W 64 M10
Wharfe → *U.K.* 53°51N 1°9W 12 D6
Wharfedale *U.K.* 54°6N 2°1W 12 C5
Wharton *N.J.*, *U.S.A.* 40°54N 74°35W 83 F10
Wharton *Pa.*, *U.S.A.* 41°31N 78°1W 82 E6
Wharton *Tex.*, *U.S.A.* 29°19N 96°6W 84 G6
Wharton Basin *Ind. Oc.* 20°0S 92°0E 64 K1
Wheatland *Calif.*, *U.S.A.* 39°1N 121°25W 78 F5
Wheatland *Wyo.*,
  U.S.A. 42°3N 104°58W 76 E11
Wheatley *Canada* 42°6N 82°27W 82 D2
Wheaton *Md.*, *U.S.A.* 39°3N 77°3W 81 F15
Wheaton *Minn.*, *U.S.A.* 45°48N 96°30W 80 C5
Wheelbarrow Pk.
  U.S.A. 37°26N 116°5W 78 H10
Wheeler *Oreg.*, *U.S.A.* 45°41N 123°53W 76 D2
Wheeler *Tex.*, *U.S.A.* 35°27N 100°16W 84 D4
Wheeler → *Canada* 57°2N 67°13W 73 A6
Wheeler L. *U.S.A.* 34°48N 87°23W 85 D11
Wheeler Pk. *N. Mex.*,
  U.S.A. 36°34N 105°25W 77 H11
Wheeler Pk. *Nev.*,
  U.S.A. 38°57N 114°15W 76 G6
Wheeler Ridge *U.S.A.* 35°0N 118°57W 79 L8
Wheelersburg *U.S.A.* 38°44N 82°51W 81 F12
Wheeling *U.S.A.* 40°4N 80°43W 82 F4
Whernside *U.K.* 54°14N 2°24W 12 C5
Whiddy I. *Ireland* 51°41N 9°31W 10 E2
Whiskey Jack L.
  Canada 58°23N 101°55W 71 B8
Whiskeytown-Shasta-Trinity △
  U.S.A. 40°45N 122°15W 76 F2
Whistleduck Cr. →
  Australia 20°15S 135°18E 62 C2
Whistler *Canada* 50°7N 122°58W 70 C4
Whitby *Canada* 43°52N 78°56W 82 C6
Whitby *U.K.* 54°29N 0°37W 12 C7
White → *Ark.*, *U.S.A.* 33°57N 91°5W 84 E9
White → *Ind.*, *U.S.A.* 38°25N 87°45W 80 F10
White → *S. Dak.*, *U.S.A.* 43°42N 99°27W 80 D4
White → *Tex.*, *U.S.A.* 33°14N 100°56W 84 E4
White → *Utah*, *U.S.A.* 40°4N 109°41W 76 F9
White → *Vt.*, *U.S.A.* 43°37N 72°20W 83 C12
White → *Wash.*, *U.S.A.* 47°12N 122°15W 78 C4
White, L. *Australia* 21°9S 128°56E 60 D4
White B. *Canada* 50°0N 56°35W 73 C8
White Bird *U.S.A.* 45°46N 116°18W 76 D5
White Butte *U.S.A.* 46°23N 103°18W 80 B2
White City *U.S.A.* 32°56S 143°10E 63 E3
White Cliffs *Australia* 30°50S 143°10E 63 E3
White Hall *U.S.A.* 39°26N 90°24W 80 F8
White Haven *U.S.A.* 41°4N 75°47W 83 E9
White Horse, Vale of
  U.K. 51°37N 1°30W 13 F6
White I. = Whakaari
  N.Z. 37°30S 177°13E 59 B6
White L. *Canada* 45°18N 76°31W 83 A8
White L. *U.S.A.* 29°44N 92°30W 84 G8
White Lake *Canada* 45°21N 76°29W 83 A8
White Mountain Peak
  U.S.A. 37°38N 118°15W 77 H4
White Mts. *Calif.*,
  U.S.A. 37°30N 118°15W 78 H8
White Mts. *N.H.*,
  U.S.A. 44°15N 71°15W 83 B13
White Mts. △ *Australia* 20°43S 145°12E 62 C4
White Nile = Nil el Abyad →
  Sudan 15°38N 32°31E 51 E12
White Otter L. *Canada* 49°5N 91°55W 72 C1
White Pass *U.S.A.* 46°38N 121°24W 78 D5
White Plains *U.S.A.* 41°2N 73°46W 83 E11
White River *Canada* 48°35N 85°20W 72 C2
White River *U.S.A.* 43°34N 100°45W 80 D3
White Rock *Canada* 49°2N 122°48W 78 A4
White Rock *U.S.A.* 35°50N 106°12W 77 J10
White Russia = Belarus ■
  Europe 53°30N 27°0E 17 B14
White Sands △ *U.S.A.* 32°46N 106°20W 77 K10
White Sea = Beloye More
  Russia 66°30N 38°0E 18 A6
White Sulphur Springs *Mont.*,
  U.S.A. 46°33N 110°54W 76 C8
White Sulphur Springs *W. Va.*,
  U.S.A. 37°48N 80°18W 81 G13
White Swan *U.S.A.* 46°23N 120°44W 78 D6
Whitecliffs *N.Z.* 43°26S 171°55E 59 E3
Whitecourt *Canada* 54°10N 115°45W 70 C5
Whiteface Mt. *U.S.A.* 44°22N 73°54W 83 B11
Whitefield *U.S.A.* 44°23N 71°37W 83 B13
Whitefish *U.S.A.* 48°25N 114°20W 76 B6
Whitefish B. *U.S.A.* 46°40N 84°55W 72 C3
Whitefish L. *Canada* 62°41N 106°48W 71 A7
Whitefish Pt. *U.S.A.* 46°45N 84°59W 81 B11
Whitegull, L. = Goélands, L. aux
  Canada 55°27N 64°17W 73 A7
Whitehall *Mich.*, *U.S.A.* 43°24N 86°21W 80 D10
Whitehall *Mont.*, *U.S.A.* 45°52N 112°6W 76 C7
Whitehall *N.Y.*, *U.S.A.* 43°33N 73°24W 83 C11
Whitehall *Wis.*, *U.S.A.* 44°22N 91°19W 80 C8

Whitehaven *U.K.* 54°33N 3°35W 12 C4
Whitehorse *Canada* 60°43N 135°3W 70 A1
Whitemark *Australia* 40°7S 148°3E 63 G4
Whiteriver *U.S.A.* 33°50N 109°58W 77 K9
Whitesand → *Canada* 60°9N 115°45W 70 A5
Whitesands *S. Africa* 34°23S 20°50E 56 E3
Whitesboro *N.Y.*, *U.S.A.* 43°7N 75°18W 83 D9
Whitesboro *Tex.*, *U.S.A.* 33°39N 96°54W 84 E6
Whiteshell △ *Canada* 50°0N 95°40W 71 C9
Whiteville *U.S.A.* 34°20N 78°42W 85 D15
Whitewater *U.S.A.* 42°50N 88°44W 80 D9
Whitewater Baldy
  U.S.A. 33°20N 108°39W 77 K9
Whitewater L. *Canada* 50°50N 89°10W 72 B2
Whitewood *Australia* 21°28S 143°30E 62 C3
Whitewood *Canada* 50°20N 102°20W 71 C8
Whithorn *U.K.* 54°44N 4°26W 11 G4
Whitianga *N.Z.* 36°47S 175°41E 59 B5
Whitman *U.S.A.* 42°5N 70°56W 83 D14
Whitney *Canada* 45°31N 78°14W 82 A6
Whitney, Mt. *U.S.A.* 36°35N 118°18W 78 J8
Whitney Point *U.S.A.* 42°20N 75°58W 83 D9
Whitstable *U.K.* 51°21N 1°3E 13 F9
Whitsunday I. *Australia* 20°15S 149°4E 62 b
Whitsunday Islands △
  Australia 20°15S 149°0E 62 b
Whittier *Alaska*, *U.S.A.* 60°47N 148°41W 74 C10
Whittier *Calif.*, *U.S.A.* 33°58N 118°2W 79 M8
Whittlesea *Australia* 37°27S 145°9E 63 F4
Wholdaia L. *Canada* 60°43N 104°20W 71 A8
Whyalla *Australia* 33°2S 137°30E 63 E2
Wiang Kosai △ *Thailand* 17°54N 99°29E 38 D2
Wiang Sa *Thailand* 18°34N 100°42E 38 C3
Wiarton *Canada* 44°40N 81°10W 82 B3
Wiay *U.K.* 57°24N 7°13W 11 D1
Wibaux *U.S.A.* 46°59N 104°11W 76 C11
Wichian Buri *Thailand* 15°39N 101°7E 38 E3
Wichita *U.S.A.* 37°42N 97°20W 80 G5
Wichita Falls *U.S.A.* 33°54N 98°30W 84 E5
Wick *U.K.* 58°26N 3°5W 11 C5
Wickenburg *U.S.A.* 33°58N 112°44W 77 K7
Wickepin *Australia* 32°50S 117°30E 61 F2
Wickham *Australia* 20°42S 117°11E 60 D2
Wickham, C. *Australia* 39°35S 143°57E 63 F3
Wickliffe *U.S.A.* 41°36N 81°28W 82 E3
Wicklow *Ireland* 52°59N 6°3W 10 D5
Wicklow □ *Ireland* 52°57N 6°25W 10 D5
Wicklow Hd. *Ireland* 52°58N 6°0W 10 D6
Wicklow Mts. *Ireland* 52°58N 6°26W 10 C5
Wicklow Mts. △ *Ireland* 53°6N 6°21W 10 C5
Widgeegoara Cr. →
  Australia 28°51S 146°34E 63 D4
Widgiemooltha
  Australia 31°30S 121°34E 61 F3
Widnes *U.K.* 53°23N 2°45W 12 D5
Wieluń *Poland* 51°15N 18°34E 17 C10
Wien *Austria* 48°12N 16°22E 16 D9
Wiener Neustadt *Austria* 47°49N 16°16E 16 E9
Wiesbaden *Germany* 50°4N 8°14E 16 C5
Wigan *U.K.* 53°33N 2°38W 12 D5
Wiggins *Colo.*, *U.S.A.* 40°14N 104°4W 76 F11
Wiggins *Miss.*, *U.S.A.* 30°51N 89°8W 85 F10
Wight, I. of *U.K.* 50°41N 1°17W 13 G6
Wigston *U.K.* 52°35N 1°6W 13 E6
Wigton *U.K.* 54°50N 3°10W 12 C4
Wigtown *U.K.* 54°53N 4°27W 11 G4
Wigtown B. *U.K.* 54°46N 4°15W 11 G4
Wik and Wikway People ◇
  Australia 13°55S 142°28E 62 A3
Wilber *U.S.A.* 40°29N 96°58W 80 E5
Wilberforce *Canada* 45°2N 78°13W 82 A6
Wilberforce, C. *Australia* 11°54S 136°35E 62 A2
Wilburton *U.S.A.* 34°55N 95°19W 84 D7
Wilcannia *Australia* 31°30S 143°26E 63 E3
Wilcox *U.S.A.* 41°35N 78°41W 82 E6
Wildrose *U.S.A.* 36°14N 117°11W 79 J9
Wildspitze *Austria* 46°53N 10°53E 16 E6
Wilge → *S. Africa* 27°3S 28°20E 57 D4
Wilhelm II Coast *Antarctica* 68°0S 90°0E 5 C7
Wilhelmshaven *Germany* 53°31N 8°7E 16 B5
Wilhelmstal *Namibia* 21°58S 16°21E 56 C2
Wilis *Indonesia* 7°51S 111°48E 37 G15
Wilkes-Barre *U.S.A.* 41°15N 75°53W 83 E9
Wilkes Land *Antarctica* 69°0S 120°0E 5 D8
Wilkie *Canada* 52°27N 108°42W 71 C7
Wilkinsburg *U.S.A.* 40°26N 79°52W 82 F5
Wilkinson Lakes
  Australia 29°40S 132°39E 61 E5
Willandra Creek →
  Australia 33°22S 145°52E 63 E4
Willapa B. *U.S.A.* 46°40N 124°0W 76 C1
Willapa Hills *U.S.A.* 46°35N 123°25W 78 D3
Willard *U.S.A.* 41°3N 82°44W 82 E2
Willare Bridge Roadhouse
  Australia 18°35S 123°38E 60 C3
Willcox *U.S.A.* 32°15N 109°50W 77 K9
Willemstad *Curaçao* 12°5N 68°55W 89 D6
William → *Canada* 59°8N 109°19W 71 B7
William 'Bill' Dannelly Res.
  U.S.A. 32°6N 87°24W 85 E11
William Creek *Australia* 28°58S 136°22E 63 D2
Williams *Australia* 33°2S 116°52E 61 F2
Williams *Ariz.*, *U.S.A.* 35°15N 112°11W 77 J7
Williams *Calif.*, *U.S.A.* 39°9N 122°9W 78 F4
Williams Harbour
  Canada 52°33S 55°47W 73 B8
Williams Lake *Canada* 52°10N 122°10W 70 C4
Williamsburg *Ky.*,
  U.S.A. 36°44N 84°10W 81 G11
Williamsburg *Pa.*,
  U.S.A. 40°28N 78°12W 82 F6
Williamsburg *Va.*,
  U.S.A. 37°16N 76°43W 81 G15
Williamson *N.Y.*, *U.S.A.* 43°14N 77°11W 82 C7
Williamson *W. Va.*,
  U.S.A. 37°41N 82°17W 81 G12
Williamsport *U.S.A.* 41°15N 77°1W 82 E7
Williamston *U.S.A.* 35°51N 77°4W 85 D16
Williamstown *Australia* 37°51S 144°52E 63 F4
Williamstown *Ky.*,
  U.S.A. 38°38N 84°34W 81 F11

Williamstown *Mass.*,
  U.S.A. 42°43N 73°12W 83 D11
Williamstown *N.Y.*,
  U.S.A. 43°26N 75°53W 83 C9
Willimantic *U.S.A.* 41°43N 72°13W 83 E12
Willingboro *U.S.A.* 40°3N 74°54W 81 E16
Williston *S. Africa* 31°20S 20°53E 56 E3
Williston *Fla.*, *U.S.A.* 29°23N 82°27W 85 G13
Williston *N. Dak.*, *U.S.A.* 48°9N 103°37W 80 A2
Williston L. *Canada* 56°0N 124°0W 70 B4
Willits *U.S.A.* 39°25N 123°21W 76 G2
Willmar *U.S.A.* 45°7N 95°3W 80 C6
Willmore Wilderness △
  Canada 53°45N 119°30W 70 C5
Willoughby *U.S.A.* 41°39N 81°24W 82 E3
Willow Bunch *Canada* 49°20N 105°35W 71 D7
Willow L. *Canada* 62°10N 119°8W 70 A5
Willow Wall, The *China* 42°10N 122°0E 35 C12
Willowick *U.S.A.* 41°38N 81°28W 82 E3
Willowlake → *Canada* 62°42N 123°8W 70 A4
Willowmore *S. Africa* 33°15S 23°30E 56 E3
Willows *U.S.A.* 39°31N 122°12W 78 F4
Willowvale = Gatyana
  S. Africa 32°16S 28°31E 57 E4
Wills, L. *Australia* 21°25S 128°51E 60 D4
Wills Cr. → *Australia* 22°43S 140°2E 62 C3
Willsboro *U.S.A.* 44°21N 73°24W 83 B11
Willunga *Australia* 35°15S 138°30E 63 F2
Wilmette *U.S.A.* 42°4N 87°42W 80 D10
Wilmington *Australia* 32°39S 138°7E 63 E2
Wilmington *Del.*,
  U.S.A. 39°45N 75°33W 81 F16
Wilmington *N.C.*,
  U.S.A. 34°14N 77°55W 85 D16
Wilmington *Ohio*,
  U.S.A. 39°27N 83°50W 81 F12
Wilmington *Vt.*, *U.S.A.* 42°52N 72°52W 83 D12
Wilmslow *U.K.* 53°19N 2°13W 12 D5
Wilpena Cr. →
  Australia 31°25S 139°29E 63 E2
Wilsall *U.S.A.* 45°59N 110°38W 76 D8
Wilson *N.C.*, *U.S.A.* 35°44N 77°55W 85 D16
Wilson *N.Y.*, *U.S.A.* 43°19N 78°50W 82 C6
Wilson *Pa.*, *U.S.A.* 40°41N 75°15W 83 F9
Wilson → *Australia* 16°48S 128°16E 60 C4
Wilson Bluff *Australia* 31°41S 129°0E 61 F4
Wilson Inlet *Australia* 35°0S 117°22E 61 G2
Wilsons Promontory
  Australia 38°59S 146°23E 63 F4
Wilton *U.S.A.* 47°10N 100°47W 80 B3
Wilton → *Australia* 14°45S 134°33E 62 A1
Wiltshire □ *U.K.* 51°18N 1°53W 13 F6
Wiltz *Lux.* 49°57N 5°55E 15 E5
Wiluna *Australia* 26°36S 120°14E 61 E3
Wimborne Minster *U.K.* 50°48N 1°59W 13 G6
Wimmera → *Australia* 36°8S 141°56E 63 F3
Winam G. *Kenya* 0°20S 34°15E 54 C3
Winburg *S. Africa* 28°30S 27°2E 56 D4
Winchendon *U.S.A.* 42°41N 72°3W 83 D12
Winchester *U.K.* 51°4N 1°18W 13 F6
Winchester *Conn.*,
  U.S.A. 41°53N 73°9W 83 E11
Winchester *Idaho*,
  U.S.A. 46°14N 116°38W 76 C5
Winchester *Ind.*, *U.S.A.* 40°10N 84°59W 81 E11
Winchester *Ky.*, *U.S.A.* 37°59N 84°11W 81 G11
Winchester *N.H.*,
  U.S.A. 42°46N 72°23W 83 D12
Winchester *Nev.*, *U.S.A.* 36°7N 115°7W 79 J11
Winchester *Tenn.*,
  U.S.A. 35°11N 86°7W 85 D11
Winchester *Va.*, *U.S.A.* 39°11N 78°10W 81 F14
Wind → *U.S.A.* 43°12N 108°12W 76 E9
Wind Cave △ *U.S.A.* 43°32N 103°17W 80 D2
Wind River Range
  U.S.A. 43°0N 109°30W 76 E9
Windamere, L. *Australia* 32°48S 149°51E 63 B4
Windau = Ventspils
  Latvia 57°25N 21°32E 9 H19
Windber *U.S.A.* 40°14N 78°50W 82 F6
Winder *U.S.A.* 34°0N 83°45W 85 D13
Windermere *U.S.A.* 54°23N 75°9W 12 C5
Windhoek *Namibia* 22°35S 17°4E 56 C2
Windidda ◇ *Australia* 26°23S 122°12E 61 E3
Windjana Gorge △
  Australia 17°51S 125°0E 60 C3
Windom *U.S.A.* 43°52N 95°7W 80 D6
Windorah *Australia* 25°24S 142°36E 62 D3
Window Rock *U.S.A.* 35°41N 109°3W 77 J9
Windrush → *U.K.* 51°43N 1°24W 13 F6
Windsor *Australia* 33°37S 150°50E 63 E5
Windsor *N.S.*, *Canada* 44°59N 64°5W 73 D7
Windsor *Ont.*, *Canada* 42°18N 83°0W 82 D2
Windsor *U.K.* 51°29N 0°36W 13 F7
Windsor *Calif.*, *U.S.A.* 38°33N 122°49W 76 G2
Windsor *Colo.*, *U.S.A.* 40°29N 104°54W 76 F11
Windsor *Conn.*, *U.S.A.* 41°50N 72°39W 83 E12
Windsor *Mo.*, *U.S.A.* 38°32N 93°31W 80 F7
Windsor *N.Y.*, *U.S.A.* 42°5N 75°37W 83 D9
Windsor *Vt.*, *U.S.A.* 43°29N 72°24W 83 C12
Windsor & Maidenhead □
  U.K. 51°29N 0°40W 13 F7
Windsorton *S. Africa* 28°16S 24°44E 56 D3
Windward Is. *W. Indies* 13°0N 61°0W 89 D7
Windward Passage = Vientos,
  Paso de los *Caribbean* 20°0N 74°0W 89 C5
Winefred L. *Canada* 55°30N 110°30W 71 B6
Winfield *U.S.A.* 37°15N 96°59W 80 G5
Wingate Mts. *Australia* 14°25S 130°40E 60 B5
Wingellina = Irrunytju
  Australia 26°3S 128°56E 61 E4
Wingham *Australia* 31°48S 152°22E 63 E5
Wingham *Canada* 43°55N 81°20W 82 C3
Winisk → *Canada* 55°17N 85°5W 72 A2
Winisk L. *Canada* 52°55N 87°22W 72 B2
Wink *U.S.A.* 31°45N 103°9W 84 F3
Winkler *Canada* 49°10N 97°56W 71 D9
Winlock *U.S.A.* 46°30N 122°56W 78 D4
Winneba *Ghana* 5°25N 0°36W 50 G5
Winnebago, L. *U.S.A.* 44°0N 88°26W 80 D9

Winnecke Cr. →
  Australia 18°35S 131°34E 60 C5
Winnemucca *U.S.A.* 40°58N 117°44W 76 F5
Winnemucca L. *U.S.A.* 40°7N 119°21W 76 F4
Winner *U.S.A.* 43°22N 99°52W 80 D4
Winnett *U.S.A.* 47°0N 108°21W 76 C9
Winnfield *U.S.A.* 31°56N 92°38W 84 F8
Winnibigoshish, L.
  U.S.A. 47°27N 94°13W 80 B6
Winnipeg *Canada* 49°54N 97°9W 71 D9
Winnipeg → *Canada* 50°38N 96°19W 71 C9
Winnipeg, L. *Canada* 52°0N 97°0W 71 C9
Winnipeg Beach *Canada* 50°30N 96°58W 71 C9
Winnipegosis *Canada* 51°39N 99°55W 71 C9
Winnipegosis L. *Canada* 52°30N 100°0W 71 C9
Winnipesaukee, L.
  U.S.A. 43°38N 71°21W 83 C13
Winnisquam L. *U.S.A.* 43°33N 71°31W 83 C13
Winnsboro *La.*, *U.S.A.* 32°10N 91°43W 84 E9
Winnsboro *S.C.*, *U.S.A.* 34°23N 81°5W 85 D14
Winnsboro *Tex.*, *U.S.A.* 32°58N 95°17W 84 E7
Winokapau, L. *Canada* 53°15N 62°50W 73 B7
Winona *Minn.*, *U.S.A.* 44°3N 91°39W 80 C8
Winona *Miss.*, *U.S.A.* 33°29N 89°44W 85 E10
Winooski *U.S.A.* 44°29N 73°11W 83 B11
Winooski → *U.S.A.* 44°32N 73°17W 83 B11
Winschoten *Neths.* 53°9N 7°3E 15 A7
Winsford *U.K.* 53°12N 2°31W 12 D5
Winslow = Bainbridge Island
  U.S.A. 47°38N 122°32W 78 C4
Winslow *U.S.A.* 35°2N 110°42W 77 J8
Winsted *U.S.A.* 41°55N 73°4W 83 E11
Winston-Salem *U.S.A.* 36°6N 80°15W 85 C14
Winter Garden *U.S.A.* 28°34N 81°35W 85 G14
Winter Haven *U.S.A.* 28°1N 81°44W 85 G14
Winter Park *U.S.A.* 28°36N 81°20W 85 G14
Winterhaven *U.S.A.* 32°44N 114°38W 79 N12
Winters *U.S.A.* 38°32N 121°58W 78 G5
Winterset *U.S.A.* 41°20N 94°1W 80 E6
Wintersville *U.S.A.* 40°23N 80°42W 82 F4
Winterswijk *Neths.* 51°58N 6°43E 15 C6
Winterthur *Switz.* 47°30N 8°44E 20 C8
Winthrop *U.S.A.* 48°28N 120°10W 76 B3
Winton *Australia* 22°24S 143°3E 62 C3
Winton *N.Z.* 46°8S 168°20E 59 G2
Wirlyajarrayi ◇
  Australia 21°45S 132°35E 60 D5
Wirrulla *Australia* 32°24S 134°31E 63 E1
Wisbech *U.K.* 52°41N 0°9E 13 E8
Wisconsin □ *U.S.A.* 44°45N 89°30W 80 C9
Wisconsin → *U.S.A.* 43°0N 91°15W 80 D9
Wisconsin Rapids
  U.S.A. 44°23N 89°49W 80 C9
Wisdom *U.S.A.* 45°37N 113°27W 76 D7
Wiseman *U.S.A.* 67°25N 150°6W 74 B9
Wishaw *U.K.* 55°46N 3°54W 11 F5
Wishek *U.S.A.* 46°16N 99°33W 80 B4
Wisła → *Poland* 54°22N 18°55E 17 A10
Wismar *Germany* 53°54N 11°29E 16 B6
Wisner *U.S.A.* 41°59N 96°55W 80 E5
Witbank = eMalahleni
  S. Africa 25°51S 29°14E 57 D4
Witdraai *S. Africa* 26°58S 20°48E 56 D3
Witham *U.K.* 51°48N 0°40E 13 F8
Witham → *U.K.* 52°59N 0°2W 12 E7
Withernsea *U.K.* 53°44N 0°1E 12 D8
Witjira △ *Australia* 26°22S 135°37E 63 D2
Witless Bay *Canada* 47°17N 52°50W 73 C9
Witney *U.K.* 51°48N 1°28W 13 F6
Witnossob → *Namibia* 23°55S 18°45E 56 D3
Witriver *S. Africa* 25°20S 31°0E 57 D5
Wittenberge *Germany* 53°0N 11°45E 16 B6
Wittenoom *Australia* 22°15S 118°20E 60 D2
Witu *Kenya* 2°23S 40°26E 54 C5
Witvlei *Namibia* 22°23S 18°32E 56 C2
Wiwon *N. Korea* 40°54N 126°3E 35 D14
Wkra → *Poland* 52°27N 20°44E 17 B11
Wlingi *Indonesia* 8°5S 112°25E 37 H15
Włocławek *Poland* 52°40N 19°3E 17 B10
Włodawa *Poland* 51°33N 23°31E 17 C12
Woburn *U.S.A.* 42°29N 71°9W 83 D13
Wodian *China* 32°50N 112°35E 34 H7
Wodonga *Australia* 36°5S 146°50E 63 F4
Wokam *Indonesia* 5°45S 134°28E 37 F8
Woking *U.K.* 51°19N 0°34W 13 F7
Wokingham *U.S.A.* 51°24N 0°49W 13 F7
Wokingham □ *U.K.* 51°25N 0°51W 13 F7
Wolf → *Canada* 60°17N 132°33W 70 A2
Wolf Creek *U.S.A.* 47°0N 112°4W 76 C7
Wolf L. *Canada* 60°24N 131°40W 70 A2
Wolf Point *U.S.A.* 48°5N 105°39W 76 B11
Wolfe Creek Crater △
  Australia 19°10S 127°47E 60 C4
Wolfe I. *Canada* 44°7N 76°20W 83 B8
Wolfeboro *U.S.A.* 43°35N 71°13W 83 C13
Wolfsberg *Austria* 46°50N 14°52E 16 E8
Wolfsburg *Germany* 52°25N 10°48E 16 B6
Wolin *Poland* 53°50N 14°37E 16 B8
Wollaston, Is. *Chile* 55°40S 67°30W 96 H3
Wollaston L. *Canada* 58°7N 103°10W 71 B8
Wollaston Lake *Canada* 58°3N 103°33W 71 B8
Wollaston Pen. *Canada* 69°30N 115°0W 68 D9
Wollongong *Australia* 34°25S 150°54E 63 E5
Wolmaransstad *S. Africa* 27°12S 25°59E 56 D4
Wolseley *S. Africa* 33°26S 19°7E 56 E2
Wolsey *U.S.A.* 44°25N 98°28W 80 C4
Wolstenholme, C.
  Canada 62°35N 77°30W 66 C12
Wolvega *Neths.* 52°52N 6°0E 15 B6
Wolverhampton *U.K.* 52°35N 2°7W 13 E5
Wondai *Australia* 26°20S 151°49E 63 D5
Wongalarroo L. *Australia* 31°32S 144°0E 63 E3
Wongan Hills *Australia* 30°51S 116°37E 61 F2
Wonju *S. Korea* 37°22N 127°58E 35 F14
Wonosari *Indonesia* 7°58S 110°36E 37 G14
Wonosobo *Indonesia* 7°22S 109°54E 37 G13
Wonowon *Canada* 56°44N 121°48W 70 B4
Wŏnsan *N. Korea* 39°11N 127°27E 35 E14
Wonthaggi *Australia* 38°37S 145°37E 63 F4
Wood Buffalo △ *Canada* 59°0N 113°41W 70 B6
Wood Is. *Australia* 16°24S 123°19E 60 C3

Wood L. *Canada* 55°17N 103°17W **71** B8
Woodah, I. *Australia* 13°27S 136°10E **62** A2
Woodbourne *U.S.A.* 41°46N 74°36W **83** E10
Woodbridge *Canada* 43°47N 79°36W **82** C5
Woodbridge *U.K.* 52°6N 1°20E **13** E9
Woodburn *Australia* 29°6S 153°23E **63** A5
Woodburn *U.S.A.* 45°9N 122°51W **76** D2
Woodenbong *Australia* 28°24S 152°39E **63** D5
Woodend *Australia* 37°20S 144°33E **63** F4
Woodford *Australia* 26°58S 152°47E **63** D5
Woodfords *U.S.A.* 38°47N 119°50W **78** G7
Woodlake *U.S.A.* 36°25N 119°6W **78** J7
Woodland *Calif., U.S.A.* 38°41N 121°46W **78** G5
Woodland *Maine, U.S.A.* 45°9N 67°25W **81** C20
Woodland *Pa., U.S.A.* 41°0N 78°21W **82** F6
Woodland *Wash., U.S.A.* 45°54N 122°45W **78** E4
Woodland Caribou △ *Canada* 51°0N 94°45W **71** C10
Woodlands *Singapore* 1°26N 103°46E **39** d
Woodlands, The *U.S.A.* 30°9N 95°29W **84** F7
Woodonga *Australia* 36°10S 146°50E **63** F4
Woodridge *Canada* 49°20N 96°9W **71** D9
Woodroffe, Mt. *Australia* 26°20S 131°45E **61** E5
Woods, L. *Australia* 17°50S 133°30E **62** B1
Woods, L. of the *N. Amer.* 49°15N 94°45W **71** D10
Woods Bay *Canada* 45°8N 79°59W **82** A5
Woodstock *Australia* 19°35S 146°50E **62** B4
Woodstock *N.B., Canada* 46°11N 67°37W **73** C6
Woodstock *Ont., Canada* 43°10N 80°45W **82** C4
Woodstock *U.K.* 51°51N 1°20W **13** F6
Woodstock *Ill., U.S.A.* 42°19N 88°27W **80** D9
Woodstock *N.Y., U.S.A.* 42°2N 74°7W **83** D10
Woodstock *Vt., U.S.A.* 43°37N 72°31W **83** C12
Woodsville *U.S.A.* 44°9N 72°2W **83** B13
Woodview *Canada* 44°35N 78°8W **82** B6
Woodville *N.Z.* 40°20S 175°53E **59** D5
Woodville *Miss., U.S.A.* 31°6N 91°18W **84** F9
Woodville *Tex., U.S.A.* 30°47N 94°25W **84** F7
Woodward *U.S.A.* 36°26N 99°24W **84** C5
Woody *U.S.A.* 35°42N 118°50W **79** K8
Woody → *Canada* 52°31N 100°51W **71** C8
Woolacombe *U.K.* 51°10N 4°13W **13** F3
Woolamai, C. *Australia* 38°30S 145°23E **63** F4
Wooler *U.K.* 55°33N 2°1W **12** B5
Woolgoolga *Australia* 30°6S 153°11E **63** E5
Woomera *Australia* 31°5S 136°50E **63** E2
Woonsocket *R.I., U.S.A.* 42°0N 71°31W **83** E13
Woonsocket *S. Dak., U.S.A.* 44°3N 98°17W **80** C4
Wooramel → *Australia* 25°47S 114°10E **61** E1
Wooramel Roadhouse *Australia* 25°45S 114°17E **61** E1
Wooroonooran △ *Australia* 16°25S 146°1E **62** B4
Wooster *U.S.A.* 40°48N 81°56W **82** F3
Worcester *S. Africa* 33°39S 19°27E **56** E2
Worcester *U.K.* 52°11N 2°12W **13** E5
Worcester *Mass., U.S.A.* 42°16N 71°48W **83** D13
Worcester *N.Y., U.S.A.* 42°36N 74°45W **83** D10
Worcestershire □ *U.K.* 52°13N 2°10W **13** E5
Workington *U.K.* 54°39N 3°33W **12** C4
Worksop *U.K.* 53°18N 1°7W **12** D6
Workum *Neths.* 52°59N 5°26E **15** B5
Worland *U.S.A.* 44°1N 107°57W **76** D10
Worms *Germany* 49°37N 8°21E **16** D5
Worsley *Canada* 56°31N 119°8W **70** B5
Wortham *U.S.A.* 31°47N 96°28W **84** F6
Worthing *Barbados* 13°5N 59°35W **89** g
Worthing *U.K.* 50°49N 0°21W **13** G7
Worthington *Minn., U.S.A.* 43°37N 95°36W **80** D6
Worthington *Pa., U.S.A.* 40°50N 79°38W **82** F5
Wosi *Indonesia* 0°15S 128°0E **37** E7
Wote *Kenya* 1°47S 37°38E **54** C4
Wotjalum ○ *Australia* 16°30S 123°45E **60** C3
Wotjobaluk ○ *Australia* 37°0S 142°0E **63** C3
Wou-han = Wuhan *China* 30°31N 114°18E **33** E11
Wousi = Wuxi *China* 31°33N 120°18E **33** E13
Wowoni *Indonesia* 4°5S 123°5E **37** E6
Wrangel I. = Vrangelya, Ostrov *Russia* 71°0N 180°0E **29** B18
Wrangell *U.S.A.* 56°28N 132°23W **70** B2
Wrangell Mts. *U.S.A.* 61°30N 142°0W **68** E3
Wrath, C. *U.K.* 58°38N 5°1W **11** C3
Wray *U.S.A.* 40°5N 102°13W **76** F12
Wrekin, The *U.K.* 52°41N 2°32W **13** E5
Wrens *U.S.A.* 33°12N 82°23W **85** E13
Wrexham *U.K.* 53°3N 3°0W **12** D4
Wrexham □ *U.K.* 53°1N 2°58W **12** D5
Wright *Fla., U.S.A.* 30°27N 86°38W **85** F11
Wright *Wyo., U.S.A.* 43°45N 105°28W **76** E11
Wright Pt. *Canada* 43°48N 81°44W **82** C3
Wrightson, Mt. *U.S.A.* 31°42N 110°51W **77** L8
Wrightwood *U.S.A.* 34°22N 117°38W **79** L9
Wrigley *Canada* 63°16N 123°37W **68** E7
Wrocław *Poland* 51°5N 17°5E **17** C9
Września *Poland* 52°21N 17°36E **17** B9
Wu Jiang → *China* 29°40N 107°20E **32** F10
Wu Kau Tang *China* 22°32N 114°14E **33** a
Wu'an *China* 36°40N 114°15E **34** F8
Wubalanji ○ *Australia* 15°28S 133°1E **60** C5
Wubin *Australia* 30°6S 116°37E **61** F2
Wubu *China* 37°28N 110°42E **34** F6
Wuchang *China* 44°55N 127°5E **35** B14
Wuchuan *China* 41°5N 111°28E **34** D6
Wuda *China* 39°29N 106°42E **34** E4
Wuding He → *China* 37°2N 110°23E **34** F6
Wudinna *Australia* 33°0S 135°22E **63** E2
Wudu *China* 33°22N 104°54E **34** H3
Wuguishan *China* 22°25N 113°25E **33** a

Wuhe *China* 33°10N 117°50E **35** H9
Wuhsi = Wuxi *China* 31°33N 120°18E **33** E13
Wuhu *China* 31°22N 118°21E **33** E12
Wukari *Nigeria* 7°51N 9°42E **50** G7
Wulajie *China* 44°6N 126°33E **35** B14
Wular L. *India* 34°20N 74°30E **43** B6
Wuliang *Indonesia* 7°27S 131°0E **37** F8
Wulumuchi = Ürümqi *China* 43°45N 87°45E **32** C6
Wundanyi *Kenya* 3°24S 38°22E **54** C4
Wunnummin L. *Canada* 52°55N 89°10W **72** B2
Wuntho *Burma* 23°55N 95°45E **41** H19
Wupatki △ *U.S.A.* 35°35N 111°20W **77** J8
Wuppertal *Germany* 51°16N 7°12E **16** C4
Wuppertal *S. Africa* 32°13S 19°12E **56** E2
Wuqing *China* 39°23N 117°4E **35** E9
Wurralibi ○ *Australia* 15°33S 128°3E **60** C4
Wurtsboro *U.S.A.* 41°35N 74°29W **83** E10
Würzburg *Germany* 49°46N 9°55E **16** D5
Wushan *China* 34°43N 104°53E **34** G3
Wushi *China* 41°9N 79°13E **32** C4
Wutai *China* 38°40N 113°12E **34** E7
Wutai Shan *China* 39°3N 113°32E **34** E7
Wuting = Huimin *China* 37°27N 117°28E **35** F9
Wutonghaolai *China* 42°50N 120°5E **35** C11
Wutongqiao *China* 29°22N 103°50E **32** F9
Wuwei *China* 37°57N 102°34E **32** D9
Wuxi *China* 31°33N 120°18E **33** E13
Wuxiang *China* 36°49N 112°50E **34** F7
Wuyang *China* 33°25N 113°35E **34** H7
Wuyi *China* 37°46N 115°56E **34** F8
Wuyi Shan *China* 27°0N 117°0E **33** F12
Wuyuan *China* 41°2N 108°20E **34** D5
Wuzhai *China* 38°54N 111°48E **34** E6
Wuzhi Shan *China* 18°45N 109°45E **38** C7
Wuzhong *China* 38°2N 106°12E **34** E4
Wuzhou *China* 23°30N 111°18E **33** G11
Wuzishan = Tongshi *China* 18°30N 109°20E **38** C7
Wyaaba Cr. → *Australia* 16°27S 141°35E **62** B3
Wyalkatchem *Australia* 31°17S 117°22E **61** F2
Wyalusing *U.S.A.* 41°40N 76°16W **83** E8
Wyandotte *U.S.A.* 42°12N 83°9W **81** D12
Wyandra *Australia* 27°12S 145°56E **63** D4
Wyangala, L. *Australia* 33°54S 149°0E **63** E4
Wyara, L. *Australia* 28°42S 144°14E **63** D3
Wycheproof *Australia* 36°5S 143°17E **63** F3
Wycliffe Well *Australia* 20°48S 134°14E **62** C1
Wye → *U.K.* 51°38N 2°40W **13** F5
Wyemandoo *Australia* 28°28S 118°29E **61** E2
Wymondham *U.K.* 52°35N 1°7E **13** E9
Wymore *U.S.A.* 40°7N 96°40W **80** E6
Wyndham *Australia* 15°33S 128°3E **60** C4
Wyndham *N.Z.* 46°20S 168°51E **59** G2
Wynne *U.S.A.* 35°14N 90°47W **85** D9
Wynyard *Australia* 41°5S 145°44E **63** G4
Wynyard *Canada* 51°45N 104°10W **71** C8
Wyola L. *Australia* 29°8S 130°17E **61** E5
Wyoming *Canada* 42°57N 82°7W **82** D2
Wyoming □ *U.S.A.* 43°0N 107°30W **76** E10
Wyomissing *U.S.A.* 40°20N 75°59W **83** F9
Wyong *Australia* 33°14S 151°24E **63** E5
Wytheville *U.S.A.* 36°57N 81°5W **81** G13

X

Xaafuun *Somali Rep.* 10°25N 51°16E **47** E5
Xaafuun, Ras *Somali Rep.* 10°27N 51°24E **47** E5
Xaçmaz *Azerbaijan* 41°31N 48°42E **19** F8
Xai-Xai *Mozam.* 25°6S 33°31E **57** D5
Xaignabouri = Sayaboury *Laos* 19°15N 101°45E **38** C3
Xainza *China* 30°58N 88°35E **32** E6
Xalapa *Mexico* 19°32N 96°55W **87** D5
Xangongo *Angola* 16°45S 15°5E **56** B2
Xankändi *Azerbaijan* 39°52N 46°49E **44** C5
Xanthi *Greece* 41°10N 24°58E **23** D11
Xanxerê *Brazil* 26°53S 52°23W **95** B5
Xapuri *Brazil* 10°35S 68°35W **92** F5
Xar Moron He → *China* 43°25N 120°35E **35** C11
Xátiva *Spain* 38°59N 0°32W **21** C5
Xau, L. *Botswana* 21°15S 24°44E **56** C3
Xavantina *Brazil* 21°15S 52°48W **95** A5
Xebert *China* 44°2N 122°0E **35** B12
Xenia *U.S.A.* 39°41N 83°56W **81** F12
Xeropotamos → *Cyprus* 34°42N 32°33E **25** E11
Xhora *S. Africa* 31°55S 28°38E **57** E4
Xhumo *Botswana* 21°7S 24°35E **56** C3
Xi Jiang → *China* 22°5N 113°20E **33** G11
Xi Ujimqin Qi *China* 44°32N 117°40E **35** B9
Xi Xian *China* 36°41N 110°58E **34** F6
Xia Xian *China* 35°8N 111°12E **34** G6
Xiachengzi *China* 44°40N 130°18E **35** B16
Xiajin *China* 36°56N 116°0E **34** F9
Xiamen *China* 24°25N 118°4E **33** D12
Xi'an *China* 34°15N 109°0E **34** G5
Xian Xian *China* 38°12N 116°6E **34** E9
Xiang Jiang → *China* 28°55N 112°50E **33** F11
Xiang Khouang *Laos* 19°17N 103°25E **38** C4
Xiangcheng *China* 33°50N 113°27E **34** H7
Xiangfan *China* 32°2N 112°8E **33** E11
Xianggang = Hong Kong □ *China* 22°11N 114°14E **33** a
Xianghuang Qi *China* 42°2N 113°50E **34** C7
Xiangning *China* 35°58N 110°50E **34** G6
Xiangquan *China* 36°30N 113°1E **34** F7
Xiangquan He = Sutlej → *Pakistan* 29°23N 71°3E **42** E4
Xiangshui *China* 34°12N 119°33E **35** G10
Xiangtan *China* 27°51N 112°54E **33** F11
Xiantao *China* 30°25N 113°25E **33** E11
Xianyang *China* 34°20N 108°40E **34** G5
Xiao Hinggan Ling *China* 49°0N 127°0E **33** B14

Xiao Xian *China* 34°15N 116°55E **34** G9
Xiaoshan *China* 30°12N 120°18E **33** E13
Xiaowutai Shan *China* 39°51N 114°59E **34** E8
Xiashan = Zhanjiang *China* 21°15N 110°20E **33** G11
Xiawa *China* 42°35N 120°38E **35** C11
Xiayi *China* 34°15N 116°10E **34** G9
Xichang *China* 27°51N 102°19E **32** F9
Xichuan *China* 33°0N 111°30E **34** H6
Xifei He → *China* 32°45N 116°40E **34** H9
Xifeng *Gansu, China* 35°40N 107°40E **34** G4
Xifeng *Liaoning, China* 42°42N 124°45E **35** C13
Xifengzhen = Xifeng *China* 35°40N 107°40E **34** G4
Xigazê *China* 29°5N 88°45E **32** F6
Xihe *China* 34°2N 105°20E **34** G3
Xihua *China* 33°45N 114°30E **34** H8
Xili Shuiku *China* 22°36N 113°57E **33** a
Xiliao He → *China* 43°32N 123°35E **35** C12
Xilinhot *China* 43°52N 116°2E **34** C9
Ximana *Mozam.* 19°24S 33°58E **55** F3
Ximiao *China* 40°59N 100°12E **32** C9
Xin Xian = Xinzhou *China* 38°22N 112°46E **34** E7
Xinavane *Mozam.* 25°2S 32°47E **57** D5
Xinbin *China* 41°40N 125°2E **35** D13
Xing Xian *China* 38°27N 111°7E **34** E6
Xingcheng *China* 40°40N 120°45E **35** D11
Xinghe *China* 40°55N 113°55E **34** D7
Xinghua *China* 32°58N 119°48E **35** H10
Xinglong *China* 40°25N 117°30E **35** D9
Xingping *China* 34°20N 108°28E **34** G5
Xingtai *China* 37°3N 114°32E **34** F8
Xingu → *Brazil* 1°30S 51°53W **93** D8
Xingxingxia *China* 41°47N 95°0E **32** C8
Xingyang *China* 34°45N 112°52E **34** G7
Xingyi *China* 25°3N 104°59E **32** F9
Xinhe *China* 37°30N 115°15E **34** F8
Xining *China* 36°34N 101°40E **32** D9
Xinjiang *China* 35°34N 111°11E **34** G6
Xinjiang Uygur Zizhiqu □ *China* 42°0N 86°0E **32** C6
Xinjin = Pulandian *China* 39°25N 121°58E **35** E11
Xinkai He → *China* 43°32N 123°35E **35** C12
Xinken *China* 22°39N 113°36E **33** a
Xinle *China* 38°25N 114°40E **34** E8
Xinlitun *China* 42°0N 122°8E **35** D12
Xinmin *China* 41°59N 122°50E **35** D12
Xintai *China* 35°55N 117°45E **35** G9
Xinwan *China* 22°47N 113°40E **33** a
Xinxiang *China* 35°18N 113°50E **34** G7
Xinyang *China* 32°6N 114°3E **33** E11
Xinyi *China* 34°23N 118°21E **35** G10
Xinzhan *China* 43°50N 127°18E **35** C14
Xinzheng *China* 34°20N 113°45E **34** G7
Xinzhou *Hainan, China* 19°43N 109°17E **38** C7
Xinzhou *Shanxi, China* 38°22N 112°46E **34** E7
Xiongyuecheng *China* 40°12N 122°5E **35** D12
Xiping *Henan, China* 33°22N 114°5E **34** H8
Xiping *Henan, China* 33°25N 111°8E **34** H6
Xique-Xique *Brazil* 10°50S 42°40W **93** F10
Xisha Qundao = Paracel Is. *S. China Sea* 15°50N 112°0E **36** A4
Xiuyan *China* 40°18N 123°11E **35** D12
Xixabangma Feng *China* 28°20N 85°40E **43** E11
Xixia *China* 33°25N 111°29E **34** H6
Xixiang *Guangdong, China* 22°34N 113°52E **33** a
Xixiang *Shaanxi, China* 33°0N 107°44E **34** H4
Xixón = Gijón *Spain* 43°32N 5°42W **21** A3
Xiyang *China* 37°38N 113°38E **34** F7
Xizang Zizhiqu □ *China* 32°0N 88°0E **32** C3
Xlendi *Malta* 36°1N 14°12E **25** C1
Xochob *Mexico* 19°21N 89°48W **87** D7
Xuan Loc *Vietnam* 10°56N 107°14E **39** G6
Xuanhua *China* 40°40N 115°2E **34** D8
Xuanwei *China* 26°15N 103°59E **32** F9
Xuchang *China* 34°2N 113°48E **34** G7
Xun Xian *China* 35°42N 114°33E **34** G8
Xunyang *China* 32°48N 109°22E **34** H5
Xunyi *China* 35°8N 108°20E **34** G5
Xúquer → *Spain* 39°5N 0°10W **21** C5
Xushui *China* 39°2N 115°40E **34** E8
Xuwen *China* 20°20N 110°10E **33** G11
Xuyi *China* 32°55N 118°32E **35** H10
Xuzhou *China* 34°18N 117°10E **35** G9
Xylophagou *Cyprus* 34°54N 33°51E **25** E12

Y

Ya Xian = Sanya *China* 18°14N 109°29E **38** C7
Yaamba *Australia* 23°8S 150°22E **62** C5
Ya'an *China* 29°58N 103°5E **32** F9
Yaapeet *Australia* 35°45S 142°3E **63** F3
Yablonovyy Khrebet *Russia* 53°0N 114°0E **29** D12
Yablonovyy Ra. = Yablonovyy Khrebet *Russia* 53°0N 114°0E **29** D12
Yabrai Shan *China* 39°40N 103°0E **34** E2
Yabrūd *Syria* 33°58N 36°39E **46** B5
Yabucoa *Puerto Rico* 18°3N 65°53W **89** d
Yacheng *China* 18°22N 109°6E **38** D7
Yacuiba *Bolivia* 22°0S 63°43W **94** A3
Yacuma → *Bolivia* 13°38S 65°23W **92** F5
Yadgir *India* 16°45N 77°5E **40** L10
Yadkin  *U.S.A.* 35°23N 80°4W **85** D14
Yaeyama-Rettō *Japan* 24°30N 123°40E **31** M1
Yagasa Cluster *Fiji* 18°57S 178°28W **59** a
Yağdnoye *Russia* 62°33N 149°40E **29** C15
Yahila *Dem. Rep. of the Congo* 0°13N 24°28E **54** B1
Yahk *Canada* 49°6N 116°10W **70** D5
Yahuma *Dem. Rep. of the Congo* 1°0N 23°10E **52** D4
Yaita *Japan* 36°48N 139°56E **31** F9
Yaiza *Canary Is.* 28°57N 13°46W **24** F6

Yakeshi *China* 49°17N 120°44E **33** B13
Yakima *U.S.A.* 46°36N 120°31W **76** C3
Yakima → *U.S.A.* 46°15N 119°14W **76** C3
Yakishiri-Jima *Japan* 44°26N 141°25E **30** B10
Yakobi I. *U.S.A.* 58°0N 136°30W **70** B1
Yakovlevka *Russia* 44°26N 133°28E **30** B6
Yaku-Shima *Japan* 30°20N 130°30E **31** J5
Yakumo *Japan* 42°15N 140°16E **30** C10
Yakutat *U.S.A.* 59°33N 139°44W **68** F4
Yakutat B. *U.S.A.* 59°45N 140°45W **74** D11
Yakutia = Sakha □ *Russia* 66°0N 130°0E **29** C14
Yakutsk *Russia* 62°5N 129°50E **29** C13
Yala *Thailand* 6°33N 101°18E **39** J3
Yalata *Australia* 31°59S 132°26E **61** F5
Yalata ○ *Australia* 31°35S 132°7E **61** F5
Yalboroo *Australia* 20°50S 148°40E **62** b
Yale *U.S.A.* 43°8N 82°48W **82** C2
Yalgorup △ *Australia* 32°39S 115°38E **61** F2
Yalinga *C.A.R.* 6°33N 23°10E **52** C4
Yalkabul, Pta. *Mexico* 21°32N 88°37W **87** C7
Yalleroi *Australia* 24°3S 145°42E **62** C4
Yalobusha → *U.S.A.* 33°33N 90°10W **85** E9
Yalong *China* 18°12N 109°42E **38** C7
Yalong Jiang → *China* 26°40N 101°55E **32** F9
Yalova *Turkey* 40°41N 29°15E **23** D13
Yalpirakinu ○ *Australia* 22°24S 132°15E **60** D5
Yalta *Ukraine* 44°30N 34°10E **19** F5
Yalu Jiang → *China* 39°55N 124°19E **35** E13
Yam *Australia* 9°54S 142°46E **62** a
Yam Ha Melah = Dead Sea *Asia* 31°30N 35°30E **46** D4
Yam Kinneret *Israel* 32°45N 35°35E **46** C4
Yamada *Japan* 33°33N 130°49E **31** H5
Yamagata *Japan* 38°15N 140°15E **30** E10
Yamagata □ *Japan* 38°30N 140°0E **30** E10
Yamaguchi *Japan* 34°10N 131°32E **31** G5
Yamaguchi □ *Japan* 34°20N 131°40E **31** G5
Yamal, Poluostrov *Russia* 71°0N 70°0E **28** B8
Yamal Pen. = Yamal, Poluostrov *Russia* 71°0N 70°0E **28** B8
Yamanashi □ *Japan* 35°40N 138°40E **31** G9
Yamantau, Gora *Russia* 54°15N 58°6E **18** D10
Yamato Ridge *Sea of Japan* 39°20N 135°0E **30** E7
Yamba *Australia* 29°26S 153°23E **63** D5
Yambarran Ra. *Australia* 15°10S 130°25E **60** C5
Yâmbiô *Sudan* 4°35N 28°16E **51** H11
Yambol *Bulgaria* 42°30N 26°30E **23** C12
Yamburg *Russia* 68°21N 77°8E **28** C8
Yamdena *Indonesia* 7°45S 131°20E **37** F8
Yame *Japan* 33°13N 130°35E **31** H5
Yamethin *Burma* 20°29N 96°18E **41** J20
Yamma Yamma, L. *Australia* 26°16S 141°20E **63** D3
Yamoussoukro *Ivory C.* 6°49N 5°17W **50** G4
Yampa → *U.S.A.* 40°32N 108°59W **76** F9
Yampi Sd. *Australia* 16°8S 123°38E **60** C3
Yampil *Moldova* 48°15N 28°15E **17** D15
Yampol = Yampil *Moldova* 48°15N 28°15E **17** D15
Yamuna → *India* 25°30N 81°53E **43** G9
Yamunanagar *India* 30°7N 77°17E **42** D7
Yamzho Yumco *China* 28°48N 90°35E **32** F7
Yana → *Russia* 71°30N 136°0E **29** B14
Yanagawa *Japan* 33°10N 130°24E **31** H5
Yanai *Japan* 33°58N 132°7E **31** H6
Yan'an *China* 36°35N 109°26E **34** F5
Yanaul *Russia* 56°25N 55°0E **18** C10
Yanbu 'al Baḥr *Si. Arabia* 24°0N 38°5E **44** F3
Yanchang *China* 36°43N 110°1E **34** F6
Yancheng *Henan, China* 33°35N 114°0E **34** H8
Yancheng *Jiangsu, China* 33°23N 120°8E **35** H11
Yanchep *Australia* 31°33S 115°37E **61** F2
Yanchi *China* 37°48N 107°20E **34** F4
Yanchuan *China* 36°51N 110°10E **34** F6
Yanco Cr. → *Australia* 35°14S 145°35E **63** F4
Yandeyarra ○ *Australia* 21°17S 118°24E **60** D2
Yandicoogina *Australia* 22°49S 119°12E **60** D2
Yandoon *Burma* 17°0N 95°40E **41** L19
Yang Xian *China* 33°15N 107°30E **34** H4
Yang-yang *S. Korea* 38°4N 128°38E **35** E15
Yangambi *Dem. Rep. of the Congo* 0°47N 24°24E **54** B1
Yangcheng *China* 35°28N 112°22E **34** G7
Yangch'ü = Taiyuan *China* 37°52N 112°33E **34** F7
Yanggao *China* 40°21N 113°55E **34** D7
Yanggu *China* 36°8N 115°43E **34** F8
Yangjiang *China* 21°50N 111°59E **33** G11
Yangliuqing *China* 39°2N 117°5E **35** E9
Yangon = Rangoon *Burma* 16°45N 96°20E **41** L20
Yangpingguan *China* 32°58N 106°5E **34** H4
Yangquan *China* 37°58N 113°31E **34** F7
Yangtse = Chang Jiang → *China* 31°48N 121°10E **33** E13
Yangtze Kiang = Chang Jiang → *China* 31°48N 121°10E **33** E13
Yangyuan *China* 40°1N 114°10E **34** D8
Yangzhou *China* 32°21N 119°26E **33** E12
Yanji *China* 42°59N 129°30E **35** C15
Yankton *U.S.A.* 42°53N 97°23W **80** D5
Yankunytjatjara-Antakirinja ○ *Australia* 27°20S 134°30E **63** A1
Yanonge *Dem. Rep. of the Congo* 0°35N 24°38E **54** B1
Yanqi *China* 42°5N 86°35E **32** C6
Yanqing *China* 40°30N 115°58E **34** D8
Yanshan *China* 38°4N 117°22E **35** E9
Yanshou *China* 45°28N 128°22E **35** B15
Yantabulla *Australia* 29°21S 145°0E **63** D4
Yantai *China* 37°34N 121°22E **35** F11
Yantian *China* 22°35N 114°16E **33** a
Yantongshan *China* 43°18N 126°0E **35** C14
Yanuca *Fiji* 18°24S 178°0E **59** a
Yanzhou *China* 35°35N 116°49E **34** G9
Yao Noi, Ko *Thailand* 8°7N 98°37E **39** a
Yao Xian *China* 34°55N 108°59E **34** G5
Yao Yai, Ko *Thailand* 8°0N 98°35E **39** a

Yaoundé *Cameroon* 3°50N 11°35E **52** D2
Yaowan *China* 34°15N 118°3E **35** G10
Yap *Pac. Oc.* 9°30N 138°10E **64** G5
Yapen *Indonesia* 1°50S 136°0E **37** E9
Yapen, Selat *Indonesia* 1°20S 136°10E **37** E9
Yapero *Indonesia* 4°59S 137°11E **37** E9
Yappar → *Australia* 18°22S 141°16E **62** B3
Yapuparra ○ *Australia* 27°15S 126°20E **61** E4
Yaqaga *Fiji* 16°35S 178°36E **59** a
Yaqui → *Mexico* 27°37N 110°39W **86** B2
Yar-Sale *Russia* 66°50N 70°50E **28** C8
Yaraka *Australia* 24°53S 144°3E **62** C3
Yaransk *Russia* 57°22N 47°49E **18** C8
Yare → *U.K.* 52°35N 1°38E **13** E9
Yaremcha *Ukraine* 48°27N 24°33E **17** D13
Yarensk *Russia* 62°11N 49°15E **18** B8
Yarí → *Colombia* 0°20S 72°20W **92** D4
Yarkand = Shache *China* 38°20N 77°10E **32** D4
Yarkant He → *China* 40°26N 80°59E **32** C5
Yarker *Canada* 44°23N 76°46W **83** B8
Yarkhun → *Pakistan* 36°17N 72°30E **43** A5
Yarlung Ziangbo Jiang = Brahmaputra → *Asia* 23°40N 90°35E **43** H13
Yarmouth *Canada* 43°50N 66°7W **73** D6
Yarmūk → *Syria* 32°42N 35°40E **46** C4
Yaroslavl *Russia* 57°35N 39°55E **18** C6
Yarqa, W. → *Egypt* 30°0N 33°49E **46** F2
Yarra Yarra Lakes *Australia* 29°40S 115°45E **61** E2
Yarram *Australia* 38°29S 146°39E **63** F4
Yarraman *Australia* 26°50S 152°0E **63** D5
Yarras *Australia* 31°25S 152°20E **63** E5
Yarrie *Australia* 20°40S 120°12E **60** D3
Yartsevo *Russia* 60°20N 90°0E **29** C10
Yarumal *Colombia* 6°58N 75°24W **92** B3
Yasawa *Fiji* 16°47S 177°31E **59** a
Yasawa Group *Fiji* 17°0S 177°23E **59** a
Yaselda *Belarus* 52°7N 26°28E **17** B14
Yasin *Pakistan* 36°24N 73°23E **43** A5
Yasinski, L. *Canada* 53°16N 77°35W **72** B4
Yasinya *Ukraine* 48°16N 24°21E **17** D13
Yasothon *Thailand* 15°50N 104°10E **38** E5
Yass *Australia* 34°49S 148°54E **63** E4
Yāsūj *Iran* 30°31N 51°31E **45** D6
Yatağan *Turkey* 37°20N 28°10E **23** F13
Yates Center *U.S.A.* 37°53N 95°44W **80** G6
Yathkyed L. *Canada* 62°40N 98°0W **71** A9
Yatsushiro *Japan* 32°30N 130°40E **31** H5
Yatta Plateau *Kenya* 2°0S 38°0E **54** C4
Yauco *Puerto Rico* 18°2N 66°51W **89** d
Yavari → *Peru* 4°21S 70°2W **92** D4
Yávaros *Mexico* 26°42N 109°31W **86** B3
Yavatmal *India* 20°20N 78°15E **40** J11
Yavne *Israel* 31°52N 34°45E **46** D3
Yavoriv *Ukraine* 49°55N 23°20E **17** D12
Yavorov = Yavoriv *Ukraine* 49°55N 23°20E **17** D12
Yawatahama *Japan* 33°27N 132°24E **31** H6
Yawri B. *S. Leone* 8°22N 13°0W **50** G3
Yaxian = Sanya *China* 18°14N 109°29E **38** C7
Yazd *Iran* 31°55N 54°27E **45** D7
Yazd □ *Iran* 32°0N 55°0E **45** D7
Yazd-e Khvāst *Iran* 31°31N 52°7E **45** D7
Yazman *Pakistan* 29°8N 71°45E **42** E4
Yazoo → *U.S.A.* 32°22N 90°54W **85** E9
Yazoo City *U.S.A.* 32°51N 90°25W **85** E9
Ybycuí *Paraguay* 26°5S 56°46W **94** B4
Ybytyruzú △ *Paraguay* 25°51S 56°11W **95** B4
Ye *Burma* 15°15N 97°15E **38** E1
Ye Xian *China* 33°35N 113°25E **34** H7
Yebyu *Burma* 14°15N 98°13E **38** E2
Yecheng *China* 37°54N 77°26E **32** D4
Yecheon *S. Korea* 36°39N 128°27E **35** F15
Yecla *Spain* 38°35N 1°5W **21** C5
Yécora *Mexico* 28°20N 108°58W **86** B3
Yedintsy = Edineţ *Moldova* 48°9N 27°18E **17** D14
Yegros *Paraguay* 26°20S 56°25W **94** B4
Yehbuah *Indonesia* 8°23S 114°45E **37** J17
Yehuda, Midbar *Israel* 31°35N 35°15E **46** D4
Yei *Sudan* 4°9N 30°40E **51** H12
Yekaterinburg *Russia* 56°50N 60°30E **28** D7
Yelarbon *Australia* 28°33S 150°38E **63** D5
Yelets *Russia* 52°40N 38°30E **18** D6
Yelin = Lingshui *China* 18°27N 110°0E **38** C8
Yelizavetgrad = Kirovohrad *Ukraine* 48°35N 32°20E **19** E5
Yelizovo *Russia* 53°11N 158°23E **29** D16
Yell *U.K.* 60°35N 1°5W **11** A7
Yell Sd. *U.K.* 60°33N 1°15W **11** A7
Yellow = Huang He → *China* 37°55N 118°50E **35** F10
Yellow Sea *China* 35°0N 123°0E **35** G12
Yellowhead Pass *Canada* 52°53N 118°25W **70** C5
Yellowknife *Canada* 62°27N 114°29W **70** A6
Yellowknife → *Canada* 62°31N 114°19W **70** A6
Yellowstone *U.S.A.* 47°59N 103°59W **76** C12
Yellowstone △ *U.S.A.* 44°40N 110°30W **76** D8
Yellowstone L. *U.S.A.* 44°27N 110°22W **76** D8
Yelsk *Belarus* 51°50N 29°10E **17** C15
Yemen ■ *Asia* 15°0N 44°0E **47** E3
Yen Bai *Vietnam* 21°42N 104°52E **38** B5
Yenangyaung *Burma* 20°30N 95°0E **41** J19
Yenbo = Yanbu 'al Baḥr *Si. Arabia* 24°0N 38°5E **44** F3
Yenda *Australia* 34°13S 146°14E **63** E4
Yeni Erenköy = Yialousa *Cyprus* 35°32N 34°10E **25** D13
Yenice *Turkey* 39°55N 27°17E **23** E12
Yenisey → *Russia* 71°50N 82°40E **28** B9
Yeniseysk *Russia* 58°27N 92°13E **29** D10
Yeniseyskiy Zaliv *Russia* 72°20N 81°0E **28** B9
Yenyuka *Russia* 57°57N 121°15E **29** D13
Yeo → *U.K.* 51°2N 2°49W **13** G5
Yeo, L. *Australia* 28°0S 124°30E **61** E3
Yeo I. *Canada* 45°24N 81°48W **82** A3
Yeola *India* 20°2N 74°30E **40** J9

Yeong-wol *S. Korea* 37°11N 128°28E **35** F15
Yeongcheon *S. Korea* 35°58N 128°56E **35** G15
Yeongdeok *S. Korea* 36°24N 129°22E **35** F15
Yeongdong *S. Korea* 36°10N 127°46E **35** F14
Yeongju *S. Korea* 36°50N 128°40E **35** F15
Yeosu *S. Korea* 34°47N 127°45E **35** G14
Yeotmal = Yavatmal
　India 20°20N 78°15E **40** J11
Yeovil *U.K.* 50°57N 2°38W **13** G5
Yeppoon *Australia* 23°5S 150°47E **62** C5
Yerbent *Turkmenistan* 39°30N 58°50E **28** F6
Yerbogachen *Russia* 61°16N 108°0E **29** C11
Yerevan *Armenia* 40°10N 44°31E **44** A5
Yerington *U.S.A.* 38°59N 119°10W **76** G4
Yermo *U.S.A.* 34°54N 116°50W **79** L10
Yerólakkos *Cyprus* 35°11N 33°15E **25** D12
Yeropol *Russia* 65°15N 168°40E **29** C17
Yeroskipos *Cyprus* 34°46N 32°28E **25** E11
Yershov *Russia* 51°23N 48°27E **19** D8
Yerushalayim = Jerusalem
　Israel/West Bank 31°47N 35°10E **46** D4
Yes Tor *U.K.* 50°41N 4°0W **13** G4
Yesan *S. Korea* 36°41N 126°51E **35** F14
Yeso *U.S.A.* 34°26N 104°37W **77** J11
Yessey *Russia* 68°29N 102°10E **29** C11
Yetman *Australia* 28°56S 150°48E **63** D5
Yeu, Î. d' *France* 46°42N 2°20W **20** C2
Yevpatoriya *Ukraine* 45°15N 33°20E **19** E5
Yeysk *Russia* 46°40N 38°12E **19** E6
Yezd = Yazd *Iran* 31°55N 54°27E **45** D7
Ygatimí *Paraguay* 24°5S 55°40W **95** A4
Yhati *Paraguay* 25°45S 56°35W **94** B4
Yhú *Paraguay* 25°0S 56°0W **95** B4
Yí → *Uruguay* 33°7S 57°8W **94** C4
Yi He → *China* 34°10N 118°8E **35** G10
Yi Xian *Hebei, China* 39°20N 115°30E **34** E8
Yi Xian *Liaoning, China* 41°30N 121°22E **35** D11
Yialiás → *Cyprus* 35°9N 33°44E **25** D12
Yialousa *Cyprus* 35°32N 34°10E **25** D13
Yibin *China* 28°45N 104°32E **32** F9
Yichang *China* 30°40N 111°20E **33** E11
Yicheng *China* 35°42N 111°40E **34** G6
Yichuan *China* 36°2N 110°10E **34** F6
Yichun *China* 47°44N 128°52E **33** B14
Yidu *China* 36°43N 118°28E **35** F10
Yijun *China* 35°28N 109°8E **34** G5
Yıldız Dağları *Turkey* 41°48N 27°36E **23** D12
Yilehuli Shan *China* 51°20N 124°20E **33** A13
Yima *China* 34°44N 111°53E **34** G6
Yimianpo *China* 45°7N 128°2E **35** B15
Yin Xu *China* 36°8N 114°10E **34** F8
Yi'nan *China* 35°31N 118°24E **35** G10
Yinchuan *China* 38°30N 106°15E **34** E4
Yindarlgooda, L.
　Australia 30°40S 121°52E **61** F3
Yindjibarndi ☼ *Australia* 22°0S 118°35E **60** D2
Ying He → *China* 32°30N 116°30E **34** H9
Ying Xian *China* 39°32N 113°10E **34** E7
Yingkou *China* 40°37N 122°18E **35** D12
Yingpanshui *China* 37°26N 104°18E **34** F3
Yingualyalya ☼
　Australia 18°49S 129°12E **60** C4
Yining *China* 43°58N 81°10E **32** C5
Yiningarra ☼ *Australia* 20°53S 129°27E **60** D4
Yinmabin *Burma* 22°10N 94°55E **41** H19
Yirga Alem *Ethiopia* 6°48N 38°22E **47** F2
Yirrkala *Australia* 12°14S 136°56E **62** A2
Yishan *China* 24°28N 108°38E **32** G10
Yishui *China* 35°47N 118°30E **35** G10
Yishun *Singapore* 1°26N 103°51E **39** d
Yitong *China* 43°13N 125°20E **35** C13
Yixing *China* 31°21N 119°48E **33** E12
Yiyang *Henan, China* 34°27N 112°10E **34** G7
Yiyang *Hunan, China* 28°35N 112°18E **33** F11
Yli-Kitka *Finland* 66°8N 28°30E **8** C23
Ylitornio *Finland* 66°19N 23°39E **8** C20
Ylivieska *Finland* 64°4N 24°28E **8** D21
Yoakum *U.S.A.* 29°17N 97°9W **84** G6
Yog Pt. *Phil.* 14°6N 124°12E **37** B6
Yogyakarta *Indonesia* 7°49S 110°22E **37** G14
Yogyakarta □ *Indonesia* 7°48S 110°22E **37** G14
Yoho △ *Canada* 51°25N 116°30W **70** C5
Yojoa, L. de *Honduras* 14°53N 88°0W **88** D2
Yok Don △ *Vietnam* 12°50N 107°40E **38** F6
Yokadouma *Cameroon* 3°26N 14°55E **52** D2
Yokkaichi *Japan* 34°55N 136°38E **31** G8
Yoko *Cameroon* 5°32N 12°20E **52** C2
Yokohama *Japan* 35°27N 139°28E **31** G9
Yokosuka *Japan* 35°20N 139°40E **31** G9
Yokote *Japan* 39°20N 140°30E **30** E10
Yola *Nigeria* 9°10N 12°29E **51** G8
Yolaina, Cordillera de
　Nic. 11°30N 84°0W **88** D3
Yólöten *Turkmenistan* 37°18N 62°21E **45** B9
Yom → *Thailand* 15°35N 100°1E **38** E3
Yonago *Japan* 35°25N 133°19E **31** G6
Yonaguni-Jima *Japan* 24°27N 123°0E **31** M1
Yonan *N. Korea* 37°55N 126°11E **35** F14
Yonezawa *Japan* 37°57N 140°4E **30** F10
Yong-in *S. Korea* 37°14N 127°12E **35** F14
Yong Peng *Malaysia* 2°0N 103°3E **39** M4
Yong Sata *Thailand* 7°8N 99°41E **39** J2
Yongamp'o *N. Korea* 39°56N 124°23E **35** E13
Yong'an *China* 25°59N 117°25E **33** F12
Yongcheng *China* 38°17N 102°0E **32** D9
Yongcheng *China* 33°55N 116°20E **34** H9
Yongdeng *China* 36°38N 103°25E **34** F2
Yonghe *China* 36°46N 110°25E **34** F6
Yŏnghŭng *N. Korea* 39°31N 127°18E **35** E14
Yongji *China* 34°52N 110°28E **34** G6
Yongji *Shanxi, China* 34°52N 110°28E **34** G6
Yongnian *China* 36°47N 114°29E **34** F8
Yongning *China* 38°15N 106°14E **34** E4
Yongzhou *China* 26°17N 111°37E **33** F11
Yonibana *S. Leone* 8°30N 12°19E **50** G3
Yonkers *U.S.A.* 40°56N 73°52W **83** F11
Yonne → *France* 48°23N 2°58E **20** B5
York *Australia* 31°52S 116°47E **61** F2
York *U.K.* 53°58N 1°6W **12** D6
York *Ala., U.S.A.* 32°29N 88°18W **85** E10

York *Nebr., U.S.A.* 40°52N 97°36W **80** E5
York *Pa., U.S.A.* 39°58N 76°44W **81** F15
York, City of □ *U.K.* 53°58N 1°6W **12** D6
York, C. *Australia* 10°42S 142°31E **62** A3
York, Kap *Greenland* 75°55N 66°25W **69** B18
York, Vale of *U.K.* 54°15N 1°25W **12** C6
York Sd. *Australia* 15°0S 125°5E **60** C4
Yorke Pen. *Australia* 34°50S 137°40E **63** E2
Yorkshire Dales △ *U.K.* 54°12N 2°10E **12** C5
Yorkshire Wolds *U.K.* 54°8N 0°31W **12** C7
Yorkton *Canada* 51°11N 102°28W **71** C8
Yorkville *U.S.A.* 38°52N 123°13W **78** G3
Yoro *Honduras* 15°9N 87°7W **88** C2
Yoron-Jima *Japan* 27°2N 128°26E **31** L4
Yos Sudarso, Pulau = Dolak,
　Pulau *Indonesia* 8°0S 138°30E **37** F9
Yosemite △ *U.S.A.* 37°45N 119°40W **78** H7
Yosemite Village
　U.S.A. 37°45N 119°35W **78** H7
Yoshino-Kumano △
　Japan 34°12N 135°55E **31** H8
Yoshkar Ola *Russia* 56°38N 47°55E **18** C8
Yotvata *Israel* 29°55N 35°2E **46** F4
Youbou *Canada* 48°53N 124°13W **78** B3
Youghal *Ireland* 51°56N 7°52W **10** E4
Youghal B. *Ireland* 51°55N 7°49W **10** E4
Young *Australia* 34°19S 148°18E **63** E4
Young *Canada* 51°47N 105°45W **71** C7
Young *Uruguay* 32°44S 57°36W **94** C4
Young I. *Antarctica* 66°25S 162°24E **5** C11
Younghusband, L.
　Australia 30°50S 136°5E **63** E2
Younghusband Pen.
　Australia 36°0S 139°25E **63** F2
Youngstown *Canada* 51°35N 111°10W **71** C6
Youngstown *N.Y., U.S.A.* 43°15N 79°3W **82** C5
Youngstown *Ohio, U.S.A.* 41°6N 80°39W **82** E4
Youngsville *U.S.A.* 41°51N 79°19W **82** E5
Youngwood *U.S.A.* 40°14N 79°34W **82** F5
Youyu *China* 40°10N 112°20E **34** D7
Yozgat *Turkey* 39°51N 34°47E **19** G5
Ypacaraí *Paraguay* 25°18S 57°19W **94** B4
Ypané → *Paraguay* 23°29S 57°19W **94** A4
Ypres = Ieper *Belgium* 50°51N 2°53E **15** D2
Yreka *U.S.A.* 41°44N 122°38W **76** F2
Ystad *Sweden* 55°26N 13°50E **9** J15
Ysyk-Köl = Balykchy
　Kyrgyzstan 42°26N 76°12E **32** C4
Ysyk-Köl *Kyrgyzstan* 42°25N 77°15E **28** E8
Ythan → *U.K.* 57°19N 1°59W **11** D7
Ytyk-Kyuyel *Russia* 62°30N 133°45E **29** C14
Yu Jiang → *China* 23°22N 110°3E **33** G11
Yü Shan *Taiwan* 23°25N 120°52E **33** G13
Yu Xian = Yuzhou
　China 34°10N 113°28E **34** G7
Yu Xian *Hebei, China* 39°50N 114°35E **34** E8
Yu Xian *Shanxi, China* 38°5N 113°20E **34** E7
Yuan Jiang → *China* 28°55N 111°50E **33** F11
Yuanping *China* 38°42N 112°46E **34** E7
Yuanqu *China* 35°18N 111°40E **34** G6
Yuanyang *China* 35°3N 113°58E **34** G7
Yuba → *U.S.A.* 39°8N 121°36W **78** F5
Yuba City *U.S.A.* 39°8N 121°37W **78** F5
Yūbari *Japan* 43°4N 141°59E **30** C10
Yūbetsu *Japan* 44°13N 143°50E **30** B11
Yueyang *China* 29°21N 113°5E **33** F9
Yugorenok *Russia* 59°47N 137°40E **29** D14
Yukon *U.S.A.* 35°31N 97°45W **84** D6
Yukon → *U.S.A.* 62°32N 163°54W **74** C7
Yukon Flats *U.S.A.* 66°40N 145°45W **74** B10
Yukon Territory □
　Canada 63°0N 135°0W **68** E5
Yukta *Russia* 63°26N 105°42E **29** C11
Yukuhashi *Japan* 33°44N 130°59E **31** H5
Yulara *Australia* 25°10S 130°55E **61** E5
Yulin *Hainan, China* 18°10N 109°31E **38** C7
Yulin *Shaanxi, China* 38°20N 109°30E **34** E5
Yuma *Ariz., U.S.A.* 32°43N 114°37W **79** N12
Yuma *Colo., U.S.A.* 40°8N 102°43W **76** F12
Yuma, B. de *Dom. Rep.* 18°20N 68°35W **89** C6
Yumbe *Uganda* 3°28N 31°15E **54** B3
Yumbi
　Dem. Rep. of the Congo 1°12S 26°15E **54** C2
Yumen *China* 39°50N 97°30E **32** D8
Yun Xian *China* 32°50N 110°46E **34** H6
Yuna *Australia* 28°20S 115°0E **61** E2
Yuncheng *Henan, China* 35°36N 115°57E **34** G8
Yuncheng *Shanxi, China* 35°2N 111°0E **34** G6
Yungang Shiku *China* 40°5N 113°0E **34** D7
Yungas *Bolivia* 17°0S 66°0W **92** G5
Yungay *Chile* 37°10S 72°5W **94** D1
Yunkanjini ☼ *Australia* 22°33S 131°6E **60** D5
Yunling Shan *China* 28°30N 98°50E **32** F8
Yunnan □ *China* 25°0N 102°0E **32** G8
Yunta *Australia* 32°34S 139°36E **63** E2
Yunxi *China* 33°0N 110°22E **34** H6
Yunyang *China* 33°0N 112°45E **33** E11
Yupanqui Basin *Pac. Oc.* 19°0S 101°0W **65** J17
Yuraygir △ *Australia* 29°45S 153°15E **63** D5
Yurga *Russia* 55°42N 84°51E **28** D9
Yurimaguas *Peru* 5°55S 76°7W **92** E3
Yurubí △ *Venezuela* 10°26N 68°42W **89** D6
Yuscarán *Honduras* 13°58N 86°45W **88** D2
Yushe *China* 37°4N 112°58E **34** F7

Yushu *Jilin, China* 44°43N 126°38E **35** B14
Yushu *Qinghai, China* 33°5N 96°55E **32** E8
Yutai *China* 35°0N 116°45E **34** G9
Yutian *Hebei, China* 39°53N 117°45E **35** E9
Yutian *Sinkiang-Uigur,*
　China 36°52N 81°42E **32** D5
Yuxarı Qarabağ =
　Nagorno-Karabakh □
　Azerbaijan 39°55N 46°45E **44** B5
Yuxi *China* 24°30N 102°35E **32** G9
Yuzawa *Japan* 39°10N 140°30E **30** E10
Yuzhno-Kurilsk *Russia* 44°1N 145°51E **29** E15
Yuzhno-Sakhalinsk
　Russia 46°58N 142°45E **33** B17
Yuzhnyy □ *Russia* 44°0N 40°0E **28** E5
Yuzhou *China* 34°10N 113°28E **34** G7
Yvetot *France* 49°37N 0°44E **20** B4

Z

Zaanstad *Neths.* 52°27N 4°50E **15** B4
Zāb al Kabīr → *Iraq* 36°1N 43°24E **44** C4
Zāb aş Şaghīr → *Iraq* 35°17N 43°29E **44** C4
Zabaykalsk *Russia* 49°40N 117°25E **29** E12
Zabol *Iran* 31°0N 61°32E **45** D9
Zābol □ *Afghan.* 32°0N 67°0E **40** D5
Zābolī *Iran* 27°10N 61°35E **45** E9
Zabrze *Poland* 50°18N 18°50E **17** C10
Zacapa *Guatemala* 14°59N 89°31W **88** C2
Zacapu *Mexico* 19°50N 101°43W **86** D4
Zacatecas *Mexico* 22°47N 102°35W **86** C4
Zacatecas □ *Mexico* 23°0N 103°0W **86** C4
Zacatecoluca *El Salv.* 13°29N 88°51W **88** D2
Zachary *U.S.A.* 30°39N 91°9W **84** F9
Zacoalco de Torres
　Mexico 20°14N 103°35W **86** C4
Zacualtipán *Mexico* 20°39N 98°36W **87** C5
Zadar *Croatia* 44°8N 15°14E **16** F8
Zadetkyi Kyun *Burma* 10°0N 98°25E **39** G2
Zafarqand *Iran* 33°11N 52°29E **45** C7
Zafra *Spain* 38°26N 6°30W **21** C2
Żagań *Poland* 51°39N 15°22E **16** C8
Zagaoua *Chad* 15°30N 22°24E **51** E10
Zagazig *Egypt* 30°40N 31°30E **51** B12
Zāghen *Iran* 33°30N 48°42E **45** C6
Zagreb *Croatia* 45°50N 15°58E **16** F9
Zāgros, Kūhhā-ye *Iran* 33°45N 48°5E **45** C6
Zagros Mts. = Zāgros, Kūhhā-ye
　Iran 33°45N 48°5E **45** C6
Zahamena △ *Madag.* 17°37S 48°49E **57** B8
Zāhedān *Fārs, Iran* 28°46N 53°52E **45** D7
Zāhedān *Sīstān va Balūchestān,*
　Iran 29°30N 60°50E **45** D9
Zahlah *Lebanon* 33°52N 35°50E **46** B4
Zaïre = Congo → *Africa* 6°4S 12°24E **52** F2
Zaječar *Serbia* 43°53N 22°18E **23** C10
Zaka *Zimbabwe* 20°20S 31°29E **57** C5
Zakamensk *Russia* 50°23N 103°17E **29** D11
Zakhodnaya Dzvina =
　Daugava → *Latvia* 57°4N 24°3E **9** H21
Zākhū *Iraq* 37°10N 42°50E **44** B4
Zakinthos = Zakynthos
　Greece 37°47N 20°54E **23** F9
Zakopane *Poland* 49°18N 19°57E **17** D10
Zakros *Greece* 35°6N 26°10E **25** D8
Zakynthos *Greece* 37°47N 20°54E **23** F9
Zalaegerszeg *Hungary* 46°53N 16°47E **17** E9
Zalantun *China* 48°0N 122°43E **33** B13
Zalari *Russia* 53°33N 102°30E **29** D11
Zalău *Romania* 47°12N 23°3E **17** E12
Zaleshchiki = Zalishchyky
　Ukraine 48°45N 25°45E **17** D13
Zalew Wiślany *Poland* 54°20N 19°50E **17** A10
Zalishchyky *Ukraine* 48°45N 25°45E **17** D13
Zama L. *Canada* 58°45N 119°5W **70** B5
Zambeke
　Dem. Rep. of the Congo 2°8N 25°17E **54** B2
Zambeze → *Africa* 18°35S 36°20E **55** F4
Zambezi = Zambeze →
　Africa 18°35S 36°20E **55** F4
Zambezi *Zambia* 13°30S 23°15E **53** G4
Zambezi △ *Zimbabwe* 17°54S 25°41E **55** F2
Zambezi □ *Mozam.* 16°15S 37°30E **55** F4
Zambia ■ *Africa* 15°0S 28°0E **55** F2
Zamboanga *Phil.* 6°59N 122°3E **37** C6
Zamora *Mexico* 19°59N 102°16W **86** D4
Zamora *Spain* 41°30N 5°45W **21** B3
Zamość *Poland* 50°43N 23°15E **17** C12
Zanda *China* 31°32N 79°50E **32** E4
Zandvoort *Neths.* 52°22N 4°32E **15** B4
Zanesville *U.S.A.* 39°56N 82°1W **82** G2
Zangābād *Iran* 38°26N 46°44E **44** B5
Zangue → *Mozam.* 17°50S 35°21E **55** F4
Zanjān *Iran* 36°40N 48°35E **45** B6
Zanjān □ *Iran* 37°20N 49°30E **45** B6
Zanjān → *Iran* 37°8N 47°47E **45** B6
Zante = Zakynthos
　Greece 37°47N 20°54E **23** F9
Zanthus *Australia* 31°2S 123°50E **61** F3
Zanzibar *Tanzania* 6°12S 39°12E **54** D4
Zaouiet El-Kala = Bordj Omar
　Driss *Algeria* 28°10N 6°40E **50** C7
Zaouiet Reggâne *Algeria* 26°32N 0°3E **50** C6
Zaoyang *China* 32°10N 112°45E **33** E11
Zaozhuang *China* 34°50N 117°35E **35** G9
Zap Suyu = Zāb al Kabīr →
　Iraq 36°1N 43°24E **44** B4
Zapadnaya Dvina = Daugava →
　Latvia 57°4N 24°3E **9** H21
Západné Beskydy *Europe* 49°30N 19°0E **17** D10
Zapala *Argentina* 39°0S 70°5W **96** D2
Zapaleri, Cerro *Bolivia* 22°49S 67°11W **94** A2
Zapata *U.S.A.* 26°55N 99°16W **84** H5
Zapolyarnyy *Russia* 69°26N 30°51E **8** B24
Zapopán *Mexico* 20°43N 103°24W **86** C4
Zaporizhzhya *Ukraine* 47°50N 35°10E **19** E6
Zaporozhye = Zaporizhzhya
　Ukraine 47°50N 35°10E **19** E6
Zara *Turkey* 39°58N 37°43E **44** B3

Zaragoza *Coahuila,*
　Mexico 28°29N 100°55W **86** B4
Zaragoza *Nuevo León,*
　Mexico 23°58N 99°46W **87** C5
Zaragoza *Spain* 41°39N 0°53W **21** B5
Zarand *Kermān, Iran* 30°46N 56°34E **45** D8
Zarand *Markazī, Iran* 35°18N 50°25E **45** C6
Zaranj *Afghan.* 30°55N 61°55E **40** D2
Zarasai *Lithuania* 55°40N 26°20E **9** J22
Zárate *Argentina* 34°7S 59°0W **94** C4
Zard, Kūh-e *Iran* 32°22N 50°4E **45** C6
Zāreh *Iran* 35°7N 49°9E **45** C6
Zaria *Nigeria* 11°0N 7°40E **50** F7
Zarneh *Iran* 33°55N 46°10E **44** C5
Zaros *Greece* 35°8N 24°54E **25** D6
Zarqā', Nahr az →
　Jordan 32°10N 35°37E **46** C4
Zarrīn *Iran* 32°46N 54°37E **45** C7
Zaruma *Ecuador* 3°40S 79°38W **92** D3
Żary *Poland* 51°37N 15°10E **16** C8
Zarzis *Tunisia* 33°31N 11°2E **51** B8
Zaskar → *India* 34°13N 77°20E **43** B7
Zaskar Mts. *India* 33°15N 77°30E **43** C7
Zastron *S. Africa* 30°18S 27°7E **56** E4
Zāvareh *Iran* 33°29N 52°28E **45** C7
Zave *Zimbabwe* 17°6S 30°1E **57** B5
Zavitinsk *Russia* 50°10N 129°20E **29** D13
Zavodovski I. *Antarctica* 56°0S 27°45W **5** B1
Zawiercie *Poland* 50°30N 19°24E **17** C10
Zāwiyat al Bayḍā = Al Bayḍā
　Libya 32°50N 21°44E **51** B10
Zāyā *Iraq* 33°33N 44°13E **44** C5
Zāyandeh → *Iran* 32°35N 52°0E **45** C7
Zaysan *Kazakhstan* 47°28N 84°52E **32** B5
Zaysan Köli *Kazakhstan* 48°0N 83°0E **28** E9
Zayü *China* 28°48N 97°27E **41** E20
Zazafotsy *Madag.* 21°11S 46°21E **57** C8
Zbarazh *Ukraine* 49°43N 25°44E **17** D13
Zdolbuniv *Ukraine* 50°30N 26°15E **17** C14
Zduńska Wola *Poland* 51°37N 18°59E **17** C10
Zeballos *Canada* 49°59N 126°50W **70** D3
Zebediela *S. Africa* 24°20S 29°17E **57** C4
Zeebrugge *Belgium* 51°19N 3°12E **15** C3
Zeehan *Australia* 41°52S 145°25E **63** G4
Zeeland *Neths.* 51°30N 3°50E **15** C3
Zeerust *S. Africa* 25°31S 26°4E **56** D4
Zefat *Israel* 32°58N 35°29E **46** C4
Zehak *Iran* 30°53N 61°42E **45** D9
Zeil, Mt. *Australia* 23°30S 132°23E **60** D5
Zeila = Saylac
　Somali Rep. 11°21N 43°30E **47** E3
Zeist *Neths.* 52°5N 5°15E **15** B5
Zeitz *Germany* 51°2N 12°7E **16** C7
Zelenogorsk *Russia* 60°12N 29°43E **8** F23
Zelenograd *Russia* 56°1N 37°12E **18** C6
Zelenople *U.S.A.* 40°48N 80°8W **82** F4
Zémio *C.A.R.* 5°2N 25°5E **54** A2
Zempoala *Mexico* 19°27N 96°23W **87** D5
Zemun *Serbia* 44°51N 20°25E **23** B9
Zenica *Bos.-H.* 44°10N 17°57E **23** B7
Žepče *Bos.-H.* 44°28N 18°2E **23** B8
Zevenaar *Neths.* 51°56N 6°5E **15** C6
Zeya *Russia* 53°48N 127°14E **29** D13
Zeya → *Russia* 51°42N 128°53E **29** D13
Zêzere → *Portugal* 39°28N 8°20W **21** C1
Zghartā *Lebanon* 34°21N 35°53E **46** A4
Zgorzelec *Poland* 51°10N 15°0E **16** C8
Zhabinka *Belarus* 52°13N 24°2E **17** B13
Zhambyl = Taraz
　Kazakhstan 42°54N 71°22E **32** C3
Zhangaözen *Kazakhstan* 43°18N 52°48E **19** F9
Zhangagazaly *Kazakhstan* 45°48N 62°6E **28** E7
Zhangbei *China* 41°10N 114°45E **34** D8
Zhangguangcai Ling
　China 45°0N 129°0E **35** B15
Zhangjiabian *China* 22°33N 113°28E **33** a
Zhangjiakou *China* 40°48N 114°55E **34** D8
Zhangye *China* 38°50N 100°23E **32** D9
Zhangzhou *China* 24°30N 117°35E **33** G12
Zhanhua *China* 37°40N 118°8E **35** F10
Zhanjiang *China* 21°15N 110°20E **33** G11
Zhannetty, Ostrov
　Russia 76°43N 158°0E **29** B16
Zhao Xian *China* 37°43N 114°45E **34** F8
Zhaocheng *China* 36°22N 111°38E **34** F6
Zhaoqing *China* 23°0N 112°20E **33** G11
Zhaotong *China* 27°20N 103°44E **32** F9
Zhaoyang Hu *China* 35°4N 116°47E **34** G9
Zhaoyuan *Heilongjiang,*
　China 45°27N 125°0E **35** B13
Zhaoyuan *Shandong,*
　China 37°20N 120°23E **35** F11
Zhari Namco *China* 31°6N 85°36E **32** E6
Zhashkiv *Ukraine* 49°15N 30°5E **17** D16
Zhashui *China* 33°40N 109°8E **34** H5
Zhayylma *Kazakhstan* 51°37N 61°33E **28** D7
Zhayyq → *Kazakhstan* 47°0N 51°48E **19** E9
Zhdanov = Mariupol
　Ukraine 47°5N 37°31E **19** E6
Zhecheng *China* 34°7N 115°20E **34** G8
Zhejiang □ *China* 29°0N 120°0E **33** F13
Zheleznodorozhnyy
　Russia 62°35N 50°55E **18** B9
Zheleznogorsk-Ilimskiy
　Russia 56°34N 104°8E **29** D11
Zhen'an *China* 33°27N 109°9E **34** H5
Zhenlai *China* 38°4N 122°39E **35** B12
Zhenping *China* 33°10N 112°16E **34** H7
Zhenyuan *China* 35°5N 107°30E **34** G4
Zhetiqara *Kazakhstan* 52°11N 61°12E **28** D7
Zhezqazghan *Kazakhstan* 47°44N 67°40E **28** E7
Zhidan *China* 36°48N 108°48E **34** F5
Zhigansk *Russia* 66°48N 123°27E **29** C13
Zhilinda *Russia* 70°0N 114°20E **29** C12

Zhmerynka *Ukraine* 49°2N 28°2E **17** D15
Zhob *Pakistan* 31°20N 69°31E **42** D3
Zhob → *Pakistan* 32°4N 69°50E **42** C3
Zhodzina *Belarus* 54°5N 28°17E **17** A15
Zhokhova, Ostrov
　Russia 76°4N 152°40E **29** B16
Zhongba *China* 29°39N 84°10E **32** F5
Zhongdian *China* 27°48N 99°42E **32** F8
Zhongning *China* 37°29N 105°40E **34** F3
Zhongshan *Antarctica* 69°0S 39°50E **5** C6
Zhongshan *China* 22°26N 113°20E **33** a
Zhongtiao Shan *China* 35°0N 111°10E **34** G6
Zhongwei *China* 37°30N 105°12E **34** F3
Zhongyang *China* 37°20N 111°11E **34** F6
Zhosaly *Kazakhstan* 45°29N 64°4E **28** E7
Zhoucun *China* 36°47N 117°48E **35** F9
Zhouchang *China* 39°40N 123°0E **35** E12
Zhoukou *China* 33°38N 114°38E **34** H8
Zhoukoudian *China* 39°41N 115°56E **34** E8
Zhouzhi *China* 34°10N 108°12E **34** G5
Zhovkva *Ukraine* 50°4N 23°58E **17** C12
Zhuanghe *China* 39°40N 123°0E **35** E12
Zhucheng *China* 36°0N 119°27E **35** G10
Zhugqu *China* 33°40N 104°30E **34** H3
Zhuhai *China* 22°17N 113°34E **33** a
Zhujiang Kou *China* 22°20N 113°45E **33**
Zhumadian *China* 32°59N 114°2E **33** E11
Zhuo Xian = Zhuozhou
　China 39°28N 115°58E **34** E8
Zhuolu *China* 40°20N 115°12E **34** E8
Zhuozhou *China* 39°28N 115°58E **34** E8
Zhuozi *China* 41°0N 112°25E **34** D7
Zhuzhou *China* 27°49N 113°12E **33** F11
Zhytomyr *Ukraine* 50°20N 28°40E **17** C15
Zhytomyr □ *Ukraine* 50°50N 28°10E **17** C15
Ziarat *Pakistan* 30°25N 67°49E **42** D2
Zibo *China* 36°47N 118°3E **35** F10
Zichang *China* 37°18N 109°40E **34** F5
Zidi = Wandhari
　Pakistan 27°42N 66°48E **42** F2
Zielona Góra *Poland* 51°57N 15°31E **16** C8
Zierikzee *Neths.* 51°40N 3°55E **15** C3
Zigong *China* 29°15N 104°48E **32** F9
Ziguéy *Chad* 14°43N 15°50E **51** F8
Ziguinchor *Senegal* 12°35N 16°20W **50** F2
Zihuatanejo *Mexico* 17°39N 101°33W **86** D4
Žilina *Slovak Rep.* 49°12N 18°42E **17** D10
Zillah *Libya* 28°30N 17°33E **51** C9
Zima *Russia* 54°0N 102°5E **29** D11
Zimapán *Mexico* 20°45N 99°21W **87** C5
Zimba *Zambia* 17°20S 26°11E **55** F2
Zimbabwe *Zimbabwe* 20°16S 30°54E **55** G3
Zimbabwe ■ *Africa* 19°0S 30°0E **55** F3
Zimnicea *Romania* 43°40N 25°22E **17** G13
Zinave △ *Mozam.* 21°35S 33°40E **57** C5
Zinder *Niger* 13°48N 9°0E **50** F7
Zinga *Tanzania* 9°16S 38°49E **55** D4
Zion △ *U.S.A.* 37°15N 113°5W **77** H7
Ziros *Greece* 35°5N 26°8E **25** D8
Zirreh, Gowd-e *Afghan.* 29°45N 62°0E **40** E3
Zitácuaro *Mexico* 19°24N 100°22W **86** D4
Zitundo *Mozam.* 26°48S 32°47E **57** D5
Ziwa Magharibi = Kagera □
　Tanzania 2°0S 31°30E **54** C3
Ziway, L. *Ethiopia* 8°0N 38°50E **47** F2
Ziyang *China* 32°32N 108°31E **34** H5
Zlatograd *Bulgaria* 41°22N 25°7E **23** D11
Zlatoust *Russia* 55°10N 59°40E **18** C10
Zlín *Czech Rep.* 49°14N 17°40E **17** D9
Zmeinogorsk *Kazakhstan* 51°10N 82°13E **28** D9
Znojmo *Czech Rep.* 48°50N 16°2E **16** D9
Zobeyrī *Iran* 34°10N 46°40E **44** C5
Zobia *Dem. Rep. of the Congo* 3°0N 25°59E **54** B2
Zoetermeer *Neths.* 52°3N 4°30E **15** B4
Zohreh → *Iran* 30°16N 51°15E **45** D6
Zolochiv *Ukraine* 49°45N 24°51E **17** D13
Zomba *Malawi* 15°22S 35°19E **55** F4
Zongo
　Dem. Rep. of the Congo 4°20N 18°35E **52** D3
Zonguldak *Turkey* 41°28N 31°50E **19** F5
Zonqor Pt. *Malta* 35°52N 14°34E **25** D2
Zorritos *Peru* 3°43S 80°40W **92** D2
Zouar *Chad* 20°30N 16°32E **51** D8
Zouérate = Zouîrât
　Mauritania 22°44N 12°21W **50** D3
Zouîrât *Mauritania* 22°44N 12°21W **50** D3
Zoutkamp *Neths.* 53°20N 6°18E **15** A6
Zrenjanin *Serbia* 45°22N 20°23E **23** B9
Ẓufār *Oman* 17°40N 54°0E **47** D5
Zug *Switz.* 47°10N 8°31E **20** C8
Zugspitze *Germany* 47°25N 10°59E **16** E6
Zuid-Holland □ *Neths.* 52°0N 4°35E **15** C4
Zuidbeveland *Neths.* 51°30N 3°50E **15** C3
Zuidhorn *Neths.* 53°15N 6°23E **15** A6
Zula *Eritrea* 15°17N 39°40E **47** D2
Zumbo *Mozam.* 15°35S 30°26E **55** F3
Zumpango *Mexico* 19°48N 99°6W **87** D5
Zunhua *China* 40°18N 117°58E **35** D9
Zuni Pueblo *U.S.A.* 35°4N 108°51W **77** J9
Zunyi *China* 27°42N 106°53E **32** F10
Zuoquan *China* 37°1N 113°27E **34** F7
Zurbāṭīyah *Iraq* 33°9N 46°3E **44** C5
Zürich *Switz.* 47°22N 8°32E **20** C8
Zutphen *Neths.* 52°9N 6°12E **15** B6
Zuurberg △ *S. Africa* 33°12S 25°32E **56** E4
Zuwārah *Libya* 32°58N 12°1E **51** B8
Žúzan *Iran* 34°22N 59°53E **45** C9
Zvishavane *Zimbabwe* 20°17S 30°2E **55** G3
Zvolen *Slovak Rep.* 48°33N 19°10E **17** D10
Zwettl *Austria* 48°35N 15°9E **16** D8
Zwickau *Germany* 50°44N 12°30E **16** C7
Zwolle *Neths.* 52°31N 6°6E **15** B6
Zwolle *U.S.A.* 31°38N 93°39W **84** F8
Żyrardów *Poland* 52°3N 20°28E **17** B11
Zyryan *Kazakhstan* 49°43N 84°20E **28** E9
Zyryanka *Russia* 65°45N 150°51E **29** C16
Zyryanovsk = Zyryan
　Kazakhstan 49°43N 84°20E **28** E9
Żywiec *Poland* 49°42N 19°10E **17** D10